175 YEARS OF DICTIONARY PUBLISHING

Collins

175 YEARS OF DICTIONARY PUBLISHING

Dictionary

of the

English Language

HarperCollins Publishers
Westerhill Road
Bishopbriggs
Glasgow
G64 2QT
Great Britain

First Edition 2010

Reprint 10 9 8 7 6 5 4 3 2 1 0

© HarperCollins Publishers 2010

HOME EDITION
ISBN 978-0-00-733756-9

EXPORT EDITION
ISBN 978-0-00-741250-1

www.collinslanguage.com

A catalogue record for this book is available from the
British Library

Typeset by Davidson Publishing Solutions, Glasgow

Printed in India by Gopsons Papers Ltd

Acknowledgements
We would like to thank those authors and publishers
who kindly gave permission for copyright material
to be used in the Collins Word Web. We would also
like to thank Times Newspapers Ltd for providing
valuable data.

EDITORIAL STAFF

Editors
Ian Brookes
Robert Groves
Mary O'Neill
Anne Robertson

Essays written by
Duncan Black
Gerry Breslin
Ian Brookes
Justin Crozier
Patrick Goldsmith
Barry Grossman
Robert Groves
Orin Hargraves
Andrew Holmes
Michael Munro
Cerwyss O'Hare
Mary O'Neill
Vincent Ooi
Anne Robertson
Fraser Sutherland
Peter Trudgill
Kate Wild

Computing Support
Thomas Callan

For the publisher
Gerry Breslin
Lucy Cooper
Kerry Ferguson
Elaine Higgleton

Foreword

Collins Dictionary of the English Language offers something more than a traditional dictionary. Not only does it provide a clear and reliable guide to English spelling and usage, but it also gives the user an insight into some of the most important and interesting aspects of English language and literature.

What sets this dictionary apart from others is the inclusion of more than two hundred full-page articles about different aspects of English, interspersed at regular intervals throughout the dictionary text. These cover a variety of topics and give a wealth of information, all presented in a highly readable form. One of the recurring themes is the history of the English language, with some articles outlining key stages in the story of the language and others highlighting the role that different languages have played in the development of English; another recurring theme is the variety of English: articles focus on the different types of English that are spoken around the world, including the different dialects spoken within the United Kingdom and North America; other essays look at the subject of communication in a broader sense, covering such topics as Braille, sign language, and the NATO alphabet; there are also articles about some perennial grammatical controversies, so that you can become better informed about such topics as splitting the infinitive or when to use *less* and *fewer*; finally, there are articles providing succinct accounts of key literary movements and genres and the life and works of important literary figures from Geoffrey Chaucer through to JK Rowling.

These articles greatly enhance the experience of browsing through the dictionary, as well as offering a useful point of reference and summarizing some important concepts. Moreover, they are not the only places where you will find information that goes beyond the scope of a standard dictionary: at the opening of each letter of the alphabet there is a short article explaining the origins and cultural significance of that letter.

That is not to take anything away from the dictionary itself, of course. As with every Collins dictionary, the text has been prepared by drawing on the evidence provided by the 2.5-billion-word Collins corpus. This vast database of English, drawn from sources in every English-speaking part of the world, provides the editors with statistical evidence about the relative frequency of words in the language and reveals the ways that each word is typically spelt and used. It also provides evidence about which words are increasing in use, helping lexicographers to track the arrival into the language of new terms such as *carbon capture*, *microblog*, and *staycation*. Indeed, such is the importance of the corpus to the way that dictionaries are produced that we have even made it the subject of one of our full-page articles.

The English language never stands still, and so there is always a need for new dictionaries to keep track of its latest changes, recording both newly coined words and changes in the way that existing words are used. Moreover, the language is currently evolving more rapidly than ever, thanks largely to advances in communications technology. The internet has allowed the voices of individual bloggers to reach mass audiences, while email and text messaging have become ubiquitous as forms of communication, challenging many received ideas about grammar and spelling. Knowing that the dictionary has been prepared with the help of the Collins corpus allows you to be confident that you are accessing an up-to-the-minute and reliable guide to English. Yet the presence of so many additional features in *Collins Dictionary of the English Language* also means that using the dictionary will be a stimulating and enjoyable experience.

Using this Dictionary

Main entry words printed in blue, in large bold type, eg

> **abbey**

All main entry words, including abbreviations and combining forms, in one alphabetical sequence, eg

> **abbot**
> **abbreviate**
> **ABC**[1]
> **ABC**[2]
> **abdicate**

Variant spellings shown in full, eg

> **adrenalin** *or* **adrenaline**

Note: where the spellings -ize and -ization are used at the end of a word, the alternative forms -ise and -isation are equally acceptable.

Pronunciations given in brackets for words that are difficult or confusing; the word is respelt as it is pronounced, with the stressed syllable in bold type, eg

> **antipodes** (an-**tip**-pod-deez)

Parts of speech shown in italics as an abbreviation, eg

> **ablaze** *adj*

When a word can be used as more than one part of speech, the change of part of speech is shown after an arrow, eg

> **adept** *adj* **1** proficient in something requiring skill ▷ *n* **2** a person skilled in something

Parts of speech may be combined for words, eg

> **awash** *adv, adj* washed over by water

Irregular parts or confusing forms of verbs, nouns, adjectives, and adverbs shown in bold type, eg

> **begin** *vb* -ginning, -gan, -gun
> **regret** *vb* -gretting, -gretted
> **anniversary** *n, pl* -ries
> **angry** *adj* -grier, -griest
> **well** *adv* better, best

Meanings separated by numbers, eg

> **absorb** *vb* **1** to soak up a liquid **2** to
> engage the interest of someone **3** to
> receive the force of an impact ...

Phrases and idioms are included in the meanings of the main entry word, eg

> **hand** ... **22 keep one's hand in** to
> continue to practise something **23**
> **(near) at hand** very close **24 on hand**
> close by; available

Related words shown in the same paragraph as the main entry word, eg

> **absurd** *adj* obviously senseless or
> illogical; ridiculous **absurdity** *n*
> **absurdly** *adv*

Note: where the meaning of a related word is not given, it may be understood from
the main entry word, or from another related word.

Usage notes comment on matters of usage and correctness, eg

> **USAGE**
> The use of *to* after *acquiesce* was
> formerly regarded as incorrect, but is
> now acceptable.

Word origins give the historical origins of words, eg

> **acerbic** (ass-**sir**-bik) *adj* harsh or bitter:
> *an acerbic critic*
> **WORD ORIGIN** Latin *acerbus* sharp, sour

Cross-references shown in black bold, eg

> **aetiology** (ee-tee-**ol**-a-jee) *n* same as
> **etiology**

List of Essays by Page Order

List of Essays by Theme

Literature and the Arts

Communication, Jargon and Terminology

Aspects of Language

List of Abbreviations

AD	anno Domini		*med*	medicine
adj	adjective		*meteorol*	meteorology
adv	adverb		*mil*	military
anat	anatomy		*n*	noun
archit	architecture		N	North
astrol	astrology		*naut*	nautical
Austral	Australia(n)		NZ	New Zealand
BC	before Christ		*photog*	photography
biol	biology		*pl*	plural
Brit	British		*prep*	preposition
chem	chemistry		*pron*	pronoun
conj	conjunction		*psychol*	psychology
E	East		®	trademark
eg	for example		RC	Roman Catholic
esp.	especially		S	South
etc.	et cetera		*Scot*	Scottish
fem	feminine		*sing*	singular
foll.	followed		US	United States
geom	geometry		*vb*	verb
interj	interjection		W	West
masc	masculine		*zool*	zoology

Aa

The origins of the letter A can be traced back to the Semitic family of languages, which includes Hebrew and Phoenician, where the opening letter of the alphabet was shaped like an ox's head and called *aleph*, after the Hebrew word for an ox.

The Greeks borrowed this opening letter, although they rotated it so that the two horns of the ox which had previously stuck out to the side now protruded downwards and looked more like legs than horns. The Greeks also changed the sound that the letter represented from a glottal stop (which is not used in Greek) to a vowel. It then became called *alpha* (A,α), and along with the second letter *beta*, it came to represent an entire series of letters or 'alphabet'.

The letter was later adapted by the Romans as part of the set of letters that was used to write Latin and which forms the basis of the modern English alphabet.

The position of A at the head of the alphabet means that the letter has come to represent primacy. For students, an A represents the highest available mark; in the jargon of sociologists, people in senior professional and managerial jobs are categorized as A's; and before the arrival of compact discs and downloads, the A-side of a record was the side which held the track considered most suitable for radio play.

In some cases the letter A is just a convenient place to start, rather than necessarily showing that something is the most important thing of its type. When we say that a car helps you to get from A to B, there is no suggestion that you are going from the best place to a place that is somehow inferior, and if a book is described as an A to Z, it simply means that it covers every aspect of its particular theme.

Just occasionally things that were designated as A are stripped of their primacy by historical developments. For example, the main trunk roads in Britain were called A roads, but these days you might be quicker to take the motorway.

On the whole, however, it is much better to be on the A list or a member of the A team than to be on any other list or team that is named after a letter.

---

a *or* **A** *n, pl* **a's, A's** *or* **As 1** the first letter of the English alphabet **2 from A to B** from one place to another: *I just want a car that takes me from A to B* **3 from A to Z** from start to finish

a *adj (indefinite article)* **1** used preceding a singular count noun that has not been mentioned before: *a book; a great shame* **2** used preceding a noun or adjective of quantity: *a litre of wine; a great amount has been written; I swim a lot and walk much more* **3** each or every; per: *I saw him once a week for six weeks*

A 1 *music* the sixth note of the scale of C major **2** ampere(s) **3** atomic: *an A-bomb*

Å angstrom unit

a- *or before a vowel* **an-** *prefix* not or without: *atonal; asexual; anaemia*
   WORD ORIGIN Greek

A1, A-1 *or* **A-one** *adj informal* first-class, excellent

A4 *n* a standard paper size, 297 × 210 mm

AA 1 Alcoholics Anonymous **2** (in Britain and South Africa) Automobile Association

AAA *Brit* (formerly) Amateur Athletic Association

A & R artists and repertoire

aardvark *n* a S African anteater with long ears and snout
   WORD ORIGIN obsolete Afrikaans: earth pig

AB 1 able-bodied seaman **2** Alberta

ab- *prefix* away from or opposite to: *abnormal*
   WORD ORIGIN Latin

aback *adv* **taken aback** startled or disconcerted

abacus (**ab**-a-cuss) *n* a counting device consisting of a frame holding beads on metal rods
   WORD ORIGIN Latin

abaft *adv, adj naut* closer to the stern of a ship
   WORD ORIGIN Old English *be* by + *æftan* behind

abalone (ab-a-**lone**-ee) *n* an edible sea creature with a shell lined with mother-of-pearl
   WORD ORIGIN American Spanish *abulón*

abandon *vb* **1** to desert or leave: *he had already abandoned his first wife* **2** to give up completely: *did you abandon all attempts at contact with the boy?* **3** to give oneself over completely to an emotion ▷ *n* **4 with abandon** uninhibitedly and without restraint **abandonment** *n*
   WORD ORIGIN Old French *a bandon* under one's control

abandoned *adj* **1** no longer used or occupied: *four people were found dead in an abandoned vehicle* **2** wild and uninhibited: *that fluffy abandoned laugh*

abase *vb* **abasing, abased** ● **abase oneself** to make oneself humble **abasement** *n*
   WORD ORIGIN Old French *abaissier*

abashed *adj* embarrassed and ashamed
   WORD ORIGIN Old French *esbair* to be astonished

abate *vb* **abating, abated** to make or become less strong: *the tension has abated in recent months* **abatement** *n*
   WORD ORIGIN Old French *abatre* to beat down

abattoir (**ab**-a-twahr) *n* a slaughterhouse
   WORD ORIGIN French *abattre* to fell

abbacy *n, pl* **-cies** the office or jurisdiction of an abbot or abbess
   WORD ORIGIN Church Latin *abbatia*

abbé (**ab**-bay) *n* a French abbot or other clergyman

abbess *n* the nun in charge of a convent
   WORD ORIGIN Church Latin *abbatissa*

abbey *n* **1** a church associated with a community of monks or nuns **2** a community of monks or nuns **3** a building inhabited by monks or nuns
   WORD ORIGIN Church Latin *abbatia* ABBACY

abbot *n* the head of an abbey of monks
   WORD ORIGIN Aramaic *abbā* father

abbreviate *vb* **-ating, -ated 1** to shorten a word by leaving out some letters **2** to cut short **abbreviation** *n*
   WORD ORIGIN Latin *brevis* brief

ABC¹ *n* **1** the alphabet **2** an alphabetical guide **3** the basics of something

a

ABC² Australian Broadcasting Corporation

abdicate *vb* **-cating, -cated 1** to give up the throne formally **2** to give up one's responsibilities **abdication** *n*
WORD ORIGIN Latin *abdicare* to disclaim

abdomen *n* the part of the body that contains the stomach and intestines **abdominal** *adj*
WORD ORIGIN Latin

abdominoplasty *n* the surgical removal of excess skin and fat from the abdomen

abduct *vb* to remove (a person) by force; kidnap **abduction** *n* **abductor** *n*
WORD ORIGIN Latin *abducere* to lead away

abeam *adv, adj* at right angles to the length of a ship or aircraft

Aberdeen Angus *n* a black hornless breed of beef cattle originating in Scotland

aberrant *adj* not normal, accurate, or correct: *aberrant behaviour*

aberration *n* **1** a sudden change from what is normal, accurate, or correct **2** a brief lapse in control of one's thoughts or feelings: *he suddenly had a mental aberration*
WORD ORIGIN Latin *aberrare* to wander away

abet *vb* **abetting, abetted** to help or encourage in wrongdoing
WORD ORIGIN Old French *abeter* to lure on

abeyance *n* **in abeyance** put aside temporarily
WORD ORIGIN Old French *abeance*, literally: a gaping after

abhor *vb* **-horring, -horred** to detest utterly
WORD ORIGIN Latin *abhorrere* to shudder at

abhorrent *adj* hateful or disgusting **abhorrence** *n*

abide *vb* **1** to tolerate: *I can't abide stupid people* **2** to last or exist for a long time: *these instincts, while subdued in the individual, may abide in the race* **3** **abide by** to act in accordance with: *he must abide by the findings of the report* **4** *archaic* to live
WORD ORIGIN Old English *ābīdan*, from *a-* (intensive) + *bīdan* to wait

abiding *adj* lasting for ever: *an abiding interest in history*

ability *n, pl* **-ties 1** possession of the necessary skill or power to do something **2** great skill or competence: *his ability as a speaker was legendary*
WORD ORIGIN Latin *habilitas*

abject *adj* **1** utterly miserable: *one Mexican in five lives in abject poverty* **2** lacking all self-respect **abjectly** *adv*
WORD ORIGIN Latin *abjectus* thrown away

abjure *vb* **-juring, -jured** to renounce or deny under oath **abjuration** *n*
WORD ORIGIN Latin *abjurare*

ablation *n* **1** the surgical removal of an organ or part **2** the wearing away of a rock or glacier **3** the melting of a part, such as the heat shield of a space re-entry vehicle
WORD ORIGIN Latin *ablatus* carried away

ablaze *adj* **1** on fire **2** brightly illuminated: *the sky was ablaze with the*

stars shining bright **3** emotionally aroused: *his eyes were ablaze with anger*

able *adj* **1** having the necessary power, skill, or opportunity to do something **2** capable or talented
WORD ORIGIN Latin *habilis* easy to hold

-able *suffix forming adjectives* able to be acted upon as specified: *washable* **-ably** *suffix forming adverbs* **-ability** *suffix forming nouns*
WORD ORIGIN Latin *-abilis, -ibilis*

able-bodied *adj* strong and healthy

able-bodied seaman *or* **able seaman** *n* a seaman who is trained in certain skills

abled *adj* having a range of physical powers as specified: *less abled; differently abled*

ableism (**ay**-bel-iz-zum) *n* discrimination against disabled or handicapped people

able rating *n* (in Britain) a seaman of the lowest rank in a navy

ablutions *pl n* the act of washing: *after the nightly ablutions, I settled down to read*
WORD ORIGIN Latin *abluere* to wash away

ably *adv* competently or skilfully

ABM antiballistic missile

abnegation *n* the act of giving something up
WORD ORIGIN Latin *abnegare* to deny

abnormal *adj* differing from the usual or typical **abnormality** *n* **abnormally** *adv*

aboard *adv, adj, prep* on, in, onto, or into (a ship, plane, or train)

abode *n* one's home
WORD ORIGIN from ABIDE

abolish *vb* to do away with (laws, regulations, or customs)
WORD ORIGIN Latin *abolere* to destroy

abolition *n* **1** the act of doing away with something: *the abolition of slavery* **2** **Abolition** the ending of slavery **abolitionist** *n, adj*

A-bomb *n* short for **atomic bomb**

abominable *adj* very bad or unpleasant: *I think that what is being done here is utterly abominable* **abominably** *adv*

abominable snowman *n* a large creature, like a man or an ape, that is said to live in the Himalayas
WORD ORIGIN translation of Tibetan *metohkangmi* foul snowman

abominate *vb* **-nating, -nated** to dislike intensely **abomination** *n*
WORD ORIGIN Latin *abominari* to regard as an ill omen

aboriginal *adj* existing in a place from the earliest known period

Aboriginal *adj* **1** of or relating to (esp. Australian) Aborigines ▷ *n* **2** an Aborigine

aborigine (ab-or-**rij**-in-ee) *n Brit, Austral, & NZ* an original inhabitant of a country or region, esp. Australia
WORD ORIGIN Latin *aborigines* the name of the inhabitants of Latium in pre-Roman times

Aborigine *n* a member of a dark-skinned people who were already living in Australia when European settlers arrived

abort *vb* **1** (of a pregnancy) to end before the fetus is viable **2** to perform an

abortion on a pregnant woman **3** to end a plan or process before completion
WORD ORIGIN Latin *abortare*

abortion *n* **1** an operation to end pregnancy **2** the premature ending of a pregnancy when a fetus is expelled from the womb before it can live independently **3** the failure of a mission or project **4** *informal* something that is grotesque **abortionist** *n*

abortion pill *n* a drug used to terminate a pregnancy in its earliest stage

abortive *adj* failing to achieve its purpose

abound *vb* **1** to exist in large numbers **2** **abound in** to have a large number of
WORD ORIGIN Latin *abundare* to overflow

about *prep* **1** relating to or concerning **2** near to **3** carried on: *I haven't any money about me* **4** on every side of ▷ *adv* **5** near in number, time, or degree; approximately **6** nearby **7** here and there: *there were some fifteen other people scattered about on the first floor* **8** all around; on every side **9** in or to the opposite direction **10** in rotation: *turn and turn about* **11** used to indicate understatement: *it's about time somebody told the truth on that subject* **12** **about to** on the point of; intending to: *she was about to get in the car* **13** **not about to** determined not to: *we're not about to help her out* ▷ *adj* **14** active: *he was off the premises well before anyone was up and about*
WORD ORIGIN Old English *abūtan*, *onbūtan* on the outside of

about-turn *or US* **about-face** *n* **1** a complete change of opinion or direction **2** a reversal of the direction in which one is facing

above *prep* **1** higher than; over **2** greater than in quantity or degree: *above average* **3** superior to or higher than in quality, rank, or ability **4** too high-minded for: *he considered himself above the task of working* **5** too respected for; beyond: *his fleet was above suspicion* **6** too difficult to be understood by: *a discussion that was way above my head* **7** louder or higher than (other noise) **8** in preference to **9** **above all** most of all; especially ▷ *adv* **10** in or to a higher place: *the hills above* **11** in a previous place (in something written or printed) **12** higher in rank or position ▷ *n* **13** **the above** something previously mentioned ▷ *adj* **14** appearing in a previous place (in something written or printed): *for a copy of the free brochure write to the above address*
WORD ORIGIN Old English *abufan*

above board *adj* completely honest and open

abracadabra *n* a word used in magic spells, which is supposed to possess magic powers
WORD ORIGIN Latin

abrasion *n* **1** a scraped area on the skin; graze **2** *geog* the erosion of rock by rock fragments scratching and scraping it
WORD ORIGIN Latin *abradere* to scrape away

abrasive *adj* **1** rude and unpleasant in manner **2** tending to rub or scrape; rough ▷ *n* **3** a substance used for cleaning, smoothing, or polishing

abreast *adj* **1** alongside each other and facing in the same direction: *the two cars were abreast* **2 abreast of** up to date with

abridge *vb* **abridging, abridged** to shorten a written work by taking out parts **abridgment** *or* **abridgement** *n*
WORD ORIGIN Late Latin *abbreviare*

abroad *adv* **1** to or in a foreign country **2** generally known or felt: *there is a new spirit abroad*

abrogate *vb* **-gating, -gated** to cancel (a law or an agreement) formally **abrogation** *n*
WORD ORIGIN from Latin *ab-* away + *rogare* to propose a law

abrupt *adj* **1** sudden or unexpected: *an abrupt departure* **2** rather rude in speech or manner **abruptly** *adv* **abruptness** *n*
WORD ORIGIN Latin *abruptus* broken off

abs *pl n* abdominal muscles

abscess (**ab**-sess) *n* **1** a swelling containing pus as a result of inflammation ▷ *vb* **2** to form a swelling containing pus **abscessed** *adj*
WORD ORIGIN Latin *abscessus* literally: a throwing off

abscissa *n, pl* **-scissas** *or* **-scissae** *maths* (in a two-dimensional system of Cartesian coordinates) the distance from the vertical axis measured parallel to the horizontal axis
WORD ORIGIN New Latin *linea abscissa* a cut-off line

abscond *vb* to run away unexpectedly
WORD ORIGIN Latin *abscondere* to conceal

abseil (**ab**-sale) *vb* **1** to go down a steep drop by a rope fastened at the top and tied around one's body ▷ *n* **2** an instance of abseiling
WORD ORIGIN German *abseilen*

absence *n* **1** the state of being away **2** the time during which a person or thing is away **3** the fact of being without something

absent *adj* **1** not present in a place or situation **2** lacking **3** not paying attention ▷ *vb* **4 absent oneself** to stay away **absently** *adv*
WORD ORIGIN Latin *absens*

absentee *n* a person who should be present but is not

absenteeism *n* persistent absence from work or school

absent-minded *adj* inattentive or forgetful **absent-mindedly** *adv*

absinthe *n* a strong, green, alcoholic drink, originally containing wormwood
WORD ORIGIN Greek *apsinthion* wormwood

absolute *adj* **1** total and complete: *he ordered an immediate and absolute ceasefire* **2** with unrestricted power and authority: *she has absolute control with fifty per cent of the shares* **3** undoubted or certain: *I was telling the absolute truth* **4** not dependent on or relative to anything else **5** pure; unmixed: *absolute alcohol* ▷ *n* **6** a principle or rule believed to be unfailingly correct **7 the Absolute** *philosophy* that which is totally unconditioned, perfect, or complete
WORD ORIGIN Latin *absolutus*

absolutely *adv* **1** completely or perfectly ▷ *interj* **2** yes indeed, certainly

absolute majority *n* a number of votes totalling over 50 per cent, such as the total number of votes that beats the combined opposition

absolute pitch *n* the ability to identify the pitch of a note, or to sing a given note, without reference to one previously sounded

absolute zero *n physics* the lowest temperature theoretically possible, at which the particles that make up matter would be at rest: equivalent to $-273.15°C$ or $-459.67°F$

absolution *n Christianity* a formal forgiveness of sin pronounced by a priest

absolutism *n* a political system in which a monarch or dictator has unrestricted power

absolve *vb* **-solving, -solved** to declare to be free from blame or sin
WORD ORIGIN Latin *absolvere*

absorb *vb* **1** to soak up a liquid **2** to engage the interest of someone **3** to receive the force of an impact **4** *physics* to take in radiant energy and retain it **5** to take in or incorporate: *this country has absorbed almost one million refugees* **absorbent** *adj* **absorbing** *adj*
WORD ORIGIN Latin *absorbere* to suck

absorption *n* **1** the process of absorbing something or the state of being absorbed **2** *physiol* the process by which nutrients enter the tissues of an animal or a plant **absorptive** *adj*

abstain *vb* **1** (usually foll. by *from*) to choose not to do or partake of something: *you will be asked to abstain from food prior to your general anaesthetic* **2** to choose not to vote **abstainer** *n*
WORD ORIGIN Latin *abstinere*

abstemious (ab-**steem**-ee-uss) *adj* taking very little alcohol or food **abstemiously** *adv* **abstemiousness** *n*
WORD ORIGIN Latin *abstemius*

abstention *n* **1** the formal act of not voting **2** the act of abstaining from something, such as drinking alcohol

abstinence *n* the practice of choosing not to do something one would like **abstinent** *adj*

abstract *adj* **1** referring to ideas or qualities rather than material objects: *an abstract noun* **2** not applied or practical; theoretical: *he was frustrated by the highly abstract mathematics being taught* **3** of art in which the subject is represented by shapes and patterns rather than by a realistic likeness ▷ *n* **4** a summary **5** an abstract painting or sculpture **6** an abstract word or idea **7 in the abstract** without referring to specific circumstances ▷ *vb* **8** to summarize **9** to remove or extract
WORD ORIGIN Latin *abstractus* drawn off

abstracted *adj* lost in thought; preoccupied **abstractedly** *adv*

abstraction *n* **1** a general idea rather than a specific example: *these absurd philosophical abstractions continued to bother him* **2** the quality of being abstract or abstracted

abstruse *adj* not easy to understand
WORD ORIGIN Latin *abstrusus* concealed

absurd *adj* obviously senseless or illogical; ridiculous **absurdity** *n* **absurdly** *adv*
WORD ORIGIN Latin *absurdus*

abundance *n* **1** a great amount **2** degree of plentifulness **3 in abundance** in great amounts: *they had fish and fruit in abundance* **abundant** *adj*
WORD ORIGIN Latin *abundare* to abound

abundantly *adv* **1** very: *he made his disagreement with the prime minister abundantly clear* **2** plentifully; in abundance

abuse *n* **1** prolonged ill-treatment of or violence towards someone: *child abuse* **2** insulting comments **3** improper use: *an abuse of power* ▷ *vb* **abusing, abused** **4** to take advantage of dishonestly: *these two ministers had abused their position for financial gain* **5** to ill-treat violently: *he had been sexually abused as a child* **6** to speak insultingly or cruelly to **abuser** *n*
WORD ORIGIN Latin *abuti* to misuse

abusive *adj* rude or insulting: *he was alleged to have used abusive language towards spectators* **abusively** *adv*

abut *vb* **abutting, abutted** to be next to or touching
WORD ORIGIN Old French *abouter*

abutment *n* a construction that supports the end of a bridge

abysmal *adj informal* extremely bad **abysmally** *adv*
WORD ORIGIN Medieval Latin *abysmus* abyss

abyss *n* **1** a very deep hole in the ground **2** a frightening or threatening situation: *the abyss of revolution and war ahead*
WORD ORIGIN Greek *abussos* bottomless

Ac *chem* actinium

AC 1 alternating current **2** athletic club

a/c 1 account **2** account current

acacia (a-**kay**-sha) *n* a shrub or tree with small yellow or white flowers
WORD ORIGIN Greek *akakia*

academic *adj* **1** relating to a college or university **2** (of pupils) having an aptitude for study **3** relating to studies such as languages and pure science rather than technical or professional studies **4** of theoretical interest only: *the argument is academic* ▷ *n* **5** a member of the teaching or research staff of a college or university **academically** *adv*

academy *n, pl* **-mies 1** a society for the advancement of literature, art, or science **2** a school for training in a particular skill: *sixteen hundred students would also spend their first year at the military academy* **3** (in Scotland) a secondary school
WORD ORIGIN Greek *akadēmeia* the place where Plato taught

Acadian *adj* **1** denoting or relating to Acadia or its inhabitants ▷ *n* **2** any of the early French settlers in Nova Scotia. See also **Cajun**

acanthus *n* **1** a plant with large spiny leaves and spikes of white or purplish flowers **2** a carved ornament based on the leaves of the acanthus plant
WORD ORIGIN Greek *akantha* thorn

ACAS (in Britain) Advisory Conciliation and Arbitration Service

ACC (in New Zealand) Accident Compensation Corporation

acc. 1 *grammar* accusative **2** account

accede *vb* **-ceding, -ceded • accede to 1** to agree to **2** to take up (an office or position): *he acceded to the throne after his Irish exile*
WORD ORIGIN Latin *accedere*

accelerando *adv music* with increasing speed
WORD ORIGIN Italian

accelerate *vb* **-ating, -ated 1** to move or cause to move more quickly **2** to cause to happen sooner than expected
WORD ORIGIN Latin *accelerare*

acceleration *n* **1** the act of increasing speed **2** the rate of increase of speed or the rate of change of velocity

accelerator *n* **1** a pedal in a motor vehicle that is pressed to increase speed **2** *physics* a machine for increasing the speed and energy of charged particles

accent *n* **1** the distinctive style of pronunciation of a person or group from a particular area, country, or social background **2** a mark used in writing to indicate the prominence of a syllable or the way a vowel is pronounced **3** particular emphasis: *there will be an accent on sport and many will enjoy rowing* **4** the stress on a syllable or musical note ▷ *vb* **5** to lay particular emphasis on
WORD ORIGIN Latin *accentus*

accentuate *vb* **-ating, -ated** to stress or emphasize **accentuation** *n*

accept *vb* **1** to take or receive something offered **2** to agree to **3** to consider something as true **4** to tolerate or resign oneself to **5** to take on the responsibilities of: *he asked if I would become his assistant and I accepted that position* **6** to receive someone into a community or group **7** to receive something as adequate or valid
WORD ORIGIN Latin *acceptare*

acceptable *adj* **1** able to be endured; tolerable: *in war killing is acceptable* **2** good enough; adequate: *he found the article acceptable* **acceptability** *n* **acceptably** *adv*

acceptance *n* **1** the act of accepting something **2** favourable reception **3** belief or agreement

accepted *adj* commonly approved or recognized: *the accepted wisdom about old age*

access *n* **1** a means of approaching or entering a place **2** the condition of allowing entry, for example entry to a building by wheelchairs or prams **3** the right or opportunity to use something or enter a place: *the bourgeoisie gained access to political power* **4** the opportunity or right to see or approach someone: *my ex-wife sabotages my access to the children* ▷ *vb* **5** to obtain information from a computer
WORD ORIGIN Latin *accedere* to accede

accessible *adj* **1** easy to approach, enter, or use **2** easy to understand: *the most accessible opera by Wagner* **accessibility** *n*

accession *n* the act of taking up an office or position: *the 40th anniversary of her accession to the throne*

accessory *n, pl* **-ries 1** a supplementary part or object **2** a small item, such as a bag or belt, worn or carried by someone to complete his or her outfit **3** a person who is involved in a crime but who was not present when it took place
WORD ORIGIN Late Latin *accessorius*

access road *n* a road providing a way to a particular place or on to a motorway

access time *n* the time required to retrieve a piece of stored information from a computer

accident *n* **1** an unpleasant event that causes damage, injury, or death **2** an unforeseen event or one without apparent cause: *they had met in town by accident*
WORD ORIGIN Latin *accidere* to happen

accidental *adj* **1** occurring by chance or unintentionally ▷ *n* **2** *music* a symbol denoting a sharp, flat, or natural that is not a part of the key signature
accidentally *adv*

accident-prone *adj* (of a person) often involved in accidents

acclaim *vb* **1** to applaud or praise: *the highly acclaimed children's TV series* **2** to acknowledge publicly: *he was immediately acclaimed the new prime minister* ▷ *n* **3** an enthusiastic expression of approval
WORD ORIGIN Latin *acclamare*

acclamation *n* **1** an enthusiastic reception or display of approval **2** *Canad* an instance of being elected without opposition **3 by acclamation** by a majority without a ballot

acclimatize *or* **-tise** *vb* **-tizing, -tized** *or* **-tising, -tised** to adapt to a new climate or environment **acclimatization** *or* **-tisation** *n*

accolade *n* **1** an award, praise, or honour **2** a touch on the shoulder with a sword conferring knighthood
WORD ORIGIN Latin *ad-* to + *collum* neck

accommodate *vb* **-dating, -dated 1** to provide with lodgings **2** to have room for **3** to do a favour for **4** to adjust or become adjusted; to adapt
WORD ORIGIN Latin *accommodare*

accommodating *adj* willing to help; obliging

accommodation *n* a place in which to sleep, live, or work

accommodation address *n Brit* an address on letters to a person who cannot or does not wish to receive mail at a permanent address

accompaniment *n* **1** something that accompanies something else **2** *music* a supporting part for an instrument, a band, or an orchestra

accompanist *n* a person who plays a musical accompaniment

accompany *vb* **-nies, -nying, -nied 1** to go with (someone) **2** to happen or exist at the same time as **3** to provide a musical accompaniment for
WORD ORIGIN Old French *accompaignier*

accomplice *n* a person who helps someone else commit a crime
WORD ORIGIN Late Latin *complex* partner

accomplish *vb* **1** to manage to do; achieve: *most infants accomplish it immediately* **2** to complete
WORD ORIGIN Latin *complere* to fill up

accomplished *adj* **1** expert or proficient: *an accomplished liar* **2** successfully completed

accomplishment *n* **1** the successful completion of something **2** something successfully completed **3** (*often pl*) personal abilities or skills

accord *n* **1** agreement or harmony **2** a formal agreement between groups or nations: *the Paris peace accords* **3 of one's own accord** voluntarily or willingly **4 with one accord** unanimously ▷ *vb* **5** to grant: *she was at last accorded her true status* **6 accord with** to fit in with or be consistent with
WORD ORIGIN Latin *ad-* to + *cor* heart

accordance *n* **in accordance with** conforming to or according to: *food is prepared in accordance with Jewish laws*

according *adv* **1 according to a** as stated by: *according to her, they were once engaged* **b** in conformity with: *work hours varied according to the tides* **2 according as** depending on whether

accordingly *adv* **1** in an appropriate manner **2** consequently

accordion *n* a box-shaped musical instrument played by moving the two sides apart and together, and pressing a keyboard or buttons to produce the notes **accordionist** *n*
WORD ORIGIN German *Akkordion*

accost *vb* to approach, stop, and speak to
WORD ORIGIN Latin *ad-* to + *costa* side, rib

account *n* **1** a report or description **2** a person's money held in a bank **3** a statement of financial transactions with the resulting balance **4** part or behalf: *I am sorry that you suffered on my account* **5 call someone to account** to demand an explanation from someone **6 give a good** *or* **bad account of oneself** to perform well or fail to perform well **7 of no account** of little importance or value **8 on account of** because of **9 take account of** *or* **take into account** to take into consideration; allow for ▷ *vb* **10** to consider as: *the evening was accounted a major step forward by all concerned*
WORD ORIGIN Old French *acont*

accountable *adj* responsible to someone or for some action **accountability** *n*

accountant *n* a person who maintains and audits business accounts **accountancy** *n*

account for *vb* **1** to give reasons for **2** to explain or count up what has been spent

accounting *n* the skill or practice of maintaining and auditing business accounts

accoutrements (ak-**koo**-tra-ments) *or* US **accouterments** (ak-**koo**-ter-ments) *pl n* clothing and equipment for a particular activity
WORD ORIGIN Old French *accoustrer* to equip

accredit *vb* **1** to give official recognition to **2** to send (a diplomat) with official credentials to a particular country **3** to certify as meeting required standards **4** to attribute (a quality or an action) to (a person) **accreditation** *n*
WORD ORIGIN French *accréditer*

Word Histories
part 1

Aardvark is an obsolete Afrikaans word meaning 'earth pig', from *aarde*, meaning 'earth' and *vark*, meaning 'pig'. With its long ears and snout and its stout body, the aardvark does look rather like a pig, but pigs and aardvarks belong to totally separate animal families.

The phrase **above board** is in origin a gambling term. It is an allusion to the fact that it is difficult for a player to cheat at cards when his hands are above the 'board' or gambling table and therefore clearly visible to the other players.

The original **Academy**, in Greek *Akadēmeia*, was an olive grove outside ancient Athens where the philosopher Plato taught in the 4th century BC.

An **adder** was originally 'a nadder', from the Old English *naedre*, 'serpent', but over the course of time the 'n' transferred from the noun to the article. This is quite a common linguistic shift, and happened with several other English words, including **apple**.

Algebra: The term *al-jabr* is taken from the title of an Arabic book on mathematics by the 9th-century Muslim mathematician *al-Khwārizmī*, the *Kitab al-jabr wa al-muqābulah*. In Arabic *al-jabr* means 'reunion' or 'integration'. When the book was later translated into Latin, 'al-jabr' became 'algebra'.

The word **alligator** comes from Spanish *el lagarto*, meaning 'the lizard'.

Amazon is one of the world's oldest examples of folk etymology. The popular explanation is that the word comes from the Greek *a* + *mazos*, 'without a breast', as these ferocious woman warriors were supposed to cut or burn off a breast so that they could draw their bows further. It's more likely, however, that the word comes from the name of a Scythian tribe, with the breast explanation being the Greeks' attempt to make sense of the name of this particular people.

Amethyst comes from Greek *amethustos* meaning 'not drunk'. It was thought in ancient times that anyone wearing or touching an amethyst would not become drunk. Wine goblets were sometimes carved from amethyst.

Amok comes from the Malay word *amoq* meaning 'a furious assault'.

The first people to wear **anoraks** were Eskimos. In the Eskimo language, *anoraq* means 'a piece of clothing' and denotes a long, hooded jacket made from fur such as sealskin or caribou skin.

Apocalypse: This word comes from Greek *apokaluptein*, which means 'to reveal or disclose'. An apocalypse is a prophetic disclosure of something that is going to happen, such as the description of the end of the world given in the last book of the Bible, the 'Revelation of St John the Divine', which is also known as 'the Apocalypse'.

An **apple** was originally 'a napple', but over the course of time the N transferred from the noun to the article. This is quite a common linguistic shift, and happened with several other English words, such as **adder**.

Apricot: This word has a long and interesting history. It comes originally from the Latin word *praecox*, meaning 'early ripening'. From Latin it was borrowed into Greek, and then into Arabic as *al-birqūq*, denoting the apricot, which flowers and ripens earlier than the peach. From Arabic, it came back to Europe as Portuguese *albricoque*, and from Portuguese into English as the 'apricock', later altered to 'apricot'.

The word **arctic** comes from the Greek adjective *arktikos*, meaning 'relating to a bear' (Greek *arktos*). In Greek *arktikos* also meant 'relating to the Great Bear,' the constellation which can be seen in the northern sky and which points towards the Pole Star.

Armageddon comes from the Hebrew words *har megiddōn*, 'the mountain district of Megiddo'. Megiddo, which is in northern Israel, was the site of several battles in Old Testament times.

a

accretion (ak-**kree**-shun) *n* **1** a gradual increase in size, through growth or addition **2** something added, such as an extra layer
WORD ORIGIN Latin *accretio*

accrue *vb* -**cruing**, -**crued** **1** (of money or interest) to increase gradually over a period of time **2 accrue to** to fall naturally to: *some advantage must accrue to the weaker party*
WORD ORIGIN Latin *accrescere*

accumulate *vb* -**lating**, -**lated** to gather together in an increasing quantity; collect **accumulative** *adj*
WORD ORIGIN Latin *accumulare* to heap up

accumulation *n* **1** something that has been collected **2** the collecting together of things

accumulator *n* **1** *Austral & Brit* a rechargeable device for storing electrical energy **2** *Brit horse racing* a collective bet on successive races, with both stake and winnings being carried forward to accumulate progressively

accuracy *n* faithful representation of the truth: *care is taken to ensure the accuracy of the content*

accurate *adj* faithfully representing the truth: *all the information was accurate* **accurately** *adv*
WORD ORIGIN Latin *accurare* to perform with care

accursed (a-**curse**-id) *adj* **1** under a curse **2** hateful or detestable

accusation *n* **1** an allegation that a person is guilty of some wrongdoing **2** a formal charge brought against a person **accusatory** *adj*

accusative *n grammar* a grammatical case in some languages that identifies the direct object of a verb

accuse *vb* -**cusing**, -**cused** to charge a person with wrongdoing **accuser** *n* **accusing** *adj* **accusingly** *adv*
WORD ORIGIN Latin *accūsāre*

accused *n* **the accused** *law* the defendant appearing on a criminal charge

accustom *vb* **accustom oneself to** to become familiar with or used to from habit or experience
WORD ORIGIN Old French *acostumer*

accustomed *adj* **1** usual or customary: *he parked his motorcycle in its accustomed place* **2 accustomed to a** used to **b** in the habit of

ace *n* **1** a playing card with one symbol on it **2** *informal* an expert: *an American stock car ace* **3** *tennis* a winning serve that the opponent fails to reach **4** a fighter pilot who has destroyed several enemy aircraft ▷ *adj* **5** *informal* superb or excellent: *an ace tennis player*
WORD ORIGIN Latin *as* a unit

acerbic (ass-**sir**-bik) *adj* harsh or bitter: *an acerbic critic*
WORD ORIGIN Latin *acerbus* sharp, sour

acerbity *n, pl* -**ties** **1** bitter speech or temper **2** bitterness of taste

acetaldehyde (ass-it-**tal**-dee-hide) *n chem* a colourless volatile liquid, used as a solvent

acetate (**ass**-it-tate) *n* **1** *chem* any salt or ester of acetic acid **2** Also: **acetate rayon** a synthetic textile fibre made from cellulose acetate

acetic (ass-**see**-tik) *adj chem* of, containing, or producing acetic acid or vinegar
WORD ORIGIN Latin *acetum* vinegar

acetic acid *n chem* a strong-smelling colourless liquid used to make vinegar

acetone (**ass**-it-tone) *n chem* a strong-smelling colourless liquid used as a solvent for paints and lacquers

acetylene (ass-**set**-ill-een) *n chem* a colourless soluble flammable gas used in welding metals

ache *vb* **aching**, **ached** **1** to feel or be the source of a continuous dull pain **2** to suffer mental anguish ▷ *n* **3** a continuous dull pain
WORD ORIGIN Old English *ācan*

achieve *vb* **achieving**, **achieved** to gain by hard work or effort **achiever** *n*
WORD ORIGIN Old French *achever* to bring to an end

achievement *n* **1** something that has been accomplished by hard work, ability, or heroism **2** the successful completion of something

Achilles heel (ak-**kill**-eez) *n* a small but fatal weakness
WORD ORIGIN *Achilles* in Greek mythology was killed by an arrow in his unprotected heel

Achilles tendon *n* the fibrous cord that connects the muscles of the calf to the heel bone

achromatic *adj* **1** without colour **2** refracting light without breaking it up into its component colours **3** *music* involving no sharps or flats **achromatically** *adv*

acid *n* **1** *chem* one of a class of compounds, corrosive and sour when dissolved in water, that combine with a base to form a salt **2** *slang* LSD **3** a sour-tasting substance ▷ *adj* **4** *chem* of, from, or containing acid **5** sharp or sour in taste **6** sharp in speech or manner **acidly** *adv*
WORD ORIGIN Latin *acidus*

Acid House or **Acid** *n* a type of funk-based, electronically edited disco music of the late 1980s, which has hypnotic sound effects and which is associated with hippy culture and the use of the drug ecstasy
WORD ORIGIN *acid* (LSD) + *House* music

acidic *adj* containing acid

acidify *vb* -**fies**, -**fying**, -**fied** to convert into acid **acidification** *n*

acidity *n* **1** the quality of being acid **2** the amount of acid in a solution

acid rain *n* rain containing pollutants released into the atmosphere by burning coal or oil

acid reflux *n* the regurgitation of stomach acid into the oesophagus, causing heartburn

acid test *n* a rigorous and conclusive test of worth or value
WORD ORIGIN from the testing of gold with nitric acid

acknowledge *vb* -**edging**, -**edged** **1** to recognize or admit the truth of a statement **2** to show recognition of a person by a greeting or glance **3** to make known that a letter or message has been received **4** to express

gratitude for (a favour or compliment)
WORD ORIGIN Old English *oncnāwan* to recognize

acknowledgment or **acknowledgement** *n* **1** the act of acknowledging something or someone **2** something done or given as an expression of gratitude

acme (**ak**-mee) *n* the highest point of achievement or excellence
WORD ORIGIN Greek *akmē*

acne (**ak**-nee) *n* a skin disease in which pus-filled spots form on the face
WORD ORIGIN New Latin

acolyte *n* **1** a follower or attendant **2** *Christianity* a person who assists a priest
WORD ORIGIN Greek *akolouthos*

aconite *n* **1** a poisonous plant with hoodlike flowers **2** dried aconite root, used as a narcotic
WORD ORIGIN Greek *akoniton*

acorn *n* the fruit of the oak tree, consisting of a smooth nut in a cuplike base
WORD ORIGIN Old English *æcern*

acoustic *adj* **1** of sound, hearing, or acoustics **2** (of a musical instrument) without electronic amplification **3** designed to absorb sound: *acoustic tiles* **acoustically** *adv*
WORD ORIGIN Greek *akouein* to hear

acoustics *n* **1** the scientific study of sound ▷ *pl n* **2** the characteristics of a room or auditorium determining how well sound can be heard within it

acquaint *vb* **acquaint with** to make (someone) familiar with
WORD ORIGIN Latin *accognoscere* to know well

acquaintance *n* **1** a person whom one knows slightly **2** slight knowledge of a person or subject **3 make the acquaintance of** to come into social contact with **4** the people one knows: *an actress of my acquaintance*

acquainted *adj* **1** on terms of familiarity but not intimacy **2 acquainted with** familiar with: *she became acquainted with the classics of Chinese literature*

acquiesce (ak-wee-**ess**) *vb* -**escing**, -**esced** to agree to what someone wants **acquiescence** *n* **acquiescent** *adj*
WORD ORIGIN Latin *acquiescere*

▤ USAGE
▤ The use of *to* after *acquiesce* was
▤ formerly regarded as incorrect, but is
▤ now acceptable.

acquire *vb* -**quiring**, -**quired** to get or develop (something such as an object, trait, or ability) **acquirement** *n*
WORD ORIGIN Latin *acquirere*

acquired taste *n* **1** a liking for something at first considered unpleasant **2** the thing liked

acquisition *n* **1** something acquired, often to add to a collection **2** the act of acquiring something

acquisitive *adj* eager to gain material possessions **acquisitively** *adv* **acquisitiveness** *n*

acquit *vb* -**quitting**, -**quitted** **1** to pronounce someone not guilty: *he's been acquitted of negligence* **2** to behave in a

particular way: *she acquitted herself well in the meeting* **acquittal** *n*
WORD ORIGIN Old French *aquiter*

acre *n* **1** a unit of area equal to 4840 square yards (4046.86 square metres) **2 acres** *informal* a large amount: *acres of skin*
WORD ORIGIN Old English *æcer*

acreage (**ake**-er-rij) *n* land area in acres

acrid (**ak**-rid) *adj* **1** unpleasantly strong-smelling **2** sharp in speech or manner **acridity** *n* **acridly** *adv*
WORD ORIGIN Latin *acer* sharp, sour

acrimony *n* bitterness and resentment felt about something **acrimonious** *adj*
WORD ORIGIN Latin *acrimonia*

acrobat *n* an entertainer who performs gymnastic feats requiring skill, agility, and balance **acrobatic** *adj* **acrobatically** *adv*
WORD ORIGIN Greek *akrobatēs* one who walks on tiptoe

acrobatics *pl n* the skills or feats of an acrobat

acronym *n* a word made from the initial letters of other words, for example UNESCO for the *United Nations Educational, Scientific, and Cultural Organization*
WORD ORIGIN Greek *akros* outermost + *onoma* name

acrophobia *n* abnormal fear of being at a great height
WORD ORIGIN Greek *akron* summit + *phobos* fear

acropolis (a-**crop**-pol-liss) *n* the citadel of an ancient Greek city
WORD ORIGIN Greek *akros* highest + *polis* city

across *prep* **1** from one side to the other side of **2** on or at the other side of ▷ *adv* **3** from one side to the other **4** on or to the other side
WORD ORIGIN Old French *a croix* crosswise

across-the-board *adj* affecting everyone in a particular group or place equally: *across-the-board tax cuts*

acrostic *n* a number of lines of writing, such as a poem, in which the first or last letters form a word or proverb
WORD ORIGIN Greek *akros* outermost + *stikhos* line of verse

acrylic *adj* **1** made of acrylic ▷ *n* **2** a man-made fibre used for clothes and blankets **3** a kind of paint made from acrylic acid
WORD ORIGIN Latin *acer* sharp + *olere* to smell

acrylic acid *n chem* a strong-smelling colourless corrosive liquid

acrylic resin *n chem* any of a group of polymers of acrylic acid, used as synthetic rubbers, in paints, and as plastics

act *n* **1** something done **2** a formal decision reached or law passed by a law-making body: *an act of parliament* **3** a major division of a play or opera **4** a short performance, such as a sketch or dance **5** a pretended attitude: *she appeared calm but it was just an act* **6 get in on the act** *informal* to become involved in something in order to share the benefit **7 get one's act together** *informal* to organize oneself ▷ *vb* **8** to do

something **9** to perform (a part or role) in a play, film, or broadcast **10** to present (a play) on stage **11 act for** to be a substitute for: *Mr Lewis was acting for the head of the department* **12 act as** to serve the function of: *she is acting as my bodyguard* **13** to behave: *she acts as though she really hates you* **14** to behave in an unnatural way ▷ See also **act up**
WORD ORIGIN Latin *actum* a thing done

ACT Australian Capital Territory

acting *n* **1** the art of an actor ▷ *adj* **2** temporarily performing the duties of: *the acting president has declared a state of emergency*

actinide series *n chem* a series of 15 radioactive elements with increasing atomic numbers from actinium to lawrencium

actinium *n chem* a radioactive element of the actinide series, occurring as a decay product of uranium. Symbol: Ac
WORD ORIGIN Greek *aktis* ray

action *n* **1** doing something for a particular purpose **2** something done on a particular occasion **3** a lawsuit **4** movement during some physical activity **5** the operating mechanism in a gun or machine **6** the way in which something operates or works **7** *slang* the main activity in a place **8** the events that form the plot of a story or play **9** activity, force, or energy **10** a minor battle **11 actions** behaviour **12 out of action** not functioning

actionable *adj law* giving grounds for legal action

action painting *n* an art form in which paint is thrown, smeared, dripped, or spattered on the canvas

action replay *n* the rerunning of a small section of a television tape, for example of a sporting event

action stations *pl n* the positions taken up by individuals in preparation for battle or for some other activity

activate *vb* -**vating, -vated 1** to make something active **2** *physics* to make something radioactive **3** *chem* to increase the rate of a reaction **activation** *n*

active *adj* **1** busy and energetic **2** energetically involved in or working hard for: *active in the peace movement* **3** happening now and energetically: *the plan is under active discussion* **4** functioning or causing a reaction: *the active ingredient is held within the capsule* **5** (of a volcano) erupting periodically **6** *grammar* denoting a form of a verb used to indicate that the subject is performing the action, for example *kicked* in *The boy kicked the football* ▷ *n* **7** *grammar* the active form of a verb **actively** *adv*

active list *n mil* a list of officers available for full duty

active service *n* military duty in an operational area

activist *n* a person who works energetically to achieve political or social goals **activism** *n*

activity *n* **1** the state of being active **2** lively movement **3** *pl* -**ties** any specific action or pursuit: *he was engaged in political activities abroad*

act of God *n law* a sudden occurrence caused by natural forces, such as a flood

actor *or fem* **actress** *n* a person who acts in a play, film, or broadcast

actual *adj* existing in reality or as a matter of fact
WORD ORIGIN Latin *actus* act

≡ **USAGE**
≡ The excessive use of *actual* and *actually*
≡ should be avoided. They are
≡ unnecessary in sentences such as *in*
≡ *actual fact, he is forty-two,* and *he did*
≡ *actually go to the play but did not enjoy it.*

actuality *n, pl* -**ties** reality

actually *adv* as an actual fact; really

actuary *n, pl* -**aries** a person qualified to calculate commercial risks and probabilities involving uncertain future events, esp. in such contexts as life assurance **actuarial** *adj*
WORD ORIGIN Latin *actuarius* one who keeps accounts

actuate *vb* -**ating, -ated 1** to start up a mechanical device **2** to motivate someone
WORD ORIGIN Medieval Latin *actuare*

act up *vb informal* to behave in a troublesome way

acuity (ak-**kew**-it-ee) *n* keenness of vision or thought
WORD ORIGIN Latin *acutus* acute

acumen (**ak**-yew-men) *n* the ability to make good decisions
WORD ORIGIN Latin: sharpness

acupuncture *n* a medical treatment involving the insertion of needles at various parts of the body to stimulate the nerve impulses **acupuncturist** *n*
WORD ORIGIN Latin *acus* needle + PUNCTURE

acute *adj* **1** severe or intense: *acute staff shortages* **2** penetrating in perception or insight **3** sensitive or keen: *it was amazing how acute your hearing got in the bush* **4** (of a disease) sudden and severe **5** *maths* (of an angle) of less than 90° **6** (of a hospital or bed) intended to accommodate short-term patients ▷ *n* **7** an acute accent **acutely** *adv* **acuteness** *n*
WORD ORIGIN Latin *acutus*

acute accent *n* the mark (´), used in some languages to indicate that the vowel over which it is placed is pronounced in a certain way

ad *n informal* an advertisement

AD (indicating years numbered from the supposed year of the birth of Christ) in the year of the Lord
WORD ORIGIN Latin *anno Domini*

ad- *prefix* **1** to or towards: *adverb* **2** near or next to: *adrenal*
WORD ORIGIN Latin

Ada *n* a high-level computer programming language, used esp. for military systems
WORD ORIGIN after Ada, Countess of Lovelace, pioneer in computer programming

adage (**ad**-ij) *n* a traditional saying that is generally accepted as being true
WORD ORIGIN Latin *adagium*

adagietto *music adv* **1** slowly, but more quickly than adagio ▷ *n, pl* -**tos 2** a movement or piece to be performed fairly slowly

adagio (ad-**dahj**-yo) *music adv* **1** slowly ▷ *n, pl* **-gios** **2** a movement or piece to be performed slowly
WORD ORIGIN Italian

Adam *n* **1** *Bible* the first man created by God **2** **not know someone from Adam** to not know someone at all

adamant *adj* unshakable in determination or purpose **adamantly** *adv*
WORD ORIGIN Greek *adamas* unconquerable

Adam's apple *n* the projecting lump of thyroid cartilage at the front of a person's neck

adapt *vb* **1** to adjust (something or oneself) to different conditions **2** to change something to suit a new purpose **adaptable** *adj* **adaptability** *n*
WORD ORIGIN Latin *adaptare*

adaptation *n* **1** something that is produced by adapting something else: *a TV adaptation of a Victorian novel* **2** the act of adapting

adaptor *or* **adapter** *n* **1** a device used to connect several electrical appliances to a single socket **2** any device for connecting two parts of different sizes or types

ADC aide-de-camp

add *vb* **1** to combine (numbers or quantities) so as to make a larger number or quantity **2** to join something to something else so as to increase its size, effect, or scope: *these new rules will add an extra burden on already overworked officials* **3** to say or write something further **4** **add in** to include ▶ See also **add up**
WORD ORIGIN Latin *addere*

addendum *n, pl* **-da** something added on, esp. an appendix to a book or magazine

adder *n* a small poisonous snake with a black zigzag pattern along the back
WORD ORIGIN Old English *nædre*

addict *n* **1** a person who is unable to stop taking narcotic drugs **2** *informal* a person who is devoted to something: *he's a telly addict* **addictive** *adj*
WORD ORIGIN Latin *addictus* given over

addicted *adj* **1** dependent on a narcotic drug **2** *informal* devoted to something: *I'm a news freak and addicted to BBC Breakfast News* **addiction** *n*

addition *n* **1** the act of adding **2** a person or thing that is added **3** a mathematical operation in which the total of two or more numbers or quantities is calculated **4** **in addition (to)** besides; as well (as) **additional** *adj* **additionally** *adv*

additive *n* any substance added to something, such as food, to improve it or prevent deterioration

addled *adj* **1** confused or unable to think clearly **2** (of eggs) rotten
WORD ORIGIN Old English *adela* filth

add-on *n* a feature that can be added to a standard model to give increased benefits

address *n* **1** the place at which someone lives **2** the conventional form by which the location of a building is described **3** a formal speech **4** *computers* a number giving the location of a piece of stored information ▷ *vb* **5** to mark (a letter or parcel) with an address **6** to speak to **7** to direct one's attention to (a problem or an issue) **8** **address oneself to a** to speak or write to **b** to apply oneself to: *we have got to address ourselves properly to this problem*
WORD ORIGIN Latin *ad-* to + *directus* direct

addressee *n* a person to whom a letter or parcel is addressed

adduce *vb* **-ducing, -duced** to mention something as evidence
WORD ORIGIN Latin *adducere* to lead to

add up *vb* **1** to calculate the total of (two or more numbers or quantities) **2** *informal* to make sense: *there's something about it that doesn't add up* **3** **add up to** to amount to

adenoidal *adj* having a nasal voice or impaired breathing because of enlarged adenoids

adenoids (**ad**-in-oidz) *pl n* a mass of tissue at the back of the throat
WORD ORIGIN Greek *adenoeidēs* glandular

adept *adj* **1** proficient in something requiring skill ▷ *n* **2** a person skilled in something **adeptness** *n*
WORD ORIGIN Latin *adipisci* to attain

adequate *adj* just enough in amount or just good enough in quality **adequacy** *n* **adequately** *adv*
WORD ORIGIN Latin *ad-* to + *aequus* equal

à deux (ah **duh**) *adj, adv* of or for two people
WORD ORIGIN French

ADHD *med* attention deficit hyperactivity disorder

adhere *vb* **-hering, -hered** **1** to stick to **2** to act according to (a rule or agreement) **3** to be a loyal supporter of (something)
WORD ORIGIN Latin *adhaerere*
≡ **USAGE**
≡ See at **adhesion**.

adherent *n* **1** a supporter or follower ▷ *adj* **2** sticking or attached **adherence** *n*

adhesion *n* **1** the quality or condition of sticking together **2** *pathol* the joining together of two structures or parts of the body that are normally separate, for example after surgery
≡ **USAGE**
≡ *Adhesion* is preferred when talking ≡ about sticking or holding fast in a ≡ physical sense. *Adherence* is preferred ≡ when talking about attachment to a ≡ political party, cause, etc.

adhesive *n* **1** a substance used for sticking things together ▷ *adj* **2** able or designed to stick to things

ad hoc *adj, adv* for a particular purpose only
WORD ORIGIN Latin: to this

adieu (a-**dew**) *interj, n, pl* **adieux** *or* **adieus** (a-**dewz**) goodbye
WORD ORIGIN French

ad infinitum *adv* endlessly: *we would not be able to sustain the currency ad infinitum*
WORD ORIGIN Latin

adipose *adj* of or containing fat; fatty: *adipose tissue*
WORD ORIGIN Latin *adeps* fat

adj. adjective

adjacent *adj* **1** near or next: *the schools were adjacent but there were separate doors* **2** *geom* (of a side of a right-angled triangle) lying between a specified angle and the right angle
WORD ORIGIN Latin *ad-* near + *jacere* to lie

adjective *n* a word that adds information about a noun or pronoun **adjectival** *adj*
WORD ORIGIN Latin *nomen adjectivum* attributive noun

adjoin *vb* to be next to and joined onto **adjoining** *adj*

adjourn *vb* **1** to close a court at the end of a session **2** to postpone or be postponed temporarily **3** *informal* to go elsewhere: *can we adjourn to the dining room?* **adjournment** *n*
WORD ORIGIN Old French *ajourner* to defer to an arranged day

adjudge *vb* **-judging, -judged** to declare someone to be something specified: *my wife was adjudged to be the guilty party*

adjudicate *vb* **-cating, -cated** **1** to give a formal decision on a dispute **2** to serve as a judge, for example in a competition **adjudication** *n* **adjudicator** *n*
WORD ORIGIN Latin *adjudicare*

adjunct *n* **1** something added that is not essential **2** a person who is subordinate to another
WORD ORIGIN Latin *adjunctus* adjoined

adjure *vb* **-juring, -jured** **1** to command someone to do something **2** to appeal earnestly to someone **adjuration** *n*
WORD ORIGIN Latin *adjurare*

adjust *vb* **1** to adapt to a new environment **2** to alter slightly, so as to be accurate or suitable **3** *insurance* to determine the amount payable in settlement of a claim **adjustable** *adj* **adjuster** *n*
WORD ORIGIN Old French *adjuster*

adjustment *n* **1** a slight alteration **2** the act of adjusting

adjutant (**aj**-oo-tant) *n* an officer in an army who acts as administrative assistant to a superior
WORD ORIGIN Latin *adjutare* to aid

ad-lib *vb* **-libbing, -libbed** **1** to improvise a speech or piece of music without preparation ▷ *adj* **2** improvised: *ad-lib studio chat* ▷ *n* **3** an improvised remark ▷ *adv* **ad lib** **4** spontaneously or freely
WORD ORIGIN short for Latin *ad libitum*, literally: according to pleasure

Adm. *Brit* Admiral

adman *n, pl* **-men** *informal* a man who works in advertising

admin *n* *informal* administration

administer *vb* **1** to manage (an organization or estate) **2** to organize and put into practice: *anyone can learn to administer the test procedure* **3** to give medicine to someone **4** to supervise the taking of (an oath)
WORD ORIGIN Latin *administrare*

administrate *vb* **-trating, -trated** to manage an organization

administration *n* **1** management of the affairs of an organization **2** the people who administer an organization **3** a government: *the first non-communist administration in the country's history* **4** the

Words from Literature
part 1

accoucheur *n* a male midwife or doctor
> I think my sister must have had some general idea
> that I was a young offender whom an Accoucheur
> Policeman had taken up (on my birthday) and
> delivered over to her
> *Great Expectations* Charles Dickens

addled *adj* confused and unable to think properly
> But she counted and counted till she got that addled
> *The Adventures of Huckleberry Finn* Mark Twain

admiration *n* amazement or wonder
> lifting up his hands and eyes by way of admiration
> *Gulliver's Travels* Jonathan Swift

afeard *adj* afraid
> shake it – and don't be afeard
> *The Adventures of Huckleberry Finn* Mark Twain

affect *v* to follow
> Hadst thou affected sweet divinity
> *Doctor Faustus* 5.2 Christopher Marlowe

aground *adv* when a boat runs aground, it touches the
ground in a shallow part of the water and gets stuck
> what kep' you? – boat get aground?
> *The Adventures of Huckleberry Finn* Mark Twain

ague *n* a fever in which the patient has alternate hot
and cold shivering fits
> his exposure to the wet and cold had brought on
> fever and ague
> *Oliver Twist* Charles Dickens

alchemy *adj* false or worthless
> all wealth alchemy
> *The Sun Rising* John Donne

all alike *phrase* the same all the time
> Love, all alike
> *The Sun Rising* John Donne

alow and aloft *phrase* alow means in the lower part or
bottom, and aloft means on the top, so alow and aloft
means on the top and in the bottom or throughout
> Someone's turned the chest out alow and aloft
> *Treasure Island* Robert Louis Stevenson

ambuscade *n* ambuscade is not a proper word
> Tom means an ambush, which is when a group
> of people attack their enemies, after hiding and
> waiting for them and so we would lie in
> ambuscade, as he called it
> *The Adventures of Huckleberry Finn* Mark Twain

amiable *adj* likeable or pleasant
> Such amiable qualities must speak for themselves
> *Pride and Prejudice* Jane Austen

amulet *n* a charm thought to drive away evil spirits.
> uttered phrases at once occult and familiar,
> like the amulet worn on the heart
> *Silas Marner* George Eliot

amusement *n* a strange and disturbing puzzle
> this was an amusement the other way
> *Robinson Crusoe* Daniel Defoe

ancient *n* an ancient was the flag displayed on a ship
to show which country it belongs to. It is also called
the ensign
> her ancient and pendants out
> *Robinson Crusoe* Daniel Defoe

antic *adj* horrible or grotesque
> armed and dressed after a very antic manner
> *Gulliver's Travels* Jonathan Swift

antics *n* an old word meaning clowns, or people who
do silly things to make other people laugh
> And point like antics at his triple crown
> *Doctor Faustus* 3.2 Christopher Marlowe

appanage *n* a living allowance
> As if loveliness were not the special prerogative
> of woman – her legitimate appanage and heritage!
> *Jane Eyre* Charlotte Brontë

append *verb* to attach or add to
> and these words appended
> *Treasure Island* Robert Louis Stevenson

act of administering something, such as medicine or an oath **administrative** adj

administrator n a person who administers an organization or estate

admirable (ad-mer-a-bl) adj deserving or inspiring admiration: *the boldness of the undertaking is admirable* **admirably** adv

admiral n **1** Also called: **admiral of the fleet** a naval officer of the highest rank **2** any of various brightly coloured butterflies **WORD ORIGIN** Arabic *amīr-al* commander of

Admiralty n Brit the former government department in charge of the Royal Navy

admire vb **-miring, -mired** to respect and approve of (a person or thing) **admiration** n **admirer** n **admiring** adj **admiringly** adv **WORD ORIGIN** Latin *admirari* to wonder at

admissible adj law allowed to be brought as evidence in court

admission n **1** permission or the right to enter **2** permission to join an organization **3** the price charged for entrance **4** a confession: *she was, by her own admission, not educated*

admit vb **-mitting, -mitted 1** to confess or acknowledge (a crime or mistake) **2** to concede (the truth of something) **3** to allow (someone) to enter **4** to take (someone) in to a hospital for treatment: *he was admitted for tests* **5 admit to** to allow someone to participate in something **6 admit of** to allow for: *these rules admit of no violation* **WORD ORIGIN** Latin *admittere*

admittance n **1** the right to enter **2** the act of entering a place

admittedly adv it must be agreed: *my research is admittedly incomplete*

admixture n **1** a mixture **2** an ingredient

admonish vb to reprimand sternly **admonition** n **admonitory** adj **WORD ORIGIN** Latin *admonere*

ad nauseam (ad **naw**-zee-am) adv to a boring or sickening extent: *she went on and on ad nauseam about her divorce* **WORD ORIGIN** Latin: to (the point of) nausea

ado n fuss: *without further ado* **WORD ORIGIN** Middle English *at do* a to-do

adobe (ad-**oh**-bee) n **1** a sun-dried brick **2** the claylike material from which such bricks are made **3** a building made of such bricks **WORD ORIGIN** Spanish

adolescence n the period between puberty and adulthood **WORD ORIGIN** Latin *adolescere* to grow up

adolescent adj **1** of or relating to adolescence **2** informal (of behaviour) immature ▷ n **3** an adolescent person

Adonis n a handsome young man **WORD ORIGIN** name of a handsome youth in Greek myth

adopt vb **1** law to take someone else's child as one's own **2** to choose (a plan or method) **3** to choose (a country or name) to be one's own **adoptee** n **adoption** n **WORD ORIGIN** Latin *adoptare*

adoptive adj **1** acquired or related by adoption: *an adoptive father* **2** of or relating to adoption

adorable adj very attractive; lovable

adore vb **adoring, adored 1** to love intensely or deeply **2** informal to like very much: *I adore being in the country* **3** to worship a god with religious rites **adoration** n **adoring** adj **adoringly** adv **WORD ORIGIN** Latin *adorare*

adorn vb to decorate; increase the beauty of **adornment** n **WORD ORIGIN** Latin *adornare*

ADP automatic data processing

adrenal (ad-**reen**-al) adj anat **1** on or near the kidneys **2** of or relating to the adrenal glands **WORD ORIGIN** Latin *ad-* near + *renes* kidneys

adrenal glands pl n anat two endocrine glands covering the upper surface of the kidneys

adrenalin or **adrenaline** n biochem a hormone secreted by the adrenal gland in response to stress. It increases heart rate, pulse rate, and blood pressure

adrift adj, adv **1** drifting **2** without a clear purpose **3** informal off course, wrong: *it was obvious that something had gone adrift*

adroit adj quick and skilful in how one behaves or thinks **adroitly** adv **adroitness** n **WORD ORIGIN** French *à droit* rightly

adsorb vb (of a gas or vapour) to condense and form a thin film on a surface **adsorbent** adj **adsorption** n **WORD ORIGIN** Latin *ad-* to + *sorbere* to drink in

ADT Atlantic Daylight Time

adulation n uncritical admiration **WORD ORIGIN** Latin *adulari* to flatter

adult n **1** a mature fully grown person, animal, or plant ▷ adj **2** having reached maturity; fully developed **3** suitable for or typical of adult people: *she had very adult features* **4** sexually explicit: *adult films* **adulthood** n **WORD ORIGIN** Latin *adultus* grown up

adulterate vb **-ating, -ated** to spoil something by adding inferior material **adulteration** n **WORD ORIGIN** Latin *adulterare*

adulterer or fem **adulteress** n a person who has committed adultery

adultery n, pl **-teries** sexual unfaithfulness of a husband or wife **adulterous** adj **WORD ORIGIN** Latin *adulterium*

adv. adverb

advance vb **-vancing, -vanced 1** to go or bring forward **2** to make progress: *this student has advanced in reading and writing* **3** to further a cause: *an association founded to advance the interests of ex-soldiers* **4 advance on** to move towards someone in a threatening manner **5** to present an idea for consideration **6** to lend a sum of money ▷ n **7** a forward movement **8** improvement or progress: *the greatest advance in modern medicine* **9** a loan of money **10** a payment made before it is legally due **11** an increase in price: *any advance on fifty pounds?* **12 in advance** beforehand: *you have to pay in*

advance **13 in advance of** ahead of in time or development ▷ adj **14** done or happening before an event: *advance warning* ▶ See also **advances** **WORD ORIGIN** Latin *abante* from before

advanced adj **1** at a late stage in development **2** not elementary: *he was taking the advanced class in economics*

Advanced level n Brit a formal name for **A level**

advancement n promotion in rank or status

advances pl n approaches made to a person with the hope of starting a romantic or sexual relationship

advantage n **1** a more favourable position or state **2** benefit or profit: *they could make this work to their advantage* **3** tennis the point scored after deuce **4 take advantage of a** to use a person unfairly **b** to use an opportunity **5 to advantage** to good effect: *her hair was shaped to display to advantage her superb neck* **WORD ORIGIN** Latin *abante* from before

advantaged adj in a superior social or financial position

advantageous adj likely to bring benefits **advantageously** adv

advection n physics the transferring of heat in a horizontal stream of gas **WORD ORIGIN** Latin *ad-* to + *vehere* to carry

advent n an arrival: *the advent of the personal computer* **WORD ORIGIN** Latin *ad-* to + *venire* to come

Advent n the season that includes the four Sundays before Christmas

Adventist n a member of a Christian group that believes in the imminent return of Christ

adventitious adj added or appearing accidentally **WORD ORIGIN** Latin *adventicius* coming from outside

adventure n **1** a risky undertaking, the ending of which is uncertain: *our African adventure* **2** exciting or unexpected events **WORD ORIGIN** Latin *advenire* to happen to (someone), arrive

adventure playground n Brit, Austral, & NZ a playground for children that contains building materials and other equipment to build with or climb on

adventurer or fem **adventuress** n **1** a person who seeks money or power by unscrupulous means **2** a person who seeks adventure

adventurism n recklessness in politics or finance

adventurous adj daring or enterprising

adverb n a word that modifies a sentence, verb, adverb, or adjective, for example easily, very, and happily in They could easily envy the very happily married couple **adverbial** adj **WORD ORIGIN** Latin *adverbium*, literally: added word

adversary (**ad**-verse-er-ree) n, pl **-saries** an opponent in a fight, disagreement, or sporting contest **WORD ORIGIN** Latin *adversus* against

adverse adj **1** unfavourable to one's interests: *adverse effects* **2** antagonistic or hostile **adversely** adv **WORD ORIGIN** Latin *ad-* towards + *vertere* to turn

adversity *n, pl* **-ties** very difficult or hard circumstances

advert *n informal* an advertisement

advertise *vb* **-tising, -tised 1** to present or praise (goods or a service) to the public, in order to encourage sales **2** to make (a vacancy, an event, or an article for sale) publicly known **advertiser** *n* **advertising** *n*
WORD ORIGIN Latin *advertere* to turn one's attention to

advertisement *n* any public announcement designed to sell goods or publicize an event

advice *n* **1** recommendation as to an appropriate choice of action **2** formal notification of facts
WORD ORIGIN Latin *ad* to + *visum* view

advisable *adj* sensible and likely to achieve the desired result **advisability** *n*

advise *vb* **-vising, -vised 1** to offer advice to **2** to inform or notify **adviser** *or* **advisor** *n*
WORD ORIGIN Latin *ad-* to + *videre* to see

advised *adj* thought-out: *ill-advised*

advisedly (ad-**vize**-id-lee) *adv* deliberately; after careful consideration: *I use the word advisedly*

advisory *adj* **1** able to offer advice ▷ *n, pl* **-ries 2** a statement giving advice or a warning **3** a person or organization that gives advice: *the Prime Minister's media advisory*

advocaat *n* a liqueur with a raw egg base
WORD ORIGIN Dutch

advocacy *n* active support of a cause or course of action

advocate *vb* **-cating, -cated 1** to recommend a course of action publicly ▷ *n* **2** a person who upholds or defends a cause or course of action **3** a person who speaks on behalf of another in a court of law **4** *Scots Law* a barrister
WORD ORIGIN Latin *advocare* to call, summon

adware *n computers* **1** software that collects information about a user's browsing patterns in order to display relevant advertisements **2** software that is produced with advertisements embedded within it

adze *or US* **adz** *n* a tool with a blade at right angles to the handle, used for shaping timber
WORD ORIGIN Old English *adesa*

AEA Atomic Energy Authority

AEC *US* Atomic Energy Commission

AEEU (in Britain) Amalgamated Engineering and Electrical Union

aegis (**ee**-jiss) *n* **under the aegis of** with the sponsorship or protection of
WORD ORIGIN Greek *aigis* shield of Zeus

aeolian harp (ee-**oh**-lee-an) *n* a musical instrument that produces sounds when the wind passes over its strings
WORD ORIGIN after *Aeolus,* god of winds in Greek myth

aeon *or US* **eon** (**ee**-on) *n* **1** an immeasurably long period of time **2** the longest division of geological time
WORD ORIGIN Greek *aiōn*

aerate *vb* **-ating, -ated** to put gas into a liquid, for example when making a fizzy drink **aeration** *n*

aerial *n* **1** the metal pole or wire on a television or radio which transmits or receives signals ▷ *adj* **2** in, from, or operating in the air **3** extending high into the air **4** of or relating to aircraft
WORD ORIGIN Greek *aēr* air

aerial top dressing *n* NZ spreading of fertilizer from an aeroplane onto remote areas

aero-, aeri- *or* **aer-** *combining form* **1** relating to aircraft **2** relating to air, atmosphere, or gas
WORD ORIGIN Greek *aēr* air

aerobatics *n* spectacular manoeuvres, such as loops or rolls, performed by aircraft
WORD ORIGIN AERO- + (ACRO)BATICS

aerobe *n biol* an organism that requires oxygen to survive
WORD ORIGIN Greek *aēr* air + *bios* life

aerobic *adj* designed for or relating to aerobics: *aerobic exercise*

aerobics *n* exercises to increase the amount of oxygen in the blood and strengthen the heart and lungs

aerodrome *n* a small airport

aerodynamics *n* the study of how air flows around moving objects **aerodynamic** *adj* **aerodynamicist** *n*

aero engine *n* an engine for an aircraft

aerofoil *n* a part of an aircraft, such as the wing, designed to give lift in flight

aerogram *n* an air-mail letter on a single sheet of light paper that seals to form an envelope

aeronautics *n* the study or practice of flight through the air **aeronautical** *adj*

aeroplane *or US & Canad* **airplane** *n* a heavier-than-air powered flying vehicle with fixed wings
WORD ORIGIN AERO- + Greek *planos* wandering

aerosol *n* a small metal pressurized can from which a substance can be dispensed in a fine spray
WORD ORIGIN AERO- + SOL(UTION)

aerospace *n* **1** the earth's atmosphere and space beyond ▷ *adj* **2** of rockets or space vehicles: *the aerospace industry*

aesthete *or US* **esthete** (**eess**-theet) *n* a person who has or who pretends to have a highly developed appreciation of beauty

aesthetic *or US* **esthetic** (iss-**thet**-ik) *adj* **1** relating to the appreciation of art and beauty ▷ *n* **2** a principle or set of principles relating to the appreciation of art and beauty **aesthetically** *or US* **esthetically** *adv* **aestheticism** *or US* **estheticism** *n*
WORD ORIGIN Greek *aisthanomai* to perceive, feel

aesthetics *or US* **esthetics** *n* **1** the branch of philosophy concerned with the study of the concepts of beauty and taste **2** the study of the rules and principles of art

aether *n* same as **ether** (senses 2, 3)

aetiology (ee-tee-**ol**-a-jee) *n* same as **etiology**

a.f. audio frequency

afar *n* **from afar** from or at a great distance

affable *adj* showing warmth and friendliness **affability** *n* **affably** *adv*
WORD ORIGIN Latin *affabilis*

affair *n* **1** an event or happening: *the Irangate affair* **2** a sexual relationship outside marriage **3** a thing to be done or attended to: *my wife's career is her own affair* **4** something previously specified: *lunch was a subdued affair*
WORD ORIGIN Old French *à faire* to do

affairs *pl n* **1** personal or business interests **2** matters of public interest: *foreign affairs*

affect¹ *vb* **1** to influence (someone or something): *the very difficult conditions continued to affect our performance* **2** (of pain or disease) to attack: *the virus can spread to affect the heart muscle* **3** to move someone emotionally: *the experience has affected him deeply*
WORD ORIGIN Latin *afficere*

affect² *vb* **1** to put on a show of: *he affects a certain disinterest* **2** to wear or use by preference: *he likes to be called Captain John and affects a nautical cap*
WORD ORIGIN Latin *affectare* to strive after

affectation *n* an attitude or manner put on to impress others

affected *adj* **1** behaving or speaking in a manner put on to impress others **2** pretended: *an affected indifference*

affecting *adj* arousing feelings of pity; moving

affection *n* **1** fondness or tenderness for a person or thing **2 affections** feelings of love; emotions: *I was angry with her for playing with their affections*

affectionate *adj* having or displaying tenderness, affection, or warmth **affectionately** *adv*

affectless *adj* **1** showing no emotion or concern for others **2** not causing any emotion: *an affectless novel*

affianced (af-**fie**-anst) *adj* old-fashioned engaged to be married
WORD ORIGIN Medieval Latin *affidare* to trust (oneself) to

affidavit (af-fid-**dave**-it) *n law* a written statement made under oath
WORD ORIGIN Medieval Latin, literally: he declares on oath

affiliate *vb* **-ating, -ated 1** (of a group) to link up with a larger group ▷ *n* **2** a person or organization that is affiliated with another **affiliation** *n*
WORD ORIGIN Medieval Latin *affiliatus* adopted as a son

affinity *n, pl* **-ties 1** a feeling of closeness to and understanding of a person **2** a close similarity in appearance, structure, or quality **3** a chemical attraction
WORD ORIGIN Latin *affinis* bordering on, related

affirm *vb* **1** to declare to be true **2** to state clearly one's support for (an idea or belief) **affirmation** *n*
WORD ORIGIN Latin *ad-* to + *firmare* to make firm

affirmative *adj* **1** indicating agreement: *an affirmative answer* ▷ *n* **2** a word or phrase indicating agreement, such as *yes*

affix *vb* **1** to attach or fasten ▷ *n* **2** a word or syllable added to a word to produce a

derived or inflected form, such as *-ment* in *establishment*
WORD ORIGIN Medieval Latin *affixare*

afflict *vb* to cause someone suffering or unhappiness
WORD ORIGIN Latin *affligere* to knock against

affliction *n* **1** something that causes physical or mental suffering **2** a condition of great distress or suffering

affluent *adj* having plenty of money
affluence *n*
WORD ORIGIN Latin *ad-* to + *fluere* to flow

affluent society *n* a society in which the material benefits of prosperity are widely available

afford *vb* **1 can afford** to be able to do or spare something without risking financial difficulties or undesirable consequences: *she can't afford to be choosy* **2** to give or supply: *afford me an opportunity to judge for myself* **affordable** *adj* **affordability** *n*
WORD ORIGIN Old English *geforthian* to further, promote

afforest *vb* to plant trees on
afforestation *n*
WORD ORIGIN Medieval Latin *afforestare*

affray *n Brit, Austral, & NZ* a noisy fight in a public place
WORD ORIGIN Vulgar Latin *exfridare* (unattested) to break the peace

affront *n* **1** a deliberate insult ▷ *vb* **2** to hurt someone's pride or dignity
WORD ORIGIN Old French *afronter* to strike in the face

afghan *n NZ* a type of biscuit

Afghan *adj* **1** of Afghanistan ▷ *n* **2** a person from Afghanistan **3** the language of Afghanistan

Afghan hound *n* a large slim dog with long silky hair

aficionado (af-fish-yo-**nah**-do) *n, pl* **-dos** an enthusiastic fan of a sport or interest
WORD ORIGIN Spanish

afield *adv* **far afield** far away: *they used to travel as far afield as Hungary*

aflame *adv, adj* **1** in flames **2** deeply aroused: *his face was aflame with self-contempt and embarrassment*

afloat *adj* **1** floating **2** free of debt: *his goal is to keep the company afloat* **3** aboard ship ▷ *adv* **4** floating **5** free of debt **6** aboard ship; at sea

afoot *adj, adv* happening; in operation: *I had no suspicion of what was afoot*

afore *adv, prep, conj old-fashioned or dialect* before

aforementioned *adj* mentioned before

aforesaid *adj* referred to previously

aforethought *adj* premeditated: *malice aforethought*

a fortiori (**eh** for-tee-**or**-rye) *adv* for similar but more convincing reasons
WORD ORIGIN Latin

afraid *adj* **1** feeling fear or apprehension **2** regretful: *I'm afraid I lost my temper*
WORD ORIGIN Middle English *affraied*

afresh *adv* once more

African *adj* **1** of Africa ▷ *n* **2** a person from Africa

Africana *pl n* objects of cultural or historical interest from Africa

African-American *n* **1** an American of African descent ▷ *adj* **2** of African-Americans, their history, or their culture

Africander *n* a breed of humpbacked cattle originally from southern Africa
WORD ORIGIN Afrikaans *Afrikander*

African time *n S African slang* unpunctuality

African violet *n* a flowering house plant with pink or purple flowers and hairy leaves

Afrikaans *n* one of the official languages of South Africa, descended from Dutch
WORD ORIGIN Dutch

Afrikaner *n* a White South African whose native language is Afrikaans

Afro *n, pl* **-ros** a frizzy bushy hairstyle

Afro- *combining form* indicating Africa or African: *Afro-Caribbean*

Afro-American *n, adj* same as **African-American**

aft *adv, adj* at or towards the rear of a ship or aircraft
WORD ORIGIN shortened from ABAFT

after *prep* **1** following in time or place **2** in pursuit of: *he was after my mother's jewellery* **3** concerning: *he asked after Laura* **4** considering: *you seem all right after what happened last night* **5** next in excellence or importance to **6** in imitation of; in the manner of **7** in accordance with: *a man after his own heart* **8** with the same name as: *the street is named after the designer of the church* **9** *US* past (the hour of): *fifteen after twelve* **10 after all a** in spite of everything: *I was, after all, a suspect* **b** in spite of expectations or efforts **11 after you** please go before me ▷ *adv* **12** at a later time; afterwards ▷ *conj* **13** at a time later than the time when: *she arrived after the reading had begun* ▷ *adj* **14** *naut* further aft: *the after cabin*
WORD ORIGIN Old English *æfter*

afterbirth *n* the placenta and fetal membranes expelled from the mother's womb after childbirth

aftercare *n* **1** the help and support given to a person discharged from a hospital or prison **2** the regular care required to keep something in good condition

afterdamp *n* a poisonous gas formed after the explosion of firedamp in a coal mine

aftereffect *n* any result occurring some time after its cause

afterglow *n* **1** the glow left after the source of a light has disappeared, for example after sunset **2** a pleasant feeling remaining after an enjoyable experience

afterlife *n* life after death

aftermath *n* effects or results of an event considered collectively: *the aftermath of the weekend violence*
WORD ORIGIN *after* + Old English *mæth* a mowing

afternoon *n* the period between noon and evening

afterpains *pl n* pains caused by contraction of a woman's womb after childbirth

afters *n informal* the sweet course of a meal

aftersales *n* any customer service that follows the sale of a product
after-sales *adj*

aftershave *n* a scented lotion applied to a man's face after shaving

aftershock *n* one of a series of minor tremors occurring after the main shock of an earthquake

aftertaste *n* a taste that lingers on after eating or drinking

afterthought *n* **1** something thought of after the opportunity to use it has passed **2** an addition to something already completed

afterwards *or* **afterward** *adv* later
WORD ORIGIN Old English *æfterweard*

Ag *chem* silver
WORD ORIGIN Latin *argentum*

again *adv* **1** another or a second time: *I want to look at that atlas again* **2** once more in a previously experienced state or condition: *he pictured her again as she used to be* **3** in addition to the original amount: *twice as much again* **4** on the other hand **5** moreover or furthermore: *she is beautiful and, again, intelligent* **6 again and again** continually or repeatedly
WORD ORIGIN Old English *ongegn* opposite to

against *prep* **1** standing or leaning beside: *he leaned against a tree* **2** opposed to or in disagreement with **3** in contrast to: *his complexion was a sickly white against the black stubble of his beard* **4** coming in contact with: *rain rattled against the window* **5** having an unfavourable effect on: *the system works against you when you don't have money* **6** as a protection from: *a safeguard against bacteria* **7** in exchange for or in return for: *the dollar has gained very slightly against the yen* **8 as against** as opposed to; as compared with
WORD ORIGIN Middle English *ageines*

agape *adj* **1** (of the mouth) wide open **2** (of a person) very surprised

agar (**ayg**-ar) *or* **agar-agar** *n* a jelly-like substance obtained from seaweed and used as a thickener in food
WORD ORIGIN Malay

agaric *n* any fungus with gills on the underside of the cap, such as a mushroom
WORD ORIGIN Greek *agarikon*

agate (**ag**-git) *n* a hard semiprecious form of quartz with striped colouring
WORD ORIGIN Greek *akhatēs*

agave (a-**gave**-vee) *n* a tropical American plant with tall flower stalks and thick leaves
WORD ORIGIN Greek *agauos* illustrious

age *n* **1** the length of time that a person or thing has existed **2** a period or state of human life **3** the latter part of human life **4** a period of history marked by some feature **5 ages** *informal* a long time **6 come of age** to become legally responsible for one's actions (usually at 18 years) ▷ *vb* **ageing** *or* **aging, aged 7** to become old: *skin type changes as one ages* **8** to appear or cause to appear older: *the years had not aged her in any way*
WORD ORIGIN Latin *aetas*

Words from Shakespeare
part 1

abate *v* to lessen or diminish
There lives within the very flame of love
A kind of wick or snuff that will abate it
Hamlet 4.7

abate *v* to shorten
Abate thy hours *A Midsummer Night's Dream* 3.2

abate *v* to deprive
She hath abated me of half my train *King Lear* 2.4

abjure *v* to renounce or give up
This rough magic I here abjure *The Tempest* 5.1

abroad *adv* elsewhere or everywhere
You have heard of the news abroad *King Lear* 2.1

abrogate *v* to put an end to
so it shall praise you to abrogate scurrility
Love's Labours Lost 4.2

abuse *n* deception or fraud
What should this mean? Are all the rest come
back?
Or is it some abuse, and no such thing? *Hamlet* 4.7

abuse *n* insult or offence
I will be deaf to pleading and excuses
Nor tears nor prayers shall purchase our abuses
Romeo and Juliet 3.1

abuser *n* someone who betrays, a betrayer
I ... do attach thee
For an abuser of the world *Othello* 1.2

accent *n* language
In states unborn, and accents yet unknown
Julius Caesar 3.1

accident *n* an event or something that happened
think no more of this night's accidents
A Midsummer Night's Dream 4.1

accommodate *v* to equip or to give someone the
equipment to do something
The safer sense will ne'er accommodate
His master thus. *King Lear* 4.6

according *adj* sympathetic or ready to agree within
the scope of choice
Lies my consent and fair according voice
Romeo and Juliet 1.2

account *n* judgement (by God) or reckoning
No reckoning made, but sent to my account
With all my imperfections on my head
Hamlet 1.5

accountant *adj* answerable or accountable
his offence is ...
Accountant to the law *Measure for Measure* 2.4

ace *n* one or first. It refers to the lowest score on a dice
No die, but an ace, for him; for he is but one.
Less than an ace, man; for he is dead; he is
nothing. *A Midsummer Night's Dream* 5.1

acquit *v* to be rid of or free of. It is related to the
verb *quit*
I am glad I am so acquit of this tinderbox
The Merry Wives of Windsor 1.3

afeard *adj* afraid or frightened
Nothing afeard of what thyself didst make
Macbeth 1.3

affiance *n* confidence or trust
O how hast thou with jealousy infected
The sweetness of affiance *Henry V* 2.2

affinity *n* important connections, or relationships
with important people
The Moor replies
That he you hurt is of great fame in Cyprus,
And great affinity *Othello* 3.1

agnize *v* to recognize or acknowledge something
I do agnize
A natural and prompt alacrity I find in hardness
Othello 1.3

ague *n* a fever in which the patient has hot and cold
shivers one after the other
This is some monster of the isle with four legs,
who hath got ... an ague *The Tempest* 2.2

aged *adj* 1 (**ay**-jid) advanced in years; old 2 (rhymes with **raged**) being at the age of: *a girl aged thirteen is missing*

ageing or **aging** *n* 1 the fact or process of growing old ▷ *adj* 2 becoming or appearing older

ageism or **agism** *n* discrimination against people on the grounds of age **ageist** or **agist** *n*

ageless *adj* 1 apparently never growing old 2 seeming to have existed for ever; eternal: *an ageless profession*

agency *n, pl* **-cies** 1 an organization providing a specific service: *an advertising agency* 2 the business or functions of an agent 3 action or power by which something happens: *the intervention of a human agency in the sequence of events* **WORD ORIGIN** Latin *agere* to do

agenda *n* 1 a schedule or list of items to be attended to, for example at a meeting 2 *US & Canad* an appointment diary with room for storing addresses, telephone numbers, etc. **WORD ORIGIN** Latin: things to be done

agent *n* 1 a person who arranges business for other people, esp. for actors or singers 2 a spy 3 a substance which causes change in other substances: *an emulsifying agent* 4 someone or something which causes an effect: *the agent of change*

agent noun *n* a noun representing a person or thing performing the action of a verb: *performer, suspender*

agent provocateur (azh-on prov-vok-at-**tur**) *n, pl* **agents provocateurs** (azh-on prov-vok-at-**tur**) a person employed by the authorities to tempt people to commit illegal acts and so be discredited or punished **WORD ORIGIN** French

age-old *adj* very old; ancient

agglomerate *vb* **-ating, -ated** 1 to form or be formed into a mass ▷ *n* 2 a volcanic rock consisting of fused angular fragments of rock **WORD ORIGIN** Latin *agglomerare*

agglomeration *n* a confused mass or cluster

agglutinate *vb* **-nating, -nated** to stick as if with glue **agglutination** *n* **WORD ORIGIN** Latin *agglutinare*

aggrandize or **-dise** *vb* **-dizing, -dized** or **-dising, -dised** to make greater in size, power, or rank **aggrandizement** or **-disement** *n* **WORD ORIGIN** Old French *aggrandir*

aggravate *vb* **-vating, -vated** 1 to make (a disease, situation, or problem) worse 2 *informal* to annoy **aggravating** *adj* **aggravation** *n* **WORD ORIGIN** Latin *aggravare* to make heavier

aggravated *adj law* (of a criminal offence) made more serious by its circumstances

aggregate *n* 1 an amount or total formed from separate units 2 *geol* a rock, such as granite, consisting of a mixture of minerals 3 the sand and stone mixed with cement and water to make concrete ▷ *adj* 4 formed of separate units collected into a whole ▷ *vb* **-gating, -gated** 5 to combine or be combined into a whole 6 to amount to (a particular number) **aggregation** *n* **WORD ORIGIN** Latin *aggregare* to add to a flock or herd

aggression *n* 1 violent and hostile behaviour 2 an unprovoked attack **aggressor** *n* **WORD ORIGIN** Latin *aggredi* to attack

aggressive *adj* 1 full of anger or hostility 2 forceful or determined: *an aggressive salesman* **aggressively** *adv* **aggressiveness** *n*

aggrieved *adj* upset and angry **WORD ORIGIN** Latin *aggravare* to aggravate

aggro *n Brit, Austral, & NZ slang* aggressive behaviour **WORD ORIGIN** from *aggravation*

aghast *adj* overcome with amazement or horror **WORD ORIGIN** Old English *gæstan* to frighten

agile *adj* 1 quick in movement; nimble 2 mentally quick or acute **agility** *n* **WORD ORIGIN** Latin *agilis*

agin *prep dialect* against or opposed to: *he gave the usual line of talk agin the government* **WORD ORIGIN** obsolete *again* against

agitate *vb* **-tating, -tated** 1 to excite, disturb, or trouble 2 to shake or stir (a liquid) 3 to attempt to stir up public opinion for or against something **agitated** *adj* **agitatedly** *adv* **agitation** *n* **agitator** *n* **WORD ORIGIN** Latin *agitare*

agitprop *n* political agitation and propaganda **WORD ORIGIN** Russian *Agitpropbyuro*

aglitter *adj* sparkling or glittering

aglow *adj* glowing

aglu or **agloo** *n Canad* a breathing hole made in ice by a seal **WORD ORIGIN** Inuit

AGM annual general meeting

agnostic *n* 1 a person who believes that it is impossible to know whether God exists 2 a person who claims that the answer to some specific question cannot be known with certainty ▷ *adj* 3 of or relating to agnostics **agnosticism** *n* **WORD ORIGIN** A- + *gnostic* having knowledge

ago *adv* in the past: *fifty years ago* **WORD ORIGIN** Old English *āgān* to pass away

USAGE

The use of *ago* with *since* (*it's ten years ago since he wrote the novel*) is redundant and should be avoided: *it is ten years since he wrote the novel*.

agog *adj* eager or curious: *Marcia would be agog to hear his news* **WORD ORIGIN** Old French *en gogues* in merriments

agonize or **-nise** *vb* **-nizing, -nized** or **-nising, -nised** 1 to worry greatly 2 to suffer agony **agonizing** or **-nising** *adj* **agonizingly** or **-nisingly** *adv*

agony *n, pl* **-nies** acute physical or mental pain **WORD ORIGIN** Greek *agōnia* struggle

agony aunt *n* a person who replies to readers' letters in an agony column

agony column *n* a newspaper or magazine feature offering advice on readers' personal problems

agoraphobia *n* a pathological fear of being in public places **agoraphobic** *adj, n* **WORD ORIGIN** Greek *agora* marketplace + *phobos* fear

AGR advanced gas-cooled reactor

agrarian *adj* of or relating to land or agriculture **agrarianism** *n* **WORD ORIGIN** Latin *ager* field

agree *vb* **agreeing, agreed** 1 to be of the same opinion 2 to give assent; consent 3 to be consistent 4 **agree on** to reach a joint decision about: *the ministers agreed on a strategy* 5 **agree with** to be agreeable or suitable to (one's health or appearance): *marriage and motherhood must agree with you* 6 to concede: *the unions have agreed that the results of appraisal are relevant* 7 *grammar* to be the same in number, gender, and case as a connected word **WORD ORIGIN** Old French *a gre* at will

agreeable *adj* 1 pleasant and enjoyable 2 prepared to consent: *I cannot say that she was agreeable to the project but she was resigned* **agreeably** *adv*

agreement *n* 1 the act or state of agreeing 2 a legally enforceable contract

agribusiness *n* 1 the use of intensive methods to increase profits in agriculture 2 all of the businesses that process, distribute, and support farm products **WORD ORIGIN** *agri(culture)* + *business*

agriculture *n* the rearing of crops and livestock; farming **agricultural** *adj* **agriculturalist** *n* **WORD ORIGIN** Latin *ager* field + *cultura* cultivation

agrimony *n* a plant with small yellow flowers and bitter-tasting bristly fruits **WORD ORIGIN** Greek *argemōnē* poppy

agrochemical *n* a chemical used in agriculture

agrodolce (ag-gro-**dole**-chay) *n* an Italian sweet-and-sour sauce **WORD ORIGIN** Italian

agronomy (ag-**ron**-om-mee) *n* the science of land cultivation, soil management, and crop production **agronomist** *n* **WORD ORIGIN** Greek *agros* field + *nemein* to manage

aground *adv* onto the bottom of shallow water: *they felt a jolt as the ship ran aground*

ague (**aig**-yew) *n* 1 old-fashioned malarial fever with shivering 2 a fit of shivering **WORD ORIGIN** Old French (*fievre*) *ague* acute fever

ah *interj* an exclamation expressing pleasure, pain, sympathy, etc.

aha *interj* an exclamation expressing triumph, surprise, etc.

ahead *adv* 1 at or in the front; before 2 forwards: *go straight ahead* 3 **get ahead** to achieve success: *I was young and hungry to get ahead* ▷ *adj* 4 in a leading position: *he is ahead in the polls*

ahem *interj* a clearing of the throat, used to attract attention or express doubt

ahi *n* another name for **yellowfin tuna** **WORD ORIGIN** Hawaiian

ahoy *interj naut* a shout made to call a ship or to attract attention

AI 1 artificial insemination 2 artificial intelligence

aid *n* **1** money, equipment, or services provided for people in need; assistance **2** a person or device that helps or assists ▷ *vb* **3** to help financially or in other ways **WORD ORIGIN** Latin *adjutare* to help

Aid *or* **-aid** *n combining form* denoting a charitable organization that raises money for a particular cause: *Band Aid*

AID formerly, artificial insemination by donor

aide *n* an assistant: *a senior aide to the Prime Minister*

aide-de-camp (aid-de-**kom**) *n, pl* **aides-de-camp** (aid-de-**kom**) a military officer serving as personal assistant to a senior **WORD ORIGIN** French: camp assistant

AIDS acquired immunodeficiency syndrome: a viral disease that destroys the body's ability to fight infection

AIH artificial insemination by husband

ail *vb literary* **1** to trouble or afflict **2** to feel unwell **WORD ORIGIN** Old English *eglan*

aileron (**ale**-er-on) *n* a hinged flap on the back of an aircraft wing which controls rolling **WORD ORIGIN** French *aile* wing

ailing *adj* unwell or unsuccessful over a long period: *an ailing company*

ailment *n* a slight illness

aim *vb* **1** to point (a weapon or missile) or direct (a blow or remark) at a particular person or object **2** to propose or intend: *they aim to provide full and equal rights to all groups* ▷ *n* **3** the action of directing something at an object **4** intention or purpose **5 take aim** to point a weapon or missile at a person or object **WORD ORIGIN** Latin *aestimare* to estimate

aimless *adj* having no purpose or direction **aimlessly** *adv*

ain't *not standard* am not, is not, are not, have not, *or* has not: *it ain't fair*

air *n* **1** the mixture of gases that forms the earth's atmosphere. It consists chiefly of nitrogen, oxygen, argon, and carbon dioxide **2** the space above and around the earth; sky ▶ Related adjective: **aerial 3** a distinctive quality, appearance, or manner: *I thought he had an air of elegance and celebrity about him* **4** a simple tune **5** transportation in aircraft: *I went off to Italy by air and train* **6 in the air** in circulation; current: *a sense of expectation is in the air* **7 into thin air** leaving no trace behind **8 on the air** in the act of broadcasting on radio or television **9 up in the air** uncertain ▷ *vb* **10** to make known publicly: *these issues will be aired at a ministerial meeting* **11** to expose to air or dry or ventilate **12** (of a television or radio programme) to be broadcast ▶ See also **airs** **WORD ORIGIN** Greek *aēr*

airbag *n* a safety device in a car, consisting of a bag that inflates automatically in an accident to protect the driver or passenger

air base *n* a centre from which military aircraft operate

airborne *adj* **1** carried by air **2** (of aircraft) flying; in the air

air brake *n* a brake in heavy vehicles that is operated by compressed air

airbrush *n* **1** an atomizer which sprays paint by means of compressed air ▷ *vb* **2** to paint using an airbrush **3** to improve the image of (a person or thing) by hiding defects beneath a bland exterior

air chief marshal *n* a very senior officer in an air force

air commodore *n* a senior officer in an air force

air conditioning *n* a system for controlling the temperature and humidity of the air in a building **air-conditioned** *adj* **air conditioner** *n*

aircraft *n, pl* **-craft** any machine capable of flying, such as a glider or aeroplane

aircraft carrier *n* a warship with a long flat deck for the launching and landing of aircraft

aircraftman *n, pl* **-men** a serviceman of the most junior rank in an air force **aircraftwoman** *fem n*

air cushion *n* **1** an inflatable cushion **2** the pocket of air that supports a hovercraft

Airedale *n* a large terrier with rough tan-coloured hair and a black patch covering most of the back

airfield *n* a place where aircraft can land and take off

air force *n* the branch of a nation's armed services that is responsible for air warfare

air gun *n* a gun fired by means of compressed air

airhead *n slang* a person who is stupid or incapable of serious thought

air hostess *n chiefly Brit* a female flight attendant on an airline

airily *adv* in a light-hearted and casual manner

airing *n* **1** exposure to air or warmth for drying or ventilation **2** exposure to public debate: *both these notions got an airing during the campaign*

airing cupboard *n* a heated cupboard in which laundry is aired and kept dry

airless *adj* lacking fresh air; stuffy

air letter *n* same as **aerogram**

airlift *n* **1** the transportation by air of troops or cargo when other routes are blocked ▷ *vb* **2** to transport by an airlift

airline *n* an organization that provides scheduled flights for passengers or cargo

airliner *n* a large passenger aircraft

airlock *n* **1** a bubble of air blocking the flow of liquid in a pipe **2** an airtight chamber between places that do not have the same air pressure, such as in a spacecraft or submarine

airmail *n* **1** the system of sending mail by aircraft **2** mail sent by aircraft

airman *or fem* **airwoman** *n, pl* **-men** *or* **-women** a person serving in an air force

air marshal *n* **1** a senior Royal Air Force officer of equivalent rank to a vice admiral in the Royal Navy **2** the rank of a Royal New Zealand Air Force officer when Chief of the Defence Force

Air Miles *pl n Brit* points awarded on buying flight tickets and certain other products which can be used to pay for other flights

airplane *n US & Canad* an aeroplane

airplay *n* the broadcast performances of a record on radio

air pocket *n* a small descending air current that causes an aircraft to lose height suddenly

airport *n* a landing and taking-off area for civil aircraft, with facilities for aircraft maintenance and passenger arrival and departure

air pump *n* a device for pumping air into or out of something

air rage *n* aggressive behaviour by an airline passenger that endangers the safety of the crew and other passengers

air raid *n* an attack by enemy aircraft in which bombs are dropped

air rifle *n* a rifle fired by means of compressed air

airs *pl n* manners put on to impress people: *we're poor and we never put on airs*

airship *n* a lighter-than-air self-propelled aircraft

airsick *adj* nauseated from travelling in an aircraft

airside *n* the part of an airport nearest the aircraft

airspace *n* the atmosphere above a particular country, regarded as its territory

airspeed *n* the speed of an aircraft relative to the air in which it moves

airstrip *n* a cleared area for the landing and taking-off of aircraft

air terminal *n* a building in a city from which air passengers are transported to an airport

airtight *adj* **1** sealed so that air cannot enter **2** having no weak points: *your reasoning is airtight and your evidence sound*

airtime *n* the time allocated to a particular programme, topic, or type of material on radio or television

air vice-marshal *n* a senior officer in an air force

airwaves *pl n informal* radio waves used in radio and television broadcasting

airway *n* an air route used regularly by aircraft

airworthy *adj* (of an aircraft) safe to fly **airworthiness** *n*

airy *adj* **airier, airiest 1** spacious and well ventilated **2** light-hearted and casual **3** having little basis in reality; fanciful: *airy assurances*

aisle (rhymes with **mile**) *n* a passageway separating seating areas in a church, theatre, or cinema, or separating rows of shelves in a supermarket **WORD ORIGIN** Latin *ala* wing

aitchbone *n* a cut of beef from the rump bone **WORD ORIGIN** Middle English *nache-bone*

ajar *adj, adv* (of a door) slightly open **WORD ORIGIN** Old English *cierran* to turn

AK Alaska

AK-47 *n trademark* same as **Kalashnikov**

akimbo *adv* (**with**) **arms akimbo** with hands on hips and elbows turned outwards **WORD ORIGIN** Middle English *in kenebowe* in keen (ie sharp) bow

a

akin *adj* akin to similar or very close to: *the technique is akin to impressionist painting*

Al *chem* aluminium

AL Alabama

à la *prep* in the manner or style of: *laced with Gothic allusion à la David Lynch* **WORD ORIGIN** French

alabaster *n* a kind of white stone used for making statues and vases **WORD ORIGIN** Greek *alabastros*

à la carte *adj, adv* (of a menu) having dishes individually priced **WORD ORIGIN** French

alacrity *n* speed or eagerness: *I accepted the invitation with alacrity* **WORD ORIGIN** Latin *alacer* lively

à la mode *adj* fashionable **WORD ORIGIN** French

alarm *n* **1** fear aroused by awareness of danger **2** a noise warning of danger: *there had been no time to put on life jackets or to sound the alarm* **3** a device that transmits a warning **4** short for **alarm clock** ▷ *vb* **5** to fill with fear **6** to fit or activate a burglar alarm on (a house, car, etc.) **alarming** *adj* **WORD ORIGIN** Old Italian *all'arme* to arms

alarm clock *n* a clock that sounds at a set time to wake a person up

alarmist *n* **1** a person who alarms others needlessly ▷ *adj* **2** causing needless alarm

alas *adv* **1** unfortunately or regrettably: *the answer, alas, is that they cannot get any for the moment* ▷ *interj* **2** old-fashioned an exclamation of grief or alarm **WORD ORIGIN** Old French *ha las!*

alb *n* a long white linen robe worn by a Christian priest **WORD ORIGIN** Latin *albus* white

albacore *n* a tuna found in warm seas which is valued as a food fish **WORD ORIGIN** Arabic *al-bakrah*

Albanian *adj* **1** of Albania ▷ *n* **2** a person from Albania **3** the language of Albania

albatross *n* **1** a large sea bird with very long wings **2** *golf* a score of three strokes under par for a hole **WORD ORIGIN** Portuguese *alcatraz* pelican

albeit *conj* even though: *these effects occur, albeit to a lesser degree* **WORD ORIGIN** Middle English *al be it* although it be (that)

albino *n, pl* **-nos** a person or animal with white or almost white hair and skin and pinkish eyes **albinism** *n* **WORD ORIGIN** Latin *albus* white

Albion *n* *poetic* Britain or England **WORD ORIGIN** Latin

album *n* **1** a book with blank pages, for keeping photographs or stamps in **2** a long-playing record **WORD ORIGIN** Latin: blank tablet

albumen *n* **1** egg white **2** *biochem* same as **albumin** **WORD ORIGIN** Latin *albus* white

albumin *or* **albumen** *n* *biochem* a water-soluble protein found in blood plasma, egg white, milk, and muscle

alchemy *n* a medieval form of chemistry concerned with trying to change base metals into gold and to find an elixir to prolong life indefinitely **alchemist** *n* **WORD ORIGIN** Arabic *al* the + *kīmiyā'* transmutation

alcohol *n* **1** a colourless flammable liquid present in intoxicating drinks **2** intoxicating drinks generally **WORD ORIGIN** Arabic *al-kuhl* powdered antimony

alcohol-free *adj* **1** (of beer or wine) containing only a trace of alcohol **2** (of a period of time) during which no alcohol is taken: *an alcohol-free evening*

alcoholic *n* **1** a person who is addicted to alcohol ▷ *adj* **2** of or relating to alcohol

alcoholism *n* a condition in which dependence on alcohol harms a person's health and everyday life

alcopop *n* *informal* an alcoholic drink that tastes like a soft drink **WORD ORIGIN** ALCO(HOL) + POP¹ (sense 9)

alcove *n* a recess in the wall of a room **WORD ORIGIN** Arabic *al-qubbah* the vault

aldehyde *n* *chem* any organic compound containing the group –CHO, derived from alcohol by oxidation **WORD ORIGIN** New Latin *al(cohol) dehyd(rogenatum)* dehydrogenated alcohol

alder *n* a tree with toothed leaves and conelike fruits, often found in damp places **WORD ORIGIN** Old English *alor*

alderman *n, pl* **-men** **1** (formerly, in England and Wales) a senior member of a local council, elected by other councillors **2** (in the US, Canada & Australia) a member of the governing body of a city **WORD ORIGIN** Old English *ealdor* chief + *mann* man

ale *n* **1** a beer fermented in an open vessel using yeasts that rise to the top of the brew **2** (formerly) an alcoholic drink that is unflavoured by hops **3** *Brit* another word for **beer** **WORD ORIGIN** Old English *alu, ealu*

alehouse *n* *old-fashioned* a public house

alembic *n* **1** an obsolete type of container used for distillation **2** anything that distils or purifies things **WORD ORIGIN** Arabic *al-anbīq* the still

alert *adj* **1** watchful and attentive **2** alert to aware of ▷ *n* **3** a warning or the period during which a warning remains in effect **4** on the alert watchful ▷ *vb* **5** to warn of danger **6** to make aware of a fact **alertness** *n* **WORD ORIGIN** Italian *all'erta* on the watch

A level *n* **1** *Brit* the advanced level of a subject taken for the General Certificate of Education **2** a pass in a subject at A level

Alexander technique *n* a technique for improving posture by becoming more aware of it **WORD ORIGIN** after Frederick Matthias Alexander, Australian actor

alfalfa *n* a plant widely used for feeding farm animals **WORD ORIGIN** Arabic *al-fasfasah*

alfresco *adj, adv* in the open air **WORD ORIGIN** Italian: in the cool

algae (**al**-jee) *pl n, sing* **alga** (**al**-ga) plants which grow in water or moist ground, and which have no true stems, roots, or leaves **WORD ORIGIN** Latin *alga* seaweed

algebra *n* a branch of mathematics in which symbols are used to represent numbers **algebraic** *adj* **WORD ORIGIN** Arabic *al-jabr* the reunion of broken parts

ALGOL *n* an early computer programming language designed for mathematical and scientific purposes **WORD ORIGIN** *alg(orithmic) o(riented) l(anguage)*

Algonquin *or* **Algonkin** *n* **1** a member of a North American Indian people formerly living along the St Lawrence and Ottawa Rivers in Canada **2** the language of this people

algorism *n* the Arabic or decimal system of counting **WORD ORIGIN** from *al-Khuwārizmi*, 9th-century Persian mathematician

algorithm *n* a logical arithmetical or computational procedure for solving problems **WORD ORIGIN** changed from ALGORISM

alias *adv* **1** also known as: *Iris florentina, alias orris root* ▷ *n, pl* **-ases** **2** a false name **WORD ORIGIN** Latin: otherwise

alibi *n, pl* **-bis** **1** *law* a plea of being somewhere else when a crime was committed **2** *informal* an excuse ▷ *vb* **-biing, -bied** **3** to provide someone with an alibi **WORD ORIGIN** Latin: elsewhere

Alice band *n* a band worn across the head to hold the hair back from the face

alien *adj* **1** foreign **2** from another world **3** alien to repugnant or opposed to: *these methods are alien to the world of politics* ▷ *n* **4** a person who is a citizen of a country other than the one in which he or she lives **5** a being from another world **6** a person who does not seem to fit in with his or her environment **WORD ORIGIN** Latin *alienus*

alienable *adj* *law* able to be transferred to another owner

alienate *vb* **-ating, -ated** **1** to cause a friend to become unfriendly or hostile **2** *law* to transfer the ownership of property to another person **alienation** *n*

alight¹ *vb* **alighting, alighted** *or* **alit** **1** to step out of a vehicle or off a horse: *we alighted on Vladivostok station* **2** to land: *we saw thirty goldfinches alighting on the ledge* **WORD ORIGIN** Old English *ālīhtan*

alight² *adj, adv* **1** on fire **2** illuminated: *the lamp on the desk was alight*

align (a-**line**) *vb* **1** to bring (a person or group) into agreement with the policy of another **2** to place (two objects) in a particular position in relation to each other **alignment** *n* **WORD ORIGIN** Old French *à ligne* into line

alike *adj* **1** similar: *they were thought to be very alike* ▷ *adv* **2** in the same way: *they even dressed alike* **3** considered together: *players and spectators alike* **WORD ORIGIN** Old English *gelīc*

alimentary *adj* of or relating to nutrition

A History of Scrabble

Scrabble, in its current form, is a game for two to four players or, occasionally, teams. Each player draws seven tiles at the start of the game and players take turns to form words on the board. After the first word is played, every word formed must touch or intersect a word already on the board, incorporating the tile at the crossover point in the new word. When letters have been played, they are replaced at each turn by drawing tiles from a bag to make up a full rack of seven. High scores may be achieved by using the rarer, high-value letters (especially the 'power tiles' of J, Q, X, and Z), by forming words on premium squares on the board (special coloured squares that double or triple the value of the letter or word originally played on them), and by playing all seven letters at once to achieve a 50-point bonus. The key to successful Scrabble is constant awareness of the various opportunities for forming words on the board. When words are formed in ways other than simple intersection or expansion, more than one new word is created in the process, giving scope for a much higher score. The main ways of doing this are known as 'hooking' (adding a letter to the start or finish of an existing word and building a new word at right angles) and 'tagging' (playing a word parallel to an existing word and creating a series of two-letter words in the process). Expert players will also be aware of the usefulness of 'blocking' (playing words that do not allow the opponent to 'hook' and 'tag' in this way). It is also worth remembering that several categories of words are ineligible for Scrabble, and these include hyphenated words, multiple-word phrases, and capitalized words.

Scrabble was invented in the 1930s by American Alfred Butts. Mr Butts was an architect by trade and a word-games enthusiast in his spare time. He called his original invention Lexiko, and based the frequency of letters used in his game on how often they occurred in newspaper headlines. This early version differed from the game we know as Scrabble in several fundamental ways. For example, players did not use a board and there was no point-scoring system to speak of (for this same reason, high-scoring 'power tiles' were not yet part of the game). Mr Butts tried for many years to market his invention, but with little success. It was the time of the Great Depression, and economic enterprises were difficult to get off the ground. As the years went by, Mr Butts refined his game, and it came to resemble more closely the game we know today as Scrabble. His refinements included the addition of a board and premium squares that allowed higher scoring if words were played on them. But commercial success eluded him. Fortuitously, Mr Butts met James Brunot, who was interested in the game, bought the rights, and began to market it after he formed a company in the 1940s. The game had been through several different names, including 'It' and 'Criss-Crosswords', but finally the name 'Scrabble' was agreed. However, Scrabble was no overnight success, and the game did not sell particularly well at first. Its breakthrough moment was its discovery by Jack Strauss. Mr Strauss was the president of Macy's department store, and after he played and enjoyed Scrabble while on vacation, he ensured Macy's began to stock and promote the game. After this nationwide exposure, Scrabble went on to enjoy huge success, and by the 1960s was established as one of the most popular boardgames in the world.

Alfred Butts died in 1993, but his legacy is a wildly popular and globally successful game. Around 100 million sets have been sold worldwide since the game was first marketed, and Scrabble can be played not only in English, but also Arabic, Danish, Dutch, Finnish, Portuguese, Russian, and Yiddish. And in case you were wondering, the highest-ever score for a single word played in Scrabble was 392 for CAZIQUES, played by Karl Khoshnaw of Richmond, Surrey, in 1982.

alimentary canal *n* the tubular passage in the body through which food is passed and digested

alimony *n law* an allowance paid under a court order by one spouse to another after separation **WORD ORIGIN** Latin *alimonia* sustenance

A-line *adj* (of a skirt) slightly flared

aliphatic *adj chem* (of an organic compound) having an open chain structure **WORD ORIGIN** Greek *aleiphar* oil

aliquant *adj maths* denoting or belonging to a number that is not an exact divisor of a given number **WORD ORIGIN** Latin *aliquantus* somewhat

aliquot *adj maths* denoting or belonging to an exact divisor of a number **WORD ORIGIN** Latin: several

A list *n* **1** the most socially desirable category ▷ *adj* **A-list 2** of the most socially desirable category: *an A-list event*

alive *adj* **1** living; having life **2** in existence: *he said that he would keep the company alive, no matter what* **3** lively **4 alive to** aware of **5 alive with** swarming with: *the rocky shoreline was alive with birds* **WORD ORIGIN** Old English *on life* in life

alkali (**alk**-a-lie) *n chem* a substance that combines with acid and neutralizes it to form a salt **WORD ORIGIN** Arabic *al-qili* the ashes (of saltwort)

alkaline *adj chem* having the properties of or containing an alkali **alkalinity** *n*

alkaloid *n chem* any of a group of organic compounds containing nitrogen. Many are poisonous and some are used as drugs

alkane *n chem* any saturated hydrocarbon with the general formula CnH_2n+2

alkene *n chem* any unsaturated hydrocarbon with the general formula CnH_2n

all *determiner* **1** the whole quantity or number (of): *all the banks agree; we're all to blame* **2** every one of a class: *almost all animals sneeze* ▷ *adj* **3** the greatest possible: *in all seriousness* **4** any whatever: *I'm leaving out all question of motive for the time being* **5 all along** since the beginning **6 all but** nearly **7 all in all** everything considered **8 all over a** finished **b** everywhere in or on: *we send them all over the world* **c** *informal* typically: *that's him all over* **9 all the** so much (more or less) than otherwise: *the need for new drugs is all the more important* **10 at all** used for emphasis: *my throat's no better at all* **11 be all for** *informal* to be strongly in favour of **12 for all** in spite of: *for all his cynicism, he's at heart a closet idealist* **13 in all** altogether: *there were five in all* ▷ *adv* **14** (in scores of games) each: *the score was two all* ▷ *n* **15 give one's all** to make the greatest possible effort **WORD ORIGIN** Old English *eall*

Allah *n* the name of God in Islam

allay *vb* to reduce (fear, doubt, or anger) **WORD ORIGIN** Old English *ālecgan* to put down

all clear *n* a signal indicating that danger is over

allegation *n* an unproved assertion or accusation

allege *vb* **-leging, -leged** to state without proof **WORD ORIGIN** Latin *allegare* to dispatch on a mission

alleged *adj* stated but not proved: *the spot where the alleged crime took place* **allegedly** (al-**lej**-id-lee) *adv*

allegiance *n* loyalty or dedication to a person, cause, or belief **WORD ORIGIN** Old French *lige* liege

allegory *n, pl* **-ries** a story, poem, or picture with an underlying meaning as well as the literal one **allegorical** *adj* **allegorize** or **-rise** *vb* **WORD ORIGIN** Greek *allēgorein* to speak figuratively

allegretto *music adv* **1** fairly quickly or briskly ▷ *n, pl* **-tos 2** a piece or passage to be performed fairly quickly or briskly **WORD ORIGIN** Italian

allegro *music adv* **1** in a brisk lively manner ▷ *n, pl* **-gros 2** a piece or passage to be performed in a brisk lively manner **WORD ORIGIN** Italian

allele (al-**leel**) *n* any of two or more genes that are responsible for alternative characteristics, such as smooth or wrinkled seeds in peas

alleluia *interj* praise the Lord! **WORD ORIGIN** Hebrew *halleluyah*

allergen (**al**-ler-jen) *n* a substance capable of causing an allergic reaction **allergenic** *adj*

allergic *adj* **1** having or caused by an allergy **2 allergic to** *informal* having a strong dislike of: *father and son seemed to have been allergic to each other from the start*

allergy *n, pl* **-gies 1** extreme sensitivity to a substance such as a food or pollen, which causes the body to react to any contact with it **2** *informal* a strong dislike for something **WORD ORIGIN** Greek *allos* other + *ergon* activity

alleviate *vb* **-ating, -ated** to lessen (pain or suffering) **alleviation** *n* **WORD ORIGIN** Latin *levis* light

≡ USAGE
≡ See at **ameliorate**.

alley *n* **1** a narrow passage between or behind buildings **2 a** a building containing lanes for tenpin bowling **b** a long narrow wooden lane down which the ball is rolled in tenpin bowling **3** a path in a garden, often lined with trees **WORD ORIGIN** Old French *alee*

alleyway *n* a narrow passage with buildings or walls on both sides

all found *adv* (of charges for accommodation) including meals, heating, and other living expenses

Allhallows *n* same as **All Saints' Day**

alliance *n* **1** the state of being allied **2** a formal relationship between two or more countries or political parties to work together **3** the countries or parties involved **WORD ORIGIN** Old French *alier* to ally

allied *adj* **1** united by a common aim or common characteristics: *the allied areas of telepathy and clairvoyance* **2 Allied** relating to the countries that fought against Germany and Japan in the Second World War: *the Allied bombing of German cities*

alligator *n* a large reptile of the southern US, similar to the crocodile but with a shorter broader snout **WORD ORIGIN** Spanish *el lagarto* the lizard

all in *adj* **1** *informal* exhausted **2** (of wrestling) with no style forbidden ▷ *adv* **3** with all expenses included

alliteration *n* the use of the same sound at the start of words occurring together, as in *round the rugged rock the ragged rascal ran* **alliterative** *adj* **WORD ORIGIN** Latin *litera* letter

allocate *vb* **-cating, -cated** to assign to someone or for a particular purpose **allocation** *n* **WORD ORIGIN** Latin *locus* a place

allopathy (al-**lop**-ath-ee) *n med* an orthodox method of treating disease, by using drugs that produce an effect opposite to the effect of the disease being treated, as contrasted with homeopathy **allopathic** *adj* **WORD ORIGIN** Greek *allos* other + *pathos* suffering

allot *vb* **-lotting, -lotted** to assign as a share or for a particular purpose **WORD ORIGIN** Old French *lot* portion

allotment *n* **1** *Brit* a small piece of land rented by a person to grow vegetables on **2** a portion allotted **3** distribution

allotrope *n chem* any of two or more physical forms in which an element can exist

allotropy *n chem* the existence of an element in two or more physical forms **allotropic** *adj* **WORD ORIGIN** Greek *allos* other + *tropos* manner

all-out *adj informal* using one's maximum powers: *an all-out attack on inflation*

allow *vb* **1** to permit someone to do something **2** to set aside: *I allowed plenty of time* **3** to acknowledge (a point or claim) **4 allow for** to take into account **allowable** *adj* **WORD ORIGIN** Late Latin *allaudare* to extol

allowance *n* **1** an amount of money given at regular intervals **2** (in Britain) an amount of a person's income that is not subject to income tax **3 make allowances for a** to treat or judge someone less severely because he or she has special problems **b** to take into account in one's plans

alloy *n* **1** a mixture of two or more metals ▷ *vb* **2** to mix metals in order to obtain a substance with a desired property **WORD ORIGIN** Latin *alligare* to bind

all-purpose *adj* useful for many purposes

all right *adj* **1** acceptable or satisfactory: *is everything all right?* **2** unharmed; safe: *I'm going to check if he's all right* ▷ *interj* **3** an expression of approval or agreement ▷ *adv* **4** satisfactorily **5** safely **6** without doubt: *it was him all right*

≡ USAGE
≡ See at **alright**.

all-round *adj* **1** having many skills; versatile: *an all-round player* **2** of broad scope; comprehensive: *we cannot do without up-to-date and all-round training*

all-rounder *n* a person with many skills and abilities

All Saints' Day *n* a Christian festival celebrated on November 1 to honour all the saints

All Souls' Day *n* RC *Church* a day of prayer (November 2) for the dead in purgatory

allspice *n* a spice used in cooking, which comes from the berries of a tropical American tree

all-time *adj informal* unsurpassed at a particular time: *one of boxing's all-time greats*

allude *vb* **-luding, -luded** ● **allude to** to refer indirectly to
WORD ORIGIN Latin *alludere*
USAGE
Avoid confusion with **elude**.

allure *n* attractiveness or appeal
WORD ORIGIN Old French *alurer* to lure

alluring *adj* extremely attractive

allusion *n* an indirect reference

alluvial *adj* **1** of or relating to alluvium ▷ *n* **2** same as **alluvium**

alluvium *n, pl* **-via** a fertile soil consisting of mud, silt, and sand deposited by flowing water
WORD ORIGIN Latin

ally *n, pl* **-lies 1** a country, person, or group with an agreement to support another ▷ *vb* **-lies, -lying, -lied 2 ally oneself with** to agree to support another country, person, or group
WORD ORIGIN Latin *ligare* to bind

alma mater *n* the school, college, or university that one attended
WORD ORIGIN Latin: bountiful mother

almanac *n* a yearly calendar with detailed information on matters like anniversaries and phases of the moon
WORD ORIGIN Late Greek *almenikhiaka*

almighty *adj* **1** having power over everything **2** *informal* very great: *there was an almighty bang* ▷ *n* **3 the Almighty** God

almond *n* an edible oval nut with a yellowish-brown shell, which grows on a small tree
WORD ORIGIN Greek *amugdalē*

almoner *n* Brit a former name for a hospital social worker
WORD ORIGIN Old French *almosne* alms

almost *adv* very nearly

alms (**ahmz**) *pl n* old-fashioned donations of money or goods to the poor
WORD ORIGIN Greek *eleēmosunē* pity

almshouse *n* Brit (formerly) a house, financed by charity, which offered accommodation to the poor

aloe *n* **1** a plant with fleshy spiny leaves **2 aloes** a bitter drug made from aloe leaves
WORD ORIGIN Greek

aloe vera *n* a plant producing a juice which is used to treat skin and hair

aloft *adv* **1** in the air **2** *naut* in the rigging of a ship
WORD ORIGIN Old Norse *ā lopt*

alone *adj* **1** without anyone or anything else ▷ *adv* **2** without anyone or anything else **3 leave someone** or **something alone** to refrain from annoying someone or interfering with something **4 let alone** not to mention: *it looked inconceivable that he could run again, let alone be elected*
WORD ORIGIN Old English *al one* all (entirely) one

along *prep* **1** over part or all of the length of: *we were going along the railway tracks* ▷ *adv* **2** moving forward: *they were roaring along at 40mph* **3** in company with another or others: *let them go along for the ride* **4 along with** together with: *I'm including the good days along with the bad*
WORD ORIGIN Old English *andlang*
USAGE
See at **plus**.

alongside *prep* **1** close beside ▷ *adv* **2** near the side of something

aloof *adj* distant or haughty in manner
WORD ORIGIN obsolete *a loof* to windward

alopecia (al-loh-**pee**-sha) *n* loss of hair, usually due to illness
WORD ORIGIN Greek *alōpekia* mange in foxes

aloud *adv* in an audible voice

alp *n* **1** a high mountain **2 the Alps** a high mountain range in S central Europe
WORD ORIGIN Latin *Alpes*

alpaca *n* **1** a South American mammal related to the llama, with dark shaggy hair **2** wool or cloth made from this hair
WORD ORIGIN South American Indian *allpaca*

alpenstock *n* a strong stick with an iron tip used by hikers and mountain climbers
WORD ORIGIN German

alpha *n* **1** the first letter in the Greek alphabet (A, α) **2** *Brit* the highest grade in an examination or for a piece of academic work **3 alpha and omega** the first and last

alphabet *n* a set of letters in fixed conventional order, used in a writing system
WORD ORIGIN *alpha* + *beta*, the first two letters of the Greek alphabet

alphabetical *adj* in the conventional order of the letters of an alphabet **alphabetically** *adv*

alphabetize *or* **-ise** *vb* **-izing, -ized** *or* **-ising, -ised** to put in alphabetical order **alphabetization** *or* **-isation** *n*

alphanumeric *adj* consisting of alphabetical and numerical symbols

alpha particle *n* *physics* a positively charged particle, emitted during some radioactive transformations

alpha ray *n* *physics* a stream of alpha particles

alpine *adj* **1** of high mountains **2 Alpine** of the Alps ▷ *n* **3** a plant grown on or native to mountains

alpinist *n* a mountain climber

already *adv* **1** before the present time **2** before an implied or expected time

alright *adj, interj, adv* not standard same as **all right**

USAGE
The form *alright*, though very common, is still considered by many people to be wrong or less acceptable than *all right*.

Alsatian *n* a large wolflike dog

also *adv* in addition; too
WORD ORIGIN Old English *alswā*

also-ran *n* a loser in a race, competition, or election

Alta. Alberta

altar *n* **1** the table used for Communion in Christian churches **2** a raised structure on which sacrifices are offered and religious rites performed
WORD ORIGIN Latin *altus* high

altarpiece *n* a painting or a decorated screen set above and behind the altar in a Christian church

alter *vb* to make or become different; change
WORD ORIGIN Latin *alter* other

alteration *n* a change or modification

altercation *n* a noisy argument
WORD ORIGIN Latin *altercari* to quarrel

alter ego *n* **1** a hidden side to one's personality **2** a very close friend
WORD ORIGIN Latin: other self

alternate *vb* **-nating, -nated 1** to occur by turns **2** to interchange regularly or in succession ▷ *adj* **3** occurring by turns **4** every second (one) of a series: *alternate days* **5** being a second choice **alternately** *adv* **alternation** *n*
WORD ORIGIN Latin *alternare*

alternate angles *pl n* *geom* two angles at opposite ends and on opposite sides of a line intersecting two other lines

alternating current *n* an electric current that reverses direction at frequent regular intervals

alternative *n* **1** a possibility of choice between two or more things **2** either or any of such choices ▷ *adj* **3** presenting a choice between two or more possibilities **4** of a lifestyle etc. that is less conventional or materialistic than is usual **alternatively** *adv*

alternative energy *n* a form of energy obtained from natural resources like waves and wind

alternative medicine *n* the treatment of disease by unconventional methods like homeopathy, and involving attention to the patient's emotional wellbeing

alternator *n* an electrical machine that generates an alternating current

although *conj* in spite of the fact that

altimeter (al-**tim**-it-er) *n* an instrument that measures altitude
WORD ORIGIN Latin *altus* high + **-METER**

altitude *n* height, esp. above sea level
WORD ORIGIN Latin *altus* high, deep

alto *n, pl* **-tos 1** short for **contralto 2** the highest adult male voice **3** a singer with an alto voice **4** a musical instrument, for instance a saxophone, that is the second or third highest in its family ▷ *adj* **5** denoting such an instrument, singer, or voice: *an alto flute*
WORD ORIGIN Italian: high

altogether *adv* **1** completely: *an altogether different message* **2** on the whole:

a

this is not altogether a bad thing **3** in total: *altogether, 25 aircraft took part* ▷ *n* **4 in the altogether** *informal* naked

alt.rock *n* a genre of rock music regarded by fans as being outside the mainstream

altruism *n* unselfish concern for the welfare of others **altruist** *n* **altruistic** *adj*
WORD ORIGIN Italian *altrui* others

alum *n chem* a double sulphate of aluminium and potassium, used in manufacturing and in medicine
WORD ORIGIN Latin *alumen*

aluminium *or US & Canad* **aluminum** *n chem* a light malleable silvery-white metallic element that does not rust. Symbol: Al

aluminize *or* -**ise** *vb* -**nizing, -nized** *or* -**nising, -nised** to cover with aluminium

alumnus (al-**lumm**-nuss) *or fem* **alumna** (al-**lumm**-na) *n, pl* -**ni** (-**nie**) *or* -**nae** (-**nee**) *chiefly US & Canad* a graduate of a school or college
WORD ORIGIN Latin: nursling, pupil

alveolus (al-**vee**-ol-luss) *n, pl* -**li** (-**lie**) any small pit, cavity, or saclike dilation, such as a honeycomb cell, a tooth socket, or the tiny air sacs in the lungs
WORD ORIGIN Latin: a little hollow

always *adv* **1** without exception: *she was always at the top of her form in school work* **2** continually: *you're always shouting or whining* **3** in any case: *they're all adults, they can always say no*
WORD ORIGIN Old English *ealne weg* all the way

alyssum *n* a garden plant with clusters of small white flowers
WORD ORIGIN Greek *alussos* curing rabies

Alzheimer's disease (**alts**-hime-erz) *n* a disorder of the brain resulting in a progressive decline in intellectual and physical abilities and eventual dementia
WORD ORIGIN after A. *Alzheimer*, German physician

am *vb* (*with "I" as subject*) a form of the present tense of **be**
WORD ORIGIN Old English *eam*

Am *chem* americium

AM 1 amplitude modulation **2** (in Britain) Member of the National Assembly for Wales

Am. America(n)

a.m. before noon
WORD ORIGIN Latin *ante meridiem*

amah *n* (in the East, formerly) a nurse or maidservant
WORD ORIGIN Portuguese *ama*

amakwerekwere *n S African informal, derogatory* a term used by Black people to refer to foreign Africans
WORD ORIGIN from Xhosa *ama*, a plural prefix, + *kwerekwere* imitative of unintelligible sound

amalgam *n* **1** a blend or combination **2** an alloy of mercury with another metal: *dental amalgam*
WORD ORIGIN Medieval Latin *amalgama*

amalgamate *vb* -**mating, -mated 1** to combine or unite **2** to alloy (a metal) with mercury **amalgamation** *n*

amandla (a-**mand**-la) *n S African* a political slogan calling for power to the Black population
WORD ORIGIN Nguni (language group of southern Africa): power

amanuensis (am-man-yew-**en**-siss) *n, pl* -**ses** (-**seez**) a person who copies manuscripts or takes dictation
WORD ORIGIN Latin *servus a manu* slave at hand

amaranth *n* **1** *poetic* an imaginary flower that never fades **2** a lily-like plant with small green, red, or purple flowers
WORD ORIGIN Greek *a-* not + *marainein* to fade

amaretti *pl n* Italian almond biscuits
WORD ORIGIN Italian *amaro* bitter

amaryllis *n* a lily-like plant with large red or white flowers and a long stalk
WORD ORIGIN *Amaryllis*, Greek name for a shepherdess

amass *vb* to accumulate or collect: *the desire to amass wealth*
WORD ORIGIN Latin *ad-* to + *massa* mass

amateur *n* **1** a person who engages in a sport or other activity as a pastime rather than as a profession **2** a person unskilled in a subject or activity ▷ *adj* **3** doing something out of interest, not for money **4** amateurish **amateurism** *n*
WORD ORIGIN Latin *amator* lover

amateurish *adj* lacking skill

amatory *adj* of or relating to romantic or sexual love
WORD ORIGIN Latin *amare* to love

amaut *or* **amowt** *n Canad* a hood on an Inuit woman's parka for carrying a child

amaze *vb* **amazing, amazed** to fill with surprise; astonish **amazement** *n* **amazing** *adj* **amazingly** *adv*
WORD ORIGIN Old English *āmasian*

Amazon *n* **1** a strong and powerful woman **2** *Greek myth* one of a race of women warriors of Scythia **Amazonian** *adj*
WORD ORIGIN Greek

ambassador *n* **1** a diplomat of the highest rank, sent to another country as permanent representative of his or her own country **2** a representative or messenger: *he saw himself as an ambassador for the game* **ambassadorial** *adj*
WORD ORIGIN Old Provençal *ambaisador*

amber *n* **1** a yellow translucent fossilized resin, used in jewellery ▷ *adj* **2** brownish-yellow
WORD ORIGIN Arabic *'anbar* ambergris

ambergris (**am**-ber-greece) *n* a waxy substance secreted by the sperm whale, which is used in making perfumes
WORD ORIGIN Old French *ambre gris* grey amber

ambidextrous *adj* able to use both hands with equal ease
WORD ORIGIN Latin *ambi-* both + *dexter* right hand

ambience *or* **ambiance** *n* the atmosphere of a place

ambient *adj* **1** surrounding: *low ambient temperatures* **2** creating a relaxing atmosphere: *ambient music*
WORD ORIGIN Latin *ambi-* round + *ire* to go

ambiguity *n, pl* -**ties 1** the possibility of interpreting an expression in more than one way **2** an ambiguous situation or expression: *the ambiguities of feminine identity*

ambiguous *adj* having more than one possible interpretation **ambiguously** *adv*
WORD ORIGIN Latin *ambigere* to go around

ambit *n* limits or boundary
WORD ORIGIN Latin *ambire* to go round

ambition *n* **1** strong desire for success **2** something so desired; a goal
WORD ORIGIN Latin *ambitio* a going round (of candidates)

ambitious *adj* **1** having a strong desire for success **2** requiring great effort or ability: *ambitious plans*

ambivalence (am-**biv**-a-lenss) *n* the state of feeling two conflicting emotions at the same time **ambivalent** *adj*

amble *vb* -**bling, -bled 1** to walk at a leisurely pace ▷ *n* **2** a leisurely walk or pace
WORD ORIGIN Latin *ambulare* to walk

ambrosia *n* **1** something delightful to taste or smell **2** *classical myth* the food of the gods
WORD ORIGIN Greek: immortality

ambulance *n* a motor vehicle designed to carry sick or injured people
WORD ORIGIN Latin *ambulare* to walk

ambulatory *adj* **1** of or relating to walking **2** able to walk ▷ *n, pl* -**ries 3** a place for walking in, such as a cloister

ambush *n* **1** the act of waiting in a concealed position to make a surprise attack **2** an attack from such a position ▷ *vb* **3** to attack suddenly from a concealed position
WORD ORIGIN Old French *embuschier* to position in ambush

ameliorate (am-**meal**-yor-rate) *vb* -**rating, -rated** to make (something) better **amelioration** *n*
WORD ORIGIN Latin *melior* better

USAGE
Ameliorate is often wrongly used where *alleviate* is meant. *Ameliorate* should be used to mean 'improve', not 'make easier to bear', so one should talk about *alleviating* pain or hardship, not *ameliorating* it.

amen *interj* so be it: used at the end of a prayer
WORD ORIGIN Hebrew: certainly

amenable (a-**mean**-a-bl) *adj* likely or willing to cooperate
WORD ORIGIN Latin *minare* to drive (cattle)

amend *vb* to make small changes to something such as a piece of writing or a contract, in order to improve it: *he has amended the basic design*
WORD ORIGIN Old French *amender*

amendment *n* an improvement or correction

amends *pl n* **make amends for** to compensate for some injury or insult

amenity *n, pl* -**ties** a useful or enjoyable feature: *all kinds of amenities including horse riding and golf*
WORD ORIGIN Latin *amoenus* agreeable

amenorrhoea *or esp. US* **amenorrhea** (aim-men-or-**ree**-a) *n* abnormal absence of menstruation
WORD ORIGIN Greek *a-* not + *mēn* month + *rhein* to flow

A History of English – Origins

E nglish is a funny word. It seems to refer to England, a country that is just one part of the United Kingdom and whose population accounts for as little as 11 per cent of the total number of speakers of the English language. Furthermore, the word *English* derives from the name of only one of the Germanic speakers who brought their language to the British Isles in the fifth century AD, and not even the tribe that was originally most dominant.

The original speakers of 'English' came from modern-day Germany. English belongs to the Germanic family of languages, a sub-set of the Indo-European family that includes Modern German, Danish, Dutch, Norwegian, Swedish, and Icelandic, among others. The ancient Germans were always a problem for the Roman Empire, but they were fierce warriors and Rome hired some Germans as mercenaries to keep the extremities of the Empire in line: extremities like that Britannia place they had recently acquired. The mercenaries came mainly from three different Germanic tribes: the Angles, the Saxons, and the Jutes. Not long after they arrived the Roman Empire collapsed and the mercenaries stayed. They re-conquered the Britons and renamed them the Welsh, which in their language meant 'foreigners'.

The three tribes initially stayed divided into Angles and Saxons (the Jutes seem to have been absorbed by the Angles), and even within their own tribes they formed separate and competitive kingdoms. East Anglia, for instance, was an ancient Anglian Kingdom, as was Northumberland. There was also an Anglian kingdom called Mercia, which means 'land of the border people', though it was in the Midlands. The Saxons, too, were divided, as evidenced by place-names like *Essex* ('Land of the East Saxons'), *Wessex* ('Land of the West Saxons'), *Sussex* ('Land of the South Saxons'), and *Middlesex* ('Land of the Middle Saxons').

As they came from different tribes, the Angles and Saxons brought different dialects of the ancient Germanic language. It is likely these dialects would have been mutually intelligible with each other and with those still in use on the Continent, but they were probably more distinct than present-day regional accents. We now collectively refer to all the dialects spoken in Britain as *Old English* or *Anglo-Saxon*, though most of the surviving written evidence is in the West Saxon dialect. Modern English, however, shows more Anglian influence, so Old English can appear more alien to modern readers than it would have if Mercian, for instance, had won out.

Though at first glance Anglo-Saxon looks like a foreign language, a close look reveals that many words we use every day have changed little in the past thousand years. In the following passage from the Old English poem *Beowulf* Anglo-Saxon words are glossed in italics:

Him se yldestra   andswarode
him the eldest   answered
werodes wisa   wordhord onleac
the company's leader   [his] word-hoard unlocked
'We synt gumcynnes   Geata leode
'*We are men   of the Geatish people*
ond Higelaces   heorthgeneatas.
and Higelac's   hearth-companions.
Wæs min fæder   folcum gecythed,
My father was   known among his folk
æthele ordfruma   Ecgtheow haten.
a noble war-leader   named Ecgtheow.
Gebad wintra worn   ær he on weg hwurfe,
He lived many winters   ere he went on his way,
gamol of geardum.'
old of years.'

Certain words are instantly recognizable: *him, word, we, he, on*; others have changed so little that their meanings are quite obvious: *hord* (hoard), *ond* (and), *fæder* (father), *folcum* (folk). Some words have equivalents in modern English, but they have changed enough that the connection is not immediately obvious: *gecythed* means 'known', and survives in the present-day adjective *uncouth*; *gebad* means 'lived' or 'stayed', and survives in *bide* and *abide*; *geardum* is a form of the word *gear*, 'year' – Anglo-Saxon *ge* – often becomes *ye* in Modern English. Only a handful of words in the passage, then, are truly unfamiliar: *werodes* (a company of men); *ordfruma* (war-leader); *æthele* (noble).

a

Amen-Ra *n* an Egyptian god with a ram's head

American *adj* **1** of the United States of America or the American continent ▷ *n* **2** a person from the United States of America or the American continent

American football *n* a game similar to rugby, played by two teams of eleven players

American Indian *n* **1** a member of any of the original peoples of America ▷ *adj* **2** of any of these peoples

Americanism *n* an expression or custom that is characteristic of the people of the United States

Americanize *or*-**ise** *vb* -**izing**, -**ized** *or* -**ising**, -**ised** to make American in outlook or form

americium *n chem* a white metallic element artificially produced from plutonium. Symbol: Am
WORD ORIGIN from *America* (where it was first produced)

amethyst (**am**-myth-ist) *n* **1** a purple or violet variety of quartz used as a gemstone ▷ *adj* **2** purple or violet
WORD ORIGIN Greek *amethustos* not drunken

Amex (**aah**-mex) **1** *trademark* American Express **2** American Stock Exchange

Amharic *n* the official language of Ethiopia

amiable *adj* having a pleasant nature; friendly **amiability** *n* **amiably** *adv*
WORD ORIGIN Latin *amicus* friend

amicable *adj* characterized by friendliness: *ideally the parting should be amicable* **amicability** *n* **amicably** *adv*
WORD ORIGIN Latin *amicus* friend

amid *or* **amidst** *prep* in the middle of; among
WORD ORIGIN Old English *on middan* in the middle

amide *n chem* **1** any organic compound containing the group –CONH₂ **2** an inorganic compound having the general formula M(NH₂)ₓ, where M is a metal atom
WORD ORIGIN from *ammonia*

amidships *adv naut* at, near, or towards the centre of a ship

amine (am-**mean**) *n chem* an organic base formed by replacing one or more of the hydrogen atoms of ammonia by organic groups
WORD ORIGIN from *ammonium*

amino acid (am-**mean**-oh) *n chem* any of a group of organic compounds containing the **amino group**, –NH₂, and one or more carboxyl groups, –COOH, esp. one that is a component of protein

amir (am-**meer**) *n* same as **emir**
WORD ORIGIN Arabic

amiss *adv* **1** wrongly or badly: *anxious not to tread amiss* **2** **take something amiss** to be offended by something ▷ *adj* **3** wrong or faulty
WORD ORIGIN Middle English *a mis*, from *mis* wrong

amity *n formal* friendship
WORD ORIGIN from Latin *amicus* friend

ammeter *n* an instrument for measuring an electric current in amperes
WORD ORIGIN *am(pere)* + -**METER**

ammo *n informal* ammunition

ammonia *n* **1** a colourless strong-smelling gas containing hydrogen and nitrogen **2** a solution of this in water
WORD ORIGIN ultimately from a substance found near the shrine of the Roman-Egyptian god Jupiter *Ammon*

ammonite *n* the fossilized spiral shell of an extinct sea creature
WORD ORIGIN Medieval Latin *cornu Ammonis* horn of Ammon

ammonium *adj chem* of or containing the chemical group NH₄– or the ion NH₄⁺

ammunition *n* **1** bullets, bombs, and shells that can be fired from or as a weapon **2** facts that can be used in an argument
WORD ORIGIN Latin *munitio* fortification

amnesia *n* a partial or total loss of memory **amnesiac** *adj, n*
WORD ORIGIN Greek: forgetfulness

amnesty *n, pl* -**ties** **1** a general pardon for offences against a government **2** a period during which a law is suspended, to allow people to confess to crime or give up weapons without fear of prosecution
WORD ORIGIN Greek *a*- not + *mnasthai* to remember

amniocentesis *n, pl* -**ses** removal of amniotic fluid from the womb of a pregnant woman in order to detect possible abnormalities in the fetus
WORD ORIGIN *amnion* + Greek *kentēsis* a pricking

amnion *n, pl* -**nia** the innermost of two membranes enclosing an embryo **amniotic** *adj*
WORD ORIGIN Greek: a little lamb

amniotic fluid *n* the fluid surrounding the fetus in the womb

amoeba *or US* **ameba** (am-**mee**-ba) *n, pl* -**bae** (-bee) *or* -**bas** a microscopic single-cell creature that is able to change its shape
WORD ORIGIN Greek *ameibein* to change

amok *or* **amuck** *adv* **run amok** to run about in a violent frenzy
WORD ORIGIN Malay *amoq* furious assault

among *or* **amongst** *prep* **1** in the midst of: *she decided to dwell among the Greeks* **2** in the group, class, or number of: *he is among the top trainers* **3** to each of: *the stakes should be divided among the players* **4** with one another within a group: *sort it out among yourselves*
WORD ORIGIN Old English *amang*
▤ USAGE
▤ See at **between**.

amoral (aim-**mor**-ral) *adj* without moral standards or principles **amorality** *n*
▤ USAGE
▤ *Amoral* is often wrongly used where ▤ *immoral* is meant. *Immoral* should be ▤ used to talk about the breaking of ▤ moral rules, *amoral* about people who ▤ have no moral code or about places or ▤ situations where moral ▤ considerations do not apply.

amorous *adj* feeling, displaying, or relating to sexual love or desire
WORD ORIGIN Latin *amor* love

amorphous *adj* **1** lacking a definite shape **2** of no recognizable character or type
WORD ORIGIN Greek *a*- not + *morphē* shape

amortize *or*-**tise** *vb* -**tizing**, -**tized** *or* -**tising**, -**tised** *finance* to pay off (a debt) gradually by periodic transfers to a sinking fund
WORD ORIGIN Latin *ad* to + *mors* death

amount *n* **1** extent or quantity ▷ *vb* **2** **amount to** to be equal or add up to
WORD ORIGIN Old French *amonter* to go up
▤ USAGE
▤ The use of a plural noun after *amount* ▤ *of* (an amount of bananas; the amount of ▤ refugees) should be avoided: *a quantity of* ▤ *bananas; the number of refugees.*

amour *n* a secret love affair
WORD ORIGIN Latin *amor* love

amour-propre (am-moor-**prop**-ra) *n* self-esteem

amp *n* **1** an ampere **2** *informal* an amplifier

amperage *n* the strength of an electric current measured in amperes

ampere (**am**-pair) *n* the basic unit of electric current
WORD ORIGIN after A. M. *Ampère*, French physicist & mathematician

ampersand *n* the character &, meaning *and*
WORD ORIGIN shortened from *and per se and*, that is, the symbol & by itself (represents) *and*

amphetamine (am-**fet**-am-mean) *n* a drug used as a stimulant
WORD ORIGIN shortened from chemical name

amphibian *n* **1** an animal, such as a newt, frog, or toad, that lives on land but breeds in water **2** a vehicle that can travel on both water and land

amphibious *adj* **1** living or operating both on land and in or on water **2** relating to a military attack launched from the sea against a shore
WORD ORIGIN Greek *amphibios* having a double life

amphitheatre *or US* **amphitheater** *n* a circular or oval building without a roof, in which tiers of seats rise from a central open arena
WORD ORIGIN Greek *amphitheatron*

amphora (**am**-for-ra) *n, pl* -**phorae** (-for-ree) an ancient Greek or Roman jar with two handles and a narrow neck
WORD ORIGIN Greek *amphi*- on both sides + *phoreus* bearer

ample *adj* **1** more than sufficient: *there is already ample evidence* **2** large: *ample helpings of stewed pomegranates and pears*
WORD ORIGIN Latin *amplus*

amplifier *n* an electronic device used to increase the strength of a current or sound signal

amplify *vb* -**fies**, -**fying**, -**fied** **1** *electronics* to increase the strength of (a current or sound signal) **2** to explain in more detail **3** to increase the size, extent, or effect of **amplification** *n*
WORD ORIGIN Latin *amplificare*

amplitude *n* **1** greatness of extent **2** *physics* the maximum displacement

from the zero or mean position of a wave or oscillation
WORD ORIGIN Latin *amplus* spacious

amplitude modulation *n electronics* a method of transmitting information using radio waves in which the amplitude of the carrier wave is varied in accordance with the amplitude of the input signal

amply *adv* fully or generously: *she was amply rewarded for it*

ampoule *or US* **ampule** *n med* a small glass container in which liquids for injection are sealed
WORD ORIGIN French

ampulla *n, pl* **-pullae 1** *anat* the dilated end part of certain tubes in the body **2** *Christianity* a container for the wine and water, or the oil, used in church
WORD ORIGIN Latin

amputate *vb* **-tating, -tated** to cut off (a limb or part of a limb) for medical reasons **amputation** *n*
WORD ORIGIN Latin *am-* around + *putare* to prune

amputee *n* a person who has had a limb amputated

amuck *adv* same as **amok**

amulet *n* a trinket or jewel worn as a protection against evil
WORD ORIGIN Latin *amuletum*

amuse *vb* **amusing, amused 1** to cause to laugh or smile **2** to entertain or keep interested **amusing** *adj* **amusingly** *adv*
WORD ORIGIN Old French *amuser* to cause to be idle

amusement *n* **1** the state of being amused **2** something that amuses or entertains someone

amusement arcade *n* a large room with coin-operated electronic games and fruit machines

amusement park *n* a large open-air entertainment area with rides and stalls

amylase *n* an enzyme present in saliva that helps to change starch into sugar

an *adj* (*indefinite article*) same as **a**: used before an initial vowel sound: *an old man; an hour*
WORD ORIGIN Old English *ān* one

≡ USAGE
≡*An* was formerly often used before ≡words that begin with *h* and are ≡unstressed on the first syllable: *an* ≡*hotel; an historic meeting*: sometimes the ≡initial *h* was not pronounced. This ≡usage is now becoming obsolete.

an- *prefix* see **a-**

Anabaptist *n* **1** a member of a 16th-century Protestant movement that believed in adult baptism ▷ *adj* **2** of this movement
WORD ORIGIN Late Greek *anabaptizein* to baptize again

anabolic steroid *n* a synthetic steroid hormone used to stimulate muscle and bone growth

anabolism *n biol* a metabolic process in which body tissues are synthesized from food
WORD ORIGIN Greek *anabolē* a rising up

anachronism (an-**nak**-kron-iz-zum) *n* **1** the representation of something in a historical context in which it could not have occurred or existed **2** a person or

thing that seems to belong to another time **anachronistic** *adj*
WORD ORIGIN Greek *ana* against + *khronos* time

anaconda *n* a large S American snake which squeezes its prey to death
WORD ORIGIN probably from Sinhalese *henakandayā* whip snake

anaemia *or US* **anemia** (an-**neem**-ee-a) *n* a deficiency of red blood cells or their haemoglobin content, resulting in paleness and lack of energy
WORD ORIGIN Greek *an* without + *haima* blood

anaemic *or US* **anemic** *adj* **1** having anaemia **2** pale and sickly-looking **3** lacking vitality

anaerobe *n biol* an organism that does not require oxygen **anaerobic** *adj*
WORD ORIGIN Greek *an* not + *aēr* air + *bios* life

anaesthesia *or US* **anesthesia** (an-niss-**theez**-ee-a) *n* loss of bodily feeling caused by disease or accident or by drugs such as ether: called **general anaesthesia** when consciousness is lost and **local anaesthesia** when only a specific area of the body is involved
WORD ORIGIN Greek

anaesthetic *or US* **anesthetic** (an-niss-**thet**-ik) *n* **1** a substance that causes anaesthesia ▷ *adj* **2** causing anaesthesia

anaesthetist (an-**neess**-thet-ist) *n Brit* a doctor who administers anaesthetics

anaesthetize, anaesthetise *or US* **anesthetize** *vb* **-tizing, -tized** *or* **-tising, -tised** to cause to feel no pain by administering an anaesthetic

Anaglypta *n trademark* a thick embossed wallpaper, designed to be painted

anagram *n* a word or phrase made by rearranging the letters of another word or phrase
WORD ORIGIN Greek *anagrammatizein* to transpose letters

anal (**ain**-al) *adj* of or relating to the anus
WORD ORIGIN New Latin *analis*

analgesia *n* the absence of pain
WORD ORIGIN Greek

analgesic (an-nal-**jeez**-ik) *n* **1** a drug that relieves pain ▷ *adj* **2** pain-relieving: *an analgesic balm*

analog *n US & computers* same as **analogue**

≡ USAGE
≡The spelling *analog* is a US variant of ≡*analogue* in all its senses, and is also ≡the generally preferred spelling in the ≡computer industry.

analogize *or* **-gise** *vb* **-gizing, -gized** *or* **-gising, -gised 1** to use analogy in argument **2** to reveal analogy between (one thing and another)

analogous *adj* similar in some respects
WORD ORIGIN Greek *analogos* proportionate

≡ USAGE
≡The use of *with* after *analogous* should ≡be avoided: *swimming has no event that is* ≡*analogous to* (not *with*) *the 100 metres in* ≡*athletics.*

analogue *or US* **analog** *n* **1** a physical object or quantity used to measure or represent another quantity

2 something that is analogous to something else ▷ *adj* **3** displaying information by means of a dial
≡ USAGE
≡See at **analog**.

analogy *n, pl* **-gies 1** a similarity, usually in a limited number of features **2** a comparison made to show such a similarity **analogical** *adj*
WORD ORIGIN Greek *analogia*

anal-retentive *adj* (of a person) excessively fussy and concerned with order and minute details

analyse *or US* **-lyze** (an-nal-lize) *vb* **-lysing, -lysed** *or* **-lyzing, -lyzed 1** to examine (something) in detail in order to discover its meaning or essential features **2** to break (something) down into its components **3** to psychoanalyse (someone)

analysis (an-**nal**-liss-iss) *n, pl* **-ses** (-seez) **1** the separation of a whole into its parts for study or interpretation **2** a statement of the results of this **3** short for **psychoanalysis**
WORD ORIGIN Greek *analusis* a dissolving

analyst *n* **1** a person who is skilled in analysis **2** a psychoanalyst

analytical *or* **analytic** *adj* relating to or using analysis **analytically** *adv*

anaphylactic shock *n* a severe, sometimes fatal, reaction to a substance to which a person has an extreme sensitivity, often involving respiratory difficulty and circulation failure
WORD ORIGIN Greek *ana* again + *phulaxis* guarding

anarchism *n* a doctrine advocating the abolition of government and its replacement by a social system based on voluntary cooperation

anarchist *n* **1** a person who advocates anarchism **2** a person who causes disorder or upheaval **anarchistic** *adj*

anarchy (**an**-ark-ee) *n* **1** general lawlessness and disorder **2** the absence of government **anarchic** *adj*
WORD ORIGIN Greek *an* without + *arkh-* leader

anastigmat *n* a lens corrected for astigmatism **anastigmatic** *adj*

anathema (an-**nath**-im-a) *n* a detested person or thing: *the very colour was anathema to him*
WORD ORIGIN Greek: something accursed

anathematize *or* **-tise** *vb* **-tizing, -tized** *or* **-tising, -tised** to curse

anatomist *n* an expert in anatomy

anatomy *n, pl* **-mies 1** the science of the physical structure of animals and plants **2** the structure of an animal or plant **3** *informal* a person's body: *the male anatomy* **4** a detailed analysis: *an anatomy of the massacre* **anatomical** *adj*
WORD ORIGIN Greek *ana* up + *temnein* to cut

ANC African National Congress: South African political movement instrumental in bringing an end to apartheid

ancestor *n* **1** a person in former times from whom one is descended **2** a forerunner: *the immediate ancestor of rock and roll is rhythm and blues*
WORD ORIGIN Latin *antecedere* to go before

ancestral adj of or inherited from ancestors

ancestry n, pl -tries **1** family descent: of Japanese ancestry **2** origin or roots: a vehicle whose ancestry dated back to the 1950s

anchor n **1** a hooked device attached to a boat by a cable and dropped overboard to fasten the boat to the sea bottom **2** a source of stability or security: a spiritual anchor **3** anchors slang the brakes of a motor vehicle: he rammed on the anchors ▷ vb **4** to use an anchor to hold (a boat) in one place **5** to fasten securely: we anchored his wheelchair to a rock **WORD ORIGIN** Greek ankura

anchorage n a place where boats can be anchored

anchor ice n Canad ice that forms at the bottom of a lake or river

anchorite n a person who chooses to live in isolation for religious reasons **WORD ORIGIN** Greek anakhōrein to retire

anchorman or **anchorwoman** n **1** a broadcaster in a central studio, who links up and presents items from outside camera units and reporters in other studios **2** the last person to compete in a relay team

anchovy (an-chov-ee) n, pl -vies a small marine food fish with a salty taste **WORD ORIGIN** Spanish anchova

ancien régime (on-syan ray-zheem) n **1** the political and social system of France before the 1789 Revolution **2** a former system **WORD ORIGIN** French: old regime

ancient adj **1** dating from very long ago **2** very old **3** of the far past, esp. before the collapse of the Western Roman Empire (476 AD) ▷ n **4** ancients people who lived very long ago, such as the Romans and Greeks **WORD ORIGIN** Latin ante before

ancillary adj **1** supporting the main work of an organization: hospital ancillary workers **2** used as an extra or supplement: I had a small ancillary sleeping tent **WORD ORIGIN** Latin ancilla female servant

and conj **1** in addition to: plants and birds **2** as a consequence: she fell downstairs and broke her neck **3** afterwards: she excused herself and left **4** used for emphasis or to indicate repetition or continuity: they called again and again **5** used to express a contrast between instances of something: there are jobs and jobs **6** informal used in place of to in infinitives after verbs such as try, go, and come: come and see us again; go and wash your hands **WORD ORIGIN** Old English

≡ **USAGE**
≡ See at **try**.

andante (an-dan-tay) music adv **1** moderately slowly ▷ n **2** a passage or piece to be performed moderately slowly **WORD ORIGIN** Italian andare to walk

andantino (an-dan-tee-no) music adv **1** slightly faster than andante ▷ n, pl -nos **2** a passage or piece to be performed in this way

andiron n either of a pair of metal stands for supporting logs in a fireplace

WORD ORIGIN Old French andier

and/or conj not standard either one or the other or both

≡ **USAGE**
≡ Many people think that and/or is only
≡ acceptable in legal and commercial
≡ contexts. In other contexts, it is better
≡ to use or both: many drinkers lose their jobs
≡ or their driving licences or both (not their jobs
≡ and/or their driving licences).

androgen n any of the steroids that promote the development of male sexual organs and certain male sexual characteristics **WORD ORIGIN** Greek anēr man + -gen (suffix) producing

androgynous adj having both male and female characteristics **WORD ORIGIN** Greek anēr man + gunē woman

android n a robot resembling a human being **WORD ORIGIN** Late Greek androeidēs manlike

andrology (an-drol-la-jee) n the branch of medicine concerned with diseases and conditions specific to men **andrologist** n **WORD ORIGIN** Greek anēr man + -LOGY

anecdote n a short amusing account of an incident **anecdotal** adj **WORD ORIGIN** Greek anekdotos not published

anemia n US anaemia

anemometer n an instrument for recording wind speed

anemone (an-nem-on-ee) n a flowering plant with white, purple, or red flowers **WORD ORIGIN** Greek: windflower

aneroid barometer n a device for measuring air pressure, consisting of a partially evacuated chamber, in which variations in pressure cause a pointer on the lid to move **WORD ORIGIN** Greek a not + nēros wet

anesthesia n US anaesthesia

aneurysm or **aneurism** (an-new-riz-zum) n med a permanent swelling of a blood vessel **WORD ORIGIN** Greek aneurunein to dilate

anew adv **1** once more **2** in a different way

angel n **1** a spiritual being believed to be an attendant or messenger of God **2** a conventional representation of an angel as a human being with wings **3** informal a person who is kind, pure, or beautiful **4** informal an investor in a theatrical production **WORD ORIGIN** Greek angelos messenger

angel cake or esp. US **angel food cake** n a very light sponge cake

angelfish n, pl -fish or -fishes a South American aquarium fish with large fins

angelic adj **1** very kind, pure, or beautiful **2** of or relating to angels **angelically** adv

angelica (an-jell-ik-a) n a plant whose candied stalks are used in cookery **WORD ORIGIN** Medieval Latin (herba) angelica angelic herb

Angelus (an-jell-uss) n RC Church **1** prayers recited in the morning, at midday, and in the evening **2** the bell signalling the times of these prayers **WORD ORIGIN** Latin Angelus domini

nuntiavit Mariae the angel of the Lord brought tidings to Mary

anger n **1** a feeling of extreme annoyance or displeasure ▷ vb **2** to make (someone) angry **WORD ORIGIN** Old Norse angr grief

angina (an-jine-a) or **angina pectoris** (peck-tor-riss) n a sudden intense pain in the chest caused by a momentary lack of adequate blood supply to the heart muscle **WORD ORIGIN** Greek ankhonē a strangling

angle¹ n **1** the space between or shape formed by two straight lines or surfaces that meet **2** the divergence between two such lines or surfaces, measured in degrees **3** a recess or corner **4** point of view ▷ vb -gling, -gled **5** to move in or place at an angle **6** to write (an article) from a particular point of view **WORD ORIGIN** Latin angulus corner

angle² vb -gling, -gled **1** to fish with a hook and line **2** angle for to try to get by hinting: he's just angling for sympathy **WORD ORIGIN** Old English angul fish-hook

angler n a person who fishes with a hook and line

Angles pl n a race from N Germany who settled in E and N England in the 5th and 6th centuries AD **WORD ORIGIN** Latin Anglus a person from Angul, Germany

Anglican adj **1** of or relating to the Church of England ▷ n **2** a member of the Anglican Church **Anglicanism** n **WORD ORIGIN** Latin Anglicus English, of the Angles

Anglicism n an expression or custom that is peculiar to the English

anglicize or -**cise** vb -cizing, -cized or -cising, -cised to make or become English in outlook or form

angling n the art or sport of fishing with a hook and line

Anglo n, pl -glos **1** US a White inhabitant of the US who is not of Latin extraction **2** Canad an English-speaking Canadian

Anglo- combining form English or British: the history of Anglo-German relations **WORD ORIGIN** Medieval Latin Anglii the English

Anglo-French adj **1** of England and France **2** of the Anglo-French language ▷ n **3** the Norman-French language of medieval England

Anglo-Indian adj **1** of England and India **2** denoting or relating to Anglo-Indians ▷ n **3** a person of mixed British and Indian descent **4** an English person who has lived for a long time in India

Anglo-Norman adj **1** of or relating to the Norman conquerors of England or their language ▷ n **2** a Norman inhabitant of England after 1066 **3** the Anglo-French language

Anglophile n a person who admires England or the English

Anglo-Saxon n **1** a member of any of the West Germanic tribes that settled in Britain from the 5th century AD

SCRABBLE
Two-Letter Words

There are 124 two-letter words in Collins Scrabble Tournament and Club Word List. Two-letter words are useful for 'tagging', allowing you to play parallel to letters already on the board. This will rack you up lots of points, especially if you manage to get your Q, Z, X, or J onto a triple. Although you don't have to know the meaning of the words you table in Scrabble, it may make this list easier to memorize. So if you don't know your *xi* from your *za*, read on...

AA volcanic rock
AB abdominal muscle
AD short form of advertisement
AE Scots word meaning one or a single
AG agriculture
AH expression of pleasure, pain, or sympathy
AI the three-toed sloth
AL Asian shrub or tree
AM part of the verb to be
AN the indefinite article used before an initial vowel sound
AR the letter R
AS while, because, since
AT used to indicate location or position
AW expression of disapproval, commiseration, or appeal
AX US spelling of axe
AY yes
BA the soul represented as a bird with a human head
BE exist, live
BI short for bisexual
BO exclamation used to startle or surprise
BY near to, at the side of, via; a bye
CH obsolete form of I
DA Burmese knife
DE of or from
DI plural form of deus
DO perform, complete; a party
EA dialect word for river
ED education
EE Scots word for eye

EF the letter F
EH exclamation of surprise or inquiry
EL elevated railway
EM printing meaurement
EN printing measurement
ER expression of hesitation
ES the letter S
ET past tense of eat
EX former spouse or partner
FA variant spelling of fah
FE charge, fee
FY variant spelling of fie
GI martial arts suit
GO to move or proceed; a turn or attempt
GU musical instrument
HA exclamation of derision, triumph, or surprise
HE male person or animal
HI hello
HM expression of thoughtful consideration
HO exclamation used to attract attention
ID unconscious primitive instincts
IF in case that; an uncertainty or condition
IN inside, within; a way of approaching a person
IO cry of joy or grief
IS part of the verb to be
IT nonhuman thing
JA yes
JO Scots word for a sweetheart
KA ancient Egyptian spirit
KI Japanese martial art
KO Maori digging-stick

KY Scots word for cows
LA variant spelling of lah
LI Chinese unit of length
LO look!
MA word for mother
ME refers to the speaker or writer
MI musical term
MM expression of satisfaction
MO short for moment
MU 12th Greek letter
MY of or belonging to the speaker or writer
NA Scots word for no
NE not, nor
NO expression of denial, refusal, etc
NU 13th Greek letter
NY nigh; to approach
OB objection
OD hypothetical force
OE grandchild
OF belonging to
OH exclamation of surprise, pain, etc
OI exclamation used to attract attention
OM intonation chanted as a mantra
ON not off; the side of the field on which the batsman stands
OO Scots word for wool
OP short for operation
OR conjunction used to join alternatives; gold
OS bone
OU South African slang for a man
OW exclamation of pain
OX adult castrated bull

OY grandchild
PA word for father
PE 17th Hebrew letter
PI 16th Greek letter
PO chamberpot
QI vital energy believed to circulate in the body
RE musical term
SH exclamation to request silence
SI musical term
SO variant spelling of soh
ST exclamation to request silence
TA thank you
TE musical term
TI variant spelling of te
TO towards, in the direction of
UG cause loathing in, hate
UH expression of uncertainty
UM sound of hesitation
UN dialect variant of one
UP in a higher place; a rise or success
UR sound of hesitation
US refers to the speaker or writer and another
UT syllable used for the note C
WE refers to the speaker or writer and another
WO archaic spelling of woe
XI 14th Greek letter
XU monetary unit
YA you
YE archaic word for you
YO expression of greeting
YU jade
ZA pizza
ZO Tibetan breed of cattle

2 any White person whose native language is English **3** same as **Old English 4** *informal* plain, blunt, and often rude English ▷ *adj* **5** of the Anglo-Saxons or the Old English language **6** of the White Protestant culture of Britain and the US

angora *n* **1** a variety of goat, cat, or rabbit with long silky hair **2** the hair of the angora goat or rabbit **3** cloth made from this hair
WORD ORIGIN *Angora*, former name of Ankara, in Turkey

Angostura Bitters *pl n trademark* a bitter tonic, used as a flavouring in alcoholic drinks
WORD ORIGIN from *Angostura* in Venezuela

angry *adj* **-grier, -griest 1** feeling or expressing annoyance or rage **2** severely inflamed: *he had angry welts on his forehead* **3** dark and stormy: *angry waves* **angrily** *adv*

USAGE
It was formerly considered incorrect to talk about being *angry at* a person, but this use is now acceptable.

angst *n* a feeling of anxiety
WORD ORIGIN German

angstrom *n* a unit of length equal to 10^{-10} metre, used to measure wavelengths
WORD ORIGIN after Anders J. *Ångström*, Swedish physicist

anguish *n* great mental pain
WORD ORIGIN Latin *angustus* narrow

anguished *adj* feeling or showing great mental pain: *anguished cries*

angular *adj* **1** lean and bony: *his angular face* **2** having an angle or angles **3** measured by an angle: *angular momentum* **angularity** *n*

anhydride *n chem* a substance that combines with water to form an acid

anhydrous *adj chem* containing no water
WORD ORIGIN Greek *an* without + *hudōr* water

anil *n* a West Indian shrub which is a source of indigo
WORD ORIGIN Arabic *an-nīl*, the indigo

aniline *n chem* a colourless oily poisonous liquid, obtained from coal tar and used for making dyes, plastics, and explosives

animal *n* **1** *zool* any living being that is capable of voluntary movement and possesses specialized sense organs **2** any living being other than a human being **3** any living being with four legs **4** a cruel or coarse person **5** *facetious* a person or thing: *there's no such animal* ▷ *adj* **6** of or from animals **7** of or relating to physical needs or desires
WORD ORIGIN Latin *animalis* (adjective) living, breathing

animalcule *n* a microscopic animal

animal husbandry *n* the science of breeding, rearing, and caring for farm animals

animalism *n* **1** preoccupation with physical matters; sensuality **2** the doctrine that human beings lack a spiritual nature

animality *n* **1** the animal instincts of human beings **2** the state of being an animal

animalize *or* **-ise** *vb* **-izing, -ized** *or* **-ising, -ised** to make (a person) brutal or sensual

animal magnetism *n* the quality of being sexually attractive

animal rights *pl n* the rights of animals to be protected from human abuse

animal spirits *pl n* outgoing and boisterous enthusiasm
WORD ORIGIN from a vital force once supposed to be dispatched by the brain to all points of the body

animate *vb* **-mating, -mated 1** to give life to **2** to make lively **3** to produce (a story) as an animated cartoon ▷ *adj* **4** having life
WORD ORIGIN Latin *anima* breath, spirit

animated *adj* **1** interesting and lively **2** (of a cartoon) made by using animation **animatedly** *adv*

animated cartoon *n* a film produced by photographing a series of gradually changing drawings, which give the illusion of movement when the series is projected rapidly

animation *n* **1** the techniques used in the production of animated cartoons **2** liveliness and enthusiasm: *there's an animation in her that is new*

animator *n* a person who makes animated cartoons

animism *n* the belief that natural objects possess souls **animist** *n, adj* **animistic** *adj*
WORD ORIGIN Latin *anima* breath, spirit

animosity *n, pl* **-ties** a powerful dislike or hostility
WORD ORIGIN see ANIMUS

animus *n* intense dislike; hatred
WORD ORIGIN Latin: mind, spirit

anion (**an-eye-on**) *n* an ion with negative charge **anionic** *adj*
WORD ORIGIN Greek *ana-* up + *ienai* to go

anise (**an-niss**) *n* a Mediterranean plant with liquorice-flavoured seeds
WORD ORIGIN Greek *anison*

aniseed *n* the liquorice-flavoured seeds of the anise plant, used for flavouring

ankh *n* a T-shaped cross with a loop on the top, which symbolized eternal life in ancient Egypt
WORD ORIGIN Egyptian *'nh* life, soul

ankle *n* **1** the joint connecting the leg and the foot **2** the part of the leg just above the foot
WORD ORIGIN Old Norse

anklet *n* an ornamental chain worn round the ankle

ankylosis (ang-kill-**loh**-siss) *n* abnormal immobility of a joint, caused by a fibrous growth within the joint
WORD ORIGIN Greek *ankuloun* to crook

anna *n* a former Indian coin worth one sixteenth of a rupee
WORD ORIGIN Hindi *ānā*

annals *pl n* **1** yearly records of events **2** regular reports of the work of a society or other organization **annalist** *n*
WORD ORIGIN Latin (*libri*) *annales* yearly (books)

anneal *vb* to toughen (glass or metal) by heat treatment
WORD ORIGIN Old English *onǣlan*

annelid *n* a worm with a segmented body, such as the earthworm
WORD ORIGIN Latin *anulus* ring

annex *vb* **1** to seize (territory) by conquest or occupation **2** to take without permission **3** to join or add (something) to something larger **annexation** *n*
WORD ORIGIN Latin *annectere* to attach to

annexe *or esp.* US **annex** *n* **1** an extension to a main building **2** a building used as an addition to a main one nearby

annihilate *vb* **-lating, -lated 1** to destroy (a place or a group of people) completely **2** *informal* to defeat totally in an argument or a contest **annihilation** *n*
WORD ORIGIN Latin *nihil* nothing

anniversary *n, pl* **-ries 1** the date on which an event, such as a wedding, occurred in some previous year **2** the celebration of this
WORD ORIGIN Latin *annus* year + *vertere* to turn

anno Domini *adv* in the year of our Lord

annotate *vb* **-tating, -tated** to add critical or explanatory notes to a written work **annotation** *n*
WORD ORIGIN Latin *nota* mark

announce *vb* **-nouncing, -nounced 1** to make known publicly **2** to proclaim **3** to declare the arrival of (a person) **4** to be a sign of: *snowdrops announced the arrival of spring* **announcement** *n*
WORD ORIGIN Latin *annuntiare*

announcer *n* a person who introduces programmes on radio or television

annoy *vb* **1** to irritate or displease **2** to harass sexually **annoyance** *n* **annoying** *adj*
WORD ORIGIN Latin *in odio* (*esse*) (to be) hated

annual *adj* **1** occurring or done once a year: *the union's annual conference* **2** lasting for a year: *the annual subscription* ▷ *n* **3** a plant that completes its life cycle in one year **4** a book published once every year **annually** *adv*
WORD ORIGIN Latin *annus* year

annualize *or* **-ise** *vb* **-izing, -ized** *or* **-ising, -ised** to calculate (a rate) for or as if for a year

annuity *n, pl* **-ties** a fixed sum payable at specified intervals over a period
WORD ORIGIN Latin *annuus* annual

annul *vb* **-nulling, -nulled** to declare (a contract or marriage) invalid
WORD ORIGIN Latin *nullus* not any

annular (**an-new-lar**) *adj* ring-shaped
WORD ORIGIN Latin *anulus* ring

annular eclipse *n* an eclipse of the sun in which a ring of sunlight can be seen surrounding the shadow of the moon

annulate (**an-new-lit**) *adj* having, composed of, or marked with rings
WORD ORIGIN Latin *anulus* ring

annulment *n* the formal declaration that a contract or marriage is invalid

Annunciation *n* **1 the Annunciation** the announcement by the angel Gabriel to the Virgin Mary of her conception of Christ **2** the festival commemorating this, on March 25 (Lady Day)
WORD ORIGIN Latin *annuntiare* to

announce

anode *n electronics* the positive electrode in an electrolytic cell or in an electronic valve
WORD ORIGIN Greek *anodos* a way up

anodize *or* **-dise** *vb* **-dizing, -dized** *or* **-dising, -dised** *chem* to coat (a metal) with a protective oxide film by electrolysis

anodyne *n* **1** something that relieves pain or distress ▷ *adj* **2** neutral **3** capable of relieving pain or distress
WORD ORIGIN Greek *an-* without + *odunē* pain

anoint *vb* to smear with oil as a sign of consecration
WORD ORIGIN Latin *inunguere*

anointing of the sick *n RC Church* a sacrament in which a person who is dying is anointed by a priest

anomalous *adj* different from the normal or usual order or type
WORD ORIGIN Greek *an-* not + *homalos* even

anomaly (an-**nom**-a-lee) *n, pl* **-lies** something that deviates from the normal; an irregularity

anomie *or* **anomy** (**an**-oh-mee) *n sociol* lack of social or moral standards
WORD ORIGIN Greek *a-* without + *nomos* law

anon *adv old-fashioned or informal* soon: *you shall see him anon*
WORD ORIGIN Old English *on āne* in one, that is, immediately

anon. anonymous

anonymize *or* **-ise** *vb* **-izing, -ized** *or* **-ising, -ised** to organize in a way that preserves anonymity: *anonymized AIDS screening*

anonymous *adj* **1** by someone whose name is unknown or withheld: *an anonymous letter* **2** having no known name: *an anonymous writer* **3** lacking distinguishing characteristics: *an anonymous little town* **4 Anonymous** of an organization that helps applicants who remain anonymous: *Alcoholics Anonymous* **anonymity** *n*
WORD ORIGIN Greek *an-* without + *onoma* name

anorak *n* **1** a waterproof hip-length jacket with a hood **2** *Brit informal* a socially inept person with a hobby considered to be boring
WORD ORIGIN Greenland Inuktitut *ánorâq*

anorexia *or* **anorexia nervosa** *n* a psychological disorder characterized by fear of becoming fat and refusal to eat **anorexic** *adj, n*
WORD ORIGIN Greek *an-* without + *orexis* appetite

another *adj* **1** one more: *they don't have the right to demand another chance* **2** different: *you'll have to find another excuse* ▷ *pron* **3** one more: *help yourself to another* **4** a different one: *one way or another*
WORD ORIGIN originally *an other*

answer *vb* **1** to reply or respond (to) by word or act **2** to be responsible (to a person) **3** to reply correctly to (a question) **4** to respond or react: *a dog that answers to the name of Pugg* **5** to meet the requirements of **6** to give a defence of

(a charge) ▷ *n* **7** a reply to a question, request, letter, or article **8** a solution to a problem **9** a reaction or response
WORD ORIGIN Old English *andswaru*

answerable *adj* **answerable for** *or* **to** responsible for or accountable to

answer back *vb* to reply rudely (to)

answering machine *n* a device for answering a telephone automatically and recording messages

ant *n* a small often wingless insect, living in highly organized colonies
WORD ORIGIN Old English *ǣmette*

antacid *chem n* **1** a substance used to treat acidity in the stomach ▷ *adj* **2** having the properties of this substance

antagonism *n* openly expressed hostility

antagonist *n* an opponent or adversary **antagonistic** *adj*

antagonize *or* **-nise** *vb* **-nizing, -nized** *or* **-nising, -nised** to arouse hostility in: *it was not prudent to antagonize a hired killer*
WORD ORIGIN Greek *anti-* against + *agōn* contest

antalkali (ant-**alk**-a-lie) *n chem* a substance that neutralizes alkalis

Antarctic *n* **1 the Antarctic** the area around the South Pole ▷ *adj* **2** of this region
WORD ORIGIN Greek *antarktikos*

Antarctic Circle *n* the imaginary circle around the earth at latitude 66° 32′ S

ante *n* **1** the stake put up before the deal in poker by the players **2** *informal* a sum of money representing a person's share **3 up the ante** *informal* to increase the costs or risks involved in an action ▷ *vb* **-teing, -ted** *or* **-teed 4** to place (one's stake) in poker **5 ante up** *informal* to pay
WORD ORIGIN Latin: before

ante- *prefix* before in time or position: *antediluvian; antechamber*
WORD ORIGIN Latin

anteater *n* a mammal with a long snout used for eating termites

antecedent *n* **1** an event or circumstance that happens or exists before another **2** *grammar* a word or phrase to which a relative pronoun, such as *who*, refers **3 antecedents** a person's ancestors and past history ▷ *adj* **4** preceding in time or order
WORD ORIGIN Latin *antecedere* to go before

antechamber *n* an anteroom

antedate *vb* **-dating, -dated 1** to be or occur at an earlier date than **2** to give (something) a date that is earlier than the actual date

antediluvian *adj* **1** belonging to the ages before the biblical Flood **2** old-fashioned
WORD ORIGIN Latin *ante-* before + *diluvium* flood

antelope *n, pl* **-lopes** *or* **-lope** any of a group of graceful deerlike mammals of Africa and Asia, which have long legs and horns
WORD ORIGIN Late Greek *antholops* a legendary beast

antenatal *adj* before birth; during pregnancy: *an antenatal clinic*

antenna *n* **1** *pl* **-nae** one of a pair of mobile feelers on the heads of insects, lobsters, and certain other creatures **2** *pl* **-nas** an aerial: *TV antennas*
WORD ORIGIN Latin: sail yard

antepenultimate *adj* **1** third from last ▷ *n* **2** anything that is third from last

ante-post *adj* *Brit* (of a bet) placed before the runners in a race are confirmed

anterior *adj* **1** at or towards the front **2** earlier
WORD ORIGIN Latin

anteroom *n* a small room leading into a larger room, often used as a waiting room

anthem *n* **1** a song of loyalty or devotion: *a national anthem* **2** a piece of music for a choir, usually set to words from the Bible
WORD ORIGIN Late Latin *antiphona* antiphon

anther *n bot* the part of the stamen of a flower which contains the pollen
WORD ORIGIN Greek *anthos* flower

ant hill *n* a mound of soil built by ants around the entrance to their nest

anthology *n, pl* **-gies** a collection of poems or other literary pieces by various authors **anthologist** *n*
WORD ORIGIN Greek *anthos* flower + *legein* to collect

anthracite *n* a hard coal that burns slowly with little smoke or flame but intense heat
WORD ORIGIN Greek *anthrax* coal

anthrax *n* a dangerous infectious disease of cattle and sheep, which can be passed to humans
WORD ORIGIN Greek: carbuncle

anthropocentric *adj* regarding the human being as the most important factor in the universe
WORD ORIGIN Greek *anthrōpos* human being + Latin *centrum* centre

anthropoid *adj* **1** resembling a human being ▷ *n* **2** an ape, such as the chimpanzee, that resembles a human being

anthropology *n* the study of human origins, institutions, and beliefs **anthropological** *adj* **anthropologist** *n*
WORD ORIGIN Greek *anthrōpos* human being + *logos* word

anthropomorphism *n* the attribution of human form or personality to a god, animal, or object **anthropomorphic** *adj*

anthropomorphous *adj* shaped like a human being
WORD ORIGIN Greek *anthrōpos* human being + *morphē* form

anti *informal adj* **1** opposed to a party, policy, or attitude ▷ *n* **2** an opponent of a party, policy, or attitude

anti- *prefix* **1** against or opposed to: *antiwar* **2** opposite to: *anticlimax* **3** counteracting or neutralizing: *antifreeze*
WORD ORIGIN Greek

anti-aircraft *adj* for defence against aircraft attack

antiballistic missile *n* a missile designed to destroy a ballistic missile in flight

antibiotic *n* **1** a chemical substance

capable of destroying bacteria ▷ *adj* **2** of or relating to antibiotics

antibody *n, pl* **-bodies** a protein produced in the blood which destroys bacteria

Antichrist *n* **1** *New Testament* the chief enemy of Christ **2** an enemy of Christ or Christianity

anticipate *vb* **-pating, -pated 1** to foresee and act in advance of: *he anticipated some probing questions* **2** to look forward to **3** to make use of (something, such as one's salary) before receiving it **4** to mention (part of a story) before its proper time **anticipatory** *adj*

WORD ORIGIN Latin *ante-* before + *capere* to take

USAGE
The use of *anticipate* to mean *expect* should be avoided.

anticipation *n* the act of anticipating; expectation, premonition, or foresight: *smiling in happy anticipation*

anticlerical *adj* opposed to the power and influence of the clergy in politics

anticlimax *n* a disappointing conclusion to a series of events **anticlimactic** *adj*

anticline *n geol* a fold of rock raised up into a broad arch so that the strata slope down on both sides

anticlockwise *adv, adj* in the opposite direction to the rotation of the hands of a clock

anticoagulant (an-tee-koh-**ag**-yew-lant) *n* a substance that prevents the clotting of blood

antics *pl n* absurd acts or postures
WORD ORIGIN Italian *antico* something grotesque (from fantastic carvings found in ruins of ancient Rome)

anticyclone *n meteorol* an area of moving air of high pressure in which the winds rotate outwards

antidepressant *n* **1** a drug used to treat depression ▷ *adj* **2** of or relating to such a drug

antidote *n* **1** *med* a substance that counteracts a poison **2** anything that counteracts a harmful condition: *exercise may be a good antidote to insomnia*
WORD ORIGIN Greek *anti-* against + *didonai* to give

antifreeze *n* a liquid added to water to lower its freezing point, used in the radiator of a motor vehicle to prevent freezing

antigen (**an**-tee-jen) *n* a substance, usually a toxin, that causes the body to produce antibodies
WORD ORIGIN *anti(body)* + *-gen* (suffix) producing

antihero *n, pl* **-roes** a central character in a novel, play, or film, who lacks the traditional heroic virtues

antihistamine *n* a drug that neutralizes the effects of histamine, used in the treatment of allergies

antiknock *n* a substance added to motor fuel to reduce knocking in the engine caused by too rapid combustion

antilogarithm *n maths* a number corresponding to a given logarithm

antimacassar *n* a cloth put over the back of a chair to prevent it getting dirty
WORD ORIGIN *anti-* + *Macassar* (oil)

antimatter *n physics* a hypothetical form of matter composed of antiparticles

antimony (**an**-tim-mon-ee) *n chem* a silvery-white metallic element that is added to alloys to increase their strength. Symbol: Sb
WORD ORIGIN Medieval Latin *antimonium*

antinomy (**an**-tin-nom-ee) *n, pl* **-mies** contradiction between two laws or principles that are reasonable in themselves
WORD ORIGIN Greek *anti-* against + *nomos* law

antinovel *n* a type of prose fiction in which conventional elements of the novel are rejected

antinuclear *adj* opposed to nuclear weapons or nuclear power

antioxidant *n chem* a substance that slows down the process of oxidation

antiparticle *n nuclear physics* an elementary particle that has the same mass as its corresponding particle, but opposite charge and opposite magnetism

antipasto *n, pl* **-tos** an appetizer in an Italian meal
WORD ORIGIN Italian: before food

antipathy (an-**tip**-a-thee) *n* a feeling of strong dislike or hostility **antipathetic** *adj*
WORD ORIGIN Greek *anti-* against + *patheia* feeling

antipersonnel *adj* (of weapons or bombs) designed to be used against people rather than equipment

antiperspirant *n* a substance applied to the skin to reduce or prevent perspiration

antiphon *n* a hymn sung in alternate parts by two groups of singers
WORD ORIGIN Greek *anti-* against + *phōnē* sound

antipodes (an-**tip**-pod-deez) *pl n* **1** any two places that are situated diametrically opposite one another on the earth's surface **2** **the Antipodes** Australia and New Zealand **antipodean** *adj*
WORD ORIGIN Greek plural of *antipous* having the feet opposite

antipope *n* a pope set up in opposition to the one chosen by church laws

antipyretic *adj* **1** reducing fever ▷ *n* **2** a drug that reduces fever

antiquarian *adj* **1** collecting or dealing with antiquities or rare books ▷ *n* **2** an antiquary

antiquary *n, pl* **-quaries** a person who collects, deals in, or studies antiques or ancient works of art

antiquated *adj* obsolete or old-fashioned
WORD ORIGIN Latin *antiquus* ancient

antique *n* **1** a decorative object or piece of furniture, of an earlier period, that is valued for its beauty, workmanship, and age ▷ *adj* **2** made in an earlier period **3** *informal* old-fashioned
WORD ORIGIN Latin *antiquus* ancient

antiquity *n, pl* **-ties 1** great age **2** the far distant past **3** **antiquities** objects dating from ancient times

antiracism *n* the policy of challenging racism or promoting racial tolerance **antiracist** *n, adj*

antirrhinum *n* a two-lipped flower of various colours, such as the snapdragon
WORD ORIGIN Greek *anti-* like, imitating + *rhis* nose

antiscorbutic *adj* preventing or curing scurvy

anti-Semitic *adj* discriminating against Jews **anti-Semite** *n* **anti-Semitism** *n*

antiseptic *adj* **1** preventing infection by killing germs ▷ *n* **2** an antiseptic substance

antiserum *n* blood serum containing antibodies used to treat or provide immunity to a disease

antishake *adj* (of photographic equipment) reducing the blurring caused by movement of the person taking a photograph

antisocial *adj* **1** avoiding the company of other people **2** (of behaviour) annoying or harmful to other people

antisocial behaviour order *n* a civil order made against a troublesome individual which restricts his or her activities or movements

antistatic *adj* reducing the effects of static electricity

antitank *adj* (of weapons) designed to destroy military tanks

antithesis (an-**tith**-iss-iss) *n, pl* **-ses** (-seez) **1** the exact opposite **2** *rhetoric* the placing together of contrasting ideas or words to produce an effect of balance, such as *where gods command, mere mortals must obey* **antithetical** *adj*
WORD ORIGIN Greek *anti-* against + *tithenai* to place

antitoxin *n* an antibody that acts against a toxin **antitoxic** *adj*

antitrades *pl n* winds blowing in the opposite direction from and above the trade winds

antitrust *adj US, Austral, & S African* (of laws) opposing business monopolies

antivirus *adj* **1** relating to software designed to protect computer files from viruses ▷ *n* **2** such a piece of software

antler *n* one of a pair of branched horns on the heads of male deer
WORD ORIGIN Old French *antoillier*

antonym *n* a word that means the opposite of another
WORD ORIGIN Greek *anti-* opposite + *onoma* name

antrum *n, pl* **-tra** *anat* a natural cavity, esp. in a bone
WORD ORIGIN Latin: cave

Anubis *n* an Egyptian god with a jackal's head

anus (**ain**-uss) *n* the opening at the end of the alimentary canal, through which faeces are discharged
WORD ORIGIN Latin

anvil *n* a heavy iron block on which metals are hammered into particular shapes
WORD ORIGIN Old English *anfealt*

anxiety *n, pl* **-ties 1** a state of uneasiness

Canadian English

Does Canadian English exist? In one way, the term needs no defence. Canada has three coasts and the second-largest land mass in the world, and people have lived there for millennia. It has a longer constitutional history than most modern nation-states. It follows that Canadian English should assume a characteristic form.

Yet the term is arguable, if only because in the postmodern global age the very concept of the nation is debatable. English has acquired new varieties, especially in South and Southeast Asia and in Africa, which may not correspond to political boundaries. At the same time, the exponential growth of the Internet and satellite communications has made general English omnipresent and, some would say, omnipotent. The proper question may be: Is there English or Englishes? A compromise-minded Canadian might answer 'Both'.

Culture and the human brain shape how and what each person speaks; the confluence of history, geography, and climate forms a people. Evolving out of British and French colonies, Canadians adopted innumerable British legal, political, and administrative terms. After settlement, the population that stretched westward to the Pacific across rivers, lakes, marsh, prairie, and mountain needed names for the new plants and animals they found. In this, they were greatly aided by the native peoples' nomenclature. Some nouns at the core of common compounds in Canadian English – *beaver, berry, bush, cod, caribou, deer, duck, ground, log, maple, moose* – testify to the encounter with the wilderness. The climate naturally brought forth compounds based on *cold, frost, ice,* and *winter.*

After many wars, peace treaties, and political or diplomatic wrangles of all kinds, English Canada accommodated itself to its French speakers, and also rejected the alternative of the US republican model. Such a history has spawned many terms. In the nineteenth and twentieth centuries, waves of immigrants brought their traditions and their words: the Chinese who helped build the Canadian Pacific Railway across prairie and mountain, and later operated the only restaurants in little towns, the Ukrainians who ploughed the western plains, the Italians and Portuguese who toiled in the construction trades.

Canadian English is a hybrid. With many exceptions, it follows the British spelling pattern, a colonial inheritance. With some exceptions, it follows the standard northern form of US pronunciation, partly because of the Loyalists who fled north after the Revolutionary War, mainly because of the immensely long border Canada and the United States share. Similarly, many words, including sports terms, are not Canadianisms but North Americanisms, even though they may be more used north of the border that used to be called conventionally, and a little misleadingly, the *Forty-Ninth Parallel.* The tendency of *Canucks* to use synonyms or alternate spellings of a word can suggest that they possess a larger vocabulary than they actually do.

Even given the similarities to the speech and lexicon of the United States and the United Kingdom, national differences emerged, some due to federal government laws. A national sales tax was termed the *GST (Goods and Services Tax)*, not the *VAT.* Also departing from British English, a Canadian *overpass* carried one stream of highway traffic above another, not a *flyover*, and a road junction that took traffic around a central island was a *rotary*, not a *roundabout.* Metrication ensured that Canadian measures of weights, distances, dimensions, and temperature emulated those of European, not US or traditional Imperial standards.

To these were added such distinctively Canadian words as *loonie* and *toonie*, the one- and two-dollar coins; *parkette*, a small urban park; and *parkade*, a parking garage. Since household power is often generated by hydroelectricity, householders pay *hydro* bills. *Unemployment insurance* benefits, once informally called *pogey*, became *employment insurance*. A person who buys a cup of coffee with two helpings of cream and sugar is buying a *double-double* or, if alcoholically inclined, a *mickey*, a half-bottle, of liquor, *Calgary red-eye*, a drink of beer and tomato juice, or even a *two-four*, a case of 24 bottles of beer. Dog-owners strolling in a parkette are expected to obey *stoop and scoop* regulations to pick up their pets' excrement. Canadians like to laugh at their American cousins for being litigious yet they are, if anything, equally legalistic.

a

about what may happen **2** eagerness: *she was uneasy with his mixture of diffidence and anxiety to please*

anxious *adj* **1** worried and tense **2** causing anxiety: *he was anxious about the enormity of the task ahead* **3** intensely desiring: *both sides were anxious for a deal* **anxiously** *adv*
WORD ORIGIN Latin *anxius*

any *determiner* **1** one, some, or several, no matter how much or what kind: *the jar opener fits over the top of any bottle or jar; have you left me any?* **2** even the smallest amount or even one: *we can't answer any questions; don't give her any* **3** whatever or whichever: *police may board any bus or train* **4** an indefinite or unlimited amount or number: *he would sign cheques for any amount of money* ▷ *adv* **5** to even the smallest extent: *the outcome wouldn't have been any different*
WORD ORIGIN Old English *ænig*

anybody *pron* same as **anyone**

anyhow *adv* same as **anyway**

anyone *pron* **1** any person: *is anyone there?* **2** a person of any importance: *is he anyone?*

anything *pron* **1** any object, event, or action whatever: *they'll do anything to please you* ▷ *adv* **2** in any way: *it is not a computer nor anything like a computer* **3** **anything but** not at all: *the result is anything but simple*

anyway *adv* **1** at any rate; nevertheless **2** in any manner **3** carelessly

anywhere *adv* **1** in, at, or to any place **2** **get anywhere** to be successful: *we will not get anywhere by being negative*

anzac *n* NZ a type of biscuit

Anzac *n* (in the First World War) a soldier serving with the Australian and New Zealand Army Corps

Anzac Day April 25, a public holiday in Australia and New Zealand commemorating the Anzac landing at Gallipoli in 1915

AOB (on the agenda for a meeting) any other business

aorta (eh-**or**-ta) *n* the main artery of the body, which carries oxygen-rich blood from the heart
WORD ORIGIN Greek *aortē* something lifted

apace *adv literary* quickly: *repairs to the grid continued apace*

Apache *n, pl* **Apaches** or **Apache** a member of a Native American people of the southwestern US and N Mexico
WORD ORIGIN Mexican Spanish

apart *adj, adv* **1** to or in pieces: *he took a couple of cars apart and rebuilt them* **2** separate in time, place, or position: *my father and myself stood slightly apart from them* **3** individual or distinct: *a nation apart* **4** not being taken into account: *early timing difficulties apart, they encountered few problems* **5** **apart from** other than: *apart from searching the house there is little more we can do*
WORD ORIGIN Old French *a part* at (the) side

apartheid *n* (formerly) the official government policy of racial segregation in South Africa
WORD ORIGIN Afrikaans *apart* + *-heid*

-hood

apartment *n* **1** any room in a building, usually one of several forming a suite, used as living accommodation **2** *chiefly US & Canad* Also called (Brit): **flat** a set of rooms forming a home within a building usually incorporating other similar homes
WORD ORIGIN French *appartement*

apathy *n* lack of interest or enthusiasm **apathetic** *adj*
WORD ORIGIN Greek *a-* without + *pathos* feeling

ape *n* **1** an animal, such as a chimpanzee or gorilla, which is closely related to human beings and the monkeys, and which has no tail **2** a stupid, clumsy, or ugly man ▷ *vb* **aping, aped** **3** to imitate **apelike** *adj*
WORD ORIGIN Old English *apa*

apeman *n, pl* **-men** an extinct primate thought to have been the forerunner of true humans

aperient (ap-**peer**-ee-ent) *med adj* **1** having a mild laxative effect ▷ *n* **2** a mild laxative
WORD ORIGIN Latin *aperire* to open

aperitif (ap-per-rit-**teef**) *n* an alcoholic drink taken before a meal
WORD ORIGIN French

aperture *n* **1** a hole or opening **2** an opening in a camera or telescope that controls the amount of light entering it
WORD ORIGIN Latin *aperire* to open

apex *n* the highest point
WORD ORIGIN Latin: point

APEX Advance Purchase Excursion: a reduced fare for journeys booked a specified period in advance

aphasia *n* a disorder of the central nervous system that affects the ability to use and understand words
WORD ORIGIN Greek *a-* not + *phanai* to speak

aphelion (ap-**heel**-lee-on) *n, pl* **-lia** (-lee-a) *astron* the point in the orbit of a planet or comet when it is farthest from the sun
WORD ORIGIN Greek *apo-* from + *hēlios* sun

aphid (**eh**-fid) or **aphis** (**eh**-fiss) *n, pl* **aphids** or **aphides** (**eh**-fid-deez) a small insect which feeds by sucking the juices from plants
WORD ORIGIN New Latin

aphorism *n* a short clever saying expressing a general truth
WORD ORIGIN Greek *aphorizein* to define

aphrodisiac (af-roh-**diz**-zee-ak) *n* **1** a substance that arouses sexual desire ▷ *adj* **2** arousing sexual desire
WORD ORIGIN Greek *aphrodisios* belonging to Aphrodite, goddess of love

Aphrodite *n Greek myth* the goddess of love

apiary (**ape**-yar-ee) *n, pl* **-aries** a place where bees are kept **apiarist** *n*
WORD ORIGIN Latin *apis* bee

apical (**ape**-ik-kl) *adj* of, at, or being an apex

apiculture *n* the breeding and care of bees **apiculturist** *n*
WORD ORIGIN Latin *apis* bee + CULTURE

apiece *adv* each: *they had another cocktail apiece and then went down to dinner*

apish (**ape**-ish) *adj* **1** stupid or foolish

2 resembling an ape

aplomb (ap-**plom**) *n* calm self-possession
WORD ORIGIN French: uprightness

apocalypse *n* **1** the end of the world **2** an event of great destructive violence **apocalyptic** *adj*
WORD ORIGIN Greek *apo-* away + *kaluptein* to hide

Apocalypse *n* **the Apocalypse** *Bible* the Book of Revelation, the last book of the New Testament

Apocrypha (ap-**pok**-rif-fa) *pl n* **the Apocrypha** the 14 books included as an appendix to the Old Testament, which are not accepted as part of the Hebrew scriptures
WORD ORIGIN Late Latin *apocrypha (scripta)* hidden (writings), from Greek *apokruptein* to hide away

apocryphal *adj* of questionable authenticity: *the paranoid and clearly apocryphal story*

apogee (**ap**-oh-jee) *n* **1** *astron* the point in its orbit around the earth when the moon or a satellite is farthest from the earth **2** the highest point: *the concept found its apogee in Renaissance Italy*
WORD ORIGIN Greek *apogaios* away from the earth

apolitical *adj* not concerned with political matters

Apollo *n classical myth* the god of the sun, music, and medicine

apologetic *adj* showing or expressing regret **apologetically** *adv*

apologetics *n* the branch of theology concerned with the reasoned defence of Christianity

apologia *n* a formal written defence of a cause

apologist *n* a person who offers a formal defence of a cause

apologize or **-gise** *vb* **-gizing, -gized** or **-gising, -gised** to say that one is sorry for some wrongdoing

apology *n, pl* **-gies** **1** an expression of regret for some wrongdoing **2** same as **apologia** **3** **an apology for** a poor example of: *an apology for a man*
WORD ORIGIN Greek *apologia* a verbal defence, speech

apophthegm (**ap**-poth-em) *n* a short clever saying expressing a general truth
WORD ORIGIN Greek *apophthengesthai* to speak frankly

apoplectic *adj* **1** of apoplexy **2** *informal* furious

apoplexy *n med* a stroke
WORD ORIGIN Greek *apoplēssein* to cripple by a stroke

apostasy (ap-**poss**-stass-ee) *n, pl* **-sies** abandonment of one's religious faith, political party, or cause
WORD ORIGIN Greek *apostasis* desertion

apostate *n* **1** a person who has abandoned his or her religion, political party, or cause ▷ *adj* **2** guilty of apostasy

a posteriori (eh poss-steer-ee-**or**-rye) *adj logic* involving reasoning from effect to cause
WORD ORIGIN Latin: from the latter

apostle *n* **1** one of the twelve disciples chosen by Christ to preach his gospel

2 an ardent supporter of a cause or movement
WORD ORIGIN Greek *apostolos* a messenger

apostolic (ap-poss-**stoll**-ik) *adj* **1** of or relating to the Apostles or their teachings **2** of or relating to the pope

Apostolic See *n* the see of the pope, at Rome

apostrophe¹ (ap-**poss**-trof-fee) *n* the punctuation mark (') used to indicate the omission of a letter or letters, such as *he's* for *he has* or *he is*, and to form the possessive, as in *John's father*
WORD ORIGIN Greek *apostrephein* to turn away

apostrophe² *n rhetoric* a digression from a speech to address an imaginary or absent person or thing
WORD ORIGIN Greek: a turning away

apostrophize *or*-**phise** *vb* -phizing, -phized *or*-phising, -phised *rhetoric* to address an apostrophe to

apothecary *n, pl* -caries *old-fashioned* a chemist
WORD ORIGIN Late Latin *apothecarius* warehouseman

apotheosis (ap-poth-ee-**oh**-siss) *n, pl* -ses (-seez) **1** a perfect example: *it was the apotheosis of elitism* **2** elevation to the rank of a god
WORD ORIGIN Greek

appal *or US* **appall** *vb* -palling, -palled to fill with horror; terrify
WORD ORIGIN Old French *appalir* to turn pale

appalling *adj* **1** causing dismay, horror, or revulsion **2** very bad **appallingly** *adv*

apparatus *n* **1** a collection of equipment used for a particular purpose **2** any complicated device, system, or organization: *the whole apparatus of law enforcement*
WORD ORIGIN Latin

apparel (ap-**par**-rel) *n old-fashioned* clothing
WORD ORIGIN Latin *parare* to prepare

apparent *adj* **1** readily seen or understood; obvious **2** seeming as opposed to real: *he frowned in apparent bewilderment* **apparently** *adv*
WORD ORIGIN Latin *apparere* to appear

apparition *n* a ghost or ghostlike figure
WORD ORIGIN Latin *apparere* to appear

appeal *vb* **1** to make an earnest request **2 appeal to** to attract, please, or interest **3** *law* to apply to a higher court to review (a case or issue decided by a lower court) **4** to resort to a higher authority to change a decision **5** to call on in support of an earnest request: *he appealed for volunteers to help in relief work* **6** *cricket* to request the umpire to declare a batsman out ▷ *n* **7** an earnest request for money or help **8** the power to attract, please, or interest people **9** *law* a request for a review of a lower court's decision by a higher court **10** an application to a higher authority to change a decision that has been made **11** *cricket* a request to the umpire to declare the batsman out
WORD ORIGIN Latin *appellare* to entreat

appealing *adj* attractive or pleasing

appear *vb* **1** to come into sight **2** to seem: *it appears that no one survived the crash* **3** to come into existence: *a rash and small sores appeared around the shoulder and neck* **4** to perform: *she hadn't appeared in a film for almost fifty years* **5** to be present in court before a magistrate or judge: *two men have appeared in court in London charged with conspiracy* **6** to be published or become available: *both books appeared in 1934*
WORD ORIGIN Latin *apparere*

appearance *n* **1** a sudden or unexpected arrival of someone or something at a place **2** the introduction or invention of something: *the appearance of credit cards* **3** an act or instance of appearing: *it will be his fiftieth appearance for his country* **4** the way a person or thing looks: *I spotted a man of extraordinary appearance* **5 keep up appearances** to maintain the public impression of wellbeing or normality **6 put in an appearance** to attend an event briefly **7 to all appearances** apparently: *to all appearances they seemed enthralled by what he was saying*

appease *vb* -peasing, -peased **1** to pacify (someone) by yielding to his or her demands **2** to satisfy or relieve (a feeling) **appeasement** *n*
WORD ORIGIN Old French *apaisier*

appellant *law n* **1** a person who appeals to a higher court to review the decision of a lower court ▷ *adj* **2** same as **appellate**

appellate (ap-**pell**-it) *adj law* **1** of appeals **2** (of a tribunal) having the power to review appeals

appellation *n formal* a name or title

append *vb formal* to add as a supplement: *a series of notes appended to his translation of the poems*
WORD ORIGIN Latin *pendere* to hang

appendage *n* a secondary part attached to a main part

appendicectomy *or esp. US, Canad, & Austral* **appendectomy** *n, pl* -mies surgical removal of the appendix
WORD ORIGIN *appendix* + Greek *tomē* a cutting

appendicitis *n* inflammation of the appendix, causing abdominal pain

appendix (ap-**pen**-dix) *n, pl* -dices (-diss-seez) *or*-dixes **1** separate additional material at the end of a book **2** *anat* a short thin tube, closed at one end and attached to the large intestine at the other end
WORD ORIGIN Latin

appertain *vb* **appertain to** to belong to, relate to, or be connected with
WORD ORIGIN Latin *ad-* to + *pertinere* to pertain

appetence *or* **appetency** *n, pl* -tences *or*-tencies a craving or desire
WORD ORIGIN Latin *appetentia*

appetite *n* **1** a desire for food or drink **2** a liking or willingness: *he had an insatiable appetite for publicity*
WORD ORIGIN Latin *appetere* to desire ardently

appetizer *or*-iser *n* a small amount of food or drink taken at the start of a meal to stimulate the appetite

appetizing *or*-ising *adj* stimulating the appetite; looking or smelling delicious

applaud *vb* **1** to show approval of by clapping one's hands **2** to express approval of: *we applaud her determination and ambition*
WORD ORIGIN Latin *applaudere*

applause *n* appreciation shown by clapping one's hands

apple *n* **1** a round firm fruit with red, yellow, or green skin and crisp whitish flesh, that grows on trees **2 apple of one's eye** a person that one loves very much
WORD ORIGIN Old English *æppel*

apple-pie bed *n* a bed made with the sheets folded so as to prevent the person from entering it

apple-pie order *n* **in apple-pie order** *informal* very tidy

applet *n computers* a computing program that runs within a page on the World Wide Web
WORD ORIGIN *app(lication program)* + *-let* small or lesser

appliance *n* a machine or device that has a specific function

applicable *adj* appropriate or relevant

applicant *n* a person who applies for something, such as a job or grant

application *n* **1** a formal request, for example for a job **2** the act of applying something to a particular use: *you can make practical application of this knowledge to everyday living* **3** concentrated effort: *success would depend on their talent and application* **4** the act of putting something, such as a lotion or paint, onto a surface

applicator *n* a device for applying cosmetics, medication, or some other substance

applied *adj* put to practical use: *applied mathematics*

appliqué (ap-**plee**-kay) *n* a kind of decoration in which one material is cut out and sewn or fixed onto another
WORD ORIGIN French: applied

apply *vb* -plies, -plying, -plied **1** to make a formal request for something, such as a job or a loan **2** to put to practical use: *he applied his calligrapher's skill* **3** to put onto a surface: *the hand lotion should be applied whenever possible throughout the day* **4** to be relevant or appropriate: *he had been involved in research applied to flying wing aircraft* **5 apply oneself** to concentrate one's efforts or faculties
WORD ORIGIN Latin *applicare* to attach to

appoint *vb* **1** to assign officially to a job or position **2** to fix or decide (a time or place for an event) **3** to equip or furnish: *it was a beautifully appointed room with rows and rows of books* **appointee** *n*
WORD ORIGIN Old French *apointer* to put into a good state

appointment *n* **1** an arrangement to meet a person **2** the act of placing someone in a job or position **3** the person appointed **4** the job or position to which a person is appointed **5 appointments** fixtures or fittings

apportion *vb* to divide out in shares

apposite *adj* suitable or appropriate: *an apposite saying*
WORD ORIGIN Latin *ad-* near + *ponere* to put

a

apposition *n* a grammatical construction in which a noun or group of words is placed after another to modify its meaning, for example *my friend the mayor*

appraisal *n* an assessment of the worth or quality of a person or thing

appraise *vb* **-praising, -praised** to assess the worth, value, or quality of **WORD ORIGIN** Old French *aprisier*

≡ **USAGE**
Appraise is sometimes wrongly used where *apprise* is meant: *they had been apprised* (not *appraised*) *of my arrival.*

appreciable *adj* enough to be noticed; significant **appreciably** *adv*

appreciate *vb* **-ating, -ated 1** to value highly: *we appreciate his music* **2** to be aware of and understand: *I can fully appreciate how desperate you must feel* **3** to feel grateful for: *we do appreciate all you do for us* **4** to increase in value **WORD ORIGIN** Latin *pretium* price

appreciation *n* **1** gratitude **2** awareness and understanding of a problem or difficulty **3** sensitive recognition of good qualities, as in art **4** an increase in value

appreciative *adj* feeling or expressing appreciation **appreciatively** *adv*

apprehend *vb* **1** to arrest and take into custody **2** to grasp (something) mentally; understand **WORD ORIGIN** Latin *apprehendere* to lay hold of

apprehension *n* **1** anxiety or dread **2** the act of arresting **3** understanding

apprehensive *adj* fearful or anxious about the future

apprentice *n* **1** someone who works for a skilled person for a fixed period in order to learn his or her trade ▷ *vb* **-ticing, -ticed 2** to take or place as an apprentice **apprenticeship** *n* **WORD ORIGIN** Old French *aprendre* to learn

apprise *or* **-prize** *vb* **-prising, -prised** *or* **-prizing, -prized** to make aware: *I needed to apprise the students of the dangers involved* **WORD ORIGIN** French *apprendre* to teach; learn

≡ **USAGE**
≡ See at **appraise**.

appro *n* **on appro** *informal* on approval

approach *vb* **1** to come close or closer to **2** to make a proposal or suggestion to **3** to begin to deal with (a matter) ▷ *n* **4** the act of coming close or closer **5** a proposal or suggestion made to a person **6** the way or means of reaching a place; access **7** a way of dealing with a matter **8** an approximation **9** the course followed by an aircraft preparing for landing **approachable** *adj* **WORD ORIGIN** Latin *ad-* to + *prope* near

approach road *n* NZ & S African a smaller road leading into a major road

approbation *n* approval

appropriate *adj* **1** right or suitable ▷ *vb* **-ating, -ated 2** to take for one's own use without permission **3** to put (money) aside for a particular purpose **appropriately** *adv* **WORD ORIGIN** Latin *ad-* to + *proprius* one's own

appropriation *n* **1** the act of putting money aside for a particular purpose **2** money put aside for a particular purpose

approval *n* **1** consent **2** a favourable opinion **3 on approval** (of articles for sale) with an option to be returned without payment if unsatisfactory: *each volume in the collection will be sent to you on approval*

approve *vb* **-proving, -proved 1** to consider fair, good, or right **2** to authorize or agree to **WORD ORIGIN** Latin *approbare*

approx. approximate or approximately

approximate *adj* **1** almost but not quite exact ▷ *vb* **-mating, -mated 2 approximate to a** to come close to **b** to be almost the same as **approximately** *adv* **approximation** *n* **WORD ORIGIN** Latin *ad-* to + *proximus* nearest

appurtenances *pl n* minor or additional features or possessions **WORD ORIGIN** Old French *apartenance* secondary thing

APR annual percentage rate

Apr. April

après-ski (ap-ray-**skee**) *n* social activities after a day's skiing

apricot *n* **1** a yellowish-orange juicy fruit which resembles a small peach ▷ *adj* **2** yellowish-orange **WORD ORIGIN** Latin *praecox* early-ripening

April *n* the fourth month of the year **WORD ORIGIN** Latin *Aprilis*

April fool *n* a victim of a practical joke played on April 1 (**April Fools' Day** or **All Fools' Day**)

a priori (eh pry-**or**-rye) *adj logic* involving reasoning from cause to effect **WORD ORIGIN** Latin: from the previous

apron *n* **1** a garment worn over the front of the body to protect one's clothes **2** a hard-surfaced area at an airport or hangar for manoeuvring and loading aircraft **3** the part of a stage extending in front of the curtain **4 tied to someone's apron strings** dependent on or dominated by someone **WORD ORIGIN** Old French *naperon* little cloth

apropos (ap-prop-**poh**) *adj* **1** appropriate ▷ *adv* **2** by the way; incidentally **3 apropos of** with regard to **WORD ORIGIN** French *à propos* to the purpose

apse *n* an arched or domed recess at the east end of a church **WORD ORIGIN** Greek *apsis* a fitting together

apsis (**ap**-siss) *n, pl* **apsides** (**ap**-sid-deez) *astron* either of two points lying at the extremities of the elliptical orbit of a planet or satellite **WORD ORIGIN** see APSE

apt *adj* **1** having a specified tendency: *they are apt to bend the rules* **2** suitable or appropriate **3** quick to learn: *she was turning out to be a more apt pupil than he had expected* **aptly** *adv* **aptness** *n* **WORD ORIGIN** Latin *aptus* fitting

APT *Brit* Advanced Passenger Train

apteryx *n* same as **kiwi** (sense 1) **WORD ORIGIN** Greek *a-* without + *pteron* wing

aptitude *n* natural tendency or ability

aqua *adj* short for **aquamarine** **WORD ORIGIN** Latin: water

aqua fortis *n obsolete* nitric acid **WORD ORIGIN** Latin: strong water

aqualung *n* an apparatus for breathing underwater, consisting of a mouthpiece attached to air cylinders

aquamarine *n* **1** a clear greenish-blue gemstone ▷ *adj* **2** greenish-blue **WORD ORIGIN** Latin *aqua marina* sea water

aquaplane *n* **1** a board on which a person stands to be towed by a motorboat for sport ▷ *vb* **-planing, -planed 2** to ride on an aquaplane **3** (of a motor vehicle) to skim uncontrollably on a thin film of water

aqua regia (**ak**-wa **reej**-ya) *n* a mixture of nitric acid and hydrochloric acid **WORD ORIGIN** New Latin: royal water; referring to its use in dissolving gold, the royal metal

aquarium *n, pl* **aquariums** *or* **aquaria 1** a tank in which fish and other underwater creatures are kept **2** a building containing such tanks **WORD ORIGIN** Latin *aquarius* relating to water

Aquarius *n astrol* the eleventh sign of the zodiac: the Water Carrier **WORD ORIGIN** Latin

aquatic *adj* **1** growing or living in water **2** *sport* performed in or on water ▷ *n* **3** an aquatic animal or plant **4 aquatics** water sports **WORD ORIGIN** Latin *aqua* water

aquatint *n* a print like a watercolour, produced by etching copper with acid **WORD ORIGIN** Italian *acqua tinta* dyed water

aqua vitae (**ak**-wa **vee**-tie) *n old-fashioned* brandy **WORD ORIGIN** Medieval Latin: water of life

aqueduct *n* a structure, often a bridge, that carries water across a valley or river **WORD ORIGIN** Latin *aqua* water + *ducere* to convey

aqueous *adj* **1** of, like, or containing water **2** produced by the action of water **WORD ORIGIN** Latin *aqua* water

aqueous humour *n physiol* the watery fluid in the eyeball, between the cornea and the lens

aquifer *n* a deposit of rock, such as sandstone, containing water that can be used to supply wells **WORD ORIGIN** Latin *aqua* water + *ferre* to carry

aquiline *adj* **1** (of a nose) curved like an eagle's beak **2** of or like an eagle **WORD ORIGIN** Latin *aquila* eagle

Ar *chem* argon

AR Arkansas

Arab *n* **1** a member of a Semitic people originally from Arabia ▷ *adj* **2** of the Arabs **WORD ORIGIN** Arabic *'Arab*

SCRABBLE
Three-Letter Words, part 1
AAH–BOO

There are 1292 allowable three-letter words in the Collins Scrabble Tournament and Club Word List. Even if you don't plan to learn them all, the ones containing Q, Z, X, and J are well worth knowing. Some of the highest Scrabble scores come from hooking one of these letters on a triple-letter square so that, by scoring it in both directions, the letter ends up worth six times its face value. All it takes is a *qis* or a *xis* to *zap* your opponent in this *jeu*!

AAH exclamation of pleasure, satisfaction, etc
AAL Asian shrub or tree
AAS plural form of aa
ABA type of cloth from Syria
ABB yarn used in weaving
ABO offensive word for Aborigine
ABS plural form of ab
ABY pay the penalty for
ACE playing card
ACH Scots expression of surprise
ACT something done, deed
ADD combine
ADO fuss, trouble
ADS plural form of ad
ADZ heavy hand tool
AFF Scots word for off
AFT at or towards the rear
AGA Ottoman military commander
AGE length of time
AGO in the past
AGS plural form of ag
AHA exclamation of triumph, surprise, etc
AHI the yellowfin tuna
AHS plural form of ah
AIA nursemaid in East
AID assistance or support
AIL trouble, afflict
AIM point or direct at target
AIN Scots word for own
AIR the mixture of gases forming the earth's atmosphere
AIS plural form of ai

AIT islet, esp in a river
AKA New Zealand vine
AKE old spelling of ache
ALA wing
ALB Christian priest's robe
ALE kind of beer
ALF uncultivated Australian
ALL the whole quantity of something
ALP high mountain
ALS plural form of al
ALT musical term
AMA wet nurse
AMI male friend
AMP ampere
AMU atomic mass unit
ANA in equal quantities
AND conjunction used to express addition
ANE Scots word for one
ANI type of tropical American bird
ANN payment to a parish minister's widow
ANT small insect
ANY one or some
APE primate
APO type of protein
APP short for application program
APT suitable, appropriate
ARB short form of arbitrageur
ARC part of a circle or curve
ARD primitive plough
ARE 100 square metres
ARF barking sound
ARK the boat built by Noah
ARM upper limb
ARS plural form of ar

ART creation of works of beauty
ARY dialect form of any
ASH substance left after burning
ASK request an answer from
ASP small poisonous snake
ASS donkey
ATE part of the verb to eat
ATT old Siamese coin
AUA the yellow-eye mullet
AUE Maori exclamation of pain, distress, etc
AUF old word for oaf
AUK northern sea bird
AVA Scots word for at all
AVE welcome or farewell
AVO Macao currency unit
AWA Scots word for away
AWE wonder and respect mixed with dread
AWL pointed tool
AWN bristles growing from certain grasses
AXE tool with a sharp blade
AYE yes
AYS plural form of ay
AYU small Japanese fish
AZO chemistry term
BAA sound of a sheep
BAC baccalaureate
BAD not good
BAG flexible container
BAH expression of contempt or disgust
BAL balmoral, an ankle-high shoe
BAM cheat, hoax
BAN prohibit or forbid
BAP large soft bread roll

BAR length of metal, etc
BAS plural form of ba
BAT club used to hit the ball in sports
BAY semicircular indentation of a shoreline
BED piece of furniture
BEE insect that makes honey
BEG solicit (money, etc)
BEL unit for comparing two power levels
BEN mountain peak
BES variant of beth, 2nd Hebrew letter
BET wager
BEY Ottoman official
BEZ part of deer's horn
BIB cloth worn by babies
BID offer to buy something, esp in competition
BIG of considerable size, number, etc
BIN container for rubbish
BIO short for biography
BIS twice
BIT small piece or portion
BIZ short for business
BOA large snake
BOB move up and down repeatedly
BOD person
BOG wet spongy ground
BOH exclamation used to startle or surprise
BOI lesbian who dresses like a boy
BOK S African antelope
BON good
BOO shout of disapproval

arabesque (ar-ab-**besk**) *n* **1** a ballet position in which one leg is raised behind and the arms are extended **2** *arts* an elaborate design of intertwined leaves, flowers, and scrolls **3** an ornate piece of music
WORD ORIGIN Italian *arabesco* in the Arabic style

Arabian *adj* **1** of Arabia or the Arabs ▷ *n* **2** same as **Arab**

Arabic *n* **1** the language of the Arabs ▷ *adj* **2** of this language, the Arabs, or Arabia

Arabic numerals *pl n* the symbols 1, 2, 3, 4, 5, 6, 7, 8, 9, 0, used to represent numbers

arable *adj* (of land) suitable for growing crops on
WORD ORIGIN Latin *arare* to plough

arachnid (ar-**rak**-nid) *n* an eight-legged insect-like creature, such as a spider, scorpion, or tick
WORD ORIGIN Greek *arakhnē* spider

arak *n* same as **arrack**

Aramaic *n* an ancient Semitic language spoken in parts of Syria and the Lebanon

Aran *adj* (of knitwear) knitted in a complicated pattern traditional to the Aran Islands off the west coast of Ireland

arbiter *n* **1** a person empowered to judge in a dispute **2** a person with influential opinions about something: *the customer must be the ultimate arbiter of quality*

arbitrary *adj* **1** not done according to any plan or for any particular reason **2** without consideration for the wishes of others: *the arbitrary power of the king* **arbitrarily** *adv*

arbitrate *vb* **-trating, -trated** to settle (a dispute) by arbitration **arbitrator** *n*
WORD ORIGIN Latin *arbitrari* to give judgment

arbitration *n* the hearing and settlement of a dispute by an impartial referee chosen by both sides

arbor¹ *n* US same as **arbour**

arbor² *n* a revolving shaft or axle in a machine
WORD ORIGIN Latin: tree

arboreal (ahr-**bore**-ee-al) *adj* **1** of or resembling a tree **2** living in or among trees

arboretum (ahr-bore-**ee**-tum) *n, pl* **-ta** (-ta) a botanical garden where rare trees or shrubs are cultivated
WORD ORIGIN Latin *arbor* tree

arboriculture *n* the cultivation of trees or shrubs
WORD ORIGIN Latin *arbor* tree + CULTURE

arbor vitae (ahr-bore **vee**-tie) *n* an evergreen tree
WORD ORIGIN New Latin: tree of life

arbour *or* US **arbor** *n* a shelter in a garden shaded by trees or climbing plants
WORD ORIGIN Latin *herba* grass

arbutus (ar-**byew**-tuss) *n* an evergreen shrub with berries like strawberries
WORD ORIGIN Latin

arc *n* **1** something curved in shape **2** *maths* a section of a circle or other curve **3** *electronics* a stream of very bright light that forms when an electric current flows across a small gap between two electrodes ▷ *vb* **4** to form an arc
WORD ORIGIN Latin *arcus* bow, arch

ARC AIDS-related complex: relatively mild symptoms suffered in the early stages of infection with the AIDS virus

arcade *n* **1** a covered passageway lined with shops **2** a set of arches and their supporting columns
WORD ORIGIN Latin *arcus* bow, arch

Arcadian *literary adj* **1** rural, in an idealized way ▷ *n* **2** a person who leads a quiet simple country life
WORD ORIGIN *Arcadia*, rural district of Ancient Greece

arcane *adj* very mysterious
WORD ORIGIN Latin *arcanus* secret

arch¹ *n* **1** a curved structure that spans an opening or supports a bridge or roof **2** something curved **3** the curved lower part of the foot ▷ *vb* **4** to form an arch
WORD ORIGIN Latin *arcus* bow, arc

arch² *adj* **1** knowing or superior **2** coyly playful: *he gave an arch smile to indicate his pride* **archly** *adv*
WORD ORIGIN independent use of ARCH-

arch- *or* **archi-** *combining form* chief or principal: *archbishop; archenemy*
WORD ORIGIN Greek *arkhein* to rule

archaeobotany *n* the study of plant remains found at archaeological sites **archaeobotanist** *n*

archaeology *or* **archeology** *n* the study of ancient cultures by the scientific analysis of physical remains **archaeological** *or* **archeological** *adj* **archaeologist** *or* **archeologist** *n*
WORD ORIGIN Greek *arkhaiologia* study of what is ancient

archaeopteryx *n* an extinct primitive bird with teeth, a long tail, and well-developed wings
WORD ORIGIN Greek *arkhaios* ancient + *pterux* winged creature

archaeozoology *n* the study of animal remains found at archaeological sites **archaeozoologist** *n*

archaic (ark-**kay**-ik) *adj* **1** of a much earlier period **2** out of date or old-fashioned **3** (of a word or phrase) no longer in everyday use **archaically** *adv*
WORD ORIGIN Greek *arkhē* beginning

archaism (**ark**-kay-iz-zum) *n* an archaic word or style **archaistic** *adj*

archangel (**ark**-ain-jell) *n* an angel of the highest rank

archbishop *n* a bishop of the highest rank

archbishopric *n* the rank, office, or diocese of an archbishop

archdeacon *n* a church official ranking just below a bishop **archdeaconry** *n*

archdiocese *n* the diocese of an archbishop

archduchess *n* **1** a woman who holds the rank of archduke **2** the wife or widow of an archduke

archduchy *n, pl* **-duchies** the territory ruled by an archduke or archduchess

archduke *n* a duke of high rank, esp. one from Austria

archenemy *n, pl* **-mies** a chief enemy

archeology *n* same as **archaeology**

archer *n* a person who shoots with a bow and arrow
WORD ORIGIN Latin *arcus* bow

archery *n* the art or sport of shooting with a bow and arrow

archetype (**ark**-ee-type) *n* **1** a perfect or typical specimen **2** an original model; prototype **archetypal** *adj*
WORD ORIGIN Greek *arkhetupos* first-moulded

archidiaconal (ark-ee-die-**ak**-on-al) *adj* of an archdeacon or his office

archiepiscopal (ark-ee-ip-**piss**-kop-al) *adj* of an archbishop or his office

Archimedes' principle (ark-ee-**mee**-deez) *n physics* the principle that the apparent loss in weight of an object immersed in a fluid is equal to the weight of the displaced fluid
WORD ORIGIN after *Archimedes*, Greek mathematician & physicist

archipelago (ark-ee-**pel**-a-go) *n, pl* **-gos** **1** a group of islands **2** a sea full of small islands
WORD ORIGIN Greek *arkhi-* chief + *pelagos* sea

architect *n* **1** a person qualified to design and supervise the construction of buildings **2** any planner or creator: *you will be the architect of your own future*
WORD ORIGIN Greek *arkhi-* chief + *tektōn* workman

architecture *n* **1** the style in which a building is designed and built: *Gothic architecture* **2** the science of designing and constructing buildings **3** the structure or design of anything: *computer architecture* **architectural** *adj*

architrave (**ark**-ee-trave) *n archit* **1** a beam that rests on top of columns **2** a moulding around a doorway or window opening
WORD ORIGIN Italian, from *arch-* + *trave* beam

archive (**ark**-ive) *n* **1** a place where records or documents are kept **2** *archives* a collection of records or documents **3** *computers* data put on tape or disk for long-term storage ▷ *vb* **4** to store in an archive

archivist (**ark**-iv-ist) *n* a person in charge of archives

archway *n* a passageway under an arch

arctic *adj informal* very cold; freezing

Arctic *n* **1** the Arctic the area around the North Pole ▷ *adj* **2** of this region
WORD ORIGIN Greek *arktikos* northern, literally: pertaining to (the constellation of) the Bear

Arctic Circle *n* the imaginary circle around the earth at latitude 66° 32´ N

arctic hare *n* a large hare of the Canadian Arctic whose fur turns white in winter

arctic willow *n* a low-growing shrub of the Canadian Arctic

arc welding *n* a technique in which metal is welded by heat generated by an electric arc

ardent *adj* **1** passionate **2** intensely enthusiastic **ardently** *adv*
WORD ORIGIN Latin *ardere* to burn

ardour *or* US **ardor** *n* **1** emotional warmth; passion **2** intense enthusiasm
WORD ORIGIN Latin *ardere* to burn

arduous *adj* difficult to accomplish; strenuous
WORD ORIGIN Latin *arduus* steep, difficult

are[1] *vb* the plural form of the present tense of **be**: used as the singular form with *you*
WORD ORIGIN Old English *aron*

are[2] *n* a unit of measure equal to one hundred square metres
WORD ORIGIN Latin *area* piece of ground

area *n* 1 a section, part, or region 2 a part having a specified function: *reception area* 3 the size of a two-dimensional surface 4 a subject field: *the area of literature* 5 a sunken area giving access to a basement 6 any flat, curved, or irregular expanse of a surface 7 range or scope
WORD ORIGIN Latin: level ground, threshing floor

area school *n* NZ a school in a rural area that includes primary and post-primary classes

arena *n* 1 a seated enclosure where sports events take place 2 the area of an ancient Roman amphitheatre where gladiators fought 3 a sphere of intense activity: *the political arena*
WORD ORIGIN Latin *harena* sand

aren't are not

areola *n, pl* **-lae** or **-las** a small circular area, such as the coloured ring around the human nipple
WORD ORIGIN Latin

Ares *n Greek myth* the god of war

arête *n* a sharp ridge separating valleys
WORD ORIGIN French: fishbone

Argentine or **Argentinian** *adj* 1 of Argentina ▷ *n* 2 a person from Argentina

argon *n chem* an unreactive odourless element of the rare gas series, forming almost 1 per cent of the atmosphere. Symbol: Ar
WORD ORIGIN Greek *argos* inactive

argosy *n, pl* **-sies** *old-fashioned or poetic* a large merchant ship, or a fleet of such ships
WORD ORIGIN Italian *Ragusea (nave)* (ship) of Ragusa, a former name for Dubrovnik

argot (**ahr**-go) *n* slang or jargon peculiar to a particular group
WORD ORIGIN French

argue *vb* **-guing, -gued** 1 to try to prove by presenting reasons 2 to debate 3 to quarrel 4 to persuade: *we argued her out of going* 5 to suggest: *her looks argue despair* **arguable** *adj* **arguably** *adv*
WORD ORIGIN Latin *arguere* to make clear, accuse

argument *n* 1 a quarrel 2 a discussion 3 a point presented to support or oppose a proposition

argumentation *n* the process of reasoning methodically

argumentative *adj* likely to argue

argy-bargy or **argie-bargie** *n, pl* **-bargies** *Brit informal* a squabbling argument
WORD ORIGIN Scots

aria (**ah**-ree-a) *n* an elaborate song for solo voice in an opera or choral work
WORD ORIGIN Italian

arid *adj* 1 having little or no rain 2 uninteresting **aridity** *n*
WORD ORIGIN Latin *aridus*

Aries *n astrol* the first sign of the zodiac: the Ram
WORD ORIGIN Latin

aright *adv* correctly or properly

arise *vb* **arising, arose, arisen** 1 to come into being: *the opportunity for action did not arise* 2 to come into notice: *people can seek answers to their problems as and when they arise* 3 **arise from** to happen as a result of 4 *old-fashioned* to get or stand up
WORD ORIGIN Old English *ārīsan*

aristocracy *n, pl* **-cies** 1 a class of people of high social rank 2 government by this class 3 a group of people considered to be outstanding in a particular sphere of activity
WORD ORIGIN Greek *aristos* best + *kratein* to rule

aristocrat *n* a member of the aristocracy

aristocratic *adj* 1 of the aristocracy 2 grand or elegant

Aristotelian (ar-riss-tot-**eel**-ee-an) *adj* of Aristotle, 4th-century BC Greek philosopher, or his philosophy

arithmetic *n* 1 the branch of mathematics concerned with numerical calculations, such as addition, subtraction, multiplication, and division 2 calculations involving numerical operations 3 knowledge of or skill in arithmetic: *even simple arithmetic was beyond him* ▷ *adj also* **arithmetical** 4 of or using arithmetic **arithmetically** *adv* **arithmetician** *n*
WORD ORIGIN Greek *arithmos* number

arithmetic mean *n* the average value of a set of terms, expressed as their sum divided by their number: *the arithmetic mean of 3, 4, and 8 is 5*

arithmetic progression *n* a sequence, each term of which differs from the preceding term by a constant amount, such as 3, 6, 9, 12

ark *n Bible* the boat built by Noah, which survived the Flood
WORD ORIGIN Latin *arca* box, chest

Ark *n Judaism* 1 Also called: **Holy Ark** the cupboard in a synagogue in which the Torah scrolls are kept 2 Also called: **Ark of the Covenant** a chest containing the laws of the Jewish religion, regarded as the most sacred symbol of God's presence among the Hebrew people

arm[1] *n* 1 (in humans, apes, and monkeys) either of the upper limbs from the shoulder to the wrist 2 the sleeve of a garment 3 the side of a chair on which one's arm can rest 4 a subdivision or section of an organization: *the London-based arm of a Swiss bank* 5 something resembling an arm in appearance or function: *the arm of a record player* 6 power or authority: *the long arm of the law* 7 **arm in arm** with arms linked 8 **at arm's length** at a distance 9 **with open arms** with warmth and hospitality
WORD ORIGIN Old English

arm[2] *vb* 1 to supply with weapons 2 to prepare (an explosive device) for use 3 to provide (a person or thing) with something that strengthens, or protects: *you will be armed with all the information you will ever need* ▶ See also **arms** > **armed** *adj*
WORD ORIGIN Latin *arma* arms, equipment

armada *n* 1 a large number of ships 2 **the Armada** the great fleet sent by Spain against England in 1588
WORD ORIGIN Medieval Latin *armata* fleet, armed forces

armadillo *n, pl* **-los** a small S American burrowing mammal covered in strong bony plates
WORD ORIGIN Spanish *armado* armed (man)

Armageddon *n* 1 *New Testament* the final battle between good and evil at the end of the world 2 a catastrophic and extremely destructive conflict
WORD ORIGIN Hebrew *har megiddōn*, mountain district of *Megiddo* (in N Palestine)

armament *n* 1 **armaments** the weapon equipment of a military vehicle, ship, or aircraft 2 preparation for war
WORD ORIGIN Latin *armamenta* equipment

armature *n* 1 a revolving structure in an electric motor or generator, wound with the coils that carry the current 2 *sculpture* a framework to support the clay or other material used in modelling
WORD ORIGIN Latin *armatura* armour, equipment

armchair *n* 1 an upholstered chair with side supports for the arms ▷ *adj* 2 taking no active part: *we are, on the whole, a nation of armchair athletes*

armed forces *pl n* all the military forces of a nation or nations

armful *n* as much as can be held in the arms: *armfuls of lovely flowers*

armhole *n* the opening in a piece of clothing through which the arm passes

armistice (**arm**-miss-stiss) *n* an agreement between opposing armies to stop fighting
WORD ORIGIN Latin *arma* arms + *sistere* to stop

Armistice Day *n* the anniversary of the signing of the armistice that ended the First World War, on November 11, 1918

armlet *n* a band or bracelet worn around the arm

armorial *adj* of or relating to heraldry or heraldic arms

armour or US **armor** *n* 1 metal clothing worn by medieval warriors for protection in battle 2 *mil* armoured fighting vehicles in general 3 the protective metal plates on a tank or warship 4 protective covering, such as the shell of certain animals 5 a quality or attitude that gives protection ▷ *vb* 6 to equip or cover with armour
WORD ORIGIN Latin *armātūra* armour, equipment

armoured or US **armored** *adj* 1 having a protective covering 2 consisting of armoured vehicles: *an armoured brigade*

armourer or US **armorer** *n* 1 a person who makes or mends arms and armour 2 a person in charge of small arms in a military unit

armour plate *n* a tough heavy steel for protecting warships and vehicles **armour-plated** *adj*

armoury *or US* **armory** *n, pl* **-mouries** *or* **-mories** 1 a secure storage place for weapons 2 military supplies 3 resources on which to draw: *modern medicine has a large armoury of drugs for the treatment of mental illness*

armpit *n* 1 the hollow beneath the arm where it joins the shoulder 2 *slang* an extremely unpleasant place: *the armpit of the Mediterranean*

armrest *n* the part of a chair or sofa that supports the arm

arms *pl n* 1 weapons collectively 2 military exploits: *prowess in arms* 3 the heraldic symbols of a family or state 4 **take up arms** to prepare to fight 5 **under arms** armed and prepared for war 6 **up in arms** prepared to protest strongly

army *n, pl* **-mies** 1 the military land forces of a nation 2 a large number of people or animals **WORD ORIGIN** Medieval Latin *armata* armed forces

aroha *n NZ* love, compassion, or affection **WORD ORIGIN** Māori

aroma *n* 1 a distinctive pleasant smell 2 a subtle pervasive quality or atmosphere **WORD ORIGIN** Greek: spice

aromatherapy *n* the use of fragrant essential oils as a treatment in alternative medicine, often to relieve tension

aromatic *adj* 1 having a distinctive pleasant smell 2 *chem* (of an organic compound) having an unsaturated ring of atoms, usually six carbon atoms ▷ *n* 3 something, such as a plant or drug, that gives off a fragrant smell

arose *vb* the past tense of **arise**

around *prep* 1 situated at various points in: *cameramen were positioned around the auditorium* 2 from place to place in: *he had spent twenty-five minutes driving around Amsterdam* 3 somewhere in or near 4 approximately in: *around 1980* ▷ *adv* 5 in all directions from a point of reference: *there wasn't a house for miles around* 6 in the vicinity, esp. restlessly but idly: *I couldn't hang around too long* 7 in no particular place or direction: *a few tropical fish tanks dotted around* 8 *informal* present in some unknown or unspecified place 9 *informal* available: *cancer drugs have been around for years* 10 **have been around** *informal* to have gained considerable experience of a worldly or social nature

USAGE
In American English, *around* is usually used instead of *round* in adverbial and prepositional senses, except in a few fixed phrases such as *all year round*. The use of *around* in adverbial senses is less common in British English.

arouse *vb* **arousing, aroused** 1 to produce (a reaction, emotion, or response) 2 to awaken from sleep **arousal** *n*

arpeggio (arp-**pej**-ee-oh) *n, pl* **-gios** a chord whose notes are played or sung in rapid succession **WORD ORIGIN** Italian

arquebus (**ark**-wee-bus) *n* a portable long-barrelled gun dating from the 15th century **WORD ORIGIN** Middle Dutch *hakebusse* hook gun

arrack *or* **arak** *n* a coarse alcoholic drink distilled in Eastern countries from grain or rice **WORD ORIGIN** Arabic *'araq* sweat, sweet juice

arraign (ar-**rain**) *vb* 1 to bring (a prisoner) before a court to answer a charge 2 to accuse **arraignment** *n* **WORD ORIGIN** Old French *araisnier* to accuse

arrange *vb* **-ranging, -ranged** 1 to plan in advance: *my parents had arranged a surprise party* 2 to arrive at an agreement: *they had arranged to go to the cinema* 3 to put into a proper or systematic order 4 to adapt (a musical composition) for performance in a certain way **WORD ORIGIN** Old French *a-* to + *rangier* to put in a row, range

arrangement *n* 1 a preparation or plan made for an event: *travel arrangements* 2 an agreement or a plan to do something 3 a thing composed of various ordered parts: *a flower arrangement* 4 the form in which things are arranged 5 an adaptation of a piece of music for performance in a different way

arrant *adj* utter or downright: *that's the most arrant nonsense I've ever heard* **WORD ORIGIN** Middle English variant of *errant* (wandering, vagabond)

arras *n* a tapestry wall-hanging **WORD ORIGIN** *Arras*, a town in N France

array *n* 1 an impressive display or collection 2 an orderly arrangement, such as of troops in battle order 3 *computers* a data structure in which elements may be located by index numbers 4 *poetic* rich clothing ▷ *vb* 5 to arrange in order 6 to dress in rich clothing **WORD ORIGIN** Old French *arayer* to arrange

arrears *pl n* 1 money owed 2 **in arrears** late in paying a debt **WORD ORIGIN** Latin *ad* to + *retro* backwards

arrest *vb* 1 to take (a person) into custody 2 to slow or stop the development of 3 to catch and hold (one's attention) ▷ *n* 4 the act of taking a person into custody 5 **under arrest** being held in custody by the police 6 the slowing or stopping of something: *a cardiac arrest* **WORD ORIGIN** Latin *ad* at, to + *restare* to stand firm, stop

arresting *adj* attracting attention; striking

arrival *n* 1 the act of arriving 2 a person or thing that has just arrived 3 *informal* a recently born baby

arrive *vb* **-riving, -rived** 1 to reach a place or destination 2 **arrive at** to come to (a conclusion, idea, or decision) 3 to occur: *the crisis he predicted then has now arrived* 4 *informal* to be born 5 *informal* to attain success **WORD ORIGIN** Latin *ad* to + *ripa* river bank

arrivederci (ar-reeve-a-**der**-chee) *interj* goodbye **WORD ORIGIN** Italian

arrogant *adj* having an exaggerated opinion of one's own importance or ability **arrogance** *n* **arrogantly** *adv* **WORD ORIGIN** Latin *arrogare* to claim as one's own

arrogate *vb* **-gating, -gated** to claim or seize without justification **arrogation** *n* **WORD ORIGIN** Latin *arrogare*

arrow *n* 1 a long slender pointed weapon, with feathers at one end, that is shot from a bow 2 an arrow-shaped sign or symbol used to show the direction to a place **WORD ORIGIN** Old English *arwe*

arrowhead *n* the pointed tip of an arrow

arrowroot *n* an easily digestible starch obtained from the root of a West Indian plant

arse *or US & Canad* **ass** *n taboo* the buttocks or anus **WORD ORIGIN** Old English *ærs*

arsehole *or US & Canad* **asshole** *n taboo* 1 the anus 2 a stupid or annoying person

arsenal *n* 1 a building in which arms and ammunition are made or stored 2 a store of anything regarded as weapons: *this new weapon in the medical arsenal* **WORD ORIGIN** Arabic *dār* house + *siñ'ah* manufacture

arsenic *n* 1 a toxic metalloid element. Symbol: As 2 a nontechnical name for **arsenic trioxide**, a highly poisonous compound used as a rat poison and insecticide ▷ *adj also* **arsenical** 3 of or containing arsenic **WORD ORIGIN** Syriac *zarnīg*

arson *n* the crime of intentionally setting fire to property **arsonist** *n* **WORD ORIGIN** Latin *ardere* to burn

art *n* 1 the creation of works of beauty or other special significance 2 works of art collectively 3 human creativity as distinguished from nature 4 skill: *she was still new to the art of bargaining* 5 any branch of the visual arts, esp. painting 6 **get something down to a fine art** to become proficient at something through practice ▶ See also **arts** **WORD ORIGIN** Latin *ars* craftsmanship

Art Deco (art **deck**-oh) *n* a style of design, at its height in the 1930s, characterized by geometrical shapes **WORD ORIGIN** French *art décoratif*

artefact *or* **artifact** *n* something made by human beings, such as a tool or a work of art **WORD ORIGIN** Latin *ars* skill + *facere* to make

Artemis *n Greek myth* the goddess of hunting

arterial *adj* 1 of or affecting an artery 2 being a major route: *an arterial road*

arteriosclerosis (art-ear-ee-oh-skler-oh-siss) *n* thickening and loss of elasticity of the walls of the arteries. Nontechnical name: **hardening of the arteries**

artery *n, pl* **-teries** 1 any of the tubes that carry oxygenated blood from the

Words from Literature
part 2

approver *n* an approver is someone who gives evidence against someone he used to work with
> Mr. Noah Claypole: receiving a free pardon from the Crown in consequence of being admitted approver against Fagin
> *Oliver Twist* Charles Dickens

areas *n* the areas is the space, below street level, in front of the basement of a house
> The Dodger had a vicious propensity, too, of pulling the caps from the heads of small boys and tossing them down areas
> *Oliver Twist* Charles Dickens

artificially *adv* artfully or cleverly
> and he with a sharp flint sharpened very artificially
> *Gulliver's Travels* Jonathan Swift

artist *n* a skilled workman
> This man was a most ingenious artist
> *Gulliver's Travels* Jonathan Swift

assizes *n* assizes were regular court sessions which a visiting judge was in charge of
> you shall hang at the next assizes
> *Treasure Island* Robert Louis Stevenson

attraction *n* gravitation, or Newton's theory of gravitation
> he predicted the same fate to attraction
> *Gulliver's Travels* Jonathan Swift

aver *v* to aver is to claim something strongly
> for Jem Rodney, the mole catcher, averred that one evening as he was returning homeward
> *Silas Marner* George Eliot

baby *n* a doll, which is a child's toy that looks like a small person
> and skilful dressing her baby
> *Gulliver's Travels* Jonathan Swift

bagatelle *n* a game rather like billiards or pool
> Breakfast had been ordered at a pleasant little tavern, a mile or so away upon the rising ground beyond the green; and there was a bagatelle board in the room, in case we should desire to unbend our minds after the solemnity.
> *Great Expectations* Charles Dickens

bah *int* an exclamation of frustration or anger
> "Bah," said Scrooge.
> *A Christmas Carol* Charles Dickens

bairn *n* a northern word for child
> Who has taught you those fine words, my bairn?
> *Wuthering Heights* Emily Brontë

bait *v* to bait means to stop on a journey to take refreshment
> So, when they stopped to bait the horse, and ate and drank and enjoyed themselves, I could touch nothing that they touched, but kept my fast unbroken.
> *David Copperfield* Charles Dickens

balustrade *n* a row of vertical columns that form railings
> but I mean to say you might have got a hearse up that staircase, and taken it broadwise, with the splinter-bar towards the wall, and the door towards the balustrades: and done it easy
> *A Christmas Carol* Charles Dickens

bandbox *n* a large lightweight box for carrying bonnets or hats
> I am glad I bought my bonnet, if it is only for the fun of having another bandbox
> *Pride and Prejudice* Jane Austen

barren *n* a stretch or expanse of barren land
> a line of upright stones, continued the length of the barren
> *Wuthering Heights* Emily Brontë

basin *n* a basin was a cup without a handle
> who is drinking his tea out of a basin
> *Wuthering Heights* Emily Brontë

heart to various parts of the body **2** a major road or means of communication **WORD ORIGIN** Latin *arteria*

artesian well (art-**teez**-yan) *n* a well receiving water from a higher altitude, so the water is forced to flow upwards **WORD ORIGIN** from Old French *Arteis* Artois (in N France) where such wells were common

Artex *n trademark, Brit* a type of coating for walls and ceilings that gives a textured finish

art form *n* a recognized mode or medium of artistic expression

artful *adj* **1** cunning **2** skilful in achieving a desired end **artfully** *adv*

arthritis *n* inflammation of a joint or joints, causing pain and stiffness **arthritic** *adj, n* **WORD ORIGIN** Greek *arthron* joint

arthropod *n* a creature, such as an insect or a spider, which has jointed legs and a hard case on its body **WORD ORIGIN** Greek *arthron* joint + *pous* foot

artic *n Brit informal* an articulated lorry

artichoke *n* **1** Also called: **globe artichoke** the flower head of a thistle-like plant, cooked as a vegetable **2** same as **Jerusalem artichoke** **WORD ORIGIN** Arabic *al-kharshūf*

article *n* **1** a written composition in a magazine or newspaper **2** an item or object **3** a clause in a written document **4** *grammar* any of the words *a, an,* or *the* **WORD ORIGIN** Latin *articulus* small joint

articled *adj* bound by a written contract, such as one that governs a period of training: *an articled clerk*

articular *adj* of or relating to joints **WORD ORIGIN** Latin *articulus* small joint

articulate *adj* **1** able to express oneself fluently and coherently **2** distinct, clear, or definite: *his amiable and articulate campaign attracted support* **3** *zool* possessing joints ▷ *vb* **-lating, -lated 4** to speak clearly and distinctly **5** to express coherently in words **articulately** *adv* **WORD ORIGIN** Latin *articulare* to divide into joints

articulated lorry *n* a large lorry in two separate sections connected by a pivoted bar

articulation *n* **1** the expressing of an idea in words **2** the process of articulating a speech sound or the sound so produced **3** a being jointed together **4** *zool* a joint between bones or arthropod segments

artifact *n* same as **artefact**

artifice *n* **1** a clever trick **2** skill or cleverness **WORD ORIGIN** Latin *ars* skill + *facere* to make

artificer (art-**tiff**-iss-er) *n* a skilled craftsman

artificial *adj* **1** man-made; not occurring naturally **2** made in imitation of a natural product: *artificial flavourings* **3** not sincere **artificiality** *n* **artificially** *adv* **WORD ORIGIN** Latin *artificialis* belonging to art

artificial insemination *n* introduction of semen into the womb by means other than sexual intercourse

artificial intelligence *n* the branch of computer science aiming to produce machines which can imitate intelligent human behaviour

artificial respiration *n* any method of restarting a person's breathing after it has stopped

artillery *n* **1** large-calibre guns **2** military units specializing in the use of such guns **WORD ORIGIN** Old French *artillier* to equip with weapons

artisan *n* a skilled workman; craftsman **artisanal** *adj* **WORD ORIGIN** French

artist *n* **1** a person who produces works of art such as paintings or sculpture **2** a person who is skilled at something **3** same as **artiste** ▷ **artistic** *adj* **artistically** *adv*

artiste *n* a professional entertainer such as a singer or dancer

artistry *n* **1** artistic ability **2** great skill

artless *adj* **1** free from deceit or cunning: *artless generosity* **2** natural or unpretentious **artlessly** *adv*

Art Nouveau (ahr noo-**voh**) *n* a style of art and architecture of the 1890s, characterized by sinuous outlines and stylized natural forms **WORD ORIGIN** French: new art

arts *pl n* **1** **the arts** the nonscientific branches of knowledge **2** see **fine art 3** cunning schemes

artwork *n* all the photographs and illustrations in a publication

arty *adj* **artier, artiest** *informal* having an affected interest in art **artiness** *n*

arum lily *n* a plant with a white funnel-shaped leaf surrounding a yellow spike of flowers

Aryan (**air**-ree-an) *n* **1** (in Nazi ideology) a non-Jewish person of the Nordic type **2** a person supposedly descended from the Indo-Europeans ▷ *adj* **3** of Aryans **WORD ORIGIN** Sanskrit *ārya* of noble birth

as *conj* **1** while or when: *he arrived just as the band finished the song* **2** in the way that: *they had talked and laughed as only the best of friends can* **3** that which; what: *George did as he was asked* **4** (of) which fact or event (referring to the previous statement): *to become wise, as we all know, is not easy* **5** **as it were** in a way; in a manner of speaking: *he was, as it were, on probation* **6** since; seeing that **7** for instance ▷ *adv, conj* **8** used to indicate amount or extent in comparisons: *he was as fat as his mum and dad* ▷ *prep* **9** in the role of; being: *my task, as his physician, is to do the best that I can* **10** **as for** or **to** with reference to **11** **as if** or **though** as it would be if: *she felt as if she had been run over by a bulldozer* **12** **as (it) is** in the existing state of affairs **WORD ORIGIN** Old English *alswā* likewise

⸻ USAGE
See at **like**.

As *chem* arsenic

ASA 1 (in Britain) Amateur Swimming Association **2** (in Britain) Advertising Standards Authority

asafoetida *n* a strong-smelling plant resin used as a spice in Eastern cookery **WORD ORIGIN** Medieval Latin *asa* gum + Latin *foetidus* evil-smelling

a.s.a.p. as soon as possible

asbestos *n* a fibrous mineral which does not burn, formerly widely used as a heat-resistant material **WORD ORIGIN** Greek: inextinguishable

asbestosis *n* inflammation of the lungs resulting from inhalation of asbestos fibre

ASBO *Brit* antisocial behaviour order

ascend *vb* **1** to go or move up **2** to slope upwards **3** **ascend the throne** to become king or queen **WORD ORIGIN** Latin *ascendere*

ascendancy or **ascendance** *n* the condition of being dominant: *when hardliners were in the ascendancy last winter*

ascendant or **ascendent** *adj* **1** dominant or influential ▷ *n* **2** *astrol* the sign of the zodiac that is rising on the eastern horizon at a particular moment **3** **in the ascendant** increasing in power or influence

ascension *n* the act of ascending

Ascension Day *n Christianity* the 40th day after Easter, when the Ascension of Christ into Heaven is celebrated

ascent *n* **1** the act of ascending **2** an upward slope

ascertain *vb* to find out definitely **ascertainment** *n* **WORD ORIGIN** Old French *acertener* to make certain

ascetic (ass-**set**-tik) *n* **1** a person who abstains from worldly comforts and pleasures ▷ *adj* **2** rigidly abstinent and self-denying **WORD ORIGIN** Greek *askētikos*

ASCII (**ass**-kee) *n* a code for transmitting data between computers **WORD ORIGIN** A(merican) S(tandard) C(ode for) I(nformation) I(nterchange)

ascorbic acid (ass-**core**-bik) *n* a vitamin that occurs in citrus fruits, tomatoes, and green vegetables, and which prevents and cures scurvy. Also called: **vitamin C** **WORD ORIGIN** A- + SCORBUTIC

ascribe *vb* **-cribing, -cribed 1** to attribute, as to a particular origin: *headaches which may be ascribed to stress* **2** to consider that (a particular quality) is possessed by something or someone: *specific human qualities are ascribed to each of the four elements* **ascription** *n* **WORD ORIGIN** Latin *ad* in addition + *scribere* to write

⸻ USAGE
Ascribe is sometimes used where *subscribe* is meant: I do not subscribe (not *ascribe*) to this view.

aseptic (eh-**sep**-tik) *adj* free from harmful bacteria

asexual (eh-**sex**-yew-al) *adj* **1** having no apparent sex or sex organs **2** (of reproduction) not involving sexual activity **asexually** *adv*

ash[1] *n* **1** the powdery substance formed when something is burnt **2** fine particles of lava thrown out by an erupting volcano **WORD ORIGIN** Old English *æsce*

ash² *n* a tree with grey bark and winged seeds
WORD ORIGIN Old English *æsc*

ashamed *adj* 1 overcome with shame or remorse 2 unwilling through fear of humiliation or shame: *she'd be ashamed to admit to jealousy*
WORD ORIGIN Old English *āscamod*

ash can *n US* a dustbin

ashen *adj* pale with shock

ashes *pl n* 1 remains after burning 2 the remains of a human body after cremation

Ashes *pl n* **the Ashes** a cricket trophy competed for by England and Australia since 1882
WORD ORIGIN from a mock obituary of English cricket after a great Australian victory

ashlar *or* **ashler** *n* 1 a square block of cut stone for use in building 2 a thin dressed stone used to face a wall
WORD ORIGIN Old French *aisselier* crossbeam

ashore *adv* towards or on land

ashram *n* a religious retreat where a Hindu holy man lives
WORD ORIGIN Sanskrit *āśrama*

ashtray *n* a dish for tobacco ash and cigarette ends

Ash Wednesday *n* the first day of Lent, named from the Christian custom of sprinkling ashes on penitents' heads

ashy *adj* **ashier, ashiest** 1 pale greyish 2 covered with ash

Asian *adj* 1 of Asia 2 *Brit* of the Indian subcontinent ▷ *n* 3 a person from Asia 4 *Brit* a person from the Indian subcontinent or a descendant of one
≡USAGE
≡The use of *Asian* or *Asiatic* as a noun can ≡be offensive and should be avoided.

Asian pear *n* an apple-shaped pear with crisp juicy flesh

Asiatic *adj* Asian
≡USAGE
≡See at **Asian**.

aside *adv* 1 to one side 2 out of other people's hearing: *her mother took her aside for a serious talk* 3 out of mind: *she pushed aside her fears of being beaten or killed* 4 into reserve: *a certain amount must also be put aside for defence and government* ▷ *n* 5 a remark not meant to be heard by everyone present 6 a remark that is not connected with the subject being discussed

asinine (ass-in-nine) *adj* 1 obstinate or stupid 2 of or like an ass
WORD ORIGIN Latin *asinus* ass

ask *vb* 1 to say or write (something) in a form that requires an answer: *I asked him his name; 'do you think we'll have trouble landing?' he asked* 2 to make a request or demand: *the chairman asked for a show of hands* 3 to invite 4 to inquire about: *I pretended to be lost and asked for directions* 5 to expect: *is that too much to ask?*
▷ **WORD ORIGIN** Old English *āscian*

ask after *vb* to make polite inquiries about the health of: *he asked after you*

askance (ass-**kanss**) *adv* **look askance at a** to look at with an oblique glance **b** to regard with suspicion

WORD ORIGIN origin unknown

askew *adv, adj* towards one side; crooked

ask for *vb* 1 to seek to speak to 2 to request 3 *informal* to behave in a manner that is regarded as inviting (something): *you were asking for trouble there*

asking price *n* the price suggested by a seller

aslant *adv* 1 at a slant ▷ *prep* 2 slanting across

asleep *adj* 1 in or into a state of sleep 2 (of limbs) numb 3 *informal* not listening or paying attention

ASLEF (in Britain) Associated Society of Locomotive Engineers and Firemen

asp *n* a small viper of S Europe
WORD ORIGIN Greek *aspis*

asparagus *n* the young shoots of a plant of the lily family, which can be cooked and eaten
WORD ORIGIN Greek *asparagos*

aspartame *n* an artificial sweetener

aspect *n* 1 a distinct feature or element in a problem or situation 2 a position facing a particular direction: *the room's east-facing aspect* 3 appearance or look: *a room with a somewhat gloomy aspect*
WORD ORIGIN Latin *ad-* to, at + *specere* to look

aspen *n* a poplar tree whose leaves quiver in the wind
WORD ORIGIN Old English *æspe*

asperity (ass-**per**-rit-ee) *n, pl* **-ties** roughness or sharpness of temper
WORD ORIGIN Latin *asper* rough

aspersion *n* **cast aspersions on** to make disparaging or malicious remarks about
WORD ORIGIN Latin *aspergere* to sprinkle

asphalt *n* 1 a black tarlike substance used in road-surfacing and roofing materials ▷ *vb* 2 to cover with asphalt
WORD ORIGIN Greek *asphaltos*, probably from *a-* not + *sphallein* to cause to fall; referring to its use as a binding agent

asphodel *n* a plant with clusters of yellow or white flowers

asphyxia (ass-**fix**-ee-a) *n* unconsciousness or death caused by lack of oxygen
WORD ORIGIN Greek *a-* without + *sphuxis* pulse

asphyxiate *vb* **-ating, -ated** to smother or suffocate **asphyxiation** *n*

aspic *n* a savoury jelly based on meat or fish stock, used as a mould for meat or vegetables
WORD ORIGIN French

aspidistra *n* a house plant with long tapered evergreen leaves
WORD ORIGIN Greek *aspis* shield

aspirant *n* a person who aspires, such as to a powerful position

aspirate *phonetics vb* **-rating, -rated** 1 to pronounce (a word or syllable) with an initial h ▷ *n* 2 the sound represented in English and several other languages as h

aspiration *n* 1 a strong desire or aim 2 *phonetics* the pronunciation of an aspirated consonant **aspirational** *adj*

aspirator *n* a device for removing fluids from a body cavity by suction

aspire *vb* **-piring, -pired** to yearn for something or hope to do or be something: *it struck him as bizarre that*

somebody could aspire to be a dental technician **aspiring** *adj*
WORD ORIGIN Latin *aspirare* to breathe upon

aspirin *n, pl* **-rin** *or* **-rins** 1 a drug used to relieve pain and fever 2 a tablet of aspirin
WORD ORIGIN German

ass¹ *n* 1 a mammal resembling the horse but with longer ears 2 a foolish person
WORD ORIGIN Old English *assa*

ass² *n US & Canad taboo* same as **arse**
WORD ORIGIN Old English *ærs*

assagai *n* same as **assegai**

assail *vb* 1 to attack violently 2 to criticize strongly 3 to disturb: *he was assailed by a dizzy sensation* **assailant** *n*
WORD ORIGIN Latin *assilire* to leap on

assassin *n* a murderer of a prominent person
WORD ORIGIN Arabic *hashshāshīn*, plural of *hashshāsh* one who eats hashish

assassinate *vb* **-nating, -nated** to murder (a prominent person) **assassination** *n*

assault *n* 1 a violent attack, either physical or verbal ▷ *vb* 2 to attack violently
WORD ORIGIN Old French *asaut*

assault and battery *n criminal law* a threat of attack to another person followed by actual attack

assault course *n* an obstacle course designed to give soldiers practice in negotiating hazards

assay *vb* 1 to analyse (a substance, such as gold) to find out how pure it is ▷ *n* 2 an analysis of the purity of an ore or precious metal
WORD ORIGIN Old French *assai*

assegai *or* **assagai** *n, pl* **-gais** a sharp light spear used in southern Africa
WORD ORIGIN Arabic *az zaghayah*

assemblage *n* 1 a collection or group of things 2 the act of assembling

assemble *vb* **-bling, -bled** 1 to collect or gather together 2 to put together the parts of (a machine)
WORD ORIGIN Old French *assembler*

assembler *n* 1 a person or thing that assembles 2 a computer program that converts a set of low-level symbolic data into machine language

assembly *n, pl* **-blies** 1 a number of people gathered together for a meeting 2 the act of assembling

assembly line *n* a sequence of machines and workers in a factory assembling a product

assemblyman *n, pl* **-men** a member of a legislative assembly

assent *n* 1 agreement, consent ▷ *vb* 2 to agree
WORD ORIGIN Latin *assentiri*

assert *vb* 1 to state or declare 2 to insist upon (one's rights, etc.) 3 **assert oneself** to speak and act forcefully
WORD ORIGIN Latin *asserere* to join to oneself

assertion *n* 1 a positive statement, usually made without evidence 2 the act of asserting

assertive *adj* confident and direct in dealing with others **assertively** *adv* **assertiveness** *n*

assess vb **1** to judge the worth or importance of **2** to estimate the value of (income or property) for taxation purposes **assessment** n
WORD ORIGIN Latin *assidere* to sit beside

assessor n **1** a person who values property for taxation or insurance purposes **2** a person with technical expertise called in to advise a court **3** a person who evaluates the merits of something

asset n **1** a thing or person that is valuable or useful **2** any property owned by a person or company
WORD ORIGIN Latin *ad-* to + *satis* enough

asset-stripping n *commerce* the practice of taking over a failing company at a low price and then selling the assets piecemeal **asset-stripper** n

asseverate vb **-ating, -ated** *formal* to declare solemnly **asseveration** n
WORD ORIGIN Latin *asseverare* to do (something) earnestly

assiduous adj **1** hard-working **2** done with care **assiduity** n **assiduously** adv
WORD ORIGIN Latin *assidere* to sit beside

assign vb **1** to select (someone) for a post or task **2** to give a task or duty (to someone) **3** to attribute to a specified cause **4** to set apart (a place or time) for a particular function or event: *to assign a day for the meeting* **5** *law* to transfer (one's right, interest, or title to property) to someone else
WORD ORIGIN Latin *assignare*

assignation (ass-sig-**nay**-shun) n a secret arrangement to meet, esp. one between lovers
WORD ORIGIN Latin *assignatio* a marking out

assignment n **1** something that has been assigned, such as a task **2** the act of assigning **3** *law* the transfer to another person of a right, interest, or title to property

assimilate vb **-lating, -lated 1** to learn and understand (information) thoroughly **2** to adjust or become adjusted: *they became assimilated to German culture* **3** to absorb (food) **assimilable** adj **assimilation** n
WORD ORIGIN Latin *ad-* to + *similis* like

assist vb **1** to give help or support ▷n **2** *sport* a pass by a player which enables another player to score a goal
WORD ORIGIN Latin *assistere* to stand by

assistance n help or support

assistant n **1** a helper or subordinate **2** same as **shop assistant** ▷adj **3** junior or deputy: *assistant manager*

assistant referee n *soccer* the official name for **linesman** (sense 1)

assizes *pl* n *Brit* (formerly in England and Wales) the sessions of the principal court in each county
WORD ORIGIN Latin *assidere* to sit beside

assoc. association

associate vb **-ating, -ated 1** to connect in the mind **2** to mix socially: *addicts are driven to associate with criminals* **3 be associated** or **associate oneself with** to be involved with (a group) because of shared views: *she had long been associated with the far right* ▷n **4** a partner in business **5** a companion or friend

▷adj **6** having partial rights or subordinate status: *an associate member* **7** joined with in business: *an associate director*
WORD ORIGIN Latin *ad-* to + *sociare* to join

association n **1** a group of people with a common interest **2** the act of associating or the state of being associated **3** friendship: *their association still had to remain a secret* **4** a mental connection of ideas or feelings: *the place contained associations for her*

association football n same as **soccer**

associative adj *maths* (of an operation such as multiplication or addition) producing the same answer regardless of the way the elements are grouped, for example $(2 \times 3) \times 4 = 2 \times (3 \times 4)$

assonance n the rhyming of vowel sounds but not consonants, as in *time* and *light*
WORD ORIGIN Latin *assonare* to sound

assorted adj **1** consisting of various kinds mixed together **2** matched: *an ill-assorted childless couple*
WORD ORIGIN Old French *assorter*

assortment n a collection of various things or sorts

asst assistant

assuage (ass-**wage**) vb **-suaging, -suaged** to relieve (grief, pain, or thirst)
WORD ORIGIN Latin *suavis* pleasant

assume vb **-suming, -sumed 1** to take to be true without proof **2** to undertake or take on: *every general staff officer was able to assume control of the army* **3** to make a pretence of: *the man had assumed a debonair attitude* **4** to take on: *her eyes assumed a scared haunted look*
WORD ORIGIN Latin *ad-* to + *sumere* to take up

assumed name n a false name used by someone to disguise his or her identity

assuming conj if it is assumed or taken for granted: *assuming the first two phases were successful, the third phase would follow*

assumption n **1** something that is taken for granted **2** the act of assuming power or possession
WORD ORIGIN Latin *assumptio* a taking up

Assumption n *Christianity* the taking up of the Virgin Mary into heaven when her earthly life was ended

assurance n **1** a statement or assertion intended to inspire confidence **2** feeling of confidence; certainty **3** insurance that provides for events that are certain to happen, such as death

assure vb **-suring, -sured 1** to promise or guarantee **2** to convince: *they assured me that they had not seen the document* **3** to make (something) certain **4** *chiefly Brit* to insure against loss of life
WORD ORIGIN Latin *ad-* to + *securus* secure

assured adj **1** confident or self-assured **2** certain to happen **3** *chiefly Brit* insured **assuredly** (a-**sure**-id-lee) adv

Assyrian n an inhabitant of ancient Assyria, a kingdom of Mesopotamia

AST Atlantic Standard Time

astatine n *chem* a radioactive element occurring naturally in minute amounts

or artificially produced by bombarding bismuth with alpha particles. Symbol: At
WORD ORIGIN Greek *astatos* unstable

aster n a plant with white, blue, purple, or pink daisy-like flowers
WORD ORIGIN Greek: star

asterisk n **1** a star-shaped character (*) used in printing or writing to indicate a footnote etc. ▷vb **2** to mark with an asterisk
WORD ORIGIN Greek *asteriskos* a small star

astern adv, adj *naut* **1** at or towards the stern of a ship **2** backwards **3** behind a vessel

asteroid n any of the small planets that orbit the sun between Mars and Jupiter
WORD ORIGIN Greek *asteroeidēs* starlike

asthma (**ass**-ma) n an illness causing difficulty in breathing **asthmatic** adj, n
WORD ORIGIN Greek

astigmatic adj relating to or affected with astigmatism
WORD ORIGIN Greek *a-* without + *stigma* spot, focus

astigmatism (eh-**stig**-mat-tiz-zum) n a defect of a lens, esp. of the eye, causing it not to focus properly

astir adj **1** out of bed **2** in motion

astonish vb to surprise greatly **astonishing** adj **astonishment** n
WORD ORIGIN Latin *ex-* out + *tonare* to thunder

astound vb to overwhelm with amazement **astounding** adj
WORD ORIGIN Old French *estoner*

astraddle prep astride

astrakhan n **1** a fur made of the dark curly fleece of lambs from Astrakhan in Russia **2** a cloth resembling this

astral adj **1** relating to or resembling the stars **2** of the spirit world
WORD ORIGIN Greek *astron* star

astray adj, adv out of the right or expected way
WORD ORIGIN Old French *estraier* to stray

astride adj **1** with a leg on either side **2** with legs far apart ▷prep **3** with a leg on either side of

astringent adj **1** causing contraction of body tissue **2** checking the flow of blood from a cut **3** severe or harsh ▷n **4** an astringent drug or lotion **astringency** n
WORD ORIGIN Latin *astringens* drawing together

astro- *combining form* indicating a star or stars: *astrology*
WORD ORIGIN Greek

astrolabe n an instrument formerly used to measure the altitude of stars and planets
WORD ORIGIN Greek *astron* star + *lambanein* to take

astrology n the study of the alleged influence of the stars, planets, sun, and moon on human affairs **astrologer** or **astrologist** n **astrological** adj
WORD ORIGIN Greek *astron* star + *logos* word, account

astronaut n a person trained for travelling in space
WORD ORIGIN Greek *astron* star + *nautēs* sailor

Word Histories
part 2

The word **arsenal** came into English from Italian, but it has its origin in Arabic. In Arabic a *dār al-sīn'ah* is a workshop or factory. This word was borrowed from Arabic into Italian as *arsenale*, meaning 'dockyard'. And it was in the sense of 'dockyard' that it came into English, only later coming to have the meaning of an arms and ammunition store.

Asparagus was transformed by folk etymology into 'sparrowgrass' from the 17th century until the 19th, with the original form being regarded as stuffy or pedantic during this period. Unusually for a folk etymology, however, 'sparrowgrass' has now died out.

Assassin: The source of this word is the Arabic word *hashshāshīn*, meaning 'people who take hashish'. The word comes from the name of a feared medieval Muslim sect who allegedly ate or smoked hashish before embarking on missions to murder those they considered their enemies, Crusaders and Muslim leaders alike.

Avocado comes from the Aztec word *ahuacatl*, meaning 'testicle' as well as 'avocado'. The fruit was given this name by the Aztecs because of its shape. The word entered Mexican Spanish as *aguacate*, and changed to 'avocado' under the influence of the Spanish word *avocado* meaning 'advocate'.

Ballot comes from Italian *ballotta* meaning 'little ball'. In medieval Venice, votes were cast by dropping black or white pebbles or balls into a box.

Banal: In Old French, the adjective *banal* referred to the mill, bakery, etc. that was owned by the local lord and that all his tenants had to use. The word 'banal' therefore came to mean 'common to everyone' and from that, 'commonplace' or 'ordinary'.

Bandy comes from Old French *bander* meaning 'to hit a ball backwards and forwards in tennis'. The word 'bandy' also denotes an old form of tennis that is no longer played.

Bawdy: *Bawd* is an old word for a 'brothel keeper'. It comes from an old French word *baud* meaning 'merry' or 'lively'. Bawdy stories are therefore the sort that contain lighthearted references to sexual activity, such as might be associated with brothels.

Bayonet: Bayonets were first made in the 16th century in the town of *Bayonne* in southwestern France, and it is from the name of the town that they take their name.

Bedlam: The Hospital of St. Mary of Bethlehem in London was an institution where the insane or mentally ill were cared for. Its name was colloquially shortened to *Bethlem* or *Bedlam*, from which the word 'bedlam' comes.

Belfry derives from the Old French word *berfrei*, meaning 'tower' – originally a siege tower – and has nothing to do with bells. The 'l' in the English word is due to folk etymology, associating towers with the bells hung in the church variety.

Berserk comes from the Old Norse word *berserkr*, denoting a Viking warrior who wore a shirt (*serkr*) made from the skin of a bear (*björn*). Berserkrs worked themselves into a frenzy before going into battle, from which comes the notion of someone 'going berserk'.

Bikini: The bikini takes its name from the *Bikini* Atoll in the Marshall Islands in the Pacific Ocean, where an atom-bomb was exploded in 1946. The bikini was given its name because it was said that the effect on men caused by women wearing bikinis was as explosive and devastating as the effect of the atom-bomb.

A **bonfire** is literally a 'bone-fire'. Bones were used as fuel in the Middle Ages.

Boycott: Captain Charles Boycott (1832–1897) was a retired British army officer who became an estate manager in Ireland. When in 1880 he was asked to reduce his tenants' rents after a bad harvest, he refused and tried to have some of the tenants evicted. For this, the tenants refused to have anything further to do with him, and he left Ireland shortly afterwards.

a

astronautics *n* the science and technology of space flight **astronautical** *adj*

astronomical *or* **astronomic** *adj* **1** enormously large **2** of astronomy **astronomically** *adv*

astronomical unit *n* a unit of distance equal to the average distance between the earth and the sun (1.495×10^{11}m)

astronomy *n* the scientific study of heavenly bodies **astronomer** *n* **WORD ORIGIN** Greek *astron* star + *nomos* law

astrophysics *n* the study of the physical and chemical properties of celestial bodies **astrophysical** *adj* **astrophysicist** *n*

Astroturf *n trademark* a brand of artificial grass **WORD ORIGIN** from the *Astro(dome)*, sports stadium where it was first used + *turf*

astute *adj* quick to notice or understand **astutely** *adv* **astuteness** *n* **WORD ORIGIN** Latin *astutus*

asunder *adv, adj literary* into parts or pieces; apart

asylum *n* **1** refuge granted to a political refugee from a foreign country **2** (formerly) a mental hospital **WORD ORIGIN** Greek *asulon*

asymmetric bars (**ass**-sim-met-rik, **ay**-sim-met-rik) *pl n gymnastics* a pair of bars parallel to each other but at different heights, used for various exercises

asymmetry *n* lack of symmetry **asymmetric** *or* **asymmetrical** *adj*

asymptote (**ass**-im-tote) *n* a straight line that is closely approached but never met by a curve **asymptotic** *adj* **WORD ORIGIN** Greek *asumptōtos* not falling together

at *prep* **1** indicating location or position: *she had planted a vegetable garden at the back* **2** towards; in the direction of: *she was staring at the wall behind him* **3** indicating position in time: *we arrived at 12.30* **4** engaged in: *the innocent laughter of children at play* **5** during the passing of: *she works at night as a nurse's aide* **6** for; in exchange for: *crude oil is selling at its lowest price since September* **7** indicating the object of an emotion: *I'm angry at you because you were rude to me* **WORD ORIGIN** Old English *æt*

At *chem* astatine

at. **1** atmosphere **2** atomic

atavism (**at**-a-viz-zum) *n* **1** the recurrence of primitive characteristics that were present in distant ancestors but not in more recent ones **2** reversion to a former type **atavistic** *adj* **WORD ORIGIN** Latin *atavus* great-grandfather's grandfather, ancestor

ataxia *n pathol* lack of muscular coordination **ataxic** *adj* **WORD ORIGIN** Greek

ate *vb* the past tense of **eat**

atelier (**at**-tell-yay) *n* an artist's studio

atheism (**aith**-ee-iz-zum) *n* the belief that there is no God **atheist** *n* **WORD ORIGIN** Greek *a-* without + *theos* god

Athena *or* **Athene** *n Greek myth* the goddess of wisdom

atherosclerosis *n, pl* **-ses** a disease in which deposits of fat cause the walls of the arteries to thicken **atherosclerotic** *adj* **WORD ORIGIN** Greek *athērōma* tumour + SCLEROSIS

athlete *n* **1** a person trained to compete in sports or exercises **2** *chiefly Brit* a competitor in track-and-field events **WORD ORIGIN** Greek *athlos* a contest

athlete's foot *n* a fungal infection of the skin of the foot

athletic *adj* **1** physically fit or strong **2** of or for an athlete or athletics **athletically** *adv* **athleticism** *n*

athletics *pl n Austral & Brit* track-and-field events

at-home *n Austral & Brit* a social gathering in a person's home

athwart *prep* **1** across ▷ *adv* **2** transversely; from one side to another

atigi *n* a type of parka worn by the Inuit in Canada

Atlantic *adj* of the Atlantic Ocean, the world's second largest ocean, bounded by the Arctic, the Antarctic, America, and Europe and Africa **WORD ORIGIN** Greek *(pelagos) Atlantikos* (the sea) of Atlas (so called because it lay beyond the Atlas Mountains)

Atlanticism *n* belief in close economic and military cooperation between Europe and the United States **Atlanticist** *n*

Atlantis *n* (in ancient legend) a continent said to have sunk beneath the Atlantic west of Gibraltar

atlas *n* a book of maps **WORD ORIGIN** because *Atlas*, a Titan in Greek mythology, was shown supporting the heavens in 16th-century books of maps

atmosphere *n* **1** the mass of gases surrounding the earth or any other heavenly body **2** the air in a particular place **3** a pervasive feeling or mood: *the atmosphere was tense* **4** a unit of pressure equal to the normal pressure of the air at sea level **atmospheric** *adj* **atmospherically** *adv* **WORD ORIGIN** Greek *atmos* vapour + *sphaira* sphere

atmospherics *pl n* radio interference caused by electrical disturbance in the atmosphere

atoll *n* a circular coral reef surrounding a lagoon **WORD ORIGIN** *atollon*, native name in the Maldive Islands

atom *n* **1 a** the smallest unit of matter which can take part in a chemical reaction **b** this entity as a source of nuclear energy **2** a very small amount **WORD ORIGIN** Greek *atomos* that cannot be divided

atom bomb *n* same as **atomic bomb**

atomic *adj* **1** of or using atomic bombs or atomic energy **2** of atoms **atomically** *adv*

atomic bomb *or* **atom bomb** *n* a type of bomb in which the energy is provided by nuclear fission

atomic energy *n* same as **nuclear energy**

atomic mass unit *n* a unit of mass that is equal to one twelfth of the mass of an atom of carbon-12

atomic number *n* the number of protons in the nucleus of an atom of an element

atomic theory *n* any theory in which matter is regarded as consisting of atoms

atomic weight *n* the ratio of the average mass per atom of an element to one twelfth of the mass of an atom of carbon-12

atomize *or* **-ise** *vb* **-izing, -ized** *or* **-ising, -ised** **1** to separate into free atoms **2** to reduce to fine particles or spray **3** to destroy by nuclear weapons

atomizer *or* **-iser** *n* a device for reducing a liquid to a fine spray

atonal (eh-**tone**-al) *adj* (of music) not written in an established key **atonality** *n*

atone *vb* **atoning, atoned** to make amends (for a sin, crime, or wrongdoing)

atonement *n* **1** something done to make amends for wrongdoing **2** *Christian theol* the reconciliation of humankind with God through the sacrificial death of Christ **WORD ORIGIN** Middle English *at onement* in harmony

atop *prep* on top of

atrium *n, pl* **atria** **1** *anat* the upper chamber of each half of the heart **2** a central hall that extends through several storeys in a modern building **3** the open main court of an ancient Roman house **atrial** *adj* **WORD ORIGIN** Latin

atrocious *adj* **1** extremely cruel or wicked **2** horrifying or shocking **3** *informal* very bad **atrociously** *adv* **WORD ORIGIN** Latin *atrox* dreadful

atrocity *n* **1** behaviour that is wicked or cruel **2** *pl* **-ties** an act of extreme cruelty

atrophy (**at**-trof-fee) *n, pl* **-phies** **1** a wasting away of a physical organ or part **2** a failure to grow ▷ *vb* **-phies, -phying, -phied** **3** to waste away **WORD ORIGIN** Greek *atrophos* ill-fed

atropine *n* a poisonous alkaloid obtained from deadly nightshade **WORD ORIGIN** New Latin *atropa* deadly nightshade

attach *vb* **1** to join, fasten, or connect **2** to attribute or ascribe: *he attaches particular importance to the proposed sale* **3** **attach oneself** *or* **be attached to** to become associated with or join **WORD ORIGIN** Old French *atachier*

attaché (at-**tash**-shay) *n* a specialist attached to a diplomatic mission **WORD ORIGIN** French

attaché case *n* a flat rectangular briefcase for carrying papers

attached *adj* **1** married, engaged, or in an exclusive sexual relationship **2** **attached to** fond of

attachment *n* **1** affection or regard for **2** an accessory that can be fitted to a device to change what it can do

attack *vb* **1** to launch a physical assault (against) **2** to criticize vehemently **3** to set about (a job or problem) with vigour **4** to affect adversely: *BSE attacks the animal's brain* **5** to take the initiative in a game or sport ▷ *n* **6** the act of attacking **7** any sudden appearance of a disease or

symptoms: *a bad attack of mumps* **attacker** *n*
WORD ORIGIN Old Italian *attaccare*

attain *vb* **1** to manage to do or get (something): *the country attained economic growth* **2** to reach **attainable** *adj*
WORD ORIGIN Latin *attingere*

attainment *n* an achievement or the act of achieving something

attar *n* a perfume made from damask roses
WORD ORIGIN Persian *'atir* perfumed

attempt *vb* **1** to make an effort (to do or achieve something); try ▷ *n* **2** an endeavour to achieve something; effort **3 attempt on someone's life** an attack on someone with the intention to kill
WORD ORIGIN Latin *attemptare*

≡ USAGE
≡ *Attempt* should not be used in the
≡ passive when followed by an
≡ infinitive: *attempts were made to find a*
≡ *solution* (not *a solution was attempted to be*
≡ *found*).

attend *vb* **1** to be present at (an event) **2** to go regularly to a school, college, etc. **3** to look after: *the actors lounged in their canvas chairs, attended by sycophants* **4** to pay attention **5 attend to** to apply oneself to: *I've a few things I must attend to*
WORD ORIGIN Latin *attendere* to stretch towards

attendance *n* **1** the act of attending **2** the number of people present **3** regularity in attending

attendant *n* **1** a person who assists, guides, or provides a service ▷ *adj* **2** associated: *nuclear power and its attendant dangers* **3** being in attendance

attendee *n* a person who is present at a specified event

attention *n* **1** concentrated direction of the mind **2** consideration, notice, or observation **3** detailed care or treatment **4** the alert position in military drill **5 attentions** acts of courtesy: *the attentions of men seemed to embarrass her*

attentive *adj* **1** paying close attention **2** considerately helpful: *at society parties he is attentive to his wife* **attentively** *adv* **attentiveness** *n*

attenuated *adj* **1** weakened **2** thin and extended **attenuation** *n*
WORD ORIGIN Latin *attenuare* to weaken

attest *vb* **1** to affirm or prove the truth of **2** to bear witness to (an act or event) **attestation** *n*
WORD ORIGIN Latin *testari* to bear witness

attested *adj Brit* (of cattle) certified to be free from a disease, such as tuberculosis

attic *n* a space or room within the roof of a house
WORD ORIGIN from the *Attic* style of architecture

attire *n* clothes, esp. fine or formal ones
WORD ORIGIN Old French *atirier* to put in order

attired *adj* dressed in a specified way

attitude *n* **1** the way a person thinks and behaves **2** a position of the body **3** *informal* a hostile manner **4** the orientation of an aircraft or spacecraft in relation to some plane or direction
WORD ORIGIN Latin *aptus* apt

attitudinize *or* **-nise** *vb* **-nizing, -nized** *or* **-nising, -nised** to adopt a pose or opinion for effect

attorney *n* **1** a person legally appointed to act for another **2** US a lawyer
WORD ORIGIN Old French *atourner* to direct to

attorney general *n, pl* **attorneys general** *or* **attorney generals** a chief law officer of some governments

attract *vb* **1** to arouse the interest or admiration of **2** (of a magnet) to draw (something) closer by exerting a force on it
WORD ORIGIN Latin *attrahere* to draw towards

attraction *n* **1** the act or quality of attracting **2** an interesting or desirable feature: *the Scottishness of Scott is an attraction, but by no means his only merit* **3** an object or place that people visit for interest: *this carefully preserved tourist attraction* **4** (of a magnet) a force by which one object attracts another

attractive *adj* appealing to the senses or mind **attractively** *adv* **attractiveness** *n*

attribute *vb* **-uting, -uted** **1 attribute to** to regard as belonging to or produced by: *a play attributed to William Shakespeare* ▷ *n* **2** a quality or feature representative of a person or thing **attributable** *adj* **attribution** *n*
WORD ORIGIN Latin *attribuere* to associate with

attributive *adj grammar* (of an adjective) coming before the noun modified

attrition *n* constant wearing down to weaken or destroy: *a war of attrition*
WORD ORIGIN Latin *atterere* to weaken

attune *vb* **-tuning, -tuned** to adjust or accustom (a person or thing)

ATV all-terrain vehicle: a vehicle with wheels designed to travel on rough ground

atypical (eh-**tip**-ik-kl) *adj* not typical **atypically** *adv*

Au *chem* gold
WORD ORIGIN Latin *aurum*

aubergine (**oh**-bur-zheen) *n Brit* the dark purple fruit of a tropical plant, cooked and eaten as a vegetable
WORD ORIGIN French, from Arabic *al-bādindjān*

aubrietia (aw-**bree**-sha) *n* a trailing purple-flowered rock plant
WORD ORIGIN after Claude *Aubriet*, painter of flowers and animals

auburn *adj* (of hair) reddish-brown
WORD ORIGIN (originally meaning: blond) Latin *albus* white

auction *n* **1** a public sale at which articles are sold to the highest bidder ▷ *vb* **2** to sell by auction
WORD ORIGIN Latin *auctio* an increasing

auctioneer *n* a person who conducts an auction

audacious *adj* **1** recklessly bold or daring **2** impudent or presumptuous **audacity** *n*
WORD ORIGIN Latin *audax* bold

audible *adj* loud enough to be heard **audibility** *n* **audibly** *adv*
WORD ORIGIN Latin *audire* to hear

audience *n* **1** a group of spectators or listeners at a concert or play **2** the people reached by a book, film, or radio or television programme **3** a formal interview
WORD ORIGIN Latin *audire* to hear

audio *adj* **1** of or relating to sound or hearing **2** of or for the transmission or reproduction of sound
WORD ORIGIN Latin *audire* to hear

audio book *n* a reading of a book recorded on tape

audio frequency *n* a frequency in the range 20 hertz to 20 000 hertz, audible to the human ear

audiometer (aw-dee-**om**-it-er) *n* an instrument for testing hearing

audiotypist *n* a typist trained to type from a dictating machine **audiotyping** *n*

audiovisual *adj* involving both hearing and sight: *audiovisual teaching aids*

audit *n* **1** an official inspection of business accounts, conducted by an independent qualified accountant **2** any thoroughgoing assessment or review: *an audit of their lifestyle* ▷ *vb* **auditing, audited** **3** to examine (business accounts) officially
WORD ORIGIN Latin *audire* to hear

audition *n* **1** a test of a performer's or musician's ability for a particular role or job ▷ *vb* **2** to test or be tested in an audition
WORD ORIGIN Latin *audire* to hear

auditor *n* a person qualified to audit accounts
WORD ORIGIN Latin *auditor* a hearer

auditorium *n, pl* **-toriums** *or* **-toria** **1** the area of a concert hall or theatre in which the audience sits **2** US & Canad a building for public meetings
WORD ORIGIN Latin

auditory *adj* of or relating to hearing
WORD ORIGIN Latin *audire* to hear

au fait (oh **fay**) *adj* **1** (usually foll. by *with*) fully informed (about) **2** expert
WORD ORIGIN French: to the point

auf Wiedersehen (owf **vee**-der-zay-en) *interj* goodbye
WORD ORIGIN German

Aug. August

Augean (aw-**jee**-an) *adj* extremely dirty or corrupt
WORD ORIGIN from *Augeas*, in Greek mythology, king whose filthy stables Hercules cleaned in one day

auger *n* a pointed tool for boring holes
WORD ORIGIN Old English *nafugār* nave (ie hub of a wheel) spear

aught *pron old-fashioned or literary* anything whatever: *for aught I know*
WORD ORIGIN Old English *āwiht*

augment *vb* to make or become greater in number or strength **augmentation** *n*
WORD ORIGIN Latin *augere* to increase

augmented reality *n* an artificial environment created through the combination of real-world and computer-generated data

au gratin (oh **grat**-tan) *adj* cooked with a topping of breadcrumbs and sometimes cheese
WORD ORIGIN French

augur *vb* to be a good or bad sign of future events: *a double fault on the opening point did not augur well*
WORD ORIGIN Latin: diviner of omens

augury *n* **1** the foretelling of the future **2** *pl* -ries an omen

august *adj* dignified and imposing
WORD ORIGIN Latin *augustus*

August *n* the eighth month of the year
WORD ORIGIN Latin, after the emperor *Augustus*

Augustan *adj* **1** of the Roman emperor Augustus Caesar or the poets writing during his reign **2** of any literary period noted for refinement and classicism

auk *n* a northern sea bird with a heavy body, short wings, and black-and-white plumage
WORD ORIGIN Old Norse *ālka*

auld lang syne *n* times past
WORD ORIGIN Scots, literally: old long since

aunt *n* **1** a sister of one's father or mother **2** the wife of one's uncle **3** a child's term of address for a female friend of the parents
WORD ORIGIN Latin *amita* a father's sister

auntie *or* **aunty** *n*, *pl* -ies *informal* an aunt

Aunt Sally *n*, *pl* -lies **1** a figure used in fairgrounds as a target **2** any target for insults or criticism

au pair *n* a young foreign woman who does housework in return for board and lodging
WORD ORIGIN French

aura *n*, *pl* auras *or* aurae **1** a distinctive air or quality associated with a person or thing **2** any invisible emanation
WORD ORIGIN Greek: breeze

aural *adj* of or using the ears or hearing
aurally *adv*
WORD ORIGIN Latin *auris* ear

aureate *adj literary* **1** covered with gold **2** (of a style of writing or speaking) excessively elaborate
WORD ORIGIN Latin *aurum* gold

aureole *or* **aureola** *n* **1** a ring of light surrounding the head of a figure represented as holy; halo **2** the sun's corona, visible as a faint halo during eclipses
WORD ORIGIN Latin *aurum* gold

au revoir (oh riv-**vwahr**) *interj* goodbye
WORD ORIGIN French

auric *adj* of or containing gold in the trivalent state
WORD ORIGIN Latin *aurum* gold

auricle *n* **1** the upper chamber of the heart **2** the outer part of the ear
auricular *adj*
WORD ORIGIN Latin *auris* ear

auricula *n*, *pl* -lae *or* -las an alpine primrose with leaves shaped like a bear's ear
WORD ORIGIN Latin *auris* ear

auriferous *adj* containing gold
WORD ORIGIN Latin *aurum* gold + *ferre* to bear

aurochs *n*, *pl* -rochs a recently extinct European wild ox
WORD ORIGIN German

aurora *n*, *pl* -ras *or* -rae **1** an atmospheric phenomenon of bands of light sometimes seen in the polar regions **2** *poetic* the dawn
WORD ORIGIN Latin: dawn

aurora australis *n* the aurora seen around the South Pole
WORD ORIGIN New Latin: southern aurora

aurora borealis *n* the aurora seen around the North Pole
WORD ORIGIN New Latin: northern aurora

auscultation *n* the listening to of the internal sounds of the body, usually with a stethoscope, to help with medical diagnosis
WORD ORIGIN Latin *auscultare* to listen attentively

auspices (aw-spiss-siz) *pl n* **under the auspices of** with the support and approval of
WORD ORIGIN Latin *auspicium* augury from birds

auspicious *adj* showing the signs of future success

⧉ USAGE
The use of *auspicious* to mean 'very special' (as in *this auspicious occasion*) should be avoided.

Aussie *n*, *adj informal* Australian

austere *adj* **1** stern or severe: *his austere and serious attitude to events* **2** self-disciplined or ascetic: *an extraordinarily austere and puritanical organization* **3** severely simple or plain: *the austere backdrop of grey*
WORD ORIGIN Greek *austēros* astringent

austerity *n*, *pl* -ties **1** the state of being austere **2** reduced availability of luxuries and consumer goods

austral *adj* of or from the south
WORD ORIGIN Latin *auster* the south wind

Austral. **1** Australasia **2** Australia(n)

Australasian *adj* of Australia, New Zealand, and neighbouring islands

Australia Day *n* public holiday in Australia on January 26

Australian *adj* **1** of Australia ▷ *n* **2** a person from Australia

Austrian *adj* **1** of Austria ▷ *n* **2** a person from Austria

autarchy (**aw**-tar-kee) *n*, *pl* -chies absolute power or autocracy
WORD ORIGIN Greek *autarkhia*

autarky (**aw**-tar-kee) *n*, *pl* -kies a policy of economic self-sufficiency
WORD ORIGIN Greek *autarkeia*

authentic *adj* **1** of undisputed origin or authorship; genuine **2** reliable or accurate **3** *music* using period instruments, scores, and playing techniques **authentically** *adv*
authenticity *n*
WORD ORIGIN Greek *authentikos*

authenticate *vb* -cating, -cated to establish as genuine **authentication** *n*

author *n* **1** a person who writes a book, article, or other written work **2** an originator or creator
WORD ORIGIN Latin *auctor*

authoritarian *adj* **1** insisting on strict obedience to authority ▷ *n* **2** a person who insists on strict obedience to authority **authoritarianism** *n*

authoritative *adj* **1** recognized as being reliable: *the authoritative book on Shakespeare* **2** possessing authority; official **authoritatively** *adv*

authority *n*, *pl* -ties **1** the power to command, control, or judge others **2** a person or group with this power: *a third escapee turned himself in to the authorities* **3** a decision-making organization or government department: *the local authority* **4** an expert in a particular field **5** official permission: *he had no authority to negotiate* **6** a position that has the power to command, control, or judge others: *people in authority* **7** **on good authority** from reliable evidence **8** confidence resulting from expertise
WORD ORIGIN Latin *auctor* author

authorize *or* **-ise** *vb* -izing, -ized *or* -ising, -ised **1** to give authority to **2** to give official permission for
authorization *or* -isation *n*

Authorized Version *n* **the Authorized Version** an English translation of the Bible published in 1611

authorship *n* **1** the origin or originator of a written work or plan **2** the profession of writing

autism *n psychiatry* abnormal self-absorption, usually affecting children, characterized by lack of response to people and limited ability to communicate **autistic** *adj*
WORD ORIGIN Greek *autos* self

auto *n*, *pl* -tos *US & Canad informal* short for **automobile**

auto- *or sometimes before a vowel* **aut-** *combining form* **1** self; of or by the same one: *autobiography* **2** self-propelling: *automobile*
WORD ORIGIN Greek *autos* self

autobahn *n* a motorway in German-speaking countries
WORD ORIGIN German, from *Auto* car + *Bahn* road

autobiography *n*, *pl* -phies an account of a person's life written by that person **autobiographer** *n* **autobiographical** *adj*

autoclave *n* an apparatus for sterilizing objects by steam under pressure
WORD ORIGIN AUTO- + Latin *clavis* key

autocracy *n*, *pl* -cies government by an individual with unrestricted authority

autocrat *n* **1** a ruler with absolute authority **2** a dictatorial person **autocratic** *adj* **autocratically** *adv*
WORD ORIGIN AUTO- + Greek *kratos* power

autocross *n* a sport in which cars race over a circuit of rough grass

Autocue *n trademark* an electronic television prompting device displaying a speaker's script, unseen by the audience

auto-da-fé (aw-toe-da-**fay**) *n*, *pl* **autos-da-fé** **1** *history* the ceremonial passing of sentence on heretics by the Spanish Inquisition **2** the burning to death of heretics
WORD ORIGIN Portuguese, literally: act of the faith

autofocus *n* a camera system in which the lens is focused automatically

Words from Shakespeare part 2

alarm, alarum *n* a call to arms or a signal for soldiers to prepare to fight
> Whence cometh this alarum and the noise?
> *Henry VI part 1* 1.4

Albion *n* England
> but I will sell my dukedom,
> To buy a slobbery and a dirty farm In that nook-shotten isle of Albion *Henry V* 3.5

all of all *phrase* everything, or the sum of all things
> The very all of all *Love's Labours Lost* 5.1

amend *v* to get better or to heal
> at his touch ...They presently amend *Macbeth* 4.3

anchor *v* to concentrate on something or fix on it
> My invention ... Anchors on Isabel
> *Measure for Measure* 2.4

anon *adv* soon
> You shall see anon how the murderer gets the love of Gonzago's wife *Hamlet* 3.2

antic *adj* weird or strange
> I'll charm the air to give a sound
> While you perform your antic round *Macbeth* 4.1

antic *n* a clown or a strange, unattractive creature
> If black, why nature, drawing an antic,
> Made a foul blot *Much Ado About Nothing* 3.1

apace *adv* quickly
> Come apace *As You Like It* 3.3

apparel *n* clothes or clothing
> one suit of apparel *Hamlet* 3.2

appliance *n* a cure
> Diseases desperate grown
> By desperate appliance are relieved *Hamlet* 4.3

argument *n* a topic of conversation or the subject
> Why 'tis the rarest argument of wonder that hath shot out in our latter times
> *All's Well That Ends Well* 2.3

arrant *adj* absolute, complete
> Fortune, that arrant whore *King Lear* 2.4

arras *n* a tapestry, a large cloth with a picture sewn on it using coloured thread
> Behind the arras I'll convey myself
> To hear the process *Hamlet* 3.3

art *n* knowledge
> Their malady convinces
> The great essay of art *Macbeth* 4.3

art *n* skill
> He ... gave you such a masterly report
> For art and exercise in your defence *Hamlet* 4.7

art *n* magic
> Now I want
> Spirits to enforce, art to enchant
> *The Tempest* 5 Epilogue

attend (on/upon) *v* to wait for or to expect
> Tarry I here, I but attend on death
> *Two Gentlemen of Verona* 3.1

auditor *n* a member of an audience or someone who listens
> I'll be an auditor *A Midsummer Night's Dream* 3.1

aught *n* anything
> if my love thou holdest at aught *Hamlet* 4.3

aunt *n* an old woman or someone who talks a lot or a gossip
> The wisest aunt telling the saddest tale
> *A Midsummer Night's Dream* 2.1

aunt *n* a mistress or a prostitute
> the thrush and the jay
> Are summer songs for me and my aunts
> While we lie tumbling in the hay
> *The Winter's Tale* 4.3

avaunt *int* go away!
> Avaunt, you curs! *King Lear* 3.6

a

autogiro or **autogyro** *n, pl* **-ros** a self-propelled aircraft resembling a helicopter but with an unpowered rotor

autograph *n* **1** a handwritten signature of a famous person ▷ *vb* **2** to write one's signature on or in
WORD ORIGIN AUTO- + Greek *graphein* to write

automat *n US* a vending machine

automate *vb* **-mating, -mated** to make (a manufacturing process) automatic

automatic *adj* **1** (of a device or mechanism) able to activate or regulate itself **2** (of a process) performed by automatic equipment **3** done without conscious thought **4** (of a firearm) utilizing some of the force of each explosion to reload and fire continuously **5** occurring as a necessary consequence: *the certificate itself carries no automatic legal benefits* ▷ *n* **6** an automatic firearm **7** a motor vehicle with automatic transmission **automatically** *adv*
WORD ORIGIN Greek *automatos* acting independently

automatic pilot *n* **1** a device that automatically maintains an aircraft on a preset course **2** on automatic pilot repeating an action or process without thought

automatic transmission *n* a transmission system in a motor vehicle in which the gears change automatically

automation *n* the use of automatic, often electronic, methods to control industrial processes

automaton *n, pl* **-tons** or **-ta 1** a mechanical device operating under its own power **2** a person who acts mechanically
WORD ORIGIN Greek *automatos* spontaneous

automobile *n US & Canad* a motorcar

automotive *adj* **1** relating to motor vehicles **2** self-propelling

autonomous *adj* **1** having self-government **2** independent of others
WORD ORIGIN AUTO- + Greek *nomos* law

autonomy *n, pl* **-mies 1** the right or state of self-government **2** freedom to determine one's own actions and behaviour
WORD ORIGIN Greek *autonomia*

autopilot *n* an automatic pilot

autopsy *n, pl* **-sies** examination of a corpse to determine the cause of death
WORD ORIGIN Greek *autopsia* seeing with one's own eyes

autoroute *n* a motorway in French-speaking countries
WORD ORIGIN French, from *auto* car + *route* road

autostrada *n* a motorway in Italian-speaking countries
WORD ORIGIN Italian, from *auto* car + *strada* road

autosuggestion *n* a process in which a person unconsciously supplies the means of influencing his or her own behaviour or beliefs

autumn *n* **1** the season of the year between summer and winter **2** a period of late maturity followed by a decline **autumnal** *adj*
WORD ORIGIN Latin *autumnus*

aux. auxiliary

auxiliaries *pl n* foreign troops serving another nation

auxiliary *adj* **1** secondary or supplementary **2** supporting ▷ *n, pl* **-ries 3** a person or thing that supports or supplements
WORD ORIGIN Latin *auxilium* help

auxiliary verb *n* a verb used to indicate the tense, voice, or mood of another verb, such as *will* in *I will go*

AV (of the Bible) Authorized Version

av. 1 average **2** avoirdupois

avail *vb* **1** to be of use, advantage, or assistance (to) **2** avail oneself of to make use of ▷ *n* **3** use or advantage: *to no avail*
WORD ORIGIN Latin *valere* to be strong

available *adj* **1** obtainable or accessible **2** able to be contacted and willing to talk: *a spokesman insisted she was not available for comment* **availability** *n* **availably** *adv*

avalanche *n* **1** a fall of large masses of snow and ice down a mountain **2** a sudden or overwhelming quantity of anything
WORD ORIGIN French

avant- (**av**-ong) *prefix* belonging to the avant-garde of a field: *avant-jazz*

avant-garde (av-ong-**gard**) *n* **1** those artists, writers, or musicians whose techniques and ideas are in advance of those generally accepted ▷ *adj* **2** using ideas or techniques in advance of those generally accepted
WORD ORIGIN French: vanguard

avarice (**av**-a-riss) *n* extreme greed for wealth **avaricious** *adj*
WORD ORIGIN Latin *avere* to crave

avast *interj naut* stop! cease!
WORD ORIGIN probably Dutch *hou'vast* hold fast

avatar *n* **1** *Hinduism* the appearance of a god in human or animal form **2** *computers* graphical representation of a person in a virtual environment, such as an online role-playing game
WORD ORIGIN Sanskrit *avatāra* a going down

Ave (**ah**-vay) or **Ave Maria** (ma-**ree**-a) *n* same as **Hail Mary**
WORD ORIGIN Latin: hail, Mary!

Ave. avenue

avenge *vb* **avenging, avenged** to inflict a punishment in retaliation for (harm done) or on behalf of (the person harmed) **avenger** *n*
WORD ORIGIN Latin *vindicare*

≡ USAGE
≡ The use of *avenge* with a reflexive
≡ pronoun was formerly considered
≡ incorrect, but is now acceptable: *she*
≡ *avenged herself on the man who killed her*
≡ *daughter.*

avenue *n* **1** a wide street **2** a road bordered by two rows of trees **3** a line of approach: *the United States was exhausting every avenue to achieve a diplomatic solution*
WORD ORIGIN French, from *avenir* to come to

aver (av-**vur**) *vb* **averring, averred** to state to be true **averment** *n*
WORD ORIGIN Latin *verus* true

average *n* **1** the typical or normal amount or quality **2** the result obtained by adding the numbers or quantities in a set and dividing the total by the number of members in the set **3** on average usually or typically ▷ *adj* **4** usual or typical **5** calculated as an average **6** mediocre or inferior ▷ *vb* **-aging, -aged 7** to calculate or estimate the average of **8** to amount to or be on average
WORD ORIGIN Middle English *averay* loss arising from damage to ships, ultimately from Arabic *awār* damage

averse *adj* opposed: *he's not averse to publicity, of the right kind*
WORD ORIGIN Latin *avertere* to turn from

aversion *n* **1** extreme dislike or disinclination **2** a person or thing that arouses this

avert *vb* **1** to turn away: *he had to avert his eyes* **2** to ward off: *a final attempt to avert war*
WORD ORIGIN Latin *avertere* to turn from

Avesta *n* a collection of sacred writings of Zoroastrianism

avian (**aiv**-ee-an) *adj* of or like a bird: *the treatment of avian diseases*
WORD ORIGIN Latin *avis* bird

avian flu *n* another name for **bird flu**
WORD ORIGIN Latin *avis* bird

aviary *n, pl* **aviaries** a large enclosure in which birds are kept
WORD ORIGIN Latin *avis* bird

aviation *n* the art or science of flying aircraft
WORD ORIGIN Latin *avis* bird

aviator *n old-fashioned* the pilot of an aircraft **aviatrix** *fem n*

avid *adj* **1** very keen or enthusiastic: *he is an avid football fan* **2** eager: *avid for economic development* **avidity** *n* **avidly** *adv*
WORD ORIGIN Latin *avere* to long for

avocado *n, pl* **-dos** a pear-shaped tropical fruit with a leathery green skin and greenish-yellow flesh
WORD ORIGIN Spanish *aguacate*

avocation *n* **1** *Brit, Austral, & NZ, old-fashioned* a person's regular job **2** *formal* a hobby
WORD ORIGIN Latin *avocare* to distract

avocet *n* a long-legged shore bird with a long slender upward-curving bill
WORD ORIGIN Italian *avocetta*

avoid *vb* **1** to refrain from doing **2** to prevent from happening **3** to keep out of the way of **avoidable** *adj* **avoidably** *adv* **avoidance** *n*
WORD ORIGIN Old French *esvuidier*

avoirdupois or **avoirdupois weight** (av-er-de-**poise**) *n* a system of weights based on the pound, which contains 16 ounces
WORD ORIGIN Old French *aver de peis* goods of weight

avow *vb* **1** to state or affirm **2** to admit openly **avowal** *n* **avowed** *adj* **avowedly** (a-**vow**-id-lee) *adv*
WORD ORIGIN Latin *advocare* to call upon

avuncular *adj* (of a man) friendly, helpful, and caring towards someone younger
WORD ORIGIN Latin *avunculus* (maternal) uncle

await *vb* **1** to wait for **2** to be in store for

awake *adj* **1** not sleeping **2** alert or aware: *awake to the danger* ▷ *vb* **awaking, awoke** *or* **awaked, awoken** *or* **awaked 3** to emerge or rouse from sleep **4** to become or cause to become alert **WORD ORIGIN** Old English *awacan*

☰ **USAGE**
☰ See at **wake**.

awaken *vb* **1** to awake **2** to cause to be aware of: *anxieties awakened by reunification*

awakening *n* the start of a feeling or awareness in someone: *a picture of an emotional awakening*

award *vb* **1** to give (something) for merit **2** *law* to declare to be entitled, such as by decision of a court ▷ *n* **3** something awarded, such as a prize **4** *law* the decision of an arbitrator or court **WORD ORIGIN** Old French *eswarder* to decide after investigation

aware *adj* **1** **aware of** knowing about: *he's at least aware of the problem* **2** informed: *they are becoming more politically aware every day* **awareness** *n* **WORD ORIGIN** Old English *gewær*

awash *adv, adj* washed over by water

away *adv* **1** from a particular place: *I saw them walk away and felt absolutely desolated* **2** in or to another, a usual, or a proper place: *he decided to put the car away in the garage* **3** at a distance: *keep away from the windows* **4** out of existence: *the pillars rotted away* **5** indicating motion or distance from a normal or proper place: *the child shook her head and looked away* **6** continuously: *he continued to scribble away* ▷ *adj* **7** not present: *he had been away from home for years* **8** distant: *the castle was farther away than he had thought* **9** *sport* played on an opponent's ground **WORD ORIGIN** Old English *on weg* on way

awayday *n* a day trip taken for pleasure **WORD ORIGIN** from *awayday ticket* a special-rate day return by train

awe *n* **1** wonder and respect mixed with dread ▷ *vb* **awing, awed 2** to inspire with reverence or dread **WORD ORIGIN** Old Norse *agi*

aweigh *adj naut* (of an anchor) no longer hooked into the bottom

awesome *adj* **1** inspiring or displaying awe **2** *slang* excellent or outstanding

awestruck *adj* overcome or filled with awe

awful *adj* **1** very bad or unpleasant **2** *informal* considerable or great: *that's an awful lot of money, isn't it?* **3** *obsolete* inspiring

reverence or dread ▷ *adv* **4** *not standard* very: *I'm working awful hard on my lines*

awfully *adv* **1** in an unpleasant way **2** *informal* very: *we were both awfully busy*

awhile *adv* for a brief period

awkward *adj* **1** clumsy or ungainly **2** embarrassed: *he was awkward and nervous around girls* **3** difficult to deal with: *the lawyer was in an awkward situation* **4** difficult to use or handle: *it was small but heavy enough to make it awkward to carry* **5** embarrassing: *there were several moments of awkward silence* **awkwardly** *adv* **awkwardness** *n* **WORD ORIGIN** Old Norse *öfugr* turned the wrong way round

awl *n* a pointed hand tool for piercing wood, leather, etc. **WORD ORIGIN** Old English *æl*

awn *n* any of the bristles growing from the flowering parts of certain grasses and cereals **WORD ORIGIN** Old English *agen* ear of grain

awning *n* a canvas roof supported by a frame to give protection against the weather **WORD ORIGIN** origin unknown

awoke *vb* a past tense and (now rare or dialectal) past participle of **awake**

awoken *vb* a past participle of **awake**

AWOL (**eh**-woll) *adj mil* absent without leave but without intending to desert

awry (a-**rye**) *adv, adj* **1** with a twist to one side; askew: *my neck was really awry after the journey* **2** amiss or faulty: *if a gear gets stuck, the whole system goes awry* **WORD ORIGIN** Middle English *on wry*

axe *or US* **ax** *n, pl* **axes 1** a hand tool with one side of its head sharpened to a cutting edge, used for felling trees and splitting timber **2 an axe to grind** a favourite topic one wishes to promote **3** *informal* a severe cut in spending or in the number of staff employed ▷ *vb* **axing, axed 4** *informal* to dismiss (employees), restrict (expenditure), or terminate (a project) **WORD ORIGIN** Old English *æx*

axes[1] *n* the plural of **axis**

axes[2] *n* the plural of **axe**

axial *adj* **1** forming or of an axis **2** in, on, or along an axis **axially** *adv*

axil *n* the angle where the stalk of a leaf joins a stem **WORD ORIGIN** Latin *axilla* armpit

axiom *n* **1** a generally accepted principle **2** a self-evident statement **WORD ORIGIN** Greek *axios* worthy

axiomatic *adj* **1** containing axioms **2** self-evident or obvious **axiomatically** *adv*

axis (**ax**-iss) *n, pl* **axes** (**ax**-eez) **1** a real or imaginary line about which a body can rotate or about which an object or geometrical construction is symmetrical **2** one of two or three reference lines used in coordinate geometry to locate a point in a plane or in space **WORD ORIGIN** Latin

axle *n* a shaft on which a wheel or pair of wheels revolves **WORD ORIGIN** Old Norse *öxull*

axolotl *n* an aquatic salamander of N America **WORD ORIGIN** Mexican Indian: water doll

ayah *n* (in parts of the former British Empire) a native maidservant or nursemaid **WORD ORIGIN** Hindi *āyā*

ayatollah *n* one of a class of Islamic religious leaders in Iran **WORD ORIGIN** Arabic *aya* sign + *allah* God

aye *or* **ay** *interj* **1** *Brit, Austral, & NZ* yes ▷ *n* **2** an affirmative vote or voter **WORD ORIGIN** probably from I, expressing assent

Ayrshire *n* one of a breed of brown-and-white dairy cattle **WORD ORIGIN** *Ayrshire*, district of Scotland

AZ Arizona

azalea (az-**zale**-ya) *n* a garden shrub grown for its showy flowers **WORD ORIGIN** Greek *azaleos* dry

azimuth *n* **1** the arc of the sky between the zenith and the horizon **2** *surveying* the horizontal angle of a bearing measured clockwise from the north **WORD ORIGIN** Arabic *as-samt* the path

Aztec *n* **1** a member of a Mexican Indian race who established a great empire, overthrown by the Spanish in the early 16th century **2** the language of the Aztecs ▷ *adj* **3** of the Aztecs or their language **WORD ORIGIN** *Aztlan*, their traditional place of origin, literally: near the cranes

azure *n* **1** the deep blue colour of a clear blue sky **2** *poetic* a clear blue sky ▷ *adj* **3** deep blue **WORD ORIGIN** Arabic *lāzaward* lapis lazuli

Bb

The letter B is the second letter and the first consonant in the English alphabet. It came into the Roman alphabet from the Greek letter *beta* (B, β), which in turn had come from the Semitic letter *beth*, whose name means 'house'. Scholars have speculated that the letter *beth* was based on a pictorial representation of a house, and was originally a square with a gap to represent a doorway. In the modern letter B, the doorway has been closed up and there is no way to move from one of the letter's twin chambers into the other – a design that could not be countenanced by any reputable architect.

Although second place out of twenty-six ought to be a position of some distinction, poor B does tend to suffer from comparison with its illustrious neighbour A when it comes to cultural associations.

A celebrity who is regarded as being on the B-list is likely to be crushed at not having made the A-list, rather than looking down with disdain upon the lowly C-listers. While B roads might offer a picturesque view, travellers who use them are not likely to make rapid progress. The B-side of a record was (with a few notable exceptions) the home for novelty tracks and instrumentals, and rarely made acquaintance with the stylus of a record player. B movies were low-budget films that padded out a double-bill in the heyday of the cinema, and which were never likely to garner Academy Awards, however fondly they may be remembered by film aficionados.

In academic parlance as well, the letter B indicates something of secondary importance. As a grade for an examination it is satisfactory but suggests a performance that falls short of the highest quality. Even in the names of academic degrees, the letter stands for the Latin *Baccalaureus* which indicates a basic Bachelor's degree (as in 'B.A.' and 'B.Sc.') – an achievement not to be sneered at, but comparing unfavourably with the letters M and D that signify a masters degree and a doctorate respectively.

b or **B** *n, pl* **b's**, **B's** or **Bs 1** the second letter of the English alphabet **2 from A to B** see **a** (sense 2)

b *cricket* **a** bowled **b** bye

B 1 *music* the seventh note of the scale of C major **2** the second in a series, class, or rank **3** *chem* boron **4** *chess* bishop

b. born

Ba *chem* barium

BA 1 Bachelor of Arts **2** British Airways

baa *vb* **baaing, baaed 1** (of a sheep) to make a characteristic bleating sound ▷ *n* **2** the cry made by a sheep

baas *n S African* a boss
WORD ORIGIN Afrikaans

baaskap *n* (in South Africa) control by Whites of non-Whites
WORD ORIGIN Afrikaans

babaco *n* a greenish-yellow egg-shaped fruit

babble *vb* **-bling, -bled 1** to talk in a quick, foolish, or muddled way **2** to make meaningless sounds: *children first gurgle and babble at random* **3** to disclose secrets carelessly **4** *literary* (of streams) to make a low murmuring sound ▷ *n* **5** muddled or foolish speech **6** a murmuring sound **babbler** *n* **babbling** *n*
WORD ORIGIN probably imitative

babe *n* **1** a baby **2 babe in arms** *informal* a naive or inexperienced person **3** *slang* a girl, esp. an attractive one

babel (**babe**-el) *n* **1** a confusion of noises or voices **2** a scene of noise and confusion
WORD ORIGIN from the confusion of languages on the tower of *Babel* (Genesis 11:1–10)

babiche *n Canad* thongs or lacings of rawhide

baboon *n* a medium-sized monkey with a long face, large teeth, and a fairly long tail
WORD ORIGIN Middle English *babewyn* gargoyle

baby *n, pl* **-bies 1** a newborn child **2** the youngest or smallest of a family or group **3** a recently born animal **4** an immature person **5** *slang* a sweetheart **6** a project of personal concern **7 be left holding the baby** to be left with a responsibility ▷ *adj* **8** comparatively small of its type: *baby carrots* ▷ *vb* **-bies, -bying, -bied 9** to treat like a baby **babyhood** *n* **babyish** *adj*
WORD ORIGIN probably childish reduplication

baby bonus *n Canad informal* Family Allowance

baby-sit *vb* **-sitting, -sat** to act or work as a baby-sitter **baby-sitting** *n, adj*

baby-sitter *n* a person who takes care of a child while the parents are out

baccalaureate (back-a-**law**-ree-it) *n* the university degree of Bachelor of Arts
WORD ORIGIN Medieval Latin *baccalarius* bachelor

baccarat (**back**-a-rah) *n* a card game in which two or more punters gamble against the banker
WORD ORIGIN French *baccara*

bacchanalian (back-a-**nail**-ee-an) *adj literary* (of a party) unrestrained and involving a great deal of drinking and sometimes sexual activity
WORD ORIGIN from *Bacchus*, Greek & Roman god of wine

Bacchus *n classical myth* the god of wine; Dionysus

baccy *n Brit informal* tobacco

bach (**batch**) NZ *n* **1** a small holiday cottage ▷ *vb* **2** to look after oneself when one's spouse is away

bachelor *n* **1** an unmarried man **2** a person who holds a first degree from a university or college **bachelorhood** *n*
WORD ORIGIN Old French *bacheler* youth, squire

Bachelor of Arts *n* a person with a first degree from a university or college, usually in the arts

bacillary *adj* of or caused by bacilli

bacillus (bass-**ill**-luss) *n, pl* **-li** (-lie) a rod-shaped bacterium, esp. one causing disease
WORD ORIGIN Latin *baculum* walking stick

back *n* **1** the rear part of the human body, from the neck to the pelvis **2** the spinal column **3** the part or side of an

Alice Munro

Alice Munro, *née* Laidlaw, was born in the small town of Wingham in southwestern Ontario near Lake Huron, acronymically called *Sowesto*, which became the setting for many of her short stories. After her marriage, she moved with her husband to British Columbia, where she lived for 20 years, chiefly in Victoria. After a divorce and remarriage, she returned to the region of her birth and upbringing.

Munro gained her first fame as a fiction writer in Canada, but international acclaim gradually followed, and she became published in prestigious magazines, most frequently in *The New Yorker*. She became a multiple winner of awards, including the most important Canadian awards for fiction, the Governor General's (thrice) and the Giller Prize (twice), not to mention the Man Booker International Prize. Like Mavis Gallant, the author is unusual in that she achieved artistic and commercial success solely for short stories, not novels. The nearest thing to a conventional novel in her body of work are the stories with recurring characters in *Lives of Girls and Women* (1971) and *Who Do You Think You Are?* (1978, published in the United States and United Kingdom as *The Beggar Maid: Stories of Flo and Rose*). But her stories, typically between 7,000 and 8,000 words, have the fully-imagined solidity and well-roundedness of the best novels.

Although she has experimented with structural devices, Munro writes classic short stories that revolve around an evocative central metaphor and end in subtle denouements. Her people typically come from the rural or small-town lower middle class, and their stories are usually told by a woman (after all, one of her collections is called *Lives of Girls and Women*) who struggles with coming-of-age dilemmas, reverts or refers to her own or others' troubled past, or mulls over the vagaries and instability of families, friends, or romantic partners. One wag once said a generic Munro story ought to bear the title 'Aunt Maude in the Nursing Home', failing to recognize how expertly she expands local, apparently trivial detail into the universally significant. Often sombre and meditative, here and there

with dramatically heightened lyricism, the stories are leavened at intervals with wry, or what Scots call 'pawky', (sly) humour. Always she is interested in what, in the story 'Differently', a character calls 'accidental clarity'.

Munro has never attempted to disguise or downplay her Canadian settings or cultural references in a quest to acquire new readers. Thus she can unselfconsciously speak of *Maclean's*, the national newsmagazine, or observe that Canadians don't use the US *pocketbook* (Canadian *purse*) in ways that do not require awkward explanation. Just as notable is how she deftly inserts smoothly idiomatic dialogue into the narrative, always revealing character or advancing the story's exposition. The same is true of her habit of slotting in a passage from a popular song or piece of verse.

Shame or guilt, acknowledged or not, often form the subtext of the stories, and a complex ambiguity is a thematic constant, echoed in such book titles as *Dance of the Happy Shades* (1968), *Something I've Been Meaning to Tell You* (1974), *Who Do You Think You Are?* (1978), and *Open Secrets* (1994). Even the wisdom or propriety of telling or hearing a story is typified in a story title, 'What Do You Want to Know For?'

Although not a recluse, Munro has been a very intensely private person, so it was something of a surprise when she published *View from Castle Rock: Stories* (2006), which traced her paternal family's history from its origins in the Ettrick Valley in Scotland, where an ancestor was a friend of James Hogg, author of *Memoirs and Confessions of a Justified Sinner*. But self-revelation was strictly limited, her view being that, as she says in her Foreword, 'You could say that such stories pay more attention to the truth of a life than fiction usually does. But not enough to swear on'.

Elsewhere, in the title story 'The Progress of Love' (1986), she makes a character invent an episode in her parents' life together and then say, 'How hard it is for me to believe that I made that up. It seems so much the truth it is the truth; it's what I believe about them'. This could be her artistic credo.

object opposite the front **4** the part of anything less often seen or used **5** *ball games* a defensive player or position **6 at the back of one's mind** not in one's conscious thoughts **7 behind someone's back** secretly or deceitfully **8 put** *or* **get someone's back up** to annoy someone **9 turn one's back on someone** to refuse to help someone ▷ *vb* **10** to move or cause to move backwards **11** to provide money for (a person or enterprise) **12** to bet on the success of: *to back a horse* **13** to provide (a pop singer) with a musical accompaniment **14** (foll. by *on* or *onto*) to have the back facing (towards): *his garden backs onto a school* **15** (of the wind) to change direction anticlockwise ▷ *adj* **16** situated behind: *back garden* **17** owing from an earlier date: *back rent* **18** remote: *a back road* ▷ *adv* **19** at, to, or towards the rear **20** to or towards the original starting point or condition: *I went back home* **21** in reply or retaliation: *to hit someone back* **22** in concealment or reserve: *to keep something back* **23 back and forth** to and fro **24 back to front a** in reverse **b** in disorder ▸ See also **back down, back off**, etc.
WORD ORIGIN Old English *bæc*

backbencher *n* a Member of Parliament who does not hold office in the government or opposition

backbite *vb* **-biting, -bit, -bitten** *or* **-bit** to talk spitefully about an absent person **backbiter** *n*

back boiler *n* Brit a tank at the back of a fireplace for heating water

backbone *n* **1** the spinal column **2** strength of character **3** *computers* a central section that connects segments of a network

back-breaking *adj* (of work) exhausting

backburn *Austral & NZ vb* **1** to clear (an area of bush) by creating a fire that burns in the opposite direction from the wind **2** to prevent a bush fire from spreading by clearing an area of land in front of it ▷ *n* **3** the act or result of backburning

back catalogue *n* a musician's previous recordings, as opposed to their current recordings

backchat *n* informal impudent replies

backcloth *n* a painted curtain at the back of a stage set. Also called: **backdrop**

backcomb *vb* to comb (the hair) towards the roots to give more bulk to a hairstyle

back country *n* Austral & NZ land far away from settled areas

backdate *vb* **-dating, -dated** to make (a document) effective from a date earlier than its completion

back door *n* a means of entry to a job or position that is secret or obtained through influence

back down *vb* to withdraw an earlier claim

backer *n* a person who gives financial or other support

backfire *vb* **-firing, -fired 1** (of a plan or scheme) to fail to have the desired effect **2** (of an internal-combustion engine) to make a loud noise as a result of an explosion of unburnt gases in the exhaust system

backgammon *n* a game for two people played on a board with pieces moved according to throws of the dice
WORD ORIGIN *back* + obsolete *gammon* game

background *n* **1** the events or circumstances that help to explain something **2** a person's social class, education, or experience **3** the part of a scene furthest from the viewer **4** an inconspicuous position: *in the background* **5** the space behind the chief figures or objects in a picture

backhand *n* **1** *tennis, etc.* a stroke made from across the body with the back of the hand facing the direction of the stroke **2** the side on which backhand strokes are made

backhanded *adj* **1** (of a blow or shot) performed with the arm moving from across the body **2** ambiguous or implying criticism: *a backhanded compliment*

backhander *n* **1** slang a bribe **2** a backhanded stroke or blow

backing *n* **1** support **2** something that forms or strengthens the back of something **3** musical accompaniment for a pop singer

backing dog *n* NZ a dog that moves a flock of sheep by jumping on their backs

backlash *n* **1** a sudden and adverse reaction **2** a recoil between interacting badly fitting parts in machinery

backlog *n* an accumulation of things to be dealt with

backlot *n* an area outside a film or television studio used for outdoor filming

back number *n* **1** an old issue of a newspaper or magazine **2** *informal* a person or thing considered to be old-fashioned

back off *vb* **1** to retreat **2** to abandon (an intention or objective)

back office *n* **1** the administrative staff of a financial institution or other business ▷ *adj* **2** of or relating to such staff: *back-office operations*

back out *vb* (often foll. by *of*) to withdraw from (an agreement)

backpack *n* **1** a rucksack ▷ *vb* **2** to go hiking or travelling with a backpack **backpacker** *n*

back passage *n* the rectum

back-pedal *vb* **-pedalling, -pedalled** *or* US **-pedaling, -pedaled** to retract or modify a previous opinion or statement

back room *n* **1** a place where secret research or planning is done ▷ *adj* **back-room 2** of or relating to secret research or planning: *back-room boys*

back seat *n* informal a less important or responsible position: *lyricism took a back seat to drama*

back-seat driver *n* informal a person who offers unwanted advice

backside *n* informal the buttocks

backslide *vb* **-sliding, -slid** to relapse into former bad habits or vices **backslider** *n*

backspace *vb* **-spacing, -spaced** to move a typewriter carriage or computer cursor backwards

backspin *n* sport a backward spin given to a ball to reduce its speed at impact

backstabbing *n* treacherous actions or remarks that are likely to cause harm to a person **backstabber** *n* **backstab** *vb*

backstage *adv* **1** behind the stage in a theatre ▷ *adj* **2** situated backstage

backstairs *or* **backstair** *adj* underhand: *backstairs gossip*

backstreet *n* **1** a street in a town far from the main roads ▷ *adj* **2** denoting secret or illegal activities: *a backstreet abortion*

backstroke *n* swimming a stroke performed on the back, using backward circular strokes of each arm

backtrack *vb* **1** to go back along the same route one has just travelled **2** to retract or reverse one's opinion or policy

back up *vb* **1** to support **2** *computers* to make a copy of (a data file), esp. as a security copy **3** (of traffic) to become jammed behind an obstruction ▷ *n* **backup 4** support or reinforcement **5** a reserve or substitute ▷ *adj* **backup 6** able to be substituted: *a backup copy*

backward *adj* **1** directed towards the rear **2** retarded in physical, material, or intellectual development **3** reluctant or bashful ▷ *adv* **4** same as **backwards** ▷ **backwardness** *n*

backwards *or* **backward** *adv* **1** towards the rear **2** with the back foremost **3** in the reverse of the usual direction **4** into a worse state: *the Gothic novel's been going backwards since Radcliffe* **5 bend over backwards** informal to make a special effort to please someone

backwash *n* **1** water washed backwards by the motion of oars or a ship **2** an unpleasant aftereffect of an event or situation

backwater *n* **1** an isolated or backward place or condition **2** a body of stagnant water connected to a river

backwoods *pl n* **1** any remote sparsely populated place **2** partially cleared, sparsely populated forests **backwoodsman** *n*

back yard *n* **1** a yard at the back of a house, etc. **2 in one's own back yard a** close at hand **b** involving or implicating one

bacon *n* **1** meat from the back and sides of a pig, dried, salted, and often smoked **2 bring home the bacon** informal **a** to achieve success **b** to provide material support
WORD ORIGIN Old French

bacteria *pl n, sing* **-rium** a large group of microorganisms, many of which cause disease **bacterial** *adj*
WORD ORIGIN Greek *baktron* rod

bacteriology *n* the study of bacteria **bacteriologist** *n*

Bactrian camel *n* a two-humped camel
WORD ORIGIN *Bactria*, ancient country of Asia

bad *adj* **worse, worst 1** not good; of poor quality **2** lacking skill or talent: *I'm so bad at that sort of thing* **3** harmful: *smoking is bad for you* **4** evil or immoral **5** naughty or mischievous **6** rotten or decayed: *a bad egg* **7** severe: *a bad headache* **8** incorrect or faulty: *bad grammar* **9** sorry or upset: *I feel bad about saying no* **10** unfavourable or distressing: *bad news* **11** offensive or unpleasant: *bad language* **12** not valid: *a bad cheque* **13** not recoverable: *a bad debt* **14 badder, baddest** *slang* good; excellent **15 not bad** or **not so bad** *informal* fairly good **16 too bad** *informal* (often used dismissively) regrettable ▷ *n* **17** unfortunate or unpleasant events: *you've got to take the good with the bad* ▷ *adv* **18** *not standard* badly: *to want something bad* **badness** *n* **WORD ORIGIN** Middle English

bad blood *n* a feeling of intense hatred or hostility between people

bade or **bad** *vb* a past tense of **bid**

badge *n* **1** a distinguishing emblem or mark worn to show membership or achievement **2** any revealing feature or mark **WORD ORIGIN** Old French *bage*

badger *n* **1** a stocky burrowing mammal with a black and white striped head ▷ *vb* **2** to pester or harass **WORD ORIGIN** probably from *badge*

badinage (bad-in-nahzh) *n* playful and witty conversation **WORD ORIGIN** French

badly *adv* **worse, worst 1** poorly; inadequately **2** unfavourably: *our plan worked out badly* **3** severely: *badly damaged* **4** very much: *he badly needed to improve his image* **5 badly off** poor

badminton *n* a game played with rackets and a shuttlecock which is hit back and forth across a high net **WORD ORIGIN** *Badminton* House, Glos

BAF British Athletics Federation

Bafana bafana (bah-**fan**-na) *pl n S African* the South African national soccer team **WORD ORIGIN** from Nguni (language group of southern Africa) *bafana* the boys

baffle *vb* **-fling, -fled 1** to perplex ▷ *n* **2** a mechanical device to limit or regulate the flow of fluid, light, or sound **bafflement** *n* **baffling** *adj* **WORD ORIGIN** origin unknown

bag *n* **1** a flexible container with an opening at one end **2** the contents of such a container **3** a piece of luggage **4** a handbag **5** a loose fold of skin under the eyes **6** any sac in the body of an animal **7** *offensive slang* an ugly or bad-tempered woman: *an old bag* **8** the amount of game taken by a hunter **9 in the bag** *slang* assured of succeeding ▷ *vb* **bagging, bagged 10** to put into a bag **11** to bulge or cause to bulge **12** to capture or kill, as in hunting **13** *informal* to succeed in securing: *he bagged the best chair* ▷ See also **bags** **WORD ORIGIN** probably Old Norse *baggi*

bagatelle *n* **1** something of little value **2** a board game in which balls are struck into holes **3** a short piece of music **WORD ORIGIN** French

bagel (**bay**-gl) *n* a hard ring-shaped bread roll **WORD ORIGIN** Yiddish *beygel*

baggage *n* **1** suitcases packed for a journey **2** an army's portable equipment **3** *informal* previous knowledge or experience that may have an influence in new circumstances: *cultural baggage* **WORD ORIGIN** Old French *bagage*

baggy *adj* **-gier, -giest** (of clothes) hanging loosely **bagginess** *n*

bag lady *n* a homeless woman who carries around all her possessions in shopping bags

bagpipes *pl n* a musical wind instrument in which sounds are produced in reed pipes by air from an inflated bag

bags *pl n* **1** *informal* a lot ▷ *interj* **2** Also: **bags I** *children's slang Brit & NZ* an indication of the desire to do, be, or have something

bah *interj* an expression of contempt or disgust

bail[1] *law n* **1** a sum of money deposited with the court as security for a person's reappearance in court **2** the person giving such security **3 jump bail** to fail to reappear in court after bail has been paid **4 stand** or **go bail** to act as surety for someone ▷ *vb* **5** (foll. by *out*) to obtain the release of (a person) from custody by depositing money with the court **WORD ORIGIN** Old French: custody

bail[2] or **bale** *vb* **bail out** to remove water from (a boat). See also **bail out** **WORD ORIGIN** Old French *baille* bucket

bail[3] *n* **1** *cricket* either of two small wooden bars across the tops of the stumps **2** a partition between stalls in a stable or barn **3** *Austral & NZ* a framework in a cow shed used to secure the head of a cow during milking **4** a movable bar on a typewriter that holds the paper against the roller **WORD ORIGIN** Old French *baile* stake

bailey *n* the outermost wall or court of a castle **WORD ORIGIN** Old French *baille* enclosed court

Bailey bridge *n* a temporary bridge that can be rapidly assembled **WORD ORIGIN** after Sir Donald Coleman *Bailey*, its designer

bailiff *n* **1** *Brit* a sheriff's officer who serves writs and summonses **2** the agent of a landlord or landowner **WORD ORIGIN** Old French *baillif*

bailiwick *n* **1** *law* the area over which a bailiff has power **2** a person's special field of interest **WORD ORIGIN** *bailie* magistrate + obsolete *wick* district

bail out or **bale out** *vb* **1** *informal* to help (a person or organization) out of a predicament **2** to make an emergency parachute jump from an aircraft

bail up *vb* **1** *Austral & NZ informal* to confine (a cow) or (of a cow) to be confined by the head in a bail. See **bail**[3]. **2** *Austral history* (of a bushranger) to hold under guard in order to rob **3** *Austral* to submit to robbery without offering resistance **4** *Austral informal* to accost or detain, esp. in conversation; buttonhole

bain-marie (ban-mar-ee) *n, pl* **bains-marie** a container for holding hot water, in which sauces and other dishes are gently cooked or kept warm **WORD ORIGIN** French: bath of Mary

bairn *n Scot & N English* a child **WORD ORIGIN** Old English *bearn*

bait *n* **1** something edible fixed to a hook or in a trap to attract fish or animals **2** an enticement ▷ *vb* **3** to put a piece of food on or in (a hook or trap) **4** to persecute or tease **5** to set dogs upon (a bear or badger) **WORD ORIGIN** Old Norse *beita* to hunt

USAGE
The phrase *with bated breath* is sometimes wrongly spelled *with baited breath*.

baize *n* a feltlike woollen fabric, usually green, which is used for the tops of billiard and card tables **WORD ORIGIN** Old French *bai* reddish-brown

bake *vb* **baking, baked 1** to cook by dry heat in an oven **2** to cook bread, pastry, or cakes **3** to make or become hardened by heat **4** *informal* to be extremely hot **WORD ORIGIN** Old English *bacan*

bakeapple *n* cloudberry

baked beans *pl n* haricot beans, baked and tinned in tomato sauce

Bakelite (**bake**-a-lite) *n trademark* any of a class of resins used as electric insulators and for making plastics **WORD ORIGIN** after L. H. *Baekeland*, inventor

baker *n* a person who makes or sells bread, cakes, etc.

baker's dozen *n* thirteen

bakery *n, pl* **-eries** a place where bread, cakes, etc. are made or sold

baking powder *n* a powdered mixture that contains sodium bicarbonate and cream of tartar: used in baking as a raising agent

bakkie (**buck**-ee) *n S African* a small truck with an enclosed cab and an open goods area at the back **WORD ORIGIN** Afrikaans *bak* container

baksheesh *n* (in some Eastern countries) money given as a tip or present **WORD ORIGIN** Persian *bakhshīsh*

Balaclava or **Balaclava helmet** *n* a close-fitting woollen hood that covers the ears and neck **WORD ORIGIN** after *Balaklava*, in the Crimea

balalaika *n* a Russian musical instrument with a triangular body and three strings **WORD ORIGIN** Russian

balance *n* **1** stability of mind or body: *lose one's balance* **2** a state of being in balance **3** harmony in the parts of a whole **4** the power to influence or control: *the balance of power* **5** something that remains: *the balance of what you owe* **6** *accounting* **a** the matching of debit and credit totals in an account **b** a difference between such totals **7** a weighing device **8 in the balance** in an undecided condition **9 on balance** after weighing up all the factors ▷ *vb* **-ancing, -anced 10** to weigh in or as if

b

in a balance **11** to be or come into equilibrium **12** to bring into or hold in equilibrium **13** to compare the relative weight or importance of **14** to arrange so as to create a state of harmony **15** *accounting* to compare or equalize the credit and debit totals of (an account) **WORD ORIGIN** Latin *bilanx* having two scales

balance of payments *n* the difference in value between a nation's total payments to foreign countries and its total receipts from foreign countries

balance of power *n* the equal distribution of military and economic power among countries

balance of trade *n* the difference in value between exports and imports of goods

balance sheet *n* a statement that shows the financial position of a business

balcony *n, pl* **-nies 1** a platform projecting from a building with a balustrade along its outer edge, often with access from a door **2** an upper tier of seats in a theatre or cinema **WORD ORIGIN** Italian *balcone*

bald *adj* **1** having no hair or fur, esp. of a man having no hair on the scalp **2** lacking natural covering **3** plain or blunt: *the bald facts* **4** (of a tyre) having a worn tread **baldly** *adv* **baldness** *n* **WORD ORIGIN** Middle English *ballede*

balderdash *n* stupid or illogical talk **WORD ORIGIN** origin unknown

balding *adj* becoming bald

bale¹ *n* **1** a large bundle of hay or goods bound by ropes or wires for storage or transportation ▷ *vb* **baling, baled 2** to make (hay) or put (goods) into a bale or bales **WORD ORIGIN** Old High German *balla* ball

bale² *vb* **baling, baled** same as **bail²**

baleen *n* whalebone **WORD ORIGIN** Latin *balaena* whale

baleen whale *n* same as **whalebone whale**

baleful *adj* harmful, menacing, or vindictive **balefully** *adv*

bale out *vb* same as **bail out**

balk *or* **baulk** *vb* **1** to stop short: *the horse balked at the jump* **2** to recoil: *France balked at the parliament having a veto* **3** to thwart, check, or foil: *he was balked in his plans* **WORD ORIGIN** Old English *balca* ridge

Balkan *adj* of any of the countries of the Balkan Peninsula in SE Europe, between the Adriatic and Aegean Seas

ball¹ *n* **1** a spherical or nearly spherical mass: *a ball of wool* **2** a round or roundish object used in various games **3** a single delivery of the ball in a game **4** any more or less rounded part of the body: *the ball of the foot* **5** **have the ball at one's feet** to have the chance of doing something **6** **on the ball** *informal* alert; informed **7** **play ball** *informal* to cooperate **8** **set** *or* **keep the ball rolling** to initiate or maintain the progress of an action, discussion, or project ▷ *vb* **9** to form into a ball ▶ See also **balls, balls-up** **WORD ORIGIN** Old Norse *böllr*

ball² *n* **1** a lavish or formal social function for dancing **2** **have a ball** *informal* to have a very enjoyable time **WORD ORIGIN** Late Latin *ballare* to dance

ballad *n* **1** a narrative song or poem often with a chorus that is repeated **2** a slow sentimental song **WORD ORIGIN** Old Provençal *balada* song accompanying a dance

ballade *n* **1** *prosody* a verse form consisting of three stanzas and an envoy, all ending with the same line **2** *music* a romantic instrumental composition

ball-and-socket joint *n anat* a joint in which a rounded head fits into a rounded cavity, allowing a wide range of movement

ballast *n* **1** a substance, such as sand, used to stabilize a ship when it is not carrying cargo **2** crushed rock used for the foundation of a road or railway track ▷ *vb* **3** to give stability or weight to **WORD ORIGIN** probably Low German

ball bearing *n* **1** an arrangement of steel balls placed between moving parts of a machine in order to reduce friction **2** a metal ball used in such an arrangement

ball boy *or fem* **ball girl** *n* (in tennis) a person who retrieves balls that go out of play

ball cock *n* a device consisting of a floating ball and valve for regulating the flow of liquid into a tank or cistern

ballerina *n* a female ballet dancer **WORD ORIGIN** Italian

ballet *n* **1** a classical style of expressive dancing based on precise conventional steps **2** a theatrical representation of a story performed by ballet dancers **balletic** *adj* **WORD ORIGIN** Italian *balletto* a little dance

ball game *n* **1** a game played with a ball **2** *US & Canad* a game of baseball **3** *informal* a state of affairs: *a whole new ball game*

ballistic missile *n* a launched weapon which is guided automatically in flight but falls freely at its target

ballistics *n* the study of the flight of projectiles, often in relation to firearms **ballistic** *adj* **WORD ORIGIN** Greek *ballein* to throw

ballocks *pl n, interj* same as **bollocks**

balloon *n* **1** an inflatable rubber bag used as a plaything or party decoration **2** a large bag inflated with a lighter-than-air gas, designed to rise and float in the atmosphere with a basket for carrying passengers **3** an outline containing the words or thoughts of a character in a cartoon ▷ *vb* **4** to fly in a balloon **5** to swell or increase rapidly in size: *the cost of health care has ballooned* **balloonist** *n* **WORD ORIGIN** Italian dialect *ballone* ball

ballot *n* **1** the practice of selecting a representative or course of action by voting **2** the number of votes cast in an election **3** the actual vote or paper indicating a person's choice ▷ *vb* **-loting, -loted 4** to vote or ask for a vote from: *we balloted the members on this issue*

5 to vote for or decide on something by ballot **WORD ORIGIN** Italian *ballotta* a little ball

ballot box *n* a box into which voting papers are dropped on completion

ballot paper *n* a paper used for voting

ballpark *n* **1** *US & Canad* a stadium used for baseball games **2** *informal* approximate range: *in the right ballpark*

ballpoint *or* **ballpoint pen** *n* a pen which has a small ball bearing as a writing point

ballroom *n* a large hall for dancing

ballroom dancing *n* social dancing in couples to music in conventional rhythms, such as the waltz

balls *pl n taboo slang* **1** the testicles **2** nonsense **3** courage and determination **ballsy** *adj*

balls-up *taboo slang n* **1** something botched or muddled ▷ *vb* **balls up 2** to muddle or botch

bally *adj, adv* Brit, old-fashioned slang extreme or extremely: *a bally nuisance; he's too bally charming for his own good*

ballyhoo *n informal* unnecessary or exaggerated fuss **WORD ORIGIN** origin unknown

balm *n* **1** an aromatic substance obtained from certain tropical trees and used for healing and soothing **2** something comforting or soothing: *her calmness was like a balm to my troubled mind* **3** an aromatic herb, lemon balm **WORD ORIGIN** Latin *balsamum* balsam

balmy *adj* **balmier, balmiest 1** (of weather) mild and pleasant **2** same as **barmy**

baloney *or* **boloney** *n informal* nonsense **WORD ORIGIN** Bologna (sausage)

balsa (**bawl**-sa) *n* **1** a tree of tropical America which yields light wood **2** Also: **balsawood** the light wood of this tree, used for making rafts, models, etc. **WORD ORIGIN** Spanish: raft

balsam *n* **1** an aromatic resin obtained from various trees and shrubs and used in medicines and perfumes **2** any plant yielding balsam **3** a flowering plant, such as busy lizzie **WORD ORIGIN** Greek *balsamon*

balti (**boll**-ti, **bahl**-ti) *n* a spicy Indian dish served in a metal dish **WORD ORIGIN** probably from the *Baltistan* region of Pakistan

Baltic (**bawl**-tik) *adj* of the Baltic Sea in N Europe or the states bordering it

baluster *n* a set of posts supporting a rail **WORD ORIGIN** French *balustre*

balustrade *n* an ornamental rail supported by a set of posts **WORD ORIGIN** French

bamboo *n* a tall treelike tropical grass with hollow stems which are used to make canes, furniture, etc. **WORD ORIGIN** probably from Malay *bambu*

bamboozle *vb* **-zling, -zled** *informal* **1** to cheat; mislead **2** to confuse **bamboozlement** *n* **WORD ORIGIN** origin unknown

SCRABBLE
Three-Letter Words, part 2
BOP–EEL

BOP dance to pop music
BOR neighbour
BOS plural form of bo
BOT larva of a botfly
BOW lower head as sign of respect
BOX container
BOY male child
BRA brassiere
BRO family member
BRR used to suggest shivering
BRU South African word for friend
BUB youngster
BUD swelling on a plant
BUG insect
BUM buttocks
BUN sweet bread roll or cake
BUR washer fitting around the end of a rivet
BUS large motor vehicle
BUT except, only
BUY acquire by paying money
BYE goodbye
BYS plural form of by
CAA Scots word for call
CAB taxi
CAD dishonourable man
CAG short for cagoule
CAM device that converts a circular motion
CAN be able to
CAP covering for the head
CAR motor vehicle
CAT furry mammal
CAW cry of a crow or raven
CAY small low island
CAZ short for casual
CEE 3rd letter of the alphabet
CEL short for celluloid
CEP another name for porcino
CHA tea
CHE dialectal form of I

CHI 22nd letter of the Greek alphabet
CID leader
CIG short for cigarette
CIS chemistry term
CIT town dweller
CLY steal or seize
COB male swan
COD large food fish
COG tooth on the rim of a gearwheel
COL high mountain pass
CON deceive, swindle
COO make a soft murmuring sound
COP copper
COR exclamation of surprise or admiration
COS cosine
COT baby's bed with high sides
COW female bovine animal
COX coxswain
COY affectedly shy or modest
COZ archaic word for cousin
CRU vineyard
CRY shed tears
CUB the young of some animals
CUD partially digested food
CUE signal to an actor or musician to begin
CUM with
CUP drinking vessel
CUR mongrel dog
CUT divide with a sharp instrument
CUZ cousin
CWM geology term
DAB pat lightly
DAD word for father
DAE Scots word for do
DAG cut daglocks from sheep
DAH term used in Morse code
DAK system of mail delivery

DAL decalitre
DAM barrier built across a river to create a lake
DAN judo term
DAP flyfishing with a floss silk line
DAS plural form of da
DAW jackdaw
DAY period of 24 hours
DEB debutante
DEE Scots word for die
DEF very good
DEG water (a plant, etc)
DEI plural form of deus
DEL differential operator
DEN home of a wild animal
DEV Hindu god
DEW drops of water that form on the ground
DEX dextroamphetamine
DEY commanders of the Janissaries of Algiers
DIB fish with a bobbing bait
DID part of the verb to do
DIE cease living
DIF short for difference
DIG cut into earth, esp with a spade
DIM badly lit
DIN loud unpleasant noise
DIP plunge briefly into liquid
DIS treat someone with contempt
DIT term used in Morse code
DIV stupid or foolish person
DOB (as in dob in) inform against
DOC doctor
DOD cut the hair of
DOE female deer
DOF South African word for stupid
DOG domesticated four-legged mammal

DOH musical term
DOL unit of pain intensity
DOM title given to monks
DON put on (clothing)
DOO Scots word for dove
DOP tot of alcoholic drink
DOR European dung beetle
DOS plural form of do
DOT small round mark
DOW Arab vessel
DOY beloved person
DRY lacking moisture
DSO Tibetan breed of cattle
DUB give (a person or place) a name
DUD ineffectual person
DUE something owed
DUG part of the verb to dig
DUH response implying that the speaker is stupid
DUI plural form of duo
DUN brownish-grey
DUO duet
DUP open
DUX the top pupil in a class or school
DYE colouring substance
DZO Tibetan breed of cattle
EAN give birth
EAR organ of hearing
EAS plural form of ea
EAT chew and swallow food
EAU drainage channel
EBB (of tide water) flow back
ECH Shakespearean word for eke out
ECO short for ecology
ECU French coin
EDH character of the runic alphabet
EDS plural form of ed
EEK expression indicating shock
EEL snakelike fish

b

ban vb **banning, banned 1** to prohibit or forbid officially ▷ n **2** an official prohibition
WORD ORIGIN Old English bannan to proclaim

banal (ban-nahl) adj lacking originality **banality** n
WORD ORIGIN Old French: common to all

banana n a crescent-shaped fruit that grows on a tropical or subtropical treelike plant
WORD ORIGIN Spanish or Portuguese, of African origin

banana republic n informal a small politically unstable country whose economy is dominated by foreign interests

band¹ n **1** a group of musicians playing together, esp. on brass or percussion instruments **2** a group of people having a common purpose: a band of revolutionaries ▷ vb **3** (foll. by together) to unite
WORD ORIGIN French bande

band² n **1** a strip of some material, used to hold objects together: a rubber band **2** a strip of fabric used as an ornament or to reinforce clothing **3** a stripe of contrasting colour or texture **4** a driving belt in machinery **5** physics a range of frequencies or wavelengths between two limits ▷ vb **6** to fasten or mark with a band
WORD ORIGIN Old French bende

bandage n **1** a piece of material used to dress a wound or wrap an injured limb ▷ vb **-daging, -daged 2** to cover or wrap with a bandage
WORD ORIGIN French bande strip

bandanna or **bandana** n a large brightly-coloured handkerchief or neckerchief
WORD ORIGIN Hindi bāndhnū tie-dyeing

B & B bed and breakfast

bandbox n a lightweight usually cylindrical box for hats

bandeau (ban-doe) n, pl **-deaux** (-doze) a narrow ribbon worn round the head
WORD ORIGIN French

banderole n **1** a narrow flag usually with forked ends **2** a ribbon-like scroll bearing an inscription
WORD ORIGIN Old French

bandicoot n **1** an Australian marsupial with a long pointed muzzle and a long tail **2 bandicoot rat** any of three burrowing rats of S and SE Asia
WORD ORIGIN Telugu (language of SE India) pandikokku

bandit n a robber, esp. a member of an armed gang **banditry** n
WORD ORIGIN Italian bandito

bandmaster n the conductor of a band

bandolier n a shoulder belt with small pockets for cartridges
WORD ORIGIN Old French bandouliere

band saw n a power-operated saw consisting of an endless toothed metal band running over two wheels

bandsman n, pl **-men** a player in a musical band

bandstand n a roofed outdoor platform for a band

bandwagon n **jump** or **climb on the bandwagon** to join a popular party or movement that seems assured of success

bandwidth n the range of frequencies used for transmitting electronic information

bandy adj **-dier, -diest 1** Also: **bandy-legged** having legs curved outwards at the knees **2** (of legs) curved outwards at the knees ▷ vb **-dies, -dying, -died 3** to exchange (words), sometimes in a heated manner **4 bandy about** to use (a name, term, etc.) frequently
WORD ORIGIN probably from Old French bander to hit back and forth

bane n a person or thing that causes misery or distress: the bane of my life **baneful** adj
WORD ORIGIN Old English bana

bang n **1** a short loud explosive noise, such as the report of a gun **2** a hard blow or loud knock **3** taboo slang an act of sexual intercourse **4 with a bang** successfully: the party went with a bang ▷ vb **5** to hit or knock, esp. with a loud noise **6** to close (a door) noisily **7** to make or cause to make a loud noise, as of an explosion **8** taboo slang to have sexual intercourse with ▷ adv **9 with a sudden impact**: the car drove bang into a lamppost **10** precisely: bang in the middle
WORD ORIGIN Old Norse bang, banga hammer

banger n **1** Austral & Brit informal an old decrepit car **2** slang a sausage **3** a firework that explodes loudly

Bangladeshi adj **1** of Bangladesh ▷ n **2** a person from Bangladesh

bangle n a bracelet worn round the arm or sometimes round the ankle
WORD ORIGIN Hindi bangrī

banian n same as **banyan**

banish vb **1** to send into exile **2** to drive away: it's the only way to banish weeds from the garden **banishment** n
WORD ORIGIN Old French banir

banisters or **bannisters** pl n the railing and supporting balusters on a staircase
WORD ORIGIN altered from BALUSTER

banjo n, pl **-jos** or **-joes** a stringed musical instrument with a long neck and a circular drumlike body **banjoist** n
WORD ORIGIN US pronunciation of earlier bandore

bank¹ n **1** an institution offering services, such as the safekeeping and lending of money at interest **2** the building used by such an institution **3** the funds held by a banker or dealer in some gambling games **4** any supply, store, or reserve: a data bank ▷ vb **5** to deposit (cash or a cheque) in a bank **6** to transact business with a bank
▶ See also **bank on**
WORD ORIGIN probably from Italian banca bench, moneychanger's table

bank² n **1** a long raised mass, esp. of earth **2** a slope, as of a hill **3** the sloping side and ground on either side of a river ▷ vb **4** to form into a bank or mound **5** to cover (a fire) with ashes and fuel so that it will burn slowly **6** (of an aircraft) to tip to one side in turning
WORD ORIGIN Scandinavian

bank³ n **1** an arrangement of similar objects in a row or in tiers ▷ vb **2** to arrange in a bank
WORD ORIGIN Old French banc bench

bankable adj likely to ensure financial success: a bankable star **bankability** n

bank account n an arrangement whereby a customer deposits money at a bank and may withdraw it when it is needed

bank card n any plastic card issued by a bank, such as a cash card or a cheque card

banker¹ n **1** a person who owns or manages a bank **2** the keeper of the bank in various gambling games

banker² n Austral & NZ informal a stream almost overflowing its banks: the creek was running a banker

banker's order n same as **standing order** (sense 1)

bank holiday n (in Britain) a public holiday when banks are closed by law

banking n the business engaged in by a bank

banknote n a piece of paper money issued by a central bank

bank on vb to rely on

bankrupt n **1** a person, declared by a court to be unable to pay his or her debts, whose property is sold and the proceeds distributed among the creditors **2** a person no longer having a particular quality: a spiritual bankrupt ▷ adj **3** declared insolvent **4** financially ruined **5** no longer having a particular quality: morally bankrupt ▷ vb **6** to make bankrupt **bankruptcy** n
WORD ORIGIN Old Italian banca BANK¹ + rotta broken

banksia n an Australian evergreen tree or shrub

banner n **1** a long strip of material displaying a slogan, advertisement, etc. **2** a placard carried in a demonstration **3** Also called: **banner headline** a large headline in a newspaper extending across the page **4** an advertisement, often animated, that extends across the width of a web page
WORD ORIGIN Old French baniere

bannock n Scot a round flat cake made from oatmeal or barley
WORD ORIGIN Old English bannuc

banns pl n the public announcement of an intended marriage
WORD ORIGIN plural of obsolete bann proclamation

banquet n **1** an elaborate formal dinner often followed by speeches ▷ vb **-queting, -queted 2** to hold or take part in a banquet
WORD ORIGIN Italian banco a table

banshee n (in Irish folklore) a female spirit whose wailing warns of a coming death
WORD ORIGIN Irish Gaelic bean sídhe woman of the fairy mound

bantam n **1** a small breed of domestic fowl **2** a small but aggressive person
WORD ORIGIN after Bantam, village in Java, said to be the original home of this fowl

bantamweight n a professional boxer weighing up to 118 lb (53.5 kg) or an amateur weighing up to 119 lb (54 kg)

banter vb **1** to tease jokingly ▷ n **2** teasing or joking conversation
WORD ORIGIN origin unknown

Bantu n **1** a group of languages of Africa **2** pl **-tu** or **-tus** offensive a Black speaker of a Bantu language ▷ adj **3** of the Bantu languages or the peoples who speak them
WORD ORIGIN Bantu Ba-ntu people

Bantustan n offensive formerly, an area reserved for occupation by a Black African people. Official name: **homeland**
WORD ORIGIN Bantu + Hindi -stan country of

banyan or **banian** n an Indian tree whose branches grow down into the soil forming additional trunks
WORD ORIGIN Hindi baniyā

baobab (**bay-oh-bab**) n an African tree with a massive grey trunk, short angular branches, and large pulpy fruit
WORD ORIGIN probably from a native African word

bap n Brit a large soft bread roll
WORD ORIGIN origin unknown

baptism n a Christian religious rite in which a person is immersed in or sprinkled with water as a sign of being cleansed from sin and accepted as a member of the Church **baptismal** adj

baptism of fire n **1** any introductory ordeal **2** a soldier's first experience of battle

Baptist n **1** a member of a Protestant denomination that believes in the necessity of adult baptism by immersion **2** **the Baptist** John the Baptist ▷ adj **3** of the Baptist Church

baptize or **-tise** vb **-tizing, -tized** or **-tising, -tised 1** Christianity to immerse (a person) in water or sprinkle water on (him or her) as part of the rite of baptism **2** to give a name to
WORD ORIGIN Greek baptein to bathe, dip

bar[1] n **1** a rigid usually straight length of metal, wood, etc. used as a barrier or structural part **2** a solid usually rectangular block of any material: a bar of soap **3** anything that obstructs or prevents: a bar to women's mobility **4** a counter or room where alcoholic drinks are served **5** a narrow band or stripe, as of colour or light **6** a heating element in an electric fire **7** see **Bar 8** the place in a court of law where the accused stands during trial **9** music a group of beats that is repeated with a consistent rhythm throughout a piece of music **10** football, etc. same as **crossbar 11** heraldry a narrow horizontal line across a shield **12** **behind bars** in prison ▷ vb **barring, barred 13** to secure with a bar: to bar the door **14** to obstruct: the fallen tree barred the road **15** to exclude: he was barred from membership of the club **16** to mark with a bar or bars ▷ prep **17** except for
WORD ORIGIN Old French barre

bar[2] n a unit of pressure equal to 10^5 newtons per square metre
WORD ORIGIN Greek baros weight

Bar n **1** **the Bar** barristers collectively **2** **be called to the Bar** Brit to become a barrister

barachois n (in the Atlantic Provinces of Canada) a shallow lagoon formed by a sand bar

barb n **1** a cutting remark **2** a point facing in the opposite direction to the main point of a fish-hook, harpoon, etc.

3 a beardlike growth, hair, or projection ▷ vb **4** to provide with a barb or barbs **barbed** adj
WORD ORIGIN Latin barba beard

barbarian n **1** a member of a primitive or uncivilized people **2** a coarse or vicious person ▷ adj **3** uncivilized or brutal

barbaric adj primitive or brutal

barbarism n **1** a brutal, coarse, or ignorant act **2** the condition of being backward, coarse, or ignorant **3** a substandard word or expression

barbarity n, pl **-ties 1** the state of being barbaric or barbarous **2** a vicious act

barbarous adj **1** uncivilized: a barbarous and uninhabitable jungle **2** brutal or cruel: the barbarous tortures inflicted on them
WORD ORIGIN Greek barbaros barbarian, non-Greek

barbecue n **1** a grill on which food is cooked over hot charcoal, usually out of doors **2** food cooked over hot charcoal, usually out of doors **3** a party or picnic at which barbecued food is served ▷ vb **-cuing, -cued 4** to cook on a grill, usually over charcoal
WORD ORIGIN American Spanish barbacoa frame made of sticks

barbed wire n strong wire with sharp points protruding at close intervals

barbel n **1** a long thin growth that hangs from the jaws of certain fishes, such as the carp **2** a freshwater fish with such a growth
WORD ORIGIN Latin barba beard

barbell n a long metal rod to which heavy discs are attached at each end for weightlifting

barber n a person whose business is cutting men's hair and shaving beards
WORD ORIGIN Latin barba beard

barberry n, pl **-ries** a shrub with orange or red berries
WORD ORIGIN Arabic barbāris

barbican n a walled defence to protect a gate or drawbridge of a fortification
WORD ORIGIN Old French barbacane

barbiturate n a derivative of barbituric acid used in medicine as a sedative

barbituric acid n a crystalline solid used in the preparation of barbiturate drugs
WORD ORIGIN German Barbitursäure

Barbour n trademark, Brit a waterproof waxed jacket

barcarole or **barcarolle** n **1** a Venetian boat song **2** an instrumental composition resembling this
WORD ORIGIN French

bar chart or **graph** n a diagram consisting of vertical or horizontal bars whose lengths are proportional to amounts or quantities

bar code n an arrangement of numbers and parallel lines on a package, which can be electronically scanned at a checkout to give the price of the goods

bard n **1** archaic or literary a poet **2 a** (formerly) an ancient Celtic poet **b** a poet who wins a verse competition at a Welsh eisteddfod **3** **the Bard** William Shakespeare, English playwright and poet
WORD ORIGIN Scottish Gaelic

bare adj **1** unclothed: used esp. of a part of the body **2** without the natural, conventional, or usual covering: bare trees **3** lacking appropriate furnishings, etc.: a bare room **4** simple: the bare facts **5** just sufficient: the bare minimum ▷ vb **baring, bared 6** to uncover **bareness** n
WORD ORIGIN Old English bær

bareback adj, adv (of horse-riding) without a saddle

bare-faced or **barefaced** adj obvious or shameless: a bare-faced lie

barefoot or **barefooted** adj, adv with the feet uncovered

bareheaded adj, adv with the head uncovered

bare-knuckle adj **1** without boxing gloves **2** aggressive and without reservations

barely adv **1** only just: barely enough **2** scantily: barely furnished

☰**USAGE**
☰See at **hardly**.

bargain n **1** an agreement establishing what each party will give, receive, or perform in a transaction **2** something acquired or received in such an agreement **3** something bought or offered at a low price **4** **drive a hard bargain** to forcefully pursue one's own profit in a transaction **5** **into the bargain** besides ▷ vb **6** to negotiate the terms of an agreement or transaction
WORD ORIGIN Old French bargaigne

bargain for vb to anticipate

bargain on vb to rely or depend on

barge n **1** a flat-bottomed boat, used for transporting freight, esp. on canals **2** a boat, often decorated, used in pageants, etc. ▷ vb **barging, barged** informal **3** (foll. by into) to bump into **4** to push one's way violently **5** (foll. by into or in) to interrupt rudely: he barged into our conversation
WORD ORIGIN Medieval Latin barga

bargee n Brit a person in charge of a barge

bargepole n **1** a long pole used to propel a barge **2** **not touch with a bargepole** informal to refuse to have anything to do with

bariatric adj of or relating to the treatment of obesity: bariatric surgery
WORD ORIGIN Greek baros weight + iatrikos of healing

barista (**bar-ee-sta**) n a person who makes and sells coffee in a coffee bar

baritone n **1** the second lowest adult male voice **2** a singer with such a voice
WORD ORIGIN Greek barus low + tonos tone

barium (**bare-ee-um**) n chem a soft silvery-white metallic chemical element. Symbol: Ba
WORD ORIGIN Greek barus heavy

barium meal n a preparation of barium sulphate, which is opaque to X-rays, used in X-ray examination of the alimentary canal

bark[1] n **1** the loud harsh cry of a dog or certain other animals ▷ vb **2** (of a dog or other animal) to make its typical cry **3** to shout in an angry tone: he barked an order **4** **bark up the wrong tree** informal to misdirect one's attention or efforts
WORD ORIGIN Old English beorcan

b

b

bark² *n* **1** an outer protective layer of dead corklike cells on the trunks of trees ▷ *vb* **2** to scrape or rub off (skin), as in an injury **3** to remove the bark from (a tree)
WORD ORIGIN Old Norse *börkr*

barker *n* a person at a fairground who loudly addresses passers-by to attract customers

barking *slang chiefly Brit adj* **1** mad or crazy ▷ *adv* **2** extremely: *barking mad*

barley *n* **1** a tall grasslike plant with dense bristly flower spikes, widely cultivated for grain **2** the grain of this grass used in making beer and whisky and for soups
WORD ORIGIN Old English *bere*

barleycorn *n* a grain of barley, or barley itself

barley sugar *n* a brittle clear amber-coloured sweet

barley water *n* a drink made from an infusion of barley

barm *n* the yeasty froth on fermenting malt liquors
WORD ORIGIN Old English *bearm*

barmaid *n* a woman who serves in a pub

barman *n, pl* **-men** a man who serves in a pub

bar mitzvah *Judaism n* **1** a ceremony marking the 13th birthday of a boy and his assumption of religious obligations ▷ *adj* **2** (of a Jewish boy) having undergone this ceremony
WORD ORIGIN Hebrew: son of the law

barmy *adj* **-mier, -miest** *slang* insane
WORD ORIGIN originally, full of BARM, frothing, excited

barn *n* a large farm outbuilding, chiefly for storing grain, but also for livestock
WORD ORIGIN Old English *bere* barley + *ærn* room

barnacle *n* a marine shellfish that lives attached to rocks, ship bottoms, etc.
barnacled *adj*
WORD ORIGIN Old French *bernac*

barnacle goose *n* a goose with a black-and-white head and body
WORD ORIGIN it was formerly believed that the goose developed from a shellfish

barn dance *n* **1** *US & Canad* a party with square-dancing **2** *Brit* a progressive round country dance

barney *n informal* a noisy fight or argument
WORD ORIGIN origin unknown

barn owl *n* an owl with a pale brown-and-white plumage and a heart-shaped face

barnstorm *vb* **1** *chiefly US & Canad* to tour rural districts making speeches in a political campaign **2** to tour rural districts putting on shows
barnstorming *n, adj*

barnyard *n* a yard adjoining a barn

barograph *n meteorol* a barometer that automatically keeps a record of changes in atmospheric pressure
WORD ORIGIN Greek *baros* weight + *graphein* to write

barometer *n* an instrument for measuring atmospheric pressure, used to determine weather or altitude

changes **barometric** *adj*
WORD ORIGIN Greek *baros* weight + *metron* measure

baron *n* **1** a member of the lowest rank of nobility in the British Isles **2** a powerful businessman or financier: *a press baron* **baronial** *adj*
WORD ORIGIN Old French

baroness *n* **1** a woman holding the rank of baron **2** the wife or widow of a baron

baronet *n* a commoner who holds the lowest hereditary British title
baronetcy *n*

barony *n, pl* **-nies** the domain or rank of a baron

baroque (bar-**rock**) *n* **1** a highly ornate style of architecture and art, popular in Europe from the late 16th to the early 18th century **2** a highly ornamented 17th-century style of music ▷ *adj* **3** ornate in style
WORD ORIGIN French from Portuguese *barroco* imperfectly shaped pearl

barque (**bark**) *n* **1** a sailing ship, esp. one with three masts **2** *poetic* any boat
WORD ORIGIN Old Provençal *barca*

barrack¹ *vb* to house (soldiers) in barracks

barrack² *vb* **1** *Brit, Austral, & NZ informal* to criticize loudly or shout against (a team or speaker) **2** *Austral & NZ* (foll. by *for*) to shout encouragement for (a team)
WORD ORIGIN Irish: to boast

barracks *pl n* **1** a building or group of buildings used to accommodate military personnel **2** a large and bleak building
WORD ORIGIN French *baraque*

barracuda (bar-rack-**kew**-da) *n, pl* **-da** or **-das** a tropical fish which feeds on other fishes
WORD ORIGIN American Spanish

barrage (bar-**rahzh**) *n* **1** a continuous delivery of questions, complaints, etc. **2** *mil* the continuous firing of artillery over a wide area **3** a construction built across a river to control the water level
WORD ORIGIN French *barrer* to obstruct

barrage balloon *n* a balloon tethered by cables, often with net suspended from it, used to deter low-flying air attack

barramundi *n* edible Australian fish

barre (**bar**) *n* a rail at hip height used for ballet practice
WORD ORIGIN French

barrel *n* **1** a cylindrical container, usually with rounded sides and flat ends, and held together by metal hoops **2** a unit of capacity of varying amount in different industries **3** the tube through which the bullet of a firearm is fired **4 over a barrel** *informal* powerless ▷ *vb* **-relling, -relled** or *US* **-reling, -reled** **5** to put into a barrel or barrels
WORD ORIGIN Old French *baril*

barrel organ *n* a musical instrument played by turning a handle

barren *adj* **1** incapable of producing offspring **2** unable to support the growth of crops, fruit, etc.: *barren land* **3** unprofitable or unsuccessful: *Real Madrid have had a barren two seasons* **4** dull
barrenness *n*
WORD ORIGIN Old French *brahain*

barricade *n* **1** a barrier, esp. one erected hastily for defence ▷ *vb* **-cading, -caded** **2** to erect a barricade across (an entrance)
WORD ORIGIN Old French *barrique* a barrel

barrier *n* **1** anything that blocks a way or separates, such as a gate **2** anything that prevents progress: *a barrier of distrust* **3** anything that separates or hinders union: *a language barrier*
WORD ORIGIN Old French *barre* bar

barrier cream *n* a cream used to protect the skin

barrier reef *n* a long narrow ridge of coral, separated from the shore by deep water

barring *prep* unless something occurs; except for

barrister *n* a lawyer who is qualified to plead in the higher courts
WORD ORIGIN from BAR¹

barrow¹ *n* **1** same as **wheelbarrow** **2** a handcart used by street traders
WORD ORIGIN Old English *bearwe*

barrow² *n* a heap of earth placed over a prehistoric tomb
WORD ORIGIN Old English *beorg*

barrow boy *n Brit* a man who sells goods from a barrow

Bart. Baronet

barter *vb* **1** to trade goods or services in exchange for other goods or services, rather than for money ▷ *n* **2** trade by the exchange of goods
WORD ORIGIN Old French *barater* to cheat

baryon (**bar**-ree-on) *n* an elementary particle that has a mass greater than or equal to that of the proton
WORD ORIGIN Greek *barus* heavy

baryta (bar-**rite**-a) *n* a compound of barium, such as barium oxide
WORD ORIGIN Greek *barus* heavy

barytes (bar-**rite**-eez) *n* a colourless or white mineral: a source of barium
WORD ORIGIN Greek *barus* heavy

basal *adj* **1** at, of, or constituting a base **2** fundamental

basal metabolic rate *n* the amount of energy consumed by an animal's body at rest

basalt (**bass**-awlt) *n* a dark volcanic rock
basaltic *adj*
WORD ORIGIN Greek *basanitēs* touchstone

bascule *n* a drawbridge that operates by a counterbalanced weight
WORD ORIGIN French: seesaw

base¹ *n* **1** the bottom or supporting part of anything **2** the fundamental principle or part: *agriculture was the economic base of the city's growth* **3** a centre of operations, organization, or supply **4** a starting point: *the new discovery became the base for further research* **5** the main ingredient of a mixture: *to use rice as a base in cookery* **6** *chem* a compound that combines with an acid to form a salt **7** the lower side or face of a geometric construction **8** *maths* the number of units in a counting system that is equivalent to one in the next higher counting place: *10 is the base of the decimal system* **9** a starting or finishing point in any of various games ▷ *vb* **basing, based**

A Brief History of Literature
part 1

Rousseau and Darwin both suggested that homo sapiens possibly sang before the invention of speech. Whether or not that is true, the earliest literature is certainly a species of song: poetry long predates literary prose, and the earliest poetry, we now know, was sung. At this period, there was no 'free verse'; all poetry was organized in some way, usually by metre (rhyme was at first a decorative, incidental feature, and only became a major organizing principle of English verse in the Middle Ages), and the purpose of poetry was apparently mnemonic. There was no such thing as writing, so the only way a society could preserve its collected knowledge, history, culture, and traditions, was through verse. Poetry, being language organized into regular rhythmic patterns (and probably tied to a familiar melody), was easier to remember than prose.

This worked so well that epics – long narrative poems that tell a historically and culturally significant story – survived centuries, even millennia, preserving incidents from the distant past before finally being committed to writing and 'preserved' in a permanent form. The *Iliad*, attributed to Homer (though he was merely the poet who sang the version we know), narrates a conflict from an age when the Greeks were likely a disunified band of sea-faring marauders, not unlike the Vikings would be later, and their future of scholarship, philosophy, art, and literature would have been inconceivable. The Old English epic *Beowulf* was committed to writing about the year 1000 AD, but the society it depicts existed before the Angles, Saxons, and Jutes ever departed the Continent en masse for the British Isles; there is no mention of 'England' or 'English', for these things did not exist in the time of Beowulf and Hrothgar.

But poetry had failings as an historical record as well. In the first place, its very usefulness could have delayed the development of a sophisticated writing system in certain cultures. Ancient Germanic peoples had a runic alphabet from at least the first century AD, but this was never used to write continuous prose or even poetry, and the main preserve of Germanic culture and history continued to be oral recitation until they were converted to Christianity by missionaries after the fall of the Roman Empire in the fifth century. The more important failing of oral history is that it does not preserve fact as we understand it today, and it certainly does not 'preserve' many details.

If we wish to read *Beowulf*, we must either learn Old English, or read a translation, because the *Beowulf* we know is written in an ancient form of English that is no longer spoken. However, that language is contemporary to the time when it was written down, rather than the age it describes. In an oral culture, one would not tell a tale in a language no one speaks; the older forms of the language would certainly have been forgotten anyway. Other, more salient details that get conveniently 'updated' as time moves forward are things like weapons, names, and place-names, even the structure of society. As society develops, its poetry preserves what remains important and discards what is not. That there is no permanent, written record makes this more than possible. Thus Homer's Greeks do not resemble the sea-faring raiders they must have been, but are sophisticated and *sedentary*. Similarly, the 1,168 ships catalogued in Book II of our *Iliad* may be permanent to us, but would not have been to an oral culture. As certain kingdoms, tribes, and families disappeared or fell out of prominence, they would cease to be recounted in new performances of the Catalogue, their places taken by more recently emerged or newly prosperous names, even if they could not historically have participated in the Trojan War.

And yet, for all its failings, poetry remained a useful and popular medium for millennia, giving the many peoples of the world a means of preserving their history when no other method was available, and providing a culturally unifying activity: the recitation of an epic would have been a public event, like a concert or a piece of theatre today, and there would have been no 'antisocial' private reading by individuals.

And, as we shall see, the entertainment value and aesthetic value of poetry ensured its continued survival and popularity throughout the age of writing and print, and into the digital age.

b

10 (foll. by *on* or *upon*) to use as a basis for **11** (foll. by *at* or *in*) to station, post, or place **WORD ORIGIN** Latin *basis* pedestal

base² *adj* **1** dishonourable or immoral: *base motives* **2** of inferior quality or value: *a base coin* **3** debased; counterfeit: *base currency* **WORD ORIGIN** Late Latin *bassus* of low height

baseball *n* **1** a team game in which the object is to score runs by batting the ball and running round all four bases **2** the ball used in this game

baseless *adj* not based on fact

baseline *n* **1** a value or starting point on an imaginary scale with which other things are compared **2** a line at each end of a tennis court that marks the limit of play

baseliner *n tennis* a player who plays most of his or her shots from the back of court

basement *n* a partly or wholly underground storey of a building

base metal *n* a common metal such as copper or lead, that is not a precious metal

base rate *n* **1** the rate of interest used by a bank as a basis for its lending rates **2** the rate at which the Bank of England lends to other financial organizations, which effectively controls interest rates throughout the UK

bases¹ *n* the plural of **basis**

bases² *n* the plural of **base¹**

bash *informal vb* **1** to strike violently or crushingly **2** (foll. by *into*) to crash into ▷ *n* **3** a heavy blow **4 have a bash** *informal* to make an attempt **WORD ORIGIN** origin unknown

bashful *adj* shy or modest **bashfully** *adv* **WORD ORIGIN** *bash*, short for ABASH

-bashing *combining form informal* or *slang* **a** indicating a malicious attack on members of a group: *union-bashing* **b** indicating an activity undertaken energetically: *Bible-bashing* **-basher** *n combining form*

basic *adj* **1** of or forming a base or basis **2** elementary or simple: *a few basic facts* **3** excluding additions or extras: *basic pay* **4** *chem* of or containing a base ▷ *n* **5 basics** fundamental principles, facts, etc. **basically** *adv*

BASIC *n* a computer programming language that uses common English terms **WORD ORIGIN** *b(eginner's) a(ll-purpose) s(ymbolic) i(nstruction) c(ode)*

basic slag *n* a slag produced in steel-making, containing calcium phosphate

basil *n* an aromatic herb used for seasoning food **WORD ORIGIN** Greek *basilikos* royal

basilica *n* **1** a Roman building, used for public administration, which is rectangular with two aisles and a rounded end **2** a Christian church of similar design **WORD ORIGIN** Greek *basilikē oikia* the king's house

basilisk *n* (in classical legend) a serpent that could kill by its breath or glance **WORD ORIGIN** Greek *basiliskos* royal child

basin *n* **1** a round wide container open at the top **2** the amount a basin will hold **3** a washbasin or sink **4** any partially enclosed area of water where ships or boats may be moored **5** the catchment area of a particular river **6** a depression in the earth's surface **WORD ORIGIN** Old French *bacin*

basis *n, pl* **bases 1** something that underlies, supports, or is essential to an idea, belief, etc. **2** a principle on which something depends **WORD ORIGIN** Greek: step

bask *vb* (foll. by *in*) **1** to lie in or be exposed (to pleasant warmth or sunshine) **2** to enjoy (approval or favourable conditions) **WORD ORIGIN** Old Norse *bathask* to bathe

basket *n* **1** a container made of interwoven strips of wood or cane **2** the amount a basket will hold **3** *basketball* **a** the high horizontal hoop through which a player must throw the ball to score points **b** a point scored in this way **WORD ORIGIN** Middle English

basketball *n* a team game in which points are scored by throwing the ball through a high horizontal hoop

basket weave *n* a weave of yarns, resembling that of a basket

basketwork *n* same as **wickerwork**

basking shark *n* a very large plankton-eating shark, which often floats at the sea surface

basmati rice *n* a variety of long-grain rice with slender aromatic grains, used for savoury dishes **WORD ORIGIN** Hindi: aromatic

basque *n* a tight-fitting bodice for women **WORD ORIGIN** origin unknown

Basque *n* **1** a member of a people living in the W Pyrenees in France and Spain **2** the language of the Basques ▷ *adj* **3** of the Basques **WORD ORIGIN** Latin *Vasco*

bas-relief *n* sculpture in which the figures project slightly from the background **WORD ORIGIN** Italian *basso rilievo*

bass¹ (base) *n* **1** the lowest adult male voice **2** a singer with such a voice **3** *informal* same as **bass guitar** or **double bass** ▷ *adj* **4** of the lowest range of musical notes: *the system is engineered to give good bass sound from very small speakers* **5** denoting a musical instrument that is lowest or second lowest in pitch in its family: *bass trombone* **6** of or relating to a bass guitar or double bass: *the band is unusual in that it has two bass players* **7** of or written for a singer with the lowest adult male voice: *the bass soloist in next week's performance of Handel's 'Messiah'* **WORD ORIGIN** Middle English *bas*

bass² (rhymes with **gas**) *n* **1** various Australian freshwater and sea fish **2** a European spiny-finned freshwater fish **WORD ORIGIN** Middle English

bass clef (base) *n* the clef that establishes F a fifth below middle C on the fourth line of the staff

bass drum (base) *n* a large drum of low pitch

basset hound *n* a smooth-haired dog with short legs and long ears **WORD ORIGIN** French *bas* low

bass guitar (base) *n* an electric guitar with the same pitch and tuning as a double bass

bassinet *n* a wickerwork or wooden cradle or pram, usually hooded **WORD ORIGIN** French: little basin

basso *n, pl* **-sos** or **-si** a singer with a bass voice **WORD ORIGIN** Late Latin *bassus* low

bassoon *n* a woodwind instrument that produces a range of low sounds **bassoonist** *n* **WORD ORIGIN** Italian *basso* deep

bastard *n* **1** *informal, offensive* an obnoxious or despicable person **2** *archaic or offensive* a person born of parents not married to each other **3** *informal* something extremely difficult or unpleasant ▷ *adj* **4** *archaic or offensive* illegitimate by birth **5** counterfeit; spurious **bastardy** *n* **WORD ORIGIN** Old French *bastart*

bastardize or **-ise** *vb* **-izing, -ized** or **-ising, -ised 1** to debase **2** to declare illegitimate

baste¹ *vb* **basting, basted** to sew with loose temporary stitches **WORD ORIGIN** Old French *bastir* to build

baste² *vb* **basting, basted** to moisten (meat) during cooking with hot fat **WORD ORIGIN** origin unknown

baste³ *vb* **basting, basted** to thrash **WORD ORIGIN** origin unknown

bastinado *n, pl* **-does 1** a punishment or torture by beating on the soles of the feet with a stick ▷ *vb* **-doing, -doed 2** to beat (a person) in this way **WORD ORIGIN** Spanish *baston* stick

bastion *n* **1** a projecting part of a fortification **2** a thing or person regarded as defending a principle or way of life: *a bastion of anti-communism* **WORD ORIGIN** French *bastille* fortress

bat¹ *n* **1** any of various types of club used to hit the ball in certain sports **2** *cricket* a batsman **3 off one's own bat a** of one's own accord **b** by one's own unaided efforts ▷ *vb* **batting, batted 4** to strike with or as if with a bat **5** *cricket, etc.* to take a turn at batting **WORD ORIGIN** Old English *batt* club

bat² *n* **1** a nocturnal mouselike flying animal with leathery wings **2 blind as a bat** having extremely poor eyesight **WORD ORIGIN** Scandinavian

bat³ *vb* **batting, batted 1** to flutter (one's eyelids) **2 not bat an eyelid** *informal* to show no surprise **WORD ORIGIN** probably from obsolete *bate* flutter, beat

batch *n* **1** a group of similar objects or people dispatched or dealt with at the same time **2** the bread, cakes, etc. produced at one baking ▷ *vb* **3** to group (items) for efficient processing **WORD ORIGIN** Middle English *bache*

batch processing *n* a system by which the computer programs of several users are submitted as a single batch

bated *adj* **with bated breath** in suspense or fear

bath *n* **1** a large container in which to wash the body **2** the act of washing in such a container **3** the amount of water in a bath **4 baths** a public swimming

pool **5 a** a liquid in which something is immersed as part of a chemical process, such as developing photographs **b** the vessel containing such a liquid ▷ *vb* **6** *Brit* to wash in a bath
WORD ORIGIN Old English *bæth*

Bath chair *n* a wheelchair for invalids

bath cube *n* a cube of soluble scented material for use in a bath

bathe *vb* **bathing, bathed 1** to swim in open water for pleasure **2** to apply liquid to (the skin or a wound) in order to cleanse or soothe **3** *chiefly US & Canad* to wash in a bath **4** to spread over: *bathed in moonlight* ▷ *n* **5** *Brit* a swim in open water **bather** *n*
WORD ORIGIN Old English *bathian*

bathos (bay-thoss) *n* a sudden ludicrous descent from exalted to ordinary matters in speech or writing **bathetic** *adj*
WORD ORIGIN Greek: depth

bathrobe *n* **1** a loose-fitting garment for wear before or after a bath or swimming **2** *US & Canad* a dressing gown

bathroom *n* **1** a room with a bath or shower, washbasin, and toilet **2** *US & Canad* a toilet

bathyscaph or **bathyscaphe** *n* a deep-sea diving vessel for observation
WORD ORIGIN Greek *bathus* deep + *skaphē* light boat

bathysphere *n* a strong steel deep-sea diving sphere, lowered by cable
WORD ORIGIN Greek *bathus* deep + *sphere*

batik (bat-teek) *n* **a** a process of printing fabric in which areas not to be dyed are covered by wax **b** fabric printed in this way
WORD ORIGIN Javanese: painted

batman *n, pl* **-men** an officer's servant in the armed forces
WORD ORIGIN Old French *bat* packsaddle

baton *n* **1** a thin stick used by the conductor of an orchestra or choir **2** *athletics* a short bar transferred from one runner to another in a relay race **3** a police officer's truncheon **4** a short stick or something shaped like one
WORD ORIGIN French

baton round *n* same as **plastic bullet**

bats *adj informal* mad or eccentric

batsman *n, pl* **-men** *cricket, etc.* a person who bats or specializes in batting

battalion *n* a military unit comprised of three or more companies
WORD ORIGIN French *bataillon*

batten¹ *n* **1** a strip of wood used to strengthen something or make it secure **2** a strip of wood used for holding a tarpaulin in place over a hatch on a ship ▷ *vb* **3** to strengthen or fasten with battens
WORD ORIGIN French *bâton* stick

batten² *vb* (foll. by *on*) to thrive at the expense of (someone else)
WORD ORIGIN probably from Old Norse *batna* to improve

batter¹ *vb* **1** to hit repeatedly **2** to damage or injure, as by blows, heavy wear, etc. **3** to subject (someone, usually a close relative) to repeated physical violence **battered** *adj* **batterer** *n* **battering** *n*
WORD ORIGIN Middle English *bateren*

batter² *n* a mixture of flour, eggs, and milk, used in cooking
WORD ORIGIN Middle English *bater*

batter³ *n* *baseball, etc.* a player who bats

battering ram *n* (esp. formerly) a large beam used to break down fortifications

battery *n, pl* **-teries 1** two or more primary cells connected to provide a source of electric current **2** a number of similar things occurring together: *a battery of questions* **3** *criminal law* unlawful beating or wounding of a person **4** *chiefly Brit* a series of cages for intensive rearing of poultry **5** a fortified structure on which artillery is mounted ▷ *adj* **6** kept in a series of cages for intensive rearing: *battery hens*
WORD ORIGIN Latin *battuere* to beat

battle *n* **1** a fight between large armed forces **2** conflict or struggle ▷ *vb* **-tling, -tled 3** to fight in or as if in military combat: *shop stewards battling to improve conditions at work* **4** to struggle: *she battled through the crowd*
WORD ORIGIN Latin *battuere* to beat

battle-axe *n* **1** a domineering woman **2** (formerly) a large broad-headed axe

battle cruiser *n* a high-speed warship with lighter armour than a battleship, but of the same size

battle cry *n* **1** a slogan used to rally the supporters of a campaign, movement, etc. **2** a shout uttered by soldiers going into battle

battledore *n* **1** Also called: **battledore and shuttlecock** an ancient racket game **2** a light racket used in this game
WORD ORIGIN Middle English *batyldoure*

battledress *n* the ordinary uniform of a soldier

battlefield or **battleground** *n* the place where a battle is fought

battlement *n* a wall with gaps, originally for firing through
WORD ORIGIN Old French *bataille* battle

battle royal *n* **1** a fight involving many combatants **2** a long violent argument

battleship *n* a large heavily armoured warship

batty *adj* **-tier, -tiest** *slang* **1** crazy **2** eccentric: *a batty OAP*
WORD ORIGIN from BAT²

bauble *n* a trinket of little value
WORD ORIGIN Old French *baubel* plaything

baud *n* *computers* a unit used to measure the speed of transmission of electronic data
WORD ORIGIN after J. M. E. *Baudot*, inventor

bauera *n* small evergreen Australian shrub

Bauhaus (bow-house) *adj* of a school of architecture and applied arts in Germany in the 1920s and 30s characterized by a functionalist approach to design
WORD ORIGIN German: building house

baulk *vb, n* same as **balk**

bauxite *n* a claylike substance that is the chief source of aluminium
WORD ORIGIN (Les) *Baux* in southern France, where originally found

bawdy *adj* **bawdier, bawdiest** (of language, writing, etc.) containing humorous references to sex **bawdily** *adv* **bawdiness** *n*
WORD ORIGIN Old French *baud* merry

bawdyhouse *n* *archaic* a brothel

bawl *vb* **1** to cry noisily **2** to shout loudly ▷ *n* **3** a loud shout or cry **bawling** *n*
WORD ORIGIN imitative

bay¹ *n* a stretch of shoreline that curves inwards
WORD ORIGIN Old French *baie*

bay² *n* **1** a recess in a wall **2** an area set aside for a particular purpose: *a sick bay; a loading bay* **3** same as **bay window 4** an area off a road in which vehicles may park or unload **5** a compartment in an aircraft: *the bomb bay*
WORD ORIGIN Old French *baee* gap

bay³ *n* **1** a deep howl of a hound or wolf **2 at bay a** forced to turn and face attackers: *the stag at bay* **b** at a safe distance: *to keep his mind blank and his despair at bay* ▷ *vb* **3** to howl in deep prolonged tones
WORD ORIGIN Old French *abaiier* to bark

bay⁴ *n* **1** a Mediterranean laurel tree with glossy aromatic leaves **2 bays** a wreath of bay leaves
WORD ORIGIN Latin *baca* berry

bay⁵ *adj* **1** reddish-brown ▷ *n* **2** a reddish-brown horse
WORD ORIGIN Latin *badius*

bayberry *n, pl* **-ries** a tropical American tree that yields an oil used in making bay rum. Also: **bay**

bay leaf *n* the dried leaf of a laurel, used for flavouring in cooking

bayonet *n* **1** a blade that can be attached to the end of a rifle and used as a weapon ▷ *vb* **-neting, -neted** or **-netting, -netted 2** to stab or kill with a bayonet
WORD ORIGIN *Bayonne*, a port in France, where it originated

bay rum *n* an aromatic liquid, used in medicines and cosmetics, which was originally obtained by distilling bayberry leaves with rum

bay window *n* a window projecting from a wall

bazaar *n* **1** a sale, esp. one in aid of charity **2** (esp. in the Orient) a market area, esp. a street of small stalls
WORD ORIGIN Persian *bāzār*

bazooka *n* a portable rocket launcher that fires a projectile capable of piercing armour
WORD ORIGIN after a pipe instrument devised by an American comedian

BB *Brit* Boys' Brigade

B2B business-to-business; denoting trade between commercial organizations rather than between businesses and private customers

BBC British Broadcasting Corporation

BBQ barbecue

BC 1 (indicating years numbered back from the supposed year of the birth of Christ) before Christ **2** British Columbia

BCE (used, esp. by non-Christians, in numbering years BC) before Common Era

BCG *trademark* Bacillus Calmette-Guérin (antituberculosis vaccine)

b

BD Bachelor of Divinity

BDS Bachelor of Dental Surgery

be *vb, present sing 1st person* **am**; *2nd person* **are**; *3rd person* **is**; *present pl* **are**; *past sing 1st person* **was**; *2nd person* **were**; *3rd person* **was**; *past pl* **were**; *present participle* **being**; *past participle* **been**. **1** to exist; live: *I think, therefore I am* **2** to pay a visit; go: *have you been to Spain?* **3** to take place: *my birthday was last Thursday* **4** used as a linking verb between the subject of a sentence and its complement: *John is a musician; honey is sweet; the dance is on Saturday* **5** forms the progressive present tense: *the man is running* **6** forms the passive voice of all transitive verbs: *a good film is being shown on television tomorrow* **7** expresses intention, expectation, or obligation: *the president is to arrive at 9.30* **WORD ORIGIN** Old English *bēon*

Be *chem* beryllium

BE Bachelor of Engineering

be- *prefix forming verbs mainly from nouns* **1** to surround or cover: *befog* **2** to affect completely: *bedazzle* **3** to consider as or cause to be: *befriend* **4** to provide or cover with: *bejewel* **5** *(from verbs)* at, for, against, on, or over: *bewail* **WORD ORIGIN** Old English *be-, bi-* by

beach *n* **1** an area of sand or pebbles sloping down to the sea or a lake ▷ *vb* **2** to run or haul (a boat) onto a beach **WORD ORIGIN** origin unknown

beachcomber *n* a person who searches shore debris for anything of worth

beachhead *n mil* an area of shore captured by an attacking army, on which troops and equipment are landed

beacon *n* **1** a signal fire or light on a hill or tower, used formerly as a warning of invasion **2** a lighthouse **3** a radio or other signal marking a flight course in air navigation **4** same as **Belisha beacon** **WORD ORIGIN** Old English *beacen* sign

bead *n* **1** a small pierced piece of glass, wood, or plastic that may be strung with others to form a necklace, rosary, etc. **2** a small drop of moisture **3** a small metal knob acting as the sight of a firearm ▷ *vb* **4** to decorate with beads **beaded** *adj* **WORD ORIGIN** Old English *bed* prayer

beading *n* a narrow rounded strip of moulding used for edging furniture

beadle *n* **1** *Brit* (formerly) a minor parish official who acted as an usher **2** *Scot* a church official who attends the minister **WORD ORIGIN** Old English *bydel*

beady *adj* **beadier, beadiest** small, round, and glittering: *beady eyes*

beagle *n* a small hound with a smooth coat, short legs, and drooping ears **WORD ORIGIN** origin unknown

beak¹ *n* **1** the projecting horny jaws of a bird **2** *slang* a person's nose **beaky** *adj* **WORD ORIGIN** Latin *beccus*

beak² *n Brit, Austral, & NZ slang* a judge, magistrate, or headmaster **WORD ORIGIN** originally thieves' jargon

beaker *n* **1** a tall drinking cup **2** a lipped glass container used in laboratories **WORD ORIGIN** Old Norse *bikarr*

beam *n* **1** a broad smile **2** a ray of light **3** a narrow flow of electromagnetic radiation or particles: *an electron beam* **4** a long thick piece of wood, metal, etc. used in building **5** the central shaft of a plough to which all the main parts are attached **6** the breadth of a ship at its widest part **7** **off (the) beam** *informal* mistaken or irrelevant ▷ *vb* **8** to smile broadly **9** to send out or radiate **10** to divert or aim (a radio signal, light, etc.) in a certain direction: *the concert was beamed live from Geneva* **WORD ORIGIN** Old English

beam-ends *pl n* **on one's beam-ends** out of money

bean *n* **1** the seed or pod of various climbing plants, eaten as a vegetable **2** any of various beanlike seeds, such as coffee **3** **full of beans** *informal* full of energy and vitality **4** **not have a bean** *slang* to be without money **WORD ORIGIN** Old English *bēan*

beanbag *n* **1** a small cloth bag filled with dried beans and thrown in games **2** a very large cushion filled with polystyrene granules and used as a seat

bean curd *n* same as **tofu**

beanfeast *n Brit informal* any festive or merry occasion

beanie *n Brit, Austral, & NZ* close-fitting woollen hat

beano *n, pl* **beanos** *Brit, old-fashioned slang* a celebration or party

beanpole *n slang* a tall thin person

beansprout *n* a small edible shoot grown from a bean seed, often used in Chinese dishes

bear¹ *vb* **bearing, bore, borne** **1** to support or hold up **2** to bring: *to bear gifts* **3** to accept the responsibility of: *to bear a heavier burden of taxation* **4** to give birth to **5** to produce by natural growth: *to bear fruit* **6** to tolerate or endure **7** to stand up to; sustain: *his story does not bear scrutiny* **8** to hold in the mind: *to bear a grudge* **9** to show or be marked with: *he still bears the scars* **10** to have, be, or stand in (relation or comparison): *her account bears no relation to the facts* **11** to move in a specified direction: *bear left* **12** **bring to bear** to bring into effect ▷ See also **bear down on, bear on**, etc. **WORD ORIGIN** Old English *beran*

▤ **USAGE**
▤ When *bear* means 'give birth to', the
▤ past participle used to form the
▤ passive voice can be either *born* or
▤ *borne*. When it is followed by the
▤ preposition *by*, *borne* should be used:
▤ *babies borne by American surrogates*. In all
▤ other cases the past participle should
▤ be *born*: *I was born in Glasgow; the baby born
▤ to hairdresser Maxine.*

bear² *n, pl* **bears** or **bear** **1** a large heavily-built mammal with a long shaggy coat **2** a bearlike animal, such as the koala **3** an ill-mannered person **4** *stock exchange* a person who sells shares in anticipation of falling prices to make a profit on repurchase **5** **like a bear with a sore head** *informal* bad-tempered, irritable **WORD ORIGIN** Old English *bera*

bearable *adj* endurable; tolerable

bear-baiting *n history* an entertainment in which dogs attacked a chained bear

beard *n* **1** the hair growing on the lower parts of a man's face **2** any similar growth in animals ▷ *vb* **3** to oppose boldly: *I bearded my formidable employer in her den* **bearded** *adj* **WORD ORIGIN** Old English

bear down on *vb* **1** to press down on **2** to approach (someone) in a determined manner

bearer *n* **1** a person or thing that carries, presents, or upholds something **2** a person who presents a note or bill for payment

bear hug *n* a rough tight embrace

bearing *n* **1** (foll. by *on* or *upon*) relevance to: *it has no bearing on this problem* **2** a part of a machine supporting another part, and usually reducing friction **3** the act of producing fruit or young **4** a person's general social conduct **5** the angular direction of a point measured from a known position **6** the position, as of a ship, fixed with reference to two or more known points **7** **bearings** a sense of one's relative position: *I lost my bearings in the dark* **8** *heraldry* a device on a heraldic shield

bear on *vb* to be relevant to

bear out *vb* to show to be truthful: *the witness will bear me out*

bearskin *n* **1** the pelt of a bear **2** a tall fur helmet worn by certain British Army regiments

bear up *vb* to cope with hardships: *they are bearing up well under the pressure*

bear with *vb* to be patient with

beast *n* **1** a large wild animal **2** a brutal or uncivilized person **3** savage nature or characteristics: *the beast in man* **WORD ORIGIN** Latin *bestia*

beastly *adj informal* **-lier, -liest** unpleasant; disagreeable

beat *vb* **beating, beat, beaten** or **beat** **1** to strike with a series of violent blows **2** to move (wings) up and down **3** to throb rhythmically **4** *cookery* to stir or whisk vigorously **5** to shape (metal) by repeated blows **6** *music* to indicate (time) by one's hand or a baton **7** to produce (a sound) by striking a drum **8** to overcome or defeat: *he was determined to beat his illness* **9** to form (a path or track) by repeated use **10** to arrive, achieve, or finish before (someone or something): *she beat her team mate fair and square* **11** (foll. by *back, down,* or *off,* etc.) to drive, push, or thrust **12** to scour (woodlands or undergrowth) to rouse game for shooting **13** *slang* to puzzle or baffle: *it beats me* ▷ *n* **14** a stroke or blow **15** the sound made by a stroke or blow **16** a regular throb **17** an assigned route, as of a policeman **18** the basic rhythmic unit in a piece of music **19** pop or rock music characterized by a heavy rhythmic beat ▷ *adj* **20** *slang* totally exhausted ▷ See also **beat down, beat up** ▷ **beating** *n* **WORD ORIGIN** Old English *bēatan*

beatbox *n* **1** a drum machine ▷ *vb* **2** to simulate percussion instruments with the voice, esp. in hip-hop music **beatboxing** *n*

beat down *vb* **1** (of the sun) to shine intensely **2** *informal* to force or persuade (a seller) to accept a lower price

West Midlands Dialect

In 2008 a university research study concluded that the speech of people from the West Midlands was the least admired of all the accents in the United Kingdom. Even people who said nothing at all made a better impression.

The accent of the region around Birmingham is often characterized as being nasal and monotonous. Typically, vowels expand in length, so that *I* becomes 'oi' and *you* becomes 'yow'. This has the effect of slowing down a person's speech, possibly suggesting a concomitant slowness of thought. In addition, the voice tends to become lower and to fall away as it reaches the end of a sentence, which may suggest a lack of confidence and enthusiasm on the part of the speaker.

However, there is some evidence that the low esteem in which other Britons hold the West Midlands accent is due in some part to social prejudice. People from overseas exhibit a more mixed response to the accent, and have even pronounced it to be friendly in tone. Even native speakers have found it alluring at times. Conservative politician Alan Clark famously commented in his diaries that his political nemesis Clare Short had 'a lovely Brummie accent'. Beauty is in the ear of beholder.

Of course, the word *Brummie* denotes specifically the accent of the city of Birmingham (coming from city's local name of *Brummagem*, which is affectionately shortened to *Brum*). Yet, as with other regions that appear to be monolithic to outsiders, the West Midlands in fact accommodates a range of different ways of speaking. People from Worcester or Leamington Spa are likely to express alarm at any suggestion that they might have a Brummie accent.

One of the more distinctive accents of the region is that of the Black Country, the region to the northwest of Birmingham. The inhabitants of this area are known as 'Yam Yams' (a reference to the way that they say 'you am' or 'y'am' instead of 'you are'). In this accent, the vowel 'a' is often transformed into 'o', so that *hand* becomes *hond* and *laugh* becomes *loff*. Workers in the region's factories were typically urged to 'gi 'it some 'ommer' ('hit it hard').

Like their neighbours in Birmingham, people from the Black Country may call a baby a *babby*, and talk about a *chimley* rather than a chimney, while something that is very good may be described as *bostin'*. The habit of eating *chicklings* (fried pig's intestines) is not, however, one that many people outside of the Black Country seem anxious to share.

It has been said that this dialect preserves aspects of Anglo-Saxon speech that have been lost from Standard English. A notable example of this is the way that the present participle form of verbs ends in '-en' rather than '-ing', so that a Black Country native might say 'I'm just goen to the shops'.

Elements of Early English have also been detected in the dialect of the Potteries, the region around Stoke-on-Trent, a little further to the north, which is famous for its ceramic industry. Words such as *nesh* ('excessively sensitive to the cold') and *clemmed* ('hungry' or 'starving') can be traced back to Anglo-Saxon and Norse words, and have survived in local speech to the present day.

The Potteries were the setting of a sequence of novels by local-born writer Arnold Bennett (1867–1931), who occasionally constructs dialogue in which characters drop into the local dialect, saying things like, 'Dost mean to say as they thought as I 'ud give 'em a hundred pound towards th' new organ?' However, this sort of dialogue is probably best taken as an attempt to imbue a story with local flavour rather than as a serious attempt to reconstruct the vernacular of the area. Those who subscribe to the view that the West Midlands is home to the least palatable of all the British accents would no doubt recoil from the idea of having to read very much that was written in the local dialect.

b

beater n **1** a device used for beating: *a carpet beater* **2** a person who rouses wild game

beatific adj *literary* **1** displaying great happiness **2** having a divine aura
WORD ORIGIN Latin *beatus*

beatify (bee-at-if-fie) vb **-fies, -fying, -fied 1** *RC Church* to declare (a deceased person) to be among the blessed in heaven: the first step towards canonization **2** to make extremely happy **beatification** n

beatitude n supreme blessedness or happiness
WORD ORIGIN Latin *beatitudo*

Beatitude n *Christianity* any of the blessings on the poor, meek, etc. in the Sermon on the Mount

Beat movement n a group of US writers who emerged in the 1950s, noted for their rejection of the social and political systems of the West and their espousal of alternative lifestyles

beatnik n a young person in the late 1950s who rebelled against conventional attitudes and styles of dress
WORD ORIGIN BEAT (noun) + -NIK

beat up *informal* vb **1** to inflict severe physical damage on (someone) by striking or kicking repeatedly ▷ n **2** *Austral & NZ* a small matter deliberately exaggerated ▷ adj **beat-up 3** dilapidated

beau (boh) n, pl **beaux** or **beaus** (bohz) **1** *chiefly US* a boyfriend **2** a man who is greatly concerned with his appearance
WORD ORIGIN French

Beaufort scale n *meteorol* a scale for measuring wind speeds, ranging from 0 (calm) to 12 (hurricane)
WORD ORIGIN after Sir Francis *Beaufort*, who devised it

Beaujolais n a red or white wine from southern Burgundy in France

beauteous adj *poetic* beautiful

beautician n a person who works in a beauty salon

beautiful adj **1** being very attractive to look at **2** highly enjoyable; very pleasant **beautifully** adv

beautify vb **-fies, -fying, -fied** to make beautiful **beautification** n

beauty n, pl **-ties 1** the combination of all the qualities of a person or thing that delight the senses and mind **2** a very attractive woman **3** *informal* an outstanding example of its kind **4** *informal* an advantageous feature: *the beauty of this job is the short hours*
WORD ORIGIN Latin *bellus* handsome

beauty queen n a woman who has been judged the most beautiful in a contest

beauty salon or **parlour** n an establishment that provides services such as hairdressing, facial treatment, and massage

beauty spot n **1** a place of outstanding beauty **2** a small dark-coloured spot formerly worn on a lady's face as decoration

beaver n **1** a large amphibious rodent with soft brown fur, a broad flat tail, and webbed hind feet **2** its fur **3** a tall

hat made of this fur ▷ vb **4 beaver away** to work very hard and steadily
WORD ORIGIN Old English *beofor*

bebop n same as **bop**
WORD ORIGIN imitative of the rhythm

becalmed adj (of a sailing ship) motionless through lack of wind

became vb the past tense of **become**

because conj **1** on account of the fact that: *because it's so cold we'll go home* **2 because of** on account of: *I lost my job because of her*
WORD ORIGIN Middle English *bi cause*
USAGE
See at **reason**.

bechamel sauce (bay-sham-ell) n a thick white sauce flavoured with onion and seasonings
WORD ORIGIN after the Marquis of *Béchamel*, its inventor

beck¹ n **at someone's beck and call** having to be constantly available to do as someone asks
WORD ORIGIN Middle English *becnen* to beckon

beck² n (in N England) a stream
WORD ORIGIN Old English *becc*

beckon vb **1** to summon with a gesture **2** to lure: *fame beckoned*
WORD ORIGIN Old English *bīecnan*

become vb **-coming, -came, -come 1** to come to be: *he became Prime Minister last year* **2** (foll. by *of*) to happen to: *what became of him?* **3** to suit: *that dress becomes you*
WORD ORIGIN Old English *becuman* happen

becoming adj suitable or appropriate: *his conduct was not becoming to the rank of officer*

becquerel (beck-a-rell) n the SI unit of activity of a radioactive source
WORD ORIGIN after A. H. *Becquerel*, physicist

bed n **1** a piece of furniture on which to sleep **2** a plot of ground in which plants are grown **3** the bottom of a river, lake, or sea **4** any underlying structure or part **5** a layer of rock **6 get out of bed on the wrong side** *informal* to begin the day in a bad mood **7 go to bed with** to have sexual intercourse with ▷ vb **bedding, bedded 8** (foll. by *down*) to go to or put into a place to sleep or rest **9** to have sexual intercourse with **10** to place firmly into position: *the poles were bedded in concrete* **11** *geol* to form or be arranged in a distinct layer **12** to plant in a bed of soil
WORD ORIGIN Old English *bedd*

BEd Bachelor of Education

bed and breakfast n *chiefly Brit* overnight accommodation and breakfast

bedaub vb to smear over with something sticky or dirty

bedbug n a small blood-sucking wingless insect that infests dirty houses

bedclothes pl n coverings for a bed

bedding n **1** bedclothes, sometimes with a mattress **2** litter, such as straw, for animals **3** the distinct layered deposits of rocks

bedeck vb to cover with decorations

bedevil (bid-dev-ill) vb **-illing, -illed** or *US* **-iling, -iled 1** to harass or torment **2** to throw into confusion **bedevilment** n

bedfellow n **1** a temporary associate **2** a person with whom one shares a bed

bedlam n a noisy confused situation
WORD ORIGIN from Hospital of St Mary of *Bethlehem*, a former mental hospital in London

bed linen n sheets and pillowcases for a bed

Bedouin n **1** pl **-ins** or **-in** a nomadic Arab tribesman of the deserts of Arabia, Jordan, and Syria **2** a wanderer
WORD ORIGIN Arabic *badw* desert

bedpan n a shallow container used as a toilet by people who are not well enough to leave bed

bedraggled adj with hair or clothing that is untidy, wet, or dirty

bedridden adj unable to leave bed because of illness

bedrock n **1** the solid rock beneath the surface soil **2** basic principles or facts

bedroom n **1** a room used for sleeping ▷ adj **2** containing references to sex: *a bedroom comedy*

Beds Bedfordshire

bedside n **1** the area beside a bed ▷ adj **2** placed at or near the side of the bed: *the bedside table*

bedsit or **bedsitter** n a furnished sitting room with a bed

bedsore n an ulcer on the skin, caused by a lengthy period of lying in bed due to illness

bedspread n a top cover on a bed

bedstead n the framework of a bed

bedstraw n a plant with small white or yellow flowers

bed-wetting n involuntarily urinating in bed

bee¹ n **1** a four-winged insect that collects nectar and pollen to make honey and wax **2 have a bee in one's bonnet** to be obsessed with an idea
WORD ORIGIN Old English *bīo*

bee² n a social gathering to carry out a communal task: *quilting bee*
WORD ORIGIN probably from Old English *bēn* boon

Beeb n **the Beeb** *Brit informal* the BBC

beech n **1** a tree with smooth greyish bark **2** the hard wood of this tree **3** see **copper beech**
WORD ORIGIN Old English *bēce*

beechnut n the small brown triangular edible nut of the beech tree

beef n **1** the flesh of a cow, bull, or ox **2** *slang* a complaint ▷ vb **3** *slang* to complain ▸ See also **beef up**
WORD ORIGIN Old French *boef*, from Latin *bos* ox

beefburger n a flat fried or grilled cake of minced beef; hamburger

beefcake n *slang* musclemen as displayed in photographs

beefeater n a yeoman warder of the Tower of London

beef tea n a drink made by boiling pieces of lean beef

beef tomato or **beefsteak tomato** n a type of large fleshy tomato

beef up *vb informal* to strengthen

beefy *adj* **beefier, beefiest 1** *informal* muscular **2** like beef **beefiness** *n*

beehive *n* a structure in which bees are housed

beekeeper *n* a person who keeps bees for their honey **beekeeping** *n*

beeline *n* **make a beeline for** to speedily take the most direct route to

Beelzebub (bee-**ell**-zib-bub) *n* Satan or any devil
WORD ORIGIN Hebrew *bá'al zebūb*, literally: lord of flies

been *vb* the past participle of **be**

beep *n* **1** a high-pitched sound, like that of a car horn ▷ *vb* **2** to make or cause to make such a noise
WORD ORIGIN imitative

beer *n* **1** an alcoholic drink brewed from malt, sugar, hops, and water **2** a glass, can, or bottle containing this drink
WORD ORIGIN Old English *beor*

beer and skittles *n informal* enjoyment or pleasure

beer parlour *n Canad* a licensed place in which beer is sold and drunk

beery *adj* **beerier, beeriest** smelling or tasting of beer

beeswax *n* **1** a wax produced by honeybees for making honeycombs **2** this wax after refining, used in polishes, etc.

beet *n* a plant with an edible root and leaves, such as the sugar beet and beetroot
WORD ORIGIN Old English *bēte*

beetle[1] *n* **1** an insect with a hard wing-case closed over its back for protection ▷ *vb* **-tling, -tled 2** (foll. by *along* or *off*, etc.) *informal* to scuttle or scurry
WORD ORIGIN Old English *bitela*

beetle[2] *vb* **-tling, -tled** to overhang; jut: *the eaves of the roof beetled out over the windows* **beetling** *adj*
WORD ORIGIN origin unknown

beetle-browed *adj* having bushy or overhanging eyebrows

beetroot *n* a variety of the beet plant with a dark red root that may be eaten as a vegetable, in salads, or pickled

beet sugar *n* the sucrose obtained from sugar beet

befall *vb* **-falling, -fell, -fallen** *archaic or literary* to happen to
WORD ORIGIN Old English *befeallan*

befit *vb* **-fitting, -fitted** to be appropriate to or suitable for **befitting** *adj*

before *conj* **1** earlier than the time when **2** rather than: *she'll resign before she agrees to it* ▷ *prep* **3** preceding in space or time; in front of; ahead of: *they stood before the altar* **4** in the presence of: *to be brought before a judge* **5** in preference to: *to put friendship before money* ▷ *adv* **6** previously **7** in front
WORD ORIGIN Old English *beforan*

beforehand *adj, adv* early; in advance

befriend *vb* to become a friend to

befuddled *adj* stupefied or confused, as through alcoholic drink

beg *vb* **begging, begged 1** to ask for money or food in the street **2** to ask formally, humbly, or earnestly: *I beg forgiveness; I beg to differ* **3** **beg the question** to put forward an argument that assumes the very point it is supposed to establish, or that depends on some other questionable assumption **4** **go begging** to be unwanted or unused
WORD ORIGIN probably from Old English *bedecian*

began *vb* the past tense of **begin**

beget *vb* **-getting, -got** or **-gat, -gotten** or **-got** *old-fashioned* **1** to cause or create: *repetition begets boredom* **2** to father
WORD ORIGIN Old English *begietan*

beggar *n* **1** a person who lives by begging **2** *chiefly Brit* a fellow: *lucky beggar!* ▷ *vb* **3** **beggar description** to be impossible to describe **beggarly** *adj*

begin *vb* **-ginning, -gan, -gun 1** to start (something) **2** to bring or come into being **3** to start to say or speak **4** to have the least capacity to do something: *it doesn't even begin to address the problem* **beginner** *n*
WORD ORIGIN Old English *beginnan*

beginner's luck *n* exceptional luck supposed to attend a beginner

beginning *n* **1** a start **2 beginnings** an early part or stage **3** the place where or time when something starts **4** an origin; source

begone *interj* go away!

begonia *n* a tropical plant with ornamental leaves and waxy flowers
WORD ORIGIN after Michel *Bégon*, patron of science

begot *vb* a past tense and past participle of **beget**

begotten *vb* a past participle of **beget**

begrudge *vb* **-grudging, -grudged 1** to envy (someone) the possession of something **2** to give or allow unwillingly: *he begrudged her an apology*

beguile (big-**gile**) *vb* **-guiling, -guiled** to charm (someone) into doing something he or she would not normally do

beguiling *adj* charming, often in a deceptive way

beguine (big-**geen**) *n* **1** a dance of South American origin **2** music for this dance
WORD ORIGIN French *béguin* flirtation

begum (**bay**-gum) *n* (in certain Muslim countries) a woman of high rank
WORD ORIGIN Turkish *begim*

begun *vb* the past participle of **begin**

behalf *n* **on** or *US & Canad* **in behalf of** in the interest of or for the benefit of
WORD ORIGIN Old English *be* by + *halfe* side

behave *vb* **-having, -haved 1** to act or function in a particular way **2** to conduct oneself in a particular way: *the baby behaved very well* **3** to conduct oneself properly
WORD ORIGIN Middle English

behaviour or *US* **behavior** *n* **1** manner of behaving **2** *psychol* the response of an organism to a stimulus **behavioural** or *US* **behavioral** *adj*

behavioural science *n* the scientific study of the behaviour of organisms

behaviourism or *US* **behaviorism** *n* a school of psychology that regards objective observation of the behaviour of organisms as the only valid subject for study **behaviourist** or *US* **behaviorist** *adj, n*

behead *vb* to remove the head from
WORD ORIGIN Old English *behēafdian*

beheld *vb* the past of **behold**

behemoth (bee-**hee**-moth) *n* a huge person or thing
WORD ORIGIN Hebrew *běhēmāh* beast, name given to a huge beast in the Bible (Job 40:15)

behest *n* an order or earnest request: *I came at her behest*
WORD ORIGIN Old English *behǣs*

behind *prep* **1** in or to a position further back than **2** in the past in relation to: *I want to leave the past behind me* **3** late according to: *running behind schedule* **4** concerning the circumstances surrounding: *the reasons behind his departure* **5** supporting: *I'm right behind you in your application* ▷ *adv* **6** in or to a position further back **7** remaining after someone's departure: *she left her books behind* **8** in arrears: *to fall behind with payments* ▷ *adj* **9** in a position further back ▷ *n* **10** *informal* the buttocks
WORD ORIGIN Old English *behindan*

behindhand *adj, adv* **1** in arrears **2** backward **3** late

behold *vb* **-holding, -held** *archaic or literary* to look (at); observe **beholder** *n*
WORD ORIGIN Old English *bihealdan*

beholden *adj* indebted; obliged: *I am beholden to you*

behove *vb* **-hoving, -hoved** *archaic* to be necessary or fitting for: *it behoves me to warn you*
WORD ORIGIN Old English *behōfian*

beige *adj* pale creamy-brown
WORD ORIGIN Old French

being *n* **1** the state or fact of existing **2** essential nature; self **3** something that exists or is thought to exist: *a being from outer space* **4** a human being

bejewelled or *US* **bejeweled** *adj* decorated with jewels

bel *n* a unit for comparing two power levels or measuring the intensity of a sound, equal to 10 decibels
WORD ORIGIN after A. G. Bell, scientist

belabour or *US* **belabor** *vb* to attack verbally or physically

belated *adj* late or too late: *belated greetings* **belatedly** *adv*

belay *vb* **-laying, -layed 1** *naut* to secure a line to a pin or cleat **2** *naut* to stop **3** *mountaineering* to secure (a climber) by fixing a rope round a rock or piton
WORD ORIGIN Old English *belecgan*

belch *vb* **1** to expel wind from the stomach noisily through the mouth **2** to expel or be expelled forcefully: *smoke belching from factory chimneys* ▷ *n* **3** an act of belching
WORD ORIGIN Old English *bialcan*

beleaguered *adj* **1** struggling against difficulties or criticism: *the country's beleaguered health system* **2** besieged by an enemy: *a ship bringing food to the beleaguered capital of Monrovia*
WORD ORIGIN BE- + obsolete *leaguer* a siege

belfry *n, pl* **-fries 1** the part of a tower or steeple in which bells are hung **2** a tower or steeple
WORD ORIGIN Germanic

b

Belgian *adj* **1** of Belgium ▷ *n* **2** a person from Belgium

belgium sausage *n* NZ large smooth bland sausage

Belial (bee-lee-al) *n* the devil or Satan
WORD ORIGIN Hebrew *balīyya'al* worthless

belie *vb* **-lying, -lied 1** to show to be untrue: *the facts belied the theory* **2** to misrepresent: *the score belied the closeness of the match* **3** to fail to justify: *the promises were soon belied*
WORD ORIGIN Old English *belēogan*

belief *n* **1** trust or confidence: *belief in the free market* **2** opinion; conviction: *it's my firm belief* **3** a principle, etc. accepted as true, often without proof **4** religious faith

believe *vb* **-lieving, -lieved 1** to accept as true or real: *I believe God exists* **2** to think, assume, or suppose: *I believe you know my father* **3** to accept the statement or opinion of (a person) as true **4** to have religious faith **5 believe in** to be convinced of the truth or existence of: *I don't believe in ghosts* **believable** *adj* **believer** *n*
WORD ORIGIN Old English *beliefan*

Belisha beacon (bill-**lee**-sha) *n* Brit a flashing orange globe mounted on a striped post, indicating a pedestrian crossing
WORD ORIGIN after L. Hore-Belisha, politician

belittle *vb* **-tling, -tled** to treat (something or someone) as having little value or importance

bell *n* **1** a hollow, usually metal, cup-shaped instrument that emits a ringing sound when struck **2** the sound made by such an instrument **3** an electrical device that rings or buzzes as a signal **4** something shaped like a bell **5** Brit slang a telephone call **6 ring a bell** to sound familiar; recall something previously experienced
WORD ORIGIN Old English *belle*

belladonna *n* **1** a drug obtained from deadly nightshade **2** same as **deadly nightshade**
WORD ORIGIN Italian, literally: beautiful lady; supposed to refer to its use as a cosmetic

bell-bottoms *pl n* trousers that flare from the knee **bell-bottomed** *adj*

belle *n* a beautiful woman, esp. the most attractive woman at a function: *the belle of the ball*
WORD ORIGIN French

belles-lettres (bell-**let**-tra) *n* literary works, particularly essays and poetry
WORD ORIGIN French

bellicose *adj* warlike; aggressive
WORD ORIGIN Latin *bellum* war

belligerence *n* the act or quality of being belligerent or warlike

belligerent *adj* **1** marked by readiness to fight **2** relating to or engaged in a war ▷ *n* **3** a person or country engaged in war
WORD ORIGIN Latin *bellum* war + *gerere* to wage

bell jar *n* a bell-shaped glass cover used to protect flower arrangements or cover apparatus to confine gases in experiments

bellow *vb* **1** to make a loud deep cry like that of a bull **2** to shout in anger ▷ *n* **3** the characteristic noise of a bull **4** a loud deep roar
WORD ORIGIN probably from Old English *bylgan*

bellows *n* **1** a device consisting of an air chamber with flexible sides that is used to create and direct a stream of air **2** a flexible corrugated part, such as that connecting the lens system of some cameras to the body
WORD ORIGIN plural of Old English *belig* belly

bell pull *n* a handle or cord pulled to operate a bell

bell push *n* a button pressed to operate an electric bell

bell-ringer *n* a person who rings church bells or musical handbells
bell-ringing *n*

bells and whistles *pl n* attractive but nonessential additional features
WORD ORIGIN from the bells and whistles which used to decorate fairground organs

belly *n, pl* **-lies 1** the part of the body of a vertebrate containing the intestines and other organs **2** the stomach **3** the front, lower, or inner part of something **4 go belly up** informal to die, fail, or end ▷ *vb* **-lies, -lying, -lied 5** to swell out; bulge
WORD ORIGIN Old English *belig*

bellyache *n* **1** informal a pain in the abdomen ▷ *vb* **-aching, -ached 2** slang to complain repeatedly

bellybutton *n* informal the navel

belly dance *n* **1** a sensuous dance performed by women, with undulating movements of the abdomen ▷ *vb* **belly-dance, -dancing, -danced 2** to dance thus **belly dancer** *n*

belly flop *n* **1** a dive into water in which the body lands horizontally ▷ *vb* **belly-flop, -flopping, -flopped 2** to perform a belly flop

bellyful *n* **1** slang more than one can tolerate **2** as much as one wants or can eat

belly laugh *n* a loud deep hearty laugh

belong *vb* **1** (foll. by *to*) to be the property of **2** (foll. by *to*) to be bound to (a person, organization, etc.) by ties of affection, association, membership, etc.: *the nations concerned belonged to NATO* **3** (foll. by *to, under,* or *with,* etc.) to be classified with: *it belongs to a different class of comets* **4** (foll. by *to*) to be a part of: *this lid belongs to that tin* **5** to have a proper or usual place **6** informal to be acceptable, esp. socially
WORD ORIGIN Middle English *belongen*

belonging *n* a secure relationship: *they have a strong sense of belonging*

belongings *pl n* the things that a person owns or has with him or her

beloved *adj* **1** dearly loved ▷ *n* **2** a person who is dearly loved

below *prep* **1** at or to a position lower than; under **2** less than **3** unworthy of; beneath ▷ *adv* **4** at or to a lower position **5** at a later place in something written **6** archaic on earth or in hell
WORD ORIGIN Middle English *bilooghe*

belt *n* **1** a band of leather or cloth worn around the waist **2** an area where a specific thing is found; zone: *a belt of high pressure* **3** same as **seat belt 4** a band of flexible material between rotating shafts or pulleys to transfer motion or transmit goods: *a fan belt; a conveyer belt* **5** informal a sharp blow **6 below the belt** informal unscrupulous or cowardly **7 tighten one's belt** to reduce expenditure **8 under one's belt** as part of one's experience: *he had a string of successes under his belt* ▷ *vb* **9** to fasten with or as if with a belt **10** to hit with a belt **11** slang to give (someone) a sharp blow **12** (foll. by *along*) slang to move very fast
WORD ORIGIN Old English

belter *n* slang an outstanding person or event: *a belter of a match*

belt out *vb* informal to sing (a song) loudly

belt up *vb* **1** slang to stop talking **2** to fasten with a belt

beluga (bill-**loo**-ga) *n* a large white sturgeon of the Black and Caspian Seas, from which caviar and isinglass are obtained
WORD ORIGIN Russian *byeluga*

belvedere *n* a building designed and situated to look out on pleasant scenery
WORD ORIGIN Italian: beautiful sight

BEM British Empire Medal

bemoan *vb* to lament: *he's always bemoaning his fate*

bemused *adj* puzzled or confused

ben *n* Scot, Irish a mountain peak: *Ben Lomond*
WORD ORIGIN Gaelic *beinn*

bench *n* **1** a long seat for more than one person **2 the bench a** a judge or magistrate sitting in court **b** judges or magistrates collectively **3** a long and strong worktable
WORD ORIGIN Old English *benc*

benchmark *n* **1** a mark on a fixed object, used as a reference point in surveying **2** a criterion by which to measure something: *the speech was a benchmark of his commitment*

bench press *n* an exercise in which a person pushes a barbell upwards while lying flat on a bench

bend¹ *vb* **bending, bent 1** to form a curve **2** to turn from a particular direction: *the road bends right* **3** (often foll. by *down,* etc.) to incline the body **4** to submit: *to bend before public opinion* **5** to turn or direct (one's eyes, steps, or attention) **6 bend someone's ear** informal to complain (to someone) for a long time **7 bend the rules** informal to ignore or change rules to suit oneself ▷ *n* **8** a curved part **9** the act of bending **10 round the bend** Brit slang mad **bendy** *adj*
WORD ORIGIN Old English *bendan*

bend² *n* heraldry a diagonal line across a shield
WORD ORIGIN Old English: a band, strip

bender *n* informal **1** a drinking bout **2** a shelter made from plastic sheeting and woven branches

bends *pl n* **the bends** informal decompression sickness

Words from Shakespeare
part 3

aye *adv* always or ever
Whose state and honour I for aye allow
Richard II 5.2

baffle *v* to be disgraced in public or humiliated
I am disgraced, impeached, and baffled here
Richard II 1.1

bald *adj* trivial or silly
I knew 'twould be a bald conclusion
The Comedy of Errors 2.2

ban *n* a curse or an evil spell
Sometimes with lunatic bans... Enforce their
charity *King Lear* 2.3

barren *adj* empty or hollow
now I let go your hand, I am barren.
Twelfth Night 1.3

base *adj* unworthy or dishonourable
civet is of a baser birth than tar *As You Like It* 3.2

bawdy *adj* obscene or rude
Bloody, bawdy villain! *Hamlet* 2.2

bear in hand *phrase* to take advantage of or fool
This I made good to you In our last conference,
passed in probation with you
How you were borne in hand *Macbeth* 3.1

beard *v* to oppose or confront someone
Com'st thou to beard me in Denmark? *Hamlet* 2.2

beard, in someone's *phrase* said to someone's face
I will verify as much in his beard *Henry V* 3.2

beaver *n* a visor on a battle helmet
O yes, my lord, he wore his beaver up *Hamlet* 1.2

become *v* to suit
Nothing in his life became him like the leaving it
Macbeth 1.4

bed, brought to *phrase* to give birth
His wife but yesternight was brought to bed
Titus Andronicus 4.2

bedabbled *adj* sprinkled
Bedabbled with the dew, and torn with briers
A Midsummer Night's Dream 3.2

bedlam *n* the hospital of St Mary of Bethlehem,
London, which was a place the insane were sent to
The country give me proof and precedent
Of Bedlam beggars *King Lear* 2.3

bed-swerver *n* someone who was unfaithful in
marriage, an adulterer
she's
A bed-swerver *The Winter's Tale* 2.1

befall *v* to happen, occur or take place
In this same interlude it doth befall
That I present
a wall *A Midsummer Night's Dream* 5.1

behoof *n* advantage or benefit
All our surgeons
Convent in their behoof *Two Noble Kinsmen* 1.4

beldam *n* a witch or old woman
Have I not reason, beldams as you are? *Macbeth* 3.5

belike *adv* probably, perhaps or presumably
belike he likes it not *Hamlet* 3.2

bent *n* preference or direction
Let me work,
For I can give his humour true bent,
And I will bring him to the Capitol *Julius Caesar* 2.1

bent *adj* determined to do something
for now I am bent to know
By the worst means the worst. *Macbeth* 3.4

beshrew *v* to curse or wish evil on someone
much beshrew my manners and my pride
If Hermia meant to say Lysander lied
A Midsummer Night's Dream 2.2

betime(s) *adv* early
To business that we love we rise betime
Antony and Cleopatra 4.4

bend sinister *n heraldry* a diagonal line across a shield, indicating a bastard line

beneath *prep* **1** below; under **2** too trivial for: *beneath his dignity* ▷ *adv* **3** below; underneath
WORD ORIGIN Old English *beneothan*

Benedictine *n* **1** a monk or nun of the Christian order of Saint Benedict **2** a liqueur first made by Benedictine monks ▷ *adj* **3** of Saint Benedict or his order

benediction *n* **1** a prayer for divine blessing **2** a Roman Catholic service in which the congregation is blessed with the sacrament **benedictory** *adj*
WORD ORIGIN Latin *benedictio*

benefaction *n* **1** the act of doing good, particularly donating to charity **2** the donation or help given
WORD ORIGIN Latin *bene* well + *facere* to do

benefactor *n* a person who supports a person or institution by giving money **benefactress** *fem n*

benefice *n Christianity* a Church office that provides its holder with an income
WORD ORIGIN Latin *beneficium* benefit

beneficent (bin-**eff**-iss-ent) *adj* charitable; generous **beneficence** *n*
WORD ORIGIN Latin *beneficus*

beneficial *adj* helpful or advantageous
WORD ORIGIN Latin *beneficium* kindness

beneficiary *n, pl* **-ciaries 1** a person who gains or benefits **2** *law* a person entitled to receive funds or property under a trust, will, etc.

benefit *n* **1** something that improves or promotes **2** advantage or sake: *I'm doing this for your benefit* **3** a payment made by an institution or government to a person who is ill, unemployed, etc. **4** a theatrical performance or sports event to raise money for a charity ▷ *vb* **-fiting, -fited** *or US* **-fitting, -fitted 5** to do or receive good; profit
WORD ORIGIN Latin *bene facere* to do well

benefit society *n US* same as **friendly society**

benevolence *n* **1** inclination to do good **2** an act of kindness **benevolent** *adj*

Bengali *n* **1** a member of a people living chiefly in Bangladesh and West Bengal **2** the language of this people ▷ *adj* **3** of Bengal or the Bengalis

benighted *adj* lacking cultural, moral, or intellectual enlightenment

benign (bin-**nine**) *adj* **1** showing kindliness **2** favourable: *a stroke of benign fate* **3** *pathol* (of a tumour, etc.) able to be controlled **benignly** *adv*
WORD ORIGIN Latin *benignus*

benignant *adj* **1** kind or gracious **2** same as **benign** (senses 2, 3) ▷ **benignancy** *n*

benignity (bin-**nig**-nit-tee) *n, pl* **-ties** kindliness

bent *adj* **1** not straight; curved **2** *slang* **a** dishonest; corrupt: *bent officials* **b** *Austral & Brit offensive slang* homosexual **3 bent on** determined to pursue (a course of action) ▷ *n* **4** personal inclination or aptitude: *he had a strong practical bent in his nature*

Benthamism *n* the utilitarian philosophy of Jeremy Bentham, which holds that the ultimate goal of society should be to promote the greatest happiness of the greatest number **Benthamite** *n, adj*

bento *or* **bento box** *n* a thin box, made of plastic or lacquered wood, divided into compartments, which contain small separate dishes comprising a Japanese meal, esp. lunch
WORD ORIGIN Japanese *bento* box lunch

bentwood *n* **1** wood bent in moulds, used mainly for furniture ▷ *adj* **2** made from such wood: *a bentwood chair*

benumb *vb* **1** to make numb or powerless **2** to stupefy (the mind, senses, will, etc.): *the work benumbed their minds and crushed their spirits*

benzene *n* a flammable poisonous liquid used as a solvent, insecticide, etc.
WORD ORIGIN from *benzoin*, a fragrant resin from certain Asiatic trees

benzine *n* a volatile liquid obtained from coal tar and used as a solvent

bequeath *vb* **1** *law* to dispose of (property) as in a will **2** to hand down: *the author bequeaths no solutions*
WORD ORIGIN Old English *becwethan*

bequest *n* **1** the act of gifting money or property in a will **2** money or property that has been gifted in a will

berate *vb* **-rating, -rated** to scold harshly

Berber *n* **1** a member of a Muslim people of N Africa **2** the language of this people ▷ *adj* **3** of the Berbers

berberis *n* a shrub with red berries
WORD ORIGIN Medieval Latin

berceuse (bare-**suhz**) *n* **1** a lullaby **2** an instrumental piece suggestive of this
WORD ORIGIN French

bereaved *adj* having recently lost a close relative or friend through death **bereavement** *n*
WORD ORIGIN Old English *bereafian* to deprive

bereft *adj* (foll. by *of*) deprived: *a government bereft of ideas*

beret (**ber**-ray) *n* a round flat close-fitting brimless cap
WORD ORIGIN French

berg¹ *n* short for **iceberg**

berg² *n S African* a mountain

bergamot *n* **1** a small Asian tree with sour pear-shaped fruit **2 essence of bergamot** a fragrant essential oil from the fruit rind of this plant, used in perfumery
WORD ORIGIN French *bergamote*

beri-beri *n* a disease caused by a dietary deficiency of thiamine (vitamin B_1)
WORD ORIGIN Sinhalese

berk *or* **burk** *n Brit, Austral, & NZ slang* a stupid person; fool
WORD ORIGIN *Berkshire Hunt*, rhyming slang for *cunt*

berkelium *n chem* an artificial radioactive element. Symbol: Bk
WORD ORIGIN after *Berkeley*, California, where it was discovered

Berks Berkshire

berm *n NZ* narrow grass strip between the road and the footpath in a residential area

Bermuda shorts *pl n* shorts that come down to the knees
WORD ORIGIN after *Bermudas*, islands in NW Atlantic

Bernoulli principle *n physics* the principle that the pressure in a moving fluid becomes less as the speed rises
WORD ORIGIN after Daniel *Bernoulli*, mathematician & physicist

berry *n, pl* **-ries** a small round fruit that grows on bushes or trees and is often edible
WORD ORIGIN Old English *berie*

berserk *adj* **go berserk** to become violent or destructive
WORD ORIGIN Icelandic *björn* bear + *serkr* shirt

berth *n* **1** a bunk in a ship or train **2** *naut* a place assigned to a ship at a mooring **3** *naut* sufficient room for a ship to manoeuvre **4 give a wide berth to** to keep clear of ▷ *vb* **5** *naut* to dock (a ship) **6** to provide with a sleeping place **7** *naut* to pick up a mooring in an anchorage
WORD ORIGIN probably from BEAR¹

beryl *n* a transparent hard mineral, used as a source of beryllium and as a gemstone
WORD ORIGIN Greek *bērullos*

beryllium *n* a toxic silvery-white metallic element. Symbol: Be
WORD ORIGIN Greek *bērullos*

beseech *vb* **-seeching, -sought** *or* **-seeched** to ask earnestly; beg
WORD ORIGIN Middle English; see BE-, SEEK

beset *vb* **-setting, -set 1** to trouble or harass constantly **2** to surround or attack from all sides

beside *prep* **1** next to; at, by, or to the side of **2** as compared with **3** away from: *beside the point* **4 beside oneself** overwhelmed; overwrought: *beside oneself with grief* ▷ *adv* **5** at, by, to, or along the side of something or someone
WORD ORIGIN Old English *be sīdan*

besides *adv* **1** in addition ▷ *prep* **2** apart from; even considering ▷ *conj* **3** anyway; moreover

besiege *vb* **-sieging, -sieged 1** to surround with military forces to bring about surrender **2** to hem in **3** to overwhelm, as with requests

besmirch *vb* to tarnish (someone's name or reputation)

besom *n* a broom made of a bundle of twigs tied to a handle
WORD ORIGIN Old English *besma*

besotted *adj* **1** having an irrational passion for a person or thing **2** stupefied with alcohol

besought *vb* a past of **beseech**

bespatter *vb* **1** to splash with dirty water **2** to dishonour or slander

bespeak *vb* **-speaking, -spoke, -spoken** *or* **-spoke 1** to indicate or suggest: *imitation bespeaks admiration* **2** to engage or ask for in advance: *she was bespoke to a family in the town*

bespectacled *adj* wearing spectacles

bespoke *adj chiefly Brit* **1** (esp. of a suit) made to the customer's specifications **2** making or selling such suits: *a bespoke tailor*

best *adj* **1** the superlative of **good 2** most excellent of a particular group, category, etc. **3** most suitable, desirable, etc. ▷ *adv* **4** the superlative of **well 5** in a manner surpassing all others; most attractively, etc. ▷ *n* **6 the best** the most outstanding or excellent person, thing, or group in a category **7** the utmost effort: *I did my best* **8** a person's finest clothes **9 at best a** in the most favourable interpretation **b** under the most favourable conditions **10 for the best a** for an ultimately good outcome **b** with good intentions **11 get the best of** to defeat or outwit **12 make the best of** to cope as well as possible with ▷ *vb* **13** to defeat **WORD ORIGIN** Old English *betst*

bestial *adj* **1** brutal or savage **2** of or relating to a beast **WORD ORIGIN** Latin *bestia* beast

bestiality *n, pl* **-ties 1** brutal behaviour, character, or action **2** sexual activity between a person and an animal

bestiary *n, pl* **-aries** a medieval collection of descriptions of animals

bestir *vb* **-stirring, -stirred** to cause (oneself) to become active

best man *n* the male attendant of the bridegroom at a wedding

bestow *vb* to present (a gift) or confer (an honour) **bestowal** *n*

bestrew *vb* **-strewing, -strewed, -strewn** *or* **-strewed** to scatter or lie scattered over (a surface)

bestride *vb* **-striding, -strode** to have or put a leg on either side of

bestseller *n* a book or other product that has sold in great numbers **bestselling** *adj*

bet *n* **1** the act of staking a sum of money or other stake on the outcome of an event **2** the stake risked **3** a course of action: *your best bet is to go by train* **4** *informal* an opinion: *my bet is that you've been up to no good* ▷ *vb* **betting, bet** *or* **betted 5** to make or place a bet with (someone) **6** to stake (money, etc.) in a bet **7** *informal* to predict (a certain outcome): *I bet she doesn't turn up* **8 you bet** *informal* of course **WORD ORIGIN** probably short for *abet*

beta *n* **1** the second letter in the Greek alphabet (B, β) **2** the second in a group or series

beta-blocker *n* a drug that decreases the activity of the heart: used in the treatment of high blood pressure and angina pectoris

beta-carotene *n biochem* the most important form of the plant pigment carotene, which occurs in milk, vegetables, and other foods and, when eaten by man and animals, is converted in the body to vitamin A

betake *vb* **-taking, -took, -taken** ● **betake oneself** *formal* to go or move: *he betook himself to the public house*

beta particle *n* a high-speed electron or positron emitted by a nucleus during radioactive decay or nuclear fission

betatron *n* a type of particle accelerator for producing high-energy beams of electrons

betel (**bee**-tl) *n* an Asian climbing plant, the leaves and nuts of which can be chewed **WORD ORIGIN** Malayalam (language of SW India) *vettila*

bête noire (bet **nwahr**) *n, pl* **bêtes noires** a person or thing that one particularly dislikes or dreads **WORD ORIGIN** French, literally: black beast

betide *vb* **-tiding, -tided** to happen or happen to: *woe betide us if we're not ready on time* **WORD ORIGIN** BE- + obsolete *tide* to happen

betoken *vb* to indicate; signify

betray *vb* **1** to hand over or expose (one's nation, friend, etc.) treacherously to an enemy **2** to disclose (a secret or confidence) treacherously **3** to reveal unintentionally: *his singing voice betrays his origins* **betrayal** *n* **betrayer** *n* **WORD ORIGIN** Latin *tradere* to hand over

betroth *vb archaic* to promise to marry or to give in marriage **betrothal** *n* **WORD ORIGIN** Middle English *betreuthen*

betrothed *old-fashioned adj* **1** engaged to be married ▷ *n* **2** the person to whom one is engaged

better *adj* **1** the comparative of **good 2** more excellent than others **3** more suitable, attractive, etc. **4** improved or fully recovered in health **5 the better part of** a large part of ▷ *adv* **6** the comparative of **well 7** in a more excellent manner **8** in or to a greater degree **9 better off** in more favourable circumstances, esp. financially **10 had better** would be sensible, etc. to: *I had better be off* ▷ *n* **11 the better** something that is the more excellent, useful, etc. of two such things **12 betters** people who are one's superiors, esp. in social standing **13 get the better of** to defeat or outwit ▷ *vb* **14** to improve upon **WORD ORIGIN** Old English *betera*

better half *n humorous* one's spouse

betterment *n* improvement

better-off *adj* reasonably wealthy: *Catalonia aims to attract better-off tourists*

betting shop *n* (in Britain) a licensed bookmaker's premises not on a racecourse

between *prep* **1** at a point intermediate to two other points in space, time, etc. **2** in combination; together: *between them, they saved enough money to buy a car* **3** confined to: *between you and me* **4** indicating a linking relation or comparison **5** indicating alternatives, strictly only two alternatives ▷ *adv also* **in between 6** between one specified thing and another **WORD ORIGIN** Old English *betwēonum*

USAGE
After *distribute* and words with a similar meaning, *among* should be used rather than *between*: *this enterprise issued shares which were distributed among its workers.*

betwixt *prep, adv* **1** *archaic* between **2 betwixt and between** in an intermediate or indecisive position

bevel *n* **1** a slanting edge ▷ *vb* **-elling, -elled** *or* US **-eling, -eled 2** to be inclined; slope **3** to cut a bevel on (a piece of timber, etc.) **WORD ORIGIN** Old French *baer* to gape

bevel gear *n* a toothed gear meshed with another at an angle to it

beverage *n* any drink other than water **WORD ORIGIN** Old French *bevrage*

beverage room *n Canad* same as **beer parlour**

bevvy *n, pl* **-vies** *dialect* **1** an alcoholic drink **2** a session of drinking **WORD ORIGIN** probably from Old French *bevee, buvee* drinking

bevy *n, pl* **bevies** a flock; a group **WORD ORIGIN** origin unknown

bewail *vb* to express great sorrow over; lament

beware *vb* **-waring, -wared** (often foll. by *of*) to be wary (of); be on one's guard (against) **WORD ORIGIN** be (imperative) + obsolete *war* wary

bewilder *vb* to confuse utterly; puzzle **bewildering** *adj* **bewilderment** *n* **WORD ORIGIN** BE- + obsolete *wilder* to lose one's way

bewitch *vb* **1** to attract and fascinate **2** to cast a spell over **bewitching** *adj* **WORD ORIGIN** Middle English *bewicchen*

bey *n* **1** (in modern Turkey) a title of address, corresponding to Mr **2** (in the Ottoman Empire) a title given to provincial governors **WORD ORIGIN** Turkish: lord

beyond *prep* **1** at or to a point on the other side of: *beyond those hills* **2** outside the limits or scope of ▷ *adv* **3** at or to the other or far side of something **4** outside the limits of something ▷ *n* **5 the beyond** the unknown, esp. life after death **WORD ORIGIN** Old English *begeondan*

bezel *n* **1** the sloping edge of a cutting tool **2** the slanting face of a cut gem **3** a groove holding a gem, watch crystal, etc. **WORD ORIGIN** French *biseau*

bezique *n* a card game for two or more players **WORD ORIGIN** French *bésigue*

B/F *or* **b/f** *book-keeping* brought forward

BFPO British Forces Post Office

Bh *chem* bohrium

Bhagavad-Gita (bug-a-vad-**geet**-a) *n* a sacred Hindu text composed about 200 BC **WORD ORIGIN** Sanskrit: song of the Blessed One

bhaji *n, pl* **bhaji** *or* **bhajis** an Indian savoury made of chopped vegetables mixed in a spiced batter and deep-fried **WORD ORIGIN** Hindi

bhang *n* a preparation of Indian hemp used as a narcotic and intoxicant **WORD ORIGIN** Hindi

bhangra *n* a type of traditional Punjabi folk music combined with elements of Western pop music **WORD ORIGIN** Hindi

bhp brake horsepower

Bi *chem* bismuth

bi- *combining form* **1** having two: *bifocal* **2** occurring or lasting for two: *biennial* **3** on both sides, directions, etc.: *bilateral* **4** occurring twice during: *biweekly*

b

5 *chem* **a** denoting a compound containing two identical cyclical hydrocarbon systems: *biphenyl* **b** indicating an acid salt of a dibasic acid: *sodium bicarbonate* **WORD ORIGIN** Latin *bis* twice

biannual *adj* occurring twice a year **biannually** *adv*

bias *n* **1** mental tendency, esp. prejudice **2** a diagonal cut across the weave of a fabric **3** *bowls* a bulge or weight inside one side of a bowl that causes it to roll in a curve ▷ *vb* **-asing, -ased** *or* **-assing, -assed 4** to cause to have a bias; prejudice **biased** *or* **biassed** *adj* **WORD ORIGIN** Old French *biais*

bias binding *n* a strip of material used for binding hems

biaxial *adj* (esp. of a crystal) having two axes

bib *n* **1** a piece of cloth or plastic worn to protect a very young child's clothes while eating **2** the upper front part of some aprons, dungarees, etc. **WORD ORIGIN** Middle English *bibben* to drink

bibcock *n* a tap with a nozzle bent downwards

bibelot (**bib**-loh) *n* an attractive or curious trinket **WORD ORIGIN** Old French *beubelet*

bibl. 1 bibliographical **2** bibliography

Bible *n* **1 the Bible** the sacred writings of the Christian religion, comprising the Old and New Testaments **2 bible** a book regarded as authoritative: *this guide has long been regarded as the hill walkers' bible* **biblical** *adj* **WORD ORIGIN** Greek *biblion* book

Bible Belt *n* those states of the S US where Protestant fundamentalism is dominant

bibliography *n, pl* **-phies 1** a list of books on a subject or by a particular author **2** a list of sources used in a book, etc. **3** the study of the history, etc. of literary material **bibliographer** *n* **WORD ORIGIN** Greek *biblion* book + *graphein* to write

bibliophile *n* a person who collects or is fond of books **WORD ORIGIN** Greek *biblion* book + *philos* loving

bibulous *adj literary* addicted to alcohol **WORD ORIGIN** Latin *bibere* to drink

bicameral *adj* (of a legislature) consisting of two chambers **WORD ORIGIN** BI- + Latin *camera* chamber

bicarb *n* short for **bicarbonate of soda**

bicarbonate *n* a salt of carbonic acid

bicarbonate of soda *n* sodium bicarbonate used as medicine or a raising agent in baking

bicentenary *or US* **bicentennial** *adj* **1** marking a 200th anniversary ▷ *n, pl* **-naries 2** a 200th anniversary

biceps *n, pl* **-ceps** *anat* a muscle with two origins, esp. the muscle that flexes the forearm **WORD ORIGIN** BI- + Latin *caput* head

bicker *vb* to argue over petty matters; squabble **WORD ORIGIN** origin unknown

bicolour, bicoloured *or US* **bicolor, bicolored** *adj* two-coloured

bicuspid *adj* **1** having two points ▷ *n* **2** a bicuspid tooth

bicycle *n* **1** a vehicle with a metal frame and two wheels, one behind the other, pedalled by the rider ▷ *vb* **-cling, -cled 2** to ride a bicycle **WORD ORIGIN** BI- + Greek *kuklos* wheel

bid *vb* **bidding; bad, bade,** *or* **bid; bidden** *or* **bid 1** to offer (an amount) in an attempt to buy something **2** to say (a greeting): *to bid farewell* **3** to order: *do as you are bid!* **4** *bridge, etc.* to declare how many tricks one expects to make ▷ *n* **5 a** an offer of a specified amount **b** the price offered **6 a** the quoting by a seller of a price **b** the price quoted **7** an attempt, esp. to attain power **8** *bridge, etc.* the number of tricks a player undertakes to make **bidder** *n* **WORD ORIGIN** Old English *biddan*

biddable *adj* obedient

bidding *n* **1** an order or command: *she had done his bidding* **2** an invitation; summons: *he knew to knock and wait for bidding before he entered* **3** the bids in an auction, card game, etc.

biddy *n, pl* **-dies** *informal* a woman, esp. an old gossipy one **WORD ORIGIN** pet form of *Bridget*

biddy-bid, biddy-biddy *n, pl* **-bids, -biddies** NZ a low-growing plant with hooked burrs

bide *vb* **biding, bided** *or* **bode, bided 1** *archaic or dialect* to remain **2 bide one's time** to wait patiently for an opportunity **WORD ORIGIN** Old English *bīdan*

bidet (**bee**-day) *n* a small low basin for washing the genital area **WORD ORIGIN** French: small horse

biennial *adj* **1** occurring every two years ▷ *n* **2** a plant that completes its life cycle in two years

bier *n* a stand on which a corpse or a coffin rests before burial **WORD ORIGIN** Old English *bēr*

biff *slang n* **1** a blow with the fist ▷ *vb* **2** to give (someone) such a blow **WORD ORIGIN** probably imitative

bifid *adj* divided into two by a cleft in the middle **WORD ORIGIN** BI- + Latin *findere* to split

bifocal *adj* having two different focuses, esp. (of a lens) permitting near and distant vision

bifocals *pl n* a pair of spectacles with bifocal lenses

bifurcate *vb* **-cating, -cated 1** to fork into two branches ▷ *adj* **2** forked into two branches **bifurcation** *n* **WORD ORIGIN** BI- + Latin *furca* fork

big *adj* **bigger, biggest 1** of great or considerable size, weight, number, or capacity **2** having great significance; important **3** important through having power, wealth, etc. **4 a** elder: *my big brother* **b** grown-up **5** generous: *that's very big of you* **6** extravagant; boastful: *big talk* **7 too big for one's boots** conceited; unduly self-confident **8** in an advanced stage of pregnancy: *big with child* **9 in a big way** in a very grand or enthusiastic way ▷ *adv informal* **10** boastfully; pretentiously: *he talks big* **11** on a grand scale: *think big*

WORD ORIGIN origin unknown

bigamy *n* the crime of marrying a person while still legally married to someone else **bigamist** *n* **bigamous** *adj* **WORD ORIGIN** BI- + Greek *gamos* marriage

big-bang theory *n* a cosmological theory that suggests that the universe was created as the result of a massive explosion

Big Brother *n* a person or organization that exercises total dictatorial control **WORD ORIGIN** from the novel *1984* by George Orwell

big business *n* large commercial organizations collectively

big end *n* the larger end of a connecting rod in an internal-combustion engine

big game *n* large animals that are hunted or fished for sport

bighead *n informal* a conceited person **big-headed** *adj*

bight *n* **1** a long curved shoreline **2** the slack part or a loop in a rope **WORD ORIGIN** Old English *byht*

big name *informal n* **1** a famous person ▷ *adj* **big-name 2** famous

bigot *n* a person who is intolerant, esp. regarding religion, politics, or race **bigoted** *adj* **bigotry** *n* **WORD ORIGIN** Old French

big shot *n informal* an important person

Big Smoke *n* **the Big Smoke** *informal* a big city, esp. London

big stick *n informal* force or the threat of force

big time *n* **the big time** *informal* the highest level of a profession, esp. entertainment **big-timer** *n*

big top *n informal* the main tent of a circus

bigwig *n informal* an important person

bijou (**bee**-zhoo) *n, pl* **-joux** (**-zhooz**) **1** something small and delicately worked ▷ *adj* **2** small but tasteful: *a bijou residence* **WORD ORIGIN** French: a jewel

bike *n informal* a bicycle or motorcycle

biker *n* a person who rides a motorcycle

biker jacket *n* a short, close-fitting leather jacket often worn by motorcyclists

bikini *n* a woman's brief two-piece swimming costume **WORD ORIGIN** after *Bikini* atoll, from a comparison between the devastating effect of the atom-bomb test and the effect caused by women wearing bikinis

bilateral *adj* affecting or undertaken by two parties; mutual

bilberry *n, pl* **-ries** a blue or blackish edible berry that grows on a shrub **WORD ORIGIN** probably Scandinavian

bilby *n, pl* **-bies** an Australian marsupial with long pointed ears and grey fur

bile *n* **1** a greenish fluid secreted by the liver to aid digestion of fats **2** irritability or peevishness **WORD ORIGIN** Latin *bilis*

bilge *n* **1** *informal* nonsense **2** *naut* the bottom of a ship's hull **3** the dirty water that collects in a ship's bilge **WORD ORIGIN** probably variant of *bulge*

Words from Literature
part 3

battalia *n* the order of battle
    till I saw part of his army in battalia
    Gulliver's Travels Jonathan Swift

battery *n* a battery is a fort or a place where guns are positioned
    You bring the lot to me, at that old Battery over yonder
    Great Expectations Charles Dickens

battledore and shuttlecock *n* the game battledore and shuttlecock was an early version of the game now known as badminton. The aim of the early game was simply to keep the shuttlecock from hitting the ground.
    Battledore and shuttlecock's a wery good game when you an't the shuttlecock and two lawyers the battledores, in which case it gets too excitin' to be pleasant
    Pickwick Papers Charles Dickens

beadle *n* a beadle was a local official who had power over the poor
    But these impertinences were speedily checked by the evidence of the surgeon, and the testimony of the beadle
    Oliver Twist Charles Dickens

bearings *pl n* the bearings of a place are the measurements or directions that are used to find or locate it
    the bearings of the island
    Treasure Island Robert Louis Stevenson

beaufet *n* a beaufet was a sideboard
    and sweet-cake from the beaufet
    Emma Jane Austen

beck *n* a beck is a small stream
    a beck which follows the bend of the glen
    Wuthering Heights Emily Brontë

bedight *v* to decorate
    and bedight with Christmas holly stuck into the top.
    A Christmas Carol Charles Dickens

Bedlam *n* Bedlam was a lunatic asylum in London which had statues carved by Caius Gabriel Cibber at its entrance
    Bedlam, and those carved maniacs at the gates
    The Prelude William Wordsworth

beeves *n* oxen or castrated bulls, which are animals used for pulling vehicles or carrying things
    to deliver in every morning six beeves
    Gulliver's Travels Jonathan Swift

begot *v* to create or cause
    Begot in thee
    On His Mistress John Donne

behoof *n* behoof means benefit
    "Yes, young man," said he, releasing the handle of the article in question, retiring a step or two from my table, and speaking for the behoof of the landlord and waiter at the door
    Great Expectations Charles Dickens

berth *n* a berth is a bed on a boat
    this is the berth for me
    Treasure Island Robert Louis Stevenson

bever *n* a snack, or small portion of food, eaten between main meals
    that buys me thirty meals a day and ten bevers
    Doctor Faustus 2.1 Christopher Marlowe

bilge water *n* the bilge is the widest part of a ship's bottom, and the bilge water is the dirty water that collects there
    no gush of bilge-water had turned it to fetid puddle
    Jane Eyre Charlotte Brontë

bill *n* an old term meaning a prescription. A prescription is the piece of paper on which your doctor writes an order for medicine and which you give to a chemist to get the medicine
    Are not thy bills hung up as monuments
    Doctor Faustus 1.1 Christopher Marlowe

b

bilharzia (bill-**hart**-see-a) *n* a disease caused by infestation of the body with blood flukes
WORD ORIGIN after T. *Bilharz*, who discovered the blood fluke

biliary *adj* of bile, the ducts that convey bile, or the gall bladder

bilingual *adj* 1 able to speak two languages 2 expressed in two languages **bilingualism** *n*

bilious *adj* 1 nauseous; sick: *a bilious attack* 2 *informal* bad-tempered; irritable: *the regime's most persistent and bilious critic* 3 (of a colour) harsh and offensive
WORD ORIGIN Latin *biliosus* full of bile

bilk *vb* to cheat or deceive, esp. to avoid making payment to **bilker** *n*
WORD ORIGIN perhaps variant of *balk*

bill¹ *n* 1 a statement of money owed for goods or services supplied 2 a draft of a proposed new law presented to a law-making body 3 a printed notice or advertisement 4 *US & Canad* a piece of paper money; note 5 any list of items, events, etc. such as a theatre programme ▷ *vb* 6 to send or present an account for payment to (a person) 7 to advertise by posters 8 to schedule as a future programme: *next week they will discuss what are billed as new ideas for economic reform* 9 **fit** or **fill the bill** *informal* to be suitable or adequate
WORD ORIGIN Late Latin *bulla* document

bill² *n* 1 the projecting jaws of a bird; beak ▷ *vb* 2 **bill and coo** (of lovers) to kiss and whisper amorously
WORD ORIGIN Old English *bile*

billabong *n* *Austral* a pool in the bed of a stream with an interrupted water flow
WORD ORIGIN Aboriginal

billboard *n* a hoarding

billet¹ *vb* **-leting, -leted** 1 to assign a lodging to (a soldier) ▷ *n* 2 accommodation, esp. for a soldier, in civilian lodgings 3 *Austral & NZ* a person who is billeted
WORD ORIGIN Old French *billette*, from *bulle* a document

billet² *n* 1 a chunk of wood, esp. for fuel 2 a small bar of iron or steel
WORD ORIGIN Old French *billette* a little log

billet-doux (bill-ee-**doo**) *n, pl* **billets-doux** (bill-ee-**dooz**) *old-fashioned or jocular* a love letter
WORD ORIGIN French: a sweet letter

billhook *n* a tool with a hooked blade, used for chopping, etc.

billiards *n* a game in which a long cue is used to propel balls on a table
WORD ORIGIN Old French *billard* curved stick

billion *n, pl* **-lions** or **-lion** 1 one thousand million: 1 000 000 000 or 10⁹ 2 (in Britain, originally) one million million: 1 000 000 000 000 or 10¹² 3 (often pl) *informal* an extremely large but unspecified number: *billions of dollars* **billionth** *adj, n*
WORD ORIGIN French

billionaire *n* a person who has money or property worth at least a billion pounds, dollars, etc.

bill of exchange *n* a document instructing a third party to pay a stated sum at a designated date or on demand

bill of fare *n* a menu

bill of health *n* 1 a certificate that confirms the health of a ship's company 2 **clean bill of health** *informal* **a** a good report of one's physical condition **b** a favourable account of a person's or a company's financial position

bill of lading *n* a document containing full particulars of goods shipped

billow *n* 1 a large sea wave 2 a swelling or surging mass, as of smoke or sound ▷ *vb* 3 to rise up or swell out **billowing** *adj, n* **billowy** *adj*
WORD ORIGIN Old Norse *bylgja*

billy or **billycan** *n, pl* **-lies** or **-lycans** a metal can or pot for boiling water, etc. over a campfire
WORD ORIGIN Scots *billypot*

billy goat *n* a male goat

biltong *n* *S African* strips of meat dried and cured in the sun
WORD ORIGIN Afrikaans

bimbo *n, pl* **-bos** *slang* an attractive but empty-headed young woman
WORD ORIGIN Italian: little child

bimetallic *adj* consisting of two metals

bimetallism *n* the use of two metals, esp. gold and silver, in fixed relative values as the standard of value and currency **bimetallist** *n*

bin *n* 1 a container for rubbish, etc. 2 a large container for storing something in bulk, such as coal, grain, or bottled wine ▷ *vb* **binning, binned** 3 to put in a rubbish bin: *I bin my junk mail without reading it*
WORD ORIGIN Old English *binne* basket

binary (**bine**-a-ree) *adj* 1 composed of two parts 2 *maths, computers* of or expressed in a system with two as its base 3 *chem* containing atoms of two different elements ▷ *n, pl* **-ries** 4 something composed of two parts
WORD ORIGIN Late Latin *binarius*

binary star *n* a system of two stars revolving around a common centre of gravity

bind *vb* **binding, bound** 1 to make secure, such as with a rope 2 to unite with emotional ties or commitment 3 to place (someone) under legal or moral obligation 4 to place under certain constraints: *bound by the rules* 5 to stick together or cause to stick: *egg binds fat and flour* 6 to enclose and fasten (the pages of a book) between covers 7 to provide (a garment) with an edging 8 (foll. by *up*) to bandage ▷ *n* 9 *informal* a difficult or annoying situation
WORD ORIGIN Old English *bindan*

binder *n* 1 a firm cover for holding loose sheets of paper together 2 a person who binds books 3 something used to fasten or tie, such as rope or twine 4 *obsolete* a machine for cutting and binding grain into sheaves

bindery *n, pl* **-eries** a place in which books are bound

binding *n* 1 anything that binds or fastens 2 the covering of a book ▷ *adj* 3 imposing an obligation or duty

bind over *vb* to place (a person) under a legal obligation, esp. to keep the peace

bindweed *n* a plant that twines around a support

binge *n* *informal* 1 a bout of excessive eating or drinking 2 excessive indulgence in anything
WORD ORIGIN probably dialect: to soak

binge drinking *n* the practice of drinking excessive amounts of alcohol regularly

bingo *n* a gambling game in which numbers called out are covered by players on their individual cards. The first to cover a given arrangement is the winner
WORD ORIGIN origin unknown

binnacle *n* a housing for a ship's compass
WORD ORIGIN Late Latin *habitaculum* dwelling-place

binocular *adj* involving or intended for both eyes: *binocular vision*
WORD ORIGIN BI- + Latin *oculus* eye

binoculars *pl n* an optical instrument for use with both eyes, consisting of two small telescopes joined together

binomial *n* 1 a mathematical expression consisting of two terms, such as 3x + 2y ▷ *adj* 2 referring to two names or terms
WORD ORIGIN BI- + Latin *nomen* name

binomial theorem *n* a general mathematical formula that expresses any power of a binomial without multiplying out, as in $(a+b)^2 = a^2 + 2ab + b^2$

bio- *combining form* 1 indicating life or living organisms: *biogenesis* 2 indicating a human life or career: *biography*
WORD ORIGIN Greek *bios* life

bioastronautics *n* the study of the effects of space flight on living organisms

biochemistry *n* the study of the chemical compounds, reactions, etc. occurring in living organisms **biochemical** *adj* **biochemist** *n*

biocide *n* a substance used to destroy living things
WORD ORIGIN BIO- + Latin *caedere* to kill

biocoenosis or *US* **biocenosis** (bye-oh-see-**no**-siss) *n* the relationships between animals and plants subsisting together
WORD ORIGIN BIO- + Greek *koinōsis* sharing

biodegradable *adj* (of sewage and packaging) capable of being decomposed by natural means **biodegradability** *n*

biodiesel *n* a biofuel intended for use in diesel engines

biodiversity *n* the existence of a wide variety of plant and animal species in their natural environments

bioengineering *n* the design and manufacture of aids, such as artificial limbs, to help people with disabilities

biofuel *n* fuel derived from renewable biological resources

biogas *n* gaseous fuel produced by the fermentation of organic waste

biogenesis *n* the principle that a living organism must originate from a similar parent organism

biogenic (bye-oh-**jen**-ik) *adj* originating from a living organism

biography *n, pl* **-phies 1** an account of a person's life by another person **2** such accounts collectively **biographer** *n* **biographical** *adj*
WORD ORIGIN BIO- + Greek *graphein* to write

biol. 1 biological **2** biology

biological *adj* **1** of or relating to biology **2** (of a detergent) containing enzymes that remove natural stains, such as blood or grass **biologically** *adv*

biological clock *n* an inherent timing mechanism that controls the rhythmic repetition of processes in living organisms, such as sleeping

biological control *n* the control of destructive organisms, esp. insects, by nonchemical means, such as introducing a natural predator of the pest

biological warfare *n* the use of living organisms or their toxic products to induce death or incapacity in humans

biology *n* the study of living organisms **biologist** *n*

biomass *n* the total number of living organisms in a given area

biomechanics *n* the study of the mechanics of the movement of living organisms

biomedicine *n* **1** the medical and biological study of the effects of unusual environmental stress **2** the study of herbal remedies

biometric *adj* relating to the analysis of biological data using mathematical and statistical methods, especially for purposes of identification: *biometric passport*

biometry *or* **biometrics** *n* the analysis of biological data using mathematical and statistical methods, especially for purposes of identification

bionic *adj* **1** of or relating to bionics **2** (in science fiction) having physical functions augmented by electronic equipment
WORD ORIGIN BIO- + *(electro)nic*

bionics *n* **1** the study of biological functions in order to develop electronic equipment that operates similarly **2** the replacement of limbs or body parts by artificial electronically powered parts

biophysics *n* the physics of biological processes and the application of methods used in physics to biology **biophysical** *adj* **biophysicist** *n*

biopic (**bye**-oh-pick) *n informal* a film based on the life of a famous person
WORD ORIGIN bio(graphical) + pic(ture)

biopsy *n, pl* **-sies** examination of tissue from a living body to determine the cause or extent of a disease
WORD ORIGIN BIO- + Greek *opsis* sight

biorhythm *n* a complex recurring pattern of physiological states, believed to affect physical, emotional, and mental states

bioscope *n* **1** a kind of early film projector **2** *S African* a cinema

biosphere *n* the part of the earth's surface and atmosphere inhabited by living things

biosynthesis *n* the formation of complex compounds by living organisms **biosynthetic** *adj*

biotech *n* short for **biotechnology**

biotechnology *n* the use of microorganisms, such as cells or bacteria, in industry and technology

bioterrorism *n* the use of viruses, bacteria, etc. by terrorists **bioterrorist** *n*

biotin *n* a vitamin of the B complex, abundant in egg yolk and liver
WORD ORIGIN Greek *biotē* life

bipartisan *adj* consisting of or supported by two political parties

bipartite *adj* **1** consisting of or having two parts **2** affecting or made by two parties: *a bipartite agreement*

biped (**bye**-ped) *n* **1** any animal with two feet ▷ *adj also* **bipedal 2** having two feet
WORD ORIGIN BI- + Latin *pes* foot

biplane *n* an aeroplane with two sets of wings, one above the other

bipolar *adj* **1** having two poles **2** having two extremes **bipolarity** *n*

birch *n* **1** a tree with thin peeling bark and hard close-grained wood **2** the birch a bundle of birch twigs or a birch rod used, esp. formerly, for flogging offenders ▷ *vb* **3** to flog with the birch
WORD ORIGIN Old English *bierce*

bird *n* **1** a two-legged creature with feathers and wings, which lays eggs and can usually fly ▶ Related adjective: **avian 2** *slang chiefly Brit* a girl or young woman **3** *informal* a person: *he's a rare bird* **4** a bird in the hand something definite or certain **5** birds of a feather people with the same ideas or interests **6** kill two birds with one stone to accomplish two things with one action
WORD ORIGIN Old English *bridd*

bird flu *n* a form of influenza occurring in poultry caused by a virus capable of spreading to humans

birdie *n* **1** *informal* a bird **2** *golf* a score of one stroke under par for a hole

birdlime *n* a sticky substance smeared on twigs to catch small birds

bird of paradise *n* a songbird of New Guinea, the male of which has brilliantly coloured plumage

bird of prey *n* a bird, such as a hawk or owl, that hunts other animals for food

birdseed *n* a mixture of various kinds of seeds for feeding cage birds

bird's-eye view *n* **1** a view seen from above **2** a general or overall impression of something

bird-watcher *n* a person who studies wild birds in their natural surroundings

biretta *n* *RC Church* a stiff square clerical cap
WORD ORIGIN Italian *berretta*

Biro *n, pl* **-ros** *trademark* a kind of ballpoint pen

birth *n* **1** the process of bearing young; childbirth **2** the act of being born **3** the beginning of something; origin **4** ancestry: *of noble birth* **5** give birth to **a** to bear (offspring) **b** to produce or originate (an idea, plan, etc.)
WORD ORIGIN Old Norse *byrth*

birth certificate *n* an official form stating the time and place of a person's birth

birth control *n* limitation of childbearing by means of contraception

birthday *n* **1** an anniversary of the day of one's birth **2** the day on which a person was born

birthmark *n* a blemish on the skin formed before birth

birth mother *n* the woman who gives birth to a child, regardless of whether she is the genetic mother or subsequently brings up the child

birthplace *n* the place where someone was born or where something originated

birth rate *n* the ratio of live births to population, usually expressed per 1000 population per year

birthright *n* privileges or possessions that a person has or is believed to be entitled to as soon as he or she is born

biscuit *n* **1** a small flat dry sweet or plain cake **2** porcelain that has been fired but not glazed ▷ *adj* **3** pale brown or yellowish-grey
WORD ORIGIN Old French *(pain) biscuit* twice-cooked (bread)

bisect *vb* **1** *maths* to divide into two equal parts **2** to cut or split into two **bisection** *n*
WORD ORIGIN BI- + Latin *secare* to cut

bisexual *adj* **1** sexually attracted to both men and women **2** showing characteristics of both sexes ▷ *n* **3** a bisexual person **bisexuality** *n*

bishop *n* **1** a clergyman having spiritual and administrative powers over a diocese **2** a chessman capable of moving diagonally
WORD ORIGIN Greek *episkopos* overseer

bishopric *n* the see, diocese, or office of a bishop

bismuth *n* *chem* a brittle pinkish-white metallic element. Some compounds are used in alloys and in medicine. Symbol: Bi
WORD ORIGIN German *Wismut*

bison *n, pl* **-son** an animal of the cattle family with a massive head, shaggy forequarters, and a humped back
WORD ORIGIN Germanic

bisque[1] *n* a thick rich soup made from shellfish
WORD ORIGIN French

bisque[2] *adj* **1** pink-to-yellowish-tan ▷ *n* **2** *ceramics* same as **biscuit** (sense 2)
WORD ORIGIN shortened from *biscuit*

bistable *adj* (of an electronic system) having two stable states

bistro *n, pl* **-tros** a small restaurant
WORD ORIGIN French

bit[1] *n* **1** a small piece, portion, or quantity **2** a short time or distance **3** a bit rather; somewhat: *a bit stupid* **4** a bit of rather: *a bit of a fool* **5** bit by bit gradually **6** do one's bit to make one's expected contribution
WORD ORIGIN Old English *bite* action of biting

bit[2] *n* **1** a metal mouthpiece on a bridle for controlling a horse **2** a cutting or drilling tool, part, or head in a brace, drill, etc.
WORD ORIGIN Old English *bita*

b

bit³ *vb* the past tense of **bite**

bit⁴ *n maths, computers* **1** a single digit of binary notation, represented either by 0 or by 1 **2** the smallest unit of information, indicating the presence or absence of a single feature **WORD ORIGIN** *b(inary + dig)it*

bitch *n* **1** a female dog, fox, or wolf **2** *slang, offensive* a malicious or spiteful woman **3** *informal* a difficult situation or problem ▷ *vb* **4** *informal* to complain; grumble **WORD ORIGIN** Old English *bicce*

bitchy *adj* **bitchier, bitchiest** *informal* spiteful or malicious **bitchiness** *n*

bite *vb* **biting, bit, bitten 1** to grip, cut off, or tear with the teeth or jaws **2** (of animals or insects) to injure by puncturing (the skin) with the teeth or fangs **3** (of corrosive material) to eat away or into **4** to smart or cause to smart; sting **5** *angling* (of a fish) to take the bait or lure **6** to take firm hold of or act effectively upon: *turn the screw till it bites the wood* **7** *slang* to annoy or worry: *what's biting her?* ▷ *n* **8** the act of biting **9** a thing or amount bitten off **10** a wound or sting inflicted by biting **11** *angling* an attempt by a fish to take the bait or lure **12** a snack **13** a stinging or smarting sensation **biter** *n* **WORD ORIGIN** Old English *bītan*

biting *adj* **1** piercing; keen: *a biting wind* **2** sarcastic; incisive

bitmap *n computers* a picture created by colour or shading on a visual display unit

bit part *n* a very small acting role with few lines to speak

bitstream *n computers* a sequence of digital data transmitted electronically

bitten *vb* the past participle of **bite**

bitter *adj* **1** having an unpalatable harsh taste, as the peel of an orange **2** showing or caused by hostility or resentment **3** difficult to accept: *a bitter blow* **4** sarcastic: *bitter words* **5** bitingly cold: *a bitter night* ▷ *n* **6** Brit beer with a slightly bitter taste **bitterly** *adv* **bitterness** *n* **WORD ORIGIN** Old English *biter*

bittern *n* a large wading marsh bird with a booming call **WORD ORIGIN** Old French *butor*

bitters *pl n* bitter-tasting spirits flavoured with plant extracts

bittersweet *adj* **1** tasting of or being a mixture of bitterness and sweetness **2** pleasant but tinged with sadness

bitty *adj* **-tier, -tiest** lacking unity; disjointed **bittiness** *n*

bitumen *n* a sticky or solid substance that occurs naturally in asphalt and tar and is used in road surfacing **bituminous** *adj* **WORD ORIGIN** Latin

bituminous coal *n* a soft black coal that burns with a smoky yellow flame

bivalve *n* **1** a sea creature, such as an oyster or mussel, that has a shell consisting of two hinged valves and breathes through gills ▷ *adj* **2** of these molluscs

bivouac *n* **1** a temporary camp, as used by soldiers or mountaineers ▷ *vb* **-acking, -acked 2** to make a temporary camp **WORD ORIGIN** French

biz *n informal* business

bizarre *adj* odd or unusual, esp. in an interesting or amusing way **WORD ORIGIN** Italian *bizzarro* capricious

Bk *chem* berkelium

BL 1 *chiefly Brit* Bachelor of Law **2** Bachelor of Letters **3** Barrister-at-Law

blab *vb* **blabbing, blabbed** to divulge (secrets) indiscreetly **WORD ORIGIN** Germanic

blabber *n* **1** a person who blabs ▷ *vb* **2** to talk without thinking **WORD ORIGIN** Middle English *blabberen*

black *adj* **1** having no hue, owing to the absorption of all or almost all light; of the colour of coal **2** without light **3** without hope; gloomy: *the future looked black* **4** dirty or soiled **5** angry or resentful: *black looks* **6** unpleasant in a cynical or macabre manner: *black comedy* **7** (of coffee or tea) without milk or cream **8** wicked or harmful: *a black lie* ▷ *n* **9** the darkest colour; the colour of coal **10** a dye or pigment producing this colour **11** black clothing, worn esp. in mourning: *she was in black, as though in mourning* **12** complete darkness: *the black of the night* **13** in the black in credit or without debt ▷ *vb* **14** same as **blacken 15** to polish (shoes or boots) with blacking **16** *Brit, Austral, & NZ* (of trade unionists) to organize a boycott of (specified goods, work, etc.) ▶ See also **blackout** ▷ **blackness** *n* **blackish** *adj* **WORD ORIGIN** Old English *blæc*

Black *n* **1** a member of a dark-skinned race ▷ *adj* **2** of or relating to a Black person or Black people

black-and-blue *adj* (of the skin) bruised, as from a beating

black-and-white *n* **1** a photograph, film, etc. in black, white, and shades of grey, rather than in colour **2** in black and white **a** in print or writing **b** in extremes: *he always sees things in black and white*

black-backed gull *n* a large common black-and-white European gull

blackball¹ *vb* **1** to vote against **2** to exclude (someone) from a group, etc. **WORD ORIGIN** from *black ball*, used formerly to veto

blackball² *n NZ* a hard boiled sweet with black-and-white stripes

black bear *n* **1** a bear inhabiting forests of North America **2** a bear of central and E Asia

black belt *n judo, karate, etc.* **a** a black belt that signifies that the wearer has reached a high standard in martial art **b** a person entitled to wear this

blackberry *n, pl* **-ries** a small blackish edible fruit that grows on a woody bush with thorny stems. Also called: **bramble**

BlackBerry *n trademark* a hand-held device for sending and receiving e-mail

blackbird *n* a common European thrush, the male of which has black plumage and a yellow bill

blackboard *n* a hard or rigid surface made of a smooth usually dark substance, used for writing or drawing on with chalk, esp. in teaching

black box *n informal* a flight recorder

blackcap *n* a brownish-grey warbler, the male of which has a black crown

blackcock *n* the male of the black grouse

Black Country *n* **the Black Country** the formerly heavily industrialized West Midlands of England

blackcurrant *n* a very small blackish edible fruit that grows in bunches on a bush

blackdamp *n* air that is low in oxygen content and high in carbon dioxide as a result of an explosion in a mine

Black Death *n* **the Black Death** a form of bubonic plague in Europe and Asia during the 14th century

black economy *n Brit, Austral, & NZ* that portion of the income of a nation that remains illegally undeclared

blacken *vb* **1** to make or become black or dirty **2** to damage (someone's reputation); discredit: *they planned to blacken my father's name*

black eye *n* bruising round the eye

Black Friar *n* a Dominican friar

blackguard (**blag**-gard) *n* an unprincipled contemptible person **WORD ORIGIN** originally, lowest group at court

blackhead *n* **1** a black-tipped plug of fatty matter clogging a pore of the skin **2** a bird with black plumage on the head

black hole *n astron* a hypothetical region of space resulting from the collapse of a star and surrounded by a gravitational field from which neither matter nor radiation can escape

black ice *n* a thin transparent layer of new ice on a road

blacking *n* any preparation for giving a black finish to shoes, metals, etc.

blackjack¹ *n* pontoon or a similar card game **WORD ORIGIN** *black + jack* (the knave)

blackjack² *n chiefly US & Canad* a truncheon of leather-covered lead with a flexible shaft **WORD ORIGIN** *black + jack* (implement)

black lead *n* same as **graphite**

blackleg *n Brit* **1** a person who continues to work or does another's job during a strike ▷ *vb* **-legging, -legged 2** to refuse to join a strike

blacklist *n* **1** a list of people or organizations considered untrustworthy or disloyal ▷ *vb* **2** to put (someone) on a blacklist

black magic *n* magic used for evil purposes

blackmail *n* **1** the act of attempting to obtain money by threatening to reveal shameful information **2** the use of unfair pressure in an attempt to influence someone ▷ *vb* **3** to obtain or attempt to obtain money by intimidation **4** to attempt to influence (a person) by unfair pressure **blackmailer** *n* **WORD ORIGIN** *black +* Old English *māl* terms

Mavis Gallant

Born in Montreal to English parents, Mavis Gallant attended many schools, the first one all-French. She lost her father while young and, after work as a newspaper journalist and a brief marriage, went to Europe in 1950 and settled in Paris. All these dislocations anticipated those of her characters in many stories. They may be Canadian, British, French, Spanish, or German; often they are tourists, expatriates, refugees, or exiles; they may live in or visit Montreal, Paris, Berlin, Madrid, Geneva, or the Riviera; often they have troubled relationships with spouses or parents.

Gallant obsessively made up stories as a child, and as an adult wrote them for years, piling them up in a picnic hamper, before she attempted to get them published. As she says in the Preface to the massive *Selected Stories of Mavis Gallant* (1996), 'The fear that I inherited a flawed legacy, a vocation without the competence to sustain it, haunted me from early youth.' When she did attempt to get published, her work was quickly accepted by the *New Yorker:* all but one of the *Selected Stories* first appeared in it. She returned to her journalistic roots with the essays and reviews in *Paris Notebooks* (1986), including a sardonic chronology of the unofficial strikes and chaotic demonstrations that paralyzed Paris in May 1968, and a brilliantly insightful account of the sensational case of Gabrielle Russier, a French schoolteacher who became romantically involved with a teenage student. Although possessing a deep knowledge of French society denied to most expatriates, Gallant retained a sense of the individual's essential strangeness.

The stories, sometimes novella-length and structured in sections, occasionally linked in a series, are told in a detached voice in which much is concealed beneath the surface; her objective, pellucid style never calls attention to itself or gets in the way of narrative. An independent, self-determined woman, Gallant never dwells on her own struggles, even in works that have autobiographical correlatives like the novel *A Fairly Good Time* (1970) and the collection *Home Truths* (1981). The recipient of many awards and honorary doctorates, she remained anchored in Paris, except for a year as a Writer-in-Residence at the University of Toronto.

Paris Notebooks contains wonderful zingers. The nineteenth-century Baron de Mareste 'was witty, clever, worldly, cultivated, erudite, elegant, and intelligent – in short, an obsolescent species of Parisian.' Jean Giraudoux 'was on strained terms with his wife – she was a quarrelsome pessimist, as women are apt to become when married to philandering optimists.' The stories' openings are no less ironic, and instantly put the reader in the picture. 'The End of the World' begins, 'I never like to leave Canada, because I'm disappointed every time. I've felt disappointed about places I haven't even seen.' 'In the Tunnel' starts, 'Sarah's father was a born widower.' The title story of *From the Fifteenth District* (1979) commences, 'Although an epidemic of haunting, widely reported, spread through the Fifteenth District of our city last summer, only three acceptable complaints were lodged with the police.' Violent events are related flatly. In 'Speck's Idea' a Parisian art dealer's first gallery 'was blown up by Basque separatists, who had mistaken it for a travel agency exploiting the beauty of their coast.'

Gallant's endings are no less accomplished. 'Varieties of Exile', (which could have been the title of *Selected Stories*), ends, 'All this business of putting life through a sieve and then discarding it was another variety of exile; I knew that even then, but it seemed quite right and perfectly natural.' At the end of 'The Chosen Husband', Gallant writes, 'She and Marie were Montreal girls, not trained to accompany heroes, or to hold out for dreams, but just to be patient.' In 'Rue de Lille', Juliette 'was knitting squares of wool to be sewn together to make a blanket; there was always, somewhere, a flood or an earthquake or a flow of refugees, and those who outlasted jeopardy had to be covered.'

In *Paris Notebooks*, writing of the Belgian-born writer Marguerite Yourcenar, Gallant notes, 'Writers who choose domicile in a foreign place, for whatever reason, usually treat their native language as a delicate timepiece, making certain it runs exactly and that no dust gets inside.' She could be speaking of herself.

b

Black Maria (mar-**rye**-a) *n* a police van for transporting prisoners

black mark *n* a discredit noted against someone

black market *n* a place or a system for buying or selling goods or currencies illegally, esp. in violation of controls or rationing **black marketeer** *n*

black mass *n* a blasphemous travesty of the Christian Mass, used in black magic

blackout *n* **1** (in wartime) the putting out or hiding of all lights as a precaution against a night air attack **2** a momentary loss of consciousness, vision, or memory **3** a temporary electrical power failure **4** the prevention of information broadcasts: *a news blackout* ▷ *vb* **black out 5** to put out (lights) **6** to lose vision, consciousness, or memory temporarily **7** to stop (news, a television programme, etc.) from being broadcast

black pepper *n* a dark-coloured hot seasoning made from the dried berries and husks of the pepper plant

Black Power *n* a movement of Black people to obtain equality with Whites

black pudding *n* Brit a black sausage made from pig's blood, suet, etc.

Black Rod *n* (in Britain) the chief usher of the House of Lords and of the Order of the Garter

black sheep *n* a person who is regarded as a disgrace or failure by his or her family or peer group

Blackshirt *n* a member of the Italian Fascist party before and during the Second World War

blacksmith *n* a person who works iron with a furnace, anvil, and hammer

black spot *n* **1** a place on a road where accidents frequently occur **2** an area where a particular situation is exceptionally bad: *an unemployment black spot*

blackthorn *n* a thorny shrub with black twigs, white flowers, and small sour plumlike fruits

black tie *n* **1** a black bow tie worn with a dinner jacket ▷ *adj* **black-tie 2** denoting an occasion when a dinner jacket should be worn

Black Watch *n* **the Black Watch** the Royal Highland Regiment in the British Army

black widow *n* an American spider, the female of which is highly venomous and commonly eats its mate

bladder *n* **1** anat a membranous sac, usually containing liquid, esp. the urinary bladder **2** a hollow bag made of leather, etc. which becomes round when filled with air or liquid **3** a hollow saclike part in certain plants, such as seaweed **bladdery** *adj*
WORD ORIGIN Old English *blǣdre*

blade *n* **1** the part of a sharp weapon, tool, or knife, that forms the cutting edge **2** the thin flattish part of a propeller, oar, or fan **3** the flattened part of a leaf, sepal, or petal **4** the long narrow leaf of a grass or related plant
WORD ORIGIN Old English *blæd*

blag *vb* **blagging, blagged** Brit slang **1** to obtain by wheedling or cadging **2** to steal or rob

WORD ORIGIN origin unknown

blain *n* a blister, blotch, or sore on the skin
WORD ORIGIN Old English *blegen*

blame *vb* **blaming, blamed 1** to consider (someone) responsible for: *I blame her for the failure* **2** (foll. by on) to put responsibility for (something) on (someone): *she blames the failure on me* **3** **be to blame** to be at fault ▷ *n* **4** responsibility for something that is wrong: *they must take the blame for the failure* **5** an expression of condemnation: *analysts lay the blame on party activists* **blamable** or **blameable** *adj* **blameless** *adj*
WORD ORIGIN Late Latin *blasphemare* to blaspheme

blameworthy *adj* deserving blame **blameworthiness** *n*

blanch *vb* **1** to whiten **2** to become pale, as with sickness or fear **3** to prepare meat or vegetables by plunging them in boiling water **4** to cause (celery, chicory, etc.) to grow white from lack of light
WORD ORIGIN Old French *blanc* white

blancmange (blam-**monzh**) *n* a jelly-like dessert of milk, stiffened usually with cornflour
WORD ORIGIN Old French *blanc manger* white food

bland *adj* **1** dull and uninteresting: *the bland predictability of the film* **2** (of food, drink, etc.) flavourless **3** smooth in manner: *he looked at his visitor with a bland smile* **blandly** *adv*
WORD ORIGIN Latin *blandus* flattering

blandish *vb* to persuade by mild flattery; coax
WORD ORIGIN Latin *blandiri*

blandishments *pl n* flattery intended to coax or cajole

blank *adj* **1** (of a writing surface) not written on **2** (of a form, etc.) with spaces left for details to be filled in **3** without ornament or break: *a blank wall* **4** empty or void: *a blank space* **5** showing no interest or expression: *a blank look* **6** lacking ideas or inspiration: *his mind went blank* ▷ *n* **7** an empty space **8** an empty space for writing in **9** the condition of not understanding: *my mind went a complete blank* **10** a mark, often a dash, in place of a word **11** same as **blank cartridge 12 draw a blank** to get no results from something ▷ *vb* **13** (foll. by out) to cross out, blot, or obscure **14 blank something out** to refuse to think about something; to clear something from one's mind **15** slang to ignore: *the crowd blanked her for the first four numbers* **blankly** *adv*
WORD ORIGIN Old French *blanc* white

blank cartridge *n* a cartridge containing powder but no bullet

blank cheque *n* **1** a signed cheque on which the amount payable has not been specified **2** complete freedom of action

blanket *n* **1** a large piece of thick cloth for use as a bed covering **2** a concealing cover, as of smoke, leaves, or snow ▷ *adj* **3** applying to or covering a wide group or variety of people, conditions, situations, etc.: *a blanket ban on all supporters travelling to away matches* ▷ *vb* **-keting, -keted 4** to cover as if with

a blanket **5** to cover a wide area; give blanket coverage to
WORD ORIGIN Old French *blancquete*

blanket stitch *n* a strong reinforcing stitch for the edges of blankets

blank verse *n* unrhymed verse

blare *vb* **blaring, blared 1** to sound loudly and harshly **2** to proclaim loudly: *the newspaper headlines blared the news* ▷ *n* **3** a loud harsh noise
WORD ORIGIN Middle Dutch *bleren*

blarney *n* flattering talk
WORD ORIGIN after the *Blarney* Stone in SW Ireland, said to endow whoever kisses it with skill in flattery

blasé (blah-**zay**) *adj* indifferent or bored, esp. through familiarity
WORD ORIGIN French

blaspheme *vb* **-pheming, -phemed 1** to speak disrespectfully of (God or sacred things) **2** to utter curses **blasphemer** *n*
WORD ORIGIN Greek *blasphēmos* evil-speaking

blasphemy *n, pl* **-mies** behaviour or language that shows disrespect for God or sacred things **blasphemous** *adj*

blast *n* **1** an explosion, such as that caused by dynamite **2** the charge used in a single explosion **3** a sudden strong gust of wind or air **4** a sudden loud sound, such as that made by a trumpet **5** a violent verbal outburst, esp. critical **6** slang a very enjoyable or thrilling experience: *the party was a blast* **7 at full blast** at maximum speed, volume, etc. ▷ *interj* **8** slang an exclamation of annoyance ▷ *vb* **9** to blow up (a rock, tunnel, etc.) with explosives **10** to make or cause to make a loud harsh noise **11** to criticize severely
WORD ORIGIN Old English *blǣst*

blasted *adj, adv* slang extreme or extremely: *a blasted idiot*

blast furnace *n* a furnace for smelting using a blast of preheated air

blastoff *n* **1** the launching of a rocket under its own power ▷ *vb* **blast off 2** (of a rocket) to be launched

blatant (**blay**-tant) *adj* **1** glaringly obvious: *a blatant lie* **2** offensively noticeable: *their blatant disregard for my feelings* **blatantly** *adv*
WORD ORIGIN coined by Edmund Spenser, poet

blather *vb, n* same as **blether**

blaze[1] *n* **1** a strong fire or flame **2** a very bright light or glare **3** an outburst (of passion, patriotism, etc.) ▷ *vb* **blazing, blazed 4** to burn fiercely **5** to shine brightly **6** to become stirred, as with anger or excitement **7 blaze away** to shoot continuously ▶ See also **blazes**
WORD ORIGIN Old English *blæse*

blaze[2] *n* **1** a mark, usually indicating a path, made on a tree **2** a light-coloured marking on the face of an animal ▷ *vb* **blazing, blazed 3** to mark (a tree, path, etc.) with a blaze **4 blaze a trail** to explore new territories, areas of knowledge, etc.
WORD ORIGIN probably from Middle Low German *bles* white marking

blaze[3] *vb* **blazing, blazed** ● **blaze something abroad** to make something widely known

blazer *n* a fairly lightweight jacket, often in the colours of a sports club, school, etc.

blazes *pl n slang, euphemistic* hell

blazon *vb* **1** to proclaim publicly: *the newspaper photographs were blazoned on the front pages* **2** *heraldry* to describe or colour (heraldic arms) conventionally ▷ *n* **3** *heraldry* a coat of arms
WORD ORIGIN Old French *blason* coat of arms

bleach *vb* **1** to make or become white or colourless by exposure to sunlight, or by the action of chemical agents ▷ *n* **2** a bleaching agent
WORD ORIGIN Old English *blǣcan*

bleaching powder *n* a white powder consisting of chlorinated calcium hydroxide

bleak *adj* **1** exposed and barren **2** cold and raw **3** offering little hope; dismal: *a bleak future* **bleakly** *adv* **bleakness** *n*
WORD ORIGIN Old English *blāc* pale

bleary *adj* **blearier, bleariest 1** with eyes dimmed, by tears or tiredness: *a few bleary hacks* **2** indistinct or unclear **blearily** *adv*

bleary-eyed *or* **blear-eyed** *adj* with eyes blurred, such as with old age or after waking

bleat *vb* **1** (of a sheep, goat, or calf) to utter its plaintive cry **2** to whine ▷ *n* **3** the characteristic cry of sheep, goats, and calves **4** a weak complaint or whine
WORD ORIGIN Old English *blǣtan*

bleed *vb* **bleeding, bled 1** to lose or emit blood **2** to remove or draw blood from (a person or animal) **3** (of plants) to exude (sap or resin), esp. from a cut **4** *informal* to obtain money, etc. from (someone), esp. by extortion **5** to draw liquid or gas from (a container or enclosed system) **6 my heart bleeds for you** I am sorry for you: often used ironically
WORD ORIGIN Old English *blēdan*

bleeding *adj, adv Brit slang* extreme or extremely: *a bleeding fool*

bleep *n* **1** a short high-pitched signal made by an electrical device **2** same as **bleeper** ▷ *vb* **3** to make a bleeping signal **4** to call (someone) by means of a bleeper
WORD ORIGIN imitative

bleeper *n* a small portable radio receiver that makes a bleeping signal

blemish *n* **1** a defect; flaw; stain ▷ *vb* **2** to spoil or tarnish
WORD ORIGIN Old French *blemir* to make pale

blench *vb* to shy away, as in fear
WORD ORIGIN Old English *blencan* to deceive

blend *vb* **1** to mix or mingle (components) **2** to mix (different varieties of tea, whisky, etc.) **3** to look good together; harmonize **4** (esp. of colours) to shade gradually into each other ▷ *n* **5** a mixture produced by blending
WORD ORIGIN Old English *blandan*

blende *n* a mineral consisting mainly of zinc sulphide: the chief source of zinc

blender *n* an electrical kitchen appliance for pureeing vegetables, etc.

blenny *n, pl* **-nies** a small fish of coastal waters with a tapering scaleless body and long fins
WORD ORIGIN Greek *blennos* slime

bless *vb* **blessing, blessed** *or* **blest 1** to make holy by means of a religious rite **2** to give honour or glory to (a person or thing) as holy **3** to call upon God to protect **4** to worship or adore (God) **5 be blessed with** to be endowed with: *she is blessed with immense energy* **6 bless me!** an exclamation of surprise **7 bless you!** said to a person who has just sneezed
WORD ORIGIN Old English *blǣdsian* to sprinkle with sacrificial blood

blessed *adj* **1** made holy **2** *RC Church* (of a person) beatified by the pope **3** bringing great happiness or good fortune: *he was blessed with good looks* **4** *euphemistic* damned: *I'm blessed if I know*

blessing *n* **1** the act of invoking divine protection or aid **2** approval; good wishes **3** a happy event

blest *vb* a past of **bless**

blether *Scot vb* **1** to speak foolishly at length ▷ *n* **2** foolish talk **3** a person who blethers
WORD ORIGIN Old Norse *blathr* nonsense

blew *vb* the past tense of **blow**

blight *n* **1** a person or thing that spoils or prevents growth **2** any plant disease characterized by withering and shrivelling without rotting **3** a fungus or insect that causes blight in plants **4** an ugly urban district ▷ *vb* **5** to cause to suffer a blight **6** to frustrate or disappoint: *blighted love* **7** to destroy: *the event blighted her life*
WORD ORIGIN origin unknown

blighter *n Brit, Austral, & NZ informal* a despicable or irritating person or thing

Blighty *n Brit, Austral, & NZ slang* **1** (used especially by troops serving abroad) Britain; home **2** *pl* **Blighties** (esp. in the First World War) a wound that causes the recipient to be sent home to Britain
WORD ORIGIN Hindi *bilāyatī* foreign land

blimey *interj Brit & NZ slang* an exclamation of surprise or annoyance
WORD ORIGIN short for *gorblimey* God blind me

blimp¹ *n* **1** a small nonrigid airship **2** *films* a soundproof cover fixed over a camera during shooting
WORD ORIGIN probably from *(type)* B-limp

blimp² *n chiefly Brit* a person who is stupidly complacent and reactionary. Also called: **Colonel Blimp**
WORD ORIGIN a cartoon character

blind *adj* **1** unable to see **2** unable or unwilling to understand: *she is blind to his faults* **3** not determined by reason: *blind hatred* **4** acting or performed without control or preparation **5** done without being able to see, relying on instruments for information **6** hidden from sight: *a blind corner* **7** closed at one end: *a blind alley* **8** completely lacking awareness or consciousness: *a blind stupor* **9** having no openings: *a blind wall* ▷ *adv* **10** without being able to see ahead or using only instruments: *flying blind* **11** without adequate information: *we* bought the house blind **12 blind drunk** *informal* very drunk ▷ *vb* **13** to deprive of sight permanently or temporarily **14** to deprive of good sense, reason, or judgment **15** to darken; conceal **16** to overwhelm by showing detailed knowledge: *he tried to blind us with science* ▷ *n* **17** a shade for a window **18** any obstruction or hindrance to sight, light, or air **19** a person, action, or thing that serves to deceive or conceal the truth **blinding** *adj* **blindly** *adv* **blindness** *n*
WORD ORIGIN Old English

‖ **USAGE**
‖ See at **disabled**.

blind alley *n* **1** an alley open at one end only **2** *informal* a situation in which no further progress can be made

blind date *n informal* a prearranged social meeting between two people who have not met before

blindfold *vb* **1** to prevent (a person or animal) from seeing by covering the eyes ▷ *n* **2** a piece of cloth used to cover the eyes ▷ *adj, adv* **3** having the eyes covered with a cloth
WORD ORIGIN Old English *blindfellian* to strike blind

blind man's buff *n* a game in which a blindfolded person tries to catch and identify the other players
WORD ORIGIN obsolete *buff* a blow

blind spot *n* **1** a small oval-shaped area of the retina which is unable to see **2** a place where vision is obscured **3** a subject about which a person is ignorant or prejudiced

blindworm *n* same as **slowworm**

bling *adj slang* **1** flashy, ostentatious, glitzy, etc. ▷ *n* **2** ostentatious jewellery

blink *vb* **1** to close and immediately reopen (the eyes), usually involuntarily **2** to shine intermittently or unsteadily ▷ *n* **3** the act or an instance of blinking **4** a glance; glimpse **5 on the blink** *slang* not working properly
WORD ORIGIN variant of BLENCH

blinker *vb* **1** to provide (a horse) with blinkers **2** to obscure or be obscured with or as with blinkers

blinkered *adj* **1** considering only a narrow point of view **2** (of a horse) wearing blinkers

blinkers *pl n Austral & Brit* leather side pieces attached to a horse's bridle to prevent sideways vision

blinking *adj, adv informal* extreme or extremely: *a blinking idiot*

blip *n* **1** a repetitive sound, such as the kind produced by an electronic device **2** the spot of light on a radar screen indicating the position of an object **3** a temporary irregularity in the performance of something
WORD ORIGIN imitative

bliss *n* **1** perfect happiness; serene joy **2** the joy of heaven **blissful** *adj* **blissfully** *adv*
WORD ORIGIN Old English *blīths*

B list *n* **1** a category slightly below the most socially desirable ▷ *adj* **B-list 2** of the category slightly below the most socially desirable: *B-list celebrities*

blister *n* **1** a small bubble on the skin filled with a watery fluid **2** a swelling

b

containing air or liquid, such as on a painted surface ▷ *vb* **3** to have or cause to have blisters **4** to attack verbally with great scorn **blistering** *adj*
WORD ORIGIN Old French *blestre*

blithe *adj* **1** heedless; casual and indifferent **2** very happy or cheerful **blithely** *adv*
WORD ORIGIN Old English *blīthe*

blithering *adj informal* stupid; foolish: *you blithering idiot*
WORD ORIGIN variant of *blethering*

BLitt Bachelor of Letters
WORD ORIGIN Latin *Baccalaureus Litterarum*

blitz *n* **1** a violent and sustained attack by enemy aircraft **2** any intensive attack or concerted effort ▷ *vb* **3** to attack suddenly and intensively
WORD ORIGIN see BLITZKRIEG

Blitz *n* **the Blitz** the systematic bombing of Britain in 1940–41 by the German Air Force

blitzkrieg *n* a swift intensive military attack designed to defeat the opposition quickly
WORD ORIGIN German: lightning war

blizzard *n* a blinding storm of wind and snow
WORD ORIGIN origin unknown

bloat *vb* **1** to cause to swell, as with a liquid or air **2** to cause to be puffed up, as with conceit **3** to cure (fish, esp. herring) by half drying in smoke **bloated** *adj*
WORD ORIGIN Old Norse *blautr* soaked

bloater *n Brit* a herring that has been salted in brine, smoked, and cured

blob *n* **1** a soft mass or drop **2** a spot of colour, ink, etc. **3** an indistinct or shapeless form or object
WORD ORIGIN imitative

bloc *n* a group of people or countries combined by a common interest
WORD ORIGIN French

block *n* **1** a large solid piece of wood, stone, etc. **2** such a piece on which particular tasks may be done, as chopping, cutting, etc. **3** a large building of offices, flats, etc. **4** a group of buildings in a city bounded by intersecting streets on each side **5** an obstruction or hindrance: *a writer with a block* **6** one of a set of wooden or plastic cubes as a child's toy **7** *slang* a person's head **8** a piece of wood, metal, etc. engraved for printing **9** a casing housing one or more freely rotating pulleys. See also **block and tackle 10** a quantity considered as a single unit ▷ *vb* **11** to obstruct or impede by introducing an obstacle: *lorry drivers had blocked the routes to Paris* **12** to impede, retard, or prevent (an action or procedure) **13** to stamp (a title or design) on (a book cover, etc.) **14** *cricket* to play (a ball) defensively
▶ See also **block out** ▷ **blockage** *n*
WORD ORIGIN Dutch *blok*

blockade *n* **1** *mil* the closing off of a port or region to prevent the passage of goods ▷ *vb* **-ading, -aded 2** to impose a blockade on

block and tackle *n* a hoisting device in which a rope or chain is passed around a pair of blocks containing one or more pulleys

blockboard *n* a type of plywood consisting of strips of wood sandwiched between layers of veneer

blockbuster *n informal* **1** a film, novel, etc. that has been or is expected to be highly successful **2** a large bomb used to demolish extensive areas

blockhead *n* a stupid person **blockheaded** *adj*

blockie *n Austral* an owner of a small property, esp. a farm

block letter *n* a plain capital letter. Also called: **block capital**

block out *vb* **1** to plan or describe (something) in a general fashion **2** to prevent the entry or consideration of (something)

blog *n informal* a journal written on-line and accessible to users of the internet. Full name: **weblog** ▷ **blogger** *n* **blogging** *n*

blogosphere *n informal* a collective term for the weblogs on the internet

bloke *n Brit, Austral, & NZ informal* a man **blokeish** or **blokey** *adj*
WORD ORIGIN Shelta

blonde or *masc* **blond** *adj* **1** (of hair) fair **2** (of a person) having fair hair and a light complexion ▷ *n* **3** a person having light-coloured hair and skin **blondeness** or *masc* **blondness** *n*
WORD ORIGIN Old French

blood *n* **1** a reddish fluid in vertebrates that is pumped by the heart through the arteries and veins ▶ Related adjective: **haemal 2** bloodshed, esp. when resulting in murder: *they were responsible for the spilling of blood throughout the country* **3** lifeblood **4** relationship through being of the same family, race, or kind; kinship **5** the blood royal or noble descent: *a prince of the blood* **6** flesh and blood **a** near kindred or kinship, esp. that between a parent and child **b** human nature: *it's more than flesh and blood can stand* **7** in one's blood as a natural or inherited characteristic or talent **8** newcomers viewed as an invigorating force: *new blood* **9** in cold blood showing no passion; ruthlessly **10** make one's blood boil to cause to be angry or indignant **11** make one's blood run cold to fill with horror ▷ *vb* **12** *hunting* to cause (young hounds) to taste the blood of a freshly killed quarry **13** to initiate (a person) to war or hunting
WORD ORIGIN Old English *blōd*

blood-and-thunder *adj* denoting melodramatic behaviour

blood bank *n* a place where blood is stored until required for transfusion

blood bath *n* a massacre

blood brother *n* a man or boy who has sworn to treat another as his brother, often in a ceremony in which their blood is mingled

blood count *n* determination of the number of red and white blood corpuscles in a specific sample of blood

blood-curdling or **bloodcurdling** *adj* terrifying

blood donor *n* a person who gives blood to be used for transfusion

blood group *n* any one of the various groups into which human blood is classified

blood heat *n* the normal temperature of the human body, 98.4°F or 37°C

bloodhound *n* a large hound, formerly used in tracking and police work

bloodless *adj* **1** without blood: *bloodless surgery* **2** conducted without violence: *a bloodless coup* **3** anaemic-looking; pale **4** lacking vitality; lifeless: *the bloodless ambience of supermarkets*

blood-letting *n* **1** bloodshed, esp. in a feud **2** the former medical practice of removing blood

bloodlust *n* a desire for violence and carnage

blood money *n* **1** money obtained by ruthlessly sacrificing others **2** money paid to a hired murderer **3** compensation paid to the relatives of a murdered person

blood orange *n* a variety of orange, the pulp of which is dark red when ripe

blood poisoning *n* same as **septicaemia**

blood pressure *n* the pressure exerted by the blood on the inner walls of the blood vessels

blood relation or **relative** *n* a person related by birth

bloodshed *n* slaughter; killing

bloodshot *adj* (of an eye) inflamed

blood sport *n* any sport involving the killing of an animal

bloodstained *adj* discoloured with blood

bloodstock *n* thoroughbred horses

bloodstream *n* the flow of blood through the vessels of a living body

bloodsucker *n* **1** an animal that sucks blood, esp. a leech **2** *informal* a person who preys upon another person, esp. by extorting money

bloodthirsty *adj* **-thirstier, -thirstiest** taking pleasure in bloodshed or violence

blood vessel *n* a tube through which blood travels in the body

bloody *adj* **bloodier, bloodiest 1** covered with blood **2** marked by much killing and bloodshed: *a bloody war* **3** cruel or murderous: *a bloody tyrant* ▷ *adj, adv* **4** *slang* extreme or extremely: *a bloody fool; a bloody good idea* ▷ *vb* **bloodies, bloodying, bloodied 5** to stain with blood

Bloody Caesar *n* a drink consisting of vodka, juice made from clams and tomatoes, Worcester sauce and Tabasco

Bloody Mary *n* a drink consisting of tomato juice and vodka

bloody-minded *adj Brit & NZ informal* deliberately obstructive and unhelpful

bloom *n* **1** a blossom on a flowering plant **2** the state or period when flowers open **3** a healthy or flourishing condition; prime **4** a youthful or healthy glow **5** a fine whitish coating on the surface of fruits or leaves ▷ *vb* **6** (of flowers) to open **7** to bear flowers **8** to flourish or grow **9** to be in a healthy, glowing condition
WORD ORIGIN Germanic

bloomer *n Brit informal* a stupid mistake; blunder
WORD ORIGIN from BLOOMING

Word Histories
part 3

Brandy is short for 'brandywine', which comes from Dutch *brandewijn* meaning 'burnt wine' or 'distilled wine'.

Brass monkey: A popular explanation for the phrase 'cold enough to freeze the balls off a brass monkey' unfolds a story of surprising delicacy: naval cannonballs were stacked on a brass triangle known as a 'monkey'. Freezing temperatures would cause the brass to contract at a different rate from the iron cannonballs, causing the balls to roll off. Sadly, this picturesque story is untrue – earlier versions of the phrase use 'freeze the tail off a brass monkey', so the allusion is simply to metal objects becoming cold and brittle – or perhaps even to temperatures so cold that even metal animals would suffer frostbite in their vulnerable extremities.

Bric-a-brac: This word came into English from French. The French word itself comes from an obsolete phrase *à bric et à brac* meaning 'at random'.

Bridegroom: A bridegroom, obviously, has nothing to do with horses. This example of folk etymology occurred in the 16th century when the last element of the Old English term *brideguma* – 'bride-man', or 'suitor' – was changed to 'groom', meaning 'lad' or 'boy', which had not yet acquired an equine association.

Buck: Urban folklore maintains that 'buck', in the sense of a US dollar, is a racist term denoting the value for which male slaves were traded. This is untrue, however; the 'bucks' that were used as currency in early America were buckskins, which trappers valued at a dollar each in trade.

Bungalow comes from Hindi *banglā* meaning 'of Bengal'. A bungalow was originally a house of the style generally occupied by Europeans in Bengal, a one-storey house with a verandah round it and a thatched roof.

Cabal: A popular explanation of the origin of 'cabal' is that the word is an acronym of the names of five of Charles II's ministers who were heavily involved in political intrigue in 1673: Clifford, Arlington, Buckingham, Ashley, and Lauderdale. This attractive story inverts the actual order of events, however. 'Cabal', derived ultimately from Hebrew, and related to the mystical offshoot of Judaism, *kabbala*, was already in use in English, though not very common. The fact that the names of the plotting ministers happened to fit as an acrostic of 'cabal' is a happy coincidence for the 17th-century wit who made the link. This highlights an interesting linguistic point: while acronyms – deriving words from a set of initials – are virtually unknown before the 20th century, acrostics – fitting the initials of a set of words to an existing word – have been around for centuries.

Calculate comes from the Latin word *calculare* meaning 'to count using small stones', from *calculus*, meaning a 'stone' or 'pebble'. The Romans used pebbles to count with.

Calendar: This word comes from medieval Latin *kalendārium*, meaning 'account book'. The word 'kalendarium' itself comes from Latin *kalendae*, the 'calends', the first day of the month in the Roman calendar and the day on which interest on debts was due.

Candidate: *Candidatus* in Latin means 'white-robed'. In ancient Rome, candidates for public office wore white togas.

The word **cardinal** comes from Latin *cardo*, meaning 'hinge'. When something is important, other things can be said to hinge on it.

Catacombs: *Catacumbas* was the name given to the underground cemetery built below the Basilica of St Sebastian near Rome. In the course of time, the name was applied to similar cemeteries elsewhere.

Catamaran: A catamaran was originally a type of raft found in India, made by tying three logs together. The word 'catamaran' comes from Tamil *kattumaram*, which means 'tied logs'.

bloomers pl n **1** informal women's baggy knickers **2** (formerly) loose trousers gathered at the knee, worn by women **WORD ORIGIN** after Mrs A. Bloomer, social reformer

blooming adv, adj Brit informal extreme or extremely: blooming painful **WORD ORIGIN** euphemistic for bloody

blossom n **1** the flower or flowers of a plant, esp. producing edible fruit **2** the period of flowering ▷ vb **3** (of plants) to flower **4** to come to a promising stage **WORD ORIGIN** Old English blōstm

blot n **1** a stain or spot, esp. of ink **2** something that spoils **3** a stain on one's character ▷ vb **blotting, blotted 4** to stain or spot **5** to cause a blemish in or on: he blotted his copybook by missing a penalty **6** to soak up (excess ink, etc.) by using blotting paper **7** blot out **a** to darken or hide completely: the mist blotted out the sea **b** to block from one's mind: to blot out the memories **WORD ORIGIN** Germanic

blotch n **1** an irregular spot or discoloration ▷ vb **2** to become or cause to become marked by such discoloration **blotchy** adj **WORD ORIGIN** probably from botch, influenced by blot

blotter n a sheet of blotting paper

blotting paper n a soft absorbent paper, used for soaking up surplus ink

blotto adj Brit, Austral, & NZ slang extremely drunk **WORD ORIGIN** from blot (verb)

blouse n **1** a woman's shirtlike garment **2** a waist-length belted jacket worn by soldiers ▷ vb **blousing, bloused 3** to hang or cause to hang in full loose folds **WORD ORIGIN** French

blouson (**blew**-zon) n a short loose jacket with a tight-fitting waist **WORD ORIGIN** French

blow¹ vb **blowing, blew, blown 1** (of a current of air, the wind, etc.) to be or cause to be in motion **2** to move or be carried by or as if by wind **3** to expel (air, etc.) through the mouth or nose **4** to breathe hard; pant **5** to inflate with air or the breath **6** (of wind, etc.) to make a roaring sound **7** to cause (a musical instrument) to sound by forcing air into it **8** (often foll. by up, down, or in, etc.) to explode, break, or disintegrate completely **9** electronics (of a fuse or valve) to burn out because of excessive current **10** to shape (glass, etc.) by forcing air or gas through the material when molten **11** slang to spend (money) freely **12** slang to use (an opportunity) ineffectively **13** slang to expose or betray (a secret) **14** past participle **blowed** informal same as **damn 15** blow hot and cold informal to keep changing one's attitude towards someone or something **16** blow one's top informal to lose one's temper ▷ n **17** the act or an instance of blowing **18** the sound produced by blowing **19** a blast of air or wind **20** Brit slang cannabis ▶ See also **blow away, blow out,** etc. **WORD ORIGIN** Old English blāwan

blow² n **1** a powerful or heavy stroke with the fist, a weapon, etc. **2** a sudden setback: the scheme was dealt a blow by the introduction of martial law **3** an attacking action: a blow for freedom **4** come to blows **a** to fight **b** to result in a fight **WORD ORIGIN** probably Germanic

blow away vb slang **1** to kill by shooting **2** to defeat utterly

blow-by-blow adj explained in great detail: a blow-by-blow account

blow-dry vb **-dries, -drying, -dried 1** to style (the hair) while drying it with a hand-held hair dryer ▷ n **2** this method of styling hair

blower n **1** a mechanical device, such as a fan, that blows **2** informal a telephone

blowfly n, pl **-flies** a fly that lays its eggs in meat

blowhole n **1** the nostril of a whale **2** a hole in ice through which seals, etc. breathe **3** a vent for air or gas **4** geol a hole in a cliff top leading to a sea cave

blowie n Austral informal a bluebottle

blown vb a past participle of **blow**

blow out vb **1** (of a flame) to extinguish or be extinguished **2** (of a tyre) to puncture suddenly **3** (of an oil or gas well) to lose oil or gas in an uncontrolled manner ▷ n **blowout 4** a sudden burst in a tyre **5** the uncontrolled escape of oil or gas from a well **6** slang a large filling meal

blow over vb **1** to be forgotten **2** to cease or be finished: the crisis blew over

blowpipe n **1** a long tube from which poisoned darts, etc. are shot by blowing **2** a tube for blowing air into a flame to intensify its heat **3** an iron pipe used to blow glass into shape

blowsy adj **blowsier, blowsiest 1** (of a woman) slovenly or sluttish **2** (of a woman) ruddy in complexion **WORD ORIGIN** dialect blowze beggar girl

blowtorch or **blowlamp** n a small burner that produces a very hot flame, used to remove old paint, soften metal, etc.

blow up vb **1** to explode or cause to explode **2** to inflate with air **3** to increase the importance of (something): an affair blown up out of all proportions **4** informal to lose one's temper **5** informal to reprimand (someone) **6** informal to enlarge (a photograph) **7** to come into existence with sudden force: a crisis had blown up ▷ n **blow-up 8** informal an enlarged photograph

blowy adj **blowier, blowiest** windy

blubber n **1** the fatty tissue of aquatic mammals such as the whale **2** informal flabby body fat ▷ vb **3** to sob without restraint **WORD ORIGIN** probably imitative

bludge Austral & NZ informal vb **bludging, bludged 1** (foll. by on) to scrounge from **2** to evade work ▷ n **3** a very easy task

bludgeon n **1** a stout heavy club, typically thicker at one end ▷ vb **2** to hit as if with a bludgeon **3** to force; bully; coerce **WORD ORIGIN** origin unknown

blue n **1** the colour of a clear unclouded sky **2** anything blue, such as blue clothing or blue paint: she is clothed in blue **3** a sportsman who represents or has represented Oxford or Cambridge University **4** Brit informal a Tory **5** Austral & NZ slang an argument or fight **6** Also: **bluey** Austral & NZ slang a court summons **7** Austral & NZ informal a mistake **8** out of the blue unexpectedly ▷ adj **bluer, bluest 9** of the colour blue; of the colour of a clear unclouded sky **10** (of the flesh) having a purple tinge from cold **11** depressed or unhappy **12** pornographic: blue movies ▷ vb **blueing** or **bluing, blued 13** to make or become blue or bluer **14** old-fashioned, informal to spend extravagantly or wastefully: I consoled myself by blueing my royalty cheque ▶ See also **blues** > **blueness** n **WORD ORIGIN** Old French bleu

blue baby n a baby born with a bluish tinge to the skin because of lack of oxygen in the blood

bluebell n a woodland plant with blue bell-shaped flowers

blueberry n, pl **-ries** a very small blackish edible fruit that grows on a North American shrub

bluebird n a North American songbird with a blue plumage

blue blood n royal or aristocratic descent

bluebook n **1** (in Britain) a government publication, usually the report of a commission **2** (in Canada) an annual statement of government accounts

bluebottle n **1** a large fly with a dark-blue body; blowfly **2** Austral & NZ informal a Portuguese man-of-war

blue cheese n cheese containing a blue mould, such as Stilton or Danish blue

blue chip n **1** finance a stock considered reliable ▷ adj **blue-chip 2** denoting something considered to be a valuable asset

blue-collar adj denoting manual industrial workers

blue-eyed boy n informal a favourite

blue funk n slang a state of great terror

blue heeler n Austral & NZ informal a dog that controls cattle by biting their heels

bluenose n US slang a puritanical or prudish person **2** Also: **bluenoser** (sometimes cap) Canad informal a native or inhabitant of Nova Scotia

blue pencil n **1** deletion or alteration of the contents of a book or other work ▷ vb **blue-pencil, -cilling, -cilled** or US **-ciling, -ciled 2** to alter or delete parts of (a book, film, etc.)

blue peter n a signal flag of blue with a white square at the centre, displayed by a vessel about to leave port

blueprint n **1** an original description of a plan or idea that explains how it is expected to work **2** a photographic print of plans, technical drawings, etc. consisting of white lines on a blue background

blue ribbon n **1** a badge awarded as the first prize in a competition **2** (in Britain) a badge of blue silk worn by members of the Order of the Garter

blues pl n the blues **1** a feeling of depression or deep unhappiness **2** a type of folk song originating among Black Americans

blue-screen adj relating to a film technique in which actors are filmed against a blue screen so that special effects can be added later

blue-sky *adj* of research done for theoretical reasons rather than for practical application

bluestocking *n usually disparaging* a scholarly or intellectual woman **WORD ORIGIN** from the blue worsted stockings worn by members of an 18th-century literary society

bluetit *n* a small European bird with a blue crown, wings, and tail and yellow underparts

bluetongue *n* an Australian lizard with a blue tongue

Bluetooth *n trademark* a short-range radio technology that allows wireless communication between computers, mobile phones, etc.

blue whale *n* a very large bluish-grey whale: the largest mammal

bluff¹ *vb* 1 to pretend to be confident in order to influence (someone) ▷ *n* 2 deliberate deception to create the impression of a strong position 3 **call someone's bluff** to challenge someone to give proof of his or her claims **WORD ORIGIN** Dutch *bluffen* to boast

bluff² *n* 1 a steep promontory, bank, or cliff 2 *Canad* a clump of trees on the prairie; copse ▷ *adj* 3 good-naturedly frank and hearty **WORD ORIGIN** probably from Middle Dutch *blaf* broad

bluish *or* **blueish** *adj* slightly blue

blunder *n* 1 a stupid or clumsy mistake ▷ *vb* 2 to make stupid or clumsy mistakes 3 to act clumsily; stumble **blundering** *n, adj* **WORD ORIGIN** Scandinavian

blunderbuss *n* an obsolete gun with wide barrel and flared muzzle **WORD ORIGIN** Dutch *donderbus* thunder gun

blunt *adj* 1 (esp. of a knife) lacking sharpness 2 not having a sharp edge or point: *a blunt instrument* 3 (of people, manner of speaking, etc.) straightforward and uncomplicated ▷ *vb* 4 to make less sharp 5 to diminish the sensitivity or perception of: *prison life has blunted his mind* **bluntly** *adv* **WORD ORIGIN** Scandinavian

blur *vb* blurring, blurred 1 to make or become vague or less distinct 2 to smear or smudge 3 to make (the judgment, memory, or perception) less clear; dim ▷ *n* 4 something vague, hazy, or indistinct 5 a smear or smudge **blurred** *adj* **blurry** *adj* **WORD ORIGIN** perhaps variant of *blear*

blurb *n* a promotional description, such as on the jackets of books **WORD ORIGIN** coined by G. Burgess, humorist & illustrator

blurt *vb* (foll. by *out*) to utter suddenly and involuntarily **WORD ORIGIN** probably imitative

blush *vb* 1 to become suddenly red in the face, esp. from embarrassment or shame ▷ *n* 2 a sudden reddening of the face, esp. from embarrassment or shame 3 a rosy glow 4 same as **rosé** **WORD ORIGIN** Old English *blȳscan*

blusher *n* a cosmetic applied to the cheeks to give a rosy colour

bluster *vb* 1 to speak loudly or in a bullying way 2 (of the wind) to be gusty ▷ *n* 3 empty threats or protests **blustery** *adj* **WORD ORIGIN** probably from Middle Low German *blüsteren* to blow violently

BM 1 Bachelor of Medicine 2 British Museum

BMA British Medical Association

BMI *n* body mass index: an index used to indicate whether or not a person is a healthy weight for his or her height

B-movie *n* a film originally made as a supporting film, now considered a genre in its own right

BMR basal metabolic rate

BMus Bachelor of Music

BMX *n* 1 bicycle motocross: stunt riding over an obstacle course on a bicycle 2 a bicycle designed for bicycle motocross

BO 1 *informal* body odour 2 box office

boa *n* 1 a large nonvenomous snake of Central and South America that kills its prey by constriction 2 a woman's long thin scarf of feathers or fur **WORD ORIGIN** Latin

boab (**boh**-ab) *n Austral informal* short for **baobab**

boa constrictor *n* a very large snake of tropical America and the West Indies that kills its prey by constriction

boar *n* 1 an uncastrated male pig 2 a wild pig **WORD ORIGIN** Old English *bār*

board *n* 1 a long wide flat piece of sawn timber 2 a smaller flat piece of rigid material for a specific purpose: *ironing board* 3 **a** a group of people who officially administer a company, trust, etc. **b** any other official group, such as examiners or interviewers 4 a person's meals, provided regularly for money 5 stiff cardboard or similar material, used for the outside covers of a book 6 a flat thin rectangular sheet of composite material, such as chipboard 7 *naut* the side of a ship 8 a portable surface for indoor games such as chess or backgammon 9 **go by the board** *informal* to be in disuse, neglected, or lost 10 **on board** on or in a ship, aeroplane, etc. ▷ *vb* 11 to go aboard (a train or other vehicle) 12 to attack (a ship) by forcing one's way aboard 13 (foll. by *up* or *in*, etc.) to cover with boards 14 to receive meals and lodging in return for money 15 **board out** to arrange for (someone, esp. a child) to receive food and lodging away from home 16 (in ice hockey and box lacrosse) to bodycheck an opponent against the boards ▶ See also **boards** **WORD ORIGIN** Old English *bord*

boarder *n Brit* a pupil who lives at school during term time

boarding *n* 1 the act of embarking on an aircraft, train, ship, etc. 2 a structure of boards 3 timber boards collectively 4 (in ice hockey and box lacrosse) an act of bodychecking an opponent against the boards

boarding house *n* a private house that provides accommodation and meals for paying guests

boarding school *n* a school providing living accommodation for pupils

boardroom *n* a room where the board of directors of a company meets

boards *pl n* 1 a wooden wall forming the enclosure in which ice hockey or box lacrosse is played 2 **the boards** the stage

boast *vb* 1 to speak in excessively proud terms of one's possessions, talents, etc. 2 to possess (something to be proud of): *a team which boasts five current world record holders* ▷ *n* 3 a bragging statement 4 something that is bragged about: *this proved to be a false boast* **WORD ORIGIN** origin unknown

boastful *adj* tending to boast

boat *n* 1 a small vessel propelled by oars, paddle, sails, or motor 2 *informal* a ship 3 see **gravy boat, sauce boat** 4 **in the same boat** sharing the same problems 5 **miss the boat** to lose an opportunity 6 **rock the boat** *informal* to cause a disturbance in the existing situation ▷ *vb* 7 to travel or go in a boat, esp. as recreation **WORD ORIGIN** Old English *bāt*

boater *n* a stiff straw hat with a straight brim and flat crown

boathouse *n* a shelter by the edge of a river, lake, etc. for housing boats

boating *n* rowing, sailing, or cruising in boats as a form of recreation

boatman *n, pl* -men a man who works on, hires out, or repairs boats

boatswain (**boh**-sn) *n naut* same as **bosun**

boat train *n* a train scheduled to take passengers to or from a particular ship

bob¹ *vb* bobbing, bobbed 1 to move or cause to move up and down repeatedly, such as while floating in water 2 to move or cause to move with a short abrupt movement, esp. of the head 3 **bob up** to appear or emerge suddenly ▷ *n* 4 a short abrupt movement, as of the head **WORD ORIGIN** origin unknown

bob² *n* 1 a hairstyle in which the hair is cut short evenly all round the head 2 a dangling weight on a pendulum or plumb line ▷ *vb* bobbing, bobbed 3 to cut (the hair) in a bob **WORD ORIGIN** Middle English *bobbe* bunch of flowers

bob³ *n, pl* bob *Brit, Austral, & NZ informal* (formerly) a shilling: *two bob* **WORD ORIGIN** origin unknown

bobbejaan *n S African* 1 a baboon 2 a large black spider 3 a monkey wrench **WORD ORIGIN** Afrikaans

bobbin *n* a reel on which thread or yarn is wound **WORD ORIGIN** Old French *bobine*

bobble *n* 1 a tufted ball, usually woollen, that is used for decoration ▷ *vb* -bling, -bled 2 (of a ball) to bounce erratically because of an uneven playing surface **WORD ORIGIN** from BOB¹

bobby *n, pl* -bies *Brit informal* a British policeman **WORD ORIGIN** after *Robert Peel*, who set up the Metropolitan Police Force

b

bobby pin *n US, Canad, Austral, & NZ* a metal hairpin

bobotie (ba-**boot**-ee) *n S African* a traditional Cape dish of curried minced meat
WORD ORIGIN probably from Malay

bobsleigh *n* **1** a sledge for racing down a steeply banked ice-covered run ▷ *vb* **2** to ride on a bobsleigh

bobtail *n* **1** a docked tail **2** an animal with such a tail ▷ *adj also* **bobtailed** **3** having the tail cut short

bocconcini (bok-on-**chee**-nee) *pl n* small bite-sized pieces of mozzarella cheese
WORD ORIGIN Italian

Boche (**bosh**) *n offensive slang* a German, esp. a German soldier
WORD ORIGIN French

bod *n informal* **1** a person: *he's a queer bod* **2** short for **body** (sense 1)
WORD ORIGIN short for *body*

bode[1] *vb* **boding, boded** to be an omen of (good or ill); portend
WORD ORIGIN Old English *bodian*

bode[2] *vb* a past tense of **bide**

bodega *n* a shop in a Spanish-speaking country that sells wine
WORD ORIGIN Spanish

bodge *vb* **bodging, bodged** *Brit, Austral, & NZ informal* to make a mess of; botch

bodice *n* **1** the upper part of a woman's dress, from the shoulder to the waist **2** a tight-fitting corset worn laced over a blouse, or (formerly) as a woman's undergarment
WORD ORIGIN originally Scots *bodies*, plural of *body*

bodily *adj* **1** relating to the human body ▷ *adv* **2** by taking hold of the body: *he threw him bodily from the platform* **3** in person; in the flesh

bodkin *n* a blunt large-eyed needle
WORD ORIGIN origin unknown

body *n, pl* **bodies 1** the entire physical structure of an animal or human ▸ Related adjective: **corporal 2** the trunk or torso **3** a corpse **4** a group regarded as a single entity: *a local voluntary body* **5** the main part of anything: *the body of a car* **6** a separate mass of water or land **7** the flesh as opposed to the spirit **8** fullness in the appearance of the hair **9** the characteristic full quality of certain wines **10** *informal* a person: *all the important bodies from the council were present* **11** a woman's one-piece undergarment **12 keep body and soul together** to manage to survive
WORD ORIGIN Old English *bodig*

bodyboard *n* a small polystyrene surfboard **bodyboarder** *n*

body building *n* regular exercising designed to enlarge the muscles

bodycheck *ice hockey, etc. n* **1** obstruction of another player ▷ *vb* **2** to deliver a bodycheck to (an opponent)

bodyguard *n* a person or group of people employed to protect someone

body language *n* the communication of one's thoughts or feelings by the position or movements of one's body rather than by words

body politic *n* **the body politic** the people of a nation or the nation itself considered as a political entity

body search *n* **1** a search by police, customs officials, etc. that involves examination of a prisoner's or suspect's bodily orifices ▷ *vb* **body-search 2** to search (a prisoner or suspect) in this manner

body shop *n* a repair yard for vehicle bodywork

body snatcher *n* (formerly) a person who robbed graves and sold the corpses for dissection

body stocking *n* **1** a one-piece undergarment for women, covering the torso **2** a tightly-fitting garment covering the whole of the body, worn esp. for dancing or exercising

body warmer *n* a sleeveless quilted jerkin, worn as an outer garment

bodywork *n* the external shell of a motor vehicle

Boer *n* a descendant of any of the Dutch or Huguenot colonists who settled in South Africa
WORD ORIGIN Dutch

boere- *combining form S African* rustic or country-style
WORD ORIGIN from Afrikaans *boer* a farmer

boeremeisie (**boor**-a-may-see) *n S African* a country girl of Afrikaans stock

boereseun (**boor**-a-see-oon) *n S African* a country boy of Afrikaans stock

boerewors (**boor**-a-vorss) *n S African* a traditional home-made farmer's sausage

boffin *n informal, old-fashioned* a scientist or expert
WORD ORIGIN origin unknown

bog *n* **1** a wet spongy area of land **2** *slang* a toilet **boggy** *adj* **bogginess** *n*
WORD ORIGIN Gaelic *bogach* swamp

bog down *vb* **bogging, bogged** to impede physically or mentally

bogey *or* **bogy** *n* **1** an evil or mischievous spirit **2** something that worries or annoys **3** *golf* a score of one stroke over par on a hole **4** *slang* a piece of dried mucus from the nose
WORD ORIGIN probably obsolete *bug* an evil spirit

bogeyman *n, pl* **-men** a frightening person, real or imaginary, used as a threat, esp. to children

boggle *vb* **-gling, -gled 1** to be surprised, confused, or alarmed: *the mind boggles at the idea* **2** to hesitate or be evasive when confronted with a problem
WORD ORIGIN probably Scots

bogie *or* **bogy** *n* an assembly of wheels forming a pivoted support at either end of a railway coach
WORD ORIGIN origin unknown

bogle (**boh**-gul) *n* a rhythmic dance performed to ragga music
WORD ORIGIN origin unknown

bog-standard *adj Brit & Irish slang* completely ordinary; run-of-the-mill

bogus (**boh**-guss) *adj* not genuine
WORD ORIGIN origin unknown

bogy *n, pl* **-gies** same as **bogey** or **bogie**

bohemian *n* **1** a person, esp. an artist or writer, who lives an unconventional life ▷ *adj* **2** unconventional in appearance, behaviour, etc. **bohemianism** *n*

bohrium *n chem* an element artificially produced in minute quantities. Symbol: Bh
WORD ORIGIN after N. *Bohr*, physicist

boil[1] *vb* **1** to change or cause to change from a liquid to a vapour so rapidly that bubbles of vapour are formed in the liquid **2** to reach or cause to reach boiling point **3** to cook or be cooked by the process of boiling **4** to bubble and be agitated like something boiling: *the sea was boiling* **5** to be extremely angry ▷ *n* **6** the state or action of boiling ▸ See also **boil away, boil down, boil over**
WORD ORIGIN Latin *bullire* to bubble

boil[2] *n* a red painful swelling with a hard pus-filled core caused by infection of the skin
WORD ORIGIN Old English *bȳle*

boil away *vb* to cause (liquid) to evaporate completely by boiling or (of liquid) to evaporate completely

boil down *vb* **1** to reduce or be reduced in quantity by boiling **2 boil down to** to be the essential element in

boiler *n* **1** a closed vessel in which water is heated to provide steam to drive machinery **2** a domestic device to provide hot water, esp. for central heating

boilermaker *n* a person who works with metal in heavy industry

boiler suit *n Brit* a one-piece overall

boiling point *n* **1** the temperature at which a liquid boils **2** *informal* the condition of being angered or highly excited

boil over *vb* **1** to overflow or cause to overflow while boiling **2** to burst out in anger or excitement

boisterous *adj* **1** noisy and lively; unruly **2** (of the sea, etc.) turbulent or stormy
WORD ORIGIN Middle English *boistuous*

bold *adj* **1** courageous, confident, and fearless **2** immodest or impudent: *she gave him a bold look* **3** *Irish* (of a child) naughty; badly behaved **4** standing out distinctly; conspicuous: *a figure carved in bold relief* **boldly** *adv* **boldness** *n*
WORD ORIGIN Old English *beald*

bole *n* the trunk of a tree
WORD ORIGIN Old Norse *bolr*

bolero *n, pl* **-ros 1** a Spanish dance, usually in triple time **2** music for this dance **3** a short open jacket not reaching the waist
WORD ORIGIN Spanish

boll *n* the rounded seed capsule of flax, cotton, etc.
WORD ORIGIN Dutch *bolle*

bollard *n* **1** *Austral & Brit* a small post marking a kerb or traffic island or barring cars from entering **2** a strong wooden or metal post on a wharf, quay, etc. used for securing mooring lines
WORD ORIGIN perhaps from *bole*

bollocks *or* **ballocks** *taboo slang pl n* **1** the testicles ▷ *n* **2** nonsense; rubbish ▷ *interj* **3** an exclamation of annoyance, disbelief, etc.
WORD ORIGIN Old English *beallucas*

English as a Lingua Franca

English is very often used in business meetings by people of different nationalities who have no other language in common. This is English used as a lingua franca. There's been an idea around for some time that this kind of English is actually morphing into something with its own grammar and vocabulary, a whole new variety of English.

There are already many varieties of English. US English is generally reckoned to be a different variety from UK English. We can tell whether somebody comes from Texas or from Newcastle from their accent and the words they use, and also from their grammar – for example, 'y'all' isn't common in Newcastle. But people in the UK have no trouble understanding US-made soaps, and TV has done a lot to bring these two varieties closer together. The Australian English of 'Neighbours' is also familiar to viewers in the UK.

If English as a lingua franca really is a separate variety, then what is it like? One point might be a tendency to drop the 'third-person' –s ending, so that business people may say things like 'she like, he buy'.

Another would be widespread use of 'false friends' like *actually* being used with their source language meanings rather than their standard English ones – *now*, in the case of *actually*. Yet another would be a reluctance to use idiomatic language like 'go in for' or 'bring something to the table'.

But all these are features of the English of learners. Proponents of ELF claim that there are more non-native speakers than native speakers using English. But it seems very unlikely that they are all using English in the same way. If any organization set out to draw up rules for ELF, it would only be able to identify a small set of common denominators.

One such attempt is Globish, which aims to promote a boiled-down, no-nonsense language for international business people to communicate in. It seems to assume that a lingua franca needs to be simple. But business is anything but simple. Terms like 'feasibility study' or 'cash-flow projection' crop up when people aren't otherwise using any English at all, because these terms are more familiar in English than in the language that's being used. Dictionaries of business English contain thousands of phrases that are almost exclusively used in a business context. Globish has a vocabulary of 1,500 words. It would tax a six-year old to say everything they wanted using only that number of words, let alone somebody discussing, say, whether or not to build a new airport.

English originated as a lingua franca. It developed as a tool to help the Norman French communicate with their Anglo-Saxon subjects, which is why it has parallel terms that other languages don't seem to need: the cooked meat/live animal distinction, pork/pig, beef/cow, etc, is pretty superfluous. And although it went through a process of rationalization in some respects (for example, you don't have to learn if it's *la chaise* or *le livre*, just that it's *the* chair, *the* book) it hasn't been *simple* at any stage in its existence. Languages are complex because the lives their speakers lead are complex.

If someone who speaks nothing but English tries to talk to a learner of English, even a proficient one, without making any allowances, then they make life very difficult for the learner. It isn't just the more colourful idioms like 'pull the other one' that aren't obvious. Much more difficult to understand are combinations of really common words like 'come up with, take it out on'. English gets a lot of mileage out of stringing one-syllable words together.

It pays to be aware of what the person you're talking to is likely to understand, and adjust accordingly. This is one major reason why the teaching of foreign languages is vital, to put English speakers on the receiving end so they understand the potential problems. It seems unlikely that Globish or English as a Lingua Franca will be taught in UK or US schools any time soon, so we have to hope that the teaching of French, German, Spanish, and Chinese will open students' eyes to other people's problems.

b

Bolshevik n **1** (formerly) a Russian Communist **2** any Communist **3** informal, offensive any political radical, esp. a revolutionary **Bolshevism** n **Bolshevist** adj, n
WORD ORIGIN Russian Bol'shevik majority

bolshie or **bolshy** Brit & NZ informal adj **1** difficult to manage; rebellious **2** politically radical or left-wing ▷ n, pl -shies **3** any political radical
WORD ORIGIN from BOLSHEVIK

bolster vb **1** to support or strengthen: the government were unwilling to bolster sterling ▷ n **2** a long narrow pillow **3** any pad or support
WORD ORIGIN Old English

bolt[1] n **1** a bar that can be slid into a socket to lock a door, gate, etc. **2** a metal rod or pin that has a head and a screw thread to take a nut **3** a flash (of lightning) **4** a sudden movement, esp. in order to escape **5** an arrow, esp. for a crossbow **6 a bolt from the blue** a sudden, unexpected, and usually unwelcome event **7 shoot one's bolt** to exhaust one's efforts ▷ vb **8** to run away suddenly **9** to secure or lock with or as if with a bolt **10** to attach firmly one thing to another by means of a nut and bolt **11** to eat hurriedly: bolting your food may lead to indigestion **12** (of a horse) to run away without control **13** (of vegetables) to produce flowers and seeds too soon ▷ adv **14 bolt upright** stiff and rigid
WORD ORIGIN Old English: arrow

bolt[2] or **boult** vb **1** to pass (flour, a powder, etc.) through a sieve **2** to examine and separate
WORD ORIGIN Old French bulter

bolt hole n a place of escape

bomb n **1** a hollow projectile containing explosive, incendiary, or other destructive substance **2** an object in which an explosive device has been planted: a car bomb **3** chiefly Brit slang a large sum of money: it cost a bomb **4** slang a disastrous failure: the new play was a total bomb **5 like a bomb** informal with great speed or success **6 the bomb** a hydrogen or an atom bomb considered as the ultimate destructive weapon ▷ vb **7** to attack with a bomb or bombs; drop bombs (on) **8** (foll. by along) informal to move or drive very quickly **9** slang to fail disastrously. See also **bomb out** > **bombing** n
WORD ORIGIN Greek bombos booming noise

bombard vb **1** to attack with concentrated artillery fire or bombs **2** to attack persistently **3** to attack verbally, esp. with questions **4** physics to direct high-energy particles or photons against (atoms, nuclei, etc.) **bombardment** n
WORD ORIGIN Old French bombarde stone-throwing cannon

bombardier n **1** Brit a noncommissioned rank in the Royal Artillery **2** US the member of a bomber aircrew responsible for releasing the bombs

Bombardier n Canad trademark a snow tractor, usually having caterpillar tracks at the rear and skis at the front

bombast n pompous and flowery language **bombastic** adj
WORD ORIGIN Medieval Latin bombax cotton

Bombay duck n a fish that is eaten dried with curry dishes as a savoury
WORD ORIGIN through association with Bombay (now Mumbai), port in India

bombazine n a twill fabric, usually of silk and worsted, formerly worn dyed black for mourning
WORD ORIGIN Latin bombyx silk

bomber n **1** a military aircraft designed to carry out bombing missions **2** a person who plants bombs

bomb out vb informal fail disastrously

bombshell n a shocking or unwelcome surprise

bona fide (bone-a **fide**-ee) adj **1** genuine: a bona fide manuscript **2** undertaken in good faith: a bona fide agreement
WORD ORIGIN Latin

bonanza n **1** sudden and unexpected luck or wealth **2** US & Canad a mine or vein rich in ore
WORD ORIGIN Spanish: calm sea, hence, good luck

bonbon n a sweet
WORD ORIGIN French

bond n **1** something that binds, fastens, or holds together **2** something that brings or holds people together; tie: a bond of friendship **3 bonds** something that restrains or imprisons **4** a written or spoken agreement, esp. a promise: a marriage bond **5** chem a means by which atoms are combined in a molecule **6** finance a certificate of debt issued in order to raise funds **7** S African the conditional pledging of property, esp. a house, as security for the repayment of a loan **8** law a written acknowledgment of an obligation to pay a sum or to perform a contract **9 in bond** commerce securely stored until duty is paid ▷ vb **10** to hold or be held together; bind **11** to form a friendship **12** to put or hold (goods) in bond
WORD ORIGIN Old Norse band

bondage n **1** a sexual practice in which one partner is tied or chained up **2** slavery **3** subjection to some influence or duty

bonded adj **1** finance consisting of, secured by, or operating under a bond or bonds **2** commerce in bond

bond paper n superior quality writing paper

bondservant n a serf or slave

bone n **1** any of the various structures that make up the skeleton in most vertebrates **2** the porous rigid tissue of which these parts are made **3** something consisting of bone or a bonelike substance **4 bones** the human skeleton **5** a thin strip of plastic, etc. used to stiffen corsets and brassieres **6 close to** or **near the bone** risqué or indecent **7 have a bone to pick** to have grounds for a quarrel **8 make no bones about a** to be direct and candid about **b** to have no scruples about **9 the bare bones** the essentials ▷ vb **boning, boned 10** to remove the bones from (meat for cooking, etc.) **11** to stiffen (a

corset, etc.) by inserting bones ▶ See also **bone up on** > **boneless** adj
WORD ORIGIN Old English bān

bone china n a type of fine porcelain containing powdered bone

bone-dry adj informal completely dry

bone-idle adj extremely lazy

bone meal n dried and ground animal bones, used as a fertilizer or in stock feeds

boneshaker n slang a decrepit or rickety vehicle

bone up on vb informal to study intensively

bonfire n a large outdoor fire
WORD ORIGIN Middle English bone-fire, from the use of bones as fuel

bongo n, pl -gos or -goes a small bucket-shaped drum, usually one of a pair, played by beating with the fingers
WORD ORIGIN American Spanish

bonhomie (bon-om-**mee**) n exuberant friendliness
WORD ORIGIN French

bonito (ba-**nee**-toh) n, pl -os **1** a small tunny-like marine food fish **2** a related fish, whose flesh is dried and flaked and used in Japanese cookery

bonk vb informal **1** to have sexual intercourse **2** to hit **bonking** n
WORD ORIGIN probably imitative

bonkers adj Brit, Austral, & NZ slang mad; crazy
WORD ORIGIN origin unknown

bon mot (bon **moh**) n, pl bons mots a clever and fitting remark
WORD ORIGIN French, literally: good word

bonnet n **1** the hinged metal cover over a motor vehicle's engine **2** any of various hats tied with ribbons under the chin **3** (in Scotland) a soft cloth cap
WORD ORIGIN Old French bonet

bonny adj -nier, -niest **1** Scot & N English dialect beautiful: a bonny lass **2** good or fine
WORD ORIGIN Latin bonus

bonsai n, pl -sai an ornamental tree or shrub grown in a small shallow pot in order to stunt its growth
WORD ORIGIN Japanese bon bowl + sai to plant

bonsela (bon-**sell**-a) n S African informal a small gift of money
WORD ORIGIN Zulu ibanselo gift

bonus n something given, paid, or received above what is due or expected
WORD ORIGIN Latin: good

bon voyage interj a phrase used to wish a traveller a pleasant journey
WORD ORIGIN French

bony adj bonier, boniest **1** resembling or consisting of bone **2** thin **3** having many bones

boo interj **1** a shout uttered to express dissatisfaction or contempt **2** an exclamation uttered to startle someone ▷ vb booing, booed **3** to shout 'boo' at (someone or something) as an expression of disapproval

boob slang n **1** Brit, Austral, & NZ an embarrassing mistake; blunder **2** a female breast **3** Austral a prison

▷ *vb* **4** *Brit, Austral, & NZ* to make a blunder **WORD ORIGIN** from *booby*

boobook (boo-book) *n* a small spotted Australian brown owl

booby *n, pl* **-bies 1** *old-fashioned* an ignorant or foolish person **2** a tropical marine bird related to the gannet **WORD ORIGIN** Latin *balbus* stammering

booby prize *n* a mock prize given to the person with the lowest score in a competition

booby trap *n* **1** a hidden explosive device primed so as to be set off by an unsuspecting victim **2** a trap for an unsuspecting person, esp. one intended as a practical joke

boodle *n slang* money or valuables, esp. when stolen, counterfeit, or used as a bribe **WORD ORIGIN** Dutch *boedel* possessions

boogie *vb* **-gieing, -gied** *slang* to dance to fast pop music **WORD ORIGIN** origin unknown

boogie board *n* another name for **bodyboard**

boogie-woogie *n* a style of piano jazz using blues harmonies **WORD ORIGIN** perhaps imitative

boohai *n NZ informal* **1** a very remote area **2 up the boohai** very mistaken or astray **WORD ORIGIN** from the remote township of *Puhoi*

boohoo *vb* **-hooing, -hooed 1** to sob or pretend to sob noisily ▷ *n, pl* **-hoos 2** distressed or pretended sobbing

book *n* **1** a number of printed pages bound together along one edge and protected by covers **2** a written work or composition, such as a novel **3** a number of sheets of paper bound together: *an account book* **4 books** a record of the transactions of a business or society **5** the libretto of an opera or musical **6** a major division of a written composition, such as of a long novel or of the Bible **7** a number of tickets, stamps, etc. fastened together along one edge **8** a record of betting transactions **9 a closed book** a subject that is beyond comprehension: *art remains a closed book to him* **10 bring to book** to reprimand or require (someone) to give an explanation of his or her conduct **11 by the book** according to the rules **12 in someone's good or bad books** regarded by someone with favour or disfavour **13 throw the book at someone a** to charge someone with every relevant offence **b** to inflict the most severe punishment on someone ▷ *vb* **14** to reserve (a place, passage, etc.) or engage the services of (someone) in advance **15** (of a police officer) to take the name and address of (a person) for an alleged offence with a view to prosecution **16** (of a football referee) to take the name of (a player) who has broken the rules seriously ▷ See also **book in WORD ORIGIN** Old English *bōc*

bookcase *n* a piece of furniture containing shelves for books

book club *n* a club that sells books at low prices to members, usually by mail order

book end *n* one of a pair of supports for holding a row of books upright

bookie *n informal* short for **bookmaker**

book in *vb chiefly Brit & NZ* to register one's arrival at a hotel

booking *n* **1** *Brit, Austral, & NZ* a reservation, as of a table or seat **2** *theatre* an engagement of a performer

bookish *adj* **1** fond of reading; studious **2** forming opinions through reading rather than experience

book-keeping *n* the skill or occupation of systematically recording business transactions **book-keeper** *n*

booklet *n* a thin book with paper covers

bookmaker *n* a person who as an occupation accepts bets, esp. on horse racing **bookmaking** *n*

bookmark *n* **1** a strip of some material put between the pages of a book to mark a place **2** *computers* an identifier put on a website that enables the user to return to it quickly and easily ▷ *vb* **3** *computers* to identify and store a website so that one can return to it quickly and easily

bookstall *n* a stall or stand where periodicals, newspapers, or books are sold

bookworm *n* **1** a person devoted to reading **2** a small insect that feeds on the binding paste of books

Boolean algebra (boo-lee-an) *n* a system of symbolic logic devised to codify nonmathematical logical operations: used in computers **WORD ORIGIN** after George *Boole*, mathematician

boom¹ *vb* **1** to make a loud deep echoing sound **2** to prosper vigorously and rapidly: *business boomed* ▷ *n* **3** a loud deep echoing sound **4** a period of high economic growth **WORD ORIGIN** imitative

boom² *n* **1** *naut* a spar to which the foot of a sail is fastened to control its position **2** a pole carrying an overhead microphone and projected over a film or television set **3** a barrier across a waterway **WORD ORIGIN** Dutch: tree

boomer *n Austral* a large male kangaroo

boomerang *n* **1** a curved wooden missile of Australian Aborigines which can be made to return to the thrower **2** an action or statement that recoils on its originator ▷ *vb* **3** (of a plan) to recoil unexpectedly, harming its originator **WORD ORIGIN** Aboriginal

boomslang *n* a large greenish venomous tree-living snake of southern Africa **WORD ORIGIN** Afrikaans

boon¹ *n* something extremely useful, helpful, or beneficial **WORD ORIGIN** Old Norse *bōn* request

boon² *adj* close or intimate: *boon companion* **WORD ORIGIN** Latin *bonus* good

boongary (boong-gar-ree) *n* a tree kangaroo of NE Queensland, Australia

boor *n* an ill-mannered, clumsy, or insensitive person **boorish** *adj* **WORD ORIGIN** Old English *gebūr* dweller, farmer

boost *n* **1** encouragement or help: *a boost to morale* **2** an upward thrust or push **3** an increase or rise ▷ *vb* **4** to encourage or improve: *to boost morale* **5** to cause to rise; increase: *we significantly boosted our market share* **6** to advertise on a big scale **WORD ORIGIN** origin unknown

booster *n* **1** a supplementary injection of a vaccine given to ensure that the first injection will remain effective **2** a radio-frequency amplifier to strengthen signals **3** the first stage of a multistage rocket

boot¹ *n* **1** an outer covering for the foot that extends above the ankle **2** an enclosed compartment of a car for holding luggage **3** *informal* a kick: *he gave the door a boot* **4 lick someone's boots** to behave flatteringly towards someone **5 put the boot in** *slang* **a** to kick a person when already down **b** to finish something off with unnecessary brutality **6 the boot** *slang* dismissal from employment ▷ *vb* **7** to kick **8** to start up (a computer) **9 boot out** *informal* **a** to eject forcibly **b** to dismiss from employment **WORD ORIGIN** Middle English *bote*

boot² *n* **to boot** as well; in addition **WORD ORIGIN** Old English *bōt* compensation

boot camp *n* a centre for juvenile offenders, with strict discipline and hard physical exercise

bootee *n* a soft boot for a baby, esp. a knitted one

booth *n, pl* **booths 1** a small partially enclosed cubicle **2** a stall, esp. a temporary one at a fair or market **WORD ORIGIN** Scandinavian

bootleg *vb* **-legging, -legged 1** to make, carry, or sell (illicit goods, esp. alcohol) ▷ *adj* **2** produced, distributed, or sold illicitly **bootlegger** *n* **WORD ORIGIN** smugglers carried bottles of liquor concealed in their boots

bootless *adj* of little or no use; vain; fruitless **WORD ORIGIN** Old English *bōtlēas*

bootlicker *n informal* one who seeks favour by grovelling to someone in authority

booty¹ *n, pl* **-ties** any valuable article or articles obtained as plunder **WORD ORIGIN** Old French *butin*

booty² *n slang* the buttocks, esp. those of an attractive female **WORD ORIGIN** from *butt* the buttocks

booze *informal n* **1** alcoholic drink ▷ *vb* **boozing, boozed 2** to drink alcohol, esp. in excess **boozy** *adj* **WORD ORIGIN** Middle Dutch *būsen*

boozer *n informal* **1** a person who is fond of drinking **2** *Brit, Austral, & NZ* a bar or pub

booze-up *n Brit, Austral, & NZ slang* a drinking spree

bop *n* **1** a form of jazz with complex rhythms and harmonies ▷ *vb* **bopping, bopped 2** *informal* to dance to pop music **bopper** *n* **WORD ORIGIN** from BEBOP

bora *n Austral* an Aboriginal ceremony **WORD ORIGIN** from a native Australian language

boracic *adj* same as **boric**

borage *n* a Mediterranean plant with star-shaped blue flowers
WORD ORIGIN Arabic *abū 'āraq* literally: father of sweat

borax *n* a white mineral in crystalline form used in making glass, soap, etc.
WORD ORIGIN Persian *būrah*

Bordeaux *n* a red or white wine produced around Bordeaux in SW France

border *n* **1** the dividing line between political or geographic regions **2** a band or margin around or along the edge of something **3** a design around the edge of something **4** a narrow strip of ground planted with flowers or shrubs: *a herbaceous border* ▷ *vb* **5** to provide with a border **6 a** to be adjacent to; lie along the boundary of **b** to be nearly the same as; verge on: *a story that borders on the unbelievable*
WORD ORIGIN Old French *bort* side of a ship

borderland *n* **1** land located on or near a boundary **2** an indeterminate state or condition

borderline *n* **1** a dividing line **2** an indeterminate position between two conditions: *the borderline between love and friendship* ▷ *adj* **3** on the edge of one category and verging on another: *a borderline failure*

Borders *pl n* **the Borders** the area straddling the border between England and Scotland

bore[1] *vb* **boring, bored 1** to produce (a hole) with a drill, etc. **2** to produce (a tunnel, mine shaft, etc.) by drilling ▷ *n* **3** a hole or tunnel in the ground drilled in search of minerals, oil, etc. **4 a** the hollow of a gun barrel **b** the diameter of this hollow; calibre
WORD ORIGIN Old English *borian*

bore[2] *vb* **boring, bored 1** to tire or make weary by being dull, repetitious, or uninteresting ▷ *n* **2** a dull or repetitious person, activity, or state **bored** *adj* **boring** *adj*
WORD ORIGIN origin unknown

bore[3] *n* a high wave moving up a narrow estuary, caused by the tide
WORD ORIGIN Old Norse *bāra*

bore[4] *vb* the past tense of **bear**[1]

boreal forest (**bore**-ee-al) *n* the forest of northern latitudes, esp. in Scandinavia, Canada, and Siberia, consisting mainly of spruce and pine
WORD ORIGIN Latin *boreas* the north wind

boredom *n* the state of being bored

boree (**baw**-ree) *n* *Austral* same as **myall**

boric *adj* of or containing boron

boric acid *n* a white soluble crystalline solid used as a mild antiseptic

born *vb* **1** a past participle of **bear**[1] (sense 4) **2** **not have been born yesterday** not to be gullible or foolish ▷ *adj* **3** possessing certain qualities from birth: *a born musician* **4** being in a particular social status at birth: *ignobly born*
≡ USAGE
≡ Care should be taken not to use *born*
≡ where *borne* is intended: *he had borne*
≡ (not *born*) *his ordeal with great courage: the*
≡ *following points should be borne in mind.*

born-again *adj* **1** having experienced conversion, esp. to evangelical Christianity **2** showing the enthusiasm of someone newly converted to any cause: *a born-again romantic* ▷ *n* **3** a person with fervent enthusiasm for a newfound cause

borne *vb* a past participle of **bear**[1]
≡ USAGE
≡ See at **born**.

boron *n* *chem* a hard almost colourless crystalline metalloid element that is used in hardening steel. Symbol: B
WORD ORIGIN *bor(ax)* + *(carb)on*

boronia *n* an Australian aromatic flowering shrub

borough *n* **1** a town, esp. (in Britain) one that forms the constituency of an MP or that was originally incorporated by royal charter **2** any of the constituent divisions of Greater London or New York City
WORD ORIGIN Old English *burg*

borrow *vb* **1** to obtain (something, such as money) on the understanding that it will be returned to the lender **2** to adopt (ideas, words, etc.) from another source **borrower** *n* **borrowing** *n*
WORD ORIGIN Old English *borgian*
≡ USAGE
≡ The use of *off* after *borrow* was formerly
≡ considered incorrect, but is now
≡ acceptable in informal contexts.

borscht or **borsch** *n* a Russian soup based on beetroot
WORD ORIGIN Russian *borshch*

borstal *n* (formerly, in Britain) a prison for offenders aged 15 to 21
WORD ORIGIN after *Borstal*, village in Kent where the first institution was founded

borzoi *n* a tall dog with a narrow head and a long coat
WORD ORIGIN Russian: swift

bosh *n* *Brit, Austral, & NZ informal* meaningless talk or opinions; nonsense
WORD ORIGIN Turkish *boş* empty

Bosnian *adj* **1** from Bosnia ▷ *n* **2** a person from Bosnia

bosom *n* **1** the chest or breast of a person, esp. the female breasts **2** a protective centre or part: *the bosom of the family* **3** the breast considered as the seat of emotions ▷ *adj* **4** very dear: *a bosom friend*
WORD ORIGIN Old English *bōsm*

boss[1] *informal n* **1** a person in charge of or employing others ▷ *vb* **2** to employ, supervise, or be in charge of **3** **boss around** or **about** to be domineering or overbearing towards
WORD ORIGIN Dutch *baas* master

boss[2] *n* a raised knob or stud, esp. an ornamental one on a vault, shield, etc.
WORD ORIGIN Old French *boce*

bossa nova *n* **1** a dance similar to the samba, originating in Brazil **2** music for this dance
WORD ORIGIN Portuguese

bossy *adj* **bossier, bossiest** *informal* domineering, overbearing, or authoritarian **bossiness** *n*

bosun or **boatswain** (**boh**-sn) *n* an officer who is responsible for the maintenance of a ship and its equipment

bot. **1** botanical **2** botany

botany *n, pl* **-nies** the study of plants, including their classification, structure, etc. **botanical** or **botanic** *adj* **botanist** *n*
WORD ORIGIN Greek *botanē* plant

botch *vb* **1** to spoil through clumsiness or ineptitude **2** to repair badly or clumsily ▷ *n* also **botch-up 3** a badly done piece of work or repair
WORD ORIGIN origin unknown

both *adj* **1** two considered together: *both parents were killed during the war* ▷ *pron* **2** two considered together: *both are to blame* ▷ *conj* **3** not just one but also the other of two (people or things): *both Darren and Keith enjoyed the match*
WORD ORIGIN Old Norse *bāthir*

bother *vb* **1** to take the time or trouble: *don't bother to come with me* **2** to give annoyance, pain, or trouble to **3** to trouble (a person) by repeatedly disturbing; pester ▷ *n* **4** a state of worry, trouble, or confusion **5** a person or thing that causes fuss, trouble, or annoyance **6** *informal* a disturbance or fight: *a spot of bother* ▷ *interj* **7** *Brit, Austral, & NZ* an exclamation of slight annoyance
WORD ORIGIN origin unknown

bothersome *adj* causing bother

bothy *n, pl* **bothies** *chiefly Scot* **1** a hut used for temporary shelter **2** (formerly) a farm worker's quarters
WORD ORIGIN perhaps from *booth*

Botox *n trademark* **1** a preparation of botulinum toxin used to treat muscle spasm and to remove wrinkles ▷ *vb* **2** to apply Botox to (a person or a part of the body)
WORD ORIGIN from BOT(ULINUM) (T)OX(IN)

bottle *n* **1** a container, often of glass and usually cylindrical with a narrow neck, for holding liquids **2** the amount such a container will hold **3** *Brit slang* courage; nerve: *you don't have the bottle* **4** **the bottle** *informal* drinking of alcohol, esp. to excess ▷ *vb* **5** to put or place in a bottle or bottles
▶ See also **bottle up**
WORD ORIGIN Late Latin *buttis* cask

bottle bank *n* a large container into which members of the public can throw glass bottles and jars for recycling

bottle-feed *vb* **-feeding, -fed** to feed (a baby) with milk from a bottle

bottle-green *adj* dark green

bottleneck *n* **1** a narrow stretch of road or a junction at which traffic is or may be held up **2** something that holds up progress

bottlenose dolphin *n* a grey or greenish dolphin with a bottle-shaped snout

bottle party *n* a party to which guests bring drink

bottler *n* *Austral & NZ, old-fashioned informal* an exceptional person or thing

bottle shop *n* *Austral & NZ* a shop licensed to sell alcohol for drinking elsewhere

bottle store *n* *S African* a shop licensed to sell alcohol for drinking elsewhere

The Terminology of Computers

Compared to a computer, the internal combustion engine is a model of simplicity. A computer is not merely a machine, but an intricate system involving, among other things, silicon *chips*, a *motherboard*, a *central processing unit* or *CPU*, and a *hard disk*. Each has subparts with names often involving letters, numbers, sometimes fused into opaque acronyms. Moreover, the system's *peripherals* – the *monitor, printer, keyboard, mouse,* and *modem* – become as vital as the part that does the actual computing and each, too, has its specific terminology. No wonder, then, that the advent of the computer spawned a universe of *technobabble*.

Even the evolution of the computer since the Second World War launched an assembly line of terms. First were the hugely expensive *mainframes*, some as big as rooms, then, in the 1980s, the revolution of the affordable *personal computer* or *PC*, which set the computer on the desks and tabletops of individuals to deploy *applications* like *spreadsheets, databases,* and *word processing*. Innumerable innovations and refinements appeared, then were bettered by others; brands of *programming languages, hardware, software,* and *operating systems* battled for supremacy.

To link these computers, telephone lines and *fibre optic cables* became the physical conduits. At first, the linkage took the form of *networks* used by military personnel and academics, the dawn of the *internet*. After the personal computer spread the *cybernetic* wealth to one person at a time, and *hack* and *hacker* acquired new senses, the *World Wide Web* was devised, permitting the use of unique addresses, *URLs* (*Universal Resource Locators*). Meanwhile, *dial-up* modems, linked by remote *servers*, were succeeded by faster *broadband* connections. Users could use a *search engine* on the World Wide Web to locate whatever *home page* or *Web site* they wanted, and find an answer to nearly any question they asked. They could play *computer games* non-stop and communicate *e-mail* messages across oceans and continents. Everyone was connected to everything, and *internet cafés* could be found everywhere.

Nor was this all. The storage capacity of chips vastly increased, and some computers physically shrank to the size of a *notebook* or *laptop*, or to the dimensions of hand-held devices, *personal digital assistants*, that were a byproduct of *wireless technology*. The computer or its simulacrum was literally everywhere. No communications technology – not the telegraph or telephone, not radio or television – had advanced so far so rapidly.

Once computer networks had passed out of the hands of specialists and experts, and their use was no longer the province of technologically savvy, stereotypically obsessive *geeks* and *nerds,* it followed that countries, organizations, and corporations would seek to exploit them for the purposes of politics, promotion, or propaganda, or commercially through advertisements. The rise of digital technology brought movies, television, and the telephone inside the computer, and led many to predict the death of printed books, magazines, and newspapers. Some companies sought to move applications and data storage away from the individual's computer and house them on demand in the virtually unlimited portion of *cyberspace* known as *the cloud*.

When the personal computer began to become a mass consumer item like the pop-up toaster, *computer literacy* was a necessity, and some feared the demise of literacy itself among the young. As it turns out, the fact that most people will read this breathless survey of computer terms without an explanation of each new word shows how far *computerspeak* has saturated our ordinary discourse. Young people are writing or *texting* more than they ever have, communicating through *social networks*, interactive *blogs*, and of course by e-mail.

As communication, e-mail is astonishingly effective, but prone to mishaps like the ill-advised or inadvertent use of the *send button*, or by the transmission of jokes that are taken much too seriously. To correct the latter, the *emoticon* or *smiley* was invented, for example : -) to indicate a humorous intention. If this is the lighter side of computer use, the darker side is exposed by those who maliciously spread *viruses*, surreptitiously collect user information, or seek to cripple an enemy's network. A new, sometimes justified suspicion has invaded human communication. We have to see yet whether our cybernetic world will end up being : -) or :-(

bottle tree *n* an Australian tree with a bottle-shaped swollen trunk

bottle up *vb* to restrain (powerful emotion)

bottom *n* **1** the lowest, deepest, or farthest removed part of a thing: *the bottom of a hill* **2** the least important or successful position: *the bottom of a class* **3** the ground underneath a sea, lake, or river **4** the underneath part of a thing **5** the buttocks **6 at bottom** in reality; basically **7 be at the bottom of** to be the ultimate cause of **8 get to the bottom of** to discover the real truth about ▷ *adj* **9** lowest or last
WORD ORIGIN Old English *botm*

bottomless *adj* **1** unlimited; inexhaustible: *bottomless resources* **2** very deep: *bottomless valleys*

bottom line *n* **1** the conclusion or main point of a process, discussion, etc. **2** the last line of a financial statement that shows the net profit or loss of a company or organization

bottom out *vb* to reach the lowest point and level out: *consumer spending has bottomed out*

botulism *n* severe food poisoning resulting from the toxin **botulin**, produced in imperfectly preserved food
WORD ORIGIN Latin *botulus* sausage

bouclé *n* a curled or looped yarn or fabric giving a thick knobbly effect
WORD ORIGIN French: curly

boudoir (**boo**-dwahr) *n* a woman's bedroom or private sitting room
WORD ORIGIN French, literally: room for sulking in

bouffant (**boof**-fong) *adj* (of a hairstyle) having extra height and width through backcombing
WORD ORIGIN French *bouffer* to puff up

bougainvillea *n* a tropical climbing plant with flowers surrounded by showy red or purple bracts
WORD ORIGIN after L. A. de *Bougainville*, navigator

bough *n* any of the main branches of a tree
WORD ORIGIN Old English *bōg* arm, twig

bought *vb* the past of **buy**

bouillon (**boo**-yon) *n* a thin clear broth or stock
WORD ORIGIN French *bouillir* to boil

boulder *n* a smooth rounded mass of rock shaped by erosion
WORD ORIGIN Scandinavian

boulder clay *n* an unstratified glacial deposit of fine clay, boulders, and pebbles

boules (**bool**) *n* a game, popular in France, in which metal bowls are thrown to land as close as possible to a target ball
WORD ORIGIN French: balls

boulevard *n* a wide usually tree-lined road in a city
WORD ORIGIN Middle Dutch *bolwerc* bulwark; because originally often built on the ruins of an old rampart

boult *vb* same as **bolt²**

bounce *vb* **bouncing, bounced** **1** (of a ball, etc.) to rebound from an impact **2** to cause (a ball, etc.) to hit a solid surface and spring back **3** to move or cause to move suddenly; spring: *I bounced down the stairs* **4** *slang* (of a bank) to send (a cheque) back or (of a cheque) to be sent back unredeemed because of lack of funds in the account ▷ *n* **5** the action of rebounding from an impact **6** a leap or jump **7** springiness **8** *informal* vitality; vigour **bouncy** *adj*
WORD ORIGIN probably imitative

bounce back *vb* to recover one's health, good spirits, confidence, etc. easily

bouncer *n* **1** *slang* a person employed at a club, disco, etc. to prevent unwanted people from entering and to eject drunks or troublemakers **2** *cricket* a ball bowled so that it bounces high on pitching

bouncing *adj* vigorous and robust: *a bouncing baby*

Bouncy Castle *n trademark* a very large inflatable model, usually of a castle, on which children may bounce at fairs, etc.

bound¹ *vb* **1** the past of **bind** ▷ *adj* **2** tied as if with a rope **3** restricted or confined: *housebound* **4** certain: *it's bound to happen* **5** compelled or obliged: *they agreed to be bound by the board's recommendations* **6** (of a book) secured within a cover or binding **7 bound up with** closely or inextricably linked with

bound² *vb* **1** to move forwards by leaps or jumps **2** to bounce; spring away from an impact ▷ *n* **3** a jump upwards or forwards **4** a bounce, as of a ball
WORD ORIGIN Old French *bondir*

bound³ *vb* **1** to place restrictions on; limit: *bounded by tradition* **2** to form a boundary of ▷ *n* **3** see **bounds**
▷ **boundless** *adj*
WORD ORIGIN Old French *bonde*

bound⁴ *adj* going or intending to go towards: *homeward bound*
WORD ORIGIN Old Norse *buinn*, past participle of *būa* prepare

boundary *n, pl* **-ries** **1** something that indicates the farthest limit, such as of an area **2** *cricket* **a** the marked limit of the playing area **b** a stroke that hits the ball beyond this limit, scoring four or six runs

bounden *adj old-fashioned* morally obligatory: *bounden duty*

bounder *n old-fashioned Brit slang* a morally reprehensible person; cad

bounds *pl n* **1** a limit; boundary: *their jealousy knows no bounds* **2** something that restricts or controls, esp. the standards of a society: *within the bounds of good taste*

bountiful *or* **bounteous** *adj literary* **1** plentiful; ample: *a bountiful harvest* **2** giving freely; generous

bounty *n, pl* **-ties** **1** *literary* generosity; liberality **2** something provided in generous amounts: *nature's bounty* **3** a reward or premium by a government
WORD ORIGIN Latin *bonus* good

bouquet *n* **1** a bunch of flowers, esp. a large carefully arranged one **2** the aroma of wine
WORD ORIGIN French: thicket

bouquet garni *n, pl* **bouquets garnis** a bunch of herbs tied together and used for flavouring soups, stews, or stocks
WORD ORIGIN French

bourbon (**bur**-bn) *n* a whiskey distilled, chiefly in the US, from maize
WORD ORIGIN after *Bourbon* county, Kentucky, where it was first made

bourgeois (**boor**-zhwah) *often disparaging adj* **1** characteristic of or comprising the middle class **2** conservative or materialistic in outlook **3** (in Marxist thought) dominated by capitalism ▷ *n, pl* **-geois** **4** a member of the middle class, esp. one regarded as being conservative and materialistic
WORD ORIGIN Old French *borjois* citizen

bourgeoisie (boor-zhwah-**zee**) *n* **the bourgeoisie 1** the middle classes **2** (in Marxist thought) the capitalist ruling class

bourn *n chiefly S Brit* a stream
WORD ORIGIN Old French *bodne* limit

bourrée (**boor**-ray) *n* **1** a traditional French dance in fast duple time **2** music for this dance
WORD ORIGIN French

Bourse (**boorss**) *n* a stock exchange, esp. of Paris
WORD ORIGIN French: purse

bout *n* **1 a** a period of time spent doing something, such as drinking **b** a period of illness: *a bad bout of flu* **2** a boxing, wrestling, or fencing match
WORD ORIGIN obsolete *bought* turn

boutique *n* a small shop, esp. one that sells fashionable clothes
WORD ORIGIN French

bouzouki *n* a Greek long-necked stringed musical instrument related to the mandolin
WORD ORIGIN Modern Greek

bovine *adj* **1** of or relating to cattle **2** dull, sluggish, or ugly
WORD ORIGIN Latin *bos* ox

bow¹ (rhymes with **cow**) *vb* **1** to lower (one's head) or bend (one's knee or body) as a sign of respect, greeting, agreement, or shame **2** to comply or accept: *bow to the inevitable* **3 bow and scrape** to behave in a slavish manner ▷ *n* **4** a lowering or bending of the head or body as a mark of respect, etc. **5 take a bow** to acknowledge applause ▶ See also **bow out**
WORD ORIGIN Old English *būgan*

bow² (rhymes with **know**) *n* **1** a decorative knot usually having two loops and two loose ends **2** a long stick across which are stretched strands of horsehair, used for playing a violin, viola, cello, etc. **3** a weapon for shooting arrows, consisting of an arch of flexible wood, plastic, etc. bent by a string fastened at each end **4** something that is curved, bent, or arched ▷ *vb* **5** to form or cause to form a curve or curves
WORD ORIGIN Old English *boga* arch, bow

bow³ (rhymes with **cow**) *n* **1** *chiefly naut* the front end or part of a vessel **2** *rowing* the oarsman at the bow
WORD ORIGIN probably Low German *boog*

bowdlerize *or* **-ise** *vb* **-izing, -ized** *or* **-ising, -ised** to remove passages or words regarded as indecent from (a play, novel, etc.) **bowdlerization** *or* **-isation** *n*
WORD ORIGIN after Thomas *Bowdler*, editor who expurgated Shakespeare

bowel *n* **1** an intestine, esp. the large intestine in man **2 bowels** entrails **3 bowels** the innermost part: *the bowels of the earth*
WORD ORIGIN Latin *botellus* a little sausage

bower *n* a shady leafy shelter in a wood or garden
WORD ORIGIN Old English *būr* dwelling

bowerbird *n* a brightly coloured songbird of Australia and New Guinea

bowie knife *n* a stout hunting knife
WORD ORIGIN after Jim *Bowie*, Texan adventurer

bowl¹ *n* **1** a round container open at the top, used for holding liquid or serving food **2** the amount a bowl will hold **3** the hollow part of an object, esp. of a spoon or tobacco pipe
WORD ORIGIN Old English *bolla*

bowl² *n* **1 a** a wooden ball used in the game of bowls **b** a large heavy ball with holes for gripping used in the game of bowling ▷ *vb* **2** to roll smoothly or cause to roll smoothly along the ground **3** *cricket* **a** to send (a ball) from one's hand towards the batsman **b** Also: **bowl out** to dismiss (a batsman) by delivering a ball that breaks his wicket **4** to play bowls **5 bowl along** to move easily and rapidly, as in a car ▸ See also **bowl over, bowls**
WORD ORIGIN French *boule*

bow-legged *adj* having legs that curve outwards at the knees

bowler¹ *n* **1** a person who bowls in cricket **2** a player at the game of bowls

bowler² *n* a stiff felt hat with a rounded crown and narrow curved brim
WORD ORIGIN after John *Bowler*, hatter

bowline *n naut* **1** a line used to keep the sail taut against the wind **2** a knot used for securing a loop that will not slip at the end of a piece of rope
WORD ORIGIN probably from Middle Low German *bōlīne*

bowling *n* **1** a game in which a heavy ball is rolled down a long narrow alley at a group of wooden pins **2** *cricket* the act of delivering the ball to the batsman

bowl over *vb* **1** *informal* to surprise (a person) greatly, in a pleasant way **2** to knock down

bowls *n* a game played on a very smooth area of grass in which opponents roll biased wooden bowls as near a small bowl (the jack) as possible

bow out *vb* to retire or withdraw gracefully

bowsprit *n naut* a spar projecting from the bow of a sailing ship
WORD ORIGIN Middle Low German *bōch* BOW³ + *sprēt* pole

bowstring *n* the string of an archer's bow

bow tie *n* a man's tie in the form of a bow

bow window *n* a curved bay window

bow-wow *n* **1** a child's word for **dog** **2** an imitation of the bark of a dog

box¹ *n* **1** a container with a firm base and sides and sometimes a removable or hinged lid **2** the contents of such a container **3** a separate compartment for a small group of people, as in a theatre **4** a compartment for a horse in a stable or a vehicle **5** a section of printed matter on a page, enclosed by lines or a border **6** a central agency to which mail is addressed and from which it is collected or redistributed: *a post-office box* **7** same as **penalty box** **8** **the box** *Brit informal* television ▷ *vb* **9** to put into a box ▸ See also **box in** ▸ **boxlike** *adj*
WORD ORIGIN Greek *puxos* BOX³

box² *vb* **1** to fight (an opponent) in a boxing match **2** to engage in boxing **3** to hit (esp. a person's ears) with the fist ▷ *n* **4** a punch with the fist, esp. on the ear
WORD ORIGIN origin unknown

box³ *n* a slow-growing evergreen tree or shrub with small shiny leaves
WORD ORIGIN Greek *puxos*

boxer *n* **1** a person who boxes **2** a medium-sized dog with smooth hair and a short nose

boxer shorts or **boxers** *pl n* men's underpants shaped like shorts but with a front opening

box girder *n* a girder that is hollow and square or rectangular in shape

box in *vb* to prevent from moving freely

boxing *n* the act, art, or profession of fighting with the fists

Boxing Day *n* the first day after Christmas (in Britain, traditionally and strictly, the first weekday), observed as a holiday
WORD ORIGIN from the former custom of giving Christmas boxes to tradesmen on this day

box jellyfish *n* a highly venomous jellyfish with a cuboid body that lives in Australian tropical waters

box junction *n* (in Britain) a road junction marked with yellow crisscross lines which vehicles may only enter when their exit is clear

box lacrosse *n Canad* lacrosse played indoors

box number *n* a number used as an address for mail, esp. one used by a newspaper for replies to an advertisement

box office *n* **1** an office at a theatre, cinema, etc. where tickets are sold **2** the public appeal of an actor or production ▷ *adj* **box-office 3** relating to the sales at the box office

box pleat *n* a flat double pleat made by folding under the fabric on either side

boxroom *n* a small room in which boxes, cases, etc. may be stored

box spring *n* a coiled spring contained in a boxlike frame, used for mattresses, chairs, etc.

boxwood *n* the hard yellow wood of the box tree, used to make tool handles, etc. See **box³**

boy *n* **1** a male child **2** a man regarded as immature or inexperienced **3** *S African, offensive* a Black male servant **boyhood** *n* **boyish** *adj*
WORD ORIGIN origin unknown

boycott *vb* **1** to refuse to deal with (an organization or country) as a protest against its actions or policy ▷ *n* **2** an instance or the use of boycotting
WORD ORIGIN after Captain *Boycott*,

Irish land agent, a victim of such practices for refusing to reduce rents

boyfriend *n* a male friend with whom a person is romantically or sexually involved

Boyle's law *n* the principle that the pressure of a gas varies inversely with its volume at constant temperature
WORD ORIGIN after Robert *Boyle*, scientist

boy scout *n* see **Scout**

BP 1 blood pressure **2** British Pharmacopoeia

bpi bits per inch (used of a computer tape)

Bq *physics* becquerel

Br *chem* bromine

Br. 1 Breton **2** Britain **3** British

bra *n* a woman's undergarment for covering and supporting the breasts
WORD ORIGIN from *brassiere*

braaivleis (**brye**-flayss) *S African n* **1** a grill on which food is cooked over hot charcoal, usually outdoors **2** an outdoor party at which food like this is served ▷ *vb* **3** to cook (food) on in this way. Also: **braai**
WORD ORIGIN Afrikaans

brace *n* **1** something that steadies, binds, or holds up another thing **2** a beam or prop, used to stiffen a framework **3** a hand tool for drilling holes **4** a pair, esp. of game birds **5** either of a pair of characters, { }, used for connecting lines of printing or writing **6** see **braces** ▷ *vb* **bracing, braced 7** to steady or prepare (oneself) before an impact **8** to provide, strengthen, or fit with a brace
WORD ORIGIN Latin *bracchia* arms

brace and bit *n* a hand tool for boring holes, consisting of a cranked handle into which a drilling bit is inserted

bracelet *n* an ornamental chain or band worn around the arm or wrist
WORD ORIGIN Latin *bracchium* arm

bracelets *pl n slang* handcuffs

braces *pl n* **1** *Brit & NZ* a pair of straps worn over the shoulders for holding up the trousers **2** an appliance of metal bands and wires for correcting unevenness of teeth

brachiopod (**brake**-ee-oh-pod) *n* an invertebrate sea animal with a shell consisting of two valves
WORD ORIGIN Greek *brakhiōn* arm + *pous* foot

brachium (**brake**-ee-um) *n, pl* **brachia** (**brake**-ee-a) *anat* the arm, esp. the upper part
WORD ORIGIN Latin *bracchium* arm

bracing *adj* refreshing: *the bracing climate*

bracken *n* **1** a fern with large fronds **2** a clump of these ferns
WORD ORIGIN Scandinavian

bracket *n* **1** a pair of characters, [ ], ( ), or { }, used to enclose a section of writing or printing **2** a group or category falling within certain defined limits: *the lower income bracket* **3** an L-shaped or other support fixed to a wall to hold a shelf, etc. ▷ *vb* **-eting, -eted 4** to put (written or printed matter) in brackets **5** to group or class together
WORD ORIGIN Latin *braca* breeches

b

brackish adj (of water) slightly salty
WORD ORIGIN Middle Dutch brac

bract n a leaf, usually small and scaly, growing at the base of a flower
WORD ORIGIN Latin bractea thin metal plate

brad n a small tapered nail with a small head
WORD ORIGIN Old English brord point

brae n Scot a hill or slope
WORD ORIGIN Middle English bra

brag vb **bragging, bragged 1** to speak arrogantly and boastfully: he'll probably go around bragging to his friends ▷ n **2** boastful talk or behaviour **3** a card game similar to poker
WORD ORIGIN origin unknown

braggart n a person who boasts loudly or exaggeratedly

Brahma n **1** a Hindu god, the Creator **2** same as **Brahman** (sense 2)

Brahman n, pl **-mans 1** Also: **Brahmin** a member of the highest or priestly caste in the Hindu caste system **2** Hinduism the ultimate and impersonal divine reality of the universe **Brahmanic** adj
WORD ORIGIN Sanskrit: prayer

braid vb **1** to interweave (hair, thread, etc.) **2** to decorate with an ornamental trim or border ▷ n **3** a length of hair that has been braided **4** narrow ornamental tape of woven silk, wool, etc. **braiding** n
WORD ORIGIN Old English bregdan

Braille n a system of writing for the blind consisting of raised dots interpreted by touch
WORD ORIGIN after Louis Braille, its inventor

brain n **1** the soft mass of nervous tissue within the skull of vertebrates that controls and coordinates the nervous system **2** (often pl) informal intellectual ability: he's got brains **3** informal an intelligent person **4** on the brain informal constantly in mind: I had that song on the brain **5** the brains informal a person who plans and organizes something: the brains behind the bid ▷ vb **6** slang to hit (someone) hard on the head
WORD ORIGIN Old English brægen

brainchild n informal an idea or plan produced by creative thought

braindead adj **1** having suffered brain death **2** informal stupid

brain death n complete stoppage of breathing due to irreparable brain damage

brain drain n informal the emigration of scientists, technologists, academics, etc.

brainfood n any foodstuff containing nutrients thought to promote brain function

brainless adj stupid or foolish

brainstorm n **1** informal a sudden mental aberration **2** a sudden and violent attack of insanity **3** informal same as **brainwave**

brainstorming n a thorough discussion to solve problems or create ideas

brains trust n a group of knowledgeable people who discuss topics in public or on radio or television

brain-teaser n informal a difficult problem

brainwash vb to cause (a person) to alter his or her beliefs, by methods based on isolation, sleeplessness, etc. **brainwashing** n

brainwave n informal a sudden idea or inspiration

brain wave n a fluctuation of electrical potential in the brain

brainy adj **brainier, brainiest** informal clever; intelligent

braise vb **braising, braised** to cook (food) slowly in a closed pan with a small amount of liquid
WORD ORIGIN Old French brese live coals

brak¹ (bruck) n S African a crossbred dog; mongrel
WORD ORIGIN Dutch

brak² (bruck) adj S African (of water) slightly salty; brackish
WORD ORIGIN Afrikaans

brake¹ n **1** a device for slowing or stopping a vehicle **2** something that slows down or stops progress: he put a brake on my enthusiasm ▷ vb **braking, braked 3** to slow down or cause to slow down, by or as if by using a brake
WORD ORIGIN Middle Dutch braeke

brake² n Brit an area of dense undergrowth; thicket
WORD ORIGIN Old English bracu

brake horsepower n the rate at which an engine does work, measured by the resistance of an applied brake

brake light n a red light at the rear of a motor vehicle that lights up when the brakes are applied

brake shoe n a curved metal casting that acts as a brake on a wheel

bramble n **1** a prickly plant or shrub such as the blackberry **2** Scot, N English, & NZ a blackberry **brambly** adj
WORD ORIGIN Old English bræmbel

bran n husks of cereal grain separated from the flour
WORD ORIGIN Old French

branch n **1** a secondary woody stem extending from the trunk or main branch of a tree **2** one of a number of shops, offices, or groups that belongs to a central organization: he was transferred to their Japanese branch **3** a subdivision or subsidiary section of something larger or more complex: branches of learning ▷ vb **4** to divide, then develop in different directions **branchlike** adj
WORD ORIGIN Late Latin branca paw

branch off vb to diverge from the main way, road, topic, etc.

branch out vb to expand or extend one's interests

brand n **1** a particular product or a characteristic that identifies a particular producer **2** a trade name or trademark **3** a particular kind or variety **4** an identifying mark made, usually by burning, on the skin of animals as a proof of ownership **5** an iron used for branding animals **6** a mark of disgrace **7** archaic or poetic a flaming torch ▷ vb **8** to label, burn, or mark with or as if with a brand **9** to label (someone): he was branded a war criminal
WORD ORIGIN Old English: fire

brandish vb to wave (a weapon, etc.) in a triumphant or threatening way
WORD ORIGIN Old French brandir

brand-new adj absolutely new

brandy n, pl **-dies** an alcoholic spirit distilled from wine
WORD ORIGIN Dutch brandewijn

brandy snap n a crisp sweet biscuit, rolled into a cylinder

brash adj **1** tastelessly or offensively loud, or showy: brash modernization **2** impudent or bold: I thought it was very brash of her to ask me **brashness** n
WORD ORIGIN origin unknown

brass n **1** an alloy of copper and zinc **2** an object, ornament, or utensil made of brass **3 a** the large family of wind instruments including the trumpet, trombone, etc. made of brass **b** instruments of this family forming a section in an orchestra **4** same as **top brass 5** N English dialect money **6** Brit an engraved brass memorial tablet in a church **7** informal bold self-confidence; nerve
WORD ORIGIN Old English bræs

brass band n a group of musicians playing brass and percussion instruments

brasserie n a bar or restaurant serving drinks and cheap meals
WORD ORIGIN French brasser to stir

brass hat n Brit informal a top-ranking official, esp. a military officer

brassica n any plant of the cabbage and turnip family
WORD ORIGIN Latin: cabbage

brassiere n same as **bra**
WORD ORIGIN French

brass rubbing n an impression of an engraved brass tablet made by rubbing a paper placed over it with heelball or chalk

brass tacks pl n **get down to brass tacks** informal to discuss the realities of a situation

brassy adj **brassier, brassiest 1** brazen or flashy **2** like brass, esp. in colour **3** (of sound) harsh and strident

brat n a child, esp. one who is unruly
WORD ORIGIN origin unknown

bravado n an outward display of self-confidence
WORD ORIGIN Spanish bravada

brave adj **1** having or displaying courage, resolution, or daring **2** fine; splendid: a brave sight ▷ n **3** a warrior of a Native American tribe of N America ▷ vb **braving, braved 4** to confront with resolution or courage: she braved the 21 miles of Lake Tahoe **bravery** n
WORD ORIGIN Italian bravo

bravo interj **1** well done! ▷ n **2** pl **-vos** a cry of 'bravo' **3** pl **-voes** or **-vos** a hired killer or assassin
WORD ORIGIN Italian

bravura n **1** a display of boldness or daring **2** music brilliance of execution
WORD ORIGIN Italian

brawl n **1** a loud disagreement or fight ▷ vb **2** to quarrel or fight noisily
WORD ORIGIN probably from Dutch brallen to boast

Leonard Cohen

Leonard Cohen was a poet before he was a singer and songwriter; it was only in 1968 and the release of his first album when he was 34 that he decisively turned toward public performances and studio recordings. But the distinction between activities was never clear: the poems were lyrical, and the songs merely required music to make them complete poems.

Born in the affluent Westmount district of Montreal, Cohen was nine when his merchant father died. After he graduated from McGill University and published his first book *Let Us Compare Mythologies* (1956), he intermittently studied in Montreal and New York before, abandoning academe, he decamped to the Greek island of Hydra. There he began the first of the serious romantic relationships that marked his life; a second relationship more than a decade later resulted in a son and a daughter. He was also writing two novels, *The Favourite Game* (1963), about a poet's formative years, and the beautifully written though thematically incoherent *Beautiful Losers* (1966).

What followed were several decades of waxing and waning popularity, worldwide concert tours and memorable album releases alternating with long periods of reclusion. Another paradox of his career was the fusion of his Talmudic inheritance and immersion in Buddhism, especially under a Zen master at Mount Baldy near Los Angeles. As a poet, he became acclaimed in Canada with *The Spice-Box of Earth* (1961); as a performer or influential songwriter he became more famous in Europe than in North America. His work, whether performed by himself or many other vocalists, became heard on airwaves and film soundtracks everywhere, culminating late in his career with the song *Hallelujah*, which was well nigh omnipresent in 2008, some 24 years after its first release.

Cohen was shrewd in choosing gifted producers, arrangers, and back-up singers, and it's often been remarked that his progress was assisted by older and perhaps wiser mentors, beginning with his Montreal friend, the poet Irving Layton. What's certain is that multiple influences – the Beat movement, Greek myths, Zen koans, Biblical prophecy, and the psalms of David – have nourished his work. Cohen's persona of dignity, reserve, and world-weariness has been matched by witty self-deprecation. He refused a Governor General's Award for Poetry in 1969, declaring that 'the poems themselves forbid it absolutely', and has often made fun of his singing voice, a rumbling gravelly bass. In *Tower of Song*, he jokes that he was 'born with the gift/ Of a golden voice'. When he was named best male vocalist in Canada in 1993, he commented at a ceremony that 'only in a country like this with a voice like mine could I receive such an award'. In the dirges and waltzes of Cohen's work, dichotomies make entrances and exits: rootedness versus wandering, action versus contemplation, mind versus body, power versus victimhood. Poems of devotion to women, implicitly praising himself, are balanced by poems of self-loathing. Equating loss with creativity, pain with beauty, the lines and titles of his poems and songs are tinged with erotic melancholy and edged with existential irony: *Dance Me to the End of Love; Death of a Ladies' Man; Hey, That's No Way To Say Goodbye; Sisters of Mercy; Closing Time; Bird on the Wire; Ain't No Cure For Love.* He pillories his ego, yet claims attention.

In some respects a private man, Cohen occasionally erupted into the news. He was caught in the middle when, after entertaining at Israeli tank emplacements during the Yom Kippur War in 1973, he later sympathized with both sides in the Palestinian-Israeli conflicts. In 2005 he sued his business managers for allegedly misappropriating millions of dollars in income, claiming that they had left him nearly impoverished. These were distractions from what was, after all, his proper business: writing the poems and songs that have become permanent parts of the Canadian consciousness and the annals of popular song. In *Book of Longing* (2006), a collection of poems, ballads, and amateurish but effective drawings, he writes, 'I am this thing that needs to sing.'

brawn n **1** strong well-developed muscles **2** physical strength **3** *Brit & NZ* a seasoned jellied loaf made from the head of a pig **brawny** adj
WORD ORIGIN Old French *braon* meat

bray vb **1** (of a donkey) to utter its characteristic loud harsh sound **2** to utter something with a loud harsh sound ▷ n **3** the loud harsh sound uttered by a donkey **4** a similar loud sound
WORD ORIGIN Old French *braire*

braze vb **brazing, brazed** to join (two metal surfaces) by fusing brass between them
WORD ORIGIN Old French: to burn

brazen adj **1** shameless and bold **2** made of or resembling brass **3** having a ringing metallic sound ▷ vb **4** **brazen it out** to face and overcome a difficult or embarrassing situation boldly or shamelessly **brazenly** adv

brazier[1] (**bray**-zee-er) n a portable metal container for burning charcoal or coal
WORD ORIGIN French *braise* live coals

brazier[2] n a worker in brass

brazil n **1** the red wood of various tropical trees of America **2** same as **brazil nut**
WORD ORIGIN Old Spanish *brasa* glowing coals; referring to the redness of the wood

Brazilian adj **1** of Brazil ▷ n **2** a person from Brazil

brazil nut n a large three-sided nut of a tropical American tree

breach n **1** a breaking of a promise, obligation, etc. **2** any serious disagreement or separation **3** a crack, break, or gap ▷ vb **4** to break (a promise, law, etc.) **5** to break through or make an opening or hole in
WORD ORIGIN Old English *bræc*
USAGE
≡ See at **breech**.

breach of promise n law (formerly) failure to carry out one's promise to marry

breach of the peace n law an offence against public order causing an unnecessary disturbance of the peace

bread n **1** a food made from a dough of flour or meal mixed with water or milk, usually raised with yeast and then baked **2** necessary food **3** slang money ▷ vb **4** to cover (food) with breadcrumbs before cooking
WORD ORIGIN Old English *brēad*

bread and butter n informal a means of support; livelihood

breadboard n **1** a wooden board on which bread is sliced **2** an experimental arrangement of electronic circuits

breadfruit n, pl **-fruits** or **-fruit** a tree of the Pacific Islands, whose edible round fruit has a texture like bread when baked

breadline n **on the breadline** impoverished; living at subsistence level

breadth n **1** the extent or measurement of something from side to side **2** openness and lack of restriction, esp.

of viewpoint or interest; liberality
WORD ORIGIN Old English *brād* broad

breadwinner n a person supporting a family with his or her earnings

break vb **breaking, broke, broken** **1** to separate or become separated into two or more pieces **2** to damage or become damaged so as not to work **3** to burst or cut the surface of (skin) **4** to fracture (a bone) in (a limb, etc.) **5** to fail to observe (an agreement, promise, or law): *they broke their promise* **6** to reveal or be revealed: *she broke the news gently* **7** (foll. by *with*) to separate oneself from **8** to stop for a rest: *to break a journey* **9** to bring or come to an end: *the winter weather broke at last* **10** to weaken or overwhelm or be weakened or overwhelmed, as in spirit: *he felt his life was broken by his illness* **11** to cut through or penetrate: *silence broken by shouts* **12** to improve on or surpass: *she broke three world records* **13** (often foll. by *in*) to accustom (a horse) to the bridle and saddle, to being ridden, etc. **14** (foll. by *of*) to cause (a person) to give up (a habit): *this cure will break you of smoking* **15** to weaken the impact or force of: *this net will break his fall* **16** to decipher: *to break a code* **17** to lose the order of: *to break ranks* **18** to reduce to poverty or the state of bankruptcy **19** to come into being: *light broke over the mountains* **20** (foll. by *into*) **a** to burst into (song, laughter, etc.) **b** to change to (a faster pace) **21** to open with explosives: *to break a safe* **22 a** (of waves) to strike violently against **b** (of waves) to collapse into foam or surf **23** snooker to scatter the balls at the start of a game **24** boxing, wrestling (of two fighters) to separate from a clinch **25** (of the male voice) to undergo a change in register, quality, and range at puberty **26** to interrupt the flow of current in (an electrical circuit) **27 break camp** to pack up and leave a camp **28 break even** to make neither a profit nor a loss **29 break the mould** to make a change that breaks an established habit or pattern ▷ n **30** the act or result of breaking; fracture **31** a brief rest **32** a sudden rush, esp. to escape: *they made a sudden break for freedom* **33** any sudden interruption in a continuous action **34** Brit & NZ a short period between classes at school **35** a (short) holiday **36** informal a fortunate opportunity, esp. to prove oneself **37** informal a piece of good or bad luck **38** billiards, snooker a series of successful shots during one turn **39** snooker the opening shot that scatters the placed balls **40** a discontinuity in an electrical circuit **41 break of day** the dawn ▸ See also **breakaway, break down,** etc. **breakable** adj
WORD ORIGIN Old English *brecan*

breakage n **1** the act or result of breaking **2** compensation or allowance for goods damaged while in use, transit, etc.

breakaway n **1** loss or withdrawal of a group of members from an association, club, etc. **2** Austral a stampede of cattle, esp. at the smell of water ▷ adj **3** dissenting: *a breakaway faction* ▷ vb **break away** **4** to leave hastily or escape **5** to withdraw or quit

break dance n **1** an acrobatic dance style associated with hip-hop music, originating in the 1980s ▷ vb **break-dance, -dancing, -danced** **2** to perform a break dance **break dancing** n

break down vb **1** to cease to function; become ineffective **2** to give way to strong emotion or tears **3** to crush or destroy **4** to have a nervous breakdown **5** to separate into component parts: *with exercise the body breaks down fat to use as fuel* **6** to separate or cause to separate into simpler chemical elements; decompose **7** to analyse or be subjected to analysis ▷ n **breakdown** **8** an act or instance of breaking down; collapse **9** same as **nervous breakdown** **10** an analysis of something into its parts

breaker n **1** a large sea wave with a white crest or one that breaks into foam on the shore **2** a citizens' band radio operator

breakfast n **1** the first meal of the day ▷ vb **2** to eat breakfast
WORD ORIGIN BREAK + FAST[2]

break in vb **1** to enter a building, illegally, esp. by force **2** to interrupt **3** to accustom (a person or animal) to normal duties or practice **4** to use or wear (new shoes or new equipment) until comfortable or running smoothly ▷ n **break-in** **5** the act of illegally entering a building, esp. by thieves

breaking point n the point at which something or someone gives way under strain

breakneck adj (of speed or pace) excessively fast and dangerous

break off vb **1** to sever or detach **2** to end (a relationship or association) **3** to stop abruptly

break out vb **1** to begin or arise suddenly: *fighting broke out between the two factions* **2** to make an escape, esp. from prison **3 break out in** to erupt in (a rash or spots) ▷ n **break-out** **4** an escape, esp. from prison

break through vb **1** to penetrate **2** to achieve success after lengthy efforts ▷ n **breakthrough** **3** a significant development or discovery

break up vb **1** to separate or cause to separate **2** to put an end to (a relationship) or (of a relationship) to come to an end **3** to dissolve or cause to dissolve: *the meeting broke up at noon* **4** Brit (of a school) to close for the holidays ▷ n **break-up** **5** a separation or disintegration

breakwater n a massive wall built out into the sea to protect a shore or harbour from the force of waves

bream n, pl **bream** **1** a freshwater fish covered with silvery scales **2** a food fish of European seas **3** a food fish of Australasian seas
WORD ORIGIN Old French *bresme*

breast n **1** either of the two soft fleshy milk-secreting glands on a woman's chest **2** the front part of the body from the neck to the abdomen; chest **3** the corresponding part in certain other mammals **4** the source of human emotions **5** the part of a garment that covers the breast **6 make a clean breast of something** to divulge truths about oneself ▷ vb *literary* **7** to reach the summit of: *breasting the mountain top* **8** to confront boldly; face: *breast the storm* **WORD ORIGIN** Old English *brēost*

breastbone *n* same as **sternum**

breast-feed *vb* **-feeding, -fed** to feed (a baby) with milk from the breast; suckle

breastplate *n* a piece of armour covering the chest

breaststroke *n* a swimming stroke in which the arms are extended in front of the head and swept back on either side

breastwork *n fortifications* a temporary defensive work, usually breast-high

breath *n* **1** the taking in and letting out of air during breathing **2** a single instance of this **3** the air taken in or let out during breathing **4** the vapour, heat, or odour of air breathed out **5** a slight gust of air **6** a short pause or rest **7** a suggestion or slight evidence; suspicion: *trembling at the least breath of scandal* **8** a whisper or soft sound **9 catch one's breath a** to rest until breathing is normal **b** to stop breathing momentarily from excitement, fear, etc. **10 out of breath** gasping for air after exertion **11 save one's breath** to avoid useless talk **12 take someone's breath away** to overwhelm someone with surprise, etc. **13 under one's breath** in a quiet voice or whisper **WORD ORIGIN** Old English *brǣth*

breathable *adj* **1** (of air) fit to be breathed **2** (of material) allowing air to pass through so that perspiration can evaporate

Breathalyser *or* **-lyzer** *n Brit trademark* a device for estimating the amount of alcohol in the breath **breathalyse** *or* **-lyze** *vb* **WORD ORIGIN** breath + (an)alyser

breathe *vb* **breathing, breathed** **1** to take in oxygen and give out carbon dioxide; respire **2** to exist; be alive **3** to rest to regain breath or composure **4** (esp. of air) to blow lightly **5** to exhale or emit: *the dragon breathed fire* **6** to impart; instil: *a change that breathed new life into Polish industry* **7** to speak softly; whisper **8 breathe again** *or* **freely** *or* **easily** to feel relief **9 breathe one's last** to die

breather *n informal* a short pause for rest

breathing *n* **1** the passage of air into and out of the lungs to supply the body with oxygen **2** the sound this makes

breathing space *n* a short period during which a difficult situation temporarily becomes less severe: *the cut in interest rates creates a breathing space for struggling businesses*

breathless *adj* **1** out of breath; gasping, etc. **2** holding one's breath or having it taken away by excitement, etc. **3** (esp. of the atmosphere) motionless and stifling **breathlessness** *n*

breathtaking *adj* causing awe or excitement

breath test *n* a chemical test of a driver's breath to determine the amount of alcohol consumed

bred *vb* the past of **breed**

bredie (**breed**-ee) *n S African* a meat and vegetable stew **WORD ORIGIN** Portuguese *bredo* ragout

breech *n* **1** the buttocks **2** the part of a firearm behind the barrel **WORD ORIGIN** Old English *brēc*, plural of *brōc* leg covering

▤ **USAGE**
▤ *Breech* is sometimes wrongly used as a
▤ verb where *breach* is meant: *the barrier/*
▤ *agreement was breached* (not *breeched*).

breech delivery *n* birth of a baby with the feet or buttocks appearing first

breeches *pl n* trousers extending to the knee or just below, worn for riding, etc.

breeches buoy *n* a pulley device with a life buoy and pair of breeches attached, which is used as a means of transference between ships or rescue from the sea

breed *vb* **breeding, bred** **1** to produce new or improved strains of (domestic animals and plants) **2** to produce or cause to produce by mating **3** to bear (offspring) **4** to bring up; raise: *she was city bred* **5** to produce or be produced: *the agreement bred confidence between the two* ▷ *n* **6** a group of animals, esp. domestic animals, within a species, that have certain clearly defined characteristics **7** a kind, sort, or group: *he was a gentleman, a breed not greatly admired* **8** a lineage or race **breeder** *n* **WORD ORIGIN** Old English *brēdan*

breeder reactor *n* a nuclear reactor that produces more fissionable material than it uses

breeding *n* **1** the process of producing plants or animals by controlled methods of reproduction **2** the process of bearing offspring **3** the result of good upbringing or training

breeze¹ *n* **1** a gentle or light wind **2** *informal* an easy task ▷ *vb* **breezing, breezed** **3** to move quickly or casually: *he breezed into the room* **WORD ORIGIN** probably from Old Spanish *briza*

breeze² *n* ashes of coal, coke, or charcoal **WORD ORIGIN** French *braise* live coals

breeze block *n* a light building brick made from the ashes of coal, coke, etc. bonded together by cement

breezy *adj* **breezier, breeziest** **1** fresh; windy **2** casual or carefree

Bren gun *n* an air-cooled gas-operated light machine gun **WORD ORIGIN** after *Br*(no), Czech Republic, and *En*(field), England, where it was made

brent *or esp. US* **brant** *n* a small goose with dark grey plumage and a short neck

brethren *pl n archaic* a plural of **brother**

▤ **USAGE**
▤ This plural of *brother*, which has
▤ existed since at least 1200 AD, is now
▤ archaic in English. It is, however, used
▤ between fellow members of a
▤ religious group or order, or sometimes
▤ between fellow members of a group,
▤ political party, or community with
▤ shared interests: *Iranian Shia brethren*
▤ *across the border; Baker's Republican*
▤ *brethren; his sporting brethren.*

Breton *adj* **1** of Brittany ▷ *n* **2** a person from Brittany **3** the Celtic language of Brittany

breve *n* an accent (˘) placed over a vowel to indicate that it is short or is pronounced in a specified way **WORD ORIGIN** Latin *brevis* short

breviary *n, pl* **-ries** *RC Church* a book of psalms, hymns, prayers, etc. to be recited daily **WORD ORIGIN** Latin *brevis* short

brevity *n* **1** a short duration; brief time **2** lack of verbosity **WORD ORIGIN** Latin *brevitas*

brew *vb* **1** to make (beer, ale, etc.) from malt and other ingredients by steeping, boiling, and fermentation **2** to prepare (a drink, such as tea) by infusing **3** to devise or plan: *to brew a plot* **4** to be in the process of being brewed **5** to be about to happen or forming: *a rebellion was brewing* ▷ *n* **6** a beverage produced by brewing, esp. tea or beer **7** an instance of brewing: *last year's brew* **brewer** *n* **WORD ORIGIN** Old English *brēowan*

brewery *n, pl* **-eries** a place where beer, ale, etc. is brewed

briar¹ *or* **brier** *n* **1** a shrub of S Europe, with a hard woody root (briarroot) **2** a tobacco pipe made from this root **WORD ORIGIN** French *bruyère*

briar² *n* same as **brier¹**

bribe *vb* **bribing, bribed** **1** to promise, offer, or give something, often illegally, to (a person) to receive services or gain influence ▷ *n* **2** a reward, such as money or favour, given or offered for this purpose **bribery** *n* **WORD ORIGIN** Old French *briber* to beg

bric-a-brac *n* miscellaneous small ornamental objects **WORD ORIGIN** French

brick *n* **1** a rectangular block of baked or dried clay, used in building construction **2** the material used to make such blocks **3** any rectangular block: *a brick of ice cream* **4** bricks collectively **5** *informal* a reliable, trustworthy, or helpful person **6 drop a brick** *Brit & NZ informal* to make a tactless or indiscreet remark ▷ *vb* **7** (foll. by *in, up, over*) to construct, line, pave, fill, or wall up with bricks: *they bricked up access to the historic pillar* **WORD ORIGIN** Middle Dutch *bricke*

brickbat *n* **1** blunt criticism **2** a piece of brick used as a weapon **WORD ORIGIN** BRICK + BAT¹

bricklayer *n* a person who builds with bricks

brick-red *adj* reddish-brown

bridal *adj* of a bride or a wedding **WORD ORIGIN** Old English *brȳdealu* bride ale

bride *n* a woman who has just been or is about to be married **WORD ORIGIN** Old English *brȳd*

bridegroom *n* a man who has just been or is about to be married **WORD ORIGIN** Old English *brȳdguma*

bridesmaid *n* a girl or young woman who attends a bride at her wedding

bridge¹ *n* **1** a structure that provides a way over a railway, river, etc. **2** a platform from which a ship is piloted

b

and navigated **3** the hard ridge at the upper part of the nose **4** a dental plate containing artificial teeth that is secured to natural teeth **5** a piece of wood supporting the strings of a violin, guitar, etc. ▷*vb* **bridging, bridged 6** to build or provide a bridge over (something) **7** to connect or reduce the distance between: *talks aimed at bridging the gap between the two sides* **WORD ORIGIN** Old English *brycg*

bridge² *n* a card game for four players, based on whist, in which the trump suit is decided by bidding between the players **WORD ORIGIN** origin unknown

bridgehead *n mil* a fortified or defensive position at the end of a bridge nearest to the enemy

bridgework *n* a partial denture attached to the surrounding teeth

bridging loan *n* a loan made to cover the period between two transactions, such as the buying of another house before the sale of the first is completed

bridle *n* **1** headgear for controlling a horse, consisting of straps and a bit and reins **2** something that curbs or restrains ▷*vb* **-dling, -dled 3** to show anger or indignation: *he bridled at the shortness of her tone* **4** to put a bridle on (a horse) **5** to restrain; curb **WORD ORIGIN** Old English *brigdels*

bridle path *n* a path suitable for riding or leading horses

Brie (**bree**) *n* a soft creamy white cheese **WORD ORIGIN** *Brie*, region in N France

brief *adj* **1** short in duration **2** short in length or extent; scanty: *a brief bikini* **3** terse or concise ▷*n* **4** a condensed statement or written synopsis **5** *law* a document containing all the facts and points of law of a case by which a solicitor instructs a barrister to represent a client **6** *RC Church* a papal letter that is less formal than a bull **7** Also called: **briefing** instructions **8 hold a brief for** to argue for; champion **9 in brief** in short; to sum up ▷*vb* **10** to prepare or instruct (someone) by giving a summary of relevant facts **11** *English law* **a** to instruct (a barrister) by brief **b** to retain (a barrister) as counsel **briefly** *adv* **WORD ORIGIN** Latin *brevis*

briefcase *n* a flat portable case for carrying papers, books, etc.

briefs *pl n* men's or women's underpants without legs

brier¹ *or* **briar** *n* any of various thorny shrubs or other plants, such as the sweetbrier **WORD ORIGIN** Old English *brēr, brǣr*

brier² *n* same as **briar¹**

brig¹ *n naut* a two-masted square-rigged ship **WORD ORIGIN** from BRIGANTINE

brig² *n Scot & N English* a bridge

Brig. Brigadier

brigade *n* **1** a military formation smaller than a division and usually commanded by a brigadier **2** a group of people organized for a certain task: *a rescue brigade* **WORD ORIGIN** Old French

brigadier *n* a senior officer in an army, usually commanding a brigade

brigalow *n Austral* a type of acacia tree **WORD ORIGIN** from a native Australian language

brigand *n* a bandit, esp. a member of a gang operating in mountainous areas **WORD ORIGIN** Old French

brigantine *n* a two-masted sailing ship **WORD ORIGIN** Old Italian *brigantino* pirate ship

bright *adj* **1** emitting or reflecting much light; shining **2** (of colours) intense or vivid **3** full of promise: *a bright future* **4** lively or cheerful **5** quick-witted or clever ▷*adv* **6** brightly: *the light burned bright in his office* **brightly** *adv* **brightness** *n* **WORD ORIGIN** Old English *beorht*

brighten *vb* **1** to make or become bright or brighter **2** to make or become cheerful

brill *n, pl* **brill** *or* **brills** a European flatfish similar to the turbot **WORD ORIGIN** probably Cornish *brȳthel* mackerel

brilliance *or* **brilliancy** *n* **1** great brightness **2** excellence in physical or mental ability **3** splendour

brilliant *adj* **1** shining with light; sparkling **2** (of a colour) vivid **3** splendid; magnificent: *a brilliant show* **4** of outstanding intelligence or intellect ▷*n* **5** a diamond cut with many facets to increase its sparkle **WORD ORIGIN** French *brillant* shining

brilliantine *n* a perfumed oil used to make the hair smooth and shiny **WORD ORIGIN** French

brim *n* **1** the upper rim of a cup, bowl, etc. **2** a projecting edge of a hat ▷*vb* **brimming, brimmed 3** to be full to the brim: *he saw the tears that brimmed in her eyes* **brimless** *adj* **WORD ORIGIN** Middle High German *brem*

brimful *adj* (foll. by *of*) completely filled with

brimstone *n obsolete* sulphur **WORD ORIGIN** Old English *brynstān*

brindled *adj* brown or grey streaked with a darker colour: *a brindled dog* **WORD ORIGIN** Middle English *brended*

brine *n* **1** a strong solution of salt and water, used for pickling **2** *literary* the sea or its water **WORD ORIGIN** Old English *brīne*

bring *vb* **bringing, brought 1** to carry, convey, or take (something or someone) to a designated place or person **2** to cause to happen: *responsibility brings maturity* **3** to cause to come to mind: *it brought back memories* **4** to cause to be in a certain state, position, etc.: *the punch brought him to his knees* **5** to make (oneself): *she couldn't bring herself to do it* **6** to sell for: *the painting brought a large sum* **7** *law* **a** to institute (proceedings, charges, etc.) **b** to put (evidence, etc.) before a tribunal ▶ See also **bring about, bring down,** etc. **WORD ORIGIN** Old English *bringan*

bring about *vb* to cause to happen: *a late harvest brought about by bad weather*

bring-and-buy sale *n Brit & NZ* an informal sale, often for charity, to

which people bring items for sale and buy those that others have brought

bring down *vb* to cause to fall

bring forth *vb* to give birth to

bring forward *vb* **1** to move (a meeting or event) to an earlier date or time **2** to present or introduce (a subject) for discussion **3** *book-keeping* to transfer (a sum) to the top of the next page or column

bring in *vb* **1** to yield (income, profit, or cash) **2** to introduce (a legislative bill, etc.) **3** to return (a verdict)

bring off *vb* to succeed in achieving (something difficult)

bring out *vb* **1** to produce, publish, or have (a book) published **2** to expose, reveal, or cause to be seen: *he brought out the best in me* **3** (foll. by *in*) to cause (a person) to become covered with (a rash, spots, etc.)

bring over *vb* to cause (a person) to change allegiances

bring round *vb* **1** to restore (a person) to consciousness after a faint **2** to convince (another person) of an opinion or point of view

bring to *vb* to restore (a person) to consciousness: *the smelling salts brought her to*

bring up *vb* **1** to care for and train (a child); rear **2** to raise (a subject) for discussion; mention **3** to vomit (food)

brinjal *n S African & Indian* dark purple tropical fruit, cooked and eaten as a vegetable **WORD ORIGIN** Portuguese *berinjela*

brink *n* **1** the edge or border of a steep place **2** the land at the edge of a body of water **3 on the brink of** very near; on the point of: *on the brink of disaster* **WORD ORIGIN** Middle Dutch *brinc*

brinkmanship *n* the practice of pressing a dangerous situation to the limit of safety in order to win an advantage

briny *adj* **brinier, briniest 1** of or like brine; salty ▷*n* **2 the briny** *informal* the sea

brio *n* liveliness; vigour **WORD ORIGIN** Italian

briquette *n* a small brick made of compressed coal dust, used for fuel **WORD ORIGIN** French

brisk *adj* **1** lively and quick; vigorous: *brisk trade* **2** invigorating or sharp: *brisk weather* **3** practical and businesslike: *his manner was brisk* **briskly** *adv* **WORD ORIGIN** probably variant of BRUSQUE

brisket *n* beef from the breast of a cow **WORD ORIGIN** probably Scandinavian

brisling *n* same as **sprat** **WORD ORIGIN** Norwegian

bristle *n* **1** any short stiff hair, such as on a pig's back **2** something resembling these hairs: *toothbrush bristle* ▷*vb* **-tling, -tled 3** to stand up or cause to stand up like bristles **4** to show anger or indignation: *she bristled at the suggestion* **5** to be thickly covered or set: *the hedges bristled with blossom* **bristly** *adj* **WORD ORIGIN** Old English *byrst*

Brit *n informal* a British person

Epic and Romance

In everyday usage, *epic* probably means anything that is long and grand, and *romance* denotes a love-story; both terms, however, also refer to ancient literary genres.

Justified or not, the word 'epic' is likely to be used in describing long, serious films or pieces of (especially classical) music, such as Coppola's *Godfather* trilogy or Scorsese's *Gangs of New York* and Wagner's famous Ring Cycle, as well as less weighty works like Tolkien's *Lord of the Rings*, the *Star Wars* series, rock or pop music double-albums such as Pink Floyd's *The Wall*, and occasionally even the latest Harry Potter film. Like *tragedy*, which also began as the name of a genre of classical literature, *epic* is bandied about so frequently that only the vaguest of criteria (usually the length of the work) unites everything attached to it.

The word *epic* comes from ancient Greek *epikos*, an adjective derived from *epos*, 'speech, song'. The original epics were long narrative poems that were recited or sung before an audience and told of the deeds of a hero, and usually an episode important in the national history, such as the founding of the nation, or the defeat of an enemy. The *Iliad* is the classic example in Greek, telling the story of Achilles' heroic death and the Greek victory at the Trojan War. The Roman epic is the *Aeneid*, which tells of Aeneas, who escaped the Trojan defeat and sailed to Italy to found what would become the Roman Empire. *Beowulf* is the epic of Old English; other major epics are the Mesopotamian *Gilgamesh*, the German *Nibelungenlied*, and the Norse sagas.

Because epics record part of a culture's history (or its perceived history) and yet regularly contain fantastic or supernatural elements, they have influenced both historical, fantasy, and even horror writing. Though the Greeks developed prose historical writing, many medieval 'histories' were written in verse, and consciously followed the conventions of epic poetry. As mentioned above, Tolkien's fantasy *Lord of the Rings* is very conscious of epic style, and has copious references to *Beowulf* and the *Iliad*. More recently, Wolfgang Petersen's film *Troy* (2004) presents a version of the *Iliad* with all supernatural elements removed, making it closer to a *historical epic* (an epic perceived as solely based upon fact), and Michael Crichton's novel *The Eaters of the Dead* (1976) takes a similar approach to *Beowulf*.

The *romance* may be seen as a development of the *epic* genre. There was once a great deal of theorizing about how the two forms are related, with scholars such as WP Ker arguing that the *epic* always glorifies the society, while the *romance* celebrates the individual. Any consistent set of features of the *romance* is frustrated by the fact that a large and disparate group of works have claimed that name.

The word *romance* ultimately comes from Latin *romanicus* and means 'Roman'; the same word refers to the Medieval and Modern languages descended from Latin, such as French, Italian, Portuguese, and Spanish. A major difference between *epic* and *romance* is that epics tend to be ancient (being composed before and up to the fall of the Roman Empire) and romances tend to be medieval. Like the epic, romances were originally composed in verse, and they told of historical or quasi-historical figures and deeds. Romance is associated with the three great 'Matters' (that is, areas of subject matter) of the Middle Ages: The *Matter of Rome* (actually stories of Alexander the Great); the *Matter of France* (stories of Charlemagne); and the *Matter of Britain* (Arthurian Legend). The differences in Ancient and Medieval prosodic and narrative conventions accounts for some of the dissimilarity between epic and romance. However, a more important difference is that, whereas many epics were composed orally, romances were all composed in writing.

A great many verse romances from Middle English survive today, including *King Horn*, *Havelok the Dane*, *Sir Orfeo*, and *Sir Gawain and the Green Knight*. Thomas Mallory's *Morte Darthur* was composed in prose, yet it obeys most of the other conventions of romance, takes Arthurian Legend as its subject matter, and even uses much of the typical 'formulaic' vocabulary of romance, which was originally devised for purely prosodic reasons. Thus the romance genre came to have a major impact on the *novel* as a genre, establishing stylistic, linguistic, and subject matter conventions for early prose fiction. Even today, most European languages call the novel a *roman*.

b

Brit. 1 Britain **2** British

Britannia *n* a female warrior carrying a trident and wearing a helmet, personifying Great Britain

Britannia metal *n* an alloy of tin with antimony and copper

Britannic *adj* of Britain; British: *Her Britannic Majesty*

britches *pl n* same as **breeches**

British *adj* **1** of Britain or the British Commonwealth **2** denoting the English language as spoken and written in Britain ▷ *pl n* **3 the British** the people of Britain

British Summer Time *n* a time set one hour ahead of Greenwich Mean Time: used in Britain from the end of March to the end of October, providing an extra hour of daylight in the evening. Abbrev: **BST**

Briton *n* **1** a native or inhabitant of Britain **2** *history* any of the early Celtic inhabitants of S Britain
WORD ORIGIN of Celtic origin

brittle *adj* **1** easily cracked or broken; fragile **2** curt or irritable: *a brittle reply* **3** hard or sharp in quality: *a brittle laugh* **brittly** *adv*
WORD ORIGIN Old English *brēotan* to break

broach *vb* **1** to initiate or introduce (a topic) for discussion **2** to tap or pierce (a container) to draw off (a liquid) **3** to open in order to begin to use ▷ *n* **4** a spit for roasting meat
WORD ORIGIN Latin *brochus* projecting

broad *adj* **1** having great breadth or width **2** of vast extent: *broad plains* **3** not detailed; general **4** clear and open: *broad daylight* **5** obvious: *broad hints* **6** tolerant: *a broad view* **7** extensive: *broad support* **8** vulgar or coarse **9** strongly marked: *he spoke broad Australian English* ▷ *n* **10** *slang chiefly US & Canad* a woman **11 the Broads** in East Anglia, a group of shallow lakes connected by a network of rivers **broadly** *adv*
WORD ORIGIN Old English *brād*

B-road *n* a secondary road in Britain

broadband *n* a telecommunications technique that uses a wide range of frequencies to allow messages to be sent simultaneously

broad bean *n* the large edible flattened seed of a Eurasian bean plant

broadcast *n* **1** a transmission or programme on radio or television ▷ *vb* **-casting, -cast** *or* **-casted 2** to transmit (announcements or programmes) on radio or television **3** to take part in a radio or television programme **4** to make widely known throughout an area: *to broadcast news* **5** to scatter (seed, etc.) **broadcaster** *n* **broadcasting** *n*

broaden *vb* to make or become broad or broader; widen

broad gauge *n* a railway track with a greater distance between the lines than the standard gauge of 56½ inches

broad-leaved *adj* denoting trees other than conifers; having broad rather than needle-shaped leaves

broadloom *adj* of or designating carpets woven on a wide loom

broad-minded *adj* **1** tolerant of opposing viewpoints; liberal **2** not easily shocked

broadsheet *n* a newspaper in a large format

broadside *n* **1** a strong or abusive verbal or written attack **2** *naval* the simultaneous firing of all the guns on one side of a ship **3** *naut* the entire side of a ship ▷ *adv* **4** with a broader side facing an object

broadsword *n* a broad-bladed sword used for cutting rather than stabbing

brocade *n* **1** a rich fabric woven with a raised design ▷ *vb* **-cading, -caded 2** to weave with such a design
WORD ORIGIN Spanish *brocado*

broccoli *n* a variety of cabbage with greenish flower heads
WORD ORIGIN Italian

brochette (brosh-**ett**) *n* a skewer used for holding pieces of meat or vegetables while grilling
WORD ORIGIN Old French *brochete*

brochure *n* a pamphlet or booklet, esp. one containing introductory information or advertising
WORD ORIGIN French

broderie anglaise *n* open embroidery on white cotton, fine linen, etc.
WORD ORIGIN French: English embroidery

broekies (**brook**-eez) *pl n* *S African informal* underpants
WORD ORIGIN Afrikaans

brogue[1] *n* a sturdy walking shoe, often with ornamental perforations
WORD ORIGIN Irish Gaelic *bróg*

brogue[2] *n* a broad gentle-sounding dialectal accent, esp. that used by the Irish in speaking English
WORD ORIGIN origin unknown

broil *vb* same as **grill** (sense 1)
WORD ORIGIN Old French *bruillir*

broiler *n* a young tender chicken suitable for roasting

broke *vb* **1** the past tense of **break** ▷ *adj* **2** *informal* having no money

broken *vb* **1** the past participle of **break** ▷ *adj* **2** fractured, smashed, or splintered **3** interrupted; disturbed: *broken sleep* **4** not functioning **5** (of a promise or contract) violated; infringed **6** (of the speech of a foreigner) imperfectly spoken: *broken English* **7** Also: **broken-in** made tame by training **8** exhausted or weakened, as through ill-health or misfortune

broken chord *n* same as **arpeggio**

broken-down *adj* **1** worn out, as by age or long use; dilapidated **2** not in working order

brokenhearted *adj* overwhelmed by grief or disappointment

broken home *n* a family which does not live together because the parents are separated or divorced

broker *n* **1** an agent who buys or sells goods, securities, etc.: *insurance broker* **2** a person who deals in second-hand goods
WORD ORIGIN Anglo-French *brocour* broacher

brokerage *n* commission charged by a broker

broker-dealer *n* same as **stockbroker**

brolga *n* a large grey Australian crane with a trumpeting call. Also called: **native companion**

brolly *n, pl* **-lies** *Brit, Austral, & NZ informal* an umbrella

bromide *n* **1** *chem* any compound of bromine with another element or radical **2** a dose of sodium or potassium bromide given as a sedative **3** a boring, meaningless, or obvious remark

bromide paper *n* a type of photographic paper coated with an emulsion of silver bromide

bromine *n* *chem* a dark red liquid chemical element that gives off a pungent vapour. Symbol: Br
WORD ORIGIN Greek *brōmos* bad smell

bronchial *adj* of or relating to both of the bronchi or the smaller tubes into which they divide

bronchiole *n* any of the smallest bronchial tubes

bronchitis *n* inflammation of the bronchial tubes, causing coughing and difficulty in breathing

bronchus (**bronk**-uss) *n, pl* **bronchi** (**bronk**-eye) either of the two main branches of the windpipe
WORD ORIGIN Greek *bronkhos*

bronco *n, pl* **-cos** (in the US and Canada) a wild or partially tamed horse
WORD ORIGIN Mexican Spanish

brontosaurus *n* a very large plant-eating four-footed dinosaur that had a long neck and long tail
WORD ORIGIN Greek *brontē* thunder + *sauros* lizard

bronze *n* **1** an alloy of copper and smaller proportions of tin **2** a statue, medal, or other object made of bronze ▷ *adj* **3** made of or resembling bronze **4** yellowish-brown ▷ *vb* **bronzing, bronzed 5** (esp. of the skin) to make or become brown; tan
WORD ORIGIN Italian *bronzo*

Bronze Age *n* a phase of human culture, lasting in Britain from about 2000 to 500 BC during which weapons and tools were made of bronze

bronze medal *n* a medal awarded as third prize

brooch *n* an ornament with a hinged pin and catch, worn fastened to clothing
WORD ORIGIN Old French *broche*

brood *n* **1** a number of young animals, esp. birds, produced at one hatching **2** all the children in a family: often used jokingly ▷ *vb* **3** (of a bird) to sit on or hatch eggs **4** to think long and unhappily about something: *he brooded on his failure to avert the confrontation* **brooding** *n, adj*
WORD ORIGIN Old English *brōd*

broody *adj* **broodier, broodiest 1** moody; introspective **2** (of poultry) wishing to sit on or hatch eggs **3** *informal* (of a woman) wishing to have a baby

brook[1] *n* a natural freshwater stream
WORD ORIGIN Old English *brōc*

brook[2] *vb* to bear; tolerate: *she would brook no opposition*
WORD ORIGIN Old English *brūcan*

broom *n* **1** a type of long-handled sweeping brush **2** a yellow-flowered

b

shrub **3 a new broom** a newly appointed official, etc. eager to make radical changes **WORD ORIGIN** Old English *brōm*

broomstick *n* the long handle of a broom

bros. *or* **Bros.** brothers

broth *n* a soup made by boiling meat, vegetables, etc. in water **WORD ORIGIN** Old English

brothel *n* a house where men pay to have sexual intercourse with prostitutes **WORD ORIGIN** short for *brothel-house*, from Middle English *brothel* useless person

brother *n* **1** a man or boy with the same parents as another person ▸ Related adjective: **fraternal 2** a man belonging to the same group, trade union, etc. as another or others; fellow member **3** comrade; friend **4** *Christianity* a member of a male religious order **WORD ORIGIN** Old English *brōthor*

brotherhood *n* **1** fellowship **2** an association, such as a trade union **3** the state of being a brother

brother-in-law *n, pl* **brothers-in-law 1** the brother of one's wife or husband **2** the husband of one's sister

brotherly *adj* of or like a brother, esp. in showing loyalty and affection

brougham (**brew-am**) *n* a horse-drawn closed carriage with a raised open driver's seat in front **WORD ORIGIN** after Lord *Brougham*

brought *vb* the past of **bring**

brouhaha *n* loud confused noise **WORD ORIGIN** French

brow *n* **1** the part of the face from the eyes to the hairline; forehead **2** same as **eyebrow 3** the jutting top of a hill **WORD ORIGIN** Old English *brū*

browbeat *vb* **-beating, -beat, -beaten** to frighten (someone) with threats

brown *adj* **1** of the colour of wood or the earth **2** (of bread) made from wheatmeal or wholemeal flour **3** deeply tanned ▸ *n* **4** the colour of wood or the earth **5** anything brown, such as brown paint or brown clothing: *clad in brown* ▸ *vb* **6** to make or become brown or browner, for example as a result of cooking **brownish** *adj* **WORD ORIGIN** Old English *brūn*

brown bear *n* a large ferocious brownish bear of N America, Europe, and Asia

brown coal *n* same as **lignite**

browned-off *adj informal chiefly Brit* thoroughly bored and depressed

brownfield *adj* relating to an urban area which has previously been built on: *brownfield sites*

Brownian motion *n physics* the random movement of particles in a fluid, caused by continuous bombardment from molecules of the fluid **WORD ORIGIN** after Robert *Brown*, physicist

brownie *n* **1** (in folklore) an elf said to do helpful work, esp. household chores, at night **2** a small square nutty chocolate cake

Brownie Guide *or* **Brownie** *n* a member of the junior branch of the Guides

Brownie point *n* a notional mark to one's credit for being seen to do the right thing

browning *n Brit* a substance used to darken gravies

brown paper *n* a kind of coarse unbleached paper used for wrapping

brown rice *n* unpolished rice, in which the grains retain the outer yellowish-brown layer (bran)

Brown Shirt *n* **1** (in Nazi Germany) a storm trooper **2** a member of any fascist party or group

brown trout *n* a common brownish trout

browse *vb* **browsing, browsed 1** to look through (a book or articles for sale) in a casual leisurely manner **2** *computers* to read hypertext, esp. on the World Wide Web **3** (of deer, goats, etc.) to feed upon vegetation by continual nibbling ▸ *n* **4** an instance of browsing **WORD ORIGIN** French *broust* bud

browser *n computers* a software package that enables a user to read hypertext, esp. on the World Wide Web

brucellosis *n* an infectious disease of cattle, goats, and pigs, caused by bacteria and transmittable to humans **WORD ORIGIN** after Sir David *Bruce*, bacteriologist

bruise *vb* **bruising, bruised 1** to injure (body tissue) without breaking the skin, usually with discoloration, or (of body tissue) to be injured in this way **2** to hurt (someone's feelings) **3** to damage (fruit) ▸ *n* **4** a bodily injury without a break in the skin, usually with discoloration **WORD ORIGIN** Old English *brȳsan*

bruiser *n informal* a strong tough person, esp. a boxer or a bully

brumby *n, pl* **-bies** *Austral* **1** a wild horse **2** an unruly person **WORD ORIGIN** origin unknown

brunch *n* a meal eaten late in the morning, combining breakfast with lunch **WORD ORIGIN** BR(EAKFAST) + (L)UNCH

brunette *n* a girl or woman with dark brown hair **WORD ORIGIN** French

brunt *n* the main force or shock of a blow, attack, etc.: *the town bore the brunt of the earthquake*

bruschetta (broo-**sket**-ta) *n* an Italian open sandwich of toasted bread topped with olive oil and tomatoes, olives, etc. **WORD ORIGIN** Italian

brush[1] *n* **1** a device made of bristles, hairs, wires, etc. set into a firm back or handle: used to apply paint, groom the hair, etc. **2** the act of brushing **3** a brief encounter, esp. an unfriendly one **4** the bushy tail of a fox **5** an electric conductor, esp. one made of carbon, that conveys current between stationary and rotating parts of a generator, motor, etc. ▸ *vb* **6** to clean, scrub, or paint with a brush **7** to apply or remove with a brush or brushing movement **8** to touch lightly and briefly ▸ See also **brush aside, brush off, brush up WORD ORIGIN** Old French *broisse*

brush[2] *n* a thick growth of shrubs and small trees; scrub **WORD ORIGIN** Old French *broce*

brush aside *or* **away** *vb* to dismiss (a suggestion or an idea) without consideration; disregard

brushed *adj textiles* treated with a brushing process to raise the nap and give a softer and warmer finish: *brushed nylon*

brush off *slang vb* **1** to dismiss and ignore (a person), esp. curtly ▸ *n* **brushoff 2** give someone the brushoff to reject someone

brush turkey *n* a bird of New Guinea and Australia resembling the domestic fowl, with black plumage

brush up *vb* **1** (often foll. by *on*) to refresh one's knowledge or memory of (a subject) ▸ *n* **brush-up 2** *Brit* the act of tidying one's appearance: *have a wash and brush-up*

brushwood *n* **1** cut or broken-off tree branches, twigs, etc. **2** same as **brush**[2]

brushwork *n* a characteristic manner of applying paint with a brush: *Rembrandt's brushwork*

brusque *adj* blunt or curt in manner or speech **brusquely** *adv* **brusqueness** *n* **WORD ORIGIN** Italian *brusco* sour

Brussels sprout *n* a vegetable like a tiny cabbage

brut (**broot**) *adj* (of champagne or sparkling wine) very dry

brutal *adj* **1** cruel; vicious; savage **2** harsh or severe **3** extremely honest or frank in speech or manner **brutality** *n* **brutally** *adv*

brutalism *n* an austere architectural style of the 1950s on, characterized by the use of exposed concrete and angular shapes

brutalize *or* **-ise** *vb* **-izing, -ized** *or* **-ising, -ised 1** to make or become brutal **2** to treat (someone) brutally **brutalization** *or* **-isation** *n*

brute *n* **1** a brutal person **2** any animal except man; beast ▸ *adj* **3** wholly instinctive or physical, like that of an animal: *cricket is not a game of brute force* **4** without reason or intelligence **5** coarse and grossly sensual **WORD ORIGIN** Latin *brutus* irrational

brutish *adj* **1** of or resembling a brute; animal **2** coarse; cruel; stupid

bryony *n, pl* **-nies** a herbaceous climbing plant with greenish flowers and red or black berries **WORD ORIGIN** Greek *bruōnia*

Brythonic (brith-**on**-ik) *n* **1** the S group of Celtic languages, consisting of Welsh, Cornish, and Breton ▸ *adj* **2** of this group of languages **WORD ORIGIN** Welsh *Brython* Celt

BS 1 Bachelor of Surgery **2** British Standard(s)

BSc Bachelor of Science

BSE bovine spongiform encephalopathy: a fatal virus disease of cattle

BSI British Standards Institution

B-side *n* the less important side of a gramophone record

BSL British Sign Language

BST British Summer Time

Bt Baronet

BT British Telecom

btu or **BThU** British thermal unit

bubble n **1** a small globule of air or a gas in a liquid or a solid **2** a thin film of liquid forming a ball around air or a gas: *a soap bubble* **3** a dome, esp. a transparent glass or plastic one **4** an unreliable scheme or enterprise ▷ vb **-bling, -bled 5** to form bubbles **6** to move or flow with a gurgling sound **7 bubble over** to express an emotion freely: *she was bubbling over with excitement* **WORD ORIGIN** probably Scandinavian

bubble and squeak n *Brit, Austral, & NZ* a dish of boiled cabbage and potatoes fried together

bubble bath n **1** a substance used to scent, soften, and foam in bath water **2** a bath with such a substance

bubble car n *Brit* a small car of the 1950s with a transparent bubble-shaped top

bubble gum n a type of chewing gum that can be blown into large bubbles

bubble wrap n a type of polythene wrapping containing many small air pockets, used to protect breakable goods

bubbly adj **-blier, -bliest 1** lively; animated; excited **2** full of or resembling bubbles ▷ n **3** *informal* champagne

bubo (byew-boh) n, pl **-boes** *pathol* inflammation and swelling of a lymph node, esp. in the armpit or groin **bubonic** (bew-**bonn**-ik) adj **WORD ORIGIN** Greek *boubōn* groin

bubonic plague n an acute infectious disease characterized by the formation of buboes

buccaneer n a pirate, esp. in the Caribbean in the 17th and 18th centuries **WORD ORIGIN** French *boucanier*

buck[1] n **1** the male of the goat, hare, kangaroo, rabbit, and reindeer **2** *archaic* a spirited young man **3** the act of bucking ▷ vb **4** (of a horse or other animal) to jump vertically, with legs stiff and back arched **5** (of a horse, etc.) to throw (its rider) by bucking **6** *informal* to resist or oppose obstinately: *bucking the system* ▶ See also **buck up** **WORD ORIGIN** Old English *bucca* he-goat

buck[2] n *US, Canad, Austral, & NZ informal* a dollar **WORD ORIGIN** origin unknown

buck[3] n **pass the buck** *informal* to shift blame or responsibility onto another **WORD ORIGIN** probably from *buckhorn knife*, placed before a player in poker to indicate that he was the next dealer

bucket n **1** an open-topped cylindrical container with a handle **2** the amount a bucket will hold **3** a bucket-like part of a machine, such as the scoop on a mechanical shovel **4 kick the bucket** *slang* to die ▷ vb **-eting, -eted 5** (often foll. by *down*) (of rain) to fall very heavily **WORD ORIGIN** Old English *būc*

bucket shop n **1** *chiefly Brit* a travel agency specializing in cheap airline tickets **2** an unregistered firm of stockbrokers that engages in fraudulent speculation

buckle n **1** a clasp for fastening together two loose ends, esp. of a belt or strap ▷ vb **-ling, -led 2** to fasten or be fastened with a buckle **3** to bend or cause to bend out of shape, esp. as a result of pressure or heat **WORD ORIGIN** Latin *buccula* cheek strap

buckle down vb *informal* to apply oneself with determination

buckler n a small round shield worn on the forearm **WORD ORIGIN** Old French *bocler*

Bucks Buckinghamshire

buckshee adj *Brit slang* without charge; free **WORD ORIGIN** from BAKSHEESH

buckshot n large lead pellets used for hunting game

buckskin n **1** a strong greyish-yellow suede leather, originally made from deerskin **2 buckskins** trousers made f buckskin

buckteeth pl n projecting upper front teeth **buck-toothed** adj

buckthorn n a thorny shrub whose berries were formerly used as a purgative

buck up vb *informal* **1** to make or become more cheerful or confident **2** to make haste

buckwheat n **1** a type of small black seed used as animal fodder and in making flour **2** the flour obtained from such seeds **WORD ORIGIN** Middle Dutch *boecweite*

bucolic (byew-**koll**-ik) adj **1** of the countryside or country life; rustic **2** of or relating to shepherds; pastoral ▷ n **3** a pastoral poem **WORD ORIGIN** Greek *boukolos* cowherd

bud n **1** a swelling on the stem of a plant that develops into a flower or leaf **2** a partially opened flower: *rosebud* **3** any small budlike outgrowth: *taste buds* **4 nip something in the bud** to put an end to something in its initial stages ▷ vb **budding, budded 5** (of plants and some animals) to produce buds **6** *horticulture* to graft (a bud) from one plant onto another **WORD ORIGIN** Middle English *budde*

Buddhism n a religion founded by the Buddha that teaches that all suffering can be brought to an end by overcoming greed, hatred, and delusion **Buddhist** n, adj

budding adj beginning to develop or grow: *a budding actor*

buddleia n a shrub which has long spikes of purple flowers **WORD ORIGIN** after A. *Buddle*, botanist

buddy n, pl **-dies 1** *chiefly US & Canad informal* a friend **2** a volunteer who helps and supports a person suffering from AIDS ▷ vb **-dies, -dying, -died 3** to act as a buddy to (a person suffering from AIDS) **WORD ORIGIN** probably variant of BROTHER

budge vb **budging, budged 1** to move slightly: *he refuses to budge off that chair* **2** to change or cause to change opinions: *nothing would budge him from this idea*

WORD ORIGIN Old French *bouger*

budgerigar n a small cage bird bred in many different-coloured varieties **WORD ORIGIN** Aboriginal

budget n **1** a plan of expected income and expenditure over a specified period **2** the total amount of money allocated for a specific purpose during a specified period ▷ adj **3** inexpensive: *a budget hotel* ▷ vb **-eting, -eted 4** to enter or provide for in a budget **5** to plan the expenditure of (money or time) **budgetary** adj **WORD ORIGIN** Latin *bulga* leather pouch

Budget n **the Budget** an annual estimate of British government expenditures and revenues and the financial plans for the following financial year

budget deficit n the amount by which government spending exceeds income from taxation, etc.

budgie n *informal* same as **budgerigar**

buff[1] n **1** a soft thick flexible undyed leather **2** a cloth or pad of material used for polishing **3 in the buff** *informal* completely naked ▷ adj **4** dull yellowish-brown **5** *informal* in a condition of high physical fitness and body tone ▷ vb **6** to clean or polish (a metal, floor, shoes, etc.) with a buff **WORD ORIGIN** Late Latin *bufalus* buffalo

buff[2] n *informal* an expert on or devotee of a given subject: *an opera buff* **WORD ORIGIN** from the buff-coloured uniforms worn by volunteer firemen in New York City

buffalo n, pl **-loes** or **-lo 1** a type of cattle with upward-curving horns **2** same as **water buffalo 3** *US & Canad* a bison **WORD ORIGIN** Greek *bous* ox

buffer[1] n **1** one of a pair of spring-loaded steel pads at the ends of railway vehicles and railway tracks that reduces shock on impact **2** a person or thing that lessens shock or protects from damaging impact, circumstances, etc. **3** *chem* **a** a substance added to a solution to resist changes in its acidity or alkalinity **b** Also called: **buffer solution** a solution containing such a substance **4** *computers* a device for temporarily storing data ▷ vb **5** to cushion; provide a buffer for **WORD ORIGIN** from BUFFET[2]

buffer[2] n *Brit informal* a stupid or bumbling person, esp. a man: *an old buffer* **WORD ORIGIN** origin unknown

buffer state n a small and usually neutral state between two rival powers

buffet[1] (boof-fay, buff-ay) n **1** a counter where light refreshments are served **2** a meal at which guests help themselves from a number of dishes **WORD ORIGIN** French

buffet[2] (buff-it) vb **-feting, -feted 1** to knock against or about; batter: *the ship was buffeted by strong winds* **2** to hit, esp. with the fist ▷ n **3** a blow, esp. with a hand **WORD ORIGIN** Old French *buffeter*

buffet car (boof-fay) n *Brit* a railway coach where light refreshments are served

Words from Shakespeare
part 4

bevy *n* type or sort
  many more of the same bevy *Hamlet* 5.2

blazon *v* to display or show something
  that thy skill be more to blazon it
  Romeo and Juliet 2.6

blind *adj* reckless or not concerned about consequences
  are you yet to your own souls so blind
  That two you will war with God by murdering me
  Richard III 1.4

bombast *n* wool stuffing (used in a cushion, for example) and so it came to mean something padded out or long-winded
  How now my sweet creature of bombast
  Henry IV part 1 2.4

bond *n* a contract or legal deed
  Well, then, your bond, and let me see
  Merchant of Venice 1.3

bottom *n* essence, main point or intent
  Now I see
  The bottom of your purpose
  All's Well That Ends Well 3.7

bounteously *adv* plentifully, abundantly
  I prithee, and I'll pay thee bounteously
  Twelfth Night 1.2

brace *n* a couple or two
  Have lost a brace of kinsmen *Romeo and Juliet* 5.3

brand *v* to mark permanantly
  the wheeled seat
  Of fortunate Caesar ... branded his baseness that
  ensued *Anthony and Cleopatra* 4.14

brave *adj* fine, excellent or splendid
  O brave new world
  That has such people in't
  The Tempest 5.1

brine *n* sea-water
  He shall drink nought brine, for I'll not show him
  Where the quick freshes are *The Tempest* 3.2

brow *n* appearance
  doth hourly grow
  Out of his brows *Hamlet* 3.3

burden *n* a chorus
  I would sing my song without a burden
  As You Like It 3.2

buttons, in one's *phrase* clear, easy to see
  Tis in his buttons he will carry't
  The Merry Wives of Windsor 3.2

cable *n* scope or reach
  The law ... Will give her cable *Othello* 1.2

cadent *adj* falling or dropping
  With cadent tears fret channels in her cheeks
  King Lear 1.4

canker *v* to decay, become corrupt
  And, as with age his body uglier grows,
  So his mind cankers *The Tempest* 4.1

canon, from the *phrase* out of order, improper
  Twas from the canon *Coriolanus* 3.1

cap-a-pie *adv* from head to foot, completely
  I am courtier cap-a-pie *The Winter's Tale* 4.4

carbonadoed *adj* cut or scored (scratched) with a knife
  it is your carbonadoed *All's Well That Ends Well* 4.5

carouse *v* to drink at length, party
  They cast their caps up and carouse together
  Anthony and Cleopatra 4.12

carrack *n* a large old ship, a galleon
  Faith, he tonight hath boarded a land-carrack
  Othello 1.2

cassock *n* a military cloak, long coat
  half of the which dare not shake the snow from off
  their cassocks lest they shake themselves to pieces
  All's Well That Ends Well 4.3

catastrophe *n* conclusion or end
  pat he comes, like the catastrophe of the old
  comedy *King Lear* 1.2

buffoon n a person who amuses others by silly behaviour **buffoonery** n
WORD ORIGIN Latin *bufo* toad

bug n **1** any of various insects having piercing and sucking mouthparts **2** *chiefly US & Canad* any insect **3** *informal* a minor illness caused by a germ or virus **4** *informal* a small error, esp. in a computer or computer program **5** *informal* an obsessive idea or hobby **6** *informal* a concealed microphone used for recording conversations in spying **7** *Austral* a flattish edible shellfish ▷ *vb* **bugging, bugged** *informal* **8** to irritate or upset (someone) **9** to conceal a microphone in (a room or telephone)
WORD ORIGIN origin unknown

bugbear n a thing that causes obsessive anxiety
WORD ORIGIN obsolete *bug* an evil spirit + BEAR[2]

bugger n **1** *taboo slang* a person or thing considered to be unpleasant or difficult **2** *slang* a humorous or affectionate term for someone: *a friendly little bugger* **3** a person who practises buggery ▷ *vb* **4** *slang* to tire; weary **5** to practise buggery with ▷ *interj* **6** *taboo slang* an exclamation of annoyance or disappointment
WORD ORIGIN Medieval Latin *Bulgarus* Bulgarian heretic

bugger about or **around** *vb slang* **1** to fool about and waste time **2** to create difficulties for: *they really buggered me about when I tried to get my money back*

bugger off *vb taboo slang* to go away; depart

bugger up *vb slang* to spoil or ruin (something)

buggery n *Brit, Austral, & NZ* anal intercourse

buggy n, pl **-gies 1** a light horse-drawn carriage having two or four wheels **2** a lightweight folding pram for babies or young children
WORD ORIGIN origin unknown

bugle *music* n **1** a brass instrument used chiefly for military calls ▷ *vb* **-gling, -gled 2** to play or sound (on) a bugle **bugler** n
WORD ORIGIN short for *bugle horn* ox horn, from Latin *buculus* bullock

build *vb* **building, built 1** to make or construct by joining parts or materials: *more than 100 bypasses have been built in the past decade* **2** to establish and develop: *it took ten years to build the business* **3** to make in a particular way or for a particular purpose: *she's built for speed, not stamina* **4** (often foll. by *up*) to increase in intensity ▷ *n* **5** physical form, figure, or proportions: *he has an athletic build*
WORD ORIGIN Old English *byldan*

builder n a person who constructs houses and other buildings

building n **1** a structure, such as a house, with a roof and walls **2** the business of building houses, etc.

building society n a cooperative banking enterprise where money can be invested and mortgage loans made available

build up *vb* **1** to construct (something) gradually, systematically, and in stages **2** to increase by degrees: *he steadily built up a power base* **3** to prepare for or gradually approach a climax ▷ *n* **build-up 4** a progressive increase in number or size: *the build-up of industry* **5** a gradual approach to a climax **6** extravagant publicity or praise, esp. as a campaign

built *vb* the past of **build**

built-in *adj* **1** included as an essential part: *a built-in cupboard* **2** essential: *a built-in instinct*

built-up *adj* **1** having many buildings: *a built-up area* **2** increased by the addition of parts: *built-up heels*

bulb n **1** same as **light bulb 2** the onion-shaped base of the stem of some plants, which sends down roots **3** a plant, such as a daffodil, which grows from a bulb **4** any bulb-shaped thing **bulbous** *adj*
WORD ORIGIN Greek *bolbos* onion

Bulgarian *adj* **1** of Bulgaria ▷ *n* **2** a person from Bulgaria **3** the language of Bulgaria

bulge n **1** a swelling or an outward curve on a normally flat surface **2** a sudden increase in number, esp. of population ▷ *vb* **bulging, bulged 3** to swell outwards **bulging** *adj*
WORD ORIGIN Latin *bulga* bag

bulimia n a disorder characterized by compulsive overeating followed by vomiting **bulimic** *adj, n*
WORD ORIGIN Greek *bous* ox + *limos* hunger

bulk n **1** volume or size, esp. when great **2** the main part: *he spends the bulk of his time abroad* **3** a large body, esp. of a person **4** the part of food which passes unabsorbed through the digestive system **5 in bulk** in large quantities: *how frequently do you buy food in bulk for your family?* ▷ *vb* **6 bulk large** to be or seem important or prominent
WORD ORIGIN Old Norse *bulki* cargo

≡ USAGE
≡ The use of a plural noun after *bulk* was
≡ formerly considered incorrect, but is
≡ now acceptable.

bulk buying n the purchase of goods in large amounts, often at reduced prices

bulkhead n any upright partition in a ship or aeroplane
WORD ORIGIN probably from Old Norse *bálkr* partition + HEAD

bulky *adj* **bulkier, bulkiest** very large and massive, esp. so as to be unwieldy **bulkiness** n

bull[1] n **1** a male of domestic cattle, esp. one that is sexually mature **2** the male of various other animals including the elephant and whale **3** a very large, strong, or aggressive person **4** *stock exchange* a speculator who buys in anticipation of rising prices in order to make a profit on resale **5** *chiefly Brit* same as **bull's-eye** (senses 1, 2) **6 like a bull in a china shop** clumsy **7 take the bull by the horns** to face and tackle a difficulty without shirking
WORD ORIGIN Old English *bula*

bull[2] n a ludicrously self-contradictory or nonsensical statement
WORD ORIGIN origin unknown

bull[3] n a formal document issued by the pope

WORD ORIGIN Latin *bulla* round object

bull bars *pl* n a large protective metal grille on the front of some vehicles, esp. four-wheel-drive vehicles

bulldog n a thickset dog with a broad head and a muscular body

bulldog clip n a clip for holding papers together, consisting of two metal clamps and a spring

bulldoze *vb* **-dozing, -dozed 1** to move, demolish, or flatten with a bulldozer **2** *informal* to coerce (someone) into doing something by intimidation
WORD ORIGIN origin unknown

bulldozer n a powerful tractor fitted with caterpillar tracks and a blade at the front, used for moving earth

bullet n a small metallic missile used as the projectile of a gun or rifle
WORD ORIGIN French *boulette* little ball

bulletin n **1** a broadcast summary of the news **2** an official statement on a matter of public interest **3** a periodical published by an organization for its members
WORD ORIGIN Italian *bulla* papal edict

bulletin board n **1** *US* same as **notice board 2** *computers* a type of data-exchange system by which messages can be sent and read

bullfight n a public show, popular in Spain, in which a matador baits and usually kills a bull in an arena **bullfighter** n **bullfighting** n

bullfinch n a common European songbird with a black head and, in the male, a pinkish breast

bullfrog n any of various large frogs having a loud deep croak

bullion n gold or silver in the form of bars and ingots
WORD ORIGIN Anglo-French: mint

bull-necked *adj* having a short thick neck

bullock n a gelded bull; steer
WORD ORIGIN Old English *bulluc*

bullring n an arena for staging bullfights

bull's-eye n **1** the small central disc of a target or a dartboard **2** a shot hitting this **3** *informal* something that exactly achieves its aim **4** a peppermint-flavoured boiled sweet **5** a small circular window **6** a thick disc of glass set into a ship's deck, etc. to admit light **7** the glass boss at the centre of a sheet of blown glass **8 a** a convex lens used as a condenser **b** a lamp or lantern containing such a lens

bullshit *taboo slang* n **1** exaggerated or foolish talk; nonsense ▷ *vb* **-shitting, -shitted 2** to talk bullshit to: *don't bullshit me*

bull terrier n a terrier with a muscular body and a short smooth coat

bully n, pl **-lies 1** a person who hurts, persecutes, or intimidates weaker people ▷ *vb* **-lies, -lying, -lied 2** to hurt, intimidate, or persecute (a weaker or smaller person) ▷ *interj* **3 bully for you** or **him, etc.** *informal* well done! bravo!: now usually used sarcastically
WORD ORIGIN originally, sweetheart, fine fellow, swaggering coward, probably from Middle Dutch *boele* lover

b

bully beef *n* canned corned beef
WORD ORIGIN French *bœuf bouilli* boiled beef

bully-off *hockey n* **1** the method of restarting play in which two opposing players stand with the ball between them and strike their sticks together three times before trying to hit the ball ▷ *vb* **bully off 2** to restart play with a bully-off
WORD ORIGIN origin unknown

bulrush *n* **1** a tall reedlike marsh plant with brown spiky flowers **2** *Bible* same as **papyrus** (sense 1)
WORD ORIGIN Middle English *bulrish*

bulwark *n* **1** a wall or similar structure used as a fortification; rampart **2** a person or thing acting as a defence
WORD ORIGIN Middle High German *bolwerk*

bum¹ *n Brit, Austral, & NZ slang* the buttocks or anus
WORD ORIGIN origin unknown

bum² *informal n* **1** a disreputable loafer or idler **2** a tramp; hobo ▷ *vb* **bumming, bummed 3** to get by begging; cadge: *to bum a lift* **4 bum around** to spend time to no good purpose; loaf ▷ *adj* **5** of poor quality; useless: *he hit a bum note*
WORD ORIGIN probably from German *bummeln* to loaf

bumbag *n* a small bag worn on a belt around the waist

bumble *vb* **-bling, -bled 1** to speak or do in a clumsy, muddled, or inefficient way **2** to move in a clumsy or unsteady way **bumbling** *adj, n*
WORD ORIGIN origin unknown

bumblebee *n* a large hairy bee
WORD ORIGIN obsolete *bumble* to buzz

bumf *or* **bumph** *n Brit, Austral, & NZ* **1** *informal* official documents or forms **2** *slang* toilet paper
WORD ORIGIN short for *bumfodder*

bump *vb* **1** to knock or strike (someone or something) with a jolt **2** to travel or proceed in jerks and jolts **3** to hurt by knocking ▷ *n* **4** an impact; knock; jolt; collision **5** a dull thud from an impact or collision **6** a lump on the body caused by a blow **7** a raised uneven part, such as on a road surface ▷ See also **bump into, bump off, bump up** ▷ **bumpy** *adj*
WORD ORIGIN probably imitative

bumper¹ *n* a horizontal bar attached to the front and rear of a vehicle to protect against damage from impact

bumper² *n* **1** a glass or tankard, filled to the brim, esp. as a toast **2** an unusually large or fine example of something ▷ *adj* **3** unusually large, fine, or abundant: *a bumper crop*
WORD ORIGIN probably obsolete *bump* to bulge

bumph *n* same as **bumf**

bump into *vb informal* to meet (someone) by chance

bumpkin *n* an awkward simple rustic person: *a country bumpkin*
WORD ORIGIN probably from Dutch

bump off *vb slang* to murder (someone)

bumptious *adj* offensively self-assertive or conceited
WORD ORIGIN probably *bump* + *fractious*

bump up *vb informal* to increase (prices) by a large amount

bun *n* **1** a small sweetened bread roll, often containing currants or spices **2** a small round cake **3** a hairstyle in which long hair is gathered into a bun shape at the back of the head
WORD ORIGIN origin unknown

bunch *n* **1** a number of things growing, fastened, or grouped together: *a bunch of grapes; a bunch of keys* **2** a collection; group: *a bunch of queries* **3** a group or company: *a bunch of cowards* ▷ *vb* **4** to group or be grouped into a bunch
WORD ORIGIN origin unknown

bundle *n* **1** a number of things or a quantity of material gathered or loosely bound together: *a bundle of sticks* **2** something wrapped or tied for carrying; package **3** *biol* a collection of strands of specialized tissue such as nerve fibres **4** *bot* a strand of conducting tissue within plants ▷ *vb* **-dling, -dled 5** (foll. by *out, off,* or *into,* etc.) to cause (someone) to go, esp. roughly or unceremoniously: *she bundled them unceremoniously out into the garden* **6** to push or throw (something), esp. in a quick untidy way: *the soiled items were bundled into a black plastic bag*
WORD ORIGIN probably from Middle Dutch *bundel*

bundle up *vb* to make (something) into a bundle or bundles

bundu *n S African & Zimbabwean slang* a largely uninhabited wild region far from towns
WORD ORIGIN from a Bantu language

bun fight *n Brit, Austral, & NZ slang* a tea party

bung *n* **1** a stopper, esp. of cork or rubber, used to close something such as a cask or flask **2** same as **bunghole** ▷ *vb* **3** (foll. by *up*) *informal* to close or seal (something) with or as if with a bung **4** *Brit, Austral, & NZ slang* to throw (something) somewhere in a careless manner; sling
WORD ORIGIN Middle Dutch *bonghe*

bungalow *n* a one-storey house
WORD ORIGIN Hindi *banglā* (house) of Bengali type

bungee jumping *or* **bungy jumping** *n* a sport in which a person jumps from a high bridge, tower, etc. to which he or she is connected by a rubber rope
WORD ORIGIN from *bungie*, slang word for India rubber

bunghole *n* a hole in a cask or barrel through which liquid can be drained

bungle *vb* **-gling, -gled 1** to spoil (an operation) through clumsiness or incompetence; botch ▷ *n* **2** a clumsy or unsuccessful performance; blunder **bungler** *n* **bungling** *adj, n*
WORD ORIGIN origin unknown

bunion *n* an inflamed swelling of the first joint of the big toe
WORD ORIGIN origin unknown

bunk¹ *n* **1** a narrow shelflike bed fixed along a wall, esp. in a caravan or ship **2** same as **bunk bed**
WORD ORIGIN probably from *bunker*

bunk² *n informal* same as **bunkum**

bunk³ *n* **do a bunk 1** *Brit, Austral, & NZ slang* to make a hurried and secret

departure **2** *Brit, NZ, & S African* be absent without permission
WORD ORIGIN origin unknown

bunk bed *n* one of a pair of beds constructed one above the other to save space

bunker *n* **1** an obstacle on a golf course, usually a sand-filled hollow bordered by a ridge **2** an underground shelter **3** a large storage container for coal, etc.
WORD ORIGIN Scots *bonkar*

bunkum *n* empty talk; nonsense
WORD ORIGIN after *Buncombe*, North Carolina, alluded to in an inane speech by its Congressional representative

bunny *n, pl* **-nies** a child's word for **rabbit**
WORD ORIGIN Scottish Gaelic *bun* rabbit's tail

bunny girl *n* a night-club hostess whose costume includes a rabbit-like tail and ears

Bunsen burner *n* a gas burner consisting of a metal tube with an adjustable air valve at the base
WORD ORIGIN after R. W. *Bunsen*, chemist

bunting¹ *n* decorative flags, pennants, and streamers
WORD ORIGIN origin unknown

bunting² *n* a songbird with a short stout bill
WORD ORIGIN origin unknown

bunya *n* a tall dome-shaped Australian coniferous tree

bunyip *n Austral* a legendary monster said to live in swamps and lakes
WORD ORIGIN from a native Australian language

buoy *n* **1** a brightly coloured floating object anchored to the sea bed for marking moorings, navigable channels, or obstructions in the water ▷ *vb* **2** (foll. by *up*) to prevent from sinking: *the life belt buoyed him up* **3** to raise the spirits of; hearten: *exports are on the increase, buoyed by a weak dollar* **4** *naut* to mark (a channel or obstruction) with a buoy or buoys
WORD ORIGIN probably Germanic

buoyant *adj* **1** able to float in or rise to the surface of a liquid **2** (of a liquid or gas) able to keep a body afloat **3** thriving: *a buoyant economy* **4** cheerful or resilient **buoyancy** *n*

bur *or* **burr** *n* **1** a seed case or flower head with hooks or prickles **2** any plant that produces burs
WORD ORIGIN probably from Old Norse

burble *vb* **-bling, -bled 1** to make or utter with a bubbling sound; gurgle **2** to talk quickly and excitedly
WORD ORIGIN probably imitative

burbot *n, pl* **-bots** *or* **-bot** a freshwater fish of the cod family that has barbels around its mouth
WORD ORIGIN Old French *bourbotte*

burden¹ *n* **1** something that is carried; load **2** something that is difficult to bear ▷ Related adjective: **onerous** *vb* **3** to put or impose a burden on; load **4** to weigh down; oppress **burdensome** *adj*
WORD ORIGIN Old English *byrthen*

burden² *n* **1** a line of words recurring at the end of each verse of a song **2** the

theme of a speech, book, etc.
WORD ORIGIN Old French *bourdon* droning sound

burdock *n* a weed with large heart-shaped leaves, and burlike fruits
WORD ORIGIN BUR + DOCK⁴

bureau (byew-roe) *n, pl* -reaus *or* -reaux (-rose) **1** an office or agency, esp. one providing services for the public **2** *US* a government department **3** *chiefly Brit* a writing desk with pigeonholes and drawers against which the writing surface can be closed when not in use **4** *US* a chest of drawers
WORD ORIGIN French

bureaucracy *n, pl* -cies **1** a rigid system of administration based upon organization into bureaus, division of labour, a hierarchy of authority, etc. **2** government by such a system **3** government officials collectively **4** any administration in which action is impeded by unnecessary official procedures

bureaucrat *n* **1** an official in a bureaucracy **2** an official who adheres rigidly to bureaucracy **bureaucratic** *adj*

bureau de change *n* a place where foreign currencies can be exchanged
WORD ORIGIN French

burette *or US* **buret** *n* a graduated glass tube with a stopcock on one end for dispensing known volumes of fluids
WORD ORIGIN Old French *buire* ewer

burgeon *vb* to develop or grow rapidly; flourish
WORD ORIGIN Old French *burjon*

burger *n informal* same as **hamburger**

burgh *n* (in Scotland until 1975) a town with a degree of self-government
WORD ORIGIN Scots form of *borough*

burgher *n archaic* a citizen, esp. one from the Continent
WORD ORIGIN German *Bürger* or Dutch *burger*

burglar *n* a person who illegally enters a property to commit a crime
WORD ORIGIN Medieval Latin *burglator*

burglary *n, pl* -ries the crime of entering a building as a trespasser to commit theft or another offence

burgle *vb* -gling, -gled to break into (a house, shop, etc.)

burgomaster *n* the chief magistrate of a town in Austria, Belgium, Germany, or the Netherlands
WORD ORIGIN Dutch *burgemeester*

Burgundy *n* **1** a red or white wine produced in the Burgundy region, around Dijon in France ▷ *adj* **2 burgundy** dark purplish-red

burial *n* the burying of a dead body

burin (byoor-in) *n* a steel chisel used for engraving metal, wood, or marble
WORD ORIGIN French

burk *n Brit slang* same as **berk**

burka *n* another spelling of **burqa**

burl *or* **birl** *n informal* **1** *Scot, Austral, & NZ* an attempt; try: *give it a burl* **2** *Austral & NZ* a ride in a car
WORD ORIGIN from Scots *birl* to spin or turn

burlesque *n* **1** an artistic work, esp. literary or dramatic, satirizing a subject by caricaturing it **2** *US & Canad theatre* a

bawdy comedy show of the late 19th and early 20th centuries ▷ *adj* **3** of or characteristic of a burlesque
WORD ORIGIN Italian *burla* a jest

burly *adj* -lier, -liest large and thick of build; sturdy
WORD ORIGIN Germanic

burn¹ *vb* **burning, burnt** *or* **burned 1** to be or set on fire **2** to destroy or be destroyed by fire **3** to damage, injure, or mark by heat: *he burnt his hand* **4** to die or put to death by fire **5** to be or feel hot: *my forehead is burning* **6** to smart or cause to smart: *brandy burns your throat* **7** to feel strong emotion, esp. anger or passion **8** to use for the purposes of light, heat, or power: *to burn coal* **9** to form by or as if by fire: *to burn a hole* **10** to char or become charred: *the toast is burning* **11** to record data on (a compact disc) **12 burn one's bridges** *or* **boats** to commit oneself to a particular course of action with no possibility of turning back **13 burn one's fingers** to suffer from having meddled or interfered ▷ *n* **14** an injury caused by exposure to heat, electrical, chemical, or radioactive agents **15** a mark caused by burning
▷ See also **burn out**
WORD ORIGIN Old English *beornan*

burn² *n Scot & N English* a small stream
WORD ORIGIN Old English *burna*

burner *n* the part of a stove or lamp that produces flame or heat

burning *adj* **1** intense; passionate **2** urgent; crucial: *a burning problem*

burning glass *n* a convex lens for concentrating the sun's rays to produce fire

burnish *vb* to make or become shiny or smooth by friction; polish
WORD ORIGIN Old French *brunir* to make brown

burnous *n* a long circular cloak with a hood, worn esp. by Arabs
WORD ORIGIN Arabic *burnus*

burn out *vb* **1** to become or cause to become inoperative as a result of heat or friction: *the clutch burnt out* ▷ *n* **burnout 2** total exhaustion and inability to work effectively as a result of excessive demands or overwork

burnt *vb* **1** a past of **burn¹** ▷ *adj* **2** affected by or as if by burning; charred

burp *n* **1** *informal* a belch ▷ *vb* **2** *informal* to belch **3** to cause (a baby) to belch
WORD ORIGIN imitative

burqa *or* **burka** *n* a long enveloping garment worn by Muslim women in public, covering all but the wearer's eyes
WORD ORIGIN from Arabic

burr *n* **1** the soft trilling sound given to the letter (r) in some English dialects **2** a whirring or humming sound **3** a rough edge left on metal or paper after cutting **4** a small hand-operated drill
WORD ORIGIN origin unknown

burrawang *n* an Australian plant with fern-like flowers and an edible nut

burrow *n* **1** a hole dug in the ground by a rabbit or other small animal ▷ *vb* **2** to dig (a tunnel or hole) in, through, or under ground **3** to move through a place by or as if by digging **4** to delve deeply: *he burrowed into his coat pocket* **5** to

live in or as if in a burrow
WORD ORIGIN probably variant of *borough*

bursar *n* a treasurer of a school, college, or university
WORD ORIGIN Medieval Latin *bursarius* keeper of the purse

bursary *n, pl* -ries **1** a scholarship or grant awarded esp. in Scottish and New Zealand schools and universities **2** *NZ* a state examination for senior pupils at secondary school

burst *vb* **bursting, burst 1** to break or cause to break open or apart suddenly and noisily; explode **2** to come or go suddenly and forcibly: *he burst into the room* **3** to be full to the point of breaking open: *bursting at the seams* **4** (foll. by *into*) to give vent to (something) suddenly or loudly: *she burst into song* ▷ *n* **5** an instance of breaking open suddenly; explosion **6** a break; breach: *there was a burst in the pipe* **7** a sudden increase of effort; spurt: *a burst of speed* **8** a sudden and violent occurrence or outbreak: *a burst of applause*
WORD ORIGIN Old English *berstan*

burton *n* **go for a burton** *Brit & NZ slang* **a** to be broken, useless, or lost **b** to die
WORD ORIGIN origin unknown

bury *vb* **buries, burying, buried 1** to place (a corpse) in a grave **2** to place (something) in the earth and cover it with soil **3** to cover (something) from sight; hide **4** to occupy (oneself) with deep concentration: *he buried himself in his work* **5** to dismiss (a feeling) from the mind: *they decided to bury any hard feelings*
WORD ORIGIN Old English *byrgan*

bus *n* **1** a large motor vehicle designed to carry passengers between stopping places along a regular route **2** *informal* a car or aircraft that is old and shaky **3** *electronics, computers* an electrical conductor used to make a common connection between several circuits ▷ *vb* **bussing, bussed** *or* **busing, bused 4** to travel or transport by bus **5** *chiefly US & Canad* to transport (children) by bus from one area to another in order to create racially integrated schools
WORD ORIGIN short for OMNIBUS

busby *n, pl* -bies a tall fur helmet worn by certain British soldiers
WORD ORIGIN origin unknown

bush¹ *n* **1** a dense woody plant, smaller than a tree, with many branches; shrub **2** a dense cluster of such shrubs; thicket **3** something resembling a bush, esp. in density: *a bush of hair* **4 the bush** an uncultivated area covered with trees or shrubs in Australia, Africa, New Zealand, and Canada **5** *Canad* an area on a farm on which timber is grown and cut **6 beat about the bush** to avoid the point at issue
WORD ORIGIN Germanic

bush² *n* **1** a thin metal sleeve or tubular lining serving as a bearing ▷ *vb* **2** to fit a bush to (a casing or bearing)
WORD ORIGIN Middle Dutch *busse* box

bushbaby *n, pl* -babies a small agile tree-living mammal with large eyes and a long tail

bushed *adj informal* extremely tired; exhausted

Words from Literature
part 4

black cap *n* a judge wore a black cap when he was about to sentence a prisoner to death
> The judge assumed the black cap, and the prisoner still stood with the same air and gesture.
> *Oliver Twist* Charles Dickens

black gentleman *n* this was another word for the devil
> for she is as impatient as the black gentleman
> *Emma* Jane Austen

boot-jack *n* a wooden device to help take boots off
> The speaker appeared to throw a boot-jack, or some such article, at the person he addressed
> *Oliver Twist* Charles Dickens

booty *n* treasure or prizes
> would be inclined to give up their booty in payment of the dead man's debts
> *Treasure Island* Robert Louis Stevenson

Bow Street runner *phrase* Bow Street runners were the first British police force, set up by the author Henry Fielding in the eighteenth century
> as would have convinced a judge or a Bow Street runner
> *Treasure Island* Robert Louis Stevenson

brawn *n* brawn is a dish of meat which is set in jelly
> Heaped up upon the floor, to form a kind of throne, were turkeys, geese, game, poultry, brawn, great joints of meat, sucking-pigs
> *A Christmas Carol* Charles Dickens

bray *v* when a donkey brays, it makes a loud, harsh sound
> and she doesn't bray like a jackass
> *The Adventures of Huckleberry Finn* Mark Twain

break *v* in order to train a horse you first have to break it
> "If a high-mettled creature like this," said he, "can't be broken by fair means, she will never be good for anything
> *Black Beauty* Anna Sewell

bullyragging *n* bullyragging is an old word which means bullying. To bullyrag someone is to threaten or force someone to do something they don't want to do
> and a lot of loafers bullyragging him for sport
> *The Adventures of Huckleberry Finn* Mark Twain

but *prep* except for (this)
> but this, all pleasures fancies be
> *The Good-Morrow* John Donne

by hand *phrase* by hand was a common expression of the time meaning that baby had been fed either using a spoon or a bottle rather than by breast-feeding
> My sister, Mrs. Joe Gargery, was more than twenty years older than I, and had established a great reputation with herself... because she had bought me up 'by hand'
> *Great Expectations* Charles Dickens

bye-spots *n* bye-spots are lonely places
> and bye-spots of tales rich with indigenous produce
> *The Prelude* William Wordsworth

calico *n* plain white fabric made from cotton
> There was two old dirty calico dresses
> *The Adventures of Huckleberry Finn* Mark Twain

camp-fever *n* another word for the disease typhus
> during a severe camp-fever
> *Emma* Jane Austen

cant *n* cant is insincere or empty talk
> "Man," said the Ghost, "if man you be in heart, not adamant, forbear that wicked cant until you have discovered What the surplus is, and Where it is."
> *A Christmas Carol* Charles Dickens

canty *adj* lively, full of life
> My mother lived til eighty, a canty dame to the last
> *Wuthering Heights* Emily Brontë

canvas *v* to discuss
> We think so very differently on this point, Mr Knightley, that there can be no use in canvassing it
> *Emma* Jane Austen

bushel *n Brit* an obsolete unit of dry or liquid measure equal to 8 gallons (36.4 litres)
WORD ORIGIN Old French *boissel*

bush jacket *n* a casual jacket with four patch pockets and a belt

bush line *n Canad* an airline operating in the bush country of Canada's northern regions

bush lot *n Canad* same as **bush¹** (sense 5)

bushman *n, pl* **-men** *Austral & NZ* a person who lives or travels in the bush

Bushman *n, pl* **-men** a member of a hunting and gathering people of southern Africa
WORD ORIGIN Afrikaans *boschjesman*

bush pilot *n Canad* a pilot who operates a plane in the bush country

bush sickness *n NZ* a disease of animals caused by mineral deficiency in old bush country **bush-sick** *adj*

bush telegraph *n* a means of spreading rumour or gossip

bush tucker *n Austral* **a** any wild animal, insect, plant, etc. traditionally used as food by Australian Aborigines **b** a style of cooking using these ingredients

bushveld *n S African* bushy countryside
WORD ORIGIN Afrikaans

bushwalking *n Austral* the leisure activity of walking in the bush **bushwalker** *n*

bushy *adj* **bushier, bushiest** **1** (of hair) thick and shaggy **2** covered or overgrown with bushes

business *n* **1** the purchase and sale of goods and services **2** a commercial or industrial establishment **3** a trade or profession **4** commercial activity: *the two countries should do business with each other* **5** proper or rightful concern or responsibility: *mind your own business* **6** an affair; matter: *it's a dreadful business* **7** serious work or activity: *get down to business* **8** a difficult or complicated matter: *it's a business trying to see him* **9 mean business** to be in earnest
WORD ORIGIN Old English *bisignis* care, attentiveness

businesslike *adj* efficient and methodical

businessman *or fem* **businesswoman** *n, pl* **-men** *or* **-women** a person engaged in commercial or industrial business, usually an owner or executive

business park *n* an area specially designated to accommodate business offices, light industry, etc.

business rate *n* a tax levied on businesses, based on the value of their premises

business school *n* an institution that offers courses to managers in aspects of business, such as marketing, finance, and law

busker *n* a person who entertains for money in streets or stations **busk** *vb*
WORD ORIGIN perhaps from Spanish *buscar* to look for

busman's holiday *n informal* a holiday spent doing the same as one does at work

bust¹ *n* **1** a woman's bosom **2** a sculpture of the head, shoulders, and upper chest of a person
WORD ORIGIN Italian *busto* a sculpture

bust² *informal vb* **busting, busted** *or* **bust** **1** to burst or break **2** (of the police) to raid or search (a place) or arrest (someone) **3** *US & Canad* to demote in military rank ⊳ *adj* **4** broken **5 go bust** to become bankrupt
WORD ORIGIN from *burst*

bustard *n* a bird with a long strong legs, a heavy body, a long neck, and speckled plumage

bustle¹ *vb* **-tling, -tled** **1** (often foll. by *about*) to hurry with a great show of energy or activity ⊳ *n* **2** energetic and noisy activity **bustling** *adj*
WORD ORIGIN probably obsolete *buskle* to prepare

bustle² *n* a cushion or framework worn by women in the late 19th century at the back in order to expand the skirt
WORD ORIGIN origin unknown

bust-up *informal n* **1** a serious quarrel, esp. one ending a relationship **2** *Brit, Austral, & NZ* a disturbance or brawl ⊳ *vb* **bust up 3** to quarrel and part **4** to disrupt (a meeting), esp. violently

busy *adj* **busier, busiest** **1** actively or fully engaged; occupied **2** crowded with or characterized by activity **3** (of a telephone line) in use; engaged ⊳ *vb* **busies, busying, busied 4** to make or keep (someone, esp. oneself) busy; occupy **busily** *adv*
WORD ORIGIN Old English *bisig*

busybody *n, pl* **-bodies** a meddlesome, prying, or officious person

but *conj* **1** contrary to expectation: *he cut his hand but didn't cry* **2** in contrast; on the contrary: *I like seafood but my husband doesn't* **3** other than: *we can't do anything but wait* **4** without it happening: *we never go out but it rains* ⊳ *prep* **5** except: *they saved all but one* **6 but for** were it not for: *but for you, we couldn't have managed* ⊳ *adv* **7** only: *I can but try; he was but a child* ⊳ *n* **8** an objection: *ifs and buts*
WORD ORIGIN Old English *būtan* without, except

but and ben *n Scot* a two-roomed cottage consisting of an outer room (**but**) and an inner room (**ben**)
WORD ORIGIN Old English *būtan* outside + *binnan* inside

butane (**byew**-tane) *n* a colourless gas used in the manufacture of rubber and fuels
WORD ORIGIN from *butyl*

butch *adj slang* (of a woman or man) markedly or aggressively masculine
WORD ORIGIN from *butcher*

butcher *n* **1** a person who sells meat **2** a person who kills animals for meat **3** a brutal murderer ⊳ *vb* **4** to kill and prepare (animals) for meat **5** to kill (people) at random or brutally **6** to make a mess of; botch
WORD ORIGIN Old French *bouchier*

butcherbird *n* an Australian magpie that impales its prey on thorns

butchery *n, pl* **-eries** **1** senseless slaughter **2** the business of a butcher

butler *n* the head manservant of a household, in charge of the wines, table, etc.

WORD ORIGIN Old French *bouteille* bottle

butt¹ *n* **1** the thicker or blunt end of something, such as the stock of a rifle **2** the unused end of a cigarette or cigar; stub **3** *chiefly US & Canad slang* the buttocks
WORD ORIGIN Middle English

butt² *n* **1** a person or thing that is the target of ridicule or teasing **2** *shooting, archery* **a** a mound of earth behind the target **b butts** the target range
WORD ORIGIN Old French *but*

butt³ *vb* **1** to strike (something or someone) with the head or horns **2** (foll. by *in* or *into*) to intrude, esp. into a conversation; interfere ⊳ *n* **3** a blow with the head or horns
WORD ORIGIN Old French *boter*

butt⁴ *n* a large cask for collecting or storing liquids
WORD ORIGIN Late Latin *buttis* cask

butte (**byewt**) *n US & Canad* an isolated steep flat-topped hill
WORD ORIGIN Old French *bute* mound behind a target

butter *n* **1** an edible fatty yellow solid made from cream by churning **2** any substance with a butter-like consistency, such as peanut butter ⊳ *vb* **3** to put butter on or in (something) ▸ See also **butter up** > **buttery** *adj*
WORD ORIGIN Greek *bous* cow + *turos* cheese

butter bean *n* a large pale flat edible bean

buttercup *n* a small bright yellow flower

butterfingers *n informal* a person who drops things by mistake or fails to catch things

butterflies *pl n informal* a nervous feeling in the stomach

butterfly *n, pl* **-flies** **1** an insect with a slender body and brightly coloured wings **2** a swimming stroke in which the arms are plunged forward together in large circular movements **3** a person who never settles with one interest or occupation for long
WORD ORIGIN Old English *buttorflēoge*

butterfly nut *n* same as **wing nut**

buttermilk *n* the sourish liquid remaining after the butter has been separated from milk

butterscotch *n* a hard brittle toffee made with butter, brown sugar, etc.

butter up *vb* to flatter

buttery *n, pl* **-teries** *Brit* (in some universities) a room in which food and drink are sold to students
WORD ORIGIN Latin *butta* cask

buttock *n* **1** either of the two large fleshy masses that form the human rump **2** the corresponding part in some mammals
WORD ORIGIN perhaps from Old English *buttuc* round slope

button *n* **1** a disc or knob of plastic, wood, etc. attached to a garment, which fastens two surfaces together by passing through a buttonhole **2** a small disc that operates a door bell or machine when pressed **3** a small round object, such as a sweet or badge **4 not worth a button** *Brit* of no value; useless

▷ *vb* **5** to fasten (a garment) with a button or buttons
WORD ORIGIN Old French *boton*

buttonhole *n* **1** a slit in a garment through which a button is passed to fasten two surfaces together **2** a flower worn pinned to the lapel or in the buttonhole ▷ *vb* **-holing, -holed 3** to detain (a person) in conversation

button mushroom *n* an unripe mushroom

button up *vb* **1** to fasten (a garment) with a button or buttons **2** *informal* to conclude (business) satisfactorily: *we've got it all buttoned up*

buttress *n* **1** a construction, usually of brick or stone, built to support a wall **2** any support or prop ▷ *vb* **3** to support (a wall) with a buttress **4** to support or sustain: *his observations are buttressed by the most recent scholarly research*
WORD ORIGIN Old French *bouter* to thrust

butty *n, pl* **-ties** *chiefly N English dialect* a sandwich: *a jam butty*
WORD ORIGIN from *buttered (bread)*

butyl (**byew**-tile) *adj* of or containing any of four isomeric forms of the group C_4H_9-: *butyl rubber*
WORD ORIGIN Latin *butyrum* butter

buxom *adj* (of a woman) healthily plump, attractive, and full-bosomed
WORD ORIGIN Middle English *buhsum* compliant

buy *vb* **buying, bought 1** to acquire (something) by paying a sum of money for it; purchase **2** to be capable of purchasing: *money can't buy love* **3** to acquire by any exchange or sacrifice: *the rise in interest rates was just to buy time until the weekend* **4** to bribe (someone) **5** *slang* to accept (something) as true **6** (foll. by *into*) to purchase shares of (a company) ▷ *n* **7** a purchase: *a good buy*. See also **buy in, buy into**, etc.
WORD ORIGIN Old English *bycgan*

USAGE
The use of *off* after *buy* as in *I bought this off my neighbour* was formerly considered incorrect, but is now acceptable in informal contexts.

buyer *n* **1** a person who buys; customer **2** a person employed to buy merchandise for a shop or factory

buy in *vb* to purchase (goods) in large quantities

buy into *vb* to agree with (an argument or theory)

buy off *vb* to pay (someone) to drop a charge or end opposition

buy-out *n* **1** the purchase of a company, often by its former employees ▷ *vb* **buy**

out 2 to purchase the ownership of a company or property from (someone)

buy up *vb* **1** to purchase all that is available of (something) **2** to purchase a controlling interest in (a company)

buzz *n* **1** a rapidly vibrating humming sound, such as of a bee **2** a low sound, such as of many voices in conversation **3** *informal* a telephone call **4** *informal* a sense of excitement ▷ *vb* **5** to make a vibrating sound like that of a prolonged z **6** (of a place) to be filled with an air of excitement: *the city buzzed with the news* **7** to summon (someone) with a buzzer **8** *informal* to fly an aircraft very low over (people, buildings, or another aircraft) **9 buzz about** or **around** to move around quickly and busily
WORD ORIGIN imitative

buzzard *n* a bird of prey with broad wings and tail and a soaring flight
WORD ORIGIN Latin *buteo* hawk

buzzer *n* an electronic device that produces a buzzing sound as a signal

buzzkill or **buzzkiller** *n* *informal* someone or something that stops people from enjoying themselves

buzz off *vb* *Austral & Brit informal* to go away; depart

buzz word *n* *informal* a word, originally from a particular jargon, which becomes a popular vogue word

by *prep* **1** used to indicate the performer of the action of a passive verb: *seeds eaten by the birds* **2** used to indicate the person responsible for a creative work: *three songs by Britten* **3** via; through: *enter by the back door* **4** used to indicate a means used: *he frightened her by hiding behind the door* **5** beside; next to; near: *a tree by the stream* **6** passing the position of; past: *I drove by the place she works* **7** not later than; before: *return the books by Tuesday* **8** used to indicate extent: *it is hotter by five degrees* **9** multiplied by: *four by three equals twelve* **10** during the passing of: *by night* **11** placed between measurements of the various dimensions of something: *a plank fourteen inches by seven* ▷ *adv* **12** near: *the house is close by* **13** away; aside: *he put some money by each week* **14** passing a point near something; past: *he drove by* ▷ *n, pl* **byes 15** same as **bye¹**
WORD ORIGIN Old English *bī*

by and by *adv* presently or eventually

by and large *adv* in general; on the whole

bye¹ *n* **1** *sport* status of a player or team who wins a preliminary round by virtue of having no opponent **2** *cricket* a run scored off a ball not struck by the batsman **3 by the bye**

incidentally; by the way
WORD ORIGIN variant of *by*

bye² or **bye-bye** *interj informal* goodbye

by-election or **bye-election** *n* an election held during the life of a parliament to fill a vacant seat

bygone *adj* past; former: *a bygone age*

bygones *pl n* **let bygones be bygones** to agree to forget past quarrels

bylaw or **bye-law** *n* a rule made by a local authority
WORD ORIGIN probably Scandinavian

by-line *n* **1** a line under the title of an article in a newspaper or magazine, giving the author's name **2** same as **touchline**

BYO, BYOG *n* *Austral & NZ* an unlicensed restaurant at which diners may bring their own alcoholic drink
WORD ORIGIN *bring your own (grog)*

bypass *n* **1** a main road built to avoid a city **2** a secondary pipe, channel, or appliance through which the flow of a substance, such as gas or electricity, is redirected **3** a surgical operation in which the blood flow is redirected away from a diseased or blocked part of the heart ▷ *vb* **4** to go around or avoid (a city, obstruction, problem, etc.) **5** to proceed without reference to (regulations or a superior); get round; avoid

by-play *n* secondary action in a play, carried on apart while the main action proceeds

by-product *n* **1** a secondary or incidental product of a manufacturing process **2** a side effect

byre *n* *Brit* a shelter for cows
WORD ORIGIN Old English *bȳre*

byroad *n* a secondary or side road

bystander *n* a person present but not involved; onlooker; spectator

byte *n* *computers* a group of bits processed as one unit of data
WORD ORIGIN origin unknown

byway *n* a secondary or side road, esp. in the country

byword *n* **1** a person or thing regarded as a perfect example of something: *their name is a byword for quality* **2** a common saying; proverb

Byzantine *adj* **1** of Byzantium, an ancient Greek city on the Bosphorus **2** of the Byzantine Empire, the continuation of the Roman Empire in the East **3** of the style of architecture developed in the Byzantine Empire, with massive domes, rounded arches, and mosaics **4** (of attitudes, methods, etc.) inflexible or complicated ▷ *n* **5** an inhabitant of Byzantium

b

Cc

The letter C is the third letter of the English alphabet. It has its origins in gamma (Γ,γ), which was the third letter of the Greek alphabet, and which is the ancestor of both C and G. In the Roman alphabet, the letter C became differentiated from G, and also acquired a different sound, being used for the hard /k/ sound which in Greek had been indicated by kappa (Κ,κ).

In English, C still represents this hard sound, but in front of I and E it also represents the soft /s/ sound, thus giving the letter a schizophrenic nature which can make it a slippery customer when it comes to spelling. One of the best-known rules of English spelling, the rule that I comes before E, is reversed when this pair come after the letter C.

On purely phonetic grounds, C is in fact redundant in English: it can always be substituted by K or S, and the combination CH could be shown by TSH. Yet this has not stopped C from being one of the more frequently distributed letters in the language: only S is more common as an initial letter for English words.

C can designate the third item in a series, although the letter is not defined by its position in the alphabet in quite the same way that B is. Having said this, it is undeniably worse to be a C-list celebrity than a B-lister. Being classified as 'C' can mark something out as average when the system has five tiers (as is the case with occupational groupings, when C designates clerical and skilled manual workers), but in a three-tier system, being a C is as bad as it gets.

In Roman numerals, C stands for one hundred (being the initial letter of *centum*, the Latin word for a hundred), and this is connected with the familiar use of the letter as an abbreviation for a hundred years or 'century', whether before a number (as in 'C21') or after (as in '21c').

C is also one of several letters that have come to be used as a euphemism for a word that people would rather not say out loud. People who feel it is unlucky to talk about 'cancer' might choose to refer to this disease as 'the big C'.

C 1 centi- 2 *cricket* caught 3 cubic 4 the speed of light in free space

C 1 *music* the first note of a major scale containing no sharps or flats (**C major**) 2 *chem* carbon 3 Celsius 4 centigrade 5 century: C20 6 coulomb 7 the Roman numeral for 100 8 a high-level computer programming language

c. (used preceding a date) about: *c. 1800* **WORD ORIGIN** Latin *circa*

Ca *chem* calcium

CA 1 California 2 Central America 3 Chartered Accountant

ca. (used preceding a date) about: *ca. 1930* **WORD ORIGIN** Latin *circa*

cab *n* 1 a taxi 2 the enclosed driver's compartment of a lorry, bus, or train **WORD ORIGIN** from *cabriolet*

cabal (kab-**bal**) *n* 1 a small group of political plotters 2 a secret plot or conspiracy **WORD ORIGIN** French *cabale*

cabaret (kab-a-**ray**) *n* 1 a floor show of dancing and singing at a nightclub or restaurant 2 a place providing such entertainment **WORD ORIGIN** French: tavern

cabbage *n* 1 a vegetable with a large head of green or reddish-purple leaves 2 *informal* a person who is unable to move or think, as a result of brain damage: *he can only exist as a cabbage who must be cared for by his relatives*

WORD ORIGIN Norman French *caboche* head

cabbage tree *n* NZ a palm-like tree with a bare trunk and spiky leaves

cabbage white *n* a large white butterfly whose larvae feed on cabbage leaves

cabbie or **cabby** *n, pl* **-bies** *informal* a taxi driver

caber *n* Scot a heavy section of trimmed tree trunk tossed in competition at Highland games **WORD ORIGIN** Gaelic *cabar* pole

Cabernet Sauvignon (kab-er-**nay** so-veen-yon) *n* a dry red wine produced in the Bordeaux region of France and elsewhere **WORD ORIGIN** French

cabin *n* 1 a room used as living quarters in a ship or boat 2 a small simple dwelling: *a log cabin* 3 the enclosed part of an aircraft in which the passengers or crew sit **WORD ORIGIN** Late Latin *capanna* hut

cabin boy *n* a boy who waits on the officers and passengers of a ship

cabin cruiser *n* a motorboat with a cabin

cabinet *n* a piece of furniture containing shelves, cupboards, or drawers for storage or display: *a filing cabinet; a cocktail cabinet* **WORD ORIGIN** Old French *cabine* cabin

Cabinet *n* a committee of senior government ministers or advisers to a president

cabinet-maker *n* a person who makes fine furniture **cabinet-making** *n*

cabin fever *n* Canad acute depression resulting from being isolated or sharing cramped quarters

cable *n* 1 a strong thick rope of twisted hemp or wire 2 a bundle of wires covered with plastic or rubber that conducts electricity 3 a telegram sent abroad by submarine cable or telephone line 4 Also called: **cable stitch** a knitted design which resembles a twisted rope ▷ *vb* **-bling, -bled** 5 to send (someone) a message by cable **WORD ORIGIN** Late Latin *capulum* halter

cable car *n* a vehicle that is pulled up a steep slope by a moving cable

cablegram *n* a more formal name for **cable** (sense 3)

cable television *n* a television service in which the subscriber's television is connected to a central receiver by cable

caboodle *n* **the whole caboodle** *informal* the whole lot **WORD ORIGIN** origin unknown

caboose *n* 1 US & Canad a railway car at the rear of a train, used as quarters for the crew 2 Canad a mobile building used as a cookhouse or

New Zealand English

The English language first arrived in New Zealand in the 19th century, brought by British settlers. What writer Frank Arthur Swinnerton identified in 1912 as a regional variation of English (he described it as a 'carefully modulated murmur') had been in existence since the previous century, and had its roots in Scottish, English, and Irish dialects. English spoken on New Zealand's North Island is non-rhotic, however some of the southernmost parts of the South Island have a more rhotic dialect in which an 'r' is pronounced after a vowel and before a consonant. This regional variation is most likely attributable to the Scottish ancestry of many of the area's inhabitants, and dialectical differences between other regions are slight.

Modern New Zealand English is distinguished from other forms of World English by lexical rather than grammatical means, by way of the huge influence of the indigenous Maori language, or *te reo Maori* (commonly abbreviated to *te reo*) on its vocabulary. *Te reo Maori* is a Polynesian language with varying degrees of linguistic links to Tahitian, Samoan, and Hawaiian, and is an official language of New Zealand alongside English. New Zealand's progressive social approach to integration demonstrated by movements such as *Kohanga Reo* (which aims to preserve the language) has led to the indigenous culture becoming much more integrated since the 1980s. Many loan words from Maori are used in New Zealand English, including *kia ora* (a standard spoken greeting), *hongi* (a non-verbal greeting when noses are touched together), *whakapapa* (genealogy), and *haka* (the war dance famously performed by New Zealand's All Blacks rugby team before matches). Maori words are especially dominant when describing indigenous flora and fauna (many of which were a necessity, as there were no equivalents in European zoology or botany) such as the *kakapo* (one of New Zealand's many flightless birds, the most notable being the *kiwi*), the *tarakihi* (a fish), and the *manuka* plant. The cross-pollination of the two languages is illustrated best by such chimeric words as *half-pie*. This deceptively English-sounding phrase stems from *half-pai*, incorporating the English word *half* and the Maori word *pai*, which means *good*.

In terms of pronunciation, New Zealand English is superficially related to Australian English, and vowel sounds are the easiest way to distinguish the two. In New Zealand English, 'i' [ə] sounds are pronounced in a way that makes them closer to the British English 'u', in sharp contrast to the Australian ɪ. In contrast, the 'e' sound in, for example, *dress*, *dead*, or *get*, is pronounced more closely to 'i' in New Zealand. And the 'a' sound in *bat* or *cat* most closely resembles 'e' (or ɛ in the International Phonetic Alphabet). Aside from vowel sounds, a crucial step is to be aware that the 'wh-' combination used in so many Maori words is pronounced as an 'f' sound, so for example *wharenui* would be pronounced 'far-en-oo-ee'. Most significantly, the historical trend by previous generations of Anglicising Maori words (especially placenames) has been reversed. Maori placenames can usually be broken down into their component parts, for example Kaikoura on the South Island is composed of *kai* (meaning *food* when used separately, but when used as part of a place name it is indicative of a place where a food source abounded) and *koura* (meaning *crayfish*). So, literally translated, Kaikoura means the place where crayfish were plentiful and eaten.

Cultural vocabulary specific to New Zealand that does not have its roots in Maori includes *bach* (a beach hut), *boohai* (somewhere remote, insignificant, or thoroughly lost – the etymology is based on a mispronunciation of the township of Puhoi), *jandals* (flip-flops), *jellymeat* (pet food), and *morepork* (a small owl). Some regional variations are that *dairy* is used to mean delicatessen or corner shop, *judder bar* is used instead of *speed bump*, and *gumboots* tends to be used to describe waterproof boots instead of *Wellington boots* or *wellies*. And, as a further distinction from Australian English, bush walking is known as *tramping*. Plus there are the inevitable specificities when brand names become genericized and are used exclusively in everyday speech. In New Zealand's case, *Tippex* or *white-out fluid* is known as *Twink*.

bunkhouse for a work crew
WORD ORIGIN Dutch *cabûse*

cabriolet (kab-ree-oh-**lay**) *n* a small two-wheeled horse-drawn carriage with a folding hood
WORD ORIGIN French: a little skip; referring to the lightness of movement

cacao (kak-**kah**-oh) *n* a tropical American tree with seed pods (**cacao beans**) from which cocoa and chocolate are prepared
WORD ORIGIN Mexican Indian *cacauatl* cacao beans

cachalot *n* the sperm whale
WORD ORIGIN Portuguese *cachalote*

cache (kash) *n* a hidden store of weapons, provisions, or treasure
WORD ORIGIN French *cacher* to hide

cachet (kash-shay) *n* prestige or distinction: *a Mercedes carries a certain cachet*
WORD ORIGIN French

cachou *n* a lozenge eaten to sweeten the breath
WORD ORIGIN Malay *kāchu*

cack-handed *adj informal* clumsy: *I open cans in a very cack-handed way*
WORD ORIGIN dialect *cack* excrement

cackle *vb* -ling, -led **1** to laugh shrilly **2** (of a hen) to squawk with shrill broken notes ▷ *n* **3** the sound of cackling **cackling** *adj*
WORD ORIGIN probably imitative

cacophony (kak-**koff**-on-ee) *n* harsh discordant sound: *a cacophony of barking* **cacophonous** *adj*
WORD ORIGIN Greek *kakos* bad + *phōnē* sound

cactus *n, pl* -tuses *or* -ti a thick fleshy desert plant with spines but no leaves
WORD ORIGIN Greek *kaktos* type of thistle

cad *n old-fashioned, informal* a man who behaves dishonourably **caddish** *adj*
WORD ORIGIN from *caddie*

cadaver (kad-**dav**-ver) *n med* a corpse
WORD ORIGIN Latin

cadaverous *adj* pale, thin, and haggard

caddie *n* **1** a person who carries a golfer's clubs ▷ *vb* -dying, -died **2** to act as a caddie
WORD ORIGIN from *cadet*

caddis fly *n* an insect whose larva (the **caddis worm**) lives underwater in a protective case of silk, sand, and stones

caddy¹ *n, pl* -dies *chiefly Brit* a small container for tea
WORD ORIGIN Malay *kati*

caddy² *n, pl* -dies, *vb* -dies, -dying, -died same as **caddie**

cadence (**kade**-enss) *n* **1** the rise and fall in the pitch of the voice **2** the close of a musical phrase
WORD ORIGIN Latin *cadere* to fall

cadenza *n* a complex solo passage in a piece of music
WORD ORIGIN Italian

cadet *n* a young person training for the armed forces or the police
WORD ORIGIN French

cadge *vb* cadging, cadged *informal* to get (something) from someone by taking advantage of his or her generosity **cadger** *n*
WORD ORIGIN origin unknown

cadi *n* a judge in a Muslim community
WORD ORIGIN Arabic *qāḍī* judge

cadmium *n chem* bluish-white metallic element found in zinc ores and used in electroplating and alloys. Symbol: Cd
WORD ORIGIN Latin *cadmia* zinc ore

cadre (**kah**-der) *n* a small group of people selected and trained to form the core of a political organization or military unit
WORD ORIGIN Latin *quadrum* square

caecum *or US* **cecum** (**seek**-um) *n, pl* -ca (-ka) the pouch at the beginning of the large intestine
WORD ORIGIN short for Latin *intestinum caecum* blind intestine

Caenozoic *adj* same as **Cenozoic**

Caerphilly *n* a creamy white mild-flavoured cheese

Caesar (**seez**-ar) *n* **1** a Roman emperor **2** any emperor or dictator
WORD ORIGIN after Gaius Julius *Caesar*, Roman general & statesman **3** short for **Caesar salad**

Caesarean, Caesarian *or US* **Cesarean** (siz-**zair**-ee-an) *n* short for **Caesarean section**

Caesarean section *n* surgical incision into the womb in order to deliver a baby
WORD ORIGIN from the belief that Julius Caesar was delivered in this way

Caesar salad *n* a salad of lettuce, cheese, and croutons with a dressing of olive oil, garlic, and lemon juice
WORD ORIGIN after *Caesar* Cardini, its inventor

caesium *or US* **cesium** *n chem* a silvery-white metallic element used in photocells. Symbol: Cs
WORD ORIGIN Latin *caesius* bluish-grey

caesura (siz-**your**-ra) *n, pl* -ras *or* -rae (-ree) a pause in a line of verse
WORD ORIGIN Latin: a cutting

café *n* **1** a small or inexpensive restaurant that serves drinks and snacks or light meals **2** *S African* a corner shop
WORD ORIGIN French

cafeteria *n* a self-service restaurant
WORD ORIGIN American Spanish: coffee shop

caff *n slang* a café

caffeine *n* a stimulant found in tea, coffee, and cocoa
WORD ORIGIN German *Kaffee* coffee

caftan *n* same as **kaftan**

cage *n* **1** an enclosure made of bars or wires, for keeping birds or animals in **2** the enclosed platform of a lift in a mine ▷ *vb* caging, caged **3** to confine in a cage **caged** *adj*
WORD ORIGIN Latin *cavea* enclosure

cagey *adj* cagier, cagiest *informal* reluctant to go into details; wary: *he is cagey about what he paid for the business* **cagily** *adv*
WORD ORIGIN origin unknown

cagoule (kag-**gool**) *n Brit* a lightweight hooded waterproof jacket
WORD ORIGIN French

cahoots *pl n* **in cahoots** *informal* conspiring together: *the loan sharks were in cahoots with the home-improvement companies*
WORD ORIGIN origin unknown

caiman *n, pl* -mans same as **cayman**

cairn *n* a mound of stones erected as a memorial or marker
WORD ORIGIN Gaelic *carn*

cairngorm *n* a smoky yellow or brown quartz gemstone
WORD ORIGIN *Cairn Gorm* (blue cairn), mountain in Scotland

caisson (**kayss**-on) *n* a watertight chamber used to carry out construction work under water
WORD ORIGIN French

cajole *vb* -joling, -joled to persuade by flattery; coax: *he allowed himself to be cajoled into staying on* **cajolery** *n*
WORD ORIGIN French *cajoler*

Cajun *n* **1** a native of Louisiana descended from 18th-century Acadian immigrants **2** the dialect of French spoken by such people **3** the music of this ethnic group ▷ *adj* **4** denoting or relating to such people, their language, or their music
WORD ORIGIN from ACADIAN

cake *n* **1** a sweet food baked from a mixture of flour, sugar, eggs, etc. **2** a flat compact mass of something: *a cake of soap* **3** **have one's cake and eat it** to enjoy both of two incompatible alternatives **4** **piece of cake** *informal* something that is easy to do **5** **sell like hot cakes** *informal* to be sold very quickly: *commercial novels sell like hot cakes* ▷ *vb* caking, caked **6** to form into a hardened mass or crust: *there was blood caked an inch thick on the walls*
WORD ORIGIN Old Norse *kaka*

cal. calorie (small)

Cal. **1** Calorie (large) **2** California

calabash *n* **1** a large round gourd that grows on a tropical American tree **2** a bowl made from the dried hollow shell of a calabash
WORD ORIGIN obsolete French *calabasse*

calabrese (kal-lab-**bray**-zee) *n* a kind of green sprouting broccoli
WORD ORIGIN Italian: from *Calabria* (region of SW Italy)

calamari *n* squid cooked for eating, esp. cut into rings and fried in batter
WORD ORIGIN from Italian, plural of *calamaro* squid

calamine *n* a pink powder consisting chiefly of zinc oxide, used to make soothing skin lotions and ointments
WORD ORIGIN Medieval Latin *calamina*

calamitous *adj* resulting in or from disaster: *the country's calamitous economic decline*

calamity *n, pl* -ties a disaster or misfortune
WORD ORIGIN Latin *calamitas*

calcareous (kal-**care**-ee-uss) *adj* of or containing calcium carbonate
WORD ORIGIN Latin *calx* lime

calciferol *n* a substance found in fish oils and used in the treatment of rickets. Also called: **vitamin D₂**
WORD ORIGIN *calcif(erous* + *ergost)erol*, a substance in plants that is a source of vitamin D

calciferous *adj* producing salts of calcium, esp. calcium carbonate

calcify *vb* **-fies, -fying, -fied** to harden by the depositing of calcium salts **calcification** *n*
WORD ORIGIN Latin *calx* lime

calcine *vb* **-cining, -cined** to oxidize (a substance) by heating **calcination** *n*
WORD ORIGIN Medieval Latin *calcinare* to heat

calcite *n* a colourless or white form of calcium carbonate

calcium *n* *chem* a soft silvery-white metallic element found in bones, teeth, limestone, and chalk. Symbol: Ca
WORD ORIGIN Latin *calx* lime

calcium carbonate *n* a white crystalline salt found in limestone, chalk, and pearl, used to make cement

calcium hydroxide *n* a white crystalline alkali used to make mortar and soften water

calcium oxide *n* same as **quicklime**

calculable *adj* able to be computed or estimated

calculate *vb* **-lating, -lated 1** to solve or find out by a mathematical procedure or by reasoning **2** to aim to have a particular effect: *this ad campaign is calculated to offend*
WORD ORIGIN Latin *calculare*, from *calculus* pebble used as a counter

calculated *adj* **1** undertaken after considering the likelihood of success: *a calculated gamble* **2** carefully planned: *a calculated and callous murder*

calculating *adj* selfishly scheming

calculation *n* **1** the act or result of calculating **2** selfish scheming: *there was an element of calculation in her insistence on arriving after dark*

calculator *n* a small electronic device for doing mathematical calculations

calculus *n* **1** the branch of mathematics dealing with infinitesimal changes to a variable number or quantity **2** *pl* **-li** *pathol* same as **stone** (sense 7)
WORD ORIGIN Latin: pebble

Caledonian *adj* Scottish
WORD ORIGIN from *Caledonia*, the Roman name for Scotland

calendar *n* **1** a chart showing a year divided up into months, weeks, and days **2** a system for determining the beginning, length, and divisions of years: *the Jewish calendar* **3** a schedule of events or appointments: *concerts were an important part of the social calendar of the Venetian nobility*
WORD ORIGIN Latin *kalendae* the calends

calender *n* **1** a machine in which paper or cloth is smoothed by passing it between rollers ▷ *vb* **2** to smooth in such a machine
WORD ORIGIN French *calandre*

calends or **kalends** *pl n* (in the ancient Roman calendar) the first day of each month
WORD ORIGIN Latin *kalendae*

calendula *n* a plant with orange-and-yellow rayed flowers
WORD ORIGIN Medieval Latin

calf[1] *n, pl* **calves 1** a young cow, bull, elephant, whale, or seal **2** same as **calfskin**
WORD ORIGIN Old English *cealf*

calf[2] *n, pl* **calves** the back of the leg between the ankle and the knee
WORD ORIGIN Old Norse *kálfi*

calf love *n* adolescent infatuation

calfskin *n* fine leather made from the skin of a calf

calibrate *vb* **-brating, -brated** to mark the scale or check the accuracy of (a measuring instrument) **calibration** *n*

calibre or *US* **caliber** (**kal**-lib-ber) *n* **1** a person's ability or worth: *a poet of Wordsworth's calibre* **2** the diameter of the bore of a gun or of a shell or bullet
WORD ORIGIN Arabic *qālib* shoemaker's last, mould

calico *n* a white or unbleached cotton fabric
WORD ORIGIN *Calicut*, town in India

californium *n* *chem* a radioactive metallic element produced artificially. Symbol: Cf
WORD ORIGIN after the University of California, where it was discovered

caliper *n US* same as **calliper**

caliph *n* *Islam* the title of the successors of Mohammed as rulers of the Islamic world
WORD ORIGIN Arabic *khalifa* successor

caliphate *n* the office, jurisdiction, or reign of a caliph

calisthenics *n* same as **callisthenics**

call *vb* **1** to name: *a town called Eyemouth* **2** to describe (someone or something) as being: *they called him a Hitler* **3** to speak loudly so as to attract attention **4** to telephone: *he left a message for Lynch to call him* **5** to summon: *a doctor must be called immediately* **6** to pay someone a visit: *the social worker called and she didn't answer the door* **7** to arrange: *the meeting was called for the lunch hour* **8 call someone's bluff** see **bluff**[1] (sense 3) ▷ *n* **9** a cry or shout **10** the cry made by a bird or animal **11** a communication by telephone **12** a short visit: *I paid a call on an old friend* **13** a summons or invitation: *the police and fire brigade continued to respond to calls* **14** need, demand, or desire: *a call for economic sanctions* **15** allure or fascination: *the call of the open road* **16 on call** available when summoned: *there's a doctor on call in town*
▸ See also **call for, call in**, etc. **caller** *n*
WORD ORIGIN Old English *ceallian*

call box *n* a soundproof enclosure for a public telephone

call centre *n* *Brit, Austral, & NZ* an office where staff carry out an organization's telephone transactions

call for *vb* **1** to require: *appendicitis calls for removal of the appendix* **2** to come and fetch

call girl *n* a prostitute with whom appointments are made by telephone

calligraphy *n* beautiful handwriting **calligrapher** *n* **calligraphic** *adj*
WORD ORIGIN Greek *kallos* beauty + -GRAPHY

call in *vb* **1** to summon to one's assistance: *she called in a contractor to make the necessary repairs* **2** to pay a brief visit **3** to demand payment of (a loan): *if the share price continues to drop, some banks may call in their loans*

calling *n* **1** a strong urge to follow a particular profession or occupation, esp.

a caring one **2** a profession or occupation, esp. a caring one

Calliope *n* *Greek myth* the Muse of epic poetry

calliper or *US* **caliper** *n* **1** a metal splint for supporting the leg **2** a measuring instrument consisting of two steel legs hinged together
WORD ORIGIN variant of *calibre*

callisthenics or **calisthenics** *n* light exercises designed to promote general fitness **callisthenic** or **calisthenic** *adj*
WORD ORIGIN Greek *kalli-* beautiful + *sthenos* strength

call off *vb* **1** to cancel or abandon: *the strike has now been called off* **2** to order (a dog or a person) to stop attacking someone

call on or **upon** *vb* to make an appeal or request to: *church leaders called on political leaders to resume the discussions*

callous *adj* showing no concern for other people's feelings **callously** *adv* **callousness** *n*
WORD ORIGIN Latin *callosus*

calloused *adj* covered in calluses

call out *vb* **1** to shout loudly **2** to summon to one's assistance: *the army and air force have been called out to help drop food packets* **3** to order (workers) to strike

callow *adj* young and inexperienced: *a callow youth*
WORD ORIGIN Old English *calu*

call up *vb* **1** to summon for active military service **2** to cause one to remember ▷ *n* **call-up 3** a general order to report for military service

callus *n, pl* **-luses** an area of hard or thickened skin on the hand or foot
WORD ORIGIN Latin *callum* hardened skin

calm *adj* **1** not showing or not feeling agitation or excitement **2** not ruffled by the wind: *a flat calm sea* **3** (of weather) windless ▷ *n* **4** a peaceful state ▷ *vb* **5** (often foll. by *down*) to make or become calm **calmly** *adv* **calmness** *n*
WORD ORIGIN Late Latin *cauma* heat, hence a rest during the heat of the day

Calor Gas *n trademark, Brit* butane gas liquefied under pressure in portable containers for domestic use

caloric (kal-**or**-ik) *adj* of heat or calories

calorie *n* **1** a unit of measure for the energy value of food **2** Also: **small calorie** the quantity of heat required to raise the temperature of 1 gram of water by 1°C
WORD ORIGIN Latin *calor* heat

Calorie *n* **1** Also: **large calorie** a unit of heat, equal to one thousand calories **2** the amount of a food capable of producing one calorie of energy

calorific *adj* of calories or heat

calumniate *vb* **-ating, -ated** to make false or malicious statements about (someone)

calumny *n, pl* **-nies** a false or malicious statement; slander
WORD ORIGIN Latin *calumnia* slander

Calvary *n* *Christianity* the place just outside the walls of Jerusalem where Jesus Christ was crucified
WORD ORIGIN Latin *calvaria* skull

calve *vb* **calving, calved** to give birth to a calf

calves *n* the plural of **calf**

Calvinism *n* the theological system of Calvin, the 16th-century French theologian, stressing predestination and salvation solely by God's grace **Calvinist** *n, adj* **Calvinistic** *adj*

calypso *n, pl* **-sos** a West Indian song with improvised topical lyrics **WORD ORIGIN** probably from *Calypso*, sea nymph in Greek mythology

calyx (**kale**-ix) *n, pl* **calyxes** *or* **calyces** (**kal**-iss-seez) the outer leaves that protect the developing bud of a flower **WORD ORIGIN** Latin: shell, husk

calzone (kal-**zone**-ee) *n* a folded pizza filled with cheese, tomatoes, etc.

cam *n* a part of an engine that converts a circular motion into a to-and-fro motion **WORD ORIGIN** Dutch *kam* comb

camaraderie *n* familiarity and trust between friends **WORD ORIGIN** French

camber *n* a slight upward curve to the centre of a road surface **WORD ORIGIN** Latin *camurus* curved

Cambodian *adj* **1** of Cambodia ▷ *n* **2** a person from Cambodia

Cambrian *adj geol* of the period of geological time about 600 million years ago

cambric *n* a fine white linen fabric **WORD ORIGIN** Flemish *Kamerijk* Cambrai

Cambs Cambridgeshire

camcorder *n* a combined portable video camera and recorder

came *vb* the past tense of **come**

camel *n* either of two humped mammals, the dromedary and Bactrian camel, that can survive long periods without food or water in desert regions **WORD ORIGIN** Greek *kamēlos*

camellia (kam-**meal**-ya) *n* an ornamental shrub with glossy leaves and white, pink, or red flowers **WORD ORIGIN** after G. J. Kamel, Jesuit missionary

camel's hair *or* **camelhair** *n* soft cloth, usually tan in colour, which is made from camel's hair and is used to make coats

Camembert (**kam**-mem-bare) *n* a soft creamy cheese **WORD ORIGIN** *Camembert*, village in Normandy

cameo *n, pl* **cameos 1** a brooch or ring with a profile head carved in relief **2** a small but important part in a film or play played by a well-known actor or actress **WORD ORIGIN** Italian *cammeo*

camera *n* **1** a piece of equipment used for taking photographs or pictures for television or cinema **2 in camera** in private **WORD ORIGIN** Greek *kamara* vault

cameraman *n, pl* **-men** a man who operates a camera for television or cinema

camera obscura *n* a darkened room with an opening through which images of outside objects are

projected onto a flat surface **WORD ORIGIN** New Latin

camera phone *n* a mobile phone incorporating a camera

camiknickers *pl n Brit* a woman's undergarment consisting of knickers attached to a camisole top

camisole *n* a woman's bodice-like garment with shoulder straps **WORD ORIGIN** French

camomile *or* **chamomile** (**kam**-mo-mile) *n* a sweet-smelling plant used to make herbal tea **WORD ORIGIN** Greek *khamaimēlon* earth-apple (referring to the scent of the flowers)

camouflage (**kam**-moo-flahzh) *n* **1** the use of natural surroundings or artificial aids to conceal or disguise something ▷ *vb* **-flaging, -flaged 2** to conceal by camouflage **WORD ORIGIN** French

camp[1] *n* **1** a place where people stay in tents **2** a collection of huts and other buildings used as temporary lodgings for military troops or for prisoners of war **3** a group that supports a particular doctrine: *the socialist camp* ▷ *vb* **4** to stay in a camp **camper** *n* **camping** *n* **WORD ORIGIN** Latin *campus* field

camp[2] *informal adj* **1** effeminate or homosexual **2** consciously artificial, vulgar, or affected ▷ *vb* **3 camp it up** to behave in a camp manner **WORD ORIGIN** origin unknown

campaign *n* **1** a series of coordinated activities designed to achieve a goal **2** *mil* a number of operations aimed at achieving a single objective ▷ *vb* **3** to take part in a campaign: *he paid tribute to all those who'd campaigned for his release* **campaigner** *n* **WORD ORIGIN** Latin *campus* field

campanile (camp-an-**neel**-lee) *n* a bell tower, usually one not attached to another building **WORD ORIGIN** Italian

campanology *n* the art of ringing bells **campanologist** *n* **WORD ORIGIN** Late Latin *campana* bell

campanula *n* a plant with blue or white bell-shaped flowers **WORD ORIGIN** New Latin: a little bell

camp bed *n* a lightweight folding bed

camp follower *n* **1** a person who supports a particular group or organization without being a member of it **2** a civilian who unofficially provides services to military personnel

camphor *n* a sweet-smelling crystalline substance obtained from the wood of the **camphor tree**, which is used medicinally and in mothballs **WORD ORIGIN** Arabic *kāfūr*

camphorated *adj* impregnated with camphor

campion *n* a red, pink, or white European wild flower **WORD ORIGIN** origin unknown

camp oven *n Austral & NZ* a heavy metal pot or box with a lid, used for baking over an open fire

camp site *n* a place where people can stay in tents

campus *n, pl* **-puses** the grounds and buildings of a university or college **WORD ORIGIN** Latin: field

camshaft *n* a part of an engine consisting of a rod to which cams are attached

can[1] *vb, past* **could 1** be able to: *make sure he can breathe easily* **2** be allowed to: *you can swim in the large pool* **WORD ORIGIN** Old English *cunnan*

☰ USAGE
☰ See at **may**.

can[2] *n* **1** a metal container, usually sealed, for food or liquids ▷ *vb* **canning, canned 2** to put (something) into a can **WORD ORIGIN** Old English *canne*

Can. 1 Canada **2** Canadian

Canada Day *n* (in Canada) July 1, a public holiday marking the anniversary of the day in 1867 when Canada became a dominion

Canada goose *n* a greyish-brown North American goose with a black neck and head

Canada jay *n* a grey jay of northern N America, notorious for stealing

Canadian *adj* **1** of Canada ▷ *n* **2** a person from Canada

Canadiana *pl n* objects relating to Canadian history and culture

Canadian football *n* a game like American football played on a grass field between teams of 12 players

Canadianism *n* **1** the Canadian national character or spirit **2** a linguistic feature peculiar to Canada or Canadians

Canadianize *or* **-ise** *vb* **-izing, -ized** *or* **-ising, -ised** to make Canadian

Canadian Shield *n* the wide area of Precambrian rock extending over most of central and E Canada: rich in minerals

Canadien *or fem* **Canadienne** (kan-ad-ee-**en**) *n* a French Canadian **WORD ORIGIN** French: Canadian

canaille (kan-**nye**) *n* the masses or rabble **WORD ORIGIN** French, from Italian *canaglia* pack of dogs

canal *n* **1** an artificial waterway constructed for navigation or irrigation **2** a passage or duct in a person's body: *the alimentary canal* **WORD ORIGIN** Latin *canna* reed

canalize *or* **-lise** *vb* **-lizing, -lized** *or* **-lising, -lised 1** to give direction to (a feeling or activity) **2** to convert into a canal **canalization** *or* **-lisation** *n*

canapé (**kan**-nap-pay) *n* a small piece of bread or toast spread with a savoury topping **WORD ORIGIN** French: sofa

canard *n* a false report **WORD ORIGIN** French: a duck

canary *n, pl* **-naries** a small yellow songbird often kept as a pet

canasta *n* a card game like rummy, played with two packs of cards **WORD ORIGIN** Spanish: basket (because two packs, or a basketful, of cards are required)

cancan *n* a lively high-kicking dance performed by a female group **WORD ORIGIN** French

Words from Literature
part 5

capital *adj* excellent or extremely good
for it's capital, so shady, light, and big
Little Women Louisa May Alcott

capstan *n* a device used on a ship to lift sails and anchors
capstans going, ships going out to sea, and unintelligible sea creatures roaring curses over the bulwarks at respondent lightermen
Great Expectations Charles Dickens

case-bottle *n* a square bottle designed to fit with others into a case
The spirit being set before him in a huge case-bottle, which had originally come out of some ship's locker
The Old Curiosity Shop Charles Dickens

casement *n* a word meaning window
The teacher in Nicholas Nickleby misspells window showing what a bad teacher he is.
"W-i-n, win, d-e-r, der, winder, a casement."
Nicholas Nickleby Charles Dickens

cataleptic *adj* a cataleptic fit is one in which the victim goes into a trancelike state and remains still for a long time
It was at this point in their history that Silas's cataleptic fit occurred during the prayer-meeting
Silas Marner George Eliot

cauldron *n* a large cooking pot made of metal
stirring a large cauldron which seemed to be full of soup
Alice's Adventures in Wonderland Lewis Carroll

cephalic *adj* to do with the head
with ink composed of a cephalic tincture
Gulliver's Travels Jonathan Swift

chaise and four *n* a closed four-wheel carriage pulled by four horses
he came down on Monday in a chaise and four to see the place
Pride and Prejudice Jane Austen

chamberlain *n* the main servant in a household
In those times a bed was always to be got there at any hour of the night, and the chamberlain, letting me in at his ready wicket, lighted the candle next in order on his shelf
Great Expectations Charles Dickens

characters *n* distinguishing marks
Impressed upon all forms the characters
The Prelude William Wordsworth

chary *adj* cautious
I should have been chary of discussing my guardian too freely even with her
Great Expectations Charles Dickens

cherish *v* to cheer or brighten
some philosophic song of Truth that cherishes our daily life
The Prelude William Wordsworth

chickens' meat *phrase* an old term which means chickens' feed or food
I had shook a bag of chickens' meat out in that place
Robinson Crusoe Daniel Defoe

chimera *n* an unrealistic idea or a wish which is unlikely to be fulfilled
with many other wild impossible chimeras
Gulliver's Travels Jonathan Swift

chine *n* a cut of meat that includes part or all of the backbone of the animal
and they found hams and chines uncut
Silas Marner George Eliot

chits *n* a slang word which means girls
I hate affected, niminy-piminy chits!
Little Women Louisa May Alcott

chop *v* to come suddenly or accidentally upon
if I had chopped upon them
Robinson Crusoe Daniel Defoe

C

cancel *vb* **-celling, -celled** *or US* **-celing, -celed 1** to stop (something that has been arranged) from taking place **2** to mark (a cheque or stamp) with an official stamp to prevent further use **3 cancel out** to make ineffective by having the opposite effect: *economic vulnerability cancels out any possible political gain* **cancellation** *n*
WORD ORIGIN Late Latin *cancellare* to strike out, make like a lattice

cancer *n* **1** a serious disease resulting from a malignant growth or tumour, caused by abnormal and uncontrolled cell division **2** a malignant growth or tumour **3** an evil influence that spreads dangerously: *their country would remain a cancer of instability* **cancerous** *adj*
WORD ORIGIN Latin: crab, creeping tumour

Cancer *n* **1** *astrol* the fourth sign of the zodiac; the Crab **2 tropic of Cancer** see **tropic** (sense 1)
WORD ORIGIN Latin

candela (kan-**dee**-la) *n* the SI unit of luminous intensity (the amount of light a source gives off in a given direction)
WORD ORIGIN Latin: candle

candelabrum *or* **candelabra** *n, pl* **-bra, -brums,** *or* **-bras** a large branched holder for candles or overhead lights
WORD ORIGIN Latin *candela* candle

candid *adj* honest and straightforward in speech or behaviour **candidly** *adv*
WORD ORIGIN Latin *candere* to be white

candidate *n* **1** a person seeking a job or position **2** a person taking an examination **3** a person or thing regarded as suitable or likely for a particular fate or position: *someone who smokes, drinks, or eats too much is a candidate for heart disease* **candidacy** *or* **candidature** *n*
WORD ORIGIN Latin *candidatus* clothed in white

candied *adj* coated with or cooked in sugar: *candied peel*

candle *n* **1** a stick or block of wax or tallow surrounding a wick, which is burned to produce light **2 burn the candle at both ends** to exhaust oneself by doing too much
WORD ORIGIN Latin *candela*

candlelight *n* the light from a candle or candles **candlelit** *adj*

Candlemas *n Christianity* February 2, the Feast of the Purification of the Virgin Mary

candlepower *n* the luminous intensity of a source of light: now expressed in candelas

candlestick *or* **candleholder** *n* a holder for a candle

candlewick *n* cotton with a tufted pattern, used to make bedspreads and dressing gowns

candour *or US* **candor** *n* honesty and straightforwardness of speech or behaviour
WORD ORIGIN Latin *candor*

candy *n, pl* **-dies** *chiefly US & Canad* a sweet or sweets
WORD ORIGIN Arabic *qand* cane sugar

candyfloss *n Brit* a light fluffy mass of spun sugar, held on a stick

candy-striped *adj* having narrow coloured stripes on a white background

candytuft *n* a garden plant with clusters of white, pink, or purple flowers

cane *n* **1** the long flexible stems of the bamboo or any similar plant **2** strips of such stems, woven to make wickerwork **3** a bamboo stem tied to a garden plant to support it **4** a flexible rod used to beat someone **5** a slender walking stick ▷ *vb* **caning, caned 6** to beat with a cane
WORD ORIGIN Greek *kanna*

cane sugar *n* the sugar that is obtained from sugar cane

cane toad *n* a large toad used to control insects and other pests of sugar cane plantations

canine (**kay**-nine) *adj* **1** of or like a dog ▷ *n* **2** a sharp-pointed tooth between the incisors and the molars
WORD ORIGIN Latin *canis* dog

canister *n* a metal container for dry food
WORD ORIGIN Latin *canistrum* basket woven from reeds

canker *n* **1** an ulceration or ulcerous disease **2** something evil that spreads and corrupts
WORD ORIGIN Latin *cancer* cancerous sore

cannabis *n* a drug obtained from the dried leaves and flowers of the hemp plant
WORD ORIGIN Greek *kannabis*

canned *adj* **1** preserved in a can **2** *informal* recorded in advance: *canned carols*

cannelloni *or* **canneloni** *pl n* tubular pieces of pasta filled with meat or cheese
WORD ORIGIN Italian

cannery *n, pl* **-neries** a place where foods are canned

cannibal *n* **1** a person who eats human flesh **2** an animal that eats the flesh of other animals of its kind **cannibalism** *n*
WORD ORIGIN Spanish *Canibales* natives of Cuba and Haiti

cannibalize *or* **-ise** *vb* **-izing, -ized** *or* **-ising, -ised** to use parts from (one machine or vehicle) to repair another

canning *n* the process of sealing food in cans to preserve it

cannon *n, pl* **-nons** *or* **-non 1** a large gun consisting of a metal tube mounted on a carriage, formerly used in battles **2** an automatic aircraft gun **3** *billiards* a shot in which the cue ball strikes two balls successively ▷ *vb* **4 cannon into** to collide with
WORD ORIGIN Italian *canna* tube

cannonade *n* continuous heavy gunfire

cannonball *n* a heavy metal ball fired from a cannon

cannon fodder *n* men regarded as expendable in war

cannot *vb* can not

canny *adj* **-nier, -niest** shrewd or cautious **cannily** *adv*
WORD ORIGIN from *can* (in the sense: to know how)

canoe *n* a light narrow open boat, propelled by one or more paddles **canoeist** *n*
WORD ORIGIN Carib

canoeing *n* the sport of rowing or racing in a canoe

canon[1] *n* a priest serving in a cathedral
WORD ORIGIN Late Latin *canonicus* person living under a rule

canon[2] *n* **1** *Christianity* a Church decree regulating morals or religious practices **2** a general rule or standard: *the Marx-Engels canon* **3** a list of the works of an author that are accepted as authentic: *the Yeats canon* **4** a piece of music in which a melody in one part is taken up in one or more other parts successively
WORD ORIGIN Greek *kanōn* rule

canonical *adj* **1** conforming with canon law **2** included in a canon of writings

canonical hour *n RC Church* one of the seven prayer times appointed for each day

canonicals *pl n* the official clothes worn by clergy when taking services

canonize *or* **-ise** *vb* **-izing, -ized** *or* **-ising, -ised** *RC Church* to declare (a dead person) to be a saint **canonization** *or* **-isation** *n*

canon law *n* the body of laws of a Christian Church

canoodle *vb* **-dling, -dled** *slang* to kiss and cuddle
WORD ORIGIN origin unknown

canopied *adj* covered with a canopy: *canopied niches*

canopy *n, pl* **-pies 1** an ornamental awning above a bed or throne **2** a rooflike covering over an altar, niche, or door **3** any large or wide covering: *the thick forest canopy* **4** the part of a parachute that opens out **5** the transparent hood of an aircraft cockpit
WORD ORIGIN Greek *kōnōpeion* bed with a mosquito net

cant[1] *n* **1** insincere talk concerning religion or morals **2** specialized vocabulary of a particular group, such as thieves or lawyers ▷ *vb* **3** to use cant: *canting hypocrites*
WORD ORIGIN probably from Latin *cantare* to sing

cant[2] *n* **1** a tilted position ▷ *vb* **2** to tilt or overturn: *the engine was canted to one side*
WORD ORIGIN perhaps from Latin *canthus* iron hoop round a wheel

can't *vb* can not

cantabile (kan-**tah**-bill-lay) *adv music* flowing and melodious
WORD ORIGIN Italian

cantaloupe *or* **cantaloup** *n Brit* a kind of melon with sweet-tasting orange flesh
WORD ORIGIN *Cantaluppi*, near Rome, where first cultivated in Europe

cantankerous *adj* quarrelsome or bad-tempered
WORD ORIGIN origin unknown

cantata (kan-**tah**-ta) *n* a musical setting of a text, consisting of arias, duets, and choruses
WORD ORIGIN Italian

canteen *n* **1** a restaurant attached to a workplace or school **2** a box containing a set of cutlery
WORD ORIGIN Italian *cantina* wine cellar

canter *n* **1** a gait of horses that is faster than a trot but slower than a gallop ▷ *vb* **2** (of a horse) to move at a canter
WORD ORIGIN short for *Canterbury trot*, the pace at which pilgrims rode to Canterbury

canticle *n* a short hymn with words from the Bible
WORD ORIGIN Latin *canticulum*

cantilever *n* a beam or girder fixed at one end only
WORD ORIGIN origin unknown

cantilever bridge *n* a bridge made of two cantilevers which meet in the middle

canto (**kan**-toe) *n, pl* **-tos** a main division of a long poem
WORD ORIGIN Italian: song

canton *n* a political division of a country, such as Switzerland
WORD ORIGIN Old French: corner

Cantonese *adj* **1** of Canton, a port in SE China ▷ *n* **2** *pl* **-nese** a person from Canton **3** the Chinese dialect of Canton

cantonment (kan-**toon**-ment) *n* a permanent military camp in British India
WORD ORIGIN Old French *canton* corner

cantor *n* *Judaism* a man employed to lead synagogue services
WORD ORIGIN Latin: singer

Canuck *n, adj* *US & Canad informal* Canadian
WORD ORIGIN origin unknown

canvas *n* **1** a heavy cloth of cotton, hemp, or jute, used to make tents and sails and for painting on in oils **2** an oil painting done on canvas **3** **under canvas** in a tent: *sleeping under canvas*
WORD ORIGIN Latin *cannabis* hemp

canvass *vb* **1** to try to persuade (people) to vote for a particular candidate or party in an election **2** to find out the opinions of (people) by conducting a survey ▷ *n* **3** the activity of canvassing
canvasser *n* **canvassing** *n*
WORD ORIGIN probably from obsolete sense of *canvas* (to toss someone in a canvas sheet, hence, to criticize)

canyon *n* a deep narrow steep-sided valley
WORD ORIGIN Spanish *cañon*

canyoning *n* the sport of travelling down a river situated in a canyon by a variety of means including scrambling, swimming, and abseiling

caoutchouc (**cow**-chook) *n* same as **rubber¹** (sense 1)
WORD ORIGIN from S American Indian

cap *n* **1** a soft close-fitting covering for the head **2** *sport* a cap given to someone selected for a national team **3** a small flat lid: *petrol cap* **4** a small amount of explosive enclosed in paper and used in a toy gun **5** a contraceptive device placed over the mouth of the womb **6** an upper financial limit **7** **cap in hand** humbly ▷ *vb* **capping, capped 8** to cover or top with something: *a thick cover of snow capped the cars* **9** *sport* to select (a player) for a national team:

Australia's most capped player **10** to impose an upper level on (a tax): *charge capping* **11** *informal* to outdo or excel: *capping anecdote with anecdote*
WORD ORIGIN Late Latin *cappa* hood

CAP (in the EU) Common Agricultural Policy

cap. capital

capability *n, pl* **-ties** the ability or skill to do something

capable *adj* **1** having the ability or skill to do something: *a side capable of winning the championship* **2** competent and efficient: *capable high achievers*
capably *adv*
WORD ORIGIN Latin *capere* to take

capacious *adj* having a large capacity or area
WORD ORIGIN Latin *capere* to take

capacitance *n* *physics* **1** the ability of a capacitor to store electrical charge **2** a measure of this

capacitor *n* *physics* a device for storing a charge of electricity

capacity *n, pl* **-ties 1** the ability to contain, absorb, or hold something **2** the maximum amount something can contain or absorb: *filled to capacity* **3** the ability to do something: *his capacity to elicit great loyalty* **4** a position or function: *acting in an official capacity* **5** the maximum output of which an industry or factory is capable: *the refinery had a capacity of three hundred thousand barrels a day* **6** *physics* same as **capacitance** ▷ *adj* **7** of the maximum amount or number possible: *a capacity crowd*
WORD ORIGIN Latin *capere* to take

caparisoned (kap-**par**-riss-sond) *adj* (esp. of a horse) magnificently decorated or dressed
WORD ORIGIN Old Spanish *caparazón* saddlecloth

cape¹ *n* a short sleeveless cloak
WORD ORIGIN Late Latin *cappa*

cape² *n* a large piece of land that juts out into the sea
WORD ORIGIN Latin *caput* head

Cape *n* **the Cape 1** the Cape of Good Hope **2** the SW region of South Africa's Cape Province

caper *n* **1** a high-spirited escapade ▷ *vb* **2** to skip about light-heartedly
WORD ORIGIN probably from CAPRIOLE

capercaillie *or* **capercailzie** (kap-per-**kale**-yee) *n* a large black European woodland grouse
WORD ORIGIN Scottish Gaelic *capull coille* horse of the woods

capers *pl n* the pickled flower buds of a Mediterranean shrub, used in making sauces
WORD ORIGIN Greek *kapparis* caper plant

capillarity *n* *physics* a phenomenon caused by surface tension that results in the surface of a liquid rising or falling in contact with a solid

capillary (kap-**pill**-a-ree) *n, pl* **-laries 1** *anat* one of the very fine blood vessels linking the arteries and the veins ▷ *adj* **2** (of a tube) having a fine bore **3** *anat* of the capillaries
WORD ORIGIN Latin *capillus* hair

capital¹ *n* **1** the chief city of a country, where the government meets **2** the

total wealth owned or used in business by an individual or group **3** wealth used to produce more wealth by investment **4** **make capital out of** to gain advantage from: *to make political capital out of the hostage situation* **5** a capital letter ▷ *adj* **6** *law* involving or punishable by death: *a capital offence* **7** denoting the large letter used as the initial letter in a sentence, personal name, or place name **8** *Brit, Austral, & NZ, old-fashioned* excellent or first-rate: *a capital dinner*
WORD ORIGIN Latin *caput* head

capital² *n* the top part of a column or pillar
WORD ORIGIN Old French *capitel*, from Latin *caput* head

capital gain *n* profit from the sale of an asset

capital goods *pl n* *econ* goods that are themselves utilized in the production of other goods

capitalism *n* an economic system based on the private ownership of industry

capitalist *adj* **1** based on or supporting capitalism: *capitalist countries* ▷ *n* **2** a supporter of capitalism **3** a person who owns a business **capitalistic** *adj*

capitalize *or* **-ise** *vb* **-izing, -ized** *or* **-ising, -ised 1 capitalize on** to take advantage of: *to capitalize on the available opportunities* **2** to write or print (words) in capital letters **3** to convert (debt or earnings) into capital stock **capitalization** *or* **-isation** *n*

capital levy *n* a tax on capital or property as contrasted with a tax on income

capitally *adv old-fashioned* in an excellent manner; admirably

capital punishment *n* the punishment of death for committing a serious crime

capital stock *n* **1** the value of the total shares that a company can issue **2** the total capital existing in an economy at a particular time

capitation *n* a tax of a fixed amount per person
WORD ORIGIN Latin *caput* head

capitulate *vb* **-lating, -lated** to surrender under agreed conditions
capitulation *n*
WORD ORIGIN Medieval Latin *capitulare* to draw up under headings

capo *n, pl* **-pos** a device fitted across the strings of a guitar or similar instrument so as to raise the pitch
WORD ORIGIN Italian *capo tasto* head stop

capoeira (kap-poo-**eer**-uh) *n* a combination of martial art and dance, which originated among African slaves in 19th-century Brazil
WORD ORIGIN from Portuguese

capon (**kay**-pon) *n* a castrated cock fowl fattened for eating
WORD ORIGIN Latin *capo*

caponata (kap-uh-**nah**-tuh) *n* a dish of fried seasoned aubergine and other vegetables, served as an appetizer
WORD ORIGIN Italian

cappuccino (kap-poo-**cheen**-oh) *n, pl* **-nos** coffee with steamed milk, usually

sprinkled with powdered chocolate
WORD ORIGIN Italian

caprice (kap-**reess**) *n* **1** a sudden change of attitude or behaviour **2** a tendency to have such changes
WORD ORIGIN Italian *capriccio* a shiver, caprice

capricious *adj* having a tendency to sudden unpredictable changes of attitude or behaviour **capriciously** *adv*

Capricorn *n* **1** *astrol* the tenth sign of the zodiac; the Goat **2** tropic of Capricorn see **tropic** (sense 1)
WORD ORIGIN Latin *caper* goat + *cornu* horn

capriole *n* **1** an upward but not forward leap made by a horse ▷ *vb* **-oling, -oled 2** to perform a capriole
WORD ORIGIN Latin *capreolus, caper* goat

caps. capital letters

capsicum *n* a kind of pepper used as a vegetable or ground to produce a spice
WORD ORIGIN Latin *capsa* box

capsize *vb* **-sizing, -sized** (of a boat) to overturn accidentally
WORD ORIGIN origin unknown

capstan *n* a vertical rotating cylinder round which a ship's rope or cable is wound
WORD ORIGIN Old Provençal *cabestan*

capstone *n* same as **copestone** (sense 2)

capsule *n* **1** a soluble gelatine case containing a dose of medicine **2** *bot* a plant's seed case that opens when ripe **3** *anat* a membrane or sac surrounding an organ or part **4** see **space capsule** ▷ *adj* **5** very concise: *capsule courses*
WORD ORIGIN Latin *capsa* box

capsulize *or* **-ise** *vb* **-izing, -ized** *or* **-ising, -ised 1** to state (information) in a highly condensed form **2** to enclose in a capsule

Capt. Captain

captain *n* **1** the person in charge of a ship, boat, or civil aircraft **2** a middle-ranking naval officer **3** a junior officer in the army **4** the leader of a team or group ▷ *vb* **5** to be captain of **captaincy** *n*
WORD ORIGIN Latin *caput* head

caption *n* **1** a title, brief explanation, or comment accompanying a picture ▷ *vb* **2** to provide with a caption
WORD ORIGIN Latin *captio* a seizing

captious *adj* tending to make trivial criticisms
WORD ORIGIN Latin *captio* a seizing

captivate *vb* **-vating, -vated** to attract and hold the attention of; enchant **captivating** *adj*
WORD ORIGIN Latin *captivus* captive

captive *n* **1** a person who is kept in confinement ▷ *adj* **2** kept in confinement **3** (of an audience) unable to leave
WORD ORIGIN Latin *captivus*

captivity *n* the state of being kept in confinement

captor *n* a person who captures a person or animal

capture *vb* **-turing, -tured 1** to take by force **2** to succeed in representing (something elusive) in words, pictures, or music: *today's newspapers capture the mood of the nation* **3** *physics* (of an atomic

nucleus) to acquire (an additional particle) ▷ *n* **4** the act of capturing or the state of being captured
WORD ORIGIN Latin *capere* to take

capuchin (**kap**-yew-chin) *n* a S American monkey with a cowl of thick hair on the top of its head
WORD ORIGIN Italian *cappuccio* hood

Capuchin *n* **1** a friar belonging to a branch of the Franciscan Order founded in 1525 ▷ *adj* **2** of this order
WORD ORIGIN Italian *cappuccio* hood

capybara *n* the largest living rodent, found in S America

car *n* **1** a motorized road vehicle designed to carry a small number of people **2** the passenger compartment of a cable car, airship, lift, or balloon **3** *US & Canad* a railway carriage
WORD ORIGIN Latin *carra, carrum* two-wheeled wagon

caracal *n* a lynx with reddish fur, which inhabits deserts of N Africa and S Asia
WORD ORIGIN Turkish *kara kūlāk* black ear

carafe (kar-**raff**) *n* a wide-mouthed bottle for water or wine
WORD ORIGIN Arabic *gharrāfah* vessel

carambola *n* a yellow edible star-shaped fruit that grows on a Brazilian tree
WORD ORIGIN Spanish

caramel *n* **1** a chewy sweet made from sugar and milk **2** burnt sugar, used for colouring and flavouring food
WORD ORIGIN French

caramelize *or* **-ise** *vb* **-izing, -ized** *or* **-ising, -ised** to turn into caramel

carapace *n* the thick hard upper shell of tortoises and crustaceans
WORD ORIGIN Spanish *carapacho*

carat *n* **1** a unit of weight of precious stones, equal to 0.20 grams **2** a measure of the purity of gold in an alloy, expressed as the number of parts of gold in 24 parts of the alloy
WORD ORIGIN Arabic *qīrāt* weight of four grains

caravan *n* **1** a large enclosed vehicle designed to be pulled by a car or horse and equipped to be lived in **2** (in some Eastern countries) a company of traders or other travellers journeying together
WORD ORIGIN Persian *kārwān*

caravanning *n* travelling or holidaying in a caravan

caravanserai *n* (in some Eastern countries, esp. formerly) a large inn enclosing a courtyard, providing accommodation for caravans
WORD ORIGIN Persian *kārwānsarāī* caravan inn

caraway *n* a Eurasian plant with seeds that are used as a spice in cooking
WORD ORIGIN Arabic *karawyā*

carb *n* *informal* short for **carbohydrate**

carbide *n* *chem* a compound of carbon with a metal

carbine *n* a type of light rifle
WORD ORIGIN French *carabine*

carbohydrate *n* any of a large group of energy-producing compounds, including sugars and starches, that contain carbon, hydrogen, and oxygen

carbolic acid *n* a disinfectant derived from coal tar

carbon *n* **1** a nonmetallic element occurring in three forms, charcoal, graphite, and diamond, and present in all organic compounds. Symbol: C **2** short for **carbon paper** or **carbon copy**
WORD ORIGIN Latin *carbo* charcoal

carbonaceous *adj* of, resembling, or containing carbon

carbonate *n* a salt or ester of carbonic acid

carbonated *adj* (of a drink) containing carbon dioxide; fizzy

carbon black *n* powdered carbon produced by partial burning of natural gas or petroleum, used in pigments and ink

carbon capture *n* the removal and storage of carbon dioxide emissions from power plants and factories, instead of releasing it into the atmosphere

carbon copy *n* **1** a duplicate obtained by using carbon paper **2** *informal* a person or thing that is identical or very similar to another

carbon dating *n* a technique for finding the age of organic materials, such as wood, based on their content of radioactive carbon

carbon dioxide *n* a colourless odourless incombustible gas formed during breathing, and used in fire extinguishers and in making fizzy drinks

carbon footprint *n* a measure of the amount of carbon dioxide released into the atmosphere through a single endeavour or through the activities of a person, company, etc. over a given period

carbonic *adj* containing carbon

carbonic acid *n* a weak acid formed when carbon dioxide combines with water

carboniferous *adj* yielding coal or carbon

Carboniferous *adj* *geol* of the period of geological time about 330 million years ago, during which coal seams were formed

carbonize *or* **-ise** *vb* **-izing, -ized** *or* **-ising, -ised 1** to turn into carbon as a result of partial burning **2** to coat (a substance) with carbon **carbonization** *or* **-isation** *n*

carbon monoxide *n* a colourless odourless poisonous gas formed by the incomplete burning of carbon compounds; part of the gases that come from a vehicle's exhaust

carbon-neutral *adj* not affecting the overall volume of carbon dioxide in the atmosphere

carbon offset *n* a compensatory measure made by an individual or company for carbon emissions, such as tree planting

carbon paper *n* a thin sheet of paper coated on one side with a dark waxy pigment, containing carbon, used to make a duplicate of something as it is typed or written

Word Histories
part 4

Caterpillar: Strange as it may seem, a caterpillar is, in terms of its word origins, a type of cat. The word comes from Old Norman French *catepelose*, meaning 'hairy cat'.

Chameleon: Although it may not much look like one, a chameleon is, in terms of its word origins, a type of lion, a 'ground lion'. The word comes from two Greek words, *khamai*, meaning 'on the ground', and *leōn* meaning 'lion'.

Chapel: According to legend, St Martin of Tours once gave half his cloak to a beggar. This cloak (Latin *cappella*) was kept as a relic and the place where it was kept also became known as the 'cappella' or, in Old French, *chapelle*. The use of this word then spread to other places of worship.

As **chav** has sprung into widespread use, various explanations have been proffered – abbreviations of Chatham Average or Cheltenam Average, or an acronym of Council Housed And Violent, for example. The word has a much older origin, in fact, deriving from the Romany term for a youth or boy: *chavi*. 'Chav', therefore, seems to have been around for a long time, but has only recently come to prominence in the media.

Chess: The purpose of the game of chess may be to capture your opponent's king, but in terms of word origins, a player's aim is really to kill the king: 'checkmate' comes from the Arabic phrase *shāh māt*, meaning 'the king is dead'.

Cheetah comes from Hindi *cītā*, which is derived from Sanskrit *citrakāya*, meaning 'leopard', from *citra*, meaning 'bright' or 'speckled', and *kāya*, meaning 'body'.

Chocolate: Europeans were first introduced to chocolate at the court of the Aztec king Montezuma in the 16th century. 'Chocolate' or *xocolatl* was a bitter Aztec drink made from cocoa beans. The name *xocolatl* means 'bitter water', from Aztec *xococ*, meaning 'bitter', and *atl*, meaning 'water'.

Cigar came into English from Spanish, but it probably originally comes from Mayan (a Central American language) *sicar*, meaning 'to smoke'.

Cockroach: A cockroach is neither a male fowl nor a freshwater fish – nor is it a combination of the two! Rather, the recognisable English elements were used to make the Spanish *cucaracha* a more familiar word. An older folk etymology derived 'cockroach' from the slang term for excrement, 'caca'.

Coffee comes, via Italian, from Turkish *kahve*, from Arabic *qahwah*, meaning 'wine' or 'coffee'.

Companion: A companion was originally someone you liked enough to share a meal with. The Latin word *companio* consists of the roots *com-*, meaning 'with' or 'together', and *panis*, meaning 'bread'.

Condom: The invention of the condom is often attributed to a certain Dr Condom. Unfortunately, while the story is persistent, no written record of the good doctor has yet been found. The origins of 'condom' thus remain shrouded in darkness; perhaps the most likely suggestion is that the word derives from the Italian *guantone*, a 'little glove' – as in the contemporary safe-sex slogan, 'no glove, no love'.

Cop is popularly supposed to be an acronym for Constable On Patrol. Like most supposed acronym etymologies, however, there is no truth in it. 'Cop' as a noun is simply a shortened form of 'copper', from the dialect verb 'cop', 'to seize' as in 'it's a fair cop, guv!'

Crap is often derived from one Thomas Crapper (1837–1910), an English plumber who invented the ball-and-suction device used in modern flush toilets. While Crapper was a real figure, 'crap', as both verb and noun, predates Crapper's 1882 invention. The word comes from Old English, and was applied to a wide variety of rubbish or discarded material before it was applied to defecation. Crapper, however, may have been responsible for the slang term for a toilet, in large part because his name sounded like an agent noun of the established verb. See **hooker** for a similar instance of fortuitous etymology.

carbon tax *n* a tax on the emissions caused by the burning of coal, gas, and oil, aimed at reducing the production of greenhouse gases

carbon tetrachloride *n* a colourless nonflammable liquid used as a solvent, cleaning fluid, and insecticide

car boot sale *n* a sale of goods from car boots in a site hired for the occasion

Carborundum *n trademark* an abrasive material consisting of silicon carbide

carboxyl group *or* **radical** *n chem* the chemical group –COOH: the functional group in organic acids

carboy *n* a large bottle protected by a basket or box
WORD ORIGIN Persian *qarāba*

carbuncle *n* a large painful swelling under the skin like a boil
WORD ORIGIN Latin *carbo* coal

carburettor *or US & Canad* **carburetor** *n* a device in an internal-combustion engine that mixes petrol with air and regulates the intake of the mixture into the engine

carcass *or* **carcase** *n* **1** the dead body of an animal **2** *informal* a person's body: *ask that person to move his carcass*
WORD ORIGIN Old French *carcasse*

carcinogen *n* a substance that produces cancer **carcinogenic** *adj*
WORD ORIGIN Greek *karkinos* cancer

carcinoma *n, pl* **-mas** *or* **-mata** a malignant tumour
WORD ORIGIN Greek *karkinos* cancer

card¹ *n* **1** a piece of stiff paper or thin cardboard used for identification, reference, proof of membership, or sending greetings or messages: *a Christmas card* **2** one of a set of small pieces of cardboard, marked with figures or symbols, used for playing games or for fortune-telling **3** a small rectangle of stiff plastic with identifying numbers for use as a credit card, cheque card, or charge card **4** *old-fashioned informal* a witty or eccentric person ▶ See also **cards**
WORD ORIGIN Greek *khartēs* leaf of papyrus

card² *n* **1** a machine or tool for combing fibres of cotton or wool to disentangle them before spinning ▷ *vb* **2** to process with such a machine or tool
WORD ORIGIN Latin *carduus* thistle

cardamom *n* a spice that is obtained from the seeds of a tropical plant
WORD ORIGIN Greek *kardamon* cress + *amōmon* an Indian spice

cardboard *n* a thin stiff board made from paper pulp

card-carrying *adj* being an official member of an organization: *a card-carrying Conservative*

cardholder *n* a person who owns a credit or debit card

cardiac *adj* of or relating to the heart
WORD ORIGIN Greek *kardia* heart

cardigan *n* a knitted jacket
WORD ORIGIN after 7th Earl of *Cardigan*

cardinal *n* **1** any of the high-ranking clergymen of the Roman Catholic Church who elect the pope and act as his chief counsellors ▷ *adj* **2** fundamentally important; principal
WORD ORIGIN Latin *cardo* hinge

cardinal number *n* a number denoting quantity but not order in a group, for example one, two, or three

cardinal points *pl n* the four main points of the compass: north, south, east, and west

cardinal virtues *pl n* the most important moral qualities, traditionally justice, prudence, temperance, and fortitude

card index *n* an index in which each item is separately listed on systematically arranged cards

cardiogram *n* an electrocardiogram. See **electrocardiograph**

cardiograph *n* an electrocardiograph **cardiographer** *n* **cardiography** *n*

cardiology *n* the branch of medicine dealing with the heart and its diseases **cardiologist** *n*

cardiothoracic *adj* of or relating to the heart or the chest

cardiovascular *adj* of or relating to the heart and the blood vessels

cards *n* **1** any game played with cards, or card games generally **2** **lay one's cards on the table** to declare one's intentions openly **3** **on the cards** likely to take place: *a military coup was on the cards* **4** **play one's cards right** to handle a situation cleverly

cardsharp *or* **cardsharper** *n* a professional card player who cheats

card vote *n Brit & NZ* a vote by delegates in which each delegate's vote counts as a vote by all his or her constituents

care *vb* **caring**, **cared** **1** to be worried or concerned: *he does not care what people think about him* **2** to like (to do something): *anybody care to go out?* **3** **care for a** to look after or provide for: *it is still largely women who care for dependent family members* **b** to like or be fond of: *he did not care for his concentration to be disturbed; I don't suppose you could ever care for me seriously* **4** **I couldn't care less** I am completely indifferent ▷ *n* **5** careful or serious attention; caution: *treat all raw meat with extreme care to avoid food poisoning* **6** protection or charge: *the children are now in the care of a state orphanage* **7** trouble or worry: *his mind turned towards money cares* **8** **care of** (written on envelopes) at the address of **9** **in** *or* **into care** *Brit & NZ* (of a child) made the legal responsibility of a local authority or the state by order of a court **10** **take care** to be careful **11** **take care of** to look after: *women have to take greater care of themselves during pregnancy*
WORD ORIGIN Old English *cearian*

careen *vb* to tilt over to one side
WORD ORIGIN Latin *carina* keel

career *n* **1** the series of jobs in a profession or occupation that a person has through his or her life: *a career in child psychology* **2** the part of a person's life spent in a particular occupation or type of work: *a school career punctuated with exams* ▷ *vb* **3** to rush in an uncontrolled way ▷ *adj* **4** having chosen to dedicate his or her life to a particular occupation: *a career soldier*
WORD ORIGIN Latin *carrus* two-wheeled wagon

careerist *n* a person who seeks to advance his or her career by any means possible **careerism** *n*

carefree *adj* without worry or responsibility

careful *adj* **1** cautious in attitude or action **2** very exact and thorough **carefully** *adv* **carefulness** *n*

careless *adj* **1** done or acting with insufficient attention **2** unconcerned in attitude or action **carelessly** *adv* **carelessness** *n*

carer *n* a person who looks after someone who is ill or old, often a relative: *the group offers support for the carers of those with dementia*

caress *n* **1** a gentle affectionate touch or embrace ▷ *vb* **2** to touch gently and affectionately
WORD ORIGIN Latin *carus* dear

caret (**kar**-ret) *n* a symbol (‸) indicating a place in written or printed matter where something is to be inserted
WORD ORIGIN Latin: there is missing

caretaker *n* **1** a person employed to look after a place or thing ▷ *adj* **2** performing the duties of an office temporarily: *a caretaker administration*

careworn *adj* showing signs of stress or worry

cargo *n, pl* **-goes** *or esp. US* **-gos** goods carried by a ship, aircraft, or other vehicle
WORD ORIGIN Spanish *cargar* to load

cargo pants *or* **trousers** *pl n* loose trousers with a large external pocket on the side of each leg

Carib *n* **1** *pl* **-ibs** *or* **-ib** a member of a group of Native American peoples of NE South America and the S West Indies **2** any of the languages of these peoples
WORD ORIGIN Spanish *Caribe*

Caribbean *adj* of the Caribbean Sea, bounded by Central America, South America, and the West Indies, or the surrounding countries and islands

caribou *n, pl* **-bou** *or* **-bous** a large North American reindeer
WORD ORIGIN from a Native American language

caricature *n* **1** a drawing or description of a person which exaggerates characteristic features for comic effect **2** a description or explanation of something that is so exaggerated or over-simplified that it is difficult to take seriously: *the classic caricature of the henpecked husband* ▷ *vb* **-turing, -tured** **3** to make a caricature of
WORD ORIGIN Italian *caricatura* a distortion

caries (**care**-reez) *n* tooth decay
WORD ORIGIN Latin: decay

carillon (kar-**rill**-yon) *n* **1** a set of bells hung in a tower and played either from a keyboard or mechanically **2** a tune played on such bells
WORD ORIGIN French

caring *adj* **1** feeling or showing care and compassion for other people **2** of or relating to professional social or medical care: *the caring professions*

carjack *vb* to attack (a driver in a car) in order to rob the driver or to steal the car for another crime
WORD ORIGIN CAR + (HI)JACK

cark *vb* **cark it** *Austral & NZ slang* to die

Carmelite *n* **1** a Christian friar or nun belonging to the order of Our Lady of Carmel ▷ *adj* **2** of this order
WORD ORIGIN after Mount *Carmel*, in Palestine, where the order was founded

carminative *adj* **1** able to relieve flatulence ▷ *n* **2** a carminative drug
WORD ORIGIN Latin *carminare* to card wool, comb out

carmine *adj* vivid red
WORD ORIGIN Arabic *qirmiz* kermes

carnage *n* extensive slaughter of people
WORD ORIGIN Latin *caro* flesh

carnal *adj* of a sexual or sensual nature: *carnal knowledge* **carnality** *n*
WORD ORIGIN Latin *caro* flesh

carnation *n* a cultivated plant with clove-scented white, pink, or red flowers
WORD ORIGIN Latin *caro* flesh

carnelian *n* a reddish-yellow variety of chalcedony, used as a gemstone
WORD ORIGIN Old French *corneline*

carnet (**kar**-nay) *n* a customs licence permitting motorists to take their cars across certain frontiers
WORD ORIGIN French: notebook

carnival *n* **1** a festive period with processions, music, and dancing in the street **2** a travelling funfair
WORD ORIGIN Old Italian *carnelevare* a removing of meat (referring to the Lenten fast)

carnivore (**car**-niv-vore) *n* **1** a meat-eating animal **2** *informal* an aggressively ambitious person **carnivorous** (**car-niv**-or-uss) *adj*
WORD ORIGIN Latin *caro* flesh + *vorare* to consume

carob *n* the pod of a Mediterranean tree, used as a chocolate substitute
WORD ORIGIN Arabic *al kharrūbah*

carol *n* **1** a joyful religious song sung at Christmas ▷ *vb* -olling, -olled *or US* -oling, -oled **2** to sing carols **3** to sing joyfully
WORD ORIGIN Old French

carotene *n* *biochem* any of four orange-red hydrocarbons, found in many plants, converted to vitamin A in the liver
WORD ORIGIN from Latin *carota* carrot

carotid (kar-**rot**-id) *n* **1** either of the two arteries that supply blood to the head and neck ▷ *adj* **2** of either of these arteries
WORD ORIGIN Greek *karoun* to stupefy; so named because pressure on them produced unconsciousness

carousal *n* a merry drinking party

carouse *vb* -rousing, -roused to have a merry drinking party: *carousing with friends*
WORD ORIGIN German (*trinken*) *gar aus* (to drink) right out

carousel (kar-roo-**sell**) *n* **1** a revolving conveyor for luggage at an airport or for slides for a projector **2** *US & Canad* a merry-go-round
WORD ORIGIN Italian *carosello*

carp¹ *n, pl* carp *or* carps a large freshwater food fish
WORD ORIGIN Old French *carpe*

carp² *vb* to complain or find fault **carping** *adj, n*
WORD ORIGIN Old Norse *karpa* to boast

carpaccio (kar-**patch**-ee-oh) *n* an Italian dish of thin slices of raw meat or fish
WORD ORIGIN Italian

carpal *n* a wrist bone
WORD ORIGIN Greek *karpos* wrist

car park *n* an area or building reserved for parking cars

carpel *n* the female reproductive organ of a flowering plant
WORD ORIGIN Greek *karpos* fruit

carpenter *n* a person who makes or repairs wooden structures
WORD ORIGIN Latin *carpentarius* wagon-maker

carpentry *n* the skill or work of a carpenter

carpet *n* **1** a heavy fabric for covering floors **2** a covering like a carpet: *a carpet of leaves* **3 on the carpet** *informal* being or about to be reprimanded **4 sweep something under the carpet** to conceal or keep silent about something that one does not want to be discovered ▷ *vb* -peting, -peted **5** to cover with a carpet or a covering like a carpet
WORD ORIGIN Latin *carpere* to pluck, card

carpetbag *n* a travelling bag made of carpeting

carpetbagger *n* **1** a politician who seeks office in a place where he or she has no connections **2** *Brit* a person who makes a short-term investment in a mutual savings or life-assurance organization in order to benefit from free shares issued following the organization's conversion to a public limited company

carpeting *n* carpet material or carpets in general

carpet snake *n* a large nonvenomous Australian snake with a carpet-like pattern on its back

car phone *n* a telephone that operates by cellular radio for use in a car

carport *n* a shelter for a car, consisting of a roof supported by posts

carpus *n, pl* -pi the set of eight bones of the human wrist
WORD ORIGIN Greek *karpos*

carrageen *n* an edible red seaweed of North America and N Europe
WORD ORIGIN *Carragheen*, near Waterford, Ireland

carriage *n* **1** *Brit, Austral, & NZ* one of the sections of a train for passengers **2** the way a person holds and moves his or her head and body **3** a four-wheeled horse-drawn passenger vehicle **4** the moving part of a machine, such as a typewriter, that supports and shifts another part **5** the charge made for conveying goods
WORD ORIGIN Old French *cariage*

carriage clock *n* a style of portable clock, originally used by travellers

carriageway *n* **1** *Brit* the part of a road along which traffic passes in one direction: *the westbound carriageway of the M4* **2** *NZ* the part of a road used by vehicles

carrier *n* **1** a person, vehicle, or organization that carries something: *armoured personnel carriers* **2** a person or animal that, without suffering from a disease, is capable of transmitting it to others **3** short for **aircraft carrier**

carrier bag *n* *Brit* a large plastic or paper bag for carrying shopping

carrier pigeon *n* a homing pigeon used for carrying messages

carrion *n* dead and rotting flesh
WORD ORIGIN Latin *caro* flesh

carrion crow *n* a scavenging European crow with a completely black plumage and bill

carrot *n* **1** a long tapering orange root vegetable **2** something offered as an incentive
WORD ORIGIN Greek *karōton*

carroty *adj* (of hair) reddish-orange

carry *vb* -ries, -rying, -ried **1** to take from one place to another **2** to have with one habitually, for example in one's pocket or handbag: *to carry a donor card* **3** to transmit or be transmitted: *to carry disease* **4** to have as a factor or result: *the charge of desertion carries a maximum penalty of twenty years* **5** to be pregnant with: *women carrying Down's Syndrome babies* **6** to hold (one's head or body) in a specified manner: *she always wears a sari and carries herself like an Indian* **7** to secure the adoption of (a bill or motion): *the resolution was carried by fewer than twenty votes* **8** (of a newspaper or television or radio station) to include in the contents: *several papers carried front-page pictures of the Russian president* **9** *maths* to transfer (a number) from one column of figures to the next **10** to travel a certain distance or reach a specified point: *his faint voice carried no farther than the front few rows* **11 carry the can** *informal* to take all the blame for something ▸ See also **carry away, carry forward**, etc.
WORD ORIGIN Latin *carrum* transport wagon

carry away *vb* be *or* get carried away to be engrossed in or fascinated by something to the point of losing self-control: *he could be carried away by his own rhetoric*

carrycot *n* a light portable bed for a baby, with handles and a hood, which usually also serves as the body of a pram

carry forward *vb* to transfer (an amount) to the next column, page, or accounting period

carry off *vb* **1** to lift and take (someone or something) away: *the German striker was carried off after snapping an Achilles tendon* **2** to win: *who will carry off this year's honours is unclear* **3** to handle (a situation) successfully: *he had the presence and social ability to carry off the job* **4** to cause to die: *the circulatory disorder which carried off other members of his family*

carry on *vb* **1** to continue: *we'll carry on exactly where we left off* **2** to do, run, or take part in: *the vast trade carried on in the city* **3** *informal* to cause a fuss: *I don't want to carry on and make a big scene* ▷ *n* **carry-on** **4** *informal chiefly Brit* a fuss

carry out *vb* **1** to follow (an order or instruction) **2** to accomplish (a task): *to carry out repairs*

carry over *vb* to extend from one period or situation into another: *major debts carried over from last year*

carry through *vb* to bring to completion: *these are difficult policies to carry through*

carsick *adj* nauseated from riding in a car

cart *n* 1 an open horse-drawn vehicle, usually with two wheels, used to carry goods or passengers 2 any small vehicle that is pulled or pushed by hand ▷ *vb* 3 to carry, usually with some effort: *men carted bricks and tiles and wooden boards* ▶ See also **cart off**
WORD ORIGIN Old Norse *kartr*

carte blanche *n* complete authority: *she's got carte blanche to redecorate*
WORD ORIGIN French: blank paper

cartel *n* an association of competing firms formed in order to fix prices
WORD ORIGIN German *Kartell*

Cartesian *adj* of René Descartes, 17th-century French philosopher and mathematician, or his works
WORD ORIGIN *Cartesius*, Latin form of Descartes

Cartesian coordinates *pl n* a set of numbers that determine the location of a point in a plane or in space by its distance from two fixed intersecting lines

carthorse *n* a large heavily built horse kept for pulling carts or for farm work

Carthusian *n* 1 a Christian monk or nun belonging to a strict monastic order founded in 1084 ▷ *adj* 2 of this order
WORD ORIGIN Latin *Carthusia* Chartreuse, near Grenoble

cartilage (**kar**-till-ij) *n* a strong flexible tissue forming part of the skeleton **cartilaginous** *adj*
WORD ORIGIN Latin *cartilago*

cart off *vb* to take (someone) somewhere forcefully: *we had been carted off to the security police building*

cartography *n* the art of making maps or charts **cartographer** *n* **cartographic** *adj*
WORD ORIGIN French *carte* map, chart

carton *n* 1 a cardboard box or container 2 a container of waxed paper in which drinks are sold
WORD ORIGIN Italian *carta* card

cartoon *n* 1 a humorous or satirical drawing in a newspaper or magazine 2 same as **comic strip** 3 same as **animated cartoon** > **cartoonist** *n*
WORD ORIGIN Italian *cartone* pasteboard

cartouche *n* 1 an ornamental tablet or panel in the form of a scroll 2 (in ancient Egypt) an oblong or oval figure containing royal or divine names
WORD ORIGIN French: scroll, cartridge

cartridge *n* 1 a metal casing containing an explosive charge and bullet for a gun 2 the part of the pick-up of a record player that converts the movements of the stylus into electrical signals 3 a sealed container of film or tape, or ink for a special kind of pen
WORD ORIGIN from French *cartouche*

cartridge belt *n* a belt with loops or pockets for holding cartridges

cartridge clip *n* a metallic container holding cartridges for an automatic gun

cartridge paper *n* a type of heavy rough drawing paper

cartwheel *n* 1 a sideways somersault supported by the hands with legs outstretched 2 the large spoked wheel of a cart

carve *vb* **carving, carved** 1 to cut in order to form something: *carving wood* 2 to form (something) by cutting: *the statue which was carved by Michelangelo* 3 to slice (cooked meat) ▶ See also **carve out, carve up** > **carver** *n*
WORD ORIGIN Old English *ceorfan*

carve out *vb informal* to make or create: *to carve out a political career*

carvery *n, pl* **-veries** a restaurant where customers pay a set price for unrestricted helpings of carved meat and other food

carve up *vb* 1 to divide or share out: *in 1795, Poland was carved up between three empires* ▷ *n* **carve-up** 2 the division or sharing out of something: *a territorial carve-up*

carving *n* a figure or design produced by carving stone or wood

carving knife *n* a long-bladed knife for carving cooked meat

carwash *n* a place fitted with equipment for automatically washing cars

caryatid (kar-ree-**at**-id) *n* a supporting column in the shape of a female figure
WORD ORIGIN Greek *Karuatides* priestesses of Artemis at *Karuai* (Caryae), in Laconia

Casanova *n* a promiscuous man
WORD ORIGIN after Giovanni *Casanova*, Italian adventurer

casbah *n* the citadel of a North African city
WORD ORIGIN Arabic *kasba* citadel

cascade *n* 1 a waterfall or series of waterfalls over rocks 2 something flowing or falling like a waterfall: *a cascade of luxuriant hair* ▷ *vb* **-cading, -caded** 3 to flow or fall in a cascade: *rays of sunshine cascaded down*
WORD ORIGIN Italian *cascare* to fall

cascading style sheet *n computers* a file recording style details, such as fonts, colours, etc. that ensures style is consistent over all the pages of a website

cascara *n* the bark of a N American shrub, used as a laxative
WORD ORIGIN Spanish: bark

case¹ *n* 1 a single instance or example of something: *cases of teenage pregnancies* 2 a matter for discussion: *the case before the Ethics Committee* 3 a specific condition or state of affairs: *a sudden-death play-off in the case of a draw* 4 a set of arguments supporting an action or cause: *I put my case before them* 5 a person or problem dealt with by a doctor, social worker, or solicitor 6 **a** an action or lawsuit: *a rape case* **b** the evidence offered in court to support a claim: *he will try to show that the case against his client is largely circumstantial* 7 *grammar* a form of a noun, pronoun, or adjective

showing its relation to other words in the sentence: *the accusative case* 8 *informal* an amusingly eccentric person 9 **in any case** no matter what 10 **in case** so as to allow for the possibility that: *the President has ordered a medical team to stand by in case hostages are released* 11 **in case of** in the event of: *in case of a future conflict*
WORD ORIGIN Old English *casus* (grammatical) case, associated with Old French *cas* a happening; both from Latin *cadere* to fall

case² *n* 1 a container, such as a box or chest 2 a suitcase 3 a protective outer covering ▷ *vb* **casing, cased** 4 *slang* to inspect carefully (a place one plans to rob)
WORD ORIGIN Latin *capsa* box

case-hardened *adj* having been made callous by experience: *a case-hardened senior policewoman*

case history *n* a record of a person's background or medical history

casein *n* a protein found in milk, which forms the basis of cheese
WORD ORIGIN Latin *caseus* cheese

case law *n* law established by following judicial decisions made in earlier cases

caseload *n* the number of cases that someone like a doctor or social worker deals with at any one time

casement *n* a window that is hinged on one side
WORD ORIGIN probably from Old French *encassement* frame

case study *n* an analysis of a group or person in order to make generalizations about a larger group or society as a whole

casework *n* social work based on close study of the personal histories and circumstances of individuals and families **caseworker** *n*

cash *n* 1 banknotes and coins, rather than cheques 2 *informal* money: *strapped for cash* ▷ *adj* 3 of, for, or paid in cash: *cash hand-outs* ▷ *vb* 4 to obtain or pay banknotes or coins for (a cheque or postal order) ▶ See also **cash in on**
WORD ORIGIN Old Italian *cassa* money box

cash-and-carry *adj* operating on a basis of cash payment for goods that are taken away by the purchaser: *the cash-and-carry wholesalers*

cashback *n* 1 a discount offered in return for immediate payment 2 a service by which a customer in a shop can draw out cash on a debit card

cash-book *n book-keeping* a journal in which all money transactions are recorded

cash card *n* a card issued by a bank or building society which can be inserted into a cash dispenser in order to obtain money

cash crop *n* a crop produced for sale rather than for subsistence

cash desk *n* a counter or till in a shop where purchases are paid for

cash discount *n* a discount granted to a purchaser who pays within a specified period

cash dispenser *n* a computerized device outside a bank which supplies

Words from Shakespeare
part 5

cautel *n* a trick or a deceptive act
Perhaps he loves you now
And now no soil not cautel doth besmirch
Hamlet 1.2

celerity *n* speed, swiftness
Hence hath offence his quick celerity
When it is borne in high authority
Measure for Measure 4.2

chafe *n* anger or temper
this Herculean Roman does become
The carriage of his chafe *Anthony and Cleopatra* 1.3

chanson *n* a song
The first row of the pious chanson will show you
more *Hamlet* 2.2

chapman *n* a trader or merchant
Not uttered by base sale of chapman's tongues
Love's Labours Lost 2.1

chaps, chops *n* a word for jaws
Which ne'er shook hands nor bade farewell to him
Till he unseamed him from the nave to th' chops
Macbeth 1.2

chattels *n* one's moveable possessions.
She is my goods, my chattels
The Taming of the Shrew 3.3

chide *v* to tell off or reprimand
Now I but chide, but I should use thee worse
A Midsummer Night's Dream 3.2

chinks *n* cash or money
he that can lay hold of her
Shall have the chinks *Romeo and Juliet* 1.5

choleric *adj* quick to become angry
therewithal unruly waywardness that infirm and
choleric years bring with them *King Lear* 1.1

chuff *n* a miser, someone who clings to his or her
money
ye fat chuffs *Henry IV* part I 2.2

cipher *n* nothing
Mine were the very cipher of a function
Measure for Measure 2.2

circummured *adj* surrounded with a wall
He hath a garden circummured with brick
Measure for Measure 4.1

civet *n* a type of scent or perfume
Give me an ounce of civet *King Lear* 4.6

clamorous *adj* noisy or boisterous
Be clamorous and leap all civil bounds
Twelfth Night 1.4

clangour, clangor *n* ringing
Like to a dismal clangour heard from far
Henry VI part III 2.3

cleave *v* to stick to something or be faithful to it
Thy thoughts I cleave to *The Tempest* 4.1

clock and clock, 'twixt *phrase* from hour to hour,
without stopping or continuously
To weep 'twixt clock and clock *Cymbeline* 3.4

close *adj* hidden
Stand close; this is the same Athenian
A Midsummer Night's Dream 3.2

cloud on one's face, a *n* a troubled, unhappy
expression
He has cloud in's face *Anthony and Cleopatra* 3.2

cloy *v* to satisfy an appetite
Other women cloy
The appetites they feed *Anthony and Cleopatra* 2.2

cock-a-hoop, set *phrase* become free of everything
You will set cock-a-hoop *Romeo and Juliet* 1.5

colours *n* battle-flags or banners
we support the approbation of those that weep this
lamentable divorce under her colours *Cymbeline* 1.5

combustion *n* disorder or chaos
prophesying ... Of dire combustion and confused
events *Macbeth* 2.3

cash when a special card is inserted and the user's code number keyed in

cashew *n* an edible kidney-shaped nut
WORD ORIGIN S American Indian *acajú*

cash flow *n* the movement of money into and out of a business

cashier¹ *n* a person responsible for handling cash in a bank, shop, or other business
WORD ORIGIN French *casse* money chest

cashier² *vb* to dismiss with dishonour from the armed forces
WORD ORIGIN Latin *quassare* to QUASH

cash in on *vb informal* to gain profit or advantage from: *trying to cash in on the dispute*

cashmere *n* a very fine soft wool obtained from goats
WORD ORIGIN from *Kashmir*, in SW central Asia

cash on delivery *n* a system involving cash payment to the carrier on delivery of merchandise. Abbrev: **COD**

cash register *n* a till that has a mechanism for displaying and adding the prices of the goods sold

casing *n* a protective case or covering

casino *n, pl* **-nos** a public building or room where gambling games are played
WORD ORIGIN Italian

cask *n* **1** a strong barrel used to hold alcoholic drink **2** *Austral* a cubic carton containing wine, with a tap for dispensing
WORD ORIGIN Spanish *casco* helmet

casket *n* **1** a small box for valuables **2** *US* a coffin
WORD ORIGIN probably from Old French *cassette* little box

Cassandra *n* someone whose prophecies of doom are unheeded
WORD ORIGIN Trojan prophetess in Greek mythology

cassava *n* a starch obtained from the root of a tropical American plant, used to make tapioca
WORD ORIGIN West Indian *caçábi*

casserole *n* **1** a covered dish in which food is cooked slowly, usually in an oven, and served **2** a dish cooked and served in this way: *beef casserole* ▷ *vb* **-roling, -roled** **3** to cook in a casserole
WORD ORIGIN French

cassette *n* a plastic case containing a reel of film or magnetic tape
WORD ORIGIN French: little box

cassia *n* **1** a tropical plant whose pods yield a mild laxative **2 cassia bark** a cinnamon-like spice obtained from the bark of a tropical Asian tree
WORD ORIGIN Greek *kasia*

cassock *n* an ankle-length garment, usually black, worn by some Christian priests
WORD ORIGIN Italian *casacca* a long coat

cassowary *n, pl* **-waries** a large flightless bird of Australia and New Guinea
WORD ORIGIN Malay *kěsuari*

cast *n* **1** the actors in a play collectively **2 a** an object made of material that has been shaped, while molten, by a mould **b** the mould used to shape such an object **3** *surgery* a rigid casing made of plaster of Paris for immobilizing broken

bones while they heal **4** a sort, kind, or style: *people of an academic cast of mind* **5** a slight squint in the eye ▷ *vb* **casting, cast 6** to select (an actor) to play a part in a play or film **7** to give or deposit (a vote) **8** to express (doubts or aspersions) **9** to cause to appear: *a shadow cast by the grandstand; the gloom cast by the recession* **10 a** to shape (molten material) by pouring it into a mould **b** to make (an object) by such a process **11** to throw (a fishing line) into the water **12** to throw with force: *cast into a bonfire* **13** to direct (a glance): *he cast his eye over the horse-chestnut trees* **14** to roll or throw (a dice) **15 cast aside** to abandon or reject: *cast aside by her lover* **16 cast a spell a** to perform magic **b** to have an irresistible influence ▸ See also **cast around, cast back**, etc.
WORD ORIGIN Old Norse *kasta*

castanets *pl n* a musical instrument, used by Spanish dancers, consisting of curved pieces of hollow wood, held between the fingers and thumb and clicked together
WORD ORIGIN Spanish *castañeta*, from *castaña* chestnut

cast around *or* **about** *vb* to make a mental or visual search: *he cast around for a job*

castaway *n* a person who has been shipwrecked

cast back *vb* to turn (the mind) to the past

cast down *vb* to make (a person) feel discouraged or dejected

caste *n* **1** any of the four major hereditary classes into which Hindu society is divided **2** social rank
WORD ORIGIN Latin *castus* pure, not polluted

castellated *adj* having turrets and battlements, like a castle
WORD ORIGIN Medieval Latin *castellare* to fortify as a castle

caster *n* same as **castor**

caster sugar *n* finely ground white sugar

castigate *vb* **-gating, -gated** to find fault with or reprimand (a person) harshly **castigation** *n*
WORD ORIGIN Latin *castigare* to correct

casting *n* an object that has been cast in metal from a mould

casting vote *n* the deciding vote used by the chairperson of a meeting when an equal number of votes are cast on each side

cast iron *n* **1** iron containing so much carbon that it is brittle and must be cast into shape rather than wrought ▷ *adj* **cast-iron 2** made of cast iron **3** definite or unchallengeable: *cast-iron guarantees*

castle *n* **1** a large fortified building or set of buildings, often built as a residence for a ruler or nobleman in medieval Europe **2** same as **rook²**
WORD ORIGIN Latin: *castellum*

castle in the air *or* **in Spain** *n* a hope or desire unlikely to be realized

cast-off *adj* **1** discarded because no longer wanted or needed: *cast-off clothing* ▷ *n* **2** a person or thing that has been discarded because no longer wanted or

needed ▷ *vb* **cast off 3** to discard (something no longer wanted or needed) **4** to untie a ship from a dock **5** to knot and remove (a row of stitches, esp. the final row) from the needle in knitting

cast on *vb* to make (a row of stitches) on the needle in knitting

castor *n* a small swivelling wheel fixed to a piece of furniture to enable it to be moved easily in any direction

castor oil *n* an oil obtained from the seeds of an Indian plant, used as a lubricant and purgative

castrate *vb* **-trating, -trated 1** to remove the testicles of **2** to deprive of vigour or masculinity **castration** *n*
WORD ORIGIN Latin *castrare*

castrato *n, pl* **-ti** *or* **-tos** (in 17th- and 18th-century opera) a male singer whose testicles were removed before puberty, allowing the retention of a soprano or alto voice
WORD ORIGIN Italian

casual *adj* **1** being or seeming careless or nonchalant: *he was casual about security* **2** occasional or irregular: *casual workers* **3** shallow or superficial: *casual relationships* **4** for informal wear: *a casual jacket* **5** happening by chance or without planning: *a casual comment* ▷ *n* **6** an occasional worker **casually** *adv*
WORD ORIGIN Latin *casus* event, chance

casuals *pl n* **1** informal clothing **2** *Brit* young men wearing expensive casual clothes who go to football matches in order to start fights

casualty *n, pl* **-ties 1** a person who is killed or injured in an accident or war **2** the hospital department where victims of accidents are given emergency treatment **3** a person or thing that has suffered as the result of a particular event or circumstance: *583 job losses with significant casualties among public-sector employees*

casuarina (kass-yew-a-**reen**-a) *n* an Australian tree with jointed green branches
WORD ORIGIN from Malay *kěsuari*, referring to the resemblance of the branches to the feathers of the cassowary

casuistry *n* reasoning that is misleading or oversubtle **casuist** *n*
WORD ORIGIN Latin *casus* case

cat *n* **1** a small domesticated mammal with thick soft fur and whiskers **2** a wild animal related to the cat, such as the lynx, lion, or tiger ▸ Related adjective: **feline 3** **let the cat out of the bag** to disclose a secret **4 raining cats and dogs** raining very heavily **5 set the cat among the pigeons** to stir up trouble **catlike** *adj*
WORD ORIGIN Latin *cattus*

catabolism *n biol* a metabolic process in which complex molecules are broken down into simple ones with the release of energy **catabolic** *adj*
WORD ORIGIN Greek *kata-* down + *ballein* to throw

cataclysm (**kat**-a-kliz-zum) *n* **1** a violent upheaval of a social, political, or military nature: *the cataclysm of the Second World War* **2** a disaster such as an

earthquake or a flood **cataclysmic** *adj*
WORD ORIGIN Greek *katakluzein* to flood

catacombs (**kat**-a-koomz) *pl n* an underground burial place consisting of tunnels with side recesses for tombs
WORD ORIGIN Late Latin *catacumbas* cemetery near Rome

catafalque (**kat**-a-falk) *n* a raised platform on which a body lies in state before or during a funeral
WORD ORIGIN Italian *catafalco*

Catalan *adj* **1** of Catalonia ▷ *n* **2** a language of Catalonia in NE Spain **3** a person from Catalonia

catalepsy *n* a trancelike state in which the body is rigid **cataleptic** *adj*
WORD ORIGIN Greek *katalēpsis* a seizing

catalogue *or US* **catalog** *n* **1** a book containing details of items for sale **2** a list of all the books of a library **3** a list of events, qualities, or things considered as a group: *a catalogue of killings* ▷ *vb* **-loguing, -logued** *or* **-loging, -loged 4** to enter (an item) in a catalogue **5** to list a series of (events, qualities, or things): *the report catalogues two decades of human-rights violations* **cataloguer** *n*
WORD ORIGIN Greek *katalegein* to list

catalpa *n* a tree of N America and Asia with bell-shaped whitish flowers
WORD ORIGIN Carolina Creek (a Native American language) *kutuhlpa* winged head

catalyse *or US* **-lyze** *vb* **-lysing, -lysed** *or* **-lyzing, -lyzed** to influence (a chemical reaction) by catalysis

catalysis *n* acceleration of a chemical reaction by the action of a catalyst **catalytic** *adj*
WORD ORIGIN Greek *kataluein* to dissolve

catalyst *n* **1** a substance that speeds up a chemical reaction without itself undergoing any permanent chemical change **2** a person or thing that causes an important change to take place: *a catalyst for peace*

catalytic converter *n* a device which uses catalysts to reduce the quantity of poisonous substances emitted by the exhaust of a motor vehicle

catalytic cracker *n* a unit in an oil refinery in which mineral oils are converted into fuels by a catalytic process

catamaran *n* a boat with twin parallel hulls
WORD ORIGIN Tamil *kattumaram* tied timber

catamite *n* a boy kept as a homosexual partner
WORD ORIGIN Latin *Catamitus*, variant of *Ganymedes* Ganymede, cupbearer to the gods in Greek mythology

catapult *n* **1** a Y-shaped device with a loop of elastic fastened to the ends of the prongs, used by children for firing stones **2** a device used to launch aircraft from a warship ▷ *vb* **3** to shoot forwards or upwards violently: *traffic catapulted forward with a roar* **4** to cause (someone) suddenly to be in a particular situation: *catapulted to stardom*
WORD ORIGIN Greek *kata-* down + *pallein* to hurl

cataract *n* **1** *pathol* **a** a condition in which the lens of the eye becomes partially or totally opaque **b** the opaque area **2** a large waterfall
WORD ORIGIN Greek *katarassein* to dash down

catarrh (**kat-tar**) *n* excessive mucus in the nose and throat, often experienced during or following a cold **catarrhal** *adj*
WORD ORIGIN Greek *katarrhein* to flow down

catastrophe (**kat-ass**-trof-fee) *n* a great and sudden disaster or misfortune **catastrophic** *adj*
WORD ORIGIN Greek *katastrephein* to overturn

catatonia *n* a form of schizophrenia in which the sufferer experiences stupor, with outbreaks of excitement **catatonic** *adj*
WORD ORIGIN Greek *kata-* down + *tonos* tension

cat burglar *n* a burglar who enters buildings by climbing through upper windows

catcall *n* a shrill whistle or cry of disapproval or derision

catch *vb* **catching, caught 1** to seize and hold **2** to capture (a person or a fish or animal) **3** to surprise in an act: *two boys were caught stealing* **4** to reach (a bus, train, or plane) in time to board it **5** to see or hear: *you'll have to be quick if you want to catch her DJ-ing* **6** to be infected with (an illness) **7** to entangle or become entangled **8** to attract (someone's attention, imagination, or interest) **9** to comprehend or make out: *you have to work hard to catch his tone and meaning* **10** to reproduce (a quality) accurately in a work of art **11** (of a fire) to start burning **12** *cricket* to dismiss (a batsman) by catching a ball struck by him before it touches the ground **13 catch at a** to attempt to grasp **b** to take advantage of (an opportunity) **14 catch it** *informal* to be punished ▷ *n* **15** a device such as a hook, for fastening a door, window, or box **16** the total number of fish caught **17** *informal* a concealed or unforeseen drawback **18** an emotional break in the voice **19** *informal* a person considered worth having as a husband or wife **20** *cricket* the act of catching a ball struck by a batsman before it touches the ground, resulting in him being out
▷ See also **catch on, catch out, catch up**
WORD ORIGIN Latin *capere* to seize

catchcry *n, pl* **-cries** *Austral* a well-known, frequently used phrase, esp. one associated with a particular group

catching *adj* infectious

catchment *n* **1** a structure in which water is collected **2** all the people served by a school or hospital in a particular catchment area

catchment area *n* **1** the area of land draining into a river, basin, or reservoir **2** the area served by a particular school or hospital

catch on *vb informal* **1** to become popular or fashionable **2** to understand: *I was slow to catch on to what she was trying to tell me*

catch out *vb informal chiefly Brit* to trap (someone) in an error or a lie

catchpenny *adj Brit* designed to have instant appeal without regard for quality

catch phrase *n* a well-known phrase or slogan associated with a particular entertainer or other celebrity

catch-22 *n* a situation in which a person is frustrated by a set of circumstances that prevent any attempt to escape from them
WORD ORIGIN from the title of a novel by J Heller

catch up *vb* **1 be caught up in** to be unwillingly or accidentally involved in: *hundreds of civilians have been caught up in the clashes* **2 catch up on** *or* **with** to bring (something) up to date: *he had a lot of paperwork to catch up on* **3 catch up with** to reach or pass (someone or something): *she ran to catch up with him*

catchword *n* a well-known and frequently used phrase or slogan

catchy *adj* **catchier, catchiest** (of a tune) pleasant and easily remembered

catechism (**kat**-tik-kiz-zum) *n* instruction on the doctrine of a Christian Church by a series of questions and answers
WORD ORIGIN Greek *katēkhizein* to catechize

catechize *or* **-echise** *vb* **-echizing, -echized** *or* **-echising, -echised 1** to instruct in Christianity using a catechism **2** to question (someone) thoroughly **catechist** *n*
WORD ORIGIN Greek *katēkhizein*

categorical *or* **categoric** *adj* absolutely clear and certain: *he was categorical in his denial* **categorically** *adv*

categorize *or* **-rise** *vb* **-rizing, -rized** *or* **-rising, -rised** to put in a category **categorization** *or* **-risation** *n*

category *n, pl* **-ries** a class or group of things or people with some quality or qualities in common
WORD ORIGIN Greek *katēgoria* assertion

cater *vb* **1** to provide what is needed or wanted: *operating theatres that can cater for open-heart surgery* **2** to provide food or services: *chef is pleased to cater for vegetarians and vegans*
WORD ORIGIN Anglo-Norman *acater* to buy

caterer *n* a person whose job is to provide food for social events such as parties and weddings

catering *n* the supplying of food for a social event

caterpillar *n* **1** the wormlike larva of a butterfly or moth **2** *trademark* Also: **caterpillar track** an endless track, driven by cogged wheels, used to propel a heavy vehicle such as a bulldozer
WORD ORIGIN probably from Old French *catepelose* hairy cat

caterwaul *vb* **1** to make a yowling noise like a cat ▷ *n* **2** such a noise
WORD ORIGIN imitative

catfish *n, pl* **-fish** *or* **-fishes** a freshwater fish with whisker-like barbels around the mouth

catgut *n* a strong cord made from dried animals' intestines, used to string musical instruments and sports rackets

catharsis (kath-**thar**-siss) n **1** the relief of strong suppressed emotions, for example through drama or psychoanalysis **2** evacuation of the bowels, esp. with the use of a laxative **WORD ORIGIN** Greek *kathairein* to purge, purify

cathartic adj **1** causing catharsis ▷ n **2** a drug that causes catharsis

Cathay n a literary or archaic name for China **WORD ORIGIN** Medieval Latin *Cataya*

cathedral n the principal church of a diocese **WORD ORIGIN** Greek *kathedra* seat

Catherine wheel n a firework that rotates, producing sparks and coloured flame **WORD ORIGIN** after St *Catherine* of Alexandria, martyred on a spiked wheel

catheter (**kath**-it-er) n a slender flexible tube inserted into a body cavity to drain fluid **WORD ORIGIN** Greek *kathienai* to insert

cathode n electronics the negative electrode in an electrolytic cell or in an electronic valve or tube **WORD ORIGIN** Greek *kathodos* a descent

cathode rays pl n a stream of electrons emitted from the surface of a cathode in a valve

cathode-ray tube n a valve in which a beam of electrons is focused onto a fluorescent screen to produce a visible image, used in television receivers and visual display units

catholic adj (of tastes or interests) covering a wide range **WORD ORIGIN** Greek *katholikos* universal

Catholic Christianity adj **1** of the Roman Catholic Church ▷ n **2** a member of the Roman Catholic Church **Catholicism** n

cation (**kat**-eye-on) n a positively charged ion **WORD ORIGIN** Greek *kata-* down + *ienai* to go

catkin n a drooping flower spike found on trees such as the birch, hazel, and willow **WORD ORIGIN** obsolete Dutch *katteken* kitten

catmint n a Eurasian plant with scented leaves that attract cats. Also: **catnip**

catnap n **1** a short sleep or doze ▷ vb **-napping, -napped 2** to sleep or doze for a short time or intermittently

cat-o'-nine-tails n, pl **-tails** a rope whip with nine knotted thongs, formerly used to inflict floggings as a punishment

cat's cradle n a game played by making patterns with a loop of string between the fingers

catseyes pl n trademark, Brit, Austral, & NZ glass reflectors set into the road at intervals to indicate traffic lanes by reflecting light from vehicles' headlights

cat's paw n a person used by someone else to do unpleasant things for him or her **WORD ORIGIN** from the tale of a monkey who used a cat's paw to draw chestnuts out of a fire

cattle pl n domesticated cows and bulls ▷ Related adjective: **bovine WORD ORIGIN** Old French *chatel* chattel

cattle-cake n concentrated food for cattle in the form of cakelike blocks

cattle-grid or NZ **cattle-stop** n a grid covering a hole dug in a road to prevent livestock crossing while allowing vehicles to pass unhindered

catty adj **-tier, -tiest** informal spiteful: *her remarks were amusing and only slightly catty* **cattiness** n

catwalk n **1** a narrow pathway over the stage of a theatre or along a bridge **2** a narrow platform where models display clothes in a fashion show

Caucasian or **Caucasoid** adj **1** of the predominantly light-skinned racial group of humankind ▷ n **2** a member of this group

caucus n, pl **-cuses 1** a local committee or faction of a political party **2** a political meeting to decide future plans **3** NZ a formal meeting of all MPs of one party **WORD ORIGIN** probably of Native American origin

caudal adj zool at or near the tail or back part of an animal's body **WORD ORIGIN** Latin *cauda* tail

caught vb the past of **catch**

caul n anat a membrane sometimes covering a child's head at birth **WORD ORIGIN** Old French *calotte* close-fitting cap

cauldron or **caldron** n a large pot used for boiling **WORD ORIGIN** Latin *caldarium* hot bath

cauliflower n a vegetable with a large head of white flower buds surrounded by green leaves **WORD ORIGIN** Italian *caoli fiori* cabbage flowers

cauliflower ear n permanent swelling and distortion of the ear, caused by repeated blows usually received in boxing

caulk vb to fill in (cracks) with paste or some other material **WORD ORIGIN** Latin *calcare* to trample

causal adj of or being a cause: *a causal connection* **causally** adv

causation or **causality** n **1** the production of an effect by a cause **2** the relationship of cause and effect

causative adj producing an effect: *bright lights seem to be a causative factor in some migraines*

cause n **1** something that produces a particular effect **2** grounds for action; justification: *there is cause for concern* **3** an aim or principle which an individual or group is interested in and supports: *the Socialist cause* ▷ vb **causing, caused 4** to be the cause of **causeless** adj **WORD ORIGIN** Latin *causa*

cause célèbre (**kawz** sill-**leb**-ra) n, pl **causes célèbres** (**kawz** sill-**leb**-ras) a controversial legal case, issue, or person **WORD ORIGIN** French

causeway n a raised path or road across water or marshland **WORD ORIGIN** Middle English *cauciwey* paved way

caustic adj **1** capable of burning or corroding by chemical action: *caustic soda* **2** bitter and sarcastic: *caustic critics* ▷ n **3** chem a caustic substance **caustically** adv **WORD ORIGIN** Greek *kaiein* to burn

caustic soda n same as **sodium hydroxide**

cauterize or **-ise** vb **-izing, -ized** or **-ising, -ised** to burn (a wound) with heat or a caustic agent to prevent infection **cauterization** or **-isation** n **WORD ORIGIN** Greek *kaiein* to burn

caution n **1** care or prudence, esp. in the face of danger **2** warning: *a word of caution* **3** law chiefly Brit a formal warning given to a person suspected of an offence ▷ vb **4** to warn or advise: *he cautioned against an abrupt turnaround* **cautionary** adj **WORD ORIGIN** Latin *cautio*

cautious adj showing or having caution **cautiously** adv

cavalcade n a procession of people on horseback or in cars **WORD ORIGIN** Italian *cavalcare* to ride on horseback

cavalier adj **1** showing haughty disregard; offhand ▷ n **2** old-fashioned a gallant or courtly gentleman **WORD ORIGIN** Late Latin *caballarius* rider

Cavalier n a supporter of Charles I during the English Civil War

cavalry n the part of an army originally mounted on horseback, but now often using fast armoured vehicles **cavalryman** n **WORD ORIGIN** Italian *cavaliere* horseman

cave n a hollow in the side of a hill or cliff, or underground **WORD ORIGIN** Latin *cavus* hollow

caveat (**kav**-vee-at) n **1** law a formal notice requesting the court not to take a certain action without warning the person lodging the caveat **2** a caution **WORD ORIGIN** Latin: let him beware

cave in vb **1** to collapse inwards **2** informal to yield completely under pressure: *the government caved in to the revolutionaries' demands* ▷ n **cave-in 3** the sudden collapse of a roof or piece of ground

caveman n, pl **-men 1** a prehistoric cave dweller **2** informal a man who is primitive or brutal in behaviour

cavern n a large cave **WORD ORIGIN** Latin *cavus* hollow

cavernous adj like a cavern in vastness, depth, or hollowness: *the cavernous building*

caviar or **caviare** n the salted roe of the sturgeon, regarded as a delicacy and usually served as an appetizer **WORD ORIGIN** Turkish *havyār*

cavil vb **-illing, -illed** or US **-iling, -iled 1** to raise annoying petty objections ▷ n **2** a petty objection **WORD ORIGIN** Latin *cavillari* to jeer

caving n the sport of climbing in and exploring caves **caver** n

cavity n, pl **-ties 1** a hollow space **2** dentistry a decayed area on a tooth **WORD ORIGIN** Latin *cavus* hollow

cavort vb to skip about; caper

Stephen Leacock

What attracted great comedians like Groucho Marx, Jack Benny, and Charlie Chaplin to Stephen Leacock's humour was likely not its surface geniality but the violent anarchy that underpinned it. The way that the characters in his comic sketches leap-frog, or are catapulted, from one absurdity to another was bound to appeal to them.

Nor was the apparent contradiction between bland-ness and chaos the only one in Leacock's busy life. Achieving fame as a humourist, he was also a popular historian and biographer who wrote studies of Charles Dickens and Mark Twain. For many years heading the Economics (then called Political Economy) Department at McGill University, he authored a much-reprinted textbook called *Elements of Political Science* (1906). A workaholic, a staunch Tory Imperialist, and a social conservative, he believed that progress could best be measured by our kindness to each other. The gently satirical portrait of 'Mariposa' in *Sunshine Sketches of a Little Town* (1912) is balanced by a sharper treatment of how wealth and status work in *Arcadian Adventures with the Idle Rich* (1914).

Born in Hampshire in 1869, he was six years old when his large family immigrated to Canada, settling on an unproductive farm near Orillia (Mariposa's orig-inal) on Lake Couchiching north of Toronto. His father was an abusive alcoholic, but Leacock gained a good private-school education thanks to the remittances of an English grandfather. He paid his way through uni-versity in Toronto by reluctantly toiling as a school-master. His prosperity only became assured when, after gaining a doctorate in Chicago, he joined McGill; his books averaged one a year for the rest of his life. Tragedy impinged: his wife died in 1925, making him solely responsible for their only child, who suffered from a genetic disorder retarding his physical growth. His son's health remained a constant worry. To his great bitterness, Leacock, a gifted lecturer, was forcibly retired from McGill in 1936. The remaining eight years of his life were darkened by loneliness and depression, only relieved by summers at his home in Orillia.

Throughout his career, hard work and comedy were Leacock's emotional compensation and consolation. A visiting curate, Melpomenus Jones in *Literary Lapses* (1910), is too timid to tear himself away from his hosts' home and, after endlessly drinking tea and looking at family photographs, eventually dies there. In 'Boarding House Geometry', a landlady 'is a parallelogram – that is, an oblong angular figure, which cannot be described, but which is equal to anything'. In *Nonsense Novels* (1911), 'Hannah of the Highlands' is 'gathering lobsters in the burn that ran through the Glen'. In 'Gertrude the Governess: or Simple Seventeen' the famous line, 'Lord Ronald said nothing; he flung himself from the room, flung himself upon his horse and rode madly off in all directions' is almost topped in *Short Circuits* (1928) by the heroine 'Margaret Overproof', whose 'graceful neck sloped away in all directions till it reached her bust, which stopped it'. In *Moonbeams from the Larger Lunacy* (1915) he writes of 'Ram Spudd: The New-World Singer. Is He Divinely Inspired? Or Is He Not? At any Rate We Discovered Him.' He explodes travel-writing conventions in *My Discovery of England* (1922). '"New Orleans," writes another visitor, "opened her arms to me and bestowed upon me the soft and languorous kiss of the Caribbean." This statement may or may not be true: but in any case it hardly seems the fair thing to mention it.' As for the United Kingdom, Leacock notes that 'The Gulf Stream, as it nears the shores of the British Isles and feels the propinquity of Ireland, rises into the air, turns into soup, and comes down on London.'

In the mock-humble Preface to *Nonsense Novels*, Leacock hopes that 'this little book may bring some passing amusement in hours of idleness, or some brief respite when the sadness of the heart or the sufferings of the body forbid the perusal of worthier things.' His readers did get amusement and respite. Leacock came to be honoured by a Canadian postage stamp in 1969, and an annual award for the best book of humour is named after him. It is virtually certain that he would have made fun of both.

caw *n* **1** the cry of a crow, rook, or raven ▷ *vb* **2** to make this cry
WORD ORIGIN imitative

cay *n* a small low island or bank of sand and coral fragments
WORD ORIGIN Spanish *cayo*

cayenne pepper *or* **cayenne** *n* a very hot red spice made from the dried seeds of capsicums
WORD ORIGIN S American Indian *quiynha*

cayman *or* **caiman** *n, pl* **-mans** a tropical American reptile similar to an alligator
WORD ORIGIN Carib

caz *adj slang* short for **casual**

CB 1 Citizens' Band **2** Commander of the Order of the Bath

CBC Canadian Broadcasting Corporation

CBE Commander of the Order of the British Empire (a Brit. title)

CBI Confederation of British Industry

cc *or* **c.c. 1** carbon copy **2** cubic centimetre

CC 1 County Council **2** Cricket Club

CCS cascading style sheet

CCTV closed-circuit television

cd candela

Cd *chem* cadmium

CD compact disc

CDI compact disc interactive: a system for storing a mix of software, data, audio, and compressed video for interactive use under processor control

C.diff *or* **C.difficile** Clostridium difficile

Cdn. Canadian

CD player *n* a device for playing compact discs

Cdr Commander

CD-R compact disk recordable

CD-ROM compact disc read-only memory: a compact disc used with a computer system as a read-only optical disc

CD-RW compact disk read-write

CDT Central Daylight Time

CD-video *n* a compact-disc player that, when connected to a television and a hi-fi, produces high-quality stereo sound and synchronized pictures from a compact disc

Ce *chem* cerium

cease *vb* **ceasing, ceased 1** to bring or come to an end ▷ *n* **2 without cease** without stopping
WORD ORIGIN Latin *cessare*

ceasefire *n* a temporary period of truce

ceaseless *adj* without stopping
ceaselessly *adv*

cedar *n* **1** a coniferous tree with needle-like evergreen leaves and barrel-shaped cones **2** the sweet-smelling wood of this tree
WORD ORIGIN Greek *kedros*

cede *vb* **ceding, ceded** to transfer or surrender (territory or legal rights)
WORD ORIGIN Latin *cedere* to yield

cedilla *n* a character (,) placed underneath a *c*, esp. in French or Portuguese, indicating that it is to be pronounced (s), not (k)
WORD ORIGIN Spanish: little *z*

Ceefax *n trademark* (in Britain) the BBC teletext service

ceilidh (**kay**-lee) *n* an informal social gathering in Scotland or Ireland with folk music and country dancing
WORD ORIGIN Gaelic

ceiling *n* **1** the inner upper surface of a room **2** an upper limit set on something such as a payment or salary **3** the upper altitude to which an aircraft can climb
WORD ORIGIN origin unknown

celandine *n* a wild plant with yellow flowers
WORD ORIGIN Greek *khelidōn* swallow; the plant's season was believed to parallel the migration of swallows

celebrant *n* a person who performs or takes part in a religious ceremony

celebrate *vb* **-brating, -brated 1** to hold festivities: *let's celebrate!* **2** to hold festivities to mark (a happy event, birthday, or anniversary) **3** to perform (a solemn or religious ceremony) **4** to praise publicly: *the novel is justly celebrated as a masterpiece* **celebration** *n* **celebratory** *adj*
WORD ORIGIN Latin *celeber* numerous, renowned

celebrated *adj* well known: *the celebrated musician*

celebrity *n, pl* **-ties 1** a famous person **2** the state of being famous

celeriac (sill-**ler**-ree-ak) *n* a variety of celery with a large turnip-like root

celerity (sill-**ler**-rit-tee) *n formal* swiftness
WORD ORIGIN Latin *celeritas*

celery *n* a vegetable with long green crisp edible stalks
WORD ORIGIN Greek *selinon* parsley

celesta *n* an instrument like a small piano in which key-operated hammers strike metal plates
WORD ORIGIN French *céleste* heavenly

celestial *adj* **1** heavenly or divine: *celestial music* **2** of or relating to the sky or space: *celestial objects such as pulsars and quasars*
WORD ORIGIN Latin *caelum* heaven

celestial equator *n* an imaginary circle lying on the celestial sphere in a plane perpendicular to the earth's axis

celestial sphere *n* an imaginary sphere of infinitely large radius enclosing the universe

celibate *adj* **1** unmarried or abstaining from sex, esp. because of a religious vow of chastity ▷ *n* **2** a celibate person **celibacy** *n*
WORD ORIGIN Latin *caelebs* unmarried

cell *n* **1** *biol* the smallest unit of an organism that is able to function independently **2** a small simple room in a prison, convent, or monastery **3** any small compartment, such as a cell of a honeycomb **4** a small group operating as the core of a larger organization: *Communist cells* **5** a device that produces electrical energy by chemical action **6** *US & Canad* a cellular telephone
WORD ORIGIN Latin *cella* room, storeroom

cellar *n* **1** an underground room, usually used for storage **2** a place where wine is stored **3** a stock of bottled wines
WORD ORIGIN Latin *cellarium* food store

cellarage *n* **1** the area of a cellar **2** a charge for storing goods in a cellar

cello (**chell**-oh) *n, pl* **-los** a large low-pitched musical instrument of the violin family, held between the knees and played with a bow **cellist** *n*
WORD ORIGIN short for *violoncello*

Cellophane *n trademark* a thin transparent material made from cellulose that is used as a protective wrapping, esp. for food
WORD ORIGIN *cellulose* + Greek *phainein* to shine, appear

cellular *adj* **1** of, consisting of, or resembling a cell or cells: *cellular changes* **2** woven with an open texture: *cellular blankets* **3** designed for or using cellular radio: *cellular phones*

cellular radio *n* radio communication, used esp. in car phones, based on a network of transmitters each serving a small area known as a cell

cellulite *n* fat deposits under the skin alleged to resist dieting

celluloid *n* **1** a kind of plastic made from cellulose nitrate and camphor, used to make toys and, formerly, photographic film **2** the cinema or films generally: *a Shakespeare play committed to celluloid*

cellulose *n* the main constituent of plant cell walls, used in making paper, rayon, and plastics

cellulose acetate *n* a nonflammable material used to make film, lacquers, and artificial fibres

cellulose nitrate *n* a compound used in plastics, lacquers, and explosives

Celsius *adj* denoting a measurement on the Celsius scale
WORD ORIGIN after Anders *Celsius*, astronomer who invented it

Celsius scale *n* a scale of temperature in which 0° represents the melting point of ice and 100° represents the boiling point of water

Celt (kelt) *n* **1** a person from Scotland, Ireland, Wales, Cornwall, or Brittany **2** a member of a people who inhabited Britain, Gaul, and Spain in pre-Roman times
WORD ORIGIN Latin *Celtae* the Celts

Celtic (**kel**-tik, **sel**-tik) *n* **1** a group of languages that includes Gaelic, Welsh, and Breton ▷ *adj* **2** of the Celts or the Celtic languages

cement *n* **1 a** a fine grey powder made of limestone and clay, mixed with water and sand to make mortar or concrete **b** mortar or concrete **2** something that unites, binds, or joins things or people: *bone cement; the cement of fear and hatred of the Left* **3** *dentistry* a material used for filling teeth ▷ *vb* **4** to join, bind, or cover with cement **5** to make (a relationship) stronger: *this would cement a firm alliance between the army and rebels*
WORD ORIGIN Latin *caementum* stone from the quarry

cemetery *n, pl* **-teries** a place where dead people are buried: *a military cemetery*
WORD ORIGIN Greek *koimētērion* room for sleeping

cenotaph n a monument honouring soldiers who died in a war
WORD ORIGIN Greek *kenos* empty + *taphos* tomb

Cenozoic or **Caenozoic** (see-no-**zoh**-ik) adj geol of the most recent geological era, beginning 65 million years ago, characterized by the development and increase of the mammals
WORD ORIGIN Greek *kainos* recent + *zōion* animal

censer n a container for burning incense

censor n 1 a person authorized to examine films, letters, or publications, in order to ban or cut anything considered obscene or objectionable ▷ vb 2 to ban or cut portions of (a film, letter, or publication)
WORD ORIGIN Latin *censere* to consider

censorious adj harshly critical

censorship n the practice or policy of censoring films, letters, or publications

censure n 1 severe disapproval ▷ vb -suring, -sured 2 to criticize (someone or something) severely
WORD ORIGIN Latin *censere* to assess

census n, pl -suses an official periodic count of a population including such information as sex, age, and occupation
WORD ORIGIN Latin *censere* to assess

cent n a monetary unit worth one hundredth of the main unit of currency in many countries
WORD ORIGIN Latin *centum* hundred

cent. 1 central 2 century

centaur n Greek myth a creature with the head, arms, and torso of a man, and the lower body and legs of a horse
WORD ORIGIN Greek *kentauros*

centavo n, pl -vos a monetary unit worth one hundredth of the main unit of currency in Portugal and many Latin American countries
WORD ORIGIN Spanish: one hundredth part

centenarian n a person who is at least 100 years old

centenary (sen-**teen**-a-ree) n, pl -naries chiefly Brit a 100th anniversary or the celebration of one. US equivalent: **centennial**
WORD ORIGIN Latin *centum* hundred

center n, vb US same as **centre**

centesimal n 1 one hundredth ▷ adj 2 of or divided into hundredths
WORD ORIGIN Latin *centum* hundred

centi- prefix 1 denoting one hundredth: *centimetre* 2 a hundred: *centipede*
WORD ORIGIN Latin *centum* hundred

centigrade adj same as **Celsius**

USAGE
Although still used in meteorology, *centigrade*, when indicating the Celsius scale of temperature, is now usually avoided in other scientific contexts because of its possible confusion with the hundredth part of a grade.

centigram or **centigramme** n one hundredth of a gram

centilitre or US **centiliter** n a measure of volume equivalent to one hundredth of a litre

centime (**son**-teem) n a monetary unit worth one hundredth of the main unit of currency in a number of countries
WORD ORIGIN Latin *centum* hundred

centimetre or US **centimeter** n a unit of length equal to one hundredth of a metre

centipede n a small wormlike creature with many legs

central adj 1 of, at, or forming the centre of something: *eastern and central parts of the country* 2 main or principal: *a central issue* **centrally** adv **centrality** n

central bank n a national bank that acts as the government's banker, controls credit, and issues currency

Central European Time n the standard time adopted by Western European countries one hour ahead of Greenwich Mean Time, corresponding to British Summer Time. Abbrev: **CET**

central government n the government of a whole country, as opposed to the smaller organizations that govern counties, towns, and districts

central heating n a system for heating a building by means of radiators or air vents connected to a central source of heat **centrally heated** adj

centralism n the principle of bringing a country or an organization under central control **centralist** adj

centralize or -**ise** vb -izing, -ized or -ising, -ised to bring (a country or an organization) under central control **centralization** or -**isation** n

central locking n a system by which all the doors of a motor vehicle are locked automatically when the driver's door is locked manually

central nervous system n the part of the nervous system of vertebrates that consists of the brain and spinal cord

central processing unit n the part of a computer that performs logical and arithmetical operations on the data

central reservation n Brit & NZ the strip that separates the two sides of a motorway or dual carriageway

centre or US **center** n 1 the middle point or part of something 2 a place where a specified activity takes place: *a shopping centre* 3 a person or thing that is a focus of interest: *the centre of a long-running dispute* 4 a place of activity or influence: *the parliament building was the centre of resistance* 5 a political party or group that favours moderation 6 sport a player who plays in the middle of the field rather than on a wing ▷ vb -tring, -tred or US -tering, -tered 7 to put in the centre of something 8 **centre on** to have as a centre or main theme: *the summit is expected to centre on expanding the role of the UN*
WORD ORIGIN Greek *kentron* needle, sharp point

centreboard or US **centerboard** n a supplementary keel for a sailing boat or dinghy

centrefold or US **centerfold** n a large coloured illustration, often a photograph of a naked or scantily

dressed young woman, folded to form the centre pages of a magazine

centre forward n sport the middle player in the forward line of a team

centre half or **centre back** n soccer a defender who plays in the middle of the defence

centre of gravity n the point in an object around which its mass is evenly distributed

centre pass n hockey a push or hit made in any direction to start the game

centrepiece or US **centerpiece** n 1 the most important item of a group of things: *she was the centrepiece of this conference* 2 an ornament for the centre of a table

centrifugal (sent-**riff**-few-gl) adj 1 moving or tending to move away from a centre 2 of or operated by centrifugal force: *centrifugal extractors*
WORD ORIGIN Greek *kentron* centre + Latin *fugere* to flee

centrifugal force n a force that acts outwards on any body that rotates or moves along a curved path

centrifuge n a machine that separates substances by the action of centrifugal force

centripetal (sent-**rip**-it-al) adj moving or tending to move towards a centre
WORD ORIGIN Greek *kentron* centre + Latin *petere* to seek

centripetal force n a force that acts inwards on any body that rotates or moves along a curved path

centrist n a person who holds moderate political views

centurion n (in ancient Rome) the officer in command of a century
WORD ORIGIN Latin *centurio*

century n, pl -ries 1 a period of 100 years 2 a score of 100 runs in cricket 3 (in ancient Rome) a unit of foot soldiers, originally consisting of 100 men
WORD ORIGIN Latin *centuria*

CEO chief executive officer

cephalopod (**seff**-a-loh-pod) n a sea mollusc with a head and tentacles, such as the octopus
WORD ORIGIN Greek *kephalē* head + *pous* foot

ceramic n 1 a hard brittle material made by heating clay to a very high temperature 2 an object made of this material ▷ adj 3 made of ceramic: *ceramic tiles*
WORD ORIGIN Greek *keramos* potter's clay

ceramics n the art of producing ceramic objects **ceramicist** or **ceramist** n

Cerberus (**sir**-ber-uss) n Greek myth a three-headed dog who guarded the entrance to Hades

cere n a soft waxy swelling, containing the nostrils, at the base of the upper beak of a parrot
WORD ORIGIN Latin *cera* wax

cereal n 1 any grass that produces an edible grain, such as oat, wheat, or rice 2 the grain produced by such a plant 3 a breakfast food made from this grain, usually eaten mixed with milk
WORD ORIGIN Latin *cerealis* concerning agriculture

cerebellum (serr-rib-**bell**-lum) *n, pl* **-lums** *or* **-la** (-la) the back part of the brain, which controls balance and muscular coordination
WORD ORIGIN Latin

cerebral (**serr**-rib-ral) *adj* **1** of the brain: *a cerebral haemorrhage* **2** involving intelligence rather than emotions or instinct: *the cerebral joys of the literary world*

cerebral palsy *n* a condition in which the limbs and muscles are permanently weak, caused by damage to the brain

cerebrate (**serr**-rib-rate) *vb* **-brating, -brated** *usually facetious* to use the mind; think **cerebration** *n*

cerebrospinal *adj* of the brain and spinal cord: *a sample of cerebrospinal fluid*

cerebrovascular (serr-rib-roh-**vass**-kew-lar) *adj* of the blood vessels and blood supply of the brain

cerebrum (**serr**-rib-rum) *n, pl* **-brums** *or* **-bra** (-bra) the main part of the human brain, associated with thought, emotion, and personality
WORD ORIGIN Latin: the brain

ceremonial *adj* **1** of ceremony or ritual ▷ *n* **2** a system of formal rites; ritual **ceremonially** *adv*

ceremonious *adj* excessively polite or formal **ceremoniously** *adv*

ceremony *n, pl* **-nies 1** a formal act or ritual performed for a special occasion: *a wedding ceremony* **2** formally polite behaviour **3 stand on ceremony** to insist on or act with excessive formality
WORD ORIGIN Latin *caerimonia* what is sacred

Ceres *n* the Roman goddess of agriculture

cerise (ser-**reess**) *adj* cherry-red
WORD ORIGIN French: cherry

cerium *n chem* a steel-grey metallic element found only in combination with other elements. Symbol: Ce
WORD ORIGIN from *Ceres* (an asteroid)

CERN Conseil Européen pour la Recherche Nucléaire: a European organization for research in high-energy particle physics

cert *n* **a dead cert** *informal* something that is certain to happen or to be successful

cert. certificate

certain *adj* **1** positive and confident about something: *he was certain they would agree* **2** definitely known: *it is by no means certain the tomb still exists* **3** sure or bound: *the cuts are certain to go ahead* **4** some but not much: *a certain amount* **5** particular: *certain aspects* **6** named but not known: *a running commentary by a certain Mr Fox* **7 for certain** without doubt
WORD ORIGIN Latin *certus* sure

certainly *adv* without doubt: *he will certainly be back*

certainty *n* **1** the condition of being certain **2** *pl* **-ties** something established as inevitable

certifiable *adj* considered to be legally insane

certificate *n* an official document stating the details of something such as birth, death, or completion of an academic course
WORD ORIGIN Old French *certifier* to certify

certified *adj* **1** holding or guaranteed by a certificate: *a certified acupuncturist* **2** declared legally insane

certify *vb* **-fies, -fying, -fied 1** to confirm or attest to **2** to guarantee (that certain required standards have been met) **3** to declare legally insane **certification** *n*
WORD ORIGIN Latin *certus* certain + *facere* to make

certitude *n formal* confidence or certainty

cervical smear *n med* a smear taken from the neck (cervix) of the womb for detection of cancer

cervix *n, pl* **cervixes** *or* **cervices 1** the lower part of the womb that extends into the vagina **2** *anat* the neck **cervical** *adj*
WORD ORIGIN Latin

cesium *n US* same as **caesium**

cessation *n* an ending or pause: *a cessation of hostilities*
WORD ORIGIN Latin *cessare* to be idle

cession *n* the act of ceding territory or legal rights
WORD ORIGIN Latin *cedere* to yield

cesspool *or* **cesspit** *n* a covered tank or pit for collecting and storing sewage or waste water
WORD ORIGIN Old French *souspirail* air vent

CET Central European Time

cetacean (sit-**tay**-shun) *n* a sea creature such as a whale or dolphin, which belongs to a family of fish-shaped mammals and breathes through a blowhole
WORD ORIGIN Greek *kētos* whale

cetane (**see**-tane) *n* a colourless liquid hydrocarbon, used as a solvent
WORD ORIGIN Latin *cetus* whale

cetane number *n* a measure of the quality of a diesel fuel expressed as the percentage of cetane in it

cf compare
WORD ORIGIN Latin *confer*

Cf *chem* californium

CF Canadian Forces

CFB Canadian Forces Base

CFC chlorofluorocarbon

CFL Canadian Football League

CFS chronic fatigue syndrome

cg centigram

CGI computer-generated image(s)

cgs units *pl n* a metric system of units based on the centimetre, gram, and second: for scientific and technical purposes, replaced by SI units

CH Companion of Honour (a Brit. title)

ch. 1 chapter **2** church

Chablis (**shab**-lee) *n* a dry white wine made around Chablis, France

cha-cha *or* **cha-cha-cha** *n* **1** a modern ballroom dance from Latin America **2** music for this dance
WORD ORIGIN American (Cuban) Spanish

chaconne *n* a musical form consisting of a set of variations on a repeated melodic bass line

chad *n* the small pieces removed during the punching of holes in punch cards, printer paper, etc.

chafe *vb* **chafing, chafed 1** to make sore or worn by rubbing **2** to be annoyed or impatient: *the lower castes are chafing against 20 years of servitude*
WORD ORIGIN Old French *chaufer* to warm

chafer *n* a large slow-moving beetle
WORD ORIGIN Old English *ceafor*

chaff[1] *n* **1** grain husks separated from the seeds during threshing **2** something of little worth; rubbish: *you had to be a very perceptive listener to sort the wheat from the chaff of his discourse*
WORD ORIGIN Old English *ceaf*

chaff[2] *vb* to tease good-naturedly
WORD ORIGIN probably slang variant of *chafe*

chaffinch *n* a small European songbird with black-and-white wings and, in the male, a reddish body and blue-grey head
WORD ORIGIN Old English *ceaf* CHAFF[1] + *finc* finch

chafing dish *n* a dish with a heating apparatus beneath it, for cooking or keeping food warm at the table

chagrin (**shag**-grin) *n* a feeling of annoyance and disappointment
WORD ORIGIN French

chagrined *adj* annoyed and disappointed

chain *n* **1** a flexible length of metal links, used for fastening, binding, or connecting, or in jewellery **2 chains** anything that restricts or restrains someone: *bound by the chains of duty* **3** a series of connected facts or events **4** a number of establishments, such as hotels or shops, that have the same owner or management **5** *chem* a number of atoms or groups bonded together so that the resulting molecule, ion, or radical resembles a chain **6** a row of mountains or islands ▷ *vb* **7** to restrict, fasten, or bind with or as if with a chain: *the demonstrators chained themselves to railings*
WORD ORIGIN Latin *catena*

chain gang *n US* a group of convicted prisoners chained together

chain letter *n* a letter, often with a request for or promise of money, that is sent to many people who are asked to send copies to other people

chain mail *n* same as **mail**[2]

chain reaction *n* **1** a series of events, each of which causes the next **2** a chemical or nuclear reaction in which the product of one step triggers the following step

chain saw *n* a motor-driven saw in which the cutting teeth form links in a continuous chain

chain-smoke *vb* **-smoking, -smoked** to smoke continuously, lighting one cigarette from the preceding one **chain smoker** *n*

chair *n* **1** a seat with a back and four legs, for one person to sit on **2** an official position of authority or the person holding it: *the chair of the Security Council* **3** a professorship **4 in the chair** presiding over a meeting **5 the chair** *informal* the electric chair ▷ *vb* **6** to preside over (a meeting)
WORD ORIGIN Greek *kathedra*

Canadian French

When the Royal Commission on Bilingualism and Biculturalism, commonly known as the *Bi and Bi Commission*, presented its final report in 1969, it concluded that French-speakers were far from being equal linguistic partners in the Canadian Confederation. Outside Quebec, governments underserved and underrepresented them. The solution was to give French and English equal status, ideally remaking Canada into a bilingual country.

The federal government, then led by the fluently bilingual Pierre Trudeau, responded quickly. It passed legislation making French and English official languages, which had many implications for the public service, schools, and the court system. It promoted French-immersion educational programs, and decreed that there be bilingual labelling and packaging for consumer products: cornflour would have to also call itself *fécule de maïs*.

Opposition to this was spearheaded by unlikely bedfellows. Separatist or nationalist forces in Quebec wanted *Québécois* to be French-speaking *Maîtres Chez Nous*, 'Masters in Our Own House', preferably of ethnic stock that was *pure laine*, pure-wool authentic. The word Québécois itself expressed the new nationalism; Quebeckers traditionally were called *Canadiens*. Quebec passed legislation to ensure that French dominated the school and workplace. Indifferent to the rights of the French minority in other provinces, the Québécois wanted their own, self-contained *nation*, though in Canada there was debate about whether the word meant a people or an autonomous state. Meanwhile, some in the English majority outside Quebec were outraged that cereal boxes now came in two languages, and that the Latin name *Nova Scotia* was translated as *Nouvelle Écosse*. Occasionally, English resistance stemmed from anti-French bigotry. More commonly, it reflected the libertarian or populist view that government had no business dictating what language people used.

Eventually, French became the dominant language of Quebec in fact and law and more prevalent in the federal civil service. Bilingualism increased somewhat in Canada, and immigrants tended to adopt the prevailing language of the communities in which they settled. A bit more than 80 per cent of the Quebec population remains French-speaking, and about 80 per cent of the Canadian population as a whole speaks English, notwithstanding pockets of French in the Maritime Provinces, Ontario, and Manitoba.

Canadian French, which contains archaisms, like *piastres* for dollars, and is less clearly articulated than standard French, derives from the speech of early colonists, who mainly came from northwestern France, especially Normandy. It has idiosyncrasies, such as *une blonde* for a girlfriend, or *le courriel* for e-mail. It borrows from aboriginal languages and from English (*le boss*). English also intervenes in *joual*, the dialect of the urban working class. The omnipresent English *eh* is paralleled by the French *hein*. Yet a Quebec traffic sign may say *ARRÊT*, not *STOP*, and use *stationnement* to denote parking. There are, too, regional varieties of Canadian: the *Acadian French* of Atlantic Canada, and the *Métis French* of the prairies that, mixed with Cree, became another language, *Michif*.

French pervades Canadian culture from the official to the informal. Any Canadian history lesson will make reference to the *voyageur*, the fur-trading canoeman, or the *habitant*, a land-owning peasant: the student may root for the *Habs*, nickname for the Montreal Canadiens hockey team. Even the most stubborn English speaker is likely to pronounce French-derived words (*clique, niche, tuque*) the French way. Drivers are accustomed to constructions such as *CITY CENTRE-VILLE*, and such French noun + adjective constructions in hotel names as the *Fairmont Chateau Laurier*, or government departments like *Health Canada* (French *Santé Canada*) or Industry Canada (French *Industrie Canada*). Observers of the political scene take note of the *péquistes*, members of the *Parti Québécois*. With no self-consciousness, English Montrealers use *dépanneur* for a convenience store, call a college a CEGEP ('say-jep', short for *collège d'enseignement général et professionnel*), use the Québécois swear-word *Tabernacle*, and travel by *Metro*, the subway. On Christmas Eve, a cook in British Columbia may say she's going to bake a *tourtière*, the traditional Québécois meat pie.

C

chairlift *n* a series of chairs suspended from a moving cable for carrying people up a slope

chairman *n, pl* **-men** a person who is in charge of a company's board of directors or a meeting **chairwoman** *fem n* **chairmanship** *n*

USAGE
Chairman can seem inappropriate when applied to a woman, while chairwoman can be offensive. Chair and chairperson can be applied to either a man or a woman; chair is generally preferred to chairperson.

chaise (**shaze**) *n* a light horse-drawn carriage with two wheels
WORD ORIGIN French

chaise longue (**long**) *n, pl* **chaise longues** *or* **chaises longues** a couch with a back and a single armrest
WORD ORIGIN French

chalcedony (kal-**sed**-don-ee) *n, pl* **-nies** a form of quartz composed of very fine crystals, often greyish or blue in colour
WORD ORIGIN Greek *khalkēdōn* a precious stone

chalet *n* **1** a type of Swiss wooden house with a steeply sloping roof **2** a similar house used as a ski lodge or holiday home
WORD ORIGIN French

chalice (**chal**-liss) *n* **1** *poetic* a drinking cup or goblet **2** *Christianity* a gold or silver goblet containing the wine at communion
WORD ORIGIN Latin *calix* cup

chalk *n* **1** a soft white rock consisting of calcium carbonate **2** a piece of chalk, either white or coloured, used for writing and drawing on blackboards **3 as different as chalk and cheese** *informal* totally different **4 not by a long chalk** *informal* by no means: *you haven't finished by a long chalk* ▷ *vb* **5** to draw or mark with chalk **chalky** *adj*
WORD ORIGIN Latin *calx* limestone

chalk up *vb informal* **1** to score or register: *the home side chalked up a 9-1 victory* **2** to charge or credit (money) to an account

challenge *n* **1** a demanding or stimulating situation **2** a call to engage in a contest, fight, or argument **3** a questioning of a statement or fact **4** a demand by a sentry for identification or a password **5** *law* a formal objection to a juror ▷ *vb* **-lenging, -lenged 6** to invite or call (someone) to take part in a contest, fight, or argument **7** to call (a decision or action) into question **8** to order (a person) to stop and be identified **9** *law* to make formal objection to (a juror) **challenger** *n* **challenging** *adj*
WORD ORIGIN Latin *calumnia* calumny

challenged *adj* disabled as specified: *physically challenged; mentally challenged*

chalybeate (kal-**lib**-bee-it) *adj* containing or impregnated with iron salts: *a natural chalybeate spring rises at the edge of the lake*
WORD ORIGIN Greek *khalups* iron

chamber *n* **1** a meeting hall, usually one used for a legislative or judicial assembly **2** a room equipped for a particular purpose: *a decompression*

chamber 3 a legislative or judicial assembly: *the Senate, the upper chamber of Canada's parliament* **4** *old-fashioned or poetic* a room in a house, esp. a bedroom **5** a compartment or cavity: *the heart chambers* **6** a compartment for a cartridge or shell in a gun ▷ See also **chambers**
WORD ORIGIN Greek *kamara* vault

chamberlain *n history* an officer who managed the household of a king or nobleman
WORD ORIGIN Old French *chamberlayn*

chambermaid *n* a woman employed to clean bedrooms in a hotel

chamber music *n* classical music to be performed by a small group of musicians

Chamber of Commerce *n* an organization of local business people to promote, regulate, and protect their interests

chamber pot *n* a bowl for urine, formerly used in bedrooms

chambers *pl n* **1** a judge's room for hearing private cases not taken in open court **2** (in England) the set of rooms used as offices by a barrister

chameleon (kam-**meal**-yon) *n* a small lizard with long legs that is able to change colour to blend in with its surroundings
WORD ORIGIN Greek *khamai* on the ground + *leōn* lion

chamfer (**cham**-fer) *n* **1** a bevelled surface at an edge or corner ▷ *vb* **2** to cut a chamfer on or in
WORD ORIGIN Old French *chant* edge + *fraindre* to break

chamois *n, pl* **-ois 1** (**sham**-wah) a small mountain antelope of Europe and SW Asia **2** (**sham**-ee) a soft suede leather made from the skin of this animal or from sheep or goats **3** (**sham**-ee) Also: **chamois leather, shammy, chammy** a piece of such leather or similar material, used for cleaning and polishing
WORD ORIGIN Old French

chamomile (**kam**-mo-mile) *n* same as **camomile**

champ¹ *vb* **1** to chew noisily **2 champ at the bit** *informal* to be restless or impatient to do something
WORD ORIGIN probably imitative

champ² *n informal* short for **champion** (sense 1)

champagne *n* **1** a white sparkling wine produced around Reims and Épernay, France ▷ *adj* **2** denoting a luxurious lifestyle: *a champagne capitalist*
WORD ORIGIN Champagne, region of France

champers (**sham**-perz) *n slang* champagne

champion *n* **1** a person, plant, or animal that has defeated all others in a competition: *the Olympic 100 metres champion* **2** someone who defends a person or cause: *a champion of the downtrodden* ▷ *vb* **3** to support: *he unceasingly championed equal rights and opportunities* ▷ *adj* **4** *N English dialect* excellent **championship** *n*
WORD ORIGIN Latin *campus* field

chance *n* **1** the extent to which something is likely to happen; probability **2** an opportunity or occasion to do something: *a chance to escape rural poverty* **3** a risk or gamble: *the government is not in the mood to take any more chances* **4** the unknown and unpredictable element that causes something to happen in one way rather than another: *in Buddhism there is no such thing as chance or coincidence* **5 by chance** without planning: *by chance she met an old school friend* **6 on the off chance** acting on the slight possibility: *he had called on the agents on the off chance that he might learn something of value* ▷ *vb* **chancing, chanced 7** to risk or hazard: *a few picnickers chanced the perilous footpath* **8** to do something without planning to: *I chanced to look down* **9 chance on** or **upon** to discover by accident: *I chanced upon a copy of this book*
WORD ORIGIN Latin *cadere* to occur

chancel *n* the part of a church containing the altar and choir
WORD ORIGIN Latin *cancelli* lattice

chancellery *or* **chancellory** *n, pl* **-leries** *or* **-lories 1** *Austral & Brit* the residence or office of a chancellor **2** *US* the office of an embassy or consulate
WORD ORIGIN Anglo-French *chancellerie*

chancellor *n* **1** the head of government in several European countries **2** *US* the president of a university **3** *Brit, Austral, & Canad* the honorary head of a university **chancellorship** *n*
WORD ORIGIN Late Latin *cancellarius* porter

Chancellor of the Exchequer *n Brit* the cabinet minister responsible for finance

Chancery *n* (in England) the Lord Chancellor's court, a division of the High Court of Justice
WORD ORIGIN shortened from CHANCELLERY

chancre (**shang**-ker) *n pathol* a painless ulcer that develops as a primary symptom of syphilis
WORD ORIGIN French

chancy *adj* **chancier, chanciest** *informal* uncertain or risky

chandelier (shan-dill-**eer**) *n* an ornamental hanging light with branches and holders for several candles or bulbs
WORD ORIGIN French

chandler *n* a dealer in a specified trade or merchandise: *a ship's chandler* **chandlery** *n*
WORD ORIGIN Old French *chandelier* dealer in candles

change *n* **1** the fact of becoming different **2** variety or novelty: *they wanted to print some good news for a change* **3** a different set, esp. of clothes **4** money exchanged for its equivalent in a larger denomination or in a different currency **5** the balance of money when the amount paid is larger than the amount due **6** coins of a small denomination ▷ *vb* **changing, changed 7** to make or become different **8** to replace with or exchange for another: *the Swedish Communist Party changed its name to the Left Party* **9** to give and receive (something) in return: *slaves and masters*

changed places **10** to give or receive (money) in exchange for its equivalent sum in a smaller denomination or different currency **11** to put on other clothes **12** to get off one bus, train, or airliner and on to another: *there's no direct train, so you'll need to change at York* ▸ See also **change down, changeover, change up** ▹ **changeless** *adj*
WORD ORIGIN Latin *cambire* to exchange, barter

changeable *adj* changing often **changeability** *n*

change down *vb* to select a lower gear when driving

changeling *n* a child believed to have been exchanged by fairies for the parents' real child

change of life *n* the menopause

changeover *n* **1** a complete change from one system, attitude, or product to another ▹ *vb* **change over 2** to swap places or activities: *the train crews changed over at the frontier*

change up *vb* to select a higher gear when driving

channel *n* **1** a band of radio frequencies assigned for the broadcasting of a radio or television signal **2** a path for an electrical signal or computer data **3** a means of access or communication: *reports coming through diplomatic channels* **4** a broad strait connecting two areas of sea **5** the bed or course of a river, stream, or canal **6** a navigable course through an area of water **7** a groove ▹ *vb* **-nelling, -nelled** *or US* **-neling, -neled 8** to direct or convey through a channel or channels: *tunnels that channel the pilgrims into the area; to channel funds abroad*
WORD ORIGIN Latin *canalis* pipe, conduit

Channel *n* **the Channel** the English Channel

channel-hop *vb* **-hopping, -hopped** to change television channels repeatedly using a remote control device

chant *vb* **1** to repeat (a slogan) over and over **2** to sing or recite (a psalm) ▹ *n* **3** a rhythmic or repetitious slogan repeated over and over, usually by more than one person **4** a religious song with a short simple melody in which several words or syllables are sung on one note
WORD ORIGIN Latin *canere* to sing

chanter *n* the pipe on a set of bagpipes on which the melody is played

chanticleer *n* a name for a cock, used in fables
WORD ORIGIN Old French *chanter cler* to sing clearly

chanty *n, pl* **-ties** same as **shanty²**

Chanukah *or* **Hanukkah** (**hah**-na-ka) *n* an eight-day Jewish festival, held in December, commemorating the rededication of the temple by Judas Maccabaeus
WORD ORIGIN Hebrew

chaos *n* complete disorder or confusion **chaotic** *adj* **chaotically** *adv*
WORD ORIGIN Greek *khaos*

chap *n informal* a man or boy
WORD ORIGIN from Old English *cēapman* pedlar

chapati *or* **chapatti** *n* (in Indian cookery) a kind of flat thin unleavened bread
WORD ORIGIN Hindi

chapel *n* **1** a place of worship with its own altar, in a church or cathedral **2** a similar place of worship in a large house or institution **3** (in England and Wales) a Nonconformist place of worship **4** (in Scotland) a Roman Catholic church **5** the members of a trade union in a newspaper office, printing house, or publishing firm
WORD ORIGIN Latin *cappa* cloak: originally the sanctuary where the cloak of St Martin was kept

chaperone (**shap**-per-rone) *n* **1** an older person who accompanies and supervises a young person or young people on social occasions ▹ *vb* **-oning, -oned 2** to act as a chaperone to
WORD ORIGIN Old French *chape* hood

chaplain *n* a clergyman attached to a chapel, military body, or institution **chaplaincy** *n*
WORD ORIGIN Late Latin *cappella* chapel

chaplet *n* a garland worn on the head
WORD ORIGIN Old French *chapelet*

chapman *n, pl* **-men** *old-fashioned* a travelling pedlar
WORD ORIGIN Old English *cēapman*

chapped *adj* (of the skin) raw and cracked, through exposure to cold
WORD ORIGIN probably Germanic

chappie *n informal* a man or boy

chaps *pl n* leather leggings without a seat, worn by cowboys
WORD ORIGIN shortened from Spanish *chaparejos*

chapter *n* **1** a division of a book **2** a period in a life or history: *the latest chapter in the long and complex tale of British brewing* **3** a sequence of events: *a chapter of accidents* **4** a branch of some societies or clubs **5** a group of the canons of a cathedral **6** **chapter and verse** exact authority for an action or statement
WORD ORIGIN Latin *caput* head

char¹ *vb* **charring, charred** to blacken by partial burning
WORD ORIGIN short for *charcoal*

char² *Brit informal n* **1** short for **charwoman** ▹ *vb* **charring, charred 2** to clean other people's houses as a job
WORD ORIGIN Old English *cerr* turn of work

char³ *n Brit old-fashioned slang* tea
WORD ORIGIN Chinese *ch'a*

char⁴ *n, pl* **char** *or* **chars** a troutlike fish of cold lakes and northern seas
WORD ORIGIN origin unknown

charabanc (**shar**-rab-bang) *n Brit, old-fashioned* a coach for sightseeing
WORD ORIGIN French: wagon with seats

character *n* **1** the combination of qualities distinguishing an individual person, group of people, or place: *the unique charm and character of this historic town* **2** a distinguishing quality or characteristic: *bodily movements of a deliberate character* **3** reputation, esp. good reputation: *a man of my Dad's character and standing in the community* **4** an attractively unusual or interesting quality: *the little town was full of life and character* **5** a person represented in a play, film, or story **6** an unusual or amusing person: *quite a character* **7** *informal* a person: *a flamboyant character* **8** a single letter, numeral, or symbol used in writing or printing **9** **in** *or* **out of character** typical *or* not typical of the apparent character of a person **characterless** *adj*
WORD ORIGIN Greek *kharaktēr* engraver's tool

character assassination *n* an attempt to destroy someone's good reputation by slander or deliberate misrepresentation of his or her views: *he described the accusation as 'an appalling piece of character assassination'*

characteristic *n* **1** a distinguishing feature or quality **2** *maths* the integral part of a logarithm: *the characteristic of 2.4771 is 2* ▹ *adj* **3** typical or representative of someone or something: *the prime minister fought with characteristic passion* **characteristically** *adv*

characterization *or* **-isation** *n* **1** the description or portrayal of a person by an actor or writer: *a novel full of rich characterization and complex plotting* **2** the act or an instance of characterizing

characterize *or* **-ise** *vb* **-izing, -ized** *or* **-ising, -ised 1** to be a characteristic of: *the violence that characterized the demonstrations* **2** to describe: *we have made what I would characterize as outstanding progress*

charade (shar-**rahd**) *n* an absurd pretence
WORD ORIGIN French

charades *n* a game in which one team acts out each syllable of a word or phrase, which the other team has to guess

charcoal *n* **1** a black form of carbon made by partially burning wood or other organic matter **2** a stick of this used for drawing **3** a drawing done in charcoal ▹ *adj* **4** Also: **charcoal-grey** very dark grey
WORD ORIGIN origin unknown

Chardonnay (**shar**-don-nay) *n* a white wine produced in the Burgundy region of France and elsewhere
WORD ORIGIN French

charge *vb* **charging, charged 1** to ask (an amount of money) as a price **2** to enter a debit against a person's account for (a purchase) **3** to accuse (someone) formally of a crime in a court of law **4** to make a rush at or sudden attack upon **5** to fill (a glass) **6** to cause (an accumulator or capacitor) to take and store electricity **7** to fill or saturate with liquid or gas: *old mine workings charged with foul gas* **8** to fill with a feeling or mood: *the emotionally charged atmosphere* **9** *formal* to command or assign: *the president has charged his foreign minister with trying to open talks* ▹ *n* **10** a price charged for something; cost **11** a formal accusation of a crime in a court of law **12** an onrush or attack **13** custody or guardianship: *in the charge of the police* **14** a person or thing committed to someone's care: *a nanny reported the cruel father of one of her charges to social workers* **15 a** a cartridge or shell **b** the explosive required to fire a gun **16** *physics* **a** the attribute of matter responsible for all electrical phenomena, existing in two forms, positive and negative **b** the total amount of electricity stored in a capacitor or an accumulator **17 in charge of** in control of and responsible for: *in charge of defence and foreign affairs* **WORD ORIGIN** Old French *chargier* to load

chargeable *adj* **1** liable to be taxed or charged **2** liable to result in a legal charge

charge card *n* a card issued by a chain store, shop, or organization, that enables customers to obtain goods and services for which they pay later

chargé d'affaires (shar-zhay daf-**fair**) *n*, *pl* **chargés d'affaires** (**shar**-zhay daf-**fair**) **1** the temporary head of a diplomatic mission in the absence of the ambassador or minister **2** the head of a small or unimportant diplomatic mission **WORD ORIGIN** French

charge hand *n* a workman ranked just below a foreman

charge nurse *n* a nurse in charge of a hospital ward

charger *n* **1** a device for charging a battery **2** (in the Middle Ages) a warhorse

char-grilled *adj* (of food) grilled over charcoal

chariot *n* a two-wheeled horse-drawn vehicle used in ancient times for wars and races **WORD ORIGIN** Old French *char* car

charioteer *n* a chariot driver

charisma (kar-**rizz**-ma) *n* the quality or power of an individual to attract, influence, or inspire people **charismatic** (kar-rizz-**mat**-ik) *adj* **WORD ORIGIN** Greek *kharis* grace, favour

charismatic movement *n* Christianity a group that believes in divine gifts such as instantaneous healing and uttering unintelligible sounds while in a religious ecstasy

charitable *adj* **1** kind or lenient in one's attitude towards others **2** of or for charity: *a charitable organization* **charitably** *adv*

charity *n* **1** *pl* **-ties** an organization set up to provide help to those in need **2** the giving of help, such as money or food, to those in need **3** help given to those in need; alms **4** a kindly attitude towards people **WORD ORIGIN** Latin *caritas* affection

charlady *n*, *pl* **-ladies** Brit same as **charwoman**

charlatan (**shar**-lat-tan) *n* a person who claims expertise that he or she does not have **WORD ORIGIN** Italian *ciarlare* to chatter

Charles' law *n* physics the principle that the volume of a gas varies in proportion to its temperature at constant pressure **WORD ORIGIN** after Jacques *Charles*, physicist

charleston *n* a lively dance of the 1920s **WORD ORIGIN** after *Charleston*, South Carolina

charlie *n* Brit old-fashioned informal a fool

charlock *n* a weed with hairy leaves and yellow flowers **WORD ORIGIN** Old English *cerlic*

charlotte *n* a dessert made with fruit and bread or cake crumbs: *apple charlotte* **WORD ORIGIN** French

charm *n* **1** the quality of attracting, fascinating, or delighting people **2** a trinket worn on a bracelet **3** a small object worn for supposed magical powers **4** a magic spell ▷ *vb* **5** to attract, fascinate, or delight **6** to influence or obtain by personal charm: *you can easily be charmed into changing your mind* **7** to protect as if by magic: *a charmed life* **charmer** *n* **charmless** *adj* **WORD ORIGIN** Latin *carmen* song

charming *adj* delightful or attractive **charmingly** *adv*

charm offensive *n* a concentrated attempt to gain favour by being helpful and obliging

charnel house *n* (formerly) a building or vault for the bones of the dead **WORD ORIGIN** Latin *carnalis* fleshly

charollais (**sharr**-ol-lay) *n* a breed of large white beef cattle **WORD ORIGIN** Monts du *Charollais*, E France

chart *n* **1** a graph, table, or sheet of information in the form of a diagram **2** a map of the sea or the stars **3 the charts** informal the weekly lists of the bestselling pop records or the most popular videos ▷ *vb* **4** to plot the course of **5** to make a chart of **6** to appear in the pop charts **WORD ORIGIN** Greek *khartēs* papyrus

charter *n* **1** a formal document granting or demanding certain rights or liberties: *a children's charter* **2** the fundamental principles of an organization: *the UN Charter* **3** the hire or lease of transportation for private use ▷ *vb* **4** to lease or hire by charter **5** to grant a charter to **WORD ORIGIN** Latin *charta* leaf of papyrus

chartered accountant *n* an accountant who has passed the examinations of the Institute of Chartered Accountants

Chartism *n* English history a movement (1838–48) for social and political reforms, demand for which was presented to Parliament in charters **Chartist** *n*, *adj*

chartreuse (shar-**truhz**) *n* a green or yellow liqueur made from herbs **WORD ORIGIN** after *La Grande Chartreuse*, monastery near Grenoble, where the liqueur is produced

charwoman *n*, *pl* **-women** Brit a woman whose job is to clean other people's houses

chary (**chair**-ee) *adj* **charier, chariest** wary or careful: *chary of interfering* **WORD ORIGIN** Old English *cearig*

Charybdis (kar-**rib**-diss) *n* **1** a ship-devouring monster in classical mythology, identified with a whirlpool off the coast of Sicily **2 between Scylla and Charybdis** see **Scylla**

chase¹ *vb* **chasing, chased 1** to pursue (a person or animal) persistently or quickly **2** to force (a person or animal) to leave a place **3** informal to court (someone) in an unsubtle manner **4** informal to rush or run: *chasing around*

the world **5** informal to pursue (something or someone) energetically in order to obtain results or information ▷ *n* **6** the act or an instance of chasing a person or animal **WORD ORIGIN** Latin *capere* to take

chase² *vb* **chasing, chased** to engrave or emboss (metal) **WORD ORIGIN** Old French *enchasser*

chaser *n* a drink drunk after another of a different kind, for example beer after whisky

chasm (**kaz**-zum) *n* **1** a very deep crack in the ground **2** a wide difference in interests or feelings: *a deep chasm separating science from politics* **WORD ORIGIN** Greek *khasma*

chassis (**shass**-ee) *n*, *pl* **chassis** (**shass**-eez) the steel frame, wheels, and mechanical parts of a vehicle **WORD ORIGIN** French

chaste *adj* **1** abstaining from sex outside marriage or from all sexual intercourse **2** (of conduct or speech) pure, decent, or modest: *a chaste kiss on the forehead* **3** simple in style: *chaste furniture* **chastely** *adv* **chastity** *n* **WORD ORIGIN** Latin *castus* pure

chasten (**chase**-en) *vb* to subdue (someone) by criticism **WORD ORIGIN** Latin *castigare*

chastise *vb* **-tising, -tised 1** to scold severely **2** old-fashioned to punish by beating **chastisement** *n* **WORD ORIGIN** Middle English *chastisen*

chasuble (**chazz**-yew-bl) *n* Christianity a long sleeveless robe worn by a priest when celebrating Mass **WORD ORIGIN** Late Latin *casubla* garment with a hood

chat *n* **1** an informal conversation ▷ *vb* **chatting, chatted 2** to have an informal conversation ▸ See also **chat up** **WORD ORIGIN** short for *chatter*

chateau (**shat**-toe) *n*, *pl* **-teaux** (-toe) or **-teaus** a French country house or castle **WORD ORIGIN** French

chatelaine (**shat**-tell-lane) *n* (formerly) the mistress of a large house or castle **WORD ORIGIN** French

chatline *n* a telephone service enabling callers to join in general conversation with each other

chatroom *n* a site on the internet where users have group discussions by electronic mail

chat show *n* a television or radio show in which guests are interviewed informally

chattels *pl n* old-fashioned possessions **WORD ORIGIN** Old French *chatel* personal property

chatter *vb* **1** to speak quickly and continuously about unimportant things **2** (of birds or monkeys) to make rapid repetitive high-pitched noises **3** (of the teeth) to click together rapidly through cold or fear ▷ *n* **4** idle talk or gossip **5** the high-pitched repetitive noise made by a bird or monkey **WORD ORIGIN** imitative

chatterbox *n* informal a person who talks a great deal, usually about unimportant things

Words from Literature
part 6

chute *n* a narrow channel
> One morning about day-break, I found a canoe
> and crossed over a chute to the main shore
> *The Adventures of Huckleberry Finn* Mark Twain

circumspection *n* careful observation of events and
circumstances; caution
> I honour your circumspection
> *Pride and Prejudice* Jane Austen

clamber *v* to climb somewhere with difficulty,
usually using your hands and your feet
> he clambered up and down stairs
> *Treasure Island* Robert Louis Stevenson

clime *n* climate
> no season knows nor clime
> *The Sun Rising* John Donne

clinched *adj* clenched
> the tops whereof I could but just reach with my
> fist clinched
> *Gulliver's Travels* Jonathan Swift

close chair *n* a sedan chair, which is a covered chair
which has room for one person. The sedan chair is
carried on two poles by two men, one in front and one
behind
> persuaded even the Empress herself to let me hold
> her in her close chair
> *Gulliver's Travels* Jonathan Swift

clown *n* peasant or person who lives off the land
> In ancient days by emperor and clown
> *Ode on a Nightingale* John Keats

coalheaver *n* a coalheaver loaded coal onto ships
using a spade
> Good, strong, wholesome medicine, as was given
> with great success to two Irish labourers and a
> coalheaver
> *Oliver Twist* Charles Dickens

coal-whippers *n* men who worked at docks using
machines to load coal onto ships
> here, were colliers by the score and score, with the
> coal-whippers plunging off stages on deck
> *Great Expectations* Charles Dickens

cobweb *n* the net which a spider makes for catching
insects
> the walls and ceilings were all hung round with
> cobwebs
> *Gulliver's Travels* Jonathan Swift

coddle *v* to treat someone too kindly or protect them
too much
> and I've been coddling the fellow as if I'd been his
> grandmother
> *Little Women* Louisa May Alcott

coil *n* noise or fuss or disturbance
> What a coil is there?
> *Doctor Faustus* 4.7 Christopher Marlowe

collar *v* a slang term which means to capture
> In this sentence, it means he stole it [the money]
> he collared it
> *The Adventures of Huckleberry Finn* Mark Twain

colling *n* an old word which means embracing
and kissing
> and no clasping and colling at all
> *Tess of the D'Urbervilles* Thomas Hardy

colloquy *n* a formal conversation or dialogue
> Such colloquies have occupied many a pair of
> pale-faced weavers
> *Silas Marner* George Eliot

comfit *n* confits are sugar-covered pieces of fruit or
nut eaten as sweets
> and pulled out a box of comfits
> *Alice's Adventures in Wonderland* Lewis Carroll

chattering classes n the chattering classes informal, often derogatory the members of the educated sections of society who enjoy discussion of political, social, and cultural issues

chatty adj -tier, -tiest 1 (of a person) fond of friendly, informal conversation; talkative 2 (of a letter) informal and friendly; gossipy

chat up vb Austral & Brit informal to talk flirtatiously to (someone) with a view to starting a romantic or sexual relationship

chauffeur n 1 a person employed to drive a car for someone ▷ vb 2 to act as driver for (someone) **chauffeuse** fem n **WORD ORIGIN** French: stoker

chauvinism (**show**-vin-iz-zum) n an irrational belief that one's own country, race, group, or sex is superior: male chauvinism **chauvinist** n, adj **chauvinistic** adj **WORD ORIGIN** after Nicolas Chauvin, French soldier under Napoleon

chav n Brit slang, derogatory a young working-class person who dresses in casual sports clothes

cheap adj 1 costing relatively little; inexpensive 2 of poor quality; shoddy: planks of cheap, splintery pine 3 not valued highly; not worth much: promises are cheap 4 informal mean or despicable: a cheap jibe ▷ n 5 on the cheap Brit informal at a low cost ▷ adv 6 at a low cost **cheaply** adv **cheapness** n **WORD ORIGIN** Old English ceap barter, price

cheapen vb 1 to lower the reputation of; degrade 2 to reduce the price of

cheap-jack n informal a person who sells cheap and shoddy goods

cheapskate n informal a miserly person

cheat vb 1 to defraud: he cheated her out of millions 2 to act dishonestly in order to gain some advantage or profit 3 **cheat on** informal to be unfaithful to (one's spouse or lover) ▷ n 4 a person who cheats 5 a fraud or deception **WORD ORIGIN** short for escheat

check vb 1 to examine, investigate, or make an inquiry into 2 to slow the growth or progress of 3 to stop abruptly 4 to correspond or agree: that all checks with our data here ▷ n 5 a test to ensure accuracy or progress 6 a means to ensure against fraud or error 7 a break in progress; stoppage 8 US same as **cheque** 9 chiefly US & Canad the bill in a restaurant 10 a pattern of squares or crossed lines 11 a single square in such a pattern 12 chess the state or position of a king under direct attack 13 **in check** under control or restraint ▷ interj 14 chiefly US & Canad an expression of agreement ▸ See also **check in**, **check out**, etc. **WORD ORIGIN** Old French eschec a check at chess

checked adj having a pattern of squares

checker n US & Canad 1 same as **chequer** 2 same as **draughtsman** (sense 3)

checkered adj US & Canad same as **chequered**

checkers n US & Canad same as **draughts**

check in vb 1 a to register one's arrival at a hotel or airport b to register the arrival of (guests or passengers) at a hotel or airport ▷ n **check-in** 2 a the formal registration of arrival at a hotel or airport b the place where one registers one's arrival at a hotel or airport

check list n a list to be referred to for identification or verification

checkmate n 1 chess the winning position in which an opponent's king is under attack and unable to escape 2 utter defeat ▷ vb -mating, -mated 3 chess to place the king of (one's opponent) in checkmate 4 to thwart or defeat **WORD ORIGIN** Arabic shāh māt the king is dead

check out vb 1 to pay the bill and leave a hotel 2 to investigate, examine, or look at: he asked if he could check out the old man's theory; start the evening off by checking out one of the in bars in the city ▷ n **checkout** 3 a counter in a supermarket, where customers pay

checkpoint n a place where vehicles or travellers are stopped for identification or inspection

checkup n a thorough examination to see if a person or thing is in good condition

check up on vb to investigate the background of

Cheddar n a firm orange or yellowy-white cheese **WORD ORIGIN** Cheddar, village in Somerset, where it was originally made

cheek n 1 either side of the face below the eye 2 informal impudence, boldness, or lack of respect 3 informal a buttock 4 **cheek by jowl** close together 5 **turn the other cheek** to refuse to retaliate ▷ vb 6 Brit, Austral, & NZ informal to speak or behave disrespectfully to someone **WORD ORIGIN** Old English ceace

cheekbone n the bone at the top of the cheek, just below the eye

cheeky adj cheekier, cheekiest disrespectful; impudent **cheekily** adv **cheekiness** n

cheep n 1 the short weak high-pitched cry of a young bird ▷ vb 2 to utter a cheep **WORD ORIGIN** imitative

cheer vb 1 to applaud or encourage with shouts 2 **cheer up** to make or become happy or hopeful; comfort or be comforted ▷ n 3 a shout of applause or encouragement 4 a feeling of cheerfulness: the news brought little cheer **WORD ORIGIN** Middle English (in the sense: face, welcoming aspect), from Greek kara head

cheerful adj 1 having a happy disposition 2 pleasantly bright: a cheerful colour 3 ungrudging: a cheerful giver **cheerfully** adv **cheerfulness** n

cheerio interj 1 informal a farewell greeting ▷ n 2 Austral & NZ a small red cocktail sausage

cheerleader n a person who leads a crowd in cheers, usually at sports events

cheerless adj dreary or gloomy

cheers interj informal chiefly Brit 1 a drinking toast 2 a farewell greeting 3 an expression of gratitude

cheery adj cheerier, cheeriest cheerful **cheerily** adv

cheese[1] n 1 a food made from coagulated milk curd 2 a block of this **WORD ORIGIN** Latin caseus

cheese[2] n **big cheese** slang an important person **WORD ORIGIN** perhaps from Hindi chiz thing

cheeseburger n a hamburger with a slice of cheese melted on top of it

cheesecake n 1 a dessert with a biscuit-crumb base covered with a sweet cream-cheese mixture and sometimes with a fruit topping 2 slang magazine photographs of naked or scantily dressed women

cheesecloth n a light, loosely woven cotton cloth

cheesed off adj Brit, Austral, & NZ slang bored, disgusted, or angry **WORD ORIGIN** origin unknown

cheeseparing adj 1 mean or miserly ▷ n 2 meanness or miserliness

cheesy adj cheesier, cheesiest 1 like cheese 2 informal (of a smile) broad but possibly insincere 3 informal in poor taste: a cheesy game show

cheetah n a large fast-running wild cat of Africa and SW Asia, which has a light brown coat with black spots **WORD ORIGIN** Hindi cītā

chef n a cook, usually the head cook, in a restaurant or hotel **WORD ORIGIN** French

chef-d'oeuvre (shay-**durv**) n, pl **chefs-d'oeuvre** (shay-**durv**) a masterpiece **WORD ORIGIN** French

Chelsea Pensioner n an inhabitant of the Chelsea Royal Hospital in SW London, a home for old and infirm soldiers

chem. 1 chemical 2 chemist 3 chemistry

chemical n 1 any substance used in or resulting from a reaction involving changes to atoms or molecules ▷ adj 2 of or used in chemistry 3 of, made from, or using chemicals: a chemical additive found in many foods **chemically** adv

chemical engineering n the applications of chemistry in industrial processes **chemical engineer** n

chemical warfare n warfare using weapons such as gases and poisons

chemin de fer (shem-**man** de **fair**) n a gambling game, a variation of baccarat **WORD ORIGIN** French: railway, referring to the fast tempo of the game

chemise (shem-**meez**) n a woman's old-fashioned loose-fitting slip or dress **WORD ORIGIN** Late Latin camisa

chemist n 1 Brit, Austral, & NZ a shop selling medicines and cosmetics 2 Brit, Austral, & NZ a qualified dispenser of prescribed medicines 3 a specialist in chemistry **WORD ORIGIN** Medieval Latin alchimista alchemist

chemistry n the branch of science concerned with the composition, properties, and reactions of substances

chemotherapy *n* the treatment of disease, often cancer, by means of chemicals

chenille (shen-**neel**) *n* **1** a thick soft tufty yarn **2** a fabric made of this **WORD ORIGIN** French

cheque *or US* **check** *n* a written order to someone's bank to pay money from his or her account to the person to whom the cheque is made out **WORD ORIGIN** from *check* (in the sense: means of verification)

cheque book *n* a book of detachable blank cheques issued by a bank

cheque card *n* Brit a plastic card issued by a bank guaranteeing payment of a customer's cheques

chequer *or US* **checker** *n* a piece used in Chinese chequers ▸ See also **chequers** **WORD ORIGIN** Middle English: chessboard

chequered *or US* **checkered** *adj* **1** marked by varied fortunes: *a chequered career* **2** marked with alternating squares of colour

chequers *or US* **checkers** *n* the game of draughts

cherish *vb* **1** to cling to (an idea or feeling): *cherished notions* **2** to care for **WORD ORIGIN** Latin *carus* dear

Cherokee *n* **1** a member of a Native American people, formerly of the Appalachian mountains, now living chiefly in Oklahoma **2** the language of this people

cheroot (sher-**root**) *n* a cigar with both ends cut off squarely **WORD ORIGIN** Tamil *curuttu* curl, roll

cherry *n, pl* **-ries 1** a small round soft fruit with red or blackish skin and a hard stone **2** the tree on which this fruit grows ▸ *adj* **3** deep red: *cherry lips* **WORD ORIGIN** Greek *kerasios*

cherry tomato *n* a miniature tomato, slightly bigger than a cherry

cherub *n, pl* **cherubs** *or (for sense 1)* **cherubim 1** Christianity an angel, often represented as a winged child **2** an innocent or sweet child **cherubic** (chair-**roo**-bik) *adj* **WORD ORIGIN** Hebrew *kērūbh*

chervil *n* an aniseed-flavoured herb **WORD ORIGIN** Old English *cerfelle*

Cheshire cheese *n* a mild white or pale orange cheese with a crumbly texture

chess *n* a game of skill for two players using a chessboard on which chessmen are moved, with the object of checkmating the opponent's king **WORD ORIGIN** Old French *esches*, plural of *eschec* check

chessboard *n* a square board divided into 64 squares of two alternating colours, for playing chess

chessman *n, pl* **-men** a piece used in chess **WORD ORIGIN** Middle English *chessemeyne* chess company

chest *n* **1** the front of the body, from the neck to the waist **2** **get something off one's chest** *informal* to unburden oneself of worries or secrets by talking about them **3** a heavy box for storage or shipping: *a tea chest* **WORD ORIGIN** Greek *kistē* box

chesterfield *n* **1** a large couch with high padded sides and back **2** Canad any sofa or couch **WORD ORIGIN** after a 19th-century Earl of Chesterfield

chestnut *n* **1** a reddish-brown edible nut **2** the tree that this nut grows on **3** a horse of a reddish-brown colour **4** *informal* an old or stale joke ▸ *adj* **5** dark reddish-brown: *chestnut hair* **WORD ORIGIN** Greek *kastanea*

chest of drawers *n* a piece of furniture consisting of a set of drawers in a frame

chesty *adj* **chestier, chestiest** Brit *informal* suffering from or symptomatic of chest disease: *chesty colds* **chestiness** *n*

cheval glass (shev-**val**) *n* a full-length mirror mounted so as to swivel within a frame **WORD ORIGIN** French *cheval* support (literally: horse)

chevalier (shev-a-**leer**) *n* **1** a member of the French Legion of Honour **2** a chivalrous man **WORD ORIGIN** Medieval Latin *caballarius* horseman

Cheviot *n* a large British sheep with a heavy medium-length fleece **WORD ORIGIN** Cheviot Hills on borders of England & Scotland

chevron (**shev**-ron) *n* a V-shaped pattern, such as those worn on the sleeve of a military uniform to indicate rank **WORD ORIGIN** Old French

chew *vb* **1** to work the jaws and teeth in order to grind (food) ▸ *n* **2** the act of chewing **3** something that is chewed, such as a sweet or a piece of tobacco **WORD ORIGIN** Old English *ceowan*

chewing gum *n* a flavoured gum which is chewed but not swallowed

chew over *vb* to consider carefully

chewy *adj* **chewier, chewiest** of a consistency requiring a lot of chewing

chez (**shay**) *prep* at the home of **WORD ORIGIN** French

chianti (kee-**ant**-ee) *n* a dry red wine produced in Tuscany, Italy

chiaroscuro (kee-ah-roh-**skew**-roh) *n, pl* **-ros** the distribution of light and shade in a picture **WORD ORIGIN** Italian *chiaro* clear + *oscuro* obscure

chic (**sheek**) *adj* **1** stylish or elegant ▸ *n* **2** stylishness or elegance **WORD ORIGIN** French

chicane (shik-**kane**) *n* an obstacle placed on a motor-racing circuit to slow the cars down **WORD ORIGIN** French *chicaner* to quibble

chicanery *n* trickery or deception

chick *n* **1** a baby bird, esp. a domestic fowl **2** *slang* a young woman **WORD ORIGIN** short for *chicken*

chicken *n* **1** a domestic fowl bred for its flesh or eggs **2** the flesh of this bird used for food **3** *slang* a coward ▸ *adj* **4** *slang* cowardly **WORD ORIGIN** Old English *ciecen*

chicken feed *n* *slang* a trifling amount of money

chicken-hearted *adj* easily frightened; cowardly

chicken out *vb* *informal* to fail to do something through cowardice

chickenpox *n* an infectious viral disease, usually affecting children, which produces an itchy rash

chicken wire *n* wire netting

chickpea *n* an edible hard yellow pealike seed **WORD ORIGIN** Latin *cicer*

chickweed *n* a common garden weed with small white flowers

chicory *n* **1** a plant grown for its leaves, which are used in salads, and for its roots **2** the root of this plant, roasted, dried, and used as a coffee substitute **WORD ORIGIN** Greek *kikhōrion*

chide *vb* **chiding, chided** old-fashioned to rebuke or scold **WORD ORIGIN** Old English *cīdan*

chief *n* **1** the head of a group or body of people **2** the head of a tribe ▸ *adj* **3** most important: *the chief suspects* **4** highest in rank: *the Chief Constable* **WORD ORIGIN** Latin *caput* head

chiefly *adv* **1** especially or essentially **2** mainly or mostly

chief petty officer *n* a senior noncommissioned officer in a navy

chieftain *n* the leader of a tribe or clan **WORD ORIGIN** Late Latin *capitaneus* commander

chief technician *n* a noncommissioned officer in the Royal Air Force

chiffchaff *n* a European warbler with a yellowish-brown plumage **WORD ORIGIN** imitative

chiffon (**shif**-fon) *n* a fine see-through fabric of silk or nylon **WORD ORIGIN** French *chiffe* rag

chiffonier *or* **chiffonnier** (shiff-on-**near**) *n* **1** a tall elegant chest of drawers **2** a wide low open-fronted cabinet **WORD ORIGIN** French

chignon (**sheen**-yon) *n* a roll or knot of long hair pinned up at the back of the head **WORD ORIGIN** French

chigoe (**chig**-go) *n* a tropical flea that burrows into the skin. Also: **chigger** **WORD ORIGIN** Carib *chigo*

chihuahua (chee-**wah**-wah) *n* a tiny short-haired dog, originally from Mexico **WORD ORIGIN** after Chihuahua, state in Mexico

chilblain *n* an inflammation of the fingers or toes, caused by exposure to cold **WORD ORIGIN** CHILL (noun) + BLAIN

child *n, pl* **children 1** a young human being; boy or girl **2** a son or daughter ▸ Related adjective: **filial 3** a childish or immature person **4** the product of an influence or environment: *a child of the Army* **5** **with child** old-fashioned pregnant **childless** *adj* **childlessness** *n* **WORD ORIGIN** Old English *cild*

childbearing *n* **1** the process of giving birth to a child ▸ *adj* **2** **of childbearing age** of an age when women are able to give birth to children

child benefit *n* Brit a regular government payment to parents of children up to a certain age

childbirth *n* the act of giving birth to a child ▸ Related adjective: **natal**

childhood *n* the time or condition of being a child

childish *adj* **1** immature or silly: *childish fighting over who did what* **2** of or like a child: *childish illnesses*

childlike *adj* like a child, for example in being innocent or trustful

child minder *n* a person who looks after children whose parents are working

children *n* the plural of **child**

child's play *n informal* something that is easy to do

chill *n* **1** a feverish cold **2** a moderate coldness **3** a feeling of coldness resulting from a cold or damp environment or from sudden fear ▷ *vb* **4** to make (something) cool or cold: *chilled white wine* **5** to cause (someone) to feel cold or frightened **6** *informal* to calm oneself ▷ *adj* **7** unpleasantly cold: *chill winds* **chilling** *adj* **chillingly** *adv* **WORD ORIGIN** Old English *ciele*

chilled or **chilled-out** *adj informal* relaxed or easy-going in character or behaviour

chiller *n* **1** short for **spine-chiller** **2** a cooling or refrigerating device

chilli or **chili** *n* **1** *pl* **chillies** or **chilies** the small red or green hot-tasting pod of a type of capsicum, used in cookery, often in powdered form **2** short for **chilli con carne**
WORD ORIGIN Mexican Indian

chilli con carne *n* a highly seasoned Mexican dish of meat, onions, beans, and chilli powder
WORD ORIGIN Spanish: chilli with meat

chill out *informal vb* **1** to relax, esp. after energetic dancing at a rave ▷ *adj* **chill-out** **2** suitable for relaxation after energetic dancing: *a chill-out area*

chilly *adj* **-lier, -liest** **1** causing or feeling moderately cold **2** without warmth; unfriendly: *a chilly reception*

chilly bin *n NZ informal* a portable insulated container for packing food and drink in ice

Chiltern Hundreds *pl n* (in Britain) a nominal office that an MP applies for in order to resign his seat

chime *n* **1** the musical ringing sound made by a bell or clock ▷ *vb* **chiming, chimed** **2** (of a bell) to make a clear musical ringing sound **3** (of a clock) to indicate (the time) by chiming
WORD ORIGIN Latin *cymbalum* cymbal

chime in *vb* to say something just after someone else has spoken

chimera (kime-**meer**-a) *n* **1** a wild and unrealistic dream or idea **2** *Greek myth* a fire-breathing monster with the head of a lion, body of a goat, and tail of a serpent
WORD ORIGIN Greek *khimaira* she-goat

chimerical *adj* wildly fanciful or imaginary

chime with *vb* to agree or be consistent with

chimney *n* a hollow vertical structure that carries smoke or steam away from a fire or engine
WORD ORIGIN Greek *kaminos* oven

chimney breast *n* the walls surrounding the base of a chimney or fireplace

chimneypot *n* a short pipe on the top of a chimney

chimney stack *n* the part of a chimney sticking up above a roof

chimney sweep *n* a person who cleans soot from chimneys

chimp *n informal* short for **chimpanzee**

chimpanzee *n* an intelligent small black ape of central W Africa
WORD ORIGIN African dialect

chin *n* the front part of the face below the mouth
WORD ORIGIN Old English *cinn*

china¹ *n* **1** ceramic ware of a type originally from China **2** dishes or ornamental objects made of china
WORD ORIGIN Persian *chīnī*

china² *n Brit & S African informal* a friend or companion
WORD ORIGIN from cockney rhyming slang *china plate* mate

china clay *n* same as **kaolin**

Chinaman *n, pl* **-men** *old-fashioned or offensive* a man from China

Chinatown *n* a section of a town or city outside China with a mainly Chinese population

chinchilla *n* **1** a small S American rodent bred in captivity for its soft silvery-grey fur **2** the fur of this animal
WORD ORIGIN Spanish

chine *n* **1** a cut of meat including part of the backbone ▷ *vb* **chining, chined** **2** to cut (meat) along the backbone
WORD ORIGIN Old French *eschine*

Chinese *adj* **1** of China ▷ *n* **2** *pl* **-nese** a person from China or a descendant of one **3** any of the languages of China

Chinese chequers *n* a game played with marbles or pegs on a six-pointed star-shaped board

Chinese lantern *n* a collapsible lantern made of thin paper

Chinese leaves *pl n* the edible leaves of a Chinese cabbage

Chinese puzzle *n* a complicated puzzle or problem

chink¹ *n* a small narrow opening: *a chink of light*
WORD ORIGIN Old English *cine* crack

chink² *vb* **1** to make a light ringing sound ▷ *n* **2** a light ringing sound
WORD ORIGIN imitative

chinless wonder *n Brit informal* a person, usually upper-class, lacking strength of character

chinoiserie (sheen-**wahz**-a-ree) *n* **1** a style of decorative art based on imitations of Chinese motifs **2** objects in this style
WORD ORIGIN French *chinois* Chinese

Chinook *n* **1** *pl* **-nook** or **-nooks** a member of a Native American people of the Pacific coast of N America **2** the language of this people

Chinook salmon *n* a Pacific salmon valued as a food fish

chinos (**chee**-nohz) *pl n* trousers made of a kind of hard-wearing cotton
WORD ORIGIN *chino*, the cloth; origin unknown

chintz *n* a printed patterned cotton fabric with a glazed finish, used for curtains and chair coverings
WORD ORIGIN Hindi *chīnt*

chintzy *adj* **chintzier, chintziest** **1** of or covered with chintz **2** (of a room or house) decorated in an excessively fussy or twee way

chinwag *n Brit, Austral, & NZ informal* a chat

chip *n* **1** a thin strip of potato fried in deep fat **2** *US, Canad, Austral, & NZ* a potato crisp **3** *electronics* a tiny wafer of semiconductor material, such as silicon, processed to form an integrated circuit **4** a counter used to represent money in gambling games **5** a small piece removed by chopping, cutting, or breaking **6** a mark left where a small piece has been broken off something **7 chip off the old block** *informal* a person who resembles one of his or her parents in personality **8 have a chip on one's shoulder** *informal* to be resentful or bear a grudge **9 when the chips are down** *informal* at a time of crisis ▷ *vb* **chipping, chipped** **10** to break small pieces from
WORD ORIGIN Old English *cipp*

chip and PIN *n* a system for authorizing credit- or debit-card payment requiring the purchaser to enter a personal identification number

chipboard *n* thin rigid board made of compressed wood particles

chip in *vb informal* **1** to contribute to a common fund **2** to interrupt with a remark

chipmunk *n* a squirrel-like striped burrowing rodent of North America and Asia
WORD ORIGIN from a Native American language

chipolata *n chiefly Brit* a small sausage
WORD ORIGIN Italian *cipolla* onion

Chippendale *adj* (of furniture) by or in the style of Thomas Chippendale, with Chinese and Gothic motifs, curved legs, and massive carving

chipset *n* a highly integrated circuit on the motherboard of a computer that controls many of its data transfer functions

chiropody (kir-**rop**-pod-ee) *n* the treatment of minor foot complaints like corns **chiropodist** *n*

chiropractic (kire-oh-**prak**-tik) *n* a system of treating bodily disorders by manipulation of the spine **chiropractor** *n*
WORD ORIGIN Greek *kheir* hand + *praktikos* practical

chirp *vb* **1** (of some birds and insects) to make a short high-pitched sound **2** *Brit, Austral, & NZ* to speak in a lively fashion ▷ *n* **3** a chirping sound
WORD ORIGIN imitative

chirpy *adj* **chirpier, chirpiest** *informal* lively and cheerful **chirpiness** *n*

chirrup *vb* **1** (of some birds) to chirp repeatedly ▷ *n* **2** a chirruping sound
WORD ORIGIN variant of *chirp*

chisel *n* **1** a metal tool with a sharp end for shaping wood or stone ▷ *vb* **-elling, -elled** or *US* **-eling, -eled** **2** to carve or form with a chisel
WORD ORIGIN Latin *caesus* cut

The Influence of Greek on English

It is estimated that around 5% of all English words originally come from Greek. This may be fewer than come from Latin, French, or Anglo-Saxon, but the influence of Greek is by no means negligible.

The ancient Greeks are widely regarded as the originators of democracy, philosophy, theatre, and the entire Western cultural tradition. It is natural, therefore, that the language of writers such as Homer, Plato, and Aristotle should have had an influence on the cultures that followed it.

Moreover, even after Greek civilization had passed its peak, and the Romans had established themselves as the dominant power in the Mediterranean, the Greek language continued to be used throughout the Eastern part of the Roman Empire. Importantly, it was in Greek that the books of the New Testament were written, and so much of the vocabulary of the Church has been influenced by this language, with words such as 'church', 'apostle', 'bible', 'priest', and 'bishop' all having Greek origins.

The Greek alphabet is not identical with the modern English alphabet, and the differences between the two can often be an indicator of whether or not a word has a Greek origin. The letters J, Q, W, and F do not have direct equivalents in the Greek alphabet, and so words that contain these letters are unlikely to come from Greek. On the other hand, the letter combinations CH and PH suggest a Greek origin, as these correspond to the Greek letters chi and phi. The letter Y being used with the short /ɪ/ sound is another characteristically Greek feature, and represents the Greek letter upsilon in English words such as 'chrysanthemum' and 'chlorophyll'.

For many words that have come into English from Greek, it is possible to trace a line of descent from the Greek language through Latin and Old French into English. Thus the Greek word *aer* was taken from Greek into Latin, and then emerged in Old French as *air*, the form in which it reached English in the 13th century.

In other cases, English has borrowed vocabulary directly from Greek, without the intervention of Latin and French. The so-called 'English Renaissance' of the 16th and 17th centuries witnessed a renewed admiration for Greek and Roman culture, and Greek and Latin were regarded as having the necessary authority to be used as sources of new words, especially when it came to supplying scientific terminology.

The vocabulary of medicine is especially indebted to Greek. The suffixes '-itis' (indicating an inflammation), '-osis' (indicating a diseased condition), '-phobia' (indicating an irrational fear), and '-mania' (indicating an irrational enthusiasm) are all derived from Greek, and moreover are typically combined with other Greek words to produce the names of medical conditions. Thus 'arthritis' draws on *arthron*, the Greek word for a joint, and 'pyromania' makes use of *pur*, the word for fire.

Greek provides many of the prefixes that generate the words used in scientific discourse. The Greek names for numbers are behind the series of prefixes 'mono-', 'di-', 'tri-', 'tetra-', 'penta-', and 'hexa-' that are familiar from the names of many chemical compounds. Greek is also behind the names of some of the better known chemical elements: 'hydrogen' was coined from two Greek words and literally means 'producing water', while 'oxygen' means 'producing acid'. Even the names of the sciences themselves are invariably Greek: the suffix '-ology' is derived from *logos*, meaning 'word' or 'study', and so biology is literally 'the study of life', pathology is 'the study of suffering', and so on.

Other areas of scholarship besides the sciences draw on Greek. Much of the terminology of literary criticism – including words such as *catharsis, hubris, irony, character,* and *pathos* – is Greek, having being fixed by Aristotle in his influential work *The Poetics*.

However, the Greek influence in English is not restricted to the world of scholarship. Greek elements are found in numerous words in everyday use. We would not talk about a planet (which literally means 'wanderer'), a helicopter ('spiral wing'), a telephone ('far sound'), a photograph ('light writing'), or numerous other things were it not for Greek.

chiselled *or US* **chiseled** *adj* finely or sharply formed: *chiselled angular features*

chit[1] *n* a short official note, such as a memorandum, requisition, or receipt. Also: **chitty**
WORD ORIGIN Hindi *cittha* note

chit[2] *n Brit, Austral, & NZ, old-fashioned* a pert or impudent girl
WORD ORIGIN Middle English: young animal, kitten

chitchat *n* chat or gossip

chitin (**kite**-in) *n* the tough substance forming the outer layer of the bodies of arthropods
WORD ORIGIN Greek *khitōn* tunic

chitterlings *pl n* the intestines of a pig or other animal prepared as food
WORD ORIGIN origin unknown

chivalrous *adj* gallant or courteous **chivalrously** *adv*

chivalry *n* **1** courteous behaviour, esp. by men towards women **2** the medieval system and principles of knighthood **chivalric** *adj*
WORD ORIGIN Old French *chevalier* knight

chives *pl n* the long slender hollow leaves of a small Eurasian plant, used in cooking for their onion-like flavour
WORD ORIGIN Latin *caepa* onion

chivvy *vb* **-vies, -vying, -vied** *Brit* to harass or nag
WORD ORIGIN probably from *Chevy Chase*, a Scottish ballad

chloral hydrate *n* a colourless crystalline solid used as a sedative

chlorate *n chem* any salt containing the ion ClO_3

chloride *n chem* **1** any compound of chlorine and another element and radical **2** any salt or ester of hydrochloric acid

chlorinate *vb* **-ating, -ated 1** to disinfect (water) with chlorine **2** *chem* to combine or treat (a substance) with chlorine: *chlorinated hydrocarbons* **chlorination** *n*

chlorine *n* a poisonous strong-smelling greenish-yellow gaseous element, used in water purification and as a disinfectant, and, combined with sodium, to make common salt. Symbol: Cl

chloro- *combining form* green
WORD ORIGIN Greek *khlōros*

chlorofluorocarbon *n chem* any of various gaseous compounds of carbon, hydrogen, chlorine, and fluorine, used as refrigerants and aerosol propellants, some of which break down the ozone in the atmosphere

chloroform *n* a sweet-smelling liquid, used as a solvent and cleansing agent, and formerly as an anaesthetic
WORD ORIGIN CHLORO- + *formyl*: see FORMIC ACID

chlorophyll *or US* **chlorophyl** *n* the green colouring matter of plants, which enables them to convert sunlight into energy
WORD ORIGIN CHLORO- + Greek *phullon* leaf

chloroplast *n biol* one of the parts of a plant cell that contains chlorophyll
WORD ORIGIN CHLORO- + Greek *plastos* formed

chock *n* **1** a block or wedge of wood used to prevent the sliding or rolling of a heavy object ▷ *vb* **2** to fit with or secure by a chock
WORD ORIGIN origin unknown

chock-a-block *adj* filled to capacity

chock-full *adj* completely full

chocolate *n* **1** a food made from roasted ground cacao seeds, usually sweetened and flavoured **2** a sweet or drink made from this ▷ *adj* **3** deep brown **chocolaty** *adj*
WORD ORIGIN Aztec *xocolatl*

choice *n* **1** the act of choosing or selecting **2** the opportunity or power of choosing: *parental choice* **3** a person or thing chosen or that may be chosen: *the president's choice as the new head of the CIA* **4** an alternative action or possibility: *they had no choice but to accept* **5** a range from which to select: *a choice of weapons* ▷ *adj* **6** of high quality: *choice government jobs* **7** carefully chosen: *a few choice words* **8** vulgar: *choice language*
WORD ORIGIN Old French *choisir* to choose

choir *n* **1** an organized group of singers, usually for singing in church **2** the part of a church, in front of the altar, occupied by the choir
WORD ORIGIN Latin *chorus*

choirboy *n* a boy who sings in a church choir

choke *vb* **choking, choked 1** to hinder or stop the breathing of (a person or animal) by strangling or smothering **2** to have trouble in breathing, swallowing, or speaking **3** to block or clog up: *the old narrow streets become choked to a standstill* **4** to hinder the growth of: *weeds would outgrow and choke the rice crop* ▷ *n* **5** a device in a vehicle's engine that enriches the petrol-air mixture by reducing the air supply
WORD ORIGIN Old English *ācēocian*

choke back *vb* to suppress (tears or anger)

choked *adj informal* disappointed or angry: *I still feel choked about him leaving*

choker *n* a tight-fitting necklace

choke up *vb* **1** to block completely **2 choked up** *informal* overcome with emotion

choko *n, pl* **-kos** *Austral & NZ* the pear-shaped fruit of a tropical American vine, eaten as a vegetable
WORD ORIGIN Brazilian Indian

choler (**kol**-ler) *n archaic* anger or bad temper
WORD ORIGIN Greek *kholē* bile

cholera (**kol**-ler-a) *n* a serious infectious disease causing severe diarrhoea and stomach cramps, caught from contaminated water or food
WORD ORIGIN Greek *kholē* bile

choleric *adj* bad-tempered

cholesterol (kol-**lest**-er-oll) *n* a fatty alcohol found in all animal fats, tissues, and fluids, an excess of which is thought to contribute to heart and artery disease
WORD ORIGIN Greek *kholē* bile + *stereos* solid

chomp *vb* to chew (food) noisily

chook *n informal chiefly Austral & NZ* a hen or chicken

choose *vb* **choosing, chose, chosen 1** to select (a person, thing, or course of action) from a number of alternatives **2** to like or please: *when she did choose to reveal her secret, the group were initially hushed* **3** to consider it desirable or proper: *I don't choose to read that sort of book*
WORD ORIGIN Old English *ceosan*

choosy *adj* **choosier, choosiest** *informal* fussy; hard to please

chop[1] *vb* **chopping, chopped 1** (often foll. by *down* or *off*) to cut (something) with a blow from an axe or other sharp tool **2** to cut into pieces **3** *boxing, karate* to hit (an opponent) with a short sharp blow **4** *Brit, Austral, & NZ informal* to dispense with or reduce **5** *sport* to hit (a ball) sharply downwards ▷ *n* **6** a cutting blow **7** a slice of mutton, lamb, or pork, usually including a rib **8** *sport* a sharp downward blow or stroke **9 the chop** *slang* dismissal from employment
WORD ORIGIN variant of *chap*: see CHAPPED

chop[2] *vb* **chopping, chopped 1** chop and change to change one's mind repeatedly **2** chop logic to use excessively subtle or involved argument
WORD ORIGIN Old English *ceapian* to barter

chop chop *adv pidgin English* quickly

chopper *n* **1** *informal* **a** helicopter **2** *chiefly Brit* a small hand axe **3** a butcher's cleaver **4** a type of bicycle or motorcycle with very high handlebars **5** *NZ* a child's bicycle

choppy *adj* **-pier, -piest** (of the sea) fairly rough **choppiness** *n*

chops *pl n Brit, Austral, & NZ informal* **1** the jaws or cheeks **2 lick one's chops** to anticipate something with pleasure
WORD ORIGIN origin unknown

chopsticks *pl n* a pair of thin sticks of ivory, wood, or plastic, used for eating Chinese or other East Asian food
WORD ORIGIN pidgin English, from Chinese

chop suey *n* a Chinese-style dish of chopped meat, bean sprouts, and other vegetables in a sauce
WORD ORIGIN Chinese *tsap sui* odds and ends

choral *adj* of or for a choir

chorale (kor-**rahl**) *n* **1** a slow stately hymn tune **2** *chiefly US* a choir or chorus
WORD ORIGIN German *Choralgesang* choral song

chord[1] *n* **1** *maths* a straight line connecting two points on a curve **2** *anat* same as **cord 3 strike** *or* **touch a chord** to bring about an emotional response, usually of sympathy
WORD ORIGIN Greek *khordē* string

chord[2] *n* the simultaneous sounding of three or more musical notes
WORD ORIGIN short for *accord*

chordate *n* any animal that has a long fibrous rod just above the gut to support the body, such as the vertebrates

chore *n* **1** a small routine task **2** an unpleasant task
WORD ORIGIN Old English *cerr* a turn of work

chorea (kor-**ree**-a) *n* a disorder of the nervous system characterized by uncontrollable brief jerky movements **WORD ORIGIN** Greek *khoreia* dance

choreograph *vb* to compose the steps and dances for (a piece of music or ballet)

choreography *n* **1** the composition of steps and movements for ballet and other dancing **2** the steps and movements of a ballet or dance **choreographer** *n* **choreographic** *adj* **WORD ORIGIN** Greek *khoreia* dance + -GRAPHY

chorister *n* a singer in a church choir

chortle *vb* -**tling**, -**tled 1** to chuckle with amusement ▷ *n* **2** an amused chuckle **WORD ORIGIN** coined by Lewis Carroll

chorus *n, pl* -**ruses 1** a large choir **2** a piece of music to be sung by a large choir **3** a part of a song repeated after each verse **4** something expressed by many people at once: *a chorus of boos* **5** the noise made by a group of birds or small animals: *the dawn chorus* **6** a group of singers or dancers who perform together in a show **7** (in ancient Greece) a group of actors who commented on the action of a play **8** (in Elizabethan drama) the actor who spoke the prologue and epilogue **9 in chorus** in unison ▷ *vb* **10** to sing or say together **WORD ORIGIN** Greek *khoros*

chorus girl *n* a young woman who dances or sings in the chorus of a show or film

chose *vb* the past tense of **choose**

chosen *vb* **1** the past participle of **choose** ▷ *adj* **2** selected for some special quality: *the chosen one*

chough (**chuff**) *n* a large black bird of the crow family **WORD ORIGIN** origin unknown

choux pastry (**shoo**) *n* a very light pastry made with eggs **WORD ORIGIN** French *pâte choux* cabbage dough

chow *n* **1** a thick-coated dog with a curled tail, originally from China **2** *informal* food **WORD ORIGIN** pidgin English

chowder *n* a thick soup containing clams or fish **WORD ORIGIN** French *chaudière* kettle

chow mein *n* a Chinese-American dish consisting of chopped meat or vegetables fried with noodles **WORD ORIGIN** from Chinese

chrism *n* consecrated oil used for anointing in some churches **WORD ORIGIN** Greek *khriein* to anoint

Christ *n* **1** Jesus of Nazareth (Jesus Christ), regarded by Christians as the Messiah of Old Testament prophecies **2** the Messiah of Old Testament prophecies **3** an image or picture of Christ ▷ *interj* **4** *taboo slang* an oath expressing annoyance or surprise **WORD ORIGIN** Greek *khristos* anointed one

christen *vb* **1** same as **baptize 2** to give a name to (a person or thing) **3** *informal* to use for the first time **christening** *n* **WORD ORIGIN** Old English *cristnian*

Christendom *n* all Christian people or countries

Christian *n* **1** a person who believes in and follows Jesus Christ **2** *informal* a person who displays the virtues of kindness and mercy encouraged in the teachings of Jesus Christ ▷ *adj* **3** of Jesus Christ, Christians, or Christianity **4** kind or good

Christian Era *n* the period beginning with the year of Christ's birth

Christianity *n* **1** the religion based on the life and teachings of Christ **2** Christian beliefs or practices **3** same as **Christendom**

Christianize or -**ise** *vb* -**izing**, -**ized** or -**ising**, -**ised 1** to convert to Christianity **2** to fill with Christian principles, spirit, or outlook **Christianization** or -**isation** *n*

Christian name *n* a personal name formally given to Christians at baptism: loosely used to mean a person's first name

Christian Science *n* the religious system founded by Mary Baker Eddy (1866), which emphasizes spiritual regeneration and healing through prayer **Christian Scientist** *n*

Christmas *n* **1 a** *Christianity* a festival commemorating the birth of Christ, held by most Churches to have occurred on December 25 **b** Also: **Christmas Day** December 25, as a day of secular celebrations when gifts and greetings are exchanged ▷ *adj* **2** connected with or taking place at the time of year when this festival is celebrated: *the Christmas holidays* **Christmassy** *adj* **WORD ORIGIN** Old English *Crīstes mæsse* Mass of Christ

Christmas box *n* a tip or present given at Christmas, esp. to postmen or tradesmen

Christmas Eve *n* the evening or the whole day before Christmas Day

Christmas pudding *n* *Austral & Brit* a rich steamed pudding containing suet, dried fruit, and spices

Christmas rose *n* an evergreen plant with white or pink winter-blooming flowers

Christmas tree *n* an evergreen tree or an imitation of one, decorated as part of Christmas celebrations

chromate *n* *chem* any salt or ester of chromic acid

chromatic *adj* **1** of or in colour or colours **2** *music* **a** involving the sharpening or flattening of notes or the use of such notes **b** of the chromatic scale **chromatically** *adv* **WORD ORIGIN** Greek *khrōma* colour

chromatics *n* the science of colour

chromatic scale *n* a twelve-note scale including all the semitones of the octave

chromatin *n* *biochem* the part of the nucleus of a cell that forms the chromosomes and can easily be dyed **WORD ORIGIN** from *chrome*

chromatography *n* the technique of separating and analysing the components of a mixture of liquids or gases by slowly passing it through an adsorbing material

WORD ORIGIN Greek *khrōma* colour + -GRAPHY

chrome *n* **1** same as **chromium 2** anything plated with chromium ▷ *vb* **chroming, chromed 3** to plate with chromium **WORD ORIGIN** Greek *khrōma* colour

chromite *n* a brownish-black mineral which is the only commercial source of chromium

chromium *n* *chem* a hard grey metallic element, used in steel alloys and electroplating to increase hardness and corrosion resistance. Symbol: Cr **WORD ORIGIN** from *chrome*

chromosome *n* any of the microscopic rod-shaped structures that appear in a cell nucleus during cell division, consisting of units (genes) that are responsible for the transmission of hereditary characteristics **WORD ORIGIN** Greek *khrōma* colour + *sōma* body

chromosphere *n* a gaseous layer of the sun's atmosphere extending from the photosphere to the corona

chronic *adj* **1** (of a disease) developing slowly or lasting for a long time **2** (of a bad habit or bad behaviour) having continued for a long time; habitual: *chronic drug addiction* **3** very serious or severe: *chronic food shortages* **4** *Brit, Austral, & NZ informal* very bad: *the play was chronic* **chronically** *adv* **WORD ORIGIN** Greek *khronos* time

chronic fatigue syndrome *n* a condition characterized by painful muscles and general weakness sometimes persisting long after a viral illness

chronicle *n* **1** a record of events in chronological order ▷ *vb* -**cling**, -**cled 2** to record in or as if in a chronicle **chronicler** *n* **WORD ORIGIN** Greek *khronika* annals

chronological *adj* **1** (of a sequence of events) arranged in order of occurrence **2** relating to chronology **chronologically** *adv*

chronology *n, pl* -**gies 1** the arrangement of dates or events in order of occurrence **2** the determining of the proper sequence of past events **3** a table of events arranged in order of occurrence **chronologist** *n* **WORD ORIGIN** Greek *khronos* time + -LOGY

chronometer *n* a timepiece designed to be accurate in all conditions **WORD ORIGIN** Greek *khronos* time + -METER

chrysalis (**kriss**-a-liss) *n* an insect in the stage between larva and adult, when it is in a cocoon **WORD ORIGIN** Greek *khrusos* gold

chrysanthemum *n* a garden plant with large round flowers made up of many petals **WORD ORIGIN** Greek *khrusos* gold + *anthemon* flower

chub *n, pl* **chub** or **chubs** a common freshwater game fish of the carp family with a dark greenish body **WORD ORIGIN** origin unknown

chubby *adj* -**bier**, -**biest** plump and round **chubbiness** *n* **WORD ORIGIN** perhaps from *chub*

chuck¹ *vb* **1** *informal* to throw carelessly **2** *informal* (sometimes foll. by *in* or *up*) to give up; reject: *he chucked in his job* **3** to pat (someone) affectionately under the chin **4** *Austral & NZ informal* to vomit ▷ *n* **5** a throw or toss **6** a pat under the chin ▸ See also **chuck off, chuck out** WORD ORIGIN origin unknown

chuck² *n* **1** Also: **chuck steak** a cut of beef from the neck to the shoulder blade **2** a device that holds a workpiece in a lathe or a tool in a drill WORD ORIGIN variant of *chock*

chuck³ *n W Canad* **1** a large body of water **2** Also: **saltchuck** the sea WORD ORIGIN Chinook

chuckle *vb* **-ling, -led** **1** to laugh softly or to oneself ▷ *n* **2** a partly suppressed laugh WORD ORIGIN probably from *chuck* cluck

chuck off *vb* (often foll. by *at*) *Austral & NZ informal* to abuse or make fun of

chuck out *vb informal* to throw out

chuddies *pl n Indian informal* underpants

chuff *vb* to move while making a puffing sound, as a steam engine WORD ORIGIN imitative

chuffed *adj informal* pleased or delighted: *I suppose you're feeling pretty chuffed* WORD ORIGIN origin unknown

chug *n* **1** a short dull sound like the noise of an engine ▷ *vb* **chugging, chugged** **2** (esp. of an engine) to operate or move with this sound: *lorries chug past* WORD ORIGIN imitative

chukka or **chukker** *n polo* a period of continuous play, usually 7½ minutes WORD ORIGIN Hindi *cakkar*

chum *n* **1** *informal* a close friend ▷ *vb* **chumming, chummed** **2** **chum up with** to form a close friendship with WORD ORIGIN probably from *chamber fellow*

chummy *adj* **-mier, -miest** *informal* friendly **chummily** *adv* **chumminess** *n*

chump *n* **1** *informal* a stupid person **2** a thick piece of meat **3** a thick block of wood **4** **off one's chump** *Brit slang* crazy WORD ORIGIN origin unknown

chunk *n* **1** a thick solid piece of something **2** a considerable amount WORD ORIGIN variant of CHUCK²

chunky *adj* **chunkier, chunkiest** **1** thick and short **2** containing thick pieces **3** *chiefly Brit* (of clothes, esp. knitwear) made of thick bulky material **chunkiness** *n*

church *n* **1** a building for public Christian worship **2** religious services held in a church **3** a particular Christian denomination **4** Christians collectively **5** the clergy as distinguished from the laity **6** **Church** institutional religion as a political or social force: *conflict between Church and State* WORD ORIGIN Greek *kuriakon* (*dōma*) the Lord's (house)

churchgoer *n* a person who attends church regularly

churchman *n, pl* **-men** a clergyman

Church of England *n* the reformed established state Church in England, with the sovereign as its temporal head

Church of Scotland *n* the established Presbyterian church in Scotland

churchwarden *n* **1** *Church of England, Episcopal Church* a lay assistant of a parish priest **2** an old-fashioned long-stemmed tobacco pipe made of clay

churchyard *n* the grounds round a church, used as a graveyard

churl *n* **1** a surly ill-bred person **2** *archaic* a farm labourer WORD ORIGIN Old English *ceorl*

churlish *adj* surly and rude

churn *n* **1** a machine in which cream is shaken to make butter **2** a large container for milk ▷ *vb* **3** to stir (milk or cream) vigorously in order to make butter **4** to move about violently: *a hot tub of churning water* WORD ORIGIN Old English *ciern*

churn out *vb informal* to produce (something) rapidly and in large numbers

chute¹ (**shoot**) *n* a steep sloping channel or passage down which things may be dropped WORD ORIGIN Old French *cheoite* fallen

chute² *n informal* short for **parachute**

chutney *n* a pickle of Indian origin, made from fruit, vinegar, spices, and sugar: *mango chutney* WORD ORIGIN Hindi *catni*

chutzpah (**hoots**-pa) *n informal* unashamed self-confidence; impudence WORD ORIGIN Yiddish

chyle *n* a milky fluid formed in the small intestine during digestion WORD ORIGIN Greek *khulos* juice

chyme *n* the thick fluid mass of partially digested food that leaves the stomach WORD ORIGIN Greek *khumos* juice

chypre (**sheep**-ra) *n* a perfume made from sandalwood WORD ORIGIN French: Cyprus

Ci curie

CI Channel Islands

CIA Central Intelligence Agency; a US bureau responsible for espionage and intelligence activities

ciabatta (cha-**bat**-ta) *n* a type of bread made with olive oil WORD ORIGIN Italian: slipper

cicada (sik-**kah**-da) *n* a large broad insect, found in hot countries, that makes a high-pitched drone WORD ORIGIN Latin

cicatrix (**sik**-a-trix) *n, pl* **cicatrices** (sik-a-**trice**-eez) the tissue that forms in a wound during healing; scar WORD ORIGIN Latin: scar

cicerone (siss-a-**rone**-ee) *n, pl* **-nes** or **-ni** *literary* a person who guides and informs sightseers WORD ORIGIN after *Cicero*, Roman orator

CID (in Britain) Criminal Investigation Department; the detective division of a police force

cider *n* an alcoholic drink made from fermented apple juice WORD ORIGIN Hebrew *shēkhār* strong drink

cigar *n* a tube-like roll of cured tobacco leaves for smoking WORD ORIGIN Spanish *cigarro*

cigarette *n* a thin roll of shredded tobacco in thin paper, for smoking WORD ORIGIN French: a little cigar

cilantro (sil-**lan**-tro) *n chiefly US & Canad* a European plant, cultivated for its aromatic seeds and leaves, used in flavouring foods. Also called: **coriander** WORD ORIGIN Spanish

cilium *n, pl* **cilia** *biol* **1** any of the short threads projecting from a cell or organism, whose rhythmic beating causes movement **2** an eyelash **ciliary** *adj* WORD ORIGIN Latin

C in C *mil* Commander in Chief

cinch (**sinch**) *n* **1** *informal* an easy task **2** *slang* a certainty WORD ORIGIN Spanish *cincha* saddle girth

cinchona (sing-**kone**-a) *n* **1** a South American tree or shrub with medicinal bark **2** its dried bark which yields quinine **3** a drug made from cinchona bark WORD ORIGIN after the Countess of *Chinchón*

cincture *n literary* something, such as a belt or girdle, that goes around another thing WORD ORIGIN Latin *cingere* to gird

cinder *n* **1** a piece of material that will not burn, left after burning coal or wood **2 cinders** ashes WORD ORIGIN Old English *sinder*

Cinderella *n* a poor, neglected, or unsuccessful person or thing WORD ORIGIN after *Cinderella*, the heroine of a fairy tale

cine camera *n* a camera for taking moving pictures

cinema *n* **1** a place designed for showing films **2 the cinema a** the art or business of making films **b** films collectively **cinematic** *adj* WORD ORIGIN shortened from *cinematograph*

cinematograph *n chiefly Brit* a combined camera, printer, and projector **cinematographer** *n* **cinematographic** *adj* WORD ORIGIN Greek *kinēma* motion + -GRAPH

cinematography *n* the technique of making films: *he won an Oscar for his stunning cinematography*

cineraria *n* a garden plant with daisy-like flowers WORD ORIGIN Latin *cinis* ashes

cinerarium *n, pl* **-raria** a place for keeping the ashes of the dead after cremation **cinerary** *adj* WORD ORIGIN Latin *cinerarius* relating to ashes

cinnabar *n* **1** a heavy red mineral containing mercury **2** a large red-and-black European moth WORD ORIGIN Greek *kinnabari*

cinnamon *n* the spice obtained from the aromatic bark of a tropical Asian tree WORD ORIGIN Hebrew *qinnamown*

cinquefoil *n* **1** a plant with five-lobed compound leaves **2** an ornamental

How does a word get into a dictionary?

One of the questions most frequently asked of lexicographers (after the one about whether that word beginning with F is in your dictionary) is 'How does a word find its way into the dictionary?' After all, not every word that has ever been invented or written down appears in every English dictionary. There must be some process that determines which words are included and at what point a newly coined word is considered to have become part of the language.

There is no central body that rules on whether a word is officially a part of the English language, and so each dictionary publisher is free to make its own decisions about which words to include and which to exclude. There can be a considerable difference in the policies adopted, with some publishers being more conservative while others are keen to add as many current terms as possible. Moreover, not every dictionary covers the same number of words, so the criteria for inclusion will be more rigorous for some books than for others: you would not expect to find as many words in a pocket-sized dictionary as you would in one that costs three times as much and needs both hands to pick it up.

For a new word to be considered for inclusion in a dictionary it must first come to the attention of the editors, and this can happen in three main ways. Firstly, most dictionaries have some sort of language-monitoring programme in which people scan the media for words that may be entering use. Words which are not currently included in the dictionary are then fed into a database. Secondly, computers can be used to scan large chunks of electronically stored text and check against the dictionary for words that are not already included. This sort of computer program is called a 'monitor corpus', and can process text more quickly and accurately than a human reader, although it is no good at judging how worthwhile the results of its searches are. Finally, new words are sometimes submitted to dictionaries by members of the public who are keen to see a favourite word given the stamp of authenticity that a dictionary provides. (Words in the latter category may be treated with some caution by dictionary editors. Reasons such as 'I made this word up and all my friends find it highly amusing' or 'It would help me score highly at Scrabble' are unlikely to cut much ice. Nevertheless, editors are always on the lookout for genuine new words.)

When a new edition of a dictionary is due to be published, editors will review the words that have been suggested by these sources and look for objective evidence to determine which words are most deserving of inclusion. This objective evidence is provided by a large database of language called a 'corpus', which contains millions or even billions of words taken from a balanced range of sources – from spoken and written language, from different English-speaking regions, and covering different subject areas. Editors can see how many times a word shows up in a corpus and what sort of places these are. By and large, the more times a word appears, the more likely it is to go into the dictionary, but editors will also take account of such matters as whether the word is restricted to a particular group of speakers or a particular window in time. Words whose use is restricted in this way may need a higher overall number of occurrences to be considered worth adding.

After making their selection of words, editors will then compile dictionary entries for these, including information on how the word is pronounced, to what grammatical class it belongs, what its origins are, and what it means, as well as any other information that a user may find necessary. The word is then ready to take its place in the published work alongside the other members of the lexicon.

Yet even after a word has been included in a dictionary, it may not stay there for ever. Editors are constantly seeking to ensure that their dictionary reflects current usage, and a word that turns out to be a short-lived phenomenon may be removed to help make room for the next wave of words clamouring to be allowed in.

carving in the form of five arcs arranged in a circle
WORD ORIGIN Latin *quinquefolium* plant with five leaves

Cinque Ports *pl n* an association of ports on the SE coast of England, with certain ancient duties and privileges

cipher *or* **cypher** (**sife**-er) *n* **1** a method of secret writing using substitution of letters according to a key **2** a secret message **3** the key to a secret message **4** a person or thing of no importance **5** *obsolete* the numeral zero ▷ *vb* **6** to put (a message) into secret writing
WORD ORIGIN Arabic *sifr* zero

circa (**sir**-ka) *prep* (used with a date) approximately; about: *circa 1788*
WORD ORIGIN Latin

circadian *adj* of biological processes that occur regularly at 24-hour intervals
WORD ORIGIN Latin *circa* about + *dies* day

circle *n* **1** a curved line surrounding a central point, every point of the line being the same distance from the centre **2** the figure enclosed by such a curve **3** something formed or arranged in the shape of a circle: *they ran round in little circles* **4** a group of people sharing an interest, activity, or upbringing: *his judgment is well respected in diplomatic circles* **5** *theatre* the section of seats above the main level of the auditorium **6** a process or chain of events or parts that forms a connected whole; cycle **7 come full circle** to arrive back at one's starting point ▷ *vb* **-cling, -cled 8** to move in a circle (around) **9** to enclose in a circle
WORD ORIGIN Latin *circus*

circlet *n* a small circle or ring, esp. a circular ornament worn on the head
WORD ORIGIN Old French *cerclet* little circle

circuit *n* **1** a complete route or course, esp. one that is circular or that lies around an object **2** a complete path through which an electric current can flow **3 a** a periodical journey around an area, as made by judges or salesmen **b** the places visited on such a journey **4** a motor-racing track **5** *sport* a series of tournaments in which the same players regularly take part: *the professional golf circuit* **6** a number of theatres or cinemas under one management
WORD ORIGIN Latin *circum* around + *ire* to go

circuit breaker *n* a device that stops the flow of current in an electrical circuit if there is a fault

circuitous (sir-**kew**-it-uss) *adj* indirect and lengthy: *a circuitous route*

circuitry (**sir**-kit-tree) *n* **1** the design of an electrical circuit **2** the system of circuits used in an electronic device

circular *adj* **1** of or in the shape of a circle **2** travelling in a circle **3** (of an argument) not valid because a statement is used to prove the conclusion and the conclusion to prove the statement **4** (of letters or announcements) intended for general distribution ▷ *n* **5** a letter or advertisement sent to a large number of people at the same time **circularity** *n*

circularize *or* **-ise** *vb* **-izing, -ized** *or* **-ising, -ised** to distribute circulars to

circular saw *n* a power-driven saw in which a circular disc with a toothed edge is rotated at high speed

circulate *vb* **-lating, -lated 1** to send, go, or pass from place to place or person to person: *rumours were circulating that he was about to resign* **2** to move through a circuit or system, returning to the starting point: *regular exercise keeps the blood circulating around the body* **3** to move around the guests at a party, talking to different people: *it wasn't like her not to circulate among all the guests* **circulatory** *adj*
WORD ORIGIN Latin *circulari*

circulation *n* **1** the flow of blood from the heart through the arteries, and then back through the veins to the heart, where the cycle is renewed **2** the number of copies of a newspaper or magazine that are sold **3** the distribution of newspapers or magazines **4** sending or moving around: *the circulation of air* **5 in circulation a** (of currency) being used by the public **b** (of people) active in a social or business context

circum- *prefix* around; on all sides: *circumlocution*
WORD ORIGIN Latin

circumcise *vb* **-cising, -cised 1** to remove the foreskin of (a male) **2** to cut or remove the clitoris of (a female) **3** to perform such an operation as a religious rite on (someone) **circumcision** *n*
WORD ORIGIN Latin CIRCUM- + *caedere* to cut

circumference *n* **1** the boundary of a specific area or figure, esp. of a circle **2** the distance round this **circumferential** *adj*
WORD ORIGIN Latin CIRCUM- + *ferre* to bear

circumflex *n* a mark (^) placed over a vowel to show that it is pronounced in a particular way, for instance as a long vowel in French
WORD ORIGIN Latin CIRCUM- + *flectere* to bend

circumlocution *n* **1** an indirect way of saying something **2** an indirect expression **circumlocutory** *adj*

circumnavigate *vb* **-gating, -gated** to sail, fly, or walk right around **circumnavigation** *n*

circumscribe *vb* **-scribing, -scribed 1** *formal* to limit or restrict within certain boundaries: *the President's powers are circumscribed by the Constitution* **2** *geom* to draw a geometric figure around (another figure) so that the two are in contact but do not intersect **circumscription** *n*
WORD ORIGIN Latin CIRCUM- + *scribere* to write

circumspect *adj* cautious and careful not to take risks **circumspection** *n* **circumspectly** *adv*
WORD ORIGIN Latin CIRCUM- + *specere* to look

circumstance *n* **1** an occurrence or condition that accompanies or influences a person or event **2** unplanned events and situations which cannot be controlled: *a victim of circumstance* **3 pomp and circumstance**

formal display or ceremony **4 under** *or* **in no circumstances** in no case; never **5 under the circumstances** because of conditions
WORD ORIGIN Latin CIRCUM- + *stare* to stand

circumstantial *adj* **1** (of evidence) strongly suggesting something but not proving it **2** fully detailed

circumstantiate *vb* **-ating, -ated** to prove by giving details

circumvent *vb* *formal* **1** to avoid or get round (a rule, restriction, etc.) **2** to outwit (a person) **circumvention** *n*
WORD ORIGIN Latin CIRCUM- + *venire* to come

circus *n, pl* **-cuses 1** a travelling company of entertainers such as acrobats, clowns, trapeze artists, and trained animals **2** a public performance given by such a company **3** *Brit* an open place in a town where several streets meet **4** *informal* a hectic or well-published situation: *her second marriage turned into a media circus* **5** (in ancient Rome) an open-air stadium for chariot races or public games **6** a travelling group of professional sportsmen: *the Formula One circus*
WORD ORIGIN Greek *kirkos* ring

cirque (sirk) *n* a steep-sided semicircular hollow found in mountainous areas

cirrhosis (sir-**roh**-siss) *n* a chronic progressive disease of the liver, often caused by drinking too much alcohol
WORD ORIGIN Greek *kirrhos* orange-coloured

cirrocumulus (sirr-oh-**kew**-myew-luss) *n, pl* **-li** (-lie) a high cloud of ice crystals grouped into small separate globular masses

cirrostratus (sirr-oh-**strah**-tuss) *n, pl* **-ti** (-tie) a uniform layer of cloud above about 6000 metres

cirrus *n, pl* **-ri 1** a thin wispy cloud found at high altitudes **2** a plant tendril **3** a slender tentacle in certain sea creatures
WORD ORIGIN Latin: curl

CIS Commonwealth of Independent States

cisalpine *adj* on this (the southern) side of the Alps, as viewed from Rome

cisco *n, pl* **-coes** *or* **-cos** a whitefish, esp. the lake herring of cold deep lakes of North America
WORD ORIGIN from a Native American language

cissy *n, pl* **-sies**, *adj* same as **sissy**

Cistercian *n* **1** a Christian monk or nun belonging to an especially strict Benedictine order ▷ *adj* **2** of or relating to this order
WORD ORIGIN Cîteaux, original home of the order

cistern *n* **1** a water tank, esp. one which holds water for flushing a toilet **2** an underground reservoir
WORD ORIGIN Latin *cista* box

citadel *n* a fortress in a city
WORD ORIGIN Latin *civitas*

citation *n* **1** an official commendation or award, esp. for bravery **2** the quoting of a book or author **3** a quotation

139 | cite – clan

cite vb **citing, cited 1** to quote or refer to (a passage, book, or author) **2** to bring forward as proof **3** to summon to appear before a court of law **4** to mention or commend (someone) for outstanding bravery **5** to enumerate: *the president cited the wonders of the American family*
WORD ORIGIN Old French *citer* to summon

citified adj *often disparaging* having the customs, manners, or dress of city people

citizen n **1** a native or naturalized member of a state or nation **2** an inhabitant of a city or town

citizenry n citizens collectively

Citizens' Band n a range of radio frequencies for use by the public for private communication

citizenship n the condition or status of a citizen, with its rights and duties

citrate n any salt or ester of citric acid

citric adj of or derived from citrus fruits or citric acid

citric acid n a weak acid found especially in citrus fruits and used as a flavouring (E330)

citron n **1** a lemon-like fruit of a small Asian tree **2** the candied rind of this fruit, for decorating foods
WORD ORIGIN Latin *citrus* citrus tree

citronella n **1** a tropical Asian grass with lemon-scented leaves **2** the aromatic oil obtained from this grass

citrus fruit n juicy, sharp-tasting fruit such as oranges, lemons, or limes
WORD ORIGIN Latin *citrus* citrus tree

city n, pl **cities 1** any large town **2** (in Britain) a town that has received this title from the Crown **3** the people of a city collectively **4** (in the US and Canada) a large town with its own government established by charter from the state or provincial government
WORD ORIGIN Latin *civis* citizen

City n **the City** Brit **1** the area in central London in which the United Kingdom's major financial business is transacted **2** the various financial institutions in this area

city editor n **1** Brit (on a newspaper) the editor in charge of business news **2** US & Canad (on a newspaper) the editor in charge of local news

city-state n *ancient history* a state consisting of a sovereign city and its dependencies

civet (**siv**-vit) n **1** a spotted catlike mammal of Africa and S Asia **2** the musky fluid produced by this animal, used in perfumes
WORD ORIGIN Arabic *zabād* civet perfume

civic adj of a city or citizens **civically** adv

civic centre n Brit & NZ a complex of public buildings, including recreational facilities and offices of local government

civics n the study of the rights and responsibilities of citizenship

civil adj **1** of or occurring within the state or between citizens: *civil unrest* **2** of or relating to the citizen as an individual: *civil rights* **3** not part of the military,

legal, or religious structures of a country: *civil aviation* **4** polite or courteous: *he seemed very civil and listened politely* **civilly** adv
WORD ORIGIN Latin *civis* citizen

civil defence n the organizing of civilians to deal with enemy attacks and natural disasters

civil disobedience n a nonviolent protest, such as a refusal to obey laws or pay taxes

civil engineer n a person qualified to design and construct public works, such as roads or bridges **civil engineering** n

civilian n **1** a person who is not a member of the armed forces or police ▷ adj **2** not relating to the armed forces or police: *civilian clothes*

civility n, pl **-ties 1** polite or courteous behaviour **2 civilities** polite words or actions

civilization or **-lisation** n **1** the total culture and way of life of a particular people, nation, region, or period **2** a human society that has a complex cultural, political, and legal organization **3** the races collectively who have achieved such a state **4** cities or populated areas, as contrasted with sparsely inhabited areas **5** intellectual, cultural, and moral refinement

civilize or **-lise** vb **-lizing, -lized** or **-lising, -lised 1** to bring out of barbarism into a state of civilization **2** to refine, educate, or enlighten **civilized** or **-lised** adj

civil law n **1** the law of a state, relating to private and civilian affairs **2** a system of law based on that of ancient Rome

civil liberties pl n a person's rights to freedom of speech and action

civil list n (in Britain) the annual amount given by Parliament to the royal household and the royal family

civil marriage n *law* a marriage performed by an official other than a clergyman

civil partnership n a legal union, similar to a marriage, between two people of the same sex

civil rights pl n the personal rights of the individual citizen to have equal treatment and equal opportunities

civil servant n a member of the civil service

civil service n the service responsible for the public administration of the government of a country

civil war n war between people of the same country

civvies pl n Brit, Austral, & NZ slang civilian clothes as opposed to uniform

civvy street n *slang* civilian life

CJD Creutzfeldt-Jakob disease: a fatal virus disease that affects the central nervous system

cl centilitre

Cl *chem* chlorine

clack n **1** the sound made by two hard objects striking each other ▷ vb **2** to make this sound
WORD ORIGIN imitative

clad vb a past of **clothe**

cladding n **1** the material used to cover the outside of a building **2** a protective metal coating attached to another metal
WORD ORIGIN special use of CLAD

cladistics n a method of grouping animals by measurable likenesses
WORD ORIGIN Greek *klados* branch

claim vb **1** to assert as a fact: *he had claimed to be too ill to return* **2** to demand as a right or as one's property: *you can claim housing benefit to help pay your rent* **3** to call for or need: *this problem claims our attention* **4** to cause the death of: *violence which has claimed at least fifty lives* **5** to succeed in obtaining; win: *she claimed her fifth European tour victory with a closing round of 64* ▷ n **6** an assertion of something as true or real **7** an assertion of a right; a demand for something as due **8** a right or just title to something: *a claim to fame* **9** anything that is claimed, such as a piece of land staked out by a miner **10 a** a demand for payment in connection with an insurance policy **b** the sum of money demanded **claimant** n
WORD ORIGIN Latin *clamare* to shout

clairvoyance n the alleged power of perceiving things beyond the natural range of the senses
WORD ORIGIN French: clear-seeing

clairvoyant n **1** a person claiming to have the power to foretell future events ▷ adj **2** of or possessing clairvoyance

clam n an edible shellfish with a hinged shell. See also **clam up**
WORD ORIGIN earlier *clamshell* shell that clamps

clamber vb **1** to climb awkwardly, using hands and feet ▷ n **2** a climb performed in this manner
WORD ORIGIN probably variant of *climb*

clammy adj **-mier, -miest** unpleasantly moist and sticky **clammily** adv **clamminess** n
WORD ORIGIN Old English *clǣman* to smear

clamour or US **clamor** n **1** a loud protest **2** a loud and persistent noise or outcry ▷ vb **3 clamour for** to demand noisily **4** to make a loud noise or outcry **clamorous** adj
WORD ORIGIN Latin *clamare* to cry out

clamp[1] n **1** a mechanical device with movable jaws for holding things together tightly **2** see **wheel clamp** ▷ vb **3** to fix or fasten with a clamp **4** to immobilize (a car) by means of a wheel clamp
WORD ORIGIN Dutch or Low German *klamp*

clamp[2] n a mound of a harvested root crop, covered with straw and earth to protect it from winter weather
WORD ORIGIN Middle Dutch *klamp* heap

clamp down vb **1 clamp down on a** to become stricter about **b** to suppress (something regarded as undesirable) ▷ n **2 clampdown** a sudden restriction placed on an activity

clam up vb **clamming, clammed** *informal* to keep or become silent

clan n **1** a group of families with a common surname and a common ancestor, esp. among Scottish

Highlanders **2** an extended family related by ancestry or marriage: *America's leading political clan, the Kennedys* **3** a group of people with common characteristics, aims, or interests **clansman** *n*
WORD ORIGIN Scottish Gaelic *clann*

clandestine *adj formal* secret and concealed: *a base for clandestine activities* **clandestinely** *adv*
WORD ORIGIN Latin *clam* secretly

clang *vb* **1** to make a loud ringing noise, as metal does when it is struck ▷ *n* **2** a ringing metallic noise
WORD ORIGIN Latin *clangere*

clanger *n* **drop a clanger** *informal* to make a very noticeable mistake

clangour *or US* **clangor** *n* a loud continuous clanging sound **clangorous** *adj*
WORD ORIGIN Latin *clangor*

clank *n* **1** an abrupt harsh metallic sound ▷ *vb* **2** to make such a sound
WORD ORIGIN imitative

clannish *adj* (of a group) tending to exclude outsiders: *the villagers can be very clannish*

clap¹ *vb* **clapping, clapped** **1** to applaud by striking the palms of one's hands sharply together **2** to place or put quickly or forcibly: *in former times he would have been clapped in irons or shot* **3** to strike (a person) lightly with an open hand as in greeting **4** to make a sharp abrupt sound like two objects being struck together **5** **clap eyes on** *informal* to catch sight of ▷ *n* **6** the act or sound of clapping **7** a sharp abrupt sound, esp. of thunder **8** a light blow
WORD ORIGIN Old English *clæppan*

clap² *n slang* gonorrhoea
WORD ORIGIN Old French *clapier* brothel

clapped out *adj informal* worn out; dilapidated

clapper *n* **1** a small piece of metal hanging inside a bell, which causes it to sound when struck against the side **2** **like the clappers** *Brit informal* extremely quickly: *he left, pedalling like the clappers*

clapperboard *n* a pair of hinged boards clapped together during film shooting to help in synchronizing sound and picture

claptrap *n informal* foolish or pretentious talk: *pseudo-intellectual claptrap*

claque *n formal* **1** a group of people hired to applaud **2** a group of fawning admirers
WORD ORIGIN French *claquer* to clap

claret (klar-rit) *n* **1** a dry red wine, esp. one from Bordeaux ▷ *adj* **2** purplish-red
WORD ORIGIN Latin *clarus* clear

clarify *vb* **-fies, -fying, -fied** **1** to make or become clear or easy to understand **2** to make or become free of impurities, esp. by heating: *clarified butter* **clarification** *n*
WORD ORIGIN Latin *clarus* clear + *facere* to make

clarinet *n* a keyed woodwind instrument with a single reed **clarinettist** *n*
WORD ORIGIN French *clarinette*

clarion *n* **1** an obsolete high-pitched trumpet **2** its sound
WORD ORIGIN Latin *clarus* clear

clarion call *n* strong encouragement to do something

clarity *n* clearness
WORD ORIGIN Latin *claritas*

clash *vb* **1** to come into conflict **2** to be incompatible **3** (of dates or events) to coincide **4** (of colours or styles) to look ugly or incompatible together: *patterned fabrics which combine seemingly clashing shades to great effect* **5** to make a loud harsh sound, esp. by striking together ▷ *n* **6** a collision or conflict **7** a loud harsh noise
WORD ORIGIN imitative

clasp *n* **1** a fastening, such as a catch or hook, for holding things together **2** a firm grasp or embrace ▷ *vb* **3** to grasp or embrace tightly **4** to fasten together with a clasp
WORD ORIGIN origin unknown

clasp knife *n* a large knife with blades which fold into the handle

class *n* **1** a group of people sharing a similar social and economic position **2** the system of dividing society into such groups **3** a group of people or things sharing a common characteristic **4 a** a group of pupils or students who are taught together **b** a meeting of a group of students for tuition **5** a standard of quality or attainment: *second class* **6** *informal* excellence or elegance, esp. in dress, design, or behaviour: *a full-bodied red wine with real class* **7** *biol* one of the groups into which a phylum is divided, containing one or more orders **8** **in a class of its own** *or* **in a class by oneself** without an equal for ability, talent, etc. ▷ *adj* **9** *informal* excellent, skilful, or stylish: *a class act* ▷ *vb* **10** to place in a class
WORD ORIGIN Latin *classis* class, rank

class-conscious *adj* aware of belonging to a particular social rank

classic *adj* **1** serving as a standard or model of its kind; typical: *it is a classic symptom of iron deficiency* **2** of lasting interest or significance because of excellence: *the classic work on Central America* **3** characterized by simplicity and purity of form: *a classic suit* ▷ *n* **4** an author, artist, or work of art of the highest excellence **5** a creation or work considered as definitive
WORD ORIGIN Latin *classicus* of the first rank

classical *adj* **1** of or in a restrained conservative style: *it had been built in the 18th century in a severely classical style* **2** *music* **a** in a style or from a period marked by stability of form, intellectualism, and restraint **b** denoting serious art or music in general **3** of or influenced by ancient Greek and Roman culture **4** of the form of a language historically used for formal and literary purposes: *classical Chinese* **5** (of an education) based on the humanities and the study of Latin and Greek **classically** *adv*

classic car *n chiefly Brit* a car that is more than 25 years old

classicism *n* **1** an artistic style based on Greek and Roman models, showing emotional restraint and regularity of form **2** knowledge of the culture of ancient Greece and Rome **classicist** *n*

classics *pl n* **1** the study of ancient Greek and Roman literature and culture **2** **the classics a** those works of literature regarded as great or lasting **b** the ancient Greek and Latin languages

classification *n* **1** placing things systematically in categories **2** a division or category in a classifying system **classificatory** *adj*
WORD ORIGIN French

classified *adj* **1** arranged according to some system of classification **2** *government* (of information) not available to people outside a restricted group, esp. for reasons of national security

classify *vb* **-fies, -fying, -fied** **1** to arrange or order by classes **2** *government* to declare (information) to be officially secret **classifiable** *adj*

classless *adj* **1** not belonging to a class **2** distinguished by the absence of economic or social distinctions: *a classless society*

classmate *n* a friend or contemporary in the same class of a school

classroom *n* a room in a school where lessons take place

classy *adj* **classier, classiest** *informal* stylish and sophisticated **classiness** *n*

clatter *vb* **1** to make a rattling noise, as when hard objects hit each other ▷ *n* **2** a rattling sound or noise
WORD ORIGIN Old English *clatrung* clattering

clause *n* **1** a section of a legal document such as a will or contract **2** *grammar* a group of words, consisting of a subject and a predicate including a finite verb, that does not necessarily constitute a sentence **clausal** *adj*
WORD ORIGIN Latin *clausula* conclusion

claustrophobia *n* an abnormal fear of being in a confined space **claustrophobic** *adj*
WORD ORIGIN Latin *claustrum* cloister + -PHOBIA

clavichord *n* an early keyboard instrument with a very soft tone
WORD ORIGIN Latin *clavis* key + *chorda* string

clavicle *n* either of the two bones connecting the shoulder blades with the upper part of the breastbone; the collarbone
WORD ORIGIN Latin *clavis* key

claw *n* **1** a curved pointed nail on the foot of birds, some reptiles, and certain mammals **2** a similar part in some invertebrates, such as a crab's pincer ▷ *vb* **3** to scrape, tear, or dig with claws or nails: *she clawed his face with her fingernails* **4** to achieve (something) only after overcoming great difficulties: *he clawed his way to power and wealth; settlers attempting to claw a living from the desert*
WORD ORIGIN Old English *clawu*

claw back *vb* **1** to get back (something) with difficulty **2** to recover (a part of a grant or allowance) in the form of a tax or financial penalty

Indian English

By a conservative count, India has 415 languages. English is one of them.

After the United States, India has more English speakers than any other country – more than 90 million of them – who generally use it as a second or even third language. To them may be added many millions in Bangladesh and Pakistan, as well as millions more in other countries. The British were on the subcontinent from the seventeenth century onward as traders, colonizers, missionaries, soldiers, and administrators, culminating in the ninteenth- and twentieth-century Imperial *Raj* (reign). Even after independence in 1947, the use of English did not decline. In fact, it grew with the rise of the internet, satellite communications, and India-based call centres for foreign companies' tele-marketing and technical support.

Statistics are always in flux, and generalizations always hazardous, in the second most populous country on earth. Twenty-two Indian languages have more than a million native speakers. That fact alone guarantees that the Indian English spoken by a bilingual or multilingual person will reflect a native language, whether it be Hindi, the official, most widely spoken one or, in order of population, Bengali, Telugu, Marathi, Tamil, Urdu, and Gujarati. Though spelling usually follows British English, which also may confer social prestige on its users, Indian English differs in many ways. Its syntax, usages, and pronunciations are rich pickings for comedians though Indians also make fun of themselves, helped by the habit of using seemingly pompous formulations such as beginning a business letter with '*Respected Sir*' and ending it with '*Please do the needful*', or asking, '*What is your good name, sir?*'

Word order may appear wrenched to non-Indian ears. Some short words like *also*, *but*, and *only* may be tagged for emphasis at the end of sentences, or repeated: '*We talked about books only only.*' Like *only*, *itself* can emphasize time and place: '*Can we discuss the topic next week itself?*' A question may end, '*yes?*' '*no?*' or '*isn't it?*' To distinguish between male and female, a cousin may be a *cousin brother* or a *cousin sister*: '*He is your cousin brother, isn't it?*' Compounding words often occurs: a *time-pass* is time spent purposelessly or unexcitingly: '*That course was a real time-pass.*' Likewise, word-shortening: *enthusiasm* is *enthu*, fundamentals are *fundas*. Though Indians are no more profane than other English-speakers, *damn* is used much more frequently.

The progressive tense is much used, as in '*Chanda is wearing sari*' and '*You have seen?*' The definite or indefinite article is often dropped: '*She was often guest.*' Rhyming phrases abound, as in the title of a famous Anglo-Indian dictionary, whose shortened form was *Hobson-Jobson*. A person older than oneself may be respectfully addressed as *aunty* or *uncle*, or the suffix *–ji* or the Urdu-derived *sahib* tacked on to a name or title: '*Swami-ji*', '*Begum Sahib*'.

Hindi often intervenes, as in *wallah*, to denote an occupation or activity, as in *tiffin-wallah*, a person who delivers snacks or lunches. Indians are expert at mixing or switching from one language or social context to another. Since *since* and *for* is the same in Hindi, *since* is often used for the latter: '*I have been ill since two weeks.*' Hindi in fact has fused with English to form the hybrid language *Hinglish*, one common word of which is *yaar*, a buddy or companion. Pronunciation varies much from the north to the south but Indians, like most Canadians, generally pronounce the *r* before consonants or at the end of words. *V* and *w* often sound the same. They often pronounce weak vowels as full ones, and stress the syllable rather than longer rhythmic units, lending speech a sing-song quality.

Outside the country, India has loaned many words to standard English. From Hindi: *shampoo*. From Malayalam: *ginger*. From Sanskrit: *guru, yoga, pariah*. From Tamil: *curry*. So it goes: *bamboo, mango, bungalow, chintz, juggernaut, pundit* ... Culturally, international enthusiasm for Indian food has made terms for breads and snacks (*chapatti, samosas, pakoras*), spice mixtures (*masala*), and *tandoori* chicken familiar to restaurant-goers and home cooks alike. The fame of the Indian movie industry has also grown mightily, as witness *Bollywood*, which blends *Bombay* and *Hollywood*. Bombay has officially been renamed *Mumbai*, taken from Sanskrit and Marathi words. The new name may take a while to catch on.

clay *n* **1** a very fine-grained earth, soft when moist and hardening when baked, used to make bricks and pottery **2** earth or mud **3** *poetic* the material of the human body **clayey, clayish,** *or* **claylike** *adj*
WORD ORIGIN Old English *clæg*

claymore *n* a large two-edged broadsword used formerly by Scottish Highlanders
WORD ORIGIN Gaelic *claidheamh mōr* great sword

clay pigeon *n* a disc of baked clay hurled into the air from a machine as a target for shooting

Clayton's *adj Austral & NZ informal* acting as an imitation or substitute: *this latest ploy is simply a Clayton's resignation*
WORD ORIGIN from the trademark of a non-alcoholic drink marketed as 'the drink you have when you're not having a drink'

CLC Canadian Labour Congress

clean *adj* **1** free from dirt or impurities: *clean water* **2** habitually hygienic and neat **3** morally sound: *clean living* **4** without objectionable language or obscenity: *good clean fun* **5** without anything in it or on it: *a clean sheet of paper* **6** causing little contamination or pollution: *rape seed oil may provide a clean alternative to petrol* **7** recently washed; fresh **8** thorough or complete: *a clean break with the past* **9** skilful and done without fumbling; dexterous: *a clean catch* **10** *sport* played fairly and without fouls **11** free from dishonesty or corruption: *clean government* **12** simple and streamlined in design: *the clean lines and colourful simplicity of these ceramics* **13** (esp. of a driving licence) showing or having no record of offences **14** *slang* **a** innocent **b** not carrying illegal drugs, weapons, etc. ▷ *vb* **15** to make or become free of dirt: *he wanted to help me clean the room* ▷ *adv* **16** in a clean way **17** *not standard* completely: *she clean forgot to face the camera* **18** **come clean** *informal* to make a revelation or confession ▷ *n* **19** the act or an instance of cleaning: *the fridge could do with a clean* ▸ See also **clean up**
WORD ORIGIN Old English *clǣne*

clean-cut *adj* **1** clearly outlined **2** wholesome in appearance

cleaner *n* **1** a person, device, or substance that removes dirt **2** a shop or firm that provides a dry-cleaning service **3** **take someone to the cleaners** *informal* to rob or defraud someone

cleanly (kleen-lee) *adv* **1** easily or smoothly **2** in a fair manner ▷ *adj* (klen-lee), **-lier, -liest 3** habitually clean or neat **cleanliness** *n*

cleanse *vb* **cleansing, cleansed 1** to remove dirt from **2** to remove evil or guilt from **cleanser** *n*

clean-shaven *adj* (of men) having the facial hair shaved off

clean sheet *n sport* an instance of conceding no goals or points in a match

clean-tech *informal adj* **1** using clean technology ▷ *n* **2** same as **clean technology**

clean technology *n* techniques that minimize the damage caused to the environment as a result of manufacturing processes

clean up *vb* **1** to make (something) free from dirt **2** to make tidy or presentable **3** to rid (a place) of undesirable people or conditions **4** *informal* to make a great profit ▷ *n* **cleanup 5** the process of cleaning up

clear *adj* **1** free from doubt or confusion: *clear evidence of police thuggery* **2** certain in the mind; sure: *I am still not clear about what they can and cannot do* **3** easy to see or hear; distinct **4** perceptive; alert: *clear thinking* **5** evident or obvious: *it is not clear how he died* **6** transparent: *clear glass doors* **7** free from darkness or obscurity; bright **8** (of sounds or the voice) not harsh or hoarse **9** even and pure in tone or colour **10** free of obstruction; open: *a clear path runs under the trees* **11** (of weather) free from dullness or clouds **12** without blemish or defect: *a clear skin* **13** free of suspicion, guilt, or blame: *a clear conscience* **14** (of money) without deduction; net **15** free from debt or obligation **16** without qualification or limitation; complete: *a clear lead* ▷ *adv* **17** in a clear or distinct manner **18** completely **19** **clear of** out of the way of: *once we were clear of the harbour we headed east* ▷ *n* **20** **in the clear** free of suspicion, guilt, or blame ▷ *vb* **21** to free from doubt or confusion **22** to rid of objects or obstructions **23** to make or form (a path) by removing obstructions **24** to move or pass by or over without contact: *he cleared the fence easily* **25** to make or become free from darkness or obscurity **26** to rid (one's throat) of phlegm **27 a** (of the weather) to become free from dullness, fog, or rain **b** (of mist or fog) to disappear **28** (of a cheque) to pass through one's bank and be charged against one's account **29** to free from impurity or blemish **30** to obtain or give (clearance) **31** to prove (someone) innocent of a crime or mistake **32** to permit (someone) to see or handle classified information **33** to make or gain (money) as profit **34** to discharge or settle (a debt) **35** **clear the air** to sort out a misunderstanding ▸ See also **clear away, clear off,** etc. **clearly** *adv*
WORD ORIGIN Latin *clarus*

clearance *n* **1** the act of clearing: *slum clearance* **2** permission for a vehicle or passengers to proceed **3** official permission to have access to secret information or areas **4** space between two parts in motion

clearance sale *n* a sale in which a shop sells off unwanted goods at reduced prices

clear away *vb* to remove (dishes, etc.) from the table after a meal

clear-cut *adj* **1** easy to distinguish or understand: *there is no clear-cut distinction between safe and unsafe areas of the city* **2** clearly outlined

clearing *n* an area with few or no trees or shrubs in wooded or overgrown land

clearing bank *n* (in Britain) any bank that makes use of the central clearing house in London

clearing house *n* **1** *banking* an institution where cheques and other commercial papers drawn on member banks are cancelled against each other so that only net balances are payable **2** a central agency for the collection and distribution of information or materials

clear off *vb informal* to go away: often used as a command

clear out *vb* **1** to remove and sort the contents of (a room or container) **2** *informal* to go away: often used as a command ▷ *n* **clear-out 3** an act of clearing someone or something out

clear up *vb* **1** to put (a place or thing that is disordered) in order **2** to explain or solve (a mystery or misunderstanding) **3** (of an illness) to become better **4** (of the weather) to become brighter

clearway *n Austral & Brit* a stretch of road on which motorists may stop only in an emergency

cleat *n* **1** a wedge-shaped block attached to a structure to act as a support **2** a piece of wood or iron with two projecting ends round which ropes are fastened
WORD ORIGIN Germanic

cleavage *n* **1** the space between a woman's breasts, as revealed by a low-cut dress **2** a division or split **3** (of crystals) the act of splitting or the tendency to split along definite planes so as to make smooth surfaces

cleave¹ *vb* **cleaving; cleft, cleaved,** *or* **clove; cleft, cleaved,** *or* **cloven 1** to split apart: *cleave the stone along the fissures* **2** to make by or as if by cutting: *a two-lane highway that cleaved its way through the northern extremities of the Everglades*
WORD ORIGIN Old English *clēofan*

cleave² *vb* **cleaving, cleaved** to cling or stick: *a farmhouse cleaved to the hill*
WORD ORIGIN Old English *cleofian*

cleaver *n* a heavy knife with a square blade, used for chopping meat

cleavers *n* a plant with small white flowers and sticky fruits
WORD ORIGIN Old English *clīfe*

clef *n music* a symbol placed at the beginning of each stave indicating the pitch of the music written after it
WORD ORIGIN French

cleft *n* **1** a narrow opening in a rock **2** an indentation or split ▷ *adj* **3** **in a cleft stick** in a very difficult position ▷ *vb* **4** a past of **cleave¹**

cleft palate *n* a congenital crack in the mid line of the hard palate

clematis *n* a climbing plant grown for its large colourful flowers
WORD ORIGIN Greek *klēma* vine twig

clemency *n* mercy

clement *adj* **1** (of the weather) mild **2** merciful
WORD ORIGIN Latin *clemens* mild

clementine *n* a citrus fruit resembling a tangerine
WORD ORIGIN French

clench *vb* **1** to close or squeeze together (the teeth or a fist) tightly **2** to grasp or grip firmly ▷ *n* **3** a firm grasp or grip
WORD ORIGIN Old English *beclencan*

clerestory (clear-store-ee) *n, pl* **-ries** a row of windows in the upper part of the wall of the nave of a church above the roof of the aisle **clerestoried** *adj*
WORD ORIGIN clear + storey

clergy *n, pl* **-gies** priests and ministers as a group
WORD ORIGIN see CLERK

clergyman *n, pl* **-men** a member of the clergy

cleric *n* a member of the clergy

clerical *adj* **1** of clerks or office work: *a clerical job* **2** of or associated with the clergy: *a Lebanese clerical leader*

clerical collar *n* a stiff white collar with no opening at the front, worn by the clergy in certain Churches

clerihew *n* a form of comic or satiric verse, consisting of two couplets and containing the name of a well-known person
WORD ORIGIN after E. *Clerihew* Bentley, who invented it

clerk *n* **1** an employee in an office, bank, or court who keeps records, files, and accounts **2** *US & Canad* a hotel receptionist **3** *archaic* a scholar ▷ *vb* **4** to work as a clerk **clerkship** *n*
WORD ORIGIN Greek *klērikos* cleric, from *klēros* heritage

clerk of works *n* an employee who oversees building work

clever *adj* **1** displaying sharp intelligence or mental alertness **2** skilful with one's hands **3** smart in a superficial way **4** *Brit informal* sly or cunning **cleverly** *adv* **cleverness** *n*
WORD ORIGIN Middle English *cliver*

clianthus *n* a plant of Australia and New Zealand with clusters of ornamental scarlet flowers
WORD ORIGIN probably from Greek *kleos* glory + *anthos* flower

cliché (klee-shay) *n* an expression or idea that is no longer effective because of overuse **clichéd** *or* **cliché'd** *adj*
WORD ORIGIN French

click *n* **1** a short light often metallic sound ▷ *vb* **2** to make a clicking sound: *cameras clicked and whirred* **3** Also: **click on** *computers* to press and release (a button on a mouse) or select (a particular function) by pressing and releasing a button on a mouse **4** *informal* to become suddenly clear: *it wasn't until I saw the photograph that everything clicked into place* **5** *slang* (of two people) to get on well together: *I met him at a dinner party and we clicked straight away* **6** *slang* to be a great success: *the film cost so much that if it hadn't clicked at the box office we'd have been totally wiped out*
WORD ORIGIN imitative

client *n* **1** someone who uses the services of a professional person or organization **2** a customer **3** *computers* a program or work station that requests data from a server
WORD ORIGIN Latin *cliens* retainer

clientele (klee-on-tell) *n* customers or clients collectively

cliff *n* a steep rock face, esp. along the seashore
WORD ORIGIN Old English *clif*

cliffhanger *n* a film, game, etc. which is exciting and full of suspense because its outcome is uncertain **cliffhanging** *adj*

climacteric *n* **1** same as **menopause** **2** the period in the life of a man corresponding to the menopause, during which sexual drive and fertility diminish
WORD ORIGIN Greek *klimakter* rung of a ladder

climate *n* **1** the typical weather conditions of an area **2** an area with a particular kind of climate **3** a prevailing trend: *the current economic climate* **climatic** *adj* **climatically** *adv*
WORD ORIGIN Greek *klima* inclination, region

USAGE
Climatic is sometimes wrongly used where *climactic* is meant. *Climatic* should be used to talk about things relating to climate; *climactic* is used to describe something which forms a climax.

climax *n* **1** the most intense or highest point of an experience or of a series of events: *a striking climax to the year's efforts to promote tourism* **2** a decisive moment in a dramatic or other work: *the film has a climax set atop a gale-swept lighthouse* **3** an orgasm ▷ *vb* **4** *not standard* to reach or bring to a climax **climactic** *adj*
WORD ORIGIN Greek *klimax* ladder

climb *vb* **1** to go up or ascend (stairs, a mountain, etc.) **2** to move or go with difficulty: *she climbed through a window* **3** to rise to a higher point or intensity: *I grew increasingly delirious as my temperature climbed* **4** to increase in value or amount: *the number could eventually climb to half-a-million* **5** to ascend in social position: *he climbed the ranks of the organization* **6** (of plants) to grow upwards by twining, using tendrils or suckers **7** to incline or slope upwards: *the road climbed up through the foothills* **8** **climb into** *informal* to put on or get into: *I climbed into the van* ▷ *n* **9** the act or an instance of climbing **10** a place or thing to be climbed, esp. a route in mountaineering **climbable** *adj* **climber** *n* **climbing** *n, adj*
WORD ORIGIN Old English *climban*

climb down *vb* **1** to retreat (from an opinion or position) **2** **climb-down** **2** a retreat from an opinion or position

clime *n* *poetic* a region or its climate

clinch *vb* **1** to settle (an argument or agreement) decisively **2** to secure (a nail) by bending the protruding point over **3** to engage in a clinch, as in boxing or wrestling ▷ *n* **4** the act of clinching **5** *boxing, wrestling* a movement in which one or both competitors hold on to the other to avoid punches or regain wind **6** *slang* a lovers' embrace
WORD ORIGIN variant of *clench*

clincher *n* *informal* something decisive, such as a fact, argument, or point scored

cling *vb* **clinging**, **clung** **1** (often foll. by *to*) to hold fast or stick closely (to something) **2** to be emotionally overdependent on **3** to continue to do or believe in: *he clings to the belief that people are capable of change* **clinging** *or* **clingy** *adj*
WORD ORIGIN Old English *clingan*

clingfilm *n* *Brit* a thin polythene material used for wrapping food

clinic *n* **1** a place in which outpatients are given medical treatment or advice **2** a similar place staffed by specialist physicians or surgeons: *I have an antenatal clinic on Friday afternoon* **3** *Brit & NZ* a private hospital or nursing home **4** the teaching of medicine to students at the bedside
WORD ORIGIN Greek *klinē* bed

clinical *adj* **1** of or relating to the observation and treatment of patients directly: *clinical trials of a new drug* **2** of or relating to a clinic **3** logical and unemotional: *they have a somewhat clinical attitude to their children's upbringing* **4** (of a room or buildings) plain, simple, and usually unattractive **clinically** *adv*

clinical thermometer *n* a thermometer for measuring the temperature of the body

clink¹ *vb* **1** to make a light sharp metallic sound ▷ *n* **2** such a sound
WORD ORIGIN perhaps from Middle Dutch *klinken*

clink² *n* *slang* prison
WORD ORIGIN after *Clink*, a former prison in London

clinker *n* the fused coal left over in a fire or furnace
WORD ORIGIN Dutch *klinker* a type of brick

clinker-built *adj* (of a boat or ship) with a hull made from overlapping planks
WORD ORIGIN obsolete *clinker* a nailing together, probably from *clinch*

Clio *n* *Greek myth* the Muse of history

clip¹ *vb* **clipping**, **clipped** **1** to cut or trim with scissors or shears **2** to remove a short section from (a film or newspaper) **3** *Austral & Brit* to punch a hole in (something, esp. a ticket) **4** *informal* to strike with a sharp, often slanting, blow **5** to shorten (a word) **6** *slang* to obtain (money) by cheating ▷ *n* **7** the act of clipping **8** a short extract from a film **9** something that has been clipped **10** *informal* a sharp, often slanting, blow: *a clip on the ear* **11** *informal* speed: *proceeding at a smart clip* **12** *Austral & NZ* the total quantity of wool shorn, as in one place or season
WORD ORIGIN Old Norse *klippa* to cut

clip² *n* **1** a device for attaching or holding things together **2** an article of jewellery that can be clipped onto a dress or hat **3** short for **paperclip** or **cartridge clip** ▷ *vb* **clipping**, **clipped** **4** to attach or hold together with a clip
WORD ORIGIN Old English *clyppan* to embrace

clipboard *n* a portable writing board with a clip at the top for holding paper

clip joint *n* *slang* a nightclub in which customers are overcharged

clipped *adj* (of speech) abrupt, clearly pronounced, and using as few words as possible

clipper *n* a fast commercial sailing ship

clippers *pl n* a tool used for clipping and cutting

clippie *n* *Brit old-fashioned informal* a bus conductress

clipping *n* something cut out, esp. an article from a newspaper

clique (kleek) *n* a small exclusive group of friends or associates **cliquey, cliquy,** or **cliquish** *adj*
WORD ORIGIN French

clit *n taboo Slang* short for **clitoris**

clitoris (klit-or-riss) *n* a small sexually sensitive organ at the front of the vulva **clitoral** *adj*
WORD ORIGIN Greek *kleitoris*

Cllr councillor

cloaca (kloh-ake-a) *n, pl* **-cae** a cavity in most animals, except higher mammals, into which the alimentary canal and the genital and urinary ducts open
WORD ORIGIN Latin: sewer

cloak *n* 1 a loose sleeveless outer garment, fastened at the throat and falling straight from the shoulders 2 something that covers or conceals ▷ *vb* 3 to hide or disguise 4 to cover with or as if with a cloak
WORD ORIGIN Medieval Latin *clocca* cloak, bell

cloak-and-dagger *adj* of or involving mystery and secrecy

cloakroom *n* 1 a room in which coats may be left temporarily 2 *Brit, euphemistic* a toilet

clobber¹ *vb informal* 1 to batter 2 to defeat utterly 3 to criticize severely
WORD ORIGIN origin unknown

clobber² *n Brit, Austral, & NZ informal* personal belongings, such as clothes
WORD ORIGIN origin unknown

cloche (klosh) *n* 1 *Brit, Austral, & NZ* a small glass or plastic cover for protecting young plants 2 a woman's close-fitting hat
WORD ORIGIN French: bell

clock¹ *n* 1 a device for showing the time, either through pointers that revolve over a numbered dial, or through a display of figures 2 a device with a dial for recording or measuring 3 the downy head of a dandelion that has gone to seed 4 short for **time clock** 5 *informal* same as **speedometer** or **mileometer** 6 *Brit slang* the face 7 **round the clock** all day and all night ▷ *vb* 8 to record (time) with a stopwatch, esp. in the calculation of speed 9 *Brit, Austral, & NZ slang* to strike, esp. on the face or head 10 *informal* to turn back the mileometer on (a car) illegally so that its mileage appears less 11 *Brit slang* to see or notice
WORD ORIGIN Medieval Latin *clocca* bell

clock² *n* an ornamental design on the side of a sock
WORD ORIGIN origin unknown

clock in *or* **on** *vb* to register one's arrival at work on an automatic time recorder

clock out *or* **off** *vb* to register one's departure from work on an automatic time recorder

clock up *vb* to record or reach (a total): *he has now clocked up over 500 games for the club*

clockwise *adv, adj* in the direction in which the hands of a clock rotate

clockwork *n* 1 a mechanism similar to that of a spring-driven clock, as in a wind-up toy 2 **like clockwork** with complete regularity and precision

clod *n* 1 a lump of earth or clay 2 *Brit, Austral, & NZ* a dull or stupid person **cloddish** *adj*
WORD ORIGIN Old English

clodhopper *n informal* 1 a clumsy person 2 **clodhoppers** large heavy shoes

clog *vb* **clogging, clogged** 1 to obstruct or become obstructed with thick or sticky matter 2 to encumber 3 to stick in a mass ▷ *n* 4 a wooden or wooden-soled shoe
WORD ORIGIN origin unknown

cloisonné (klwah-zon-nay) *n* a design made by filling in a wire outline with coloured enamel
WORD ORIGIN French

cloister *n* 1 a covered pillared walkway within a religious building 2 a place of religious seclusion, such as a monastery ▷ *vb* 3 to confine or seclude in or as if in a monastery
WORD ORIGIN Medieval Latin *claustrum* monastic cell, from Latin *claudere* to close

cloistered *adj* sheltered or protected

clomp *n, vb* same as **clump** (senses 2, 3)

clone *n* 1 a group of organisms or cells of the same genetic constitution that have been reproduced asexually from a single plant or animal 2 *informal* a person who closely resembles another 3 *slang* a mobile phone that has been given the electronic identity of an existing mobile phone, so that calls made on it are charged to that owner ▷ *vb* **cloning, cloned** 4 to produce as a clone 5 *informal* to produce near copies of (a person) 6 *slang* to give (a mobile phone) the electronic identity of an existing mobile phone so that calls made on it are charged to that owner **cloning** *n*
WORD ORIGIN Greek *klōn* twig, shoot

clonk *vb* 1 to make a loud dull thud 2 *informal* to hit ▷ *n* 3 a loud thud
WORD ORIGIN imitative

close¹ *vb* **closing, closed** 1 to shut: *he lay back and closed his eyes* 2 to bar, obstruct, or fill up (an entrance, a hole, etc.): *the blockades had closed major roads, railways, and border crossings* 3 to cease or cause to cease giving service: *both stores closed at 9 p.m.; the Shipping Company closed its offices in Bangkok* 4 to end; terminate: *'Never,' she said, so firmly that it closed the subject* 5 (of agreements or deals) to complete or be completed successfully 6 to come closer (to): *he was still in second place but closing fast on the leader* 7 to take hold: *his small fingers closed around the coin* 8 *stock exchange* to have a value at the end of a day's trading, as specified: *the pound closed four-and-a-half cents higher* 9 to join the ends or edges of something: *to close a circuit* ▷ *n* 10 the act of closing 11 the end or conclusion: *the close of play* 12 (rhymes with **dose**) *Brit* a courtyard or quadrangle enclosed by buildings 13 *Scot* the entry from the street to a tenement building ▶ See also **close down, close in,** etc.
WORD ORIGIN Latin *claudere*

close² *adj* 1 near in space or time 2 intimate: *we were such close friends in those days* 3 near in relationship: *the dead man*
seems to have had no close relatives 4 careful, strict, or searching: *their research will not stand up to close scrutiny* 5 having the parts near together: *a close formation* 6 near to the surface; short: *an NCO's haircut, cropped close on top, shaved clean at sides and back* 7 almost equal: *a close game* 8 not deviating or varying greatly from something: *a close resemblance* 9 confined or enclosed 10 oppressive, heavy, or airless: *damp, close weather* 11 strictly guarded: *he had been placed in close arrest* 12 secretive or reticent 13 miserly; not generous 14 restricted as to public admission or membership ▷ *adv* 15 closely; tightly 16 near or in proximity **closely** *adv* **closeness** *n*
WORD ORIGIN Old French *clos*

closed *adj* 1 blocked against entry 2 only admitting a selected group of people; exclusive: *he had a fairly closed circle of friends* 3 not open to question or debate 4 *maths* **a** (of a curve or surface) completely enclosing an area or volume **b** (of a set) made up of members on which a specific operation, such as addition, gives as its result another existing member of the set

closed circuit *n* a complete electrical circuit through which current can flow

closed-circuit television *n* a television system used within a limited area such as a building

close down *vb* 1 to stop operating or working: *the factory closed down many years ago* ▷ *n* **close-down** 2 *Brit & NZ radio, television* the end of a period of broadcasting

closed shop *n Brit, Austral, & NZ* (formerly) a place of work in which all workers had to belong to a particular trade union

close harmony *n* a type of singing in which all parts except the bass lie close together

close in *vb* 1 (of days) to become shorter with the approach of winter 2 **close in on** to advance on so as to encircle or surround

close quarters *pl n* **at close quarters a** engaged in hand-to-hand combat **b** very near together

close season *n* 1 the period of the year when it is illegal to kill certain game or fish 2 *sport* the period of the year when there is no domestic competition

close shave *n informal* a narrow escape

closet *n* 1 *US & Austral* a small cupboard 2 a small private room 3 short for **water closet** ▷ *adj* 4 private or secret: *a closet homosexual* ▷ *vb* **-eting, -eted** 5 to shut away in private, esp. in order to talk: *he was closeted with the President*
WORD ORIGIN Old French *clos* enclosure

close-up *n* 1 a photograph or film or television shot taken at close range 2 a detailed or intimate view or examination ▷ *vb* **close up** 3 to shut entirely: *every other shop front seemed to be closed up* 4 to draw together: *the ranks closed up and marched on* 5 (of wounds) to heal completely

close with *vb* to engage in battle with (an enemy)

Clostridium difficile *n* a bacterium of the human intestine which is a

Scouse Dialect

The name 'Scouse' is commonly given to the dialect and slang used by natives of the city of Liverpool, who are correspondingly known as 'Scousers'. The word itself seems to have been around since the middle of the nineteenth century, and is believed to derive from the older term 'lobscouse', which was a sailor's stew containing meat, vegetables, hardtack, and no doubt anything else the ship's cook could get his hands on.

How did this come to be associated with Liverpool? The city has a long history as a major port, with many of its native sons going to sea or working on the docks, and many of its incomers from other places having been sailors too. Like any large port, the city imbibed a little of the influences of the many nationalities that were wafted in on its great river, in this case the Mersey, but the strongest influences on the way people spoke in Liverpool were undoubtedly Irish, and to a lesser extent Scots and Welsh. A glance at the more common surnames in the city to this day will quickly reveal the Celtic origins of many of its natives.

In the second half of the twentieth century Liverpool natives benefited from a gradual loosening of the hold of Received Pronunciation on the ways in which it was deemed proper to speak in public. Regional accents became acceptable, and in the case of Scouse, even fashionable, with the rise to global fame of The Beatles and other exponents of the 'Mersey Sound' of the 1960s. Television also exposed most of Britain to the Liverpool accent in comedies such as 'The Liver Birds', dramas such as 'The Boys from the Blackstuff', and in the patter of Scouse comedians such as Ken Dodd, Jimmy Tarbuck, and Alexei Sayle. In the 1990s, southerner Harry Enfield's TV sketches featuring the belligerent and excitable 'Scousers', forever advising one another to 'Calm down!' Were seen as more affectionate than scurrilous even in the city itself.

Liverpool has also made its mark in the game of football, with its two major teams, Liverpool and Everton, usually managing to maintain a place at the highest levels while dividing the city into the opposing camps of *rednoses* (supporters of Liverpool, who usually play in a red strip) and *bluenoses* (fans of Everton, who usually play in blue).

Apart from such local rivalries, Scousers are known for being chatty, friendly, and approachable, and the local language is full of affectonate terms of address such as *la* or *lar*, meaning 'pal' (which has largely supplanted the earlier *wack* or *wacker*), *queen* (used to a woman), and *kidder* (applied to anyone). A Scouser who is pleased about something will say that he is *made up*. If he likes you he may describe you as *sound*.

This is not to say that more unpleasant attitudes and perceptions do not occur in Scouse. If a Scouser is in a bad mood, he or she may be said to *have a cob on* and you might be told to *do one* ('get lost'). If he or she wishes to denigrate an individual, then terms such as *scally* ('rascal' or 'rogue') and *soft lad* (a foolish or gullible person) may be called into play. *Scallies* who deal in *knockoff* (stolen goods) are likely to come to the attention of the *bizzies* or *scuffers* (the police).

If you are unfortunate enough not to have been born within the city, but in the surrounding hinterland, then Scousers may show you a lack of respect. If you come from elsewhere in Lancashire you may be categorized as a *Lanky*, or if you are assessed as being deficient in the urban sophistication of the city-dweller, you may be stigmatized as a *woolyback*. Perhaps worst of all, if you originate in the rival north-western metropolis, Manchester, you are liable to be dismissed as a *Manc*.

A characteristic of Scouse is the tendency to shorten words and add the suffix *-y* or *-ie*. This has created such terms as *leccy* ('electricity'), which turns up in phrases like *pay the leccy* and *the leccy's cut off*, and *Corpy* (the city Corporation, a well-known source of employment and services). Similarly 'Christmas' becomes *Chrizzie*, a present is a *prezzie*, and one's best pal is your *bezzie mate*.

common cause of colitis in hospital patients. Often shortened to: **C.diff**, **C.difficile**

closure *n* **1** the act of closing or the state of being closed **2** something that closes or shuts **3** a procedure by which a debate may be stopped and an immediate vote taken **4** *chiefly US* **a** a resolution of a significant event or relationship in a person's life **b** the sense of contentment experienced after such a resolution

clot *n* **1** a soft thick lump formed from liquid **2** *informal* a stupid person ▷ *vb* **clotting, clotted 3** to form soft thick lumps
WORD ORIGIN Old English *clott*

cloth *n, pl* **cloths 1** a fabric formed by weaving, felting, or knitting fibres **2** a piece of such fabric used for a particular purpose **3 the cloth** the clergy
WORD ORIGIN Old English *clāth*

clothe *vb* **clothing, clothed** *or* **clad 1** to put clothes on **2** to provide with clothes **3** to cover or envelop (something) so as to change its appearance: *a small valley clothed in thick woodland*
WORD ORIGIN Old English *clāthian*

clothes *pl n* **1** articles of dress **2** *chiefly Brit* short for **bedclothes**
WORD ORIGIN Old English *clāthas*, plural of *clāth* cloth

clotheshorse *n* **1** a frame on which to hang laundry for drying or airing **2** a person who is extremely concerned with his or her appearance

clothesline *n* a piece of rope from which clean washing is hung to dry

clothes peg *n* a small wooden or plastic clip for attaching washing to a clothesline

clothier *n* a person who makes or sells clothes or cloth

clothing *n* **1** garments collectively **2** something that covers or clothes

clotted cream *n Brit* a thick cream made from scalded milk

cloud *n* **1** a mass of water or ice particles visible in the sky **2** a floating mass of smoke, dust, etc. **3** a large number of insects or other small animals in flight **4** something that darkens, threatens, or carries gloom **5 in the clouds** not in contact with reality **6 on cloud nine** *informal* elated; very happy **7 under a cloud a** under reproach or suspicion **b** in a state of gloom or bad temper ▷ *vb* **8** to make or become more difficult to see through: *my glasses kept clouding up; mud clouded the water* **9** to confuse or impair: *his judgment was no longer clouded by alcohol* **10** to make or become gloomy or depressed: *insanity clouded the last years of his life* ▶ See also **cloud over** ▷ **cloudless** *adj*
WORD ORIGIN Old English *clūd* rock, hill

cloudburst *n* a heavy fall of rain

cloud chamber *n physics* an apparatus for detecting high-energy particles by observing their tracks through a chamber containing a supersaturated vapour

cloud-cuckoo-land *n* a place of fantasy or impractical ideas

cloud over *vb* **1** (of the sky or weather)

to become cloudy: *it was clouding over and we thought it would rain* **2** (of a person's face or eyes) to suddenly look gloomy or depressed: *Grace's face clouded over and she turned away*

cloudy *adj* **cloudier, cloudiest 1** covered with cloud or clouds **2** (of liquids) opaque or muddy **3** confused or unclear **cloudily** *adv* **cloudiness** *n*

clout *n* **1** *informal* a fairly hard blow **2** power or influence ▷ *vb* **3** *informal* to hit hard
WORD ORIGIN Old English *clūt* piece of cloth

clove¹ *n* a dried closed flower bud of a tropical tree, used as a spice
WORD ORIGIN Latin *clavus* nail

clove² *n* a segment of a bulb of garlic
WORD ORIGIN Old English *clufu* bulb

clove³ *vb* a past tense of **cleave¹**

clove hitch *n* a knot used to fasten a rope to a spar or a larger rope

cloven *vb* **1** a past participle of **cleave¹** ▷ *adj* **2** split or divided

cloven hoof *or* **foot** *n* the divided hoof of a pig, goat, cow, or deer

clover *n* **1** a plant with three-lobed leaves and dense flower heads **2 in clover** *informal* in ease or luxury
WORD ORIGIN Old English *clǣfre*

clown *n* **1** a comic entertainer, usually bizarrely dressed and made up, appearing in the circus **2** an amusing person **3** a clumsy rude person ▷ *vb* **4** to behave foolishly **5** to perform as a clown **clownish** *adj*
WORD ORIGIN origin unknown

cloying *adj* so sweet or pleasurable that it ultimately becomes sickly: *cloying sentimentality* **cloyingly** *adv*
WORD ORIGIN Middle English *cloy* originally to nail, hence, to obstruct

club *n* **1** a group or association of people with common aims or interests **2** the building used by such a group **3** a stout stick used as a weapon **4** a stick or bat used to strike the ball in various sports, esp. golf **5** an establishment or regular event at which people dance to records; disco: *a new weekly club with resident DJ* **6** a building in which members go to meet, dine, read, etc. **7** *chiefly Brit* an organization, esp. in a shop, set up as a means of saving **8** a playing card marked with one or more black trefoil symbols **9** short for **Indian club** ▷ *vb* **clubbing, clubbed 10** to beat with a club **11 club together** to combine resources or efforts for a common purpose
WORD ORIGIN Old Norse *klubba*

club class *n* **1** a class of air travel which is less luxurious than first class but more luxurious than economy class ▷ *adj* **club-class 2** of this class of air travel

club foot *n* a congenital deformity of the foot

clubhouse *n* the premises of a sports or other club, esp. a golf club

club root *n* a fungal disease of cabbages and related plants, in which the roots become thickened and distorted

cluck *n* **1** the low clicking noise made by a hen ▷ *vb* **2** (of a hen) to make a

clicking sound **3** to express (a feeling) by making a similar sound: *the landlady was clucking feverishly behind them*
WORD ORIGIN imitative

clue *n* **1** something that helps to solve a problem or unravel a mystery **2 not have a clue a** to be completely baffled **b** to be ignorant or incompetent ▷ *adj* **3 clued-up** shrewd and well-informed
WORD ORIGIN variant of **clew** ball of thread

clueless *adj slang* helpless or stupid

clump *n* **1** a small group of things or people together **2** a dull heavy tread ▷ *vb* **3** to walk or tread heavily **4** to form into clumps **clumpy** *adj*
WORD ORIGIN Old English *clympe*

clumsy *adj* **-sier, -siest 1** lacking in skill or physical coordination: *an extraordinarily clumsy player* **2** badly made or done **3** said or done without thought or tact: *I took the clumsy hint and left* **clumsily** *adv* **clumsiness** *n*
WORD ORIGIN Middle English *clumse* to benumb

clung *vb* the past of **cling**

clunk *n* **1** a dull metallic sound ▷ *vb* **2** to make such a sound
WORD ORIGIN imitative

cluster *n* **1** a number of things growing, fastened, or occurring close together **2** a number of people or things grouped together ▷ *vb* **3** to gather or be gathered in clusters
WORD ORIGIN Old English *clyster*

clutch¹ *vb* **1** to seize with or as if with hands or claws **2** to grasp or hold firmly **3 clutch at** to attempt to get hold or possession of ▷ *n* **4** a device that enables two revolving shafts to be joined or disconnected, esp. one that transmits the drive from the engine to the gearbox in a vehicle **5** the pedal which operates the clutch in a car **6** a firm grasp **7 clutches a** hands or claws in the act of clutching: *his free kick escaped the clutches of the rival goalkeeper* **b** power or control: *rescued from the clutches of the Gestapo*
WORD ORIGIN Old English *clyccan*

clutch² *n* **1** a set of eggs laid at the same time **2** a group, bunch, or cluster: *a clutch of gloomy economic reports*
WORD ORIGIN Old Norse *klekja* to hatch

clutch bag *n* a handbag without handles

clutter *vb* **1** to scatter objects about (a place) in an untidy manner ▷ *n* **2** an untidy heap or mass of objects **3** a state of untidiness
WORD ORIGIN Middle English *clotter*

Clydesdale *n* a heavy powerful carthorse, originally from Scotland

cm centimetre

Cm *chem* curium

Cmdr Commander

CND Campaign for Nuclear Disarmament

CNS *biol* central nervous system

Co *chem* cobalt

CO 1 Colorado **2** Commanding Officer

Co.¹ *or* **CO. 1** Company **2 and co.** *informal* and the rest of them: *Harold and co.*

Co.² County

co- *prefix* **1** together; joint or jointly: *coproduction* **2** indicating partnership or equality: *co-star; copilot* **3** to the same or a similar degree: *coextend* **4** (in mathematics and astronomy) of the complement of an angle: *cosecant* **WORD ORIGIN** Latin; see COM-

c/o **1** care of **2** *book-keeping* carried over

coach *n* **1** a large comfortable single-decker bus used for sightseeing or long-distance travel **2** a railway carriage **3** a large four-wheeled enclosed carriage, usually horse-drawn **4** a trainer or instructor: *the coach of the Mexican national team* **5** a tutor who prepares students for examinations ▷ *vb* **6** to train or teach **coaching** *n* **WORD ORIGIN** from *Kocs*, village in Hungary where horse-drawn coaches were first made

coachman *n, pl* **-men** the driver of a horse-drawn coach or carriage

coachwork *n* the body of a car

coagulate (koh-**ag**-yew-late) *vb* **-lating, -lated** to change from a liquid into a soft semisolid mass; clot **coagulant** *n* **coagulation** *n* **WORD ORIGIN** Latin *coagulare*

coal *n* **1** a compact black or dark brown rock consisting largely of carbon formed from partially decomposed vegetation: a fuel and a source of coke, coal gas, and coal tar **2** one or more lumps of coal **3** **coals to Newcastle** something supplied to a place where it is already plentiful **WORD ORIGIN** Old English *col*

coalesce (koh-a-**less**) *vb* **-lescing, -lesced** to unite or come together in one body or mass **coalescence** *n* **coalescent** *adj* **WORD ORIGIN** Latin *co-* together + *alescere* to increase

coalface *n* the exposed seam of coal in a mine

coalfield *n* an area rich in deposits of coal

coal gas *n* a mixture of gases produced by the distillation of bituminous coal and used for heating and lighting

coalition (koh-a-**lish**-un) *n* a temporary alliance, esp. between political parties **WORD ORIGIN** Latin *coalescere* to coalesce

coal scuttle *n* a container for holding coal for a domestic fire

coal tar *n* a black tar, produced by the distillation of bituminous coal, used for making drugs and chemical products

coal tit *n* a small songbird with a black head with a white patch on the nape

coaming *n* a raised frame round a ship's hatchway for keeping out water **WORD ORIGIN** origin unknown

coarse *adj* **1** rough in texture or structure **2** unrefined or indecent: *coarse humour* **3** of inferior quality **coarsely** *adv* **coarseness** *n* **WORD ORIGIN** origin unknown

coarse fish *n* *Brit* a freshwater fish that is not of the salmon family **coarse fishing** *n*

coarsen *vb* to make or become coarse

coast *n* **1** the place where the land meets the sea **2** **the coast is clear** *informal* the obstacles or dangers are gone ▷ *vb* **3** to move by momentum or force of gravity, without the use of power **4** to proceed without great effort: *they coasted to a 31-9 win in the pairs* **coastal** *adj* **WORD ORIGIN** Latin *costa* side, rib

coaster *n* **1** a small mat placed under a bottle or glass to protect a table **2** *Brit* a small ship used for coastal trade

coastguard *n* **1** an organization which aids shipping, saves lives at sea, and prevents smuggling **2** a member of this

coastline *n* the outline of a coast

coat *n* **1** an outer garment with sleeves, covering the body from the shoulders to below the waist **2** the hair, wool, or fur of an animal **3** any layer that covers a surface ▷ *vb* **4** to cover with a layer **WORD ORIGIN** Old French *cote*

coat hanger *n* a curved piece of wood, wire, or plastic, fitted with a hook and used to hang up clothes

coating *n* a layer or film spread over a surface: *a thick coating of breadcrumbs*

coat of arms *n* the heraldic emblem of a family or organization

coat of mail *n* *history* a protective garment made of linked metal rings or plates

coax *vb* **1** to persuade (someone) gently **2** to obtain (something) by persistent coaxing **3** to work on (something) carefully and patiently so as to make it function as desired: *I watched him coax the last few drops of beer out of his glass* **WORD ORIGIN** obsolete *cokes* a fool

coaxial (koh-**ax**-ee-al) *adj* **1** *electronics* (of a cable) transmitting by means of two concentric conductors separated by an insulator **2** having a common axis

cob *n* **1** a male swan **2** a thickset type of horse **3** the stalk of an ear of maize **4** *Austral & Brit* a round loaf of bread **5** *Brit* a hazel tree or hazelnut **WORD ORIGIN** origin unknown

cobalt *n* *chem* a brittle hard silvery-white metallic element used in alloys. Symbol: Co **WORD ORIGIN** Middle High German *kobolt* goblin; from the miners' belief that goblins placed it in the silver ore

cobber *n* *Austral or old-fashioned NZ informal* a friend **WORD ORIGIN** dialect *cob* to take a liking to someone

cobble *n* a cobblestone

cobbled *adj* (of a street or road) paved with cobblestones

cobbler *n* a person who makes or mends shoes **WORD ORIGIN** origin unknown

cobblers *pl n* *Brit, Austral, & NZ slang* nonsense **WORD ORIGIN** rhyming slang *cobblers' awls* balls

cobblestone *n* a rounded stone used for paving **WORD ORIGIN** from *cob*

cobble together *vb* **-bling, -bled** to put together clumsily: *a coalition cobbled together from parties with widely differing aims*

cobia (**koh**-bee-a) *n* a large dark-striped game fish of tropical and subtropical seas

COBOL *n* a high-level computer programming language designed for general commercial use **WORD ORIGIN** *co(mmon) b(usiness) o(riented) l(anguage)*

cobra *n* a highly venomous hooded snake of tropical Africa and Asia **WORD ORIGIN** Latin *colubra* snake

cobweb *n* **1** a web spun by certain spiders **2** a single thread of such a web **cobwebbed** *adj* **cobwebby** *adj* **WORD ORIGIN** Old English (*ātor*)*coppe* spider

cobwebs *pl n* mustiness, confusion, or obscurity: *her election dusted away the cobwebs that normally surround the presidency*

coca *n* the dried leaves of a S American shrub which contain cocaine **WORD ORIGIN** S American Indian *kúka*

Coca-Cola *n trademark* a carbonated soft drink

cocaine *n* an addictive drug derived from coca leaves, used as a narcotic and local anaesthetic

coccyx (**kok**-six) *n, pl* **coccyges** (kok-**sije**-eez) *anat* a small triangular bone at the base of the spine in human beings and some apes **coccygeal** *adj* **WORD ORIGIN** Greek *kokkux* cuckoo, from its likeness to a cuckoo's beak

cochineal *n* a scarlet dye obtained from a Mexican insect, used for colouring food **WORD ORIGIN** Greek *kokkos* kermes berry

cochlea (**kok**-lee-a) *n, pl* **-leae** (-lee-ee) *anat* the spiral tube in the internal ear, which converts sound vibrations into nerve impulses **cochlear** *adj* **WORD ORIGIN** Greek *kokhlias* snail

cock *n* **1** a male bird, esp. of domestic fowl **2** a stopcock **3** *taboo slang* a penis **4** the hammer of a gun **5** *Brit informal* friend: used as a term of address ▷ *vb* **6** to draw back the hammer of (a gun) so that it is ready to fire **7** to lift and turn (part of the body) in a particular direction ▶ See also **cockup** **WORD ORIGIN** Old English *cocc*

cockabully *n* a small fresh-water fish of New Zealand **WORD ORIGIN** Māori *kokopu*

cockade *n* a feather or rosette worn on the hat as a badge **WORD ORIGIN** French *coq* cock

cock-a-hoop *adj* *Brit, Austral, & NZ* in very high spirits **WORD ORIGIN** origin unknown

cock-a-leekie *n* a Scottish soup of chicken boiled with leeks

cock-and-bull story *n* *informal* an obviously improbable story, esp. one used as an excuse

cockatiel *n* a crested Australian parrot with a greyish-brown and yellow plumage

cockatoo *n, pl* **-toos** a light-coloured crested parrot of Australia and the East Indies **WORD ORIGIN** Malay *kakatua*

cockatrice *n* a legendary monster that could kill with a glance **WORD ORIGIN** Late Latin *calcatrix* trampler

cockchafer *n* a large flying beetle **WORD ORIGIN** COCK + *chafer* beetle

cocked hat n **1** a hat with three corners and a turned-up brim **2 knock into a cocked hat** slang to outdo or defeat

cockerel n a young domestic cock, less than a year old

cocker spaniel n a small spaniel
WORD ORIGIN from *cocking* hunting woodcocks

cockeyed adj informal **1** crooked or askew **2** foolish or absurd **3** cross-eyed

cockfight n a fight between two gamecocks fitted with sharp metal spurs

cockie, cocky n, pl **-kies** Austral & NZ informal a cockatoo

cockle n **1** an edible bivalve shellfish **2** its shell **3 warm the cockles of one's heart** to make one feel happy
WORD ORIGIN Greek *konkhule* mussel

cockleshell n **1** the rounded shell of the cockle **2** a small light boat

cockney n **1** a native of London, esp. of its East End **2** the urban dialect of London or its East End ▷ adj **3** characteristic of cockneys or their dialect
WORD ORIGIN Middle English *cokeney* cock's egg, later applied contemptuously to townsmen

cockpit n **1** the compartment in an aircraft for the pilot and crew **2** the driver's compartment in a racing car **3** naut a space in a small vessel containing the wheel and tiller **4** the site of many battles or conflicts: *the south of the country is a cockpit of conflicting interests* **5** an enclosure used for cockfights

cockroach n a beetle-like insect which is a household pest
WORD ORIGIN Spanish *cucaracha*

cockscomb n same as **coxcomb**

cocksure adj overconfident or arrogant
WORD ORIGIN origin unknown

cocktail n **1** a mixed alcoholic drink **2** an appetizer of seafood or mixed fruits **3** any combination of diverse elements: *Central America was a cocktail of death, poverty, and destruction*
WORD ORIGIN origin unknown

cockup Austral & Brit slang n **1** something done badly ▷ vb **cock up 2** to ruin or spoil

cocky adj **cockier, cockiest** excessively proud of oneself **cockily** adv **cockiness** n

coco n, pl **-cos** the coconut palm
WORD ORIGIN Portuguese: grimace

cocoa or **cacao** n **1** a powder made by roasting and grinding cocoa beans **2** a hot or cold drink made from cocoa powder
WORD ORIGIN from CACAO

cocoa bean n a cacao seed

cocoa butter n a fatty solid obtained from cocoa beans and used for confectionery and toiletries

coconut n **1** the fruit of a type of palm tree (**coconut palm**), which has a thick fibrous oval husk and a thin hard shell enclosing edible white flesh. The hollow centre is filled with a milky fluid (**coconut milk**) **2** the flesh of the coconut

coconut matting n coarse matting made from the husk of the coconut

cocoon n **1** a silky protective covering produced by a silkworm or other insect larva, in which the pupa develops **2** a protective covering ▷ vb **3** to wrap in or protect as if in a cocoon
WORD ORIGIN Provençal *coucoun* eggshell

cocotte n a small fireproof dish in which individual portions of food are cooked and served
WORD ORIGIN French

cod[1] n, pl **cod** or **cods** a large food fish
WORD ORIGIN probably Germanic

cod[2] adj Brit slang having the character of an imitation or parody: *the chorus were dressed in exuberant cod-medieval costumes*
WORD ORIGIN origin unknown

COD cash (in the US, collect) on delivery

coda (**kode**-a) n music the final part of a musical movement or work
WORD ORIGIN Italian: tail

coddle vb **-dling, -dled 1** to pamper or overprotect **2** to cook (eggs) in water just below boiling point
WORD ORIGIN origin unknown

code n **1** a system of letters, symbols, or prearranged signals, by which information can be communicated secretly or briefly **2** a set of principles or rules: *a code of practice* **3** a system of letters or digits used for identification purposes: *area code; tax code* ▷ vb **coding, coded 4** to translate or arrange into a code
WORD ORIGIN Latin *codex* book, wooden block

codeine (**kode**-een) n a drug made mainly from morphine, used as a painkiller and sedative
WORD ORIGIN Greek *kōdeia* head of a poppy

codex (**koh**-dex) n, pl **-dices** (-diss-seez) a volume of manuscripts of an ancient text
WORD ORIGIN Latin: wooden block, book

codfish n, pl **-fish** or **-fishes** a cod

codger n Brit, Austral, & NZ informal an old man
WORD ORIGIN probably variant of *cadger*

codicil (**cod**-iss-ill) n law an addition to a will
WORD ORIGIN from CODEX

codify (**kode**-if-fie) vb **-fies, -fying, -fied** to organize or collect together (rules or procedures) systematically **codification** n

codling n a young cod

cod-liver oil n an oil extracted from fish, rich in vitamins A and D

codpiece n history a bag covering the male genitals, attached to breeches
WORD ORIGIN obsolete *cod* scrotum

codswallop n Brit, Austral, & NZ slang nonsense
WORD ORIGIN origin unknown

coeducation n the education of boys and girls together **coeducational** adj

coefficient n **1** maths a number or constant placed before and multiplying another quantity: *the coefficient of the term 3xyz is 3* **2** physics a number or constant used to calculate the behaviour of a given substance under specified conditions

coelacanth (**seel**-a-kanth) n a primitive marine fish, thought to be extinct until a living specimen was discovered in 1938
WORD ORIGIN Greek *koilos* hollow + *akanthos* spine

coelenterate (seel-**lent**-a-rate) n any invertebrate that has a saclike body with a single opening, such as a jellyfish or coral
WORD ORIGIN Greek *koilos* hollow + *enteron* intestine

coeliac or US **celiac** n a person who suffers from coeliac disease ▷ adj of or related to the abdomen
WORD ORIGIN Greek *koilia* belly

coeliac disease (**seel**-ee-ak) n a disease which makes the digestion of food difficult
WORD ORIGIN Greek *koilia* belly

coenobite (**seen**-oh-bite) n a member of a religious order in a monastic community
WORD ORIGIN Greek *koinos* common + *bios* life

coequal adj, n equal

coerce (koh-**urss**) vb **-ercing, -erced** to compel or force **coercion** n
WORD ORIGIN Latin *co-* together + *arcere* to enclose

coercive adj using force or authority to make a person do something against his or her will

coeval (koh-**eev**-al) adj **1** contemporary **2** n a contemporary **coevally** adv
WORD ORIGIN Latin *co-* together + *aevum* age

coexist vb **1** to exist together at the same time or in the same place **2** to exist together in peace despite differences **coexistence** n **coexistent** adj

coextensive adj covering the same area, either literally or figuratively: *the concepts of 'the nation' and 'the people' are not coextensive*

C of E Church of England

coffee n **1** a drink made from the roasted and ground seeds of a tall tropical shrub **2** Also called: **coffee beans** the beanlike seeds of this shrub **3** the shrub yielding these seeds ▷ adj **4** medium-brown
WORD ORIGIN Turkish *kahve*, from Arabic *qahwah* coffee, wine

coffee bar n a café; snack bar

coffee house n a place where coffee is served, esp. one that was a fashionable meeting place in 18th-century London

coffee mill n a machine for grinding roasted coffee beans

coffee table n a small low table

coffee-table book n a large expensive illustrated book

coffer n **1** a chest for storing valuables **2 coffers** a store of money **3** an ornamental sunken panel in a ceiling or dome
WORD ORIGIN Greek *kophinos* basket

cofferdam n a watertight enclosure pumped dry to enable construction work or ship repairs to be done

coffered adj (of a ceiling or dome) decorated with ornamental sunken panels

Words from Literature
part 7

come out *v* when a girl came out in society it meant she was of marriageable age. In order to 'come out' girls were expecting to attend balls and other parties during a season
> The younger girls formed hopes of coming out a year or two sooner than they might otherwise have done
> *Pride and Prejudice* Jane Austen

commit *v* to arrest or stop
> Commit the rascals
> *Doctor Faustus* 4.7 Christopher Marlowe

commodious *adj* commodious means convenient
> the most commodious and effectual ways
> *Gulliver's Travels* Jonathan Swift

commons *n* an old term meaning food shared with others
> his pauper assistants ranged themselves behind him; the gruel was served out; and a long grace was said over the short commons.
> *Oliver Twist* Charles Dickens

complacency *n* a desire to please others. Today complacency means feeling pleased with oneself without good reason.
> Twas thy power that raised the first complacency in me
> *The Prelude* William Wordsworth

complaisance *n* complaisance was eagerness to please
> we cannot wonder at his complaisance
> *Pride and Prejudice* Jane Austen

complaisant *adj* polite
> extremely cheerful and complaisant to their guest
> *Gulliver's Travels* Jonathan Swift

conning *n* learning by heart
> Or conning more
> *The Prelude* William Wordsworth

consequent *n* consequence
> as avarice is the necessary consequent of old age
> *Gulliver's Travels* Jonathan Swift

consort *n* a concert
> The King, who delighted in music, had frequent consorts at Court
> *Gulliver's Travels* Jonathan Swift

conversible *adj* easy to talk to, companionable
> He can be a conversible companion
> *Pride and Prejudice* Jane Austen

copper *n* a large pot than can be heated directly over a fire
> He gazed in stupefied astonishment on the small rebel for some seconds, and then clung for support to the copper
> *Oliver Twist* Charles Dickens

copper-stick *n* the long piece of wood used to stir washing in the copper (or boiler) which was usually the biggest cooking pot in the house
> It was Christmas Eve, and I had to stir the pudding for next day, with a copper-stick, from seven to eight by the Dutch clock
> *Great Expectations* Charles Dickens

counting-house *n* a place where accountants work
> Once upon a time - of all the good days in the year, on Christmas Eve - old Scrooge sat busy in his counting-house
> *A Christmas Carol* Charles Dickens

courtier *n* someone who attends the king or queen, a member of the court
> next the ten courtiers;
> *Alice's Adventures in Wonderland* Lewis Carroll

covey *n* a flock of partridges
> and will save all of the best covies for you
> *Pride and Prejudice* Jane Austen

cow *v* to frighten or intimidate
> it cowed me more than the pain
> *Treasure Island* Robert Louis Stevenson

cozen *v* to trick or deceive
> Do you remember, sir, how you cozened me
> *Doctor Faustus* 4.7 Christopher Marlowe

coffin *n* a box in which a corpse is buried or cremated
WORD ORIGIN Latin *cophinus* basket

cog *n* **1** one of the teeth on the rim of a gearwheel **2** a gearwheel, esp. a small one **3** an unimportant person in a large organization or process
WORD ORIGIN Scandinavian

cogent (**koh**-jent) *adj* forcefully convincing **cogency** *n*
WORD ORIGIN Latin *co-* together + *agere* to drive

cogitate (**koj**-it-tate) *vb* **-tating, -tated** to think deeply about (something) **cogitation** *n* **cogitative** *adj*
WORD ORIGIN Latin *cogitare*

cognac (**kon**-yak) *n* high-quality French brandy

cognate *adj* **1** derived from a common original form: *cognate languages* **2** related to or descended from a common ancestor ▷ *n* **3** a cognate word or language **4** a relative **cognation** *n*
WORD ORIGIN Latin *co-* same + *gnatus* born

cognition *n formal* **1** the processes of getting knowledge, including perception, intuition, and reasoning **2** the results of such a process **cognitive** *adj*
WORD ORIGIN Latin *cognoscere* to learn

cognizance *or* **cognisance** *n formal* **1** knowledge or understanding **2** **take cognizance of** to take notice of **3** the range or scope of knowledge or understanding **cognizant** *or* **cognisant** *adj*
WORD ORIGIN Latin *cognoscere* to learn

cognomen (kog-**noh**-men) *n, pl* **-nomens** *or* **-nomina** (-**nom**-min-a) *formal* **1** a nickname **2** a surname **3** an ancient Roman's third name or nickname
WORD ORIGIN Latin: additional name

cognoscenti (kon-yo-**shen**-tee) *pl n, sing* **-te** (-tee) connoisseurs
WORD ORIGIN obsolete Italian

cogwheel *n* same as **gearwheel**

cohabit *vb* to live together as husband and wife without being married **cohabitation** *n*
WORD ORIGIN Latin *co-* together + *habitare* to live

cohabitee *n* a person who lives with, and has a sexual and romantic relationship with, someone to whom he or she is not married

cohere *vb* **-hering, -hered** **1** to hold or stick firmly together **2** to be logically connected or consistent
WORD ORIGIN Latin *co-* together + *haerere* to cling

coherent *adj* **1** logical and consistent **2** capable of intelligible speech **3** cohering or sticking together **4** *physics* (of two or more waves) having the same frequency and a constant fixed phase difference **coherence** *n*

cohesion *n* **1** sticking together **2** *physics* the force that holds together the atoms or molecules in a solid or liquid **cohesive** *adj*

cohort *n* **1** a band of associates **2** a tenth part of an ancient Roman Legion
WORD ORIGIN Latin *cohors* yard, company of soldiers

coif *n* **1** a close-fitting cap worn in the Middle Ages **2** a hairstyle ▷ *vb* **coiffing, coiffed** **3** to arrange (the hair)
WORD ORIGIN Late Latin *cofea* helmet, cap

coiffeur *n* a hairdresser **coiffeuse** *fem n*
WORD ORIGIN French

coiffure *n* a hairstyle
WORD ORIGIN French

coil¹ *vb* **1** to wind or be wound into loops **2** to move in a winding course ▷ *n* **3** something wound in a connected series of loops **4** a single loop of such a series **5** a contraceptive device in the shape of a coil, inserted in the womb **6** an electrical conductor wound into a spiral, to provide inductance
WORD ORIGIN Old French *coillir* to collect together

coil² *n* **mortal coil** the troubles of the world
WORD ORIGIN coined by William Shakespeare

coin *n* **1** a metal disc used as money **2** metal currency collectively ▷ *vb* **3** to invent (a new word or phrase) **4** to make or stamp (coins) **5** **coin it in** *or* **coin money** *informal* to make money rapidly
WORD ORIGIN Latin *cuneus* wedge

coinage *n* **1** coins collectively **2** the currency of a country **3** a newly invented word or phrase **4** the act of coining

coincide *vb* **-ciding, -cided** **1** to happen at the same time **2** to agree or correspond exactly: *what she had said coincided exactly with his own thinking* **3** to occupy the same place in space
WORD ORIGIN Latin *co-* together + *incidere* to occur

coincidence *n* **1** a chance occurrence of simultaneous or apparently connected events **2** a coinciding

coincident *adj* **1** having the same position in space or time **2** **coincident with** in exact agreement with

coincidental *adj* resulting from coincidence; not intentional **coincidentally** *adv*

coir *n* coconut fibre, used in making rope and matting
WORD ORIGIN Malayalam (a language of SW India) *kāyar* rope

coitus (**koh**-it-uss) *or* **coition** (koh-**ish**-un) *n* sexual intercourse **coital** *adj*
WORD ORIGIN Latin *coire* to meet

coke¹ *n* **1** a solid fuel left after gas has been distilled from coal ▷ *vb* **coking, coked** **2** to become or convert into coke
WORD ORIGIN probably *dialect colk* core

coke² *n slang* cocaine

Coke *n trademark* short for **Coca-Cola**

col *n* the lowest point of a ridge connecting two mountain peaks
WORD ORIGIN French: neck

Col. Colonel

cola *n* **1** a soft drink flavoured with an extract from the nuts of a tropical tree **2** the W African tree whose nuts contain this extract
WORD ORIGIN probably variant of W African *kolo* nut

colander *n* a bowl with a perforated bottom for straining or rinsing foods
WORD ORIGIN Latin *colum* sieve

cold *adj* **1** low in temperature: *the cold March wind; cans of cold beer* **2** not hot enough: *eat your food before it gets cold!* **3** lacking in affection or enthusiasm **4** not affected by emotion: *the cold truth* **5** dead **6** (of a trail or scent in hunting) faint **7** (of a colour) giving the impression of coldness **8** *slang* unconscious **9** *informal* (of a seeker) far from the object of a search **10** denoting the contacting of potential customers without previously approaching them to establish their interest: *cold mailing* **11** **cold comfort** little or no comfort **12** **have** *or* **get cold feet** to be or become fearful or reluctant **13** **in cold blood** deliberately and without mercy **14** **leave someone cold** *informal* to fail to excite or impress someone **15** **throw cold water on** *informal* to discourage ▷ *n* **16** the absence of heat **17** a viral infection of the nose and throat characterized by catarrh and sneezing **18** the sensation caused by loss or lack of heat **19** **(out) in the cold** *informal* neglected or ignored ▷ *adv* **20** *informal* unrehearsed or unprepared: *he played his part cold* **coldly** *adv* **coldness** *n*
WORD ORIGIN Old English *ceald*

cold-blooded *adj* **1** callous or cruel **2** *zool* (of all animals except birds and mammals) having a body temperature that varies according to the temperature of the surroundings

cold chisel *n* a toughened steel chisel

cold cream *n* a creamy preparation used for softening and cleansing the skin

cold frame *n* an unheated wooden frame with a glass top, used to protect young plants

cold front *n meteorol* the boundary line between a warm air mass and the cold air pushing it from beneath and behind

cold-hearted *adj* lacking in feeling or warmth **cold-heartedness** *n*

cold shoulder *informal* ▷ *n* **1** **give someone the cold shoulder** to snub someone ▷ *vb* **cold-shoulder** **2** to treat with indifference

cold snap *n* a short period of cold and frosty weather

cold sore *n* a cluster of blisters near the lips, caused by a virus

cold storage *n* **1** the storage of things in a refrigerated place **2** *informal* a state of temporary disuse: *the idea has been in cold storage ever since*

cold sweat *n informal* coldness and sweating as a bodily reaction to fear or nervousness

cold turkey *n slang* a method of curing drug addiction by the sudden withdrawal of all doses

cold war *n* a state of political hostility between two countries without actual warfare

cole *n* any of various plants such as the cabbage and rape
WORD ORIGIN Latin *caulis* cabbage

coleslaw *n* a salad dish of shredded raw cabbage in a dressing

WORD ORIGIN Dutch *koolsalade* cabbage salad

coley *n Brit* an edible fish with white or grey flesh
WORD ORIGIN perhaps from *coalfish*

colic *n* severe pains in the stomach and bowels **colicky** *adj*
WORD ORIGIN Greek *kolon* COLON²

colitis (koh-**lie**-tiss) *n* inflammation of the colon, usually causing diarrhoea and lower abdominal pain

collaborate *vb* **-rating, -rated 1** to work with another or others on a joint project **2** to cooperate with an enemy invader **collaboration** *n* **collaborative** *adj* **collaborator** *n*
WORD ORIGIN Latin *com-* together + *laborare* to work

collage (kol-**lahzh**) *n* **1** an art form in which various materials or objects are glued onto a surface to make a picture **2** a picture made in this way **3** a work, such as a piece of music, created by combining unrelated styles **collagist** *n*
WORD ORIGIN French

collagen *n* a protein found in cartilage and bone that yields gelatine when boiled
WORD ORIGIN Greek *kolla* glue

collapse *vb* **-lapsing, -lapsed 1** to fall down or cave in suddenly **2** to fail completely: *a package holiday company which collapsed last year* **3** to fall down from lack of strength, exhaustion, or illness: *he collapsed with an asthma attack* **4** to sit down and rest because of tiredness or lack of energy: *she collapsed in front of the telly when she got home* **5** to fold compactly, esp. for storage ▷ *n* **6** the act of falling down or falling to pieces **7** a sudden failure or breakdown
WORD ORIGIN Latin *collabi* to fall in ruins

collapsible *adj* able to be folded up for storage

collar *n* **1** the part of a garment round the neck **2** a band of leather, rope, or metal placed around an animal's neck **3** *biol* a ringlike marking around the neck of a bird or animal **4** a cut of meat, esp. bacon, from the neck of an animal **5** a ring or band around a pipe, rod, or shaft ▷ *vb Brit, Austral, & NZ informal* **6** to seize; arrest **7** to catch in order to speak to **8** to take for oneself
WORD ORIGIN Latin *collum* neck

collarbone *n* same as **clavicle**

collate *vb* **-lating, -lated 1** to examine and compare carefully **2** to gather together and put in order **collator** *n*
WORD ORIGIN Latin *com-* together + *latus* brought

collateral *n* **1** security pledged for the repayment of a loan **2** a person, animal, or plant descended from the same ancestor as another but through a different line ▷ *adj* **3** descended from a common ancestor but through different lines **4** additional but subordinate: *a spokeswoman said that there was no collateral information to dispute the assurances the government had been given* **5** situated or running side by side: *collateral ridges of mountains*
WORD ORIGIN Latin *com-* together + *lateralis* of the side

collateral damage *n mil* unintentional civilian casualties or damage to civilian property caused by military action: *to minimize collateral damage maximum precision in bombing is required*

collation *n* **1** the act or result of collating **2** *formal* a light meal

colleague *n* a fellow worker, esp. in a profession
WORD ORIGIN Latin *collega*

collect¹ *vb* **1** to gather together or be gathered together **2** to gather (objects, such as stamps) as a hobby or for study **3** to go to a place to fetch (a person or thing) **4** to receive payments of (taxes, dues, or contributions) **5** to regain control of (oneself or one's emotions)
WORD ORIGIN Latin *com-* together + *legere* to gather

collect² *n Christianity* a short prayer said during certain church services
WORD ORIGIN Medieval Latin *oratio ad collectam* prayer at the assembly

collected *adj* **1** calm and self-controlled **2** brought together into one book or set of books: *the collected works of Dickens*

collection *n* **1** things collected or accumulated **2** a group of people **3** the act or process of collecting **4** a selection of clothes usually presented by a particular designer **5** a sum of money collected, as in church **6** a regular removal of letters from a postbox

collective *adj* **1** done by or characteristic of individuals acting as a group: *the army's collective wisdom regarding peacekeeping* ▷ *n* **2** a group of people working together on an enterprise and sharing the benefits from it **collectively** *adv*

collective bargaining *n* negotiation between a trade union and an employer on the wages and working conditions of the employees

collective noun *n* a noun that is singular in form but that refers to a group of people or things, as *crowd* or *army*

≡ USAGE
Collective nouns are usually used with singular verbs: *the family is on holiday; General Motors is mounting a big sales campaign.* In British usage, however, plural verbs are sometimes employed in this context, esp. where reference is being made to a collection of individual objects or people rather than to the group as a unit: *the family are all on holiday.* Care should be taken that the same collective noun is not treated as both singular and plural in the same sentence: *the family is well and sends its best wishes* or *the family are all well and send their best wishes,* but not *the family is well and send their best wishes.*

collectivism *n* the theory that the state should own all means of production **collectivist** *adj*

collectivize or **-vise** *vb* **-vizing, -vized** or **-vising, -vised** to organize according to the theory of collectivism **collectivization** or **-visation** *n*

collector *n* **1** a person who collects objects as a hobby **2** a person employed to collect debts, rents, or tickets

collector's item *n* an object highly valued by collectors for its beauty or rarity

colleen *n Irish* a girl
WORD ORIGIN Irish Gaelic *cailín*

college *n* **1** an institution of higher or further education that is not a university **2** a self-governing section of certain universities **3** *Brit & NZ* a name given to some secondary schools **4** an organized body of people with specific rights and duties: *the president is elected by an electoral college* **5** a body organized within a particular profession, concerned with regulating standards **6** the staff and students of a college
WORD ORIGIN Latin *collega* colleague

collegian *n* a member of a college

collegiate *adj* **1** of a college or college students **2** (of a university) composed of various colleges

collide *vb* **-liding, -lided 1** to crash together violently **2** to conflict or disagree
WORD ORIGIN Latin *com-* together + *laedere* to strike

collie *n* a silky-haired dog used for herding sheep and cattle
WORD ORIGIN Scots, probably from earlier *colie* black

collier *n chiefly Brit* **1** a coal miner **2** a ship designed to carry coal

colliery *n, pl* **-lieries** *chiefly Brit* a coal mine and its buildings

collision *n* **1** a violent crash between moving objects **2** the conflict of opposed ideas or wishes
WORD ORIGIN Latin *collidere* to collide

collision course *n* **1** a trajectory of movement likely to result in a collision **2** a course of action likely to result in a serious disagreement or confrontation: *the union is on an inevitable collision course with the government*

collocate *vb* **-cating, -cated** (of words) to occur together regularly **collocation** *n*

colloid *n* a mixture of particles of one substance suspended in a different substance **colloidal** *adj*
WORD ORIGIN Greek *kolla* glue

collop *n* a small slice of meat
WORD ORIGIN Scandinavian

colloquial *adj* suitable for informal speech or writing **colloquially** *adv*

colloquialism *n* **1** a colloquial word or phrase **2** the use of colloquial words and phrases

colloquium *n, pl* **-quiums** or **-quia** an academic conference or seminar
WORD ORIGIN Latin; see COLLOQUY

colloquy *n, pl* **-quies** *formal* a conversation or conference **colloquist** *n*
WORD ORIGIN Latin *com-* together + *loqui* to speak

collude *vb* **-luding, -luded** to cooperate secretly or dishonestly with someone
WORD ORIGIN Latin *colludere* to conspire

collusion *n* secret or illegal agreement or cooperation **collusive** *adj*

collywobbles *pl n slang* **1** an intense feeling of nervousness **2** an upset stomach
WORD ORIGIN probably from *colic* + *wobble*

C

cologne *n* a perfumed toilet water
WORD ORIGIN *Cologne*, Germany, where it was first manufactured

colon[1] *n, pl* **-lons** the punctuation mark (:) used before an explanation or an example, a list, or an extended quotation
WORD ORIGIN Greek *kōlon* limb, clause

colon[2] *n, pl* **-lons** *or* **-la** the part of the large intestine connected to the rectum **colonic** *adj*
WORD ORIGIN Greek *kolon* large intestine

colonel *n* a senior commissioned officer in the army or air force **colonelcy** *n*
WORD ORIGIN Old Italian *colonnello* column of soldiers

colonial *adj* **1** of or inhabiting a colony or colonies **2** of a style of architecture popular in North America in the 17th and 18th centuries: *a colonial mansion* **3** *Austral* of a style of architecture popular during Australia's colonial period ▷ *n* **4** an inhabitant of a colony

colonial goose *n* NZ, old-fashioned stuffed roast mutton

colonialism *n* the policy of acquiring and maintaining colonies, esp. for exploitation **colonialist** *n, adj*

colonist *n* a settler in or inhabitant of a colony

colonize *or* **-nise** *vb* **-nizing, -nized** *or* **-nising, -nised 1** to establish a colony in (an area) **2** to settle in (an area) as colonists **colonization** *or* **-nisation** *n*

colonnade *n* a row of evenly spaced columns, usually supporting a roof **colonnaded** *adj*
WORD ORIGIN French *colonne* column

colony *n, pl* **-nies 1** a group of people who settle in a new country but remain under the rule of their homeland **2** the territory occupied by such a settlement **3** a group of people with the same nationality or interests, forming a community in a particular place: *an artists' colony* **4** *zool* a group of the same type of animal or plant living or growing together **5** *bacteriol* a group of microorganisms when grown on a culture medium
WORD ORIGIN Latin *colere* to cultivate, inhabit

colophon *n* a publisher's symbol on a book
WORD ORIGIN Greek *kolophōn* a finishing stroke

color *n, vb* US same as **colour**

Colorado beetle *n* a black-and-yellow beetle that is a serious pest of potatoes
WORD ORIGIN *Colorado*, state of central US

coloration *or* **colouration** *n* arrangement of colours: *a red coloration of the eyes*

coloratura *n music* **1** a part for a solo singer which has much complicated ornamentation of the basic melody **2** a soprano who specializes in such music
WORD ORIGIN obsolete Italian, literally: colouring

colossal *adj* **1** very large in size: *the turbulent rivers and colossal mountains of New Zealand* **2** very serious or significant: *a colossal legal blunder*

colossus *n, pl* **-si** *or* **-suses 1** a very large statue **2** a huge or important person or thing
WORD ORIGIN Greek *kolossos*

colostomy *n, pl* **-mies** an operation to form an opening from the colon onto the surface of the body, for emptying the bowel
WORD ORIGIN COLON[2] + Greek *stoma* mouth

colour *or* US **color** *n* **1** a property of things that results from the particular wavelengths of light which they reflect or give out, producing a sensation in the eye **2** a colour, such as a red or green, that possesses hue, as opposed to black, white, or grey **3** a substance, such as a dye, that gives colour **4** the skin complexion of a person **5** the use of all the colours in painting, drawing, or photography **6** the distinctive tone of a musical sound **7** details which give vividness or authenticity: *I walked the streets and absorbed the local colour* **8** semblance or pretext: *under colour of* ▷ *vb* **9** to apply colour to (something) **10** to influence or distort: *anger coloured her judgment* **11** to become red in the face, esp. when embarrassed or annoyed **12** to give a convincing appearance to: *he coloured his account of what had happened*
▸ See also **colours**
WORD ORIGIN Latin *color*

colour bar *n* racial discrimination by whites against non-whites

colour-blind *adj* **1** unable to distinguish between certain colours, esp. red and green **2** not discriminating on grounds of skin colour: *colour-blind policies* **colour blindness** *n*

coloured *or* US **colored** *adj* having a colour or colours other than black or white: *coloured glass bottles; a peach-coloured outfit with matching hat*

Coloured *or* US **Colored** *n* **1** offensive a person who is not White **2** in South Africa, a person of racially mixed parentage or descent ▷ *adj* **3** *S African* of mixed White and non-White parentage

colourful *or* US **colorful** *adj* **1** with bright or richly varied colours **2** vivid or distinctive in character

colouring *or* US **coloring** *n* **1** the application of colour **2** something added to give colour **3** appearance with regard to shade and colour **4** the colour of a person's complexion

colourless *or* US **colorless** *adj* **1** without colour: *a colourless gas* **2** dull and uninteresting: *a colourless personality* **3** grey or pallid in tone or hue: *a watery sun hung low in the colourless sky*

colours *or* US **colors** *pl n* **1** the flag of a country, regiment, or ship **2** *Brit sport* a badge or other symbol showing membership of a team, esp. at a school or college **3** **nail one's colours to the mast** to commit oneself publicly to a course of action **4** **show one's true colours** to display one's true nature or character

colour sergeant *n* a sergeant who carries the regimental, battalion, or national colours

colour supplement *n Brit* an illustrated magazine accompanying a newspaper

colt *n* **1** a young male horse or pony **2** *sport* a young and inexperienced player
WORD ORIGIN Old English: young ass

coltsfoot *n, pl* **-foots** a weed with yellow flowers and heart-shaped leaves

columbine *n* a plant that has brightly coloured flowers with five spurred petals
WORD ORIGIN Medieval Latin *columbina herba* dovelike plant

column *n* **1** an upright pillar usually having a cylindrical shaft, a base, and a capital **2** a form or structure in the shape of a column: *a column of smoke* **3** a vertical division of a newspaper page **4** a regular feature in a paper: *a cookery column* **5** a vertical arrangement of numbers **6** *mil* a narrow formation in which individuals or units follow one behind the other **columnar** *adj*
WORD ORIGIN Latin *columna*

columnist *n* a journalist who writes a regular feature in a newspaper

com- *or* **con-** *prefix* used with a main word to mean together; with; jointly: *commingle*
WORD ORIGIN Latin, from *cum* with

coma *n* a state of unconsciousness from which a person cannot be aroused, caused by injury, disease, or drugs
WORD ORIGIN Greek *kōma* heavy sleep

Comanche (kom-**man**-chee) *n, pl* **-ches** *or* **-che** a member of a N American Indian people, formerly living in the plains to the east of the Rockies, now chiefly in Oklahoma

comatose *adj* **1** in a coma **2** sound asleep

comb *n* **1** a toothed instrument for disentangling or arranging hair **2** a tool or machine that cleans and straightens wool or cotton **3** a fleshy serrated crest on the head of a domestic fowl **4** a honeycomb ▷ *vb* **5** to use a comb on **6** to search with great care: *police combed the streets for the missing girl*
WORD ORIGIN Old English *camb*

combat *n* **1** a fight or struggle ▷ *vb* **-bating, -bated 2** to fight: *a coordinated approach to combating the growing drugs problem* **combative** *adj*
WORD ORIGIN Latin *com-* with + *battuere* to beat

combatant *n* **1** a person taking part in a combat ▷ *adj* **2** engaged in or ready for combat

combat trousers *or* **combats** *pl n* loose casual trousers with large pockets on the sides of the legs

combe *n* same as **coomb**

comber *n* a long curling wave

combination *n* **1** the act of combining or state of being combined **2** people or things combined **3** the set of numbers or letters that opens a combination lock **4** a motorcycle with a sidecar **5** *maths* an arrangement of the members of a set into specified groups without regard to order in the group

combination lock *n* a lock that can only be opened when a set of dials is turned to show a specific sequence of numbers or letters

Language Communities in Canada
part 1

One stock Canadian phrase is *founding peoples*, taken to be the French and the English, whose leaders brought about the Canadian constitution in 1867. Though true in the narrow political sense, it's misleading in that it ignores the many native peoples living in the northernmost parts of North America prior to European contact. As well, 'English' implicitly means 'English speakers', and is thus a linguistic, not an ethnic, category. Given the early Scottish prominence in land exploration and the fur trade, it could be argued that the ethnic Scots, not the English, were one of the two founding peoples.

About the French there is less ambiguity. French explorers and settlers formed a beachhead in what is now the Maritimes during the 17th century, and their descendents became the *Acadians*. In 1755-63 the British expelled many Acadians to other colonies along the Atlantic seaboard, an early example of ethnic cleansing. Some settled in Louisiana, where they became the distinctive people known as *Cajuns*. Yet, with a strong homing instinct, some exiles returned to Acadia.

In the previous century, southern Quebec, *New France,* was settled, and French explorers and fur traders mapped much of the northern part of the continent. After the British conquest of North America and the American Revolution, French Canadians by the early 1800s were on the move westward to the Prairies, where they intermarried with aboriginals, creating a new people, the *Métis.*

As these italicized words suggest, French indelibly affected Canadian English, and not just in the names of ethnic groups and places on the map. Going east to west, one encounters *aboiteau*, a sluice gate in a marshland dike; *gaspereau*, the alewife; *rappie pie* and *tourtière*, kinds of meat pie, the former made with grated potatoes; *sugar pie* (a direct translation of *tarte au sucre*) made from brown or maple sugar; *concession*, especially in Ontario, a tract of surveyed farmland that is divided into lots; *snye*, a side channel of a river, and, on the Prairies, *coulee,* a deep, steep-sided ravine formed by heavy rain or melting snow. To keep one's head warm in winter and hot in summer, there's the *toque*, a knitted woollen cap.

Despite the best efforts of federally-minded politicians in the past, Canada is far from being bilingual from coast to coast to (Arctic) coast. Yet no English speaker can avoid using French-derived words like *prairie* and *portage*. Even apart from such common terms, an *Anglo-Quebecker* will comfortably use a word like *dépanneur*, a convenience store, and an Ontarian in a restaurant will happily or unhappily order *poutine*, a mixture of chipped potatoes and cheese curds swimming in gravy. In Quebec, the mix of two languages can produce delightful hybrids; there, one can order a *hot dog steamé.*

In law, politics, and government, the development of British institutions has uneasily coexisted with the *French fact*, the awareness of Francophones as a distinct, unassimilated group. An older, more melancholy phrase for the parallel peoples of Canada is *two solitudes*, after the namesake novel by Hugh MacLennan. In any event, Canadians are forever wrangling about whether Quebec is a *nation*, a people sharing a history and culture, or a *nation* considered as a separate autonomous political entity. But the paired languages on coins and postage stamps, on the backs of cereal boxes, and in every manner of corporate and federal government logo (*Postes Canada Canada Post*), remind citizens that they live in a paradoxically unified yet historically dualistic country.

A visitor might come to the conclusion that Canada is a nation of phones: *Anglophones,* English-speakers; *Francophones*, French-speakers; and, in Quebec, *allophones,* speakers whose first language is neither French nor English. Immigration will ensure that Canada, like many other Western countries, will become increasingly multicultural. In turn, Canadian English will incorporate words not just from French – which, after all, it has been doing since the times of settlement – but from the languages of southern and eastern Europe, and those from every corner of Africa, Asia, and the Americas. Despite this trend, the fact that, following the Norman Conquest of England in 1066, English in general has owed much of its vocabulary to French has only been reinforced by the Canadian historical experience. It is hard to imagine a time when this will not be the case.

combinations *pl n Brit* a one-piece undergarment with long sleeves and legs

combine *vb* **-bining, -bined 1** to join together **2** to form a chemical compound ▷ *n* **3** an association of people or firms for a common purpose **4** short for **combine harvester**
WORD ORIGIN Latin *com-* together + *bini* two by two

combine harvester *n* a machine used to reap and thresh grain in one process

combings *pl n* the loose hair or fibres removed by combing, esp. from animals

combining form *n* a part of a word that occurs only as part of a compound word, such as *anthropo-* in *anthropology*

combo *n, pl* **-bos** a small group of jazz musicians

combustible *adj* capable of igniting and burning easily

combustion *n* **1** the process of burning **2** a chemical reaction in which a substance combines with oxygen to produce heat and light
WORD ORIGIN Latin *comburere* to burn up

come *vb* **coming, came, come 1** to move towards a place considered near to the speaker or hearer: *come and see me as soon as you can* **2** to arrive or reach: *turn left and continue until you come to a cattle-grid; he came to Britain in the 1920s* **3** to occur: *Christmas comes but once a year* **4** to happen as a result: *no good will come of this* **5** to occur to the mind: *the truth suddenly came to me* **6** to reach a specified point, state, or situation: *a dull brown dress that came down to my ankles; he'd come to a decision* **7** to be produced: *it also comes in other colours* **8 come from** to be or have been a resident or native (of): *my mother comes from Greenock* **9** to become: *it was like a dream come true* **10** *slang* to have an orgasm **11** *Brit & NZ informal* to play the part of: *don't come the innocent with me* **12** (*subjunctive use*) when a specified time arrives: *come next August* **13 as ... as they come** the most characteristic example of a type: *he's an arrogant swine and as devious as they come* **14 come again?** *informal* what did you say? **15 come to light** to be revealed ▷ *interj* **16** an exclamation expressing annoyance or impatience: *come now!* ▸ See also **come about, come across**, etc.
WORD ORIGIN Old English *cuman*

come about *vb* to happen

come across *vb* **1** to meet or find by accident **2** to communicate the intended meaning or impression **3 come across as** to give a certain impression

come at *vb* to attack: *he came at me with an axe*

comeback *n informal* **1** a return to a former position or status **2** a response or retaliation ▷ *vb* **come back 3** to return, esp. to the memory **4** to become fashionable again

come between *vb* to cause the estrangement or separation of (two people)

come by *vb* to find or obtain, esp. accidentally: *Graham filled him in on how he came by the envelope*

Comecon (**kom**-meek-on) *n* (formerly) an economic league of Soviet-oriented Communist nations
WORD ORIGIN Co(uncil for) M(utual) Econ(omic Aid)

comedian *or fem* **comedienne** *n* **1** an entertainer who tells jokes **2** a person who performs in comedy

comedown *n* **1** a decline in status or prosperity **2** *informal* a disappointment ▷ *vb* **come down 3** (of prices) to become lower **4** to reach a decision: *a 1989 court ruling in favour of three councils who wanted Sunday trading banned* **5** to be handed down by tradition or inheritance **6 come down with** to begin to suffer from (illness) **7 come down on** to reprimand sharply **8 come down to** to amount to: *at the end the case came down to the one simple issue* **9 come down in the world** to lose status or prosperity

comedy *n, pl* **-dies 1** a humorous film, play, or broadcast **2** such works as a genre **3** the humorous aspect of life or of events **4** (in classical literature) a play which ends happily
WORD ORIGIN Greek *kōmos* village festival + *aeidein* to sing

come forward *vb* **1** to offer one's services **2** to present oneself

come-hither *adj informal* flirtatious and seductive: *a come-hither look*

come in *vb* **1** to prove to be: *it came in useful* **2** to become fashionable or seasonable **3** to finish a race (in a certain position) **4** to be received: *reports of more deaths came in today* **5** (of money) to be received as income **6** to be involved in a situation: *where do I come in?* **7 come in for** to be the object of: *she came in for a lot of criticism*

come into *vb* **1** to enter **2** to inherit

comely *adj* **-lier, -liest** old-fashioned good-looking **comeliness** *n*
WORD ORIGIN Old English *cȳmlīc* beautiful

come of *vb* to result from: *nothing came of it*

come off *vb* **1** to emerge from a situation in a certain position: *the people who have come off worst are the poor* **2** *informal* to take place **3** *informal* to have the intended effect: *it was a gamble that didn't come off*

come-on *n* **1** *informal* a lure or enticement ▷ *vb* **come on 2** (of power or water) to start running or functioning **3** to make progress: *my plants are coming on nicely* **4** to begin: *I think I've got a cold coming on* **5** to make an entrance on stage **6** to make a certain impression: *he comes on like a hard man* **7 come on to** *informal* to make sexual advances to

come out *vb* **1** to be made public or revealed: *it was only then that the truth came out* **2** to be published or put on sale: *their latest album which came out last month* **3** Also: **come out of the closet** to reveal something formerly concealed, esp. that one is a homosexual **4** *chiefly Brit* to go on strike **5** to declare oneself: *the report has come out in favour of maintaining child benefit* **6** to end up or turn out: *this wine consistently came out top in our tastings; the figures came out exactly right* **7 come out in** to become covered with (a rash or spots) **8 come out with** to say or disclose: *she came out with a remark that left me speechless* **9** to enter society formally

come over *vb* **1** to influence or affect: *I don't know what's come over me* **2** to communicate the intended meaning or impression **3** to give a certain impression **4** to change sides or opinions **5** *informal* to feel a particular sensation: *it makes him come over slightly queasy*

come round *vb* **1** to recover consciousness **2** to change one's opinion

comestibles *pl n* food
WORD ORIGIN Latin *comedere* to eat up

comet *n* a heavenly body that travels round the sun, leaving a long bright trail behind it
WORD ORIGIN Greek *komētēs* long-haired

come through *vb* to survive or endure (an illness or difficult situation) successfully

come to *vb* **1** to regain consciousness **2** to amount to (a total figure)

come up *vb* **1** to be mentioned or arise: *we hope that the difficulties that have arisen in the past will not keep coming up* **2** to be about to happen: *the club has important games coming up* **3 come up against** to come into conflict with **4 come up in the world** to rise in status **5 come up to** to meet a standard **6 come up with** to produce or propose: *he has a knack for coming up with great ideas*

come upon *vb* to meet or encounter unexpectedly

comeuppance *n informal* deserved punishment
WORD ORIGIN from *come up* (in the sense: to appear before a court)

comfit *n* a sugar-coated sweet
WORD ORIGIN Latin *confectum* something prepared

comfort *n* **1** a state of physical ease or well-being **2** relief from suffering or grief **3** a person or thing that brings ease **4 comforts** things that make life easier or more pleasant: *the comforts of home* ▷ *vb* **5** to soothe or console **6** to bring physical ease to **comforting** *adj*
WORD ORIGIN Latin *con-* (intensive) + *fortis* strong

comfortable *adj* **1** giving comfort; relaxing **2** free from trouble or pain **3** *informal* well-off financially **4** not afraid or embarrassed: *he was not comfortable expressing sympathy* **comfortably** *adv*

comforter *n* **1** a person or thing that comforts **2** *Brit* a baby's dummy **3** *Brit* a woollen scarf

comfrey *n* a tall plant with bell-shaped blue, purple, or white flowers
WORD ORIGIN Latin *conferva* water plant

comfy *adj* **-fier, -fiest** *informal* comfortable

comic *adj* **1** humorous; funny **2** of or relating to comedy ▷ *n* **3** a comedian **4** a magazine containing comic strips
WORD ORIGIN Greek *kōmikos*

comical *adj* causing amusement, often because of being ludicrous or ridiculous: *an enthusiasm comical to behold* **comically** *adv*

comic opera n an opera with speech and singing that tells an amusing story

comic strip n a sequence of drawings in a newspaper or magazine, telling a humorous story or an adventure

coming adj 1 (of time or events) approaching or next: *in the coming weeks* 2 likely to be important in the future: *he was regarded as a coming man at the Foreign Office* 3 **have it coming to one** informal to deserve what one is about to suffer ▷ n 4 arrival or approach

comity n, pl **-ties** formal friendly politeness, esp. between different countries **WORD ORIGIN** Latin *comis* affable

comma n the punctuation mark (,) indicating a slight pause and used where there is a list of items or to separate the parts of a sentence **WORD ORIGIN** Greek *komma* clause

command vb 1 to order or compel 2 to have authority over 3 to deserve and get: *a public figure who commands almost universal respect* 4 to look down over: *the house commands a magnificent view of the sea and the islands* ▷ n 5 an authoritative instruction that something must be done 6 the authority to command 7 knowledge; control: *a fluent command of French* 8 a military or naval unit with a specific function 9 *computers* a part of a program consisting of a coded instruction to the computer to perform a specified function **WORD ORIGIN** Latin *com-* (intensive) + *mandare* to order

commandant n an officer in charge of a place or group of people

commandeer vb 1 to seize for military use 2 to take as if by right: *he commandeered the one waiting taxi outside the station* **WORD ORIGIN** Afrikaans *kommandeer*

commander n 1 an officer in command of a military group or operation 2 a middle-ranking naval officer 3 a high-ranking member of some orders of knights

commander-in-chief n, pl **commanders-in-chief** the supreme commander of a nation's armed forces

commanding adj 1 being in charge: *the commanding officer* 2 in a position or situation where success looks certain: *a commanding lead* 3 having the air of authority: *a commanding voice* 4 having a wide view

commandment n a divine command, esp. one of the Ten Commandments in the Old Testament

commando n, pl **-dos** or **-does** a a military unit trained to make swift raids in enemy territory b a member of such a unit **WORD ORIGIN** Dutch *commando* command

commedia dell'arte (kom-**made**-ee-a dell-**art**-tay) n a form of improvised comedy popular in Italy in the 16th century, with stock characters and a stereotyped plot **WORD ORIGIN** Italian

commemorate vb **-rating, -rated** to honour or keep alive the memory of: *a series of events to commemorate the end of the* Second World War **commemoration** n **commemorative** adj **WORD ORIGIN** Latin *com-* (intensive) + *memorare* to remind

commence vb **-mencing, -menced** to begin **WORD ORIGIN** Latin *com-* (intensive) + *initiare* to begin

commencement n 1 the beginning; start 2 *US & Canad* a graduation ceremony

commend vb 1 to praise in a formal manner: *the judge commended her bravery* 2 to recommend: *he commended the scheme warmly* 3 to entrust: *I commend my child to your care* **commendable** adj **commendation** n **WORD ORIGIN** Latin *com-* (intensive) + *mandare* to entrust

commensurable adj 1 measurable by the same standards 2 *maths* a having a common factor b having units of the same dimensions and being related by whole numbers **commensurability** n

commensurate adj 1 corresponding in degree, size, or value 2 commensurable **WORD ORIGIN** Latin *com-* same + *mensurare* to measure

comment n 1 a remark, criticism, or observation 2 a situation or event that expresses some feeling: *a sad comment on the nature of many relationships* 3 talk or gossip 4 a note explaining or criticizing a passage in a text 5 **no comment** I decline to say anything about the matter ▷ vb 6 to remark or express an opinion **WORD ORIGIN** Latin *commentum* invention

commentariat n the journalists and broadcasters who analyse and comment on current affairs **WORD ORIGIN** from COMMENTATOR + PROLETARIAT

commentary n, pl **-taries** 1 a spoken accompaniment to an event, broadcast, or film 2 a series of explanatory notes on a subject

commentate vb **-tating, -tated** to act as a commentator

≡ **USAGE**
≡ The verb *commentate*, derived from
≡ *commentator*, is sometimes used as a
≡ synonym for *comment on* or *provide a*
≡ *commentary for*. It is not yet fully
≡ accepted as standard, though
≡ widespread in sports reporting and
≡ journalism.

commentator n 1 a person who provides a spoken commentary for a broadcast, esp. of a sporting event 2 an expert who reports on and analyses a particular subject

commerce n 1 the buying and selling of goods and services 2 *literary* social relations **WORD ORIGIN** Latin *commercium*

commercial adj 1 of or engaged in commerce: *commercial exploitation of sport* 2 sponsored or paid for by an advertiser: *commercial radio* 3 having profit as the main aim: *this is a more commercial, accessible album than its predecessor* ▷ n 4 a radio or television advertisement

commercialism n 1 the principles and practices of commerce 2 exclusive or inappropriate emphasis on profit

commercialize or **-ise** vb **-izing, -ized** or **-ising, -ised** 1 to make commercial 2 to exploit for profit, esp. at the expense of quality **commercialization** or **-isation** n

commercial traveller n a travelling salesman

commie n, pl **-mies**, adj informal & offensive Communist

commingle vb **-gling, -gled** to mix or be mixed

commis (kom-iss, kom-ee) adj Brit (of a waiter or chef) apprentice: *the commis chef* **WORD ORIGIN** French

commiserate vb **-ating, -ated** (usually foll. by *with*) to express sympathy or pity (for) **commiseration** n **WORD ORIGIN** Latin *com-* together + *miserari* to bewail

commissar n formerly, an official responsible for political education in Communist countries

commissariat n a military department in charge of food supplies **WORD ORIGIN** Medieval Latin *commissarius* commissary

commissary n, pl **-saries** 1 *US* a shop supplying food or equipment, as in a military camp 2 a representative or deputy **WORD ORIGIN** Medieval Latin *commissarius* official in charge

commission n 1 an order for a piece of work, esp. a work of art or a piece of writing 2 a duty given to a person or group to perform 3 the fee or percentage paid to a salesperson for each sale made 4 a group of people appointed to perform certain duties: *a new parliamentary commission on defence* 5 the act of committing a sin or crime 6 *mil* the rank or authority officially given to an officer 7 authority to perform certain duties 8 **in** or **out of commission** in or not in working order ▷ vb 9 to place an order for: *a report commissioned by the United Nations; a new work commissioned by the BBC Symphony Orchestra* 10 *mil* to give a commission to 11 to prepare (a ship) for active service 12 to grant authority to **WORD ORIGIN** Latin *committere* to commit

commissionaire n chiefly Brit a uniformed doorman at a hotel, theatre, or cinema **WORD ORIGIN** French

commissioned officer n a military officer holding a rank by a commission

commissioner n 1 an appointed official in a government department or other organization 2 a member of a commission

commit vb **-mitting, -mitted** 1 to perform (a crime or error) 2 to hand over or allocate: *a marked reluctance to commit new money to business* 3 to pledge to a cause or a course of action 4 to send (someone) to prison or hospital 5 **commit to memory** to memorize 6 **commit to paper** to write down **WORD ORIGIN** Latin *committere* to join

commitment n 1 dedication to a cause or principle 2 an obligation, responsibility, or promise that restricts

C

freedom of action **3** the act of committing or state of being committed

committal *n* the official consignment of a person to a prison or mental hospital

committed *adj* having pledged oneself to a particular belief or course of action: *a committed pacifist*

committee *n* a group of people appointed to perform a specified service or function
WORD ORIGIN Middle English *committen* to entrust

commode *n* **1** a chair with a hinged flap concealing a chamber pot **2** a chest of drawers
WORD ORIGIN French

commodious *adj* with plenty of space
WORD ORIGIN Latin *commodus* convenient

commodity *n, pl* **-ties** something that can be bought or sold
WORD ORIGIN Latin *commoditas* suitability

commodore *n* **1** *Brit* a senior commissioned officer in the navy **2** the president of a yacht club
WORD ORIGIN probably from Dutch *commandeur*

common *adj* **1** frequently encountered: *a fairly common plant; this disease is most common in kittens and young cats* **2** widespread among people in general: *common practice* **3** belonging to two or more people: *we share common interests* **4** belonging to the whole community: *common property* **5** low-class, vulgar, or coarse **6** *maths* belonging to two or more: *the lowest common denominator* **7** not belonging to the upper classes: *the common people* **8** common or garden *informal* ordinary ▷ *n* **9** a piece of open land belonging to all the members of a community **10** in common shared, in joint use ▷ See also **Commons**
▷ **commonly** *adv*
WORD ORIGIN Latin *communis* general

commonality *n, pl* **-ties** **1** the sharing of common attributes **2** the ordinary people

commonalty *n, pl* **-ties** **1** the ordinary people **2** the members of an incorporated society

common cold *n* same as **cold** (sense 17)

commoner *n* a person who does not belong to the nobility

common fraction *n* same as **simple fraction**

common law *n* **1** law based on judges' decisions and custom, as distinct from written laws ▷ *adj* **common-law 2** (of a relationship) regarded as a marriage through being long-standing

Common Market *n* a former name for **European Union**

commonplace *adj* **1** so common or frequent as not to be worth commenting on: *foreign holidays have now become commonplace* **2** dull or unoriginal: *a commonplace observation* ▷ *n* **3** a cliché **4** an ordinary thing
WORD ORIGIN translation of Latin *locus communis* argument of wide application

common room *n chiefly Brit & Austral* a sitting room for students or staff in schools or colleges

commons *pl n* **1** *Brit* shared food or rations **2** short commons reduced rations

Commons *n* the Commons same as **House of Commons**

common sense *n* **1** good practical understanding ▷ *adj* **common-sense 2** inspired by or displaying this

common time *n music* a time signature with four crotchet beats to the bar; four-four time: *a dance in common time*

commonwealth *n* the people of a state or nation viewed politically

Commonwealth *n* the Commonwealth **a** Official name: the Commonwealth of Nations an association of sovereign states that are or at some time have been ruled by Britain **b** the official title of the federated states of Australia

commotion *n* noisy disturbance
WORD ORIGIN Latin *com-* (intensive) + *movere* to move

communal *adj* **1** belonging to or used by a community as a whole **2** of a commune **communally** *adv*

communautaire (kom-**myune**-aw-ter) *adj* supporting the principles of the European Union
WORD ORIGIN French: community

commune¹ *n* **1** a group of people living together and sharing possessions and responsibilities **2** the smallest district of local government in Belgium, France, Italy, and Switzerland
WORD ORIGIN Latin *communia* things held in common

commune² *vb* **-muning, -muned**
● commune with **a** to experience strong emotion for: *communing with nature* **b** to talk intimately with
WORD ORIGIN Old French *comuner* to hold in common

communicable *adj* **1** capable of being communicated **2** (of a disease) capable of being passed on easily

communicant *n Christianity* a person who receives Communion

communicate *vb* **-cating, -cated 1** to exchange (thoughts) or make known (information or feelings) by speech, writing, or other means **2** (usually foll. by *to*) to transmit (to): *the reaction of the rapturous audience communicated itself to the performers* **3** to have a sympathetic mutual understanding **4** *Christianity* to receive Communion **communicator** *n* **communicative** *adj*
WORD ORIGIN Latin *communicare* to share

communicating *adj* making or having a direct connection from one room to another: *the suite is made up of three communicating rooms; the communicating door*

communication *n* **1** the exchange of information, ideas, or feelings **2** something communicated, such as a message **3** communications means of travelling or sending messages

communication cord *n Brit* a chain in a train which may be pulled by a passenger to stop the train in an emergency

communion *n* **1** a sharing of thoughts, emotions, or beliefs **2** communion with strong feelings for: *private communion with nature* **3** a religious group with shared beliefs and practices: *the Anglican communion*
WORD ORIGIN Latin *communis* common

Communion *n Christianity* **1** a ritual commemorating Christ's Last Supper by the consecration of bread and wine **2** the consecrated bread and wine. Also called: **Holy Communion**

communiqué (kom-**mune**-ik-kay) *n* an official announcement
WORD ORIGIN French

communism *n* the belief that private ownership should be abolished and all work and property should be shared by the community **communist** *n, adj*
WORD ORIGIN French *communisme*

Communism *n* **1** a political movement based upon the writings of Karl Marx that advocates communism **2** the political and social system established in countries with a ruling Communist Party **Communist** *n, adj*

community *n, pl* **-ties** **1** all the people living in one district **2** a group of people with shared origins or interests: *the local Jewish community* **3** a group of countries with certain interests in common **4** the public; society **5** a group of interdependent plants and animals inhabiting the same region
WORD ORIGIN Latin *communis* common

community centre *n* a building used by a community for social gatherings or activities

community charge *n* in Britain, the formal name for **poll tax**

community college *n US & Canad* a nonresidential college offering two-year courses of study

community service *n* organized unpaid work intended for the good of the community: often used as a punishment for minor criminals

commutative *adj maths* giving the same result irrespective of the order of the numbers or symbols

commutator *n* a device used to change alternating electric current into direct current

commute *vb* **-muting, -muted 1** to travel some distance regularly between one's home and one's place of work **2** *law* to reduce (a sentence) to one less severe **3** to substitute **4** to pay (an annuity or pension) at one time, instead of in instalments ▷ *n* **5** a journey made by commuting **commutable** *adj* **commutation** *n*
WORD ORIGIN Latin *com-* mutually + *mutare* to change

commuter *n* a person who regularly travels a considerable distance to work

compact¹ *adj* **1** closely packed together **2** neatly fitted into a restricted space **3** concise; brief ▷ *vb* **4** to pack closely together ▷ *n* **5** a small flat case containing a mirror and face powder **compactly** *adv* **compactness** *n*
WORD ORIGIN Latin *com-* together + *pangere* to fasten

compact² *n* a contract or agreement
WORD ORIGIN Latin *com-* together + *pacisci* to contract

Language Communities in Canada
part 2

W hat the speakers of aboriginal languages lack in population size – less than one per cent of Canadians – they make up in rich diversity.

Although the First Nations peoples who live on reserves are on average much younger than other Canadians and their birth rate is three times higher, many of the languages they inherited are endangered. These languages belong to at least 10 families, a few of which encompass numerous languages and dialects. A few, like Algonquian and Athapaskan, may have an enormous geographical sprawl. In its various forms the Algonquian language Cree, which has the largest number of native speakers, is in use from British Columbia to Labrador. Algonquian languages embrace the Mi'kmaq of the Maritimes, the Ojibwa of Ontario, and the Blackfoot of the Prairies. The Athabaskan family, which includes 16 languages within Canada, with Dene the most spoken of them, stretches east from British Columbia to Manitoba and north to the Yukon and the Northwest Territories.

There are regional concentrations: the Siouan family of the Prairies, and the historically important Iroquoian family of southwestern Quebec and southern Ontario, which includes such tribes as the Mohawk, Oneida, Cayuga, Onondaga, and Seneca. The Salish, Tsimshian, and Wakashan families are centred in British Columbia: as is frequently the case, such peoples embrace many languages, and few speakers of them. Belonging to no families are languages that linguists call isolates, such as Haida, spoken in the Queen Charlotte Islands off the northern coast of British Columbia, and Tlingit, spoken in British Columbia and the Yukon, both of which have fewer than 200 speakers. To such depressing statistics can be added the fact that both the Beothuk people of Newfoundland and their language became extinct in the early nineteenth century. We know nothing of what was spoken by the Dorset, a Paleo-Eskimo culture that preceded the arrival of the Inuit in the Arctic.

The fact that native peoples possessed oral cultures, preliterate in the sense of not possessing alphabets or European writing systems, does not mean they lacked forms of graphic communication. The beaded wampum belts of Iroquoian peoples and the birchbark scrolls of the Ojibwa were symbolic and mnemonic devices, the Mi'kmaq had hieroglyphics, and many sites with pictographs (rock paintings) and petroglyphs (rock carvings) can be found across Canada, notably in British Columbia and near Peterborough, Ontario, where hundreds of petroglyphs were carved into crystalline limestone, likely by an Algonquian people between 900 and 1400 AD.

So dire in some respects, European contact with aboriginals was linguistically fertile, spawning hybrid languages like the Michif of the Métis on the Prairies, a mixture of French and Plains Cree. On the Pacific Northwest coast, Chinook Jargon developed, a pidgin lingua franca used by traders, trappers, in the workplace, and in mixed-marriage households, and drew on French and local languages. Some Chinook Jargon migrated into general Canadian English as place names and in such terms as *skookum* (strong, impressive), *potlatch* (ceremonial gift-giving), and *saltchuck* (saltwater).

When Europeans arrived, English became the beneficiary of many words and terms relating to North American plants, animals, geographical features, tools, and transportation. Eventually, some aboriginal languages began to be written, largely thanks to an early nineteenth-century British missionary and amateur linguist named James Evans. Influenced by the Devanagari script used in British India and Pitman shorthand, Evans developed a syllabic writing system that modified the consonants and associated vowels by using orientation: for example, in Cree, the consonant *p* has the shape of a chevron which, depending on the vowel, may point upward, downward, left, or right. The peoples Evans worked with readily adopted his systems and, over time, and in other hands, Canadian syllabics became used for some First Nations languages, and for Inuktitut in the Arctic.

First Nations, *Métis*, and *Inuit* are essentially political terms. Yet each is composed of nations, if we think of a nation as an aboriginal people of common ancestry who share certain social, cultural, or linguistic constants. When people of European origins invented writing systems to record aboriginal speech it could be considered a form of historical redress. What had been destroyed so often was now preserved.

compact disc n a small digital audio disc on which the sound is read by an optical laser system

companion n **1** a person who associates with or accompanies someone: *a travelling companion* **2** a woman paid to live or travel with another woman **3** a guidebook or handbook **4** one of a pair **companionship** n
WORD ORIGIN Late Latin *companio* one who eats bread with another

companionable adj friendly and pleasant to be with **companionably** adv

companionway n a ladder from one deck to another in a ship

company n, pl **-nies 1** a business organization **2** a group of actors **3** a small unit of troops **4** the officers and crew of a ship **5** the fact of being with someone: *I enjoy her company* **6** a number of people gathered together **7** a guest or guests **8** a person's associates **9** **keep someone company** to accompany someone **10** **part company** to disagree or separate
WORD ORIGIN see COMPANION

company sergeant-major n mil the senior noncommissioned officer in a company

comparable adj **1** worthy of comparison **2** able to be compared (with) **comparability** n

comparative adj **1** relative: *despite the importance of his discoveries, he died in comparative poverty* **2** involving comparison: *comparative religion* **3** grammar the form of an adjective or adverb that indicates that the quality denoted is possessed to a greater extent. In English the comparative is marked by the suffix *-er* or the word *more* ▷ n **4** the comparative form of an adjective or adverb **comparatively** adv

compare vb **-paring, -pared 1** to examine in order to observe resemblances or differences: *the survey compared the health of three groups of children* **2** **compare to** to declare to be like: *one ambulance driver compared the carnage to an air crash* **3** (usually foll. by *with*) to resemble: *his storytelling compares with the likes of Le Carré* **4** to bear a specified relation when examined: *this full-flavoured white wine compares favourably with more expensive French wines* **5** **compare notes** to exchange opinions ▷ n **6** **beyond compare** without equal
WORD ORIGIN Latin *com-* together + *par* equal

comparison n **1** a comparing or being compared **2** likeness or similarity: *there is no comparison at all between her and Catherine* **3** grammar the positive, comparative, and superlative forms of an adjective or adverb **4** **in comparison to** or **with** compared to **5** **bear** or **stand comparison with** to be able to be compared with (something else), esp. favourably: *his half-dozen best novels can stand comparison with anyone's*

compartment n **1** one of the sections into which a railway is sometimes divided **2** a separate section: *filing the information away in some compartment of his mind* **3** a small storage space: *the ice-making compartment of the fridge*
WORD ORIGIN French *compartiment*

compartmentalize or **-ise** vb **-izing, -ized** or **-ising, -ised** to put into categories or sections

compass n **1** an instrument for finding direction, with a magnetized needle which points to magnetic north **2** limits or range: *within the compass of a normal sized book such a comprehensive survey is not possible* **3** **compasses** an instrument used for drawing circles or measuring distances, that consists of two arms, joined at one end
WORD ORIGIN Latin *com-* together + *passus* step

compassion n a feeling of distress and pity for the suffering or misfortune of another
WORD ORIGIN Latin *com-* with + *pati* to suffer

compassionate adj showing or having compassion **compassionately** adv

compassionate leave n leave from work granted on the grounds of family illness or bereavement

compatible adj **1** able to exist together harmoniously **2** consistent: *his evidence is fully compatible with the other data* **3** (of pieces of equipment) capable of being used together **compatibility** n
WORD ORIGIN Late Latin *compati* to suffer with

compatriot n a fellow countryman or countrywoman
WORD ORIGIN French *compatriote*

compel vb **-pelling, -pelled 1** to force (to be or do something) **2** to obtain by force: *his performance compelled attention*
WORD ORIGIN Latin *com-* together + *pellere* to drive

compelling adj **1** arousing strong interest: *a compelling new novel* **2** convincing: *compelling evidence*

compendious adj brief but comprehensive

compendium n, pl **-diums** or **-dia 1** Brit a selection of different table games in one container **2** a concise but comprehensive summary
WORD ORIGIN Latin: a saving, literally: something weighed

compensate vb **-sating, -sated 1** to make amends to (someone), esp. for loss or injury **2** to cancel out the effects of (something): *the car's nifty handling fails to compensate for its many flaws* **3** to serve as compensation for (injury or loss) **compensatory** adj
WORD ORIGIN Latin *compensare*

compensation n **1** payment made as reparation for loss or injury **2** the act of making amends for something

compere Brit, Austral, & NZ n **1** a person who introduces a stage, radio, or television show ▷ vb **-pering, -pered 2** to be the compere of
WORD ORIGIN French: godfather

compete vb **-peting, -peted 1** to take part in (a contest or competition) **2** to strive (to achieve something or to be successful): *able to compete on the international market*
WORD ORIGIN Latin *com-* together + *petere* to seek

competence or **competency** n **1** the ability to do something well or effectively **2** a sufficient income to live on **3** the state of being legally competent or qualified

competent adj **1** having sufficient skill or knowledge: *he was a very competent engineer* **2** suitable or sufficient for the purpose: *it was a competent performance, but hardly a remarkable one* **3** having valid legal authority: *lawful detention after conviction by a competent court*
WORD ORIGIN Latin *competens*

competition n **1** the act of competing; rivalry: *competition for places was keen* **2** an event in which people compete **3** the opposition offered by competitors **4** people against whom one competes

competitive adj **1** involving rivalry: *the increasingly competitive computer industry* **2** characterized by an urge to compete: *her naturally competitive spirit* **3** of good enough value to be successful against commercial rivals: *we offer worldwide flights at competitive prices* **competitiveness** n

competitor n a person, team, or firm that competes

compile vb **-piling, -piled 1** to collect and arrange (information) from various sources **2** computers to convert (commands from a computer) from the language used by the person using it into machine code suitable for the computer, using a compiler **compilation** n
WORD ORIGIN Latin *com-* together + *pilare* to thrust down, pack

compiler n **1** a person who compiles information **2** a computer program that converts a high-level programming language into the machine language used by a computer

complacency n extreme self-satisfaction **complacent** adj **complacently** adv

complain vb **1** to express resentment or displeasure **2** **complain of** to state that one is suffering from a pain or illness: *he complained of breathing trouble and chest pains* **3** to make a formal protest: *he complained to the police about his rowdy neighbours*
WORD ORIGIN Latin *com-* (intensive) + *plangere* to bewail

complainant n law a plaintiff

complaint n **1** the act of complaining **2** a reason for complaining **3** a mild illness or disorder **4** a formal protest

complaisant (kom-**play**-zant) adj willing to please or oblige **complaisance** n
WORD ORIGIN Latin *complacere* to please greatly

complement n **1** a person or thing that completes something **2** a complete amount or number: *a full complement of staff nurses and care assistants* **3** the officers and crew needed to man a ship **4** grammar a word or words added to the verb to complete the meaning of the predicate in a sentence, as *a fool* in *He is a fool* or *that he would come* in *I hoped that he would come* **5** maths the angle that when added to a specified angle produces a right angle ▷ vb **6** to complete or form a complement to
WORD ORIGIN Latin *com-* (intensive) + *plere* to fill

USAGE
Avoid confusion with **compliment**.

complementary adj 1 forming a complete or balanced whole 2 forming a complement

complementary medicine n same as **alternative medicine**

complete adj 1 thorough; absolute: it was a complete shambles 2 perfect in quality or kind: he is the complete modern footballer 3 finished 4 having all the necessary parts 5 **complete with** having as an extra feature or part: a mansion complete with swimming pool ▷ vb -pleting, -pleted 6 to finish 7 to make whole or perfect **completely** adv **completion** n
WORD ORIGIN Latin complere to fill up

complex adj 1 made up of interconnected parts 2 intricate or complicated 3 maths of or involving complex numbers ▷ n 4 a whole made up of related parts: a leisure complex including a gymnasium, squash courts, and a 20-metre swimming pool 5 psychoanal a group of unconscious feelings that influences a person's behaviour 6 informal an obsession or phobia: I have never had a complex about my height
WORD ORIGIN Latin com- together + plectere to braid

USAGE
Complex is sometimes used where complicated is meant. Complex should be used to say only that something consists of several parts rather than that, because something consists of many parts, it is difficult to understand or analyse.

complex fraction n maths a fraction in which the numerator or denominator or both contain fractions

complexion n 1 the colour and general appearance of the skin of a person's face 2 character or nature: the political complexion of the government
WORD ORIGIN Latin complexio a combination

complexity n, pl -ties 1 the state or quality of being intricate or complex 2 something complicated

complex number n any number of the form a + bi, where a and b are real numbers and i = √−1

compliance n 1 complying 2 a tendency to do what others want **compliant** adj

complicate vb -cating, -cated to make or become complex or difficult to deal with
WORD ORIGIN Latin complicare to fold together

complicated adj difficult to understand or deal with
USAGE
See at **complex**.

complication n 1 something which makes a situation more difficult to deal with: an added complication is the growing concern for the environment 2 a medical condition arising as a consequence of another

complicity n, pl -ties the fact of being an accomplice in a crime

compliment n 1 an expression of praise 2 **compliments** formal greetings ▷ vb

3 to express admiration for
WORD ORIGIN Italian complimento
USAGE
Avoid confusion with **complement**.

complimentary adj 1 expressing praise 2 free of charge: a complimentary drink

comply vb -plies, -plying, -plied to act in accordance (with a rule, order, or request)
WORD ORIGIN Spanish cumplir to complete

component n 1 a constituent part or feature of a whole 2 maths one of a set of two or more vectors whose resultant is a given vector ▷ adj 3 forming or functioning as a part or feature: over 60 component parts
WORD ORIGIN Latin componere to put together

comport vb formal 1 **comport oneself** to behave in a specified way 2 **comport with** to suit or be appropriate to **comportment** n
WORD ORIGIN Latin comportare to collect

compose vb -posing, -posed 1 to put together or make up 2 to be the component elements of 3 to create (a musical or literary work) 4 to calm (oneself) 5 to arrange artistically 6 printing to set up (type)
WORD ORIGIN Latin componere to put in place

composed adj (of people) in control of their feelings

composer n a person who writes music

composite adj 1 made up of separate parts 2 (of a plant) with flower heads made up of many small flowers, such as the dandelion 3 maths capable of being factorized: a composite function ▷ n 4 something composed of separate parts 5 a composite plant
WORD ORIGIN Latin compositus well arranged

Composite adj of a style of classical architecture which combines elements of the Ionic and Corinthian styles

composite school n Canad a secondary school which offers both academic courses and vocational training

composition n 1 the act of putting together or composing 2 something composed 3 the things or parts which make up a whole 4 a work of music, art, or literature 5 the harmonious arrangement of the parts of a work of art 6 a written exercise; an essay 7 printing the act or technique of setting up type

compositor n a person who arranges type for printing

compos mentis adj sane
WORD ORIGIN Latin

compost n 1 a mixture of decaying plants and manure, used as a fertilizer 2 soil mixed with fertilizer, used for growing plants ▷ vb 3 to make (vegetable matter) into compost
WORD ORIGIN Latin compositus put together

composure n the state of being calm or unworried

compote n fruit stewed with sugar or in a syrup
WORD ORIGIN French

compound[1] n 1 chem a substance that contains atoms of two or more chemical elements held together by chemical bonds 2 any combination of two or more parts, features, or qualities 3 a word formed from two existing words or combining forms ▷ vb 4 to combine so as to create a compound 5 to make by combining parts or features: the film's score is compounded from surging strings, a heavenly chorus and jazzy saxophones 6 to intensify by an added element: the problems of undertaking relief work are compounded by continuing civil war 7 law to agree not to prosecute in return for payment: to compound a crime ▷ adj 8 composed of two or more parts or elements 9 music with a time in which the number of beats per bar is a multiple of three: such tunes are usually in a form of compound time, for example six-four **compoundable** adj
WORD ORIGIN Latin componere to put in order

compound[2] n a fenced enclosure containing buildings, such as a camp for prisoners of war
WORD ORIGIN Malay kampong village

compound fracture n a fracture in which the broken bone pierces the skin

compound interest n interest paid on a sum and its accumulated interest

comprehend vb 1 to understand 2 to include **comprehensible** adj
WORD ORIGIN Latin comprehendere

comprehension n 1 understanding 2 inclusion

comprehensive adj 1 of broad scope or content 2 (of car insurance) providing protection against most risks, including third-party liability, fire, theft, and damage 3 Brit of the comprehensive school system ▷ n 4 Brit a comprehensive school

comprehensive school n Brit a secondary school for children of all abilities

compress vb 1 to squeeze together 2 to condense ▷ n 3 a cloth or pad applied firmly to some part of the body to cool inflammation or relieve pain
WORD ORIGIN Latin comprimere

compression n 1 the act of compressing 2 the reduction in volume and increase in pressure of the fuel mixture in an internal-combustion engine before ignition

compressor n a device that compresses a gas

comprise vb -prising, -prised 1 to be made up of: the group comprised six French diplomats, five Italians, and three Bulgarians 2 to form or make up: women comprised 57 per cent of all employees, but less than 10 per cent of managers
WORD ORIGIN French compris included
USAGE
The use of of after comprise should be avoided: the library comprises (not comprises of) 500 000 books and manuscripts.

compromise (kom-prom-mize) n 1 settlement of a dispute by concessions on each side: everyone pleaded for compromise; the compromise was only reached after hours of hard bargaining 2 the terms of such a settlement 3 something

midway between different things ▷ *vb* -**mising, -mised 4** to settle (a dispute) by making concessions **5** to put (oneself or another person) in a dishonourable position ▷ *adj* **6** being, or having the nature or, a compromise: *a compromise solution* **compromising** *adj*
WORD ORIGIN Latin *compromittere* to promise at the same time

comptroller *n* a financial controller

compulsion *n* **1** an irresistible urge to perform some action **2** compelling or being compelled
WORD ORIGIN Latin *compellere* to compel

compulsive *adj* **1** resulting from or acting from a compulsion **2** irresistible or absorbing **compulsively** *adv*

compulsory *adj* required by regulations or laws

compulsory purchase *n* the enforced purchase of a property by a local authority or government department

compunction *n* a feeling of guilt or regret
WORD ORIGIN Latin *compungere* to sting

computation *n* a calculation involving numbers or quantities **computational** *adj*

compute *vb* -**puting, -puted** to calculate (an answer or result), often by using a computer
WORD ORIGIN Latin *computare*

computer *n* an electronic device that processes data according to a set of instructions

computer game *n* a game played on a home computer by manipulating a joystick or keys in response to the graphics on the screen

computerize or -**ise** *vb* -**izing, -ized** or -**ising, -ised 1** to equip with a computer **2** to control or perform (operations) by means of a computer **computerization** or -**isation** *n*

computing *n* **1** the activity of using computers and writing programs for them **2** the study of computers and their application

comrade *n* **1** a fellow member of a union or a socialist political party **2** a companion **comradely** *adj* **comradeship** *n*
WORD ORIGIN French *camarade*

con[1] *informal n* **1** same as **confidence trick** ▷ *vb* **conning, conned 2** to swindle or defraud

con[2] *n* see **pros and cons**
WORD ORIGIN Latin *contra* against

con[3] *n slang* a convict

Con *politics* Conservative

con- *prefix* see **com-**

concatenation *n formal* a series of linked events
WORD ORIGIN Latin *com-* together + *catena* chain

concave *adj* curving inwards like the inside surface of a ball **concavity** *n*
WORD ORIGIN Latin *concavus* arched

conceal *vb* **1** to cover and hide **2** to keep secret **concealment** *n*
WORD ORIGIN Latin *com-* (intensive) + *celare* to hide

concede *vb* -**ceding, -ceded 1** to admit (something) as true or correct **2** to give

up or grant (something, such as a right) **3** to acknowledge defeat in (a contest or argument)
WORD ORIGIN Latin *concedere*

conceit *n* **1** an excessively high opinion of oneself **2** *literary* a far-fetched or clever comparison
WORD ORIGIN see CONCEIVE

conceited *adj* having an excessively high opinion of oneself **conceitedness** *n*

conceivable *adj* capable of being understood, believed, or imagined **conceivably** *adv*

conceive *vb* -**ceiving, -ceived 1** to imagine or think **2** to consider in a certain way: *we must do what we conceive to be right* **3** to form in the mind **4** to become pregnant
WORD ORIGIN Latin *concipere* to take in

concentrate *vb* -**trating, -trated 1** to focus all one's attention, thoughts, or efforts on something: *she tried hard to concentrate, but her mind kept flashing back to the previous night* **2** to bring or come together in large numbers or amounts in one place: *a flawed system that concentrates power in the hands of the few* **3** to make (a liquid) stronger by removing water from it ▷ *n* **4** a concentrated substance **concentrated** *adj*
WORD ORIGIN Latin *com-* same + *centrum* centre

concentration *n* **1** intense mental application **2** the act of concentrating **3** something that is concentrated **4** the amount or proportion of a substance in a mixture or solution

concentration camp *n* a prison camp for civilian prisoners, as in Nazi Germany

concentric *adj* having the same centre: *concentric circles*
WORD ORIGIN Latin *com-* same + *centrum* centre

concept *n* an abstract or general idea: *one of the basic concepts of quantum theory*
WORD ORIGIN Latin *concipere* to conceive

conception *n* **1** a notion, idea, or plan **2** the fertilization of an egg by a sperm in the Fallopian tube followed by implantation in the womb **3** origin or beginning: *the gap between the conception of an invention and its production*
WORD ORIGIN Latin *concipere* to conceive

conceptual *adj* of or based on concepts

conceptualize or -**ise** *vb* -**izing, -ized** or -**ising, -ised** to form a concept or idea of **conceptualization** or -**isation** *n*

concern *n* **1** anxiety or worry: *the current concern over teenage pregnancies* **2** something that is of interest or importance to a person **3** regard or interest: *a scrupulous concern for client confidentiality* **4** a business or firm ▷ *vb* **5** to worry or make anxious **6** to involve or interest: *he had converted the building into flats without concerning himself with the niceties of planning permission* **7** to be relevant or important to
WORD ORIGIN Latin *com-* together + *cernere* to sift

concerned *adj* **1** interested or involved: *I have spoken to the person concerned and he has no recollection of saying such a thing* **2** worried or anxious: *we are increasingly concerned for her safety*

concerning *prep* about; regarding

concert *n* **1** a performance of music by players or singers in front of an audience **2** **in concert a** working together **b** (of musicians or singers) performing live
WORD ORIGIN Latin *com-* together + *certare* strive

concerted *adj* decided or planned by mutual agreement: *a concerted effort*

concertina *n* **1** a small musical instrument similar to an accordion ▷ *vb* -**naing, -naed 2** to collapse or fold up like a concertina
WORD ORIGIN from *concert*

concerto (kon-**chair**-toe) *n, pl* -**tos** or -**ti** (-tee) a large-scale composition for an orchestra and one or more soloists
WORD ORIGIN Italian

concert pitch *n* the internationally agreed pitch to which concert instruments are tuned for performance

concession *n* **1** any grant of rights, land, or property by a government, local authority, or company **2** a reduction in price for a certain category of person: *fare concessions for senior citizens* **3** the act of yielding or conceding **4** something conceded **5** *Canad* **a** a land subdivision in a township survey **b** same as **concession road** ▷ **concessionary** *adj*
WORD ORIGIN Latin *concedere* to concede

concessionaire *n* someone who holds a concession

concession road *n Canad* one of a series of roads separating concessions in a township

conch *n, pl* **conchs** or **conches 1** a marine mollusc with a large brightly coloured spiral shell **2** its shell
WORD ORIGIN Greek *konkhē* shellfish

concierge (kon-see-**airzh**) *n* (esp. in France) a caretaker in a block of flats
WORD ORIGIN French

conciliate *vb* -**ating, -ated** to try to end a disagreement with or pacify (someone) **conciliator** *n*
WORD ORIGIN Latin *conciliare* to bring together

conciliation *n* **1** the act of conciliating **2** a method of helping the parties in a dispute to reach agreement, esp. divorcing or separating couples to part amicably

conciliatory *adj* intended to end a disagreement

concise *adj* brief and to the point **concisely** *adv* **conciseness** or **concision** *n*
WORD ORIGIN Latin *concidere* to cut short

conclave *n* **1** a secret meeting **2** *RC Church* a private meeting of cardinals to elect a new pope
WORD ORIGIN Latin *clavis* key

conclude *vb* -**cluding, -cluded 1** to decide by reasoning: *the investigation concluded that key data for the paper were faked* **2** to come or bring to an end: *the festival concludes on December 19th* **3** to arrange or settle finally: *officials have refused to comment on the failure to conclude an agreement*
WORD ORIGIN Latin *concludere*

conclusion *n* **1** a final decision, opinion, or judgment based on reasoning: *the obvious conclusion is that*

A History of English – Viking Invaders

The English language was first brought to Britain by Germanic tribes, most notably the Angles, Saxons, and Jutes. These tribes would eventually be conquered by the Normans, but two centuries before that, a different group of Northern invaders moved into Britain, leaving a lasting effect on the English language.

From about 800 AD Danish invaders began attacking the British Isles, particularly the Anglo-Saxon kingdoms in what is now England. This was not the first Danish import to the British Isles. The principal Anglo-Saxon epic poem, *Beowulf*, tells of the Danish king Hrothgar, whose stronghold is attacked by a monster; England and the English are not mentioned in the poem at all.

The Anglo-Saxons would not have been too far estranged linguistically or culturally from their attackers – although centuries of prosperity and conversion to Christianity probably aggravated any internecine enmity the two tribes might have felt – and the Anglo-Saxon poem known as *The Battle of Maldon* depicts the Saxons and the Danes taunting each other in what seems to be a mutually intelligible language. The Anglo-Saxons were unable to repel these Viking invaders completely, and the Danes succeeded in occupying much of what is now the East Midlands.

Had the Anglo-Saxons been more similar to the Danes, they might have simply assimilated with their invaders, and the Viking invasion might have had little or no effect on the English language. However, their languages were not necessarily as close as the Old English poems indicate.

Like the Danes, the Angles, Saxons, and Jutes were Germanic peoples, and they spoke a Germanic language. However, the Anglo-Saxons spoke a West Germanic language, and the Danes a North Germanic one.

One of the lasting effects of the Viking invasion is place-names. Anglo-Saxon had its own conventions for naming settlements; *burg*, an ancient West Germanic word meaning a fortified town or citadel, was common, and survives in various forms in names like *Edinburgh*, *Middlesbrough*, *Peterborough*, and even *Canterbury*. The Danes brought their own words; in particular, any place-name ending in *–by* or *–thorpe* (both Old Norse words for 'settlement'), such as *Grimsby* or *Scunthorpe*, probably used to be a Danish colony.

The Danes also brought some entirely new vocabulary which replaced their Anglo-Saxon equivalents and became the Modern English words we know today: *law* comes from Old Norse *lög*; the Anglo-Saxon word was *æ*; *window* comes from Norse *vindauga*; the Anglo-Saxon word was *eagþyrel*; and *sky* comes from Norse *skȳ*; the Anglo-Saxon word was *lyft*. The Danes gave us our modern plural pronoun *they* and plural possessive *their* as well; Anglo-Saxon used *hie* and *hiera*.

Old Norse also had different pronunciation conventions than Old English. This meant that even when the two languages had a word in common, there was a Danish and an English way of pronouncing it. An example of this was *shirt*, which in Old English was written *scyrte* (pronounced with an 'sh' sound) and in Old Norse was *skyrte* (pronounced with 'sk' as written). Both words referred to a garment we would call a 'tunic', something that covered one from the torso down to below the waist. Both versions of the word survive in modern English, but now refer to two different garments.

But the most interesting change is the creation of the word *she*. Old English for *she* was *heo*; Old Norse would have been something like *hun*. So where did *she* come from? Well, in Old English, the first of two consecutive vowels was given the most stress: *hEo*; in Old Norse, the second vowel was stressed: *heO*. Anglo-Saxons living under the Danes must have started pronouncing *heo* with a Danish accent. Eventually, the first vowel was so shortened it became a semi-consonant: *hyo*. When 'h' and 'y' occur together, eventually an 'sh' sound results. In Middle English, we see this word written *sho* or *scho*. Eventually, the 'o' raised to present-day 'e', probably passing through an intermediate stage (like *scha*) that has not been recorded.

something is being covered up **2** end or ending **3** outcome or result: *if you take that strategy to its logical conclusion you end up with communism* **4** **in conclusion** finally **5** **jump to conclusions** to come to a conclusion too quickly, without sufficient thought or evidence

conclusive *adj* putting an end to doubt: *there is no conclusive proof of this* **conclusively** *adv*

concoct *vb* **1** to make by combining different ingredients **2** to invent or make up (a story or plan) **concoction** *n*
WORD ORIGIN Latin *coquere* to cook

concomitant *adj* **1** existing or along with (something else): *the concomitant health gains* ▷ *n* **2** something that is concomitant
WORD ORIGIN Latin *com-* with + *comes* companion

concord *n* **1** agreement or harmony **2** peaceful relations between nations **3** *music* a harmonious combination of musical notes **concordant** *adj*
WORD ORIGIN Latin *com-* same + *cor* heart

concordance *n* **1** a state of harmony or agreement **2** an alphabetical list of words in a literary work, with the context and often the meaning

concordat *n* *formal* a treaty or agreement, such as one between the Vatican and another state
WORD ORIGIN Latin *concordatum* something agreed

concourse *n* **1** a large open space in a public place, where people can meet: *a crowded concourse at Heathrow Airport* **2** a crowd
WORD ORIGIN Latin *concurrere* to run together

concrete *n* **1** a building material made of cement, sand, stone, and water that hardens to a stonelike mass ▷ *vb* **-creting, -creted** **2** to cover with concrete ▷ *adj* **3** made of concrete **4** specific as opposed to general **5** relating to things that can be perceived by the senses, as opposed to abstractions
WORD ORIGIN Latin *concrescere* to grow together

concretion *n* **1** a solidified mass **2** the act of solidifying

concubine (kon-kew-bine) *n* **1** old-fashioned a woman living with a man as his wife, but not married to him **2** a secondary wife in polygamous societies **concubinage** *n*
WORD ORIGIN Latin *concumbere* to lie together

concupiscence (kon-**kew**-piss-enss) *n* *formal* strong sexual desire **concupiscent** *adj*
WORD ORIGIN Latin *concupiscere* to covet

concur *vb* **-curring, -curred** to agree; be in accord
WORD ORIGIN Latin *concurrere* to run together

concurrence *n* **1** agreement **2** simultaneous occurrence

concurrent *adj* **1** taking place at the same time or place **2** meeting at, approaching, or having a common point: *concurrent lines* **3** in agreement **concurrently** *adv*

concuss *vb* to injure (the brain) by a fall or blow
WORD ORIGIN Latin *concutere* to disturb greatly

concussion *n* **1** a brain injury caused by a blow or fall, usually resulting in loss of consciousness **2** violent shaking

condemn *vb* **1** to express strong disapproval of **2** to pronounce sentence on in a court of law **3** to force into a particular state: *a system that condemns most of our youngsters to failure* **4** to judge or declare (something) unfit for use **5** to indicate the guilt of: *everything the man had said condemned him, morally if not technically* **condemnation** *n* **condemnatory** *adj*
WORD ORIGIN Latin *condemnare*

condensation *n* **1** anything that has condensed from a vapour, esp. on a window **2** the act of condensing, or the state of being condensed

condense *vb* **-densing, -densed** **1** to express in fewer words **2** to increase the density of; concentrate **3** to change from a gas to a liquid or solid
WORD ORIGIN Latin *condensare*

condensed milk *n* milk thickened by evaporation, with sugar added

condenser *n* **1** an apparatus for reducing gases to their liquid or solid form by the removal of heat **2** same as **capacitor** **3** a lens that concentrates light

condescend *vb* **1** to behave patronizingly towards (one's supposed inferiors) **2** to do something as if it were beneath one's dignity **condescending** *adj* **condescension** *n*
WORD ORIGIN Church Latin *condescendere*

condiment *n* any seasoning for food, such as salt, pepper, or sauces
WORD ORIGIN Latin *condire* to pickle

condition *n* **1** a particular state of being: *the human condition; the van is in very poor condition* **2** **conditions** circumstances: *worsening weather conditions; the government pledged to improve living and working conditions* **3** a necessary requirement for something else to happen: *food is a necessary condition for survival* **4** a restriction or a qualification **5** a term of an agreement: *the conditions of the lease are set out* **6** state of physical fitness, esp. good health: *she is in a serious condition in hospital; out of condition* **7** an ailment: *a heart condition* **8** **on condition that** provided that ▷ *vb* **9** to accustom or alter the reaction of (a person or animal) to a particular stimulus or situation **10** to treat with a conditioner **11** to make fit or healthy **12** to influence or determine the form that something takes: *he argued that the failure of Latin American industry was conditioned by international economic structures* **conditioning** *n, adj*
WORD ORIGIN Latin *con-* together + *dicere* to say

conditional *adj* **1** depending on other factors **2** *grammar* expressing a condition on which something else depends, for example 'If he comes' is a conditional clause in the sentence 'If he comes I shall go'

conditioner *n* a thick liquid used when washing to make hair or clothes feel softer

condo *n, pl* **-dos** *US & Canad informal* a condominium building or apartment

condolence *n* sympathy expressed for someone in grief or pain **condole** *vb*
WORD ORIGIN Latin *com-* together + *dolere* to grieve

condom *n* a rubber sheath worn on the penis or in the vagina during sexual intercourse to prevent conception or infection
WORD ORIGIN origin unknown

condominium *n, pl* **-ums** **1** *Austral, US, & Canad* **a** an apartment building in which each apartment is individually owned **b** an apartment in such a building **2** joint rule of a state by two or more other states
WORD ORIGIN Latin *com-* together + *dominium* ownership

condone *vb* **-doning, -doned** to overlook or forgive (an offence or wrongdoing)
WORD ORIGIN Latin *com-* (intensive) + *donare* to donate

condor *n* a very large rare S American vulture
WORD ORIGIN S American Indian *kuntur*

conducive *adj* (often foll. by *to*) likely to lead to or produce (a result)
WORD ORIGIN Latin *com-* together + *ducere* to lead

conduct *n* **1** behaviour **2** the management or handling of an activity or business ▷ *vb* **3** to carry out: *the police are conducting an investigation into the affair* **4** **conduct oneself** to behave (oneself) **5** to control (an orchestra or choir) by the movements of the hands or a baton **6** to accompany and guide (people or a party): *a conducted tour* **7** to transmit (heat or electricity)
WORD ORIGIN Latin *com-* together + *ducere* to lead

conductance *n* the ability of a specified body to conduct electricity

conduction *n* the transmission of heat or electricity

conductivity *n* the property of transmitting heat, electricity, or sound

conductor *n* **1** a person who conducts an orchestra or choir **2** an official on a bus who collects fares **3** *US, Canad, & NZ* a railway official in charge of a train **4** something that conducts electricity or heat **conductress** *fem n*

conduit (kon-**dew**-it) *n* **1** a route or system for transferring things from one place to another: *a conduit for smuggling cocaine into the United States* **2** a channel or tube for carrying a fluid or electrical cables **3** a means of access or communication
WORD ORIGIN Latin *conducere* to lead

cone *n* **1** a geometric solid consisting of a circular or oval base, tapering to a point **2** a cone-shaped wafer shell used to contain ice cream **3** the scaly fruit of a conifer tree **4** *Brit, Austral, & NZ* a plastic cone used as a temporary traffic marker on roads **5** a type of cell in the retina, sensitive to colour and bright light
WORD ORIGIN Greek *kōnus* pine cone, geometrical cone

coney n same as **cony**

confab n informal a conversation

confabulation n formal a conversation **WORD ORIGIN** Latin confabulari to talk together

confection n 1 any sweet food, such as a cake or a sweet 2 old-fashioned an elaborate piece of clothing **WORD ORIGIN** Latin confectio a preparing

confectioner n a person who makes or sells confectionery

confectionery n, pl -eries 1 sweets and chocolates collectively: a drop in confectionery sales 2 the art or business of a confectioner

confederacy n, pl -cies a union of states or people joined for a common purpose **confederal** adj **WORD ORIGIN** Late Latin confoederatio agreement

confederate n 1 a state or individual that is part of a confederacy 2 an accomplice or conspirator ▷ adj 3 united; allied ▷ vb -ating, -ated 4 to unite in a confederacy **WORD ORIGIN** Late Latin confoederare to unite by a league

Confederate adj of or supporting those American states which withdrew from the USA in 1860–61, leading to the American Civil War

confederation n 1 a union or alliance of states or groups 2 confederating or being confederated 3 a federation

confer vb -ferring, -ferred 1 to discuss together 2 to grant or give: the power conferred by wealth **conferment** n **conferrable** adj **WORD ORIGIN** Latin com- together + ferre to bring

conference n a meeting for formal consultation or discussion **WORD ORIGIN** Medieval Latin conferentia

confess vb 1 to admit (a fault or crime) 2 to admit to be true, esp. reluctantly 3 Christianity to declare (one's sins) to God or to a priest, so as to obtain forgiveness **WORD ORIGIN** Latin confiteri to admit

confession n 1 something confessed 2 an admission of one's faults, sins, or crimes 3 **confession of faith** a formal public statement of religious beliefs

confessional n 1 Christianity a small room or enclosed stall in a church where a priest hears confessions ▷ adj 2 of or suited to a confession

confessor n 1 Christianity a priest who hears confessions and gives spiritual advice 2 history a person who demonstrates his Christian religious faith by the holiness of his life: Edward the Confessor

confetti n small pieces of coloured paper thrown at weddings **WORD ORIGIN** Italian

confidant or fem **confidante** n a person to whom private matters are confided **WORD ORIGIN** French confident

confide vb -fiding, -fided 1 **confide in** to tell (something) in confidence to 2 formal to entrust into another's keeping **WORD ORIGIN** Latin confidere

confidence n 1 trust in a person or thing 2 belief in one's own abilities 3 trust or a trustful relationship: she won first the confidence, then the admiration, of her bosses 4 something confided, such as a secret 5 **in confidence** as a secret

confidence trick n a swindle in which the swindler gains the victim's trust in order to cheat him or her

confident adj 1 having or showing certainty: we are now confident that this technique works 2 sure of oneself **confidently** adv **WORD ORIGIN** Latin confidere to have complete trust in

confidential adj 1 spoken or given in confidence 2 entrusted with another's secret affairs: a confidential secretary 3 suggestive of intimacy: a halting, confidential manner **confidentiality** n **confidentially** adv

confiding adj trusting: a close and confiding relationship **confidingly** adv

configuration n 1 the arrangement of the parts of something 2 the form or outline of such an arrangement **WORD ORIGIN** Late Latin configurare to model on something

confine vb -fining, -fined 1 to keep within bounds 2 to restrict the free movement of: a nasty dose of flu which confined her to bed for days ▷ n 3 **confines** boundaries or limits **WORD ORIGIN** Latin finis boundary

confinement n 1 being confined 2 the period of childbirth

confirm vb 1 to prove to be true or valid 2 to reaffirm (something), so as to make (it) more definite: she confirmed that she is about to resign as leader of the council 3 to strengthen: this cruise confirmed my first impressions of the boat's performance 4 to formally make valid 5 to administer the rite of confirmation to **WORD ORIGIN** Latin confirmare

confirmation n 1 the act of confirming 2 something that confirms 3 a rite in several Christian churches that admits a baptized person to full church membership

confirmed adj long-established in a habit or condition: a confirmed bachelor

confiscate vb -cating, -cated to seize (property) by authority **confiscation** n **WORD ORIGIN** Latin confiscare to seize for the public treasury

conflagration n a large destructive fire **WORD ORIGIN** Latin com- (intensive) + flagrare to burn

conflate vb -flating, -flated to combine or blend into a whole **conflation** n **WORD ORIGIN** Latin conflare to blow together

conflict n 1 opposition between ideas or interests 2 a struggle or battle ▷ vb 3 to be incompatible **conflicting** adj **WORD ORIGIN** Latin confligere to combat

confluence n 1 a place where rivers flow into one another 2 a gathering **confluent** adj **WORD ORIGIN** Latin confluere to flow together

conform vb 1 to comply with accepted standards, rules, or customs 2 (usually foll. by with) to be like or in accordance

with: people tend to absorb ideas that conform with their existing beliefs, and reject those that do not **WORD ORIGIN** Latin confirmare to strengthen

conformation n 1 the general shape of an object 2 the arrangement of the parts of an object

conformist adj 1 **a** (of a person) behaving or thinking like most other people rather than in an original or unconventional way: a shy and conformist type of boy **b** (of an organization or society) expecting everyone to behave in the same way: the school was a dull, conformist place for staff and students alike ▷ n 2 a person who behaves or thinks like most other people rather than in an original or unconventional way

conformity n, pl -ities 1 compliance in actions or behaviour with certain accepted rules, customs, or standards 2 likeness

confound vb 1 to astound or bewilder 2 to fail to distinguish between 3 **confound it!** damn it! **WORD ORIGIN** Latin confundere to mingle, pour together

confounded adj 1 informal damned: what a confounded nuisance! 2 bewildered; confused: her silent, utterly confounded daughter

confrere (kon-frair) n a colleague: their Gallic confreres **WORD ORIGIN** Medieval Latin confrater

confront vb 1 (of a problem or task) to present itself to 2 to meet face to face in hostility or defiance 3 to present (someone) with something, esp. in order to accuse or criticize: she finally confronted him with her suspicions **WORD ORIGIN** Latin com- together + frons forehead

confrontation n a serious argument or fight

Confucianism n the teachings of Confucius (551–479 BC), the ancient Chinese philosopher, which emphasize moral order **Confucian** n, adj **Confucianist** n

confuse vb -fusing, -fused 1 to fail to distinguish between one thing and another 2 to perplex or disconcert 3 to make unclear: he confused his talk with irrelevant detail 4 to throw into disorder **confusing** adj **confusingly** adv **WORD ORIGIN** Latin confundere to pour together

confused adj 1 lacking a clear understanding of something 2 disordered and difficult to understand or make sense of: a confused dream

confusion n 1 mistaking one person or thing for another 2 bewilderment 3 lack of clarity 4 disorder

confute vb -futing, -futed to prove to be wrong **confutation** n **WORD ORIGIN** Latin confutare to check, silence

conga n 1 a Latin American dance performed by a number of people in single file 2 a large single-headed drum played with the hands ▷ vb -gaing, -gaed 3 to dance the conga **WORD ORIGIN** from American Spanish

congeal *vb* to change from a liquid to a semisolid state
WORD ORIGIN Latin *com-* together + *gelare* to freeze

congenial *adj* **1** friendly, pleasant, or agreeable: *he found the Botanic Gardens a most congenial place for strolling* **2** having a similar disposition or tastes **congeniality** *n*
WORD ORIGIN *con-* (same) + *genial*

congenital *adj* (of an abnormal condition) existing at birth but not inherited: *congenital heart disease* **congenitally** *adv*
WORD ORIGIN Latin *con-* together + *genitus* born

conger *n* a large sea eel
WORD ORIGIN Greek *gongros*

congested *adj* **1** crowded to excess **2** clogged or blocked **congestion** *n*
WORD ORIGIN Latin *congerere* to pile up

conglomerate *n* **1** a large corporation made up of many different companies **2** a thing composed of several different elements **3** a type of rock consisting of rounded pebbles or fragments held together by silica or clay ▷ *vb* **-ating, -ated 4** to form into a mass ▷ *adj* **5** made up of several different elements **6** (of rock) consisting of rounded pebbles or fragments held together by silica or clay **conglomeration** *n*
WORD ORIGIN Latin *conglomerare* to roll up

congratulate *vb* **-lating, -lated 1** to express one's pleasure to (a person) at his or her success or good fortune **2 congratulate oneself** to consider oneself clever or fortunate (as a result of): *she congratulated herself on her own business acumen* **congratulatory** *adj*
WORD ORIGIN Latin *congratulari*

congratulations *pl n, interj* expressions of pleasure or joy on another's success or good fortune

congregate *vb* **-gating, -gated** to collect together in or as a crowd
WORD ORIGIN Latin *congregare* to collect into a flock

congregation *n* a group of worshippers **congregational** *adj*

Congregationalism *n* a system of Protestant church government in which each church is self-governing **Congregationalist** *adj, n*

congress *n* a formal meeting of representatives for discussion **congressional** *adj*
WORD ORIGIN Latin *com-* together + *gradi* to walk

Congress *n* the federal legislature of the US, consisting of the House of Representatives and the Senate **Congressional** *adj* **Congressman** *n* **Congresswoman** *fem n*

congruent *adj* **1** agreeing or corresponding **2** *geom* identical in shape and size: *congruent triangles* **congruence** *n*
WORD ORIGIN Latin *congruere* to agree

congruous *adj formal* **1** appropriate or in keeping: *an elegant, though not altogether congruous, wing was added to the house in 1735* **2** corresponding or agreeing: *this finding is congruous with Adam's 1982 study* **congruity** *n*
WORD ORIGIN Latin *congruere* to agree

conical *adj* in the shape of a cone

conic section *n* a figure, either a circle, ellipse, parabola, or hyperbola, formed by the intersection of a plane and a cone

conifer *n* a tree or shrub bearing cones and evergreen leaves, such as the fir or larch **coniferous** *adj*
WORD ORIGIN Latin *conus* cone + *ferre* to bear

conjecture *n* **1** the formation of conclusions from incomplete evidence **2** a guess ▷ *vb* **-turing, -tured 3** to form (an opinion or conclusion) from incomplete evidence **conjectural** *adj*
WORD ORIGIN Latin *conjicere* to throw together

conjoin *vb* to join or become joined

conjoined twins *pl n* the technical name for **Siamese twins**

conjugal (kon-jew-gal) *adj* of marriage: *conjugal rights*
WORD ORIGIN Latin *conjunx* wife or husband

conjugate *vb* (kon-jew-gate), **-gating, -gated 1** *grammar* to give the inflections of (a verb) **2** (of a verb) to undergo inflection according to a specific set of rules **3** *formal* to combine: *a country in which conjugating Marxism with Christianity has actually been tried* ▷ *n* (kon-jew-git) **4** *formal* something formed by conjugation: *haemoglobin is a conjugate of a protein with an iron-containing pigment*
WORD ORIGIN Latin *com-* together + *jugare* to connect

conjugation *n* **1** *grammar* **a** inflection of a verb for person, number, tense, voice, and mood **b** the complete set of the inflections of a given verb **2** a joining

conjunction *n* **1** joining together **2** simultaneous occurrence of events **3** a word or group of words that connects words, phrases, or clauses; for example *and*, *if*, and *but* **4** *astron* the apparent nearness of two heavenly bodies to each other **conjunctional** *adj*

conjunctiva *n, pl* **-vas** or **-vae** the delicate mucous membrane that covers the eyeball and inner eyelid **conjunctival** *adj*
WORD ORIGIN New Latin *membrana conjunctiva* the conjunctive membrane

conjunctive *adj* **1** joining or joined **2** used as a conjunction: *a conjunctive adverb* ▷ *n* **3** a word or words used as a conjunction
WORD ORIGIN Latin *conjungere* to join

conjunctivitis *n* inflammation of the conjunctiva

conjuncture *n* a combination of events, esp. one that leads to a crisis

conjure *vb* **-juring, -jured 1** to make (something) appear, as if by magic **2** to perform tricks that appear to be magic **3** to summon (a spirit or demon) by magic **4** *formal or literary* to appeal earnestly to: *I conjure you by all which you profess: answer me!* **conjuring** *n*
WORD ORIGIN Latin *conjurare* to swear together

conjure up *vb* **1** to create an image in the mind: *the name Versailles conjures up a past of sumptuous grandeur* **2** to produce as if from nowhere: *he conjured up a fabulous opening goal*

conjuror or **conjurer** *n* a person who performs magic tricks for people's entertainment

conk *Brit, Austral, & NZ slang n* **1** the head or nose ▷ *vb* **2** to strike (someone) on the head or nose
WORD ORIGIN probably changed from *conch*

conker *n* same as **horse chestnut** (sense 2)

conkers *n Brit* a game in which a player swings a horse chestnut (conker), threaded onto a string, against that of another player to try to break it
WORD ORIGIN dialect *conker* snail shell, originally used in the game

conk out *vb informal* **1** (of a machine or car) to break down **2** to become tired or fall asleep suddenly
WORD ORIGIN origin unknown

con man *n informal* a person who swindles someone by means of a confidence trick

connect *vb* **1** to link or be linked: *high blood pressure is closely connected to heart disease* **2** to put into telephone communication with **3** (of two public vehicles) to have the arrival of one timed to occur just before the departure of the other, for the convenience of passengers **4** to associate in the mind: *he had always connected sex with violence* **5** to relate by birth or marriage: *she was distantly connected with the Wedgwood family* **connective** *adj*
WORD ORIGIN Latin *connectere* to bind together

connection or **connexion** *n* **1** a relationship or association **2** a link or bond **3** a link between two components in an electric circuit **4 a** an opportunity to transfer from one public vehicle to another **b** the vehicle scheduled to provide such an opportunity **5** an influential acquaintance **6** a relative **7** logical sequence in thought or expression **8** a telephone link **9** *slang* a supplier of illegal drugs, such as heroin **10 in connection with** with reference to: *a number of people have been arrested in connection with the explosion*

connective tissue *n* body tissue that supports organs, fills spaces between them, and forms tendons and ligaments

conning tower *n* the raised observation tower containing the periscope on a submarine
WORD ORIGIN *con* to steer a ship

connivance *n* encouragement or permission of wrongdoing

connive *vb* **-niving, -nived 1 connive at** to allow or encourage wrongdoing by ignoring it **2** to conspire
WORD ORIGIN Latin *connivere* to blink, hence, leave uncensured

connoisseur (kon-noss-**sir**) *n* a person with special knowledge of the arts, food, or drink
WORD ORIGIN French

connotation *n* an additional meaning or association implied by a word: *the German term carries a connotation of elitism* **connote** *vb*
WORD ORIGIN Latin *con-* + together *notare* to mark, note

Common Mistakes

In some ways this title is an oxymoron. In language, once something becomes common, it stops being a mistake, and starts to become acceptable. There's always resistance of course: last-ditch defenders of the status quo of forty years before, when they were at school and had to do lots of exercises to make sure they avoided the linguistic faux pas that might exclude them from the job they most wanted, those very same faux pas that they now read and hear all the time. Of course, teachers continue to mark children's work wrong, and finding a surplus apostrophe in 'its' can still produce a feeling of superiority. This particular mistake hasn't yet reached the point where it becomes the norm, but its time is near.

We get used to being corrected. We learn early in our lives that we can be wrong. If language were left to three-year olds, irregular verbs would have been eliminated generations ago; small children regularize rigorously, deducing patterns and producing logical forms like 'I falled over'. That stops once children realize that older and taller people don't say falled. They hear 'fell' so often that it becomes clear that *falled* is only for babies, and it's therefore shunned. Language is acquired by imitation and deduction, and nobody wants to stand out as odd.

At school the correction process continues, and the sources become both our peers and our teachers. Often there's a lot of difference between the way our peers and our teachers speak. Sometimes children end up able to speak in two ways, so that they can be comfortable using a regional variety with their local friends, and a more standard variety elsewhere. It would be a mistake for them to use either variety with the wrong people. To say 'Put wood in th'ole' outside Lancashire would draw blank looks, but to say 'Close the door' would be out of place where your friends express this differently.

Regional varieties have their own sets of consistent rules, as do social varieties. And there are generational varieties, too. Grammar books for foreign learners used to devote pages to the differences between *might have* and *may have*. There used to be a difference between 'They might have been killed' and 'They may have been killed', but this difference has now largely disappeared. 'A large number of people' is gradually being overtaken by 'A large amount of people'. As for *less* as against *fewer*, a cartoon summarized this situation by showing a checkout aisle with a sign above it saying 'Five items or fewer for pedants'.

There is no Academy for the English Language to compare with the bodies which supposedly control other languages. This leads to a small amount of confusion over whether it's better to write *-ise* words with a z or an s, and whether judgment should have an e or not, but English is held together by a consensus. English is astonishingly consistent, considering how widely it's used. But like all languages, it's organic, and it has evolved. It hasn't been conjured out of the void ready made. Like everything else that evolves, it has weak points which are constantly being challenged and which may change faster than others. It has areas of frank confusion: who can say for certain what the 'correct' usages are for lay, lie, laid and lain?

Of course it's possible to draw up a list of common errors, and this plays to our fear of being wrong. Nobody likes to be embarrassed by being shown up, whether by using a spellchecker uncritically, or by making grammatical mistakes. The many websites and books devoted to explaining dark secrets like dangling participles and how to avoid them, or why begging the question is so often used incorrectly, underline how common these 'mistakes' are, which means that they are in fact part of the consensus. If the media are/is full of dangling participles, then we are obviously able to cope with them so efficiently that we don't even notice them. ('Scrambling over the gate, the smell hit him in the face' may be amusing, but it isn't really ambiguous, because everybody knows that smells don't scramble over gates.)

There's a lot of debate about the evidence for evolution, but some of the best evidence for it is right here, in language. Latin evolved into the Romance languages, Elizabethan English evolved into modern English, and our own Englishes are evolving as we study them. This all happened because people always make 'mistakes', all the time, everywhere, in every age, and that's the engine that drives language change.

C

connubial (kon-**new**-bee-al) *adj formal* of marriage: *connubial bliss*
WORD ORIGIN Latin *conubium* marriage

conquer *vb* **1** to defeat (an opponent or opponents) **2** to overcome (a difficulty or feeling) **3** to gain possession of (a place) by force or war **conquering** *adj* **conqueror** *n*
WORD ORIGIN Latin *conquirere* to search for

conquest *n* **1** the act of conquering **2** a person or thing that has been conquered **3** a person whose affections have been won

conquistador *n, pl* **-dors** or **-dores** one of the Spanish conquerors of Mexico and Peru in the 16th century
WORD ORIGIN Spanish: conqueror

Cons. Conservative

consanguineous *adj formal* related by birth **consanguinity** *n*
WORD ORIGIN Latin *con-* with + *sanguis* blood

conscience *n* **1** the sense of right and wrong that governs a person's thoughts and actions **2** a feeling of guilt: *he showed no hint of conscience over the suffering he had inflicted* **3** in (all) conscience in fairness **4** on one's conscience causing feelings of guilt
WORD ORIGIN Latin *conscire* to know

conscience-stricken *adj* feeling guilty because of having done something wrong

conscientious *adj* **1** painstaking or thorough in one's work **2** governed by conscience **conscientiously** *adv* **conscientiousness** *n*

conscientious objector *n* a person who refuses to serve in the armed forces on moral or religious grounds

conscious *adj* **1** alert and awake **2** aware of one's surroundings and of oneself **3** aware (of something): *he was conscious of a need to urinate* **4** deliberate or intentional: *a conscious attempt* **5** of the part of the mind that is aware of a person's self, surroundings, and thoughts, and that to a certain extent determines choices of action: *the conscious is only a small part of the mind* ▷ *n* **6** the conscious part of the mind **consciously** *adv* **consciousness** *n*
WORD ORIGIN Latin *com-* with + *scire* to know

conscript *n* **1** a person who is enrolled for compulsory military service ▷ *vb* **2** to enrol (someone) for compulsory military service
WORD ORIGIN Latin *conscriptus* enrolled

conscription *n* compulsory military service

consecrate *vb* **-crating, -crated 1** to make or declare sacred or for religious use **2** to devote or dedicate (something) to a specific purpose **3** *Christianity* to sanctify (bread and wine) to be received as the body and blood of Christ **consecration** *n*
WORD ORIGIN Latin *consecrare*

consecutive *adj* following in order without interruption; successive: *three consecutive nights of rioting* **consecutively** *adv*
WORD ORIGIN Latin *consequi* to pursue

consensus *n* general or widespread agreement
WORD ORIGIN Latin *consentire* to agree

≡ USAGE
Since *consensus* refers to a collective opinion, the words of *opinion* in the phrase *consensus of opinion* are redundant and should therefore be avoided.

consent *n* **1** agreement, permission, or approval **2** age of consent the age at which sexual intercourse is permitted by law ▷ *vb* **3** to permit or agree (to) **consenting** *adj*
WORD ORIGIN Latin *consentire* to agree

consequence *n* **1** a logical result or effect **2** significance or importance: *we said little of consequence to each other; a woman of little consequence* **3** in consequence as a result **4** take the consequences to accept whatever results from one's action

consequent *adj* **1** following as an effect **2** following as a logical conclusion
WORD ORIGIN Latin *consequens* following closely

≡ USAGE
See at **consequential**.

consequential *adj* **1** important or significant **2** following as a result

≡ USAGE
Although both *consequential* and *consequent* can refer to something which happens as the result of something else, *consequent* is more common in this sense in modern English: *the new measures were put into effect, and the consequent protest led to the dismissal of those responsible*.

consequently *adv* as a result; therefore

conservancy *n* environmental conservation

conservation *n* **1** protection and careful management of the environment and natural resources **2** protection from change, loss, or injury **3** *physics* the principle that the quantity of a specified aspect of a system, such as momentum or charge, remains constant **conservationist** *n*

conservative *adj* **1** favouring the preservation of established customs and values, and opposing change **2** moderate or cautious: *a conservative estimate* **3** conventional in style: *people in this area are conservative in their tastes* ▷ *n* **4** a conservative person **conservatism** *n*

Conservative *adj* **1** of or supporting the Conservative Party, the major right-wing political party in Britain, which believes in private enterprise and capitalism **2** of or supporting a similar right-wing party in other countries ▷ *n* **3** a supporter or member of the Conservative Party

conservatoire (kon-**serv**-a-twahr) *n* a school of music
WORD ORIGIN French

conservatory *n, pl* **-tories 1** a greenhouse attached to a house **2** a conservatoire

conserve *vb* **-serving, -served 1** to protect from harm, decay, or loss **2** to preserve (fruit or other food) with sugar ▷ *n* **3** fruit preserved by cooking in sugar

WORD ORIGIN Latin *conservare* to keep safe

consider *vb* **1** to be of the opinion that **2** to think carefully about (a problem or decision) **3** to bear in mind: *Corsica is well worth considering for those seeking a peaceful holiday in beautiful surroundings* **4** to have regard for or care about: *you must try to consider other people's feelings more* **5** to discuss (something) in order to make a decision **6** to look at: *he considered her and she forced herself to sit calmly under his gaze*
WORD ORIGIN Latin *considerare* to inspect closely

considerable *adj* **1** large enough to reckon with: *a considerable number of people* **2** a lot of: *he was in considerable pain* **considerably** *adv*

considerate *adj* thoughtful towards other people

consideration *n* **1** careful thought **2** a fact to be taken into account when making a decision **3** thoughtfulness for other people **4** payment for a service **5** take into consideration to bear in mind **6** under consideration being currently discussed

considered *adj* **1** presented or thought out with care: *a considered opinion* **2** thought of in a specified way: *highly considered*

considering *conj, prep* **1** taking (a specified fact) into account: *considering the mileage the car had done, it was lasting well* ▷ *adv* **2** *informal* taking into account the circumstances: *it's not bad considering*

consign *vb* **1** to give into the care or charge of **2** to put irrevocably: *those events have been consigned to history* **3** to put (in a specified place or situation): *only a few months ago such demands would have consigned the student leaders to prisons and labour camps* **4** to address or deliver (goods): *a cargo of oil drilling equipment consigned to Saudi Arabia* **consignee** *n* **consignor** *n*
WORD ORIGIN Latin *consignare* to put one's seal to, sign

consignment *n* **1** a shipment of goods **2** the act or an instance of consigning: *the goods are sent to Hong Kong for onward consignment to customers in the area*

consist *vb* **1** consist of to be made up of: *a match consists of seven games* **2** consist in to have as its main or only part: *his madness, if he is mad, consists in believing that he is a sundial*
WORD ORIGIN Latin *consistere* to stand firm

consistency *n, pl* **-encies 1** degree of thickness or smoothness **2** being consistent

consistent *adj* **1** holding to the same principles **2** in agreement **consistently** *adv*

consolation *n* **1** a person or thing that is a comfort in a time of sadness or distress **2** a consoling or being consoled

consolation prize *n* something given to console the loser of a game

console¹ *vb* **-soling, -soled** to comfort (someone) in sadness or distress **consolable** *adj*
WORD ORIGIN Latin *consolari*

console² *n* **1** a panel of controls for electronic equipment **2** a cabinet for a television or audio equipment **3** an ornamental bracket used to support a wall fixture **4** the desklike case of an organ, containing the pedals, stops, and keys

WORD ORIGIN Old French *consolateur* one that provides support

consolidate *vb* **-dating, -dated 1** to make or become stronger or more stable **2** to combine into a whole **consolidation** *n* **consolidator** *n*

WORD ORIGIN Latin *consolidare* to make firm

consommé (kon-**som**-may) *n* a thin clear meat soup

WORD ORIGIN French

consonance *n formal* agreement or harmony

consonant *n* **1 a** a speech sound made by partially or completely blocking the breath streams, for example *b* or *f* **b** a letter representing this ▷ *adj* **2** consonant with in keeping or agreement with: *an individualistic style of religion, more consonant with liberal society* **3** harmonious: *this highly-dissonant chord is followed by a more consonant one*

WORD ORIGIN Latin *consonare* to sound at the same time

consort *vb* **1 consort with** to keep company with ▷ *n* **2** a husband or wife of a reigning monarch **3** a small group of voices or instruments

WORD ORIGIN Latin *consors* partner

consortium *n, pl* **-tia** an association of business firms

WORD ORIGIN Latin: partnership

conspectus *n formal* a survey or summary

WORD ORIGIN Latin: a viewing

conspicuous *adj* **1** clearly visible **2** noteworthy or striking: *conspicuous bravery* **conspicuously** *adv*

WORD ORIGIN Latin *conspicuus*

conspiracy *n, pl* **-cies 1** a secret plan to carry out an illegal or harmful act **2** the act of making such plans

conspire *vb* **-spiring, -spired 1** to plan a crime together in secret **2** to act together as if by design: *the weather and the recession conspired to hit wine production and sales* **conspirator** *n* **conspiratorial** *adj*

WORD ORIGIN Latin *conspirare* to plot together

constable *n* a police officer of the lowest rank

WORD ORIGIN Late Latin *comes stabuli* officer in charge of the stable

constabulary *n, pl* **-laries** *chiefly Brit* the police force of an area

constant *adj* **1** continuous: *she has endured constant criticism, mockery, and humiliation* **2** unchanging: *the average speed of the winds remained constant over this period* **3** faithful ▷ *n* **4** *maths, physics* a quantity or number which remains invariable: *the velocity of light is a constant* **5** something that is unchanging **constancy** *n* **constantly** *adv*

WORD ORIGIN Latin *constare* to be steadfast

constellation *n* **1** a group of stars which form a pattern and are given a name **2** a group of people or things: *the constellation of favourable circumstances*

WORD ORIGIN Latin *com-* together + *stella* star

consternation *n* a feeling of anxiety or dismay

constipated *adj* unable to empty one's bowels

WORD ORIGIN Latin *constipare* to press closely together

constipation *n* a condition in which emptying one's bowels is difficult

constituency *n, pl* **-cies 1** the area represented by a Member of Parliament **2** the voters in such an area

constituent *n* **1** a person living in an MP's constituency **2** a component part ▷ *adj* **3** forming part of a whole: *the constituent parts of the universe* **4** having the power to make or change a constitution of a state: *a constituent assembly*

WORD ORIGIN Latin *constituere* to constitute

constitute *vb* **-tuting, -tuted 1** to form or make up: *the amazing range of crags that constitute the Eglwyseg Mountains* **2** to set up (an institution) formally

WORD ORIGIN Latin *com-* (intensive) + *statuere* to place

constitution *n* **1** the principles on which a state is governed **2 the Constitution** (in certain countries) the statute embodying such principles **3** a person's state of health **4** the make-up or structure of something: *changes in the very constitution of society*

constitutional *adj* **1** of a constitution **2** authorized by or in accordance with the Constitution of a nation: *constitutional monarchy* **3** inherent in the nature of a person or thing: *a constitutional sensitivity to cold* ▷ *n* **4** a regular walk taken for the good of one's health **constitutionally** *adv*

constitutive *adj* **1** forming a part of something **2** with the power to appoint or establish

constrain *vb* **1** to compel or force: *he felt constrained to apologize* **2** to limit, restrict, or inhibit: *the mobility of workers is constrained by the serious housing shortage*

WORD ORIGIN Latin *constringere* to bind together

constrained *adj* embarrassed or unnatural: *his constrained expression*

constraint *n* **1** something that limits a person's freedom of action **2** repression of natural feelings **3** a forced unnatural manner

constrict *vb* **1** to make smaller or narrower by squeezing **2** to limit or restrict **constrictive** *adj*

WORD ORIGIN Latin *constringere* to tie up together

constriction *n* **1** a feeling of tightness in some part of the body, such as the chest **2** a narrowing **3** something that constricts

constrictor *n* **1** a snake that coils around and squeezes its prey to kill it **2** a muscle that contracts an opening

construct *vb* **1** to build or put together **2** *geom* to draw (a figure) to specified requirements **3** to compose (an argument or sentence) ▷ *n* **4** a complex idea resulting from the combination of

simpler ideas **5** something formulated or built systematically **constructor** *n*

WORD ORIGIN Latin *construere* to build

construction *n* **1** the act of constructing or manner in which a thing is constructed **2** something that has been constructed **3** the business or work of building houses or other structures **4** *formal* an interpretation: *the financial markets will put the worst possible construction on any piece of news which might affect them* **5** *grammar* the way in which words are arranged in a sentence, clause, or phrase **constructional** *adj*

constructive *adj* **1** useful and helpful: *constructive criticism* **2** *law* deduced by inference; not openly expressed **constructively** *adv*

construe *vb* **-struing, -strued 1** to interpret the meaning of (something): *her indifference was construed as rudeness* **2** to analyse the grammatical structure of (a sentence) **3** to combine (words) grammatically **4** *old-fashioned* to translate literally

WORD ORIGIN Latin *construere* to build

consul *n* **1** an official representing a state in a foreign country **2** one of the two chief magistrates in ancient Rome **consular** *adj* **consulship** *n*

WORD ORIGIN Latin

consulate *n* **1** the workplace and official home of a consul **2** the position or period of office of a consul

consult *vb* **1** to ask advice from or discuss matters with (someone): *he never consults his wife about what he's about to do* **2** to refer to for information: *he consulted his watch*

WORD ORIGIN Latin *consultare*

consultant *n* **1** a specialist doctor with a senior position in a hospital **2** a specialist who gives expert professional advice **consultancy** *n*

consultation *n* **1** the act of consulting **2** a meeting for discussion or the seeking of advice **consultative** *adj*

consulting *adj* acting as an adviser on professional matters: *consulting engineers*

consulting room *n* a room in which a doctor sees patients

consume *vb* **-suming, -sumed 1** to eat or drink **2** to use up **3** to destroy: *the ship blew up and was consumed by flames* **4** to obsess: *he was consumed with jealousy over the ending of their affair* **consumable** *adj* **consuming** *adj*

WORD ORIGIN Latin *com-* (intensive) + *sumere* to take up

consumer *n* a person who buys goods or uses services

consumer durables *pl n* manufactured products that have a relatively long life, such as cars or televisions

consumer goods *pl n* goods bought for personal needs rather than those required for the production of other goods or services

consumerism *n* **1** the belief that a high level of consumer spending is desirable and beneficial to the economy: *the obsessive consumerism of the 80s* **2** protection of the rights of consumers

consummate *vb* (kon-**sum**-mate), **-mating, -mated 1** to make (a

marriage) legal by sexual intercourse **2** to complete or fulfil ▷ *adj* (kon-**sum**-mit) **3** supremely skilled: *a consummate craftsman* **4** complete or extreme: *consummate skill; consummate ignorance* **consummation** *n*
WORD ORIGIN Latin *consummare* to complete

consumption *n* **1** the quantity of something consumed or used: *for such a powerful car, fuel consumption is modest* **2** the act of eating or drinking something: *this meat is unfit for human consumption* **3** *econ* purchase of goods and services for personal use **4** *old-fashioned* tuberculosis of the lungs

consumptive *adj* **1** wasteful or destructive **2** of tuberculosis of the lungs ▷ *n* **3** a person with tuberculosis of the lungs

cont. continued

contact *n* **1** the state or act of communication: *the airport lost contact with the plane shortly before the crash* **2** the state or act of touching: *rugby is a game of hard physical contact* **3** an acquaintance who might be useful in business **4** a connection between two electrical conductors in a circuit **5** a person who has been exposed to a contagious disease ▷ *vb* **6** to come or be in communication or touch with
WORD ORIGIN Latin *contingere* to touch on all sides

contact lens *n* a small lens placed on the eyeball to correct defective vision

contagion *n* **1** the passing on of disease by contact **2** a contagious disease **3** a corrupting influence that tends to spread
WORD ORIGIN Latin *contagio* infection

contagious *adj* **1** (of a disease) capable of being passed on by contact **2** (of a person) capable of passing on a transmissible disease **3** spreading from person to person: *contagious enthusiasm*

contain *vb* **1** to hold or be capable of holding: *the bag contained a selection of men's clothing* **2** to have as one of its ingredients or constituents: *tea and coffee both contain appreciable amounts of caffeine* **3** to consist of: *the book contains 13 very different and largely separate chapters* **4** to check or restrain (feelings or behaviour) **5** to prevent from spreading or going beyond fixed limits: *the blockade was too weak to contain the French fleet* **containable** *adj*
WORD ORIGIN Latin *continere*

container *n* **1** an object used to hold or store things in **2** a large standard-sized box for transporting cargo by lorry or ship

containerize *or* **-ise** *vb* **-izing, -ized** *or* **-ising, -ised** **1** to pack (cargo) in large standard-sized containers **2** to fit (a port, ship, or lorry) to carry goods in standard-sized containers **containerization** *or* **-isation** *n*

containment *n* the prevention of the spread of something harmful

contaminate *vb* **-nating, -nated** **1** to make impure; pollute **2** to make radioactive **contaminant** *n* **contamination** *n*
WORD ORIGIN Latin *contaminare* to defile

contemn *vb* *formal* to regard with contempt
WORD ORIGIN Latin *contemnere*

contemplate *vb* **-plating, -plated** **1** to think deeply about **2** to consider as a possibility **3** to look at thoughtfully **4** to meditate **contemplation** *n*
WORD ORIGIN Latin *contemplare*

contemplative *adj* **1** of or given to contemplation ▷ *n* **2** a person dedicated to religious contemplation

contemporaneous *adj* happening at the same time **contemporaneity** *n*

contemporary *adj* **1** existing or occurring at the present time **2** living or occurring in the same period **3** modern in style or fashion **4** of approximately the same age ▷ *n, pl* **-raries** **5** a person or thing living at the same time or of approximately the same age as another
WORD ORIGIN Latin *com-* together + *temporarius* relating to time

≡ **USAGE**
≡ Since *contemporary* can mean either of
≡ the same period or of the present
≡ period, it is best to avoid this word
≡ where ambiguity might arise as in *a*
≡ *production* of Othello *in contemporary dress.*
≡ *Modern dress* or *Elizabethan dress* should
≡ be used in such contexts to avoid
≡ ambiguity.

contempt *n* **1** scorn **2** hold in contempt to scorn or despise **3** deliberate disrespect for the authority of a court of law: *contempt of court*
WORD ORIGIN Latin *contemnere* to scorn

contemptible *adj* deserving to be despised or hated: *a contemptible lack of courage*

contemptuous *adj* showing or feeling strong dislike or disrespect **contemptuously** *adv*

contend *vb* **1 contend with** to deal with **2** to assert **3** to compete or fight **4** to argue earnestly **contender** *n*
WORD ORIGIN Latin *contendere* to strive

content[1] *n* **1 contents** everything inside a container **2 contents** a list of chapters at the front of a book **3** the meaning or substance of a piece of writing, often as distinguished from its style or form **4** the amount of a substance contained in a mixture: *the water vapour content of the atmosphere*
WORD ORIGIN Latin *contentus* contained

content[2] *adj* **1** satisfied with things as they are **2** willing to accept a situation or a proposed course of action ▷ *vb* **3** to satisfy (oneself or another person) ▷ *n* **4** peace of mind **contentment** *n*
WORD ORIGIN Latin *contentus* contented, having restrained desires

contented *adj* satisfied with one's situation or life **contentedly** *adv* **contentedness** *n*

contention *n* **1** disagreement or dispute **2** a point asserted in argument **3 bone of contention** a point of dispute
WORD ORIGIN Latin *contentio*

contentious *adj* **1** causing disagreement **2** tending to quarrel **contentiousness** *n*

contest *n* **1** a game or match in which people or teams compete **2** a struggle

for power or control ▷ *vb* **3** to dispute: *he has said he will contest the verdict* **4** to take part in (a contest or struggle for power): *all parties which meet the legal requirements will be allowed to contest the election* **contestable** *adj*
WORD ORIGIN Latin *contestari* to introduce a lawsuit

contestant *n* a person who takes part in a contest

context *n* **1** the circumstances relevant to an event or fact **2** the words before and after a word or passage in a piece of writing that contribute to its meaning: *taken out of context, lines like these sound ridiculous, but, as part of a scrupulously written play, they are just right* **contextual** *adj*
WORD ORIGIN Latin *com-* together + *texere* to weave

contiguous *adj* *formal* very near or touching
WORD ORIGIN Latin *contiguus*

continent[1] *n* one of the earth's large landmasses (Asia, Australia, Africa, Europe, North and South America, and Antarctica) **continental** *adj*
WORD ORIGIN Latin *terra continens* continuous land

continent[2] *adj* **1** able to control one's bladder and bowels **2** sexually restrained **continence** *n*
WORD ORIGIN Latin *continere* to contain, retain

Continent *n* **the Continent** the mainland of Europe as distinct from the British Isles **Continental** *adj*

continental breakfast *n* a light breakfast of coffee and rolls

continental climate *n* a climate with hot summers, cold winters, and little rainfall, typical of the interior of a continent

continental drift *n* *geol* the theory that the earth's continents drift gradually over the surface of the planet, due to currents in its mantle

continental quilt *n* *Brit* a large quilt used as a bed cover in place of the top sheet and blankets

continental shelf *n* the gently sloping shallow sea bed surrounding a continent

contingency *n, pl* **-cies** **1** an unknown or unforeseen future event or condition **2** something dependent on a possible future event

contingent *n* **1** a group of people with a common interest, that represents a larger group: *a contingent of European scientists* **2** a military group that is part of a larger force: *the force includes a contingent of the Foreign Legion* ▷ *adj* **3** (foll. by *on* or *upon*) dependent on (something uncertain) **4** happening by chance
WORD ORIGIN Latin *contingere* to touch, befall

continual *adj* **1** occurring without interruption **2** recurring frequently **continually** *adv*
WORD ORIGIN Latin *continuus* uninterrupted

≡ **USAGE**
≡ See at **continuous**.

continuance *n* **1** the act of continuing **2** duration

Words from Shakespeare
part 6

comely *adj* lovely, beautiful, graceful
O, what a world is this, when what is comely
Envenoms him that bears it! *As You Like It* 2.3

commend *v* send greetings to someone
Commend me to my brother *Measure for Measure* 1.4

compact *n* an agreement or a contract
what compact mean you to have with us?
Julius Caesar 3.1

compass *n* range or scope
you would sound me from my lowest note to the
top of my compass *Hamlet* 3.2

compass *v* to achieve, bring about or make happen
How now shall this be compassed?
Canst thou bring me to the party? *The Tempest* 3.2

compatible *adj* sensitive
I am very comptible, even to the least sinister
usage. *Twelfth Night* 1.5

confederacy *n* a group of people usually joined
together to commit a crime (another word for
conspiracy)
Lo, she is one of this confederacy!
A Midsummer Night's Dream 3.2

confound *v* to confuse or mix up; to stop or prevent
A million fail, confounding oath on oath.
A Midsummer Night's Dream 3.2

contagion *n* disease or poison
hell itself breathes out
Contagion to this world *Hamlet* 3.2

contumely *n* an insult
the proud man's contumely *Hamlet* 3.1

counterfeit *v* to copy or imitate
Meantime your cheeks do counterfeit our roses
Henry VI part I 2.4

counterfeit *v* to pretend or make believe
I will counterfeit the bewitchment of some popular
man *Coriolanus*

coz *n* a shortened form of cousin
sweet my coz, be merry *As You Like It* 1.2

cozenage, coz'nage *n* cheating or deception
Thrown out his angle for my proper life,
And with such coz'nage *Hamlet* 5.2

crave *v* to beg or request
I crave your pardon *The Comedy of Errors* 1.2

crotchet *n* a strange idea or whim
thou hast some strange crotchets in thy head now
The Merry Wives of Windsor 2.1

cuckold *n* a man whose wife has been unfaithful to him
As there is no true cuckold but calamity
Twelfth Night 1.5

cuffs, go to *phrase* to fight
the player went to cuffs in the question *Hamlet* 2.2

cup *v* to pour drink or fill glasses with alcohol
cup us til the world go round
Anthony and Cleopatra 2.7

cur *n* insult meaning dog or coward
Out, dog! out, cur! Thou drivest me past the bounds
Of maiden's patience
A Midsummer Night's Dream 3.2

curiously *adv* carefully or skilfully
The sleeves curiously cut *The Taming of the Shrew* 4.3

curry *v* to flatter or to praise someone more than they
are worth
I would curry with Master Shallow that no man
could better command his servants
Henry IV part II 5.1

custom *n* a habit or a usual practice
Hath not old custom made this life more sweet
Than that of painted pomp? *As You Like It* 2.1

cutpurse *n* a thief. Men used to carry their money
in a small bag (purse) that hung from their belts;
thieves would cut the purse from the belt and steal
their money
A cutpurse of the empire and the rule *Hamlet* 3.4

continuation n **1** the act of continuing **2** a part or thing added, such as a sequel **3** a renewal of an interrupted action or process

continue vb **-tinuing, -tinued 1** to remain or cause to remain in a particular condition or place **2** to carry on (doing something): *we continued kissing; heavy fighting continued until Thursday afternoon* **3** to resume after an interruption: *we'll continue after lunch* **4** to go on to a further place: *the road continues on up the hill*
WORD ORIGIN Latin *continuare* to join together

continuity n, pl **-ties 1** a smooth development or sequence **2** the arrangement of scenes in a film so that they follow each other logically and without breaks

continuo n, pl **-tinuos** *music* a continuous bass accompaniment played usually on a keyboard instrument
WORD ORIGIN Italian

continuous adj **1** without end: *a continuous process* **2** not having any breaks or gaps in it: *a continuous line of boats; continuous rain* **continuously** adv
WORD ORIGIN Latin *continuus*

≡ USAGE
≡ Both *continual* and *continuous* can be
≡ used to say that something continues
≡ without interruption, but only
≡ *continual* can correctly be used to say
≡ that something keeps happening
≡ repeatedly.

continuum n, pl **-tinua** or **-tinuums** a continuous series or whole, no part of which is noticeably different from the parts immediately next to it, although the ends or extremes of it are very different from each other: *the continuum from minor misbehaviour to major crime*
WORD ORIGIN Latin

contort vb to twist or bend out of shape **contortion** n
WORD ORIGIN Latin *contortus* intricate

contortionist n a performer who contorts his or her body to entertain others

contour n **1** an outline **2** same as **contour line** ▷ vb **3** to shape so as to form or follow the contour of something
WORD ORIGIN Italian *contornare* to sketch

contour line n a line on a map or chart joining points of equal height or depth

contra- *prefix* **1** against or contrasting: *contraceptive* **2** (in music) lower in pitch: *contrabass*
WORD ORIGIN Latin *contra* against

contraband n **1** smuggled goods ▷ adj **2** (of goods) smuggled
WORD ORIGIN Spanish *contrabanda*

contraception n the deliberate use of artificial or natural means to prevent pregnancy
WORD ORIGIN CONTRA- + CONCEPTION

contraceptive n **1** a device, such as a condom, that is used to prevent pregnancy ▷ adj **2** providing or relating to contraception: *the contraceptive pill*

contract n **1** a formal agreement between two or more parties **2** a document setting out a formal agreement ▷ vb **3** to make a formal agreement with (a person or company) to do or deliver (something) **4** to enter into (a relationship or marriage) formally: *she had contracted an alliance with a wealthy man* **5** to make or become smaller, narrower, or shorter **6** to become affected by (an illness) **7** to draw (muscles) together or (of muscles) to be drawn together **8** to shorten (a word or phrase) by omitting letters or syllables, usually indicated in writing by an apostrophe **contractible** adj
WORD ORIGIN Latin *contractus* agreement

contract bridge n the most common variety of bridge, in which only tricks bid and won count towards the game

contraction n **1** a contracting or being contracted **2** a shortening of a word or group of words, often marked by an apostrophe, for example *I've come* for *I have come* **3 contractions** *med* temporary shortening and tensing of the uterus during pregnancy and labour

contractor n a person or firm that supplies materials or labour for other companies

contract out vb *Brit* to agree not to take part in a scheme

contractual adj of or in the nature of a contract

contradict vb **1** to declare the opposite of (a statement) to be true **2** (of a fact or statement) to suggest that (another fact or statement) is wrong **contradiction** n
WORD ORIGIN Latin *contra-* against + *dicere* to speak

contradictory adj (of facts or statements) inconsistent

contradistinction n a distinction made by contrasting different qualities **contradistinctive** adj

contraflow n a flow of road traffic going alongside but in an opposite direction to the usual flow

contralto n, pl **-tos** or **-ti 1** the lowest female voice **2** a singer with such a voice
WORD ORIGIN Italian

contraption n *informal* a strange-looking device or gadget
WORD ORIGIN origin unknown

contrapuntal adj *music* of or in counterpoint
WORD ORIGIN Italian *contrappunto* counterpoint

contrariwise adv **1** from a contrasting point of view **2** in the opposite way

contrary n, pl **-ries 1 on** or **to the contrary** in opposition to what has just been said or implied ▷ adj **2** opposed; completely different: *a contrary view, based on equally good information* **3** perverse; obstinate **4** (of the wind) unfavourable ▷ adv **contrary to 5** in opposition or contrast to: *contrary to popular belief* **6** in conflict with: *contrary to nature* **contrariness** n
WORD ORIGIN Latin *contrarius* opposite

contrast n **1** a difference which is clearly seen when two things are compared **2** a person or thing showing differences when compared with another **3** the degree of difference between the colours in a photograph or television picture ▷ vb **4** to compare or be compared in order to show the differences between (things): *he contrasts that society with contemporary America* **5 contrast with** to be very different from: *her speed of reaction contrasted with her husband's vagueness* **contrasting** adj
WORD ORIGIN Latin *contra-* against + *stare* to stand

contravene vb **-vening, -vened** *formal* to break (a rule or law) **contravention** n
WORD ORIGIN Latin *contra-* against + *venire* to come

contretemps (kon-tra-tahn) n, pl **-temps** an embarrassing minor disagreement
WORD ORIGIN French

contribute vb **-buting, -buted** (often foll. by *to*) **1** to give (support or money) for a common purpose or fund **2** to supply (ideas or opinions) **3 contribute to** to be partly responsible for: *his own unconvincing play contributed to his defeat* **4** to write (an article) for a publication **contribution** n **contributory** adj **contributor** n
WORD ORIGIN Latin *contribuere* to collect

contrite adj full of guilt or regret **contritely** adv **contrition** n
WORD ORIGIN Latin *contritus* worn out

contrivance n **1** an ingenious device **2** an elaborate or deceitful plan **3** the act or power of contriving

contrive vb **-triving, -trived 1** to make happen: *he had already contrived the murder of King Alexander* **2** to devise or construct ingeniously: *he contrived a plausible reason to fly back to London; he contrived a hook from a bent nail*
WORD ORIGIN Old French *controver*

control n **1** power to direct something: *the province is mostly under guerrilla control* **2** a curb or check: *import controls* **3 controls** instruments used to operate a machine **4** a standard of comparison used in an experiment **5** an experiment used to verify another by having all aspects identical except for the one that is being tested ▷ vb **-trolling, -trolled 6** to have power over: *the gland which controls the body's metabolic rate* **7** to limit or restrain: *he could not control his jealousy* **8** to regulate or operate (a machine) **9** to restrict the authorized supply of (certain drugs) **controllable** adj
WORD ORIGIN Old French *conteroller* to regulate

controller n **1** a person who is in charge **2** a person in charge of the financial aspects of a business

control tower n a tall building at an airport from which air traffic is controlled

controversy n, pl **-sies** argument or debate concerning a matter about which there is strong disagreement **controversial** adj
WORD ORIGIN Latin *contra-* against + *vertere* to turn

contumacy (kon-tume-mass-ee) n, pl **-cies** *literary* obstinate disobedience **contumacious** (kon-tume-may-shuss) adj
WORD ORIGIN Latin *contumax* obstinate

contumely (kon-tume-mill-ee) n, pl **-lies** *literary* **1** scornful or insulting treatment **2** a humiliating insult
WORD ORIGIN Latin *contumelia*

contusion *n formal* a bruise **contuse** *vb*
WORD ORIGIN Latin *contusus* bruised

conundrum *n* **1** a puzzling question or problem **2** a riddle whose answer contains a pun
WORD ORIGIN origin unknown

conurbation *n* a large heavily populated urban area formed by the growth and merging of towns
WORD ORIGIN Latin *con-* together + *urbs* city

convalesce *vb* **-lescing, -lesced** to recover health after an illness or operation
WORD ORIGIN Latin *com-* (intensive) + *valescere* to grow strong

convalescence *n* **1** gradual return to health after illness or an operation **2** the period during which such recovery occurs **convalescent** *n, adj*

convection *n* the transmission of heat caused by movement of molecules from cool regions to warmer regions of lower density
WORD ORIGIN Latin *convehere* to bring together

convector *n* a heating device which gives out hot air

convene *vb* **-vening, -vened** to gather or summon for a formal meeting
WORD ORIGIN Latin *convenire* to assemble

convener or **convenor** *n* a person who calls or chairs a meeting: *the shop stewards' convener at the factory* **convenership** or **convenorship** *n*

convenience *n* **1** the quality of being suitable or convenient **2 at your convenience** at a time suitable to you **3** an object that is useful: *a house with every modern convenience* **4** *euphemistic chiefly Brit* a public toilet

convenience food *n* food that needs little preparation and can be used at any time

convenient *adj* **1** suitable or opportune **2** easy to use **3** nearby
WORD ORIGIN Latin *convenire* to be in accord with

convent *n* **1** a building where nuns live **2** a school in which the teachers are nuns **3** a community of nuns
WORD ORIGIN Latin *conventus* meeting

conventicle *n Brit & US history* a secret or unauthorized religious meeting
WORD ORIGIN Latin *conventiculum*

convention *n* **1** the established view of what is thought to be proper behaviour **2** an accepted rule or method: *a convention used by printers* **3** a formal agreement or contract between people and nations **4** a large formal assembly of a group with common interests
WORD ORIGIN Latin *conventio* an assembling

conventional *adj* **1** following the accepted customs and lacking originality **2** established by accepted usage or general agreement **3** (of weapons or warfare) not nuclear **conventionally** *adv*

conventionality *n, pl* **-ties 1** the quality of being conventional **2** something conventional

conventionalize or **-ise** *vb* **-izing, -ized** or **-ising, -ised** to make conventional

converge *vb* **-verging, -verged 1** to move towards or meet at the same point **2** (of opinions or effects) to move towards a shared conclusion or result **convergence** *n* **convergent** *adj*
WORD ORIGIN Latin *com-* together + *vergere* to incline

conversant *adj* **conversant with** having knowledge or experience of
WORD ORIGIN Latin *conversari* to keep company with

conversation *n* informal talk between two or more people

conversational *adj* **1** of or used in conversation: *conversational French* **2** resembling informal spoken language: *the author's easy, conversational style*

conversationalist *n* a person with a specified ability at conversation: *a brilliant conversationalist*

conversation piece *n* something, such as an unusual object, that provokes conversation

converse¹ *vb* **-versing, -versed** to have a conversation
WORD ORIGIN Latin *conversari* to keep company with

converse² *adj* **1** reversed or opposite ▷ *n* **2** a statement or idea that is the opposite of another **conversely** *adv*
WORD ORIGIN Latin *conversus* turned around

conversion *n* **1** a change or adaptation **2** *maths* a calculation in which a weight, volume, or distance is worked out in a different system of measurement: *the conversion from Fahrenheit to Celsius* **3** a change to another belief or religion **4** *rugby* a score made after a try by kicking the ball over the crossbar from a place kick
WORD ORIGIN Latin *conversio* a turning around

convert *vb* **1** to change or adapt **2** to cause (someone) to change in opinion or belief **3** to change (a measurement) from one system of units to another **4** to change (money) into a different currency **5** *rugby* to make a conversion after (a try) ▷ *n* **6** a person who has been converted to another belief or religion **converter** or **convertor** *n*
WORD ORIGIN Latin *convertere* to turn around, alter

convertible *adj* **1** capable of being converted **2** *finance* (of a currency) freely exchangeable into other currencies ▷ *n* **3** a car with a folding or removable roof

convex *adj* curving outwards like the outside surface of a ball **convexity** *n*
WORD ORIGIN Latin *convexus* vaulted, rounded

convey *vb* **1** to communicate (information) **2** to carry or transport from one place to another **3** (of a channel or path) to transfer or transmit **4** *law* to transfer (the title to property) **conveyable** *adj* **conveyor** *n*
WORD ORIGIN Old French *conveier*

conveyance *n* **1** *old-fashioned* a vehicle **2** *law* **a** a transfer of the legal title to property **b** the document effecting such a transfer **3** the act of conveying: *the*

conveyance of cycles on peak hour trains **conveyancer** *n*

conveyancing *n* the branch of law dealing with the transfer of ownership of property

conveyor belt *n* an endless moving belt driven by rollers and used to transport objects, esp. in a factory

convict *vb* **1** to declare (someone) guilty of an offence ▷ *n* **2** a person serving a prison sentence
WORD ORIGIN Latin *convictus* convicted

conviction *n* **1** a firmly held belief or opinion **2** an instance of being found guilty of a crime: *he had several convictions for petty theft* **3** a convincing or being convinced **4 carry conviction** to be convincing

convince *vb* **-vincing, -vinced** to persuade by argument or evidence **convinced** *adj* **convincible** *adj* **convincing** *adj*
WORD ORIGIN Latin *convincere* to demonstrate incontrovertibly

convivial *adj* sociable or lively: *a convivial atmosphere; convivial company* **conviviality** *n*
WORD ORIGIN Late Latin *convivialis*

convocation *n formal* a large formal meeting

convoke *vb* **-voking, -voked** *formal* to call together
WORD ORIGIN Latin *convocare*

convoluted *adj* **1** coiled or twisted **2** (of an argument or sentence) complex and difficult to understand

convolution *n* **1** a coil or twist **2** an intricate or confused matter or condition **3** a convex fold in the surface of the brain

convolvulus *n, pl* **-luses** or **-li** a twining plant with funnel-shaped flowers and triangular leaves
WORD ORIGIN Latin: bindweed

convoy *n* a group of vehicles or ships travelling together
WORD ORIGIN Old French *convoier* to convey

convulse *vb* **-vulsing, -vulsed 1** to shake or agitate violently **2** (of muscles) to undergo violent spasms **3** *informal* to be overcome (with laughter or rage) **4** to disrupt the normal running of: *student riots have convulsed India* **convulsive** *adj*
WORD ORIGIN Latin *con-* together + *vellere* to pluck, pull

convulsion *n* **1** a violent muscular spasm **2** a violent upheaval **3 convulsions** *informal* uncontrollable laughter: *I was in convulsions*

cony or **coney** *n, pl* **-nies** or **-neys** *Brit* **1** a rabbit **2** rabbit fur
WORD ORIGIN Latin *cuniculus* rabbit

coo *vb* **cooing, cooed 1** (of a dove or pigeon) to make a soft murmuring sound **2** bill and coo to murmur softly or lovingly ▷ *n* **3** a cooing sound ▷ *interj* **4** *Brit slang* an exclamation of surprise or amazement **cooing** *adj, n*
WORD ORIGIN imitative

cooee *interj* **1** *Brit, Austral, & NZ* a call used to attract attention **2** *Austral & NZ* **within cooee** within calling distance: *the school was within cooee of our house*
WORD ORIGIN Aboriginal

cook vb **1** to prepare (food) by heating or (of food) to be prepared in this way **2** slang to alter or falsify (figures or accounts): she had cooked the books ▷ n **3** a person who prepares food for eating ▸ See also **cook up**
WORD ORIGIN Latin coquere

cook-chill n a method of food preparation used by caterers, in which cooked dishes are chilled rapidly and reheated as required

cooker n **1** chiefly Brit an apparatus for cooking heated by gas or electricity **2** Brit an apple suitable for cooking but not for eating raw

cookery n the art or practice of cooking ▸ Related adjective: **culinary**

cookery book or **cookbook** n a book containing recipes for cooking

cookie n, pl **cookies 1** US & Canad a biscuit **2** that's the way the cookie crumbles informal that is how things inevitably are **3** informal a person: a real tough cookie
WORD ORIGIN Dutch koekje little cake

cook up vb informal to invent (a story or scheme)

cool adj **1** moderately cold: it should be served cool, even chilled **2** comfortably free of heat: it was one of the few cool days that summer **3** calm and unemotional: a cool head **4** indifferent or unfriendly: the idea met with a cool response **5** calmly impudent **6** informal (of a large sum of money) without exaggeration: a cool million **7** informal sophisticated or elegant **8** (of a colour) having violet, blue, or green predominating **9** informal marvellous ▷ vb **10** to make or become cooler **11** to calm down ▷ n **12** coolness: in the cool of the evening **13** slang calmness; composure: he lost his cool and wantonly kicked the ball away **coolly** adv **coolness** n
WORD ORIGIN Old English cōl

coolant n a fluid used to cool machinery while it is working

cool drink n S African a soft drink

cooler n a container for making or keeping things cool

coolibah n an Australian eucalypt that grows beside rivers
WORD ORIGIN Aboriginal

coolie n old-fashioned, offensive an unskilled Oriental labourer
WORD ORIGIN Hindi kulī

cooling tower n a tall hollow structure in a factory or power station, inside which hot water cools as it trickles down

coomb or **coombe** n a short valley or deep hollow
WORD ORIGIN Old English cumb

coon n **1** informal short for **raccoon** **2** offensive slang a Negro or Australian Aborigine **3** S African, offensive a person of mixed race

coop[1] n **1** a cage or pen for poultry or small animals ▷ vb **2** coop up to confine in a restricted place
WORD ORIGIN Latin cupa basket, cask

coop[2] or **co-op** (koh-op) n Brit, Austral, & NZ a cooperative society or a shop run by a cooperative society

cooper n a person who makes or repairs barrels or casks

cooperate or **co-operate** vb **1** to work or act together **2** to assist or be willing to assist **cooperation** or **co-operation** n
WORD ORIGIN Latin co- with + operari to work

cooperative or **co-operative** adj **1** willing to cooperate **2** (of an enterprise or farm) owned and managed collectively ▷ n **3** a cooperative organization

cooperative society n a commercial enterprise owned and run by customers or workers, in which the profits are shared among the members

coopt or **co-opt** (koh-**opt**) vb to add (someone) to a group by the agreement of the existing members
WORD ORIGIN Latin cooptare to choose, elect

coordinate or **co-ordinate** vb -nating, -nated **1** to bring together and cause to work together efficiently ▷ n **2** maths any of a set of numbers defining the location of a point with reference to a system of axes ▷ adj **3** of or involving coordination **4** of or involving the use of coordinates: coordinate geometry **coordination** or **co-ordination** n **coordinator** or **co-ordinator** n
WORD ORIGIN Latin co- together + ordinatio arranging

coordinates or **co-ordinates** pl n clothes designed to be worn together

coot n **1** a small black water bird **2** Brit, Austral, & NZ a foolish person
WORD ORIGIN probably Low German

cop slang n **1** a policeman **2** not much cop of little value or worth ▷ vb copping, copped **3** to take or seize **4** cop it to get into trouble or be punished: he copped it after he was spotted driving a car without a seat belt ▸ See also **cop out**
WORD ORIGIN perhaps from Old French caper to seize

copal n a resin used in varnishes

copartner n a partner or associate **copartnership** n

cope[1] vb coping, coped **1** to deal successfully (with): well-nourished people cope better with stress **2** to tolerate or endure: the ability to cope with his pain
WORD ORIGIN Old French coper to strike, cut

cope[2] n a large ceremonial cloak worn by some Christian priests
WORD ORIGIN Late Latin cappa hooded cloak

cope[3] vb coping, coped to provide (a wall) with a coping
WORD ORIGIN probably from French couper to cut

copeck n same as **kopeck**

Copernican (kop-**per**-nik-an) adj of the theory that the earth and the planets rotate round the sun
WORD ORIGIN after Copernicus, astronomer

copestone n **1** Also called: coping stone a stone used to form a coping **2** the stone at the top of a building or wall

copier n a person or machine that copies

copilot n the second pilot of an aircraft

coping n a layer of rounded or sloping bricks on the top of a wall

coping saw n a handsaw with a U-shaped frame, used for cutting curves in wood

copious (**kope**-ee-uss) adj existing or produced in large quantities **copiously** adv
WORD ORIGIN Latin copiosus

cop out slang vb **1** to avoid taking responsibility or committing oneself ▷ n cop-out **2** a way or an instance of avoiding responsibility or commitment
WORD ORIGIN probably from COP

copper[1] n **1** a soft reddish metallic element, used in such alloys as brass and bronze. Symbol: Cu **2** informal any copper or bronze coin **3** chiefly Brit a large metal container used to boil water ▷ adj **4** reddish-brown
WORD ORIGIN Latin Cyprium aes Cyprian metal, from Greek Kupris Cyprus

copper[2] n Brit slang a policeman
WORD ORIGIN from COP (verb)

copper beech n a European beech with reddish leaves

copper-bottomed adj financially reliable
WORD ORIGIN from the practice of coating the bottom of ships with copper to prevent the timbers rotting

copperhead n a poisonous snake with a reddish-brown head

copperplate n **1** an elegant handwriting style **2** a polished copper plate engraved for printing **3** a print taken from such a plate

copper sulphate n a blue crystalline copper salt used in electroplating and in plant sprays

coppice n a small group of trees or bushes growing close together
WORD ORIGIN Old French copeiz

copra n the dried oil-yielding kernel of the coconut
WORD ORIGIN Malayalam (a language of SW India) koppara coconut

copse n same as **coppice**
WORD ORIGIN from COPPICE

Copt n **1** a member of the Coptic Church, a part of the Christian Church which was founded in Egypt **2** an Egyptian descended from the ancient Egyptians
WORD ORIGIN Coptic kyptios Egyptian

Coptic n **1** the language of the Copts, descended from Ancient Egyptian and surviving only in the Coptic Church ▷ adj **2** of the Copts or the Coptic Church

copula n, pl -las or -lae a verb, such as be, that is used to link the subject with the complement of a sentence, as in he became king
WORD ORIGIN Latin: bond

copulate vb -lating, -lated to have sexual intercourse **copulation** n
WORD ORIGIN Latin copulare to join together

copy n, pl copies **1** a thing made to look exactly like another **2** a single specimen of a book, magazine, or record of which there are many others exactly the same: my copy of 'Death on the Nile' **3** written material for printing **4** the text of an advertisement **5** journalism informal suitable material for an article: disasters are always good copy ▷ vb copies, copying, copied **6** to make a copy (of)

Words from Literature
part 8

cravat *n* a folded cloth that a man wears wrapped around his neck as a decorative item of clothing
> we'd 'a' slept in our cravats to-night
> *The Adventures of Huckleberry Finn* Mark Twain

crock and dirt *phrase* an old expression meaning soot and dirt
> and the mare catching cold at the door, and the boy grimed with crock and dirt
> *Great Expectations* Charles Dickens

crockery *n* pottery
> By one of the parrots was a cat made of crockery
> *The Adventures of Huckleberry Finn* Mark Twain

crooked sixpence *phrase* it was considered unlucky to have a bent sixpence
> You've got the beauty, you see, and I've got the luck, so you must keep me by you for your crooked sixpence
> *Silas Marner* George Eliot

cross *prep* across
> The two great streets, which run cross and divide it into four quarters
> *Gulliver's Travels* Jonathan Swift

culpable *adj* if you are culpable for something it means you are to blame
> deep are the sorrows that spring from false ideas for which no man is culpable.
> *Silas Marner* George Eliot

cultured *adj* cultivated
> Nor less when spring had warmed the cultured Vale
> *The Prelude* William Wordsworth

cupidity *n* greed
> These people hated me with the hatred of cupidity and disappointment.
> *Great Expectations* Charles Dickens

curricle *n* an open two-wheeled carriage with one seat for the driver and space for a single passenger
> and they saw a lady and a gentleman in a curricle
> *Pride and Prejudice* Jane Austen

cynosure *n* something that strongly attracts attention or admiration
> Then I thought of Eliza and Georgiana; I beheld one the cynosure of a ballroom, the other the inmate of a convent cell
> *Jane Eyre* Charlotte Brontë

dalliance *n* someone's dalliance with something is a brief involvement with it
> nor sporting in the dalliance of love
> *Doctor Faustus* Chorus Christopher Marlowe

darkling *adv* darkling is an archaic way of saying in the dark
> Darkling I listen
> *Ode to a Nightingale* John Keats

delf-case *n* a sideboard for holding dishes and crockery
> at the pewter dishes and delf-case
> *Wuthering Heights* Emily Brontë

determin *v* to end
> and be out of vogue when that was determined
> *Gulliver's Travels* Jonathan Swift

determine *v* to determine can mean to learn or find especially by investigation or experience
> All the sensitive feelings it wounded so cruelly, all the shame and misery it kept alive within my breast, became more poignant as I thought of this; and I determined that the life was unendurable
> *David Copperfield* Charles Dickens

Deuce *n* a slang term for the Devil
> "Ah, I dare say I did. Deuce take me," he added suddenly, "I know I did. I find I am not quite unscrewed yet."
> *Great Expectations* Charles Dickens

diabolical *adj* diabolical means devilish or evil
> and with a thousand diabolical expressions
> *Treasure Island* Robert Louis Stevenson

direction *n* address
> Elizabeth was not surprised at it, as Jane had written the direction remarkably ill
> *Pride and Prejudice* Jane Austen

7 to act or try to be like another **WORD ORIGIN** Latin *copia* abundance

copybook *n* **1** a book of specimens of handwriting for imitation **2** blot one's copybook *informal* to spoil one's reputation by a mistake or indiscretion ▷ *adj* **3** done exactly according to the rules **4** trite or unoriginal

copycat *n informal* a person who imitates or copies someone

copyist *n* **1** a person who makes written copies **2** an imitator: *although the songs are derivative, it is unfair to dismiss the band as mere copyists*

copyright *n* **1** the exclusive legal right to reproduce and control an original literary, musical, or artistic work ▷ *vb* **2** to take out a copyright on ▷ *adj* **3** protected by copyright

copy typist *n* a typist who types from written or typed drafts rather than dictation

copywriter *n* a person employed to write advertising copy

coquette *n* a woman who flirts **coquetry** *n* **coquettish** *adj* **WORD ORIGIN** French

coracle *n* a small round boat made of wicker covered with skins **WORD ORIGIN** Welsh *corwgl*

coral *n* **1** the stony substance formed by the skeletons of marine animals called polyps, often forming an island or reef **2** any of the polyps whose skeletons form coral ▷ *adj* **3** orange-pink **WORD ORIGIN** Greek *korallion*

cor anglais *n, pl* **cors anglais** *music* an alto woodwind instrument of the oboe family **WORD ORIGIN** French: English horn

corbel *n archit* a stone or timber support sticking out of a wall **WORD ORIGIN** Old French: a little raven

corbie *n Scot* a raven or crow **WORD ORIGIN** Latin *corvus*

cord *n* **1** string or thin rope made of twisted strands **2** *anat* a structure in the body resembling a rope: *the vocal cords* **3** a ribbed fabric like corduroy **4** *US, Canad, Austral, & NZ* an electrical flex **5** a unit for measuring cut wood, equal to 128 cubic feet ▷ *adj* **6** (of fabric) ribbed ▸ See also **cords** **WORD ORIGIN** Greek *khordē*

cordate *adj* heart-shaped

corded *adj* **1** tied or fastened with cord **2** (of a fabric) ribbed: *white corded silk* **3** (of muscles) standing out like cords

cordial *adj* **1** warm and friendly: *a cordial atmosphere* **2** heartfelt or sincere: *I developed a cordial dislike for the place* ▷ *n* **3** a drink with a fruit base: *lime cordial* **cordially** *adv* **WORD ORIGIN** Latin *cor* heart

cordiality *n* warmth of feeling

cordite *n* a smokeless explosive used in guns and bombs **WORD ORIGIN** from *cord*, because of its stringy appearance

cordless *adj* (of an electrical appliance such as a kettle or telephone) powered by an internal battery or kept in a holder which is connected to the mains, so that there is no cable connecting the appliance itself to the electrical mains

cordon *n* **1** a chain of police, soldiers, or vehicles guarding an area **2** an ornamental braid or ribbon **3** *horticulture* a fruit tree trained to grow as a single stem bearing fruit ▷ *vb* **4** cordon off to put or form a cordon round **WORD ORIGIN** Old French: a little cord

cordon bleu (**bluh**) *adj* (of cookery or cooks) of the highest standard: *a cordon bleu chef* **WORD ORIGIN** French: blue ribbon

cordon sanitaire *n* **1** a line of buffer states shielding a country **2** a guarded line isolating an infected area **WORD ORIGIN** French, literally: sanitary line

cords *pl n* trousers made of corduroy

corduroy *n* a heavy cotton fabric with a velvety ribbed surface **WORD ORIGIN** origin unknown

corduroys *pl n* trousers made of corduroy

core *n* **1** the central part of certain fleshy fruits, containing the seeds **2** the central or essential part of something: *the historic core of the city* **3** a piece of magnetic soft iron inside an electromagnet or transformer **4** *geol* the central part of the earth **5** a cylindrical sample of rock or soil, obtained by the use of a hollow drill **6** *physics* the region of a nuclear reactor containing the fissionable material **7** *computers* the main internal memory of a computer ▷ *vb* **coring, cored 8** to remove the core from (fruit) **WORD ORIGIN** origin unknown

corella *n* a white Australian cockatoo

co-respondent *n* a person with whom someone being sued for divorce is claimed to have committed adultery

corgi *n* a short-legged sturdy dog **WORD ORIGIN** Welsh *cor* dwarf + *ci* dog

coriander *n* a European plant, cultivated for its aromatic seeds and leaves, used in flavouring foods **WORD ORIGIN** Greek *koriannon*

Corinthian *adj* **1** of Corinth, a port in S Greece **2** of a style of classical architecture characterized by a bell-shaped capital with carved leaf-shaped ornaments ▷ *n* **3** a person from Corinth

cork *n* **1** the thick light porous outer bark of a Mediterranean oak **2** a piece of cork used as a stopper **3** *bot* the outer bark of a woody plant ▷ *vb* **4** to stop up (a bottle) with a cork **WORD ORIGIN** probably from Arabic *qurq*

corkage *n* a charge made at a restaurant for serving wine bought elsewhere

corked *adj* (of wine) spoiled through being stored in a bottle with a decayed cork

corker *n old-fashioned slang* a splendid or outstanding person or thing

corkscrew *n* **1** a device for pulling corks from bottles, usually consisting of a pointed metal spiral attached to a handle ▷ *adj* **2** like a corkscrew in shape ▷ *vb* **3** to move in a spiral or zigzag course

corm *n* the scaly bulblike underground stem of certain plants **WORD ORIGIN** Greek *kormos* tree trunk

cormorant *n* a large dark-coloured long-necked sea bird **WORD ORIGIN** Old French *corp* raven + *-mareng* of the sea

corn[1] *n* **1** a cereal plant such as wheat, oats, or barley **2** the grain of such plants **3** *US, Canad, Austral, & NZ* maize **4** *slang* something unoriginal or oversentimental **WORD ORIGIN** Old English

corn[2] *n* a painful hardening of the skin around a central point in the foot, caused by pressure **WORD ORIGIN** Latin *cornu* horn

corn circle *n* same as **crop circle**

corncob *n* the core of an ear of maize, to which the kernels are attached

corncrake *n* a brown bird with a harsh grating cry

cornea (**korn**-ee-a) *n* the transparent membrane covering the eyeball **corneal** *adj* **WORD ORIGIN** Latin *cornu* horn

corned beef *n* cooked beef preserved in salt

cornelian *n* same as **carnelian**

corner *n* **1** the place or angle formed by the meeting of two converging lines or surfaces **2** the space within the angle formed, as in a room **3** the place where two streets meet **4** a sharp bend in a road **5** a remote place: *far-flung corners of the world* **6** any secluded or private place **7** *sport* a free kick or shot taken from the corner of the field **8** cut corners to take the shortest or easiest way at the expense of high standards **9** turn the corner to pass the critical point of an illness or a difficult time ▷ *adj* **10** on or in a corner: *a corner seat* ▷ *vb* **11** to force (a person or animal) into a difficult or inescapable position **12** (of a vehicle or its driver) to turn a corner **13** to obtain a monopoly of **WORD ORIGIN** Latin *cornu* point, horn

corner shop *n* a small general shop serving a neighbourhood

cornerstone *n* **1** an indispensable part or basis: *the food we eat is one of the cornerstones of good health* **2** a stone at the corner of a wall

cornet *n* **1** a brass instrument of the trumpet family **2** *Brit* a cone-shaped ice-cream wafer **cornetist** *n* **WORD ORIGIN** Latin *cornu* horn

corn exchange *n* a building where corn is bought and sold

cornflakes *pl n* a breakfast cereal made from toasted maize

cornflour *n* **1** a fine maize flour, used for thickening sauces **2** *NZ* fine wheat flour

cornflower *n* a small plant with blue flowers

cornice (**korn**-iss) *n* **1** a decorative moulding round the top of a wall or building **2** *archit* the projecting mouldings at the top of a column **WORD ORIGIN** Old French

Cornish *adj* **1** of Cornwall ▷ *n* **2** a Celtic language of Cornwall, extinct by 1800 ▷ *pl n* **3** the Cornish the people of Cornwall

Cornish pasty *n* a pastry case with a filling of meat and vegetables

cornucopia (korn-yew-**kope**-ee-a) *n* **1** a great abundance: *a cornucopia of rewards* **2** a symbol of plenty, consisting of a horn overflowing with fruit and flowers
WORD ORIGIN Latin *cornu copiae* horn of plenty

corny *adj* **cornier, corniest** *slang* unoriginal or oversentimental

corolla *n* the petals of a flower collectively
WORD ORIGIN Latin: garland

corollary (kor-**oll**-a-ree) *n, pl* **-laries 1** a proposition that follows directly from another that has been proved **2** a natural consequence
WORD ORIGIN Latin *corollarium* money paid for a garland

corona (kor-**rone**-a) *n, pl* **-nas** or **-nae** (-nee) **1** a circle of light around a luminous body, usually the moon **2** the outermost part of the sun's atmosphere, visible as a faint halo during a total eclipse **3** a long cigar with blunt ends **4** *bot* a crownlike part of some flowers on top of the seed or on the inner side of the corolla **5** *physics* an electrical glow appearing around the surface of a charged conductor
WORD ORIGIN Latin: crown

coronary (kor-ron-a-ree) *adj* **1** *anat* of the arteries that supply blood to the heart ▷ *n, pl* **-naries 2** a coronary thrombosis
WORD ORIGIN Latin *coronarius* belonging to a wreath or crown

coronary thrombosis *n* a condition where the blood flow to the heart is blocked by a clot in a coronary artery

coronation *n* the ceremony of crowning a monarch
WORD ORIGIN Latin *coronare* to crown

coronavirus *n* a type of airborne virus accounting for 10–30% of all colds
WORD ORIGIN from its corona-like appearance under an electron microscope

coroner *n* a public official responsible for the investigation of violent, sudden, or suspicious deaths
WORD ORIGIN Anglo-French *corouner*

coronet *n* **1** a small crown worn by princes or peers **2** a band of jewels worn as a headdress
WORD ORIGIN Old French *coronete*

corpora *pl n* the plural of **corpus**

corporal¹ *n* a noncommissioned officer in an army
WORD ORIGIN Old French *caporal*, from Latin *caput* head

corporal² *adj* of the body
WORD ORIGIN Latin *corpus* body

corporal punishment *n* physical punishment, such as caning

corporate *adj* **1** relating to business corporations: *corporate finance* **2** shared by a group **3** forming a corporation; incorporated
WORD ORIGIN Latin *corpus* body

corporation *n* **1** a large business or company **2** a city or town council **3** *informal* a large paunch
corporative *adj*

corporatism *n* organization of a state on the lines of a business enterprise, with substantial government management of the economy

corporeal (kore-**pore**-ee-al) *adj* of the physical world rather than the spiritual
WORD ORIGIN Latin *corpus* body

corps (kore) *n, pl* **corps 1** a military unit with a specific function: *medical corps* **2** an organized body of people: *the diplomatic corps*
WORD ORIGIN French

corps de ballet *n* the members of a ballet company
WORD ORIGIN French

corpse *n* a dead body, esp. of a human being
WORD ORIGIN Latin *corpus*

corpulent *adj* fat or plump
corpulence *n*
WORD ORIGIN Latin *corpulentus*

corpus *n, pl* **-pora** a collection of writings, such as one by a single author or on a specific topic: *the corpus of Marxist theory*
WORD ORIGIN Latin: body

corpuscle *n* a red blood cell (see **erythrocyte**) or white blood cell (see **leucocyte**) **corpuscular** *adj*
WORD ORIGIN Latin *corpusculum* a little body

corral *US & Canad n* **1** an enclosure for cattle or horses ▷ *vb* **-ralling, -ralled 2** to put in a corral
WORD ORIGIN Spanish

corrasion *n geol* erosion of rocks caused by fragments transported over them by water, wind, or ice
WORD ORIGIN Latin *corradere* to scrape together

correct *adj* **1** free from error; true: *the correct answer* **2** in conformity with accepted standards: *in most cultures there is a strong sense of correct sexual conduct* ▷ *vb* **3** to make free from or put right errors **4** to indicate the errors in (something) **5** to rebuke or punish in order to improve: *I stand corrected* **6** to make conform to a standard **correctly** *adv* **correctness** *n*
WORD ORIGIN Latin *corrigere* to make straight

correction *n* **1** an act or instance of correcting **2** an alteration correcting something: *corrections to the second proofs* **3** a reproof or punishment **correctional** *adj*

corrective *adj* intended to put right something that is wrong: *corrective action*

correlate *vb* **-lating, -lated 1** to place or be placed in a mutual relationship: *water consumption is closely correlated to the number of people living in a house* ▷ *n* **2** either of two things mutually related **correlation** *n*

correlative *adj* **1** having a mutual relationship **2** *grammar* (of words, usually conjunctions) corresponding to each other and occurring regularly together, for example *neither* and *nor*

correspond *vb* **1** to be consistent or compatible (with) **2** to be similar (to) **3** to communicate (with) by letter **corresponding** *adj* **correspondingly** *adv*
WORD ORIGIN Latin *com-* together + *respondere* to respond

correspondence *n* **1** communication by letters **2** the letters exchanged in this way **3** relationship or similarity

correspondence course *n* a course of study conducted by post

correspondent *n* **1** a person who communicates by letter **2** a person employed by a newspaper or news service to report on a special subject or from a foreign country

corridor *n* **1** a passage in a building or a train **2** a strip of land or airspace that provides access through the territory of a foreign country **3** **corridors of power** the higher levels of government or the Civil Service
WORD ORIGIN Old Italian *corridore*, literally: place for running

corrie *n* (in Scotland) a circular hollow on the side of a hill
WORD ORIGIN Gaelic *coire* cauldron

corrigendum (kor-rij-**end**-um) *n, pl* **-da** (-da) **1** an error to be corrected **2** a slip of paper inserted into a book after printing, listing corrections
WORD ORIGIN Latin: that which is to be corrected

corroborate *vb* **-rating, -rated** to support (a fact or opinion) by giving proof **corroboration** *n* **corroborative** *adj*
WORD ORIGIN Latin *com-* (intensive) + *roborare* to make strong

corroboree *n Austral* **1** an Aboriginal gathering or dance of festive or warlike character **2** *informal* any noisy gathering
WORD ORIGIN Aboriginal

corrode *vb* **-roding, -roded 1** to eat away or be eaten away by chemical action or rusting **2** to destroy gradually: *rumours corroding the public's affection for the royal family*
WORD ORIGIN Latin *corrodere* to gnaw to pieces

corrosion *n* **1** the process by which something, esp. a metal, is corroded **2** the result of corrosion **corrosive** *adj*

corrugate *vb* **-gating, -gated** to fold into alternate grooves and ridges **corrugation** *n*
WORD ORIGIN Latin *corrugare*

corrugated iron *n* a thin sheet of iron or steel, formed with alternating ridges and troughs

corrupt *adj* **1** open to or involving bribery or other dishonest practices: *corrupt practices* **2** morally depraved **3** (of a text or data) made unreliable by errors or alterations ▷ *vb* **4** to make corrupt **corruptive** *adj*
WORD ORIGIN Latin *corruptus* spoiled

corruptible *adj* capable of being corrupted

corruption *n* **1** dishonesty and illegal behaviour **2** the act of corrupting morally or sexually **3** the process of rotting or decaying **4** an unintentional or unauthorized alteration in a text or data **5** an altered form of a word

corsage (kore-**sahzh**) *n* a small bouquet worn on the bodice of a dress
WORD ORIGIN Old French *cors* body

corsair *n* **1** a pirate **2** a pirate ship **3** a privateer
WORD ORIGIN Old French *corsaire*

corse n archaic a corpse

corselet n **1** a woman's one-piece undergarment, combining corset and bra **2** a piece of armour to cover the trunk
WORD ORIGIN Old French cors bodice

corset n **1** a close-fitting undergarment worn by women to shape the torso **2** a similar garment worn by either sex to support and protect the back **corsetry** n
WORD ORIGIN Old French: a little bodice

cortege (kore-**tayzh**) n a funeral procession
WORD ORIGIN Italian corteggio

cortex (kore-tex) n, pl -tices (-tiss-seez) anat the outer layer of the brain or some other internal organ **cortical** adj
WORD ORIGIN Latin: bark, outer layer

cortisone n a steroid hormone used in treating rheumatoid arthritis, allergies, and skin diseases
WORD ORIGIN corticosterone, a hormone

corundum n a hard mineral used as an abrasive, and of which the ruby and white sapphire are precious forms
WORD ORIGIN Tamil kuruntam

coruscate vb -cating, -cated formal to emit flashes of light; sparkle **coruscating** adj **coruscation** n
WORD ORIGIN Latin coruscare to flash

corvette n a lightly armed escort warship
WORD ORIGIN perhaps from Middle Dutch corf

corymb n bot a flat-topped flower cluster with the stems growing progressively shorter towards the centre
WORD ORIGIN Greek korumbos cluster

cos¹ or **cos lettuce** n a lettuce with a long slender head and crisp leaves
WORD ORIGIN after Kos, the Aegean island of its origin

cos² cosine

cosec (koh-sek) cosecant

cosecant (koh-**seek**-ant) n (in trigonometry) the ratio of the length of the hypotenuse to that of the opposite side in a right-angled triangle

cosh chiefly Brit n **1** a heavy blunt weapon, often made of hard rubber ▷ vb **2** to hit on the head with a cosh
WORD ORIGIN Romany kosh

cosignatory n, pl -ries a person or country that signs a document jointly with others

cosine (koh-sine) n (in trigonometry) the ratio of the length of the adjacent side to that of the hypotenuse in a right-angled triangle
WORD ORIGIN see CO-, SINE

cosmetic n **1** anything applied to the face or body in order to improve the appearance ▷ adj **2** done or used to improve the appearance of the face or body **3** improving in appearance only: glossy brochures are part of a cosmetic exercise
WORD ORIGIN Greek kosmētikos, from kosmein to arrange

cosmetic surgery n surgery performed to improve the appearance, rather than for medical reasons

cosmic adj **1** of or relating to the whole universe: the cosmic order **2** occurring in or coming from outer space: cosmic dust

cosmogony n, pl -nies the study of the origin of the universe
WORD ORIGIN Greek kosmos world + gonos creation

cosmology n the study of the origin and nature of the universe **cosmological** adj **cosmologist** n
WORD ORIGIN Greek kosmos world + -LOGY

cosmonaut n the Russian name for an astronaut
WORD ORIGIN Russian kosmonavt, from Greek kosmos universe + nautēs sailor

cosmopolitan adj **1** composed of people or elements from many different countries or cultures **2** having lived and travelled in many countries **3** sophisticated and cultured ▷ n **4** a cosmopolitan person **cosmopolitanism** n
WORD ORIGIN Greek kosmos world + politēs citizen

cosmos n the universe considered as an ordered system
WORD ORIGIN Greek kosmos order

Cossack n **1** a member of a S Russian people, famous as horsemen and dancers ▷ adj **2** of the Cossacks: a Cossack dance
WORD ORIGIN Russian kazak vagabond

cosset vb -seting, -seted to pamper or pet
WORD ORIGIN origin unknown

cost n **1** the amount of money, time, or energy required to obtain or produce something **2** suffering or sacrifice: these were crucial truths which rugby never grasped, to its cost **3** the amount paid for a commodity by its seller: to sell at cost **4** costs law the expenses of a lawsuit **5** at all costs regardless of any cost or effort involved **6** at the cost of at the expense of losing: they eventually triumphed, but at the cost of many lives ▷ vb **costing, cost 7** to be obtained or obtainable in exchange for: calls cost 36p a minute cheap rate, 48p at other times **8** to involve the loss or sacrifice of: a fall which almost cost him his life **9** costing, costed to estimate the cost of producing something
WORD ORIGIN Latin constare to stand at, cost

cost accounting n the recording and controlling of all the costs involved in running a business **cost accountant** n

costal adj of the ribs

cost-effective adj providing adequate financial return in relation to outlay

costermonger n Brit a person who sells fruit and vegetables from a barrow in the street
WORD ORIGIN costard a kind of apple + monger trader

costive adj old-fashioned having or causing constipation
WORD ORIGIN Old French costivé

costly adj -lier, -liest **1** expensive **2** involving great loss or sacrifice: a bitter and costly war **costliness** n

cost of living n the average cost of the basic necessities of life, such as food, housing, and clothing

costume n **1** a style of dressing, including all the clothes and accessories, typical of a particular

country or period **2** the clothes worn by an actor or performer: a jester's costume **3** short for **swimming costume** ▷ vb -tuming, -tumed **4** to provide with a costume: she was costumed by many of the great Hollywood designers **costumed** adj
WORD ORIGIN Italian: dress, custom

costume jewellery n inexpensive but attractive jewellery

costumier n a maker or supplier of theatrical or fancy dress costumes

cosy or US **cozy** adj -sier, -siest or US -zier, -ziest **1** warm and snug **2** intimate and friendly: a cosy chat ▷ n, pl -sies or US -zies **3** a cover for keeping things warm: a tea cosy **cosiness** or US **coziness** n
WORD ORIGIN Scots

cot¹ n **1** a bed with high sides for a baby or very young child **2** a small portable bed
WORD ORIGIN Hindi khāt bedstead

cot² n **1** literary or archaic a small cottage **2** a cote
WORD ORIGIN Old English

cot³ cotangent

cotangent n (in trigonometry) the ratio of the length of the adjacent side to that of the opposite side in a right-angled triangle

cot death n the unexplained sudden death of a baby while asleep

cote or **cot** n a small shelter for birds or animals
WORD ORIGIN Old English

coterie (kote-er-ee) n a small exclusive group of friends or people with common interests
WORD ORIGIN French

cotoneaster (kot-tone-ee-**ass**-ter) n a garden shrub with red berries

cottage n a small simple house, usually in the country **cottager** n
WORD ORIGIN from COT²

cottage cheese n a mild soft white cheese made from skimmed milk curds

cottage industry n a craft industry in which employees work at home

cottage pie n a dish of minced meat topped with mashed potato

cottaging n Brit, Austral, & NZ slang homosexual activity between men in a public lavatory
WORD ORIGIN from cottage (in the sense: a public lavatory)

cotter¹ n machinery a bolt or wedge that is used to secure parts of machinery
WORD ORIGIN Middle English cotterel

cotter² n Scot & history a farm labourer occupying a cottage and land rent-free
WORD ORIGIN see COT²

cotter pin n machinery a split pin used to hold parts together and fastened by having the ends spread apart after it is inserted

cotton n **1** the soft white downy fibre surrounding the seeds of a plant grown in warm climates, used to make cloth and thread **2** cloth or thread made from cotton fibres **cottony** adj
WORD ORIGIN Arabic qutn

cotton bud n a small stick with cotton wool tips used for cleaning the ears, applying make-up, etc.

Australian English

As with other forms of World English, Australian English has developed its own vocabulary and linguistic conventions. The first form of English to arrive in Australia was British English, which was spoken by deportees and the staff of penal colonies and their families. The Cockney dialect was predominant in the colonies of New South Wales and Tasmania (known at the time as Van Diemen's Land), and Irish and Scots dialects were also strong influences. Convicts ceased to be transported to Australia in the 19th century, but immigration continued apace, and Americanized language was also introduced during several gold rushes of the 19th century. This economic migration dwarfed the numbers of convicts who had been shipped to Australia, and the legacy of US English persists in everyday Australian vocabulary such as *freeway* and words such as *bonzer*, which is believed to be a contracted form of *bonanza*.

Present day Australian English is spoken with a non-rhotic accent, and regional variations are more easily identified by differing vocabularies rather than accents or pronunciation. These differences can vary from state to state in subtle ways, such as the terminology used for beer glasses (what is known as a *middy* in New South Wales is called a *pot* in Victoria). Vocabulary used nationwide in Australian English (or *Strine*, as it is affectionately known – the word is a play on the pronunciation of 'Australian' in a broad Aussie accent) includes *tucker* (meaning 'food'), *ocker* (a term for a boorish Aussie male, derived originally from a nickname for *Oscar*), *bush* (uncultivated rural areas) and *dinkum* (meaning 'work', also used in the idiom *fair dinkum*, which means 'genuine' or 'honestly'). Diminutive forms of words are also used widely. For example, 'afternoon' become *arvo*, 'university' becomes *uni*, 'barbecue' becomes *barbie* (or *barby*), and 'football' *footie* (or *footy*).

Naturally, Australian English reflects the country's culture. The central position of sport in Australian life is reflected in terms such as to *barrack for* (to shout support for a team or a person, especially a sports player). Australian English often demonstrates another of its proud cultural traditions, namely calling a spade a spade. This is usually done with no small degree of self-aware humour, and is illustrated perfectly by the use of *barbecue stopper* as a colloquialism for a *faux pas*, and *spit the dummy* to describe an outburst or tantrum. Some claim that the well-known word *pom* (a derogatory term for the British) is derived from the initials on prisoner uniforms ('Prisoner Of [Her] Majesty'). However, there is little historical evidence to support this. A more plausible explanation is that *pom* and *pommy* exist as shortened forms of the bright-red fruit *pomegranate* (referring to the British propensity to burn in the sun).

In everyday speech, Australian English often relies on rhyming slang. Much of this is identical to its British counterpart, no doubt because much of it arrived with nineteenth-century migrants and deportees. But the slang has put down roots in Australia, not least because of the informality of Australian English and its consequent wealth of slang of all kinds. There are interesting equivalents to cockney terms, as with *goanna* and *joanna*, both of which rely on idiosyncrasies of the two accents to rhyme with 'piano'. The influence of sport is also demonstrated by the use of tennis player *Adrian Quist* as a rhyme for *pissed* ('drunk').

Words from Aboriginal languages have been integrated into Australian English in Anglicized forms, mainly as a source of vocabulary for flora (*jarrah*), fauna (*kangaroo*, *kookaburra*, *dingo*), and place names (such as the Sydney suburbs of *Parramatta* and *Woolloomooloo*, and Australia's capital city *Canberra*). *Didgeridoo* is not, as is widely believed, an Aboriginal word, and is most likely an onomatopoeic invention.

cotton on *vb informal* to understand or realize the meaning (of): *it has taken the world 20 years to cotton on to this idea*

cotton wool *n* absorbent fluffy cotton, used for surgical dressings and to apply creams to the skin

cotyledon (kot-ill-**ee**-don) *n* the first leaf produced by a plant embryo
WORD ORIGIN Greek *kotulē* cup

couch *n* 1 a piece of upholstered furniture for seating more than one person 2 a bed on which patients of a doctor or a psychoanalyst lie during examination or treatment ▷ *vb* 3 to express in a particular style of language: *a proclamation couched in splendidly archaic phraseology* 4 *archaic* (of an animal) to crouch, as when preparing to leap
WORD ORIGIN Old French *coucher* to lay down

couchette (koo-**shett**) *n* a bed converted from seats on a train or ship
WORD ORIGIN French

couch grass *n* a grassy weed which spreads quickly

couch potato *n slang* a physically lazy person, esp. one who spends most of the day in front of the television

cougan *n Austral slang* a drunk and rowdy person

cougar (koo-gar) *n* same as **puma**
WORD ORIGIN from S American Indian

cough *vb* 1 to expel air abruptly and noisily from the lungs 2 (of an engine or other machine) to make a sound similar to this ▷ *n* 3 an act or sound of coughing 4 an illness which causes frequent coughing
WORD ORIGIN Old English *cohhetten*

cough up *vb* 1 *informal* to give up (money or information) 2 to bring up into the mouth by coughing: *to cough up blood*

could *vb* 1 used to make the past tense of **can¹** 2 used to make the subjunctive mood of **can¹**, esp. in polite requests or conditional sentences: *could I have a word with you, please?* 3 used to indicate the suggestion of a course of action: *we could make a fortune from selling players, but that would not be in the long-term interests of the club* 4 used to indicate a possibility: *it could simply be a spelling mistake*
WORD ORIGIN Old English *cūthe*

couldn't could not

coulis (koo-lee) *n* a thin purée of vegetables or fruit, usually served as a sauce surrounding a dish: *rum truffle cake with raspberry coulis*
WORD ORIGIN French: purée

coulomb (koo-lom) *n* the SI unit of electric charge
WORD ORIGIN after C. A. de *Coulomb*, physicist

coulter (kole-ter) *n* a vertical blade on a plough in front of the ploughshare
WORD ORIGIN Latin *culter* ploughshare, knife

council *n* 1 a group meeting for discussion or consultation 2 a legislative or advisory body: *the United Nations Security Council* 3 *Brit* the local governing authority of a town or county 4 *Austral* the local governing authority

of a district or shire ▷ *adj* 5 of or provided by a local council: *a council house*
WORD ORIGIN Latin *concilium* assembly

≡ USAGE
≡ Avoid confusion with **counsel**.

councillor *or US* **councilor** *n* a member of a council

≡ USAGE
≡ Avoid confusion with **counsellor**.

council tax *n* (in Britain) a tax based on the relative value of property levied to fund local council services

counsel *n* 1 advice or guidance 2 discussion or consultation: *when it was over they took counsel of their consciences* 3 a barrister or group of barristers who conduct cases in court and advise on legal matters ▷ *vb* -**selling**, -**selled** *or US* -**seling**, -**seled** 4 to give advice or guidance to 5 to recommend or urge **counselling** *or US* **counseling** *n*
WORD ORIGIN Latin *consilium* deliberating body

≡ USAGE
≡ Avoid confusion with **council**.

counsellor *or US* **counselor** *n* 1 an adviser 2 *US* a lawyer who conducts cases in court

≡ USAGE
≡ Avoid confusion with **councillor**.

count¹ *vb* 1 to say numbers in ascending order up to and including: *count from one to ten* 2 to add up or check (each thing in a group) in order to find the total: *he counted the money he had left* 3 to be important: *it's the thought that counts* 4 to consider: *he can count himself lucky* 5 to take into account or include: *the time he'd spent in prison on remand counted towards his sentence* 6 not counting excluding 7 *music* to keep time by counting beats ▷ *n* 8 the act of counting 9 the number reached by counting: *a high pollen count* 10 *law* one of a number of charges 11 keep or lose count to keep or fail to keep an accurate record of items or events 12 out for the count unconscious ▷ See also **count against**, **countdown**, etc. **countable** *adj*
WORD ORIGIN Latin *computare* to calculate

count² *n* a middle-ranking European nobleman
WORD ORIGIN Latin *comes* associate

count against *vb* to have an effect or influence that makes something more unlikely: *his age counts against him getting promotion*

countdown *n* the act of counting backwards to zero to time exactly an operation such as the launching of a rocket

countenance *n* 1 *literary* the face or facial expression ▷ *vb* -**nancing**, -**nanced** 2 to support or tolerate
WORD ORIGIN Latin *continentia* restraint, control

counter¹ *n* 1 a long flat surface in a bank or shop, on which business is transacted 2 a small flat disc used in board games 3 a disc or token used as an imitation coin 4 under the counter (of the sale of goods) illegal
WORD ORIGIN Latin *computare* to compute

counter² *n* an apparatus for counting things

counter³ *vb* 1 to say or do (something) in retaliation or response 2 to oppose or act against 3 to return the attack of (an opponent) ▷ *adv* 4 in an opposite or opposing direction or manner 5 run counter to to be in direct contrast with ▷ *adj* 6 opposing or opposite ▷ *n* 7 something that is contrary or opposite to something else 8 an opposing action 9 a return attack, such as a blow in boxing
WORD ORIGIN Latin *contra* against

counter- *prefix* 1 against or opposite: *counterattack* 2 complementary or corresponding: *counterpart*
WORD ORIGIN Latin *contra*

counteract *vb* to act against or neutralize **counteraction** *n* **counteractive** *adj*

counterattack *n* 1 an attack in response to an attack ▷ *vb* 2 to make a counterattack (against)

counterbalance *n* 1 a weight or influence that balances or neutralizes another ▷ *vb* -**ancing**, -**anced** 2 to act as a counterbalance to

counterbid *n* a bid made in response to a bid from another party, offering more favourable terms to the seller

counterblast *n* an aggressive response to a verbal attack

counterclockwise *adv, adj US & Canad* same as **anticlockwise**

counterespionage *n* activities to counteract enemy espionage

counterfeit *adj* 1 made in imitation of something genuine with the intent to deceive or defraud: *counterfeit currency* 2 pretended: *counterfeit friendship* ▷ *n* 3 an imitation designed to deceive or defraud ▷ *vb* 4 to make a fraudulent imitation of 5 to feign: *surprise is an easy emotion to counterfeit*
WORD ORIGIN Old French *contrefait*

counterfoil *n Brit* the part of a cheque or receipt kept as a record

counterintelligence *n* activities designed to frustrate enemy espionage

countermand *vb* to cancel (a previous order)
WORD ORIGIN Old French *contremander*

countermeasure *n* action taken to counteract some other action

counterpane *n* a bed covering
WORD ORIGIN Medieval Latin *culcita puncta* quilted mattress

counterpart *n* 1 a person or thing complementary to or corresponding to another 2 a duplicate of a legal document

counterpoint *n* 1 the harmonious combining of two or more parts or melodies 2 a melody or part combined in this way ▷ *vb* 3 to set in contrast
WORD ORIGIN Old French *contrepoint* an accompaniment set against the notes of a melody

counterpoise *vb* -**poising**, -**poised** to oppose with something of equal weight or effect: *counterpoising humour and horror*

counterproductive *adj* having an effect opposite to the one intended

countersign *vb* 1 to sign (a document already signed by another) as

C

confirmation ▷ *n* **2** the signature so written

countersink *vb* **-sinking, -sank, -sunk** to drive (a screw) into a shaped hole so that its head is below the surface

countertenor *n* **1** an adult male voice with an alto range **2** a singer with such a voice

counterterrorism *n* activities intended to prevent terrorist acts or to eradicate terrorist groups **counterterrorist** *adj*

countess *n* **1** a woman holding the rank of count or earl **2** the wife or widow of a count or earl

countless *adj* too many to count

count noun *n* a noun that may be preceded by an indefinite article and can be used in the plural, such as *telephone* or *thing*

count on *vb* to rely or depend on

count out *vb* **1** *informal* to exclude **2** to declare (a boxer) defeated when he has not risen from the floor within ten seconds

countrified *adj* having an appearance or manner associated with the countryside rather than a town

country *n, pl* **-tries 1** an area distinguished by its people, culture, language, or government **2** the territory of a nation or state **3** the people of a nation or state **4** the part of the land that is away from cities or industrial areas **5** a person's native land **6** same as **country and western 7 across country** not keeping to roads **8 go to the country** *Brit & NZ* to dissolve Parliament and hold a general election **WORD ORIGIN** Medieval Latin *contrata* (*terra*) (land) lying opposite

country and western *or* **country music** *n* popular music based on American White folk music

country club *n* a club in the country, which has sporting and social facilities

country dance *n* a type of British folk dance performed in rows or circles

countryman *n, pl* **-men 1** a person from one's own country **2** *Brit, Austral, & NZ* a person who lives in the country **countrywoman** *fem n*

countryside *n* land away from the cities

county *n, pl* **-ties 1** (in some countries) a division of a country ▷ *adj* **2** *Brit informal* upper-class **WORD ORIGIN** Old French *conté* land belonging to a count

coup (**koo**) *n* **1** a brilliant and successful action **2** a coup d'état **WORD ORIGIN** French

coup de grâce (**koo** de **grahss**) *n, pl* **coups de grâce** (**koo** de **grahss**) a final or decisive action **WORD ORIGIN** French

coup d'état (**koo** day-**tah**) *n, pl* **coups d'état** (**kooz** day-**tah**) a sudden violent or illegal overthrow of a government **WORD ORIGIN** French

coupé (**koo**-pay) *n* a sports car with two doors and a sloping fixed roof **WORD ORIGIN** French *carrosse coupé* cut-off carriage

couple *n* **1** two people who are married or romantically involved **2** two

partners in a dance or game **3** **a couple of a** a pair of: *a couple of guys* **b** *informal* a few: *a couple of weeks* ▷ *pron* **4** **a couple a** two **b** *informal* a few: *give him a couple* ▷ *vb* **-pling, -pled 5** to connect or link: *an ingrained sense of shame, coupled with a fear of ridicule* **6** *literary* to have sexual intercourse **WORD ORIGIN** Latin *copula* a bond

couplet *n* two successive lines of verse, usually rhyming and of the same metre

coupling *n* a device for connecting things, such as railway cars or trucks

coupon *n* **1** a piece of paper entitling the holder to a discount or free gift **2** a detachable slip that can be used as a commercial order form **3** *Brit* a football pools entry form **WORD ORIGIN** Old French *colpon* piece cut off

courage *n* **1** the ability to face danger or pain without fear **2 the courage of one's convictions** the confidence to act according to one's beliefs **WORD ORIGIN** Latin *cor* heart

courageous *adj* showing courage **courageously** *adv*

courgette *n* a type of small vegetable marrow **WORD ORIGIN** French

courier *n* **1** a person who looks after and guides travellers **2** a person paid to deliver urgent messages **WORD ORIGIN** Latin *currere* to run

course *n* **1** a complete series of lessons or lectures: *a training course* **2** a sequence of medical treatment prescribed for a period of time: *a course of antibiotics* **3** an onward movement in time or space: *during the course of his career he worked with many leading actors* **4** a route or direction taken: *the ships were blown off course by a gale* **5** the path or channel along which a river moves **6** an area on which a sport is played or a race is held: *a golf course* **7** any of the successive parts of a meal **8** a continuous, usually horizontal layer of building material, such as bricks or tiles, at one level in a building **9** a mode of conduct or action: *the safest course of action was to do nothing* **10** the natural development of a sequence of events: *allow the fever to run its course* **11** a period of time: *over the course of the last two years* **12** **as a matter of course** as a natural or normal consequence or event **13** **in the course of** in the process of **14 in due course** at the natural or appropriate time **15 of course a** (*adv*) as expected; naturally **b** (*interj*) certainly; definitely ▷ *vb* **coursing, coursed 16** (of a liquid) to run swiftly **17** to hunt with hounds that follow the quarry by sight and not scent **WORD ORIGIN** Latin *cursus* a running

coursebook *n* a book that is used as part of an educational course

courser¹ *n* **1** a person who courses hounds **2** a hound trained for coursing

courser² *n* *literary* a swift horse; steed **WORD ORIGIN** Old French *coursier*

coursework *n* work done by a student and assessed as part of an educational course

coursing *n* hunting with hounds trained to hunt game by sight

court *n* **1** *law* **a** a judicial body which hears and makes decisions on legal cases **b** the room or building in which such a body meets **2** a marked area used for playing a racket game **3** an area of ground wholly or partly surrounded by walls or buildings **4** a name given to some short streets, blocks of flats, or large country houses as a part of their address: *Carlton Court* **5** the residence or retinue of a sovereign **6** any formal assembly held by a sovereign **7 go to court** to take legal action **8 hold court** to preside over a group of admirers **9 out of court** without a trial or legal case **10 pay court to** to give flattering attention to ▷ *vb* **11** to attempt to gain the love of **12** to pay attention to (someone) in order to gain favour **13** to try to obtain (something): *he has not courted controversy, but he has certainly attracted it* **14** to make oneself open or vulnerable to: *courting disaster* **WORD ORIGIN** Latin *cohors* cohort

court card *n* (in a pack of playing cards) a king, queen, or jack **WORD ORIGIN** earlier *coat-card*, from the decorative coats worn by the figures depicted

courteous *adj* polite and considerate in manner **courteously** *adv* **courteousness** *n* **WORD ORIGIN** Middle English *corteis* with courtly manners

courtesan (kore-tiz-**zan**) *n history* a mistress or high-class prostitute **WORD ORIGIN** Old French *courtisane*

courtesy *n, pl* **-sies 1** politeness; good manners **2** a courteous act or remark **3 by courtesy of** with the consent of **WORD ORIGIN** Old French *corteis* courteous

courthouse *n* a public building in which courts of law are held

courtier *n* an attendant at a royal court

courtly *adj* **-lier, -liest 1** ceremoniously polite **2** of or suitable for a royal court **courtliness** *n*

court martial *n, pl* **court martials** *or* **courts martial 1** the trial of a member of the armed forces charged with breaking military law ▷ *vb* **court-martial, -tialling, -tialled** *or US* **-tialing, -tialed 2** to try by court martial

courtship *n* the courting of an intended spouse or mate

court shoe *n* a low-cut shoe for women, without laces or straps

courtyard *n* an open area of ground surrounded by walls or buildings

couscous (**kooss**-kooss) *n* **1** a type of semolina used in North African cookery **2** a spicy North African dish, consisting of steamed semolina served with a stew **WORD ORIGIN** Arabic *kouskous*

cousin *n* the child of one's aunt or uncle. Also called: **first cousin** **WORD ORIGIN** Latin *consobrinus*

couture (koo-**toor**) *n* **1** high-fashion designing and dressmaking ▷ *adj* **2** relating to high fashion design and dress-making: *couture clothes* **WORD ORIGIN** French: sewing

couturier *n* a person who designs fashion clothes for women **WORD ORIGIN** French

C

covalency *or US* **covalence** *n chem* **1** the ability to form a bond in which two atoms share a pair of electrons **2** the number of covalent bonds which a particular atom can make with others **covalent** *adj*

cove[1] *n* a small bay or inlet
WORD ORIGIN Old English *cofa*

cove[2] *n old-fashioned, slang* a fellow; chap
WORD ORIGIN probably from Romany *kova*

coven (kuv-ven) *n* a meeting of witches
WORD ORIGIN Latin *convenire* to come together

covenant (kuv-ven-ant) *n* **1** *chiefly Brit* a formal agreement to make an annual payment to charity **2** *law* a formal sealed agreement **3** *Bible* God's promise to the Israelites and their commitment to worship him alone ▷ *vb* **4** to agree by a legal covenant **covenanter** *n*
WORD ORIGIN Latin *convenire* to come together, agree

Covenanter *n Scots history* a person upholding either of two 17th-century covenants to establish and defend Presbyterianism

Coventry *n* **send someone to Coventry** to punish someone by refusing to speak to him or her
WORD ORIGIN after *Coventry*, England

cover *vb* **1** to place something over so as to protect or conceal **2** to put a garment on; clothe **3** to extend over or lie thickly on the surface of: *the ground was covered with dry leaves* **4** (sometimes foll. by *up*) to screen or conceal; hide from view **5** to travel over **6** to protect (an individual or group) by taking up a position from which fire may be returned if those being protected are fired upon **7** to keep a gun aimed at **8 a** to insure against loss or risk **b** to provide for (loss or risk) by insurance **9** to include or deal with: *the course covers accounting, economics, statistics, law, and computer applications* **10** to act as reporter or photographer on (a news event) for a newspaper or magazine **11** (of a sum of money) to be enough to pay for (something) **12** *music* to record a cover version of **13** *sport* to guard or obstruct (an opponent, team-mate, or area) **14 cover for** to deputize for (a person) **15** (foll. by *for* or *up for*) to provide an alibi (for): *can my men count on your friends at City Hall to cover for us?* ▷ *n* **16** anything which covers **17** a blanket or bedspread **18** the outside of a book or magazine **19** a pretext or disguise: *he claimed UN resolutions were being used as a cover for planned American aggression* **20** an envelope or other postal wrapping: *under plain cover* **21** an individual table setting **22** insurance **23** a cover version **24 the covers** *cricket* the area roughly at right angles to the pitch on the off side and about halfway to the boundary **25 break cover** to come out from a shelter or hiding place **26 take cover** to make for a place of safety or shelter **27 under cover** protected or in secret ▶ See also **cover-up** ▷ **covering** *adj, n*
WORD ORIGIN Latin *cooperire* to cover completely

coverage *n journalism* the amount of reporting given to a subject or event

cover charge *n* a fixed service charge added to the bill in a restaurant

cover girl *n* an attractive woman whose picture appears on the cover of a magazine

covering letter *n* an accompanying letter sent as an explanation

coverlet *n* same as **bedspread**

cover note *n Austral & Brit* a temporary certificate from an insurance company giving proof of a current policy

covert *adj* **1** concealed or secret ▷ *n* **2** a thicket or woodland providing shelter for game **3** *ornithol* any of the small feathers on the wings and tail of a bird that surround the bases of the larger feathers **covertly** *adv*
WORD ORIGIN Old French: covered

cover-up *n* **1** concealment or attempted concealment of a mistake or crime ▷ *vb* **cover up** **2** to cover completely **3** to attempt to conceal (a mistake or crime)

cover version *n* a version by a different artist of a previously recorded musical item

covet *vb* **-eting, -eted** to long to possess (something belonging to another person)
WORD ORIGIN Latin *cupiditas* cupidity

covetous *adj* jealously longing to possess something **covetously** *adv* **covetousness** *n*

covey (kuv-vee) *n* **1** a small flock of grouse or partridge **2** a small group of people
WORD ORIGIN Old French *cover* to sit on, hatch

cow[1] *n* **1** the mature female of cattle **2** the mature female of various other mammals, such as the elephant or whale **3** *not in technical use* any domestic species of cattle **4** *informal, offensive* a disagreeable woman
WORD ORIGIN Old English *cū*

cow[2] *vb* to frighten or subdue with threats
WORD ORIGIN Old Norse *kūga* to oppress

coward *n* a person who is easily frightened and avoids dangerous or difficult situations **cowardly** *adj*
WORD ORIGIN Latin *cauda* tail

cowardice *n* lack of courage

cowbell *n* a bell hung around a cow's neck

cowboy *n* **1** (in the US and Canada) a ranch worker who herds and tends cattle, usually on horseback **2** a conventional character of Wild West folklore or films **3** *Brit, Austral, NZ informal* an irresponsible or unscrupulous worker or businessman **cowgirl** *fem n*

cowcatcher *n US & Canad* a fender on the front of a locomotive to clear the track of animals or other obstructions

cow cocky *n Austral & NZ* a one-man dairy farmer

cower *vb* to cringe or shrink in fear
WORD ORIGIN Middle Low German *kūren* to lie in wait

cowl *n* **1** a loose hood **2** a monk's hooded robe **3** a cover fitted to a chimney to increase ventilation and prevent draughts **cowled** *adj*
WORD ORIGIN Latin *cucullus* hood

cowlick *n* a tuft of hair over the forehead

cowling *n* a streamlined detachable metal covering around an engine

co-worker *n* a fellow worker: *these habits can drive your boss and co-workers crazy*

cow parsley *n* a hedgerow plant with umbrella-shaped clusters of white flowers

cowpat *n* a pool of cow dung

cowpox *n* a contagious disease of cows, the virus of which is used to make smallpox vaccine

cowrie *n, pl* **-ries** the glossy brightly-marked shell of a marine mollusc
WORD ORIGIN Hindi *kaurī*

cowslip *n* a European wild plant with yellow flowers
WORD ORIGIN Old English *cūslyppe*, from *cū* cow + *slyppe* slime, dung

cox *n* **1** a coxswain ▷ *vb* **2** to act as coxswain of (a boat)

coxcomb *or* **cockscomb** *n* **1** the comb of a domestic cock **2** *informal* a conceited dandy

coxswain (kok-sn) *n* the person who steers a lifeboat or rowing boat
WORD ORIGIN *cock* a ship's boat + SWAIN

coy *adj* **1** affectedly shy and modest **2** unwilling to give information **coyly** *adv* **coyness** *n*
WORD ORIGIN Latin *quietus* quiet

coyote (koy-ote-ee) *n, pl* **-otes** *or* **-ote** a small wolf of the deserts and prairies of North America
WORD ORIGIN Mexican Indian *coyotl*

coypu *n, pl* **-pus** *or* **-pu** a beaver-like amphibious rodent, bred for its fur
WORD ORIGIN From a Native American language, *kóypu*

cozen *vb literary* to cheat or trick **cozenage** *n*
WORD ORIGIN originally a cant term

Cpl *Corporal*

CPU *computers* central processing unit

Cr *chem* chromium

crab *n* **1** an edible shellfish with five pairs of legs, the first pair modified into pincers **2** short for **crab louse 3 catch a crab** *rowing* to make a stroke in which the oar misses the water or digs too deeply, causing the rower to fall backwards
WORD ORIGIN Old English *crabba*

crab apple *n* a kind of small sour apple

crabbed *adj* **1** (of handwriting) cramped and hard to read **2** bad-tempered
WORD ORIGIN probably from *crab*, because of its sideways movement & *crab apple*, because of its sourness

crabby *adj* **-bier, -biest** bad-tempered

crab louse *n* a parasitic louse living in the pubic area of humans

crack *vb* **1** to break or split without complete separation of the parts **2** to break with a sudden sharp sound **3** to make or cause to make a sudden sharp sound: *the coachman cracked his whip* **4** (of the voice) to become harsh or change pitch suddenly **5** *informal* to fail or break down: *he had cracked under the strain of losing his job* **6** to yield or cease to resist: *he had cracked under torture* **7** to hit with a forceful or resounding blow

Word Histories
part 5

Cravat came into English from French *cravate*, but ultimately comes from Serbo-Croat *Hrvat*. meaning 'Croat'. Croat mercenaries in the French army during the Thirty Years War were noted for the linen scarves they wore.

Crayfish: A crayfish isn't really a fish, of course, nor was it when it entered the English language from Old French. Folk etymology has transformed *crevice*, 'crab', to 'crayfish' to render the word for this aquatic creature more intelligible to English speakers.

Cringe: To 'cringe' comes from Old English *cringan* meaning 'to yield in battle'.

Currant: Currants originally came from Corinth in Greece. The word 'currant' is from early English *rayson of Corannte*, which translates Norman French *raisin de Corauntz*, meaning 'grape from Corinth'.

Dachshund is a German word meaning 'badger-dog', from *Dachs*, meaning 'badger', and *Hund*, meaning 'dog'. (*Hund* is related to the English word 'hound'.) Dachshunds were originally bred to hunt badgers.

Daft and **deft** both come from Old English *gedæfte*, meaning 'gentle'.

Daisy comes from Old English *dæges ēage*, meaning 'day's eye'. The flower was given this name because it opens in the daytime and closes at night.

Dean comes, via Old French, from Latin *decanus*, meaning 'someone in charge of ten people', from Latin *decem*, meaning 'ten'. The chapter of a cathedral or collegiate church consisted of ten canons.

In medieval times, **dismal** (from Latin *dies mali*, meaning 'evil days') was the name given to the 24 days of the year (two in each month) that were believed to be unlucky.

Dope comes from Dutch *doop*, meaning 'a thick sauce'.

Dunce: In medieval times, the followers of the 13th-century theologian John Duns Scotus were called 'Dunses'. They were ridiculed by later philosophers as opponents of learning, and so the term came to be applied to those incapable of learning.

Earmark: The notion of 'earmarking' something comes from the practice of putting identification marks on the ears of domestic or farm animals.

Earwig comes from Old English *earwicga*, meaning 'ear insect'. It was once believed that earwigs would creep into people's ears.

Easter: Although Easter is a Christian festival, its name comes from Old English *Eostre*, the name of a pre-Christian Germanic goddess whose festival was celebrated at the spring equinox.

The word **Eavesdrop** comes from Old English *yfesdrype*, meaning 'water dripping from the eaves'. The 'eavesdrop' was the ground around a house where the water dripped down from the eaves, and an 'eavesdropper' was someone who would stand outside in the rain in the eavesdrop to hear what was being said inside the house.

Electricity comes from the Greek word *ēlektron*, meaning 'amber'. The ancient Greeks had found out that if you rub a piece of amber, it will attract small particles by the force that we now understand to be electricity.

Emu is from Portuguese *ema*, meaning 'ostrich'. The name was also applied to the birds we now know as the cassowary and the rhea, since emus, cassowaries and rheas all bear some resemblance to ostriches.

Era: In Latin *aera* means 'copper counters'. The word came to mean 'a number', and hence 'a number of years reckoned from a particular point in time'.

Fad is sometimes supposed to be an acronym of For A Day. While this fits nicely, like most acronymic word origins, it isn't actually true. 'Fad' has been around for much longer than the suggested acronym, and is a shortened version of an earlier slang term, 'fiddle-faddle'.

8 to break into or force open: *it'll take me longer if I have to crack the safe myself* **9** to solve or decipher (a code or problem) **10** *informal* to tell (a joke) **11** to break (a molecule) into smaller molecules or radicals by heat or catalysis as in the distillation of petroleum **12** to open (a bottle) for drinking **13 crack it** *informal* to achieve something ▷ *n* **14** a sudden sharp noise **15** a break or fracture without complete separation of the two parts **16** a narrow opening or fissure **17** *informal* a sharp blow **18 crack of dawn** daybreak **19** a broken or cracked tone of voice **20** *informal* an attempt **21** *informal* a gibe or joke **22** *slang* a highly addictive form of cocaine **23** *chiefly Irish informal* fun; informal entertainment **24 a fair crack of the whip** *informal* a fair chance or opportunity ▷ *adj* **25** *slang* first-class or excellent: *crack troops* ▸ See also **crack down, crack up**

WORD ORIGIN Old English *cracian*

crackbrained *adj* idiotic or crazy: *a crackbrained scheme*

crack down *vb* **1 crack down on** to take severe measures against ▷ *n* **crackdown** **2** severe or repressive measures

cracked *adj* **1** damaged by cracking **2** harsh-sounding **3** *informal* crazy

cracked wheat *n* whole wheat cracked between rollers so that it will cook more quickly

cracker *n* **1** a thin crisp unsweetened biscuit **2** a decorated cardboard tube, pulled apart with a bang, containing a paper hat and a joke or a toy **3** a small explosive firework **4** *slang* an excellent or notable thing or person

crackers *adj* *Brit & NZ slang* insane

cracking *adj* **1 get cracking** *informal* to start doing something immediately **2 a cracking pace** *informal* a high speed ▷ *adv, adj* **3** *Brit informal* first-class: *five cracking good saves* ▷ *n* **4** the oil-refining process in which heavy oils are broken down into smaller molecules by heat or catalysis

crackle *vb* **-ling, -led** **1** to make small sharp popping noises ▷ *n* **2** a crackling sound **crackly** *adj*

crackling *n* **1** a series of small sharp popping noises **2** the crisp browned skin of roast pork

crackpot *informal* *n* **1** an eccentric person ▷ *adj* **2** eccentric: *crackpot philosophies*

crack up *vb* **1** *informal* to have a physical or mental breakdown **2** to begin to break into pieces: *there are worrying reports of buildings cracking up as the earth dries out and foundations move* **3 not all it is cracked up to be** *informal* not as good as people have claimed it to be ▷ *n* **crackup** **4** *informal* a physical or mental breakdown

-cracy *n combining form* indicating a type of government or rule: *plutocracy; mobocracy.* See also **-crat**

WORD ORIGIN Greek *kratos* power

cradle *n* **1** a baby's bed on rockers **2** a place where something originates: *the cradle of civilization* **3** a supporting framework or structure **4** a platform or trolley in which workmen are suspended on the side of a building or ship ▷ *vb* **-dling, -dled** **5** to hold gently as if in a cradle

WORD ORIGIN Old English *cradol*

cradle-snatcher *n informal* a person who marries or has a sexual relationship with someone much younger than himself or herself

craft *n* **1** an occupation requiring skill or manual dexterity **2** skill or ability **3** cunning or guile **4** *pl* **craft** a boat, ship, aircraft, or spacecraft ▷ *vb* **5** to make skilfully

WORD ORIGIN Old English *cræft* skill, strength

craftsman *or fem* **craftswoman** *n, pl* **-men** *or* **-women** **1** a skilled worker **2** a skilled artist **craftsmanship** *n*

crafty *adj* **-tier, -tiest** skilled in deception **craftily** *adv* **craftiness** *n*

crag *n* a steep rugged rock or peak **craggy** *adj*

WORD ORIGIN Celtic

craic *n* an Irish spelling of **crack** (sense 23)

crake *n zool* a bird of the rail family, such as the corncrake

WORD ORIGIN Old Norse *krāka* crow or *krākr* raven

cram *vb* **cramming, crammed** **1** to force (more people or things) into (a place) than it can hold **2** to eat or feed to excess **3** *chiefly Brit* to study hard just before an examination

WORD ORIGIN Old English *crammian*

crammer *n* a person or school that prepares pupils for an examination

cramp[1] *n* **1** a sudden painful contraction of a muscle **2** temporary stiffness of a muscle group from overexertion: *writer's cramp* **3** severe stomach pain **4** a clamp for holding masonry or timber together ▷ *vb* **5** to affect with a cramp

WORD ORIGIN Old French *crampe*

cramp[2] *vb* **1** to confine or restrict **2 cramp someone's style** *informal* to prevent someone from impressing another person or from behaving naturally: *shyness will cramp their style*

WORD ORIGIN Middle Dutch *crampe* hook

cramped *adj* **1** closed in **2** (of handwriting) small and irregular

crampon *n* a spiked iron plate strapped to a boot for climbing on ice

WORD ORIGIN French

cranberry *n, pl* **-ries** a sour edible red berry

WORD ORIGIN Low German *kraanbere* crane berry

crane *n* **1** a machine for lifting and moving heavy objects, usually by suspending them from a movable projecting arm **2** a large wading bird with a long neck and legs ▷ *vb* **craning, craned** **3** to stretch out (the neck) in order to see something

WORD ORIGIN Old English *cran*

crane fly *n* a fly with long legs, slender wings, and a narrow body

cranesbill *n* a plant with pink or purple flowers

cranial *adj* of or relating to the skull

craniology *n* the scientific study of the human skull

WORD ORIGIN Greek *kranion* skull + -LOGY

cranium *n, pl* **-niums** *or* **-nia** *anat* **1** the skull **2** the part of the skull that encloses the brain

WORD ORIGIN Greek *kranion*

crank *n* **1** a device for transmitting or converting motion, consisting of an arm projecting at right angles from a shaft **2** a handle incorporating a crank, used to start an engine or motor **3** *informal* an eccentric or odd person ▷ *vb* **4** to turn with a crank **5** to start (an engine) with a crank

WORD ORIGIN Old English *cranc*

crankcase *n* the metal case that encloses the crankshaft in an internal-combustion engine

crankpin *n* a short cylindrical pin in a crankshaft, to which the connecting rod is attached

crankshaft *n* a shaft with one or more cranks, to which the connecting rods are attached

cranky *adj* **-kier, -kiest** *informal* **1** eccentric **2** bad-tempered **crankiness** *n*

cranny *n, pl* **-nies** a narrow opening

WORD ORIGIN Old French *cran*

crap[1] *slang n* **1** nonsense **2** junk **3** *taboo* faeces ▷ *vb* **crapping, crapped** **4** *taboo* to defecate **crappy** *adj*

WORD ORIGIN Middle English *crappe* chaff

crap[2] *n* same as **craps**

crape *n* same as **crepe**

craps *n* **1** a gambling game played with two dice **2 shoot craps** to play this game

WORD ORIGIN probably from *crabs* lowest throw at dice

crapulent *or* **crapulous** *adj literary* given to or resulting from excessive eating or drinking **crapulence** *n*

WORD ORIGIN Latin *crapula* drunkenness

crash *n* **1** a collision involving a vehicle or vehicles **2** a sudden descent of an aircraft as a result of which it crashes **3** a sudden loud noise **4** a breaking and falling to pieces **5** the sudden collapse of a business or stock exchange ▷ *vb* **6** to cause (a vehicle or aircraft) to collide with another vehicle, the ground, or some other object or (of vehicles or aircraft) to be involved in a collision **7** to make or cause to make a loud smashing noise **8** to drop with force and break into pieces with a loud noise **9** to break or smash into pieces with a loud noise **10** (of a business or stock exchange) to collapse or fail suddenly **11** to move violently or noisily **12** (of a computer system or program) to fail suddenly because of a malfunction **13** *Austral & Brit informal* to gate-crash ▷ *adj* **14** requiring or using great effort in order to achieve results quickly: *a crash course*

WORD ORIGIN probably Middle English *crasen* to smash + *dasshen* to strike

crash barrier *n* a safety barrier along the centre of a motorway, around a racetrack, or at the side of a dangerous road

crash dive *n* **1** a sudden steep emergency dive by a submarine ▷ *vb* **crash-dive, -diving, -dived** **2** to perform a crash dive

crash helmet *n* a helmet worn by motorcyclists to protect the head in case of a crash

crashing *adj informal* extreme: *a crashing bore*

crash-land *vb* (of an aircraft) to land in an emergency, causing damage **crash-landing** *n*

crash out *vb informal* **1** to go to sleep or become unconscious **2** to be eliminated from a competition in a way that brings disgrace or embarrassment

crash team *n* a medial team with special equipment who can arrive quickly to treat a patient having a heart attack

crass *adj* stupid and insensitive: *the enquiry is crass and naive* **crassly** *adv* **crassness** *n*
WORD ORIGIN Latin *crassus* thick

-crat *n combining form* indicating a supporter or member of a particular form of government: *autocrat; democrat* **-cratic** *or* **-cratical** *adj combining form*
WORD ORIGIN Greek *-kratēs*

crate *n* **1** a large container made of wooden slats, used for packing goods **2** *slang* an old car or aeroplane ▷ *vb* **crating, crated 3** to put in a crate **crateful** *n*
WORD ORIGIN Latin *cratis* wickerwork

crater *n* **1** the bowl-shaped opening in a volcano or a geyser **2** a cavity made by the impact of a meteorite or an explosion **3** a roughly circular cavity on the surface of the moon and some planets ▷ *vb* **4** to make or form craters in (a surface, such as the ground) **cratered** *adj*
WORD ORIGIN Greek *kratēr* mixing bowl

cravat *n* a scarf worn round the neck instead of a tie
WORD ORIGIN French *cravate*

crave *vb* **craving, craved 1** to desire intensely: *a vulnerable, unhappy girl who craved affection* **2** *formal* to beg or plead for: *may I crave your lordship's indulgence?* **craving** *n*
WORD ORIGIN Old English *crafian*

craven *adj* **1** cowardly ▷ *n* **2** a coward
WORD ORIGIN Middle English *cravant*

craw *n* **1** the crop of a bird **2** the stomach of an animal **3 stick in one's craw** *informal* to be difficult for one to agree with or accept
WORD ORIGIN Middle English

crawfish *n, pl* **-fish** *or* **-fishes** same as **crayfish**

crawl *vb* **1** to move on one's hands and knees **2** (of insects, worms, or snakes) to creep slowly **3** to move very slowly **4** to act in a servile manner **5** to be or feel as if covered with crawling creatures: *the kind of smile that made your hair stand on end and your flesh crawl* ▷ *n* **6** a slow creeping pace or motion **7** *swimming* a stroke in which the feet are kicked like paddles while each arm in turn reaches forward and pulls back through the water
WORD ORIGIN probably from Old Norse *krafla*

crayfish *or esp. US* **crawfish** *n, pl* **-fish** *or* **-fishes** an edible shellfish like a lobster
WORD ORIGIN Old French *crevice* crab

crayon *n* **1** a small stick or pencil of coloured wax or clay ▷ *vb* **2** to draw or colour with a crayon
WORD ORIGIN Latin *creta* chalk

craze *n* **1** a short-lived fashion or enthusiasm ▷ *vb* **crazing, crazed 2** to make mad **3** *ceramics, metallurgy* to develop or cause to develop fine cracks: *you must prevent the drill crazing the glazed surface of the tile*
WORD ORIGIN probably from Old Norse

crazed *adj* **1** wild and uncontrolled in behaviour **2** (of porcelain) having fine cracks

crazy *adj* **-zier, -ziest** *informal* **1** ridiculous **2 crazy about** extremely fond of: *he was crazy about me* **3** extremely annoyed or upset **4** insane **crazily** *adv* **craziness** *n*

crazy paving *n Brit, Austral, & NZ* a form of paving on a path, made of irregular slabs of stone

creak *vb* **1** to make or move with a harsh squeaking sound ▷ *n* **2** a harsh squeaking sound **creaky** *adj* **creakiness** *n*
WORD ORIGIN imitative

cream *n* **1** the fatty part of milk, which rises to the top **2** a cosmetic or medication that resembles cream in consistency **3** any of various foods resembling or containing cream **4** the best part of something **5 cream sherry** a full-bodied sweet sherry ▷ *adj* **6** yellowish-white ▷ *vb* **7** to beat (foodstuffs) to a light creamy consistency **8** to remove the cream from (milk) **9** to prepare or cook (foodstuffs) with cream or milk **10 cream off** to take away the best part of **creamy** *adj*
WORD ORIGIN Late Latin *cramum*

cream cheese *n* a type of very rich soft white cheese

creamer *n chiefly Brit* a powdered milk substitute for coffee

creamery *n, pl* **-eries** a place where dairy products are made or sold

cream of tartar *n* a purified form of the tartar produced in wine-making, an ingredient in baking powder

crease *n* **1** a line made by folding or pressing **2** a wrinkle or furrow, esp. on the face **3** *cricket* any of four lines near each wicket marking positions for the bowler or batsman ▷ *vb* **creasing, creased 4** to make or become wrinkled or furrowed **creasy** *adj*
WORD ORIGIN Middle English *crēst*

create *vb* **-ating, -ated 1** to cause to come into existence **2** to be the cause of **3** to appoint to a new rank or position **4** *Brit slang* to make an angry fuss
WORD ORIGIN Latin *creare*

creation *n* **1** a creating or being created **2** something brought into existence or created

Creation *n Christianity* **1** God's act of bringing the universe into being **2** the universe as thus brought into being by God

creationism *n* the doctrine that ascribes the origins of all things to God's acts of creation rather than to evolution **creationist** *n, adj*

creative *adj* **1** having the ability to create **2** imaginative or inventive ▷ *n* **3** a creative person, esp. one who devises advertising campaigns **creativity** *n*

creator *n* a person who creates

Creator *n* **the Creator** God

creature *n* **1** an animal, bird, or fish **2** a person **3** a person or thing controlled by another

crèche *n* **1** a day nursery for very young children **2** a supervised play area provided for young children for short periods
WORD ORIGIN French

cred *n slang* short for **credibility**

credence (kreed-enss) *n* belief in the truth or accuracy of a statement: *the question is, how much credence to give to their accounts?*
WORD ORIGIN Latin *credere* to believe

credentials *pl n* **1** something that entitles a person to credit or confidence **2** a document giving evidence of the bearer's identity or qualifications

credibility gap *n* the difference between claims or statements made and the true facts

credible *adj* **1** capable of being believed; convincing: *there is no credible evidence* **2** trustworthy or reliable: *the latest claim is the only one to involve a credible witness* **credibility** *n*
WORD ORIGIN Latin *credere* to believe

credit *n* **1 a** the system of allowing customers to receive goods or services before payment **b** the time allowed for paying for such goods or services **2** reputation for trustworthiness in paying debts **3 a** the positive balance in a person's bank account **b** the sum of money that a bank makes available to a client in excess of any deposit **4** a sum of money or equivalent purchasing power, available for a person's use **5** *accounting* **a** acknowledgment of a sum of money by entry on the right-hand side of an account **b** an entry or total of entries on this side **6** praise or approval, as for an achievement or quality: *you must give him credit for his perseverance* **7** a person or thing who is a source of praise or approval: *he is a credit to his family* **8** influence or reputation based on the good opinion of others: *he acquired credit within the community* **9** belief or confidence in someone or something: *this theory is now gaining credit among the scientific community* **10** *education* **a** distinction awarded to an examination candidate obtaining good marks **b** certification that a section of an examination syllabus has been satisfactorily completed **11 on credit** with payment to be made at a future date ▷ *vb* **-iting, -ited 12** *accounting* **a** to enter (an item) as a credit in an account **b** to acknowledge (a payer) by making such an entry **13 credit with** to give credit for: *credit us with some intelligence* **14** to believe ▸ See also **credits**
WORD ORIGIN Latin *credere* to believe

creditable *adj* deserving praise or honour **creditably** *adv*

credit account n Brit a credit system in which shops allow customers to obtain goods and services before payment

credit card n a card issued by banks or shops, allowing the holder to buy on credit

credit crunch n a period during which there is a sudden reduction in the availability of credit from banks, mortgage lenders, etc.

creditor n a person or company to whom money is owed

credit rating n an evaluation of the ability of a person or business to repay money lent

credits pl n a list of people responsible for the production of a film, programme, or record

creditworthy adj (of a person or a business) regarded as deserving credit on the basis of earning power and previous record of debt repayment **creditworthiness** n

credo n, pl **-dos** a creed

credulity n willingness to believe something on little evidence

credulous adj 1 too willing to believe: he has convinced only a few credulous American intellectuals 2 arising from or showing credulity: credulous optimism **WORD ORIGIN** Latin credere to believe

creed n 1 a system of beliefs or principles 2 a formal statement of the essential parts of Christian belief **WORD ORIGIN** Latin credo I believe

creek n 1 a narrow inlet or bay 2 US, Canad, Austral, & NZ a small stream or tributary 3 **up the creek** slang in a difficult position **WORD ORIGIN** Old Norse kriki nook

creel n a wickerwork basket used by fishermen **WORD ORIGIN** Scots

creep vb **creeping, crept** 1 to move quietly and cautiously 2 to crawl with the body near to or touching the ground 3 to have the sensation of something crawling over the skin, from fear or disgust: she makes my flesh creep 4 (of plants) to grow along the ground or over rocks ▷ n 5 a creeping movement 6 slang an obnoxious or servile person **WORD ORIGIN** Old English crēopan

creeper n 1 a plant, such as ivy, that grows by creeping 2 US & Canad same as **tree creeper**

creeps pl n **give someone the creeps** informal to give someone a feeling of fear or disgust

creepy adj **creepier, creepiest** informal causing a feeling of fear or disgust **creepiness** n

creepy-crawly n, pl **-crawlies** Brit informal a small crawling creature

cremate vb **-mating, -mated** to burn (a corpse) to ash **cremation** n **WORD ORIGIN** Latin cremare

crematorium n, pl **-riums** or **-ria** a building where corpses are cremated

crème de la crème n the very best: the crème de la crème of cities **WORD ORIGIN** French

crème de menthe n a liqueur flavoured with peppermint

WORD ORIGIN French

crenellated or US **crenelated** adj having battlements **crenellation** or US **crenelation** n **WORD ORIGIN** Late Latin crena a notch

creole n 1 a language developed from a mixture of different languages which has become the main language of a place ▷ adj 2 of or relating to a creole **WORD ORIGIN** Spanish

Creole n 1 (in the West Indies and Latin America) a native-born person of mixed European and African descent 2 (in the Gulf States of the US) a native-born person of French descent 3 the French creole spoken in the Gulf States ▷ adj 4 of or relating to any of these peoples: Creole cooking

creosote n 1 a thick dark liquid made from coal tar and used for preserving wood 2 a colourless liquid made from wood tar and used as an antiseptic ▷ vb **-soting, -soted** 3 to treat with creosote **WORD ORIGIN** Greek kreas flesh + sōtēr preserver

crepe (krayp) n 1 a thin light fabric with a crinkled texture 2 a very thin pancake, often folded around a filling 3 a type of rubber with a wrinkled surface, used for the soles of shoes **WORD ORIGIN** French

crepe paper n paper with a crinkled texture, used for decorations

crept vb the past of **creep**

crepuscular adj 1 of or like twilight 2 (of animals) active at twilight **WORD ORIGIN** Latin crepusculum dusk

Cres. Crescent

crescendo (krish-end-oh) n, pl **-dos** 1 a gradual increase in loudness 2 a musical passage that gradually gets louder ▷ adv 3 gradually getting louder **WORD ORIGIN** Italian

crescent n 1 the curved shape of the moon when in its first or last quarter 2 chiefly Brit & NZ a crescent-shaped street ▷ adj 3 crescent-shaped **WORD ORIGIN** Latin crescere to grow

cress n a plant with strong-tasting leaves, used in salads and as a garnish **WORD ORIGIN** Old English cressa

crest n 1 the top of a mountain, hill, or wave 2 a tuft or growth of feathers or skin on the top of a bird's or animal's head 3 a heraldic design or figure used on a coat of arms and elsewhere 4 an ornamental plume or emblem on top of a helmet ▷ vb 5 to come or rise to a high point 6 to lie at the top of 7 to reach the top of (a hill or wave) **crested** adj **WORD ORIGIN** Latin crista

crestfallen adj disappointed or disheartened

Cretaceous adj geol of the period of geological time about 135 million years ago, at the end of which the dinosaurs died out **WORD ORIGIN** Latin creta chalk

cretin n 1 informal a very stupid person 2 no longer in technical use a person who is mentally handicapped and physically deformed because of a thyroid deficiency **cretinism** n **cretinous** adj **WORD ORIGIN** French from Latin Christianus Christian, alluding to the humanity of such people despite their handicaps

cretonne n a heavy printed cotton or linen fabric, used in furnishings **WORD ORIGIN** French

crevasse n a deep open crack in a glacier **WORD ORIGIN** French

crevice n a narrow crack or gap in rock **WORD ORIGIN** Latin crepare to crack

crew¹ n 1 the people who man a ship or aircraft 2 a group of people working together: a film crew 3 informal any group of people ▷ vb 4 to serve as a crew member on a ship or boat **WORD ORIGIN** Middle English crue reinforcement, from Latin crescere to increase

crew² vb archaic a past of **crow²**

crew cut n a closely cut haircut for men

crewel n a loosely twisted worsted yarn, used in embroidery **crewelwork** n **WORD ORIGIN** origin unknown

crew neck n a plain round neckline **crew-neck** or **crew-necked** adj

crib n 1 a piece of writing stolen from elsewhere 2 a translation or list of answers used by students, often dishonestly 3 a baby's cradle 4 a rack or manger for fodder 5 a model of the manger scene at Bethlehem 6 short for **cribbage** 7 NZ a small holiday house ▷ vb **cribbing, cribbed** 8 to copy (someone's work) dishonestly 9 to confine in a small space **WORD ORIGIN** Old English cribb

cribbage n a card game for two to four players, who each try to win a set number of points before the others **WORD ORIGIN** origin unknown

crib-wall n NZ a retaining wall built against an earth bank

crick informal n 1 a painful muscle spasm or cramp in the neck or back ▷ vb 2 to cause a crick in **WORD ORIGIN** origin unknown

cricket¹ n 1 a game played by two teams of eleven players using a ball, bats, and wickets 2 **not cricket** informal not fair play **cricketer** n **WORD ORIGIN** Old French criquet wicket

cricket² n a jumping insect like a grasshopper, which produces a chirping sound by rubbing together its forewings **WORD ORIGIN** Old French criquer to creak, imitative

cried vb the past of **cry**

crier n an official who makes public announcements

crime n 1 an act prohibited and punished by law 2 unlawful acts collectively 3 informal a disgraceful act: to be a woman writing music is neither a crime against nature nor a freakish rarity **WORD ORIGIN** Latin crimen

criminal n 1 a person guilty of a crime ▷ adj 2 of or relating to crime or its punishment 3 informal senseless or disgraceful **criminally** adv **criminality** n

criminalize or **-ise** vb **-izing, -ized** or **-ising, -ised** 1 to make (an action or activity) criminal 2 to treat (a person) as a criminal

Received Pronunciation

People learning British English all around the world are normally taught to pronounce it in Received Pronunciation (RP for short), the accent whose most famous speaker is Queen Elizabeth II. Those learners of English that subsequently arrive on the shores of Britain as tourists or to work or study may be dismayed by the disparity between the English they have learned and that which they encounter on the streets of Glasgow, or even London. RP is, at least in its purest form, spoken by less than 3% of the population of Britain. It is used by far more people outside Britain as a model accent for teaching English. Although not widely used in Britain, it has the advantage of being widely understood (it is 'received' in the sense of 'widely accepted', like 'received wisdom'). Speakers of the divergent accents of British English might at times have difficulty understanding each other, but everyone can understand RP. Its status as a 'standard' accent is reflected in its use by most British English dictionaries to show how words should be pronounced.

Unlike most accents of English, RP gives no clues to where a speaker comes from. It is a 'prestige accent', indicating the superior social and educational background of the speaker. In decades past, RP was the sole preserve of members of the upper class, likely to have been educated at one of the 'better' schools, typically followed by Oxford or Cambridge University. The erosion of Britain's class structures throughout the 20th century has allowed the accent to be acquired by people outside the upper-class elite and today might simply indicate a high level of education.

Linguists argue over the accuracy and usefulness of terms like 'the Queen's English'. However, most agree that different groups within RP can be identified, including the conservative variety used by the Queen, and a contemporary type, used by younger speakers such as the trendy London set of the 1980s that included Diana, soon to be Princess of Wales. Like all accents, it is constantly evolving. The accents of upper-class characters in British films from the 1940s can sound comically old-fashioned to us now. Recent studies of 50 years of Queen Elizabeth's Christmas broadcasts have demonstrated the ways in which she has modified her accent. The most notable change is in the pronunciation of the letter 'a' from /e/ ('thet bleck cet on the met') to /æ/ ('that black cat on the mat'), which led one commentator to joke that the Queen's accent has been changing since the days when coal was delivered to Buckingham Palace 'in sex'.

RP is young, as British English accents go. It emerged in the 19th century from the speech of the upper classes of the south east of England (as the base of political and economic power). Massive reforms had opened education to the lower classes for the first time, so that possession of an education was no longer sufficient to signal membership of the elite. The upper classes had, for centuries, used a variety of regional accents, but a non-regional accent became the new means of signalling social superiority. Regional accents were increasingly seen as 'incorrect', and it was necessary for the socially ambitious to modify and, if possible, eradicate their accent's regional features (such as 'H-dropping' – 'ouse' as opposed to 'house'). George Bernard Shaw's 1913 play 'Pygmalion' (and the Hollywood version, 'My Fair Lady') exemplify the association of RP with correctness, and the redemptive possibilities that its acquisition might offer. Eliza Doolittle's life is transformed once she sheds her Cockney speech, and the former flower-seller from the gutter is accepted into polite society.

Increasingly, regional accents feature in all walks of life, and are well represented in the media. It is no longer necessary to have an RP accent to achieve professional success or social status. Some linguists suggest that it has become disadvantageous to have an RP accent and that, in a reversal of fortune, speakers might modify their accents with regional features. It is at least true to say that regional accents are no longer a barrier to attainment in most spheres of British life.

criminology *n* the scientific study of crime **criminologist** *n*
WORD ORIGIN Latin *crimen* crime + -LOGY

crimp *vb* 1 to fold or press into ridges 2 to curl (hair) tightly with curling tongs 3 *chiefly US informal* to restrict or hinder: *a slowdown in the US economy could crimp some big Swedish concerns' profits* ▷ *n* 4 the act or result of crimping
WORD ORIGIN Old English *crympan*

Crimplene *n trademark* a crease-resistant synthetic fabric

crimson *adj* deep purplish-red
WORD ORIGIN Arabic *qirmizi kermes* (dried bodies of insects used to make a red dye)

cringe *vb* **cringing, cringed** 1 to shrink or flinch in fear: *he cringed and shrank against the wall* 2 to behave in a submissive or timid way: *women who cringe before abusive husbands* 3 *informal* to be very embarrassed: *I cringe every time I see that old photo of me* ▷ *n* 4 the act of cringing
WORD ORIGIN Old English *cringan* to yield in battle

crinkle *vb* **-kling, -kled** 1 to become slightly creased or folded ▷ *n* 2 a crease or fold **crinkly** *adj*
WORD ORIGIN Old English *crincan* to bend

crinoline *n* a petticoat stiffened with hoops to make the skirt stand out
WORD ORIGIN Latin *crinis* hair + *lino* flax

cripple *n offensive* 1 a person who is lame or disabled 2 a person with a mental or social problem: *an emotional cripple* ▷ *vb* **-pling, -pled** 3 to make a cripple of 4 to damage (something) **crippled** *adj* **crippling** *adj*
WORD ORIGIN Old English *crypel*

crisis *n, pl* **-ses** 1 a crucial stage or turning point in the course of anything 2 a time of extreme trouble or danger
WORD ORIGIN Greek *krisis* decision

crisp *adj* 1 fresh and firm: *a crisp green salad* 2 dry and brittle: *bake until crisp and golden brown* 3 clean and neat: *crisp white cotton* 4 (of weather) cold but invigorating: *a crisp autumn day* 5 clear and sharp: *the telescope is designed to provide the first crisp images of distant galaxies* 6 lively or brisk: *the service is crisp and efficient* ▷ *n* 7 *Brit* a very thin slice of potato fried till crunchy ▷ *vb* 8 to make or become crisp **crisply** *adv* **crispness** *n*
WORD ORIGIN Latin *crispus* curled

crispbread *n* a thin dry biscuit made of wheat or rye

crispy *adj* **crispier, crispiest** hard and crunchy **crispiness** *n*

crisscross *vb* 1 to move in or mark with a crosswise pattern ▷ *adj* 2 (of lines) crossing one another in different directions

criterion *n, pl* **-ria** *or* **-rions** a standard by which something can be judged or decided
WORD ORIGIN Greek *kritērion*

USAGE
Criteria, the plural of *criterion*, is not acceptable as a singular noun: *this criterion is not valid; these criteria are not valid*.

critic *n* 1 a professional judge of art, music, or literature 2 a person who finds fault and criticizes
WORD ORIGIN Greek *kritēs* judge

critical *adj* 1 very important or dangerous: *this was a critical moment in her career* 2 so seriously ill or injured as to be in danger of dying: *he is in a critical condition in hospital* 3 fault-finding or disparaging: *the article is highly critical of the government* 4 examining and judging analytically and without bias: *he submitted the plans to critical examination* 5 of a critic or criticism 6 *physics* denoting a constant value at which the properties of a system undergo an abrupt change: *the critical temperature above which the material loses its superconductivity* 7 (of a nuclear power station or reactor) having reached a state in which a nuclear chain reaction becomes self-sustaining **critically** *adv*

criticism *n* 1 fault-finding or censure 2 an analysis of a work of art or literature 3 the occupation of a critic 4 a work that sets out to analyse

criticize *or* **-cise** *vb* **-cizing, -cized** *or* **-cising, -cised** 1 to find fault with 2 to analyse (something)

critique *n* 1 a critical essay or commentary 2 the act or art of criticizing
WORD ORIGIN French

croak *vb* 1 (of a frog or crow) to make a low hoarse cry 2 to utter or speak with a croak 3 *slang* to die ▷ *n* 4 a low hoarse sound **croaky** *adj*
WORD ORIGIN Old English *crācettan*

Croatian (kroh-**ay**-shun) *adj* 1 of Croatia ▷ *n* 2 a person from Croatia 3 the dialect of Serbo-Croat spoken in Croatia

crochet (kroh-shay) *vb* **-cheting, -cheted** 1 to make (a piece of needlework) by looping and intertwining thread with a hooked needle ▷ *n* 2 work made by crocheting
WORD ORIGIN French: small hook

crock¹ *n* an earthenware pot or jar
WORD ORIGIN Old English *crocc* pot

crock² *n* **old crock** *Brit, Austral, & NZ slang* a person or thing that is old or broken-down
WORD ORIGIN Scots

crockery *n* china dishes or earthenware vessels collectively

crocodile *n* 1 a large amphibious tropical reptile 2 *Brit, Austral, & NZ informal* a line of people, esp. schoolchildren, walking two by two
WORD ORIGIN Greek *krokodeilos* lizard

crocodile tears *pl n* an insincere show of grief
WORD ORIGIN from the belief that crocodiles wept over their prey to lure further victims

crocus *n, pl* **-cuses** a plant with white, yellow, or purple flowers in spring
WORD ORIGIN Greek *krokos* saffron

croft *n* a small farm worked by one family in Scotland **crofter** *n* **crofting** *adj, n*
WORD ORIGIN Old English

croissant (**krwah**-son) *n* a flaky crescent-shaped bread roll
WORD ORIGIN French

cromlech *n Brit* 1 a circle of prehistoric standing stones 2 *no longer in technical use* a dolmen
WORD ORIGIN Welsh

crone *n* a witchlike old woman
WORD ORIGIN Old French *carogne* carrion

crony *n, pl* **-nies** a close friend
WORD ORIGIN Greek *khronios* long-lasting

crook *n* 1 *informal* a dishonest person 2 a bent or curved place or thing: *she held the puppy in the crook of her arm* 3 a bishop's or shepherd's staff with a hooked end ▷ *adj* 4 *Austral & NZ informal* a ill b of poor quality c unpleasant; bad 5 **go (off) crook** *Austral & NZ informal* to lose one's temper 6 **go crook at** *or* **on** *Austral & NZ informal* to rebuke or upbraid ▷ *vb* 7 to bend or curve
WORD ORIGIN Old Norse *krokr* hook

crooked *adj* 1 bent or twisted 2 set at an angle 3 *informal* dishonest or illegal **crookedly** *adv* **crookedness** *n*

croon *vb* to sing, hum, or speak in a soft low tone **crooner** *n*
WORD ORIGIN Middle Dutch *crōnen* to groan

crop *n* 1 a cultivated plant, such as a cereal, vegetable, or fruit plant 2 the season's total yield of farm produce 3 any group of things appearing at one time: *a remarkable crop of new Scottish plays* 4 the handle of a whip 5 short for **riding crop** 6 a pouchlike part of the gullet of a bird, in which food is stored or prepared for digestion 7 a short cropped hairstyle ▷ *vb* **cropping, cropped** 8 to cut (something) very short 9 to produce or harvest as a crop 10 (of animals) to feed on (grass) 11 to clip part of (the ear or ears) of (an animal), esp. for identification ▶ See also **crop up**
WORD ORIGIN Old English *cropp*

crop circle *n* a pattern made up of ring shapes formed by the unexplained flattening of cereals growing in a field

cropper *n* **come a cropper** *informal* a to fail completely b to fall heavily

crop top *n* a short T-shirt or vest that reveals the wearer's midriff

crop up *vb informal* to occur or appear unexpectedly

croquet (**kroh**-kay) *n* a game played on a lawn in which balls are hit through hoops
WORD ORIGIN French

croquette (kroh-**kett**) *n* a fried cake of mashed potato, meat, or fish
WORD ORIGIN French

crosier *n* same as **crozier**

cross *vb* 1 to move or go across (something): *she crossed the street to the gallery* 2 to meet and pass: *further south, the way is crossed by Brewer Street* 3 *Brit & NZ* to draw two parallel lines across (a cheque) and so make it payable only into a bank account 4 to mark with a cross or crosses 5 to cancel or delete with a cross or with lines: *she crossed out the first three words* 6 to place across or crosswise: *he sat down and crossed his legs* 7 to make the sign of the cross upon as a blessing 8 to annoy or anger (someone) by challenging or opposing their wishes and plans 9 to interbreed or cross-fertilize 10 *football* to pass (the ball) from a wing to the middle of the field **11** (of each of two letters in the post) to be sent before the other is received **12** (of telephone lines) to interfere with each other so that several callers are connected together at one time **13 cross one's fingers** to fold one finger across another in the hope of bringing good luck **14 cross one's heart** to promise by making the sign of a cross over one's heart **15 cross one's mind** to occur to one briefly or suddenly ▷ *n* **16** a structure, symbol, or mark consisting of two intersecting lines **17** an upright post with a bar across it, used in ancient times as a means of execution **18** a representation of the Cross on which Jesus Christ was executed as an emblem of Christianity **19** a symbol (×) used as a signature or error mark **20 the sign of the cross** a sign made with the hand by some Christians to represent the Cross **21** a medal or monument in the shape of a cross **22** the place in a town or village where a cross has been set up **23** *biol* **a** the process of crossing; hybridization **b** a hybrid **24** a mixture of two things **25** a hindrance or misfortune: *we've all got our own cross to bear* **26** *football* a pass of the ball from a wing to the middle of the field ▷ *adj* **27** angry **28** lying or placed across: *a cross beam* **crossly** *adv* **crossness** *n* **WORD ORIGIN** Latin *crux*

Cross *n* **the Cross a** the cross on which Jesus Christ was crucified **b** Christianity

cross- *combining form* **1** indicating action from one individual or group to another: *cross-cultural; cross-refer* **2** indicating movement or position across something: *crosscurrent; crosstalk* **3** indicating a crosslike figure or intersection: *crossbones*

crossbar *n* **1** a horizontal beam across a pair of goalposts **2** the horizontal bar on a man's bicycle

cross-bench *n Brit* a seat in Parliament for a member belonging to neither the government nor the opposition **cross-bencher** *n*

crossbill *n* a finch that has a bill with crossed tips

crossbow *n* a weapon consisting of a bow fixed across a wooden stock, which releases an arrow when the trigger is pulled

crossbreed *vb* **-breeding, -bred 1** to produce (a hybrid animal or plant) by crossing two different species ▷ *n* **2** a hybrid animal or plant

crosscheck *vb* **1** to check the accuracy of (something) by using a different method ▷ *n* **2** a crosschecking

cross-country *adj, adv* **1** by way of open country or fields ▷ *n* **2** a long race held over open ground

crosscut *vb* **-cutting, -cut 1** to cut across ▷ *adj* **2** cut across ▷ *n* **3** a transverse cut or course

cross-examine *vb* **-examining, -examined 1** *law* to question (a witness for the opposing side) in order to check his or her testimony **2** to question closely or relentlessly **cross-examination** *n* **cross-examiner** *n*

cross-eyed *adj* with one or both eyes turning inwards towards the nose

cross-fertilize or **-lise** *vb* **-lizing, -lized** or **-lising, -lised** to fertilize (an animal or plant) by fusion of male and female reproductive cells from different individuals of the same species **cross-fertilization** or **-lisation** *n*

crossfire *n* **1** *mil* gunfire crossing another line of fire **2** a lively exchange of ideas or opinions

crosshatch *vb* *drawing* to shade with two or more sets of parallel lines that cross one another

crossing *n* **1** a place where a street, railway, or river may be crossed **2** the place where one thing crosses another **3** a journey across water

cross-legged *adj* sitting with the legs bent and the knees pointing outwards

crosspatch *n* *informal* a bad-tempered person **WORD ORIGIN** *cross* + obsolete *patch* fool

cross-ply *adj* (of a tyre) having the fabric cords in the outer casing running diagonally to stiffen the sidewalls

cross-purposes *pl n* **at cross-purposes** misunderstanding each other in a discussion

cross-question *vb* to cross-examine

cross-refer *vb* **-referring, -referred** to refer from one part of something to another

cross-reference *n* **1** a reference within a text to another part of the text ▷ *vb* **-referencing, -referenced 2** to cross-refer

crossroad *n US & Canad* **1** a road that crosses another road **2** a road that connects one main road to another

crossroads *n* **1** the point at which roads cross one another **2 at the crossroads** at the point at which an important choice has to be made

cross section *n* **1** *maths* a surface formed by cutting across a solid, usually at right angles to its longest axis **2** a random sample regarded as representative: *a cross section of society* **cross-sectional** *adj*

cross-stitch *n* an embroidery stitch made from two crossing stitches

crosstalk *n* **1** *Brit* rapid or witty talk **2** unwanted signals transferred between communication channels

crosswalk *n uS & Canad* a place marked where pedestrians may cross a road

crosswise or **crossways** *adj* **1** across **2** in the shape of a cross ▷ *adv* **3** across: *slice the celery crosswise* **4** in the shape of a cross

crossword puzzle or **crossword** *n* a puzzle in which vertically and horizontally crossing words suggested by clues are written into a grid of squares

crotch *n* **1** the forked part of the human body between the legs **2** the corresponding part of a pair of trousers or pants **3** any forked part formed by the joining of two things: *the crotch of the tree* **crotched** *adj* **WORD ORIGIN** probably variant of CRUTCH

crotchet *n* *music* a note having the time value of a quarter of a semibreve **WORD ORIGIN** Old French *crochet* little hook

crotchety *adj* *informal* bad-tempered

crouch *vb* **1** to bend low with the legs and body pulled close together ▷ *n* **2** this position **WORD ORIGIN** Old French *crochir* to become bent like a hook

croup¹ (**kroop**) *n* a throat disease of children, with a hoarse cough and laboured breathing **WORD ORIGIN** Middle English: to cry hoarsely, probably imitative

croup² (**kroop**) *n* the hindquarters of a horse **WORD ORIGIN** Old French *croupe*

croupier (**kroop**-ee-ay) *n* a person who collects bets and pays out winnings at a gambling table **WORD ORIGIN** French

crouton *n* a small piece of fried or toasted bread served in soup **WORD ORIGIN** French

crow¹ *n* **1** a large black bird with a harsh call **2 as the crow flies** in a straight line **WORD ORIGIN** Old English *crāwa*

crow² *vb* **1** past **crowed** or **crew** (of a cock) to utter a shrill squawking sound **2** to boast about one's superiority **3** (of a baby) to utter cries of pleasure ▷ *n* **4** a crowing sound **WORD ORIGIN** Old English *crāwan*

crowbar *n* a heavy iron bar used as a lever

crowd *n* **1** a large number of things or people gathered together **2** a particular group of people: *we got to know a French crowd from Lyons* **3 the crowd** the masses ▷ *vb* **4** to gather together in large numbers **5** to press together into a confined space **6** to fill or occupy fully **7** *informal* to make (someone) uncomfortable by coming too close **crowded** *adj* **WORD ORIGIN** Old English *crūdan*

crowd-pleaser *n* a person or thing that appeals to a large proportion of an audience **crowd-pleasing** *adj*

crown *n* **1** a monarch's ornamental headdress, usually made of gold and jewels **2** a wreath for the head, given as an honour **3** the highest or central point of something arched or curved: *the crown of the head* **4 a** the enamel-covered part of a tooth projecting beyond the gum **b** a substitute crown, usually of gold or porcelain, fitted over a decayed or broken tooth **5** a former British coin worth 25 pence **6** the outstanding quality or achievement: *the last piece is the crown of the evening* ▷ *vb* **7** to put a crown on the head of (someone) to proclaim him or her monarch **8** to put on the top of **9** to reward **10** to form the topmost part of **11** to put the finishing touch to (a series of events): *he crowned a superb display with three goals* **12** to attach a crown to (a tooth) **13** *Brit, Austral, & NZ slang* to hit over the head **14** *draughts* to promote (a draught) to a king by placing another draught on top of it **WORD ORIGIN** Greek *korōnē*

Crown *n* **the Crown** the power or institution of the monarchy

crown colony *n* a British colony controlled by the Crown

crown court *n* a local criminal court in England and Wales

Crown Derby *n* a type of fine porcelain made at Derby

crown jewels *pl n* the jewellery used by a sovereign on ceremonial occasions

crown-of-thorns *n* a starfish with a spiny outer covering that feeds on living coral

crown prince *n* the male heir to a sovereign throne **crown princess** *n*

crow's feet *pl n* wrinkles at the outer corners of the eye

crow's nest *n* a lookout platform fixed at the top of a ship's mast

crozier or **crosier** *n* a hooked staff carried by bishops as a symbol of office
WORD ORIGIN Old French *crossier* staff-bearer

crucial *adj* **1** of exceptional importance **2** *Brit slang* very good **crucially** *adv*
WORD ORIGIN Latin *crux* cross

cruciate *adj* shaped or arranged like a cross **cruciately** *adv*
WORD ORIGIN Latin *crux* cross

cruciate ligament *n anat* either of a pair of ligaments that cross each other in the knee

crucible *n* a pot in which metals or other substances are melted
WORD ORIGIN Medieval Latin *crucibulum* night lamp

crucifix *n* a model cross with a figure of Christ upon it
WORD ORIGIN Church Latin *crucifixus* the crucified Christ

crucifixion *n* a method of execution by fastening to a cross, normally by the hands and feet

Crucifixion *n* **1** the Crucifixion the crucifying of Christ **2** a representation of this

cruciform *adj* shaped like a cross

crucify *vb* **-fies, -fying, -fied 1** to put to death by crucifixion **2** to treat cruelly **3** *slang* to defeat or ridicule totally
WORD ORIGIN Latin *crux* cross + *figere* to fasten

crud *n slang* a sticky or encrusted substance **cruddy** *adj*
WORD ORIGIN earlier form of CURD

crude *adj* **1** rough and simple: *crude farm implements* **2** tasteless or vulgar **3** in a natural or unrefined state ▷ *n* **4** short for **crude oil** ▷ **crudely** *adv* **crudity** or **crudeness** *n*
WORD ORIGIN Latin *crudus* bloody, raw

crude oil *n* unrefined petroleum

crudités (**crew-dit-tay**) *pl n* a selection of raw vegetables often served with a variety of dips before a meal
WORD ORIGIN French *crudité* rawness

cruel *adj* **1** deliberately causing pain without pity **2** causing pain or suffering **cruelly** *adv* **cruelty** *n*
WORD ORIGIN Latin *crudelis*

cruet *n* **1** a small container for pepper, salt, etc. at table **2** a set of such containers on a stand
WORD ORIGIN Old French *crue* flask

cruise *n* **1** a sail taken for pleasure, stopping at various places ▷ *vb* **cruising,**

cruised 2 to sail about from place to place for pleasure **3** (of a vehicle, aircraft, or ship) to travel at a moderate and efficient speed **4** to proceed steadily or easily: *they cruised into the final of the qualifying competition*
WORD ORIGIN Dutch *kruisen* to cross

cruise missile *n* a low-flying subsonic missile that is guided throughout its flight

cruiser *n* **1** a large fast warship armed with medium-calibre weapons **2** Also called: **cabin cruiser** a motorboat with a cabin

cruiserweight *n* a professional boxer weighing up to 195 pounds (88.5 kg)

crumb *n* **1** a small fragment of bread or other dry food **2** a small bit or scrap: *a crumb of comfort*
WORD ORIGIN Old English *cruma*

crumble *vb* **-bling, -bled 1** to break into crumbs or fragments **2** to fall apart or decay ▷ *n* **3** a baked pudding consisting of stewed fruit with a crumbly topping: *rhubarb crumble* **crumbly** *adj* **crumbliness** *n*

crumby *adj* **crumbier, crumbiest 1** full of crumbs **2** same as **crummy**

crummy *adj* **-mier, -miest** *slang* **1** of very bad quality: *a crummy hotel* **2** unwell: *I felt really crummy*
WORD ORIGIN variant spelling of *crumby*

crumpet *n* **1** a light soft yeast cake, eaten buttered **2** *chiefly Brit slang* sexually attractive women collectively
WORD ORIGIN origin unknown

crumple *vb* **-pling, -pled 1** to crush or become crushed into untidy wrinkles or creases **2** to collapse in an untidy heap: *her father lay crumpled on the floor* ▷ *n* **3** an untidy crease or wrinkle **crumply** *adj*
WORD ORIGIN obsolete *crump* to bend

crunch *vb* **1** to bite or chew with a noisy crushing sound **2** to make a crisp or brittle sound ▷ *n* **3** a crunching sound **4 the crunch** *informal* the critical moment or situation **crunchy** *adj* **crunchiness** *n*
WORD ORIGIN imitative

crupper *n* **1** a strap that passes from the back of a saddle under a horse's tail **2** the horse's rump
WORD ORIGIN Old French *crupiere*

crusade *n* **1** any of the medieval military expeditions undertaken by European Christians to recapture the Holy Land from the Muslims **2** a vigorous campaign in favour of a cause ▷ *vb* **-sading, -saded 3** to take part in a crusade **crusader** *n*
WORD ORIGIN Latin *crux* cross

cruse *n* a small earthenware container for liquids
WORD ORIGIN Old English *crūse*

crush *vb* **1** to press or squeeze so as to injure, break, or put out of shape **2** to break or grind into small pieces **3** to control or subdue by force **4** to extract (liquid) by pressing: *crush a clove of garlic* **5** to defeat or humiliate utterly **6** to crowd together ▷ *n* **7** a dense crowd **8** the act of crushing **9** *informal* an infatuation: *I had a teenage crush on my French teacher* **10** a drink made by crushing fruit: *orange crush*
WORD ORIGIN Old French *croissir*

crush barrier *n* a barrier put up to separate sections of large crowds and prevent crushing

crust *n* **1** the hard outer part of bread **2** the baked shell of a pie or tart **3** any hard outer layer: *a thin crust of snow* **4** the solid outer shell of the earth ▷ *vb* **5** to cover with or form a crust
WORD ORIGIN Latin *crusta* hard surface, rind

crustacean *n* **1** an animal with a hard outer shell and several pairs of legs, which usually lives in water, such as a crab or lobster ▷ *adj* **2** of crustaceans
WORD ORIGIN Latin *crusta* shell

crusty *adj* **crustier, crustiest 1** having a crust **2** rude or irritable **crustiness** *n*

crutch *n* **1** a long staff with a rest for the armpit, used by a lame person to support the weight of the body **2** something that supports **3** *Brit* same as **crotch** (sense 1)
WORD ORIGIN Old English *crycc*

crutchings *pl n Austral & NZ* the wool clipped from a sheep's hindquarters

crux *n, pl* **cruxes** or **cruces** a crucial or decisive point
WORD ORIGIN Latin: cross

cry *vb* **cries, crying, cried 1** to shed tears **2** to make a loud vocal sound, usually to express pain or fear or to appeal for help **3** to utter loudly or shout **4** (of an animal or bird) to utter loud characteristic sounds **5 cry for** to appeal urgently for ▷ *n, pl* **cries 6** a fit of weeping **7** the act or sound of crying **8** the characteristic utterance of an animal or bird **9** an urgent appeal: *a cry for help* **10** a public demand: *a cry for more law and order on the streets* **11 a far cry from** something very different from **12 in full cry a** in eager pursuit **b** in the middle of talking or doing something ▶ See also **cry off**
WORD ORIGIN Old French *crier*

crying *adj* **a crying shame** something that demands immediate attention

cry off *vb informal* to withdraw from an arrangement

cryogenics *n* the branch of physics concerned with very low temperatures and their effects **cryogenic** *adj*
WORD ORIGIN Greek *kruos* cold + *-genēs* born

crypt *n* a vault or underground chamber, such as one beneath a church, used as a burial place
WORD ORIGIN Greek *kruptē*

cryptic *adj* having a hidden or secret meaning; puzzling: *no-one knew what he meant by that cryptic remark* **cryptically** *adv*
WORD ORIGIN Greek *kruptos* concealed

cryptogam *n bot* a plant that reproduces by spores not seeds
WORD ORIGIN Greek *kruptos* hidden + *gamos* marriage

cryptography *n* the art of writing in and deciphering codes **cryptographer** *n* **cryptographic** *adj*
WORD ORIGIN Greek *kruptos* hidden + -GRAPHY

crystal *n* **1** a solid with a regular internal structure and symmetrical arrangement of faces **2** a single grain of a crystalline substance **3** a very clear and brilliant glass **4** something made

Marshall McLuhan

During his early career, Marshall McLuhan was a student of classical rhetoric and Renaissance literature. A teacher at the University of Toronto for many years, McLuhan was a devout Roman Catholic convert with deeply conservative tendencies. Given this background, he might have been expected to deplore the modern world in many ways yet, as a moral imperative, he was determined to make sense of it. This he did in bestselling books marked by a hectic style in which cryptic aphorisms, which he called *probes*, were rapidly piled one upon the other. The style mirrored his view that, in our media-saturated age, transitions and continuity have been lost, and juxtapositions ruled. McLuhan's packrat accumulation of salient facts and images, his apparent immodesty, and the oracular fervour with which he declaimed his conclusions, made him suspect to more cautious scholars. To some observers, he was a genius; to others, a humbug.

His status in academe was not assisted by the fact that he became in the 1960s a darling of the US media for his rapid-fire monologues and, in the process, one of the most-quoted thinkers of the twentieth century. Advertising agencies and media conglomerates rushed to exploit his insights, despite the comically caustic comments he had once made about their products in *The Mechanical Bride: Folklore of Industrial Man*. This incurably bookish man became associated with the notion that, as a technology, print culture was doomed, and that we had entered a tribal universe wired to our senses and synapses.

Born in Edmonton, educated in Winnipeg and at Cambridge University, McLuhan was influenced by the work of James Joyce, with whom he shared a love of puns, and that of the literary critics IA Richards and FR Leavis. He became a friend of Wyndham Lewis, the Canadian-born novelist and Vorticist painter. In Toronto, he collaborated with the US anthropologist Edmund Carpenter, with whom he edited the journal *Explorations*, and acquired a mentor in the historian Harold Innis, one of whose books, *The Bias of Communication,* anticipated McLuhan's memorable phrase, 'The medium is the message.' Some of his book titles, whole or in part, became catchphrases and, for some of his readers, bywords: *The Gutenberg Galaxy: The Making of Typographic Man* (in which he may have anticipated the use of *surf* to mean the quick movement from site to site on the World Wide Web); *Understanding Media: The Extensions of Man* (in which 'The medium is the message' appears); *The Medium is the Massage: An Inventory of Effects; War and Peace in the Global Village*; and *From Cliché to Archetype*.

As in GK Chesterton, a writer McLuhan much admired, his style relies on inverted clichés and calculated paradoxes, which can seem by turns penetrating or facile. 'Money is the poor man's credit card' and 'Invention is the mother of necessities.' Or 'We look at the present through a rear-view mirror. We march backwards into the future' and 'Today each of us lives several hundred years in a decade.' Or 'All advertising advertises advertising' and 'When a thing is current, it creates currency.' Any author might fear the possibility that 'The future of the book is the blurb.' But one is impressed by the self-knowledge of 'I may be wrong, but I'm never in doubt.'

After his death, the University of Toronto repaid the fame he had gained it by attempting to dismantle the Centre for Culture and Technology he had established there. But perhaps Marshall McLuhan could have no successor. For *global village* alone, even for the less well-known *global theatre*, he earned neologistic immortality.

McLuhan's nearest, though still remote, Canadian rival as a coiner of new words and phrases has been the Vancouver writer and visual artist Douglas Coupland, who invented *McJob* for a low-paying, often temporary, job taken by a person who is qualified to hold one with much better prospects. *McJob* appears in his novel *Generation X*, whose title itself became a catchword for the generation born between the early 1960s and the mid-1970s that succeeded the Baby Boomers. From an earlier and much different generation, McLuhan became an unlikely prophet of the postmodern world.

of crystal **5** crystal glass articles collectively **6** *electronics* a crystalline element used in certain electronic devices, such as a detector or oscillator ▷ *adj* **7** bright and clear: *the crystal waters of the pool*
WORD ORIGIN Greek *krustallos* ice, crystal

crystal ball *n* the glass globe used in crystal gazing

crystal gazing *n* **1** the act of staring into a crystal ball supposedly in order to see future events **2** the act of trying to foresee or predict **crystal gazer** *n*

crystalline *adj* **1** of or like crystal or crystals **2** clear

crystallize, crystalize *or* **-ise** *vb* **-izing, -ized** *or* **-ising, -ised 1** to make or become definite **2** to form into crystals **3** to preserve (fruit) in sugar **crystallization, crystalization** *or* **-isation** *n*

crystallography *n* the science of crystal structure

crystalloid *n* a substance that in solution can pass through a membrane

crystal meth *n informal* crystal methamphetamine, a concentrated and highly potent form of methamphetamine with dangerous side effects

Cs *chem* caesium

CSA (in Britain) Child Support Agency

CSE (formerly, in Britain) Certificate of Secondary Education: an examination the first grade pass of which was an equivalent to a GCE O level

CS gas *n* a gas causing tears and painful breathing, used to control civil disturbances
WORD ORIGIN initials of its US inventors, Ben Carson and Roger Staughton

CST Central Standard Time

CT Connecticut

CT scanner *n* an X-ray machine that can produce cross-sectional images of the soft tissues
WORD ORIGIN *c*(omputerized) *t*(omography) scanner

CTV Canadian Television (Network Limited)

Cu *chem* copper
WORD ORIGIN Late Latin *cuprum*

cu. cubic

cub *n* **1** the young of certain mammals, such as the lion or bear **2** a young or inexperienced person ▷ *vb* **cubbing, cubbed 3** to give birth to (cubs)
WORD ORIGIN origin unknown

Cub *n* short for **Cub Scout**

Cuban *adj* **1** from Cuba ▷ *n* **2** a person from Cuba

cubbyhole *n* a small enclosed space or room
WORD ORIGIN dialect *cub* cattle pen

cube *n* **1** an object with six equal square faces **2** the product obtained by multiplying a number by itself twice: *the cube of 2 is 8* ▷ *vb* **cubing, cubed 3** to find the cube of (a number) **4** to cut into cubes
WORD ORIGIN Greek *kubos*

cube root *n* the number or quantity whose cube is a given number or quantity: *2 is the cube root of 8*

cubic *adj* **1 a** having three dimensions **b** having the same volume as a cube with length, width, and depth each measuring the given unit: *a cubic metre* **2** having the shape of a cube **3** *maths* involving the cubes of numbers

cubicle *n* an enclosed part of a large room, screened for privacy
WORD ORIGIN Latin *cubiculum*

cubic measure *n* a system of units for the measurement of volumes

cubism *n* a style of art, begun in the early 20th century, in which objects are represented by geometrical shapes **cubist** *adj, n*

cubit *n* an ancient measure of length based on the length of the forearm
WORD ORIGIN Latin *cubitum* elbow, cubit

cuboid *adj* **1** shaped like a cube ▷ *n* **2** *maths* a geometric solid whose six faces are rectangles

Cub Scout *or* **Cub** *n* a member of a junior branch of the Scout Association

cuckold *literary or old-fashioned n* **1** a man whose wife has been unfaithful to him ▷ *vb* **2** to make a cuckold of
WORD ORIGIN Middle English *cukeweld*

cuckoo *n, pl* **cuckoos 1** a migratory bird with a characteristic two-note call, noted for laying its eggs in the nests of other birds ▷ *adj* **2** *informal* insane or foolish
WORD ORIGIN Old French *cucu*, imitative

cuckoopint *n* a plant with arrow-shaped leaves, purple flowers, and red berries

cuckoo spit *n* a white frothy mass produced on plants by the larvae of some insects

cucumber *n* **1** a long fruit with thin green rind and crisp white flesh, used in salads **2 as cool as a cucumber** calm and self-possessed
WORD ORIGIN Latin *cucumis*

cud *n* **1** partially digested food which a ruminant brings back into its mouth to chew again **2 chew the cud** to think deeply
WORD ORIGIN Old English *cudu*

cuddle *vb* **-dling, -dled 1** to hug or embrace fondly **2 cuddle up** to lie close and snug ▷ *n* **3** a fond hug **cuddly** *adj*
WORD ORIGIN origin unknown

cudgel *n* a short thick stick used as a weapon
WORD ORIGIN Old English *cycgel*

cue¹ *n* **1** a signal to an actor or musician to begin speaking or playing **2** a signal or reminder **3 on cue** at the right moment ▷ *vb* **cueing, cued 4** to give a cue to
WORD ORIGIN perhaps from the letter *q*, used in an actor's script to represent Latin *quando* when

cue² *n* **1** a long tapering stick used to hit the balls in billiards, snooker, or pool ▷ *vb* **cueing, cued 2** to hit (a ball) with a cue
WORD ORIGIN variant of QUEUE

cuff¹ *n* **1** the end of a sleeve **2** *US, Canad, Austral, & NZ* a turn-up on trousers **3 off the cuff** *informal* impromptu: *he delivers many speeches off the cuff*
WORD ORIGIN Middle English *cuffe* glove

cuff² *Brit, Austral, & NZ vb* **1** to strike with an open hand ▷ *n* **2** a blow with an open hand
WORD ORIGIN origin unknown

cuff link *n* one of a pair of decorative fastenings for shirt cuffs

cuisine (quiz-**zeen**) *n* **1** a style of cooking: *Italian cuisine* **2** the range of food served in a restaurant
WORD ORIGIN French

cul-de-sac *n, pl* **culs-de-sac** *or* **cul-de-sacs** a road with one end blocked off
WORD ORIGIN French: bottom of the bag

culinary *adj* of the kitchen or cookery
WORD ORIGIN Latin *culina* kitchen

cull *vb* **1** to choose or gather **2** to remove or kill (the inferior or surplus) animals from a herd ▷ *n* **3** the act of culling
WORD ORIGIN Latin *colligere* to gather together

culminate *vb* **-nating, -nated** to reach the highest point or climax: *the parade culminated in a memorial service* **culmination** *n*
WORD ORIGIN Latin *culmen* top

culottes *pl n* women's flared trousers cut to look like a skirt
WORD ORIGIN French

culpable *adj* deserving blame **culpability** *n*
WORD ORIGIN Latin *culpa* fault

culprit *n* the person guilty of an offence or misdeed
WORD ORIGIN Anglo-French *culpable* guilty + *prit* ready

cult *n* **1** a specific system of religious worship **2** a sect devoted to the beliefs of a cult **3** devoted attachment to a person, idea, or activity **4** a popular fashion: *the bungee-jumping cult* ▷ *adj* **5** very popular among a limited group of people: *a cult TV series*
WORD ORIGIN Latin *cultus* cultivation, refinement

cultish *adj* intended to appeal to a small group of fashionable people

cultivate *vb* **-vating, -vated 1** to prepare (land) to grow crops **2** to grow (plants) **3** to develop or improve (something) by giving special attention to it: *he tried to cultivate a reputation for fairness* **4** to try to develop a friendship with (a person)
WORD ORIGIN Latin *colere* to till

cultivated *adj* well-educated: *a civilized and cultivated man*

cultivation *n* **1** the act of cultivating **2** culture or refinement

cultivator *n* a farm implement used to break up soil and remove weeds

culture *n* **1** the ideas, customs, and art of a particular society **2** a particular civilization at a particular period **3** a developed understanding of the arts **4** development or improvement by special attention or training: *physical culture* **5** the cultivation and rearing of plants or animals **6** a growth of bacteria for study ▷ *vb* **-turing, -tured 7** to grow (bacteria) in a special medium **cultural** *adj*
WORD ORIGIN Latin *colere* to till

cultured *adj* **1** showing good taste or manners **2** artificially grown or synthesized

cultured pearl *n* a pearl artificially grown in an oyster shell

culture shock *n sociol* the feelings of isolation and anxiety experienced by a person on first coming into contact with a culture very different from his or her own

culvert *n* a drain or pipe that crosses under a road or railway
WORD ORIGIN origin unknown

cum *prep* with: *a small living-cum-dining room*
WORD ORIGIN Latin

cumbersome *or* **cumbrous** *adj* 1 awkward because of size or shape 2 difficult because of complexity: *the cumbersome appeals procedure*

cumin *or* **cummin** *n* 1 the spicy-smelling seeds of a Mediterranean herb, used in cooking 2 the plant from which these seeds are obtained
WORD ORIGIN Greek *kuminon*

cummerbund *n* a wide sash worn round the waist, esp. with a dinner jacket
WORD ORIGIN Hindi *kamarband*, from Persian *kamar* loins + *band* band

cumquat *n* same as **kumquat**

cumulative (**kew**-myew-la-tiv) *adj* growing in amount, strength, or effect by small steps: *the cumulative effect of twelve years of war*

cumulus (**kew**-myew-luss) *n, pl* **-li** (-lie) a thick or billowing white or dark grey cloud
WORD ORIGIN Latin: mass

cuneiform (**kew**-nif-form) *n* 1 an ancient system of writing using wedge-shaped characters ▷ *adj* 2 written in cuneiform
WORD ORIGIN Latin *cuneus* wedge

cunjevoi *n Austral* 1 a plant of tropical Asia and Australia with small flowers, cultivated for its edible rhizome 2 a sea squirt

cunnilingus *n* the kissing and licking of a woman's genitals by her sexual partner
WORD ORIGIN Latin *cunnus* vulva + *lingere* to lick

cunning *adj* 1 clever at deceiving 2 made with skill ▷ *n* 3 cleverness at deceiving 4 skill or ingenuity
WORD ORIGIN Old English *cunnende*

cunt *n taboo* 1 the female genitals 2 *offensive slang* a stupid or obnoxious person
WORD ORIGIN Middle English

cup *n* 1 a small bowl-shaped drinking container with a handle 2 the contents of a cup 3 something shaped like a cup: *a bra with padded cups* 4 a cup-shaped trophy awarded as a prize 5 a sporting contest in which a cup is awarded to the winner 6 a mixed drink with fruit juice or wine as a base: *claret cup* 7 one's lot in life: *his cup of bitterness was full to overflowing* 8 **someone's cup of tea** *informal* someone's chosen or preferred thing ▷ *vb* **cupping, cupped** 9 to form (the hands) into the shape of a cup 10 to hold in cupped hands
WORD ORIGIN Old English *cuppe*

cupboard *n* a piece of furniture or a recess with a door, for storage

cupboard love *n* a show of love put on in order to gain something

Cup Final *n* 1 the annual final of the FA or Scottish Cup soccer competition 2 the final of any cup competition

Cupid *n* 1 the Roman god of love, represented as a winged boy with a bow and arrow 2 a picture or statue of Cupid
WORD ORIGIN Latin *cupido* desire

cupidity (kew-**pid**-it-ee) *n formal* strong desire for wealth or possessions
WORD ORIGIN Latin *cupere* to long for

cupola (**kew**-pol-la) *n* 1 a domed roof or ceiling 2 a small dome on the top of a roof 3 an armoured revolving gun turret on a warship
WORD ORIGIN Latin *cupa* tub

cupreous (**kew**-pree-uss) *adj* of or containing copper
WORD ORIGIN Latin *cuprum* copper

cupric (**kew**-prick) *adj* of or containing copper in the divalent state

cupronickel (kew-proh-**nik**-el) *n* a copper alloy containing up to 40 per cent nickel

cup tie *n Brit sport* an eliminating match between two teams in a cup competition

cur *n* 1 a vicious mongrel dog 2 a contemptible person
WORD ORIGIN Middle English *kurdogge*

curable *adj* capable of being cured **curability** *n*

curaçao (kew-rah-so) *n* an orange-flavoured liqueur

curacy (**kew**-rah-see) *n, pl* **-cies** the work or position of a curate

curare (kew-**rah**-ree) *n* a poisonous resin obtained from a South American tree, used as a muscle relaxant in medicine
WORD ORIGIN Carib *kurari*

curate *n* a clergyman who assists a vicar or parish priest
WORD ORIGIN Medieval Latin *cura* spiritual oversight

curative *adj* 1 able to cure ▷ *n* 2 something able to cure

curator *n* the person in charge of a museum or art gallery **curatorial** *adj* **curatorship** *n*
WORD ORIGIN Latin: one who cares

curb *n* 1 something that restrains or holds back 2 a horse's bit with an attached chain or strap, used to check the horse 3 a raised edge that strengthens or encloses ▷ *vb* 4 to control or restrain ▶ See also **kerb**
WORD ORIGIN Latin *curvus* curved

curcumin *n* a yellow pigment, present in turmeric, that is an antioxidant and has anti-inflammatory properties

curd *n* 1 coagulated milk, used in making cheese or as a food 2 any similar substance: *bean curd*
WORD ORIGIN origin unknown

curd cheese *n* a mild smooth white cheese made from skimmed milk curds

curdle *vb* **-dling, -dled** 1 to turn into curd; coagulate 2 **make someone's blood curdle** to fill someone with horror

cure *vb* **curing, cured** 1 to get rid of (an ailment or problem) 2 to restore

(someone) to health 3 to preserve (meat or fish) by salting or smoking 4 to preserve (leather or tobacco) by drying 5 to vulcanize (rubber) ▷ *n* 6 a restoration to health 7 medical treatment that restores health 8 a means of restoring health or improving a situation 9 a curacy
WORD ORIGIN Latin *cura* care

cure-all *n* something supposed to cure all ailments or problems

curette *or* **curet** *n* 1 a surgical instrument for scraping tissue from body cavities ▷ *vb* **-retting, -retted** 2 to scrape with a curette **curettage** *n*
WORD ORIGIN French

curfew *n* 1 a law which states that people must stay inside their houses after a specific time at night 2 the time set as a deadline by such a law 3 *history* the ringing of a bell at a fixed time, as a signal for putting out fires and lights
WORD ORIGIN Old French *cuevrefeu* cover the fire

Curia *n, pl* **-riae** the court and government of the Roman Catholic Church **curial** *adj*
WORD ORIGIN Latin

curie *n* the standard unit of radioactivity
WORD ORIGIN after Pierre *Curie*, French physicist

curio (**kew**-ree-oh) *n, pl* **-rios** a rare or unusual thing valued as a collector's item
WORD ORIGIN from *curiosity*

curiosity *n, pl* **-ties** 1 eagerness to know or find out 2 a rare or unusual thing

curious *adj* 1 eager to learn or know 2 eager to find out private details 3 unusual or peculiar **curiously** *adv*
WORD ORIGIN Latin *curiosus* taking pains over something

curium (**kew**-ree-um) *n chem* a silvery-white metallic radioactive element artificially produced from plutonium. Symbol: Cm
WORD ORIGIN after Pierre & Marie *Curie*, French physicists

curl *vb* 1 to twist (hair) or (of hair) to grow in coils or ringlets 2 to twist into a spiral or curve 3 to play the game of curling 4 **curl one's lip** to show contempt by raising a corner of the lip ▷ *n* 5 a coil of hair 6 a curved or spiral shape ▶ See also **curl up** > **curly** *adj*
WORD ORIGIN probably from Middle Dutch *crullen*

curler *n* 1 a pin or small tube for curling hair 2 a person who plays curling

curlew *n* a large wading bird with a long downward-curving bill
WORD ORIGIN Old French *corlieu*

curlicue *n* an intricate ornamental curl or twist
WORD ORIGIN *curly* + CUE²

curling *n* a game played on ice, in which heavy stones with handles are slid towards a target circle

curl up *vb* 1 to lie or sit with legs drawn up 2 to be embarrassed or horrified

curmudgeon *n* a bad-tempered or mean person **curmudgeonly** *adj*
WORD ORIGIN origin unknown

currajong *n* same as **kurrajong**

currant *n* **1** a small dried seedless raisin **2** a small round acid berry, such as the redcurrant
WORD ORIGIN earlier *rayson of Corannte* raisin of Corinth

currawong *n* an Australian songbird
WORD ORIGIN Aboriginal

currency *n, pl* **-cies 1** the system of money or the actual coins and banknotes in use in a particular country **2** general acceptance or use: *ideas that had gained currency during the early 1960s*
WORD ORIGIN Latin *currere* to run, flow

current *adj* **1** of the immediate present: *current affairs; the current economic climate* **2** most recent or up-to-date: *the current edition* **3** commonly accepted: *current thinking on this issue* **4** circulating and valid at present: *current coins* ▷ *n* **5** a flow of water or air in a particular direction **6** *physics* a flow or rate of flow of electric charge through a conductor **7** a general trend or drift: *two opposing currents of thought* **currently** *adv*
WORD ORIGIN Latin *currere* to run, flow

current account *n* a bank account from which money may be drawn at any time using a chequebook or computerized card

curriculum *n, pl* **-la** or **-lums 1** all the courses of study offered by a school or college **2** a course of study in one subject at a school or college: *the history curriculum* **curricular** *adj*
WORD ORIGIN Latin: course

curriculum vitae (vee-tie) *n, pl* **curricula vitae** an outline of someone's educational and professional history, prepared for job applications
WORD ORIGIN Latin: the course of one's life

curry¹ *n, pl* **-ries 1** a dish of Indian origin consisting of meat or vegetables in a hot spicy sauce **2** curry seasoning or sauce **3 curry powder** a mixture of spices for making curry ▷ *vb* **-ries, -rying, -ried 4** to prepare (food) with curry powder
WORD ORIGIN Tamil *kari* sauce, relish

curry² *vb* **-ries, -rying, -ried 1** to groom (a horse) **2** to dress (leather) after it has been tanned **3 curry favour** to ingratiate oneself with an important person
WORD ORIGIN Old French *correer* to make ready

currycomb *n* a ridged comb used for grooming horses

curse *vb* **cursing, cursed 1** to swear or swear at (someone) **2** to call on supernatural powers to bring harm to (someone or something) ▷ *n* **3** a profane or obscene expression, usually of anger **4** an appeal to a supernatural power for harm to come to a person **5** harm resulting from a curse **6** something that causes great trouble or harm **7 the curse** *informal* menstruation or a menstrual period
WORD ORIGIN Old English *cursian*

cursed *adj* **1** under a curse: *he is now sick after being cursed by the witch doctor* **2 cursed with** having (something unfortunate or unwanted): *their new-born son had been cursed with a genetic defect*

cursive *adj* **1** of handwriting or print in which letters are joined in a flowing style ▷ *n* **2** a cursive letter or printing type
WORD ORIGIN Medieval Latin *cursivus* running

cursor *n* **1** a movable point of light that shows a specific position on a visual display unit **2** the sliding part of a slide rule or other measuring instrument

cursory *adj* hasty and usually superficial **cursorily** *adv*
WORD ORIGIN Late Latin *cursorius* of running

curt *adj* so blunt and brief as to be rude **curtly** *adv* **curtness** *n*
WORD ORIGIN Latin *curtus* cut short

curtail *vb* **1** to cut short: *the opening round was curtailed by heavy rain* **2** to restrict: *a plan to curtail drinks advertising* **curtailment** *n*
WORD ORIGIN obsolete *curtal* to dock

curtain *n* **1** a piece of material hung at an opening or window to shut out light or to provide privacy **2** a hanging cloth that conceals all or part of a theatre stage from the audience **3** the end of a scene or a performance in the theatre, marked by the fall or closing of the curtain **4** the rise or opening of the curtain at the start of a performance **5** something forming a barrier or screen: *a curtain of rain* ▷ *vb* **6** to shut off or conceal with a curtain **7** to provide with curtains
WORD ORIGIN Late Latin *cortina*

curtain call *n theatre* a return to the stage by performers to receive applause

curtain-raiser *n* **1** *theatre* a short play performed before the main play **2** a minor event happening before a major one

curtains *pl n informal* death or ruin; the end

curtsy or **curtsey** *n, pl* **-sies** or **-seys 1** a woman's formal gesture of respect made by bending the knees and bowing the head ▷ *vb* **-sies, -sying, -sied** or **-seys, -seying, -seyed 2** to make a curtsy
WORD ORIGIN variant of *courtesy*

curvaceous *adj informal* having a curved shapely body

curvature *n* the state or degree of being curved

curve *n* **1** a continuously bending line with no straight parts **2** something that curves or is curved **3** curvature **4** *maths* a system of points whose coordinates satisfy a given equation **5** a line representing data on a graph ▷ *vb* **curving, curved 6** to form into or move in a curve **curvy** *adj*
WORD ORIGIN Latin *curvare* to bend

curvet *n* **1** a horse's low leap with all four feet off the ground ▷ *vb* **-vetting, -vetted** or **-veting, -veted 2** to make such a leap
WORD ORIGIN Latin *curvare* to bend

curvilinear *adj* consisting of or bounded by a curved line

cuscus *n, pl* **-cuses** a large nocturnal possum of N Australia and New Guinea
WORD ORIGIN probably from a native word in New Guinea

cushion *n* **1** a bag filled with a soft material, used to make a seat more comfortable **2** something that provides comfort or absorbs shock **3** the resilient felt-covered rim of a billiard table ▷ *vb* **4** to protect from injury or shock **5** to lessen the effects of **6** to provide with cushions **cushiony** *adj*
WORD ORIGIN Latin *culcita* mattress

cushy *adj* **cushier, cushiest** *informal* easy: *a cushy job*
WORD ORIGIN Hindi *khush* pleasant

cusp *n* **1** a small point on the grinding or chewing surface of a tooth **2** a point where two curves meet **3** *astrol* any division between houses or signs of the zodiac **4** *astron* either of the points of a crescent moon
WORD ORIGIN Latin *cuspis* pointed end

cuss *informal n* **1** a curse or oath **2** an annoying person ▷ *vb* **3** to swear or swear at

cussed (kuss-id) *adj informal* **1** obstinate: *the older she got the more cussed she became* **2** same as **cursed** ▷ **cussedness** *n*

custard *n* **1** a sauce made of milk and sugar thickened with cornflour **2** a baked sweetened mixture of eggs and milk
WORD ORIGIN Middle English *crustade* kind of pie

custodian *n* the person in charge of a public building **custodianship** *n*

custody *n, pl* **-dies 1** the act of keeping safe **2** imprisonment prior to being tried **custodial** *adj*
WORD ORIGIN Latin *custos* guard, defender

custom *n* **1** a long-established activity, action, or festivity: *the custom of serving port after dinner* **2** the long-established habits or traditions of a society **3** a usual practice or habit: *she held his hand more tightly than was her custom in public* **4** regular use of a shop or business ▷ *adj* **5** made to the specifications of an individual customer: *a custom car; custom-tailored suits* ▶ See also **customs**
WORD ORIGIN Latin *consuetudo*

customary *adj* **1** usual **2** established by custom **customarily** *adv* **customariness** *n*

custom-built or **-made** *adj* made according to the specifications of an individual customer

customer *n* **1** a person who buys goods or services **2** *informal* a person with whom one has to deal: *a tricky customer*

custom house *n* a government office where customs are collected

customize or **-ise** *vb* **-izing, -ized** or **-ising, -ised** to make (something) according to a customer's individual requirements

customs *n* **1** duty charged on imports or exports **2** the government department responsible for collecting this **3** the area at a port, airport, or border where baggage and freight are examined for dutiable goods

cut *vb* **cutting, cut 1** to open up or penetrate (a person or thing) with a sharp instrument **2** (of a sharp instrument) to penetrate or open up (a person or thing) **3** to divide or be divided with or as if with a sharp

South African English

English in South Africa is only one of eleven official languages. There are two European languages that were imported by settlers – English and Afrikaans. Afrikaans is very closely related to Dutch, and used to be called Cape Dutch, but it was given the status of a separate language in 1925. English has borrowed a number of words from Afrikaans, and one Afrikaans loan word in particular is very well known because of its status as the opening word in many English dictionaries: *aardvark*. Other well-known loan words include *commando* which comes from the Afrikaans *kommando*, and *trek*, which came originally from the Middle Dutch *tekken*. Still others relate to the animals and geography of South Africa, eg *eland*, *springbok*, *veld*, and *kraal*.

Afrikaans has a longer history in South Africa than English. The Dutch had been there for 150 years when the English took over in 1806, and both European groups have now been there for a further two centuries. Afrikaans may be a little more different from Dutch than South African English is from international English. Some estimates put the vocabulary difference between Afrikaans and Dutch at about 15 per cent, although Dutch speakers are said to be able to understand Afrikaans with little effort. In any case, the length of time a language has been spoken outside its home territory has little bearing on whether it's considered a different language. English, Spanish, Portuguese, and French have not been renamed in their ex-colonies, despite the fact that Brazilian Portuguese is clearly different from the Portuguese of Portugal, Angola, or Mozambique. It should also not be forgotten that the identity of Afrikaans is intrinsically bound up with the apartheid regime – the word *apartheid* itself crossed from Afrikaans into mainstream English as a result of the official policy formerly enforced in South Africa.

When a language is exported to a different part of the world it starts to accumulate new vocabulary items. Dried beef – beef jerky – is called *biltong* in South Africa, a cinema is a *bioscope*, traffic lights are *robots*, a truck is a *bakkie*, and an off-licence is a *bottle store*. White South Africans use *shame!* with a variety of meanings that are puzzling to a speaker of British English. White South Africans also use *just now* in a way that is quite unlike its use in the UK; it means *in a bit*. The interjection *ja well no fine* can indicate reluctant acceptance in a range of situations. There are obvious pronunciation differences, but none of them any more or less remarkable than differences between Birmingham and London within the United Kingdom. There are new coinages which may find their way out of the country: a *vuvuzela* is a kind of horn that's blown at football matches, which became more widely known as a result of the 2010 World Cup.

South African slang is as ripe and evocative as that of other varieties of English. *Zola Budd*, the South African athlete whose controversial tripping of American athlete Mary Decker in the 1984 Olympic 3,000 metres earned her a place in the history books, means 'taxi' in South African slang. To be synonymous with speed and nippiness seems somehow more appropriate than with a 'potato' which is what *Zola Budd* meant in 1980s Cockney rhyming slang ('spud').

But all these differences are curiosities. Since only just over eight per cent of the population of South Africa speak English as their first language, English really comes into its own as a lingua franca, for example between speakers of Xhosa and Afrikaans. It's readily available in cinemas, on the television, in schools and at universities, and the South African government is well aware of its usefulness for international trade and development. For anybody who wants to get a quick idea of what standard South African English is like, a quick look at online newspapers shows that it is developing, changing, in a state of flux – but it's the same state of flux that English is in all round the world.

instrument **4** to trim **5** to abridge or shorten **6** to reduce or restrict: *cut your intake of fried foods* **7** to form or shape by cutting **8** to reap or mow **9** *sport* to hit (the ball) so that it spins and swerves **10** to hurt the feelings of (a person): *her rudeness cut me to the core* **11** *informal* to pretend not to recognize **12** *informal* to absent oneself from without permission: *he found the course boring, and was soon cutting classes* **13** to stop (doing something): *cut the nonsense* **14** to dilute or adulterate: *heroin cut with talcum powder* **15** to make a sharp or sudden change in direction: *the path cuts to the right just after you pass the quarry* **16** to grow (teeth) through the gums **17** *films* **a** to call a halt to a shooting sequence **b** **cut to** to move quickly to (another scene) **18** *films* to edit (film) **19** to switch off (a light or engine) **20** to make (a commercial recording): *he cut his first solo album in 1971* **21** *cards* **a** to divide (the pack) at random into two parts after shuffling **b** to pick cards from a spread pack to decide the dealer or who plays first **22** **cut a dash** to make a stylish impression **23** **cut a person dead** *informal* to ignore a person completely **24** **cut and run** *informal* to escape quickly from a difficult situation **25** **cut both ways** **a** to have both good and bad effects **b** to serve both sides of an argument **26** **cut it fine** *informal* to allow little margin of time or space **27** **cut no ice** *informal* to fail to make an impression **28** **cut one's teeth on** *informal* to get experience from ▷ *n* **29** the act of cutting **30** a stroke or incision made by cutting **31** a piece cut off **32** a channel or path cut or hollowed out **33** a reduction: *a pay cut* **34** a deletion in a text, film, or play **35** *informal* a portion or share **36** the style in which hair or a garment is cut **37** a direct route; short cut **38** *sport* a stroke which makes the ball spin and swerve **39** *films* an immediate transition from one shot to the next **40** *Brit* a canal **41** **a cut above** *informal* superior to; better than ▷ *adj* **42** made or shaped by cutting **43** reduced by cutting: *the shop has hundreds of suits, all at cut prices* **44** adulterated or diluted **45** **cut and dried** *informal* settled in advance ▸ See also **cut across, cutback**, etc.
WORD ORIGIN probably from Old Norse

cut across *vb* **1** to go against (ordinary restrictions or expectations): *this dilemma has cut across class divisions* **2** to cross or traverse

cutaneous (kew-**tane**-ee-uss) *adj* of the skin
WORD ORIGIN Latin *cutis* skin

cutaway *adj* (of a drawing or model) having part of the outside omitted to reveal the inside

cutback *n* **1** a decrease or reduction ▷ *vb* **cut back** **2** to shorten by cutting **3** (often foll. by *on*) to make a reduction: *we may cut back on other expenditure*

cut down *vb* **1** to fell **2** (often foll. by *on*) to make a reduction: *cut down on the amount of salt you eat* **3** to kill **4** **cut someone down to size** to cause someone to feel less important or to be less conceited

cute *adj* **1** appealing or attractive **2** *informal* clever or shrewd **cuteness** *n*
WORD ORIGIN from ACUTE

cut glass *n* **1** glass with patterns cut into the surface ▷ *adj* **cut-glass** **2** upper-class; refined: *Victoria with her cut-glass accent*

cuticle (**kew**-tik-kl) *n* **1** hardened skin round the base of a fingernail or toenail **2** same as **epidermis**
WORD ORIGIN Latin *cuticula* skin

cut in *vb* **1** to interrupt **2** to move in front of another vehicle, leaving too little space

cutlass *n* a curved one-edged sword formerly used by sailors
WORD ORIGIN French *coutelas*

cutler *n* a person who makes or sells cutlery
WORD ORIGIN Latin *culter* knife

cutlery *n* knives, forks, and spoons, used for eating

cutlet *n* **1** a small piece of meat taken from the neck or ribs **2** a flat croquette of chopped meat or fish
WORD ORIGIN Old French *costelette* a little rib

cut off *vb* **1** to remove or separate by cutting **2** to stop the supply of **3** to interrupt (a person who is speaking), esp. during a telephone conversation **4** to bring to an end **5** to disinherit: *cut off without a penny* **6** to intercept so as to prevent retreat or escape ▷ *n* **cutoff** **7** the point at which something is cut off; limit **8** *chiefly US* a short cut **9** a device to stop the flow of a fluid in a pipe

cut out *vb* **1** to shape by cutting **2** to delete or remove **3** *informal* to stop doing (something) **4** (of an engine) to cease to operate suddenly **5** (of an electrical device) to switch off, usually automatically **6** **be cut out for** to be suited or equipped for: *you're not cut out for this job* **7** **have one's work cut out** to have as much work as one can manage ▷ *n* **cutout** **8** a device that automatically switches off a circuit or engine as a safety device **9** something that has been cut out from something else

cut-price *or esp. US* **cut-rate** *adj* **1** at a reduced price **2** offering goods or services at prices below the standard price

cutter *n* **1** a person or tool that cuts **2** a small fast boat

cut-throat *adj* **1** fierce or ruthless in competition: *the cut-throat world of international finance* **2** (of a card game) played by three people: *cut-throat poker* ▷ *n* **3** a murderer **4** *Brit & NZ* a razor with a long blade that folds into its handle

cutting *n* **1** an article cut from a newspaper or magazine **2** a piece cut from a plant for rooting or grafting **3** a passage cut through high ground for a road or railway **4** the editing process of a film ▷ *adj* **5** (of a remark) likely to hurt the feelings **6** keen; piercing: *a cutting wind* **7** designed for cutting: *the hatchet's blade is largely stone, but its cutting edge is made of copper*

cutting edge *n* the leading position in any field; forefront: *the cutting edge of space technology*

cuttlefish *n, pl* **-fish** *or* **-fishes** a flat squidlike mollusc which squirts an inky fluid when in danger
WORD ORIGIN Old English *cudele*

cut up *vb* **1** to cut into pieces **2** *informal* (of a driver) to overtake or pull in front of (another driver) in a dangerous manner **3** **be cut up** *informal* to be very upset **4** **cut up rough** *Brit informal* to become angry or violent

CV curriculum vitae

cwm (**koom**) *n* (in Wales) a valley
WORD ORIGIN Welsh

cwt hundredweight

cyanic acid *n* a colourless poisonous volatile liquid acid

cyanide *n* any of a number of highly poisonous substances containing a carbon-nitrogen group of atoms

cyanogen *n* a poisonous colourless flammable gas
WORD ORIGIN Greek *kuanos* dark blue

cyanosis *n pathol* a blue discoloration of the skin, caused by a deficiency of oxygen in the blood
WORD ORIGIN Greek *kuanos* dark blue

cyber- *combining form* indicating computers: *cyberspace*
WORD ORIGIN from CYBERNETICS

cybercafé *n* a café equipped with computer terminals which customers can use to access the internet
WORD ORIGIN CYBER- + CAFÉ

cybernetics *n* the branch of science in which electronic and mechanical systems are studied and compared to biological systems **cybernetic** *adj*
WORD ORIGIN Greek *kubernētēs* steersman

cyberspace *n* the hypothetical environment which contains all the data stored in computers
WORD ORIGIN CYBER- + SPACE

cybersquatting *n* the practice of registering an internet domain name that is likely to be wanted by another person or organization in the hope that it can be sold to them for a profit **cybersquatter** *n*

cyclamen (**sik**-la-men) *n* a plant with white, pink, or red flowers, with turned-back petals
WORD ORIGIN Greek *kuklaminos*

cycle *vb* **-cling, -cled** **1** to ride a bicycle **2** to occur in cycles ▷ *n* **3** *Brit, Austral, & NZ* a bicycle **4** *US* a motorcycle **5** a complete series of recurring events **6** the time taken or needed for one such series **7** a single complete movement in an electrical, electronic, or mechanical process **8** a set of plays, songs, or poems about a figure or event **cycling** *n*
WORD ORIGIN Greek *kuklos*

cyclical *or* **cyclic** *adj* **1** occurring in cycles **2** *chem* (of an organic compound) containing a closed ring of atoms

cyclist *n* a person who rides a bicycle

cyclo- *or before a vowel* **cycl-** *combining form* **1** indicating a circle or ring: *cyclotron* **2** *chem* denoting a cyclical compound: *cyclopropane*
WORD ORIGIN Greek *kuklos* cycle

cyclometer (sike-**lom**-it-er) *n* a device that records the number of revolutions made by a wheel and the distance travelled

cyclone *n* **1** a body of moving air below normal atmospheric pressure, which often brings rain **2** a violent tropical storm **cyclonic** *adj*
WORD ORIGIN Greek *kuklōn* a turning around

cyclopedia *or* **cyclopaedia** *n* same as **encyclopedia**

Cyclops *n, pl* **Cyclopes** *or* **Cyclopses** *classical myth* one of a race of giants having a single eye in the middle of the forehead
WORD ORIGIN Greek *Kuklōps* round eye

cyclotron *n* an apparatus, used in atomic research, which accelerates charged particles by means of a strong vertical magnetic field

cyder *n* same as **cider**

cygnet *n* a young swan
WORD ORIGIN Latin *cygnus* swan

cylinder *n* **1** a solid or hollow body with circular equal ends and straight parallel sides **2** a container or other object shaped like a cylinder **3** the chamber in an internal-combustion engine within which the piston moves **4** the rotating mechanism of a revolver, containing cartridge chambers **cylindrical** *adj*
WORD ORIGIN Greek *kulindein* to roll

cymbal *n* a percussion instrument consisting of a round brass plate which is struck against another or hit with a stick **cymbalist** *n*

WORD ORIGIN Greek *kumbē* something hollow

cyme *n bot* a flower cluster which has a single flower on the end of each stem and of which the central flower blooms first **cymose** *adj*
WORD ORIGIN Greek *kuma* anything swollen

Cymric (**kim**-rik) *adj* **1** of Wales ▷ *n* **2** the Celtic language of Wales

cynic (**sin**-ik) *n* a person who believes that people always act selfishly
WORD ORIGIN Greek *kuōn* dog

Cynic *n* a member of an ancient Greek philosophical school that had contempt for worldly things **Cynicism** *n*

cynical *adj* **1** believing that people always act selfishly **2** sarcastic or sneering **cynically** *adv*

cynicism *n* the attitude or beliefs of a cynic

cynosure (**sin**-oh-zyure) *n literary* a centre of interest or attention
WORD ORIGIN Greek *Kunosoura* dog's tail (name of the constellation of Ursa Minor)

cypher (**sife**-er) *n, vb* same as **cipher**

cypress *n* **1** an evergreen tree with dark green leaves **2** the wood of this tree
WORD ORIGIN Greek *kuparissos*

Cypriot *adj* **1** of Cyprus ▷ *n* **2** a person from Cyprus **3** the dialect of Greek spoken in Cyprus

Cyrillic *adj* of the Slavic alphabet devised supposedly by Saint Cyril, now used primarily for Russian and Bulgarian

cyst (**sist**) *n* **1** *pathol* an abnormal membranous sac containing fluid or diseased matter **2** *anat* any normal sac in the body
WORD ORIGIN Greek *kustis* pouch, bag

cystic fibrosis *n* a congenital disease, usually affecting young children, which causes breathing disorders and malfunctioning of the pancreas

cystitis (siss-**tite**-iss) *n* inflammation of the bladder, causing a desire to urinate frequently, accompanied by a burning sensation

-cyte *n combining form* indicating a cell: *leucocyte*
WORD ORIGIN Greek *kutos* vessel

cytology (site-**ol**-a-jee) *n* the study of plant and animal cells **cytological** *adj* **cytologically** *adv* **cytologist** *n*

cytoplasm *n* the protoplasm of a cell excluding the nucleus **cytoplasmic** *adj*

czar (**zahr**) *n* same as **tsar**

Czech *adj* **1** of the Czech Republic ▷ *n* **2** a person from the Czech Republic **3** the language of the Czech Republic

Czechoslovak *or* **Czechoslovakian** *adj* **1** of the former Czechoslovakia ▷ *n* **2** a person from the former Czechoslovakia

Dd

The letter D is the fourth letter of the English alphabet. It was adapted by the Romans from the Greek letter delta (Δ,δ), which in turn came from the Semitic letter daleth. In Hebrew, the word *daleth* means 'tent door', which gives a clue to the origins of the triangular shape of the Greek letter. (The use of a triangle to represent the letter D can still be seen in the Star of David, which is composed of two triangles, each representing the opening letter of King David's name.)

The shape of the letter was modified in the Roman alphabet from a triangle into the form in which it is used in the modern English alphabet.

Any object replicating the letter's semicircular shape can be referred to as a D. A D-ring is a metal clip with one straight edge and one curved edge that forms part of a harness, while the semicircular area on a snooker table in which the cue ball is placed at the start of play is known as the 'D'.

In pre-decimal British currency a lower-case 'd' was an abbreviation for a penny (the Latin equivalent of this low-value coin being a *denarius*). An upper-case letter D can be an abbreviation for either of the Latin words *Deus* (God) or *Dominus* (Lord), and this is the significance of the letter in abbreviations such as AD ('in the year of our Lord'), DG ('by the grace of God'), and DV ('God willing').

In American sport, by contrast, D has become a popular abbreviation for 'defense', and fans wishing to inspire their team's defensive players can sometimes be seen brandishing a cardboard cutout of the letter D along with a picture of a fence. Knowing this may help non-Americans to understand how an American rock band could have taken on the name of 'Tenacious D'.

The letter D is also found in the expression 'D-day', a name given to the day appointed for some major undertaking. The original D-day was, of course, the date set for the Allied invasion of occupied Europe – 6 June 1944. The choice of the letter for that occasion is supposed to have been an arbitrary one, based solely on the fact that D is the first letter of the word 'day'.

---

d 1 *physics* density **2** deci-

D 1 *music* the second note of the scale of C major **2** *chem* deuterium **3** the Roman numeral for 500

d. 1 *Brit & NZ* (before decimalization) penny *or* pennies
WORD ORIGIN Latin *denarius* **2** died **3** daughter

dab¹ *vb* **dabbing, dabbed 1** to pat lightly and quickly **2** to apply with short tapping strokes: *dabbing antiseptic on cuts* ▷ *n* **3** a small amount of something soft or moist **4** a light stroke or tap **5 dabs** *slang chiefly Brit* fingerprints
WORD ORIGIN imitative

dab² *n* a small European flatfish covered with rough toothed scales
WORD ORIGIN Anglo-French *dabbe*

dabble *vb* **-bling, -bled 1** to be involved in an activity in a superficial way: *she dabbles in right-wing politics* **2** to splash (one's toes or fingers) in water **dabbler** *n*
WORD ORIGIN probably from Dutch *dabbelen*

dab hand *n informal* a person who is particularly skilled at something: *a dab hand with a needle and thread*
WORD ORIGIN origin unknown

dace *n, pl* **dace** *or* **daces** a European freshwater fish of the carp family
WORD ORIGIN Old French *dars* dart

dachshund *n* a small dog with short legs and a long body
WORD ORIGIN German *Dachs* badger + *Hund* dog

dactyl *n prosody* a metrical foot of three syllables, one long followed by two short **dactylic** *adj*
WORD ORIGIN Greek *daktulos* finger, comparing the finger's three joints to the three syllables

dad *or* **daddy** *n informal* father
WORD ORIGIN from child's *da da*

Dada *or* **Dadaism** *n* an art movement of the early 20th century that systematically used arbitrary and absurd concepts **Dadaist** *n, adj*
WORD ORIGIN French: hobbyhorse

daddy-longlegs *n informal* **1** *Brit* crane fly **2** a small web-spinning spider with long legs

dado (**day-doe**) *n, pl* **-does** *or* **-dos 1** the lower part of an interior wall, often separated by a rail, that is decorated differently from the upper part **2** *archit* the part of a pedestal between the base and the cornice
WORD ORIGIN Italian: die, die-shaped pedestal

daemon (**deem-on**) *n* same as **demon**

daffodil *n* **1** a spring plant with yellow trumpet-shaped flowers ▷ *adj* **2** brilliant yellow
WORD ORIGIN variant of Latin *asphodelus* asphodel

daft *adj informal chiefly Brit* **1** foolish or crazy **2 daft about** very enthusiastic about: *he's daft about football*
WORD ORIGIN Old English *gedæfte* gentle, foolish

dag *NZ n* **1** the dried dung on a sheep's rear **2** *informal* an amusing person ▷ *pl n* **3 rattle one's dags** *informal* hurry up ▷ *vb* **4** to remove the dags from a sheep
WORD ORIGIN origin unknown

dagga (**duhh-a**) *n S African* a local name for marijuana
WORD ORIGIN probably from Khoi (language of southern Africa) *daxa*

dagger *n* **1** a short knifelike weapon with a double-edged pointed blade **2** a character (†) used to indicate a cross-reference **3 at daggers drawn** in a state of open hostility **4 look daggers** to glare with hostility
WORD ORIGIN origin unknown

daggy *adj Austral & NZ informal* **1** untidy; dishevelled: *he turned up wearing a daggy tracksuit* **2** eccentric: *his daggy hobby of collecting novelty tea towels*

daguerreotype (**dag-gair-oh-type**) *n* a type of early photograph produced on chemically treated silver
WORD ORIGIN after L. *Daguerre*, its inventor

The Language of Food

Boeuf bourgignon is beef stew in red wine, but *boeuf bourgignon* sounds better. The words we use affect our tastebuds, and even phrases like *Chinese food* and *Indian food* accumulate a cluster of associations (*fried rice, curry*). Since the nineteenth century, the prestige language of gastronomy, and even the concept of the restaurant, was French. The Italians added the populist touch, and in every large city in the world one can find their *pasta* and *pizza*.

In the 1950s, typical British or American home cooks would cautiously rub a garlic clove around a salad bowl; a few decades later they were cooking dishes that called for 40 cloves of the stuff. Somerset Maugham, who once said that if one wanted to eat well in England one should breakfast three times a day, might be startled by the contemporary range of offerings in an English *wine bar* or *gastropub*. Indeed, sensuous menu descriptions of dishes in dining places often amount to *gastroporn*.

About the 1970s the era began of *celebrity chefs*, bestselling ethnic cookbooks, miracle weight-loss diets, and cable TV channels devoted exclusively to food. The interest in food, not just as sustenance but as hedonism, was heralded by James Beard and by Julia Child in the United States, and by Elizabeth David in Britain. Cooking and dining began to be signatures of middle-class lifestyles, especially of *foodies*, and trends quickly succeeded one another: at first timidly with Swiss *fondue*, then in full spate with heart-healthy Mediterranean and soy-centred vegetarian dishes. For those who had the leisure, *brunch* became a Sunday-morning institution. People rushed to buy the *Beaujolais nouveau*. The *street food* and *haute cuisine* of every region of the world clamoured for attention, and found a following: Southeast Asia (*pad thai*), Latin America (*tortillas*), the West Indies (*jerk chicken*), and the Middle East (*felafel*). The food of minorities, which might be shaped, say, by Jewish or Muslim dietary laws, or simply be the improvisations of poverty (*soul food*), invaded the middle-class supermarket. As the suburbanite continued to fire up the backyard *barbecue*, American regional styles came into vogue: *Cajun* and *Creole* cooking from Louisiana (*gumbo*), or Tex-Mex from the Southwest (*chili con carne*). Among the more refined, a specialized vocabulary of synaesthetic terms (*notes, finish*) and improbable allusions (*vanilla, saddle leather*) grew up to describe the tastes of wines, beers, cheeses, and malt whiskies. The white Westerner's tolerance for fiery sauces and treatments based on members of the capsicum family soared and racks of herbs and spices swelled. The addiction to caffeinated stimulants (coffee, tea, chocolate) became such that the global coffee industry was said to rank next to petroleum in dollar value.

The late Industrial Revolution had brought huge advances in the storage, shipping, and preserving of fruit and vegetables grown in farflung places, from *kiwi fruit* to *iceberg lettuce*. Yet by the twenty-first century, long-distance production and mass consumption inspired the opposite reaction, an emphasis on long-roasting or simmering *slow food*, and of local produce that was consumed by *locovores*. But Westerners were still gobbling or guzzling the *fast food* or *junk food* Americans had invented a century earlier: *French fries, hot dogs, hamburgers, milkshakes, ice cream, popcorn, Coca-Cola*, and *Pepsi-Cola*. They began their day with *cornflakes*.

Despite the tidal wave of new terms, British and American English stubbornly retained differences for common words: a British *tin* remained the American *can*, the *courgette* the *zucchini*, the *aubergine* the *eggplant*, the *sweet biscuit* the *cookie*. A *muffin* was a small domed cake in America, but a flat circular bread in England, but if Americans ate the latter, they ate an *English muffin*. Other confusables abounded: *yams* and *sweet potatoes*, *rice* and *wild rice*, the fungus *truffle* and the chocolate *truffle*.

Customarily, food always marked not just cultural differences, but spawned a wealth of metaphors and analogies, such as 'the greatest thing since sliced bread'. (As a term, though not as a packaged bakery item, *sliced bread* first appeared in 1958). *Spam*, the 1930s *luncheon meat*, notorious as army grub during the Second World War, became the 1990s term for unwanted, mass-posted e-mail advertisements. Spam has always been something of a *mystery meat*.

dahlia (**day**-lya) *n* a garden plant with showy flowers
WORD ORIGIN after Anders *Dahl*, botanist

Dáil Éireann (doil **air**-in) *or* **Dáil** *n* (in the Republic of Ireland) the lower chamber of parliament
WORD ORIGIN Irish *dáil* assembly + *Éireann* of Eire

daily *adj* **1** occurring every day or every weekday: *there have been daily airdrops of food, blankets, and water* **2** of or relating to a single day or to one day at a time: *her home help comes in on a daily basis* ▷ *adv* **3** every day ▷ *n, pl* **-lies** **4** *Austral & Brit* a daily newspaper **5** *Brit informal* a woman employed to clean someone's house
WORD ORIGIN Old English *dæglic*

dainty *adj* **-tier, -tiest** **1** delicate, pretty, or elegant: *dainty little pink shoes* ▷ *n, pl* **-ties** **2** *Brit* a small choice cake or sweet **daintily** *adv*
WORD ORIGIN Old French *deintié*

daiquiri (**dak**-eer-ee) *n, pl* **-ris** an iced drink containing rum, lime juice, and sugar
WORD ORIGIN after *Daiquiri*, town in Cuba

dairy *n, pl* **dairies** **1** a company or shop that sells milk and milk products **2** a place where milk and cream are stored or made into butter and cheese **3** food containing milk or milk products: *I can't eat dairy* **4** *NZ* small shop selling groceries and milk often outside normal trading hours ▷ *adj* **5** of milk or milk products: *dairy produce*
WORD ORIGIN Old English *dæge* servant girl

dairy cattle *n* cows reared mainly for their milk

dairy farm *n* a farm where cows are kept mainly for their milk

dairymaid *n* *Brit, Austral, & NZ* (formerly) a woman employed to milk cows

dairyman *n* *Brit, Austral, & S African* a man employed to look after cows

dais (**day**-iss) *n* a raised platform in a hall or meeting place used by a speaker
WORD ORIGIN Old French *deis*

daisy *n, pl* **-sies** a small low-growing flower with a yellow centre and pinkish-white petals
WORD ORIGIN Old English *dægesēge* day's eye

daisy chain *n* a string of daisies joined together by their stems to make a necklace

daisywheel *n* a flat disc in a word processor with radiating spokes for printing characters

dal¹ *n* same as **dhal**

dal² decalitre(s)

Dalai Lama *n* the chief lama and (until 1959) ruler of Tibet

dale *n* an open valley
WORD ORIGIN Old English *dæl*

dalliance *n* *old-fashioned* flirtation

dally *vb* **-lies, -lying, -lied** **1** *old-fashioned* to waste time or dawdle **2** **dally with** to deal frivolously with: *to dally with someone's affections*
WORD ORIGIN Anglo-French *dalier* to gossip

Dalmatian *n* a large dog with a smooth white coat and black spots

dam¹ *n* **1** a barrier built across a river to create a lake **2** a lake created by such a barrier ▷ *vb* **damming, dammed** **3** to block up (a river) by a dam
WORD ORIGIN probably from Middle Low German

dam² *n* the female parent of an animal such as a sheep or horse
WORD ORIGIN variant of *dame*

dam³ decametre(s)

damage *vb* **-aging, -aged** **1** to harm or injure ▷ *n* **2** injury or harm caused to a person or thing **3** *informal* cost: *what's the damage?* **damaging** *adj*
WORD ORIGIN Latin *damnum* injury, loss

damages *pl n* *law* money awarded as compensation for injury or loss

damask *n* a heavy fabric with a pattern woven into it, used for tablecloths, curtains, etc.
WORD ORIGIN *Damascus*, where fabric originally made

dame *n* *slang* a woman
WORD ORIGIN Latin *domina* lady

Dame *n* (in Britain) the title of a woman who has been awarded the Order of the British Empire or another order of chivalry

damn *interj* **1** *slang* an exclamation of annoyance ▷ *adv* **2** *slang Also* **damned** extremely ▷ *adj* **3** *slang Also* **damned** extreme: *a damn good idea* ▷ *vb* **4** to condemn as bad or worthless **5** to curse **6** (of God) to condemn to hell or eternal punishment **7** to prove (someone) guilty **8** **damn with faint praise** to praise so unenthusiastically that the effect is condemnation ▷ *n* **9** **not give a damn** *informal* not care **damning** *adj*
WORD ORIGIN Latin *damnum* loss, injury

damnable *adj* very unpleasant or annoying **damnably** *adv*

damnation *interj* **1** an exclamation of anger ▷ *n* **2** *theol* eternal punishment

damned *adj* **1** condemned to hell ▷ *adv, adj slang* **2** extreme or extremely **3** used to indicate amazement or refusal: *I'm damned if I'll do it!*

damnedest *n* **do one's damnedest** *informal* to do one's best: *I'm doing my damnedest to make myself clear*

damp *adj* **1** slightly wet ▷ *n* **2** slight wetness; moisture ▷ *vb* **3** to make slightly wet **4** **damp down a** to reduce the intensity of (someone's emotions or reactions): *they attempted to damp down protests* **b** to reduce the flow of air to (a fire) to make it burn more slowly **damply** *adv* **dampness** *n*
WORD ORIGIN Middle Low German: steam

dampcourse *or* **damp-proof course** *n* a layer of waterproof material built into the base of a wall to prevent moisture rising

dampen *vb* **1** to reduce the intensity of **2** to make damp

damper *n* **1** **put a damper on** to produce a depressing or inhibiting effect on **2** a movable plate to regulate the draught in a stove or furnace **3** the pad in a piano or harpsichord that deadens the vibration of each string as its key is

released **4** *chiefly Austral & NZ* any of various unleavened loaves and scones, typically cooked on an open fire

damsel *n* *archaic or poetic* a young woman
WORD ORIGIN Old French *damoisele*

damson *n* a small blue-black edible plumlike fruit that grows on a tree
WORD ORIGIN Latin *prunum damascenum* Damascus plum

dan *n* *judo, karate* **1** any of the 10 black-belt grades of proficiency **2** a competitor entitled to dan grading
WORD ORIGIN Japanese

dance *vb* **dancing, danced** **1** to move the feet and body rhythmically in time to music **2** to perform (a particular dance): *to dance a tango* **3** to skip or leap **4** to move in a rhythmic way: *their reflection danced in the black waters* **5** **dance attendance on** someone to carry out someone's slightest wish in an overeager manner ▷ *n* **6** a social meeting arranged for dancing **7** a series of rhythmic steps and movements in time to music **8** a piece of music in the rhythm of a particular dance **dancer** *n* **dancing** *n, adj*
WORD ORIGIN Old French *dancier*

dancehall *n* a style of dance-oriented reggae

D and C *n* *med* dilatation of the cervix and curettage of the uterus: a minor operation to clear the womb or remove tissue for diagnosis

dandelion *n* a wild plant with yellow rayed flowers and deeply notched leaves
WORD ORIGIN Old French *dent de lion* tooth of a lion, referring to its leaves

dander *n* **get one's dander up** *Brit, Austral, & NZ slang* to become angry
WORD ORIGIN from *dandruff*

dandified *adj* dressed like or resembling a dandy

dandle *vb* **-dling, -dled** to move (a young child) up and down on one's knee
WORD ORIGIN origin unknown

dandruff *n* loose scales of dry dead skin shed from the scalp
WORD ORIGIN origin unknown

dandy *n, pl* **-dies** **1** a man who is greatly concerned with the elegance of his appearance ▷ *adj* **-dier, -diest** **2** *informal* very good or fine
WORD ORIGIN origin unknown

dandy-brush *n* a stiff brush used for grooming a horse

Dane *n* a person from Denmark

danger *n* **1** the possibility that someone may be injured or killed **2** someone or something that may cause injury or harm **3** a likelihood that something unpleasant will happen: *the danger of flooding*
WORD ORIGIN Middle English *daunger* power, hence power to inflict injury

danger money *n* extra money paid to compensate for the risks involved in dangerous work

dangerous *adj* likely or able to cause injury or harm **dangerously** *adv*

dangle *vb* **-gling, -gled** **1** to hang loosely **2** to display (something attractive) as an enticement
WORD ORIGIN probably imitative

Danish *adj* **1** of Denmark ▷ *n* **2** the language of Denmark

Danish blue *n* a white cheese with blue veins and a strong flavour

Danish pastry *n* a rich puff pastry filled with apple, almond paste, etc. and topped with icing

dank *adj* (esp. of cellars or caves) unpleasantly damp and chilly
WORD ORIGIN probably from Old Norse

dapper *adj* (of a man) neat in appearance and slight in build
WORD ORIGIN Middle Dutch

dappled *adj* **1** marked with spots of a different colour; mottled **2** covered in patches of light and shadow
WORD ORIGIN origin unknown

dapple-grey *n* a horse with a grey coat and darker coloured spots

Darby and Joan *n chiefly Brit* a happily married elderly couple
WORD ORIGIN couple in 18th-century ballad

dare *vb* **daring, dared** **1** to be courageous enough to try (to do something) **2** to challenge (someone) to do something risky **3 I dare say a** it is quite possible **b** probably ▷ *n* **4** a challenge to do something risky
WORD ORIGIN Old English *durran*

≡ **USAGE**
≡ When used negatively or
≡ interrogatively, *dare* does not usually
≡ add -*s*: *he dare not come; dare she come?*
≡ When used negatively in the past
≡ tense, however, *dare* usually adds -*d*: *he*
≡ *dared not come.*

daredevil *n* **1** a recklessly bold person ▷ *adj* **2** recklessly bold or daring

daring *adj* **1** willing to do things that may be dangerous ▷ *n* **2** the courage to do things that may be dangerous
daringly *adv*

dark *adj* **1** having little or no light **2** (of a colour) reflecting little light: *dark brown* **3** (of hair or skin) brown or black **4** (of thoughts or ideas) gloomy or sad **5** sinister or evil: *a dark deed* **6** sullen or angry: *a dark scowl* **7** secret or mysterious: *keep it dark* ▷ *n* **8** absence of light; darkness **9** night or nightfall **10 in the dark** in ignorance **darkly** *adv* **darkness** *n*
WORD ORIGIN Old English *deorc*

dark age *n* a period of ignorance or barbarism

Dark Ages *pl n* the period of European history between 500 and 1000 AD

darken *vb* **1** to make or become dark or darker **2** to make gloomy, angry, or sad

dark horse *n* a person who reveals little about himself or herself, esp. someone who has unexpected talents

darkroom *n* a darkened room in which photographs are developed

darling *n* **1** a person very much loved: used as a term of address **2** a favourite: *the darling of the gossip columns* ▷ *adj* **3** beloved **4** pleasing: *a darling film*
WORD ORIGIN Old English *dēorling*

darn[1] *vb* **1** to mend a hole in (a knitted garment) with a series of interwoven stitches ▷ *n* **2** a patch of darned work on a garment
WORD ORIGIN origin unknown

darn[2] *interj, adj, adv, vb, n euphemistic* same as **damn**

darnel *n* a weed that grows in grain fields
WORD ORIGIN origin unknown

dart *n* **1** a small narrow pointed missile that is thrown or shot, as in the game of darts **2** a sudden quick movement **3** a tapered tuck made in dressmaking ▷ *vb* **4** to move or throw swiftly and suddenly **darting** *adj*
WORD ORIGIN Germanic

dartboard *n* a circular board used as the target in the game of darts

darts *n* a game in which darts are thrown at a dartboard

Darwinism or **Darwinian theory** *n* the theory of the origin of animal and plant species by evolution **Darwinian** *adj, n* **Darwinist** *n, adj*
WORD ORIGIN after Charles *Darwin*, English naturalist

dash *vb* **1** to move hastily; rush **2** to hurl; crash: *deep-sea rollers dashing spray over jagged rocks* **3** to frustrate: *prospects for peace have been dashed* ▷ *n* **4** a sudden quick movement **5** a small amount: *a dash of milk* **6** a mixture of style and courage: *the commander's dash did not impress him* **7** the punctuation mark (—), used to indicate a change of subject **8** the symbol (–), used in combination with the symbol **dot** (.) in Morse code ▷ See also **dash off**
WORD ORIGIN Middle English *daschen, dassen*

dashboard *n* the instrument panel in a car, boat, or aircraft

dasher *n Canad* one of the boards surrounding an ice-hockey rink

dashing *adj* stylish and attractive: *a splendidly dashing character*

dash off *vb* to write down or finish off hastily

dassie *n S African* a hyrax, esp. a rock hyrax
WORD ORIGIN Afrikaans

dastardly *adj old-fashioned* mean and cowardly
WORD ORIGIN Middle English *dastard* dullard

dasyure (**dass**-ee-your) *n* a small marsupial of Australia, New Guinea, and adjacent islands

DAT digital audio tape

dat. dative

data *n* **1** a series of observations, measurements, or facts; information **2** *computers* the numbers, digits, characters, and symbols operated on by a computer
WORD ORIGIN Latin: (things) given

≡ **USAGE**
≡ Although now often used as a
≡ singular noun, *data* is in fact a plural.

database *n* **1** a store of information in a form that can be easily handled by a computer **2** a large store of information: *a database of knowledge*

data capture *n* a process for converting information into a form that can be handled by a computer

data processing *n* a sequence of operations performed on data, esp. by a computer, in order to extract or interpret information

date[1] *n* **1** a specified day of the month **2** the particular day or year when an event happened **3 a** an appointment, esp. with a person to whom one is romantically or sexually attached **b** the person with whom the appointment is made **4 to date** up to now ▷ *vb* **dating, dated 5** to mark (a letter or cheque) with the date **6** to assign a date of occurrence or creation to **7** to reveal the age of: *that dress dates her* **8** to make or become old-fashioned: *it's the freshest look this year but may date quickly* **9** *informal chiefly US & Canad* to be a boyfriend or girlfriend of **10 date from** or **date back to** to have originated at (a specified time)
WORD ORIGIN Latin *dare* to give, as in *epistula data Romae* letter handed over at Rome

≡ **USAGE**
≡ See at **year**.

date[2] *n* the dark-brown, sweet-tasting fruit of the date palm
WORD ORIGIN Greek *daktulos* finger

dated *adj* unfashionable; outmoded

dateless *adj* likely to remain fashionable or interesting regardless of age

dateline *n journalism* information placed at the top of an article stating the time and place the article was written

Date Line *n* short for **International Date Line**

date palm *n* a tall palm grown in tropical regions for its fruit

date rape *n* the act of a man raping a woman or pressuring her into having sex while they are on a date together

dative *n grammar* the grammatical case in certain languages that expresses the indirect object
WORD ORIGIN Latin *dativus*

datum *n, pl* **-ta** a single piece of information usually in the form of a fact or statistic
WORD ORIGIN Latin: something given

daub *vb* **1** to smear (paint or mud) quickly or carelessly over a surface **2** to paint (a picture) clumsily or badly ▷ *n* **3** a crude or badly done painting: *a typical child's daub*
WORD ORIGIN Old French *dauber* to paint

daughter *n* **1** a female child **2** a girl or woman who comes from a certain place or is connected with a certain thing: *a daughter of the church* ▷ *adj* **3** *biol* denoting a cell, chromosome, etc. produced by the division of one of its own kind **4** *physics* (of a nuclide) formed from another nuclide by radioactive decay **daughterly** *adj*
WORD ORIGIN Old English *dohtor*

daughter-in-law *n, pl* **daughters-in-law** the wife of one's son

daunting *adj* intimidating or worrying: *this project grows more daunting every day*
WORD ORIGIN Latin *domitare* to tame

dauntless *adj* fearless; not discouraged

dauphin (**daw**-fin) *n* formerly, the eldest son of the king of France
WORD ORIGIN Old French: originally a family name

davenport *n* **1** *chiefly Brit* a writing desk with drawers at the side **2** *Austral, US, & Canad* a large sofa
WORD ORIGIN sense 1 supposedly after Captain *Davenport*, who commissioned the first ones

davit (**dav**-vit) *n* a crane, usually one of a pair, on the side of a ship for lowering or hoisting a lifeboat **WORD ORIGIN** Anglo-French *daviot*, from *Davi* David

Davy Jones's locker *n* the ocean's bottom, regarded as the grave of those lost or buried at sea **WORD ORIGIN** origin unknown

Davy lamp *n* same as **safety lamp** **WORD ORIGIN** after Sir Humphrey *Davy*, chemist

dawdle *vb* **-dling, -dled** to walk slowly or lag behind **WORD ORIGIN** origin unknown

dawn *n* **1** daybreak **2** the beginning of something ▷ *vb* **3** to begin to grow light after the night **4** to begin to develop or appear **5 dawn on** or **upon** to become apparent (to someone) **WORD ORIGIN** Old English *dagian* to dawn

dawn chorus *n* the singing of birds at dawn

day *n* **1** the period of 24 hours from one midnight to the next **2** the period of light between sunrise and sunset **3** the part of a day occupied with regular activity, esp. work **4** a period or point in time: *in days gone by; in Shakespeare's day* **5** a day of special observance: *Christmas Day* **6** a time of success or recognition: *his day will come* **7 all in a day's work** part of one's normal activity **8 at the end of the day** in the final reckoning **9 call it a day** to stop work or other activity **10 day in, day out** every day without changing **11 that'll be the day a** that is most unlikely to happen **b** I look forward to that ▶ Related adjective: **diurnal** **WORD ORIGIN** Old English *dæg*

daybreak *n* the time in the morning when light first appears

day centre *n* a place that provides care where elderly or disabled people can spend the day

daydream *n* **1** a pleasant fantasy indulged in while awake ▷ *vb* **2** to indulge in idle fantasy **daydreamer** *n*

Day-Glo *adj* (of a colour) luminous in daylight: *Day-Glo pink* **WORD ORIGIN** from a trade name for a brand of fluorescent paint

daylight *n* **1** light from the sun **2** daytime **3** daybreak **4 see daylight** to realize that the end of a difficult task is approaching ▶ See also **daylights**

daylight robbery *n informal* blatant overcharging

daylights *pl n informal* **1 beat the living daylights out of someone** to beat someone soundly **2 scare the living daylights out of someone** to frighten someone greatly

daylight-saving time *n* time set one hour ahead of the local standard time, to provide extra daylight in the evening in summer

Day of Atonement *n* same as **Yom Kippur**

day release *n Brit* a system whereby workers go to college one day a week for vocational training

day return *n* a reduced fare for a train or bus journey travelling both ways in one day

day room *n* a communal living room in a hospital or similar institution

daytime *n* the time from sunrise to sunset

day-to-day *adj* routine; everyday

daze *vb* **dazing, dazed 1** to cause to be in a state of confusion or shock ▷ *n* **2** a state of confusion or shock: *in a daze* **dazed** *adj* **WORD ORIGIN** Old Norse *dasa*

dazzle *vb* **-zling, -zled 1** to impress greatly: *she was dazzled by his wit* **2** to blind for a short time by sudden excessive light: *he passed two cars and they dazzled him with their headlights* ▷ *n* **3** bright light that dazzles **dazzling** *adj* **dazzlingly** *adv* **WORD ORIGIN** from *daze*

dB or **db** decibel(s)

Db *chem* dubnium

DBE Dame (Commander of the Order) of the British Empire

DC 1 direct current **2** District of Columbia

DCC digital compact cassette: a magnetic tape cassette on which sound can be recorded digitally

DD Doctor of Divinity

D-day *n* the day selected for the start of some operation **WORD ORIGIN** after D(ay)-day, the day of the Allied invasion of Europe on June 6, 1944

DDS or **DDSc** Doctor of Dental Surgery or Science

DDT *n* dichlorodiphenyltrichloroethane; an insecticide, now banned in many countries

DE Delaware

de- *prefix* **1** indicating removal: *dethrone* **2** indicating reversal: *declassify* **3** indicating departure from: *decamp* **WORD ORIGIN** Latin

deacon *n Christianity* **1** (in episcopal churches) an ordained minister ranking immediately below a priest **2** (in some Protestant churches) a lay official who assists the minister **WORD ORIGIN** Greek *diakonos* servant

deactivate *vb* **-vating, -vated** to make (a bomb or other explosive device) harmless

dead *adj* **1** no longer alive **2** no longer in use or finished: *a dead language; a dead match* **3** unresponsive **4** (of a limb) numb **5** complete or absolute: *there was dead silence* **6** *informal* very tired **7** (of a place) lacking activity **8** *electronics* **a** drained of electric charge **b** not connected to a source of electric charge **9** *sport* (of a ball) out of play **10 dead from the neck up** *informal* stupid **11 dead to the world** *informal* fast asleep ▷ *n* **12** a period during which coldness or darkness is most intense: *the dead of winter* ▷ *adv* **13** *informal* extremely: *dead easy* **14** suddenly and abruptly: *stop dead* **15** dead on exactly right **WORD ORIGIN** Old English *dēad*

deadbeat *n informal* a lazy or socially undesirable person

dead beat *adj informal* exhausted

dead duck *n slang* something that is doomed to failure

deaden *vb* to make (something) less intense: *drugs deaden the pain; heavy curtains deadened the echo* **deadening** *adj*

dead end *n* **1** a cul-de-sac **2** a situation in which further progress is impossible: *efforts to free the hostages had reached a dead end*

deadhead *n US & Canad* **1** *informal* a person who does not pay on a bus, at a game, etc. **2** *informal* a commercial vehicle travelling empty **3** *slang* a dull person **4** *US & Canad* a totally or partially submerged log floating in a lake

dead heat *n* a tie for first place between two or more participants in a race or contest

dead letter *n* **1** a letter that cannot be delivered or returned due to lack of information **2** a law or rule that is no longer enforced

deadline *n* a time or date by which a job or task must be completed

deadlock *n* a point in a dispute at which no agreement can be reached

deadlocked *adj* having reached a deadlock

dead loss *n informal* a useless person or thing

deadly *adj* **-lier, -liest 1** likely to cause death: *deadly poison* **2** *informal* extremely boring ▷ *adv, adj* **3** like or suggestive of death: *deadly pale* ▷ *adv* **4** extremely: *she was being deadly serious*

deadly nightshade *n* a poisonous plant with purple bell-shaped flowers and black berries

dead man's handle or **pedal** *n* a safety device which only allows equipment to operate when a handle or pedal is being pressed

dead march *n* solemn funeral music played to accompany a procession

dead-nettle *n* a plant with leaves like nettles but without stinging hairs

deadpan *adj* **1** deliberately emotionless ▷ *adv* **2** in a deliberately emotionless manner

dead reckoning *n* a method of establishing one's position using the distance and direction travelled

dead set *adv* firmly decided: *he is dead set on leaving*

dead soldier or **marine** *n informal* an empty beer or spirit bottle

dead weight *n* **1** a heavy weight or load **2** the difference between the loaded and the unloaded weights of a ship

dead wood *n informal* people or things that are no longer useful

deaf *adj* **1** unable to hear **2 deaf to** refusing to listen or take notice of **deafness** *n* **WORD ORIGIN** Old English *dēaf* **≡ USAGE** **≡** See at **disabled**.

deaf-and-dumb *adj offensive* unable to hear or speak

deafblind *adj* unable to hear or see

deafen *vb* to make deaf, esp. momentarily by a loud noise **deafening** *adj*

deaf-mute *n* a person who is unable to hear or speak

Words from Shakespeare
part 7

dainty *adj* splendid, fine
Why, that's my dainty Ariel! *The Tempest* 5.1

dally *v* to play with or tease
They that dally nicely with words may quickly make them wanton *Twelfth Night* 3.1

damask *n* a light-red or pink colour
Twas just the difference
Betwixt the constant red and mingled damask
As You Like It 3.5

dare *v* to challenge or, confront
He goes before me, and still dares me on
A Midsummer Night's Dream 3.3

dare *v* to present, deliver or inflict
all that fortune, death, and danger dare *Hamlet* 4.4

darkly *adv* secretly or cunningly
I will go darkly to work with her
Measure for Measure 5.1

daw *n* an idiot or fool. After the jackdaw, a bird believed to be stupid
Yea, just so much as you may take upon a knife's point and choke a daw withal
Much Ado About Nothing 3.1

debile *adj* weak or feeble
And debile minister great power
All's Well That Ends Well 2.3

deboshed *adj* corrupted or debauched
Men so disordered, deboshed and bold *King Lear* 1.4

decoct *v* to heat up or warm something
Can sodden water,
A drench for sur-rein'd jades ... Decoct their cold blood to such valiant heat? *Henry V* 3.5

deep-revolving *adj* deep-thinking, meditating
The deep-revolving Buckingham
No more shall be the neighbour to my counsels
Richard III 4.2

defect *n* shortcoming or something that is not right
Being unprepared
Our will became the servant to defect *Macbeth* 2.1

degree *n* rank, standing or station
Should a like language use to all degrees,
And mannerly distinguishment leave out
Betwixt the prince and beggar *The Winter's Tale* 2.1

deify *v* to worship as a God
all ... deifying the name of Rosalind *As You Like It* 3.2

delated *adj* detailed
the scope
Of these delated articles *Hamlet* 1.2

delicate *adj* of fine quality or valuable
thou wast a spirit too delicate *The Tempest* 1.2

demise *v* to transmit, give or convey
what state ... Canst thou demise to any child of mine? *Richard III* 4.4

deplore *v* to express with grief or sorrow
Never more
Will I my master's tears to you deplore
Twelfth Night 3.1

depose *v* to make someone take an oath, or swear something to be true
Depose him in the justice of his cause *Richard II* 1.3

depositary *n* a trustee
Made you ... my depositary *King Lear* 2.4

derive *v* to come from or to descend from. It usually applies to people
No part of it is mine,
This shame derives itself from unknown loins.
Much Ado About Nothing 4.1

derive *v* to inherit
Treason is not inherited ,Or, if we derive it from our friends
What's that to me? *As You Like It* 1.3

deal¹ n **1** an agreement or transaction **2** a particular type of treatment received: *a fair deal* **3** a large amount: *the land alone is worth a good deal* **4** *cards* a player's turn to distribute the cards **5 big deal** *slang* an important matter: often used sarcastically ▷ *vb* **dealing, dealt** (**delt**) **6** to inflict (a blow) on **7** *slang* to sell any illegal drug **8 deal in** to engage in commercially **9 deal out** to apportion or distribute ▶ See also **deal with** WORD ORIGIN Old English *dǣlan*

deal² n **1** a plank of softwood timber **2** the sawn wood of various coniferous trees WORD ORIGIN Middle Low German *dele* plank

dealer n **1** a person or organization whose business involves buying and selling things **2** *slang* a person who sells illegal drugs **3** *cards* the person who distributes the cards

dealings pl n business relations with a person or organization

dealt vb the past of **deal¹**

deal with vb **1** to take action on: *he was not competent to deal with the legal aspects* **2** to be concerned with: *I do not wish to deal with specifics* **3** to do business with

dean n **1** the chief administrative official of a college or university faculty **2** *chiefly Church of England* the chief administrator of a cathedral or collegiate church WORD ORIGIN Late Latin *decanus* one set over ten people

deanery n, pl **-eries 1** a place where a dean lives **2** the parishes presided over by a rural dean

dear n **1** (often used in direct address) someone regarded with affection ▷ *adj* **2** beloved; precious **3 a** highly priced **b** charging high prices **4** a form of address used at the beginning of a letter before the name of the recipient: *Dear Mr Anderson* **5 dear to** important or close to ▷ *interj* **6** an exclamation of surprise or dismay: *oh dear, I've broken it* ▷ *adv* **7** dearly: *her errors have cost her dear* **dearly** adv WORD ORIGIN Old English *dēore*

dearth (**dirth**) n an inadequate amount; scarcity WORD ORIGIN Middle English *derthe*

death n **1** the permanent end of life in a person or animal **2** an instance of this: *his sudden death* **3** ending or destruction **4 at death's door** likely to die soon **5 catch one's death (of cold)** *informal* to contract a severe cold **6 like death warmed up** *informal* looking or feeling very ill or very tired **7 put to death** to execute **8 to death a** until dead **b** very much: *I had probably scared him to death* WORD ORIGIN Old English *dēath*

deathbed n the bed in which a person dies or is about to die

deathblow n a thing or event that destroys hope

death certificate n a document signed by a doctor certifying the death of a person and stating the cause of death if known

death duty n (in Britain) the former name for **inheritance tax**

death knell n something that heralds death or destruction

deathless adj everlasting because of fine qualities: *highbrow, deathless, and often endless prose*

deathly adj **1** resembling death: *a deathly pallor* **2** deadly

death mask n a cast taken from the face of a person who has recently died

death rate n the ratio of deaths in an area or group to the population of that area or group

death row n US part of a prison where convicts awaiting execution are imprisoned

death's-head n a human skull or a picture of one used to represent death or danger

death trap n a place or vehicle considered very unsafe

death warrant n **1** the official authorization for carrying out a sentence of death **2 sign one's (own) death warrant** to cause one's own destruction

deathwatch beetle n a beetle that bores into wood and produces a tapping sound

deb n *informal* a debutante

debacle (day-**bah**-kl) n something that ends in a disastrous failure, esp. because it has not been properly planned WORD ORIGIN French

debar vb **-barring, -barred** to prevent (someone) from doing something ≡ USAGE ≡ See at **disbar**.

debase vb **-basing, -based** to lower in quality, character, or value **debasement** n WORD ORIGIN see DE-, BASE²

debatable adj not absolutely certain: *her motives are highly debatable*

debate n **1** a discussion **2** a formal discussion, as in a parliament, in which opposing arguments are put forward ▷ *vb* **-bating, -bated 3** to discuss (something) formally **4** to consider (possible courses of action) WORD ORIGIN Old French *debatre*

debauch (dib-**bawch**) vb to make someone bad or corrupt, esp. sexually WORD ORIGIN Old French *desbaucher* to corrupt

debauched adj immoral; sexually corrupt

debauchery n excessive drunkenness or sexual activity

debenture n a long-term bond, bearing fixed interest and usually unsecured, issued by a company or governmental agency **debentured** adj WORD ORIGIN Latin *debentur mihi* there are owed to me

debenture stock n shares issued by a company, guaranteeing a fixed return at regular intervals

debilitate vb **-tating, -tated** to make gradually weaker **debilitation** n **debilitating** adj WORD ORIGIN Latin *debilis* weak

debility n, pl **-ties** a state of weakness, esp. caused by illness

debit n **1** the money, or a record of the money, withdrawn from a person's bank account **2** *accounting* **a** acknowledgment of a sum owing by entry on the left side of an account **b** an entry or the total of entries on this side ▷ *vb* **-iting, -ited 3** to charge (an account) with a debt: *they had debited our account* **4** *accounting* to record (an item) as a debit in an account WORD ORIGIN Latin *debitum* debt

debit card n a card issued by a bank or building society enabling customers to pay for goods by inserting it into a computer-controlled device at the place of sale, which is connected through the telephone network to the bank or building society

debonair or **debonnaire** adj (of a man) confident, charming, and well-dressed WORD ORIGIN Old French

debouch vb **1** (esp. of troops) to move into a more open space **2** (of a river, glacier, etc.) to flow into a larger area or body **debouchment** n WORD ORIGIN Old French *dé-* from + *bouche* mouth

debrief vb to interrogate (a soldier, diplomat, astronaut, etc.) on the completion of a mission **debriefing** n

debris (**deb**-ree) n **1** fragments of something destroyed; rubble **2** a mass of loose stones and earth WORD ORIGIN French

debt n **1** a sum of money owed **2 bad debt** a debt that is unlikely to be paid **3 in debt** owing money **4 in someone's debt** grateful to someone for his or her help: *I couldn't have managed without you – I'm in your debt* WORD ORIGIN Latin *debitum*

debt of honour n a debt that is morally but not legally binding

debtor n a person who owes money

debug vb **-bugging, -bugged** *informal* **1** to locate and remove defects in (a computer program) **2** to remove concealed microphones from (a room or telephone)

debunk vb *informal* to expose the falseness of: *many commonly held myths are debunked by the book* **debunker** n WORD ORIGIN DE- + BUNK²

debut (**day**-byoo) n the first public appearance of a performer WORD ORIGIN French

debutante (**day**-byoo-tont) n a young upper-class woman who is formally presented to society WORD ORIGIN French

Dec. December

decade n a period of ten years WORD ORIGIN Greek *deka* ten

decadence (**deck**-a-denss) n a decline in morality or culture **decadent** adj WORD ORIGIN Medieval Latin *decadentia* a falling away

decaf (**dee**-kaf) *informal* n **1** decaffeinated coffee ▷ *adj* **2** decaffeinated

decaffeinated (dee-**kaf**-fin-ate-id) adj with the caffeine removed: *decaffeinated tea*

decagon n *geom* a figure with ten sides **decagonal** adj

WORD ORIGIN Greek *deka* ten + *gōnia* angle

decahedron (deck-a-**heed**-ron) *n* a solid figure with ten plane faces **decahedral** *adj*
WORD ORIGIN Greek *deka* ten + *hedra* base

decalitre *or US* **decaliter** *n* a measure of volume equivalent to 10 litres

Decalogue *n* same as **Ten Commandments**
WORD ORIGIN Greek *deka* ten + *logos* word

decametre *or US* **decameter** *n* a unit of length equal to ten metres

decamp *vb* to leave secretly or suddenly

decant *vb* **1** to pour (a liquid, esp. wine) from one container to another **2** *chiefly Brit* to rehouse (people) while their homes are being renovated
WORD ORIGIN Medieval Latin *de-* from + *canthus* spout, rim

decanter *n* a stoppered bottle into which a drink is poured for serving

decapitate *vb* **-tating, -tated** to behead **decapitation** *n*
WORD ORIGIN Latin *de-* from + *caput* head

decapod *n* **1** a creature, such as a crab, with five pairs of walking limbs **2** a creature, such as a squid, with eight short tentacles and two longer ones
WORD ORIGIN Greek *deka* ten + *pous* foot

decarbonize *or* **-ise** *vb* **-izing, -ized** *or* **-ising, -ised** to remove carbon from (an internal-combustion engine) **decarbonization** *or* **-isation** *n*

decathlon *n* an athletic contest in which each athlete competes in ten different events **decathlete** *n*
WORD ORIGIN Greek *deka* ten + *athlon* contest

decay *vb* **1** to decline gradually in health, prosperity, or quality **2** to rot or cause to rot **3** *physics* (of an atomic nucleus) to undergo radioactive disintegration ▷ *n* **4** the process of something rotting: *too much sugar can cause tooth decay* **5** the state brought about by this process **6** *physics* disintegration of a nucleus, occurring spontaneously or as a result of electron capture
WORD ORIGIN Latin *de-* from + *cadere* to fall

decease *n formal* death
WORD ORIGIN Latin *decedere* to depart

deceased *adj formal* **1** dead ▷ *n* **2** a dead person: *the deceased*

deceit *n* behaviour intended to deceive

deceitful *adj* full of deceit

deceive *vb* **-ceiving, -ceived** **1** to mislead by lying **2** **deceive oneself** to refuse to acknowledge something one knows to be true **3** to be unfaithful to (one's sexual partner)
WORD ORIGIN Latin *decipere* to ensnare, cheat

decelerate *vb* **-ating, -ated** to slow down **deceleration** *n*
WORD ORIGIN DE- + (AC)CELERATE

December *n* the twelfth month of the year
WORD ORIGIN Latin: the tenth month (the Roman year originally began with March)

decencies *pl n* generally accepted standards of good behaviour

decency *n* conformity to the prevailing standards of what is right

decennial *adj* **1** lasting for ten years **2** occurring every ten years

decent *adj* **1** conforming to an acceptable standard or quality: *a decent living wage; he's made a few decent films* **2** polite or respectable: *he's a decent man* **3** fitting or proper: *that's the decent thing to do* **4** conforming to conventions of sexual behaviour **5** *informal* kind; generous: *she was pretty decent to me* **decently** *adv*
WORD ORIGIN Latin *decens* suitable

decentralize *or* **-ise** *vb* **-izing, -ized** *or* **-ising, -ised** to reorganize into smaller local units **decentralization** *or* **-isation** *n*

deception *n* **1** the act of deceiving someone or the state of being deceived **2** something that deceives; trick

deceptive *adj* likely or designed to deceive **deceptively** *adv* **deceptiveness** *n*

deci- *combining form* denoting one tenth: *decimetre*
WORD ORIGIN Latin *decimus* tenth

decibel *n* a unit for comparing two power levels or measuring the intensity of a sound
WORD ORIGIN DECI- + BEL

decide *vb* **-ciding, -cided** **1** to reach a decision: *we must decide on suitable action; he decided to stay on* **2** to cause to reach a decision **3** to settle (a question): *possible profits decided the issue* **4** to influence the outcome of (a contest) decisively: *the goal that decided the match came just before half-time*
WORD ORIGIN Latin *decidere* to cut off

decided *adj* **1** definite or noticeable: *a decided improvement* **2** strong and definite: *he has decided views on the matter* **decidedly** *adv*

deciduous *adj* **1** (of a tree) shedding all leaves annually **2** (of antlers or teeth) being shed at the end of a period of growth
WORD ORIGIN Latin *deciduus* falling off

decilitre *or US* **deciliter** *n* a measure of volume equivalent to one tenth of a litre

decimal *n* **1** a fraction written in the form of a dot followed by one or more numbers, for example .2 = $^2/_{10}$ ▷ *adj* **2** relating to or using powers of ten **3** expressed as a decimal
WORD ORIGIN Latin *decima* a tenth

decimal currency *n* a system of currency in which the units are parts or powers of ten

decimalize *or* **-ise** *vb* **-izing, -ized** *or* **-ising, -ised** to change (a system or number) to the decimal system **decimalization** *or* **-isation** *n*

decimal point *n* the dot between the unit and the fraction of a number in the decimal system

decimal system *n* a number system with a base of ten, in which numbers are expressed by combinations of the digits 0 to 9

decimate *vb* **-mating, -mated** to destroy or kill a large proportion of **decimation** *n*
WORD ORIGIN Latin *decimare*

USAGE
You would talk about the whole of something being *decimated*, not a part: *disease decimated the population*, not *disease decimated most of the population*.

decimetre *or US* **decimeter** *n* a unit of length equal to one tenth of a metre

decipher *vb* **1** to make out the meaning of (something obscure or illegible) **2** to convert from code into plain text **decipherable** *adj*

decision *n* **1** a choice or judgment made about something **2** the act of making up one's mind **3** the ability to make quick and definite decisions
WORD ORIGIN Latin *decisio* a cutting off

decisive *adj* **1** having great influence on the result of something: *the decisive goal was scored in the closing minutes* **2** having the ability to make quick decisions **decisively** *adv* **decisiveness** *n*

deck *n* **1** an area of a ship that forms a floor, at any level **2** a similar area in a bus **3** same as **tape deck** **4** *US & Austral* a pack of playing cards **5** **clear the decks** *informal* to prepare for action, as by removing obstacles ▷ *vb* **6** *slang* to knock (a person) to the ground
WORD ORIGIN Middle Dutch *dec* a covering

deck chair *n* a folding chair with a wooden frame and a canvas seat

decking *n* a wooden deck or platform, esp. one in a garden for deck chairs, etc.

deckle edge *n* a rough edge on paper, often left as ornamentation **deckle-edged** *adj*
WORD ORIGIN the *deckle* is the frame that holds the pulp in paper making

deck out *vb* to make more attractive by decorating: *the village was decked out in the blue-and-white flags*

declaim *vb* **1** to speak loudly and dramatically **2** **declaim against** to protest against loudly and publicly **declamation** *n* **declamatory** *adj*
WORD ORIGIN Latin *declamare*

declaration *n* **1** a firm, emphatic statement **2** an official announcement or statement **declaratory** *adj*

declare *vb* **-claring, -clared** **1** to state firmly and forcefully **2** to announce publicly or officially: *a state of emergency has been declared* **3** to state officially that (someone or something) is as specified: *he was declared fit to play* **4** to acknowledge (dutiable goods or income) for tax purposes **5** *cards* to decide (the trump suit) by making the winning bid **6** *cricket* to bring an innings to an end before the last batsman is out **7** **declare for** *or* **against** to state one's support or opposition for something
WORD ORIGIN Latin *declarare* to make clear

declassify *vb* **-fies, -fying, -fied** to state officially that (information or a document) is no longer secret **declassification** *n*

declension *n grammar* changes in the form of nouns, pronouns, or adjectives to show case, number, and gender
WORD ORIGIN Latin *declinatio* a bending aside, hence variation

declination *n* **1** *astron* the angular distance of a star or planet north or south from the celestial equator **2** the

d

angle made by a compass needle with the direction of the geographical north pole

decline *vb* **-clining, -clined 1** to become smaller, weaker, or less important **2** to politely refuse to accept or do (something) **3** *grammar* to list the inflections of (a noun, pronoun, or adjective) ▷ *n* **4** a gradual weakening or loss
WORD ORIGIN Latin *declinare* to bend away

declivity *n, pl* **-ties** a downward slope **declivitous** *adj*
WORD ORIGIN Latin *declivitas*

declutch *vb* to disengage the clutch of a motor vehicle

decoct *vb* to extract the essence from (a substance) by boiling **decoction** *n*
WORD ORIGIN Latin *decoquere* to boil down

decode *vb* **-coding, -coded** to convert from code into ordinary language **decoder** *n*

decoke *vb* **-coking, -coked** same as **decarbonize**

décolletage (day-kol-**tahzh**) *n* a low-cut dress or neckline
WORD ORIGIN French

décolleté (day-**kol**-tay) *adj* **1** (of a woman's garment) low-cut ▷ *n* **2** a low-cut neckline
WORD ORIGIN French

decommission *vb* to dismantle or remove from service (a nuclear reactor, weapon, ship, etc. which is no longer required)

decompose *vb* **-posing, -posed 1** to rot **2** to break up or separate into constituent parts **decomposition** *n*

decompress *vb* **1** to free from pressure **2** to return (a diver) to normal atmospheric pressure **decompression** *n*

decompression sickness *n* a disorder characterized by severe pain and difficulty in breathing caused by a sudden and sustained change in atmospheric pressure

decongestant *n* a drug that relieves nasal congestion

decontaminate *vb* **-nating, -nated** to make (a place or object) safe by removing poisons, radioactivity, etc. **decontamination** *n*

decor (**day**-core) *n* a style or scheme of interior decoration and furnishings in a room or house
WORD ORIGIN French

decorate *vb* **-rating, -rated 1** to make more attractive by adding some ornament or colour **2** to paint or wallpaper **3** to confer a mark of distinction, esp. a medal, upon **decorative** *adj* **decorator** *n*
WORD ORIGIN Latin *decorare*

Decorated style *or* **architecture** *n* a 14th-century style of English architecture characterized by the ogee arch, geometrical tracery, and floral decoration

decoration *n* **1** an addition that makes something more attractive or ornate **2** the way in which a room or building is decorated **3** something, esp. a medal, conferred as a mark of honour

decorous (**deck**-or-uss) *adj* polite, calm, and sensible in behaviour
decorously *adv* **decorousness** *n*
WORD ORIGIN Latin *decorus*

decorum (dik-**core**-um) *n* polite and socially correct behaviour

decoy *n* **1** a person or thing used to lure someone into danger **2** an image of a bird or animal, used to lure game into a trap or within shooting range ▷ *vb* **3** to lure into danger by means of a decoy
WORD ORIGIN probably from Dutch *de kooi* the cage

decrease *vb* **-creasing, -creased 1** to make or become less in size, strength, or quantity ▷ *n* **2** a lessening; reduction **3** the amount by which something has been diminished **decreasing** *adj* **decreasingly** *adv*
WORD ORIGIN Latin *decrescere* to grow less

decree *n* **1** a law made by someone in authority **2** a judgment of a court ▷ *vb* **decreeing, decreed 3** to order by decree
WORD ORIGIN Latin *decretum* ordinance

decree absolute *n* the final decree in divorce proceedings, which leaves the parties free to remarry

decree nisi *n* a provisional decree in divorce proceedings, which will later be made absolute unless cause is shown why it should not
WORD ORIGIN Latin *nisi* unless

decrepit *adj* weakened or worn out by age or long use **decrepitude** *n*
WORD ORIGIN Latin *crepare* to creak

decretal *n RC Church* a papal decree
WORD ORIGIN Late Latin *decretalis*

decry *vb* **-cries, -crying, -cried** to express open disapproval of
WORD ORIGIN Old French *descrier*

decrypt *vb* **1** to decode (a message) with or without previous knowledge of its key **2** to make intelligible (a television or other signal) that has been deliberately distorted for transmission. See also **encrypt** > **decryption** *n*
WORD ORIGIN DE- + (EN)CRYPT

dedicate *vb* **-cating, -cated 1** to devote (oneself or one's time) wholly to a special purpose or cause **2** to inscribe or address (a book, piece of music, etc.) to someone as a token of affection or respect **3** to play (a record) on radio for someone as a greeting **4** to set apart for sacred uses
WORD ORIGIN Latin *dedicare* to announce

dedicated *adj* **1** devoted to a particular purpose or cause **2** *computers* designed to fulfil one function

dedication *n* **1** wholehearted devotion **2** an inscription in a book dedicating it to a person

deduce *vb* **-ducing, -duced** to reach (a conclusion) by reasoning from evidence; work out **deducible** *adj*
WORD ORIGIN Latin *de-* away + *ducere* to lead

deduct *vb* to subtract (a number, quantity, or part)
WORD ORIGIN Latin *deducere* to deduce

deductible *adj* **1** capable of being deducted **2** *US* tax-deductible

deduction *n* **1** the act or process of subtracting **2** something that is deducted **3** *logic* **a** a process of

reasoning by which a conclusion necessarily follows from a set of general premises **b** a conclusion reached by this process **deductive** *adj*

deed *n* **1** something that is done **2** a notable achievement **3** action as opposed to words **4** *law* a legal document, esp. one concerning the ownership of property
WORD ORIGIN Old English *dēd*

deed box *n* a strong box in which deeds and other documents are kept

deed poll *n law* a deed made by one party only, esp. to change one's name

deejay *n informal* a disc jockey
WORD ORIGIN from the initials DJ

deem *vb* to judge or consider: *common sense is deemed to be a virtue*
WORD ORIGIN Old English *dēman*

deep *adj* **1** extending or situated far down from a surface: *a deep ditch* **2** extending or situated far inwards, backwards, or sideways **3** of a specified dimension downwards, inwards, or backwards: *six metres deep* **4** coming from or penetrating to a great depth **5** difficult to understand **6** of great intensity: *deep doubts* **7** **deep in** totally absorbed in: *deep in conversation* **8** (of a colour) intense or dark **9** low in pitch: *a deep laugh* **10** **go off the deep end** *informal* to lose one's temper **11** **in deep water** *informal* in a tricky position or in trouble ▷ *n* **12** any deep place on land or under water **13** **the deep a** *poetic* the ocean **b** *cricket* the area of the field relatively far from the pitch **14** the most profound, intense, or central part: *the deep of winter* ▷ *adv* **15** late: *deep into the night* **16** profoundly or intensely: *deep down I was afraid it was all my fault* **deeply** *adv*
WORD ORIGIN Old English *dēop*

deepen *vb* to make or become deeper or more intense

deep-freeze *n* **1** same as **freezer** ▷ *vb* **-freezing, -froze, -frozen 2** to freeze or keep in a deep-freeze

deep-fry *vb* **-fries, -frying, -fried** to cook in hot oil deep enough to completely cover the food

deep-laid *adj* (of a plan) carefully worked out and kept secret

deep-rooted *or* **deep-seated** *adj* (of ideas, beliefs, etc.) firmly fixed or held

deep-vein thrombosis *n* a blood clot in one of the major veins, usually in the legs or pelvis

deer *n, pl* **deer** *or* **deers** a large hoofed mammal
WORD ORIGIN Old English *dēor* beast

deerstalker *n* a cloth hat with peaks at the front and back and earflaps

de-escalate *vb* to reduce the intensity of (a problem or situation) **de-escalation** *n*

def *adj* **deffer, deffest** *slang* very good
WORD ORIGIN perhaps from *definitive*

deface *vb* **-facing, -faced** to deliberately spoil the surface or appearance of **defacement** *n*

de facto *adv* **1** in fact ▷ *adj* **2** existing in fact, whether legally recognized or not
WORD ORIGIN Latin

Words from Literature
part 9

discover *v* to make known or announce
the Emperor would discover the secret while
I was out of his power
Gulliver's Travels Jonathan Swift

dissemble *v* to hide or conceal
dissemble nothing
On His Mistress John Donne

dissolve *v* to dissolve here means to release from
life, to die
Fade far away, dissolve, and quite forget
Ode on a Nightingale John Keats

distrain *v* to distrain is to seize the property of
someone who is in debt in compensation for the
money owed
for he's threatening to distrain for it
Silas Marner George Eliot

Divan *n* a Divan was originally a Turkish council
of state – the name was transferred to the couches
they sat on and is used to mean this in English
Mr Brass applauded this picture very much,
and the bed being soft and comfortable,
Mr Quilp determined to use it, both as a sleeping
place by night and as a kind of Divan by day.
The Old Curiosity Shop Charles Dickens

divorcement *n* separation
By all pains which want and divorcement hath
On His Mistress John Donne

dog in the manger, a *phrase* this phrase describes
someone who prevents you from enjoying something
that they themselves have no need for
You are a dog in the manger, Cathy, and desire
no one to be loved but yourself
Wuthering Heights Emily Brontë

dolorifuge *n* dolorifuge is a word which Thomas
Hardy invented. It means pain-killer or comfort
as a species of dolorifuge
Tess of the D'Urbervilles Thomas Hardy

dome *n* building
that river and that mouldering dome
The Prelude William Wordsworth

domestic *n* here domestic means a person's
management of the house
to give some account of my domestic
Gulliver's Travels Jonathan Swift

dunce *n* a dunce is another word for idiot
Do you take me for a dunce? Go on?
Alice's Adventures in Wonderland Lewis Carroll

ecod *int* a slang exclamation meaning "oh God!"
"Ecod," replied Wemmick, shaking his head,
"that's not my trade."
Great Expectations Charles Dickens

egg-hot *n* an egg-hot (see also 'flip' and 'negus')
was a hot drink made from beer and eggs, sweetened
with nutmeg
She fainted when she saw me return, and made a
little jug of egg-hot afterwards to console us while
we talked it over.
David Copperfield Charles Dickens

encore *n* an encore is a short extra performance at
the end of a longer one, which the entertainer gives
because the audience has enthusiastically asked for it
we want a little something to answer encores
with, anyway
The Adventures of Huckleberry Finn Mark Twain

equipage *n* an elegant and impressive carriage
and besides, the equipage did not answer to any
of their neighbours
Pride and Prejudice Jane Austen

exordium *n* an exordium is the opening part of a speech
"Now, Handel," as if it were the grave beginning of
a portentous business exordium, he had suddenly
given up that tone
Great Expectations Charles Dickens

expect *v* to wait for
to expect his farther commands
Gulliver's Travels Jonathan Swift

defalcate *vb* **-cating, -cated** *law* to make wrong use of funds entrusted to one **defalcation** *n*
WORD ORIGIN Medieval Latin *defalcare* to cut off

defame *vb* **-faming, -famed** to attack the good reputation of **defamation** *n* **defamatory** (dif-**fam**-a-tree) *adj*
WORD ORIGIN Latin *diffamare* to spread by unfavourable report

default *n* **1** a failure to do something, esp. to meet a financial obligation or to appear in court **2** *computers* an instruction to a computer to select a particular option unless the user specifies otherwise **3 by default** happening because something else has not happened: *they gained a colony by default because no other European power wanted it* **4 in default of** in the absence of ▷ *vb* **5** to fail to fulfil an obligation, esp. to make payment when due **defaulter** *n*
WORD ORIGIN Old French *defaillir* to fail

defeat *vb* **1** to win a victory over **2** to thwart or frustrate: *this accident has defeated all his hopes of winning* ▷ *n* **3** the act of defeating or state of being defeated
WORD ORIGIN Old French *desfaire* to undo, ruin

defeatism *n* a ready acceptance or expectation of defeat **defeatist** *n, adj*

defecate *vb* **-cating, -cated** to discharge waste from the body through the anus **defecation** *n*
WORD ORIGIN Latin *defaecare*

defect *n* **1** an imperfection or blemish ▷ *vb* **2** to desert one's country or cause to join the opposing forces **defection** *n* **defector** *n*
WORD ORIGIN Latin *deficere* to forsake, fail

defective *adj* imperfect or faulty: *defective hearing*

defence *or US* **defense** *n* **1** resistance against attack **2** something that provides such resistance **3** an argument or piece of writing in support of something that has been criticized or questioned **4** a country's military resources **5** *law* a defendant's denial of the truth of a charge **6** *law* the defendant and his or her legal advisers collectively **7** *sport* the players in a team whose function is to prevent the opposing team from scoring **8** **defences** fortifications **defenceless** *or US* **defenseless** *adj*
WORD ORIGIN Latin *defendere* to defend

defend *vb* **1** to protect from harm or danger **2** to support in the face of criticism: *I spoke up to defend her* **3** to represent (a defendant) in court **4** to protect (a title or championship) against a challenge **defender** *n*
WORD ORIGIN Latin *defendere* to ward off

defendant *n* a person accused of a crime

defensible *adj* capable of being defended because believed to be right **defensibility** *n*

defensive *adj* **1** intended for defence **2** guarding against criticism or exposure of one's failings: *he can be highly defensive and wary* ▷ *n* **3 on the defensive** in a position of defence, as in being ready to reject criticism **defensively** *adv*

defer¹ *vb* **-ferring, -ferred** to delay until a future time; postpone: *payment was deferred indefinitely* **deferment** *or* **deferral** *n*
WORD ORIGIN Old French *differer* to be different, postpone

defer² *vb* **-ferring, -ferred** ● **defer to** to comply with the wishes (of)
WORD ORIGIN Latin *deferre* to bear down

deference *n* polite and respectful behaviour

deferential *adj* showing respect **deferentially** *adv*

defiance *n* open resistance to authority or opposition **defiant** *adj*

defibrillator *n med* an apparatus for stopping fibrillation of the heart by application of an electric current

deficiency *n, pl* **-cies 1** the state of being deficient **2** a lack or shortage

deficiency disease *n* any condition, such as scurvy, caused by a lack of vitamins or other essential substances

deficient *adj* **1** lacking something essential **2** inadequate in quantity or quality
WORD ORIGIN Latin *deficere* to fall short

deficit *n* the amount by which a sum is lower than that expected or required
WORD ORIGIN Latin: there is lacking

defile¹ *vb* **-filing, -filed 1** to make foul or dirty **2** to make unfit for ceremonial use **defilement** *n*
WORD ORIGIN Old French *defouler* to trample underfoot, abuse

defile² *n* a narrow pass or gorge: *the sandy defile of Wadi Rum*
WORD ORIGIN French *défiler* to file off

define *vb* **-fining, -fined 1** to describe the nature of **2** to state precisely the meaning of **3** to show clearly the outline of: *the picture was sharp and cleanly defined* **4** to fix with precision; specify: *define one's duties* **definable** *adj*
WORD ORIGIN Latin *definire* to set bounds to

definite *adj* **1** firm, clear, and precise: *I have very definite views on this subject* **2** having precise limits or boundaries **3** known for certain: *it's definite that they have won* **definitely** *adv*
WORD ORIGIN Latin *definitus* limited, distinct

definite article *n grammar* the word 'the'

definition *n* **1** a statement of the meaning of a word or phrase **2** a description of the essential qualities of something **3** the quality of being clear and distinct **4** sharpness of outline

definitive *adj* **1** final and unable to be questioned or altered: *a definitive verdict* **2** most complete, or the best of its kind: *the book was hailed as the definitive Dickens biography* **definitively** *adv*

deflate *vb* **-flating, -flated 1** to collapse or cause to collapse through the release of gas **2** to take away the self-esteem or conceit from **3** to cause deflation of (an economy)
WORD ORIGIN DE- + (IN)FLATE

deflation *n* **1** *econ* a reduction in economic activity resulting in lower levels of output and investment **2** a feeling of sadness following excitement **deflationary** *adj*

deflect *vb* to turn or cause to turn aside from a course **deflection** *n* **deflector** *n*
WORD ORIGIN Latin *deflectere*

deflower *vb literary* to deprive (a woman) of her virginity

defoliate *vb* **-ating, -ated** to deprive (a plant) of its leaves **defoliant** *n* **defoliation** *n*
WORD ORIGIN Latin *de-* from + *folium* leaf

deforestation *n* the cutting down or destruction of forests

deform *vb* to put (something) out of shape or spoil its appearance
WORD ORIGIN Latin *de-* from + *forma* shape beauty

deformed *adj* disfigured or misshapen

deformity *n, pl* **-ties 1** *pathol* a distortion of an organ or part **2** the state of being deformed

defraud *vb* to cheat out of money, property, or a right to do something

defray *vb* to provide money to cover costs or expenses **defrayal** *n*
WORD ORIGIN Old French *deffroier* to pay expenses

defrock *vb* to deprive (a priest) of ecclesiastical status

defrost *vb* **1** to make or become free of frost or ice **2** to thaw (frozen food) by removing from a deep-freeze

deft *adj* quick and skilful in movement; dexterous **deftly** *adv* **deftness** *n*
WORD ORIGIN Middle English variant of *daft* (in the sense: gentle)

defunct *adj* no longer existing or working properly
WORD ORIGIN Latin *defungi* to discharge (one's obligations), die

defuse *or US sometimes* **defuze** *vb* **-fusing, -fused** *or* **-fuzing, -fuzed 1** to remove the fuse of (an explosive device) **2** to reduce the tension in (a difficult situation): *I said it in a bid to defuse the situation*

≡ **USAGE**
≡ Avoid confusion with **diffuse**.

defy *vb* **-fies, -fying, -fied 1** to resist openly and boldly **2** to elude in a baffling way: *his actions defy explanation* **3** *formal* to challenge (someone to do something)
WORD ORIGIN Old French *desfier*

degenerate *adj* **1** having deteriorated to a lower mental, moral, or physical level ▷ *n* **2** a degenerate person ▷ *vb* **-ating, -ated 3** to become degenerate **degeneracy** *n*
WORD ORIGIN Latin *degener* departing from its kind, ignoble

degeneration *n* **1** the process of degenerating **2** *biol* the loss of specialization or function by organisms

degenerative *adj* (of a disease or condition) getting steadily worse

degrade *vb* **-grading, -graded 1** to reduce to dishonour or disgrace **2** to reduce in status or quality **3** *chem* to decompose into atoms or smaller molecules **degradation** *n* **degrading** *adj*
WORD ORIGIN Latin *de-* from + *gradus* rank, degree

degree *n* **1** a stage in a scale of relative amount or intensity: *this task involved a greater degree of responsibility* **2** an academic award given by a university or

college on successful completion of a course **3** *grammar* any of the forms of an adjective used to indicate relative amount or intensity **4** a unit of temperature. Symbol: ° **5** a measure of angle equal to one three-hundred-and-sixtieth of the circumference of a circle. Symbol: ° **6** a unit of latitude or longitude. Symbol: ° **7 by degrees** little by little; gradually
WORD ORIGIN Latin *de-* down + *gradus* step

dehisce *vb* **-hiscing, -hisced** (of the seed capsules of some plants) to burst open spontaneously **dehiscence** *n* **dehiscent** *adj*
WORD ORIGIN Latin *dehiscere* to split open

dehumanize or **-ise** *vb* **-izing, -ized** or **-ising, -ised 1** to deprive of the qualities thought of as being best in human beings, such as kindness **2** to make (an activity) mechanical or routine **dehumanization** or **-isation** *n*

dehydrate *vb* **-drating, -drated 1** to remove water from (food) in order to preserve it **2 be dehydrated** (of a person) to become weak or ill through losing too much water from the body **dehydration** *n*

de-ice *vb* **de-icing, de-iced** to free of ice **de-icer** *n*

deify (**day**-if-fie) *vb* **-fies, -fying, -fied** to treat or worship (someone or something) as a god **deification** *n*
WORD ORIGIN Latin *deus* god + *facere* to make

deign (**dane**) *vb* to do something that one considers beneath one's dignity: *she did not deign to reply*
WORD ORIGIN Latin *dignari* to consider worthy

deindustrialization or **-sation** *n* a decline in the importance of a country's manufacturing industry

deism (**dee**-iz-zum) *n* belief in the existence of God based only on natural reason, without reference to revelation **deist** *n, adj* **deistic** *adj*

deity (**dee**-it-ee) *n, pl* **-ties 1** a god or goddess **2** the state of being divine
WORD ORIGIN Latin *deus* god

Deity *n* **the Deity** God

déjà vu (**day**-zhah **voo**) *n* a feeling of having experienced before something that is happening at the present moment
WORD ORIGIN French: already seen

dejected *adj* in low spirits; downhearted **dejectedly** *adv* **dejection** *n*
WORD ORIGIN Latin *deicere* to cast down

de jure *adv* according to law
WORD ORIGIN Latin

deke *Canad slang vb* **deking, deked 1** (in ice hockey or box lacrosse) to draw (a defending player) out of position by faking a shot or movement ▷ *n* **2** such a shot or movement
WORD ORIGIN from *decoy*

dekko *n Brit, Austral, & NZ slang* **have a dekko** have a look
WORD ORIGIN Hindi *dekhnā* to see

delay *vb* **1** to put (something) off to a later time **2** to slow up or cause to be late **3 a** to hesitate in doing something **b** to deliberately take longer than

necessary to do something ▷ *n* **4** the act of delaying **5** a period of inactivity or waiting before something happens or continues
WORD ORIGIN Old French *des-* off + *laier* to leave

delectable *adj* delightful or very attractive
WORD ORIGIN Latin *delectare* to delight

delectation *n formal* great pleasure and enjoyment

delegate *n* **1** a person chosen to represent others at a conference or meeting ▷ *vb* **-gating, -gated 2** to entrust (duties or powers) to another person **3** to appoint as a representative
WORD ORIGIN Latin *delegare* to send on a mission

delegation *n* **1** a group chosen to represent others **2** the act of delegating

delete *vb* **-leting, -leted** to remove or cross out (something printed or written) **deletion** *n*
WORD ORIGIN Latin *delere*

deleterious (del-lit-**eer**-ee-uss) *adj formal* harmful or injurious
WORD ORIGIN Greek *dēlētērios*

Delft *n* tin-glazed earthenware which originated in Delft in the Netherlands, typically with blue decoration on a white ground. Also: **delftware**

deliberate *adj* **1** carefully thought out in advance; intentional **2** careful and unhurried: *a deliberate gait* ▷ *vb* **-ating, -ated 3** to consider (something) deeply; think over **deliberately** *adv* **deliberative** *adj*
WORD ORIGIN Latin *deliberare* to consider well

deliberation *n* **1** careful consideration **2** calmness and absence of hurry **3 deliberations** formal discussions

delicacy *n, pl* **-cies 1** fine or subtle quality, construction, etc.: *delicacy of craftsmanship* **2** fragile or graceful beauty **3** something that is considered particularly nice to eat **4** frail health **5** refinement of feeling, manner, or appreciation: *the delicacy of the orchestra's playing* **6** need for careful or tactful treatment

delicate *adj* **1** fine or subtle in quality or workmanship **2** having a fragile beauty **3** (of colour, smell, or taste) pleasantly subtle **4** easily damaged; 'fragile **5** precise or sensitive in action **6** requiring tact: *a delicate matter* **7** showing consideration for the feelings of other people **delicately** *adv*
WORD ORIGIN Latin *delicatus* affording pleasure

delicatessen *n* a shop selling unusual or imported foods, often already cooked or prepared
WORD ORIGIN German *Delikatessen* delicacies

delicious *adj* **1** very appealing to taste or smell **2** extremely enjoyable **deliciously** *adv*
WORD ORIGIN Latin *deliciae* delights

delight *n* **1** extreme pleasure **2** something or someone that causes this ▷ *vb* **3** to please greatly **4 delight in** to take great pleasure in **delightful** *adj* **delightfully** *adv*
WORD ORIGIN Latin *delectare* to please

delighted *adj* greatly pleased

delimit *vb* **-iting, -ited** to mark or lay down the limits of **delimitation** *n*

delineate (dill-**lin**-ee-ate) *vb* **-ating, -ated 1** to show by drawing **2** to describe in words **delineation** *n*
WORD ORIGIN Latin *delineare* to sketch out

delinquent *n* **1** someone, esp. a young person, who breaks the law ▷ *adj* **2** repeatedly breaking the law **delinquency** *n*
WORD ORIGIN Latin *delinquens* offending

deliquesce *vb* **-quescing, -quesced** (esp. of certain salts) to dissolve in water absorbed from the air **deliquescence** *n* **deliquescent** *adj*
WORD ORIGIN Latin *deliquescere* to melt away

delirious *adj* **1** suffering from delirium **2** wildly excited and happy **deliriously** *adv*

delirium *n* **1** a state of excitement and mental confusion, often with hallucinations **2** violent excitement
WORD ORIGIN Latin: madness

delirium tremens (**trem**-enz) *n* a severe condition characterized by delirium and trembling, caused by chronic alcoholism
WORD ORIGIN New Latin: trembling delirium

deliver *vb* **1** to carry (goods or mail) to a destination **2** to hand over: *the tenants were asked to deliver up their keys* **3** to aid in the birth of (offspring) **4** to present (a lecture or speech) **5** to release or rescue (from captivity or danger) **6** to strike (a blow) suddenly **7** *informal* Also: **deliver the goods** to produce something promised **deliverance** *n*
WORD ORIGIN Latin *de-* from + *liberare* to free

delivery *n, pl* **-eries 1 a** the act of delivering goods or mail **b** something that is delivered **2** the act of giving birth to a baby **3** manner or style in public speaking: *her delivery was clear and humorous* **4** *cricket* the act or manner of bowling a ball **5** *S African* a semi-official slogan for the provision of services to previously disadvantaged communities

dell *n chiefly Brit* a small wooded hollow
WORD ORIGIN Old English

delouse *vb* **-lousing, -loused** to rid (a person or animal) of lice

Delphic *adj* obscure or ambiguous, like the ancient Greek oracle at Delphi

delphinium *n, pl* **-iums** or **-ia** a large garden plant with spikes of blue flowers
WORD ORIGIN Greek *delphis* dolphin

delta *n* **1** the fourth letter in the Greek alphabet (Δ, δ) **2** the flat area at the mouth of some rivers where the main stream splits up into several branches

delude *vb* **-luding, -luded** to make someone believe something that is not true
WORD ORIGIN Latin *deludere*

deluge (**del**-lyooj) *n* **1** a great flood of water **2** torrential rain **3** an overwhelming number ▷ *vb* **-uging, -uged 4** to flood **5** to overwhelm
WORD ORIGIN Latin *diluere* to wash away

Deluge n the Deluge same as the **Flood**

delusion n **1** a mistaken idea or belief **2** the state of being deluded **delusive** adj **delusory** adj

de luxe adj rich or sumptuous; superior in quality: a de luxe hotel
WORD ORIGIN French

delve vb **delving, delved 1** to research deeply or intensively (for information) **2** old-fashioned to dig
WORD ORIGIN Old English delfan

demagnetize or **-ise** vb **-izing, -ized** or **-ising, -ised** to remove magnetic properties **demagnetization** or **-isation** n

demagogue or US sometimes **demagog** n a political agitator who attempts to win support by appealing to the prejudice and passions of the mob **demagogic** adj **demagogy** n
WORD ORIGIN Greek dēmagōgos people's leader

demand vb **1** to request forcefully **2** to require as just, urgent, etc.: the situation demands intervention **3** to claim as a right ▷ n **4** a forceful request **5** something that requires special effort or sacrifice: demands upon one's time **6** econ willingness and ability to purchase goods and services **7** in demand sought after; popular **8** on demand as soon as requested: the funds will be available on demand
WORD ORIGIN Latin demandare to commit to

demanding adj requiring a lot of skill, time, or effort: a demanding relationship

demarcation n the act of establishing limits or boundaries, esp. between the work performed by members of different trade unions
WORD ORIGIN Spanish demarcar to appoint the boundaries of

demean vb **1** to undermine the status or dignity of (someone or something) **2** demean oneself to do something unworthy of one's status or character: there is no doubt that he will lose face with the boss by having to demean himself in this way
WORD ORIGIN DE- + MEAN²

demeanour or US **demeanor** n the way a person behaves
WORD ORIGIN Old French de- (intensive) + mener to lead

demented adj mad; insane **dementedly** adv
WORD ORIGIN Late Latin dementare to drive mad

dementia (dim-**men**-sha) n a state of serious mental deterioration
WORD ORIGIN Latin: madness

demerara sugar n brown crystallized cane sugar from the West Indies
WORD ORIGIN after Demerara, a region of Guyana

demerit n **1** a fault or disadvantage **2** US & Canad a mark given against a student for failure or misconduct

demesne (dim-**mane**) n **1** land surrounding a house or manor **2** property law the possession of one's own property or land **3** a region or district; domain
WORD ORIGIN Old French demeine

Demeter n Greek myth the goddess of agriculture

demi- combining form **1** half: demirelief **2** of less than full size, status, or rank: demigod
WORD ORIGIN Latin dimidius half

demigod n **1 a** a being who is part mortal, part god **b** a lesser deity **2** a godlike person

demijohn n a large bottle with a short narrow neck, often encased in wickerwork
WORD ORIGIN probably from French dame-jeanne

demilitarize or **-rise** vb **-rizing, -rized** or **-rising, -rised** to remove all military forces from (an area): demilitarized zone **demilitarization** or **-risation** n

demimonde n **1** (esp. in the 19th century) a class of women considered to be outside respectable society because of promiscuity **2** any group considered not wholly respectable
WORD ORIGIN French: half-world

demise n **1** the eventual failure of something originally successful **2** euphemistic, formal death **3** property law a transfer of an estate by lease ▷ vb **-mising, -mised 4** property law to transfer for a limited period; lease
WORD ORIGIN Old French demis dismissed

demi-sec adj (of wines) medium-sweet

demisemiquaver n music a note with the time value of one thirty-second of a semibreve

demist vb to make or become free of condensation **demister** n

demo n, pl **-os** informal **1** short for **demonstration** (sense 1) **2** a demonstration record or tape

demob vb **-mobbing, -mobbed** Brit, Austral, & NZ informal to demobilize

demobilize or **-lise** vb **-lizing, -lized** or **-lising, -lised** to release from the armed forces **demobilization** or **-lisation** n

democracy n, pl **-cies 1** a system of government or organization in which the citizens or members choose leaders or make other important decisions by voting **2** a country in which the citizens choose their government by voting
WORD ORIGIN Greek dēmokratia

democrat n a person who believes in democracy

Democrat n US politics a member or supporter of the Democratic Party, the more liberal of the two main political parties in the US **Democratic** adj

democratic adj of or relating to a country, organization, or system in which leaders are chosen or decisions are made by voting **democratically** adv

demodulation n electronics the process by which an output wave or signal is obtained having the characteristics of the original modulating wave or signal

demography n the study of population statistics, such as births and deaths **demographic** adj
WORD ORIGIN Greek dēmos the populace + -GRAPHY

demolish vb **1** to tear down or break up (buildings) **2** to put an end to; destroy: I demolished her argument in seconds **3** facetious to eat up: he demolished the whole cake **demolisher** n **demolition** n
WORD ORIGIN Latin demoliri to throw down

demon n **1** an evil spirit **2** a person, obsession, etc. thought of as evil or persistently tormenting **3** a person extremely skilful in or devoted to a given activity: a demon at cricket **demonic** adj
WORD ORIGIN Greek daimōn spirit, fate

demonetize or **-tise** vb **-tizing, -tized** or **-tising, -tised** to withdraw from use as currency **demonetization** or **-tisation** n

demoniac or **demoniacal** adj **1** appearing to be possessed by a devil **2** suggesting inner possession or inspiration: the demoniac fire of genius **3** frantic or frenzied: demoniac activity **demoniacally** adv

demonize or **-ise** vb **-izing, -ized** or **-ising, -ised 1** to make into a demon **2** to describe as evil or guilty: America is demonized by many in France

demonolatry n the worship of demons
WORD ORIGIN demon + Greek latreia worship

demonology n the study of demons or demonic beliefs
WORD ORIGIN demon + -LOGY

demonstrable adj able to be proved **demonstrably** adv

demonstrate vb **-strating, -strated 1** to show or prove by reasoning or evidence **2** to display and explain the workings of (a machine, product, etc.) **3** to reveal the existence of: the adult literacy campaign demonstrated the scale of educational deprivation **4** to show support or opposition by public parades or rallies
WORD ORIGIN Latin demonstrare to point out

demonstration n **1** a march or public meeting to demonstrate opposition to something or support for something **2** an explanation, display, or experiment showing how something works **3** proof or evidence leading to proof

demonstrative adj **1** tending to show one's feelings freely and openly **2** grammar denoting a word used to point out the person or thing referred to, such as this and those **3** demonstrative of giving proof of **demonstratively** adv

demonstrator n **1** a person who demonstrates how a device or machine works **2** a person who takes part in a public demonstration

demoralize or **-ise** vb **-izing, -ized** or **-ising, -ised** to deprive (someone) of confidence or enthusiasm: she had been demoralized and had just given up **demoralization** or **-isation** n

demote vb **-moting, -moted** to lower in rank or position **demotion** n
WORD ORIGIN DE- + (PRO)MOTE

demotic adj of or relating to the common people
WORD ORIGIN Greek dēmotikos

demur vb **-murring, -murred 1** to show reluctance; object ▷ n **2** without demur without objecting
WORD ORIGIN Latin demorari to linger

Thomas Chandler Haliburton

I f Washington Irving was the first great exponent of American humour, it can be fairly claimed that Thomas Chandler Haliburton founded its most typical form, the tale told in a democratic idiomatic voice, a voice that Mark Twain brought to a stylistic pinnacle and on which stand-up comedians later founded their routines. Americans had used a composite dialect humour before Haliburton came along, but it was left to this British colonial to root it in a fully realized character. Haliburton was a Nova Scotia boy when British privateers attacked American shipping in the Atlantic during the War of 1812 and grew up with a fixed gaze on the new republic to the south. In his hands, Sam Slick became its emblematic figure.

Haliburton published *The Clockmaker; or The Sayings of Samuel Slick of Slickville* in three series (1836-40). In them, the local Squire Poker accompanies the Connecticut traveling salesman Sam Slick as he journeys around Nova Scotia, peddling clocks to a citizenry whom he regards as gullible, backward-looking, and lazy-minded. By the third series, Slick rather improbably becomes a US attaché to the Court of St. James. A patriot ('I guess we are the greatest nation on the face of the airth, and the most enlightened too'), Slick tells the Squire that the besetting sin of the *Blue Noses* (Nova Scotians) is false pride, 'the ruin of this country, I hope I may be skinned if it tante' (ain't). When the Squire chides Slick about the US slave trade, Slick turns the tables: 'I guess you needn't twitt [sic] me with our slave-sales, for we deal only in blacks; but blue nose approbates no distinction in colours, when reduced to poverty, is reduced to slavery, and is sold - *a White Nigger.*'

Haliburton was born in 1796 in Windsor, an Annapolis Valley town, where he got a good college education and became a successful lawyer and investor. A public-spirited bon vivant, for three years he sat in the colony's legislature; he termed the appointed executive council 'twelve dignified, deep read, pensioned old ladies, but filled with prejudices and whims like all other antiquated spinsters'. Appointed a judge, he served for 27 years. Meanwhile, in 1848, Nova Scotia had become the first British colony to achieve a government responsible to its electorate. Socially progressive in many ways, opposed to the sectarianism of his time, Haliburton used his writing skill and considerable powers of invective to oppose anything that smacked of radicalism or liberalism. He continued his Tory ways in England, where he became a Member of Parliament and was the first British colonial to be awarded an honorary doctorate by Oxford University. He died in 1865.

Each episode of *The Clockmaker* is pointed by a moral or maxim, and in fact the entire book amounts to a database of vivid proverbs like 'The bigger the house, the bigger the fools that be in it.' Haliburton, not Lewis Carroll, popularized the phrase *mad as a hatter*, and Slick is garrulously expert at *soft sawder*, flattery: Haliburton first used the term. Slick says of a 'desperate sour' innkeeper's wife: '...if she goes to act ugly, I'll give her a dose of "soft sawder," that will take the frown out of her frontispiece, and make her dial-plate as smooth as a lick of copal varnish.' Such linguistic flair may have been why the book was hugely popular on both sides of the Atlantic. It was only one of his many books, including histories, anthologies, and political pamphlets; they were often written in haste, and uneven in quality. He mined his character in *Sam Slick's Wise Saws and Modern Instances; Or, What He Said, Did, and Invented* (1853) but *The Clockmaker* remains his monument. In Sam Slick, he created a Yankee go-getter folk hero who has endured as a stereotype of the ambitious, arrogant American. Yet he also admired Americans for their enterprise and capacity for change. When the Squire says, 'Mr. Slick, like all his countrymen whom I have seen, felt that his own existence was invested in that of the Constitution of the United States' it is, allowing for exaggeration, as true now as it was then.

demure *adj* quiet, reserved, and rather shy **demurely** *adv* **demureness** *n*
WORD ORIGIN perhaps from Old French *demorer* to delay, linger

demutualize *or* **-ise** *vb* **-izing, -ized** *or* **-ising, -ised** (of a mutual savings or life-assurance organization) to convert to a public limited company **demutualization** *or* **-isation** *n*

demystify *vb* **-fies, -fying, -fied** to remove the mystery from: *he attempted to demystify the contemporary jargon of psychology* **demystification** *n*

den *n* **1** the home of a wild animal; lair **2** *chiefly US* a small secluded room in a home, often used for a hobby **3** a place where people indulge in criminal or immoral activities: *a den of iniquity*
WORD ORIGIN Old English *denn*

denarius (din-**air**-ee-uss) *n, pl* **-narii** (-**nair**-ee-eye) a silver coin of ancient Rome, often called a penny in translation
WORD ORIGIN Latin

denary (**dean**-a-ree) *adj* calculated by tens; decimal
WORD ORIGIN Latin *denarius*

denationalize *or* **-ise** *vb* **-izing, -ized** *or* **-ising, -ised** to transfer (an industry or a service) from public to private ownership **denationalization** *or* **-isation** *n*

denature *vb* **-turing, -tured** **1** to change the nature of **2** to make (alcohol) unfit to drink by adding another substance

dendrology *n* the study of trees
WORD ORIGIN Greek *dendron* tree + -LOGY

dene *or* **dean** *n chiefly Brit* a narrow wooded valley

dengue (**deng**-gee) *n* a viral disease transmitted by mosquitoes, characterized by headache, fever, pains in the joints, and a rash
WORD ORIGIN probably of African origin

denial *n* **1** a statement that something is not true **2** a rejection of a request **3** *psychol* a process by which painful thoughts are not permitted into the consciousness

denier (**den**-yer) *n* a unit of weight used to measure the fineness of silk and man-made fibres
WORD ORIGIN Old French: coin

denigrate *vb* **-grating, -grated** to criticize (someone or something) unfairly **denigration** *n* **denigrator** *n*
WORD ORIGIN Latin *denigrare* to make very black

denim *n* **1** a hard-wearing cotton fabric used for jeans, skirts, etc. **2** **denims** jeans made of denim
WORD ORIGIN French (*serge*) *de Nîmes* (serge) of Nîmes, in S France

denizen *n* **1** a person, animal, or plant that lives or grows in a particular place **2** an animal or plant established in a place to which it is not native
WORD ORIGIN Old French *denzein*

denominate *vb* **-nating, -nated** to give a specific name to; designate
WORD ORIGIN Latin *denominare*

denomination *n* **1** a group which has slightly different beliefs from other groups within the same faith **2** a unit in a system of weights, values, or measures: *coins of small denomination have been withdrawn* **3** a name given to a class or group; classification
denominational *adj*

denominator *n* the number below the line in a fraction, as 8 in ⅞

denote *vb* **-noting, -noted** **1** to be a sign or indication of: *these contracts denote movement on the widest possible scale* **2** (of a word or phrase) to have as a literal or obvious meaning **denotation** *n*
WORD ORIGIN Latin *denotare* to mark

denouement (day-**noo**-mon) *n* the final outcome or solution in a play or other work
WORD ORIGIN French

denounce *vb* **-nouncing, -nounced** **1** to condemn openly or vehemently **2** to give information against
WORD ORIGIN Latin *denuntiare* to make an official proclamation, threaten

dense *adj* **1** thickly crowded or closely packed **2** difficult to see through: *dense clouds of smoke* **3** *informal* stupid or dull **4** (of a film, book, etc.) difficult to follow or understand: *the content should be neither too dense nor too abstract* **densely** *adv*
WORD ORIGIN Latin *densus* thick

density *n, pl* **-ties** **1** the degree to which something is filled or occupied: *an average population density* **2** *physics* a measure of the compactness of a substance, expressed as its mass per unit volume **3** a measure of a physical quantity per unit of length, area, or volume

dent *n* **1** a hollow in the surface of something ▷ *vb* **2** to make a dent in
WORD ORIGIN variant of *dint*

dental *adj* of or relating to the teeth or dentistry
WORD ORIGIN Latin *dens* tooth

dental floss *n* a waxed thread used to remove particles of food from between the teeth

dental surgeon *n* same as **dentist**

dentate *adj* having teeth or toothlike notches
WORD ORIGIN Latin *dentatus*

dentifrice (**den**-tif-riss) *n* paste or powder for cleaning the teeth
WORD ORIGIN Latin *dens* tooth + *fricare* to rub

dentine (**den**-teen) *n* the hard dense tissue that forms the bulk of a tooth
WORD ORIGIN Latin *dens* tooth

dentist *n* a person qualified to practise dentistry
WORD ORIGIN French *dentiste*

dentistry *n* the branch of medicine concerned with the teeth and gums

dentition *n* the typical arrangement, type, and number of teeth in a species
WORD ORIGIN Latin *dentitio* a teething

denture *n* (*often pl*) a partial or full set of artificial teeth
WORD ORIGIN French *dent* tooth

denude *vb* **-nuding, -nuded** **1** to make bare; strip: *the atrocious weather denuded the trees* **2** *geol* to expose (rock) by the erosion of the layers above **denudation** *n*

denumerable *adj maths* countable

denunciation *n* open condemnation; denouncing
WORD ORIGIN Latin *denuntiare* to proclaim

deny *vb* **-nies, -nying, -nied** **1** to declare (a statement) to be untrue **2** to refuse to give or allow: *we have been denied permission* **3** to refuse to acknowledge: *the baron denied his wicked son*
WORD ORIGIN Latin *denegare*

deodar *n* a Himalayan cedar with drooping branches
WORD ORIGIN Hindi

deodorant *n* a substance applied to the body to prevent or disguise the odour of perspiration

deodorize *or* **-ise** *vb* **-izing, -ized** *or* **-ising, -ised** to remove or disguise the odour of **deodorization** *or* **-isation** *n*

deoxyribonucleic acid *n* same as **DNA**

depart *vb* **1** to leave **2** to differ or deviate: *to depart from the original concept*
WORD ORIGIN Old French *departir*

departed *adj euphemistic* dead

department *n* **1** a specialized division of a large business organization, hospital, university, etc. **2** a major subdivision of the administration of a government **3** an administrative division in several countries, such as France **4** *informal* a specialized sphere of activity: *wine-making is my wife's department* **departmental** *adj*
WORD ORIGIN French *département*

department store *n* a large shop divided into departments selling many kinds of goods

departure *n* **1** the act of departing **2** a divergence from previous custom, rule, etc. **3** a course of action or venture: *the album represents a new departure for them*

depend *vb* **depend on a** to put trust (in); rely (on) **b** to be influenced or determined (by): *the answer depends on four main issues* **c** to rely (on) for income or support
WORD ORIGIN Latin *dependere* to hang from

dependable *adj* reliable and trustworthy **dependability** *n* **dependably** *adv*

dependant *n* a person who depends on another for financial support
≡ USAGE
≡ Avoid confusion with **dependent**.

dependence *n* **1** the state of relying on something in order to be able to survive or operate properly **2** reliance or trust: *they had a bond between them of mutual dependence and trust*

dependency *n, pl* **-cies** **1** a territory subject to a state on which it does not border **2** *psychol* overreliance on another person or on a drug

dependent *adj* **1** depending on a person or thing for aid or support **2** **dependent on** *or* **upon** influenced or conditioned by
≡ USAGE
≡ Avoid confusion with **dependant**.

depict *vb* **1** to represent by drawing, painting, etc. **2** to describe in words **depiction** *n*
WORD ORIGIN Latin *depingere*

depilatory (dip-**pill**-a-tree) *adj* **1** able or serving to remove hair ▷ *n, pl* **-ries** **2** a chemical used to remove hair
WORD ORIGIN Latin *depilare* to pull out the hair

deplete vb -pleting, -pleted **1** to use up (supplies or money) **2** to reduce in number **depletion** n
WORD ORIGIN Latin *deplere* to empty out

deplorable adj very bad or unpleasant **deplorably** adv

deplore vb -ploring, -plored to express or feel strong disapproval of
WORD ORIGIN Latin *deplorare* to weep bitterly

deploy vb to organize (troops or resources) into a position ready for immediate and effective action **deployment** n
WORD ORIGIN Latin *displicare* to unfold

deponent n law a person who makes a statement on oath
WORD ORIGIN Latin *deponens* putting down

depopulate vb -lating, -lated to cause to be reduced in population **depopulation** n

deport vb **1** to remove forcibly from a country **2 deport oneself** to behave in a specified manner
WORD ORIGIN Latin *deportare* to carry away, banish

deportation n the act of expelling someone from a country

deportee n a person deported or awaiting deportation

deportment n the way in which a person moves and stands: *she had the manners and deportment of a great lady*
WORD ORIGIN Old French *deporter* to conduct (oneself)

depose vb -posing, -posed **1** to remove from an office or position of power **2** law to testify on oath
WORD ORIGIN Latin *deponere* to put aside

deposit vb -iting, -ited **1** to put down **2** to entrust (money or valuables) for safekeeping **3** to place (money) in a bank account or other savings account **4** to lay down naturally: *the river deposits silt* ▷ n **5** a sum of money placed in a bank account or other savings account **6** money given in part payment for goods or services **7** an amount of a substance left on a surface as a result of a chemical or geological process
WORD ORIGIN Latin *depositus* put down

deposit account n Brit a bank account that earns interest

depositary n, pl -taries a person or group to whom something is entrusted for safety

deposition n **1** law the sworn statement of a witness used in court in his or her absence **2** the act of deposing **3** the act of depositing **4** something deposited
WORD ORIGIN Late Latin *depositio* a laying down, testimony

depositor n a person who places or has money on deposit in a bank or similar organization: *panic-stricken depositors*

depository n, pl -ries **1** a store where furniture, valuables, etc. can be kept for safety **2** same as **depositary**

depot (**dep**-oh) n **1** a place where goods and vehicles are kept when not in use **2** US, Canad, & NZ a bus or railway station
WORD ORIGIN French

depraved adj morally bad; corrupt

WORD ORIGIN Latin *depravare* to distort, corrupt

depravity n, pl -ties moral corruption

deprecate vb -cating, -cated to express disapproval of **deprecation** n **deprecatory** adj
WORD ORIGIN Latin *deprecari* to avert, ward off
⌁ **USAGE**
⌁ Avoid confusion with **depreciate**.

depreciate vb -ating, -ated **1** to decline in value or price **2** to deride or criticize **depreciatory** adj
WORD ORIGIN Latin *de-* down + *pretium* price
⌁ **USAGE**
⌁ Avoid confusion with **deprecate**.

depreciation n **1** accounting the reduction in value of a fixed asset through use, obsolescence, etc. **2** a decrease in the exchange value of a currency **3** the act or an instance of belittling

depredation n plundering; pillage
WORD ORIGIN Latin *depraedare* to pillage

depress vb **1** to make sad and gloomy **2** to lower (prices) **3** to push down **depressing** adj **depressingly** adv
WORD ORIGIN Old French *depresser*

depressant adj **1** med able to reduce nervous or functional activity; sedative ▷ n **2** a depressant drug

depressed adj **1** low in spirits; downcast **2** suffering from economic hardship, such as unemployment: *the current depressed conditions* **3** pressed down or flattened

depression n **1** a mental state in which a person has feelings of gloom and inadequacy **2** an economic condition in which there is substantial unemployment, low output and low investment; slump **3** meteorol a mass of air below normal atmospheric pressure, which often causes rain **4** a sunken place

Depression n **the Depression** the worldwide economic depression of the early 1930s

depressive adj causing sadness and lack of energy

deprive vb -priving, -prived ● **deprive of** to prevent from having or enjoying **deprivation** n
WORD ORIGIN Latin *de-* from + *privare* to deprive of

deprived adj lacking adequate living conditions, education, etc.: *deprived ghettos*

dept department

depth n **1** the distance downwards, backwards, or inwards **2** intensity of emotion or feeling **3** the quality of having a high degree of knowledge, insight, and understanding **4** intensity of colour **5** lowness of pitch **6 depths a** a remote inaccessible region: *the depths of the forest* **b** the most severe part: *the depths of depression* **c** a low moral state **7 out of one's depth a** in water deeper than one is tall **b** beyond the range of one's competence or understanding
WORD ORIGIN Middle English *dep* deep

depth charge n a bomb used to attack submarines that explodes at a preset depth of water

deputation n a body of people appointed to represent others

depute vb -puting, -puted to appoint (someone) to act on one's behalf
WORD ORIGIN Late Latin *deputare* to assign, allot

deputize or -**tise** vb -tizing, -tized or -tising, -tised (usually foll. by *for*) to act as deputy

deputy n, pl -ties a person appointed to act on behalf of another
WORD ORIGIN Old French *deputer* to appoint

derail vb to cause (a train or tram) to go off the rails **derailment** n

derailleur (dee-**rail**-yer) n a type of gear-change mechanism for bicycles

deranged adj **1** mad, or behaving in a wild and uncontrolled way **2** in a state of disorder **derangement** n
WORD ORIGIN from Old French *desrengier* to disorder, disturb

derby n, pl -bies US & Canad a bowler hat

Derby n, pl -bies **1 the Derby** an annual horse race for three-year-olds, run at Epsom Downs, Surrey **2 local derby** a sporting event between teams from the same area
WORD ORIGIN after the Earl of *Derby*, who founded the race in 1780

deregulate vb -lating, -lated to remove regulations or controls from **deregulation** n

derelict adj **1** abandoned or unused and falling into ruins ▷ n **2** a social outcast or vagrant
WORD ORIGIN Latin *derelinquere* to abandon

dereliction n **1** the state of being abandoned **2 dereliction of duty** wilful neglect of one's duty

derestrict vb Brit, Austral, & NZ to make (a road) free from speed limits **derestriction** n

deride vb -riding, -rided to speak of or treat with contempt or ridicule **derision** n
WORD ORIGIN Latin *deridere* to laugh to scorn

de rigueur (de rig-**gur**) adj required by fashion
WORD ORIGIN French, literally: of strictness

derisive adj mocking or scornful **derisively** adv

derisory adj too small or inadequate to be considered seriously: *the shareholders have dismissed the offer as derisory*

derivation n the origin or descent of something, such as a word

derivative adj **1** based on other sources; not original ▷ n **2** a word, idea, etc. that is derived from another **3** maths the rate of change of one quantity with respect to another

derive vb -riving, -rived to draw or be drawn (from) in source or origin
WORD ORIGIN Old French *deriver* to spring from

dermatitis n inflammation of the skin
WORD ORIGIN Greek *derma* skin

dermatology n the branch of medicine concerned with the skin **dermatologist** n
WORD ORIGIN Greek *derma* skin + -LOGY

d

d

derogate *vb* -gating, -gated ● derogate from to cause to seem inferior; detract from **derogation** *n*
WORD ORIGIN Latin *derogare* to diminish

derogatory (dir-**rog**-a-tree) *adj* expressing or showing a low opinion of someone or something

derrick *n* **1** a simple crane that has lifting tackle slung from a boom **2** the framework erected over an oil well to enable drill tubes to be raised and lowered
WORD ORIGIN after *Derrick*, famous hangman

derring-do *n archaic or literary* a daring spirit or deed
WORD ORIGIN Middle English *durring don* daring to do

derv *n Brit* diesel oil, when used for road transport
WORD ORIGIN d(iesel) e(ngine) r(oad) v(ehicle)

dervish *n* a member of a Muslim religious order noted for a frenzied, ecstatic, whirling dance
WORD ORIGIN Persian *darvīsh* mendicant monk

desalination *n* the process of removing salt, esp. from sea water

descale *vb* to remove the hard coating which sometimes forms inside kettles, pipes, etc.

descant *n* **1** a tune played or sung above a basic melody ▷ *adj* **2** of the highest member in a family of musical instruments: *a descant clarinet*
WORD ORIGIN Latin *dis-* apart + *cantus* song

descend *vb* **1** to move down (a slope, staircase, etc.) **2** to move or fall to a lower level, pitch, etc. **3** be descended from to be connected by a blood relationship to **4** descend on to visit unexpectedly **5** descend to to stoop to (unworthy behaviour)
WORD ORIGIN Latin *descendere*

descendant *n* a person or animal descended from an individual, race, or species

descendent *adj* descending

descent *n* **1** the act of descending **2** a downward slope **3** a path or way leading downwards **4** derivation from an ancestor; family origin **5** a decline or degeneration

describe *vb* -scribing, -scribed **1** to give an account of (something or someone) in words **2** to trace the outline of (a circle, etc.)
WORD ORIGIN Latin *describere* to copy off, write out

description *n* **1** a statement or account that describes someone or something **2** the act of describing **3** sort, kind, or variety: *antiques of every description*

descriptive *adj* describing something: *it was a very descriptive account of the play* **descriptively** *adv*

descry *vb* -scries, -scrying, -scried **1** to catch sight of **2** to discover by looking carefully
WORD ORIGIN Old French *descrier* to proclaim

desecrate *vb* -crating, -crated to violate the sacred character of (an object or place) **desecration** *n*
WORD ORIGIN DE- + (CON)SECRATE

desegregate *vb* -gating, -gated to end racial segregation in (a school or other public institution) **desegregation** *n*

deselect *vb* **1** *computers* to cancel (a highlighted selection of data) on a computer screen **2** *Brit politics* (of a constituency organization) to refuse to select (an MP) for re-election **deselection** *n*

desensitize or **-tise** *vb* -tizing, -tized or -tising, -tised to make insensitive or less sensitive: *the patient was desensitized to the allergen; to desensitize photographic film*

desert[1] *n* a region that has little or no vegetation because of low rainfall
WORD ORIGIN Church Latin *desertum*

desert[2] *vb* **1** to abandon (a person or place) without intending to return **2** *chiefly mil* to leave (a post or duty) with no intention of returning **deserted** *adj* **deserter** *n* **desertion** *n*
WORD ORIGIN Latin *deserere*

desertification *n* a process by which fertile land turns into desert

desert island *n* a small uninhabited island in the tropics

deserts *pl n* get one's just deserts get the punishment one deserves
WORD ORIGIN Old French *deserte* something deserved

deserve *vb* -serving, -served to be entitled to or worthy of
WORD ORIGIN Latin *deservire* to serve devotedly

deserved *adj* rightfully earned **deservedly** (diz-**zerv**-id-lee) *adv*

deserving *adj* worthy of a reward, help, or praise

deshabille (day-zab-**beel**) or **dishabille** *n* the state of being partly dressed
WORD ORIGIN French *déshabillé*

desi *Indian English adj* **1** indigenous or local ▷ *n* **2** *informal* a person considered to be of South Asian origin
WORD ORIGIN Hindi

desiccate *vb* -cating, -cated to remove most of the water from; dry **desiccated** *adj* **desiccation** *n*
WORD ORIGIN Latin *desiccare* to dry up

design *vb* **1** to work out the structure or form of (something), by making a sketch or plans **2** to plan and make (something) artistically **3** to intend (something) for a specific purpose: *the move is designed to reduce travelling costs* ▷ *n* **4** a sketch, plan, or preliminary drawing **5** the arrangement or features of an artistic or decorative work: *he built it to his own design* **6** a finished artistic or decorative creation **7** the art of designing **8** an intention; purpose **9** have designs on to plot to gain possession of
WORD ORIGIN Latin *designare* to mark out, describe

designate (**dez**-zig-nate) *vb* -nating, -nated **1** to give a name to or describe as: *vessels sunk during battle are designated as war graves* **2** to select (someone) for an office or duty; appoint ▷ *adj* **3** appointed, but not yet in office: *a Prime Minister designate*
WORD ORIGIN Latin *designatus* marked out

designated driver *n* a person who volunteers not to drink alcohol at a social event, in order to drive people who have been drinking

designation *n* **1** something that designates, such as a name **2** the act of designating

designedly (dee-**zine**-id-lee) *adv* by intention

designer *n* **1** a person who draws up original sketches or plans from which things are made ▷ *adj* **2** designed by a well-known fashion designer: *a wardrobe full of designer clothes* **3** having an appearance of fashionable trendiness: *designer stubble*

designing *adj* cunning and scheming

desirable *adj* **1** worth having or doing: *a desirable lifestyle* **2** arousing sexual desire **desirability** *n* **desirably** *adv*

desire *vb* -siring, -sired **1** to want very much **2** *formal* to request: *we desire your company at the wedding of our daughter* ▷ *n* **3** a wish or longing **4** sexual appetite **5** a person or thing that is desired
WORD ORIGIN Latin *desiderare*

desirous *adj* (usually foll. by *of*) having a desire for: *deeply desirous of regaining the leadership*

desist *vb* to stop doing: *please desist from talking*
WORD ORIGIN Latin *desistere*

desk *n* **1** a piece of furniture with a writing surface and usually drawers **2** a service counter in a public building, such as a hotel **3** the section of a newspaper or television station responsible for a particular subject: *the picture desk*
WORD ORIGIN Medieval Latin *desca* table

deskill *vb* **1** to mechanize or computerize (a job) thereby reducing the skill required to do it **2** to deprive (employees) of the opportunity to use their skills **deskilling** *n*

desktop *n* **1** the main screen display on a personal computer ▷ *adj* **2** (esp. of a computer system) for use at a desk

desktop publishing *n* a computer system which combines text and graphics and presents them in a professional-looking printed format

desolate *adj* **1** uninhabited and bleak **2** made uninhabitable; devastated **3** without friends, hope, or encouragement **4** gloomy or dismal; depressing ▷ *vb* -lating, -lated **5** to deprive of inhabitants **6** to make barren; devastate **7** to make wretched or forlorn **desolately** *adv* **desolateness** *n*
WORD ORIGIN Latin *desolare* to leave alone

desolation *n* **1** ruin or devastation **2** solitary misery; wretchedness

despair *n* **1** total loss of hope ▷ *vb* **2** to lose or give up hope: *we must not despair of finding a peaceful solution*
WORD ORIGIN Old French *despoir* hopelessness

despatch *vb, n* same as **dispatch**

desperado *n, pl* -does or -dos a reckless person ready to commit any violent illegal act
WORD ORIGIN probably pseudo-Spanish

Tolkien –
The Alternative Modernism

There would seem to be nothing 'modernist' about the epic-length fantasy *The Lord of the Rings* or its author. *LOTR* has a unified plot and a linear narrative presented in chronological order, while modernists preferred multiple, fragmented points-of-view, and jarring transitions between narrative time periods. Also, Fantasy by nature often takes an imaginary or mythical past as its setting or subject, whereas the High Modernists took contemporary reality, or even the imagined future, as their subject. But John Ranald Reuel Tolkein also fought in the First World War, the cataclysm that kicked off Modernism, and he was a contemporary of the greatest Modernist authors, Joyce among them. So could *Lord of the Rings* have anything in common with *Ulysses*?

Modernism's most characteristic feature is a fragmented point-of-view. Apart from its 'main' text (the named and numbered chapters), *The Lord of the Rings* includes a substantial prologue and six appendices, each of which exist within the imagined world of Middle Earth. Though the main chapters would appear to be a unified novel (especially if one ignores Tolkien's footnotes), the additional materials provide a kind of 'frame narrative', suggesting the novel is actually a translation of *The Red Book of Westmarch*, a fictional manuscript written largely by the hobbits, with contributions from other characters. A 'frame narrative' is not exclusively 'modernist'; in fact, it was popular in the Middle Ages (it features in Chaucer's *Canterbury Tales* and Boccaccio's *Decameron*), which is certainly where Tolkien encountered it. However, the frame narrative allows Tolkien to achieve a subtle fragmentation of perspective in *Lord of the Rings*.

The novel opens in an ordinary story-telling mode: 'When Mr. Bilbo Baggins of Bag End announced that he would shortly be celebrating his eleventy-first birthday with a party of special magnificence, there was much talk and excitement in Hobbiton.' The most noticeable thing about this sentence is the word *eleventy-first*, which has a comic, rather than an epic effect on the text.

Frodo is present at all the events in *The Fellowship of the Ring*, and can be taken to be the main 'author' of these chapters. As hobbits are not 'epic' heroes, Frodo's sentences are personal, impressionistic and relatively short, even at sombre times: 'The Company of the Ring stood silent beside the tomb of Balin. Frodo thought of Bilbo and his long friendship with the dwarf, and of Balin's visit to the Shire long ago. In that dusty chamber in the mountains it seemed a thousand years ago and on the other side of the world.' Also, his word order is consistent with Twentieth-Century English.

Several chapters in *The Two Towers* involve no hobbits at all, but only Gimli, Legolas, and Aragorn – the likeliest 'author' of these segments. Aragorn is a traditional 'epic' hero, and is partial to long, periodic sentences, frequent use of the colon and semi-colon, and archaic vocabulary that are not common in the 'hobbit' chapters:

At last as the afternoon was waning they came to the eaves of the forest, and in an open glade among the first trees they found the place of the great burning: the ashes were still hot and smoking. Beside it was a great pile of helms and mail, cloven shields, and broken swords, bows and darts and other gear of war. Upon a stake in the middle was set a goblin head; upon its shattered helm the white badge could still be seen.

In this archaic passage, predicates precede subjects and adverbial phrases precede their objects. It evokes the 'epic' language found in ancient poetry. This heightened language disappears, however, when we rejoin Frodo and Sam, or Merry and Pippin. Though it is not the novel's most striking feature, the subtle variation of tone betrays what Tolkien would have us believe is a variety of sources and authors underlying the apparently unified whole. Though he almost certainly derived it from his vast knowledge of medieval literature, the effect is nearly the same as of a modernist text: knowledge is internalized and dependent upon discernible, individual points of view which, though they can be organized into a unified, authoritative whole, still show their sutures.

desperate *adj* **1** willing to do anything to improve one's situation **2** (of an action) undertaken as a last resort **3** very grave: *in desperate agony* **4** having a great need or desire: *I was desperate for a child* **desperately** *adv*
WORD ORIGIN Latin *desperare* to have no hope

desperation *n* **1** desperate recklessness **2** the state of being desperate

despicable *adj* deserving contempt **despicably** *adv*

despise *vb* **-pising, -pised** to look down on with contempt
WORD ORIGIN Latin *despicere* to look down

despite *prep* in spite of
WORD ORIGIN Old French *despit*

despoil *vb formal* to plunder **despoliation** *n*
WORD ORIGIN Latin *despoliare*

despondent *adj* dejected or depressed **despondency** *n* **despondently** *adv*
WORD ORIGIN Latin *despondere* to lose heart

despot *n* any person in power who acts tyrannically **despotic** *adj* **despotically** *adv*
WORD ORIGIN Greek *despotēs* lord, master

despotism *n* **1** absolute or tyrannical government **2** tyrannical behaviour

dessert *n* the sweet course served at the end of a meal
WORD ORIGIN French

dessertspoon *n* a spoon between a tablespoon and a teaspoon in size

destination *n* the place to which someone or something is going

destined (**dess**-tinnd) *adj* **1** certain to be or do something: *the school is destined to close this summer* **2** heading towards a specific destination: *some of the oil was destined for Eastern Europe*
WORD ORIGIN Latin *destinare* to appoint

destiny *n, pl* **-nies** **1** the future destined for a person or thing **2** the predetermined course of events **3** the power that predetermines the course of events
WORD ORIGIN Old French *destinee*

destitute *adj* lacking the means to live; totally impoverished **destitution** *n*
WORD ORIGIN Latin *destituere* to leave alone

de-stress *vb* to become or cause to become less stressed or anxious

destroy *vb* **1** to ruin; demolish **2** to put an end to **3** to kill (an animal) **4** to crush or defeat
WORD ORIGIN Latin *destruere* to pull down

destroyer *n* **1** a small heavily armed warship **2** a person or thing that destroys

destructible *adj* capable of being destroyed

destruction *n* **1** the act of destroying something or state of being destroyed **2** a cause of ruin
WORD ORIGIN Latin *destructio* a pulling down

destructive *adj* **1** causing or capable of causing harm, damage, or injury **2** intended to discredit, esp. without positive suggestions or help: *destructive speeches against the platform* **destructively** *adv*

desuetude (diss-**syoo**-it-tude) *n formal* the condition of not being in use
WORD ORIGIN Latin *desuescere* to lay aside a habit

desultory (**dez**-zl-tree) *adj* **1** passing or jumping from one thing to another; disconnected: *desultory conversation* **2** occurring in a random way: *a desultory thought* **desultorily** *adv*
WORD ORIGIN Latin *de-* from + *salire* to jump

detach *vb* **1** to disengage and separate **2** *mil* to send (a regiment, officer, etc.) on a special assignment **detachable** *adj*
WORD ORIGIN Old French *destachier*

detached *adj* **1** *Brit, Austral, & S African* separate or standing apart: *a detached farmhouse* **2** showing no emotional involvement: *she continued to watch him in her grave and detached manner*

detachment *n* **1** the state of not being personally involved in something **2** *mil* a small group of soldiers separated from the main group

detail *n* **1** an item that is considered separately **2** an item considered to be unimportant: *a mere detail* **3** treatment of individual parts: *the census provides a considerable amount of detail* **4** a small section of a work of art often enlarged to make the smaller features more distinct **5** *chiefly mil* **a** personnel assigned a specific duty **b** the duty **6** **in detail** including all the important particulars ▷ *vb* **7** to list fully **8** *chiefly mil* to select (personnel) for a specific duty
WORD ORIGIN Old French *detailler* to cut in pieces

detailed *adj* having many details

detain *vb* **1** to delay (someone) **2** to force (someone) to stay: *the police detained him for questioning* **detainee** *n* **detainment** *n*
WORD ORIGIN Latin *detinere*

detect *vb* **1** to perceive or notice: *to detect a note of sarcasm* **2** to discover the existence or presence of: *to detect alcohol in the blood* **detectable** *adj* **detector** *n*
WORD ORIGIN Latin *detegere* to uncover

detection *n* **1** the act of noticing, discovering, or sensing something **2** the act or process of extracting information

detective *n* **a** a police officer who investigates crimes **b** same as **private detective**

detente (day-**tont**) *n* the easing of tension between nations
WORD ORIGIN French

detention *n* **1** imprisonment, esp. of a suspect awaiting trial **2** a form of punishment in which a pupil is detained after school

detention centre *n* a place where young people may be detained for short periods of time by order of a court

deter *vb* **-terring, -terred** to discourage or prevent someone from doing something by instilling fear or doubt in them
WORD ORIGIN Latin *deterrere*

detergent *n* **1** a chemical substance used for washing clothes, dishes, etc. ▷ *adj* **2** having cleansing power
WORD ORIGIN Latin *detergens* wiping off

deteriorate *vb* **-rating, -rated** to become worse **deterioration** *n*
WORD ORIGIN Latin *deterior* worse

determinant *adj* **1** serving to determine or affect ▷ *n* **2** a factor that controls or influences what will happen **3** *maths* a square array of elements that represents the sum of certain products of these elements

determinate *adj* definitely limited or fixed

determination *n* **1** the condition of being determined; resoluteness **2** the act of making a decision

determine *vb* **-mining, -mined** **1** to settle (an argument or a question) conclusively **2** to find out the facts about (something): *the tests determined it was in fact cancer* **3** to fix in scope, extent, etc.: *to determine the degree of the problem* **4** to make a decision
WORD ORIGIN Latin *determinare* to set boundaries to

determined *adj* firmly decided **determinedly** *adv*

determiner *n grammar* a word, such as a number, article, or personal pronoun, that determines the meaning of a noun phrase

determinism *n* the theory that human choice is not free, but is decided by past events **determinist** *n, adj*

deterrent *n* **1** something that deters **2** a weapon or set of weapons held by one country to deter another country attacking ▷ *adj* **3** tending to deter **deterrence** *n*
WORD ORIGIN Latin *deterrens* hindering

detest *vb* to dislike intensely **detestable** *adj*
WORD ORIGIN Latin *detestari*

detestation *n* intense hatred

dethrone *vb* **-throning, -throned** to remove from a throne or deprive of any high position **dethronement** *n*

detonate *vb* **-nating, -nated** to make (an explosive device) explode or (of an explosive device) to explode **detonation** *n*
WORD ORIGIN Latin *detonare* to thunder down

detonator *n* a small amount of explosive or a device used to set off an explosion

detour *n* a deviation from a direct route or course of action
WORD ORIGIN French

detoxify *vb* **-fies, -fying, -fied** to remove poison from **detoxification** *n*

detract *vb* **detract from** to make (something) seem less good, valuable, or impressive: *I wouldn't want to detract from your triumph* **detractor** *n* **detraction** *n*
WORD ORIGIN Latin *detrahere* to pull away, disparage

USAGE
Detract is sometimes wrongly used where *distract* is meant: *a noise distracted* (not *detracted*) *my attention.*

detriment *n* disadvantage or damage **detrimental** *adj* **detrimentally** *adv*
WORD ORIGIN Latin *detrimentum* a rubbing off

detritus (dit-**trite**-uss) *n* **1** a loose mass of stones and silt worn away from rocks

2 debris **detrital** *adj*
WORD ORIGIN Latin: a rubbing away

de trop (de **troh**) *adj* unwanted or unwelcome: *I know when I'm de trop, so I'll leave you two together*
WORD ORIGIN French

detumescence *n* the subsidence of a swelling
WORD ORIGIN Latin *detumescere* to cease swelling

deuce (**dyewss**) *n* **1** *tennis* a tied score that requires one player to gain two successive points to win the game **2** a playing card or dice with two spots
WORD ORIGIN Latin *duo* two

deus ex machina *n* an unlikely development introduced into a play or film to resolve the plot

deuterium *n* a stable isotope of hydrogen. Symbol: D or ²H
WORD ORIGIN Greek *deuteros* second

deuterium oxide *n* same as **heavy water**

Deutschmark (**doytch**-mark) *or* **Deutsche Mark** (**doytch**-a) *n* a former monetary unit of Germany
WORD ORIGIN German: German mark

deutzia (**dyewt**-see-a) *n* a shrub with clusters of pink or white flowers

devalue *vb* **-valuing, -valued 1** to reduce the exchange value of (a currency) **2** to reduce the value of (something or someone) **devaluation** *n*

devastate *vb* **-tating, -tated** to damage (a place) severely or destroy it **devastation** *n*
WORD ORIGIN Latin *devastare*

devastated *adj* shocked and extremely upset **devastating** *adj* **devastatingly** *adv*

develop *vb* **1** to grow or bring to a later, more elaborate, or more advanced stage **2** to come or bring into existence: *the country has developed a consumer society* **3** to make or become gradually clearer or more widely known **4** to follow as a result of something: *Cubism developed from attempts to give painting a more intellectual concept of form* **5** to contract (an illness) **6** to improve the value or change the use of (land) **7** to exploit the natural resources of (a country or region) **8** *photog* to treat (a photographic plate or film) to produce a visible image
WORD ORIGIN Old French *desveloper* to unwrap

developer *n* **1** a person who develops property **2** *photog* a chemical used to develop photographs or films

developing country *n* a poor or nonindustrial country that is seeking to develop its resources by industrialization

development *n* **1** the process of growing or developing **2** the product of developing **3** an event or incident that changes a situation **4** an area of land that has been developed **developmental** *adj*

development area *n* (in Britain) an area which has experienced economic depression and which is given government assistance to establish new industry

deviant *adj* **1** deviating from what is considered acceptable behaviour ▷ *n* **2** a

person whose behaviour deviates from what is considered to be acceptable **deviance** *n*

deviate *vb* **-ating, -ated 1** to differ from others in belief or thought **2** to depart from one's usual or previous behaviour **deviation** *n*
WORD ORIGIN Late Latin *deviare* to turn aside from the direct road

device *n* **1** a machine or tool used for a particular purpose **2** *euphemistic* a bomb **3** a scheme or plan **4** a design or emblem **5 leave someone to his or her own devices** to leave someone alone to do as he or she wishes
WORD ORIGIN Old French *devis* contrivance + *devise* intention

devil *n* **1** *theol* **the Devil** the chief spirit of evil and enemy of God **2** any evil spirit **3** a person regarded as wicked **4** a person: *lucky devil* **5** a person regarded as daring: *be a devil!* **6** *informal* something difficult or annoying **7 between the devil and the deep blue sea** between equally undesirable alternatives **8 give the devil his due** to acknowledge the talent or success of an unpleasant person **9 talk of the devil!** used when an absent person who has been the subject of conversation arrives unexpectedly **10 the devil** used as an exclamation to show surprise or annoyance: *what the devil is she doing here?* ▷ *vb* **-villing, -villed** *or US* **-viling, -viled 11** to prepare (food) by coating with a highly flavoured spiced mixture **12** *chiefly Brit* to do routine literary work for a lawyer or author
WORD ORIGIN Greek *diabolos* enemy, accuser

devilish *adj* **1** of or like a devil; fiendish ▷ *adv, adj* **2** *informal* extreme or extremely: *devilish good food* **devilishly** *adv*

devil-may-care *adj* happy-go-lucky; reckless

devilment *n* mischievous conduct

devilry *n* **1** reckless fun or mischief **2** wickedness

devil's advocate *n* a person who takes an opposing or unpopular point of view for the sake of argument

devious *adj* **1** insincere and dishonest **2** (of a route or course of action) indirect **deviously** *adv*
WORD ORIGIN Latin *devius* lying to one side of the road

devise *vb* **-vising, -vised** to work out (something) in one's mind
WORD ORIGIN Old French *deviser* to divide

devoid *adj* **devoid of** completely lacking in a particular quality: *she was a woman totally devoid of humour*
WORD ORIGIN Old French *devoider* to remove

devolution *n* a transfer of authority from a central government to regional governments **devolutionist** *n, adj*
WORD ORIGIN Medieval Latin *devolutio* a rolling down

devolve *vb* **-volving, -volved** to pass or cause to pass to a successor or substitute, as duties or power
WORD ORIGIN Latin *devolvere* to roll down

Devon *n* a breed of large red cattle originally from Devon

Devonian *adj* **1** *geol* of the period of geological time about 405 million years ago **2** of or relating to Devon

devote *vb* **-voting, -voted** to apply or dedicate (one's time, money, or effort) to a particular purpose
WORD ORIGIN Latin *devovere* to vow

devoted *adj* feeling or demonstrating loyalty or devotion: *he was clearly devoted to his family* **devotedly** *adv*

devotee (dev-vote-**tee**) *n* **1** a person fanatically enthusiastic about a subject or activity **2** a zealous follower of a religion

devotion *n* **1** strong attachment to or affection for someone or something **2** religious zeal; piety **3 devotions** religious observance or prayers **devotional** *adj*

devour *vb* **1** to eat up greedily **2** to engulf and destroy **3** to read avidly **devouring** *adj*
WORD ORIGIN Latin *devorare* to gulp down

devout *adj* **1** deeply religious **2** sincere; heartfelt: *a devout confession* **devoutly** *adv*
WORD ORIGIN Latin *devotus* faithful

dew *n* drops of water that form on the ground or on a cool surface at night from vapour in the air **dewy** *adj*
WORD ORIGIN Old English *dēaw*

dewberry *n, pl* **-berries** a type of bramble with blue-black fruits

dewclaw *n* a nonfunctional claw on a dog's leg

Dewey Decimal System *n* a system of library book classification with ten main subject classes
WORD ORIGIN after Melvil *Dewey*, educator

dewlap *n* a loose fold of skin hanging under the throat in cattle, dogs, etc.
WORD ORIGIN Middle English *dew* + *lap* hanging flap

dew-worm *n* *US & Canad* a large earthworm used as fishing bait

dewy-eyed *adj* innocent and inexperienced

dexter *adj* of or on the right side of a shield, etc. from the bearer's point of view
WORD ORIGIN Latin

dexterity *n* **1** skill in using one's hands **2** mental quickness
WORD ORIGIN Latin *dexteritas* aptness, readiness

dexterous *adj* possessing or done with dexterity **dexterously** *adv*

dextrin *or* **dextrine** *n* a sticky substance obtained from starch: used as a thickening agent in food
WORD ORIGIN French *dextrine*

dextrose *n* a glucose occurring in fruit, honey, and in the blood of animals

DFC (in Britain) Distinguished Flying Cross

dg decigram

DH *Brit* Department of Health

dhal *or* **dal** *n* **1** the nutritious pealike seed of a tropical shrub **2** a curry made from lentils or other pulses
WORD ORIGIN Hindi *dāl*

dharma *n* **1** *Hinduism* moral law or behaviour **2** *Buddhism* ideal truth
WORD ORIGIN Sanskrit

d

dhoti *n, pl* **-tis** a long loincloth worn by men in India
WORD ORIGIN Hindi

DI *Brit* Donor Insemination: a method of making a woman pregnant by transferring sperm from a man other than her husband or regular partner using artificial means

di- *prefix* **1** twice; two; double: *dicotyledon* **2** containing two specified atoms or groups of atoms: *carbon dioxide*
WORD ORIGIN Greek

diabetes (die-a-**beet**-eez) *n* a medical condition in which the body is unable to control the level of sugar in the blood
WORD ORIGIN Greek: a passing through

diabetic *n* **1** a person who has diabetes ▷ *adj* **2** of or having diabetes **3** suitable for people suffering from diabetes: *diabetic chocolate*

diabolic *adj* of the Devil; satanic
WORD ORIGIN Greek *diabolos* devil

diabolical *adj informal* **1** unpleasant or annoying: *the weather was diabolical* **2** extreme: *diabolical cheek* **3** same as **diabolic** ▷ **diabolically** *adv*

diabolism *n* **a** witchcraft or sorcery **b** worship of devils **diabolist** *n*

diaconate *n* the position or period of office of a deacon **diaconal** *adj*
WORD ORIGIN Late Latin *diaconatus*

diacritic *n* a sign placed above or below a character or letter to indicate phonetic value or stress
WORD ORIGIN Greek *diakritikos* serving to distinguish

diadem *n old-fashioned* a small jewelled crown or headband, usually worn by royalty: *a gold diadem*
WORD ORIGIN Greek: royal headdress

diaeresis *or esp. US* **dieresis** (die-**air**-iss-iss) *n, pl* **-ses** (-seez) the mark (¨) placed over the second of two adjacent vowels to indicate that it is to be pronounced separately, as in *naïve*
WORD ORIGIN Greek: a division

diagnose *vb* **-nosing, -nosed** to determine by diagnosis

diagnosis (die-ag-**no**-siss) *n, pl* **-ses** (-seez) the discovery and identification of diseases from the examination of symptoms **diagnostic** *adj*
WORD ORIGIN Greek: a distinguishing

diagonal *adj* **1** *maths* connecting any two vertices in a polygon that are not adjacent **2** slanting ▷ *n* **3** a diagonal line, plane, or pattern **diagonally** *adv*
WORD ORIGIN Greek *dia-* through + *gōnia* angle

diagram *n* a sketch or plan showing the form or workings of something **diagrammatic** *adj*
WORD ORIGIN Greek *diagraphein* to mark out

dial *n* **1** the face of a clock or watch, marked with divisions representing units of time **2** the graduated disc on a measuring instrument **3** the control on a radio or television set used to change the station **4** a numbered disc on the front of some telephones ▷ *vb* **dialling, dialled** *or US* **dialing, dialed 5** to try to establish a telephone connection with (someone) by operating the dial or buttons on a telephone
WORD ORIGIN Latin *dies* day

dialect *n* a form of a language spoken in a particular geographical area **dialectal** *adj*
WORD ORIGIN Greek *dialektos* speech, dialect

dialectic *n* **1** logical debate by question and answer to resolve differences between two views **2** the art of logical argument **dialectical** *adj*
WORD ORIGIN Greek *dialektikē (tekhnē)* (the art) of argument

dialling tone *or US, Canad, Austral, & NZ* **dial tone** *n* a continuous sound heard on picking up a telephone receiver, indicating that a number can be dialled

dialogue *or US sometimes* **dialog** *n* **1** conversation between two people **2** a conversation in a literary or dramatic work **3** a discussion between representatives of two nations or groups
WORD ORIGIN Greek *dia-* between + *legein* to speak

dialysis (die-**al**-iss-iss) *n, pl* **-ses** (-seez) **1** *med* the filtering of blood through a semipermeable membrane to remove waste products **2** the separation of the particles in a solution by filtering through a semipermeable membrane **dialyser** *or* **-lyzer** *n* **dialytic** *adj*
WORD ORIGIN Greek *dialuein* to tear apart, dissolve

diamagnetism *n* the phenomenon exhibited by substances that are repelled by both poles of a magnet

diamanté (die-a-**man**-tee) *adj* decorated with glittering bits of material, such as sequins
WORD ORIGIN French

diameter *n* **a** a straight line through the centre of a circle or sphere **b** the length of such a line
WORD ORIGIN Greek *dia-* through + *metron* measure

diametric *or* **diametrical** *adj* **1** of or relating to a diameter **2** completely opposed: *the diametric opposition of the two camps* **diametrically** *adv*

diamond *n* **1** a usually colourless exceptionally hard precious stone of crystallized carbon **2** *geom* a figure with four sides of equal length forming two acute and two obtuse angles **3** a playing card marked with one or more red diamond-shaped symbols **4** *baseball* the playing field ▷ *adj* **5** (of an anniversary) the sixtieth: *diamond wedding*
WORD ORIGIN Latin *adamas* the hardest iron or steel, diamond

Diana *n* the Roman goddess of hunting

diapason (die-a-**pay**-zon) *n music* **1** either of two stops found throughout the range of a pipe organ **2** the range of an instrument or voice
WORD ORIGIN Greek *dia pasōn* through all (the notes)

diaper *n US & Canad* a nappy
WORD ORIGIN Medieval Greek *diaspros* pure white

diaphanous (die-**af**-fan-uss) *adj* (of fabrics) fine and translucent
WORD ORIGIN Greek *diaphanēs* transparent

diaphoretic *n* **1** a drug that causes perspiration or sweat ▷ *adj* **2** relating to or causing perspiration or sweat

diaphragm (**die**-a-fram) *n* **1** *anat* the muscular partition that separates the abdominal cavity and chest cavity **2** same as **cap** (sense 5) **3** a device to control the amount of light entering an optical instrument **4** a thin vibrating disc which converts sound to electricity or vice versa, as in a microphone or loudspeaker
WORD ORIGIN Greek *dia-* across + *phragma* fence

diapositive *n* a positive transparency; slide

diarist *n* a person who writes a diary that is subsequently published

diarrhoea *or esp. US* **diarrhea** (die-a-**ree**-a) *n* frequent discharge of abnormally liquid faeces
WORD ORIGIN Greek *dia-* through + *rhein* to flow

diary *n, pl* **-ries 1** a book containing a record of daily events, appointments, or observations **2** a written record of daily events, appointments, or observations
WORD ORIGIN Latin *dies* day

Diaspora (die-**ass**-spore-a) *n* **1** the dispersion of the Jews after the Babylonian conquest of Palestine **2** a dispersion of people originally belonging to one nation
WORD ORIGIN Greek: a scattering

diastase (**die**-ass-stayss) *n* an enzyme that converts starch into sugar **diastasic** *adj*
WORD ORIGIN Greek *diastasis* a separation

diastole (die-**ass**-stoh-lee) *n* dilation of the chambers of the heart **diastolic** *adj*

diatom *n* a microscopic unicellular alga
WORD ORIGIN Greek *diatomos* cut in two

diatomic *adj* containing two atoms

diatonic *adj* of or relating to any scale of five tones and two semitones produced by playing the white keys of a keyboard instrument
WORD ORIGIN Greek *diatonos* extending

diatribe *n* a bitter critical attack
WORD ORIGIN Greek *dia-* through + *tribein* to rub

dibble *n* a small hand tool used to make holes in the ground for bulbs, seeds, or roots
WORD ORIGIN origin unknown

dice *n, pl* **dice 1** a small cube, each of whose sides has a different number of spots (1 to 6), used in games of chance ▷ *vb* **dicing, diced 2** to cut (food) into small cubes **3** **dice with death** to take a risk
WORD ORIGIN originally plural of DIE²

dicey *adj* **dicier, diciest** *informal* dangerous or tricky

dichotomy (die-**kot**-a-mee) *n, pl* **-mies** division into two opposed groups or parts **dichotomous** *adj*
WORD ORIGIN Greek *dicha* in two + *temnein* to cut

USAGE
Dichotomy should always refer to a division of some kind into two groups. It is sometimes used to refer to a puzzling situation which seems to involve a contradiction, but this use is generally thought to be incorrect.

Words from Shakespeare
part 8

descry *v* to see or catch sight of
The news is true, my lord. He is descried
Anthony and Cleopatra 3.7

desert *n* worth or merit
That dost in vile misproson shackle up
My love and her desert *All's Well That Ends Well* 2.3

design *v* to indicate or point out
we shall see
Justice design the victor's chivalry *Richard II* 1.1

designment *n* a plan or undertaking
The desperate tempest hath so bang'd the Turks,
That their designment halts *Othello* 2.1

despite *v* to spite or attempt to thwart a plan
Only to despite them I will endeavour anything
Much Ado About Nothing 2.2

device *n* a plan, plot or trick
Excellent, I smell a device *Twelfth Night* 2.3

disable *v* to devalue or make little of
he disabled my judgement *As You Like It* 5.4

discandy *v* to melt away or dissolve
The hearts ... do discandy, melt their sweets
Anthony and Cleopatra 4.12

disciple *v* to teach or train
He ... was
Discipled of the bravest *All's Well That Ends Well* 1.2

discommend *v* to criticize
my dialect which you discommend so much
King Lear 2.2

discourse *n* conversation, talk or chat
which part of it I'll waste
With such discourse as
I not doubt shall make it
Go quick away *The Tempest* 5.1

discover *v* to reveal or show
the Prince discovered to Claudio that he loved my
niece *Much Ado About Nothing* 1.2

disliken *v* to disguise, make unlike
disliken
The truth of your own seeming
The Winter's Tale 4.4

dismantle *v* to remove or take away
Commit a thing so monstrous to dismantle
So many folds of favour *King Lear* 1.1

disponge *v* to pour out or rain down
The poisonous damp of night disponge upon me
Anthony and Cleopatra 4.9

distrain *v* to confiscate something
My father's goods are all distrained and sold
Richard II 2.3

divers *adj* various
I will give out divers schedules of my beauty
Twelfth Night 1.5

doff *v* to get rid of or dispose
make our women fight
To doff their dire distresses *Macbeth* 4.3

dog *v* to follow someone or something closely
I will rather leave to see Hector than not to dog him
Troilus and Cressida 5.1

dotage *n* infatuation
Her dotage now I do begin to pity
A Midsummer Night's Dream 4.1

dotard *n* an old fool
I speak not like a dotard nor a fool
Much Ado About Nothing 5.1

dote *v* to love, cherish, care without seeing any fault
And won her soul; and she, sweet lady, dotes,
Devoutly dotes, dotes in idolatry
A Midsummer Night's Dream 1.1

doublet *n* a man's close-fitting jacket with short skirt
Lord Hamlet, with his doublet all unbraced
Hamlet 2.1

dichromatic *adj* having two colours
WORD ORIGIN Greek *di-* double + *khrōma* colour

dick *n slang* 1 *taboo* a penis 2 **clever dick** an opinionated person
WORD ORIGIN *Dick* familiar form of *Richard*

dickens *n* **the dickens** *informal* used as an exclamation to show surprise, confusion, or annoyance: *what the dickens do you think you're doing?*
WORD ORIGIN from the name *Dickens*

Dickensian *adj* 1 of Charles Dickens (1812–70), British novelist 2 denoting poverty, distress, and exploitation, as depicted in the novels of Dickens

dicky¹ *n, pl* **dickies** a false shirt front
WORD ORIGIN from *Dick*, name

dicky² *adj* **dickier**, **dickiest** *Brit & NZ informal* shaky or weak: *a dicky heart*
WORD ORIGIN origin unknown

dicky-bird *n* a child's word for a bird

dicky-bow *n Brit* a bow tie

dicotyledon (die-kot-ill-**leed**-on) *n* a flowering plant with two seed leaves

dictate *vb* **-tating**, **-tated** 1 to say (words) aloud for another person to transcribe 2 to seek to impose one's will on others ▷ *n* 3 an authoritative command 4 a guiding principle: *the dictates of reason*
WORD ORIGIN Latin *dictare* to say repeatedly

dictation *n* 1 the act of dictating words to be taken down in writing 2 the words dictated

dictator *n* 1 a ruler who has complete power 2 a person who behaves in a tyrannical manner **dictatorship** *n*

dictatorial *adj* 1 of or pertaining to a dictator 2 tyrannical; overbearing **dictatorially** *adv*

diction *n* the manner of pronouncing words and sounds
WORD ORIGIN Latin *dicere* to speak

dictionary *n, pl* **-aries** 1 a a book that consists of an alphabetical list of words with their meanings b a similar book giving equivalent words in two languages 2 a reference book listing terms and giving information about a particular subject
WORD ORIGIN Late Latin *dictio* word

dictum *n, pl* **-tums** *or* **-ta** 1 a formal statement; pronouncement 2 a popular saying or maxim
WORD ORIGIN Latin

did *vb* the past tense of **do¹**

didactic *adj* intended to teach or instruct people: *an Impressionist work can be as didactic in its way as a sermon* **didactically** *adv* **didacticism** *n*
WORD ORIGIN Greek *didaktikos* skilled in teaching

diddle *vb* **-dling**, **-dled** *informal* to swindle **diddler** *n*
WORD ORIGIN Jeremy *Diddler*, a scrounger in a 19th-century play

didgeridoo *n* an Australian Aboriginal deep-toned wind instrument
WORD ORIGIN imitative

didn't did not

die¹ *vb* **dying**, **died** 1 (of a person, animal, or plant) to cease all biological activity permanently 2 (of something inanimate) to cease to exist 3 to lose strength, power, or energy by degrees 4 to stop working: *the engine died* 5 **be dying** to be eager (for something or to do something) 6 **be dying of** *informal* to be nearly overcome with (laughter, boredom, etc.) 7 **die hard** to change or disappear only slowly: *old loyalties die hard* 8 **to die for** *informal* highly desirable: *a salary to die for* ▶ See also **die down**, **die out**
WORD ORIGIN Old English *dīegan*

≡ **USAGE**
≡ It was formerly considered incorrect to use the preposition *from* after *die*, but *of* and *from* are now both acceptable: *he died of/from his injuries.*

die² *n* 1 a shaped block used to cut or form metal 2 a casting mould 3 same as **dice** (sense 1) 4 **the die is cast** an irrevocable decision has been taken
WORD ORIGIN Latin *dare* to give, play

die down *vb* 1 to lose strength or power by degrees 2 to become calm: *the storm has died down now*

die-hard *or* **diehard** *n* a person who resists change

dieldrin *n* a highly toxic crystalline insecticide

dielectric *n* 1 a substance of very low electrical conductivity; insulator ▷ *adj* 2 having the properties of a dielectric
WORD ORIGIN Greek *dia-* through + ELECTRIC

die out *or* **off** *vb* to become extinct or disappear after a gradual decline

dieresis (die-**air**-iss-iss) *n, pl* **-ses** (-seez) same as **diaeresis**

diesel *n* 1 same as **diesel engine** 2 a vehicle driven by a diesel engine 3 *informal* diesel oil
WORD ORIGIN after R. *Diesel*, engineer

diesel-electric *n* a locomotive with a diesel engine driving an electric generator

diesel engine *n* an internal-combustion engine in which oil is ignited by compression

diesel oil *or* **fuel** *n* a fuel obtained from petroleum distillation, used in diesel engines

diet¹ *n* 1 the food that a person or animal regularly eats 2 a specific allowance or selection of food, to control weight or for health reasons: *a high-fibre diet* ▷ *vb* 3 to follow a special diet so as to lose weight ▷ *adj* 4 suitable for eating with a weight-reduction diet: *diet soft drinks* **dietary** *adj* **dieter** *n*
WORD ORIGIN Greek *diaita* mode of living

diet² *n* a legislative assembly in some countries
WORD ORIGIN Medieval Latin *dieta* public meeting

dietary fibre *n* the roughage in fruits and vegetables that aids digestion

dietetic *adj* prepared for special dietary requirements

dietetics *n* the study of diet, nutrition, and the preparation of food

dietician *n* a person qualified to advise people about healthy eating

differ *vb* 1 to be dissimilar in quality, nature, or degree 2 to disagree
WORD ORIGIN Latin *differre* to scatter, be different

difference *n* 1 the state or quality of being unlike 2 a disagreement or argument 3 the result of the subtraction of one number or quantity from another 4 **make a difference** to have an effect 5 **split the difference a** to compromise **b** to divide a remainder equally

different *adj* 1 partly or completely unlike 2 new or unusual 3 not identical or the same; other: *he wears a different tie every day* **differently** *adv*
≡ **USAGE**
≡ The constructions *different from*, *different to*, and *different than* are all found in the works of writers of English during the past. Nowadays, however, the most widely acceptable preposition to use after *different* is *from*. *Different to* is common in British English, but is considered by some people to be incorrect, or less acceptable. *Different than* is a standard construction in American English. As, however, this idiom is not regarded as totally acceptable in British usage, it is preferable either to use *different from*: *this result is only slightly different from that obtained in the US* or to rephrase the sentence: *this result differs only slightly from that in the US.*

differential *adj* 1 of, relating to, or using a difference 2 *maths* involving differentials ▷ *n* 3 a factor that differentiates between two comparable things 4 *maths* a minute difference between values in a scale 5 *chiefly Brit* the difference between rates of pay for different types of labour, esp. within a company or industry

differential calculus *n* the branch of mathematics concerned with derivatives and differentials

differential gear *n* the gear in the driving axle of a road vehicle that permits one driving wheel to rotate faster than the other when cornering

differentiate *vb* **-ating**, **-ated** 1 to perceive or show the difference (between) 2 to make (one thing) distinct from other such things 3 *maths* to determine the derivative of a function or variable **differentiation** *n*

difficult *adj* 1 not easy to do, understand, or solve 2 not easily pleased or satisfied: *a difficult patient* 3 full of hardships or trials: *he had recently had a difficult time with his job as a self-employed builder*

difficulty *n, pl* **-ties** 1 the state or quality of being difficult 2 a task or problem that is hard to deal with 3 a troublesome or embarrassing situation: *in financial difficulties* 4 an objection or obstacle: *you're just making difficulties* 5 lack of ease; awkwardness: *he could run only with difficulty*
WORD ORIGIN Latin *difficultas*

diffident *adj* lacking self-confidence; shy **diffidence** *n* **diffidently** *adv*
WORD ORIGIN Latin *dis-* not + *fidere* to trust

diffract *vb* to cause to undergo diffraction **diffractive** *adj*

diffraction *n* **1** *physics* a deviation in the direction of a wave at the edge of an obstacle in its path **2** the formation of light and dark fringes by the passage of light through a small aperture
WORD ORIGIN Latin *diffringere* to shatter

diffuse *vb* **-fusing, -fused 1** to spread over a wide area **2** *physics* to cause to undergo diffusion ▷ *adj* **3** spread out over a wide area **4** lacking conciseness **diffusible** *adj* **diffuser** *n*
WORD ORIGIN Latin *diffusus* spread abroad

≡ USAGE
≡ Avoid confusion with **defuse**.

diffusion *n* **1** the act of diffusing or the fact of being diffused; dispersion **2** *physics* the random thermal motion of atoms and molecules in gases, liquids, and some solids **3** *physics* the transmission or reflection of light, in which the radiation is scattered in many directions

dig *vb* **digging, dug 1** to cut into, break up, and turn over or remove (earth), esp. with a spade **2** to excavate (a hole or tunnel) by digging, usually with an implement or (of animals) with claws **3** to obtain by digging: *dig out potatoes* **4** to find by effort or searching: *he dug out a mini cassette from his pocket* **5** *informal* to like or understand **6** (foll. by *in* or *into*) to thrust or jab ▷ *n* **7** the act of digging **8** an archaeological excavation **9** a thrust or poke **10** a cutting remark
▶ See also **dig in**
WORD ORIGIN Middle English *diggen*

digest *vb* **1** to subject (food) to a process of digestion **2** to absorb mentally ▷ *n* **3** a shortened version of a book, report, or article **digestible** *adj*
WORD ORIGIN Latin *digerere* to divide

digestion *n* **1** the process of breaking down food into easily absorbed substances **2** the body's system for doing this

digestive *adj* relating to digestion

digger *n* a machine used for excavation

dig in *vb* **1** to mix (compost or fertilizer) into the soil by digging **2** *informal* to begin to eat vigorously **3** *informal* (of soldiers) to dig a trench and prepare for an enemy attack **4 dig one's heels in** *informal* to refuse to move or be persuaded

digit (**dij**-it) *n* **1** a finger or toe **2** any numeral from 0 to 9
WORD ORIGIN Latin *digitus* toe, finger

digital *adj* **1** displaying information as numbers rather than with a dial **2** representing data as a series of numerical values **3** of or possessing digits **digitally** *adv*

digital audio tape *n* magnetic tape on which sound is recorded digitally, giving high-fidelity reproduction

digital clock *or* **watch** *n* a clock or watch in which the time is indicated by digits rather than by hands on a dial

digital computer *n* a computer in which the input consists of numbers, letters, and other characters that are represented internally in binary notation

digitalis *n* a drug made from foxglove leaves: used as a heart stimulant

WORD ORIGIN Latin: relating to a finger (from the shape of the foxglove flowers)

digital recording *n* a sound recording process that converts audio or analogue signals into a series of pulses

digital switchover *n* the process of changing the method of transmitting television from analogue to digital format

digital television *n* television in which the picture information is transmitted in digital form and decoded at the television receiver

digitate *adj* **1** (of leaves) having leaflets in the form of a spread hand **2** (of animals) having digits

digitize *or* **-ise** *vb* **-izing, -ized** *or* **-ising, -ised** to transcribe (data) into a digital form for processing by a computer **digitizer** *or* **-iser** *n*

dignified *adj* calm, impressive, and worthy of respect

dignify *vb* **-fies, -fying, -fied 1** to add distinction to: *the meeting was dignified by the minister* **2** to add a semblance of dignity to by the use of a pretentious name or title: *she dignifies every plant with its Latin name*
WORD ORIGIN Latin *dignus* worthy + *facere* to make

dignitary *n, pl* **-taries** a person of high official position or rank

dignity *n, pl* **-ties 1** serious, calm, and controlled behaviour or manner **2** the quality of being worthy of honour **3** sense of self-importance: *he considered the job beneath his dignity*
WORD ORIGIN Latin *dignus* worthy

digraph *n* two letters used to represent a single sound, such as *gh* in *tough*

digress *vb* to depart from the main subject in speech or writing **digression** *n*
WORD ORIGIN Latin *digressus* turned aside

digs *pl n Brit, Austral, & S African informal* lodgings
WORD ORIGIN from *diggings*, perhaps referring to where one digs or works

dihedral *adj* having or formed by two intersecting planes

dilapidated *adj* (of a building) having fallen into ruin **dilapidation** *n*
WORD ORIGIN Latin *dilapidare* to waste

dilate *vb* **-lating, -lated** to make or become wider or larger: *her eyes dilated in the dark* **dilation** *or* **dilatation** *n*
WORD ORIGIN Latin *dilatare* to spread out

dilatory (**dill**-a-tree) *adj* tending or intended to waste time **dilatorily** *adv* **dilatoriness** *n*
WORD ORIGIN Late Latin *dilatorius*

dildo *n, pl* **-dos** an object used as a substitute for an erect penis
WORD ORIGIN origin unknown

dilemma *n* a situation offering a choice between two equally undesirable alternatives
WORD ORIGIN Greek *di-* double + *lēmma* proposition

≡ USAGE
≡ The use of *dilemma* to refer to a problem that seems incapable of a solution is considered by some people to be incorrect.

dilettante (dill-it-**tan**-tee) *n, pl* **-tantes** *or* **-tanti** a person whose interest in a subject is superficial rather than serious **dilettantism** *n*
WORD ORIGIN Italian

diligent *adj* **1** careful and persevering in carrying out tasks or duties **2** carried out with care and perseverance: *a diligent approach to work* **diligence** *n* **diligently** *adv*
WORD ORIGIN Latin *diligere* to value

dill *n* a sweet-smelling herb used for flavouring
WORD ORIGIN Old English *dile*

dilly-dally *vb* **-lies, -lying, -lied** *Brit, Austral, & NZ informal* to dawdle or waste time
WORD ORIGIN reduplication of *dally*

dilute *vb* **-luting, -luted 1** to make (a liquid) less concentrated by adding water or another liquid **2** to make (someone's power, idea, or role) weaker or less effective: *socialists used their majority in parliament to dilute legislation crucial to developing a market economy* ▷ *adj* **3** *chem* (of a solution) having a low concentration **dilution** *n*
WORD ORIGIN Latin *diluere*

diluvian *or* **diluvial** *adj* of a flood, esp. the great Flood described in the Old Testament
WORD ORIGIN Latin *diluere* to wash away

dim *adj* **dimmer, dimmest 1** badly lit **2** not clearly seen; faint: *a dim figure in the doorway* **3** not seeing clearly: *eyes dim with tears* **4** *informal* mentally dull **5** not clear in the mind; obscure: *a dim awareness* **6** lacking in brightness or lustre: *a dim colour* **7 take a dim view of** to disapprove of ▷ *vb* **dimming, dimmed 8** to become or cause to become dim **9** to cause to seem less bright **10** *US & Canad* same as **dip** (sense 4) > **dimly** *adv* **dimness** *n*
WORD ORIGIN Old English *dimm*

dime *n* a coin of the US and Canada worth ten cents
WORD ORIGIN Latin *decem* ten

dimension *n* **1** an aspect or factor: *the attack brought a whole new dimension to the bombing campaign* **2** dimensions scope or extent **3** (*often pl*) a measurement of the size of something in a particular direction **dimensional** *adj*
WORD ORIGIN Latin *dimensio* an extent

dimer *n chem* a molecule made up of two identical molecules bonded together

diminish *vb* **1** to make or become smaller, fewer, or less **2** *music* to decrease (a minor interval) by a semitone **3** to reduce in authority or status
WORD ORIGIN Latin *deminuere* to make smaller + archaic *minish* to lessen

diminuendo *music n, pl* **-dos 1 a** a gradual decrease in loudness **b** a passage which gradually decreases in loudness ▷ *adv* **2** gradually decreasing in loudness
WORD ORIGIN Italian

diminution *n* reduction in size, volume, intensity, or importance
WORD ORIGIN Latin *deminutio*

diminutive *adj* **1** very small; tiny **2** *grammar* **a** denoting an affix added to a word to convey the meaning *small* or *unimportant* or to express affection, as for example, the suffix *-ette* in French **b** denoting a word formed by the addition of a diminutive affix ▷ *n* **3** *grammar* a diminutive word or affix **diminutiveness** *n*

dimmer *n* **1** a device for dimming an electric light **2** *US* **a** a dipped headlight on a road vehicle **b** a parking light on a car

dimple *n* **1** a small natural dent on the cheeks or chin ▷ *vb* **-pling, -pled 2** to produce dimples by smiling **WORD ORIGIN** Middle English *dympull*

dimwit *n informal* a stupid person **dim-witted** *adj*

din *n* **1** a loud unpleasant confused noise ▷ *vb* **dinning, dinned 2 din something into someone** to instil something into someone by constant repetition **WORD ORIGIN** Old English *dynn*

dinar (**dee**-nahr) *n* a monetary unit of various Balkan, Middle Eastern, and North African countries **WORD ORIGIN** Latin *denarius* a Roman coin

dine *vb* **dining, dined 1** to eat dinner **2 dine on** *or* **off** to make one's meal of: *the guests dined on roast beef* **WORD ORIGIN** Old French *disner*

diner *n* **1** a person eating a meal in a restaurant **2** *chiefly US & Canad* a small cheap restaurant **3** short for **dining car**

dinette *n* an alcove or small area for use as a dining room

ding *n* *Austral dated & NZ informal* a small dent in a vehicle

ding-dong *n* **1** the sound of a bell **2** a violent exchange of blows or words **WORD ORIGIN** imitative

dinges (**ding**-uss) *n* *S African informal* a jocular word for something whose name is unknown or forgotten; thingumabob **WORD ORIGIN** Dutch *ding* thing

dinghy (**ding**-ee, **ding**-gee) *n, pl* **-ghies** a small boat, powered by sail, oars, or outboard motor **WORD ORIGIN** Hindi or Bengali *dingi*

dingle *n* a small wooded hollow or valley **WORD ORIGIN** origin unknown

dingo *n, pl* **-goes** an Australian native wild dog **WORD ORIGIN** Aboriginal

dingy (**din**-jee) *adj* **-gier, -giest 1** *Brit, Austral, & NZ* dull, neglected, and drab: *he waited in this dingy little outer office* **2** shabby and discoloured: *she was wearing dingy white overalls* **dinginess** *n* **WORD ORIGIN** origin unknown

dining car *n* a railway coach in which meals are served

dining room *n* a room where meals are eaten

dinkum *adj* *Austral & NZ informal* genuine or right: *a fair dinkum offer* **WORD ORIGIN** English dialect: work

dinky *adj* **dinkier, dinkiest** *chiefly Brit informal* small and neat; dainty **WORD ORIGIN** dialect *dink* neat

dinky-di *adj* *Austral informal* typical **WORD ORIGIN** variant of DINKUM

dinner *n* **1** the main meal of the day, eaten either in the evening or at midday **2** a formal social occasion at which an evening meal is served **WORD ORIGIN** Old French *disner* to dine

dinner jacket *n* a man's semiformal black evening jacket without tails

dinner service *n* a set of matching dishes suitable for serving a meal

dinosaur *n* any of a large order of extinct prehistoric reptiles many of which were gigantic **WORD ORIGIN** Greek *deinos* fearful + *sauros* lizard

dint *n* **by dint of** by means of: *by dint of their own efforts* **WORD ORIGIN** Old English *dynt* a blow

diocesan *adj* of or relating to a diocese

diocese (**die**-a-siss) *n* the district over which a bishop has control **WORD ORIGIN** Greek *dioikēsis* administration

diode *n* **1** a semiconductor device for converting alternating current to direct current **2** an electronic valve with two electrodes between which a current can flow only in one direction **WORD ORIGIN** Greek *di-* double + *hodos* a way, road

dioecious (die-**eesh**-uss) *adj* (of plants) having the male and female reproductive organs on separate plants **WORD ORIGIN** Greek *di-* twice + *oikia* house

Dionysian (die-on-**niz**-zee-an) *adj* wild or orgiastic **WORD ORIGIN** from *Dionysus*, Greek god of wine

Dionysus *n* *Greek myth* the god of wine

dioptre *or US* **diopter** (die-**op**-ter) *n* a unit for measuring the refractive power of a lens **WORD ORIGIN** Greek *dia-* through + *opsesthai* to see

diorama *n* **1** a miniature three-dimensional scene, in which models of figures are seen against a background **2** a picture made up of illuminated translucent curtains, viewed through an aperture **WORD ORIGIN** Greek *dia-* through + *horama* view

dioxide *n* an oxide containing two oxygen atoms per molecule

dip *vb* **dipping, dipped 1** to plunge or be plunged quickly or briefly into a liquid **2** to put one's hands into something, esp. to obtain an object: *she dipped into her handbag looking for change* **3** to slope downwards **4** to switch (car headlights) from the main to the lower beam **5** to undergo a slight decline, esp. temporarily: *sales dipped in November* **6** to immerse (farm animals) briefly in a chemical to rid them of insects **7** to lower or be lowered briefly: *she dipped her knee in a curtsy* ▷ *n* **8** the act of dipping **9** a brief swim **10** a liquid chemical in which farm animals are dipped **11** a depression, esp. in a landscape **12** a momentary sinking down **13** a creamy mixture into which pieces of food are dipped before being eaten ▶ See also **dip into** **WORD ORIGIN** Old English *dyppan*

Dip Ed (in Britain) Diploma in Education

diphtheria (dif-**theer**-ree-a) *n* a contagious disease producing fever and difficulty in breathing and swallowing **WORD ORIGIN** Greek *diphthera* leather; from the membrane that forms in the throat

diphthong *n* a vowel sound, occupying a single syllable, in which the speaker's tongue moves continuously from one position to another, as in the pronunciation of *a* in late **WORD ORIGIN** Greek *di-* double + *phthongos* sound

dip into *vb* **1** to draw upon: *he dipped into his savings* **2** to read passages at random from (a book or journal)

diploid *adj* *biol* denoting a cell or organism with pairs of homologous chromosomes **WORD ORIGIN** Greek *di-* double + *-ploos* -fold

diploma *n* a document conferring a qualification or recording successful completion of a course of study **WORD ORIGIN** Latin: official document, literally: letter folded double

diplomacy *n* **1** the conduct of the relations between nations by peaceful means **2** skill in the management of international relations **3** tact or skill in dealing with people

diplomat *n* an official, such as an ambassador, engaged in diplomacy

diplomatic *adj* **1** of or relating to diplomacy **2** skilled in negotiating between nations **3** tactful in dealing with people **diplomatically** *adv* **WORD ORIGIN** French *diplomatique* concerning the documents of diplomacy; see DIPLOMA

diplomatic immunity *n* the freedom from legal action and exemption from taxation which diplomats have in the country where they are working

dipole *n* **1** two equal but opposite electric charges or magnetic poles separated by a small distance **2** a molecule that has two such charges or poles **dipolar** *adj*

dipper *n* **1** a ladle used for dipping **2** a songbird that inhabits fast-flowing streams

diprotodont (die-**pro**-toe-dont) *n* a marsupial with fewer than three upper incisor teeth on each side of the jaw

dipsomania *n* a compulsive desire to drink alcoholic beverages **dipsomaniac** *n, adj* **WORD ORIGIN** Greek *dipsa* thirst + *mania* madness

dipstick *n* a rod with notches on it dipped into a container to indicate the fluid level

dip switch *n* a device for dipping headlights on a vehicle

dipterous *adj* having two wings or winglike parts **WORD ORIGIN** Greek *dipteros* two-winged

diptych (**dip**-tik) *n* a painting on two hinged panels **WORD ORIGIN** Greek *di-* double + *ptuchē* a panel

dire *adj* disastrous, urgent, or terrible: *he was now in dire financial straits* **WORD ORIGIN** Latin *dirus* ominous

direct *adj* **1** shortest; straight: *a direct route* **2** without intervening people: *they secretly arranged direct links to their commanders* **3** honest; frank: *he was polite but very direct* **4** diametric: *the direct opposite* **5** in an unbroken line of descent: *a direct*

Singaporean English

Singaporean English is a new variety of English (NVE), alongside other established NVEs such as Indian English, Filipino English, and Nigerian English. Unlike older varieties of English (OVEs) such as British English, Australian English, or US English, NVEs historically emerged primarily through the classroom rather than the home, incorporating the attendant cultures of a multiracial population, and complementing the other languages of the country.

Singaporean English very much displays NVE characteristics. According to the latest Singapore General Household Survey (2005), English is the predominant language of the home for only 28.7% Chinese, 13.0% Malay, and 39% Indian residents respectively. It complements the predominant use of Mandarin Chinese (47.2%) and Chinese dialects (23.9%) for Chinese residents, Malay (86.8%) for Malay residents, and Tamil (36.8%) and Malay (10.6%) for Indian residents in the home respectively. Despite this, English is the predominant language of instruction in learning institutions and can be considered the *de facto* national language (which constitutionally, and so *de jure*, is Malay). English is the leading language of administration, education, public signage, and everyday interaction, and the link language for the 3.73 million residents which comprise 74.2% Chinese, 13.4% Malay, and 9.2% Indians respectively. Many Singaporeans are bilingual or trilingual.

English as a linguistic entity in the country may be divided into three parts: standard English (which usually means standard British/US English), High Singaporean English (educated, 'standard' Singaporean English), and Low Singaporean English (colloquial Singaporean English, also popularly known as 'Singlish'). Standard English is the benchmark set in grammar books, dictionaries, classroom texts, official media, and print materials. The local high variety comprises linguistic expressions that are acceptable in various situations. The norms represented in these expressions are not often immediately noticeable; they tend to be an 'invisible' cross between standard English and a local language or cultural notion. The low variety is acceptable only in informal situations and is the popular colloquial variety found in casual conversations, some TV comedy programmes, many online personal blogs, and informal online discussion forums.

The high variety includes such terms as *handphone* (for mobile phone), *killer litter* (heavy objects thrown from high rise buildings that can injure passers-by below), and *Singapore Girl* (advertising depiction of Singapore Airline's flight stewardesses). Another example is *red packet* (Chinese *hong bao*) which is a red/pink envelope containing money given during auspicious occasions; it is a term shared with other NVEs such as Hong Kong English and Malaysian English. The expression *sleep late*, as in 'I like to sleep late at 3am', corresponds to the idea of staying up late at night in both Malay (*tidur lewat*) and Chinese (*wǎn shuì*). However, an OVE which has the song title 'I like to sleep late in the morning' makes it clear that one gets up late in the morning.

Low variety terms include *kiasu* (from Hokkien Chinese, to mean 'afraid to lose out'), *cut* ('to overtake': 'His car cut mine') and *blur* ('dazed'). The low variety is mainly influenced by Chinese (especially Mandarin or Hokkien) and/or Malay grammar structures and words. It is popularly characterized by particles such as *lah, leh, lor,* and *meh* whose various intonations express different attitudinal meanings at the end of a sentence. In the expression *Referee kayu meh?*, the Malay term *kayu* ('wood') metaphorically means 'block-headed/dim-witted' and the Chinese dialect particle *meh* (depending on the tone) can indicate surprise, scepticism, sarcasm, or disbelief. Thus the sentence loosely translates as follows: 'I can't believe that the referee is as stupid/dim-witted as you say he is.'

Proficient Singaporean English speakers should have the ability to shift between standard English, the high variety, and the low variety to suit the occasion. On the other hand, less educated speakers can access only the low variety. There are both advocates and opponents of the low variety: advocates refer to its indispensable cultural identity, but opponents (including educationists and some prominent politicians) warn that it could be a 'handicap' for the local populace to master standard English for international communication.

descendant ▷ *adv* **6** directly; straight ▷ *vb* **7** to conduct or control the affairs of **8** to give orders with authority to (a person or group) **9** to tell (someone) the way to a place **10** to address (a letter, parcel, etc.) **11** to address (a look or remark) at someone: *the look she directed at him was one of unconcealed hatred* **12 a** to provide guidance to (actors, cameramen, etc.) in (a play or film) **b** to supervise the making or staging of (a film or play) **directness** *n*
WORD ORIGIN Latin *dirigere* to guide

direct access *n* a method of reading data from a computer file without reading through the file from the beginning

direct current *n* an electric current that flows in one direction only

direct debit *n* an order given to a bank or other financial institution by an account holder to pay an amount of money from the account to a specified person or company at regular intervals

direction *n* **1** the course or line along which a person or thing moves, points, or lies **2** management or guidance: *the campaign was successful under his direction* **3** the work of a stage or film director

directional *adj* **1** of or showing direction **2** *electronics* (of an aerial) transmitting or receiving radio waves more effectively in some directions than in others

directions *pl n* instructions for doing something or for reaching a place

directive *n* an instruction; order

directly *adv* **1** in a direct manner **2** at once; without delay **3** immediately or very soon: *I'll do that directly* ▷ *conj* **4** as soon as: *we left directly the money arrived*

direct object *n grammar* a noun, pronoun, or noun phrase denoting the person or thing receiving the direct action of a verb. For example, *a book* in *They bought Anne a book*

director *n* **1** a person or thing that directs or controls **2** a member of the governing board of a business, trust, etc. **3** the person responsible for the artistic and technical aspects of the making of a film or television programme **directorial** *adj* **directorship** *n*

directorate *n* **1** a board of directors **2** the position of director

director-general *n, pl* **directors-general** a person in overall charge of certain large organizations

directory *n, pl* **-ries 1** a book listing names, addresses, and telephone numbers of individuals or business companies **2** *computers* an area of a disk containing the names and locations of the files it currently holds

direct speech *n* the reporting of what someone has said by quoting the exact words

direct tax *n* a tax paid by the person or organization on which it is levied

dirge *n* **1** a chant of lamentation for the dead **2** any mournful song
WORD ORIGIN Latin *dirige* direct (imperative), opening word of antiphon used in the office of the dead

dirigible (**dir**-rij-jib-bl) *adj* **1** able to be steered ▷ *n* **2** same as **airship**
WORD ORIGIN Latin *dirigere* to direct

dirk *n* a dagger, formerly worn by Scottish Highlanders
WORD ORIGIN Scots *durk*

dirndl *n* **1** a woman's dress with a full gathered skirt and fitted bodice **2** a gathered skirt of this kind
WORD ORIGIN from German

dirt *n* **1** any unclean substance, such as mud; filth **2** loose earth; soil **3** packed earth, cinders, etc. used to make a racetrack **4** obscene speech or writing **5** *informal* harmful gossip
WORD ORIGIN Old Norse *drit* excrement

dirt-cheap *adj, adv* at an extremely low price

dirt-poor *adj chiefly US* extremely poor

dirt track *n* a racetrack made of packed earth or cinders

dirty *adj* **dirtier, dirtiest 1** covered or marked with dirt; filthy **2** causing one to become grimy: *a dirty job* **3** (of a colour) not clear and bright **4** unfair, dishonest, or unkind: *dirty tricks* **5 a** obscene: *dirty jokes* **b** sexually clandestine: *a dirty weekend* **6** revealing dislike or anger: *a dirty look* **7** (of weather) rainy or stormy **8 dirty work** unpleasant or illicit activity ▷ *n* **9 do the dirty on** *informal* to behave meanly towards ▷ *vb* **dirties, dirtying, dirtied 10** to make dirty; soil **dirtiness** *n*

dirty bomb *n informal* a bomb made from nuclear waste combined with conventional explosives that is capable of spreading radioactive material over a wide area

dis *vb* **disses, dissing, dissed** *slang chiefly US* same as **diss**

dis- *prefix* **1** indicating reversal: *disconnect* **2** indicating negation or lack: *dissimilar; disgrace* **3** indicating removal or release: *disembowel*

disability *n, pl* **-ties 1** a severe physical or mental illness that restricts the way a person lives his or her life **2** something that disables someone

disable *vb* **-abling, -abled** to make ineffective, unfit, or incapable **disablement** *n*

disabled *adj* lacking one or more physical powers, such as the ability to walk or to coordinate one's movements
≡ **USAGE**
≡ The use of *the disabled, the blind*, etc. can
≡ be offensive and should be avoided.
≡ Instead you should talk about *disabled*
≡ *people, blind people*, etc.

disabuse *vb* **-abusing, -abused** to rid (someone) of a mistaken idea: *Arnold felt unable to disabuse her of her prejudices*

disaccharide (die-**sack**-a-ride) *n* a sugar, such as sucrose, whose molecules consist of two linked monosaccharides

disadvantage *n* **1** an unfavourable or harmful circumstance **2 at a disadvantage** in a less favourable position than other people: *he continued to insist that he was at a disadvantage at the hearings* **disadvantageous** *adj*

disadvantaged *adj* socially or economically deprived

disaffected *adj* having lost loyalty to or affection for someone or something; alienated: *three million disaffected voters* **disaffection** *n*

disagree *vb* **-greeing, -greed 1** to have differing opinions or argue about (something) **2** to fail to correspond; conflict **3** to cause physical discomfort to: *curry disagrees with me*

disagreeable *adj* **1** (of an incident or situation) unpleasant **2** (of a person) bad-tempered or disobliging **disagreeably** *adv*

disagreement *n* **1** refusal or failure to agree **2** a difference between results, totals, etc. which shows that they cannot all be true **3** an argument

disallow *vb* to reject as untrue or invalid; cancel

disappear *vb* **1** to cease to be visible; vanish **2** to go away or become lost, esp. without explanation **3** to cease to exist: *the pain has disappeared* **disappearance** *n*

disappoint *vb* **1** to fail to meet the expectations or hopes of; let down **2** to prevent the fulfilment of (a plan, etc.); frustrate **disappointed** *adj* **disappointing** *adj*
WORD ORIGIN Old French *desapointier*

disappointment *n* **1** the feeling of being disappointed **2** a person or thing that disappoints

disapprobation *n* disapproval

disapprove *vb* **-proving, -proved** to consider wrong or bad **disapproval** *n* **disapproving** *adj*

disarm *vb* **1** to deprive of weapons **2** to win the confidence or affection of **3** (of a country) to decrease the size and capability of one's armed forces

disarmament *n* the reduction of fighting capability by a country

disarming *adj* removing hostility or suspicion **disarmingly** *adv*

disarrange *vb* **-ranging, -ranged** to throw into disorder **disarrangement** *n*

disarray *n* **1** confusion and lack of discipline **2** extreme untidiness ▷ *vb* **3** to throw into confusion

disassociate *vb* **-ating, -ated** same as **dissociate** ▷ **disassociation** *n*

disaster *n* **1** an accident that causes great distress or destruction **2** something, such as a project, that fails or has been ruined **disastrous** *adj* **disastrously** *adv*
WORD ORIGIN Italian *disastro*

disavow *vb* to deny connection with or responsibility for (something) **disavowal** *n*

disband *vb* to stop or cause to stop functioning as a unit or group **disbandment** *n*

disbar *vb* **-barring, -barred** to deprive (a barrister) of the right to practise
≡ **USAGE**
≡ *Disbar* is sometimes wrongly used
≡ where *debar* is meant: *he was debarred*
≡ (not *disbarred*) *from attending meetings.*

disbelieve *vb* **-lieving, -lieved 1** to reject (a person or statement) as being untruthful **2 disbelieve in** to have no faith or belief in: *to disbelieve in the supernatural* **disbelief** *n*

disburse *vb* **-bursing, -bursed** to pay out **disbursement** *n*
WORD ORIGIN Old French *desborser*

≡ USAGE
≡ *Disburse* is sometimes wrongly used
≡ where *disperse* is meant: *the police used*
≡ *water cannon to disperse* (not *disburse*) *the*
≡ *crowd.*

disc *n* **1** a flat circular object **2** a gramophone record **3** *anat* a circular flat structure in the body, esp. between the vertebrae **4** *computers* same as **disk**
WORD ORIGIN Latin *discus* discus

discard *vb* to get rid of (something or someone) as useless or undesirable
WORD ORIGIN DIS- + *card* (the playing card)

disc brake *n* a brake in which two pads rub against a flat disc

discern *vb* to see or be aware of (something) clearly **discernible** *adj*
WORD ORIGIN Latin *discernere* to divide

discerning *adj* having or showing good judgment **discernment** *n*

discharge *vb* **-charging, -charged 1** to release or allow to go **2** to dismiss (someone) from duty or employment **3** to fire (a gun) **4** to cause to pour forth: *the scar was red and swollen and began to discharge pus* **5** to remove (the cargo) from a boat, etc.; unload **6** to meet the demands of (a duty or responsibility) **7** to relieve oneself of (a debt) **8** *physics* to take or supply electrical current from (a cell or battery) ▷ *n* **9** something that is discharged **10** dismissal or release from an office, job, etc. **11** a pouring out of a fluid; emission **12** *physics* a conduction of electricity through a gas

disciple (diss-**sipe**-pl) *n* **1** a follower of the doctrines of a teacher **2** one of the personal followers of Christ during his earthly life
WORD ORIGIN Latin *discipulus* pupil

disciplinarian *n* a person who practises strict discipline

disciplinary *adj* of or imposing discipline; corrective

discipline *n* **1** the practice of imposing strict rules of behaviour on other people **2** the ability to behave and work in a controlled manner **3** a particular area of academic study ▷ *vb* **-plining, -plined 4** to improve or attempt to improve the behaviour of (oneself or someone else) by training or rules **5** to punish
WORD ORIGIN Latin *disciplina* teaching

disciplined *adj* able to behave and work in a controlled way

disc jockey *n* a person who announces and plays recorded pop records on a radio programme or at a disco

disclaim *vb* **1** to deny (responsibility for or knowledge of something) **2** to give up (any claim to)

disclaimer *n* a statement denying responsibility for or knowledge of something

disclose *vb* **-closing, -closed 1** to make (information) known **2** to allow to be seen: *she agreed to disclose the contents of the box* **disclosure** *n*

disco *n, pl* **-cos 1** a nightclub for dancing to amplified pop records **2** an occasion at which people dance to amplified pop

records **3** mobile equipment for providing music for a disco
WORD ORIGIN from DISCOTHEQUE

discography *n, pl* **-phies** a classified list of gramophone records

discolour *or US* **discolor** *vb* to change in colour; to fade or stain **discoloration** *n*

discomfit *vb* **-fiting, -fited** to make uneasy or confused **discomfiture** *n*
WORD ORIGIN Old French *desconfire* to destroy

discomfort *n* **1** a mild pain **2** a feeling of worry or embarrassment **3 discomforts** conditions that cause physical uncomfortableness: *the physical discomforts of pregnancy*

discommode *vb* **-moding, -moded** to cause inconvenience **discommodious** *adj*
WORD ORIGIN DIS- + obsolete *commode* to suit

discompose *vb* **-posing, -posed** to disturb or upset someone **discomposure** *n*

disconcert *vb* to disturb the confidence or self-possession of; upset, embarrass, or take aback **disconcerting** *adj*

disconnect *vb* **1** to undo or break the connection between (two things) **2** to stop the supply of (gas or electricity to a building) ▷ *n* **3** a lack of connection: disconnection: *a disconnect between political discourse and the public* **disconnection** *n*

disconnected *adj* (of speech or ideas) not logically connected

disconsolate *adj* sad beyond comfort **disconsolately** *adv*
WORD ORIGIN Medieval Latin *disconsolatus*

discontent *n* lack of contentment, as with one's condition or lot in life **discontented** *adj* **discontentedly** *adv*

discontinue *vb* **-nuing, -nued** to come or bring to an end; stop

discontinuous *adj* characterized by interruptions; intermittent **discontinuity** *n*

discord *n* **1** lack of agreement or harmony between people **2** harsh confused sounds **3** a combination of musical notes that lacks harmony
WORD ORIGIN Latin *discors* at variance

discordant *adj* **1** at variance; disagreeing **2** harsh in sound; inharmonious **discordance** *n*

discotheque *n* same as **disco**
WORD ORIGIN French

discount *vb* **1** to leave (something) out of account as being unreliable, prejudiced, or irrelevant **2** to deduct (an amount or percentage) from the price of something ▷ *n* **3** a deduction from the full amount of a price **4 at a discount** below the regular price

discountenance *vb* **-nancing, -nanced** to make (someone) ashamed or confused

discourage *vb* **-raging, -raged 1** to deprive of the will or enthusiasm to persist in something **2** to oppose by expressing disapproval **discouragement** *n* **discouraging** *adj*

discourse *n* **1** conversation **2** a formal treatment of a subject in speech or writing ▷ *vb* **-coursing, -coursed 3** to

speak or write (about) at length
WORD ORIGIN Medieval Latin *discursus* argument

discourteous *adj* showing bad manners; rude **discourteously** *adv* **discourtesy** *n*

discover *vb* **1** to be the first to find or find out about **2** to learn about for the first time **3** to find after study or search **discoverer** *n*

discovery *n, pl* **-veries 1** the act of discovering **2** a person, place, or thing that has been discovered

discredit *vb* **-diting, -dited 1** to damage the reputation of (someone) **2** to cause (an idea) to be disbelieved or distrusted ▷ *n* **3** something that causes disgrace **discreditable** *adj*

discreet *adj* **1** careful to avoid embarrassment when dealing with secret or private matters **2** unobtrusive: *there was a discreet entrance down a side alley* **discreetly** *adv*
WORD ORIGIN Old French *discret*

≡ USAGE
≡ Avoid confusion with **discrete**.

discrepancy *n, pl* **-cies** a conflict or variation between facts, figures, or claims **discrepant** *adj*
WORD ORIGIN Latin *discrepare* to differ in sound

≡ USAGE
≡ *Discrepancy* is sometimes wrongly used
≡ where *disparity* is meant. A *discrepancy*
≡ exists between things which ought to
≡ be the same; it can be small but is
≡ usually significant. A *disparity* is a
≡ large difference between measurable
≡ things such as age, rank, or wages.

discrete *adj* separate or distinct **discreteness** *n*
WORD ORIGIN Latin *discretus* separated

≡ USAGE
≡ Avoid confusion with **discreet**.

discretion (diss-**kresh**-on) *n* **1** the quality of behaving so as to avoid social embarrassment or distress **2** freedom or authority to make judgments and to act as one sees fit: *at his discretion* **discretionary** *adj*

discriminate *vb* **-nating, -nated 1** to make a distinction against or in favour of a particular person or group **2** to recognize or understand a difference: *to discriminate between right and wrong* **discriminating** *adj*
WORD ORIGIN Latin *discriminare* to divide

discrimination *n* **1** unfair treatment of a person, racial group, or minority **2** subtle appreciation in matters of taste **3** the ability to see fine distinctions

discriminatory *adj* based on prejudice

discursive *adj* passing from one topic to another
WORD ORIGIN Latin *discursus* a running to and fro

discus *n* *field sports* a disc-shaped object with a heavy middle, thrown by athletes
WORD ORIGIN Greek *diskos*

discuss *vb* **1** to consider (something) by talking it over **2** to treat (a subject) in speech or writing **discussion** *n*
WORD ORIGIN Latin *discutere* to dash to pieces

disdain n 1 a feeling of superiority and dislike; contempt ▷ vb 2 to refuse or reject with disdain: *he disdained domestic conventions* **disdainful** adj **disdainfully** adv
WORD ORIGIN Old French *desdeign*

disease n an unhealthy condition in a person, animal, or plant which is caused by bacteria or infection **diseased** adj
WORD ORIGIN Old French *desaise*

diseconomy n *econ* a disadvantage, such as higher costs, resulting from the scale on which a business operates

disembark vb to land or cause to land from a ship, aircraft, or other vehicle **disembarkation** n

disembodied adj 1 lacking a body 2 seeming not to be attached to or come from anyone **disembodiment** n

disembowel vb -welling, -welled or US -weling, -weled to remove the entrails of **disembowelment** n

disempower vb to deprive (a person) of power or authority **disempowerment** n

disenchanted adj disappointed and disillusioned (with something) **disenchantment** n

disenfranchise vb -chising, -chised to deprive (someone) of the right to vote or of other rights of citizenship

disengage vb -gaging, -gaged 1 to release from a connection 2 mil to withdraw from close action **disengagement** n

disentangle vb -gling, -gled 1 to release from entanglement or confusion 2 to unravel or work out **disentanglement** n

disequilibrium n a loss or absence of stability or balance

disestablish vb to deprive (a church or religion) of established status **disestablishment** n

disfavour or US **disfavor** n 1 disapproval or dislike 2 the state of being disapproved of or disliked

disfigure vb -guring, -gured to spoil the appearance or shape of **disfigurement** n

disfranchise vb -chising, -chised same as **disenfranchise**

disgorge vb -gorging, -gorged 1 to vomit 2 to discharge (contents)

disgrace n 1 a condition of shame, loss of reputation, or dishonour 2 a shameful person or thing 3 exclusion from confidence or trust: *he was sent home in disgrace* ▷ vb -gracing, -graced 4 to bring shame upon (oneself or others) **disgraceful** adj **disgracefully** adv

disgruntled adj sulky or discontented: *the disgruntled home supporters* **disgruntlement** n
WORD ORIGIN DIS- + obsolete *gruntle* to complain

disguise vb -guising, -guised 1 to change the appearance or manner in order to conceal the identity of (someone or something) 2 to misrepresent (something) in order to obscure its actual nature or meaning ▷ n 3 a mask, costume, or manner that disguises 4 the state of being disguised **disguised** adj
WORD ORIGIN Old French *desguisier*

disgust n 1 a great loathing or distaste ▷ vb 2 to sicken or fill with loathing

disgusted adj **disgusting** adj
WORD ORIGIN Old French *desgouster* to sicken

dish n 1 a container used for holding or serving food, esp. an open shallow container 2 the food in a dish 3 a particular kind of food 4 short for **dish aerial** 5 *informal* an attractive person ▷ See also **dish out, dish up**
WORD ORIGIN Old English *disc*

dishabille (diss-a-**beel**) n same as **deshabille**

dish aerial n a large disc-shaped aerial with a concave reflector, used to receive signals in radar, radio telescopes, and satellite broadcasting

disharmony n lack of agreement or harmony **disharmonious** adj

dishcloth n a cloth for washing dishes

dishearten vb to weaken or destroy the hope, courage, or enthusiasm of **disheartened** adj **disheartening** adj

dishevelled or US **disheveled** adj (of a person's hair, clothes, or general appearance) disordered and untidy
WORD ORIGIN Old French *deschevelé*

dishonest adj not honest or fair **dishonestly** adv **dishonesty** n

dishonour or US **dishonor** vb 1 to treat with disrespect 2 to refuse to pay (a cheque) ▷ n 3 a lack of honour or respect 4 a state of shame or disgrace 5 something that causes a loss of honour **dishonourable** adj **dishonourably** adv

dish out vb 1 *informal* to distribute 2 **dish it out** to inflict punishment

dish up vb to serve (food)

dishwasher n a machine for washing and drying dishes, cutlery, etc.

dishwater n 1 water in which dishes have been washed 2 **like dishwater** (of tea) very weak

dishy adj **dishier, dishiest** *informal* good-looking

disillusion vb 1 to destroy the illusions or false ideas of (someone) ▷ n also **disillusionment** 2 the state of being disillusioned

disillusioned adj disappointed at finding out reality does not match one's ideals

disincentive n something that discourages someone from behaving or acting in a particular way

disinclined adj unwilling or reluctant **disinclination** n

disinfect vb to rid of harmful germs by cleaning with a chemical substance **disinfection** n

disinfectant n a substance that destroys harmful germs

disinformation n false information intended to mislead

disingenuous adj dishonest and insincere **disingenuously** adv

disinherit vb -iting, -ited *law* to deprive (an heir) of inheritance **disinheritance** n

disintegrate vb -grating, -grated 1 to lose cohesion; break up: *the business disintegrated* 2 (of an object) to break into fragments; shatter 3 *physics* a to undergo nuclear fission or include

nuclear fission in **b** same as **decay** (sense 3) > **disintegration** n

disinter vb -terring, -terred 1 to dig up 2 to bring to light; expose

disinterested adj 1 free from bias; objective 2 *not standard* feeling or showing a lack of interest; uninterested **disinterest** n

USAGE
Many people consider that the use of *disinterested* to mean not interested is incorrect and that *uninterested* should be used.

disjointed adj having no coherence; disconnected: *a disjointed conversation*

disjunctive adj serving to disconnect or separate

disk n 1 *chiefly US & Canad* same as **disc** 2 *computers* a storage device, consisting of a stack of plates coated with a magnetic layer, which rotates rapidly as a single unit
WORD ORIGIN see DISC

disk drive n *computers* the controller and mechanism for reading and writing data on computer disks

dislike vb -liking, -liked 1 to consider unpleasant or disagreeable ▷ n 2 a feeling of not liking something or someone

dislocate vb -cating, -cated 1 to displace (a bone or joint) from its normal position 2 to disrupt or shift out of place **dislocation** n

dislodge vb -lodging, -lodged to remove (something) from a previously fixed position

disloyal adj not loyal; deserting one's allegiance or duty **disloyalty** n

dismal adj 1 gloomy and depressing 2 *informal* of poor quality **dismally** adv
WORD ORIGIN Medieval Latin *dies mali* unlucky days

dismantle vb -tling, -tled 1 to take apart piece by piece 2 to cause (an organization or political system) to stop functioning by gradually reducing its power or purpose
WORD ORIGIN Old French *desmanteler*

dismay vb 1 to fill with alarm or depression ▷ n 2 a feeling of alarm or depression
WORD ORIGIN Old French *des-* (intensive) + *esmayer* to frighten

dismember vb 1 to remove the limbs of 2 to cut to pieces **dismemberment** n

dismiss vb 1 to remove (an employee) from a job 2 to allow (someone) to leave 3 to put out of one's mind; no longer think about 4 (of a judge) to state that (a case) will not be brought to trial 5 *cricket* to bowl out (a side) for a particular number of runs **dismissal** n **dismissive** adj
WORD ORIGIN Latin *dis-* from + *mittere* to send

dismount vb to get off a horse or bicycle

disobedient adj refusing to obey **disobedience** n

disobey vb to neglect or refuse to obey (a person or an order)

disobliging adj unwilling to help

disorder n 1 a state of untidiness and disorganization 2 public violence or rioting 3 an illness **disordered** adj

Samuel Johnson

Samuel Johnson is undoubtedly the best-known figure in the history of English dictionary-making. His fame as a lexicographer derives from *A Dictionary of the English Language*, which was published in 1755 and was the first coherent attempt to define the language in its entirety. Although he is widely known as 'Doctor Johnson', he was not a medical man, nor even a university graduate. His doctorate was an honorary one, awarded by Trinity College Dublin after the compilation of his dictionary.

Johnson was born in Lichfield, Staffordshire, in 1709, where his father owned a bookshop. As an infant he contracted scrofula, which affected his appearance and left him partially deaf and also blind in one eye. It is perhaps not surprising that he became more comfortable around books than people.

He attended Oxford University, but left in order to assist his dying father. Unable to make a success of his father's business, he worked as a schoolteacher, during which time he started to write. In 1737, he moved to London, earning his living as a journalist, poet, and editor.

He first created a plan for compiling a dictionary in 1747, having secured a contract for 1500 guineas from a syndicate of booksellers. Over the next eight years he worked on the project from his house in London's Gough Square, employing assistants to help him with the more mundane tasks.

Johnson had originally estimated that he could complete the work in three years. (He was undaunted when a friend pointed out that it has taken a panel of forty French experts over forty years to compile a comparable dictionary: "Let me see; forty times forty is sixteen hundred. As three to sixteen hundred, so is the proportion of an Englishman to a Frenchman.") Nevertheless, the work proved more difficult than he had imagined and forced him to limit his ambition for the book. He had thought that the entire English language could be brought to conform to a set of rules, but was forced to conclude in the end that the best he could do was merely to describe the way that language is used.

The finished dictionary included over 42,000 entries and extended over two large volumes. The title page boasts that Johnson has teased out the 'different significations' of words and deduced their definitions from their origins, as well as illustrating their meanings by quotations from 'the best writers'. Indeed, the plundering of English literature to provide copious examples of how words are used is one of the great achievements of the dictionary. Another great achievement of the dictionary was to contribute to the standardization of English spelling, which had hitherto been left largely to the taste and discretion of the writer.

These days, Johnson's dictionary is remembered for its flashes of humour, such as when he defines oats as 'a grain which in England is generally given to horses, but in Scotland supports the people' or a patron as 'a wretch who supports with insolence, and is paid with flattery'.

Yet in spite of the reputation it achieved, the dictionary was not infallible, Johnson's resources being limited and his interests lying more in the literary matters than in technical accuracy. When asked why he had offered an incorrect definition of the word 'pastern' he had to confess, "Ignorance, madam, ignorance." The task of compilation left Johnson to reflect that perfection was not something that should be looked for in a dictionary: "Dictionaries are like watches. The worst is better than none, and the best cannot be expected to go quite true."

The publication of the dictionary led to the award of a state pension from George III, which finally gave Johnson a measure of financial security. His later publications included the fable *Rasselas* (1759), a critical edition of *The Plays of William Shakespeare* (1765), and the ten-volume *Lives of the Most Eminent English Poets* (1779–81). Besides his fame as a lexicographer, he is also known as one of England's greatest wits and conversationalists – a reputation guaranteed by his biographer James Boswell, who recorded many of Johnson's sayings in his *Journal of a Tour to the Hebrides* (1785) and *The Life of Samuel Johnson* (1791).

disorderly *adj* **1** untidy and disorganized **2** uncontrolled; unruly **3** *law* violating public peace

disorganize *or* **-ise** *vb* **-izing, -ized** *or* **-ising, -ised** to disrupt the arrangement or system of **disorganization** *or* **-isation** *n*

disorientate *or* **disorient** *vb* **-tating, -tated** *or* **-enting, -ented** to cause (someone) to lose his or her bearings **disorientation** *n*

disown *vb* to deny any connection with (someone)

disparage *vb* **-aging, -aged** to speak contemptuously of **disparagement** *n* **disparaging** *adj*
WORD ORIGIN Old French *desparagier*

disparate *adj* utterly different in kind **disparity** *n*
WORD ORIGIN Latin *disparare* to divide

☰ USAGE
☰ See at **discrepancy**.

dispassionate *adj* not influenced by emotion; objective **dispassionately** *adv*

dispatch *or* **despatch** *vb* **1** to send off to a destination or to perform a task **2** to carry out (a duty or task) promptly **3** to murder ▷ *n* **4** an official communication or report, sent in haste **5** a report sent to a newspaper by a correspondent **6** murder **7** **with dispatch** quickly
WORD ORIGIN Italian *dispacciare*

dispatch rider *n* *Brit, Austral, & NZ* a motorcyclist who carries dispatches

dispel *vb* **-pelling, -pelled** to disperse or drive away
WORD ORIGIN Latin *dispellere*

dispensable *adj* not essential; expendable

dispensary *n, pl* **-ries** a place where medicine is prepared and given out

dispensation *n* **1** the act of distributing or dispensing **2** *chiefly RC Church* permission to dispense with an obligation of church law **3** any exemption from an obligation **4** the ordering of life and events by God

dispense *vb* **-pensing, -pensed** **1** to distribute in portions **2** to prepare and distribute (medicine) **3** to administer (the law, etc.) **4** **dispense with** to do away with or manage without **dispenser** *n*
WORD ORIGIN Latin *dispendere* to weigh out

☰ USAGE
☰ *Dispense with* is sometimes wrongly
☰ used where *dispose of* is meant: *this task*
☰ *can be disposed of* (not *dispensed with*)
☰ *quickly and easily*.

dispensing optician *n* see **optician** (sense 2)

disperse *vb* **-persing, -persed** **1** to scatter over a wide area **2** to leave or cause to leave a gathering: *police dispersed rioters* **3** to separate (light) into its different wavelengths **4** to separate (particles) throughout a solid, liquid, or gas **dispersal** *or* **dispersion** *n*
WORD ORIGIN Latin *dispergere* to scatter widely

☰ USAGE
☰ See at **disburse**.

dispirit *vb* to make downhearted **dispirited** *adj* **dispiriting** *adj*

displace *vb* **-placing, -placed** **1** to move (something) from its usual place **2** to remove (someone) from a post or position of authority

displaced person *n* a person forced from his or her home or country, esp. by war or revolution

displacement *n* **1** the act of displacing **2** *physics* the weight or volume of liquid displaced by an object submerged or floating in it **3** *maths* the distance measured in a particular direction from a reference point. Symbol: *s*

display *vb* **1** to show **2** to reveal or make evident: *to display anger* ▷ *n* **3** the act of exhibiting or displaying **4** something displayed **5** an exhibition **6** *electronics* a device capable of representing information visually, as on a screen **7** *zool* a pattern of behaviour by which an animal attracts attention while courting, defending its territory, etc.
WORD ORIGIN Anglo-French *despleier* to unfold

displease *vb* **-pleasing, -pleased** to annoy or offend (someone) **displeasure** *n*

disport *vb* **disport oneself** to indulge oneself in pleasure
WORD ORIGIN Anglo-French *desporter*

disposable *adj* **1** designed for disposal after use: *disposable cigarette lighters* **2** available for use if needed: *disposable capital*

disposal *n* **1** the act or means of getting rid of something **2** **at one's disposal** available for use

dispose *vb* **-posing, -posed** **1** **dispose of a** to throw away **b** to give, sell, or transfer to another **c** to deal with or settle: *I disposed of that problem right away* **d** to kill **2** to arrange or place in a particular way: *around them are disposed the moulded masks of witch doctors*
WORD ORIGIN Latin *disponere* to set in different places

☰ USAGE
☰ See at **dispense**.

disposed *adj* **1** willing or eager (to do something): *few would feel disposed to fault his judgment* **2** having an inclination as specified (towards someone or something): *my people aren't too well disposed towards defectors*

disposition *n* **1** a person's usual temperament **2** a tendency or habit **3** arrangement; layout

dispossess *vb* to deprive (someone) of (a possession) **dispossessed** *adj* **dispossession** *n*

disproportion *n* lack of proportion or equality

disproportionate *adj* out of proportion **disproportionately** *adv*

disprove *vb* **-proving, -proved** to show (an assertion or claim) to be incorrect

dispute *n* **1** a disagreement between workers and their employer **2** an argument between two or more people **3** **beyond dispute** unable to be questioned or denied: *it's beyond dispute that tensions already existed between them* ▷ *vb* **-puting, -puted** **4** to argue or quarrel about (something) **5** to doubt the validity of **6** to fight over

possession of **disputation** *n* **disputatious** *adj*
WORD ORIGIN Latin *disputare* to discuss

disqualify *vb* **-fies, -fying, -fied** **1** to officially ban (someone) from doing something: *he was disqualified from driving for ten years* **2** to make ineligible, as for entry to an examination **disqualification** *n*

disquiet *n* **1** a feeling of anxiety or uneasiness ▷ *vb* **2** to make (someone) anxious **disquieting** *adj* **disquietude** *n*

disquisition *n* a formal written or oral examination of a subject

disregard *vb* **1** to give little or no attention to; ignore ▷ *n* **2** lack of attention or respect

disrepair *n* the condition of being worn out or in poor working order

disreputable *adj* having or causing a bad reputation **disreputably** *adv*

disrepute *n* a loss or lack of good reputation

disrespect *n* contempt or lack of respect **disrespectful** *adj*

disrobe *vb* **-robing, -robed** *literary* to undress

disrupt *vb* to interrupt the progress of **disruption** *n* **disruptive** *adj*
WORD ORIGIN Latin *disruptus* burst asunder

diss *vb* *slang chiefly US* to treat (a person) with contempt
WORD ORIGIN from DISRESPECT

dissatisfied *adj* displeased or discontented **dissatisfaction** *n*

dissect *vb* **1** to cut open (a corpse) to examine it **2** to examine critically and minutely: *the above conclusion causes one to dissect that policy more closely* **dissection** *n*
WORD ORIGIN Latin *dissecare*

dissemble *vb* **-bling, -bled** to conceal one's real motives or emotions by pretence **dissembler** *n*
WORD ORIGIN Latin *dissimulare*

disseminate *vb* **-nating, -nated** to spread (information, ideas, etc.) widely **dissemination** *n*
WORD ORIGIN Latin *disseminare*

dissension *n* disagreement and argument
WORD ORIGIN Latin *dissentire* to dissent

dissent *vb* **1** to disagree **2** *Christianity* to reject the doctrines of an established church ▷ *n* **3** a disagreement **4** *Christianity* separation from an established church **dissenter** *n* **dissenting** *adj*
WORD ORIGIN Latin *dissentire* to disagree

Dissenter *n* *Christianity chiefly Brit* a Protestant who refuses to conform to the established church

dissentient *adj* dissenting from the opinion of the majority

dissertation *n* **1** a written thesis, usually required for a higher degree **2** a long formal speech
WORD ORIGIN Latin *dissertare* to debate

disservice *n* a harmful action

dissident *n* **1** a person who disagrees with a government or a powerful organization ▷ *adj* **2** disagreeing or dissenting **dissidence** *n*
WORD ORIGIN Latin *dissidere* to be remote from

d

dissimilar *adj* not alike; different **dissimilarity** *n*

dissimulate *vb* **-lating, -lated** to conceal one's real feelings by pretence **dissimulation** *n*

dissipate *vb* **-pating, -pated 1** to waste or squander **2** to scatter or break up
WORD ORIGIN Latin *dissipare* to disperse

dissipated *adj* showing signs of overindulgence in alcohol or other physical pleasures

dissipation *n* **1** the process of dissipating **2** unrestrained indulgence in physical pleasures

dissociate *vb* **-ciating, -ciated 1 dissociate oneself from** to deny or break an association with (a person or organization) **2** to regard or treat as separate **dissociation** *n*

dissoluble *adj* same as **soluble** > **dissolubility** *n*
WORD ORIGIN Latin *dissolubilis*

dissolute *adj* leading an immoral life
WORD ORIGIN Latin *dissolutus* loose

dissolution *n* **1** the act of officially breaking up an organization or institution **2** the act of officially ending a formal agreement, such as a marriage **3** the formal ending of a meeting or assembly, such as a Parliament

dissolve *vb* **-solving, -solved 1** to become or cause to become liquid; melt **2** to officially break up (an organization or institution) **3** to formally end: *the campaign started as soon as Parliament was dissolved last month* **4** to collapse emotionally: *she dissolved in loud tears* **5** *films, television* to fade out one scene and replace with another to make two scenes merge imperceptibly
WORD ORIGIN Latin *dissolvere* to make loose

dissonance *n* a lack of agreement or harmony between things: *this dissonance of colours* **dissonant** *adj*

dissuade *vb* **-suading, -suaded** to deter (someone) by persuasion from doing something or believing in something **dissuasion** *n*
WORD ORIGIN Latin *dissuadere*

dissyllable *or* **disyllable** *n* a word of two syllables **dissyllabic** *or* **disyllabic** *adj*

distaff *n* the rod on which flax is wound for spinning
WORD ORIGIN Old English *distæf*

distaff side *n* the female side of a family

distance *n* **1** the space between two points or places **2** the state of being apart **3** a distant place **4** remoteness in manner **5 the distance** the most distant part of the visible scene **6 go the distance a** *boxing* to complete a bout without being knocked out **b** to complete an assigned task or responsibility **7 keep one's distance** to maintain a reserved attitude to another person ▷ *vb* **-tancing, -tanced 8 distance oneself from** *or* **be distanced from** to separate oneself or be separated mentally from

distance learning *n* a teaching system involving video and written material for studying at home

distant *adj* **1** far-off; remote **2** far apart **3** separated by a specified distance: *five kilometres distant* **4** apart in relationship: *a distant cousin* **5** going to a faraway place **6** remote in manner; aloof **7** abstracted: *a distant look entered her eyes* **distantly** *adv*
WORD ORIGIN Latin *dis-* apart + *stare* to stand

distaste *n* a dislike of something offensive

distasteful *adj* unpleasant or offensive **distastefulness** *n*

distemper¹ *n* a highly contagious viral disease that can affect young dogs
WORD ORIGIN Latin *dis-* apart + *temperare* to regulate

distemper² *n* **1** paint mixed with water, glue, etc. which is used for painting walls ▷ *vb* **2** to paint with distemper
WORD ORIGIN Latin *dis-* (intensive) + *temperare* to mingle

distend *vb* to expand by pressure from within; swell **distensible** *adj* **distension** *n*
WORD ORIGIN Latin *distendere*

distich (**diss**-stick) *n* *prosody* a unit of two verse lines
WORD ORIGIN Greek *di-* two + *stikhos* row, line

distil *or US* **distill** *vb* **-tilling, -tilled 1** to subject to or obtain by distillation **2** to give off (a substance) in drops **3** to extract the essence of
WORD ORIGIN Latin *de-* down + *stillare* to drip

distillation *n* **1** the process of evaporating a liquid and condensing its vapour **2** Also: **distillate** a concentrated essence

distiller *n* a person or company that makes spirits

distillery *n*, *pl* **-eries** a place where alcoholic drinks are made by distillation

distinct *adj* **1** not the same; different: *these two areas produce wines with distinct characteristics* **2** clearly seen, heard, or recognized: *it is not possible to draw a distinct line between the two categories; there's a distinct smell of burning* **3** clear and definite: *there is a distinct possibility of rain* **4** obvious: *a distinct improvement* **distinctly** *adv*
WORD ORIGIN Latin *distinctus*

distinction *n* **1** the act of distinguishing or differentiating **2** a distinguishing feature **3** the state of being different or distinguishable **4** special honour, recognition, or fame **5** excellence of character **6** a symbol of honour or rank

distinctive *adj* easily recognizable; characteristic **distinctively** *adv* **distinctiveness** *n*

distingué (diss-**tang**-gay) *adj* distinguished or noble
WORD ORIGIN French

distinguish *vb* **1** to make, show, or recognize a difference: *I have tried to distinguish between fact and theory* **2** to be a distinctive feature of: *what distinguishes the good teenage reader from the less competent one?* **3** to make out by hearing, seeing, or tasting: *she listened but could distinguish nothing except the urgency of their discussion*

4 distinguish oneself to make oneself noteworthy **distinguishable** *adj* **distinguishing** *adj*
WORD ORIGIN Latin *distinguere* to separate

distinguished *adj* **1** dignified in appearance or behaviour **2** highly respected: *a distinguished historian*

distort *vb* **1** to alter or misrepresent (facts) **2** to twist out of shape; deform **3** *electronics* to reproduce or amplify (a signal) inaccurately **distorted** *adj* **distortion** *n*
WORD ORIGIN Latin *distorquere* to turn different ways

distract *vb* **1** to draw (a person or his or her attention) away from something **2** to amuse or entertain
WORD ORIGIN Latin *distrahere* to pull in different directions
≡ USAGE
≡ See at **detract**.

distracted *adj* unable to concentrate because one's mind is on other things

distraction *n* **1** something that diverts the attention **2** something that serves as an entertainment **3** mental turmoil

distrain *vb* *law* to seize (personal property) to enforce payment of a debt **distraint** *n*
WORD ORIGIN Latin *di-* apart + *stringere* to draw tight

distrait (diss-**tray**) *adj* absent-minded or abstracted
WORD ORIGIN French

distraught (diss-**trawt**) *adj* upset or agitated
WORD ORIGIN obsolete *distract*

distress *n* **1** extreme unhappiness or worry **2** great physical pain **3** financial trouble ▷ *vb* **4** to upset badly **5 in distress** in dire need of help **distressing** *adj* **distressingly** *adv*
WORD ORIGIN Latin *districtus* divided in mind

distressed *adj* **1** much troubled; upset **2** in great physical pain **3** in financial difficulties **4** (of furniture or fabric) having signs of ageing artificially applied

distributary *n*, *pl* **-taries** one of several outlet streams draining a river, esp. on a delta

distribute *vb* **-uting, -uted 1** to hand out or deliver (leaflets, mail, etc.) **2** to share (something) among the members of a particular group
WORD ORIGIN Latin *distribuere*

distribution *n* **1** the delivering of leaflets, mail, etc. to individual people or organizations **2** the sharing out of something among a particular group **3** the arrangement or spread of anything over an area, space, or period of time: *the unequal distribution of wealth* **4** *commerce* the process of satisfying the demand for goods and services

distributive *adj* **1** of or relating to distribution **2** *maths* of the rule that the same result is produced when multiplication is performed on a set of numbers as when performed on the members of the set individually

distributor *n* **1** a wholesaler who distributes goods to retailers in a

d

specific area **2** the device in a petrol engine that sends the electric current to the sparking plugs

district *n* **1** an area of land regarded as an administrative or geographical unit **2** an area which has recognizable or special features: *an upper-class residential district*
WORD ORIGIN Medieval Latin *districtus* area of jurisdiction

district court judge *n* *Austral & NZ* a judge presiding over a lower court

district nurse *n* (in Britain) a nurse who attends to patients in their homes within a particular district

distrust *vb* **1** to regard as untrustworthy ▷ *n* **2** a feeling of suspicion or doubt **distrustful** *adj*

disturb *vb* **1** to intrude on; interrupt **2** to upset or worry **3** to disarrange; muddle **4** to inconvenience **disturbing** *adj* **disturbingly** *adv*
WORD ORIGIN Latin *disturbare*

disturbance *n* **1** an interruption or intrusion **2** an unruly outburst in public

disturbed *adj psychiatry* emotionally upset, troubled, or maladjusted

disunite *vb* **-niting, -nited** to cause disagreement among **disunion** *n* **disunity** *n*

disuse *n* the state of being neglected or no longer used; neglect

disused *adj* no longer used

disyllable *n* same as **dissyllable**

ditch *n* **1** a narrow channel dug in the earth for drainage or irrigation ▷ *vb* **2** *slang* to abandon or discard: *she ditched her boyfriend last month*
WORD ORIGIN Old English *dīc*

dither *vb* **1** *chiefly Brit & NZ* to be uncertain or indecisive ▷ *n* **2** *chiefly Brit* a state of indecision or agitation **ditherer** *n* **dithery** *adj*
WORD ORIGIN Middle English *didder*

dithyramb *n* (in ancient Greece) a passionate choral hymn in honour of Dionysus **dithyrambic** *adj*
WORD ORIGIN Greek *dithurambos*

ditto *n, pl* **-tos 1** the above; the same: used in lists to avoid repetition, and represented by the mark (,,) placed under the thing repeated ▷ *adv* **2** in the same way
WORD ORIGIN Italian (dialect) *detto* said

ditty *n, pl* **-ties** a short simple song or poem
WORD ORIGIN Latin *dictare* to say repeatedly

ditzy *or* **ditsy** *adj* **ditzier, ditziest** *or* **ditsier, ditsiest** *slang* silly and scatterbrained
WORD ORIGIN perhaps from DOTTY + DIZZY

diuretic (die-yoor-et-ik) *n* a drug that increases the flow of urine
WORD ORIGIN Greek *dia-* through + *ourein* to urinate

diurnal (die-urn-al) *adj* **1** happening during the day or daily **2** (of animals) active during the day
WORD ORIGIN Latin *diurnus*

diva *n, pl* **-vas** *or* **-ve** a distinguished female singer; prima donna
WORD ORIGIN Latin: a goddess

divalent *adj chem* having two valencies or a valency of two **divalency** *n*

divan *n* **a** a low bed with a thick base under the mattress **b** a couch with no back or arms
WORD ORIGIN Turkish *dīvān*

dive *vb* **diving, dived** *or US* **dove, dived 1** to plunge headfirst into water **2** (of a submarine or diver) to submerge under water **3** (of a bird or aircraft) to fly in a steep nose-down descending path **4** to move quickly in a specified direction: *he dived for the door* **5 dive in** *or* **into a** to put (one's hand) quickly or forcefully into **b** to start doing (something) enthusiastically ▷ *n* **6** a headlong plunge into water **7** the act of diving **8** a steep nose-down descent of a bird or aircraft **9** *slang* a disreputable bar or club
WORD ORIGIN Old English *dȳfan*

dive bomber *n* a military aircraft designed to release bombs on a target during a dive **dive-bomb** *vb*

diver *n* **1** a person who works or explores underwater **2** a person who dives for sport **3** a large diving bird of northern oceans with a straight pointed bill and webbed feet

diverge *vb* **-verging, -verged 1** to separate and go in different directions **2** to be at variance; differ: *the two books diverge in setting and in style* **3** to deviate (from a prescribed course) **divergence** *n* **divergent** *adj*
WORD ORIGIN Latin *dis-* apart + *vergere* to turn

diverse *adj* **1** having variety; assorted **2** different in kind
WORD ORIGIN Latin *diversus* turned in different directions

diversify *vb* **-fies, -fying, -fied 1** to create different forms of; vary **2** (of an enterprise) to vary (products or operations) in order to expand or reduce the risk of loss **diversification** *n*
WORD ORIGIN Latin *diversus* different + *facere* to make

diversion *n* **1** *chiefly Brit* an official detour used by traffic when a main route is closed **2** something that distracts someone's attention or concentration **3** the act of diverting from a specified course **4** a pleasant or amusing pastime or activity **diversionary** *adj*

diversity *n* **1** the quality of being different or varied **2** a point of difference

divert *vb* **1** to change the course or direction of (traffic) **2** to distract the attention of **3** to entertain or amuse
WORD ORIGIN Latin *divertere* to turn aside

diverticulitis *n* inflammation of pouches in the wall of the colon, causing lower abdominal pain
WORD ORIGIN Latin *deverticulum* path, track

divertimento *n, pl* **-ti** a piece of entertaining music in several movements
WORD ORIGIN Italian

divest *vb* **1** to strip (of clothes) **2** to deprive of a role, function, or quality: *the chairman felt duty-bound to stay with the*

company after it was divested of all its aviation interests
WORD ORIGIN earlier *devest*

divide *vb* **-viding, -vided 1** to separate into parts **2** to share or be shared out in parts **3** to disagree or cause to disagree: *experts are divided over the plan* **4** to keep apart or be a boundary between **5** to categorize or classify **6** to calculate how many times one number can be contained in another ▷ *n* **7** a division or split **8** *chiefly US & Canad* an area of high ground separating drainage basins
WORD ORIGIN Latin *dividere* to force apart

dividend *n* **1** a portion of a company's profits paid to its shareholders **2** an extra benefit: *Saudi progressives saw a dividend to the crisis* **3** *maths* a number to be divided by another number
WORD ORIGIN Latin *dividendum* what is to be divided

divider *n* a screen placed so as to divide a room into separate areas

dividers *pl n* compasses with two pointed arms, used for measuring or dividing lines

divination *n* the art of discovering future events as though by supernatural powers

divine *adj* **1** of God or a god **2** godlike **3** *informal* splendid or perfect ▷ *n* **4** a priest who is learned in theology ▷ *vb* **-vining, -vined 5** to discover (something) by intuition or guessing **divinely** *adv* **diviner** *n*
WORD ORIGIN Latin *divus* a god

diving bell *n* a diving apparatus with an open bottom, supplied with compressed air from above

diving board *n* a platform from which swimmers may dive

diving suit *n* a waterproof suit used for diving with a detachable helmet and an air supply

divining rod *n* a forked twig said to move when held over ground in which water or metal is to be found

divinity *n, pl* **-ties 1** the study of religion **2** a god or goddess **3** the state of being divine

divisible *adj* capable of being divided **divisibility** *n*

division *n* **1** the separation of something into two or more distinct parts **2** the act of dividing or sharing out **3** one of the parts into which something is divided **4** the mathematical operation of dividing **5** a difference of opinion **6** a part of an organization that has been made into a unit for administrative or other reasons **7** a formal vote in Parliament **8** one of the groups of teams that make up a football or other sports league **9** *army* a major formation containing the necessary arms to sustain independent combat **10** *biol* one of the major groups into which the plant kingdom is divided, corresponding to a phylum **divisional** *adj*
WORD ORIGIN Latin *dividere* to divide

division sign *n* the symbol ÷, placed between two numbers to indicate that the first number should be divided by the second, as in $12 ÷ 6 = 2$

divisive (div-vice-iv) *adj* tending to cause disagreement: *he played an*

King James English

As a monument of English prose, the *King James Bible* or *Authorized Version* stands alone. Designed as a bulky tome for public worship, not private reading, a colossal commercial failure at first, it eventually became the bestselling English book of all time. When James I commissioned nearly 50 Church of England clergyman scholars in 1604 to embark on its creation, he and they meant it to reconcile the conflicting claims of Roman Catholicism and Puritanism, and to uphold the rule of kings and bishops. Instead, it was the majesty of its language that prevailed.

One of the very rare collaborative masterpieces, it not only marked the high-tide mark of Elizabethan and Jacobean writing, but signalled the end of a century in which Middle English had moved rapidly into Modern English. Yet, with its *verily* and *it came to pass*, its *-th* verb endings (*goeth, sayeth*), its use of *thou* for *you* in the second person singular, and *thereof* for *it* or *its* (*then shall he eat thereof* not *then shall he eat it*), the Bible's language was archaic even when it was published in 1611. It tended to use elegant variations of words rather than simple repetition, and slowed readers or hearers with its multiple *ands* and *ofs*, and its copious punctuation. Yet, by way of William Tyndale's Bible (1525–1530), it also used such plainspoken idioms as *apple of his eye, the salt of the earth, the powers that be, my brother's keeper,* and *lick the dust*. Nonetheless, it may have been its slow pacing, Latinisms, and formality that produced its enduring attraction. Despite its now-familiar rubric 'Translated out of the Original Tongues and with the Former Translations diligently compared', the making of the King James Bible involved more comparison than direct translation from Hebrew, Aramaic, Greek, and Latin. Its composition bore all the signs of stylistic craft.

Given the vast task at hand, the notorious unwieldiness of committees, and the chaotic nature of the process, it seems in the colloquial sense of the word miraculous that the job ever got done. The Bible-drafting committees aimed to accurately reproduce the authentic Word of God but, whether they were aware of it or not, their text embeds a virtual anthology of literary forms and genres: tales, histories, gnomic or visionary poems, dramas, letters, sermons, hymns, prayers, parables – even a wedding idyll. For many generations to come, these forms framed not only how sermons, hymns, and prayers were composed, but how even writers who called themselves atheists or agnostics expressed their narratives and lyrics. Long before and after the Bible's text became standardized in 1769 and large print runs made low prices possible, church attendance and home Bible reading saturated writers' consciousness. The spiritual words of faith and belief became the words by which they understood everyday reality.

The impact the King James Bible made on the English language was not in its grammar or new words – Shakespeare, who died five years after its completion, coined many more – but its stately cadences, and even more so, the amazing aptness of its phraseology. Just as the decline of classical education meant that allusions to Greek and Roman myths could not be readily understood, the rise of secularism tended to deprive Biblical phrases of their powerful context. However, hundreds of phrases retain currency. The linguist David Crystal has noted that in the *Gospel According to St. Matthew* alone appear such evergreen expressions as *man shall not live by bread alone; the salt of the earth; O ye of little faith; cast your pearls before swine; seek and ye shall find; the blind lead the blind; suffer little children; den of thieves; render... unto Caesar the things that are Caesar's;* and *the sign of the times*. The phrases' evocative power reaches to the twentieth century in the titles of famous novels, such as John Steinbeck's *The Grapes of Wrath* (*Revelation of St. John the Divine*), and Ernest Hemingway's *The Sun Also Rises* (*Ecclesiastes, or The Preacher*).

Those who spurn the King James Bible because it is Christian, or even religious, turn their backs not only on the history of English since 1611, but on the language's lexical and rhetorical resources.

important role in *defusing potentially divisive issues*

divisor *n* a number to be divided into another number

divorce *n* **1** the legal ending of a marriage **2** a separation, esp. one that is permanent ▷ *vb* **-vorcing, -vorced** **3** to separate or be separated by divorce **4** to remove or separate
WORD ORIGIN Latin *divertere* to separate

divorcee *or masc* **divorcé** *n* a person who is divorced

divot *n* a small piece of turf

divulge *vb* **-vulging, -vulged** to make known: *I am not permitted to divulge his name* **divulgence** *n*
WORD ORIGIN Latin *divulgare*

divvy[1] *vb* **-vies, -vying, -vied** • **divvy up** *informal* to divide and share

divvy[2] *n, pl* **-vies** *Brit, dialect* a stupid person

Diwali (duh-**wah**-lee) *n* an annual Hindu festival honouring Lakshmi, the goddess of wealth

Dixie *n* the southern states of the US. Also called: **Dixieland**
WORD ORIGIN origin unknown

DIY *or* **d.i.y.** *Brit, Austral, & NZ* do-it-yourself

dizzy *adj* **-zier, -ziest** **1** feeling giddy **2** unable to think clearly; confused **3** tending to cause giddiness or confusion ▷ *vb* **-zies, -zying, -zied** **4** to cause to feel giddy or confused **dizzily** *adv* **dizziness** *n*
WORD ORIGIN Old English *dysig* silly

DJ *or* **dj** **1** disc jockey **2** *Brit* dinner jacket

djinni *or* **djinny** *n, pl* **djinn** same as **jinni**

dl decilitre(s)

DLitt *or* **DLit** **1** Doctor of Letters **2** Doctor of Literature
WORD ORIGIN Latin *Doctor Litterarum*

DLL *computers* dynamic link library: a set of programs that can be activated and then discarded by other programs

dm decimetre(s)

DM Deutschmark

DMus Doctor of Music

DNA deoxyribonucleic acid, the main constituent of the chromosomes of all organisms

DNA fingerprinting *or* **DNA profiling** *n* same as **genetic fingerprinting**

D-notice *n Austral & Brit* an official notice sent to newspapers prohibiting the publication of certain security information
WORD ORIGIN from their administrative classification letter

do[1] *vb* **does, doing, did, done** **1** to perform or complete (a deed or action): *we do a fair amount of entertaining* **2** to be adequate: *it's not what I wanted but it will have to do* **3** to provide: *this hotel only does bed and breakfast* **4** to make tidy or elegant: *he watched her do her hair* **5** to improve: *that style does nothing for you* **6** to find an answer to (a problem or puzzle) **7** to conduct oneself: *do as you want* **8** to cause or produce: *herbal teas have active ingredients that can do good* **9** to give or grant: *do me a favour* **10** to work at as a course of study or a job **11** to mimic **12** to achieve a particular speed,

amount, or rate: *this computer system can do 40 different cross checks; this car can do sixty miles to the gallon* **13 a** used to form questions: *do you like it?* **b** used to intensify positive statements and commands: *tensions do exist* **c** used to form negative statements or commands: *do not talk while I'm talking!* **d** used to replace an earlier verb: *he drinks much more than I do* **14** *informal* to visit (a place) as a tourist: *we plan to do the States this year* **15** *slang* to serve (a period of time) as a prison sentence **16** *informal* to cheat or rob: *I was done out of ten pounds* **17** *slang* **a** to arrest **b** to convict of a crime: *he was done for 3 years for housebreaking* **18** *slang chiefly Brit* to assault **19** *slang* to take or use (drugs) **20 make do** to manage with whatever is available ▷ *n, pl* **dos** *or* **do's** **21** *informal chiefly Brit & NZ* a party or other social event **22 do's and don'ts** *informal* rules
▸ See also **do away with, do by**, etc.
WORD ORIGIN Old English *dōn*

do[2] *n, pl* **dos** *music* same as **doh**

do away with *vb* to get rid of (someone or something)

Doberman pinscher *or* **Doberman** *n* a large dog with a glossy black-and-tan coat
WORD ORIGIN after L. *Dobermann*, dog breeder

dob in *vb* **dobbing, dobbed** *Austral & NZ informal* **1** to inform against **2** to contribute to a fund

do by *vb* to treat in the manner specified: *he felt badly done by*

doc *n informal* same as **doctor**

DOC (in New Zealand) Department of Conservation

docile *adj* (of a person or animal) easily controlled **docilely** *adv* **docility** *n*
WORD ORIGIN Latin *docilis* easily taught

dock[1] *n* **1** an enclosed area of water where ships are loaded, unloaded, or repaired **2** a wharf or pier ▷ *vb* **3** to moor or be moored at a dock **4** to link (two spacecraft) or (of two spacecraft) to be linked together in space
WORD ORIGIN Middle Dutch *docke*

dock[2] *vb* **1** to deduct (an amount) from (a person's wages) **2** to remove part of (an animal's tail) by cutting through the bone
WORD ORIGIN Middle English *dok*

dock[3] *n* an enclosed space in a court of law where the accused person sits or stands
WORD ORIGIN Flemish *dok* sty

dock[4] *n* a weed with broad leaves
WORD ORIGIN Old English *docce*

docker *n Brit* a person employed to load and unload ships

docket *n* **1** *chiefly Brit* a label on a package or other delivery, stating contents, delivery instructions, etc. ▷ *vb* **-eting, -eted** **2** to fix a docket to (a package or other delivery)
WORD ORIGIN origin unknown

dockyard *n* a place where ships are built or repaired

Doc Martens *pl n trademark* a brand of lace-up boots with thick lightweight resistant soles

doctor *n* **1** a person licensed to practise medicine **2** a person who has been

awarded a doctorate **3** *chiefly US & Canad* a person licensed to practise dentistry or veterinary medicine ▷ *vb* **4** to change in order to deceive: *she confessed to having doctored the figures* **5** to poison or drug (food or drink) **6** to castrate (an animal) **doctoral** *adj*
WORD ORIGIN Latin: teacher

doctorate *n* the highest academic degree in any field of knowledge

doctrinaire *adj* stubbornly insistent on the application of a theory without regard to practicality

doctrine (**dock**-trin) *n* **1** a body of teachings of a religious, political, or philosophical group **2** a principle or body of principles that is taught or advocated **doctrinal** *adj*
WORD ORIGIN Latin *doctrina* teaching

docudrama *n* a film or television programme based on true events, presented in a dramatized form

document *n* **1** a piece of paper that provides an official record of something ▷ *vb* **2** to record or report (something) in detail **3** to support (a claim) with evidence
WORD ORIGIN Latin *documentum* a lesson

documentary *n, pl* **-ries** **1** a film or television programme presenting the facts about a particular subject ▷ *adj* **2** of or based on documents: *vital documentary evidence has been found*

documentation *n* documents supplied as proof or evidence of something

docu-soap *n* a television documentary series presenting the lives of the people filmed as entertainment

dodder *vb* to move unsteadily **dodderer** *n* **doddery** *adj*
WORD ORIGIN variant of earlier *dadder*

doddle *n Brit, Austral, & NZ informal* something easily accomplished: *the test turned out to be a doddle*
WORD ORIGIN origin unknown

dodecagon (doe-**deck**-a-gon) *n* a polygon with twelve sides
WORD ORIGIN Greek *dōdeka* twelve + *gōnia* angle

dodecahedron (doe-deck-a-**heed**-ron) *n* a solid figure with twelve plane faces

dodge *vb* **dodging, dodged** **1** to avoid being hit, caught, or seen by moving suddenly **2** to evade by cleverness or trickery: *the Government will not be able to dodge the issue* ▷ *n* **3** a cunning and deceitful trick
WORD ORIGIN origin unknown

Dodgem *n trademark* a small electric car driven and bumped against similar cars in a rink at a funfair

dodger *n* a person who evades a duty or obligation

dodgy *adj* **dodgier, dodgiest** *Brit, Austral & NZ informal* **1** dangerous, risky, or unreliable: *he's in a very dodgy political position* **2** untrustworthy: *they considered him a very dodgy character*

dodo *n, pl* **dodos** *or* **dodoes** **1** a large extinct bird that could not fly **2 as dead as a dodo** no longer existing
WORD ORIGIN Portuguese *duodo* stupid

do down *vb* to belittle or humiliate: *the moderate constructionist does not wish to do science down*

doe *n, pl* **does** *or* **doe** the female of the deer, hare, or rabbit
WORD ORIGIN Old English *dā*

DOE (in Britain) Department of the Environment

doek (rhymes with **book**) *n S African informal* a square of cloth worn on the head by women
WORD ORIGIN Afrikaans

doer *n* an active or energetic person

does *vb* third person singular of the present tense of **do¹**

doff *vb* to take off or lift (one's hat) in salutation
WORD ORIGIN Old English *dōn of*

do for *vb informal* **1** to cause the ruin, death, or defeat of: *I'm done for if this error comes to light* **2** to do housework for **3** **do well for oneself** to thrive or succeed

dog *n* **1** a domesticated canine mammal occurring in many different breeds **2** any other member of the dog family, such as the dingo or coyote ▸ Related adjective: **canine 3** the male of animals of the dog family **4** *informal* a person: *you lucky dog!* **5** *US & Canad informal* something unsatisfactory or inferior **6 a dog's life** a wretched existence **7 dog eat dog** ruthless competition **8 like a dog's dinner** dressed smartly and ostentatiously ▸ *vb* **dogging, dogged 9** to follow (someone) closely **10** to trouble: *dogged by ill health* ▸ See also **dogs**
WORD ORIGIN Old English *docga*

dog box *n Austral & NZ informal* same as **doghouse**

dogcart *n* a light horse-drawn two-wheeled cart

dog collar *n* **1** a collar for a dog **2** *informal* a clerical collar

dog days *pl n Brit, Austral, & NZ* the hottest period of the summer
WORD ORIGIN in ancient times reckoned from the heliacal rising of the Dog Star

doge (**doje**) *n* (formerly) the chief magistrate of Venice or Genoa
WORD ORIGIN Latin *dux* leader

dog-eared *adj* **1** (of a book) having pages folded down at the corner **2** shabby or worn

dog-end *n Brit, Austral, & NZ informal* a cigarette end

dogfight *n* **1** close-quarters combat between fighter aircraft **2** any rough fight

dogfish *n, pl* **-fish** *or* **-fishes** a small shark

dogged (**dog-gid**) *adj* obstinately determined **doggedly** *adv* **doggedness** *n*

doggerel *n* poorly written, usually comic, verse
WORD ORIGIN Middle English *dogerel* worthless

doggo *adv* **lie doggo** *informal* to hide and keep quiet
WORD ORIGIN probably from *dog*

doggy *or* **doggie** *n, pl* **-gies 1** a child's word for a **dog** ▸ *adj* **-gier, -giest 2** of or like a dog **3** fond of dogs: *I suppose dogs are all right but doggy folk can be real bores*

doggy bag *n* a bag in which leftovers from a meal may be taken away, supposedly for the diner's dog

doghouse *n* **1** *US & Canad* a kennel **2 in the doghouse** *informal* in disfavour

dogie, dogy *or* **dogey** (**dohg**-ee) *n, pl* **-gies** *or* **-geys** *US & Canad* a motherless calf
WORD ORIGIN from *dough-guts*, because they were fed on flour-and-water paste

dog in the manger *n* a person who prevents others from using something he has no use for

dogleg *n* a sharp bend

dogma *n* a doctrine or system of doctrines proclaimed by authority as true
WORD ORIGIN Greek: opinion

dogmatic *adj* habitually stating one's opinions in a forceful or arrogant manner **dogmatically** *adv* **dogmatism** *n*

do-gooder *n informal* a well-intentioned but naive or impractical person

dog paddle *n* a swimming stroke in which the hands are paddled in imitation of a swimming dog. Also called: **doggy paddle**

dogs *pl n* **1 the dogs** *Austral & Brit informal* greyhound racing **2 go to the dogs** *informal* to go to ruin physically or morally **3 let sleeping dogs lie** to leave things undisturbed

dogsbody *n, pl* **-bodies** *informal* a person who carries out boring or unimportant tasks for others

dog-tired *adj informal* exhausted

dogwatch *n* either of two watches aboard ship, from four to six pm or from six to eight pm

doh *or* **do** *n music* (in tonic sol-fa) the first note of any ascending major scale

doily *or* **doyley** *n, pl* **-lies** *or* **-leys** a decorative lacelike paper mat laid on a plate
WORD ORIGIN after *Doily*, a London draper

do in *vb slang* **1** to kill **2** to exhaust

doings *pl n* **1** deeds or actions: *her brother's doings upset her terribly* ▸ *n* **2** *informal* anything of which the name is not known or is left unsaid: *do you have the doings to open this?*

do-it-yourself *n* the practice of constructing and repairing things oneself

Dolby *n trademark* a system used in tape recorders which reduces noise level on recorded or broadcast sound

doldrums *n* **the doldrums 1 a** a feeling of depression **b** a state of inactivity **2** a belt of sea along the equator noted for absence of winds
WORD ORIGIN probably from Old English *dol* dull

dole *n* **1 the dole** *Brit, Austral, & NZ informal* money received from the state while unemployed **2 on the dole** *Brit, Austral, & NZ informal* receiving benefit while unemployed ▸ *vb* **doling, doled 3 dole out** to distribute in small quantities
WORD ORIGIN Old English *dāl* share

dole bludger *n Austral & NZ informal* a person who chooses to live off unemployment benefit

doleful *adj* dreary or mournful **dolefully** *adv* **dolefulness** *n*
WORD ORIGIN from Latin *dolere* to lament

doll *n* **1** a small model of a human being, used as a toy **2** *slang* a pretty girl or young woman
WORD ORIGIN probably from *Doll*, pet name for *Dorothy*

dollar *n* the standard monetary unit of various countries
WORD ORIGIN Low German *daler*

dollop *n informal* an amount of food served in a lump: *he shook the bottle and added a large dollop of ketchup*
WORD ORIGIN origin unknown

doll up *vb slang* **get dolled up** to dress (oneself) in a stylish or showy manner

dolly *n, pl* **-lies 1** a child's word for a **doll** (sense 1) **2** *films, television* a wheeled support on which a camera may be mounted **3** Also called: **dolly bird** *slang chiefly Brit* an attractive and fashionable girl

dolman sleeve *n* a sleeve that is very wide at the armhole and tapers to a tight wrist
WORD ORIGIN Turkish *dolaman* a winding round

dolmen *n* a prehistoric monument consisting of a horizontal stone supported by vertical stones, thought to be a tomb
WORD ORIGIN French

dolomite *n* a mineral consisting of calcium magnesium carbonate
WORD ORIGIN after Déodat de *Dolomieu*, mineralogist

dolphin *n* a sea mammal of the whale family, with a long pointed snout
WORD ORIGIN Greek *delphis*

dolphinarium *n* an aquarium for dolphins, esp. one in which they give public displays

dolt *n* a stupid person **doltish** *adj*
WORD ORIGIN probably related to Old English *dol* stupid

domain *n* **1** a particular area of activity or interest **2** land under one ruler or government **3** *computers* a group of computers that have the same suffix in their names on the internet, specifying the country, type of institution, etc. where they are located **4** *NZ* a public park
WORD ORIGIN French *domaine*

dome *n* **1** a rounded roof built on a circular base **2** something shaped like this
WORD ORIGIN Latin *domus* house

domed *adj* shaped like a dome

domestic *adj* **1** of one's own country or a specific country: *the domestic economy was generally better* **2** of the home or family **3** enjoying home or family life: *she was never a very domestic sort of person* **4** intended for use in the home: *the kitchen was equipped with all the latest domestic appliances* **5** (of an animal) bred or kept as a pet or for the supply of food ▸ *n* **6** a household servant **domestically** *adv*
WORD ORIGIN Latin *domesticus* belonging to the house

domesticate *vb* **-cating, -cated 1** to bring or keep (wild animals or plants) under control or cultivation **2** to accustom (someone) to home life **domestication** *n*

d

domesticity *n, pl* **-ties 1** home life **2** devotion to home life

domestic science *n* the study of cooking, needlework, and other household skills

domicile (**dom**-miss-ile) *n* **1** *formal* a person's regular dwelling place **2** *law* the country in which a person has his or her permanent legal residence **domiciliary** *adj*
WORD ORIGIN Latin *domus* house

domiciled *adj* living in a particular place: *the holding company was domiciled in Bermuda*

dominant *adj* **1** having control, authority, or influence: *a dominant leader* **2** main or chief: *coal is still, worldwide, the dominant fuel* **3** *genetics* (in a pair of genes) designating the gene that produces a particular character in an organism **dominance** *n*

dominate *vb* **-nating, -nated 1** to control or govern **2** to tower above (surroundings): *the building had been designed to dominate the city skyscape* **3** to predominate in **dominating** *adj* **domination** *n*
WORD ORIGIN Latin *dominari* to be lord over

dominee (**doom**-in-nee) *n* S African a minister of the Dutch Reformed Church
WORD ORIGIN Dutch, from Latin *dominus* master

domineering *adj* acting arrogantly or tyrannically
WORD ORIGIN Dutch *domineren*

Dominican *n* **1** a friar or nun of the Christian order founded by Saint Dominic ▷ *adj* **2** of the Dominican order

dominion *n* **1** control or authority **2** the land governed by one ruler or government **3** (formerly) a self-governing division of the British Empire
WORD ORIGIN Latin *dominium* ownership

domino[1] *n, pl* **-noes** a small rectangular block marked with dots, used in dominoes
WORD ORIGIN Italian, perhaps from *domino!* master!, said by the winner

domino[2] *n, pl* **-noes** or **-nos** a large hooded cloak worn with an eye mask at a masquerade
WORD ORIGIN Latin *dominus* lord, master

dominoes *n* a game in which dominoes with matching halves are laid together

don[1] *vb* **donning, donned** to put on (clothing)
WORD ORIGIN Middle English

don[2] *n* **1** *Brit* a member of the teaching staff at a university or college **2** a Spanish gentleman or nobleman **3** (in the Mafia) the head of a family
WORD ORIGIN Latin *dominus* lord

donate *vb* **-nating, -nated** to give (something) to a charity or other organization

donation *n* **1** the act of donating **2** a contribution to a charity or other organization
WORD ORIGIN Latin *donum* gift

donder S African slang *vb* **1** to beat (someone) up ▷ *n* **2** a wretch; swine
WORD ORIGIN Dutch *donderen* to swear, bully

done *vb* **1** the past participle of **do**[1] ▷ *interj* **2** an expression of agreement: *£60 seems reasonable, done!* ▷ *adj* **3** (of a task) completed **4** (of food) cooked enough **5** used up: *the milk is done* **6** Brit, Austral, & NZ socially acceptable: *the done thing* **7** *informal* cheated or tricked **8 done in** or **up** *informal* exhausted

doner kebab *n* a dish of grilled minced lamb, served in a split slice of unleavened bread
WORD ORIGIN Turkish *döner* rotating

dongle *n* computers **1** a plug-in device that allows a computer user to access the internet via mobile broadband **2** an electronic device that accompanies software to prevent the unauthorized copying of programs

donjon *n* the heavily fortified central tower of a castle
WORD ORIGIN archaic variant of *dungeon*

Don Juan *n* a successful seducer of women
WORD ORIGIN after the legendary Spanish philanderer

donkey *n* **1** a long-eared member of the horse family **2** a person who is considered to be stupid or stubborn
WORD ORIGIN origin unknown

donkey jacket *n* Brit, Austral, & NZ a man's thick hip-length jacket with a waterproof panel across the shoulders

donkey's years *pl n* *informal* a long time

donkey-work *n* uninteresting groundwork

donnish *adj* resembling a university don; pedantic or fussy

donor *n* **1** *med* a person who gives blood or organs for use in the treatment of another person **2** a person who makes a donation
WORD ORIGIN Latin *donare* to give

donor card *n* a card carried by someone to show that the body parts specified may be used for transplants after the person's death

Don Quixote (**don** kee-**hoe**-tee) *n* an impractical idealist
WORD ORIGIN after the hero of Miguel de Cervantes' novel *Don Quixote de la Mancha*

don't do not

doodle *vb* **-dling, -dled 1** to scribble or draw aimlessly ▷ *n* **2** a shape or picture drawn aimlessly
WORD ORIGIN originally, a foolish person

doom *n* **1** death or a terrible fate ▷ *vb* **2** to destine or condemn to death or a terrible fate
WORD ORIGIN Old English *dōm*

doomsday or **domesday** *n* **1** the day on which the Last Judgment will occur **2** any dreaded day
WORD ORIGIN Old English *dōmes dæg* Judgment Day

doona *n* Austral a large quilt used as a bed cover in place of the top sheet and blankets

door *n* **1** a hinged or sliding panel for closing the entrance to a building, room, or cupboard **2** a doorway or entrance **3** a means of access or escape: *the door to happiness* **4 lay something at someone's door** to blame someone for

something **5 out of doors** in the open air
WORD ORIGIN Old English *duru*

doorjamb *n* one of the two vertical posts that form the sides of a door frame. Also called: **doorpost**

doorman *n, pl* **-men** a man employed to be on duty at the main entrance of a large building

doormat *n* **1** a mat, placed at an entrance, for wiping dirt from shoes **2** *informal* a person who offers little resistance to being treated badly

doorstep *n* **1** a step in front of a door **2** *informal* a thick slice of bread

doorstop *n* a heavy object or one fixed to the floor, which prevents a door from closing or from striking a wall

door-to-door *adj* **1** (of selling) from one house to the next **2** (of a journey) direct

doorway *n* an opening into a building or room

doosra (**dooz**-ruh) *n* cricket a delivery bowled by an off-spinner that turns the opposite way from an off-break
WORD ORIGIN Urdu, Hindi

dop *n* S African informal a tot or small drink, usually alcoholic
WORD ORIGIN Afrikaans

dope *n* **1** *slang* an illegal drug, such as cannabis **2** a drug administered to a person or animal to affect performance in a race or other sporting competition **3** *informal* a slow-witted person **4** confidential information **5** a thick liquid, such as a lubricant ▷ *vb* **doping, doped 6** to administer a drug to
WORD ORIGIN Dutch *doop* sauce

dopey or **dopy** *adj* **dopier, dopiest 1** *informal* half-asleep, as when under the influence of a drug **2** *slang* silly

doppelgänger (**dop**-pl-geng-er) *n* legend a ghostly duplicate of a living person
WORD ORIGIN German *Doppelgänger* double-goer

Doppler effect *n* a change in the apparent frequency of a sound or light wave as a result of relative motion between the observer and the source
WORD ORIGIN after C. J. *Doppler*, physicist

dorba *n* Austral informal a stupid, inept, or clumsy person

Doric *adj* **1** of a style of classical architecture characterized by a heavy fluted column and a simple capital ▷ *n* **2** a rustic dialect, esp. a Scots one
WORD ORIGIN Doris, in ancient Greece

dormant *adj* **1** temporarily quiet, inactive, or not being used **2** *biol* alive but in a resting condition **dormancy** *n*
WORD ORIGIN Latin *dormire* to sleep

dormer or **dormer window** *n* a window that is built upright in a sloping roof
WORD ORIGIN Latin *dormitorium* dormitory

dormitory *n, pl* **-ries 1** a large room, esp. at a school, containing several beds **2** a building, esp. at a college, providing living accommodation ▷ *adj* **3** Austral & Brit denoting an area from which most of the residents commute to work: *the swelling suburban dormitory areas*
WORD ORIGIN Latin *dormitorium*, from *dormire* to sleep

Native Canadians

Many Canadian English words stem from aboriginal languages: *Canada* itself derives from a *Huron* word meaning 'village'. The first aboriginal speakers lived when the concepts of country or province did not exist, much less international borders. No language family existed entirely within Canada, but spilled over into what are now the United States and other countries. Hence, Eskimo-Aleut extended into Alaska, Siberian Russia, and Greenland. The tribes of the Pacific Northwest, such as the Haida, Tsimshian, Nootka, and Coast Salish, knew nothing of anything shaped like the political units British Columbia and Washington State. The speakers of Siouan, Algonquian, and Athapaskan languages on the prairies and subarctic forests did not understand themselves to live within our political units. Nor, in what is now Eastern Canada, did speakers in the Iroquoian group, or the sprawling Algonquian family that included the Cree and Ojibwa.

It didn't take long for explorers and settlers to alter and adopt native terms for the strange flora, fauna, geographical features, tools, and means of transportation they encountered. The same is true of innumerable place names.

This pattern of naming and claiming was equally true in New England and other parts of colonial America. However, the relatively small *Native Canadian* population disproportionately counts more in the culture, politics, and society of contemporary Canada than *Native Americans* tends to in the United States. Hence, common words with aboriginal origins may carry a greater weight of connotation in Canada. By *chipmunk* (Ojibwa), *toboggan* and *caribou* (Mi'kmaq), *skunk* and *moose* (Abenaki), *sockeye* salmon (Salishan), *teepee* (Sioux), *igloo* and *kayak* (Inuktitut); a Canadian may mean the same thing as a non-Canadian, but the range of cultural reference is different.

The contact between Native and newcomer was linguistically rewarding, even yielding a pidgin, *Chinook Jargon*, based on Chinook, Salishan, English, and French, and used by traders on the north Pacific coast. Chinook Jargon in turn gave Canadian English *muckymuck*, a pompous person, often an official, and *skoo-*

kum, excellent or impressive. Invasions by white Europeans, and the wars between European powers, catastrophically affected aboriginal lives, as did an imported disease, smallpox. Combinations of factors sometimes even led to a people's extinction, such as that of the *Beothuk* in Newfoundland. Entire populations were displaced; the Huron, who lived around Lake Simcoe in what is now Ontario, ended up north of Quebec City and, changing their name to *Wyandot*, in Oklahoma. In public policy and administration, a host of terms arose. A parcel of land set aside for aboriginals is a *reserve* (US *reservation*), and in recent decades the agreements assigning *treaty rights* have been endlessly interpreted to resolve *land claims*. A policy of assimilation, which some have termed cultural genocide, once led federal authorities to wrench children from their homes and send them to faraway Christian-run *residential schools*.

The attempts in recent decades to redress historical injustices have had linguistic implications. The names of various tribes became respelled to reflect, not European corruptions, but original pronunciations. The *Micmac* of Atlantic Canada became the *Mi'kmaq*; *Algonquian*, the language group, became *Algonkian*; *Algonquin*, the tribe, became *Algonkin*. More outlandishly to English ears, the Coast Salish of British Columbia became the *Sne Nay Muxw*.

The Constitution Act of 1982 recognized three aboriginal peoples. In the Act's vocabulary, *First Nation*, which began to be used in official parlance in the 1970s, is virtually synonymous with *tribe*. *Nation* often became attached to names of the communities previously termed *bands*. Of the two other peoples, the western Canadian *Métis*, of mixed Native and European, often French, origins, acquired official status as a term; the *Inuit* of Arctic Canada were no longer *Eskimos*. To further confuse matters, aboriginals more informally are called *First Peoples*.

When Christopher Columbus made landfall and encountered aboriginals, he thought he had reached India. Despite this geographical howler, the misnomer *Indian* is still widely used, even by the people Columbus misnamed.

Dormobile n trademark a vanlike vehicle specially equipped for living in while travelling

dormouse n, pl **-mice** a small rodent resembling a mouse with a furry tail **WORD ORIGIN** origin unknown

dorp n S African a small town or village **WORD ORIGIN** Dutch

dorsal adj anat, zool of or on the back **WORD ORIGIN** Latin dorsum back

dory n, pl **-ries** a spiny-finned food fish. Also called: **John Dory** **WORD ORIGIN** French dorée gilded

DOS computers disk operating system

dose n 1 a specific quantity of a medicine taken at one time 2 informal something unpleasant to experience: a dose of the cold 3 the total energy of radiation absorbed 4 slang a sexually transmitted infection ▷ vb **dosing, dosed** 5 to administer a quantity of medicine to (someone) **dosage** n **WORD ORIGIN** Greek dosis a giving

dosh n slang money

dosing strip n (in New Zealand) an area for treating dogs suspected of having hydatid disease

doss slang vb 1 **doss down** to sleep on a makeshift bed 2 to pass time aimlessly: I doss around a lot ▷ n 3 a task requiring little effort **WORD ORIGIN** origin unknown

dosshouse n slang a cheap lodging house for homeless people

dossier (**doss**-ee-ay) n a collection of papers about a subject or person **WORD ORIGIN** French

dot n 1 a small round mark 2 the small round mark used to represent the short sound in Morse code 3 **on the dot** at exactly the arranged time ▷ vb **dotting, dotted** 4 to mark with a dot 5 to scatter or intersperse: there are numerous churches dotted around Rome 6 **dot one's i's and cross one's t's** informal to pay meticulous attention to detail **WORD ORIGIN** Old English dott head of a boil

dotage n feebleness of mind as a result of old age **WORD ORIGIN** Middle English doten to dote

dotard n a person who is feeble-minded through old age

dotcom or **dot.com** n a company that conducts most of its business on the internet **WORD ORIGIN** from .com, the domain name suffix of businesses trading on the internet

dote vb **doting, doted** • **dote on** or **upon** to love (someone or something) to an excessive degree **doting** adj **WORD ORIGIN** Middle English doten

dotterel n a shore bird with reddish-brown underparts and white bands around the head and neck **WORD ORIGIN** Middle English dotrelle

dottle n the tobacco left in a pipe after smoking **WORD ORIGIN** obsolete dot lump

dotty adj **-tier, -tiest** slang slightly crazy **dottiness** n **WORD ORIGIN** from dot

double adj 1 as much again in size, strength, number, etc.: a double scotch 2 composed of two equal or similar parts 3 designed for two users: a double bed 4 folded in half: the blanket had been folded double 5 stooping: she was bent double over the flower bed 6 ambiguous: a double meaning 7 false, deceitful, or hypocritical: double standards 8 music (of an instrument) sounding an octave lower: a double bass ▷ adv 9 twice over: that's double the amount requested ▷ n 10 twice the size, strength, number, etc. 11 a double measure of spirits 12 a person who closely resembles another person 13 a bet on two horses in different races in which any winnings from the first race are placed on the horse in the later race 14 **at** or **on the double** quickly or immediately ▷ vb **-bling, -bled** 15 to make or become twice as much 16 to bend or fold so that one part covers another 17 to play two parts or serve two roles 18 to turn sharply 19 bridge to make a call that will double certain scoring points if the preceding bid becomes the contract 20 **double for** to act as substitute for ▶ See also **double back, doubles, double up** ▷ **doubler** n **WORD ORIGIN** Latin duplus twofold

double agent n a spy employed by two enemy countries at the same time

double back vb to go back in the opposite direction: I doubled back searching for the track

double-barrelled or US **-barreled** adj 1 (of a gun) having two barrels 2 Brit (of a surname) having hyphenated parts

double bass n a stringed instrument, the largest and lowest member of the violin family

double-breasted adj (of a garment) having overlapping fronts

double-check vb to make certain by checking again

double chin n a fold of fat under the chin

double cream n Austral & Brit thick cream with a high fat content

double-cross vb 1 to cheat or betray ▷ n 2 an instance of double-crossing

double-dealing n treacherous or deceitful behaviour

double-decker n 1 chiefly Brit a bus with two passenger decks one on top of the other ▷ adj 2 informal having two layers: a double-decker sandwich

double-double n 1 chiefly US & Canad basketball the feat of scoring 10 or more in each of two classes of quantifiable positive action (such as points, assists, rebounds, etc.) 2 Canad a cup of coffee served with two helpings of cream and sugar

double Dutch n informal speech or writing that is difficult to understand: it was double Dutch to me

double-edged adj 1 (of a remark) malicious in intent though apparently complimentary 2 (of a knife) having a cutting edge on either side of the blade

double entendre (**doob**-bl on-**tond**-ra) n a word or phrase with two interpretations, esp. with one meaning that is rude **WORD ORIGIN** obsolete French

double entry n a book-keeping system in which a transaction is entered as a debit in one account and as a credit in another

double glazing n a window consisting of two layers of glass separated by a space, fitted to reduce heat loss

double Gloucester (**glost**-er) n a smooth orange-red cheese with a mild flavour

double-jointed adj (of a person) having unusually flexible joints

double knitting n a medium thickness of knitting wool

double negative n a grammatical construction, considered incorrect, in which two negatives are used where one is needed, for example I wouldn't never have believed it

double-park vb to park (a vehicle) alongside another vehicle, causing an obstruction

double pneumonia n pneumonia affecting both lungs

double-quick adj 1 very quick ▷ adv 2 in a very quick manner

doubles n a game between two pairs of players

double standard n a set of principles that allows greater freedom to one person or group than to another

doublet (**dub**-lit) n history a man's close-fitting jacket, with or without sleeves **WORD ORIGIN** Old French

double take n a delayed reaction by a person to a remark or situation: she did a double take when he said he was leaving

double talk n deceptive or ambiguous talk

doublethink n the acceptance of conflicting facts or principles at the same time

double time n 1 Brit, Austral, & NZ a doubled wage rate sometimes paid for overtime work 2 music two beats per bar

double up vb 1 to bend or cause to bend in two: she was doubled up with stomach cramps 2 to share with other people: we only took two cars, so we had to double up

double whammy n informal a devastating setback made up of two elements

doubloon n a former Spanish gold coin **WORD ORIGIN** Spanish doblón

doubly adv 1 to or in a greater degree, quantity, or measure: I have to be doubly careful 2 in two ways: the defence debate was doubly complicated

doubt n 1 uncertainty about the truth, facts, or existence of something 2 an unresolved difficulty or point 3 **give someone the benefit of the doubt** accept that someone is speaking the truth 4 **no doubt** almost certainly ▷ vb 5 to be inclined to disbelieve: I doubt that we are late 6 to distrust or be suspicious of: he doubted their motives **doubter** n **WORD ORIGIN** Latin dubitare to hesitate

USAGE Where a clause follows doubt in a positive sentence, it was formerly considered correct to use whether: (I doubt whether he will come), but now if and *that* are also acceptable. In negative statements, *doubt* is followed by *that*: *I do not doubt that he is telling the truth*. In such sentences, *but* (*I do not doubt but that he is telling the truth*) is redundant.

doubtful *adj* 1 unlikely or improbable: *it's doubtful that I will marry again* 2 unsure or uncertain: *I was doubtful about some of his ideas* **doubtfully** *adv* **doubtfulness** *n*

USAGE
It was formerly considered correct to use *whether* after *doubtful* (*it is doubtful whether he will come*), but now *if* and *that* are also acceptable.

doubtless *adv* probably or almost certainly: *somebody will know and doubtless somebody will ring us*

douche (**doosh**) *n* 1 a stream of water directed onto or into the body for cleansing or medical purposes 2 an instrument for applying a douche ▷ *vb* **douching, douched** 3 to cleanse or treat by means of a douche **WORD ORIGIN** French

dough *n* 1 a thick mixture of flour and water or milk, used for making bread, pastry, or biscuits 2 *slang* money **WORD ORIGIN** Old English *dāg*

doughnut *n* a small cake of sweetened dough cooked in hot fat

doughty (**dowt**-ee) *adj* -tier, -tiest *old-fashioned* brave and determined **WORD ORIGIN** Old English *dohtig*

do up *vb* 1 to wrap and make into a bundle: *he did up the parcel* 2 to fasten: *to do up one's blouse* 3 to renovate or redecorate

dour (**doo**-er, **dow**-er) *adj* sullen and unfriendly **dourness** *n* **WORD ORIGIN** probably from Latin *durus* hard

douse or **dowse** (rhymes with **mouse**) *vb* **dousing, doused** or **dowsing, dowsed** 1 to drench with water or other liquid 2 to put out (a light) **WORD ORIGIN** origin unknown

dove *n* 1 a bird with a heavy body, small head, and short legs 2 *politics* a person opposed to war **WORD ORIGIN** Old English *dūfe*

dovecote or **dovecot** *n* a box, shelter, or part of a house built for doves or pigeons to live in

dove-grey *adj* greyish-brown

dovetail *n* 1 Also called: **dovetail joint** a wedge-shaped joint used to fit two pieces of wood tightly together ▷ *vb* 2 to fit together closely or neatly: *her resignation dovetails well with the new structure*

dowager *n* a woman possessing property or a title obtained from her dead husband **WORD ORIGIN** Old French *douagiere*

dowdy *adj* -dier, -diest wearing dull and unfashionable clothes **dowdily** *adv* **dowdiness** *n* **WORD ORIGIN** Middle English *dowd* slut

dowel *n* a wooden or metal peg that fits into two corresponding holes to join larger pieces of wood or metal together **WORD ORIGIN** Middle Low German *dövel* plug

dower *n* 1 the life interest in a part of her husband's estate allotted to a

widow by law 2 *archaic* a dowry **WORD ORIGIN** Latin *dos* gift

dower house *n* a house for the use of a widow, often on her deceased husband's estate

do with *vb* 1 **could do with** need or would benefit from: *I could do with some royal treatment* 2 **have to do with** to be associated with: *his illness has a lot to do with his failing the exam* 3 **to do with** concerning; related to: *this book has to do with the occult*

do without *vb* to manage without

down[1] *prep* 1 from a higher to a lower position in or on 2 at a lower or further level or position on, in, or along: *I wandered down the corridor* ▷ *adv* 3 at or to a lower level or position: *he bent down* 4 indicating lowering or destruction: *to bring down an aircraft* 5 indicating intensity or completion: *calm down and mind your manners* 6 immediately: *cash down* 7 on paper: *she copied it down* 8 away from a more important place: *he came down from head office* 9 reduced to a state of lack: *he was down to his last pound* 10 lacking a specified amount: *down several pounds* 11 lower in price 12 from an earlier to a later time: *the ring was handed down from my grandmother* 13 to a finer state: *to grind down* 14 *sport* being a specified number of points or goals behind an opponent 15 (of a person) being inactive, owing to illness: *down with the cold* ▷ *adj* 16 depressed or unhappy: *he seems very down today* ▷ *vb* 17 *informal* to eat or drink quickly 18 to fell (someone or something) ▷ *n* 19 **have a down on** *informal* to feel hostile towards: *you seem to have a down on the family tonight* **WORD ORIGIN** Old English *dūne* from the hill

down[2] *n* soft fine feathers **downy** *adj* **WORD ORIGIN** Old Norse *dūnn*

down-and-out *n* 1 a person who is homeless and destitute ▷ *adj* 2 without any means of support; destitute

downbeat *adj informal* 1 depressed or gloomy: *she was in one of her downbeat moods* 2 casual and restrained: *the chairman's statement was decidedly downbeat* ▷ *n* 3 *music* the first beat of a bar

downcast *adj* 1 sad and dejected 2 (of the eyes) directed downwards

downer *n slang* 1 a barbiturate, tranquilizer, or narcotic 2 **on a downer** in a state of depression

downfall *n* 1 a sudden loss of position or reputation 2 the cause of this

downgrade *vb* -grading, -graded to reduce in importance or value

downhearted *adj* sad and discouraged

downhill *adj* 1 going or sloping down ▷ *adv* 2 towards the bottom of a hill 3 **go downhill** *informal* to deteriorate

Downing Street *n* the British prime minister or the British government **WORD ORIGIN** after the street in London which contains the official residence of the prime minister and the chancellor of the exchequer

download *vb* 1 to transfer (data) from the memory of one computer to that of another ▷ *n* 2 a file transferred in this way

down-market *adj* cheap, popular, and of poor quality

down payment *n* the deposit paid on an item purchased on hire-purchase, mortgage, etc.: *an initial down payment is usually required*

downpour *n* a heavy continuous fall of rain

downright *adv* 1 extremely: *it's just downright cruel* ▷ *adj* 2 absolute; utter: *Crozier is a downright thief*

down-river *adj, adv* nearer the mouth of a river

downs *pl n* an area of low grassy hills, esp. in S England

downshifting *n* the practice of simplifying one's lifestyle and becoming less materialistic

downside *n* the disadvantageous aspect of a situation: *the downside of capitalism*

downsize *vb* 1 to reduce the number of people employed by (a company) 2 to reduce the size of or produce a smaller version of (something)

Down's syndrome *or esp. US, Canad, & Austral* **Down syndrome** *n pathol* a genetic disorder characterized by mental impairment and physical abnormalities, including a flattish face and a vertical fold of skin at the inner edge of the eye **WORD ORIGIN** after John *Langdon*-*Down*, physician

downstairs *adv* 1 down the stairs; to or on a lower floor ▷ *n* 2 a lower or ground floor

downstream *adv, adj* in or towards the lower part of a stream; with the current

downtime *n commerce* time during which a computer or other machine is not working

down-to-earth *adj* sensible or practical

downtown *chiefly US, Canad, & NZ n* 1 the central or lower part of a city, esp. the main commercial area ▷ *adv* 2 towards, to, or into this area

downtrodden *adj* oppressed and lacking the will to resist

downturn *n* a drop in the success of an economy or a business

down under *informal n* 1 Australia or New Zealand ▷ *adv* 2 in or to Australia or New Zealand

downward *adj* 1 descending from a higher to a lower level, condition, or position ▷ *adv* 2 same as **downwards** > **downwardly** *adv*

downwards or **downward** *adv* 1 from a higher to a lower level, condition, or position 2 from an earlier time or source to a later one

downwind *adv, adj* in the same direction towards which the wind is blowing; with the wind from behind

dowry *n, pl* -ries the property brought by a woman to her husband at marriage **WORD ORIGIN** Latin *dos*

dowse (rhymes with **cows**) *vb* **dowsing, dowsed** to search for underground water or minerals using a divining rod **dowser** *n* **WORD ORIGIN** origin unknown

doxology *n, pl* -gies a hymn or verse of praise to God

d

d

WORD ORIGIN Greek *doxologos* uttering praise

doyen (**doy**-en) *n* the senior member of a group, profession, or society **doyenne** (doy-**en**) *fem n*
WORD ORIGIN French

doze *vb* **dozing, dozed 1** to sleep lightly or for a short period **2 doze off** to fall into a light sleep ▷ *n* **3** a short sleep
WORD ORIGIN probably from Old Norse *dūs* lull

dozen *adj, n* twelve **dozenth** *adj*
WORD ORIGIN Latin *duodecim*

dozy *adj* **dozier, doziest 1** feeling sleepy **2** *Brit informal* stupid and slow-witted

DP displaced person

DPB (in New Zealand) Domestic Purposes Benefit

dpi *computers* dots per inch

DPP (in Britain) Director of Public Prosecutions

Dr 1 Doctor **2** Drive

drab *adj* **drabber, drabbest 1** dull and dreary **2** light olive-brown **drabness** *n*
WORD ORIGIN Old French *drap* cloth

drachm (**dram**) *n Brit* a unit of liquid measure equal to one eighth of a fluid ounce (3.55 ml)
WORD ORIGIN variant of DRAM

drachma *n, pl* **-mas** or **-mae** a former monetary unit of Greece
WORD ORIGIN Greek *drakhmē* a handful

draconian *adj* severe or harsh: *draconian measures were taken by the government*
WORD ORIGIN after *Draco*, Athenian statesman

draft *n* **1** a preliminary outline of a letter, book, or speech **2** a written order for payment of money by a bank **3** *US & Austral* selection for compulsory military service ▷ *vb* **4** to write a preliminary outline of a letter, book, or speech **5** to send (personnel) from one place to another to carry out a specific job **6** *chiefly US* to select for compulsory military service ▷ *n, vb* **7** *US* same as **draught**
WORD ORIGIN variant of DRAUGHT

drag *vb* **dragging, dragged 1** to pull with force along the ground **2** to trail on the ground **3** to persuade (someone) to go somewhere: *he didn't want to come so I had to drag him along* **4** to move (oneself) slowly and with difficulty: *I had to drag myself out of bed this morning* **5** to linger behind: *she dragged along behind her mother* **6** to search (a river) with a dragnet or hook **7** to draw (on a cigarette) **8** *computers* to move (a graphics image) from one place to another on the screen by manipulating a mouse with its button held down **9 drag away** or **from** to force (oneself) to come away from something interesting: *I was completely spellbound and couldn't drag myself away from the film* **10 drag on** or **out** to last or be prolonged tediously: *winter dragged on* **11 drag one's feet** *informal* to act with deliberate slowness ▷ *n* **12** a person or thing that slows up progress **13** *informal* a tedious or boring thing: *it was a drag having to walk two miles to the station every day* **14** *informal* a draw on a cigarette **15** an implement, such as a dragnet, used for dragging **16** *aeronautics* the resistance to the motion of a body

passing through air **17 in drag** (of a man) wearing women's clothes, usually as a form of entertainment ▶ See also **drag up**
WORD ORIGIN Old English *dragan* to draw

draggle *vb* **-gling, -gled** to make or become wet or dirty by trailing on the ground
WORD ORIGIN Middle English

dragnet *n* a net used to scour the bottom of a pond or river when searching for something

dragoman *n, pl* **-mans** or **-men** (in some Middle Eastern countries) a professional interpreter or guide
WORD ORIGIN Arabic *targumān*

dragon *n* **1** a mythical monster that resembles a large fire-breathing lizard **2** *informal* a fierce woman **3 chase the dragon** *slang* to smoke opium or heroin
WORD ORIGIN Greek *drakōn*

dragonfly *n, pl* **-flies** a brightly coloured insect with a long slender body and two pairs of wings

dragoon *n* **1** a heavily armed cavalryman ▷ *vb* **2** to coerce or force: *we were dragooned into participating*
WORD ORIGIN French *dragon*

drag race *n* a race in which specially built or modified cars or motorcycles are timed over a measured course **drag racing** *n*

drag up *vb informal* to revive (an unpleasant fact or story)

drain *n* **1** a pipe that carries off water or sewage **2** a cause of a continuous reduction in energy or resources: *the expansion will be a drain on resources* **3** a metal grid on a road or pavement through which rainwater flows **4 down the drain** wasted ▷ *vb* **5** to draw off or remove (liquid) from **6** to flow (away) or filter (off) **7** to dry or be emptied as a result of liquid running off or flowing away **8** to drink the entire contents of (a glass or cup) **9** to make constant demands on (energy or resources); exhaust **10** (of a river) to carry off the surface water from (an area)
WORD ORIGIN Old English *drēahnian*

drainage *n* **1** a system of pipes, drains, or ditches used to drain water or other liquids **2** the process or a method of draining

draining board *n* a grooved surface at the side of a sink, used for draining washed dishes

drainpipe *n* a pipe for carrying off rainwater or sewage

drake *n* the male of a duck
WORD ORIGIN origin unknown

dram *n* **1** a small amount of spirits, such as whisky **2** a unit of weight equal to one sixteenth of an ounce (avoirdupois)
WORD ORIGIN Greek *drakhmē*; see DRACHMA

drama *n* **1** a serious play for theatre, television, or radio **2** plays in general, as a form of literature **3** the art of writing, producing, or acting in a play **4** a situation that is exciting or highly emotional
WORD ORIGIN Greek: something performed

dramatic *adj* **1** of or relating to drama **2** like a drama in suddenness or effectiveness: *the government's plan has had a dramatic effect on employment in television* **3** acting or performed in a flamboyant way: *he spread his hands in a dramatic gesture of helplessness* **dramatically** *adv*

dramatics *n* **1** the art of acting or producing plays ▷ *pl n* **2** exaggerated, theatrical behaviour

dramatis personae (**drah**-mat-tiss per-**soh**-nigh) *pl n* the characters in a play
WORD ORIGIN New Latin

dramatist *n* a playwright: *Austria's greatest living dramatist*

dramatize or **-tise** *vb* **-tizing, -tized** or **-tising, -tised 1** to rewrite (a book or story) in a form suitable for performing on stage **2** to express (something) in a dramatic or exaggerated way: *he dramatizes his illness* **dramatization** or **-tisation** *n*

drank *vb* the past tense of **drink**

drape *vb* **draping, draped 1** to cover with material or fabric **2** to hang or arrange in folds **3** to place casually: *he draped his arm across the back of the seat* ▶ See also **drapes**
WORD ORIGIN Old French *draper*

draper *n Brit* a person who sells fabrics and sewing materials

drapery *n, pl* **-peries 1** fabric or clothing arranged and draped **2** fabrics and cloth collectively

drapes *pl n Austral, NZ, US, & Canad* material hung at an opening or window to shut out light or to provide privacy

drastic *adj* strong and severe: *the police are taking drastic measures against car thieves* **drastically** *adv*
WORD ORIGIN Greek *drastikos*

drat *interj slang* an exclamation of annoyance
WORD ORIGIN probably alteration of *God rot*

draught or *US* **draft** *n* **1** a current of cold air, usually one coming into a room or vehicle **2** a portion of liquid to be drunk, esp. a dose of medicine **3** a gulp or swallow: *she took a deep draught then a sip* **4 on draught** (of beer) drawn from a cask **5** one of the flat discs used in the game of draughts. US and Canad equivalent: **checker 6 feel the draught** to be short of money ▷ *adj* **7** (of an animal) used for pulling heavy loads: *horses are specialized draught animals*
WORD ORIGIN probably Old Norse *drahtr*

draught beer *n* beer stored in a cask

draughtboard *n* a square board divided into 64 squares, used for playing draughts

draughts *n* a game for two players using a draughtboard and 12 draughtsmen each
WORD ORIGIN plural of *draught* (in obsolete sense: a chess move)

draughtsman or *US* **draftsman** *n, pl* **-men 1** a person employed to prepare detailed scale drawings of equipment, machinery, or buildings **2** a person skilled in drawing **3** *US and Canad* equivalent: **checker** *Brit* a flat disc used in the game of draughts **draughtsmanship** *n*

Charles Dickens

Several years ago, an episode of *The Simpsons* introduced the character of Homer's mother, who had gone unmentioned throughout the series only to appear out of nowhere with a convenient explanation of her previous absence. Assessing the situation, Lisa remarks that it is 'like something out of Dickens...or Melrose Place'. It is telling that an author of Dickens' stature can be compared to a tawdry soap opera, even if only for comic effect. Much of Victorian literature was concerned with feeling, with 'sensibility' or 'sentiment', which is not always to modern tastes.

Charles Dickens is perhaps the most prominent novelist of the Victorian Period, the era in literary history which roughly corresponds to the reign of Queen Victoria (1837-1901). In this era, taste in novels had become something quite different from its inception.

As a form of literature, the novel traces its origin to Cervantes' *Don Quixote* (though prose fiction dates back at least to Ancient Greece), but the genre did not take off in the English-speaking world until the eighteenth century. In this period, the Age of Reason, there was an emphasis on realism, with many novels, such as Daniel Defoe's *Moll Flanders*, purporting to be 'true' histories of actual persons. However, what we may think of as the 'art of fiction' was not highly developed in this period, with plots especially being 'episodic' and lacking any real unity or narrative structure.

By the beginning of the nineteenth century, the essential criteria for a successful novel as we know it today began to be established, including a unified plot with exposition, rising and falling action, a climax, and a resolution. However, another trend in literature had also taken hold: the so-called Novel of Sensibility.

'Sensibility' refers to a vogue, beginning in the latter half of the eighteenth century, for literature that provokes an emotional response in the reader, exemplified perhaps by the novels of Samuel Richardson. Jane Austen's debut, *Sense and Sensibility*, marks a reaction to this trend and a return to reason which Austen was to continue throughout her career. However, by the Victorian Period, popular tastes had returned to sensibility, which we now call sentimentality.

That we can speak of 'popular' taste in literature at all is a mark of the great social progress that was made in the Victorian Period. Whereas in previous eras, literacy had been the province of the socially elite or the clergy, in the nineteenth century, in part owing to technological advances in printing, an unprecedented number of 'common' people were able to read, and writers and publishers alike competed for them.

To be sure, Dickens was a talented writer; his books, such as *Oliver Twist*, *Great Expectations*, and *A Tale of Two Cities*, are among the most famous in English literature, and his characters are so memorable as to have generated new words themselves. *Bumbledom*, meaning 'self-importance in a minor office', comes from the character Bumble in *Oliver Twist*. *Dolly Varden*, a type of women's hat, is named for the character in *Barnaby Rudge*. *Gamp*, which is British slang for an umbrella, comes from Sarah Gamp, the nurse in *Martin Chuzzlewit*, who carried a faded umbrella. *David Copperfield* gives a *Micawber*, as well as the prototype for a biography. Thus Holden Caulfield warns his readers not to expect 'all that David Copperfield stuff' in the first paragraph of JD Salinger's *The Catcher in the Rye*, and the vampire Louis asks, on beginning his own life story, 'Shall we begin like David Copperfield? I am born? I grow up?' in Anne Rice's *Interview with the Vampire*. Although his greatest triumph is certainly that *Dickensian* does not mean merely 'of Charles Dickens or his works' but more often denotes depictions of poverty and social injustice, such as a *Dickensian orphanage*.

That said, Dickens did not write without an audience in mind. Most of his works were published serially, and the necessity of ending chapters with a cliffhanger (to get readers to buy the next instalment) can make his plots seem contrived, to say nothing of his sentimental scenes such as Little Nell's death in *The Old Curiosity Shop* or Sydney Carton's self-sacrifice at the end of *A Tale of Two Cities*. This and many other suspiciously convenient plot points (such as Magwitch turning out to be both Pip's benefactor and Estrella's father in *Great Expectations*) can render this renowned author – and much of Victorian fiction – a little too close to soap opera for modern tastes.

draughty or US **drafty** adj **draughtier, draughtiest** or US **draftier, draftiest** exposed to draughts of air **draughtily** adv **draughtiness** n

draw vb **drawing, drew, drawn 1** to sketch (a picture, pattern, or diagram) with a pen or pencil **2** to cause (a person or thing) to move closer or further away from a place by pulling **3** to bring, take, or pull (something) out of a container: *he drew a gun and laid it on the table* **4** to take (something) from a particular source: *the inhabitants drew water from the well two miles away* **5** to move in a specified direction: *he drew alongside me* **6** to attract: *she drew enthusiastic audiences from all over the country* **7** to formulate or decide: *he drew similar conclusions* **8** to cause to flow: *the barman nodded and drew two pints* **9** to choose or be given by lottery: *Brazil have drawn Spain in the semi-final of the Cup* **10** (of two teams or contestants) to finish a game with an equal number of points **11** archery to bend (a bow) by pulling the string **12** to cause (pus) to discharge from an abscess or wound ▷ n **13** a raffle or lottery **14** informal a person, place, show, or event that attracts a large audience **15** a contest or game ending in a tie ▶ See also **drawback, draw in**, etc. **WORD ORIGIN** Old English *dragan*

drawback n **1** a disadvantage or hindrance ▷ vb **draw back 2** to move backwards: *the girl drew back as though in pain* **3** to turn aside from an undertaking: *the prime minister drew back from his original intention*

drawbridge n a bridge that may be raised to prevent access or to enable vessels to pass

drawer n **1** a sliding box-shaped part of a piece of furniture used for storage **2** a person or thing that draws

drawers pl n old-fashioned an undergarment worn on the lower part of the body

draw in vb **1** (of a train) to arrive at a station **2 the nights are drawing in** the hours of daylight are becoming shorter

drawing n **1** a picture or plan made by means of lines on a surface **2** the art of making drawings

drawing pin n Brit & NZ a short tack with a broad smooth head used for fastening papers to a drawing board or other surface

drawing room n a room where visitors are received and entertained

drawl vb **1** to speak slowly with long vowel sounds ▷ n **2** the way of speech of someone who drawls **drawling** adj **WORD ORIGIN** probably frequentative of *draw*

drawn vb **1** the past participle of **draw** ▷ adj **2** haggard, tired, or tense in appearance

draw off vb to cause (a liquid) to flow from something

draw on vb **1** to make use of from a source or fund: *they are able to draw on a repertoire of around 400 songs* **2** (of a period of time) to come near or pass by: *summer draws on; time draws on*

draw out vb **1** (of a train) to leave a station **2** to encourage (someone) to talk freely: *therapy groups will continue to draw her out* **3 draw out of** to find out (information) from

drawstring n a cord run through a hem around an opening, so that when it is pulled tighter, the opening closes

draw up vb **1** to prepare and write out: *the signatories drew up a draft agreement* **2** (of a vehicle) to come to a halt

dray n a low cart used for carrying heavy loads **WORD ORIGIN** Old English *dræge* dragnet

dread vb **1** to anticipate with apprehension or terror ▷ n **2** great fear **WORD ORIGIN** Old English *ondrǣdan*

dreadful adj **1** extremely disagreeable or shocking **2** extreme: *there were dreadful delays* **dreadfully** adv

dreadlocks pl n hair worn in the Rastafarian style of tightly curled strands

dreadnought n **1** a type of battleship with heavy guns **2** a heavy overcoat

dream n **1** an imagined series of events experienced in the mind while asleep **2** a daydream: *the dream of success turning into a nightmare* **3** a goal or aim: *Unity has been their constant dream* **4** a wonderful person or thing: *her house is a dream* ▷ vb **dreaming, dreamed** or **dreamt 5** to experience (a dream) **6** to indulge in daydreams **7** to be unrealistic: *you're dreaming if you think we can win* **8 dream of** to consider the possibility of: *she would not dream of taking his advice* **9 dream of** or **about** to have an image of or fantasy about: *they often dream about what life will be like for them on the outside* ▷ adj **10** beautiful or pleasing: *a dream kitchen* **dreamer** n **WORD ORIGIN** Old English *drēam* song

dream team n informal a group of people regarded as having the perfect combination of talents

dream ticket n a combination of two people, esp. candidates in an election, that is considered to be ideal

dream up vb to formulate in the imagination: *a character dreamed up by a scriptwriter*

dreamy adj **dreamier, dreamiest 1** vague or impractical: *she was wild-eyed and dreamy* **2** relaxing or gentle: *I felt this dreamy contentment* **3** informal wonderful or impressive: *he drives a dreamy Jaguar* **dreamily** adv **dreaminess** n

dreary adj **drearier, dreariest** dull or uninteresting: *there are long streets of dreary red houses spreading everywhere* **drearily** adv **dreariness** n **WORD ORIGIN** Old English *drēorig* gory

dredge¹ n **1** a machine used to scoop or suck up silt or mud from a river bed or harbour ▷ vb **dredging, dredged 2** to remove silt or mud from (a river bed or harbour) by means of a dredge **3** to search for (a submerged object) with or as if with a dredge **dredger** n **WORD ORIGIN** origin unknown

dredge² vb **dredging, dredged** to sprinkle (food) with a substance, such as flour **dredger** n **WORD ORIGIN** Old French *dragie*

dredge up vb informal to remember (something obscure or half-forgotten): *I didn't retain you to dredge up unfortunate incidents from my past*

dregs pl n **1** solid particles that settle at the bottom of some liquids **2 the dregs** the worst or most despised elements: *the dregs of colonial society* **WORD ORIGIN** Old Norse *dregg*

drench vb **1** to make completely wet **2** to give medicine to (an animal) **drenching** n, adj **WORD ORIGIN** Old English *drencan* to cause to drink

Dresden or **Dresden china** n delicate and decorative porcelain made near Dresden, Germany

dress n **1** a one-piece garment worn by a woman or girl, with a skirt and bodice and sometimes sleeves **2** complete style of clothing: *contemporary dress* ▷ adj **3** suitable for a formal occasion: *he was wearing a dress shirt* ▷ vb **4** to put clothes on **5** to put on formal clothes **6** to apply protective covering to (a wound) **7** to cover (a salad) with dressing **8** to prepare (meat, poultry, or fish) for selling or cooking by cleaning or gutting **9** to put a finish on (the surface of stone, metal, or other building material) ▶ See also **dress up** **WORD ORIGIN** Old French *drecier* to arrange

dressage (**dress**-ahzh) n **a** the method of training horses to perform manoeuvres as a display of obedience **b** the manoeuvres performed **WORD ORIGIN** French

dress circle n the first gallery in a theatre

dress code n a set of rules regarding the style of dress acceptable in an office, restaurant, etc.

dresser¹ n **1** a piece of furniture with shelves and cupboards, used for storing or displaying dishes **2** US a chest of drawers **WORD ORIGIN** Old French *drecier* to arrange

dresser² n **1** a person who dresses in a specified way: *Lars was a meticulous, elegant dresser* **2** theatre a person employed to assist performers with their costumes

dressing n **1** a sauce for food: *salad dressing* **2** US & Canad same as **stuffing** (sense 1) **3** a covering for a wound **4** manure or fertilizer spread on land **5** a gluey material used for stiffening paper, textiles, etc.

dressing-down n informal a severe reprimand

dressing gown n a loose-fitting garment worn over one's pyjamas or nightdress

dressing room n a room used for changing clothes and applying make-up, esp. a backstage room in a theatre

dressing table n a piece of bedroom furniture with a mirror and a set of drawers

dressmaker n a person who makes clothes for women **dressmaking** n

dress rehearsal n **1** the last rehearsal of a play, opera, or show using costumes, lighting, and other effects **2** any full-scale practice: *astronauts are in* *the midst of a two day dress rehearsal of their launch countdown*

dress shirt *n* a man's evening shirt, worn as part of formal evening dress

dress suit *n* a man's evening suit

dress up *vb* **1** to put on glamorous or stylish clothes **2** to put fancy dress on: *the guests dressed up like cowboys* **3** to disguise (something) to make it more attractive or acceptable: *the offer was simply an old one dressed up in new terms*

dressy *adj* **dressier, dressiest 1** (of clothes or occasions) elegant **2** (of people) dressing stylishly **dressiness** *n*

drew *vb* the past tense of **draw**

drey or **dray** *n Austral & Brit* a squirrel's nest
WORD ORIGIN origin unknown

dribble *vb* **-bling, -bled 1** to flow or allow to flow in a thin stream or drops **2** to allow saliva to trickle from the mouth **3** (in football, hockey, etc.) to propel (the ball) by kicking or tapping in quick succession ▷ *n* **4** a small quantity of liquid falling in drops or flowing in a thin stream **5** a small supply: *there's only a dribble of milk left* **6** an act or instance of dribbling **dribbler** *n*
WORD ORIGIN obsolete *drib*, variant of *drip*

dribs and drabs *pl n informal* small occasional amounts

dried *vb* the past of **dry**

drier¹ *adj* a comparative of **dry**

drier² *n* same as **dryer¹**

driest *adj* a superlative of **dry**

drift *vb* **1** to be carried along by currents of air or water **2** to move aimlessly from one place or activity to another **3** to wander away from a fixed course or point **4** (of snow) to pile up in heaps ▷ *n* **5** something piled up by the wind or current, as a snowdrift **6** a general movement or development: *there has been a drift away from family control* **7** the main point of an argument or speech: *I was beginning to get his drift* **8** the extent to which a vessel or aircraft is driven off course by winds, etc. **9** a current of water created by the wind
WORD ORIGIN Old Norse

drifter *n* **1** a person who moves aimlessly from place to place **2** a boat used for drift-net fishing

drift net *n* a fishing net that is allowed to drift with the tide

driftwood *n* wood floating on or washed ashore by the sea

drill¹ *n* **1** a machine or tool for boring holes **2** *mil* training in procedures or movements, as for parades **3** strict and often repetitious training **4** *informal* correct procedure: *he knows the drill as well as anybody* ▷ *vb* **5** to bore a hole in (something) with or as if with a drill **6** to instruct or be instructed in military procedures or movements **7** to teach by rigorous exercises or training
WORD ORIGIN Middle Dutch *drillen*

drill² *n* **1** a machine for planting seeds in rows **2** a furrow in which seeds are sown **3** a row of seeds planted by means of a drill ▷ *vb* **4** to plant (seeds) by means of a drill
WORD ORIGIN origin unknown

drill³ *n* a hard-wearing cotton cloth, used for uniforms
WORD ORIGIN German *Drillich*

drill⁴ *n* a W African monkey, related to the mandrill
WORD ORIGIN from a West African word

drilling platform *n* an offshore structure that supports a drilling rig

drilling rig *n* the complete machinery, equipment, and structures needed to drill an offshore oil well

drily or **dryly** *adv* in a dry manner

drink *vb* **drinking, drank, drunk 1** to swallow (a liquid) **2** to consume alcohol, esp. to excess **3** to bring (oneself) into a specified condition by consuming alcohol: *he drank himself senseless every night* **4 drink someone's health** to wish someone health or happiness with a toast **5 drink in** to pay close attention to: *I drank in what the speaker said* **6 drink to** to drink a toast to: *I drank to their engagement* ▷ *n* **7** liquid suitable for drinking **8** a portion of liquid for drinking **9** alcohol, or the habit of drinking too much of it **drinkable** *adj* **drinker** *n*
WORD ORIGIN Old English *drincan*

drink-driving *adj* of or relating to driving a car after drinking alcohol: *a drink-driving offence*

drip *vb* **dripping, dripped 1** to fall or let fall in drops ▷ *n* **2** a drop of liquid **3** the falling of drops of liquid **4** the sound made by falling drops **5** *informal* a weak or foolish person **6** *med* a device that administers a liquid drop by drop into a vein
WORD ORIGIN Old English *dryppan*

drip-dry *adj* **1** (of clothes or fabrics) designed to dry without creases if hung up when wet ▷ *vb* **-dries, -drying, -dried 2** to dry or become dry thus

drip-feed *vb* **-feeding, -fed 1** to feed (someone) a liquid drop by drop, usually through a vein ▷ *n* **2** same as **drip** (sense 6)

dripping *n* the fat that comes from meat while it is being roasted

drive *vb* **driving, drove, driven 1** to guide the movement of (a vehicle) **2** to transport or be transported in a vehicle **3** to goad into a specified state: *the black despair that finally drove her to suicide* **4** to push or propel: *he drove the nail into the wall with a hammer* **5** *sport* to hit (a ball) very hard and straight **6** *golf* to strike (the ball) with a driver **7** to chase (game) from cover **8 drive home** to make (a point) clearly understood by emphasis ▷ *n* **9** a journey in a driven vehicle **10** a road for vehicles, esp. a private road leading to a house **11** a special effort made by a group of people for a particular purpose: *a charity drive* **12** energy, ambition, or initiative **13** *psychol* a motive or interest: *sex drive* **14** a sustained and powerful military offensive **15** the means by which power is transmitted in a machine **16** *sport* a hard straight shot or stroke
WORD ORIGIN Old English *drīfan*

drive at *vb informal* to intend or mean: *he had no idea what she was driving at*

drive-by *n informal* an incident in which a person is shot at by a person in a moving vehicle

drive-in *n* **1** a cinema, restaurant, etc. offering a service where people remain in their cars while using the service provided ▷ *adj* **2** denoting a cinema, etc. of this kind

drivel *n* **1** foolish talk ▷ *vb* **-velling, -velled** or *US* **-veling, -veled 2** to speak foolishly **3** to allow (saliva) to flow from the mouth
WORD ORIGIN Old English *dreflian* to slaver

driven *vb* the past participle of **drive**

driver *n* **1** a person who drives a vehicle **2** *golf* a long-shafted club with a large head and steep face, used for tee shots

driver's licence *n Canad & Austral* an official document authorizing a person to drive a motor vehicle. Also called (in Britain and certain other countries): **driving licence**

drive-thru *n* **1** a takeaway restaurant, bank, etc. designed so that customers can use it without leaving their cars ▷ *adj* **2** denoting a restaurant, etc. of this kind

drive-time *n* **1** the time of day when many people are driving to or from work, considered as a broadcasting slot ▷ *adj* **2** of this time of day: *the daily drive-time show*

driveway *n* a path for vehicles connecting a building to a public road

driving licence *n* an official document authorizing a person to drive a motor vehicle

drizzle *n* **1** very light rain ▷ *vb* **-zling, -zled 2** to rain lightly **drizzly** *adj*
WORD ORIGIN Old English *drēosan* to fall

droll *adj* quaintly amusing **drollery** *n* **drolly** *adv*
WORD ORIGIN French *drôle* scamp

dromedary (**drom**-mid-er-ee) *n, pl* **-daries** a camel with a single hump
WORD ORIGIN Greek *dromas* running

drone¹ *n* **1** a male honeybee **2** a person who lives off the work of others
WORD ORIGIN Old English *drān*

drone² *vb* **droning, droned 1** to make a monotonous low dull sound **2 drone on** to talk in a monotonous tone without stopping ▷ *n* **3** a monotonous low dull sound **4** a single-reed pipe in a set of bagpipes
WORD ORIGIN related to DRONE¹

drongo *n* a tropical songbird with a glossy black plumage, a forked tail, and a stout bill

drool *vb* **1 drool over** to show excessive enthusiasm for or pleasure in **2** same as **drivel** (senses 2, 3)
WORD ORIGIN probably alteration of DRIVEL

droop *vb* **1** to sag, as from weakness or lack of support **2** to be overcome by weariness: *her eyelids drooped as if she were falling asleep* **drooping** *adj*
WORD ORIGIN Old Norse *drūpa*

droopy *adj* hanging or sagging downwards: *a droopy moustache*

drop *vb* **dropping, dropped 1** to fall or allow (something) to fall vertically **2** to decrease in amount, strength, or value **3** to fall to the ground, as from exhaustion **4** to sink to a lower position, as on a scale **5** to mention

d

casually: *he dropped a hint* **6** to set down (passengers or goods): *can you drop me at the hotel?* **7** *informal* to send: *drop me a letter* **8** to discontinue: *can we drop the subject?* **9** *informal* to be no longer friendly with: *I dropped him when I discovered his political views* **10** to leave out in speaking: *he has a tendency to drop his h's* **11** (of animals) to give birth to (offspring) **12** *sport* to omit (a player) from a team **13** to lose (a game or point) **14 drop back** to progress more slowly than other people going in the same direction **15 drop in** or **by** *informal* to pay someone a casual visit ▷ *n* **16** a small quantity of liquid forming a round shape **17** a small quantity of liquid **18** a small round sweet: *a lemon drop* **19** a decrease in amount, strength, or value **20** the vertical distance that anything may fall **21** the act of unloading troops or supplies by parachute ▸ See also **drop off, dropout, drops**
WORD ORIGIN Old English *dropian*

drop curtain *n* *theatre* a curtain that can be raised and lowered onto the stage

droplet *n* a very small drop of liquid

drop off *vb* **1** to set down (passengers or goods) **2** *informal* to fall asleep **3** to decrease or decline: *sales dropped off during our period of transition*

dropout *n* **1** a person who rejects conventional society **2** a student who does not complete a course of study ▷ *vb* **drop out 3** to abandon or withdraw (from an institution or group)

dropper *n* a small tube with a rubber part at one end for drawing up and dispensing drops of liquid

droppings *pl n* the dung of certain animals, such as rabbits or birds

drops *pl n* any liquid medication applied by means of a dropper

drop scone *n* a flat spongy cake made by dropping a spoonful of batter on a hot griddle

dropsy *n* an illness in which watery fluid collects in the body **dropsical** *adj*
WORD ORIGIN Middle English *ydropesie*, from Greek *hudōr* water

drosky or **droshky** *n, pl* **-kies** an open four-wheeled carriage, formerly used in Russia
WORD ORIGIN Russian *drozhki*

dross *n* **1** the scum formed on the surfaces of molten metals **2** anything of inferior quality: *we can't publish this dross*
WORD ORIGIN Old English *drōs* dregs

drought (rhymes with **out**) *n* a prolonged period of time during which no rain falls
WORD ORIGIN Old English *drūgoth*

drove¹ *vb* the past tense of **drive**

drove² *n* **1** a herd of livestock being driven together **2** a moving crowd of people
WORD ORIGIN Old English *drāf* herd

drover *n* a person who drives sheep or cattle

drown *vb* **1** to die or kill by immersion in liquid **2** to drench thoroughly **3** to make (a sound) impossible to hear by making a loud noise

WORD ORIGIN probably from Old English *druncnian*

drowse *vb* **drowsing, drowsed** to be sleepy, dull, or sluggish
WORD ORIGIN probably from Old English *drūsian* to sink

drowsy *adj* **drowsier, drowsiest**
1 feeling sleepy **2** peaceful and quiet: *row upon row of windows looked out over drowsy parkland* **drowsily** *adv* **drowsiness** *n*

drubbing *n* an utter defeat, as in a contest: *the Communists received a drubbing*
WORD ORIGIN probably from Arabic *dáraba* to beat

drudge *n* **1** a person who works hard at an uninteresting task ▷ *vb* **drudging, drudged 2** to work at such tasks
WORD ORIGIN origin unknown

drudgery *n* uninteresting work that must be done

drug *n* **1** any substance used in the treatment, prevention, or diagnosis of disease **2** a chemical substance, such as a narcotic, taken for the effects it produces ▷ *vb* **drugging, drugged 3** to administer a drug to (a person or animal) in order to induce sleepiness or unconsciousness **4** to mix a drug with (food or drink): *who drugged my wine?*
WORD ORIGIN Old French *drogue*

drug addict *n* a person who is dependent on narcotic drugs

druggist *n* *US & Canad* a pharmacist

drugstore *n* *US & Canad* a pharmacy where a wide variety of goods are available

Druid *n* a member of an ancient order of Celtic priests **Druidic** or **Druidical** *adj*
WORD ORIGIN Latin *druides*

drum *n* **1** a percussion instrument sounded by striking a skin stretched across the opening of a hollow cylinder **2** the sound produced by a drum **3** an object shaped like a drum: *an oil drum* **4** same as **eardrum** ▷ *vb* **drumming, drummed 5** to play (music) on a drum **6** to tap rhythmically or regularly: *he drummed his fingers on the desk* **7** to fix in someone's mind by constant repetition: *my father always drummed into us how privileged we were* ▸ See also **drum up** > **drummer** *n*
WORD ORIGIN Middle Dutch *tromme*

drumbeat *n* the sound made by beating a drum

drumhead *n* the part of a drum that is struck

drum machine *n* a synthesizer programmed to reproduce the sound of percussion instruments

drum major *n* the noncommissioned officer in the army who is in command of the drums and the band when paraded together

drum majorette *n* a girl who marches at the head of a procession, twirling a baton

drumstick *n* **1** a stick used for playing a drum **2** the lower joint of the leg of a cooked fowl

drum up *vb* to obtain (support or business) by making requests or canvassing

drunk *vb* **1** the past participle of **drink** ▷ *adj* **2** intoxicated with alcohol to the

extent of losing control over normal functions **3** overwhelmed by strong influence or emotion: *he was half drunk with satisfaction at his victory over the intruder* ▷ *n* **4** a person who is drunk or drinks habitually to excess
WORD ORIGIN Old English *druncen*, past participle of *drincan* to drink

drunkard *n* a person who is frequently or habitually drunk

drunken *adj* **1** intoxicated with alcohol **2** habitually drunk **3** caused by or relating to alcoholic intoxication: *a drunken argument* **drunkenly** *adv* **drunkenness** *n*

drupe *n* a fleshy fruit with a stone, such as the peach or cherry
WORD ORIGIN Greek *druppa* olive

dry *adj* **drier, driest** or **dryer, dryest**
1 lacking moisture **2** having little or no rainfall **3** having the water drained away or evaporated: *a dry gully for the most part of the year* **4** not providing milk: *a dry cow* **5** (of the eyes) free from tears **6** *Brit, Austral, & NZ informal* thirsty **7** eaten without butter or jam: *a dry cracker* **8** (of wine) not sweet **9** dull and uninteresting: *a dry subject* **10** (of humour) subtle and sarcastic **11** prohibiting the sale of alcoholic liquor: *a dry district* ▷ *vb* **dries, drying, dried 12** to make or become dry **13** to preserve (food) by removing the moisture ▸ See also **dry out, dry up** > **dryness** *n*
WORD ORIGIN Old English *drȳge*

dryad *n, pl* **dryads** or **dryades** (**dry**-ad-deez) *Greek myth* a wood nymph
WORD ORIGIN Greek *druas*

dry battery *n* an electric battery composed of dry cells

dry cell *n* an electric cell in which the electrolyte is in the form of a paste to prevent it from spilling

dry-clean *vb* to clean (clothes, etc.) with a solvent other than water **dry-cleaner** *n* **dry-cleaning** *n*

dry dock *n* a dock that can be pumped dry to permit work on a ship's bottom

dryer¹ *n* any device that removes moisture by heating or by hot air

dryer² *adj* same as **drier¹**

dry ice *n* solid carbon dioxide used as a refrigerant

dryly *adv* same as **drily**

dry out *vb* **1** to make or become dry **2** to undergo or cause to undergo treatment for alcoholism or drug addiction

dry rot *n* **1** crumbling and drying of timber, caused by certain fungi **2** a fungus causing this decay

dry run *n* *informal* a rehearsal

dry stock *n* *NZ* cattle raised for meat

dry-stone *adj* (of a wall) made without mortar

dry up *vb* **1** to make or become dry **2** to dry (dishes, cutlery, etc.) with a tea towel after they have been washed **3** (of a resource) to come to an end **4** *informal* to stop speaking: *she suddenly dried up in the middle of her speech*

DSC *Brit mil* Distinguished Service Cross
DSO *Brit mil* Distinguished Service Order
DSS *Brit* Department of Social Security

Words from Shakespeare
part 9

dowager *n* a widow
Like to a step-dame or a dowage
A Midsummer Night's Dream 1.1

dowdy *n* an ugly woman
Dido was a dowdy *Romeo and Juliet* 2.4

dower, dowery *n* the riches or property given by the father of a bride to her husband-to-be
Thy truth then by they dower *King Lear* 1.1

dram *n* a tiny amount
Why, everything adheres together that no dram of a scruple *Twelfth Night* 3.4

drift *n* a plan, scheme or intention
Shall Romeo by my letters know our drift
Romeo and Juliet 4.1

dropsied *adj* pretentious
Where great additions swell's and virtues none
It is a dropsied honour *All's Well That Ends Well* 2.3

drudge *n* a slave, servant
If I be his cuckold, he's my drudge
All's Well That Ends Well 1.3

dwell *v* to exist, to be
I'd rather dwell in my necessity
Merchant of Venice 1.3

earnest *adj* a pledge to pay or a payment in advance for an earnest of a greater honour
He bade me from him call thee Thane of Cawdor
Macbeth 1.3

ecstasy *n* madness
This is the very ecstasy of love *Hamlet* 2.1

edict *n* law or declaration
It stands as an edict in destiny.
A Midsummer Night's Dream 1.1

egall *adj* equal
companions
Whose souls do bear an egall yoke of love
Merchant of Venice 2.4

easel, eisel *n* vinegar
Woo't drink up eisel? *Hamlet* 5.1

eke, eke out *v* to add to, to increase
Still be kind
And eke out our performance with your mind
Henry V Chorus

elbow, out at *phrase* in poor condition, as when jacket sleeves are worn at the elbow which shows that it is an old jacket
He cannot, sir. He's out at elbow
Measure for Measure 2.1

element *n* formerly thought to be the things from which all things were made. They were four elements: air, earth, water and fire
Does not our lives consist of the four elements?
Twelfth Night 2.3

elf *v* to tangle
I'll ... elf all my hairs in knots *King Lear* 2.3

embassy *n* a message
We'll once more hear Orsino's embassy.
Twelfth Night 1.5

emphasis *n* a forceful expression or strong statement
What is he whose grief
Bears such an emphasis *Hamlet* 5.1

empiric *n* an untrained doctor, sometimes also called a quack
we must not ... prostitute our past-cure malady
To empirics *All's Well That Ends Well* 2.1

emulate *adj* envious
pricked on by a most emulate pride *Hamlet* 1.1

enchant *v* to put a magic spell on
Damn'd as thou art, thou hast enchanted her,
For I'll refer me to all things of sense *Othello* 1.2

enclog *v* to hinder something or to provide an obstacle to it
Traitors enscarped to enclog the guitless keel
Othello 1.2

DSW (in New Zealand) Department of Social Welfare

DTP *computers* desktop publishing

DT's *informal* delirium tremens

dual *adj* having two parts, functions, or aspects: *dual controls; dual nationality* **duality** *n*
WORD ORIGIN Latin *duo* two

dual carriageway *n Brit, Austral, & NZ* a road with a central strip of grass or concrete to separate traffic travelling in opposite directions

dub¹ *vb* **dubbing, dubbed** to give (a person or place) a name or nickname: *he is dubbed a racist despite his strong denials*
WORD ORIGIN Old English *dubbian*

dub² *vb* **dubbing, dubbed 1** to provide (a film) with a new soundtrack in a different language **2** to provide (a film or tape) with a soundtrack ▷ *n* **3** *music* a style of reggae record production involving exaggeration of instrumental parts, echo, etc.
WORD ORIGIN shortened from DOUBLE

dubbin *n* a kind of thick grease applied to leather to soften it and make it waterproof
WORD ORIGIN *dub* to dress leather

dubious (dew-bee-uss) *adj* **1** not entirely honest, safe, or reliable: *this allegation was at best dubious and at worst an outright fabrication* **2** unsure or undecided: *she felt dubious about the entire proposition* **3** of doubtful quality or worth: *she had the dubious honour of being taken for his mother* **dubiety** (dew-**by**-it-ee) *n* **dubiously** *adv*
WORD ORIGIN Latin *dubius* wavering

dubnium *n chem* an element produced in minute quantities by bombarding plutonium with high-energy neon ions. Symbol: Db
WORD ORIGIN after *Dubna* in Russia, where it was first reported

ducal (**duke**-al) *adj* of a duke

ducat (**duck**-it) *n* a former European gold or silver coin
WORD ORIGIN Old Italian *ducato*

duchess *n* **1** a woman who holds the rank of duke **2** the wife or widow of a duke
WORD ORIGIN Old French *duchesse*

duchy *n, pl* **duchies** the area of land owned or ruled by a duke or duchess
WORD ORIGIN Old French *duche*

duck¹ *n, pl* **ducks** *or* **duck 1** a water bird with short legs, webbed feet, and a broad blunt bill **2** the flesh of this bird used for food **3** the female of such a bird **4** *cricket* a score of nothing **5** **like water off a duck's back** without effect: *I reprimanded him but it was like water off a duck's back*
WORD ORIGIN Old English *dūce*

duck² *vb* **1** to move (the head or body) quickly downwards, to escape being seen or avoid a blow **2** to plunge suddenly under water **3** *informal* to dodge (a duty or responsibility)
WORD ORIGIN Middle English

duck-billed platypus *n* see **platypus**

duckling *n* a young duck

ducks and drakes *n* **1** a game in which a flat stone is bounced across the surface of water **2** **play ducks and**

drakes with *informal* to use recklessly: *he has played ducks and drakes with his life*

duct *n* **1** a tube, pipe, or channel through which liquid or gas is sent **2** a tube in the body through which liquid such as tears or bile can pass
WORD ORIGIN Latin *ducere* to lead

ductile *adj* (of a metal) able to be shaped into sheets or drawn out into threads **ductility** *n*
WORD ORIGIN Latin *ductilis*

dud *informal adj* **1** an ineffectual person or thing: *they had the foresight to pick on someone who was not a total dud* ▷ *adj* **2** bad or useless: *a dud cheque*
WORD ORIGIN origin unknown

dude *n informal* **1** *US & Canad* a man: *he was a black dude in his late twenties* **2** *chiefly US & Canad old-fashioned* a dandy **3** *Western US & Canad* a city dweller who spends his or her holiday on a ranch
WORD ORIGIN origin unknown

dudgeon *n* **in high dudgeon** angry or resentful: *the scientist departed in high dudgeon*
WORD ORIGIN origin unknown

due *adj* **1** expected to happen, be done, or arrive at a particular time: *he is due to return on Thursday* **2** immediately payable: *the balance is now due* **3** owed as a debt: *they finally agreed to pay her the money she was due* **4** fitting or proper: *he was found guilty of driving without due care and attention* **5** **due to** happening or existing as a direct result of someone or something else: *the cause of death was chronic kidney failure due to diabetes* ▷ *n* **6** something that is owed or required **7** **give someone his** *or* **her due** to acknowledge someone's good points: *I'll give him his due, he's resourceful* ▷ *adv* **8** directly or exactly: *due west*
WORD ORIGIN Latin *debere* to owe

USAGE
The use of *due to* as a compound preposition (*the performance has been cancelled due to bad weather*) was formerly considered incorrect, but is now acceptable.

duel *n* **1** a formal fight between two people using guns, swords, or other weapons to settle a quarrel ▷ *vb* **duelling, duelled** *or US* **dueling, dueled 2** to fight in a duel **duellist** *n*
WORD ORIGIN Latin *duellum*, poetical variant of *bellum* war

duenna *n* (esp. in Spain) an elderly woman acting as chaperone to girls
WORD ORIGIN Spanish *dueña*

dues *pl n* membership fees paid to a club or organization: *union dues*

duet *n* a piece of music sung or played by two people **duettist** *n*
WORD ORIGIN Latin *duo* two

duff *adj* **1** *chiefly Brit informal* broken or useless: *my car had a duff clutch* ▷ *vb* **2** *golf informal* to bungle (a shot) **3** **duff up** *Brit slang* to beat (someone) severely
WORD ORIGIN probably from *duffer*

duffel *or* **duffle** *n* same as **duffel coat**
WORD ORIGIN after *Duffel*, Belgian town

duffel bag *n* a cylinder-shaped canvas bag fastened with a drawstring

duffel coat *n* a wool coat usually with a hood and fastened with toggles

duffer *n informal* a dull or incompetent person
WORD ORIGIN origin unknown

dug¹ *vb* the past of **dig**

dug² *n* a teat or udder of a female animal
WORD ORIGIN Scandinavian

dugite (**doo**-gyte) *n* a medium-sized Australian venomous snake

dugong *n* a whalelike mammal found in tropical waters
WORD ORIGIN Malay *duyong*

dugout *n* **1** a canoe made by hollowing out a log **2** *Brit* (at a sports ground) the covered bench where managers and substitutes sit **3** *mil* a covered shelter dug in the ground to provide protection

duiker *or* **duyker** (**dike**-er) *n, pl* **-kers** *or* **-ker** a small African antelope
WORD ORIGIN Dutch: diver

du jour (doo zhoor) *adj informal* currently fashionable
WORD ORIGIN French, literally: of the day

duke *n* **1** a nobleman of the highest rank **2** the prince or ruler of a small principality or duchy **dukedom** *n*
WORD ORIGIN Latin *dux* leader

dulcet (**dull**-sit) *adj* (of a sound) soothing or pleasant: *she smiled and, in dulcet tones, told me I would be next*
WORD ORIGIN Latin *dulcis* sweet

dulcimer *n* a tuned percussion instrument consisting of a set of strings stretched over a sounding board and struck with hammers
WORD ORIGIN Old French *doulcemer*

dull *adj* **1** not interesting: *the finished article would make dull reading* **2** slow to learn or understand **3** (of an ache) not intense: *I have a dull ache in the middle of my back* **4** (of weather) not bright or clear **5** not lively or energetic: *she appeared, looking dull and apathetic* **6** (of colour) lacking brilliance **7** (of the blade of a knife) not sharp **8** (of a sound) not loud or clear: *his head fell back to the carpet with a dull thud* ▷ *vb* **9** to make or become dull **dullness** *n* **dully** *adv*
WORD ORIGIN Old English *dol*

dullard *n old-fashioned* a dull or stupid person

dulse *n* a seaweed with large red edible fronds
WORD ORIGIN Irish *duilesc* seaweed

duly *adv* **1** in a proper manner: *my permit was duly stamped* **2** at the proper time: *the photographer duly arrived*

dumb *adj* **1** lacking the power to speak **2** lacking the power of human speech: *the event was denounced as cruelty to dumb animals* **3** temporarily unable to speak: *I was struck dumb when I heard the news* **4** done or performed without speech: *I looked at her in dumb puzzlement* **5** *informal* stupid or slow to understand ▶ See also **dumb down** ▷ **dumbly** *adv*
WORD ORIGIN Old English

dumbbell *n* **1** a short bar with a heavy ball or disc at either end, used for physical exercise **2** *slang chiefly US & Canad* a stupid person

dumb down *vb* to make (something) less intellectually demanding or sophisticated: *a move to dumb down its news coverage*

dumbfounded *adj* speechless with amazement: *she sat open-mouthed and dumbfounded*
WORD ORIGIN *dumb + (con)found*

dumb show *n* meaningful gestures without speech

dumbstruck *adj* temporarily speechless through shock or surprise

dumbwaiter *n* **1** a lift for carrying food, etc. from one floor of a building to another **2** *Brit* **a** a stand placed near a dining table to hold food **b** a revolving circular tray placed on a table to hold food

dumdum *or* **dumdum bullet** *n* a soft-nosed bullet that expands on impact and causes large and serious wounds
WORD ORIGIN after *Dum-Dum*, town near Calcutta where originally made

dummy *n, pl* -**mies 1** a large model that looks like a human being, used for displaying clothes in a shop, as a target, etc. **2** a copy of an object, often lacking some essential feature of the original **3** *slang* a stupid person **4** *bridge* **a** the hand exposed on the table by the declarer's partner and played by the declarer **b** the declarer's partner **5** a rubber teat for babies to suck ▷ *adj* **6** imitation or substitute: *you can train them with dummy bombs and live ammunition*
WORD ORIGIN from *dumb*

dummy run *n* a practice or test carried out to test if any problems remain: *we'll do a dummy run on the file to see if the program works*

dump *vb* **1** to drop or let fall in a careless manner: *he dumped the books on the bed* **2** *informal* to abandon (someone or something) without proper care: *the unwanted babies were dumped in orphanages* **3** to dispose of (nuclear waste) **4** *commerce* to sell (goods) in bulk and at low prices, usually in another country, in order to keep prices high in the home market **5** *computers* to record (the contents of the memory) on a storage device at a series of points during a computer run ▷ *n* **6** a place where rubbish is left **7** *informal* a dirty, unattractive place: *you're hardly in this dump out of choice* **8** *mil* a place where weapons or supplies are stored
WORD ORIGIN probably from Old Norse

dumpling *n* **1** a small ball of dough cooked and served with stew **2** a round pastry case filled with fruit: *an apple dumpling*
WORD ORIGIN obsolete *dump* lump

dumps *pl n* **down in the dumps** *informal* feeling depressed and miserable
WORD ORIGIN probably from Middle Dutch *domp* haze

dumpy *adj* **dumpier, dumpiest** short and plump
WORD ORIGIN perhaps related to DUMPLING

dun¹ *vb* **dunning, dunned 1** to press (a debtor) for payment ▷ *n* **2** a demand for payment
WORD ORIGIN origin unknown

dun² *adj* brownish-grey
WORD ORIGIN Old English *dunn*

dunce *n* *Brit, Austral, & NZ* a person who is stupid or slow to learn

WORD ORIGIN *Dunses*, term of ridicule applied to the followers of John *Duns Scotus*, scholastic theologian

dunderhead *n* *Brit, Austral, & NZ* a slow-witted person
WORD ORIGIN probably from Dutch *donder* thunder + HEAD

dune *n* a mound or ridge of drifted sand
WORD ORIGIN Middle Dutch

dung *n* the faeces from large animals
WORD ORIGIN Old English: prison

dungarees *pl n* trousers with a bib attached
WORD ORIGIN *Dungrī*, district of Bombay, where the fabric used originated

dungeon *n* a prison cell, often underground
WORD ORIGIN Old French *donjon*

dunghill *n* a heap of dung

dunk *vb* **1** to dip (a biscuit or piece of bread) in a drink or soup before eating it **2** to put (something) in liquid: *dunk the garment in the dye for 15 minutes* **3** *basketball* to drop (the ball) through the hoop after having leapt high enough to have the hands above the rim ▷ *n* **4** *basketball* a scoring shot in which one player drops the ball through the hoop after having leapt high enough to have the hands above the rim
WORD ORIGIN Old High German *dunkōn*

dunlin *n* a small sandpiper, of northern and arctic regions, with a brown back and a black breast
WORD ORIGIN from DUN²

dunnock *n* same as **hedge sparrow**
WORD ORIGIN from DUN²

dunny *n, pl* -**nies** *Austral or old-fashioned NZ informal* a toilet
WORD ORIGIN of obscure origin

duo *n, pl* **duos 1** two singers or musicians who sing or play music together as a pair **2** *informal* two people who have something in common or do something together: *when they're together they make an impressive duo*
WORD ORIGIN Latin: two

duodecimal *adj* relating to twelve or twelfths
WORD ORIGIN Latin *duodecim* twelve

duodenum (dew-oh-**deen**-um) *n* the first part of the small intestine, just below the stomach **duodenal** *adj*
WORD ORIGIN Medieval Latin *intestinum duodenum digitorum* intestine of twelve fingers' length

duologue *or US sometimes* **duolog** *n* a part or all of a play in which the speaking roles are limited to two actors
WORD ORIGIN DUO + (MONO)LOGUE

DUP (in Northern Ireland) Democratic Unionist Party

dupe *vb* **duping, duped 1** to deceive or cheat: *you duped me into doing exactly what you wanted* ▷ *n* **2** a person who is easily deceived
WORD ORIGIN French

duple *adj* **1** same as **double 2** *music* having two beats in a bar
WORD ORIGIN Latin *duplus* double

duplex *n* **1** *US & Canad* **a** an apartment on two floors **b** *US & Austral* a semidetached house ▷ *adj* **2** having two parts
WORD ORIGIN Latin: twofold

duplicate *adj* **1** copied exactly from an original: *he had a duplicate key to the front door* ▷ *n* **2** an exact copy **3** **in duplicate** in two exact copies: *submit the draft in duplicate, please* ▷ *vb* -**cating, -cated 4** to make an exact copy of **5** to do again (something that has already been done) **duplication** *n* **duplicator** *n*
WORD ORIGIN Latin *duplicare* to double

duplicity *n* deceitful behaviour: *he is a man of duplicity, who turns things to his advantage*
WORD ORIGIN Old French *duplicite*

durable *adj* strong and long-lasting: *the car's body was made of a light but durable plastic* **durability** *n*
WORD ORIGIN Latin *durare* to last

durable goods *pl n* goods that do not require frequent replacement. Also called: **durables**

duration *n* the length of time that something lasts
WORD ORIGIN Latin *durare* to last

durbar *n* **a** (formerly) the court of a native ruler or a governor in India **b** a reception at such a court
WORD ORIGIN Hindi *darbār*

duress *n* physical or moral pressure used to force someone to do something: *confessions obtained under duress*
WORD ORIGIN Latin *durus* hard

during *prep* throughout or within the limit of (a period of time)
WORD ORIGIN Latin *durare* to last

dusk *n* the time just before nightfall when it is almost dark
WORD ORIGIN Old English *dox*

dusky *adj* **duskier, duskiest 1** dark in colour: *her gold earrings gleamed against her dusky cheeks* **2** dim or shadowy: *the dusky room was crowded with absurd objects* **duskily** *adv* **duskiness** *n*

dust *n* **1** small dry particles of earth, sand, or dirt **2** **bite the dust a** to stop functioning: *my television has finally bitten the dust* **b** to fall down dead **3** **shake the dust off one's feet** to depart angrily **4** **throw dust in someone's eyes** to confuse or mislead someone ▷ *vb* **5** to remove dust from (furniture) by wiping **6** to sprinkle (something) with a powdery substance: *serve dusted with brown sugar and cinnamon*
WORD ORIGIN Old English *dūst*

dustbin *n* a large, usually cylindrical, container for household rubbish

dust bowl *n* a dry area in which the surface soil is exposed to wind erosion

dustcart *n* *chiefly Brit & NZ* a lorry for collecting household rubbish

dust cover *n* **1** same as **dustsheet 2** same as **dust jacket**

duster *n* a cloth used for dusting

dust jacket *or* **cover** *n* a removable paper cover used to protect a book

dustman *n, pl* -**men** *Brit* a man whose job is to collect household rubbish

dust mite *n* one of two varieties of mites that feed on shed human skin cells and whose excrement is a household allergen

dustpan *n* a short-handled shovel into which dust is swept from floors

dustsheet *n* a large cloth cover used to protect furniture from dust

dust-up n informal a fight or argument

dusty adj **dustier, dustiest 1** covered with dust **2** (of a colour) tinged with grey

Dutch adj **1** of the Netherlands ▷ n **2** the language of the Netherlands ▷ pl n **3** the Dutch the people of the Netherlands ▷ adv **4 go Dutch** informal to go on an outing where each person pays his or her own expenses

Dutch auction n an auction in which the price is lowered by stages until a buyer is found

Dutch barn n Brit a farm building with a steel frame and a curved roof

Dutch courage n false courage gained from drinking alcohol

Dutch elm disease n a fungal disease of elm trees

Dutchman or fem **Dutchwoman** n, pl **-men** or **-women** a person from the Netherlands

Dutch oven n **1** an iron or earthenware container with a lid, used for stews, etc. **2** a metal box, open in front, for cooking in front of an open fire

Dutch treat n informal an outing where each person pays his or her own expenses

Dutch uncle n informal a person who criticizes or scolds frankly and severely

duteous adj formal or archaic dutiful or obedient

dutiable adj (of goods) requiring payment of duty

dutiful adj doing what is expected: she is a responsible and dutiful mother **dutifully** adv

duty n, pl **-ties 1** the work performed as part of one's job: it is his duty to supervise the memorial services **2** a obligation to fulfil one's responsibilities: it's my duty as a doctor to keep it confidential **3** a government tax on imports **4 on** or **off duty** at (or not at) work
WORD ORIGIN Anglo-French dueté

duty-bound adj morally obliged to do something: we are duty-bound to take whatever measures are necessary

duty-free adj, adv with exemption from customs or excise duties

duty-free shop n a shop, esp. at an airport, that sells duty-free goods

duvet (**doo**-vay) n same as **continental quilt**
WORD ORIGIN French

DVD Digital Versatile or Video Disk: a type of compact disc that can store large amounts of video and audio information

DVLA Brit Driver and Vehicle Licensing Agency

DVT deep-vein thrombosis

dwaal n S African a state of absent-mindedness; a daze
WORD ORIGIN Afrikaans

dwang n NZ & S African a short piece of wood inserted in a timber-framed wall

dwarf vb **1** to cause (someone or something) to seem small by being much larger ▷ adj **2** (of an animal or plant) much below the average size for the species: a dwarf evergreen shrub ▷ n, pl **dwarfs** or **dwarves 3** a person who is smaller than average size **4** (in folklore) a small ugly manlike creature, often possessing magical powers
WORD ORIGIN Old English dweorg

dwell vb **dwelling, dwelt** or **dwelled** formal, literary to live as a permanent resident **dweller** n
WORD ORIGIN Old English dwellan to seduce, get lost

dwelling n formal, literary a place of residence

dwell on or **upon** vb to think, speak, or write at length about (something)

dwindle vb **-dling, -dled** to grow less in size, strength, or number
WORD ORIGIN Old English dwīnan

Dy chem dysprosium

dye n **1** a colouring substance **2** the colour produced by dyeing ▷ vb **dyeing, dyed 3** to colour (hair or fabric) by applying a dye **dyer** n
WORD ORIGIN Old English dēag

dyed-in-the-wool adj having strong and unchanging attitudes or opinions: he's a dyed-in-the-wool communist

dying vb **1** the present participle of **die**[1] ▷ adj **2** occurring at the moment of death: in accordance with his dying wish **3** (of a person or animal) very ill and likely to die soon **4** becoming less important or less current: coal mining is a dying industry

dyke[1] n esp. US **dike** n **1** a wall built to prevent flooding **2** a ditch **3** Scot a dry-stone wall
WORD ORIGIN Old English dic ditch

dyke[2] or **dike** n slang a lesbian
WORD ORIGIN origin unknown

dynamic adj **1** (of a person) full of energy, ambition, or new ideas **2** relating to a force of society, history, or the mind that produces a change: the government needs a more dynamic policy towards the poor **3** physics relating to energy or forces that produce motion **dynamically** adv
WORD ORIGIN Greek dunamis power

dynamics n **1** the branch of mechanics concerned with the forces that change or produce the motions of bodies

▷ pl n **2** those forces that produce change in any field or system **3** music the various degrees of loudness called for in a performance

dynamism n great energy or enthusiasm

dynamite n **1** an explosive made of nitroglycerine **2** informal a dangerous or exciting person or thing: she's still dynamite ▷ vb **-miting, -mited 3** to mine or blow (something) up with dynamite
WORD ORIGIN Greek dunamis power

dynamo n, pl **-mos** a device for converting mechanical energy into electricity
WORD ORIGIN short for dynamoelectric machine

dynamoelectric adj of the conversion of mechanical energy into electricity or vice versa

dynamometer (dine-a-**mom**-it-er) n an instrument for measuring mechanical power or force

dynast n a hereditary ruler
WORD ORIGIN Greek dunasthai to be powerful

dynasty n, pl **-ties 1** a series of rulers of a country from the same family **2** a period of time during which a country is ruled by the same family **dynastic** adj
WORD ORIGIN Greek dunastēs dynast

dysentery n infection of the intestine which causes severe diarrhoea
WORD ORIGIN Greek dusentera bad bowels

dysfunction n **1** med any disturbance or abnormality in the function of an organ or part **2** (esp. of a family) failure to show the characteristics or fulfil the purposes accepted as normal or beneficial **dysfunctional** adj

dyslexia n a developmental disorder that causes learning difficulty with reading, writing, and numeracy **dyslexic** adj, n
WORD ORIGIN Greek dus- not + lexis word

dysmenorrhoea or esp. US **dysmenorrhea** n painful or difficult menstruation
WORD ORIGIN Greek dus- bad + rhoia a flowing

dyspepsia n indigestion **dyspeptic** adj, n
WORD ORIGIN Greek dus- bad + pepsis digestion

dysprosium n chem a metallic element of the lanthanide series. Symbol: Dy
WORD ORIGIN Greek dusprositos difficult to get near

dystrophy (**diss**-trof-fee) n see **muscular dystrophy**
WORD ORIGIN Greek dus- not + trophē food

Anthony Burgess and Postmodernism

Anthony Burgess, for better or worse, is best known for *A Clockwork Orange*, a long novella set in an unspecified future Britain where delinquent youths speak an impenetrable slang largely based upon Russian (evidence of cold-war anxiety) while the government enacts draconian measures to tackle crime. Though a rewarding read in itself, the book's fame is actually the result of Stanley Kubrick's infamous film adaptation.

Postmodernism takes modernism as its starting point, and if James Joyce exemplifies high modernism in prose, then we can look for no better representative of postmodern prose than Burgess, who took a copy of *Finnegans Wake* with him to the front in World War II. As such, he joins a very elite list of six people whom we know have both read *and understood* the *Wake*: Burgess himself, fellow post-modernist and Joyce's former secretary Samuel Beckett, mythologist and Joyce aficionado Joseph Campbell (who wrote the famous *Skeleton Key to Finnegans Wake*), the scholar John Bishop, of the University of California at Berkeley, who has written many books on the *Wake*, and the popular authors Tom Robbins and Phillip K Dick, both of whom reference the *Wake* in their novels.

Burgess was, among other things, a skilled linguist; as such he was in a privileged position to understand Joyce's final work, and with his strong background in Slavic languages, he was one of the first to point out the influence of Russian in *Finnegans Wake*. Perhaps without early exposure to Joyce, Burgess would never have dared to create a narrative told exclusively in a fictitious variety of English built on anachronisms and inter-lingual portmanteaus, leaving the onus on his readers to find their own way through it. But such is Burgess's *A Clockwork Orange*, the whole of which is a first-person narrative told in an invented slang called *Nadsat*. The name is derived from the Russian suffix equivalent to English *-teen*. It is comprised of modified Russian vocabulary, rhyming slang, and completely invented words. The story immediately plunges the reader into this slang from the first line. Though the syntax is non-standard, it is intelligible, and some of the slang used is English, such as *flip* and *bastard*. However, *rassoodock*, meaning 'mind', comes from Russian *rassudok* 'sanity', and *droog* comes from Russian *drüg* 'friend'. Even the name of the milk bar, *Korova*, comes from the Russian word for 'cow'. Other slang words used include *mesto*, Russian for 'place', *skorry*, from Russian *skori* 'quick', *vesch*, Russian for 'thing', *moloko*, Russian for 'milk', *peet*, from Russian *pit* 'drink', and *mozg*, Russian for 'brain'. Even the apparently English word *horrorshow* actually comes from Russian *khorosho* 'good'.

This total language immersion in an alien tongue also served Burgess in less well-known novels, such as *Nothing Like the Sun* and *A Dead Man in Deptford*, his fictionalized accounts of the lives of Shakespeare and Christopher Marlowe, respectively. Both books attempt to re-create Elizabethan English as it might have been used by someone other than a skilled professional writer. *Deptford*, for example, is narrated by a minor actor who was Marlowe's sometime lover; and the prose, though rich and allusive, is meandering and often difficult to follow. The first sentence uses 51 words to mean 'You probably guess that a lot of this story is made up, though it's based on things I actually saw'. And yet it gives us the flavour of affected, periodic diction that was certainly a feature of sixteenth-century English, as well as alluding to Shakespeare's *Macbeth*, referencing contemporary linguistic facts, such as the now-archaic form *oft* coexisting with *often*, and illustrating poetic techniques like alliteration with the phrase 'heap of happenings'. The awkward construction 'Eye to eye knowledge of' uses *eye* as both noun and verb (a common practice in Early Modern English). It also recalls the phrase 'see eye to eye', meaning 'agree' (implying a discussion about whether the narrator will disagree with his readers, his subject, or historical fact). 'Eye to eye' can also mean 'face to face' addressing the narrator's lack of an intimate relationship with his subject. Manipulating language with such subtlety is the legacy of Modernism; mixing it with bawdy humour and employing it in popular fiction, however, is the cornerstone of postmodernism.

Ee

The letter E is the fifth letter of the English alphabet. It has its origins in the Greek letter *epsilon* (E,ε) which literally means 'plain E' and contrasted with the letter *eta* (H,η) which made a longer sound. It is believed that *epsilon* was derived from an earlier Semitic letter associated with a person at prayer, and the outstretched hands of the praying figure may perhaps survive in the horizontal lines at the top and bottom of the modern E.

E can designate the fifth item in a series, and in a five-tier grading system anything designated E belongs in the lowest twenty per cent. Thus an E grade in an examination is unlikely to be a cause for celebration.

E is the most frequently occurring of all letters in English, as well as in French and many other languages. This makes all the more remarkable the achievement of the French writer Georges Perec, who managed to write an entire novel without using a single letter E. (He later made up for this by writing another novel which used no vowels except for E.)

In the game of Scrabble there are twelve E's in play – more than any other letter. However, such is the value of the letter in building words that players of the game are seldom displeased to find an E on their rack.

In science, E is a symbol for energy, and Albert Einstein famously said that $E = mc^2$, defining the energy of a body in terms of its mass and the speed of light.

E is also associated with Europe. 'E numbers' are the European Union's identification codes for food additives, and generally regarded as something to be wary of, and the symbol for the euro, the currency of most European Union countries, is a form of this letter (€).

The letter E took on a whole new significance in the rave culture of the early 1990s as an informal name for the drug ecstasy.

Around the same time, a still more pervasive use for the letter was emerging: a synonym for electronic communication. This began with the abbreviation of 'electronic mail' to 'e-mail'. Before long, the letter E (usually in its lower-case form) was being used in front of numerous other words to indicate an operation carried out by the electronic transfer of data, as in 'e-business', 'e-banking', and 'e-learning'.

---

e *maths* a number used as the base of natural logarithms. Approximate value: 2.718 282...

E 1 *music* the third note of the scale of C major **2** East(ern) **3** English **4** *physics* **a** energy **b** electromotive force **5** *slang* the drug ecstasy or an ecstasy tablet

e- *prefix* electronic: *e-mail; e-tailer*

E- *prefix* used with a number following it to indicate that something, such as a food additive, conforms to an EU standard

each *adj* **1** every one of two or more people or things considered individually: *each year* ▷ *pron* **2** every one of two or more people or things: *each had been given one room to design* ▷ *adv* **3** for, to, or from each person or thing: *twenty pounds each* **4** **each other** (of two or more people) each one to or at the other or others; one another: *they stared at each other* **WORD ORIGIN** Old English *ǣlc*

⧉ **USAGE**
⧉ *Each* is a singular pronoun and
⧉ should be used with a singular form
⧉ of a verb: *each of the candidates was* (not
⧉ *were*) *interviewed separately*. See also at
⧉ **either**.

eager *adj* very keen to have or do something **eagerly** *adv* **eagerness** *n* **WORD ORIGIN** Latin *acer* sharp, keen

eagle *n* **1** a large bird of prey with broad wings and strong soaring flight **2** *golf* a score of two strokes under par for a hole **WORD ORIGIN** Latin *aquila*

eagle-eyed *adj* having very sharp eyesight

eaglet *n* a young eagle

ear¹ *n* **1** the part of the body with which a person or animal hears **2** the external visible part of the ear **3** the ability to hear musical and other sounds and interpret them accurately: *a good ear for languages* **4** willingness to listen: *they are always willing to lend an ear* **5** **be all ears** to be prepared to listen attentively to something **6** **fall on deaf ears** to be ignored: *his words fell on deaf ears* **7** **in one ear and out the other** heard but quickly forgotten or ignored **8** **out on one's ear** *informal* dismissed suddenly and unpleasantly **9** **play by ear** to play without written music **10** **play it by ear** *informal* to make up one's plan of action as one goes along **11** **turn a deaf ear to** to be deliberately unresponsive to: *many countries have turned a deaf ear to their cries for help* **12** **up to one's ears in** *informal* deeply involved in **WORD ORIGIN** Old English *ēare*

ear² *n* the part of a cereal plant, such as wheat or barley, that contains the seeds **WORD ORIGIN** Old English *ēar*

earache *n* pain in the ear

earbash *vb Brit, Austral, & NZ informal* to talk incessantly **earbashing** *n*

eardrum *n* the thin membrane separating the external ear from the middle ear

earful *n informal* a scolding or telling-off

earl *n* (in Britain) a nobleman ranking below a marquess and above a viscount **earldom** *n* **WORD ORIGIN** Old English *eorl*

Earl Grey *n* a variety of China tea flavoured with oil of bergamot

ear lobe *n* the soft hanging lowest part of the human ear

early *adj* **-lier, -liest 1** occurring or arriving before the correct or expected time **2** in the first part of a period of time: *early April* **3** near the beginning of the development or history of something: *early Britain was very primitive; early models of this car rust easily* ▷ *adv* **4** occurring or arriving before the correct or expected time **5** in the first part of a period of time **6** near the beginning of the development or history of something: *early in the war* **WORD ORIGIN** Old English *ǣrlīce*

Early English *n* a style of architecture used in England in the 12th and 13th centuries, characterized by narrow pointed arches and ornamental intersecting stonework in windows

earmark *vb* **1** to set (something) aside for a specific purpose ▷ *n* **2** a feature that enables the nature of something to be identified: *it had all the earmarks of a disaster*

earn *vb* **1** to gain or be paid (money) in return for work **2** to acquire or deserve through one's behaviour or action: *you've earned a good night's sleep* **3** to make (money) as interest or profit: *her savings earned 8% interest* **earner** *n* **WORD ORIGIN** Old English *earnian*

earnest[1] *adj* **1** serious and sincere, often excessively so ▷ *n* **2 in earnest** with serious or sincere intentions **earnestly** *adv* **earnestness** *n* **WORD ORIGIN** Old English *eornost*

earnest[2] *n Brit, Austral, & NZ, old-fashioned* a part payment given in advance as a guarantee of the remainder, esp. to confirm a contract **WORD ORIGIN** Old French *erres* pledges

earnings *pl n* money earned

earphone *n* a small device connected to a radio or tape recorder and worn over the ear, so that a person can listen to a broadcast or tape without anyone else hearing it

ear-piercing *adj* extremely loud or shrill

earplug *n* a piece of soft material placed in the ear to keep out noise or water

earring *n* a piece of jewellery worn in or hanging from the ear lobe

earshot *n* the range within which a sound can be heard: *out of earshot*

ear-splitting *adj* extremely loud or shrill

earth *n* **1** (*sometimes cap*) the planet that we live on, the third planet from the sun, the only one on which life is known to exist ▸ Related adjective: **terrestrial 2** the part of the surface of this planet that is not water **3** the soil in which plants grow **4** the hole in which a fox lives **5** a wire in a piece of electrical equipment through which electricity can escape into the ground if a fault develops **6 come down to earth** to return to reality from a daydream or fantasy **7 on earth** used for emphasis: *what on earth happened?* ▷ *vb* **8** to fit (a piece of electrical equipment) with an earth **WORD ORIGIN** Old English *eorthe*

earthbound *adj* **1** unable to leave the surface of the earth **2** lacking in imagination

earthen *adj* made of earth or baked clay: *an earthen floor*

earthenware *n* dishes and other objects made of baked clay: *an earthenware flowerpot*

earthly *adj* **-lier, -liest 1** of life on earth as opposed to any heavenly or spiritual state **2** *informal* conceivable or possible: *what earthly reason would they have for lying?*

earthquake *n* a series of vibrations at the earth's surface caused by movement of the earth's crust

earth science *n* any science, such as geology, concerned with the structure, age, etc. of the earth

earth-shattering *adj* very surprising or shocking: *an earth-shattering event*

earthwards *adv* towards the earth

earthwork *n* **1** excavation of earth, as in engineering construction **2** a fortification made of earth

earthworm *n* a common worm that burrows in the soil

earthy *adj* **earthier, earthiest 1** open and direct in the treatment of sex, excretion, etc. **2** of or like earth: *earthy colours* **earthiness** *n*

earwig *n* a thin brown insect with pincers at the tip of its abdomen **WORD ORIGIN** Old English *ēarwicga*, from *ēare* ear + *wicga* beetle

ease *n* **1** lack of difficulty **2** freedom from discomfort or worry **3** rest, leisure, or relaxation **4** freedom from poverty: *a life of leisure and ease* **5 at ease a** *mil* (of a soldier) standing in a relaxed position with the feet apart **b** in a relaxed attitude or frame of mind ▷ *vb* **easing, eased 6** to make or become less difficult or severe: *the pain gradually eased* **7** to move into or out of a place or situation slowly and carefully **8 ease off** *or* **up** to lessen or cause to lessen in severity, pressure, tension, or strain: *the rain eased off* **WORD ORIGIN** Old French *aise*

easel *n* a frame on legs, used for supporting an artist's canvas, a display, or a blackboard **WORD ORIGIN** Dutch *ezel* ass

easily *adv* **1** without difficulty **2** without doubt; by far: *easily the most senior Chinese leader to visit the West*

USAGE
See at **easy**.

east *n* **1** one of the four cardinal points of the compass, at 90° clockwise from north **2** the direction along a line of latitude towards the sunrise **3 the east** any area lying in or towards the east ▷ *adj* **4** situated in, moving towards, or facing the east **5** (esp. of the wind) from the east ▷ *adv* **6** in, to, or towards the east **WORD ORIGIN** Old English *ēast*

East *n* **1 the East a** the southern and eastern parts of Asia **b** (esp. formerly) the countries in Eastern Europe and Asia which are or have been under Communist rule ▷ *adj* **2** of or denoting the eastern part of a country or region

eastbound *adj* going towards the east

Easter *n* **1** *Christianity* a festival commemorating the Resurrection of Christ ▷ *adj* **2** taking place at the time of the year when this festival is celebrated: *the Easter holidays* **WORD ORIGIN** Old English *ēastre*

Easter egg *n* a chocolate egg given at Easter

easterly *adj* **1** of or in the east ▷ *adv, adj* **2** towards the east **3** from the east: *an easterly breeze*

eastern *adj* **1** situated in or towards the east **2** facing or moving towards the east **3** (*sometimes cap*) of or characteristic of the east or East **easternmost** *adj*

Easterner *n* a person from the east of a country or region

eastern hemisphere *n* the half of the globe that contains Europe, Asia, Africa, and Australia

eastings *pl n* a series of numbers in a grid reference indicating the distance eastwards from a given meridian

eastward *adj, adv also* **eastwards 1** towards the east ▷ *n* **2** the eastward part or direction

easy *adj* **easier, easiest 1** not difficult; simple: *the house is easy to keep clean* **2** free from pain, care, or anxiety: *an easy life* **3** tolerant and undemanding; easy-going **4** defenceless or readily fooled: *easy prey* **5** moderate and not involving any great effort: *an easy ride* **6** *informal* ready to fall in with any suggestion made: *he wanted to do something and I was easy about it* **7** *informal* pleasant and not involving any great effort to enjoy: *easy on the eye* ▷ *adv* **8 go easy on a** to avoid using too much of: *he'd tried to go easy on the engines* **b** to treat less severely than is deserved: *go easy on him, he's just a kid* **9 take it easy** to relax and avoid stress or undue hurry **easiness** *n* **WORD ORIGIN** Old French *aisié*

USAGE
Easy should only be used as an adverb in certain set phrases: *to take it easy; easy does it*. Where a fixed expression is not involved, the usual adverbial form of *easy* is preferred: *this polish goes on more easily* (not *easier*) *than the other*.

easy chair *n* a comfortable upholstered armchair

easy-going *adj* relaxed in manner or attitude; very tolerant

eat *vb* **eating, ate, eaten 1** to take (food) into the mouth and swallow it **2** to have a meal: *sometimes we eat out of doors* **3** *informal* to make anxious or worried: *what's eating you?* **4 eat away** *or* **into** *or* **up** to destroy or use up partly or wholly: *inflation ate into the firm's profits* ▸ See also **eat out, eat up** ▷ **eater** *n* **WORD ORIGIN** Old English *etan*

eatable *adj* fit or suitable for eating

eating *n* **1** food in relation to its quality or taste: *these add up to lots of vitamins and minerals, and good eating* ▷ *adj* **2** suitable for eating uncooked: *eating apples*

eat out *vb* to eat at a restaurant

eat up *vb* **1** to eat or consume entirely: *eat up these potatoes* **2** *informal* to affect severely: *I was eaten up by jealousy*

eau de Cologne (oh de kol-**lone**) *n* full form of **cologne** **WORD ORIGIN** French: water of Cologne

eau de vie (oh de **vee**) *n* brandy or a similar alcoholic drink **WORD ORIGIN** French: water of life

eaves *pl n* the edge of a sloping roof that overhangs the walls **WORD ORIGIN** Old English *efes*

eavesdrop *vb* **-dropping, -dropped** to listen secretly to a private conversation **eavesdropper** *n*
WORD ORIGIN Old English *yfesdrype* water dripping from the eaves

eavestrough *n Canad* a gutter at the eaves of a building

ebb *vb* **1** (of the sea or the tide) to flow back from its highest point **2** to fall away or decline: *her anger ebbed away* ▷ *n* **3** the flowing back of the tide from high to low water **4 at a low ebb** in a weak state: *her creativity was at a low ebb*
WORD ORIGIN Old English *ebba* ebb-tide

ebony *n* **1** a very hard dark-coloured wood used to make furniture, etc. ▷ *adj* **2** very deep black
WORD ORIGIN Greek *ebenos*

e-book *n* a book in electronic form

ebullient *adj* full of enthusiasm or excitement **ebullience** *n*
WORD ORIGIN Latin *ebullire* to bubble forth, be boisterous

EC 1 European Commission **2** European Community: a former name for the European Union

eccentric *adj* **1** unconventional or odd **2** (of circles) not having the same centre ▷ *n* **3** a person who behaves unconventionally or oddly **eccentrically** *adv*
WORD ORIGIN Greek *ek-* away from + *kentron* centre

eccentricity *n* **1** unconventional or odd behaviour **2** *pl* **-ties** an unconventional or odd habit or act

ecclesiastic *n* **1** a member of the clergy ▷ *adj* **2** of or relating to the Christian Church or its clergy
WORD ORIGIN Greek *ekklēsia* assembly

ecclesiastical *adj* of or relating to the Christian Church or its clergy

ECG electrocardiogram

echelon (**esh-a-lon**) *n* **1** a level of power or responsibility: *the upper echelons of society* **2** *mil* a formation in which units follow one another but are spaced out sideways to allow each a line of fire ahead
WORD ORIGIN French *échelon* rung of a ladder

echidna (**ik-kid-na**) *n, pl* **-nas, -nae** (**-nee**) an Australian spiny egg-laying mammal. Also called: **spiny anteater**

echinoderm (**ik-kine-oh-durm**) *n* a sea creature with a five-part symmetrical body, such as a starfish or sea urchin
WORD ORIGIN Greek *ekhinos* sea urchin + *derma* skin

echo *n, pl* **-oes 1 a** the reflection of sound by a solid object **b** a sound reflected by a solid object **2** a repetition or imitation of someone else's opinions **3** something that brings back memories: *an echo of the past* **4** the signal reflected back to a radar transmitter by an object ▷ *vb* **-oing, -oed 5** (of a sound) to be reflected off an object in such a way that it can be heard again **6** (of a place) to be filled with a sound and its echoes: *the church echoed with singing* **7** (of people) to repeat or imitate (what someone else has said): *his conclusion echoed that of Jung* **echoing** *adj*
WORD ORIGIN Greek *ēkhō*

echo chamber *n* a room with walls that reflect sound, used to create an echo effect

echolocation *n* the discovery of an object's position by measuring the time taken for an echo to return from it

echo sounder *n* a navigation device that determines depth by measuring the time taken for a pulse of sound to reach the sea bed and for the echo to return

éclair *n* a finger-shaped cake of choux pastry, filled with cream and coated with chocolate
WORD ORIGIN French: lightning (probably because it does not last long)

eclampsia *n pathol* a serious condition that can develop towards the end of a pregnancy, causing high blood pressure, swelling, and convulsions

eclectic *adj* **1** composed of elements selected from a wide range of styles, ideas, or sources: *the eclectic wine list includes bottles from all round the world* **2** selecting elements from a wide range of styles, ideas, or sources: *an eclectic approach that takes the best from all schools of psychology* ▷ *n* **3** a person who takes an eclectic approach **eclecticism** *n*
WORD ORIGIN Greek *eklegein* to select

eclipse *n* **1** the obscuring of one star or planet by another. A **solar eclipse** occurs when the moon passes between the sun and the earth; a **lunar eclipse** when the earth passes between the sun and the moon **2** a loss of importance, power, or fame: *communism eventually went into eclipse* ▷ *vb* **eclipsing, eclipsed 3** to overshadow or surpass **4** (of a star or planet) to hide (another planet or star) from view
WORD ORIGIN Greek *ekleipsis* a forsaking

ecliptic *n astron* the great circle on the celestial sphere representing the apparent annual path of the sun relative to the stars

eco- *combining form* denoting ecology or ecological: *ecotourism*

E.coli (**ee-koal-eye**) *n* a common bacterium often found in the intestines
WORD ORIGIN shortened from *Escherichia coli*, after Theodor *Escherich*, paediatrician

ecological *adj* **1** of or relating to ecology **2** tending or intended to benefit or protect the environment: *an ecological approach to agriculture* **ecologically** *adv*

ecology *n* the study of the relationships between people, animals, and plants, and their environment **ecologist** *n*
WORD ORIGIN Greek *oikos* house

e-commerce *or* **ecommerce** *n* business transactions conducted on the internet

econ. economy

economic *adj* **1** of or relating to an economy or economics **2** *Austral & Brit* capable of being produced or operated for profit **3** *informal* inexpensive or cheap

economical *adj* **1** not requiring a lot of money to use: *low fuel consumption makes this car very economical* **2** (of a person) spending money carefully and sensibly **3** using no more time, effort, or resources than is necessary **4 economical with the truth** *euphemistic* deliberately withholding information **economically** *adv*

economics *n* **1** the study of the production and consumption of goods and services and the commercial activities of a society ▷ *pl n* **2** financial aspects: *the economics of health care*

economist *n* a person who specializes in economics

economize *or* **-mise** *vb* **-mizing, -mized** *or* **-mising, -mised** to reduce expense or waste: *people are being advised to economize on fuel use*

economy *n, pl* **-mies 1** the system by which the production, distribution, and consumption of goods and services is organized in a country or community: *the rural economy* **2** the ability of a country to generate wealth through business and industry: *unless the economy improves, more jobs will be lost* **3** careful use of money or resources to save expense, time, or energy **4** an instance of this: *we can make economies by reusing envelopes* ▷ *adj* **5** denoting a class of air travel that is cheaper than first-class **6** offering a larger quantity for a lower price: *an economy pack*
WORD ORIGIN Greek *oikos* house + *nemein* to manage

economy-class syndrome *n* a deep-vein thrombosis that has developed in the legs or pelvis of a person travelling for a long time in cramped conditions
WORD ORIGIN reference to the restricted legroom of cheaper seats on passenger aircraft

economy of scale *n econ* a fall in average costs resulting from an increase in the scale of production

ecosystem *n ecology* the system of relationships between animals and plants and their environment

ecotourism *n* tourism designed to contribute to the protection of the environment or at least minimize damage to it **ecotourist** *n*

ecru *adj* pale creamy-brown
WORD ORIGIN French

ecstasy *n, pl* **-sies 1** a state of extreme delight or joy **2** *slang* a strong drug that acts as a stimulant and can cause hallucinations **ecstatic** *adj* **ecstatically** *adv*
WORD ORIGIN Greek *ekstasis* displacement, trance

ECT electroconvulsive therapy: the treatment of depression and some other mental disorders by passing a current of electricity through the brain, producing a convulsion

ectomorph *n physiol* a person with a thin body build. See also **endomorph, mesomorph** ▷ **ectomorphic** *adj*
WORD ORIGIN Greek *ektos* outside + *morphē* shape

ectopic *adj med* (of an organ or other body part) congenitally displaced or abnormally positioned
WORD ORIGIN Greek *ektopos* out of position

ectoplasm *n* (in spiritualism) the substance that supposedly is emitted from the body of a medium during a trance
WORD ORIGIN Greek *ektos* outside + *plasma* something moulded

Science Fiction

Science fiction sounds as if it ought to be fiction with a scientific theme, but quite a lot of writing that is classified as science fiction barely has any science in it at all. Time travel stories are often reckoned to be science fiction, when the only 'science' is the police box/whirlpool that enables the characters to travel through time. It's simpler to say that science fiction is anything that finds its way into the science fiction section of a shop. So it's the market that decides what counts as science fiction. Fantasy books and films sit alongside *The Lord of the Rings*, Sci-Fi books and films sit alongside *I, Robot* and *Jurassic Park*. As with any categories, there are members which so clearly belong in that category that they define it, and then there are the cases where a shop might just hedge its bets and put them in both sections.

Sci-Fi has a slightly nerdy aftertaste to it. It conjures up *Star Trek* conventions, Terry Pratchett groupies, and *Star Wars* action figures. And what's the Sci-Fi equivalent of George Eliot's *Middlemarch*? What's the respectable, universally admired cornerstone of Sci-Fi, full of insight, vision and deep characterization?

Disneyland and others profit well from Jules Verne. But although you can describe Verne as prescient (up to a point: it wouldn't do you much good to be fired at the moon out of an enormous cannon, for example), the only one of his books that's deep is *20,000 Leagues Under the Sea*. HG Wells wrote gripping stories, but his characters are not memorable, and sadly we could go through the whole canon of Sci-Fi authors and put a line through a very large number of them.

There are a few non-nerdy classics, but none involve aliens or space travel. Dystopias seem to be a more fertile ground for producing real literature. Aldous Huxley's *Brave New World*, Ray Bradbury's *Fahrenheit 451* and George Orwell's *1984* are not just Sci-Fi books; they help define society. Sometimes the ironies are unintentional: Orwell's *Big Brother* is now a relatively harmless reality TV programme.

The growth in the comic-book Sci-Fi of aliens and interplanetary travel broadly coincided with the space race. After the launch of the first satellite, Sputnik, in 1957, it became clear that humans would soon be able to visit the Moon and confirm or disprove all the stories about it written since Lucian's second-century *A True Story*. Once the moon landings had been achieved, it seemed that anything was possible, and everybody expected the pace to speed up, with a mission to Mars following soon after the Apollo programme. We now know better, but all those writers at the time whose imaginations were fired by the expectation of contact with other civilizations were cruelly disappointed. Money was not poured into space exploration, and the future took on a completely different aspect from what the Sci-Fi writers imagined. On the one hand, reality disappointed; on the other, it totally confounded expectation. The internet was not part of post-war Sci-Fi, and neither was genetic engineering, because it took a long time for the discovery of DNA and its implications to become clear. Films like *Gattaca* and *The Matrix* could not have been made before the last decade of the 20th century, because they could not have been imagined. The science that underpins them hadn't yet become available to Sci-Fi writers.

Sci-Fi dates very quickly. This is because the pace of change in the world has accelerated enormously in recent decades. Many of these changes are the result of advances in technology and medicine, but the undesirable by-products of civilization – global warming, the ozone hole, the death of coral reefs – also play a part. Post-apocalyptic Sci-Fi like *The Chrysalids* by John Wyndham used to assume global nuclear war, but this generation's fear is global warming.

But it isn't only writing about the future that is affected by changes in the real world. The development in science is also opening up new ways for us to find out more about the past. As we use new scientific tools in archaeology, we discover more about how our ancestors lived, and we see that we may need to change our ideas even about the relatively recent past. A glance at any historical film made forty years ago shows how our ideas of the past can be just as wide of the mark as our ideas about the future. It may be that any fiction which is not set in the present is a kind of Sci-Fi. The next time you go into Waterstone's, you may find that the whole shop has been classified as Sci-Fi.

ecumenical *adj* **1** of or relating to the Christian Church throughout the world **2** tending to promote unity among Christian churches
WORD ORIGIN Greek *oikoumenikos* of the inhabited world

ecumenism or **ecumenicism** *n* the aim of unity among Christian churches throughout the world

eczema (**ek**-sim-a, ig-**zeem**-a) *n pathol* a condition in which the skin becomes inflamed and itchy
WORD ORIGIN Greek *ek-* out + *zein* to boil

ed. **1** edition **2** editor

Edam *n* a round yellow Dutch cheese with a red waxy covering
WORD ORIGIN after *Edam*, in Holland

eddo (**ed**-doh) *n, pl* **eddoes** same as **taro**

eddy *n, pl* **-dies 1** a circular movement of air, water, or smoke ▷ *vb* **-dies, -dying, -died 2** to move with a gentle circular motion; swirl gently
WORD ORIGIN probably from Old Norse

edelweiss (**ade**-el-vice) *n* a small white alpine flower
WORD ORIGIN German: noble white

edema (id-**deem**-a) *n, pl* **-mata** same as **oedema**

Eden *n* **1** Also called: **Garden of Eden** *Bible* the garden in which Adam and Eve were placed at the Creation **2** a place of great delight or contentment
WORD ORIGIN Hebrew *'ēdhen* place of pleasure

edentate *n* **1** a mammal with few or no teeth, such as an armadillo or a sloth ▷ *adj* **2** denoting such a mammal
WORD ORIGIN Latin *edentatus* lacking teeth

edge *n* **1** a border or line where something ends or begins: *the edge of the city* **2** a line along which two faces or surfaces of a solid meet **3** the sharp cutting side of a blade **4** keenness, sharpness, or urgency: *there was a nervous edge to his voice* **5 have the edge on** to have a slight advantage over **6 on edge** nervous and irritable **7 set someone's teeth on edge** to make someone acutely irritated ▷ *vb* **edging, edged 8** to make, form, or be an edge or border for: *a pillow edged with lace* **9** to move very gradually in a particular direction: *I edged through to the front of the crowd*
WORD ORIGIN Old English *ecg*

edgeways or *esp. US & Canad* **edgewise** *adv* **1** with the edge forwards or uppermost **2 get a word in edgeways** to interrupt a conversation in which someone else is talking continuously

edging *n* anything placed along an edge for decoration

edgy *adj* **edgier, edgiest** nervous, irritable, or anxious **edginess** *n*

edible *adj* fit to be eaten; eatable **edibility** *n*
WORD ORIGIN Latin *edere* to eat

edict (**ee**-dikt) *n* a decree or order given by any authority
WORD ORIGIN Latin *edicere* to declare

edifice (**ed**-if-iss) *n* **1** a large or impressive building **2** an elaborate system of beliefs and institutions: *the crumbling edifice of Communist rule*
WORD ORIGIN Latin *aedificare* to build

edify (**ed**-if-fie) *vb* **-fies, -fying, -fied** to inform or instruct (someone) with a view to improving his or her morals or understanding **edification** *n* **edifying** *adj*
WORD ORIGIN Latin *aedificare* to build

edit *vb* **editing, edited 1** to prepare (text) for publication by checking and improving its accuracy or clarity **2** to be in charge of (a newspaper or magazine) **3** to prepare (a film, tape, etc.) by rearranging or selecting material **4 edit out** to remove (a section) from a text, film, etc.

edition *n* **1** a particular version of a book, newspaper, or magazine produced at one time: *the revised paperback edition* **2** a single television or radio programme which forms part of a series: *the first edition goes on the air in 30 minutes*

editor *n* **1** a person who edits **2** a person in overall charge of a newspaper or magazine **3** a person in charge of one section of a newspaper or magazine: *the Political Editor* **4** a person in overall control of a television or radio programme **editorship** *n*
WORD ORIGIN Latin *edere* to publish

editorial *n* **1** an article in a newspaper expressing the opinion of the editor or publishers ▷ *adj* **2** of editing or editors: *an editorial meeting* **3** relating to the contents and opinions of a magazine or newspaper: *the paper's editorial policy* **editorially** *adv*

EDP electronic data processing

EDT Eastern Daylight Time

educate *vb* **-cating, -cated 1** to teach (someone) over a long period of time so that he or she acquires knowledge and understanding of a range of subjects **2** to send (someone) to a particular educational establishment: *he was educated at mission schools* **3** to teach (someone) about a particular matter: *a campaign to educate people to the dangers of smoking* **educative** *adj*
WORD ORIGIN Latin *educare* to rear, educate

educated *adj* **1** having an education, esp. a good one **2** displaying culture, taste, and knowledge **3 educated guess** a guess that is based on experience

education *n* **1** the process of acquiring knowledge and understanding **2** knowledge and understanding acquired through study and training: *education is the key to a good job* **3** the process of teaching, esp. at a school, college, or university **4** the theory of teaching and learning **educational** *adj* **educationally** *adv* **educationalist** or **educationist** *n*

Edwardian *adj* of or in the reign of King Edward VII of Great Britain and Ireland (1901–10)

EEC European Economic Community: a former name for the European Union

EEG electroencephalogram

eel *n* a slimy snakelike fish
WORD ORIGIN Old English *ǣl*

e'er *adv poetic* short for **ever**

eerie *adj* **eerier, eeriest** strange and frightening **eerily** *adv*

WORD ORIGIN probably from Old English *earg* cowardly

efface *vb* **-facing, -faced 1** to obliterate or make dim: *nothing effaced the memory* **2** to rub out or erase **3 efface oneself** to make oneself inconspicuous **effacement** *n*
WORD ORIGIN French *effacer* to obliterate the face

effect *n* **1** a change or state of affairs caused by something or someone: *the gales have had a serious effect on the crops* **2** power to influence or produce a result: *the wine had little effect on him* **3** the condition of being operative: *a new law has come into effect* **4** the overall impression: *the whole effect is one of luxury* **5** basic meaning or purpose: *words to that effect* **6** an impression, usually a contrived one: *he paused for effect* **7** a physical phenomenon: *the greenhouse effect* **8 in effect** for all practical purposes: *in effect he has no choice* **9 take effect** to begin to produce results ▷ *vb* **10** to cause (something) to take place: *a peace treaty was effected*
WORD ORIGIN Latin *efficere* to accomplish

effective *adj* **1** producing a desired result: *an effective vaccine against HIV* **2** officially coming into operation: *the new rates become effective at the end of May* **3** impressive: *a highly effective speech* **4** in reality, although not officially or in theory: *he is in effective control of the company* **effectively** *adv* **effectiveness** *n*

effects *pl n* **1** personal belongings **2** lighting, sounds, etc. to accompany a stage, film, or broadcast production

effectual *adj* **1** producing the intended result **2** (of a document etc.) having legal force **effectually** *adv*

effeminate *adj* (of a man) displaying characteristics regarded as typical of a woman **effeminacy** *n*
WORD ORIGIN Latin *femina* woman

effervescent *adj* **1** (of a liquid) giving off bubbles of gas **2** (of a person) lively and enthusiastic **effervescence** *n*
WORD ORIGIN Latin *effervescere* to foam up

effete (if-**feet**) *adj* weak, powerless, and decadent
WORD ORIGIN Latin *effetus* exhausted by bearing young

efficacious *adj* producing the intended result **efficacy** *n*
WORD ORIGIN Latin *efficere* to achieve

efficient *adj* working or producing effectively without wasting effort, energy, or money **efficiency** *n* **efficiently** *adv*
WORD ORIGIN Latin *efficiens* effecting

effigy (**ef**-fij-ee) *n, pl* **-gies 1** a statue or carving of someone, often as a memorial: *a 14th-century wooden effigy of a knight* **2** a crude representation of someone, used as a focus for contempt: *an effigy of the president was set on fire*
WORD ORIGIN Latin *effingere* to portray

efflorescence *n* **1** the blooming of flowers on a plant **2** a brief period of high-quality artistic activity
WORD ORIGIN Latin *efflorescere* to blossom

effluent n liquid discharged as waste, for instance from a factory or sewage works
WORD ORIGIN Latin *effluere* to flow out

effluvium n, pl **-via** an unpleasant smell, such as the smell of decaying matter
WORD ORIGIN Latin: a flowing out

efflux n 1 the process of flowing out 2 something that flows out

effort n 1 physical or mental energy needed to do something 2 a determined attempt to do something 3 achievement or creation: *his earliest literary efforts* **effortless** adj **effortlessly** adv
WORD ORIGIN Latin *fortis* strong

effrontery n insolence or boldness
WORD ORIGIN Late Latin *effrons* putting forth one's forehead

effusion n 1 an unrestrained verbal expression of emotions or ideas 2 a sudden pouring out: *small effusions of blood*
WORD ORIGIN Latin *effundere* to shed

effusive adj enthusiastically showing pleasure, gratitude, or approval **effusively** adv **effusiveness** n

EFL English as a Foreign Language

EFTA European Free Trade Association

EFTPOS electronic funds transfer at point of sale

eg or **e.g.** for example
WORD ORIGIN Latin *exempli gratia*

egalitarian adj 1 expressing or supporting the idea that all people should be equal ▷ n 2 a person who believes that all people should be equal **egalitarianism** n
WORD ORIGIN French *égal* equal

egg n 1 the oval or round object laid by the females of birds, reptiles, and other creatures, containing a developing embryo 2 a hen's egg used for food 3 a type of cell produced in the body of a female animal which can develop into a baby if fertilized by a male reproductive cell 4 **have egg on one's face** *informal* to have been made to look ridiculous 5 **put all one's eggs in one basket** to rely entirely on one action or decision, with no alternative in case of failure
WORD ORIGIN Old Norse

egg cup n a small cup for holding a boiled egg

egghead n *informal* an intellectual person

eggnog n a drink made of raw eggs, milk, sugar, spice, and brandy or rum
WORD ORIGIN egg + nog strong ale

egg on vb to encourage (someone) to do something foolish or daring
WORD ORIGIN Old English *eggian*

eggplant n US, Canad, Austral, & NZ a dark purple tropical fruit, cooked and eaten as a vegetable

eggshell n 1 the hard porous outer layer of a bird's egg ▷ adj 2 (of paint) having a very slight sheen

ego n, pl **egos** 1 the part of a person's self that is able to recognize that person as being distinct from other people and things 2 a person's opinion of his or her own worth: *men with fragile egos*
WORD ORIGIN Latin: I

egocentric adj thinking only of one's own interests and feelings **egocentricity** n

Egoli (eh-**goh**-li) n an informal name for Johannesburg
WORD ORIGIN from Zulu *eGoli* place of gold

egomania n an obsessive concern with fulfilling one's own needs and desires, regardless of the effect on other people **egomaniac** n

egotism or **egoism** n concern only for one's own interests and feelings **egotist** or **egoist** n **egotistical**, **egoistical** or **egotistic**, **egoistic** adj

ego trip n *informal* something that a person does in order to boost his or her self-image

egregious (ig-**greej**-uss) adj shockingly bad: *egregious government waste*
WORD ORIGIN Latin *egregius* outstanding (literally: standing out from the herd)

egress (ee-**gress**) n *formal* 1 the act of going out 2 a way out or exit
WORD ORIGIN Latin *egredi* to come out

egret (ee-**grit**) n a wading bird like a heron, with long white feathery plumes
WORD ORIGIN Old French *aigrette*

Egyptian adj 1 of Egypt 2 of the ancient Egyptians ▷ n 3 a person from Egypt 4 a member of an ancient people who established an advanced civilization in Egypt 5 the language of the ancient Egyptians

Egyptology n the study of the culture of ancient Egypt **Egyptologist** n

eh interj 1 an exclamation used to ask for repetition or confirmation 2 Canad & E Scot a filler phrase used to make a pause in speaking, or add slight emphasis: *it's broken, eh, so I can't play for six weeks*

eider or **eider duck** n a large sea duck of the N hemisphere
WORD ORIGIN Old Norse *æthr*

eiderdown n a thick warm cover for a bed, filled with soft feathers, originally the breast feathers of the female eider duck

Eid-ul-Adha (eed-ool-**ah**-da) n an annual Muslim festival, marking the end of the pilgrimage to Mecca
WORD ORIGIN from Arabic *id ul adha* festival of sacrifice

Eid-ul-Fitr (eed-ool-**feet**-er) n an annual Muslim festival, marking the end of Ramadan
WORD ORIGIN from Arabic *id ul fitr* festival of fast-breaking

eight n 1 the cardinal number that is the sum of one and seven 2 a numeral, 8 or VIII, representing this number 3 something representing or consisting of eight units 4 *rowing* **a** a light narrow boat rowed by eight people **b** the crew of such a boat ▷ adj 5 amounting to eight: *eight apples* **eighth** adj, n
WORD ORIGIN Old English *eahta*

eighteen n 1 the cardinal number that is the sum of ten and eight 2 a numeral, 18 or XVIII, representing this number 3 something representing or consisting of 18 units ▷ adj 4 amounting to eighteen: *eighteen months* **eighteenth** adj, n

eightfold adj 1 having eight times as many or as much 2 composed of eight parts ▷ adv 3 by eight times as many or as much

eightsome reel n a lively Scottish country dance for eight people

eighty n, pl **eighties** 1 the cardinal number that is the product of ten and eight 2 a numeral, 80 or LXXX, representing this number 3 something representing or consisting of 80 units ▷ adj 4 amounting to eighty: *eighty miles* **eightieth** adj, n

eina (**ay**-na) interj S African an exclamation of pain
WORD ORIGIN Khoi (language of southern Africa)

einsteinium n *chem* a radioactive metallic element artificially produced from plutonium. Symbol: Es
WORD ORIGIN after Albert *Einstein*, physicist

Eire n Ireland or the Republic of Ireland
WORD ORIGIN Irish Gaelic

EIS Educational Institute of Scotland

eisteddfod (ice-**sted**-fod) n a Welsh festival with competitions in music, poetry, drama, and art
WORD ORIGIN Welsh: session

either adj, pron 1 one or the other (of two): *we were offered either fish or beef* 2 both one and the other: *we sat at either end of a long settee* ▷ conj 3 used preceding two or more possibilities joined by *or*: *it must be stored either in the fridge or in a cool place* ▷ adv 4 likewise: *I don't eat meat and my husband doesn't either* 5 used to qualify or modify a previous statement: *he wasn't exactly ugly, but he wasn't an oil painting either*
WORD ORIGIN Old English *ægther*

USAGE
Either should be followed by a singular verb: *either is good; either of these books is useful.* Care should be taken to avoid ambiguity when using *either* to mean *both* or *each*, as in the following sentence: *a ship could be moored on either side of the channel.* Agreement between the verb and its subject in *either...or...* constructions follows the pattern given for *neither...nor...* See at **neither**.

ejaculate vb **-lating, -lated** 1 to discharge semen from the penis while having an orgasm 2 *literary* to say or shout suddenly **ejaculation** n **ejaculatory** adj
WORD ORIGIN Latin *ejaculari* to hurl out

eject vb 1 to push or send out forcefully 2 to compel (someone) to leave a place or position 3 to leave an aircraft rapidly in mid-flight, using an ejector seat **ejection** n **ejector** n
WORD ORIGIN Latin *ejicere*

ejector seat or **ejection seat** n a seat in a military aircraft that throws the pilot out in an emergency

eke out vb **eking, eked** 1 to make (a supply) last for a long time by using as little as possible 2 to manage to sustain (a living) despite having barely enough food or money
WORD ORIGIN obsolete *eke* to enlarge

elaborate adj 1 very complex because of having many different parts: *elaborate equipment* 2 having a very complicated e

design: *elaborate embroidery* ▷ *vb* **-rating, -rated 3 elaborate on** to describe in more detail: *he did not elaborate on his plans* **4** to develop (a plan or theory) in detail **elaborately** *adv* **elaboration** *n*
WORD ORIGIN Latin *elaborare* to take pains

élan (ale-an) *n* style and liveliness
WORD ORIGIN French

eland (eel-and) *n* a large spiral-horned antelope of southern Africa
WORD ORIGIN Dutch: elk

elapse *vb* **elapsing, elapsed** (of time) to pass by
WORD ORIGIN Latin *elabi* to slip away

elastane *n* a synthetic fibre that is able to return to its original shape after being stretched

elastic *adj* **1** capable of returning to its original shape after stretching, compression, or other distortion **2** capable of being adapted to meet the demands of a particular situation: *an elastic interpretation of the law* **3** made of elastic ▷ *n* **4** tape, cord, or fabric containing flexible rubber **elastically** *adv* **elasticated** *adj* **elasticity** *n*
WORD ORIGIN Greek *elastikos* propellent

elastic band *n* a rubber band

elated *adj* extremely happy and excited **elatedly** *adv*
WORD ORIGIN Latin *elatus* carried away

elation *n* a feeling of great happiness and excitement

elbow *n* **1** the joint between the upper arm and the forearm **2** the part of a garment that covers the elbow ▷ *vb* **3** to push with one's elbow or elbows: *she elbowed him aside; he elbowed his way to the bar*
WORD ORIGIN Old English *elnboga*

elbow grease *n facetious* vigorous physical labour, esp. hard rubbing

elbow room *n* sufficient scope to move or to function

elder¹ *adj* **1** (of one of two people) born earlier ▷ *n* **2** an older person: *have some respect for your elders* **3** a senior member of a tribe, who has authority **4** (in certain Protestant Churches) a member of the church who has certain administrative, teaching, or preaching powers
WORD ORIGIN Old English *eldra*

elder² *n* a shrub or small tree with clusters of small white flowers and dark purple berries
WORD ORIGIN Old English *ellern*

elderberry *n, pl* **-ries 1** the fruit of the elder **2** same as **elder²**

elderly *adj* **1** rather old ▷ *pl n* **2 the elderly** old people

elder statesman *n* a respected influential older person, esp. a politician

eldest *adj* (of a person, esp. a child) oldest
WORD ORIGIN Old English *eldesta*

El Dorado (el dor-**rah**-doe) *n* **1** a fabled city in South America, supposedly rich in treasure **2** Also: **eldorado** any place of great riches or fabulous opportunity
WORD ORIGIN Spanish: the golden (place)

eldritch *adj poetic Scot* unearthly or weird
WORD ORIGIN origin unknown

elect *vb* **1** to choose (someone) to fill a position by voting for him or her: *she was elected President in 1990* **2** to choose or decide: *those who elected to stay* ▷ *adj* **3** voted into office but not yet having taken over from the current office-bearer: *the President elect* ▷ *pl n* **4 the elect** any group of people specially chosen for some privilege **electable** *adj*
WORD ORIGIN Latin *eligere* to select

election *n* **1 a** a process whereby people vote for a person or party to fill a position: *last month's presidential election* **b** short for **general election 2** the gaining of political power or taking up of a position in an organization as a result of being voted for: *he will be seeking election as the President of Romania*

electioneering *n* the act of taking an active part in a political campaign, for example by canvassing

elective *adj* **1** of or based on selection by vote: *an elective office* **2** not compulsory or necessary: *an elective hysterectomy*

elector *n* **1** someone who is eligible to vote in an election **2** (in the Holy Roman Empire) any of the German princes who were entitled to elect a new emperor: *the Elector of Hanover*

electoral *adj* of or relating to elections: *the electoral system* **electorally** *adv*

electoral register *n* the official list of all the people in an area who are eligible to vote in elections

electorate *n* **1** all the people in an area or country who have the right to vote in an election **2** the rank or territory of an elector of the Holy Roman Empire

electric *adj* **1** produced by, transmitting, or powered by electricity: *an electric fire* **2** very tense or exciting: *the atmosphere was electric* ▷ *n* **3 electrics** *Brit* an electric circuit or electric appliances
WORD ORIGIN Greek *ēlektron* amber (because friction causes amber to become electrically charged)
Ξ **USAGE**
Ξ See at **electronic**.

electrical *adj* of or relating to electricity **electrically** *adv*
Ξ **USAGE**
Ξ See at **electronic**.

electrical engineering *n* the branch of engineering concerned with practical applications of electricity and electronics **electrical engineer** *n*

electric blanket *n* a blanket fitted with an electric heating element, used to warm a bed

electric chair *n* (in the US) a chair for executing criminals by passing a strong electric current through them

electric eel *n* an eel-like South American freshwater fish, which can stun or kill its prey with a powerful electric shock

electric field *n physics* a region of space surrounding a charged particle within which another charged particle experiences a force

electric guitar *n* an electrically amplified guitar

electrician *n* a person trained to install and repair electrical equipment

electricity *n* **1** a form of energy associated with stationary or moving electrons, ions, or other charged particles **2** the supply of electricity to houses, factories, etc. for heating, lighting, etc.

electric shock *n* pain and muscular spasms caused by an electric current passing through the body

electrify *vb* **-fies, -fying, -fied 1** to adapt or equip (a system or device) to work by electricity: *the whole track has now been electrified* **2** to provide (an area) with electricity **3** to startle or excite intensely **electrification** *n*

electrifying *adj* very exciting and surprising

electro- *combining form* electric or electrically: *electroconvulsive*
WORD ORIGIN Greek *ēlektron* amber; see ELECTRIC

electrocardiograph *n* an instrument for making tracings (**electrocardiograms**) recording the electrical activity of the heart

electrocute *vb* **-cuting, -cuted** to kill or injure by an electric shock **electrocution** *n*
WORD ORIGIN ELECTRO- + (EXE)CUTE

electrode *n* a small piece of metal used to take an electric current to or from a power source, piece of equipment, or living body

electrodynamics *n* the branch of physics concerned with the interactions between electrical and mechanical forces

electroencephalograph (ill-lek-tro-en-**sef**-a-loh-graf) *n* an instrument for making tracings (**electroencephalograms**) recording the electrical activity of the brain

electrolysis (ill-lek-**troll**-iss-iss) *n* **1** the process of passing an electric current through a liquid in order to produce a chemical reaction in the liquid **2** the destruction of living tissue, such as hair roots, by an electric current

electrolyte *n* a solution or molten substance that conducts electricity **electrolytic** *adj*

electromagnet *n* a magnet consisting of a coil of wire wound round an iron core through which a current is passed

electromagnetic *adj* **1** of or operated by an electromagnet **2** of or relating to electromagnetism **electromagnetically** *adv*

electromagnetism *n* magnetism produced by an electric current

electromotive *adj physics* of or producing an electric current

electromotive force *n physics* **1** a source of energy that can cause current to flow in an electrical circuit **2** the rate at which energy is drawn from such a source when a unit of current flows through the circuit, measured in volts

electron *n physics* an elementary particle in all atoms that has a negative electrical charge

electronegative *adj physics* **1** having a negative electric charge **2** tending to gain or attract electrons

Robert Burns: Biography

Unquestionably Scotland's most famous poet, Robert Burns is also considered Scotland's National Bard. Writing principally in the Scots dialect, he was a key influence on the Romantic movement and his works have been widely referenced in literature by authors as diverse as John Steinbeck (who took the title *Of Mice And Men* from *To A Mouse*) and MR James (in his story *Whistle, And I'll Come To You*). His life and works are celebrated in Scotland on 'Burns Night' on January 25th (his birthday) and no New Year party would be complete without a rendition of his *Auld Lang Syne*.

Burns was born in 1759 in Alloway, Ayrshire. He was to be the eldest of seven children and he grew up working on his family's farm. From an early age, relationships with women proved particularly fertile grounds for Burns's inspiration. Nelly Kilpatrick was an early muse and the inspiration for *Handsome Nell*, which he wrote at 15. He had numerous affairs throughout his life and fathered many children, both legitimate and illegitimate. In 1785, he had his first child, Elizabeth, by one of his mother's servants, Elizabeth Paton. This event prompted his *A Poet's Welcome To His Love Begotten Daughter* (also known as *A Welcome to a Bastart Wean*). He also fathered twins with Jean Armour out of wedlock, and as a result suffered public censure. While separated from Jean Armour, Burns had an affair with Mary Campbell and planned to emigrate to the West Indies (as illustrated by his *Will ye go to the Indies, my Mary?*). However, Burns married Jean Armour in 1788, and they were to have nine children together.

In 1786, he published his collection *Poems, Chiefly in the Scottish dialect*. This work (which came to be known as 'the Kilmarnock edition') was very success-ful, and includes some of his most celebrated poems, including *The Cotter's Saturday Night*, *Address to the Deil*, and *To a Mouse*. Abandoning his plans for emigration, Burns went to Edinburgh, where he was hailed as a 'ploughman poet' before a larger edition ('the Edinburgh edition') was published. However, Burns did not discover a means to allow him to write full time and he returned to Ayrshire and took a lease on a farm in Dumfries.

Shortly after, he became an Excise officer and this employment was to be the inspiration behind his poems *Extemporaneous Effusion On being appointed to an Excise division* (1789) and *The De'il's Awa' wi' th' Exciseman* (1792). The irony of his adopting such a profession was clearly not lost on Burns, the latter work concerning as it does an Excise officer tempted away by Satan, thus allowing alcohol smugglers to ply their trade.

In 1790, Burns wrote *Tam O'Shanter*. This folklore-infused tale of witches and devilry is one of his best-known works, and its recitation in full is a key part of a Burns Night celebration (as is *Address to a Haggis*). Another key poem is *Scots Wha Hae* (1793), which was inspired by the speech given by Robert the Bruce to his troops before the Battle of Bannockburn. Burns had political sympathies with revolutionary causes and his support for independence in the American colonies and for the revolution in France caused further controversy (having already faced public disapproval based on his lifestyle). However, these same sympathies led him to be seen as a people's poet in Russia, where he remains a celebrated figure.

In 1795, Burns became ill with rheumatic fever, and he died in 1796. His final child (son Maxwell) was born on the day of his funeral.

electronic *adj* **1** (of a device, circuit, or system) containing transistors, silicon chips, etc., which control the current passing through it **2** making use of electronic systems: *electronic surveillance devices* **electronically** *adv*

USAGE
Electronic refers to equipment, such as television sets, computers, etc. in which the current is controlled by transistors, valves, and similar components. *Electrical* is used in a more general sense to refer to the use of electricity as a whole as opposed to other forms of energy: *electrical engineering; an electrical appliance. Electric* can be used interchangeably with *electrical*, but is often restricted to the description of particular devices or to concepts relating to the flow of current: *electric fire; electric charge.*

electronic paper or **ink** *n* a material used in e-readers, consisting of black particles suspended in white fluid which become visible in response to an electronic charge

electronic publishing *n* the publication of information on discs, magnetic tape, etc. so that it can be accessed by computer

electronics *n* the technology concerned with the development, behaviour, and applications of devices and circuits, for example televisions and computers, which make use of electronic components such as transistors or silicon chips

electron microscope *n* a powerful microscope that uses electrons, rather than light, to produce a magnified image

electronvolt *n physics* a unit of energy equal to the work done on an electron accelerated through a potential difference of 1 volt

electroplate *vb* **-plating, -plated 1** to coat (an object) with metal by dipping it in a special liquid through which an electric current is passed ▷ *n* **2** electroplated articles collectively

electropositive *adj physics* **1** having a positive electric charge **2** tending to release electrons

electrostatics *n* the branch of physics concerned with static electricity **electrostatic** *adj*

elegant *adj* **1** attractive and graceful or stylish **2** cleverly simple and clear: *an elegant summary* **elegance** *n* **elegantly** *adv*
WORD ORIGIN Latin *elegans* tasteful

elegiac *adj literary* sad, mournful, or plaintive

elegy (**el**-lij-ee) *n, pl* **-gies** a mournful poem or song, esp. a lament for the dead
WORD ORIGIN Greek *elegos* lament

USAGE
Avoid confusion with **eulogy**.

element *n* **1** one of the fundamental components making up a whole **2** *chem* any of the known substances that cannot be separated into simpler substances by chemical means **3** a distinguishable section of a social group: *liberal elements in Polish society* **4** a degree: *an element of truth* **5** a metal part in an electrical device, such as a kettle, that changes the electric current into heat **6** one of the four substances (earth, air, water, and fire) formerly believed to make up the universe **7** *maths* any of the members of a set **8** in one's element in a situation in which one is happy and at ease: *she was in her element behind the wheel* **9** elements **a** the basic principles of something **b** weather conditions, esp. wind, rain, and cold: *only 200 braved the elements*
WORD ORIGIN Latin *elementum*

elemental *adj* of or like basic and powerful natural forces or passions

elementary *adj* **1** simple, basic, and straightforward: *elementary precautions* **2** involving only the most basic principles of a subject: *elementary mathematics*

elementary particle *n physics* any of several entities, such as electrons, neutrons, or protons, that are less complex than atoms

elementary school *n* **1** *Brit* same as **primary school 2** *US & Canad* a state school for the first six to eight years of a child's education

elephant *n* **1** a very large four-legged animal that has a very long flexible nose called a trunk, large ears, and two ivory tusks, and lives in Africa or India **2** elephant in the room an obvious truth deliberately ignored by all parties in a situation
WORD ORIGIN Greek *elephas*

elephantiasis (el-lee-fan-**tie**-a-siss) *n pathol* a skin disease, caused by parasitic worms, in which the affected parts of the body become extremely enlarged

elephantine *adj* like an elephant, esp. in being huge, clumsy, or ponderous

elevate *vb* **-vating, -vated 1** to raise in rank or status: *she had elevated flirting to an art form* **2** to lift to a higher place: *this action elevates the upper back*
WORD ORIGIN Latin *elevare*

elevated *adj* **1** higher than normal: *elevated cholesterol levels* **2** (of ideas or pursuits) on a high intellectual or moral level: *elevated discussions about postmodernism* **3** (of land or part of a building) higher than the surrounding area

elevation *n* **1** the act of elevating someone or something: *his elevation to the peerage* **2** height above sea level **3** a raised area **4** a scale drawing of one side of a building

elevator *n* **1** *Austral, US, & Canad* a lift for carrying people **2** a mechanical hoist

eleven *n* **1** the cardinal number that is the sum of ten and one **2** a numeral, 11 or XI, representing this number **3** something representing or consisting of 11 units **4** a team of 11 players in football, cricket, etc. ▷ *adj* **5** amounting to eleven: *eleven years* **eleventh** *adj, n*
WORD ORIGIN Old English *endleofan*

eleven-plus *n* (in Britain, esp. formerly) an examination taken by children aged 10 or 11 that determines the type of secondary education they will be given

elevenses *pl n Brit, Austral, S Africa, & NZ informal* a mid-morning snack

eleventh hour *n* **1** the latest possible time ▷ *adj* **eleventh-hour 2** done at the latest possible time: *an eleventh-hour rescue*

elf *n, pl* **elves** (in folklore) a small mischievous fairy
WORD ORIGIN Old English *ælf*

elfin *adj* **1** small and delicate: *her elfin features* **2** of or relating to elves

elicit *vb* **1** to bring about (a response or reaction): *her remarks elicited a sharp retort* **2** to draw out (information) from someone: *a phone call elicited the fact that she had just awakened*
WORD ORIGIN Latin *elicere*

elide *vb* **eliding, elided** to omit (a syllable or vowel) from a spoken word
WORD ORIGIN Latin *elidere* to knock

eligible *adj* **1** meeting the requirements or qualifications needed: *he may be eligible for free legal services* **2** old-fashioned desirable as a spouse **eligibility** *n*
WORD ORIGIN Latin *eligere* to elect

eliminate *vb* **-nating, -nated 1** to get rid of (something or someone unwanted, unnecessary, or not meeting the requirements needed): *he can be eliminated from the list of suspects* **2** to remove (a competitor or team) from a contest, esp. following a defeat: *they were eliminated in the third round* **3** *slang* to murder in cold blood: *Stalin had thousands of his former comrades eliminated* **elimination** *n*
WORD ORIGIN Latin *eliminare* to turn out of the house

USAGE
Eliminate is sometimes wrongly used to talk about avoiding the repetition of something undesirable: *we must prevent* (not *eliminate*) *further mistakes of this kind.*

elision *n* omission of a syllable or vowel from a spoken word
WORD ORIGIN Latin *elidere* to elide

elite (ill-**eet**) *n* the most powerful, rich, or gifted members of a group or community

elitism *n* **1** the belief that society should be governed by a small group of people who are superior to everyone else **2** pride in being part of an elite **elitist** *n, adj*

elixir (ill-**ix**-er) *n* **1** an imaginary substance that is supposed to be capable of prolonging life and changing base metals into gold **2** a liquid medicine mixed with syrup
WORD ORIGIN Arabic *al iksīr*

Elizabethan *adj* **1** of or in the reign of Queen Elizabeth I of England (1558–1603) ▷ *n* **2** a person who lived during the reign of Queen Elizabeth I

elk *n* a very large deer of N Europe and Asia with broad flat antler

ellipse *n* an oval shape resembling a flattened circle

ellipsis (ill-**lip**-siss) *n, pl* **-ses** (-seez) **1** the omission of a word or words from a sentence **2** *printing* three dots (...) indicating an omission
WORD ORIGIN Greek *elleipein* to leave out

ellipsoid *n geom* a surface whose plane sections are ellipses or circles

elliptical or **elliptic** *adj* **1** oval-shaped **2** (of speech or writing) obscure or ambiguous

elm *n* **1** a tall tree with broad leaves **2** the hard heavy wood of this tree **WORD ORIGIN** Old English

elocution *n* the art of speaking clearly in public **elocutionist** *n*
WORD ORIGIN Latin *e-* out + *loqui* to speak

elongate (eel-long-gate) *vb* **-gating, -gated** to make or become longer **elongation** *n*
WORD ORIGIN Latin *e-* away + *longe* (adverb) far

elope *vb* **eloping, eloped** (of two people) to run away secretly to get married **elopement** *n*
WORD ORIGIN Anglo-French *aloper*

eloquence *n* the ability to speak or write in a skilful and convincing way

eloquent *adj* **1** (of speech or writing) fluent and persuasive **2** (of a person) able to speak in a fluent and persuasive manner **3** visibly or vividly expressive: *he raised an eloquent eyebrow* **eloquently** *adv*
WORD ORIGIN Latin *e-* out + *loqui* to speak

else *adv* **1** in addition or more: *what else do you want to know?* **2** other or different: *it was unlike anything else that had happened* **3 or else a** if not, then: *tell us soon or else we shall go mad* **b** *informal* or something terrible will result: used as a threat: *do it our way or else*
WORD ORIGIN Old English *elles*

elsewhere *adv* in or to another place

ELT English Language Teaching

elucidate *vb* **-dating, -dated** to make (something obscure or difficult) clear **elucidation** *n*
WORD ORIGIN Late Latin *elucidare* to enlighten

elude *vb* **eluding, eluded 1** to avoid or escape from (someone or something) **2** to fail to be understood or remembered by: *the mysteries of commerce elude me*
WORD ORIGIN Latin *eludere* to deceive

elusive *adj* **1** difficult to find or catch **2** difficult to remember or describe **elusiveness** *n*

elver *n* a young eel
WORD ORIGIN variant of *eelfare* eel-journey

elves *n* the plural of **elf**

Elysium (ill-liz-zee-um) *n* **1** *Greek myth* the dwelling place of the blessed after death **2** a state or place of perfect bliss **Elysian** *adj*
WORD ORIGIN Greek *Êlusion pedion* blessed fields

emaciated (im-mace-ee-ate-id) *adj* extremely thin through illness or lack of food **emaciation** *n*
WORD ORIGIN Latin *macer* thin

e-mail *or* **email** (ee-mail) *n* **1** the transmission of messages from one computer terminal to another ▷ *vb* **2** to contact (a person) by e-mail **3** to send (a message) by e-mail

emanate (em-a-nate) *vb* **-nating, -nated** to come or seem to come from someone or something: *an aura of power emanated from him* **emanation** *n*
WORD ORIGIN Latin *emanare* to flow out

emancipate *vb* **-pating, -pated** to free from social, political, or legal restrictions **emancipation** *n*
WORD ORIGIN Latin *emancipare* to give independence (to a son)

emasculate *vb* **-lating, -lated** to deprive of power or strength **emasculation** *n*
WORD ORIGIN Latin *emasculare* to remove the testicles

embalm *vb* to preserve (a corpse) by the use of chemicals and oils
WORD ORIGIN Old French *embaumer*

embankment *n* a man-made ridge of earth or stone that carries a road or railway or prevents a river or lake from overflowing

embargo *n, pl* **-goes 1** an order by a government or international body prohibiting trade with a country: *the world trade embargo against Iraq* ▷ *vb* **-going, -goed 2** to place an official prohibition on
WORD ORIGIN Spanish

embark *vb* **1** to go on board a ship or aircraft **2 embark on** to begin (a new project or venture) **embarkation** *n*
WORD ORIGIN Old Provençal *embarcar*

embarrass *vb* **1** to make (someone) feel shy, ashamed, or guilty about something **2** to cause political problems for (a government or party) **3** to cause to have financial difficulties **embarrassed** *adj* **embarrassing** *adj* **embarrassingly** *adv* **embarrassment** *n*
WORD ORIGIN Italian *imbarrare* to confine within bars

embassy *n, pl* **-sies 1** the residence or place of business of an ambassador **2** an ambassador and his or her assistants and staff
WORD ORIGIN Old Provençal *ambaisada*

embattled *adj* **1** (of a country) involved in fighting a war, esp. when surrounded by enemies **2** facing many problems and difficulties: *the embattled Mayor*

embed *vb* **-bedding, -bedded 1** to fix firmly in a surrounding solid mass: *the boy has shrapnel embedded in his spine* **2** to fix (an attitude or idea) in a society or in someone's mind: *corruption was deeply embedded in the ruling party*

embellish *vb* **1** to make (something) more attractive by adding decorations **2** to make (a story) more interesting by adding details which may not be true **embellishment** *n*
WORD ORIGIN Old French *embelir*

ember *n* a smouldering piece of coal or wood remaining after a fire has died
WORD ORIGIN Old English *ǣmyrge*

embezzle *vb* **-zling, -zled** to steal (money) that belongs to the company or organization that one works for **embezzlement** *n* **embezzler** *n*
WORD ORIGIN Anglo-French *embeseiller* to destroy

embittered *adj* feeling anger and despair as a result of misfortune: *embittered by poverty* **embitterment** *n*

emblazon (im-blaze-on) *vb* **1** to decorate with a coat of arms, slogan, etc.: *a jacket emblazoned with his band's name* **2** to proclaim or publicize: *I am not sure he would want his name emblazoned in my column*

emblem *n* an object or design chosen to symbolize an organization or idea **emblematic** *adj*
WORD ORIGIN Greek *emblēma* insertion

embody *vb* **-bodies, -bodying, -bodied 1** to be an example of or express (an idea or other abstract concept) **2** to include as part of a whole: *the proposal has been embodied in a draft resolution* **embodiment** *n*

embolden *vb* to make bold

embolism *n pathol* the blocking of a blood vessel by a blood clot, air bubble, etc.

embolus *n, pl* **-li** *pathol* a blood clot, air bubble, or other stoppage that blocks a small blood vessel
WORD ORIGIN Greek *embolos* stopper

emboss *vb* to mould or carve a decoration on (a surface) so that it stands out from the surface
WORD ORIGIN Old French *embocer*

embrace *vb* **-bracing, -braced 1** to clasp (someone) with one's arms as an expression of affection or a greeting **2** to accept eagerly **3** to include or be made up of: *a church that embraces two cultures* ▷ *n* **4** an act of embracing
WORD ORIGIN Latin *im-* in + *bracchia* arms

embrasure *n* **1** an opening for a door or window which is wider on the inside of the wall than on the outside **2** an opening in a battlement or wall, for shooting through
WORD ORIGIN French

embrocation *n* a lotion rubbed into the skin to ease sore muscles
WORD ORIGIN Greek *brokhē* a moistening

embroider *vb* **1** to do decorative needlework on (a piece of cloth or a garment) **2** to add imaginary details to (a story) **embroiderer** *n*
WORD ORIGIN Old French *embroder*

embroidery *n* **1** decorative needlework, usually on cloth or canvas **2** the act of adding imaginary details to a story

embroil *vb* to involve (oneself or another person) in problems or difficulties **embroilment** *n*
WORD ORIGIN French *embrouiller*

embryo (em-bree-oh) *n, pl* **-bryos 1** an unborn animal or human being in the early stages of development, in humans up to approximately the end of the second month of pregnancy **2** something in an early stage of development: *the embryo of a novel*
WORD ORIGIN Greek *embruon*

embryology *n* the scientific study of embryos

embryonic *adj* **1** of or relating to an embryo **2** in an early stage

emend *vb* to make corrections or improvements to (a text) **emendation** *n*
WORD ORIGIN Latin *e-* out + *mendum* a mistake

emerald n **1** a green transparent variety of beryl highly valued as a gem ▷ adj **2** bright green
WORD ORIGIN Greek *smaragdos*

Emerald Isle n poetic Ireland

emerge vb **emerging, emerged 1** to come into view out of something: *two men emerged from the pub* **2** to come out of a particular state of mind or way of existence: *she emerged from the trance* **3** to come to the end of a particular event or situation: *no party emerged from the election with a clear majority* **4** to become apparent, esp. as the result of a discussion or investigation: *it emerged that he had been drinking* **5** to come into existence over a long period of time: *a new style of dance music emerged in the late 1980s* **emergence** n **emergent** adj
WORD ORIGIN Latin *emergere* to rise up from

emergency n, pl **-cies 1** an unforeseen or sudden occurrence, esp. of danger demanding immediate action **2 state of emergency** a time of crisis, declared by a government, during which normal laws and civil rights can be suspended ▷ adj **3** for use in an emergency: *the emergency exit* **4** made necessary because of an emergency: *emergency surgery*

emeritus (im-**mer**-rit-uss) adj retired, but retaining one's title on an honorary basis: *a professor emeritus*
WORD ORIGIN Latin *merere* to deserve

emery n a hard greyish-black mineral used for smoothing and polishing
WORD ORIGIN Greek *smuris* powder for rubbing

emery board n a strip of cardboard coated with crushed emery, for filing one's fingernails

emetic (im-**met**-ik) n **1** a substance that causes vomiting ▷ adj **2** causing vomiting
WORD ORIGIN Greek *emetikos*

EMF electromotive force

emigrate vb **-grating, -grated** to leave one's native country to settle in another country: *they emigrated to Spain* **emigrant** n, adj **emigration** n
WORD ORIGIN Latin *emigrare*

émigré (**em**-mig-gray) n someone who has left his or her native country for political reasons
WORD ORIGIN French

eminence n **1** the state of being well-known and well-respected **2** a piece of high ground

Eminence n **Your** or **His Eminence** a title used to address or refer to a cardinal

éminence grise (em-in-nonss **greez**) n, pl **éminences grises** a person who wields power and influence unofficially
WORD ORIGIN French, literally: grey eminence, originally applied to Père Joseph, secretary of Cardinal Richelieu

eminent adj well-known and well-respected
WORD ORIGIN Latin *eminere* to stand out

eminently adv extremely: *eminently sensible*

emir (em-**meer**) n an independent ruler in the Islamic world **emirate** n
WORD ORIGIN Arabic *'amīr* commander

emissary n, pl **-saries** an agent sent on a mission by a government or head of state
WORD ORIGIN Latin *emissarius*

emission n **1** the act of giving out heat, light, a smell, etc. **2** energy or a substance given out by something: *exhaust emissions from motor vehicles*

emit vb **emitting, emitted 1** to give or send forth (heat, light, a smell, etc.) **2** to produce (a sound)
WORD ORIGIN Latin *emittere* to send out

Emmental (**em**-men-tahl) n a hard Swiss cheese with holes in it
WORD ORIGIN after *Emmenthal*, valley in Switzerland

emollient adj **1** (of skin cream or lotion) having a softening effect **2** helping to avoid confrontation; calming: *his emollient political style* ▷ n **3** a cream or lotion that softens the skin
WORD ORIGIN Latin *emollire* to soften

emolument n fees or wages from employment
WORD ORIGIN Latin *emolumentum* benefit; originally, fee paid to a miller

emote vb **emoting, emoted** to display exaggerated emotion, as if acting

emoticon (im-**mote**-ik-kon) n computers same as **smiley** (sense 2)
WORD ORIGIN EMOT(ION) + ICON

emotion n **1** any strong feeling, such as joy or fear **2** the part of a person's character based on feelings rather than thought: *the conflict between emotion and logic*
WORD ORIGIN Latin *emovere* to disturb

emotional adj **1** of or relating to the emotions: *emotional abuse* **2** influenced by feelings rather than rational thinking: *he was too emotional to be a good doctor* **3** appealing to the emotions: *emotional appeals for public support* **4** showing one's feelings openly, esp. when upset: *he became very emotional and burst into tears* **emotionalism** n **emotionally** adv

emotive adj tending or designed to arouse emotion

≡ **USAGE**
≡ *Emotional* is preferred to *emotive* when
≡ describing a display of emotion:
≡ *he was given an emotional* (not *emotive*)
≡ *welcome*.

empathize or **-thise** vb **-thizing, -thized** or **-thising, -thised** (often foll. by *with*) to sense and understand someone else's feelings as if they were one's own

empathy n the ability to sense and understand someone else's feelings as if they were one's own **empathic** adj
WORD ORIGIN Greek *empatheia* affection, passion

emperor n a man who rules an empire
WORD ORIGIN Latin *imperare* to command

emperor penguin n a very large Antarctic penguin with orange-yellow patches on its neck

emphasis n, pl **-ses 1** special importance or significance given to something, such as an object or idea **2** stress on a particular syllable, word, or phrase in speaking
WORD ORIGIN Greek

emphasize or **-sise** vb **-sizing, -sized** or **-sising, -sised** to give emphasis or prominence to: *to emphasize her loyalty*

emphatic adj **1** expressed, spoken, or done forcefully: *an emphatic denial of the allegations* **2** forceful and positive: *he was emphatic about his desire for peace talks* **emphatically** adv
WORD ORIGIN Greek *emphainein* to display

emphysema (em-fiss-**see**-ma) n pathol a condition in which the air sacs of the lungs are grossly enlarged, causing breathlessness
WORD ORIGIN Greek *emphusēma* a swelling up

empire n **1** a group of countries under the rule of a single person or sovereign state **2** a large industrial organization that is controlled by one person: *the heiress to a jewellery empire*
WORD ORIGIN Latin *imperare* to command

empire-builder n informal a person who seeks extra power by increasing the number of his or her staff **empire-building** n, adj

empirical adj derived from experiment, experience, and observation rather than from theory or logic: *there is no empirical data to support this claim* **empirically** adv
WORD ORIGIN Greek *empeirikos* practised

empiricism n philosophy the doctrine that all knowledge derives from experience **empiricist** n

emplacement n a prepared position for an artillery gun

employ vb **1** to hire (someone) to do work in return for money **2** to keep busy or occupy: *she was busily employed cutting the grass* **3** to use as a means: *you can employ various methods to cut your heating bills* ▷ n **4 in the employ of** doing regular paid work for: *he is in the employ of The Sunday Times* **employable** adj
WORD ORIGIN Old French *emploier*

employee or US **employe** n a person who is hired to work for someone in return for payment

employer n a person or company that employs workers

employment n **1** the act of employing or state of being employed **2** a person's work or occupation **3** the availability of jobs for the population of a town, country, etc.: *the party's commitment to full employment*

emporium n, pl **-riums** or **-ria** old-fashioned a large retail shop with a wide variety of merchandise
WORD ORIGIN Latin, from Greek *emporos* merchant

empower vb to give (someone) the power or authority to do something

empowerment n **1** the giving or delegation of power; authority **2** S African a semi-official slogan for the empowering of previously disadvantaged populations

empress n **1** a woman who rules an empire **2** the wife or widow of an emperor
WORD ORIGIN Latin *imperatrix*

empty adj **-tier, -tiest 1** containing nothing **2** without inhabitants;

The Influence of French on English

The Norman conquest of English has a lot to answer for. Anyone who compares wordlists of French and English may be forgiven for thinking that one is a dialect of the other. One estimate has it that a third of English words have a direct or indirect French derivation. Pronunciation and word order differ substantially, but even here French makes itself seen and heard. English speakers grapple with a naturalized French phrase like *déjà vu,* sometimes humourously, as when the baseball catcher Yogi Berra remarked 'It's like deja vu all over again.' The French pattern of word + adjective recurs in formulations like the *Secretary General* of the United Nations and the *Governor General* of Canada. Even French gender inflections infiltrate English in the different spellings of the male *blond* and the female *blonde.*

For the English and French, it's been an *entente,* not always *cordiale.* French purists have long defended the classical standards of their language, as witness the founding of the Académie française in 1637. It's been a losing battle, not just because of the twentieth-century dominance of English in the European Community, and indeed throughout the world, but because French itself departs from the standard academic model within France from north to south, in lands once controlled by France such as French Canada, Louisiana, and Haiti, and in current overseas *départements* like Martinique, Guadeloupe, and French Guiana.

Long before William the Conqueror invaded England in 1066, English and French had borrowed words from each other. After the Conquest, French became for the nobility and the emerging middle class the language of government, law, and public administration, with regional variants of Old English spoken by the larger population. Over several centuries, the two merged. One consequence of this *marriage of convenience* (a loan, or more or less literal, translation of *mariage de convenance*) was that English became Latinized. French became the main conduit for innumerable words of Latin or, more remotely, Greek origins, either directly or indirectly in words borrowed from such other Latin-derived languages as Spanish and Italian. This process was further augmented in the seventeenth century and after by scientists who adopted, adapted, or coined a vast neo-Latin terminology.

But French also supplanted Latin as the international language of diplomacy for many years, and survives in terms like *ambassador, attaché,* and *chargé d'affaires.* Nations that seek a *rapprochement* move from hostility to *détente* to an *entente.* Especially useful in diplomacy, French is rich in terms describing emotional states and personal relationships, leading English to borrow them heavily to make up for its lack of felicity in such matters; hence we speak of a *ménage à trois,* a *cri de cœur,* a *crime of passion* (*crime passionel*). Over the centuries, French became the prestige language of the arts (*art deco, roman fleuve*), women's fashion and dress (*crêpe de Chine, décolletage*), and *cuisine* (we *blanch* carrots and *sauté* onions). Ballet dancers perform *pirouettes, jetés,* and the *pas de deux*; when Midwestern Americans want apple pie with ice cream they order the pie *à la mode.* We drink an *apéritif* and then, after eating too much, finish with a *digestif.* A would-be sophisticate or humorist lards sentences with *au contraire, apropos,* and *je ne sais quoi,* and no intellectual with *amour-propre* who wishes to be *au courant* dares to ignore new currents of thought emerging from the Sorbonne: it might be the next *structuralism* or *deconstructionism.*

The huge number of French and English words that are spelled similarly or the same is simultaneously a blessing and a curse to the language learner. It delivers a large and instant vocabulary, yet lays traps for the unwary in the form of *faux amis.* These treacherous friends can turn the speaker into an unwitting comedian, or someone apparently afflicted with a rare brain disorder. Reading from English to French, *patron* is a boss or benefactor, and a client; *formidable* is wonderful or impressive, and dreadful; *seize* is to forcibly take hold of someone or something, and the number sixteen; *pain* is physical distress, and bread; *chat* is to talk informally, and a cat.

Luckily, *RSVP* (*Répondez, s'il vous plaît*) means the same in both French and English. There is no bidding French *adieu.*

e

unoccupied **3** without purpose, substance, or value: *he contemplated yet another empty weekend* **4** insincere or trivial: *empty words* **5** *informal* drained of energy or emotion **6** *maths, logic* (of a set or class) containing no members ▷ *vb* **-ties, -tying, -tied 7** to make or become empty **8** to remove from something: *they emptied out the remains of the tin of paint* ▷ *n, pl* **-ties 9** an empty container, esp. a bottle **emptiness** *n*
WORD ORIGIN Old English *æmtig*

empty-handed *adj* having gained nothing: *the robbers ran off empty-handed*

empty-headed *adj* silly or incapable of serious thought

empyrean (em-pie-**ree**-an) *n poetic* the sky or the heavens
WORD ORIGIN Greek *empuros* fiery

EMS European Monetary System: the system enabling some EU members to coordinate their exchange rates

emu *n* a large Australian long-legged bird that cannot fly
WORD ORIGIN Portuguese *ema* ostrich

EMU 1 European Monetary Union **2** Economic and Monetary Union

emulate *vb* **-lating, -lated** to imitate (someone) in an attempt to do as well as or better than him or her **emulation** *n* **emulator** *n*
WORD ORIGIN Latin *aemulus* competing with

emulsifier *n* a substance that helps to combine two liquids, esp. a water-based liquid and an oil

emulsify *vb* **-fies, -fying, -fied** to make or form into an emulsion

emulsion *n* **1** a mixture of two liquids in which particles of one are suspended evenly throughout the other **2** *photog* a light-sensitive coating for paper or film **3** a type of water-based paint
WORD ORIGIN Latin *emulgere* to milk out

enable *vb* **-abling, -abled 1** to provide (someone) with the means or opportunity to do something **2** to make possible: *to enable the best possible chance of cure*

enabling act *n* a legislative act giving certain powers to a person or organization

enact *vb* **1** to establish by law: *plans to enact a bill of rights* **2** to perform (a story or play) by acting **enactment** *n*

enamel *n* **1** a coloured glassy coating on the surface of articles made of metal, glass, or pottery **2** an enamel-like paint or varnish **3** the hard white substance that covers teeth ▷ *vb* **-elling, -elled** or US **-eling, -eled 4** to decorate or cover with enamel
WORD ORIGIN Old French *esmail*

enamoured or US **enamored** *adj* **enamoured of a** in love with **b** very fond of and impressed by: *he is not enamoured of Moscow*
WORD ORIGIN Latin *amor* love

en bloc *adv* as a whole; all together
WORD ORIGIN French

enc. 1 enclosed **2** enclosure

encamp *vb formal* to set up a camp **encampment** *n*

encapsulate *vb* **-lating, -lated 1** to put in a concise form; summarize **2** to

enclose in, or as if in, a capsule **encapsulation** *n*

encase *vb* **-casing, -cased** to enclose or cover completely: *her arms were encased in plaster* **encasement** *n*

encephalitis (en-sef-a-**lite**-iss) *n* inflammation of the brain **encephalitic** *adj*
WORD ORIGIN Greek *en-* in + *kephalē* head

encephalogram *n* an electroencephalogram
WORD ORIGIN Greek *en-* in + *kephalē* head + *gramma* drawing

enchant *vb* **1** to delight and fascinate **2** to cast a spell on **enchanted** *adj* **enchantment** *n* **enchanter** *n* **enchantress** *fem n*
WORD ORIGIN Latin *incantare* to chant a spell

enchilada (en-chill-**lah**-da) *n* a Mexican dish consisting of a tortilla filled with meat, served with chilli sauce

encircle *vb* **-cling, -cled** to form a circle round **encirclement** *n*

enclave *n* a part of a country entirely surrounded by foreign territory: *a Spanish enclave*
WORD ORIGIN Latin *in-* in + *clavis* key

enclose *vb* **-closing, -closed 1** to surround completely: *the house enclosed a courtyard* **2** to include along with something else: *he enclosed a letter with the parcel*

enclosed *adj* kept separate from the normal everyday activities of the outside world: *an enclosed community of nuns*

enclosure *n* **1** an area of land enclosed by a fence, wall, or hedge **2** something, such as a cheque, enclosed with a letter

encode *vb* **-coding, -coded** to convert (a message) into code

encomium *n* a formal expression of praise
WORD ORIGIN Latin

encompass *vb* **1** to enclose within a circle; surround **2** to include all of: *the programme encompasses the visual arts, music, literature, and drama*

encore *interj* **1** again: used by an audience to demand a short extra performance ▷ *n* **2** an extra song or piece performed at a concert in response to enthusiastic demand from the audience
WORD ORIGIN French

encounter *vb* **1** to meet (someone) unexpectedly **2** to be faced with: *he had rarely encountered such suffering* **3** to meet (an opponent or enemy) in a competition or battle ▷ *n* **4** a casual or unexpected meeting **5** a game or battle: *a fierce encounter between the army and armed rebels*
WORD ORIGIN Latin *in-* in + *contra* against, opposite

encourage *vb* **-raging, -raged 1** to give (someone) the confidence to do something **2** to stimulate (something or someone) by approval or help **encouragement** *n* **encouraging** *adj*
WORD ORIGIN French *encourager*

encroach *vb* to intrude gradually on someone's rights or on a piece of land **encroachment** *n*

WORD ORIGIN Old French *encrochier* to seize

encrust *vb* to cover (a surface) with a layer of something, such as jewels or ice **encrustation** *n*

encrypt *vb* **1** to put (a message or data) into a coded form **2** to distort (a television or other signal) so that it cannot be received without the use of specific equipment. See also **decrypt** ▷ **encryption** *n*
WORD ORIGIN Greek *en-* in + *kruptos* hidden

encumber *vb* **1** to hinder or impede: *neither was greatly encumbered with social engagements* **2** to burden with a load or with debts
WORD ORIGIN Old French *en-* into + *combre* a barrier

encumbrance *n* something that impedes or is burdensome

encyclical (en-**sik**-lik-kl) *n* a letter sent by the pope to all Roman Catholic bishops
WORD ORIGIN Greek *kuklos* circle

encyclopedia or **encyclopaedia** *n* a book or set of books, often in alphabetical order, containing facts about many different subjects or about one particular subject
WORD ORIGIN Greek *enkuklios* general + *paideia* education

encyclopedic or **encyclopaedic** *adj* (of knowledge or information) very full and thorough; comprehensive

end *n* **1** one of the two extreme points of something such as a road **2** the surface at one of the two extreme points of an object: *a pencil with a rubber at one end* **3** the extreme extent or limit of something: *the end of the runway* **4** the most distant place or time that can be imagined: *the ends of the earth* **5** the act or an instance of stopping doing something or stopping something from continuing: *I want to put an end to all the gossip* **6** the last part of something: *at the end of the story* **7** a remnant or fragment: *cigarette ends* **8** death or destruction **9** the purpose of an action: *he will only use you to achieve his own ends* **10** *sport* either of the two defended areas of a playing field **11 in the end** finally **12 make ends meet** to have just enough money to meet one's needs **13 no end** used for emphasis: *these moments give me no end of trouble* **14 on end** *informal* without pause or interruption: *for months on end* **15 the end** *slang* the worst, esp. beyond the limits of endurance ▷ *vb* **16** to bring or come to a finish **17 end it all** *informal* to commit suicide ▶ See also **end up**
WORD ORIGIN Old English *ende*

endanger *vb* to put in danger

endangered *adj* (of a species of animal) in danger of becoming extinct

endear *vb* to cause to be liked: *his wit endeared him to a great many people* **endearing** *adj*

endearment *n* an affectionate word or phrase

endeavour or US **endeavor** *formal vb* **1** to try (to do something) ▷ *n* **2** an effort to do something
WORD ORIGIN Middle English *endeveren*

endemic *adj* present within a localized area or only found in a particular group of people: *he found 100 species of plant endemic to that ridge* **WORD ORIGIN** Greek *en-* in + *dēmos* the people

ending *n* **1** the last part or conclusion of something: *the film has a happy ending* **2** the tip or end of something: *nerve endings*

endive *n* a plant with crisp curly leaves, used in salads **WORD ORIGIN** Old French

endless *adj* **1** having no end; eternal or infinite **2** continuing too long or continually recurring: *an endless stream of visitors* **endlessly** *adv*

endmost *adj* nearest the end

endocrine *adj* of or denoting a gland that secretes hormones directly into the blood stream, or a hormone secreted by such a gland **WORD ORIGIN** Greek *endon* within + *krinein* to separate

endogenous (en-**dodge**-in-uss) *adj* *biol* developing or originating from within

endometrium (end-oh-**meet**-tree-um) *n* the mucous membrane lining the womb **endometrial** *adj* **WORD ORIGIN** Greek *endon* within + *mētra* womb

endomorph *n* *physiol* a person with a fat and heavy body build. See also **ectomorph, mesomorph** > **endomorphic** *adj* **WORD ORIGIN** Greek *endon* within + *morphē* shape

endorphin *n* any of a group of chemicals found in the brain, which have an effect similar to morphine

endorsation *n* *Canad* approval or support

endorse *vb* -**dorsing**, -**dorsed** **1** to give approval or support to **2** to sign the back of (a cheque) to specify the payee **3** *chiefly Brit* to record a conviction on (a driving licence) **endorsement** *n* **WORD ORIGIN** Old French *endosser* to put on the back

endoscope *n* *med* a long slender medical instrument used for examining the interior of hollow organs **endoscopy** *n*

endoskeleton *n* *zool* an internal skeleton, such as the bony skeleton of vertebrates

endothermic *adj* (of a chemical reaction) involving or requiring the absorption of heat

endow *vb* **1** to provide with a source of permanent income, esp. by leaving money in a will **2 endowed with** provided with or possessing (a quality or talent) **WORD ORIGIN** Old French *endouer*

endowment *n* **1** the money given to an institution, such as a hospital **2** a natural talent or quality

endowment assurance or **insurance** *n* a kind of life insurance that pays a specified sum directly to the policyholder at a designated date or to his or her beneficiary should he or she die before this date

endpaper *n* either of two leaves at the front and back of a book pasted to the inside of the cover

end product *n* the final result of a process

end up *vb* **1** to arrive at a place by a roundabout route or without intending to: *the van somehow ended up in Bordeaux* **2** to arrive at a particular condition or situation without expecting to: *I thought I was going to hate it, but I ended up enjoying myself*

endurance *n* the ability to withstand prolonged hardship

endure *vb* -**during**, -**dured** **1** to bear (hardship) patiently **2** to tolerate or put up with: *I cannot endure your disloyalty any longer* **3** to last for a long time **endurable** *adj* **WORD ORIGIN** Latin *indurare* to harden

enduring *adj* long-lasting

endways *or esp. US & Canad* **endwise** *adv* having the end forwards or upwards

enema (**en**-im-a) *n* *med* a quantity of fluid inserted into the rectum to empty the bowels, for example before an operation **WORD ORIGIN** Greek: injection

enemy *n, pl* -**mies** **1** a person who is hostile or opposed to a person, group, or idea **2** a hostile nation or people **3** something that harms or opposes something: *oil is an enemy of the environment* ▶ Related adjective: **inimical** *adj* **4** of or belonging to an enemy: *enemy troops* **WORD ORIGIN** Latin *inimicus* hostile

energetic *adj* **1** having or showing energy and enthusiasm: *an energetic campaigner for democracy* **2** involving a lot of movement and physical effort: *energetic exercise* **energetically** *adv*

energize *or* -**gise** *vb* -**gizing**, -**gized** *or* -**gising**, -**gised** to stimulate or enliven

energy *n, pl* -**gies** **1** capacity for intense activity; vigour **2** intensity or vitality of action or expression; forcefulness **3** *physics* the capacity to do work and overcome resistance **4** a source of power, such as electricity **WORD ORIGIN** Greek *energeia* activity

energy drink *n* a soft drink designed to boost the drinker's energy levels

enervate *vb* -**vating**, -**vated** to deprive of strength or vitality **enervating** *adj* **enervation** *n* **WORD ORIGIN** Latin *enervare* to remove the nerves from

enfant terrible (**on**-fon ter-**reeb**-la) *n, pl* **enfants terribles** a talented but unconventional or indiscreet person **WORD ORIGIN** French, literally: terrible child

enfeeble *vb* -**bling**, -**bled** to make (someone or something) weak

enfilade *mil* *n* **1** a burst of gunfire sweeping from end to end along a line of troops ▶ *vb* -**lading**, -**laded** **2** to attack with an enfilade **WORD ORIGIN** French *enfiler* to thread on string

enfold *vb* **1** to cover (something) by, or as if by, wrapping something round it: *darkness enfolded the city* **2** to embrace or hug

enforce *vb* -**forcing**, -**forced** **1** to ensure that (a law or decision) is obeyed **2** to impose (obedience) by, or as if by, force **enforceable** *adj* **enforcement** *n*

enfranchise *vb* -**chising**, -**chised** to grant (a person or group of people) the right to vote **enfranchisement** *n*

Eng. **1** England **2** English

engage *vb* -**gaging**, -**gaged** **1** Also: **be engaged** (usually foll. by *in*) to take part or participate: *he engaged in criminal and illegal acts; they were engaged in espionage* **2** to involve (a person or his or her attention) intensely: *there's nothing to engage the intellect in this film* **3** to employ (someone) to do something **4** to promise to do something **5** *mil* to begin a battle with **6** to bring (part of a machine or other mechanism) into operation, esp. by causing components to interlock **7 engage in conversation** to start a conversation with **WORD ORIGIN** Old French *en-* in + *gage* a pledge

engaged *adj* **1** having made a promise to get married **2** (of a telephone line or a toilet) already being used

engagement *n* **1** a business or social appointment **2** the period when a couple has agreed to get married but the wedding has not yet taken place **3** a limited period of employment, esp. in the performing arts **4** a battle

engagement ring *n* a ring worn by a woman engaged to be married

engaging *adj* pleasant and charming **engagingly** *adv*

engender *vb* to produce (a particular feeling, atmosphere, or situation) **WORD ORIGIN** Latin *ingenerare*

engine *n* **1** any machine designed to convert energy into mechanical work, esp. one used to power a vehicle **2** a railway locomotive **WORD ORIGIN** Latin *ingenium* nature, talent

engineer *n* **1** a person trained in any branch of engineering **2** a person who repairs and maintains mechanical or electrical devices **3** a soldier trained in engineering and construction work **4** an officer responsible for a ship's engines **5** *US & Canad* a train driver ▶ *vb* **6** to cause or plan (an event or situation) in a clever or devious manner **7** to design or construct as a professional engineer

engineering *n* the profession of applying scientific principles to the design and construction of engines, cars, buildings, bridges, roads, and electrical machines

English *adj* **1** of England or the English language ▶ *n* **2** the principal language of Britain, Ireland, Australia, New Zealand, the US, Canada, and several other countries ▶ *pl n* **3 the English** the people of England

English breakfast *n* a breakfast including cooked food, such as bacon and eggs

Englishman *or fem* **Englishwoman** *n, pl* -**men** *or* -**women** a person from England

engorge *vb* -**gorging**, -**gorged** *pathol* to clog or become clogged with blood **engorgement** *n*

engrave vb -graving, -graved **1** to carve or etch a design or inscription into (a surface) **2** to print (designs or characters) from a plate into which they have been cut or etched **3** to fix deeply or permanently in the mind **engraver** n
WORD ORIGIN en- in + obsolete grave to carve

engraving n **1** a printing surface that has been engraved **2** a print made from this

engross (en-**groce**) vb to occupy the attention of (someone) completely **engrossing** adj
WORD ORIGIN en- in + Latin grossus thick

engulf vb **1** to immerse, plunge, or swallow up: engulfed by flames **2** to overwhelm: a terrible fear engulfed her

enhance vb -hancing, -hanced to improve or increase in quality, value, or power: grilling on the barbecue enhances the flavour **enhancement** n **enhancer** n
WORD ORIGIN Old French enhaucier

enigma n something or someone that is mysterious or puzzling **enigmatic** adj **enigmatically** adv
WORD ORIGIN Greek ainissesthai to speak in riddles

enjoin vb **1** to order (someone) to do something **2** to impose (a particular kind of behaviour) on someone: the sect enjoins poverty on its members **3** law to prohibit (someone) from doing something by an injunction
WORD ORIGIN Old French enjoindre

enjoy vb **1** to receive pleasure from **2** to have or experience (something, esp. something good): many fat people enjoy excellent health **3** **enjoy oneself** to have a good time **enjoyable** adj **enjoyably** adv **enjoyment** n
WORD ORIGIN Old French enjoir

enlarge vb -larging, -larged **1** to make or grow larger **2** **enlarge on** to speak or write about in greater detail **enlargement** n **enlarger** n

enlighten vb to give information or understanding to **enlightening** adj

enlightened adj **1** rational and having beneficial effects: an enlightened approach to social welfare **2** (of a person) tolerant and unprejudiced

enlightenment n the act of enlightening or the state of being enlightened

enlist vb **1** to enter the armed forces **2** to obtain (someone's help or support) **enlistment** n

enlisted adj (of a man or woman in the US Army or Navy) being below the rank of an officer

enliven vb to make lively, cheerful, or bright **enlivening** adj

en masse adv all together; as a group
WORD ORIGIN French

enmeshed adj deeply involved: enmeshed in turmoil

enmity n a feeling of hostility or ill will
WORD ORIGIN Latin inimicus hostile

ennoble vb -bling, -bled **1** to make (someone) a member of the nobility **2** to make (someone or his or her life) noble or dignified: poverty does not ennoble people

ennui (on-**nwee**) n literary boredom and dissatisfaction resulting from lack of activity or excitement
WORD ORIGIN French

enormity n **1** extreme wickedness **2** pl -ties an act of great wickedness **3** the vastness or extent of a problem or difficulty

⋮ **USAGE**
⋮ In modern English, it is common to
⋮ talk about the enormity of something
⋮ such as a task or a problem, but one
⋮ should not talk about the enormity of
⋮ an object or area: distribution is a problem
⋮ because of India's enormous size (not India's
⋮ enormity).

enormous adj unusually large in size, extent, or degree **enormously** adv
WORD ORIGIN Latin e- out of, away from + norma rule, pattern

enough adj **1** as much or as many as necessary **2** **that's enough!** used to stop someone behaving in a particular way ▷ pron **3** an adequate amount or number: I don't know enough about the subject to be able to speak about it ▷ adv **4** as much as necessary **5** fairly or quite: that's a common enough experience **6** very: used to give emphasis to the preceding word: funnily enough, I wasn't alarmed **7** just adequately: he sang well enough
WORD ORIGIN Old English genōh

en passant (on pass-**on**) adv in passing: references made en passant
WORD ORIGIN French

enquire vb -quiring, -quired same as **inquire** ▷ **enquiry** n

enrage vb -raging, -raged to make extremely angry

enraptured adj filled with delight and fascination

enrich vb **1** to improve or increase the quality or value of: his poetry has vastly enriched the English language **2** to improve in nutritional value, colour, or flavour: a sauce enriched with beer **3** to make wealthy or wealthier **enriched** adj **enrichment** n

enrol or US **enroll** vb -rolling, -rolled to become or cause to become a member **enrolment** or US **enrollment** n

en route adv on or along the way
WORD ORIGIN French

ensconce vb -sconcing, -sconced to settle firmly or comfortably
WORD ORIGIN Middle English en- in + sconce fortification

ensemble (on-**som**-bl) n **1** all the parts of something considered as a whole **2** the complete outfit of clothes a person is wearing **3** a group of musicians or actors performing together **4** music a passage in which all or most of the performers are playing or singing at once
WORD ORIGIN French: together

enshrine vb -shrining, -shrined to contain and protect (an idea or right) in a society, legal system, etc.: the university's independence is enshrined in its charter

enshroud vb to cover or hide (an object) completely, as if by draping something over it: fog enshrouded the forest

ensign n **1** a flag flown by a ship to indicate its nationality **2** any flag or banner **3** (in the US Navy) a commissioned officer of the lowest rank **4** (formerly, in the British infantry) a commissioned officer of the lowest rank
WORD ORIGIN Latin insignia badges

enslave vb -slaving, -slaved to make a slave of (someone) **enslavement** n

ensnare vb -snaring, -snared **1** to trap or gain power over (someone) by dishonest or underhand means **2** to catch (an animal) in a snare

ensue vb -suing, -sued **1** to happen next **2** to occur as a consequence: if glaucoma is not treated, blindness can ensue **ensuing** adj
WORD ORIGIN Latin in- in + sequi to follow

en suite adj, adv (of a bathroom) connected to a bedroom and entered directly from it: an en-suite bathroom; a room with a bathroom en suite
WORD ORIGIN French, literally: in sequence

ensure or esp. US **insure** vb -suring, -sured **1** to make certain: we must ensure that similar accidents do not happen again **2** to make safe or protect: female athletes should take extra iron to ensure against anaemia

ENT med ear, nose, and throat

entablature n archit the part of a classical building supported by the columns, consisting of an architrave, a frieze, and a cornice
WORD ORIGIN Italian intavolatura something put on a table, hence, something laid flat

entail vb **1** to bring about or impose inevitably: few women enter marriage knowing what it really entails **2** Brit, Austral, & NZ property law to restrict the ability to inherit (a piece of property) to designated heirs
WORD ORIGIN Middle English en- in + taille limitation

entangle vb -gling, -gled **1** to catch very firmly in something, such as a net or wire: a fishing line had entangled his legs **2** to involve in a complicated series of problems or difficulties: he entangles himself in contradictions **3** to involve in a troublesome relationship: she kept getting entangled with unsuitable boyfriends **entanglement** n

entente (on-**tont**) n short for **entente cordiale**
WORD ORIGIN French: understanding

entente cordiale (cord-ee-**ahl**) n a friendly understanding between two or more countries
WORD ORIGIN French: cordial understanding

enter vb **1** to come or go into (a particular place): he entered the room **2** to join (a party or organization) **3** to become involved in or take part in: 1500 schools entered the competition **4** to become suddenly present or noticeable in: a note of anxiety entered his voice **5** to record (an item) in a journal or list **6** theatre to come on stage: used as a stage direction: enter Joseph **7** to begin (a new process or period of time): the occupation of the square has entered its eleventh day
WORD ORIGIN Latin intrare

enteric (en-**ter**-ik) adj of the intestines
WORD ORIGIN Greek enteron intestine

Neologisms

Modern English may not be so modern. Some date the English spoken today from the Elizabethan Age (the late 1500s), or from the Jacobean years of the early 1600s. Others date it from the late 1600s, when Sir Isaac Newton and his contemporaries revolutionized science or, about a century later, from the Industrial Revolution's steam power, factories, and mass manufacturing: both led to a vast expansion of technical vocabulary. Alternatively, some trace it from the standardizing spellings of Samuel Johnson's dictionary in 1755. What we can say is that the nineteenth and twentieth centuries greatly accelerated the pace by which new words entered the language.

Each industrial improvement, innovation, or invention in transportation and power generation (*railways*, steam and *diesel*-powered ships, *automobiles, aircraft*, *atomic energy* and *nuclear* power, *space exploration*) and communications (the *postage stamp, telegraph, telephone, radio, movies, television, satellite transmission, personal computers*, and the *internet*) supplied new words. Political and social movements such as *fascism*, *Communism*, and *religious fundamentalism*, and *feminists*' and minority groups' struggle for social equality enlarged the lexicon, as did two *World Wars* of unprecedented size and scope, bridged by the *Great Depression*.

These and lesser wars – in Vietnam, the Persian Gulf and Middle East, Africa, South Asia, and *Yugoslavia*, not to mention the *Cold War* – rearranged national borders and displaced entire populations. In the aftermath of wars or of hardship in home countries, millions became refugees or emigrants. Such huge demographic shifts, as well as *social mobility* within countries, fed countless words into English, as did, after the Second World War, the quickening of such colossal economies as China, Russia, and phoenix-like Japan and Germany. New words followed the money.

By the twenty-first century, anxiety about the *Bomb's* potential for global annihilation largely had been replaced by fear of attacks from *terrorists*. Concern over the world's deteriorating *ecology* mounted, especially about *climate change* and *global warming*, leading to a search for *alternative energy sources* like *solar power* or *wind power*. Words or senses of words like *open marriage, speed,* and *self-help* pointed respectively to altered gender relations, the spread of *street drugs*, and *pop psychology*. No widespread new word or phrase could arrive without its abbreviation or acronym.

Although syntax and spelling mainly did not change, English usage became much more informal. The *internal migration* to cities meant that urban speech replaced rural dialects. As a consequence of two World Wars, the United States grew into a military and economic superpower. The American dominance in technology, commerce, and *pop culture*, especially *youth culture*, dating from the *Jazz Age*, ensured that its slang and jargon spread across the globe, together with a democratic informality of usage. This trend toward the colloquial in fact began much earlier with the rise of mass-circulation newspapers and magazines and later through movies and the *broadcast* media. To some, the old classics-based education and class-based manners and mores were *elitist*, patriarchal, or imperialistic. Whereas taboo words had been sex-related, the new taboos involved race. The *f-word* became vulgar at most, while the *n-word* became taboo. Semantic shifts also occurred: *gay* now meant 'homosexual', not 'light-hearted'.

In the Victorian era, the British Empire had covered a quarter of the earth's surface. In a long process that transpired before, during, and after its dissolution, its constituent parts evolved distinctive dialects or varieties of English in Ireland, Scotland, Australia, New Zealand, Canada, the West Indies, and the Indian subcontinent.

English is the world's most widely distributed language. It is an official language of India and the *European Community*. It prevails in *air traffic control*, *software* and *hardware* development, and in *globalization* and international trade. The online use of English on *Web sites* and in *e-mail* messages greatly outweighs any other language. The future of English, this strange blend of the Graeco-Latin and the Germanic, may depend on whether it will become *World English* or, like Latin, it will splinter into separate languages.

enter into vb **1** to be an important factor in (a situation or plan): *money doesn't enter into it: it's a matter of principle* **2** to start to do or be involved in (a process or series of events): *the government will not enter into negotiations with terrorists*

enteritis (en-ter-**rite**-iss) n inflammation of the small intestine

enterprise n **1** a business firm **2** a project or undertaking, esp. one that requires boldness or effort **3** boldness and energy **WORD ORIGIN** Old French *entreprendre* to undertake

enterprising adj full of boldness and initiative **enterprisingly** adv

entertain vb **1** to provide amusement for (a person or audience) **2** to show hospitality to (guests) **3** to consider (an idea or suggestion) **WORD ORIGIN** Old French *entre-* mutually + *tenir* to hold

entertainer n a person who entertains, esp. professionally

entertaining adj **1** interesting, amusing, and enjoyable ▷ n **2** the provision of hospitality to guests: *the smart kitchen is perfect for entertaining*

entertainment n **1** enjoyment and interest: *a match of top-quality entertainment and goals* **2** an act or show that entertains, or such acts and shows collectively

enthral or US **enthrall** (en-**thrawl**) vb **-thralling, -thralled** to hold the attention or interest of **enthralling** adj **enthralment** or US **enthrallment** n

enthrone vb **-throning, -throned 1** to place (a person) on a throne in a ceremony to mark the beginning of his or her new role as a monarch or bishop **2** to give an important or prominent position to (something): *the religious fundamentalism now enthroned in American life* **enthronement** n

enthuse vb **-thusing, -thused** to feel or cause to feel enthusiasm

enthusiasm n ardent and lively interest or eagerness: *your enthusiasm for literature* **WORD ORIGIN** Greek *enthousiazein* to be possessed by a god

enthusiast n a person who is very interested in and keen on something **enthusiastic** adj **enthusiastically** adv

entice vb **-ticing, -ticed** to attract (someone) away from one place or activity to another **enticement** n **enticing** adj **WORD ORIGIN** Old French *enticier*

entire adj made up of or involving all of something, including every detail, part, or aspect **entirely** adv **WORD ORIGIN** Latin *integer* whole

entirety n, pl **-ties 1** all of a person or thing: *you must follow this diet for the entirety of your life* **2** **in its entirety** as a whole

entitle vb **-tling, -tled 1** to give (someone) the right to do or have something **2** to give a name or title to (a book or film) **entitlement** n

entity n, pl **-ties** something that exists in its own right and not merely as part of a bigger thing

WORD ORIGIN Latin *esse* to be

entomb vb **1** to place (a corpse) in a tomb **2** to bury or trap: *a circulatory system entombed in fat* **entombment** n

entomology n the study of insects **entomological** adj **entomologist** n **WORD ORIGIN** Greek *entomon* insect

entourage (**on**-toor-ahzh) n a group of people who assist or travel with an important or well-known person **WORD ORIGIN** French *entourer* to surround

entozoon (en-toe-**zoe**-on) n, pl **-zoa** (-**zoe**-a) a parasite, such as a tapeworm, that lives inside another animal

entrails pl n **1** the internal organs of a person or animal; intestines **2** the innermost parts of anything **WORD ORIGIN** Latin *interanea* intestines

entrance[1] n **1** something, such as a door or gate, through which it is possible to enter a place **2** the act of coming into a place, esp. with reference to the way in which it is done: *she made a sudden startling entrance* **3** *theatre* the act of appearing on stage **4** the right to enter a place: *he refused her entrance because she was carrying her Scottie dog* **5** ability or permission to join or become involved with a group or organization: *entrance to the profession should be open to men and women alike* ▷ adj **6** necessary in order to enter something: *they have paid entrance fees for English-language courses*

entrance[2] vb **-trancing, -tranced** to fill with delight **entrancement** n **entrancing** adj

entrant n a person who enters a university, competition, etc.

entrap vb **-trapping, -trapped 1** to trick (someone) into danger or difficulty **2** to catch in a trap **entrapment** n

entreat vb to ask (someone) earnestly to do something **WORD ORIGIN** Old French *entraiter*

entreaty n, pl **-treaties** an earnest request or plea

entrecote (**on**-tra-coat) n a steak of beef cut from between the ribs **WORD ORIGIN** French

entrée (**on**-tray) n **1** the right to enter a place **2** a dish served before a main course **3** *chiefly US* the main course **WORD ORIGIN** French

entrench vb **1** to fix or establish firmly: *the habit had become entrenched* **2** *mil* to fortify (a position) by digging trenches around it **entrenchment** n

entrepreneur n the owner of a business who attempts to make money by risk and initiative **entrepreneurial** adj **WORD ORIGIN** French

entropy (en-trop-ee) n **1** *formal* lack of pattern or organization **2** *physics* a thermodynamic quantity that represents the amount of energy present in a system that cannot be converted into work because it is tied up in the atomic structure of the system **WORD ORIGIN** Greek *entropē* a turning towards

entrust vb **1** to give (someone) a duty or responsibility: *Miss Conway, who was entrusted with the child's education* **2** to put (something) into the care of someone: *he stole all the money we had entrusted to him*

USAGE It is usually considered incorrect to talk about *entrusting* someone *to do* something: *the army cannot be trusted* (not *entrusted*) *to carry out orders.*

entry n, pl **-tries 1** something, such as a door or gate, through which it is possible to enter a place **2** the act of coming in to a place, esp. with reference to the way in which it is done **3** the right to enter a place: *he was refused entry to Britain* **4** the act of joining an organization or group: *Britain's entry into the EU* **5** a brief note, article, or group of figures in a diary, book, or computer file **6** a quiz form, painting, etc. submitted in an attempt to win a competition **7** a person, horse, car, etc. entering a competition ▷ adj **8** necessary in order to enter something: *entry fee*

entwine vb **-twining, -twined** to twist together or round something else

E number n any of a series of numbers with the prefix E- indicating a specific food additive recognized by the EU

enumerate vb **-ating, -ated 1** to name or list one by one **2** to count **3** *Canad* to compile the voting list for an area **enumeration** n **enumerator** n **WORD ORIGIN** Latin *e-* out + *numerare* to count

enunciate vb **-ating, -ated 1** to pronounce (words) clearly **2** to state precisely or formally **enunciation** n **WORD ORIGIN** Latin *enuntiare* to declare

enuresis (en-yoo-**reece**-iss) n involuntary urination, esp. during sleep **WORD ORIGIN** Greek *en-* in + *ouron* urine

envelop vb to cover, surround, or enclose **envelopment** n **WORD ORIGIN** Old French *envoluper*

envelope n **1** a flat covering of paper, that can be sealed, used to enclose a letter, etc. **2** any covering, wrapper, or enclosing structure: *an envelope of filo pastry* **3** *geom* a curve that is tangential to each one of a group of curves **WORD ORIGIN** French *envelopper* to wrap round

enviable adj so desirable or fortunate that it is likely to cause envy **enviably** adv

envious adj feeling, showing, or resulting from envy **enviously** adv

environment (en-**vire**-on-ment) n **1** the surroundings in which a person, animal, or plant lives **2** *ecology* **the environment** the natural world of land, sea, air, plants, and animals: *nuclear waste must be prevented from leaking into the environment* **environmental** adj **WORD ORIGIN** French *environs* surroundings

environmentalist n a person concerned with the protection and preservation of the natural environment

environs pl n a surrounding area, esp. the outskirts of a city

envisage or US **envision** vb **-aging, -aged** or **-ioning, -ioned** to believe to be possible or likely in the future: *the commission envisages a mix of government and private funding* **WORD ORIGIN** French *en-* in + *visage* face

USAGE
It was formerly considered incorrect to use a clause after *envisage* as in *it is envisaged that the new centre will cost £40 million*, but this use is now acceptable.

envoy *n* **1** a messenger or representative **2** a diplomat ranking next below an ambassador
WORD ORIGIN French *envoyer* to send

envy *n, pl* **-vies 1** a feeling of discontent aroused by someone else's possessions, achievements, or qualities **2** something that causes envy: *their standards are the envy of the world* ▷ *vb* **-vies, -vying, -vied 3** to wish that one had the possessions, achievements, or qualities of (someone else) **envyingly** *adv*
WORD ORIGIN Latin *invidia*

enzyme *n* any of a group of complex proteins, that act as catalysts in specific biochemical reactions **enzymatic** *adj*
WORD ORIGIN Greek *en-* in + *zumē* leaven

Eocene (**ee**-oh-seen) *adj* of the epoch of geological time about 55 million years ago
WORD ORIGIN Greek *ēos* dawn + *kainos* new

Eolithic *adj* of the early period of the Stone Age, when crude stone tools were used

EP *n* an extended-play gramophone record, which is 7 inches in diameter and has a longer recording on each side than a single does

epaulette *n* a piece of ornamental material on the shoulder of a garment, esp. a military uniform
WORD ORIGIN French

épée (**ep**-pay) *n* a straight-bladed sword used in fencing

ephedrine (**eff**-fid-dreen) *n* an alkaloid used for the treatment of asthma and hay fever
WORD ORIGIN *Ephedra*, genus of plants which produce it

ephemera (if-**fem**-a-ra) *pl n* items designed to last only for a short time, such as programmes or posters

ephemeral *adj* lasting only for a short time
WORD ORIGIN Greek *hēmera* day

epic *n* **1** a long exciting book, poem, or film, usually telling of heroic deeds **2** a long narrative poem telling of the deeds of a legendary hero ▷ *adj* **3** very large or grand: *a professional feud of epic proportions*
WORD ORIGIN Greek *epos* word, song

epicene *adj* (esp. of a man) having characteristics or features that are not definitely male or female
WORD ORIGIN Greek *epikoinos* common to many

epicentre *or US* **epicenter** *n* the point on the earth's surface immediately above the origin of an earthquake
WORD ORIGIN Greek *epi* above + *kentron* point

epicure *n* a person who enjoys good food and drink **epicurism** *n*
WORD ORIGIN after *Epicurus*, Greek philosopher, who held that pleasure is the highest good

epicurean *adj* **1** devoted to sensual pleasures, esp. food and drink ▷ *n* **2** same as **epicure** ▷ **epicureanism** *n*

epidemic *n* **1** a widespread occurrence of a disease **2** a rapid development or spread of something: *an epidemic of rape* ▷ *adj* **3** (esp. of a disease) affecting many people in an area: *stress has now reached epidemic proportions*
WORD ORIGIN Greek *epi* among + *dēmos* people

epidemiology (ep-pid-deem-ee-ol-a-jee) *n* the branch of medical science concerned with the occurrence and control of diseases in populations **epidemiologist** *n*

epidermis *n* the thin protective outer layer of the skin **epidermal** *adj*
WORD ORIGIN Greek *epi* upon + *derma* skin

epidural (ep-pid-**dure**-al) *adj* **1** on or over the outermost membrane covering the brain and spinal cord (**dura mater**) ▷ *n* **2 a** an injection of anaesthetic into the space outside the outermost membrane enveloping the spinal cord **b** anaesthesia produced by this method
WORD ORIGIN from *dura mater*

epiglottis *n* a thin flap of cartilage at the back of the mouth that covers the entrance to the larynx during swallowing
WORD ORIGIN Greek *epi* upon + *glōtta* tongue

epigram *n* **1** a witty remark **2** a short poem with a witty ending **epigrammatic** *adj*
WORD ORIGIN Greek *epi* upon + *graphein* to write

epigraph *n* **1** a quotation at the beginning of a book **2** an inscription on a monument or building
WORD ORIGIN Greek *epi* upon + *graphein* to write

epilepsy *n* a disorder of the central nervous system which causes periodic loss of consciousness and sometimes convulsions
WORD ORIGIN Greek *epi* upon + *lambanein* to take

epileptic *adj* **1** of or having epilepsy ▷ *n* **2** a person who has epilepsy

epilogue *n* a short concluding passage or speech at the end of a book or play
WORD ORIGIN Greek *epi* upon + *logos* word, speech

epiphany (ip-**piff**-a-nee) *n, pl* **-nies** a moment of great or sudden revelation
WORD ORIGIN Greek *epiphaneia* an appearing

Epiphany *n, pl* **-nies** a Christian festival held on January 6 commemorating, in the Western church, the manifestation of Christ to the Magi and, in the Eastern church, the baptism of Christ

episcopacy (ip-**piss**-kop-a-see) *n* **1** government of a Church by bishops **2** *pl* **-cies** same as **episcopate**

episcopal (ip-**piss**-kop-al) *adj* of or relating to bishops
WORD ORIGIN Greek *episkopos* overseer

Episcopal Church *n* (in Scotland and the US) a self-governing branch of the Anglican Church

episcopalian *adj also* **episcopal 1** practising or advocating Church government by bishops ▷ *n* **2** an advocate of such Church government

Episcopalian (ip-piss-kop-**pale**-ee-an) *adj* **1** of or relating to the Episcopal Church ▷ *n* **2** a member of this Church **Episcopalianism** *n*

episcopate (ip-**piss**-kop-it) *n* **1** the office, status, or term of office of a bishop **2** bishops collectively

episiotomy (ip-peez-ee-**ot**-tom-ee) *n, pl* **-tomies** an operation involving cutting into the area between the genitals and the anus sometimes performed during childbirth to make the birth easier

episode *n* **1** an event or series of events **2** any of the sections into which a novel or a television or radio serial is divided
WORD ORIGIN Greek *epi* in addition + *eisodios* coming in

episodic *adj* **1** resembling or relating to an episode **2** occurring at irregular and infrequent intervals

epistemology (ip-iss-stem-**ol**-a-jee) *n* the theory of knowledge, esp. the critical study of its validity, methods, and scope **epistemological** *adj* **epistemologist** *n*
WORD ORIGIN Greek *epistēmē* knowledge

epistle *n* **1** *formal or humorous* a letter **2** a literary work in letter form, esp. a poem
WORD ORIGIN Greek *epistolē*

Epistle *n New Testament* any of the letters written by the apostles

epistolary *adj* **1** of or relating to letters **2** (of a novel) presented in the form of a series of letters

epitaph *n* **1** a commemorative inscription on a tombstone **2** a commemorative speech or written passage
WORD ORIGIN Greek *epi* upon + *taphos* tomb

epithelium *n, pl* **-lia** *anat* a cellular tissue covering the external and internal surfaces of the body **epithelial** *adj*
WORD ORIGIN Greek *epi* upon + *thēlē* nipple

epithet *n* a word or short phrase used to describe someone or something: *these tracks truly deserve that overworked epithet 'classic'*
WORD ORIGIN Greek *epitithenai* to add

epitome (ip-**pit**-a-mee) *n* **1** a person or thing that is a typical example of a characteristic or class: *the epitome of rural tranquillity* **2** a summary, esp. of a written work
WORD ORIGIN Greek *epitemnein* to abridge

epitomize *or* **-mise** *vb* **-mizing, -mized** *or* **-mising, -mised** to be or make a perfect or typical example of

EPNS electroplated nickel silver

epoch (**ee**-pok) *n* **1** a long period of time marked by some predominant characteristic: *the cold-war epoch* **2** the beginning of a new or distinctive period: *the invention of nuclear weapons marked an epoch in the history of warfare* **3** *geol* a unit of time within a period during which a series of rocks is formed **epochal** *adj*
WORD ORIGIN Greek *epokhē* cessation

epoch-making *adj* very important or significant

eponymous (ip-**pon**-im-uss) *adj* **1** (of a person) being the person after whom a literary work, film, etc. is named: *the eponymous heroine in the film of Jane Eyre* **2** (of a literary work, film, etc.) named after its central character or creator: *The Stooges' eponymous debut album* **WORD ORIGIN** Greek *epōnumos* giving a significant name

epoxy *chem adj* **1** of or containing an oxygen atom joined to two different groups that are themselves joined to other groups **2** of or consisting of an epoxy resin ▷ *n, pl* **epoxies** **3** an epoxy resin **WORD ORIGIN** Greek *epi* upon + OXY(GEN)

epoxy resin *n* a tough resistant thermosetting synthetic resin, used in laminates and adhesives

EPROM *n computers* erasable programmable read-only memory: a storage device that can be reprogrammed to hold different data

Epsom salts *pl n* a medicinal preparation of hydrated magnesium sulphate, used to empty the bowels **WORD ORIGIN** after *Epsom*, a town in England

equable (**ek**-wab-bl) *adj* **1** even-tempered and reasonable **2** (of a climate) not varying much throughout the year, and neither very hot nor very cold **equably** *adv* **WORD ORIGIN** Latin *aequabilis*

equal *adj* **1** identical in size, quantity, degree, or intensity **2** having identical privileges, rights, or status **3** applying in the same way to all people or in all circumstances: *equal rights* **4** equal to having the necessary strength, ability, or means for: *she was equal to any test the corporation put to her* ▷ *n* **5** a person or thing equal to another ▷ *vb* **equalling, equalled** *or US* **equaling, equaled** **6** to be equal to; match **7** to make or do something equal to: *he has equalled his world record in the men's 100 metres* **equally** *adv* **WORD ORIGIN** Latin *aequalis*

⌇ USAGE
⌇ The use of *more equal* as in *from now on*
⌇ *their relationship will be a more equal one* is
⌇ acceptable in modern English usage.
⌇ *Equally* is preferred to *equally as* in
⌇ sentences such as *reassuring the victims is*
⌇ *equally important*. *Just as* is preferred to
⌇ *equally as* in sentences such as *their*
⌇ *surprise was just as great as his*.

equality *n, pl* **-ties** the state of being equal

equalize *or* **-ise** *vb* **-izing, -ized** *or* **-ising, -ised** **1** to make equal or uniform **2** (in a sport) to reach the same score as one's opponent or opponents **equalization** *or* **-isation** *n* **equalizer** *or* **-iser** *n*

equal opportunity *n* the offering of employment or promotion equally to all, without discrimination as to sex, race, colour, etc.

equanimity *n* calmness of mind or temper; composure **WORD ORIGIN** Latin *aequus* even + *animus* mind, spirit

equate *vb* **equating, equated** **1** to make or regard as equivalent **2** *maths* to form an equation from **equatable** *adj*

equation *n* **1** a mathematical statement that two expressions are equal **2** a situation or problem in which a number of different factors need to be considered: *this plan leaves human nature out of the equation* **3** the act of equating **4** *chem* a representation of a chemical reaction using symbols of the elements

equator *n* an imaginary circle around the earth at an equal distance from the North Pole and the South Pole **WORD ORIGIN** Medieval Latin (*circulus*) *aequator* (*diei et noctis*) (circle) that equalizes (the day and night)

equatorial *adj* of, like, or existing at or near the equator

equerry (**ek**-kwer-ee) *n, pl* **-ries** *Brit* an officer of the royal household who acts as a personal attendant to a member of the royal family **WORD ORIGIN** Old French *escuirie* group of squires

equestrian *adj* **1** of or relating to horses and riding **2** on horseback: *an equestrian statue of the Queen* **equestrianism** *n* **WORD ORIGIN** Latin *equus* horse

equidistant *adj* equally distant

equilateral *adj* **1** having all sides of equal length ▷ *n* **2** a geometric figure having all sides of equal length

equilibrium *n, pl* **-ria** **1** a stable condition in which forces cancel one another **2** a state of mental and emotional balance; composure **WORD ORIGIN** Latin *aequi-* equal + *libra* balance

equine *adj* of or like a horse **WORD ORIGIN** Latin *equus* horse

equinoctial *adj* **1** relating to or occurring at an equinox ▷ *n* **2** a storm at or near an equinox

equinox *n* either of the two occasions when day and night are of equal length, around March 21 and September 23 **WORD ORIGIN** Latin *aequi-* equal + *nox* night

equip *vb* **equipping, equipped** **1** to provide with supplies, components, etc.: *the car comes equipped with a catalytic converter* **2** to provide with abilities, understanding, etc.: *stress is something we are all equipped to cope with* **WORD ORIGIN** Old French *eschiper* to fit out (a ship)

equipment *n* **1** a set of tools or devices used for a particular purpose: *communications equipment* **2** an act of equipping

equipoise *n* the state of being perfectly balanced; equilibrium

equitable *adj* fair and reasonable **equitably** *adv*

equitation *n* the study of riding and horsemanship **WORD ORIGIN** Latin *equitare* to ride

equities *pl n* same as **ordinary shares**

equity *n, pl* **-ties** **1** the quality of being impartial; fairness **2** *law* a system of using principles of natural justice and fair conduct to reach a judgment when common law is inadequate or inappropriate **3** the difference in value between a person's debts and the value of the property on which they are secured: *negative equity*

WORD ORIGIN Latin *aequus* level, equal

Equity *n Brit, Austral, & NZ* the actors' trade union

equivalent *n* **1** something that has the same use or function as something else: *Denmark's equivalent to Silicon Valley* ▷ *adj* **2** equal in value, quantity, significance, etc. **3** having the same or a similar effect or meaning **equivalence** *n* **WORD ORIGIN** Latin *aequi-* equal + *valere* to be worth

equivocal *adj* **1** capable of varying interpretations; ambiguous **2** deliberately misleading or vague **3** of doubtful character or sincerity: *the party's commitment to genuine reform is equivocal* **equivocally** *adv* **WORD ORIGIN** Latin *aequi-* equal + *vox* voice

equivocate *vb* **-cating, -cated** to use vague or ambiguous language in order to deceive someone or to avoid telling the truth **equivocation** *n* **equivocator** *n*

er *interj* a sound made when hesitating in speech

Er *chem* erbium

ER Queen Elizabeth **WORD ORIGIN** Latin *Elizabeth Regina*

era *n* **1** a period of time considered as distinctive; epoch **2** an extended period of time measured from a fixed point: *the Communist era* **3** *geol* a major division of time **WORD ORIGIN** Latin *aera* counters, pieces of brass money

eradicate *vb* **-cating, -cated** to destroy or get rid of completely: *measures to eradicate racism* **eradicable** *adj* **eradication** *n* **eradicator** *n* **WORD ORIGIN** Latin *e-* out + *radix* root

erase *vb* **erasing, erased** **1** to destroy all traces of: *he could not erase the memory of his earlier defeat* **2** to rub or wipe out (something written) **3** to remove sound or information from (a magnetic tape or disk) **erasable** *adj* **WORD ORIGIN** Latin *e-* out + *radere* to scrape

eraser *n* an object, such as a piece of rubber, for erasing something written

erasure *n* **1** an erasing **2** the place or mark where something has been erased

Erato *n Greek myth* the Muse of love poetry

erbium *n chem* a soft silvery-white element of the lanthanide series of metals. Symbol: Er **WORD ORIGIN** after *Ytterby*, Sweden

ere *conj, prep poetic* before **WORD ORIGIN** Old English *ǣr*

e-reader *n* a hand-held device for displaying e-books

erect *vb* **1** to build **2** to raise to an upright position **3** to found or form: *the caricature of socialism erected by Lenin* ▷ *adj* **4** upright in posture or position **5** *physiol* (of the penis, clitoris, or nipples) firm or rigid after swelling with blood, esp. as a result of sexual excitement **erection** *n* **WORD ORIGIN** Latin *erigere* to set up

erectile *adj physiol* (of an organ, such as the penis) capable of becoming erect

eremite (**air**-rim-mite) *n* a Christian hermit **WORD ORIGIN** Greek *erēmos* lonely

SCRABBLE
Three-Letter Words, part 3
EEN–GOV

EEN Scots form of eye
EFF say the word 'fuck'
EFS plural form of ef
EFT newt
EGG oval or round object laid by female birds
EGO conscious mind of an individual
EHS plural form of eh
EIK Scots form of eke
EKE increase, enlarge, or lengthen
ELD old age
ELF small mischievous fairy
ELK large deer of N Europe and Asia
ELL unit of length equal to approximately 45 inches
ELM tree with serrated leaves
ELS plural form of el
ELT young female pig
EME uncle
EMO type of music
EMS plural form of em
EMU large flightless bird
END come to a finish
ENE variant of even
ENG phonetics symbol
ENS existence in the most general abstract sense
EON long period of time
ERA period of time
ERE before
ERF plot of land for building purposes
ERG unit of work or energy
ERK aircraftman
ERN archaic variant of earn
ERR make a mistake
ERS bitter vetch
ESS the letter S
EST treatment that helps people achieve psychological growth
ETA 7th Greek letter

ETH character of the runic alphabet
EUK itch
EVE evening or day before an event
EVO evening
EWE female sheep
EWK itch
EWT archaic form of newt
EXO excellent
EYE organ of sight
FAA Scots word for fall
FAB excellent
FAD short-lived fashion
FAE Scots word for from
FAG slang word for cigarette
FAH musical term
FAN object used to create a current of air
FAP drunk
FAR at, to, or from a great distance
FAS plural form of fa
FAT having excess flesh on the body
FAW gypsy
FAX electronic system for sending documents
FAY fairy or sprite
FED FBI agent
FEE charge
FEG segment from an orange
FEH Hebrew coin
FEM feminine
FEN flat marshy land
FER same as far
FES plural form of fe
FET fetch
FEU right of use of land
FEW not many
FEY whimsically strange
FEZ brimless tasselled cap
FIB trivial lie
FID spike for separating strands of rope

FIE exclamation of disapproval
FIG soft pear-shaped fruit
FIL Shakespearean word for the shaft of a vehicle
FIN the organs of locomotion in fish
FIR tree
FIT be appropriate for
FIX make or become firm, stable, or secure
FIZ make a hissing sound
FLU viral infection
FLY move through the air on wings
FOB short watch chain
FOE enemy, opponent
FOG mass of condensed water vapour in the air
FOH expression of disgust
FON fool
FOP man excessively concerned with fashion
FOR in the place of, in favour of
FOU Scots word for full
FOX reddish-brown bushy-tailed animal
FOY loyalty
FRA brother: a title given to an Italian monk or friar
FRO back or from
FRY cook in fat or oil
FUB put off, fob
FUD rabbit's tail
FUG hot stale atmosphere
FUM mythological phoenix
FUN enjoyment or amusement
FUR soft hair of a mammal
GAB talk or chatter
GAD go about in search of pleasure
GAE Scots word for go
GAG choke or retch
GAL girl

GAM school of whales
GAN archaic word for begin
GAP break or opening
GAR pike-like fish
GAS airlike substance that is not liquid or solid
GAT pistol or revolver
GAU district set up by the Nazi Party
GAY homosexual
GED Scots word for pike
GEE mild exclamation of surprise
GEL jelly-like substance
GEM precious stone or jewel
GEN information
GEO small fjord or gully
GET obtain or receive
GEY intensifier
GHI clarified butter
GIB metal wedge
GID disease of sheep
GIE Scots word for give
GIF obsolete word for if
GIG single performance by musicians
GIN spirit flavoured with juniper berries
GIO gully, creek
GIP pain, torture
GIS plural form of gi
GIT contemptible person
GJU musical instrument
GNU ox-like antelope
GOA Tibetan gazelle
GOB lump of a soft substance
GOD worshipped spirit
GOE Spenserian word for go
GON geometrical grade
GOO sticky substance
GOR God!
GOS plural form of go
GOT part of the verb to get
GOV short for governor

ergo *conj* therefore
WORD ORIGIN Latin

ergonomic *adj* **1** designed to minimize effort and discomfort **2** of or relating to ergonomics

ergonomics *n* the study of the relationship between workers and their environment
WORD ORIGIN Greek *ergon* work + (ECO) NOMICS

ergot *n* **1** a disease of a cereal, such as rye, caused by a fungus **2** the dried fungus used in medicine
WORD ORIGIN French: spur (of a cock)

Erin *n archaic or poetic* Ireland
WORD ORIGIN Irish Gaelic *Éirinn*

ermine *n, pl* **-mines** or **-mine** **1** the stoat in northern regions, where it has a white winter coat **2** the fur of this animal, used to trim state robes of judges, nobles, etc.
WORD ORIGIN Medieval Latin *Armenius (mus)* Armenian (mouse)

erne or **ern** *n* a fish-eating sea eagle
WORD ORIGIN Old English *earn*

Ernie *n* (in Britain) a machine that randomly selects winning numbers of Premium Bonds
WORD ORIGIN acronym of Electronic Random Number Indicator Equipment

erode *vb* **eroding, eroded** **1** to wear down or away **2** to deteriorate or cause to deteriorate
WORD ORIGIN Latin *e-* away + *rodere* to gnaw

erogenous (ir-**roj**-in-uss) *adj* sensitive to sexual stimulation: *an erogenous zone*
WORD ORIGIN Greek *erōs* love + *-genēs* born

erosion *n* **1** the wearing away of rocks or soil by the action of water, ice, or wind **2** a gradual lessening or reduction: *an erosion of national sovereignty* **erosive** or **erosional** *adj*

erotic *adj* of, concerning, or arousing sexual desire or giving sexual pleasure **erotically** *adv*
WORD ORIGIN Greek *erōs* love

erotica *pl n* explicitly sexual literature or art

eroticism *n* **1** erotic quality or nature **2** the use of sexually arousing symbolism in literature or art **3** sexual excitement or desire

err *vb* **1** to make a mistake **2** to sin
WORD ORIGIN Latin *errare*

errand *n* **1** a short trip to get or do something for someone **2 run an errand** to make such a trip
WORD ORIGIN Old English *ǣrende*

errant *adj* **1** behaving in a way considered to be unacceptable: *an errant schoolboy* **2** old-fashioned or literary wandering in search of adventure: *a knight errant* **errantry** *n*
WORD ORIGIN Latin *iter* journey

erratic *adj* **1** irregular or unpredictable: *his increasingly erratic behaviour* ▷ *n* **2** *geol* a rock that has been transported by glacial action **erratically** *adv*
WORD ORIGIN Latin *errare* to wander

erratum *n, pl* **-ta** an error in writing or printing
WORD ORIGIN Latin

erroneous *adj* based on or containing an error or errors; incorrect **erroneously** *adv*

error *n* **1** a mistake, inaccuracy, or misjudgment **2** the act or state of being wrong or making a misjudgment: *the plane was shot down in error* **3** the amount by which the actual value of a quantity might differ from an estimate: *a 3% margin of error*
WORD ORIGIN Latin

ersatz (**air**-zats) *adj* made in imitation of something more expensive: *ersatz coffee*
WORD ORIGIN German *ersetzen* to substitute

Erse *n, adj* Irish Gaelic
WORD ORIGIN Lowland Scots *Erisch* Irish

erstwhile *adj* **1** former ▷ *adv* **2** *archaic* formerly

eruct or **eructate** *vb formal* to belch **eructation** *n*
WORD ORIGIN Latin *e-* out + *ructare* to belch

erudite (**air**-rude-ite) *adj* having or showing great academic knowledge **erudition** *n*
WORD ORIGIN Latin *erudire* to polish

erupt *vb* **1** (of a volcano) to throw out molten lava, ash, and steam in a sudden and violent way **2** to burst forth suddenly and violently: *riots erupted across the country* **3** (of a group of people) to suddenly become angry and aggressive: *the meeting erupted in fury* **4** (of a blemish) to appear on the skin **eruptive** *adj* **eruption** *n*
WORD ORIGIN Latin *e-* out + *rumpere* to burst

erysipelas (air-riss-**sip**-ill-ass) *n* an acute disease of the skin, with fever and raised purplish patches
WORD ORIGIN Greek *erusi-* red + *-pelas* skin

erythrocyte (ir-**rith**-roe-site) *n* a red blood cell that transports oxygen through the body
WORD ORIGIN Greek *eruthros* red + *kutos* hollow vessel

Es *chem* einsteinium

escalate *vb* **-lating, -lated** to increase or be increased in size, seriousness, or intensity **escalation** *n*
WORD ORIGIN from *escalator*

escalator *n* a moving staircase consisting of stair treads fixed to a conveyor belt
WORD ORIGIN Latin *scala* ladder

escalope (**ess**-kal-lop) *n* a thin slice of meat, usually veal
WORD ORIGIN Old French: shell

escapade *n* a mischievous act or adventure
WORD ORIGIN French

escape *vb* **-caping, -caped** **1** to get away or break free from (confinement) **2** to manage to avoid (something dangerous, unpleasant, or difficult) **3** (of gases, liquids, etc.) to leak gradually **4** to elude; be forgotten by: *those little round cakes whose name escapes me* ▷ *n* **5** the act of escaping or state of having escaped **6** a way of avoiding something difficult, dangerous, or unpleasant: *his frequent illnesses provided an escape from intolerable stress* **7** a means of relaxation or relief: *he found temporary escape through the local cinema* **8** a leakage of gas or liquid

WORD ORIGIN Late Latin *e-* out + *cappa* cloak

escapee *n* a person who has escaped from prison

escapement *n* the mechanism in a clock or watch which connects the hands to the pendulum or balance

escape road *n* a small road leading off a steep hill, into which a car can be driven if the brakes fail

escape velocity *n* the minimum velocity necessary for a particle, space vehicle, etc. to escape from the gravitational field of the earth or other celestial body

escapism *n* an inclination to retreat from unpleasant reality, for example through fantasy **escapist** *n, adj*

escapologist *n* an entertainer who specializes in freeing himself or herself from chains, ropes, etc. **escapology** *n*

escarpment *n* the long continuous steep face of a ridge or mountain
WORD ORIGIN French *escarpement*

eschatology (ess-cat-**tol**-a-jee) *n* the branch of theology concerned with the end of the world **eschatological** *adj*
WORD ORIGIN Greek *eskhatos* last

escheat (iss-**cheat**) *law n* **1** formerly, the return of property to the state in the absence of legal heirs **2** the property so reverting ▷ *vb* **3** to obtain (land) by escheat
WORD ORIGIN Old French *escheoir* to fall to the lot of

eschew (iss-**chew**) *vb* to avoid doing or being involved in (something disliked or harmful) **eschewal** *n*
WORD ORIGIN Old French *eschiver*

escort *n* **1** people or vehicles accompanying another to protect or guard them **2** a person who accompanies someone of the opposite sex on a social occasion ▷ *vb* **3** to act as an escort to
WORD ORIGIN French *escorte*

escritoire (ess-kree-**twahr**) *n* a writing desk with compartments and drawers
WORD ORIGIN Medieval Latin *scriptorium* writing room in a monastery

escudo (ess-**kew**-doe) *n, pl* **-dos** a former monetary unit of Portugal
WORD ORIGIN Spanish: shield

esculent *formal adj* **1** edible ▷ *n* **2** any edible substance
WORD ORIGIN Latin *esculentus* good to eat

escutcheon *n* **1** a shield displaying a coat of arms **2 blot on one's escutcheon** a stain on one's honour
WORD ORIGIN Latin *scutum* shield

Eskimo *n* **1** *pl* **-mos** or **-mo** a member of a group of peoples who live in N Canada, Greenland, Alaska, and E Siberia **2** the language of these peoples ▷ *adj* **3** of the Eskimos
WORD ORIGIN Algonquian *esquimawes*

USAGE
The peoples native to the area from western Greenland to NW Canada prefer to be called *Inuit* rather than *Eskimo*.

ESN *Brit* educationally subnormal; formerly used to designate a child who needs special schooling

esoteric (ee-so-**ter**-rik) *adj* understood by only a small number of people, esp. because they have special knowledge **esoterically** *adv*
WORD ORIGIN Greek *esōterō* inner

ESP extrasensory perception

esp. especially

espadrille (**ess**-pad-drill) *n* a light canvas shoe with a braided cord sole
WORD ORIGIN French

espalier (ess-**pal**-yer) *n* **1** a shrub or fruit tree trained to grow flat **2** the trellis on which such plants are grown
WORD ORIGIN French

esparto or **esparto grass** *n, pl* **-tos** any of various grasses of S Europe and N Africa, used to make ropes, mats, etc.
WORD ORIGIN Greek *spartos* a kind of rush

especial *adj formal* same as **special**
WORD ORIGIN Latin *specialis* individual

≡ USAGE
≡ *Especial* and *especially* have a more
≡ limited use than *special* and *specially*.
≡ *Special* is preferred to *especial* when the
≡ sense is one of being out of the
≡ ordinary: *a special lesson; he has been*
≡ *specially trained*. *Special* is also used when
≡ something is referred to as being for a
≡ particular purpose: *the word was specially*
≡ *underlined for you*. Where an idea of
≡ pre-eminence or individuality is
≡ involved, either *especial* or *special* may
≡ be used: *he is my especial* (or *special*) *friend*;
≡ *he is especially* (or *specially*) *good at his job*.
≡ In informal English, however, *special* is
≡ usually preferred in all contexts.

especially *adv* **1** particularly: *people are dying, especially children and babies* **2** more than usually: *an especially virulent disease*

Esperanto *n* an international artificial language **Esperantist** *n, adj*
WORD ORIGIN literally: the one who hopes, pseudonym of Dr L. L. Zamenhof, its Polish inventor

espionage (**ess**-pyon-ahz) *n* **1** the use of spies to obtain secret information, esp. by governments **2** the act of spying
WORD ORIGIN French *espionnage*

esplanade *n* a long open level stretch of ground, esp. beside the seashore or in front of a fortified place
WORD ORIGIN French

espousal *n* **1** adoption or support: *his espousal of the free market* **2** old-fashioned a marriage or engagement ceremony

espouse *vb* **-pousing, -poused 1** to adopt or give support to (a cause, ideal, etc.) **2** old-fashioned (esp. of a man) to marry
WORD ORIGIN Latin *sponsare*

espresso *n, pl* **-sos** coffee made by forcing steam or boiling water through ground coffee
WORD ORIGIN Italian: pressed

esprit (ess-**pree**) *n* spirit, liveliness, or wit
WORD ORIGIN French

esprit de corps (de **kore**) *n* consciousness of and pride in belonging to a particular group
WORD ORIGIN French

espy *vb* **espies, espying, espied** to catch sight of
WORD ORIGIN Old French *espier*

Esq. esquire

esquire *n* **1** *chiefly Brit* a title of respect placed after a man's name and usually shortened to *Esq.*: *I Davies, Esquire* **2** (in medieval times) the attendant of a knight
WORD ORIGIN Late Latin *scutarius* shield bearer

essay *n* **1** a short literary composition on a single subject **2** a short piece of writing on a subject done as an exercise by a student **3** an attempt ▷ *vb* **4** *formal* to attempt: *he essayed a faint smile*
WORD ORIGIN Old French *essai* an attempt

essayist *n* a person who writes essays

essence *n* **1** the most important and distinctive feature of something, which determines its identity **2** a concentrated liquid used to flavour food **3 in essence** essentially **4 of the essence** vitally important
WORD ORIGIN Latin *esse* to be

essential *adj* **1** vitally important; absolutely necessary: *it is essential to get this finished on time* **2** basic or fundamental: *she translated the essential points of the lecture into English* ▷ *n* **3** something fundamental or indispensable **essentially** *adv*

essential oil *n* any of various volatile oils in plants, which have the odour or flavour of the plant from which they are extracted

EST 1 Eastern Standard Time **2** electric-shock treatment

est. 1 established **2** estimate(d)

establish *vb* **1** to create or set up (an organization, link, etc.): *the regime wants to establish better relations with neighbouring countries* **2** to become firmly associated with a particular activity or reputation: *the play that established him as a major dramatist* **3** to prove: *a test to establish if your baby has any chromosomal disorder* **4** to cause (a principle) to be accepted: *our study establishes the case for further research*
WORD ORIGIN Latin *stabilis* firm, stable

Established Church *n* a church, such as the Church of England, that is recognized as the official church of a country

establishment *n* **1** the act of establishing or state of being established **2 a** a business organization or other institution **b** a place of business **3** the people employed by an organization

Establishment *n* **the Establishment** a group of people having authority within a society: usually seen as conservative

estate *n* **1** a large piece of landed property, esp. in the country **2** *Austral & Brit* a large area of land with houses or factories built on it: *an industrial estate* **3** *law* property or possessions, esp. of a deceased person **4** *history* any of the orders or classes making up a society
WORD ORIGIN Latin *status* condition

estate agent *n* *Austral & Brit* a person whose job is to help people buy and sell houses and other property

estate car *n* *Brit* a car which has a long body with a door at the back end and luggage space behind the rear seats

estate duty *n* a former name for **inheritance tax**

esteem *n* **1** admiration and respect ▷ *vb* **2** to have great respect or high regard for (someone) **3** *formal* to judge or consider: *I should esteem it a kindness* **esteemed** *adj*
WORD ORIGIN Latin *aestimare* to assess the worth of

ester *n* *chem* a compound produced by the reaction between an acid and an alcohol
WORD ORIGIN German

estimable *adj* worthy of respect

estimate *vb* **-mating, -mated 1** to form an approximate idea of (size, cost, etc.); calculate roughly **2** to form an opinion about; judge **3** to submit an approximate price for a job to a prospective client ▷ *n* **4** an approximate calculation **5** a statement of the likely charge for certain work **6** an opinion **estimator** *n*
WORD ORIGIN Latin *aestimare* to assess the worth of

estimation *n* **1** a considered opinion; judgment: *overall, he went up in my estimation* **2** the act of estimating

Estonian *adj* **1** from Estonia ▷ *n* **2** a person from Estonia

estranged *adj* **1** no longer living with one's husband or wife: *his estranged wife* **2** having quarrelled and lost touch with one's family or friends: *I am estranged from my son* **estrangement** *n*
WORD ORIGIN from Latin *extraneus* foreign

estuary *n, pl* **-aries** the widening channel of a river where it nears the sea **estuarine** *adj*
WORD ORIGIN Latin *aestus* tide

ET *Brit* Employment Training: a government scheme offering training in technology and business skills for unemployed people

ETA estimated time of arrival

e-tail (**ee**-tail) *n* retail conducted via the internet

et al. 1 and elsewhere
WORD ORIGIN Latin *et alibi* **2** and others
WORD ORIGIN Latin *et alii*

etc. et cetera

et cetera or **etcetera** (et **set**-ra) *adv* **1** and the rest; and others; or the like **2** and so forth
WORD ORIGIN Latin *et* and + *cetera* the other (things)

≡ USAGE
≡ It is unnecessary to use *and* before *etc.*
≡ as *etc.* (*et cetera*) already means *and other*
≡ *things*. The repetition of *etc.* as in *he*
≡ *brought paper, ink, notebooks, etc. etc.* is
≡ avoided except in informal contexts.

etceteras *pl n* miscellaneous extra things or people

etch *vb* **1** to wear away the surface of a metal, glass, etc. by the action of an acid **2** to cut a design or pattern into a printing plate with acid **3** to imprint vividly: *the scene is etched on my mind* **etcher** *n*
WORD ORIGIN Dutch *etsen*

etching *n* **1** the art or process of preparing or printing etched designs **2** a print made from an etched plate

eternal *adj* **1** without beginning or end; lasting for ever **2** unchanged by time: *eternal truths* **3** seemingly unceasing: *his eternal whingeing* **4** of or like God or a god: *the Eternal Buddha* **eternally** *adv*
WORD ORIGIN Latin *aeternus*

eternal triangle *n* an emotional or sexual relationship in which there are conflicts between a man and two women or a woman and two men

eternity *n, pl* **-ties 1** endless or infinite time **2** a seemingly endless period of time: *it seemed an eternity before he could feel his heart beating again* **3** the timeless existence after death **4** the state of being eternal

eternity ring *n* a ring given as a token of lasting affection, esp. one set all around with stones to symbolize continuity

ethane *n* a flammable gaseous alkane obtained from natural gas and petroleum: used as a fuel
WORD ORIGIN from *ethyl*

ethanoic acid *n* same as **acetic acid**

ethanol *n* same as **alcohol** (sense 1)

ethene *n* same as **ethylene**

ether *n* **1** a colourless sweet-smelling liquid used as a solvent and anaesthetic **2** the substance formerly believed to fill all space and to transmit electromagnetic waves **3** the upper regions of the atmosphere; clear sky. Also (for senses 2 and 3): **aether**
WORD ORIGIN Greek *aithein* to burn

ethereal (eth-**eer**-ee-al) *adj* **1** extremely delicate or refined **2** heavenly or spiritual **ethereally** *adv*
WORD ORIGIN Greek *aithēr* ether

ethic *n* a moral principle or set of moral values held by an individual or group
WORD ORIGIN Greek *ēthos* custom

ethical *adj* **1** of or based on a system of moral beliefs about right and wrong **2** in accordance with principles of professional conduct **3** of or relating to ethics **ethically** *adv*

ethics *pl n* **1** a code of behaviour, esp. of a particular group, profession, or individual: *business ethics* **2** the moral fitness of a decision, course of action, etc. ▷ *n* **3** the study of the moral value of human conduct

Ethiopian *adj* **1** of Ethiopia ▷ *n* **2** a person from Ethiopia

ethnic *or* **ethnical** *adj* **1** of or relating to a human group with racial, religious, and linguistic characteristics in common **2** characteristic of another culture, esp. a peasant one: *ethnic foodstuffs* **ethnically** *adv*
WORD ORIGIN Greek *ethnos* race

ethnic cleansing *n* the practice, by the dominant ethnic group in an area, of removing other ethnic groups by expulsion or extermination

ethnocentric *adj* of or relating to the belief that one's own nation, culture, or group is intrinsically superior **ethnocentricity** *n*

ethnology *n* the branch of anthropology that deals with races and peoples and their relations to one another **ethnological** *adj* **ethnologist** *n*

ethos (**eeth**-oss) *n* the distinctive spirit and attitudes of a people, culture, etc.
WORD ORIGIN Greek

ethyl (**eth**-ill) *adj* of, consisting of, or containing the monovalent group C_2H_5-
WORD ORIGIN from *ether*

ethyl alcohol *n* same as **alcohol** (sense 1)

ethylene *or* **ethene** *n* a colourless flammable gaseous alkene used to make polythene and other chemicals

etiolate (ee-tee-oh-late) *vb* **-lating, -lated 1** *formal* to become or cause to become weak **2** *bot* to make a green plant paler through lack of sunlight **etiolation** *n*
WORD ORIGIN French *étioler* to make pale

etiology *n, pl* **-gies 1** the study of causation **2** the study of the cause of diseases **etiological** *adj*
WORD ORIGIN Greek *aitia* cause + -LOGY

etiquette *n* **1** the customs or rules of behaviour regarded as correct in social life **2** a conventional code of practice in certain professions
WORD ORIGIN French

étude (ay-tewd) *n music* a short composition for a solo instrument, esp. intended to be played as an exercise or to demonstrate virtuosity
WORD ORIGIN French: study

etymology *n, pl* **-gies 1** the study of the sources and development of words **2** an account of the source and development of a word **etymological** *adj* **etymologist** *n*
WORD ORIGIN Greek *etumon* basic meaning + -LOGY

Eu *chem* europium

EU European Union

eucalyptus *or* **eucalypt** *n, pl* **-lyptuses, -lyptus** *or* **-lypts** any of a mostly Australian genus of trees, widely cultivated for timber and gum, and for the medicinal oil in their leaves (**eucalyptus oil**)
WORD ORIGIN Greek *eu-* well + *kaluptos* covered

Eucharist (**yew**-kar-ist) *n* **1** the Christian sacrament commemorating Christ's Last Supper by the consecration of bread and wine **2** the consecrated elements of bread and wine **Eucharistic** *adj*
WORD ORIGIN Greek *eukharistos* thankful

Euclidean *or* **Euclidian** (yew-**klid**-ee-an) *adj* denoting a system of geometry based on the rules of Euclid, 3rd-century BC Greek mathematician

eugenics (yew-**jen**-iks) *n* the study of methods of improving the human race, esp. by selective breeding **eugenic** *adj* **eugenically** *adv* **eugenicist** *n*
WORD ORIGIN Greek *eugenēs* well-born

eulogize *or* **-gise** *vb* **-gizing, -gized** *or* **-gising, -gised** to praise (a person or thing) highly in speech or writing **eulogistic** *adj*

eulogy *n, pl* **-gies 1** a speech or piece of writing praising a person or thing, esp. a person who has recently died **2** high praise
WORD ORIGIN Greek *eulogia* praise
≡ USAGE
≡ Avoid confusion with **elegy**.

eunuch *n* a man who has been castrated, esp. (formerly) a guard in a harem
WORD ORIGIN Greek *eunoukhos* bedchamber attendant

euphemism *n* an inoffensive word or phrase substituted for one considered offensive or upsetting, such as *departed* for *dead* **euphemistic** *adj* **euphemistically** *adv*
WORD ORIGIN Greek *eu-* well + *phēmē* speech

euphonious *adj* pleasing to the ear

euphonium *n* a brass musical instrument with four valves, resembling a small tuba
WORD ORIGIN *euph(ony + harm)onium*

euphony *n, pl* **-nies** a pleasing sound, esp. in speech
WORD ORIGIN Greek *eu-* well + *phōnē* voice

euphoria *n* a feeling of great but often unjustified or exaggerated happiness **euphoric** *adj*
WORD ORIGIN Greek *eu-* well + *pherein* to bear

Eur. **1** Europe **2** European

Eurasian *adj* **1** of Europe and Asia **2** of mixed European and Asian descent ▷ *n* **3** a person of mixed European and Asian descent

eureka (yew-**reek**-a) *interj* an exclamation of triumph on discovering or solving something
WORD ORIGIN Greek *heurēka* I have found (it)

euro *n, pl* **euros** the unit of the European Union's single currency

Euro- *combining form* Europe or European

Eurocentric *adj* chiefly concerned with Europe and European culture: *a Eurocentric view of British history*

Euroland *or* **Eurozone** *n* the geographical area containing the countries that have joined the European single currency

European *adj* **1** of Europe ▷ *n* **2** a person from Europe **3** a person of European descent **4** an advocate of closer links between the countries of Europe, esp. those in the European Union **Europeanism** *n*

European Community *or* **European Economic Community** *n* former names for **European Union**

European Union *n* an economic organization of W European states, which have some shared monetary, social, and political goals

Europhile (**you**-roh-file) *n* **1** a person who admires Europe or the European Union ▷ *adj* **2** marked by admiration of Europe or the European Union

europium *n chem* a silvery-white element of the lanthanide series. Symbol: Eu
WORD ORIGIN after *Europe*

Euro-sceptic *n* **1** (in Britain) a person who is opposed to closer links with the European Union ▷ *adj* **2** (in Britain) opposing closer links with the European Union: *three Euro-sceptic MPs*

Eurozone *n* same as **Euroland**

Eustachian tube *n* a tube that connects the middle ear with the

Words from Shakespeare
part 10

endure *v* to allow or to permit
and will endure
Our setting down before't. *Macbeth* 5.4

enfranchise *v* to set something free
Do this or this;
Take in that kingdom and enfranchise that;
Perform't, or else we damn thee.
Anthony and Cleopatra 1.1

engage *v* to pledge or to promise
This to be true I do engage my life *As You Like It* 5.4

engaol *v* to lock up or put in prison
Within my mouth you have engaoled my tongue
Richard II 1.3

engine *n* a plot, device or a machine
their promises, enticements, oaths, tokens, and all
these engines, of lust, are not the things they go
under *All's Well That Ends Well* 3.5

englut *v* to swallow up or eat whole
For certainly thou art so near the gulf,
Thou needs must be englutted. *Henry V* 4.3

enjoined *adj* joined together for the same reason
Of enjoined penitents
There's four or five *All's Well That Ends Well* 3.5

entertain *v* to welcome or receive
Approach, rich Ceres, her to entertain.
The Tempest 4.1

entertain *v* to cherish, hold in high regard or to respect
and I quake,
Lest thou a feverous life shouldst entertain
And six or seven winters more respect
Than a perpetual honour. *Measure for Measure* 3.1

envious *adj* spiteful or vindictive
he shall appear to the envious a scholar
Measure for Measure 3.2

ere *prep* before
ere this I should ha' fatted all the region kites
Hamlet 2.2

err *v* to go astray, to make a mistake
And as he errs, doting on Hermia's eyes
A Midsummer Night's Dream 1.1

erst *adv* once or before
that erst brought sweetly forth
The freckled cowslip, *Henry V* 5.2

eschew *v* to deliberately avoid doing something
What cannot be eschewed must be embraced
The Merry Wives of Windsor 5.5

escote *v* to pay for, support
How are they escoted? *Hamlet* 2.2

estimable *adj* appreciative
I could not with such estimable wonder over-far
believe that *Twelfth Night* 2.1

extenuate *v* to lessen
Which by no means we may extenuate
A Midsummer Night's Dream 1.1

fain *adv* gladly or willingly
I would fain prove so *Hamlet* 2.2

fall *n* (in a voice or music) going higher and lower
and so die
That strain again! it had a dying fall:
Twelfth Night 1.1

false *adj* treacherous
this is counter, you false Danish dogs! *Hamlet* 4.5

fare *v* to get on or manage
I fare well *The Taming of the Shrew* Introduction 2

feign *v* to make up, pretend or fake
It is the more like to be feigned *Twelfth Night* 1.5

fie *int* an exclamation of disgust
Fie, that you'll say so! *Twelfth Night* 1.3

figure *v* to symbolize or look like
Wings and no eyes, figure unheedy haste
A Midsummer Night's Dream 1.1

pharynx and equalizes the pressure between the two sides of the eardrum **WORD ORIGIN** after Bartolomeo *Eustachio*, anatomist

Euterpe *n Greek myth* the Muse of lyric poetry

euthanasia *n* the act of killing someone painlessly, esp. to relieve suffering from an incurable illness **WORD ORIGIN** Greek: easy death

eV electronvolt

evacuate *vb* -ating, -ated **1** to send away from a dangerous place to a safe place: *200 people were evacuated from their homes because of the floods* **2** to empty (a place) of people because it has become dangerous: *the entire street was evacuated until the fire was put out* **3** *physiol* to discharge waste from the body evacuation *n* evacuee *n* **WORD ORIGIN** Latin *evacuare* to empty

evade *vb* evading, evaded **1** to get away from or avoid (imprisonment, captors, etc.) **2** to get around, shirk, or dodge (the law, a duty, etc.) **3** to avoid answering (a question) **WORD ORIGIN** Latin *evadere* to go forth

evaluate *vb* -ating, -ated to find or judge the quality or value of something evaluation *n* **WORD ORIGIN** French *évaluer*

evanesce *vb* -nescing, -nesced *formal* to fade gradually from sight **WORD ORIGIN** Latin *evanescere*

evanescent *adj formal* quickly fading away; ephemeral or transitory evanescence *n*

evangelical *Christianity adj* **1** of or following from the Gospels **2** of certain Protestant sects which emphasize salvation through faith alone and a belief in the absolute authority of the Bible ▷ *n* **3** a member of an evangelical sect **4** displaying missionary zeal in promoting something evangelicalism *n* evangelically *adv* **WORD ORIGIN** Greek *evangelion* good news

evangelism *n* the practice of spreading the Christian gospel

evangelist *n* a preacher, sometimes itinerant evangelistic *adj*

Evangelist *n* any of the writers of the Gospels: Matthew, Mark, Luke, or John

evangelize *or* -lise *vb* -lizing, -lized *or* -lising, -lised to preach the Christian gospel (to) evangelization *or* -lisation *n*

evaporate *vb* -rating, -rated **1** to change from a liquid or solid to a vapour **2** to become less and less and finally disappear: *faith in the government evaporated rapidly after the election* evaporable *adj* evaporation *n* **WORD ORIGIN** Latin *e-* out + *vapor* steam

evaporated milk *n* thick unsweetened tinned milk from which some of the water has been removed

evasion *n* **1** the act of evading something, esp. a duty or responsibility, by cunning or illegal means: *tax evasion* **2** cunning or deception used to dodge a question, duty, etc.

evasive *adj* **1** seeking to evade; not straightforward: *an evasive answer* **2** avoiding or seeking to avoid trouble or difficulties: *evasive action* evasively *adv*

eve *n* **1** the evening or day before some special event **2** the period immediately before an event: *on the eve of the Second World War* **3** *poetic or old-fashioned* evening **WORD ORIGIN** variant of EVEN²

Eve *n Bible* the first woman, created by God from Adam's rib

even¹ *adj* **1** level and regular; flat **2** on the same level: *make sure the surfaces are even with one another* **3** regular and unvarying: *an even pace* **4** equally balanced between two sides **5** equal in number, quantity, etc. **6** (of a number) divisible by two **7** denoting alternatives, events, etc. that have an equal probability: *they have a more than even chance of winning the next election* **8** having scored the same number of points **9** even money *or* evens a bet in which the winnings are exactly the same as the amount staked **10** get even with *informal* to exact revenge on; settle accounts with ▷ *adv* **11** used to suggest that the content of a statement is unexpected or paradoxical: *it's chilly in Nova Scotia, even in August* **12** used to intensify a comparative adjective or adverb: *an even greater demand* **13** used to introduce a word that is stronger and more accurate than one already used: *a normal, even inevitable aspect of ageing* **14** used preceding a hypothesis to emphasize that whether or not the condition is fulfilled, the statement remains valid: *the remark didn't call for an answer even if he could have thought of one* **15** even so in spite of any assertion to the contrary; nevertheless **16** even though despite the fact that ▸ See also **even out, even up** > evenly *adv* evenness *n* **WORD ORIGIN** Old English *efen*

even² *n poetic or old-fashioned* **1** eve **2** evening **WORD ORIGIN** Old English *æfen*

even-handed *adj* fair; impartial

evening *n* **1** the latter part of the day, esp. from late afternoon until nightfall ▷ *adj* **2** of or in the evening: *the evening meal* **WORD ORIGIN** Old English *æfnung*

evening class *n Brit, Austral, & NZ* an educational class for adults, held during the evening

evening dress *n* clothes for a formal occasion during the evening

evening primrose *n* a plant with yellow flowers that open in the evening

evening star *n* a planet, usually Venus, seen shining brightly just after sunset

even out *vb* to make or become even, by the removal of bumps, inequalities, etc.

evensong *n Church of England* the daily evening service. Also called: **Evening Prayer**

event *n* **1** anything that takes place, esp. something important **2** a planned and organized occasion: *the wedding was one of the social events of the year* **3** any one contest in a sporting programme **4** in any event *or* at all events whatever happens **5** in the event when it came to the actual or final outcome: *in the event, neither of them turned up* **6** in the event of if (such a thing) happens **7** in the event that if it should happen that

WORD ORIGIN Latin *evenire* to happen

even-tempered *adj* calm and not easily angered

eventful *adj* full of exciting or important incidents

eventide *n archaic or poetic* evening

eventing *n Brit, Austral, & NZ* riding competitions (esp. **three-day events**), usually involving cross-country riding, jumping, and dressage

eventual *adj* happening or being achieved at the end of a situation or process: *the Fascists' eventual victory in the Spanish Civil War* eventually *adv*

eventuality *n, pl* -ties a possible occurrence or result: *I was utterly unprepared for such an eventuality*

even up *vb* to make or become equal

ever *adv* **1** at any time: *it was the fourth fastest time ever* **2** always: *ever present* **3** used to give emphasis: *tell him to put to sea as soon as ever he can* **4** ever so *or* ever such *informal chiefly Brit* used to give emphasis: *I'm ever so sorry* **WORD ORIGIN** Old English *æfre*

evergreen *adj* **1** (of certain trees and shrubs) bearing foliage throughout the year ▷ *n* **2** an evergreen tree or shrub

everlasting *adj* **1** never coming to an end; eternal **2** lasting so long or occurring so often as to become tedious everlastingly *adv*

evermore *adv* all time to come

every *adj* **1** each without exception: *they were winning every battle* **2** the greatest or best possible: *there is every reason to believe in the sincerity of their commitment* **3** each: *every 20 years* **4** every bit as *informal* just as: *she's every bit as clever as you* **5** every other each alternate: *every other month* **WORD ORIGIN** Old English *æfre* ever + *ælc* each

everybody *pron* every person; everyone
USAGE
See at **everyone**.

everyday *adj* **1** commonplace or usual **2** happening each day **3** suitable for or used on ordinary days

Everyman *n* the ordinary person; common man **WORD ORIGIN** after the central figure in a medieval morality play

everyone *pron* every person; everybody
USAGE
Everyone and *everybody* are interchangeable, as are *no one* and *nobody*, and *someone* and *somebody*. Care should be taken to distinguish between *everyone* and *someone* as single words and *every one* and *some one* as two words, the latter form correctly being used to refer to each individual person or thing in a particular group: *every one of them is wrong*.

everything *pron* **1** the whole; all things: *everything had been carefully packed* **2** the thing that is most important: *work was everything to her*

everywhere *adv* to or in all parts or places

evict *vb* to expel (someone) legally from his or her home or land eviction *n* **WORD ORIGIN** Latin *evincere* to vanquish utterly

evidence *n* **1** something which provides ground for belief or disbelief: *there is no evidence that depression is inherited* **2** *law* matter produced before a court of law in an attempt to prove or disprove a point in issue **3** in evidence on display; apparent ▷ *vb* -dencing, -denced **4** to show clearly; demonstrate: *you evidenced no talent for music*

evident *adj* easy to see or understand **evidently** *adv*
WORD ORIGIN Latin *videre* to see

evidential *adj* of, serving as, or based on evidence **evidentially** *adv*

evil *n* **1** a force or power that brings about wickedness and harm: *the battle between good and evil* **2** a wicked or morally wrong act or thing: *the evil of racism* ▷ *adj* **3** (of a person) deliberately causing great harm and misery; wicked: *an evil dictator* **4** (of an act, idea, etc.) causing great harm and misery; morally wrong: *what you did was deeply evil* **5** very unpleasant: *it was fascinating to see people vanish as if we had some very evil smell* **evilly** *adv*
WORD ORIGIN Old English *yfel*

evildoer *n* a person who does evil **evildoing** *n*

evil eye *n* the evil eye a look superstitiously supposed to have the power of inflicting harm

evince *vb* **evincing, evinced** *formal* to show or display (a quality or feeling) clearly: *a humility which he had never evinced in earlier days*
WORD ORIGIN Latin *evincere* to overcome
▤ USAGE
▤ *Evince* is sometimes wrongly used ▤ where *evoke* is meant: *the proposal evoked* ▤ (not *evinced*) *a storm of protest*.

eviscerate *vb* -ating, -ated to remove the internal organs of; disembowel **evisceration** *n*
WORD ORIGIN Latin *e-* out + *viscera* entrails

evocation *n* the act of evoking **evocative** *adj*

evoke *vb* **evoking, evoked** **1** to call or summon up (a memory or feeling) from the past **2** to provoke or bring about: *his sacking evoked a huge public protest*
WORD ORIGIN Latin *evocare* to call forth
▤ USAGE
▤ See at **evince** and **invoke**.

evolution *n* **1** *biol* a gradual change in the characteristics of a population of animals or plants over successive generations **2** a gradual development, esp. to a more complex form **evolutionary** *adj*
WORD ORIGIN Latin *evolutio* an unrolling

evolve *vb* **evolving, evolved** **1** to develop gradually **2** (of animal or plant species) to undergo evolution
WORD ORIGIN Latin *evolvere* to unfold

e-voting *n* the application of electronic technology to cast and count votes in an election

ewe *n* a female sheep
WORD ORIGIN Old English *ēowu*

ewer *n* a large jug with a wide mouth
WORD ORIGIN Latin *aqua* water

ex¹ *prep finance* excluding or without: *ex dividend*
WORD ORIGIN Latin: out of, from

ex² *n, pl* **exes** *informal* one's former wife or husband

ex- *prefix* **1** out of, outside, or from: *exit* **2** former: *his glamorous ex-wife*
WORD ORIGIN Latin

exacerbate (ig-**zass**-er-bate) *vb* -bating, -bated to make (pain, emotion, or a situation) worse **exacerbation** *n*
WORD ORIGIN Latin *acerbus* bitter

exact *adj* **1** correct in every detail; strictly accurate **2** precise, as opposed to approximate **3** based on measurement and the formulation of laws: *forecasting floods is not an exact science* ▷ *vb* **4** to obtain or demand as a right, esp. through force or strength: *the rebels called for revenge to be exacted for the killings*
WORD ORIGIN Latin *exigere* to demand

exacting *adj* making rigorous or excessive demands

exaction *n* *formal* **1** the act of obtaining or demanding money as a right **2** a sum or payment exacted

exactitude *n* the quality of being exact; precision

exactly *adv* **1** with complete accuracy and precision: *I don't know exactly where they live* **2** in every respect: *he looks exactly like his father* ▷ *interj* **3** just so! precisely!

exaggerate *vb* -rating, -rated **1** to regard or represent as greater than is true **2** to make greater or more noticeable **exaggerated** *adj* **exaggeratedly** *adv* **exaggeration** *n*
WORD ORIGIN Latin *exaggerare* to heap up

exalt *vb* **1** to praise highly **2** to raise to a higher rank **exalted** *adj* **exaltation** *n*
WORD ORIGIN Latin *exaltare* to raise
▤ USAGE
▤ *Exalt* is sometimes wrongly used ▤ where *exult* is meant: *he was exulting* ▤ (not *exalting*) *in his win earlier that day*.

exam *n* short for **examination**

examination *n* **1** the act of examining **2** *education* exercises, questions, or tasks set to test a person's knowledge and skill **3** *med* physical inspection of a patient **4** *law* the formal questioning of a person on oath

examine *vb* -mining, -mined **1** to inspect carefully or in detail; investigate **2** *education* to test a person's knowledge of a subject by written or oral questions **3** *med* to investigate a patient's state of health **4** *law* to formally question someone on oath **examinee** *n* **examiner** *n*
WORD ORIGIN Latin *examinare* to weigh

example *n* **1** a specimen that is typical of its group; sample: *a fine example of Georgian architecture* **2** a particular event, object, or person that demonstrates a point or supports an argument, theory, etc.: *Germany is a good example of how federalism works in practice* **3** a person, action, or thing that is worthy of imitation **4** a punishment or the person punished regarded as a warning to others **5** for example as an illustration
WORD ORIGIN Latin *exemplum*

exasperate *vb* -rating, -rated to cause great irritation to **exasperated** *adj* **exasperating** *adj* **exasperation** *n*
WORD ORIGIN Latin *exasperare* to make rough

ex cathedra *adj, adv* **1** with the authority of one's official position **2** *RC Church* (of doctrines of faith or morals) defined by the pope as infallibly true
WORD ORIGIN Latin: from the chair

excavate *vb* -vating, -vated **1** to unearth (buried objects) methodically to discover information about the past **2** to make a hole in something by digging into it or hollowing it out: *one kind of shrimp excavates a hole for itself* **excavation** *n* **excavator** *n*
WORD ORIGIN Latin *excavare* to make hollow

exceed *vb* **1** to be greater in degree or quantity **2** to go beyond the limit of (a restriction)
WORD ORIGIN Latin *excedere* to go beyond

exceedingly *adv* very; extremely

excel *vb* -celling, -celled **1** to be better than; surpass **2** excel in or at to be outstandingly good at
WORD ORIGIN Latin *excellere* to rise up

excellence *n* the quality of being exceptionally good

Excellency or **Excellence** *n, pl* -lencies or -lences Your or His or Her Excellency a title used to address a high-ranking official, such as an ambassador

excellent *adj* exceptionally good; outstanding

except *prep* **1** Also: except for not including; apart from: *everyone except Jill laughed* **2** except that but for the fact that ▷ *vb* **3** to leave out or exclude
WORD ORIGIN Latin *excipere* to take out

excepting *prep* except
▤ USAGE
▤ The use of *excepting* is considered by ▤ many people to be acceptable only ▤ after *not, only, always*, or *without*. ▤ Elsewhere *except* is preferred: *every* ▤ *country agreed to the proposal except* (not ▤ *excepting*) *Spain; he was well again except for* ▤ (not *excepting*) *a slight pain in his chest*.

exception *n* **1** anything excluded from or not conforming to a general rule or classification **2** take exception to to make objections to

exceptionable *adj* open to objection

exceptional *adj* **1** forming an exception **2** having much more than average intelligence, ability, or skill **exceptionally** *adv*

excerpt *n* **1** a passage taken from a book, speech, etc.; extract ▷ *vb* **2** to take a passage from a book, speech, etc.
WORD ORIGIN Latin *excerptum* (something) picked out

excess *n* **1** the state or act of going beyond normal or permitted limits **2** an immoderate or abnormal amount **3** the amount, number, etc. by which one thing exceeds another **4** behaviour regarded as too extreme or immoral to be acceptable: *a life of sex, drugs, and drunken excess* **5** excesses acts or actions that are unacceptably cruel or immoral: *one of the bloodiest excesses of a dictatorial regime* **6** in excess of more than **7** to excess to an extreme or unhealthy extent: *he had started to drink to excess* ▷ *adj* **8** more than normal, necessary, or permitted: *excess fat* **excessive** *adj* **excessively** *adv*
WORD ORIGIN Latin *excedere* to go beyond

e

excess luggage or **baggage** n luggage that is more in weight or number of pieces than an airline, etc. will carry free

exchange vb -changing, -changed 1 (of two or more people, governments, etc.) to give each other (something similar) at the same time: *they nervously exchanged smiles* 2 to replace (one thing) with another, esp. to replace unsatisfactory goods: *could I exchange this for a larger size, please?* ▷ n 3 the act of exchanging 4 anything given or received as an equivalent or substitute for something else 5 an argument 6 Also called: **telephone exchange** a centre in which telephone lines are interconnected 7 a place where securities or commodities are traded, esp. by brokers or merchants 8 a transfer of sums of money of equivalent value, as between different currencies 9 the system by which commercial debts are settled, esp. by bills of exchange, without direct payment of money **exchangeable** adj
WORD ORIGIN Latin *cambire* to barter

exchange rate n the rate at which the currency unit of one country may be exchanged for that of another

Exchequer n government (in Britain and certain other countries) the accounting department of the Treasury
WORD ORIGIN Old French *eschequier* counting table

excise¹ n 1 a tax on goods, such as spirits, produced for the home market 2 Brit that section of the government service responsible for the collection of excise, now the Board of Customs and Excise
WORD ORIGIN Latin *assidere* to sit beside, assist in judging

excise² vb -cising, -cised 1 to delete a passage from a book 2 to remove an organ or part surgically **excision** n
WORD ORIGIN Latin *excidere* to cut down

exciseman n, pl -men Brit (formerly) a government agent who collected excise and prevented smuggling

excitable adj nervous and easily excited **excitability** n

excite vb -citing, -cited 1 to make (a person) feel so happy that he or she is unable to relax because he or she is looking forward eagerly to something: *he was excited at the long-awaited arrival of a son* 2 to cause or arouse (an emotion, response, etc.): *the idea strongly excited his interest* 3 to arouse sexually 4 physiol to cause a response in (an organ, tissue, or part) 5 physics to raise (an atom, molecule, etc.) to a higher energy level **excited** adj **excitedly** adv
WORD ORIGIN Latin *exciere* to stimulate

excitement n 1 the state of being excited 2 a person or thing that excites

exciting adj causing excitement; stirring; stimulating **excitingly** adv

exclaim vb to cry out or speak suddenly or excitedly, as from surprise, delight, horror, etc.
WORD ORIGIN Latin *exclamare*

exclamation n 1 an abrupt or excited cry or utterance 2 the act of exclaiming **exclamatory** adj

exclamation mark or US **point** n the punctuation mark (!) used after exclamations and forceful commands

exclude vb -cluding, -cluded 1 to keep out; prevent from entering 2 to leave out of consideration **exclusion** n
WORD ORIGIN Latin *excludere*

excluding prep excepting

exclusive adj 1 excluding or incompatible with anything else: *these two theories are mutually exclusive* 2 not shared: *exclusive rights* 3 used or lived in by a privileged minority, esp. a fashionable clique: *an exclusive skiing resort* 4 not including the numbers, dates, etc. mentioned 5 **exclusive of** except for; not taking account of 6 **exclusive to** limited to; found only in ▷ n 7 a story reported in only one newspaper **exclusively** adv **exclusivity** or **exclusiveness** n

excommunicate vb -cating, -cated to expel (someone) from membership of a church and ban him or her from taking part in its services **excommunication** n
WORD ORIGIN Late Latin *excommunicare* to exclude from the community

excoriate vb -ating, -ated 1 literary to censure severely 2 to strip skin from a person or animal **excoriation** n
WORD ORIGIN Late Latin *excoriare* to strip, flay

excrement n waste matter discharged from the body; faeces **excremental** adj
WORD ORIGIN Latin *excernere* to sift, excrete

excrescence n something that protrudes, esp. an outgrowth from a part of the body **excrescent** adj
WORD ORIGIN Latin *excrescrere* to grow out

excreta (ik-**skree**-ta) pl n urine and faeces discharged from the body

excrete vb -creting, -creted to discharge waste matter, such as urine, sweat, or faeces, from the body **excretion** n **excretory** adj
WORD ORIGIN Latin *excernere* to discharge

excruciating adj 1 unbearably painful; agonizing 2 hard to bear: *never had an afternoon passed with such excruciating slowness* **excruciatingly** adv
WORD ORIGIN Latin *excruciare* to torture

exculpate vb -pating, -pated to free from blame or guilt
WORD ORIGIN Latin *ex* from + *culpa* fault

excursion n a short outward and return journey, esp. for sightseeing, etc.; outing
WORD ORIGIN Latin *excurrere* to run out

excuse n 1 an explanation offered to justify an action which has been criticized or as a reason for not fulfilling an obligation, etc. ▷ vb -cusing, -cused 2 to put forward a reason or justification for (an action, fault, or offending person) 3 to pardon (a person) or overlook (a fault) 4 to free (someone) from having to carry out a task, obligation, etc.: *a doctor's letter excusing him from games at school* 5 to allow to leave 6 **be excused** euphemistic to go to the toilet 7 **excuse me!** an expression used to catch someone's attention or to apologize for an interruption, disagreement, etc. **excusable** adj

WORD ORIGIN Latin *ex* out + *causa* cause, accusation

ex-directory adj Brit & NZ not listed in a telephone directory by request

execrable (**eks**-sik-rab-bl) adj of very poor quality **execrably** adv
WORD ORIGIN see EXECRATE

execrate vb -crating, -crated 1 to feel and express loathing and hatred of (someone or something) 2 to curse (a person or thing) **execration** n
WORD ORIGIN Latin *exsecrari* to curse

executable adj computers 1 (of a program) able to be run ▷ n 2 a file containing a program that will run as soon as it is opened

execute vb -cuting, -cuted 1 to put a condemned person to death 2 to carry out or accomplish 3 to produce or create (a work of art) 4 law to render (a deed) effective, for example by signing it 5 to carry out the terms of (a contract, will, etc.) **executer** n
WORD ORIGIN Old French *executer*

execution n 1 the act of executing 2 the carrying out or undergoing of a sentence of death 3 the manner in which something is performed; technique

executioner n a person whose job is to kill people who have been sentenced to death

executive n 1 a person or group responsible for the administration of a project or business 2 the branch of government responsible for carrying out laws, decrees, etc. ▷ adj 3 having the function of carrying plans, orders, laws, etc. into effect: *the executive producer* 4 of or for executives: *the executive car park* 5 informal very expensive or exclusive: *executive cars*

executor n law a person appointed by someone to ensure that the conditions set out in his or her will are carried out **executorial** adj **executrix** fem n

exegesis (eks-sij-**jee**-siss) n, pl -ses (-seez) explanation of a text, esp. of the Bible
WORD ORIGIN Greek *exēgeisthai* to interpret

exemplar n 1 a person or thing to be copied; model 2 a typical specimen; example
WORD ORIGIN Latin *exemplum* example

exemplary adj 1 so good as to be an example worthy of imitation 2 (of a punishment) extremely harsh, so as to discourage others from committing a similar crime

exemplify vb -fies, -fying, -fied 1 to show by example 2 to serve as an example of **exemplification** n
WORD ORIGIN Latin *exemplum* example + *facere* to make

exempt adj 1 not subject to an obligation, tax, etc. ▷ vb 2 to release (someone) from an obligation, tax, etc. **exemption** n
WORD ORIGIN Latin *exemptus* removed

exequies (**eks**-sik-weez) pl n, sing -quy funeral rites
WORD ORIGIN Latin *exequiae*

exercise n 1 physical exertion, esp. for training or keeping fit 2 an activity

The Language of Robert Burns

Robert Burns was probably the greatest ambassa-dor of the Scots language of his day, and possibly the greatest ambassador Scots has ever had (though nowadays he must compete with the likes of Hugh MacDiarmid and Irvine Welsh). His poems and songs, especially his shorter ones, are known throughout the world, and he is the author of perhaps the best-known and least-understood lyric in the world.

Although an eighteenth-century poet and roughly contemporary with Samuel Johnson, Burns is more associated with Romanticism, and even sentimental-ism, than the Age of Reason; to this end his friends and supporters characterized him as the 'heaven-taught ploughman poet', though in actual fact he was as intel-ligent and as meticulous in his poetic style as any of the Enlightenment writers.

How we think of Burns depends greatly upon where we are in the world. Among the Scottish Diaspora, Burns is a cultural hero, and may be associated with his patriotic songs, such as *Scots Wha Hae*.

In Burns' homeland, he remains the National Poet, and an icon to be sure; however, a younger audience is likely to associate him with 'tartanry' and a kitschy faux-nationalism which obsesses over the romanti-cized relics of Scotland's past while leaving aside the question of its future. This opinion is sustained by the continual reciting of a small number of well-known lyrics like *To a Mouse* and the *Address to a Haggis* (the mandatory Burns Supper reading), at the expense of the poet's longer, more accomplished works.

Supporters of Burns in Scotland point out the wit and humour of works like *Tam o'Shanter* (itself rather overplayed), but perhaps both sides of the argument would be surprised to learn that Burns also composed in standard 'English' English, even when writing in his 'nationalist' mode, as in *Here Stewarts Once in Triumph Reign'd*.

Here Stewarts once in triumph reign'd,
And laws for Scotland's weal ordain'd;
But now unroof'd their palace stands,
Their sceptre's fall'n to other hands.

The above passage contains not one distinctly Scottish feature, other than its praising of the Stewart dynasty (and Scotland's former independence): the ending of the past participles in -*d* instead of -*ed* was common in the eighteenth century, when the -*ed* end-ing could still be pronounced as a full syllable when spelled out; the unfamiliar word *weal*, meaning some-thing like 'commonwealth', was standard English for the time.

This should hardly come as a surprise. Burns was a talented poet, and we like to think of poets as artists, but he was still a man with a mind to make money. The potential audience for his poetry was much greater south of the Border, and Burns was careful that his verse, like blended whisky, would suit palates through-out the English-speaking world. If we examine his Scots poems, we find the dialect words often need little or no glossing: context reveals their meaning, or they turn out to be mere re-spellings in the Scottish pro-nunciation, as in *cowran* for 'cowering'. Though we would expect Burns' dialect to be Ayrshire, it is in fact not heavily 'regional', beyond being Scots, which pre-vented his poetry being rejected by speakers of rival varieties, such as those of Edinburgh and Aberdeen. Finally, Burns' use of an intelligible form of Scots may actually have been a selling point in England, backing up his cultivated image as a 'heaven-taught plough-man' and providing a folksy, sentimental alternative to the hyper-educated, elitist verse of the Enlightenment.

Whatever the case, one telling indicator of Burns' enduring international popularity remains: every New Year's Eve (called Hogmanay in Scotland), the entire English-speaking world gathers at the stroke of mid-night to sing Burns' most famous song, *Auld Lang Syne* – indeed, one of the most well-known songs ever written – even though they may not understand all the words.

planned to achieve a particular purpose: *the group's meeting was mainly an exercise in mutual reassurance* **3** a set of movements, tasks, etc. designed to improve or test one's ability or fitness **4** the use or practice of (a right, power, or authority) **5** *mil* a manoeuvre or simulated combat operation ▷ *vb* **-cising, -cised 6** to put into use; make use of: *we urge all governments involved to exercise restraint* **7** to take exercise or perform exercises **8** to practise using in order to develop or train: *to exercise one's voice* **9** to worry or vex: *Western governments have been exercised by the need to combat international terrorism* **10** *mil* to carry out simulated combat, manoeuvres, etc. **exerciser** *n*
WORD ORIGIN Latin *exercere* to drill

exert *vb* **1** to use influence, authority, etc. forcefully or effectively **2 exert oneself** to make a special effort
WORD ORIGIN Latin *exserere* to thrust out

exertion *n* **1** effort or exercise, esp. physical effort: *the sudden exertion of running for a bus* **2** the act or an instance of using one's influence, powers, or authority: *the exertion of parental authority*

exeunt (**eks**-see-unt) they go out: used as a stage direction
WORD ORIGIN Latin

exfoliate *vb* **-ating, -ated 1** to peel off in scales or layers **2** to remove dead cells from the skin by washing with a granular cosmetic preparation **exfoliation** *n*

ex-gratia (eks-**gray**-sha) *adj* given as a favour where no legal obligation exists: *an ex-gratia payment*
WORD ORIGIN New Latin: out of kindness

exhale *vb* **-haling, -haled 1** to expel breath or smoke from the lungs; breathe out **2** to give off or be given off as gas, fumes, etc.: *the crater exhaled smoke* **exhalation** *n*
WORD ORIGIN Latin *exhalare*

exhaust *vb* **1** to tire out **2** to use up totally **3** to discuss a topic so thoroughly that no more remains to be said ▷ *n* **4** gases ejected from an engine as waste products **5** the parts of an engine through which waste gases pass **exhausted** *adj* **exhaustible** *adj*
WORD ORIGIN Latin *exhaurire* to draw out

exhaustion *n* **1** extreme tiredness **2** the act of exhausting or state of being exhausted

exhaustive *adj* very thorough; comprehensive **exhaustively** *adv*

exhibit *vb* **1** to display (a work of art) to the public **2** to show (a quality or feeling): *they exhibited extraordinary courage* ▷ *n* **3** an object exhibited to the public **4** *law* a document or object produced in court as evidence **exhibitor** *n*
WORD ORIGIN Latin *exhibere* to hold forth

exhibition *n* **1** a public display of art, skills, etc. **2** the act of exhibiting or the state of being exhibited: *an exhibition of bad temper* **3 make an exhibition of oneself** to behave so foolishly that one attracts public attention

exhibitionism *n* **1** a compulsive desire to attract attention to oneself **2** a compulsive desire to expose one's genitals publicly **exhibitionist** *n*

exhilarate *vb* **-rating, -rated** to make (someone) feel lively and cheerful **exhilaration** *n*
WORD ORIGIN Latin *exhilarare*

exhilarating *adj* causing strong feelings of excitement and happiness

exhort *vb* *formal* to urge (someone) earnestly **exhortation** *n*
WORD ORIGIN Latin *exhortari*

exhume (ig-**zyume**) *vb* **-huming, -humed** *formal* to dig up something buried, esp. a corpse **exhumation** *n*
WORD ORIGIN Latin *ex* out + *humus* the ground

exigency *n, pl* **-gencies** *formal* **1** an urgent demand or need **2** an emergency **exigent** *adj*
WORD ORIGIN Latin *exigere* to require

exiguous *adj formal* scanty or meagre **exiguity** *n*
WORD ORIGIN Latin *exiguus*

exile *n* **1** a prolonged, usually enforced absence from one's country **2** a person banished or living away from his or her country ▷ *vb* **-iling, -iled 3** to expel (someone) from his or her country; banish
WORD ORIGIN Latin *exsilium*

exist *vb* **1** to have being or reality; be: *does God exist?* **2** to only just be able to keep oneself alive, esp. because of poverty or hunger **3** to be living; live **4** to be present under specified conditions or in a specified place **existing** *adj*
WORD ORIGIN Latin *exsistere* to step forth

existence *n* **1** the fact or state of being real, live, or actual **2** a way of life, esp. a poor or hungry one **3** everything that exists **existent** *adj*

existential *adj* **1** of or relating to existence, esp. human existence **2** of or relating to existentialism

existentialism *n* a philosophical movement stressing personal experience and responsibility of the individual, who is seen as a free agent **existentialist** *adj, n*

exit *n* **1** a way out **2** the act of going out **3** *theatre* the act of going offstage **4** *Austral & Brit* a point at which vehicles may leave or join a motorway ▷ *vb* **exiting, exited 5** to go away or out; depart **6** *theatre* to go offstage: used as a stage direction: *exit bleeding from the room*
WORD ORIGIN Latin *exire* to go out

exocrine *adj* of or denoting a gland, such as the sweat gland, that discharges its product through a duct
WORD ORIGIN Greek *exō* outside + *krinein* to separate

exodus (**eks**-so-duss) *n* the departure of a large number of people
WORD ORIGIN Greek *ex* out + *hodos* way

Exodus *n* *Bible* the second book of the Old Testament, containing a description of the departure of the Israelites from Egypt

ex officio (eks off-**fish**-ee-oh) *adv, adj* by right of position or office
WORD ORIGIN Latin

exonerate *vb* **-ating, -ated** to clear (someone) of blame or a criminal charge **exoneration** *n*
WORD ORIGIN Latin *exonerare* to free from a burden

exorbitant *adj* (of prices, demands, etc.) excessively great or high: *an exorbitant rent* **exorbitantly** *adv*
WORD ORIGIN Latin *ex* out, away + *orbita* track

exorcize *or* **-cise** *vb* **-cizing, -cized** *or* **-cising, -cised** to expel (evil spirits) by prayers and religious rites **exorcism** *n* **exorcist** *n*
WORD ORIGIN Greek *ex* out + *horkos* oath

exoskeleton *n* *zool* the protective or supporting structure covering the outside of the body of many animals, for example insects or crabs

exothermic *adj* (of a chemical reaction) involving or leading to the giving off of heat

exotic *adj* **1** having a strange allure or beauty **2** originating in a foreign country; not native ▷ *n* **3** a non-native plant **exotically** *adv*
WORD ORIGIN Greek *exō* outside

exotica *pl n* exotic objects, esp. as a collection

expand *vb* **1** to make or become greater in extent, size, or scope **2** to spread out; unfold **3 expand on** to go into more detail about (a story or subject) **4** to become increasingly relaxed, friendly, and talkative **5** *maths* to express a function or expression as the sum or product of terms **expandable** *adj*
WORD ORIGIN Latin *expandere* to spread out

expanse *n* an uninterrupted wide area; stretch: *a large expanse of water*

expansible *adj* able to expand or be expanded

expansion *n* **1** the act of expanding **2** an increase or development, esp. in the activities of a company

expansionism *n* the practice of expanding the economy or territory of a country **expansionist** *n, adj*

expansive *adj* **1** wide or extensive **2** friendly, open, and talkative **expansiveness** *n*

expat *adj, n* short for **expatriate**

expatiate (iks-**pay**-shee-ate) *vb* **-ating, -ated ● expatiate on** *formal* to speak or write at length on (a subject) **expatiation** *n*
WORD ORIGIN Latin *exspatiari* to digress

expatriate (eks-**pat**-ree-it) *adj* **1** living away from one's native country: *an expatriate American* **2** exiled ▷ *n* **3** a person living away from his or her native country **4** an exile **expatriation** *n*
WORD ORIGIN Latin *ex* out, away + *patria* native land

expect *vb* **1** to regard as likely **2** to look forward to or be waiting for **3** to require (something) as an obligation: *he expects an answer by January* **4 be expecting** *informal* to be pregnant
WORD ORIGIN Latin *exspectare* to watch for

expectancy *n* **1** something expected, esp. on the basis of a norm: *a life expectancy of 78* **2** anticipation or expectation

expectant *adj* **1** expecting or hopeful **2 a** pregnant **b** married to or living with a woman who is pregnant: *an expectant father* **expectantly** *adv*

expectation *n* **1** the state of expecting or of being expected **2** something looked forward to, whether feared or hoped for **3** belief that someone should behave in a particular way: *women with expectations of old-fashioned gallantry*

expectorant *med adj* **1** helping to bring up phlegm from the respiratory passages ▷ *n* **2** an expectorant medicine

expectorate *vb* **-rating, -rated** *formal* to cough up and spit out (phlegm from the respiratory passages) **expectoration** *n*
WORD ORIGIN Latin *expectorare* to drive from the breast, expel

expediency *or* **expedience** *n, pl* **-encies** *or* **-ences 1** the use of methods that are advantageous rather than fair or just **2** appropriateness or suitability

expedient (iks-**pee**-dee-ent) *n* **1** something that achieves a particular purpose: *income controls were used only as a short-term expedient* ▷ *adj* **2** useful or advantageous in a given situation: *they only talk about human rights when it is politically expedient*
WORD ORIGIN Latin *expediens* setting free; see EXPEDITE

expedite *vb* **-diting, -dited** *formal* **1** to hasten the progress of **2** to do quickly
WORD ORIGIN Latin *expedire* to free the feet

expedition *n* **1** an organized journey or voyage, esp. for exploration **2** the people and equipment comprising an expedition **3** a pleasure trip or excursion: *an expedition to the seaside* **expeditionary** *adj*
WORD ORIGIN Latin *expedire* to prepare, expedite

expeditious *adj* done quickly and efficiently

expel *vb* **-pelling, -pelled 1** to drive out with force **2** to dismiss from a school, club, etc. permanently
WORD ORIGIN Latin *expellere*

expend *vb formal* to spend or use up (time, energy, or money)
WORD ORIGIN Latin *expendere* to weigh out, pay

expendable *adj* **1** not worth preserving **2** able to be sacrificed to achieve an objective, esp. a military one

expenditure *n* **1** something expended, esp. money **2** the amount expended

expense *n* **1** a particular payment of money; expenditure **2** the amount of money needed to buy or do something; cost **3 expenses** money spent in the performance of a job, etc. **4** something requiring money for its purchase or upkeep **5 at the expense of** to the detriment of
WORD ORIGIN Latin *expensus* weighed out

expense account *n* **1** an arrangement by which an employee's expenses are refunded by his or her employer **2** a record of such expenses

expensive *adj* costing a great deal of money **expensiveness** *n*

experience *n* **1** direct personal participation or observation of something: *his experience of prison life* **2** a particular incident, feeling, etc. that a person has undergone **3** accumulated knowledge, esp. of practical matters ▷ *vb* **-encing, -enced 4** to participate in or undergo **5** to be moved by; feel
WORD ORIGIN Latin *experiri* to prove

experienced *adj* skilful or knowledgeable as a result of having done something many times before

experiential *adj philosophy* relating to or derived from experience

experiment *n* **1** a test or investigation to provide evidence for or against a theory: *a scientific experiment* **2** the trying out of a new idea or method ▷ *vb* **3** to carry out an experiment or experiments **experimentation** *n* **experimenter** *n*
WORD ORIGIN Latin *experiri* to test

experimental *adj* **1** relating to, based on, or having the nature of an experiment **2** trying out new ideas or methods **experimentally** *adv*

expert *n* **1** a person who has extensive skill or knowledge in a particular field ▷ *adj* **2** skilful or knowledgeable **3** of, involving, or done by an expert **expertly** *adv*
WORD ORIGIN Latin *expertus* known by experience

expertise (eks-per-**teez**) *n* special skill, knowledge, or judgment
WORD ORIGIN French

expiate *vb* **-ating, -ated** *formal* to make amends for (a sin or wrongdoing) **expiation** *n*
WORD ORIGIN Latin *expiare*

expiration *n* **1** the finish of something; expiry **2** the act, process, or sound of breathing out **expiratory** *adj*

expire *vb* **-piring, -pired 1** to finish or run out; come to an end **2** to breathe out air **3** to die
WORD ORIGIN Latin *exspirare* to breathe out

expiry *n, pl* **-ries** a coming to an end, esp. of the period of a contract

explain *vb* **1** to make something easily understandable, esp. by giving a clear and detailed account of it **2** to justify or attempt to justify by giving reasons for one's actions **3 explain away** to offer excuses or reasons for (mistakes)
WORD ORIGIN Latin *explanare* to flatten, make clear

explanation *n* **1** the reason or reasons why a particular event or situation happened: *there is no reasonable explanation for her behaviour* **2** a detailed account or description: *a 90-minute explanation of his love of jazz*

explanatory *adj* serving or intended to serve as an explanation

expletive (iks-**plee**-tiv) *n* an exclamation or swearword expressing emotion rather than meaning
WORD ORIGIN Latin *explere* to fill up

explicable *adj* capable of being explained

explicate *vb* **-cating, -cated** *formal* to make clear; explain **explication** *n*
WORD ORIGIN Latin *explicare* to unfold

explicit *adj* **1** precisely and clearly expressed, leaving nothing to implication: *an explicit commitment to democracy* **2** leaving little to the imagination; graphically detailed: *the film contains some sexually explicit scenes* **3** (of a person) expressing something in a precise and clear way, so as to leave no doubt about what is meant **explicitly** *adv*
WORD ORIGIN Latin *explicitus* unfolded

explode *vb* **-ploding, -ploded 1** to burst with great violence; blow up **2** (of a gas) to undergo a sudden violent expansion as a result of a fast chemical or nuclear reaction **3** to react suddenly or violently with emotion **4** (esp. of a population) to increase rapidly **5** to show (a theory, etc.) to be baseless
WORD ORIGIN Latin *explodere* to drive off by clapping

exploit *vb* **1** to take advantage of a person or situation for one's own ends **2** to make the best use of ▷ *n* **3** a notable deed or feat **exploitation** *n* **exploiter** *n*
WORD ORIGIN Old French: accomplishment

exploitative *adj* tending to take advantage of a person or situation for one's own ends

explore *vb* **-ploring, -plored 1** to examine or investigate, esp. systematically **2** to travel into an unfamiliar region, esp. for scientific purposes **exploration** *n* **exploratory** *or* **explorative** *adj* **explorer** *n*
WORD ORIGIN Latin *ex* out + *plorare* to cry aloud

explosion *n* **1** an exploding **2** a violent release of energy resulting from a rapid chemical or nuclear reaction **3** a sudden or violent outburst of activity, noise, emotion, etc. **4** a rapid increase

explosive *adj* **1** able or likely to explode **2** potentially violent: *an explosive situation* ▷ *n* **3** a substance capable of exploding **explosiveness** *n*

expo *n, pl* **-pos** short for **exposition** (sense 3)

exponent *n* **1** a person who advocates an idea, cause, etc.: *an exponent of free speech* **2** a person who is a skilful performer of some activity: *one of the greatest modern exponents of the blues* **3** *maths* a number placed as a superscript to another number indicating how many times the number is to be used as a factor
WORD ORIGIN Latin *exponere* to expound

exponential *adj* **1** *maths* of or involving numbers raised to an exponent **2** *informal* very rapid **exponentially** *adv*

export *n* **1** the sale of goods and services to a foreign country: *a ban on the export of arms* **2 exports** goods or services sold to a foreign country ▷ *vb* **3** to sell goods or services or transport goods to a foreign country **exporter** *n*
WORD ORIGIN Latin *exportare* to carry away

expose *vb* **-posing, -posed 1** to uncover (something previously covered) **2** to reveal the truth about (someone or something), esp. when it is shocking or scandalous: *an MP whose private life was recently exposed in the press* **3** to leave (a person or thing) unprotected in a potentially harmful situation: *workers were exposed to relatively low doses of radiation* **4 expose someone to** to give someone an introduction to or experience of (something new) **5** *photog* to subject (a film) to light **6 expose oneself** to display one's sexual organs in public **WORD ORIGIN** Latin *exponere* to set out

exposé (iks-**pose**-ay) *n* the bringing of a scandal, crime, etc. to public notice **WORD ORIGIN** French

exposed *adj* **1** not concealed; displayed for viewing: *the exposed soles of his shoes* **2** without shelter from the elements **3** vulnerable: *the enemy attacked our army's exposed flank*

exposition *n* **1** a systematic explanation of a subject **2** the act of expounding or setting out a viewpoint **3** a large public exhibition **4** *music* the first statement of the themes of a movement **WORD ORIGIN** Latin *exponere* to display

expository *adj* explanatory

ex post facto *adj* having retrospective effect **WORD ORIGIN** Latin *ex* from + *post* afterwards + *factus* done

expostulate *vb* -lating, -lated
● **expostulate with** to reason or argue with, esp. in order to dissuade or as a protest **expostulation** *n* **expostulatory** *adj* **WORD ORIGIN** Latin *expostulare* to require

exposure *n* **1** the state of being exposed to, or lacking protection from, something: *the body cannot cope with sudden exposure to stress* **2** the revealing of the truth about someone or something, esp. when it is shocking or scandalous: *the exposure of a loophole in the tax laws* **3** the harmful effect on a person's body caused by lack of shelter from the weather, esp. the cold **4** appearance before the public, as on television **5** *photog* **a** the act of exposing a film to light **b** an area on a film that has been exposed **6** *photog* **a** the intensity of light falling on a film multiplied by the time for which it is exposed **b** a combination of lens aperture and shutter speed used in taking a photograph

exposure meter *n* *photog* an instrument for measuring the intensity of light so that suitable camera settings can be chosen

expound *vb* to explain a theory, belief, etc. in detail **WORD ORIGIN** Latin *exponere* to set forth

express *vb* **1** to state (an idea or feeling) in words; utter: *two record labels have expressed an interest in signing the band* **2** to show (an idea or feeling): *his body and demeanour expressed distrust* **3** to indicate through a symbol or formula **4** to squeeze out (juice, etc.) **5 express oneself** to communicate one's thoughts or ideas ▷ *adj* **6** explicitly stated **7** deliberate and specific: *she came with the express purpose of causing a row* **8** of or for rapid transportation of people, mail, etc. ▷ *n* **9** a fast train stopping at only a few stations **10** *chiefly US & Canad* a system for sending mail rapidly ▷ *adv* **11** using a system for rapid transportation of people, mail, etc.: *please send this letter express: it's very urgent!* **expressible** *adj* **WORD ORIGIN** Latin *exprimere* to force out

expression *n* **1** the transforming of ideas into words **2** a showing of emotion without words **3** communication of emotion through music, painting, etc. **4** a look on the face that indicates mood or emotion **5** a particular phrase used conventionally to express something **6** *maths* a variable, function, or some combination of these **expressionless** *adj*

expressionism *n* an early 20th-century artistic and literary movement which sought to express emotions rather than to represent the physical world **expressionist** *n, adj*

expression mark *n* *music* one of a set of symbols indicating how a piece or passage is to be performed

expressive *adj* **1** of or full of expression **2 expressive of** showing or suggesting: *looks expressive of hatred and revenge*

expressly *adv* **1** definitely **2** deliberately and specifically

expressway *n* *chiefly US* a motorway

expropriate *vb* -ating, -ated *formal* (of a government or other official body) to take (money or property) away from its owners **expropriation** *n* **expropriator** *n* **WORD ORIGIN** Medieval Latin *expropriare* to deprive of possessions

expulsion *n* the act of expelling or the fact of being expelled **expulsive** *adj* **WORD ORIGIN** Latin *expellere* to expel

expunge (iks-**sponge**) *vb* -punging, -punged *formal* to remove all traces of: *he had tried to expunge his failure from his mind* **WORD ORIGIN** Latin *expungere* to blot out

expurgate (**eks**-per-gate) *vb* -gating, -gated to amend a piece of writing by removing sections thought to be offensive **expurgation** *n* **expurgator** *n* **WORD ORIGIN** Latin *expurgare* to clean out

exquisite *adj* **1** extremely beautiful or attractive **2** showing unusual delicacy and craftsmanship **3** sensitive or discriminating: *exquisite manners* **4** intensely felt: *exquisite joy* **exquisitely** *adv* **WORD ORIGIN** Latin *exquisitus* excellent

ex-serviceman *or fem* **ex-servicewoman** *n, pl* -men *or* -women a person who has served in the armed forces

extant *adj* still in existence; surviving **WORD ORIGIN** Latin *exstans* standing out

≡ **USAGE**
≡ *Extant* is sometimes wrongly used
≡ simply to say that something exists,
≡ without any connotation of survival:
≡ *plutonium is perhaps the deadliest element in*
≡ *existence* (not the *deadliest element extant*).

extemporaneous *adj* spoken or performed without preparation **extemporaneously** *adv*

extempore (iks-**temp**-or-ee) *adj, adv* without planning or preparation **WORD ORIGIN** Latin *ex tempore* instantaneously

extemporize *or* -**rise** *vb* -rizing, -rized *or* -rising, -rised to perform or speak without preparation **extemporization** *or* -**risation** *n* **extemporizer** *or* -**riser** *n*

extend *vb* **1** to make bigger or longer than before: *they extended the house by*

building a conservatory **2** to reach to a certain distance or in a certain direction: *the suburbs extend for many miles* **3** to last for a certain time: *in Norway maternity leave extends to 52 weeks* **4** to broaden the meaning or scope of: *the law was extended to ban all guns* **5** to make something exist or be valid for longer than before: *her visa was extended for three months* **6** to present or offer: *a tradition of extending asylum to refugees* **7** to straighten or stretch out (part of the body): *she extended a hand in welcome* **8 extend oneself** to make use of all one's ability or strength, often because forced to: *she'll have to really extend herself if she wants to win* **extendable** *adj* **WORD ORIGIN** Latin *extendere* to stretch out

extended family *n* a social unit in which parents, children, grandparents, and other relatives live as a family unit

extensible *adj* capable of being extended

extension *n* **1** a room or rooms added to an existing building **2** a development that includes or affects more people or things than before: *an extension of democracy within the EU* **3** an additional telephone connected to the same line as another **4** an extra period of time in which something continues to exist or be valid: *an extension of the contract for another 2 years* ▷ *adj* **5** denoting something that can be extended or that extends another object: *an extension ladder* **6** of or relating to the provision of teaching and other facilities by a school or college to people who cannot attend full-time courses

extensive *adj* **1** covering a large area: *extensive moorland* **2** very great in effect: *the bomb caused extensive damage* **3** containing many details, ideas, or items on a particular subject: *an extensive collection of modern art* **extensively** *adv*

extensor *n* any muscle that stretches or extends an arm, leg, or other part of the body

extent *n* **1** the length, area, or size of something **2** the scale or seriousness of a situation or difficulty: *the extent of the damage* **3** the degree or amount to which something applies: *to a certain extent that's true*

extenuate *vb* -ating, -ated *formal* to make an offence or fault less blameworthy, by giving reasons that partly excuse it **extenuating** *adj* **extenuation** *n* **WORD ORIGIN** Latin *extenuare* to make thin

exterior *n* **1** a part or surface that is on the outside **2** the outward appearance of a person: *Jim's grumpy exterior concealed a warm heart* **3** a film scene shot outside ▷ *adj* **4** of, situated on, or suitable for the outside **5** coming or acting from outside or abroad **WORD ORIGIN** Latin comparative of *exterus* on the outside

exterior angle *n* an angle of a polygon contained between one side extended and the adjacent side

exterminate *vb* -nating, -nated to destroy a group or type of people,

Scottish English
part 1

If you look in a dictionary of Old English, you will find that *Scot-land* is defined as 'Ireland'. In Anglo-Saxon times, *Scotland* was the name of the island off the west coast of England, and the people who lived there were called the *Scottas* (Latin *Scotti*). The people north of the River Tweed were the Picts. The Scotti moved into present-day Scotland when the kingdom of Dál Riata expanded into Argyll from Northern Ireland in the late 6th century AD.

The Scotti spoke a Celtic language, the ancestor of modern Scottish Gaelic. The language we call *Scots*, however, is a Germanic language. Politically, Scots is recognized as a minority language by the European Union; linguistically speaking, there are still many who do not accept Scots as a separate language, considering it rather a dialect of English. This is, however, precisely how Scots began.

The Scots language derives from the Northern varieties of Old and Middle English. It was probably introduced into what is now Scotland in the 7th century when the Northumbrians (who were Angles) gained control of the Pictish stronghold called 'Din Eidyn', meaning 'fortress on the hill'. The Northumbrians kept the second element of this name, but they translated the common Celtic word *din* ('fortress') into their own word *burg* and moved it to the end of the place-name, as was their convention, to create *Edinburgh*. Later, as the Celtic-speakers retreated further into the Highlands and their language became more obscure to the English and Lowland Scots, people began to assume that *Edinburgh* meant 'Edwin's burg' - a logical assumption, as Edwin was a famous Northumbrian King, but ultimately a mistaken folk etymology. In any case, the Old English historian Bede lists Edinburgh as part of the Kingdom of Northumbria in 731, so at least from the 700s Edinburgh was an 'English' city (some argue it still is today).

Though much of the early history of Scotland is dominated by Celts and the pre-Celtic Picts, the Anglians of the Lothian region soon became the dominant force in the south of the country, expanded throughout the Central Belt into the former territory of Dál Riata and up the east coast as far as the Doric-speaking regions of the Grampians and Aberdeenshire. Though it may seem ironic, English became the language of the Scottish court, and the earliest poems recounting the exploits of Scotland's heroes William Wallace and Robert the Bruce are written in it.

Throughout the Middle Ages there were still Gaelic-speakers in Scotland, especially in rural communities and in the Highlands and Islands; nor were the two languages completely isolated from each other. Until the 16th century, the word 'Scottis' referred to the Gaelic language; what we now call 'Scots' was then known as 'Inglis' (the Northern word for 'English'). 'Scots' was not used to denote the Germanic language spoken largely in the Lowlands until after the disastrous Battle of Flodden in 1513. John Barbour, author of the epic poem *The Brus* (1375) proclaims he is writing in 'Inglis', as does the poet known as 'Blind Hary', who wrote *The Wallace* about a century later. Gavin Douglas, however, who completed his translation of Virgil's *Aeneid* soon after Flodden, calls his language 'Scottis', and so it has been known ever since.

Because Scotland was united with England under King James I (formerly James VI of Scotland) less than a century after this, Scots was never fully codified or established as an official national standard. Today there is no single variety of Scots we would think of as the most typical or representative. Scottish Nationalists who seek to make Scots the official language of Scotland face an unpleasant choice between either selecting one of the three most prominent varieties (Edinburgh, Glaswegian, or Doric), all of which are heavily influenced by contact with 'English' English, or (as they have usually done) synthesize an artificial language - kind of a Scottish Esperanto - which unites features from all main dialects and uses as few 'English' words as possible, and which nobody actually speaks.

However, standardized or not, Scots is still a living part of communication in Scotland, and the medium of many recent works of Scottish literature, and certainly a much nearer relative of English than Frisian.

animals, or plants completely **extermination** n **exterminator** n **WORD ORIGIN** Latin *exterminare* to drive away

external adj **1** of, situated on, or suitable for the outside: *there was damage to the house's external walls* **2** coming or acting from outside: *most ill health is caused by external influences* **3** of or involving foreign nations: *Hong Kong's external trade* **4** anat situated on or near the outside of the body: *the external ear* **5** brought into an organization to do a task which must be done impartially, esp. one involving testing or checking: *external examiners* **6** of or relating to someone taking a university course, but not attending a university: *an external degree* ▷ n **7 externals** obvious circumstances or aspects, esp. superficial ones: *despite the war, the externals of life in the city remain normal* **externality** n **externally** adv **WORD ORIGIN** Latin *externus*

externalize or **-ise** vb **-izing, -ized** or **-ising, -ised** to express (thoughts or feelings) in words or actions **externalization** or **-isation** n

extinct adj **1** (of an animal or plant species) having died out **2** no longer in existence, esp. because of social changes: *shipbuilding is virtually extinct in Scotland* **3** (of a volcano) no longer liable to erupt **WORD ORIGIN** Latin *exstinguere* to extinguish

extinction n **1** the dying out of a plant or animal species **2** the end of a particular way of life or type of activity

extinguish vb **1** to put out (a fire or light) **2** to remove or destroy entirely **extinguishable** adj **extinguisher** n **WORD ORIGIN** Latin *exstinguere*

extirpate (**eks**-ter-pate) vb **-pating, -pated** to remove or destroy completely: *the Romans attempted to extirpate the Celtic religion* **extirpation** n **WORD ORIGIN** Latin *exstirpare* to root out

extol or US **extoll** vb **-tolling, -tolled** to praise lavishly **WORD ORIGIN** Latin *extollere* to elevate

extort vb to obtain money or favours by intimidation, violence, or the misuse of authority **extortion** n **WORD ORIGIN** Latin *extorquere* to wrest away

extortionate adj (of prices, profits, etc.) much higher than is fair **extortionately** adv

extra adj **1** more than is usual, expected or needed; additional ▷ n **2** a person or thing that is additional **3** something for which an additional charge is made **4** films a person temporarily engaged, usually for crowd scenes **5** cricket a run not scored from the bat **6** an additional edition of a newspaper ▷ adv **7** unusually; exceptionally **WORD ORIGIN** probably from *extraordinary*

extra- prefix outside or beyond an area or scope: *extracellular; extraterrestrial* **WORD ORIGIN** Latin

extract vb **1** to pull out or uproot by force **2** to remove from a container **3** to derive (pleasure, information, etc.) from some source **4** informal to obtain (money, information, etc.) from someone who is not willing to provide it: *a confession extracted by force* **5** to obtain (a substance) from a material or the ground by mining, distillation, digestion, etc.: *oil extracted from shale* **6** to copy out (an article, passage, etc.) from a publication ▷ n **7** something extracted, such as a passage from a book, etc. **8** a preparation containing the concentrated essence of a substance **extractive** adj **extractor** n **WORD ORIGIN** Latin *extrahere* to draw out

≡ **USAGE**
≡ *Extract* is sometimes wrongly used ≡ where *extricate* would be better: *he will* ≡ *find it difficult extricating* (not *extracting*) ≡ *himself from this situation.*

extraction n **1** the act or an instance of extracting **2** the removal of a tooth by a dentist: *few patients need an extraction* **3** the origin or ancestry of a person: *he is of German extraction*

extractor fan n a fan used to remove stale air from a room

extracurricular adj not part of the normal courses taken by students: *her free time is devoted to extracurricular duties*

extradite vb **-diting, -dited** to hand over an alleged offender to the country where the crime took place for trial: *an agreement to extradite him to Hong Kong* **extraditable** adj **extradition** n **WORD ORIGIN** Latin *ex* away + *traditio* a handing over

extrajudicial adj **1** outside the ordinary course of legal proceedings: *extrajudicial evidence* **2** beyond the jurisdiction or authority of the court: *an extrajudicial opinion*

extramarital adj occurring between a married person and a person other than his or her spouse: *an extramarital affair*

extramural adj connected with but outside the normal courses of a university or college **WORD ORIGIN** Latin *extra* beyond + *murus* wall

extraneous (iks-**train**-ee-uss) adj not essential or relevant to the situation or subject being considered **WORD ORIGIN** Latin *extraneus* external

extraordinary adj **1** very unusual or surprising: *the extraordinary sight of my grandfather wearing a dress* **2** having some special or extreme quality: *an extraordinary first novel* **3** (of a meeting, ambassador, etc.) specially called or appointed to deal with one particular topic **extraordinarily** adv **WORD ORIGIN** Latin *extraordinarius* beyond what is usual

extraordinary rendition n the process by which a country seizes a terrorist suspect and then transports him or her for interrogation to a country where due process of law is unlikely to be respected

extrapolate (iks-**trap**-a-late) vb **-lating, -lated 1** to infer something not known from the known facts, using logic and reason **2** maths to estimate the value of a function or measurement beyond the known values, by the extension of a curve **extrapolation** n **WORD ORIGIN** EXTRA- + -*polate*, as in *interpolate*

extrasensory adj of or relating to extrasensory perception

extrasensory perception n the supposed ability to obtain information without the use of normal senses of sight, hearing, etc.

extravagant adj **1** spending more than is reasonable or affordable **2** costing more than is reasonable or affordable: *an extravagant gift* **3** going beyond usual or reasonable limits: *extravagant expectations* **4** (of behaviour or gestures) extreme, esp. in order to make a particular impression: *an extravagant display of affection* **5** very elaborate and impressive: *extravagant costumes* **extravagance** n **WORD ORIGIN** Latin *extra* beyond + *vagari* to wander

extravaganza n **1** an elaborate and lavish entertainment **2** any fanciful display, literary composition, etc. **WORD ORIGIN** Italian: *extravagance*

extravert adj, n same as **extrovert**

extreme adj **1** of a high or the highest degree or intensity **2** exceptionally severe or unusual: *people can survive extreme conditions* **3** (of an opinion, political group, etc.) beyond the limits regarded as acceptable; fanatical **4** farthest or outermost ▷ n **5** either of the two limits of a scale or range **6** go to extremes to be unreasonable in speech or action **7** in the extreme to the highest or furthest degree: *the effect was dramatic in the extreme* **extremely** adv **WORD ORIGIN** Latin *extremus* outermost

extreme sport n any of various sports with a high risk of injury or death

extreme unction n RC Church a former name for **anointing of the sick**

extremist n **1** a person who favours or uses extreme or violent methods, esp. to bring about political change ▷ adj **2** holding extreme opinions or using extreme methods **extremism** n

extremity n, pl **-ties 1** the farthest point **2** an unacceptable or extreme nature or degree: *the extremity of his views alienated other nationalists* **3** an extreme condition, such as misfortune **4 extremities** hands and feet

extricate vb **-cating, -cated** to free from a difficult or complicated situation or place **extricable** adj **extrication** n **WORD ORIGIN** Latin *extricare*

≡ **USAGE**
≡ See at **extract**.

extrinsic adj **1** not an integral or essential part **2** originating or acting from outside **extrinsically** adv **WORD ORIGIN** Latin *exter* outward + *secus* alongside

extroversion n psychol the directing of one's interests outwards, esp. towards making social contacts

extrovert adj **1** lively and outgoing **2** psychol concerned more with external reality than inner feelings ▷ n **3** a person who has these characteristics **extroverted** adj **WORD ORIGIN** *extro-* (variant of EXTRA-, contrasting with *intro-*) + Latin *vertere* to turn

extrude vb **-truding, -truded 1** to squeeze or force out **2** to produce moulded sections of plastic, metal, etc. by forcing through a shaped die **extruded** *adj* **extrusion** *n*

WORD ORIGIN Latin *extrudere* to thrust out

exuberant *adj* **1** full of vigour and high spirits **2** (of vegetation) growing thickly; flourishing **exuberance** *n*

WORD ORIGIN Latin *exuberans* abounding

exude *vb* **-uding, -uded 1** (of a liquid or smell) to seep or flow out slowly and steadily **2** to seem to have (a quality or feeling) to a great degree: *the Chancellor exuded confidence* **exudation** *n*

WORD ORIGIN Latin *exsudare*

exult *vb* to be joyful or jubilant **exultation** *n* **exultant** *adj*

WORD ORIGIN Latin *exsultare* to jump for joy

≡ USAGE
≡ See at **exalt**.

eye *n* **1** the organ of sight in humans and animals **2** the external part of an eye, often including the area around it **3** (often pl) the ability to see or record what is happening: *the eyes of an entire nation were upon us* **4** a look, glance, or gaze **5** attention or observation: *his new shirt caught my eye* **6** the ability to judge or appreciate something: *his shrewd eye for talent* **7** (often pl) opinion, judgment, or authority: *in the eyes of the law* **8** a dark spot on a potato from which new shoots can grow **9** a small hole, such as the one at the blunt end of a sewing needle **10** a small area of calm in the centre of a storm, hurricane, or tornado **11** all eyes *informal* acutely vigilant **12** an eye for an eye justice consisting of an equivalent action to the original wrong or harm **13** have eyes for to be interested in **14** in one's mind's eye

imagined or remembered vividly **15** in the public eye exposed to public curiosity **16** keep an eye on to take care of **17** keep an eye open *or* out for to watch with special attention for **18** keep one's eyes peeled *or* skinned to watch vigilantly **19** look someone in the eye to look openly and without embarrassment at someone **20** make eyes at someone to look at someone in an obviously attracted manner **21** more than meets the eye hidden motives, meanings, or facts **22** my eye! *old-fashioned informal* nonsense! **23** see eye to eye with to agree with **24** set *or* lay *or* clap eyes on to see: *I never laid eyes on him again* **25** turn a blind eye to *or* close one's eyes to to pretend not to notice **26** up to one's eyes in extremely busy with **27** with an eye to with the intention of **28** with one's eyes open in full knowledge of all the facts ▷ *vb* **eyeing** *or* **eying, eyed 29** to look at carefully or warily ▸ See also **eye up** ▷ **eyeless** *adj* **eyelike** *adj*

WORD ORIGIN Old English *ēage*

eyeball *n* **1** the entire ball-shaped part of the eye **2** eyeball to eyeball in close confrontation ▷ *vb* **3** *slang* to stare at

eyebrow *n* **1** the bony ridge over each eye **2** the arch of hair on this ridge **3** raise an eyebrow to show doubt or disapproval

eye-catching *adj* very striking and tending to catch people's attention **eye-catcher** *n*

eye dog *n* NZ a dog trained to control sheep by staring at them

eyeful *n* **1** *slang* a good look at or view of something **2** *slang* an attractive sight, esp. a woman **3** an amount of liquid, dust, etc. that has got into someone's eye

eyeglass *n* a lens for aiding defective vision

eyelash *n* any of the short hairs that grow from the edge of the eyelids

eyelet *n* **1** a small hole for a lace or cord to be passed through **2** a small metal ring reinforcing such a hole

eyelevel *adj* level with a person's eyes: *an eyelevel oven*

eyelid *n* either of the two folds of skin that cover an eye when it is closed

eyeliner *n* a cosmetic used to outline the eyes

eye-opener *n* *informal* something startling or revealing

eyepiece *n* the lens in a microscope, telescope, etc. into which the person using it looks

eye shadow *n* a coloured cosmetic worn on the upper eyelids

eyesight *n* the ability to see: *poor eyesight*

eyesore *n* something very ugly

eyestrain *n* fatigue or irritation of the eyes, caused by tiredness or a failure to wear glasses

eyetooth *n, pl* **-teeth 1** either of the two canine teeth in the upper jaw **2** give one's eyeteeth for to go to any lengths to achieve or obtain (something)

eye up *vb informal* to look at (someone) in a way that indicates sexual interest

eyewash *n* **1** a lotion for the eyes **2** *informal* nonsense; rubbish

eyewitness *n* a person present at an event who can describe what happened

eyrie *n* **1** the nest of an eagle, built in a high inaccessible place **2** any high isolated place

WORD ORIGIN Latin *area* open field, hence, nest

Ff

The letter F is the sixth letter of the English alphabet. The sound that it represents has its nearest equivalent in the Greek alphabet in the letter *phi* (Φ,φ), but F has its origins in another Greek character called *digamma*. This was formed by superimposing one letter *gamma* on another to produce a character with two horizontal strokes emerging from a vertical stem. In Classical Greek, the *digamma* had been discarded from the alphabet, but it remained in use as a numeral. It was not forgotten, however, and emerged in the Roman alphabet as F, while *phi* was discarded.

The lower-case version of this letter is unusual in being of three-quarter height and having a cross-stroke. The shape of the letter can create problems in typography by causing it to run into following letters, and some fonts get around this by representing the combinations 'fi' and 'fl' by a single character or 'glyph'.

The letter F has found use as an abbreviation in various technical subjects. In biology, it represents a 'filial generation': to a geneticist the children of a parent are referred to as the 'F1 generation', the grandchildren as the 'F2 generation', and so on. In photography, meanwhile, a lower-case form of the letter is used as an abbreviation for 'focal length', and the lower the 'f-number' of a lens, the faster it is. To a historian, however, the letter F is more likely to call to mind 'the three F's', which were the items for which the Irish land reformers agitated in the late 19th century, these being fixity of tenure, free sale, and fair rent.

In modern times the letter F has been brought into some disrepute by the fact that it is the first letter of a notoriously offensive word, which is often referred to as 'the F word'. However, quite a different picture of the letter F is revealed in Jane Austen's *Sense and Sensibility*. After Elinor Dashwood is suspected of having formed an attachment to Edward Ferrars, she is subjected to teasing in the form of frequent allusions to the initial letter of Mr Ferrars' surname: 'The letter F-- had been likewise invariably brought forward, and found productive of such countless jokes, that its character as the wittiest letter in the alphabet had been long established with Elinor.'

---

f¹ *physics* frequency

f², **f/** or **f:** f-number

F 1 *music* the fourth note of the scale of C major **2** Fahrenheit **3** farad(s) **4** *chem* fluorine **5** *physics* force **6** franc(s)

f. or **F. 1** fathom(s) **2** female **3** *grammar* feminine **4** *pl* **ff.** following (page)

fa *n music* same as **fah**

FA (in Britain) Football Association

F.A.B. *interj Brit informal* an expression of agreement to, or acknowledgement of, a command
WORD ORIGIN from British television series, *Thunderbirds*

Fabian (**fay**-bee-an) *adj* **1** of the Fabian Society, which aims to establish socialism gradually and democratically ▷ *n* **2** a member of the Fabian Society **Fabianism** *n*
WORD ORIGIN after *Fabius*, Roman general, who wore out Hannibal's strength while avoiding a pitched battle

fable *n* **1** a short story, often one with animals as characters, that illustrates a moral **2** an unlikely story which is usually untrue **3** a story about mythical characters or events
WORD ORIGIN Latin *fabula* story

fabled *adj* well-known from anecdotes and stories rather than experience

Fablon *n trademark* a brand of adhesive-backed plastic used for covering surfaces

fabric *n* **1** any cloth made from yarn or fibres by weaving or knitting **2** the structure that holds a system together: *the fabric of society* **3** the walls, floor, and roof of a building
WORD ORIGIN Latin *faber* craftsman

fabricate *vb* **-cating, -cated 1** to invent a story or lie: *fabricated reports about the opposition* **2** to make or build **fabrication** *n*
WORD ORIGIN Latin *fabrica* workshop

fabulous *adj* **1** *informal* extremely good **2** almost unbelievable: *a city of fabulous wealth* **3** told of in fables and legends: *a fabulous horned creature* **fabulously** *adv*
WORD ORIGIN Latin *fabulosus* celebrated in fable

facade (fass-**sahd**) *n* **1** the front of a building **2** a front or deceptive outer appearance

face *n* **1** the front of the head from the forehead to the lower jaw **2 a** one's expression: *as his eyes met hers his face sobered* **b** a distorted expression to show disgust or defiance: *she was pulling a face at him* **3** the front or main side of an object, building, etc. **4** the surface of a clock or watch that has the numbers or hands on it **5** the functional side of an object, such as a tool or playing card **6** the exposed area of a mine from which coal or metal can be mined **7** *Brit slang* a well-known or important person **8 in the face of** in spite of: *a determined character in the face of adversity* **9 lose face** to lose one's credibility **10 on the face of it** to all appearances **11 put a good** or **brave face on** to maintain a cheerful appearance despite misfortune **12 save face** to keep one's good reputation **13 set one's face against** to oppose with determination **14 to someone's face** directly and openly ▷ *vb* **facing, faced 15** to look towards **16** to be opposite **17** to be confronted by: *they were faced with the prospect of high inflation* **18** to provide with a surface of a different material ▶ See also **face up to**
WORD ORIGIN Latin *facies* form

Facebook *n* a popular social networking site

face card *n* a playing card showing a king, queen, or jack

faceless *adj* without individual identity or character: *faceless government officials*

face-lift *n* **1** cosmetic surgery for tightening sagging skin and smoothing wrinkles on the face **2** an outward improvement designed to give a more

Scottish English
part 2

Scots began as a Northern Variety of Middle English. English was already present in what is now Scotland from the 7th century AD, when the Anglian kingdom of Northumbria annexed *Din Eidyn* and renamed it *Edinburgh*.

For the next several centuries, as Northumbrian English became established in the Lothian region, there would not have been a distinctly 'Scottish' variety of English; rather, the language was just another variety of Northern English. Later, however, when Scotland became politically distinct from England, the language which was still called 'Inglis' began to develop features peculiar to Scotland.

The earliest form of Scots for which we have evidence is called Older Scots, and it made its literary debut in 1375, when John Barbour, Archdeacon of Aberdeen (though he was probably born in Galloway) composed *The Brus*, an epic poem recounting the history of Scotland's King Robert the Bruce, who defeated the English King at Bannockburn in 1314. Barbour called his language 'Inglis' (English), and many of the features of Older Scots are practically identical to the features of Northern Middle English: the use of *quh-* for words that begin *wh-* in the South (*quha* for *who*; *quhen* for *when*, etc); *y-* in place of *th-* or the character *thorn* (þ) (*ye* for *þe* or *the*; *yat* for *þat* or *that*); the vowel *a* where *o* would be expected in the Modern English (*bat* for *boat*). Certain features are similar to Northern Middle English, but have developed in a specific way. As with Northern Middle English, Older Scots uses the *-s* inflection for the third person present singular of verbs; however, Scots prefers *-is* or *-ys* to *-es* (*haldis* instead of *haldes*). This inflection is also used for the plural and genitive singular of nouns, so that, viewed in isolation, the word *baris* can mean '[s/he] bears [it]', '[the] bears', or '[the] bear's [thing]'. Older Scots also tends to have the character yogh (ȝ) where Southern Middle English and Modern English have *y* (ȝ*eit* for *yet*; ȝ*our* for *your*) and *ch* where English has *gh* (*richt* for *right*). And one of the most distinctive features of Older Scots is the addition of the letter *i* immediately after a vowel to make it 'long' (Modern English uses *e* after the next consonant, as in *rat* versus *rate*).

Some of these features can be seen in the following passage from the *Brus*:

> *Ye Brus lap on and yidder raid*
> *And thocht for owtyn mar letting*
> *For to qwyt hym his discoueryng.*
> *Yidder he raid but langer let*
> *And with Schyr Ihone ye Cumyn met*
> *In ye Freris at ye hye awter*
> *And schawyt him with lauchand cher*
> *Ye endentur, syne with a knyff*
> *Rycht in yat sted hym reft ye lyff.*

We clearly see *raid* for 'road', *thocht* for 'thought', *mar* for 'more', and *ye* and *yidder* for 'ye' and 'thither'. Also evident is the suffix *-and* in place of *-ing* in the word *lauchand* ('laughing'), which is also common in Northern Middle English.

Alongside these linguistic features there is a Scots vocabulary. Again, some words are shared with Northern English: *mekill* ('large'), *gat(e)* ('road'), *till* ('to') are all common in Northern England (there is still a Micklegate in York), and all derive from Old Norse. Norse also gave Scots some words which do not occur in England, such as *kirk* ('church'), *thole* ('suffer'), and *wicht* ('mighty'). The most striking thing about the vocabulary, though, is the absence of Gaelic words. Apart from place-names and geographical features like *loch*, *brae*, and *craig*, the vocabulary of Scots is entirely Germanic. The linguistic picture of medieval Scotland, then, is one of English dominant in the Central Belt, largely identical to Northern Middle English, but with peculiar spelling and (probably) pronunciation, and some vocabulary borrowed from the recent invaders from Scandinavia (whom Scotland managed to push out about a century before the English did).

Writing in Older Scots is scarce: largely represented by *The Brus* and three other major poetical works of the 14th century, two of which, the *Legends of the Saints* and the *Buik of Alexander*, were once attributed to Barbour, and the third, Andrew of Wyntoun's *Cronikill*, is a historical work in verse.

modern appearance: *the stadium was given a face-lift*

facer *n Brit old-fashioned informal* a difficulty or problem

face-saving *adj* preventing damage to one's reputation **face-saver** *n*

facet *n* **1** an aspect of something, such as a personality **2** any of the surfaces of a cut gemstone
WORD ORIGIN French *facette* little face

facetious (fass-**see**-shuss) *adj* joking, or trying to be amusing, esp. at inappropriate times **facetiously** *adv*
WORD ORIGIN Old French *facetie* witticism

face up to *vb* to accept an unpleasant fact or reality

face value *n* apparent worth or meaning: *only a fool would take it at face value*

facia (**fay**-shee-a) *n, pl* **-ciae** (-shee-ee) same as **fascia**

facial *adj* **1** of the face ▷ *n* **2** a beauty treatment for the face **facially** *adv*

facile (**fass**-ile) *adj* **1** (of a remark, argument, etc.) overly simple and showing lack of real thought **2** easily performed or achieved: *a facile winner of his only race this year*
WORD ORIGIN Latin *facilis* easy

facilitate *vb* **-tating, -tated** to make easier the progress of: *the agreement helped facilitate trade between the countries* **facilitation** *n*

facility *n, pl* **-ties 1 facilities** the means or equipment needed for an activity: *leisure and shopping facilities* **2** the ability to do things easily and well **3** skill or ease: *grown human beings can forget with remarkable facility*
WORD ORIGIN Latin *facilis* easy

facing *n* **1** a piece of material used esp. to conceal the seam of a garment **2 facings** contrasting collar and cuffs on a jacket **3** an outer layer of material applied to the surface of a wall

facsimile (fak-**sim**-ill-ee) *n* **1** an exact copy **2** same as **fax** (senses 1, 2)
WORD ORIGIN Latin *fac simile!* make something like it!

fact *n* **1** an event or thing known to have happened or existed **2** a truth that can be proved from experience or observation **3** a piece of information **4 after** or **before the fact** *criminal law* after or before the commission of the offence **5 as a matter of fact** or **in fact** in reality or actuality **6 fact of life** an inescapable truth, esp. an unpleasant one. See also **facts of life**
WORD ORIGIN Latin *factum* something done

faction¹ *n* **1** a small group of people within a larger body, but differing from it in certain aims and ideas **2** strife within a group **factional** *adj*
WORD ORIGIN Latin *factio* a making

faction² *n* a dramatized presentation of actual events
WORD ORIGIN blend of FACT + FICTION

factious *adj* inclined to quarrel and cause divisions: *a factious political party is unelectable*
⸗ USAGE
⸗ See at **fractious**.

factitious *adj* artificial rather than natural
WORD ORIGIN Latin *facticius*

factor *n* **1** an element that contributes to a result: *reliability was an important factor in the success of the car* **2** *maths* any whole number that will divide exactly into a given number, for example 2 and 3 are factors of 6 **3** a quantity by which an amount is multiplied or divided to become that number of times bigger or smaller: *production increased by a factor of 3* **4** *med* any of several substances that participate in the clotting of blood: *factor VIII* **5** a level on a scale of measurement: *suntan oil with a factor of 5* **6** (in Scotland) the manager of an estate
WORD ORIGIN Latin: one who acts
⸗ USAGE
⸗ *Factor* (sense 1) should only be used to
⸗ refer to something which contributes
⸗ to a result. It should not be used to
⸗ refer to a part of something such as
⸗ a plan or arrangement; instead a
⸗ word such as *component* or *element*
⸗ should be used.

factorial *maths n* **1** the product of all the whole numbers from one to a given whole number ▷ *adj* **2** of factorials or factors

factorize or **-rise** *vb* **-rizing, -rized** or **-rising, -rised** *maths* to resolve a whole number into factors **factorization** or **-risation** *n*

factory *n, pl* **-ries** a building where goods are manufactured in large quantities
WORD ORIGIN Late Latin *factorium*, from *facere* to make

factory farm *n Brit, Austral, & NZ* a farm in which animals are given foods that increase the amount of meat, eggs, or milk they yield **factory farming** *n*

factory ship *n* a vessel that processes fish supplied by a fleet

factotum *n* a person employed to do all kinds of work
WORD ORIGIN Latin *fac!* do! + *totum* all

facts of life *pl n* the details of sexual behaviour and reproduction

factual *adj* concerning facts rather than opinions or theories: *a factual report* **factually** *adv*

faculty *n, pl* **-ties 1** one of the powers of the mind or body, such as memory, sight, or hearing **2** any ability or power, either inborn or acquired: *his faculties of reasoning were considerable* **3 a** a department within a university or college **b** its staff **c** *chiefly US & Canad* all the teaching staff of a university, school, or college
WORD ORIGIN Latin *facultas* capability

fad *n informal* **1** an intense but short-lived fashion: *the skateboard fad* **2** a personal whim **faddish** *adj*
WORD ORIGIN origin unknown

faddy *adj* **-dier, -diest** unreasonably fussy, particularly about food

fade *vb* **fading, faded 1** to lose brightness, colour, or strength **2 fade away** or **out** to vanish slowly
WORD ORIGIN Middle English *fade* dull

fade in or **out** *vb* (of vision or sound in a film or broadcast) to increase or decrease gradually

faeces or *esp. US* **feces** (**fee**-seez) *pl n* bodily waste matter discharged through the anus **faecal** or *esp. US* **fecal** (**fee**-kl) *adj*
WORD ORIGIN Latin: dregs

Faeroese or **Faroese** (fair-oh-**eez**) *adj* **1** of the Faeroes, islands in the N Atlantic ▷ *n* **2** *pl* **-ese** a person from the Faeroes **3** the language of the Faeroes

faff about *vb Brit & S African informal* to dither or fuss
WORD ORIGIN origin unknown

fag¹ *n* **1** *informal* a boring or tiring task: *weeding was a fag* **2** *Brit* (esp. formerly) a young public school boy who performs menial chores for an older boy ▷ *vb* **fagging, fagged 3** *Brit* to do menial chores in a public school
WORD ORIGIN origin unknown

fag² *n slang* a cigarette
WORD ORIGIN origin unknown

fag³ *n offensive slang chiefly US & Canad* short for **faggot²**

fag end *n* **1** the last and worst part: *another dull game at the fag end of the football season* **2** *Brit & NZ informal* the stub of a cigarette

fagged *adj informal* exhausted by hard work. Also: **fagged out**

faggot¹ or *esp. US* **fagot** *n* **1** *Brit, Austral, & NZ* a ball of chopped liver bound with herbs and bread **2** a bundle of sticks
WORD ORIGIN from Old French

faggot² *n offensive slang* a male homosexual
WORD ORIGIN special use of FAGGOT¹

fah *n music* (in tonic sol-fa) the fourth note of any ascending major scale

Fahrenheit (**far**-ren-hite) *adj* of or measured according to the scale of temperature in which 32° represents the melting point of ice and 212° the boiling point of water
WORD ORIGIN after Gabriel *Fahrenheit*, physicist

faïence (**fie**-ence) *n* tin-glazed earthenware
WORD ORIGIN *Faenza*, N Italy, where made

fail *vb* **1** to be unsuccessful in an attempt **2** to stop operating **3** to judge or be judged as being below the officially accepted standard required in a course or examination **4** to prove disappointing or useless to someone: *the government has failed the homeless* **5** to neglect or be unable to do something: *he failed to repair the car* **6** to go bankrupt ▷ *n* **7** a failure to attain the required standard **8 without fail a** regularly or without exception: *use this shampoo once a week without fail* **b** definitely: *they agreed to enforce the embargo without fail*
WORD ORIGIN Latin *fallere* to disappoint

failing *n* **1** a weak point ▷ *prep* **2 failing that** alternatively: *your doctor will normally be able to advise you or, failing that, one of the self-help agencies*

fail-safe *adj* **1** designed to return to a safe condition in the event of a failure or malfunction **2** safe from failure

failure *n* **1** the act or an instance of failing **2** someone or something that is unsuccessful: *he couldn't help but regard his own son as a failure* **3** the fact of something required or expected not being done or not happening: *his failure to appear at the meeting* **4** a halt in normal operation: *heart failure* **5** a decline or loss of something: *crop failure* **6** the fact of not reaching the required standard in an examination or test

fain *adv old-fashioned* gladly or willingly
WORD ORIGIN Old English *fægen*

faint *adj* **1** lacking clarity, brightness, or volume: *her voice was very faint* **2** feeling dizzy or weak **3** lacking conviction or force: *a faint attempt to smile* ▷ *vb* **4** to lose consciousness ▷ *n* **5** a sudden loss of consciousness **faintly** *adv*
WORD ORIGIN Old French *faindre* to be idle

faint-hearted *adj* lacking courage and confidence

fair¹ *adj* **1** reasonable and just: *a move towards fair trade* **2** in agreement with rules **3** light in colour: *her fair skin* **4** *old-fashioned* young and beautiful: *a fair maiden* **5** quite good: *a fair attempt at making a soufflé* **6** quite large: *they made a fair amount of money* **7** (of the tide or wind) favourable to the passage of a ship or plane **8** fine or cloudless **9** **fair and square** in a correct or just way ▷ *adv* **10** in a fair way **11** absolutely or squarely: *he was caught fair off his guard* **fairness** *n*
WORD ORIGIN Old English *fæger*

fair² *n* **1** a travelling entertainment with sideshows, rides, and amusements **2** an exhibition of goods produced by a particular industry to promote business: *the Frankfurt book fair*
WORD ORIGIN Latin *feriae* holidays

fair copy *n* a neat copy, without mistakes or alterations, of a piece of writing

fair game *n* a person regarded as a justifiable target for criticism or ridicule

fairground *n* an open space used for a fair

fairing *n* a metal structure fitted around parts of an aircraft, car, etc. to reduce drag
WORD ORIGIN *fair* to streamline

Fair Isle *n* an intricate multicoloured knitted pattern
WORD ORIGIN after one of the Shetland Islands where this type of pattern originated

fairly *adv* **1** to a moderate degree or extent: *in the Philippines labour is fairly cheap* **2** to a great degree or extent: *the folder fairly bulged with documents* **3** as deserved: *the pound was fairly valued against the Deutschmark*

fair play *n* a conventional standard of honourable behaviour

fair sex *n* **the fair sex** *old-fashioned* women collectively

fair trade *n* the practice of buying goods from producers in the developing world at a guaranteed price

fairway *n* **1** (on a golf course) the mown areas between tees and greens **2** *naut* a part of a river or sea on which ships may sail

fair-weather *adj* not reliable in difficult situations: *a fair-weather friend*

fairy *n, pl* **fairies 1** an imaginary supernatural being with magical powers **2** *offensive slang* a male homosexual
WORD ORIGIN Old French *faerie* fairyland, from *feie* fairy

fairy floss *n Austral* a light fluffy mass of spun sugar, held on a stick. Also called: **candy floss**

fairy godmother *n* a generous friend who appears unexpectedly and offers help in time of trouble

fairyland *n* **1** an imaginary place where fairies live **2** an enchanted or wonderful place

fairy lights *pl n* small coloured electric bulbs used as decoration, esp. on a Christmas tree

fairy penguin *n* a small penguin with a bluish head and back, found on the Australian coast

fairy ring *n* a ring of dark grass caused by fungi

fairy tale or **story** *n* **1** a story about fairies or magical events **2** a highly improbable account: *his report was little more than a fairy tale* ▷ *adj* **fairy-tale 3** of or like a fairy tale: *a fairy-tale wedding* **4** highly improbable: *a fairy-tale account of his achievements*

fait accompli (**fate** ak-**kom**-plee) *n* something already done and beyond alteration: *they had to accept the invasion as a fait accompli*
WORD ORIGIN French

faith *n* **1** strong belief in something, esp. without proof **2** a specific system of religious beliefs **3** complete confidence or trust, such as in a person or remedy **4** allegiance to a person or cause **5 bad faith** dishonesty **6 good faith** honesty
WORD ORIGIN Latin *fides* trust, confidence

faithful *adj* **1** remaining true or loyal **2** maintaining sexual loyalty to one's lover or spouse **3** consistently reliable: *my old, but faithful, four-cylinder car* **4** accurate in detail: *a faithful translation of the book* ▷ *pl n* **the faithful 5 a** the believers in a religious faith **b** loyal followers **faithfully** *adv* **faithfulness** *n*

faith healing *n* treatment of a sick person through the power of religious faith **faith healer** *n*

faithless *adj* treacherous or disloyal

fajitas (fa-**hee**-taz) *pl n* a Mexican dish of soft tortillas wrapped around fried strips of meat or vegetables
WORD ORIGIN Mexican Spanish

fake *vb* **faking, faked 1** to cause something not genuine to appear real or more valuable by fraud **2** to pretend to have (an illness, emotion, etc.) ▷ *n* **3** an object, person, or act that is not genuine ▷ *adj* **4** not genuine: *fake fur*
WORD ORIGIN probably from Italian *facciare* to make or do

fakir (**fay**-keer) *n* **1** a Muslim religious ascetic who spurns worldly possessions **2** a Hindu holy man
WORD ORIGIN Arabic *faqīr* poor

falcon *n* a type of bird of prey that can be trained to hunt other birds and small animals
WORD ORIGIN Late Latin *falco* hawk

falconry *n* **1** the art of training falcons to hunt **2** the sport of hunting with falcons **falconer** *n*

fall *vb* **falling, fell, fallen 1** to descend by the force of gravity from a higher to a lower place **2** to drop suddenly from an upright position **3** to collapse to the ground **4** to become less or lower in number or quality: *inflation fell by one percentage point* **5** to slope downwards **6** to be badly wounded or killed **7** to give in to attack: *in 1939 Barcelona fell to the Nationalists* **8** to lose power or status **9** to pass into a specified condition: *I fell asleep* **10** to adopt a downhearted expression: *his face fell and he pouted like a child* **11** (of night or darkness) to begin **12** to occur at a specified time: *Christmas falls on a Sunday* **13** to give in to temptation or sin **14 fall apart a** to break owing to long use or poor construction: *the chassis is falling apart* **b** to become disorganized and ineffective: *since you resigned, the office has fallen apart* **15 fall short** to prove inadequate **16 fall short of** to fail to reach (a standard) ▷ *n* **17** an instance of falling **18** an amount of something, such as snow or soot, that has fallen **19** a decrease in value or number **20** a decline in status or importance: *the town's fall from prosperity* **21** a capture or overthrow: *the fall of Budapest in February 1945* **22** *wrestling* a scoring move, pinning both shoulders of one's opponent to the floor for a specified period **23** *chiefly US* autumn ▸ See also **fall about, fall away, falls**, etc.
WORD ORIGIN Old English *feallan*

Fall *n* **the Fall** *theol* the state of mankind's innate sinfulness following Adam's sin of disobeying God

fall about *vb* to laugh uncontrollably

fallacy *n, pl* **-cies 1** an incorrect or misleading notion based on inaccurate facts or faulty reasoning: *the fallacy underlying the government's industrial policy* **2** reasoning that is unsound **fallacious** *adj*
WORD ORIGIN Latin *fallere* to deceive

fall away *vb* **1** to slope down: *the ground fell away sharply to the south* **2** to decrease in size or intensity: *obstacles to all-party talks are falling away with amazing speed*

fall back *vb* **1** to retreat **2 fall back on** to have to choose (a less acceptable alternative): *they had to fall back on other lines of defence*

fall behind *vb* **1** to fail to keep up **2** to be in arrears, such as with a payment

fall down *vb* **1** to drop suddenly or collapse **2** to fail to meet requirements **3** (of an argument or idea) to fail at a specific point: *in one area only did the case fall down*

fallen *vb* **1** the past participle of **fall** ▷ *adj* **2** *old-fashioned* (of a woman) having had sex outside marriage **3** killed in battle

fall for *vb* **1** to become strongly attracted to (someone) **2** to be deceived by (a lie or trick)

fall guy *n informal* **1** the victim of a confidence trick **2** a person who is publicly blamed for something, though it may not be his or her fault

fallible *adj* **1** (of a person) liable to make mistakes **2** capable of error: *our*

all-too-fallible economic indicators
fallibility *n*
WORD ORIGIN Latin *fallere* to deceive

fall in *vb* **1** to collapse **2** to get into line or formation in a display, march, or procession **3 fall in with a** to meet and join **b** to agree with or support (a person or a suggestion)

falling star *n informal* a meteor

fall off *vb* **1** to drop unintentionally to the ground from (a bicycle, horse, etc.) **2** to decrease in size or intensity: *demand for beef began to fall off*

fall on *vb* **1** to attack (an enemy) **2** to meet with (something unpleasant): *his family had fallen on hard times* **3** to affect: *a horrified hush fell on the company* **4 fall on one's feet** to emerge unexpectedly well from a difficult situation

Fallopian tube *n* either of a pair of slender tubes through which eggs pass from the ovaries to the uterus in female mammals
WORD ORIGIN after Gabriello *Fallopio*, anatomist

fallout *n* **1** radioactive material in the atmosphere following a nuclear explosion **2** unpleasant circumstances following an event: *the political fallout of the riots* ▷ *vb* **fall out 3** *informal* to disagree and quarrel: *I hope we don't fall out over this issue* **4** to leave a military formation

fallow¹ *adj* (of land) left unseeded after being ploughed to regain fertility for a future crop
WORD ORIGIN Old English *fealga*

fallow² *adj* light yellowish-brown
WORD ORIGIN Old English *fealu*

fallow deer *n* a deer that has a reddish coat with white spots in summer

falls *pl n* a waterfall

fall through *vb* to fail before completion: *his transfer deal fell through*

fall to *vb* **1** to become the responsibility of: *it fell to the Prime Minister to announce the plans* **2** to begin (some activity, such as eating, working, or fighting)

false *adj* **1** not in accordance with the truth or facts: *false allegations* **2** not real or genuine but intended to seem so: *false teeth* **3** misleading or deceptive: *their false promises* **4** forced or insincere: *false cheer* **5** based on mistaken ideas **falsely** *adv* **falseness** *n*
WORD ORIGIN Latin *falsus*

false alarm *n* a situation that appears to be dangerous but turns out not to be: *air-raid sirens sounded once but it turned out to be a false alarm*

falsehood *n* **1** the quality of being untrue **2** a lie

false pretences *pl n* **under false pretences** so as to mislead people about one's true intentions

false start *n athletics & swimming* an occasion when one competitor starts a race before the starter's signal has been given, which means that all competitors have to be recalled and the race restarted

falsetto *n, pl* **-tos** a voice pitch higher than one's normal range
WORD ORIGIN Italian

falsies *pl n informal* pads worn to exaggerate the size of a woman's breasts

falsify *vb* **-fies, -fying, -fied** to make a report or evidence false by alteration in order to deceive **falsification** *n*
WORD ORIGIN Latin *falsus* false + *facere* to make

falsity *n, pl* **-ties 1** the state of being false **2** a lie

falter *vb* **1** to be hesitant, weak, or unsure **2** (of a machine) to lose power or strength in an uneven way: *the engine began to falter and the plane lost height* **3** to speak nervously and without confidence **4** to stop moving smoothly and start moving unsteadily: *as he neared the house his steps faltered* **faltering** *adj*
WORD ORIGIN origin unknown

fame *n* the state of being widely known or recognized
WORD ORIGIN Latin *fama* report

famed *adj* extremely well-known: *a nation famed for its efficiency*

familial *adj formal* of or relating to the family

familiar *adj* **1** well-known **2** frequent or common: *it was a familiar argument* **3 familiar with** well acquainted with **4** friendly and informal **5** more intimate than is acceptable ▷ *n* **6** an animal or bird believed to share with a witch her supernatural powers **7** a friend **familiarly** *adv* **familiarity** *n*
WORD ORIGIN Latin *familia* family

familiarize *or* **-rise** *vb* **-rizing, -rized** *or* **-rising, -rised** to make (oneself or someone else) fully aware of a particular subject **familiarization** *or* **-risation** *n*

family *n, pl* **-lies 1** a social group consisting of parents and their offspring ▶ Related adjective: **familial 2** one's wife or husband and one's children **3** one's children **4** a group descended from a common ancestor **5** all the people living together in one household **6** any group of related objects or beings: *a family of chemicals* **7** *biol* one of the groups into which an order is divided, containing one or more genera: *the cat family* ▷ *adj* **8** of or suitable for a family or any of its members: *films for a family audience* **9 in the family way** *informal* pregnant
WORD ORIGIN Latin *familia*

Family Allowance *n* **1** in Britain, a former name for **child benefit 2** (in Canada) an allowance formerly paid by the Federal Government to the parents of dependent children

family assistance *n* (in New Zealand) a tax credit given to families on the basis of their income and family size

family doctor *n Brit, Austral, & NZ informal* same as **general practitioner**

family man *n* **1** a man with a wife and children **2** a man who loves his family and spends a lot of time with them

family name *n* a surname, esp. when regarded as representing a family's good reputation

family planning *n* the control of the number of children in a family by the use of contraceptives

family tree *n* a chart showing the relationships between individuals in a family over many generations

famine *n* a severe shortage of food
WORD ORIGIN Latin *fames* hunger

famish *vb* **be famished** *or* **famishing** to be very hungry
WORD ORIGIN Latin *fames* hunger

famous *adj* known to or recognized by many people
WORD ORIGIN Latin *famosus*

famously *adv* **1** well-known: *her famously relaxed manner* **2** very well: *the two got on famously*

fan¹ *n* **1** any device for creating a current of air, esp. a rotating machine of blades attached to a central hub **2** a hand-held object, usually made of paper, which creates a draught of cool air when waved **3** something shaped like such a fan, such as the tail of certain birds ▷ *vb* **fanning, fanned 4** to create a draught of air in the direction of someone or something **5 fan out** to spread out in the shape of a fan: *the troops fanned out along the beach*
WORD ORIGIN Latin *vannus*

fan² *n* a person who admires or is enthusiastic about a pop star, actor, sport, or hobby: *he was a big fan of Woody Allen*
WORD ORIGIN from *fanatic*

fanatic *n* **1** a person whose enthusiasm for something, esp. a political or religious cause, is extreme **2** *informal* a person devoted to a particular hobby or pastime ▷ *adj also* **fanatical 3** excessively enthusiastic **fanatically** *adv* **fanaticism** *n*
WORD ORIGIN Latin *fanaticus* belonging to a temple, hence, inspired by a god, frenzied

fanbase *n* a body of admirers of a particular pop singer, sports team, etc.

fan belt *n* the belt that drives a cooling fan in a car engine

fancier *n* a person with a keen interest in the thing specified: *a pigeon fancier*

fanciful *adj* **1** not based on fact **2** made in a curious or imaginative way: *fanciful architecture* **3** guided by unrestrained imagination: *fanciful tales of fairy folk* **fancifully** *adv*

fan club *n* **1** an organized group of admirers of a particular pop singer or star **2 be a member of someone's fan club** *informal* to approve of someone strongly

fancy *adj* **-cier, -ciest 1** special, unusual, and elaborate **2** (often used ironically) superior in quality **3** (of a price) higher than expected ▷ *n, pl* **-cies 4** a sudden spontaneous idea **5** a sudden or irrational liking for a person or thing **6** *old-fashioned or literary* a person's imagination ▷ *vb* **-cies, -cying, -cied 7** *Brit informal* to be physically attracted to (another person) **8** *informal* to have a wish for **9** to picture in the imagination **10** to think or suppose: *I fancy I am redundant here* **11 fancy oneself** to have a high opinion of oneself ▷ *interj* **12** Also: **fancy that!** an exclamation of surprise **fancily** *adv*
WORD ORIGIN Middle English *fantsy*

Geordie Dialect

To those who come from the rest of the United Kingdom, the word *Geordie* may conjure up the whole of the North-East of England from the River Tees to the Scottish border. To those within the North-East, however, the word has a narrower meaning, and refers exclusively to the language of Tyneside. A native of Newcastle would be apt to refer to the people of nearby Wearside as *Mackems* (after the Wearsiders' saying concerning ships that 'we mak 'em and they [the Tynesiders] tak 'em [out to sea]'). Inhabitants of the more distant Teesside are known as *Smoggies* (a name that reflects the pollution associated with the local chemical industry), although someone from Hartlepool is more specifically a *Monkeyhanger* (referring to the story that during the Napoleonic wars the townspeople executed a shipwrecked ape for being a French spy).

Although a true Geordie may only come from the area around Newcastle and Gateshead, all of the dialects spoken in North-East England have much in common. Indeed, many of the dialect words of the North-East are common to other Northern versions of English. You might equally hear the words *aye* ('yes'), *badly* ('ill'), and *nowt* ('nothing') from a native of Yorkshire, while words such as *baary* ('fine'), *bairn* ('child'), and *hoaching* ('full of people') are also used by Scots.

Many words that are characteristic of the Geordie dialect are simply Standard English words that have altered vowel sounds: *talk* and *walk* become *taak* and *waak*; *make* and *take* become *mak* and *tak* or *mek* and *tek*; *cow* and *now* become *coo* and *noo*; *dead* and *head* become *deed* and *heed*; and *down* and *town* become *doon* and *toon*. The letter 'v' makes a frequent appearance in Geordie dialectal forms as *to* becomes *tiv* and *do* becomes *div*, while another common transformation involves the letter 'y' following an initial consonant, as when *boot* becomes *byeut* and *cook* becomes *cyeuk*.

Characteristic Geordie pronouns include *yous*, which acts as a plural form of *you*, and *wor* meaning 'our'. The latter is often used before a name as a sign of affection, as in 'wor Jackie', the nickname of Newcastle football legend Jackie Milburn.

It may say something about the warmth of the North-Eastern character that the dialect is rich with terms of approval. A person described as *bonny* is good-looking, while if you call someone *canny* you are more likely to be referring to their agreeable personality. The word *pet* is often used as a friendly form of address, and a special friend might be called a *hinny* (an altered form of 'honey').

A greeting may be followed by the exclamation *howay*, meaning 'let's go' or 'come on' (which is probably familiar from the chant of 'Howay the lads', used by the supporters in the 'Toon Army' to urge on the players of Newcastle United). This is not to be confused with *hadaway*, which has the opposite meaning of 'go away', and is used in expressions of dismissal.

As with other regions, there are some distinctive words for local delicacies. *Panhaggerty* is a dish made by frying up leftover meat and potatoes; a *stottie* is a wedge of bread cut from a flat round loaf, usually filled with meat or cheese; while a *singing hinny* is a kind of currant bun (so called from noise it makes while being cooked on a griddle).

The traditional coalmining industry was responsible for words such as *yacker* ('a miner'), *gallowa* ('a pit pony'), and *caunch* ('a mound of earth'). In his spare time, a miner might have kept pigeons in a *ducket* ('dovecot') or *cree* ('shed'). However, the decline of the coal industry has meant that many words of the miners' jargon (known as 'Pitmatic') have now become obsolete.

Nowadays, Newcastle is noted for its lively nightlife (although drinking has always played a major part in the mythology of the area). Revellers can enjoy a *bottle of broon* (a bottle of Newcastle Brown Ale, also fondly referred to as a *bottle of dog*), with the result that they may become *peevy*, *bladdered*, or *palatick* - the Geordie dialect is not lacking in synonyms for 'drunk'.

fancy dress *n* clothing worn for a party at which people dress up to look like a particular animal or character

fancy-free *adj* free from commitments, esp. marriage

fancy goods *pl n* small decorative gifts

fancy man *n* *old-fashioned slang* a woman's lover

fancy woman *n* *old-fashioned slang* a man's lover

fancywork *n* ornamental needlework

fandango *n, pl* **-gos 1** a lively Spanish dance **2** music for this dance
WORD ORIGIN Spanish

fanfare *n* a short rousing tune played on brass instruments
WORD ORIGIN French

fang *n* **1** the long pointed tooth of a poisonous snake through which poison is injected **2** the canine tooth of a meat-eating mammal
WORD ORIGIN Old English: what is caught, prey

fanjet *n* same as **turbofan**

fanlight *n* a semicircular window over a door or another window

fanny *n, pl* **-nies** *slang* **1** *Austral & Brit taboo* the female genitals **2** *chiefly US & Canad* the buttocks
WORD ORIGIN origin unknown

fantail *n* **1** a breed of domestic pigeon with a large tail like a fan **2** a fly-catching bird of Australia, New Zealand, and SE Asia with a broad fan-shaped tail

fantasia *n* **1** any musical work not composed in a strict form **2** a mixture of popular tunes arranged as a continuous whole
WORD ORIGIN Italian: fancy

fantasize *or* **-sise** *vb* **-sizing, -sized** *or* **-sising, -sised** to imagine pleasant but unlikely events

fantastic *adj* **1** *informal* excellent **2** *informal* very large in degree or amount: *a fantastic amount of money* **3** strange or exotic in appearance: *fantastic costumes* **4** difficult to believe or unlikely to happen **fantastically** *adv*

fantasy *n, pl* **-sies 1** a far-fetched idea **2** imagination unrestricted by reality **3** a daydream **4** fiction with a large fantasy content **5** *music* same as **fantasia** ▷ *adj* **6** of a competition in which a participant selects players for an imaginary, ideal team and points are awarded according to the actual performances of the chosen players: *fantasy football*
WORD ORIGIN Greek *phantazein* to make visible

fan vaulting *n* *archit* vaulting with ribs that radiate like those of a fan from the top part of a pillar

fanzine (**fan**-zeen) *n* a magazine produced by fans of a specific interest, football club, etc. for fellow fans

FAQ *n* *computers* frequently asked question *or* questions: a text file containing basic information on a particular subject

far *adv* **farther, farthest** *or* **further, furthest 1** at, to, or from a great distance **2** at or to a remote time: *as far back as 1984* **3** by a considerable degree: *far greater* **4** **as far as a** to the degree or extent that **b** to the distance or place of **c** *informal* with reference to **5** **by far** by a considerable margin **6** **far and away** by a very great margin: *far and away the ugliest building in the city* **7** **far and wide** in a great many places over a large area **8** **go far a** to be successful **b** to be sufficient or last long: *her wages didn't go far* **9** **go too far** to go beyond reasonable limits: *the press have gone too far this time* **10** **so far a** up to the present moment **b** up to a certain point, extent, or degree ▷ *adj* **11** distant in space or time: *the far south* **12** extending a great distance **13** more distant: *over in the far corner* **14** **far from** by no means: *the battle is far from over*
WORD ORIGIN Old English *feorr*

farad *n* *physics* the SI unit of electric capacitance
WORD ORIGIN after Michael *Faraday*, physicist

faraway *adj* **1** very distant **2** dreamy or absent-minded: *a faraway look in his eyes*

farce *n* **1** a humorous play involving characters in unlikely and ridiculous situations **2** the style of comedy of this kind **3** a ludicrous situation: *the game degenerated into farce* **farcical** *adj* **farcically** *adv*
WORD ORIGIN Latin *farcire* to stuff, interpolate passages (in plays)

fare *n* **1** the amount charged or paid for a journey in a bus, train, or plane **2** a paying passenger **3** a range of food and drink: *marvellous picnic fare* ▷ *vb* **faring, fared 4** to get on (in a specified way): *he fared well in the exam*
WORD ORIGIN Old English *faran*

Far East *n* the countries of E Asia **Far Eastern** *adj*

fare stage *n* **1** a section of a bus journey for which a set charge is made **2** the bus stop marking the end of such a section

farewell *interj* **1** *old-fashioned* goodbye ▷ *n* **2** the act of saying goodbye and leaving ▷ *vb* **3** *NZ* to say goodbye ▷ *adj* **4** parting or closing: *the President's farewell speech*

far-fetched *adj* unlikely to be true

far-flung *adj* **1** distributed over a wide area **2** far distant or remote

farinaceous *adj* containing starch or having a starchy texture
WORD ORIGIN Latin *far* coarse meal

farm *n* **1** a tract of land, usually with a house and buildings, cultivated as a unit or used to rear livestock **2** a unit of land or water devoted to the growing or rearing of some particular type of fruit, animal, or fish: *a salmon farm; an ostrich farm* ▷ *vb* **3 a** to cultivate land **b** to rear animals or fish on a farm **4** to do agricultural work as a way of life **5** to collect and keep the profits from a tax district or business ▶ See also **farm out**
WORD ORIGIN Old French *ferme* rented land

farmed *adj* (of fish or game) reared on a farm rather than caught in the wild

farmer *n* a person who owns or manages a farm

farmers' market *n* a market at which farm produce is sold directly to the public by the producer

farm hand *n* a person who is hired to work on a farm

farmhouse *n* a house attached to a farm

farming *n* the business or skill of agriculture

farmland *n* land that is used for or suitable for farming

farm out *vb* **1** to send (work) to be done by another person or firm **2** (of the state) to put a child into the care of a private individual

farmstead *n* a farm and its main buildings

farmyard *n* the small area of land enclosed by or around the farm buildings

far-off *adj* distant in space or time: *a far-off land*

far-out *adj* **1** very unusual or strange: *the idea was so far-out it was ludicrous* **2** *informal* wonderful

farrago (far-**rah**-go) *n, pl* **-gos** *or* **-goes** a hotchpotch or mixture, esp. a ridiculous or unbelievable one: *a farrago of patriotic nonsense*

far-reaching *adj* extensive in influence, effect, or range

farrier *n* *chiefly Brit* a person who shoes horses
WORD ORIGIN Latin *ferrarius* smith

farrow *n* **1** a litter of piglets ▷ *vb* **2** (of a sow) to give birth to a litter
WORD ORIGIN Old English *fearh*

far-seeing *adj* having wise judgment

far-sighted *adj* **1** able to look forward and plan ahead **2** *US* long-sighted

fart *taboo n* **1** an emission of intestinal gas from the anus ▷ *vb* **2** to break wind
WORD ORIGIN Middle English *farten*

farther *adv* **1** to or at a greater distance in space or time **2** in addition ▷ *adj* **3** more distant or remote in space or time
WORD ORIGIN Middle English

≡ **USAGE**
≡ *Farther, farthest, further,* and *furthest* can
≡ all be used to refer to literal distance,
≡ but *further* and *furthest* are regarded as
≡ more correct for figurative senses
≡ denoting greater or additional
≡ amount, time, etc.: *further to my letter.*
≡ *Further* and *furthest* are also preferred
≡ for figurative distance.

farthermost *adj* most distant or remote

farthest *adv* **1** to or at the greatest distance in space or time ▷ *adj* **2** most distant or remote in space or time
WORD ORIGIN Middle English *ferthest*

farthing *n* a former British coin worth a quarter of an old penny
WORD ORIGIN Old English *fēorthing*

farthingale *n* a hoop worn under skirts in the Elizabethan period
WORD ORIGIN Old Spanish *verdugo* rod

fasces (**fass**-eez) *pl n, sing* **-cis** (-siss) (in ancient Rome) a bundle of rods containing an axe with its blade pointing out; a symbol of a magistrate's power
WORD ORIGIN Latin

fascia *or* **facia** (**fay**-shee-a) *n, pl* **-ciae** (-shee-ee) **1** the flat surface above a shop window **2** *archit* a flat band or

surface **3** *Brit* the outer panel which surrounds the instruments and dials of a motor vehicle
WORD ORIGIN Latin: band

fascinate *vb* **-nating, -nated** to attract and delight by arousing interest **fascinating** *adj* **fascinatingly** *adv* **fascination** *n*
WORD ORIGIN Latin *fascinum* a bewitching

≡ **USAGE**
≡ A person can be fascinated *by* or *with*
≡ another person or thing. It is correct
≡ to speak of someone's fascination *with*
≡ a person or thing; you can also say a
≡ person or thing has a fascination *for*
≡ someone.

Fascism (**fash-iz-zum**) *n* **1** the authoritarian and nationalistic political movement in Italy (1922–43) **2** any ideology or movement like this **Fascist** *n, adj*
WORD ORIGIN Italian *fascio* political group

fashion *n* **1** style in clothes, hairstyles, behaviour, etc. that is popular at a particular time **2** the way that something happens or is done: *conversing in a very animated fashion* **3 after a fashion** in some way, but not very well: *he apologized, after a fashion, for his haste* ▷ *vb* **4** to form, make, or shape: *he had fashioned a crude musical instrument*
WORD ORIGIN Latin *facere* to make

fashionable *adj* **1** popular with a lot of people at a particular time **2** popular among well-off or famous people: *the fashionable Côte d'Azur* **fashionably** *adv*

fast¹ *adj* **1** acting or moving quickly **2** accomplished in or lasting a short time **3** adapted to or allowing for rapid movement: *the fast lane* **4** (of a clock or watch) indicating a time in advance of the correct time **5** given to a life of expensive and exciting activities: *the desire for a fast life* **6** firmly fixed, fastened, or shut **7** (of colours and dyes) not likely to fade **8** *photog* very sensitive and able to be used in low-light conditions **9 fast friends** devoted and loyal friends **10 pull a fast one** *informal* to play an unscrupulous trick ▷ *adv* **11** quickly **12 fast asleep** in a deep sleep **13** firmly and tightly: *stuck fast* **14 play fast and loose** to behave in an insincere or unreliable manner
WORD ORIGIN Old English *fæst* strong, tight

fast² *vb* **1** to go without food for a period of time, esp. for religious reasons ▷ *n* **2** a period of fasting
WORD ORIGIN Old English *fæstan*

fast-breeder reactor *n* a nuclear reactor that produces more fissionable material (plutonium) than it consumes for the purposes of generating electricity

fasten *vb* **1** to make or become secure or joined **2** to close by fixing firmly in place or locking **3 fasten on a** to direct one's attention in a concentrated way towards: *the mind needs such imagery to fasten on to* **b** to take a firm hold on **fastener** *n*
WORD ORIGIN Old English *fæstnian*

fastening *n* something that fastens something, such as a clasp or lock

fast food *n* food, such as hamburgers, that is prepared and served very quickly

fastidious *adj* **1** paying great attention to neatness, detail, and order: *a fastidious dresser* **2** excessively concerned with cleanliness **fastidiously** *adv* **fastidiousness** *n*
WORD ORIGIN Latin *fastidiosus* scornful

fast lane *n* **1** the outside lane on a motorway for overtaking or travelling fast **2** *informal* the quickest but most competitive route to success: *the hectic pace of life in the corporate fast lane*

fastness *n* *Brit & Austral, literary* a stronghold or safe place that is hard to get to

fast-track *adj* **1** taking the quickest but most competitive route to success or personal advancement: *a fast-track marketer's dream* ▷ *vb* **2** to speed up the progress of (a project or person)

fat *adj* **fatter, fattest** **1** having more flesh on the body than is thought necessary or desirable; overweight **2** (of meat) containing a lot of fat **3** thick or wide: *his obligatory fat cigar* **4** profitable or productive: *fat years for the farmers are few and far between* **5 a fat chance** *slang* unlikely to happen **6 a fat lot of good** *slang* not at all good or useful ▷ *n* **7** extra or unwanted flesh on the body **8** a greasy or oily substance obtained from animals or plants and used in cooking **9 the fat is in the fire** an action has been taken from which disastrous consequences are expected **10 the fat of the land** the best that is obtainable **fatless** *adj* **fatness** *n*
WORD ORIGIN Old English *fætt* crammed

fatal *adj* **1** resulting in death: *a fatal accident* **2** resulting in unfortunate consequences: *Gorbachov's second fatal mistake* **fatally** *adv*
WORD ORIGIN Latin *fatum* fate

fatalism *n* the belief that all events are decided in advance by God or Fate so that human beings are powerless to alter their destiny **fatalist** *n* **fatalistic** *adj* **fatalistically** *adv*

fatality *n, pl* **-ties** a death caused by an accident or disaster

fate *n* **1** the ultimate force that supposedly predetermines the course of events **2** the inevitable fortune that happens to a person or thing **3** death or downfall: *Custer met his fate at Little Bighorn*
WORD ORIGIN Latin *fatum*

fated *adj* **1** certain to be or do something: *he was always fated to be a musician* **2** doomed to death or destruction

fateful *adj* having important, and usually disastrous, consequences **fatefully** *adv*

Fates *pl n classical myth* the goddesses who control human destiny

fathead *n informal* a stupid person **fatheaded** *adj*

father *n* **1** a male parent **2** a person who founds a line or family; forefather **3** a man who starts, creates, or invents something: *the father of democracy in Costa Rica* **4** a leader of an association or council: *the city fathers* ▷ *vb* **5** (of a man)

to be the biological cause of the conception and birth of (a child) **fatherhood** *n*
WORD ORIGIN Old English *fæder*

Father *n* **1** God **2** a title used for Christian priests **3** any of the early writers on Christian doctrine

Father Christmas *n* same as **Santa Claus**

father-in-law *n, pl* **fathers-in-law** the father of one's wife or husband

fatherland *n* a person's native country

fatherly *adj* kind or protective, like a father

Father's Day *n* a day celebrated in honour of fathers

fathom *n* **1** a unit of length, used in navigation, equal to six feet (1.83 metres) ▷ *vb* **2** to understand by thinking carefully about: *I couldn't fathom his intentions* **fathomable** *adj*
WORD ORIGIN Old English *fæthm*

fathomless *adj* too deep or difficult to fathom

fatigue (**fat-eeg**) *n* **1** extreme physical or mental tiredness **2** the weakening of a material caused by repeated stress or movement **3** the duties of a soldier that are not military **4 fatigues** a soldier's clothing for nonmilitary or battlefield duties ▷ *vb* **-tiguing, -tigued** **5** to make or become weary or exhausted
WORD ORIGIN Latin *fatigare* to tire

fat stock *n* livestock fattened and ready for market

fatten *vb* to grow or cause to grow fat or fatter **fattening** *adj*

fatty *adj* **-tier, -tiest** **1** containing or derived from fat **2** greasy or oily ▷ *n, pl* **-ties** **3** *informal* a fat person

fatty acid *n* any of a class of organic acids some of which, such as stearic acid, are found in animal or vegetable fats

fatuity *n, pl* **-ties** **1** foolish thoughtlessness **2** a fatuous remark

fatuous *adj* foolish, inappropriate, and showing no thought **fatuously** *adv*
WORD ORIGIN Latin *fatuus*

faucet (**faw-set**) *n* **1** a tap fitted to a barrel **2** *US & Canad* a tap
WORD ORIGIN Old French *fausset*

fault *n* **1** responsibility for something wrong **2** a defect or failing: *they shut the production line to remedy a fault* **3** a weakness in a person's character **4** *geol* a fracture in the earth's crust with displacement of the rocks on either side **5** *tennis, squash, etc.* a serve that bounces outside the proper service court or fails to get over the net **6** (in showjumping) a penalty mark for failing to clear, or refusing, a fence **7 at fault** to be to blame for something wrong **8 find fault with** to seek out minor imperfections in **9 to a fault** more than is usual or necessary: *generous to a fault* ▷ *vb* **10** to criticize or blame **11** *geol* to undergo or cause to undergo a fault **faultless** *adj* **faultlessly** *adv*
WORD ORIGIN Latin *fallere* to fail

fault-finding *n* continual criticism

faulty *adj* **faultier, faultiest** badly designed or not working properly: *a faulty toaster*

faun *n* (in Roman legend) a creature with the head and torso of a man and the legs, ears, and horns of a goat **WORD ORIGIN** Latin *Faunus*, god of forests

fauna *n, pl* **-nas** *or* **-nae** all the animal life of a given place or time: *the fauna of the Arctic* **WORD ORIGIN** Late Latin *Fauna*, a goddess of living things

faux pas (foe **pah**) *n, pl* **faux pas** (foe **pahz**) a socially embarrassing action or mistake **WORD ORIGIN** French

favour *or US* **favor** *n* **1** an approving attitude: *the company looked with favour on his plan* **2** an act done out of goodwill or generosity **3** bias at the expense of others: *his fellow customs officers, showing no favour, demanded to see his luggage* **4 in** or **out of favour** regarded with approval or disapproval **5 in favour of a** approving **b** to the benefit of ▷ *vb* **6** to prefer **7** to show bias towards (someone) at the expense of others: *parents sometimes favour the youngest child in the family* **8** to support or agree with (something): *he favours the abolition of capital punishment* **favoured** *or US* **favored** *adj* **WORD ORIGIN** Latin *favere* to protect

favourable *or US* **favorable** *adj* **1** advantageous, encouraging, or promising: *a favourable climate for business expansion* **2** giving consent or approval **favourably** *or US* **favorably** *adv*

favourite *or US* **favorite** *adj* **1** most liked ▷ *n* **2** a person or thing regarded with especial preference or liking **3** *sport* a competitor thought likely to win **WORD ORIGIN** Latin *favere* to protect

favouritism *or US* **favoritism** *n* the practice of giving special treatment to a person or group: *favouritism in the allocation of government posts*

fawn¹ *n* **1** a young deer aged under one year ▷ *adj* **2** pale greyish-brown **WORD ORIGIN** Latin *fetus* offspring

fawn² *vb* **fawn on 1** to seek attention from (someone) by insincere flattery: *it makes me sick to see the way you fawn on that awful woman* **2** (of a dog) to try to please (someone) by a show of extreme friendliness **fawning** *adj* **WORD ORIGIN** Old English *fægnian* to be glad

fax *n* **1** an electronic system for transmitting an exact copy of a document **2** a document sent by this system **3** Also called: **fax machine, facsimile machine** a machine which transmits and receives exact copies of documents ▷ *vb* **4** to send (a document) by this system **WORD ORIGIN** short for *facsimile*

fazed *adj* worried or disconcerted **WORD ORIGIN** Old English *fēsian*

FBI (in the US) Federal Bureau of Investigation

FC (in Britain) Football Club

FD Defender of the Faith: the title of the British sovereign as head of the Church of England **WORD ORIGIN** Latin *Fidei Defensor*

Fe *chem* iron **WORD ORIGIN** Latin *ferrum*

fealty *n, pl* **-ties** (in feudal society) the loyalty sworn to a lord by his tenant or servant **WORD ORIGIN** Latin *fidelitas* fidelity

fear *n* **1** a feeling of distress or alarm caused by danger or pain that is about to happen **2** something that causes fear **3** possibility or likelihood: *there is no fear of her agreeing to that* **4 no fear** *informal* certainly not ▷ *vb* **5** to be afraid of (someone or something) **6** *formal* to be sorry: *I fear the children were not very good yesterday* **7 fear for** to feel anxiety about **fearless** *adj* **fearlessly** *adv* **WORD ORIGIN** Old English *fær*

fearful *adj* **1** afraid and full of fear **2** frightening or causing fear: *the ship hit a fearful storm* **3** *informal* very bad: *they were making a fearful noise* **fearfully** *adv*

fearsome *adj* terrible or frightening

feasible *adj* able to be done: *a manned journey to Mars is now feasible* **feasibility** *n* **feasibly** *adv* **WORD ORIGIN** Anglo-French *faisable*

feast *n* **1** a large and special meal for many people **2** something extremely pleasing: *a feast of colour* **3** an annual religious celebration ▷ *vb* **4** to take part in a feast **5** to give a feast to **6 feast on** to eat a large amount of: *down come hundreds of vultures to feast on the remains* **7 feast one's eyes on** to look at (someone or something) with a great deal of attention and pleasure **WORD ORIGIN** Latin *festus* joyful

Feast of Tabernacles *n* same as **Sukkoth**

feat *n* a remarkable, skilful, or daring action: *an extraordinary feat of engineering* **WORD ORIGIN** Anglo-French *fait*

feather *n* **1** any of the flat light structures that form the plumage of birds, each consisting of a shaft with soft thin hairs on either side **2 feather in one's cap** a cause for pleasure at one's achievements ▷ *vb* **3** to fit, cover, or supply with feathers **4** *rowing* to turn an oar parallel to the water between strokes, in order to lessen wind resistance **5 feather one's nest** to collect possessions and money to make one's life comfortable, often dishonestly **feathered** *adj* **feathery** *adj* **WORD ORIGIN** Old English *fether*

feather bed *n* **1** a mattress filled with feathers or down ▷ *vb* **featherbed, -bedding, -bedded 2** to pamper or spoil (someone)

featherbedding *n* the practice of working in a factory or office deliberately slowly and inefficiently so that more workers are employed than are necessary

featherbrain *n* an empty-headed or forgetful person **featherbrained** *adj*

featherweight *n* **1** a professional or an amateur boxer weighing up to 126 pounds (57 kg) **2** something very light or of little importance: *a featherweight politician*

feature *n* **1 features** any one of the parts of the face, such as the nose, chin, or mouth **2** a prominent or distinctive part of something: *regular debates were a feature of our final year* **3** the main film in a cinema programme **4** an item appearing regularly in a newspaper or magazine **5** a prominent story in a newspaper ▷ *vb* **-turing, -tured 6** to have as a feature or make a feature of: *this cooker features a fan-assisted oven* **7** to give special prominence to: *the film features James Mason as Rommel* **featureless** *adj* **WORD ORIGIN** Anglo-French *feture*

Feb. February

febrile (**fee**-brile) *adj formal* **1** very active and nervous: *increasingly febrile activity at the Stock Exchange* **2** of or relating to fever **WORD ORIGIN** Latin *febris* fever

February *n, pl* **-aries** the second month of the year **WORD ORIGIN** Latin *Februarius mensis* month of expiation

feckless *adj* irresponsible and lacking character and determination: *her feckless brother was always in debt* **WORD ORIGIN** obsolete *feck* value, effect

fecund *adj literary* **1** fertile or capable of producing many offspring **2** intellectually productive or creative: *an extraordinarily fecund year even by Mozart's standards* **fecundity** *n* **WORD ORIGIN** Latin *fecundus*

fed *vb* the past of **feed**

federal *adj* **1** of a form of government in which power is divided between one central and several regional governments **2** of the central government of a federation **3** *Austral* of a style of house built around the time of Federation **federalism** *n* **federalist** *n, adj* **WORD ORIGIN** Latin *foedus* league

Federal *adj* of or supporting the Union government during the American Civil War

Federal Government *n* the national government of a federated state, such as that of Canada located in Ottawa or of Australia in Canberra

federalize *or* **-lise** *vb* **-lizing, -lized** *or* **-lising, -lised 1** to unite in a federal union **2** to subject to federal control **federalization** *or* **-lisation** *n*

federate *vb* **-rating, -rated** to unite in a federal union **federative** *adj*

federation *n* **1** the union of several provinces, states, etc. **2** any alliance or association of organizations which have freely joined together for a common purpose: *a federation of twenty regional unions*

fed up *adj informal* annoyed or bored

fee *n* **1** a charge paid to be allowed to do something: *many people resent the licence fee* **2** a payment asked by professional people for their services **3** *property law* an interest in land that can be inherited. The interest can be with unrestricted rights (**fee simple**) or restricted (**fee tail**) **WORD ORIGIN** Old French *fie*

feeble *adj* **1** lacking in physical or mental strength **2** not effective or convincing: *feeble excuses for Scotland's latest defeat* **feebly** *adv* **WORD ORIGIN** Old French *feble*

feeble-minded *adj* unable to think or understand effectively

feed *vb* **feeding, fed 1** to give food to (a person or an animal) **2** to give

Word Histories
part 6

Female: Interestingly, the original form of 'female' was unconnected to 'male'. It was *femelle*, a French diminutive of the Latin *femina*, and was applied to young women or girls. Folk etymology intervened after the word had entered the English language, and altered the word to make it an obvious counterpart of 'male'.

Ferret comes from Old French *furet* meaning 'little thief', from Latin *fūr*, meaning 'thief', a Latin root also found in 'furtive'.

Flak is formed from the first letters 'fl-a-k' of the component parts of the German word for an anti-aircraft gun, *Fliegerabwehrkanone*, literally an 'aircraft defence gun'.

Friday: Friday, in Old English *Frīgedæg*, is 'Freya's day'. Freya was the Norse goddess of love.

Gay, meaning 'homosexual', is sometimes said to be an acronym of Good As You, representing a coded statement of equality with heterosexuals. This is a false etymology, however, as the word's evolution can be traced to its early association with sexual acts. Prostitutes of both sexes were described as 'gay' in the 19th century because they wore brightly coloured clothing to attract custom. Accordingly, a 'gay boy' was a male prostitute; the association with homosexuality seems to have grown out of this, subsequently becoming a sort of codeword by which homosexual men could identify each other.

Golf is sometimes held up as an acronym rooted in spectacular male chauvinism: Gentlemen Only, Ladies Forbidden. While this may indeed represent the values of conservative clubhouses, the explanation is entirely false. 'Golf' is found in written sources from the 15th century, and probably derives from a Middle Dutch word *colf*, meaning a club.

Gorilla comes from Greek *Gorillai*, the name the ancient Greeks gave to a supposed African tribe with hairy bodies.

Greyhound: Greyhounds can be several different colours – their 'greyness' is the result of folk etymology altering the Old English *grighund* 'bitch-dog'.

Gym: Originally the word 'gymkhana' did not apply to horse-riding but to other sporting and athletic activities. Hindi *gend-khānā* literally means a 'ball house' or 'racket court', and that is where sports activities were held. *Gend* was altered to 'gym' under the influence of words like 'gymnastics'.

Halloween means 'holy evening', from Old English *halig*, meaning 'holy', and *æfen*, meaning 'evening'. Halloween is the evening before All Saints' Day, November 1.

Hamburger: Hamburgers are named after their city of origin, *Hamburg* in Germany. Similarly Frankfurters are sausages from the town of Frankfurt. The word 'hamburger' has nothing to do with 'ham', but the 'burger' part has now been taken as a noun in its own right, on the basis of which we now have 'beefburgers', 'cheeseburgers', and so on.

Harlot is sometimes traced to Arlette, the unmarried mother of William the Conqueror (William was known as William the Bastard prior to 1066). But the word originally meant a vagabond, and was usually applied to males; this is how Chaucer uses it. The prostitute sense doesn't appear in print until the 16th century. The word's development seems to be similar to that of 'tramp', which acquired the sense of a promiscuous woman by the 1920s.

Health: In origin, 'health' (Old English *hælth*) is the noun related to the adjective 'hale' (as in the phrase 'hale and hearty'), in the same way as 'warmth' is related to 'warm' and 'depth' is related to 'deep'. 'Health' is 'haleness' or 'wholeness'. To drink to someone's health is to drink a toast to their wellbeing.

Hippopotamus: A hippopotamus is literally a 'water horse'. The word comes from Greek *hippos*, meaning 'horse', and *potamos*, meaning 'river'.

(something) as food: *people feeding bread to their cattle* **3** to eat food: *red squirrel feed in the pines* **4** to supply or prepare food for **5** to provide what is needed for the continued existence, operation, or growth of: *illustrations which will feed an older child's imagination; pools fed by waterfalls* ▷ *n* **6** the act of feeding **7** food, esp. that given to animals or babies **8** *Brit, Austral, & NZ informal* a meal **WORD ORIGIN** Old English *fēdan*

feedback *n* **1** information in response to an inquiry or experiment: *considerable feedback from the customers* **2** the return of part of the output of an electronic circuit to its input **3** the return of part of the sound output of a loudspeaker to the microphone, so that a high-pitched whine is produced

feeder *n* **1** a device used to feed an animal, child, or sick person **2** an animal or a person who feeds: *these larvae are voracious feeders* **3** a road, rail, or air service that links outlying areas to the main network **4** a tributary or channel of a river

feel *vb* **feeling, felt** **1** to have a physical or emotional sensation of: *he felt a combination of shame and relief* **2** to become aware of or examine by touching **3** Also: **feel in one's bones** to sense by intuition **4** to believe or think: *I felt I got off pretty lightly* **5** **feel for** to show compassion towards **6** **feel like** to have an inclination (for something or doing something): *I feel like going to the cinema* **7** **feel up to** to be fit enough for (something or doing something) ▷ *n* **8** the act of feeling **9** an impression: *all this mixing and matching has a French feel to it* **10** the sense of touch **11** an instinctive ability: *a feel for art* **WORD ORIGIN** Old English *fēlan*

feeler *n* **1** an organ on an insect's head that is sensitive to touch **2** **put out feelers** to make informal suggestions or remarks designed to probe the reactions of others

feeling *n* **1** an emotional reaction: *a feeling of discontent* **2** **feelings** emotional sensitivity: *I don't want to hurt your feelings* **3** instinctive appreciation and understanding: *your feeling for language* **4** an intuitive understanding that cannot be explained: *I began to have a sinking feeling that I was not going to get rid of her* **5** opinion or view: *it was his feeling that the report was a misinterpretation of what had been said* **6** capacity for sympathy or affection: *moved by feeling for his fellow citizens* **7 a** the ability to experience physical sensations: *he has no feeling in his left arm* **b** the sensation so experienced **8** the impression or mood created by something: *a feeling of excitement in the air* **9** **bad feeling** resentment or anger between people, for example after an argument or an injustice: *his refusal may have triggered bad feeling between the two men* **feelingly** *adv*

feet *n* **1** the plural of **foot** **2** **be run** or **rushed off one's feet** to be very busy **3** **feet of clay** a weakness that is not widely known **4** **have** or **keep one's feet on the ground** to be practical and reliable **5** **put one's feet up** to take a rest **6** **stand on one's own feet** to be

independent **7** **sweep off one's feet** to fill with enthusiasm

feign (**fane**) *vb* to pretend to experience (a particular feeling): *he didn't have to feign surprise* **feigned** *adj* **WORD ORIGIN** Old French *feindre*

feint[1] (**faint**) *n* **1** a misleading movement designed to distract an opponent, such as in boxing or fencing ▷ *vb* **2** to make a feint **WORD ORIGIN** Old French *feindre* to feign

feint[2] (**faint**) *n* *printing* paper that has pale lines across it for writing on **WORD ORIGIN** variant of *faint*

feisty (**fie-stee**) *adj* **feistier, feistiest** *informal* **1** showing courage or spirit **2** *US & Canad* frisky **3** *US & Canad* irritable **WORD ORIGIN** from dialect *feist* small dog

feldspar or **felspar** *n* a hard mineral that is the main constituent of igneous rocks **feldspathic** or **felspathic** *adj* **WORD ORIGIN** German *feldspath*

felicitations *pl n, interj* expressions of pleasure at someone's success or good fortune; congratulations

felicitous *adj* appropriate and well-chosen: *a felicitous combination of architectural styles*

felicity *n* **1** great happiness and pleasure **2** the quality of being pleasant or desirable: *small moments of architectural felicity amidst acres of monotony* **3** *pl* **-ties** an appropriate and well-chosen remark: *Nietzsche's verbal felicities are not lost in translation* **WORD ORIGIN** Latin *felicitas* happiness

feline *adj* **1** of or belonging to the cat family **2** like a cat, esp. in stealth or grace ▷ *n* **3** any member of the cat family **felinity** *n* **WORD ORIGIN** Latin *feles* cat

fell[1] *vb* the past tense of **fall**

fell[2] *vb* **1** to cut down (a tree) **2** to knock down (a person), esp. in a fight **WORD ORIGIN** Old English *fellan*

fell[3] *adj* **in one fell swoop** in one single action or on one single occasion: *they arrested all the hooligans in one fell swoop* **WORD ORIGIN** Middle English *fel*

fell[4] *n* *Scot & N English* a mountain, hill, or moor **WORD ORIGIN** Old Norse *fjall*

fell[5] *n* an animal's skin or hide with its hair **WORD ORIGIN** Old High German *fel* skin

fellatio (fill-**lay**-shee-oh) *n* a sexual activity in which the penis is stimulated by the partner's mouth **WORD ORIGIN** Latin *fellare* to suck

felloe or **felly** *n, pl* **-loes** or **-lies** a segment or the whole rim of a wooden wheel **WORD ORIGIN** Old English *felge*

fellow *n* **1** a man or boy **2** a comrade or associate **3** a person in the same group or condition: *he earned the respect of his fellows at Dunkirk* **4** a member of the governing body at any of various universities or colleges **5** (in Britain) a postgraduate research student ▷ *adj* **6** in the same group or condition: *a conversation with a fellow passenger* **WORD ORIGIN** Old English *fēolaga*

Fellow *n* a senior member of an academic institution

fellow feeling *n* sympathy existing between people who have shared similar experiences

fellowship *n* **1** the state of sharing mutual interests or activities **2** a society of people sharing mutual interests or activities **3** companionship or friendship **4** *education* a financed research post providing study facilities

fellow traveller *n* *history* a person who sympathized with the Communist Party but was not a member of it

felon *n* *criminal law* (formerly) a person who committed a serious crime **WORD ORIGIN** Old French: villain

felony *n, pl* **-nies** *criminal law* (formerly) a serious crime, such as murder or arson **felonious** *adj*

felspar *n* same as **feldspar**

felt[1] *vb* the past of **feel**

felt[2] *n* a matted fabric of wool, made by working the fibres together under pressure **WORD ORIGIN** Old English

felt-tip pen *n* a pen with a writing point made from pressed fibres

fem. **1** female **2** feminine

female *adj* **1** of the sex producing offspring **2** of or characteristic of a woman **3** (of reproductive organs such as the ovary and carpel) capable of producing reproductive cells (**gametes**) that are female **4** (of flowers) not having parts in which pollen is produced (**stamens**) **5** (of a mechanical component) having an opening into which a projecting male component can be fitted ▷ *n* **6** a female person, animal, or plant **WORD ORIGIN** Latin *femina* a woman

feminine *adj* **1** possessing qualities considered typical of or appropriate to a woman **2** of women **3** *grammar* denoting a gender of nouns that includes some female animate things **femininity** *n* **WORD ORIGIN** Latin *femina* a woman

feminism *n* a doctrine or movement that advocates equal rights for women **feminist** *n, adj*

femme fatale (**fam** fat-**tahl**) *n, pl* **femmes fatales** (**fam** fat-**tahlz**) an alluring or seductive woman who leads men into dangerous or difficult situations by her charm **WORD ORIGIN** French

femto- *combining form* denoting 10^{-15}: *femtometer* **WORD ORIGIN** Danish *femten* fifteen

femur (**fee**-mer) *n, pl* **femurs** or **femora** (**fee**-mer-ra) the thighbone **femoral** *adj* **WORD ORIGIN** Latin: thigh

fen *n* *Brit* low-lying flat marshy land **WORD ORIGIN** Old English *fenn*

fence *n* **1** a barrier that encloses an area such as a garden or field, usually made of posts connected by wire rails or boards **2** an obstacle for a horse to jump in steeplechasing or showjumping **3** *slang* a dealer in stolen property **4** *machinery* a guard or guide, esp. in a circular saw or plane **5** (**sit**) **on the fence** (to be) unwilling to commit oneself ▷ *vb* **fencing, fenced 6** to construct a fence on or around (a piece of land) **7 fence in** *or* **off** to close in *or* separate off with or as if with a fence **8** to fight using swords or foils **9** to argue cleverly but evasively: *they fenced for a while, weighing each other up* **WORD ORIGIN** Middle English *fens*, from *defens* defence

fencing *n* **1** the sport of fighting with swords or foils **2** materials used for making fences

fend *vb* **1 fend for oneself** to look after oneself; be independent **2 fend off** to defend oneself against (verbal or physical attack) **WORD ORIGIN** Middle English *fenden*

fender *n* **1** a low metal barrier that stops coals from falling out of a fireplace **2** a soft but solid object, such as a coil of rope, hung over the side of a vessel to prevent damage when docking **3** *US & Canad* the wing of a car

fenestration *n* the arrangement of windows in a building **WORD ORIGIN** Latin *fenestra* window

feng shui (**fung shway**) *n* the Chinese art of deciding the best design or position of a grave, building, etc. in order to bring good luck **WORD ORIGIN** Chinese *feng* wind + *shui* water

Fenian (**feen**-yan) *n* (formerly) a member of an Irish revolutionary organization founded to fight for an independent Ireland **Fenianism** *n* **WORD ORIGIN** after *Fianna*, legendary band of Irish warriors

fenland *n* *Brit* an area of low-lying flat marshy land

fennel *n* a fragrant plant whose seeds, leaves, and root are used in cookery **WORD ORIGIN** Old English *fenol*

fenugreek *n* a Mediterranean plant grown for its heavily scented seeds **WORD ORIGIN** Old English *fēnogrēcum*

feoff (**feef**) *n* same as **fief** **WORD ORIGIN** Anglo-French

feral *adj* **1** (of animals and plants) existing in a wild state, esp. after being domestic or cultivated **2** savage **WORD ORIGIN** Latin *ferus* savage

ferment *n* **1** excitement and unrest caused by change or uncertainty **2** any substance, such as yeast, that causes fermentation ▷ *vb* **3** to undergo or cause to undergo fermentation **WORD ORIGIN** Latin *fermentum* yeast
☰USAGE
☰See at **foment.**

fermentation *n* a chemical reaction in which an organic molecule splits into simpler substances, esp. the conversion of sugar to ethyl alcohol by yeast

fermium *n* *chem* an element artificially produced by neutron bombardment of plutonium. Symbol: Fm **WORD ORIGIN** after Enrico *Fermi*, physicist

fern *n* a flowerless plant with roots, stems, and long feathery leaves that reproduces by releasing spores **ferny** *adj* **WORD ORIGIN** Old English *fearn*

ferocious *adj* savagely fierce or cruel **ferocity** *n*

WORD ORIGIN Latin *ferox*

ferret *n* **1** a small yellowish-white animal related to the weasel and bred for hunting rats and rabbits ▷ *vb* **-reting, -reted 2** to hunt rabbits or rats with ferrets **3** to search around **4 ferret out a** to drive from hiding **b** to find by determined investigation: *she could ferret out little knowledge of his background* **WORD ORIGIN** Latin *fur* thief

ferric *adj* of or containing iron in the trivalent state **WORD ORIGIN** Latin *ferrum* iron

Ferris wheel *n* a large vertical fairground wheel with hanging seats for riding on **WORD ORIGIN** after G. W. G. *Ferris*, American engineer

ferroconcrete *n* same as **reinforced concrete**

ferrous *adj* of or containing iron in the divalent state **WORD ORIGIN** Latin *ferrum* iron

ferruginous (fur-**rooj**-in-uss) *adj* (of a mineral or rock) containing iron **WORD ORIGIN** Latin *ferrum* iron

ferrule *n* a metal ring or cap placed over the end of a stick for added strength **WORD ORIGIN** Latin *viria* bracelet

ferry *n, pl* **-ries 1** a boat for transporting passengers and vehicles across a body of water, esp. as a regular service **2** such a service ▷ *vb* **-ries, -rying, -ried 3** to transport or go by ferry **4** to transport (passengers or goods) on a regular basis **ferryman** *n* **WORD ORIGIN** Old English *ferian* to carry

fertile *adj* **1** capable of producing offspring, crops, or vegetation **2** *biol* capable of growth and development: *fertile seeds* **3** highly productive: *a fertile imagination* **4** *physics* (of a substance) able to be transformed into fissile or fissionable material **fertility** *n* **WORD ORIGIN** Latin *fertilis*

fertilize *or* **-lise** *vb* **-lizing, -lized** *or* **-lising, -lised 1** to provide (an animal or plant) with sperm or pollen to bring about fertilization **2** to supply (soil) with nutrients **fertilization** *or* **-lisation** *n*

fertilizer *or* **-liser** *n* any substance, such as manure, added to soil to increase its productivity

fervent *or* **fervid** *adj* intensely sincere and passionate **fervently** *adv* **WORD ORIGIN** Latin *fervere* to boil

fervour *or US* **fervor** *n* great intensity of feeling or belief **WORD ORIGIN** Latin *fervere* to boil

fescue *n* a pasture and lawn grass with stiff narrow leaves **WORD ORIGIN** Old French *festu*

fest *n* an event at which the emphasis is on a particular activity: *fashion fest* **WORD ORIGIN** German: festival

fester *vb* **1** to grow worse and increasingly hostile: *the bitterness which had been festering beneath the surface* **2** (of a wound) to form pus **3** to rot and decay: *rubbish festered in the heat* **WORD ORIGIN** Old French *festre* suppurating sore

festival *n* **1** an organized series of special events and performances: *the Edinburgh Festival* **2** a day or period set aside for celebration **WORD ORIGIN** Latin *festivus* joyful

festive *adj* of or like a celebration **WORD ORIGIN** Latin *festivus* joyful

festivity *n, pl* **-ties 1** happy celebration: *a spirit of joy and festivity* **2 festivities** celebrations

festoon *vb* **1** to drape with decorations: *Christmas trees festooned with fairy lights* ▷ *n* **2** a decorative chain of flowers or ribbons suspended in loops **WORD ORIGIN** Italian *festone* ornament for a feast

feta *n* a white Greek cheese made from sheep's or goat's milk **WORD ORIGIN** Modern Greek

fetal alcohol syndrome *n* a condition in newborn babies caused by excessive alcohol intake by the mother during pregnancy: characterized by various defects including mental retardation

fetch[1] *vb* **1** to go after and bring back **2** to be sold for (a certain price): *Impressionist pictures fetch very high prices* **3** *informal* to give someone a blow or slap **4 fetch and carry** to perform menial tasks **WORD ORIGIN** Old English *feccan*

fetch[2] *n* the ghost or apparition of a living person **WORD ORIGIN** origin unknown

fetching *adj* *informal* attractive: *a fetching dress*

fetch up *vb* **1** *US & NZ informal* to arrive or end up **2** *slang* to vomit food

fete (**fate**) *n* **1** an event, usually outdoors, with stalls, competitions, etc., held to raise money for charity ▷ *vb* **feting, feted 2** to honour and entertain (someone) publicly: *the President was feted with an evening of music and dancing* **WORD ORIGIN** French

fetid *or* **foetid** *adj* having a stale and unpleasant smell **WORD ORIGIN** Latin *fetere* to stink

fetish *n* **1 a** a form of behaviour in which a person derives sexual satisfaction from handling an object **b** any object that is involved in such behaviour **2** any object, activity, etc. to which one is excessively devoted: *cleanliness is almost a fetish with her* **3** an object that is believed to have magical powers **fetishism** *n* **fetishist** *n* **WORD ORIGIN** Portuguese *feitiço* sorcery

fetlock *n* **1** the back part of a horse's leg, just behind the hoof **2** the tuft of hair growing from this part **WORD ORIGIN** Middle English *fetlak*

fetter *n* **1 fetters** checks or restraints: *free from the fetters of religion* **2** a chain fixed around a prisoner's ankle ▷ *vb* **3** to prevent from behaving freely and naturally: *fettered by bureaucracy* **4** to tie up in fetters **WORD ORIGIN** Old English *fetor*

fettle *n* **in fine fettle** in good spirits or health **WORD ORIGIN** Old English *fetel* belt

fetus *or* **foetus** (**fee**-tuss) *n, pl* **-tuses** the embryo of a mammal in the later

stages of development **fetal** or **foetal** adj
WORD ORIGIN Latin: offspring

feu n Scots Law a right to the use of land in return for a fixed annual payment (**feu duty**)
WORD ORIGIN Old French

feud n **1** long and bitter hostility between two families, clans, or individuals ▷ vb **2** to carry on a feud
WORD ORIGIN Old French feide

feudal adj of or characteristic of feudalism
WORD ORIGIN Medieval Latin feudum fief

feudalism n the legal and social system in medieval Europe, in which people were given land and protection by a lord in return for which they worked and fought for him. Also called: **feudal system**

fever n **1** an abnormally high body temperature, accompanied by a fast pulse rate, shivering, and nausea ▸ Related adjective: **febrile 2** any disease characterized by a high temperature **3** intense nervous excitement: she waited in a fever of anxiety
WORD ORIGIN Latin febris

feverish or **fevered** adj **1** suffering from fever **2** in a state of nervous excitement: a feverish scramble to buy shares **feverishly** adv

fever pitch n a state of intense excitement

few adj **1** hardly any: few homes had telephones in Paris in the 1930s **2 a few** a small number of: a few days ago **3 a good few** informal several **4 few and far between** scarce **5 quite a few** informal several
WORD ORIGIN Old English fēawa

≣ **USAGE**
≣ See at **less**.

fey adj **1** vague and whimsically strange **2** having the ability to look into the future
WORD ORIGIN Old English fæge marked out for death

fez n, pl **fezzes** a round red brimless hat with a flat top and a tassel hanging from it. Formerly worn by men in Turkey and some Arab countries
WORD ORIGIN Turkish

ff. and the following (pages, lines, etc.)

fiancé or fem **fiancée** (fee-on-say) n a person who is engaged to be married
WORD ORIGIN Old French fiancier to promise, betroth

fiasco n, pl **-cos** or **-coes** an action or attempt that fails completely in a ridiculous or disorganized way: the invasion of Cuba ended in a fiasco
WORD ORIGIN Italian: flask; sense development obscure

fiat (fie-at) n **1** an official order issued without the consultation of those expected to obey it: the junta ruled by fiat **2** official permission
WORD ORIGIN Latin: let it be done

fib n **1** a trivial and harmless lie ▷ vb **fibbing, fibbed 2** to tell such a lie **fibber** n
WORD ORIGIN origin unknown

fibre or US **fiber** n **1** a natural or synthetic thread that may be spun into yarn **2** a threadlike animal or plant tissue: a simple network of nerve fibres **3** a fibrous substance that helps the body digest food: fruits, vegetables, grains, lentils, and beans are high in fibre **4** strength of character: moral fibre **5** essential substance or nature: my every fibre sang out in sudden relief **fibrous** adj
WORD ORIGIN Latin fibra filament, entrails

fibreboard n a building material made of compressed wood

fibreglass n **1** material consisting of matted fine glass fibres, used as insulation **2** a light strong material made by bonding fibreglass with a synthetic resin, used for boats and car bodies

fibre optics n the transmission of information by light along very thin flexible fibres of glass **fibre optic** adj

fibril (**fibe**-rill) n a small fibre

fibrillation n uncontrollable twitching of muscle fibres, esp. those of the heart

fibrin n a white insoluble elastic protein formed when blood clots

fibrinogen (fib-**rin**-no-jen) n biol a soluble plasma protein involved in blood clotting

fibro n Austral a mixture of cement and asbestos fibre, used in sheets for building. Short for: **fibrocement**

fibroid (**fibe**-royd) adj **1** anat (of structures or tissues) containing or resembling fibres ▷ n **2** a harmless tumour composed of fibrous connective tissue

fibrosis (fibe-**roh**-siss) n the formation of an abnormal amount of fibrous tissue

fibrositis (fibe-roh-**site**-iss) n inflammation of fibrous tissue, esp. of the back muscles, causing pain and stiffness

fibula (**fib**-yew-la) n, pl **-lae** (-lee) or **-las** the outer and thinner of the two bones between the knee and ankle of the human leg **fibular** adj
WORD ORIGIN Latin: a clasp

fiche (**feesh**) n a sheet of film for storing publications in miniature form

fickle adj **1** changeable in purpose, affections, etc.: notoriously fickle voters **2** (of the weather) changing often and suddenly **fickleness** n
WORD ORIGIN Old English ficol deceitful

fiction n **1** literary works invented by the imagination, such as novels **2** an invented story or explanation: the fiction that the Baltic states freely joined the USSR **3** law something assumed to be true for the sake of convenience, though probably false **fictional** adj
WORD ORIGIN Latin fictio a fashioning

fictionalize or **-lise** vb **-lizing, -lized** or **-lising, -lised** to make into fiction

fictitious adj **1** not genuine: rumours of false accounting and fictitious loans had surrounded the bank for years **2** of or in fiction

fiddle n **1** informal or disparaging the violin **2** a violin played as a folk instrument **3** Brit & NZ informal a dishonest action or scheme **4 on the fiddle** informal engaged in an illegal or fraudulent undertaking **5 fit as a fiddle** informal in very good health **6 play second fiddle** informal to undertake a role that is less important or powerful than someone else's ▷ vb **-dling, -dled 7** to play (a tune) on the fiddle **8** informal to do (something) by illegal or dishonest means **9** informal to falsify (accounts) **10 fiddle with** to move or touch (something) restlessly or nervously **11 fiddle about** or **around** informal to waste time
WORD ORIGIN Old English fithele

fiddle-faddle interj old-fashioned nonsense
WORD ORIGIN reduplication of fiddle

fiddler n **1** a person who plays the fiddle **2** a small burrowing crab **3** informal a person who dishonestly alters something or lies in order to get money

fiddlesticks interj an expression of annoyance or disagreement

fiddling adj small or unimportant

fiddly adj **-dlier, -dliest** small and awkward to do or handle

fidelity n, pl **-ties 1** faithfulness to one's spouse or lover **2** loyalty to a person, belief, or cause **3** accuracy in reporting detail: an account of the invasion written with objectivity and fidelity **4** electronics the degree to which an amplifier or radio accurately reproduces the input signal
WORD ORIGIN Latin fides faith

fidget vb **-dgeting, -dgeted 1** to move about restlessly **2 fidget with** to make restless or uneasy movements with (something): he broke off, fidgeting with the papers, unable to meet their gaze ▷ n **3** a person who fidgets **4 the fidgets** a state of restlessness: these youngsters are very highly strung and tend to get the fidgets **fidgety** adj
WORD ORIGIN earlier fidge

fiduciary (fid-**yewsh**-ya-ree) law n **1** a person bound to act for someone else's benefit, as a trustee ▷ adj **2** of or relating to a trust or trustee
WORD ORIGIN Latin fiducia trust

fie interj obsolete or facetious an exclamation of disapproval
WORD ORIGIN Old French fi

fief (**feef**) n (in feudal Europe) land granted by a lord in return for military service
WORD ORIGIN Old French fie

fiefdom n **1** (in Feudal Europe) the property owned by a lord **2** an area over which a person has influence or authority

field n **1** an area of uncultivated grassland; meadow **2** a piece of cleared land used for pasture or growing crops **3** a marked off area on which sports or athletic competitions are held **4** an area that is rich in minerals or other natural resources: an oil field **5 a** all the competitors in a competition **b** the competitors in a competition excluding the favourite **6** a battlefield **7** cricket the fielders collectively **8** a wide expanse of land covered by some substance such as snow or lava **9** an area of human activity or knowledge: the most distinguished physicist in the field of quantum physics **10** a place away from the laboratory or classroom where practical work is done **11** the

Words from Literature
part 10

familiar *n* familiars are spirits or devils who come to someone when they are called
I'll turn all the lice about thee into familiars
Doctor Faustus 1.4 Christopher Marlowe

fantod *n* a state of nervous irritability
It most give me the fantods
The Adventures of Huckleberry Finn Mark Twain

farthing *n* a farthing was an old unit of British currency which was worth a quarter of a penny
"Not a farthing less. A great many back-payments are included in it, I assure you."
A Christmas Carol Charles Dickens

farthingale *n* a hoop worn under a skirt to extend it
A bell with an old voice – which I dare say in its time had often said to the house, Here is the green farthingale
Great Expectations Charles Dickens

favour *n* an old word which means ribbon
A group of humble mourners entered the gate: wearing white favours
Oliver Twist Charles Dickens

feigned *adj* pretend
not my feigned page
On His Mistress John Donne

fence *n* a fence is someone who receives and sells stolen goods
"What are you up to? Ill-treating the boys, you covetous, avaricious, in-sa-ti-a-ble old fence?"
Oliver Twist Charles Dickens

fess *adj* an old word which means pleased or proud
You'll be fess enough, my poppet
Tess of the D'Urbervilles Thomas Hardy

fettered *adj* fettered means bound in chains or chained
"You are fettered," said Scrooge, trembling. " Tell me why?"
A Christmas Carol Charles Dickens

fidge *v* to fidget
Look, Jim, how my fingers fidges
Treasure Island Robert Louis Stevenson

finger-post *n* a sign-post showing the direction to different places
"The gallows," continued Fagin, "the gallows, my dear, is an ugly finger-post, which points out a very short and sharp turning that has stopped many a bold fellow's career on the broad highway."
Oliver Twist Charles Dickens

fire-irons *n* tools kept by the side of the fire to either cook with or look after the fire
the fire-irons came first
Alice's Adventures in Wonderland Lewis Carroll

fire-plug *n* another word for a fire hydrant
The pony looked with great attention into a fire-plug, which was near him, and appeared to be quite absorbed in contemplating it
The Old Curiosity Shop Charles Dickens

flank *n* the side of an animal
And all her silken flanks with garlands dressed
Ode on a Grecian Urn John Keats

flip *n* a flip is a drink made from warmed ale, sugar, spice and beaten egg
The events of the day, in combination with the twins, if not with the flip, had made Mrs. Micawber hysterical, and she shed tears as she replied
David Copperfield Charles Dickens

flit *v* to flit means to move quickly
and if he had meant to flit to Thrushcross Grange
Wuthering Heights Emily Brontë

floorcloth *n* a hard-wearing piece of canvas used instead of carpet
This avenging phantom was ordered to be on duty at eight on Tuesday morning in the hall (it was two feet square, as charged for floorcloth)
Great Expectations Charles Dickens

surface or background of something, such as a flag **12** *physics* In full: **field of force** the region surrounding a body, such as a magnet, within which it can exert a force on another similar body not in contact with it **13 play the field** *informal* to have many romantic relationships before getting married ▷ *adj* **14** *mil* of equipment or personnel for operations in the field: *field guns* ▷ *vb* **15** *sport* to catch or return (the ball) as a fielder **16** *sport* to send (a player or team) onto the field to play **17** *sport* (of a player or team) to act or take turn as a fielder or fielders **18** *informal* to deal successfully with (a question or remark) **WORD ORIGIN** Old English *feld*

field day *n* **1** *informal* an opportunity or occasion for unrestrained action, esp. if previously denied or restricted: *the revelations gave the press a field day* **2** *mil* a day devoted to manoeuvres or exercises

fielder *n cricket, etc.* a member of the fielding side

field event *n* a competition, such as the discus, that takes place on a field as opposed to the track

fieldfare *n* a type of large thrush **WORD ORIGIN** Old English *feldefare*

field glasses *pl n* binoculars

field hockey *n US & Canad* hockey played on a field, as distinguished from ice hockey

field marshal *n* an officer holding the highest rank in certain armies

fieldmouse *n, pl* **-mice** a nocturnal mouse that lives in woods and fields

field officer *n* an officer holding the rank of major, lieutenant colonel, or colonel

fieldsman *n, pl* **-men** *cricket* a fielder

field sports *pl n* sports carried on in the countryside, such as hunting or fishing

field trip *n* an expedition, esp. by students, to study something at first hand

fieldwork *n mil* a temporary structure used in defending a place or position

field work *n* an investigation made in the field as opposed to the classroom or laboratory **field worker** *n*

fiend (**feend**) *n* **1** an evil spirit **2** a cruel or wicked person **3** *informal* a person who is extremely interested in or fond of something: *a fitness fiend* **fiendish** *adj* **fiendishly** *adv* **WORD ORIGIN** Old English *fēond*

Fiend *n* **the Fiend** the devil

fierce *adj* **1** very aggressive or angry: *a fierce dog* **2** intense or strong: *a fierce wind* **fiercely** *adv* **WORD ORIGIN** Latin *ferus*

fiery (**fire-ee**) *adj* **fierier, fieriest 1** consisting of or like fire: *a fiery explosion* **2** displaying strong passion, esp. anger: *a fiery speech* **3** (of food) very spicy **fierily** *adv* **fieriness** *n*

fiesta *n* (esp. in Spain and Latin America) a religious festival or carnival **WORD ORIGIN** Spanish

FIFA (**fee-fa**) International Association Football Federation **WORD ORIGIN** French *Fédération Internationale de Football Association*

fife *n* a small high-pitched flute, often used in military bands **WORD ORIGIN** Old High German *pfifa*

fifteen *n* **1** the cardinal number that is the sum of ten and five **2** a numeral, 15 or XV, representing this number **3** something representing or consisting of 15 units **4** a Rugby Union team ▷ *adj* **5** amounting to fifteen: *fifteen trees* **fifteenth** *adj, n*

fifth *adj* **1** of or being number five in a series ▷ *n* **2** one of five equal parts of something **3** *music* the interval between a note and the note three-and-a-half tones higher or lower than it **4** an additional high gear fitted to some vehicles, esp. certain sports cars

fifth column *n* any group that secretly helps the enemies of its own country or organization **fifth columnist** *n*

fifty *n, pl* **-ties 1** the cardinal number that is the product of ten and five **2** a numeral, 50 or L, representing this number **3** something representing or consisting of 50 units ▷ *adj* **4** amounting to fifty: *fifty bodies* **fiftieth** *adj, n*

fifty-fifty *adj, adv informal* **1** in equal parts **2** just as likely to happen as not to happen: *a fifty-fifty chance of survival*

fig *n* **1** a soft sweet fruit full of tiny seeds, which grows on a tree **2 not care** or **give a fig** not to care at all: *he did not give a fig for his enemies* **WORD ORIGIN** Latin *ficus* fig tree

fig. 1 figurative(ly) **2** figure

fight *vb* **fighting, fought 1** to struggle against (an enemy) in battle or physical combat **2** to struggle to overcome or destroy: *to fight drug trafficking* **3** to carry on (a battle or contest) **4** to make (one's way) somewhere with difficulty: *they fought their way upstream* **5 fight for** to uphold (a cause) by struggling: *fight for your rights* **6 fight it out** to struggle or compete until a decisive result is obtained **7 fight shy of** to avoid: *they fought shy of direct involvement in the conflict* ▷ *n* **8** a battle **9** a quarrel or contest **10** a boxing match **11 put up a fight** to offer resistance **fighting** *n* **WORD ORIGIN** Old English *feohtan*

fighter *n* **1** a professional boxer **2** a person who has determination **3** *mil* an armed aircraft for destroying other aircraft

fighting chance *n* a slight chance of success dependent on a struggle

fight off *vb* **1** to drive away (an attacker) **2** to struggle to avoid: *to fight off infection*

fig leaf *n* **1** a representation of a leaf of the fig tree used in sculpture to cover the genitals of nude figures **2** anything used to conceal something thought to be shameful: *the agreement was a fig leaf for Hitler's violation of the treaty*

figment *n* **a figment of one's imagination** something nonexistent and only imagined by someone **WORD ORIGIN** Latin *fingere* to shape

figuration *n* ornamentation

figurative *adj* **1** (of language) abstract, imaginative, or symbolic; not literal **2** (of art) involving realistic representation of people and things **figuratively** *adv*

figure *n* **1** a written symbol for a number **2** an amount expressed in numbers **3 figures** calculations with numbers **4** visible shape or form; outline **5** a slim bodily shape: *it's not good for your figure* **6** a well-known person: *a public figure* **7** a representation in painting or sculpture, esp. of the human body **8** an illustration or diagram in a text **9** a decorative pattern **10** a fixed set of movements in dancing or skating **11** *geom* any combination of points, lines, curves, or planes **12** *music* a characteristic short pattern of notes **13 figure of fun** a person who is often laughed at by other people ▷ *vb* **-uring, -ured 14** to calculate (sums or amounts) **15** *US, Canad, Austral, & NZ informal* to consider **16** to be included or play a part: *a house which figures in several of White's novels* **17** *informal* to be consistent with expectation: *Small-time crook, earns most of his cash as an informer. – That figures* **WORD ORIGIN** Latin *figura* a shape

figured *adj* **1** decorated with a design: *a chair upholstered in figured velvet* **2** *music* ornamental

figurehead *n* **1** a person who is formally the head of a movement or an organization, but has no real authority **2** a carved bust on the bow of some sailing vessels

figure of speech *n* an expression, such as a simile, in which words do not have their literal meaning

figure out *vb informal* to work out, solve, or understand: *I can't figure him out*

figure skating *n* ice skating in which the skater traces outlines of selected patterns **figure skater** *n*

figurine *n* a small carved or moulded figure **WORD ORIGIN** French

filament *n* **1** the thin wire inside a light bulb that emits light **2** *electronics* a high-resistance wire forming the cathode in some valves **3** a single strand of fibre **4** *bot* the stalk of a stamen **filamentary** *adj* **WORD ORIGIN** Latin *filum* thread

filbert *n* the brown edible nuts of the hazel **WORD ORIGIN** after St *Philbert*, because the nuts are ripe around his feast day, August 22

filch *vb* to steal in small amounts **WORD ORIGIN** Middle English *filchen* to steal, attack

file¹ *n* **1** a folder or box used to keep documents in order **2** the documents, etc. kept in this way **3** documents or information about a specific subject or person: *the doctor handed him his file* **4** a line of people in marching formation, one behind another **5** *computers* an organized collection of related records **6 on file** recorded for reference, as in a file ▷ *vb* **filing, filed 7** to place (a document) in a file **8** to place (a legal document) on public or official record **9** to bring a lawsuit, esp. for divorce **10** to submit (a report or story) to a newspaper **11** to march or walk in a line **WORD ORIGIN** Latin *filum* a thread

file² *n* **1** a hand tool consisting of a steel blade with small cutting teeth on its

faces, used for shaping or smoothing ▷ *vb* **filing, filed 2** to shape or smooth (a surface) with a file
WORD ORIGIN Old English *fīl*

file sharing *n* the practice of sharing computer data or space on a network

filial *adj* of or suitable to a son or daughter: *filial duty*
WORD ORIGIN Latin *filius* son

filibuster *n* **1** the process of obstructing legislation by means of long speeches so that time runs out and a vote cannot be taken **2** a legislator who engages in such obstruction ▷ *vb* **3** to obstruct (legislation) with such delaying tactics
WORD ORIGIN probably from Dutch *vrijbuiter* pirate

filigree *n* **1** delicate ornamental work of gold or silver wire ▷ *adj* **2** made of filigree
WORD ORIGIN Latin *filum* thread + *granum* grain

filings *pl n* shavings or particles removed by a file: *iron filings*

Filipino (fill-lip-**pee**-no) *adj* **1** of the Philippines ▷ *n, pl* **-nos 2** Also (fem): **Filipina** a person from the Philippines

fill *vb* (often foll. by *up*) **1** to make or become full **2** to occupy the whole of: *their supporters filled the entire stand* **3** to plug (a gap or crevice) **4** to meet (a requirement or need) satisfactorily: *this book fills a major gap* **5** to cover (a page or blank space) with writing or drawing **6** to hold and perform the duties of (an office or position) **7** to appoint or elect an occupant to (an office or position) ▷ *n* **8** one's **fill** sufficient for one's needs or wants ▶ See also **fill in, fill out, fill up**
WORD ORIGIN Old English *fyllan*

filler *n* **1** a paste used for filling in cracks or holes in a surface before painting **2** *journalism* an item to fill space between more important articles

fillet *n* **1** a piece of boneless meat or fish **2** a thin strip of ribbon or lace worn in the hair or around the neck **3** *archit* a narrow flat moulding ▷ *vb* **-leting, -leted 4** to cut or prepare (meat or fish) as a fillet
WORD ORIGIN Latin *filum* thread

fill in *vb* **1** to complete (a form) **2** to act as a substitute **3** to put material into (a hole) so as to make it level with a surface **4** *informal* to give (a person) fuller details

filling *n* **1** a substance or thing used to fill something: *a sandwich filling* **2** *dentistry* a substance that fills a gap or cavity of a tooth ▷ *adj* **3** (of food or a meal) substantial and satisfying

filling station *n* *chiefly Brit* a place where petrol and other supplies for motorists are sold

fillip *n* **1** something that adds stimulation or enjoyment **2** the action of holding a finger towards the palm with the thumb and suddenly releasing it with a snapping sound
WORD ORIGIN imitative

fill out *vb* **1** to fill in (a form or application) **2** to make or become plumper, thicker, or rounder **3** to make more substantial: *he filled out his speech with a few jokes*

fill up *vb* **1** to complete (a form or application) **2** to make or become full

filly *n, pl* **-lies** a young female horse
WORD ORIGIN Old Norse *fylja*

film *n* **1 a** a sequence of images projected onto a screen, creating the illusion of movement **b** a form of entertainment in such a sequence of images ▶ Related adjective: **cinematic 2** a thin flexible strip of cellulose coated with a photographic emulsion, used to make negatives and slides **3** a thin coating, covering, or layer: *a fine film of dust covered the floor* **4** a thin sheet of any material, as of plastic for packaging ▷ *vb* **5 a** to photograph with a movie or video camera **b** to make a film of (a screenplay or event) **6 film over** to cover or become covered with a thin layer ▷ *adj* **7** of or relating to films or the cinema
WORD ORIGIN Old English *filmen* membrane

filmic *adj* of or suggestive of films or the cinema **filmically** *adv*

film star *n* a popular film actor or actress

film strip *n* a strip of film composed of different images projected separately as slides

filmy *adj* **filmier, filmiest** very thin and almost transparent: *a shirt of filmy black chiffon* **filmily** *adv* **filminess** *n*

filo *or* **filo pastry** (**feel**-o) *n* a type of flaky Greek pastry in very thin sheets
WORD ORIGIN Modern Greek *phullon* leaf

Filofax *n* trademark a type of loose-leaf ring binder, used as a portable personal filing system

filter *n* **1** a substance, such as paper or sand, that allows fluid to pass but retains solid particles **2** any device containing such a substance, esp. a tip on the mouth end of a cigarette **3** any electronic or acoustic device that blocks signals of certain frequencies while allowing others to pass **4** any transparent disc of gelatine or glass used to reduce the intensity of given frequencies from the light leaving a lamp or entering a camera **5** *Brit* a traffic signal which permits vehicles to turn either left or right when the main signals are red ▷ *vb* **6** Also: **filter out** to remove or separate (particles) from (a liquid or gas) by a filter **7** Also: **filter through** to pass through a filter or something like a filter
WORD ORIGIN Medieval Latin *filtrum* piece of felt used as a filter

filter out *or* **through** *vb* to become known gradually: *the crowd broke up when the news filtered through*

filter paper *n* a porous paper used for filtering liquids

filter tip *n* **1** an attachment to the mouth end of a cigarette for trapping impurities **2** a cigarette with such an attachment **filter-tipped** *adj*

filth *n* **1** disgusting dirt and muck **2** offensive material or language **filthiness** *n* **filthy** *adj*
WORD ORIGIN Old English *fȳlth*

filtrate *n* **1** a liquid or gas that has been filtered ▷ *vb* **-trating, -trated 2** to filter **filtration** *n*

WORD ORIGIN Medieval Latin *filtrare* to filter

fin *n* **1** any of the winglike projections from a fish's body enabling it to balance and swim **2** *Brit* a vertical surface to which the rudder is attached at the rear of an aeroplane **3** a swimmer's flipper **finned** *adj*
WORD ORIGIN Old English *finn*

fin. 1 finance **2** financial

finagle (fin-**nay**-gl) *vb* **-gling, -gled** *informal* to use or achieve by craftiness or trickery
WORD ORIGIN origin unknown

final *adj* **1** of or occurring at the end; last **2** having no possibility of further discussion, action, or change: *a final decision* ▷ *n* **3** a deciding contest between the winners of previous rounds in a competition ▶ See also **finals** > **finality** *n* **finally** *adv*
WORD ORIGIN Latin *finis* limit, boundary

finale (fin-**nah**-lee) *n* the concluding part of a dramatic performance or musical composition
WORD ORIGIN Italian

finalist *n* a contestant who has reached the last stage of a competition

finalize *or* **-lise** *vb* **-lizing, -lized** *or* **-lising, -lised** to put into final form; settle: *plans have yet to be finalized* **finalization** *or* **-lisation** *n*
⁞ **USAGE**
⁞ Although *finalize* has been in
⁞ widespread use for some time, many
⁞ speakers and writers still prefer to use
⁞ *complete, conclude,* or *make final,* esp. in
⁞ formal contexts.

finals *pl n* **1** the deciding part of a competition **2** *education Brit & S African* the last examinations in an academic course

finance *vb* **-nancing, -nanced 1** to provide or obtain funds for (a project or large purchase) ▷ *n* **2** the system of money, credit, and investment **3** management of money, loans, or credits: *the dangerous political arena of public-sector finance* **4** funds or the provision of funds **5 finances** money resources: *the company's crumbling finances*
WORD ORIGIN Old French *finer* to end, settle by payment

financial *adj* **1** of or relating to finance, finances, or people who manage money **2** *Austral & NZ informal* having ready money **financially** *adv*

financial year *n* any annual accounting period

financier *n* a person who is engaged in large-scale financial operations

finch *n* a small songbird with a short strong beak
WORD ORIGIN Old English *finc*

find *vb* **finding, found 1** to discover by chance **2** to discover by search or effort **3** to realize or become aware: *I have found that if you make the effort then people will be more willing to help you* **4** to consider (someone or something) to have a particular quality: *his business partner had found that odd* **5** to experience (a particular feeling): *she found comfort in his words* **6** *law* to pronounce (the defendant) guilty or not guilty **7** to reach (a target) **8** to provide, esp. with difficulty: *we'll find room for you too* **9 find one's feet** to become capable or confident ▷ *n* **10** a person or thing that is found, esp. a valuable discovery: *the archaeological find of the century* **WORD ORIGIN** Old English *findan*

finder *n* **1** a small telescope fitted to a larger one **2** a person or thing that finds **3** *photog* short for **viewfinder**

finding *n* the conclusion reached after an inquiry or investigation

find out *vb* **1** to learn something that one did not already know **2 find someone out** to discover that someone has been dishonest or deceitful

fine[1] *adj* **1** very good **2** superior in skill: *a fine doctor* **3** (of weather) clear and dry **4** *informal* quite well: *I felt fine* **5** satisfactory: *as far as we can tell, everything is fine* **6** of delicate or careful workmanship: *fine porcelain* **7** subtle: *too fine a distinction* **8** very thin or slender: *fine soft hair* **9** very small: *fine print* **10** (of edges or blades) sharp **11** fancy, showy, or smart **12** good-looking **13** *ironic* disappointing or terrible: *a fine mess!* ▷ *adv* **14** *informal* very well: *that's what we've always done, and it suits us just fine* ▷ *vb* **fining, fined 15** to make (something) finer or thinner **16 fine down** to make (a theory or criticism) more precise or exact **finely** *adv* **WORD ORIGIN** Latin *finis* end, boundary, as in *finis honorum* the highest degree of honour

fine[2] *n* **1** a payment imposed as a penalty ▷ *vb* **fining, fined 2** to impose a fine on **WORD ORIGIN** Old French *fin*

fine art *n* **1** art produced chiefly to appeal to the sense of beauty **2** any of the fields in which such art is produced, such as painting, sculpture, and engraving

fine-drawn *adj* **1** (of arguments or distinctions) subtle **2** (of wire) drawn out until very fine

finery *n* elaborate or showy decoration, esp. clothing and jewellery: *the actress dressed up in her finery*

fines herbes (feenz **airb**) *pl n* finely chopped mixed herbs, used to flavour omelettes **WORD ORIGIN** French

finespun *adj* **1** spun or drawn out to a fine thread **2** excessively subtle or concerned with minute detail: *a finespun theological debate*

finesse (fin-**ness**) *n* **1** elegant and delicate skill **2** subtlety and tact in handling difficult situations: *a lack of diplomatic finesse* **3** *bridge, whist* an attempt to win a trick when opponents hold a high card in the suit led by playing a lower card ▷ *vb* **-nessing, -nessed 4** to bring about with finesse **5** *bridge, whist* to play (a card) as a finesse **WORD ORIGIN** Old French

fine-tooth comb *or* **fine-toothed comb** *n* **1** a comb with fine teeth set closely together **2 go over with a fine-tooth comb** to examine very thoroughly

fine-tune *vb* **-tuning, -tuned** to make fine adjustments to (something) so that it works really well

finger *n* **1** one of the four long jointed parts of the hand **2** the part of a glove made to cover a finger **3** something that resembles a finger in shape or function **4** a quantity of liquid in a glass as deep as a finger is wide **5 get** or **pull one's finger out** *Brit & NZ informal* to begin or speed up activity, esp. after initial delay **6 put one's finger on** to identify precisely **7 put the finger on** *informal* to inform on or identify, esp. for the police **8 twist around one's little finger** to have easy and complete influence over ▷ *vb* **9** to touch or manipulate with the fingers; handle **10** to use one's fingers in playing (a musical instrument) **11** *informal chiefly US* to identify as a criminal or suspect **fingerless** *adj* **WORD ORIGIN** Old English

fingerboard *n* the long strip of hard wood on a violin, guitar, etc. upon which the strings are stopped by the fingers

finger bowl *n* a small bowl of water for rinsing the fingers at table during a meal, esp. at a formal dinner

fingering *n* **1** the technique of using one's fingers in playing a musical instrument **2** the numerals in a musical part indicating this

fingernail *n* a thin hard clear plate covering part of the upper surface of the end of each finger

fingerprint *n* **1** an impression of the pattern of ridges on the inner surface of the end of each finger and thumb ▷ *vb* **2** to take an inked impression of the fingerprints of (a person) **3** to take a sample of the DNA of (a person)

fingerstall *n* a protective covering for a finger

fingertip *n* **1** the end of a finger **2 have at one's fingertips** to know thoroughly

finicky *or* **finicking** *adj* **1** extremely fussy **2** overelaborate or ornate: *finicky designer patterns* **WORD ORIGIN** earlier *finical*, from FINE[1]

finis *n* the end: used at the end of books **WORD ORIGIN** Latin

finish *vb* **1** to bring to an end; conclude or stop **2** to be at or come to the end; use up **3** to bring to a desired or complete condition **4** to put a particular surface texture on (wood, cloth, or metal) **5 finish off a** to complete by doing the last part of: *he finished off his thesis last week* **b** to destroy or defeat completely: *he finished off Faldo at the 16th hole* **6 finish with** to end a relationship with (someone) ▷ *n* **7** the final stage or part; end **8** death or absolute defeat **9** the surface texture of wood, cloth, or metal **10** a thing or event that completes **WORD ORIGIN** Latin *finire*

finishing school *n* a private school for girls that teaches social skills and polite behaviour

finite (**fine**-ite) *adj* **1** having limits in size, space, or time: *finite supplies of fossil fuels* **2** *maths, logic* having a countable number of elements **3** *grammar* denoting any form of a verb inflected for person, number, and tense **WORD ORIGIN** Latin *finitus* limited

Finn *n* a person from Finland

finnan haddock *or* **haddie** *n* a smoked haddock **WORD ORIGIN** *Findon*, town near Aberdeen

Finnish *adj* **1** of Finland ▷ *n* **2** the language of Finland

fino (**fee**-no) *n* a very dry sherry **WORD ORIGIN** Spanish: fine

fiord (**fee**-ord) *n* same as **fjord**

fipple flute *n* an end-blown flute with a plug (**fipple**) at the mouthpiece, such as the recorder or flageolet

fir *n* a pyramid-shaped tree with needle-like leaves and erect cones **WORD ORIGIN** Old English *furh*

fire *n* **1** the state of combustion producing heat, flames, and often smoke **2** *Brit* burning coal or wood, esp. in a hearth to heat a room **3** a destructive uncontrolled burning that destroys buildings, crops, etc. **4** an electric or gas device for heating a room **5** the act of shooting weapons **6** passion and enthusiasm: *her questions brought new fire to the debate* **7 catch fire** to start burning **8 on fire a** burning **b** ardent or eager **9 open fire** to start firing a gun, artillery, etc. **10 play with fire** to be involved in something risky **11 set fire to** *or* **set on fire a** to ignite **b** to arouse or excite **12 under fire** being attacked, such as by weapons or by harsh criticism ▷ *vb* **firing, fired 13** to discharge (a firearm) **14** to detonate (an explosive device) **15** *informal* to dismiss from employment **16** to ask a lot of questions quickly in succession **17** *ceramics* to bake in a kiln to harden the clay **18** to kindle or be kindled **19** (of an internal-combustion engine) to produce an electrical spark which causes the fuel to burn and the engine to start **20** to provide with fuel **21** to arouse to strong emotion: *he fired his team mates with enthusiasm* **WORD ORIGIN** Old English *fȳr*

fire alarm *n* a device to give warning of fire

firearm *n* a weapon, such as a pistol, that fires bullets

fireball *n* **1** ball-shaped lightning **2** the hot ionized gas at the centre of a nuclear explosion **3** a large bright meteor **4** *slang* an energetic person

firebomb *n* a bomb that is designed to cause fires

firebrand *n* a person who arouses passionate political feelings, often causing trouble

firebreak *n* a strip of open land in a forest to stop the advance of a fire

firebrick *n* a heat-resistant brick, used for lining furnaces, flues, and fireplaces

fire brigade *n* *Austral & Brit* an organized body of firefighters

fire clay *n* a heat-resistant clay used in making firebricks and furnace linings

firecracker *n* a firework which produces a loud bang

firedamp *n* *Brit, Austral, & NZ* an explosive mixture of hydrocarbons, chiefly methane, formed in coal mines

firedog *n* same as **andiron**

fire door *n* a door made of noncombustible material that prevents a fire spreading within a building

The Language of the Credit Crunch

The economic downturn has seen a mixture of terminology from the worlds of economics, banking, and trading dominate the media, and jargon that was previously restricted to financial circles and the pages of *The Economist* has found its way into news headlines and the English language at large.

This linguistic bleed-through began with the *sub-prime* crisis, which concerned the negative effects of widespread lending to borrowers at a high risk of default (the borrowers themselves were perceived to be sub-par, not the loans provided). The link to the US mortgage market brought to the world's attention *Freddie Mac* and *Fannie Mae*, the twin American institutions traditionally associated with mortgage lending, but not widely known outside North America.

As *sub-prime* gave way to the more generally applied term *credit crunch*, and eventually to the umbrella term *economic downturn*, other financial vocabulary thrust into the headlines included *deleveraging* (when a company is forced to dispose of its assets to pay off debts), *dry powder* (simply put: company cash reserves), *decoupling* (emerging markets not following the performance of their developed counterparts, such as the US economy), and *T-bill* (short for *Treasury bill*, a form of US government bond). As banks and other institutions had been trading in debts, trading terminology such as *CDS's* (credit default swaps) and *derivatives* (financial instruments with a price determined by the commodity, currency, etc, to which they are linked) were examined in the media. Some even became the unlikeliest of buzzwords, such as *quantitative easing*.

For the avoidance of doubt, *quantitative easing* is the printing of money by a government. This money is then used to buy up government bonds. (This process is distinct from *qualitative easing*, which is a form of financial stimulus brought about by a country altering its portfolio to investments perceived as less risky). In common use alongside *quantitative easing* was the new sense of the modifier *toxic*, which has now come to be descriptive of any bad asset, defaulted loan, or financial liability in the wake of the downturn, with *toxic bank* serving as a synonym for a *bad bank*, i.e. one that is set up to hold bad or underperforming assets. A key word used when describing the banking crisis was *recapitalizing*, relating as it did to providing banks and institutions with enough capital to survive after excessive losses.

While most of this terminology had already existed within the financial sphere for many years, the economic downturn also yielded to the English language a dividend of neologisms. Some were taken directly from the names of governmental financial stimulus packages, for example the US provided *TARP* (the Troubled Asset Relief Program) and *TALF* (the Term Asset-backed securities Loan Facility). And, since the economic crisis defined the *zeitgeist*, its effects and vocabulary could not avoid gradually filtering into lifestyle supplements, throwing up such terms as *staycation* (spending a holiday at home to save money), *recessionista*, *frugalista*, and *austerity chic* (buzzwords applied to those adapting the world of fashion to the downturn) and the sociological phenomenon *luxury shame* (the understandable reluctance to flaunt one's wealth in difficult economic times).

Large-scale financial impropriety by individuals, meanwhile, brought to the world's attention *feeder funds* (funds conducting their business through another *master fund*) and the workings of *Ponzi schemes* (named after Charles Ponzi, these fraudulent investment schemes do not pay back to their investors from actual profit, but from their own money or that paid by alternate investors). The chief perpetrator of the latter (Bernard Madoff) was labelled with a portmanteau word originally coined in the 1930s: *bankster*.

Some of the recent coinages are not without humour, however, such as *ninja loan* (No Income, No Job or Assets) or *vulture capitalist* (a none-too-complimentary variation on *venture capitalist*). There have even been loan words brought into English, such as *kreppa*, the Icelandic word for crisis, now applied to the recession.

fire drill n a rehearsal of procedures for escape from a fire

fire-eater n 1 a performer who pretends to swallow flaming rods 2 a very quarrelsome person

fire engine n a vehicle that carries firefighters and firefighting equipment to a fire

fire escape n a metal staircase or ladder on the outside of a building for escape in the event of fire

fire-extinguisher n a portable device for spraying water, foam, or powder to extinguish a fire

firefighter n a person whose job is to put out fires and rescue people endangered by them **firefighting** adj, n

firefly n, pl **-flies** a beetle that glows in the dark

fireguard n a screen made of wire mesh put before an open fire to protect against sparks

fire hall n Canad a fire station

fire hydrant n an outlet from a water main in the street, from which firefighters can draw water in an emergency

fire irons pl n a shovel, poker, and tongs for tending a domestic fire

fireman n, pl **-men** 1 a man whose job is to put out fires and rescue people endangered by them 2 (on steam trains) the man who stokes the fire

fireplace n an open recess at the base of a chimney for a fire; hearth

fireplug n chiefly US & NZ same as **fire hydrant**

fire power n mil the amount of fire that can be delivered by a unit or weapon

fire raiser n Brit a person who deliberately sets fire to property **fire raising** n

fire ship n history a ship loaded with explosives, set on fire and left to drift among an enemy's warships

fireside n the hearth

fire station n a building where firefighting vehicles and equipment are stationed

firetrap n a building that would burn easily or one without fire escapes

firewall n computers software that prevents unauthorized access to a computer network from the internet

firewater n informal any alcoholic spirit

firework n a device containing chemicals that is ignited to produce coloured sparks and sometimes bangs

fireworks pl n 1 a show in which fireworks are let off 2 informal an outburst of temper 3 an exciting and impressive performance, speech, or piece of writing: Dickens' verbal fireworks

firing n 1 a discharge of a firearm 2 the process of baking ceramics in a kiln 3 something used as fuel

firing line n 1 mil the positions from which fire is delivered 2 the leading or most vulnerable position in an activity: the manager is in the firing line after a string of bad results

firing squad n a group of soldiers appointed to shoot a condemned criminal dead

firkin n 1 a small wooden barrel or similar container 2 Brit a unit of capacity equal to nine gallons
WORD ORIGIN Middle Dutch vierde fourth

firm¹ adj 1 not soft or yielding to a touch or pressure 2 securely in position 3 definitely established: a firm agreement 4 having determination or strength: if you are firm and consistent she will come to see things your way ▷ adv 5 **stand firm** to refuse to give in ▷ vb 6 to make or become firm: to firm up flabby thighs **firmly** adv **firmness** n
WORD ORIGIN Latin firmus

firm² n 1 a business company 2 Brit slang a gang of criminals or football hooligans
WORD ORIGIN Spanish firma signature

firmament n literary the sky or the heavens
WORD ORIGIN Late Latin firmamentum

first adj 1 earliest in time or order 2 rated, graded, or ranked above all other levels: the First Lord of the Admiralty 3 denoting the lowest forward gear in a motor vehicle 4 music denoting the highest voice part in a chorus or one of the sections of an orchestra: the first violin ▷ n 5 the person or thing coming before all others 6 the beginning or outset 7 education chiefly Brit an honours degree of the highest class 8 the lowest forward gear in a motor vehicle ▷ adv 9 before anything else: I would advise you to try surgery first 10 for the first time: this story first came to public attention in January 1984
WORD ORIGIN Old English fyrest

first aid n immediate medical assistance given in an emergency

first-born adj 1 eldest of the children in a family ▷ n 2 the eldest child in a family

first class n 1 the class or grade of the best or highest value, rank, or quality ▷ adj **first-class** 2 of the best or highest class or grade 3 excellent 4 denoting the most comfortable class of accommodation in a hotel, aircraft, or train 5 denoting mail that is handled faster than second-class mail ▷ adv **first-class** 6 by first-class mail, transport, etc.

first-day cover n philately an envelope postmarked on the first day of the issue of its stamps

first-degree burn n a burn in which the skin surface is red and painful

first floor n 1 the storey of a building immediately above the one at ground level 2 US the storey at ground level

first-foot Scot & NZ n 1 the first person to enter a household in the New Year ▷ vb 2 to visit (someone) as first-foot **first-footing** n

first fruits pl n 1 the first results or profits of an undertaking 2 fruit that ripens first

first-hand adj 1 obtained directly from the original source ▷ adv 2 directly from the original source 3 **at first hand** directly

First Lady n (in the US) the wife of the president

firstly adv same as **first** (sense 9)

first mate n an officer second in command to the captain of a merchant ship

First Minister n 1 the chief minister of the Scottish Parliament 2 the chief minister of the Northern Ireland Assembly

First Nation n one of the formally recognized Canadian aboriginal communities

first night n the first public performance of a play or other production

first offender n a person convicted of a criminal offence for the first time

first officer n same as **first mate**

First Peoples pl n Canad a collective term for the Native Canadian peoples, the Inuit, and the Métis

first person n the form of a pronoun or verb used by the speaker to refer to himself or herself, or a group including himself or herself

first-person shooter n a computer game in which the player aims and shoots at targets, and the graphics displayed are seen from the viewpoint of the shooter

first-rate adj of the best quality; excellent

First Secretary n the chief minister of the National Assembly for Wales

firth n a narrow inlet of the sea, esp. in Scotland
WORD ORIGIN Old Norse fjörthr fjord

fiscal adj 1 of or relating to government finances, esp. tax revenues ▷ n 2 (in Scotland) same as **procurator fiscal**
WORD ORIGIN Latin fiscalis concerning the state treasury

fish n, pl **fish** or **fishes** 1 a cold-blooded animal with a backbone, gills, and usually fins and a skin covered in scales, that lives in water ▶ Related adjective: **piscine** 2 the flesh of fish used as food 3 **cold fish** a person who shows little emotion 4 **drink like a fish** to drink alcohol to excess 5 **have other fish to fry** to have other more important concerns 6 **like a fish out of water** ill at ease in an unfamiliar situation ▷ vb 7 to attempt to catch fish 8 to fish in (a particular area of water): the first trawler to fish these waters 9 to grope for and find with some difficulty: he fished a cigarette from his pocket 10 **fish for** to seek (something) indirectly: he was fishing for compliments
WORD ORIGIN Old English fisc

fishcake n a fried flattened ball of flaked fish mixed with mashed potatoes

fisherman n, pl **-men** a person who fishes as a profession or for sport

fishery n, pl **-eries** 1 a the industry of catching, processing, and selling fish b a place where this is carried on 2 a place where fish are reared

fish-eye lens n photog a lens with a highly curved front that covers almost 180°

fishfinger n an oblong piece of fish coated in breadcrumbs

fishing n the occupation of catching fish

fishing rod n a long tapered flexible pole for use with a fishing line and, usually, a reel

fishmeal *n* ground dried fish used as feed for farm animals or as a fertilizer

fishmonger *n* *chiefly Brit* a seller of fish

fishnet *n* an open mesh fabric resembling netting, sometimes used for tights or stockings

fishplate *n* a flat piece of metal joining one rail or beam to the next, esp. on railway tracks

fishtail *n* a nozzle having a long narrow slot at the top, placed over a Bunsen burner to produce a thin fanlike flame

fishwife *n*, *pl* **-wives** a coarse or bad-tempered woman with a loud voice

fishy *adj* **fishier, fishiest 1** of or suggestive of fish **2** *informal* suspicious or questionable: *something a bit fishy about his explanation* **fishily** *adv*

fissile *adj* **1** capable of undergoing nuclear fission **2** tending to split

fission *n* **1** the act or process of splitting into parts **2** *biol* a form of asexual reproduction involving a division into two or more equal parts **3** the splitting of atomic nuclei with the release of a large amount of energy **fissionable** *adj* **WORD ORIGIN** Latin *fissio* a splitting

fissure (**fish**-er) *n* any long narrow cleft or crack, esp. in a rock **WORD ORIGIN** Latin *fissus* split

fist *n* a hand with the fingers clenched into the palm **WORD ORIGIN** Old English *fȳst*

fisticuffs *pl n* fighting with the fists **WORD ORIGIN** probably from obsolete *fisty* with the fist + CUFF²

fistula (**fist**-yew-la) *n* *pathol* a long narrow ulcer **WORD ORIGIN** Latin: tube, ulcer

fit¹ *vb* **fitting, fitted 1** to be appropriate or suitable for **2** to be of the correct size or shape (for) **3** to adjust in order to make appropriate **4** to try clothes on and note any adjustments needed **5** to make competent or ready: *the experience helped to fit him for the task* **6** to correspond with the facts or circumstances: *this part doesn't fit in with the rest of his theory* ▷ *adj* **fitter, fittest 7** appropriate **8** in good health **9** worthy or suitable: *houses fit for human habitation* ▷ *n* **10** the manner in which something fits: *the suit was an excellent fit* ▶ See also **fit in**, **fit out** ▷ **fitly** *adv* **fitness** *n* **WORD ORIGIN** probably from Middle Dutch *vitten*

fit² *n* **1** a sudden attack or convulsion, such as an epileptic seizure **2** a sudden short burst or spell: *fits of laughter; a fit of pique* **3** **in fits and starts** in spasmodic spells **4** **have a fit** *informal* to become very angry **WORD ORIGIN** Old English *fitt* conflict

fitful *adj* occurring in irregular spells **fitfully** *adv*

fit in *vb* **1** to give a place or time to (someone or something) **2** to belong or conform, esp. after adjustment

fitment *n* **1** an accessory attached to a machine **2** *chiefly Brit* a detachable part of the furnishings of a room

fit out *vb* to equip: *he started to fit out a ship in secret*

fitted *adj* **1** designed for excellent fit: *a fitted suit* **2** (of a carpet) covering a floor completely **3 a** (of furniture) built to fit a particular space **b** (of a kitchen, bathroom, etc.) having equipment and furniture built or selected to suit the measurements of the room **4** (of sheets) having ends that are elasticated to fit tightly over a mattress

fitter *n* **1** a person who is skilled in the installation and adjustment of machinery **2** a person who fits garments

fitting *adj* **1** appropriate or proper ▷ *n* **2** an accessory or part **3** the trying-on of clothes so that they can be adjusted to fit **4** **fittings** furnishings or accessories in a building **fittingly** *adv*

five *n* **1** the cardinal number that is the sum of one and four **2** a numeral, 5 or V, representing this number **3** something representing or consisting of five units ▷ *adj* **4** amounting to five: *five years* ▶ See also **fives** **WORD ORIGIN** Old English *fīf*

five-eighth *n* **1** *Austral* (in rugby) a player positioned between the scrum-half and the inside-centre **2** *NZ* (in rugby) either of two players positioned between the halfback and the centre

fivefold *adj* **1** having five times as many or as much **2** composed of five parts ▷ *adv* **3** by five times as many or as much

fivepins *n* a bowling game played esp. in Canada

fiver *n* *Brit, Austral, & NZ informal* a five-pound or five-dollar note

fives *n* a ball game similar to squash but played with bats or the hands

fix *vb* **1** to make or become firm, stable, or secure **2** to repair **3** to attach or place permanently: *fix the mirror to the wall* **4** to settle definitely or decide upon: *the meeting is fixed for the 12th* **5** to direct (the eyes, etc.) steadily: *she fixed her eyes upon the jewels* **6** *informal* to unfairly influence the outcome of: *the fight was fixed by the promoter* **7** *informal* to put a stop to the activities of (someone): *the Party was determined to fix him* **8** *informal* to prepare: *let me fix you a drink* **9** *photog* to treat (a film, plate, or paper) with fixer to make the image permanent **10** to convert (atmospheric nitrogen) into nitrogen compounds **11** *slang* to inject a narcotic drug ▷ *n* **12** *informal* a difficult situation **13** the reckoning of a navigational position of a ship by radar, etc. **14** *slang* an injection of a narcotic ▶ See also **fix up** **WORD ORIGIN** Latin *fixus* fixed

fixation *n* **1** an obsessive interest in something **2** *psychol* a strong attachment of a person to another person or an object in early life **3** *chem* the conversion of nitrogen in the air into a compound, esp. a fertilizer **fixated** *adj*

fixative *n* **1** a fluid sprayed over drawings to prevent smudging **2** a liquid used to hold objects, esp. dentures, in place **3** a substance added to a perfume to make it less volatile

fixed *adj* **1** attached or placed so as to be immovable **2** stable: *fixed rates* **3** unchanging and appearing artificial: *a fixed smile* **4** established as to relative position: *a fixed point* **5** always at the same time **6** (of ideas) firmly maintained **7** *informal* equipped or provided for, esp. with money or possessions **8** *informal* illegally arranged: *a fixed trial* **fixedly** (**fix**-id-lee) *adv*

fixed star *n* an extremely distant star that appears to be almost stationary

fixer *n* **1** *photog* a solution used to make an image permanent **2** *slang* a person who makes arrangements, esp. illegally

fixity *n*, *pl* **-ties** the state or quality of a person's gaze, attitude, or concentration not changing or weakening: *a remarkable fixity of purpose*

fixture *n* **1** an object firmly fixed in place, esp. a household appliance **2** something or someone regarded as fixed in a particular place or position **3 a** a sports match **b** the date of it

fix up *vb* **1** to arrange **2** **fix up with** to provide with: *can you fix me up with tickets?*

fizz *vb* **1** to make a hissing or bubbling sound **2** (of a drink) to produce bubbles of carbon dioxide ▷ *n* **3** a hissing or bubbling sound **4** releasing of small bubbles of gas by a liquid **5** any effervescent drink **fizzy** *adj* **fizziness** *n* **WORD ORIGIN** imitative

fizzle *vb* **-zling, -zled 1** to make a hissing or bubbling sound **2** **fizzle out** *informal* to fail or die out, esp. after a promising start **WORD ORIGIN** probably from obsolete *fist* to break wind

fjord (fee-**ord**) *n* a long narrow inlet of the sea between high cliffs, esp. in Norway **WORD ORIGIN** Norwegian, from Old Norse *fjörthr*

FL Florida

fl. fluid

flab *n* unsightly or unwanted fat on the body **WORD ORIGIN** from *flabby*

flabbergasted *adj* *informal* completely astonished **WORD ORIGIN** origin unknown

flabby *adj* **-bier, -biest 1** having flabby flesh **2** loose or limp **3** weak and lacking purpose: *flabby hesitant leaders* **flabbiness** *n* **WORD ORIGIN** alteration of *flappy*, from *flap*

flaccid (**flak**-sid) *adj* soft and limp **flaccidity** *n* **WORD ORIGIN** Latin *flaccidus*

flag¹ *n* **1** a piece of cloth often attached to a pole, used as an emblem or for signalling **2** a code inserted into a computer file to distinguish certain information ▷ *vb* **flagging, flagged 3** to mark with a tag or sticker **4** *NZ* to give up an activity **5** **flag down** to signal (a vehicle) to stop **6** **flag up** bring something to someone's attention **WORD ORIGIN** origin unknown

flag² *n* same as **iris** (sense 2) **WORD ORIGIN** origin unknown

flag³ *vb* **flagging, flagged 1** to lose enthusiasm or energy **2** to become limp **flagging** *adj* **WORD ORIGIN** origin unknown

flag[4] *n* short for **flagstone**

flag day *n* Brit a day on which money is collected by a charity and small stickers are given to contributors

flagellate *vb* (**flaj**-a-late), **-lating, -lated** **1** to whip, esp. in religious penance or for sexual pleasure ▷ *adj* (**flaj**-a-lit) **2** possessing one or more flagella **3** like a whip **flagellation** *n*
WORD ORIGIN Latin *flagellare* to whip

flagellum (flaj-**jell**-lum) *n, pl* **-la** (-la) or **-lums 1** biol a long whiplike outgrowth that acts as an organ of movement **2** bot a long thin shoot or runner
WORD ORIGIN Latin: a little whip

flageolet (flaj-a-**let**) *n* a high-pitched musical instrument of the recorder family
WORD ORIGIN French

flag fall *n* Austral the minimum charge for hiring a taxi, to which the rate per kilometre is added

flagged *adj* paved with flagstones

flag of convenience *n* a foreign flag flown by a ship registered in that country to gain financial or legal advantage

flag of truce *n* a white flag indicating an invitation to an enemy to negotiate

flagon *n* **1** a large bottle of wine, cider, etc. **2** a narrow-necked jug for containing liquids
WORD ORIGIN Late Latin *flasco* flask

flagpole or **flagstaff** *n* a pole on which a flag is flown

flagrant (**flayg**-rant) *adj* openly outrageous: *flagrant violation of international law* **flagrancy** *n*
WORD ORIGIN Latin *flagrare* to blaze, burn

flagship *n* **1** a ship aboard which the commander of a fleet is quartered **2** the most important ship belonging to a shipping company **3** the most modern or impressive product or asset of an organization: *the company has opened its own flagship store*

flagstone *n* a flat slab of hard stone for paving
WORD ORIGIN Old Norse *flaga* slab

flag up *vb* to bring (something) to someone's attention; point out

flag-waving *n* informal an emotional appeal to patriotic feeling

flail *n* **1** a tool formerly used for threshing grain by hand ▷ *vb* **2** to wave about wildly: *arms flailing, they staggered about* **3** to beat with or as if with a flail
WORD ORIGIN Latin *flagellum* whip

flair *n* **1** natural ability: *she has a flair for languages* **2** originality and stylishness: *to dress with flair*
WORD ORIGIN French

flak *n* **1** anti-aircraft fire **2** severe criticism: *most of the flak was directed at the umpire*
WORD ORIGIN German Fl(ieger)a(bwehr)k(anone) aircraft defence gun

flake[1] *n* **1** a small thin piece chipped off an object or substance **2** a small piece: *flakes of snow* **3** slang an eccentric or unreliable person ▷ *vb* **flaking, flaked** **4** to peel or cause to peel off in flakes **5** to break into small thin pieces: *bake for 30 minutes, or until the fish is firm and flakes easily* **flaky** *adj*
WORD ORIGIN from Old Norse

flake[2] *n* (in Australia) the commercial name for the meat of the gummy shark

flake out *vb* informal to collapse or fall asleep from exhaustion

flak jacket *n* a reinforced sleeveless jacket for protection against gunfire or shrapnel

flambé (**flahm**-bay) *vb* **flambéeing, flambéed** to cook or serve (food) in flaming brandy
WORD ORIGIN French

flamboyant *adj* **1** behaving in a very noticeable, extravagant way: *a flamboyant jazz pianist* **2** very bright and showy **flamboyance** *n*
WORD ORIGIN French: flaming

flame *n* **1** a hot luminous body of burning gas coming in flickering streams from burning material **2** flames the state of burning: *half the building was in flames* **3** intense passion: *the flame of love* **4** informal an abusive message sent by e-mail ▷ *vb* **flaming, flamed 5** to burn brightly **6** to become red or fiery: *colour flamed in Sally's cheeks* **7** to become angry or excited **8** informal to send (someone) an abusive message by e-mail
WORD ORIGIN Latin *flamma*

flamenco *n, pl* **-cos 1** a rhythmic Spanish dance accompanied by a guitar and vocalist **2** music for this dance
WORD ORIGIN Spanish

flame-thrower *n* a weapon that ejects a stream or spray of burning fluid

flaming *adj* **1** burning with flames **2** glowing brightly **3** very angry and heated: *a flaming row* **4** informal extreme; damned: *what the flaming hell do you think you're doing?* ▷ *adv* **5** informal extremely; damned: *I was flaming mad about what happened*

flamingo *n, pl* **-gos** or **-goes** a large pink wading bird with a long neck and legs
WORD ORIGIN Portuguese *flamengo*

flammable *adj* easily set on fire; inflammable **flammability** *n*

USAGE
Flammable and *inflammable* are interchangeable when used of the properties of materials. *Flammable* is, however, often preferred for warning labels as there is less likelihood of misunderstanding (*inflammable* being sometimes taken to mean *not flammable*). *Inflammable* is preferred in figurative contexts: *this could prove to be an inflammable situation*.

flan *n* an open sweet or savoury tart
WORD ORIGIN French

flange *n* a projecting collar or rim on an object for strengthening it or for attaching it to another object
WORD ORIGIN origin unknown

flank *n* **1** the side of a man or animal between the ribs and the hip **2** a cut of beef from the flank **3** the side of a naval or military formation ▷ *vb* **4** to be positioned at the side of (a person or thing)
WORD ORIGIN Old French *flanc*

flannel *n* **1** Brit a small piece of towelling cloth used to wash the face **2** a soft light woollen fabric used for clothing **3** flannels trousers made of flannel **4** Brit informal evasive talk that avoids giving any commitment or direct answer ▷ *vb* **-nelling, -nelled** or US **-neling, -neled 5** Brit informal to flatter or talk evasively
WORD ORIGIN Welsh *gwlân* wool

flannelette *n* a cotton imitation of flannel, used to make sheets and nightdresses

flap *vb* **flapping, flapped 1** to move backwards and forwards or up and down, like a bird's wings in flight ▷ *n* **2** the action of or noise made by flapping **3** a piece of material attached at one edge and usually used to cover an opening, such as on a pocket **4** a hinged section of an aircraft wing that is raised or lowered to control the aircraft's speed **5** informal a state of panic or agitation
WORD ORIGIN probably imitative

flapjack *n* **1** Brit a chewy biscuit made with rolled oats **2** NZ a small thick pancake

flapper *n* (in the 1920s) a lively young woman who dressed and behaved unconventionally

flare *vb* **flaring, flared 1** to burn with an unsteady or sudden bright flame: *camp fires flared like beacons in the dark* **2** (of temper, violence, or trouble) to break out suddenly **3** to spread outwards from a narrow to a wider shape ▷ *n* **4** an unsteady flame **5** a sudden burst of flame **6 a** a blaze of light used to illuminate, signal distress, alert, etc. **b** the device producing such a blaze **7** flares trousers with legs that flare out at the bottom **flared** *adj*
WORD ORIGIN origin unknown

flare up *vb* **1** to burst suddenly into fire **2** informal to burst into anger

flash *n* **1** a sudden short blaze of intense light or flame **2** a sudden occurrence of a particular emotion or experience: *a flash of anger* **3** a very brief time: *in a flash he was inside and locked the door behind him* **4** a short unscheduled news announcement **5** Austral & Brit an emblem on a uniform or vehicle to identify its military formation **6** photog short for **flashlight 7** flash in the pan a project, person, etc. that enjoys only short-lived success ▷ *adj* **8** informal ostentatious or vulgar **9** brief and rapid: *a flash fire* ▷ *vb* **10** to burst or cause to burst suddenly into flame **11** to shine with a bright light suddenly or repeatedly **12** to move very fast **13** to come rapidly (into the mind or vision) **14 a** to signal very fast: *a warning was flashed onto a computer screen in the cockpit* **b** to signal by use of a light, such as car headlights **15** informal to display in a boastful and extravagant way: *flashing banknotes around* **16** informal to show briefly **17** Brit slang to expose oneself indecently **flasher** *n*
WORD ORIGIN origin unknown

flashback *n* a scene in a book, play, or film that shows earlier events

flashbulb *n* photog a small light bulb that produces a bright flash of light

Jane Austen, the British Regency, and the End of Reason

It is a view universally adopted that a single woman in possession of a Jane Austen novel must be in want of a man. But Jane Austen is not a mere precursor to *chick lit* or any other genre of fiction aimed only at women. In fact, Ms Austen's novels outshine those of many of her predecessors, contemporaries, and followers in accomplishment, wit, and understanding.

Historically, Jane Austen belongs to the British Regency, the period between 1811 and 1820, when the Prince of Wales reigned as Prince Regent during the incapacity of George III. This era was a transition between the eighteenth century and the Victorian Period, and Austen's work can be seen as the last stand of a still-new literary style based on wit, reason, and realism, before Victorian tastes ushered in the verbose and sentimental prose of popular fiction.

Though the eighteenth century saw great development in the English novel, it was not until the Victorian Period that a set of accepted criteria emerged, much of which is still in place today, at least in mainstream fiction. Victorian and post-Victorian readers expect a unified plot, rather than the episodic ones of eighteenth-century writers like Defoe. This Austen can deliver, as well as character and motive. Where Austen differs from the Victorians is in her lack of excessive adjectives and decorous language intended to elicit an emotional reaction from the reader. Even by present-day standards Austen's prose can seem more like reportage than narration. There is little evocative description; we are not given a complete *visual* picture of Regency England. Even the famous 'Pemberley House' of *Pride and Prejudice* is merely 'a large, handsome, stone building' situated before a row of wooded hills and behind a stream. A more sentimental writer would have given fuller descriptions of the place, and an author in the Gothic tradition (the natural successor of Sentimentalism) might well have devoted more than a page to creating a grand old house.

Austen does give us a convincing picture of Regency *manners*. Indeed, Austen exemplifies the *novel of manners*, a sub-genre which focuses on the social customs of a particular class or social sphere. Therein lies her genius and appeal: she proves a subtle satirist and a master of irony; her quasi-detached, matter-of-fact style becomes a precise tool for dissecting her society, and generally prevents her over-telling her jokes. For example, Mrs Bennet is characterized through her own words and actions alone. Austen never *tells* us that she is a ridiculous hypocrite; she *shows* us.

The main target of Austen's satire is the socio-economic situation of genteel women. Before we criticize Austen's novels for being too much concerned with marriage, we should consider what they tell us about marriage in this period. The eighteenth century saw the rise of the merchant class as a powerful economic force. Previously wealth had been created through the ownership of land; now it was created in trade. This led to members of the landed gentry gradually losing their wealth while members of the merchant class grew rich enough to buy titles and estates. The two classes began intermarrying, the gentility replenishing their wealth while the merchants gained higher social status.

Austen's heroines are frequently daughters of impoverished gentry (as was Austen herself); their plight is that they are educated and accomplished, but with little fortune and no title; they are not usually seen as desirable either to the upwardly mobile merchants or the fortune-hunting upper-gentility. Yet without a suitable marriage, they will end up with no means of economic support. It is not just their emotional happiness at stake: it is their material future.

Austen's unflinching portrayal of this situation may elevate her to feminist literature, the more so because of the richness and realism of her heroines. Austen's women earn their happy endings through intelligence (Elizabeth Bennet), morality (Fanny Price), or by turning away from pride and conceit (Emma Woohouse), romanticism (Marianne Dashwood), or Gothic melodrama (Catherine Morland) in favour of reason and virtue. In this respect, Austen is a successor to Samuel Johnson, a last flag-bearer of the Age of Reason against the encroaching melodrama that would take hold in the Victorian Era.

flash drive *n* a portable computer hard drive and data storage device

flash flood *n* a sudden short-lived flood

flashing *n* a weatherproof material used to cover the joins in a roof

flashlight *n* **1** *photog* the brief bright light emitted by a flashbulb **2** *chiefly US & Canad* a torch

flash point *n* **1** a critical time beyond which a situation will inevitably erupt into violence **2** the lowest temperature at which the vapour above a liquid can be ignited

flashy *adj* **flashier, flashiest** showy in a vulgar way: *a loud and flashy tie* **flashily** *adv* **flashiness** *n*

flask *n* **1** same as **vacuum flask** **2** a small flat container for alcoholic drink designed to be carried in a pocket **3** a bottle with a narrow neck, esp. used in a laboratory **WORD ORIGIN** Medieval Latin *flasca*, *flasco*

flat¹ *adj* **flatter, flattest 1** horizontal or level: *roofs are now flat instead of slanted* **2** even or smooth: *a flat surface* **3** lying stretched out at full length **4** (of a tyre) deflated **5** (of shoes) having an unraised heel **6** without qualification; total: *a flat rejection* **7** fixed: *a flat rate* **8** unexciting: *a picture curiously flat in tone* **9** without variation or emotion: *a flat voice* **10** (of drinks) no longer fizzy **11** (of a battery) fully discharged **12** (of paint) without gloss **13** *music* a denoting a note that has been lowered in pitch by one chromatic semitone: *B flat* **b** (of an instrument, voice, etc.) out of tune by being too low in pitch ▷ *adv* **14** in or into a level or flat position: *the boat was knocked almost flat* **15** completely: *flat broke* **16** exactly: *in three months flat* **17** *music* **a** lower than a standard pitch **b** too low in pitch: *singing flat* **18** **fall flat (on one's face)** to fail to achieve a desired effect **19** **flat out** *informal* with maximum speed and effort ▷ *n* **20** a flat object or part **21** low-lying land, esp. a marsh **22** a mud bank exposed at low tide **23** *music* **a** an accidental that lowers the pitch of a note by one semitone. Symbol: ♭ **b** a note affected by this accidental **24** *theatre* a wooden frame covered with painted canvas, used to form part of a stage setting **25** a punctured car tyre **26** **the flat** *chiefly Brit* the season of flat racing **flatly** *adv* **WORD ORIGIN** Old Norse *flatr*

flat² *n* **1** a set of rooms forming a home entirely on one floor of a building ▷ *vb* **flatting, flatted 2** *Austral & NZ* to share a flat **3** **go flatting** *Austral & NZ* to leave home to share a flat **WORD ORIGIN** Old English *flett* floor, hall, house

flatboat *n* a flat-bottomed boat for transporting goods on a canal

flatfish *n, pl* **-fish** or **-fishes** a sea fish, such as the sole, which has a flat body with both eyes on the uppermost side

flat-footed *adj* **1** having less than the usual degree of arching in the insteps of the feet **2** *informal* clumsy or insensitive

flathead *n* a common Australian flatfish

flatiron *n* (formerly) an iron for pressing clothes that was heated by being placed on a stove

flatlet *n* *Brit, Austral, & S African* a small flat

flatmate *n* a person with whom one shares a flat

flat-pack *adj* (of furniture, etc.) supplied in pieces in a flat box for assembly by the buyer

flat racing *n* the racing of horses on racecourses without jumps

flatscreen *n* a slimline television set or computer monitor with a flat screen

flat spin *n* **1** an aircraft spin in which the longitudinal axis is more nearly horizontal than vertical **2** *informal* a state of confusion

flatten *vb* **1** to make or become flat or flatter **2** *informal* **a** to knock down or injure **b** to crush or subdue

flatter *vb* **1** to praise insincerely, esp. in order to win favour **2** to show to advantage: *she wore a simple green cotton dress which she knew flattered her* **3** to make (a person) appear more attractive than in reality: *a portrait that flattered him* **4** to cater to the vanity of (a person): *I was flattered by her praise* **5** **flatter oneself** to believe, perhaps mistakenly, something good about oneself **flatterer** *n* **WORD ORIGIN** Old French *flater* to lick, fawn upon

flattery *n, pl* **-teries** excessive or insincere praise

flattie *n* *NZ & S African informal* flat tyre

flatulent *adj* suffering from or caused by too much gas in the stomach or intestines **flatulence** *n* **WORD ORIGIN** Latin *flatus* blowing

flatworm *n* a worm, such as a tapeworm, with a flattened body

flaunt *vb* to display (oneself or one's possessions) arrogantly: *flaunting his new car* **WORD ORIGIN** origin unknown

⦚ USAGE
Flaunt is sometimes wrongly used where *flout* is meant: *they must be prevented from flouting (not flaunting) the law.*

flautist (**flaw**-tist) *n* a flute player **WORD ORIGIN** Italian *flautista*

flavour or *US* **flavor** *n* **1** taste perceived in food or liquid in the mouth **2** a distinctive quality or atmosphere: *Rome has its own particular flavour* ▷ *vb* **3** to give flavour to: *salmon flavoured with dill* **flavourless** or *US* **flavorless** *adj* **WORD ORIGIN** Old French *flaour*

flavouring or *US* **flavoring** *n* a substance used to flavour food

flaw *n* **1** an imperfection or blemish **2** a mistake in something that makes it invalid: *a flaw in the system* **flawed** *adj* **flawless** *adj* **WORD ORIGIN** probably from Old Norse *flaga* stone slab

flax *n* **1** a plant that has blue flowers and is cultivated for its seeds and the fibres of its stems **2** its fibres, made into linen fabrics **3** *NZ* a perennial plant producing a fibre that is used by Māoris

for decorative work and weaving baskets **WORD ORIGIN** Old English *fleax*

flaxen *adj* **1** of flax **2** (of hair) pale yellow

flay *vb* **1** to strip off the skin of, esp. by whipping **2** to criticize severely **WORD ORIGIN** Old English *flēan*

flea *n* **1** a small wingless jumping insect feeding on the blood of mammals and birds **2** **flea in one's ear** *informal* a sharp rebuke **WORD ORIGIN** Old English *flēah*

fleabite *n* **1** the bite of a flea **2** a slight annoyance or discomfort

flea-bitten *adj* **1** bitten by or infested with fleas **2** *informal* shabby or decrepit: *a flea-bitten hotel*

flea market *n* an open-air market selling cheap second-hand goods

fleapit *n* *informal* a shabby cinema or theatre

fleck *n* **1** a small marking or streak **2** a small or tiny piece of something: *a fleck of grit* ▷ *vb* **3** to speckle: *a grey suit flecked with white* **WORD ORIGIN** probably from Old Norse *flekkr* stain, spot

fled *vb* the past of **flee**

fledged *adj* **1** (of young birds) able to fly **2** qualified and competent: *a fully fledged doctor* **WORD ORIGIN** Old English *-flycge*, as in *unflycge* unfledged

fledgling or **fledgeling** *n* **1** a young bird that has grown feathers ▷ *adj* **2** new or inexperienced: *Poland's fledgling market economy*

flee *vb* **fleeing, fled 1** to run away from (a place, danger, etc.) **2** to run or move quickly **WORD ORIGIN** Old English *flēon*

fleece *n* **1** the coat of wool that covers a sheep **2** the wool removed from a sheep at one shearing **3** sheepskin or a fabric with soft pile, used as a lining for coats, etc. **4** *Brit* a jacket or top made of this fabric **5** a warm outdoor jacket or top made from a polyester fabric with a brushed nap ▷ *vb* **fleecing, fleeced 6** to defraud or overcharge **7** same as **shear** (sense 1) **WORD ORIGIN** Old English *flēos*

fleecy *adj* of or resembling fleece ▷ *n, pl* **-ies 2** *NZ informal* a person who collects fleeces after shearing and prepares them for baling

fleet¹ *n* **1** a number of warships organized as a tactical unit **2** all the ships of a nation or company: *the British merchant fleet* **3** a number of vehicles under the same ownership **WORD ORIGIN** Old English *flēot* ship, flowing water

fleet² *adj* rapid in movement **WORD ORIGIN** probably from Old English *flēotan* to float

fleet chief petty officer *n* a noncommissioned officer in a navy

fleeting *adj* rapid and soon passing: *a fleeting moment* **fleetingly** *adv*

Fleet Street *n* **1** the street in London where many newspaper offices were formerly situated **2** British national newspapers collectively: *Fleet Street's obsession with the Royal Family*

Fleming *n* a person from Flanders or Flemish-speaking Belgium

Flemish *adj* 1 of Flanders, in Belgium ▷ *n* 2 one of the two official languages of Belgium ▷ *pl n* 3 **the Flemish** the people from Flanders or Flemish-speaking Belgium

flesh *n* 1 the soft part of the body of an animal or human, esp. muscular tissue ▸ Related adjective: **carnal** 2 *informal* excess weight; fat 3 the meat of animals as opposed to that of fish or, sometimes, fowl 4 the thick soft part of a fruit or vegetable 5 **the flesh** sexuality or sensuality: *pleasures of the flesh* 6 **flesh and blood** human beings or human nature: *it is almost more than flesh and blood can bear* 7 **in the flesh** in person; actually present 8 **one's own flesh and blood** one's own family 9 **press the flesh** *informal* to shake hands with large numbers of people, esp. in political campaigning **WORD ORIGIN** Old English *flǣsc*

flesh-coloured *adj* yellowish-pink

fleshly *adj* **-lier, -liest** 1 relating to sexuality or sensuality: *the fleshly implications of their love* 2 worldly as opposed to spiritual

flesh out *vb* to expand on or give more details to: *further meetings will be needed to flesh out the agreement*

fleshpots *pl n* places, such as brothels and strip clubs, where sexual desires are catered to **WORD ORIGIN** from the Biblical use as applied to Egypt (Exodus 16:3)

flesh wound *n* a wound affecting superficial tissues

fleshy *adj* **fleshier, fleshiest** 1 plump 2 resembling flesh 3 *bot* (of some fruits) thick and pulpy **fleshiness** *n*

fleur-de-lys or **fleur-de-lis** (**flur**-de-**lee**) *n, pl* **fleurs-de-lys** or **fleurs-de-lis** (**flur**-de-**leez**) a representation of a lily with three distinct petals **WORD ORIGIN** Old French *flor de lis* lily flower

flew *vb* the past tense of **fly**[1]

flews *pl n* the fleshy hanging upper lip of a bloodhound or similar dog **WORD ORIGIN** origin unknown

flex *n* 1 *Austral & Brit* a flexible insulated electric cable: *a coiled kettle flex* ▷ *vb* 2 to bend 3 to bend and stretch (a muscle) **WORD ORIGIN** Latin *flexus* bent, winding

flexible *adj* 1 able to be bent easily without breaking 2 adaptable to changing circumstances: *flexible working arrangements* **flexibility** *n* **flexibly** *adv*

flexitime *n* a system permitting flexibility of working hours at the beginning or end of the day, provided an agreed total is worked

flibbertigibbet *n* *old-fashioned* an irresponsible, silly, gossipy person **WORD ORIGIN** origin unknown

flick *vb* 1 to touch or move with the finger or hand in a quick jerky movement 2 to move with a short sudden movement, often repeatedly 3 **flick through** to look at (a book or magazine) quickly or idly ▷ *n* 4 a tap or quick stroke **WORD ORIGIN** imitative

flicker *vb* 1 to give out an unsteady or irregular light 2 to move quickly to and fro ▷ *n* 3 an unsteady or brief light 4 a brief or faint indication of emotion: *a flicker of fear in his voice* **WORD ORIGIN** Old English *flicorian*

flick knife *n* a knife with a retractable blade that springs out when a button is pressed

flicks *pl n* *slang, old-fashioned* the cinema

flier *n* same as **flyer**

flight[1] *n* 1 a journey by aircraft 2 the act or manner of flying 3 a group of flying birds or aircraft 4 an aircraft flying on a scheduled journey 5 a set of stairs between one landing and the next 6 **flight of fancy** an idea that is imaginative but not practical 7 small plastic or feather fins at the rear of an arrow or dart which make it stable in flight **WORD ORIGIN** Old English *flyht*

flight[2] *n* 1 the act of running away, esp. from danger 2 **put to flight** to cause to run away 3 **take (to) flight** to run away **WORD ORIGIN** Old English *flyht* (unattested)

flight attendant *n* a person who attends to the needs of passengers on a commercial flight

flight deck *n* 1 the crew compartment in an airliner 2 the upper deck of an aircraft carrier from which aircraft take off

flightless *adj* (of certain birds and insects) unable to fly

flight lieutenant *n* a junior commissioned officer in an air force

flight recorder *n* an electronic device in an aircraft for storing information concerning its performance in flight. It is often used to determine the cause of a crash. Also called: **black box**

flight sergeant *n* a noncommissioned officer in an air force

flighty *adj* **flightier, flightiest** frivolous and not very reliable or serious **flightiness** *n*

flimsy *adj* **-sier, -siest** 1 not strong or substantial 2 light and thin: *a flimsy gauze mask* 3 not very convincing: *flimsy evidence* **flimsily** *adv* **flimsiness** *n* **WORD ORIGIN** origin unknown

flinch *vb* 1 to draw back suddenly from pain or something unpleasant 2 **flinch from** to avoid: *I wouldn't flinch from saying that to his face* **WORD ORIGIN** Old French *flenchir*

fling *vb* **flinging, flung** 1 to throw with force 2 to move or go hurriedly or violently: *she flung her arms open wide* 3 to put or send without warning: *they used to fling me in jail* 4 to put (something) somewhere hurriedly or carelessly 5 **fling oneself into** to apply oneself with enthusiasm to ▷ *n* 6 a short spell of self-indulgent enjoyment 7 a brief romantic or sexual relationship 8 a vigorous Scottish country dance: *a Highland fling* **WORD ORIGIN** from Old Norse

flint *n* 1 a very hard stone that produces sparks when struck with steel 2 any piece of flint, esp. one used as a primitive tool 3 a small piece of an

iron alloy, used in cigarette lighters **flinty** *adj* **WORD ORIGIN** Old English

flintlock *n* an obsolete gun in which the powder was lit by a spark produced by a flint

flip *vb* **flipping, flipped** 1 to throw (something light or small) carelessly 2 to turn (something) over: *flip the fish on its back* 3 to turn (a device or machine) on or off by quickly pressing a switch 4 to throw (an object such as a coin) so that it turns in the air 5 to buy and sell an asset (often property) quickly for profit 6 (in Britain) to change the designation of an MP's primary and secondary residences in order to maximize a claim from public funds 7 **flip through** to look at (a book or magazine) idly 8 Also: **flip one's lid** *slang* to fly into an emotional outburst ▷ *n* 9 a snap or tap, usually with the fingers ▷ *adj* 10 *informal* flippant or pert **WORD ORIGIN** probably imitative

flipchart *n* a large pad of paper mounted on a stand, used in giving lectures, etc.

flip-flop *n* *Brit & S African* a rubber-soled sandal attached to the foot by a thong between the big toe and the next toe **WORD ORIGIN** reduplication of *flip*

flippant *adj* treating serious matters with inappropriate light-heartedness or lack of respect **flippancy** *n* **WORD ORIGIN** probably from *flip*

flipper *n* 1 the flat broad limb of seals, whales, and other aquatic animals specialized for swimming 2 either of a pair of rubber paddle-like devices worn on the feet as an aid in swimming

flirt *vb* 1 to behave as if sexually attracted to someone 2 (foll. by *with*) to consider lightly; toy with: *he had often flirted with the idea of emigrating* ▷ *n* 3 a person who flirts **flirtation** *n* **flirtatious** *adj* **WORD ORIGIN** origin unknown

flit *vb* **flitting, flitted** 1 to fly or move along rapidly and lightly 2 to pass quickly: *a shadow flitted across his face* 3 *Scot & N English dialect* to move house 4 *Brit informal* to leave hurriedly and stealthily in order to avoid debts ▷ *n* 5 the act of flitting 6 **do a flit** *NZ informal* to abandon rented accommodation **WORD ORIGIN** Old Norse *flytja* to carry

flitch *n* a side of pork salted and cured **WORD ORIGIN** Old English *flicce*

flitter *vb* *rare* same as **flutter**

float *vb* 1 to rest on the surface of a fluid without sinking 2 to move lightly or freely across a surface or through air or water 3 to move about aimlessly, esp. in the mind: *a pleasant image floated into his mind* 4 **a** to launch (a commercial enterprise, etc.) **b** to offer for sale on the stock market 5 *finance* to allow (a currency) to fluctuate against other currencies ▷ *n* 6 an inflatable object that helps people learning to swim stay afloat 7 *angling* an indicator attached to a baited line that moves when a fish bites 8 a long rigid boatlike structure, of which there are usually two, attached to an aircraft instead of wheels so that it can land on and take off from water **9** a decorated lorry that is part of a procession **10** a small delivery vehicle: *a milk float* **11** *Austral & NZ* a vehicle for transporting horses **12** a sum of money used to cover small expenses or provide change **13** the hollow floating ball of a ball cock **WORD ORIGIN** Old English *flotian*

floatation *n* same as **flotation**

floating *adj* **1** (of a population) moving about; not settled **2** (of an organ or part) displaced or abnormally movable: *a floating kidney* **3** (of a voter) not committed to one party **4** *finance* **a** (of capital) available for current use **b** (of a currency) free to fluctuate against other currencies

floating rib *n* a lower rib not attached to the breastbone

floats *pl n theatre* footlights

flocculent *adj* like tufts of wool **flocculence** *n* **WORD ORIGIN** Latin *floccus* tuft of wool

flock¹ *n* **1** a group of animals of one kind, esp. sheep or birds **2** a large number of people **3** a congregation of Christians regarded as the responsibility of a member of the clergy ▷ *vb* **4** to gather together or move in large numbers **WORD ORIGIN** Old English *flocc*

flock² *n* **1** waste from fabrics such as cotton or wool, used for stuffing mattresses ▷ *adj* **2** (of wallpaper) having a velvety raised pattern **WORD ORIGIN** Latin *floccus* tuft of wool

floe *n* a sheet of floating ice **WORD ORIGIN** probably from Norwegian *flo* slab, layer

flog *vb* **flogging, flogged** **1** to beat harshly, esp. with a whip or stick **2** (sometimes foll. by *off*) *informal* to sell **3** *Austral & NZ informal* to steal **4** **flog a dead horse** *chiefly Brit* to waste one's energy **flogging** *n* **WORD ORIGIN** probably from Latin *flagellare*

flood *n* **1** an overflowing of water on an area that is normally dry **2** a large amount of water **3** the rising of the tide from low to high water ▸ Related adjectives: **diluvial, diluvian** **4** a large amount: *a flood of letters* **5** *theatre* short for **floodlight** ▷ *vb* **6** to cover or become covered with water **7** to fill to overflowing **8** to put a large number of goods on sale on (a market) at the same time, often at a cheap price: *the US was flooded with cheap televisions* **9** to flow or surge: *the memories flooded back* **10** to supply excess petrol to (a petrol engine) so that it cannot work properly **11** to bleed profusely from the womb **flooding** *n* **WORD ORIGIN** Old English *flōd*

Flood *n* **the Flood** *Old Testament* the flood from which Noah and his family and livestock were saved in the ark (Genesis 7–8)

floodgate *n* **1** a gate used to control the flow of water **2** **floodgates** controls against an outpouring of emotion: *it had opened the floodgates of her anxiety*

floodlight *n* **1** a lamp that casts a broad intense light, used in the theatre or to illuminate sports grounds or the

exterior of buildings ▷ *vb* **-lighting, -lit** **2** to illuminate by floodlight

flood plain *n geog* a flat area bordering a river, made of sediment deposited during flooding

floor *n* **1** the lower surface of a room **2** a storey of a building **3** a flat bottom surface: *the ocean floor* **4** that part of a legislative hall in which debate is conducted **5** a minimum limit: *a wages floor for low-paid employees* **6** **have the floor** to have the right to speak in a debate or discussion ▷ *vb* **7** to knock to the ground **8** *informal* to disconcert or defeat **WORD ORIGIN** Old English *flōr*

floorboard *n* one of the boards forming a floor

floored *adj* covered with a floor: *an attic floored with pine planks*

flooring *n* **1** the material used in making a floor: *pine flooring* **2** a floor

floor plan *n* a scale drawing of the arrangement of rooms on one floor of a building

floor show *n* a series of entertainments, such as singing and dancing, in a nightclub

floozy, floozie *or* **floosie** *n, pl* **-zies** *or* **-sies** *slang, old-fashioned* a woman considered to be disreputable or immoral **WORD ORIGIN** origin unknown

flop *vb* **flopping, flopped** **1** to bend, fall, or collapse loosely or carelessly **2** *informal* to fail: *his first big film flopped* **3** to fall or move with a sudden noise ▷ *n* **4** *informal* a complete failure **5** the act of flopping **floppy** *adj* **WORD ORIGIN** variant of *flap*

floppy disk *n* a flexible magnetic disk that stores data in the memory of a digital computer

flora *n* all the plant life of a given place or time **WORD ORIGIN** *Flora*, Roman goddess of flowers

floral *adj* decorated with or consisting of flowers or patterns of flowers

Florentine *adj* **1** of Florence, a city in central Italy ▷ *n* **2** a person from Florence

floret (**flaw**-ret) *n* a small flower forming part of a composite flower head **WORD ORIGIN** Old French *florete*

floribunda *n* a type of rose whose flowers grow in large clusters **WORD ORIGIN** New Latin *floribundus* flowering freely

florid *adj* **1** having a red or flushed complexion **2** very ornate and extravagant: *florid prose* **WORD ORIGIN** Latin *floridus* blooming

florin *n* a former British, Australian, and New Zealand coin, equivalent to ten pence or twenty cents **WORD ORIGIN** Old Italian *fiorino* Florentine coin

florist *n* a person or shop selling flowers

floss *n* **1** fine silky fibres, such as those obtained from silkworm cocoons **2** see **dental floss** ▷ *vb* **3** to clean (between the teeth) with dental floss **flossy** *adj* **WORD ORIGIN** probably from Old French

flosche down

flotation *or* **floatation** *n* the launching or financing of a commercial enterprise by bond or share issues

flotilla *n* a small fleet or a fleet of small ships **WORD ORIGIN** Spanish *flota* fleet

flotsam *n* **1** floating wreckage from a ship **2** **flotsam and jetsam** **a** odds and ends **b** *Brit* homeless or vagrant people **WORD ORIGIN** Anglo-French *floteson*

flounce¹ *vb* **flouncing, flounced** **1** to move or go with emphatic movements ▷ *n* **2** the act of flouncing **WORD ORIGIN** Scandinavian

flounce² *n* an ornamental frill on a garment or tablecloth **WORD ORIGIN** Old French *froncir* to wrinkle

flounder¹ *vb* **1** to struggle to move or stay upright, esp. in water or mud **2** to behave or speak in an awkward, confused way **WORD ORIGIN** probably a blend of FOUNDER + BLUNDER

USAGE
Flounder is sometimes wrongly used where *founder* is meant: *the project foundered (not floundered) because of a lack of funds.*

flounder² *n, pl* **-der** *or* **-ders** an edible flatfish **WORD ORIGIN** Scandinavian

flour *n* **1** a powder prepared by grinding grain, esp. wheat ▷ *vb* **2** to sprinkle (food or utensils) with flour **floury** *adj* **WORD ORIGIN** Middle English *flur* 'flower', i.e. best part

flourish *vb* **1** to be active, successful, or widespread; prosper **2** to be at the peak of development **3** to wave (something) dramatically ▷ *n* **4** a dramatic waving or sweeping movement: *he created a flourish with an imaginary wand* **5** an ornamental curly line in writing **6** a fancy or extravagant action or part of something: *he took his tie off with a flourish* **flourishing** *adj* **WORD ORIGIN** Latin *florere* to flower

flout (rhymes with **out**) *vb* to deliberately disobey (a rule, law, etc.) **WORD ORIGIN** probably from Middle English *flouten* to play the flute

USAGE
See at **flaunt**.

flow *vb* **1** (of liquids) to move in a stream **2** (of blood, electricity, etc.) to circulate **3** to move steadily and smoothly: *a golf club with rich-looking cars flowing into it* **4** to be produced effortlessly: *words flowed from him in a steady stream* **5** to hang freely: *her hair loose and flowing down her back* **6** to be abundant: *at the buffet lunch, wine flowed like water* **7** (of tide water) to rise ▷ *n* **8** the act, rate, or manner of flowing: *the abundant flow of water through domestic sprinklers* **9** a continuous stream or discharge **10** the advancing of the tide **WORD ORIGIN** Old English *flōwan*

flow chart *or* **sheet** *n* a diagram showing a sequence of operations in an industrial process, computer program, etc.

flower *n* **1** the part of a plant that is, usually, brightly coloured, and quickly fades, producing seeds **2** a plant grown

Eponyms

E ponyms, words derived from personal names, are so common in English that it's a wonder we don't run out of names.

We have scientific units of measurement (*watt, volt, ampere*, the *Mach number*) and laws (*Boyle's law, Heisenberg's Uncertainty Principle*), as well as satirical laws like the *Peter Principle* ('In a hierarchy, every employee tends to rise to his level of incompetence"), *Parkinson's Law* ('Work expands so as to fill the time available for its completion'), and *Murphy's Law* ('Anything that can go wrong will go wrong.'). One doesn't have to be a character in Jonathan Swift's *Gulliver's Travels* to be a *Liliputian*, a *Brobdingnagian*, or a *yahoo*. Botanists and zoologists coin genus-and-species names likewise, but tend to be more fanciful (one has named a lichen *Caloplaca obamae*). The periodic table is crowded with chemical elements named after scientists: *curium, mendelevium, rutherfordium, einsteinium*; the name Alfred Nobel, the Swedish inventor of dynamite, became attached to both *nobelium* and the *Nobel Prize*. Since there are lots of minerals in Canada, Canadian geologists disproportionately lend their names to them: *cernyite, dawsonite, donnayite, ferrierite, gunningite, hawleyite, loganite, satterlyite, steacyite*; less explicable is why so many mineral eponyms, from *zaccagnaite* to *zoisite*, start with z.

Innumerable places are named after their founders or other notables, and the titles of books, films, and TV series (*Huckleberry Finn, Harper, Seinfeld*) refer not merely to the main character in one of them, but to the work, film, or series itself. The list goes on. Sexual deviations: *sadism, masochism*. Clothing: *cardigan, derby, stetson*. Berries, flowers, fruits, trees: *loganberry, narcissus*, the *Bartlett pear*, the *Douglas* fir. Typefaces: *Bodoni, Caslon*. Psychoanalysis: the *Oedipus complex*. Big bottles for wine: *jeroboam, nebuchadnezzar*. Parts of the body, literal or proverbial: *Adam's apple, Achilles heel*. Trade names that became generic terms: *Ferris wheel, diesel*. Musical instruments: *saxophone, sousaphone*. Food and drink: *lobster Newburg, beef Stroganoff, eggs benedict, melba toast*, the *martini*. Religions and denominations: *Lutheranism, Buddhism, Christianity*.

Guns: *colt, derringer, Uzi*. Movements, ideologies, and philosophies: *Marxism, Platonism*. National personifications: *Uncle Sam, John Bull*. Other personifications, too: someone can be a *Don Juan*, a *Jezebel*, a *Polyanna*, a *Scrooge*, an *Uncle Tom*, an *Horatio Alger*, or a bipolar *Jekyll and Hyde*. Adjectives depict qualities of a famous author's work: *Orwellian, Kafkaesque, Dickensian, Machiavellian*. Then there are the jokers of language use: *Spoonerisms*, said by or attributed to the Oxford don, the Rev William Archibald Spooner ("It is kisstomary to cuss the bride"), the movie mogul Samuel Goldwyn's *Goldwynisms* ("Let's have some new clichés"), and *Yogiisms*, after the baseball catcher Yogi Berra ("You can observe a lot by watching.").

The most interesting eponyms are common words in which no trace of their origin remains. It's easy enough to guess which Greek and Roman gods and goddesses engendered *panic, saturnine, hermetic, martial, plutocracy, mercuric*, and *erotic*. Yet many originals and causes remain obscure. Agrarian protest and political machinations were the basis of at least two eponyms. *Boycott* draws on the name of a nineteenth-century land agent, Capt. CC Boycott, whose Irish tenants ostracized him. To *gerrymander* is to redraw an electoral map for partisan purposes. The word comes from the Massachusetts Governor Elbridge Gerry, whose redrawn map had the shape of a salamander. It did not come from someone named Gerry Mander.

The convention that diseases were named after their describers has a built-in ambiguity. So far as we know, Burrill B Crohn, the American pathologist who described *Crohn's disease*, did not have Crohn's disease, nor did the German neurologists Hans Gerhard Creutzfeldt and Alfons Maria Jakob have *Creutzfeldt-Jakob disease*. We may not be aware that the British army officer Henry Shrapnel invented *shrapnel*, that the blind French educator Louis Braille devised *braille*, and that the forename Robert partly yielded *bobolink* and Patrick the *paddy wagon*. The original *dunce* was the medieval Scottish theologian *Duns Scotus*. Sometimes eponyms are libellous.

for its colourful flowers ▶ Related adjective: **floral 3** the best or finest part: *in the flower of her youth* **4 in flower** with flowers open ▷ *vb* **5** to produce flowers; bloom **6** to reach full growth or maturity: *liberty only flowers in times of peace*
WORD ORIGIN Latin *flos*

flowered *adj* decorated with flowers or a floral design

flowerpot *n* a pot in which plants are grown

flowery *adj* **1** decorated with flowers or floral patterns **2** (of language or style) containing elaborate literary expressions **floweriness** *n*

flown *vb* the past participle of **fly¹**

fl. oz. fluid ounce(s)

Flt Lt Flight Lieutenant

Flt Sgt Flight Sergeant

flu *n informal* short for **influenza**

fluctuate *vb* **-ating, -ated** to change frequently and erratically: *share prices fluctuated wildly throughout the day* **fluctuation** *n*
WORD ORIGIN Latin *fluctus* a wave

flue *n* a passage or pipe in a chimney, used to carry off smoke, gas, or hot air
WORD ORIGIN origin unknown

fluent *adj* **1** able to speak or write with ease: *they spoke fluent English; fluent in French* **2** spoken or written with ease **fluency** *n* **fluently** *adv*
WORD ORIGIN Latin *fluere* to flow

fluff *n* **1** soft light particles, such as the down of cotton or wool **2** *informal* a mistake, esp. in speaking or reading lines ▷ *vb* **3** to make or become soft and puffy **4** *informal* to make a mistake in performing **fluffy** *adj* **fluffiness** *n*
WORD ORIGIN probably from earlier *flue* downy matter

fluid *n* **1** a substance, such as a liquid or gas, that can flow and has no fixed shape ▷ *adj* **2** capable of flowing and easily changing shape **3** constantly changing or apt to change **fluidity** *n*
WORD ORIGIN Latin *fluere* to flow

fluid ounce *n* **1** *Brit* a unit of liquid measure equal to one twentieth of an Imperial pint (28.4 ml) **2** *US* a unit of liquid measure equal to one sixteenth of a US pint (29.6 ml)

fluke¹ *n* an accidental stroke of luck **fluky** *adj*
WORD ORIGIN origin unknown

fluke² *n* **1** the flat triangular point of an anchor **2** either of the two lobes of the tail of a whale
WORD ORIGIN perhaps a special use of FLUKE³ (in the sense: a flounder, flatfish)

fluke³ *n* any parasitic flatworm, such as the liver fluke
WORD ORIGIN Old English *flōc*

flume *n* **1** a narrow sloping channel for water **2** an enclosed water slide at a swimming pool

flummery *n informal* silly or trivial talk
WORD ORIGIN Welsh *llymru*

flummox *vb* to puzzle or confuse
WORD ORIGIN origin unknown

flung *vb* the past of **fling**

flunk *vb US, Canad, Austral, NZ, & S African*

informal to fail (an examination, course, etc.)
WORD ORIGIN origin unknown

flunky or **flunkey** *n, pl* **flunkies** or **flunkeys 1** a manservant who wears ceremonial dress **2** a person who performs small unimportant tasks for a powerful or important person in the hope of being rewarded
WORD ORIGIN origin unknown

fluor (**flew**-or) *n* same as **fluorspar**
WORD ORIGIN Latin: a flowing; so called from its use as a metallurgical flux

fluoresce *vb* **-rescing, -resced** to exhibit fluorescence
WORD ORIGIN back formation from FLUORESCENCE

fluorescence *n* **1** *physics* the emission of light from atoms or molecules that are bombarded by particles, such as electrons, or by radiation from a separate source **2** the radiation emitted as a result of fluorescence **fluorescent** *adj*
WORD ORIGIN from *fluor*

fluorescent lamp *n* a lamp in which ultraviolet radiation from an electrical gas discharge causes a thin layer of phosphor on a tube's inside surface to fluoresce

fluoridate *vb* **-dating, -dated** to add fluoride to (water) as protection against tooth decay **fluoridation** *n*

fluoride *n chem* any compound containing fluorine and another element or radical

fluorinate *vb* **-nating, -nated** to treat or combine with fluorine **fluorination** *n*

fluorine *n chem* a poisonous strong-smelling pale yellow gas that is the most reactive of all the elements. Symbol: F

fluoroscopy (floor-**oss**-kop-ee) *n* same as **radioscopy**

fluorspar, fluor *or US & Canad* **fluorite** *n* a white or colourless mineral, consisting of calcium fluoride in crystalline form: the chief ore of fluorine

flurry *n, pl* **-ries 1** a short rush of vigorous activity or movement **2** a light gust of wind or rain, or fall of snow ▷ *vb* **-ries, -rying, -ried 3** to confuse or bewilder
WORD ORIGIN obsolete *flurr* to scatter

flush¹ *vb* **1** to blush or cause to blush **2** to send water quickly through (a pipe or a toilet) so as to clean it **3** to elate: *she was flushed with excitement* ▷ *n* **4** a rosy colour, esp. in the cheeks **5** a sudden flow, such as of water **6** a feeling of elation: *in the flush of victory* **7** freshness: *in the first flush of youth* **flushed** *adj*
WORD ORIGIN perhaps from FLUSH³

flush² *adj* **1** level with another surface **2** *informal* having plenty of money ▷ *adv* **3** so as to be level
WORD ORIGIN probably from FLUSH¹ (in the sense: spring out)

flush³ *vb* to drive out of a hiding place
WORD ORIGIN Middle English *flusshen*

flush⁴ *n* (in poker and similar games) a hand containing only one suit
WORD ORIGIN Latin *fluxus* flux

fluster *vb* **1** to make or become nervous

or upset ▷ *n* **2** a nervous or upset state
WORD ORIGIN from Old Norse

flute *n* **1** a wind instrument consisting of a tube of wood or metal with holes in the side stopped either by the fingers or keys. The breath is directed across a mouth hole in the side **2** a tall narrow wineglass, used esp. for champagne ▷ *vb* **fluting, fluted 3** to utter in a high-pitched tone **fluty** *adj*
WORD ORIGIN Old French *flahute*

fluted *adj* having decorated grooves

fluting *n* a design or decoration of flutes on a column

flutter *vb* **1** to wave rapidly **2** (of birds or butterflies) to flap the wings **3** to move with an irregular motion **4** *pathol* (of the heart) to beat abnormally rapidly **5** to move about restlessly ▷ *n* **6** a quick flapping or vibrating motion **7** a state of nervous excitement or confusion **8** excited interest **9** *Brit informal* a modest bet **10** *pathol* an abnormally rapid beating of the heart **11** *electronics* a slow variation in pitch in a sound-reproducing system
WORD ORIGIN Old English *floterian* to float to and fro

fluvial (**flew**-vee-al) *adj* of or relating to a river
WORD ORIGIN Latin *fluvius* river

flux *n* **1** continuous change or instability **2** a flow or discharge **3** a substance mixed with a metal oxide to assist in fusion **4** *physics* **a** the rate of flow of particles, energy, or a fluid **b** the strength of a field in a given area: *magnetic flux*
WORD ORIGIN Latin *fluxus* a flow

fly¹ *vb* **flies, flying, flew, flown 1** to move through the air on wings or in an aircraft **2** to control the flight of (an aircraft) **3** to float, flutter, display, or be displayed in the air: *the Red Cross flag flew at each corner of the compound* **4** to transport or be transported through the air by aircraft, wind, etc. **5** to move very quickly or suddenly: *the front door flew open* **6** to pass quickly: *how time flies* **7** to escape from (an enemy or a place) **8 fly a kite** to release information or take a step in order to test public opinion **9 fly at** to attack (someone) **10 fly high** *informal* to have a high aim **11 let fly** *informal* to lose one's temper: *a young child letting fly at you in a sudden moment of temper* ▷ *n, pl* **flies 12** Also: **flies** a closure that conceals a zip, buttons, or other fastening, as on trousers **13** a flap forming the entrance to a tent **14 flies** *theatre* the space above the stage, used for storing scenery
WORD ORIGIN Old English *flēogan*

fly² *n, pl* **flies 1** a small insect with two pairs of wings **2** any of various similar but unrelated insects, such as the dragonfly **3** *angling* a lure made from a fish-hook attached with feathers to resemble a fly **4 fly in the ointment** *informal* a slight flaw that detracts from value or enjoyment **5 fly on the wall** a person who watches others, while not being noticed himself or herself **6 there are no flies on him** or **her** *informal* he or she is no fool
WORD ORIGIN Old English *flēoge*

fly³ *adj slang chiefly Brit* sharp and cunning

WORD ORIGIN origin unknown

flyaway *adj* **1** (of hair) very fine and soft **2** frivolous or light-hearted: *a flyaway remark*

flyblown *adj* **1** covered with blowfly eggs **2** in a dirty and bad condition

fly-by-night *informal adj* **1** unreliable or untrustworthy, esp. in money matters ▷ *n* **2** an untrustworthy person

flycatcher *n* a small insect-eating songbird

flyer *or* **flier** *n* **1** a small advertising leaflet **2** a person or thing that flies or moves very fast **3** *old-fashioned* an aircraft pilot

fly-fishing *n angling* fishing using artificial flies as lures

flying *n* **1** the act of piloting, navigating, or travelling in an aircraft ▷ *adj* **2** hurried and brief: *a flying visit* **3** fast or built for speed: *Australia's flying fullback* **4** hanging, waving, or floating freely: *flags flying proudly*

flying boat *n* a seaplane in which the fuselage consists of a hull that provides buoyancy

flying buttress *n* an arch and vertical column that supports a wall from the outside

flying colours *pl n* conspicuous success; triumph: *they passed with flying colours*

flying fish *n* a fish of warm and tropical seas, with winglike fins used for gliding above the water

flying fox *n* **1** a large fruit bat of tropical Africa and Asia **2** *Austral & NZ* a platform suspended from an overhead cable, used for transporting people or materials

flying officer *n* a junior commissioned officer in an air force

flying saucer *n* an unidentified disc-shaped flying object alleged to come from outer space

flying squad *n* a small group of police or soldiers ready to move into action quickly

flying start *n* **1** any promising beginning: *a flying start to the new financial year* **2** a start to a race in which the competitor is already travelling at speed as he or she passes the starting line

flyleaf *n, pl* **-leaves** the inner leaf of the endpaper of a book

flyover *n* an intersection of two roads at which one is carried over the other by a bridge

flypaper *n* paper with a sticky and poisonous coating, hung up to trap flies

fly-past *n* a ceremonial flight of aircraft over a given area

fly sheet *n* a piece of canvas drawn over the ridgepole of a tent to form an outer roof

fly spray *n* a liquid used to destroy flies, sprayed from an aerosol

flyweight *n* a professional or an amateur boxer weighing up to 112 pounds (51 kg)

flywheel *n* a heavy wheel that regulates the speed of a machine

Fm *chem* fermium

FM frequency modulation

f-number *n photog* the ratio of the effective diameter of a lens to its focal length

foal *n* **1** the young of a horse or related animal ▷ *vb* **2** to give birth to (a foal) **WORD ORIGIN** Old English *fola*

foam *n* **1** a mass of small bubbles of gas formed on the surface of a liquid **2** frothy saliva **3** a light spongelike solid used for insulation, packing, etc. ▷ *vb* **4** to produce or cause to produce foam **5 foam at the mouth** to be very angry **foamy** *adj* **WORD ORIGIN** Old English *fām*

fob *n* **1** a chain by which a pocket watch is attached to a waistcoat **2** a small pocket in a man's waistcoat, for holding a watch **WORD ORIGIN** Germanic

f.o.b. *or* **FOB** *commerce* free on board

fob off *vb* **fobbing, fobbed** **1** to pretend to satisfy (a person) with lies or excuses **2** to sell or pass off (inferior goods) as valuable **WORD ORIGIN** probably from German *foppen* to trick

focal *adj* **1** of or relating to a focus **2** situated at or measured from the focus

focal length *n* the distance from the focal point of a lens or mirror to the surface of the mirror or the centre of the lens

focal point *n* **1** the point where the rays of light from a lens or mirror meet **2** the centre of attention or interest: *a focal point for the new high-technology industries*

focus (*foe*-kuss) *vb* **-cusing, -cused** *or* **-cussing, -cussed** **1** to adjust one's eyes or an instrument on an object so that its image is clear **2** to concentrate ▷ *n, pl* **-cuses** *or* **-ci** (-sigh, -kye, -kee) **3** a point of convergence of light or sound waves, or a point from which they appear to diverge **4 in focus** (of an object or image being viewed) clear and sharp **5 out of focus** (of an object or image being viewed) blurred and fuzzy **6** same as **focal point** *or* **focal length** **7** *optics* the state of an optical image when it is distinct or the state of an instrument producing this image **8** a point upon which attention or activity is concentrated: *the focus was on health and education* **9** *geom* a fixed reference point on the concave side of a conic section, used when defining its eccentricity **WORD ORIGIN** Latin: hearth, fireplace

focus group *n* a group of people gathered by a market research company to discuss and assess a product or service

fodder *n* bulk feed for livestock, esp. hay or straw **WORD ORIGIN** Old English *fōdor*

foe *n formal or literary* an enemy **WORD ORIGIN** Old English *fāh* hostile

FoE *or* **FOE** Friends of the Earth

foetid *adj* same as **fetid**

foetus *n, pl* **-tuses** same as **fetus**

fog *n* **1** a mass of droplets of condensed water vapour suspended in the air, often greatly reducing visibility **2** *photog* a blurred area on a developed negative, print, or transparency ▷ *vb*

fogging, fogged **3** to envelop or become enveloped with or as if with fog **foggy** *adj* **WORD ORIGIN** probably from Old Norse

fog bank *n* a distinct mass of fog, esp. at sea

fogbound *adj* prevented from operating by fog

fogey *or* **fogy** *n, pl* **-geys** *or* **-gies** an extremely old-fashioned person: *a stick-in-the-mud old fogey* **fogeyish** *or* **fogyish** *adj* **WORD ORIGIN** origin unknown

foghorn *n* a large horn sounded at intervals as a warning to ships in fog

foible *n* a slight peculiarity or minor weakness: *he was intolerant of other people's foibles* **WORD ORIGIN** obsolete French form of *faible* feeble

foil¹ *vb* to baffle or frustrate (a person or an attempt) **WORD ORIGIN** Middle English *foilen* to trample

foil² *n* **1** metal in the form of very thin sheets **2** a person or thing setting off another thing to advantage: *mint sauce is an excellent foil to lamb* **WORD ORIGIN** Latin *folia* leaves

foil³ *n* a light slender flexible sword tipped by a button, used in fencing **WORD ORIGIN** origin unknown

foist *vb* **foist on** to force (someone) to have or experience (something): *the tough economic policies which have been foisted on the developing world* **WORD ORIGIN** probably from obsolete Dutch *vuisten* to enclose in one's hand

fold¹ *vb* **1** to bend double so that one part covers another **2** to bring together and intertwine (the arms or legs) **3 fold up** to enclose in a surrounding material **4** *literary* to clasp (a person) in one's arms **5** Also: **fold in** to mix (ingredients) by gently turning one over the other with a spoon **6** *informal* (of a business, organization, or project) to fail or go bankrupt ▷ *n* **7** a piece or section that has been folded **8** a mark, crease, or hollow made by folding **9** a bend in stratified rocks that results from movements within the earth's crust **WORD ORIGIN** Old English *fealdan*

fold² *n* **1** *Brit, Austral and S African* a small enclosure for sheep **2** a church or the members of it **WORD ORIGIN** Old English *falod*

folder *n* a binder or file for holding loose papers

folding door *n* a door with two or more vertical hinged leaves that can be folded one against another

foliaceous *adj* **1** like a leaf **2** *geol* consisting of thin layers **WORD ORIGIN** Latin *foliaceus*

foliage *n* **1** the green leaves of a plant **2** leaves together with the stems, twigs, and branches they are attached to, esp. when used for decoration **WORD ORIGIN** Old French *fuellage*

foliation *n* **1** *bot* **a** the process of producing leaves **b** the state of being in leaf **2** a leaflike decoration

folio *n, pl* **-lios** **1** a sheet of paper folded

in half to make two leaves for a book **2** a book of the largest common size made up of such sheets **3 a** a leaf of paper numbered on the front side only **b** the page number of a book **4** NZ a collection of related material ▷ *adj* **5** of or made in the largest book size, common esp. in early centuries of European printing: *the entire series is being reissued, several in the original folio format* **WORD ORIGIN** Latin *in folio* in a leaf

folk *pl n* **1** people in general, esp. those of a particular group or class: *ordinary folk* **2** Also: **folks** *informal* members of one's family; relatives ▷ *n* **3** *informal* short for **folk music 4** a people or tribe ▷ *adj* **5** originating from or traditional to the common people of a country: *folk art* **WORD ORIGIN** Old English *folc*

folk dance *n* **1** a traditional country dance **2** music for such a dance

folk etymology *n* the gradual change in the form of a word through the influence of a more familiar word, as for example *crayfish* from its Middle English form *crevis*

folklore *n* the traditional beliefs of a people as expressed in stories and songs

folk music *n* **1** music that is passed on from generation to generation **2** a piece written in the style of this music

folk song *n* **1** a song handed down among the common people **2** a modern song like this **folk singer** *n*

folksy *adj* **-sier, -siest** simple and unpretentious, sometimes in an artificial way

follicle *n* any small sac or cavity in the body, esp. one from which a hair grows **follicular** *adj* **WORD ORIGIN** Latin *folliculus* small bag

follow *vb* **1** to go or come after **2** to accompany: *he followed Isabel everywhere* **3** to be a logical or natural consequence of **4** to keep to the course or track of **5** to act in accordance with: *follow the rules below and it will help you a great deal* **6** to accept the ideas or beliefs of **7** to understand (an explanation) **8** to have a keen interest in: *he's followed the singer's career for more than 25 years* **9** to choose to receive someone's updates on the Twitter website ▶ See also **follow-on, follow through, follow up** **WORD ORIGIN** Old English *folgian*

follower *n* **1** a person who accepts the teachings of another: *a follower of Nietzsche* **2** a supporter, such as of a sport or team

following *adj* **1** about to be mentioned **2** next in time **3** (of winds or currents) moving in the same direction as a vessel ▷ *prep* **4** as a result of: *uncertainty following the collapse of communism* ▷ *n* **5** a group of supporters or enthusiasts
USAGE
The use of *following* to mean as a result of is very common in journalism, but should be avoided in other kinds of writing.

follow-on *cricket n* **1** an immediate second innings forced on a team scoring a prescribed number of runs fewer than its opponents in the first innings ▷ *vb* **follow on 2** to play a follow-on: *England had to follow on*

follow through *vb* **1** to continue an action or series of actions until finished **2** *sport* to continue a stroke, kick, etc. after striking the ball ▷ *n* **follow-through 3** *sport* continuation of a kick, stroke, etc. after striking the ball: *Faldo's controlled follow-through*

follow up *vb* **1** to investigate (a person, evidence, etc.) closely **2** to continue (action) after a beginning, esp. to increase its effect ▷ *n* **follow-up 3** something done to reinforce an initial action: *a routine follow-up to his operation*

folly *n, pl* **-lies 1** the quality of being foolish **2** a foolish action, idea, etc. **3** an imitation castle, temple, etc. built as a decoration in a large garden or park **WORD ORIGIN** Old French *folie* madness

foment (foam-ent) *vb* to encourage or stir up (trouble) **fomentation** *n* **WORD ORIGIN** Latin *fomentum* a poultice
USAGE
Both *foment* and *ferment* can be used to talk about stirring up trouble: *he was accused of fomenting/fermenting unrest.* Only *ferment* can be used intransitively or as a noun: *his anger continued to ferment* (not *foment*); *rural areas were unaffected by the ferment in the cities.*

fond *adj* **1 fond of** having a liking for **2** loving and affectionate: *his fond parents* **3** (of hopes or wishes) cherished but unlikely to be realized **fondly** *adv* **fondness** *n* **WORD ORIGIN** Middle English *fonnen* to be foolish

fondant *n* (a sweet made from) a thick flavoured paste of sugar and water **WORD ORIGIN** French

fondle *vb* **-dling, -dled** to touch or stroke tenderly **WORD ORIGIN** obsolete *fond* to fondle

fondue *n* a Swiss dish, consisting of melted cheese into which small pieces of bread are dipped **WORD ORIGIN** French: melted

font¹ *n* a large bowl in a church for baptismal water **WORD ORIGIN** Latin *fons* fountain

font² *n* *printing* same as **fount²**

fontanelle *or esp. US* **fontanel** *n anat* a soft membranous gap between the bones of a baby's skull **WORD ORIGIN** Old French *fontanele* a little spring

food *n* any substance that can be taken into the body by a living organism and changed into energy and body tissue ▶ Related adjective: **gastronomy** **WORD ORIGIN** Old English *fōda*

food chain *n* *ecology* a series of organisms in a community, each member of which feeds on another in the chain and is in turn eaten

food group *n* any of the categories into which different foods may be placed according to the type of nourishment they supply

foodie *n* *informal* a person with a keen interest in food and cookery

food poisoning *n* an acute illness caused by food that is contaminated by bacteria

food processor *n* a machine for chopping, mixing, or liquidizing food

foodstuff *n* any substance that can be used as food

fool¹ *n* **1** a person who lacks sense or judgment **2** a person who is made to appear ridiculous **3** (formerly) a professional jester living in a royal or noble household **4 play** *or* **act the fool** to deliberately act foolishly ▷ *vb* **5** to deceive (someone), esp. in order to make them look ridiculous **6 fool around** *or* **about with** *informal* to act or play with irresponsibly or aimlessly **7** to speak or act in a playful or jesting manner **WORD ORIGIN** Latin *follis* bellows

fool² *n* *chiefly Brit* a dessert made from a puree of fruit with cream **WORD ORIGIN** perhaps from FOOL¹

foolery *n* foolish behaviour

foolhardy *adj* **-hardier, -hardiest** recklessly adventurous **foolhardily** *adv* **foolhardiness** *n* **WORD ORIGIN** Old French *fol* foolish + *hardi* bold

foolish *adj* very silly, unwise, or absurd **foolishly** *adv* **foolishness** *n*

foolproof *adj* *informal* **1** incapable of going wrong; infallible: *a foolproof identification system* **2** (of machines etc.) guaranteed to function as intended despite human misuse or error

foolscap *n* *chiefly Brit* a standard paper size, 34.3 × 43.2 cm **WORD ORIGIN** from the watermark of a fool's (i.e. dunce's) *cap*, formerly used on it

fool's errand *n* a fruitless undertaking

fool's gold *n* a yellow-coloured mineral, such as pyrite, that is sometimes mistaken for gold

fool's paradise *n* a state of happiness based on false hopes or beliefs

foosball *n* US & Canad a game in which opponents on either side of a purpose-built table attempt to strike a ball into the other side's goal by moving horizontal bars with miniatures of footballers attached

foot *n, pl* **feet 1** the part of the leg below the ankle joint that is in contact with the ground during standing and walking **2** the part of a garment covering a foot **3** a unit of length equal to 12 inches (0.3048 metre) **4** the bottom, base, or lower end of something: *at the foot of the hill; the foot of the page* **5** old-fashioned infantry **6** *prosody* a group of two or more syllables in which one syllable has the major stress, forming the basic unit of poetic rhythm **7 one foot in the grave** *informal* near to death **8 on foot** walking **9 put one's best foot forward** to try to do one's best **10 put one's foot down** *informal* to act firmly **11 put one's foot in it** *informal* to make an embarrassing and tactless mistake **12 under foot** on the ground ▷ *vb* **13 foot it** *informal* to travel on foot **14 foot the bill** to pay the entire cost of something ▶ See also **feet** ▷ **footless** *adj* **WORD ORIGIN** Old English *fōt*
USAGE
In front of another noun, the plural for the unit of length is *foot*: *a 20-foot putt; his 70-foot ketch.* Foot can also be used instead of *feet* when mentioning

William Shakespeare

There is little argument that William Shakespeare is the greatest writer in the English language. Four hundred years after his death his work still casts a huge shadow over the rest of English literature. Indeed, there are few areas of human endeavour where one figure towers so obviously above all others.

Shakespeare was born in 1564 in Stratford-upon-Avon. Not much is known of his early life other than that he married Anne Hathaway in 1582 and that the couple had three children. At some point in the 1580s he moved to London where he worked as an actor. By 1594 he had already acquired a reputation as a poet and playwright. He joined a theatrical troupe called the Lord Chamberlain's Company (later renamed The King's Men) with whom he enjoyed great success, and helped found the Globe Theatre. Around 1613 he retired to Stratford, where he died in 1616.

In 1623 the first collected edition of his plays, known as *The First Folio*, was published (although unauthorized editions of individual plays circulated during his lifetime). Scholars continue to debate the authenticity of some of his work, but he is widely accepted as the author of 37 plays, four long narrative poems and a series of 154 sonnets.

The plays can be broadly divided into historical plays (including *Henry V* and *Richard III*), tragedies (including *Hamlet* and *King Lear*), and comedies (including *Twelfth Night* and *As You Like It*), although later works such as *The Tempest* defy easy classification.

The plots of these plays were not original but drew on existing works and chronicles. Shakespeare's genius lay in his ability to transform this material, heightening the drama, creating vivid characters, and imbuing their speech with memorable poetry.

In view of the enduring reputation that his works have enjoyed, there are a surprising number of mysteries concerning the man who created them. Nothing at all is known of his whereabouts between 1585 and 1592. There is no record that he ever travelled outside England, yet many of his plays are set in continental Europe. Nor is it easy to explain how a man of his apparently ordinary background could have created such an extraordinary body of work – a fact that has led some to believe that the plays were not written by the actor from Stratford at all. Such issues have been fruitful ground for scholarly argument, but much that has been written about the man remains speculation.

What is not in doubt is the stature of the work. Shakespeare's plays remain among the most frequently performed and best-loved in English literature. Successive generations of directors and actors have sought to reinterpret them and make them relevant for their own times. Shakespeare's home town of Stratford is a Mecca for tourists and theatregoers, and is home to the Royal Shakespeare Company, which specializes in performing his work. A recreation of the Globe Theatre was opened in London in 1997 and attempts to present Shakespeare's plays in the atmosphere in which the original playgoers would have witnessed them.

Even for people who have no interest in the theatre, Shakespeare's influence continues to be felt. Characters from his plays have become bywords for certain types of individual. When we talk of an amorous man as a 'Romeo' or describe a well-built and jovial person as being 'Falstaffian', we are invoking Shakespeare's creations.

Shakespeare is especially notable for his linguistic inventiveness. Over 2,000 words that occur in his writings are not recorded before him, and a surprisingly large proportion of these are still in common use. Some selections of his more eye-catching vocabulary are included in other parts of this book.

Many phrases from his works have become the currency of everyday speech. It is to Shakespeare that we owe 'to the manner born' (from *Hamlet*), 'pound of flesh' (*The Merchant of Venice*), 'the dogs of war' (*Julius Caesar*), 'sea change' (*The Tempest*), 'salad days' (*Antony and Cleopatra*), 'pomp and circumstance' (*Othello*), and 'more sinned against than sinning' (*King Lear*). As one of Jane Austen's characters says, 'Shakespeare one gets acquainted with without knowing how. It is a part of an Englishman's constitution.'

a quantity and in front of words like *tall*: *four foot of snow; he is at least six foot tall.*

footage *n* **1** a length of film **2** the sequences of filmed material: *footage of refugees leaving the city*

foot-and-mouth disease *n* a highly infectious viral disease of cattle, pigs, sheep, and goats, in which blisters form in the mouth and on the feet

football *n* **1** any of various games played with a ball in which two teams compete to kick, head, or propel the ball into each other's goal **2** the ball used in any of these games **footballer** *n*

football pools *pl n* same as **pools**

footbridge *n* a narrow bridge for the use of pedestrians

footfall *n* the sound of a footstep

foothills *pl n* relatively low hills at the foot of a mountain

foothold *n* **1** a secure position from which further progress may be made: *a firm foothold in Europe's telecommunications market* **2** a ledge or other place where a foot can be securely positioned, as during climbing

footing *n* **1** basis or foundation: *on a sound financial footing* **2** the relationship between two people or groups: *on an equal footing* **3** a secure grip by or for the feet

footle *vb* **-ling, -led** *chiefly Brit informal* to loiter aimlessly **footling** *adj*
WORD ORIGIN probably from French *foutre* to copulate with

footlights *pl n* *theatre* lights set in a row along the front of the stage floor

footloose *adj* free to go or do as one wishes

footman *n, pl* **-men** a male servant in uniform

footnote *n* a note printed at the bottom of a page

footpad *n* *old-fashioned* a highwayman, on foot rather than horseback

footpath *n* **1** a narrow path for walkers only **2** *Austral* a raised space alongside a road, for pedestrians

footplate *n* *chiefly Brit* a platform in the cab of a locomotive on which the crew stand to operate the controls

footprint *n* **1** an indentation or outline of the foot on a surface **2** the shape and size of the area something occupies: *enlarging the footprint of the building*

footsie *n* *informal* flirtation involving the touching together of feet

footsore *adj* having sore or tired feet, esp. from much walking

footstep *n* **1** a step in walking **2** the sound made by walking **3** a footmark **4 follow in someone's footsteps** to continue the example of another

footstool *n* a low stool used for supporting the feet of a seated person

footwear *n* anything worn to cover the feet

footwork *n* the way in which the feet are used, for example in sports or dancing: *nimble footwork*

fop *n* a man who is excessively concerned with fashion **foppery** *n* **foppish** *adj*
WORD ORIGIN perhaps from Middle English *foppe* fool

for *prep* **1** directed or belonging to: *a bottle of beer for himself* **2** to the advantage of: *he spelt it out for her* **3** in the direction of: *he headed for the door* **4** over a span of (time or distance): *she considered him coolly for a moment* **5** in favour of: *support for the war* **6** in order to get: *for a bit of company* **7** designed to meet the needs of: *the instructions are for right-handed players* **8** at a cost of: *two dishes for one* **9** in place of: *she had to substitute for her mother because they woke late* **10** because of: *dancing for joy* **11** regarding the usual characteristics of: *unusually warm for the time of year* **12** concerning: *our idea for the last scene* **13** as being: *do you take me for an idiot?* **14** at (a specified time): *multiparty elections are planned for next year* **15** to do or take part in: *two guests for dinner* **16** in the duty or task of: *that's for you to decide* **17** in relation to; as it affects: *it's too hard for me* **18** in order to preserve or retain: *fighting for survival* **19** as a direct equivalent to: *word for word* **20** in order to become or enter: *training for the priesthood* **21** in exchange for: *the cash was used to pay for food, shelter, and medical supplies* **22** for all see all (sense 12) **23 for it** *Austral & Brit informal* liable for punishment or blame: *you'll be for it if you get caught* ⊳ *conj* **24** *formal* because or seeing that: *implausibility cries aloud, and this is a pity, for much of the narrative is entertaining*
WORD ORIGIN Old English

forage (for-ridge) *vb* **-aging, -aged** **1** to search for food **2** to obtain by searching about: *she foraged for her shoes* ⊳ *n* **3** food for horses or cattle, esp. hay or straw **4** the act of searching for food or provisions
WORD ORIGIN Old French *fourrage*

forage cap *n* a cap with a flat round crown and a visor, worn by soldiers when not in battle or on parade

foramen (for-**ray**-men) *n, pl* **-ramina** (-**ram**-in-a) *or* **-ramens** *anat* a natural hole, esp. one in a bone through which nerves pass
WORD ORIGIN Latin

forasmuch as *conj* *old-fashioned or legal* seeing that or since

foray *n* **1** a short raid or incursion **2** a first attempt or new undertaking: *his first foray into films*
WORD ORIGIN Middle English *forrayen* to pillage

forbade *or* **forbad** *vb* the past tense of **forbid**

forbear¹ *vb* **-bearing, -bore, -borne** to cease or refrain (from doing something) **forbearance** *n*
WORD ORIGIN Old English *forberan*

forbear² *n* same as **forebear**

forbid *vb* **-bidding, -bade** *or* **-bad, -bidden** *or* **-bid** to prohibit or refuse to allow
WORD ORIGIN Old English *forbēodan*
USAGE
It was formerly considered incorrect to talk of *forbidding* someone *from* doing something, but in modern usage either *from* or *to* can be used: *he was forbidden from entering/to enter the building.*

forbidding *adj* severe and threatening

in appearance or manner: *a very large and forbidding building*

forbore *vb* the past tense of **forbear¹**

forborne *vb* the past participle of **forbear¹**

force¹ *n* **1** strength or power: *the force of the impact had thrown him into the fireplace* **2** exertion or the use of exertion against a person or thing that resists: *they used force and repression against those who opposed their policies* **3** *physics* an influence that changes a body from a state of rest to one of motion or changes its rate of motion. Symbol: F **4 a** intellectual or moral influence: *the Superintendent acknowledged the force of the Chief Constable's argument* **b** a person or thing with such influence: *Hitler quickly became the decisive force behind German foreign policy* **5** drive or intensity: *he reacted with frightening speed and force* **6** a group of people organized for particular duties or tasks: *a UN peacekeeping force* **7 in force a** (of a law) having legal validity **b** in great strength or numbers ⊳ *vb* **forcing, forced 8** to compel (a person, group, etc.) to do something through effort, superior strength, etc.: *forced into an arranged marriage* **9** to acquire or produce through effort, superior strength, etc.: *he forced a smile* **10** to propel or drive despite resistance **11** to break down or open (a lock, door, etc.) **12** to impose or inflict: *a series of opposition strikes forced the appointment of a coalition government* **13** to cause (plants or farm animals) to grow at an increased rate
WORD ORIGIN Latin *fortis* strong

force² *n* (in N England) a waterfall
WORD ORIGIN Old Norse *fors*

forced *adj* **1** done because of force: *forced labour* **2** false or unnatural: *forced jollity* **3** due to an emergency: *a forced landing*

force-feed *vb* **-feeding, -fed** to force (a person or animal) to swallow food

forceful *adj* **1** strong, emphatic, and confident: *a forceful speech* **2** effective **forcefully** *adv*

forcemeat *n* a mixture of chopped ingredients used for stuffing
WORD ORIGIN from *force* (see FARCE) + *meat*

forceps *n, pl* **-ceps** a surgical instrument in the form of a pair of pincers
WORD ORIGIN Latin *formus* hot + *capere* to seize

forcible *adj* **1** involving physical force **2** convincing or effective: *a strong shrewd mind and a steady forcible manner* **forcibly** *adv*

ford *n* **1** a shallow area in a river that can be crossed by car, on horseback, etc. ⊳ *vb* **2** to cross (a river) over a shallow area **fordable** *adj*
WORD ORIGIN Old English

fore *adj* **1** at, in, or towards the front: *the fore foot* ⊳ *n* **2** the front part **3 fore and aft** located at both ends of a vessel: *two double cabins fore and aft* **4 to the fore** to the front or prominent position ⊳ *interj* **5** a golfer's shouted warning to a person in the path of a flying ball
WORD ORIGIN Old English

fore- *prefix* **1** before in time or rank: *foregoing* **2** at or near the front: *foreground*
WORD ORIGIN Old English

forearm¹ *n* the part of the arm from the

elbow to the wrist

forearm² vb to prepare or arm beforehand

forebear or **forbear** n an ancestor

foreboding n a strong feeling that something bad is about to happen

forecast vb **-casting, -cast** or **-casted** **1** to predict or calculate (weather, events, etc.), in advance ▷ n **2** a statement predicting the weather **3** a prediction **forecaster** n

forecastle, fo'c's'le or **fo'c'sle** (**foke**-sl) n the raised front part of a ship

foreclose vb **-closing, -closed** law to take possession of property bought with borrowed money because repayment has not been made: *the banks have been reluctant to foreclose on troubled borrowers* **foreclosure** n
WORD ORIGIN Old French *for-* out + *clore* to close

forecourt n a courtyard in front of a building, such as one in a filling station

forefather n an ancestor

forefinger n the finger next to the thumb. Also called: **index finger**

forefoot n, pl **-feet** either of the front feet of an animal

forefront n **1** the most active or prominent position: *at the forefront of medical research* **2** the very front

foregather or **forgather** vb to gather together or assemble

forego¹ vb **-going, -went, -gone** to precede in time, place, etc.
WORD ORIGIN Old English *foregān*

forego² vb **-going, -went, -gone** same as **forgo**

foregoing adj (esp. of writing or speech) going before; preceding

foregone conclusion n an inevitable result

foreground n **1** the part of a view, esp. in a picture, nearest the viewer **2** an important or prominent position

forehand tennis, squash, etc. adj **1** (of a stroke) made so that the racket is held with the wrist facing the direction of play ▷ n **2** a forehand stroke

forehead n the part of the face between the natural hairline and the eyes
WORD ORIGIN Old English *forhēafod*

foreign adj **1** of, located in, or coming from another country, area, or people **2** dealing or concerned with another country, area, or people: *the Foreign Minister* **3** not familiar; strange **4** in an abnormal place or position: *a foreign body in the food*
WORD ORIGIN Latin *foris* outside

foreigner n **1** a person from a foreign country **2** an outsider

foreign minister or **secretary** n (in Britain) a cabinet minister who is responsible for a country's dealings with other countries

foreign office n (in Britain) the ministry of a country that is concerned with dealings with other states

foreknowledge n knowledge of something before it actually happens

foreleg n either of the front legs of an

animal

forelock n a lock of hair growing or falling over the forehead

foreman n, pl **-men 1** a person who supervises other workmen **2** law the leader of a jury

foremast n the mast nearest the bow of a ship

foremost adj **1** first in time, place, or importance: *Germany's foremost conductor* ▷ adv **2** first in time, place, or importance
WORD ORIGIN Old English *formest*, from *forma* first

forename n first name

forenoon n the daylight hours before noon

forensic (for-**ren**-sik) adj used in or connected with a court of law **forensically** adv
WORD ORIGIN Latin *forensis* public

forensic medicine n the application of medical knowledge for the purposes of the law, such as in determining the cause of death

foreordain vb to determine (events, etc.) in the future

forepaw n either of the front feet of a land mammal that does not have hooves

foreplay n sexual stimulation before intercourse

forerunner n **1** a person or thing that existed or happened before another and is similar in some way: *a forerunner of the surrealist painters* **2** a person or thing that is a sign of what will happen in the future

foresail n the main sail on the foremast of a ship

foresee vb **-seeing, -saw, -seen** to see or know beforehand **foreseeable** adj

foreshadow vb to show, indicate, or suggest in advance

foreshore n the part of the shore between high- and low-tide marks

foreshorten vb to see or draw (an object) from such an angle that it appears to be shorter than it really is

foresight n **1** the ability to anticipate and provide for future needs **2** the front sight on a firearm

foreskin n anat the fold of skin covering the tip of the penis

forest n **1** a large wooded area with a thick growth of trees and plants **2** a group of narrow or tall objects standing upright: *a forest of waving arms* **3** NZ an area planted with pines or other trees that are not native to the country **forested** adj
WORD ORIGIN Medieval Latin *forestis* unfenced woodland, from Latin *foris* outside

forestall vb to delay, stop, or guard against beforehand: *an action forestalling any further talks*
WORD ORIGIN Middle English *forestallen* to waylay

forestation n the planting of trees over a wide area

forester n a person skilled in forestry or in charge of a forest

forestry n the science or skill of

growing and maintaining trees in a forest, esp. to obtain wood

foretaste n an early but limited experience of something to come

foretell vb **-telling, -told** literary to correctly predict (an event, a result, etc.) beforehand

forethought n thoughtful planning for future events: *a little forethought can avoid a lot of problems later*

foretoken n a sign of a future event

for ever or **forever** adv **1** without end **2** at all times **3** informal for a long time: *I could go on for ever about similar incidents*

forewarn vb to warn beforehand

foreword n an introductory statement to a book

forfeit (for-fit) n **1** something lost or given up as a penalty for a fault, mistake, etc. ▷ vb **2** to lose as a forfeit ▷ adj **3** lost as a forfeit **forfeiture** n
WORD ORIGIN Old French *forfet* offence

forgather vb same as **foregather**

forgave vb the past tense of **forgive**

forge¹ n **1** a place in which metal is worked by heating and hammering; smithy **2** a furnace used for heating metal ▷ vb **forging, forged 3** to shape (metal) by heating and hammering **4** to make a fraudulent imitation of (a signature, money, a painting, etc.) **5** to create (an alliance, relationship, etc.) **forger** n
WORD ORIGIN Old French *forgier* to construct

forge² vb **forging, forged 1** to move at a steady pace **2 forge ahead** to increase speed or progress; take the lead
WORD ORIGIN origin unknown

forgery n, pl **-geries 1** an illegal copy of a painting, banknote, antique, etc. **2** the crime of making a fraudulent imitation

forget vb **-getting, -got, -gotten 1** to fail to remember (someone or something once known) **2** to neglect, either by mistake or on purpose **3** to leave behind by mistake **4 forget oneself** to act in an uncharacteristically unrestrained or unacceptable manner: *behave yourself or I might forget myself and slap your wrists* **forgettable** adj
WORD ORIGIN Old English *forgietan*

forgetful adj **1** tending to forget **2 forgetful of** inattentive to or neglectful of: *Fiona, forgetful of the time, was still in bed* **forgetfully** adv

forget-me-not n a low-growing plant with clusters of small blue flowers

forgive vb **-giving, -gave, -given 1** to stop feeling anger and resentment towards (a person) or at (an action that has caused upset or harm) **2** to pardon (a mistake) **3** to free from (a debt)
WORD ORIGIN Old English *forgiefan*

forgiveness n the act of forgiving or the state of being forgiven

forgiving adj willing to forgive

forgo or **forego** vb **-going, -went, -gone** to give up or do without
WORD ORIGIN Old English *forgān*

forgot vb **1** the past tense of **forget** **2** old-fashioned or dialect a past participle of **forget**

forgotten vb a past participle of **forget**

fork *n* **1** a small tool with long thin prongs on the end of a handle, used for lifting food to the mouth **2** a larger similar-shaped gardening tool, used for lifting or digging **3 forks** the part of a bicycle that links the handlebars to the front wheel **4 a** (of a road, river, etc.) a division into two or more branches **b** the point where the division begins **c** such a branch ▷ *vb* **5** to pick up, dig, etc. with a fork **6** to be divided into two or more branches **7** to take one or other branch at a fork in a road, etc. **WORD ORIGIN** Latin *furca*

forked *adj* **1** having a fork or forklike parts **2** zigzag: *forked lightning*

fork-lift truck *n* a vehicle with two moveable arms at the front that can be raised and lowered for transporting and unloading goods

fork out *vb slang* to pay, esp. with reluctance

forlorn *adj* **1** lonely, unhappy, and uncared-for **2** (of a place) having a deserted appearance **3** desperate and without any expectation of success: *a final, apparently forlorn attempt to save the war-torn country* **forlornly** *adv* **WORD ORIGIN** Old English *forloren* lost

forlorn hope *n* **1** a hopeless enterprise **2** a faint hope **WORD ORIGIN** changed (by folk etymology) from Dutch *verloren hoop* lost troop

form *n* **1** the shape or appearance of something **2** a visible person or animal **3** the particular mode in which a thing or person appears: *wood in the form of paper* **4** a type or kind: *abortion was widely used as a form of birth control* **5** physical or mental condition **6** a printed document, esp. one with spaces in which to fill details or answers **7** the previous record of a horse, athlete, etc. **8** *Brit slang* a criminal record **9** *education chiefly Brit & NZ* a group of children who are taught together **10** manners and etiquette: *it is considered bad form not to wear a tie* **11** the structure and arrangement of a work of art or piece of writing as distinguished from its content **12** a bench **13** a hare's nest **14** any of the various ways in which a word may be spelt or inflected ▷ *vb* **15** to give shape to or take shape, esp. a particular shape **16** to come or bring into existence: *glaciers dammed the valley bottoms with debris behind which lakes have formed* **17** to make or construct or be made or constructed **18** to train or mould by instruction or example **19** to acquire or develop: *they've formed this impression; we formed a bond* **20** to be an element of: *they had formed part of a special murder unit* **WORD ORIGIN** Latin *forma* shape, model

formal *adj* **1** of or following established conventions: *formal talks; a formal announcement* **2** characterized by conventional forms of ceremony and behaviour: *a small formal dinner party* **3** suitable for occasions organized according to conventional ceremony: *formal cocktail frocks* **4** methodical and organized: *a formal approach* **5** (of education and training) given officially at a school, college, etc.: *he had no formal training in maths* **6** symmetrical in form: *a formal garden* **7** relating to the form or structure of something as distinguished from its substance or content: *they addressed the formal elements of the structure of police work* **8** *philosophy* logically deductive rather than based on facts and observation **formally** *adv* **WORD ORIGIN** Latin *formalis*

formaldehyde (for-**mal**-de-hide) *n* a colourless poisonous strong-smelling gas, used as formalin and in synthetic resins. Also: **methanal** **WORD ORIGIN** *form(ic)* + *aldehyde*

formalin *n* a solution of formaldehyde in water, used as a disinfectant and as a preservative for biological specimens

formalism *n* concerned with outward appearances and structure at the expense of content **formalist** *n*

formality *n, pl* **-ties 1** something done as a requirement of custom or good manners: *he dealt with the formalities regarding the cremation* **2** a necessary procedure without real effect: *trials were often a mere formality with the verdict decided beforehand* **3** strict observance of ceremony

formalize *or* **-ise** *vb* **-izing, -ized** *or* **-ising, -ised 1** to make official or valid **2** to give a definite form to **formalization** *or* **-isation** *n*

format *n* **1** the shape, size, and general appearance of a publication **2** style or arrangement, such as of a television programme: *a chat-show format* **3** *computers* the arrangement of data on disk or magnetic tape to comply with a computer's input device ▷ *vb* **-matting, -matted 4** to arrange in a specified format **WORD ORIGIN** Latin *formatus* formed

formation *n* **1** the act of having or taking form or existence **2** something that is formed **3** the manner in which something is arranged **4** an arrangement of people or things acting as a unit, such as a troop of soldiers **5** a series of rocks or clouds of a particular structure or shape

formative *adj* **1** of or relating to formation, development, or growth: *formative years at school* **2** shaping or moulding: *the formative influence on his life*

former *adj* **1** belonging to or occurring in an earlier time: *a grotesque parody of a former greatness* **2** having been at a previous time: *the former prime minister* ▷ *n* **3 the former** the first or first mentioned of two

formerly *adv* in the past

Formica *n trademark* a hard laminated plastic used esp. for heat-resistant surfaces

formic acid *n* an acid derived from ants **WORD ORIGIN** Latin *formica* ant

formidable *adj* **1** frightening because very difficult to deal with or overcome: *the Finnish winter presents formidable problems to drivers* **2** extremely impressive: *a formidable Juventus squad* **formidably** *adv* **WORD ORIGIN** Latin *formido* fear

formless *adj* without a definite shape or form

formula (**form**-yew-la) *n, pl* **-las** *or* **-lae** (-lee) **1** a group of letters, numbers, or other symbols which represents a mathematical or scientific rule **2** a plan or set of rules for doing or producing something: *a formula for peace in the Middle East* **3** an established form of words, as used in religious ceremonies, legal proceedings, etc. **4** a powder used to make a milky drink for babies **5** *motor racing* the category in which a car competes, judged according to engine size **formulaic** *adj* **WORD ORIGIN** Latin *forma* form

formulary *n, pl* **-laries** a book of prescribed formulas

formulate *vb* **-lating, -lated 1** to express in a formula **2** to plan or describe precisely and clearly: *formulate a regional energy strategy* **formulation** *n*

fornicate *vb* **-cating, -cated** to have sexual intercourse without being married **fornicator** *n* **WORD ORIGIN** Latin *fornix* vault, brothel situated therein

fornication *n* voluntary sexual intercourse outside marriage

forsake *vb* **-saking, -sook, -saken 1** to withdraw support or friendship from **2** to give up (something valued or enjoyed) **WORD ORIGIN** Old English *forsacan*

forsooth *adv old-fashioned* in truth or indeed **WORD ORIGIN** Old English *forsōth*

forswear *vb* **-swearing, -swore, -sworn 1** to reject or renounce with determination **2** to testify falsely in a court of law **WORD ORIGIN** Old English *forswearian*

forsythia (for-**syth**-ee-a) *n* a shrub with yellow flowers which appear in spring before the leaves **WORD ORIGIN** after William *Forsyth*, botanist

fort *n* **1** a fortified building or position **2 hold the fort** *informal* to keep things in operation during someone's absence **WORD ORIGIN** Latin *fortis* strong

forte[1] (for-tay) *n* something at which a person excels: *cooking is his forte* **WORD ORIGIN** Latin *fortis* strong

forte[2] *adv music* loudly **WORD ORIGIN** Italian

forth *adv* **1** *formal or old-fashioned* forward, out, or away: *running back and forth across the street; Christopher Columbus set forth on his epic voyage of discovery* **2 and so forth** and so on **WORD ORIGIN** Old English

forthcoming *adj* **1** about to appear or happen: *the forthcoming elections* **2** given or made available **3** (of a person) willing to give information

forthright *adj* direct and outspoken

forthwith *adv* at once

fortification *n* **1** the act of fortifying **2 fortifications** walls, mounds, etc. used to strengthen the defences of a place

fortified wine *n* wine mixed with a small amount of brandy or alcohol, such as port or sherry

fortify *vb* **-fies, -fying, -fied 1** to make (a place) defensible, such as by building walls **2** to strengthen physically, mentally, or morally: *the news fortified their resolve to succeed* **3** to increase the

Words from Shakespeare
part 11

filch *v* if you filch something you steal it
With cunning hast thou filch'd my daughter's heart
A Midsummer Night's Dream 1.1

flout *v* to scorn something
Why will you suffer her to flout me thus?
A Midsummer Night's Dream 3.2

fond *adj* foolish
Shall we their fond pageant see?
A Midsummer Night's Dream 3.2

footing *n* landing on shore, arrival, disembarkation
Whose footing here anticipates our thoughts
A se'nnight's speed. *Othello* 2.1

footing *n* support
there your charity would have lacked footing
The Winter's Tale 3.3

forsooth *adv* in truth, certainly, truly
I had rather, forsooth, go before you like a man
The Merry Wives of Windsor 3.2

forswear *v* to lie, swear falsely or break your word
he swore a thing to me on Monday night, which he
forswore on Tuesday morning
Much Ado About Nothing 5.1

freshes *n* a fresh water stream
He shall drink nought brine, for I'll not show him
Where the quick freshes are. *The Tempest* 3.2

furlong *n* a measure of distance. It is the equivalent of
one eighth of a mile
Now would I give a thousand furlongs of sea for an
acre of barren ground *The Tempest* 1.1

gabardine *n* a cloak
My best way is to creep under his gabardine
The Tempest 2.2

gage *n* a challenge to duel or fight
There is my gage, Aumerle, in gage to thine
Richard II 4.1

gait *n* your way of walking or step
I know her by her gait *The Tempest* 4.1

gall *v* to annoy or irritate
Let it not gall your patience, good Iago,
That I extend my manners *Othello* 2.1

gambol *v* to frolic or play
Hop in his walks, and gambol in his eyes
A Midsummer Night's Dream 3.1

gaskins *pl n* trousers
or, if both break, your gaskins fall.
Twelfth Night 1.5

gentle *adj* noble or well-born
thrice-gentle Cassio! *Othello* 3.4

glass *n* a mirror
no woman's face remember
Save from my glass, mine own *The Tempest* 3.1

gleek *v* to make a joke or jibe
Nay, I can gleek upon occasion
A Midsummer Night's Dream 3.1

gust *n* taste, desire or enjoyment.
We still say that if you do something with
gusto you do it with enjoyment or enthusiasm
the gust he hath in quarrelling *Twelfth Night* 1.3

habit *n* clothes
You know me by my habit *Henry V* 3.6

heaviness *n* sadness or grief
So sorrow's heaviness doth heavier grow
For debt that bankrupt sleep doth sorrow owe
A Midsummer Night's Dream 3.2

heavy *adj* sad or sorrowful
Away from light steals home my heavy son
Romeo and Juliet 1.1

hie *v* to hurry
My husband hies him home
All's Well That Ends Well 4.4

hollowly *adv* insincerely
If hollowly invert
What best is boded me to mischief!
The Tempest 3.1

nutritious value of (a food), such as by adding vitamins
WORD ORIGIN Latin *fortis* strong + *facere* to make

fortissimo *adv music* very loudly
WORD ORIGIN Italian

fortitude *n* calm and patient courage in trouble or pain
WORD ORIGIN Latin *fortitudo* courage

fortnight *n* a period of 14 consecutive days
WORD ORIGIN Old English *fēowertīene niht* fourteen nights

fortnightly *chiefly Brit adj* **1** occurring or appearing once each fortnight ▷ *adv* **2** once a fortnight

FORTRAN *n* a high-level computer programming language designed for mathematical and scientific purposes
WORD ORIGIN *for(mula) tran(slation)*

fortress *n* a large fort or fortified town
WORD ORIGIN Latin *fortis* strong

fortuitous (for-**tyew**-it-uss) *adj* happening by chance, esp. by a lucky chance **fortuitously** *adv*
WORD ORIGIN Latin *fortuitus*

fortunate *adj* **1** having good luck **2** occurring by good luck **fortunately** *adv*

fortune *n* **1** a very large sum of money **2** luck, esp. when favourable **3** (*often pl*) a person's destiny **4** a power regarded as being responsible for human affairs **5** wealth or material prosperity
WORD ORIGIN Latin *fors* chance

fortune-teller *n* a person who claims to predict events in other people's lives

forty *n*, *pl* **-ties 1** the cardinal number that is the product of ten and four **2** a numeral, 40 or XL, representing this number **3** something representing or consisting of 40 units ▷ *adj* **4** amounting to forty: *forty pages* **fortieth** *adj, n*

forty-ninth parallel *n Canad informal* the border with the USA, which is in part delineated by the parallel line of latitude at 49°N

forty winks *n informal* a short light sleep

forum *n* **1** a meeting or medium for the open discussion of subjects of public interest **2** (in ancient Roman cities) an open space serving as a marketplace and centre of public business **3** (in South Africa) a pressure group of leaders and representatives
WORD ORIGIN Latin

forward *adj* **1** directed or moving ahead **2** at, in, or near the front **3** overfamiliar or disrespectful **4** well developed or advanced **5** of or relating to the future or favouring change ▷ *n* **6** an attacking player in any of various sports, such as soccer ▷ *adv* **7** same as **forwards** ▷ *vb* **8** to send (a letter, etc.) on to an ultimate destination **9** to advance or promote: *the veneer of street credibility he had used to forward his career*
WORD ORIGIN Old English *foreweard*

forwards *or* **forward** *adv* **1** towards or at a place ahead or in advance, esp. in space but also in time **2** towards the front

fosse *or* **foss** *n* a ditch or moat, esp. one

dug as a fortification
WORD ORIGIN Latin *fossa*

fossick *vb Austral & NZ* **1** to search for gold or precious stones in abandoned workings, rivers, etc. **2** to search for, through, or in something; to forage
WORD ORIGIN probably from English dialect *fussock* to bustle about

fossil *n* **1** remains of a plant or animal that existed in a past geological age, occurring in the form of mineralized bones, shells, etc. ▷ *adj* **2** of, like, or being a fossil
WORD ORIGIN Latin *fossilis* dug up

fossil fuel *n* fuel, such as coal or oil, formed from the decayed remains of prehistoric animals and plants

fossilize *or* **-ise** *vb* **-izing, -ized** *or* **-ising, -ised 1** to convert or be converted into a fossil **2** to become out-of-date or inflexible: *fossilized political attitudes*

foster *adj* **1** of or involved in the bringing up of a child not one's own: *foster care* ▷ *vb* **2** to bring up (a child not one's own) **3** to promote the growth or development of: *Catherine fostered knowledge and patronized the arts* **fostering** *n*
WORD ORIGIN Old English *fōstrian* to feed

fought *vb* the past of **fight**

foul *adj* **1** offensive or loathsome: *a foul deed* **2** stinking or dirty **3** full of dirt or offensive matter **4** (of language) obscene or vulgar **5** unfair: *by fair or foul means* **6** (of weather) unpleasant **7** very bad-tempered and irritable: *he was in a foul mood* **8** *informal* disgustingly bad ▷ *n* **9** *sport* a violation of the rules ▷ *vb* **10** to make dirty or polluted **11** to make or become entangled **12** to make or become clogged **13** *sport* to commit a foul against (an opponent) ▷ *adv* **14** **fall foul of** to come into conflict with
WORD ORIGIN Old English *fūl*

foul-mouthed *adj* habitually using swearwords and bad language

foul play *n* **1** violent activity, esp. murder **2** a violation of the rules in a game

foul up *vb* **1** *informal* to mismanage or bungle **2** to contaminate **3** to block or choke ▷ *n* **foul-up 4** a state of disorder resulting from mistakes or carelessness: *a foul-up by their computers*

found¹ *vb* the past of **find**

found² *vb* **1** to bring into being or establish (something, such as an institution) **2** to lay the foundation of **3** **founded on** to have a basis in: *a political system founded on fear* **founder** *n* **founding** *adj*
WORD ORIGIN Latin *fundus* bottom

found³ *vb* **1** to cast (metal or glass) by melting and pouring into a mould **2** to make (articles) in this way **founder** *n*
WORD ORIGIN Latin *fundere* to melt

foundation *n* **1** the basic experience, idea, or attitude on which a way of life or belief is based: *respect for the law is the foundation of commercial society* **2** a construction below the ground that distributes the load of a building, wall, etc. **3** the base on which something stands **4** the act of founding **5** an endowment for the support of an

institution, such as a college **6** an institution supported by an endowment **7** a cosmetic used as a base for make-up

foundation stone *n* a stone laid at a ceremony to mark the foundation of a new building

founder *vb* **1** to break down or fail: *his negotiations have foundered on economic grounds* **2** (of a ship) to sink **3** to sink into or become stuck in soft ground **4** (of a horse) to stumble or go lame
WORD ORIGIN Old French *fondrer* to submerge

USAGE
Founder is sometimes wrongly used where *flounder* is meant: *this unexpected turn of events left him floundering* (not *foundering*).

foundling *n chiefly Brit* an abandoned baby whose parents are not known
WORD ORIGIN Middle English *foundeling*

foundry *n, pl* **-ries** a place where metal is melted and cast

fount¹ *n* **1** *poetic* a spring or fountain **2** a source or supply: *a fount of knowledge*
WORD ORIGIN from *fountain*

fount² *n printing chiefly Brit* a complete set of type of one style and size
WORD ORIGIN Old French *fonte* a founding, casting

fountain *n* **1** an ornamental feature in a pool or lake consisting of a jet of water forced into the air by a pump **2** a jet or spray of water **3** a natural spring of water **4** a source or supply: *a fountain of many new ideas about the causes of cancer* **5** a cascade of sparks, lava, etc.
WORD ORIGIN Latin *fons* spring

fountainhead *n* a principal or original source

fountain pen *n* a pen supplied with ink from a container inside it

four *n* **1** the cardinal number that is the sum of one and three **2** a numeral, 4 or IV, representing this number **3** something representing or consisting of four units **4** *cricket* a score of four runs, obtained by hitting the ball so that it crosses the boundary after hitting the ground **5** *rowing* **a** a rowing boat propelled by four oarsmen **b** the crew of such a rowing boat ▷ *adj* **6** amounting to four: *four zones*
WORD ORIGIN Old English *fēower*

four-by-four *n* a vehicle with four-wheel drive

fourfold *adj* **1** having four times as many or as much **2** composed of four parts ▷ *adv* **3** by four times as many or as much

four-in-hand *n* a carriage drawn by four horses and driven by one driver

four-letter word *n* any of several short English words referring to sex or excrement: regarded generally as offensive or obscene

four-poster *n* a bed with posts at each corner supporting a canopy and curtains

fourscore *adj old-fashioned* eighty

foursome *n* **1** a group of four people **2** *golf* a game between two pairs of players

foursquare *adv* **1** squarely or firmly

▷ *adj* **2** solid and strong **3** forthright and uncompromising

four-stroke *adj* designating an internal-combustion engine in which the piston makes four strokes for every explosion

fourteen *n* **1** the cardinal number that is the sum of ten and four **2** a numeral, 14 or XIV, representing this number **3** something representing or consisting of 14 units ▷ *adj* **4** amounting to fourteen: *fourteen points* **fourteenth** *adj, n*

fourth *adj* **1** of or being number four in a series **2** denoting the highest forward gear in a motor vehicle ▷ *n* **3** the highest forward gear in a motor vehicle

fourth dimension *n* **1** the dimension of time, which in addition to three spatial dimensions specifies the position of a point or particle **2** the concept in science fiction of an extra dimension **fourth-dimensional** *adj*

fourth estate *n* the press

four-wheel drive *n* a system in which all four wheels are connected to the source of power

fowl *n* **1** a domesticated bird such as a hen **2** any other bird that is used as food or hunted as game **3** the meat of fowl **4** *old-fashioned* a bird ▷ *vb* **5** to hunt or snare wild birds **WORD ORIGIN** Old English *fugol*

fox *n, pl* **foxes** or **fox 1** a doglike wild animal with a pointed muzzle and a bushy tail **2** its reddish-brown or grey fur **3** a person who is cunning and sly ▷ *vb* **4** *informal* to confuse or puzzle **WORD ORIGIN** Old English

foxglove *n* a tall plant with purple or white flowers

foxhole *n mil* a small pit dug to provide shelter against enemy fire

foxhound *n* a breed of short-haired terrier, originally kept for hunting foxes

fox-hunting *n* the activity of hunting foxes with hounds

foxtrot *n* **1** a ballroom dance with slow and quick steps **2** music for this ▷ *vb* **-trotting, -trotted 3** to perform this dance

foxy *adj* **foxier, foxiest 1** of or resembling a fox, esp. in craftiness **2** reddish-brown **foxily** *adv* **foxiness** *n*

foyer (**foy**-ay) *n* an entrance hall in a hotel, theatre, or cinema **WORD ORIGIN** French: fireplace

fp forte-piano

FP 1 fire plug **2** freezing point

Fr 1 *Christianity* **a** Father **b** Frater **WORD ORIGIN** Latin *brother* **2** *chem* francium

fr. 1 franc **2** from

fracas (**frak**-ah) *n* a noisy quarrel or fight **WORD ORIGIN** French

fraction *n* **1** *maths* a numerical quantity that is not a whole number **2** any part or subdivision **3** a very small proportion or amount of something **4** *chem* a component of a mixture separated by distillation **fractional** *adj* **fractionally** *adv* **WORD ORIGIN** Latin *fractus* broken

fractional distillation or

fractionation *n chem* the process of separating the constituents of a liquid mixture by heating it and condensing the components separately according to their different boiling points

fractious *adj* (esp. of children) easily upset and angered, often due to tiredness **WORD ORIGIN** obsolete *fraction* discord

USAGE
Fractious is sometimes wrongly used where *factious* is meant: *this factious (not fractious) dispute has split the party still further.*

fracture *n* **1** breaking, esp. the breaking or cracking of a bone ▷ *vb* **-turing, -tured 2** to break **fractural** *adj* **WORD ORIGIN** Latin *frangere* to break

fragile *adj* **1** able to be broken or damaged easily **2** in a weakened physical state: *you're looking a bit fragile this morning* **fragility** *n* **WORD ORIGIN** Latin *fragilis*

fragment *n* **1** a piece broken off **2** an incomplete piece: *fragments of information* ▷ *vb* **3** to break into small pieces or different parts **fragmentation** *n* **WORD ORIGIN** Latin *fragmentum*

fragmentary *adj* made up of small or unconnected pieces: *fragmentary evidence to support his theory*

fragrance *n* **1** a pleasant smell **2** a perfume or scent

fragrant *adj* having a pleasant smell **WORD ORIGIN** Latin *fragrare* to emit a smell

frail *adj* **1** physically weak and delicate **2** easily damaged: *the frail aircraft* **3** easily tempted **WORD ORIGIN** Old French *frele*

frailty *n* **1** physical or moral weakness **2** *pl* **-ties** an inadequacy or fault resulting from moral weakness

frame *n* **1** an open structure that gives shape and support to something, such as a building **2** an enclosing case or border into which something is fitted: *the window frame* **3** the system around which something is built up: *caught up in the frame of the revolution* **4** the structure of the human body **5** one of a series of exposures on film used in making motion pictures **6** a television picture scanned by electron beams at a particular frequency **7** *snooker* **a** a single game in a match **b** a wooden triangle used to arrange the red balls in formation before the start of a game **8** short for **cold frame 9** *slang* a frame-up **10 frame of mind** a state of mind: *in a complacent frame of mind* ▷ *vb* **framing, framed 11** to construct by fitting parts together **12** to create and develop (plans or a policy) **13** to construct (a statement) in a particular kind of language **14** to provide or enclose with a frame **15** *slang* to conspire to incriminate (someone) on a false charge **WORD ORIGIN** Old English *framian* to avail

frame of reference *n* **1** a set of standards that determines behaviour **2** any set of planes or curves, such as the three coordinate axes, used to locate a point in space

frame-up *n slang* a conspiracy to

incriminate someone on a false charge

framework *n* **1** a particular set of beliefs, ideas, or rules referred to in order to solve a problem: *a moral framework* **2** a structure supporting something

franc *n* the standard monetary unit of Switzerland, various African countries, and formerly of France and Belgium **WORD ORIGIN** Latin *Rex Francorum* King of the Franks, inscribed on 14th-century francs

franchise *n* **1** the right to vote, esp. for a member of parliament **2** any exemption, privilege, or right granted by a public authority **3** *commerce* authorization granted to a distributor to sell a company's goods ▷ *vb* **-chising, -chised 4** *commerce chiefly US & Canad* to grant (a person, firm, etc.) a franchise **WORD ORIGIN** Old French *franchir* to set free

Franciscan *n* **1** a member of a Christian religious order of friars or nuns founded by Saint Francis of Assisi ▷ *adj* **2** of this order

francium *n chem* an unstable radioactive element of the alkali-metal group. Symbol: Fr **WORD ORIGIN** from *France*, because first found there

Franco- *combining form* indicating France or French: *the Franco-Prussian war* **WORD ORIGIN** Medieval Latin *Francus*

frangipani (fran-jee-**pah**-nee) *n* **1** an Australian evergreen tree with large yellow fragrant flowers **2** a tropical shrub with fragrant white or pink flowers

frank *adj* **1** honest and straightforward in speech or attitude ▷ *vb* **2** to put a mark on (a letter), ensuring free carriage ▷ *n* **3** an official mark stamped to a letter ensuring free delivery **frankly** *adv* **frankness** *n* **WORD ORIGIN** Medieval Latin *francus* free

Frank *n* a member of the West Germanic peoples who in the late 4th century AD gradually conquered most of Gaul **WORD ORIGIN** Old English *Franca*

Frankenstein *n* a creation or monster that brings disaster and is beyond the control of its creator. Also called: **Frankenstein's monster** **WORD ORIGIN** after Baron *Frankenstein*, who created a monster from parts of corpses in the novel by Mary Shelley

frankfurter *n* a smoked sausage of pork or beef **WORD ORIGIN** short for German *Frankfurter Wurst* sausage from Frankfurt

frankincense *n* an aromatic gum resin burnt as incense **WORD ORIGIN** Old French *franc* free, pure + *encens* incense

Frankish *n* **1** the ancient West Germanic language of the Franks ▷ *adj* **2** of the Franks or their language

frantic *adj* **1** distracted with fear, pain, joy, etc. **2** hurried and disorganized: *frantic activity* **frantically** *adv* **WORD ORIGIN** Latin *phreneticus* mad

frappé *adj* (esp. of drinks) chilled **WORD ORIGIN** French

fraternal *adj* **1** of a brother; brotherly

2 designating twins that developed from two separate fertilized ova **fraternally** *adv*
WORD ORIGIN Latin *frater* brother

fraternity *n, pl* **-ties 1** a body of people united in interests, aims, etc. **2** friendship between groups of people **3** *US & Canad* a society of male students

fraternize *or* **-nise** *vb* **-nizing, -nized** *or* **-nising, -nised** to associate on friendly terms: *fraternizing with the customers is off-limits* **fraternization** *or* **-nisation** *n*

fratricide *n* **1** the act of killing one's brother **2** a person who kills his or her brother **fratricidal** *adj*
WORD ORIGIN Latin *frater* brother + *caedere* to kill

Frau (rhymes with *how*) *n, pl* **Frauen** *or* **Fraus** a German form of address equivalent to *Mrs* or *Ms*
WORD ORIGIN German

fraud *n* **1** deliberate deception or cheating intended to gain an advantage **2** an act of such deception **3** *informal* a person who acts in a false or deceitful way
WORD ORIGIN Latin *fraus*

fraudster *n* a person who commits a fraud; swindler

fraudulent *adj* **1** acting with intent to deceive **2** proceeding from fraud **fraudulence** *n*
WORD ORIGIN Latin *fraudulentus*

fraught (frawt) *adj* **1** fraught with involving or filled with: *we expected the trip to be fraught with difficulties* **2** tense or anxious
WORD ORIGIN Middle Dutch *vrachten*

Fräulein (froy-line) *n, pl* **-lein** *or* **-leins** a German form of address equivalent to *Miss*
WORD ORIGIN German

fray¹ *n* **1** *Brit, Austral, & NZ* a noisy quarrel or brawl **2 the fray** any challenging conflict: *at the height of the run-glut Warne entered the fray*
WORD ORIGIN short for *affray*

fray² *vb* **1** to wear away into loose threads, esp. at an edge **2** to make or become strained or irritated
WORD ORIGIN French *frayer* to rub

frazil (fray-zil) *n* small pieces of ice that form in water moving turbulently enough to prevent the formation of a sheet of ice
WORD ORIGIN French *fraisil* cinders

frazzle *n informal* the state of being exhausted: *worn to a frazzle*
WORD ORIGIN probably from Middle English *faselen* to fray

freak *n* **1** a person, animal, or plant that is abnormal or deformed **2** an object, event, etc. that is abnormal: *a statistical freak* **3** *informal* a person whose appearance or behaviour is very unusual **4** *informal* a person who is very enthusiastic about something specified: *a health freak* ▷ *adj* **5** abnormal or unusual: *a freak accident* **freakish** *adj* **freaky** *adj*
WORD ORIGIN origin unknown

freak out *vb informal* to be or cause to be in a heightened emotional state

freckle *n* **1** a small brownish spot on the skin ▷ *vb* **-ling, -led 2** to mark or become marked with freckles **freckled** *adj*
WORD ORIGIN Old Norse *freknur* freckles

free *adj* **freer, freest 1** able to act at will; not under compulsion or restraint **2** not enslaved or confined **3** (of a country) independent **4** (of a translation) not exact or literal **5** provided without charge: *free school meals* **6** not occupied or in use; available: *is this seat free?* **7** (of a person) not busy **8** open or available to all **9** not fixed or joined; loose: *the free end* **10** without obstruction or blockage: *the free flow of capital* **11** *chem* chemically uncombined: *free nitrogen* **12 free and easy** casual or tolerant **13 free from** not subject to: *free from surveillance* **14 free with** using or giving (something) a lot: *he was free with his tongue* **15 make free with** to behave too familiarly towards ▷ *adv* **16** in a free manner **17** without charge or cost ▷ *vb* **freeing, freed 18** to release or liberate **19** to remove obstructions or impediments from **20** to make available or usable: *capital freed by the local authority* **21 free of** *or* **from** to relieve or rid of (obstacles, pain, etc.) **freely** *adv*
WORD ORIGIN Old English *frēo*

-free *adj combining form* free from: *duty-free; nuclear-free zones*

freebie *n slang* something provided without charge

freeboard *n* the space or distance between the deck of a vessel and the water line

freebooter *n* a pirate
WORD ORIGIN Dutch *vrijbuit* booty

freeborn *adj history* not born in slavery

Free Church *n chiefly Brit* any Protestant Church other than the Established Church

freecycle *n* **1** an informal network of citizens who promote recycling online by offering one another unwanted items free of charge ▷ *vb* **2** to recycle (an unwanted item) by offering it free of charge

freediving *n* the sport or activity of diving without the aid of breathing apparatus

freedman *n, pl* **-men** *history* a man freed from slavery

freedom *n* **1** the state of being free, esp. to enjoy political and civil liberties **2** exemption or immunity: *freedom from government control* **3** liberation, such as from slavery **4** the right or privilege of unrestricted access: *freedom of the skies* **5** self-government or independence **6** the power to order one's own actions **7** ease or frankness of manner

free enterprise *n* an economic system in which commercial organizations compete for profit with little state control

free fall *n* **1** the part of a parachute descent before the parachute opens **2** free descent of a body in which gravity is the only force acting on it

free-for-all *n informal* a disorganized brawl or argument involving all those present

free hand *n* **1** unrestricted freedom to act: *the president must be able to deal with foreign hostilities with a free hand* ▷ *adj, adv* **freehand 2** (done) by hand without the use of guiding instruments

freehold *property law n* **1** tenure of property for life without restrictions ▷ *adj* **2** of or held by freehold **freeholder** *n*

free house *n Brit* a public house not bound to sell only one brewer's products

free kick *n soccer* an unopposed kick of the ball awarded for a foul or infringement

freelance *n* **1** a self-employed person doing specific pieces of work for various employers ▷ *vb* **-lancing, -lanced 2** to work as a freelance ▷ *adj, adv* **3** of or as a freelance
WORD ORIGIN originally applied to a mercenary soldier

freeloader *n slang* a person who habitually depends on others for food, accommodation, etc.

free love *n old-fashioned* the practice of having sexual relationships outside marriage, often several relationships at the same time

freeman *n, pl* **-men** a person who has been given the freedom of a city as an honour in return for public service

free-market *adj* denoting an economic system which allows supply and demand to regulate prices and wages

Freemason *n* Also called: **Mason** a member of a widespread secret order whose members are pledged to help each other **Freemasonry** *n*

free-range *adj* kept or produced in natural conditions: *free-range eggs*

freesia *n* a plant with fragrant tubular flowers
WORD ORIGIN after F. H. T. *Freese*, physician

free space *n* a region that has no gravitational and electromagnetic fields

freestanding *adj* not attached to or supported by another object

freestyle *n* **1** a competition, such as in swimming, in which each participant may use a style of his or her choice **2** Also called: **all-in wrestling** a style of professional wrestling with no internationally agreed set of rules

freethinker *n* a person who forms his or her ideas independently of authority, esp. in matters of religion

free trade *n* international trade that is free of such government interference as protective tariffs and import quotas

free verse *n* unrhymed verse without a fixed rhythm

Freeview *n trademark* (in Britain) a free service providing digital terrestrial television

freeway *n US & Austral* a motorway

freewheel *vb* **1** to travel downhill on a bicycle without pedalling ▷ *n* **2** a device in the rear hub of a bicycle wheel that permits it to rotate freely while the pedals are stationary

freewheeling *adj* behaving in a relaxed spontaneous manner, without any long-term plans or commitments: *he had to change his freewheeling lifestyle after*

Words from Literature
part 11

fly-driver *n* a fly-driver is the driver of a carriage drawn by a single horse
>The fly-drivers, among whom I inquired next, were equally jocose and equally disrespectful
>*David Copperfield* Charles Dickens

fob *n* a small pocket in which a watch is kept
>"Certain," replied the man, drawing a gold watch from his fob
>*Oliver Twist* Charles Dickens

folly *n* folly means foolishness or stupidity
>the folly of beginning a work
>*Robinson Crusoe* Daniel Defoe

fond *adj* foolish
>Fond worldling
>*Doctor Faustus* 5.2 Christopher Marlowe

fondness *n* silly or foolish affection
>They have no fondness for their colts or foals
>*Gulliver's Travels* Jonathan Swift

for his fancy *phrase* for his liking or as he wanted
>and as I did not obey quick enough for his fancy
>*Treasure Island* Robert Louis Stevenson

forlorn *adj* lost or very upset
>you are from that day forlorn
>*Gulliver's Travels* Jonathan Swift

foster-sister *n* a foster-sister was someone brought up by the same nurse or in the same household
>I had been his foster-sister
>*Wuthering Heights* Emily Brontë

fox-fire *n* fox-fire is a weak glow that is given off by decaying, rotten wood
>what we must have was a lot of them rotten chunks that's called fox-fire
>*The Adventures of Huckleberry Finn* Mark Twain

frozen sea *phrase* the Arctic Ocean
>into the frozen sea
>*Gulliver's Travels* Jonathan Swift

gainsay *v* to gainsay something is to say it isn't true or to deny it
>"So she had," cried Scrooge. "You're right. I'll not gainsay it, Spirit. God forbid!"
>*A Christmas Carol* Charles Dickens

gaiters *n* gaiters were leggings made of a cloth or piece of leather which covered the leg from the knee to the ankle
>Mr Knightley was hard at work upon the lower buttons of his thick leather gaiters
>*Emma* Jane Austen

galluses *n* galluses is an old spelling of gallows, and here means suspenders. Suspenders are straps worn over someone's shoulders and fastened to their trousers to prevent the trousers falling down
>and home-knit galluses
>*The Adventures of Huckleberry Finn* Mark Twain

galoot *n* a sailor but also a clumsy person
>and maybe a galoot on it chopping
>*The Adventures of Huckleberry Finn* Mark Twain

gayest *adj* the most lively and bright or merry
>Beth played her gayest march
>*Little Women* Louisa May Alcott

gem *n* jewellery
>the mountain shook off turf and flower, had only heath for raiment and crag for gem
>*Jane Eyre* Charlotte Brontë

giddy *adj* giddy means dizzy
>and I wish you wouldn't keep appearing and vanishing so suddenly; you make one quite giddy.
>*Alice's Adventures in Wonderland* Lewis Carroll

gig *n* a light two-wheeled carriage
>when a gig drove up to the garden gate: out of which there jumped a fat gentleman
>*Oliver Twist* Charles Dickens

his son was born

free will *n* **1** the ability to make a choice without outside coercion or pressure: *you walked in here of your own free will* **2** *philosophy* the belief that human behaviour is an expression of personal choice and is not determined by physical forces, Fate, or God

Free World *n* the non-Communist countries collectively

freeze *vb* **freezing, froze, frozen 1** to change from a liquid to a solid by the reduction of temperature, such as water to ice **2** to preserve (food) by subjection to extreme cold **3** to cover or become covered with ice **4** to fix fast or become fixed (to something) because of frost **5** to feel or cause to feel the effects of extreme cold **6** to die of extreme cold **7** to become motionless through fear, shock, etc. **8** to cause (moving film) to stop at a particular frame **9** to fix (prices, incomes, etc.) at a particular level **10** to forbid by law the exchange or collection of (loans, assets, etc.) ▷ *n* **11** the act of freezing or state of being frozen **12** *meteorol* a spell of temperatures below freezing point **13** the fixing of incomes, prices, etc. by legislation **WORD ORIGIN** Old English *frēosan*

freeze-dry *vb* **-dries, -drying, -dried** to preserve (food) by rapid freezing and drying in a vacuum

freeze out *vb* to prevent (someone) from being involved in an activity, conversation, etc. by being unfriendly or reserved

freezer *n* an insulated cabinet for cold-storage of perishable foods

freezing *adj informal* very cold

freezing point *n* the temperature below which a liquid turns into a solid

freezing works *n Austral & NZ* a slaughterhouse at which animals are slaughtered and carcasses frozen, esp. for export

freight (**frate**) *n* **1 a** commercial transport of goods **b** the cargo transported **c** the cost of this **2** *chiefly Brit* a ship's cargo or part of it ▷ *vb* **3** to transport (goods) by freight **4** to load with goods for transport **WORD ORIGIN** Middle Dutch *vrecht*

freighter *n* a ship or aircraft designed for transporting cargo

French *adj* **1** of France ▷ *n* **2** the official language of France and an official language of Switzerland, Belgium, Canada, and certain other countries ▷ *pl n* **3 the French** the people of France **WORD ORIGIN** Old English *Frencisc* French, Frankish

French beans *pl n* green beans, the pods of which are eaten

French bread *n* white bread in a long, thin, crusty loaf

French Canadian *n* a Canadian citizen whose native language is French

French chalk *n* a variety of talc used to mark cloth or remove grease stains

French dressing *n* a salad dressing made from oil and vinegar with seasonings

French fries *pl n chiefly US & Canad* potato chips

French horn *n music* a valved brass wind instrument with a coiled tube

Frenchify *vb* **-fies, -fying, -fied** *informal* to make or become French in appearance, etc.

French letter *n* *Brit & NZ slang* a condom

Frenchman *or fem* **Frenchwoman** *n, pl* **-men** *or* **-women** a person from France

French polish *n* a shellac varnish for wood, giving a high gloss

French seam *n* a seam in which the edges are enclosed

French windows *pl n* a window extending to floor level, used as a door

frenetic (frin-**net**-ik) *adj* wild, excited, and uncontrolled **frenetically** *adv* **WORD ORIGIN** Greek *phrenitis* insanity

frenzy *n, pl* **-zies 1** violent or wild and uncontrollable behaviour **2** excited or agitated activity: *a frenzy of speculation* **frenzied** *adj* **WORD ORIGIN** Late Latin *phrenesis* madness, from Greek *phren* mind

Freon *n trademark* any of a group of gas or liquid chemical compounds of methane with chlorine and fluorine: used in propellants, aerosols, and solvents

frequency *n, pl* **-cies 1** the number of times that an event occurs within a given period **2** the state of being frequent **3** *physics* the number of times a wave repeats itself in a given time

frequency distribution *n* statistical data arranged to show the frequency with which the possible values of a variable occur

frequency modulation *n* a method of transmitting information by varying the frequency of the carrier wave in accordance with the amplitude of the input signal

frequent *adj* **1** happening often **2** habitual ▷ *vb* **3** to visit often: *a spa town frequented by the Prussian nobility* **frequently** *adv* **WORD ORIGIN** Latin *frequens* numerous

frequentative *grammar adj* **1** denoting a verb or an affix meaning repeated action ▷ *n* **2** a frequentative verb or affix

fresco *n, pl* **-coes** *or* **-cos 1** a method of wall-painting using watercolours on wet plaster **2** a painting done in this way **WORD ORIGIN** Italian: fresh plaster

fresh *adj* **1** newly made, acquired, etc. **2** not thought of before; novel: *fresh ideas* **3** most recent: *fresh allegations* **4** further or additional: *a fresh supply* **5** (of food) not canned or frozen **6** (of water) not salty **7** bright and clear: *a fresh morning* **8** (of a wind) cold and fairly strong **9** not tired; alert **10** not worn or faded: *the fresh colours of spring* **11** having a healthy or ruddy appearance **12** having recently come (from somewhere): *cakes fresh from the oven* **13** youthful or inexperienced **14** *informal* overfamiliar or disrespectful ▷ *adv* **15** recently: *a delicious fresh-baked cake* **freshly** *adv* **freshness** *n* **WORD ORIGIN** Old English *fersc*

freshen *vb* **1** to make or become fresh or fresher **2** (of the wind) to become

stronger **3 freshen up** to wash and tidy up one's appearance: *I'll go and freshen up*

fresher *or* **freshman** *n, pl* **-ers** *or* **-men** *Brit & US* a first-year student at college or university

freshet *n* **1** the sudden overflowing of a river **2** a stream of fresh water emptying into the sea

freshwater *adj* of or living in fresh water

fret¹ *vb* **fretting, fretted 1** to worry: *he would fret about the smallest of problems* **2** to rub or wear away **3** to feel or give annoyance ▷ *n* **4** a state of irritation or anxiety **WORD ORIGIN** Old English *fretan* to eat

fret² *n* **1** a repetitive geometrical figure used for ornamentation ▷ *vb* **fretting, fretted 2** to ornament with fret or fretwork **WORD ORIGIN** Old French *frete* interlaced design used on a shield

fret³ *n* a small metal bar set across the fingerboard of a musical instrument, such as a guitar, as a guide to fingering **WORD ORIGIN** origin unknown

fretful *adj* irritable or upset **fretfully** *adv*

fret saw *n* a fine-toothed saw with a long thin narrow blade, used for cutting designs in thin wood or metal

fretwork *n* decorative geometrical carving in wood

Freudian (**froy**-dee-an) *adj* of or relating to Sigmund Freud (1856–1939), Austrian psychiatrist, or his ideas **Freudianism** *n*

Freudian slip *n* a slip of the tongue that may reveal an unconscious wish

Fri. Friday

friable (**fry**-a-bl) *adj* easily broken up **friability** *n* **WORD ORIGIN** Latin *friare* to crumble

friar *n* a member of a male Roman Catholic religious order **WORD ORIGIN** Latin *frater* brother

friar's balsam *n* a compound with a camphor-like smell, used as an inhalant to relieve bronchitis

friary *n, pl* **-aries** a house of friars

fricassee *n* stewed meat, esp. chicken or veal, served in a thick white sauce **WORD ORIGIN** Old French

fricative *n* **1** a consonant produced by friction of breath through a partly closed mouth, such as (f) or (z) ▷ *adj* **2** relating to or being a fricative **WORD ORIGIN** Latin *fricare* to rub

friction *n* **1** a resistance encountered when one body moves relative to another body with which it is in contact **2** the act of rubbing one object against another **3** disagreement or conflict **frictional** *adj* **WORD ORIGIN** Latin *fricare* to rub

Friday *n* the sixth day of the week **WORD ORIGIN** Old English *Frīgedæg* day of Freya, Norse goddess

fridge *n* a cabinet for keeping food and drink cool. In full: **refrigerator**

fried *vb* the past of **fry¹**

friend *n* **1** a person known well to another and regarded with liking, affection, and loyalty **2** an ally in a fight or cause **3** a patron or supporter:

our cause has many influential friends throughout Europe ▷ *vb* **4** to choose to be friends with someone on the social networking site Facebook **5 make friends (with)** to become friendly (with) **friendless** *adj* **friendship** *n*
WORD ORIGIN Old English *frēond*

Friend *n* a member of the Society of Friends; Quaker

friendly *adj* **-lier, -liest 1** showing or expressing liking, goodwill, or trust **2** on the same side; not hostile **3** tending to help or support ▷ *n, pl* **-lies 4** *sport* a match played for its own sake and not as part of a competition **friendliness** *n*

-friendly *adj combining form* helpful, easy, or good for the person or thing specified: *a user-friendly computer system; the development of an environment-friendly weedkiller*

friendly society *n Brit* an association of people who pay regular dues in return for old-age pensions, sickness benefits, etc.

frier *n* a fryer

fries *pl n* short for **French fries**

Friesian (**free**-zhan) *n* any of several breeds of black-and-white dairy cattle

frieze (**freeze**) *n* **1** a sculptured or decorated band on a wall **2** *archit* the horizontal band between the architrave and cornice of a classical temple
WORD ORIGIN French *frise*

frigate (**frig**-it) *n* **1** a fast warship, smaller than a destroyer **2** a medium-sized warship of the 18th and 19th centuries
WORD ORIGIN French *frégate*

fright *n* **1** sudden fear or alarm **2** a sudden alarming shock **3** *informal* a very strange or unattractive person or thing
WORD ORIGIN Old English *fryhto*

frighten *vb* **1** to terrify or scare **2** to force (someone) to do something from fear **frightening** *adj*

frightful *adj* **1** very alarming or horrifying **2** annoying or disagreeable: *a frightful pair of socks* **3** *informal* extreme: *a frightful mess* **frightfully** *adv*

frigid (**frij**-id) *adj* **1** (esp. of a woman) lacking sexual responsiveness **2** very cold: *the frigid air* **3** formal or stiff in behaviour or temperament **frigidity** *n*
WORD ORIGIN Latin *frigidus* cold

frill *n* **1** a long narrow strip of fabric with many folds in it attached at one edge of something as a decoration **2** an unnecessary part of something added to make it more attractive or interesting: *no fuss, no frills, just a purity of sound and clarity of vision* **frilly** or **frilled** *adj*
WORD ORIGIN origin unknown

frilled lizard *n* a large tree-living Australian lizard with an erectile fold of skin around the neck

fringe *n* **1** hair cut short and hanging over the forehead **2** an ornamental edge of hanging threads, tassels, etc. **3** an outer edge: *London's southern fringe* **4** the minor and less important parts of an activity or organization: *two agents on the fringes of espionage activity* **5** a small group of people within a larger body,

but differing from it in certain aims and ideas: *the radical fringe of the Green Party* ▷ *adj* **6** (of theatre) unofficial or unconventional ▷ *vb* **fringing, fringed 7** to form a border for: *sandy paths fringing the water's edge* **8** to decorate with a fringe: *tinsel fringed the desk*
WORD ORIGIN Latin *fimbria* fringe, border

fringe benefit *n* a benefit given in addition to a regular salary or wage

fringed *adj* **1** (of clothes, curtains, etc.) decorated with a fringe **2 fringed with** or **by** bordered with or by: *a field fringed with trees*

frippery *n, pl* **-peries 1** showy but useless ornamentation **2** unimportant or trivial matters
WORD ORIGIN Old French *frepe* frill, rag

Frisbee *n trademark* a light plastic disc thrown with a spinning motion for recreation

Frisian (**free**-zhan) *n* **1** a language spoken in the NW Netherlands **2** a speaker of this language ▷ *adj* **3** of this language or its speakers
WORD ORIGIN Latin *Frisii* people of northern Germany

frisk *vb* **1** to leap, move about, or act in a playful manner **2** *informal* to search (someone) by feeling for concealed weapons, etc. ▷ *n* **3** a playful movement **4** *informal* an instance of frisking a person
WORD ORIGIN Old French *frisque*

frisky *adj* **friskier, friskiest** lively, high-spirited, or playful **friskily** *adv*

frisson (**freess**-on) *n* a short sudden feeling of fear or excitement
WORD ORIGIN French

fritter *n* a piece of food, such as apple, that is dipped in batter and fried in deep fat
WORD ORIGIN Latin *frigere* to fry

fritter away *vb* to waste: *he did not fritter away his energy on trivialities*
WORD ORIGIN obsolete *fitter* to break into small pieces

frivolous *adj* **1** not serious or sensible in content, attitude, or behaviour **2** unworthy of serious or sensible treatment: *frivolous distractions* **frivolity** *n*
WORD ORIGIN Latin *frivolus*

frizz *vb* **1** (of hair) to form or cause (hair) to form tight curls ▷ *n* **2** hair that has been frizzed **frizzy** *adj*
WORD ORIGIN French *friser* to curl

frizzle¹ *vb* **-zling, -zled 1** to form (hair) into tight crisp curls ▷ *n* **2** a tight curl
WORD ORIGIN probably related to Old English *frīs* curly

frizzle² *vb* **-zling, -zled** to cook or heat until crisp or shrivelled up
WORD ORIGIN probably blend of *fry* + *sizzle*

frock *n old-fashioned* **1** a girl's or woman's dress **2** a loose garment, formerly worn by peasants
WORD ORIGIN Old French *froc*

frock coat *n* a man's skirted coat, as worn in the 19th century

frog¹ *n* **1** a smooth-skinned tailless amphibian with long back legs used for jumping **2 a frog in one's throat** phlegm on the vocal cords, hindering

speech
WORD ORIGIN Old English *frogga*

frog² *n* a military style fastening on a coat consisting of a button and a loop **frogging** *n*
WORD ORIGIN origin unknown

frog³ *n* horny material in the centre of the sole of a horse's foot
WORD ORIGIN origin unknown

frogman *n, pl* **-men** a swimmer equipped with a rubber suit, flippers, and breathing equipment for working underwater

frogmarch *n* **1** a method of carrying a resisting person in which each limb is held and the victim is face downwards ▷ *vb* **2** to carry in a frogmarch or cause to move forward unwillingly

frogspawn *n* a jelly-like substance containing a frog's eggs

frolic *vb* **-icking, -icked 1** to run and play in a lively way ▷ *n* **2** lively and merry behaviour **3** a light-hearted occasion
WORD ORIGIN Dutch *vrolijk*

frolicsome *adj* merry and playful

from *prep* **1** indicating the original location, situation, etc.: *from America* **2** in a period of time starting at: *from 1950 to the current year* **3** indicating the distance between two things or places: *60 miles from the Iraqi border* **4** indicating a lower amount: *from 5 to 6* **5** showing the model of: *drawn from life* **6** used with a verbal noun to denote prohibition, etc.: *she was banned from smoking at meetings* **7** because of: *five hundred horses collapsed from exhaustion*
WORD ORIGIN Old English *fram*

fromage frais (**from**-ahzh **fray**) *n* a low-fat soft cheese with a smooth light texture
WORD ORIGIN French: fresh cheese

frond *n* **1** the compound leaf of a fern **2** the leaf of a palm
WORD ORIGIN Latin *frons*

front *n* **1** that part or side that is forward, or most often seen or used **2** a position or place directly before or ahead **3** the beginning, opening, or first part **4** the position of leadership **5** a promenade at a seaside resort **6** *mil* **a** the total area in which opposing armies face each other **b** the space in which a military unit is operating **7** *meteorol* the dividing line between two different air masses **8** an outward appearance: *he put on a bold front* **9** *informal* a business or other activity serving as a respectable cover for another, usually criminal, organization **10** Also called: **front man** a nominal leader of an organization **11** a particular field of activity: *on the economic front* **12** a group of people with a common goal: *the National Liberation Front* ▷ *adj* **13** of, at, or in the front ▷ *vb* **14** to face (onto) **15** to be a front of or for **16** to appear as a presenter in (a television show) **17** to be the leader of (a band) on stage
WORD ORIGIN Latin *frons* forehead, foremost part

frontage *n* **1** the facade of a building or the front of a plot of ground **2** the extent of the front of a shop, plot of land, etc.

frontal *adj* **1** of, at, or in the front **2** of or relating to the forehead
WORD ORIGIN Latin *frons* forehead

front bench *n* (in Britain) the leadership of either the Government or Opposition in the House of Commons or in various other legislative assemblies **front-bencher** *n*

frontier *n* **1** the region of a country bordering on another or a line marking such a boundary **2** the edge of the settled area of a country **3 frontiers** the limit of knowledge in a particular field: *twenty years ago, laser spectroscopy was on the frontiers of chemical research*
WORD ORIGIN Old French *front* part which is opposite

frontispiece *n* an illustration facing the title page of a book
WORD ORIGIN Late Latin *frontispicium* facade

frontrunner *n* *informal* the leader or a favoured contestant in a race or election

frosh *n* *US & Canad informal* a freshman

frost *n* **1** a white deposit of ice particles **2** an atmospheric temperature of below freezing point, producing this deposit ▷ *vb* **3** to cover with frost **4** to kill or damage (plants) with frost
WORD ORIGIN Old English

frostbite *n* destruction of tissues, esp. of the fingers, ears, toes, and nose, by freezing **frostbitten** *adj*

frosted *adj* (of glass) having the surface roughened so that it cannot be seen through clearly

frosting *n* *chiefly US & Canad* icing

frosty *adj* **frostier, frostiest** **1** characterized by frost: *the frosty air* **2** covered by frost **3** unfriendly or disapproving: *a frosty reception from the bank manager* **frostily** *adv* **frostiness** *n*

froth *n* **1** a mass of small bubbles of air or a gas in a liquid **2** a mixture of saliva and air bubbles formed at the lips in certain diseases, such as rabies **3** trivial but superficially attractive ideas or entertainment ▷ *vb* **4** to produce or cause to produce froth **frothy** *adj*
WORD ORIGIN Old Norse *frotha*

frown *vb* **1** to wrinkle one's brows in worry, anger, or concentration **2 frown on** to disapprove of: *smoking at work is frowned on* ▷ *n* **3** the act of frowning **4** a look of disapproval or displeasure
WORD ORIGIN Old French *froigner*

frowsty *adj* **frowstier, frowstiest** *Brit* stale or musty
WORD ORIGIN from *frowzy*

frowzy *or* **frowsy** *adj* **frowzier, frowziest** *or* **frowsier, frowsiest** **1** slovenly or unkempt in appearance **2** musty and stale
WORD ORIGIN origin unknown

froze *vb* the past tense of **freeze**

frozen *vb* **1** the past participle of **freeze** ▷ *adj* **2** turned into or covered with ice **3** killed or stiffened by extreme cold **4** (of food) preserved by a freezing process **5 a** (of prices or wages) officially fixed at a certain level **b** (of business assets) not convertible into cash **6** motionless: *she was frozen in horror*

FRS (in Britain) Fellow of the Royal Society

fructify *vb* **-fies, -fying, -fied** to bear or cause to bear fruit
WORD ORIGIN Latin *fructus* fruit + *facere* to produce

fructose *n* a crystalline sugar occurring in honey and many fruits
WORD ORIGIN Latin *fructus* fruit

frugal (**froo-gl**) *adj* **1** economical in the use of money or resources; thrifty **2** meagre and inexpensive: *a frugal meal* **frugality** *n* **frugally** *adv*
WORD ORIGIN Latin *frugi* useful, temperate

fruit *n* **1** any fleshy part of a plant that supports the seeds and is edible, such as the strawberry **2** *bot* the ripened ovary of a flowering plant, containing one or more seeds **3** any plant product useful to man, including grain and vegetables **4 fruits** the results of an action or effort, esp. if pleasant: *they have enjoyed the fruits of a complete victory* ▷ *vb* **5** to bear fruit
WORD ORIGIN Latin *fructus* enjoyment, fruit

fruiterer *n* *chiefly Brit & Austral* a person who sells fruit

fruit fly *n* **1** a small fly that feeds on and lays its eggs in plant tissues **2** a similar fly that feeds on plant sap, decaying fruit, etc. and is widely used in genetic experiments

fruitful *adj* **1** producing good and useful results: *a fruitful relationship* **2** bearing much fruit **fruitfully** *adv*

fruition (**froo-ish-on**) *n* **1** the fulfilment of something worked for or desired **2** the act or condition of bearing fruit
WORD ORIGIN Latin *frui* to enjoy

fruitless *adj* **1** producing nothing of value: *a fruitless debate* **2** without fruit **fruitlessly** *adv*

fruit machine *n* *Brit & NZ* a coin-operated gambling machine that pays out money when a particular combination of diagrams, usually of fruit, appears on a screen

fruit salad *or* **cocktail** *n* a dish consisting of pieces of different kinds of fruit

fruit sugar *n* same as **fructose**

fruity *adj* **fruitier, fruitiest** **1** of or like fruit **2** (of a voice) mellow or rich **3** *informal chiefly Brit* referring humorously to things relating to sex **fruitiness** *n*

frump *n* a woman who dresses in a dull and old-fashioned way **frumpy** *or* **frumpish** *adj*
WORD ORIGIN Middle Dutch *verrompelen* to wrinkle

frustrate *vb* **-trating, -trated** **1** to upset or anger (a person) by presenting difficulties that cannot be overcome: *his lack of ambition frustrated me* **2** to hinder or prevent (the efforts, plans, or desires) of **frustrating** *adj* **frustration** *n*
WORD ORIGIN Latin *frustrare* to cheat

frustrated *adj* dissatisfied or unfulfilled

frustum *n, pl* **-tums** *or* **-ta** *geom* the part of a solid, such as a cone or pyramid, contained between the base and a plane parallel to the base that intersects the solid

WORD ORIGIN Latin: piece

fry¹ *vb* **fries, frying, fried** **1** to cook or be cooked in fat or oil, usually over direct heat ▷ *n, pl* **fries** **2** Also: **fry-up** *informal* a dish of mixed fried food ▸ See also **fries** > **fryer** *or* **frier** *n*
WORD ORIGIN Latin *frigere*

fry² *pl n* **1** the young of various species of fish **2** see **small fry**
WORD ORIGIN Old French *freier* to spawn

frying pan *n* **1** a long-handled shallow pan used for frying **2 out of the frying pan into the fire** from a bad situation to a worse one

FSH *biol* follicle-stimulating hormone: a hormone secreted by the pituitary gland

f-stop *n* *photog* any of the lens aperture settings of a camera

ft. foot or feet

ftp file transfer protocol: a standard protocol for transferring files across a network, esp. the internet

fuchsia (**fyew-sha**) *n* an ornamental shrub with hanging purple, red, or white flowers
WORD ORIGIN after Leonhard *Fuchs*, botanist

fuck *taboo vb* **1** to have sexual intercourse with (someone) ▷ *n* **2** an act of sexual intercourse **3** *slang* a partner in sexual intercourse **4 not give a fuck** not to care at all ▷ *interj* **5** *offensive* an expression of strong disgust or anger **fucking** *n, adj, adv*
WORD ORIGIN Germanic

fuck off *vb* *offensive taboo slang* to go away

fuck up *vb* *offensive taboo slang* to make a mess of (something)

fuddle *vb* **-dling, -dled** **1** to cause to be confused or intoxicated ▷ *n* **2** a confused state **fuddled** *adj*
WORD ORIGIN origin unknown

fuddy-duddy *n, pl* **-dies** *informal* a person, esp. an elderly one, who is extremely conservative or dull
WORD ORIGIN origin unknown

fudge¹ *n* a soft sweet made from sugar, butter, and milk
WORD ORIGIN origin unknown

fudge² *vb* **fudging, fudged** **1** to make (an issue or problem) less clear deliberately **2** to avoid making a firm statement or decision
WORD ORIGIN origin unknown

fuel *n* **1** any substance burned for heat or power, such as coal or petrol **2** the material that produces energy by fission in a nuclear reactor **3 add fuel to** to make (a difficult situation) worse ▷ *vb* **fuelling, fuelled** *or US* **fueling, fueled** **4** to supply with or receive fuel **5** to intensify or make worse (a feeling or situation): *the move is bound to fuel speculation*
WORD ORIGIN Old French *feu* fire

fuel cell *n* a cell in which chemical energy is converted directly into electrical energy

fug *n* *chiefly Brit & NZ* a hot stale atmosphere **fuggy** *adj*
WORD ORIGIN origin unknown

fugitive (**fyew-jit-iv**) *n* **1** a person who flees, esp. from arrest or pursuit ▷ *adj*

Organize or Organise?

Many speakers of British English are apt to be concerned about the Americanization of their language. The argument runs that American English is a bastardized form of the language, informed by a philistine culture, and so any influence that it exerts on the mother tongue must be a baleful one. Diehard Brits are forever on the lookout for Americanisms such as *thru* or *aluminum* appearing in print, and ready to go into battle to defend the purity of their language.

Among the most treasured emblems of this perceived British purity is the practice of spelling words such as *organise* and *realise* with an 's', while those flashy Americans insist on spelling the words with that ridiculously attention-seeking letter 'z'. Woe betide any dictionary or computer spellchecker that should come down on the side of the Americans.

It is certainly true that most people in Britain are taught at school to use the 's' spelling for these words. It is also true that American English blithely spells these words with a 'z' and does not give house room to the idea that they might be spelt any other way. (Canadian writers generally line up alongside the Americans in this dispute, but in Australia, New Zealand, and South Africa the 's' form is the preferred spelling.)

Yet Britons who grow up with the understanding that *organise* and *realise* are correct, and that *organize* and *realize* are barbarisms, often get a surprise when they find that many British publishers (including all of the major dictionaries published in the United Kingdom) opt for 'z' as the primary spelling form for these words. The dictionaries do allow the 's' form as a variant, but provide this as a secondary option. Cue outraged letters about declining standards and selling out to American cultural imperialism.

The standard reply of the British dictionary publisher is that the 'z' spelling represents the most useful consensus: the alternative 's' form is unacceptable to Americans, but there has historically been some tolerance for the 'z' spellings in other countries. Apologists for the 'z' can also point to the fact that the suffix in verbs such as *organize* has its origins in Greek. In Greek words such as *baptizein* ('to baptize') and *katēchizein* ('to instruct'), the letter zeta was used rather than sigma. If these words were adopted into Latin, the letter 'z' was used to represent the Greek zeta. It was only when the words moved into French that the 's' form took precedence. So the dictionary publishers can feel a little smug about their position and claim that there is also a good historical case for giving priority to 'z'.

However, anyone who is persuaded by this argument to adopt the 'z' spelling in English should be careful not to take things too far. There are a number of common words where a 'z' should never be used. These include *advertise*, *advise*, *comprise*, *compromise*, *devise*, *exercise*, *improvise*, *supervise*, *surprise*, and *televise*. In these words, the ending is not a suffix but an integral part of the word. The rule of thumb is that if you are not left with a word after you remove the ending, you should spell the word with an 's'. (This does not hold true for *advertise*, but remember that *advert* is a modern abbreviation of *advertisement*).

Devotees of the television series *Inspector Morse* may even recall an episode where the Oxford-educated detective uses this controversy about *organize* and *organise* to attempt to catch a murderer. Morse observes that the person who wrote an incriminating letter adopts the 's' spelling, which he – being intimately familiar with the practices of British dictionaries – regards as a mark of illiteracy. He then ensures that the suspects each use plenty of words that end in '-ize' in their statements, so that the writer of the incriminating letter may be identified. The idea that individual practice in this regard is a reliable indicator of a person's education is a far-fetched one – there are many factors that may affect the preference of non-American writers – but it is certainly true that most individuals have a marked preference for one form or the other.

f

2 fleeing **3** not permanent; fleeting
WORD ORIGIN Latin *fugere* to take flight

fugu *n* any of various marine pufferfish eaten in Japan once certain lethally poisonous parts have been removed
WORD ORIGIN Japanese

fugue (fyewg) *n* a musical form consisting of a theme repeated above or below the continuing first statement **fugal** *adj*
WORD ORIGIN French

Führer *n* a leader: the title used by Hitler as Nazi dictator
WORD ORIGIN German

-ful *suffix* **1** full of or characterized by: *painful; restful* **2** able or tending to: *useful* **3** as much as will fill the thing specified: *mouthful*

fulcrum *n, pl* **-crums** *or* **-cra** the pivot about which a lever turns
WORD ORIGIN Latin: foot of a couch

fulfil *or US* **fulfill** *vb* **-filling, -filled** **1** to bring about the achievement of (a desire or promise) **2** to carry out (a request or order) **3** to satisfy (demands or conditions) **4 fulfil oneself** to achieve one's potential **fulfilment** *or* US **fulfillment** *n*
WORD ORIGIN Old English *fulfyllan*

full[1] *adj* **1** holding as much or as many as possible **2** abundant in supply: *full of enthusiasm* **3** having consumed enough food or drink **4** (of the face or figure) rounded or plump **5** complete: *the full amount* **6** with all privileges or rights: *full membership* **7** *music* powerful or rich in volume and sound **8** (of a garment) containing a large amount of fabric **9 full of** engrossed with: *she had been full of her own plans lately* **10 full of oneself** full of pride or conceit **11 full up** filled to capacity ▷ *adv* **12** completely or entirely **13** directly or right: *she hit him full in the face* **14 full well** very or extremely well: *we knew full well that she was watching every move we made* ▷ *n* **15 in full** without omitting or shortening **16 to the full** thoroughly or fully **fullness** *or esp.* US **fulness** *n*
WORD ORIGIN Old English

full[2] *vb* to make (cloth) more compact during manufacture through shrinking and beating
WORD ORIGIN Old French *fouler*

fullback *n soccer, hockey, & rugby* a defensive player

full-blooded *adj* **1** vigorous or enthusiastic **2** (esp. of horses) having ancestors of a single race or breed

full-blown *adj* fully developed

full board *n* the daily provision by a hotel of bed, breakfast, and midday and evening meals

full-bodied *adj* having a full rich flavour or quality: *a full-bodied vintage port*

fuller's earth *n* a natural absorbent clay used for fulling cloth

full-frontal *adj informal* exposing the genitals to full view

full house *n* **1** a theatre filled to capacity **2** (in bingo) the set of numbers needed to win

full-length *adj* **1** (of a mirror, portrait, etc.) showing the complete human figure **2** not abridged

full moon *n* the phase of the moon

when it is visible as a fully illuminated disc

full-on *adj informal* complete; unrestrained: *full-on military intervention*

full-scale *adj* **1** (of a plan) of actual size **2** using all resources; all-out

full stop *n* the punctuation mark (.) used at the end of a sentence and after abbreviations. Also called (esp. US and Canad): **period**

full-time *adj* **1** for all of the normal working week: *a full-time job* ▷ *adv* **full time 2** on a full-time basis: *she worked full time until she was 72* ▷ *n* **full time 3** *soccer, rugby, & hockey* the end of the game

full toss *or* **pitch** *n cricket* a bowled ball that reaches the batsman without bouncing

fully *adv* **1** to the greatest degree or extent **2** amply or adequately **3** at least: *fully a hundred people*

fully-fashioned *adj* (of stockings or knitwear) shaped and seamed so as to fit closely

fulmar *n* a heavily-built Arctic sea bird with a short tail
WORD ORIGIN Scandinavian

fulminate *vb* **-nating, -nated** ● **fulminate against** to criticize or denounce angrily **fulmination** *n*
WORD ORIGIN Latin *fulmen* lightning that strikes

fulsome *adj* **1** exaggerated and elaborate, and often sounding insincere: *fulsome praise* **2** *not standard* extremely complimentary

fumble *vb* **-bling, -bled 1** to use the hands clumsily or grope about blindly: *fumbling for a cigarette* **2** to say or do awkwardly ▷ *n* **3** the act of fumbling
WORD ORIGIN probably Scandinavian

fume *vb* **fuming, fumed 1** to be overcome with anger or fury **2** to give off (fumes) or (of fumes) to be given off, esp. during a chemical reaction **3** to treat with fumes ▷ *n* **4** (*often pl*) pungent or toxic vapour, gas, or smoke: *exhaust fumes*
WORD ORIGIN Latin *fumus* smoke, vapour

fumigate (fyew-mig-gate) *vb* **-gating, -gated** to treat (something contaminated) with fumes **fumigation** *n*
WORD ORIGIN Latin *fumus* smoke + *agere* to drive

fun *n* **1** pleasant, enjoyable, and light-hearted activity or amusement **2 for** *or* **in fun** for amusement or as a joke **3 make fun of** *or* **poke fun at** to ridicule or tease ▷ *adj* **4** (of a person) amusing and likeable **5** (of a place or activity) amusing and enjoyable
WORD ORIGIN obsolete *fon* to make a fool of

function *n* **1** the intended role or purpose of a person or thing **2** an official or formal social gathering **3** a factor, the precise nature of which depends upon another thing in some way: *muscle breakdown is a function of vitamin E deficiency* **4** *maths* a quantity, the value of which depends on the varying value of another quantity **5** a sequence of operations that a computer or calculator performs when a specified key is

pressed ▷ *vb* **6** to operate or work **7 function as** to perform the action or role of (something or someone else)
WORD ORIGIN Latin *functio*

functional *adj* **1** of or performing a function **2** practical rather than decorative **3** in working order **4** *med* affecting a function of an organ without structural change **functionally** *adv*

functional food *n* a food containing additives which provide extra nutritional value. Also called: **nutraceutical**

functionalism *n* the theory that the form of a thing should be determined by its use **functionalist** *n, adj*

functionary *n, pl* **-aries** a person acting in an official capacity, such as for a government; official

fund *n* **1** a reserve of money set aside for a certain purpose **2** a supply or store of something ▷ *vb* **3** to provide money to **4** *finance* to convert (short-term debt) into long-term debt bearing fixed interest ► See also **funds** ► **funder** *n*
WORD ORIGIN Latin *fundus* the bottom, piece of land

fundamental *adj* **1** essential or primary: *fundamental mathematical concepts* **2** basic: *a fundamental error* ▷ *n* **3 fundamentals** the most important and basic parts of a subject or activity **4** the lowest note of a harmonic series **fundamentally** *adv*

fundamentalism *n* **1** *Christianity* the view that the Bible is literally true **2** *Islam* a movement favouring strict observance of Islamic law **fundamentalist** *n, adj*

fundamental particle *n physics* same as **elementary particle**

fundholding *n* the system in which general practitioners may choose to receive a fixed budget from which they pay for non-urgent hospital treatment and drug costs for patients

fundi (foon-dee) *n S African* an expert
WORD ORIGIN Nguni (language group of southern Africa) *umfindisi*

funding *n* **1** the provision of money for a project or organization **2** the amount of money provided

fundraiser *n* **1** a person involved in organizing fundraising activities **2** an event held to raise money for a cause

fundraising *n* **1** the activity involved in raising money for a cause ▷ *adj* **2** of, for, or relating to fundraising: *a fundraising disco*

funds *pl n* money that is readily available

funeral *n* **1** a ceremony at which a dead person is buried or cremated **2 it's your funeral** *informal* a mistake has been made and you alone will be responsible for its consequences ▷ *adj* **3** of or for a funeral **funerary** *adj*
WORD ORIGIN Latin *funus*

funeral director *n* an undertaker

funeral parlour *n* a place where the dead are prepared for burial or cremation

funereal (fyew-**neer**-ee-al) *adj* suggestive of a funeral; gloomy or sombre **funereally** *adv*

funfair n Brit an amusement park with machines to ride on and stalls

fungicide n a substance used to destroy fungi
WORD ORIGIN FUNGUS + Latin *caedere* to kill

fungoid adj resembling a fungus

fungous adj appearing suddenly and spreading quickly like a fungus

fungus n, pl **fungi** or **funguses** a plant without leaves, flowers, or roots, that reproduces by spores, including moulds, yeasts, and mushrooms **fungal** adj
WORD ORIGIN Latin

funicular (fyew-**nik**-yew-lar) n a railway up the side of a mountain, consisting of two cars at either end of a cable passing round a driving wheel at the summit. Also called: **funicular railway**
WORD ORIGIN Latin *funis* rope

funk¹ old-fashioned Brit n **1** a state of nervousness, fear, or depression **2** a coward ▷ vb **3** to avoid doing (something) through fear
WORD ORIGIN origin unknown

funk² n a type of Black dance music with a strong beat
WORD ORIGIN from *funky*

funky adj **-kier, -kiest** (of jazz or pop) having a strong beat
WORD ORIGIN from obsolete *funk* to smoke tobacco, perhaps referring to music that is smelly, i.e. earthy

funnel n **1** a tube with a wide mouth tapering to a small hole, used for pouring liquids into narrow openings **2** a chimney of a ship or steam train ▷ vb **-nelling, -nelled** or US **-neling, -neled 3** to move or cause to move through, or as if through, a funnel
WORD ORIGIN Old Provençal *fonilh*

funnel-web n Austral a large poisonous black spider that builds funnel-shaped webs

funny adj **-nier, -niest 1** causing amusement or laughter; humorous **2** peculiar or odd **3** informal faint or ill: *this smell is making me feel a bit funny* **4** funny business informal suspicious or dubious behaviour **funnily** adv **funniness** n

funny bone n a sensitive area near the elbow where the nerve is close to the surface of the skin

fur n **1** the dense coat of fine silky hairs on many mammals **2** the skin of certain animals, with the hair left on **3** a garment made of fur **4** make the fur fly to cause a scene or disturbance **5** informal a whitish coating on the tongue, caused by illness **6** Brit a deposit on the insides of water pipes or kettles, caused by hard water ▷ vb **furring, furred 7** Also: **fur up** to cover or become covered with a furlike deposit
WORD ORIGIN Old French *fuerre* sheath

furbelow n old-fashioned **1** a pleated or gathered piece of material used as a decoration on a woman's garment; ruffle **2 furbelows** showy ornamentation
WORD ORIGIN French dialect *farbella* a frill

furbish vb formal to brighten up or renovate
WORD ORIGIN Old French *fourbir* to polish

furcate vb **-cating, -cated 1** to divide into two parts ▷ adj **2** forked: *furcate branches* **furcation** n
WORD ORIGIN Latin *furca* a fork

Furies pl n, sing **Fury** classical myth the goddesses of vengeance, who pursued unpunished criminals

furious adj **1** extremely angry or annoyed **2** violent or unrestrained, such as in speed or energy: *fast and furious dance routines* **furiously** adv

furl vb to roll up (an umbrella, flag, or sail) neatly and securely
WORD ORIGIN Old French *ferm* tight + *lier* to bind

furlong n a unit of length equal to 220 yards (201.168 metres)
WORD ORIGIN Old English *furlang*, from *furh* furrow + *lang* long

furlough (**fur**-loh) n leave of absence from military or other duty
WORD ORIGIN Dutch *verlof*

furnace n **1** an enclosed chamber in which heat is produced to destroy refuse or smelt ores **2** informal a very hot place
WORD ORIGIN Latin *fornax*

furnish vb **1** to provide (a house or room) with furniture, etc. **2** to supply or provide **furnished** adj
WORD ORIGIN Old French *fournir*

furnishings pl n furniture, carpets, and fittings with which a room or house is furnished

furniture n the large movable articles, such as chairs and tables, that equip a room or house
WORD ORIGIN Old French *fournir* to equip

furore (fyew-**ror**-ee) n a very angry or excited reaction by people to something: *the furore over 'The Satanic Verses'*
WORD ORIGIN Latin *furor* frenzy

furrier n a person who makes or sells fur garments
WORD ORIGIN Middle English *furour*

furrow n **1** a long narrow trench made in the ground by a plough **2** any long deep groove, esp. a deep wrinkle on the forehead ▷ vb **3** to become wrinkled **4** to make furrows in (land)
WORD ORIGIN Old English *furh*

furry adj **-rier, -riest** like or covered with fur or something furlike

further adv **1** in addition **2** to a greater degree or extent **3** to or at a more advanced point **4** to or at a greater distance in time or space ▷ adj **5** additional **6** more distant or remote in time or space ▷ vb **7** to assist the progress of (something) **furtherance** n
WORD ORIGIN Old English *furthor*
USAGE
See at **farther**.

further education n (in Britain, Australia, and South Africa) formal education beyond school other than at university

furthermore adv in addition

furthest adv **1** to the greatest degree or extent **2** to or at the greatest distance in time or space; farthest ▷ adj **3** most distant in time or space; farthest

furtive adj sly, cautious, and secretive **furtively** adv
WORD ORIGIN Latin *furtivus* stolen

fury n, pl **-ries 1** violent anger **2** uncontrolled violence: *the fury of the sea* **3** an outburst of violent anger **4** a person with a violent temper **5** like fury old-fashioned with great energy, strength, or power
WORD ORIGIN Latin *furere* to be furious

Fury n, pl **-ries** see **Furies**

furze n gorse **furzy** adj
WORD ORIGIN Old English *fyrs*

fuse¹ or US **fuze** n **1** a lead containing an explosive for detonating a bomb ▷ vb **fusing, fused** or US **fuzing, fuzed 2** to equip with such a fuse
WORD ORIGIN Latin *fusus* spindle

fuse² n **1** a protective device for safeguarding electric circuits, containing a wire that melts and breaks the circuit when the current exceeds a certain value ▷ vb **fusing, fused 2** Brit to fail or cause to fail as a result of a fuse blowing **3** to equip (a plug or circuit) with a fuse **4** to join or become combined: *the two ideas fused in his mind* **5** to unite or become united by melting **6** to become or cause to become liquid, esp. by the action of heat
WORD ORIGIN Latin *fusus* melted, cast

fuselage (**fyew**-zill-lahzh) n the main body of an aircraft
WORD ORIGIN French

fusible adj capable of being melted

fusilier (fyew-zill-**leer**) n (formerly) an infantryman armed with a light musket: a term still used in the names of certain British regiments
WORD ORIGIN French

fusillade (fyew-zill-**lade**) n **1** a rapid continual discharge of firearms **2** a sudden outburst of criticism, questions, etc.
WORD ORIGIN French *fusiller* to shoot

fusilli (foo-**zee**-li) n pasta in the form of short spirals
WORD ORIGIN Italian

fusion n **1** the act or process of melting together **2** something produced by fusing **3** a kind of popular music that is a blend of two or more styles, such as jazz and funk **4** something new created by a mixture of qualities, ideas, or things **5** see **nuclear fusion** ▷ adj **6** relating to a style of cooking that combines traditional Western techniques and ingredients with those used in Eastern cuisine
WORD ORIGIN Latin *fusio* a melting

fuss n **1** needless activity and worry **2** complaint or objection: *it was silly to make a fuss over seating arrangements* **3** an exhibition of affection or admiration: *when I arrived my nephews made a big fuss of me* ▷ vb **4** to worry unnecessarily **5** to be excessively concerned over trivial matters **6** to bother (a person) **7** fuss over to show great or excessive concern or affection for
WORD ORIGIN origin unknown

fusspot n informal a person who is difficult to please and complains often

fussy adj **fussier, fussiest 1** inclined to

fuss **2** very particular about detail **3** overelaborate: *a fussy, overdecorated palace* **fussily** *adv*

fustian *n* **1** (formerly) a hard-wearing fabric of cotton mixed with flax or wool **2** pompous talk or writing **WORD ORIGIN** Old French *fustaigne*

fusty *adj* **-tier, -tiest 1** smelling of damp or mould **2** old-fashioned **fustiness** *n* **WORD ORIGIN** Middle English *fust* wine cask

futile (**fyew**-tile) *adj* **1** useless or having no chance of success **2** foolish and of no value: *her futile remarks began to annoy me* **futility** *n* **WORD ORIGIN** Latin *futtilis* pouring out easily

futon (**foo**-tonn) *n* a Japanese padded quilt, laid on the floor as a bed

future *n* **1** the time yet to come **2** undetermined events that will occur in that time **3** the condition of a person or thing at a later date **4** prospects: *he had faith in its future* **5** *grammar* a tense of verbs used when the action specified has not yet taken place **6 in future** from now on ▷ *adj* **7** that is yet to come or be **8** of or expressing time yet to come **9** destined to become **10** *grammar* in or denoting the future as a tense of verbs ▶ See also **futures** **WORD ORIGIN** Latin *futurus* about to be

future perfect *grammar adj* **1** denoting a tense of verbs describing an action that will have been performed by a certain time ▷ *n* **2** the future perfect tense

futures *pl n* commodities bought or sold at an agreed price for delivery at a specified future date

futurism *n* an early 20th-century artistic movement making use of the characteristics of the machine age **futurist** *n, adj*

futuristic *adj* **1** of design or technology that appears to belong to some future time **2** of futurism

futurity *n, pl* **-ties 1** future **2** a future event

futurology *n* the study or prediction of the future of mankind

fuzz[1] *n* a mass or covering of fine or curly hairs, fibres, etc. **WORD ORIGIN** probably from Low German *fussig* loose

fuzz[2] *n Brit, Austral, & NZ slang* the police or a policeman **WORD ORIGIN** origin unknown

fuzzy *adj* **fuzzier, fuzziest 1** of, like, or covered with fuzz **2** unclear, blurred, or distorted: *some fuzzy pictures from a Russian radar probe* **3** (of hair) tightly curled **fuzzily** *adv* **fuzziness** *n*

fwd forward

FX *films informal* special effects **WORD ORIGIN** a phonetic respelling of *effects*

Mark Twain and Regional Realism

Before the fourteenth century, if a piece of English writing displayed a regional 'accent', one could assume that the author or (more likely) the scribe came from that region. Then Geoffrey Chaucer composed *The Reeve's Tale* in which characters speak in a distinctly 'Northern' style. But this does not mean that Chaucer or his scribes came from the Northeast of England: only the characters do. This is the earliest use of a regional accent for characterization in English literature.

By the nineteenth century, authors like Sir Walter Scott and Charlotte Brontë were using regional English in their works; yet Mark Twain's *The Adventures of Huckleberry Finn* must still have created quite a stir. *Huck Finn* is the sequel to Twain's *The Adventures of Tom Sawyer*, which is regarded as a classic of children's literature. In *Tom Sawyer*, the characters speak in regional dialect, but the narration is in standard English. *Huck Finn*, however, is a first-person narrative; the entire novel is told in the main character's local patois. It was certainly a daring step to write an entire novel in a variety of English with which only a minority of English speakers would be familiar; however, it lends an authenticity Huck's story that would have been difficult to achieve otherwise.

In the United States, nineteenth-century fiction began to return to Realism, in contrast to the sentimentality of Victorian literature. Though Twain was not above outlandish plots and fantastic events, *The Adventures of Huckleberry Finn* aspires to realism, and the regional dialect is used not simply because it is more evocative, but because it is more *accurate*. Twain gives the reader Huck's uncensored, untranslated thoughts; and in doing so, creates a portrait of the antebellum American South that is far more convincing (and troubling) than that of his nearest competitor: the sentimental *Uncle Tom's Cabin* by Harriet Beecher Stowe.

Supporters of *Huckleberry Finn* consider it to be an anti-slavery novel. However, Twain's realistic style has left him open to accusations of the opposite; even on a fair and balanced reading, it is not possible to say what Twain's opinion of slavery and African-Americans really was. Even if he were nominally an abolitionist, his views might, by present-day standards, still seem racist.

Among the evidence against the novel is the use of a certain racial slur more than 200 times. The word, though highly offensive to us, was however the historically accurate term applied to African chattel slaves in antebellum America. Using it may simply be part of Twain's realism.

More controversial is the characterization of the escaped slave, Jim, who is, together with Huck, one of the two principal characters of the book. He is taken seriously as a human being, with real feelings (in a famous scene Huck hurts Jim's feelings and has to apologize, something most of Huck's contemporaries would never have done). Being a runaway slave, he risks his freedom and his life when he helps a doctor care for the injured Tom Sawyer – a sacrifice not less affecting, but far less melodramatic than anything Stowe ever created.

However, Jim is also depicted as superstitious (he once mistakes Huck for a ghost and consults a giant hairball for predictions of the future), ignorant (he refuses to believe in the French language), and strangely compliant (he submits to an elaborate and ridiculous scheme to 'free' him, involving spiders in his bed and 'messages' to be written in his own blood, when Tom Sawyer and Huck could simply have unlocked his shed during the night). While Jim's illiteracy and lack of education are historically accurate, the superstition and complaisance – apparently included for comic effect – make it seem like Twain is laughing at Jim.

This, however, is the nature of Realism: when the author views a subject from a neutral perspective, judgement ultimately resides with the reader. We are certainly right to be disturbed by the treatment of Jim and by the world he inhabits; and, whatever Twain's own opinions were, *The Adventures of Huckleberry Finn* functions as a scathing attack on antebellum America.

Gg

The letter G is the seventh letter of the English alphabet. It has its origins in the Greek letter *gamma* (Γ,γ). In the Roman alphabet *gamma* became a C, and this letter originally did double duty for the sounds /k/ and /g/ before the G was introduced to remove the confusion.

The Greek writer Plutarch even tells us the name of the person who invented the letter G. This was one Spurius Carvilius Ruga, a Roman schoolteacher who lived in the 3rd century BC, and was presumably called 'Ruca' before he came up with the new letter by adding an extra stroke to the C.

Like its cousin C, the letter G later acquired a soft sound when it occurred in front of the letters I and E, so that in an English word such as 'gorgeous' it can now represent two quite different sounds.

The lower-case form of letter G can be written in two different ways. Most printed fonts adopt a more ornate form with two closed loops (g), while in handwriting the tail usually remains open.

In music, the letters from A to G are used to represent notes. The 'G clef' is another name for the treble clef, in which the second line from the bottom is used for the note G, and the familiar symbol for the treble clef is in fact a modified form of the letter G. The G-string is the lowest string on a violin, although it can also refer to a scanty item of underwear not much thicker than a violin string.

To a scientist, an italic *g* is the symbol for acceleration due to gravity. The effect that this acceleration has on a body is sometimes referred to as a 'g-force', and astronauts wear 'g-suits' to counter this effect.

The letter G is also widely used in the names of various associations of the most powerful industrial nations. At the first meeting of such a body in 1975, the leaders of six countries were involved, and this grouping became known as the 'Group of Six' or 'G6' for short. As time has gone on more countries have been invited to join the club, and so the countries who attend such summits are now referred to as the G8 or, at less exclusive meetings, the G20.

---

g 1 gallon(s) **2** gram(s) **3** acceleration due to gravity

G 1 *music* the fifth note of the scale of C major **2** gravity **3** good **4** giga- **5** *slang* grand (a thousand pounds or dollars)

G8 Group of Eight

G20 Group of Twenty: an international organization established to promote global economic stability

Ga *chem* gallium

GA Georgia

gab *informal vb* **gabbing, gabbed 1** to talk a lot, esp. about unimportant things ▷ *n* **2** idle talk **3 gift of the gab** the ability to talk easily and persuasively
WORD ORIGIN probably from Irish Gaelic *gob* mouth

gabardine *or* **gaberdine** *n* **1** a strong twill cloth used esp. for raincoats **2** a coat made of this cloth
WORD ORIGIN Old French *gauvardine* pilgrim's garment

gabble *vb* **-bling, -bled 1** to speak rapidly and indistinctly: *the interviewee started to gabble furiously* ▷ *n* **2** rapid and indistinct speech
WORD ORIGIN Middle Dutch *gabbelen*

gable *n* the triangular upper part of a wall between the sloping ends of a ridged roof **gabled** *adj*
WORD ORIGIN probably from Old Norse *gafl*

gad *vb* **gadding, gadded** (foll. by *about* or *around*) to go about in search of pleasure
WORD ORIGIN obsolete *gadling* companion

gadabout *n informal* a person who restlessly seeks amusement

gadfly *n, pl* **-flies 1** a large fly that bites livestock **2** a constantly irritating person
WORD ORIGIN obsolete *gad* sting

gadget *n* a small mechanical device or appliance **gadgetry** *n*
WORD ORIGIN perhaps from French *gâchette* trigger

gado-gado *n* an Indonesian dish of cooked mixed vegetables and hard-boiled eggs served with a peanut sauce
WORD ORIGIN Bahasa Indonesia

gadoid (**gay**-doid) *adj* **1** of or belonging to the cod family of marine fishes ▷ *n* **2** any gadoid fish
WORD ORIGIN New Latin *gadus* cod

gadolinium *n chem* a silvery-white metallic element of the rare-earth group. Symbol: Gd
WORD ORIGIN after Johan *Gadolin*, mineralogist

gadzooks *interj archaic* a mild oath
WORD ORIGIN perhaps from *God's hooks* the nails of the cross, from *Gad*, archaic euphemism for *God*

Gael (**gayl**) *n* a Gaelic-speaker of Scotland, Ireland, or the Isle of Man **Gaeldom** *n*
WORD ORIGIN Gaelic *Gaidheal*

Gaelic (**gal**-lik, **gay**-lik) *n* **1** any of the closely related Celtic languages of Scotland, Ireland, or the Isle of Man ▷ *adj* **2** of the Celtic people of Scotland, Ireland, or the Isle of Man, or their language

gaff[1] *n* **1** *angling* a pole with a hook attached for landing large fish **2** *naut* a spar hoisted to support a fore-and-aft sail
WORD ORIGIN Provençal *gaf* boat hook

gaff[2] *n* **blow the gaff** *Brit slang* to give away a secret
WORD ORIGIN origin unknown

gaffe *n* something said or done that is socially upsetting or incorrect
WORD ORIGIN French

gaffer *n* **1** *informal chiefly Brit* a boss or foreman **2** an old man: often used affectionately **3** *informal* the senior electrician on a television or film set
WORD ORIGIN from *godfather*

gag[1] *vb* **gagging, gagged 1** to choke as if about to vomit or as if struggling for breath **2** to stop up (a person's mouth), usually with a piece of cloth, to prevent them from speaking or crying out **3** to deprive of free speech ▷ *n* **4** something, usually a piece of cloth, stuffed into or

tied across the mouth **5** any restraint on free speech **6** a device for keeping the jaws apart: *a dentist's gag*
WORD ORIGIN Middle English *gaggen*

gag² *informal n* **1** a joke, usually one told by a professional comedian ▷ *vb* **gagging, gagged 2** to tell jokes
WORD ORIGIN origin unknown

gaga (**gah**-gah) *adj informal* **1** confused and suffering some memory loss as a result of old age **2** foolishly doting: *she's gaga over him*
WORD ORIGIN French

gage¹ *n* (formerly) a glove or other object thrown down to indicate a challenge to fight
WORD ORIGIN Old French

gage² *n, vb* **gaging, gaged** *US* same as **gauge**

gaggle *n* **1** *informal* a group of people gathered together **2** a flock of geese
WORD ORIGIN Germanic

gaiety *n, pl* **-ties 1** a state of lively good spirits **2** festivity; merrymaking
≡ USAGE
≡ See at **gay**.

gaily *adv* **1** in a lively manner; cheerfully **2** with bright colours

gain *vb* **1** to acquire (something desirable) **2** to increase, improve, or advance: *wholesale prices gained 5.6 percent* **3** to get to; reach: *gaining the top of the hill* **4** (of a watch or clock) to become or be too fast **5 gain on** to get nearer to or catch up on ▷ *n* **6** something won or acquired; profit; advantage: *a clear gain would result* **7** an increase in size or amount **8** *electronics* the ratio of the output signal of an amplifier to the input signal, usually measured in decibels
WORD ORIGIN Old French *gaaignier*

gainful *adj* useful or profitable
gainfully *adv*

gainsay *vb* **-saying, -said** *archaic or literary* to deny or contradict
WORD ORIGIN Middle English *gainsaien*, from *gain-* against + *saien* to say

gait *n* **1** manner of walking **2** (of horses and dogs) the pattern of footsteps at a particular speed, such as a trot
WORD ORIGIN variant of *gate*

gaiters *pl n* cloth or leather coverings for the legs or ankles
WORD ORIGIN French *guêtre*

gal *n slang* a girl

gala (**gah**-la) *n* **1** a special social occasion, esp. a special performance **2** *chiefly Brit* a sporting occasion with competitions in several events: *next week's sports gala*
WORD ORIGIN Old French *galer* to make merry

galactic *adj* of the Galaxy or other galaxies

galaxy *n, pl* **-axies 1** a star system held together by gravitational attraction **2** a collection of brilliant people or things: *a galaxy of legal talent*
WORD ORIGIN Middle English (in the sense: the Milky Way); from Greek *gala* milk

Galaxy *n* **the Galaxy** the spiral galaxy that contains the solar system. Also called: **Milky Way**

gale *n* **1** a strong wind, specifically one of force 8 on the Beaufort scale **2 gales** a loud outburst: *gales of laughter*
WORD ORIGIN origin unknown

galena *or* **galenite** *n* a soft bluish-grey mineral consisting of lead sulphide: the chief source of lead
WORD ORIGIN Latin: lead ore

Galia melon *n* a kind of melon with a raised network texture on the skin and sweet flesh

gall¹ (**gawl**) *n* **1** *informal* bold impudence: *she was stunned I had the gall to ask* **2** a feeling of great bitterness **3** *physiol obsolete* same as **bile**
WORD ORIGIN Old Norse

gall² (**gawl**) *vb* **1** to annoy or irritate **2** to make the skin sore by rubbing ▷ *n* **3** something that causes annoyance **4** a sore on the skin caused by rubbing
WORD ORIGIN Germanic

gall³ (**gawl**) *n* an abnormal outgrowth on a tree or plant caused by parasites
WORD ORIGIN Latin *galla*

gallant *adj* **1** persistent and courageous in the face of overwhelming odds: *a gallant fight* **2** (of a man) making a show of polite attentiveness to women **3** having a reputation for bravery: *Police Medal for gallant and meritorious services* ▷ *n* **4** *history* a young man who tried to impress women with his fashionable clothes or daring acts
gallantly *adv*
WORD ORIGIN Old French *galer* to make merry

gallantry *n* **1** showy, attentive treatment of women **2** great bravery in war or danger

gall bladder *n* a muscular sac, attached to the liver, that stores bile

galleon *n* a large three-masted sailing ship used from the 15th to the 18th centuries
WORD ORIGIN Spanish *galeón*

gallery *n, pl* **-leries 1** a room or building for displaying works of art **2** a balcony running along the inside wall of a church, hall, or other building **3** *theatre* **a** an upper floor that projects from the rear and contains the cheapest seats **b** the audience seated there **4** an underground passage in a mine or cave **5** a group of spectators, for instance at a golf match **6 play to the gallery** to try to gain approval by appealing to popular taste
WORD ORIGIN Old French *galerie*

galley *n* **1** the kitchen of a ship, boat, or aircraft **2** a ship propelled by oars or sails, used in ancient or medieval times
WORD ORIGIN Old French *galie*

galley slave *n* **1** a criminal or slave forced to row in a galley **2** *informal* a drudge

Gallic *adj* **1** French **2** of ancient Gaul or the Gauls

Gallicism *n* a word or idiom borrowed from French

gallinaceous *adj* of an order of birds, including poultry, pheasants, and grouse, that have a heavy rounded body
WORD ORIGIN Latin *gallina* hen

galling (**gawl**-ing) *adj* annoying or bitterly humiliating

gallium *n chem* a silvery metallic element used in high-temperature thermometers and low-melting alloys. Symbol: Ga
WORD ORIGIN Latin *gallus* cock, translation of French *coq* in the name of its discoverer, *Lecoq* de Boisbaudran

gallivant *vb* to go about in search of pleasure
WORD ORIGIN perhaps from *gallant*

gallon *n* **1** *Brit* a unit of liquid measure equal to 4.55 litres **2** *US* a unit of liquid measure equal to 3.79 litres
WORD ORIGIN Old Northern French *galon*

gallop *vb* **1** (of a horse) to run fast with a two-beat stride in which all four legs are off the ground at once **2** to ride (a horse) at a gallop **3** to move or progress rapidly ▷ *n* **4** the fast two-beat gait of horses **5** a galloping
WORD ORIGIN Old French *galoper*

Galloway *n* a breed of black cattle originally bred in Galloway
WORD ORIGIN after *Galloway*, district of SW Scotland

gallows *n, pl* **-lowses** *or* **-lows 1** a wooden structure consisting of two upright posts with a crossbeam, used for hanging criminals **2 the gallows** execution by hanging
WORD ORIGIN Old Norse *galgi*

gallstone *n* a small hard mass formed in the gall bladder or its ducts

Gallup Poll *n* a sampling of the views of a representative cross section of the population, usually used to forecast voting
WORD ORIGIN after G. H. *Gallup*, statistician

galop *n* **1** a 19th-century dance in quick duple time **2** music for this dance
WORD ORIGIN French

galore *adj* in abundance: *there were bargains galore*
WORD ORIGIN Irish Gaelic *go leór* to sufficiency

galoshes *pl n Brit, Austral, & NZ* a pair of waterproof overshoes
WORD ORIGIN Old French *galoche* wooden shoe

galumph *vb Brit, Austral, & NZ informal* to leap or move about clumsily or joyfully
WORD ORIGIN probably a blend of GALLOP + TRIUMPH

galvanic *adj* **1** of or producing an electric current by chemical means, such as in a battery **2** *informal* stimulating, startling, or energetic

galvanize *or* **-nise** *vb* **-nizing, -nized** *or* **-nising, -nised 1** to stimulate into action **2** to cover (metal) with a protective zinc coating **3** to stimulate by an electric current **galvanization** *or* **-nisation** *n*
WORD ORIGIN after Luigi *Galvani*, physiologist

galvanometer *n* a sensitive instrument for detecting or measuring small electric currents

gambit *n* **1** an opening remark or action intended to gain an advantage **2** *chess* an opening move in which a piece, usually a pawn, is sacrificed to gain an advantageous position
WORD ORIGIN Italian *gambetto* a tripping up

g

gamble *vb* **-bling, -bled 1** to play games of chance to win money or prizes **2** to risk or bet (something) on the outcome of an event or sport **3 gamble away** to lose by gambling **4 gamble on** to act with the expectation of: *she has gambled on proving everyone wrong* ▷ *n* **5** a risky act or venture **6** a bet or wager **gambler** *n* **gambling** *n*
WORD ORIGIN probably variant of GAME[1]

gamboge (gam-**boje**) *n* a gum resin obtained from a tropical Asian tree, used as a yellow pigment and as a purgative
WORD ORIGIN from *Cambodia*, where first found

gambol *vb* **-bolling, -bolled** *or US* **-boling, -boled 1** to jump about playfully; frolic ▷ *n* **2** playful jumping about; frolicking
WORD ORIGIN French *gambade*

game[1] *n* **1** an amusement for children **2** a competitive activity with rules **3** a single period of play in such an activity **4** (in some sports) the score needed to win **5** a single contest in a series; match **6** short for **computer game 7** style or ability in playing a game: *in the second set his overall game improved markedly* **8** an activity that seems to operate according to unwritten rules: *the political game of power* **9** an activity undertaken in a spirit of playfulness: *people who regard life as a game* **10** wild animals, birds, or fish, hunted for sport or food **11** the flesh of such animals, used as food **12** an object of pursuit: *fair game* **13** *informal* a trick or scheme: *what's his game?* **14 games** an event consisting of various sporting contests, usually in athletics: *Commonwealth Games* **15 give the game away** to reveal one's intentions or a secret **16 on the game** *slang* working as a prostitute **17 play the game** to behave fairly **18 the game is up** the scheme or trick has been found out and so cannot succeed ▷ *adj* **19** *informal* full of fighting spirit; plucky **20** *informal* prepared or willing: *I'm always game for a new sensation* ▷ *vb* **gaming, gamed 21** to play games of chance for money; gamble **gamely** *adv* **gameness** *n*
WORD ORIGIN Old English *gamen*

game[2] *adj Brit, Austral, & NZ* lame: *he had a game leg*
WORD ORIGIN probably from Irish *cam* crooked

gamekeeper *n Brit* a person employed to take care of game on an estate

game plan *n* **1** *US & Canad* a strategy for playing a particular game **2** any plan or strategy

gamer *n* a person who plays computer games

games console *n* a small machine, linked to a television set, used for playing video games

gamesmanship *n informal* the art of winning by cunning practices without actually cheating

gamester *n* a gambler

gamete (gam-**eet**) *n* a cell that can fuse with another in reproduction **gametic** *or* **gametal** *adj*
WORD ORIGIN Greek *gametē* wife

gamey *or* **gamy** *adj* **gamier, gamiest** having the smell or flavour of game

gamin *n* a street urchin
WORD ORIGIN French

gamine (gam-**een**) *n* a slim and boyish girl or young woman
WORD ORIGIN French

gaming *n* gambling

gamma *n* the third letter in the Greek alphabet (Λ, λ)

gamma radiation *n* electromagnetic radiation of shorter wavelength and higher energy than X-rays

gamma rays *pl n* streams of gamma radiation

gammon *n* **1** cured or smoked ham **2** the hindquarter of a side of bacon
WORD ORIGIN Old French *gambe* leg

gammy *adj* **-mier, -miest** *Brit & NZ slang* (of the leg) lame
WORD ORIGIN dialect variant of GAME[2]

gamp *n Brit informal* an umbrella
WORD ORIGIN after Mrs *Gamp* in Dickens' *Martin Chuzzlewit*

gamut *n* **1** entire range or scale: *a rich gamut of facial expressions* **2** *music* **a** a scale **b** the whole range of notes
WORD ORIGIN Medieval Latin, from *gamma*, the lowest note of the hexachord as established by Guido d'Arezzo + *ut* (now, doh), the first of the notes of the scale *ut, re, mi, fa, sol, la, si*

gamy *adj* same as **gamey**

gander *n* **1** a male goose **2** *informal* a quick look: *have a gander*
WORD ORIGIN Old English *gandra, ganra*

gang[1] *n* **1** a group of people who go around together, often to commit crime **2** an organized group of workmen ▷ *vb* **3** to become or act as a gang ▶ See also **gang up on**
WORD ORIGIN Old English: journey

gang[2] *vb Scot* to go or walk
WORD ORIGIN Old English *gangan*

gangbang *n slang* sexual intercourse between one woman and several men one after the other, esp. against her will

gangland *n* the criminal underworld

gangling *or* **gangly** *adj* lanky and awkward in movement
WORD ORIGIN see GANG[2]

ganglion *n, pl* **-glia** *or* **-glions** a collection of nerve cells outside the brain and spinal cord **ganglionic** *adj*
WORD ORIGIN Greek: cystic tumour

gangplank *n naut* a portable bridge for boarding and leaving a ship

gangrene *n* decay of body tissue caused by the blood supply being interrupted by disease or injury **gangrenous** *adj*
WORD ORIGIN Greek *gangraina* an eating sore

gangsta rap *n* a style of rap music originating from US Black street culture
WORD ORIGIN phonetic rendering of GANGSTER

gangster *n* a member of an organized gang of criminals **gangsterism** *n*

gangue *n* valueless material in an ore
WORD ORIGIN German *Gang* vein of metal, course

gang up on *or* **against** *vb informal* to combine in a group against

gangway *n* **1** *Brit* an aisle between rows of seats **2** same as **gangplank 3** an opening in a ship's side to take a gangplank

gannet *n* **1** a heavily built white sea bird **2** *Brit slang* a greedy person
WORD ORIGIN Old English *ganot*

ganoid *adj* **1** (of the scales of certain fishes) consisting of an inner bony layer covered with an enamel-like substance **2** (of a fish) having such scales ▷ *n* **3** a ganoid fish
WORD ORIGIN Greek *ganos* brightness

gantry *n, pl* **-tries** a large metal framework used to support something, such as a travelling crane, or to position a rocket on its launch pad
WORD ORIGIN Latin *cantherius* supporting frame, pack ass

gaol (jayl) *n, vb Austral & Brit* same as **jail** ▷ **gaoler** *n*

gap *n* **1** a break or opening in something **2** an interruption or interval **3** a difference in ideas or viewpoint: *the generation gap* **gappy** *adj*
WORD ORIGIN Old Norse: chasm

gape *vb* **gaping, gaped 1** to stare in wonder with the mouth open **2** to open the mouth wide, as in yawning **3** to be or become wide open: *a hole gaped in the roof* **gaping** *adj*
WORD ORIGIN Old Norse *gapa*

gap year *n* a year's break between leaving school and starting further education

garage *n* **1** a building used to keep cars **2** a place where cars are repaired and petrol is sold ▷ *vb* **-aging, -aged 3** to put or keep a car in a garage
WORD ORIGIN French

garage sale *n* a sale of household items held at a person's home, usually in the garage

garb *n* **1** clothes, usually the distinctive dress of an occupation or group: *modern military garb* ▷ *vb* **2** to clothe
WORD ORIGIN Old French *garbe* graceful contour

garbage *n* **1** *US, Austral, & NZ* household waste **2** worthless rubbish or nonsense
WORD ORIGIN probably from Anglo-French

garbled *adj* (of a story, message, etc.) jumbled and confused
WORD ORIGIN Old Italian *garbellare* to strain, sift

garçon (garss-**on**) *n* a waiter
WORD ORIGIN French

garda *n, pl* **gardaí** a member of the police force of the Republic of Ireland
WORD ORIGIN Irish Gaelic: guard

garden *n* **1** an area of land usually next to a house, for growing flowers, fruit, or vegetables ▶ Related adjective: **horticultural 2** Also: **gardens** a cultivated area of land open to the public: *Kensington Gardens* **3 lead someone up the garden path** *informal* to mislead or deceive someone ▷ *vb* **4** to work in or take care of a garden **gardener** *n* **gardening** *n*
WORD ORIGIN Old French *gardin*

garden centre *n* a place where plants and gardening tools and equipment are sold

Norfolk Dialect

The Norfolk dialect is the northernmost of all the Southern dialects of England. In the west of the dialect area, just to the south of the Wash, there is a very clear dialect boundary. This coincides with the county line and the river Nene, and is the major boundary between the Southern and the Northern dialect areas of England – as soon as you cross from Norfolk into Sutton Bridge you hear people saying 'bootter, oopp, coopp' for *butter, up, cup*. A little further to the south, the western dialect boundary is less dramatic, being a boundary with other Southern dialects. However, here it does not coincide exactly with the county boundary – some people in the Norfolk Fens speak dialects more typical of Wisbech, Cambridge, and Northampton rather than Norfolk. This is because the Fens were mainly uninhabited until relatively recently, and when they were drained, people moved in from the west, south, and east. The location of the modern dialect boundary reflects the extent to which people moved in from Norfolk, crossing the Ouse and heading towards the Nene. The southern boundary, between the Norfolk and Suffolk dialect areas, is even less significant. Both counties are part of the East Anglian area and the dialects are very similar, although there are lexical differences between them: splinters are called *shivers* in Norfolk, *slivers* in Suffolk; a snail is known as a *dodman* in Norfolk, a *hodmedod* in Suffolk; and the term *left-couch* 'left-handed' is confined to Norfolk. The Norfolk and Suffolk dialect boundary coincides mostly with the county boundary, the line of the Little Ouse and the Waveney. But much of north-eastern Suffolk is basically Norfolk-speaking rather than Suffolk-speaking: Beccles, Bungay, and Lowestoft are places which look to Norwich rather than Ipswich.

Norfolk is a big county, and there are also differences within the area. Gorse is known as *whinbush* in western Norfolk but *furbush* (or *furrabush*) in the east. A mould-board on a plough is called a *plat* in northern Norfolk but a *breast* in the south. And the urban dialects of Norwich, Kings Lynn, Yarmouth, and Lowestoft all have their own distinctive characteristics.

Some Norfolk 'dialect words' are basically general English words with a distinctive local pronunciation. *Trosh'n* is not really a Norfolk dialect word but simply the English word *threshing* with a distinctive Norfolk pronunciation. So is *troshel* ('threshold'). *Blar* ('cry') is a local form of *blare,* the word *duzzy* ('foolish') is the Norfolk variant of *dizzy* (which comes from Old English *dysig* meaning 'foolish'), and *brotch* or *brawtch* ('open') is simply the local way of saying *broach*.

Some of Norfolk's local vocabulary can be traced back to the multilingual history of the region. Because of its Danish heritage, Norfolk dialect has a number of words of Scandinavian origin, such as *staithe,* meaning 'landing stage', *carr* ('a bog overgrown with brushwood'), and *marram* ('sea grass') – the modern Danish word is *marehalm,* which literally means 'sea reed'. *Dag* ('dew') is Scandinavian – the modern Norwegian word is *dogg* – and so is *dow* ('dove, pigeon'). *Grup* ('a small trench, often at the side of the road') seems to be the same word as the Norwegian *grop* meaning 'pothole'.

Words of Dutch origin stem from the massive numbers of Dutch or Flemish-speaking 'Strangers' who arrived in Norfolk as religious refugees in the sixteenth century (when one-third of the population of Norwich were foreigners). Norwich has open areas called *plains* rather than *squares; dwile* ('floorcloth') comes from the Dutch *dweil,* with the same meaning; *fye out* ('clean up') may be connected to Dutch *vegen* meaning 'to sweep'; and *push* ('boil, pimple') is probably derived from Dutch *puist.*

As far as grammar is concerned, Norfolk, like Suffolk, lacks the third-person present tense singular ending -*s*, so people say *he go, she sing,* and *he like her, do he?* And they use *that* rather than *it: That's raining.* The dialect has imperatives such as *Slow you down!* and *Shut you up!* Norfolk folk indicate the second person plural by using the form *together: Come you on, together!* And *do* is used as a conjunction meaning 'otherwise': *You better go to bed now, do you'll be tired in the morning.*

garden city *n Brit* a planned town of limited size surrounded by countryside

gardenia (gar-**deen**-ya) *n* **1** a large fragrant waxy white flower **2** the evergreen shrub on which it grows
WORD ORIGIN after Dr Alexander *Garden*, botanist

gardening leave *n chiefly Brit informal* a period during which an employee who is about to leave a company continues to receive a salary but does not work

garfish *n* **1** a freshwater fish with a long body and very long toothed jaws **2** a sea fish with similar characteristics

gargantuan *adj* huge or enormous
WORD ORIGIN after *Gargantua*, a giant in Rabelais' *Gargantua and Pantagruel*

USAGE
Some people think that *gargantuan* should only be used to describe things connected with food: *a gargantuan meal; his gargantuan appetite.*

gargle *vb* **-gling, -gled 1** to rinse the mouth and throat with (a liquid) by slowly breathing out through the liquid ▷ *n* **2** the liquid used for gargling **3** the act or sound of gargling
WORD ORIGIN Old French *gargouille* throat

gargoyle *n* (on ancient buildings) a waterspout below the roof, carved in the form of a grotesque face or figure
WORD ORIGIN Old French *gargouille* gargoyle, throat

garish *adj* crudely bright or colourful **garishly** *adv* **garishness** *n*
WORD ORIGIN obsolete *gaure* to stare

garland *n* **1** a wreath of flowers and leaves worn round the head or neck or hung up ▷ *vb* **2** to decorate with a garland or garlands
WORD ORIGIN Old French *garlande*

garlic *n* the bulb of a plant of the onion family, with a strong taste and smell, made up of small segments which are used in cooking **garlicky** *adj*
WORD ORIGIN Old English *gārlēac*

garment *n* an article of clothing
WORD ORIGIN Old French *garniment*

garner *vb* to collect or gather: *the financial rewards garnered by his book*
WORD ORIGIN Latin *granum* grain

garnet *n* a red semiprecious gemstone
WORD ORIGIN Old French *grenat* red, from *pome grenate* pomegranate

garnish *vb* **1** to decorate (food) with something to add to its appearance or flavour ▷ *n* **2** a decoration for food
WORD ORIGIN Old French *garnir* to adorn, equip

garret *n* an attic in a house
WORD ORIGIN Old French *garite* watchtower

garrison *n* **1** soldiers who guard a base or fort **2** the place itself ▷ *vb* **3** to station (soldiers) in (a fort or base)
WORD ORIGIN Old French *garir* to defend

garrotte *or* **garotte** *n* **1** a Spanish method of execution by strangling **2** a cord, wire, or iron collar, used to strangle someone ▷ *vb* **-rotting, -rotted 3** to execute with a garrotte
WORD ORIGIN Spanish *garrote*

garrulous *adj* constantly chattering; talkative **garrulousness** *n*

WORD ORIGIN Latin *garrire* to chatter

garter *n* **1** a band, usually of elastic, worn round the leg to hold up a sock or stocking **2** *US & Canad* a suspender
WORD ORIGIN Old French *gartier*

Garter *n* **the Order of the Garter** the highest order of British knighthood

garter stitch *n* knitting in which all the rows are knitted in plain stitch

gas *n, pl* **gases** *or* **gasses 1** an airlike substance that is neither liquid nor solid at room temperature and atmospheric pressure **2** a fossil fuel in the form of a gas, used as a source of heat **3** an anaesthetic in the form of a gas **4** *mining* firedamp or the explosive mixture of firedamp and air **5** *US, Canad, Austral, NZ* petrol **6** a poisonous gas used in war **7** *informal* idle talk or boasting **8** *slang* an entertaining person or thing: *Monterey was a gas for musicians and fans alike* **9** *US informal* gas generated in the alimentary canal ▷ *vb* **gases** *or* **gasses, gassing, gassed 10** to subject to gas fumes so as to make unconscious or to suffocate **11** *informal* to talk a lot; chatter
WORD ORIGIN coined from Greek *khaos* atmosphere

gasbag *n informal* a person who talks too much

gas chamber *n* an airtight room which is filled with poison gas to kill people

gaseous *adj* of or like a gas

gash *n* **1** a long deep cut ▷ *vb* **2** to make a long deep cut in
WORD ORIGIN Old French *garser* to scratch, wound

gasholder *n* a large tank for storing gas before distributing it to users

gasify *vb* **-fies, -fying, -fied** to change into a gas **gasification** *n*

gasket *n* a piece of paper, rubber, or metal sandwiched between the faces of a metal joint to provide a seal
WORD ORIGIN probably from French *garcette* rope's end

gaslight *n* **1** a lamp in which light is produced by burning gas **2** the light produced by such a lamp

gasman *n, pl* **-men** a man employed to read household gas meters and install or repair gas fittings, etc.

gas mask *n* a mask fitted with a chemical filter to protect the wearer from breathing in harmful gases

gas meter *n* a device for measuring and recording the amount of gas passed through it

gasoline *or* **gasolene** *n US & Canad* petrol

gasometer (gas-**som**-it-er) *n* same as **gasholder**

gasp *vb* **1** to draw in the breath sharply or with difficulty **2** to utter breathlessly ▷ *n* **3** a short convulsive intake of breath
WORD ORIGIN Old Norse *geispa* to yawn

gas ring *n* a circular metal pipe with several holes in it fed with gas for cooking

gassy *adj* **-sier, -siest** filled with, containing, or like gas **gassiness** *n*

gastric *adj* of the stomach

gastric juice *n* a digestive fluid secreted by the stomach

gastric ulcer *n* an ulcer on the lining of the stomach

gastritis *n* inflammation of the lining of the stomach, causing vomiting or gastric ulcers

gastroenteritis *n* inflammation of the stomach and intestine, causing vomiting and diarrhoea

gastronomy *n* the art of good eating **gastronomic** *adj*
WORD ORIGIN Greek *gastēr* stomach + *nomos* law

gastropod *n* a mollusc, such as a snail or whelk, that has a single flat muscular foot, eyes on stalks, and usually a spiral shell
WORD ORIGIN Greek *gastēr* stomach + *-podos* -footed

gasworks *n* a factory in which coal gas is made

gate *n* **1** a movable barrier, usually hinged, for closing an opening in a wall or fence **2 a** the number of people admitted to a sporting event or entertainment **b** the total entrance money received from them **3** an exit at an airport by which passengers get to an aircraft **4** *electronics* a circuit with one or more input terminals and one output terminal, the output being determined by the combination of input signals **5** a slotted metal frame that controls the positions of the gear lever in a motor vehicle
WORD ORIGIN Old English *geat*

gateau (**gat**-toe) *n, pl* **-teaux** (-toes) a large rich layered cake
WORD ORIGIN French

gate-crash *vb informal* to gain entry to (a party) without invitation **gate-crasher** *n*

gatehouse *n* a building at or above a gateway

gate-leg table *or* **gate-legged table** *n* a table with leaves supported by hinged legs that can swing back to let the leaves hang from the frame

gateway *n* **1** an entrance that may be closed by a gate **2** a means of entry or access: *his only gateway to the outside world* **3** *computers* hardware and software that connect incompatible computer networks, allowing them to communicate

gather *vb* **1** to come or bring together **2** to increase gradually in (pace, speed, or momentum) **3** to prepare oneself for a task or challenge by collecting one's thoughts, strength, or courage **4** to learn from information given; conclude: *this is pretty important, I gather* **5** to draw (fabric) into small folds or tucks **6** to pick or harvest (crops) ▷ *n* **7 gathers** small folds or tucks in fabric
WORD ORIGIN Old English *gadrian*

gathering *n* a group of people, usually meeting for some particular purpose: *the Braemar Highland Gathering*

GATT General Agreement on Tariffs and Trade: a former name for the World Trade Organization

gauche (**gohsh**) *adj* socially awkward
WORD ORIGIN French

gaucho (gow-choh) *n, pl* **-chos** a cowboy of the South American pampas
WORD ORIGIN American Spanish

gaudy *adj* **gaudier, gaudiest** vulgarly bright or colourful **gaudily** *adv* **gaudiness** *n*
WORD ORIGIN from *gaud* trinket

gauge (gayj) *vb* **gauging, gauged 1** to estimate or judge (people's feelings or reactions) **2** to measure using a gauge ▷ *n* **3** an instrument for measuring quantities: *a petrol gauge* **4** a scale or standard of measurement **5** a standard for estimating people's feelings or reactions: *a gauge of public opinion* **6** the diameter of the barrel of a gun **7** the distance between the rails of a railway track
WORD ORIGIN from Old French

Gaul *n* a native of ancient Gaul

gaunt *adj* **1** bony and emaciated in appearance **2** (of a place) bleak or desolate: *the gaunt disused flour mill* **gauntness** *n*
WORD ORIGIN origin unknown

gauntlet[1] *n* **1** a long heavy protective glove **2** a medieval armoured glove **3 take up the gauntlet** to accept a challenge
WORD ORIGIN Old French *gantelet*

gauntlet[2] *n* **run the gauntlet** to be exposed to criticism or harsh treatment
WORD ORIGIN Swedish *gatlopp* passageway

gauss (rhymes with **mouse**) *n, pl* **gauss** the cgs unit of magnetic flux density
WORD ORIGIN after K. F. *Gauss*, mathematician

Gauteng *n* a province of N South Africa

gauze *n* a transparent, loosely woven cloth, often used for surgical dressings **gauzy** *adj*
WORD ORIGIN French *gaze*

gave *vb* the past tense of **give**

gavel (gav-vl) *n* a small hammer used by a judge, auctioneer, or chairman to call for order or attention
WORD ORIGIN origin unknown

gavotte *n* **1** an old formal dance in quadruple time **2** music for this dance
WORD ORIGIN French

gawk *vb* **1** to stare stupidly ▷ *n* **2** a clumsy stupid person
WORD ORIGIN Old Danish *gaukr*

gawky *adj* **gawkier, gawkiest** clumsy and awkward

gawp *vb slang* to stare stupidly **gawper** *n*
WORD ORIGIN Middle English *galpen*

gay *adj* **1** homosexual **2** carefree and merry: *with gay abandon* **3** bright and cheerful: *smartly dressed in gay colours* ▷ *n* **4** a homosexual, esp. a homosexual man: *solidarity amongst lesbians and gays*
WORD ORIGIN Old French *gai*

≡ USAGE
≡ *Gayness* is the state of being
≡ homosexual. The noun which refers
≡ to the state of being carefree and
≡ merry is *gaiety*.

gaydar *n informal* the supposed ability of a homosexual person to determine whether or not another person is homosexual

gayness *n* homosexuality

gaze *vb* **gazing, gazed 1** to look long and steadily at someone or something ▷ *n* **2** a long steady look
WORD ORIGIN Swedish dialect *gasa* to gape at

gazebo (gaz-zee-boh) *n, pl* **-bos** a summerhouse or pavilion with a good view
WORD ORIGIN perhaps a pseudo-Latin coinage based on *gaze*

gazelle *n* a small graceful fawn-coloured antelope of Africa and Asia
WORD ORIGIN Arabic *ghazāl*

gazette *n* an official newspaper that gives lists of announcements, for instance in legal or military affairs
WORD ORIGIN French

gazetteer *n* a book or section of a book that lists and describes places

gazump *vb Austral & Brit informal* to raise the price of a house after agreeing a price verbally with an intending buyer
WORD ORIGIN origin unknown

gazunder *vb Brit informal* to reduce an offer on a house immediately before exchanging contracts, having earlier agreed a higher price with (the seller) **gazunderer** *n*

GB 1 Great Britain **2** Also: **Gb** gigabyte

GBH (in Britain and South Africa) grievous bodily harm

GC George Cross (a British award for bravery)

GCE 1 (formerly in Britain) General Certificate of Education **2** *informal* a pass in a GCE examination

GCSE 1 (in Britain) General Certificate of Secondary Education; an examination in specified subjects which replaced the GCE O level and CSE **2** *informal* a pass in a GCSE examination

Gd *chem* gadolinium

g'day *interj Austral & NZ informal* same as **good day**

GDP gross domestic product

Ge *chem* germanium

gear *n* **1** a set of toothed wheels that engages with another or with a rack in order to change the speed or direction of transmitted motion **2** a mechanism for transmitting motion by gears **3** the setting of a gear to suit engine speed or direction: *a higher gear; reverse gear* **4** clothing or personal belongings **5** equipment for a particular task: *police in riot gear* **6 in** or **out of gear** with the gear mechanism engaged or disengaged ▷ *vb* **7** to prepare or organize for something: *to gear for war* ▶ See also **gear up**
WORD ORIGIN Old Norse *gervi*

gearbox *n* the metal casing enclosing a set of gears in a motor vehicle

gearing *n* a system of gears designed to transmit motion

gear lever or *US & Canad* **gearshift** *n* a lever used to engage or change gears in a motor vehicle

gear up *vb* to prepare for an activity: *to gear up for a massive relief operation*

gearwheel *n* one of the toothed wheels in the gears of a motor vehicle

gecko *n, pl* **geckos** a small tropical lizard
WORD ORIGIN Malay *ge'kok*

gee *interj US & Canad informal* a mild exclamation of surprise, admiration, etc. Also: **gee whizz**
WORD ORIGIN euphemism for *Jesus*

geebung (gee-bung) *n* **1** an Australian tree or shrub with an edible but tasteless fruit **2** the fruit of this tree

geek *n informal* a boring and unattractive person **geeky** *adj*
WORD ORIGIN perhaps from Scottish *geck* fool

geelbek (heel-bek) *n S African* an edible marine fish with yellow jaws
WORD ORIGIN Afrikaans *geel* yellow + *bek* mouth

geese *n* the plural of **goose**[1]

geezer *n Brit, Austral, & NZ informal* a man
WORD ORIGIN probably dialect pronunciation of *guiser*, a mummer

Geiger counter (guy-ger) or **Geiger-Müller counter** *n* an instrument for detecting and measuring radiation
WORD ORIGIN after Hans *Geiger*, physicist

geisha (gay-sha) *n* a professional female companion for men in Japan, trained in music, dancing, and conversation
WORD ORIGIN Japanese

gel (jell) *n* **1** a thick jelly-like substance, esp. one used to keep a hairstyle in shape ▷ *vb* **gelling, gelled 2** to become a gel **3** same as **jell 4** to apply gel to (one's hair)
WORD ORIGIN from *gelatine*

gelatine (jell-a-teen) or **gelatin** *n* a clear water-soluble protein made by boiling animal hides and bones, used in cooking, photography, etc.
WORD ORIGIN Latin *gelare* to freeze

gelatinous (jill-at-in-uss) *adj* with a thick, semi-liquid consistency

geld *vb* **gelding, gelded** or **gelt** to castrate (a horse or other animal)
WORD ORIGIN Old Norse *gelda*

gelding *n* a castrated male horse
WORD ORIGIN Old Norse *geldingr*

gelignite *n* a type of dynamite used for blasting
WORD ORIGIN GELATINE + Latin *ignis* fire

gem *n* **1** a precious stone used for decoration ▶ Related adjective: **lapidary 2** a person or thing regarded as precious or special: *a perfect gem of a hotel*
WORD ORIGIN Latin *gemma* bud, precious stone

gemfish *n* an Australian food fish with a delicate flavour

Gemini *n astrol* the third sign of the zodiac; the Twins
WORD ORIGIN Latin

gemsbok (hemss-bok) *n S African* same as **oryx**
WORD ORIGIN Afrikaans

gemstone *n* a precious or semiprecious stone, esp. one which has been cut and polished

gen *n Brit, Austral, & NZ informal* information: *I want to get as much gen as I can about the American market* ▶ See also **gen up on**
WORD ORIGIN from *gen(eral information)*

Gen. General

gendarme (zhahn-darm) *n* a member of the French police force
WORD ORIGIN French

gender *n* **1** the state of being male, female, or neuter **2** the classification of nouns in certain languages as masculine, feminine, or neuter
WORD ORIGIN Latin *genus* kind

gene (jean) *n* a unit composed of DNA forming part of a chromosome, by which inherited characteristics are transmitted from parent to offspring
WORD ORIGIN German *Gen*

genealogy (jean-ee-al-a-jee) *n* **1** the direct descent of an individual or group from an ancestor **2** *pl* **-gies** a chart showing the descent of an individual or group **genealogical** *adj* **genealogist** *n*
WORD ORIGIN Greek *genea* race

genera (jen-er-a) *n* a plural of **genus**

general *adj* **1** common or widespread: *general goodwill* **2** of, affecting, or including all or most of the members of a group **3** not specialized or specializing: *a general hospital* **4** including various or miscellaneous items: *general knowledge* **5** not definite; vague: *the examples used will give a general idea* **6** highest in authority or rank: *the club's general manager* ▷ *n* **7** a very senior military officer **8 in general** generally; mostly or usually
WORD ORIGIN Latin *generalis*

general anaesthetic *n* a substance that causes general anaesthesia. See **anaesthesia**

general election *n* an election in which representatives are chosen in all constituencies of a state

generalissimo *n, pl* **-mos** a supreme commander of combined armed forces
WORD ORIGIN Italian

generality *n* **1** *pl* **-ties** a general principle or observation: *speaking in generalities* **2** *old-fashioned* the majority: *the generality of mankind*

generalization *or* **-lisation** *n* a principle or statement based on specific instances but applied generally: *the argument sinks to generalizations and name-calling*

generalize *or* **-lise** *vb* **-lizing, -lized** *or* **-lising, -lised** **1** to form general principles or conclusions from specific instances **2** to speak in generalities **3** to make widely used or known: *generalized violence*

generally *adv* **1** usually; as a rule: *these protests have generally been peaceful* **2** commonly or widely: *it's generally agreed he has performed well* **3** not specifically; broadly: *what are your thoughts generally about the war?*

general practitioner *n* a doctor who does not specialize but has a general medical practice in which he or she treats all illnesses

general-purpose *adj* having a variety of uses: *general-purpose cooking oil*

general staff *n* officers who assist commanders in the planning and execution of military operations

general strike *n* a strike by all or most of the workers of a country

generate *vb* **-rating, -rated** to produce or create
WORD ORIGIN Latin *generare* to beget

generation *n* **1** all the people of approximately the same age: *the younger generation* **2** a successive stage in descent of people or animals: *passed on from generation to generation* **3** the average time between two generations of a species, about 35 years for humans: *an alliance which has lasted a generation* **4** a specified stage of development: *the next generation of fighter aircraft* **5** production, esp. of electricity or heat

generation gap *n* the difference in outlook and the lack of understanding between people of different generations

generation X *n* people born between the mid-1960s and mid-1970s who are highly educated and underemployed
WORD ORIGIN from the novel *Generation X: Tales for an Accelerated Culture* by Douglas Coupland

generative *adj* capable of producing or originating something

generator *n* a device for converting mechanical energy into electrical energy

generic (jin-ner-ik) *adj* of a whole class, or group, or genus **generically** *adv*
WORD ORIGIN Latin *genus* kind, race

generous *adj* **1** ready to give freely; unselfish **2** free from pettiness in character and mind **3** large or plentiful: *a generous donation* **generously** *adv* **generosity** *n*
WORD ORIGIN Latin *generosus* nobly born

genesis (jen-iss-iss) *n, pl* **-ses** (-seez) the beginning or origin of anything
WORD ORIGIN Greek

Genesis *n Bible* the first book of the Old Testament, containing a description of the creation of the world

gene therapy *n genetics* the replacement or alteration of defective genes in order to prevent the occurrence of inherited diseases

genetic (jin-net-tik) *adj* of genetics, genes, or the origin of something **genetically** *adv*
WORD ORIGIN from *genesis*

genetically modified *adj* (of an organism) having DNA which has been altered for the purpose of improvement or correction of defects

genetic code *n biochem* the order in which the four nucleic acid bases of DNA are arranged in the molecule for transmitting genetic information to the cells

genetic engineering *n* alteration of the genetic structure of an organism in order to produce more desirable traits

genetic fingerprinting *n* the use of a person's unique pattern of DNA, which can be obtained from blood, saliva, or tissue, as a means of identification **genetic fingerprint** *n*

genetics *n* the study of heredity and variation in organisms **geneticist** *n*

genial (jean-ee-al) *adj* cheerful, easy-going, and friendly **geniality** *n* **genially** *adv*
WORD ORIGIN Latin *genius* guardian deity

genie (jean-ee) *n* (in fairy tales) a servant who appears by magic and fulfils a person's wishes
WORD ORIGIN Arabic *jinni* demon

Genie *n Canad* an award given by the Academy of Canadian Cinema and Television in recognition of Canadian cinematic achievements

genital *adj* of the sexual organs or reproduction
WORD ORIGIN Latin *genitalis* concerning birth

genitals *or* **genitalia** (jen-it-ail-ya) *pl n* the external sexual organs

genitive *n grammar* a grammatical case in some languages used to indicate a relation of ownership or association
WORD ORIGIN Latin *genetivus* relating to birth

genius (jean-yuss) *n, pl* **-uses** **1** a person with exceptional ability in a particular subject or activity **2** such ability **3** a person considered as exerting influence of a certain sort: *the evil genius behind the drug-smuggling empire*
WORD ORIGIN Latin

genocide (jen-no-side) *n* the deliberate killing of a people or nation **genocidal** *adj*
WORD ORIGIN Greek *genos* race + Latin *caedere* to kill

genome *n* **1** the full complement of genetic material within an organism **2** all the genes comprising a haploid set of chromosomes
WORD ORIGIN from GENE + CHROMOSOME

genomics *n* the branch of molecular genetics concerned with the study of genomes

genotoxic *adj* harmful to genetic material

genre (zhahn-ra) *n* **1** a kind or type of literary, musical, or artistic work: *the mystery and supernatural genres* **2** a kind of painting depicting incidents from everyday life
WORD ORIGIN French

gent *n Brit, Austral, & NZ informal* short for **gentleman**

genteel *adj* **1** overly concerned with being polite **2** respectable, polite, and well-bred **genteelly** *adv*
WORD ORIGIN French *gentil* well-born

gentian (jen-shun) *n* a mountain plant with blue or purple flowers
WORD ORIGIN Latin *gentiana*

gentian violet *n* a violet-coloured solution used as an antiseptic and in the treatment of burns

Gentile *n* **1** a person who is not a Jew ▷ *adj* **2** not Jewish
WORD ORIGIN Latin *gentilis* belonging to the same tribe

gentility *n, pl* **-ties** **1** noble birth or ancestry **2** respectability and good manners
WORD ORIGIN Old French *gentilite*

gentle *adj* **1** kind and calm in character **2** temperate or moderate: *gentle autumn rain* **3** soft; not sharp or harsh: *gentle curves* **gentleness** *n* **gently** *adv*
WORD ORIGIN Latin *gentilis* belonging to the same family

Words from Literature
part 12

gladsome *adj* gladsome is an old word meaning glad or happy
> Nobody ever stopped him in the street to say, with gladsome looks
> *A Christmas Carol* Charles Dickens

glen *n* a small valley; the word is used commonly in Scotland
> a beck which follows the bend of the glen
> *Wuthering Heights* Emily Brontë

gravel *v* an old term which means to baffle or defeat someone
> gravelled the pastors of the German Church
> *Doctor Faustus* 1.1 Christopher Marlowe

grinder *n* a grinder was a private tutor
> but that when he had had the happiness of marrying Mrs Pocket very early in his life, he had impaired his prospects and taken up the calling of a Grinder
> *Great Expectations* Charles Dickens

gruel *n* a thin, watery cornmeal or oatmeal soup
> and the little saucepan of gruel (Scrooge had a cold in his head) upon the hob.
> *A Christmas Carol* Charles Dickens

guinea, half a *n* ten shillings and sixpence
> but lay out half a guinea at Ford's
> *Emma* Jane Austen

gull *v* an old term which means to fool or deceive someone
> Hush, I'll gull him supernaturally
> *Doctor Faustus* 3.4 Christopher Marlowe

gunnel *n* the gunnel, gunwale or gunwhale, is the upper edge of a boat's side
> But he put his foot on the gunnel and rocked her
> *The Adventures of Huckleberry Finn* Mark Twain

Gytrash *n* an omen of misfortune to the superstitious, usually taking the form of a hound
> I remembered certain of Bessie's tales, wherein figured a North-of-England spirit, called a 'Gytrash'
> *Jane Eyre* Charlotte Brontë

hackney-cabriolet *n* a two-wheeled carriage with four seats for hire and pulled by a horse
> A hackney-cabriolet was in waiting; with the same vehemence which she had exhibited in addressing Oliver, the girl pulled him in with her, and drew the curtains close.
> *Oliver Twist* Charles Dickens

hackney-coach *n* a four-wheeled horse-drawn vehicle for hire
> The twilight was beginning to close in, when Mr. Brownlow alighted from a hackney-coach at his own door, and knocked softly.
> *Oliver Twist* Charles Dickens

haggler *n* someone who travels from place to place selling small goods and items
> when I be plain Jack Durbeyfield, the haggler
> *Tess of the D'Urbervilles* Thomas Hardy

halter *n* a rope or strap used to lead an animal or to tie it up
> I had of course long been used to a halter and a headstall
> *Black Beauty* Anna Sewell

hamlet *n* a small village or a group of houses in the countryside
> down from the hamlet
> *Treasure Island* Robert Louis Stevenson

hand-barrow *n* a device for carrying heavy objects. It is like a wheelbarrow except that it has handles, rather than wheels, for moving the barrow
> his sea chest following behind him in a hand-barrow
> *Treasure Island* Robert Louis Stevenson

handspike *n* a stick which was used as a lever
> a bit of stick like a handspike
> *Treasure Island* Robert Louis Stevenson

haply *adv* by chance; perhaps
> And haply the Queen-Moon is on her throne
> *Ode to a Nightingale* John Keats

gentlefolk *pl n old-fashioned* people regarded as being of good breeding

gentleman *n, pl* **-men 1** a cultured, courteous, and well-bred man **2** a man who comes from a family of high social position **3** a polite name for a man **gentlemanly** *adj*

gentrification *n* a process by which the character of a traditionally working-class area is made fashionable by middle-class people **gentrify** *vb*

gentry *n Brit, old-fashioned* people just below the nobility in social rank **WORD ORIGIN** Old French *genterie*

gents *n Austral & Brit informal* a men's public toilet

genuflect *vb* to bend the knee as a sign of reverence or deference, esp. in church **genuflection** *n*
WORD ORIGIN Latin *genu* knee + *flectere* to bend

genuine *adj* **1** real and exactly what it appears to be: *a genuine antique* **2** sincerely felt: *genuine concern* **3** (of a person) honest and without pretence **genuinely** *adv* **genuineness** *n*
WORD ORIGIN Latin *genuinus* inborn

gen up on *vb* **genning, genned** *Austral & Brit informal* to become, or make someone else, fully informed about

genus (**jean**-uss) *n, pl* **genera** *or* **genuses 1** *biol* one of the groups into which a family is divided, containing one or more species **2** a class or group
WORD ORIGIN Latin: race

geocentric *adj* **1** having the earth as a centre **2** measured as from the centre of the earth

geodesic *adj* **1** relating to the geometry of curved surfaces ▷ *n* **2** the shortest line between two points on a curved surface

geodesy *n* the study of the shape and size of the earth
WORD ORIGIN Greek *gē* earth + *daiein* to divide

geography *n* **1** the study of the earth's surface, including physical features, climate, and population **2** the physical features of a region **geographer** *n* **geographical** *or* **geographic** *adj* **geographically** *adv*
WORD ORIGIN Greek *gē* earth + -GRAPHY

geology *n* **1** the study of the origin, structure, and composition of the earth **2** the geological features of an area **geologist** *n* **geological** *adj* **geologically** *adv*
WORD ORIGIN Greek *gē* earth + -LOGY

geometric *or* **geometrical** *adj* **1** of geometry **2** consisting of shapes used in geometry, such as circles, triangles, and straight lines: *geometric design* **geometrically** *adv*

geometric progression *n* a sequence of numbers, each of which differs from the succeeding one by a constant ratio, for example 1, 2, 4, 8

geometry *n* the branch of mathematics concerned with points, lines, curves, and surfaces **geometrician** *n*
WORD ORIGIN Greek *geōmetrein* to measure the land

geophysics *n* the study of the earth's physical properties and the physical forces which affect it **geophysical** *adj* **geophysicist** *n*

Geordie *Brit n* **1** a person from Tyneside **2** the Tyneside dialect ▷ *adj* **3** of Tyneside: *a Geordie accent*

George Cross *n* a British award for bravery, usually awarded to civilians

georgette (jor-**jet**) *n* a thin crepe dress material
WORD ORIGIN after Mme *Georgette*, a French dressmaker

Georgian *adj* **1** of or in the reigns of any of the kings of Great Britain and Ireland called George **2** denoting a style of architecture or furniture prevalent in Britain in the 18th century: *an elegant Georgian terrace in Edinburgh*

geospatial *adj* of or relating to the relative position of things on the earth's surface

geostationary *adj* (of a satellite) orbiting so as to remain over the same point on the earth's surface

geotechnical *adj* relating to the application of technology to engineering problems caused by geological factors

geothermal *adj* of or using the heat in the earth's interior

geranium *n* a cultivated plant with scarlet, pink, or white flowers
WORD ORIGIN Latin: cranesbill

gerbil (**jur**-bill) *n* a small rodent with long back legs, often kept as a pet
WORD ORIGIN French *gerbille*

geriatric *adj* **1** of geriatrics or old people ▷ *n* **2** an old person, esp. as a patient

geriatrics *n* the branch of medicine concerned with illnesses affecting old people

germ *n* **1** a tiny living thing, esp. one that causes disease: *a diphtheria germ* **2** the beginning from which something may develop: *the germ of a book*
WORD ORIGIN Latin *germen* sprout, seed

German *adj* **1** of Germany ▷ *n* **2** a person from Germany **3** the official language of Germany, Austria, and parts of Switzerland

germane *adj* relevant: *the studies provided some evidence germane to these questions*
WORD ORIGIN Latin *germanus* of the same race

Germanic *n* **1** the ancient language from which English, German, and the Scandinavian languages developed ▷ *adj* **2** of this ancient language or the languages that developed from it **3** characteristic of German people or things: *Germanic-looking individuals*

germanium *n chem* a brittle grey metalloid element that is a semiconductor and is used in transistors. Symbol: Ge
WORD ORIGIN after *Germany*

German measles *n* same as **rubella**

German shepherd dog *n* same as **Alsatian**

germ cell *n* a sexual reproductive cell

germicide *n* a substance used to destroy germs
WORD ORIGIN *germ* + Latin *caedere* to kill

germinal *adj* **1** of or in the earliest stage of development: *the germinal phases of the case* **2** of germ cells

germinate *vb* **-nating, -nated** to grow or cause to grow **germination** *n*
WORD ORIGIN Latin *germinare* to sprout

germ warfare *n* the military use of disease-spreading bacteria against an enemy

gerontology *n* the scientific study of ageing and the problems of old people **gerontologist** *n*
WORD ORIGIN Greek *gerōn* old man + -LOGY

gerrymandering *n* the practice of dividing the constituencies of a voting area so as to give one party an unfair advantage
WORD ORIGIN from Elbridge *Gerry*, US politician + (sala)*mander*, from the salamander-like outline of a reshaped electoral district

gerund (**jer**-rund) *n* a noun formed from a verb, ending in -*ing*, denoting an action or state, for example *running*
WORD ORIGIN Latin *gerundum* something to be carried on

gesso (**jess**-oh) *n* plaster used for painting or in sculpture
WORD ORIGIN Italian: chalk

Gestapo *n* the secret state police of Nazi Germany
WORD ORIGIN German *Ge(heime) Sta(ats) po(lizei)* secret state police

gestation *n* **1** the process of carrying and developing babies in the womb during pregnancy, or the time during which this process takes place **2** the process of developing a plan or idea in the mind
WORD ORIGIN Latin *gestare* to bear

gesticulate *vb* **-lating, -lated** to make expressive movements with the hands and arms, usually while talking **gesticulation** *n*
WORD ORIGIN Latin *gesticulari*

gesture *n* **1** a movement of the hands, head, or body to express or emphasize an idea or emotion **2** something said or done to indicate intention, or as a formality: *a gesture of goodwill* ▷ *vb* **-turing, -tured 3** to make expressive movements with the hands and arms
WORD ORIGIN Latin *gestus*

get *vb* **getting, got 1** to come into possession of **2** to bring or fetch **3** to catch (an illness) **4** to become: *they get frustrated and angry* **5** to cause to be done or to happen: *he got a wart removed; to get steamed up* **6** to hear or understand: *did you get that joke?* **7** to reach (a place or point): *we could not get to the airport in time* **8** to catch (a bus or train) **9** to persuade: *she was trying to get him to give secrets away* **10** *informal* to annoy: *you know what really gets me?* **11** *informal* to baffle: *now you've got me* **12** *informal* to hit: *a bit of grenade got me on the left hip* **13** *informal* to be revenged on **14** *informal* to start: *we got talking about it; it got me thinking* ▷ *n* **15** *Brit slang* same as **git** ▶ See also **get about, get across**, etc.
WORD ORIGIN Old English *gietan*

get about *or* **around** *vb* **1** to be socially active **2** (of news or a rumour) to circulate

get across *vb* to make (something) understood

get at vb **1** to gain access to: *to get at the information on these disks* **2** to imply or mean: *it is hard to see quite what he is getting at* **3** to annoy or criticize persistently: *people who know they're being got at*

get away vb **1** to escape or leave **2** get away with to do (something wrong) without being caught or punished ▷ *interj* **3** an exclamation of disbelief ▷ *n* **getaway 4** the act of escaping, usually by criminals ▷ *adj* **getaway 5** used to escape: *the getaway car was abandoned*

get back vb **1** to have (something) returned to one **2** to return to a former state or activity: *get back to normal* **3** get back at to retaliate against **4** get one's own back *informal* to get one's revenge

get by vb *informal* to manage in spite of difficulties: *he saw for himself what people did to get by*

get in vb **1** to arrive **2** to be elected **3** get in on to join in (an activity)

get off vb **1** to leave (a bus, train, etc.) **2** to escape the consequences of or punishment for an action: *the real culprits have got off scot-free* **3** get off with *Austral & Brit informal* to begin a romantic or sexual relationship with

get on vb **1** to enter (a bus, train, etc.) **2** to have a friendly relationship: *he had a flair for getting on with people* **3** to grow old: *he was getting on in years* **4** (of time) to elapse: *the time was getting on* **5** to make progress: *how are the children getting on?* **6** get on with to continue to do: *you can get on with whatever you were doing before* **7** getting on for approaching (a time, age, or amount): *getting on for half a century ago*

get out vb **1** to leave or escape **2** to become known **3** to gain something of significance or value: *that's all I got out of it* **4** get out of to avoid: *to get out of doing the dishes*

get over vb **1** to recover from (an illness or unhappy experience) **2** to overcome (a problem) **3** get over with to bring (something necessary but unpleasant) to an end: *better to get it over with*

get round vb **1** to overcome (a problem or difficulty) **2** (of news or a rumour) to circulate **3** *informal* to gain the indulgence of (someone) by praise or flattery: *a child who learned to get round everybody and have her own way* **4** get round to to come to (a task) eventually: *I will get round to paying the bill*

get through vb **1** to complete (a task or process) **2** to use up (money or supplies) **3** to succeed in (an examination or test) **4** get through to **a** to succeed in making (someone) understand **b** to contact (someone) by telephone

get-together n **1** *informal* a small informal social gathering ▷ *vb* **get together 2** to meet socially or in order to have a discussion

get up vb **1** to get out of bed **2** get up to *informal* to be involved in: *I don't know what those guys got up to down there* ▷ *n* **get-up 3** *informal* a costume or outfit

get-up-and-go n *informal* energy or drive

geyser (geez-er) n **1** a spring that discharges steam and hot water **2** *Brit & S African* a domestic gas water heater

WORD ORIGIN Icelandic *Geysir*

ghastly adj **-lier, -liest 1** *informal* very unpleasant **2** deathly pale **3** horrible: *a ghastly accident*
WORD ORIGIN Old English *gāstlīc* spiritual

ghat n **1** (in India) stairs leading down to a river **2** (in India) a place of cremation **3** (in India) a mountain pass
WORD ORIGIN Hindi

GHB gamma hydroxybutyrate: a substance with anaesthetic properties, used medically as a sedative and also as a recreational drug

ghee (gee) n clarified butter, used in Indian cookery
WORD ORIGIN Hindi *ghī*

gherkin n a small pickled cucumber
WORD ORIGIN Dutch *agurkkijn*

ghetto n, pl **-tos** or **-toes** an area that is inhabited by people of a particular race, religion, nationality, or class
WORD ORIGIN Italian

ghetto blaster n *informal* a large portable CD player or cassette recorder with built-in speakers

ghettoize or **-ise** vb **-izing, -ized** or **-ising, -ised** to confine (someone or something) to a particular area or category: *to ghettoize women as housewives* **ghettoization** or **-isation** n

ghillie n same as **gillie**

ghost n **1** the disembodied spirit of a dead person, supposed to haunt the living **2** a faint trace: *the ghost of a smile on his face* **3** a faint secondary image in an optical instrument or on a television screen ▷ *vb* **4** short for **ghostwrite**
WORD ORIGIN Old English *gāst*

ghost gum n *Austral* a eucalyptus with a white trunk and branches

ghostly adj **-lier, -liest** frightening in appearance or effect: *ghostly noises*

ghost town n a town that used to be busy but is now deserted

ghostwrite vb **-writing, -wrote, -written** to write (an article or book) on behalf of a person who is then credited as author **ghostwriter** n

ghoul (gool) n **1** a person who is interested in morbid or disgusting things **2** a demon that eats corpses **ghoulish** adj **ghoulishly** adv
WORD ORIGIN Arabic *ghūl*

GHQ *mil* General Headquarters

GI[1] n, pl **GIs** or **GI's** *US informal* a soldier in the US Army
WORD ORIGIN abbreviation of *government issue*

GI[2] see **glycaemic index**

giant n **1** a mythical figure of superhuman size and strength **2** a person or thing of exceptional size, ability, or importance: *industrial giants* ▷ *adj* **3** remarkably large **4** (of an atom or ion or its structure) having large numbers of particles present in a crystal lattice, with each particle exerting a strong force of attraction on those near to it
WORD ORIGIN Greek *gigas*

giant panda n see **panda**

gibber[1] (jib-ber) vb to talk in a fast and unintelligible manner

WORD ORIGIN imitative

gibber[2] (gib-ber) n *Austral* **1** a boulder **2** barren land covered with stones
WORD ORIGIN Aboriginal

gibberish n rapid incomprehensible talk; nonsense

gibbet (jib-bit) n a gallows
WORD ORIGIN Old French *gibet*

gibbon (gib-bon) n a small agile ape of the forests of S Asia
WORD ORIGIN French

gibbous (gib-bus) adj (of the moon) more than half but less than fully illuminated
WORD ORIGIN Latin *gibba* hump

gibe (jibe) n, vb **gibing, gibed** same as **jibe**[1]
WORD ORIGIN perhaps from Old French *giber* to treat roughly

giblets (jib-lits) pl n the gizzard, liver, heart, and neck of a fowl
WORD ORIGIN Old French *gibelet* stew of game birds

gidday, g'day interj *Austral & NZ* an expression of greeting

giddy adj **-dier, -diest 1** feeling weak and unsteady on one's feet, as if about to faint **2** happy and excited: *a state of giddy expectation* **giddiness** n
WORD ORIGIN Old English *gydig* mad, frenzied, possessed by God

GIF *computers* **a** graphic interchange format: a standard compressed file format used for pictures **b** a picture held in this format

gift n **1** something given to someone: *a birthday gift* **2** a special ability or power: *a gift for caricature*
WORD ORIGIN Old English: payment for a wife, dowry

gifted adj having natural talent or aptitude: *that era's most gifted director*

giftwrap vb **-wrapping, -wrapped** to wrap (a gift) in decorative wrapping paper

gig[1] n **1** a single performance by jazz or pop musicians ▷ *vb* **gigging, gigged 2** to play gigs
WORD ORIGIN origin unknown

gig[2] n a light open two-wheeled one-horse carriage
WORD ORIGIN origin unknown

gig[3] n *computers informal* short for **gigabyte**

giga- prefix **1** denoting 10^9: *gigavolt* **2** *computers* denoting 2^{30}: *gigabyte*
WORD ORIGIN Greek *gigas* giant

gigabyte n *computers* one thousand and twenty-four megabytes

gigantic adj extremely large: *the most gigantic gold paperweight ever*
WORD ORIGIN Greek *gigantikos*

giggle vb **-gling, -gled** to laugh nervously or foolishly ▷ *n* **2** a nervous or foolish laugh **3** *informal* an amusing person or thing **giggly** adj
WORD ORIGIN imitative

gigolo (jig-a-lo) n, pl **-los** a man who is paid by an older woman to be her escort or lover
WORD ORIGIN French

gigot n *chiefly Brit* a leg of lamb or mutton
WORD ORIGIN French

gild vb **gilding**, **gilded** or **gilt** 1 to cover with a thin layer of gold 2 to make (something) appear golden: *the morning sun gilded the hills* 3 **gild the lily a** to adorn unnecessarily something already beautiful **b** to praise someone excessively
WORD ORIGIN Old English *gyldan*

gill (**jill**) n a unit of liquid measure equal to one quarter of a pint (0.14 litres)
WORD ORIGIN Old French *gille* vat, tub

gillie or **ghillie** n Scot a sportsman's attendant or guide for hunting or fishing
WORD ORIGIN Scottish Gaelic *gille* boy, servant

gills (**gillz**) pl n the breathing organs of fish and other water creatures
WORD ORIGIN from Old Norse

gilt vb 1 a past of **gild** ▷ adj 2 covered with a thin layer of gold ▷ n 3 a thin layer of gold, used as decoration

gilt-edged adj denoting government securities on which interest payments and final repayments are guaranteed

gilts pl n gilt-edged securities

gimcrack (**jim**-krak) adj showy but cheap; shoddy
WORD ORIGIN origin unknown

gimlet (**gim**-let) n 1 a small hand tool with a pointed spiral tip, used for boring holes in wood ▷ adj 2 penetrating or piercing: *gimlet eyes*
WORD ORIGIN Old French *guimbelet*

gimmick n informal something designed to attract attention or publicity **gimmicky** adj **gimmickry** n
WORD ORIGIN origin unknown

gin¹ n an alcoholic drink distilled from malted grain and flavoured with juniper berries
WORD ORIGIN Dutch *genever* juniper

gin² n a noose of thin strong wire for catching small mammals
WORD ORIGIN Middle English *gyn*

gin³ n Austral, offensive an Aboriginal woman
WORD ORIGIN Aboriginal

ginger n 1 the root of a tropical plant, powdered and used as a spice or sugared and eaten as a sweet ▷ adj 2 light reddish-brown: *ginger hair* **gingery** adj
WORD ORIGIN Old French *gingivre*

ginger ale n a nonalcoholic fizzy drink flavoured with ginger extract

ginger beer n a drink made by fermenting a mixture of syrup and root ginger

gingerbread n a moist brown cake flavoured with ginger

ginger group n Brit, Austral, & NZ a group within a larger group that agitates for a more active policy

gingerly adv carefully or cautiously: *she sat gingerly on the edge of the chair*
WORD ORIGIN perhaps from Old French *gensor* dainty

ginger nut or **snap** n a hard biscuit flavoured with ginger

gingham n a cotton fabric with a checked or striped design
WORD ORIGIN Malay *ginggang* striped cloth

gingivitis (jin-jiv-**vite**-iss) n inflammation of the gums
WORD ORIGIN Latin *gingiva* gum

ginormous adj informal very large
WORD ORIGIN *gi(gantic)* + *(e)normous*

gin rummy n a version of rummy in which a player may finish if the odd cards in his hand total less than ten points
WORD ORIGIN GIN¹ + *rummy*

ginseng (**jin**-seng) n the root of a plant of China and N America, believed to have tonic and energy-giving properties
WORD ORIGIN Mandarin Chinese *jen shen*

gip (**jip**) n same as **gyp**

Gipsy n, pl **-sies** same as **Gypsy**

giraffe n a cud-chewing African mammal with a very long neck and long legs and a spotted yellowy skin
WORD ORIGIN Arabic *zarāfah*

gird vb **girding**, **girded** or **girt** 1 to put a belt or girdle around 2 **gird up one's loins** to prepare oneself for action
WORD ORIGIN Old English *gyrdan*

girder n a large steel or iron beam used in the construction of bridges and buildings

girdle n 1 a woman's elastic corset that covers the stomach and hips 2 anything that surrounds something or someone: *his girdle of supporters* 3 anat an encircling arrangement of bones: *the shoulder girdle* ▷ vb **-dling**, **-dled** 4 to surround: *a ring of volcanic ash girdling the earth*
WORD ORIGIN Old English *gyrdel*

girl n 1 a female child 2 a young woman **girlhood** n **girlish** adj
WORD ORIGIN Middle English *girle*

girlfriend n 1 a female friend with whom a person is romantically or sexually involved 2 any female friend

Girl Guide n a former name for **Guide**

girlie adj informal 1 featuring naked or scantily dressed women: *girlie magazines* 2 suited to or designed to appeal to young women: *a real girlie night out*

giro (**jire**-oh) n, pl **-ros** 1 (in some countries) a system of transferring money within a bank or post office, directly from one account into another 2 Brit informal a social-security payment by giro cheque
WORD ORIGIN Greek *guros* circuit

girt vb a past of **gird**

girth n 1 the measurement around something 2 a band fastened round a horse's middle to keep the saddle in position
WORD ORIGIN Old Norse *gjörth* belt

gist (**jist**) n the main point or meaning of something: *the gist of the letter*
WORD ORIGIN Anglo-French, as in *cest action gist en* this action consists in

git n Brit slang a contemptible person
WORD ORIGIN from *get* (in the sense: to beget, hence a bastard, fool)

give vb **giving**, **gave**, **given** 1 to present or hand (something) to someone 2 to pay (an amount of money) for a purchase 3 to grant or provide: *to give an answer* 4 to utter (a shout or cry) 5 to perform, make, or do: *the prime minister gave a speech* 6 to host (a party) 7 to sacrifice or devote: *comrades who gave their lives for their country* 8 to concede: *he was*

very efficient, I have to give him that 9 to yield or break under pressure: *something has got to give* 10 **give or take** plus or minus: *about one hundred metres, give or take five* ▷ n 11 a tendency to yield under pressure; elasticity ▷ See also **give away**, **give in**, etc. **giver** n
WORD ORIGIN Old English *giefan*

give-and-take n 1 mutual concessions and cooperation 2 a smoothly flowing exchange of ideas and talk: *a relaxed give-and-take about their past involvement*

give away vb 1 to donate as a gift 2 to reveal (a secret) 3 to present (a bride) formally to her husband in a marriage ceremony 4 **give something away** NZ to give something up ▷ n **giveaway** 5 something that reveals hidden feelings or intentions ▷ adj **giveaway** 6 very cheap or free: *a giveaway rent*

give in vb to admit defeat

given vb 1 the past participle of **give** ▷ adj 2 specific or previously stated: *priorities within the given department* 3 to be assumed: *any given place on the earth* 4 **given to** inclined to: *a man not given to undue optimism*

give off vb to send out (heat, light, or a smell)

give out vb 1 to hand out: *the bloke that was giving out those tickets* 2 to send out (heat, light, or a smell) 3 to make known: *the man who gave out the news* 4 to fail: *the engine gave out*

give over vb 1 to set aside for a specific purpose: *the amount of space given over to advertisements* 2 informal to stop doing something annoying: *tell him to give over*

give up vb 1 to stop (doing something): *I did give up smoking* 2 to resign from (a job or position) 3 to admit defeat or failure 4 to abandon (hope) 5 **give oneself up a** to surrender to the police or other authorities **b** to devote oneself completely: *she gave herself up to her work*

gizzard n the part of a bird's stomach in which hard food is broken up
WORD ORIGIN Old French *guisier* fowl's liver

glacé (**glass**-say) adj preserved in a thick sugary syrup: *glacé cherries*
WORD ORIGIN French: iced

glacial adj 1 of glaciers or ice 2 extremely cold 3 cold and unfriendly: *a glacial stare*

glacial period n same as **ice age**

glaciation n the process of covering part of the earth's surface with glaciers or masses of ice **glaciated** adj

glacier n a slowly moving mass of ice formed by an accumulation of snow
WORD ORIGIN Latin *glacies* ice

glad adj **gladder**, **gladdest** 1 happy and pleased 2 very willing: *he was only too glad to help* 3 archaic causing happiness: *glad tidings* **gladly** adv **gladness** n **gladden** vb
WORD ORIGIN Old English *glæd*

glade n an open space in a forest: *a peaceful and sheltered glade*
WORD ORIGIN origin unknown

gladiator n (in ancient Rome) a man trained to fight in arenas to provide entertainment **gladiatorial** adj
WORD ORIGIN Latin: swordsman

Jonathan Swift and Alexander Pope

Jonathan Swift and Alexander Pope were contemporaries, and friends. They were towering figures in the first half of the eighteenth century. They both wrote satirical poems and essays, but they are remembered for rather different reasons.

Alexander Pope was above all a master of the epigram. He was so adept that his phrases have been taken up and used in English without any awareness now of who originally wrote them. Consider these:

Hope springs eternal in the human breast:
Man never Is, but always To be blest.

– from *An Essay on Man* (1733), and these three, all from *An Essay on Criticism* (1711):

To err is human; to forgive, divine.
For fools rush in where angels fear to tread.
A little learning is a dangerous thing.

One of the problems with satire is that it usually has some specific target, and as such it tends to have a more restricted shelf-life than novels or plays. One of Pope's best-known works, *The Rape of the Lock,* is a very funny poem, but it needs to be read with a clear awareness of its audience and its period. Pope writes with a ;-) at the end of every line. The story is of a trivial event, dressed up as an epic, so that everything is exaggerated to make the characters even more ridiculous than they were in real life; a society girl's lock of hair was snipped off surreptitiously by a suitor. Here are the lines that describe events just seconds before the snipping:

Just then, Clarissa drew with tempting grace
A two-edged weapon from her shining case:
So Ladies in Romance assist their Knight,
Present the spear, and arm him for the fight.
He takes the gift with reverence, and extends
The little engine on his fingers' ends;
This just behind Belinda's neck he spread,
As o'er the fragrant steams she bends her head.

As with yesterday's political cartoons, as soon as the events have faded from memory, although you can see that the satire must have been hilarious at the time, you do have to put in a bit of work to appreciate it. Hence the absence of Pope's works from the shelves of most modern bookshops, which is a great pity.

In the case of Swift, few of his sayings have come to form a part of the English language, but much of what he wrote is still read today, both inside and outside the classroom. There's no doubt he was witty, but maybe not quite so pithy as Pope. Here's an example:

The reasons why so few marriages are happy, is, because young ladies spend their time in making nets, not in making cages.

His essay 'A Modest Proposal' is often used as a perfect example of irony. When it was published in 1729 it was apparently taken seriously by some people, although this seems hard to believe now: 'I have been assured by a very knowing American of my acquaintance in London, that a young healthy child well nursed is at a year old a most delicious, nourishing, and wholesome food, whether stewed, roasted, baked, or boiled, and I make no doubt that it will equally serve in a fricassee, or a ragout.' He is best known, though, for his book *Gulliver's Travels* that he wrote late in life when he himself had some considerable experience of the ways of the world. The book was published in 1726, and it was an immediate hit. Its readers would have been familiar with Defoe's best-seller *Robinson Crusoe*, published seven years before. The world was still a place with enough unexplored nooks and crannies that places inhabited by tiny people, giants, or talking horses could have seemed almost believable, and in many ways the book works like some of the episodes of *Star Trek*, where conveniently distant planets can be used to present parables about human existence. The Lilliputians, Laputa, Brobdingnag, and the land where humans are yahoos are imagined with such skill that the satirical elements and the irony take second place to the sheer imaginative power.

It is a tribute to Jonathan Swift that *Gulliver's Travels* has appeared in so many versions, some lightly disguised, some more heavily, in the two and a half centuries since it was first published. But every line in Pope's works like *The Rape of the Lock* sparkles with wit, and it's well worth reading a few footnotes to be able to laugh again at the absurdities of eighteenth-century life, so like those of our own time.

gladiolus (glad-ee-**oh**-luss) *n, pl* **-li** (-lie) a garden plant with brightly coloured funnel-shaped flowers
WORD ORIGIN Latin: a small sword

glad rags *pl n informal* one's best clothes

gladsome *adj old-fashioned* joyous or cheerful

gladwrap *Austral, NZ, & S African n* **1** *trademark* thin polythene material for wrapping ▷ *vb* **2** to wrap in gladwrap

glamorous *adj* attractive or fascinating

glamour *or US* **glamor** *n* exciting or alluring charm or beauty **glamorize** *or* **-ise** *vb*
WORD ORIGIN Scots variant of *grammar* (hence a spell, because occult practices were popularly associated with learning)

glance *n* **1** a quick look ▷ *vb* **glancing, glanced** **2** to look quickly at something **3** to be deflected off an object at an oblique angle: *the ball glanced off a spectator* **glancing** *adj*
WORD ORIGIN Middle English *glacen* to strike obliquely

≣ **USAGE**
≣ *Glance* is sometimes wrongly used
≣ where *glimpse* is meant: *he caught a*
≣ *glimpse* (not *glance*) *of her making her way*
≣ *through the crowd.*

gland *n* **1** an organ that synthesizes and secretes chemical substances for the body to use or eliminate **2** a similar organ in plants
WORD ORIGIN Latin *glans* acorn

glandular *adj* of or affecting a gland or glands

glandular fever *n* an acute infectious viral disease that causes fever, sore throat, and painful swollen lymph nodes

glare *vb* **glaring, glared** **1** to stare angrily **2** (of light or colour) to be too bright ▷ *n* **3** an angry stare **4** a dazzling light or brilliance **5 in the glare of publicity** receiving a lot of attention from the media or the public
WORD ORIGIN Middle English

glaring *adj* conspicuous or obvious: *glaring inconsistencies* **glaringly** *adv*

glasnost *n* a policy of public frankness and accountability, developed in the USSR in the 1980s under Mikhail Gorbachev
WORD ORIGIN Russian: publicity, openness

glass *n* **1** a hard brittle transparent solid, consisting of metal silicates or similar compounds **2** a drinking vessel made of glass **3** the amount contained in a drinking glass: *a glass of wine* **4** objects made of glass, such as drinking glasses and bowls
WORD ORIGIN Old English *glæs*

glass-blowing *n* the process of shaping a mass of molten glass by blowing air into it through a tube **glass-blower** *n*

glass ceiling *n* a situation in which progress, esp. promotion, appears to be possible, but restrictions or discrimination create a barrier that prevents it

glasses *pl n* a pair of lenses for correcting faulty vision, in a frame that rests on the nose and hooks behind the ears

glasshouse *n Brit & NZ* same as **greenhouse**

glassy *adj* **glassier, glassiest** **1** smooth, clear, and shiny, like glass: *the glassy sea* **2** expressionless: *that glassy look*

Glaswegian (glaz-**weej**-an) *adj* **1** of Glasgow, a city in W Scotland ▷ *n* **2** a person from Glasgow **3** the Glasgow dialect

glaucoma *n* an eye disease in which increased pressure in the eyeball causes gradual loss of sight
WORD ORIGIN Greek *glaukos* silvery, bluish-green

glaze *vb* **glazing, glazed** **1** to fit or cover with glass **2** to cover (a piece of pottery) with a protective shiny coating **3** to cover (food) with beaten egg or milk before cooking, in order to produce a shiny coating ▷ *n* **4** a protective shiny coating applied to a piece of pottery **5** a shiny coating of beaten egg or milk applied to food ▸ See also **glaze over** ▷ **glazed** *adj* **glazing** *n*
WORD ORIGIN Middle English *glasen*

glaze over *vb* to become dull through boredom or inattention: *the listener's eyes glaze over*

glazier *n* a person who fits windows or doors with glass

gleam *n* **1** a small beam or glow of light **2** a brief or dim indication: *a gleam of anticipation in his eye* ▷ *vb* **3** to shine **gleaming** *adj*
WORD ORIGIN Old English *glǣm*

glean *vb* **1** to gather (information) bit by bit **2** to gather the useful remnants of (a crop) after harvesting **gleaner** *n*
WORD ORIGIN Old French *glener*

gleanings *pl n* pieces of information that have been gleaned

glebe *n Austral & Brit* land granted to a member of the clergy as part of his or her benefice
WORD ORIGIN Latin *glaeba*

glee *n* great merriment or joy, esp. caused by the misfortune of another person
WORD ORIGIN Old English *glēo*

gleeful *adj* merry or joyful, esp. over someone else's mistake or misfortune **gleefully** *adv*

glen *n* a deep narrow mountain valley
WORD ORIGIN Scottish Gaelic *gleann*

glengarry *n, pl* **-ries** a brimless Scottish cap with a crease down the crown
WORD ORIGIN after *Glengarry*, Scotland

glib *adj* **glibber, glibbest** fluent and easy, often in an insincere or deceptive way: *there were no glib or easy answers* **glibly** *adv* **glibness** *n*
WORD ORIGIN probably from Middle Low German *glibberich* slippery

glide *vb* **gliding, glided** **1** to move easily and smoothly **2** (of an aircraft) to land without engine power **3** to fly a glider **4** to float on currents of air
WORD ORIGIN Old English *glīdan*

glider *n* **1** an aircraft that does not use an engine, but flies by floating on air currents **2** *Austral* a flying phalanger

glide time *n NZ* same as **flexitime**

gliding *n* the sport of flying in a glider

glimmer *vb* **1** (of a light) to glow faintly or flickeringly ▷ *n* **2** a faint indication: *a glimmer of hope* **3** a glow or twinkle
WORD ORIGIN Middle English

glimpse *n* **1** a brief view: *a glimpse of a rare snow leopard* **2** a vague indication: *glimpses of insecurity* ▷ *vb* **glimpsing, glimpsed** **3** to catch sight of momentarily
WORD ORIGIN Germanic

≣ **USAGE**
≣ *Glimpse* is sometimes wrongly used
≣ where *glance* is meant: *he gave a quick*
≣ *glance* (not *glimpse*) *at his watch.*

glint *vb* **1** to gleam brightly ▷ *n* **2** a bright gleam
WORD ORIGIN probably from Old Norse

glissade *n* **1** a gliding step in ballet **2** a controlled gliding down a snow slope ▷ *vb* **-sading, -saded** **3** to perform a glissade
WORD ORIGIN French

glissando *n, pl* **-dos** *music* a slide between two notes in which all intermediate notes are played
WORD ORIGIN mock Italian, from French *glisser* to slide

glisten *vb* (of a wet or glossy surface) to gleam by reflecting light: *sweat glistened above his eyes*
WORD ORIGIN Old English *glisnian*

glitch *n* a small problem that stops something from working properly
WORD ORIGIN Yiddish *glitsh* a slip

glitter *vb* **1** (of a surface) to reflect light in bright flashes **2** (of light) to be reflected in bright flashes **3** to be brilliant in a showy way: *she glitters socially* ▷ *n* **4** a sparkling light **5** superficial glamour: *the trappings and glitter of the European aristocracy* **6** tiny pieces of shiny decorative material **7** *Canad* ice formed from freezing rain **glittering** *adj* **glittery** *adj*
WORD ORIGIN Old Norse *glitra*

glitzy *adj* **glitzier, glitziest** *slang* showily attractive
WORD ORIGIN probably from German *glitzern* to glitter

gloaming *n Scot, poetic* twilight; dusk
WORD ORIGIN Old English *glōmung*

gloat *vb* to regard one's own good fortune or the misfortune of others with smug or malicious pleasure
WORD ORIGIN probably Scandinavian

glob *n informal* a rounded mass of thick fluid
WORD ORIGIN probably from *globe*, influenced by *blob*

global *adj* **1** of or applying to the whole earth: *global environmental problems* **2** of or applying to the whole of something: *a global total for local-authority revenue* **globally** *adv*

globalize *or* **-lise** *vb* **-izing, -ized** *or* **-ising, -ised** to put (something) into effect worldwide **globalization** *or* **-lisation** *n*

global warming *n* an increase in the overall temperature worldwide believed to be caused by the greenhouse effect

globe *n* **1** a sphere on which a map of the world is drawn **2 the globe** the earth **3** a spherical object, such as a glass lamp shade or fishbowl **4** *S African* an electric light bulb **WORD ORIGIN** Latin *globus*

globetrotter *n* a habitual worldwide traveller **globetrotting** *n, adj*

globular *adj* shaped like a globe or globule

globule *n* a small round drop of liquid **WORD ORIGIN** Latin *globulus*

globulin *n* a simple protein found in living tissue

glockenspiel *n* a percussion instrument consisting of tuned metal plates played with a pair of small hammers **WORD ORIGIN** German *Glocken* bells + *Spiel* play

gloom *n* 1 depression or melancholy: *all doom and gloom* 2 partial or total darkness **WORD ORIGIN** Middle English *gloumben* to look sullen

gloomy *adj* **gloomier, gloomiest** 1 despairing or sad 2 causing depression or gloom: *gloomy economic forecasts* 3 dark or dismal **gloomily** *adv*

gloop *or US* **glop** *n informal* any messy sticky fluid or substance **gloopy** *or US* **gloppy** *adj* **WORD ORIGIN** origin unknown

glorify *vb* **-fies, -fying, -fied** 1 to make (something) seem more important than it really is: *computers are just glorified adding machines* 2 to praise: *few countries have glorified success in business more than the United States* 3 to worship (God) **glorification** *n*

glorious *adj* 1 brilliantly beautiful: *in glorious colour* 2 delightful or enjoyable: *the glorious summer weather* 3 having or full of glory: *glorious successes* **gloriously** *adv*

glory *n, pl* **-ries** 1 fame, praise, or honour: *tales of glory* 2 splendour: *the glory of the tropical day* 3 something worthy of praise: *the Lady Chapel is the great glory of Lichfield* 4 adoration or worship: *the greater glory of God* ▷ *vb* **-ries, -rying, -ried** 5 **glory in** to take great pleasure in: *the workers were glorying in their new-found freedom* **WORD ORIGIN** Latin *gloria*

glory box *n Austral & NZ, old-fashioned informal* a box in which a young woman stores her trousseau

glory hole *n* an untidy cupboard or storeroom

Glos Gloucestershire

gloss[1] *n* 1 a bright shine on a surface 2 a superficially attractive appearance 3 a paint with a shiny finish 4 a cosmetic used to give a shiny appearance: *lip gloss* ▷ *vb* 5 to paint with gloss 6 **gloss over** to conceal (an error, failing, or awkward moment) by minimizing it: *don't try to gloss over bad news* **WORD ORIGIN** probably Scandinavian

gloss[2] *n* 1 an explanatory comment added to the text of a book ▷ *vb* 2 to add a gloss or glosses to **WORD ORIGIN** Latin *glossa* unusual word requiring explanatory note

glossary *n, pl* **-ries** an alphabetical list of technical or specialist words in a book, with explanations **WORD ORIGIN** Late Latin *glossarium; see* GLOSS[2]

glossy *adj* **glossier, glossiest** 1 smooth and shiny: *glossy black hair* 2 superficially attractive or sophisticated: *his glossy Manhattan flat* 3 (of a magazine) produced on expensive shiny paper

glottal stop *n phonetics* a speech sound produced by tightly closing and then opening the glottis

glottis *n* the opening at the top of the windpipe, between the vocal cords **WORD ORIGIN** Greek *glōtta* tongue

glove *n* 1 a shaped covering for the hand with individual sheaths for each finger and the thumb 2 a protective hand covering worn in sports such as boxing **WORD ORIGIN** Old English *glōfe*

glove compartment *n* a small storage area in the dashboard of a car

gloved *adj* covered by a glove or gloves: *a gloved hand*

glow *n* 1 light produced as a result of great heat 2 a steady light without flames 3 brightness of complexion 4 a feeling of wellbeing or satisfaction ▷ *vb* 5 to produce a steady light without flames 6 to shine intensely 7 to experience a feeling of wellbeing or satisfaction: *she glowed with pleasure* 8 (of the complexion) to have a strong bright colour: *his pale face glowing at the recollection* **WORD ORIGIN** Old English *glōwan*

glower (rhymes with **power**) *vb* 1 to stare angrily ▷ *n* 2 an angry stare **WORD ORIGIN** origin unknown

glowing *adj* full of praise: *a glowing tribute*

glow-worm *n* a European beetle, the females and larvae of which have organs producing a soft greenish light

gloxinia *n* a plant with white, red, or purple bell-shaped flowers **WORD ORIGIN** after Benjamin P. *Gloxin*, botanist

glucose *n* a white crystalline sugar found in plant and animal tissues **WORD ORIGIN** Greek *gleukos* sweet wine

glue *n* 1 a substance used for sticking things together ▷ *vb* **gluing** *or* **glueing, glued** 2 to join or stick together with glue 3 **glued to** paying full attention to: *golf fans will be glued to their televisions today for the Open Championship* **gluey** *adj* **WORD ORIGIN** Late Latin *glus*

glue ear *n* an accumulation of fluid in the middle ear of children, caused by infection and causing deafness

glue-sniffing *n* the practice of inhaling glue fumes to produce intoxicating or hallucinatory effects **glue-sniffer** *n*

glum *adj* **glummer, glummest** gloomy and quiet, usually because of a disappointment **glumly** *adv* **WORD ORIGIN** variant of *gloom*

glut *n* 1 an excessive supply ▷ *vb* **glutting, glutted** 2 to supply (a market) with a commodity in excess of the demand for it 3 **glut oneself** to eat or drink more than one really needs **WORD ORIGIN** probably from Old French *gloutir* to swallow

glute *n* short for **gluteus**

gluten (**gloo**-ten) *n* a sticky protein found in cereal grains, such as wheat **WORD ORIGIN** Latin: glue

gluteus *or* **glutaeus** *n* any of the three muscles of the buttock

glutinous (**gloo**-tin-uss) *adj* gluelike in texture

glutton *n* 1 someone who eats and drinks too much 2 a person who has a great capacity for something: *a glutton for work* **gluttonous** *adj* **WORD ORIGIN** Latin *gluttire* to swallow

gluttony *n* the practice of eating too much

glycaemic index *or US* **glycemic index** *n* an index indicating the effects of various foods on blood sugar. Abbrev: **GI**

glycerine (**gliss**-ser-reen) *or* **glycerin** *n* a nontechnical name for **glycerol** **WORD ORIGIN** Greek *glukeros* sweet

glycerol (**gliss**-ser-ol) *n* a colourless odourless syrupy liquid obtained from animal and vegetable fats, used as a solvent, antifreeze, and sweetener, and in explosives

glycogen (**glike**-oh-jen) *n* a starchlike carbohydrate stored in the liver and muscles of humans and animals

glycolysis (glike-**kol**-iss-iss) *n biochem* the breakdown of glucose by enzymes, with the release of energy

gm gram

GM 1 genetically modified 2 *Brit* grant-maintained

G-man *n, pl* **G-men** *US slang* an FBI agent

GMB (in Britain) General, Municipal and Boilermakers (Trade Union)

GMO genetically modified organism

GMT Greenwich Mean Time

gnarled *adj* rough, twisted, and knobbly, usually through age

gnash *vb* to grind (the teeth) together in pain or anger **WORD ORIGIN** probably from Old Norse

gnat *n* a small biting two-winged insect **WORD ORIGIN** Old English *gnætt*

gnaw *vb* 1 to bite or chew constantly so as to wear away bit by bit 2 **gnaw at** to cause constant distress or anxiety to: *uneasiness gnawed at his mind* **gnawing** *adj* **WORD ORIGIN** Old English *gnagan*

gneiss *n* a coarse-grained layered metamorphic rock **WORD ORIGIN** German *Gneis*

gnome *n* 1 an imaginary creature in fairy tales that looks like a little old man 2 a small statue of a gnome in a garden **WORD ORIGIN** French

gnomic (**no**-mik) *adj literary* of or containing short clever sayings: *gnomic pronouncements*

Gnosticism (**noss**-tiss-siz-zum) *n* a religious movement involving belief in intuitive spiritual knowledge **Gnostic** *n, adj*

GNP gross national product

gnu (**noo**) *n, pl* **gnus** *or* **gnu** a sturdy African antelope with an oxlike head **WORD ORIGIN** Xhosa *nqu*

go *vb* **goes, going, went, gone** 1 to move or proceed to or from a place: *go forward* 2 to be in regular attendance at (work, church, or a place of learning) 3 to lead to a particular place: *the path that goes right along the bank* 4 to be kept in a particular place: *where does this go?* 5 to

do or become as specified: *he went white; the gun went bang* **6** to be or continue to be in a specified state: *to go to sleep* **7** to operate or function: *the car wouldn't go* **8** to follow a specified course; fare: *I'd hate the meeting to go badly* **9** to be allotted to a particular purpose or recipient: *a third of the total budget goes on the army* **10** to be sold: *the portrait went for a fortune to a telephone bidder* **11** (of words or music) to be expressed or sung: *the song goes like this* **12** to fail or break down: *my eyesight is going; he was on lap 19 when the engine went* **13** to die: *he went quickly at the end* **14** to be spent or finished: *all tension and all hope had gone* **15** to proceed up to or beyond certain limits: *I think this is going too far* **16** to carry authority: *what Daddy says goes* **17** to endure or last out: *they go for eight or ten hours without resting* **18** not standard to say: *then she goes, 'shut up'* **19 anything goes** anything is acceptable **20 be going to** to intend or be about to: *she was afraid of what was going to happen next* **21 let go** to relax one's hold on; release **22 let oneself go a** to act in an uninhibited manner **b** to lose interest in one's appearance **23 to go** remaining: *two days to go till the holidays* ▷ *n, pl* **goes 24** an attempt: *he had a go at the furniture business* **25** a verbal or physical attack: *he couldn't resist having another go at me* **26** a turn to do something in a game: *'Your go now!' I shouted* **27** *informal* the quality of being active and energetic: *a grand old man, full of go and determination* **28 from the word go** *informal* from the very beginning **29 make a go of** *informal* to be successful in (a business venture or a relationship) **30 on the go** *informal* active and energetic ▸ See also **go about, go against**, etc.
WORD ORIGIN Old English *gān*

go about *vb* **1** to tackle (a problem or task): *he went about it in the wrong way* **2** to busy oneself with: *people have been going about their business as usual*

goad *vb* **1** to provoke (someone) to take some kind of action, usually in anger ▷ *n* **2** something that provokes someone to take some kind of action **3** a sharp pointed stick for driving cattle
WORD ORIGIN Old English *gād*

go against *vb* **1** to conflict with (someone's wishes or beliefs) **2** to be unfavourable to (a person): *a referendum would almost certainly go against them*

go-ahead *n* **1 give the go-ahead** *informal* to give permission to proceed ▷ *adj* **2** enterprising or ambitious: *prosperous and go-ahead republics*

goal *n* **1** *sport* the space into which players try to propel the ball or puck to score **2** *sport* **a** a successful attempt at scoring **b** the score so made **3** an aim or purpose: *the goal is to get homeless people on their feet* **goalless** *adj*
WORD ORIGIN origin unknown

goalie *n informal* a goalkeeper

goalkeeper *n sport* a player whose duty is to prevent the ball or puck from entering the goal

goal line *n sport* the line marking each end of the pitch, on which the goals stand

goalpost *n* **1** either of two uprights supporting the crossbar of a goal **2 move the goalposts** to change the aims of an activity to ensure the desired results

goanna *n* a large Australian lizard
WORD ORIGIN from IGUANA

goat *n* **1** an agile cud-chewing mammal with hollow horns **2 act the goat** *informal* to behave in a silly manner **3 get someone's goat** *slang* to annoy someone
WORD ORIGIN Old English *gāt*

goatee *n* a small pointed beard that does not cover the cheeks

goatherd *n* a person who looks after a herd of goats

goatskin *n* leather made from the skin of a goat

goatsucker *n US & Canad* same as **nightjar**

go-away bird *n S African* a grey lourie
WORD ORIGIN imitative

gob[1] *n* a thick mass of a soft substance
WORD ORIGIN Old French *gobe* lump

gob[2] *n Brit, Austral, & NZ slang* the mouth
WORD ORIGIN origin unknown

go back on *vb* to fail to fulfil (a promise): *he went back on his promise not to raise taxes*

gobbet *n* a chunk or lump
WORD ORIGIN Old French *gobet*

gobble[1] *vb* **-bling, -bled** to eat quickly and greedily
WORD ORIGIN probably from GOB[1]

gobble[2] *n* **1** the loud rapid gurgling sound made by a turkey ▷ *vb* **-bling, -bled 2** to make this sound
WORD ORIGIN probably imitative

gobbledegook *or* **gobbledygook** *n* pretentious or unintelligible language
WORD ORIGIN whimsical formation from GOBBLE[2]

gobbler *n informal* a turkey

go-between *n* a person who acts as a messenger between two people or groups

goblet *n* a drinking vessel with a base and stem but without handles
WORD ORIGIN Old French *gobelet* a little cup

goblin *n* a small grotesque creature in fairy tales that causes trouble for people
WORD ORIGIN Old French

gobshite *n Irish taboo slang* a stupid person
WORD ORIGIN GOB[2] + shite excrement

gobsmacked *adj Brit, Austral, & NZ slang* astonished and astounded

goby *n, pl* **-by** *or* **-bies** a small spiny-finned fish
WORD ORIGIN Latin *gobius* gudgeon

go by *vb* **1** to pass: *as time goes by* **2** to be guided by: *if my experience is anything to go by*

go-cart *n* same as **go-kart**

god *n* **1** a supernatural being, worshipped as the controller of the universe or some aspect of life, or as the personification of some force **2** an image of such a being **3** a person or thing to which excessive attention is given: *the All Blacks are gods in New Zealand* **4 the gods** the top balcony in a theatre **goddess** *fem n*

WORD ORIGIN Old English

God *n* **1** the sole Supreme Being, Creator and ruler of all, in religions such as Christianity, Judaism, and Islam ▷ *interj* **2** an oath or exclamation of surprise or annoyance

godchild *n, pl* **-children** a person who is sponsored by godparents at baptism

goddaughter *n* a female godchild

godetia *n* a garden plant with showy flowers
WORD ORIGIN after C. H. *Godet*, botanist

godfather *n* **1** a male godparent **2** the head of a Mafia family or other criminal ring

God-fearing *adj* deeply religious

godforsaken *adj* desolate or dreary: *some godforsaken village in the Himalayas*

Godhead *n* the nature and condition of being God

godless *adj* **1** wicked or unprincipled **2** not religious **godlessness** *n*

godly *adj* **-lier, -liest** deeply religious **godliness** *n*

godmother *n* a female godparent

godparent *n* a person who promises at a person's baptism to look after his or her religious upbringing

godsend *n* a person or thing that comes unexpectedly but is very welcome

godson *n* a male godchild

Godspeed *interj* an expression of good wishes for a person's safe journey and success

goer *n* a person who attends something regularly: *a church goer*

go for *vb* **1** to choose: *any politician will go for the soft option* **2** *informal* to like very much **3** to attack **4** to apply equally to: *the same might go for the other woman*

go-getter *n informal* an ambitious enterprising person **go-getting** *adj*

gogga (**hohh**-a) *n S African informal* an insect
WORD ORIGIN Nama (language of southern Africa) *xo xo*

goggle *vb* **-gling, -gled** to stare with wide-open eyes ▸ See also **goggles** ▷ **goggle-eyed** *adj*
WORD ORIGIN Middle English *gogelen* to look aside

gogglebox *n Brit slang* a television set

goggles *pl n* close-fitting protective spectacles

go-go *adj* denoting a type of dancing performed to pop music by young women wearing few clothes

Goidelic *n* **1** the group of Celtic languages, consisting of Irish Gaelic, Scottish Gaelic, and Manx ▷ *adj* **2** of this group of languages
WORD ORIGIN Old Irish *Goidel* Celt

go in for *vb* **1** to enter (a competition) **2** to take up or take part in (an activity)

going *n* **1** the condition of the ground with regard to walking or riding: *the going for the cross-country is perfect* **2** *informal* speed or progress: *not bad going for a lad of 58* ▷ *adj* **3** thriving: *the racecourse was a going concern* **4** current or accepted: *this is the going rate for graduates*

going-over *n, pl* **goings-over** *informal* **1** a thorough examination or investigation **2** a physical beating

SCRABBLE
Three-Letter Words, part 4
GOX–KAW

GOX gaseous oxygen

GOY Jewish word for a non-Jew

GUB white man

GUE musical instrument

GUL oriental carpet design

GUM flesh in which the teeth are set

GUN weapon

GUP gossip

GUR unrefined cane sugar

GUS plural form of gu

GUT intestine

GUV short for governor

GUY man or boy

GYM gymnasium

GYP swindle

HAD part of the verb to have

HAE Scots form of have

HAG ugly old woman

HAH exclamation of derision, triumph, or surprise

HAJ Muslim pilgrimage

HAM meat from a pig's thigh

HAN archaic form of have

HAO monetary unit

HAP luck, chance

HAS part of the verb to have

HAT covering for the head

HAW hawthorn berry

HAY grass cut and dried as fodder

HEH exclamation of surprise

HEM bottom edge of a garment

HEN female domestic fowl

HEP fruit of the dog rose

HER refers to a female person or animal

HES plural form of he

HET short for heterosexual

HEW cut with an axe

HEX evil spell

HEY expression of surprise or for catching attention

HIC sound of a hiccup

HID part of the verb to hide

HIE hurry

HIM refers to a male person or animal

HIN Hebrew unit of capacity

HIP part of the body between pelvis and thigh

HIS belonging to him

HIT strike, touch forcefully

HMM expression of thoughtful consideration

HOA exclamation to attract attention

HOB flat top part of a cooker

HOC Latin for this

HOD open wooden box attached to a pole

HOE long-handled tool

HOG castrated male pig

HOH cry to attract attention

HOI cry used to attract attention

HOM sacred plant

HON short for honey

HOO expression of boisterous emotion

HOP jump on one foot

HOS plural form of ho

HOT having a high temperature

HOW in what way

HOX hamstring

HOY cry used to attract attention

HUB centre of a wheel

HUE colour

HUG clasp tightly in the arms

HUH exclamation of derision

HUI meeting of Maori people

HUM low continuous vibrating sound

HUN member of Asiatic nomadic peoples

HUP cry to make a horse turn

HUT small house, shelter, or shed

HYE hurry

HYP hypotenuse

ICE water in its solid state

ICH dialect form of I

ICK expression of disgust

ICY very cold

IDE silver fish

IDS plural form of id

IFF conjunction used in logic

IFS plural form of if

IGG ignore, snub

ILK type

ILL not in good health

IMP mischievous small creature

INK coloured liquid used for writing or printing

INN pub or small hotel

INS plural form of in

ION atom

IOS plural form of io

IRE anger

IRK irritate, annoy

ISH issue, expiry

ISM doctrine, system, or practice

ISO short segment of film

ITA type of palm

ITS belonging to it

IVY evergreen climbing plant

IWI Maori tribe

JAB poke sharply

JAG cut unevenly

JAI victory (to)

JAK South and South East Asian tree

JAM pack tightly into a place

JAP splash, spatter

JAR wide-mouthed container

JAW bone in which the teeth are set

JAY bird

JEE move a horse faster

JET aircraft

JEU game

JEW obsolete offensive word meaning haggle

JIB triangular sail

JIG type of lively dance

JIN Chinese unit of weight

JIZ wig

JOB occupation

JOE Scots word for a sweetheart

JOG run at a gentle pace

JOL party

JOR movement in Indian music

JOT write briefly

JOW ring (a bell)

JOY feeling of great delight

JUD large block of coal

JUG container for liquids

JUN monetary unit

JUS right, power, or authority

JUT project or stick out

KAB ancient Hebrew measure

KAE jackdaw

KAF letter of the Hebrew alphabet

KAI food

KAK S African offensive word for faeces

KAM Shakespearean word for crooked

KAS plural form of ka

KAT shrub whose leaves have narcotic properties

KAW cry of a crow

goings-on *pl n informal* mysterious or shady activities

go into *vb* to describe or investigate in detail

goitre *or US* **goiter** (**goy**-ter) *n pathol* a swelling of the thyroid gland in the neck
WORD ORIGIN French

go-kart *n* a small four-wheeled motor vehicle, used for racing

gold *n* **1** a bright yellow precious metal, used as a monetary standard and in jewellery and plating. Symbol: Au **2** jewellery or coins made of this metal **3** short for **gold medal** ▷ *adj* **4** deep yellow
WORD ORIGIN Old English

goldcrest *n* a small bird with a bright yellow-and-black crown

gold-digger *n informal* a woman who marries or has a relationship with a man for his money

gold dust *n* **1** gold in the form of small particles or powder **2 like gold dust** in great demand because difficult to obtain: *kidney machines were like gold dust*

golden *adj* **1** made of gold: *golden bangles* **2** of the colour of gold: *golden corn* **3** *informal* very successful or destined for success: *the golden girl of British athletics* **4** excellent or valuable: *a golden opportunity for peace* **5** (of an anniversary) the fiftieth: *golden wedding; Golden Jubilee*

golden age *n* the most flourishing and outstanding period in the history of an art or nation: *the golden age of Dixieland jazz*

golden eagle *n* a large mountain eagle of the N hemisphere with golden-brown feathers

golden goal *n soccer* (in certain matches) the first goal scored in extra time, which instantly wins the match for the side scoring it

golden handshake *n informal* money given to an employee either on retirement or to compensate for loss of employment

golden hour *n* the first hour after a serious accident, when medical treatment for the victim is crucial

golden mean *n* the middle course between extremes

golden retriever *n* a retriever with silky wavy gold-coloured hair

goldenrod *n* a tall plant with spikes of small yellow flowers

golden rule *n* an important principle: *the golden rule is to start with the least difficult problems*

golden syrup *n* a light golden-coloured treacle used for sweetening food

golden wattle *n* an Australian plant with yellow flowers that yields a useful gum and bark

goldfinch *n* a European finch, the adult of which has yellow-and-black wings

goldfish *n, pl* **-fish** *or* **-fishes** a gold or orange-red freshwater fish, often kept as a pet

gold foil *n* thin gold sheet that is thicker than gold leaf

gold leaf *n* very thin gold sheet made by rolling or hammering gold and used for gilding

gold medal *n* a medal made of gold, awarded to the winner of a race or competition

gold-plated *adj* covered with a very thin coating of gold

gold rush *n* a large-scale migration of people to a territory where gold has been found

goldsmith *n* a person who makes gold jewellery and other articles

gold standard *n* a monetary system in which the basic currency unit equals a specified weight of gold

golf *n* **1** a game in which a ball is struck with clubs into a series of eighteen holes in a grassy course ▷ *vb* **2** to play golf **golfer** *n*
WORD ORIGIN origin unknown

golf club *n* **1** a long-shafted club used to strike a golf ball **2 a** an association of golf players **b** the premises of such an association

golf course *or* **links** *n* an area of ground laid out for golf

golliwog *n* a soft doll with a black face, usually made of cloth
WORD ORIGIN from a doll in a series of American children's books

golly *interj* an exclamation of mild surprise
WORD ORIGIN originally a euphemism for *God*

gonad *n* an organ in which reproductive cells are produced, such as a testis or ovary
WORD ORIGIN Greek *gonos* seed

gondola *n* **1** a long narrow flat-bottomed boat with a high ornamented stem, traditionally used on the canals of Venice **2** a moving cabin suspended from a cable, used as a ski lift
WORD ORIGIN Italian

gondolier *n* a person who propels a gondola

gone *vb* **1** the past participle of **go** ▷ *adj* **2** no longer present or no longer in existence

goner *n slang* a person who is about to die or who is beyond help

gong *n* **1** a flat circular metal disc that is hit with a hammer to give out a loud sound **2** *Brit slang* a medal
WORD ORIGIN Malay

gonorrhoea *or esp. US* **gonorrhea** (gon-or-**ree**-a) *n* a sexually transmitted disease that causes inflammation and a discharge from the genital organs
WORD ORIGIN Greek *gonos* semen + *rhoia* flux

goo *n informal* a sticky substance
WORD ORIGIN origin unknown

good *adj* **better, best 1** having admirable, pleasing, or superior qualities: *a good listener* **2** morally excellent; virtuous: *a good person* **3** beneficial: *exercise is good for the heart* **4** kindly or generous: *he is so good to us* **5** competent or talented: *she's good at physics* **6** obedient or well-behaved: *a good boy* **7** reliable or recommended: *a good make* **8** complete or thorough: *she went to have a good look round* **9** appropriate or opportune: *a good time to clear the air* **10** satisfying or enjoyable: *a good holiday* **11** newest or of the best quality: *keep the*

good dishes for guests **12** fairly large, extensive, or long: *they contain a good amount of protein* **13 as good as** virtually or practically: *the war was as good as over* ▷ *n* **14** advantage or benefit: *what is the good of it all?* **15** positive moral qualities; virtue **16 for good** for ever; permanently: *his political career was over for good* ▸ See also **goods**
WORD ORIGIN Old English *gōd*

goodbye *interj* **1** an expression used on parting ▷ *n* **2** the act of saying goodbye: *he said his goodbyes*
WORD ORIGIN from *God be with ye*

good day *interj* an expression of greeting or farewell used during the day

good-for-nothing *n* **1** an irresponsible or worthless person ▷ *adj* **2** irresponsible or worthless

Good Friday *n Christianity* the Friday before Easter, observed as a commemoration of the Crucifixion of Jesus Christ

goodies *pl n* any things considered particularly desirable

goodly *adj* **-lier, -liest** fairly large: *a goodly number of children*

good morning *interj* an expression of greeting or farewell used in the morning

good-natured *adj* tolerant and kindly

goodness *n* **1** the quality of being good ▷ *interj* **2** an exclamation of surprise

good night *interj* an expression of farewell used in the evening or at night

goods *pl n* **1** articles produced to be sold: *consumer goods* **2** movable personal property: *houses and goods are insured from fire* **3 deliver the goods** *informal* to do what is expected or required **4 have the goods on someone** *US & Canad slang* to know something incriminating about someone

Good Samaritan *n* a person who helps someone in difficulty or distress
WORD ORIGIN from a parable in Luke 10: 30–37

good-tempered *adj* tolerant and kindly

good turn *n* a helpful and friendly act

goodwill *n* **1** kindly feelings towards other people **2** the popularity and good reputation of a well-established business, considered as a valuable asset

goody *interj* **1** a child's exclamation of pleasure ▷ *n, pl* **goodies 2** *informal* the hero in a film or book. See **goodies**

goody-goody *informal n, pl* **-goodies 1** a person who behaves well in order to please people in authority ▷ *adj* **2** behaving well in order to please people in authority

gooey *adj* **gooier, gooiest** *informal* **1** sticky, soft, and often sweet **2** sentimental: *one knows the whole gooey performance is an act*

goof *vb informal* **1** to bungle or botch **2 goof off** *US & Canad* to spend time in a lazy or foolish way: *he's goofing off on the Costa del Sol*
WORD ORIGIN probably from dialect *goff* simpleton

go off *vb* **1** to stop functioning: *the heating went off* **2** to make a sudden loud noise:

a bomb went off **3** to occur as specified: *the actual launch went off perfectly* **4** *informal* (of food) to become stale or rotten **5** *Brit informal* to stop liking

goofy *adj* **goofier, goofiest** *informal* silly or ridiculous

google *vb* **1** to search for (something) on the internet using a search engine **2** to check (someone's credentials) by searching for websites containing his or her name
WORD ORIGIN from *Google*, a popular search engine on the internet

googly *n, pl* **-lies** *cricket* a ball bowled like a leg break but spinning from off to leg on pitching
WORD ORIGIN Australian English

goon *n* **1** a stupid person **2** *US informal* a hired thug
WORD ORIGIN dialect *gooney* fool; influenced by US cartoon character Alice the *goon*

go on *vb* **1** to continue or proceed **2** to take place: *there's a war going on* **3** to talk at length and annoyingly

goosander *n* a duck of Europe and North America with a dark head and white body
WORD ORIGIN probably from GOOSE[1] + Old Norse *önd* (genitive *andar*) duck

goose[1] *n, pl* **geese 1** a fairly large web-footed long-necked migratory bird **2** the female of such a bird **3** the flesh of the goose used for food **4** *informal* a silly person
WORD ORIGIN Old English *gōs*

goose[2] *vb* **goosing, goosed** *slang* to prod (someone) playfully in the bottom
WORD ORIGIN from the jabbing of a goose's bill

gooseberry *n, pl* **-ries 1** a small edible green berry with tiny hairs on the skin **2 play gooseberry** *Brit & NZ informal* to be an unwanted single person accompanying a couple

goose flesh *n* the bumpy condition of the skin due to cold or fear, in which the muscles at the base of the hair follicles contract, making the hair bristle. Also: **goose pimples**

goose-step *vb* **-stepping, -stepped** to march raising the legs high alternately while keeping the legs straight

go out *vb* **1** to go to entertainments or social functions **2** to be extinguished or cease to function: *the lights went out* **3** (of information) to be released publicly **4** (of a broadcast) to be transmitted **5 go out with** to have a romantic relationship with

go over *vb* **1** to examine very carefully **2 go over to** to change to: *he went over to the Free Orthodox Church*

gopher (**go**-fer) *n* an American burrowing rodent with wide cheek pouches
WORD ORIGIN origin unknown

Gordian knot *n* **cut the Gordian knot** to solve a complicated problem by bold or forceful action
WORD ORIGIN after *Gordius*, in Greek legend, who tied a knot that Alexander the Great cut with a sword

gore[1] *n* blood shed from a wound
WORD ORIGIN Old English *gor* dirt

gore[2] *vb* **goring, gored** (of an animal) to pierce or stab (a person or another animal) with a horn or tusk
WORD ORIGIN probably from Old English *gār* spear

gore[3] *n* a tapering piece of material in a garment, sail, or umbrella
WORD ORIGIN Old English *gāra*

gorge *n* **1** a deep narrow steep-sided valley **2 one's gorge rises** one feels disgusted or nauseated ▷ *vb* **gorging, gorged 3** Also: **gorge oneself** to eat greedily
WORD ORIGIN Latin *gurges* whirlpool

gorgeous *adj* **1** strikingly beautiful or attractive **2** *informal* warm, sunny, and very pleasant: *a gorgeous day* **gorgeously** *adv*
WORD ORIGIN Old French *gorgias* elegant

Gorgon *n* **1** *Greek myth* one of three monstrous sisters who had live snakes for hair, and were so horrifying that anyone who looked at them was turned to stone **2** *informal* a terrifying or repulsive woman
WORD ORIGIN Greek *gorgos* terrible

Gorgonzola *n* a sharp-flavoured blue-veined Italian cheese
WORD ORIGIN after *Gorgonzola*, Italian town where it originated

gorilla *n* a very large W African ape with coarse black hair
WORD ORIGIN Greek *Gorillai*, an African tribe renowned for their hairy appearance

gormless *adj* *Brit & NZ informal* stupid or dull-witted
WORD ORIGIN obsolete *gaumless*

go round *vb* to be sufficient: *there wasn't enough money to go round*

gorse *n* an evergreen shrub with small yellow flowers and prickles, which grows wild in the countryside
WORD ORIGIN Old English *gors*

gory *adj* **gorier, goriest 1** horrific or bloodthirsty: *the gory details* **2** bloody: *gory remains*

gosh *interj* an exclamation of mild surprise or wonder
WORD ORIGIN euphemistic for *God*

goshawk *n* a large swift short-winged hawk
WORD ORIGIN Old English *gōshafoc*

gosling *n* a young goose
WORD ORIGIN Old Norse *gæslingr*

go-slow *n* *Brit & NZ* a deliberate slowing of the rate of production by workers as a tactic in industrial conflict

gospel *n* **1 a** the teachings of Jesus Christ **b** the story of Christ's life and teachings **2** a doctrine held to be of great importance: *the gospel of self-help* **3** Also called: **gospel truth** unquestionable truth: *gross inaccuracies which are sometimes taken as gospel* ▷ *adj* **4** denoting a kind of religious music originating in the churches of the Black people in the Southern US
WORD ORIGIN Old English *gōdspell*, from *gōd* good + *spell* message

Gospel *n* *Christianity* any of the first four books of the New Testament, namely Matthew, Mark, Luke, and John, which tell the story of Jesus Christ

gossamer *n* **1** a very fine fabric **2** a filmy cobweb often seen on foliage or floating in the air
WORD ORIGIN probably Middle English *gos* goose + *somer* summer; referring to St Martin's summer, a period in November when goose was eaten and cobwebs abound

gossip *n* **1** idle talk, usually about other people's private lives, esp. of a disapproving or malicious nature: *office gossip* **2** an informal conversation, esp. about other people's private lives: *to have a gossip and a giggle* **3** a person who habitually talks about other people, usually maliciously ▷ *vb* **4** to talk idly or maliciously, esp. about other people's private lives **gossipy** *adj*
WORD ORIGIN Old English *godsibb* godparent, applied to a woman's female friends at the birth of a child

got *vb* **1** the past of **get 2 have got** to possess **3 have got to** must: *you have got to be prepared to work hard*

Gothic *adj* **1** of a style of architecture used in W Europe from the 12th to the 16th centuries, characterized by pointed arches, ribbed vaults, and flying buttresses **2** of a literary style featuring stories of gloom, horror, and the supernatural, popular in the late 18th century **3** of or in a heavy ornate script typeface ▷ *n* **4** Gothic architecture or art
WORD ORIGIN Greek *Gothoi*

go through *vb* **1** to experience (a difficult time or process) **2** to name or describe: *the president went through a list of government ministers* **3** to qualify for the next stage of a competition: *Belgium, Spain and Uruguay all went through from Group E* **4** to be approved: *the bill went through parliament* **5 go through with** to bring to a successful conclusion, often by persistence

gotten *vb* *chiefly US* a past participle of **get**

gouache *n* opaque watercolour paint bound with glue
WORD ORIGIN French

Gouda *n* a round mild-flavoured Dutch cheese

gouge (**gowj**) *vb* **gouging, gouged 1** to scoop or force (something) out of its position **2** to cut (a hole or groove) in something with a pointed object ▷ *n* **3** a mark or groove made by gouging
WORD ORIGIN French

goulash (**goo**-lash) *n* a rich stew seasoned with paprika, originating in Hungary
WORD ORIGIN Hungarian *gulyás hus* herdsman's meat

gourd (**goord**) *n* **1** a large hard-shelled fruit similar to a cucumber or marrow **2** a container made from a dried gourd shell
WORD ORIGIN Old French *gourde*

gourmand (**goor**-mand) *n* a person devoted to eating and drinking, usually to excess
WORD ORIGIN Old French *gourmant*

gourmet (**goor**-may) *n* an expert on good food and drink
WORD ORIGIN French

gout (gowt) *n* a disease that causes painful inflammation of certain joints, for example of the big toe **gouty** *adj*
WORD ORIGIN Latin *gutta* a drop

govern *vb* **1** to direct and control the policy and affairs of (a country or an organization) **2** to control or determine: *the international organizations governing athletics and rugby* **governable** *adj*
WORD ORIGIN Latin *gubernare* to steer

governance *n* government, control, or authority

governess *n* a woman employed in a private household to teach the children

government *n* **1** the executive policy-making body of a country or state **2** the state and its administration: *the assembled heads of state and government* **3** the system by which a country or state is ruled: *the old hard-line government* **governmental** *adj*

governor *n* **1** the chief political administrator of a region, such as a US state or a colony ▶ Related adjective: **gubernatorial 2** *Brit* the senior administrator of a school, prison, or other institution **3** *Brit informal* one's employer or father **governorship** *n*

governor general *n, pl* **governors general** *or* **governor generals** the chief representative of the British government in a Commonwealth country

go with *vb* **1** to blend or harmonize with: *the style goes well with modern art* **2** to be linked with: *respect goes with age*

go without *vb* to be denied or deprived of: *no-one should go without food*

gown *n* **1** a woman's long formal dress **2** a surgeon's overall **3** a loose wide official robe worn by clergymen, judges, lawyers, and academics
WORD ORIGIN Late Latin *gunna* garment made of fur

goy *n, pl* **goyim** *or* **goys** a Jewish word for a **Gentile**
WORD ORIGIN Yiddish

GP general practitioner

GPMU (in Britain) Graphical, Paper and Media Union

GPO (in Britain and Australia) general post office

GPS Global Positioning System: a satellite-based navigation system

Graafian follicle *n anat* a cavity in the ovary that contains a developing egg cell
WORD ORIGIN after R. de *Graaf*, anatomist

grab *vb* **grabbing, grabbed 1** to seize hold of **2** to take (food, drink, or rest) hurriedly **3** to take (an opportunity) eagerly **4** to seize illegally or unscrupulously: *land grabbing* **5** *informal* to interest or impress ▷ *n* **6** the act of grabbing
WORD ORIGIN probably from Middle Dutch *grabben*

grab bag *n* **1** a collection of miscellaneous things **2** *Austral, US, & Canad* a bag from which gifts are drawn at random

grace *n* **1** elegance and beauty of movement, form, or expression **2** a pleasing or charming quality:

architecture with few redeeming graces **3** courtesy or decency: *at least she had the grace to laugh* **4** a delay granted for the completion of a task or payment of a debt: *another year's grace* **5** *Christian theol* the free and unmerited favour of God shown towards humankind **6** a short prayer of thanks for a meal **7** **airs and graces** an affected manner **8** **with bad grace** unwillingly or grudgingly: *independence was granted with bad grace* **9** **with good grace** willingly or ungrudgingly: *to accept with good grace* ▷ *vb* **gracing, graced 10** to honour or favour: *graced by the presence of Henry Fonda* **11** to decorate or make more attractive: *bedsit walls graced by Che Guevara and James Dean*
WORD ORIGIN Latin *gratia*

Grace *n* **Your** *or* **His** *or* **Her Grace** a title used to address or refer to a duke, duchess, or archbishop

graceful *adj* having beauty of movement, style, or form **gracefully** *adv* **gracefulness** *n*

graceless *adj* **1** lacking elegance **2** lacking manners

grace note *n music* a note that ornaments a melody

Graces *pl n Greek myth* the three sister goddesses of charm and beauty

gracious *adj* **1** showing kindness and courtesy **2** characterized by elegance, ease, and indulgence: *gracious living* ▷ *interj* **3** an expression of mild surprise or wonder **graciously** *adv* **graciousness** *n*

gradation *n* **1** a series of systematic stages; gradual progression **2** a stage in such a series or progression

grade *n* **1** a place on a scale of quality, rank, or size **2** a mark or rating indicating a student's level of achievement **3** a rank or level of importance in a company or organization **4** *US, Canad, Austral, & S African* a class or year in a school **5** **make the grade** *informal* to be successful by reaching a required standard ▷ *vb* **grading, graded 6** to arrange according to quality or rank: *passes are graded from A down to E* **7** to give a grade to: *senior secretaries will need shorthand and be graded accordingly*
WORD ORIGIN Latin *gradus* step

gradient *n* **1** Also (esp. US): **grade** a sloping part of a railway, road, or path **2** Also (esp. US): **grade** a measure of the steepness of such a slope **3** a measure of the change in something, such as the angle of a curve, over a specified distance
WORD ORIGIN Latin *gradiens* stepping

gradual *adj* occurring, developing, or moving in small stages: *a gradual handover of power* **gradually** *adv*
WORD ORIGIN Latin *gradus* a step

gradualism *n* the policy of changing something gradually **gradualist** *adj*

graduate *n* **1** a person who holds a university or college degree **2** *US & Canad* a student who has completed a course of studies at a high school and received a diploma **3** same as **postgraduate** ▷ *vb* **-ating, -ated 4** to receive a degree or diploma **5** to change

by degrees: *the winds graduate from tropical storms to cyclones* **6** to mark (a measuring flask or instrument) with units of measurement
WORD ORIGIN Latin *gradus* a step

graduation *n* **1** the act of graduating from university or college **2** *US & Canad* the act of graduating from high school **3** the ceremony at which degrees and diplomas are given to graduating students **4** a mark indicating measure on an instrument or container

Graeco-Roman *or esp. US* **Greco-Roman** (greek-oh-**rome**-an) *adj* of, or showing the influence of, both Greek and Roman cultures

graffiti (graf-**fee**-tee) *n* drawings or words scribbled or sprayed on walls or posters
WORD ORIGIN Italian: little scratches

graft[1] *n* **1** *surgery* a piece of tissue transplanted to an area of the body in need of the tissue **2** a small piece of tissue from one plant that is joined to another plant so that they grow together as one ▷ *vb* **3** to transplant (tissue) to an area of the body in need of the tissue **4** to join (part of one plant) onto another plant so that they grow together as one **5** to attach or incorporate: *to graft Japanese production methods onto the American talent for innovation*
WORD ORIGIN Greek *graphein* to write

graft[2] *n* **1** *Brit informal* hard work **2** the practice of obtaining money by taking advantage of one's position ▷ *vb* **3** *informal* to work hard
WORD ORIGIN origin unknown

Grail *n* see **Holy Grail**

grain *n* **1** the small hard seedlike fruit of a cereal plant **2** a mass of such fruits gathered for food **3** cereal plants in general **4** a small hard particle: *a grain of salt* **5** a very small amount: *a grain of compassion* **6 a** the arrangement of the fibres, layers, or particles in wood, leather, or stone **b** the pattern or texture resulting from this **7 go against the grain** to be contrary to one's natural inclinations **grainy** *adj*
WORD ORIGIN Latin *granum*

gram *or* **gramme** *n* a metric unit of weight equal to one thousandth of a kilogram
WORD ORIGIN Greek *gramma* small weight

graminivorous *adj* (of an animal) grass-eating
WORD ORIGIN Latin *gramen* grass + *vorare* to swallow

grammar *n* **1** the rules of a language, that show how sentences are formed, or how words are inflected **2** the way in which grammar is used: *the teacher found errors of spelling and grammar* **3** a book on the rules of grammar
WORD ORIGIN Greek *gramma* letter

grammarian *n* a person who studies or writes about grammar for a living

grammar school *n* **1** *Brit* (esp. formerly) a secondary school for children of high academic ability **2** *US* same as **elementary school 3** *Austral* a private school, usually one controlled by a church

American English

The rise of the USA as a superpower has been matched by the emergence of its distinctive form of English. The great length of the Atlantic seaboard from Maine to Florida made it inevitable that the first European ships to venture across the ocean would bump up against the new continent. Along with hopes of economic, political, and religious betterment, the colonists, settlers, and immigrants imported their native languages. At first, in the northeast, that language was English. It was the English of New England that early in the nineteenth century led the Connecticut pedagogue Noah Webster to codify the American language, his work so influential that *Webster's* became synonymous with 'dictionary'. Webster and his rivals ensured that *centre* would be spelled *center*, *plough* would be *plow*, and *corn* would mean maize, not wheat. Speech would largely be rhotic, speakers pronouncing the *r* before a consonant (*hard*) and at the end of words (*far*). Today we hear the early lexicographers' General English echoed in primetime broadcast media and Hollywood movies.

Prior to Webster, vestiges of Elizabethan speech and British dialectical words had taken root in the rural areas of the Appalachian Mountains, and British, Irish, and French accents had fused into the varied speech of the South from Maryland to the Gulf of Mexico. Thwarted from expanding north into Canada by the stalemate of the War of 1812, the population of the new republic sprawled westward across forests and plains, eventually reaching California and even, far offshore, Hawaii. Meanwhile, the languages of conquered or displaced aboriginal peoples had fed numerous words (*squash, moccasin, opossum*) into the American lexicon. Thanks to the beckoning Atlantic seaboard, the European arrivals' languages were verbally transformed: Dutch (*boss, cookie, stoop*), French (*depot*), German (*hamburger* or *burger, frankfurter* or *frank*), and Yiddish (*dreck, chutzpah*).

Momentous political and military events transpired: Louisiana, Florida, and Alaska were purchased, and vast territories in California, the Southwest, and Texas, not to mention Guam and Puerto Rico, were won, seized, or absorbed from the Spanish Empire and Mexico. Over time, Spanish became in many places a second, or even the first, language, the *Chicanos* (Mexican Americans) gained cultural influence, and *salsa* outsold ketchup. To the Hispanics, America owes *barbecue, rodeo, canyon,* and *ranch*.

Throughout American history, the baleful effects of slavery and racial segregation made African Americans an enduring underclass, immured in rural poverty, later toiling in industrial Detroit, Chicago, and the Northeast. Blacks found relief, and later triumphed, in music, dance, and athletics. Many musical terms themselves became Americanisms: *blues, jazz, gospel, soul, rock 'n' roll, funk,* and *hip-hop*.

A fluid class structure; capitalistic, technological, and scientific innovation; and supremacy in popular culture and mass media long have made the United States a tireless coiner of jargon and specialized terminology (*split level, smart card*), idiomatic phrases (*right on!*), slang (*cathouse*), and informal words (*humdinger*). American English is also rich in euphemisms (*human resources* for *personnel, bathroom* or *restroom* for *toilet, senior citizen* or *senior* for elderly person). The automobile's twentieth-century domination brought *commuters* from home to work, where they sometimes had to *double-park* their cars. Since someone is nearly always running for office in the United States, political terms (*lame duck, filibuster*) abound. Likewise, military terms. America has often been at war, exiting a war, or thinking about getting into a war: the Vietnam War alone supplied *defoliate, fire base, grunt* (infantryman), *hack it* (manage or cope), and *napalm*. The sports – baseball, football, and basketball – that evolved or were invented spawned terms that often took on a figurative overlay: a *home run*, a *Hail Mary* pass, a *full-court press*. Less attributable is a fondness for compounds (*upfront, download*), the *-ize* ending for verbs (*accessorize, burglarize*), and nouns used as verbs (*access* a file, *profile* a person).

By the time the intellectual gadfly and word enthusiast HL Mencken published *The American Language* in 1919, his subject had become an established fact. No better illustration of the language's reach can be found than the remarkable career of *OK*, which first appeared in 1838 in Boston as a humorous abbreviation for 'oll korrect', itself humorous. It is likely the most widespread and readily recognized word in the world.

grammatical *adj* **1** of grammar **2** (of a sentence) following the rules of grammar **grammatically** *adv*

gramme *n* same as **gram**

gramophone *n* an old-fashioned type of record player
WORD ORIGIN inversion of *phonogram*

grampus *n, pl* **-puses** a dolphin-like mammal with a blunt snout
WORD ORIGIN Old French *gras* fat + *pois* fish

gran *n Brit, Austral, & NZ informal* a grandmother

granary *n, pl* **-ries 1** a building for storing threshed grain **2** a region that produces a large amount of grain
WORD ORIGIN Latin *granarium*

Granary *adj trademark* (of bread or flour) containing malted wheat grain

grand *adj* **1** large or impressive in size or appearance; magnificent: *the grand hall* **2** ambitious or important: *grand themes* **3** dignified or haughty **4** *informal* excellent or wonderful **5** comprehensive or complete: *the grand total* ▷ *n* **6** *pl* **grand** *slang* a thousand pounds or dollars **7** short for **grand piano** > **grandly** *adv*
WORD ORIGIN Latin *grandis*

grandad, granddad *or US* **granddaddy** *n, pl* **-dads** *or* **-daddies** *informal* a grandfather

grandchild *n, pl* **-children** a son or daughter of one's son or daughter

granddad *or US* **granddaddy** *n informal* see **grandad**

granddaughter *n* a daughter of one's son or daughter

grand duke *n* a prince or nobleman who rules a territory, state, or principality **grand duchess** *fem n* **grand duchy** *n*

grande dame (grond **dam**) *n* a woman regarded as the most prominent or respected member of her profession or group: *the grande dame of international fashion*
WORD ORIGIN French

grandee *n* **1** a high-ranking Spanish nobleman **2** a person who has a high rank or position: *the Party's grandees*
WORD ORIGIN Spanish *grande*

grandeur *n* **1** personal greatness, dignity, or nobility: *delusions of grandeur* **2** magnificence or splendour: *cathedral-like grandeur*

grandfather *n* the father of one's father or mother

grandfather clock *n* an old-fashioned clock in a tall wooden case that stands on the floor

grandiloquent *adj* using pompous or unnecessarily complicated language **grandiloquence** *n*
WORD ORIGIN Latin *grandiloquus*

grandiose *adj* impressive, or meant to impress: *grandiose plans for constructing a new stadium*
WORD ORIGIN French

grand jury *n law chiefly US* a jury that investigates accusations of crime to decide whether the evidence is adequate to bring a prosecution

grandma *or* **grandmama** *n informal* a grandmother

grand mal *n* a form of epilepsy in which there is loss of consciousness and violent convulsions
WORD ORIGIN French: great illness

grandmaster *n* a person who is exceptionally good at a particular activity or skill, especially chess

grandmother *n* the mother of one's father or mother

Grand National *n* an annual steeplechase for horses, run at Aintree, Liverpool

grandnephew *n* same as **great-nephew**

grandniece *n* same as **great-niece**

grand opera *n* an opera that has a serious plot and no spoken dialogue

grandpa *or* **grandpapa** *n informal* a grandfather

grandparent *n* the father or mother of one's father or mother

grand piano *n* a large piano in which the strings are arranged horizontally

Grand Prix (gron **pree**) *n* **1** an international formula one motor race **2** a very important international competitive event in other sports, such as athletics
WORD ORIGIN French: great prize

grandsire *n old-fashioned* a grandfather

grand slam *n* **1** the achievement of winning all the games or major tournaments in a sport in one season **2** see **slam²**

grandson *n* a son of one's son or daughter

grandstand *n* the main block of seats giving the best view at a sports ground

grand tour *n* **1** (formerly) an extended tour of continental Europe **2** *informal* a tour of inspection: *a grand tour of the house*

grange *n Brit* a farmhouse or country house with its farm buildings
WORD ORIGIN Anglo-French *graunge*

granite (**gran**-nit) *n* a very hard rock consisting of quartz and feldspars that is widely used for building
WORD ORIGIN Italian *granito* grained

granivorous *adj* (of an animal) grain-eating
WORD ORIGIN Latin *granum* grain + *vorare* to swallow

granny *or* **grannie** *n, pl* **-nies** *informal* a grandmother

granny flat *n* a flat in or joined on to a house, suitable for an elderly relative to live in

granny knot *n* a reef knot with the ends crossed the wrong way, making it liable to slip or jam

grant *vb* **1** to give (a sum of money or a right) formally: *to grant a 38% pay rise; only the President can grant a pardon* **2** to consent to perform or fulfil: *granting the men's request for sanctuary* **3** to admit that (something) is true: *I grant that her claims must be true* **4 take for granted a** to accept that something is true without requiring proof **b** to take advantage of (someone or something) without showing appreciation ▷ *n* **5** a sum of money provided by a government or public fund to a person

or organization for a specific purpose: *student grants*
WORD ORIGIN Old French *graunter*

Granth (**grunt**) *n* the sacred scripture of the Sikhs
WORD ORIGIN Hindi

grant-maintained school *n Brit* a school funded directly by central government

granular *adj* of, like, or containing granules: *granular materials such as powders*

granulated *adj* (of sugar) in the form of coarse grains

granule *n* a small grain of something: *gravy granules*
WORD ORIGIN Late Latin *granulum* a small grain

grape *n* a small round sweet juicy fruit with a purple or green skin, which can be eaten raw, dried to make raisins, currants, or sultanas, or used to make wine
WORD ORIGIN Old French *grape* bunch of grapes

grapefruit *n, pl* **-fruit** *or* **-fruits** a large round yellow juicy citrus fruit with a slightly bitter taste

grapeshot *n* ammunition for cannons consisting of a cluster of iron balls that scatter after firing

grapevine *n* **1** a vine grown for its grapes **2** *informal* an unofficial means of passing on information from person to person: *he'd doubtless heard rumours on the grapevine*

graph *n* a diagram showing the relation between certain sets of numbers or quantities by means of a series of dots or lines plotted with reference to a set of axes
WORD ORIGIN short for *graphic formula*

-graph *n combining form* **1** an instrument that writes or records: *tachograph* **2** a writing or record: *autograph* **-graphic** *or* **-graphical** *adj combining form* **-graphically** *adv combining form*
WORD ORIGIN Greek *graphein* to write

graphic *adj* **1** vividly described: *a graphic account of her three days in captivity* **2** of the graphic arts: *graphic design* **3** Also: **graphical** *maths* of or using a graph: *a graphic presentation* **graphically** *adv*
WORD ORIGIN Greek *graphikos*

graphic arts *pl n* the visual arts based on drawing or the use of line

graphics *n* **1** the art of drawing in accordance with mathematical rules ▷ *pl n* **2** the illustrations in a magazine or book, or in a television or film production **3** *computers* information displayed in the form of diagrams or graphs

graphite *n* a soft black form of carbon used in pencils, as a lubricant, and in some nuclear reactors
WORD ORIGIN German *Graphit*

graphology *n* the study of handwriting, usually to analyse the writer's character **graphologist** *n*

graph paper *n* paper printed with a design of small squares for drawing graphs or diagrams on

-graphy *n combining form* **1** indicating a form of writing or representing things: *calligraphy; photography* **2** indicating an

art or descriptive science: *choreography*; *topography*
WORD ORIGIN Greek *graphein* to write

grapnel *n* a device with several hooks at one end, which is used to grasp or secure an object, esp. in sailing
WORD ORIGIN Old French *grapin* a little hook

grapple *vb* -pling, -pled • **grapple with a** to try to cope with: *a difficult concept to grapple with* **b** to come to grips with (someone) in hand-to-hand combat
WORD ORIGIN Old French *grappelle* a little hook

grappling iron *n* same as **grapnel**

grasp *vb* **1** to grip firmly **2** to understand: *his failure to grasp the gravity of the crisis* ▷ *n* **3** a very firm grip **4** understanding or comprehension: *a good grasp of detail* **5** within someone's **grasp** almost certain to be accomplished or won: *he now has that prize within his grasp*
WORD ORIGIN Low German *grapsen*

grasping *adj* greedy for money

grass *n* **1** a very common green plant with jointed stems and long narrow leaves, eaten by animals such as sheep and cows, and used for lawns and sports fields **2** a particular kind of grass, such as bamboo **3** a lawn **4** *slang* marijuana **5** *Austral & Brit slang* a person who informs, usually on criminals ▷ *vb* **6** **grass on** *or* **up** *Brit slang* to inform on (someone) to the police or some other authority **7** **grass over** to cover with grass **grassy** *adj*
WORD ORIGIN Old English *græs*

grass hockey *n* (in W Canada) field hockey, as contrasted with ice hockey

grasshopper *n* an insect with long hind legs which it uses for leaping

grassland *n* **1** land covered with grass **2** pasture land

grass roots *pl n* **1** ordinary members of a group or organization, as distinct from its leaders ▷ *adj* **grassroots 2** of the ordinary members of a group or organization: *the focus of a virulent grassroots campaign*

grass snake *n* a harmless snake with a brownish-green body

grass tree *n* an Australian plant with stiff grass-like leaves and small white flowers

grass widow *n* a woman whose husband is regularly absent for a time
WORD ORIGIN perhaps an allusion to a grass bed as representing an illicit relationship

grate¹ *vb* grating, grated **1** to reduce to shreds by rubbing against a rough surface: *grated cheese* **2** to produce a harsh rasping sound by scraping against an object or surface: *the clutch plates grated* **3** **grate on** to annoy: *his manner always grated on me*
WORD ORIGIN Old French *grater*

grate² *n* **1** a framework of metal bars for holding coal or wood in a fireplace **2** same as **grating¹**
WORD ORIGIN Latin *cratis* hurdle

grateful *adj* feeling or showing thanks **gratefully** *adv*
WORD ORIGIN Latin *gratus*

grater *n* a tool with a sharp surface for grating food

gratify *vb* -fies, -fying, -fied **1** to satisfy or please (someone) **2** to yield to (a desire or whim): *all his wishes were to be gratified* **gratification** *n*
WORD ORIGIN Latin *gratus* grateful + *facere* to make

grating¹ *n* a framework of metal bars covering an opening in a wall or in the ground

grating² *adj* **1** (of a sound) rough or unpleasant **2** annoying or irritating: *his cringing obsequiousness was grating*

gratis *adv, adj* without payment; free: *the gifts are gratis*
WORD ORIGIN Latin

gratitude *n* a feeling of being grateful for gifts or favours
WORD ORIGIN Latin *gratus* grateful

gratuitous (grat-**tyoo**-it-uss) *adj* **1** unjustified or unreasonable: *gratuitous violence* **2** given or received without charge or obligation: *his gratuitous voluntary services* **gratuitously** *adv*
WORD ORIGIN Latin *gratuitus*

gratuity (grat-**tyoo**-it-ee) *n, pl* -ties money given for services rendered; tip

grave¹ *adj* (rhymes with **save**) **1** serious and worrying: *grave concern* **2** serious and solemn in appearance or behaviour: *the man looked grave and respectful* **3** (rhymes with **halve**) denoting an accent (`) over a vowel in some languages, such as French, which indicates that the vowel is pronounced in a particular way ▷ *n* (rhymes with **halve**) **4** a grave accent **gravely** *adv*
WORD ORIGIN Latin *gravis*

grave² (rhymes with **save**) *n* **1** a place where a dead person is buried ▶ Related adjective: **sepulchral 2** death: *people are smoking themselves to an early grave* **3** **make someone turn in his** *or* **her grave** to do something that would have shocked a person who is now dead
WORD ORIGIN Old English *græf*

gravel *n* **1** a mixture of rock fragments and pebbles that is coarser than sand **2** *pathol* small rough stones in the kidneys or bladder ▷ *vb* -elling, -elled *or US* -eling, -eled **3** to cover with gravel
WORD ORIGIN Old French *gravele*

gravelly *adj* **1** covered with gravel **2** (of a voice or sound) harsh and grating

graven image *n chiefly Bible* a carved image used as an idol

gravestone *n* a stone marking a grave

graveyard *n* a place where dead people are buried, esp. one by a church

graveyard slot *n television* the hours from late night until early morning when relatively few people are watching television

gravid (**grav**-id) *adj med* pregnant
WORD ORIGIN Latin *gravis* heavy

gravimeter (grav-**vim**-it-er) *n* **1** an instrument for measuring the force of gravity **2** an instrument for measuring relative density
WORD ORIGIN French *gravimètre*

gravitas (**grav**-vit-tass) *n* seriousness or solemnity
WORD ORIGIN Latin: weight

gravitate *vb* -tating, -tated **1** **gravitate towards** to be attracted or influenced by: *the mathematically inclined often gravitate towards computers* **2** *physics* to move under the influence of gravity

gravitation *n physics* **1** the force of attraction that bodies exert on one another as a result of their mass **2** the process or result of this interaction **gravitational** *adj*

gravity *n, pl* -ties **1** *physics* **a** the force that attracts bodies towards the centre of the earth, a moon, or any planet **b** same as **gravitation 2** seriousness or importance: *the gravity of the situation* **3** seriousness or solemnity of appearance or behaviour: *his priestly gravity*
WORD ORIGIN Latin *gravitas* weight

gravy *n, pl* -vies **a** the juices that come from meat during cooking **b** the sauce made by thickening and flavouring these juices
WORD ORIGIN Old French *gravé*

gravy boat *n* a small boat-shaped dish with a spout, used for serving gravy or sauce

gravy train *n slang* a job or scheme that produces a lot of money for little effort

gray *adj, n, vb chiefly US* grey

graze¹ *vb* grazing, grazed **a** (of an animal) to eat (grass or other growing plants) **b** to feed (animals) on grass or other growing plants
WORD ORIGIN Old English *grasian*

graze² *vb* grazing, grazed **1** to break the skin of (a part of the body) by scraping **2** to brush against someone gently in passing ▷ *n* **3** an injury on the skin caused by scraping
WORD ORIGIN probably a special use of GRAZE¹

grazier *n* a rancher or farmer who keeps cattle or sheep on grazing land

grazing *n* land where grass is grown for farm animals to feed upon

grease *n* **1** soft melted animal fat **2** a thick oily substance, such as the kind put on machine parts to make them work smoothly ▷ *vb* greasing, greased **3** to apply grease to: *lightly grease a baking tin* **4** **grease someone's palm** *slang* to bribe someone
WORD ORIGIN Latin *crassus* thick

greasepaint *n* theatrical make-up

greaseproof paper *n* any paper that is resistant to penetration by grease and oil, esp. one used for lining baking dishes or wrapping food

greasy *adj* greasier, greasiest **1** covered with or containing grease **2** excessively pleasant or flattering in an insincere manner **greasiness** *n*

great *adj* **1** large in size **2** large in number or amount: *the great majority* **3** larger than others of its kind: *the great white whale* **4** extreme or more than usual: *great difficulty* **5** of importance or consequence: *a great discovery* **6** of exceptional talents or achievements: *a great artist* **7** skilful: *he's a great storyteller; they are great at problem solving* **8** *informal* excellent ▷ *n* **9** **the greats** the most successful people in a particular field: *the all-time greats of golf* ▶ See also **Greats** ▷ **greatly** *adv* **greatness** *n*
WORD ORIGIN Old English *grēat*

great- *prefix* (in expressing relationship) one generation older or younger than: *great-grandmother*

great auk *n* an extinct large auk that could not fly

great-aunt *n* an aunt of one's father or mother

Great Britain *n* the mainland part of the British Isles; England, Scotland, and Wales

great circle *n maths* a circular section of a sphere that has a radius equal to the sphere's radius

greatcoat *n* a heavy overcoat

Great Dane *n* a very large dog with short smooth hair

great-nephew *n* a son of one's nephew or niece

great-niece *n* a daughter of one's nephew or niece

Greats *pl n* **1** the Honours course in classics, ancient history, and philosophy at Oxford University **2** the final examinations at the end of this course

great-uncle *n* an uncle of one's father or mother

Great War *n* same as **World War I**

greave *n* a piece of armour for the shin **WORD ORIGIN** Old French *greve*

grebe *n* a diving water bird **WORD ORIGIN** French

Grecian (**gree**-shan) *adj* of ancient Greece

greed *n* excessive desire for something, such as food or money

greedy *adj* **greedier, greediest** having an excessive desire for something, such as food or money: *greedy for personal possessions* **greedily** *adv* **WORD ORIGIN** Old English *grædig*

Greek *adj* **1** of Greece ▷ *n* **2** a person from Greece **3** the language of Greece

Greek cross *n* a cross with each of the four arms of the same length

green *adj* **1** of a colour between yellow and blue; of the colour of grass **2** covered with grass, plants, or trees: *green fields* **3** of or concerned with conservation and improvement of the environment: used in a political context: *green issues* **4** (of fruit) fresh, raw, or unripe **5** pale and sick-looking **6** inexperienced or gullible **7** **green with envy** very envious ▷ *n* **8** a colour between yellow and blue **9** anything green, such as green clothing or green ink: *printed in green* **10** a small area of grassy land: *the village green* **11** an area of smooth turf kept for a special purpose: *putting greens* **12** **greens** the leaves and stems of certain plants, eaten as a vegetable: *turnip greens* **13** **Green** a person who supports environmentalist issues **greenish** or **greeny** *adj* **greenness** *n* **WORD ORIGIN** Old English *grēne*

green beans *pl n* long narrow green beans that are cooked and eaten as a vegetable

green belt *n* a protected zone of parkland or open country surrounding a town or city

green card *n* an official permit allowing the holder permanent residence and employment, issued to foreign nationals in the US

Green Cross Code *n Brit* a code for children giving rules on road safety

greenery *n* green leaves or growing plants: *lush greenery*

green-eyed monster *n* jealousy

greenfield *adj* relating to a rural area which has not previously been built on: *greenfield factory sites*

greenfinch *n* a European finch, the male of which has olive-green feathers

green fingers *pl n* skill in growing plants

greenfly *n, pl* **-flies** a green aphid commonly occurring as a pest on plants

greengage *n* a green sweet variety of plum **WORD ORIGIN** after Sir W. *Gage*, botanist

greengrocer *n Austral & Brit* a shopkeeper who sells fruit and vegetables

greenhorn *n* an inexperienced person; novice **WORD ORIGIN** originally an animal with *green* (that is, young) horns

greenhouse *n* **1** a building with glass walls and roof where plants are grown under controlled conditions ▷ *adj* **2** relating to or contributing to the greenhouse effect: *greenhouse gases such as carbon dioxide*

greenhouse effect *n* the gradual rise in temperature in the earth's atmosphere due to heat being absorbed from the sun and being trapped by gases such as carbon dioxide in the air around the earth

greenkeeper *n* a person responsible for maintaining a golf course or bowling green

green light *n* **1** a signal to go **2** permission to proceed with a project ▷ *vb* **greenlight, -lighting, -lighted 3** to permit (a project) to proceed

green paper *n* a government document containing policy proposals to be discussed

green pepper *n* the green unripe fruit of the sweet pepper, eaten as a vegetable

greenroom *n* (esp. formerly) a backstage room in a theatre where performers rest or receive visitors

greenstick fracture *n* a fracture in which the bone is partly bent and splinters only on the outer side of the bend

greenstone *n NZ* a type of green jade used for Māori carvings and ornaments

greensward *n archaic or literary* an area of fresh green turf

green tea *n* tea made from leaves that have been dried quickly without fermenting

greenway *n US* a corridor of protected open space that is maintained for conservation, recreation, and non-motorized transportation

Greenwich Mean Time (**gren**-itch) *n* the local time of the 0° meridian passing through Greenwich, England: a basis for calculating times throughout most of the world. Abbrev: **GMT**

greet[1] *vb* **1** to address or meet with expressions of friendliness or welcome **2** to receive in a specified manner: *a direct request would be greeted coolly* **3** to be immediately noticeable to: *the scene of devastation which greeted him* **WORD ORIGIN** Old English *grētan*

greet[2] *vb Scot* to weep **WORD ORIGIN** Old English *grætan*

greeting *n* the act or words of welcoming on meeting

greetings *interj* an expression of friendly salutation

gregarious *adj* **1** enjoying the company of others **2** (of animals) living together in herds or in flocks **WORD ORIGIN** Latin *grex* flock

Gregorian calendar *n* the revision of the calendar introduced in 1582 by Pope Gregory XIII and still widely used

Gregorian chant *n* same as **plainsong**

gremlin *n* an imaginary imp jokingly blamed for malfunctions in machinery **WORD ORIGIN** origin unknown

grenade *n* a small bomb filled with explosive or gas, thrown by hand or fired from a rifle **WORD ORIGIN** Spanish *grenada* pomegranate

grenadier *n mil* **1** (in the British Army) a member of the senior regiment of infantry in the Household Brigade (the **Grenadier Guards**) **2** (formerly) a soldier trained to throw grenades **WORD ORIGIN** French

grenadine (gren-a-**deen**) *n* a syrup made from pomegranate juice, often used as an ingredient in cocktails

grevillea *n* any of various Australian evergreen trees and shrubs **WORD ORIGIN** after C. F. *Greville*, botanist

grew *vb* the past tense of **grow**

grey or US **gray** *adj* **1** of a colour between black and white; of the colour of ashes **2 a** (of hair) having partly turned white **b** (of a person) having grey hair **3** dismal, dark, or gloomy: *a grey and misty morning* **4** dull or boring: *in 1948 life generally was grey* ▷ *n* **5** a colour between black and white **6** anything grey, such as grey paint or grey clothing: *available in grey or brown* **7** a grey or whitish horse **greyness** *n* **greyish** *adj* **WORD ORIGIN** Old English *grǣg*

grey area *n* a situation or area that has no clearly defined characteristics or that falls somewhere between two categories

greyed out *adj* (of a navigation button, menu item, etc. on a computer screen) not highlighted, indicating that the function is not available

Grey Friar *n* a Franciscan friar

greyhound *n* a tall slender dog that can run very fast and is used for racing

greying *adj* becoming grey: *greying hair*

greylag or **greylag goose** *n* a large grey Eurasian goose **WORD ORIGIN** GREY + LAG, because it migrates later than other species

grey matter *n informal* intellect or brains: *those who don't have lots of grey matter*

Lewis Carroll

Lewis Carroll was a pseudonym used by the Reverend Charles Lutwidge Dodgson, who was born in 1832 in Cheshire. He taught mathematics at Christ Church College, Oxford, became the Deacon of Christ Church Cathedral in 1861, and, under the pen name of Lewis Carroll, contributed to literature some of the best known and linguistically inventive works written in the English language. His most famous books are undoubtedly *Alice's Adventures in Wonderland* (1865 – often shortened to *Alice in Wonderland*) and its sequel *Through the Looking-Glass and What Alice Found There* (1871). In both stories, a young girl finds herself transported into a bizarre, dream-like world in which she moves through a sequence of adventures. These two titles introduced a host of colourful literary creations that remain instantly recognizable to this day, including The Mad Hatter and the grinning Cheshire Cat, and English idioms such as *down the rabbit hole*. Carroll also wrote the nonsense poem *The Hunting of the Snark* (1876), while his poem *Jabberwocky* (originally part of *Through the Looking-Glass...*) is one of the most celebrated example of nonsense verse in English.

Jabberwocky was written in Sunderland and may have been inspired by the local legend of the Lambton Worm, a creature from folklore said to have terrorized the countryside before being slain by a knight returned from the Crusades, John Lambton. The poem uses nonsense words (or *nonce words*: defined by *Collins English Dictionary* as words coined for one occasion) in its playful linguistic approach. Many examples are portmanteau words, including adjectives such as *slithy* (a combination of *slimy* and *lithe*), *mimsy* (a combination of *miserable* and *flimsy*), *frabjous* (possibly a blend of *fabulous* and *joyous*), and *frumious* (which combines *fuming* and *furious*), which is descriptive of the ferocious *bandersnatch*. It also presents an assorted bestiary of imaginary creatures: besides the *bandersnatch* and the titular monster there are *raths*, *borogroves*, and *toves*. Obviously, these words have limited application to wider English, as do *beamish* (meaning both 'beam-ing' and 'happy'), *manxome* (both 'monstrous' and 'fearsome'), *snicker-snack* (an onomatopoeic word indicative of the hacking and slashing of a sword) and *tulgey* (thick and dark). However, some of the language that Carroll coined has become rooted firmly in everyday speech. *Chortle*, for example, which is an amalgam of *chuckle* and *snort*, and *galumphing* which is used to describe galloping in triumph. Some of the poem's words already existed in English, but were used in the poem to more inventive effect. *Gyre*, for example, was a verb dating back to the sixteenth century meaning 'to rotate'. However, in Carroll's poem, it has a slightly different pronunciation and uses a hard 'g'. *Burble* is also a pre-existing word established in the fourteeth century, and seems most likely to be of imitative origin, analogous to the Spanish *borbollar*, meaning 'to bubble or gush'.

It would be misleading, however, to suggest that Carroll dealt solely in the realms of nonsense. He also wrote essays, poems, and academic texts on logic and mathematics in his time. He died of pneumonia in 1898, but left his mark on the English language not only in terms of the words he added to it, but also by the manner in which his work displays the wondrous capacity of English to evolve. It is a surprise to most to learn that *chortle* was invented by an author as recently as the nineteenth century, and is an excellent illustrative example of linguistic invention for those who dismiss neologisms as 'made up' words. The English language is flexible, adaptive, and above all acquisitive, and always has room to add more words to its lexicon. A further illustration of both Carroll's inventive gift and of the English language's flexibility is the way that the word *snark* has developed. In Carroll's poem, the Snark is a creature of indeterminate physical form, but the word's make-up suggests connections with sarcasm and irritation (as in *nark*), from which developed the adjective *snarky* meaning 'rude and sarcastic'. In a final development, this adjective gave rise to a new meaning of the noun *snark*: vitriol or malicious gossip communicated via the internet.

grey squirrel *n* a grey-furred squirrel, native to E North America but now common in Britain

grid *n* **1** a network of crossing parallel lines on a map, plan, or graph paper for locating points **2 the grid** the national network of cables or pipes by which electricity, gas, or water is distributed **3** *electronics* an electrode that controls the flow of electrons between the cathode and anode of a valve **WORD ORIGIN** from *gridiron*

griddle *n* a thick round iron plate placed on top of a cooker and used to cook food **WORD ORIGIN** Old French *gridil*

gridiron *n* **1** a utensil of parallel metal bars, used to grill food **2 a** the field of play in American football **b** *informal* same as **American football** **WORD ORIGIN** Middle English *gredire*

gridlock *n* **1** obstruction of traffic caused by queues of vehicles forming across junctions and so causing queues in intersecting streets **2** a point in a dispute at which no agreement can be reached: *political gridlock* ▷ *vb* **3** (of traffic) to obstruct (an area)

grid reference *n* a series of numbers indicating the location of a point on a map

grief *n* **1** deep or intense sorrow **2** *informal* trouble or annoyance: *people were giving me grief for leaving ten minutes early* **3 come to grief** to have an unfortunate or unsuccessful end or outcome

grief-stricken *adj* deeply affected by sorrow

grievance *n* **1** a real or imaginary cause for complaint **2** a feeling of resentment at having been unfairly treated

grieve *vb* **grieving, grieved** to feel or cause to feel great sorrow or distress **grieved** *adj* **grieving** *adj* **WORD ORIGIN** Old French *grever*

grievous *adj* **1** very severe or painful: *grievous injuries* **2** very serious or worrying: *a grievous loss* **grievously** *adv*

grievous bodily harm *n criminal law* serious injury caused by one person to another

griffin, griffon *or* **gryphon** *n* a mythical winged monster with an eagle's head and a lion's body **WORD ORIGIN** Old French *grifon*

griffon *n* **1** a large vulture with pale feathers and black wings **2** a small wire-haired breed of dog **WORD ORIGIN** French

grill *vb* **1** to cook by direct heat under a grill or over a hot fire **2** *informal* to subject to relentless questioning: *the jury pool was grilled for signs of prejudice* ▷ *n* **3** a device on a cooker that radiates heat downwards for grilling food **4** a gridiron for cooking food **5** a dish of grilled food **6** see **grillroom** ▷ **grilled** *adj* **grilling** *n* **WORD ORIGIN** Latin *craticula* fine wickerwork

grille *or* **grill** *n* a metal or wooden grating, used as a screen or partition **WORD ORIGIN** Latin *craticula* fine hurdlework

grillroom *n* a restaurant specializing in grilled foods

grilse (**grillss**) *n, pl* **grilses** *or* **grilse** a salmon on its first return from the sea to fresh water **WORD ORIGIN** origin unknown

grim *adj* **grimmer, grimmest** **1** unfavourable and worrying: *grim figures on unemployment* **2** harsh and unpleasant: *grim conditions in the detention centres* **3** stern or resolute: *a grim determination to fight on* **4** *informal* unpleasant or disagreeable **grimly** *adv* **grimness** *n* **WORD ORIGIN** Old English *grimm*

grimace *n* **1** an ugly or distorted facial expression of disgust, pain, or displeasure ▷ *vb* **-macing, -maced** **2** to make a grimace **WORD ORIGIN** French

grime *n* **1** ingrained dirt ▷ *vb* **griming, grimed 2** to make very dirty: *sweat-grimed faces* **grimy** *adj* **WORD ORIGIN** Middle Dutch

grin *vb* **grinning, grinned 1** to smile broadly, showing one's teeth **2 grin and bear it** *informal* to suffer hardship without complaint ▷ *n* **3** a broad smile **grinning** *adj* **WORD ORIGIN** Old English *grennian*

grind *vb* **grinding, ground 1** to reduce to small particles by pounding or rubbing: *grinding coffee* **2** to smooth, sharpen, or polish by friction **3** (of two objects) to scrape together with a harsh rasping sound **4 an axe to grind** see **axe** (sense 2) **5 grind one's teeth** to rub one's upper and lower teeth against each other, as if chewing **6 grind to a halt** to come to an end or a standstill: *without enzymes life would grind to a halt* ▷ *n* **7** *informal* hard or tedious work: *the grind of everyday life* ▸ See also **grind down** **WORD ORIGIN** Old English *grindan*

grind down *vb* to treat harshly so as to suppress resistance: *to grind down the opposition*

grinder *n* a device for grinding substances: *an electric coffee grinder*

grindstone *n* **1** a revolving stone disc used for sharpening, grinding, or polishing things **2 keep one's nose to the grindstone** to work hard and steadily

grip *n* **1** a very tight hold: *he felt a grip at his throat* **2** the style or manner of holding something, such as a golf club or tennis racket **3** power or control over a situation, person, or activity: *rebel forces tighten their grip around the capital* **4** a travelling bag or holdall **5** a small bent clasp used to fasten the hair **6** a handle **7** a person who manoeuvres the cameras in a film or television studio **8 get** *or* **come to grips with** to face up to and deal with (a problem or subject) ▷ *vb* **gripping, gripped 9** to take a tight hold of **10** to affect strongly: *sudden panic gripped her* **11** to hold the interest or attention of: *gripped by the intensity of the film; the story gripped him* **WORD ORIGIN** Old English *gripe* grasp

gripe *vb* **griping, griped 1** *informal* to complain persistently **2** to cause sudden intense pain in the bowels ▷ *n* **3** *informal* a complaint **4 the gripes** a sudden intense pain in the bowels **WORD ORIGIN** Old English *grīpan*

grippe *n* a former name for **influenza** **WORD ORIGIN** French

gripping *adj* very interesting and exciting: *a gripping story*

grisly *adj* **-lier, -liest** causing horror or dread: *grisly murders* **WORD ORIGIN** Old English *grislic*

USAGE See at **grizzly**.

grist *n* **1** grain that is to be or that has been ground **2 grist to the mill** anything that can be turned to profit or advantage **WORD ORIGIN** Old English *grīst*

gristle *n* tough stringy animal tissue found in meat **gristly** *adj* **WORD ORIGIN** Old English

grit *n* **1** small hard particles of sand, earth, or stone **2** courage and determination ▷ *vb* **gritting, gritted 3** to cover (an icy road) with grit **4 grit one's teeth a** to rub one's upper and lower teeth against each other, as if chewing **b** to decide to carry on in a difficult situation: *he urged the Cabinet to grit its teeth and continue cutting public spending* **WORD ORIGIN** Old English *grēot*

grits *pl n* coarsely ground grain, a popular dish in the Southern US **WORD ORIGIN** Old English *grytt*

gritter *n* a vehicle that spreads grit on the roads in icy weather

gritty *adj* **-tier, -tiest 1** courageous and tough **2** covered with grit

grizzle *vb* **-zling, -zled** *Brit, Austral, & NZ informal* to whine or complain **WORD ORIGIN** Germanic

grizzled *adj* **1** (of hair) streaked or mixed with grey **2** (of a person) having grey hair

grizzly *n, pl* **-zlies** a large fierce greyish-brown bear of N America. In full: **grizzly bear**

USAGE Grizzly is sometimes wrongly used where grisly is meant: *a grisly (not grizzly) murder.*

groan *n* **1** a long deep cry of pain, grief, or disapproval **2** *informal* a grumble or complaint ▷ *vb* **3** to give a long deep cry of pain, grief, or disapproval **4** *informal* to complain or grumble **5 groan under** to be weighed down by: *chemists' shelves groan under the weight of slimming aids* **groaning** *adj, n* **WORD ORIGIN** Old English *grānian*

groat *n* a former British coin worth four old pennies **WORD ORIGIN** Middle Dutch *groot*

groats *pl n* the crushed grain of various cereals **WORD ORIGIN** Old English *grot* particle

grocer *n* a shopkeeper who sells food and other household supplies **WORD ORIGIN** Old French *grossier*

groceries *pl n* food and other household supplies

grocery *n, pl* **-ceries** the business or premises of a grocer

grog *n* **1** an alcoholic drink, usually rum, diluted with water **2** *Brit, Austral, & NZ informal* any alcoholic drink

WORD ORIGIN after Old *Grog*, nickname of Edward Vernon, British admiral, who in 1740 issued naval rum diluted with water

groggy *adj* **-gier, -giest** *informal* faint, weak, or dizzy

groin *n* **1** the part of the body where the abdomen joins the legs **2** *archit* a curved edge formed where two intersecting vaults meet
WORD ORIGIN origin unknown

grommet *n* **1** a rubber, plastic, or metal ring or eyelet **2** *med* a small tube inserted into the eardrum to drain fluid from the middle ear
WORD ORIGIN obsolete French *gourmer* bridle

groom *n* **1** a person employed to clean and look after horses **2** short for **bridegroom** ▷ *vb* **3** to clean and smarten (a horse or other animal) **4** to keep (oneself or one's appearance) clean and tidy: *carefully groomed hair* **5** to train (someone) for a particular task or occupation: *groomed for future leadership* **grooming** *n*
WORD ORIGIN Middle English *grom* manservant

groove *n* **1** a long narrow furrow cut into a surface **2** the spiral channel in a gramophone record **grooved** *adj*
WORD ORIGIN obsolete Dutch *groeve*

groovy *adj* **groovier, grooviest** *slang* attractive, fashionable, or exciting

grope *vb* **groping, groped 1** to feel about uncertainly for something **2** to find (one's way) by groping **3** to search uncertainly for a solution or expression: *the new democracies are groping for stability* **4** *slang* to fondle (someone) in a rough sexual way ▷ *n* **5** an instance of groping
WORD ORIGIN Old English *grāpian*

gros point (**groh** point) *n* **1** a cross-stitch in embroidery **2** work done in this stitch
WORD ORIGIN Old French: large point

gross *adj* **1** outrageously wrong: *gross violations of human rights* **2** very coarse or vulgar: *gross bad taste* **3** *slang* disgusting or repulsive: *I think beards are gross* **4** repulsively fat **5** with no deductions for tax or the weight of the container; total: *gross income; a gross weight of 20 000 lbs* ▷ *n* **6** *pl* **gross** twelve dozen (144) **7** the entire amount or weight ▷ *vb* **8** to earn as total revenue, before deductions **grossly** *adv*
WORD ORIGIN Old French *gros* large

gross domestic product *n* the total value of all goods and services produced domestically by a nation during a year

gross national product *n* the total value of all final goods and services produced annually by a nation: equivalent to gross domestic product plus net investment income from abroad

gross profit *n* *accounting* the difference between total revenue from sales and the total cost of purchases or materials

grotesque (groh-**tesk**) *adj* **1** strangely distorted or bizarre: *a grotesque and pervasive personality cult* **2** ugly or repulsive **3** a grotesque person or thing **4** an artistic style in which parts of human, animal, and plant forms are distorted and mixed, or a work of art in this style **grotesquely** *adv*
WORD ORIGIN Old Italian (*pittura*) *grottesca* cave (painting)

grotto *n, pl* **-toes** or **-tos** a small picturesque cave
WORD ORIGIN Old Italian *grotta*

grotty *adj* **-tier, -tiest** *Brit & NZ slang* **1** nasty or unattractive **2** in bad condition
WORD ORIGIN from *grotesque*

grouch *informal vb* **1** to complain or grumble ▷ *n* **2** a person who is always complaining **3** a persistent complaint
WORD ORIGIN Old French *grouchier*

grouchy *adj* **grouchier, grouchiest** bad-tempered

ground¹ *n* **1** the land surface **2** earth or soil **3** an area used for a particular purpose: *a cricket ground* **4** a matter for consideration or discussion: *there is no need to cover the same ground* **5** an advantage in an argument or competition: *neither side seems willing to give ground in this trial of strength* **6** the background colour of a painting **7** *US & Canad* an electrical earth **8** **grounds a** the land around a building **b** reason or justification: *the hostages should be freed on humanitarian grounds* **c** sediment or dregs: *coffee grounds* **9** **break new ground** to do something that has not been done before **10** **common ground** an agreed basis for identifying issues in an argument **11** **get something off the ground** to get something started: *to get the peace conference off the ground* **12** **into the ground** to exhaustion or excess: *he was running himself into the ground* **13** **suit someone down to the ground** *Brit informal* to be totally suitable or appropriate for someone ▷ *adj* **14** on the ground: *ground troops* ▷ *vb* **15** to confine (an aircraft or pilot) to the ground **16** *naut* to move (a ship) onto the bottom of shallow water, so that it cannot move **17** to instruct in the basics of a subject: *the student who is not grounded in the elements cannot understand the advanced teaching* **18** to provide a basis for; establish: *a scientifically grounded documentation* **19** to forbid (a child) to go out and enjoy himself or herself as a punishment **20** *US & Canad* to connect (a circuit or electrical device) to an earth
WORD ORIGIN Old English *grund*

ground² *vb* **1** the past of **grind** ▷ *adj* **2** reduced to fine particles by grinding: *ground glass*

ground bass *n music* a short melodic bass line that is repeated over and over again

ground beef *n* finely chopped beef, sometimes used to make hamburgers

ground-breaking *adj* innovative

ground control *n* the people and equipment on the ground that monitor the progress of aircraft or spacecraft

ground cover *n* dense low plants that spread over the surface of the ground

ground floor *n* the floor of a building that is level, or almost level, with the ground

grounding *n* a foundation, esp. the basic general knowledge of a subject

groundless *adj* without reason or justification: *the scare turned out to be groundless*

groundnut *n Brit* a peanut

groundsel (**grounce**-el) *n* a yellow-flowered weed
WORD ORIGIN Old English *grundeswelge*

groundsheet *n* a waterproof sheet placed on the ground in a tent to keep out damp

groundsman *n, pl* **-men** a person employed to maintain a sports ground or park

groundswell *n* a rapidly developing general feeling or opinion

ground water *n* water that has seeped through from the surface and is held underground

groundwork *n* preliminary work as a foundation or basis

group *n* **1** a number of people or things considered as a unit **2** a small band of players or singers, esp. of popular music **3** an association of business firms that have the same owner **4** *chem* two or more atoms that are bound together in a molecule and behave as a single unit: *a methyl group* –CH_3 **5** *chem* a vertical column of elements in the periodic table that all have similar properties: *the halogen group* ▷ *vb* **6** to put into or form into a group
WORD ORIGIN French *groupe*

group captain *n* a middle-ranking officer in some air forces

groupie *n slang* an ardent fan of a celebrity or of a sport or activity: *a polo groupie*

grouping *n* a set of people or organizations who act or work together to achieve a shared aim: *a pro-democracy grouping within China*

group therapy *n psychol* the treatment of people by bringing them together to share their problems in group discussion

grouse¹ *n, pl* **grouse 1** a game bird with a stocky body and feathered legs and feet **2** the flesh of this bird used for food
WORD ORIGIN origin unknown

grouse² *vb* **grousing, groused 1** to complain or grumble ▷ *n* **2** a persistent complaint
WORD ORIGIN origin unknown

grouse³ *adj Austral & NZ slang* fine or excellent
WORD ORIGIN origin unknown

grout *n* **1** a thin mortar for filling joints between tiles or masonry ▷ *vb* **2** to fill with grout
WORD ORIGIN Old English *grūt*

grove *n* a small wood or group of trees: *orange groves*
WORD ORIGIN Old English *grāf*

grovel (**grov**-el) *vb* **-elling, -elled** or *US* **-eling, -eled 1** to behave excessively humbly towards someone, esp. a superior, in an attempt to win his or her favour **2** to crawl on the floor, often in search of something: *grovelling on the floor for missing cards* **grovelling** or *US* **groveling** *adj, n*
WORD ORIGIN Middle English *on grufe* on the face

grow *vb* **growing, grew, grown 1** (of a person or animal) to increase in size and develop physically **2** (of a plant) to exist and increase in size: *an ancient meadow where wild flowers grow* **3** to produce (a plant) by planting seeds, bulbs, or cuttings, and looking after it: *many farmers have expressed a wish to grow more cotton* **4** to let (one's hair or nails) develop: *to grow a beard* **5** to increase in size or degree: *the gulf between rich and poor is growing* **6** to originate or develop: *Melbourne grew from a sheep-farming outstation and occasional port to a city* **7** to become increasingly as specified: *as the night wore on the audience grew more intolerant* ▷ See also **grow on, grow out of,** etc. **growing** *adj* **grower** *n*
WORD ORIGIN Old English *grōwan*

growing pains *pl n* **1** pains in muscles or joints sometimes experienced by growing children **2** difficulties experienced in the early stages of a new enterprise

growl *vb* **1** (of a dog or other animal) to make a low rumbling sound, usually in anger **2** to say in a gruff or angry manner: *'You're late,' he growled* **3** to make a deep rumbling sound: *his stomach growled* ▷ *n* **4** the act or sound of growling
WORD ORIGIN Old French *grouller* to grumble

grown *adj* developed or advanced: *fully grown; a grown man*

grown-up *adj* **1** having reached maturity; adult **2** of or suitable for an adult ▷ *n* **3** an adult

grow on *vb* to become progressively more acceptable or pleasant to: *I didn't like that programme at first but it has grown on me*

grow out of *vb* to become too big or mature for: *I used to be into the fifties scene but grew out of it*

growth *n* **1** the process of growing **2** an increase in size, number, or significance: *the growth of drug trafficking* **3** something grown or growing: *a thick growth of ivy* **4** any abnormal tissue, such as a tumour ▷ *adj* **5** of or relating to growth: *growth hormone*

grow up *vb* to reach maturity; become adult

groyne *n* a wall or breakwater built out from a shore to control erosion
WORD ORIGIN Old French *groign* snout

grub *n* **1** *slang* food **2** the short legless larva of certain insects, such as beetles ▷ *vb* **grubbing, grubbed 3** to search carefully for something by digging or by moving things about **4 grub up** to dig (roots or plants) out of the ground
WORD ORIGIN Germanic

grubby *adj* **-bier, -biest 1** rather dirty **2** unsavoury or morally unacceptable: *grubby activities* **grubbiness** *n*

grudge *n* **1** a persistent feeling of resentment against a person who has caused harm or upset ▷ *vb* **grudging, grudged 2** to give unwillingly: *the rich men who grudged pennies for the poor* **3** to resent or envy the success or possessions of: *none of their guests grudged them this celebration* ▷ *adj* **4** planned or carried out in order to

settle a grudge: *a grudge match*
WORD ORIGIN Old French *grouchier* to grumble

grudging *adj* felt or done unwillingly: *grudging admiration for his opponent* **grudgingly** *adv*

gruel *n* thin porridge made by boiling oatmeal in water or milk
WORD ORIGIN Old French

gruelling *or US* **grueling** *adj* extremely severe or tiring: *a gruelling journey*
WORD ORIGIN obsolete *gruel* to punish

gruesome *adj* inspiring horror and disgust
WORD ORIGIN Scandinavian

gruff *adj* **1** rough or surly in manner or speech **2** (of a voice) low and throaty **gruffly** *adv* **gruffness** *n*
WORD ORIGIN Germanic

grumble *vb* **-bling, -bled 1** to complain in a nagging way: *his neighbour grumbled about the long wait* **2** to make low rumbling sounds: *the storm grumbled in the distance* ▷ *n* **3** a complaint **4** a low rumbling sound: *a distant grumble of artillery fire* **grumbling** *adj, n*
WORD ORIGIN Middle Low German *grommelen*

grumpy *adj* **grumpier, grumpiest** sulky and bad-tempered **grumpily** *adv*
WORD ORIGIN imitative

grunge *n* **1** a style of rock music with a fuzzy guitar sound **2** a deliberately untidy and uncoordinated fashion style
WORD ORIGIN from US slang: dirt, rubbish

grungy *adj* **grungier, grungiest** *slang* **1** *chiefly US & Canad* squalid or seedy **2** (of pop music) characterized by a loud fuzzy guitar sound

grunt *vb* **1** to make a low short gruff noise, such as the sound made by a pig, or by a person to express annoyance **2** to express (something) gruffly: *he grunted his thanks* ▷ *n* **3** a low short gruff noise, such as the sound made by a pig, or by a person to express annoyance
WORD ORIGIN Old English *grunnettan*

Gruyère (grew-**yair**) *n* a hard flat pale yellow cheese with holes
WORD ORIGIN after *Gruyère*, Switzerland, where it originated

gryphon *n* same as **griffin**

GST (in Australia, New Zealand, and Canada) Goods and Services Tax

G-string *n* a strip of cloth worn between the legs and attached to a waistband

G-suit *n* a close-fitting pressurized garment that is worn by the crew of high-speed aircraft
WORD ORIGIN from *g*(ravity) suit

GT gran turismo: a touring car, usually a fast sports car with a hard fixed roof

guano (**gwah**-no) *n* the dried manure of sea birds, used as a fertilizer
WORD ORIGIN S American Indian *huano* dung

guarantee *n* **1** a formal assurance in writing that a product or service will meet certain standards or specifications **2** something that makes a specified condition or outcome certain: *there was no guarantee that there would not be another military coup* **3** same as **guaranty** ▷ *vb*

-**teeing, -teed 4** to promise or make certain: *to guarantee absolute loyalty* **5** (of a company) to provide a guarantee in writing for (a product or service) **6** to take responsibility for the debts or obligations of (another person)
WORD ORIGIN Germanic

guarantor *n* a person who gives or is bound by a guarantee or guaranty

guaranty *n, pl* **-ties 1** a pledge of responsibility for fulfilling another person's obligations in case of that person's default **2** a thing given or taken as security for a guaranty

guard *vb* **1** to watch over or shield from danger or harm; protect: *US marines who guard the American embassy* **2** to keep watch over (a prisoner) to prevent escape **3** to protect (a right or privilege) **4** to take precautions: *to guard against a possible coup attempt* ▷ *n* **5** a person or group of people who protect or watch over people or things **6** *Brit, Austral, & NZ* the official in charge of a train **7** a device or part of a machine designed to protect the user against injury **8** anything that provides protection: *a guard against future shocks* **9 off guard** having one's defences down; unprepared: *England were caught off guard as the Dutch struck two telling blows* **10 on guard** on duty to protect or watch over people or things **11 on one's guard** prepared to face danger or difficulties: *parents have been warned to be on their guard against kidnappers* **12 stand guard** (of a sentry) to keep watch
WORD ORIGIN Old French *garder* to protect

guarded *adj* cautious and avoiding any commitment: *a guarded welcome* **guardedly** *adv*

guardhouse *or* **guardroom** *n mil* a military police office in which prisoners can be detained

guardian *n* **1** one who looks after, protects, or defends someone or something: *the nation's moral guardians* **2** someone legally appointed to manage the affairs of another person, such as a child or a person who is mentally ill **guardianship** *n*

guardsman *n, pl* **-men** *mil* a member of a regiment responsible for ceremonial duties

guard's van *n Brit, Austral, & NZ* a small railway carriage in which the guard travels

guava (**gwah**-va) *n* a round tropical fruit with yellow skin and pink pulp
WORD ORIGIN from S American Indian

gubernatorial *adj chiefly US* of or relating to a governor
WORD ORIGIN Latin *gubernator* governor

gudgeon[1] *n* a small slender European freshwater fish, used as bait by anglers
WORD ORIGIN Old French *gougon*

gudgeon[2] *n* the socket of a hinge, which fits round the pin
WORD ORIGIN Old French *goujon*

guelder rose (**geld**-er) *n* a Eurasian shrub with clusters of white flowers
WORD ORIGIN from *Gelderland*, province of Holland

Guernsey (**gurn**-zee) *n* a breed of dairy cattle that produces rich creamy milk,

Scribes: the Silent Partners of the English Language

In our post-print age of electronic media, it can be easy to forget that all language was originally *oral*: it is spoken first and written second. Children learn to speak naturally by imitating their parents and other adults in their community, but no one learns to read or write except through formal instruction.

As reading and, especially, writing are such specialized skills, they are usually restricted to an elite few when a culture first moves from pure orality to literacy. Initially it is only the most highly educated members of society, the aristocrats, the clergy, the wealthy professionals, who can read and write. Yet though they may be responsible for the content of what is written, they are not the ones who commit that content to writing. That power lies with the scribes.

Scribes were professional 'copiers'; they constituted an essential part of book production before the development of printing. While kings, lords, monks, etc would all have known how to write and could have set their own words onto vellum or parchment, that would result in only a single manuscript. There were no copy-machines in the Middle Ages, and no one, not even a great author like Chaucer, had the time to copy and re-copy their work enough times to circulate it among a wide audience. This work was instead done by scribes.

Scribes played a very important role in the development of the English language. In the first place, it was scribes who recorded the few surviving Old English texts so that we can learn how much English has changed in the last 1500 years. Manuscripts from the Old English period are remarkably consistent in spelling and grammar, a result of the prominence of the West-Saxon dialect which began to emerge as a standard variety of Old English. This changed in 1066, when the Normans invaded.

Although the West-Saxon standard did not disappear immediately, during the Norman reign French was the more prestigious language, the language of the court and the ruling classes. It was during this time that Old English became Middle English, entering a period of unprecedented dialectal proliferation. By the height of the Middle English period, there was not the slightest hint of an accepted standard in English grammar, usage, spelling, or pronunciation. And it was during this period that scribes exerted their greatest influence on the development of the English language.

Scribal practice is, in fact, a source of evidence for how and when English began to change. For example, some of the earliest Middle English manuscripts are copies of Old English ones. However, the Early Middle English versions alter or simplify morphological features, such as the *ge-* prefix of preterite verbs which became *i-*, the preterite suffix inflection *-ode* which became *-ede*, and the present plural inflection *-aþ* which became *-eþ*. Some previously distinct inflections, like the dative plural *-um* became 'collapsed' into a general, 'all-purpose' inflection *-en*. Such changes reflect the evolution of English grammar and pronunciation.

Sometimes scribal practice was the result of unfamiliarity with the source language, however. The ruling Normans brought their own French-speaking scribes with them to Britain. Eventually, some of these scribes began copying English texts. When they did this, they began to apply French spelling conventions. For example, the Old English word for 'you' was *þu*. Norman French did not have the character 'þ', so this was replaced by 'th'. French also used 'ou' to make the 'long u' sound. Thus *þu* became *thou* (its modern pronunciation resulted from the Great Vowel Shift which occurred between 1400 and 1600).

Sometimes a scribe's choice was simply a mistake. One copy of Gower's *Confessio Amantis* (14th century) contains the word *athen*. This is a mistaken substitution for *ayen*, which is a Middle English form of the word *again*. This mistake occurred because the Old English form of the letter 'g' was 'ȝ'. In Middle English, this letter began to be written as 'y'. Around the same time, Northern scribes began writing 'þ' in such as way that it eventually became indistinguishable from 'y' (a practice which led to the modern-day affectation 'ye olde'). Southern scribes, however, were replacing 'þ' (and 'y' in this context) with 'th'. The scribe of the Confessio Amantis simply mistook this 'y' as representing 'þ' rather than 'g', and made what he thought was a valid substitution.

originating from Guernsey, in the Channel Islands

guerrilla or **guerilla** n a member of an irregular, politically motivated, armed force that fights regular forces **WORD ORIGIN** Spanish

guess vb **1** to form an estimate or conclusion about (something), without proper knowledge: *a competition to guess the weight of the cake* **2** to arrive at a correct estimate of (something) by guessing: *I had a notion that he guessed my thoughts* **3** *informal* to think or suppose: *I guess he must have been a great athlete* ▷ n **4** an estimate or conclusion arrived at by guessing: *we can hazard a guess at the answer* **WORD ORIGIN** probably from Old Norse

guesswork n the process of arriving at conclusions or estimates by guessing

guest n **1** a person who receives hospitality at someone else's home **2** a person who is taken out socially by someone else who pays all the expenses **3** a performer or speaker taking part in an event, show, or film by special invitation **4** a person who is staying in a hotel ▷ vb **5** to be a guest in an event, show, or film: *he guested in concert with Eric Clapton* **WORD ORIGIN** Old English *giest* guest, stranger, enemy

guesthouse n a private home or boarding house offering accommodation

guest of honour n a famous or important person who is the most important guest at a dinner or other social occasion

guff n *Brit, Austral, & NZ slang* ridiculous talk; nonsense **WORD ORIGIN** imitative

guffaw vb **1** to laugh loudly and raucously ▷ n **2** a loud raucous laugh **WORD ORIGIN** imitative

GUI (**goo**-ee) *computers* graphical user interface

guidance n help, advice, or instruction, usually from someone more experienced or more qualified: *marriage guidance*

guide n **1** a person who conducts parties of tourists around places of interest, such as museums **2** a person who leads travellers to a place, usually in a dangerous area: *a mountain guide* **3** something that can be used to gauge something or to help in planning one's actions: *starting salary was not an accurate guide to future earnings* **4** same as **guidebook 5** a book that explains the basics of a subject or skill: *a guide to higher education* ▷ vb **guiding, guided 6** to lead the way for (tourists or travellers) **7** to control the movement or course of; steer **8** to direct the affairs of (a person, team, or country): *he will stay with the club he guided to promotion to the First Division* **9** to influence (a person) in his or her actions or opinions: *to be guided by the law* **guiding** adj **WORD ORIGIN** Germanic

Guide n a member of an organization for girls that encourages discipline and practical skills

guidebook n a book which gives tourist information on a place

guided missile n a missile whose course is controlled electronically

guide dog n a dog that has been trained to lead a blind person

guideline n a principle put forward to set standards or determine a course of action: *guidelines for arms exporting*

guild n **1** an organization or club for people with shared interests **2** (in Medieval Europe) an association of men in the same trade or craft **WORD ORIGIN** Old Norse *gildi*

guilder n, pl **-ders** or **-der** a former monetary unit of the Netherlands **WORD ORIGIN** Middle Dutch *gulden*

guildhall n *Brit* a hall where members of a guild meet

guile (**gile**) n craftiness or deviousness **guileless** adj **WORD ORIGIN** Old French

guillemot (**gil**-lee-mot) n a northern oceanic black-and-white diving sea bird **WORD ORIGIN** French

guillotine n **1** a device formerly used, esp. in France, for beheading people, consisting of a weighted blade between two upright posts, which was dropped on the neck **2** a device with a blade for cutting paper ▷ vb **-tining, -tined 3** to behead with a guillotine **WORD ORIGIN** after J. I. *Guillotin*, who advocated its use

guilt n **1** the fact or state of having done wrong: *the court was unable to establish guilt* **2** remorse or self-reproach caused by feeling that one has done something wrong: *he feels no guilt about the planned cutbacks* **WORD ORIGIN** Old English *gylt*

guiltless adj free of all responsibility for wrongdoing or crime; innocent

guilty adj **guiltier, guiltiest 1** *law* judged to have committed a crime: *she has been found guilty of drug trafficking* **2** responsible for doing something wrong: *students who are guilty of cheating* **3** showing, feeling, or indicating guilt: *guilty conscience* **guiltily** adv

guinea n a former British unit of currency worth £1.05 (21 shillings), sometimes still used in quoting professional fees **WORD ORIGIN** the coin was originally made of gold from Guinea

guinea fowl n a domestic bird with a heavy rounded body and speckled feathers

guinea pig n **1** a tailless S American rodent, commonly kept as a pet or used in scientific experiments **2** a person used in an experiment **WORD ORIGIN** origin unknown

guipure (geep-**pure**) n heavy lace that has its pattern connected by threads, rather than supported on a net mesh **WORD ORIGIN** French

guise (rhymes with **size**) n **1** a false appearance: *in the guise of a wood-cutter* **2** general appearance or form: *haricot beans are best known in Britain in their popular guise of baked beans* **WORD ORIGIN** Old French

guitar n a stringed instrument with a flat back and a long neck with a fretted fingerboard, which is played by

plucking or strumming **guitarist** n **WORD ORIGIN** Spanish *guitarra*

Gulag n a system or department that silences dissidents, esp. in the former Soviet Union **WORD ORIGIN** Russian *G(lavnoye) U(pravleniye Ispravitelno-Trudovykh) Lag(erei)* Main Administration for Corrective Labour Camps

gulch n *US & Canad* a narrow ravine with a stream running through it **WORD ORIGIN** origin unknown

gulf n **1** a large deep bay **2** something that divides or separates people, such as a lack of understanding: *gradually the gulf between father and son has lessened* **WORD ORIGIN** Greek *kolpos*

Gulf War syndrome n a group of various debilitating symptoms experienced by many soldiers who served in the Gulf War of 1991, claimed to be associated with damage to the central nervous system

gull n a large sea bird with white feathers tipped with black or grey **WORD ORIGIN** Celtic

gullet n the muscular tube through which food passes from the throat to the stomach **WORD ORIGIN** Latin *gula* throat

gullible adj easily tricked; too trusting **gullibility** n

gully or **gulley** n, pl **-lies** or **-leys 1** a channel or small valley originally worn away by running water **2** *cricket* a fielding position on the off side, between the slips and point **WORD ORIGIN** French *goulet* neck of a bottle

gulp vb **1** to swallow (a drink or food) rapidly in large mouthfuls **2** to gasp or breathe in violently, for example when nervous or when swimming **3** **gulp back** to stifle or suppress: *he gulped back the tears as he said his goodbyes* ▷ n **4** the act of gulping **5** the quantity taken in a gulp **WORD ORIGIN** imitative

gum¹ n **1** a sticky substance obtained from certain plants, which hardens on exposure to air and dissolves in water **2** a substance used for sticking things together **3** short for **chewing gum** or **bubble gum 4** *chiefly Brit* a gumdrop ▷ vb **gumming, gummed 5** to stick with gum ▶ See also **gum up WORD ORIGIN** Old French *gomme*

gum² n the fleshy tissue that covers the bases of the teeth **WORD ORIGIN** Old English *gōma* jaw

gum arabic n a gum obtained from certain acacia trees, used to make ink, food thickeners, and pills

gumboil n an abscess on the gum

gumboots pl n *Brit & NZ* long rubber boots, worn in wet or muddy conditions

gumdrop n a small hard fruit-flavoured jelly-like sweet

gummy¹ adj **-mier, -miest 1** sticky or tacky **2** producing gum

gummy² adj **-mier, -miest** toothless

gumption n *Brit & NZ informal* common sense or initiative **WORD ORIGIN** origin unknown

gumtree *n* **1** any of various trees that yield gum, such as the eucalyptus **2** *up a gumtree Brit & NZ informal* in an awkward position; in difficulties

gum up *vb* **gum up the works** *informal* to spoil a plan or hinder progress

gun *n* **1** a weapon with a metallic tube or barrel from which a missile is fired, usually by force of an explosion **2** a device used to force out (a substance, such as grease or paint) under pressure: *a spray gun* **3** **jump the gun** *informal* to act prematurely **4** **stick to one's guns** *informal* to stand by one's opinions or intentions in spite of opposition ▷ *vb* **gunning, gunned 5** to press hard on the accelerator of (a vehicle's engine) **6** **gun down** to shoot (someone) with a gun ▷ *adj* **7** *NZ slang* expert: *a gun surfer* ▶ See also **gun for**
WORD ORIGIN Middle English *gonne*

gunboat *n* a small ship carrying mounted guns

gunboat diplomacy *n* diplomacy conducted by threats of military intervention

guncotton *n* a form of cellulose nitrate used as an explosive

gun dog *n* **1** a dog trained to locate or retrieve birds or animals that have been shot in a hunt **2** a dog belonging to any breed traditionally used for these activities

gunfire *n* the repeated firing of guns

gun for *vb informal* to search for (someone) in order to harm him or her in some way

gunge *n informal* a sticky or congealed substance **gungy** *adj*
WORD ORIGIN imitative

gunk *n informal* a slimy, oily, or dirty substance
WORD ORIGIN perhaps imitative

gunman *n, pl* **-men** a man who uses a gun to commit a crime

gunmetal *n* **1** a type of bronze containing copper, tin, and zinc ▷ *adj* **2** dark grey

gunnel (**gun**-nel) *n* same as **gunwale**

gunner *n* a member of the armed forces who works with, uses, or specializes in guns

gunnery *n* the art and science of the efficient design and use of large guns

gunny *n chiefly US* a coarse hard-wearing fabric, made from jute and used for sacks
WORD ORIGIN Hindi *gōnī*

gunpoint *n* **at gunpoint** being under or using the threat of being shot: *eight tourists have been kidnapped at gunpoint by unidentified men*

gunpowder *n* an explosive mixture of potassium nitrate, charcoal, and sulphur, used to make fireworks

gunrunning *n* the practice of smuggling guns and ammunition into a country **gunrunner** *n*

gunshot *n* **1** bullets fired from a gun **2** the sound of a gun being fired **3** the firing range of a gun: *within gunshot*

gunslinger *n slang* a person who can shoot very accurately and has been involved in many fights using guns,

esp. in the frontier days of the American West

gunstock *n* the wooden handle to which the barrel of a rifle is attached

gunwale (**gun**-nel) *n naut* the top of the side of a ship
WORD ORIGIN *wale*, ridge of planking originally supporting guns

gunyah *n Austral* a hut or shelter in the bush
WORD ORIGIN Aboriginal

guppy *n, pl* **-pies** a small brightly coloured tropical fish, often kept in aquariums in people's homes
WORD ORIGIN after R. J. L. *Guppy*, who gave specimens to the British Museum

gurdwara (**gurd**-wah-ra) *n* a Sikh place of worship
WORD ORIGIN from Sanskrit *guru* teacher + *dvārā* door

gurgle *vb* **-gling, -gled 1** (of water) to make low bubbling noises when flowing **2** to make low throaty bubbling noises: *the baby gurgled in delight* ▷ *n* **3** the sound of gurgling
WORD ORIGIN origin unknown

Gurkha *n* **1** a member of a Hindu people living mainly in Nepal **2** a member of a Gurkha regiment in the Indian or British Army
WORD ORIGIN Sanskrit

gurnard *n, pl* **-nard** or **-nards** a sea fish with a spiny head and long finger-like pectoral fins
WORD ORIGIN Old French *gornard* grunter

guru *n* **1** a Hindu or Sikh religious teacher or leader **2** a leader or adviser of a person or group of people: *inside a team of advertising gurus are at work*
WORD ORIGIN Hindi

Guru Granth Sahib *n* same as **Granth**

gush *vb* **1** to pour out suddenly and profusely **2** to speak or behave in an overenthusiastic manner: *I'm not about to start gushing about raspberry coulis* ▷ *n* **3** a sudden large flow of liquid **4** a sudden surge of strong feeling: *she felt a gush of pure affection for her mother*
WORD ORIGIN probably imitative

gusher *n* **1** a person who gushes **2** a spurting oil well

gushing *adj* behaving in an overenthusiastic manner: *gushing television commentators*

gusset *n* a piece of material sewn into a garment to strengthen it
WORD ORIGIN Old French *gousset*

gust *n* **1** a sudden blast of wind **2** a sudden surge of strong feeling: *a gust of joviality* ▷ *vb* **3** to blow in gusts **gusty** *adj*
WORD ORIGIN Old Norse *gustr*

gusto *n* vigorous enjoyment: *he downed a pint with gusto*
WORD ORIGIN Spanish: taste

gut *n* **1** same as **intestine 2** *slang* a stomach, esp. a fat one **3** short for **catgut 4** a silky fibrous substance extracted from silkworms and used in the manufacture of fishing tackle ▷ *vb* **gutting, gutted 5** to remove the internal organs from (a dead animal or fish) **6** (of a fire) to destroy the inside of (a building): *a local pub was gutted* ▷ *adj* **7** *informal* basic, essential, or natural:

I have a gut feeling she's after something ▶ See also **guts**
WORD ORIGIN Old English *gutt*

gutless *adj informal* lacking courage or determination

guts *pl n* **1** the internal organs of a person or an animal **2** *informal* courage, willpower, or daring **3** *informal* the inner or essential part: *the new roads have torn apart the guts of the city*

gutsy *adj* **gutsier, gutsiest** *slang* **1** bold or courageous: *the gutsy kid who lost a leg to cancer* **2** robust or vigorous: *a gutsy rendering of 'Bobby Shaftoe'*

gutta-percha *n* a whitish rubber substance, obtained from a tropical Asian tree and used in electrical insulation and dentistry
WORD ORIGIN Malay *getah* gum + *percha* gumtree

gutted *adj Brit, Austral, & NZ informal* disappointed and upset: *the supporters will be absolutely gutted if the manager leaves the club*

gutter *n* **1** a channel on the roof of a building or alongside a kerb, used to collect and carry away rainwater **2** *tenpin bowling* one of the channels on either side of an alley **3** **the gutter** a poverty-stricken, degraded, or criminal environment: *he dragged himself up from the gutter* ▷ *vb* **4** (of a candle) to flicker and be about to go out **guttering** *n*
WORD ORIGIN Latin *gutta* a drop

gutter press *n informal* the section of the popular press that concentrates on the sensational aspects of the news

guttersnipe *n Brit* a child who spends most of his or her time in the streets, usually in a slum area

guttural (**gut**-ter-al) *adj* **1** *phonetics* pronounced at the back of the throat **2** harsh-sounding
WORD ORIGIN Latin *guttur* gullet

guy[1] *n* **1** *informal* a man or boy **2** *informal* a person of either sex: *it's been very nice talking to you guys again* **3** *Brit* a crude model of Guy Fawkes, that is burnt on top of a bonfire on Guy Fawkes Day (November 5)
WORD ORIGIN short for *Guy* Fawkes, who plotted to blow up the Houses of Parliament

guy[2] *n* a rope or chain for steadying or securing something such as a tent. Also: **guyrope**
WORD ORIGIN probably Low German

guzzle *vb* **-zling, -zled** to eat or drink quickly or greedily: *the guests guzzled their way through squid with mushrooms*
WORD ORIGIN origin unknown

gybe or **jibe** (jibe) *naut vb* **gybing, gybed** or **jibing, jibed 1** (of a fore-and-aft sail) to swing suddenly from one side of a ship to the other **2** to change the course of (a ship) by letting the sail gybe ▷ *n* **3** an instance of gybing
WORD ORIGIN obsolete Dutch *gijben*

gym *n* short for **gymnasium** or **gymnastics**

gymkhana (jim-**kah**-na) *n Brit, Austral, & NZ* an event in which horses and riders take part in various races and contests
WORD ORIGIN Hindi *gend-khānā* ball house

gymnasium *n* a large room containing equipment such as bars, weights, and ropes, for physical exercise
WORD ORIGIN Greek *gumnazein* to exercise naked

gymnast *n* a person who is skilled or trained in gymnastics

gymnastics *n* **1** practice or training in exercises that develop physical strength and agility ▷ *pl n* **2** such exercises **gymnastic** *adj*

gym shoes *pl n* same as **plimsolls**

gymslip *n* a tunic formerly worn by schoolgirls as part of school uniform

gynaecology *or US* **gynecology** (guy-nee-**kol**-la-jee) *n* the branch of medicine concerned with diseases and conditions specific to women **gynaecological** *or US* **gynecological** *adj*

gynaecologist *or US* **gynecologist** *n*
WORD ORIGIN Greek *gunē* woman + -LOGY

gyp *or* **gip** *n* **give someone gyp** *Brit, Austral, & NZ slang* to cause someone severe pain: *her back's still giving her gyp*
WORD ORIGIN probably a contraction of *gee up!*

gypsophila *n* a garden plant with small white flowers

gypsum *n* a mineral used in making plaster of Paris
WORD ORIGIN Greek *gupsos*

Gypsy *or* **Gipsy** *n, pl* **-sies** a member of a travelling people scattered throughout Europe and North America
WORD ORIGIN from *Egyptian*, since they were thought to have come originally from Egypt

gyrate (jire-**rate**) *vb* **-rating, -rated** to turn round and round in a circle **gyration** *n*
WORD ORIGIN Greek *guros* circle

gyrfalcon (**jur**-fawl-kon) *n* a very large rare falcon of northern regions
WORD ORIGIN Old French *gerfaucon*

gyro *n, pl* **-ros** short for **gyroscope**

gyrocompass *n* a nonmagnetic compass that uses a motor-driven gyroscope to indicate true north
WORD ORIGIN Greek *guros* circle + COMPASS

gyroscope (**jire**-oh-skope) *n* a device containing a disc rotating on an axis that can turn freely in any direction, so that the disc maintains the same position regardless of the movement of the surrounding structure **gyroscopic** *adj*
WORD ORIGIN Greek *guros* circle + *skopein* to watch

g

The Split Infinitive

O f all the petty rules that language pedants insist on (OK, then: on which language pedants insist), the ban on the split infinitive is the best known and the least rational. It's a taboo that haunts even those who aren't quite sure what a split infinitive is.

For those who do grasp the concept, the textbook example is *Star Trek's* 'To boldly go ....' What's significant about this phrase, of course, is how well it's weathered the decades (as the 2009 'reboot' of the film franchise showed). It's memorable. It works. So what's the problem?

The answer lies in a misplaced sense of Victorian propriety. In Middle English, scribes split their infinitives like so much kindling. Thereafter, though, the construction became much rarer. Shakespeare, for example, splits an infinitive just once (and then for reasons of rhyme). It wasn't until the nineteenth century that splitting resumed in earnest – only to be banned by the language police. Great writers of the past hadn't used it much, the Victorians reasoned, so contemporary writers shouldn't either. This set the tone for the rest of the century. And despite the protests of many twentieth-century grammarians, the taboo has persisted into the new millennium.

Let's take a close look at the *Star Trek* example. It works because it places the emphasis squarely on the verb phrase – 'go where no man has gone before'. Had the screenwriters written 'To go boldly where no man has gone before', they would have emphasized the boldness rather than the trailblazing. And 'Boldly to go' just sounds forced and fussy. By splitting the infinitive, the adverb gets out of the way, allowing the root verb to work with the rest of the phrase. This establishes the crew of the *Enterprise* as explorers above all (stout-hearted though they undoubtedly are). And that's surely the point.

Linguists disagree as to whether the English infinitive can be split at all. A sentence like 'I helped carry him home' contains an infinitive (*carry*). But it's impossible to split, because there's no *to*. That suggests that *to* isn't actually part of the infinitive, but merely a helpful particle often deployed with it. Some maintain, though,

that the *naked infinitive* (like *carry* in our example) is a lesser beast than the *full infinitive* (i.e. *to carry*).

Anti-splittists cleave to that view. For them, the full infinitive is a sacred whole that mustn't be violated by anything so crude as an adverb. They perhaps have a point – an abundance of adverbs is often a sign of poor writing. And we would all, surely, balk at shoehorning a whole suite of words between the elements of the full infinitive: 'We told him to not until Christmas Day open his presents.' It's clumsy, it's ugly, and – above all – it doesn't sound like natural English.

But many split infinitives do. One of the best examples is when *really* is used for emphasis: 'To really make our mark here, we'll have to really put the hours in.' It's far from an elegant sentence. But it is the kind of thing that people say. *Really* simply doesn't belong anywhere else but smack in the middle of the infinitive: 'Really to make our mark here, we'll have to put really the hours in.' Come again? And there's no non-splitting position for phrases like *more than* in sentences like this: 'We expect profits to more than double this year.' Here, the infinitive demands to be split.

So the notion that the split infinitive is an error simply doesn't stand. But the taboo can lead to people tying themselves in knots. Indeed, some will shift adverbs to awkward places even when there's no infinitive in sight: 'He merrily danced down the street', for example, rather than the much more comfortable 'He danced merrily down the street.'

Enough is enough. We shouldn't treat the infinitive and its particle like a newborn and its mother. A brief separation will do neither any harm. In the 1990s, Kingsley Amis poured scorn on the anti-splittists, but then acknowledged that they were exactly the sort of people who end up scrutinising job applications. For that reason, he advised caution. But in the twenty-first century, we can surely afford to (ahem) not be so cautious. If an infinitive wants splitting, split it. Trust your ears. And remember the angry words of crime fiction writer Raymond Chandler to his editor: 'When I split an infinitive, God damn it, I split it so that it will remain split.'

Hh

The letter H is the eighth letter of the English alphabet. It takes its shape from the Greek letter *eta* (H,η), although that letter represented a vowel rather than a consonant in classical Greek. (The initial sound in names such as *Homer* and *Hermes* was indicated in Greek not by a letter but by a punctuation mark called a 'rough breathing' before the opening vowel.)

In early Greek, however, *eta* had represented the consonant sound /h/, deriving from the Phoenician letter *heth*, which may well have represented a fence. The idea of the fence is still evident in the solid and symmetrical shape of the letter.

Things that are shaped like a letter H can be referred to as 'zygal', an admittedly obscure adjective which literally means 'shaped like a yoke'. This refers to the yoke used to tie a pair of ploughing oxen by the necks, which had a horizontal bar joining two upright pieces.

H is one of the most phonetically flexible letters of the alphabet, and can influence the sound of the letters it follows. The letter combinations CH, TH, and SH all create sounds that are quite different from their component letters.

Another aspect of the letter that can confuse newcomers to the English language is its capacity to exist silently in words such as *hour* and *honesty*, requiring these words to be preceded by *an* instead of *a* when they require an indefinite article.

There is general agreement that the H should be silent in words such as *hour* and *honesty*, but some speakers of English are apt to leave the letter H unsounded more generally, a practice known as 'dropping your aitches', which is often taken as showing a lack of refinement, although it is widespread in some English-speaking regions.

Not least of the pronunciation controversies with which H is associated is the question of how the letter itself should be pronounced. In some communities the pronunciation 'haitch' is preferred to 'aitch', and the way that a person pronounces the letter is considered a reliable guide as to which side of Northern Ireland's sectarian divide a speaker belongs. During the Troubles, this meant that people who found themselves in hostile situations would not only have to mind their P's and Q's, but pay attention to their H's as well.

H 1 *chem* hydrogen **2** *physics* henry

h. *or* **H. 1** height **2** hour

ha¹ *or* **hah** *interj* an exclamation expressing triumph, surprise, or scorn

ha² hectare

Ha *chem* hahnium

habeas corpus (**hay**-bee-ass **kor**-puss) *n law* a writ ordering a person to be brought before a judge, so as to decide whether his or her detention is lawful **WORD ORIGIN** Latin: you may have the body

haberdasher *n Brit, Austral, & NZ* a dealer in small articles used for sewing **haberdashery** *n* **WORD ORIGIN** Anglo-French *hapertas* small items of merchandise

Haber process (**hah**-ber) *n chem* a method of making ammonia by reacting nitrogen with hydrogen at high pressure in the presence of a catalyst **WORD ORIGIN** after Fritz *Haber*, German chemist

habiliments *pl n old-fashioned* clothes **WORD ORIGIN** Old French *habillement*

habit *n* **1** a tendency to act in a particular way **2** established custom or use: *the English habit of taking tea in the* afternoon **3** an addiction to a drug **4** mental disposition or attitude: *deference was a deeply ingrained habit of mind* **5** the costume of a nun or monk **6** a woman's riding costume **WORD ORIGIN** Latin *habitus* custom

habitable *adj* fit to be lived in **habitability** *n*

habitant *n* an early French settler in Canada or Louisiana or a descendant of one, esp. a farmer

habitat *n* the natural home of an animal or plant **WORD ORIGIN** Latin: it inhabits

habitation *n* **1** occupation of a dwelling place: *unfit for human habitation* **2** *formal* a dwelling place

habit-forming *adj* tending to become a habit or addiction

habitual *adj* **1** done regularly and repeatedly: *habitual behaviour patterns* **2** by habit: *a habitual criminal* **habitually** *adv*

habituate *vb* **-ating, -ated** to accustom; get used to: *habituated to failure* **habituation** *n*

habitué (hab-**it**-yew-ay) *n* a frequent visitor to a place **WORD ORIGIN** French

hachure (**hash**-yoor) *n* shading of short lines drawn on a map to indicate the degree of steepness of a hill **WORD ORIGIN** French

hacienda (hass-ee-**end**-a) *n* (in Spanish-speaking countries) a ranch or large estate with a house on it **WORD ORIGIN** Spanish

hack¹ *vb* **1** to chop roughly or violently **2** to cut and clear (a way) through undergrowth **3** (in sport) to foul (an opposing player) by kicking his or her shins **4** *Brit & NZ informal* to tolerate **5** to manipulate a computer program skilfully, esp., to gain unauthorized access to another computer system ▷ *n* **6** a cut or gash **7** a tool, such as a pick **8** a chopping blow **9** a kick on the shins, such as in rugby **WORD ORIGIN** Old English *haccian*

hack² *n* **1** a writer or journalist who produces work fast and on a regular basis **2** a horse kept for riding, often one for hire **3** *Brit* a country ride on horseback ▷ *vb* **4** *Brit* to ride (a horse) cross-country for pleasure ▷ *adj* **5** unoriginal or of a low standard: *clumsily contrived hack verse* **WORD ORIGIN** short for *hackney*

hacker *n slang* a computer enthusiast, esp. one who through a personal computer breaks into the computer system of a company or government **hacking** *or* **hackery** *n*

hacking *adj* (of a cough) dry, painful, and harsh-sounding

hacking jacket *n* a jacket with vents at the side and sloping pockets, originally designed for wearing on horseback

hackles *pl n* **1** the hairs or feathers on the back of the neck of certain animals or birds, which rise when they are angry **2 raise someone's hackles** to make someone feel angry or hostile **WORD ORIGIN** Middle English *hakell*

hackney *n* **1** *Brit* a taxi **2** same as **hack²** (sense 2) **WORD ORIGIN** probably after *Hackney*, London, where horses were formerly raised

hackneyed (**hak**-need) *adj* (of a word or phrase) unoriginal and overused

hacksaw *n* a small saw for cutting metal

had *vb* the past of **have**

haddock *n, pl* **-dock** a North Atlantic food fish **WORD ORIGIN** origin unknown

hadedah *or* **hadeda** (**hah**-dee-dah) *n* a large grey-green S African ibis **WORD ORIGIN** imitative

Hades (**hay**-deez) *n Greek myth* **1** the underworld home of the souls of the dead **2** the god of the underworld

Hadith (**had**-dith, hah-**deeth**) *n Islam* the body of tradition and legend about Mohammed and his followers, used as a basis of Islamic law **WORD ORIGIN** Arabic

hadj *n* same as **hajj**

hadji *n, pl* **hadjis** same as **hajji**

hadn't had not

haemal *or US* **hemal** (**heem**-al) *adj* of the blood **WORD ORIGIN** Greek *haima* blood

haematic *or US* **hematic** (hee-**mat**-ik) *adj* relating to or containing blood

haematite *n* a type of iron ore which is reddish-brown when powdered

haematology *or US* **hematology** *n* the branch of medical science concerned with the blood **haematologist** *or US* **hematologist** *n* **WORD ORIGIN** Greek *haima* blood + -LOGY

haemoglobin *or US* **hemoglobin** (hee-moh-**globe**-in) *n* a protein in red blood cells that carries oxygen from the lungs to the tissues **WORD ORIGIN** Greek *haima* blood + Latin *globus* ball

haemophilia *or US* **hemophilia** (hee-moh-**fill**-lee-a) *n* a hereditary disorder, usually affecting males, in which the blood does not clot properly **haemophiliac** *n* **WORD ORIGIN** Greek *haima* blood + *philos* loving

haemorrhage *or US* **hemorrhage** (**hem**-or-ij) *n* **1** heavy bleeding from ruptured blood vessels ▷ *vb* **-rhaging, -rhaged** **2** to bleed heavily **WORD ORIGIN** Greek *haima* blood + *rhēgnunai* to burst

haemorrhoids *or US* **hemorrhoids** (**hem**-or-oydz) *pl n pathol* swollen veins in the wall of the anus **WORD ORIGIN** Greek *haimorrhoos* discharging blood

haere mai (**hire**-a-my) *interj* NZ an expression of greeting or welcome **WORD ORIGIN** Māori

hafnium *n chem* a metallic element found in zirconium ores. Symbol: Hf **WORD ORIGIN** after *Hafnia*, Latin name of Copenhagen

haft *n* the handle of an axe, knife, or dagger **WORD ORIGIN** Old English *hæft*

hag *n* **1** an unpleasant or ugly old woman **2** a witch **haggish** *adj* **WORD ORIGIN** Old English *hægtesse* witch

haggard *adj* looking tired and ill **WORD ORIGIN** Old French *hagard* wild

haggis *n* a Scottish dish made from sheep's or calf's offal, oatmeal, suet, and seasonings boiled in a skin made from the animal's stomach **WORD ORIGIN** origin unknown

haggle *vb* **-gling, -gled** to bargain or wrangle (over a price) **WORD ORIGIN** Scandinavian

hagiography *n, pl* **-phies** the writing of lives of the saints **hagiographer** *n* **WORD ORIGIN** Greek *hagios* holy + *graphein* to write

hagiology *n, pl* **-gies** literature about the lives and legends of saints **WORD ORIGIN** Greek *hagios* holy + -LOGY

hag-ridden *adj* distressed or worried

hah *interj* same as **ha¹**

ha-ha¹ *or* **haw-haw** *interj* a written representation of the sound of laughter

ha-ha² *n* a wall set in a ditch so as not to interrupt a view of the landscape **WORD ORIGIN** French

hahnium *n chem* a transuranic element artificially produced from californium. Symbol: Ha

haiku (**hie**-koo) *n, pl* **-ku** a Japanese verse form in 17 syllables **WORD ORIGIN** Japanese

hail¹ *n* **1** small pellets of ice falling from thunderclouds **2** words, ideas, missiles, etc. directed with force and in great quantity: *a hail of abuse* ▷ *vb* **3** to fall as hail: *it's hailing* **4** to fall like hail: *blows hailed down on him* **WORD ORIGIN** Old English *hægl*

hail² *vb* **1** to call out to; greet: *a voice from behind hailed him* **2** to praise, acclaim, or acknowledge: *his crew had been hailed as heroes* **3** to stop (a taxi) by shouting or gesturing **4 hail from** to come originally from: *she hails from Nova Scotia* ▷ *n* **5 within hailing distance** within hearing range ▷ *interj* **6** *poetic* an exclamation of greeting **WORD ORIGIN** Old Norse *heill* healthy

hail-fellow-well-met *adj* genial and familiar in an offensive way

Hail Mary *n RC Church* a prayer to the Virgin Mary

hailstone *n* a pellet of hail

hailstorm *n* a storm during which hail falls

hair *n* **1** any of the threadlike outgrowths on the skin of mammals **2** a mass of such outgrowths, such as on a person's head or an animal's body **3** *bot* a threadlike growth from the outer layer of a plant **4** a very small distance or margin: *he missed death by a hair* **5 get in someone's hair** *informal* to annoy someone **6 hair of the dog** an alcoholic drink taken as a cure for a hangover **7 let one's hair down** to enjoy oneself without restraint **8 not turn a hair** to show no reaction **9 split hairs** to make petty and unnecessary distinctions **hairless** *adj* **WORD ORIGIN** Old English *hær*

hairclip *n* NZ & S African a small bent metal hairpin

hairdo *n, pl* **-dos** *informal* the style of a person's hair

hairdresser *n* **1** a person who cuts and styles hair ▸ Related adjective: **tonsorial** **2** a hairdresser's premises **hairdressing** *n*

hairgrip *n chiefly Brit* a small bent clasp used to fasten the hair

hairline *n* **1** the edge of hair at the top of the forehead ▷ *adj* **2** very fine or narrow: *a hairline crack*

hairpiece *n* a section of false hair added to a person's real hair

hairpin *n* a thin U-shaped pin used to fasten the hair

hairpin bend *n* a bend in the road that curves very sharply

hair-raising *adj* very frightening or exciting

hair's-breadth *n* an extremely small margin or distance

hair shirt *n* a shirt made of horsehair cloth worn against the skin as a penance

hair slide *n* a decorative clasp used to fasten the hair

hairsplitting *n* **1** the act of making petty distinctions ▷ *adj* **2** characterized by petty distinctions

hairspring *n* a fine spring in some clocks and watches which regulates the timekeeping

hairstyle *n* the cut and arrangement of a person's hair **hairstylist** *n*

hair trigger *n* a trigger that responds to the slightest pressure

hairy *adj* **hairier, hairiest** **1** covered with hair **2** *slang* dangerous, exciting, and difficult **hairiness** *n*

hajj *or* **hadj** *n* the pilgrimage a Muslim makes to Mecca **WORD ORIGIN** Arabic

hajji *or* **hadji** *n, pl* **hajjis** *or* **hadjis** a Muslim who has made a pilgrimage to Mecca

haka *n* NZ **1** a Māori war chant accompanied by actions **2** a similar chant by a sports team

hake *n, pl* **hake** *or* **hakes** **1** an edible fish of the cod family **2** *Austral* same as **barracuda** **WORD ORIGIN** origin unknown

hakea (**hah**-kee-a) *n* an Australian tree or shrub with hard woody fruit

hakuna matata *interj African* no problem **WORD ORIGIN** from Swahili, there is no problem

h

halal or **hallal** n meat from animals that have been slaughtered according to Muslim law **WORD ORIGIN** Arabic: lawful

halberd n history a tall spear that includes an axe blade and a pick **WORD ORIGIN** Middle High German helm handle + barde axe

halcyon (**hal**-see-on) adj 1 peaceful, gentle, and calm 2 **halcyon days** a time, usually in the past, of greatest happiness or success **WORD ORIGIN** Greek alkuōn kingfisher

hale adj healthy and robust: hale and hearty **WORD ORIGIN** Old English hæl whole

half n, pl **halves** 1 either of two equal or corresponding parts that together make up a whole 2 the fraction equal to one divided by two 3 half a pint, esp. of beer 4 sport one of two equal periods of play in a game 5 a half-price ticket 6 **by half** to an excessive degree: too clever by half 7 **by halves** without being thorough: in Italy they rarely do things by halves 8 **go halves** to share expenses ▷ adj 9 denoting one of two equal parts: a half chicken ▷ adv 10 half in degree or quantity: half as much 11 partially; to an extent: half hidden in the trees 12 **not half** informal a Brit very; indeed: it isn't half hard to look at these charts b yes, indeed **WORD ORIGIN** Old English healf

half-and-half adj half one thing and half another thing

halfback n rugby a player positioned immediately behind the forwards

half-baked adj informal poorly planned: half-baked policies

half board n Brit the daily provision by a hotel of bed, breakfast, and evening meal

half-bottle n a bottle of spirits or wine that contains half the quantity of a standard bottle

half-breed n offensive a person whose parents are of different races

half-brother n the son of either one's mother or father by another partner

half-caste n offensive a person whose parents are of different races

half-cock n **go off at half-cock** or **half-cocked** to fail because of lack of preparation

half-crown or **half-a-crown** n a former British coin worth two shillings and sixpence (12½p)

half-cut adj Brit slang rather drunk

half-day n a day when one works only in the morning or only in the afternoon

half-dozen n six

half-hearted adj without enthusiasm or determination **half-heartedly** adv

half-hitch n a knot made by passing the end of a piece of rope around itself and through the loop so made

half-hour n 1 a period of 30 minutes 2 the point of time 30 minutes after the beginning of an hour **half-hourly** adv, adj

half-life n the time taken for radioactive material to lose half its radioactivity

half-light n a dim light, such as at dawn or dusk

half-mast n the halfway position of a flag on a mast as a sign of mourning

half measures pl n inadequate actions or solutions: the education system cannot be reformed by half measures

half-moon n 1 the moon when half its face is illuminated 2 the time at which a half-moon occurs 3 something shaped like a half-moon

half-nelson n a wrestling hold in which a wrestler places an arm under his opponent's arm from behind and exerts pressure with his palm on the back of his opponent's neck

halfpenny or **ha'penny** (**hayp**-nee) n, pl **-pennies** a former British coin worth half a penny

half-pie adj NZ informal badly planned; not properly thought out: a half-pie scheme **WORD ORIGIN** Māori pai good

half-pipe n a structure with a U-shaped cross section, used in skateboarding, snowboarding, Rollerblading, etc.

half-price adj, adv for half the normal price: special half-price tickets; jeans bought half-price in a sale

half-sister n the daughter of either one's mother or father by another partner

half term n Brit education a short holiday midway through a term

half-timbered adj (of a building) having an exposed timber framework filled with brick or plaster

half-time n sport an interval between the two halves of a game

half-title n the first right-hand page of a book, with only the title on it

halftone n a photographic illustration in which the image is composed of a large number of black and white dots

half-track n a vehicle with moving tracks on the rear wheels

half-truth n a partially true statement **half-true** adj

half volley n sport 1 a stroke or shot in which the ball is hit immediately after it bounces ▷ vb **half-volley** 2 to hit or kick (a ball) immediately after it bounces

halfway adv 1 at or to half the distance 2 at or towards the middle of a period of time or of an event or process 3 rather: halfway decent 4 **meet someone halfway** to compromise with someone ▷ adj 5 at the same distance from two points: the halfway line

halfway house n 1 a place to rest midway on a journey 2 the halfway stage in any process: a halfway house between the theatre and cinema is possible

halfwit n a foolish or feeble-minded person **halfwitted** adj

halibut n a large edible flatfish **WORD ORIGIN** Middle English hali holy (because it was eaten on holy days) + butte flatfish

halitosis n bad-smelling breath **WORD ORIGIN** Latin halitus breath

hall n 1 an entry area to other rooms in a house 2 a building or room for public meetings, dances, etc. 3 a residential building in a college or university 4 Brit a great house of an estate; manor 5 a large dining room in a college or university 6 the large room of a castle or stately home **WORD ORIGIN** Old English heall

hallelujah, halleluiah (hal-ee-**loo**-ya) or **alleluia** interj an exclamation of praise to God **WORD ORIGIN** Hebrew hellēl to praise + yāh the Lord

hallmark n 1 a typical feature: secrecy became the hallmark of government 2 Brit an official seal stamped on gold, silver, or platinum articles to guarantee purity and date of manufacture 3 a mark of authenticity or excellence ▷ vb 4 to stamp with a hallmark **WORD ORIGIN** after Goldsmiths' Hall in London, where items were stamped

hallo interj, n same as **hello**

halloo interj chiefly Brit a shout used to call hounds at a hunt **WORD ORIGIN** perhaps variant of hallow to encourage hounds by shouting

halloumi or **haloumi** n a salty white sheep's cheese from Greece or Turkey, usually eaten grilled **WORD ORIGIN** from Arabic haluma be mild

hallowed adj 1 regarded as holy: hallowed ground 2 respected and revered because of age, importance, or reputation: the hallowed pitch at Lord's **WORD ORIGIN** Old English hālgian to consecrate

Halloween or **Hallowe'en** n October 31, celebrated by children by dressing up as ghosts, witches, etc. **WORD ORIGIN** all hallow even all saints' eve

hallucinate vb -nating, -nated to seem to see something that is not really there **WORD ORIGIN** Latin alucinari

hallucination n the experience of seeming to see something that is not really there **hallucinatory** adj

hallucinogen n any drug that causes hallucinations **hallucinogenic** adj

hallway n an entrance area

halo (**hay**-loh) n, pl **-loes** or **-los** 1 a ring of light around the head of a sacred figure 2 a circle of refracted light around the sun or moon ▷ vb **-loes** or **-los, -loing, -loed** 3 to surround with a halo **WORD ORIGIN** Greek halōs circular threshing floor

halogen (**hal**-oh-jen) n chem any of the nonmetallic chemical elements fluorine, chlorine, bromine, iodine, and astatine, which form salts when combined with metal **WORD ORIGIN** Greek hals salt + -genēs born

halt vb 1 to come to a stop or bring (someone or something) to a stop ▷ n 2 a temporary standstill 3 a military command to stop 4 chiefly Brit a minor railway station without a building: Deeside Halt 5 **call a halt to** to put an end to **WORD ORIGIN** German halten to stop

halter n 1 a strap around a horse's head with a rope to lead it with ▷ vb 2 to put a halter on (a horse) **WORD ORIGIN** Old English hælfter

Robert Louis Stevenson

Robert Louis Balfour Stevenson was born in Edinburgh in 1850. His family trade was engineering (his father and grandfather being pioneers in lighthouse design) which he studied initially at the University of Edinburgh. He followed this with legal studies, but it was writing that he decided to pursue as a career. Stevenson's contribution to the literary world is huge, and he published a range of works in the forms of travelogues, essays, literary criticism, poetry, political writing, and plays. He also wrote many landmark novels.

Stevenson's early works detailed his travels throughout Europe, notably *An Inland Voyage* (1878), which concerned a canoeing trip down the Oise river through Belgium and France, and *Travels with a Donkey in the Cévennes* (1879). He continued his travel writing throughout his life, chronicling journeys to the United States in *The Silverado Squatters* (1883), which told of his stay at an abandoned California mining site, and *Across the Plains* (published eventually with *The Amateur Emigrant*). He also visited New Zealand and the Pacific Islands, where he was to eventually settle. (Stevenson suffered poor health as a child and endured respiratory illness throughout his life, and sought a climate that would suit his constitution.)

As a writer, Stevenson was influenced by Robert Burns, Daniel Defoe, and Sir Walter Scott. He did not believe that the realism which was fashionable in his day took account of humanity's 'nobility', and explained further the philosophical reasons for his romantic perspective in his essays from the 1880s *A Gossip on Romance*, *A Humble Remonstrance*, and *The Lantern-Bearers*. He shares themes with H Rider Haggard, John Buchan, and Joseph Conrad (who was an admirer of Stevenson's account of his Pacific travels, *In the South Seas*) and is best known for his stories that express a similar fascination with adventure and derring-do. His first widely popular work, *Treasure Island* (1883), was serialized originally in a children's magazine before its publication as a novel. Its characters of Long John Silver and protagonist Jim Hawkins are unforgettable and the story is responsible for establishing much of the iconic imagery with which pirates are associated in fiction (parrots, peg-legs, tropical islands, and 'X' marking the spot). Another major work is the historical novel *Kidnapped* (1886), which is set in the aftermath of the failed Jacobite Rising and follows the fortunes of Daniel Balfour (the character being given Stevenson's mother's maiden name). Other notable works include *The Black Arrow* (1888), set during the Wars of the Roses, and *The Master of Ballantrae* (1889), which also uses the Jacobite Rebellion as a dramatic backdrop.

Although Stevenson is famous for his 'boy's own' works, he also wrote one of the most significant and sophisticated horror stories of all time: *The Strange Case of Dr Jekyll and Mr Hyde* (1886). This tale concerns an outwardly respectable Victorian scientist who develops a potion that transforms him into Mr Hyde, a man driven by his urges with no concern for societal constraints. The book has been interpreted as a metaphor for sexual repression, a satire on Victorian values, and an attack on Stevenson's own Calvinist upbringing. Whatever the author's intention, the idea of a 'Jekyll and Hyde' has become a universally understood concept in all Western culture.

Stevenson also published children's works, such as the collection of poems *A Child's Garden of Verses* (1885) and co-wrote with his stepson Lloyd Osborne. Their collaboration yielded such novels as *The Wrecker* (1892) and the darkly comic *The Wrong Box* (1889).

In spite of moving to Samoa in 1888, he remained troubled by chronic ill-health, and he died at his home in 1894.

halterneck n a woman's top or dress which fastens behind the neck, leaving the back and arms bare

halting adj hesitant or uncertain: *she spoke halting Italian*

halve vb **halving, halved 1** to divide (something) into two equal parts **2** to reduce (the size or amount of something) by half **3** *golf* to draw with one's opponent on (a hole or round)

halyard n *naut* a line for hoisting or lowering a ship's sail or flag
WORD ORIGIN Middle English *halier*

ham¹ n smoked or salted meat from a pig's thigh
WORD ORIGIN Old English *hamm*

ham² n **1** *informal* an amateur radio operator **2** *theatre informal* an actor who overacts and exaggerates the emotions and gestures of a part ▷ adj **3** (of actors or their performances) exaggerated and overstated ▷ vb **hamming, hammed 4 ham it up** *informal* to overact
WORD ORIGIN special use of HAM¹

hamba interj S African, usually offensive go away
WORD ORIGIN Nguni (language group of southern Africa): to go

hamburger n a flat round of minced beef, often served in a bread roll
WORD ORIGIN *Hamburger steak*, steak in the fashion of *Hamburg*, Germany

ham-fisted or **ham-handed** adj *informal* very clumsy or awkward

hamlet n a small village
WORD ORIGIN Old French *hamelet*

hammer n **1** a hand tool consisting of a heavy metal head on the end of a handle, used for driving in nails, beating metal, etc. **2** the part of a gun that causes the bullet to shoot when the trigger is pulled **3** *athletics* **a** a heavy metal ball attached to a flexible wire: thrown in competitions **b** the sport of throwing the hammer **4** an auctioneer's mallet **5** the part of a piano that hits a string when a key is pressed **6 come** or **go under the hammer** to be on sale at auction **7 hammer and tongs** with great effort or energy ▷ vb **8** to hit with or as if with a hammer **9** *Brit* to criticize severely **10** *informal* to defeat heavily **11** to feel or sound like hammering: *his heart was hammering* **12 hammer in** to force (facts or ideas) into someone through repetition **13 hammer away at** to work at (something) constantly: *the paper hammered away at the same theme all the way through the campaign* ▸ See also **hammer out**
WORD ORIGIN Old English *hamor*

hammer and sickle n the emblem on the flag of the former Soviet Union, representing the industrial workers and the peasants

hammerhead n a shark with a wide flattened head

hammer out vb to produce (an agreement) with great effort

hammertoe n a condition in which the toe is permanently bent at the joint

hammock n a hanging bed made of canvas or net
WORD ORIGIN Spanish *hamaca*

hamper¹ vb to make it difficult for (someone or something) to move or progress
WORD ORIGIN origin unknown

hamper² n **1** a large basket with a lid **2** *Brit* a selection of food and drink packed as a gift
WORD ORIGIN Middle English *hanaper* a small basket

hamster n a small rodent with a stocky body, short tail, and cheek pouches
WORD ORIGIN German

hamstring n **1** one of the tendons at the back of the knee ▷ vb **-stringing, -strung 2** to make it difficult for someone to take any action
WORD ORIGIN *ham* (in the sense: leg)

hand n **1** the part of the body at the end of the arm, consisting of a thumb, four fingers, and a palm ▸ Related adjective: **manual 2** a person's style of writing: *scrolls written in her own hand* **3** the influence a person or thing has over a particular situation: *the hand of the military in shaping policy was obvious* **4** a part in some activity: *I remember with gratitude Fortune's hand in starting my collection* **5** assistance: *give me a hand with the rice* **6** a round of applause: *give a big hand to the most exciting duo in the game* **7** consent to marry someone: *he asked for her hand in marriage* **8** a manual worker **9** a member of a ship's crew **10** a pointer on a dial or gauge, esp. on a clock **11 a** the cards dealt in one round of a card game **b** one round of a card game **12** a position indicated by its location to the side of an object or the observer: *on the right hand* **13** a contrasting aspect or condition: *on the other hand* **14** source: *I had experienced at first hand many management styles* **15** a person who creates something: *a good hand at baking* **16** a unit of length equalling four inches, used for measuring the height of horses **17 by hand a** by manual rather than mechanical means **b** by messenger: *the letter was delivered by hand* **18 from hand to mouth** with no food or money in reserve: *living from hand to mouth* **19 hand in glove** in close association **20 hand over fist** steadily and quickly: *losing money hand over fist* **21 in hand a** under control **b** receiving attention: *the business in hand* **c** available in reserve: *Pakistan have a game in hand* **22 keep one's hand in** to continue to practise something **23 (near) at hand** very close **24 on hand** close by; available **25 out of hand a** beyond control **b** decisively, without possible reconsideration: *he dismissed the competition out of hand* **26 show one's hand** to reveal one's plans **27 to hand** accessible ▷ vb **28** to pass or give by the hand or hands **29 hand it to someone** to give credit to someone ▸ See also **hand down, hand on, hands**, etc.
handless adj
WORD ORIGIN Old English

handbag n a woman's small bag carried to contain personal articles

handball n a game in which two teams of seven players try to throw a ball into their opponent's goal

handbill n a small printed notice for distribution by hand

handbook n a reference manual giving practical information on a subject

handbrake n a brake in a motor vehicle operated by a hand lever

h & c hot and cold (water)

handcart n a simple cart pushed or pulled by hand, used for transporting goods

handcrafted adj made by handicraft

handcuff n **1 handcuffs** a linked pair of locking metal rings used for securing prisoners ▷ vb **2** to put handcuffs on (a person)

hand down vb **1** to pass on (knowledge, possessions, or skills) to a younger generation **2** to pass (outgrown clothes) on from one member of a family to a younger one **3** *US & Canad law* to announce (a verdict)

handful n, pl **-fuls 1** the amount that can be held in the hand **2** a small number: *a handful of parents* **3** *informal* a person or animal that is difficult to control: *as a child she was a real handful*

hand-held adj **1** held in position by the hand ▷ n **2** a device, such as a computer, that can be held in the hand

handicap n **1** a physical or mental disability **2** something that makes progress difficult **3 a** a contest in which competitors are given advantages or disadvantages in an attempt to equalize their chances **b** the advantage or disadvantage given **4** *golf* the number of strokes by which a player's averaged score exceeds par for the course ▷ vb **-capping, -capped 5** to make it difficult for (someone) to do something
WORD ORIGIN probably *hand in cap*, a lottery game in which players drew forfeits from a cap

handicapped adj physically or mentally disabled

≡ USAGE
≡ Many disabled people find the use
≡ of the word *handicapped* to describe
≡ them or their condition offensive.
≡ See **disabled**.

handicraft n **1** a skill performed with the hands, such as weaving **2** the objects produced by people with such skills

handiwork n **1** the result of someone's work or activity **2** work produced by hand

handkerchief n a small square of fabric used to wipe the nose

handle n **1** the part of an object that is held or operated in order that it may be used **2** a small lever used to open and close a door or window **3** *slang* a person's name **4** a reason for doing something: *trying to get a handle on why companies borrow money* **5 fly off the handle** *informal* to become suddenly extremely angry ▷ vb **-dling, -dled 6** to hold, move, operate, or touch with the hands **7** to have responsibility for: *she handles all their affairs personally* **8** to manage successfully: *I can handle this challenge* **9** to discuss (a subject) **10** to deal with in a specified way: *the affair was neatly handled* **11** to trade or deal in (specified merchandise): *we handle 1800 properties in Normandy* **12** to react or

respond in a specified way to operation or control: *it's light and handles well* **handling** *n*
WORD ORIGIN Old English

handlebars *pl n* a metal tube with handles at each end, used for steering a bicycle or motorcycle

handler *n* **1** a person who trains and controls an animal **2** a person who handles something: *a baggage handler*

handmade *adj* made by hand, not by machine

handmaiden *or* **handmaid** *n* **1** *old-fashioned* a female servant **2** a person or thing that serves a useful but lesser purpose: *these policies resulted in agriculture becoming the poor handmaiden of industry*

hand-me-down *n informal* an item of clothing that someone has finished with and passed on to someone else

hand on *vb* to pass (something) to the next person in a succession

hand-out *n, pl* **hand-outs 1** clothing, food, or money given to a needy person **2** a leaflet, free sample, etc. given out to publicize something **3** a piece of written information given out to the audience at a talk, lecture, etc. ▷ *vb* **hand out 4** to distribute

hand over *vb* to give up possession of or transfer (something)

hand-pick *vb* to select (a person) with great care, such as for a special job **hand-picked** *adj*

handrail *n* a rail alongside a stairway, to provide support

hands *pl n* **1 change hands** to pass from the possession of one person to another **2 have one's hands full** to be completely occupied **3 in someone's hands** in someone's control or power: *that's in the hands of the courts* **4 off one's hands** no longer one's responsibility **5 on one's hands** for which one is responsible: *what a problem case I've got on my hands* **6 wash one's hands of** to have nothing more to do with **7 win hands down** to win easily

handset *n* a telephone mouthpiece and earpiece in a single unit

hands-free *adj, n* (of) a device allowing the user to make and receive phonecalls without holding the handset

handshake *n* the act of grasping and shaking a person's hand, such as in greeting or when agreeing on a deal

handsome *adj* **1** (esp. of a man) good-looking **2** (of a building, garden, etc.) large, well-made, and with an attractive appearance: *a handsome building* **3** (of an amount of money) generous or large: *a handsome dividend* **handsomely** *adv*
WORD ORIGIN obsolete *handsom* easily handled

hands-on *adj* involving practical experience of equipment: *Navy personnel joined the 1986 expedition for hands-on operating experience*

handspring *n* a gymnastic exercise in which a person leaps forwards or backwards into a handstand and then onto his or her feet

handstand *n* the act of supporting the body on the hands in an upside-down position

hand-to-hand *adj, adv* **1** at close quarters, with fists or knives: *hand-to-hand combat; they fought hand-to-hand*

hand-to-mouth *adj* **1** with barely enough money or food to live on ▷ *adv* **2** with barely enough money or food to live on

handwork *n* work done by hand rather than by machine

handwriting *n* **1** writing by hand rather than by typing or printing **2** a person's characteristic writing style **handwritten** *adj*

handy *adj* **handier, handiest 1** conveniently within reach **2** easy to handle or use **3** good at manual work **handily** *adv*

handyman *n, pl* **-men** a man skilled at odd jobs

hang *vb* **hanging, hung 1** to fasten or be fastened from above **2** to place (something) in position, for instance by a hinge, so as to allow free movement: *to hang a door* **3** to be suspended so as to allow movement from the place where it is attached: *her long hair hung over her face* **4** to decorate with something suspended, such as pictures **5** (of cloth or clothing) to fall or flow in a particular way: *the fine gauge knit hangs loosely with graceful femininity* **6** *pt & pp* **hanged** to suspend or be suspended by the neck until dead **7** to hover: *clouds hung over the mountains* **8** to fasten to a wall: *to hang wallpaper* **9** to exhibit or be exhibited in an art gallery **10** *pt & pp* **hanged** *slang* to damn: used in mild curses or interjections **11 hang fire** to put off doing something **12 hang over** to threaten or overshadow: *the threat of war hung over the Middle East* ▷ *n* **13** the way in which something hangs **14 get the hang of something** *informal* to understand the technique of doing something ▶ See also **hang about, hang back**, etc.
WORD ORIGIN Old English *hangian*

hang about *or* **around** *vb* **1** to stand about idly somewhere **2** (foll. by *with*) to spend a lot of time in the company (of someone)

hangar *n* a large building for storing aircraft
WORD ORIGIN French: shed

hang back *vb* to be reluctant to do something

hangdog *adj* dejected, ashamed, or guilty in appearance or manner

hanger *n* same as **coat hanger**

hanger-on *n, pl* **hangers-on** an unwanted follower, esp. of a rich or famous person

hang-glider *n* an unpowered aircraft consisting of a large cloth wing stretched over a light framework from which the pilot hangs in a harness **hang-gliding** *n*

hangi (**hung**-ee) *n NZ* **1** an open-air cooking pit **2** the food cooked in it **3** the social gathering at the resultant meal
WORD ORIGIN Māori

hanging *n* **1** the act or practice of putting a person to death by suspending the body by the neck **2** a large piece of cloth hung on a wall as a decoration

hanging valley *n geog* a tributary valley that enters a main valley high up because the main valley has been deepened through erosion by a glacier

hangman *n, pl* **-men** an official who carries out a sentence of hanging

hangnail *n* a piece of skin partly torn away from the base or side of a fingernail

hang on *vb* **1** *informal* to wait: *hang on a minute, will you?* **2** to continue or persist with effort or difficulty **3** to grasp or hold **4** to depend on: *a lot hangs on its success* **5** to listen attentively to: *she hangs on every word our leader says*

hang out *vb* **1** to suspend, be suspended, or lean **2** *informal* to live or spend a lot of time in a place: *fishermen hang out in waterfront bars* **3 let it all hang out** *informal chiefly US* to relax completely; act or speak freely ▷ *n* **hang-out 4** *informal* a place where someone spends a lot of time

hangover *n* a feeling of sickness and headache after drinking too much alcohol

hang together *vb* **1** to be united **2** to be consistent: *the story simply did not hang together*

hang up *vb* **1** to replace (a telephone receiver) at the end of a conversation **2** to put on a hook or hanger ▷ *n* **hang-up 3** *informal* an emotional or psychological problem

hank *n* a loop or coil, esp. of yarn
WORD ORIGIN from Old Norse

hanker *vb* (foll. by *for* or *after*) to have a great desire for **hankering** *n*
WORD ORIGIN probably from Dutch dialect *hankeren*

hanky *or* **hankie** *n, pl* **hankies** *informal* short for **handkerchief**

hanky-panky *n informal* **1** casual sexual relations **2** mischievous behaviour
WORD ORIGIN variant of *hocus-pocus*

Hanoverian (han-no-**veer**-ee-an) *adj* of or relating to the British royal house ruling from 1714 to 1901
WORD ORIGIN after *Hanover*, Germany

Hansard *n* the official report of the proceedings of the British or Canadian parliament
WORD ORIGIN after L. *Hansard*, its original compiler

Hanseatic League (han-see-**at**-ik) *n history* a commercial organization of towns in N Germany formed in the 14th century to protect and control trade

hansom *n* formerly, a two-wheeled one-horse carriage with a fixed hood. Also called: **hansom cab**
WORD ORIGIN after its designer J. A. *Hansom*

Hants Hampshire

Hanukkah *n* same as **Chanukah**

haphazard *adj* not organized or planned **haphazardly** *adv*
WORD ORIGIN Old Norse *happ* chance, good luck + HAZARD

hapless *adj* unlucky: *the hapless victim of a misplaced murder attempt* **WORD ORIGIN** Old Norse *happ* chance, good luck

haploid *adj biol* denoting a cell or organism with unpaired chromosomes **WORD ORIGIN** Greek *haplous* single

haplotype *n genetics* a set of alleles inherited by an individual from a single parent

happen *vb* **1** to take place; occur **2** to chance (to be or do something): *I happen to know him* **3** to be the case, esp. by chance: *it happens that I know him* **4** **happen to** (of some unforeseen event, such as death) to be the experience or fate of: *if anything happens to me you will know* **WORD ORIGIN** obsolete *hap*

☰ USAGE
☰ See at **occur**.

happening *n* an event that often occurs in a way that is unexpected or hard to explain: *some strange happenings in the village recently*

happy *adj* **-pier, -piest** **1** feeling or expressing joy **2** causing joy or gladness: *the happiest day of my life* **3** fortunate or lucky: *it was a happy coincidence* **4** satisfied or content: *he seems happy to let things go on as they are* **5** willing: *I'll be happy to arrange a loan for you* **happily** *adv* **happiness** *n* **WORD ORIGIN** Old Norse *happ* chance, good luck

happy-go-lucky *adj* carefree or easy-going

hara-kiri *n* (formerly, in Japan) ritual suicide by disembowelment when disgraced or under sentence of death **WORD ORIGIN** Japanese *hara* belly + *kiri* cut

harangue *vb* **-ranguing, -rangued** **1** to address (a person or group) in an angry or forcefully persuasive way ▷ *n* **2** a forceful or angry speech **WORD ORIGIN** Old Italian *aringa* public speech

harass *vb* to trouble or annoy (someone) by repeated attacks, questions, or problems **harassed** *adj* **harassment** *n* **WORD ORIGIN** French *harasser*

harbinger (har-binge-er) *n literary* a person or thing that announces or indicates the approach of something: *a harbinger of death* **WORD ORIGIN** Old French *herbergere*

harbour *or US* **harbor** *n* **1** a sheltered port **2** a place of refuge or safety ▷ *vb* **3** to maintain secretly in the mind: *he might be harbouring a death wish* **4** to give shelter or protection to: *the government accused her of harbouring criminals* **WORD ORIGIN** Old English *herebeorg*, from *here* army + *beorg* shelter

harbour master *n* an official in charge of a harbour

hard *adj* **1** firm, solid, or rigid **2** difficult to do or understand: *a hard sum* **3** showing or requiring a lot of effort or application: *hard work* **4** unkind or unfeeling: *she's very hard, no pity for anyone* **5** causing pain, sorrow, or hardship: *the hard life of a northern settler* **6** tough or violent: *a hard man* **7** forceful: *a hard knock* **8** cool or uncompromising: *we took a long hard look at our profit factor* **9** indisputable and proven to be true: *hard facts* **10** (of water) containing calcium salts which stop soap lathering freely **11** practical, shrewd, or calculating: *he is a hard man in business* **12** harsh: *hard light* **13** (of currency) high and stable in exchange value **14** (of alcoholic drink) being a spirit rather than a wine or beer **15** (of a drug) highly addictive **16** hard-core **17** *phonetics* denoting the consonants *c* and *g* when they are pronounced as in *cat* and *got* **18** politically extreme: *the hard left* **19** **hard of hearing** slightly deaf **20** **hard up** *informal* in need of money ▷ *adv* **21** with great energy or force: *they fought so hard and well in Spain* **22** with great intensity: *thinking hard about the conversation* **23** **hard by** very close to: *Cleveland Place, hard by Bruntsfield Square* **24** **hard put (to it)** scarcely having the capacity (to do something) ▷ *n* **25** **have a hard on** *taboo slang* to have an erection of the penis **hardness** *n* **WORD ORIGIN** Old English *heard*

hard-and-fast *adj* (of rules) fixed and not able to be changed

hardback *n* **1** a book with stiff covers ▷ *adj* **2** of or denoting a hardback

hardball *n US & Canad* **1** baseball as distinct from softball **2** **play hardball** *informal* to act in a ruthless or uncompromising way

hard-bitten *adj informal* tough and determined

hardboard *n* stiff board made in thin sheets of compressed sawdust and wood pulp

hard-boiled *adj* **1** (of an egg) boiled until solid **2** *informal* tough, realistic, and unemotional

hard cash *n* money or payment in money, as opposed to payment by cheque, credit, etc.

hard copy *n* computer output printed on paper

hardcore *n* **1** a style of rock music with short fast songs and little melody **2** a type of dance music with a very fast beat

hard core *n* **1** the members of a group who most resist change **2** broken stones used to form a foundation for a road ▷ *adj* **hard-core** **3** (of pornography) showing sexual acts in explicit detail **4** extremely committed or fanatical: *a hard-core Communist*

hard disk *n computers* an inflexible disk in a sealed container

hard drive *n computers* the mechanism that handles the reading, writing, and storage of data on the hard disk

harden *vb* **1** to make or become hard; freeze, stiffen, or set **2** to make or become tough or unfeeling: *life in the camp had hardened her considerably* **3** to make or become stronger or firmer: *they hardened defences* **4** to make or become more determined or resolute: *the government has hardened its attitude to the crisis* **5** *commerce* (of prices or a market) to cease to fluctuate

hardened *adj* toughened by experience: *a hardened criminal*

hardfill *n NZ & S African* a stone waste material used for landscaping

hard-headed *adj* tough, realistic, or shrewd, esp. in business

hardhearted *adj* unsympathetic and uncaring

hardihood *n* courage or daring

hard labour *n* difficult and tiring physical work: used as a punishment for a crime in some countries

hard line *n* **1** an uncompromising policy: *a hard line on drugs* ▷ *adj* **hard-line** **2** tough and uncompromising: *a hard-line attitude to the refugee problem* **hardliner** *n*

hardly *adv* **1** scarcely; barely: *he'd hardly sipped his whisky* **2** ironic not at all: *it was hardly in the Great Train Robbery league* **3** with difficulty: *their own families would hardly recognize them*

☰ USAGE
☰ Since *hardly, scarcely*, and *barely* already
☰ have negative force, it is redundant to
☰ use another negative in the same
☰ clause: *he had hardly had* (not *he hadn't*
☰ *hardly had*) *time to think; there was scarcely*
☰ *any* (not *scarcely no*) *bread left*.

hard pad *n* (in dogs) an abnormal increase in the thickness of the foot pads: a sign of distemper

hard palate *n* the bony front part of the roof of the mouth

hard-pressed *adj* **1** under a great deal of strain and worry: *hard-pressed companies having to cut costs* **2** closely pursued

hard science *n* one of the natural or physical sciences, such as physics, chemistry, or biology

hard sell *n* an aggressive insistent technique of selling

hardship *n* **1** conditions of life that are difficult to endure **2** something that causes suffering

hard shoulder *n Brit & NZ* a surfaced verge running along the edge of a motorway and other roads for emergency stops

hardtack *n* a kind of hard saltless biscuit, formerly eaten by sailors

hardware *n* **1** metal tools or implements, esp. cutlery or cooking utensils **2** *computers* the physical equipment used in a computer system **3** heavy military equipment, such as tanks and missiles

hard-wired *adj* (of a circuit or instruction) permanently wired into a computer

hardwood *n* the wood of a deciduous tree such as oak, beech, or ash

hardy *adj* **-dier, -diest** **1** able to stand difficult conditions **2** (of plants) able to live out of doors throughout the winter **hardiness** *n* **WORD ORIGIN** Old French *hardi* emboldened

hare *n, pl* **hares** *or* **hare** **1** a mammal like a large rabbit, with longer ears and legs ▷ *vb* **haring, hared** **2** (foll. by *off* or *after*) *Austral & Brit informal* to run fast or wildly **WORD ORIGIN** Old English *hara*

harebell *n* a blue bell-shaped flower

harebrained *adj* foolish or impractical: *harebrained schemes*

harelip *n* a slight split in the mid line of the upper lip

Word Histories
part 7

Homosexual: A common example of contemporary folk etymology is the assumption that 'homosexual' can only be used to describe men. This assumption rests on the mistaken premise that the word derives from the Latin *homo*, 'man'. In fact, the derivation is from the Greek word *homos*, 'the same', and so the term applies equally to men and women.

An internet-circulated explanation for **Honeymoon** maintains that the term derives from a Babylonian custom whereby a bride's father supplied his son-in-law with mead for a month after the marriage. This is completely untrue. Mead, a drink made from fermented honey, was brewed in northern climes, not in Mesopotamia! Instead, the word alludes to the period of initial sweetness after a marriage, and acknowledges that this will not last. The 'moon' signifies either a lunar month, or the likelihood that affection will wane like the moon.

Hooker, meaning prostitute, is commonly suggested to be an eponym of the American Civil War general, 'Fighting Joe' Hooker, whose Army of the Potomac was famed for its female camp followers. While Hooker's bawdy entourage may have popularized the term, however, 'hooker' was already established as a term for prostitute by the time of the American Civil War. As with Thomas Crapper (see **crap**), Hooker's name seems to have been a happy coincidence. 'Hooker' was used from the 16th century as a term for a thief, and the prostitute sense was probably influenced by this and by the general idea of hooking – catching – clients.

Horoscope comes via Latin from Greek *hōroskopos*, meaning 'hour observer' or 'time observer', referring to the time of a person's birth. The word derives from *hōra*, meaning 'hour' or 'time', and *skopos*, meaning 'observer' (the same word as is seen in 'microscope', 'telescope', etc.).

Humble pie was originally 'umble pie' – umbles (or numbles) being the entrails of a deer. Offal, including umbles, was considered a lower-class food in medieval and Renaissance England, so after a hunt, lowly retainers would eat umble pie while higher-ranked followers would enjoy choicer cuts of meat. As 'umble' fell out of common use, folk etymology transformed it to the more recognizable 'humble'.

An **iceberg** is an 'ice mountain'. The word is a partial translation of the Dutch word *ijsberg*, from *ijs*, meaning 'ice', and *berg*, meaning 'mountain'.

The word **ignoramus** comes from *Ignoramus*, the name of an uneducated lawyer in a 17th-century play of the same name written by George Ruggle. In Latin *ignoramus* means 'we do not know'.

Infant: An infant is literally a child who is too young to have learned to talk. The word comes from Latin *infans*, meaning 'unable to speak', from *in-*, meaning 'not', and *fārī*, meaning 'to speak'.

Islam: In Arabic, *islām* means 'surrender (to God)', from the verb *aslama*, meaning 'to surrender'. The same verb also underlies the word 'Muslim', which means 'someone who surrenders (to God)'.

Isosceles comes from Greek *isos*, meaning 'equal,' and *skelos*, meaning 'leg'.

Jodhpurs are named after the town of *Jodhpur* in northwestern India.

Jubilee comes from the Hebrew word *yōbhēl* meaning a 'ram's horn'. In Old Testament times a 'jubilee' year among the Jews occurred every fifty years. In a jubilee year, fields and vineyards were left uncultivated, property that had been sold was returned to its original owner or his descendants, and people who had been sold as slaves were released from their bondage. The beginning of the jubilee was marked by the blowing of a ram's-horn trumpet.

harem *n* **1** a Muslim man's wives and concubines collectively **2** the part of an Oriental house reserved for wives and concubines
WORD ORIGIN Arabic *harīm* forbidden (place)

haricot bean *or* **haricot** (**har**-rik-oh) *n* a white edible bean, which can be dried
WORD ORIGIN French *haricot*

harissa *n* a hot paste or sauce made from chilli peppers, tomatoes, spices, and olive oil, used in North African cuisine

hark *vb* old-fashioned to listen; pay attention: *hark, the cocks are crowing*
WORD ORIGIN Old English *heorcnian*

hark back *vb* to return (to an earlier subject in speech or thought): *he keeps harking back to his music-hall days*

harlequin *n* **1** theatre a stock comic character, usually wearing a diamond-patterned multicoloured costume and a black mask ▷ *adj* **2** in varied colours
WORD ORIGIN Old French *Herlequin* leader of a band of demon horsemen

harlequinade *n* theatre a play in which harlequin has a leading role

harlot *n* literary a prostitute **harlotry** *n*
WORD ORIGIN Old French *herlot* rascal

harm *vb* **1** to injure physically, morally, or mentally ▷ *n* **2** physical, moral, or mental injury
WORD ORIGIN Old English *hearm*

harmful *adj* causing or tending to cause harm, esp. to a person's health

harmless *adj* **1** safe to use, touch, or be near **2** unlikely to annoy or worry people: *a harmless habit*

harmonic *adj* **1** of, producing, or characterized by harmony; harmonious ▷ *n* **2** music an overtone of a musical note produced when that note is played, but not usually heard as a separate note ▶ See also **harmonics** ▷ **harmonically** *adv*
WORD ORIGIN Latin *harmonicus* relating to harmony

harmonica *n* a small wind instrument in which reeds enclosed in a narrow oblong box are made to vibrate by blowing and sucking

harmonics *n* the science of musical sounds

harmonious *adj* **1** (esp. of colours or sounds) consisting of parts which blend together well **2** showing agreement, peacefulness, and friendship: *a harmonious relationship* **3** tuneful or melodious

harmonium *n* a musical keyboard instrument in which air from pedal-operated bellows causes the reeds to vibrate

harmonize *or* **-nise** *vb* **-nizing, -nized** *or* **-nising, -nised** **1** to sing or play in harmony, such as with another singer or player **2** to make or become harmonious

harmony *n, pl* **-nies** **1** a state of peaceful agreement and cooperation **2** music a pleasant combination of two or more notes sounded at the same time **3** the way parts combine well together or into a whole
WORD ORIGIN Greek *harmonia*

harness *n* **1** an arrangement of straps for attaching a horse to a cart or plough **2** something resembling this, for attaching something to a person's body: *a parachute harness* **3** **in harness** at one's routine work ▷ *vb* **4** to put a harness on (a horse or other animal) **5** to control something in order to make use of it: *learning to harness the power of your own mind*
WORD ORIGIN Old French *harneis* baggage

harp *n* **1** a large upright triangular stringed instrument played by plucking the strings with the fingers ▷ *vb* **2** **harp on** to speak in a persistent and tedious manner (about a subject) **harpist** *n*
WORD ORIGIN Old English *hearpe*

harpoon *n* **1** a barbed spear attached to a long rope and thrown or fired when hunting whales, etc. ▷ *vb* **2** to spear with a harpoon
WORD ORIGIN probably from Dutch *harpoen*

harpsichord *n* a keyboard instrument, resembling a small piano, with strings that are plucked mechanically **harpsichordist** *n*
WORD ORIGIN Late Latin *harpa* harp + Latin *chorda* string

harpy *n, pl* **-pies** a violent, unpleasant, or greedy woman
WORD ORIGIN from Greek *Harpuiai* the Harpies, literally: snatchers (mythical birdlike female monsters)

harridan *n* a scolding old woman; nag
WORD ORIGIN origin unknown

harrier¹ *n* a cross-country runner
WORD ORIGIN from *hare*

harrier² *n* a bird of prey with broad wings and long legs and tail

harrow *n* **1** an implement used to break up clods of soil ▷ *vb* **2** to draw a harrow over (land)
WORD ORIGIN from Old Norse

harrowing *adj* very upsetting or disturbing

harry *vb* **-ries, -rying, -ried** to keep asking (someone) to do something; pester
WORD ORIGIN Old English *hergian*

harsh *adj* **1** severe and difficult to cope with: *harsh winters* **2** unkind and showing no understanding: *the judge was very harsh on the demonstrators* **3** excessively hard, bright, or rough: *harsh sunlight* **4** (of sounds) unpleasant and grating **harshly** *adv* **harshness** *n*
WORD ORIGIN probably Scandinavian

hart *n, pl* **harts** *or* **hart** the male of the deer, esp. the red deer
WORD ORIGIN Old English *heorot*

hartebeest *n* a large African antelope with curved horns and a fawn-coloured coat
WORD ORIGIN Dutch

harum-scarum *adj* **1** reckless ▷ *adv* **2** recklessly ▷ *n* **3** an impetuous person
WORD ORIGIN origin unknown

harvest *n* **1** the gathering of a ripened crop **2** the crop itself **3** the season for gathering crops **4** the product of an effort or action ▷ *vb* **5** to gather (a ripened crop) **6** chiefly US to remove (an organ) from the body for transplantation
WORD ORIGIN Old English *hærfest*

harvester *n* **1** a harvesting machine, esp. a combine harvester **2** a person who harvests

harvest festival *n* **1** a Christian church service held every year to thank God for the harvest **2** any of various ceremonies celebrating the harvest in other religions

harvest moon *n* the full moon occurring nearest to the autumn equinox

harvest mouse *n* a very small reddish-brown mouse that lives in cornfields or hedgerows

has *vb* third person singular of the present tense of **have**

has-been *n* informal a person who is no longer popular or successful

hash¹ *n* **1** a dish of diced cooked meat, vegetables, etc. reheated: *corned-beef hash* **2** a reworking of old material **3** **make a hash of** informal to mess up or destroy
WORD ORIGIN Old French *hacher* to chop up

hash² *n* slang short for **hashish**

hashish (**hash**-eesh) *n* a drug made from the hemp plant, smoked for its intoxicating effects
WORD ORIGIN Arabic

hasn't has not

hasp *n* a clasp which fits over a staple and is secured by a pin, bolt, or padlock, used as a fastening
WORD ORIGIN Old English *hæpse*

hassium *n* chem an element synthetically produced in small quantities by high-energy ion bombardment. Symbol: Hs
WORD ORIGIN Latin, from *Hesse*, the German state where it was discovered

hassle informal *n* **1** a great deal of trouble **2** a prolonged argument ▷ *vb* **-sling, -sled** **3** to cause annoyance or trouble to (someone): *stop hassling me!*
WORD ORIGIN origin unknown

hassock *n* a cushion for kneeling on in church
WORD ORIGIN Old English *hassuc* matted grass

haste *n* **1** speed, esp. in an action **2** the act of hurrying in a careless manner **3** **make haste** to hurry or rush ▷ *vb* **hasting, hasted** **4** poetic to hasten
WORD ORIGIN Old French

hasten *vb* **1** to hurry or cause to hurry **2** to be anxious (to say something)

hasty *adj* **-tier, -tiest** **1** done or happening suddenly or quickly **2** done too quickly and without thought; rash **hastily** *adv*

hat *n* **1** a head covering, often with a brim, usually worn to give protection from the weather **2** informal a role or capacity: *I'm wearing my honorary consul's hat* **3** **keep something under one's hat** to keep something secret **4** **pass the hat round** to collect money for a cause **5** **take off one's hat to someone** to admire or congratulate someone
WORD ORIGIN Old English *hætt*

hatband *n* a band or ribbon around the base of the crown of a hat

hatch¹ *vb* **1** to cause (the young of various animals, esp. birds) to emerge from the egg or (of young birds, etc.) to emerge from the egg **2** (of eggs) to break and release the young animal

within **3** to devise (a plot or plan)
WORD ORIGIN Germanic

hatch² *n* **1** a hinged door covering an opening in a floor or wall **2 a** short for **hatchway b** a door in an aircraft or spacecraft **3** Also called: **serving hatch** an opening in a wall between a kitchen and a dining area **4** *informal* short for **hatchback**
WORD ORIGIN Old English *hæcc*

hatch³ *vb drawing, engraving, etc.* to mark (a figure, etc.) with fine parallel or crossed lines to indicate shading **hatching** *n*
WORD ORIGIN Old French *hacher* to chop

hatchback *n* a car with a single lifting door in the rear

hatchet *n* **1** a short axe used for chopping wood, etc. **2 bury the hatchet** to make peace or resolve a disagreement ▷ *adj* **3** narrow and sharp: *a hatchet face*
WORD ORIGIN Old French *hachette*

hatchet job *n informal* a malicious verbal or written attack

hatchet man *n informal* a person who carries out unpleasant tasks on behalf of an employer

hatchling *n* a young animal that has newly hatched from an egg

hatchway *n* an opening in the deck of a vessel to provide access below

hate *vb* **hating, hated 1** to dislike (someone or something) intensely **2** to be unwilling (to do something): *I hate to trouble you* ▷ *n* **3** intense dislike **4** *informal* a person or thing that is hated: *my own pet hate is restaurants* **hater** *n*
WORD ORIGIN Old English *hatian*

hateful *adj* causing or deserving hate

Hathor *n* an Egyptian goddess of creation

hatred *n* intense dislike

hatter *n* **1** a person who makes and sells hats **2 mad as a hatter** eccentric

hat trick *n* **1** *cricket* the achievement of a bowler in taking three wickets with three successive balls **2** any achievement of three successive goals, victories, etc.

hauberk *n history* a long sleeveless coat of mail
WORD ORIGIN Old French *hauberc*

haughty *adj* **-tier, -tiest** having or showing excessive pride or arrogance **haughtily** *adv* **haughtiness** *n*
WORD ORIGIN Latin *altus* high

haul *vb* **1** to drag or pull (something) with effort **2** to transport, such as in a lorry **3** *naut* to alter the course of (a vessel) ▷ *n* **4** the act of dragging with effort **5** a quantity of something obtained: *a good haul of fish; a huge haul of stolen goods* **6 long haul a** a long journey **b** a long difficult process
WORD ORIGIN Old French *haler*

haulage *n* **1** the business of transporting goods **2** a charge for transporting goods

haulier *n Austral & Brit* a person or firm that transports goods by road

haulm (**hawm**) *n* the stalks of beans, peas, or potatoes collectively
WORD ORIGIN Old English *healm*

haunch *n* **1** the human hip or fleshy hindquarter of an animal **2** the leg and

loin of an animal, used for food
WORD ORIGIN Old French *hanche*

haunt *vb* **1** to visit (a person or place) in the form of a ghost **2** to remain in the memory or thoughts of: *it was a belief which haunted her* **3** to visit (a place) frequently ▷ *n* **4** a place visited frequently
WORD ORIGIN Old French *hanter*

haunted *adj* **1** (of a place) frequented or visited by ghosts **2** (of a person) obsessed or worried

haunting *adj* having a quality of great beauty or sadness so as to be memorable: *a haunting melody*

hautboy (**oh**-boy) *n old-fashioned* an oboe
WORD ORIGIN French *haut* high + *bois* wood

haute couture (**oat** koo-**ture**) *n* high fashion
WORD ORIGIN French

hauteur (oat-**ur**) *n* haughtiness
WORD ORIGIN French *haut* high

Havana *n* a fine-quality hand-rolled cigar from Cuba

have *vb* **has, having, had 1** to possess: *he has a massive collection of old movies; I have an iron constitution* **2** to receive, take, or obtain: *I had a long letter* **3** to hold in the mind: *she always had a yearning to be a schoolteacher* **4** to possess a knowledge of: *I have no German* **5** to experience or be affected by: *a good way to have a change* **6** to suffer from: *to have a blood pressure problem* **7** to gain control of or advantage over: *you have me on that point* **8** slang to cheat or outwit: *I've been had* **9** to show: *have mercy on me* **10** to take part in; hold: *I had a telephone conversation* **11** to cause to be done: *have my shoes mended by Friday* **12** to eat or drink **13** *taboo slang* to have sexual intercourse with **14** to tolerate or allow: *I won't have all this noise* **15** to receive as a guest: *we have visitors* **16** to be pregnant with or give birth to (offspring) **17** used to form past tenses: *I have gone; I had gone* **18 have had it** *informal* **a** to be exhausted or killed **b** to have lost one's last chance **19 have it off** *taboo Brit slang* to have sexual intercourse **20 have to** used to express compulsion or necessity: *you'd have to wait six months* ▷ *n* **21 haves** *informal* people who have wealth, security, etc.: *the haves and the have-nots* ▶ See also **have on, have out**, etc.
WORD ORIGIN Old English *habban*

have-a-go *adj informal* (of people attempting arduous or brave tasks) brave or spirited: *have-a-go pensioner*

haven *n* **1** a place of safety **2** a harbour for shipping
WORD ORIGIN Old English *hæfen*

haven't have not

have on *vb* **1** to wear: *he'd got a long pair of trousers on* **2** to have a commitment: *what do you have on this afternoon?* **3** *informal* to trick or tease: *he's having you on* **4** to have (information, esp. when incriminating) about (a person): *she's got something on him*

have out *vb* to settle (a matter), esp. by fighting or by frank discussion: *I went to Carl's office to have it out with him*

haver *vb* **1** *Scot & N English dialect* to talk nonsense **2** to be unsure and hesitant; dither
WORD ORIGIN origin unknown

haversack *n* a canvas bag carried on the back or shoulder
WORD ORIGIN French *havresac*

have up *vb* to bring to trial: *what, and get me had up for kidnapping?*

havoc *n* **1** *informal* chaos, disorder, and confusion **2 play havoc with** to cause a great deal of damage or confusion to
WORD ORIGIN Old French *havot* pillage

haw¹ *n* the fruit of the hawthorn
WORD ORIGIN Old English *haga*

haw² *vb* **hum** (*or* **hem**) **and haw** to hesitate in speaking
WORD ORIGIN imitative

hawk¹ *n* **1** a bird of prey with short rounded wings and a long tail **2** a supporter or advocate of warlike policies ▷ *vb* **3** to hunt with falcons or hawks **hawkish** *adj* **hawklike** *adj*
WORD ORIGIN Old English *hafoc*

hawk² *vb* to offer (goods) for sale in the street or door-to-door
WORD ORIGIN from *hawker* pedlar

hawk³ *vb* **1** to clear the throat noisily **2** to force (phlegm) up from the throat
WORD ORIGIN imitative

hawker *n* a person who travels from place to place selling goods
WORD ORIGIN probably from Middle Low German *hōken* to peddle

hawk-eyed *adj* having extremely keen eyesight

hawser *n naut* a large heavy rope
WORD ORIGIN Anglo-French *hauceour*

hawthorn *n* a thorny tree or shrub with white or pink flowers and reddish fruits
WORD ORIGIN Old English *haguthorn*

hay *n* **1** grass cut and dried as fodder **2 hit the hay** *slang* to go to bed **3 make hay while the sun shines** to take full advantage of an opportunity
WORD ORIGIN Old English *hieg*

hay fever *n* an allergic reaction to pollen, which causes sneezing, runny nose, and watery eyes

haystack *or* **hayrick** *n* a large pile of hay built in the open and covered with thatch

haywire *adj* **go haywire** *informal* to stop functioning properly

hazard *n* **1** a thing likely to cause injury, loss, etc. **2** risk or likelihood of injury, loss, etc.: *evaluate the level of hazard in a situation* **3** *golf* an obstacle such as a bunker **4 at hazard** at risk ▷ *vb* **5** to risk: *hazarding the health of his crew* **6 hazard a guess** to make a guess
WORD ORIGIN Arabic *az-zahr* the die

hazard lights *or* **hazard warning lights** *pl n* the indicator lights on a motor vehicle when flashing simultaneously to indicate that the vehicle is stationary

hazardous *adj* involving great risk

haze *n* **1** *meteorol* reduced visibility as a result of condensed water vapour, dust, etc. in the air **2** confused or unclear understanding or feeling
WORD ORIGIN from *hazy*

hazel *n* **1** a shrub with edible rounded nuts ▷ *adj* **2** greenish-brown: *hazel eyes*
WORD ORIGIN Old English *hæsel*

hazelnut *n* the nut of a hazel shrub, which has a smooth shiny hard shell

hazy adj -zier, -ziest **1** (of the sky or a view) unable to be seen clearly because of dust or heat **2** dim or vague: *my memory is a little hazy on this* **hazily** adv **haziness** n
WORD ORIGIN origin unknown

Hb haemoglobin

HB *Austral & Brit* (of pencil lead) hard-black: denoting a medium-hard lead

H-bomb n short for **hydrogen bomb**

HDD hard disk drive

HD-DVD High Definition DVD: a DVD capable of storing between two and four times as much data as a standard DVD

he pron **1** (refers to) a male person or animal **2** (refers to) a person or animal of unknown or unspecified sex: *a member may vote as he sees fit* ▷ n **3** (refers to) a male person or animal: *a he-goat*
WORD ORIGIN Old English *hē*

He chem helium

HE His or Her Excellency

head n **1** the upper or front part of the body that contains the brain, eyes, mouth, nose, and ears **2** a person's mind and mental abilities: *I haven't any head for figures* **3** the most forward part of a thing: *the head of a queue* **4** the highest part of a thing; upper end: *the head of the pass* **5** something resembling a head in form or function, such as the top of a tool **6** the position of leadership or command **7** the person commanding most authority within a group or an organization **8** bot the top part of a plant, where the leaves or flowers grow in a cluster **9** a culmination or crisis: *the matter came to a head in December 1928* **10** the froth on the top of a glass of beer **11** the pus-filled tip of a pimple or boil **12** part of a computer or tape recorder that can read, write, or erase information **13** the source of a river or stream **14** the side of a coin that usually bears a portrait of the head of a monarch, etc. **15** a headland or promontory: *Beachy Head* **16** pressure of water or steam in an enclosed space **17** pl head a person or animal considered as a unit: *the cost per head of Paris's refuse collection; six hundred head of cattle* **18** a headline or heading **19** informal short for **headmaster, headmistress** or **head teacher 20** informal short for **headache 21 give someone his head** to allow someone greater freedom or responsibility **22 go to one's head a** (of an alcoholic drink) to make one slightly drunk **b** to make one conceited: *success has gone to his head* **23 head over heels (in love)** very much (in love) **24 keep one's head** to remain calm **25 not make head nor tail of** not to understand (a problem, etc.) **26 off one's head** slang very foolish or insane **27 on one's own head** at one's own risk **28 over someone's head a** to a higher authority: *the taboo of going over the head of their immediate boss* **b** beyond a person's understanding **29 put our or your or their heads together** informal to consult together **30 turn someone's head** to make someone conceited ▷ vb **31** to be at the front or top of: *Barnes headed the list* **32** to be in charge of **33** (often foll. by for) to go or cause to go (towards): *to head for the Channel ports* **34** soccer to propel

(the ball) by striking it with the head **35** to provide with a heading ▸ See also **head off, heads**
WORD ORIGIN Old English *hēafod*

headache n **1** a continuous pain in the head **2** informal any cause of worry, difficulty, or annoyance: *financial headaches*

head-banger n *Brit, Austral, & NZ slang* **1** a person who shakes his head violently to the beat of heavy-metal music **2** a crazy or stupid person

headboard n a vertical board at the head of a bed

headdress n any decorative head covering

headed adj **1** having a head or heads: *two-headed; bald-headed* **2** having a heading: *headed notepaper*

header n **1** soccer the action of striking a ball with the head **2** informal a headlong fall or dive

headfirst adv **1** with the head foremost **2** quickly and without thinking carefully: *she jumped into marriage headfirst*

headgear n hats collectively

head-hunting n **1** (of companies) the practice of actively searching for new high-level personnel, often from rival companies **2** the practice among certain peoples of removing the heads of enemies they have killed and preserving them as trophies **head-hunter** n

heading n **1** a title for a page, chapter, etc. **2** a main division, such as of a speech **3** mining a horizontal tunnel

headland n a narrow area of land jutting out into a sea

headlight or **headlamp** n a powerful light on the front of a vehicle

headline n **1** a phrase in heavy large type at the top of a newspaper or magazine article indicating the subject **2 headlines** the main points of a television or radio news broadcast

headlong adv **1** with the head foremost; headfirst **2** with great haste and without much thought: *they rushed headlong into buying a house* ▷ adj **3** hasty or reckless

headmaster or fem **headmistress** n the principal of a school

head off vb **1** to intercept and force to change direction: *police head off New Age travellers* **2** to prevent or avert: *trying to head off the prospect of civil war* **3** to depart or set out: *to head off to school*

head-on adv, adj **1** front foremost: *a head-on collision* **2** with directness or without compromise: *a head-on confrontation with the unions*

headphones pl n two small loudspeakers held against the ears, worn to listen to the radio or recorded music without other people hearing it

headquarters pl n any centre from which operations are directed

headroom or **headway** n the space below a roof or bridge which allows an object to pass or stay underneath it without touching it

heads adv with the side of a coin uppermost which has a portrait of a head on it

headship n the position or state of being a leader, esp. the head teacher of a school

headshrinker n slang a psychiatrist

headstall n the part of a bridle that fits round a horse's head

head start n an initial advantage in a competitive situation

headstone n a memorial stone at the head of a grave

headstrong adj determined to do something in one's own way and ignoring the advice of others

head teacher n the principal of a school

head-to-head adv, adj informal in direct competition

headwaters pl n the tributary streams of a river in the area in which it rises

headway n **1** progress towards achieving something: *have the police made any headway?* **2** motion forward: *we felt our way out to the open sea, barely making headway* **3** same as **headroom**

headwind n a wind blowing directly against the course of an aircraft or ship

heady adj **headier, headiest 1** (of an experience or period of time) extremely exciting **2** (of alcoholic drink, atmosphere, etc.) strongly affecting the physical senses: *a powerful, heady scent of cologne* **3** rash and impetuous

heal vb **1** (of a wound) to repair by natural processes, such as by scar formation **2** to restore (someone) to health **3** to repair (a rift in a personal relationship or an emotional wound) **healer** n **healing** n, adj
WORD ORIGIN Old English *hǣlan*

health n **1** the general condition of body and mind: *better health* **2** the state of being bodily and mentally vigorous and free from disease **3** the condition of an organization, society, etc.: *the economic health of the republics*
WORD ORIGIN Old English *hǣlth*

health camp n NZ a camp for children with health or behavioural problems

health centre n Brit the surgery and offices of the doctors in a district

health farm n a residential establishment for people wishing to improve their health by losing weight, exercising, etc.

health food n natural food, organically grown and free from additives

healthful adj same as **healthy** (senses 1, 2, 3)

health stamp n NZ a postage stamp with a small surcharge used to support health camps

health visitor n (in Britain) a nurse employed to visit mothers, their preschool children, and the elderly in their homes

healthy adj **healthier, healthiest 1** having or showing good health **2** likely to produce good health: *healthy seaside air* **3** functioning well or being sound: *this is a very healthy business to be in* **4** informal considerable: *healthy profits* **5** sensible: *a healthy scepticism about his promises* **healthily** adv **healthiness** n

heap n **1** a pile of things lying one on top of another **2** (often pl) informal a large

Words from Literature
part 13

harem *n* the part of the house where the women lived
mostly they hang round the harem
The Adventures of Huckleberry Finn Mark Twain

hautboys *n* an oboe
sausages and puddings resembling flutes and
hautboys
Gulliver's Travels Jonathan Swift

hawker *n* someone who sells goods to people as
he travels rather than from a fixed place like a shop
to buy some stockings from a hawker
Treasure Island Robert Louis Stevenson

hawser *n* a rope used to tie up or tow a ship or boat
Again among the tiers of shipping, in and out,
avoiding rusty chain-cables, frayed hempen hawsers
Great Expectations Charles Dickens

headstall *n* the part of the bridle or halter that goes
around a horse's head
I had of course long been used to a halter and
a headstall
Black Beauty Anna Sewell

hearken *v* to listen
though we sometimes stopped to lay hold of each
other and hearken
Treasure Island Robert Louis Stevenson

heartless *adj* without heart or dejected
I am not heartless
The Prelude William Wordsworth

hebdomadal *adj* weekly
It was the hebdomadal treat to which we all looked
forward from Sabbath to Sabbath
Jane Eyre Charlotte Brontë

highwayman *n* a person who stopped travellers and
robbed them
We are highwaymen
The Adventures of Huckleberry Finn Mark Twain

hinds *n* farm hands, or people who work on a farm
He called his hinds about him
Gulliver's Travels Jonathan Swift

histrionic *adj* if you refer to someone's behaviour
as histrionic, you are being critical of it because it is
dramatic and exaggerated
But the histrionic muse is the darling
The Adventures of Huckleberry Finn Mark Twain

hog *n* another word for a pig
Tom called the hogs 'ingots'
The Adventures of Huckleberry Finn Mark Twain

horrors, the *phrase* a fit, called delirium tremens,
which is caused by drinking too much alcohol
I'll have the horrors
Treasure Island Robert Louis Stevenson

huffy *adj* to be obviously annoyed or offended about
something
They will feel that more than angry speeches or
huffy actions
Little Women Louisa May Alcott

hulk *n* a prison-ship
The miserable companion of thieves and ruffians,
the fallen outcast of low haunts, the associate of
the scourings of the jails and hulks
Oliver Twist Charles Dickens

humbug *n* nonsense or rubbish
"Bah," said Scrooge. "Humbug!"
A Christmas Carol Charles Dickens

humour *n* it was believed that there were four fluids
in the body called humours which decided the
temperament of a person depending on how much
of each fluid was present
other peccant humours
Gulliver's Travels Jonathan Swift

husbandry *n* farming animals
bad husbandry were plentifully anointing their
wheels
Silas Marner George Eliot

huswife *n* a small sewing kit
but I had put my huswife on it
Emma Jane Austen

h

number or quantity ▷ *adv* **3 heaps** much: *he was heaps better* ▷ *vb* **4** to collect into a pile **5** to give freely (to): *film roles were heaped on her*
WORD ORIGIN Old English *hēap*

hear *vb* **hearing, heard 1** to perceive (a sound) with the sense of hearing **2** to listen to: *I didn't want to hear what he had to say* **3** to be informed (of something); receive information (about something): *I hear you mean to join the crusade* **4** *law* to give a hearing to (a case) **5 hear from** to receive a letter or telephone call from **6 hear! hear!** an exclamation of approval **7 hear of** to allow: *she wouldn't hear of it* **hearer** *n*
WORD ORIGIN Old English *hieran*

hearing *n* **1** the sense by which sound is perceived **2** an opportunity for someone to be listened to **3** the range within which sound can be heard; earshot **4** the investigation of a matter by a court of law

hearing aid *n* a small amplifier worn by a partially deaf person in or behind the ear to improve his or her hearing

hearing dog *n* a dog that has been trained to help a deaf person by alerting him or her to various sounds

hearken *vb archaic* to listen
WORD ORIGIN Old English *heorcnian*

hearsay *n* gossip or rumour

hearse *n* a large car used to carry a coffin at a funeral
WORD ORIGIN Latin *hirpex* harrow

heart *n* **1** a hollow muscular organ whose contractions pump the blood throughout the body **2** this organ considered as the centre of emotions, esp. love **3** tenderness or pity: *my heart went out to her* **4** courage or spirit **5** the most central part or important part: *at the heart of Italian motor racing* **6** (of vegetables such as cabbage) the inner compact part **7** the breast: *she held him to her heart* **8** a shape representing the heart, with two rounded lobes at the top meeting in a point at the bottom **9 a** a red heart-shaped symbol on a playing card **b** a card with one or more of these symbols or (*when pl*) the suit of cards so marked **10 break someone's heart** to cause someone to grieve very deeply, esp. by ending a love affair **11 by heart** by memorizing **12 have a change of heart** to experience a profound change of outlook or attitude **13 have one's heart in one's mouth** to be full of apprehension, excitement, or fear **14 have the heart** to have the necessary will or callousness (to do something): *I didn't have the heart to tell him* **15 set one's heart on something** to have something as one's ambition **16 take heart** to become encouraged **17 take something to heart** to take something seriously or be upset about something **18 wear one's heart on one's sleeve** to show one's feelings openly **19 with all one's heart** deeply and sincerely
WORD ORIGIN Old English *heorte*

heartache *n* very great sadness and emotional suffering

heart attack *n* a sudden severe malfunction of the heart

heartbeat *n* one complete pulsation of the heart

heartbreak *n* intense and overwhelming grief, esp. after the end of a love affair **heartbreaking** *adj* **heartbroken** *adj*

heartburn *n* a burning sensation in the chest caused by indigestion

hearten *vb* to encourage or make cheerful **heartening** *adj*

heart failure *n* **1** a condition in which the heart is unable to pump an adequate amount of blood to the tissues **2** sudden stopping of the heartbeat, resulting in death

heartfelt *adj* sincerely and strongly felt: *heartfelt thanks*

hearth *n* **1** the floor of a fireplace **2** this as a symbol of the home
WORD ORIGIN Old English *heorth*

heartland *n* **1** the central region of a country or continent: *we headed west towards the heartland of Tibet* **2** the area where the thing specified is most common or strongest: *Germany's industrial heartland*

heartless *adj* unkind or cruel **heartlessly** *adv*

heart-rending *adj* causing great sadness and pity: *a heart-rending story*

hearts and minds *n* the collective trust or approval of a body of people such as a populace, esp. for a foreign military force: *we must win the hearts and minds of the people*

heart-searching *n* examination of one's feelings or conscience

heartstrings *pl n often facetious* deep emotions: *tugging our heartstrings with pictures of suffering*
WORD ORIGIN originally referring to the tendons supposed to support the heart

heart-throb *n* a man, esp. a film or pop star, who is attractive to a lot of women or girls

heart-to-heart *adj* **1** (of a talk) concerned with personal problems or intimate feelings ▷ *n* **2** an intimate conversation

heart-warming *adj* inspiring feelings of happiness: *the heart-warming spectacle of a family reunion*

heartwood *n* the central core of dark hard wood in tree trunks

hearty *adj* **heartier, heartiest 1** warm, friendly, and enthusiastic **2** strongly felt: *a hearty dislike* **3** (of a meal) substantial and nourishing **heartily** *adv*

heat *vb* **1** to make or become hot or warm ▷ *n* **2** the state of being hot **3** the energy transferred as a result of a difference in temperature ▸ Related adjectives: **thermal, calorific 4** hot weather: *he loves the heat of Africa* **5** intensity of feeling: *the heat of their argument* **6** the most intense part: *in the heat of an election campaign* **7** pressure: *political heat on the government* **8** *sport* a preliminary eliminating contest in a competition **9 on** *or* **in heat** (of some female mammals) ready for mating **heating** *n*
WORD ORIGIN Old English *hǣtu*

heated *adj* impassioned or highly emotional: *a heated debate* **heatedly** *adv*

heater *n* a device for supplying heat

heath *n* **1** *Brit* a large open area, usually with sandy soil, low shrubs, and heather **2** a low-growing evergreen shrub with small bell-shaped pink or purple flowers
WORD ORIGIN Old English *hǣth*

heathen *n, pl* **-thens** *or* **-then** *old-fashioned* **1** a person who does not believe in an established religion; pagan ▷ *adj* **2** of or relating to heathen peoples
WORD ORIGIN Old English *hǣthen*

heather *n* a shrub with small bell-shaped flowers growing on heaths and mountains
WORD ORIGIN origin unknown

Heath Robinson *adj* (of a mechanical device) absurdly complicated in design for a simple function
WORD ORIGIN after William *Heath Robinson*, cartoonist

heatstroke *n* same as **sunstroke**

heat wave *n* a spell of unusually hot weather

heave *vb* **heaving, heaved 1** to lift or move (something) with a great effort **2** to throw (something heavy) with effort **3** to utter (a sigh) noisily or unhappily **4** to rise and fall heavily **5** *pt & pp* **hove** *naut* **a** to move in a specified direction: *heave her bows around and head north* **b** (of a vessel) to pitch or roll **6** to vomit or retch ▷ *n* **7** the act of heaving
WORD ORIGIN Old English *hebban*

heaven *n* **1** the place where God is believed to live and where those leading good lives are believed to go when they die **2** a place or state of happiness **3 heavens** the sky **4** Also: **heavens** God or the gods, used in exclamatory phrases: *for heaven's sake!*
WORD ORIGIN Old English *heofon*

heavenly *adj* **1** *informal* wonderful or very enjoyable: *a heavenly meal* **2** of or occurring in space: *a heavenly body* **3** of or relating to heaven

heave to *vb* to stop (a ship) or (of a ship) to stop

heavy *adj* **heavier, heaviest 1** of comparatively great weight **2** with a relatively high density: *lead is a heavy metal* **3** great in degree or amount: *heavy traffic* **4** considerable: *heavy emphasis* **5** hard to fulfil: *an exceptionally heavy demand for this issue* **6** using or consuming a lot of something quickly: *a heavy drinker* **7** deep and loud: *heavy breathing* **8** clumsy and slow: *a heavy lumbering trot* **9** (of a movement or action) with great downward force or pressure: *a heavy blow with a club* **10** solid or fat: *mountain animals acquire a heavy layer of fat* **11** not easily digestible: *a heavy meal* **12** (of cakes or bread) insufficiently raised **13** (of soil) with a high clay content **14** sad or dejected: *you feel heavy or sad afterwards* **15** (of facial features) looking sad and tired **16** (of a situation) serious and causing anxiety or sadness **17** cloudy or overcast: *heavy clouds obscured the sun* **18** (of an industry) engaged in the large-scale manufacture of large objects or extraction of raw materials **19** *mil* (of guns, etc.) large and powerful **20** dull and uninteresting: *Helen finds his friends very heavy going* **21** (of music, literature, etc.) difficult to understand or not immediately appealing **22** *slang* (of rock music) loud and having a powerful beat **23** *slang* using, or prepared to use, violence or brutality ▷ *n, pl* **heavies 24** *slang* a large strong man hired to threaten violence or deter others by his presence **25 a** a villainous role **b** an actor who plays such a part **26 the heavies** *informal* serious newspapers ▷ *adv* **27 heavily:** *time hung heavy* **heavily** *adv* **heaviness** *n* **WORD ORIGIN** Old English *hefig*

heavy-duty *adj* made to withstand hard wear, bad weather, etc.

heavy-handed *adj* acting forcefully and without care and thought

heavy-hearted *adj* sad and discouraged

heavy hydrogen *n* same as **deuterium**

heavy metal *n* a type of very loud rock music featuring guitar riffs

heavy water *n* water formed of oxygen and deuterium

heavyweight *n* **1** a professional boxer weighing over 195 pounds (88.5 kg) or an amateur weighing over 91 kg **2** a person who is heavier than average **3** *informal* an important or highly influential person

Heb. *or* **Hebr.** Hebrew (language)

Hebraic (hib-**ray**-ik) *adj* of the Hebrews or their language or culture

Hebrew *n* **1** the ancient language of the Hebrews, revived as the official language of Israel **2** a member of an ancient Semitic people; an Israelite ▷ *adj* **3** of the Hebrews or their language **WORD ORIGIN** Hebrew *'ibhrī* one from beyond (the river)

heck *interj* a mild exclamation of surprise, irritation, etc. **WORD ORIGIN** euphemistic for *hell*

heckle *vb* **-ling, -led** to interrupt (a public speaker) with comments, questions, or taunts **heckler** *n* **WORD ORIGIN** form of *hackle*

hectare *n* a unit of measure equal to one hundred ares (10 000 square metres or 2.471 acres) **WORD ORIGIN** French

hectic *adj* involving a lot of rushed activity **WORD ORIGIN** Greek *hektikos* hectic, consumptive

hector *vb* **1** to bully or torment ▷ *n* **2** a blustering bully **WORD ORIGIN** after *Hector,* legendary Trojan warrior

he'd he had *or* he would

hedge *n* **1** a row of shrubs or bushes forming a boundary **2** a barrier or protection against something, esp. against the risk of loss on an investment ▷ *vb* **hedging, hedged 3** to avoid making a decision by making noncommittal statements **4 hedge against** to guard against the risk of loss in (a bet or disagreement), by supporting the opposition as well **WORD ORIGIN** Old English *hecg*

hedgehog *n* a small mammal with a protective covering of spines

hedgerow *n* a hedge of shrubs or low trees bordering a field

hedge sparrow *n* a small brownish songbird

hedonism *n* the doctrine that the pursuit of pleasure is the most important thing in life **hedonist** *n* **hedonistic** *adj* **WORD ORIGIN** Greek *hēdonē* pleasure

heebie-jeebies *pl n* **the heebie-jeebies** *slang* nervous apprehension **WORD ORIGIN** coined by W. De Beck, cartoonist

heed *formal n* **1** careful attention: *he must have taken heed of her warning* ▷ *vb* **2** to pay close attention to (a warning or piece of advice) **WORD ORIGIN** Old English *hēdan*

heedless *adj* taking no notice; careless or thoughtless **heedlessly** *adv*

heehaw *interj* a representation of the braying sound of a donkey

heel¹ *n* **1** the back part of the foot **2** the part of a stocking or sock designed to fit the heel **3** the part of a shoe supporting the heel **4** *slang* a contemptible person **5 at one's heels** following closely behind one **6 down at heel** untidy and in poor condition **7 take to one's heels** to run off **8 kick** *or* **cool one's heels** to be kept waiting **9 to heel** under control, such as a dog walking by a person's heel ▷ *vb* **10** to repair or replace the heel of (a shoe or boot) **WORD ORIGIN** Old English *hēla*

heel² *vb* to lean to one side **WORD ORIGIN** Old English *hieldan*

heelball *n* **a** a mixture of beeswax and lampblack used by shoemakers **b** a similar substance used to take brass rubbings

heeler *n Austral & NZ* a dog that herds cattle by biting at their heels

hefty *adj* **heftier, heftiest** *informal* **1** large in size, weight, or amount **2** forceful and vigorous: *a hefty slap on the back* **3** involving a large amount of money: *a hefty fine*

hegemony (hig-**em**-on-ee) *n, pl* **-nies** domination of one state, country, or class within a group of others **WORD ORIGIN** Greek *hēgemonia*

Hegira *n* the flight of Mohammed from Mecca to Medina in 622 AD, regarded as being the starting point of the Muslim era **WORD ORIGIN** Arabic *hijrah* flight

heifer (**hef**-fer) *n* a young cow **WORD ORIGIN** Old English *heahfore*

height *n* **1** the vertical distance from the bottom of something to the top **2** the vertical distance of a place above sea level **3** relatively great distance from bottom to top **4** the topmost point; summit **5** the period of greatest intensity: *the height of the shelling* **6** an extreme example: *the height of luxury* **7 heights** extremes: *dizzy heights of success* **WORD ORIGIN** Old English *hīehthu*

heighten *vb* to make or become higher or more intense **heightened** *adj*

height of land *n US & Canad* a ridge of high ground dividing two river basins

heinous *adj* evil and shocking **WORD ORIGIN** Old French *haineus*

heir *n* the person legally succeeding to the property of a deceased person

heiress *fem n* **WORD ORIGIN** Latin *heres*

heir apparent *n, pl* **heirs apparent 1** *law* a person whose right to succeed to certain property cannot be defeated **2** a person whose succession to a role or position is extremely likely: *heir apparent to the England captaincy*

heirloom *n* an object that has been in a family for generations **WORD ORIGIN** HEIR + *lome* tool

heir presumptive *n property law* a person who expects to succeed to an estate but whose right may be defeated by the birth of an heir nearer in blood to the ancestor

heist *n slang* a robbery **WORD ORIGIN** from HOIST

held *vb* the past of **hold¹**

helical *adj* of or like a helix

helicopter *n* an aircraft, powered by rotating overhead blades, that is capable of hovering, vertical flight, and horizontal flight in any direction **WORD ORIGIN** Greek *helix* spiral + *pteron* wing

heliograph *n* an instrument with mirrors and a shutter used for sending messages in Morse code by reflecting the sun's rays **WORD ORIGIN** Greek *hēlios* sun + -GRAPHY

heliotrope *n* a plant with small fragrant purple flowers **WORD ORIGIN** Greek *hēlios* sun + *trepein* to turn

heliport *n* an airport for helicopters **WORD ORIGIN** *heli*(*copter*) + *port*

helium (**heel**-ee-um) *n chem* a very light colourless odourless inert gas. Symbol: He **WORD ORIGIN** Greek *hēlios* sun, because first detected in the solar spectrum

helix (**heel**-iks) *n, pl* **helices** (**hell**-iss-seez) *or* **helixes** a spiral **WORD ORIGIN** Greek: spiral

hell *n* **1** (in Christianity and some other religions) the place or state of eternal punishment of the wicked after death **2** (in various religions and cultures) the abode of the spirits of the dead **3** *informal* a situation that causes suffering or extreme difficulty: *war is hell* **4 come hell or high water** *informal* whatever difficulties may arise **5 for the hell of it** *informal* for the fun of it **6 from hell** *informal* denoting a person or thing that is particularly bad or alarming: *the neighbour from hell* **7 give someone hell** *informal* **a** to give someone a severe reprimand or punishment **b** to be a torment to someone **8 hell for leather** at great speed **9 the hell** *informal* **a** used for emphasis: *what the hell* **b** an expression of strong disagreement: *the hell you do!* ▷ *interj* **10** *informal* an exclamation of anger or surprise **WORD ORIGIN** Old English

he'll he will *or* he shall

hellbent *adj informal* rashly intent: *hellbent on revenge*

hellebore *n* a plant with white flowers that bloom in winter **WORD ORIGIN** Greek *helleboros*

Hellene *n* a Greek

Hellenic *adj* **1** of the Greeks or their language **2** of or relating to ancient

Greece during the classical period (776–323 BC)

Hellenism *n* **1** the principles and ideals of classical Greek civilization **2** the spirit or national character of the Greeks **Hellenist** *n*

Hellenistic *adj* of Greek civilization during the period 323–30 BC

hellfire *n* the torment of hell, imagined as eternal fire

hellish *adj informal* very unpleasant

hello, hallo *or* **hullo** *interj* **1** an expression of greeting or surprise **2** a call used to attract attention ▷ *n, pl* **-los 3** the act of saying 'hello'
WORD ORIGIN French *holà*

Hell's Angel *n* a member of a motorcycle gang noted for their lawless behaviour

helm *n* **1** *naut* the tiller or wheel for steering a ship **2** **at the helm** in a position of leadership or control **helmsman** *n*
WORD ORIGIN Old English *helma*

helmet *n* a piece of protective headgear worn by motorcyclists, soldiers, policemen, divers, etc.
WORD ORIGIN Old French

helot *n* (in ancient Greece) a serf or slave
WORD ORIGIN Greek *Heilōtes* serfs, literally: inhabitants of Helos

help *vb* **1** to assist (someone to do something) **2** to contribute to: *to help Latin America's economies* **3** to improve a situation: *a felt or rubber underlay will help* **4 a** to refrain from: *I couldn't help feeling foolish* **b** to be responsible for: *you must not blame him, he simply can't help it* **5** to serve (a customer) **6 help oneself** to take something, esp. food or drink, for oneself, without being served ▷ *n* **7** the act of helping **8** a person or thing that helps, esp. a farm worker or domestic servant **9** a remedy: *there's no help for it* ▷ *interj* **10** used to call for assistance ▶ See also **help out** ▷ **helper** *n*
WORD ORIGIN Old English *helpan*

helpful *adj* giving help **helpfully** *adv* **helpfulness** *n*

helping *n* a single portion of food

helpless *adj* **1** unable to manage independently **2** made weak: *it reduced her to helpless laughter* **helplessly** *adv* **helplessness** *n*

helpline *n* a telephone line set aside for callers to contact an organization for help with a problem

helpmate *or* **helpmeet** *n* a companion and helper, esp. a husband or wife

help out *vb* to assist (someone) by sharing the burden or cost of something

helter-skelter *adj* **1** hurried or disorganized ▷ *adv* **2** in a hurried or disorganized manner ▷ *n* **3** *Brit* a high spiral slide at a fairground
WORD ORIGIN probably imitative

hem¹ *n* **1** the bottom edge of a garment, folded under and stitched down ▷ *vb* **hemming, hemmed 2** to provide (a garment) with a hem ▶ See also **hem in**
WORD ORIGIN Old English *hemm*

hem² *n* **1** a representation of the sound of clearing the throat, used to gain attention ▷ *vb* **hemming, hemmed**

2 to make this sound **3 hem and haw** see **haw²**

he-man *n, pl* **-men** *informal* a strong man, esp. one who shows off his strength

hemi- *prefix* half: *hemisphere*
WORD ORIGIN Greek

hem in *vb* to surround and prevent from moving

hemipterous *or* **hemipteran** *adj* of an order of insects with sucking or piercing mouthparts
WORD ORIGIN Greek *hēmi* half + *pteron* wing

hemisphere *n* one half of a sphere, esp. of the earth (**northern** and **southern hemisphere**) or of the brain **hemispherical** *adj*

hemline *n* the level to which the hem of a skirt or dress hangs: *the hemline debate*

hemlock *n* a poisonous drug derived from a plant with spotted stems and small white flowers
WORD ORIGIN Old English *hymlic*

hemp *n* **1** an Asian plant with tough fibres **2** the fibre of this plant, used to make canvas and rope **3** a narcotic drug obtained from this plant **hempen** *adj*
WORD ORIGIN Old English *hænep*

hen *n* the female of any bird, esp. the domestic fowl
WORD ORIGIN Old English *henn*

henbane *n* a poisonous plant with sticky hairy leaves

hence *adv* **1** for this reason; therefore **2** from this time: *two weeks hence* **3** *archaic* from here
WORD ORIGIN Old English *hionane*

henceforth *or* **henceforward** *adv* from now on

henchman *n, pl* **-men** a person employed by someone powerful to carry out orders
WORD ORIGIN Middle English *hengestman*

henge *n* a circular monument, often containing a circle of stones, dating from the Neolithic and Bronze Ages
WORD ORIGIN from *Stonehenge*

henna *n* **1** a reddish dye, obtained from a shrub or tree of Asia and N Africa which is used to colour hair ▷ *vb* **2** to dye (the hair) with henna
WORD ORIGIN Arabic *hinnā'*

hen night *n informal* a party for women only, esp. held for a woman shortly before she is married

hen party *n informal* a party at which only women are present

henpecked *adj* (of a man) harassed by the persistent nagging of his wife

henry *n, pl* **-ry, -ries** *or* **-rys** the SI unit of electric inductance
WORD ORIGIN after Joseph Henry, physicist

hepatic *adj* of the liver
WORD ORIGIN Greek *hēpar* liver

hepatitis *n* inflammation of the liver, causing fever, jaundice, and weakness

Hephaestus *n Greek myth* the god of fire

hepta- *combining form* seven: *heptameter*

heptagon *n geom* a figure with seven sides **heptagonal** *adj*
WORD ORIGIN Greek *heptagōnos* having seven angles

heptathlon *n* an athletic contest for women in which athletes compete in seven different events

her *pron* **1** (refers to) a female person or animal: *he loves her* **2** (refers to) things personified as feminine, such as ships and nations ▷ *adj* **3** of, belonging to, or associated with her: *her hair*
WORD ORIGIN Old English *hire*

≡ **USAGE**
≡ See at **me**.

Hera *or* **Here** *n Greek myth* the queen of the gods

herald *n* **1** a person who announces important news **2** *often literary* a forerunner ▷ *vb* **3** to announce or signal the approach of: *his arrival was heralded by excited barking* **heraldic** *adj*
WORD ORIGIN Germanic

heraldry *n, pl* **-ries** the study of coats of arms and family trees

herb *n* **1** an aromatic plant that is used for flavouring in cookery, and in medicine **2** *bot* a seed-bearing plant whose parts above ground die back at the end of the growing season **herbal** *adj* **herby** *adj*
WORD ORIGIN Latin *herba* grass, green plants

herbaceous *adj* designating plants that are soft-stemmed rather than woody

herbaceous border *n* a flower bed that contains perennials rather than annuals

herbage *n* herbaceous plants collectively, esp. those on which animals graze

herbalist *n* a person who grows or specializes in the use of medicinal herbs

herbicide *n* a substance used to destroy plants, esp. weeds
WORD ORIGIN Latin *herba* plant + *caedere* to kill

herbivore (**her**-biv-vore) *n* **1** an animal that feeds only on plants **2** *informal* a liberal or idealistic person **herbivorous** (her-**biv**-or-uss) *adj*
WORD ORIGIN Latin *herba* plant + *vorare* to swallow

herculean (her-kew-**lee**-an) *adj* **1** (of a task) requiring tremendous effort or strength **2** resembling Hercules, hero of classical myth, in strength or courage

herd *n* **1** a large group of mammals, esp. cattle, living and feeding together **2** *often disparaging* a large group of people ▷ *vb* **3** to collect or be collected into, or as if into, a herd
WORD ORIGIN Old English *heord*

herd instinct *n psychol* the inborn tendency to associate with others and follow the group's behaviour

herdsman *n, pl* **-men** *chiefly Brit* a man who looks after a herd of animals

here *adv* **1** in, at, or to this place, point, case, or respect: *I am pleased to be back here* **2 here and there** at several places in or throughout an area **3 here's to** a convention used in proposing a toast **4 neither here nor there** of no relevance ▷ *n* **5** this place: *they leave here tonight*
WORD ORIGIN Old English *hēr*

hereabouts *or* **hereabout** *adv* in this region

Words from Shakespeare
part 12

holy-water, court *phrase* make empty promises, or make statements which sound good but have no real meaning
> court holy-water in a dry house is better than this rain-water out o'door *King Lear* 3.2

howsoever *adv* however
> But howsoever strange and admirable *A Midsummer Night's Dream* 5.1

humour *n* your mood, frame of mind or temperament
> it fits my humour well *As You Like It* 3.2

ill *adj* bad
> I must thank him only,
> Let my remembrance suffer ill report
> *Anthony and Cleopatra* 2.2

indistinct *adj* inseparable or unable to see a difference
> Even till we make the main and the aerial blue
> An indistinct regard. *Othello* 2.1

indulgence *n* approval
> As you from crimes would pardoned be,
> Let your indulgence set me free
> *The Tempest* Epilogue

infirmity *n* weakness or frailty
> Be not disturbed with my infirmity *The Tempest* 4.1

intelligence *n* information
> Pursue her; and for this intelligence
> If I have thanks *A Midsummer Night's Dream* 1.1

inwards *n* someone's internal organs
> the thought whereof
> Doth like a poisonous mineral gnaw my inwards
> *Othello* 2.1

issue *n* the children of a marriage
> To thine and Albany's issues,
> Be this perpetual *King Lear* 1.1

issue *n* outcome or result
> I am to pray you, not to strain my speech,
> To grosser issues *Othello*

kind *n* situation or case
> But in this kind, wanting your father's voice,
> The other must be held the worthier.
> *A Midsummer Night's Dream* 1.1

knave *n* a scoundrel
> How absolute the knave is! *Hamlet* 5.1

league *n* a distance. A league was the distance a person could walk in one hour
> From Athens is her house remote seven leagues
> *A Midsummer Night's Dream* 1.1

lief, I had as *phrase* I should like just as much
> I had as lief the town crier spoke my lines
> *Hamlet* 1.2

livery *n* a costume, outfit, uniform usually worn by a servant
> You can endure the livery of a nun
> *A Midsummer Night's Dream* 1.1

loam *n* soil containing decayed vegetable matter and therefore good for growing crops and plants
> and let him have some plaster, or some loam,
> or some rough-cast about him, to signify wall
> *A Midsummer Night's Dream* 3.1

lusty *adj* strong
> and oared
> Himself with his good arms in lusty stroke
> To th' shore *The Tempest* 2.1

maidenhead *n* chastity or virginity
> What I am, and what I would, are as secret as
> maidenhead *Twelfth Night* 1.5

mark *v* to note or pay attention to
> Where sighs and groans,
> Are made not marked *Macbeth* 4.3

marvellous *adj* very or extremely
> here's a marvellous convenient place for our
> rehearsal *A Midsummer Night's Dream* 3.1

meet *adj* right or proper
> tis most meet you should *Macbeth* 5.1

hereafter *adv* **1** *formal or law* in a subsequent part of this document, matter, or case **2** at some time in the future ▷ *n* **3 the hereafter a** life after death **b** the future

hereby *adv* (used in official statements and documents) by means of or as a result of this

hereditable *adj* same as **heritable**

hereditary *adj* **1** passed on genetically from one generation to another **2** *law* passed on to succeeding generations by inheritance

heredity (hir-**red**-it-ee) *n, pl* **-ties** the passing on from one generation to another of genetic factors that determine individual characteristics WORD ORIGIN Latin *hereditas* inheritance

Hereford *n* a hardy breed of beef cattle which has a reddish body with white markings WORD ORIGIN after *Hereford*, English city

herein *adv* *formal or law* in this place, matter, or document

hereinafter *adv* *formal or law* from this point on in this document, matter, or case

hereof *adv* *formal or law* of or concerning this

heresy (**herr**-iss-ee) *n, pl* **-sies 1** an opinion contrary to the principles of a religion **2** any belief thought to be contrary to official or established theory WORD ORIGIN Greek *hairein* to choose

heretic (**herr**-it-ik) *n* **1** *now chiefly RC Church* a person who maintains beliefs contrary to the established teachings of the Church **2** a person who holds unorthodox opinions in any field **heretical** (hir-**ret**-ik-kl) *adj*

hereto *adv* *formal or law* to this place, matter, or document

heretofore *adv* *formal or law* until now

hereupon *adv* following immediately after this; at this stage

herewith *adv* *formal* together with this: *a schedule of the event is appended herewith*

heritable *adj* capable of being inherited

heritage *n* **1** something inherited at birth **2** anything that has been carried over from the past or handed down by tradition **3** the evidence of the past, such as historical sites, considered as the inheritance of present-day society

hermaphrodite (her-**maf**-roe-dite) *n* an animal, flower, or person that has both male and female reproductive organs **hermaphroditic** *adj* WORD ORIGIN after *Hermaphroditus*, son of Hermes and Aphrodite, who merged with the nymph Salmacis to form one body

Hermes *n* *Greek myth* the messenger of the gods

hermetic *adj* sealed so as to be airtight **hermetically** *adv* WORD ORIGIN after the Greek god *Hermes*, traditionally the inventor of a magic seal

hermit *n* a person living in solitude, esp. for religious reasons WORD ORIGIN Greek *erēmos* lonely

hermitage *n* **1** the home of a hermit **2** any retreat

hermit crab *n* a small crab that lives in the empty shells of other shellfish

hernia *n* protrusion of an organ or part through the lining of the body cavity in which it is normally situated WORD ORIGIN Latin

hero *n, pl* **-roes 1** the principal male character in a novel, play, etc. **2** a man of exceptional courage, nobility, etc. **3** a man who is idealized for having superior qualities in any field WORD ORIGIN Greek *hērōs*

heroic *adj* **1** brave and courageous: *heroic work by the army engineers* **2** of, like, or befitting a hero **heroically** *adv*

heroics *pl n* behaviour or language considered too melodramatic or extravagant for the particular situation in which they are used

heroin *n* a highly addictive drug derived from morphine WORD ORIGIN probably from *hero*, referring to its aggrandizing effect on the personality

heroine *n* **1** the principal female character in a novel, play, etc. **2** a woman of exceptional courage, nobility, etc. **3** a woman who is idealized for having superior qualities in any field

heroism (**herr**-oh-izz-um) *n* great courage and bravery

heron *n* a wading bird with a long neck, long legs, and grey or white feathers WORD ORIGIN Old French *hairon*

heronry *n, pl* **-ries** a colony of breeding herons

hero worship *n* admiration for heroes or idealized people

herpes (**her**-peez) *n* any of several inflammatory skin diseases, including shingles and cold sores WORD ORIGIN Greek *herpein* to creep

herpes simplex *n* an acute viral disease causing clusters of watery blisters WORD ORIGIN New Latin: simple herpes

herpes zoster *n* same as **shingles** WORD ORIGIN New Latin: girdle herpes

Herr (**hair**) *n, pl* **Herren** a German form of address equivalent to *Mr* WORD ORIGIN German

herring *n, pl* **-rings** *or* **-ring** a food fish of northern seas, with a long silver-coloured body WORD ORIGIN Old English *hæring*

herringbone *n* a zigzag pattern consisting of short lines of V shapes

herring gull *n* a common gull that has white and grey feathers with black-tipped wings

hers *pron* **1** something belonging to her: *hers is the highest paid part-time job; the money which is rightfully hers* **2 of hers** belonging to her

herself *pron* **1 a** the reflexive form of *she* or *her*: *she busied herself at the stove* **b** used for emphasis: *none other than The Great Mother herself* **2** her normal self: *she hasn't been herself all week*

Herts Hertfordshire

hertz *n, pl* **hertz** the SI unit of frequency, equal to one cycle per second WORD ORIGIN after H. R. *Hertz*, physicist

he's he is *or* he has

hESC human embryonic stem cell

hesitant *adj* doubtful and unsure in speech or action **hesitancy** *n* **hesitantly** *adv*

hesitate *vb* **-tating, -tated 1** to be slow and uncertain in acting **2** to be reluctant (to do something): *I hesitate to use the word 'squandered'* **3** to pause during speech because of uncertainty **hesitation** *n* WORD ORIGIN Latin *haesitare*

hessian *n* a coarse jute fabric similar to sacking WORD ORIGIN after *Hesse*, Germany

hetero- *combining form* other, another, or different: *heterosexual* WORD ORIGIN Greek *heteros* other

heterodox *adj* different from established or accepted doctrines or beliefs **heterodoxy** *n* WORD ORIGIN HETERO- + Greek *doxa* opinion

heterodyne *electronics vb* **-dyning, -dyned 1** to combine (two alternating signals) so as to produce two signals with frequencies corresponding to the sum and the difference of the original frequencies ▷ *adj* **2** produced or operating by heterodyning two signals WORD ORIGIN HETERO- + Greek *dunamis* power

heterogeneous (het-er-oh-**jean**-ee-uss) *adj* varied in content; composed of different parts: *a heterogeneous collection of art* **heterogeneity** *n* WORD ORIGIN HETERO- + Greek *genos* sort

heteromorphic *adj biol* **1** differing from the normal form **2** (esp. of insects) having different forms at different stages of the life cycle **heteromorphism** *n* WORD ORIGIN HETERO- + Greek *morphē* form

heterosexual *n* **1** a person who is sexually attracted to members of the opposite sex ▷ *adj* **2** (of a person) sexually attracted to members of the opposite sex **3** (of a sexual relationship) between a man and a woman **heterosexuality** *n*

heterozygous *adj biol* having two different alleles of the same gene WORD ORIGIN HETERO- + Greek *zugōtos* yoked

het up *adj informal* agitated or excited: *he was very het up about the traffic* WORD ORIGIN dialect for *heated*

heuristic (**hew**-rist-ik) *adj* (of a method of teaching) allowing students to learn things for themselves by trial and error WORD ORIGIN Greek *heuriskein* to discover

hew *vb* **hewing, hewed, hewed** *or* **hewn 1** to chop or cut with an axe **2** to carve (something) from a substance: *a tunnel hewn out of the living rock* WORD ORIGIN Old English *hēawan*

hex *n* **1** short for **hexadecimal notation** ▷ *adj* **2** of or relating to hexadecimal notation: *hex code*

hexa- *combining form* six: *hexameter* WORD ORIGIN Greek *hex* six

hexadecimal notation *n* a number system with a base of 16, the numbers 10–15 being represented by the letters A–F

hexagon *n geom* a figure with six sides
hexagonal *adj*

hexagram *n geom* a star formed by extending the sides of a regular hexagon to meet at six points

hexameter (hek-**sam**-it-er) *n prosody* a verse line consisting of six metrical feet

hey *interj* 1 an expression of surprise or for catching attention 2 **hey presto!** an exclamation used by conjurors at the climax of a trick
WORD ORIGIN imitative

heyday *n* the time of most power, popularity, or success: *the heyday of classical composition*
WORD ORIGIN probably based on *hey*

Hf *chem* hafnium

HFEA *Brit* Human Fertilization and Embryology Authority

Hg *chem* mercury

HGV (in Britain, formerly) heavy goods vehicle

HH 1 His (or Her) Highness 2 His Holiness (title of the pope)

hi *interj informal* hello
WORD ORIGIN probably from *how are you?*

HI Hawaii

hiatus (hie-**ay**-tuss) *n, pl* **-tuses** or **-tus** a pause or an interruption in continuity: *diplomatic relations restored after a four-year hiatus*
WORD ORIGIN Latin: gap, cleft

hiatus hernia *n* protrusion of the stomach through the diaphragm at the hole for the gullet

Hib *n* Haemophilus influenzae type b: a vaccine against a specific type of bacterial meningitis, administered to children under four years of age

hibernate *vb* **-nating, -nated** (of some animals) to pass the winter in a resting state in which heartbeat, temperature, and breathing rate are very low
hibernation *n*
WORD ORIGIN Latin *hibernare* to spend the winter

Hibernia *n poetic* Ireland **Hibernian** *adj, n*

hibiscus *n, pl* **-cuses** a tropical plant with large brightly coloured flowers
WORD ORIGIN Greek *hibiskos* marsh mallow

hiccup *n* 1 a spasm of the breathing organs with a sharp coughlike sound 2 **hiccups** the state of having such spasms 3 *informal* a minor difficulty ▷ *vb* **-cuping, -cuped** or **-cupping, -cupped** 4 to make a hiccup or hiccups. Also: **hiccough**
WORD ORIGIN imitative

hick *n US, Austral, & NZ informal* an unsophisticated country person
WORD ORIGIN after *Hick*, familiar form of *Richard*

hickory *n, pl* **-ries** 1 a North American tree with edible nuts 2 the hard wood of this tree
WORD ORIGIN Native American *pawcohiccora*

hidden *vb* 1 a past participle of **hide¹** ▷ *adj* 2 not easily noticed or obscure: *hidden dangers* 3 difficult to find

hidden agenda *n* a set of motives or intentions concealed from others who might object to them

hide¹ *vb* **hiding, hid, hidden** or **hid** 1 to conceal (oneself or an object) from view or discovery: *in an attempt to hide from his wife* 2 to keep (information or one's feelings) secret 3 to obscure or cover (something) from view: *the collar hid his face* ▷ *n* 4 *Brit* a place of concealment, disguised to appear as part of its surroundings, used by hunters, bird-watchers, etc.
WORD ORIGIN Old English *hȳdan*

hide² *n* the skin of an animal, either tanned or raw
WORD ORIGIN Old English *hȳd*

hide-and-seek *n* a game in which one player covers his or her eyes while the others hide, and that player then tries to find them

hideaway *n* a hiding place or secluded spot

hidebound *adj* restricted by petty rules and unwilling to accept new ideas

hideous (**hid**-ee-uss) *adj* extremely ugly or unpleasant
WORD ORIGIN Old French *hisdos*

hide-out *n* a hiding place

hiding¹ *n* 1 a state of concealment: *in hiding* 2 **hiding place** a place of concealment

hiding² *n informal* a severe beating

hie *vb* **hieing** or **hying, hied** *archaic* or *poetic* to hurry
WORD ORIGIN Old English *hīgian* to strive

hierarchy (**hire**-ark-ee) *n, pl* **-chies** 1 a system of people or things arranged in a graded order 2 **the hierarchy** the people in power in any organization
hierarchical *adj*
WORD ORIGIN Late Greek *hierarkhēs* high priest

hieroglyphic (hire-oh-**gliff**-ik) *adj* 1 of or relating to a form of writing using picture symbols, as used in ancient Egypt ▷ *n also* **hieroglyph** 2 a symbol that is difficult to decipher 3 a picture or symbol representing an object, idea, or sound
WORD ORIGIN Greek *hieros* holy + *gluphein* to carve

hieroglyphics *n* 1 a form of writing, as used in ancient Egypt, in which pictures or symbols are used to represent objects, ideas, or sounds 2 writing that is difficult to decipher

hi-fi *n informal* 1 a set of high-quality sound-reproducing equipment 2 short for **high fidelity** ▷ *adj* 3 producing high-quality sound: *a hi-fi amplifier*

higgledy-piggledy *informal adj, adv* in a muddle
WORD ORIGIN origin unknown

high *adj* 1 being a relatively great distance from top to bottom: *a high stone wall* 2 being at a relatively great distance above sea level: *a high village* 3 being a specified distance from top to bottom: *three feet high* 4 coming up to a specified level: *waist-high* 5 being at its peak: *high summer* 6 of greater than average height: *a high ceiling* 7 greater than usual in intensity or amount: *high blood pressure; high fees* 8 (of a sound) acute in pitch 9 (of food) slightly decomposed, regarded as enhancing the flavour of game 10 towards the top of a scale of importance or quality: *high fashion* 11 intensely emotional: *high drama* 12 very cheerful: *high spirits* 13 *informal* under the influence of alcohol or drugs 14 luxurious or extravagant: *high life* 15 advanced in complexity: *high finance* 16 formal and elaborate: *High Mass* 17 **high and dry** abandoned in a difficult situation 18 **high and mighty** *informal* too confident and full of self-importance 19 **high opinion** a favourable opinion ▷ *adv* 20 at or to a height: *flying high* ▷ *n* 21 a high level 22 same as **anticyclone** 23 **on a high** *informal* a in a state of intoxication by alcohol or drugs b in a state of great excitement and happiness
WORD ORIGIN Old English *hēah*

High Arctic *n* the regions of Canada, esp. the northern islands, within the Arctic Circle

highball *n chiefly US* a long iced drink consisting of whisky with soda water or ginger ale

highbrow *often disparaging adj* 1 concerned with serious, intellectual subjects ▷ *n* 2 a person with such tastes

highchair *n* a long-legged chair with a table-like tray, used for a child at meal times

High Church *n* 1 the movement within the Church of England stressing the importance of ceremony and ritual ▷ *adj* **High-Church** 2 of or relating to this movement

high commissioner *n* the senior diplomatic representative sent by one Commonwealth country to another

high country *n* **the high country** NZ sheep pastures in the foothills of the Southern Alps

High Court *n* (in England, Wales, Australia, and New Zealand) the supreme court dealing with civil and criminal law cases

high-energy *adj* providing or inspiring a lot of energy: *a high-energy drink; a high-energy workout*

Higher *n* 1 (in Scotland) the advanced level of the Scottish Certificate of Education 2 a pass in a subject at this level: *she has got four Highers*

higher education *n* education and training at colleges, universities, and polytechnics

higher-up *n informal* a person of higher rank

highest common factor *n* the largest number that divides equally into each member of a group of numbers

high explosive *n* an extremely powerful chemical explosive, such as TNT or gelignite

highfalutin (hie-fa-**loot**-in) *adj informal* (of behaviour) excessively grand or pompous
WORD ORIGIN *-falutin* perhaps variant of *fluting*

high fidelity *n* 1 the electronic reproduction of sound with little or no distortion ▷ *adj* **high-fidelity** 2 able to produce sound with little or no distortion: *high-fidelity stereo earphones*

high-five *n slang* a gesture of greeting or congratulation in which two people slap raised palms together

high-flown *adj* extravagant or pretentious: *high-flown language*

high-flyer or **high-flier** *n* **1** a person who is extremely ambitious **2** a person of great ability in a career **high-flying** *adj, n*

high frequency *n* a radio frequency between 30 and 3 megahertz

High German *n* the standard German language

high-handed *adj* using authority in an unnecessarily forceful way **high-handedness** *n*

high jump *n* **the high jump** **a** an athletic event in which competitors have to jump over a high bar **b** *Austral & Brit informal* a severe reprimand or punishment: *I was for the high jump again*

Highland *adj* of or denoting the Highlands, a mountainous region of NW Scotland **Highlander** *n*

Highland cattle *n* a breed of cattle with shaggy reddish-brown hair and long horns

Highland fling *n* an energetic Scottish solo dance

highlands *pl n* relatively high ground

high-level language *n* a computer programming language that is close to human language

highlight *n* **1** Also called: **high spot** the most exciting or memorable part of something **2** an area of the lightest tone in a painting or photograph **3** a lightened streak in the hair produced by bleaching ▷ *vb* **4** to give emphasis to: *the prime minister repeatedly highlighted the need for lower pay*

highlighter *n* **1** a cosmetic cream or powder applied to the face to highlight the cheekbones or eyes **2** a fluorescent felt-tip pen used as a marker to emphasize a section of text without obscuring it

highly *adv* **1** extremely: *highly desirable* **2** towards the top of a scale of importance, admiration, or respect: *highly paid doctors*

highly strung or *US & Canad* **high-strung** *adj* tense and easily upset

high-maintenance *adj* **1** (of a piece of equipment, motor vehicle, etc.) requiring regular maintenance to keep it in working order **2** *informal* (of a person) requiring a high level of care and attention; demanding

High Mass *n* a solemn and elaborate Mass

high-minded *adj* having high moral principles

Highness *n* (preceded by *Your*, *His* or *Her*) a title used to address or refer to a royal person

high-octane *adj* **1** (of petrol) having a high octane number **2** *informal* dynamic or intense: *a high-octane lifestyle*

high-pitched *adj* (of a sound, esp. a voice) pitched high in tone

high-powered *adj* **1** (of machinery or equipment) powerful, advanced, and sophisticated **2** important, successful, or influential: *a high-powered business contact*

high-pressure *adj informal* (of selling) persuasive in an aggressive and persistent manner

high priest *n* the head of a cult or movement **high priestess** *fem n*

high-rise *adj* **1** of or relating to a building that has many storeys: *a high-rise estate* ▷ *n* **2** a building that has many storeys

high-risk *adj* denoting a group or area that is particularly subject to a danger

highroad *n* a main road

high school *n* a secondary school

high seas *pl n* the open seas, which are outside the authority of any one nation

high season *n* the most popular time of year at a holiday resort, etc.

high-spirited *adj* lively and wishing to have fun and excitement

high tea *n Brit* an early evening meal consisting of a cooked dish, bread, cakes, and tea

high-tech *adj* same as **hi-tech**

high technology *n* any type of sophisticated industrial process, esp. one involving electronics

high-tension *adj* (of electricity cable) carrying a powerful current

high tide *n* the sea at its highest level on the coast

high time *adv informal* the latest possible time: *it was high time she got married*

high treason *n* a serious crime directly affecting a sovereign or state

high-water mark *n* **1** the level reached by sea water at high tide or a river in flood **2** the highest or most successful stage: *the premature high-water mark of his career*

highway *n* **1** a public road that everyone may use **2** *US, Canad, Austral, & NZ* a main road, esp. one that connects towns

Highway Code *n* (in Britain) a booklet of regulations and recommendations for all road users

highwayman *n, pl* **-men** (formerly) a robber, usually on horseback, who held up travellers on public roads

hijack *vb* **1** to seize control of or divert (a vehicle or aircraft) while travelling ▷ *n* **2** an instance of hijacking: *Indonesian ferry hijack ends* **hijacker** *n*
WORD ORIGIN origin unknown

hike *vb* **hiking, hiked** **1** to walk a long way in the country, usually for pleasure **2** to raise (prices) **3** to pull up with a quick movement: *he hiked up his trouser legs* ▷ *n* **4** a long walk **5** a rise in price **hiker** *n*
WORD ORIGIN origin unknown

hilarious *adj* very funny **hilariously** *adv* **hilarity** *n*
WORD ORIGIN Greek *hilaros* cheerful

hill *n* **1** a natural elevation of the earth's surface, less high than a mountain **2** a heap or mound **3** an incline or slope **hilly** *adj*
WORD ORIGIN Old English *hyll*

hillbilly *n, pl* **-lies** **1** *usually disparaging* an unsophisticated person from the mountainous areas in the southeastern US **2** same as **country and western**
WORD ORIGIN *hill* + *Billy* (the nickname)

hillock *n* a small hill or mound

hilt *n* **1** the handle or shaft of a sword, dagger, or knife **2** **to the hilt** to the full:

he plays the role to the hilt
WORD ORIGIN Old English

hilum *n, pl* **-la** *bot* a scar on a seed marking its point of attachment to the seed vessel
WORD ORIGIN Latin: trifle

him *pron* refers to a male person or animal: *I greeted him at the hotel; I must send him a note of congratulation*
WORD ORIGIN Old English
≡ USAGE
≡ See at **me**.

himself *pron* **1 a** the reflexive form of *he* or *him*: *he secretly asked himself* **b** used for emphasis: *approved of by the Creator himself* **2** his normal self: *he was almost himself again*

hind¹ *adj* **hinder, hindmost** situated at the back: *a hind leg*
WORD ORIGIN Old English *hindan* at the back

hind² *n, pl* **hinds** or **hind** the female of the deer, esp. the red deer
WORD ORIGIN Old English

hinder¹ *vb* to get in the way of (someone or something)
WORD ORIGIN Old English *hindrian*

hinder² *adj* situated at the back
WORD ORIGIN Old English

Hindi *n* **1** a language or group of dialects of N central India **2** a formal literary dialect of this language, the official language of India
WORD ORIGIN Old Persian *Hindu* the river Indus

hindmost *adj* furthest back; last

hindquarters *pl n* the rear of a four-legged animal

hindrance *n* **1** an obstruction or snag **2** the act of hindering

hindsight *n* the ability to understand, after something has happened, what should have been done or what caused the event

Hindu *n, pl* **-dus** **1** a person who practises Hinduism ▷ *adj* **2** of Hinduism

Hinduism *n* the dominant religion of India, which involves the worship of many gods and belief in reincarnation

Hindustani *n* a group of northern Indian languages that includes Hindi and Urdu

hinge *n* **1** a device for holding together two parts, such as a door and its frame, so that one can swing freely ▷ *vb* **hinging, hinged** **2** to join or open (something) by means of a hinge **3 hinge on** to depend on: *billions of dollars of western aid hinged on the outcome of the talks* **hinged** *adj*
WORD ORIGIN probably Germanic

Hinglish *n* a variety of English incorporating elements of Hindi
WORD ORIGIN blend of HINDI + ENGLISH

hinny *n, pl* **-nies** the offspring of a male horse and a female donkey
WORD ORIGIN Greek *hinnos*

hint *n* **1** a suggestion given in an indirect or subtle manner **2** a helpful piece of advice **3** a small amount: *a hint of irony* ▷ *vb* **4** (sometimes foll. by *at*) to suggest indirectly: *a solution has been hinted at by a few politicians*
WORD ORIGIN origin unknown

The Language of Gender

Feminism, one of the great social, political, and economic revolutions of the twentieth century, embraced such issues as who did what work, how much the work earned, and whether men and women could or should be defined by nature or nurture. Its aim was to establish fairness in how women were treated and defined themselves.

That much is obvious. Less obvious are the changes feminism brought to English. English may seem to have a built-in advantage concerning sex parity because, unlike many languages, modern English typically does not assign nouns, verbs, and adjectives to the masculine, feminine, or neuter gender. Most English nouns are neuter, though Latin inflexions uneasily survive in the endings of *actress*, *waitress*, and *dominatrix*. In fairness, gender in languages like French, German, and Russian is a grammatical convention, like that by which a verb must agree in gender with its subject. In French, nothing in *la fourchette*, the table fork, confers femaleness, any more than maleness is conferred on *le soleil*, the sun.

Though feminism as an organized movement or climate of thought has been around for about two centuries, a term for it has not. *Feminism* began to be used in the late 1800s; a century later even some men called themselves feminists. Coined from *suffrage*, the right to vote, a *suffragette* (1902) was a woman who fought for female enfranchisement. *Women's movement* also dates from 1902, though the word was neglected until the 1960s, when it began to replace *women's liberation* (1966) or its disparaging form *women's lib* (1969).

As feminism gained momentum, a few coinages attempted historical redress. *History* was dubbed *herstory* to compensate for the preponderance of males in the historical record. Some feminists ransacked etymology, alleging negative bias in a word like *hysteria*, which derives from the Greek *hustera*, the womb. *Herstory* was too narrowly tendentious to catch on, but *Ms.* quickly gained acceptance as a useful neutral term for a woman who might be a *Miss* or a *Mrs*.

Within feminism, some women emphasized the distinctness of womanhood, others on what the sexes had in common, the latter reflected in the fashion for *unisex* clothing. Although *sex* and *gender* long had been used interchangeably, the former came to denote the biological state of being male or female, and the latter how society defined it. As an academic discipline, *gender studies* began to be enshrined in universities, along with its subset, *women's studies*.

Women's control over their bodies was advanced by the advent of the contraceptive *Pill* in the 1960s. A rancorous debate soon began about unwanted pregnancies. Those who thought that women were free to choose whether or not to abort an embryo termed themselves *pro-choice*; those who thought personal choice was trumped by family or religious obligations were *pro-life*. Marriage and responsibility for childcare were redefined; an unmarried couple could be *partners*. If the couple broke up, the informal equivalent of *alimony* for the married became *palimony* for the unmarried. Employers began to grant *maternity leave* or *paternity leave* to a parent after a child was born.

Another, parallel social revolution involved the private identity and public roles of homosexuals, and whether sexual orientation – *straight, gay, bisexual, transsexual* – was biologically determined or stemmed from personal preference. As a term, *lesbian* was distinguished from *gay*; lesbians adopted the gay tactic of reversing what had been an abusive term, as in *dyke* or *dike*. A group of lesbian San Francisco motorcyclists proudly called themselves *Dikes on Bikes*.

Most language changes arose not in vocabulary, but in usage. To eliminate bias, the combining form *-man* was often dropped from words: *chairman* became *chair* or *chairperson*. Men and women became *persons* or *people*. Sometimes a *-man* or *-ess* word was replaced by either a more specific or a more general term: a *repairman* became an *electrician* or *plumber*, and a *waitress* became a *server*. *Housewives* became *homemakers*. Traditionally, the personal pronouns, *he, his, him*, and *himself* were applied to both sexes. Careful writers and editors began to tiptoe around the generic *he*. They used *he or she*, or more contorted formulations like *he/she* and *s/he*. When applied to women, stereotyping adjectives such as *spunky, feisty*, and *strident* began to be shunned. No area of language use is such a minefield.

hinterland *n* **1** land lying behind a coast or the shore of a river **2** an area near and dependent on a large city, esp. a port
WORD ORIGIN German *hinter* behind + LAND

hip[1] *n* either side of the body below the waist and above the thigh
WORD ORIGIN Old English *hype*

hip[2] *n* the berry-like brightly coloured fruit of a rose bush. Also called: **rosehip**
WORD ORIGIN Old English *hēope*

hip[3] *interj* an exclamation used to introduce cheers: *hip, hip, hurrah*
WORD ORIGIN origin unknown

hip[4] *adj* **hipper, hippest** *slang* aware of or following the latest trends
WORD ORIGIN variant of earlier *hep*

hip bath *n* a portable bath in which the bather sits

hipbone *n* either of the two bones that form the sides of the pelvis

hip flask *n* a small metal flask for whisky, brandy, etc.

hip-hop *n* a US pop-culture movement originating in the 1980s, comprising rap music, graffiti, and break dancing

hippie *n* same as **hippy**[2]

hippo *n, pl* **-pos** *informal* short for **hippopotamus**

Hippocratic oath *n* an oath taken by a doctor to observe a code of medical ethics
WORD ORIGIN after *Hippocrates*, Greek physician

hippodrome *n* **1** a music hall, variety theatre, or circus **2** (in ancient Greece or Rome) an open-air course for horse and chariot races
WORD ORIGIN Greek *hippos* horse + *dromos* race

hippopotamus *n, pl* **-muses** *or* **-mi** a very large mammal with thick wrinkled skin and short legs, which lives around the rivers of tropical Africa
WORD ORIGIN Greek *hippopotamos* river horse

hippy[1] *adj* **-pier, -piest** *informal* having large hips

hippy[2] *or* **hippie** *n, pl* **-pies** (esp. during the 1960s) a person whose behaviour and dress imply a rejection of conventional values
WORD ORIGIN from HIP[4]

hipsters *pl n Brit* trousers cut so that the top encircles the hips

hire *vb* **hiring, hired 1** to acquire the temporary use of (a thing) or the services of (a person) in exchange for payment **2** to employ (a person) for wages **3** to provide (something) or the services of (oneself or others) for payment **4** **hire out** *chiefly Brit* to pay independent contractors for (work to be done) ▷ *n* **5** the act of hiring **6** **for hire** available to be hired
WORD ORIGIN Old English *hȳrian*

hireling *n disparaging* a person who works only for money

hire-purchase *n* a system in which a buyer takes possession of merchandise on payment of a deposit and completes the purchase by paying a series of instalments while the seller retains ownership until the final instalment is paid

hirsute (**her**-suit) *adj* hairy
WORD ORIGIN Latin *hirsutus* shaggy

his *adj* **1** of, belonging to, or associated with him: *his birthday* ▷ *pron* **2** something belonging to him: *his is on the left; that book is his* **3** **of his** belonging to him
WORD ORIGIN Old English

Hispanic *adj* **1** of or derived from Spain or the Spanish ▷ *n* **2** *US* a US citizen of Spanish or Latin-American descent
WORD ORIGIN Latin *Hispania* Spain

hiss *n* **1** a sound like that of a prolonged *s* **2** such a sound as an expression of dislike or disapproval ▷ *vb* **3** to utter a hiss **4** to express with a hiss: *she hissed the name* **5** to show dislike or disapproval towards (a speaker or performer) by hissing
WORD ORIGIN imitative

hissy fit *n informal* a childish temper tantrum

histamine (**hiss**-ta-meen) *n* a chemical compound released by the body tissues in allergic reactions
WORD ORIGIN Greek *histos* tissue + *amine*

histogram *n* a statistical graph that represents the frequency of values of a quantity by vertical bars of varying heights and widths
WORD ORIGIN probably *histo(ry)* + Greek *grammē* line

histology *n* the study of the tissues of an animal or plant
WORD ORIGIN Greek *histos* tissue + -LOGY

historian *n* a person who writes or studies history

historic *adj* important in history, or likely to be seen as important in the future
≡ **USAGE**
≡ A distinction is usually made
≡ between *historic* (important,
≡ significant) and *historical* (pertaining
≡ to history): *a historic decision; a historical*
≡ *perspective.*

historical *adj* **1** occurring in the past **2** describing or representing situations or people that existed in the past: *a historical novel* **3** belonging to or typical of the study of history: *historical perspective* **historically** *adv*
≡ **USAGE**
≡ See at **historic.**

historicism *n* **1** the belief that natural laws govern historical events **2** excessive respect for historical institutions, such as traditions or laws

historicity *n* historical authenticity

historiographer *n* a historian employed to write the history of a group or public institution **historiography** *n*

history *n, pl* **-ries 1** a record or account of past events and developments **2** all that is preserved of the past, esp. in written form **3** the study of interpreting past events **4** the past events or previous experiences of a place, thing, or person: *he knew the whole history of the place* **5** a play that depicts historical events
WORD ORIGIN Greek *historia* inquiry

histrionic *adj* **1** very dramatic and full of exaggerated emotion: *histrionic bursts of invective* ▷ *n* **2** **histrionics** behaviour of

this kind **histrionically** *adv*
WORD ORIGIN Latin *histrio* actor

hit *vb* **hitting, hit 1** to strike or touch (a person or thing) forcefully **2** to come into violent contact with: *a helicopter hit a Volvo* **3** to propel (a ball) by striking **4** *cricket* to score (runs) **5** to affect (a person, place, or thing) badly: *the airline says that its revenue will be hit* **6** to reach (a point or place): *the city's crime level hit new heights* **7** **hit the bottle** *slang* to start drinking excessive amounts of alcohol **8** **hit the road** *informal* to set out on a journey ▷ *n* **9** an impact or collision **10** a shot or blow that reaches its target **11** *informal* a person or thing that gains wide appeal: *those early collections made her a hit with the club set* **12** *computers slang* a single visit to a website: *over 500 000 hits a day to its site* ▷ See also **hit off, hit on, hit out at**
WORD ORIGIN Old English *hittan*

hit-and-miss *adj informal* happening in an unplanned way: *farming can be very much a hit-and-miss affair*

hit-and-run *adj* denoting a motor-vehicle accident in which the driver does not stop to give assistance or inform the police

hitch *n* **1** a temporary or minor problem or difficulty **2** a knot that can be undone by pulling against the direction of the strain that holds it ▷ *vb* **3** *informal* **a** to obtain (a ride) by hitchhiking **b** to hitchhike **4** to fasten with a knot or tie **5** **get hitched** *slang* to get married **6** **hitch up** to pull up (one's trousers, etc.) with a quick jerk
WORD ORIGIN origin unknown

hitchhike *vb* **-hiking, -hiked** to travel by getting free lifts in motor vehicles **hitchhiker** *n*

hi-tech *adj* using sophisticated, esp. electronic, technology

hither *adv old-fashioned* to or towards this place: *come hither*
WORD ORIGIN Old English *hider*

hitherto *adv formal* until this time: *fundamental questions which have hitherto been ignored*

hit list *n informal* **1** a list of people to be murdered **2** a list of targets to be eliminated: *the Treasury draws up a hit list for spending cuts*

hit man *n* a person hired by terrorists or gangsters to murder someone

hit off *vb* **hit it off** *informal* to have a good relationship with someone

hit on *or* **upon** *vb* to think of (an idea or a solution)

hit-or-miss *adj informal* unplanned or unpredictable: *hit-or-miss service.* Also: **hit-and-miss**

hit out at *vb* **1** to direct blows forcefully and vigorously at (someone) **2** to make a verbal attack upon (someone)

hit wicket *n cricket* a batsman breaking the wicket while playing a stroke and so being out

HIV human immunodeficiency virus, the cause of AIDS

hive *n* **1** a structure in which bees live **2** **hive of activity** a busy place with many people working hard
WORD ORIGIN Old English *hȳf*

hive off *vb* **hiving, hived** to transfer (part of a business, esp. the profitable part of a nationalized industry) to new ownership

hives *n pathol* an allergic reaction in which itchy red or whitish raised patches develop on the skin **WORD ORIGIN** origin unknown

HM (in Britain) Her (*or* His) Majesty

H.M.A.S. *or* **HMAS** (in Australia) Her (*or* His) Majesty's Australian Ship

HMI (in Britain) Her (*or* His) Majesty's Inspector; a government official who examines and supervises schools

hmm *interj* a sound made when considering or puzzling over something

HMRC (in Britian) Her Majesty's Revenue and Customs: a government department responsible for collecting taxes

H.M.S. *or* **HMS** (in Britain) Her (*or* His) Majesty's Ship

HMSO (in Britain) Her (*or* His) Majesty's Stationery Office

HNC (in Britain) Higher National Certificate; a qualification recognized by many national technical and professional institutions

HND (in Britain) Higher National Diploma; a qualification in a technical subject equivalent to an ordinary degree

ho *n US Black slang* a derogatory term for a woman **WORD ORIGIN** from Black or Southern US pronunciation of WHORE

Ho *chem* holmium

hoar *n* short for **hoarfrost** **WORD ORIGIN** Old English *hār*

hoard *n* **1** a store of money, food, etc. hidden away for future use ▷ *vb* **2** to save or store (money, food, etc.) **hoarder** *n* **WORD ORIGIN** Old English *hord*

≡ **USAGE**
≡ *Hoard* is sometimes wrongly written
≡ where *horde* is meant: *hordes* (not
≡ *hoards*) *of tourists*.

hoarding *n* a large board at the side of a road, used for displaying advertising posters **WORD ORIGIN** Old French *hourd* palisade

hoarfrost *n* a white layer of ice crystals formed on the ground by condensation at temperatures below freezing point

hoarse *adj* **1** (of a voice) rough and unclear through illness or too much shouting **2** having a rough and unclear voice **hoarsely** *adv* **hoarseness** *n* **WORD ORIGIN** from Old Norse

hoary *adj* **hoarier, hoariest 1** having grey or white hair **2** very old: *a hoary old problem*

hoax *n* **1** a deception, esp. a practical joke ▷ *vb* **2** to deceive or play a joke on (someone) **WORD ORIGIN** probably from *hocus* to trick

hob *n Brit* the flat top part of a cooker, or a separate flat surface, containing hotplates or burners **WORD ORIGIN** perhaps from *hub*

hobble *vb* **-bling, -bled 1** to walk with a lame awkward movement **2** to tie the legs of (a horse) together in order to restrict its movement **WORD ORIGIN** probably from Low German

hobby *n, pl* **-bies** an activity pursued in one's spare time for pleasure or relaxation **WORD ORIGIN** probably variant of the name *Robin*

hobbyhorse *n* **1** a favourite topic about which a person likes to talk at every opportunity: *public transport is his hobbyhorse* **2** a toy consisting of a stick with a figure of a horse's head at one end **3** a figure of a horse attached to a performer's waist in a morris dance

hobgoblin *n* a small, mischievous creature in fairy stories **WORD ORIGIN** *hob*, variant of the name *Rob* + GOBLIN

hobnail boots *pl n old-fashioned* heavy boots with short nails in the soles to lessen wear and tear **WORD ORIGIN** *hob* (in archaic sense: peg)

hobnob *vb* **-nobbing, -nobbed** to socialize or talk informally: *hobnobbing with the rich* **WORD ORIGIN** *hob* or *nob* to drink to one another in turns

hobo *n, pl* **-bos** *or* **-boes** *US, Canad, Austral, & NZ* a tramp or vagrant **WORD ORIGIN** origin unknown

Hobson's choice *n* the choice of taking what is offered or nothing at all **WORD ORIGIN** after Thomas *Hobson*, liveryman who gave his customers no choice

hock¹ *n* the joint in the leg of a horse or similar animal that corresponds to the human ankle **WORD ORIGIN** Old English *hōhsinu* heel sinew

hock² *n* a white wine from the German Rhine **WORD ORIGIN** German *Hochheimer*

hock³ *informal vb* **1** to pawn or pledge ▷ *n* **2 in hock a** in debt **b** in pawn **WORD ORIGIN** Dutch *hok* prison, debt

hockey *n* **1** a game played on a field by two teams of 11 players who try to hit a ball into their opponents' goal using long sticks curved at the end **2** *US & Canad* ice hockey **WORD ORIGIN** origin unknown

hocus-pocus *n informal* something said or done in order to confuse or trick someone **WORD ORIGIN** a dog Latin exclamation used by conjurors

hod *n* an open metal or plastic box attached to a pole, for carrying bricks or mortar **WORD ORIGIN** Old French *hotte* pannier

hodgepodge *n chiefly US & Canad* same as **hotchpotch**

Hodgkin's disease *n* a malignant disease that causes enlargement of the lymph nodes, spleen, and liver **WORD ORIGIN** after Thomas *Hodgkin*, physician

hoe *n* **1** a long-handled implement used to loosen the soil or to weed ▷ *vb* **hoeing, hoed 2** to scrape or weed with a hoe **WORD ORIGIN** Germanic

hog *n* **1** a castrated male pig **2** *US & Canad* any mammal of the pig family **3** *informal* a greedy person **4 go the whole hog** *slang* to do something in the most complete way possible ▷ *vb* **hogging, hogged 5** *slang* to take more than one's share of (something) **WORD ORIGIN** Old English *hogg*

Hogmanay *n* New Year's Eve in Scotland **WORD ORIGIN** probably from Old French *aguillanneuf* a New Year's Eve gift

hogshead *n* a large cask for storing alcoholic drinks **WORD ORIGIN** origin unknown

hogwash *n informal* nonsense

ho-ho *interj* a written representation of the sound of a deep laugh

ho-hum *adj informal* uninteresting or mediocre: *a ho-hum performance*

hoick *vb* **1** to raise abruptly and sharply **2** *NZ* to clear the throat and spit **WORD ORIGIN** origin unknown

hoi polloi *pl n* the ordinary people when compared to the rich or well-educated **WORD ORIGIN** Greek: the many

hoisin *n* a sweet spicy sauce of soya beans, sugar, garlic, and vinegar, used in Chinese cookery **WORD ORIGIN** from Cantonese

hoist *vb* **1** to raise or lift up, esp. by mechanical means ▷ *n* **2** any apparatus or device for lifting things **WORD ORIGIN** probably from Low German

hoity-toity *adj informal* arrogant or haughty **WORD ORIGIN** obsolete *hoit* to romp

hokey-pokey *n NZ* a brittle toffee sold in lumps

hokum *n slang chiefly US & Canad* **1** nonsense; bunk **2** obvious sentimental material in a play or film **WORD ORIGIN** probably a blend of *hocus-pocus* + *bunkum*

hold¹ *vb* **holding, held 1** to keep (an object or a person) with or within the hands or arms **2** to support: *a rope made from 1000 hairs would hold a large adult* **3** to maintain in a specified state or position: *his reputation continued to hold secure* **4** to have the capacity for: *trains designed to hold more than 400* **5** to set aside or reserve: *they will hold our tickets until tomorrow* **6** to restrain or keep back: *designed to hold dangerous criminals* **7** to remain unbroken: *if the elastic holds* **8** (of the weather) to remain dry and bright **9** to keep (the attention of): *a writer holds a reader by his temperament* **10** to arrange and cause to take place: *we must hold an inquiry* **11** to have the ownership or possession of: *she holds a degree in Egyptology* **12** to have responsibility for: *she cannot hold an elective office* **13** to be able to control the outward effects of drinking (alcohol): *he can't hold his liquor* **14** to (cause to) remain committed to (a promise, etc.) **15** to claim or believe: *some Sufis hold that all religious leaders were prophets* **16** to remain valid or true: *the categories are not the same and equivalency does not hold* **17** to consider in a specified manner: *philosophies which we hold so dear* **18** to defend successfully: *the Russians were holding the Volga front* **19** music to

sustain the sound of (a note) ▷ *n* **20** a way of holding something or the act of holding it **21** something to hold onto for support **22** controlling influence: *drugs will take a hold* **23 with no holds barred** with all limitations removed ▶ See also **hold back, hold down**, etc. **holder** *n*
WORD ORIGIN Old English *healdan*

hold² *n* the space in a ship or aircraft for storing cargo
WORD ORIGIN variant of *hole*

holdall *n Brit* a large strong travelling bag

hold back *vb* **1** to restrain (someone) or refrain from doing something: *managers declined to hold back the crowds; buyers held back in the expectation of further price decreases* **2** to withhold: *holding back the wages*

hold down *vb* **1** to restrain or control someone **2** *informal* to manage to keep (a job) **3** to prevent (wages, prices, etc.) from rising much

hold forth *vb* to speak for a long time

hold in *vb* to control or conceal (one's feelings)

holding *n* **1** land held under a lease **2** property to which the holder has legal title, such as land, stocks, or shares

holding company *n* a company that holds the controlling shares in one or more other companies

holding paddock *n Austral & NZ* a paddock in which cattle or sheep are kept temporarily, such as when awaiting sale

hold off *vb* **1** to keep (an attacker or attacking force) at a distance **2** to put off (doing something): *he held off distributing weapons*

hold on *vb* **1** to maintain a firm grasp (of something or someone) **2** *informal* to wait, esp. on the telephone **3 hold on to** to keep: *he held on to his world No. 1 ranking*

hold out *vb* **1** to offer (something) **2** to last: *I could hold out until we return home* **3** to continue to stand firm and manage to resist opposition **4 hold out for** to wait patiently for (the fulfilment of one's wishes) **5 hold out on someone** *informal* to keep from telling someone some important information

hold over *vb* to postpone: *several cases had to be held over pending further investigation*

hold-up *n* **1** an armed robbery **2** a delay: *a traffic hold-up* ▷ *vb* **hold up 3** to delay **4** to support (an object) **5** to stop and rob (someone), using a weapon **6** to exhibit or present (something) as an example: *he was held up as a model professional*

hold with *vb* to approve of: *I don't hold with divorce*

hole *n* **1** an area hollowed out in a solid **2** an opening in or through something **3** an animal's burrow **4** *informal* a fault or error: *this points to a very big hole in parliamentary security* **5** *informal* an unattractive town or other place **6** (on a golf course) any one of the divisions of a course (usually 18) represented by the distance between the tee and the sunken cup on the green into which the ball is to be played **7 in a hole** *slang* in a difficult and embarrassing situation

8 make a hole in *informal* to use a great amount of (one's money or food supply) **9 pick holes in** to point out faults in ▷ *vb* **holing, holed 10** to make a hole or holes in (something) **11** to hit (a golf ball) into a hole ▶ See **hole up** ▷ **holey** *adj*
WORD ORIGIN Old English *hol*

hole-and-corner *adj informal* furtive or secretive

hole in the heart *n* a congenital defect of the heart, in which there is an abnormal opening in the partition between the left and right halves

hole up *vb informal* to go into hiding

Holi (**holl**-lee) *n* an annual Hindu spring festival, honouring Krishna

holiday *n* **1** a period of time spent away from home for enjoyment and relaxation **2** (*often pl*) *chiefly Brit & NZ* a period in which a break is taken from work or studies for rest or recreation **3** a day on which work is suspended by law or custom, such as a bank holiday ▷ *vb* **4** *chiefly Brit* to spend a holiday
WORD ORIGIN Old English *hāligdæg* holy day

holier-than-thou *adj* offensively self-righteous

Holiness *n* (preceded by *His* or *Your*) a title reserved for the pope

holism *n* **1** the view that a whole is greater than the sum of its parts **2** (in medicine) consideration of the complete person in the treatment of disease **holistic** *adj*
WORD ORIGIN Greek *holos* whole

hollandaise sauce *n* a rich sauce of egg yolks, butter, vinegar, and lemon juice
WORD ORIGIN French *sauce hollandaise* Dutch sauce

holler *informal vb* **1** to shout or yell ▷ *n* **2** a shout or yell
WORD ORIGIN French *holà* stop!

hollow *adj* **1** having a hole or space within; not solid: *a hollow tree* **2** curving inwards: *hollow cheeks* **3** (of sounds) as if echoing in a hollow place **4** without any real value or worth: *a hollow enterprise, lacking purpose, and lacking soul* ▷ *adv* **5 beat someone hollow** *Brit & NZ informal* to defeat someone thoroughly ▷ *n* **6** a cavity or space in something **7** a dip in the land ▷ *vb* **8** (*often foll. by out*) to form a hole or cavity in **hollowly** *adv*
WORD ORIGIN Old English *holh* cave

holly *n* an evergreen tree with prickly leaves and bright red berries, used for Christmas decorations
WORD ORIGIN Old English *holegn*

hollyhock *n* a tall garden plant with spikes of colourful flowers
WORD ORIGIN *holy* + obsolete *hock* mallow

holmium *n chem* a silver-white metallic element, the compounds of which are highly magnetic. Symbol: Ho
WORD ORIGIN after *Holmia*, Latin name of Stockholm

holm oak *n* an evergreen oak tree with prickly leaves like holly

holocaust *n* **1** destruction or loss of life on a massive scale **2 the Holocaust** mass murder of the Jews in Europe by the Nazis (1940–45)

WORD ORIGIN Greek *holos* whole + *kaiein* to burn

Holocene *adj* of the current geological epoch, which began about 10 000 years ago

hologram *n* a three-dimensional photographic image produced by means of a split laser beam
WORD ORIGIN Greek *holos* whole + *grammē* line

holograph *n* a book or document handwritten by its author
WORD ORIGIN Greek *holos* whole + *graphein* to write

holography *n* the science of using lasers to produce holograms **holographic** *adj* **holographically** *adv*
WORD ORIGIN Greek *holos* whole + -GRAPHY

hols *pl n Brit & S African school slang* holidays

holster *n* a sheathlike leather case for a pistol, worn attached to a belt
WORD ORIGIN Germanic

holt *n* the lair of an otter
WORD ORIGIN from HOLD²

holy *adj* **-lier, -liest 1** of or associated with God or a deity **2** (of a person) religious and leading a virtuous life **holiness** *n*
WORD ORIGIN Old English *hālig, hǣlig*

Holy Communion *n Christianity* a church service in which people take bread and wine in remembrance of Christ's Last Supper and His atonement for the sins of the world

Holy Ghost *n* **the Holy Ghost** same as **Holy Spirit**

Holy Grail *n* **1 the Holy Grail** (in medieval legend) the bowl used by Jesus at the Last Supper **2** *informal* any ambition or goal
WORD ORIGIN *grail* from Medieval Latin *gradalis* bowl

Holy Land *n* **the Holy Land** Palestine

holy of holies *n* **1** any sacred place or a place considered as if it were sacred: *the holy of holies they called the Captain's Cabin* **2** the innermost chamber of a Jewish temple

holy orders *pl n* the status of an ordained Christian minister

Holy See *n* **the Holy See** *RC Church* the see of the pope as bishop of Rome

Holy Spirit *n* **the Holy Spirit** *Christianity* one of the three aspects of God

Holy Week *n Christianity* the week before Easter Sunday

homage *n* a public show of respect or honour towards someone or something: *the master's jazzy-classical homage to Gershwin*
WORD ORIGIN Latin *homo* man

homburg *n* a man's soft felt hat with a dented crown and a stiff upturned brim

home *n* **1** the place where one lives **2** the country or area of one's birth **3** a building or organization set up to care for people in a certain category, such as orphans or the aged **4** the place where something is invented or started: *the home of the first aircraft* **5** *sport* a team's own ground: *the match is at home* **6** *baseball, rounders, etc.* the objective towards which a player runs after striking the ball **7 at home a** in one's

Edgar Allan Poe

E dgar Allan Poe had the first prerequisite for a serious writer: an unhappy childhood.

Born in 1809 in Boston, he lost both parents before he was three years old and became the ward of a merchant and his wife in Richmond, Virginia. When this new family moved to England, he attended school for five years, mainly in Stoke Newington, now part of Greater London. After his foster parents returned to Richmond he attended university for a year. At odds with his guardian after piling up debts, he joined the army. After his foster mother died, his guardian paid his way into the United States Military Academy. Perhaps the least promising undergraduate West Point ever had, at war only with his guardian, Poe was expelled for conspicuous misconduct.

Disinherited, he began his wanderings. Although gaining popularity and prizes from time to time, he was frequently broke, and as frequently a beggar, struggling to survive in New York, Philadelphia, and Baltimore. Some of the women he adored rejected him or died. Family tragedies intruded: his elder brother, a fellow alcoholic, died; as did, from tuberculosis, his wife, a cousin he had married when she was 13 years old. In 1849, Poe died in Baltimore of unknown causes. An enemy quickly wrote that his death 'will startle many, but few will be grieved by it'.

After his death a vast critical literature grew up around his work; several of his former homes are now museums, and his first book, *Tamerlane and Other Poems*, 'By a Bostonian', became the rarest first edition in American literature, fetching $198,000 at auction.

Poe's tragic legend masks the fact that he was an astute professional writer who catered to popular tastes, a capable magazine editor who resisted regional biases, and a fearless, independent-minded book reviewer. His work – thanks to Charles Baudelaire, who began to translate it only three years after Poe's death – was at first was more popular in France than in America. Later he became hugely influential in English-speaking countries, although not in the art the author most valued, poetry. Indeed, almost every aspect of his verse is at variance with twentieth-century poetics: his melodramatic or sensationalist Romantic and Gothic obsessions, his spurning of realistic concreteness, his relentless euphony and alliteration, the parody-prone, incantatory refrains of *The Raven* ('Quoth the Raven, "Nevermore"') and the frenzied onomatopeia of *The Bells* ('the jingling and the tinkling of the bells', 'the clamor and the clanging of the bells!'). For modernists, his tour-de-forces were tour-de-farces, and his verse not poetry, but Poe-etry.

As a critic, he won more acceptance for his view that a work must embody a single effect in unified style and content, and his fierce opposition to both chauvinism ('often we find ourselves involved in the gross paradox of liking a stupid book the better, because, sure enough, the stupidity is American') and the obsequious imitation of European models. Less approved was his narrow prescription that poetry could only be the 'rhythmical creation of beauty' of a short lyric, and that sadness was the most poetical of moods.

But it is through his fiction that Poe's reputation has thrived. He pioneered the closely plotted, suspenseful detective story in stories like *The Murders in the Rue Morgue*, *The Purloined Letter*, and *The Mystery of Marie Roget* in 1843, and initiated the serial detective in his sleuth C Auguste Dupin.

Much interested in the pseudosciences of his time, he advanced speculative or science fiction with tales such as *The Narrative of Arthur Gordon Pym of Nantucket*, *A Descent into the Maelstrom*, and *The Masque of the Red Death*. The psychological novel has been extensively enriched by the stories of horror or terror, which sometimes incorporate wild humour, and in which psychotic, hallucinogenic, and hypnogogic states figure: *The Black Cat*, *The Cask of Amontillado*, *The Fall of the House of Usher*, and *The Pit and the Pendulum*. All these stories of premature burial, macabre revenge, and retribution in the aftermath of incest are not about external events but about the self-betraying mechanisms of the mind.

Although Poe's work lends itself to simplistic Freudian or Jungian analysis, and his life easily plays to our stereotypes of the mad genius and tormented artist, there were methods to his madness.

own home or country **b** at ease: *he felt more at home with the Russians* **c** receiving visitors ▷ *adj* **8** of one's home, birthplace, or native country **9** (of an activity) done in one's house: *home movies* **10** *sport* played on one's own ground: *a home game* **11** **home and dry** *Brit slang* definitely safe or successful ▷ *adv* **12** to or at home: *I came home* **13** to or on the point: *the message struck home* **14** to the fullest extent: *they drove their spears home* **15** **bring something home to someone** to make something clear to someone ▷ *vb* **homing, homed 16** (of birds) to return home accurately from a distance **17** **home in on** to be directed towards (a goal or target) **WORD ORIGIN** Old English *hām*

≣ **USAGE**
≣ See at **hone.**

homeboy *n slang* **1** a close friend **2** a member of a gang

home-brew *n* beer or other alcoholic drink brewed at home

homecoming *n* a return home, esp. after a long absence

Home Counties *pl n* the counties surrounding London

home economics *n* the study of diet, budgeting, child care, and other subjects concerned with running a home

home farm *n Brit* a farm that belonged to and provided food for a large country house

Home Guard *n* a part-time military force of volunteers recruited for the defence of the United Kingdom in the Second World War

home help *n Brit, Austral, & NZ* a person employed by a local authority to do housework in an elderly or disabled person's home

homeland *n* **1** the country from which the ancestors of a person or group came: *defending their homeland* **2** the official name in S Africa for a **Bantustan**

homeless *adj* **1** having nowhere to live ▷ *pl n* **2** **the homeless** people who have nowhere to live: *night shelters for the homeless* **homelessness** *n*

homely *adj* **-lier, -liest 1** simple, ordinary, and comfortable **2 a** *Brit* (of a person) warm and friendly **b** *chiefly US & Canad* (of a person) plain or unattractive **homeliness** *n*

home-made *adj* (esp. of foods) made at home or on the premises

Home Office *n Brit government* the department responsible for law and order, immigration, and other domestic affairs

homeopathy *or* **homoeopathy** (home-ee-**op**-ath-ee) *n* a method of treating disease by the use of small amounts of a drug that produces symptoms of the disease in healthy people **homeopath** *or* **homoeopath** (home-ee-oh-path) *n* **homeopathic** *or* **homoeopathic** *adj* **WORD ORIGIN** Greek *homoios* similar + *patheia* suffering

homeostasis *or* **homoeostasis** (hom-ee-oh-**stass**-iss) *n* the tendency of an organism to achieve a stable metabolic state by compensating automatically for violent changes in the environment and other disruptions **WORD ORIGIN** Greek *homoios* similar + *stasis* a standing

homeowner *n* a person who owns the home in which he or she lives

home page *n internet* the introductory information about a website with links to the information or services provided

Homeric (home-**mer**-rik) *adj* of or relating to Homer, Greek epic poet (circa 800 BC)

home rule *n* self-government in domestic affairs

Home Secretary *n Brit government* the head of the Home Office

homesick *adj* depressed by being away from home and family **homesickness** *n*

homespun *adj* (of philosophies or opinions) plain and unsophisticated

homestead *n* **1** a farmhouse and the adjoining land **2** (in the western US & Canada) a house and adjoining tract of land (originally often 160 acres) that was granted by the government for development as a farm

homesteader *n* (in the western US & Canada) a person who lives on and farms a homestead

homestead law *n* (in the western US & Canada) any of various laws granting certain privileges to owners of homesteads

home truths *pl n* unpleasant facts told to a person about himself or herself

home unit *n Austral & NZ* a self-contained residence that is part of a block of such residences

homeward *adj* **1** going home ▷ *adv also* **homewards 2** towards home

homework *n* **1** school work done at home **2** research or preparation

homicide *n* **1** the act of killing someone **2** a person who kills someone **homicidal** *adj* **WORD ORIGIN** Latin *homo* man + *caedere* to kill

homie *n slang chiefly US* short for **homeboy**

homily *n, pl* **-lies** a moralizing talk or piece of writing **homiletic** *adj* **WORD ORIGIN** Greek *homilia* discourse

homing *adj* **1** *zool* denoting the ability to return home after travelling great distances **2** (of a missile) capable of guiding itself onto a target

homing pigeon *n* a pigeon developed for its homing instinct, used for racing

hominid *n* **1** any member of the family of primates that includes modern man and the extinct forerunners of man ▷ *adj* **2** of or belonging to this family **WORD ORIGIN** Latin *homo* man

hominoid *adj* **1** of or like man; manlike ▷ *n* **2** a manlike animal **WORD ORIGIN** Latin *homo* man

hominy *n chiefly US* coarsely ground maize prepared as a food by boiling in milk or water **WORD ORIGIN** probably from a Native American language

homo¹ *n informal, derogatory* short for **homosexual**

homo² *n Canad informal* homogenized milk

homo- *combining form* same or like: *homologous* **WORD ORIGIN** Greek *homos* same

homogeneous (home-oh-**jean**-ee-uss) *adj* having parts or members which are all the same or which consist of only one substance: *the Arabs are not a single, homogeneous nation* **homogeneity** *n* **WORD ORIGIN** Greek *homos* same + *genos* kind

homogenize *or* **-nise** *vb* **-nizing, -nized** *or* **-nising, -nised 1** to break up the fat globules in (milk or cream) so that they are evenly distributed **2** to make different elements the same or similar: *homogenized products for a mass market*

homogenous (hom-**oj**-in-uss) *adj* having a similar structure because of common ancestry

homograph *n* a word spelt the same as another, but having a different meaning, such as *bear* (to carry) and *bear* (the animal) **WORD ORIGIN** Greek *homos* same + *graphein* to write

homologous (hom-**ol**-log-uss) *adj* **1** having a related or similar position or structure **2** *biol* (of organs and parts) having the same origin but different functions: *the wing of a bat and the arm of a monkey are homologous* **WORD ORIGIN** Greek *homos* same + *logos* ratio

homology (hom-**ol**-a-jee) *n* the condition of being homologous

homonym *n* a word pronounced and spelt the same as another, but having a different meaning, such as *novel* (a book) and *novel* (new)

homophobia *n* intense hatred or fear of homosexuals **WORD ORIGIN** *homo(sexual)* + *phobia*

homophone *n* a word pronounced the same as another, but having a different meaning or spelling or both, such as *bear* and *bare* **WORD ORIGIN** Greek *homos* same + *phōnē* sound

Homo sapiens (**home**-oh **sap**-ee-enz) *n* the name for modern man as a species **WORD ORIGIN** Latin *homo* man + *sapiens* wise

homosexual *n* **1** a person who is sexually attracted to members of the same sex ▷ *adj* **2** (of a person) sexually attracted to members of the same sex **3** (of a sexual relationship) between members of the same sex **homosexuality** *n* **WORD ORIGIN** Greek *homos* same

homozygous *adj biol* having two identical alleles of the same gene **WORD ORIGIN** Greek *homos* same + *zugōtos* yoked

homy *or esp. US* **homey** *adj* **homier, homiest** like a home; pleasant and cosy

Hon. Honourable (title)

hone *vb* **honing, honed 1** to develop and improve (a quality or ability): *a workshop to hone interview techniques* **2** to sharpen (a tool) ▷ *n* **3** a fine whetstone used for sharpening edged tools and knives **WORD ORIGIN** Old English *hān* stone

USAGE
Hone is sometimes wrongly used where *home* is meant: *this device makes it easier to home in on* (not *hone in on*) *the target.*

honest *adj* **1** truthful and moral in behaviour; trustworthy **2** open and sincere in relationships and attitudes; without pretensions **3** gained or earned fairly: *an honest income*
WORD ORIGIN Latin *honos* esteem

honestly *adv* **1** in an honest manner **2** truly: *honestly, that's all I can recall*

honesty *n, pl* **-ties 1** the quality of being truthful and trustworthy **2** a plant with flattened silvery pods which are used for indoor decoration

honey *n* **1** a sweet edible sticky substance made by bees from nectar **2** *chiefly US & Canad* a term of affection **3** *informal chiefly US & Canad* something very good of its kind: *a honey of a picture about American family life*
WORD ORIGIN Old English *huneg*

honeybee *n* a bee widely domesticated as a source of honey and beeswax

honeycomb *n* a waxy structure, constructed by bees in a hive, that consists of many six-sided cells in which honey is stored

honeydew *n* a sugary substance excreted by aphids and similar insects

honeydew melon *n* a melon with yellow skin and sweet pale flesh

honeyed *adj poetic* flattering or soothing: *honeyed words*

honeymoon *n* **1** a holiday taken by a newly married couple **2** the early period of an undertaking or activity, such as the start of a new government's term of office, when an attitude of goodwill prevails ▷ *vb* **3** to take a honeymoon **honeymooner** *n*
WORD ORIGIN traditionally, referring to the feelings of married couples as changing with the phases of the moon

honeysuckle *n* a climbing shrub with sweet-smelling white, yellow, or pink flowers
WORD ORIGIN Old English *hunigsūce*

honeytrap *n Brit informal* a scheme in which a victim is lured into a compromising sexual situation that provides the opportunity for blackmail

hongi (hong-jee) *n NZ* a Māori greeting in which people touch noses

honk *n* **1** the sound made by a motor horn **2** the sound made by a goose ▷ *vb* **3** to make or cause (something) to make a honking sound

honky-tonk *n* **1** *US & Canad slang* a cheap disreputable nightclub or dance hall **2** a style of ragtime piano-playing, esp. on a tinny-sounding piano
WORD ORIGIN rhyming compound based on HONK

honorarium *n, pl* **-iums** *or* **-ia** a voluntary fee paid for a service which is usually free
WORD ORIGIN Latin *honorarium (donum)* honorary gift

honorary *adj* **a** held or given as a mark of respect, without the usual qualifications, payment, or work: *an honorary degree* **b** (of a secretary, treasurer, etc.) unpaid

honorific *adj* showing respect: *an honorific title*

honour *or US* **honor** *n* **1** allegiance to moral principles **2** a person's good reputation and the respect they are given by other people **3 a** fame or glory **b** a person who wins fame or glory for his or her country, school, etc.: *he was an honour to his nation* **4** great respect or esteem, or an outward sign of this **5** a privilege or pleasure: *it was an honour to meet him* **6** *old-fashioned* a woman's virginity **7** *bridge, whist* any of the top four or five cards in a suit **8** *golf* the right to tee off first **9 in honour of** out of respect for **10 on one's honour** under a moral obligation ▷ *vb* **11** to hold someone in respect **12** to give (someone) special praise, attention, or an award **13** to accept and then pay (a cheque or bill) **14** to keep (one's promise); fulfil (a previous agreement)
WORD ORIGIN Latin *honor* esteem

Honour *n* (preceded by *Your, His* or *Her*) a title used to address or refer to certain judges

honourable *or US* **honorable** *adj* **1** principled **2** worthy of respect or esteem **honourably** *adv*

Honourable *adj* **the Honourable** a title of respect placed before a name: used of various officials, of the children of certain peers, and in Parliament by one member speaking of another

honours *or US* **honors** *pl n* **1** (in a university degree course) a rank or mark of the highest academic standard: *an honours degree* **2** observances of respect, esp. at a funeral **3 do the honours** to serve as host or hostess by serving food or pouring drinks

hooch (rhymes with **smooch**) *n informal* alcoholic drink, esp. illegally distilled spirits
WORD ORIGIN from a Native American language

hood¹ *n* **1** a loose head covering either attached to a coat or made as a separate garment **2** *US, Canad, & Austral* the bonnet of a car **3** the folding roof of a convertible car or a pram ▷ *vb* **4** to cover with or as if with a hood **hoodlike** *adj*
WORD ORIGIN Old English *hōd*

hood² *n slang* short for **hoodlum**

hooded *adj* **1** (of a garment) having a hood **2** (of eyes) having heavy eyelids that appear to be half-closed

hooded crow *n* a crow that has a grey body and black head, wings, and tail

hoodie *n informal* **1** a hooded sweatshirt **2** a young person who wears a hooded sweatshirt, regarded by some as a potential hooligan

hoodlum *n* a violent criminal, esp. one who is a member of a gang
WORD ORIGIN origin unknown

hoodoo *n, pl* **-doos 1** *informal* bad luck **2** *informal* a person or thing that brings bad luck **3** *chiefly US* same as **voodoo**

hoodwink *vb* to trick or deceive
WORD ORIGIN originally, to cover the eyes with a hood

hooey *n slang* nonsense
WORD ORIGIN origin unknown

hoof *n, pl* **hooves** *or* **hoofs 1** the horny covering of the end of the foot in the horse, deer, and certain other mammals **2 on the hoof a** (of livestock) alive **b** in an impromptu way: *thinking on the hoof* ▷ *vb* **3 hoof it** *slang* to walk **hoofed** *adj*
WORD ORIGIN Old English *hōf*

hoofer *n slang* a professional dancer

hoo-ha *n* a noisy commotion or fuss
WORD ORIGIN origin unknown

hook *n* **1** a curved piece of metal or plastic used to hang, hold, or pull something **2** something resembling a hook, such as a sharp bend in a river or a sharply curved strip of land **3** *boxing* a short swinging blow with the elbow bent **4** *cricket, golf* a shot that causes the ball to go to the player's left **5 by hook or by crook** by any means: *get into the charts by hook or by crook* **6 hook, line, and sinker** *informal* completely: *we fell for it hook, line, and sinker* **7 let someone off the hook** *slang* to free someone from an obligation or a difficult situation **8 sling one's hook** *Austral & Brit slang* to leave ▷ *vb* **9** to fasten with, or as if with, a hook **10** to catch (a fish) on a hook **11** *cricket, golf* to play (a ball) with a hook **12** *rugby* to obtain and pass (the ball) backwards from a scrum, using the feet
WORD ORIGIN Old English *hōc*

hookah *n* an oriental pipe for smoking marijuana or tobacco, with a long flexible stem connected to a container of water through which smoke is drawn and cooled
WORD ORIGIN Arabic *huqqah*

hooked *adj* **1** bent like a hook **2** (often foll. by *on*) **a** *slang* addicted (to): *hooked on drugs* **b** obsessed with: *hooked on football*

hooker *n* **1** *slang* a prostitute **2** *rugby* a player who uses his feet to get the ball in a scrum

Hooke's law *n physics* the principle that a solid stretches or contracts in proportion to the force placed on it, within the limits of its elasticity
WORD ORIGIN after Robert *Hooke*, physicist

hook-up *n* the linking of broadcasting equipment or stations to transmit a special programme

hookworm *n* a blood-sucking worm with hooked mouthparts

hooligan *n slang* a young person who behaves in a noisy and violent way in public **hooliganism** *n*
WORD ORIGIN origin unknown

hoon *Austral & NZ slang n* **1** a loutish youth who drives irresponsibly ▷ *vb* **2** to drive irresponsibly

hoop *n* **1** a rigid circular band of metal, plastic, or wood **2** a child's toy shaped like a hoop and rolled on the ground or whirled around the body **3** *croquet* any of the iron arches through which the ball is driven **4** a large ring through which performers or animals jump **5 go** *or* **be put through the hoops** to go through an ordeal or test ▷ *vb* **6** to surround (something) with a hoop **hooped** *adj*
WORD ORIGIN Old English *hōp*

hoopla *n Austral & Brit* a fairground game in which hoops are thrown over objects in an attempt to win them

hoopoe (hoop-oo) *n* a bird with pinkish-brown plumage with black-and-white wings and a fanlike crest
WORD ORIGIN imitative

hoop pine *n* an Australian tree or shrub with flowers in dense spikes

hooray *interj, n* same as **hurrah**

Hooray Henry (hoo-ray) *n, pl* **Hooray Henries** or **-rys** *Brit informal* a young upper-class man with an affectedly loud and cheerful manner

hoot *n* **1** the sound of a car horn **2** the cry of an owl **3** a high-pitched noise showing disapproval **4** *informal* an amusing person or thing ▷ *vb* **5** *Brit* to blow (a car horn) **6** to make a hoot **7** to jeer or yell contemptuously at someone **8** to drive (speakers or performers on stage) off by hooting
WORD ORIGIN imitative

hooter *n chiefly Brit* **1** a device that hoots, such as a car horn **2** *slang* a nose

Hoover *n* **1** *trademark* a vacuum cleaner ▷ *vb* **hoover 2** to vacuum-clean (a carpet) **3** (often foll. by *up*) to devour (something) quickly and completely

hooves *n* a plural of **hoof**

hop¹ *vb* **hopping, hopped 1** to jump forwards or upwards on one foot **2** (of frogs, birds, etc.) to move forwards in short jumps **3** to jump over something **4** *informal* to move quickly (in, on, out of, etc.): *hop into bed* **5 hop it** *Austral & Brit slang* to go away ▷ *n* **6** an instance of hopping **7** *informal* an informal dance **8** *informal* a short journey, usually in an aircraft **9 on the hop** *informal* **a** active or busy: *he keeps me on the hop* **b** unawares or unprepared: *you caught me on the hop*
WORD ORIGIN Old English *hoppian*

hop² *n* a climbing plant with green conelike flowers. See also **hops**
WORD ORIGIN Middle Dutch *hoppe*

hope *vb* **hoping, hoped 1** to desire (something), usually with some possibility of fulfilment: *you would hope for their cooperation* **2** to trust or believe: *I hope I've arranged that* ▷ *n* **3** a feeling of desire for something, usually with confidence in the possibility of its fulfilment: *the news was greeted by some as hope for further interest rate cuts* **4** a reasonable ground for this feeling: *there is hope for you yet* **5** the person, thing, situation, or event that gives cause for hope or is desired: *the young are a symbol of hope for the future*
WORD ORIGIN Old English *hopa*

hopeful *adj* **1** having, inspiring, or expressing hope ▷ *n* **2** a person considered to be on the brink of success: *a young hopeful*

hopefully *adv* **1** in a hopeful manner **2** *informal* it is hoped: *hopefully I've got a long career ahead of me*
≡ USAGE
≡ The use of *hopefully* to mean *it is hoped*
≡ used to be considered incorrect by
≡ some people but has now become
≡ acceptable in informal contexts.

hopeless *adj* **1** having or offering no hope **2** impossible to solve **3** *informal* without skill or ability: *I'm hopeless at maths* **hopelessly** *adv* **hopelessness** *n*

hopper *n* a funnel-shaped device from which solid materials can be discharged into a receptacle below

hops *pl n* the dried flowers of the hop plant, used to give a bitter taste to beer

hopscotch *n* a children's game in which a player throws a stone to land in one of a pattern of squares marked on the ground and then hops over to it to pick it up
WORD ORIGIN hop + obsolete *scotch* a line, scratch

horde *n* a very large crowd, often frightening or unpleasant
WORD ORIGIN Turkish *ordū* camp
≡ USAGE
≡ *Horde* is sometimes wrongly written
≡ where *hoard* is meant: *a hoard* (not
≡ *horde*) *of gold coins*.

horehound *n* a plant that produces a bitter juice formerly used as a cough medicine
WORD ORIGIN Old English *hārhūne*

horizon *n* **1** the apparent line that divides the earth and the sky **2 horizons** the limits of a person's interests and activities: *seeking to broaden his horizons at college* **3 on the horizon** almost certainly going to happen or be done in the future: *a new type of computer is on the horizon*
WORD ORIGIN Greek *horizein* to limit

horizontal *adj* **1** flat and level with the ground or with a line considered as a base **2** affecting or happening at one level in a system or organization: *a horizontal division of labour* ▷ *n* **3** a horizontal plane, position, or line **horizontally** *adv*

hormone *n* **1** a chemical substance produced in an endocrine gland and transported in the blood to a certain tissue, on which it has a specific effect **2** a similar substance produced by a plant that is essential for growth **3** a synthetic substance having the same effects **hormonal** *adj*
WORD ORIGIN Greek *hormōn*

horn *n* **1** either of a pair of permanent bony outgrowths on the heads of animals such as cattle and antelopes **2** any hornlike projection, such as the eyestalk of a snail **3** the antler of a deer **4** the hard substance of which horns are made **5** a musical wind instrument made from horn **6** any musical instrument consisting of a pipe or tube of brass fitted with a mouthpiece **7** a device, such as on a vehicle, for producing a warning or signalling noise **horned** *adj*
WORD ORIGIN Old English

hornbeam *n* a tree with smooth grey bark

hornbill *n* a tropical bird with a bony growth on its large beak

hornblende *n* a green-to-black mineral containing aluminium, calcium, sodium, magnesium, and iron

hornet *n* **1** a large wasp that can inflict a severe sting **2 hornet's nest** a very unpleasant situation that is difficult to deal with: *you'll stir up a hornet's nest*
WORD ORIGIN Old English *hyrnetu*

horn of plenty *n* same as **cornucopia**

hornpipe *n* **1** a solo dance, traditionally performed by sailors **2** music for this dance

horny *adj* **hornier, horniest 1** of, like, or hard as horn **2** *slang* **a** sexually aroused **b** provoking sexual arousal **c** sexually eager

horology *n* the art of making clocks and watches or of measuring time **horological** *adj*
WORD ORIGIN Greek *hōra* hour + -LOGY

horoscope *n* **1** the prediction of a person's future based on the positions of the planets, sun, and moon at the time of birth **2** a diagram showing the positions of the planets, sun, and moon at a particular time and place
WORD ORIGIN Greek *hōra* hour + *skopas* observer

horrendous *adj* very unpleasant or shocking
WORD ORIGIN Latin *horrendus* fearful

horrible *adj* **1** disagreeable and unpleasant: *a horrible hotel room* **2** causing fear, shock, or disgust: *he died a horrible death* **horribly** *adv*
WORD ORIGIN Latin *horribilis*

horrid *adj* **1** disagreeable or unpleasant: *it had been a horrid day at school* **2** *informal* (of a person) unkind and nasty: *her horrid parents*
WORD ORIGIN Latin *horridus* prickly

horrific *adj* provoking horror: *horrific injuries* **horrifically** *adv*

horrify *vb* **-fies, -fying, -fied** to cause feelings of horror in (someone); shock (someone) greatly

horror *n* **1** extreme fear or terror **2** intense hatred: *she had a horror of violence* **3** a thing or person causing fear, loathing, or distaste ▷ *adj* **4** having a frightening subject, usually concerned with the supernatural: *a horror film*
WORD ORIGIN Latin: a trembling with fear

horrors *pl n* **the horrors** *slang* a fit of nervousness or anxiety

hors d'oeuvre (or **durv**) *n, pl* **hors d'oeuvre** or **hors d'oeuvres** (or **durv**) an appetizer, usually served before the main meal
WORD ORIGIN French

horse *n* **1** a four-footed mammal with hooves, a mane, and a tail, used for riding and pulling carts, etc. ▶ Related adjectives: **equestrian, equine 2** the adult male of this species; stallion **3** *gymnastics* a padded apparatus on legs, used for vaulting **4 be** or **get on one's high horse** *informal* to act in a haughty manner **5 the horses** *informal* horse races on which bets may be placed: *an occasional flutter on the horses* **6 the horse's mouth** the most reliable source: *I'll tell you straight from the horse's mouth*. See also **horse around**
WORD ORIGIN Old English *hors*

horse around or **about** *vb informal* to play roughly or boisterously

horseback *n* a horse's back: *on horseback*

horsebox *n Brit, S African, NZ, Austral* a van or trailer used for transporting horses

horse brass *n* a decorative brass ornament, originally attached to a horse's harness

Horror

Horror in literature has its roots in traditional folk tales. Elements of the genre can be traced at least as far back as *Beowulf* and followed through the history of English literature (Shakespeare's *Macbeth*, for example, has its share of horror imagery such as gruesome murders and supernatural visitations). Horror can be a difficult genre to define, as its themes touch most (if not all) other literary genres. The word itself was coined in the 14th century and comes from the French *horreur*, which is in turn derived from the Latin *horrere*, meaning 'to bristle'. The folk tale aspect of horror is apparent in its resurrection of creatures from folklore such as the vampire, different mythical forms of which exist across most cultures, and which was popularized in the 18th century from Balkan and Eastern European legends. The word *vampire* has its roots in the German word *vampir*, originating in Serbian (the Romanian word is *strigoi*). Similarly, werewolves or lycanthropes are predominant in European myths, yet shapeshifting beliefs are recorded worldwide, particularly in Norse and Native American mythology.

The horror genre developed from the traditions of Gothic literature (it is considered by some to be a subset) and took hold as a literary form when explored by Romantic-era authors. An early example is Mary Shelley's *Frankenstein; or, A Modern Prometheus* (1818), which was written after the celebrated agreement between poets Byron, Percy and Mary Shelley, and John William Polidori, that they should all attempt to write a ghost story. This literary experiment also produced Polidori's *The Vampyre* (1819). The Romantic author most associated with the horror genre, however, is Edgar Allan Poe, whose hugely influential genre works include *The Black Cat*, *The Pit And The Pendulum*, *Murders In The Rue Morgue*, *The Fall of the House of Usher*, and *The Tell-Tale Heart*.

Robert Louis Stevenson's *The Strange Case of Dr Jekyll And Mr Hyde* (1886) was a notable horror tale published in Victorian times. This was also the era of 'Penny Dreadfuls', which were serialized stories printed on cheap pulp paper and sold for a low price. These typically featured lurid, gruesome, and sensationalist content, with the most infamous being *Varney the Vampire* (published from 1845 to 1847).

Sheridan LeFanu's vampire novella *Carmilla* (1872) was an influence on Bram Stoker, whose *Dracula* (1897) was a landmark of the genre. The novel is epistolary (meaning it is written as a series of letters or journal entries) which is a style unusual to the contemporary reader, but was a popular literary device at the time of its publication. Le Fanu also influenced MR James, a key figure in post-Victorian horror writing, who revolutionized the ghost story by using contemporary settings. Another benchmark of horror literature was WW Jacobs's short story *The Monkey's Paw*, a gruesome tale with a universal be-careful-what-you-wish-for theme.

The genre grew in strength with the publication of US author Henry James's *The Turn of the Screw*, and the writings of Ambrose Bierce (also noteworthy for his satirical *The Devil's Dictionary*) who penned such short stories as *The Damned Thing*. In the early 20th century, HP Lovecraft's works *The Call of Cthulhu* and *At The Mountains of Madness* created an entire 'mythos' (a unifying universe and mythology in which all his work was set) for his writings, one in which Old Gods lie in wait outside the fringes of humanity's limited perception.

A notable post-Lovecraft American author was Robert Bloch (who wrote the original novel upon which Alfred Hitchcock's *Psycho* is based), but the most prominent link between more Gothic-influenced forms of horror writing and the present-day mainstream bestsellers of Stephen King is the work of Richard Matheson. Just as MR James's contemporary settings for his stories had a huge impact on their effectiveness, Matheson's work took supernatural (*Stir of Echoes*) or otherworldly (*Nightmare At 20,000 Feet*) terrors and placed them in the everyday. His greatest work *I Am Legend* is arguably one of science fiction, but incorporates some elements of horror in its narrative. Matheson is also an acknowledged influence on Stephen King, who shares a theme of finding horror in the everyday, and was the first horror novelist to appear regularly on bestseller lists in the latter half of the 20th century.

horse chestnut n 1 a tree with broad leaves and brown shiny inedible nuts enclosed in a spiky case 2 the nut of this tree

horseflesh n 1 horses collectively: *Ascot's annual parade of fashion and horseflesh* 2 the flesh of a horse as food

horsefly n, pl -**flies** a large fly which sucks the blood of horses, cattle, and people

horsehair n hair from the tail or mane of a horse, used in upholstery

horse laugh n a loud and coarse laugh

horseman n, pl -**men** 1 a man who is skilled in riding 2 a man riding a horse **horsemanship** n **horsewoman** fem n

horseplay n rough or rowdy play

horsepower n a unit of power (equivalent to 745.7 watts), used to measure the power of an engine

horseradish n a plant with a white strong-tasting root, which is used to make a sauce

horse sense n same as **common sense**

horseshoe n 1 a piece of iron shaped like a U, nailed to the bottom of a horse's hoof to protect the foot 2 an object of similar shape: often regarded as a symbol of good luck

horsetail n a plant with small dark toothlike leaves

horsewhip n 1 a whip with a long thong, used for managing horses ▷ vb -**whipping, -whipped** 2 to beat (a person or animal) with such a whip

horsey or **horsy** adj **horsier, horsiest** 1 of or relating to horses: *a horsey smell* 2 devoted to horses: *the horsey set* 3 like a horse: *a horsey face*

hortatory or **hortative** adj formal encouraging
WORD ORIGIN Latin *hortari* to encourage

horticulture n the art or science of cultivating gardens **horticultural** adj **horticulturalist** or **horticulturist** n
WORD ORIGIN Latin *hortus* garden + CULTURE

Horus n an Egyptian god with a falcon's head

hosanna interj an exclamation of praise to God
WORD ORIGIN Hebrew *hōshi 'āh nnā* save now, we pray

hose¹ n 1 a flexible pipe, for conveying a liquid or gas ▷ vb **hosing, hosed** 2 to wash or water (a person or thing) with a hose
WORD ORIGIN later use of HOSE²

hose² n 1 old-fashioned stockings, socks, and tights collectively 2 history a man's garment covering the legs and reaching up to the waist
WORD ORIGIN Old English *hosa*

hoser n 1 US slang a person who swindles or deceives others 2 Canad slang an unsophisticated, esp. rural, person

hosiery n stockings, socks, and knitted underclothing collectively

hospice (**hoss**-piss) n 1 a nursing home that specializes in caring for the terminally ill 2 archaic a place of shelter for travellers, esp. one kept by a religious order
WORD ORIGIN Latin *hospes* guest

hospitable adj generous, friendly, and welcoming to guests or strangers: *charming and hospitable lodgings* **hospitably** adv
WORD ORIGIN Medieval Latin *hospitare* to receive as a guest

hospital n an institution for the medical or psychiatric care and treatment of patients
WORD ORIGIN Latin *hospes* guest

hospitality n, pl -**ties** kindness in welcoming strangers or guests

hospitalize or -**lise** vb -**lizing, -lized** or -**lising, -lised** to admit or send (a person) into a hospital **hospitalization** or -**lisation** n

hospitaller or US **hospitaler** n a member of a religious order dedicated to hospital work, ambulance services, etc.

host¹ n 1 a person who receives or entertains guests, esp. in his own home 2 the organization or country providing the facilities for a function or event: *Barcelona, host of the 1992 Olympic Games* 3 the compere of a radio or television programme 4 biol an animal or plant in or on which a parasite lives 5 computers a computer connected to a network and providing facilities to other computers and their users 6 old-fashioned the owner or manager of an inn ▷ vb 7 to be the host of (a party, programme, or event): *he's hosting a radio show*
WORD ORIGIN Latin *hospes* guest, host

host² n a great number; multitude
WORD ORIGIN Latin *hostis* stranger

Host n Christianity the bread used in Holy Communion
WORD ORIGIN Latin *hostia* victim

hostage n a person who is illegally held prisoner until certain demands are met by other people
WORD ORIGIN Old French *hoste* guest

hostel n 1 a building providing overnight accommodation at a low cost for particular groups of people, such as the homeless 2 same as **youth hostel** 3 Brit & NZ a supervised lodging house for nurses, students, etc. **hosteller** or US **hosteler** n
WORD ORIGIN Medieval Latin *hospitale* hospice

hostelry n, pl -**ries** archaic or facetious an inn

hostel school n Canad same as **residential school**

hostess n 1 a woman who receives and entertains guests, esp. in her own house 2 a woman who receives and entertains patrons of a club, restaurant, or dance hall

hostile adj 1 unfriendly and aggressive 2 opposed (to): *hostile to the referendum* 3 relating to or involving the enemies of a country
WORD ORIGIN Latin *hostis* enemy

hostility n, pl -**ties** 1 unfriendly and aggressive feelings or behaviour 2 **hostilities** acts of warfare

hot adj **hotter, hottest** 1 having a relatively high temperature 2 having a temperature higher than desirable 3 spicy or causing a burning sensation on the tongue: *hot chillies* 4 (of a temper) quick to flare up 5 (of a contest or conflict) intense 6 recent or new: *hot from the press* 7 much favoured: *a hot favourite* 8 informal having a dangerously high level of radioactivity 9 slang stolen or otherwise illegally obtained 10 (of a colour) intense; striking: *hot pink* 11 following closely: *this LP appeared hot on the heels of the debut smash* 12 informal dangerous or unpleasant: *they're making it hot for me here* 13 (in various games) very near the answer 14 **hot on** informal **a** strict about: *they are extremely hot on sloppy language* **b** particularly knowledgeable about 15 **hot under the collar** informal aroused with anger, annoyance, or resentment 16 **in hot water** informal in trouble ▶ See also **hot up** ▷ **hotly** adv
WORD ORIGIN Old English *hāt*

hot air n informal empty and usually boastful talk

hotbed n a place offering ideal conditions for the growth of an idea or activity: *a hotbed of resistance*

hot-blooded adj passionate or excitable

hot-button adj informal indicating a controversial subject that is likely to arouse strong emotions: *the hot-button issue of abortion*

hotchpotch or esp. US & Canad **hodgepodge** n a jumbled mixture
WORD ORIGIN Old French *hochepot* shake pot

hot cross bun n a yeast bun marked with a cross and traditionally eaten on Good Friday

hot-desking n the practice of not assigning permanent desks in a workplace, so that employees may work at any available desk

hot dog n a long roll split lengthways with a hot sausage inside

hotel n a commercially run establishment providing lodging and meals for guests
WORD ORIGIN French

hotelier n an owner or manager of a hotel

hotfoot adv with all possible speed: *hotfoot to the accident*

hot-gospeller n informal a revivalist preacher with a highly enthusiastic delivery

hot-headed adj impetuous, rash, or hot-tempered **hot-headedness** n

hothouse n a greenhouse in which the temperature is maintained at a fixed level

hot key n computers a single key on a computer keyboard which provides a shortcut to a function in an application

hotline n a direct telephone link between heads of government for emergency use

hot money n capital that is transferred from one financial centre to another seeking the best opportunity for short-term gain

hotplate n 1 a heated metal surface on an electric cooker 2 a portable device on which food can be kept warm

hot pool n NZ a geothermally heated pool

hotpot n a casserole of meat and vegetables covered with a layer of potatoes

hot rod n a car with an engine that has been modified to produce increased power

hot seat n 1 US slang the electric chair 2 **in the hot seat** informal in a difficult and responsible position

hotspot n 1 a place where there is a lot of exciting activity or entertainment: Birmingham's fashionable hot spots 2 an area where there is fighting or political unrest: a political hot spot in the Caucasus 3 a small area of abnormally high temperature or radioactivity 4 computers a place (esp. a public building or commercial premises) offering a wireless internet connection

hot stuff n informal 1 a person, object, or activity considered attractive, exciting, or important: they're still hot stuff 2 pornographic or erotic books, plays, films, etc.

Hottentot n 1 a race of indigenous people of South Africa which is now almost extinct 2 a member of this race 3 Also called: **Khoi Khoi** the language of this race **WORD ORIGIN** origin unknown

hotting n Brit informal the performing of high-speed stunts in a stolen car **hotter** n

hot up vb **hotting, hotted** informal to make or become more active and exciting

hot-water bottle n a rubber container, designed to be filled with hot water and used for warming a bed

hound n 1 a dog used for hunting: to ride with the hounds 2 a despicable person ▷ vb 3 to pursue, disturb, or criticize relentlessly: hounded by the press **WORD ORIGIN** Old English hund

hour n 1 a period of time equal to 60 minutes; 1/24 of a day 2 any of the points on the face of a clock or watch that indicate intervals of 60 minutes: in my hurry I mistook the hour 3 the time of day 4 the time allowed for, or used for, something: a three-and-a-half-hour test 5 the distance covered in an hour: an hour from the heart of Tokyo 6 a special moment: the decisive hour ▶ See also **hours** **WORD ORIGIN** Latin hora

hourglass n a device consisting of two transparent sections linked by a narrow channel, containing a quantity of sand that takes an hour to trickle from one section to the other

houri n, pl **-ris** (in Muslim belief) any of the nymphs of Paradise **WORD ORIGIN** Arabic haurā' woman with dark eyes

hourly adj 1 of, occurring, or done once every hour 2 measured by the hour: hourly charges 3 frequent ▷ adv 4 once every hour 5 by the hour: hourly paid 6 frequently 7 at any moment: the arrival of the men was hourly expected

hours pl n 1 an indefinite time: they play on their bikes for hours 2 a period regularly appointed for work or business 3 one's times of rising and going to bed: you keep very late hours 4 RC Church prayers recited at seven specified times of the day

Hours pl n classical myth the goddesses of the seasons

house n 1 a building used as a home; dwelling 2 the people in a house 3 a building for some specific purpose: beach house 4 a family or dynasty: the House of Windsor 5 a commercial company: auction house 6 a law-making body or the hall where it meets 7 a division of a large school: he was captain of the house rugby team 8 the audience in a theatre or cinema 9 astrol any of the 12 divisions of the zodiac 10 informal a brothel 11 **get on like a house on fire** informal (of people) to get on very well together 12 **on the house** (usually of drinks) paid for by the management 13 **put one's house in order** to settle or organize one's affairs ▷ adj 14 (of wine) sold unnamed by a restaurant, at a lower price than wines specified on the wine list: house red ▷ vb **housing, housed** 15 to give accommodation to 16 to contain or cover (something) **WORD ORIGIN** Old English hūs

house arrest n confinement to one's own home rather than in prison

houseboat n a stationary boat used as a home

housebound adj unable to leave one's house, usually because of illness

housebreaking n criminal law the act of entering a building as a trespasser for an unlawful purpose **housebreaker** n

housecoat n a woman's loose robelike garment for casual wear

housefly n, pl **-flies** a common fly often found in houses

household n 1 all the people living together in one house ▷ adj 2 relating to the running of a household: household budget

householder n a person who owns or rents a house

household name or **word** n a person or thing that is very well known

housekeeper n a person employed to run someone else's household

housekeeping n 1 the running of a household 2 money allotted for this

house lights pl n the lights in the auditorium of a theatre or cinema

housemaid n (esp. formerly) a female servant employed to do housework

housemaid's knee n a fluid-filled swelling of the kneecap

houseman n, pl **-men** med a junior doctor in a hospital

house martin n a swallow with a slightly forked tail

House music or **House** n a type of disco music of the late 1980s, based on funk, with fragments of other recordings edited in electronically

House of Commons n (in Britain and Canada) the lower chamber of Parliament

House of Keys n the lower chamber of the law-making body of the Isle of Man

House of Lords n (in Britain) the upper chamber of Parliament, composed of the peers of the realm

House of Representatives n 1 (in the US) the lower chamber of Congress, or of many state legislatures 2 (in Australia) the lower chamber of Parliament 3 the sole chamber of New Zealand's Parliament

house party n 1 a party, usually in a country house, at which guests are invited to stay for several days 2 the guests who are invited

house-proud adj excessively concerned with the appearance, cleanliness, and tidiness of one's house

houseroom n **not give something houseroom** not to want to have something in one's house

house-train vb to train (a pet) to urinate and defecate outside

housewares pl n US, Canad kitchenware and other utensils for use in the home

house-warming n a party given after moving into a new home

housewife n, pl **-wives** a woman who runs her own household and does not have a paid job **housewifely** adj

housework n the work of running a home, such as cleaning, cooking, and shopping

housing n 1 houses collectively 2 the job of providing people with accommodation 3 a part designed to contain and support a component or mechanism: the inspection panel set within the concrete housing

hove vb chiefly naut a past of **heave**

hovea n an Australian plant with purple flowers

hovel n a small house or hut that is dirty or badly in need of repair **WORD ORIGIN** origin unknown

hover vb 1 (of a bird, insect, or helicopter) to remain suspended in one place in the air 2 to linger uncertainly in a place 3 to be in an unsettled or uncertain situation or frame of mind: hovering between two options **WORD ORIGIN** Middle English hoveren

hovercraft n a vehicle that is able to travel across both land and water on a cushion of air

how adv 1 in what way, by what means: how did you spend the evening?; observing how elderly people coped 2 to what extent: they don't know how tough I am 3 how good, how well, what ... like: how good are the copies?; so that's how things are 4 **how about?** used to suggest something: how about some tea? 5 **how are you?** what is your state of health? 6 **how's that?** a what is your opinion?: we'll go out for a late-night supper – how's that? b cricket Also written: **howzat** (an appeal to the umpire) is the batsman out? **WORD ORIGIN** Old English hu

howdah n a seat for riding on an elephant's back **WORD ORIGIN** Hindi haudah

however adv 1 still; nevertheless: the book does, however, almost get funny 2 by whatever means: get there however you can 3 (with an adjective or adverb) no matter how: however low we plunge, there is always hope

howitzer n a large gun that fires shells at a steep angle **WORD ORIGIN** Czech houfnice stone-sling

howl n 1 the long, loud wailing noise made by a wolf or dog 2 a similar cry of pain or sorrow 3 a loud burst of laughter ▷ *vb* **4** to express (something) in a howl or utter such cries **5** (of the wind, etc.) to make a wailing noise **WORD ORIGIN** Middle English *houlen*

howl down *vb* to prevent (a speaker) from being heard by shouting disapprovingly

howler *n informal* a glaring mistake

howling *adj informal* great: *a howling success*

howzit *sentence substitute S African* an informal word for hello **WORD ORIGIN** from the phrase *how is it?*

hoy *interj* a cry used to attract someone's attention **WORD ORIGIN** variant of *hey*

hoyden *n old-fashioned* a wild boisterous girl; tomboy **hoydenish** *adj* **WORD ORIGIN** perhaps from Middle Dutch *heidijn* heathen

HP *or* **h.p. 1** *Brit* hire-purchase **2** horsepower

HQ *or* **h.q.** headquarters

hr hour

HRH Her (*or* His) Royal Highness

HRT 1 hormone replacement therapy **2** *Austral & NZ* high rising terminal

Hs *chem* hassium

HTML *n computers* a text description language that is used on the World Wide Web **WORD ORIGIN** hypertext markup language

HTTP *n computers* hypertext transfer protocol: a system of rules for transferring files on the internet

hub *n* **1** the central portion of a wheel, through which the axle passes **2** the central, most important, or active part of a place or organization **WORD ORIGIN** probably variant of *hob*

hubble-bubble *n* **1** same as **hookah 2** *archaic* turmoil or confusion **WORD ORIGIN** imitative

hubbub *n* **1** a confused noise of many voices **2** great confusion or excitement **WORD ORIGIN** probably from Irish *hooboobbes*

hubby *n, pl* **-bies** *informal* a husband

hubcap *n* a metal disc that fits on to and protects the hub of a wheel, esp. on a car

hubris (**hew**-briss) *n formal* pride or arrogance **hubristic** *adj* **WORD ORIGIN** Greek

huckster *n* **1** a person who uses aggressive methods of selling **2** *now rare* a person who sells small articles or fruit in the street **WORD ORIGIN** probably from Middle Dutch *hoekster*

huddle *n* **1** a small group of people or things standing or lying close together **2 go into a huddle** *informal* to have a private conference ▷ *vb* **-dling, -dled 3** (of a group of people) to crowd or nestle closely together **4** to curl up one's arms and legs close to one's body through cold or fear **WORD ORIGIN** origin unknown

hue *n* **1** the feature of colour that enables an observer to classify it as red, blue, etc. **2** a shade of a colour **WORD ORIGIN** Old English *hīw* beauty

hue and cry *n* a loud public outcry **WORD ORIGIN** Old French *hue* outcry

huff *n* **1** a passing mood of anger or resentment: *in a huff* ▷ *vb* **2** to blow or puff heavily **3** *draughts* to remove (an opponent's draught) from the board for failure to make a capture **4 huffing and puffing** empty threats or objections **huffy** *adj* **huffily** *adv* **WORD ORIGIN** imitative

hug *vb* **hugging, hugged 1** to clasp (someone or something) tightly, usually with affection **2** to keep close to (a shore or the kerb) ▷ *n* **3** a tight or fond embrace **WORD ORIGIN** probably Scandinavian

huge *adj* extremely large **hugely** *adv* **WORD ORIGIN** Old French *ahuge*

huggermugger *archaic n* **1** confusion or secrecy ▷ *adj, adv* **2** in confusion **WORD ORIGIN** origin unknown

Huguenot (**hew**-gan-oh) *n* a French Calvinist of the 16th or 17th centuries **WORD ORIGIN** French

huh *interj* an exclamation of derision, bewilderment, or inquiry

hui (**hoo**-ee) *huis, n* NZ **1** a Māori social gathering **2** a meeting to discuss Māori matters **3** any party **WORD ORIGIN** Māori

hula *n* a Hawaiian dance performed by a woman **WORD ORIGIN** Hawaiian

Hula Hoop *n trademark* a plastic hoop swung round the body by wiggling the hips

hulk *n* **1** the body of an abandoned ship **2** *disparaging* a large ungainly person or thing **WORD ORIGIN** Old English *hulc*

hulking *adj* big and ungainly

hull *n* **1** the main body of a boat **2** the outer covering of a fruit or seed such as a pea or bean **3** the leaves round the stem of a strawberry, raspberry, or similar fruit ▷ *vb* **4** to remove the hulls from (fruit or seeds) **WORD ORIGIN** Old English *hulu*

hullabaloo *n, pl* **-loos** a loud confused noise or commotion **WORD ORIGIN** *hallo* + Scots *baloo* lullaby

hullo *interj, n* same as **hello**

hum *vb* **humming, hummed 1** to make a low continuous vibrating sound **2** (of a person) to sing with the lips closed **3** to utter an indistinct sound when hesitating **4** *informal* to be in a state of feverish activity: *the town hums with activity and life* **5** *slang* to smell unpleasant **6 hum and haw** see **haw²** ▷ *n* **7** a low continuous murmuring sound **8** an unpleasant smell ▷ *interj, n* **9** an indistinct sound of hesitation **WORD ORIGIN** imitative

human *adj* **1** of or relating to people: *human occupants* **2** having the qualities of people as opposed to animals, divine beings, or machines: *human nature* **3** kind or considerate ▷ *n* **4** a human being **WORD ORIGIN** Latin *humanus*

human being *n* a man, woman, or child

humane *adj* **1** showing kindness and sympathy **2** inflicting as little pain as

possible: *a humane method of killing minke whales* **3** considered to have a civilizing effect on people: *the humane tradition of a literary education* **WORD ORIGIN** variant of *human*

humanism *n* the rejection of religion in favour of a belief in the advancement of humanity by its own efforts **humanist** *n, adj* **humanistic** *adj*

humanitarian *adj* **1** having the interests of mankind at heart ▷ *n* **2** a person who has the interests of mankind at heart **humanitarianism** *n*

humanity *n, pl* **-ties 1** the human race **2** the quality of being human **3** kindness or mercy **4 humanities** the study of literature, philosophy, and the arts

humanize *or* **-ise** *vb* **-izing, -ized** *or* **-ising, -ised** to make human or humane **humanization** *or* **-isation** *n*

humankind *n* the human race; humanity

Ξ **USAGE**
Ξ See at **mankind**.

humanly *adv* by human powers or means: *as fast as is humanly possible*

humanoid *adj* **1** like a human being in appearance ▷ *n* **2** (in science fiction) a robot or creature resembling a human being

human race *n* all men, women, and children collectively

human resources *pl n* **1** the people employed in an organization or for a service **2** (*functioning as sing*) the department in an organization that appoints or keeps records of employees

human rights *pl n* the basic rights of individuals to liberty, justice, etc.

humble *adj* **1** conscious of one's failings **2** modest and unpretentious: *humble domestic objects* **3** ordinary or not very important: *humble beginnings* ▷ *vb* **-bling, -bled 4** to cause to become humble; humiliate **humbly** *adv* **WORD ORIGIN** Latin *humilis* low

humble pie *n* **eat humble pie** to be forced to behave humbly; be humiliated **WORD ORIGIN** earlier *an umble pie*, from *numbles* offal of a deer

humbug *n* **1** *Brit* a hard peppermint sweet with a striped pattern **2** a speech or piece of writing that is obviously untrue, dishonest, or nonsense **3** a dishonest person **WORD ORIGIN** origin unknown

humdinger *n slang* **1** something unusually large **2** an excellent person or thing **WORD ORIGIN** origin unknown

humdrum *adj* ordinary, dull, and uninteresting **WORD ORIGIN** probably based on *hum*

humerus (**hew**-mer-uss) *n, pl* **-meri** (-mer-rye) the bone from the shoulder to the elbow **humeral** *adj* **WORD ORIGIN** Latin *umerus*

humid *adj* (of the weather) damp and warm **WORD ORIGIN** Latin *umidus*

humidex (**hew**-mid-ex) *n Canad* a system of measuring discomfort showing the combined effect of humidity and temperature

A History of English – Middle English

The original speakers of English were themselves invaders to the British Isles, so perhaps we shouldn't pity them too much if they were themselves conquered a couple of times.

The established Anglo-Saxon kingdoms were first conquered in a series of Viking invasions from Denmark in the ninth and tenth centuries AD. The Danish settlements were largely restricted to the present-day East Midlands and came to be known as the *Danelaw*. In their brief time here, the Danes exerted an important influence on the English language, giving us words like *window, sky,* and the plural pronoun *their*. At the close of the tenth century, the Anglo-Saxons finally managed to expel the Viking rulers and enjoyed a little over a half-century until new invaders from the North came to conquer them again.

The Normans came immediately from France, and brought a variety of the French language with them, but they, too, were originally Viking invaders. Their name has been Gallicized, but it comes from an Old Norse word meaning 'North-men'.

The Norman Invasion had such a significant influence on the development of the English language that English from the twelfth century onward is called 'Middle English'. The first major effect was increased regionalization of written English. Anglo-Saxon England had never been politically unified, so no single variety of Old English ever became the 'standard'; however, the West Saxon variety did become a kind of written standard, and most surviving Old English texts are written in West Saxon, even when the authors and scribes are Anglian or Mercian. The Normans did manage to unify England, but their official language was Norman French; the literary dominance of West Saxon effectively ended. Middle English dialects as a rule display strong evidence of the region of their author or (more frequently) their scribe. Northern dialects, for example, have the inflection *-es* or *-is/-ys* for the third person present singular: *yernes* ('yearns'), *castys* ('casts'). Midland and Southern dialects have the inflections *-eth* or *-ith*: *maketh* ('makes'), *trewith* ('believes'). Some Southern texts have initial *v* for words that begin with *f* in Modern English: *vort* ('word'), *vor* ('for').

A more lasting effect of the Norman invasion, however, was the importation of new vocabulary. Early in the reign of the Normans, English and French would have been perceived as separate languages, one courtly, one common; any borrowing that occurred would have been relatively minor. The following excerpt of the *Peterborough Chronicle* contains only three words which do not come from Old English:

This gear com Henri King to this land. Tha com Henri abbot and wreide the muneces of Burch to the king forthi that he wolde undertheden that mynstre to Clunie, swa that te king was wel neh bepaht and sende efter the muneces.

Abbot comes from Hebrew, *muneces* ('monks') comes from Ancient Greek, and *mynstre* ('minster') comes from Latin; all three of these words entered English through Christian missionaries; none come from Norman French.

Later, as Norman French became more established, the socio-political gulf between English and French narrowed, and contact between the languages increased. This famous passage from Chaucer's *Canterbury Tales* has many words that entered English through Norman French:

Whan that Aprill with his shoures soote
The droghte of March hath perced to the roote,
And bathed every veyne in swich licour
Of which vertu engendred is the flour;
Whan Zephirus eek with his sweete breeth
Inspired hath in every holt and heeth
The tendre croppes, and the yonge sun
Hath in the Ram his half cours yronne,
And smale foweles maken melodye,
That slepen al the nyght with open ye
(So priketh hem nature in hir corages)
Thanne longen folk to goon on pilgrimages.

The majority of words are still 'native' English. Also *Zephirus* comes from Greek, and *pilgrimages* is another word that will have come from missionaries. However, *perced, veyne, licour, vertu, engendred, flour, inspired, tendre, melodye, nature,* and *corages* all come from French. English now has a greater portion of everyday vocabulary derived from Romance languages than any other Germanic language, and as a result often seems quite distant from its Germanic cousins.

humidify *vb* **-fies, -fying, -fied** to make the air in (a room) more humid or damp **humidifier** *n*

humidity *n* **1** dampness **2** a measure of the amount of moisture in the air

humiliate *vb* **-ating, -ated** to hurt the dignity or pride of: *the English cricket team was humiliated by Australia* **humiliating** *adj* **humiliation** *n*
WORD ORIGIN Latin *humilis* humble

humility *n* the quality of being humble and modest

hummingbird *n* a very small brightly-coloured American bird with a long slender bill, and powerful wings that hum as they vibrate

hummock *n* a very small hill or a mound
WORD ORIGIN origin unknown

hummus *n* a creamy dip originating in the Middle East, made from puréed chickpeas
WORD ORIGIN from Turkish *humus*

humongous a variant of **humungous**

humorist *n* a person who speaks or writes in a humorous way

humorous *adj* amusing, esp. in a witty or clever way **humorously** *adv*

humour *or US* **humor** *n* **1** the quality of being funny **2** the ability to appreciate or express things that are humorous: *a sense of humour* **3** situations, speech, or writings that are humorous **4** a state of mind; mood: *in astoundingly good humour* **5** *archaic* any of various fluids in the body: *aqueous humour* ▷ *vb* **6** to be kind and indulgent to: *he decided the patient needed to be humoured* **humourless** *adj*
WORD ORIGIN Latin *humor* liquid

hump *n* **1** a rounded lump on the ground **2** a rounded deformity of the back **3** a rounded lump on the back of a camel or related animal **4** **the hump** *Brit informal* a fit of sulking: *you've got the hump today* ▷ *vb* **5** *slang* to carry or heave: *who would be responsible if they were injured humping heavy gear around?*
WORD ORIGIN probably from *humpbacked*

humpback *n* **1** same as **hunchback** **2** Also called: **humpback whale** a large whalebone whale with a hump on its back **3** Also called: **humpback bridge** *Brit* a road bridge with a sharp slope on either side **humpbacked** *adj*

humph *interj* an exclamation of annoyance or scepticism

humungous *or esp. US* **humongous** (hew-**mung**-gus) *adj informal* very large; enormous: *it was not a humungous box office hit*
WORD ORIGIN probably from *huge + enormous*

humus (**hew**-muss) *n* a dark brown or black mass of partially decomposed plant and animal matter in the soil
WORD ORIGIN Latin: soil

Humvee *n* a four-wheel drive military vehicle
WORD ORIGIN h(igh-mobility) + m(ulti-purpose) v(ehicle) + -EE

Hun *n, pl* **Huns** *or* **Hun** **1** a member of any of several Asiatic peoples who invaded the Roman Empire in the 4th and 5th centuries AD **2** *offensive, informal* (esp. in World War I) a German

WORD ORIGIN Old English *Hūnas*

hunch *n* **1** a feeling or suspicion not based on facts: *she said that she had had a hunch that the coup would not succeed* **2** same as **hump** ▷ *vb* **3** to draw (oneself or one's shoulders) up or together
WORD ORIGIN origin unknown

hunchback *n* a person who has an abnormal curvature of the spine **hunchbacked** *adj*

hundred *n, pl* **-dreds** *or* **-dred** **1** the cardinal number that is the product of ten and ten **2** a numeral, 100 or C, representing this number **3** (*often pl*) a large but unspecified number ▷ *adj* **4** amounting to a hundred: *a hundred yards* **hundredth** *adj, n*
WORD ORIGIN Old English

hundreds and thousands *pl n* tiny beads of coloured sugar, used in decorating cakes and sweets

hundredweight *n, pl* **-weights** *or* **-weight** **1** *Brit* a unit of weight equal to 112 pounds or 50.802kg **2** *US & Canad* a unit of weight equal to 100 pounds or 45.359kg **3** a metric unit of weight equal to 50 kilograms

hung *vb* **1** the past of **hang** ▷ *adj* **2** (of a parliament or jury) with no side having a clear majority **3** **hung over** *informal* suffering the effects of a hangover

‗ **USAGE**
When *hang* means 'execute', the past tense and past participle is *hanged* instead of *hung*.

Hungarian *adj* **1** of Hungary ▷ *n* **2** a person from Hungary **3** the language of Hungary

hunger *n* **1** a feeling of emptiness or weakness caused by lack of food **2** a lack of food that causes suffering or death: *refugees dying of hunger and disease* **3** desire or craving: *Europe's hunger for bullion* ▷ *vb* **4** **hunger for** to have a great desire for
WORD ORIGIN Old English *hungor*

hunger strike *n* a refusal of all food, usually by a prisoner, as a means of protest

hungry *adj* **-grier, -griest** **1** desiring food **2** (foll. by *for*) having a craving, desire, or need for: *hungry for revenge* **3** expressing greed, craving, or desire: *the media's hungry search for impact* **hungrily** *adv*

hunk *n* **1** a large piece: *a hunk of bread* **2** *slang* a well-built, sexually attractive man
WORD ORIGIN probably related to Flemish *hunke*

hunkers *pl n* haunches
WORD ORIGIN origin unknown

hunt *vb* **1** to seek out and kill (animals) for food or sport **2** **hunt down** to track in an attempt to capture (someone): *hunting down villains* **3** **hunt for** to search for: *Western companies are hunting for opportunities to invest* ▷ *n* **4** the act or an instance of hunting **5** a party organized for the pursuit of wild animals for sport **6** the members of such a party **hunting** *n*
WORD ORIGIN Old English *huntian*

huntaway *n* *NZ* a sheepdog trained to drive sheep by barking

hunter *n* **1** a person or animal that seeks out and kills or captures game **2** a

person who looks carefully for something: *a house hunter* **3** a horse or dog bred for hunting **4** a watch with a hinged metal lid or case to protect the glass

hunter-gatherer *n* a member of a society that lives by hunting and gathering naturally occurring resources

huntsman *n, pl* **-men** **1** a person who hunts **2** a person who trains hounds and manages them during a hunt

hurdle *n* **1** *athletics* one of a number of light barriers over which runners leap in certain events **2** a difficulty or problem: *the main technical hurdle is the environment* **3** **hurdles** a race involving hurdles ▷ *vb* **-dling, -dled** **4** to jump over (a hurdle or other obstacle) **hurdler** *n*
WORD ORIGIN Old English *hyrdel*

hurdy-gurdy *n, pl* **hurdy-gurdies** a mechanical musical instrument, such as a barrel organ
WORD ORIGIN probably imitative

hurl *vb* **1** to throw (something) with great force **2** to utter (something) with force; yell: *onlookers hurled abuse at them*
WORD ORIGIN probably imitative

hurling *or* **hurley** *n* a traditional Irish game resembling hockey

hurly-burly *n* great noise and activity; commotion
WORD ORIGIN obsolete *hurling* uproar

hurrah *or* **hooray** *interj, n* a cheer of joy or victory
WORD ORIGIN probably from German *hurra*

hurricane *n* a severe, often destructive storm, esp. a tropical cyclone
WORD ORIGIN Spanish *huracán*

hurricane lamp *n* a paraffin lamp with a glass covering

hurried *adj* done quickly or too quickly **hurriedly** *adv* **hurriedness** *n*

hurry *vb* **-ries, -rying, -ried** **1** to move or act, or cause to move or act, in great haste: *the umpires hurried the players off the ground* **2** to speed up the completion or progress of: *eat a small snack rather than hurry a main meal* ▷ *n* **3** haste **4** urgency or eagerness **5** **in a hurry** *informal* **a** easily: *a striking old guy, not the sort you'd forget in a hurry* **b** willingly: *he would not ease interest rates again in a hurry*
WORD ORIGIN probably imitative

hurt *vb* **hurting, hurt** **1** to cause physical or mental injury to: *is she badly hurt?* **2** to cause someone to feel pain: *my head hurt* **3** *informal* to feel pain: *she was hurting* ▷ *n* **4** physical or mental pain or suffering ▷ *adj* **5** injured or pained: *his hurt head; a hurt expression* **hurtful** *adj*
WORD ORIGIN Old French *hurter* to knock against

hurtle *vb* **-ling, -led** to move very quickly or violently
WORD ORIGIN Middle English *hurtlen*

husband *n* **1** a woman's partner in marriage ▷ *vb* **2** to use (resources, finances, etc.) economically
WORD ORIGIN Old English *hūsbonda*

husbandry *n* **1** the art or skill of farming **2** management of resources

hush *vb* **1** to make or be silent ▷ *n* **2** stillness or silence ▷ *interj* **3** a plea or

demand for silence. See also **hush up**
> hushed *adj*
WORD ORIGIN earlier *husht* quiet!

hush-hush *adj informal* (esp. of official work) secret and confidential

hush money *n slang* money given to a person to ensure that something is kept secret

hush up *vb* to suppress information or rumours about (something)

husk *n* **1** the outer covering of certain fruits and seeds ▷ *vb* **2** to remove the husk from
WORD ORIGIN probably from Middle Dutch *hūs* house

husky¹ *adj* **huskier, huskiest 1** (of a voice) slightly hoarse **2** *informal* (of a man) big and strong **huskily** *adv*
WORD ORIGIN probably from *husk*, from the toughness of a corn husk

husky² *n, pl* **huskies** an Arctic sledge dog with thick hair and a curled tail
WORD ORIGIN probably based on *eskimo*

hussar (hoo-**zar**) *n history* a member of a light cavalry regiment
WORD ORIGIN Hungarian *huszár*

hussy *n, pl* **-sies** *old-fashioned* a woman considered sexually immoral or improper
WORD ORIGIN from *hussif* housewife

hustings *pl n* the campaigns and speeches at a parliamentary election
WORD ORIGIN Old Norse *hūsthing*, from *hūs* house + *thing* assembly

hustle *vb* **-tling, -tled 1** to make (someone) move by pushing or jostling them: *he hustled her away* **2** to deal with (something) hurriedly: *they did not heedlessly hustle the tempo* **3** *US & Canad slang* (of a prostitute) to solicit clients ▷ *n* **4** lively activity and excitement
WORD ORIGIN Dutch *husselen* to shake

hustler *n US informal* a person who tries to make money or gain an advantage from every situation, often by immoral or dishonest means

hut *n* a small house or shelter
WORD ORIGIN French *hutte*

hutch *n* a cage for small animals
WORD ORIGIN Old French *huche*

hyacinth *n* a plant with bell-shaped sweet-smelling flowers
WORD ORIGIN Greek *huakinthos*

hyaena *n* same as **hyena**

hybrid *n* **1** an animal or plant resulting from a cross between two different types of animal or plant **2** a vehicle that is powered by an internal-combustion engine and another source of power **3** anything that is a mixture of two different things ▷ *adj* **4** of mixed origin **5** (of a vehicle) powered by an internal-combustion engine and another source of power
WORD ORIGIN Latin *hibrida*

hybridize *or* **-dise** *vb* **-dizing, -dized** *or* **-dising, -dised** to produce or cause (species) to produce hybrids; crossbreed **hybridization** *or* **-disation** *n*

hydatid disease (**hide**-at-id) *n* a condition caused by the presence of bladder-like cysts (**hydatids**) in the liver, lungs, or brain
WORD ORIGIN Greek *hudatis* watery sac

hydra *n* **1** a mythical many-headed serpent **2** a persistent problem: *killing the hydra of drug production is impossible* **3** a microscopic freshwater creature with a slender tubular body and tentacles around the mouth
WORD ORIGIN Greek *hudra* water serpent

hydrangea *n* an ornamental shrub with large clusters of white, pink, or blue flowers
WORD ORIGIN Greek *hudōr* water + *angeion* vessel

hydrant *n* an outlet from a water main, from which water can be tapped for fighting fires

hydrate *chem n* **1** a compound containing water chemically combined with a substance: *chloral hydrate* ▷ *vb* **-drating, -drated 2** to treat or impregnate (a substance) with water **hydration** *n*

hydraulic *adj* operated by pressure transmitted through a pipe by a liquid, such as water or oil **hydraulically** *adv*
WORD ORIGIN Greek *hudōr* water + *aulos* pipe

hydraulics *n* the study of the mechanical properties of fluids as they apply to practical engineering

hydride *n chem* a compound of hydrogen with another element

hydro¹ *n, pl* **-dros** *Brit* a hotel offering facilities for hydropathic treatment

hydro² *adj* **1** short for **hydroelectric** ▷ *n* **2** *Canad* electricity as supplied to a residence, business, etc.

hydro- *or before a vowel* **hydr-** *combining form* **1** indicating water or fluid: *hydrodynamics* **2** *chem* indicating hydrogen in a chemical compound: *hydrochloric acid*
WORD ORIGIN Greek *hudōr* water

hydrocarbon *n* a compound containing only carbon and hydrogen

hydrocephalus *n* accumulation of fluid in the cavities of the brain, causing enlargement of the head in children **hydrocephalic** *adj*
WORD ORIGIN Greek *hudōr* water + *kephalē* head

hydrochloric acid *n chem* a solution of hydrogen chloride in water: a strong acid used in many industrial and laboratory processes

hydrodynamics *n* the branch of science concerned with the mechanical properties of fluids

hydroelectric *adj* **1** generated by the pressure of falling water: *hydroelectric power* **2** of the generation of electricity by water pressure: *a hydroelectric scheme* **hydroelectricity** *n*

hydrofoil *n* **1** a fast light vessel the hull of which is raised out of the water on one or more pairs of fins **2** any of these fins

hydrogen *n chem* a colourless gas that burns easily and is the lightest element in the universe. It occurs in water and in most organic compounds. Symbol: H **hydrogenous** *adj*
WORD ORIGIN HYDRO- + -*gen* (producing); because its combustion produces water

hydrogenate (hide-**roj**-in-nate) *vb* **-ating, -ated** *chem* to combine (a substance) with hydrogen: *hydrogenated vegetable oil* **hydrogenation** *n*

hydrogen bomb *n* an extremely powerful bomb in which energy is released by fusion of hydrogen nuclei to give helium nuclei

hydrogen peroxide *n* a colourless oily unstable liquid chemical used as a hair bleach and as an antiseptic

hydrogen sulphide *n* a colourless poisonous gas with an odour of rotten eggs

hydrography (hide-**rog**-ra-fee) *n* the study of the oceans, seas, and rivers **hydrographer** *n* **hydrographic** *adj*

hydrology *n* the study of the distribution, conservation, and use of the water of the earth and its atmosphere

hydrolysis (hide-**rol**-iss-iss) *n chem* a process of decomposition in which a compound reacts with water to produce other compounds
WORD ORIGIN Greek *hudōr* water + *lusis* a loosening

hydrometer (hide-**rom**-it-er) *n* an instrument for measuring the density of a liquid

hydropathy *n* a method of treating disease by the use of large quantities of water both internally and externally **hydropathic** *adj*
WORD ORIGIN Greek *hudōr* water + *patheia* suffering

hydrophilic *adj chem* tending to dissolve in or mix with water: *a hydrophilic layer*

hydrophobia *n* **1** same as **rabies 2** (esp. of a person with rabies) a fear of drinking fluids **hydrophobic** *adj*

hydroplane *n* **1** a motorboat that raises its hull out of the water at high speeds **2** a fin on the hull of a submarine for controlling its vertical motion

hydroponics *n* a method of growing plants in gravel, etc. through which water containing the necessary nutrients is pumped
WORD ORIGIN HYDRO- + (*geo*)*ponics* science of agriculture

hydrosphere *n* the watery part of the earth's surface

hydrostatics *n* the branch of science concerned with the properties and behaviour of fluids that are not in motion **hydrostatic** *adj*

hydrotherapy *n med* the treatment of certain diseases by exercise in water

hydrous *adj* containing water

hydroxide *n chem* a compound containing a hydroxyl group or ion

hydroxyl *adj chem* of or containing the monovalent group –OH or the ion OH⁻: *forming a hydroxyl radical*

hyena *or* **hyaena** *n* a meat-eating doglike mammal of Africa and S Asia
WORD ORIGIN Greek *hus* hog

hygiene *n* **1** the principles and practices of health and cleanliness: *personal hygiene* **2** Also called: **hygienics** the science concerned with the maintenance of health **hygienic** *adj* **hygienically** *adv* **hygienist** *n*
WORD ORIGIN Greek *hugieinē*

hygrometer (hie-**grom**-it-er) *n* an instrument for measuring humidity
WORD ORIGIN Greek *hugros* wet

hygroscope *n* any device that indicates the humidity of the air without necessarily measuring it, such as an animal or vegetable fibre which contracts with moisture **WORD ORIGIN** Greek *hugros* wet + *skopein* to observe

hygroscopic *adj* (of a substance) tending to absorb water from the air

hymen *n anat* a membrane that partly covers the entrance to the vagina and is usually ruptured when sexual intercourse takes place for the first time **WORD ORIGIN** Greek: membrane

hymenopterous *adj* of or belonging to an order of insects with two pairs of membranous wings **WORD ORIGIN** Greek *humen* membrane + *pteron* wing

hymn *n* a Christian song of praise sung to God or a saint **WORD ORIGIN** Greek *humnos*

hymnal *n* a book of hymns. Also: **hymn book**

hymnody *n* 1 the composition or singing of hymns 2 hymns collectively

hymnology *n* the study of hymn composition **hymnologist** *n*

hype *slang n* 1 intensive or exaggerated publicity or sales promotion ▷ *vb* **hyping, hyped** 2 to market or promote (a commodity) using intensive or exaggerated publicity **WORD ORIGIN** origin unknown

hyped up *adj old-fashioned slang* stimulated or excited by, or as if by, drugs

hyper *adj informal* overactive or overexcited

hyper- *prefix* above, over, or in excess: *hypercritical* **WORD ORIGIN** Greek *huper* over

hyperactive *adj* (of a person) unable to relax and always in a state of restless activity

hyperbola (hie-**per**-bol-a) *n geom* a curve produced when a cone is cut by a plane at a steeper angle to its base than its side **WORD ORIGIN** Greek *huperbolē*

hyperbole (hie-**per**-bol-ee) *n* a deliberate exaggeration of speech or writing used for effect, such as *he embraced her a thousand times* **WORD ORIGIN** Greek *huper* over + *ballein* to throw

hyperbolic *or* **hyperbolical** *adj* 1 exaggerated 2 of a hyperbola or a hyperbole

hypercritical *adj* excessively critical

hyperglycaemia *or US* **hyperglycemia** (hie-per-glice-**seem**-ee-a) *n pathol* an abnormally large amount of sugar in the blood **WORD ORIGIN** Greek *huper* over + *glukus* sweet

hyperlink *computers n* 1 a word, picture, etc. in a computer document on which a user may click to move to another part of the document or to another document ▷ *vb* 2 to link (files) in this way

hypermarket *n* a huge self-service store **WORD ORIGIN** translation of French *hypermarché*

hypersensitive *adj* 1 unduly emotionally vulnerable 2 abnormally sensitive to an allergen, a drug, or high or low temperature

hypersexual *adj* 1 excessively interested in sexual activity 2 inappropriately sexualized: *hypersexual and explicit portrayals of women*

hypersonic *adj* having a speed of at least five times the speed of sound

hypertension *n pathol* abnormally high blood pressure

hypertext *n* computer software and hardware that allows users to store and view text and move between related items easily

hypertrophy (hie-**per**-trof-fee) *n, pl* **-phies** enlargement of an organ or part resulting from an increase in the size of the cells **WORD ORIGIN** Greek *huper* over + *trophē* nourishment

hyperventilation *n* an increase in the rate of breathing at rest, sometimes resulting in cramp and dizziness **hyperventilate** *vb*

hyphen *n* the punctuation mark (-), used to separate parts of compound words and between syllables of a word split between two consecutive lines **WORD ORIGIN** Greek *huphen* together

hyphenate *vb* **-ating, -ated** to separate (words) with a hyphen **hyphenation** *n*

hyphenated *adj* having two words or syllables connected by a hyphen

hypnosis *n* an artificially induced state of relaxation in which the mind is more than usually receptive to suggestion

hypnotherapy *n* the use of hypnosis in the treatment of emotional and mental problems **hypnotherapist** *n*

hypnotic *adj* 1 of or producing hypnosis or sleep 2 having an effect resembling hypnosis: *the film makes for hypnotic viewing* ▷ *n* 3 a drug that induces sleep **hypnotically** *adv* **WORD ORIGIN** Greek *hupnos* sleep

hypnotism *n* the practice of or process of inducing hypnosis **hypnotist** *n*

hypnotize *or* **-tise** *vb* **-tizing, -tized** *or* **-tising, -tised** 1 to induce hypnosis in (a person) 2 to hold the attention of (someone) completely; fascinate; mesmerize: *hypnotized by her beauty*

hypo- *or before a vowel* **hyp-** *prefix* beneath; less than: *hypodermic* **WORD ORIGIN** Greek *hupo* under

hypoallergenic *adj* not likely to cause an allergic reaction

hypocaust *n* an ancient Roman heating system in which hot air circulated under the floor and between double walls **WORD ORIGIN** Latin *hypocaustum*

hypochondria *n* abnormal anxiety concerning one's health **WORD ORIGIN** Late Latin: abdomen,

supposedly the seat of melancholy

hypochondriac *n* a person abnormally concerned about his or her health

hypocrisy (hip-**ok**-rass-ee) *n, pl* **-sies** 1 the practice of claiming to have standards or beliefs that are contrary to one's real character or actual behaviour 2 an act or instance of this

hypocrite (**hip**-oh-krit) *n* a person who pretends to be what he or she is not **hypocritical** *adj* **WORD ORIGIN** Greek *hupokrinein* to pretend

hypodermic *adj* 1 used for injecting ▷ *n* 2 a hypodermic syringe or needle

hypodermic syringe *n med* a syringe consisting of a hollow cylinder, a piston, and a hollow needle, used for withdrawing blood samples or injecting drugs under the skin

hypotension *n pathol* abnormally low blood pressure

hypotenuse (hie-**pot**-a-news) *n* the side in a right-angled triangle that is opposite the right angle **WORD ORIGIN** Greek *hupoteinousa grammē* subtending line

hypothalamus *n, pl* **-mi** an area at the base of the brain, which controls hunger, thirst, and other functions

hypothermia *n pathol* an abnormally low body temperature, as a result of exposure to cold weather

hypothesis (hie-**poth**-iss-iss) *n, pl* **-ses** (-seez) a suggested explanation for a group of facts, accepted either as a basis for further verification or as likely to be true **hypothesize** *or* **-ise** *vb* **WORD ORIGIN** Greek *hupotithenai* to propose, literally: put under

hypothetical *adj* based on assumption rather than fact or reality **hypothetically** *adv*

hyrax (**hire**-ax) *n, pl* **hyraxes** *or* **hyraces** (**hire**-a-seez) a genus of hoofed rodent-like animals

hyssop *n* 1 an aromatic plant used in herbal medicine 2 a Biblical plant, used for sprinkling in the ritual practices of the Hebrews **WORD ORIGIN** Greek *hussōpos*

hysterectomy *n, pl* **-mies** surgical removal of the womb **WORD ORIGIN** Greek *hustera* womb + *tomē* a cutting

hysteria *n* 1 a mental disorder marked by emotional outbursts and, often, symptoms such as paralysis 2 any uncontrolled emotional state, such as of panic, anger, or excitement **WORD ORIGIN** Greek *hustera* womb, from the belief that hysteria in women originated in disorders of the womb

hysteric *n* a hysterical person

hysterical *adj* 1 in a state of uncontrolled panic, anger, or excitement: *a crazy hysterical adolescent* 2 *informal* wildly funny **hysterically** *adv*

hysterics *n* 1 an attack of hysteria 2 *informal* wild uncontrollable bursts of laughter

Hz hertz

Thomas Hardy

Thomas Hardy is one of the best loved writers in the English language, forever associated with 'Wessex', the south-western corner of England that is the setting for his novels.

He was born in Dorset in 1840, the son of a stonemason and a cook. After leaving school, he became an architect, serving his apprenticeship in Dorchester before working in London for five years and then returning to Dorset in 1867. By this time he had already begun to write. His first novel failed to find a publisher, but his next attempt, *Desperate Remedies*, appeared in 1871. Success came three years later with *Far from the Madding Crowd*, and he was able to give up architecture and devote himself entirely to his writing.

In all, he published fourteen novels, including *The Return of the Native* (1878), *The Mayor of Casterbridge* (1886), *The Woodlanders* (1887), and *Tess of the D'Urbervilles* (1891). However, *Jude the Obscure* (1895) met with a hostile reception on account of its critical stance towards the institution of marriage, and after this Hardy gave up writing novels in favour of poetry. He published several collections of verse as well as a three-part verse-drama called *The Dynasts* before his death in 1928.

Although early novels such as *Under the Greenwood Tree* and (to a certain extent) *Far from the Madding Crowd* have a lighter tone, Hardy's major works are tragedies in which individuals of strong character are hounded by Fate. In *The Mayor of Casterbridge*, Michael Henchard is a successful merchant who is unable to escape the repercussions of the day in his youth when he sold his wife for five guineas at a country fair. In *Tess of the D'Urbervilles*, Tess Durbeyfield is the victim of her father's misguided attempt to restore his family's fortunes after he learns of its ancient nobility. In *Jude the Obscure*, the stonemason Jude Fawley is undone by his unrealistic desire to advance from his humble position and become a man of learning.

In the course of these dramas, the protagonists are apt to suffer from cruel quirks of fortune: they are frustrated by sudden changes in the weather, letters that go astray, and chance encounters with people from their pasts. Typical is the episode in *Far from the Madding Crowd* when a mix-up causes Fanny Robin to attend the wrong church on her wedding day and so lose her only chance of happiness. In Hardy's universe the individual is a toy in the hands of stronger powers.

The novels offer counterpoint to these tragic figures in the form of the ordinary rustics who are observed going about their business and recreation, often commenting on the action like a Greek chorus. The language of these rustics incorporates elements of Dorset dialect and is often picturesque and comical, as when the members of the Mellstock choir decry barrel organs as 'miserable dumbledores' in *Under the Greenwood Tree*, or when the mayor of Casterbridge is called 'a headstrong stunpoll' for expecting the townspeople to fall in with his plans.

The sense of place is essential to Hardy's appeal. The traditions of the countryside form vivid episodes, with white-clad maidens performing Maytime dances in *Tess of the D'Urbervilles*, girls venturing out on Midsummer's Eve hoping to catch sight of their future husbands in *The Woodlanders*, and mummers performing a Christmas play in *The Return of the Native*. More integral to the plot is the 'skimmity ride' in *The Mayor of Casterbridge*, where straw figures of an adulterous couple are paraded through the streets by a cheering mob.

Even when the Wessex countryside is not being evoked by characters or rituals, it forms an ever-present backdrop to events. *The Return of the Native* begins with an entire chapter devoted to Egdon Heath, the barren stage on which the drama will be played out, and which will endure long after the characters of the novel. The woods around Little Hintock are similarly integral to the action in *The Woodlanders*. Although Hardy created some memorable plots and characters, it is as a writer of places that he reigns supreme.

Ii

The letter I is the ninth letter of the English alphabet. It came into the Roman alphabet from the Greek letter *iota* (I,ι), which in turn had come from a Phoenician letter called *yodh*. This letter has its origins as a symbol for an arm. *Iota* was the smallest letter of the Greek alphabet, and its diminutive size gives rise to the expression 'not one iota', as an emphatic negative.

The lower-case form of the Greek differed from the modern letter I in being written without a dot. The distinctive dot (a feature shared only by the lower-case form of the related letter J) was added in the Middle Ages, when scribes found it useful to differentiate the vertical stroke of the letter I from the similar vertical strokes found in other letters. They did this by adding a short horizontal stroke or 'tittle' above the vertical line to indicate an I. Over time the size of the tittle was reduced to a mere dot.

The scribe's job of ensuring that the I's were clearly marked for a reader has an echo in a modern phrase: people who are required to make small finishing touches to a project are said to be 'dotting the I's and crossing the T's'.

The shape of the capital letter I is the simplest imaginable, being just a single vertical line. So when the Romans designed a system for writing numerals based on the letters of their alphabet, they chose I to represent the number 1. This number had previously been indicated by a simple stroke, which made it easy to keep a tally by marking notches in a stick. This system was preserved in roman numerals, with the number 'two' being written as 'II', and so on.

In recent times the letter I has become one of the most fashionable letters of the alphabet on account of its association with information technology. The Apple Corporation introduced a portable music player called the 'iPod' in 2001, and this proved so successful that the letter I has become synonymous with cutting-edge technology. The use of I was proliferated by Apple in later products such as the 'iPhone' and the website 'iTunes'. Other corporations have not been slow in exploiting the letter's new-found mystique, as when the BBC dubbed their play-on-demand service the 'iPlayer'.

i the imaginary number √−1

I¹ *pron* used by a speaker or writer to refer to himself or herself as the subject of a verb
WORD ORIGIN Old English *ic*

I² 1 *chem* iodine 2 the Roman numeral for one

I. 1 Independent 2 Institute 3 International 4 Island; Isle

IA Iowa

iamb (**eye**-am) *or* **iambus** *n, pl* **iambs** *or* **iambuses** *prosody* a metrical foot of two syllables, a short one followed by a long one
WORD ORIGIN Greek *iambos*

iambic (eye-**am**-bik) *prosody adj* 1 written in metrical units of one short and one long syllable ▷ *n* 2 an iambic foot, line, or stanza

IBA (in Britain) Independent Broadcasting Authority

Iberian *adj* 1 of Iberia, the peninsula made up of Spain and Portugal ▷ *n* 2 a person from Iberia

ibex (**ibe**-eks) *n, pl* **ibexes** *or* **ibex** a wild mountain goat with large backward-curving horns
WORD ORIGIN Latin: chamois

ibid. in the same place: used to refer to a book, page, or passage previously cited

WORD ORIGIN Latin *ibidem*

ibis (**ibe**-iss) *n, pl* **ibises** *or* **ibis** a large wading bird with a long thin curved bill
WORD ORIGIN Egyptian *hby*

Ibo (**ee**-boh) *n* 1 *pl* **Ibos** *or* **Ibo** a member of an African people of S Nigeria 2 their language

ICBM intercontinental ballistic missile

ice *n* 1 water that has frozen and become solid 2 *chiefly Brit* a portion of ice cream 3 **break the ice** to relax the atmosphere, esp. between strangers 4 **on ice** in readiness or reserve 5 **on thin ice** in a dangerous situation: *he knew he was on thin ice* 6 **the Ice** *NZ informal* Antarctica ▷ *vb* **icing, iced** 7 (foll. by *up* or *over*) to become covered with ice 8 to cover with icing 9 to cool or chill with ice
WORD ORIGIN Old English *īs*

ice age *n* any period of time during which a large part of the earth's surface was covered with ice, caused by the advance of glaciers

ice beer *n* a beer that is chilled after brewing so that any water is turned to ice and then removed

iceberg *n* 1 a large mass of ice floating in the sea 2 **tip of the iceberg** the small visible part of a problem that is much larger

WORD ORIGIN probably Middle Dutch *ijsberg* ice mountain

iceberg lettuce *n* a type of lettuce with very crisp pale leaves tightly enfolded

iceboat *n* another name for **icebreaker**

icebox *n* 1 *US & Canad* a refrigerator 2 a compartment in a refrigerator for making or storing ice 3 a container packed with ice for keeping food and drink cold

icebreaker *n* a ship designed to break a channel through ice

icecap *n* a thick mass of glacial ice that permanently covers an area

ice cream *n* a sweet frozen food, made from cream, milk, or a custard base, flavoured in various ways

iced *adj* 1 served very cold 2 covered with icing

ice field *n* a large expanse of floating sea ice

ice floe *n* a sheet of ice floating in the sea

ice hockey *n* a game like hockey played on ice by two teams wearing skates

Icelander *n* a person from Iceland

Icelandic *adj* 1 of Iceland ▷ *n* 2 the official language of Iceland

ice lolly *n* *Brit informal* a water ice or an ice cream on a stick

ice pack *n* **1** a bag or folded cloth containing crushed ice, applied to a part of the body to reduce swelling **2** same as **pack ice**

ice skate *n* **1** a boot with a steel blade fitted to the sole which enables the wearer to glide over ice ▷ *vb* **ice-skate, -skating, -skated 2** to glide over ice on ice skates **ice-skater** *n*

icewine *n Canad* a dessert wine made from grapes that have frozen before being harvested

I Ching *n* an ancient Chinese book of divination and a source of Confucian and Taoist philosophy

ichneumon (ik-**new**-mon) *n* a greyish-brown mongoose

ichthyology (ik-thi-**ol**-a-jee) *n* the study of fishes **ichthyological** *adj* **ichthyologist** *n*
WORD ORIGIN Greek *ikhthus* fish + -LOGY

icicle *n* a tapering spike of ice hanging where water has dripped
WORD ORIGIN from ICE + Old English *gicel* icicle

icing *n* **1** Also (esp. US and Canad.): **frosting** a mixture of sugar and water or egg whites used to cover and decorate cakes **2** the formation of ice on a ship or aircraft **3 icing on the cake** any unexpected extra or bonus

icing sugar *n* a very finely ground sugar used for making icing or sweets

icon *or* **ikon** *n* **1** a picture of Christ, the Virgin Mary, or a saint, venerated in the Orthodox Church **2** a picture on a computer screen representing a computer function that can be activated by moving the cursor over it **3** a person or thing regarded as a symbol of a belief or cultural movement: *a feminist icon*
WORD ORIGIN Greek *eikōn* image

iconoclast *n* **1** a person who attacks established or traditional ideas or principles **2** a destroyer of religious images or objects **iconoclastic** *adj* **iconoclasm** *n*
WORD ORIGIN Late Greek *eikōn* icon + *klastēs* breaker

icosahedron (ike-oh-sa-**heed**-ron) *n, pl* **-drons** *or* **-dra** (-dra) a solid figure with 20 faces
WORD ORIGIN Greek *eikosi* twenty + *-edron* -sided

icy *adj* **icier, iciest 1** freezing or very cold **2** covered with ice: *an icy runway* **3** cold or reserved in manner **icily** *adv* **iciness** *n*

id *n psychoanal* the primitive instincts and energies in the unconscious mind that underlie all psychological impulses
WORD ORIGIN Latin: it

ID 1 Idaho **2** identification

Id. Idaho

I'd I had *or* I would

idea *n* **1** any product of mental activity; thought **2** a scheme, intention, or plan **3** the thought of something: *the idea excites me* **4** a belief or opinion **5** a vague notion; inkling: *they had no idea of the severity of my injuries* **6** a person's conception of something: *his idea of integrity is not the same as mine* **7** aim or purpose: *the idea is to economize on transport* **8** *philosophy* (in Plato) a universal model of which all things in the same class are only imperfect imitations
WORD ORIGIN Greek: model, outward appearance

≣ USAGE
It is usually considered correct to say that someone has *the idea of doing* something, rather than *the idea to do it*: *he had the idea of taking* (not *the idea to take*) *a short holiday*.

ideal *n* **1** (*often pl*) a principle or model of ethical behaviour **2** a conception of something that is perfect **3** a person or thing considered to represent perfection **4** something existing only as an idea ▷ *adj* **5** most suitable: *they seem to have adopted an ideal man as their candidate* **6** of, involving, or existing only as an idea; imaginary: *an ideal world* **ideally** *adv*

idealism *n* **1** belief in or striving towards ideals **2** the tendency to represent things in their ideal forms, rather than as they are **3** *philosophy* the doctrine that material objects and the external world do not exist in reality, but are creations of the mind **idealist** *n* **idealistic** *adj*

idealize *or* **-lise** *vb* **-lizing, -lized** *or* **-lising, -ised** to consider or represent (something) as ideal or more nearly perfect than is true **idealization** *or* **-lisation** *n*

idée fixe (ee-day **feeks**) *n, pl* **idées fixes** (ee-day **feeks**) an idea with which a person is obsessed
WORD ORIGIN French

idem *pron, adj* the same: used to refer to an article, chapter, or book already quoted
WORD ORIGIN Latin

identical *adj* **1** that is the same: *they got the identical motel room as last year* **2** exactly alike or equal **3** (of twins) developed from a single fertilized ovum that has split into two, and thus of the same sex and very much alike **identically** *adv*
WORD ORIGIN Latin *idem* the same

identification parade *n* a group of people, including one suspected of a crime, assembled to discover whether a witness can identify the suspect

identify *vb* **-fies, -fying, -fied 1** to prove or recognize as being a certain person or thing; determine the identity of **2** (*often foll. by with*) to understand and sympathize with a person or group because one regards oneself as being similar or similarly situated **3** to consider or treat as the same **4** to connect or associate closely: *he was closely identified with the community charge* **identifiable** *adj* **identification** *n*

Identikit *n* **1** *trademark* a composite picture, assembled from descriptions given, of a person wanted by the police ▷ *adj* **2** artificially created; formulaic: *an identikit pop group* **3** stereotypical: *the identikit Scots midfield mauler*

identity *n, pl* **-ties 1** the state of being a specified person or thing: *the identity of his murderers was not immediately established* **2** the individual characteristics by which a person or thing is recognized **3** the state of being the same **4** *maths*

Also called: **identity element** a member of a set that when combined with any other member of the set, leaves it unchanged: the identity for multiplication of numbers is 1
WORD ORIGIN Latin *idem* the same

identity theft *n* the crime of fraudulently setting up and using bank accounts, credit facilities, etc. in another person's name

ideo- *combining form* of or indicating ideas: *ideology*
WORD ORIGIN from French *idéo-*, from Greek *idea* idea

ideogram *or* **ideograph** *n* a character or symbol that directly represents a concept or thing, rather than from its name
WORD ORIGIN Greek *idea* idea + *gramma* a drawing

ideology *n, pl* **-gies** the body of ideas and beliefs of a person, group, or nation **ideological** *adj* **ideologically** *adv* **ideologist** *n*
WORD ORIGIN from IDEO- + -LOGY

ides *n* (in the ancient Roman calendar) the 15th day in March, May, July, and October and the 13th of the other months
WORD ORIGIN Latin *idus*

idiocy *n, pl* **-cies 1** utter stupidity **2** a foolish act or remark

idiom *n* **1** a group of words which, when used together, have a different meaning from the one suggested by the individual words, eg *it was raining cats and dogs* **2** linguistic usage that is grammatical and natural to native speakers **3** the characteristic vocabulary or usage of a person or group **4** the characteristic artistic style of an individual or school **idiomatic** *adj*
WORD ORIGIN Greek *idios* private, separate

idiosyncrasy *n, pl* **-sies** a personal peculiarity of mind, habit, or behaviour; quirk **idiosyncratic** *adj*
WORD ORIGIN Greek *idios* private, separate + *sunkrasis* mixture

idiot *n* **1** a foolish or senseless person **2** *no longer in technical use* a person with severe mental retardation **idiotic** *adj* **idiotically** *adv*
WORD ORIGIN Greek *idiōtēs* private person, ignoramus

idle *adj* **1** not doing anything **2** not operating or being used **3** not wanting to work; lazy **4** ineffective or useless: *it would be idle to look for a solution at this stage* **5** frivolous or trivial: *idle pleasures* **6** without basis; unfounded: *idle rumours* ▷ *vb* **idling, idled 7** (*often foll. by away*) to waste or pass (time) in idleness **8** (of an engine) to run at low speed without transmitting any power **idleness** *n* **idler** *n* **idly** *adv*
WORD ORIGIN Old English *īdel*

idol (**eye**-dl) *n* **1** an object of excessive devotion or admiration **2** an image of a god used as an object of worship
WORD ORIGIN Greek *eidōlon* image

idolatry (ide-**ol**-a-tree) *n* **1** the worship of idols **2** excessive devotion or reverence **idolater** *n* **idolatrous** *adj*

idolize *or* **-lise** *vb* **-lizing, -lized** *or* **-lising, -lised 1** to love or admire excessively

2 to worship as an idol **idolization** or **-lisation** n

idyll or US sometimes **idyl** (**id**-ill) n **1** a scene or time of peace and happiness **2** a poem or prose work describing a charming rural scene or episode **idyllic** adj
WORD ORIGIN Greek *eidullion*

i.e. that is to say
WORD ORIGIN Latin *id est*

IED improvised explosive device

if conj **1** in the event that, or on condition that: *if you work hard you'll succeed* **2** used to introduce an indirect question to which the answer is either *yes* or *no*; whether: *it doesn't matter if the play is any good or not* **3** even though: *a splendid if slightly decaying house* **4** used to introduce an unfulfilled wish, with only: *if only you had told her* ▷ n **5** a condition or stipulation: *there are no hidden ifs or buts*
WORD ORIGIN Old English *gif*

iffy adj **iffier, iffiest**, *informal* full of uncertainty

igloo n, pl **-loos** a dome-shaped Inuit house, built of blocks of solid snow
WORD ORIGIN Inuktitut *igdlu*

igneous (**ig**-nee-uss) adj **1** (of rocks) formed as molten rock cools and hardens **2** of or like fire
WORD ORIGIN Latin *ignis* fire

ignis fatuus (**ig**-niss **fat**-yew-uss) n, pl **ignes fatui** (**ig**-neez **fat**-yew-eye) same as **will-o'-the-wisp**
WORD ORIGIN Medieval Latin, literally: foolish fire

ignite vb **-niting, -nited 1** to catch fire **2** to set fire to **ignitable** adj
WORD ORIGIN Latin *ignis* fire

ignition n **1** the system used to ignite the fuel in an internal-combustion engine **2** an igniting or the process of igniting

ignoble adj **1** dishonourable **2** of low birth or origins **ignobly** adv
WORD ORIGIN Latin *in-* not + *nobilis* noble

ignominy (**ig**-nom-in-ee) n, pl **-minies** disgrace or public shame: *the ignominy of being replaced* **ignominious** adj
WORD ORIGIN Latin *ignominia* disgrace

ignoramus n, pl **-muses** an ignorant person
WORD ORIGIN Latin, literally: we have no knowledge of

ignorance n lack of knowledge or education

ignorant adj **1** lacking in knowledge or education **2** rude through lack of knowledge of good manners: *an ignorant remark* **3 ignorant of** lacking in awareness or knowledge of: *ignorant of Asian culture*

ignore vb **-noring, -nored** to refuse to notice; disregard deliberately
WORD ORIGIN Latin *ignorare* not to know

iguana n a large tropical tree lizard of the W Indies and S America with a spiny back
WORD ORIGIN S American Indian *iwana*

ikebana (eek-a-**bah**-na) n the Japanese art of flower arrangement
WORD ORIGIN Japanese

ikon n same as **icon**

IL Illinois

il- prefix same as **in-¹** or **in-²**

ileum n the third and lowest part of the small intestine
WORD ORIGIN Latin: flank, groin

ilex n **1** a genus of trees or shrubs that includes holly **2** same as **holm oak**
WORD ORIGIN Latin

ilium n, pl **-ia** the uppermost and widest of the three sections of the hipbone

ilk n a type or class: *three or four others of the same ilk*
WORD ORIGIN Old English *ilca* the same family
USAGE Although the use of *ilk* to mean *a type or class* is sometimes condemned as being the result of a misunderstanding of a Scottish expression *of that ilk*, it is nevertheless well established and generally acceptable.

ill adj **worse, worst 1** not in good health **2** bad, harmful, or hostile: *ill effects* **3** promising an unfavourable outcome: *ill omen* **4 ill at ease** unable to relax ▷ n **5** evil or harm ▷ adv **6** badly, wrongly: *the title ill befits him* **7** with difficulty; hardly: *we can ill afford another scandal*
WORD ORIGIN Old Norse *illr* bad

ill. 1 illustrated **2** illustration

Ill. Illinois

I'll I will or I shall

ill-advised adj **1** (of a plan or action) badly thought out **2** (of a person) acting without reasonable care or thought

ill-bred adj lacking good manners **ill-breeding** n

ill-disposed adj unfriendly or unsympathetic

illegal adj against the law **illegally** adv **illegality** n

illegible adj unable to be read or deciphered **illegibility** n

illegitimate adj **1** born of parents who were not married to each other at the time **2** illegal; unlawful **illegitimacy** n

ill-fated adj doomed or unlucky

ill-favoured adj ugly or unattractive

ill-founded adj not based on proper proof or evidence

ill-gotten adj obtained dishonestly or illegally: *ill-gotten gains*

ill-health n the condition of being unwell

illiberal adj **1** narrow-minded or intolerant **2** not generous; mean **3** lacking in culture or refinement **illiberality** n

illicit adj **1** same as **illegal 2** forbidden or disapproved of by society: *an illicit kiss*

illiterate adj **1** unable to read and write **2** uneducated or ignorant: *linguistically illiterate* ▷ n **3** an illiterate person **illiteracy** n

ill-mannered adj having bad manners

illness n **1** a disease or indisposition **2** a state of ill health

illogical adj **1** senseless or unreasonable **2** not following logical principles **illogicality** n **illogically** adv

ill-starred adj very unlucky or unfortunate

ill-tempered adj having a bad temper

ill-timed adj done or happening at an unsuitable time

ill-treat vb to treat cruelly or harshly **ill-treatment** n

illuminant n **1** something that gives off light ▷ adj **2** giving off light

illuminate vb **-nating, -nated 1** to light up **2** to make easily understood; explain: *the report obscures rather than illuminates the most relevant facts* **3** to decorate with lights **4** to decorate (an initial letter or manuscript) with designs of gold, silver, or bright colours **illuminating** adj **illuminative** adj
WORD ORIGIN Latin *illuminare* to light up

illumination n **1** an illuminating or being illuminated **2** a source of light **3 illuminations** *chiefly Brit* lights used as decorations in streets or towns **4** the decoration in colours, gold, or silver used on some manuscripts

illumine vb **-mining, -mined** *literary* same as **illuminate**

illusion n **1** a false appearance or deceptive impression of reality: *her upswept hair gave the illusion of above average height* **2** a false or misleading idea or belief: *we may suffer from the illusion that we are special*
WORD ORIGIN Latin *illusio* deceit

illusionist n a conjuror

illusory or **illusive** adj seeming to be true, but actually false: *the economic benefits of such reforms were largely illusory*
USAGE *Illusive* is sometimes wrongly used where *elusive* is meant: *they fought hard, but victory remained elusive* (not *illusive*).

illustrate vb **-trating, -trated 1** to clarify or explain by use of examples or comparisons **2** to provide (a book or text) with pictures **3** to be an example of **illustrative** adj **illustrator** n
WORD ORIGIN Latin *illustrare* to make light, explain

illustration n **1** a picture or diagram used to explain or decorate a text **2** an example: *an illustration of the brutality of the regime* **3** the art of illustrating

illustrious adj famous and distinguished
WORD ORIGIN Latin *illustris* bright, famous

ill will n unkind feeling; hostility

IM instant messaging

I'm I am

im- prefix same as **in-¹** or **in-²**

image n **1** a mental picture of someone or something produced by the imagination or memory **2** the appearance or impression given to the public by a person or organization **3** a simile or metaphor **4** a representation of a person or thing in a work of art or literature **5** an optical reproduction of an object, formed by the lens of an eye or camera, or by a mirror **6** a person or thing that resembles another closely **7** a personification of a specified quality; epitome: *the image of good breeding* ▷ vb **-imaging, -imaged 8** to picture in the mind **9** to mirror or reflect an image of

The Influence of Arabic on English

Arabic is not just the language of the peoples of Arabia, but also the major language of the whole Islamic world. The spread of Islam from the 7th century AD brought Arabic out of the Arabian peninsula and into other areas of Asia and North Africa, and it was soon starting to leave its mark on European languages.

Between the 8th and 12th centuries, Arab scholars made great advances in science and mathematics, so when European scholars began to take an interest in such subjects it was to the Arab world that they turned for enlightenment. Thus astronomical terms such as 'zenith' (literally 'the path over one's head'), 'nadir' ('the opposite path') and 'azimuth' ('the paths') come from Arabic. In mathematics, the greatest influence of Arab scholarship was in providing a system of numbers to replace the cumbersome Roman numerals, but the Arabic language is also the source of important words such as 'zero' (from *sifr*, meaning 'empty') and 'average' (which derives from a mercantile term referring to compensation for damaged goods).

Arabic culture also permeated westwards in other ways. The conquest of Spain by the Moors brought many Arabic words into the Spanish language, and some of these words later found their way from Spanish into English, often through the intermediary of French. Our modern words 'alcove', 'jar', and 'hazard' all took this circuitous route.

Another form of contact with Arabs came through the Crusades, which saw European Christians travelling to Arabic-speaking countries in large numbers. And when Europeans were not fighting with people from the Arab world they remained in contact through trade, and the names of objects that they bought from the Arabs entered the English vocabulary, either directly or through other European languages.

Quite a few of the Arabic words that have entered English betray their origins by beginning with letters 'al-'. The word *al* is the definite article in Arabic, and often remained attached to a word when it was translated. Thus 'albatross' was originally *al-ghattās* (the white sea eagle); 'alchemy' was *al-kīmiyā'* (the transmutation); 'alcohol' was *al-kuhl* (the antimony powder);

and 'algebra' was *al-jabr* (the reunification). The words 'alfalfa', 'algorithm', 'alkali', and 'almanac' similarly retain the Arabic definite article in their modern English forms.

Among the items that Arabs sold to European merchants were various types of fruit that flourished only in warmer climates. Thus the words 'orange', 'apricot', 'lemon', and 'lime' can all be traced back to Arabic. Other foodstuffs whose names come from Arabic words include coffee, sugar, sherbet, sesame, spinach, and syrup.

The Arab traders also dealt in cloth, and the English word 'satin' comes from an Arabic form of Tseutung, the place in China from where the cloth was exported. The English words 'sequin' and 'cotton' are likewise of Arabic descent.

The example of 'satin' is a reminder that Arabic has not simply supplied its own native words, but has also acted as a conduit for words from other Asian languages to enter English. Words of Persian origin, such as 'jasmine', 'talc', and 'lilac', have come into English via Arabic, and Arabic has even been a staging post for words of Chinese origin, such as 'typhoon'.

English has long had cause to use Arabic words to describe items relating to Islamic culture. Arabic words such as 'sheikh', 'sultan', 'emir', 'mosque', and 'harem' are well established in English from travellers' tales and translations of stories such as *The Thousand and One Nights*. More recent immigration from Islamic countries has brought a sharp increase in the number of Arabic words that have been adopted into English. The names of items of clothing such as the 'jilbab' and 'burqa' and foods such as 'tahini' are no longer regarded as exotic borrowings but are considered to be standard English words. At the same time, political events have brought Arabic words such as 'fatwa', 'intifada', and 'jihad' into common parlance.

With the Islamic world playing such an important role in world events in the twenty-first century, it is probable that Arabic words will continue to feature prominently in the development of the English language.

10 to portray or describe
WORD ORIGIN Latin *imago*

imagery *n, pl* **-ries 1** figurative or descriptive language in a literary work **2** mental images **3** images collectively, esp. statues or carvings

imaginary *adj* **1** existing only in the imagination **2** *maths* relating to the square root of a negative number

imagination *n* **1** the faculty or action of producing mental images of what is not present or in one's experience **2** creative mental ability

imaginative *adj* **1** produced by or showing a creative imagination **2** having a vivid imagination

imagine *vb* **-ining, -ined 1** to form a mental image of **2** to think, believe, or guess: *I would imagine they'll be here soon* **imaginable** *adj*
WORD ORIGIN Latin *imaginari*

imaginings *pl n* speculative thoughts about what might be the case or what might happen; fantasies: *lurid imaginings*

imago (im-**may**-go) *n, pl* **imagoes** or **imagines** (im-**maj**-in-eez) a sexually mature adult insect
WORD ORIGIN Latin: likeness

imam *n Islam* **1** a leader of congregational prayer in a mosque **2** the title of some Muslim leaders
WORD ORIGIN Arabic

IMAX (**eye**-max) *n* a film projection process that produces an image ten times larger than standard

imbalance *n* a lack of balance, for instance in emphasis or proportion: *a chemical imbalance in the brain*

imbecile (**im**-biss-eel) *n* **1** *informal* an extremely stupid person **2** *old-fashioned* a person of abnormally low intelligence ▷ *adj* **3** stupid or senseless: *imbecile fanaticism* **imbecility** *n*
WORD ORIGIN Latin *imbecillus* feeble

imbed *vb* **-bedding, -bedded** same as **embed**

imbibe *vb* **-bibing, -bibed** *formal* **1** to drink (alcoholic drinks) **2** to take in or assimilate (ideas): *values she had imbibed as a child*
WORD ORIGIN Latin *imbibere*

imbroglio (imb-**role**-ee-oh) *n, pl* **-glios** a confusing and complicated situation
WORD ORIGIN Italian

imbue *vb* **-buing, -bued** to fill or inspire (with ideals or principles)
WORD ORIGIN Latin *imbuere* to stain

IMF International Monetary Fund

imitate *vb* **-tating, -tated 1** to copy the manner or style of, or take as a model: *he remains rock's most imitated guitarist* **2** to mimic or impersonate, esp. for amusement **3** to make a copy or reproduction of; duplicate **imitable** *adj* **imitator** *n*
WORD ORIGIN Latin *imitari*

imitation *n* **1** a copy of an original or genuine article **2** an instance of imitating someone: *her Coward imitations were not the best thing she did* **3** behaviour modelled on the behaviour of someone else: *to learn by imitation* ▷ *adj* **4** made to resemble something which is usually superior or more expensive: *imitation leather*

imitative *adj* **1** imitating or tending to copy **2** copying or reproducing an original, esp. in an inferior manner: *imitative painting* **3** onomatopoeic

immaculate *adj* **1** completely clean or tidy: *an immaculate pinstripe suit* **2** completely flawless: *his equestrian pedigree is immaculate* **immaculately** *adv*
WORD ORIGIN Latin *in-* not + *macula* blemish

immanent *adj* **1** present within and throughout something **2** (of God) present throughout the universe **immanence** *n*
WORD ORIGIN Latin *immanere* to remain in

immaterial *adj* **1** of no real importance or relevance **2** not formed of matter

immature *adj* **1** not fully grown or developed **2** lacking wisdom, insight, or stability because of youth **immaturity** *n*

immeasurable *adj* too great to be measured **immeasurably** *adv*

immediate *adj* **1** taking place without delay: *an immediate cut in interest rates* **2** next or nearest in space, time, or relationship: *our immediate neighbour* **3** present; current: *they had no immediate plans to close it* **immediacy** *n* **immediately** *adv*
WORD ORIGIN Latin *in-* not + *mediare* to be in the middle

immemorial *adj* having existed or happened for longer than anyone can remember: *this has been the custom since time immemorial*

immense *adj* **1** huge or vast **2** *informal* very great **immensely** *adv* **immensity** *n*
WORD ORIGIN Latin *immensus* unmeasured

immerse *vb* **-mersing, -mersed 1** to plunge or dip into liquid **2** to involve deeply: *he immersed himself in the history of Rome* **3** to baptize by dipping the whole body into water **immersion** *n*
WORD ORIGIN Latin *immergere*

immersion heater *n* an electrical device in a domestic hot-water tank for heating water

immigrant *n* a person who comes to a foreign country in order to settle there

immigration *n* the act of coming to a foreign country in order to settle there **immigrate** *vb*
WORD ORIGIN Latin *immigrare* to go into

imminent *adj* likely to happen soon **imminence** *n*
WORD ORIGIN Latin *imminere* to project over

immiscible *adj* (of liquids) incapable of being mixed: *oil and water are immiscible* **immiscibility** *n*

immobile *adj* **1** not moving **2** not able to move or be moved **immobility** *n*

immobilize *or* **-lise** *vb* **-lizing, -lized** *or* **-lising, -lised** to make unable to move or work: *a device for immobilizing steering wheels* **immobilization** *or* **-lisation** *n*

immoderate *adj* excessive or unreasonable: *immoderate consumption of alcohol* **immoderately** *adv*

immodest *adj* **1** behaving in an indecent or improper manner

2 behaving in a boastful or conceited manner **immodesty** *n*

immolate *vb* **-lating, -lated** *literary* to kill or offer as a sacrifice, esp. by fire **immolation** *n*
WORD ORIGIN Latin *immolare*

immoral *adj* **1** morally wrong; corrupt **2** sexually depraved or promiscuous **immorality** *n*

immortal *adj* **1** not subject to death or decay **2** famous for all time **3** everlasting ▷ *n* **4** a person whose fame will last for all time **5** an immortal being **immortality** *n*

immortalize *or* **-ise** *vb* **-izing, -ized** *or* **-ising, -ised 1** to give everlasting fame to: *a name immortalized by countless writers* **2** to give immortality to

immovable *or* **immoveable** *adj* **1** unable to be moved **2** unwilling to change one's opinions or beliefs **3** not affected by feeling; emotionless **4** unchanging **5** *law* (of property) consisting of land or houses **immovability** *or* **immoveability** *n* **immovably** *or* **immoveably** *adv*

immune *adj* **1** protected against a specific disease by inoculation or as the result of natural resistance **2** exempt from obligation or penalty **3** immune to secure against: *football is not immune to economic recession*
WORD ORIGIN Latin *immunis* exempt from a public service

immune system *n* the mechanism by which a body reacts to foreign materials, involving the production of antibodies

immunity *n, pl* **-ties 1** the ability of an organism to resist disease **2** freedom from prosecution, tax, etc.

immunize *or* **-nise** *vb* **-nizing, -nized** *or* **-nising, -nised** to make (someone) immune to a disease, esp. by inoculation **immunization** *or* **-nisation** *n*

immunodeficiency *n* a deficiency in or breakdown of a person's ability to fight diseases

immunology *n* the branch of medicine concerned with the study of immunity **immunological** *adj* **immunologist** *n*

immure *vb* **-muring, -mured 1** *archaic* or *literary* to imprison **2** to shut (oneself) away from society
WORD ORIGIN Latin *im-* in + *murus* wall

immutable (im-**mute**-a-bl) *adj* unchangeable or unchanging: *the immutable sequence of night and day* **immutability** *n*

imp *n* **1** a small demon **2** a mischievous child
WORD ORIGIN Old English *impa* bud, hence offspring, child

imp. 1 imperative **2** imperfect

impact *n* **1** the effect or impression made by something **2** the act of one object striking another; collision **3** the force of a collision ▷ *vb* **4** to press firmly against or into **5** impact on to have an effect on **impaction** *n*
WORD ORIGIN Latin *impactus* pushed against

impacted *adj* (of a tooth) unable to grow out because of being wedged against another tooth below the gum

impair *vb* to damage or weaken in strength or quality **impairment** *n*
WORD ORIGIN Old French *empeirer* to make worse

impala (imp-**ah**-la) *n, pl* **-las** *or* **-la** an African antelope with lyre-shaped horns
WORD ORIGIN Zulu

impale *vb* **-paling, -paled** to pierce through or fix with a sharp object: *they impaled his severed head on a spear* **impalement** *n*
WORD ORIGIN Latin *im-* on + *palus* pole

impalpable *adj formal* **1** not able to be felt by touching: *impalpable shadows* **2** difficult to understand **impalpability** *n*

impart *vb* **1** to communicate (information or knowledge) **2** to give (a specified quality): *flavouring to impart a sweet taste*
WORD ORIGIN Latin *im-* in + *partire* to share

impartial *adj* not favouring one side or the other **impartiality** *n* **impartially** *adv*

impassable *adj* (of terrain or roads) not able to be travelled through or over **impassability** *n*

impasse (**am**-pass) *n* a situation in which progress or escape is impossible
WORD ORIGIN French

impassible *adj* **1** *rare* not susceptible to pain or injury **2** impassive; unmoved **impassibility** *or* **impassibleness** *n*

impassioned *adj* full of emotion: *an impassioned plea to the United Nations*

impassive *adj* not showing or feeling emotion **impassively** *adv* **impassivity** *n*

impasto *n* the technique of applying paint thickly, so that brush marks are evident
WORD ORIGIN Italian

impatient *adj* **1** irritable at any delay or difficulty **2** restless to have or do something **impatience** *n* **impatiently** *adv*

impeach *vb* **1** *chiefly US* to charge (a public official) with an offence committed in office **2** *Austral & Brit criminal law* to accuse of treason or serious crime **3** to challenge or question (a person's honesty or honour) **impeachable** *adj* **impeachment** *n*
WORD ORIGIN Late Latin *impedicare* to entangle

impeccable *adj* without flaw or error: *impeccable manners* **impeccably** *adv*
WORD ORIGIN Latin *in-* not + *peccare* to sin

impecunious *adj formal* without money; penniless
WORD ORIGIN Latin *in-* not + *pecuniosus* wealthy

impedance (imp-**eed**-anss) *n electronics* the total effective resistance in an electric circuit to the flow of an alternating current

impede *vb* **-peding, -peded** to block or make progress or action difficult
WORD ORIGIN Latin *impedire*

impediment *n* **1** a hindrance or obstruction **2** a physical disability that makes speech or walking difficult

impedimenta *pl n* any objects that impede progress, esp. the baggage and equipment carried by an army

impel *vb* **-pelling, -pelled** **1** to urge or force (a person) to do something **2** to push, drive, or force into motion
WORD ORIGIN Latin *impellere* to drive forward

impending *adj* (esp. of something bad) about to happen
WORD ORIGIN Latin *impendere* to overhang

impenetrable *adj* **1** impossible to get through: *an impenetrable barrier* **2** impossible to understand **3** not receptive to ideas or influence: *impenetrable ignorance* **impenetrability** *n* **impenetrably** *adv*

impenitent *adj* not sorry or penitent **impenitence** *n*

imperative *adj* **1** extremely urgent; essential **2** commanding or authoritative: *an imperative tone of voice* **3** *grammar* denoting a mood of verbs used in commands ▷ *n* **4** *grammar* the imperative mood
WORD ORIGIN Latin *imperare* to command

imperceptible *adj* too slight, subtle, or gradual to be noticed **imperceptibly** *adv*

imperfect *adj* **1** having faults or errors **2** not complete **3** *grammar* denoting a tense of verbs describing continuous, incomplete, or repeated past actions ▷ *n* **4** *grammar* the imperfect tense **imperfectly** *adv*

imperfection *n* **1** the state of being imperfect **2** a fault or defect

imperial *adj* **1** of an empire, emperor, or empress **2** majestic; commanding **3** exercising supreme authority; imperious **4** (of weights or measures) conforming to the standards of a system formerly official in Great Britain ▷ *n* **5** a wine bottle holding the equivalent of eight normal bottles
WORD ORIGIN Latin *imperium* authority

imperialism *n* **1** the policy or practice of extending a country's influence over other territories by conquest, colonization, or economic domination **2** an imperial system, authority, or government **imperialist** *adj, n* **imperialistic** *adj*

imperil *vb* **-rilling, -rilled** *or US* **-riling, -riled** *formal* to put in danger

imperious *adj* used to being obeyed; domineering **imperiously** *adv*
WORD ORIGIN Latin *imperium* power

imperishable *adj* unable to disappear or be destroyed

impermanent *adj* not permanent; fleeting **impermanence** *n*

impermeable *adj* (of a substance) not allowing fluid to pass through: *an impermeable layer* **impermeability** *n*

impermissible *adj* not allowed

impersonal *adj* **1** without reference to any individual person; objective: *Buddhism began as a very impersonal doctrine* **2** without human warmth or sympathy: *an impersonal manner* **3** *grammar* **a** (of a verb) having no subject, as in *it is raining* **b** (of a pronoun) not referring to a person **impersonality** *n* **impersonally** *adv*

impersonate *vb* **-ating, -ated** **1** to pretend to be (another person) **2** to imitate the character or mannerisms of (another person) for entertainment **impersonation** *n* **impersonator** *n*

impertinent *adj* disrespectful or rude **impertinence** *n*
WORD ORIGIN Latin *impertinens* not belonging

imperturbable *adj* not easily upset; calm **imperturbability** *n* **imperturbably** *adv*

impervious *adj* **1** not letting water etc. through **2** not influenced by a feeling, argument, etc.

impetigo (imp-it-**tie**-go) *n* a contagious skin disease causing spots or pimples
WORD ORIGIN Latin: scabby eruption

impetuous *adj* **1** acting without consideration **2** done rashly or hastily **impetuosity** *n*
WORD ORIGIN Late Latin *impetuosus* violent

impetus (**imp**-it-uss) *n, pl* **-tuses** **1** an incentive or impulse **2** *physics* the force that starts a body moving or that tends to resist changes in its speed or direction once it is moving
WORD ORIGIN Latin: attack

impi *n, pl* **-pi** *or* **-pies** a group of Zulu warriors
WORD ORIGIN Nguni (language group of southern Africa) *impi* regiment, army

impiety *n* lack of respect or religious reverence

impinge *vb* **-pinging, -pinged** (often foll. by *on*) to encroach (on), affect or restrict: *international economic forces impinging on the local economy* **impingement** *n*
WORD ORIGIN Latin *impingere* to dash against

impious (**imp**-e-uss) *adj* showing a lack of respect or religious reverence

impish *adj* mischievous **impishness** *n*

implacable *adj* **1** incapable of being appeased or pacified **2** unyielding **implacability** *n* **implacably** *adv*

implant *vb* **1** to fix firmly in the mind: *to implant sound moral principles* **2** to plant or embed **3** *surgery* to graft or insert (a tissue or hormone) into the body ▷ *n* **4** anything implanted in the body, such as a tissue graft **implantation** *n*

implausible *adj* not easy to believe **implausibility** *n*

implement *vb* **1** to carry out (instructions etc.): *she refused to implement the agreed plan* ▷ *n* **2** a tool or other piece of equipment **implementation** *n*
WORD ORIGIN Late Latin *implementum*, literally: a filling up

implicate *vb* **-cating, -cated** **1** to show (someone) to be involved, esp. in a crime **2** to imply
WORD ORIGIN Latin *implicare* to involve

implication *n* **1** something that is suggested or implied **2** an act or instance of suggesting, implying, or being implied **3** a probable consequence (of something)

implicit *adj* **1** expressed indirectly: *an implicit agreement* **2** absolute and unquestioning: *implicit trust* **3** contained in, although not stated openly: *this view*

of the mind was implicit in all his work **implicitly** *adv*
WORD ORIGIN Latin *implicitus*

implied *adj* hinted at or suggested: *an implied criticism*

implode *vb* **-ploding, -ploded** to collapse inwards
WORD ORIGIN im- in + (ex)plode

implore *vb* **-ploring, -plored** to beg desperately
WORD ORIGIN Latin *implorare*

imply *vb* **-plies, -plying, -plied 1** to express or indicate by a hint; suggest **2** to suggest or involve as a necessary consequence: *a spending commitment implies a corresponding tax imposition*
WORD ORIGIN Old French *emplier*
≡ **USAGE**
≡ See at **infer**.

impolite *adj* discourteous; rude **impoliteness** *n*

impolitic *adj* ill-advised; unwise

imponderable *adj* **1** unable to be weighed or assessed ▷ *n* **2** something difficult or impossible to assess

import *vb* **1** to bring in (goods) from another country **2** *formal* to signify; mean: *to import doom* ▷ *n* **3** something imported **4** *formal* importance: *his new work is of great import* **5** meaning **6** *Canad slang* a sportsman who is not native to the area where he plays **importer** *n* **importation** *n*
WORD ORIGIN Latin *importare* to carry in

important *adj* **1** of great significance, value, or consequence **2** of social significance: *an important man in the company hierarchy* **3** of great concern: *it was important to me to know* **importance** *n* **importantly** *adv*
WORD ORIGIN Medieval Latin *importare* to signify, from Latin: to carry in
≡ **USAGE**
≡ The use of *more importantly* as in *more*
≡ *importantly, the local council is opposed to*
≡ *this proposal* has become very common,
≡ but many people still prefer to use
≡ *more important*.

importunate *adj* *formal* persistent or demanding

importune *vb* **-tuning, -tuned** *formal* to harass with persistent requests **importunity** *n*
WORD ORIGIN Latin *importunus* tiresome

impose *vb* **-posing, -posed 1** to establish (a rule, condition, etc.) as something to be obeyed or complied with **2** to force (oneself) on others **3** *printing* to arrange (pages) in the correct order for printing **4** to pass off (something) deceptively on someone **5 impose on** to take advantage of (a person or quality): *she imposed on his kindness*
WORD ORIGIN Latin *imponere* to place upon

imposing *adj* grand or impressive: *an imposing building*

imposition *n* **1** the act of imposing **2** something imposed, esp. unfairly on someone **3** the arrangement of pages for printing **4** *old-fashioned* a task set as a school punishment

impossibility *n, pl* **-ties 1** the state or quality of being impossible **2** something that is impossible

impossible *adj* **1** not able to be done or to happen **2** absurd or unreasonable **3** *informal* intolerable or outrageous: *those children are impossible* **impossibly** *adv*

impostor *or* **imposter** *n* a person who cheats or swindles by pretending to be someone else
WORD ORIGIN Late Latin *impostor* deceiver

imposture *n* *formal* deception, esp. by pretending to be someone else

impotent (**imp**-a-tent) *adj* **1** not having the power to influence people or events **2** (of a man) incapable of sexual intercourse **impotence** *n*

impound *vb* **1** to take legal possession of; confiscate **2** to confine (an animal) in a pound

impoverish *vb* **1** to make (someone) poor **2** weaken the quality of something **impoverished** *adj* **impoverishment** *n*
WORD ORIGIN Old French *empovrir*

impracticable *adj* **1** not able to be put into practice **2** unsuitable for a desired use **impracticability** *n*

impractical *adj* **1** not sensible or workable: *the use of force was viewed as impractical* **2** not having practical skills **impracticality** *n*

imprecation *n* *formal* a curse **imprecate** *vb*
WORD ORIGIN Latin *imprecari* to invoke

imprecise *adj* inexact or inaccurate **imprecision** *n*

impregnable *adj* **1** unable to be broken into or taken by force: *an impregnable fortress* **2** unable to be affected or overcome: *a confident, impregnable person* **impregnability** *n*
WORD ORIGIN Old French *imprenable*

impregnate *vb* **-nating, -nated 1** to saturate, soak, or fill throughout **2** to make pregnant **3** to imbue or permeate: *the party has been impregnated with an enthusiasm for reform* **impregnation** *n*
WORD ORIGIN Latin in- in + *praegnans* pregnant

impresario *n, pl* **-sarios** a person who runs theatre performances, concerts, etc.
WORD ORIGIN Italian

impress *vb* **1** to make a strong, lasting, or favourable impression on: *he was impressed by the standard of play* **2** to stress or emphasize **3** to imprint or stamp by pressure: *a pattern impressed in paint on the rock* ▷ *n* **4** an impressing **5** a mark produced by impressing **impressible** *adj*
WORD ORIGIN Latin *imprimere* to press into

impression *n* **1** an effect produced in the mind by a person or thing: *she was keen to create a relaxed impression* **2** a vague idea or belief: *he only had a vague impression of how it worked* **3** a strong, favourable, or remarkable effect **4** an impersonation for entertainment **5** an imprint or mark produced by pressing **6** *printing* the number of copies of a publication printed at one time

impressionable *adj* easily impressed or influenced: *the promotion of smoking to the impressionable young* **impressionability** *n*

Impressionism *n* a style of painting developed in 19th-century France, with the aim of reproducing the immediate impression or mood of things, especially the effects of light and atmosphere, rather than form or structure

impressionist *n* **1 Impressionist** an artist who painted in the style of Impressionism **2** a person who imitates the character or mannerisms of another person for entertainment

impressionistic *adj* **1 Impressionistic** of or about Impressionism **2** based on subjective observations or impressions rather than systematic study or facts: *Mitchell was making impressionistic documentaries*

impressive *adj* capable of impressing, esp. by size, magnificence, or importance **impressively** *adv*

imprimatur (imp-rim-**ah**-ter) *n* official approval for something to be printed, usually given by the Roman Catholic Church
WORD ORIGIN New Latin: let it be printed

imprint *n* **1** a mark or impression produced by pressing, printing, or stamping **2** the publisher's name and address, often with the date of publication, printed on the title page of a book ▷ *vb* **3** to produce (a mark) by pressing, printing, or stamping: *T-shirts imprinted with slogans* **4** to establish firmly; impress: *he couldn't dislodge the images imprinted on his brain*

imprison *vb* to confine in or as if in prison **imprisonment** *n*

improbable *adj* not likely or probable **improbability** *n* **improbably** *adv*

improbity *n, pl* **-ties** *formal* dishonesty or wickedness

impromptu *adj* **1** without planning or preparation; improvised ▷ *adv* **2** in a spontaneous or improvised way: *he spoke impromptu* ▷ *n* **3** a short piece of instrumental music resembling improvisation **4** something that is impromptu
WORD ORIGIN Latin *in promptu* in readiness

improper *adj* **1** indecent **2** irregular or incorrect **improperly** *adv*

improper fraction *n* a fraction in which the numerator is greater than the denominator, as $7/6$

impropriety (imp-roe-**pry**-a-tee) *n, pl* **-ties** *formal* unsuitable or slightly improper behaviour

improve *vb* **-proving, -proved 1** to make or become better in quality **2 improve on** to achieve a better standard or quality in comparison with: *both had improved on their previous performance* **improvable** *adj*
WORD ORIGIN Anglo-French *emprouer* to turn to profit

improvement *n* **1** the act of improving or the state of being improved **2** a change that makes something better or adds to its value: *home improvements* **3** *Austral & NZ* a building on a piece of land, adding to its value

improvident *adj* **1** not providing for the future **2** incautious or rash **improvidence** *n*

Collocation

Collocation is a phenomenon that is quite well known now to learners of English, but hardly known at all outside English language teaching. And that's a pity, because collocation explains a great deal. In particular, it explains how students can spend years learning grammar rules and vocabulary, and yet never actually manage to speak English in a way that sounds natural.

Collocation is what makes it possible to guess which word comes [...] Well? Which words would you expect here? Maybe *now*? *After this*? The word that's most likely to spring to mind is *next*. Somehow, we all feel we can finish off sentences people start to say to us. However irritating that may be, what it shows is that we don't create new combinations of words every time we open our mouths. It would be unbearably tiresome if everything we said was original. We'd all sound like poets, setting forth with arcane virtuosity to mingle words in ways afore unheard. The combinations we end up with are arbitrary – but fixed.

Consider the adjectives *wide* and *broad*. Is there any difference in their meaning? In some contexts they're interchangeable. Which of the two goes into the slots in these combinations:

_____ of the mark; _____ awake; company-_____; in _____ daylight; _____-angle lens; _____-screen; _____-brush.

What you see here is that in every case, only one of the words is normal. It would sound odd to use the other. This applies just as much to verbs as to adjectives. You can't *wreak* much in English – mostly *havoc*, with a little bit of *vengeance* and *revenge*, mixed in with *destruction* and *mayhem* – but hang on, shouldn't that be *murder* and *mayhem*? Of course it should. You can barely have mayhem without murder. We could probably make shift without *wreak* in the language at all; at a pinch *havoc* can be *played*, and you can get *vengeance*, in the way you can *get* most things – *get* is collocationally promiscuous, like *nice*. But collocation doesn't only apply with rare forms like this. Think about *do* and *make*. Romance languages make do (not do make, you notice) with a single verb like *faire* or *hacer*. This is good for English teachers, as it can take up several classes to 'explain' the difference (you *do* activities, and *make* things, with the following 2,000 exceptions). Try and decide which of these you *do*, and which you *make*: *appearance, business, call, comment, change, damage, difference, effort, film, harm, impact, justice, money, profit, progress, research, work*.

Well, that was easy! Now ask a foreign learner. You know the answers because you've heard them dozens, maybe hundreds, of times before. They're not determined by logic, or by meaning, but by usage: by common consensus. That's what binds words together, as much as grammar does, and all you can do to learn this is to experience it. Language is not at all like chess, with a neat board and a set of simple rules. Language, like everything organic, is extremely complex. It's evolved that way.

Perhaps the most interesting way to look at collocation is to start with a noun, and see what other words you can use it with. We can start with an infrequent word, *brunt*. A recent article in a paper said: '...it has been at the brunt of the economic downturn...'. Maybe in a few years this will become the norm. At the moment, however, it feels like a line from a spoof news programme. The consensus is still that you can *suffer, take*, and *feel the brunt* of something, but you just *can't be at the brunt* of anything. Collocational limitations don't apply only to niche words like *brunt*, though. Let's look at *invitation*. You can *accept, decline, extend, issue, refuse, receive, spurn, withdraw, rescind, reject, send*, and *rebuff* an invitation. Invitations can *arrive, pour in, prompt* something, *promise* something. They can be *attractive, formal, last-minute, open, cordial, written, express, long-standing, official, unspoken, repeated, handwritten, seductive, printed*. That covers most of the combinations that we are familiar with. If we start using other, less familiar, combinations we risk sounding peculiar.

Collocation is what allows us to communicate efficiently. By restricting the possibilities to predictable sets of words, we make sure that we're understood. Poetry is all very well, but one of its virtues is that it can be interpreted in many different ways, and that's the last thing you want in a conversation.

improvise vb -vising, -vised 1 to do or make quickly from whatever is available, without previous planning 2 to make up (a piece of music, speech, etc.) as one goes along **improvisation** n
WORD ORIGIN Latin *improvisus* unforeseen

imprudent adj not carefully thought out; rash **imprudence** n

impudent adj impertinent or insolent **impudence** n **impudently** adv
WORD ORIGIN Latin *impudens* shameless

impugn (imp-**yoon**) vb formal to challenge or attack as false **impugnment** n
WORD ORIGIN Latin *impugnare* to fight against

impulse n 1 a sudden desire or whim 2 an instinctive drive; urge: *the mothering impulse* 3 physics **a** the product of a force acting on a body and the time for which it acts **b** the change in the momentum of a body as a result of a force acting upon it 4 physiol a stimulus transmitted in a nerve or muscle
WORD ORIGIN Latin *impulsus* incitement

impulsive adj 1 tending to act without thinking first: *an impulsive man* 2 done without thinking first 3 forceful or impelling

impunity (imp-**yoon**-it-ee) n **with impunity** without punishment or unpleasant consequences
WORD ORIGIN Latin *impunis* unpunished

impure adj 1 having unwanted substances mixed in 2 immoral or obscene: *impure thoughts* 3 dirty or unclean

impurity n, pl -ties 1 an impure element or thing: *impurities in the water* 2 the quality of being impure

impute vb -puting, -puted 1 to attribute (blame or a crime) to a person 2 to attribute to a source or cause: *I impute your success to nepotism* **imputation** n
WORD ORIGIN Latin *in-* in + *putare* to think

in prep 1 inside; within: *in the room* 2 at a place where there is: *in the shade* 3 indicating a state, situation, or condition: *in silence* 4 when (a period of time) has elapsed: *come back in one year* 5 using: *written in code* 6 wearing: *the man in the blue suit* 7 with regard to (a specified activity or occupation): *in journalism* 8 while performing the action of: *in crossing the street he was run over* 9 having as purpose: *in honour of the president* 10 (of certain animals) pregnant with: *in calf* 11 into: *he fell in the water* 12 **have it in one** to have the ability (to do something) 13 **in that** or **in so far as** because or to the extent that: *it was of great help in that it gave me more confidence* ▷ adv 14 in or into a particular place; indoors: *come in* 15 at one's home or place of work: *he's not in at the moment* 16 in office or power: *the Conservatives got in at the last election* 17 so as to enclose: *block in* 18 (in certain games) so as to take one's turn of the play: *you have to get the other side out before you go in* 19 Brit (of a fire) alight 20 indicating prolonged activity, esp. by a large number: *teach-in; sit-in* 21 **have got it in for** informal to wish or intend harm towards 22 **in for**

about to experience (something, esp. something unpleasant): *they're in for a shock* 23 **in on** acquainted with or sharing in: *I was in on all his plans* 24 **in with** friendly with ▷ adj 25 fashionable; modish: *the in thing to do* ▷ n 26 **ins and outs** the detailed points or facts (of a situation)
WORD ORIGIN Old English

In chem indium

IN Indiana

in. inch(es)

in-¹, il-, im- or **ir-** prefix **a** not; non: *incredible; illegal; imperfect; irregular* **b** lack of: *inexperience*
WORD ORIGIN Latin

in-², il-, im- or **ir-** prefix in; into; towards; within; on: *infiltrate*
WORD ORIGIN from *in*

inability n the fact of not being able to do something

in absentia adv in the absence of (someone indicated)
WORD ORIGIN Latin

inaccessible adj 1 impossible or very difficult to reach 2 unable to be used or seen: *his works are inaccessible to English-speaking readers* 3 difficult to understand or appreciate: *Webern's music is still considered inaccessible* **inaccessibility** n

inaccuracy n, pl -cies 1 lack of accuracy; imprecision 2 an error or mistake **inaccurate** adj

inaction n lack of action; inertia

inactive adj 1 idle; not active 2 chem (of a substance) having little or no reactivity **inactivity** n

inadequacy n, pl -cies 1 lack or shortage 2 the state of being or feeling inferior 3 a weakness or failing: *their own failures or inadequacies*

inadequate adj 1 not enough; insufficient 2 not good enough **inadequately** adv

inadmissible adj not allowable or acceptable

inadvertent adj done unintentionally **inadvertence** n **inadvertently** adv

inadvisable adj unwise; not sensible

inalienable adj not able to be taken away or transferred to another: *the inalienable rights of the citizen*

inamorata or masc **inamorato** n, pl -tas or masc -tos literary a sweetheart or lover
WORD ORIGIN Italian *innamorata, innamorato*

inane adj senseless or silly: *inane remarks* **inanity** n
WORD ORIGIN Latin *inanis* empty

inanimate adj lacking the qualities of living beings: *inanimate objects*

inanition n formal exhaustion or weakness, as from lack of food
WORD ORIGIN Latin *inanis* empty

inapplicable adj not suitable or relevant

inapposite adj not suitable or appropriate **inappositeness** n

inappropriate adj not suitable or proper **inappropriately** adv

inapt adj 1 not apt or fitting 2 lacking skill **inaptitude** n

inarticulate adj unable to express oneself clearly or well

inasmuch as conj 1 since; because 2 in so far as

inattentive adj not paying attention **inattention** n

inaudible adj not loud enough to be heard **inaudibly** adv

inaugural adj 1 of or for an inauguration ▷ n 2 US a speech made at an inauguration

inaugurate vb -rating, -rated 1 to open or celebrate the first public use of ceremonially: *the newest electrified line was inaugurated today* 2 to formally establish (a new leader) in office 3 to begin officially or formally **inauguration** n **inaugurator** n
WORD ORIGIN Latin *inaugurare* to take omens, hence to install in office after taking auguries

inauspicious adj unlucky; suggesting an unfavourable outcome

inboard adj 1 (of a boat's motor or engine) situated within the hull 2 situated close to the fuselage of an aircraft ▷ adv 3 within the sides of, or towards the centre of, a vessel or aircraft

inborn adj existing from birth: *an inborn sense of optimism*

inbox n computers a folder in which incoming messages are stored and displayed

inbred adj 1 produced as a result of inbreeding 2 inborn or ingrained: *inbred good manners*

inbreed vb -breeding, -bred to breed from closely related individuals

inbreeding n breeding from closely related individuals

inbuilt adj (of a quality or feeling) present from the beginning: *an inbuilt prejudice*

Inc. US & Austral (of a company) incorporated

Inca n 1 pl **Inca** or **Incas** a member of a S American indigenous people whose empire, centred on Peru, lasted until the early 1530s 2 the language of this people

incalculable adj impossible to estimate or predict **incalculability** n

in camera adv in private session: *the proceedings were held in camera*
WORD ORIGIN Latin

incandescent adj 1 glowing with heat 2 (of artificial light) produced by a glowing filament **incandescence** n
WORD ORIGIN Latin *incandescere* to glow

incandescent lamp n a lamp that contains a filament which is electrically heated to incandescence

incantation n 1 ritual chanting of magic words or sounds 2 a magic spell **incantatory** adj
WORD ORIGIN Latin *incantare* to repeat magic formulas

incapable adj 1 helpless: *drunk and incapable* 2 **incapable of** lacking the ability to

incapacitate vb -tating, -tated to deprive (a person) of strength, power, or ability; disable

incapacity n, pl -ties 1 lack of power, strength, or ability 2 law legal disqualification or ineligibility

incarcerate *vb* **-rating, -rated** *formal* to confine or imprison **incarceration** *n*
WORD ORIGIN Latin *in-* in + *carcer* prison

incarnate *adj* **1** possessing human form: *a devil incarnate* **2** personified or typified: *stupidity incarnate* ▷ *vb* **-nating, -nated 3** to give a bodily or concrete form to **4** to be representative or typical of
WORD ORIGIN Late Latin *incarnare* to make flesh

incarnation *n* **1** the act of embodying or state of being embodied in human form **2** a person or thing that typifies some quality or idea

Incarnation *n Christian theol* God's coming to earth in human form as Jesus Christ

incautious *adj* (of a person or action) careless or rash

incendiary (in-**send**-ya-ree) *adj* **1** (of bombs etc.) designed to cause fires **2** tending to create strife or violence **3** relating to the illegal burning of property or goods ▷ *n, pl* **-aries 4** a bomb that is designed to start fires **5** a person who illegally sets fire to property or goods **incendiarism** *n*
WORD ORIGIN Latin *incendere* to kindle

incense¹ *n* **1** an aromatic substance burnt for its fragrant odour, esp. in religious ceremonies **2** the odour or smoke so produced ▷ *vb* **-censing, -censed 3** to burn incense to (a deity) **4** to perfume or fumigate with incense
WORD ORIGIN Church Latin *incensum*

incense² *vb* **-censing, -censed** to make very angry **incensed** *adj*
WORD ORIGIN Latin *incensus* set on fire

incentive *n* **1** something that encourages effort or action **2** an additional payment made to employees to increase production ▷ *adj* **3** encouraging greater effort: *an incentive scheme for workers*
WORD ORIGIN Latin *incentivus* setting the tune

inception *n* the beginning of a project
WORD ORIGIN Latin *incipere* to begin

incessant *adj* never stopping **incessantly** *adv*
WORD ORIGIN Latin *in-* not + *cessare* to cease

incest *n* sexual intercourse between two people who are too closely related to marry **incestuous** *adj*
WORD ORIGIN Latin *in-* not + *castus* chaste

inch *n* **1** a unit of length equal to one twelfth of a foot (2.54cm) **2** *meteorol* the amount of rain or snow that would cover a surface to a depth of one inch **3** a very small distance, degree, or amount: *neither side was prepared to give an inch* **4 every inch** in every way: *she arrived looking every inch a star* **5 inch by inch** gradually **6 within an inch of one's life** almost to death ▷ *vb* **7** to move very slowly or gradually: *I inched my way to the bar*
WORD ORIGIN Old English *ynce*

inchoate (in-**koe**-ate) *adj formal* just begun and not yet properly developed
WORD ORIGIN Latin *incohare* to make a beginning

incidence *n* **1** extent or frequency of occurrence: *the rising incidence of car fires* **2** *physics* the arrival of a beam of light or particles at a surface **3** *geom* the partial overlapping of two figures or a figure and a line

incident *n* **1** an occurrence or event, esp. a minor one **2** a relatively insignificant event that might have serious consequences **3** a public disturbance ▷ *adj* **4** *physics* (of a beam of light or particles) arriving at or striking a surface **5 incident to** *formal* likely to occur in connection with: *the dangers are incident to a policeman's job*
WORD ORIGIN Latin *incidere* to happen

incidental *adj* **1** happening in connection with or resulting from something more important **2** secondary or minor: *incidental expenses* **incidentally** *adv*

incidental music *n* background music for a film or play

incidentals *pl n* minor expenses, events, or action

incinerate *vb* **-ating, -ated** to burn up completely **incineration** *n*
WORD ORIGIN Latin *in-* to + *cinis* ashes

incinerator *n* a furnace for burning rubbish

incipient *adj formal* just starting to be or happen
WORD ORIGIN Latin *incipere* to begin

incise *vb* **-cising, -cised** to cut into with a sharp tool
WORD ORIGIN Latin *incidere* to cut into

incision *n* a cut, esp. one made during a surgical operation

incisive *adj* direct and forceful: *witty and incisive comments*

incisor *n* a sharp cutting tooth at the front of the mouth

incite *vb* **-citing, -cited** to stir up or provoke to action **incitement** *n*
WORD ORIGIN Latin *in-* in, on + *citare* to excite

incivility *n, pl* **-ties 1** rudeness **2** an impolite act or remark

incl. **1** including **2** inclusive

inclement *adj formal* (of weather) stormy or severe **inclemency** *n*

inclination *n* **1** a liking, tendency, or preference: *he showed no inclination to change his routine* **2** the degree of slope from a horizontal or vertical plane **3** a slope or slant **4** *surveying* the angular distance of the horizon below the plane of observation

incline *vb* **-clining, -clined 1** to veer from a vertical or horizontal plane; slope or slant **2** to have or cause to have a certain tendency or disposition: *that does not incline me to think that you are right* **3** to bend or lower (part of the body, esp. the head) **4 incline one's ear** to listen favourably ▷ *n* **5** an inclined surface or slope **inclined** *adj*
WORD ORIGIN Latin *inclinare* to cause to lean

inclined plane *n* a sloping plane used to enable a load to be raised or lowered by pushing or sliding, which needs less force than lifting

include *vb* **-cluding, -cluded 1** to have as part of the whole **2** to put in as part of a set, group, or category
WORD ORIGIN Latin *in-* in + *claudere* to close

inclusion *n* **1** an including or being included **2** something included

inclusive *adj* **1** including everything: *capital inclusive of profit* **2** including the limits specified: *Monday to Friday inclusive* **3** comprehensive

incognito (in-kog-**nee**-toe) *adv, adj* **1** under an assumed name or appearance ▷ *n, pl* **-tos 2** a false identity **3** a person who is incognito
WORD ORIGIN Latin *incognitus* unknown

incognizant *adj* incognizant of unaware of **incognizance** *n*

incoherent *adj* **1** unable to express oneself clearly **2** not logically connected or ordered: *an incoherent argument* **incoherence** *n*

income *n* the total amount of money earned from work or obtained from other sources over a given period of time

income support *n* (in Britain) an allowance paid by the government to people with a very low income

income tax *n* a personal tax levied on annual income

incoming *adj* **1** about to arrive **2** about to come into office

incommensurable *adj* **1** not able to be judged, measured, or compared **2** *maths* not having a common divisor other than 1, such as 2 and $\sqrt{-5}$ **incommensurability** *n*

incommensurate *adj* **1** inadequate or disproportionate: *gains incommensurate with the risk involved* **2** incommensurable

incommode *vb* **-moding, -moded** *formal* to bother, disturb, or inconvenience
WORD ORIGIN Latin *incommodus* inconvenient

incommodious *adj formal* inconveniently small; cramped

incommunicado *adv, adj* not allowed to communicate with other people, for instance while in solitary confinement
WORD ORIGIN Spanish *incomunicado*

incomparable *adj* so excellent as to be beyond or above comparison **incomparably** *adv*

incompatible *adj* not able to exist together in harmony; conflicting or inconsistent **incompatibility** *n*

incompetent *adj* **1** not having the necessary ability or skill to do something **2** *law* not legally qualified: *an incompetent witness* ▷ *n* **3** an incompetent person **incompetence** *n*

incomplete *adj* not finished or whole

incomprehension *n* inability to understand **incomprehensible** *adj*

inconceivable *adj* so unlikely to be true as to be unthinkable **inconceivability** *n*

inconclusive *adj* not giving a final decision or result

incongruous *adj* out of place; inappropriate: *an incongruous figure among the tourists* **incongruously** *adv* **incongruity** *n*

inconnu (in-kon-new) *n Canad* a whitefish of Arctic waters
WORD ORIGIN French, literally: unknown

inconsequential or **inconsequent** adj **1** unimportant or insignificant **2** not following logically as a consequence **inconsequentially** adv

inconsiderable adj **1** not worth considering; insignificant **2** not inconsiderable fairly large: he gets not inconsiderable royalties from his musicals **inconsiderably** adv

inconsiderate adj lacking in care or thought for others; thoughtless **inconsiderateness** n

inconsistent adj **1** unstable or changeable in behaviour or mood **2** containing contradictory elements: an inconsistent argument **3** not in accordance: actions inconsistent with high office **inconsistency** n

inconsolable adj very distressed **inconsolably** adv

inconspicuous adj not easily noticed or seen

inconstant adj **1** liable to change one's loyalties or opinions **2** variable: their household income is inconstant **inconstancy** n

incontestable adj impossible to deny or argue with

incontinent adj **1** unable to control the bladder and bowels **2** lacking self-restraint, esp. sexually **incontinence** n
WORD ORIGIN Latin in- not + continere to restrain

incontrovertible adj absolutely certain; undeniable **incontrovertibly** adv

inconvenience n **1** a state or instance of trouble or difficulty ▷ vb **-iencing, -ienced 2** to cause trouble or difficulty to (someone) **inconvenient** adj

incorporate vb **-rating, -rated 1** to include or be included as part of a larger unit **2** to form a united whole or mass **3** to form into a corporation ▷ adj **4** incorporated **incorporated** adj **incorporation** n
WORD ORIGIN Latin in- in + corpus body

incorporeal adj without material form, substance, or existence

incorrect adj **1** wrong: an incorrect answer **2** not proper: incorrect behaviour **incorrectly** adv

incorrigible adj (of a person or behaviour) beyond correction or reform; incurably bad **incorrigibility** n **incorrigibly** adv

incorruptible adj **1** too honest to be bribed or corrupted **2** not prone to decay or disintegration **incorruptibility** n

increase vb **-creasing, -creased 1** to make or become greater in size, degree, or frequency ▷ n **2** a rise in size, degree, or frequency **3** the amount by which something increases **4** on the increase becoming more common **increasingly** adv
WORD ORIGIN Latin in- in + crescere to grow

incredible adj **1** unbelievable **2** informal marvellous; amazing **incredibility** n **incredibly** adv

incredulity n unwillingness to believe

incredulous adj not prepared or willing to believe something

increment n **1** the amount by which something increases **2** a regular salary increase **3** maths a small positive or negative change in a variable or function **incremental** adj
WORD ORIGIN Latin incrementum increase

incriminate vb **-nating, -nated 1** to make (someone) seem guilty of a crime **2** to charge (someone) with a crime **incrimination** n **incriminatory** adj
WORD ORIGIN Late Latin incriminare to accuse

incrust vb same as **encrust**

incubate (**in**-cube-ate) vb **-bating, -bated 1** (of birds) to hatch (eggs) by sitting on them **2** to cause (bacteria) to develop, esp. in an incubator or culture medium **3** (of disease germs) to remain inactive in an animal or human before causing disease **4** to develop gradually **incubation** n
WORD ORIGIN Latin incubare

incubator n **1** med a heated enclosed apparatus for rearing premature babies **2** an apparatus for hatching birds' eggs or growing bacterial cultures

incubus (**in**-cube-uss) n, pl **-bi** or **-buses 1** a demon believed in folklore to have sexual intercourse with sleeping women **2** a nightmarish burden or worry
WORD ORIGIN Latin incubare to lie upon

inculcate vb **-cating, -cated** to fix in someone's mind by constant repetition **inculcation** n
WORD ORIGIN Latin inculcare to tread upon

inculpate vb **-pating, -pated** formal to incriminate
WORD ORIGIN Latin in- on + culpare to blame

incumbency n, pl **-cies** the office, duty, or tenure of an incumbent

incumbent formal n **1** a person who holds a particular office or position ▷ adj **2** morally binding as a duty: it is incumbent on cricketers to respect the umpire's impartiality
WORD ORIGIN Latin incumbere to lie upon

incur vb **-curring, -curred** to bring (something undesirable) upon oneself
WORD ORIGIN Latin incurrere to run into

incurable adj **1** not able to be cured: an incurable tumour **2** not able to be changed: he is an incurable romantic ▷ n **3** a person with an incurable disease **incurability** n **incurably** adv

incurious adj showing no curiosity or interest **incuriously** adv

incursion n **1** a sudden or brief invasion **2** an inroad or encroachment: a successful incursion into the American book-shop market **incursive** adj
WORD ORIGIN Latin incursio attack

ind. 1 independent **2** index **3** indicative **4** indirect **5** industrial

Ind. 1 Independent **2** India **3** Indian **4** Indiana **5** Indies

indaba (in-**dah**-ba) n **1** (among native peoples of southern Africa) a meeting to discuss a serious topic **2** S African informal a matter of concern or for discussion
WORD ORIGIN Zulu

indebted adj **1** owing gratitude for help or favours **2** owing money **indebtedness** n

indecent adj **1** morally or sexually offensive **2** unseemly or improper: indecent haste **indecency** n **indecently** adv

indecent assault n a sexual attack which does not include rape

indecent exposure n the showing of one's genitals in public

indecipherable adj impossible to read

indecisive adj **1** unable to make decisions **2** not decisive or conclusive: an indecisive argument **indecision** or **indecisiveness** n

indeed adv **1** certainly; actually: indeed, the sea featured heavily in his poems **2** truly, very: it has become a dangerous place indeed **3** in fact; what is more: it is necessary, indeed indispensable ▷ interj **4** an expression of doubt or surprise

indefatigable adj never getting tired or giving up: Mitterrand was an indefatigable organizer **indefatigably** adv
WORD ORIGIN Latin in- not + fatigare to tire

indefensible adj **1** (of behaviour or statements) unable to be justified or supported **2** (of places or buildings) impossible to defend against attack **indefensibility** n

indefinable adj difficult to describe or explain completely

indefinite adj **1** without exact limits: an indefinite number **2** vague or unclear **indefinitely** adv

indefinite article n grammar either of the words 'a' or 'an'

indelible adj **1** impossible to erase or remove **2** making indelible marks: indelible ink **indelibly** adv
WORD ORIGIN Latin in- not + delere to destroy

indelicate adj **1** offensive, embarrassing, or tasteless **2** coarse, crude, or rough **indelicacy** n

indemnify vb **-fies, -fying, -fied 1** to secure against loss, damage, or liability **2** to compensate for loss or damage **indemnification** n

indemnity n, pl **-ties 1** insurance against loss or damage **2** compensation for loss or damage **3** legal exemption from penalties incurred
WORD ORIGIN Latin in- not + damnum damage

indent vb **1** to start (a line of writing) further from the margin than the other lines **2** to order (goods) using a special order form **3** to notch (an edge or border) **4** to write out (a document) in duplicate **5** to bind (an apprentice) by indenture ▷ n **6** chiefly Brit an official order for goods, esp. foreign merchandise
WORD ORIGIN Latin in- in + dens tooth

indentation n **1** a hollow, notch, or cut, as on an edge or on a coastline **2** an indenting or being indented **3** Also: **indention** the leaving of space or the amount of space left between a margin and the start of an indented line

indenture n **1** a contract, esp. one binding an apprentice to his or her

Words from Literature
part 14

ideal *adj* imaginary
I discovered the yell was not ideal
Wuthering Heights Emily Brontë

ignis-fatuus *n* the light given out by burning marsh gases, which lead careless travellers into danger
it is madness in all women to let a secret love kindle within them, which, if unreturned and unknown, must devour the life that feeds it; and, if discovered and responded to, must lead ignis-fatuus-like, into miry wilds whence there is no extrication.
Jane Eyre Charlotte Brontë

imaginations *n* schemes or plans
soon drove out those imaginations
Gulliver's Travels Jonathan Swift

impressible *adj* impressible means open or impressionable
for Marner had one of those impressible, self-doubting natures
Silas Marner George Eliot

in good intelligence *phrase* friendly with each other
that these two persons were in good intelligence with each other
Gulliver's Travels Jonathan Swift

inanity *n* silliness or dull stupidity
Do we not wile away moments of inanity
Silas Marner George Eliot

incivility *n* rudeness or impoliteness
if it's only for a piece of incivility like to-night's
Treasure Island Robert Louis Stevenson

indigenae *n* natives or people from a certain area
an exotic that the surly indigenae will not recognise for kin
Wuthering Heights Emily Brontë

inducible *adj* unteachable
so they were the most restive and inducible
Gulliver's Travels Jonathan Swift

ingenuity *n* inventiveness
entreated me to give him something as an encouragement to ingenuity
Gulliver's Travels Jonathan Swift

ingot *n* an ingot is a lump of a valuable metal like gold, usually shaped like a brick
Tom called the hogs 'ingots'
The Adventures of Huckleberry Finn Mark Twain

inkstand *n* a pot which was put on a desk to contain either ink or pencils and pens
throwing an inkstand at the Lizard as she spoke
Alice's Adventures in Wonderland Lewis Carroll

inordinate *adj* without order. Today inordinate means 'excessive'.
Though yet untutored and inordinate
The Prelude William Wordsworth

intellectuals *n* minds
those instructions they give being too refined for the intellectuals of their workmen
Gulliver's Travels Jonathan Swift

interview *n* a meeting
By our first strange and fatal interview
On His Mistress John Donne

jack *n* a rod for turning a spit over a fire
It was a small bit of pork suspended from the kettle hanger by a string passed through a large door key, in a way known to primitive housekeepers unpossessed of jacks
Silas Marner George Eliot

jews-harp *n* a small, metal, musical instrument that is played by the mouth
A jews-harp's plenty good enough for a rat
The Adventures of Huckleberry Finn Mark Twain

jorum *n* a large bowl
while Miss Skiffins brewed such a jorum of tea, that the pig in the back premises became strongly excited
Great Expectations Charles Dickens

employer ▷ *vb* **-turing, -tured 2** to bind (an apprentice) by indenture **3** to enter into an agreement by indenture

independent *adj* **1** free from the influence or control of others **2** not dependent on anything else for function or validity **3** not relying on the support, esp. financial support, of others **4** capable of acting for oneself or on one's own **5** of or having a private income large enough to enable one to live without working: *independent means* **6** *maths* (of a variable) not dependent on another variable ▷ *n* **7** an independent person or thing **8** a politician who does not represent any political party **independence** *n* **independently** *adv*

independent school *n* a school that is neither financed nor controlled by the government or local authorities

in-depth *adj* detailed or thorough: *an in-depth analysis*

indescribable *adj* too intense or extreme for words **indescribably** *adv*

indestructible *adj* not able to be destroyed

indeterminate *adj* **1** uncertain in extent, amount, or nature **2** left doubtful; inconclusive: *an indeterminate reply* **3** *maths* **a** having no numerical meaning, as % **b** (of an equation) having more than one variable and an unlimited number of solutions **indeterminable** *adj* **indeterminacy** *n*

index (**in**-dex) *n, pl* **-dexes** *or* **-dices 1** an alphabetical list of names or subjects dealt with in a book, indicating where they are referred to **2** a file or catalogue in a library which enables a book or reference to be found **3** a number indicating the level of wages or prices as compared with some standard value **4** an indication or sign: *national birth rate was once an index of military power* **5** *maths* **a** same as **exponent b** a superscript number placed to the left of a radical sign indicating the root to be extracted: *the index of* $\sqrt[3]{8}$ *is 3* **6** a number or ratio indicating a specific characteristic or property: *refractive index* ▷ *vb* **7** to put an index in (a book) **8** to enter (a word or item) in an index **9** to make index-linked

WORD ORIGIN Latin: pointer

indexation *or* **index-linking** *n* the act of making wages, pensions, or interest rates index-linked

index finger *n* the finger next to the thumb. Also called: **forefinger**

index-linked *adj* (of pensions, wages, or interest rates) rising and falling in line with the cost of living

Indiaman *n, pl* **-men** (formerly) a merchant ship engaged in trade with India

Indian *adj* **1** of India **2** of the original inhabitants of the American continent ▷ *n* **3** a person from India **4** a person descended from the original inhabitants of the American continent

Indian club *n* a heavy bottle-shaped club, usually swung in pairs for exercise

Indian corn *n* same as **maize**

Indian file *n* same as **single file**

Indian hemp *n* same as **hemp**

Indian ink *or esp. US & Canad* **India ink** *n* a black ink made from a fine black soot

Indian summer *n* **1** a period of warm sunny weather in autumn **2** a period of tranquillity or of renewed productivity towards the end of a person's life or career

India paper *n* a thin soft opaque printing paper originally made in the Orient

Indic *adj* **1** of a branch of Indo-European consisting of many of the languages of India, including Sanskrit, Hindi, and Urdu ▷ *n* **2** this group of languages

indicate *vb* **-cating, -cated 1** to be or give a sign or symptom of: *to concede 18 goals in 7 games indicates a serious malaise* **2** to point out or show **3** to state briefly **4** to switch on the indicators in a motor vehicle to show that one is changing direction **5** (of measuring instruments) to show a reading of **6** (*usually passive*) to recommend or require: *surgery seems to be indicated for this patient* **indication** *n*

WORD ORIGIN Latin *indicare*

indicative (in-**dik**-a-tiv) *adj* **1 indicative of** suggesting: *the symptoms aren't indicative of anything serious* **2** *grammar* denoting a mood of verbs used to make a statement ▷ *n* **3** *grammar* the indicative mood

indicator *n* **1** something that acts as a sign or indication: *an indicator of the moral decline of our society* **2** a device for indicating that a motor vehicle is about to turn left or right, esp. two pairs of lights that flash **3** an instrument, such as a gauge, that registers or measures something **4** *chem* a substance used to indicate the completion of a chemical reaction, usually by a change of colour

indices (**in**-diss-seez) *n* a plural of **index**

indict (in-**dite**) *vb* to charge (a person) formally with a crime, esp. in writing **indictable** *adj*

WORD ORIGIN Latin *in-* against + *dictare* to declare

indictment *n* **1** *criminal law* a formal charge of crime, esp. in writing: *the indictment contained three similar charges against each of the defendants* **2** a serious criticism: *a scathing indictment of faith healing*

indie *n* *informal* an independent record company

indifference *n* **1** lack of concern or interest: *elite indifference to mass opinion* **2** lack of importance: *a matter of indifference to me*

indifferent *adj* **1** showing no concern or interest: *he was indifferent to politics* **2** of only average standard or quality **3** not at all good: *she had starred in several very indifferent movies* **4** unimportant **5** showing or having no preferences

WORD ORIGIN Latin *indifferens* making no distinction

indigenous (in-**dij**-in-uss) *adj* originating or occurring naturally in a country or area: *the indigenous population is under threat*

WORD ORIGIN Latin *indigenus*

indigent *adj* *formal* so poor as to lack even necessities: *the indigent widow of a fellow writer* **indigence** *n*

WORD ORIGIN Latin *indigere* to need

indigestible *adj* difficult or impossible to digest **indigestibility** *n*

indigestion *n* difficulty in digesting food, accompanied by stomach pain, heartburn, and belching

indignant *adj* feeling or showing indignation **indignantly** *adv*

WORD ORIGIN Latin *indignari* to be displeased with

indignation *n* anger aroused by something felt to be unfair or wrong

indignity *n, pl* **-ties** embarrassing or humiliating treatment

indigo *adj* **1** deep violet-blue ▷ *n, pl* **-gos** *or* **-goes 2** a dye of this colour originally obtained from plants

WORD ORIGIN Spanish *indico*, from Greek *Indikos* of India

indirect *adj* **1** done or caused by someone or something else: *indirect benefits* **2** not going in a direct course or line: *he took the indirect route home* **3** not coming straight to the point: *an indirect question* **indirectly** *adv*

indirect object *n* *grammar* the person or thing indirectly affected by the action of a verb and its direct object, as *John* in the sentence *I bought John a newspaper*

indirect speech *n* same as **reported speech**

indirect tax *n* a tax levied on goods or services which is paid indirectly by being added to the price

indiscernible *adj* not able or scarcely able to be seen

indiscipline *n* lack of discipline

indiscreet *adj* incautious or tactless in revealing secrets

indiscretion *n* **1** lack of discretion **2** an indiscreet act or remark

indiscriminate *adj* lacking discrimination or careful choice: *an indiscriminate bombing campaign* **indiscriminately** *adv* **indiscrimination** *n*

indispensable *adj* absolutely necessary: *an indispensable guide for any traveller* **indispensability** *n*

indisposed *adj* **1** sick or ill **2** unwilling **indisposition** *n*

WORD ORIGIN Latin *indispositus* disordered

indisputable *adj* beyond doubt

indissoluble *adj* permanent: *joining a political party is not an indissoluble marriage*

indistinct *adj* unable to be seen or heard clearly **indistinctly** *adv*

indistinguishable *adj* so similar as to be difficult to tell apart

indium *n* *chem* a rare soft silvery metallic element. Symbol: In

WORD ORIGIN Latin *indicum* indigo

individual *adj* **1** of, relating to, or meant for a single person or thing: *small sums from individual donors* **2** separate or distinct from others of its kind: *please mark the individual pages* **3** characterized by unusual and striking qualities ▷ *n* **4** a single person, esp. when regarded as distinct from others: *respect for the individual* **5** *informal* a person: *a most annoying individual* **6** *biol* a single animal or plant, esp. as distinct from a species **individually** *adv*

WORD ORIGIN Latin *individuus* indivisible

individualism *n* **1** the principle of leading one's life in one's own way **2** same as **laissez faire 3** egotism **individualist** *n* **individualistic** *adj*

individuality *n, pl* **-ties 1** distinctive or unique character or personality: *a house of great individuality* **2** the qualities that distinguish one person or thing from another **3** a separate existence

individualize *or* **-ise** *vb* **-izing, -ized** *or* **-ising, -ised** to make individual or distinctive in character

indivisible *adj* **1** unable to be divided **2** *maths* leaving a remainder when divided by a given number

indoctrinate *vb* **-nating, -nated** to teach (someone) systematically to accept a doctrine or opinion uncritically **indoctrination** *n*

Indo-European *adj* **1** of a family of languages spoken in most of Europe and much of Asia, including English, Russian, and Hindi ▷ *n* **2** the Indo-European family of languages

indolent *adj* lazy; idle **indolence** *n*
WORD ORIGIN Latin *indolens* not feeling pain

indomitable *adj* too strong to be defeated or discouraged: *an indomitable work ethic*
WORD ORIGIN Latin *indomitus* untamable

Indonesian *adj* **1** of Indonesia ▷ *n* **2** a person from Indonesia

indoor *adj* situated, happening, or used inside a building: *an indoor pool*

indoors *adv, adj* inside or into a building

indrawn *adj* drawn or pulled in: *he heard her indrawn breath*

indubitable (in-**dew**-bit-a-bl) *adj* beyond doubt; definite **indubitably** *adv*
WORD ORIGIN Latin *in-* not + *dubitare* to doubt

induce *vb* **-ducing, -duced 1** to persuade or use influence on **2** to cause or bring about **3** *med* to cause (labour) to begin by the use of drugs or other means **4** *logic obsolete* to draw (a general conclusion) from particular instances **5** to produce (an electromotive force or electrical current) by induction **6** to transmit (magnetism) by induction **inducible** *adj*
WORD ORIGIN Latin *inducere* to lead in

inducement *n* **1** something that encourages someone to do something **2** the act of inducing

induct *vb* **1** to bring in formally or install in a job, rank, or position **2** to initiate in knowledge of (a group or profession): *boys are inducted into the world of men*
WORD ORIGIN Latin *inductus* led in

inductance *n* the property of an electric circuit as a result of which an electromotive force is created by a change of current in the same or in a neighbouring circuit

induction *n* **1** *logic* a process of reasoning by which a general conclusion is drawn from particular instances **2** *med* the process of inducing labour **3** the process by which electrical or magnetic properties are transferred, without physical contact, from one circuit or body to another

4 a formal introduction or entry into an office or position **5** (in an internal-combustion engine) the drawing in of mixed air and fuel from the carburettor to the cylinder **inductional** *adj*

induction coil *n* a transformer for producing a high voltage from a low voltage. It consists of a soft-iron core, a primary coil of few turns, and a concentric secondary coil of many turns

induction course *n* a training course to help familiarize someone with a new job

inductive *adj* **1** *logic* of or using induction: *inductive reasoning* **2** of or operated by electrical or magnetic induction

inductor *n* a device designed to create inductance in an electrical circuit

indulge *vb* **-dulging, -dulged 1** (often foll. by *in*) to yield to or gratify (a whim or desire for): *to indulge in new clothes* **2** to allow (someone) to have or do everything he or she wants: *he had given her too much, indulged her in everything* **3** to allow (oneself) the pleasure of something: *he indulged himself* **4** *informal* to take alcoholic drink
WORD ORIGIN Latin *indulgere* to concede

indulgence *n* **1** something that is allowed because it gives pleasure; extravagance **2** the act of indulging oneself or someone else **3** liberal or tolerant treatment **4** something granted as a favour or privilege **5** RC Church a remission of the temporal punishment for sin after its guilt has been forgiven

indulgent *adj* kind or lenient, often to excess **indulgently** *adv*

industrial *adj* **1** of, used in, or employed in industry **2** with an economy relying heavily on industry: *northern industrial cities*

industrial action *n* action, such as a strike or work-to-rule, by which workers complain about their conditions

industrial estate *n* *Brit, Austral, NZ, S African* an area of land set aside for factories and warehouses

industrialism *n* an organization of society characterized by large-scale manufacturing industry rather than trade or farming

industrialist *n* a person who owns or controls large amounts of money or property in industry

industrialize *or* **-lise** *vb* **-lizing, -lized** *or* **-lising, -lised** to develop industry on a large scale in (a country or region) **industrialization** *or* **-lisation** *n*

industrial relations *pl n* the relations between management and workers

Industrial Revolution *n* **the Industrial Revolution** the transformation in the 18th and 19th centuries of Britain and other countries into industrial nations

industrious *adj* hard-working

industry *n, pl* **-tries 1** the work and process involved in manufacture: *Japanese industry increased output considerably last year* **2** a branch of commercial enterprise concerned with the

manufacture of a specified product: *the steel industry* **3** the quality of working hard
WORD ORIGIN Latin *industrius* active

Indy Car racing *n* a form of motor racing around banked oval tracks
WORD ORIGIN after the *Indianapolis 500* motor race

inebriate *n* **1** a person who is habitually drunk ▷ *adj* **2** drunk, esp. habitually **inebriation** *n*
WORD ORIGIN Latin *ebrius* drunk

inebriated *adj* drunk

inedible *adj* not fit to be eaten

ineducable (in-**ed**-yuke-a-bl) *adj* incapable of being educated, esp. on account of mental retardation

ineffable *adj* too great or intense to be expressed in words **ineffably** *adv*
WORD ORIGIN Latin *in-* not + *effabilis* utterable

ineffective *adj* having no effect or an inadequate effect

ineffectual *adj* having no effect or an inadequate effect: *the raids were costly and ineffectual*

inefficient *adj* not performing a task or function to the best advantage **inefficiency** *n*

inelegant *adj* lacking elegance or refinement

ineligible *adj* not qualified for or entitled to something

ineluctable *adj formal* impossible to avoid: *the ineluctable collapse of the coalition*
WORD ORIGIN Latin *in-* not + *eluctari* to escape

inept *adj* **1** awkward, clumsy, or incompetent **2** not suitable or fitting; out of place **ineptitude** *n*
WORD ORIGIN Latin *in-* not + *aptus* fitting

inequable *adj* **1** unfair **2** not uniform

inequality *n, pl* **-ties 1** the state or quality of being unequal **2** an instance of this **3** lack of smoothness or regularity of a surface **4** *maths* a statement indicating that the value of one quantity or expression is not equal to another

inequitable *adj* unjust or unfair

inequity *n, pl* **-ties 1** injustice or unfairness **2** something which is unjust or unfair

ineradicable *adj* impossible to remove or root out: *an ineradicable distrust of foreigners*

inert *adj* **1** without the power to move or to resist motion **2** inactive or lifeless **3** having only a limited ability to react chemically
WORD ORIGIN Latin *iners* unskilled

inertia *n* **1** a feeling of unwillingness to do anything **2** *physics* the tendency of a body to remain still or continue moving unless a force is applied to it **inertial** *adj*

inertia selling *n Brit* the illegal practice of sending unrequested goods to householders, followed by a bill for the goods if they do not return them

inescapable *adj* not able to be avoided

inessential *adj* **1** not necessary ▷ *n* **2** an unnecessary thing

inestimable *adj* too great to be calculated

inevitable *adj* **1** unavoidable; sure to happen **2** *informal* so regular as to be predictable: *the inevitable guitar solo* ▷ *n* **3** (often preceded by *the*) something that is unavoidable **inevitability** *n* **inevitably** *adv*
WORD ORIGIN Latin *in-* not + *evitare* to avoid

inexact *adj* not exact or accurate

inexcusable *adj* too bad to be justified or tolerated

inexhaustible *adj* incapable of being used up; endless

inexorable *adj* unable to be prevented from continuing or progressing: *an inexorable trend* **inexorably** *adv*
WORD ORIGIN Latin *in-* not + *exorare* to prevail upon

inexpensive *adj* not costing a lot of money

inexperienced *adj* having no knowledge or experience of a particular situation, activity, etc. **inexperience** *n*

inexpert *adj* lacking skill

inexpiable *adj* (of sin) incapable of being atoned for; unpardonable

inexplicable *adj* impossible to explain

inexpressible *adj* (of a feeling) too strong to be expressed in words

in extremis *adv* **1** in dire straits **2** at the point of death

inextricable *adj* **1** impossible to escape from: *an inextricable dilemma* **2** impossible to disentangle or separate: *an inextricable mass of twisted metal* **inextricably** *adv*

inf. **1** infantry **2** infinitive **3** informal **4** information

infallible *adj* **1** incapable of error **2** always successful: *an infallible cure* **3** (of the Pope) incapable of error in setting forth matters of doctrine on faith and morals **infallibility** *n* **infallibly** *adv*

infamous (**in**-fam-uss) *adj* well-known for something bad

infamy *n, pl* **-mies 1** the state of being infamous **2** an infamous act or event
WORD ORIGIN Latin *infamis* of evil repute

infancy *n, pl* **-cies 1** the state or period of being an infant **2** an early stage of growth or development: *virtual reality is in its infancy* **3** *law* the state or period of being a minor

infant *n* **1** a very young child; baby **2** *law* same as **minor** (sense 4) **3** *Brit* a young school child ▷ *adj* **4** of, relating to, or designed for young children: *infant school* **5** in an early stage of development: *an infant democracy*
WORD ORIGIN Latin *infans*, literally: speechless

infanta *n* **1** (formerly) a daughter of a king of Spain or Portugal **2** the wife of an infante
WORD ORIGIN Spanish and Portuguese

infante *n* (formerly) any son of a king of Spain or Portugal, except the heir to the throne
WORD ORIGIN Spanish and Portuguese

infanticide *n* **1** the act of killing an infant **2** a person who kills an infant
WORD ORIGIN INFANT + Latin *caedere* to kill

infantile *adj* **1** childishly immature **2** of infants or infancy

infantile paralysis *n* same as **poliomyelitis**

infantry *n, pl* **-tries** soldiers who fight on foot
WORD ORIGIN Italian *infanteria*

infant school *n* (in England and Wales) a school for children aged between 5 and 7

infatuate *vb* **-ating, -ated** to inspire or fill with an intense and unreasoning passion **infatuation** *n*
WORD ORIGIN Latin *infatuare*

infatuated *adj* (often foll. by *with*) carried away by an intense and unreasoning passion for someone

infect *vb* **1** to contaminate (a person or thing) with a germ or virus or its consequent disease **2** to taint or contaminate **3** to affect with an opinion or feeling as if by contagion: *even she was infected by the excitement*
WORD ORIGIN Latin *inficere* to stain

infection *n* **1** an infectious disease **2** contamination of a person or thing by a germ or virus or its consequent disease

infectious *adj* **1** (of a disease) capable of being transmitted without actual contact **2** causing or transmitting infection **3** spreading from one person to another: *infectious laughter*

infectious mononucleosis *n* same as **glandular fever**

infelicity *n, pl* **-ties** *formal* **1** something, esp. a remark or expression, that is inapt **2** the state or quality of being unhappy or unfortunate **infelicitous** *adj*

infer *vb* **-ferring, -ferred 1** to conclude by reasoning from evidence; deduce **2** *not standard* to imply or suggest
WORD ORIGIN Latin *inferre* to bring into

USAGE
The use of *infer* to mean *imply* is common in both speech and writing, but is regarded by many people as incorrect.

inference *n* **1** the act or process of reaching a conclusion by reasoning from evidence **2** an inferred conclusion or deduction

inferential *adj* of or based on inference

inferior *adj* **1** lower in quality, quantity, or usefulness **2** lower in rank, position, or status **3** of poor quality **4** lower in position **5** *printing* (of a character) printed at the foot of an ordinary character ▷ *n* **6** a person inferior to another, esp. in rank **inferiority** *n*
WORD ORIGIN Latin: lower

inferiority complex *n* *psychiatry* a disorder arising from a feeling of inferiority to others, characterized by aggressiveness or extreme shyness

infernal *adj* **1** of or relating to hell **2** *informal* irritating: *stop that infernal noise*
WORD ORIGIN Latin *infernus* lower

inferno *n, pl* **-nos 1** an intense raging fire **2** a place or situation resembling hell, because it is crowded and noisy **3** the *inferno* hell
WORD ORIGIN Late Latin *infernus* hell

infertile *adj* **1** not capable of producing offspring **2** (of soil) not productive; barren **infertility** *n*

infest *vb* to inhabit or overrun (a place, plant, etc.) in unpleasantly large numbers: *the area was infested with moles* **infestation** *n*
WORD ORIGIN Latin *infestare* to molest

infidel *n* **1** a person who has no religious belief **2** a person who rejects a specific religion, esp. Christianity or Islam ▷ *adj* **3** of unbelievers or unbelief
WORD ORIGIN Latin *infidelis* unfaithful

infidelity *n, pl* **-ties 1** sexual unfaithfulness to one's husband, wife, or lover **2** an act or instance of unfaithfulness

infield *n* **1** *cricket* the area of the field near the pitch **2** *baseball* the area of the playing field enclosed by the base lines **infielder** *n*

infighting *n* **1** rivalry or quarrelling between members of the same group or organization **2** *boxing* combat at close quarters

infiltrate *vb* **-trating, -trated 1** to enter (an organization, area, etc.) gradually and in secret, so as to gain influence or control: *they infiltrated the party structure* **2** to pass (a liquid or gas) through (a substance) by filtering or (of a liquid or gas) to pass through (a substance) by filtering **infiltration** *n* **infiltrator** *n*

infinite (**in**-fin-it) *adj* **1** having no limits or boundaries in time, space, extent, or size **2** extremely or immeasurably great or numerous: *infinite wealth* **3** *maths* having an unlimited or uncountable number of digits, factors, or terms **infinitely** *adv*

infinitesimal *adj* **1** extremely small: *an infinitesimal risk* **2** *maths* of or involving a small change in the value of a variable that approaches zero as a limit ▷ *n* **3** *maths* an infinitesimal quantity

infinitive (in-**fin**-it-iv) *n* *grammar* a form of the verb which in most languages is not inflected for tense or person and is used without a particular subject: in English, the infinitive usually consists of the word *to* followed by the verb

infinitude *n* *literary* **1** the state or quality of being infinite **2** an infinite extent or quantity

infinity *n, pl* **-ties 1** an infinitely great number or amount **2** endless time, space, or quantity **3** *maths* the concept of a value greater than any finite numerical value

infirm *adj* physically or mentally weak, esp. from old age

infirmary *n, pl* **-ries** a place for the treatment of the sick or injured; hospital

infirmity *n, pl* **-ties 1** the state of being infirm **2** physical weakness or frailty

infix *vb* **1** to fix firmly in **2** to instil or impress on the mind by repetition **infixation** *or* **infixion** *n*

in flagrante delicto (in flag-**grant**-ee dee-**lick**-toe) *adv* *chiefly law* while committing the offence
WORD ORIGIN Latin

inflame *vb* **-flaming, -flamed 1** to make angry or excited **2** to increase or intensify; aggravate **3** to produce inflammation in or become inflamed **4** to set or be set on fire

West Country Dialect

The West Country is generally taken to comprise the English counties of Cornwall, Devon, Dorset, Wiltshire, and Somerset. To non-residents this name conjures up images of cider-swilling yokels, cheerful, strong as oxen, but perhaps a little simple-minded.

It is probably unwise, however, to talk about a single West Country dialect. Cornwall has its own language, which at one time was more prevalent than English in the county. The Cornish language is now spoken only by a few hundred enthusiasts, but it is claimed to have left its mark on the speech of the county. Besides this, many dialect words were coined by workers in the county's tin mines, who coined terms such as *vug* ('a cavity in a rock') and *mundic* ('iron pyrites'), for the things they found as they went about their business.

While Cornwall was historically noted for smuggling and tin mining, Dorset and Devon fall more easily into the stereotype of farming and cider-making. Examples of the traditional dialect are preserved in the poetry of William Barnes (1801-86). Barnes was actually a serious linguist and wrote books about philology, but in his poems he took pains to write like an unstudied farm labourer, producing lines such as, 'Good morn t'ye, John. How b'ye? How b'ye? / Zoo you be gwaïn to market I do zee.' This couplet showcases two of the most striking features of the West Country dialect: *be* is used for all forms of the present tense ('you be' being used where standard English would say 'you are'), and the letter 's' is softened to become 'z'. These features are still thought of as integral to the dialect, and are likely to form the basis of the nonspecific 'Mummerset' speech beloved of actors who are cast as rustics.

RD Blackmore (1825-1900) is another writer whose works feature the regional dialect, which animates the speech of characters in works such as *Lorna Doone*, set in the area around Exmoor in Devon. A sentence such as 'Her coodn't lave 'ouze by raison of the Chirstmas bakkon comin' on, and zome o' the cider welted' presents quite a challenge to the casual reader.

Dialect also features as part of the evocation of the West Country (or 'Wessex' as he called it) in the novels of Thomas Hardy (1840-1928). Hardy regularly includes scenes in which labourers speak in the Dorset dialect, although characters of a higher social position take pains to avoid such language. In *The Mayor of Casterbridge*, Elizabeth-Jane has to learn not to refer to bees as *dumbledores* or wild hyacinths as *greggles* in order to appease her stepfather, who regards dialect words as 'those terrible marks of the beast to the truly genteel'.

Such an avoidance of dialect may fortify a character's social position, but it also deprives a person of the pleasure of using some delightful words. The West Country dialect is particularly well stocked with picturesque names for animals. An earthworm is an *angle-twitch*, while a wasp is an *appledrain*, a slug is a *dew snail*, a mistle thrush may be called a *homescreetch*, and a lapwing is a *hornywink*. Of course, the dialect has some memorable words for other things too: a stupid or feeble person may be called a *dawbake* or a *spuddle*, a molehill can be referred to as a *want knap*, and something that is dirty may be said to be *vutty*.

In the 21st century, people are less likely to pass the time talking about lapwings and molehills. As tourism has replaced agriculture as the major industry of the West Country, other regional words have become more prominent. Cornish people call the tourists who scurry busily around the county *emmets* (using an old dialect word meaning 'an ant'). Elsewhere in the region it is common to hear local people complaining about *grockles* - people from outside who come in and make life less pleasant for the permanent residents.

inflammable *adj* 1 liable to catch fire 2 easily aroused to anger or passion **inflammability** *n*

≡ **USAGE**
≡ See at **flammable**.

inflammation *n* 1 the reaction of living tissue to injury or infection, characterized by heat, redness, swelling, and pain 2 an inflaming or being inflamed

inflammatory *adj* 1 likely to provoke anger 2 characterized by or caused by inflammation

inflatable *adj* 1 capable of being inflated ▷ *n* 2 a plastic or rubber object which can be inflated

inflate *vb* **-flating, -flated** 1 to expand or cause to expand by filling with gas or air 2 to give an impression of greater importance than is justified: *something to inflate their self-esteem* 3 to cause or undergo economic inflation **WORD ORIGIN** Latin *inflare* to blow into

inflation *n* 1 an inflating or being inflated 2 *econ* a progressive increase in the general level of prices brought about by an increase in the amount of money in circulation or by increases in costs 3 *informal* the rate of increase of prices **inflationary** *adj*

inflect *vb* 1 to change (the voice) in tone or pitch 2 *grammar* to change (the form of a word) by inflection 3 to bend or curve **inflective** *adj* **WORD ORIGIN** Latin *inflectere* to curve, alter

inflection *or* **inflexion** *n* 1 change in the pitch of the voice 2 *grammar* a change in the form of a word, signalling change in such grammatical functions as tense or number 3 an angle or bend 4 an inflecting or being inflected 5 *maths* a change in curvature from concave to convex or vice versa **inflectional** *or* **inflexional** *adj*

inflexible *adj* 1 unwilling to be persuaded; obstinate 2 (of a rule etc.) firmly fixed: *inflexible schedules* 3 incapable of being bent: *inflexible joints* **inflexibility** *n*

inflict *vb* 1 to impose (something unpleasant) on 2 to deliver (a blow or wound) **infliction** *n* **inflictor** *n* **WORD ORIGIN** Latin *infligere* to strike (something) against

in-flight *adj* happening or provided during flight in an aircraft: *in-flight meals*

inflorescence *n* *bot* 1 the part of a plant that consists of the flower-bearing stalks 2 the arrangement of the flowers on the stalks 3 the process of flowering; blossoming **WORD ORIGIN** Latin *in-* into + *florescere* to bloom

inflow *n* 1 something, such as a liquid or gas, that flows in 2 the act of flowing in; influx

influence *n* 1 an effect of one person or thing on another 2 the power of a person or thing to have such an effect 3 power resulting from ability, wealth, or position 4 a person or thing with influence 5 **under the influence** *informal* drunk ▷ *vb* **-encing, -enced** 6 to have an effect upon (actions or

events) 7 to persuade or induce **WORD ORIGIN** Latin *influere* to flow into

influential *adj* having or exerting influence

influenza *n* a highly contagious viral disease characterized by fever, muscular pains, and catarrh **WORD ORIGIN** Italian: influence, hence incursion, epidemic

influx *n* 1 the arrival or entry of many people or things 2 the act of flowing in **WORD ORIGIN** Latin *influere* to flow into

info *n* *informal* short for **information**

inform *vb* 1 to give information to; tell: *he informed me that he would be free after lunch* 2 to make knowledgeable (about) or familiar (with): *he'll be informed of his rights* 3 to give incriminating information to the police 4 to impart some essential or formative characteristic to 5 to animate or inspire **informed** *adj* **WORD ORIGIN** Latin *informare* to describe

informal *adj* 1 relaxed and friendly: *an informal interview* 2 appropriate to everyday life or use rather than formal occasions: *informal clothes* 3 (of speech or writing) appropriate to ordinary conversation rather than to formal written language **informality** *n* **informally** *adv*

informant *n* a person who gives information

information *n* 1 knowledge acquired in any manner; facts 2 *computers* **a** the meaning given to data by the way it is interpreted **b** same as **data** (sense 2)

information superhighway *n* the concept of a worldwide network of computers transferring information at high speed

information technology *n* the production, storage, and communication of information using computers and electronic technology

information theory *n* the study of the processes of communication and the transmission of information

informative *adj* giving useful information

informer *n* a person who informs to the police

infra dig *adj* *informal* beneath one's dignity **WORD ORIGIN** Latin *infra dignitatem*

infrared *adj* 1 of or using rays with a wavelength just beyond the red end of the visible spectrum ▷ *n* 2 the infrared part of the spectrum **WORD ORIGIN** Latin *infra* beneath

infrasonic *adj* having a frequency below the range audible to the human ear **WORD ORIGIN** Latin *infra* beneath

infrasound *n* infrasonic waves

infrastructure *n* 1 the basic structure of an organization or system 2 the stock of facilities, services, and equipment in a country, including factories, roads, and schools, that are needed for it to function properly **WORD ORIGIN** Latin *infra* beneath

infrequent *adj* not happening often **infrequently** *adv*

infringe *vb* **-fringing, -fringed** 1 to violate or break (a law or agreement)

2 **infringe on** *or* **upon** to encroach or trespass on: *the press infringed on their privacy* **infringement** *n* **WORD ORIGIN** Latin *infringere* to break off

infuriate *vb* **-ating, -ated** to make very angry **infuriating** *adj* **infuriatingly** *adv* **WORD ORIGIN** Medieval Latin *infuriare*

infuse *vb* **-fusing, -fused** 1 to fill with (an emotion or quality) 2 to soak or be soaked in order to extract flavour **WORD ORIGIN** Latin *infundere* to pour into

infusible *adj* unable to be fused or melted **infusibility** *n*

infusion *n* 1 the act of infusing 2 a liquid obtained by infusing

ingenious (in-**jean**-ee-uss) *adj* showing cleverness and originality: *a truly ingenious invention* **WORD ORIGIN** Latin *ingenium* natural ability

ingenue (**an**-jay-new) *n* an innocent or inexperienced young woman, esp. as a role played by an actress **WORD ORIGIN** French

ingenuity (in-jen-**new**-it-ee) *n* cleverness at inventing things **WORD ORIGIN** Latin *ingenuitas* a freeborn condition; meaning influenced by INGENIOUS

ingenuous (in-**jen**-new-uss) *adj* 1 unsophisticated and trusting 2 frank and straightforward **WORD ORIGIN** Latin *ingenuus* freeborn, virtuous

ingest *vb* to take (food or liquid) into the body **ingestion** *n* **WORD ORIGIN** Latin *ingerere* to put into

ingle *n* *archaic or dialect* a fire in a room or a fireplace **WORD ORIGIN** probably Scottish Gaelic *aingeal* fire

inglenook *n* *Brit* a corner by a fireplace

inglorious *adj* dishonourable or shameful

ingoing *adj* going in; entering

ingot *n* a piece of metal cast in a form suitable for storage, usually a bar **WORD ORIGIN** origin unknown

ingrained *or* **engrained** *adj* 1 (of a habit, feeling, or belief) deeply impressed or instilled 2 (of dirt) worked into or through the fibre or pores **WORD ORIGIN** *dyed in grain* dyed with kermes through the fibre

ingratiate *vb* **-ating, -ated** to act in order to bring (oneself) into favour (with someone) **ingratiating** *adj* **WORD ORIGIN** Latin *in-* in + *gratia* favour

ingratitude *n* lack of gratitude or thanks

ingredient *n* a component of a mixture or compound, esp. in cooking **WORD ORIGIN** Latin *ingrediens* going into

ingress *n* *formal* 1 the act of going or coming in 2 the right or permission to enter **WORD ORIGIN** Latin *ingressus*

ingrowing *adj* (esp. of a toenail) growing abnormally into the flesh **ingrown** *adj*

inhabit *vb* to live or dwell in **inhabitable** *adj* **WORD ORIGIN** Latin *inhabitare*

inhabitant *n* a person or animal that is a permanent resident of a particular place or region

inhalant (in-**hale**-ant) *n* a medicinal preparation inhaled to help breathing problems

inhale *vb* **-haling, -haled** to breathe in (air, smoke, or vapour) **inhalation** *n* **WORD ORIGIN** Latin *in-* in + *halare* to breathe

inhaler *n* a container used to administer an inhalant

inharmonious *adj* lacking harmony; discordant; disagreeing

inhere *vb* **-hering, -hered ● inhere in** to be an inseparable part (of) **WORD ORIGIN** Latin *inhaerere* to stick in

inherent *adj* existing as an inseparable part **inherently** *adv*

inherit *vb* **1** to receive money, property, or a title from someone who has died **2** to receive (a characteristic) from an earlier generation by heredity **3** to receive (a position or situation) from a predecessor: *he inherited a mess* **inheritor** *n* **WORD ORIGIN** Old French *enheriter*

inheritable *adj* **1** capable of being transmitted by heredity from one generation to a later one **2** capable of being inherited

inheritance *n* **1** *law* **a** a hereditary succession to an estate or title **b** the right of an heir to succeed on the death of an ancestor **2** something inherited or to be inherited **3** the act of inheriting **4** the fact of receiving characteristics from an earlier generation by heredity

inheritance tax *n* (in Britain) a tax consisting of a percentage levied on the part of an inheritance that exceeds a specified allowance

inhibit *vb* **1** to restrain or hinder (an impulse or desire) **2** to prohibit or prevent: *an attempt to inhibit nuclear proliferation* **3** *chem* to stop, prevent, or decrease the rate of (a chemical reaction) **inhibited** *adj* **inhibitor** *n* **WORD ORIGIN** Latin *inhibere*

inhibition *n* **1** *psychol* a feeling of fear or embarrassment that stops one from behaving naturally **2** an inhibiting or being inhibited **3** the process of stopping or retarding a chemical reaction

inhospitable *adj* **1** not welcoming; unfriendly **2** (of a place or climate) not easy to live in; harsh

inhuman *adj* **1** cruel or brutal **2** not human

inhumane *adj* extremely cruel or brutal

inhumanity *n, pl* **-ties 1** lack of kindness or compassion **2** an inhumane act

inimical *adj* **1** adverse or unfavourable: *inimical to change* **2** unfriendly or hostile **WORD ORIGIN** Latin *in-* not + *amicus* friendly

inimitable *adj* impossible to imitate **inimitably** *adv*

iniquity *n, pl* **-ties 1** injustice or wickedness **2** a wicked act **iniquitous** *adj* **WORD ORIGIN** Latin *iniquus* unfair

initial *adj* **1** of or at the beginning ▷ *n* **2** the first letter of a word, esp. a person's name **3** *printing* a large letter set at the beginning of a chapter or work ▷ *vb* **-tialling, -tialled** *or US* **-tialing, -tialed 4** to sign with one's initials, esp. to indicate approval **initially** *adv* **WORD ORIGIN** Latin *initium* beginning

initiate *vb* **-ating, -ated 1** to begin or set going: *more women initiate divorce today* **2** to accept (new members) into a group, often through secret ceremonies **3** to teach the fundamentals of a skill or knowledge to (someone) ▷ *n* **4** a person who has been initiated, esp. recently **5** a beginner **initiation** *n* **initiator** *n* **WORD ORIGIN** Latin *initiare*

initiative *n* **1** a first step; a commencing move: *a peace initiative* **2** the right or power to initiate something: *it forced local people to take the initiative* **3** enterprise: *the drive and initiative to create new products* **4 on one's own initiative** without being prompted

inject *vb* **1** *med* to put (a fluid) into the body with a syringe **2** to introduce (a new element): *to inject a dose of realism into the assessment* **injection** *n* **WORD ORIGIN** Latin *injicere* to throw in

injudicious *adj* showing poor judgment; unwise

injunction *n* **1** *law* a court order not to do something **2** an authoritative command **injunctive** *adj* **WORD ORIGIN** Latin *injungere* to enjoin

injure *vb* **-juring, -jured 1** to hurt physically or mentally **2** to do wrong to (a person), esp. by an injustice: *the injured party* **3** to damage: *an opportunity to injure your reputation* **injured** *adj*

injurious *adj* **1** causing harm **2** abusive, slanderous, or libellous

injury *n, pl* **-ries 1** physical hurt **2** a specific instance of this: *a leg injury* **3** harm done to the feelings **4** damage: *inflict no injury on the wealth of the nation* **WORD ORIGIN** Latin *injuria* injustice

● **injury time** *n* *sport* playing time added at the end of a match to compensate for time spent treating injured players. Also called: **stoppage time**

injustice *n* **1** unfairness **2** an unfair action

ink *n* **1** a black or coloured liquid used for printing, writing, and drawing **2** a dark brown fluid squirted for self-concealment by an octopus or cuttlefish ▷ *vb* **3** to mark or cover with ink **4 ink in** to arrange or confirm definitely **WORD ORIGIN** Old French *enque*

inkling *n* a vague idea or suspicion **WORD ORIGIN** Middle English *inclen* to hint at

inkstand *n* a stand or tray for holding writing tools and containers for ink

inkwell *n* a small container for ink, often fitted into the surface of a desk

inky *adj* **inkier, inkiest 1** dark or black, like ink **2** stained with ink **inkiness** *n*

inlaid *adj* **1** set in another material so that the surface is smooth, such as a design in wood **2** made in this way: *an inlaid table-top*

inland *adj* **1** of or in the interior of a country or region, away from a sea or border **2** *chiefly Brit* operating within a country or region; domestic: *inland trade* ▷ *n* **3** the interior of a country or region ▷ *adv* **4** towards or into the interior of a country or region

Inland Revenue *n* (in New Zealand and formerly in Britain) a government department that collects major direct taxes, such as income tax

in-law *n* **1** a relative by marriage ▷ *adj* **2** related by marriage: *his brother-in-law*

inlay *vb* **-laying, -laid 1** to decorate (an article, esp. of furniture) by inserting pieces of wood, ivory, or metal so that the surfaces are smooth and flat ▷ *n* **2** decoration made by inlaying **3** an inlaid article **4** *dentistry* a filling shaped to fit a cavity

inlet *n* **1** a narrow strip of water extending from the sea into the land **2** a passage or valve through which a liquid or gas enters a machine

in-line skate *n* another name for **Rollerblade**

in loco parentis (par-**rent**-iss) in place of a parent: said of a person acting for a parent **WORD ORIGIN** Latin

inmate *n* a person who is confined to an institution such as a prison or hospital

inmost *adj* same as **innermost**

inn *n* a pub or small hotel providing food and accommodation **WORD ORIGIN** Old English

innards *pl n* *informal* **1** the internal organs of the body, esp. the entrails **2** the working parts of a machine **WORD ORIGIN** variant of *inwards*

innate *adj* existing from birth, rather than acquired; inborn: *his innate decency* **innately** *adv* **WORD ORIGIN** Latin *innasci* to be born in

inner *adj* **1** happening or located inside or further inside: *the door to the inner office* **2** of the mind or spirit: *her inner self* **3** exclusive or private: *the inner sanctum of the party secretariat* **4** more profound; less apparent: *the inner meaning* ▷ *n* **5** *archery* **a** the red innermost ring on a target **b** a shot which hits this ring

inner child *n* *psychol* the part of the psyche that retains the feelings as they were experienced in childhood

inner city *n* the parts of a city in or near its centre, where there are often social and economic problems

inner man *or fem* **inner woman** *n* **1** the mind or soul **2** *jocular* the stomach

innermost *adj* **1** most intimate or private: *innermost secrets* **2** furthest within

inner tube *n* an inflatable rubber tube inside a pneumatic tyre casing

inning *n* *baseball* a division of the game consisting of a turn at batting and a turn in the field for each side **WORD ORIGIN** Old English *innung* a going in

innings *n* **1** *cricket* **a** the batting turn of a player or team **b** the runs scored during such a turn **2** a period of opportunity or action

innkeeper n an owner or manager of an inn

innocence n the quality or state of being innocent **WORD ORIGIN** Latin *innocentia* harmlessness

innocent adj 1 not guilty of a particular crime 2 without experience of evil 3 harmless or innocuous 4 **innocent of** without or lacking: *innocent of prejudice* ▷ n 5 an innocent person, esp. a young child or a naive adult **innocently** adv

innocuous adj having no adverse or harmful effect **WORD ORIGIN** Latin *innocuus*

innovate vb -vating, -vated to introduce new ideas or methods **innovative** or **innovatory** adj **innovator** n **WORD ORIGIN** Latin *innovare* to renew

innovation n 1 something newly introduced, such as a new method or device 2 the act of innovating

Innu n 1 a member of an Algonquian people living in Labrador and northern Quebec 2 the Algonquian language of this people

innuendo n, pl -dos or -does an indirect or subtle reference to something rude or unpleasant **WORD ORIGIN** Latin: by hinting

Innuit (in-new-it) n same as **Inuit**

innumerable adj too many to be counted **innumerably** adv

innumerate adj having no understanding of mathematics or science **innumeracy** n

inoculate vb -lating, -lated 1 to protect against disease by injecting with a vaccine 2 to introduce (microorganisms, esp. bacteria) into (a culture medium) **inoculation** n **WORD ORIGIN** Latin *inoculare* to implant

inoffensive adj causing no harm or annoyance

inoperable adj surgery unable to be safely operated on: *an inoperable tumour*

inoperative adj not working or functioning: *continued shelling has rendered the ceasefire inoperative*

inopportune adj badly timed or inappropriate

inordinate adj 1 excessive: *an inordinate amount of time spent arguing* 2 unrestrained, as in behaviour or emotion: *inordinate anger* **inordinately** adv **WORD ORIGIN** Latin *inordinatus* disordered

inorganic adj 1 not having the structure or characteristics of living organisms 2 chem of or denoting chemical compounds that do not contain carbon 3 not resulting from or produced by growth; artificial: *inorganic fertilizers*

inorganic chemistry n the branch of chemistry concerned with the elements and compounds which do not contain carbon

inpatient n a patient who stays in a hospital for treatment

input n 1 resources, such as money, labour, or power, put into a project 2 computers the data fed into a computer ▷ vb -putting, -put 3 to enter (data) in a computer

inquest n 1 an official inquiry into an unexplained, sudden, or violent death, held by a coroner 2 informal an investigation or discussion **WORD ORIGIN** Latin *in-* into + *quaesitus* investigation

inquietude n formal restlessness or anxiety

inquire or **enquire** vb -quiring, -quired 1 to seek information (about) 2 **inquire after** to ask about the health or progress of (a person) 3 **inquire into** to make an investigation 4 **inquire of** to ask (a person) for information: *I'll inquire of my aunt when she is coming* **inquirer** or **enquirer** n **WORD ORIGIN** Latin *inquirere*

inquiry or **enquiry** n, pl -ries 1 a question 2 an investigation

inquisition n 1 a thorough investigation 2 an official inquiry, esp. one held by a jury before an officer of the Crown **inquisitional** adj

Inquisition n history an organization within the Catholic Church (1232–1820) for suppressing heresy

inquisitive adj 1 excessively curious about other people's business 2 eager to learn **inquisitively** adv **inquisitiveness** n

inquisitor n 1 a person who inquires, esp. deeply or ruthlessly 2 **Inquisitor** an officer of the Inquisition

inquisitorial adj 1 of or like an inquisition or an inquisitor 2 offensively curious **inquisitorially** adv

inquorate adj without enough people present to make a quorum

in re (in **ray**) prep in the matter of; concerning **WORD ORIGIN** Latin

INRI Jesus of Nazareth, king of the Jews (the inscription placed over Christ's head during the Crucifixion) **WORD ORIGIN** Latin *Iesus Nazarenus Rex Iudaeorum*

inroads pl n **make inroads into** to start affecting or reducing: *my gambling has made great inroads into my savings*

inrush n a sudden and overwhelming inward flow

ins. 1 inches 2 insurance

insane adj 1 mentally ill 2 stupidly irresponsible: *acting on an insane impulse* **insanely** adv

insanitary adj dirty or unhealthy

insanity n, pl -ties 1 the state of being insane 2 stupidity

insatiable (in-**saysh**-a-bl) adj impossible to satisfy **insatiability** n **insatiably** adv

inscribe vb -scribing, -scribed 1 to mark or engrave with (words, symbols, or letters) 2 to write one's name, and sometimes a brief dedication, on (a book) before giving to someone 3 to enter (a name) on a list 4 geom to draw (a geometric construction) inside another construction so that the two are in contact at as many points as possible but do not intersect **WORD ORIGIN** Latin *inscribere*

inscription n 1 something inscribed, esp. words carved or engraved on a coin, tomb, or ring 2 a signature or brief dedication in a book or on a work of art

inscrutable adj mysterious or enigmatic **inscrutability** n **WORD ORIGIN** Latin *in-* not + *scrutari* to examine

insect n 1 a small animal that has six legs and usually has wings, such as an ant, fly, or butterfly 2 (loosely) any similar invertebrate, such as a spider, tick, or centipede **WORD ORIGIN** Latin *insectum* (animal that has been) cut into

insecticide n a substance used to destroy insects **WORD ORIGIN** insect + Latin *caedere* to kill

insectivore n 1 a small mammal, such as a hedgehog or a shrew, that eats invertebrates 2 a plant or animal that eats insects **insectivorous** adj **WORD ORIGIN** insect + Latin *vorare* to swallow

insecure adj 1 anxious or uncertain 2 not adequately protected: *low-paid or insecure employment* 3 unstable or shaky **insecurity** n

inseminate vb -nating, -nated to impregnate (a female) with semen **insemination** n **WORD ORIGIN** Latin *in-* in + *semen* seed

insensate adj 1 lacking sensation or consciousness 2 insensitive or unfeeling 3 foolish

insensible adj 1 unconscious 2 without feeling 3 imperceptible 4 **insensible of** or **to** unaware of or indifferent to: *insensible to suffering* **insensibility** n

insensitive adj unaware of or ignoring other people's feelings **insensitivity** n

inseparable adj 1 constantly together because of mutual liking: *they became inseparable companions* 2 too closely connected to be separated **inseparably** adv

insert vb 1 to place or fit (something) inside something else 2 to introduce (a clause or comment) into text or a speech ▷ n 3 something inserted, esp. an advertisement in between the pages of a magazine **WORD ORIGIN** Latin *inserere* to plant in

insertion n 1 the act of inserting 2 something inserted, such as an advertisement in a newspaper

in-service adj denoting training that is given to employees during the course of employment: *an in-service course*

inset vb -setting, -set 1 to place in or within; insert ▷ n 2 something inserted 3 printing a small map or diagram set within the borders of a larger one ▷ adj 4 decorated with something inserted

inshore adj 1 in or on the water, but close to the shore: *inshore fishermen* ▷ adv, adj 2 towards the shore from the water: *the boat was forced inshore; a strong wind blowing inshore*

inside prep 1 in or to the interior of: *a bomb had gone off inside the parliament building* 2 in a period of time less than: *they took the lead inside seven minutes* ▷ adj 3 on or of the inside: *an article on the paper's inside pages* 4 by or from someone

Transitivity

odes relating to transitivity crop up in most dictionaries, especially bilingual ones. You'll almost always see something along the lines of vi, vt, or vti, vtr. Vi stands for verb, intransitive, and vt stands for verb, transitive.

Transitive verbs are verbs that have *objects*. The action of the verb is started by somebody (the *subject*, to be pedantic) who then goes on to do something to an *object*, as in 'Fred hit George'. If you stopped after 'Fred hit...' you'd feel something was missing. This feeling of incompleteness means the verb is transitive; if somebody's telling you something and they just trail off, you'll be left feeling frustrated.

Some transitive verbs can take more than one object. You can give somebody something, or give something *to* somebody. The thing you give is called a *direct object*, and the person who gets it is called an *indirect object*. This all makes perfect sense when you translate it into Spanish and realize that indirect objects are different words from direct objects. Otherwise it doesn't matter a great deal, since people who can read essays like this already know how to use both direct and indirect objects.

However, as you might expect, there are also verbs which are intransitive, which don't need (or want) an object. There aren't actually all that many verbs that are only ever intransitive. Here's a slightly edited list:

abstain ache agonize apologize
backfire behave belong blossom
chortle chatter chirp chuckle cling complain creak
crouch daydream dawdle
emigrate erupt exit fall fart fester flow frolic
gleam haggle kneel languish loom mew
quibble rant rave regress
sashay scrimp scurry sidle sizzle skulk slither
slobber sneer sniffle squirm swagger tingle toddle
twitter urinate vanish vibrate
waddle waffle wallow waver
yawn yodel yowl and zoom.

Transitive verbs outnumber intransitive verbs by about ten to one. In fact, most verbs are transitive, especially since some so-called intransitive verbs are only fakes: *allude*, for example, which gets marked intransitive in many dictionaries, is really only ever *allude to*, and it might make sense to treat it as a unit and say it's transitive. You can't sit in a corner and *allude* in the way you can sit and sulk.

Transitive verbs don't all behave in the same way. English and a few other languages have verbs that are made up of more than one word, like *put down*, *pick up*, *take out*, *go in for*, *go off with*, *look forward to*. These are usually lumped together as phrasal verbs. When you use *him*, *her*, *it* with the first three in this list everything's as it would be if you were just using *put*, *pick* or *take*: *put it down*, *pick her up*, *take it out*. But you wouldn't say *go it in for*, *go her off with*, or *look it forward to*. At first sight, the words in *go in for*, *go off with* and *look forward to* are more tightly connected than in *put down*, *pick up* and *take out*; but if you want to use a longer object, then the words *down*, *up*, and *out* can stay glued to their verbs: *I put down my hat on the chair*, *I picked up my coat*, and *I took out the rubbish*. When it comes to looking up combinations like this in a dictionary, you'll find that dictionaries cover verbs like this in different ways – you may find that you need to look in a separate section of phrasal verbs.

Another curiosity is a type of verb sometimes called *ergative*. These are transitive verbs that can be used intransitively, but when they are used intransitively the subject is more like an object. This becomes clearer with an example: *We boiled the broccoli* and *The broccoli boiled*. In the second sentence, the broccoli only boiled because somebody boiled it. There's not much difference between *The broccoli boiled* and *The broccoli was boiled*. Most verbs that can be transitive and intransitive don't work like this; *hunt* would be an example. You can hunt, or you can hunt something; but when you hunt, you aren't yourself hunted, in the way the broccoli was boiled.

Verbs combine with other words and phrases in a great variety of ways. Learner grammars and learner dictionaries are full of examples to show how different verbs can be used. Early dictionaries for learners really went to town on this, and they could have over fifty different verb patterns; so think yourself lucky if all you have to worry about is vi or vt!

within an organization, esp. illicitly: *inside information* **5** of or being the lane in a road which is nearer the side than other lanes going in the same direction: *all the lorries were in the inside lane* ▷ *adv* **6** on, in, or to the inside; indoors: *when the rain started we took our drinks inside* **7** *Brit, Austral, & NZ slang* in or into prison ▷ *n* **8** the inner side, surface, or part of something **9 inside out** with the inside facing outwards **10 know inside out** to know thoroughly ▸ See also **insides**

≡ USAGE
≡ See at **outside**.

inside job *n informal* a crime committed with the assistance of someone employed by or trusted by the victim

insider *n* a member of a group or organization who therefore has exclusive information about it

insider dealing *n* the illegal practice of a person on the stock exchange or in the civil service taking advantage of early confidential information in order to deal in shares for personal profit

insides *pl n informal* the stomach and bowels

insidious *adj* working in a subtle or apparently harmless way, but nevertheless dangerous or deadly: *an insidious virus* **insidiously** *adv* **insidiousness** *n*
WORD ORIGIN Latin *insidiae* an ambush

insight *n* **1** a penetrating understanding, as of a complex situation or problem **2** the ability to perceive clearly or deeply the inner nature of things

insignia (in-**sig**-nee-a) *n, pl* **-nias** *or* **-nia** a badge or emblem of membership, office, or honour
WORD ORIGIN Latin: badges

insignificant *adj* having little or no importance **insignificance** *n*

insincere *adj* pretending what one does not feel **insincerely** *adv* **insincerity** *n*

insinuate *vb* **-ating, -ated 1** to suggest indirectly by allusion, hints, or innuendo **2** to get (someone, esp. oneself) into a position by gradual manoeuvres: *she insinuated herself into the conversation*
WORD ORIGIN Latin *insinuare* to wind one's way into

insinuation *n* **1** an indirect or devious hint or suggestion **2** an act or the practice of insinuating

insipid *adj* **1** dull and boring **2** lacking flavour **insipidity** *n*
WORD ORIGIN Latin *in-* not + *sapidus* full of flavour

insist *vb* (often foll. by *on* or *upon*) **1** to make a determined demand (for): *he insisted on his rights* **2** to express a convinced belief (in) or assertion (of): *she insisted that she had been given permission*
WORD ORIGIN Latin *insistere* to stand upon, urge

insistent *adj* **1** making continual and persistent demands **2** demanding attention: *the chirruping of an insistent bird* **insistence** *n* **insistently** *adv*

in situ *adv, adj* in the original position
WORD ORIGIN Latin

in so far as *or* **insofar as** *prep* to the degree or extent that

insole *n* **1** the inner sole of a shoe or boot **2** a loose inner sole used to give extra warmth or to make a shoe fit

insolent *adj* rude and disrespectful **insolence** *n* **insolently** *adv*
WORD ORIGIN Latin *in-* not + *solere* to be accustomed

insoluble *adj* **1** impossible to solve **2** not able to be dissolved **insolubility** *n*

insolvent *adj* **1** unable to pay one's debts ▷ *n* **2** a person who is insolvent **insolvency** *n*

insomnia *n* inability to sleep **insomniac** *n, adj*
WORD ORIGIN Latin *in-* not + *somnus* sleep

insomuch *adv* **1** (foll. by *as* or *that*) to such an extent or degree **2** (foll. by *as*) because of the fact (that)

insouciant *adj* carefree or unconcerned **insouciance** *n*
WORD ORIGIN French

inspan *vb* **-spanning, -spanned** *chiefly S African* **1** to harness (animals) to (a vehicle); yoke **2** to press (people) into service
WORD ORIGIN Middle Dutch *inspannen*

inspect *vb* **1** to examine closely, esp. for faults or errors **2** to examine officially **inspection** *n*
WORD ORIGIN Latin *inspicere*

inspector *n* **1** an official who checks that things or places meet certain regulations and standards **2** a police officer ranking below a superintendent and above a sergeant

inspectorate *n* **1** a group of inspectors **2** the position or duties of an inspector

inspiration *n* **1** stimulation of the mind or feelings to activity or creativity **2** a person or thing that causes this state **3** an inspired idea or action **inspirational** *adj*

inspire *vb* **-spiring, -spired 1** to stimulate (a person) to activity or creativity **2** to arouse (an emotion or a reaction): *he inspires confidence*
WORD ORIGIN Latin *in-* into + *spirare* to breathe

inspired *adj* **1** brilliantly creative: *his most inspired compositions* **2** very clever and accurate: *an inspired guess*

inst. *old-fashioned* instant (this month)

instability *n* lack of steadiness or reliability

install *vb* **1** to put in and prepare (equipment) for use **2** to place (a person) formally in a position or rank **3** to settle (a person, esp. oneself) in a position or state: *Tony installed himself in an armchair*
WORD ORIGIN Medieval Latin *installare*

installation *n* **1** installing **2** equipment that has been installed **3** a place containing equipment for a particular purpose: *radar installation*

installment plan *n US Also* (*Canad*): **instalment plan**. Same as **hire-purchase**

instalment *or US* **installment** *n* **1** one of the portions into which a debt is divided for payment at regular intervals **2** a portion of something that is issued,

broadcast, or published in parts
WORD ORIGIN probably from Old French *estal* something fixed

instance *n* **1** a case or particular example **2** urgent request or order: *at the instance of* **3 for instance** as an example **4 in the first instance** in the first place; initially ▷ *vb* **-stancing, -stanced 5** to mention as an example
WORD ORIGIN Latin *instantia* a being close upon

instant *n* **1** a very brief time; moment **2** a particular moment: *at the same instant* ▷ *adj* **3** immediate **4** (of foods) able to be prepared very quickly and easily: *instant coffee* **5** urgent or pressing **6** of the present month: *a letter of the 7th instant*
WORD ORIGIN Latin *instans* present, pressing closely

instantaneous *adj* happening at once: *the applause was instantaneous* **instantaneously** *adv*

instantly *adv* immediately

instant message *n* **1** an electronic message sent in real time over a computer network ▷ *vb* **instant-message 2** to communicate with (another person) using such messages **instant messaging** *n*

instead *adv* **1** as a replacement or substitute for the person or thing mentioned **2 instead of** in place of or as an alternative to
WORD ORIGIN *in stead* in place

instep *n* **1** the middle part of the foot forming the arch between the ankle and toes **2** the part of a shoe or stocking covering this

instigate *vb* **-gating, -gated 1** to cause to happen: *to instigate rebellion* **2** to urge on to some action **instigation** *n* **instigator** *n*
WORD ORIGIN Latin *instigare*

instil *or US* **instill** *vb* **-stilling, -stilled 1** to introduce (an idea or feeling) gradually in someone's mind **2** *rare* to pour in or inject drop by drop **instillation** *n* **instiller** *n*
WORD ORIGIN Latin *instillare* to pour in a drop at a time

instinct *n* **1** the inborn tendency to behave in a particular way without the need for thought: *maternal instinct* **2** natural reaction: *my first instinct was to get out of the car* **3** intuition: *Mr Barr's mother said she knew by instinct that her son was safe*
WORD ORIGIN Latin *instinctus* roused

instinctive *or* **instinctual** *adj* done or happening without any logical thought: *an instinctive understanding of people* **instinctively** *or* **instinctually** *adv*

institute *n* **1** an organization set up for a specific purpose, especially research or teaching **2** the building where such an organization is situated **3** a rule, custom, or precedent ▷ *vb* **-tuting, -tuted 4** to start or establish **5** to install in a position or office
WORD ORIGIN Latin *instituere*, from *statuere* to place

institution *n* **1** a large important organization such as a university or bank **2** a hospital etc. for people with special needs **3** an established custom, law, or principle: *the institution of marriage*

4 *informal* a well-established person or feature: *the programme has became an institution* **5** an instituting or being instituted

institutional *adj* **1** of or relating to an institution: *institutional care* **2** dull, routine, and uniform: *institutional meals* **institutionalism** *n*

institutionalize *or* **-lise** *vb* **-lizing, -lized** *or* **-lising, -lised** **1** (*often passive*) to subject (a person) to institutional life, often causing apathy and dependence on routine **2** to make or become an institution: *institutionalized religion* **3** to place in an institution

instruct *vb* **1** to order to do something **2** to teach (someone) how to do something **3** to brief (a solicitor or barrister) **word origin** Latin *instruere*

instruction *n* **1** a direction or order **2** the process or act of teaching **instructional** *adj*

instructions *pl n* information on how to do or use something: *the plane had ignored instructions from air traffic controllers*

instructive *adj* informative or helpful

instructor *n* **1** a person who teaches something **2** *US & Canad* a college teacher ranking below assistant professor

instrument *n* **1** a tool or implement, esp. one used for precision work **2** *music* any of various devices that can be played to produce musical sounds **3** a measuring device to show height, speed, etc.: *the pilot's eyes never left his instruments* **4** *informal* a person used by another to gain an end **5** an important factor in something: *her evidence was an instrument in his arrest* **6** a formal legal document **word origin** Latin *instrumentum*

instrumental *adj* **1** helping to cause **2** played by or composed for musical instruments **3** of or done with an instrument: *instrumental error*

instrumentalist *n* a person who plays a musical instrument

instrumentation *n* **1** a set of instruments in a car etc. **2** the arrangement of music for instruments **3** the list of instruments needed for a piece of music

instrument panel *n* a panel holding the instruments in a vehicle or on a machine

insubordinate *adj* not submissive to authority **insubordination** *n*

insubstantial *adj* **1** flimsy, fine, or slight **2** imaginary or unreal

insufferable *adj* unbearable **insufferably** *adv*

insufficient *adj* not enough for a particular purpose **insufficiency** *n* **insufficiently** *adv*

insular *adj* **1** not open to change or new ideas: *theatre tradition become rather insular* **2** of or like an island **insularity** *n* **word origin** Latin *insula* island

insulate *vb* **-lating, -lated** **1** to prevent or reduce the transfer of electricity, heat, or sound by surrounding or lining with a nonconducting material **2** to isolate or set apart **insulator** *n*

word origin Late Latin *insulatus* made into an island

insulation *n* **1** material used to insulate something **2** the act of insulating

insulin (**in**-syoo-lin) *n* a hormone produced in the pancreas which controls the amount of sugar in the blood **word origin** Latin *insula* islet (of tissue in the pancreas)

insult *vb* **1** to treat or speak to rudely: *they insulted us and even threatened to kill us* ▷ *n* **2** an offensive remark or action **3** a person or thing producing the effect of an insult: *their explanation is an insult to our intelligence* **word origin** Latin *insultare* to jump upon

insuperable *adj* impossible to overcome; insurmountable **insuperability** *n*

insupportable *adj* **1** impossible to tolerate **2** incapable of being upheld or justified: *an insupportable accusation*

insurance *n* **1** the agreement by which one makes regular payments to a company who pay an agreed sum if damage, loss, or death occurs **2** the money paid for insurance or by an insurance company **3** a means of protection: *sensible insurance against heart attacks*

insurance policy *n* a contract of insurance

insure *vb* **-suring, -sured** **1** to guarantee or protect (against risk or loss) **2** (*often foll. by* *against*) to issue (a person) with an insurance policy or take out an insurance policy (on): *the players were insured against accidents* **3** *chiefly US* same as **ensure** ▷ **insurable** *adj* **insurability** *n*

insured *n* **the insured** the person covered by an insurance policy

insurer *n* a person or company that sells insurance

insurgent *adj* **1** rebellious or in revolt against an established authority ▷ *n* **2** a person who takes part in a rebellion **insurgency** *n* **word origin** Latin *insurgens* rising

insurmountable *adj* impossible to overcome: *insurmountable problems*

insurrection *n* the act of rebelling against an established authority **insurrectionist** *n, adj* **word origin** Latin *insurgere* to rise up

int. **1** internal **2** Also: **Int** international

intact *adj* not changed or damaged in any way **word origin** Latin *intactus*

intaglio (in-**tah**-lee-oh) *n, pl* **-lios** *or* **-li** **1** a seal or gem decorated with an engraved design **2** an engraved design **intagliated** *adj* **word origin** Italian

intake *n* **1** a thing or a quantity taken in: *an intake of students* **2** the act of taking in **3** the opening through which fluid or gas enters a pipe or engine

intangible *adj* **1** difficult for the mind to grasp: *intangible ideas* **2** incapable of being felt by touch **intangibility** *n*

integer *n* any positive or negative whole number or zero, as opposed to a number

with fractions or decimals **word origin** Latin: untouched

integral *adj* **1** being an essential part of a whole **2** whole or complete **3** *maths* **a** of or involving an integral **b** involving or being an integer ▷ *n* **4** *maths* the sum of a large number of minute quantities, summed either between stated limits (**definite integral**) or in the absence of limits (**indefinite integral**)

integral calculus *n* *maths* the branch of calculus concerned with the determination of integrals and their use in solving differential equations

integrand *n* *maths* a mathematical function to be integrated

integrate *vb* **-grating, -grated** **1** to make or be made into a whole **2** to amalgamate (a racial or religious group) with an existing community **3** to designate (an institution) for use by all races or groups **4** *maths* to determine the integral of a function or variable **integration** *n* **word origin** Latin *integrare*

integrated circuit *n* a tiny electronic circuit

integrity *n* **1** honesty **2** the quality of being whole or united: *respect for a state's territorial integrity* **3** the quality of being unharmed or sound: *the integrity of the cell membrane* **word origin** Latin *integritas*

integument *n* any natural protective covering, such as a skin, rind, or shell **word origin** Latin *integumentum*

intellect *n* **1** the ability to understand, think, and reason **2** a particular person's mind or intelligence, esp. a brilliant one: *his intellect is wasted on that job* **3** *informal* a person who has a brilliant mind **word origin** Latin *intellectus* comprehension

intellectual *adj* **1** of, involving, or appealing to the intellect: *intellectual literature* **2** clever or intelligent ▷ *n* **3** a person who has a highly developed intellect **intellectuality** *n* **intellectually** *adv*

intelligence *n* **1** the ability to understand, learn, and think things out quickly **2** the collection of secret information, esp. for military purposes **3** a group or department collecting military information **4** *old-fashioned* news or information **word origin** Latin *intellegere* to understand, literally: to choose between

intelligence quotient *n* a measure of the intelligence of a person calculated by dividing the person's mental age by his or her actual age and multiplying the result by 100

intelligent *adj* **1** having or showing intelligence: *an intelligent child; an intelligent guess* **2** (of a computerized device) able to initiate or modify action in the light of ongoing events **intelligently** *adv*

intelligent design *n* a theory that rejects the theory of natural selection, arguing for an intelligent cause in the form of a creator

intelligentsia n **the intelligentsia** the educated or intellectual people in a society
WORD ORIGIN Russian *intelligentsiya*

intelligible adj able to be understood **intelligibility** n

intemperate adj **1** unrestrained or uncontrolled: *intemperate remarks* **2** drinking alcohol too much or too often **3** extreme or severe: *an intemperate climate* **intemperance** n

intend vb **1** to propose or plan (something or to do something) **2** to have as one's purpose **3** to mean to express or indicate: *no criticism was intended* **4** (often foll. by *for*) to design or destine (for a certain purpose or person): *the plane was never intended for combat*
WORD ORIGIN Latin *intendere* to stretch forth

intended adj **1** planned or future ▷ n **2** *informal* a person whom one is to marry

intense adj **1** of very great force, strength, degree, or amount: *intense heat* **2** characterized by deep or forceful feelings: *an intense person* **intensely** adv **intenseness** n
WORD ORIGIN Latin *intensus* stretched

≡ **USAGE**
≡ *Intense* is sometimes wrongly used
≡ where *intensive* is meant: *the land is under*
≡ *intensive* (not *intense*) *cultivation. Intensely*
≡ is sometimes wrongly used where
≡ *intently* is meant: *he listened intently*
≡ (not *intensely*).

intensifier n a word, esp. an adjective or adverb, that intensifies the meaning of the word or phrase that it modifies, for example, *very* or *extremely*

intensify vb **-fies, -fying, -fied** to make or become intense or more intense **intensification** n

intensity n, pl **-ties 1** the state or quality of being intense **2** extreme force, degree, or amount **3** *physics* the amount or degree of strength of electricity, heat, light, or sound per unit area of volume

intensive adj **1** of or needing concentrated effort or resources: *intensive training* **2** using one specified factor more than others: *labour-intensive* **3** *agriculture* designed to increase production from a particular area: *intensive farming* **4** *grammar* (of a word) giving emphasis, for example, *very* in *the very same* **intensively** adv **intensiveness** n

≡ **USAGE**
≡ See at **intense**.

intensive care n thorough, continuously supervised treatment of an acutely ill patient in a hospital

intent n **1** something that is intended **2** *law* the will or purpose to commit a crime: *loitering with intent* **3** **to all intents and purposes** in almost every respect; virtually ▷ adj **4** having one's attention firmly fixed: *an intent look* **5** **intent on** or **upon** strongly resolved on: *intent on winning the election* **intently** adv **intentness** n
WORD ORIGIN Late Latin *intentus* aim

≡ **USAGE**
≡ See at **intense**.

intention n something intended; a plan, idea, or purpose: *he had no intention of resigning*

intentional adj done on purpose **intentionally** adv

inter (in-**ter**) vb **-terring, -terred** to bury (a corpse)
WORD ORIGIN Latin *in-* into + *terra* earth

inter- prefix **1** between or among: *international* **2** together, mutually, or reciprocally: *interdependent*
WORD ORIGIN Latin

interact vb to act on or in close relation with each other **interaction** n **interactive** adj

inter alia (in-ter **ale**-ya) adv among other things
WORD ORIGIN Latin

interbreed vb **-breeding, -bred 1** to breed within a related group so as to produce particular characteristics in the offspring **2** same as **crossbreed** (sense 1)

intercede vb **-ceding, -ceded 1** to plead in favour of **2** to act as a mediator in order to end a disagreement: *a policeman was watching the beatings without interceding*
WORD ORIGIN Latin *inter-* between + *cedere* to move

intercept vb **1** to stop or seize on the way from one place to another **2** *maths* to mark off or include (part of a line, curve, plane, or surface) between two points or lines ▷ n **3** *maths* **a** a point at which two figures intersect **b** the distance from the origin to the point at which a line, curve, or surface cuts a coordinate axis **interception** n **interceptor** n
WORD ORIGIN Latin *intercipere* to seize before arrival

intercession n **1** the act of interceding **2** a prayer offered to God on behalf of others **intercessor** n

interchange vb **-changing, -changed 1** to change places or cause to change places ▷ n **2** the act of interchanging **3** a motorway junction of interconnecting roads and bridges designed to prevent streams of traffic crossing one another **interchangeable** adj **interchangeably** adv

Intercity adj *trademark* (in Britain) denoting a fast train (service) travelling between cities

intercom n an internal communication system with loudspeakers
WORD ORIGIN short for *intercommunication*

intercommunicate vb **-cating, -cated 1** to communicate mutually **2** (of two rooms) to interconnect **intercommunication** n

intercommunion n association between Churches, involving mutual reception of Holy Communion

interconnect vb to connect with one another **interconnected** adj **interconnection** n

intercontinental adj travelling between or linking continents

intercourse n **1** the act of having sex **2** communication or dealings between individuals or groups

WORD ORIGIN Latin *intercurrere* to run between

interdenominational adj among or involving more than one denomination of the Christian Church

interdepartmental adj of or between different departments

interdependent adj dependent on one another **interdependence** n

interdict n **1** *law* an official prohibition or restraint **2** *RC Church* the exclusion of a person or place from certain sacraments, although not from communion ▷ vb **3** to prohibit or forbid **interdiction** n **interdictory** adj
WORD ORIGIN Latin *interdicere* to forbid

interdisciplinary adj involving more than one branch of learning

interest n **1** curiosity or concern about something or someone **2** the power of causing this: *to have great interest* **3** something in which one is interested; a hobby or pursuit **4** (often pl) advantage: *in one's own interests* **5** money paid for the use of credit or borrowed money: *she borrowed money at 25 per cent interest* **6** (often pl) a right, share, or claim, esp. in a business or property **7** (often pl) a group of people with common aims: *foreign interests* ▷ vb **8** to arouse the curiosity or concern of **9** to cause to become interested or involved in something
WORD ORIGIN Latin: it concerns

interested adj **1** showing or having interest **2** involved in or affected by: *a consultation paper sent to interested parties*

interest group n a group of persons who attempt to influence legislators on behalf of a particular interest

interesting adj causing interest **interestingly** adv

interface n **1** an area where two things interact or link: *the interface between Islamic culture and Western modernity* **2** an electrical circuit linking one device, esp. a computer, with another **3** *physics, chem* a surface that forms the boundary between two liquids or chemical phases that cannot be mixed ▷ vb **-facing, -faced 4** to connect or be connected with by interface **interfacial** adj

interfacing n **1** a piece of fabric sewn beneath the facing of a garment to give shape and firmness **2** same as **interlining**

interfaith adj relating to, between, or involving different religions

interfere vb **-fering, -fered 1** to try to influence other people's affairs where one is not involved or wanted **2** *physics* to produce or cause to produce interference **3 interfere with a** to clash with or hinder: *child-bearing may interfere with your career* **b** *Brit, Austral, & NZ, euphemistic* to abuse sexually **interfering** adj
WORD ORIGIN Old French *s'entreferir* to collide

interference n **1** the act of interfering **2** any undesired signal that interferes with the reception of radio waves **3** *physics* the meeting of two waves which reinforce or neutralize each other depending on whether they are in or out of phase

The British Influence on Canada

No country that was once part of the British Empire can be exempt from the legal and military terminology of the United Kingdom. Yet the impact of the local is felt at every turn.

Canada is no exception. Although *Dominion* was first applied to Virginia as an overseas British colony, its sense came to embrace self-governing polities of the British Empire, and later of the Commonwealth of Nations. The first significant use of the word came in 1867, when four colonies joined to form the *Dominion of Canada*. Newfoundland, too, had been a Dominion before it joined Canada in 1949. It's perhaps a pity that the term, officially and unofficially, has fallen into disuse.

Confusingly, the *Confederation* of 1867 resulted in a Canadian *federation*. The queen or king of the United Kingdom remains, for constitutional purposes, the *head of state*, whose representative is, federally, a *Governor General* and, in a province, a *Lieutenant Governor*. The Canadian *prime minister*, itself an inherited British term, is the *head of government*. Both the prime minister and the *premiers* of provinces are termed *first ministers* and meet from time to time to discuss intergovernmental matters at a *First Ministers' Conference*.

Canada, like the United Kingdom, has a parliament, whose workings reflect the evolution of *responsible government*, by which a cabinet is held responsible to an elected legislature and remains in power so long as its enjoys its confidence. Before this structure came to be, British criminal and civil law prevailed in North American colonies, including those that, during the *Conquest* in 1763, Britain had wrested from the French. As in so many other things, Quebec was an exception since, though it is governed by the federal *Criminal Code*, its civil law, the *Code civil*, is a much-updated legacy of French royalist and Napoleonic regimes. In Canada, a *crown attorney* or *crown prosecutor* prosecutes indictable offences, including, for example, one committed by a *found-in*, an unofficial term for someone discovered to be frequenting an illegal brothel, bar, or gambling den. A lawyer who defends an accused under common law is not merely a barrister, as in the United Kingdom, but a *barrister and solicitor*. In some provinces, a superior-court trial division is a *Queen's* (or *King's*) *Bench* and, in a few provinces, distinguished, or at least well-connected, lawyers may receive the honorific *Queen's* or *King's Counsel.*

The modified British character of Canadian institutions was due, not just to centuries of colonial administration, but to the influx of *United Empire Loyalists*, refugees who fled north from the American Revolution and its aftermath. In language use, this transfer of population, not to mention Canadian proximity to the fast-growing republic to the south, resulted in a blend of British and American spelling practices and pronunciations. Canadians are notoriously inconsistent in their usages, but most adhere to *-re* and *-our* spellings in words like *centre* and *honour,* and tend to say *zed*, not *zee*, for the letter *z*. As for *lieutenant*, they usually stand on guard for LEFtenant, not LOOtenant.

Even after branches of the armed forces were combined during *Unification* in 1968, ranks of the army, navy, and air force largely followed the British pattern. But the three main elements of the *Canadian Armed Forces*, the army, navy, and air force, are officially called *commands*. They consist of the *Land Force Command*, including the militia, *Maritime Command*, and *Air Command*. Though *Royal* was dropped in some names like the *Royal Canadian Air Force* and the *Royal Canadian Navy* after Unification, it persists in titles like the *Royal Canadian Mounted Police* (the *RCMP*), even though the *Mounties* are not particularly royal (and not usually on horseback), and in *royal commissions*, appointed by governments to enquire into, and report on, particular matters, though not perhaps on why there ought to be royal commissions.

The *Constitution Act* of 1982, including a *Charter of Rights and Freedoms,* amended, repealed, and substantially augmented the *British North America Act* passed by the British Parliament in 1867. Because the revised constitution was framed within Canada, 'brought home', a new noun and verb came to prominence in Canadian English: *patriation* and *patriate*. Although patriotism to some may appear to be an undervalued quality in Canada, at least compared to the US model, aspects of it still live on in these words.

interferon *n* *biochem* a protein made by cells that stops the development of an invading virus

interfuse *vb* **-fusing, -fused** 1 to mix or become mixed 2 to blend or fuse together **interfusion** *n*

intergalactic *adj* occurring or located between different galaxies

interim *adj* 1 temporary or provisional: *an interim government* ▷ 2 **in the interim** during the intervening time **WORD ORIGIN** Latin: meanwhile

interior *n* 1 a part or region that is on the inside: *the interior of the earth* 2 the inside of a building or room, with respect to design and decoration 3 the central area of a country or continent, furthest from the sea 4 a picture of the inside of a room or building ▷ *adj* 5 of, situated on, or suitable for the inside 6 mental or spiritual: *interior development* 7 coming or acting from within 8 of a nation's domestic affairs **WORD ORIGIN** Latin

interior angle *n* an angle of a polygon contained between two adjacent sides

interior decoration *n* 1 the decoration and furnishings of the interior of a room or house 2 Also called: **interior design** the art or business of planning this **interior decorator** *n*

interj. interjection

interject *vb* to make (a remark) suddenly or as an interruption **WORD ORIGIN** Latin *interjicere* to place between

interjection *n* a word or phrase which is used on its own and which expresses sudden emotion

interlace *vb* **-lacing, -laced** to join by lacing or weaving together: *interlaced fingers*

interlard *vb* to insert in or occur throughout: *to interlard one's writing with foreign phrases*

interlay *vb* **-laying, -laid** to insert (layers) between: *to interlay gold among the silver*

interleaf *n, pl* **-leaves** an extra leaf which is inserted

interleave *vb* **-leaving, -leaved** to insert, as blank leaves in a book, between other leaves

interleukin (in-ter-**loo**-kin) *n* *biochem* a substance obtained from white blood cells that stimulates their activity against infection and may be used to fight some forms of cancer

interline¹ *vb* **-lining, -lined** to write or print (matter) between the lines of (a text or book)

interline² *vb* **-lining, -lined** to provide (a part of a garment) with a second lining

interlining *n* the material used to interline parts of garments

interlink *vb* to connect together

interlock *vb* 1 to join or be joined firmly together ▷ *n* 2 a device used to prevent a mechanism from operating independently or unsafely

interlocutor (in-ter-**lock**-yew-ter) *n* *formal* a person who takes part in a conversation

WORD ORIGIN Latin *inter-* between + *loqui* to talk

interlocutory (in-ter-**lock**-yew-tree) *adj* 1 *law* pronounced during the course of legal proceedings; provisional: *an interlocutory injunction* 2 *formal* of dialogue; conversational

interloper (**in**-ter-lope-er) *n* a person in a place or situation where he or she has no right to be

interlude *n* 1 a period of time or different activity between longer periods or events 2 a pause between the acts of a play b a brief piece of music or other entertainment performed during this pause **WORD ORIGIN** Latin *inter-* between + *ludus* play

intermarry *vb* **-ries, -rying, -ried** 1 (of different races, religions, or social groups) to become connected by marriage 2 to marry within one's own family or tribe **intermarriage** *n*

intermediary *n, pl* **-aries** 1 a person who tries to bring about agreement between others 2 a messenger ▷ *adj* 3 acting as an intermediary 4 intermediate

intermediate *adj* 1 occurring between two points or extremes 2 (of a class, course, etc.) suitable for learners with some level of skill or competence ▷ *n* 3 something intermediate 4 *chem* a substance formed between the first and final stages of a chemical process **intermediation** *n* **WORD ORIGIN** Latin *inter-* between + *medius* middle

interment *n* a burial

intermezzo (in-ter-**met**-so) *n, pl* **-zos** or **-zi** 1 a short piece of instrumental music performed between the acts of a play or opera 2 a a short composition between two longer movements in an extended musical work b a similar composition intended for independent performance **WORD ORIGIN** Italian

interminable *adj* seemingly endless because boring: *an interminable rambling anecdote* **interminably** *adv*

intermingle *vb* **-gling, -gled** to mix together

intermission *n* an interval between parts of a play, film, etc. **WORD ORIGIN** Latin *intermittere* to leave off, cease

intermittent *adj* occurring at intervals **intermittently** *adv*

intern *vb* 1 to imprison, esp. during wartime ▷ *n* 2 *chiefly US* a trainee doctor in a hospital **internment** *n* **WORD ORIGIN** Latin *internus* internal

internal *adj* 1 of, situated on, or suitable for the inside 2 *anat* affecting or relating to the inside of the body: *internal bleeding* 3 of a nation's domestic affairs: *internal politics* 4 coming or acting from within an organization: *an internal reorganization* 5 spiritual or mental: *internal conflict* **internally** *adv* **WORD ORIGIN** Latin *internus*

internal-combustion engine *n* an engine in which power is produced by the explosion of a fuel-and-air mixture within the cylinders

international *adj* 1 of or involving two or more nations 2 controlling or legislating for several nations: *an international court* 3 available for use by all nations: *international waters* ▷ *n* 4 *sport* a a game or match between the national teams of different countries b a member of a national team **internationally** *adv*

International *n* any of several international socialist organizations

International Date Line *n* the line approximately following the 180° meridian from Greenwich on the east side of which the date is one day earlier than on the west

internationalism *n* the ideal or practice of cooperation and understanding for the good of all nations **internationalist** *n*

International Phonetic Alphabet *n* a series of signs and letters for the representation of human speech sounds

International Style or **Modernism** *n* a 20th-century architectural style characterized by undecorated straight forms and the use of glass, steel, and reinforced concrete

internecine *adj* *formal* destructive to both sides: *internecine war* **WORD ORIGIN** Latin *internecare* to destroy

internee *n* a person who is interned

internet *n* (*sometimes cap*) a large public access computer network linked to others worldwide

internist *n* a physician who specializes in internal medicine

interpenetrate *vb* **-trating, -trated** 1 to penetrate (something) thoroughly 2 to penetrate each other or one another mutually **interpenetration** *n*

interpersonal *adj* of or relating to relationships between people

interplanetary *adj* of or linking planets

interplay *n* the action and reaction of things upon each other

Interpol International Criminal Police Organization: an association of over 100 national police forces, devoted chiefly to fighting international crime

interpolate (in-**ter**-pole-ate) *vb* **-lating, -lated** 1 to insert (a comment or passage) into (a conversation or text) 2 *maths* to estimate (a value of a function) between the values already known **interpolation** *n* **WORD ORIGIN** Latin *interpolare* to give a new appearance to

interpose *vb* **-posing, -posed** 1 to place (something) between or among other things 2 to interrupt (with comments or questions) 3 to put forward so as to interrupt: *he ended the discussion by interposing a veto* **interposition** *n* **WORD ORIGIN** Latin *inter-* between + *ponere* to put

interpret *vb* 1 to explain the meaning of 2 to work out the significance of: *his remarks were widely interpreted as a promise not to raise taxes* 3 to convey the meaning of (a poem, song, etc.) in performance 4 to act as an interpreter **interpretive** *adj* **WORD ORIGIN** Latin *interpretari*

interpretation *n* **1** the act or result of interpreting or explaining **2** the particular way in which a performer expresses his or her view of a composition: *an interpretation of Mahler's fourth symphony* **3** explanation, as of a historical site, provided by the use of original objects, visual display material, etc.

interpreter *n* **1** a person who translates orally from one language into another **2** *computers* a program that translates a statement in a source program to machine language and executes it before translating and executing the next statement

interpretive centre *n* a building situated at a place of interest, such as a country park or historical site, that provides information about the site by showing videos, exhibiting objects, etc.

interracial *adj* between or among people of different races

interregnum *n, pl* **-nums** or **-na** a period between the end of one ruler's reign and the beginning of the next **interregnal** *adj* **WORD ORIGIN** Latin *inter-* between + *regnum* reign

interrelate *vb* **-lating, -lated** to connect (two or more things) or (of two or more things) to become connected to each other **interrelation** *n* **interrelationship** *n*

interrogate *vb* **-gating, -gated** to question (someone) closely **interrogation** *n* **interrogator** *n* **WORD ORIGIN** Latin *interrogare*

interrogative (in-ter-**rog**-a-tiv) *adj* **1** used in asking a question: *an interrogative pronoun* **2** of or like a question: *an interrogative look* ▷ *n* **3** an interrogative word, phrase, sentence, or construction

interrogatory (in-ter-**rog**-a-tree) *adj* **1** expressing or involving a question ▷ *n, pl* **-tories** **2** a question or interrogation

interrupt *vb* **1** to break into (a conversation or discussion) by questions or comment **2** to stop (a process or activity) temporarily **interrupted** *adj* **interruptive** *adj* **WORD ORIGIN** Latin *inter-* between + *rumpere* to break

interrupter or **interruptor** *n* a device for opening and closing an electric circuit

interruption *n* **1** something that interrupts, such as a comment or question **2** an interval or intermission **3** the act of interrupting or the state of being interrupted

interscholastic *adj* occurring between two or more schools: *an interscholastic competition*

intersect *vb* **1** (of roads or lines) to cross (each other) **2** to divide or mark off (a place, area, or surface) by passing through or across **WORD ORIGIN** Latin *intersecare* to divide

intersection *n* **1** a point at which things intersect, esp. a road junction **2** the act of intersecting or the state of being intersected **3** *maths* **a** a point or set of points common to two or more geometric figures **b** the set of elements that are common to two sets **intersectional** *adj*

intersex *n* **1** the condition of having characteristics in between those of a male and a female **2** an individual exhibiting such characteristics

intersperse *vb* **-spersing, -spersed** **1** to scatter among, between, or on **2** to mix (something) with other things scattered here and there **interspersion** *n* **WORD ORIGIN** Latin *inter-* between + *spargere* to sprinkle

interstellar *adj* between or among stars

interstice (in-**ter**-stiss) *n* (*usually pl*) **1** a small gap or crack between things **2** *physics* the space between adjacent atoms in a crystal lattice **WORD ORIGIN** Latin *interstitium* interval

intertwine *vb* **-twining, -twined** to twist together

interval *n* **1** the period of time between two events **2** *Austral & Brit* a short period between parts of a play, concert, etc. **3** *music* the difference of pitch between two notes **4** **at intervals** **a** now and then: *turn the chicken at intervals* **b** with a certain amount of space between: *the poles were placed at intervals of twenty metres* **WORD ORIGIN** Latin *intervallum*, literally: space between two palisades

intervene *vb* **-vening, -vened** **1** (often foll. by *in*) to involve oneself in a situation, esp. to prevent conflict **2** to interrupt a conversation **3** to happen so as to stop something: *he hoped to play but a serious injury intervened* **4** to come or be among or between: *ten years had intervened since he had seen Joe* **WORD ORIGIN** Latin *intervenire* to come between

intervention *n* the act of intervening, esp. to influence or alter a situation in some way **interventionist** *n, adj*

interview *n* **1** a formal discussion, esp. one in which an employer assesses a job applicant **2** a conversation in which a well-known person is asked about his or her views, career, etc. by a reporter ▷ *vb* **3** to question (someone) **interviewee** *n* **interviewer** *n* **WORD ORIGIN** Old French *entrevue*

interwar *adj* of or happening in the period between World War I and World War II

interweave *vb* **-weaving, -wove** or **-weaved, -woven** or **-weaved** to weave together

intestate *adj* **1** (of a person) not having made a will ▷ *n* **2** a person who dies without having made a will **intestacy** *n* **WORD ORIGIN** Latin *intestatus*

intestine *n* the part of the alimentary canal between the stomach and the anus. See **large intestine, small intestine** ▷ **intestinal** *adj* **WORD ORIGIN** Latin *intestinus* internal

intifada (in-tiff-**ah**-da) *n* the Palestinian uprising against Israel in the West Bank and Gaza Strip **WORD ORIGIN** Arabic

intimacy *n, pl* **-cies** **1** close or warm friendship **2** (*often pl*) intimate words or acts within a close relationship

intimate¹ *adj* **1** characterized by a close or warm personal relationship: *an intimate friend* **2** deeply personal, private, or secret **3** (of knowledge) extensive and detailed **4** *euphemistic* having sexual relations **5** having a friendly quiet atmosphere: *an intimate nightclub* ▷ *n* **6** a close friend **intimately** *adv* **WORD ORIGIN** Latin *intimus* innermost

intimate² *vb* **-mating, -mated** *formal* **1** to make (something) known in an indirect way: *he has intimated his intention to retire* **2** to announce **intimation** *n* **WORD ORIGIN** Late Latin *intimare* to proclaim

intimidate *vb* **-dating, -dated** to subdue or influence (someone) through fear **intimidating** *adj* **intimidation** *n* **WORD ORIGIN** Latin *in-* in + *timidus* fearful

into *prep* **1** to the inner part of: *they went into the house* **2** to the middle of so as to be surrounded by: *into the bushes* **3** against; up against: *he drove into a wall* **4** used to indicate the result of a change: *they turned the theatre into a garage* **5** *maths* used to indicate division: *three into six is two* **6** *informal* interested in: *I'm really into healthy food*

intolerable *adj* more than can be endured **intolerably** *adv*

intolerant *adj* refusing to accept practices and beliefs that differ from one's own **intolerance** *n*

intonation *n* **1** the sound pattern produced by variations in the voice **2** the act of intoning **3** *music* the ability to play or sing in tune **intonational** *adj*

intone *vb* **-toning, -toned** **1** to speak or recite in a monotonous tone **2** to speak with a particular tone **WORD ORIGIN** Medieval Latin *intonare*

in toto *adv* totally or entirely **WORD ORIGIN** Latin

intoxicant *n* **1** something, such as an alcoholic drink, that causes intoxication ▷ *adj* **2** causing intoxication

intoxicate *vb* **-cating, -cated** **1** (of an alcoholic drink) to make (a person) drunk **2** to stimulate or excite to a point beyond self-control **intoxicated** *adj* **intoxicating** *adj* **WORD ORIGIN** Latin *in-* in + *toxicum* poison

intoxication *n* **1** the state of being drunk **2** great excitement and exhilaration

intractable *adj* **1** (of a person) difficult to influence or direct **2** (of a problem or illness) difficult to solve or cure **intractability** *n* **intractably** *adv*

intramural *adj* *chiefly US & Canad* operating within or involving those within a school or college: *intramural sports* **WORD ORIGIN** Latin *intra-* inside + *murus* wall

intranet *n* *computers* an internal network that makes use of internet technology **WORD ORIGIN** *intra-* + INTERNET

intransigent *adj* **1** refusing to change one's attitude ▷ *n* **2** an intransigent person, esp. in politics **intransigence** *n* **WORD ORIGIN** Latin *in-* not + *transigere* to settle

intransitive adj (of a verb) not taking a direct object: *'to faint' is an intransitive verb* **intransitively** adv

intrapreneur n *Brit and US* a person who while remaining within a larger organization uses entrepreneurial skills to develop new services or systems as a subsidiary of the organization **WORD ORIGIN** *intra-* inside + *(entre)preneur*

intrauterine adj situated within the womb **WORD ORIGIN** Latin *intra-* inside + *uterus* womb

intrauterine device n a contraceptive device in the shape of a coil, inserted into the womb

intravenous (in-tra-**vee**-nuss) adj *anat* into a vein: *intravenous drug users* **intravenously** adv **WORD ORIGIN** Latin *intra-* inside + *vena* vein

in-tray n a tray used in offices for incoming letters or documents requiring attention

intrepid adj fearless or bold **intrepidity** n **intrepidly** adv **WORD ORIGIN** Latin *in-* not + *trepidus* fearful

intricate adj **1** difficult to sort out: *an intricate problem* **2** full of complicated detail: *intricate Arab mosaics* **intricacy** n **intricately** adv **WORD ORIGIN** Latin *intricare* to entangle

intrigue vb **-triguing, -trigued 1** to make interested or curious: *a question which has intrigued him for years* **2** to plot secretly or dishonestly ▷ n **3** secret plotting **4** a secret love affair **intriguing** adj **intriguingly** adv **WORD ORIGIN** French *intriguer*

intrinsic adj **1** essential to the real nature of a thing: *hedgerows are an intrinsic part of the countryside* **2** *anat* situated within or peculiar to a part: *intrinsic muscles* **intrinsically** adv **WORD ORIGIN** Latin *intrinsecus* inwardly

intro n, pl **-tros** *informal* short for **introduction**

introduce vb **-ducing, -duced 1** to present (someone) by name (to another person) **2** to present (a radio or television programme) **3** to present for consideration or approval: *he introduced the bill to Parliament in 1967* **4** to bring into use: *Latvia has introduced its own currency into circulation* **5** to insert **6 introduce to** to cause to experience for the first time: *his father introduced him to golf* **7 introduce with** to start: *he introduced his talk with some music* **introducible** adj **WORD ORIGIN** Latin *introducere* to bring inside

introduction n **1** the act of introducing something or someone **2** a preliminary part, as of a book or musical composition **3** a book that explains the basic facts about a particular subject to a beginner **4** a presentation of one person to another or others

introductory adj serving as an introduction

introit n **1** *RC Church* a short prayer said or sung as the celebrant is entering the sanctuary to celebrate Mass **2** *Church of England* a hymn or psalm sung at the beginning of a service

WORD ORIGIN Latin *introitus* entrance

introspection n the examining of one's own thoughts, impressions, and feelings **introspective** adj **WORD ORIGIN** Latin *introspicere* to look within

introversion n *psychol* the directing of interest inwards towards one's own thoughts and feelings rather than towards the external world or making social contacts

introvert adj **1** shy and quiet **2** *psychol* concerned more with inner feelings than with external reality ▷ n **3** such a person **introverted** adj **WORD ORIGIN** Latin *intro-* inward + *vertere* to turn

intrude vb **-truding, -truded** to come in or join in without being invited **WORD ORIGIN** Latin *intrudere* to thrust in

intruder n a person who enters a place without permission

intrusion n **1** the act of intruding; an unwelcome visit, etc.: *an intrusion into her private life* **2** *geol* **a** the forcing of molten rock into spaces in the overlying strata **b** molten rock formed in this way **intrusive** adj

intrust vb same as **entrust**

intuition n instinctive knowledge of or belief about something without conscious reasoning: *intuition told her something was wrong* **intuitional** adj **WORD ORIGIN** Latin *intueri* to gaze upon

intuitive adj of, possessing, or resulting from intuition: *an intuitive understanding* **intuitively** adv

Inuit n, pl **-it** or **-its** an indigenous inhabitant of North America or Greenland **WORD ORIGIN** Inuktitut, plural of *inuk* person

Inuk n a member of the Inuit people

Inuktitut n the language of the Inuit

inundate vb **-dating, -dated 1** to cover completely with water **2** to overwhelm, as if with a flood: *the police were inundated with calls* **inundation** n **WORD ORIGIN** Latin *inundare*

inured adj able to tolerate something unpleasant because one has become accustomed to it: *he became inured to the casual brutality of his captors* **inurement** n **WORD ORIGIN** Middle English *enuren* to accustom

invade vb **-vading, -vaded 1** to enter (a country or territory) by military force **2** to enter in large numbers: *the town was invaded by rugby supporters* **3** to disturb (privacy, etc.) **invader** n **WORD ORIGIN** Latin *invadere*

invalid¹ n **1** a person who is disabled or chronically ill ▷ adj **2** sick or disabled ▷ vb **3** *chiefly Brit* to dismiss (a soldier etc.) from active service because of illness **invalidism** n **WORD ORIGIN** Latin *in-* not + *validus* strong

invalid² adj **1** having no legal force: *an invalid cheque* **2** (of an argument, result, etc.) not valid because it has been based on a mistake **invalidity** n **invalidly** adv

invalidate vb **-dating, -dated 1** to make or show (an argument) to be invalid **2** to take away the legal force of (a contract) **invalidation** n

invaluable adj having great value that is impossible to calculate

invariable adj unchanging **invariably** adv

invasion n **1** the act of invading with armed forces **2** any intrusion: *an invasion of privacy* **invasive** adj

invective n abusive speech or writing **WORD ORIGIN** Late Latin *invectivus* scolding

inveigh (in-**vay**) vb *formal* **inveigh against** to make harsh criticisms against **WORD ORIGIN** Latin *invehi*, literally: to be carried in, hence assail

inveigle vb **-gling, -gled** to coax or manipulate (someone) into an action or situation **inveiglement** n **WORD ORIGIN** Old French *avogler* to blind, deceive

invent vb **1** to think up or create (something new) **2** to make up (a story, excuse, etc.) **inventor** n **WORD ORIGIN** Latin *invenire* to find

invention n **1** something that is invented **2** the act of inventing **3** creative power; inventive skill **4** *euphemistic* a lie: *his story is a malicious invention*

inventive adj creative and resourceful: *her inventive use of colour*

inventory (**in**-ven-tree) n, pl **-tories 1** a detailed list of the objects in a particular place ▷ vb **-tories, -torying, -toried 2** to make a list of **WORD ORIGIN** Medieval Latin *inventorium*

inverse adj **1** opposite in effect, sequence, direction, etc. **2** *maths* linking two variables in such a way that one increases as the other decreases ▷ n **3** the exact opposite: *the inverse of this image* **4** *maths* an inverse element

inversion n **1** the act of inverting or state of being inverted **2** something inverted, esp. a reversal of order, functions, etc.: *an inversion of their previous relationship* **inversive** adj

invert vb **1** to turn upside down or inside out **2** to reverse in effect, sequence, or direction ▷ n **3** a homosexual **invertible** adj **WORD ORIGIN** Latin *in-* in + *vertere* to turn

invertebrate n **1** any animal without a backbone, such as an insect, worm, or octopus ▷ adj **2** of or designating invertebrates

inverted commas pl n same as **quotation marks**

invest vb **1** (often foll. by *in*) to put (money) into an enterprise with the expectation of profit **2** (often foll. by *in*) to devote (time or effort to a project) **3** to give power or authority to: *invested with the powers of government* **4** (often foll. by *in*) to install someone (in an official position) **5** (foll. by *with* or *in*) to credit or provide (a person with qualities): *he was invested with great common sense* **6 invest in** to buy: *she invested in some barbecue equipment* **7 invest with** *usually poetic* to cover, as if with a coat: *when spring invests the trees with leaves* **investor** n

Edmund Spenser

Edmund Spenser was regarded in his time and to this day as one of England's greatest poets. As a public official and Protestant partisan in situ, Spenser was handed a large estate in County Cork. There he wrote the first six books of his most famous work, *The Faerie Queene.* In 1598, the Irish, who resented being displaced in their own country, burned down his castle. A year later he died in London, his fortune also in ruins.

Long before Rudyard Kipling, Spenser was a writer-imperialist. He was not just a beneficiary of a land grab, but a warrior in a ferocious conflict with Protestant England's deadly enemy, Spain, which could have used Ireland as a back entrance for conquest. Born around 1552, the son of a London cloth-maker, Spenser relied all his life on the favours of richer or mightier men, who paid for his classical schooling and a Cambridge degree, and gave him jobs. Among these men was Sir Philip Sidney, as important to him in practical matters as Chaucer's work was to his poetic education. Dedicated to Sidney but relying on European models, his first book was a collection of pastoral eclogues called *The Shepherd's Calendar*. The book succeeded among forward-looking literati, and Spenser made his way amid the intriguers and opportunists of Queen Elizabeth's court. He was secretary to Arthur Grey, Lord Deputy of Ireland, who had been dispatched there to pacify the unruly natives. After a battle at the conclusion of his savage campaign, Lord Grey massacred the Irish and Spanish troops who had surrendered. In *The Faerie Queene,* Grey becomes Arthegal, the personification of justice. Spenser's considered opinion on how to deal with the Irish was detailed in a formal paper, *View of the State of Ireland*, published after his death. If the Irish did not submit, they were to be starved or exterminated.

While Spenser lived in County Cork, his friend Sir Walter Raleigh, a poet himself and the greatest adventurer and rogue of the Elizabethan court, encouraged his labours on *The Faerie Queene,* and on the work's publication Elizabeth granted him an annual pension of 50 pounds. No wonder, because she is represented in it as the Faerie Queene herself, the white-clad Gloriana. The whole work is an allegory: the crusading Red Crosse Knight is the legendary King Arthur, and the Faeries are the English. Among the venomous villains is the dragon Errour; another is the Blatant Beast, spawn of Envy and Detraction. Doubtless there were many originals for them. However, trying to attribute Spenser's mythic figures to real-life sources is to enter a maze of symbol and sense.

Even at half the length that Spenser had intended, *The Faerie Queene* is probably the longest poem published in English. Spenser, who wrote much other verse, constructed his epic romance using the *Spenserian stanza:* nine rhyming lines, clinched by a couplet. Eight of them are in *iambic pentameter:* five metrical feet of two syllables, with the stress falling on the second syllable. The ninth line is an *alexandrine,* iambic but with an extra pair of syllables. It is a technical tour de force. Elsewhere he also proved that he could make light of formal constraints: the *Spenserian sonnet* that he pioneered allows only five rhymes in fourteen lines instead of the usual seven. Always obsessed with symmetrical numbers, he wrote his *Epithalamion,* a celebratory wedding song, in 365 long lines for the days of the year; 68 short lines for the sum of 52 weeks, 12 months, and four seasons; and 24 stanzas for each hour of the day.

For Milton, Keats, Byron, and Tennyson, Spenser was a poet's poet in his virtuoso handling of verse schemes and command of rhythmic phrasing. If *The Faerie Queene*'s words seem archaic today, that is because they were archaic even in the late sixteenth century: *forwasted* (laid waste), *eke* (also), *misweening* (misjudging), *eftsoones* (forthwith), *areeds* (appoints), and *parbreake* (vomit). He also uses common words in unfamiliar senses: *gorge* (neck), *deface* (discredit), and *pricking* (cantering). It was as if Spenser, so beset by the adversities of politics and war, resorted to creating an artificial world. In that world, English Protestant virtue always triumphed. The Irish had other ideas.

WORD ORIGIN Medieval Latin *investire* to clothe

investigate *vb* **-gating, -gated** to inquire into (a situation or problem) thoroughly in order to discover the truth: *the police are currently investigating the case* **investigative** *adj* **investigator** *n*
WORD ORIGIN Latin *investigare* to search after

investigation *n* a careful search or examination in order to discover facts

investiture *n* the formal installation of a person in an office or rank

investment *n* **1** the act of investing **2** money invested **3** something in which money is invested

investment trust *n* a financial enterprise that invests its subscribed capital in a wide range of securities for its investors' benefit

inveterate *adj* **1** deep-rooted or ingrained: *an inveterate enemy of Marxism* **2** confirmed in a habit or practice: *an inveterate gambler* **inveteracy** *n*
WORD ORIGIN Latin *inveteratus* of long standing

invidious *adj* likely to cause resentment or unpopularity
WORD ORIGIN Latin *invidia* envy

invigilate (in-**vij**-il-late) *vb* **-lating, -lated** *Brit* to supervise people who are sitting an examination **invigilation** *n* **invigilator** *n*
WORD ORIGIN Latin *invigilare* to watch over

invigorate *vb* **-rating, -rated** to give energy to or refresh **invigorating** *adj*
WORD ORIGIN Latin *in-* in + *vigor* vigour

invincible *adj* incapable of being defeated: *an army of invincible strength* **invincibility** *n* **invincibly** *adv*
WORD ORIGIN Latin *in-* not + *vincere* to conquer

inviolable *adj* that must not be broken or violated: *an inviolable oath* **inviolability** *n*

inviolate *adj* free from harm or injury **inviolacy** *n*

invisible *adj* **1** not able to be seen by the eye: *invisible radiation* **2** concealed from sight **3** *econ* relating to services, such as insurance and freight, rather than goods: *invisible earnings* **invisibility** *n* **invisibly** *adv*

invitation *n* **1** a request to attend a dance, meal, etc. **2** the card or paper on which an invitation is written

invite *vb* **-viting, -vited** **1** to ask (a person) in a friendly or polite way (to do something, attend an event, etc.) **2** to make a request for, esp. publicly or formally: *we invite applications for six scholarships* **3** to bring on or provoke: *his theory invites disaster* **4** to tempt ▷ *n* **5** *informal* an invitation
WORD ORIGIN Latin *invitare*

inviting *adj* tempting or attractive

in vitro *adv, adj* (of biological processes or reactions) happening outside the body of the organism in an artificial environment
WORD ORIGIN New Latin, literally: in glass

invocation *n* **1** the act of invoking **2** a prayer to God or another deity

asking for help, forgiveness, etc. **invocatory** *adj*

invoice *n* **1** a bill for goods and services supplied ▷ *vb* **-voicing, -voiced** **2** to present (a customer) with an invoice
WORD ORIGIN Old French *envois*, plural of *envoi* message

invoke *vb* **-voking, -voked** **1** to put (a law or penalty) into use: *chapter 8 of the UN charter was invoked* **2** to bring about: *the hills invoked a feeling of serenity* **3** to call on (God or another deity) for help, inspiration, etc. **4** to summon (a spirit) by uttering magic words
WORD ORIGIN Latin *invocare* to appeal to

USAGE *Invoke* is sometimes wrongly used where *evoke* is meant: *this proposal evoked* (not *invoked*) *a strong reaction.*

involuntary *adj* **1** carried out without one's conscious wishes; unintentional **2** *physiol* (esp. of a movement or muscle) performed or acting without conscious control **involuntarily** *adv*

involute *adj also* **involuted** **1** complex, intricate, or involved **2** rolled inwards or curled in a spiral ▷ *n* **3** *geom* the curve described by the free end of a thread as it is wound around another curve on the same plane
WORD ORIGIN Latin *involutus*

involve *vb* **-volving, -volved** **1** to include as a necessary part **2** to have an effect on: *around fifty riders were involved and some were hurt* **3** to implicate: *several people were involved in the crime* **4** to make complicated: *the situation was further involved by her disappearance* **involvement** *n*
WORD ORIGIN Latin *in-* in + *volvere* to roll

involved *adj* **1** complicated **2** involved in concerned in

invulnerable *adj* not able to be wounded or damaged **invulnerability** *n*

inward *adj* **1** directed towards the middle of something **2** situated within **3** of the mind or spirit: *inward meditation* **4** of one's own country or a specific country: *inward investment* ▷ *adv* **5** same as **inwards**

inwardly *adv* **1** within the private thoughts or feelings: *inwardly troubled, he kept smiling* **2** not aloud: *to laugh inwardly* **3** in or on the inside

inwards *or* **inward** *adv* towards the inside or middle of something

inwrought *adj* worked or woven into material, esp. decoratively

in-your-face *adj slang* aggressive and confrontational: *in-your-face advertising*

Io *chem* ionium

iodide *n chem* a compound containing an iodine atom, such as methyl iodide

iodine *n chem* a bluish-black element found in seaweed and used in medicine, photography, and dyeing. Symbol: I
WORD ORIGIN Greek *iōdēs* rust-coloured, but mistakenly derived from *ion* violet

iodize *or* **-dise** *vb* **-dizing, -dized** *or* **-dising, -dised** to treat with iodine **iodization** *or* **-disation** *n*

IOM Isle of Man

ion *n* an electrically charged atom or group of atoms formed by the loss or gain of one or more electrons
WORD ORIGIN Greek, literally: going

ion exchange *n* the process in which ions are exchanged between a solution and an insoluble solid. It is used to soften water

ionic *adj* of or in the form of ions

Ionic *adj* of a style of classical architecture characterized by fluted columns with scroll-like ornaments on the capital

ionize *or* **-ise** *vb* **-izing, -ized** *or* **-ising, -ised** to change or become changed into ions **ionization** *or* **-isation** *n*

ionosphere *n* a region of ionized layers of air in the earth's upper atmosphere, which reflects radio waves **ionospheric** *adj*

iota (eye-**oh**-ta) *n* **1** the ninth letter in the Greek alphabet (I, ι) **2** a very small amount: *I don't feel one iota of guilt*

IOU *n* a written promise or reminder to pay a debt
WORD ORIGIN representing I *owe you*

IOW Isle of Wight

IP *computers* internet protocol: a code used to label packets of data sent across the internet, identifying both the sending and the receiving computers

IPA International Phonetic Alphabet

IP address *computers* internet protocol address: a unique code that identifies each computer connected to the internet

ipecacuanha (ip-pee-kak-yew-**ann**-a) *or* **ipecac** (**ip**-pee-kak) *n* a drug made from the dried roots of a S American plant, used to cause vomiting
WORD ORIGIN S American Indian *ipekaaguéne*

iPod *n trademark* a small portable digital audio player capable of storing thousands of tracks in a variety of formats including MP3

ipso facto *adv* by that very fact or act
WORD ORIGIN Latin

IQ intelligence quotient

Ir *chem* iridium

IRA Irish Republican Army

Iranian *adj* **1** of Iran ▷ *n* **2** a person from Iran **3** a branch of the Indo-European family of languages, including Persian

Iraqi *adj* **1** of Iraq ▷ *n* **2** a person from Iraq

irascible *adj* easily angered **irascibility** *n* **irascibly** *adv*
WORD ORIGIN Latin *ira* anger

irate *adj* very angry
WORD ORIGIN Latin *iratus* enraged

ire *n literary* anger
WORD ORIGIN Latin *ira*

iridaceous (ir-rid-**day**-shuss) *adj* of or belonging to the iris family

iridescent *adj* having shimmering changing colours like a rainbow **iridescence** *n*
WORD ORIGIN Latin *irid-* iris

iridium *n chem* a hard yellowish-white chemical element that occurs in platinum ores and is used as an alloy with platinum. Symbol: Ir
WORD ORIGIN Latin *irid-* iris

iris *n* **1** the coloured muscular membrane in the eye that surrounds and controls the size of the pupil **2** a tall plant with long pointed leaves and large flowers **WORD ORIGIN** Greek: rainbow

Irish adj **1** of Ireland ▷ n **2** same as **Irish Gaelic 3** the dialect of English spoken in Ireland ▷ pl n **4 the Irish** the people of Ireland

Irish coffee n hot coffee mixed with Irish whiskey and topped with double cream

Irish Gaelic n the Celtic language of Ireland

Irishman or fem **Irishwoman** n, pl **-men** or fem or **-women** a person from Ireland

Irish moss n same as **carrageen**

irk vb to irritate or vex
   WORD ORIGIN Middle English irken to grow weary

irksome adj annoying or tiresome

iron n **1** a strong silvery-white metallic element, widely used for structural and engineering purposes. Symbol: Fe **2** a tool made of iron **3** a small electrically heated device with a weighted flat bottom for pressing clothes **4** golf a club with an angled metal head **5** a splintlike support for a malformed leg **6** great strength or resolve: a will of iron **7 strike while the iron is hot** to act at a suitable moment ▷ adj **8** made of iron **9** very hard or merciless: iron determination **10** very strong: an iron constitution ▷ vb **11** to smooth (clothes or fabric) by removing (creases) with an iron. See also **iron out, irons**
   WORD ORIGIN Old English irēn

Iron Age n a phase of human culture that began in the Middle East about 1100 BC, during which iron tools and weapons were used

ironbark n an Australian eucalyptus with hard rough bark

ironclad adj **1** covered or protected with iron: an ironclad warship **2** unable to be contradicted: ironclad proof ▷ n **3** history a large wooden 19th-century warship with armoured plating

Iron Curtain n (formerly) the guarded border between the countries of the Soviet bloc and the rest of Europe

ironic or **ironical** adj of, characterized by, or using irony **ironically** adv

ironing n clothes to be ironed

ironing board n a narrow cloth-covered board, usually with folding legs, on which to iron clothes

iron lung n an airtight metal cylinder enclosing the entire body up to the neck and providing artificial respiration

iron maiden n a medieval instrument of torture, consisting of a hinged case (often shaped in the form of a woman) lined with iron spikes

ironmaster n Brit history a manufacturer of iron

ironmonger n Brit a shopkeeper or shop dealing in hardware **ironmongery** n

iron out vb to settle (a problem or difficulty) through negotiation or discussion

iron pyrites n same as **pyrite**

iron rations pl n emergency food supplies, esp. for military personnel in action

irons pl n **1** fetters or chains **2 have several irons in the fire** to have several projects or plans at once

ironstone n **1** any rock consisting mainly of iron ore **2** a tough durable earthenware

ironwood n **1** any of various trees, such as hornbeam, with exceptionally hard wood **2** the wood of any of these trees

ironwork n work done in iron, esp. decorative work

ironworks n a building in which iron is smelted, cast, or wrought

irony n, pl **-nies 1** the mildly sarcastic use of words to imply the opposite of what they normally mean **2** a situation or result that is the direct opposite of what was expected or intended
   WORD ORIGIN Greek eirōneia

irradiate vb **-ating, -ated 1** physics to subject to or treat with light or other electromagnetic radiation **2** to make clear or bright intellectually or spiritually **3** to light up; illuminate **irradiation** n

irrational adj **1** not based on logical reasoning **2** incapable of reasoning **3** maths (of an equation or expression) involving radicals or fractional exponents **irrationality** n **irrationally** adv

irrational number n maths any real number that cannot be expressed as the ratio of two integers, such as π

irreconcilable adj not able to be resolved or settled: irreconcilable differences **irreconcilability** n

irrecoverable adj not able to be recovered

irredeemable adj **1** not able to be reformed, improved, or corrected **2** (of bonds or shares) not able to be bought back directly or paid off **3** (of paper money) not able to be converted into coin **irredeemably** adv

irredentist n a person in favour of seizing territory that was once part of his or her country **irredentism** n
   WORD ORIGIN Italian irredenta unredeemed

irreducible adj impossible to put in a reduced or simpler form **irreducibility** n

irrefutable adj impossible to deny or disprove

irregular adj **1** uneven in shape, position, arrangement, etc. **2** not conforming to accepted practice or routine **3** (of a word) not following the usual pattern of formation in a language **4** not occurring at expected or equal intervals: an irregular pulse **5** (of troops) not belonging to regular forces ▷ n **6** a soldier not in a regular army **irregularity** n **irregularly** adv

irrelevant adj not connected with the matter in hand **irrelevance** or **irrelevancy** n

irreligious adj **1** lacking religious faith **2** indifferent or opposed to religion

irremediable adj not able to be improved or cured

irremovable adj not able to be removed **irremovably** adv

irreparable adj not able to be repaired or put right: irreparable damage to his reputation **irreparably** adv

irreplaceable adj impossible to replace: acres of irreplaceable moorland were devastated

irrepressible adj not capable of being repressed, controlled, or restrained **irrepressibility** n **irrepressibly** adv

irreproachable adj blameless or faultless **irreproachability** n

irresistible adj **1** not able to be resisted or refused: irresistible pressure from the financial markets **2** extremely attractive: an irresistible woman **irresistibility** n **irresistibly** adv

irresolute adj unable to make decisions **irresolution** n

irrespective adj **irrespective of** without taking account of

irresponsible adj **1** not showing or done with due care for the consequences of one's actions or attitudes; reckless **2** not capable of accepting responsibility **irresponsibility** n **irresponsibly** adv

irretrievable adj impossible to put right or make good **irretrievability** n **irretrievably** adv

irreverence n **1** lack of due respect **2** a disrespectful remark or act **irreverent** adj

irreversible adj not able to be reversed or put right again: irreversible loss of memory **irreversibly** adv

irrevocable adj not possible to change or undo **irrevocably** adv

irrigate vb **-gating, -gated 1** to supply (land) with water through ditches or pipes in order to encourage the growth of crops **2** med to bathe (a wound or part of the body) **irrigation** n **irrigator** n
   WORD ORIGIN Latin irrigare

irritable adj **1** easily annoyed or angered **2** pathol abnormally sensitive **3** biol (of all living organisms) capable of responding to such stimuli as heat, light, and touch **irritability** n

irritant n **1** something that annoys or irritates **2** a substance that causes a part of the body to become tender or inflamed ▷ adj **3** causing irritation

irritate vb **-tating, -tated 1** to annoy or anger (someone) **2** pathol to cause (an organ or part of the body) to become inflamed or tender **3** biol to stimulate (an organ) to respond in a characteristic manner **irritation** n
   WORD ORIGIN Latin irritare to provoke

irrupt vb to enter forcibly or suddenly **irruption** n **irruptive** adj
   WORD ORIGIN Latin irrumpere

is vb third person singular of the present tense of **be**
   WORD ORIGIN Old English

ISA (**eye**-sa) n (in Britain) individual savings account

isallobar (ice-**sal**-oh-bar) n a line on a map connecting places with equal pressure changes
   WORD ORIGIN Greek isos equal + allos other + baros weight

ISBN International Standard Book Number

isinglass (ize-ing-glass) *n* **1** a gelatine made from the air bladders of freshwater fish **2** same as **mica** **WORD ORIGIN** Middle Dutch *huysenblase* sturgeon bladder

Isis *n* an Egyptian fertility goddess

Isl. **1** Island **2** Isle

Islam *n* **1** the Muslim religion teaching that there is only one God and that Mohammed is his prophet **2** Muslim countries and civilization **Islamic** *adj* **Islamist** *adj, n* **WORD ORIGIN** Arabic: surrender (to God)

island *n* **1** a piece of land that is completely surrounded by water **2** something isolated, detached, or surrounded **3** see **traffic island** ▸ Related adjective: **insular** **WORD ORIGIN** Old English *īgland*

islander *n* **1** a person who lives on an island **2** **Islander** NZ a Pacific Islander

isle *n* (except when part of a place name) a poetic name for an island

islet *n* a small island

ism *n informal, often used to show contempt* a doctrine, system, or practice, esp. one whose name ends in *-ism*, such as *communism* or *fascism*

-ism *suffix* **1** indicating a political or religious belief: *socialism; Judaism* **2** indicating a characteristic quality: *heroism* **3** indicating an action: *exorcism* **4** indicating prejudice on the basis specified: *sexism*

isn't is not

iso- *or before a vowel* **is-** *combining form* equal or identical: *isomagnetic* **WORD ORIGIN** Greek *isos* equal

isobar (ice-oh-bar) *n* **1** a line on a map connecting places of equal atmospheric pressure **2** *physics* any of two or more atoms that have the same mass number but different atomic numbers **isobaric** *adj* **isobarism** *n* **WORD ORIGIN** Greek *isobarēs* of equal weight

isochronal *or* **isochronous** *adj* **1** equal in length of time **2** occurring at equal time intervals **isochronism** *n* **WORD ORIGIN** Greek *isos* equal + *khronos* time

isohel *n* a line on a map connecting places with an equal period of sunshine **WORD ORIGIN** Greek *isos* equal + *hēlios* sun

isohyet (ice-oh-**hie**-it) *n* a line on a map connecting places having equal rainfall **WORD ORIGIN** Greek *isos* equal + *huetos* rain

isolate *vb* -lating, -lated **1** to place apart or alone **2** *chem* to obtain (a substance) in an uncombined form **3** *med* to quarantine (a person or animal) with a contagious disease **isolation** *n* **WORD ORIGIN** Latin *insulatus*, literally: made into an island

isomer (ice-oh-mer) *n chem* a substance whose molecules contain the same atoms as another but in a different arrangement **isomeric** *adj*

isometric *adj* **1** having equal dimensions or measurements **2** *physiol* relating to muscular contraction that does not produce shortening of the muscle **3** (of a three-dimensional drawing) having the three axes equally inclined and all lines drawn to scale **isometrically** *adv* **WORD ORIGIN** Greek *isometria* equal measurement

isometrics *n* a system of isometric exercises

isomorphism *n* **1** *biol* similarity of form, as in different generations of the same life cycle **2** *chem* the existence of two or more substances of different composition in a similar crystalline form **3** *maths* a one-to-one correspondence between the elements of two or more sets **isomorph** *n* **isomorphic** *or* **isomorphous** *adj*

isosceles triangle (ice-**soss**-ill-eez) *n* a triangle with two sides of equal length **WORD ORIGIN** Greek *isos* equal + *skelos* leg

isotherm (ice-oh-therm) *n* a line on a map linking places of equal temperature **WORD ORIGIN** Greek *isos* equal + *thermē* heat

isotonic *adj* **1** *physiol* (of two or more muscles) having equal tension **2** (of a drink) designed to replace the fluid and salts lost from the body during exercise

isotope (ice-oh-tope) *n* one of two or more atoms with the same number of protons in the nucleus but a different number of neutrons **isotopic** *adj* **isotopy** *n* **WORD ORIGIN** Greek *isos* equal + *topos* place

isotropic *or* **isotropous** *adj* having uniform physical properties, such as elasticity or conduction in all directions **isotropy** *n*

ISP internet service provider: a business providing its customers with connection to the internet

Israeli *adj* **1** of Israel ▸ *n, pl* **-lis** *or* **-li** **2** a person from Israel

Israelite *n Bible* a member of the ethnic group claiming descent from Jacob; a Hebrew

issue *n* **1** a topic of interest or discussion **2** an important subject requiring a decision **3** a particular edition of a magazine or newspaper **4** a consequence or result **5** *law* the descendants of a person **6** the act of sending or giving out something **7** the act of emerging; outflow **8** something flowing out, such as a river **9** **at issue** **a** under discussion **b** in disagreement **10** **force the issue** to compel decision on some matter **11** **join issue** to join in controversy **12** **take issue** to disagree ▸ *vb* -suing, -sued **13** to make (a statement etc.) publicly **14** to supply officially (with) **15** to send out or distribute **16** to publish **17** to come forth or emerge **issuable** *adj* **WORD ORIGIN** Old French *eissue* way out

isthmus (**iss**-muss) *n* a narrow strip of land connecting two relatively large land areas **WORD ORIGIN** Greek *isthmos*

it *pron* **1** refers to a nonhuman, animal, plant, or inanimate thing, or sometimes to a small baby **2** refers to something unspecified or implied or to a previous or understood clause, phrase, or word: *I knew it* **3** used to represent human life or experience in respect of the present situation: *how's it going?* **4** used as the subject of impersonal verbs: *it is snowing; it's Friday* **5** *informal* the crucial or ultimate point: *the steering failed and I thought that was it* ▸ *n* **6** *informal* **a** sexual intercourse **b** sex appeal **7** a desirable quality or ability **WORD ORIGIN** Old English *hit*

IT information technology

ITA initial teaching alphabet: a partly phonetic alphabet used to teach reading

Italian *adj* **1** of Italy ▸ *n* **2** a person from Italy **3** the official language of Italy and one of the official languages of Switzerland

Italianate *adj* Italian in style or character

italic *adj* **1** of a style of printing type in which the characters slant to the right ▸ *pl n* **2** **italics** italic type or print, used for emphasis **WORD ORIGIN** Latin *Italicus* of Italy (where it was first used)

italicize *or* **-cise** *vb* -cizing, -cized *or* -cising, -cised to print (text) in italic type **italicization** *or* **-cisation** *n*

itch *n* **1** a skin irritation causing a desire to scratch **2** a restless desire **3** any skin disorder, such as scabies, characterized by intense itching ▸ *vb* **4** to feel an irritating or tickling sensation **5** to have a restless desire (to do something): *they were itching to join the fight* **WORD ORIGIN** Old English *giccean* to itch

itchy *adj* itchier, itchiest **1** having an itch **2** **have itchy feet** to have a desire to travel **itchiness** *n*

it'd it would *or* it had

item *n* **1** a single thing in a list or collection **2** a piece of information: *a news item* **3** *book-keeping* an entry in an account **4** *informal* a couple **WORD ORIGIN** Latin: in like manner

itemize *or* **-ise** *vb* -izing, -ized *or* -ising, -ised to put on a list or make a list of **itemization** *or* **-isation** *n*

iterate *vb* -ating, -ated to say or do again **iteration** *n* **iterative** *adj* **WORD ORIGIN** Latin *iterum* again

itinerant *adj* **1** working for a short time in various places ▸ *n* **2** an itinerant worker or other person **WORD ORIGIN** Latin *iter* a journey

itinerary *n, pl* -aries **1** a detailed plan of a journey **2** a record of a journey **3** a guidebook for travellers

-itis *suffix forming nouns* indicating inflammation of a specified part: *tonsillitis* **WORD ORIGIN** Greek *-itēs* belonging to

it'll it will *or* it shall

its *adj* **1** of or belonging to it: *its left rear wheel; I can see its logical consequence* ▸ *pron* **2** something belonging to it: *its is over there*

it's it is *or* it has

itself *pron* **1 a** the reflexive form of *it*: *the cat scratched itself* **b** used for emphasis: *even the money itself won't convince me* **2** its normal or usual self: *my parrot doesn't seem itself these days*

ITV (in Britain) Independent Television

Yiddish English

Although the Jews of Europe settled in other English-speaking countries, it was the United States in which they had their greatest linguistic impact. The *Sephardim*, of Spanish and Portuguese descent, arrived in America as early as the mid-1660s, but their number was vastly eclipsed by the *Ashkenazim* of Central and Eastern Europe, who immigrated to New York and other US big cities between the 1840s and 1910. The first wave arrived from Germany, joined later by many from Poland, Ukraine, Hungary, Romania, and Russia. The language of the Ashkenazim was Yiddish, written in Hebrew but with a German core vocabulary.

Often chronically short of *shekels*, cash, and isolated in ghettos, marked out by dark clothing, Hebrew schooling, and synagogue observances, Jews surmounted barriers of snobbery and outright bigotry, whose markers were such abusive terms as *kike*, *sheeny*, and *Yid*. To the Jews, the Gentiles who surrounded them were *goys* or *goyim*, a term that, depending on the context, could be highly pejorative. The Jewish experience in America evolved against the backdrop of nineteenth-century pogroms and systemic discrimination in Europe, culminating in the twentieth century by the supreme horror of the Holocaust and, partly as a reaction, the founding of Israel as a nation-state. In America, Jews first broke into the wider society through popular music and entertainment. Although to Jews life was often no joke, comedy proved to be their safety valve, vindication, and triumph. Later, they forged a remarkable record of achievement in law, medicine, science, literature, the humanities, and in finance. In the process to acceptance or assimilation, they much enlivened language with their Yiddish-inflected English, or *Yinglish*.

Due to the hard times they endured, ghetto Jews developed what Stuart Berg Flexner has called 'a scornful fatalism', which gave birth to such expressions as 'I need it like a hole in the head' and 'I should live so long'. Yiddish English is especially rich in terms of contempt and derision. Even the words beginning with *sch-* or ending in *-ish* have a mocking or satirical sense to English ears: *schlemiel* (foolish or clumsy person), *schnook* (a dupe), *schnorrer* (a chronic borrower), *schmo* (a stupid person), as well as *putz* or *schmuck*, equivalent in standard English to the informal *jerk* or the vulgar *prick*. To this rogue's gallery could be added the lowlife *gonif*, the clumsy *klutz*, and the habitually complaining *kvetcher*. Someone could be *meshuga*, crazy. Contrariwise, someone could be a *mensch*, an upright person, a doer of *mitzvahs*, good deeds. Newcomers interjected *Nu* (Well? So?) and exclaimed *Oy* (O!). A woman could be a talkative *yenta*, whether or not she was *zaftig*, attractively full-figured. Parts of the body were vividly denoted: *tush* for buttocks, *schlong* for penis, *schnozz* for nose; to have sexual intercourse was the vulgar *schtup*.

Even as Yiddish faded as a living language it brightened standard English. Some of its repetitive rhythms were comedic gifts. Doubting someone's qualifications, a speaker of Yiddish-inflected English might say, "To his mother he's a captain. To his father he's a captain. But to a captain is he a captain?' Rhyming compounds also came into play, as in *fancy-schmancy*. In the wake of *nudnik*, a bore or annoying person, came words with *-nik* as a suffix, such as *no-goodnik* (though not *beatnik* and *Sputnik*). From a satisfying *nosh* at a *delicatessen* or *deli* came juicy *pastrami* and special senses of *corned beef* (in Britain *salt beef*) and of (in Canada) *smoked meat*. Even non-kosher supermarkets eventually began to stock *blintzes* (thin, rolled pancakes), *matzos* (crisp unleavened bread), and *lox* (smoked salmon). Religious terms like *rabbi* and *Bar mitzvah* became as mainstream as *minister* and *christening*.

The black jazz singer Billie Holiday once performed a song called *My Yiddishe Mama*. Over time, it became hard to imagine English without Yiddish-derived words. Non-Jews can comfortably say they have to *shlep* a parcel across a city; complain of a *glitch* in a process, depict a shoddy bestselling novel as *schlock* full of cloying *schmaltz;* boast that they use a special *schtick* to impress people; claim that someone is full of audacious *chutzpah; schmooze* or *kibbitz* at a social gathering; describe correct behaviour as *kosher;* and call someone a language *maven*.

IUD intrauterine device: a coil-shaped contraceptive fitted into the womb

I've I have

IVF in vitro fertilization

ivories *pl n slang* **1** the keys of a piano **2** the teeth **3** dice

ivory *n, pl* **-ries 1** a hard smooth creamy white type of bone that makes up a major part of the tusks of elephants ▷ *adj* **2** yellowish-white **ivory-like** *adj* **WORD ORIGIN** Latin *ebur*

ivory tower *n* remoteness from the realities of everyday life **ivory-towered** *adj*

IVR International Vehicle Registration

ivy *n, pl* **ivies 1** a woody climbing or trailing plant with evergreen leaves and black berry-like fruits **2** any of various other climbing or creeping plants, such as the poison ivy
WORD ORIGIN Old English *īfig*

iwi (ee-wee) *n* NZ a Māori tribe
WORD ORIGIN Māori

ixia *n* a southern African plant of the iris family with showy ornamental funnel-shaped flowers
WORD ORIGIN Greek *ixos* mistletoe

Jj

The letter J is the tenth letter of the English alphabet. The name of the letter is pronounced 'jay' in most English-speaking regions, but many Scots enunciate it as 'jai' (to distinguish it more clearly from the typical Scottish way of saying 'G').

The letter is the alphabet's new kid on the block, being one of only two English letters that were not used in the Roman alphabet (the other being W).

The Romans used the letter I both as a vowel and as a consonant (just as the corresponding letter *iota* had been used in Greek). It would not have occurred to Julius Caesar to write his first name with a J, as the letter had not yet been invented, and he would actually have written 'Iulius'.

The new letter J probably came about as an attempt to make it easier to tell when the letter I was being used as a consonant. The first stage in this process was that I was lengthened when it represented a consonant. In the 16th century a hook was added at the base of the consonantal I to make the distinction clearer, and so the letter J was formed.

However, the use of I as a consonant persisted in some quarters even after this date, and J was not fully established as a letter in its own right until the first part of the 17th century.

In the light of its late entry into the alphabet, it is not surprising that J is one of the more infrequently occurring letters in English. It is also quite particular about the company it keeps, refusing to be followed by another consonant or to occur at the end of a word (except in a few words borrowed from other languages).

In English the letter J typically represents the sound at the start of *jet* and *jump*, but other languages have used it to represent other sounds. In words of French origin, such as *jus* and *joie de vivre*, the letter has a softer /ʒ/ sound, while in Spanish words such as *junta* and *jalapeno* the letter represents a guttural /x/ more akin to the sound made by H in English. In Germanic and Slavonic languages, however, the sound of the letter is comparable to that of the English Y.

J joule(s)

ja *interj S African* yes

jab *vb* **jabbing, jabbed 1** to poke sharply ▷ *n* **2** a quick short punch **3** *informal* an injection: *a flu jab* **4** a sharp poke
WORD ORIGIN variant of *job*

jabber *vb* **1** to speak very quickly and excitedly; chatter ▷ *n* **2** quick excited chatter
WORD ORIGIN imitative

jabiru *n* a large white-and-black Australian stork

jacaranda *n* a tropical American tree with sweet-smelling wood and pale purple flowers
WORD ORIGIN from a Native American language

jack *n* **1** a mechanical device used to raise a motor vehicle or other heavy object **2** a playing card with a picture of a pageboy on it **3** *bowls* a small white bowl at which the players aim their bowls **4** *electrical engineering* a socket into which a plug can be inserted **5** a flag flown at the bow of a ship, showing nationality **6** one of the pieces used in the game of jacks **7 every man jack** everyone without exception ▸ See also **jack in, jacks, jack up**
WORD ORIGIN from short form of *John*

jackal *n* a doglike wild animal of Africa and Asia, which feeds on the decaying flesh of dead animals
WORD ORIGIN Persian *shagāl*

jackanapes *n Brit* a mischievous child
WORD ORIGIN literally: Jack of the ape, nickname of first Duke of Suffolk, whose badge showed an ape's ball and chain

jackaroo, jackeroo *n, pl* **-roos** *Austral* a trainee on a sheep station
WORD ORIGIN from *jack* man + *(kang)aroo*

jackass *n* **1** a fool **2** a male donkey **3 laughing jackass** same as **kookaburra**
WORD ORIGIN *jack* (male) + *ass*

jackboot *n* **1** a leather military boot reaching up to the knee **2** brutal and authoritarian rule

jackdaw *n* a large black-and-grey crowlike bird of Europe and Asia
WORD ORIGIN *jack* + *daw*, obsolete name for jackdaw

jacket *n* **1** a short coat with a front opening and long sleeves **2** the skin of a potato **3** same as **dust jacket**
WORD ORIGIN Old French *jaquet*

jacket potato *n* a potato baked in its skin

Jack Frost *n* frost represented as a person

jack in *vb Brit slang* to abandon (an attempt or enterprise)

jack-in-the-box *n* a toy consisting of a box containing a figure on a compressed spring, which jumps out when the lid is opened

jackknife *vb* **-knifing, -knifed 1** (of an articulated lorry) to go out of control in such a way that the trailer swings round at a sharp angle to the cab ▷ *n, pl* **-knives 2** a knife with a blade that can be folded into the handle **3** a dive in which the diver bends at the waist in midair

jack of all trades *n, pl* **jacks of all trades** a person who can do many different kinds of work; handyman

jackpot *n* **1** the most valuable prize that can be won in a gambling game **2 hit the jackpot** *informal* to be very fortunate or very successful
WORD ORIGIN probably from *jack* (playing card)

jack rabbit *n* a hare of W North America with very long hind legs and large ears
WORD ORIGIN *jackass-rabbit*, referring to its long ears

jacks *n* a game in which metal, bone, or plastic pieces are thrown and then picked up between throws of a small ball
WORD ORIGIN *jackstones*, variant of *checkstones* pebbles

Jack Tar *n chiefly literary* a sailor

jack up *vb* **1** to raise (a motor vehicle) with a jack **2** to increase (prices or salaries) **3** *NZ informal* to organize something through unorthodox channels ▷ *n* **jack-up 4** *NZ informal* something achieved dishonestly

Jacobean (jak-a-**bee**-an) *adj* of or in the reign of James I of England and Ireland (1603–25)
WORD ORIGIN Latin *Jacobus* James

Jacobite *n history* a supporter of James II and his descendants
WORD ORIGIN Latin *Jacobus* James

Jacquard (**jak**-ard) *n* a fabric with an intricate design incorporated into the weave
WORD ORIGIN after J. M. *Jacquard*, its inventor

Jacuzzi (jak-oo-zee) *n trademark* a large circular bath with a mechanism that swirls the water

jade *n* **1** an ornamental semiprecious stone, usually green in colour ▷ *adj* **2** bluish-green
WORD ORIGIN obsolete Spanish *piedra de ijada* colic stone, because it was believed to cure colic

jaded *adj* tired or bored from overindulgence or overwork

Jaffa *n Brit* a large thick-skinned orange
WORD ORIGIN after *Jaffa*, port in W Israel

jag¹ *n Scot informal* same as **jab** (sense 3)
WORD ORIGIN origin unknown

jag² *n slang* a period of uncontrolled indulgence in an activity: *all-night crying jags*
WORD ORIGIN origin unknown

jagged (**jag**-gid) *adj* having an uneven edge with sharp points
WORD ORIGIN from *jag* a sharp point

jaguar *n* a large wild cat of south and central America, with a spotted coat
WORD ORIGIN from S American Indian

jail *or* **gaol** *n* **1** a prison ▷ *vb* **2** to confine in prison
WORD ORIGIN Old French *jaiole* cage

jailbird *n informal* a person who is or has often been in jail

jailer *or* **gaoler** *n* a person in charge of a jail

jake *adj* she's jake *Austral & NZ slang* it is all right
WORD ORIGIN probably from the name *Jake*

jalopy (jal-**lop**-ee) *n, pl* **-lopies** *informal* a dilapidated old car
WORD ORIGIN origin unknown

jam¹ *vb* **jamming, jammed 1** to wedge (an object) into a tight space or against another object: *the table was jammed against the wall* **2** to fill (a place) with people or vehicles: *the surrounding roads were jammed for miles* **3** to make or become stuck or locked: *the window was jammed open* **4** *radio* to prevent the clear reception of (radio communications) by transmitting other signals on the same wavelength **5** *slang* to play in a jam session **6 jam on the brakes** to apply the brakes of a vehicle very suddenly ▷ *n* **7** a situation where a large number of people or vehicles are crowded into a place: *a traffic jam* **8** *informal* a difficult situation: *you are in a bit of a jam* **9** same as **jam session**
WORD ORIGIN probably imitative

jam² *n* a food made from fruit boiled with sugar until the mixture sets, used for spreading on bread
WORD ORIGIN perhaps from JAM¹ (the act of squeezing)

Jamaican *adj* **1** of Jamaica ▷ *n* **2** a person from Jamaica

jamb *n* a side post of a doorframe or window frame
WORD ORIGIN Old French *jambe* leg, jamb

jamboree *n* a large gathering or celebration
WORD ORIGIN origin unknown

jammy *adj* **-mier, -miest 1** covered with or tasting like jam **2** *Brit slang* lucky: *jammy so-and-sos!*

jam-packed *adj* filled to capacity

jam session *n slang* an improvised performance by jazz or rock musicians
WORD ORIGIN probably from JAM¹

Jan. January

jandal *n NZ* a rubber-soled sandal attached to the foot by a thong between the big toe and the next toe

jangle *vb* **-gling, -gled 1** to make a harsh unpleasant ringing noise **2** to produce an irritating or unpleasant effect on: *the caffeine in coffee can jangle the nerves*
WORD ORIGIN Old French *jangler*

janitor *n chiefly Scot, US, & Canad* the caretaker of a school or other building
WORD ORIGIN Latin: doorkeeper

janjaweed, janjawid (**jan**-juh-weed) *n* an armed tribal militia group in the Darfur region of Sudan
WORD ORIGIN Arabic

January *n* the first month of the year
WORD ORIGIN Latin *Januarius*

japan *n* **1** a glossy black lacquer, originally from the Orient, which is used on wood or metal ▷ *vb* **-panning, -panned 2** to varnish with japan

Japanese *adj* **1** of Japan ▷ *n* **2** *pl* **-nese** a person from Japan **3** the language of Japan

jape *n old-fashioned* a joke or prank
WORD ORIGIN origin unknown

japonica *n* **1** a Japanese shrub with red flowers and yellowish fruit **2** same as **camellia**
WORD ORIGIN New Latin *Japonia* Japan

jar¹ *n* **1** a wide-mouthed cylindrical glass container, used for storing food **2** *Brit informal* a glass of beer
WORD ORIGIN Arabic *jarrah* large earthen vessel

jar² *vb* **jarring, jarred 1** to have an irritating or unpleasant effect: *sometimes a light remark jarred on her father* **2** to be in disagreement or conflict: *their very different temperaments jarred* **3** to jolt or bump ▷ *n* **4** a jolt or shock **jarring** *adj*
WORD ORIGIN probably imitative

jardiniere *n* an ornamental pot or stand for plants
WORD ORIGIN French

jargon *n* **1** specialized language relating to a particular subject, profession, or group **2** pretentious or unintelligible language
WORD ORIGIN Old French

jarrah *n* an Australian eucalypt yielding valuable timber

jasmine *n* a shrub or climbing plant with sweet-smelling flowers
WORD ORIGIN Persian *yāsmīn*

jasper *n* a kind of quartz, usually red in colour, which is used as a gemstone and for ornamental decoration
WORD ORIGIN Greek *iaspis*

jaundice *n* yellowing of the skin and the whites of the eyes, caused by an excess of bile pigments in the blood
WORD ORIGIN French *jaune* yellow

jaundiced *adj* **1** bitter or cynical: *the financial markets are taking a jaundiced view of the Government's motives* **2** having jaundice

jaunt *n* **1** a pleasure trip or outing ▷ *vb* **2** to go on a jaunt
WORD ORIGIN origin unknown

jaunty *adj* **-tier, -tiest 1** cheerful and energetic: *he was worried beneath the jaunty air* **2** smart and attractive: *a jaunty little hat* **jauntily** *adv*
WORD ORIGIN French *gentil* noble

Java *n trademark* a computer programming language that is widely used on the internet
WORD ORIGIN after *Java* coffee from the Indonesian island, allegedly drunk by its creators

Javanese *adj* **1** of the island of Java, in Indonesia ▷ *n* **2** *pl* **-nese** a person from Java **3** the language of Java

javelin *n* a light spear thrown in a sports competition
WORD ORIGIN Old French *javeline*

jaw *n* **1** either of the bones that hold the teeth and frame the mouth **2** the lower part of the face below the mouth **3** *slang* a long chat ▷ *vb* **4** *slang* to have a long chat
WORD ORIGIN probably Old French *joue* cheek

jawbone *n* the bone in the lower jaw of a person or animal

ja well no fine *interj S African* used to indicate reluctant acceptance

jaws *pl n* **1** the mouth of a person or animal **2** the parts of a machine or tool that grip an object **3** the narrow opening of a gorge or valley **4** a dangerous or threatening position: *to snatch victory from the jaws of defeat*

jay *n* a bird of Europe and Asia with a pinkish-brown body and blue-and-black wings
WORD ORIGIN Old French *jai*

jaywalking *n* crossing the road in a dangerous or careless manner **jaywalker** *n*
WORD ORIGIN *jay* (in sense: a foolish person)

jazz *n* **1** a kind of popular music of African-American origin that has an exciting rhythm and often involves improvisation **2 and all that jazz** *slang* and other related things
WORD ORIGIN origin unknown

jazz up *vb informal* **1** to play (a piece of music) in a jazzy style **2** to make (something) appear more interesting or lively: *never seek to jazz up a plain story*

jazzy *adj* **-zier, -ziest 1** colourful and modern: *jazzy shop fronts* **2** of or like jazz

JCB *n trademark, Brit* a large machine used in building, that has a shovel on the

Words from Literature
part 15

jostle *v* to bump or push someone roughly
  being jostled himself into the kennel
  Gulliver's Travels Jonathan Swift

keepsake *n* a keepsake is a gift which reminds
someone of an event or of the person who gave it
to them.
  books and ornaments they had in their boudoirs
  at home: keepsakes that different relations had
  presented to them
  Jane Eyre Charlotte Brontë

ken *v* to know
  though little kenned the lamplighter that he
  had any company but Christmas!
  A Christmas Carol Charles Dickens

kennel *n* a gutter, which is the edge of a road next to
the pavement, where rain water collects and flows away
  being jostled himself into the kennel
  Gulliver's Travels Jonathan Swift

knock-knee *adj* slanted, at an angle.
  LOT 1 was marked in whitewashed knock-knee
  letters on the brewhouse
  Great Expectations Charles Dickens

ladylike *adj* to be ladylike is to behave in a polite,
dignified and graceful way
  No, winking isn't ladylike
  Little Women Louisa May Alcott

lapse *n* flow
  Stealing with silent lapse to join the brook
  The Prelude William Wordsworth

larry *n* an old word which means commotion or
noisy celebration
  That was all a part of the larry!
  Tess of the D'Urbervilles Thomas Hardy

lath *n* a strip of wood
  The panels shrunk, the windows cracked;
  fragments of plaster fell out of the ceiling,
  and the naked laths were shown instead
  A Christmas Carol Charles Dickens

leer *n* a leer is an unpleasant smile
  with a kind of leer
  Treasure Island Robert Louis Stevenson

lenitives *n* these are different kinds of drugs or
medicines: lenitives and palliatives were pain
relievers; aperitives were laxatives; abstersives
caused vomiting; corrosives destroyed human tissue;
restringents caused constipation; cephalalgics
stopped headaches; icterics were used as medicine
for jaundice; apophlegmatics were cough medicine,
and acoustics were cures for the loss of hearing
  lenitives, aperitives, abstersives, corrosives,
  restringents, palliatives, laxatives, cephalalgics,
  icterics, apophlegmatics, acoustics
  Gulliver's Travels Jonathan Swift

lest *conj* in case. If you do something lest something
(usually) unpleasant happens you do it to try to
prevent it happening
  She went in without knocking, and hurried
  upstairs, in great fear lest she should meet the
  real Mary Ann
  Alice's Adventures in Wonderland Lewis Carroll

levee *n* an old term for a meeting held in the morning,
shortly after the person holding the meeting has got
out of bed
  I used to attend the King's levee once or twice a week
  Gulliver's Travels Jonathan Swift

life-preserver *n* a club which had lead inside it to
make it heavier and therefore more dangerous
  and with no more suspicious articles displayed
  to view than two or three heavy bludgeons which
  stood in a corner, and a 'life-preserver' that hung
  over the chimney-piece.
  Oliver Twist Charles Dickens

front and a digger arm on the back
WORD ORIGIN initials of Joseph Cyril
Bamford, its manufacturer

jealous *adj* **1** suspicious or fearful of
being displaced by a rival **2** envious:
I was jealous of the girls who had boyfriends
3 resulting from jealousy: *my jealous tears*
jealously *adv*
WORD ORIGIN Late Latin *zelus*
emulation

jealousy *n, pl* **-ousies** the state of or an
instance of feeling jealous

jeans *pl n* casual denim trousers
WORD ORIGIN from *jean fustian* fabric
from Genoa

Jeep *n trademark* a small road vehicle with
four-wheel drive
WORD ORIGIN perhaps *general-purpose*
(*vehicle*), influenced by Eugene the *Jeep*,
creature in a comic strip

jeer *vb* **1** to be derisive towards
(someone) ▷ *n* **2** a cry of derision
jeering *adj, n*
WORD ORIGIN origin unknown

Jehovah *n* God
WORD ORIGIN Hebrew *Yahweh*

Jehovah's Witness *n* a member of
a Christian Church whose followers
believe that the end of the world is near

jejune *adj* **1** simple and unsophisticated
2 dull and uninteresting
WORD ORIGIN Latin *jejunus* empty

jejunum (jij-**june**-um) *n anat* the part
of the small intestine between the
duodenum and the ileum **jejunal** *adj*
WORD ORIGIN Latin

Jekyll and Hyde *n* a person with two
distinct personalities, one good and the
other evil
WORD ORIGIN after the character in
a novel by R. L. Stevenson

jell *vb* **1** to take on a definite form: *the
changes have had little time to jell* **2** same as
gel (sense 2)
WORD ORIGIN from *jelly*

jellaba *n* a loose robe with a hood, worn
by some Arab men
WORD ORIGIN Arabic *jallabah*

jellied *adj* prepared in a jelly: *jellied eels*

jellies *pl n slang* gelatine capsules of
temazepam, dissolved and injected as a
recreational drug
WORD ORIGIN from GELATINE

jelly *n, pl* **-lies 1** a fruit-flavoured dessert
set with gelatine **2** a food made from
fruit juice boiled with sugar until the
mixture sets, used for spreading on
bread **3** a savoury food preparation set
with gelatine ▶ See also **jellies**
▷ **jelly-like** *adj*
WORD ORIGIN Latin *gelare* to freeze

jellyfish *n, pl* **-fish** a small sea creature
with a jelly-like umbrella-shaped body
and trailing tentacles

jemmy *or US* **jimmy** *n, pl* **-mies** a short
steel crowbar, used by burglars to prise
open doors and windows
WORD ORIGIN from short form of *James*

jenny *n, pl* **-nies** a female donkey, ass, or
wren
WORD ORIGIN from the name *Jenny*

jeopardize *or* **-dise** *vb* **-dizing, -dized** *or*
-dising, -dised to put (something) at
risk: *the escalating violence that is jeopardizing
current peace moves*

jeopardy *n* danger of harm, loss, or
death: *the survival of public hospitals is in
jeopardy*
WORD ORIGIN Old French *jeu parti*,
literally: divided game, hence uncertain
issue

jerboa *n* a small rodent of Asia and
N Africa with long hind legs used for
jumping
WORD ORIGIN Arabic *yarbū'*

jeremiad *n* a long mournful complaint
WORD ORIGIN French *jérémiade*, referring
to the Lamentations of Jeremiah in the
Bible

jerepigo (jer-ree-**pee**-go) *n S African*
a sweet fortified wine similar to port
WORD ORIGIN Portuguese *jeropiga*

jerk *vb* **1** to move with an irregular or
spasmodic motion **2** to pull or push
(something) abruptly or spasmodically
▷ *n* **3** an abrupt or spasmodic movement
4 an irregular jolting motion: *the
irritating jerk that heralded a gear change*
5 *slang chiefly US & Canad* a stupid or
ignorant person
WORD ORIGIN probably variant of *yerk* to
pull stitches tight

jerkin *n* a short jacket
WORD ORIGIN origin unknown

jerky *adj* **jerkier, jerkiest** having an
irregular jolting motion: *avoid any sudden
or jerky movements* **jerkily** *adv* **jerkiness** *n*

Jerry *n old-fashioned Brit slang* **1** *pl* **-ries** a
German, esp. a German soldier
2 Germans collectively

jerry-built *adj* (of houses) built badly
with cheap materials

jerry can *n* a flat-sided can used for
carrying petrol or water
WORD ORIGIN from *Jerry* German soldier

jersey *n* **1** a knitted garment covering
the upper part of the body **2** a soft,
slightly stretchy, machine-knitted
fabric
WORD ORIGIN after *Jersey*, because of the
woollen sweaters worn by the
fishermen

Jersey *n* a breed of reddish-brown dairy
cattle that produces milk with a high
butterfat content
WORD ORIGIN after *Jersey*, island in the
English Channel

Jerusalem artichoke *n* a small
yellowish-white vegetable that grows
underground
WORD ORIGIN altered from Italian
girasole sunflower

jest *n* **1** something done or said to amuse
people **2 in jest** as a joke: *many a true word
is spoken in jest* ▷ *vb* **3** to do or say
something to amuse people
WORD ORIGIN variant of *gest* exploit

jester *n* a professional clown employed
by a king or nobleman during the
Middle Ages

Jesuit (jezz-yew-it) *n* a member of the
Society of Jesus, a Roman Catholic
religious order **Jesuitical** *adj*
WORD ORIGIN New Latin *Jesuita*

Jesus *n* **1** the founder of Christianity,
believed by Christians to be the Son of
God ▷ *interj* **2** *taboo slang* an oath
expressing intense anger or shock

jet¹ *n* **1** an aircraft driven by jet
propulsion **2** a thin stream of liquid or

gas forced out of a small hole **3** an
outlet or nozzle through which a
stream of liquid or gas is forced ▷ *vb*
jetting, jetted 4 to travel by jet aircraft
WORD ORIGIN Old French *jeter* to throw

jet² *n* a hard black mineral that is
polished and used in jewellery
WORD ORIGIN Old French *jaiet*

jet-black *adj* deep black

jetboat *n* a motorboat propelled by a jet
of water

jet engine *n* an aircraft engine that
uses jet propulsion for forward motion

jet lag *n* a feeling of fatigue and
disorientation often experienced by air
passengers who have crossed several
time zones in a short space of time

jet-propelled *adj* driven by jet
propulsion

jet propulsion *n* a method of
propulsion by which an aircraft is
moved forward by the force of the
exhaust gases ejected from the rear

jetsam *n* **1** goods thrown overboard to
lighten a ship during a storm **2 flotsam
and jetsam** see **flotsam** (sense 2)
WORD ORIGIN from *jettison*

jet set *n* rich and fashionable people
who travel widely for pleasure
jet-setter *n* **jet-setting** *adj*

jet ski *n* a small self-propelled vehicle
resembling a scooter, which skims
across water on a flat keel **jet skiing** *n*

jettison *vb* **1** to abandon or give up:
jettisoning democracy in favour of fascism
2 to throw overboard
WORD ORIGIN Latin *jactatio* a tossing
about

jetty *n, pl* **-ties 1** a landing pier or dock
2 a structure built from a shore out into
the water to protect a harbour
WORD ORIGIN Old French *jetee*
projecting part

Jew *n* **1** a person whose religion is
Judaism **2** a descendant of the ancient
Hebrews
WORD ORIGIN Hebrew *yehūdāh* Judah

jewel *n* **1** a precious or semiprecious
stone **2** a person or thing regarded as
precious or special: *a fantastic little car, a
real little jewel* **3** a gemstone used as part
of the machinery of a watch
WORD ORIGIN Old French *jouel*

jewelled *or US* **jeweled** *adj* decorated
with jewels

jeweller *or US* **jeweler** *n* a person who
buys, sells, and repairs jewellery

jewellery *or US* **jewelry** *n* objects such
as rings, necklaces, and bracelets, worn
for decoration

Jewess *n now often offensive* a woman
whose religion is Judaism

jewfish *n Austral* a freshwater catfish

Jewish *adj* of Jews or Judaism

Jewry *n* Jews collectively

jew's-harp *n* a small musical
instrument held between the teeth and
played by plucking a metal strip with
the finger

Jezebel *n* a wicked or shameless woman
WORD ORIGIN after the wife of Ahab, in
the Bible

jib¹ *n* **1** *naut* a triangular sail set in front
of the foremast **2 the cut of someone's**

jib a person's manner or style
WORD ORIGIN origin unknown

jib² vb **jibbing, jibbed** chiefly Brit **1** (of an animal) to stop short and refuse to go forwards: my animal jibbed three times **2 jib at** to object to: he jibs at any suggestion that his side are the underdogs
WORD ORIGIN origin unknown

jib³ n the projecting arm of a crane
WORD ORIGIN probably from gibbet

jibe¹ n **1** an insulting or taunting remark ▷ vb **jibing, jibed 2** to make insulting or taunting remarks

jibe² vb **jibing, jibed** informal to be in accord or be consistent: their apparent devotion hardly jibed with what he had heard about them

jibe³ vb **jibing, jibed**, n naut same as **gybe**

jiffy n, pl **jiffies** informal a very short time: won't be a jiffy!
WORD ORIGIN origin unknown

Jiffy bag n trademark a large padded envelope

jig n **1** a lively folk dance **2** music for this dance **3** a mechanical device that holds and locates a part during machining ▷ vb **jigging, jigged 4** to dance a jig **5** to move with quick jerky movements
WORD ORIGIN origin unknown

jigger n a small whisky glass

jiggered adj old-fashioned informal damned or blowed: well, I'm jiggered, so that's where it went!
WORD ORIGIN probably euphemism for buggered

jiggery-pokery n informal chiefly Brit dishonest behaviour; cheating
WORD ORIGIN Scots dialect joukery-pawkery

jiggle vb **-gling, -gled** to move with quick jerky movements
WORD ORIGIN frequentative of jig

jigsaw n **1** Also called: **jigsaw puzzle** a puzzle in which the player has to put together a picture that has been cut into irregularly shaped interlocking pieces **2** a mechanical saw with a fine steel blade for cutting along curved or irregular lines in sheets of material
WORD ORIGIN jig (to jerk up and down) + SAW¹

jihad n Islamic holy war against unbelievers

jilt vb to leave or reject (a lover) abruptly or callously
WORD ORIGIN dialect jillet flighty girl

Jim Crow n US **1** the policy or practice of segregating Black people **2** offensive a Black person
WORD ORIGIN from name of song

jingle n **1** a short catchy song used to advertise a product on radio or television **2** a light ringing sound ▷ vb **-gling, -gled 3** to make a light ringing sound
WORD ORIGIN probably imitative

jingoism n excessive and aggressive patriotism **jingoistic** or **jingoist** adj
WORD ORIGIN after the use of by Jingo! in a 19th-century song

jink vb to move quickly or jerkily in order to dodge someone: he jinked free and won a race to the line to level the scores
WORD ORIGIN Scots

jinks pl n **high jinks** boisterous or mischievous behaviour
WORD ORIGIN origin unknown

jinni or **djinni** n, pl **jinn** or **djinn** a being or spirit in Muslim belief that could take on human or animal form
WORD ORIGIN Arabic

jinx n **1** someone or something believed to bring bad luck ▷ vb **2** to bring bad luck to
WORD ORIGIN perhaps from Greek iunx wryneck, a bird used in magic

jitterbug n **1** a fast jerky American dance that was popular in the 1940s ▷ vb **-bugging, -bugged 2** to dance the jitterbug

jitters pl n **the jitters** informal a feeling of extreme nervousness experienced before an important event: I had a case of the jitters during my first two speeches
WORD ORIGIN origin unknown

jittery adj nervous

jive n **1** a lively jerky dance that was popular in the 1940s and 1950s ▷ vb **jiving, jived 2** to dance the jive **jiver** n
WORD ORIGIN origin unknown

Jnr Junior

job n **1** a person's occupation or paid employment **2** a piece of work; task **3** the performance of a task: he made a good job of the repair **4** informal a difficult task: they are having a job to fill his shoes **5** Brit, Austral, & NZ informal a crime, esp. a robbery **6 just the job** informal exactly what is required **7 make the best of a bad job** to cope as well as possible in unsatisfactory circumstances
WORD ORIGIN origin unknown

jobbing adj doing individual jobs for payment: a jobbing gardener

Jobcentre or **job centre** n (in Britain) a government office where advertisements of available jobs are displayed

Jobclub or **job club** n (in Britain) a group of unemployed people which meets every weekday and is given advice on and help with job seeking

jobless adj **1** unemployed ▷ pl n **2** people who are unemployed: the young jobless

job lot n a miscellaneous collection of articles sold together

Job's comforter n a person who adds to someone else's distress while pretending to be sympathetic
WORD ORIGIN after Job in the Bible

jobseeker's allowance n (in Britain) a social-security payment for unemployed people

job sharing n an arrangement by which a job is shared by two part-time workers

jockey n **1** a person who rides horses in races as a profession ▷ vb **2 jockey for position** to try to obtain an advantage by skilful manoeuvring
WORD ORIGIN from the name Jock

jockstrap n an elasticated belt with a pouch to support the genitals, worn by male athletes. Also called: **athletic support**
WORD ORIGIN slang jock penis

jocose (joke-**kohss**) adj old-fashioned playful or humorous **jocosely** adv
WORD ORIGIN Latin jocus joke

jocular adj **1** (of a person) often joking; good-humoured **2** (of a remark) meant lightly or humorously **jocularity** n **jocularly** adv
WORD ORIGIN Latin joculus little joke

jocund (**jok**-kund) adj literary cheerful or merry
WORD ORIGIN Latin jucundus pleasant

jodhpurs pl n trousers worn for riding, which are loose-fitting around the thighs and tight-fitting below the knees
WORD ORIGIN from Jodhpur, town in NW India

joey n Austral a young kangaroo

jog vb **jogging, jogged 1** to run at a gentle pace for exercise **2** to nudge slightly **3 jog along** to continue in a plodding way: many people jog along in second gear for the whole of their lives **4 jog someone's memory** to remind someone of something ▷ n **5** a slow run as a form of exercise **jogger** n **jogging** n
WORD ORIGIN probably variant of shog to shake

joggle vb **-gling, -gled** to shake or move with a slightly jolting motion
WORD ORIGIN frequentative of jog

jog trot n an easy bouncy pace, midway between a walk and a trot

john n slang chiefly US & Canad a toilet
WORD ORIGIN special use of the name

John Bull n England represented as a man

johnny n, pl **-nies** Brit, old-fashioned informal a chap: you legal johnnies

Johnny Canuck (kan-**nuk**) n Canad informal Canada personified as a man

joie de vivre (**zhwah** de **veev**-ra) n enjoyment of life
WORD ORIGIN French, literally: joy of living

join vb **1** to become a member of (a club or organization) **2** to become part of (a queue or list) **3** to meet (someone) as a companion: join me for a beer **4** to take part in (an activity): join the war effort **5** (of two roads or rivers) to meet and come together **6** to bring into contact: join hands **7 join forces** to combine efforts with someone ▷ n **8** a place where two things are joined together ▶ See also **join in, join up**
WORD ORIGIN Latin jungere to yoke

joined-up adj integrated by an overall strategy: joined-up government

joiner n a person whose job is making finished woodwork, such as window frames and stairs

joinery n the skill or work of a joiner

join in vb to take part in (an activity)

joint adj **1** shared by or belonging to two or more parties: the two countries have issued a joint statement ▷ n **2** anat the junction between two or more bones: a hip joint **3** a junction of two or more parts or objects: a mortar joint **4** a piece of meat suitable for roasting **5** slang a building or place of entertainment: strip joints **6** slang a cannabis cigarette **7 out of joint a** informal out of order or out of keeping: they find their routine lives out of joint with their training **b** (of a bone) knocked out of its normal position **8 put someone's nose out of joint**

see **nose** (sense 10) ▷ *vb* **9** to provide a joint or joints **10** to cut or divide (meat) into joints **jointed** *adj* **jointly** *adv*

joint-stock company *n* Brit a business firm whose capital is owned jointly by shareholders

join up *vb* to become a member of a military organization

joist *n* a beam made of timber, steel, or concrete, used as a support in the construction of floors and roofs **WORD ORIGIN** Old French *giste*

jojoba (hoe-**hoe**-ba) *n* a shrub whose seeds contain an oil used in cosmetics **WORD ORIGIN** Mexican Spanish

joke *n* **1** something that is said or done to amuse people **2** someone or something that is ridiculous: *the country's inexperienced leaders are regarded as something of a joke* **3** **no joke** informal a serious or difficult matter: *getting over mountain passes at ten thousand feet is no joke* ▷ *vb* **joking, joked** **4** to say or do something to amuse people **jokey** *adj* **jokingly** *adv* **WORD ORIGIN** Latin *jocus*

joker *n* **1** a person who jokes a lot **2** slang a person regarded without respect: *waiting for the next jokers to sign up* **3** an extra playing card in a pack, which can replace any other card in some games **4** Austral & NZ informal a chap

jol (**joll**) S African slang *n* **1** a party ▷ *vb* **jolling, jolled** **2** to have a good time **WORD ORIGIN** Dutch

jollification *n* a merry festivity

jollity *n* the condition of being jolly

jolly *adj* **-lier, -liest** **1** full of good humour **2** involving a lot of fun: *big jolly birthday parties* ▷ *adv* **3** Brit informal very: *I'm going to have a jolly good try* ▷ *vb* **-lies, -lying, -lied** **4** **jolly along** informal to try to keep (someone) cheerful by flattery or cheerful chat **WORD ORIGIN** Old French *jolif*

Jolly Roger *n* the traditional pirate flag, depicting a white skull and crossbones on a black background

jolt *n* **1** a severe shock **2** a sudden violent movement ▷ *vb* **3** to surprise or shock: *he was momentarily jolted by the news* **4** to bump against (someone or something) with a sudden violent movement **5** to move in a jerking manner **WORD ORIGIN** origin unknown

Jonah *n* a person believed to bring bad luck to those around him or her **WORD ORIGIN** after *Jonah* in the Bible

jonquil *n* a narcissus with sweet-smelling yellow or white flowers **WORD ORIGIN** French *jonquille*

Jordanian *adj* **1** of Jordan ▷ *n* **2** a person from Jordan

josh *vb* slang to joke or tease **WORD ORIGIN** origin unknown

joss stick *n* a stick of incense, giving off a sweet smell when burnt **WORD ORIGIN** *joss* (a Chinese idol) from Portuguese *deos* god

jostle *vb* **-tling, -tled** **1** to bump or push roughly: *television crews filming the scene were jostled by police* **2** to compete with someone: *jostling for power* **WORD ORIGIN** Old French *jouster* to joust

jot *vb* **jotting, jotted** **1** **jot down** to write a brief note of: *quickly jot down the answers to these questions* ▷ *n* **2** the least bit: *it makes not one jot of difference* **WORD ORIGIN** Greek *iōta* iota, smallest letter

jotter *n* a small notebook

jottings *pl n* notes jotted down

joual (**zhwahl**) *n* a nonstandard variety of Canadian French **WORD ORIGIN** French

joule (**jool**) *n* physics the SI unit of work or energy **WORD ORIGIN** after J. P. Joule, physicist

journal *n* **1** a newspaper or magazine **2** a daily record of events **WORD ORIGIN** Latin *diurnalis* daily

journalese *n* a superficial style of writing regarded as typical of newspapers and magazines

journalism *n* the profession of collecting, writing, and publishing news through newspapers and magazines or by radio and television

journalist *n* a person who writes or edits news items for a newspaper or magazine or for radio or television **journalistic** *adj*

journey *n* **1** the process of travelling from one place to another **2** the time taken or distance travelled on a journey ▷ *vb* **3** to make a journey **WORD ORIGIN** Old French *journee* a day, a day's travelling

journeyman *n, pl* **-men** a qualified craftsman who works for an employer **WORD ORIGIN** *journey* (in obsolete sense: a day's work)

joust history *n* **1** a combat with lances between two mounted knights ▷ *vb* **2** to take part in such a tournament **WORD ORIGIN** Old French *jouster*

Jove *n* **1** Jupiter (the god) **2** **by Jove** old-fashioned an exclamation of surprise or for emphasis

jovial *adj* happy and cheerful **joviality** *n* **jovially** *adv* **WORD ORIGIN** Latin *jovialis* of (the planet) Jupiter

jowl[1] *n* **1** the lower jaw **2** **cheek by jowl** see **cheek** **3** **jowls** cheeks **jowled** *adj* **WORD ORIGIN** Old English *ceafl* jaw

jowl[2] *n* fatty flesh hanging from the lower jaw **WORD ORIGIN** Old English *ceole* throat

joy *n* **1** deep happiness and contentment **2** something that brings deep happiness: *a thing of beauty is a joy for ever* **3** informal success or satisfaction: *we checked ports and airports without any joy* **WORD ORIGIN** Latin *gaudium*

joyful *adj* feeling or bringing great joy: *joyful crowds; a joyful event* **joyfully** *adv*

joyless *adj* feeling or bringing no joy

joyous *adj* extremely happy and enthusiastic **joyously** *adv*

joyride *n* a drive in a car one has stolen **joyriding** *n* **joyrider** *n*

joystick *n* the control lever of an aircraft or a computer

JP (in Britain) Justice of the Peace

JPEG (**jay-peg**) *n* computers **a** a standard compressed file format used for pictures **b** a picture held in this file format

Jr Junior

JSA jobseeker's allowance: in Britain, a payment made to unemployed people

jube *n* Austral & NZ informal same as **jujube**

jubilant *adj* feeling great joy **jubilantly** *adv* **WORD ORIGIN** Latin *jubilare* to give a joyful cry

jubilation *n* a feeling of great joy and celebration

jubilee *n* a special anniversary, esp. a 25th (**silver jubilee**) or 50th one (**golden jubilee**) **WORD ORIGIN** Old French *jubile*, ultimately from Hebrew *yōbhēl* ram's horn, used for proclamation

Judaic *adj* of Jews or Judaism

Judaism *n* the religion of the Jews, based on the Old Testament and the Talmud

Judas *n* a person who betrays a friend **WORD ORIGIN** after *Judas* Iscariot in the Bible

judder *vb* informal chiefly Brit to shake or vibrate violently: *the van juddered before it moved away* **WORD ORIGIN** probably blend of *jar* (jolt) + *shudder*

judder bar *n* NZ a raised strip across a road designed to slow down vehicles

judge *n* **1** a public official with authority to hear cases and pass sentences in a court of law **2** a person appointed to determine the result of a competition **3** a person whose opinion on a particular subject is usually reliable: *a fine judge of men* ▷ *vb* **judging, judged** **4** to determine the result of (a competition) **5** to appraise critically: *she hopes people judge her on her work rather than her appearance* **6** to decide (something) after inquiry: *we use a means test to judge the most needy cases* **7** to believe or consider: *doctors judged that the benefits of such treatment outweighed the risk* **WORD ORIGIN** Latin *judex*

judgment *or* **judgement** *n* **1** a decision formed after careful consideration: *the editorials reserve their judgment about the new political plan* **2** the verdict pronounced by a court of law **3** the ability to make critical distinctions and achieve a balanced viewpoint: *their judgment was unsound on foreign and defence issues* **4** the formal decision of the judge of a competition **5** **against one's better judgment** contrary to what one thinks is sensible: *against my better judgment, I asked for another bourbon* **6** **pass judgment** to give one's opinion, usually a critical one, on a matter

judgmental *or* **judgemental** *adj* making judgments, esp. critical ones, about other people's conduct

Judgment Day *n* Christianity the occasion of the Last Judgment by God at the end of the world

judicial *adj* **1** of judges or the administration of justice **2** showing or using good judgment: *judicial self-restraint* **judicially** *adv* **WORD ORIGIN** Latin *judicium* judgment

judiciary *n* the branch of the central authority in a country that administers justice

Parts of Speech

The parts of speech that most people are familiar with are probably noun, verb, and adjective. This is because they're fairly easy to pin down. There are more than twice as many nouns in English as all of the other parts of speech put together: there are about 6,000 verbs, 12,000 adjectives, 3,000 adverbs, and less than 200 prepositions. That leaves over 40,000 nouns. These figures are from a large bilingual dictionary. Smaller dictionaries don't have such large totals, but the proportions are similar. In education, using terms like noun and verb goes in and out of fashion. For many people, perhaps the only time they ever encounter these terms is when they use a dictionary, where the information is almost always grouped according to part of speech, even in online dictionaries.

Explanations of nouns, verbs, and adjectives often run along the lines of 'nouns are the names of people, places or things', 'verbs are doing words', 'adjectives describe nouns'. However, if we say 'pencil is a noun' this is really shorthand for 'pencil is a word that is often used in the way other words we call nouns are used'. This means that it's often found after the or a, or with an -s added to it. Individual pencils aren't nouns in the real world. It doesn't make sense to say, 'count the nouns on your desk', because there aren't any. There are only nouns in what we say or write, and they're only referred to as nouns because of the way we're using them in a particular sentence. If you say, 'I'll pencil it in for Monday', pencil is not a noun. It's a verb, because you're using it in the same way you would use write, send, bring, and other words that we normally consider to be verbs. The same is true of verbs as of nouns: you can only call a word a verb if it's being used as a verb. One of the most frequently used verbs in English is take, but in 'a new take on an old problem' it's a noun.

Adjectives are words like tall, short, long, thin. The term usually rears its head when you're learning a foreign language. This is because it's hard to explain what's going on unless you can refer to different parts of speech. In French, for example, the endings of adjectives change to match the noun they're describing. Vert is green, but 'a green skirt' is 'une jupe verte'.

Now we can move on to adverbs, prepositions, and pronouns. Adverbs often end in -ly, which is convenient, although there a few words like ugly or friendly that are adjectives. However, there are hundreds of adverbs that don't end in -ly, like very or more or soon. Adverbs usually answer the questions How? Where? and When? They're sometimes called adverbs of manner, place and time.

Prepositions are words that are positioned pre - in front of - a noun, or a phrase that includes a noun (called a noun phrase). So, under a tree, round the corner, past the shop, beyond belief. Again, as with other parts of speech, you need to look at how they're being used. You can make a list of words that are often prepositions (at, beside, by, on, over, etc) but they aren't actually prepositions until they're followed by a noun. When a word like beneath is used with a noun, as in 'beneath contempt', it's a preposition. But when it crops up in a description of a room as 'a cupboard with louvred doors beneath' then it's no longer a preposition, because there's nothing after it. In cases like this (as in he ran past) these words are being used as adverbs.

Pronouns are words that replace nouns or noun phrases. They're words like I, me and mine, you and yours, they and them and theirs. Then there are possessive adjectives like my, your and their, which are followed by nouns or noun phrases.

There are another two categories still left to look at: conjunctions and interjections. And is probably the most obvious conjunction, used for joining two ideas together, but there are a few dozen more, like although, because, if, whether, and so on. Interjections might just as well be called exclamations, which describes them better - things like oops! or ugh!, usually with an exclamation mark after them in written English.

The main point to remember about parts of speech is that they're a convenient shortcut, a way of grouping words that has been found useful over centuries. Even Shakespeare recognizes that they can be frustrating, though:

It will be proved to thy face that thou hast men
about thee that usually talk of a noun and a
verb, and such abominable words as no
Christian ear can endure to hear.

judicious *adj* having or showing good judgment: *the judicious use of charge cards* **judiciously** *adv*

judo *n* a sport derived from jujitsu, in which the two opponents try to throw or force each other on to the ground **WORD ORIGIN** Japanese *jū* gentleness + *dō* way

jug *n* a container with a handle and a small spout, used for holding and pouring liquids **WORD ORIGIN** origin unknown

jugged hare *n* hare stewed in an earthenware pot

juggernaut *n* **1** *Brit* a very large heavy lorry **2** any terrible force that demands complete self-sacrifice **WORD ORIGIN** Hindi *Jagannath* lord of the world

juggle *vb* **-gling, -gled 1** to throw and catch several objects continuously so that most are in the air at the same time **2** to keep (several activities) in progress at the same time: *women who are adept at juggling priorities* **3** to manipulate (facts or figures) to suit one's purpose **juggler** *n* **WORD ORIGIN** Old French *jogler* to perform as a jester

jugular *n* a large vein in the neck that carries blood to the heart from the head. Also called: **jugular vein** **WORD ORIGIN** Latin *jugulum* throat

juice *n* **1** a drink made from the liquid part of a fruit or vegetable: *grapefruit juice* **2** *informal* **a** petrol **b** electricity **3** juices **a** the fluids in a person's or animal's body: *digestive juices* **b** the liquid that comes out of meat when it is cooked **WORD ORIGIN** Old French *jus*

juicy *adj* **juicier, juiciest 1** full of juice **2** *informal* interesting and exciting: *juicy details*

jujitsu *n* the traditional Japanese system of unarmed self-defence **WORD ORIGIN** Japanese *jū* gentleness + *jutsu* art

juju *n* **1** a magic charm or fetish used by some tribes in W Africa **2** the power associated with a juju **WORD ORIGIN** probably from W African *djudju* evil spirit, fetish

jujube *n* a chewy sweet made of flavoured gelatine **WORD ORIGIN** Medieval Latin *jujuba*

jukebox *n* an automatic coin-operated record player **WORD ORIGIN** *juke* (from a Black American language) bawdy

jukskei *n* *S African* a game in which a peg is thrown over a fixed distance at a stake fixed into the ground **WORD ORIGIN** Afrikaans *juk* yoke + *skei* pin

Jul. July

julep *n* a sweet alcoholic drink, usually garnished with sprigs of mint

Julian calendar *n* the calendar introduced by Julius Caesar, in which leap years occur every fourth year and in every centenary year

julienne *adj* **1** (of vegetables or meat) cut into thin shreds ▷ *n* **2** a clear soup containing thinly shredded vegetables **WORD ORIGIN** French

July *n, pl* **-lies** the seventh month of the year **WORD ORIGIN** after *Julius* Caesar

jumble *n* **1** a disordered mass or state **2** articles donated for a jumble sale ▷ *vb* **-bling, -bled 3** to mix up **WORD ORIGIN** origin unknown

jumble sale *n* a sale, usually of second-hand articles, often in aid of charity

jumbo *adj* **1** *Brit, Austral, & NZ informal* very large: *jumbo prawns* ▷ *n, pl* **-bos 2** short for **jumbo jet** **WORD ORIGIN** after a famous elephant exhibited by P. T. Barnum

jumbo jet *n* *informal* a very large jet-propelled airliner

jumbuck *n* *Austral old-fashioned slang* sheep **WORD ORIGIN** from a native Australian language

jump *vb* **1** to move suddenly up into the air by using the muscles in the legs and feet **2** to move quickly: *he jumps on a No. 6 bus* **3** to jerk with astonishment or shock: *he jumped when he heard a loud noise* **4** (of prices) to rise suddenly or abruptly **5** to change quickly from one subject to another: *any other comments before I jump on to the next section?* **6** *informal* to attack without warning: *the officer was jumped by three prisoners who broke his jaw* **7** **jump down someone's throat** *informal* to speak sharply to someone **8** **jump the gun** see **gun** (sense 3) **9** **jump the queue a** to take a place in a queue ahead of people who are already queuing **b** to have an unfair advantage over other people: *squatters should not be able to jump the queue for housing* **10** **jump to it** *informal* to begin doing something immediately ▷ *n* **11** the act or an instance of jumping **12** *sport* any of several contests that involve jumping: *the long jump* **13** a sudden rise: *a 78% jump in taxable profits* **14** a sudden change from one subject to another: *stunning jumps from thought to thought* **15** a step or degree: *one jump ahead of the competition* **16** **take a running jump** *informal* a contemptuous expression of dismissal ▶ See also **jump at, jump on** **WORD ORIGIN** probably imitative

jump at *vb* to accept eagerly: *I jumped at the chance to return to English county cricket*

jumped-up *adj* *informal* having suddenly risen in significance and appearing arrogant: *a jumped-up bunch of ex-student-leaders*

jumper¹ *n* **1** *Austral & Brit* a knitted garment covering the upper part of the body **2** *US & Canad* a pinafore dress **WORD ORIGIN** obsolete *jump* man's loose jacket

jumper² *n* a person or animal that jumps

jump jet *n* *informal* a fixed-wing jet aircraft that can land and take off vertically

jump leads *pl n* two heavy cables used to start a motor vehicle with a flat battery by connecting the flat battery to the battery of another vehicle

jump on *vb* *informal* to make a sudden physical or verbal attack on: *the press really jumped on him*

jump-start *vb* **1** to start the engine of (a motor vehicle) by pushing or rolling it and then engaging the gears ▷ *n* **2** the act of starting a motor vehicle in this way

jump suit *n* a one-piece garment combining trousers and top

jumpy *adj* **jumpier, jumpiest** nervous or apprehensive

Jun. 1 June **2** Junior

junction *n* a place where roads or railway lines meet, link, or cross each other **WORD ORIGIN** Latin *junctio* a joining

juncture *n* a point in time, esp. a critical one: *trade has been halted at a crucial juncture*

June *n* the sixth month of the year **WORD ORIGIN** probably from Latin *Junius* of the goddess Juno

jungle *n* **1** a forest area in a hot country with luxuriant vegetation **2** a confused or confusing situation: *the administrative jungle* **3** a situation where there is an intense struggle for survival: *the economic jungle* **4** a type of fast electronic dance music **WORD ORIGIN** Hindi *jangal*

junior *adj* **1** lower in rank or position: *junior officers* **2** younger: *world junior champion* **3** (in England and Wales) of school children between the ages of 7 and 11 approximately **4** *US* of the third year of a four-year course at college or high school ▷ *n* **5** a person holding a low rank or position **6** a person who is younger than another person: *the man she is to marry is 20 years her junior* **7** (in England and Wales) a junior school child **8** *US* a junior student **WORD ORIGIN** Latin: younger

Junior *adj* the younger of two: usually used after a name to distinguish between two people of the same name: *Harry Connick Junior*

junior lightweight *n* a professional boxer weighing up to 130 pounds (59 kg)

juniper *n* an evergreen shrub with purple berries which are used to make gin **WORD ORIGIN** Latin *juniperus*

junk¹ *n* **1** old or unwanted objects **2** *informal* rubbish: *the sheer junk written about astrology* **3** *slang* narcotic drugs, esp. heroin **WORD ORIGIN** Middle English *jonke* old useless rope

junk² *n* a Chinese sailing boat with a flat bottom and square sails **WORD ORIGIN** Portuguese *junco*, from Javanese *jon*

junk bond *n* *finance* a security that offers a high yield but often involves a high risk of default

junket *n* **1** an excursion made by a public official and paid for out of public funds **2** a sweet dessert made of flavoured milk set with rennet **3** a feast **junketing** *n* **WORD ORIGIN** Middle English: rush basket, hence custard served on rushes

junk food *n* food with a low nutritional value

junkie *n* *informal* a drug addict

junk mail *n* unsolicited mail advertising goods or services

Juno *n* the queen of the Roman gods

junta *n* a group of military officers holding the power in a country after a revolution

WORD ORIGIN Spanish: council

Jupiter *n* **1** the king of the Roman gods **2** the largest planet

Jurassic *adj geol* of the geological period about 180 million years ago, during which dinosaurs flourished

WORD ORIGIN after the *Jura* (Mountains) in W central Europe

juridical *adj* of law or the administration of justice

WORD ORIGIN Latin *jus* law + *dicere* to say

jurisdiction *n* **1** the right or power to administer justice and to apply laws **2** the exercise or extent of such a right or power **3** authority in general: *under the jurisdiction of the referee*

WORD ORIGIN Latin *jurisdictio*

jurisprudence *n* the science or philosophy of law

WORD ORIGIN Latin *juris prudentia*

jurist *n* a person who is an expert on law

WORD ORIGIN French *juriste*

juror *n* a member of a jury

WORD ORIGIN Old French *jurer* to take an oath

jury *n, pl* **-ries 1** a group of, usually, twelve people, sworn to deliver a true verdict according to the evidence upon a case presented in a court of law **2** a group of people appointed to judge a competition

WORD ORIGIN Old French *jurer* to swear

jury box *n* an enclosure where the jury sits in a court of law

jury-rigged *adj chiefly naut* set up in a makeshift manner

WORD ORIGIN origin unknown

just *adv* **1** very recently: *the results have just been published* **2** at this very instant or in the very near future: *news is just coming in of a nuclear explosion* **3** no more than; only: *nothing fancy, just solid German fare* **4** exactly: *just the opposite* **5** barely: *the swimmers arrived just in time for the opening ceremony* **6** **just about** practically or virtually: *just about everyone* **7** **just about to** very soon going to: *it was just about to explode* **8** **just a moment** *or* **second** *or* **minute** an expression requesting someone to wait for a short time **9** **just now a** a short time ago: *as you said just now* **b** at the present time: *he needs all the support he can get just now* **c** *S African informal* in a little while **10** **just so** arranged with precision: *a cottage with the gardens and rooms all just so* ▷ *adj* **11** fair and right: *a just war* **justly** *adv* **justness** *n*

WORD ORIGIN Latin *jus* justice

≡ USAGE
≡ The use of *just* with *exactly* (*it's just exactly
≡ what they want*) is redundant and should
≡ be avoided: *it's exactly what they want.*

justice *n* **1** the quality of being just **2** the administration of law according to prescribed and accepted principles **3** a judge **4** **bring to justice** to capture, try, and punish (a criminal) **5** **do justice to** to show to full advantage: *she wore white slacks and a sleeveless blouse that did full justice to her trim figure*

WORD ORIGIN Latin *justitia*

justice of the peace *n* **1** (in Britain) a magistrate who is authorized to act as a judge in a local court of law **2** (in New Zealand) a person authorized to act in a limited judicial capacity

justifiable *adj* having a good cause or reason: *I reacted with justifiable indignation* **justifiably** *adv*

justify *vb* **-fies, -fying, -fied 1** to prove (something) to be just or valid: *the idea of the end justifying the means* **2** to defend (an action) as being warranted: *an essay justifying his conversion to Catholicism* **3** to arrange (text) when typing or printing so that both margins are straight **justification** *n*

WORD ORIGIN Latin *justificare*

jute *n* a fibre that comes from the bark of an East Indian plant, used in making rope, sacks, and mats

WORD ORIGIN Bengali *jhuto*

jut out *vb* **jutting, jutted** to stick out

WORD ORIGIN variant of JET¹

juvenile *adj* **1** young; not fully adult: *juvenile offenders* **2** of or for young people: *juvenile court* **3** immature in behaviour ▷ *n* **4** a young person

WORD ORIGIN Latin *juvenilis*

juvenile delinquent *n* a young person who is guilty of a crime **juvenile delinquency** *n*

juvenilia *pl n* works produced in an artist's youth

juxtapose *vb* **-posing, -posed** to place (two objects or ideas) close together or side by side **juxtaposition** *n*

WORD ORIGIN Latin *juxta* next to + POSITION

Kk

The letter K is the eleventh letter of the English alphabet. It has its origins in the Greek letter *kappa* (K,k), which derived from a Semitic letter representing a hand.

In the Roman alphabet the letter K was gradually superseded by C, which was found perfectly adequate to represent the hard /k/ sound. However, K was not discarded altogether. It survived in a handful of archaic words and was also used as a formal alternative to C in inscriptions.

Languages that evolved from Latin, such as French and Italian, also used C instead of K, and in these 'Romance' languages the use of K is restricted to words borrowed from other language groups. In English, the presence of a K is usually a sign that a word comes from a non-Latin source: many of the words that begin with K come from German, Japanese, Maori, or Indian languages.

Because K always indicates a hard sound, it is regarded as more aggressive than the alternative C. Its sharp angles also contrast with the smooth curve of C, and the phonic method of teaching literacy characterizes the letter as 'Kicking K'.

The letter K is not, however, entirely without spiritual associations. The letter has great significance in Sikhism, where the 'five K's' are the symbolic objects worn to show allegiance to the faith: the *kachera* (short trousers), *kangha* (comb), *kara* (bangle), *kesh* (uncut hair), and *kirpan* (short sword).

In literature, the letter K is especially associated with the nightmarish world of Franz Kafka, who gave the protagonist of *The Trial* the name of Joseph K, and also used the initial for the hero of *The Castle*.

As an abbreviation, K most commonly represents the number 1000, and is commonly used in discussions of salaries or house prices. It can also mean any unit that begins with 'kilo-' (1000 times the basic unit), as when a 10-kilometre race is referred to as a '10K'.

In baseball, however, the letter is used as shorthand for a strikeout – the most emphatic way of retiring a batter. This unusual choice can be accounted for by the fact that S was already used for 'sacrifice', but the term's survival probably owes something to the fact that the muscular nature of the letter is seen as appropriate for representing a decisive dismissal.

K 1 kelvin(s) **2** *chess* king **3** *chem* potassium
WORD ORIGIN New Latin *kalium* **4** one thousand
WORD ORIGIN from KILO- **5** *computers* a unit of 1024 words, bits, or bytes

kabaddi *n* a game in which players try to touch opposing players but avoid being captured by them

kabloona *n* a person who is not of Inuit ancestry, esp. a white person

Kaddish *n, pl* **Kaddishim** *Judaism* an ancient Jewish liturgical prayer, recited esp. by mourners
WORD ORIGIN Aramaic *qaddīsh* holy

Kaffir (**kaf**-fer) *n S African, offensive obsolete* a Black African
WORD ORIGIN Arabic *kāfir* infidel

kaftan *or* **caftan** *n* **1** a long loose garment worn by men in eastern countries **2** a woman's dress resembling this
WORD ORIGIN Turkish *qaftān*

kahawai *n* a food and game fish of New Zealand
WORD ORIGIN Māori

kai *n NZ informal* food
WORD ORIGIN Māori

kail *n* same as **kale**

kaiser (**kize**-er) *n history* a German or Austro-Hungarian emperor
WORD ORIGIN German, from Latin *Caesar* emperor

kak (**kuck**) *n S African, taboo* **1** faeces **2** rubbish
WORD ORIGIN Afrikaans

kaka *n* a parrot of New Zealand
WORD ORIGIN Māori

kakapo *n, pl* **-pos** a ground-living nocturnal New Zealand parrot that resembles an owl
WORD ORIGIN Māori

Kalashnikov *n* a Russian-made automatic rifle
WORD ORIGIN after M *Kalashnikov*, its designer

kale *n* a type of cabbage with crinkled leaves
WORD ORIGIN Old English *cāl*

kaleidoscope *n* **1** a tube-shaped toy lined with angled mirrors and containing loose pieces of coloured paper that form intricate patterns when viewed through a hole in the end **2** any complicated or rapidly changing set of colours, circumstances, etc.: *a kaleidoscope of shifting political groups and alliances* **kaleidoscopic** *adj*

WORD ORIGIN Greek *kalos* beautiful + *eidos* form + *skopein* to look at

kalends *pl n* same as **calends**

kaleyard *n Scot* a vegetable garden
WORD ORIGIN literally: cabbage garden

Kamasutra (kah-ma-**soo**-tra) *n* **the Kamasutra** an ancient Hindu text on sex
WORD ORIGIN Sanskrit *kāma* love + *sūtra* thread, rule

kamik *n* a traditional Inuit boot made of caribou hide or sealskin

kamikaze (kam-mee-**kah**-zee) *n* **1** (in World War II) a Japanese pilot who performed a suicidal mission ▷ *adj* **2** (of an action) undertaken in the knowledge that it will result in the death or injury of the person performing it: *a kamikaze attack*
WORD ORIGIN Japanese *kami* divine + *kaze* wind

Kamloops trout *n* a bright silvery rainbow trout common in British Columbia, Canada

kangaroo *n, pl* **-roos** a large Australian marsupial with powerful hind legs used for leaping
WORD ORIGIN probably Aboriginal

kangaroo court *n* an unofficial court set up by a group to discipline its members

Chaucer and Medieval English

Chaucer used to be called the 'Father of English Literature'. While we take a more balanced view of pre-Chaucerian literature now, he remains the most important English author before Shakespeare, and he is still bound up with the history of English in his time, and particularly of the emergence of a 'Standard English'.

English in Chaucer's time was not standardized; in fact, it had not been that long since the more prominent language was French, a remnant of the Norman invasion and a mark of the prestige of French in the Western world. However, English had finally become the language of court and commerce in the fourteenth century, and Chaucer's experience in these spheres of society makes it natural that he would choose to write his poetry in his native tongue.

Though Chaucer now seems to have been participating in a trend of writing in English, rather than setting one, he was more prolific and influential than most of his predecessors and many of his contemporaries. His works – particularly the famous *Canterbury Tales* – continue to be read centuries after his death and were widely disseminated during his lifetime. As a result, Chaucer, like Shakespeare after him, is the earliest recorded source for many English words: *acceptable, arrogant,* and *army* among others. As with Shakespeare, it is not certain whether Chaucer coined these words, though the high percentage of them originating from other languages suggests he was particularly ready to use foreign vocabulary to enrich his English style.

When a 'standard' English began to emerge after Chaucer's death in 1400, it was based on the 'London dialect'. One of the prevailing myths about Chaucer is that the London dialect reflected in his writing represents this standard. In fact, the language of Chaucer's manuscripts, at least in terms of spelling, is not necessarily the language of Chaucer at all, but rather of his scribes. Two manuscripts of the *Canterbury Tales* in particular – the Hengwrt and the Ellesmere – are known to be very close to the author's intended product, but in an age where spelling was not standardized, book production was entirely by hand, and scribes played an important role, we cannot consider any manuscript a completely 'accurate' representation of Chaucer's own dialect. More importantly, Chaucer's language has important differences from the Chancery English that would evolve only decades after his death and would form the true basis for Present-Day Standard English. For example, Chaucer uses *y* in some places where Present-Day English uses *g*: *yaf* for *gave*. Chancery English prefers *gaf*. Chaucer uses *wi* in some words where Present-Day English has a *u*: *swich* for *such*. Chancery English prefers *such*. Finally, Chaucer tends to use the Anglo-Saxon-derived forms of the plural possessives and pronouns: *hem* and *hir*; Chancery English prefers the Norse-derived versions *them* and *their*, which have become the Standard. Again, some of these choices may have come from Chaucer's scribes, rather than Chaucer himself, but they illustrate that the London/Kent varieties of English with which he is associated are probably not the direct ancestor of Present-Day Standard English.

What Chaucer certainly did, though, was contribute to the prestige of English. His works were respected and widely read, and would have popularized London English, possibly smoothing the road to its acceptance as a national standard.

Ironically, considering his connection with the emerging Standard English, Chaucer also represents the earliest instance of using a regional variety of English for characterization. Previous to Chaucer, if a regional form was used in a piece of writing, it meant the author or (more frequently) the scribe came from that region. However, in *The Reeve's Tale*, Chaucer has characters speak in a northern variety of English in order to contrast them with the southern characters. Imitating regional English is now a common literary device, surviving well into the present day, and has been employed in some of the most renowned works of literature, from *The Adventures of Huckleberry Finn* to the work of James Joyce and William Faulkner, right up to contemporary writers like Irvine Welsh and Anne Donovan.

kangaroo paw *n* an Australian plant with green-and-red flowers

kaolin *n* a fine white clay used in making porcelain and in some medicines
WORD ORIGIN *Kaoling,* Chinese mountain where supplies for Europe were first obtained

kapa haka *n* NZ the traditional Māori performing arts, often performed competitively
WORD ORIGIN Māori

ka pai *interj* NZ good! well done!
WORD ORIGIN Māori

kapok *n* a fluffy fibre from a tropical tree, used for stuffing pillows and padding sleeping bags
WORD ORIGIN Malay

kaput (kap-**poot**) *adj informal* ruined or broken: *the chronometer, incidentally, is kaput*
WORD ORIGIN German *kaputt*

karakul *n* **1** a sheep of central Asia, the lambs of which have soft curled dark hair **2** the fur prepared from these lambs
WORD ORIGIN Russian

karaoke *n* a form of entertainment in which members of the public sing well-known songs over a prerecorded backing tape
WORD ORIGIN Japanese *kara* empty + *ōkesutora* orchestra

karate *n* a Japanese system of unarmed combat, in which punches, chops, and kicks are made with the hands, feet, elbows, and legs
WORD ORIGIN Japanese: empty hand

karma *n Hinduism, Buddhism* a person's actions affecting his or her fate in the next reincarnation
WORD ORIGIN Sanskrit: action, effect

karoo *or* **karroo** *n, pl* **-roos** *S African* an arid semidesert plateau of Southern Africa
WORD ORIGIN Khoi (language of southern Africa) *karo* dry

kaross (ka-**ross**) *n S African* a blanket made of animal skins sewn together
WORD ORIGIN Khoi (language of southern Africa) *karos* animal-skin blanket

karri *n, pl* **-ris 1** an Australian eucalypt **2** its wood, used for building

kart *n* same as **go-kart**

kasbah *n* same as **casbah**

katipo *n, pl* **-pos** a small venomous New Zealand spider, commonly black with a red or orange stripe on the abdomen
WORD ORIGIN Māori

katydid *n* a large green grasshopper of North America
WORD ORIGIN imitative

kauri *n* a large New Zealand conifer grown for its valuable wood and resin
WORD ORIGIN Māori

kayak *n* **1** an Inuit canoe-like boat consisting of a frame covered with animal skins **2** a fibreglass or canvas-covered canoe of similar design
WORD ORIGIN Inuktitut

kazoo *n, pl* **-zoos** a cigar-shaped metal musical instrument that produces a buzzing sound when the player hums into it
WORD ORIGIN probably imitative

KBE (in Britain) Knight (Commander of the Order) of the British Empire

kbps *computers* kilobits per second

kbyte *computers* kilobyte

kcal kilocalorie

KCB (in Britain) Knight Commander of the Bath

kea *n* a large brown-green parrot of New Zealand
WORD ORIGIN Māori

kebab *n* a dish consisting of small pieces of meat and vegetables, usually threaded onto skewers and grilled
WORD ORIGIN Arabic *kabāb* roast meat

kecks *or* **keks** *pl n* N English dialect trousers
WORD ORIGIN from dialect *kicks* breeches

kedge *naut vb* **kedging, kedged 1** to move (a ship) along by hauling in on the cable of a light anchor ▷ *n* **2** a light anchor used for kedging
WORD ORIGIN Middle English *caggen* to fasten

kedgeree *n chiefly Brit* a dish consisting of rice, fish, and eggs
WORD ORIGIN Hindi *khicarī*

keek *vb, n Scot* same as **peep¹**
WORD ORIGIN probably from Middle Dutch *kīken* to look

keel *n* **1** one of the main lengthways steel or timber pieces along the base of a ship, to which the frames are fastened **2 on an even keel** working or progressing smoothly without any sudden changes
WORD ORIGIN Old Norse *kjölr*

keelhaul *vb* **1** to reprimand (someone) harshly **2** *history* to drag (someone) under the keel of a ship as a punishment

keel over *vb* **1** (of an object) to turn upside down **2** *informal* (of a person) to collapse suddenly

keelson *or* **kelson** *n* a lengthways beam fastened to the keel of a ship for strength
WORD ORIGIN probably from Low German *kielswin* keel swine

keen¹ *adj* **1** eager or enthusiastic: *a keen gardener* **2** intense or strong: *a keen interest in environmental issues* **3** intelligent, quick, and perceptive: *a keen sense of humour* **4** (of sight, smell, or hearing) capable of recognizing fine distinctions **5** (of a knife or blade) having a sharp cutting edge **6** very strong and cold: *a keen wind* **7** very competitive: *keen prices* **8 keen on** fond of; devoted to: *he is very keen on sport*
keenly *adv* **keenness** *n*
WORD ORIGIN Old English *cēne*

keen² *vb* **1** to lament the dead ▷ *n* **2** a lament for the dead
WORD ORIGIN Irish Gaelic *caoine*

keep *vb* **keeping, kept 1** to have or retain possession of (something) **2** to have temporary charge of: *he'd kept my broken beads in his pocket for me all evening* **3** to store in a customary place: *I keep it at the back of the drawer with my journal* **4** to remain or cause (someone or something) to remain in a specified state or condition: *keep still* **5** to continue or cause (someone) to continue: *keep going straight on* **6** to stay

(in, on, or at a place or position): *keep to the paths* **7** to have as part of normal stock: *they keep a small stock of first-class German wines* **8** to support (someone) financially **9** to detain (someone) **10** to be faithful to (something): *to keep a promise* **11** (of food) to stay in good condition for a certain time: *fish doesn't keep very well* **12** to observe (a religious festival) with rites or ceremonies **13** to maintain by writing regular records in: *he keeps a nature diary in his spare time* **14** to look after or maintain for use, pleasure, or profit: *an old man who kept goats and cows* **15** to associate with: *she has started keeping bad company* **16 how are you keeping?** are you well? **17 keep in with** to stay friendly with someone as they may be useful to you ▷ *n* **18** the cost of food and other everyday expense: *I have to earn my keep* **19** the main tower within the walls of a medieval castle or fortress **20 for keeps** *informal* permanently ▸ See also **keep at, keep away**, etc.
WORD ORIGIN Old English *cēpan* to observe

keep at *vb* **1** to persist in (an activity) **2** to compel (a person) to continue doing (a task)

keep away *vb* (often foll. by *from*) to prevent (someone) from going (somewhere)

keep back *vb* to refuse to reveal (something)

keep down *vb* **1** to hold (a group of people) under control **2** to cause (numbers or costs) not to increase **3** to lie low **4** to cause (food) to stay in the stomach; not vomit

keeper *n* **1** a person in charge of animals in a zoo **2** a person in charge of a museum, collection, or section of a museum **3** a person who supervises a person or thing: *the self-appointed keeper of the village conscience* **4** short for **gamekeeper, goalkeeper** or **wicketkeeper**

keep fit *n* exercises designed to promote physical fitness if performed regularly

keep from *vb* **1** to restrain (oneself or someone else) from (doing something) **2** to preserve or protect (someone) from (something): *this will keep you from falling asleep*

keeping *n* **1 in keeping with** suitable or appropriate to or for **2 out of keeping with** unsuitable or inappropriate to or for

keep off *vb* **1** to stay or cause (someone) to stay at a distance (from) **2** to avoid or cause to avoid (something): *to keep off alcohol; to keep babies off sugar* **3** to avoid or cause (someone) to avoid (a topic)

keep on *vb* **1** to persist in (doing something): *petrol consumption keeps on rising* **2** to continue to employ: *a skeleton staff of 20 is being kept on* **3 keep on about** to persist in talking about **4 keep on at** to nag (a person)

keep out *vb* **1** to remain or cause (someone) to remain outside **2 keep out of a** to cause (someone) to remain unexposed to (an unpleasant situation) **b** to avoid: *to keep out of trouble*

keepsake *n* a gift kept in memory of the giver

keep to *vb* **1** to do exactly what was expected of one: *he kept to his normal schedule* **2** to be confined to: *she kept to her bed until her flu had cleared up* **3** **keep oneself to oneself** to avoid the company of others **4** **keep to oneself a** to avoid the company of others **b** to avoid giving away (information)

keep up *vb* **1** to maintain at the present level **2** to maintain in good condition **3** **keep up with a** to maintain a pace set by (someone) **b** to remain informed about: *he liked to think he kept up with current musical trends* **c** to remain in contact with (someone) **4** **keep up with the Joneses** *informal* to compete with one's friends or neighbours in material possessions

keg *n* a small barrel in which beer is transported and stored
WORD ORIGIN Scandinavian

kelp *n* a large brown seaweed rich in iodine and potash
WORD ORIGIN origin unknown

kelpie *n* **1** (in Scottish folklore) a water spirit in the form of a horse **2** an Australian sheepdog with a smooth coat and upright ears
WORD ORIGIN origin unknown

kelson *n* same as **keelson**

kelt *n* a salmon that has recently spawned
WORD ORIGIN origin unknown

Kelt *n* same as **Celt**

kelvin *n* *physics* the basic SI unit of thermodynamic temperature
WORD ORIGIN after W. T. *Kelvin*, physicist

Kelvin scale *n* *physics* a thermodynamic temperature scale starting at absolute zero

ken *n* **1** **beyond one's ken** beyond one's range of knowledge ▷ *vb* **kenning, kenned** *or* **kent 2** *Scot & N English dialect* to know
WORD ORIGIN Old English *cennan*

kendo *n* the Japanese sport of fencing using wooden staves
WORD ORIGIN Japanese

kennel *n* **1** a hutlike shelter for a dog **2** **kennels** a place where dogs are bred, trained, or boarded ▷ *vb* **-nelling, -nelled** *or US* **-neling, -neled** to keep (a dog) in a kennel
WORD ORIGIN Latin *canis* dog

Kenyan *adj* **1** from Kenya ▷ *n* **2** a person from Kenya

kepi *n* a French military cap with a flat top and a horizontal peak
WORD ORIGIN French

kept *vb* **1** the past of **keep 2 kept woman** *or* **man** a person financially supported by someone in return for sexual favours

keratin *n* a fibrous protein found in the hair and nails

kerb *or US & Canad* **curb** *n* a line of stone or concrete forming an edge between a pavement and a roadway
WORD ORIGIN Old French *courbe* bent

kerb crawling *n* *Brit* the act of driving slowly beside a kerb to pick up a prostitute **kerb crawler** *n*

kerbstone *or US & Canad* **curbstone** *n* one of a series of stones that form a kerb

kerchief *n* a piece of cloth worn over the head or round the neck
WORD ORIGIN Old French *cuevrechef*

kerfuffle *n* *informal* a noisy and disorderly incident
WORD ORIGIN Scots *curfuffle, carfuffle*

kermes (**kur**-meez) *n* the dried bodies of female scale insects, used as a red dyestuff
WORD ORIGIN Arabic *qirmiz*

kernel *n* **1** the edible seed of a nut or fruit within the shell or stone **2** the grain of a cereal, such as wheat, consisting of the seed in a hard husk **3** the central or essential part of something: *there is a kernel of truth in these remarks*
WORD ORIGIN Old English *cyrnel* a little seed

kerosene *n* *US, Canad, Austral, & NZ* same as **paraffin** (sense 1)
WORD ORIGIN Greek *kēros* wax

Kerry *n, pl* **-ries** a small black breed of dairy cattle, originally from Ireland
WORD ORIGIN after *Kerry*, county in SW Ireland

kestrel *n* a small falcon that feeds on small animals such as mice
WORD ORIGIN Old French *cresserele*

ketch *n* a two-masted sailing ship
WORD ORIGIN Middle English *cache*

ketchup *n* a thick cold sauce, usually made of tomatoes
WORD ORIGIN Chinese *kōetsiap* brine of pickled fish

ketone (**kee**-tone) *n* *chem* any of a class of compounds with the general formula $R´COR$, where R and R´ are alkyl or aryl groups
WORD ORIGIN German *Keton*, from *Aketon* acetone

kettle *n* **1** a metal container with a handle and spout, for boiling water **2** any of various metal containers for heating liquid, cooking, etc. **3** **a different kettle of fish** a different matter entirely **4** **a fine kettle of fish** a difficult or awkward situation
WORD ORIGIN Old Norse *ketill*

kettledrum *n* a large bowl-shaped metal drum that can be tuned to play specific notes

key[1] *n* **1** a specially shaped metal instrument for moving the bolt of a lock so as to lock or unlock a door, suitcase, etc. **2** an instrument that is turned to operate a valve, clock winding mechanism, etc. **3** any of a set of levers pressed to operate a typewriter, computer, or musical keyboard instrument **4** a scale of musical notes that starts at one specific note **5** something that is crucial in providing an explanation or interpretation **6** a means of achieving a desired end: *education is the key to success in most walks of life today* **7** a list of explanations of symbols, codes, or abbreviations **8** pitch: *he spoke in a low key* ▷ *adj* **9** of great importance: *key prosecution witnesses have been giving evidence* ▷ *vb* **10** to harmonize with: *training and educational programmes uniquely keyed for local needs* **11** to adjust or fasten (something) with a key or some similar device **12** same as **keyboard** ▶ See also **key in**
WORD ORIGIN Old English *cǣg*

key[2] *n* same as **cay**

keyboard *n* **1** a set of keys on a typewriter, computer, or piano **2** a musical instrument played using a keyboard ▷ *vb* **3** to enter (text) in type using a keyboard **keyboarder** *n*

keyed up *adj* very excited or nervous

key grip *n* the person in charge of moving and setting up camera tracks and scenery in a film or television studio

keyhole *n* an opening for inserting a key into a lock

keyhole surgery *n* surgery carried out using very small instruments, performed through a narrow hole cut in the body rather than through a major incision

key in *vb* to enter (information or instructions) into a computer by means of a keyboard

key money *n* *Brit* a sum of money required from a new tenant of a house or flat before he or she moves in

Keynesian (**cane**-zee-an) *adj* of the economic theories of J M Keynes, who argued that governments should fund public works to maintain full employment, accepting if necessary the consequence of inflation

keynote *n* **1** a central or dominant idea in a speech or literary work **2** the note on which a scale or key is based ▷ *adj* **3** central or dominating: *his keynote speech to the party conference*

keypad *n* a small panel with a set of buttons for operating a Teletext system, electronic calculator, etc.

keyring *n* a metal ring, often decorative, for keeping keys on

key signature *n* *music* a group of sharps or flats at the beginning of each stave line to indicate the key

keystone *n* **1** the most important part of a process, organization, etc.: *the keystone of the government's economic policy* **2** the central stone at the top of an arch

keyword *n* *computers* a word or phrase that a computer will search for in order to locate the information or file that the computer user has requested

key worker *n* *chiefly Brit* **1** a social worker, mental health worker, or nursery nurse assigned to an individual case, patient, or child **2** (in Britain) a worker in a public sector profession considered by the government to be essential to society

kg kilogram

KG (in Britain) Knight of the Order of the Garter

KGB (formerly) the Soviet secret police
WORD ORIGIN Russian *Komitet Gosudarstvennoi Bezopasnosti* State Security Committee

khaki *adj* **1** dull yellowish-brown ▷ *n* **2** a hard-wearing fabric of this colour, used for military uniforms
WORD ORIGIN Urdu, from Persian: dusty

khan *n* a title of respect in Afghanistan and central Asia
WORD ORIGIN Turkish

kHz kilohertz

kia ora *interj* NZ a Māori greeting
WORD ORIGIN Māori

kibbutz *n, pl* **kibbutzim** a farm, factory, or other workplace in Israel, owned and run communally by its members
WORD ORIGIN Modern Hebrew *qibbūs* gathering

kibosh *n* **put the kibosh on** *slang* to put a stop to
WORD ORIGIN origin unknown

kick *vb* **1** to drive, push, or hit with the foot or feet **2** to strike out with the feet, as in swimming **3** to raise a leg high, as in dancing **4** *rugby* to score (a conversion, drop kick, or penalty) with a kick: *he kicked his third penalty* **5** (of a firearm) to recoil when fired **6** *informal* to object or resist: *school uniforms give children something to kick against* **7** *informal* to free oneself of (an addiction): *smokers who want to kick the habit* **8** **alive and kicking** *informal* active and in good health **9** **kick someone upstairs** to promote someone to a higher but effectively powerless position ▷ *n* **10** a thrust or blow with the foot **11** any of certain rhythmic leg movements used in swimming **12** the recoil of a firearm **13** *informal* an exciting effect: *we get a kick out of attacking opposing fans and overturning their buses; a few small bets just for kicks* **14** *informal* the intoxicating effect of an alcoholic drink: *a cocktail with a kick in it* **15** **kick in the teeth** *slang* a humiliating rebuff ▷ See also **kick about, kick off,** etc.
WORD ORIGIN Middle English *kiken*

kick about *or* **around** *vb informal* **1** to treat (someone) harshly **2** to discuss (ideas) informally **3** to lie neglected or forgotten: *there's a copy of that book kicking about somewhere*

kickback *n* **1** part of an income paid to a person in return for an opportunity to make a profit, often by some illegal arrangement **2** a strong reaction

kick in *vb* to start or become activated

kick off *vb* **1** to start play in a game of football by kicking the ball from the centre of the field **2** *informal* to commence (a discussion, event, etc.) ▷ *n* **kick-off 3 a** the kick that officially starts a game of football **b** the time when the first kick is due to take place **4** *informal* the time when an event is due to begin

kick out *vb informal* to dismiss (someone) or throw (someone) out forcefully

kickstand *n* a short metal bar on a motorcycle, which when kicked into a vertical position holds the cycle upright when stationary

kick-start *n* **1** Also: **kick-starter** a pedal on a motorcycle that is kicked downwards to start the engine **2** an action or event that reactivates something ▷ *vb* **3** to start (a motorcycle) with a kick-start **4** to do something bold or drastic in order to begin or improve the performance of something: *to kick-start the economy*

kick up *vb informal* to cause (trouble)

kid¹ *n* **1** *informal* a young person; child **2 a** young goat **3** soft smooth leather made from the hide of a kid ▷ *adj* **4** younger: *my kid sister* ▷ *vb* **kidding, kidded 5** (of a goat) to give birth to (young)
WORD ORIGIN from Old Norse

kid² *vb* **kidding, kidded** *informal* **1** to tease or deceive (someone) for fun **2** to fool (oneself) into believing something: *don't kid yourself that no-one else knows* **kidder** *n*
WORD ORIGIN probably from KID¹

kiddie *n informal* a child

kid gloves *pl n* **handle someone with kid gloves** to treat someone with great tact in order not to upset them

kidnap *vb* **-napping, -napped** *or US* **-naping, -naped** to capture and hold (a person), usually for ransom **kidnapper** *or US* **-naper** *n* **kidnapping** *or US* **-naping** *n*
WORD ORIGIN KID¹ + obsolete *nap* to steal

kidney *n* **1** either of two bean-shaped organs at the back of the abdominal cavity. They filter waste products from the blood, which are excreted as urine **2** the kidneys of certain animals used as food
WORD ORIGIN origin unknown

kidney bean *n* a reddish-brown kidney-shaped bean, edible when cooked

kidney machine *n* a machine carrying out the functions of damaged human kidneys

kidology *n informal* the practice of bluffing or deception in order to gain a psychological advantage over someone

kill *vb* **1** to cause the death of (a person or animal) **2** *informal* to cause (someone) pain or discomfort: *my feet are killing me* **3** to put an end to: *his infidelity had killed his marriage* **4** *informal* to quash or veto: *the main opposition party tried to kill the bill* **5** *informal* to overwhelm (someone) completely with laughter, attraction, or surprise: *her jokes really kill me* **6 kill oneself** *informal* to overexert oneself **7 kill time** to spend time on something unimportant or trivial while waiting for something: *I'm just killing time until I can talk to the other witnesses* **8 kill two birds with one stone** to achieve two results with one action ▷ *n* **9** the act of causing death at the end of a hunt or bullfight **10** the animal or animals killed during a hunt **11 in at the kill** present when something comes to a dramatic end with unpleasant results for someone else **killer** *n*
WORD ORIGIN Middle English *cullen*

killer whale *n* a black-and-white toothed whale, most common in cold seas

killing *adj* **1** *informal* very tiring: *a killing pace* **2** *informal* extremely funny **3** causing death; fatal ▷ *n* **4** the act of causing death; slaying **5 make a killing** *informal* to have a sudden financial success

killjoy *n* a person who spoils other people's pleasure

kiln *n* a large oven for burning, drying, or processing pottery, bricks, etc.
WORD ORIGIN Latin *culina* kitchen

kilo *n, pl* **kilos** short for **kilogram** or **kilometre**

kilo- *combining form* **1** denoting one thousand (10³): *kilometre* **2** (in computers) denoting 2¹⁰ (1024): *kilobyte.*
In computer usage, *kilo-* is restricted to sizes of storage (eg *kilobit*) when it means 1024: in other computer contexts it retains its usual meaning of 1000
WORD ORIGIN Greek *khilioi* thousand

kilobit *n computers* 1024 bits

kilobyte *n computers* 1024 bytes

kilocalorie *n* one thousand calories

kilocycle *n* an old word for **kilohertz**

kilogram *or* **kilogramme** *n* **1** one thousand grams **2** the basic SI unit of mass

kilohertz *n, pl* **kilohertz** one thousand hertz; one thousand cycles per second

kilojoule *n* one thousand joules

kilolitre *or US* **kiloliter** *n* a measure of volume equivalent to one thousand litres

kilometre *or US* **kilometer** *n* a unit of length equal to one thousand metres

kiloton *n* **1** one thousand tons **2** an explosive power, esp. of a nuclear weapon, equal to the power of 1000 tons of TNT

kilovolt *n* one thousand volts

kilowatt *n* one thousand watts

kilowatt-hour *n* a unit of energy equal to the work done by a power of 1000 watts in one hour

kilt *n* **1** a knee-length pleated tartan skirt-like garment, worn by men in Highland dress and by women and girls ▷ *vb* **2** to put pleats in (cloth) **kilted** *adj*
WORD ORIGIN Scandinavian

kimono (kim-**moan**-no) *n, pl* **-nos** **1** a loose wide-sleeved Japanese robe, fastened with a sash **2** a European dressing gown resembling this
WORD ORIGIN Japanese: clothing

kin *n* **1** a person's relatives collectively **2** see **next of kin**
WORD ORIGIN Old English *cyn*

kind¹ *adj* **1** considerate, friendly, and helpful: *a good, kind man; a few kind words* **2** cordial; courteous: *reprinted by kind permission*
WORD ORIGIN Old English *gecynde* natural, native

kind² *n* **1** a class or group having characteristics in common: *what kind of music do you like?* **2** essential nature or character: *differences of degree rather than of kind* **3 in kind a** (of payment) in goods or services rather than in money **b** with something of the same sort: *the government threatened to retaliate in kind to any use of nuclear weapons* **4 kind of** to a certain extent; loosely: *kind of hard; a kind of socialist* **5 of a kind** of a poorer quality or standard than is wanted or expected: *a few farmers wrest subsistence of a kind from the thin topsoil*
WORD ORIGIN Old English *gecynd* nature

▤ **USAGE**
The mixture of plural and singular constructions, although often used informally with *kind* and *sort*, should be avoided in serious writing: *children enjoy those kinds* (not *those kind*) *of stories; these sorts* (not *these sort*) *of distinctions are becoming blurred.*

kindergarten *n* a class or school for children under six years old
WORD ORIGIN from German, literally: children's garden

Herman Melville

H erman Melville did everything in reverse. Some serious novelists, achieving critical success, venture into popular genres such as detective or science fiction to extend their readership. Melville's early books like *Typee: A Peep at Polynesian Life* and *Omoo: A Narrative of Adventures in the South Seas* sold well, since they could be read as romantic nautical adventures. He then wrote the difficult books for which he is remembered.

Many fiction writers begin as poets; Melville ended as one. Thematically, he turned the optimism of the prevailing New England philosophy of Transcendentalism on its head. The world spirit that Transcendentalists espoused became for Melville the implacable indifference of the universe, with the colossal white whale of *Moby-Dick* its avatar. Extrapolating on good and evil, he resembled his close friend, Nathaniel Hawthorne, explorer of New England's shadow-side. Although most of his work is ostensibly tragic, Melville's vision appears to treat life as a cosmic joke.

Melville, who was born in New York in 1819, was descended from heroes of the American Revolution and was the son of a prosperous merchant importer who became financially ruined. After his father's death, he became a cabin boy on a transatlantic ship, then a schoolmaster. From the whaling port of New Bedford, Massachusetts, he sailed on a whaler bound for the Pacific. Melville deserted his ship in the Marquesas Islands, and briefly lived among the natives. After boarding another whaler, he did clerical work for a few months in Hawaii, then crewed aboard a frigate to Boston. All these vivid episodes can be keyed autobiographically to his novels.

Married and writing novels on a Massachusetts farm, he became a friend of Hawthorne. Readers thought *Moby-Dick*, published in 1851, was just another sea yarn. His sales began to wane; his critical reputation plummeted after *Mardi: And a Voyage Thither* and the perversely tortuous *Pierre: or, The Ambiguities* were published. In 1857, *The Confidence-Man, His Masquerade*, his last full-length novel, fared little better. He eked out an income giving public lectures, a popular entertainment at the time, and resettled in New York City, where he published a little-noticed poetry collection, *Battle Pieces and Aspects of the War* in 1866. His wife's family got him a job as a New York customs inspector, which he retained for the next 19 years. In 1876, assisted by a bequest, he published the epic poem *Clarel, A Poem and a Pilgrimage*, 18,000 lines long, which understandably found few readers. His marriage was unhappy; he was depressed and drank too much; two of his children died. He worked on the novella *Billy Budd* until his death in 1891.

Melville's reputation was resurrected in the 1920s when his works were republished and the unfinished *Billy Budd* published. A huge body of biographical and critical analyses ensued. Some focused on his mordant exposure of American hypocrisy in *The Confidence Man*, others on his largely sympathetic view of non-Westerners in early novels, the slave-ship setting of the novella *Benito Cereno*, and the variegated crew of *Moby-Dick*. Some dealt with the saintly nihilist in the short story 'Bartleby, the Scrivener', whose invariable response when asked to do anything is 'I would prefer not to.' Some declared, on the basis of *Battle Pieces and Aspects of the War*, that he is an unjustly neglected poet. Others battened on the many evocations of male beauty and conflicted male bondings in his work, which partly explains its appeal to homosexual writers and artists. Somerset Maugham thought *Moby-Dick* was one of the ten greatest novels ever written, and Benjamin Britten turned *Billy Budd* into one of his best-known operas, with a libretto co-written by EM Forster. Whether Melville, long-married and the father of four children, was homosexual, bisexual, or misanthropically heterosexual is impossible to establish.

There remains *Moby-Dick*, a densely packed sea chest of Biblical, philosophical, mythological, and metaphysical symbolism. From its famous first sentence ('Call me Ishmael') to the last two ('On the second day, a sail drew nearer, nearer, and picked me up at last. It was the devious-cruising Rachel, that in her retracing search after her missing children, only found another orphan') it is a masterpiece. As the joke has it, it is a whale of a book.

kind-hearted *adj* considerate and sympathetic

kindle *vb* **-dling, -dled 1** to set (a fire) alight or (of a fire) to start to burn **2** to arouse or be aroused: *his passions were kindled as quickly as her own* **WORD ORIGIN** Old Norse *kynda*

kindling *n* material for starting a fire, such as dry wood or straw

kindly *adj* **-lier, -liest 1** having a warm-hearted and caring nature **2** pleasant or agreeable: *a kindly climate* ▷ *adv* **3** in a considerate or humane way **4** please: *will you kindly stop prattling on about it!* **5 not take kindly to** to react unfavourably towards **kindliness** *n*

kindness *n* **1** the quality of being kind **2** a kind or helpful act

kindred *adj* **1** having similar qualities: *cholera, and other kindred diseases* **2** related by blood or marriage **3 kindred spirit** a person with whom one has something in common ▷ *n* **4** relationship by blood or marriage **5** similarity in character **6** a person's relatives collectively **WORD ORIGIN** Middle English *kinred*

kindy, kindie *n, pl* **-dies** *Austral & NZ informal* a kindergarten

kine *pl n archaic* cows or cattle **WORD ORIGIN** Old English *cȳna* of cows

kinematics (kin-nim-**mat**-iks) *n physics* the study of the motion of bodies without reference to mass or force **kinematic** *adj* **WORD ORIGIN** Greek *kinēma* movement

kinetic (kin-**net**-ik) *adj* relating to or caused by motion **kinetically** *adv* **WORD ORIGIN** Greek *kinein* to move

kinetic art *n* art, such as sculpture, that moves or has moving parts

kinetic energy *n physics* the energy of motion of a body equal to the work it would do if it were brought to rest

kinetics *n physics* the branch of mechanics concerned with the study of bodies in motion

king *n* **1** a male ruler of a country who has inherited the throne from his parents **2** a ruler or chief: *the king of the fairies* **3** a person, animal, or thing considered as the best or most important of its kind: *the king of rock and roll* **4** a playing card with a picture of a king on it **5** a chessman, able to move one square in any direction: *the object of the game is to checkmate one's opponent's king* **6** *draughts* a piece which has moved entirely across the board and been crowned and which may therefore move backwards as well as forwards **kingship** *n* **WORD ORIGIN** Old English *cyning*

kingcup *n Brit* a yellow-flowered plant; marsh marigold

kingdom *n* **1** a territory or state ruled by a king or queen **2** any of the three groups into which natural objects may be divided: the animal, plant, and mineral kingdoms **3** a place or area considered to be under the total power and control of a person, organization, or thing: *the kingdom of God*

kingfisher *n* a fish-eating bird with a greenish-blue and orange plumage **WORD ORIGIN** originally *king's fisher*

kingklip *n* an edible eel-like marine fish of S Africa **WORD ORIGIN** Afrikaans

king-of-arms *n, pl* **kings-of-arms** a person holding the highest rank of heraldic office

kingpin *n* **1** the most important person in an organization: *a Mexican narcotics kingpin* **2** a pivot pin that provides a steering joint in a motor vehicle

king post *n building* a vertical post connecting the apex of a triangular roof truss to the tie beam

king prawn *n* a large prawn, fished commercially in Australian waters

king-size *or* **king-sized** *adj* larger than a standard size

kink *n* **1** a twist or bend in something such as a rope or hair **2** *informal* a flaw or quirk in someone's personality ▷ *vb* **3** to form or cause to form a kink **WORD ORIGIN** Dutch

kinky *adj* **kinkier, kinkiest 1** *slang* given to unusual sexual practices **2** tightly looped or curled

kinsfolk *pl n* one's family or relatives

kinship *n* **1** blood relationship **2** the state of having common characteristics

kinsman *n, pl* **-men** a relation by blood or marriage **kinswoman** *fem n*

kiosk *n* **1** a small booth from which cigarettes, newspapers, and sweets are sold **2** *chiefly Brit* a public telephone box **WORD ORIGIN** French *kiosque* bandstand, from Persian *kūshk* pavilion

kip *Brit slang n* **1** sleep: *a couple of hours' kip* **2** a bed ▷ *vb* **kipping, kipped 3** to sleep or take a nap **4 kip down** to sleep in a makeshift bed **WORD ORIGIN** origin unknown

kipper *n* **1** a herring that has been cleaned, salted, and smoked ▷ *vb* **2** to cure (a herring) by salting and smoking it **WORD ORIGIN** Old English *cypera*

kirk *n Scot* a church **WORD ORIGIN** Old Norse *kirkja*

Kirsch *or* **Kirschwasser** *n* a brandy distilled from black cherries **WORD ORIGIN** German *Kirschwasser* cherry water

kismet *n* fate or destiny **WORD ORIGIN** Persian *qismat*

kiss *vb* **1** to touch with the lips as an expression of love, greeting, or respect **2** to join lips with another person as an act of love or desire **3** *literary* to touch lightly: *a long high free kick that kissed the top of the crossbar* ▷ *n* **4** a caress with the lips **5** a light touch **kissable** *adj* **WORD ORIGIN** Old English *cyssan*

kissagram *n Brit, Austral, & NZ* a greetings service in which a person is employed to present greetings by kissing the person celebrating

kiss curl *n* a circular curl of hair pressed flat against the cheek or forehead

kisser *n slang* the mouth or face

kissing crust *n NZ* the soft end of a loaf of bread where two loaves have been separated

kiss of life *n* **the kiss of life** mouth-to-mouth resuscitation in which a person

blows gently into the mouth of an unconscious person

kist *n Scot & S African* a large wooden chest

kit¹ *n* **1** a set of tools or supplies for use together or for a purpose: *a first-aid kit* **2** the container for such a set **3** a set of parts sold ready to be assembled: *a model aircraft kit* **4** *NZ* a flax basket **5** clothing and other personal effects, such as those of a soldier: *a complete set of school team kit* ▷ See also **kit out WORD ORIGIN** Middle Dutch *kitte* tankard

kit² *n NZ* a shopping bag made of string **WORD ORIGIN** Māori *kete*

kitbag *n* a canvas or other bag for a serviceman's kit

kitchen *n* a room equipped for preparing and cooking food **WORD ORIGIN** Late Latin *coquina*

kitchenette *n* a small kitchen or part of a room equipped for use as a kitchen

kitchen garden *n* a garden for growing vegetables, herbs, etc.

kitchen tea *n Austral & NZ* a party held before a wedding to which guests bring kitchen equipment as presents

kite *n* **1** a light frame covered with a thin material flown in the wind at the end of a length of string **2** a bird of prey with a long forked tail and large wings **3** a four-sided geometrical shape in which each side is equal in length to one of the sides joining it **WORD ORIGIN** Old English *cȳta*

Kite mark *n Brit* the official mark in the form of a kite on articles approved by the British Standards Institution

kith *n* **kith and kin** *old-fashioned* one's friends and relations **WORD ORIGIN** Old English *cȳthth*

kit out *or* **up** *vb* **kitting, kitted** *chiefly Brit* to provide with clothes or equipment needed for a particular activity

kitsch *n* tawdry or sentimental art or literature **kitschy** *adj* **WORD ORIGIN** from German

kitten *n* **1** a young cat **2 have kittens** *informal* to react with disapproval or anxiety: *she had kittens over the price* **WORD ORIGIN** Old French *caton*

kittenish *adj* lively and flirtatious

kittiwake *n* a type of seagull with pale grey black-tipped wings and a square-cut tail **WORD ORIGIN** imitative

kitty¹ *n, pl* **-ties** a diminutive or affectionate name for a **kitten** or **cat**

kitty² *n, pl* **-ties 1** any shared fund of money **2** the pool in certain gambling games **WORD ORIGIN** probably from KIT¹

kiwi *n, pl* **kiwis 1** a flightless bird of New Zealand with a long beak, stout legs, and no tail **2** a New Zealander **WORD ORIGIN** Māori

kiwi fruit *n* an edible fruit with a fuzzy brown skin and green flesh

kJ kilojoule(s)

kl kilolitre(s)

klaxon *n* a type of loud horn used on fire engines and ambulances as a warning signal **WORD ORIGIN** former trademark

kleinhuisie (**klayn**-hay-see) *n S African* an outside toilet
WORD ORIGIN Afrikaans, literally: little house

kleptomania *n psychol* a strong impulse to steal **kleptomaniac** *n*
WORD ORIGIN Greek *kleptein* to steal + *mania* madness

klipspringer *n* a small agile antelope of rocky regions of Africa south of the Sahara
WORD ORIGIN Afrikaans: rock jumper

kloof *n S African* a mountain pass or gorge
WORD ORIGIN Afrikaans

km kilometre(s)

km/h kilometres per hour

knack *n* **1** a skilful way of doing something **2** an ability to do something difficult with apparent ease
WORD ORIGIN probably from Middle English *knak* sharp knock

knacker *n Brit* a person who buys up old horses for slaughter
WORD ORIGIN origin unknown

knackered *adj slang* **1** extremely tired: *they'd been marching for three hours and were absolutely knackered* **2** broken or no longer functioning: *a knackered TV set*

knapsack *n* a canvas or leather bag carried strapped on the back or shoulder
WORD ORIGIN Low German *knappen* to eat + *sack* bag

knapweed *n* a plant with purplish thistle-like flowers
WORD ORIGIN Middle English *knopwed*

knave *n* **1** *cards* the jack **2** *archaic* a dishonest man **knavish** *adj*
WORD ORIGIN Old English *cnafa*

knavery *n, pl* **-eries** old-fashioned dishonest behaviour

knead *vb* **1** to work and press (a soft substance, such as dough) into a smooth mixture with the hands **2** to squeeze or press with the hands **kneader** *n*
WORD ORIGIN Old English *cnedan*

knee *n* **1** the joint of the leg between the thigh and the lower leg **2** the area around this joint **3** the upper surface of a sitting person's thigh: *a little girl being cuddled on her father's knee* **4** the part of a garment that covers the knee **5 bring someone to his knees** to force someone into submission ▷ *vb* **kneeing, kneed 6** to strike, nudge, or push with the knee
WORD ORIGIN Old English *cnēow*

kneecap *n* **1** *anat* a small flat triangular bone in front of and protecting the knee ▷ *vb* **-capping, -capped 2** (of terrorists) to shoot (a person) in the kneecap

knee-deep *adj* **1** so deep as to reach or cover the knees **2 a** sunk to the knees: *knee-deep in mud* **b** deeply involved: *knee-deep in work*

knee-high *adj* as high as the knee

knee-jerk *n* **1** *physiol* a sudden involuntary kick of the lower leg caused by a sharp tap on the tendon just below the kneecap ▷ *adj* **kneejerk 2** made or occurring as a predictable and automatic response: *a kneejerk reaction*

kneel *vb* **kneeling, knelt** or **kneeled 1** to rest, fall, or support oneself on one's knees ▷ *n* **2** the act or position of kneeling
WORD ORIGIN Old English *cnēowlian*

knees-up *n Brit informal* a party

knell *n* **1** the sound of a bell rung to announce a death or a funeral **2** something that indicates death or destruction ▷ *vb* **3** to ring a knell **4** to proclaim by a tolling bell
WORD ORIGIN Old English *cnyll*

knelt *vb* the past of **kneel**

knew *vb* the past tense of **know**

knickerbockers *pl n* loose-fitting short trousers gathered in at the knee or calf
WORD ORIGIN after Diedrich *Knickerbocker*, fictitious author of Washington Irving's *History of New York*

knickers *pl n* a woman's or girl's undergarment covering the lower trunk and having separate legs or leg-holes
WORD ORIGIN contraction of *knickerbockers*

knick-knack *n* a small ornament or trinket
WORD ORIGIN reduplication of obsolete *knack* a toy

knife *n, pl* **knives 1** a cutting instrument or weapon consisting of a sharp-edged blade of metal fitted into a handle ▷ *vb* **knifing, knifed 2** to stab or kill with a knife **knifelike** *adj*
WORD ORIGIN Old English *cnīf*

knife edge *n* **1** the sharp cutting edge of a knife **2** a critical point in the development of a situation: *and at this point the election result is still poised on a knife edge*

knight *n* **1** a man who has been given a knighthood in recognition of his achievements **2 a** (in medieval Europe) a person who served his lord as a mounted and heavily armed soldier **b** (in medieval Europe) a devoted male admirer of a noblewoman, esp. her champion in a jousting tournament **3** a chessman shaped like a horse's head, able to move either two squares horizontally and one square vertically or two squares vertically and one square horizontally ▷ *vb* **4** to make (a man) a knight
WORD ORIGIN Old English *cniht* servant

knight errant *n, pl* **knights errant** (esp. in medieval romance) a knight who wanders in search of deeds of courage, chivalry, etc. **knight errantry** *n*

knighthood *n* an honorary title given to a man by the British sovereign in recognition of his achievements

knightly *adj* of, resembling, or appropriate for a knight **knightliness** *n*

knit *vb* **knitting, knitted** or **knit 1** to make (a garment) by looping (wool) using long eyeless needles or a knitting machine **2** to join together closely **3** to draw (one's eyebrows) together ▷ *n* **4** a fabric made by knitting **knitter** *n*
WORD ORIGIN Old English *cnyttan* to tie in

knitting *n* knitted work or the process of producing it

knitwear *n* knitted clothes, such as sweaters

knives *n* the plural of **knife**

knob *n* **1** a rounded projection from a surface, such as a rotating switch on a radio **2** a rounded handle of a door or drawer **3** a small amount of butter or margarine **knoblike** *adj*
WORD ORIGIN Middle Low German *knobbe* knot in wood

knobbly *adj* having or covered with small bumps: *a curious knobbly root vegetable*

knobkerrie *n S African* a club or a stick with a rounded end
WORD ORIGIN Khoi (language of southern Africa) *kirri* stick

knock *vb* **1** to give a blow or push to **2** to rap sharply with the knuckles: *he knocked on the door of the guest room* **3** to make by striking: *he knocked a hole in the wall* **4** to collide (with) **5** to bring into a certain condition by hitting: *he was knocked unconscious in a collision* **6** *informal* to criticize adversely **7** to emit a regular banging sound as a result of a fault: *the engine was knocking badly* **8 knock on the head** to prevent the further development of (a plan) ▷ *n* **9 a** a blow, push, or rap: *he gave the table a knock* **b** the sound so caused **10** the sound of knocking in an engine or bearing **11** *informal* a misfortune, rejection, or setback **12** *informal* criticism ▶ See also **knock about, knock back**, etc.
WORD ORIGIN Old English *cnocian*

knock about or **around** *vb* **1** to wander or travel about: *I have knocked about the world through three continents* **2** (foll. by with) to associate **3** to treat brutally: *she looked knocked about, with bruises and cuts to her head* **4** to consider or discuss informally ▷ *adj* **knockabout 5** (of comedy) lively, boisterous, and physical

knock back *vb informal* **1** to drink quickly: *he fell over after knocking back eight pints of lager* **2** to cost: *lunch for two here will knock you back £50* **3** to reject or refuse: *I don't know any man who'd knock back an offer like that* ▷ *n* **knockback 4** *slang* a refusal or rejection

knock down *vb* **1** to strike to the ground with a blow, such as in boxing **2** (in auctions) to declare an article sold **3** to demolish **4** *informal* to reduce (a price) ▷ *adj* **knockdown 5** powerful: *a knockdown argument* **6** *chiefly Brit* (of a price) very cheap **7** easily dismantled: *knockdown furniture*

knocker *n* **1** a metal object attached to a door by a hinge and used for knocking **2 knockers** *slang* a woman's breasts

knock-knees *pl n* legs that are bent inwards at the knees **knock-kneed** *adj*

knock off *vb* **1** *informal* to finish work: *around ten, the day shift knocked off* **2** *informal* to make or do hastily or easily: *she knocked off 600 books in all during her long life* **3** *informal* to take (an amount) off the price of (an article): *I'll knock off 10% if you pay cash* **4** *Brit, Austral, & NZ informal* to steal **5** *slang* to kill **6** *slang* to stop doing something; used as a command: *knock it off!*

knock-on *rugby* *n* **1** the foul of playing the ball forward with the hand or arm ▷ *vb* **knock on 2** to play (the ball) forward with the hand or arm

knock-on effect *n* the indirect result of

an action or decision

knockout n **1** the act of rendering someone unconscious **2** boxing a blow that renders an opponent unable to continue after the referee has counted to ten **3** a competition in which competitors are eliminated progressively **4** informal a person or thing that is very impressive or attractive: at my youngest sister's wedding she was a knockout in navy and scarlet ▷ vb **knock out 5** to render (someone) unconscious **6** boxing to defeat (an opponent) by a knockout **7** to destroy: communications in many areas were knocked out by the earthquake **8** to eliminate from a knockout competition **9** informal to amaze: the fantastic audience reaction knocked me out

knock up vb **1** Also: **knock together** informal to make or assemble quickly: my boyfriend can knock up a wonderful lasagne **2** Brit informal to waken: to knock someone up early **3** slang to make pregnant **4** to practise before a game of tennis, squash, or badminton ▷ n **knock-up 5** a practice session at tennis, squash, or badminton

knoll n a small rounded hill
WORD ORIGIN Old English cnoll

knot n **1** a fastening formed by looping and tying pieces of rope, cord, or string **2** a tangle, such as in hair **3** a decorative bow, such as of ribbon **4** a small cluster or huddled group: a knot of passengers gathered on the platform **5** a bond: to tie the knot of friendship **6 a** a hard mass of wood where a branch joins the trunk of a tree **b** a cross section of this, visible in timber **7** a feeling of tightness, caused by tension or nervousness: a dull knot of anxiety that sat in the pit of her stomach **8** a unit of speed used by ships and aircraft, equal to one nautical mile per hour **9 at a rate of knots** very fast **10 tie someone in knots** to confuse someone completely ▷ vb **knotting, knotted 11** to tie or fasten in a knot **12** to form into a knot **13** to entangle or become entangled **knotted** adj **knotless** adj
WORD ORIGIN Old English cnotta

knothole n a hole in a piece of wood where a knot has been

knotty adj **-tier, -tiest 1** full of knots **2** extremely difficult or puzzling: a knotty problem

know vb **knowing, knew, known 1** to be or feel certain of the truth or accuracy of (a fact, answer, or piece of information) **2** to be acquainted with: I'd known him for many years, since I was seventeen **3** to have a grasp of or understand (a skill or language) **4** to understand or be aware of (something, or how to do or be something): she knew how to get on with people **5** to experience: you had to have known poverty before you could give money its true value, he claimed **6** to be intelligent, informed, or sensible enough (to do something): how did he know to send the letter in the first place? **7** to be able to distinguish: I don't know one flower from another **8 know what's what** to know how one thing or things in general work **9 you never know** things are uncertain ▷ n **10 in the know** informal

aware or informed **knowable** adj
WORD ORIGIN Old English gecnāwan

know-all n informal, disparaging a person who pretends or appears to know a lot more than other people

know-how n informal the ability to do something that is difficult or technical

knowing adj **1** suggesting secret knowledge: Paul saw the knowing look that passed between them **2** cunning or shrewd **3** deliberate **knowingly** adv **knowingness** n

knowledge n **1** the facts or experiences known by a person or group of people **2** the state of knowing **3** specific information about a subject **4 to my knowledge** as I understand it

knowledgeable or **knowledgable** adj intelligent or well-informed **knowledgeably** or **knowledgably** adv

known vb **1** the past participle of **know** ▷ adj **2** identified: consorting with known criminals

knuckle n **1** a joint of a finger **2** the knee joint of a calf or pig **3 near the knuckle** informal likely to offend people because of frankness or rudeness ▸ See also **knuckle down, knuckle under**
WORD ORIGIN Middle English

knuckle down vb **-ling, -led** informal to apply oneself conscientiously: he's never been able to knuckle down and study anything for long

knuckle-duster n a metal appliance worn over the knuckles to add force to a blow

knuckle under vb **-ling, -led** to give way under pressure or authority

knurl n a small ridge, often one of a series
WORD ORIGIN probably from knur a knot in wood

KO or **k.o.** vb **KO'ing, KO'd** or **k.o.'ing, k.o.'d 1** to knock out ▷ n, pl **KO's** or **k.o.'s 2** a knockout

koala or **koala bear** n a tree-dwelling Australian marsupial with dense grey fur
WORD ORIGIN Aboriginal

Kobe beef (koh-bi) n a grade of beef from cattle raised in Kobe, Japan, which is extremely tender and full-flavoured

koeksister (kook-sist-er) n S African a plaited doughnut deep-fried and soaked in syrup
WORD ORIGIN Afrikaans

kohanga reo, kohanga n NZ an infant class where children are taught in Māori
WORD ORIGIN Māori: language nest

kohl n a cosmetic powder used to darken the area around the eyes
WORD ORIGIN Arabic

kohlrabi (kole-**rah**-bee) n, pl **-bies** a type of cabbage with an edible stem
WORD ORIGIN Italian cavolo cabbage + rapa turnip

kokanee (coke-**can**-ee) n a freshwater salmon of lakes and rivers in W North America
WORD ORIGIN after Kokanee Creek, in British Columbia

kola n same as **cola**

kolkhoz (kol-**hawz**) n (formerly) a collective farm in the Soviet Union
WORD ORIGIN Russian

komatik (koh-ma-tik) n Canad a sledge with wooden runners and crossbars bound with animal hides
WORD ORIGIN Inuktitut

kook n US & Canad informal an eccentric or foolish person **kooky** or **kookie** adj
WORD ORIGIN probably from cuckoo

kookaburra n a large Australian kingfisher with a cackling cry
WORD ORIGIN Aboriginal

koori n, pl **-ris** an Australian Aborigine

kopeck n a former Russian monetary unit worth one hundredth of a rouble
WORD ORIGIN Russian kopeika

kopje, koppie (kop-ee) n S African a small isolated hill
WORD ORIGIN Afrikaans

Koran n the sacred book of Islam, believed by Muslims to be the infallible word of God dictated to Mohammed **Koranic** adj
WORD ORIGIN Arabic qur'ān reading, book

Korean adj **1** of Korea ▷ n **2** a person from Korea **3** the official language of North and South Korea

korma n a type of mild Indian dish consisting of meat or vegetables cooked in water, yoghurt, or cream
WORD ORIGIN from Urdu

kosher (koh-sher) adj **1** Judaism **a** conforming to religious law **b** (of food) prepared in accordance with the dietary laws **2** informal legitimate, genuine, or proper ▷ n **3** kosher food
WORD ORIGIN Yiddish

kowhai (koh-wye, koh-fye) n a small tree of New Zealand and Chile with clusters of yellow flowers
WORD ORIGIN Māori

kowtow vb **1** to be humble and very respectful (towards): the senior editors accused each other of kowtowing to his demands **2** to touch the forehead to the ground in deference ▷ n **3** the act of kowtowing
WORD ORIGIN Chinese k'o to strike, knock + t'ou head

kph kilometres per hour

Kr chem krypton

kraal n **1** a Southern African hut village surrounded by a strong fence **2** S African an enclosure for livestock
WORD ORIGIN Afrikaans, from Portuguese curral enclosure

kraken n a legendary sea monster
WORD ORIGIN Norwegian

krans (krahnss) n S African a sheer rock face
WORD ORIGIN Afrikaans

kremlin n the citadel of any Russian city
WORD ORIGIN Russian kreml

Kremlin n the central government of Russia and, formerly, the Soviet Union

krill n, pl **krill** a small shrimplike crustacean
WORD ORIGIN Norwegian kril young fish

Krishna n a Hindu god, the incarnation of Vishnu

krona n, pl **-nor** the standard monetary unit of Sweden
WORD ORIGIN Swedish, from Latin corona crown

krone (kroh-na) n, pl **-ner** (-ner) the

A Brief History of Literature
part 2

Modern poetry tends not to have rhyme and metre; it may still be thought of a collection of dreamy observations and evocative phrases that fall short of any definite meaning, and if it is perceived as 'difficult', it is probably because the symbolic language that characterizes it is so vague and personal that readers cannot interpret it.

This is not, in fact, an accurate description of the reality of modern verse, but in any case, ancient and medieval poetry is difficult for a much more concrete reason: it is highly structured. To be sure, this means the difficulty is often for the writer rather than the reader, but metre and (later) rhyme do necessitate some syntactical acrobatics that move poetic language out of the realm of familiar, everyday speech.

The metrical conventions of the poetry of any given language define its poetic diction. In modern English, we still think of metre as a strict pattern of stressed and unstressed syllables; for example, iambic pentameter (long the most common metre in English) consists of ten syllables or five metrical 'feet' comprising an unstressed followed by a stressed syllable (an *iamb*). This is the metre of Shakespeare, and it is the reason King Lear speaks the word *no* four consecutive times in Act V, scene 3 (each pair represents a *spondee*, two stressed syllables that can substitute for an iamb); and it is the reason the *-ed* ending must be stressed when Cordelia says 'For thee, oppressed king, I am cast down' in the same scene. A good portion of Shakespeare's lengthy lines stem from the constraints of metre, and it causes him to say in many words what prose might say in few.

Old English metre counted stresses but not syllables; the total length of a line could vary, as long as there were only four distinct stressed syllables, at least two of which should alliterate. To meet this requirement, poets developed a regular pattern of two nouns, adjectives, adverbs, even verbs, which merely complemented each other (and, usually, another phrase in the same sentence), which could be dropped in any line to supply two stresses, as in the following excerpts of *Beowulf*:

	Wiht unælo
grim ond grædig	gearo sona wæs

reoc ond reθe	ond on ræste genam
θritig θegna	
	The unholy creature
grim and greedy	soon was ready
savage and cruel	and from [their] rest took
thirty thanes	

The two pairs of adjectives ('grim and greedy' and 'savage and cruel') are not necessary to advance the story: without them we still have a perfectly comprehensible sentence. What they do provide, however, are two strong stresses that begin with the same letter (and the same letter as one of the stresses in the next half-line). Without these semantically superfluous phrases, the passage would not be poetry.

Automatic insertions of this kind are known as 'formulas'; they are necessary features of poetic language, for not only do they help change prose into poetry, but they are also 'ready-made', pre-existing patterns that can be learned by any aspiring poet, and they especially help spontaneous composition. In an oral society, there was never a single, 'fixed' version of a poem. Each time it was told, the story had to be composed anew. Certain facts would not be likely to change – Beowulf always defeats Grendel; the dragon always kills Beowulf – but the individual words used, the length of the poem, and other aspects would have been variable. Formulas helped poets compose acceptable verse *ex tempore*, so that all they needed to know were the main plot points and a list of formulaic phrases.

These formulas lasted well into the age of writing; they are preserved not only in *Beowulf* but in Homeric Greek and in many Middle English poems. Eventually they became so associated with poetic style that an author would use them even if they didn't need to. This affected use of poetic formulas even made it into prose. In Thomas Mallory's *Morte Darthur* there is frequent repetition of phrases like 'wit ye well', 'that noble knight', or the pattern 'full' followed by an adjective or adverb ('full loath'; 'full wight'; 'full oft'), all of which began as formulaic phrases. These and other devices give to poetry a sense of 'heightened', 'stylized' language, over and above ordinary prose, eventually becoming a requisite for all literary art.

standard monetary unit of Norway and Denmark
WORD ORIGIN Danish or Norwegian, from Latin *corona* crown

krugerrand *n* a one-ounce gold coin minted in South Africa
WORD ORIGIN Paul *Kruger,* Boer statesman + *rand*

krypton *n chem* an inert gaseous element occurring in trace amounts in air and used in fluorescent lights and lasers. Symbol: Kr
WORD ORIGIN Greek *kruptos* hidden

KS Kansas

Kt Knight

KT (in Britain) Knight of the Order of the Thistle

kt. kiloton

kudos (**kew**-doss) *n* personal fame or glory
WORD ORIGIN Greek

kudu *or* **koodoo** *n* a spiral-horned African antelope
WORD ORIGIN Afrikaans, from Khoi (language of southern Africa)

kugel (**koog**-el) *n S African* a rich, fashion-conscious, materialistic young Jewish woman
WORD ORIGIN from Yiddish *kugel,* a type of savoury pudding popular in Jewish cookery

Ku Klux Klan *n* a secret organization of White Protestant Americans who use violence against black and Jewish people **Ku Klux Klanner** *n*
WORD ORIGIN probably based on Greek *kuklos* circle + CLAN

kukri *n* a heavy, curved knife used by Gurkhas
WORD ORIGIN Hindi

kulak *n* (formerly) a property-owning Russian peasant
WORD ORIGIN Russian

kumera *or* **kumara** *n NZ* a tropical root vegetable with yellow flesh
WORD ORIGIN Māori

kümmel *n* a German liqueur flavoured with aniseed and cumin
WORD ORIGIN from German

kumquat (**kumm**-kwott) *n* a citrus fruit resembling a tiny orange
WORD ORIGIN Cantonese Chinese *kam kwat* golden orange

kung fu *n* any of various Chinese systems of martial art, esp. unarmed combat in which punches, chops, and kicks are made with the hands and feet; certain styles involve the use of weapons
WORD ORIGIN Chinese: skill; accomplishment

kura kaupapa Māori *n NZ* a primary school where the teaching is done in Māori

kurrajong *n* an Australian tree or shrub with tough fibrous bark
WORD ORIGIN from a native Australian language

kV kilovolt

kvetch *vb slang chiefly US* to complain or grumble
WORD ORIGIN Yiddish

kW kilowatt

Kwanzaa *n* an African-American festival held from December 26 until January 1
WORD ORIGIN from Swahili (*matunda ya*) *kwanza* first (fruits)

kwashiorkor *n* severe malnutrition of young children, caused by not eating enough protein
WORD ORIGIN native word in Ghana

kWh kilowatt-hour

KWIC *computers* keyword in context

KWOC *computers* keyword out of context

KY Kentucky

kyle *n Scot* a narrow strait or channel: *Kyle of Lochalsh*
WORD ORIGIN Gaelic *caol* narrow

Ll

The letter L is the twelfth letter of the English alphabet. Semitic alphabets had a letter called *lamedh*, which literally means 'whip', and this was the letter the Greeks used as the basis of their *lambda* (Λ,λ). The Greeks had various ways of writing the letter, all of which used two lines forming an acute angle. The Roman alphabet took one of the forms of *lambda* with an upright stem, and over time the acute angle developed into a right angle to give the shape of the modern letter L.

Anything that is composed of two lines that form a right angle may be referred to as 'L-shaped'. An L-shaped recession is the worst kind of economic slump, evoking a graph on which output falls sharply and then continues to scrape along the floor for a long period. Perhaps the best known use of this term is a literary one, however: Lynne Reid Banks' novel of 1960 *The L-shaped Room* was a ground-breaking story about an unmarried pregnant woman in London, which later became a successful film.

The letter L stands for 'learner', and a large red letter L on a white background is displayed on a car to indicate that the driver has not yet acquired a full licence. The associations of the letter are so strong that people who are new to any situation are often said to 'have their L-plates on', even if what they are doing has nothing to do with driving.

An even more widespread, although less obvious, use of the capital L in Britain is as the symbol for pounds sterling. The Latin equivalent of 'pound' was *libra*, and the abbreviation 'LSD' originally referred to the pre-decimal units of British currency, pounds (*librae*), shillings (*solidi*) and pence (*denarii*). After decimalization, shillings were swept away, and the abbreviation for a penny was changed from 'd' to 'p', but the symbol for a pound remained an ornate letter L with a horizontal line through it (£).

In North America, the letter L is associated with public transportation. The rapid-transit system that serves the city of Chicago is commonly referred to as 'the L', a name that derives from 'el' – a shortened form of 'elevated railroad'.

---

l litre(s)

L 1 large **2** Latin **3** learner driver **4** usually written: £ pound
WORD ORIGIN Latin *libra* **5** the Roman numeral for 50

L. *or* **l. 1** lake **2** left **3** length **4** *pl* **LL** *or* **ll** line

la *n music* same as **lah**

La *chem* lanthanum

LA 1 Los Angeles **2** Louisiana

laager *n* (in Africa) a camp defended by a circular formation of wagons
WORD ORIGIN Afrikaans *lager*

lab *n informal* short for **laboratory**

Lab *politics* Labour

label *n* **1** a piece of card or other material attached to an object to show its contents, ownership, use, or destination **2** a brief descriptive term given to a person, group, or school of thought: *we would need a handy label to explain the new company* ▷ *vb* **-belling, -belled** *or US* **-beling, -beled 3** to attach a label to **4** to describe or classify in a word or phrase
WORD ORIGIN Old French: ribbon

labial (lay-bee-al) *adj* **1** of or near the lips **2** *phonetics* relating to a speech sound made using the lips ▷ *n* **3** *phonetics* a speech sound such as English p or m, that involves the lips
WORD ORIGIN Latin *labium* lip

labiate (lay-bee-ate) *n* **1** any of a family of plants with square stems, aromatic leaves, and a two-lipped flower, such as mint or thyme ▷ *adj* **2** of this family
WORD ORIGIN Latin *labium* lip

labium (lay-bee-um) *n, pl* **-bia** (-bee-a) **1** a lip or liplike structure **2** any one of the four lip-shaped folds of the vulva
WORD ORIGIN Latin: lip

labor *n US, Austral, & sometimes Canad* same as **labour**

laboratory *n, pl* **-ries** a building or room equipped for conducting scientific research or for teaching practical science
WORD ORIGIN Latin *laborare* to work

Labor Day *n* **1** (in the US and Canada) public holiday in honour of labour, held on the first Monday in September **2** (in Australia) public holiday observed on different days in different states

laborious *adj* involving great exertion or prolonged effort **laboriously** *adv*

Labor Party *n* the main left-wing political party in Australia

labour *or US, Austral, & sometimes Canad* **labor** *n* **1** productive work, esp. physical work done for wages **2** the people involved in this, as opposed to management **3** the final stage of pregnancy, leading to childbirth **4** difficult work or a difficult job ▷ *vb* **5** to do physical work: *the girls were*

labouring madly on it **6** to work hard (for something) **7** to make one's way with difficulty: *she was now labouring down the return length* **8** to emphasize too persistently: *I have laboured the point* **9** (usually foll. by *under*) to be at a disadvantage because of a mistake or false belief: *she laboured under the illusion that I understood her*
WORD ORIGIN Latin *labor*

Labour Day *n* **1** a public holiday in honour of work, held in Britain on May 1 **2** (in New Zealand) a public holiday commemorating the introduction of the eight-hour day, held on the 4th Monday in October

laboured *or US, Austral, & sometimes Canad* **labored** *adj* undertaken with difficulty: *laboured breathing*

labourer *or US, Austral, & sometimes Canad* **laborer** *n* a person engaged in physical work

labour exchange *n Brit* the former name for a Jobcentre

Labour Party *n* **1** the main left-wing political party in a number of countries including Britain and New Zealand **2** any similar party in various other countries

labour-saving *adj* (of a method or piece of equipment) reducing the amount of work or effort needed to carry out a task

Labrador or **Labrador retriever** *n* a powerfully built dog with short dense usually black or golden hair

laburnum *n* a small ornamental tree that has clusters of yellow drooping flowers. It is highly poisonous **WORD ORIGIN** Latin

labyrinth (**lab**-er-inth) *n* **1** a mazelike network of tunnels or paths, either natural or man-made **2** any complex or confusing system **3** the interconnecting cavities of the internal ear **labyrinthine** *adj* **WORD ORIGIN** Greek *laburinthos*

lac *n* a resinous substance secreted by certain insects (**lac insects**), used in the manufacture of shellac **WORD ORIGIN** Hindi *lākh* resin

lace *n* **1** a delicate decorative fabric made from threads woven in an open web of patterns **2** a cord or string drawn through eyelets to fasten a shoe or garment ▷ *vb* **lacing, laced 3** to fasten (shoes) with a lace **4** to draw (a cord or thread) through holes as when tying shoes **5** to add a small amount of alcohol, a drug, or poison to (food or drink) **6** to intertwine; interlace **WORD ORIGIN** Latin *laqueus* noose

lacerate (**lass**-er-rate) *vb* **-ating, -ated 1** to tear (the flesh) jaggedly **2** to hurt (the feelings): *it would only lacerate an overburdened conscience* **laceration** *n* **WORD ORIGIN** Latin *lacerare* to tear

lace up *vb* **1** to fasten (clothes or footwear) with laces ▷ *adj* **lace-up 2** (of footwear) to be fastened with laces ▷ *n* **lace-up 3** a shoe or boot which fastens with a lace

lachrymal *adj* same as **lacrimal**

lachrymose *adj* **1** given to weeping; tearful **2** mournful; sad **WORD ORIGIN** Latin *lacrima* a tear

lacing *n* chiefly Brit informal a severe beating

lack *n* **1** shortage or absence of something required or desired: *a lack of confidence* ▷ *vb* **2** (often foll. by *in*) to be short (of) or have need (of): *lacking in sparkle* **WORD ORIGIN** related to Middle Dutch *laken* to be wanting

lackadaisical *adj* **1** lacking vitality and purpose **2** lazy and careless in a dreamy way **WORD ORIGIN** earlier *lackadaisy*

lackey *n* **1** a servile follower; hanger-on **2** a liveried male servant or valet **WORD ORIGIN** Catalan *lacayo, alacayo*

lacklustre or US **lackluster** *adj* lacking brilliance, force, or vitality

laconic *adj* (of a person's speech) using few words **laconically** *adv* **WORD ORIGIN** Greek *Lakōnikos* Spartan; referring to the Spartans' terseness of speech

lacquer *n* **1** a hard glossy coating made by dissolving natural or synthetic resins in a solvent that evaporates quickly **2** a black resin, obtained from certain trees, used to give a hard glossy finish to wooden furniture **3** a clear sticky substance for spraying onto the hair to hold a style in place **WORD ORIGIN** Portuguese *laca* lac

lacquered *adj* coated with lacquer

lacrimal or **lachrymal** (**lack**-rim-al) *adj* of tears or the glands that secrete tears **WORD ORIGIN** Latin *lacrima* a tear

lacrosse *n* a sport in which two teams try to propel a ball into each other's goal using long-handled sticks with a pouched net at the end **WORD ORIGIN** Canadian French: the hooked stick

lactate¹ *vb* **-tating, -tated** (of mammals) to secrete milk

lactate² *n* an ester or salt of lactic acid

lactation *n* **1** the secretion of milk from the mammary glands **2** the period during which milk is secreted

lacteal *adj* **1** of or like milk **2** (of lymphatic vessels) conveying or containing chyle ▷ *n* **3** any of the lymphatic vessels that convey chyle from the small intestine to the blood **WORD ORIGIN** Latin *lacteus* of milk

lactic *adj* relating to or derived from milk **WORD ORIGIN** Latin *lac* milk

lactic acid *n* a colourless syrupy acid found in sour milk and used as a preservative (E270) for foodstuffs

lactose *n* a white crystalline sugar occurring in milk

lacuna (lak-**kew**-na) *n, pl* **-nae** (-nee) a gap or space in a book or manuscript **WORD ORIGIN** Latin: pool, cavity

lacy *adj* **lacier, laciest** of or like lace

lad *n* **1** a boy or young man **2** informal any male **3** the lads informal a group of males **WORD ORIGIN** perhaps from Old Norse

ladder *n* **1** a portable frame consisting of two long parallel supports connected by steps, for climbing up or down **2** any system thought of as having a series of ascending stages: *the career ladder* **3** chiefly Brit a line of connected stitches that have come undone in tights or stockings ▷ *vb* **4** chiefly Brit to have or cause to have a line of undone stitches **WORD ORIGIN** Old English *hlǣdder*

ladder back *n* a chair in which the back is made of horizontal slats between two uprights

laddish *adj* Brit, Austral, & NZ informal, often derogatory characteristic of young men, esp. by being rowdy or immature

lade *vb* **lading, laded, laden** or **laded 1** to put cargo on board (a ship) or (of a ship) to take on cargo **2** (foll. by *with*) to burden or load **WORD ORIGIN** Old English *hladen* to load

laden *adj* **1** loaded **2** burdened

la-di-da or **lah-di-dah** *adj* informal affected or pretentious in speech or manners **WORD ORIGIN** mockingly imitative of affected speech

ladies or **ladies' room** *n* informal a women's public toilet

lading *n* a load; cargo; freight

ladle *n* **1** a long-handled spoon with a deep bowl for serving soup, stew, etc. ▷ *vb* **-dling, -dled 2** to serve out as with a ladle **WORD ORIGIN** Old English *hlædel*

ladle out *vb* informal to distribute (money, gifts, etc.) generously

lad mag *n* a magazine aimed at or appealing to men, focusing on fashion, gadgets, and often featuring scantily dressed women

lady *n, pl* **-dies 1** a woman regarded as having the characteristics of a good family, such as dignified manners **2** a polite name for a woman ▷ *adj* **3** female: *a lady chef* **WORD ORIGIN** Old English *hlǣfdīge*

Lady *n, pl* **-dies 1** (in Britain) a title borne by various classes of women of the peerage **2 Our Lady** a title of the Virgin Mary

ladybird *n* a small red beetle with black spots **WORD ORIGIN** after Our *Lady*, the Virgin Mary

ladyboy *n* informal a transvestite or transsexual, esp. one from the Far East

Lady Day *n* March 25, the feast of the Annunciation of the Virgin Mary: a quarter day in England, Wales, and Ireland

lady-in-waiting *n, pl* **ladies-in-waiting** a lady who attends a queen or princess

lady-killer *n* informal a man who is, or believes he is, irresistible to women

ladylike *adj* refined and fastidious

Ladyship *n* (preceded by *Your* or *Her*) a title used to address or refer to any peeress except a duchess

lady's-slipper *n* an orchid with reddish or purple flowers

lag¹ *vb* **lagging, lagged 1** (often foll. by *behind*) to hang (back) or fall (behind) in movement, progress, or development **2** to fall away in strength or intensity ▷ *n* **3** a slowing down or falling behind **4** the interval of time between two events, esp. between an action and its effect: *the time lag between mobilization and combat* **WORD ORIGIN** origin unknown

lag² *vb* **lagging, lagged 1** to wrap (a pipe, cylinder, or boiler) with insulating material to prevent heat loss ▷ *n* **2** the insulating casing of a steam cylinder or boiler **WORD ORIGIN** Scandinavian

lag³ *n* **old lag** Brit, Austral, & NZ slang a convict or ex-convict **WORD ORIGIN** origin unknown

lager *n* a light-bodied effervescent beer, fermented in a closed vessel using yeasts that sink to the bottom of the brew **WORD ORIGIN** German *Lagerbier* beer for storing

laggard *n* a person who lags behind

lagging *n* insulating material wrapped around pipes, boilers, or tanks to prevent loss of heat

lagoon *n* a body of water cut off from the open sea by coral reefs or sand bars **WORD ORIGIN** Latin *lacuna* pool

lah *n* music (in tonic sol-fa) the sixth note of any ascending major scale

laid *vb* the past of **lay¹**

laid-back *adj* relaxed in style or character

laid paper *n* paper with a regular pattern of lines impressed upon it

lain *vb* the past participle of **lie²**

Word Histories
part 8

Jumbo: *Jumbo* was the name of a famous and very large 19th-century African elephant that was used to give rides to children at London Zoo, before being sold in 1882 to Barnum and Bailey's circus.

Kamikaze comes from Japanese *kami*, meaning 'divine', and *kaze*, meaning 'wind'.

Laconic comes from the Greek word *Lakōnikos*, meaning 'Laconian' or 'Spartan'. Sparta was the capital city of the region of ancient Greece known as Laconia, and the Spartans were famous for using few words.

The word **limbo** comes from the Latin phrase *in limbo*, meaning 'on the border' (ie on the border of Hell).

Limey, a slang term for a British citizen, and particularly a serviceman, is sometimes said to be a contraction of the cockney exclamation 'Gor blimey!' Its actual derivation is equally interesting: limey is a contraction of 'lime-juicer', referring to the 19th-century practice in the British Navy of giving sailors limes to prevent scurvy.

Love, meaning a score of zero in tennis, is popularly supposed to come from the French *l'oeuf*, 'the egg', representing 0. This is an attractive story, and fits with the well-known use of 'a duck' – short for 'a duck's egg' – in cricket. Sadly, the term comes simply from the idea of 'playing for love', ie playing for the love of the game and not for victory.

Masochism derives its name from the Austrian novelist Leopold von Sacher Masoch (1836–1895), who wrote about the pleasures of masochism.

Migraine comes via French from Latin *hēmicrānia*, meaning 'pain in half the head', from Greek *hemi-*, meaning 'half', and *kranion*, meaning 'cranium, skull'.

Mile: In Roman times, a mile was equal to a thousand paces. In Latin, 'one thousand paces' is *mīlia passuum*, from *mille*, meaning 'a thousand' (the same Latin word as is found in English words such as 'millennium' and 'millimetre').

Museum comes from Greek *mouseion*, meaning the 'home of the Muses', the goddesses of the arts and sciences. The first building to be given this name was a university building built in Alexandria in Egypt about 300 BC.

Mushroom derives from the French *mousseron*, which is probably connected to 'moss'. 'Mushroom' is a classic example of folk etymology, breaking a foreign word into two recognizable elements despite the fact that neither 'mush' nor 'room' has any connection with the fungus in question.

News is sometimes supposed to be an acronym of North, East, South, West. This is nonsense, of course, as news is simply a contraction of 'new things', in line with the French *nouvelles*, but the fact that the supposed acronym is widely circulated shows just how persistent false etymologies can be.

Newt: The newt owes its name to a mistake by speakers of English round about the 15th century, who wrongly understood 'an ewt' (from Old English *eveta* or *efeta*) to be 'a newt'. In some English dialects, this mistake did not happen and newts are called 'efts', a word which looks less like its more popular cousin than it would have done in earlier times. Interestingly, the opposite process can be seen to have taken place in the name of the adder: 'an adder' comes from 'a nadder', from Old English *nǣdre*, meaning 'snake'.

Nickname: 'A nickname' was originally 'an ekename', the *eke* meaning 'addition', but the words were mistakenly divided over time, with the 'n' being assigned to the article. This is quite a common process in English, as with **newt**.

Nightmare comes from *night* and Old English *mare*, meaning 'evil spirit'.

Notch: Like 'newt', which comes from the mistaken division of 'an ewt' into 'a newt', the word 'notch' arose from the mistaken division of *an otch* (from Old French *oche*, meaning 'notch') into 'a notch'.

lair *n* **1** the resting place of a wild animal **2** *informal* a place of seclusion or hiding **WORD ORIGIN** Old English *leger*

laird *n Scot* a landowner, esp. of a large estate **WORD ORIGIN** Scots variant of *lord*

laissez faire or **laisser faire** (**less-ay fair**) *n* the policy of nonintervention, esp. by a government in commerce **WORD ORIGIN** French, literally: let (them) act

laity (**lay-it-ee**) *n* **1** people who are not members of the clergy **2** all the people who do not belong to a specific profession **WORD ORIGIN** from LAY³

lake¹ *n* an expanse of water entirely surrounded by land **WORD ORIGIN** Latin *lacus*

lake² *n* **1** a bright pigment produced by combining organic colouring matter with an inorganic compound **2** a red dye obtained by combining a metallic compound with cochineal **WORD ORIGIN** variant of *lac*

Lake District *n* a region of lakes and mountains in NW England. Also called: **Lakeland, the Lakes**

lake trout *n* a yellow-spotted trout of the Great Lakes region of Canada

lakh (**lahk**) *n* (in India) 100 000, esp. referring to this sum of rupees **WORD ORIGIN** Hindi *lākh*

lam¹ *vb* **lamming, lammed** *slang* to attack vigorously **WORD ORIGIN** Scandinavian

lam² *n* **on the lam** *US & Canad slang* **a** making an escape **b** in hiding **WORD ORIGIN** origin unknown

lama *n* a Buddhist priest or monk in Mongolia or Tibet **WORD ORIGIN** Tibetan *blama*

lamb *n* **1** the young of a sheep **2** the meat of a young sheep eaten as food **3** someone who is innocent, gentle, and good ▷ *vb* **4** (of a ewe) to give birth **WORD ORIGIN** Old English

Lamb *n* **the Lamb** a title given to Christ

lambast or **lambaste** *vb* **1** to beat severely **2** to reprimand severely **WORD ORIGIN** LAM¹ + BASTE³

lambent *adj* **1** (of a flame or light) flickering softly over a surface **2** (of wit or humour) light or brilliant **lambency** *n* **WORD ORIGIN** Latin *lambere* to lick

lambing *n* **1** the birth of lambs at the end of winter **2** the shepherd's work of tending the ewes and newborn lambs at this time

lamb's fry *n Austral & NZ* lamb's liver for cooking

lambskin *n* the skin of a lamb, usually with the wool still on, used to make coats, slippers, etc.

lame *adj* **1** disabled or crippled in the legs or feet **2** weak; unconvincing: *lame arguments* ▷ *vb* **laming, lamed** **3** to make lame **lamely** *adv* **lameness** *n* **WORD ORIGIN** Old English *lama*

lamé (**lah-may**) *n* a fabric interwoven with gold or silver threads **WORD ORIGIN** Old French *lame* gold or silver thread

lame duck *n* a person who is unable to cope without the help of other people

lament *vb* **1** to feel or express sorrow or regret (for or over) ▷ *n* **2** an expression of sorrow **3** a poem or song in which a death is lamented **lamentation** *n* **WORD ORIGIN** Latin *lamentum*

lamentable *adj* very unfortunate or disappointing **lamentably** *adv*

lamented *adj* grieved for: usually said of someone dead

lamina *n, pl* **-nae** a thin plate, esp. of bone or mineral **laminar** *adj* **WORD ORIGIN** Latin: thin plate

laminate *vb* **-nating, -nated** **1** to make (material in sheet form) by sticking together thin sheets **2** to cover with a thin sheet of material **3** to split or be split into thin sheets ▷ *n* **4** a material made by sticking sheets together ▷ *adj* **5** composed of lamina; laminated **lamination** *n*

laminated *adj* **1** composed of many layers stuck together **2** covered with a thin protective layer of plastic

lamington *n Austral & NZ* a sponge cake covered with a sweet coating

Lammas *n* August 1, formerly observed in England as a harvest festival: a quarter day in Scotland **WORD ORIGIN** Old English *hlāfmæsse* loaf mass

lamp *n* **1** a device that produces light: *an electric lamp; a gas lamp; an oil lamp* **2** a device that produces radiation, esp. for therapeutic purposes: *an ultraviolet lamp* **WORD ORIGIN** Greek *lampein* to shine

lampblack *n* a fine black soot used as a pigment in paint and ink

lampoon *n* **1** a piece of writing ridiculing a person ▷ *vb* **2** to ridicule and criticize (someone) in a lampoon **lampooner** or **lampoonist** *n* **WORD ORIGIN** French *lampon*

lamppost *n* a metal or concrete pole supporting a lamp in a street

lamprey *n* an eel-like fish with a round sucking mouth **WORD ORIGIN** Late Latin *lampreda*

LAN *computers* local area network

Lancastrian *n* **1** a person from Lancashire or Lancaster **2** a supporter of the house of Lancaster in the Wars of the Roses (1455–85) ▷ *adj* **3** of Lancashire or Lancaster **4** of the house of Lancaster

lance *n* **1** a long weapon with a pointed head used by horsemen ▷ *vb* **lancing, lanced** **2** to pierce (an abscess or boil) with a lancet **3** to pierce with or as with a lance **WORD ORIGIN** Latin *lancea*

lance corporal *n* a noncommissioned officer of the lowest rank

lanceolate *adj* narrow and tapering to a point at each end, like some leaves **WORD ORIGIN** Latin *lanceola* small lance

lancer *n* (formerly) a cavalryman armed with a lance

lancet *n* **1** a pointed surgical knife with two sharp edges **2** short for **lancet arch** or **lancet window** **WORD ORIGIN** Old French *lancette* small lance

lancet arch *n* a narrow acutely pointed arch

lancet window *n* a narrow window with a lancet arch

lancewood *n* a New Zealand tree with slender leaves

Lancs Lancashire

land *n* **1** the solid part of the surface of the earth as distinct from seas and lakes ▶ Related adjective: **terrestrial** **2** ground, esp. with reference to its use or quality: *agricultural land* **3** rural or agricultural areas: *he couldn't leave the land* **4** *law* ground owned as property **5** a country, region, or area: *to bring peace and riches to your land* ▷ *vb* **6** to come down or bring (something) down to earth after a flight or jump **7** to transfer (something) or go from a ship to the shore: *sacks of malt were landed from barges* **8** to come to or touch shore **9** *informal* to obtain: *he landed a handsomely paid job at Lloyd's* **10** *angling* to retrieve (a hooked fish) from the water **11** *informal* to deliver (a blow or punch) ▶ See also **land up** ▷ **landless** *adj* **WORD ORIGIN** Old English

land agent *n* a person in charge of a landed estate

landau (**lan-daw**) *n* a four-wheeled horse-drawn carriage with two folding hoods **WORD ORIGIN** after *Landau*, a town in Germany, where first made

landed *adj* **1** owning land: *landed gentry* **2** consisting of land: *landed property*

landfall *n* the act of sighting or nearing land, esp. from the sea

landfill *n* disposing of rubbish by covering it with earth

land girl *n* a girl or woman who does farm work, esp. in wartime

land-holder *n* a person who owns or occupies land **land-holding** *adj, n*

landing *n* **1** the floor area at the top of a flight of stairs **2** the act of coming to land, esp. after a flight or sea voyage **3** a place of disembarkation

landing field *n* an area of land on which aircraft land and from which they take off

landing gear *n* the undercarriage of an aircraft

landlady *n, pl* **-dies** **1** a woman who owns and leases property **2** a woman who owns or runs a lodging house or pub

land line *n* a telecommunications wire or cable laid over land

landlocked *adj* (of a country) completely surrounded by land

landlord *n* **1** a man who owns and leases property **2** a man who owns or runs a lodging house or pub

landlubber *n naut* any person without experience at sea

landmark *n* **1** a prominent object in or feature of a particular landscape **2** an important or unique event or development: *a landmark in scientific progress*

landmass *n* a large continuous area of land

land mine *n mil* an explosive device placed in the ground, usually detonated when someone steps on it or drives over it

landowner *n* a person who owns land **landowning** *n, adj*

landscape *n* **1** an extensive area of land regarded as being visually distinct **2** a painting, drawing, or photograph depicting natural scenery ▷ *vb* **-scaping, -scaped 3** to improve the natural features of (an area of land) **WORD ORIGIN** Middle Dutch *lantscap* region

landscape gardening *n* the art of laying out grounds in imitation of natural scenery **landscape gardener** *n*

landside *n* the part of an airport farthest from the aircraft

landslide *n* **1** Also called: **landslip a** the sliding of a large mass of rocks and soil down the side of a mountain or cliff **b** the material dislodged in this way **2** an overwhelming electoral victory

land up *vb* to arrive at a final point or condition

landward *adj* **1** lying, facing, or moving towards land **2** in the direction of the land ▷ *adv also* **landwards 3** towards land

lane *n* **1** a narrow road, esp. in the country **2** one of the parallel strips into which the carriageway of a major road or motorway is divided **3** any well-defined route or course, such as for ships or aircraft **4** one of the parallel strips into which a running track or swimming bath is divided for races **WORD ORIGIN** Old English *lane, lanu*

lang. language

language *n* **1** a system of spoken sounds or conventional symbols for communicating thought **2** the language of a particular nation or people **3** the ability to use words to communicate **4** any other means of communicating: *body language* **5** the specialized vocabulary used by a particular group: *legal language* **6** a particular style of verbal expression: *rough language* **7** computers see **programming language** **WORD ORIGIN** Latin *lingua* tongue

language laboratory *n* a room in a school or college equipped with tape recorders etc. for learning foreign languages

languid *adj* lacking energy; dreamy and inactive **languidly** *adv* **WORD ORIGIN** Latin *languere* to languish

languish *vb literary* **1** to suffer deprivation, hardship, or neglect: *she won't languish in jail for it* **2** to lose or diminish in strength or energy: *the design languished into oblivion* **3** (often foll. by *for*) to be listless with desire; pine **languishing** *adj* **WORD ORIGIN** Latin *languere*

languor (lang-ger) *n literary* a pleasant state of dreamy relaxation **languorous** *adj* **WORD ORIGIN** Latin *languere* to languish

lank *adj* **1** (of hair) straight and limp **2** thin or gaunt: *a lank bespectacled boy* **WORD ORIGIN** Old English *hlanc* loose

lanky *adj* **lankier, lankiest** ungracefully tall and thin **lankiness** *n*

lanolin *n* a yellowish sticky substance extracted from wool: used in some ointments **WORD ORIGIN** Latin *lana* wool + *oleum* oil

lantana (lan-**tay**-na) *n* a shrub with orange or yellow flowers, considered a weed in Australia

lantern *n* **1** a light with a transparent protective case **2** a raised part on top of a dome or roof which lets in light or air **3** the upper part of a lighthouse that houses the light **WORD ORIGIN** Greek *lampein* to shine

lantern jaw *n* a long hollow jaw that gives the face a drawn appearance **lantern-jawed** *adj*

lanthanide series *n chem* a class of 15 chemically related elements (**lanthanides**) with atomic numbers from 57 (lanthanum) to 71 (lutetium)

lanthanum *n chem* a silvery-white metallic element of the lanthanide series: used in electronic devices and glass manufacture. Symbol: La **WORD ORIGIN** Greek *lanthanein* to lie unseen

lanyard *n* **1** a cord worn round the neck to hold a whistle or knife **2** *naut* a line for extending or tightening rigging **WORD ORIGIN** Old French *lasne* strap

laodicean (lay-oh-**diss**-see-an) *adj* indifferent, esp. in religious matters **WORD ORIGIN** referring to the early Christians of Laodicea (Revelation 3:14–16)

lap¹ *n* **1** the area formed by the upper surface of the thighs of a seated person **2** a protected place or environment: *in the lap of luxury* **3** the part of a person's clothing that covers the lap **4** **drop in someone's lap** to give someone the responsibility for **WORD ORIGIN** Old English *læppa* flap

lap² *n* **1** one circuit of a racecourse or track **2** a stage or part of a journey **3 a** an overlapping part **b** the extent of overlap ▷ *vb* **lapping, lapped 4** to overtake (an opponent) in a race so as to be one or more circuits ahead **5** to enfold or wrap around **6** to place or lie partly or completely over, or project beyond: *deep-pile carpet that lapped against his ankles* **7** to envelop or surround with comfort, love, or peace: *she was lapped by the luxury of Seymour House* **WORD ORIGIN** probably same as LAP¹

lap³ *vb* **lapping, lapped 1** (of small waves) to wash against (the shore or a boat) with light splashing sounds **2** (often foll. by *up*) (esp. of animals) to scoop (a liquid) into the mouth with the tongue ▷ *n* **3** the act or sound of lapping ▶ See also **lap up** **WORD ORIGIN** Old English *lapian*

laparoscopy *n* an investigative surgical procedure in which an optical instrument is inserted through a small incision in the abdomen **laparoscopic** *adj* **WORD ORIGIN** Greek *lapara* flank + *skopos* target

lap dancing *n* a form of entertainment in which scantily dressed women dance erotically for individual members of the audience

lapdog *n* a small pet dog

lapel (lap-**pel**) *n* the part on the front of a jacket or coat that folds back towards the shoulders **WORD ORIGIN** from LAP¹

lapidary *n, pl* **-daries 1** a person who cuts, polishes, sets, or deals in gemstones ▷ *adj* **2** of or relating to gemstones or the work of a lapidary **WORD ORIGIN** Latin *lapidarius*, from *lapis* stone

lapis lazuli (lap-iss lazz-yew-lie) *n* a brilliant blue mineral used as a gemstone **WORD ORIGIN** Latin *lapis* stone + Medieval Latin *lazulum* azure

lap joint *n* a joint made by fastening together overlapping parts

lap of honour *n* a ceremonial circuit of a racing track by the winner of a race

Lapp *n* **1** Also: **Laplander** a member of a nomadic people living chiefly in N Scandinavia **2** the language of this people ▷ *adj* **3** of this people or their language

lappet *n* **1** a small hanging flap or piece of lace **2** *zool* a flap of flesh or membrane, such as the ear lobe or a bird's wattle **WORD ORIGIN** LAP¹ + -et (diminutive suffix)

lapse *n* **1** a temporary drop in standard as a result of forgetfulness or lack of concentration **2** a moment or instance of bad behaviour, esp. by someone who is usually well-behaved **3** a period of time sufficient for a change to take place: *the lapse between phone call and now* **4** a gradual decline to a lower degree, condition, or state: *its lapse from the tradition of Disraeli* **5** *law* the loss of some right by neglecting to exercise or renew it ▷ *vb* **lapsing, lapsed 6** to drop in standard or fail to maintain a standard **7** to decline gradually in status, condition, or degree **8** to allow to end or become no longer valid, esp. through negligence: *a bid that lapsed last July* **9** (usually foll. by *into*) to drift (into a condition): *she appeared to lapse into a brief reverie* **10** (often foll. by *from*) to turn away (from beliefs or standards) **11** (of time) to slip away **lapsed** *adj* **WORD ORIGIN** Latin *lapsus* error

laptop *adj* (of a computer) small and light enough to be held on the user's lap

lap up *vb* **1** to eat or drink **2** to accept (information or attention) eagerly: *the public are lapping up the scandal*

lapwing *n* a bird of the plover family with a crested head. Also called: **peewit** **WORD ORIGIN** Old English *hlēapewince* plover

larboard *n naut* an old word for **port²** (sense 1) **WORD ORIGIN** Middle English *laddeborde*

larceny *n, pl* **-nies** *law* theft **larcenist** *n* **WORD ORIGIN** Old French *larcin*

larch *n* **1** a coniferous tree with deciduous needle-like leaves and egg-shaped cones **2** the wood of this tree **WORD ORIGIN** Latin *larix*

lard *n* **1** the soft white fat obtained from pigs and prepared for use in cooking ▷ *vb* **2** to prepare (lean meat or poultry)

by inserting small strips of bacon or fat before cooking **3** to add unnecessary material to (speech or writing)
WORD ORIGIN Latin *laridum* bacon fat

larder *n* a room or cupboard used for storing food
WORD ORIGIN Old French *lardier*

lardy cake *n Brit* a sweet cake made of bread dough, lard, sugar, and dried fruit

large *adj* **1** having a relatively great size, quantity, or extent; big **2** of wide or broad scope, capacity, or range; comprehensive: *a large effect* ▷ *n* **3** **at large a** as a whole; in general: *both the Navy and the country at large* **b** (of a dangerous criminal or wild animal) out of captivity; free **c** in full detail ▷ *vb* **larging, larged 4 large it** *Brit slang* to enjoy oneself or celebrate in an extravagant way **largeness** *n*
WORD ORIGIN Latin *largus* ample

large intestine *n* the part of the alimentary canal consisting of the caecum, colon, and rectum

largely *adv* principally; to a great extent

large-scale *adj* **1** wide-ranging or extensive **2** (of maps and models) constructed or drawn to a big scale

largesse *or* **largess** (lar-**jess**) *n* the generous giving of gifts, favours, or money
WORD ORIGIN Old French

largish *adj* fairly large

largo *music adv* **1** in a slow and stately manner ▷ *n, pl* **-gos 2** a piece or passage to be performed in a slow and stately manner
WORD ORIGIN Italian

lariat *n US & Canad* **1** a lasso **2** a rope for tethering animals
WORD ORIGIN Spanish *la reata* the lasso

lark[1] *n* a small brown songbird, esp. the skylark
WORD ORIGIN Old English *lāwerce, lǣwerce*

lark[2] *informal n* **1** a carefree adventure or frolic **2** a harmless piece of mischief **3** an activity or job viewed with disrespect ▷ *vb* **4 lark about** to have a good time frolicking or playing pranks **larky** *adj*
WORD ORIGIN origin unknown

larkspur *n* a plant with blue, pink, or white flowers with slender spikes at the base
WORD ORIGIN LARK[1] + SPUR

larrikin *n Austral & NZ old-fashioned slang* a mischievous or unruly person

larva *n, pl* **-vae** the immature form of many insects before it develops into its adult form **larval** *adj*
WORD ORIGIN New Latin

laryngeal *adj* of or relating to the larynx

laryngitis *n* inflammation of the larynx, causing huskiness or loss of voice

larynx (**lar**-rinks) *n, pl* **larynges** (lar-**rin**-jeez) *or* **larynxes** a hollow organ forming part of the air passage to the lungs: it contains the vocal cords
WORD ORIGIN Greek *larunx*

lasagne *or* **lasagna** (laz-**zan**-ya) *n* **1** a form of pasta in wide flat sheets **2** a dish made from layers of lasagne, meat, and cheese

WORD ORIGIN Italian, from Latin *lasanum* cooking pot

lascar *n* an East Indian seaman

lascivious (lass-**iv**-ee-uss) *adj* showing or producing sexual desire; lustful **lasciviously** *adv*
WORD ORIGIN Latin *lascivia* wantonness

laser (**lay**-zer) *n* **1** a device that produces a very narrow intense beam of light, which is used for cutting very hard materials and in surgery etc. ▷ *vb* **2** to use a laser on (something), esp. as part of medical treatment **3** Also: **laser off** to remove (a tattoo, fat, etc.) with laser treatment
WORD ORIGIN from light amplification by stimulated emission of radiation

laser printer *n* a computer printer that uses a laser beam to produce characters which are then transferred to paper

lash[1] *n* **1** an eyelash **2** a sharp cutting blow from a whip **3** the flexible end of a whip ▷ *vb* **4** to hit (a person or thing) sharply with a whip, esp. formerly as punishment **5** (of rain or waves) to beat forcefully against **6** to attack (someone) with words of ridicule or scolding **7** to flick or wave sharply to and fro: *his tail lashing in irritation* **8** to urge as with a whip: *to lash the audience into a violent mood* ▷ See also **lash out**
WORD ORIGIN perhaps imitative

lash[2] *vb* to bind or secure with rope, string, or cord
WORD ORIGIN Latin *laqueus* noose

lashing[1] *n* **1** a flogging **2** a scolding

lashing[2] *n* rope, string, or cord used for binding or securing

lashings *pl n old-fashioned, informal* large amounts; lots: *lashings of cream*

lash out *vb* **1** to make a sudden verbal or physical attack **2** *informal* to spend extravagantly

lass *n* a girl or young woman
WORD ORIGIN origin unknown

Lassa fever *n* a serious viral disease of Central West Africa, characterized by high fever and muscular pains
WORD ORIGIN after *Lassa*, the Nigerian village where it was first identified

lassie *n Scot & N English informal* a little lass; girl

lassitude *n* physical or mental weariness
WORD ORIGIN Latin *lassus* tired

lasso (lass-**oo**) *n, pl* **-sos** *or* **-soes 1** a long rope with a noose at one end used for catching horses and cattle ▷ *vb* **-soing, -soed 2** to catch as with a lasso **lassoer** *n*
WORD ORIGIN Spanish, from Latin *laqueus* noose

last[1] *adj* **1** being, happening, or coming at the end or after all others **2** most recent: *last April* **3** only remaining: *that's the last one* **4** most extreme; utmost **5** least suitable or likely: *China was the last place on earth he intended to go* ▷ *adv* **6** after all others **7** most recently: *we last saw him on Thursday night* **8** as the last or latest item ▷ *n* **9** **the last a** a person or thing that is last **b** the final moment; end **10** the final appearance, mention, or occurrence: *the last of this season's visitors* **11** **at last** in the end;

finally **12 at long last** finally, after difficulty or delay
WORD ORIGIN variant of Old English *latest, lætest*

⧉ **USAGE**
Since *last* can mean either *after all others* or *most recent*, it is better to avoid using this word where ambiguity might arise, as in *her last novel*. *Final* or *latest* should be used in such contexts to avoid ambiguity.

last[2] *vb* **1** to continue to exist for a length of time: *the soccer war lasted 100 hours* **2** to be sufficient for the needs of (a person) for a length of time: *I shall make a couple of bottles to last me until next summer* **3** to remain fresh, uninjured, or unaltered for a certain time: *the flowers haven't lasted well* ▶ See also **last out**
WORD ORIGIN Old English *lēstan*

last[3] *n* the wooden or metal form on which a shoe or boot is made or repaired
WORD ORIGIN Old English *lāst* footprint

last-ditch *adj* done as a final resort: *a last-ditch attempt*

lasting *adj* existing or remaining effective for a long time

Last Judgment *n* **the Last Judgment** *theol* God's verdict on the destinies of all human beings at the end of the world

lastly *adv* **1** at the end or at the last point **2** finally

last-minute *adj* given or done at the latest possible time: *last-minute changes*

last name *n* same as **surname**

last out *vb* **1** to be sufficient for one's needs: *if the energy supply lasts out* **2** to endure or survive: *I might not last out my hours of duty*

last post *n mil* **1** a bugle call used to signal the time to retire at night **2** a similar call sounded at military funerals

last rites *pl n Christianity* religious rites for those close to death

last straw *n* a small incident, irritation, or setback that coming after others is too much to cope with

Last Supper *n* **the Last Supper** the meal eaten by Christ with his disciples on the night before his Crucifixion

lat. latitude

Lat. Latin

latch *n* **1** a fastening for a gate or door that consists of a bar that may be slid or lowered into a groove, hole, or notch **2** a spring-loaded door lock that can only be opened by a key from outside ▷ *vb* **3** to fasten, fit, or be fitted with a latch
WORD ORIGIN Old English *læccan* to seize

latchkey child *n Brit, Austral, & NZ* a child who has to let himself or herself in at home after school, as both parents are out at work

latch on *vb informal* **1** (often foll. by *to*) to attach oneself (to): *he should latch on to a man with a deal to do* **2** to understand: *it took a while to latch on to what he was trying to say*

late *adj* **1** occurring or arriving after the correct or expected time: *the plane will be late* **2** towards or near the end: *the late*

SCRABBLE
Three-Letter Words, part 5
KAY–NAE

KAY	the letter K	**LAR**	boy or young man
KEA	large parrot	**LAS**	plural form of la
KEB	Scots word meaning miscarry a lamb	**LAT**	former coin of Latvia
KED	(as in sheep ked) sheep tick	**LAV**	short for lavatory
KEF	marijuana	**LAW**	rule binding on a community
KEG	small metal beer barrel	**LAX**	not strict
KEN	know	**LAY**	part of the verb to lie
KEP	catch	**LEA**	meadow
KET	Scots word for carrion	**LED**	part of the verb to lead
KEX	type of plant	**LEE**	sheltered side
KEY	device for operating a lock	**LEG**	limb
KHI	letter of the Greek alphabet	**LEI**	(in Hawaii) garland of flowers
KID	child	**LEK**	monetary unit
KIF	marijuana	**LEP**	Spenserian word for leap
KIN	person's relatives collectively	**LES**	offensive short form of lesbian
KIP	sleep	**LET**	allow, permit
KIR	alcoholic drink	**LEU**	monetary unit
KIS	plural form of ki	**LEV**	monetary unit
KIT	outfit or equipment	**LEW**	tepid
KOA	Hawaiian tree	**LEX**	system or body of laws
KOB	antelope	**LEY**	land temporarily under grass
KOI	type of carp	**LEZ**	offensive short form of lesbian
KON	Spenserian word for know	**LIB**	short for liberation
KOP	African hill	**LID**	movable cover
KOR	ancient Hebrew unit of capacity	**LIE**	make a deliberately false statement
KOS	Indian unit of distance	**LIG**	function with free refreshments
KOW	branch, bunch of twigs	**LIN**	cease
KUE	the letter Q	**LIP**	fleshy folds at the mouth
KYE	Scots word for cows	**LIS**	fleur-de-lis
KYU	judo term	**LIT**	part of the verb to light
LAB	laboratory	**LOB**	ball struck or thrown in a high arc
LAC	(in India and Pakistan) 100,000 rupees	**LOD**	type of logarithm
LAD	boy or young man	**LOG**	portion of a felled tree
LAG	go too slowly	**LOO**	word for lavatory
LAH	musical term	**LOP**	cut away (twigs and branches)
LAM	thrash, beat		
LAP	part between the waist and knees	**LOR**	exclamation of surprise or dismay

LOS	approval, praise	**MEU**	the plant spignel
LOT	great number	**MEW**	cry of a cat
LOU	Scots word for love	**MHO**	former name for siemens
LOW	not tall or high	**MIB**	marble used in games
LOX	smoked salmon	**MIC**	short for microphone
LOY	narrow spade with a single footrest	**MID**	intermediate
LUD	lord	**MIG**	marble used in games
LUG	carry or drag with great effort	**MIL**	unit of length
LUM	chimney	**MIM**	prim
LUR	musical horn	**MIR**	Russian peasant commune
LUV	love	**MIS**	plural form of mi
LUX	unit of illumination	**MIX**	combine or blend
LUZ	supposedly indestructible bone	**MIZ**	shortened form of misery
LYE	caustic solution	**MNA**	Greek weight
LYM	bloodhound	**MOA**	large extinct flightless bird
MAA	bleat		
MAC	short for macintosh	**MOB**	disorderly crowd
MAD	mentally deranged	**MOC**	short for moccasin
MAE	(as in mae west) inflatable life jacket	**MOD**	sixties youth group
		MOE	more
MAG	short for magazine	**MOG**	short for moggy
MAK	Scots word for make	**MOI**	me
MAL	illness, pain	**MOL**	SI unit mole
MAM	word for mother	**MOM**	word for mother
MAN	adult male	**MON**	dialect variant of man
MAP	representation of the earth's surface	**MOO**	cry of a cow
MAR	spoil or impair	**MOP**	cleaning device
MAS	plural form of ma	**MOR**	layer of acidic humus
MAT	piece of fabric	**MOS**	plural form of mo
MAW	animal's mouth	**MOT**	girl or young woman
MAX	the full extent	**MOU**	Scots word for mouth
MAY	used to express possibility	**MOW**	to cut grass or crops
		MOY	coin
MED	doctor	**MOZ**	hex
MEE	Malaysian noodle dish	**MUD**	wet soft earth
MEG	short for megabyte	**MUG**	large drinking cup
MEL	pure form of honey	**MUM**	word for mother
MEM	13th letter of the Hebrew alphabet	**MUN**	dialect word for must
		MUS	plural form of mu
MEN	plural form of man	**MUT**	printing measurement
MES	plural form of me	**MUX**	spoil
MET	part of the verb to meet	**MYC**	oncogene
		NAB	arrest (someone)
		NAE	Scots word for no

afternoon **3** occurring or being at a relatively advanced time: *a late starter, his first novel was effectively his last* **4** at an advanced time in the evening or at night: *it's late, I have to get back* **5** having died recently: *her late father* **6** recent: *recollect the late defeats which your enemies have experienced* **7** former: *the late manager of the team* **8 of late** recently ▷ *adv* **9** after the correct or expected time: *Mark Wright arrived late* **10** at a relatively advanced age: *coming late to motherhood* **11** recently: *as late as in 1983, only 9 per cent of that labour force was unionized* **12 late in the day a** at a late or advanced stage **b** too late **lateness** *n*
WORD ORIGIN Old English *lǣt*

≡ **USAGE**
≡ Since *late* can mean *deceased*, many
≡ people think it is better to avoid using
≡ this word to refer to the person who
≡ held a post or position before its
≡ present holder: *the previous* (not *the late*)
≡ *editor of The Times.*

lateen *adj naut* denoting a rig with a triangular sail bent to a yard hoisted to the head of a low mast
WORD ORIGIN French *voile latine* Latin sail

Late Greek *n* the Greek language from about the 3rd to the 8th centuries AD
Late Latin *n* the form of written Latin used from the 3rd to the 7th centuries AD
lately *adv* in recent times; of late
latent *adj* lying hidden and not yet developed within a person or thing **latency** *n*
WORD ORIGIN Latin *latere* to lie hidden
later *adj, adv* **1** the comparative of **late** ▷ *adv* **2** afterwards
lateral (**lat**-ter-al) *adj* of or relating to the side or sides **laterally** *adv*
WORD ORIGIN Latin *latus* side
lateral thinking *n* a way of solving problems by apparently illogical methods
latest *adj, adv* **1** the superlative of **late** ▷ *adj* **2** most recent, modern, or new: *the latest fashions* ▷ *n* **3 at the latest** no later than the time specified
latex *n* a milky fluid produced by many plants: latex from the rubber plant is used in the manufacture of rubber
WORD ORIGIN Latin: liquid
lath *n, pl* **laths** one of several thin narrow strips of wood used as a supporting framework for plaster or tiles
WORD ORIGIN Old English *lætt*
lathe *n* a machine for shaping metal or wood by turning it against a fixed tool
WORD ORIGIN perhaps from Old Norse
lather *n* **1** foam formed by soap or detergent in water **2** foamy sweat, as produced by a horse **3** *informal* a state of agitation ▷ *vb* **4** to coat or become coated with lather **5** to form a lather **6** *informal* to beat; flog **lathery** *adj*
WORD ORIGIN Old English *lēathor* soap
Latin *n* **1** the language of ancient Rome and the Roman Empire **2** a member of any of those peoples whose languages are derived from Latin ▷ *adj* **3** of the Latin language **4** of those peoples whose languages are derived from Latin **5** of the Roman Catholic Church
WORD ORIGIN Latin *Latinus* of Latium

Latin America *n* those areas of South and Central America whose official languages are Spanish and Portuguese **Latin American** *adj, n*
latish *adj, adv* rather late
latitude *n* **1 a** an angular distance measured in degrees north or south of the equator **b** (*often pl*) a region considered with regard to its distance from the equator **2** scope for freedom of action and thought **latitudinal** *adj*
WORD ORIGIN Latin *latus* broad
latitudinarian *adj* **1** liberal, esp. in religious matters ▷ *n* **2** a person with latitudinarian views
latrine *n* a toilet in a barracks or camp
WORD ORIGIN Latin *lavatrina* bath
latter *n* **1 the latter** the second or second mentioned of two ▷ *adj* **2** near or nearer the end: *the latter half of the season* **3** more advanced in time or sequence; later
WORD ORIGIN Old English *lætra*

≡ **USAGE**
≡ *The latter* should only be used to refer
≡ to the second of two items: *many people*
≡ *choose to go by hovercraft rather than use the*
≡ *ferry, but I prefer the latter.* The last of
≡ three or more items can be referred to
≡ as *the last-named.*

latter-day *adj* present-day; modern
latterly *adv* recently; lately
lattice (**lat**-iss) *n* **1** Also called: **latticework** a framework of strips of wood or metal interlaced in a diagonal pattern **2** a gate, screen, or fence formed of such a framework **3** an array of atoms, ions, or molecules in a crystal, or an array of points indicating their positions in space ▷ *vb* **-ticing, -ticed 4** to make, adorn, or supply with a lattice **latticed** *adj*
WORD ORIGIN Old French *latte* lath
Latvian *adj* **1** from Latvia ▷ *n* **2** a person from Latvia **3** the language of Latvia
laud *literary vb* **1** to praise or glorify ▷ *n* **2** praise or glorification
WORD ORIGIN Latin *laudare* to praise
laudable *adj* deserving praise; commendable **laudability** *n* **laudably** *adv*
laudanum (**lawd**-a-num) *n* a sedative extracted from opium
WORD ORIGIN New Latin
laudatory *adj* (of speech or writing) expressing praise
laugh *vb* **1** to express amusement or happiness by producing a series of inarticulate sounds **2** to utter or express with laughter: *he laughed his derision at the play* **3** to bring or force (oneself) into a certain condition by laughter: *laughing herself silly* **4 laugh at** to make fun of; jeer at **5 laugh up one's sleeve** to laugh secretly ▷ *n* **6** the act or an instance of laughing **7** *informal* a person or thing that causes laughter: *he's a laugh, that one* **8 the last laugh** final success after previous defeat ▶ See also **laugh off** ▷ **laughingly** *adv*
WORD ORIGIN Old English *læhan, hliehhen*
laughable *adj* ridiculous because so obviously inadequate or unsuccessful
laughing gas *n* nitrous oxide used as an anaesthetic: it may cause laughter and exhilaration when inhaled

laughing stock *n* a person or thing that is treated with ridicule
laugh off *vb* to treat (something serious or difficult) lightly
laughter *n* the action or noise of laughing
WORD ORIGIN Old English *hleahtor*
launch¹ *vb* **1** to move (a vessel) into the water, esp. for the first time **2 a** to start off or set in motion: *to launch an appeal* **b** to put (a new product) on the market **3** to set (a rocket, missile, or spacecraft) into motion **4** to involve (oneself) totally and enthusiastically: *Francis launched himself into the transfer market with gusto* **5 launch into** to start talking or writing (about) **6** (usually foll. by *out*) to start (out) on a new enterprise ▷ *n* **7** an act or instance of launching **launcher** *n*
WORD ORIGIN Late Latin *lanceare* to use a lance, hence to set in motion
launch² *n* an open motorboat
WORD ORIGIN Malay *lancharan* boat, from *lanchar* speed
launch pad *or* **launching pad** *n* a platform from which a spacecraft, rocket, or missile is launched
launder *vb* **1** to wash and iron (clothes and linen) **2** to make (money illegally obtained) appear to be legally gained by passing it through foreign banks or legitimate enterprises
WORD ORIGIN Latin *lavare* to wash
Launderette *n* Brit, Austral, & NZ *trademark* an establishment where clothes can be washed and dried, using coin-operated machines. Also called (US, Canad, Austral, NZ): **Laundromat**
laundry *n, pl* **-dries 1** the clothes or linen to be laundered or that have been laundered **2** a place where clothes and linen are washed and ironed
laundry list *n* US & Canad a list of items perceived as being long
laureate (**lor**-ee-at) *adj* **1** *literary* crowned with laurel leaves as a sign of honour ▷ *n* **2** short for **poet laureate** ▷ **laureateship** *n*
WORD ORIGIN Latin *laurea* laurel
laurel *n* **1** a small Mediterranean evergreen tree with glossy leaves **2 laurels** a wreath of laurel, worn on the head as an emblem of victory or honour in classical times **3 laurels** honour, distinction, or fame **4 look to one's laurels** to be on guard against one's rivals **5 rest on one's laurels** to be satisfied with what one has already achieved and stop striving for further success
WORD ORIGIN Latin *laurus*
lav *n* Brit informal short for **lavatory**
lava *n* **1** molten rock discharged by volcanoes **2** any rock formed by the solidification of lava
WORD ORIGIN Latin *lavare* to wash
lavatorial *adj* characterized by frequent reference to excretion: *lavatorial humour*
lavatory *n, pl* **-ries** same as **toilet**
WORD ORIGIN Latin *lavare* to wash
lavender *n* **1** a plant grown for its bluish-purple flowers and as the source of a sweet-smelling oil **2** its dried flowers, used to perfume clothes ▷ *adj* **3** pale bluish-purple
WORD ORIGIN Medieval Latin *lavendula*

lavender water *n* a light perfume made from lavender

lavish *adj* **1** great in quantity or richness: *lavish banquets* **2** very generous in giving **3** extravagant; wasteful: *lavish spending habits* ▷ *vb* **4** to give or spend very generously or in great quantities **lavishly** *adv*
WORD ORIGIN Old French *lavasse* torrent

law *n* **1** a rule or set of rules regulating what may or may not be done by members of a society or community **2** a rule or body of rules made by the legislature or other authority ▶ Related adjectives: **legal, judicial, juridical 3** the control enforced by such rules: *scant respect for the rule of law* **4 the law a** the legal or judicial system **b** the profession or practice of law **c** *informal* the police or a policeman **5 law and order** the policy of strict enforcement of the law, esp. against crime and violence **6** a rule of behaviour: *an unwritten law that Nanny knows best* **7** Also called: **law of nature** a generalization based on a recurring fact or event **8** the science or knowledge of law; jurisprudence **9** a general principle, formula, or rule in mathematics, science, or philosophy: *the law of gravity* **10 the Law** the laws contained in the first five books of the Old Testament **11 go to law** to resort to legal proceedings on some matter **12 lay down the law** to speak in an authoritative manner
WORD ORIGIN Old English *lagu*

law-abiding *adj* obeying the laws: *a law-abiding citizen*

lawbreaker *n* a person who breaks the law **lawbreaking** *n, adj*

lawful *adj* allowed, recognized, or sanctioned by law; legal **lawfully** *adv*

lawgiver *n* **1** the giver of a code of laws **2** Also called: **lawmaker** a maker of laws **lawgiving** *n, adj*

lawless *adj* **1** breaking the law, esp. in a wild or violent way: *lawless butchery* **2** not having laws **lawlessness** *n*

Law Lords *pl n* (in Britain) members of the House of Lords who sit as the highest court of appeal

lawn[1] *n* an area of cultivated and mown grass
WORD ORIGIN Old French *lande*

lawn[2] *n* a fine linen or cotton fabric
WORD ORIGIN probably from *Laon*, town in France where made

lawn mower *n* a hand-operated or power-operated machine for cutting grass

lawn tennis *n* **1** tennis played on a grass court **2** same as **tennis**

lawrencium *n chem* an element artificially produced from californium. Symbol: Lr
WORD ORIGIN after E. O. *Lawrence*, physicist

lawsuit *n* a case in a court of law brought by one person or group against another

lawyer *n* a member of the legal profession who can advise clients about the law and represent them in court

lax *adj* lacking firmness; not strict **laxity** *n*
WORD ORIGIN Latin *laxus* loose

laxative *n* **1** a medicine that induces the emptying of the bowels ▷ *adj* **2** easing the emptying of the bowels
WORD ORIGIN Latin *laxare* to loosen

lay[1] *vb* **lays, laying, laid 1** to put in a low or horizontal position; cause to lie: *Mary laid a clean square of white towelling carefully on the grass* **2** to establish as a basis: *ready to lay your new fashion foundations?* **3** to place or be in a particular state or position: *underneath lay a key* **4** to regard as the responsibility of: *ridiculous attempts to lay the loss at the door of the Admiralty* **5** to put forward: *ruses by which we lay claim on one another* **6** to arrange or prepare: *she would lay her plans* **7** to place in position: *he laid a wreath* **8** (of birds, esp. the domestic hen) to produce (eggs) **9** to make (a bet) with (someone): *I'll lay money he's already gone home* **10** to arrange (a table) for a meal **11** to prepare (a fire) by arranging fuel in the grate **12** *taboo slang* to have sexual intercourse with **13 lay bare** to reveal or explain: *a century of neurophysiology has now laid bare the structures of the brain* **14 lay hold of** to seize or grasp **15 lay oneself open** to make oneself vulnerable (to criticism or attack) **16 lay open** to reveal or disclose **17 lay waste** to destroy completely ▷ *n* **18** the manner or position in which something lies or is placed **19** *taboo, slang* **a** an act of sexual intercourse **b** a sexual partner ▶ See also **lay aside, lay down**, etc.
WORD ORIGIN Old English *lecgan*

⊒ **USAGE**
⊒ In standard English, the verb *lay* can
⊒ only be used with an object, and *lie*
⊒ can only be used without one: *the*
⊒ *Queen laid a wreath; he was lying on the floor.*

lay[2] *vb* the past tense of **lie**[2]

lay[3] *adj* **1** of or involving people who are not members of the clergy **2** nonprofessional or nonspecialist
WORD ORIGIN Greek *laos* people

lay[4] *n* a short narrative poem intended to be sung
WORD ORIGIN Old French *lai*

layabout *n* a lazy person

lay aside *vb* **1** to abandon or reject **2** to put aside (one thing) in order to take up another **3** to store or reserve for future use

lay-by *n* **1** *Brit* a place where drivers can stop by the side of a main road **2** *Austral & NZ* a system of payment whereby a buyer pays a deposit on an article, which is reserved for him or her until he or she has paid the full price

lay down *vb* **1** to place on the ground or a surface **2** to sacrifice: *willing to lay down their lives for the truth* **3** to formulate (a rule or principle) **4** to record (plans) on paper **5** to store or stock: *the speed with which we lay down extra, unwanted fat*

layer *n* **1** a single thickness of something, such as a cover or a coating on a surface **2** a laying hen **3** *horticulture* a shoot that forms its own root while still attached to the parent plant ▷ *vb* **4** to form or make a layer or layers
WORD ORIGIN from LAY[1]

layette *n* a complete set of clothing, bedclothes, and other accessories for a newborn baby

WORD ORIGIN Middle Dutch *laege* box

lay figure *n* **1** an artist's jointed dummy, used esp. for studying effects of drapery **2** a person considered to be subservient or unimportant
WORD ORIGIN Dutch *leeman*, literally: joint-man

lay in *vb* to accumulate and store: *they've already laid in five hundred bottles of great vintages*

lay into *vb informal* to attack or scold severely

layman *or fem* **laywoman** *n, pl* **-men** *or* **-women 1** a person who is not a member of the clergy **2** a person who does not have specialized knowledge of a subject: *the layman's guide to nuclear power*

lay off *vb* **1** to suspend (staff) during a slack period at work **2** *informal* to leave (a person, thing, or activity) alone: *'Lay off the defence counsel bit!' he snapped* ▷ *n* **lay-off 3** a period of imposed unemployment

lay on *vb* **1** to provide or supply: *they laid on a treat for the entourage* **2 lay it on thick** *slang* to exaggerate, esp. when flattering

lay out *vb* **1** to arrange or spread out **2** to plan or design: *the main streets were laid out on a grid system* **3** to prepare (a corpse) for burial or cremation **4** *informal* to spend (money), esp. lavishly **5** *informal* to knock (someone) unconscious ▷ *n* **layout 6** the arrangement or plan of something, such as a building **7** the arrangement of printed material

lay reader *n* **1** *Church of England* a person licensed to conduct religious services other than the Eucharist **2** *RC Church* a layman chosen to read the epistle at Mass

lay up *vb* **1** *informal* to confine through illness: *laid up with a bad cold* **2** to store for future use

laze *vb* **lazing, lazed 1** to be idle or lazy **2** (often foll. by *away*) to spend (time) in idleness ▷ *n* **3** time spent lazing
WORD ORIGIN from *lazy*

lazy *adj* **lazier, laziest 1** not inclined to work or exert oneself **2** done in a relaxed manner with little effort **3** moving in a sluggish manner: *the lazy drift of the bubbles* **lazily** *adv* **laziness** *n*
WORD ORIGIN origin unknown

lazybones *n informal* a lazy person

lb 1 pound (weight)
WORD ORIGIN Latin *libra* **2** *cricket* leg bye

lbw *cricket* leg before wicket

lc 1 in the place cited
WORD ORIGIN Latin *loco citato* **2** *printing* lower case

LCD 1 liquid crystal display **2** Also: **lcd** lowest common denominator

lcm *or* **LCM** lowest common multiple

lea *n* **1** *poetic* a meadow or field **2** grassland
WORD ORIGIN Old English *lēah*

LEA (in Britain) Local Education Authority

leach *vb* **1** to remove or be removed from a substance by a liquid passing through it **2** to lose soluble substances by the action of a liquid passing through
WORD ORIGIN perhaps Old English *leccan* to water

lead[1] *vb* **leading, led 1** to show the way to (an individual or a group) by going with or ahead: *he led her into the house* **2** to guide, control, or direct: *he dismounted and led his horse back* **3** to influence someone to act, think, or behave in a certain way: *researching our family history has led her to correspond with relatives abroad* **4** to have the principal part in (something): *planners led the development of policy* **5** to go at the head of or have the top position in (something): *the pair led the field by almost two minutes* **6** (of a road or way) to be the means of reaching a place: *the footbridge leads on to a fine promenade* **7** to pass or spend: *I've led a happy life* **8** to guide or be guided by physical means: *he took her firmly by the arm and led her home* **9** to direct the course of (water, a rope, or wire) along, or as if along, a channel **10** (foll. by *with*) to have as the most important item: *the Review leads with a critique of A Place of Greater Safety* **11** *Brit music* to play first violin in (an orchestra) **12** to begin a round of cards by putting down the first card ▷ *n* **13** the first or most prominent place **14** example or leadership: *some of his children followed his lead* **15** an advantage over others: *Essex have a lead of 24 points* **16** an indication; clue: *we've got a lead on how the body got into the water* **17** a length of leather, nylon, or chain used to walk or control a dog **18** the principal role in a play, film, or other production, or the person playing such a role **19** the most important news story in a newspaper: *the shooting makes the lead in the Times* **20** the act of playing the first card in a round of cards or the card so played **21** a wire, cable, or other conductor for making an electrical connection ▷ *adj* **22** acting as a leader or lead: *lead singer* ▶ See also **lead off, lead on,** etc.
WORD ORIGIN Old English *lǣdan*

lead[2] *n* **1** a heavy toxic bluish-white metallic element: used in alloys, cable sheaths, paints, and as a radiation shield. Symbol: Pb **2 a** graphite used for drawing **b** a thin stick of this as the core of a pencil **3** a lead weight suspended on a line, used to take soundings of the depth of water **4** lead weights or shot, as used in cartridges or fishing lines **5** a thin strip of lead for holding small panes of glass or pieces of stained glass **6 leads a** thin sheets or strips of lead used as a roof covering **b** a roof covered with such sheets **7** Also called: **leading** *printing* a thin strip of metal, formerly used for spacing between lines of type ▷ *adj* **8** of, relating to, or containing lead ▷ *vb* **9** to surround, cover, or secure with lead or leads
WORD ORIGIN Old English *lēad*

leaded *adj* (of windows) made from many small panes of glass held together by lead strips

leaden *adj* **1** heavy or sluggish: *my limbs felt leaden* **2** of a dull greyish colour: *leaden November sky* **3** made of lead **4** gloomy, spiritless, or lifeless: *hollow characters and leaden dialogue*

leader *n* **1** a person who rules, guides, or inspires others; head **2** *Austral & Brit* the

leading editorial in a newspaper. Also: **leading article 3** *music* the principal first violinist of an orchestra who acts as the conductor's deputy **4** the person or animal who is leading in a race **5** the best or the most successful of its kind: *the company is a world leader in its field* **6** the leading horse or dog in a team **7** a strip of blank film or tape at the beginning of a reel **8** *bot* any of the long slender shoots that grow from the stem or branch of a tree **leadership** *n*

leaderboard *n* a board displaying the current scores of the leading competitors, esp. in a golf tournament

lead-in *n* an introduction to a subject

leading *adj* **1** principal or primary: *the leading designers* **2** in the first position: *the leading driver*

leading aircraftman *n* the rank above aircraftman in the British air force **leading aircraftwoman** *fem n*

leading light *n* an important and influential person in an organization or campaign

leading question *n* a question worded to suggest the desired answer, such as *What do you think of the horrible effects of pollution?*

leading rating *n* a rank in the Royal Navy comparable to a corporal in the army

lead off *vb* to begin

lead on *vb* to trick (someone) into believing or doing something wrong

lead pencil *n* a pencil containing a thin stick of a graphite compound

lead poisoning *n* acute or chronic poisoning by lead

lead time *n* *manufacturing* the time between the design of a product and its production

lead up to *vb* **1** to act as a preliminary or introduction to **2** to approach (a topic) gradually or cautiously

leaf *n, pl* **leaves 1** one of the flat usually green blades attached to the stem of a plant **2** the foliage of a tree or plant: *shrubs have been planted for their leaf interest* **3 in leaf** (of shrubs or trees) with all its leaves fully opened **4** a very thin sheet of metal **5** one of the sheets of paper in a book **6** a hinged, sliding, or detachable part, such as an extension to a table **7 take a leaf out of someone's book** to imitate someone in a particular course of action **8 turn over a new leaf** to begin a new and improved course of behaviour ▷ *vb* **9** (usually foll. by *through*) to turn pages casually or hurriedly without reading them **10** (of plants) to produce leaves **leafless** *adj*
WORD ORIGIN Old English *lēaf*

leafage *n* the leaves of plants

leaflet *n* **1** a sheet of printed matter distributed, usually free, for advertising or information **2** any small leaf **3** one of the divisions of a compound leaf ▷ *vb* **-leting, -leted 4** to distribute leaflets (to)

leaf mould *n* a rich soil consisting of decayed leaves

leafy *adj* **leafier, leafiest 1** covered with leaves **2** having many trees or shrubs: *a leafy suburb*

league[1] *n* **1** an association of people or nations formed to promote the interests of its members **2** an association of sporting clubs that organizes matches between member teams **3** *informal* a class or level: *the guy is not even in the same league* **4 in league (with)** working or planning together with ▷ *vb* **leaguing, leagued 5** to form or be formed into a league
WORD ORIGIN Latin *ligare* to bind

league[2] *n* an obsolete unit of distance of varying length: commonly equal to 3 miles (4.8 km)
WORD ORIGIN Late Latin *leuga, leuca*

leak *n* **1 a** a crack or hole that allows the accidental escape or entrance of liquid, gas, radiation, etc. **b** such escaping or entering liquid, etc. **2** a disclosure of secret information **3** the loss of current from an electrical conductor because of faulty insulation **4** the act or an instance of leaking **5** *slang* urination ▷ *vb* **6** to enter or escape, or allow to enter or escape, through a crack or hole **7** to make (secret information) public, esp. deliberately **leaky** *adj*
WORD ORIGIN from Old Norse

leakage *n* the act, an instance, or the result of leaking: *the leakage of 60 tonnes of oil*

lean[1] *vb* **leaning, leaned** or **leant 1** (foll. by *against, on,* or *upon*) to rest or put (something) so that it rests against a support **2** to bend or make (something) bend from an upright position **3** (foll. by *to* or *towards*) to have or express a tendency or preference ▷ *n* **4** the condition of bending from an upright position ▶ See also **lean on**
WORD ORIGIN Old English *hleonian, hlinian*

lean[2] *adj* **1** (esp. of a person) having a trim body with no surplus flesh **2** (of meat) having little or no fat **3** (of a period) sparse, difficult, or causing hardship: *these are lean days in Baghdad* ▷ *n* **4** the part of meat that contains little or no fat **leanness** *n*
WORD ORIGIN Old English *hlǣne*

leaning *n* a tendency or inclination

lean on *vb* **1** *informal* to try to influence (someone) by using threats **2** to depend on (someone) for help and advice

leant *vb* a past of **lean**[1]

lean-to *n, pl* **-tos** a building with a sloping roof attached to another building or a wall

leap *vb* **leaping, leapt** or **leaped 1** to jump suddenly from one place to another **2** (often foll. by *at*) to move or react quickly **3** to jump over ▷ *n* **4** the act of jumping **5** an abrupt or important change or increase: *a leap to full European union* **6 a leap in the dark** an action performed without knowledge of the consequences **7 by leaps and bounds** with unexpectedly rapid progress
WORD ORIGIN Old English *hlēapan*

leapfrog *n* **1** a children's game in which each player in turn leaps over the others' bent backs ▷ *vb* **-frogging, -frogged 2 a** to play leapfrog **b** to leap over (something) **3** to advance by jumps or stages

Words from Literature
part 16

lighterman *n* another word for a sailor
in and out, hammers going in ship-builders' yards, saws going at timber, clashing engines going at things unknown, pumps going in leaky ships, capstans going, ships going out to sea, and unintelligible sea creatures roaring curses over the bulwarks at respondent lightermen
Great Expectations Charles Dickens

livery *n* servants often wore a uniform known as a livery
suddenly a footman in livery came running out of the wood
Alice's Adventures in Wonderland Lewis Carroll

livid *adj* livid here means pale or ash coloured.
a dirty, livid white
Treasure Island Robert Louis Stevenson

lottery tickets *n* a popular card game
and Mrs. Philips protested that they would have a nice comfortable noisy game of lottery tickets
Pride and Prejudice Jane Austen

lower and upper worlds *phrase* the earth and the heavens are the lower and upper worlds
the changes in the lower and upper world
Gulliver's Travels Jonathan Swift

lustres *n* lustres are chandeliers. A chandelier is a large, decorative frame which holds light bulbs or candles and hangs from the ceiling
the lustres, lights, the carving and the guilding
The Prelude William Wordsworth

lynch *v* if a crowd lynch someone they kill him or her without a criminal trial
He'll never know how nigh he come to getting lynched
The Adventures of Huckleberry Finn Mark Twain

malinger *v* if someone is malingering they are pretending to be ill to avoid working
And you stand there malingering
Treasure Island Robert Louis Stevenson

manage *v* to treat with consideration
to think the honour of my own kind not worth managing
Gulliver's Travels Jonathan Swift

manhood *n* manhood means human nature
concerning the nature of manhood
Gulliver's Travels Jonathan Swift

man-trap *n* a man-trap is a set of steel jaws that snap shut when trodden on, and trap a person's leg
"Don't go to him," I called out of the window, "he's an assassin! A man-trap!"
Oliver Twist Charles Dickens

map *n* a chart of the night sky
Let maps to others, worlds on worlds have shown
The Good-Morrow John Donne

mark *v* to look at or notice
Mark but this flea, and mark in this
The Flea John Donne

maroon *n* someone who has been left in a place which is difficult to escape from, like a small island
if schooners, islands, and maroons
Treasure Island Robert Louis Stevenson

mast *n* here mast means the fruit of forest trees
a quantity of acorns, dates, chestnuts, and other mast
Gulliver's Travels Jonathan Swift

mate *v* to defeat
Where Mars did mate the warlike Carthigens
Doctor Faustus Chorus Christopher Marlowe

mealy *adj* when used to describe a face meant palid, pale or colourless
I only know two sorts of boys. Mealy boys, and beef-faced boys
Oliver Twist Charles Dickens

middling *adv* fairly or moderately
she worked me middling hard for about an hour
The Adventures of Huckleberry Finn Mark Twain

leap year *n* a calendar year of 366 days, February 29 (**leap day**) being the additional day, that occurs every four years

learn *vb* **learning, learned** *or* **learnt** **1** to gain knowledge (of something) or acquire skill in (some art or practice) **2** to memorize (something) **3** to gain by experience, example, or practice: *I learned everything the hard way* **4** (often foll. by *of* or *about*) to become informed; find out: *Captain Nelson learned of the disaster from his wireless* **learnable** *adj* **learner** *n* **WORD ORIGIN** Old English *leornian*

learned (**lurn**-id) *adj* **1** having great knowledge **2** involving or characterized by scholarship: *your learned paper on the subject*

learning *n* knowledge gained by studying

lease *n* **1** a contract by which an owner rents buildings or land to another person for a specified period **2** **a new lease of life** a prospect of renewed energy, health, or happiness ▷ *vb* **leasing, leased** **3** to let or rent (land or buildings) by lease **WORD ORIGIN** Old French *laissier* to let go

leasehold *n* **1** land or property held under a lease **2** the holding of such property under lease **leaseholder** *n*

leash *n* **1** a dog's lead **2** **straining at the leash** eagerly impatient to begin something ▷ *vb* **3** to put a leash on **WORD ORIGIN** Old French *laissier* to loose (hence to let a dog run on a leash)

least *adj, adv* **1** **the least** the superlative of **little**: *without encountering the least sign of civilization; he is the least well-educated prime minister* ▷ *adj* **2** of very little importance **3** smallest ▷ *adv* **4** **at least** if nothing else: *at least I wrote* **5** **at the least** at the minimum: *at the very least you should have some self respect* **6** **not in the least** not at all: *you're not detaining me, not in the least* **WORD ORIGIN** Old English *lǣst*, superlative of *lǣssa* less

leastways *or US & Canad* **leastwise** *adv* informal at least; anyway

leather *n* **1** the skin of an animal made smooth and flexible by tanning and removing the hair **2** **leathers** leather clothes, esp. as worn by motorcyclists ▷ *adj* **3** made of leather ▷ *vb* **4** to whip as if with a leather strap **5** to dress in leather **WORD ORIGIN** Old English *lether-* (in compound words)

leatherjacket *n* **1** any of various tropical fishes having a leathery skin **2** the tough-skinned larva of certain crane flies, which destroy the roots of grasses

leathery *adj* looking or feeling like leather, esp. in toughness

leave[1] *vb* **leaving, left** **1** to go away (from a person or place) **2** to cause to remain behind, often by mistake, in a place: *I left the paper under the table* **3** to cause to be or remain in a specified state: *the poll leaves the parties neck-and-neck* **4** to stop attending or belonging to a particular organization or institution: *at seventeen she left the convent* **5** to not eat something or not deal with something: *he left a half-eaten lunch* **6** to result in; cause:

I have been terribly hurt by women, it leaves indelible marks **7** to allow (someone) to do something without interfering: *the governor left them to it for a further few hours* **8** to be survived by (members of one's family): *he leaves a widow and one daughter* **9** to bequeath: *her adored son left his millions to an unknown half-sister* **10** to have as a remainder: *37 – 14 leaves 23* **11** **leave (someone) alone** **a** to stop annoying (someone) **b** to permit to stay or be alone ▶ See also **leave off, leave out** **WORD ORIGIN** Old English *lǣfan*

leave[2] *n* **1** permission to be absent, for instance from work: *so I asked for leave* **2** the length of such absence: *weekend leave* **3** permission to do something: *they were refused leave to appeal* **4** **on leave** officially excused from work or duty **5** **take (one's) leave of** to say farewell to **WORD ORIGIN** Old English *lēaf*

leaven (**lev**-ven) *n also* **leavening** **1** any substance, such as yeast, that produces fermentation in dough and makes it rise **2** an influence that produces a gradual change ▷ *vb* **3** to cause fermentation in (dough) **4** to spread through, causing a gradual change **WORD ORIGIN** Latin *levare* to raise

leave off *vb* **1** to stop; cease **2** to stop wearing or using

leave out *vb* to omit or exclude: *leave out everything not necessary to living*

leaves *n* the plural of **leaf**

leave-taking *n* a departing; a farewell

leavings *pl n* things left behind unwanted, such as food on a plate

Lebanese *adj* **1** from the Lebanon ▷ *n, pl* **-nese** **2** a person from the Lebanon

Lebensraum (**lay**-benz-rowm) *n* territory claimed by a nation or state because it is necessary for survival or growth **WORD ORIGIN** German: living space

lecherous (**letch**-er-uss) *adj* (of a man) having or showing strong and uncontrolled sexual desire **lecher** *n* **lechery** *n* **WORD ORIGIN** Old French *lechier* to lick

lecithin (**less**-sith-in) *n biochem* a yellow-brown compound found in plant and animal tissues, esp. egg yolk: used in making cosmetics and inks, and as an emulsifier and stabilizer (**E322**) in foods **WORD ORIGIN** Greek *lekithos* egg yolk

lectern *n* a sloping reading desk, esp. in a church **WORD ORIGIN** Latin *legere* to read

lecture *n* **1** a talk on a particular subject delivered to an audience **2** a lengthy scolding ▷ *vb* **-turing, -tured** **3** to deliver a lecture (to an audience or class) **4** to scold (someone) at length **lecturer** *n* **lectureship** *n* **WORD ORIGIN** Latin *legere* to read

led *vb* the past of **lead**[1]

LED *electronics* light-emitting diode: a semiconductor that gives out light when an electric current is applied to it

ledge *n* **1** a narrow horizontal surface that projects from a wall or window **2** a narrow shelflike projection on a cliff or mountain **WORD ORIGIN** perhaps Middle English *leggen* to lay

ledger *n* *book-keeping* the principal book in which the commercial transactions of a company are recorded **WORD ORIGIN** perhaps Middle English *leggen* to lay (because kept in a specific place)

ledger line *n* *music* a short line above or below the staff used to indicate the pitch of notes higher or lower than the range of the staff

lee *n* **1** a sheltered part or side; the side away from the direction from which the wind is blowing ▷ *adj* **2** *naut* on, at, or towards the side away from the wind: *her lee rail was awash* **WORD ORIGIN** Old English *hlēow* shelter

leech *n* **1** a worm which has a sucker at each end of the body and feeds on the blood or tissues of other animals **2** a person who lives off another person; parasite **WORD ORIGIN** Old English *lǣce*

leek *n* a vegetable of the onion family with a slender white bulb and broad flat green overlapping leaves: the national emblem of Wales **WORD ORIGIN** Old English *lēac*

leer *vb* **1** to give a sneering or suggestive look or grin ▷ *n* **2** such a look **WORD ORIGIN** Old English *hlēor* cheek

leery *adj* **leerier, leeriest** **1** *slang* (foll. by *of*) suspicious or wary **2** *now chiefly dialect* knowing or sly **WORD ORIGIN** perhaps obsolete sense (to look askance) of *leer*

lees *pl n* the sediment from an alcoholic drink **WORD ORIGIN** plural of obsolete *lee*, from Old French

leet *n* *Scot* a list of candidates for an office **WORD ORIGIN** perhaps Anglo-French *litte*, variant of **LIST**[1]

leeward *chiefly naut* *adj* **1** of, in, or moving in the direction towards which the wind blows ▷ *n* **2** the side towards the lee ▷ *adv* **3** towards the lee

leeway *n* **1** flexibility of action or expenditure: *he gave me a lot of leeway in the work I did* **2** sideways drift of a boat or aircraft

left[1] *adj* **1** denoting the side of something or someone that faces west when the front is turned towards the north **2** on the left side of the body: *I grabbed it with my left hand* **3** liberal, radical, or socialist ▷ *adv* **4** on or in the direction of the left ▷ *n* **5** a left side, direction, position, area, or part **6** **the left** the people in a political party or society who have more socialist or liberal views: *the biggest party of the French Left* **7** *boxing* **a** a blow with the left hand **b** the left hand **WORD ORIGIN** Old English: idle, weak

left[2] *vb* the past of **leave**[1]

left field *n* **1** *baseball* **a** the area of the outfield to the batter's left **b** the fielder who covers this area **2** **out of left field** unexpected or surprising: *Their proposal came out of left field* ▷ *adj* **3** *US & Canad informal* unconventional or outside the mainstream

left-hand *adj* **1** of, on, or towards the left **2** for the left hand

left-handed *adj* **1** better at using the left hand than the right **2** done with the left hand **3** designed for use by the left hand **4** awkward or clumsy **5** ambiguous or insincere: *a left-handed compliment* **6** turning from right to left; anticlockwise ▷ *adv* **7** with the left hand: *I write left-handed* **left-hander** *n*

leftist *adj* **1** of or relating to the political left or its principles ▷ *n* **2** a person who supports the political left **leftism** *n*

left-luggage office *n* Brit a place at a railway station or airport where luggage may be left for a small charge

leftover *n* **1** (*often pl*) an unused portion, esp. of cooked food ▷ *adj* **2** left as an unused portion

leftward *adj, adv also* **leftwards** on or towards the left

left-wing *adj* **1** socialist or radical: *the party ditched many of its more left-wing policies* **2** belonging to the more radical part of a political party: *a group of left-wing Conservatives* ▷ *n* **left wing 3** (*often cap*) the more radical or progressive section, esp. of a political party: *the Left Wing of the Labour Party* **4** *sport* **a** the left-hand side of the field of play **b** a player positioned in this area in certain games **left-winger** *n*

lefty *n, pl* **lefties** *informal* **1** Brit, Austral, & NZ a left-winger **2** chiefly US & Canad a left-handed person

leg *n* **1** either of the two lower limbs in humans, or any similar structure in animals, that is used for movement or support **2** the part of a garment that covers the leg **3** a lower limb of an animal, esp. the thigh, used for food: *leg of lamb* **4** something similar to a leg in appearance or function, such as one of the supports of a chair **5** a section of a journey **6** a single stage, lap, or length in a relay race **7** one of a series of games, matches, or parts of games **8** *cricket* the side of the field to the left of a right-handed batsman as he faces the bowler **9 not have a leg to stand on** *informal* to have no reasonable basis for an opinion or argument **10 on one's last legs** worn out or exhausted **11 to pull someone's leg** *informal* to tease or make fun of someone **12 shake a leg** *informal* to hurry up **13 stretch one's legs** to stand up or walk around, esp. after sitting for some time ▷ *vb* **legging, legged 14 leg it** *informal* to walk, run, or hurry
WORD ORIGIN Old Norse *leggr*

legacy *n, pl* **-cies 1** money or personal property left to someone by a will **2** something handed down to a successor
WORD ORIGIN Medieval Latin *legatia* commission

legal *adj* **1** established by or permitted by law; lawful **2** of or relating to law **3** relating to or characteristic of lawyers **legally** *adv*
WORD ORIGIN Latin *legalis*

legal aid *n* financial assistance available to people who are unable to meet the full cost of legal proceedings

legalese *n* the conventional language in which legal documents are written

legalism *n* strict adherence to the letter of the law **legalist** *n, adj* **legalistic** *adj*

legality *n, pl* **-ties** the state or quality of being legal or lawful

legalize *or* **-lise** *vb* **-lizing, -lized** *or* **-lising, -lised** to make lawful or legal **legalization** *or* **-lisation** *n*

legal tender *n* currency that a creditor must by law accept to pay a debt

legate *n* a messenger, esp. one representing the Pope
WORD ORIGIN Latin *legare* to delegate

legatee *n* the recipient of a legacy

legation *n* **1** a diplomatic mission headed by a minister **2** the official residence and office of a diplomatic minister

legato (leg-**ah**-toe) *music adv* **1** smoothly and evenly ▷ *n, pl* **-tos 2** a style of playing with no gaps between notes
WORD ORIGIN Italian

leg before wicket *n* cricket a dismissal on the grounds that a batsman has been struck on the leg by a bowled ball that otherwise would have hit the wicket. Abbrev: **lbw**

leg break *n* cricket a bowled ball that spins from leg to off on pitching

leg bye *n* cricket a run scored after the ball has hit the batsman's leg or some other part of his body, except his hand, without touching the bat. Abbrev: **lb**

legend *n* **1** a popular story handed down from earlier times which may or may not be true **2** such stories collectively **3** a person whose fame makes him or her seem exceptional: *he is a living legend* **4** modern stories about a famous person which may or may not be true: *no Garland fan could complain about sordid revelations tarnishing the legend* **5** words written on something to explain it: *a pub mirror spelling out the legend 'Saloon Bar'* **6** an explanation on a table, map, or chart, of the symbols used
WORD ORIGIN Medieval Latin *legenda* passages to be read

legendary *adj* **1** very famous: *the legendary beauty of the Alps* **2** of or relating to legend **3** described in legend: *the legendary birthplace of Aphrodite*

legerdemain (lej-er-de-**main**) *n* **1** same as **sleight of hand 2** cunning deception
WORD ORIGIN Old French: light of hand

leger line *n* same as **ledger line**

leggings *pl n* **1** an extra outer covering for the lower legs **2** close-fitting trousers for women or children

leggy *adj* **1** having unusually long legs **2** (of a plant) having a long weak stem

leghorn *n* **1** a type of Italian wheat straw that is woven into hats **2** any hat made from this straw
WORD ORIGIN English name for *Livorno*, in Italy

Leghorn (leg-**gorn**) *n* a breed of domestic fowl

legible *adj* (of handwriting) able to be read **legibility** *n* **legibly** *adv*
WORD ORIGIN Latin *legere* to read

legion *n* **1** any large military force: *the French Foreign Legion* **2** (*often pl*) any very large number **3** an infantry unit in the ancient Roman army of three to six thousand men **4** an association of veterans **legionary** *adj, n*
WORD ORIGIN Latin *legio*

legionnaire *n* (*often cap*) a member of a legion

Legionnaire's disease *n* a serious bacterial infection, with symptoms similar to pneumonia
WORD ORIGIN after the outbreak at a meeting of the American Legion in Philadelphia in 1976

legislate *vb* **-lating, -lated 1** to make or pass laws **2** to bring into effect by legislation **legislator** *n*
WORD ORIGIN Latin *lex, legis* law + *latus*, past participle of *ferre* to bring

legislation *n* **1** the act or process of making laws **2** the laws so made

legislative *adj* **1** of or relating to the process of making laws **2** having the power or function of making laws: *the election to Singapore's new legislative assembly*

legislature *n* a body of people authorized to make, amend, and repeal laws

legitimate *adj* **1** authorized by or in accordance with law: *legitimate accounting practices* **2** based on correct or acceptable principles of reasoning: *a legitimate argument* **3** (of a child) born of parents legally married to each other **4** of, relating to, or ruling by hereditary right: *under their legitimate ruling house* **5** of or relating to serious drama as distinct from films, television, or vaudeville ▷ *vb* **-mating, -mated 6** to make, pronounce, or show to be legitimate **legitimacy** *n* **legitimately** *adv*
WORD ORIGIN Medieval Latin *legitimatus* made legal

legitimize *or* **-mise** *vb* **-mizing, -mized** *or* **-mising, -mised** to make legitimate; legalize **legitimization** *or* **-misation** *n*

legless *adj* **1** without legs **2** slang very drunk

Lego *n* trademark a construction toy consisting of plastic bricks and other components that fit together
WORD ORIGIN Danish *leg godt* play well

leg-pull *n* Brit informal a practical joke

legroom *n* space to move one's legs comfortably, as in a car

leguaan *n* a large amphibious S African lizard
WORD ORIGIN Dutch, from French *l'iguane* the iguana

legume *n* **1** the pod of a plant of the pea or bean family **2** the seed from such pods, esp. beans or peas
WORD ORIGIN Latin *legere* to pick (a crop)

leguminous *adj* of or relating to any family of flowering plants having pods (or legumes) as fruits

lei *n* (in Hawaii) a garland of flowers, worn around the neck
WORD ORIGIN Hawaiian

Leics Leicestershire

leisure *n* **1** time or opportunity for relaxation or hobbies **2 at leisure a** having free time **b** not occupied **3 at one's leisure** when one has free time **leisured** *adj*
WORD ORIGIN Old French *leisir*

leisure centre *n* a building providing facilities, such as a swimming pool, gym, and café, for a range of leisure pursuits

leisurely *adj* **1** unhurried; relaxed ▷ *adv* **2** in a relaxed way **leisureliness** *n*

leitmotif or **leitmotiv** (lite-mote-eef) n **1** music a recurring melodic phrase used to suggest a character, thing, or idea **2** an often repeated image in a literary work **WORD ORIGIN** German: leading motif

lekgotla (leh-hot-luh), **kgotla** (**hot**-luh) n S African **1** a meeting place for village assemblies, court cases, and meetings of village leaders **2** a conference or business meeting **WORD ORIGIN** Sotho, Tswana

lekker adj S African slang pleasing, enjoyable, or tasty **WORD ORIGIN** Afrikaans, from Dutch

lemming n **1** a small rodent of northern and arctic regions, reputed to rush into the sea in large groups and drown **2** a member of any group following an unthinking course towards destruction **WORD ORIGIN** Norwegian

lemon n **1** a yellow oval edible fruit with juicy acidic flesh that grows on an evergreen tree in warm and tropical regions **2** slang a person or thing considered to be useless or defective ▷ adj **3** light yellow **lemony** adj **WORD ORIGIN** Arabic laymūn

lemonade n a drink made from lemon juice, sugar, and water, or from carbonated water, citric acid, and sweetener

lemon sole n an edible European flatfish

lemur n a nocturnal animal, related to the monkey, with a foxy face and long tail, found on Madagascar **WORD ORIGIN** Latin lemures ghosts

lend vb **lending**, **lent** **1** to permit the temporary use of **2** to provide (money) temporarily, often at interest **3** to contribute (some abstract quality): a painted trellis lends a classical air to any garden **4** **lend an ear** to listen **5** **lend oneself** or **itself** to be appropriate for: the building lends itself to loft conversion **lender** n **WORD ORIGIN** Old English lēnan

length n **1** the extent or measurement of something from end to end **2** a specified distance, esp. between two positions: the length of a cricket-pitch **3** a period of time, as between specified limits or moments **4** the quality, state, or fact of being long rather than short **5** a piece of something, usually longer than it is wide: a length of twine **6** (usually pl) the amount of trouble taken in doing something: to go to great lengths **7** prosody, phonetics the duration of a vowel or syllable **8** **at length a** after a long interval or period of time **b** in great detail **WORD ORIGIN** Old English lengthu

lengthen vb to make or become longer

lengthways or **lengthwise** adv, adj in, according to, or along the direction of length

lengthy adj **lengthier**, **lengthiest** very long or tiresome **lengthily** adv **lengthiness** n

lenient (lee-nee-ent) adj tolerant, not strict or severe **leniency** n **leniently** adv **WORD ORIGIN** Latin lenis soft

lenity n, pl **-ties** mercy or clemency

lens n **1** a piece of glass or other transparent material with a curved surface or surfaces, used to bring together or spread rays of light passing through it: used in cameras, telescopes, and spectacles **2** anat a transparent structure in the eye, behind the iris, that focuses images on the retina **WORD ORIGIN** Latin: lentil

lent vb the past of **lend**

Lent n Christianity the period from Ash Wednesday to Easter Saturday, during which some Christians give up doing something they enjoy **Lenten** adj **WORD ORIGIN** Old English lencten, lengten spring, literally: lengthening (of hours of daylight)

lentil n any of the small edible seeds of a leguminous Asian plant **WORD ORIGIN** Latin lens

lento music adv **1** slowly ▷ n, pl **-tos** **2** a movement or passage performed slowly **WORD ORIGIN** Italian

Leo n astrol the fifth sign of the zodiac; the Lion **WORD ORIGIN** Latin

leonine adj of or like a lion **WORD ORIGIN** Latin leo lion

leopard or fem **leopardess** n a large African and Asian mammal of the cat family, which has a tawny yellow coat with black spots. Also called: **panther** **WORD ORIGIN** Greek leōn lion + pardos panther

leotard n a tight-fitting garment covering the body from the shoulders to the thighs and worn by acrobats, ballet dancers, and people doing exercises **WORD ORIGIN** after Jules Léotard, acrobat

leper n **1** a person who has leprosy **2** a person who is avoided **WORD ORIGIN** Greek lepros scaly

lepidopteran n, pl **-terans** or **-tera** **1** an insect that has two pairs of fragile wings and develops from a caterpillar; a butterfly or moth ▷ adj also **lepidopterous** **2** denoting such an insect **WORD ORIGIN** Greek lepis scale + pteron wing

lepidopterist n a person who studies or collects moths and butterflies

leprechaun n (in Irish folklore) a mischievous elf **WORD ORIGIN** Irish Gaelic leipreachān

leprosy n pathol a chronic infectious disease, characterized by painful inflamed lumps beneath the skin and disfigurement and wasting away of affected parts **leprous** adj

lepton n physics any of a group of elementary particles with weak interactions **WORD ORIGIN** Greek leptos thin

lesbian n **1** a female homosexual ▷ adj **2** of or characteristic of lesbians **lesbianism** n **WORD ORIGIN** Lesbos, Greek Aegean island

lese-majesty (lezz-**maj**-ist-ee) n **1** an offence against the sovereign power in a state; treason **2** an act of disrespect towards authority **WORD ORIGIN** from Latin laesa majestas wounded majesty

lesion n **1** any structural change in an organ or tissue resulting from injury or disease **2** an injury or wound **WORD ORIGIN** Late Latin laesio injury

less adj **1** the comparative of **little**: less fibre **2** not standard fewer ▷ adv **3** the comparative of **little**: eat less **4** **less of** to a smaller extent or degree: it would become less of a problem **5** **no less** sometimes ironic used to indicate admiration or surprise: sculpted by a famous Frenchman, Rodin no less ▷ prep **6** minus: a two pounds-a-week rise (less tax) **WORD ORIGIN** Old English læssa, læs

≡ **USAGE**
≡ Less should not be confused with fewer.
≡ Less refers strictly only to quantity
≡ and not to number: there is less water
≡ than before. Fewer means smaller in
≡ number: there are fewer people than before.

lessee n a person to whom a lease is granted **WORD ORIGIN** Old French lesser to lease

lessen vb to make or become less

lesser adj not as great in quantity, size, or worth

lesson n **1 a** a single period of instruction in a subject **b** the content of such a period **2** material assigned for individual study **3** something from which useful knowledge or principles can be learned: one could still learn an important lesson from these masters **4** an experience that serves as a warning or example: the experience will prove a sobering lesson for the military **5** a passage of Scripture read during a church service **WORD ORIGIN** Old French leçon

lessor n a person who grants a lease of property

lest conj **1** so as to prevent any possibility that: one grabbed it lest a neighbour got there first **2** for fear that: his anxiety lest anything mar the family event **WORD ORIGIN** Old English thȳ læs the, literally: whereby less that

let¹ vb **letting**, **let** **1** to allow: a child lets a friend play with his favourite toy **2 a** an auxiliary expressing a request, proposal, or command, or conveying a warning or threat: well, let's try it; just let me catch you here again! **b** an auxiliary expressing an assumption or hypothesis: let 'a' equal 'b' **c** an auxiliary used to convey resigned acceptance of the inevitable: let the worst happen **3** to allow someone to rent (property or accommodation) **4** to cause the movement of (something) in a specified direction: this lets aluminium creep into the brain **5** **let alone** not to mention: I could hardly think, let alone find words to say **6** **let alone** or **be** stop annoying or interfering with: let the poor cat alone **7** **let go** to relax one's hold (on) **8** **let loose a** to allow (a person or animal) to leave or escape **b** informal to make (a sound) suddenly: he let loose a laugh **c** informal to fire (ammunition) from a gun ▷ n **9** Austral & Brit the act of letting property or accommodation ▶ See also **let down**, **let off**, etc. **WORD ORIGIN** Old English lǣtan to permit

let² n **1** tennis, squash a minor infringement or obstruction of the ball, requiring a point to be replayed

Toponyms

There are only so many ways that words come into being. Most of the words in the English language can be traced back to roots in other languages (chiefly Latin, Greek, French, and Anglo-Saxon). Others arise out of blending existing words together, or making up words from strings of initial letters (as in *laser* and *wysiwyg*).

Words that don't come from any of these sources are often taken from names. There are words that are named after people – often the person who invented or popularized something – such as *sandwich* and *cardigan*. These are called 'eponyms'. Then there are words that are named after places – often the place from which an object comes – which can be called 'toponyms'.

The most obvious toponyms link the place of origin to an object quite explicitly. We are accustomed to thinking of cheeses (*Camembert, Cheddar, Edam*) and wines (*Bordeaux, Chianti, Champagne*) as having names that reveal their geographical origins. Other items of food similarly boast their origins in their names: *Parma ham, Dundee cake, Worcester sauce, Turkish delight*.

Items of clothing are frequently named after the place where they were originally made or worn: think of the *Panama hat*, the *Norfolk jacket*, and the *Hawaiian shirt*. Then there are the many breeds of animal whose names indicate their place of origin. Cats can be *Manx, Persian, Siamese*, or *Abyssinian*. Amongst the more familiar breeds of dog are *Labradors, German shepherds*, and *Yorkshire terriers*. *Chihuahuas* are named after a region of Mexico, and *Rottweilers* come from the German town of Rottweil.

However, not all toponyms reveal their origins so brazenly. Some of the more interesting word histories reveal a place name lurking unexpectedly behind an everyday word. The word *denim*, for example, comes from the French phrase *de Nîmes*, because the hard-wearing cloth was originally woven in the French town of Nîmes. The word *bunkum* immortalizes Buncombe County in North Carolina, whose Congressional representative brought the place into disrepute in the early part of the 19th century by making a rambling speech about it, so that afterwards people who spoke for a long time but with little purpose were said to 'talk Bunkum'.

Places from all over the world have contributed their names to the English language: *Lima beans* are named after the capital of Peru; Venezuela is the source of *Angostura bitters*; the city of *Fez*, which gives its name to the famous brimless hat, is in Morocco; the word *coach* comes from the village of Kocs in Hungary; the Syrian capital Damascus is the origin of the word *damson*.

Even a place as notoriously unspectacular as Belgium has provided several common English words. *Brussels* is of course responsible for the *Brussels sprout*; the name of the city of *Spa* has come to be a generic word for a health resort; the town of *Duffel* has given its name to the *duffel bag* and *duffel coat*; *Mechlin* gives its name to a type of lace, and *Limburg* to a cheese; while the expression 'to meet one's Waterloo' alludes to the defeat of Napoleon in battle near the small town of *Waterloo* just to the south of Brussels.

Indeed, places such as Waterloo and Duffel can achieve a significance in language out of all proportion to their physical size. The name of *Rugby* in Warwickshire is frequently on the lips of people who have no acquaintance with the place but who are enthusiasts for the sport named after it. It is doubtful, however, whether many people who talk about rugby give much thought to the place that gave the sport its name. The same is true of the village of *Badminton* in Gloucestershire, where another sport was first played. As the words that are coined from place names become more familiar for their own sakes, so the connection with the places behind the words becomes weaker in the mind of the user.

2 without let or hindrance without obstruction
WORD ORIGIN Old English *lettan* to hinder

let down *vb* **1** to fail to satisfy the expectations of (someone); disappoint **2** to lower **3** to lengthen a garment by decreasing the hem **4** to deflate: *to let down a tyre* ▷ *n* **letdown 5** a disappointment

lethal *adj* capable of causing death
lethally *adv*
WORD ORIGIN Latin *letum* death

lethargy *n, pl* **-gies 1** sluggishness or dullness **2** an abnormal lack of energy
lethargic *adj* **lethargically** *adv*
WORD ORIGIN Greek *lēthargos* drowsy

let off *vb* **1** to excuse from (work or duties): *I'll let you off homework for a week* **2** *informal* to spare (someone) the expected punishment: *lots were let off because they couldn't be bothered to prosecute anybody* **3** to explode or fire (a bomb, gun, or firework) **4** to release (liquid, air, or steam)

let on *vb informal* **1** to reveal (a secret) **2** to pretend: *he let on that he was a pilgrim*

let out *vb* **1** to emit: *he let out a scream* **2** to allow to leave; release **3** to make (property) available for people to rent **4** to make (a garment) wider by reducing the seams **5** to reveal (a secret) ▷ *n* **let-out 6** a chance to escape

letter *n* **1** a written or printed message, usually enclosed in an envelope and sent by post **2** any of a set of conventional symbols used in writing or printing a language: character of the alphabet **3** the strict meaning of an agreement or document; exact wording: *the letter of the law* **4 to the letter** precisely: *you have to follow treatment to the letter for it to be effective* ▷ *vb* **5** to write or mark letters on (a sign) **lettering** *n*
WORD ORIGIN Latin *littera* letter of the alphabet

letter bomb *n* an explosive device in an envelope or parcel that explodes when the envelope or parcel is opened

letter box *n chiefly Brit* **1** a slot in a door through which letters are delivered **2** Also called: **pillar box, postbox** a public box into which letters and postcards are put for collection

lettered *adj* **1** well educated **2** printed or marked with letters

letterhead *n* a printed heading on stationery giving the name and address of the sender

letter of credit *n* a letter issued by a bank entitling the bearer to draw money from other banks

letterpress *n* a method of printing in which ink is transferred from raised surfaces to paper by pressure

letters *pl n* **1** literary knowledge or ability: *a man of letters* **2** literary culture in general

letters patent *pl n* see **patent** (senses 1, 3)

lettuce *n* a plant cultivated for its large edible leaves, which are used in salads
WORD ORIGIN Latin *lactuca*, from *lac* milk, because of its milky juice

let up *vb* **1** to diminish or stop **2** (foll. by *on*) *informal* to be less harsh (towards someone) ▷ *n* **let-up 3** *informal* a lessening: *there has been no let-up in the war*

leucocyte (**loo**-koh-site) *n* any of the various large white cells in the blood of vertebrates
WORD ORIGIN Greek *leukos* white + *kutos* vessel

leukaemia *or esp. US* **leukemia** (loo-**kee**-mee-a) *n* an acute or chronic disease characterized by extreme overproduction of white blood cells
WORD ORIGIN Greek *leukos* white + *haima* blood

levee¹ *n US* **1** a natural or artificial river embankment **2** a quay
WORD ORIGIN French, from Latin *levare* to raise

levee² *n* a formal reception held by a sovereign just after rising from bed
WORD ORIGIN French, from Latin *levare* to raise

level *adj* **1** on a horizontal plane **2** having an even surface **3** being of the same height as something else: *the floor of the lean-to was level with the patio* **4** equal to or even with (something or someone else): *Johnson was level with the overnight leader* **5** not exceeding the upper edge of (a spoon etc.) **6** consistent or regular: *a level pulse* **7 one's level best** the best one can do ▷ *vb* **-velling, -velled** *or US* **-veling, -veled 8** (sometimes foll. by *off*) to make horizontal or even **9** to make equal in position or status **10** to direct (an accusation or criticism) emphatically at someone **11** to focus (a look) directly at someone **12** to aim (a weapon) horizontally **13** to demolish completely ▷ *n* **14** a horizontal line or plane **15** a device, such as a spirit level, for determining whether a surface is horizontal **16** position or status in a scale of values: *a high-level delegation* **17** stage or degree of progress: *primary school level* **18** a specified vertical position: *floor level* **19** the topmost horizontal line or plane from which the height of something is calculated: *sea level* **20** a flat even surface or area of land **21** a degree or intensity reached on a measurable or notional scale: *noise level* **22 on the level** *informal* sincere or genuine
WORD ORIGIN Latin *libella*, diminutive of *libra* scales

level crossing *n Brit, Austral, & NZ* a point at which a railway line and a road cross

level-headed *adj* calm and sensible

lever *n* **1** a handle used to operate machinery **2** a bar used to move a heavy object or to prise something open **3** a rigid bar that turns on a fixed support (fulcrum) to transfer effort and motion, for instance to move a load **4** a means of exerting pressure in order to achieve an aim: *using the hostages as a lever to gain concessions from the west* ▷ *vb* **5** to open or move with a lever
WORD ORIGIN Latin *levare* to raise

leverage *n* **1** the mechanical advantage gained by using a lever **2** the ability to influence people or events: *information gives leverage*

leveraged buyout *n* a takeover bid in which a small company uses its assets, and those of the target company, to raise the loans required to finance the takeover

leveret (**lev**-ver-it) *n* a young hare
WORD ORIGIN Latin *lepus* hare

leviathan (lev-**vie**-ath-an) *n* any huge or powerful thing
WORD ORIGIN Hebrew *liwyāthān*, a Biblical sea monster

Levis *pl n trademark* denim jeans

levitate *vb* **-tating, -tated** to rise or cause to rise, suspended, in the air
levitation *n*
WORD ORIGIN Latin *levis* light

levity *n, pl* **-ties** a frivolous or too light-hearted attitude to serious matters
WORD ORIGIN Latin *levis* light

levy (**lev**-vee) *vb* **levies, levying, levied 1** to impose and collect (a tax, tariff, or fine) **2** to conscript troops for service ▷ *n, pl* **levies 3 a** the imposition and collection of taxes, tariffs, or fines **b** the money so raised **4** troops conscripted for service
WORD ORIGIN Latin *levare* to raise

lewd *adj* indecently vulgar; obscene
lewdly *adv* **lewdness** *n*
WORD ORIGIN Old English *lǣwde* lay, ignorant

lexical *adj* **1** relating to the vocabulary of a language **2** relating to a lexicon
lexically *adv*

lexicography *n* the process or profession of compiling dictionaries
lexicographer *n*

lexicon *n* **1** a dictionary, esp. one of an ancient language such as Greek **2** the vocabulary of a language or of an individual
WORD ORIGIN Greek *lexis* word

ley *n* land temporarily under grass
WORD ORIGIN variant of *lea*

Leyden jar (**lide**-en) *n physics* an early type of capacitor consisting of a glass jar with the lower part of the inside and outside coated with tinfoil
WORD ORIGIN from *Leiden*, city in the Netherlands

LGBT lesbian, gay, bisexual, and transgender

LGV (in Britain) large goods vehicle

Li *chem* lithium

liability *n, pl* **-ties 1** someone or something that is a problem or embarrassment **2** the state of being legally responsible **3** (*often pl*) sums of money owed by an organization

liable *adj* **1** probable or likely: *weak and liable to give way* **2** commonly suffering a condition: *he's liable to get colds in his chest* **3** legally obliged or responsible; answerable
WORD ORIGIN Old French *lier* to bind
USAGE
The use of *liable to* to mean *probable or likely* was formerly considered incorrect, but is now acceptable.

liaise *vb* **-aising, -aised** (usually foll. by *with*) to communicate and maintain contact with

liaison *n* **1** communication and cooperative contact between groups

2 a secretive or adulterous sexual relationship
WORD ORIGIN Old French *lier* to bind

liana *n* a woody climbing and twining plant of tropical forests
WORD ORIGIN French

liar *n* a person who tells lies

lib *n informal* liberation: used in the name of certain movements: *women's lib; gay lib*

Lib *Brit, Austral, & S African politics* Liberal

libation (lie-**bay**-shun) *n* **a** the pouring out of wine in honour of a deity **b** the wine so poured out
WORD ORIGIN Latin *libare* to pour an offering of drink

libel *n* **1** *law* the publication of something false which damages a person's reputation **2** any damaging or unflattering representation or statement ▷ *vb* **-belling, -belled** *or US* **-beling, -beled 3** *law* to make or publish a false damaging statement or representation about (a person) **libellous** *or* **libelous** *adj*
WORD ORIGIN Latin *libellus* a little book

liberal *adj* **1** having social and political views that favour progress and reform **2** generous in temperament or behaviour **3** tolerant of other people **4** using or existing in large quantities; lavish: *the world's finest gadgetry, in liberal quantities* **5** not rigid; free: *a more liberal interpretation* **6** (of an education) designed to develop general cultural interests and intellectual ability **7 Liberal** of or relating to a Liberal Party ▷ *n* **8** a person who has liberal ideas or opinions **liberalism** *n* **liberally** *adv*
WORD ORIGIN Latin *liber* free

Liberal Democrat *n* a member or supporter of the Liberal Democrats, a British centrist political party that advocates proportional representation

liberality *n, pl* **-ties 1** generosity **2** the quality of being broad-minded

liberalize *or* **-lise** *vb* **-lizing, -lized** *or* **-lising, -lised** to make (a law) less strict **liberalization** *or* **-lisation** *n*

Liberal Party *n* **1** *history* a British non-Socialist political party which advocated progress and reform **2** any similar party in various other countries **3** the main right-wing political party in Australia

liberate *vb* **-rating, -rated 1** to free (someone) from social prejudices or injustices **2** to give liberty to; make free **3** to release (a country) from enemy occupation **liberation** *n* **liberator** *n*

liberated *adj* **1** not bound by traditional sexual and social roles: *a liberated woman* **2** given liberty **3** released from enemy occupation

libertarian *n* **1** a person who believes in freedom of thought and action ▷ *adj* **2** believing in freedom of thought and action

libertine (lib-er-teen) *n* **1** a person who is promiscuous and unscrupulous ▷ *adj* **2** promiscuous and unscrupulous
WORD ORIGIN Latin *libertus* freed

liberty *n, pl* **-ties 1** the freedom to choose, think, and act for oneself **2** the right of unrestricted movement and access; freedom **3** (*often pl*) a social

action regarded as being forward or improper **4 at liberty** free or unconfined **5 at liberty to** unrestricted or authorized: *I am not at liberty to divulge his name* **6 take liberties (with)** to be overfamiliar (towards someone)
WORD ORIGIN Latin *libertas*

libidinous *adj* characterized by excessive sexual desire **libidinously** *adv*

libido (lib-**ee**-doe) *n, pl* **-dos 1** *psychoanal* psychic energy from the id **2** sexual urge or desire **libidinal** *adj*
WORD ORIGIN Latin: desire

Libra *n astrol* the seventh sign of the zodiac; the Scales
WORD ORIGIN Latin

librarian *n* a person in charge of or assisting in a library **librarianship** *n*

library *n, pl* **-braries 1** a room or building where books and other literary materials are kept **2** a collection of literary materials, films, tapes, or records, kept for borrowing or reference **3** the building or institution that houses such a collection **4** a set of books published as a series, often in a similar format **5** *computers* a collection of standard programs, usually stored on disk
WORD ORIGIN Latin *liber* book

libretto *n, pl* **-tos** *or* **-ti** a text written for an opera **librettist** *n*
WORD ORIGIN Italian: little book

Libyan *adj* **1** from Libya ▷ *n* **2** a person from Libya

lice *n* the plural of **louse**

licence *or US* **license** *n* **1** a document giving official permission to do, use, or own something **2** formal permission or exemption **3** intentional disregard of conventional rules to achieve a certain effect: *poetic licence* **4** excessive freedom
WORD ORIGIN Latin *licet* it is allowed

license *vb* **-censing, -censed 1** to grant a licence to or for **2** to give permission to or for **licensable** *adj*

licensee *n* a person who holds a licence, esp. one to sell alcoholic drink

license plate *n* the US and Canadian term for **numberplate**

licentiate *n* a person who holds a certificate of competence to practise a certain profession

licentious *adj* sexually unrestrained or promiscuous **licentiousness** *n*
WORD ORIGIN Latin *licentia* licence

lichee *n* same as **lychee**

lichen *n* any of various small mossy plants that grow in patches on tree trunks, bare ground, rocks, and stone walls
WORD ORIGIN Greek *leikhein* to lick

lich gate *n* same as **lych gate**

licit *adj formal* lawful; permitted
WORD ORIGIN Latin *licere* to be permitted

lick *vb* **1** to pass the tongue over in order to taste, wet, or clean **2** to flicker over or round (something): *flames licked the gutters* **3** *informal* **a** to defeat **b** to thrash **4 lick into shape** to put into a satisfactory condition **5 lick one's wounds** to retire after a defeat ▷ *n* **6** an instance of passing the tongue over something **7** a small amount: *a lick of paint* **8** *informal* a blow **9** *informal* a fast

pace: *a pulsating rhythm taken at a lick* **10 a lick and a promise** something hastily done, esp. a hurried wash
WORD ORIGIN Old English *liccian*

licorice *n US & Canad* same as **liquorice**

lid *n* **1** a removable or hinged cover: *a saucepan lid* **2** short for **eyelid 3 put the (tin) lid on** *informal* to put an end to **lidded** *adj*
WORD ORIGIN Old English *hlid*

lido (**lee**-doe) *n, pl* **-dos** *Brit* an open-air swimming pool or a part of a beach used by the public for swimming and sunbathing
WORD ORIGIN *Lido*, island bathing beach near Venice

lie¹ *vb* **lying, lied 1** to speak untruthfully with the intention of deceiving **2** to convey a false impression: *the camera cannot lie* ▷ *n* **3** an untrue statement deliberately used to mislead **4** something that is deliberately intended to deceive **5 give the lie to a** to disprove **b** to accuse of lying
WORD ORIGIN Old English *lyge*, *lēogan*

Ξ **USAGE**
Ξ See at **lay¹**.

lie² *vb* **lying, lay, lain 1** (often foll. by *down*) to place oneself or be in a horizontal position **2** to be situated: *I left the money lying on the table; Nepal became the only country lying between China and India* **3** to be and remain (in a particular state or condition): *others of their species lie asleep* **4** to stretch or extend: *an enormous task lies ahead* **5** (usually foll. by *in*) to exist or comprise: *her charm lies in her inner beauty* **6** (foll. by *with*) to rest (with): *the fault lies with them* ▷ *n* **7** the manner, place, or style in which something is situated **8** an animal's lair **9 lie of the land** the way in which a situation is developing ▷ See also **lie down, lie in**
WORD ORIGIN Old English *licgan*

Liebfraumilch (**leeb**-frow-milk) *n* a sweet white wine from the German Rhine
WORD ORIGIN German: from *Liebfrau* the Virgin Mary + *Milch* milk

lied (leed) *n, pl* **lieder** *music* a musical setting for solo voice and piano of a romantic or lyrical poem
WORD ORIGIN German: song

lie detector *n informal* a device used to measure any increase in blood pressure, pulse rate, etc. of someone being questioned, which is thought to indicate that the person is lying

lie down *vb* **1** to place oneself or be in a horizontal position in order to rest **2** to yield to: *never take any attack on your candidate lying down* ▷ *n* **lie-down 3** a rest

liege (leej) *adj* **1** (of a lord) owed feudal allegiance: *their liege lord* **2** (of a vassal or subject) owing feudal allegiance: *a liege subject* **3** faithful; loyal ▷ *n* **4** a liege lord **5** a subject
WORD ORIGIN Old French *lige*

lie in *vb* **1** to remain in bed late into the morning ▷ *n* **lie-in 2** a long stay in bed in the morning

lien *n law* a right to retain possession of someone else's property until a debt is paid
WORD ORIGIN Latin *ligamen* bond

lieu (lyew) *n* **in lieu of** instead of
WORD ORIGIN Old French

Lieut. lieutenant

lieutenant (lef-ten-ant, loo-ten-ant) *n*
1 a junior officer in the army, navy, or
the US police force **2** a person who acts
as principal assistant **lieutenancy** *n*
WORD ORIGIN Old French, literally:
place-holding

lieutenant colonel *n* an officer in an
army, air force, or marine corps
immediately junior to a colonel

lieutenant commander *n* an officer
in a navy immediately junior to a
commander

lieutenant general *n* a senior officer
in an army, air force, or marine corps

lieutenant governor *n* **1** a deputy
governor **2** (in Canada) the
representative of the Crown in a
province

life *n, pl* **lives 1** the state or quality that
identifies living beings, characterized
chiefly by growth, reproduction, and
response to stimuli **2** the period
between birth and death or between
birth and the present time **3** a living
person or being: *riots which claimed 22 lives*
4 the remainder or extent of one's life:
with that lady for the rest of her life **5** the
process of living: *rituals gave his life stability*
6 *informal* a sentence of life
imprisonment, usually approximating
to fifteen years **7** a characteristic state
or mode of existence: *country life is best*
8 the length of time that something is
active or functioning: *the life of a battery*
9 a present condition or mode of
existence: *they are leading a joyous life*
10 a biography **11** the sum or course of
human events and activities
12 liveliness or high spirits: *full of life*
13 a source of strength, animation, or
vitality: *he was the life of the show* **14** all
living things collectively: *there is no life on
Mars; marine life* **15 a matter of life and
death** a matter of extreme urgency
16 as large as life *informal* real and
living **17 not on your life** *informal*
certainly not **18 to the life** (of a copy of
a painting or drawing) resembling the
original exactly **19 true to life** faithful
to reality
WORD ORIGIN Old English *līf*

life assurance *n* insurance that
provides for a sum of money to be paid
to the insured person at a certain age, or
to the spouse or children on the death
of the insured. Also called: **life
insurance**

life belt *n* an inflatable ring used to keep
a person afloat when in danger of
drowning

lifeblood *n* **1** the blood vital to life
2 something that is essential for
existence, development, or success

lifeboat *n* a boat used for rescuing
people at sea

life buoy *n* a buoyant device to keep
people afloat in an emergency

life coach *n* a person whose job it is to
improve the quality of his or her
client's life, by offering advice on
professional and personal matters,
such as careers, health, personal
relationships, etc.

life cycle *n* the series of changes
occurring in each generation of an
animal or plant

lifeguard *n* a person at a beach or pool
whose job is to rescue people in danger
of drowning

life jacket *n* an inflatable sleeveless
jacket worn to keep a person afloat
when in danger of drowning

lifeless *adj* **1** inanimate; dead **2** lacking
liveliness or animation **3** unconscious

lifelike *adj* closely resembling or
representing life

lifeline *n* **1** a single means of contact or
support on which a person or an area
relies **2** a rope used for life-saving

lifelong *adj* lasting for a lifetime

life peer *n Brit* a peer whose title ceases
at his or her death

life preserver *n* **1** *Brit* a bludgeon kept
for self-defence **2** *US & Canad* a life belt
or life jacket

lifer *n informal* a prisoner sentenced to
life imprisonment

life raft *n* a raft for emergency use
at sea

life-saver *n* **1** same as **lifeguard**
2 *informal* a person or thing that gives
help in time of need **life-saving** *adj, n*

life science *n* any of the sciences
concerned with the structure and
behaviour of living organisms, such as
biology, botany, or zoology

life-size or **life-sized** *adj* representing
actual size

lifestyle *n* a set of attitudes, habits, and
possessions regarded as typical of a
particular group or an individual

life-support *adj* (of equipment or
treatment) necessary to sustain life

lifetime *n* **1** the length of time a person
is alive **2 of a lifetime** (of an
opportunity or experience) the most
important or memorable

lift *vb* **1** to rise or raise upwards to a
higher place: *the breakdown truck was lifting
the lorry* **2** to move upwards: *he slowly
lifted his hand* **3** to raise in status or
estimation: *lifted from poverty* **4** to revoke
or cancel: *the government lifted its restrictions
on imported beef* **5** to remove (plants or
underground crops) from the ground
for harvesting **6** to disappear or
disperse: *the tension lifted* **7** *informal*
to plagiarize (music or writing) ▷ *n*
8 a a compartment raised or lowered in
a vertical shaft to transport people or
goods to another floor in a building
b see **chairlift, ski lift 9** a ride in a car or
other vehicle as a passenger **10** a rise
in morale or feeling of cheerfulness
11 the act of lifting **12** the force that
lifts airborne objects
WORD ORIGIN from Old Norse

liftoff *n* the initial movement of a rocket
as it leaves its launch pad

lig *Brit slang n* **1** (esp. in the media)
a function with free entertainment
and refreshments ▷ *vb* **ligging, ligged**
2 to attend such a function **ligger** *n*
ligging *n*

ligament *n anat* a band of tough tissue
that connects various bones or cartilage
WORD ORIGIN Latin *ligare* to bind

ligature *n* **1** a link, bond, or tie **2** *printing*
a character of two or more joined
letters, such as ff **3** *music* a slur or the
group of notes connected by it ▷ *vb*
-turing, -tured 4 to bind with a ligature
WORD ORIGIN Latin *ligare* to bind

light¹ *n* **1** the natural medium,
electromagnetic radiation, that makes
sight possible **2** anything that
illuminates, such as a lamp or candle
3 see **traffic light 4** a particular type of
light: *dim yellow light* **5 a** daylight
b daybreak; dawn **6** anything that lets
in light, such as a window **7** an aspect
or view: *we have seen the world in a new light*
8 mental understanding or spiritual
insight: *suddenly he saw the light* **9** an
outstanding person: *a leading light of the
movement* **10** brightness of countenance,
esp. a sparkle in the eyes **11 a**
something that ignites, such as a spark
or flame **b** something used for igniting,
such as a match **12** see **lighthouse**
13 come to light to become known or
visible **14 in (the) light of** taking into
account **15 see the light** to understand
16 see the light (of day) a to come into
being **b** to come to public notice ▷ *adj*
17 full of light **18** (of a colour) pale: *light
blue* ▷ *vb* **lighting, lighted** or **lit 19** to
ignite **20** (often foll. by *up*) to illuminate
or cause to illuminate **21** to guide by
light ▷ See also **light up** ▷ **lightish** *adj*
WORD ORIGIN Old English *lēoht*

light² *adj* **1** not heavy; weighing
relatively little **2** relatively low in
density, strength, amount, degree, etc.:
light oil; light alloy **3** lacking sufficient
weight **4** not bulky or clumsy: *light
bedclothes* **5** not serious or difficult to
understand; entertaining: *light music*
6 graceful or agile: *light movements*
7 without strong emphasis or serious
meaning: *he gazed about with a light
inattentive smile* **8** easily digested: *a light
lunch* **9** relatively low in alcohol: *a light
wine* **10** without burdens, difficulties,
or problems: *a light heart lives longest*
11 dizzy or unclear: *a light head*
12 (of bread or cake) spongy or well
risen **13 a** (of transport) designed to
carry light loads **b** (of a vessel, aircraft,
or other transport) not loaded
14 carrying light arms or equipment:
light infantry **15** (of an industry)
producing small consumer goods
using light machinery **16 make light
of** to treat as insignificant or
unimportant ▷ *adv* **17** with little
equipment or luggage: *travelling light* ▷ *vb*
lighting, lighted or **lit 18** (esp. of birds)
to settle or land after flight **19** (foll. by
on or *upon*) to discover by chance ▷ See
also **lights** ▷ **lightish** *adj* **lightly** *adv*
lightness *n*
WORD ORIGIN Old English *lēoht*

light bulb *n* a hollow rounded glass
fitting containing a gas and a thin
metal filament that gives out light
when an electric current is passed
through it

lighten¹ *vb* **1** to make less dark **2** to
shine; glow **3** (of lightning) to flash

lighten² *vb* **1** to make or become less
heavy **2** to make or become less
burdensome **3** to make or become more
cheerful or lively

1

The Terminology of Sports in English

A sport is a zero-sum game in which a participant's gain or loss is exactly balanced by another's gain or loss. Except in cases of a tie, one always wins, and one loses. It's natural that people readily convert sports terms into metaphors in the game of life.

Even in hotly contested sports, games can be enjoyed for their own sake. Part of the pleasure is to use knowledgably a sport's peculiar, sometimes esoteric vocabulary, whether it be that of *hurling* or *Australian-rules football*. Those who report sporting events twist language, too. Since TV commentators must keep up a constant prattle, their language is often rife with mixed metaphors (*He showed he could still step up to the plate and cut the mustard*). Headline writers are fond of comic puns (*Sharks chase Ducks*) and alliteration (*Raptors handle Heat in return home*). With space at a premium, they employ numerous synonyms for *win*, and convert nouns and adjectives in unusual ways into present-tense transitive verbs: one team may *ace, pace, blank, top,* or *down* another.

When a team wins it may *rip, axe, dump, sink, whip, trip, upend, topple,* or *polish off* an opponent, and possibly *sew up* or *nail down* a *first-place finish*. If it wins unexpectedly, it may *foil, upset, shock, surprise, embarrass,* or *knock off* a favourite. If it *wins big*, it may *bomb, outclass, maul, drub, romp over, rout, bury, crush, wallop, punish, shut out, roll over, thrash, squash, shellac, clobber, humble, trample, pummel, flatten, slaughter,* or *mow down* the other side. In an easy win, the loser may be a *pushover*, as the other team *walks over, coasts past, waltzes,* or *breezes past* it. The game may be close, however; then the winner *nips, trims, clips, snips, edges, squeaks, outlasts, hold offs,* or *comes from behind.* Two teams may *even* a series. A player *inks* a contract. Even passive constructions can be forceful (*Dragons hogtied 5-0*).

Sports metaphors pervade speech. In the United States, a TV debater *hits a home run.* A union *plays ball* with an employer, since the union realizes it has two

strikes against it (baseball); either side may *call the shots* (basketball) or *fumble the ball* (football). A Canadian politician *fields* questions from reporters during a media *scrum* (rugby); in the same context, a British cabinet minister cautiously *plays a straight bat* (cricket). One notably productive US source is baseball: *strike out, play hardball, cover all the bases, out of left field,* and *rain check* have entered the general lexicon. Boxing usage is even more fertile: *hit below the belt, take the gloves off, beat someone to the punch, pull* or *roll with the punches, blow-by-blow, come out fighting* or *swinging, on the ropes,* and *down and out.* From tennis comes *the ball is in your court,* from ice hockey, *drop the gloves.*

Nowhere is the contrast between British and American English sharper than in sporting contests, beginning with the word itself. To North Americans, it is *sports*, to the English it is *sport*. *Cricket* is the quintessential English sport, though enthusiastically played in Australia, the West Indies, and the Indian subcontinent. It charms or bewilders with an arcane terminology (*out Leg before wicket,* a *mid-off* fielding position, to *cart* or *cut* the cricket ball), all the more because it superficially, deceivingly resembles baseball, with a *bowler* instead of a *pitcher,* and a *batsman* instead of a *batter.* But the English may wonder why baseball's championship is called the *World Series,* when the only non-US team in the *major leagues* is the Toronto Blue Jays. American or Canadian football as justly might be called *handball,* since hands rival feet in importance. Rugby can have *rugby league* or *rugby union* rules. In rugby, from which North American forms of football partly evolved, the equivalent of a *touchdown* is confusingly a *try.* Hockey can be played on grass, though more commonly on ice. Football, the world's most popular and widely played sport, is mainly *soccer* to North Americans.

Once a British manager was loosely quoted, "Football isn't a matter of life or death, it's much more important than that." But perhaps not more important than language.

lighter[1] *n* a small portable device for lighting cigarettes, etc.

lighter[2] *n* a flat-bottomed barge used in loading or unloading a ship **WORD ORIGIN** probably from Middle Dutch

light-fingered *adj* skilful at thieving, esp. by picking pockets

light flyweight *n* a professional boxer weighing up to 108 pounds (49 kg) or an amateur boxer weighing up to 48 kg

light-footed *adj* having a light tread

light-headed *adj* giddy; feeling faint

light-hearted *adj* cheerful or carefree in mood or disposition **light-heartedly** *adv*

light heavyweight *n* a professional boxer weighing up to 175 pounds (79.5 kg) or an amateur weighing up to 81 kg

lighthouse *n* a tower with a light to guide ships and warn of obstructions

lighting *n* **1** the apparatus for and design of artificial light effects to a stage, film, or television set **2** the act or quality of illumination

lighting-up time *n* the time when vehicles are required by law to have their lights on

light middleweight *n* a professional boxer weighing up to 154 pounds (70 kg) or an amateur boxer weighing up to 71 kg

lightning *n* **1** a flash of light in the sky caused by a discharge of electricity ▷ *adj* **2** fast and sudden: *a lightning attack* **WORD ORIGIN** variant of *lightening*

lightning conductor *or* **rod** *n* a metal rod attached to the highest part of a building to divert lightning safely to earth

light pen *n* a penlike photoelectric device that in conjunction with a computer can be used to draw lines or identify symbols on a VDU screen

light pollution *n* the glow from the lighting in streets and buildings that obscures the night sky

light rail *n* a transport system using small trains or trams

lights *pl n* the lungs of sheep, bullocks, and pigs, used for feeding pets **WORD ORIGIN** because of the light weight of the lungs

lightship *n* a moored ship equipped as a lighthouse

lights out *n* the time when residents of an institution are expected to retire to bed

light up *vb* **1** to illuminate **2** to make or become cheerful or animated: *their faces lit up and one dug the other in the ribs* **3** to light a cigarette or pipe

lightweight *adj* **1** not serious **2** of relatively light weight ▷ *n* **3** *informal* a person of little importance or influence **4** a person or animal of relatively light weight **5** a professional boxer weighing up to 135 pounds (61 kg) or an amateur weighing up to 60 kg

light welterweight *n* a professional or an amateur boxer weighing up to 140 pounds (63.5 kg)

light year *n* *astron* the distance travelled by light in one mean solar year, i.e. 9.4607×10^{15} metres

ligneous *adj* of or like wood **WORD ORIGIN** Latin *lignum* wood

lignite (**lig**-nite) *n* a brown sedimentary rock with a woody texture: used as a fuel

lignum vitae (**lig**-num **vite**-ee) *n* a tropical American tree with heavy resinous wood **WORD ORIGIN** Late Latin, literally: wood of life

like[1] *adj* **1** resembling ▷ *prep* **2** in the manner of; similar to: *she was like a child; it looks like a traffic cone* **3** such as: *a modern material, like carbon fibre* **4** characteristic of ▷ *adv* **5** in the manner of: *cheering like mad* **6** *dialect* likely ▷ *conj* **7** *not standard* as though; as if: *I don't want to make it seem like I had this bad childhood* **8** in the same way that: *she doesn't dance like you do* ▷ *n* **9** the equal or counterpart of a person or thing **10 the like** similar things: *magic, supernormal powers and the like* **11 the likes** *or* **like** of people or things similar to (someone or something specified): *the theatre was not meant for the likes of him* **WORD ORIGIN** Old English *gelīc*

≣ USAGE
The use of *like* to mean *such as* was formerly thought to be undesirable in formal writing, but has now become acceptable. It was also thought that *as* rather than *like* should be used to mean *in the same way that*, but now both *as* and *like* are acceptable: *they hunt and catch fish as/like their ancestors used to*. The use of *look like* and *seem like* before a clause, although very common, is thought by many people to be incorrect or non-standard: *it looks as though he won't come* (not *it looks like he won't come*).

like[2] *vb* **liking, liked** **1** to find enjoyable **2** to be fond of **3** to prefer or choose: *I'd like to go home* **4** to feel disposed or inclined; choose; wish: *do as you like* ▷ *n* **5** (*usually pl*) a favourable feeling, desire, or preference: *tell me your likes and dislikes* **likeable** *or* **likable** *adj* **WORD ORIGIN** Old English *līcian*

likelihood *n* chance; probability

likely *adj* **1** tending or inclined: *likely to win* **2** probable: *the likely effects of the tunnel* **3** appropriate for a purpose or activity: *a likely candidate* ▷ *adv* **4** probably or presumably **5 not likely** *informal* definitely not **WORD ORIGIN** Old Norse *līkligr*

≣ USAGE
Likely as an adverb is preceded by another, intensifying adverb, as in *it will very likely rain* or *it will most likely rain*. Its use without an intensifier, as in *it will likely rain*, is regarded as unacceptable by most users of British English, though it is common in colloquial US English.

like-minded *adj* sharing similar opinions

liken *vb* to compare

likeness *n* **1** resemblance **2** portrait **3** an imitative appearance; semblance: *in the likeness of a dragon*

likewise *adv* **1** in addition; also **2** similarly

liking *n* **1** fondness **2** what one likes or prefers: *if it's not to your liking, do let me know*

lilac *n* **1** a small tree with large sprays of purple or white sweet-smelling flowers ▷ *adj* **2** pale purple **WORD ORIGIN** Persian *nīlak* bluish

Lilliputian (lil-lip-**pew**-shun) *n* **1** a tiny person or being ▷ *adj* **2** tiny; very small **WORD ORIGIN** from *Lilliput*, an imaginary country of tiny people in Swift's *Gulliver's Travels*

Lilo *n, pl* **-los** *trademark* a type of inflatable plastic mattress

lilt *n* **1** a pleasing musical quality in a speaking voice **2** (in music) a jaunty rhythm **3** a graceful rhythmic motion ▷ *vb* **4** (of a voice, tune, or song) to rise and fall in a pleasant way **5** to move gracefully and rhythmically **lilting** *adj* **WORD ORIGIN** origin unknown

lily *n, pl* **lilies** **1** a perennial plant, such as the tiger lily, with scaly bulbs and showy white or coloured flowers **2** a water lily **WORD ORIGIN** Latin *lilium*

lily-livered *adj* *old-fashioned* cowardly

lily of the valley *n, pl* **lilies of the valley** a small plant with spikes of sweet-smelling white bell-shaped flowers

limb[1] *n* **1** an arm, leg, or wing **2** any of the main branches of a tree **3 out on a limb a** in a precarious or questionable position **b** *Brit & NZ* isolated, esp. because of unpopular opinions **limbless** *adj* **WORD ORIGIN** Old English *lim*

limb[2] *n* the apparent outer edge of the sun, a moon, or a planet **WORD ORIGIN** Latin *limbus* edge

limber[1] *adj* **1** pliant; supple **2** able to move or bend the body freely; agile **WORD ORIGIN** origin unknown

limber[2] *n* **1** part of a gun carriage, consisting of an axle, pole, and two wheels ▷ *vb* **2** to attach the limber (to a gun) **WORD ORIGIN** Middle English *lymour* shaft of a gun carriage

limber up *vb* to loosen stiff muscles by exercise

limbo[1] *n, pl* **-bos** **1** (*often cap*) RC Church (formerly) the supposed region intermediate between heaven and hell for the unbaptized **2 in limbo** not knowing the result or next stage of something and powerless to influence it **WORD ORIGIN** Medieval Latin *in limbo* on the border (of hell)

limbo[2] *n, pl* **-bos** a West Indian dance in which dancers lean backwards and pass under a horizontal bar which is gradually lowered **WORD ORIGIN** origin unknown

lime[1] *n* **1** *agriculture* calcium hydroxide spread as a dressing on acidic land ▷ *vb* **2** **liming, limed** to spread a calcium compound upon (land) **WORD ORIGIN** Old English *līm*

lime[2] *n* the green oval fruit of a small Asian citrus tree with acid fleshy pulp rich in vitamin C **WORD ORIGIN** Arabic *līmah*

lime[3] *n* a European linden tree planted for ornament **WORD ORIGIN** Old English *lind* linden

lime-green *adj* light yellowish-green

limekiln *n* a kiln in which calcium carbonate is burned to produce quicklime

limelight *n* **1 the limelight** glare of publicity: *this issue will remain in the limelight* **2 a** a type of lamp, formerly used in stage lighting, in which lime is heated to white heat **b** brilliant white light produced in this way

limerick (**lim**-mer-ik) *n* a form of comic verse consisting of five lines
WORD ORIGIN allegedly from *will you come up to Limerick?* a refrain sung between nonsense verses at a party

limestone *n* rock consisting mainly of calcium carbonate: used as a building stone and in making cement

limey *n* *US, Canad, & Austral slang* **1** a British person **2** a British sailor or ship
WORD ORIGIN from *lime-juicer*, because British sailors drank lime juice as a protection against scurvy

limit *n* **1** (*sometimes pl*) the ultimate extent or amount of something: *each soloist was stretched to his or her limit by the demands of the vocal writing* **2** (*often pl*) the boundary of a specific area: *beyond the city limits* **3** the largest quantity or amount allowed **4 the limit** *informal* a person or thing that is intolerably exasperating ▷ *vb* -**iting**, -**ited 5** to restrict **limitable** *adj*
WORD ORIGIN Latin *limes* boundary

limitation *n* **1** a restriction or controlling of quantity, quality, or achievement **2 limitations** the limit or extent of an ability to achieve something: *learn your own limitations*

limited *adj* **1** having a limit; restricted **2** without fullness or scope; narrow **3** (of governing powers or sovereignty) restricted by a constitution, laws, or an assembly: *limited government* **4** *Brit & NZ* (of a business enterprise) owned by shareholders whose liability for the enterprise's debts is restricted

limited edition *n* an edition of something, such as a book, which has been restricted to a particular number of copies

limn *vb old-fashioned* to represent in drawing or painting
WORD ORIGIN Latin *inluminare* to brighten

limousine *n* any large luxurious car
WORD ORIGIN French, literally: cloak

limp¹ *vb* **1** to walk with an uneven step, esp. with a weak or injured leg **2** to advance in a labouring or faltering manner ▷ *n* **3** an uneven walk or progress **limping** *adj, n*
WORD ORIGIN Old English *lemphealt* lame

limp² *adj* **1** lacking firmness or stiffness **2** not energetic or vital **3** (of the binding of a book) paperback **limply** *adv*
WORD ORIGIN probably Scandinavian

limpet *n* **1** a conical shellfish that clings tightly to rocks with its muscular foot ▷ *adj* **2** denoting certain weapons that are magnetically attached to their targets and resist removal: *limpet mines*
WORD ORIGIN Old English *lempedu*

limpid *adj* **1** clear or transparent **2** (of speech or writing) clear and easy to understand **limpidity** *n*
WORD ORIGIN Latin *limpidus* clear

limy¹ *adj* **limier, limiest** of, like, or smeared with birdlime

limy² *adj* **limier, limiest** of or tasting of lime (the fruit)

linage *n* **1** the number of lines in written or printed matter **2** payment according to the number of lines

linchpin *or* **lynchpin** *n* **1** a pin inserted through an axle to keep a wheel in position **2** an essential person or thing: *she was the linchpin of the experiment*
WORD ORIGIN Old English *lynis*

Lincs Lincolnshire

linctus *n, pl* -**tuses** a soothing syrupy cough mixture
WORD ORIGIN Latin *lingere* to lick

linden *n* a large tree with heart-shaped leaves and fragrant yellowish flowers. See also **lime³**
WORD ORIGIN Old English *linde* lime tree

line¹ *n* **1** a narrow continuous mark, such as one made by a pencil or brush **2** a thin indented mark or wrinkle on skin **3** a continuous length without breadth **4** a boundary: *the United Nations established a provisional demarcation line* **5** *sport* **a** a white band indicating a division on a field or track **b** a mark or imaginary mark at which a race begins or ends **6** a boundary or limit: *the invidious dividing line between universities and polytechnics* **7** the edge or contour of a shape: *the shoulder line* **8** a wire or string with a particular function: *a long washing line* **9** a telephone connection: *it was a very bad line* **10** a conducting wire, cable, or circuit for electric-power transmission or telecommunications **11** a system of travel or transportation: *a shipping line* **12** a route between two points on a railway **13** a railway track **14** a course or direction of movement: *the birds' line of flight* **15** a course of action or behaviour: *to adopt a more aggressive line* **16** a policy or prescribed way of thinking: *city commentators supported the CBI line* **17** a field of interest or activity: *heroin – that was their line* **18** straight or orderly alignment: *stand in line* **19** one kind of product or article: *a line of smart suits* **20** a row of people or things **21** a row of printed or written words **22** a unit of verse consisting of words in a single row **23** one of a number of narrow horizontal bands forming a television picture **24** *music* any of the five horizontal marks that make up the stave **25** the most forward defensive position: *the front line* **26** a formation of ships or soldiers abreast of each other **27** the combatant forces of certain armies and navies **28** *US & Canad* a queue **29 all along the line** at every stage in a series **30 draw the line (at)** to object (to) or set a limit (on): *I'm not a killer, I draw the line at that* **31 drop someone a line** to send someone a short note **32 get a line on** *informal* to obtain information about **33 in line for** likely to receive: *high achievers are in line for cash bonuses* **34 in line with** conforming to **35 lay** *or* **put on the line a** to speak frankly and directly **b** to risk (one's career or reputation) on something ▷ *vb* **lining, lined 36** to mark with a line or lines **37** to be or form a border: *the square was lined with stalls selling snacks* **38** to

place in or form a row, series, or alignment ▶ See also **lines, line-up**
> **lined** *adj*
WORD ORIGIN Old French *ligne* + Old English *līn*

line² *vb* **lining, lined 1** to attach an inside layer to **2** to cover the inside of: *the works of Shakespeare lined his walls* **3 line one's pockets** to make a lot of money, esp. dishonestly
WORD ORIGIN Latin *linum* flax

lineage (**lin**-ee-ij) *n* direct descent from an ancestor

lineal *adj* **1** being in a direct line of descent from an ancestor **2** of or derived from direct descent **3** linear
WORD ORIGIN Latin *linea* line

lineament *n* (*often pl*) a facial outline or feature
WORD ORIGIN Latin *lineare* to draw a line

linear (**lin**-ee-er) *adj* **1** of or in lines **2** of or relating to length **3** represented by a line or lines **linearity** *n*

linear measure *n* a unit or system of units for the measurement of length

lineation (lin-ee-**ay**-shun) *n* **1** the act of marking with lines **2** an arrangement of lines

line dancing *n* a form of dancing performed by rows of people to country and western music

line drawing *n* a drawing formed with lines only

linen *n* **1** a hard-wearing fabric woven from the spun fibres of flax **2** articles, such as sheets or tablecloths, made from linen cloth or from cotton
WORD ORIGIN Latin *linum* flax

line of fire *n* the flight path of a bullet discharged from a firearm

line printer *n* an electromechanical device that prints a line of characters at a time: used in printing and in computer systems

liner¹ *n* **1** a passenger ship or aircraft, esp. one that is part of a commercial fleet **2** Also called: **eyeliner** a cosmetic used to outline the eyes

liner² *n* something used as a lining: *a plastic bin liner*

lines *pl n* **1** the words of a theatrical role: *shaky sets, fluffed lines, and wooden plots* **2** *informal chiefly Brit* a marriage certificate: *marriage lines* **3** a school punishment of writing out the same sentence or phrase a specified number of times **4 read between the lines** to find an implicit meaning in addition to the obvious one

linesman *n, pl* -**men 1** an official who helps the referee or umpire in various sports, by indicating when the ball has gone out of play **2** a person who maintains railway, electricity, or telephone lines

line-up *n* **1** people or things assembled for a particular purpose: *Christmas TV line-up* **2** the members of such an assembly ▷ *vb* **line up 3** to form or organize a line-up

ling¹ *n, pl* **ling** *or* **lings** a fish with a long slender body
WORD ORIGIN probably Low German

ling² *n* heather
WORD ORIGIN Old Norse *lyng*

linger *vb* **1** to delay or prolong departure **2** to survive in a weakened condition for some time before death **3** to spend a long time doing or considering something **lingering** *adj*
WORD ORIGIN Old English *lengan* prolong

lingerie (**lan**-zher-ee) *n* women's underwear and nightwear
WORD ORIGIN French, from Latin *lineus* linen

lingo *n, pl* **-goes** *informal* any foreign or unfamiliar language or jargon
WORD ORIGIN perhaps from LINGUA FRANCA

lingua franca *n, pl* **lingua francas** *or* **linguae francae** **1** a language used for communication among people of different mother tongues **2** any system of communication providing mutual understanding
WORD ORIGIN Italian: Frankish tongue

lingual *adj* **1** *anat* of the tongue **2** articulated with the tongue **3** *rare* of language or languages **lingually** *adv*

linguist *n* **1** a person who is skilled in foreign languages **2** a person who studies linguistics
WORD ORIGIN Latin *lingua* tongue

linguistic *adj* **1** of language **2** of linguistics **linguistically** *adv*

linguistics *n* the scientific study of language

liniment *n* a medicated oily liquid applied to the skin to relieve pain or stiffness
WORD ORIGIN Latin *linere* to smear

lining *n* **1** material used to line a garment or curtain **2** any interior covering: *the lining of the womb*

link *n* **1** any of the separate rings that form a chain **2** an emotional or logical relationship between people or things; association **3** a connecting part or episode **4** a type of communications connection: *a rail link; radio link* ▷ *vb* **5** (often foll. by *up*) to connect with or as if with links **6** to connect by association
WORD ORIGIN from Old Norse

linkage *n* **1** the act of linking or the state of being linked **2** a system of links

linkman *n, pl* **-men** a presenter of a television or radio programme consisting of a number of items broadcast from different locations

links *pl n* a golf course
WORD ORIGIN Old English *hlincas*, plural of *hlinc* ridge

link-up *n* a joining together of two systems or groups

linnet *n* a brownish finch: the male has a red breast and forehead
WORD ORIGIN Old French *linotte*, from Latin *līnum* flax (because the bird feeds on flaxseeds)

lino *n* short for **linoleum**

linocut *n* **1** a design cut in relief in linoleum mounted on a block of wood **2** a print made from such a block

linoleum *n* a floor covering made of hessian or jute with a smooth decorative coating of powdered cork
WORD ORIGIN Latin *linum* flax + *oleum* oil

Linotype *n trademark* a typesetting machine that casts an entire line of text on one piece of metal

linseed *n* the seed of the flax plant
WORD ORIGIN Old English *līn* flax + *sǣd* seed

linseed oil *n* a yellow oil extracted from flax seeds and used in making paints, inks, linoleum, and varnish

lint *n* **1** an absorbent material with raised fibres on one side, used to dress wounds **2** tiny shreds of yarn or cloth; fluff
WORD ORIGIN probably Latin *linteus* made of linen, from *linum* flax

lintel *n* a horizontal beam over a door or window
WORD ORIGIN probably ultimately from Latin *limes* boundary

lion *n* **1** a large animal of the cat family found in Africa and India, with a tawny yellow coat and, in the male, a shaggy mane **2** a courageous and strong person **3** **the lion's share** the largest portion **lioness** *fem n*
WORD ORIGIN Latin *leo*

lion-hearted *adj* very brave; courageous

lionize *or* **-nise** *vb* **-nizing, -nized** *or* **-nising, -nised** to treat as a celebrity

lip *n* **1** *anat* either of the two fleshy folds surrounding the mouth **2** any structure resembling a lip, such as the rim of a jug **3** *slang* impudent talk or backchat **4** **bite one's lip** to avoid showing feelings of anger or distress **5** **keep a stiff upper lip** to maintain one's composure during a time of trouble **6** **lick** *or* **smack one's lips** to anticipate or recall something with glee or relish
WORD ORIGIN Old English *lippa*

lipase *n biochem* any of a group of enzymes that digest fat and are produced in the stomach and pancreas and occur in seeds

lipid *n biochem* any of a group of organic compounds including fats, oils, waxes, and sterols
WORD ORIGIN Greek *lipos* fat

lipo *n informal* short for **liposuction**

lipogram *n* a piece of writing in which all words containing a particular letter have been deliberately omitted

liposuction *n* a cosmetic surgical operation in which fat is removed from the body by suction

lip-read *vb* **-reading, -read** to interpret speech by lip-reading

lip-reading *n* a method used by deaf people to understand spoken words by interpreting movements of the speaker's lips **lip-reader** *n*

lip service *n* **pay lip service to** to appear to support or obey something publicly while actually disregarding it

lipstick *n* a cosmetic in the form of a stick, for colouring the lips

liquefy *vb* **-fies, -fying, -fied** (esp. of a gas) to make or become liquid **liquefaction** *n*
WORD ORIGIN Latin *liquefacere* to make liquid

liqueur (lik-**cure**) *n* a highly flavoured sweetened alcoholic spirit, intended to be drunk after a meal
WORD ORIGIN French

liquid *n* **1** a substance in a physical state which can change shape but not size ▷ *adj* **2** of or being a liquid: *liquid medicines* **3** shining and clear: *liquid sunlight days* **4** flowing, fluent, or smooth **5** (of assets) in the form of money or easily convertible into money
WORD ORIGIN Latin *liquere* to be fluid

liquidate *vb* **-dating, -dated** **1** to settle or pay off (a debt or claim) **2** to dissolve a company and divide its assets among creditors **3** to convert (assets) into cash **4** to eliminate or kill

liquidation *n* **1 a** the dissolving of a company by selling its assets to pay off its debts **b go into liquidation** (of a business firm) to have its affairs so terminated **2** destruction; elimination

liquidator *n* an official appointed to liquidate a business

liquid-crystal display *n* a display of numbers, characters, or images, esp. on a calculator, using cells containing a liquid with crystalline properties, that change their reflectivity when an electric field is applied to them

liquidity *n* the state of being able to meet financial obligations

liquidize *or* **-dise** *vb* **-dizing, -dized** *or* **-dising, -dised** **1** to make or become liquid; liquefy **2** to process (food) in a liquidizer to make it liquid

liquidizer *or* **-diser** *n* a kitchen appliance with blades for liquidizing food

liquid measure *n* a unit or system of units for measuring volumes of liquids or their containers

liquid oxygen *n* oxygen liquefied by cooling: used in rocket fuels

liquid paraffin *n* an oily liquid obtained by petroleum distillation and used as a laxative

liquor *n* **1** spirits or other alcoholic drinks **2** any liquid in which food has been cooked
WORD ORIGIN Latin *liquere* to be liquid

liquorice *or US & Canad* **licorice** (**lik**-ker-iss) *n* **1** a chewy black sweet with a strong flavour **2** the dried black root of a Mediterranean plant, used as a laxative and in confectionery
WORD ORIGIN Greek *glukus* sweet + *rhiza* root

lira *n, pl* **lire** *or* **liras** **1** a former monetary unit of Italy **2** the standard monetary unit of Turkey
WORD ORIGIN Italian, from Latin *libra* pound

lisle (rhymes with **mile**) *n* a strong fine cotton thread or fabric, formerly used to make stockings
WORD ORIGIN after *Lisle* (now Lille), in France

lisp *n* **1** a speech defect in which s and z are pronounced like the th sounds in English *thin* and *then* respectively ▷ *vb* **2** to speak with a lisp
WORD ORIGIN Old English *wlisp* lisping (imitative)

LISP *n* a high-level computer programming language suitable for work in artificial intelligence
WORD ORIGIN *lis(t) p(rocessing)*

lissom *or* **lissome** *adj* slim and graceful and agile in movement
WORD ORIGIN variant of *lithesome*, from *lithe* + *-some* of a specific nature

William Faulkner

William Faulkner was able to write short, clear, declarative sentences. It was just that sometimes he didn't choose to. Faulkner's propensity for hyperbole and grandiloquence is exaggerated, even if one sentence in *Absalom, Absalom!* does run to 1,300 words. The first sentence in the much-anthologized short story 'A Rose for Emily' is: 'When Miss Emily Grierson died, our whole town went to the funeral: the men through a sort of respectful affection for a fallen monument, the women mostly out of curiosity to see the inside of her house, which no one save an old man-servant – a combined gardener and cook – had seen in at least ten years.' The sentence is long, but each (common) word suits its first-person plural narrator.

Born in 1897 into a deep-rooted Mississippi family, Faulkner settled down in an antebellum house he'd bought in Oxford, a town he transformed into fiction, just as his Yoknapatawpha was modelled on Lafayette County, 'my own little postage stamp of native soil'. A lifelong binge drinker, often financially strapped, his jobs before and after he married his childhood sweetheart in 1929 included a comically brief career as a maladroit postmaster and extended stints as a Hollywood scriptwriter. But, as Flannery O'Connor memorably said, 'The presence alone of Faulkner in our midst makes a great difference in what the writer can and cannot permit himself to do. Nobody wants his mule and wagon stalled on the same track the Dixie Limited is roaring down.'

Without completing high school, Faulkner tried to join the American armed forces during World War I, but was rejected because he was too short. Undeterred, he went to Canada to train fecklessly with the Royal Air Force: the war ended before he could go overseas; he may not even have flown solo. Back in Oxford, he was permitted to enrol at the University of Mississippi, dropped out, took odd jobs, wrote poems and plays. He briefly worked in a bookshop in New York, and lived in New Orleans, where Sherwood Anderson befriended him. After his first novel was accepted, he spent several months in Paris. Returning to Oxford, as he always did, he embarked on the novels that were uniquely his own, beginning with *The Sound and the Fury*, quickly followed by *As I Lay Dying* and *Light in August*. Amid publishers' vacillations about his difficult books, disappointing sales, and the deaths of an infant daughter and a brother, killed in the monoplane Faulkner had given him, he also wrote short stories, some for the *Saturday Evening Post*. Nothing could stop him writing.

One scholar has noted that Faulkner identifies some 600 Yoknapatawpha residents by name. The novels are thronged with clans of impoverished black or white farm labourers, grasping *arrivistes*, and haunted aristocrats. He abruptly shifts time and perspective, stages grotesque or horrific events, and launches multiple voices on a stream of consciousness. Behind the voices is the oracular author. In this fictive world, nothing is ever forgotten. In *Absalom, Absalom!* he says a character's 'very body was an empty hall echoing with sonorous defeated names; he was not a being, an entity, he was a commonwealth. He was a barracks filled with stubborn, back-looking ghosts...'

When he became a public figure, Faulkner condemned racial segregation, a courageous act for the time (the late 1950s) and the place (the Deep South), although he thought Southerners should solve their problems themselves. Now celebrated internationally, especially in France, he had said movingly in 1950, when he received the Nobel Prize, 'I believe that man will not merely endure: he will prevail.' He might have been speaking of himself.

Always witty, Faulkner once spoke of a great writer's ruthlessness: 'The writer's only responsibility is to his art'; and wrote that 'If a writer has to rob his mother, he will not hesitate; the 'Ode on a Grecian Urn' is worth any number of old ladies.' With his fellow Nobel laureate, Ernest Hemingway, he had a mutually respectful, wary, and sometimes catty relationship. Hemingway called Faulkner 'Old Corndrinking Mellifluous' and said, 'Poor Faulkner. Does he really think big emotions come from big words? He thinks I don't know the ten-dollar words.' Faulkner certainly knew them. But he also knew the one-dollar words.

list¹ *n* **1** an item-by-item record of names or things, usually written one below the other ▷ *vb* **2** to make a list of **3** to include in a list
WORD ORIGIN Old English *līste*

list² *vb* **1** (esp. of ships) to lean to one side ▷ *n* **2** a leaning to one side: *developed a list to starboard*
WORD ORIGIN origin unknown

listed building *n* (in Britain, Australia, and New Zealand) a building protected from demolition or alteration because of its special historical or architectural interest

listen *vb* **1** to concentrate on hearing something **2** to take heed or pay attention: *listen, let me explain* **listener** *n*
WORD ORIGIN Old English *hlysnan*

listen in *vb* (often foll. by *on* or *to*) to listen secretly to; eavesdrop

listeriosis *n* a serious form of food poisoning, caused by bacteria of the genus *Listeria*
WORD ORIGIN after Joseph *Lister*, surgeon

listing *n* **1** a list or an entry in a list **2 listings** lists of films, concerts, etc. printed in newspapers and magazines, and showing details such as times and venues

listless *adj* lacking interest or energy **listlessly** *adv*
WORD ORIGIN obsolete *list* desire

list price *n* the selling price of merchandise as quoted in a catalogue or advertisement

lists *pl n* **1** *history* the enclosed field of combat at a tournament **2 enter the lists** to engage in a conflict or controversy
WORD ORIGIN plural of Old English *līste* border

lit *vb* a past of **light¹** or **light²**

lit. **1** literal(ly) **2** literary **3** literature

litany *n, pl* **-nies 1** *Christianity* a prayer consisting of a series of invocations, each followed by the same response **2** any tedious recital: *a litany of complaints*
WORD ORIGIN Late Greek *litaneia* prayer

litchi *n* same as **lychee**

lite *adj* **1** (of food or drink) containing few calories or little alcohol or fat **2** denoting a less extreme version of a person or thing: *reggae lite*
WORD ORIGIN variant spelling of LIGHT²

liter *n* US same as **litre**

literacy *n* **1** the ability to read and write **2** the ability to use language effectively

literal *adj* **1** in exact accordance with the explicit meaning of a word or text **2** word for word: *a literal translation* **3** dull or unimaginative: *she's very, very literal and flat in how she interprets what she sees* **4** true; actual ▷ *n* **5** a misprint or misspelling in a text **literally** *adv*
WORD ORIGIN Latin *littera* letter

literalism *n* the tendency to take words and statements in their literal sense **literalist** *n*

literary *adj* **1** of or characteristic of literature: *literary criticism* **2** knowledgeable about literature **3** (of a word) used chiefly in written work; not colloquial **literariness** *n*

WORD ORIGIN Latin *litterarius* concerning reading and writing

literate *adj* **1** able to read and write **2** educated ▷ *n* **3** a literate person
WORD ORIGIN Latin *litteratus* learned

literati *pl n* literary or scholarly people
WORD ORIGIN Latin

literature *n* **1** written material such as poetry, novels, or essays **2** the body of written work of a particular culture, people, or era: *Elizabethan literature* **3** written or printed matter of a particular type or genre: *medical literature* **4** the art or profession of a writer **5** *informal* printed matter on any subject
WORD ORIGIN Latin *litteratura* writing

lithe *adj* attractively graceful and supple in movement
WORD ORIGIN Old English *līthe* (in the sense: gentle; later: supple)

lithium *n chem* a soft silvery element of the alkali metal series: the lightest known metal. Symbol: Li
WORD ORIGIN Greek *lithos* stone

litho *n, pl* **-thos,** *adj, adv* short for **lithography, lithograph, lithographic** or **lithographically**

lithograph *n* **1** a print made by lithography ▷ *vb* **2** to reproduce (pictures or text) by lithography **lithographic** *adj* **lithographically** *adv*

lithography (lith-**og**-ra-fee) *n* a method of printing from a metal or stone surface on which the printing areas are made ink-receptive **lithographer** *n*
WORD ORIGIN Greek *lithos* stone + *graphein* to write

Lithuanian *adj* **1** from Lithuania ▷ *n* **2** a person from Lithuania **3** the language of Lithuania

litigant *n* a person involved in a lawsuit

litigate *vb* **-gating, -gated 1** to bring or contest a lawsuit **2** to engage in legal proceedings **litigator** *n*
WORD ORIGIN Latin *lis, lit-* lawsuit + *agere* to carry on

litigation *n* the process of bringing or contesting a lawsuit

litigious (lit-**ij**-uss) *adj* frequently going to law

litmus *n* a soluble powder obtained from lichens, which is turned red by acids and blue by alkalis. Paper treated with it (**litmus paper**) is used as an indicator in chemistry
WORD ORIGIN perhaps Scandinavian

litmus test *n* something which is regarded as a simple and accurate test of a particular thing, such as a person's attitude to an issue

litotes *n, pl* **-tes** understatement used for effect, for example 'She was not a little upset' meaning 'She was extremely upset'
WORD ORIGIN Greek *litos* small

litre *or US* **liter** *n* a measure of volume equivalent to 1 cubic decimetre
WORD ORIGIN Greek *litra* a unit of weight

litter *n* **1** small items of rubbish carelessly dropped in public places **2** a disordered or untidy collection of objects **3** a group of animals produced at one birth **4** straw or hay used as bedding for animals **5** dry material

used to line a receptacle in which a domestic cat can urinate and defecate **6** (esp. formerly) a bed or seat held between parallel poles and used for carrying people ▷ *vb* **7** to strew with litter **8** to scatter or be scattered in an untidy fashion **9** (of animals) to give birth to offspring **10** to provide (an animal) with straw or hay for bedding
WORD ORIGIN Latin *lectus* bed

litter lout Brit *or US, Canad, Austral, & NZ* **litterbug** *n* slang a person who drops refuse in public places

little *adj* **1** of small or less than average size **2** young: *a little boy* **3** endearingly familiar: *he was a sweet little man* **4** contemptible, mean, or disagreeable: *some of my best friends were little squirts* **5** of small quantity, extent, or duration: *there was little money circulating; I could see little evidence of it* ▷ *adv* **6** (usually preceded by *a*) to a small extent or degree; not a lot: *to sleep a little* **7** not at all, or hardly: *army life varied little as the years passed* **8** not much or often: *we go there very little now* **9 little by little** by small degrees ▷ *n* **10 make little of** to treat as insignificant: *one episode in their history is made little of in the guide books* **11 think little of** to have a low opinion of ▸ See also **less, lesser, least**
WORD ORIGIN Old English *lȳtel*

little people *pl n* folklore small supernatural beings, such as elves

littoral *adj* **1** of or by the shore ▷ *n* **2** a coastal region
WORD ORIGIN Latin *litus* shore

liturgy *n, pl* **-gies** the forms of public services officially prescribed by a Church **liturgical** *adj*
WORD ORIGIN Greek *leitourgia*

livable *or* **liveable** *adj* (foll. by *with*) tolerable or pleasant to live (with)

live¹ *vb* **living, lived 1** to show the characteristics of life; be alive **2** to remain alive or in existence **3** to exist in a specified way: *to live at ease* **4** to have one's home: *he went to live in Switzerland* **5** to continue or last: *his childhood had always lived inside him* **6** (foll. by *on, upon* or *by*) to support one's style of life: *forest dwellers who live by extracting rubber* **7** (foll. by *with*) to endure the effects (of a crime or mistake); tolerate **8** to pass or spend (one's life) **9** to enjoy life to the full: *he likes to live every day to the full* **10** to put into practice in one's daily life: *the freedom to live his own life as he chooses* **11 live and let live** to be tolerant ▸ See also **live down, live in,** etc.
WORD ORIGIN Old English *libban, lifian*

live² *adj* **1** alive; living **2** *radio, television* transmitted at the time of performance, rather than being prerecorded: *a live broadcast* **3** actual: *I was able to speak to a real live Hurricane pilot* **4** (of a record) recorded during a performance **5** connected to a source of electric power: *a live cable* **6** of current interest; controversial: *the document has become a live political issue* **7** loaded or capable of exploding: *a live firing exercise with a 4.5in gun* **8** (of a coal or ember) glowing or burning ▷ *adv* **9** during, at, or in the form of a live performance
WORD ORIGIN shortened from *on live* alive

live down vb to withstand people's reactions to a crime or mistake until they forget it

live in vb 1 to have one's home at the place where one works ▷ adj **live-in** 2 resident: a live-in nanny is a must; her live-in girlfriend

livelihood n one's job or other source of income

livelong (**liv**-long) adj chiefly poetic long or seemingly long: all the livelong day

lively adj -lier, -liest 1 full of life or vigour 2 vivacious or animated 3 vivid **liveliness** n

liven vb (usually foll. by up) to make or become lively; enliven

liver[1] n 1 a large glandular organ which secretes bile, balances nutrients, and removes certain poisons from the body 2 the liver of certain animals used as food **WORD ORIGIN** Old English lifer

liver[2] n a person who lives in a specified way: a fast liver

liveried adj wearing livery

liverish adj 1 informal having a disorder of the liver 2 feeling disagreeable and slightly irritable

Liverpudlian adj 1 of Liverpool, a city in NW England ▷ n 2 a person from Liverpool

liver sausage n a sausage containing liver

liverwort n a plant growing in wet places and resembling green seaweeds or leafy mosses **WORD ORIGIN** late Old English liferwyrt

livery n, pl -eries 1 the identifying uniform of a servant 2 distinctive dress or outward appearance 3 the stabling, keeping, or hiring out of horses for money **WORD ORIGIN** Old French livrée allocation

lives n the plural of **life**

livestock n animals kept on a farm

live together vb (of an unmarried couple) to live in the same house; cohabit

live up to vb to fulfil (an expectation, obligation, or principle)

live wire n 1 informal an energetic person 2 a wire carrying an electric current

livid adj 1 informal extremely angry 2 of a dark grey or purple colour: livid bruises **WORD ORIGIN** Latin livere to be black and blue

living adj 1 possessing life; not dead or inanimate 2 currently in use or valid: a living alliance 3 seeming to be real: a living doll 4 (of people or animals) existing in the present age 5 very: the living image 6 of or like everyday life: living costs 7 of or involving those now alive: one of our greatest living actors ▷ n 8 the condition of being alive 9 the manner of one's life: high living 10 one's financial means 11 Church of England a benefice

living room n a room in a private house or flat used for relaxation and entertainment

living wage n a wage adequate for a worker to live on and support a family in reasonable comfort

living will n a document that states that a person who becomes terminally ill does not want their life to be prolonged by artificial means

lizard n a reptile with an elongated body, four limbs, and a long tail **WORD ORIGIN** Latin lacerta

ll. lines (of written matter)

llama n a South American mammal of the camel family, that is used as a beast of burden and is valued for its woolly fleece **WORD ORIGIN** from a Native American language

LLB Bachelor of Laws **WORD ORIGIN** Latin Legum Baccalaureus

LLD Doctor of Laws **WORD ORIGIN** Latin Legum Doctor

LLM Master of Laws **WORD ORIGIN** Latin Legum Magister

lo interj old-fashioned look! see!: lo and behold **WORD ORIGIN** Old English lā

loach n a freshwater fish with a long narrow body and barbels around the mouth **WORD ORIGIN** Old French loche

load n 1 something to be borne or conveyed; weight 2 the amount borne or conveyed 3 something that weighs down or burdens: I have enough of a load to carry right now 4 electronics the power delivered by a machine, generator, or circuit 5 an external force applied to a component or mechanism 6 **a load of** informal a quantity of: a load of half-truths 7 **get a load of** informal to pay attention to ▷ vb 8 to place cargo or goods upon (a ship or vehicle) 9 to burden or oppress 10 to supply in abundance: other treats are loaded with fat 11 to cause to be biased: the dice are loaded 12 to put ammunition into (a firearm) 13 photog to insert film in (a camera) 14 to weight or bias (a roulette wheel or dice) 15 computers to transfer (a program) to a memory ▷ See also **loads** ▷ **loader** n **WORD ORIGIN** Old English lād course; in meaning, influenced by LADE

loaded adj 1 carrying a load 2 charged with ammunition 3 (of a question or statement) containing a hidden trap or implication 4 (of dice or a roulette wheel) weighted or otherwise biased 5 slang wealthy 6 slang chiefly US & Canad drunk

loads pl n informal (often foll. by of) a lot

loadstar n same as **lodestar**

loadstone n same as **lodestone**

loaf[1] n, pl **loaves** 1 a shaped mass of baked bread 2 any shaped or moulded mass of food, such as cooked meat 3 slang the head; common sense: use your loaf! **WORD ORIGIN** Old English hlāf

loaf[2] vb to loiter or lounge around in an idle way **WORD ORIGIN** perhaps from loafer

loafer n 1 a person who avoids work; idler 2 a moccasin-like shoe **WORD ORIGIN** perhaps German Landläufer vagabond

loam n fertile soil consisting of sand, clay, and decaying organic material **loamy** adj **WORD ORIGIN** Old English lām

loan n 1 money lent at interest for a fixed period of time 2 the act of lending: I am grateful to her for the loan of her book 3 property lent 4 **on loan** lent out; borrowed ▷ vb 5 to lend (something, esp. money) **WORD ORIGIN** Old Norse lān

loan shark n a person who lends money at an extremely high interest rate, esp. illegally

loath or **loth** (rhymes with **both**) adj (usually foll. by to) reluctant or unwilling **WORD ORIGIN** Old English lāth (in the sense: hostile)

loathe vb **loathing, loathed** to feel strong disgust for **WORD ORIGIN** Old English lāthian

loathing n strong disgust

loathsome adj causing loathing

loaves n the plural of **loaf**[1]

lob sport n 1 a ball struck or bowled in a high arc ▷ vb **lobbing, lobbed** 2 to hit or kick (a ball) in a high arc 3 informal to throw **WORD ORIGIN** probably Low German

lobar (**loh**-ber) adj of or affecting a lobe

lobate adj with or like lobes

lobby n, pl -bies 1 a room or corridor used as an entrance hall or vestibule 2 a group which attempts to influence legislators on behalf of a particular interest 3 chiefly Brit a hall in a legislative building used for meetings between legislators and members of the public 4 chiefly Brit one of two corridors in a legislative building in which members vote ▷ vb -bies, -bying, -bied 5 to attempt to influence (legislators) in the formulation of policy **WORD ORIGIN** Old High German lauba arbor

lobbyist n a person who lobbies on behalf of a particular interest

lobe n 1 any rounded projection 2 the fleshy lower part of the external ear 3 any subdivision of a bodily organ **WORD ORIGIN** Greek lobos lobe of the ear or of the liver

lobelia n a plant with blue, red, white, or yellow five-lobed flowers **WORD ORIGIN** Matthias de Lobel, botanist

lobola n S African (in southern Africa) an African custom by which a bridegroom's family makes a payment in cattle or cash to the bride's family shortly before the marriage **WORD ORIGIN** Nguni (language group of southern Africa) ukulobola to give bride price

lobotomy n, pl -mies the surgical cutting of nerves in the frontal lobe of the brain to treat severe mental disorders **WORD ORIGIN** Greek lobos lobe + tomē a cutting

lobscouse n a sailor's stew of meat, vegetables, and hardtack **WORD ORIGIN** perhaps dialect lob to boil + scouse broth

lobster n, pl -sters or -ster 1 a large edible crustacean with large pincers and a long tail, which turns red when boiled 2 its edible flesh 3 Austral informal a $20 note

lobster pot *n* a round basket made of open slats, used to catch lobsters

local *adj* **1** of or concerning a particular area **2** restricted to a particular place **3** *med* of, affecting, or confined to a limited area or part: *a local anaesthetic* **4** (of a train or bus) stopping at all stations or stops ▷ *n* **5** an inhabitant of a specified locality: *we swim, sunbathe, meet the locals, unwind* **6** *Brit informal* a pub close to one's home **locally** *adv*
WORD ORIGIN Latin *locus* place

local anaesthetic *n med* see **anaesthesia**

local authority *n* the governing body of a county, district, or region

locale (loh-**kahl**) *n* the place where something happens or has happened
WORD ORIGIN French, from Latin *locus* place

local government *n* the government of the affairs of counties, towns, and districts by locally elected political bodies

locality *n, pl* **-ties 1** a neighbourhood or area **2** the site or scene of an event

localize *or* **-lise** *vb* **-lizing, -lized** *or* **-lising, -lised** to restrict (something) to a particular place

locate *vb* **-cating, -cated 1** to discover the whereabouts of; find **2** to situate or build: *located around the corner from the church* **3** to become established or settled

location *n* **1** a site or position; situation **2** the act of locating or the state of being located: *make their location and rescue a top priority* **3** a place outside a studio where filming is done: *shot on location* **4** (in South Africa) a Black African or Coloured township
WORD ORIGIN Latin *locare* to place

loc. cit. (in textual annotation) in the place cited
WORD ORIGIN Latin *loco citato*

loch *n Scot* **1** a lake **2** a long narrow arm of the sea
WORD ORIGIN Gaelic

loci (loh-sigh) *n* the plural of **locus**

lock¹ *n* **1** a device for fastening a door, drawer, lid, etc. and preventing unauthorized access **2** a section of a canal or river closed off by gates between which the water level can be altered to aid boats moving from one level to the next **3** *Brit & NZ* the extent to which a vehicle's front wheels will turn: *they adopted more steering lock* **4** the interlocking of parts **5** a mechanism that fires a gun **6** **lock, stock, and barrel** completely; entirely **7** a wrestling hold **8** Also called: **lock forward** *rugby* a player in the second row of the scrum ▷ *vb* **9** to fasten or become fastened to prevent entry or exit **10** to secure (a building) by locking all doors and windows **11** to fix or become fixed together securely **12** to become or cause to become immovable: *just before your knees lock* **13** to clasp or entangle in a struggle or embrace ▶ See also **lock out, lock up**
WORD ORIGIN Old English *loc*

lock² *n* **1** a strand or curl of hair **2 locks** *chiefly literary* hair
WORD ORIGIN Old English *loc*

locker *n* a small compartment with a lock, used for temporarily storing clothes, valuables, or luggage

locket *n* a small hinged ornamental pendant that holds a picture or keepsake
WORD ORIGIN French *loquet* latch

lockjaw *n pathol* a nontechnical name for **trismus** or **tetanus**

lock out *vb* **1** to prevent from entering by locking a door **2** to prevent (employees) from working during an industrial dispute, by shutting them out of the premises ▷ *n* **lockout 3** the closing of a place of employment by an employer, in order to force employees to accept terms

locksmith *n* a person who makes or repairs locks

lock up *vb* **1** to imprison **2** to secure a building by locking all the doors and windows ▷ *n* **lockup 3** a jail **4** *Brit* a garage or store separate from the main premises **5** *Brit* a small shop with no attached quarters for the owner ▷ *adj* **lock-up 6** *Brit & NZ* (of premises) without living quarters: *a lock-up garage*

loco¹ *n informal* a locomotive

loco² *adj slang chiefly US* insane
WORD ORIGIN Spanish: crazy

locomotion *n* the act or power of moving
WORD ORIGIN Latin *loco* from a place + MOTION

locomotive *n* **1** a self-propelled engine for pulling trains ▷ *adj* **2** of locomotion

locum *n* a person who stands in temporarily for a doctor or clergyman
WORD ORIGIN Medieval Latin *locum tenens* (someone) holding the place (of another)

locus (loh-kuss) *n, pl* **loci 1** an area or place where something happens **2** *maths* a set of points or lines whose location satisfies, or is determined by, one or more specified conditions: *the locus of points equidistant from a given point is a circle*
WORD ORIGIN Latin

locust *n* **1** an African insect, related to the grasshopper, which travels in vast swarms, stripping large areas of vegetation **2** a North American leguminous tree with prickly branches; the carob tree
WORD ORIGIN Latin *locusta*

locution *n* **1** manner or style of speech **2** a word, phrase, or expression
WORD ORIGIN Latin *locutio* an utterance

lode *n* a vein of metallic ore
WORD ORIGIN Old English *lād* course

lodestar *n* **1** a star, esp. the North Star, used in navigation or astronomy as a point of reference **2** something that serves as a guide

lodestone *n* **1 a** magnetic iron ore **b** a piece of this, used as a magnet **2** a person or thing regarded as a focus of attraction

lodge *n* **1** *chiefly Brit* the gatekeeper's house at the entrance to the grounds of a country mansion **2** a house or cabin used occasionally by hunters, skiers, etc.: *a hunting lodge* **3** *chiefly Brit* a room used by porters in a university or college **4** a local branch of certain societies **5** a beaver's home ▷ *vb* **lodging, lodged 6** to provide or be provided with rented accommodation **7** to live temporarily in rented accommodation **8** to embed or be embedded: *the bullet lodged in his brain* **9** to leave for safety or storage: *he lodged his wages in the bank* **10** to bring (a charge or accusation) against someone: *the Brazilians lodged a complaint* **11** (often foll. by *in* or *with*) to place (authority or power) in the control (of someone)
WORD ORIGIN Old French *loge*

lodger *n* a person who pays rent in return for accommodation in someone else's home

lodging *n* **1** a temporary residence: *where might I find a night's lodging?* **2 lodgings** a rented room or rooms in another person's home

loess (loh-iss) *n* a fine-grained soil, found mainly in river valleys, originally deposited by the wind
WORD ORIGIN Swiss German *lösch* loose

loft *n* **1** the space inside a roof **2** a gallery in a church **3** a room over a stable used to store hay **4** a raised house or coop in which pigeons are kept **5** *golf* **a** the angle of the face of the club used to elevate a ball **b** the height reached by a struck ball ▷ *vb* **6** *sport* to strike or kick (a ball) high in the air
WORD ORIGIN Old Norse *lopt* air, ceiling

lofty *adj* **loftier, loftiest 1** of majestic or imposing height **2** morally admirable: *lofty ideals* **3** unpleasantly superior: *a lofty contempt* **loftily** *adv* **loftiness** *n*

log¹ *n* **1** a section of a felled tree stripped of branches **2 a** a detailed record of a voyage of a ship or aircraft **b** a record of the hours flown by pilots and aircrews **c** a book in which these records are made; logbook **3** a device consisting of a float with an attached line, formerly used to measure the speed of a ship **4 sleep like a log** to sleep without stirring ▷ *vb* **logging, logged 5** to saw logs from (trees) **6** to enter (a distance or event) in a logbook or log ▶ See also **log in, log out**
WORD ORIGIN origin unknown

log² *n* short for **logarithm**

loganberry *n, pl* **-ries** a purplish-red fruit, similar to a raspberry, that grows on a trailing prickly plant
WORD ORIGIN after J. H. *Logan*, who first grew it

logarithm *n* the exponent indicating the power to which a fixed number, the base, must be raised to obtain a given number or variable **logarithmic** *adj*
WORD ORIGIN Greek *logos* ratio + *arithmos* number

logbook *n* **1** a book containing the official record of trips made by a ship or aircraft **2** *Brit informal* the registration document of a car

loggerhead *n* **1** a large-headed turtle occurring in most seas **2 at loggerheads** engaged in dispute or confrontation
WORD ORIGIN probably dialect *logger* wooden block + HEAD

loggia (loj-ya) *n* a covered gallery on the side of a building
WORD ORIGIN Italian

Why English Spelling is so Tricky

English spelling can sometimes appear to be a chaotic affair. The spellings of words such as *choir*, *colonel*, *laugh*, and *yacht* could never be guessed from the way that the words are pronounced, and this has caused much protestation at the diabolical conventions of spelling. Some people have even called for the introduction of a simpler system.

If every letter in the alphabet represented one sound and one sound only, you could write out words very easily once you knew which letter represented which sound. Some languages (such as Italian) are indeed quite like this, and present few surprises with regard to spelling once you know how each sound is written.

But English uses about 44 different sounds to make up words, whereas there are only 26 letters to indicate these sounds. This means that there is a mismatch between sound and spelling. Some letters have to be used for more than one sound, so the letter 't' has one sound in *tin* but is part of a different sound in *thin*, while 'a' has a different sound in *mat* than it has in *mate*.

More significantly, some sounds can be represented by more than one letter or combination of letters. The vowel sound in the words *aisle*, *guy*, *might*, and *rye* is the same in each word, but the spellings used to represent this sound are quite different. Similarly, the consonant sound at the end of the words *if*, *graph*, and *rough* has the same pronunciation in each word, but is represented by different letters.

Because of this mismatch between sound and spelling, it is possible for two different words to sound the same but be spelt differently. This can lead to confusion between the two spellings, as in the example of *there*, meaning 'to that place', and *their*, meaning 'belonging to them'.

Moreover, several other factors conspire to produce oddities in English spelling. For a start, English makes use of words from many different languages. At the heart of modern English are two completely different languages – Anglo-Saxon and French – which have two different spelling systems, but which both contributed thousands of words to the language.

As English developed it borrowed words from many other languages too, including Latin, Ancient Greek, Italian, Spanish, German, Arabic, Hindi, and Japanese. Each of these languages has its own spelling system – many of which are quite different from the natural English system – and the words that English has borrowed from them often keep the spelling patterns of the original language. Some of the letter combinations used in words borrowed from French – think of *connoisseur* – and Arabic – think of *burqa* – break the usual rules of English spelling.

Another source of difficulty is that some words contain letters which are not sounded when the word is pronounced. For example, the letter 'g' is silent in *gnat*, *phlegm*, and *sign*, while 'h' is silent in *honest*, *ghost*, and *rhyme*. Often these silent letters were sounded in the original form of a word. Over many years the pronunciation of these words became simplified, but the spelling has not changed to reflect the new pronunciation.

Then there is the fact that all of the letters except 'h', 'q', and 'y' can occur both as single and double letters within a word. For example, the letter 'b' occurs as a single letter in *robin*, *habit*, and *crab*, but in *bobbin*, *rabbit*, and *ebb* the 'b' is doubled without there being any change in the pattern of pronunciation.

As if all this did not make spelling hard enough, sometimes there is not even a clear agreement about which spelling of a word is correct. Some people write *barbecue* while others prefer *barbeque*; some write *judgment* but others prefer *judgement*. One of the most common sources of variation is the difference between American English, where, for example, *center*, *color*, and *gray* are regarded as correct, and British English, which uses *centre*, *colour*, and *grey*.

Yet in spite of all of the pitfalls they present, the current spellings are deeply entrenched, and any attempt at reform would probably only cause greater confusion. Perhaps the best approach is to accept English spelling as it is, and to embrace its quirkiness.

logging *n* the work of felling, trimming, and transporting timber **logger** *n*

logic *n* **1** the branch of philosophy that analyses the patterns of reasoning **2** a particular system of reasoning **3** reasoned thought or argument, as distinguished from irrationality **4** the interdependence of a series of events or facts **5** *electronics, computers* the principles underlying the units in a computer system that produce results from data **WORD ORIGIN** Greek *logikos* concerning speech or reasoning

logical *adj* **1** relating to or characteristic of logic **2** using or deduced from the principles of logic: *a logical conclusion* **3** capable of or using clear and valid reasoning **4** reasonable because of facts or events: *the logical choice* **logically** *adv*

logic gate *n electronics* same as **gate** (sense 4)

logician *n* a person who specializes in or is skilled at logic

log in *or* **on** *vb* to gain entrance to a computer system by keying in a special command

logistics *n* the detailed planning and organization of a large complex operation, such as a military campaign **logistical** *or* **logistic** *adj* **logistically** *adv* **WORD ORIGIN** French *loger* to lodge

log jam *n chiefly US & Canad* **1** a blockage caused by the crowding together of logs floating in a river **2** a deadlock

logo (**loh**-go) *n, pl* **-os** a special design that identifies a company or an organization and appears on all its products, printed material, etc. **WORD ORIGIN** shortened from *logotype* badge, symbol

log out *vb* to exit from a computer system by keying in a special command

-logy *n combining form* **1** indicating the science or study of: *musicology* **2** indicating writing or discourse: *trilogy; phraseology* **-logical** *or* **-logic** *adj combining form* **-logist** *n combining form* **WORD ORIGIN** Greek *logos* word

loin *n* **1** the part of the body between the pelvis and the ribs **2** a cut of meat from this part of an animal ▸ See also **loins** **WORD ORIGIN** Old French *loigne*

loincloth *n* a piece of cloth covering only the loins

loins *pl n* **1** the hips and the inner surface of the legs where they join the body **2** *euphemistic* the genitals

loiter *vb* to stand or wait aimlessly or idly **WORD ORIGIN** perhaps Middle Dutch *löteren* to wobble

Lolita (low-**lee**-ta) *n* a sexually precocious young girl **WORD ORIGIN** after the character in Nabokov's novel *Lolita*

loll *vb* **1** to lounge in a lazy manner **2** to hang loosely: *a wet lolling tongue; his head lolled back and forth* **WORD ORIGIN** perhaps imitative

lollipop *n* **1** a boiled sweet stuck on a small wooden stick **2** *Brit* an ice lolly **WORD ORIGIN** perhaps dialect *lolly* the tongue + POP²

lollipop man *or* **lady** *n Brit informal* a person holding a circular sign on a pole who stops traffic to enable children to cross the road safely

lollop *vb chiefly Brit* to walk or run with a clumsy or relaxed bouncing movement **WORD ORIGIN** probably *loll* + *-op*, as in *gallop*

lolly *n, pl* **-lies** **1** *informal* a lollipop **2** *Brit* short for **ice lolly** **3** *Brit, Austral, & NZ slang* money **4** *Austral & NZ informal* a sweet **WORD ORIGIN** shortened from *lollipop*

Londoner *n* a person from London

London pride *n* a rock plant with a rosette of leaves and pink flowers

lone *adj* **1** solitary: *a lone figure* **2** isolated: *a lone isle guarded by the great Atlantic swell* **3** *Brit* unmarried or widowed: *a lone parent* **WORD ORIGIN** from the mistaken division of *alone* into *a lone*

lonely *adj* **-lier, -liest** **1** unhappy as a result of solitude **2** resulting from the state of being alone: *command can be a lonely business* **3** isolated and not much visited by people: *a lonely beach* **loneliness** *n*

lonely hearts *adj* of or for people seeking a congenial companion or marriage partner: *lonely hearts ads*

loner *n informal* a person who prefers to be alone

lonesome *adj* **1** *chiefly US & Canad* lonely **2** causing feelings of loneliness: *it was lonesome up here on the mountain*

long¹ *adj* **1** having relatively great length in space or time **2** having greater than the average or expected range, extent, or duration: *a long session of talks* **3** seeming to occupy a greater time than is really so: *she was quiet a long moment* **4** of a specified extent or duration: *trimmed to about two cms long* **5** consisting of a large number of parts: *a long list* **6** *phonetics, prosody* (of a vowel) of relatively considerable duration **7** from end to end; lengthwise **8** *finance* having large holdings of securities or commodities in anticipation of rising prices **9** **in the long run** ultimately; after or over a period of time **10** **long on** *informal* plentifully supplied or endowed with: *long on show-biz gossip* ▷ *adv* **11** for a certain time or period: *how long have we got?* **12** for or during an extensive period of time: *to talk long into the night* **13** a considerable amount of time: *long after I met you; long ago* **14** **as** *or* **so long as** **a** for or during the same length of time that **b** provided that; if ▷ *n* **15** anything that is long **16** **before long** soon **17** **for long** for a long time **18** **the long and the short of it** the essential points or facts **longish** *adj* **WORD ORIGIN** Old English *lang*

long² *vb* to have a strong desire for something or to do something: *I longed for a baby; the more I think of him the more I long to see him* **WORD ORIGIN** Old English *langian*

long. longitude

long- *adv* (in combination) for or lasting a long time: *long-established; long-lasting*

longboat *n* **1** the largest boat carried aboard a commercial ship **2** same as **longship**

longbow *n* a large powerful hand-drawn bow

long-distance *adj* **1** covering relatively long distances: *a long-distance race* **2** (of a telephone call) connecting points relatively far apart

longevity (lon-**jev**-it-ee) *n* long life **WORD ORIGIN** Latin *longus* long + *aevum* age

long face *n* a glum expression

longhand *n* ordinary handwriting, as opposed to typing or shorthand

longhorn *n* a British breed of beef cattle with long curved horns

longing *n* **1** a strong feeling of wanting something one is unlikely ever to have ▷ *adj* **2** having or showing desire: *longing glances* **longingly** *adv*

longitude *n* distance in degrees east or west of the prime meridian at 0° **WORD ORIGIN** Latin *longitudo* length

longitudinal *adj* **1** of longitude or length **2** placed or extended lengthways

long johns *pl n informal* long underpants

long jump *n* an athletic contest of jumping the greatest length from a fixed mark

long-life *adj* (of milk, batteries, etc.) lasting longer than the regular kind

long-lived *adj* living or lasting for a long time

long-playing *adj old-fashioned* of or relating to an LP

long-range *adj* **1** of or extending into the future: *a long-range economic forecast* **2** (of vehicles, aircraft, or weapons) capable of covering great distances

longship *n* a narrow open boat with oars and a square sail, used by the Vikings

longshore drift *n* the movement of material along a beach, due to waves approaching the shore at an oblique angle

longshoreman *n, pl* **-men** *US & Canad* a docker

long shot *n* **1** an undertaking, guess, or possibility with little chance of success **2** a bet against heavy odds **3** **not by a long shot** not by any means: *she wasn't beaten, not by a long shot*

long-sighted *adj* **1** able to see only distant objects in focus **2** far-sighted

long-standing *adj* existing for a long time

long-suffering *adj* enduring trouble or unhappiness without complaint

long-term *adj* **1** lasting or extending over a long time: *a long-term commitment* ▷ *n* **long term** **2** **in the long term** over a long period of time: *in the long term the cost of energy will have to go up*

longtime *adj* of long standing: *his longtime colleague; his longtime relationship with Sue*

long wave *n* a radio wave with a wavelength greater than 1000 metres

longways *or US & Canad* **longwise** *adv* lengthways

long-winded *adj* tiresomely long **long-windedness** *n*

loo *n, pl* **loos** *Brit & NZ informal* a toilet **WORD ORIGIN** perhaps from French *lieux d'aisance* water closet

loofah *n* a long rough-textured bath sponge made from the dried pod of a gourd
WORD ORIGIN Arabic *lūf*

look *vb* **1** (often foll. by *at*) to direct the eyes (towards): *he turned to look at her* **2** (often foll. by *at*) to consider: *let's look at the issues involved* **3** to give the impression of being; seem: *Luxembourg's timetable looks a winner* **4** to face in a particular direction: *Morgan's Rock looks south* **5** (foll. by *for*) to search or seek: *the department looks for reputable firms* **6** (foll. by *into*) to carry out an investigation **7** to direct a look at (someone) in a specified way: *she looks at Teresina suspiciously* **8** to match in appearance with (something): *looking your best* **9** to expect or hope (to do something): *we would look to derive a procedure that would account for most cases* **10** **look alive** or **lively** or **sharp** or **smart** to hurry up; get busy **11** **look here** an expression used to attract someone's attention or add emphasis to a statement ▷ *n* **12** an instance of looking: *a look of icy contempt* **13** a view or sight (of something): *take a look at my view* **14** (often *pl*) appearance to the eye or mind; aspect: *I'm not happy with the look of things here; better than you by the looks of it* **15** style or fashion: *the look made famous by the great Russian* ▷ *conj* **16** an expression demanding attention or showing annoyance: *look, I won't be coming back*
▶ See also **look after, look back**, etc.
looker *n*
☰ USAGE
☰ See at **like**.

look after *vb* to take care of

lookalike *n* a person or thing that is the double of another, often well-known, person or thing

look back *vb* **1** to think about the past **2** **never looked back** was extremely successful: *he became the station's first major signing and never looked back*

look down *vb* (foll. by *on* or *upon*) to treat as inferior or unimportant

look forward to *vb* to anticipate with pleasure

look-in *informal n* **1** a chance to be chosen or participate: *before anyone else gets a look-in* ▷ *vb* **look in 2** to pay a short visit

looking glass *n* a mirror

look on *vb* **1** to be a spectator **2** to consider or regard: *I just looked on her as a friend* **looker-on** *n*

lookout *n* **1** the act of watching for danger or for an opportunity: *on the lookout for attack* **2** a person or people keeping such a watch **3** a viewpoint from which a watch is kept **4** *informal* worry or concern: *that is my lookout rather than theirs* **5** *chiefly Brit* chances or prospect: *it's a bad lookout for Europe* ▷ *vb* **look out 6** to be careful **7** to watch out for: *look out particularly for oils that have been flavoured* **8** to find and take out: *little time to look out clothes that she might need* **9** (foll. by *on* or *over*) to face in a particular direction: *looking out over the courtyard*

look over *vb* **1** to inspect or examine ▷ *n* **look-over 2** an inspection

look-see *n slang* a brief inspection

look up *vb* **1** to discover or confirm by checking in a reference book **2** to improve: *things were looking up* **3** **look up to** to have respect for: *she looked up to him as a kind of father* **4** to visit (a person): *I'll look you up when I'm in town*

loom[1] *n* a machine for weaving yarn into cloth
WORD ORIGIN variant of Old English *gelōma* tool

loom[2] *vb* **1** to appear indistinctly, esp. as a tall and threatening shape **2** (of an event) to seem ominously close
WORD ORIGIN perhaps East Frisian *lomen* to move slowly

loon[1] *n US & Canad* same as **diver** (sense 3)
WORD ORIGIN Scandinavian

loon[2] *n informal* a simple-minded or stupid person

loonie *n Canad slang* **1** a Canadian dollar coin with a loon bird on one of its faces **2** the Canadian currency

loony *slang adj* **loonier, looniest 1** insane **2** foolish or ridiculous ▷ *n, pl* **loonies 3** a foolish or insane person
WORD ORIGIN shortened from *lunatic*

loop *n* **1** the rounded shape formed by a curved line that crosses itself: *a loop of the highway* **2** any round or oval-shaped thing that is closed or nearly closed **3** *electronics* a closed circuit through which a signal can circulate **4** a flight manoeuvre in which an aircraft flies vertically in a complete circle **5** a continuous strip of film or tape **6** *computers* a series of instructions in a program, performed repeatedly until some specified condition is satisfied ▷ *vb* **7** to make into a loop **8** to fasten or encircle with a loop **9** Also: **loop the loop** to fly or be flown vertically in a complete circle
WORD ORIGIN origin unknown

loophole *n* an ambiguity or omission in the law, which enables one to evade it

loopy *adj* **loopier, loopiest** *informal* slightly mad or crazy

loose *adj* **1** (of clothing) not close-fitting: *the jacket loose and unbuttoned* **2** free or released from confinement or restraint **3** not tight, fastened, fixed, or tense **4** not bundled, fastened, or put in a container: *loose tobacco* **5** inexact or imprecise: *a loose translation* **6** (of cash) accessible: *a lot of the loose money is floating around the city* **7** *old-fashioned* sexually promiscuous **8** lacking a sense of propriety: *loose talk* **9** **at a loose end** bored because one has nothing to do ▷ *n* **10** **on the loose** free from confinement or restraint **11** **the loose** *rugby* the part of play when the forwards close round the ball in a ruck or loose scrum ▷ *adv* **12** in a loose manner; loosely ▷ *vb* **loosing, loosed 13** to free or release from restraint or obligation: *he loosed the dogs* **14** to unfasten or untie: *the guards loosed his arms* **15** to make or become less strict, tight, firmly attached, or compact **16** to let fly (a bullet, arrow, or other missile) **loosely** *adv* **looseness** *n*
WORD ORIGIN Old Norse *lauss* free

loosebox *n* an enclosed stall with a door in which an animal can be kept

loose cannon *n* a person or thing, with the potential to cause considerable

damage, that appears to be out of control

loose-jointed *adj* supple and lithe

loose-leaf *adj* (of a binder) allowing the removal and addition of pages

loosen *vb* **1** to make or become less tight: *loosen and relax the ankle* **2** (often foll. by *up*) to make or become less firm, compact, or rigid: *massage is used first to loosen up the muscles* **3** to untie **4** (often foll. by *up*) to make or become less strict: *the churches loosen up on sexual teachings*

loot *n* **1** goods stolen in wartime or during riots; plunder **2** *informal* money ▷ *vb* **3** to plunder (a city) during war or riots **4** to steal (money or goods) during war or riots **looter** *n*
WORD ORIGIN Hindi *lūt*

lop *vb* **lopping, lopped** (usually foll. by *off*) **1** to cut (parts) off a tree or body **2** to cut out or eliminate any unnecessary parts: *some parts of the legislature were lopped off*
WORD ORIGIN Middle English *loppe* branches cut off

lope *vb* **loping, loped 1** to move or run with a long easy stride ▷ *n* **2** a long steady gait or stride
WORD ORIGIN Old Norse *hlaupa* to leap

lop-eared *adj* (of animals) having ears that droop

lopsided *adj* greater in weight, height, or size on one side

loquacious *adj* talkative **loquacity** *n*
WORD ORIGIN Latin *loqui* to speak

lord *n* **1** a person with power or authority over others, such as a monarch or master **2** a male member of the nobility **3** (in medieval Europe) a feudal superior **4** **my lord** a respectful form of address used to a judge, bishop, or nobleman ▷ *vb* **5** **lord it over someone** to act in a superior manner towards someone
WORD ORIGIN Old English *hlāford* bread keeper

Lord *n* **1** *Christianity* a title given to God or Jesus Christ **2** *Brit* a title given to certain male peers **3** *Brit* a title given to certain high officials and judges ▷ *interj* **4** an exclamation of dismay or surprise: *Good Lord!*

Lord Chancellor *n Brit government* the cabinet minster who is head of the judiciary and Speaker of the House of Lords

Lord Chief Justice *n* (in England and Wales) the judge who is second only to the Lord Chancellor and president of one division of the High Court of Justice

Lord Lieutenant *n* **1** (in Britain) the representative of the Crown in a county **2** (formerly) the British viceroy in Ireland

lordly *adj* **-lier, -liest 1** haughty or arrogant **2** of or suitable to a lord **lordliness** *n*

Lord Mayor *n* the mayor in the City of London, in certain other English boroughs, and in some Australian cities

Lord Privy Seal *n* (in Britain) the senior cabinet minister without official duties

Lords *n* **the Lords** short for **House of Lords**

lordship n the position or authority of a lord

Lordship n (preceded by *Your* or *His*) *Brit* a title used to address or refer to a bishop, a judge of the high court, or any peer except a duke

Lord's Prayer n **the Lord's Prayer** the prayer taught by Jesus Christ to his disciples

Lords Spiritual pl n (in Britain) the Anglican archbishops and senior bishops who are members of the House of Lords

Lord's Supper n **the Lord's Supper** same as **Holy Communion**

Lords Temporal pl n (in Britain) the peers other than bishops in their capacity as members of the House of Lords

lore n collective knowledge or wisdom on a particular subject
WORD ORIGIN Old English *lār*

lorgnette (lor-**nyet**) n a pair of spectacles or opera glasses mounted on a long handle
WORD ORIGIN French, from *lorgner* to squint

lorikeet n a small brightly coloured Australian parrot

lorry n, pl **-ries** *Brit & S African* a large motor vehicle for transporting heavy loads
WORD ORIGIN perhaps dialect *lurry* to pull

lose vb **losing**, **lost** 1 to come to be without, through carelessness or by accident or theft 2 to fail to keep or maintain: *to lose control* 3 to suffer the loss of: *he will lose his redundancy money* 4 to get rid of: *I've lost a stone this summer* 5 to fail to get or make use of: *Lysenko never lost a chance to show his erudition* 6 to be defeated in a fight or competition 7 to fail to see, hear, or understand: *she lost sight of him* 8 to waste: *so I'd lost a fortune* 9 to go astray from: *psychologists lose the trail* 10 to allow to go astray or out of sight: *he lost, at the Gare de Lyon, a case with most of his early manuscripts* 11 to cause the loss of: *I came in to have the gear attended to, which lost me a lap* 12 to absorb or engross: *lost in thought* 13 to die or cause the death of: *two lost as yacht sinks in storm* 14 to outdistance or escape from: *there's some satisfaction in knowing that they've lost us* 15 (of a timepiece) to run slow (by a specified amount)
WORD ORIGIN Old English *losian* to perish

lose out vb *informal* 1 to be defeated or unsuccessful 2 **lose out on** to fail to secure or make use of: *the yard has already lost out on a number of valuable orders this year*

loser n 1 a person or thing that loses 2 *informal* a person or thing that seems destined to fail: *he's a bit of a loser*

losing adj unprofitable or failing: *a losing streak that cost him millions*

loss n 1 the act or an instance of losing 2 the person, thing, or amount lost: *the only loss was a sleeping-bag* 3 the disadvantage or deprivation resulting from losing: *a loss of sovereignty* 4 **at a loss** a uncertain what to do; bewildered b with income less than outlay: *they cannot afford to run branches at a loss*

WORD ORIGIN Old English *lōsian* to be destroyed

loss leader n an article offered at a low price to attract customers

lost vb 1 the past of **lose** ▷ adj 2 unable to find one's way 3 unable to be found or recovered 4 confused or bewildered: *she seemed a bit lost* 5 (sometimes foll. by *on*) not used, noticed, or understood by: *not that the propaganda value of the game was lost on the authorities* 6 no longer possessed or existing: *lost credit* 7 (foll. by *in*) engrossed (in): *he remained lost in his own thoughts* 8 morally fallen: *a lost woman* 9 damned: *a lost soul*

lost cause n something with no chance of success

lot pron 1 **a lot** a great number or quantity: *not that there was a lot to tell; a lot of people* ▷ n 2 a collection of things or people: *your lot have wasted enough time* 3 destiny or fortune: *the refugees did not choose their lot* 4 any object, such as a straw or slip of paper, drawn from others at random to make a selection or choice: *they could only be split by the drawing of lots; the casting by lots* 5 the use of lots in making a choice: *chosen by lot* 6 an item or set of items for sale in an auction 7 *US, Canad, Austral, & NZ* an area of land: *to the parking lot* 8 **a bad lot** an unpleasant or disreputable person 9 **cast** or **throw in one's lot with someone** to join with voluntarily and share the fortunes of someone 10 **the lot** the entire amount or number ▷ adv 11 (preceded by *a*) *informal* to a considerable extent, degree, or amount: *steroids are used a lot in weightlifting* ▶ See also **lots**
WORD ORIGIN Old English *hlot*

loth (rhymes with **both**) adj same as **loath**

Lothario (loh-**thah**-ree-oh) n, pl **-os** a seducer
WORD ORIGIN after a character in a play

lotion n a liquid preparation having a soothing, cleansing, or antiseptic action, applied to the skin
WORD ORIGIN Latin *lotio* a washing

lots *informal* pl n 1 (often foll. by *of*) great numbers or quantities: *lots of friends; you can read lots into Nostradamus* ▷ adv 2 a great deal

lottery n, pl **-teries** 1 a method of raising money by selling tickets by which a winner is selected at random 2 a venture whose outcome is a matter of luck: *hospital treatment is a lottery*
WORD ORIGIN Middle Dutch *loterije*

lotto n 1 a game of chance similar to bingo 2 **Lotto** (in certain countries) the national lottery
WORD ORIGIN Italian

lotus n 1 (in Greek mythology) a fruit that induces dreamy forgetfulness in those who eat it 2 any of several water lilies of tropical Africa and Asia, regarded as sacred 3 a symbolic representation of such a plant
WORD ORIGIN Greek *lōtos*

lotus-eater n a person who lives in lazy forgetfulness

lotus position n a seated cross-legged position with each foot on top of the opposite thigh, used in yoga and meditation

loud adj 1 (of sound) relatively great in volume: *loud applause* 2 making or able to make sounds of relatively great volume: *a loud voice* 3 insistent and emphatic: *loud appeals* 4 (of colours or patterns) harsh to look at 5 noisy, vulgar, and offensive ▷ adv 6 in a loud manner 7 **out loud** audibly **loudly** adv **loudness** n
WORD ORIGIN Old English *hlud*

loud-hailer n a portable loudspeaker with a built-in amplifier and microphone

loudmouth n a person who talks too much, esp. in a boastful or indiscreet way **loudmouthed** adj

loudspeaker n a device for converting electrical signals into sounds

lough n *Irish* 1 a lake 2 a long narrow arm of the sea
WORD ORIGIN Irish *loch* lake

lounge n 1 a living room in a private house 2 same as **lounge bar** 3 a communal room in a hotel, ship, or airport, used for waiting or relaxing in 4 the act of lounging ▷ vb **lounging**, **lounged** 5 (often foll. by *about* or *around*) to sit or lie in a relaxed manner 6 to pass time lazily or idly
WORD ORIGIN origin unknown

lounge bar n a more expensive and comfortable bar in a pub or hotel

lounge suit n a man's suit for daytime wear

lour vb same as **lower²**

lourie (rhymes with **dowry**) or **loerie** n a type of African bird with either crimson or grey plumage
WORD ORIGIN Afrikaans, from Malay

louse n 1 pl **lice** a wingless blood-sucking insect which feeds off man and some animals 2 pl **louses** *slang* an unpleasant or dishonourable person
WORD ORIGIN Old English *lūs*

louse up vb **lousing**, **loused** *slang* to ruin or spoil

lousy adj **lousier**, **lousiest** 1 *slang* very mean or unpleasant 2 *slang* inferior or bad 3 *slang* ill or unwell 4 infested with lice

lout n a crude or oafish person; boor **loutish** adj
WORD ORIGIN perhaps Old English *lūtan* to stoop

louvre or *US* **louver** (**loo**-ver) n **a** any of a set of horizontal slats in a door or window, slanted to admit air but not rain **b** the slats and frame supporting them **louvred** or *US* **louvered** adj
WORD ORIGIN Old French *lovier*

lovage n a European herb with greenish-white flowers
WORD ORIGIN Old French *luvesche*, from Latin *ligusticum*, literally: Ligurian (plant)

love vb **loving**, **loved** 1 to have a great affection for a person or thing 2 to have passionate desire for someone 3 to like (to do something) very much ▷ n 4 an intense emotion of affection towards a person or thing 5 a deep feeling of sexual attraction 6 wholehearted liking for or pleasure in something 7 a beloved person: often used as an endearment 8 *Brit informal*

Caribbean English

One delight of visiting the Caribbean, or of living among West Indians anywhere, is the sound of voices. It may be the singsong cadence of Trinidadians, the gentle rhythms of Jamaican speech, or just the sound of an unplaceable island in the Caribbean Sea. In fact, the term *Caribbean* can even embrace Guyana and Belize on the South and North American mainlands, countries of coastal Central America, and Bermuda in the Atlantic.

On a big island such as Jamaica or Trinidad, the sounds are located on a continuum of speech and word choice. *Erudite English* takes its vocabulary of long words and phrases from the Bible and literary classics, overlaid with local pitch, stress, and tone. The spelling, choice of words, and syntax of *Standard English* generally follow British English. That version of English may be highly distinctive, as in *Jamaican English*, or provide the basis of a creole – virtually a different language, as in *Jamaican Patois*. Even those who have never set foot on the Bahamas, Grenada, or St Lucia hear the sounds in music and spoken-word poetry: *calypso*, *reggae*, *dub*, and *rap*.

A speaker may switch from one variety to another, depending on social context. Sound, lexicon, and syntax vary, too, depending on whether speakers descend from indentured servants exported to Trinidad from India, or from West Africans abducted in the slave trade. One especially finds this in the language of gastronomy, whether at home or among expatriates in Britain and North America. Thus the hungry Trinidadian or Guyanan may lunch on a goat *roti*, a flatbread enclosing curried meats and vegetables, or snack on a *double*, chickpea curry sandwiched between two small rounds of fried dough. The Jamaican seeks out *jerk* chicken or pork, in which each molecule of meat seems to have been replaced by a molecule of allspice, thyme, and scotch bonnet peppers (as distinguished from *seasoning peppers*, which impart flavour, not heat). *Ground provisions* is a generic term for staples such as yams, cassava, and plantains. The Englishes that emerged in Jamaica and elsewhere incorporated specialized terms for fruits and vegetables (such as

*ackee*s and *callaloo*), and call bananas *figs*.

Aboriginal languages such as Taino and Carib are extinct, but some Caribbean words derive from them, as do others from the languages of West Africa and the Indian subcontinent. The way Caribbean peoples speak was also influenced by British, French, and Spanish colonizers and colonists, and the impact of American culture and technology. In Jamaica, the Rastafarian movement forged a unique synthesis of messianic belief centred on the Ethiopian emperor Haile Selassie, dietary proscriptions, attachment to *ganja* (marijuana) and championship of Black pride. Trinidadian speech is saturated with words relating to the annual phantasmagoria of the Carnival festival, and to many aspects of folklore. A common Trinidadian pastime is to *lime*, to hang around and observe.

Such idiosyncrasies apart, Caribbean English has many commonalities. Customers in a bar sound like they're ordering a *bear* instead of a *beer*. In Guyana, Jamaica, Antigua, and St Kitts, the short 'o' sound tends to sound like the short 'a', so that *job* becomes *jab*. In many places, *think*, *three*, and *thanks* become *tink*, *tree*, and *tanks*, and *that*, *those*, and *there* become *dat*, *dose*, and *dere*. Commonly dropped is the verb *to be* (*she waiting*, not *she is waiting*), and the final of two or more concluding consonants, so that *stand* becomes *stan'*. The present tense may be used to refer to past time (*I work two weeks on dis job*), and the singular may stand for the plural (*My relative all live in de islands*). Rhythm is timed to syllables. People in Jamaica, Barbados, and Guyana pronounce the 'r' before a consonant and at the end of words; those in the Bahamas, Belize, Trinidad and Tobago, as well as the Windward and Leeward Islands, don't.

What the dialect poet Miguel Browne writes of Trinidadians in 'Trini Talk' could apply equally to the residents of other islands:

Man we know how to talk before we could creep.
We could out talk all odders in one clean sweep.
A Trini who cah talk will laugh instead.
And if he cah do dat, he better off dead.

a commonplace term of address, not necessarily restricted to people one knows or has regard for **9** (in tennis, squash, etc.) a score of zero **10 fall in love** to become in love **11 for love or money** in any circumstances **12 in love** feeling a strong emotional and sexual attraction **13 make love to a** to have sexual intercourse with **b** *now archaic* to court **lovable** *or* **loveable** *adj*
WORD ORIGIN Old English *lufu*

love affair *n* a romantic or sexual relationship between two people who are not married to each other

lovebird *n* any of several small African parrots often kept as cage birds

lovebite *n* a temporary red mark left on a person's skin by a partner biting or sucking it during lovemaking

love child *n euphemistic* a child whose parents have not been married to each other

loveless *adj* without love: *a loveless marriage*

love-lies-bleeding *n* a plant with drooping spikes of small red flowers

love life *n* a person's romantic or sexual relationships

lovelorn *adj* miserable because of unreturned love or unhappiness in love

lovely *adj* -lier, -liest **1** very attractive or beautiful **2** highly pleasing or enjoyable: *thanks for a lovely evening* ⊳ *n, pl* -lies **3** *slang* an attractive woman: *curvaceous lovelies* **loveliness** *n*

lovemaking *n* **1** sexual play and activity between lovers, including sexual intercourse **2** *archaic* courtship

lover *n* **1** a person having a sexual relationship with another person outside marriage **2** (*often pl*) either of the people involved in a love affair **3** someone who loves a specified person or thing: *an animal-lover*

lovesick *adj* pining or languishing because of love **lovesickness** *n*

lovey-dovey *adj* making a sentimental or showy display of affection

loving *adj* feeling or showing love and affection **lovingly** *adv*

loving cup *n* a large two-handled cup out of which people drink in turn

low¹ *adj* **1** having a relatively small distance from base to top: *a low wall* **2** of less than usual amount, degree, quality, or cost: *low score; low inflation* **3** situated at a relatively short distance above the ground, sea level, or the horizon: *heavy weather with low driving cloud* **4** (of numbers) small **5** involving or containing a relatively small amount of something: *low-alcohol summer drinks* **6** having little value or quality: *it sounds as if your self-confidence is low* **7** coarse or vulgar: *low comedy* **8** unworthy or contemptible: *Oh, that's low, Justin* **9** inferior in culture or status **10** in a weakened physical or mental state **11** with a hushed tone: *in a low, scared voice* **12** low-necked: *a low evening gown* **13** music of or having a relatively low pitch **14** (of latitudes) situated not far north or south of the equator **15** having little or no money **16** unfavourable: *he has a low opinion of Ford* **17** deep: *a low bow*

18 (of a gear) providing a relatively low speed ⊳ *adv* **19** in a low position, level, or degree: *the pilot flew low over the area* **20** at a low pitch; deeply: *he's singing very low* **21** cheaply: *the bank is having to buy high and sell low* **22 lay low a** to make (someone) fall by a blow **b** to overcome or destroy **23 lie low** to keep or be concealed or quiet ⊳ *n* **24** a low position, level, or degree: *shares hit new low* **25** an area of low atmospheric pressure; depression **lowness** *n*
WORD ORIGIN Old Norse *lāgr*

low² *n* **1** Also: **lowing** the sound uttered by cattle; moo ⊳ *vb* **2** to make a mooing sound
WORD ORIGIN Old English *hlōwan*

low-alcohol *adj* (of beer or wine) containing only a small amount of alcohol

lowborn *adj now rare* of ignoble or common parentage

lowbrow *disparaging n* **1** a person with uncultivated or nonintellectual tastes ⊳ *adj* **2** of or for such a person

Low Church *n* a section of the Church of England which stresses evangelical beliefs and practices **Low-Church** *adj*

low comedy *n* comedy characterized by slapstick and physical action

Low Countries *pl n* Belgium, Luxembourg, and the Netherlands

low-down *informal adj* **1** mean, underhand, and dishonest ⊳ *n* **lowdown 2 the lowdown** information

lower¹ *adj* **1** being below one or more other things: *the lower branches* **2** reduced in amount or value: *lower rates* **3 Lower** *geol* denoting the early part of a period or formation ⊳ *vb* **4** to cause or allow to move down: *she lowered her head* **5** to behave in a way that damages one's respect: *she'd never lowered herself enough to make a call* **6** to lessen or become less: *the cholesterol was lowered by medication* **7** to make quieter or reduce the pitch of

lower² *or* **lour** *vb* (of the sky or weather) to be overcast and menacing **lowering** *or* **louring** *adj*
WORD ORIGIN Middle English *louren* to scowl

lower case *n* (in printing) small letters, as opposed to capital letters **lower-case** *adj*

lower class *n* the class with the lowest position in society **lower-class** *adj*

lower house *n* one of the houses of a parliament that has two chambers: usually the larger and more representative

lowest common denominator *n maths* the smallest integer or polynomial that is exactly divisible by each denominator of a set of fractions

lowest common multiple *n maths* the smallest number or quantity that is exactly divisible by each member of a set of numbers or quantities

low frequency *n* any radio frequency lying between 300 and 30 kilohertz

Low German *n* a language of N Germany, spoken in rural areas

low-key *or* **low-keyed** *adj* **1** restrained or subdued **2** having a low intensity or tone

lowland *n* **1** relatively low ground **2** (*often pl*) a low generally flat region ⊳ *adj* **3** of a lowland or lowlands **lowlander** *n*

Lowland *adj* of the Lowlands or the dialects of English spoken there **Lowlander** *n*

Lowlands *pl n* a low generally flat region of S Central Scotland

lowlight *n* **1** an unenjoyable or unpleasant part of an event **2** (*usually pl*) a streak of darker colour artificially applied to the hair

lowly *adj* -lier, -liest **1** humble in position or status **2** simple and unpretentious **lowliness** *n*

Low Mass *n* a simplified form of Mass that is spoken rather than sung

low-minded *adj* having a vulgar or crude mind **low-mindedness** *n*

low-pitched *adj* **1** pitched low in tone **2** (of a roof) with a shallow slope

low profile *n* a deliberate shunning of publicity: *he kept a low profile* **low-profile** *adj*

low-spirited *adj* depressed or dejected

low-tech *adj* **1** of or using low technology **2** in the style of interior design that uses items associated with low technology

low technology *n* unsophisticated technology that is limited to the production of basic necessities

low tide *n* the tide at its lowest level or the time at which it reaches this

low water *n* **1** low tide **2** the lowest level which a stretch of water reaches

loyal *adj* **1** faithful to one's friends, country, or government **2** of or expressing loyalty: *the loyal toast* **loyally** *adv*
WORD ORIGIN Latin *legalis* legal

loyalist *n* a patriotic supporter of the sovereign or government **loyalism** *n*

Loyalist *n* (in Northern Ireland) any of the Protestants wishing to retain Ulster's link with Britain

loyalty *n, pl* -ties **1** the quality of being loyal **2** a feeling of friendship or duty towards someone or something

loyalty card *n* a swipe card issued by a supermarket or chain store to a customer, used to record credit points awarded for money spent in the store

lozenge *n* **1** *med* a medicated tablet held in the mouth until it has dissolved **2** *geom* a rhombus
WORD ORIGIN Old French *losange*

LP *n* a gramophone record of 12 inches in diameter, which holds about 20 or 25 minutes of sound on each side
WORD ORIGIN shortened from *long player*

L-plate *n Austral & Brit* a red 'L' on a white square attached to a motor vehicle to indicate that the driver is a learner

Lr *chem* lawrencium

LSD *n* lysergic acid diethylamide; an illegal hallucinogenic drug

L.S.D., £.s.d. *or* **l.s.d.** pounds, shillings, pence
WORD ORIGIN Latin *librae, solidi, denarii*

Lt Lieutenant

Ltd *Brit* Limited (Liability)

Lu *chem* lutetium

lubber *n* **1** a big, awkward, or stupid person **2** short for **landlubber**
> **lubberly** *adj, adv* **lubberliness** *n*
WORD ORIGIN probably from Old Norse

lubricant *n* a lubricating substance, such as oil

lubricate (**loo**-brik-ate) *vb* **-cating, -cated 1** to cover with an oily substance to lessen friction **2** to make greasy, slippery, or smooth **lubrication** *n*
WORD ORIGIN Latin *lubricare* to make slippery

lubricious (loo-**brish**-uss) *adj formal or literary* lewd
WORD ORIGIN Latin *lubricus* slippery

lucerne *n Austral & Brit* same as **alfalfa**

lucid *adj* **1** clear and easily understood **2** capable of clear thought, particularly between periods of insanity or delirium **3** shining or glowing **lucidity** *n* **lucidly** *adv*
WORD ORIGIN Latin *lucidus* full of light

Lucifer *n* Satan
WORD ORIGIN Latin: light-bearer, from *lux* light + *ferre* to bear

luck *n* **1** events that are subject to chance; fortune, good or bad **2** success or good fortune **3 down on one's luck** lacking good fortune to the extent of suffering hardship **4 no such luck** *informal* unfortunately not **5 try one's luck** to attempt something that is uncertain
WORD ORIGIN Middle Dutch *luc*

luckless *adj* unfortunate or unlucky

lucky *adj* **luckier, luckiest 1** having or bringing good fortune **2** happening by chance, esp. as desired **luckily** *adv*

lucky dip *n Brit, Austral, & NZ* a box filled with sawdust containing small prizes for which children search

lucrative *adj* profitable

lucre (**loo**-ker) *n usually facetious* money or wealth: *filthy lucre*
WORD ORIGIN Latin *lucrum* gain

Luddite *n Brit history* **1** any of the textile workers opposed to mechanization, who organized machine-breaking between 1811 and 1816 **2** any opponent of industrial change or innovation ▷ *adj* **3** of the Luddites
WORD ORIGIN after Ned *Ludd*, who destroyed machinery

luderick *n* an Australian fish, usually black or dark brown in colour

ludicrous *adj* absurd or ridiculous **ludicrously** *adv*
WORD ORIGIN Latin *ludus* game

ludo *n Austral & Brit* a simple board game in which players move counters forward by throwing dice
WORD ORIGIN Latin: I play

luff *vb* **1** *naut* to sail (a ship) into the wind **2** to move the jib of a crane in order to shift a load
WORD ORIGIN Old French *lof*

lug¹ *vb* **lugging, lugged** to carry or drag with great effort
WORD ORIGIN probably from Old Norse

lug² *n* **1** a projecting piece by which something is connected, supported, or lifted **2** *informal & Scot* an ear
WORD ORIGIN Scots: ear

luggage *n* suitcases, trunks, and bags
WORD ORIGIN perhaps LUG¹ + *-age*, as in *baggage*

lugger *n naut* a small working boat with an oblong sail
WORD ORIGIN origin unknown

lugubrious (loo-**goo**-bree-uss) *adj* mournful or gloomy
WORD ORIGIN Latin *lugere* to grieve

lugworm *n* a large worm which lives in burrows on sandy shores and is often used as bait by fishermen
WORD ORIGIN origin unknown

lukewarm *adj* **1** (of a liquid) moderately warm; tepid **2** lacking enthusiasm or conviction
WORD ORIGIN probably from Old English *hlēow* warm

lull *vb* **1** to soothe (a person or animal) by soft sounds or motions **2** to calm (fears or suspicions) by deception ▷ *n* **3** a short period of calm
WORD ORIGIN perhaps imitative of crooning sounds

lullaby *n, pl* **-bies** a quiet song to lull a child to sleep
WORD ORIGIN perhaps a blend of *lull* + *goodbye*

lumbago (lum-**bay**-go) *n* pain in the lower back; low backache
WORD ORIGIN Latin *lumbus* loin

lumbar *adj* relating to the lower back
WORD ORIGIN Latin *lumbus* loin

lumbar puncture *n med* insertion of a hollow needle into the lower spinal cord to withdraw fluid for diagnosis

lumber¹ *n* **1** *Brit* unwanted disused household articles **2** *chiefly US & Canad* logs; sawn timber ▷ *vb* **3** *informal* to burden with something unpleasant: *somebody gets lumbered with the extra costs* **4** to fill up with useless household articles **5** *chiefly US & Canad* to convert trees into marketable timber
WORD ORIGIN perhaps from LUMBER²

lumber² *vb* to move awkwardly and heavily **lumbering** *adj*
WORD ORIGIN Middle English *lomeren*

lumberjack *n* (esp. in North America) a person who fells trees and prepares the timber for transport

luminary *n, pl* **-naries 1 a** a famous person **b** an expert in a particular subject **2** *literary* something, such as the sun or moon, that gives off light

luminescence *n physics* the emission of light at low temperatures by any process other than burning **luminescent** *adj*

luminous *adj* **1** reflecting or giving off light: *luminous colours* **2** *not in technical use* luminescent: *luminous sparklers* **3** enlightening or wise **luminosity** *n*
WORD ORIGIN Latin *lumen* light

lump¹ *n* **1** a small solid mass without definite shape **2** *pathol* any small swelling or tumour **3** *informal* an awkward, heavy, or stupid person **4 a lump in one's throat** a tight dry feeling in one's throat, usually caused by great emotion **5 the lump** *Brit* self-employed workers in the building trade considered collectively ▷ *adj* **6** in the form of a lump or lumps: *lump sugar* ▷ *vb* **7** (often foll. by *together*) to consider as a single group, often without justification **8** to grow into lumps or become lumpy
WORD ORIGIN probably related to Scandinavian dialect: block

lump² *vb* **lump it** *informal* to accept something irrespective of personal preference: *if you don't like it, you can lump it*
WORD ORIGIN origin unknown

lumpectomy *n, pl* **-mies** surgical removal of a tumour in a breast
WORD ORIGIN *lump* + Greek *tomē* a cutting

lumpish *adj* stupid, clumsy, or heavy **lumpishness** *n*

lump sum *n* a relatively large sum of money, paid at one time

lumpy *adj* **lumpier, lumpiest** full of or having lumps **lumpiness** *n*

lunacy *n, pl* **-cies 1** foolishness **2** (formerly) any severe mental illness

lunar *adj* relating to the moon: *lunar eclipse*
WORD ORIGIN Latin *luna* the moon

lunatic *adj* **1** foolish; eccentric **2** *archaic* insane ▷ *n* **3** a foolish or annoying person **4** *archaic* a person who is insane
WORD ORIGIN Latin *luna* moon

lunatic asylum *n offensive* a home or hospital for the mentally ill

lunatic fringe *n* the members of a group who adopt views regarded as extreme

lunch *n* **1** a meal eaten during the middle of the day ▷ *vb* **2** to eat lunch
WORD ORIGIN shortened from *luncheon*

luncheon *n* a lunch, often a formal one
WORD ORIGIN probably variant of *nuncheon*, from Middle English *none* noon + *schench* drink

luncheon meat *n* a ground mixture of meat (often pork) and cereal, usually tinned

luncheon voucher *n Brit* a voucher for a specified amount issued to employees and accepted by some restaurants as payment for food

lunchroom *n US & Canad* a room where lunch is served or where students or employees may eat lunches they bring

lung *n* the part of the body that allows an animal or bird to breathe air. Humans have two lungs, contained within the chest cavity
WORD ORIGIN Old English *lungen*

lunge *n* **1** a sudden forward motion **2** *fencing* a thrust made by advancing the front foot and straightening the back leg ▷ *vb* **lunging, lunged 3** to move with a lunge **4** *fencing* to make a lunge
WORD ORIGIN French *allonger* to stretch out (one's arm)

lungfish *n, pl* **-fish** *or* **-fishes** a freshwater fish with an air-breathing lung

lupin *n* a garden plant with large spikes of brightly coloured flowers and flattened pods
WORD ORIGIN Latin *lupinus* wolfish; from the belief that it ravenously exhausted the soil

lupine *adj* of or like a wolf
WORD ORIGIN Latin *lupus* wolf

lupus *n* an ulcerous skin disease
WORD ORIGIN Latin: wolf; so called because it rapidly eats away the affected part

USAGE
In current usage the word *lupus* alone is generally understood to signify *lupus vulgaris*. *Lupus erythematosus* is normally referred to in full or by the abbreviation LE.

lurch[1] *vb* **1** to lean or tilt suddenly to one side **2** to stagger ▷ *n* **3** a lurching movement
WORD ORIGIN origin unknown

lurch[2] *n* **leave someone in the lurch** to abandon someone in trouble
WORD ORIGIN French *lourche*, a game similar to backgammon

lure *vb* **luring, lured 1** (sometimes foll. by *away* or *into*) to tempt or attract by the promise of reward ▷ *n* **2** a person or thing that lures **3** *angling* a brightly coloured artificial spinning bait **4** *falconry* a feathered decoy to which small pieces of meat can be attached
WORD ORIGIN Old French *loirre* falconer's lure

lurid *adj* **1** vivid in shocking detail; sensational: *magazines whose lurid covers sickened him* **2** glaring in colour: *a lurid red tartan* **3** horrible in savagery or violence: *reporting lurid crimes* **luridly** *adv*
WORD ORIGIN Latin *luridus* pale yellow

lurk *vb* **1** to move stealthily or be concealed, esp. for evil purposes **2** to be present in an unobtrusive way; be latent
WORD ORIGIN probably frequentative of *lour*

lurking *adj* lingering but almost unacknowledged: *it confirms a lurking suspicion*

luscious (**lush**-uss) *adj* **1** extremely pleasurable to taste or smell **2** very attractive
WORD ORIGIN perhaps short for *delicious*

lush[1] *adj* **1** (of vegetation) growing thickly and healthily **2** luxurious, elaborate, or opulent
WORD ORIGIN Latin *laxus* loose

lush[2] *n slang* an alcoholic
WORD ORIGIN origin unknown

lust *n* **1** a strong sexual desire **2** a strong desire or drive: *a lust for power* ▷ *vb* **3** (often foll. by *after* or *for*) to have a passionate desire (for) **lustful** *adj* **lustfully** *adv*
WORD ORIGIN Old English

lustre *or US* **luster** *n* **1** soft shining light reflected from a surface; sheen **2** great splendour or glory **3** a shiny metallic surface on some pottery and porcelain **lustrous** *adj*
WORD ORIGIN Latin *lustrare* to make bright

lusty *adj* **lustier, lustiest 1** healthy and full of strength and energy **2** strong or invigorating **lustily** *adv* **lustiness** *n*

lute *n* an ancient plucked stringed instrument with a long fingerboard and a body shaped like a half pear
WORD ORIGIN Arabic *al 'ūd*, literally: the wood

lutetium (loo-**tee**-shee-um) *n chem* a silvery-white metallic element of the lanthanide series. Symbol: Lu
WORD ORIGIN *Lutetia*, ancient name of Paris

Lutheran *n* **1** a follower of Martin Luther (1483–1546), German leader of the Reformation, or a member of a Lutheran Church ▷ *adj* **2** of or relating to Luther, his doctrines, or any of the Churches that follow these doctrines **Lutheranism** *n*

luvvie *or* **luvvy** *n, pl* **-vies** *facetious* a person who is involved in acting or the theatre

lux *n, pl* **lux** the SI unit of illumination
WORD ORIGIN Latin: light

luxe *n* see **de luxe**

Luxembourger *n* a person from Luxembourg

luxuriant *adj* **1** rich and abundant; lush: *luxuriant foliage* **2** very elaborate or ornate **luxuriance** *n* **luxuriantly** *adv*
WORD ORIGIN Latin *luxuriare* to abound to excess

USAGE
See at **luxurious**.

luxuriate *vb* **-ating, -ated 1 luxuriate in** to take self-indulgent pleasure in; revel in **2** to flourish profusely

luxurious *adj* **1** characterized by luxury **2** enjoying or devoted to luxury **luxuriously** *adv*

USAGE
Luxurious is sometimes wrongly used where *luxuriant* is meant: *he had a luxuriant* (not *luxurious*) *moustache; the walls were covered with a luxuriant growth of wisteria.*

luxury *n, pl* **-ries 1** indulgence in rich and sumptuous living **2** something considered an indulgence rather than a necessity ▷ *adj* **3** relating to, indicating, or supplying luxury: *a luxury hotel*
WORD ORIGIN Latin *luxuria* excess

LV (in Britain) luncheon voucher

lx lux

lyceum *n* (now chiefly in the names of buildings) a public building for events such as concerts and lectures
WORD ORIGIN Latin: a school in ancient Athens

lychee (lie-**chee**) *n* a Chinese fruit with a whitish juicy pulp
WORD ORIGIN Cantonese *lai chi*

lych gate *or* **lich gate** *n* a roofed gate to a churchyard, formerly used as a temporary shelter for a coffin
WORD ORIGIN Old English *līc* corpse

Lycra *n trademark* a synthetic elastic fabric used for tight-fitting garments, such as swimsuits

lye *n* **1** a caustic solution obtained from wood ash **2** a concentrated solution of sodium hydroxide or potassium hydroxide
WORD ORIGIN Old English *lēag*

lying *vb* the present participle of **lie**[1] or **lie**[2]

lying-in *n, pl* **lyings-in** *old-fashioned* confinement in childbirth

lymph *n* the almost colourless body fluid containing chiefly white blood cells **lymphatic** *adj*
WORD ORIGIN Latin *lympha* water

lymphatic system *n* a network of fine vessels by which lymph circulates throughout the body

lymph node *n* any of many bean-shaped masses of tissue in the lymphatic system that help to protect against infection

lymphocyte *n* a type of white blood cell
WORD ORIGIN lymph + Greek *kutos* vessel

lynch *vb* (of a mob) to kill (a person) for some supposed offence without a trial **lynching** *n*
WORD ORIGIN after Captain William Lynch of Virginia, US

lynchpin *n* same as **linchpin**

lynx *n, pl* **lynxes** *or* **lynx** a mammal of the cat family, with grey-brown mottled fur, tufted ears, and a short tail
WORD ORIGIN Greek *lunx*

lynx-eyed *adj* having keen sight

lyre *n* an ancient Greek U-shaped stringed instrument, similar to a harp but plucked with a plectrum
WORD ORIGIN Greek *lura*

lyrebird *n* an Australian bird, the male of which spreads its tail into the shape of a lyre during courtship

lyric *adj* **1 a** (of poetry) expressing the writer's personal feelings **b** (of poetry) having the form and manner of a song **2** of or relating to such poetry **3** (of a singing voice) light and melodic ▷ *n* **4** a short poem of songlike quality **5 lyrics** the words of a popular song: *Cole invests all her lyrics with a touch of drama* **lyrically** *adv*
WORD ORIGIN Greek *lura* lyre

lyrical *adj* **1** same as **lyric** (senses 1, 2) **2** enthusiastic or effusive

lyricism *n* **1** the quality or style of lyric poetry **2** emotional outpouring

lyricist *n* a person who writes the words for a song, opera, or musical

Emily Dickinson

Emily Dickinson was born in 1830. Her life was eventful, although all of the events were private. Virtually all her life was spent in the town of Amherst, Massachusetts, most of it in homes she shared with her parents, sister, and brother. Although she wrote many letters to a series of admired older men, and was a close friend of her sister-in-law, in later life she withdrew to her room, only emerging to do baking and housework, and to cultivate a luxuriant garden. Since much of her correspondence was destroyed at her own request, we don't know whether she was romantically involved with anyone. In any event, there is passion enough in her poetry.

When she died of Bright's Disease in 1886, only a tiny fraction of her work had been published. The rest, about 800 poems, was bound into manuscript 'fascicles' and found after her death. The editors of the published versions provided titles, converted her punctuation, capitalization, and half-rhymes into conventional verse forms, and sometimes even rewrote entire lines. It was not until 1955 that her complete work was published more or less as she had written it. Much scholarly work has gone into preserving her intentions, even to the extent of decoding the length and shape of her many dashes.

Certainly the appearance of her work resembles no other in nineteenth-century poetry. It is almost as if it were reproducing the motions of her mind. Her dashes could be end-stops or ellipses:

The Brain – is wider than the Sky –
For – put them side by side –
The one the other will contain
With ease – and You – beside –

In her lifetime, nobody in her Amherst circle, especially not her depressive, sickly mother or well-intentioned, politically prominent father, knew quite what to do with this white-clad wraith in their midst, but everyone acknowledged her originality.

The morbidity and violence of Dickinson's sensibility was wildly at variance with Victorian practice. The poet and novelist Thomas Bailey Aldrich remarked that 'an eccentric, dreamy, half-educated recluse in an out-of-the-way New England village (or anywhere else) cannot with impunity set at defiance the laws of gravitation and grammar'.

With the coming of the twentieth century, however, readers valued the forked lightning of her images. A snake is 'A narrow Fellow in the Grass' whose 'notice sudden is –'; 'Hope is the thing with feathers'; 'The Brain is just the weight of God –'; 'I heard a Fly buzz – when I died –'. Along with Walt Whitman, she is one of the great originals of American poetry.

Yet Dickinson was also a woman of her time and place, affected by the contrasting New England currents of Puritanism and Transcendentalism. Whether framed as prayers, declarations, riddles, or definitions, many poems are ostensibly Christian or at least quasi-religious, addressed to 'Sir' or 'Master'. Before she arrived at her own style, her early verses were sentimental and read like greetings cards, but her mature syntax was disjunctive, and her versification roughly followed the traditional metre of hymn-writers, which was in turn based on ballads:

This is my letter to the world,
That never wrote to me, –
The simple news that Nature told,
With tender majesty.

To an encouraging editor at the *Atlantic Monthly*, Dickinson once described herself: 'I am small, like the wren, and my hair is bold, like the chestnut bur, and my eyes like the sherry in the glass that the guest leaves.' She had initiated their correspondence by asking, 'Are you too deeply occupied to say if my Verse is alive?' He and others since have answered in the affirmative.

Mm

The letter M is the thirteenth letter of the English alphabet and marks the halfway point of the sequence. The Romans developed this letter from the Greek letter *mu* (M,μ). The Greek *mu* had its origins in the Semitic letter *mem*, which was originally associated with water and had an undulating shape which can still be discerned in the rise and fall of the strokes that make up the modern letter M.

With its three vertical lines, the lower-case form of M takes up more space than most letters of the alphabet. Printers who needed to take account of the varying widths of characters to calculate how many letters would fit on a line therefore used the name 'em' for the widest space that a character can occupy in a particular font (this being twice the width of an 'en').

The shape of the letter also makes it one of the more time-consuming letters to write, and medieval scribes often omitted it in their manuscripts, indicating its presence merely by a stroke above the preceding letter.

M is the Roman numeral for 1000 (the Latin word for a thousand being *mille*), and so the year 2000 is written MM. The abbreviation has not caught on more widely, however, and colloquially a thousand is more likely to be called a K (from the Greek *khilioi*) or a G (from the American slang 'grand').

Economists use the letter M to indicate the quantity of money in circulation, and the letter is attached to various numbers to designate the different ways of measuring this. M1, for example, is defined as the total value of all notes and coins in circulation as well as money that is instantly available to be withdrawn from banks.

For aficionados of James Bond, however, M will call to mind the head of the British Secret Service, played on screen by Bernard Lee and latterly by Dame Judi Dench. In real life the head of MI6 is customarily known as 'C', after Mansfield Cumming who was the service's first director when it was formed during World War I. In the Bond stories, Ian Fleming substituted the initial of Cumming's forename to come up with the soubriquet for his fictional spymaster.

---

m 1 metre(s) **2** mile(s) **3** milli- **4** million **5** minute(s)

M 1 mach **2** *currency* mark(s) **3** medium **4** mega- **5** (in Britain) motorway **6** the Roman numeral for 1000

m. 1 male **2** married **3** masculine **4** meridian **5** month

M. 1 Majesty **2** Master **3** (in titles) Member **4** *pl* **MM.** *or* **MM** Monsieur

ma *n* an informal word for mother

MA 1 Massachusetts **2** Master of Arts

ma'am *n* short for **madam** (sense 1)

maas (**mahs**) *n* S *African* thick soured milk
WORD ORIGIN Nguni (language group of southern Africa) *amasi* milk

mac *or* **mack** *n* Brit informal a mackintosh

Mac *n* chiefly US & Canad an informal term of address to a man
WORD ORIGIN Gaelic *mac* son of

macabre (mak-**kahb**-ra) *adj* strange and horrible; gruesome
WORD ORIGIN French

macadam *n* a road surface made of compressed layers of small broken stones, esp. one bound together with tar or asphalt
WORD ORIGIN after John *McAdam*, engineer

macadamia (mak-a-**day**-mee-a) *n* an Australian tree with edible nuts

WORD ORIGIN after John *Macadam*, Australian chemist

macadamize *or* **-ise** *vb* **-izing, -ized** *or* **-ising, -ised** to pave a road with macadam

macaque (mak-**kahk**) *n* any of various Asian and African monkeys with cheek pouches and either a short tail or no tail
WORD ORIGIN W African *makaku*

macaroni *n, pl* **-nis** *or* **-nies 1** pasta tubes made from wheat flour **2** (in 18th-century Britain) a man who was excessively concerned with his clothes and appearance
WORD ORIGIN Italian (dialect) *maccarone*

macaroon *n* a sweet biscuit made of ground almonds
WORD ORIGIN French *macaron*

macaw *n* a large tropical American parrot with a long tail and brightly coloured feathers
WORD ORIGIN Portuguese *macau*

mace¹ *n* **1** a ceremonial staff carried by certain officials **2** a club with a spiked metal head used in the Middle Ages
WORD ORIGIN probably Vulgar Latin *mattea*

mace² *n* a spice made from the dried outer casing of the nutmeg
WORD ORIGIN Latin *macir*

macebearer *n* a person who carries a mace in processions or ceremonies

macerate (**mass**-er-ate) *vb* **-ating, -ated** to soften or be softened by soaking **macerated** *adj* **maceration** *n*
WORD ORIGIN Latin *macerare* to soften

Mach (**mak**) *n* a unit for expressing the speed of an aircraft as a multiple of the speed of sound: *an airliner capable of cruising at Mach 2*. See also **Mach number**

machete (mash-**ett**-ee) *n* a broad heavy knife used for cutting or as a weapon
WORD ORIGIN Spanish

Machiavellian (mak-ee-a-**vel**-yan) *adj* cleverly deceitful and unscrupulous **Machiavellianism** *n*
WORD ORIGIN after *Machiavelli*, political philosopher

machinations (mak-in-**nay**-shuns) *pl n* cunning schemes or plots to gain power or harm an opponent: *the machinations of a power-hungry institution*
WORD ORIGIN Latin *machinari* to plan

machine *n* **1** an assembly of components arranged so as to perform a particular task and usually powered by electricity **2** a vehicle, such as a car or aircraft **3** a system within an organization that controls activities and policies: *the party machine* ▷ *vb* **-chining, -chined 4** to shape, cut, or make something using a machine **machinable** *adj*
WORD ORIGIN Latin *machina*

machine code *or* **language** *n* instructions for a computer in binary or hexadecimal code that require no conversion or translation by the computer

machine gun *n* **1** a rapid-firing automatic gun, using small-arms ammunition ▷*vb* **machine-gun, -gunning, -gunned 2** to shoot or fire at with a machine gun

machine-readable *adj* in a form suitable for processing by a computer

machinery *n, pl* **-eries 1** machines, machine parts, or machine systems collectively **2** the mechanism of a machine **3** the organization and procedures by which a system functions: *the machinery of international politics*

machine shop *n* a workshop in which machine tools are operated

machine tool *n* a power-driven machine, such as a lathe, for cutting and shaping metal, wood, or plastic

machinist *n* **1** a person who operates machines to cut or process materials **2** a maker or repairer of machines

machismo (mak-**izz**-moh) *n* strong or exaggerated masculinity
WORD ORIGIN Spanish *macho* male

Mach number (**mak**) *n* the ratio of the speed of a body in a particular medium to the speed of sound in that medium
WORD ORIGIN after Ernst *Mach*, physicist

macho (**match**-oh) *adj* **1** strongly or exaggeratedly masculine ▷*n* **2** strong or exaggerated masculinity
WORD ORIGIN from *machismo*

mack *n Brit informal* same as **mac**

mackerel *n, pl* **-rel** *or* **-rels** an edible sea fish
WORD ORIGIN Old French *maquerel*

mackinaw *n chiefly US & Canad* a thick short double-breasted plaid coat
WORD ORIGIN from a variant of *Mackinac*, an island in N Michigan

mackintosh *or* **macintosh** *n Brit* **1** a raincoat made of rubberized cloth **2** any raincoat
WORD ORIGIN after Charles *Macintosh*, who invented it

macramé (mak-**rah**-mee) *n* **1** the art of knotting and weaving coarse thread into patterns **2** ornaments made in this way
WORD ORIGIN Turkish *makrama* towel

macro- *or before a vowel* **macr-** *combining form* large, long, or great: *macroscopic*
WORD ORIGIN Greek *makros*

macrobiotics *n* a dietary system which advocates whole grains and vegetables grown without chemical additives **macrobiotic** *adj*
WORD ORIGIN Greek *makros* long + *biotos* life

macrocarpa *n* a large Californian coniferous tree, used in New Zealand and elsewhere as a windbreak on farms and for rough timber
WORD ORIGIN Greek *makros* large + *karpos* fruit

macrocosm *n* a complex structure, such as the universe or society, regarded as a whole

WORD ORIGIN Greek *makros kosmos* great world

macroeconomics *n* the branch of economics concerned with the relationships between aggregates, such as consumption and investment, in a large economic system **macroeconomic** *adj*

macromolecule *n* any very large molecule, such as a protein or synthetic polymer

macron *n* a mark (˘) placed over a letter to represent a long vowel
WORD ORIGIN Greek *makros* long

macroscopic *adj* **1** large enough to be visible to the naked eye **2** concerned with large units
WORD ORIGIN Greek *makros* large + *skopein* to look at

macula (**mak**-kew-la) *n, pl* **-ulae** (-yew-lee) *anat* a small spot or area of distinct colour, such as a freckle
WORD ORIGIN Latin

mad *adj* **madder, maddest 1** mentally deranged; insane **2** extremely foolish; senseless: *that was a mad thing to do!* **3** *informal* angry or annoyed: *he's mad at her for the unjust accusation* **4** extremely excited or confused: *a mad rush* **5 a** (of animals) unusually ferocious: *a mad bear* **b** (of animals) afflicted with rabies **6 like mad** *informal* with great energy, enthusiasm, or haste **7 mad about** *or* **on** *or* **over** wildly enthusiastic about or fond of **madness** *n*
WORD ORIGIN Old English *gemǣded* made insane

madam *n, pl* **madams 1** *pl* **mesdames** a polite term of address for a woman **2** a woman who runs a brothel **3** *Austral & Brit informal* a spoilt or pert girl: *she is a thoroughly precocious little madam if ever there was one*
WORD ORIGIN Old French *ma dame* my lady

madame (mad-**dam**) *n, pl* **mesdames** (may-**dam**) a French form of address equivalent to *Mrs*

madcap *adj* **1** impulsive, reckless, or unlikely to succeed: *a madcap expansion of council bureaucracy* ▷*n* **2** an impulsive or reckless person

mad cow disease *n informal* same as **BSE**

madden *vb* to make or become mad or angry **maddening** *adj*

madder *n* **1** a plant with small yellow flowers and a red fleshy root **2** a dark reddish-purple dye formerly obtained from its root **3** an artificial pigment of this colour
WORD ORIGIN Old English *mædere*

made *vb* **1** the past of **make** ▷*adj* **2** produced or shaped as specified: *handmade* **3 get** *or* **have it made** *informal* to be assured of success

Madeira (mad-**deer**-a) *n* a fortified white wine from Madeira, an island in the N Atlantic

Madeira cake *n* a type of rich sponge cake

mademoiselle (mad-mwah-**zel**) *n, pl* **mesdemoiselles** (maid-mwah-**zel**) **1** a French form of address equivalent to *Miss* **2** a French teacher or governess

made-to-measure *adj* (of a piece of clothing) made specifically to fit the person who has ordered it

made-up *adj* **1** invented or fictitious **2** wearing make-up **3** put together: *some made-up carpet shampoo* **4** (of a road) surfaced with tarmac or concrete

madhouse *n informal* **1** a state of uproar or confusion **2** *old-fashioned* a mental hospital

madly *adv* **1** in an insane or foolish manner **2** with great speed and energy **3** *informal* extremely or excessively: *she was madly in love with him*

madman *or fem* **madwoman** *n, pl* **-men** *or* **-women** a person who is insane

Madonna *n* **1** *chiefly RC Church* the Virgin Mary **2** a picture or statue of the Virgin Mary
WORD ORIGIN Italian: my lady

madras *n* a medium-hot curry: *chicken madras*
WORD ORIGIN after the *Madras* area of India

madrigal *n* a type of 16th- or 17th-century part song for unaccompanied voices **madrigalist** *n*
WORD ORIGIN Medieval Latin *matricale* primitive

maelstrom (**male**-strom) *n* **1** a large powerful whirlpool **2** any confused, violent, and destructive turmoil: *a maelstrom of adulterous passion*
WORD ORIGIN Old Dutch *malen* to whirl round + *stroom* stream

maenad (**mean**-ad) *n* **1** *classical history* a female disciple of Dionysus, the Greek god of wine **2** a frenzied woman
WORD ORIGIN Greek *mainas* madwoman

maestro (**my**-stroh) *n, pl* **-tri** *or* **-tros 1** a distinguished musician or conductor **2** any master of an art: *Milan's maestro of minimalism*
WORD ORIGIN Italian: master

mae west *n slang* an inflatable life jacket
WORD ORIGIN after *Mae West*, actress renowned for her large bust

Mafia *n* **the Mafia** a secret criminal organization founded in Sicily, and carried to the US by Italian immigrants
WORD ORIGIN Sicilian dialect, literally: hostility to the law

mafioso (maf-fee-**oh**-so) *n, pl* **-sos** *or* **-si** (-see) a member of the Mafia

mag *n* short for **magazine** (sense 1)

magazine *n* **1** a periodic paperback publication containing written pieces and illustrations **2** a television or radio programme made up of short nonfictional items **3** a metal case holding several cartridges used in some firearms **4** a rack for automatically feeding slides through a projector **5** a place for storing weapons, explosives, or military equipment
WORD ORIGIN Arabic *makhāzin* storehouses

magenta (maj-**jen**-ta) *adj* deep purplish-red
WORD ORIGIN after *Magenta*, Italy

maggot *n* the limbless larva of various insects, esp. the housefly and blowfly **maggoty** *adj*
WORD ORIGIN earlier *mathek*

m

magi (**maje**-eye) *pl n, sing* **magus** (**may**-guss) **1** see **magus 2 the three Magi** *Christianity* the wise men from the East who came to worship the infant Jesus (Matthew 2:1–12)
WORD ORIGIN see MAGUS

magic *n* **1** the supposed power to make things happen by using supernatural means **2** tricks done to entertain; conjuring **3** any mysterious or extraordinary quality or power: *the magic of Placido Domingo* **4 like magic** very quickly ▷ *adj also* **magical 5** of magic **6** possessing or considered to possess mysterious powers **7** unaccountably enchanting **8** *informal* wonderful or marvellous ▷ *vb* **-gicking, -gicked 9** to transform or produce as if by magic: *he had magicked up a gourmet meal at a moment's notice* **magically** *adv*
WORD ORIGIN Greek *magikē* witchcraft

magic away *vb* to cause to disappear as if by magic: *to magic away pollution*

magic carpet *n* (in fairy stories) a carpet which can carry people through the air

magician *n* **1** a conjuror **2** a person with magic powers

magic lantern *n* an early type of slide projector

magisterial *adj* **1** commanding and authoritative **2** of a magistrate **magisterially** *adv*
WORD ORIGIN Latin *magister* master

magistracy *n, pl* **-cies 1** the office or function of a magistrate **2** magistrates collectively

magistrate *n* **1** a public officer concerned with the administration of law **2** same as **justice of the peace 3** *Austral & NZ* a former name for **district court judge**
WORD ORIGIN Latin *magister* master

magistrates' court *n* (in England) a court that deals with minor crimes, certain civil actions, and preliminary hearings

magma *n, pl* **-mas** *or* **-mata** hot molten rock within the earth's crust which sometimes finds its way to the surface where it solidifies to form igneous rock
WORD ORIGIN Greek: salve made by kneading

Magna Carta *n English history* the charter granted by King John at Runnymede in 1215, recognizing the rights and privileges of the barons, church, and freemen
WORD ORIGIN Medieval Latin: great charter

magnanimous *adj* generous and forgiving, esp. towards a defeated enemy **magnanimity** *n* **magnanimously** *adv*
WORD ORIGIN Latin *magnanimus* great-souled

magnate *n* an influential or wealthy person, esp. in industry
WORD ORIGIN Late Latin *magnates* great men

magnesia *n* a white tasteless substance used as an antacid and laxative; magnesium oxide
WORD ORIGIN Greek *Magnēsia* of *Magnēs*, ancient mineral-rich region

magnesium *n chem* a light silvery-white metallic element that burns with a very bright white flame. Symbol: Mg
WORD ORIGIN from *magnesia*

magnet *n* **1** a piece of iron, steel, or lodestone that has the property of attracting iron to it **2** a person or thing that exerts a great attraction: *these woods are a magnet for bird watchers*
WORD ORIGIN Greek *magnēs*

magnetic *adj* **1** of, producing, or operated by means of magnetism **2** of or like a magnet **3** capable of being made into a magnet **4** exerting a powerful attraction: *political leaders of magnetic appeal* **magnetically** *adv*

magnetic disk *n* a computer storage disk

magnetic field *n* an area around a magnet in which its power of attraction is felt

magnetic mine *n* a mine which detonates when a magnetic field, such as that generated by the metal of a ship's hull, is detected

magnetic needle *n* a slender magnetized rod used in certain instruments, such as the magnetic compass, for indicating the direction of a magnetic field

magnetic north *n* the direction in which a compass needle points, at an angle from the direction of true (geographic) north

magnetic pole *n* either of two variable points on the earth's surface towards which a magnetic needle points

magnetic storm *n* a sudden severe disturbance of the earth's magnetic field, caused by emission of charged particles from the sun

magnetic tape *n* a long plastic strip coated with a magnetic substance, used to record sound or video signals or to store information in computers

magnetism *n* **1** the property of attraction displayed by magnets **2** powerful personal charm **3** the branch of physics concerned with magnetic phenomena

magnetite *n* a black magnetizable mineral that is an important source of iron

magnetize *or* **-tise** *vb* **-tizing, -tized** *or* **-tising, -tised 1** to make a substance or object magnetic **2** to attract strongly: *he was magnetized by her smile* **magnetizable** *or* **-tisable** *adj* **magnetization** *or* **-tisation** *n*

magneto (mag-**nee**-toe) *n, pl* **-tos** a small electric generator in which the magnetic field is produced by a permanent magnet, esp. one used to provide the spark in an internal-combustion engine
WORD ORIGIN short for *magnetoelectric generator*

magnetron *n* an electronic valve used with a magnetic field to generate microwave oscillations, used. esp. in radar
WORD ORIGIN *magnet* + *electron*

Magnificat *n Christianity* the hymn of the Virgin Mary (Luke 1:46–55), used as a canticle
WORD ORIGIN from its opening word

magnification *n* **1** the act of magnifying or the state of being magnified **2** the degree to which something is magnified **3** a magnified copy of something

magnificent *adj* **1** splendid or impressive in appearance **2** superb or very fine: *a magnificent performance* **magnificence** *n* **magnificently** *adv*
WORD ORIGIN Latin *magnificus* great in deeds

magnify *vb* **-fies, -fying, -fied 1** to make something look bigger than it really is, for instance by using a lens or microscope **2** to make something seem more important than it really is; exaggerate: *you are magnifying the problem out of all proportion* **3** to make something sound louder than it really is: *the stethoscope magnifies internal body sounds* **magnified** *adj*
WORD ORIGIN Latin *magnificare* to praise

magnifying glass *or* **magnifier** *n* a convex lens used to produce an enlarged image of an object

magniloquent *adj* (of speech) excessively grand, literary, and pompous **magniloquence** *n*
WORD ORIGIN Latin *magnus* great + *loqui* to speak

magnitude *n* **1** relative importance: *an evil of the first magnitude* **2** relative size or extent **3** *astron* the apparent brightness of a celestial body expressed on a numerical scale on which bright stars have a low value
WORD ORIGIN Latin *magnitudo* size

magnolia *n* an Asian and North American tree or shrub with white, pink, purple, or yellow showy flowers
WORD ORIGIN after Pierre *Magnol*, botanist

magnox *n* an alloy composed mainly of magnesium, used in fuel elements of some nuclear reactors (**magnox reactors**)
WORD ORIGIN from *mag(nesium)* n(o) ox(idation)

magnum *n, pl* **-nums** a wine bottle of twice the normal size, holding 1.5 litres
WORD ORIGIN Latin: a big thing

magnum opus *n* a great work of art or literature, esp. the greatest single work of an artist
WORD ORIGIN Latin

magpie *n* **1** a bird of the crow family with black-and-white plumage, a long tail, and a chattering call **2** any of various similar Australian birds, eg the butcherbird **3** *Brit* a person who hoards small objects
WORD ORIGIN from *Mag*, diminutive of *Margaret* + *pie*, obsolete name for the magpie

magus (**may**-guss) *n, pl* **magi** (**maje**-eye) **1** a Zoroastrian priest **2** an astrologer or magician of ancient times
WORD ORIGIN Old Persian: magician

Magyar *n* **1** a member of the main ethnic group of Hungary **2** the Hungarian language ▷ *adj* **3** of the Magyars

maharaja *or* **maharajah** *n* the head of one of the royal families which formerly ruled parts of India
WORD ORIGIN Hindi: great raja

Quebec English

Likely no jurisdiction in North America, and possibly in the world, is more language-obsessed than Quebec. The majority of Québécois are fiercely protective of French, regarding it as an inseparable part of their identity as a people. English-speaking Quebeckers, who mainly live in Montreal, but also in the Eastern Townships, the Gaspé Peninsula, and scattered parts of the province, are mindful that they belong to a linguistic majority in Canada, indeed North America: they equally insist on their rights, even as in non-linguistic matters do the even smaller minority of indigenous peoples like the Innu, Cree, Mohawks, and Inuit.

Nationalism has been a recurrent feature of Quebec society ever since the English Conquest of 1763. During and after the 1960s, it erupted, and culminated in the referendum of 1995, which narrowly defeated a proposal that Quebec seek *sovereignty-association* (a muted form of separatism in which Quebec in most respects would become politically independent) with the rest of Canada (sometimes abbreviated as *ROC*). During this period, Quebec governments enacted a series of laws proclaiming French to be the province's official language, making it predominant in the public service, the judicial system, education, commercial signs and billboards, business contracts, and employer-employee relations. The *allophones*, whose first language was neither English nor French, would be absorbed into the French mainstream, and a program of *francization* would convert large businesses into all-French enterprises. Street names were changed: *Dorchester Boulevard* became *Boulevard René-Lévesque*, replacing the name of a colonial administrator with that of a nationalist hero.

Most Québécois welcomed these measures, viewing them as a symbol of pride, and redressing the days when English-dominated companies denied equitable services to their French customers. They resented the unrequited effort many had made to learn a second language. They may have remembered the anti-French bigotry that had long been an undercurrent in Canadian history and the fact that, when the federal government took steps to encourage national bilingualism, some English Canadians, especially in Western Canada, railed against bilingual cereal boxes. For their part, English speakers and allophones vehemently opposed the measures, sure that this time it was *their* culture that was under threat. They declared that the laws violated the Canadian constitution. They jeered at the mandated removal of apostrophes from storefront signs, and termed the bureaucrats who enforced such regulations *the language police*. Some English residents left Quebec; some companies relocated their head offices.

Yet after endless, polarizing, acrimonious debates, English speakers in time felt less persecuted, and largely came to accept the fact that political, business, and cultural activities would be chiefly conducted in French. Unanticipated positive consequences resulted: the rates of bilingualism in Quebec rose among both French and English. It became not uncommon to hear speakers chatting on an assembly line or while riding on a bus switch between French and English with remarkable ease.

The English that Quebeckers continued to speak reflected political, cultural, and legal developments, further modified by the fact that English Quebeckers in Montreal were outnumbered twofold by allophones, who often were or became multilingual. They shopped at *dépanneurs*, convenience stores, and banked at *caisses*, credit unions. They pronounced *Pie IX*, as in the boulevard name, as *pi-neuf*, not *pie-nine*. Most acronyms were retained as English, as *NDG* for the Montreal district of Notre-Dame-de-Grâce. A CEGEP (*Collège d'enseignement general et professional*, a college in a system of post-secondary schools), was pronounced *say jep*. Some English words acquired senses derived from French. Anglophones asked for an *all-dressed* hot dog (a translation of *tout garni*), a hot dog with mustard, relish, and other garnishes; a *subvention* was a government grant. The English-speaker confidently ordered *pâté chinois*, knowing it was shepherd's pie. Some French terms like *poutine*, a mixture of chipped potatoes, cheese curds, and gravy, and *tourtière*, a meat pie, had already passed into wider Canadian English.

In the best of all possible worlds, everyone would speak a second language. Quebeckers and Québécois are moving in that direction.

maharani or **maharanee** n the wife of a maharaja
WORD ORIGIN Hindi: great rani

maharishi n Hinduism a teacher of religious and mystical knowledge
WORD ORIGIN Hindi: great sage

mahatma n a person revered for his holiness or wisdom: often used as a title or form of address: Mahatma Gandhi
WORD ORIGIN Sanskrit mahā great + ātman soul

mah jong or **mah-jongg** n a game of Chinese origin, played using tiles bearing various designs, in which the players try to obtain a winning combination of tiles
WORD ORIGIN Chinese, literally: sparrows

mahogany n, pl -nies 1 the hard reddish-brown wood of any of several tropical trees ▷ adj 2 reddish-brown: wonderful mahogany tones
WORD ORIGIN origin unknown

mahout (ma-howt) n (in India and the East Indies) an elephant driver or keeper
WORD ORIGIN Hindi mahāut

maid n 1 a female servant 2 archaic or literary a young unmarried girl; maiden
WORD ORIGIN form of maiden

maiden n 1 archaic or literary a young unmarried girl, esp. a virgin 2 horse racing a horse that has never won a race ▷ adj 3 unmarried: a maiden aunt 4 first or earliest: maiden voyage **maidenhood** n **maidenly** adj
WORD ORIGIN Old English mægden

maidenhair fern n a fern with delicate hairlike fronds of small pale green leaflets

maidenhead n 1 the hymen 2 virginity or maidenhood

maiden name n a woman's surname before marriage

maiden over n cricket an over in which no runs are scored

maid of honour n 1 an unmarried lady attending a queen or princess 2 US & Canad the principal unmarried attendant of a bride

maidservant n a female servant

mail[1] n 1 letters and packages transported and delivered by the post office 2 the postal system 3 a single collection or delivery of mail 4 a train, ship, or aircraft that carries mail 5 short for **e-mail** ▷ vb 6 chiefly US & Canad to send by mail 7 to contact or send by e-mail
WORD ORIGIN Old French male bag

mail[2] n flexible armour made of riveted metal rings or links **mailed** adj
WORD ORIGIN Old French maille mesh

mailbag n a large bag for transporting or delivering mail

mailbox n 1 US, Canad, & Austral a box outside a house into which the postman puts letters for the occupiers of the house 2 (on a computer) the directory in which e-mail messages are stored

mail coach n history a fast stagecoach designed primarily for carrying mail

mailing list n a register of names and addresses to which information or advertising matter is sent by post or e-mail

mailman n, pl -men US & Canad a postman

mail merge n computers a word-processing facility that can produce personalized letters by combining data from two different files

mail order n a system of buying and selling goods by post

mailshot n a posting of circulars, leaflets, or other advertising to a selected large number of people at once

maim vb to injure badly or cruelly, with some permanent damage resulting
WORD ORIGIN Old French mahaignier to wound

main adj 1 chief or principal ▷ n 2 a principal pipe or line in a system used to distribute water, electricity, or gas 3 **mains** the main distribution network for water, gas, or electricity 4 great strength or force: with might and main 5 literary the open ocean 6 **in the main** on the whole
WORD ORIGIN Old English mægen strength

mainbrace n naut 1 the rope that controls the movement of the spar of a ship's mainsail 2 **splice the mainbrace** see **splice**

main clause n grammar a clause that can stand alone as a sentence

mainframe n computers a high-speed general-purpose computer, with a large store capacity

mainland n the main part of a land mass as opposed to an island

main line n 1 railways the chief route between two points, usually fed by branch lines ▷ vb **mainline** 2 slang to inject a drug into a vein

mainly adv for the most part; principally

mainmast n naut the chief mast of a sailing vessel with two or more masts

mainsail n naut the largest and lowermost sail on the mainmast

mainspring n 1 the chief cause or motive of something: the mainspring of a dynamic economy 2 the chief spring of a watch or clock

mainstay n 1 a chief support 2 naut a rope securing a mainmast

mainstream n 1 the people or things representing the most common or generally accepted ideas and styles in a society, art form, etc.: the mainstream of academic life 2 the main current of a river ▷ adj 3 belonging to the social or cultural mainstream: mainstream American movies

mainstreeting n Canad the practice of a politician walking about a town or city to gain votes

maintain vb 1 to continue or keep in existence: we must maintain good relations with them 2 to keep in proper or good condition: an expensive car to maintain 3 to sustain or keep up a particular level or speed: he set off at a high speed, but couldn't maintain it all the way 4 to enable a person to have the money, food and other things he or she needs to live: the money maintained us for a month 5 to assert: he had always maintained that he never wanted children 6 to defend against contradiction: he maintained his innocence
WORD ORIGIN from Latin manu tenere to hold in the hand

maintenance n 1 the act of maintaining or the state of being maintained 2 the process of keeping a car, building, etc. in good condition 3 law financial provision ordered to be made by way of periodical payments or a lump sum, usually for a separated or divorced spouse

maisonette n Brit & S African a flat with more than one floor
WORD ORIGIN French, diminutive of maison house

maitre d'hotel (met-ra dote-tell) n, pl **maitres d'hotel** a head waiter
WORD ORIGIN French

maize n a type of corn grown for its large yellow edible grains, which are used for food and as a source of oil. See also **sweet corn**
WORD ORIGIN Spanish maiz

Maj. Major

majestic adj beautiful, dignified, and impressive **majestically** adv

majesty n 1 great dignity and grandeur 2 supreme power or authority
WORD ORIGIN Latin majestas

Majesty n, pl -ties (preceded by Your, His, Her or Their) a title used to address or refer to a sovereign or the wife or widow of a sovereign

Maj. Gen. Major General

majolica or **maiolica** n a type of porous pottery glazed with bright metallic oxides. It was extensively made in Renaissance Italy
WORD ORIGIN Italian, from Late Latin Majorica Majorca

major adj 1 greater in size, frequency, or importance than others of the same kind: the major political parties 2 very serious or significant: a major investigation 3 main or principal: a major road 4 music a (of a scale) having notes separated by a whole tone, except for the third and fourth notes, and seventh and eighth notes, which are separated by a semitone b of or based on the major scale: the key of D major ▷ n 5 a middle-ranking military officer 6 music a major key, chord, mode, or scale 7 a person who has reached the age of legal majority 8 US, Canad, S African, Austral, & NZ the principal field of study of a student ▷ vb 9 US, Canad, S African, Austral, & NZ to study as one's principal subject: he majored in economics
WORD ORIGIN Latin: greater

major-domo n, pl -mos the chief steward or butler of a great household
WORD ORIGIN Medieval Latin major domus head of the household

majorette n one of a group of girls who practise formation marching and baton twirling

major general n a senior military officer

majority n, pl -ties 1 the greater number or part of something 2 (in an election) the number of votes or seats by which the strongest party or candidate beats the combined opposition or the runner-up **3** the largest party or group that votes together in a meeting, council or parliament **4** the age at which a person legally becomes an adult **5 in the majority** forming or part of the group of people or things made up of more than half of a larger group

WORD ORIGIN Medieval Latin *majoritas*

≡USAGE
≡ The *majority of* can only refer to a
≡ number of things or people. When
≡ talking about an amount, *most of*
≡ should be used: *most of* (not *the majority*
≡ *of*) *the harvest was saved.*

make *vb* **making, made 1** to create, construct, establish, or draw up; bring into being: *houses made of stone; he will have to make a will* **2** to cause to do or be; compel or induce: *please make her go away* **3** to bring about or produce: *don't make a noise* **4** to carry out or perform: *he made his first trip to China in 1987; she made an obscene gesture* **5** to appoint: *they made him caretaker manager* **6** to come into a specified state or condition: *to make merry* **7** to become: *she will make a good diplomat* **8** to cause or ensure the success of: *that news has made my day* **9** to amount to: *5 and 5 make 10* **10** to earn or be paid: *they must be making a fortune* **11** to have the qualities of or be suitable for: *what makes this book such a good read?* **12** to prepare for use: *she forgot to make her bed* **13** to be the essential element in: *confidence makes a good salesman* **14** to use for a specified purpose: *they will make this town their base* **15** to deliver: *he made a very good speech* **16** to consider to be: *what time do you make it?* **17** to cause to seem or represent as being: *her girlish pigtails made her look younger than she was; she made the experience sound most unpleasant* **18** to acquire: *she doesn't make friends easily* **19** to engage in: *they made war on the Turks* **20** to travel a certain distance or to a certain place: *we can make at least three miles before it gets dark* **21** to arrive in time for: *he didn't make the first act of the play* **22** to win or score: *he made a break of 125* **23** *informal* to gain a place or position on or in: *to make the headlines* **24 make a day or night of it** to cause an activity to last a day or night **25 make eyes at** *old-fashioned* to flirt with or ogle **26 make it** *informal* **a** to be able to attend: *I'm afraid I can't make it to your party* **b** to be successful **27 make like** *slang chiefly US & Canad* **a** to imitate **b** to pretend **28 make to** *or* **as if to** *or* **as though to** to act with the intention or with a show of doing something: *she made as if to hit him* ▷ *n* **29** manufacturer; brand: *what make of car is that?* **30** the way in which something is made **31 on the make** *slang* out for profit or conquest
▸ See also **make away, make for**, etc.
maker *n*

WORD ORIGIN Old English *macian*

make away *vb* **1** to depart in haste **2 make away with a** to steal **b** to kill or get rid of

make believe *vb* **1** to pretend ▷ *n* **make-believe 2** a fantasy or pretence

make do *vb* to manage with an inferior alternative

make for *vb* **1** to head towards **2** to

prepare to attack **3** to help bring about: *this will make for a spectacular race*

make of *vb* to interpret as the meaning of: *what did she make of it all?*

make off *vb* **1** to go or run away in haste **2 make off with** to steal or abduct

make out *vb* **1** to manage to see or hear **2** to understand **3** to write out: *how shall I make out the cheque?* **4** to attempt to establish or prove: *she made me out to be a crook* **5** to pretend: *he made out that he could play the piano* **6** to manage or get on: *how did you make out in the exam?*

make over *vb* **1** to renovate or remodel: *she made over the dress to fit her sister* ▷ *n* **makeover 2** a complete remodelling **3** a series of alterations, including beauty treatments and new clothes, intended to make an improvement to someone's appearance

Maker *n* a title given to God

makeshift *adj* serving as a temporary substitute

make-up *n* **1** cosmetics, such as powder or lipstick **2** the cosmetics used by an actor to adapt his or her appearance **3** the arrangement of the parts of something **4** mental or physical constitution ▷ *vb* **make up 5** to form or constitute: *these arguments make up the case for the defence* **6** to devise or compose, sometimes with the intent to deceive: *she was well known for making up stories about herself* **7** to supply what is lacking; complete: *I'll make up the difference* **8** Also: **make it up** to settle differences amicably **9 make up for** to compensate for: *one good year can make up for several bad ones* **10** to apply cosmetics to the face **11 make up to** *informal* **a** to make friendly overtures to **b** to flirt with

makeweight *n* an unimportant person or thing added to make up a lack

making *n* **1** the act or process of producing something **2 be the making of** to cause the success of **3 in the making** in the process of becoming or being made

makings *pl n* **have the makings of** to have the potentials, qualities, or materials necessary to make or become something: *it had the makings of a classic showdown*

mako *n, pl* **makos** a powerful shark of the Atlantic and Pacific Oceans
WORD ORIGIN Māori

mal- *combining form* bad or badly; wrong or wrongly: *maladjusted; malfunction*
WORD ORIGIN Latin *malus* bad, *male* badly

malachite (**mal**-a-kite) *n* a green mineral used as a source of copper, and for making ornaments
WORD ORIGIN Greek *molokhitis*

maladjustment *n psychol* a failure to meet the demands of society, such as coping with problems and social relationships **maladjusted** *adj*

maladminister *vb* to administer badly, inefficiently, or dishonestly **maladministration** *n*

maladroit (mal-a-**droyt**) *adj* clumsy, awkward, or tactless **maladroitly** *adv* **maladroitness** *n*
WORD ORIGIN French *mal* badly + ADROIT

malady (**mal**-a-dee) *n, pl* **-dies**

old-fashioned any disease or illness
WORD ORIGIN Vulgar Latin *male habitus* in poor condition

malaise (mal-**laze**) *n* **1** a vague feeling of unease, illness, or depression **2** a complex of problems affecting a country, economy, etc.: *Belgium's political malaise*
WORD ORIGIN Old French *mal* bad + *aise* ease

malapropism *n* the comic misuse of a word by confusion with one which sounds similar, for example *under the affluence of alcohol*
WORD ORIGIN after Mrs *Malaprop* in Sheridan's play *The Rivals*

malaria *n* a disease with recurring attacks of fever, caused by the bite of some types of mosquito **malarial** *adj*
WORD ORIGIN Italian *mala aria* bad air

malarkey *n slang* nonsense or rubbish
WORD ORIGIN origin unknown

Malay *n* **1** a member of a people living chiefly in Malaysia and Indonesia **2** the language of this people ▷ *adj* **3** of the Malays or their language

Malayan *adj* **1** of Malaya ▷ *n* **2** a person from Malaya

Malaysian *adj* **1** of Malaysia ▷ *n* **2** a person from Malaysia

malcontent *n* a person who is discontented with the existing situation
WORD ORIGIN Old French

male *adj* **1** of the sex that can fertilize female reproductive cells **2** of or characteristic of a man **3** for or composed of men or boys: *a male choir* **4** (of flowers) bearing stamens but lacking a pistil **5** *electronics, engineering* having a projecting part or parts that fit into a hollow counterpart: *a male plug* ▷ *n* **6** a male person, animal, or plant **maleness** *n*
WORD ORIGIN Latin *masculus* masculine

male chauvinism *n* the belief, held by some men, that men are better and more important than women **male chauvinist** *n, adj*

malediction (mal-lid-**dik**-shun) *n* the utterance of a curse against someone or something **maledictory** *adj*
WORD ORIGIN Latin *maledictio* a reviling

malefactor (**mal**-if-act-or) *n* a criminal or wrongdoer **malefaction** *n*
WORD ORIGIN Latin *malefacere* to do evil

malevolent (mal-**lev**-a-lent) *adj* wishing evil to others; malicious **malevolence** *n* **malevolently** *adv*
WORD ORIGIN Latin *malevolens*

malfeasance (mal-**fee**-zanss) *n law* wrongful or illegal behaviour, esp. by a public official
WORD ORIGIN Old French *mal faisant* evil-doing

malformation *n* **1** the condition of being faulty or abnormal in form or shape **2** *pathol* a deformity, esp. when congenital **malformed** *adj*

malfunction *vb* **1** to fail to function properly or fail to function at all ▷ *n* **2** failure to function properly or failure to function at all

malice (**mal**-iss) *n* the desire to do harm

m

or cause mischief to others **malicious** *adj* **maliciously** *adv*
WORD ORIGIN Latin *malus* evil

malice aforethought *n law* a deliberate intention to do something unlawful

malign (mal-**line**) *vb* **1** to say unpleasant and untrue things about someone; slander ▷ *adj* **2** evil in influence or effect
WORD ORIGIN Latin *malignus* spiteful

malignant (mal-**lig**-nant) *adj* **1** seeking to harm others **2** tending to cause great harm; injurious **3** *pathol* (of a tumour) uncontrollable or resistant to therapy **malignancy** *n*
WORD ORIGIN Late Latin *malignare* to behave spitefully

malignity (mal-**lig**-nit-ee) *n* the condition of being malign or deadly

malinger (mal-**ling**-ger) *vb* to pretend to be ill, or exaggerate how ill one is, to avoid work **malingerer** *n*
WORD ORIGIN French *malingre* sickly

mall (**mawl**) *n* **1** *US, Canad, Austral, & NZ* short for **shopping mall 2** a shaded avenue, esp. one open to the public
WORD ORIGIN after *the Mall*, an avenue in St James's Park, London

mallard *n, pl* **-lard** *or* **-lards** a common N hemisphere duck, the male of which has a dark green head
WORD ORIGIN Old French *mallart*

malleable (**mal**-lee-a-bl) *adj* **1** (esp. of metal) capable of being hammered or pressed into shape without breaking **2** able to be influenced **malleability** *n* **malleably** *adv*
WORD ORIGIN Medieval Latin *malleabilis*

mallee *n* a low-growing eucalypt found in dry regions of Australia

mallet *n* **1** a hammer with a large wooden head **2** a long stick with a head like a hammer used to strike the ball in croquet or polo
WORD ORIGIN Old French *maillet* wooden hammer

mallow *n* any of a group of plants, with purple, pink, or white flowers
WORD ORIGIN Latin *malva*

malnourished *adj* physically weak due to lack of healthy food

malnutrition *n* physical weakness resulting from insufficient food or an unbalanced diet

malodorous (mal-**lode**-or-uss) *adj* having an unpleasant smell: *the malodorous sludge of Boston harbour*

malpractice *n* illegal, unethical, or negligent professional conduct

malt *n* **1** grain, such as barley, that is kiln-dried after it has been germinated by soaking in water **2** see **malt whisky** ▷ *vb* **3** to make into or become malt **4** to make from malt or to add malt to **malted** *adj* **malty** *adj*
WORD ORIGIN Old English *mealt*

Maltese *adj* **1** of Malta ▷ *n* **2** *pl* **-tese** a person from Malta **3** the language of Malta

Maltese cross *n* a cross with triangular arms that taper towards the centre, sometimes with the outer sides curving in

Malthusian (malth-**yew**-zee-an) *adj* of

the theory stating that increases in population tend to exceed increases in the food supply and that therefore sexual restraint should be exercised
WORD ORIGIN after T. R. *Malthus*, economist

maltose *n* a sugar formed by the action of enzymes on starch
WORD ORIGIN *malt* + *-ose* indicating a sugar

maltreat *vb* to treat badly, cruelly, or violently **maltreatment** *n*
WORD ORIGIN French *maltraiter*

malt whisky *n* whisky made from malted barley

malversation *n rare* professional or public misconduct
WORD ORIGIN French *malverser* to behave badly

malware *n* a computer program designed specifically to damage or disrupt a system, such as a virus

mam *n informal or dialect* same as **mother**

mama *or esp. US* **mamma** (mam-**mah**) *n old-fashioned, informal* same as **mother**
WORD ORIGIN reduplication of childish syllable *ma*

mamba *n* a very poisonous tree snake found in tropical and Southern Africa
WORD ORIGIN Zulu *im-amba*

mambo *n, pl* **-bos** a Latin American dance resembling the rumba
WORD ORIGIN American Spanish

mammal *n* a warm-blooded animal, such as a human being, dog or whale, the female of which produces milk to feed her babies **mammalian** *adj, n*
WORD ORIGIN Latin *mamma* breast

mammary *adj* of the breasts or milk-producing glands
WORD ORIGIN Latin *mamma* breast

mammary gland *n* any of the milk-producing glands in mammals, such as a woman's breast or a cow's udder

mammon *n* wealth regarded as a source of evil and corruption, personified in the New Testament as a false god (**Mammon**)
WORD ORIGIN New Testament Greek *mammōnas* wealth

mammoth *n* **1** a large extinct elephant with a hairy coat and long curved tusks ▷ *adj* **2** gigantic
WORD ORIGIN Russian *mamot*

mammy *n, pl* **-mies** *informal or dialect* same as **mother**

man *n, pl* **men 1** an adult male human being, as distinguished from a woman **2** a human being of either sex; person: *all men are born equal* **3** human beings collectively; mankind ▶ Related adjective: **anthropoid 4** a human being regarded as representative of a particular period or category: *Neanderthal man* **5** an adult male human being with qualities associated with the male, such as courage or virility: *take it like a man* **6** an employee, servant, or representative **7** a member of the armed forces who is not an officer **8** a member of a group or team **9** a husband, boyfriend, or male lover **10** a movable piece in various games, such as draughts **11** *S African slang* any

person: used as a term of address **12 as one man** with unanimous action or response **13 he's your man** he's the person needed **14 man and boy** from childhood **15 sort out the men from the boys** to discover who can cope with difficult or dangerous situations and who cannot **16 to a man** without exception ▷ *vb* **manning, manned 17** to provide with sufficient people for operation or defence **18** to take one's place at or near in readiness for action **manhood** *n*
WORD ORIGIN Old English *mann*

USAGE
The use of words ending in *-man* is avoided as implying a male in job advertisements, where sexual discrimination is illegal, and in many other contexts where a term that is not gender-specific is available, such as *salesperson, barperson, camera operator*.

Man. Manitoba

mana *n NZ* authority, influence and prestige

manacle (**man**-a-kl) *n* **1** a metal ring or chain put round the wrists or ankles, used to restrict the movements of a prisoner or convict ▷ *vb* **-cling, -cled 2** to put manacles on
WORD ORIGIN Latin *manus* hand

manage *vb* **-naging, -naged 1** to succeed in doing something: *we finally managed to sell our old house* **2** to be in charge of; administer: *the company is badly managed* **3** to have room or time for: *can you manage lunch tomorrow?* **4** to keep under control: *she disapproved of taking drugs to manage stress* **5** to struggle on despite difficulties, esp. financial ones: *most people cannot manage on a cleaner's salary* **manageable** *adj*
WORD ORIGIN Italian *maneggiare* to train (esp. horses)

management *n* **1** the people responsible for running an organization or business **2** managers or employers collectively **3** the technique or practice of managing or controlling

manager *n* **1** a person who manages an organization or business **2** a person in charge of a sports team **3** a person who controls the business affairs of an actor or entertainer **manageress** *fem n*

managerial *adj* of a manager or management

managing director *n* the senior director of a company, who has overall responsibility for the way it is run

mañana (man-**yah**-na) *n, adv* **a** tomorrow **b** some other and later time
WORD ORIGIN Spanish

man-at-arms *n, pl* **men-at-arms** a soldier, esp. a medieval soldier

manatee *n* a large plant-eating mammal occurring in tropical coastal waters of the Atlantic
WORD ORIGIN Carib *Manattouī*

Manchu *n, pl* **-chus** *or* **-chu** a member of a Mongoloid people of Manchuria, a region of NE China, who conquered China in the 17th century, ruling until 1912

Mancunian (man-**kew**-nee-an) *adj* **1** of Manchester, a city in NW England ▷ *n* **2** a person from Manchester

Words from Literature
part 17

mill *n* a mill, or treadmill, was a device for hard labour or punishment in prison
>Was you never on the mill?
>*Oliver Twist* Charles Dickens

milliner's shop *n* a shop that sold fabrics, clothing, lace and accessories; as time went on they specialized more and more in hats
>to pay their duty to their aunt and to a milliner's shop just over the way
>*Pride and Prejudice* Jane Austen

minching un' munching *phrase* how people in the north of England used to describe the way people from the south speak
>Minching un' munching!
>*Wuthering Heights* Emily Brontë

mine *n* gold
>Whether both th'Indias of spice and mine
>*The Sun Rising* John Donne

mire *n* mud
>Tis my fate to be always ground into the mire under the iron heel of oppression
>*The Adventures of Huckleberry Finn* Mark Twain

miscellany *n* a miscellany is a collection of many different kinds of things
>under that, the miscellany began
>*Treasure Island* Robert Louis Stevenson

mistarshers *n* a moustache
>when he put his hand up to his mistarshers
>*Tess of the D'Urbervilles* Thomas Hardy

morrow *n* morrow means tomorrow
>And now good-morrow to our waking souls
>*The Good-Morrow* John Donne

mortification *n* an old word for gangrene which is when part of the body decays or 'dies' because of disease
>Yes, it was a mortification – that was it
>*The Adventures of Huckleberry Finn* Mark Twain

mought *v* mought is an old spelling of might
>what you mought call me? You mought call me captain
>*Treasure Island* Robert Louis Stevenson

move me not *v* move me not means do not make me angry
>Move me not, Faustus
>*Doctor Faustus* 2.1 Christopher Marlowe

muffin-cap *n* a muffin cap is a flat cap made from wool
>the old one, remained stationary in the muffin-cap and leathers
>*Oliver Twist* Charles Dickens

mulatter *n* a mulatter was another word for mulatto, which is a person with parents who are from different races
>a mulatter, most as white as a white man
>*The Adventures of Huckleberry Finn* Mark Twain

mummery *n* an old word that meant meaningless (or pretentious) ceremony
>When they were all gone, and when Trabb and his men – but not his boy: I looked for him – had crammed their mummery into bags, and were gone too, the house felt wholesomer.
>*Great Expectations* Charles Dickens

nap *n* the woolly surface on a new item of clothing. Here the surface has been worn away so it looks bare like an old hat with the nap rubbed off
>*The Adventures of Huckleberry Finn* Mark Twain

natural *n* a person born with learning difficulties
>though he had been left to his particular care by their deceased father, who thought him almost a natural.
>*David Copperfield* Charles Dickens

natural *adj* natural meant illegitimate
>Harriet Smith was the natural daughter of somebody
>*Emma* Jane Austen

WORD ORIGIN Medieval Latin *Mancunium* Manchester

mandala *n Hindu and Buddhist art* a circular design symbolizing the universe
WORD ORIGIN Sanskrit: circle

mandarin *n* **1** (in the Chinese Empire) a member of a senior grade of the bureaucracy **2** a high-ranking official with extensive powers **3** a person of standing and influence, esp. in literary or intellectual circles **4** a small citrus fruit resembling the tangerine
WORD ORIGIN Sanskrit *mantrin* counsellor

Mandarin Chinese *or* **Mandarin** *n* the official language of China since 1917

mandate *n* **1** an official or authoritative command to carry out a particular task: *the UN force's mandate does not allow it to intervene* **2** *politics* the political authority given to a government or an elected representative through an electoral victory **3** Also: **mandated territory** (formerly) a territory administered by one country on behalf of an international body ▷ *vb* **-dating, -dated 4** to delegate authority to **5** to assign territory to a nation under a mandate
WORD ORIGIN Latin *mandare* to command

mandatory *adj* **1** obligatory; compulsory **2** having the nature or powers of a mandate **mandatorily** *adv*

mandible *n* **1** the lower jawbone of a vertebrate **2** either of the jawlike mouthparts of an insect **3** either part of the bill of a bird, esp. the lower part
WORD ORIGIN Late Latin *mandibula* jaw

mandolin *n* a musical instrument with four pairs of strings stretched over a small light body, usually played with a plectrum
WORD ORIGIN Italian *mandolino* small lute

mandrake *n* a plant with a forked root. It was formerly thought to have magic powers and a narcotic was prepared from its root
WORD ORIGIN Latin *mandragoras*

mandrel *or* **mandril** *n* **1** a spindle on which the object being worked on is supported in a lathe **2** a shaft on which a machining tool is mounted
WORD ORIGIN perhaps from French *mandrin* lathe

mandrill *n* a monkey of W Africa. The male has red and blue markings on its face and buttocks
WORD ORIGIN *man* + *drill* an Old-World monkey

mane *n* **1** the long hair that grows from the neck in such mammals as the lion and horse **2** long thick human hair **maned** *adj*
WORD ORIGIN Old English *manu*

manège (man-**nayzh**) *n* **1** the art of training horses and riders **2** a riding school
WORD ORIGIN Italian *maneggiare* to manage

maneuver *n, vb US* same as **manoeuvre**

man Friday *n* **1** a loyal male servant or assistant **2** Also: **girl Friday**, **person Friday** any person who does all the odd jobs that arise, esp. in an office

WORD ORIGIN after the native in *Robinson Crusoe*

manful *adj* determined and brave **manfully** *adv*

manganese *n chem* a brittle greyish-white metallic element used in making steel. Symbol: Mn
WORD ORIGIN probably altered form of Medieval Latin *magnesia*

mange *n* a skin disease of domestic animals, characterized by itching and loss of hair
WORD ORIGIN Old French *mangeue* itch

mangelwurzel *n* a variety of beet with a large yellowish root
WORD ORIGIN German *Mangold* beet + *Wurzel* root

manger *n* a trough in a stable or barn from which horses or cattle feed
WORD ORIGIN Old French *maingeure*

mangetout (**mawnzh**-too) *n* a variety of garden pea with an edible pod
WORD ORIGIN French: eat all

mangle¹ *vb* **-gling, -gled 1** to destroy or damage by crushing and twisting **2** to spoil **mangled** *adj*
WORD ORIGIN Norman French *mangler*

mangle² *n* **1** a machine for pressing or squeezing water out of washed clothes, consisting of two heavy rollers between which the clothes are passed ▷ *vb* **-gling, -gled 2** to put through a mangle
WORD ORIGIN Dutch *mangel*

mango *n, pl* **-goes** *or* **-gos** the egg-shaped edible fruit of a tropical Asian tree, with a smooth rind and sweet juicy flesh
WORD ORIGIN Malay *mangā*

mangrove *n* a tropical evergreen tree or shrub with intertwining aerial roots that forms dense thickets along coasts
WORD ORIGIN older *mangrow* (changed through influence of *grove*), from Portuguese *mangue*

mangy *adj* **-gier, -giest 1** having mange **2** scruffy or shabby **mangily** *adv* **manginess** *n*

manhandle *vb* **-handling, -handled 1** to handle or push someone about roughly **2** to move something by manpower rather than by machinery

manhole *n* a hole with a detachable cover, through which a person can enter a sewer or pipe to inspect or repair it

man-hour *n* a unit of work in industry, equal to the work done by one person in one hour

manhunt *n* an organized search, usually by police, for a wanted man or fugitive

mania *n* **1** an obsessional enthusiasm or liking **2** a mental disorder characterized by great or violent excitement
WORD ORIGIN Greek: madness

-mania *n combining form* indicating extreme or abnormal excitement aroused by something: *kleptomania*

maniac *n* **1** a wild disorderly person **2** a person who has a great craving for or enthusiasm for something **maniacal** (man-**eye**-ak-kl) *adj*
WORD ORIGIN Late Latin *maniacus* belonging to madness

manic *adj* **1** extremely excited or

energetic; frenzied: *manic, cavorting dancers* **2** of, involving, or affected by mania: *deep depression broken by periods of manic excitement*

manic-depressive *psychiatry adj* **1** denoting a mental disorder characterized by an alternation between extreme euphoria and deep depression ▷ *n* **2** a person afflicted with this disorder

manicure *n* **1** cosmetic care of the hands and fingernails ▷ *vb* **-curing, -cured 2** to care for the fingernails and hands **manicurist** *n*
WORD ORIGIN Latin *manus* hand + *cura* care

manifest *adj* **1** easily noticed, obvious ▷ *vb* **2** to reveal or display: *an additional symptom now manifested itself* **3** to show by the way one behaves: *he manifested great personal bravery* **4** (of a disembodied spirit) to appear in visible form ▷ *n* **5** a customs document containing particulars of a ship and its cargo **6** a list of the cargo and passengers on an aeroplane **manifestation** *n*
WORD ORIGIN Latin *manifestus* plain

manifesto *n, pl* **-tos** *or* **-toes** a public declaration of intent or policy issued by a group of people, for instance by a political party
WORD ORIGIN Italian

manifold *adj formal* **1** numerous and varied: *her talents are manifold* ▷ *n* **2** a pipe with a number of inlets or outlets, esp. one in a car engine
WORD ORIGIN Old English *manigfeald*

manikin *n* **1** a little man; dwarf or child **2** a model of the human body
WORD ORIGIN Dutch *manneken*

manila *or* **manilla** *n* a strong usually brown paper used to make envelopes
WORD ORIGIN after *Manila*, in the Philippines

man in the street *n* the average person

manioc *n* same as **cassava**
WORD ORIGIN S American Indian *mandioca*

manipulate *vb* **-lating, -lated 1** to handle or use skilfully **2** to control something or someone cleverly or deviously **manipulation** *n* **manipulator** *n* **manipulative** *adj*
WORD ORIGIN Latin *manipulus* handful

mankind *n* **1** human beings collectively **2** men collectively
USAGE Some people object to the use of *mankind* to refer to all human beings and prefer the term *humankind*.

manly *adj* **-lier, -liest 1** possessing qualities, such as vigour or courage, traditionally regarded as appropriate to a man; masculine **2** characteristic of a man **manliness** *n*

man-made *adj* made by humans; artificial

manna *n* **1** *Bible* the miraculous food which sustained the Israelites in the wilderness (Exodus 16:14–36) **2** a windfall: *manna from heaven*
WORD ORIGIN Hebrew *mān*

manned *adj* having a human staff or crew: *thirty years of manned space flight*

mannequin *n* **1** a woman who wears

the clothes displayed at a fashion show; model **2** a life-size dummy of the human body used to fit or display clothes
WORD ORIGIN French

manner *n* **1** the way a thing happens or is done **2** a person's bearing and behaviour **3** the style or customary way of doing something: *sculpture in the Greek manner* **4** type or kind **5 in a manner of speaking** in a way; so to speak **6 to the manner born** naturally fitted to a specified role or activity
WORD ORIGIN Old French *maniere*

mannered *adj* **1** (of speech or behaviour) unnaturally formal and put on to impress others **2** having manners as specified: *ill-mannered*

mannerism *n* **1** a distinctive and individual gesture or way of speaking **2** excessive use of a distinctive or affected manner, esp. in art or literature

mannerly *adj* well-mannered and polite **mannerliness** *n*

manners *pl n* **1** a person's social conduct viewed in the light of whether it is regarded as polite or acceptable or not: *his manners leave something to be desired; shockingly bad manners* **2** a socially acceptable way of behaving: *it's not manners to point*

mannish *adj* (of a woman) displaying qualities regarded as typical of a man

manoeuvre *or US* **maneuver** (man-**noo**-ver) *vb* **-vring, -vred** *or* **-vering, -vered 1** to move or do something with dexterity and skill: *she manoeuvred the car easily into the parking space* **2** to manipulate a situation in order to gain some advantage **3** to perform a manoeuvre or manoeuvres ▷ *n* **4** a movement or action requiring dexterity and skill **5** a contrived, complicated, and possibly deceptive plan or action **6 manoeuvres** military or naval exercises, usually on a large scale **7** a change in course of a ship or aircraft, esp. a complicated one **8 room for manoeuvre** the possibility of changing one's plans or behaviour if it becomes necessary or desirable **manoeuvrable** *or US* **maneuverable** *adj* **manoeuvrability** *or US* **maneuverability** *n*
WORD ORIGIN French, from Medieval Latin *manuopera* manual work

manoeuvring *or US* **maneuvering** *n* the skilful manipulation of a situation to gain some advantage

man-of-war *n, pl* **men-of-war 1** a warship **2** short for **Portuguese man-of-war**

manor *n* **1** (in medieval Europe) the lands and property controlled by a lord **2** *Brit* a large country house and its lands **3** *Brit slang* an area of operation, esp. of a local police force **manorial** *adj*
WORD ORIGIN Old French *manoir* dwelling

manor house *n chiefly Brit* a large country house, esp. one that was originally part of a medieval manor

manpower *n* the number of people needed or available for a job

manqué (**mong**-kay) *adj* unfulfilled;

would-be: *an actor manqué*
WORD ORIGIN French, literally: having missed

mansard *n* a roof with two slopes on both sides and both ends, the lower slopes being steeper than the upper
WORD ORIGIN after François *Mansart*, architect

manse *n* the house provided for a minister of some Christian denominations
WORD ORIGIN Medieval Latin *mansus* dwelling

manservant *n, pl* **menservants** a male servant, esp. a valet

mansion *n* **1** a large and imposing house **2 Mansions** *Brit* a name given to some blocks of flats as part of their address: *18 Wilton Mansions*
WORD ORIGIN Latin *mansio* a remaining

manslaughter *n law* the unlawful but not deliberately planned killing of one human being by another

mantel *n* a wooden, stone, or iron frame around a fireplace
WORD ORIGIN variant of *mantle*

mantelpiece *n* a shelf above a fireplace often forming part of the mantel. Also: **mantel shelf, chimneypiece**

manticore *n* a mythical beast with a lion's body, a scorpion's tail, and a man's head with three rows of teeth
WORD ORIGIN Persian *mardkhora* man-eater

mantilla *n* a woman's lace or silk scarf covering the shoulders and head, worn esp. in Spain
WORD ORIGIN Spanish *manta* cloak

mantis *n, pl* **-tises** *or* **-tes** a carnivorous insect resembling a grasshopper, that rests with the first pair of legs raised as if in prayer. Also: **praying mantis**
WORD ORIGIN Greek: prophet

mantissa *n* the part of a common logarithm consisting of the decimal point and the figures following it: *the mantissa of 2.4771 is .4771*
WORD ORIGIN Latin: something added

mantle *n* **1** *old-fashioned* a loose wrap or cloak **2** anything that covers completely or envelops: *a mantle of snow covered the ground* **3** the responsibilities and duties which go with a particular job or position: *he refuses to accept the mantle of leader* **4** a small mesh dome used to increase illumination in a gas or oil lamp by becoming incandescent **5** *geol* the part of the earth between the crust and the core ▷ *vb* **-tling, -tled 6** to spread over or become spread over: *mountains mantled in lush vegetation*
WORD ORIGIN Latin *mantellum* little cloak

man-to-man *adj* characterized by frankness and sincerity: *a man-to-man discussion*

mantra *n* **1** *Hinduism, Buddhism* any sacred word or syllable used as an object of concentration **2** *Hinduism* a Vedic psalm of praise
WORD ORIGIN Sanskrit: speech, instrument of thought

manual *adj* **1** of a hand or hands: *manual dexterity* **2** physical as opposed to mental: *manual labour* **3** operated or done by human labour rather than

automatic or computer-aided means: *a manual gearbox* ▷ *n* **4** a book of instructions or information **5** *music* one of the keyboards on an organ **manually** *adv*
WORD ORIGIN Latin *manus* hand

manufacture *vb* **-turing, -tured 1** to process or make goods on a large scale, esp. using machinery **2** to invent or concoct evidence, an excuse, etc. ▷ *n* **3** the production of goods, esp. by industrial processes **manufacturer** *n* **manufacturing** *n, adj*
WORD ORIGIN Latin *manus* hand + *facere* to make

manuka (**mah**-nook-a) *n* a New Zealand tree with strong elastic wood and aromatic leaves
WORD ORIGIN Māori

manuka honey *n* honey from the nectar of the manuka tree; its antibacterial agent is used for medicinal purposes. See also **UMF**

manumit (man-new-**mit**) *vb* **-mitting, -mitted** to free from slavery **manumission** *n*
WORD ORIGIN Latin *manumittere* to release

manure *n* **1** animal excrement used as a fertilizer ▷ *vb* **-nuring, -nured 2** to spread manure upon fields or soil
WORD ORIGIN Anglo-French *mainoverer*

manuscript *n* **1** a book or other document written by hand **2** the original handwritten or typed version of a book or article submitted by an author for publication
WORD ORIGIN Medieval Latin *manuscriptus* handwritten

Manx *adj* **1** of the Isle of Man ▷ *n* **2** an almost extinct Celtic language of the Isle of Man ▷ *pl n* **3 the Manx** the people of the Isle of Man **Manxman** *n* **Manxwoman** *n*
WORD ORIGIN Scandinavian

Manx cat *n* a short-haired breed of cat without a tail

many *adj* **1** a large number of; numerous: *many times; many people think the government is incompetent* ▷ *pron* **2** a number of people or things, esp. a large one: *his many supporters; have as many as you want* **3 many a** each of a considerable number of: *many a man* ▷ *n* **4 the many** the majority of mankind, esp. the common people
WORD ORIGIN Old English *manig*

Maoism *n* Communism as interpreted in the theories and policies of Mao Tse-tung (1893–1976), Chinese statesman **Maoist** *n, adj*

Māori *n* **1** *pl* **-ri** *or* **-ris** a member of the Polynesian people living in New Zealand since before the arrival of European settlers **2** the language of this people ▷ *adj* **3** of this people or their language

map *n* **1** a diagrammatic representation of the earth's surface or part of it, showing the geographical distributions or positions of features such as roads, towns, relief, and rainfall **2** a diagrammatic representation of the stars or of the surface of a celestial body **3** *maths* same as **function 4 put on the map** to make (a town or company)

m

well-known: *William Morris put Kelmscott on the map* ▷ *vb* **mapping, mapped 5** to make a map of **6** *maths* to represent or transform (a function, figure, or set) ▸ See also **map out**
WORD ORIGIN Latin *mappa* cloth

maple *n* **1** any of various trees or shrubs with five-pointed leaves and winged seeds borne in pairs **2** the hard wood of any of these trees ▸ See also **sugar maple**
WORD ORIGIN Old English *mapeltrēow* maple tree

maple leaf *n* the leaf of the maple tree, the national emblem of Canada

maple syrup *n* a very sweet syrup made from the sap of the sugar maple

map out *vb* to plan or design

mapping *n* *maths* same as **function**

maquis (mah-**kee**) *n, pl* **-quis** (-**kee**) **1** the French underground movement that fought against the German occupying forces in World War II **2** a type of shrubby, mostly evergreen, vegetation found in coastal regions of the Mediterranean area
WORD ORIGIN French

mar *vb* **marring, marred** to spoil or be the one bad feature of: *Sicily's coastline is marred by high-rise hotels*
WORD ORIGIN Old English *merran*

Mar. March

marabou *n* **1** a large black-and-white African stork **2** the soft white down of this bird, used to trim hats etc.
WORD ORIGIN Arabic *murābit* holy man

maraca (mar-**rak**-a) *n* a shaken percussion instrument, usually one of |a pair, consisting of a gourd or plastic shell filled with dried seeds or pebbles
WORD ORIGIN Brazilian Portuguese

marae (mar-**rye**) *n* NZ **1** an enclosed space in front of a Māori meeting house **2** a Māori meeting house and its buildings
WORD ORIGIN Māori

maraschino (mar-rass-**kee**-no) *n* a liqueur made from a type of sour cherry having a taste like bitter almonds
WORD ORIGIN Italian

maraschino cherry *n* a cherry preserved in maraschino

marathon *n* **1** a race on foot of 26 miles 385 yards (42.195 kilometres) **2** any long or arduous task or event ▷ *adj* **3** of or relating to a race on foot of 26 miles 385 yards (42.195 kilometres): *marathon runners* **4** long and arduous: *a marathon nine hour meeting*
WORD ORIGIN referring to the feat of the messenger said to have run 26 miles from Marathon to Athens to bring the news of victory in 490 BC

maraud *vb* to wander or raid in search of plunder **marauder** *n* **marauding** *adj*
WORD ORIGIN French *marauder* to prowl

marble *n* **1** a hard limestone rock, which usually has a mottled appearance and can be given a high polish **2** a block of marble or work of art made of marble **3** a small round glass ball used in playing marbles ▷ *vb* **-bling, -bled 4** to mottle with variegated streaks in imitation of marble **marbled** *adj*
WORD ORIGIN Greek *marmaros*

marbles *n* a game in which marbles are rolled at one another

marbling *n* **1** a mottled effect or pattern resembling marble **2** the streaks of fat in lean meat

marc *n* **1** the remains of grapes or other fruit that have been pressed for wine-making **2** a brandy distilled from these
WORD ORIGIN French

marcasite *n* **1** a pale yellow form of iron pyrites used in jewellery **2** a cut and polished form of steel used for making jewellery
WORD ORIGIN Arabic *marqashītā*

march¹ *vb* **1** to walk with very regular steps, like a soldier **2** to walk in a quick and determined manner, esp. when angry: *he marched into the kitchen without knocking* **3** to make a person or group proceed: *he was marched back to his cell* **4** (of an army, procession, etc.) to walk as an organized group: *the demonstrators marched down the main street* **5** to advance or progress steadily: *time marches on* ▷ *n* **6** a regular stride **7** a long or exhausting walk **8** the steady development or progress of something: *the continuous march of industrial development* **9** a distance covered by marching **10** an organized protest in which a large group of people walk somewhere together: *a march against racial violence* **11** a piece of music suitable for marching to **12 steal a march on** to gain an advantage over, esp. by a trick **marcher** *n* **marching** *adj*
WORD ORIGIN Old French *marchier* to tread

march² *n* **1** a border or boundary **2** the land lying along a border or boundary, often of disputed ownership
WORD ORIGIN Old French *marche*

March *n* the third month of the year
WORD ORIGIN Latin *Martius* (month) of Mars

March hare *n* a hare during its breeding season in March, noted for its wild and excitable behaviour

marching girl *n* NZ a girl who does team formation marching as a sport

marching orders *pl n* **1** *informal* dismissal, esp. from employment **2** military orders, giving instructions about a march

marchioness (marsh-on-**ness**) *n* **1** a woman who holds the rank of marquis or marquess **2** the wife or widow of a marquis or marquess
WORD ORIGIN Medieval Latin *marchionissa*

marchpane *n archaic* marzipan
WORD ORIGIN French

Mardi Gras (mar-dee **grah**) *n* the festival of Shrove Tuesday, celebrated in some cities with great revelry
WORD ORIGIN French: fat Tuesday

mare¹ *n* the adult female of a horse or zebra
WORD ORIGIN Old English *mere*

mare² (mar-**ray**) *n, pl* **maria** one of many huge dry plains on the surface of the moon or Mars, visible as dark markings
WORD ORIGIN Latin: sea

mare's-nest *n* a discovery imagined to be important but proving to be worthless

margarine *n* a butter substitute made from vegetable and animal fats
WORD ORIGIN Greek *margaron* pearl

marge *n Austral & Brit informal* margarine

margin *n* **1** an edge, rim, or border: *we came to the margin of the wood; people on the margin of society* **2** the blank space surrounding the text on a page **3** an additional amount or one beyond the minimum necessary: *the margin of victory was seven lengths; a small margin of error* **4** *chiefly Austral* a payment made in addition to a basic wage, esp. for special skill or responsibility **5** a limit beyond which something can no longer exist or function: *the margin of physical survival* **6** *econ* the minimum return below which an enterprise becomes unprofitable
WORD ORIGIN Latin *margo* border

marginal *adj* **1** of, in, on, or forming a margin **2** not important; insignificant: *he remained a rather marginal political figure* **3** close to a limit, esp. a lower limit: *marginal legal ability* **4** *econ* relating to goods or services produced and sold at the margin of profitability: *marginal cost* **5** *politics* of or designating a constituency in which elections tend to be won by small margins: *a marginal seat* **6** designating agricultural land on the edge of fertile areas ▷ *n* **7** *politics chiefly Brit & NZ* a marginal constituency **marginally** *adv*

marginalia *pl n* notes in the margin of a book, manuscript, or letter

margrave *n* (formerly) a German nobleman ranking above a count
WORD ORIGIN Middle Dutch *markgrave* count of the frontier

marguerite *n* a garden plant with flowers resembling large daisies
WORD ORIGIN French: daisy

marigold *n* any of various plants cultivated for their yellow or orange flowers
WORD ORIGIN from *Mary* (the Virgin) + *gold*

marijuana *or* **marihuana** (mar-ree-**wah**-na) *n* the dried leaves and flowers of the hemp plant, used as a drug, esp. in cigarettes
WORD ORIGIN Mexican Spanish

marimba *n* a percussion instrument consisting of a set of hardwood plates placed over tuned metal resonators, played with soft-headed sticks
WORD ORIGIN West African

marina *n* a harbour for yachts and other pleasure boats
WORD ORIGIN Latin: marine

marinade *n* **1** a mixture of oil, wine, vinegar, etc. in which meat or fish is soaked before cooking ▷ *vb* **-nading, -naded 2** same as **marinate**
WORD ORIGIN French

marinate *vb* **-nating, -nated** to soak in marinade **marinated** *adj*
WORD ORIGIN Italian *marinare* to pickle

marine *adj* **1** of, found in, or relating to the sea **2** of shipping or navigation **3** used or adapted for use at sea ▷ *n* **4** (esp. in Britain and the US) a soldier trained for land and sea combat **5** a country's shipping or navy collectively:

Words from Shakespeare
part 13

merely *adv* completely or entirely
Love is merely a madness *As You Like It* 3.2

misgraffed *adj* mismatched or unequal
Or else misgraffed in respect of years
A Midsummer Night's Dream 1.1

misprision *n* an error or mistake
Misprision in the highest degree! *Twelfth Night* 1.5

mollification *n* appeasement or a way of preventing someone getting angry
I am to hull here a little longer. Some mollification for your giant *Twelfth Night* 1.5

mouth, cold in the *phrase* dead
What, must our mouths be cold? *The Tempest* 1.1

murmur *n* rumour or hearsay
and then 'twas fresh in murmur *Twelfth Night* 1.2

murrain *n* plague, pestilence
A murrain on your monster, and the devil take your fingers! *The Tempest* 3.2

neaf *n* fist
Give me your neaf, Monsieur Mustardseed
A Midsummer Night's Dream 4.1

nice *adj* fussy or particular
An therefore, goaded with most sharp occasions,
Which lay nice manners by, I put you to
The use of your own virtues *All's Well That Ends Well* 5.1

nice *adj* critical or delicate
We're good … To set so rich a man
On the nice hazard of one doubtful hour?
Henry IV part 1

nice *adj* carefully accurate, fastidious
O relation
Too nice and yet too true! *Macbeth* 4.3

nonpareil *n* without equal, peerless
though you were crown'd
The nonpareil of beauty! *Twelfth Night* 1.5

office *n* business or work
Speak your office *Twelfth Night* 1.5

outsport *v* to overdo
Let's teach ourselves that honorable stop,
Not to outsport discretion. *Othello* 2.2

owe *v* to own, possess
Lend less than thou owest *King Lear* 1.4

paragon *v* to surpass or exceed
he hath achieved a maid
That paragons description and wild fame
Othello 2.1

pate *n* head
Back, slave, or I will break thy pate across
The Comedy of Errors 2.1

paunch *v* to stab someone (usually in the stomach). Paunch is still a common word for a stomach
Batter his skull, or paunch him with a stake
The *Tempest* 3.2

peevish *adj* irritable or easily angered
Run after that same peevish messenger *Twelfth Night* 1.5

peradventure *adv* perhaps or maybe
Peradventure this is not Fortune's work
As You Like It 1.2

perforce *adv* by force or violently
my rights and royalties,
Plucked from my arms perforce *Richard II* 2.3

personage *n* your appearance
Of what personage and years is he?
Twelfth Night 1.5

pestilence *n* plague or disease
Methought she purg'd the air of pestilence!
Twelfth Night 1.1

physic *n* medicine or a treatment
tis a physic
That's bitter to sweet end *Measure for Measure* 4.6

the merchant marine
WORD ORIGIN Latin *marinus* of the sea
mariner (**mar**-in-er) *n* a sailor
marionette *n* a puppet whose limbs are moved by strings
WORD ORIGIN French, from the name *Marion*
marital *adj* of or relating to marriage **maritally** *adv*
WORD ORIGIN Latin *maritus* married
maritime *adj* **1** of or relating to shipping **2** of, near, or living near the sea
WORD ORIGIN Latin *maritimus* of the sea
marjoram *n* a plant with sweet-scented leaves, used for seasoning food and in salads
WORD ORIGIN Medieval Latin *marjorana*
mark¹ *n* **1** a visible impression on a surface, such as a spot or scratch **2** a sign, symbol, or other indication that distinguishes something **3** a written or printed symbol, as used for punctuation **4** a letter, number, or percentage used to grade academic work **5** a thing that indicates position; marker **6** an indication of some quality: *a mark of respect* **7** a target or goal **8** impression or influence: *this book displays the mark of its author's admiration of Kafka* **9** (in trade names) a particular model or type of a vehicle, machine, etc.: *the Ford Escort Mark Two* **10** one of the temperature settings at which a gas oven can work: *bake at gas mark 5 for thirty minutes* **11** make one's mark to achieve recognition **12** on your mark or marks a command given to runners in a race to prepare themselves at the starting line **13** up to the mark meeting the desired standard ▷ *vb* **14** to make a visible impression, trace, or stain on **15** to have a tendency to become dirty, scratched, or damaged: *this material marks easily* **16** to characterize or distinguish: *the gritty determination that has marked his career* **17** to designate someone as a particular type of person: *she would now be marked as a troublemaker* **18** to label, esp. to indicate price **19** to celebrate or commemorate an occasion or its anniversary: *a series of concerts to mark the 200th anniversary of Mozart's death* **20** to pay attention to: *mark my words* **21** to observe or notice **22** to grade or evaluate academic work **23** *sport* to stay close to an opponent to hamper his or her play **24** mark off or out to set boundaries or limits on **25** mark time **a** to move the feet alternately as in marching but without advancing **b** to wait for something more interesting to happen ▸ See also **markdown, mark-up**
WORD ORIGIN Old English *mearc*
mark² *n* see **Deutschmark**
WORD ORIGIN Old English *marc* unit of weight of precious metal
markdown *n* **1** a price reduction ▷ *vb* **mark down 2** to reduce in price **3** to make a written note of: *she marked down the number of the getaway car*
marked *adj* **1** obvious or noticeable: *a marked improvement* **2** singled out, esp. as the target of attack: *a marked man* **markedly** (**mark**-id-lee) *adv*
marker *n* **1** an object used to show the position of something **2** Also called:

marker pen a thick felt-tipped pen used for drawing and colouring
market *n* **1** an occasion at which people meet to buy and sell merchandise **2** a place at which a market is held **3** the buying and selling of goods and services, esp. when unrestrained by political or social considerations: *the market has been brought into health care* **4** the trading opportunities provided by a particular group of people: *the youth market* **5** demand for a particular product **6** short for **stock market 7** be in the market for to wish to buy **8** on the market available for purchase **9** seller's or buyer's market a market characterized by excess demand (or supply) and thus favourable to sellers (or buyers) ▷ *adj* **10** of, relating to, or controlled by the buying and selling of goods and services, esp. when unrestrained by political or social considerations: *a market economy* ▷ *vb* **-keting, -keted 11** to offer or produce for sale **marketable** *adj*
WORD ORIGIN Latin *mercari* to trade
market forces *pl n* the effect of supply and demand on trading within a free market
market garden *n chiefly Brit & NZ* a place where fruit and vegetables are grown for sale **market gardener** *n*
marketing *n* the part of a business which controls the way that goods or services are sold
market maker *n stock exchange* a dealer in securities on the London Stock Exchange who can also deal with the public as a broker
marketplace *n* **1** a place where a public market is held **2** the commercial world of buying and selling
market price *n* the prevailing price at which goods may be bought or sold
market research *n* the study of customers' wants and purchases, and of the forces influencing them
market-test *vb* to put (a section of a public-sector service) out to tender, often before full privatization
market town *n chiefly Brit* the main town in an agricultural area, usually one where a market is regularly held
marking *n* **1** the arrangement of colours on an animal or plant **2** the assessment and correction of pupils' or students' written work by teachers
marksman *n, pl* **-men** a person skilled in shooting **marksmanship** *n*
mark-up *n* **1** an amount added to the cost of something to provide the seller with a profit ▷ *vb* **mark up 2** to increase the cost of something by an amount or percentage in order to make a profit
marl *n* a fine-grained rock consisting of clay, limestone, and silt used as a fertilizer **marly** *adj*
WORD ORIGIN Late Latin *margila*
marlin *n, pl* **-lin** or **-lins** a large fish with a long spear-like upper jaw, found in warm and tropical seas
WORD ORIGIN after *marlinspike* (because of its long jaw)
marlinspike or **marlinespike** (**mar**-lin-spike) *n naut* a pointed metal

tool used in separating strands of rope
WORD ORIGIN Dutch *marlijn* light rope + SPIKE
marmalade *n* a jam made from citrus fruits, esp. oranges
WORD ORIGIN Portuguese *marmelo* quince
marmoreal (mar-**more**-ee-al) *adj* of or like marble
WORD ORIGIN Latin *marmoreus*
marmoset *n* a small South American monkey with a long bushy tail
WORD ORIGIN Old French *marmouset* grotesque figure
marmot *n* any of various burrowing rodents of Europe, Asia, and North America. They are heavily built and have coarse fur
WORD ORIGIN French *marmotte*
maroon¹ *vb* **1** to abandon someone in a deserted area, esp. on an island **2** to isolate in a helpless situation: *we're marooned here until the snow stops* **marooned** *adj*
WORD ORIGIN American Spanish *cimarrón* wild
maroon² *adj* **1** dark purplish-red ▷ *n* **2** an exploding firework or flare used as a warning signal
WORD ORIGIN French: chestnut
marque (**mark**) *n* a brand of product, esp. of a car
WORD ORIGIN French
marquee *n* a large tent used for a party, exhibition, etc.
WORD ORIGIN invented singular form of MARQUISE
marquess (**mar**-kwiss) *n* **1** (in the British Isles) a nobleman ranking between a duke and an earl **2** see **marquis**
marquetry *n, pl* **-quetries** a pattern of inlaid veneers of wood or metal used chiefly as ornamentation in furniture
WORD ORIGIN Old French *marqueter* to inlay
marquis *n, pl* **-quises** or **-quis** (in various countries) a nobleman ranking above a count, corresponding to a British marquess
WORD ORIGIN Old French *marchis* count of the frontier
marquise (mar-**keez**) *n* **1** (in various countries) a marchioness **2** a gemstone cut in a pointed oval shape
WORD ORIGIN French
marram grass *n* a grass that grows on sandy shores: often planted to stabilize sand dunes
WORD ORIGIN Old Norse *marálmr*
marriage *n* **1** the state or relationship of being husband and wife: *the institution of marriage* **2** the contract made by a man and woman to live as husband and wife ▸ Related adjectives: **connubial, nuptial 3** the ceremony formalizing this union; wedding **4** a close union or relationship: *the marriage of scientific knowledge and industry*
marriageable *adj* suitable for marriage, usually with reference to age
marriage guidance *n* advice given by trained counsellors to couples who have problems in their married life
married *adj* **1** having a husband or wife **2** of marriage or married people: *married*

life ▷ *n* **3 marrieds** married people: *young marrieds*

marrow *n* **1** the fatty tissue that fills the cavities of bones **2** short for **vegetable marrow**

WORD ORIGIN Old English *mærg*

marrowfat pea *or* **marrow pea** *n* a variety of large pea

marry¹ *vb* **-ries, -rying, -ried 1** to take (someone) as one's husband or wife **2** to join or give in marriage **3** Also: **marry up** to fit together or unite; join: *their playing marries Irish traditional music and rock*

WORD ORIGIN Latin *maritare*

marry² *interj archaic* an exclamation of surprise or anger

WORD ORIGIN euphemistic for the Virgin *Mary*

Mars *n* **1** the Roman god of war **2** the fourth planet from the sun

Marseillaise (mar-say-**yaze**) *n* **the Marseillaise** the French national anthem

WORD ORIGIN French (*chanson*) *marseillaise* (song) of Marseilles (first sung in Paris by the battalion of Marseilles)

marsh *n* low poorly drained land that is wet, muddy, and sometimes flooded **marshy** *adj*

WORD ORIGIN Old English *merisc*

marshal *n* **1** (in some armies and air forces) an officer of the highest rank: *Field Marshall* **2** an officer who organizes or controls ceremonies or public events **3** US the chief police or fire officer in some states **4** (formerly in England) an officer of the royal family or court ▷ *vb* **-shalling, -shalled** *or US* **-shaling, -shaled 5** to arrange in order: *she marshalled her facts and came to a conclusion* **6** to assemble and organize people or vehicles in readiness for onward movement **7** to guide or lead, esp. in a ceremonious way: *she marshalled them towards the lecture theatre* **marshalcy** *n*

WORD ORIGIN Old French *mareschal*

marshalling yard *n railways* a place where railway wagons are shunted and made up into trains

Marshal of the Royal Air Force *n* the highest rank in the Royal Air Force

marsh gas *n* a gas largely composed of methane formed when plants decay in the absence of air

marshland *n* land consisting of marshes

marshmallow *n* a spongy pink or white sweet

marsh mallow *n* a plant that grows in salt marshes and has pale pink flowers. It was formerly used to make marshmallows

marsupial (mar-**soop**-ee-al) *n* **1** a mammal, such as a kangaroo or an opossum, the female of which carries her babies in a pouch at the front of her body until they reach a mature state ▷ *adj* **2** of or like a marsupial

WORD ORIGIN Latin *marsupium* purse

mart *n* a market or trading centre

WORD ORIGIN Middle Dutch: market

Martello tower *n* a round tower used for coastal defence, formerly much used in Europe

WORD ORIGIN after Cape *Mortella* in Corsica

marten *n, pl* **-tens** *or* **-ten 1** any of several agile weasel-like mammals with bushy tails and golden-brown to blackish fur **2** the fur of these animals

WORD ORIGIN Middle Dutch *martren*

martial *adj* of or characteristic of war, soldiers, or the military life: *martial music*

WORD ORIGIN Latin *martialis* of Mars, god of war

martial art *n* any of various philosophies and techniques of self-defence originating in the Far East, such as judo or karate

martial law *n* rule of law maintained by military forces in the absence of civil law

Martian (**marsh**-an) *adj* **1** of the planet Mars ▷ *n* **2** an inhabitant of Mars, in science fiction

martin *n* a bird of the swallow family with a square or slightly forked tail

WORD ORIGIN probably after St *Martin*, because the birds were believed to migrate at Martinmas

martinet *n* a person who maintains strict discipline

WORD ORIGIN after General *Martinet*, drillmaster under Louis XIV

martingale *n* a strap from the reins to the girth of a horse, preventing it from carrying its head too high

WORD ORIGIN French

martini *n* **1** (*often cap*) *trademark* an Italian vermouth **2** a cocktail of gin and vermouth

Martinmas *n* the feast of St Martin on November 11: a quarter day in Scotland

martyr *n* **1** a person who chooses to die rather than renounce his or her religious beliefs **2** a person who suffers greatly or dies for a cause or belief **3 a martyr to** suffering constantly from: *a martyr to arthritis* ▷ *vb* **4** to make a martyr of **martyrdom** *n*

WORD ORIGIN Late Greek *martur-* witness

marvel *vb* **-velling, -velled** *or US* **-veling, -veled 1** to be filled with surprise or wonder ▷ *n* **2** something that causes wonder

WORD ORIGIN Old French *merveille*

marvellous *or US* **marvelous** *adj* **1** excellent or splendid: *a marvellous idea* **2** causing great wonder or surprise; extraordinary: *electricity is a marvellous thing* **marvellously** *or US* **marvelously** *adv*

Marxism *n* the economic and political theories of Karl Marx (1818–83), German political philosopher, which argue that class struggle is the basic agency of historical change, and that capitalism will be superseded by communism **Marxist** *n, adj*

marzipan *n* a mixture made from ground almonds, sugar, and egg whites that is put on top of cakes or used to make sweets

WORD ORIGIN Italian *marzapane*

masala *n Indian cookery* a mixture of spices ground into a paste

masc. masculine

mascara *n* a cosmetic for darkening the eyelashes

WORD ORIGIN Spanish: mask

mascarpone (mass-car-**po**-nee) *n* a soft Italian cream cheese

WORD ORIGIN from Italian dialect *mascherpa* ricotta

mascot *n* a person, animal, or thing considered to bring good luck

WORD ORIGIN French *mascotte*

masculine *adj* **1** possessing qualities or characteristics considered typical of or appropriate to a man; manly **2** unwomanly; not feminine **3** *grammar* denoting a gender of nouns that includes some male animate things **4** *prosody* denoting a rhyme between pairs of single final stressed syllables **masculinity** *n*

WORD ORIGIN Latin *masculinus*

maser *n* a device for amplifying microwaves, working on the same principle as a laser

WORD ORIGIN m(icrowave) a(mplification by) s(timulated) e(mission of) r(adiation)

mash *n* **1** a soft pulpy mass **2** *agriculture* bran, meal, or malt mixed with warm water and used as food for horses, cattle, or poultry **3** *Brit informal* mashed potatoes ▷ *vb* **4** to beat or crush into a mash **mashed** *adj*

WORD ORIGIN Old English *mæsc-*

mask *n* **1** any covering for the whole or a part of the face worn for amusement, protection, or disguise **2** behaviour that hides one's true feelings: *his mask of detachment* **3** *surgery* a sterile gauze covering for the nose and mouth worn to minimize the spread of germs **4** a device placed over the nose and mouth to facilitate or prevent inhalation of a gas **5** a moulded likeness of a face or head, such as a death mask **6** the face or head of an animal such as a fox ▷ *vb* **7** to cover with or put on a mask **8** to hide or disguise: *a high brick wall that masked the front of the building* **9** to cover so as to protect **masked** *adj*

WORD ORIGIN Arabic *maskharah* clown

masking tape *n* an adhesive tape used to protect surfaces surrounding an area to be painted

masochism (**mass**-oh-kiz-zum) *n* **1** *psychiatry* a condition in which pleasure, esp. sexual pleasure, is obtained from feeling pain or from being humiliated **2** a tendency to take pleasure from one's own suffering **masochist** *n, adj* **masochistic** *adj*

WORD ORIGIN after Leopold von Sacher *Masoch*, novelist

mason *n* a person skilled in building with stone

WORD ORIGIN Old French *masson*

Mason *n* a Freemason

Masonic *adj* of Freemasons or Freemasonry

masonry *n* **1** stonework or brickwork **2** the craft of a mason

Masonry *n* Freemasonry

masque (**mask**) *n* a dramatic entertainment of the 16th to 17th centuries, consisting of dancing, dialogue, and song **masquer** *n*

WORD ORIGIN variant of *mask*

masquerade (mask-er-**aid**) *vb* **-ading, -aded 1** to pretend to be someone or

m

something else ▷ *n* **2** an attempt to keep secret the real identity or nature of something: *he was unable to keep up his masquerade as the war's victor* **3** a party at which the guests wear masks and costumes
WORD ORIGIN Spanish *mascara* mask

mass *n* **1** a large body of something without a definite shape **2** a collection of the component parts of something: *a mass of fibres* **3** a large amount or number, as of people **4** the main part or majority **5** the size of a body; bulk **6** *physics* a physical quantity expressing the amount of matter in a body **7** (in painting or drawing) an area of unified colour, shade, or intensity ▷ *adj* **8** done or occurring on a large scale: *mass hysteria* **9** consisting of a mass or large number, esp. of people: *a mass meeting* ▷ *vb* **10** to join together into a mass ▸ See also **masses** > **massed** *adj*
WORD ORIGIN Latin *massa*

Mass *n* **1** (in the Roman Catholic Church and certain other Christian churches) a service in which bread and wine are consecrated to represent the body and blood of Christ **2** a musical setting of parts of this service
WORD ORIGIN Church Latin *missa*

massacre (**mass**-a-ker) *n* **1** the wanton or savage killing of large numbers of people **2** *informal* an overwhelming defeat ▷ *vb* **-cring, -cred 3** to kill people indiscriminately or in large numbers **4** *informal* to defeat overwhelmingly
WORD ORIGIN Old French

massage (**mass**-ahzh) *n* **1** the kneading or rubbing of parts of the body to reduce pain or stiffness or help relaxation ▷ *vb* **-saging, -saged 2** to give a massage to **3** to manipulate statistics or evidence to produce a desired result
WORD ORIGIN French *masser* to rub

massage parlour *n* **1** a commercial establishment providing massages **2** *euphemistic* a place where men pay to have sex with prostitutes

massasauga (mass-a-**saw**-ga) *n* a North American venomous snake with a horny rattle at the end of the tail
WORD ORIGIN after the *Missisauga* River, Ontario, Canada

masses *pl n* **1 the masses** ordinary people as a group **2 masses of** *informal chiefly Brit* a great number or quantity of: *masses of food*

masseur (mass-**ur**) *or fem* **masseuse** (mass-**uhz**) *n* a person who gives massages

massif (**mass**-seef) *n* a series of connected masses of rock forming a mountain range
WORD ORIGIN French

massive *adj* **1** (of objects) large, bulky, heavy, and usually solid **2** impressive or imposing **3** intensive or considerable: *a massive overdose* **massively** *adv*
WORD ORIGIN French *massif*

mass-market *adj* of, for, or appealing to a large number of people; popular: *mass-market newspapers*

mass media *pl n* the means of communication that reach large numbers of people, such as television, newspapers, and radio

mass noun *n* a noun that refers to an extended substance rather than to each of a set of objects, eg, *water* as opposed to *lake*

mass number *n* the total number of protons and neutrons in the nucleus of an atom

mass-produce *vb* **-producing, -produced** to manufacture standardized goods on a large scale by extensive use of machinery **mass-produced** *adj* **mass-production** *n*

mass spectrometer *n* an instrument for analysing the composition of a sample of material, in which ions, produced from the sample, are separated by electric or magnetic fields according to their ratios of charge to mass

mast¹ *n* **1** *naut* a vertical pole for supporting sails, radar equipment, etc. above the deck of a ship **2** a tall upright pole used as an aerial for radio or television broadcasting: *a television mast* **3** **before the mast** *naut* as an apprentice seaman
WORD ORIGIN Old English *mæst*

mast² *n* the fruit of forest trees, such as beech or oak, used as food for pigs
WORD ORIGIN Old English *mæst*

mastaba *n* a mud-brick superstructure above tombs in ancient Egypt
WORD ORIGIN Arabic: bench

mastectomy (mass-**tek**-tom-ee) *n, pl* **-mies** surgical removal of a breast
WORD ORIGIN Greek *mastos* breast + *tomē* a cutting

master *n* **1** the man who has authority over others, such as the head of a household, the employer of servants, or the owner of slaves or animals **2** a person with exceptional skill at a certain thing: *B.B. King is a master of the blues* **3** a person who has complete control of a situation: *the master of his portfolio* **4** an original copy or tape from which duplicates are made **5** a craftsman fully qualified to practise his trade and to train others **6** a player of a game, esp. chess or bridge, who has won a specified number of tournament games **7** a highly regarded teacher or leader **8** a graduate holding a master's degree **9** the chief officer aboard a merchant ship **10** *chiefly Brit* a male teacher **11** the superior person or side in a contest **12** the heir apparent of a Scottish viscount or baron: *the Master of Ballantrae* ▷ *adj* **13** (of a craftsman) fully qualified to practise and to train others **14** overall or controlling: *master plan* **15** designating a mechanism that controls others: *master switch* **16** main or principal: *master bedroom* ▷ *vb* **17** to become thoroughly proficient in **18** to overcome or defeat
WORD ORIGIN Latin *magister* teacher

Master *n* a title of address for a boy who is not old enough to be called *Mr*

master aircrew *n* a rank in the Royal Air Force, equal to warrant officer

masterful *adj* **1** showing great skill **2** domineering or authoritarian **masterfully** *adv*

master key *n* a key that opens all the locks of a set; passkey

masterly *adj* showing great skill; expert

mastermind *vb* **1** to plan and direct a complex task or project ▷ *n* **2** a person who plans and directs a complex task or project

Master of Arts *n* a degree, usually postgraduate in a nonscientific subject, or a person holding this degree

master of ceremonies *n* a person who presides over a public ceremony, formal dinner, or entertainment, introducing the events and performers

Master of Science *n* a degree, usually postgraduate in a scientific subject, or a person holding this degree

Master of the Rolls *n* (in England) the senior civil judge in the country and the head of the Public Record Office

masterpiece *or* **masterwork** *n* **1** an outstanding work or performance **2** the most outstanding piece of work of an artist or craftsman

masterstroke *n* an outstanding piece of strategy, skill, or talent

mastery *n, pl* **-teries 1** outstanding skill or expertise **2** complete power or control: *he had complete mastery over the country*

masthead *n* **1** *naut* the highest part of a mast **2** the name of a newspaper or periodical printed at the top of the front page

mastic *n* **1** an aromatic resin obtained from a Mediterranean tree and used to make varnishes and lacquers **2** any of several putty-like substances used as a filler, adhesive, or seal
WORD ORIGIN Greek *mastikhē*

masticate *vb* **-cating, -cated** to chew food **mastication** *n*
WORD ORIGIN Greek *mastikhan* to grind the teeth

mastiff *n* a large powerful short-haired dog, usually fawn or brown with dark streaks
WORD ORIGIN Latin *mansuetus* tame

mastitis *n* inflammation of the breast

mastodon *n* an extinct elephant-like mammal
WORD ORIGIN New Latin, literally: breast-tooth, referring to the nipple-shaped projections on the teeth

mastoid *adj* **1** shaped like a nipple or breast ▷ *n* **2** a nipple-like projection of bone behind the ear **3** *informal* mastoiditis
WORD ORIGIN Greek *mastos* breast

mastoiditis *n* inflammation of the mastoid

masturbate *vb* **-bating, -bated** to fondle one's own genitals, or those of someone else, to cause sexual pleasure **masturbation** *n*
WORD ORIGIN Latin *masturbari*

mat¹ *n* **1** a thick flat piece of fabric used as a floor covering, a place to wipe one's shoes, etc. **2** a small pad of material used to protect a surface from heat or scratches from an object placed upon it **3** a large piece of thick padded material put on the floor as a surface for wrestling, gymnastics, etc. ▷ *vb* **matting, matted 4** to tangle or become tangled into a dense mass
WORD ORIGIN Old English *matte*

Augustan Literature

Centuries are convenient fictions and literary periods do not necessarily start or stop in a year ending in two zeros. The English literary eighteenth century may have begun as early as 1660, when Charles II reclaimed the throne, or after 1674, when John Milton died. It may have ended in 1796 with the Romantic manifesto of *Lyrical Ballads* by William Wordsworth and Samuel Taylor Coleridge.

However we measure it, the shape of the century is clear, at least in retrospect. Novelists took fiction in directions that set the pace for the next two centuries: Daniel Defoe and Henry Fielding for realism, Samuel Richardson for sensibility and the epistolary form, Jonathan Swift and Laurence Sterne for parody, fantasy, and satire, Horace Walpole for Gothic romance. Other prose writers were innovative, too: Joseph Addison in the personal essay, Johnson in biography (notably in his *Lives of the Poets*), and James Boswell in his biography of Johnson. Johnson created a monumental dictionary, but although all his instincts pointed toward writing permanent definitions, he was forced to take account of how language changed. In the end, this arch-Tory was, like the others, a reformer.

In a culture where the proliferation of newspapers and magazines threw up legions of versatile hacks and partisan controversialists, poets sought safe models in the marmoreal qualities of the Latin classics: Horace, Virgil, Ovid, and Juvenal. What literary historians call the 'Augustan period' loosely began when the imported, German-speaking George I acquired the throne in 1714 and decisively made England a Protestant country. From the prolific John Dryden poets inherited the heroic couplet, two rhyming lines, each with five two-syllable metrical feet, the stress falling on the second syllable. It was a form ideally suited to epigram and satire. The heroic couplet's great exponent was Alexander Pope. A Catholic commoner, deformed by infant tuberculosis, he was an outsider in obvious ways, yet found influential friends, and fame with his Latin imitations and savagely satirical work. *The Essay on Criticism*, the invective-laden *Dunciad*, and *An Essay on Man* yielded some of the language's most-quoted proverbs and catchphrases: 'A little learning is a dangerous thing', 'A bird in the hand is worth two in the bush', and 'Fools rush in where angels fear to tread'.

Pope was a friend of John Gay, whose sprightly libretto for the hugely successful *The Beggar's Opera* engaged with the subject of London's pullulating low-life. As the century proceeded, a vein of brooding pastoral melancholy surfaced, traceable in the titles of long poems such as Edward Young's *Night Thoughts*, Johnson's *The Vanity of Human Wishes*, and Thomas Gray's 'Elegy Written in a Country Churchyard'. Gray's elegy gave the language, and the writers to come, such immortal lines and phrases as 'The paths of glory lead but to the grave', 'kindred spirit', and 'Far from the madding crowd'. Solitary melancholy was counterbalanced, sometimes reinforced, by the religious-minded. Among the hymnodists was the poet William Cowper, whose work produced the enduring 'God moves in a mysterious way, / His wonders to perform', 'God made the country, and man made the town', 'Variety's the very spice of life,' and 'I am monarch of all I survey'.

Perhaps because they sought native equivalents of the classics, many authorities fell for poetic impostures, such as Thomas Chatterton with his pseudo-medieval forgeries and James Macpherson with his supposedly discovered *Ossian*, which he claimed was translated from the ancient Scots Gaelic. These were like public illnesses mirroring private maladies. Pope had Pott's disease, Swift was intermittently insane and had Ménière's disease, causing deafness, tinnitus, and vertigo. Christopher Smart, a one-off original like William Blake in the next century, was obsessed in his psalms, hymns, and *Jubilate Agno* with charismatic Christianity and Freemasonry, volubly prayed in the street, and spent time in a mental asylum. Johnson had Tourette syndrome, bad eyesight, chronic depression, and other afflictions. Chatterton, who died an apparent suicide at the age of 17, had venereal disease. Cowper was bipolar. In the eighteenth century, you didn't have to be sick to be a great writer. But apparently it helped.

mat² *adj* same as **matt**
  WORD ORIGIN French, literally: dead

matador *n* the bullfighter armed with a sword, who attempts to kill the bull
  WORD ORIGIN Spanish, from *matar* to kill

matai *n* a New Zealand tree, the wood of which is used for timber for building
  WORD ORIGIN Māori

match¹ *n* **1** a formal game or sports event in which people or teams compete **2** a person or thing able to provide competition for another: *he has met his match* **3** a person or thing that resembles, harmonizes with, or is equivalent to another: *the colours aren't a perfect match, but they're close enough; white wine is not a good match for steak* **4** a person or thing that is an exact copy or equal of another **5** a partnership between a man and a woman, as in marriage **6** a person regarded as a possible partner in marriage: *for any number of men she would have been a good match* ▷ *vb* **7** to fit parts together **8** to resemble, harmonize with, or equal one another or something else: *our bedroom curtains match the bedspread; she walked at a speed that he could barely match* **9** to find a match for **10 match with** or **against a** to compare in order to determine which is the superior **b** to arrange a competition between **matching** *adj*
  WORD ORIGIN Old English *gemæcca* spouse

match² *n* **1** a thin strip of wood or cardboard tipped with a chemical that ignites when scraped against a rough or specially treated surface **2** a fuse used to fire cannons' explosives
  WORD ORIGIN Old French *meiche*

matchbox *n* a small box for holding matches

match-fit *adj sport* in good physical condition for competing in a match

matchless *adj* unequalled

matchmaker *n* a person who introduces people in the hope that they will form a couple **matchmaking** *n, adj*

match play *n golf* scoring according to the number of holes won and lost

match point *n sport* the final point needed to win a match

matchstick *n* **1** the wooden part of a match ▷ *adj* **2** (esp. of drawn figures) thin and straight: *little matchstick men*

matchwood *n* **1** wood suitable for making matches **2** splinters

mate¹ *n* **1 a** *informal chiefly Brit, Austral, & NZ* a friend: often used as a term of address between males: *I spotted my mate Jimmy McCrae at the other end of the bar; that's all right, mate* **b** an associate or colleague: *a classmate; the governor's running mate* **2** the sexual partner of an animal **3** a marriage partner **4** *naut* any officer below the master on a commercial ship **5** (in some trades) an assistant: *a plumber's mate* **6** one of a pair of matching items ▷ *vb* **mating, mated 7** to pair (a male and female animal) or (of animals) to pair for breeding **8** to marry **9** to join as a pair
  WORD ORIGIN Low German

mate² *n, vb* **mating, mated** *chess* same as **checkmate**

mater *n Brit, humorous* mother: often used facetiously
  WORD ORIGIN Latin

material *n* **1** the substance of which a thing is made **2** cloth **3** ideas or notes that a finished work may be based on: *the material of the story resembles an incident in his own life* ▷ *adj* **4** concerned with or composed of physical matter or substance; not relating to spiritual or abstract things: *the material universe* **5** of or affecting economic or physical wellbeing: *material prosperity* **6** relevant or pertinent: *material evidence* ▸ See also **materials**
  WORD ORIGIN Latin *materia* matter

materialism *n* **1** excessive interest in and desire for money or possessions **2** the belief that only the material world exists **materialist** *n, adj* **materialistic** *adj*

materialize *or* **-lise** *vb* **-lizing, -lized** *or* **-lising, -lised 1** *not standard* to become fact; actually happen: *the promised pay rise never materialized* **2** to appear after being invisible: *trees materialized out of the gloom* **3** to take shape: *after hours of talks, a plan began to materialize* **materialization** *or* **-lisation** *n*

materially *adv* to a significant extent: *we were not materially affected*

materials *pl n* the equipment necessary for a particular activity: *building materials*

materiel (mat-ear-ee-**ell**) *n* the materials and equipment of an organization, esp. of a military force
  WORD ORIGIN French

maternal *adj* **1** of or characteristic of a mother **2** related through the mother's side of the family: *his maternal uncle* **maternally** *adv*
  WORD ORIGIN Latin *mater* mother

maternity *n* **1** motherhood **2** motherliness ▷ *adj* **3** relating to women during pregnancy or childbirth: *maternity leave*

mate's rates *pl n NZ informal* reduced charges offered to a friend or colleague

matey *adj Brit informal* friendly or intimate

math *n US & Canad informal* short for **mathematics**

mathematical *adj* **1** using, used in, or relating to mathematics **2** having the precision of mathematics **mathematically** *adv*

mathematician *n* an expert or specialist in mathematics

mathematics *n* **1** a group of related sciences, including algebra, geometry, and calculus, which use a specialized notation to study number, quantity, shape, and space **2** numerical calculations involved in the solution of a problem
  WORD ORIGIN Greek *mathēma* a science

maths *n Austral & Brit informal* short for **mathematics**

matinee (mat-in-nay) *n* an afternoon performance of a play or film
  WORD ORIGIN French

matins *n* an early morning service in various Christian Churches
  WORD ORIGIN Latin *matutinus* of the morning

matriarch (**mate**-ree-ark) *n* the female head of a tribe or family **matriarchal** *adj*
  WORD ORIGIN Latin *mater* mother + Greek *arkhein* to rule

matriarchy *n, pl* **-chies** a form of social organization in which a female is head of the family or society, and descent and kinship are traced through the female line

matrices (**may**-triss-seez) *n* a plural of **matrix**

matricide *n* **1** the act of killing one's mother **2** a person who kills his or her mother **matricidal** *adj*
  WORD ORIGIN Latin *mater* mother + *caedere* to kill

matriculate *vb* **-lating, -lated** to enrol or be enrolled in a college or university **matriculation** *n*
  WORD ORIGIN Medieval Latin *matriculare* to register

matrilineal (mat-rill-**in**-ee-al) *adj* relating to descent through the female line

matrimony *n* the state of being married **matrimonial** *adj*
  WORD ORIGIN Latin *matrimonium* wedlock

matrix (**may**-trix) *n, pl* **-trices** *or* **matrixes 1** the context or framework in which something is formed or develops: *a highly complex matrix of overlapping interests* **2** the rock in which fossils or pebbles are embedded **3** a mould, esp. one used in printing **4** *maths* a rectangular array of elements set out in rows and columns
  WORD ORIGIN Latin: womb

matron *n* **1** a staid or dignified married woman **2** a woman in charge of the domestic or medical arrangements in an institution **3** *Brit* (formerly) the administrative head of the nursing staff in a hospital **matronly** *adj*
  WORD ORIGIN Latin *matrona*

matron of honour *n, pl* **matrons of honour** a married woman attending a bride

matt *or* **matte** *adj* having a dull surface rather than a shiny one

matted *adj* tangled into a thick mass

matter *n* **1** the substance of which something, esp. a physical object, is made; material **2** substance that occupies space and has mass, as distinguished from substance that is mental or spiritual **3** substance of a specified type: *vegetable matter* **4** an event, situation, or subject: *a matter of taste; the break-in is a matter for the police* **5** a quantity or amount: *a matter of a few pounds* **6** the content of written or verbal material as distinct from its style or form **7** written material in general: *advertising matter* **8** a secretion or discharge, such as pus **9 for that matter** as regards that **10 no matter** regardless of; irrespective of: *you have to leave, no matter what she thinks* **11 the matter** wrong; the trouble: *there's nothing the matter* ▷ *vb* **12** to be of importance ▷ *interj* **no matter 13** it is unimportant
  WORD ORIGIN Latin *materia* cause, substance

matter of fact *n* **1 as a matter of fact** actually; in fact ▷ *adj* **matter-of-fact**

2 unimaginative or emotionless: *he conducted the executions in a completely matter-of-fact manner*

matting *n* a coarsely woven fabric used as a floor covering

mattock *n* a type of large pick that has one flat, horizontal end to its blade, used for loosening soil
WORD ORIGIN Old English *mattuc*

mattress *n* a large flat cushion with a strong cover, filled with cotton, foam rubber, etc. and often including coiled springs, used as a bed
WORD ORIGIN Arabic *almatrah* place where something is thrown

maturation *n* the process of becoming mature

mature *adj* **1** fully developed physically or mentally; grown-up **2** (of plans or theories) fully considered and thought-out **3** sensible and balanced in personality and emotional behaviour **4** due or payable: *a mature insurance policy* **5** (of fruit, wine, or cheese) ripe or fully aged ▷ *vb* **-turing, -tured 6** to make or become mature **7** (of bills or bonds) to become due for payment or repayment **maturity** *n*
WORD ORIGIN Latin *maturus* early, developed

matzo *n, pl* **matzos** a large very thin biscuit of unleavened bread, traditionally eaten by Jews during Passover
WORD ORIGIN Hebrew *matsāh*

maudlin *adj* foolishly or tearfully sentimental, esp. as a result of drinking
WORD ORIGIN Middle English *Maudelen* Mary Magdalene, often shown weeping

maul *vb* **1** to tear with the claws: *she was badly mauled by a lion* **2** to criticize a play, performance, etc. severely: *the film was mauled by the critics* **3** to handle roughly or clumsily ▷ *n* **4** *rugby* a loose scrum
WORD ORIGIN Latin *malleus* hammer

maunder *vb* to move, talk, or act aimlessly or idly
WORD ORIGIN origin unknown

Maundy Thursday *n Christianity* the Thursday before Easter observed as a commemoration of the Last Supper
WORD ORIGIN Latin *mandatum* commandment

mausoleum (maw-so-**lee**-um) *n* a large stately tomb
WORD ORIGIN Greek *mausōleion* the tomb of king *Mausolus*

mauve *adj* light purple
WORD ORIGIN Latin *malva* mallow

maverick *n* **1** a person of independent or unorthodox views **2** (in the US and Canada) an unbranded stray calf ▷ *adj* **3** (of a person or his or her views) independent and unorthodox
WORD ORIGIN after Samuel A. *Maverick*, Texas rancher

maw *n* the mouth, throat, or stomach of an animal
WORD ORIGIN Old English *maga*

mawkish *adj* foolishly or embarrassingly sentimental **mawkishness** *n*
WORD ORIGIN obsolete *mawk* maggot

max *n informal* **1** the most significant or greatest thing **2 to the max** to the ultimate extent

max. maximum

maxi *adj* **1** (of a garment) very long **2** large or considerable
WORD ORIGIN from *maximum*

maxilla *n, pl* **-lae 1** the upper jawbone of a vertebrate **2** any part of the mouth in insects and other arthropods **maxillary** *adj*
WORD ORIGIN Latin: jaw

maxim *n* a brief expression of a general truth, principle, or rule of conduct
WORD ORIGIN Latin *maxima*, in the phrase *maxima propositio* basic axiom

maximal *adj* of or being a maximum; the greatest possible

maximize *or* **-mise** *vb* **-mizing, -mized** *or* **-mising, -mised** to make as high or great as possible; increase to a maximum **maximization** *or* **-misation** *n*

maximum *n, pl* **-mums** *or* **-ma 1** the greatest possible amount or degree: *he gave the police the maximum of cooperation* **2** the greatest amount recorded, allowed, or reached: *keep to a maximum of two drinks a day* ▷ *adj* **3** of, being, or showing a maximum or maximums: *maximum speed*
WORD ORIGIN Latin: greatest

maxwell *n* the cgs unit of magnetic flux
WORD ORIGIN after J. C. *Maxwell*, physicist

may¹ *vb, past* **might 1** used as an auxiliary to indicate that permission is requested by or granted to someone: *she may leave* **2** used as an auxiliary to indicate the possibility that something could happen: *problems which may well have tragic consequences* **3** used as an auxiliary to indicate ability or capacity, esp. in questions: *may I help you?* **4** used as an auxiliary to indicate a strong wish: *long may she reign*
WORD ORIGIN Old English *mæg*, from *magan* to be able

USAGE
It was formerly considered correct to use *may* rather than *can* when referring to permission as in: *you may use the laboratory for your experiments*, but this use of *may* is now almost entirely restricted to polite questions such as: *may I open the window?* The use of *may* with *if* in constructions such as *your analysis may have been more credible if...* is generally regarded as incorrect, *might* being preferred: *your analysis might have been more credible if...*

may² *or* **may tree** *n Brit* same as **hawthorn**
WORD ORIGIN from *May*

May *n* the fifth month of the year
WORD ORIGIN probably from *Maia*, Roman goddess

Maya *n* **1** *pl* **-ya** *or* **-yas** a member of an indigenous people of Central America, who once had an advanced civilization **2** the language of this people **Mayan** *n, adj*

maybe *adv* perhaps

Mayday *n* the international radio distress signal
WORD ORIGIN phonetic spelling of French *m'aidez* help me

May Day *n* the first day of May, traditionally a celebration of the coming of spring: in some countries now a holiday in honour of workers

mayfly *n, pl* **-flies** a short-lived insect with large transparent wings

mayhem *n* **1** any violent destruction or confusion: *a driver caused motorway mayhem* **2** *law* the maiming of a person
WORD ORIGIN Anglo-French *mahem* injury

mayn't may not

mayonnaise *n* a thick creamy sauce made from egg yolks, oil, and vinegar
WORD ORIGIN French

mayor *n* the civic head of a municipal council in many countries **mayoral** *adj*
WORD ORIGIN Latin *maior* greater

mayoralty *n, pl* **-ties** the office or term of office of a mayor

mayoress *n* **1** *chiefly Brit* the wife of a mayor **2** a female mayor

maypole *n* a tall pole around which people dance during May-Day celebrations

May queen *n* a girl chosen to preside over May-Day celebrations

maze *n* **1** a complex network of paths or passages designed to puzzle people who try and find their way through or out of it **2** a puzzle in which the player must trace a path through a complex network of lines without touching or crossing any of them **3** any confusing network or system: *a maze of regulations*
WORD ORIGIN from *amaze*

mazurka *n* **1** a lively Polish dance in triple time **2** music for this dance
WORD ORIGIN Polish

mb millibar

Mb *computers* megabyte

MB 1 Bachelor of Medicine **2** Manitoba

MBE (in Britain) Member of the Order of the British Empire

MC 1 Master of Ceremonies **2** (in the US) Member of Congress **3** (in Britain) Military Cross

MCC (in Britain) Marylebone Cricket Club

MCh Master of Surgery
WORD ORIGIN Latin *Magister Chirurgiae*

Md *chem* mendelevium

MD 1 Doctor of Medicine
WORD ORIGIN Latin *Medicinae Doctor*
2 Managing Director **3** Maryland

MDF medium density fibreboard: a wood-substitute material used in interior decoration

MDMA methylenedioxymethamphetamine: the chemical name for the drug ecstasy

MDT (in the US and Canada) Mountain Daylight Time

me¹ *pron* (objective) **1** refers to the speaker or writer: *that hurts me* ▷ *n* **2** *informal* the personality of the speaker or writer or something that expresses it: *the real me*
WORD ORIGIN Old English *mē*

USAGE
It was formerly regarded as correct to use *I, he, she*, etc. rather than *me, him, her*, after the verb *to be*, as in: *it is I who told him*. Since both *I* and *me* can sound strange in a sentence like this, it is better to use a different construction:

m

I am the one who told him. The use of a possessive before an *-ing* form of a verb was formerly thought to be preferable to using *me*, etc. but now both forms are acceptable: *he didn't like my/me having a job of my own.*

me² *or***mi** *n music* (in tonic sol-fa) the third note of any ascending major scale

ME 1 Maine **2** Middle English **3** myalgic encephalomyelitis: see **chronic fatigue syndrome**

mea culpa (**may**-ah **cool**-pah) an acknowledgment of guilt
WORD ORIGIN Latin, literally: my fault

mead¹ *n* a wine-like alcoholic drink made from honey, often with spices added
WORD ORIGIN Old English *meodu*

mead² *n archaic or poetic* a meadow
WORD ORIGIN Old English *mǣd*

meadow *n* **1** a grassy field used for hay or for grazing animals **2** a low-lying piece of grassland, often near a river
WORD ORIGIN Old English *mædwe*

meadowsweet *n* a plant with dense heads of small fragrant cream-coloured flowers

meagre *or US* **meager** *adj* **1** not enough in amount or extent: *meagre wages* **2** thin or emaciated
WORD ORIGIN Old French *maigre*

meal¹ *n* **1** any of the regular occasions, such as breakfast or dinner, when food is served and eaten **2** the food served and eaten **3 make a meal of** *informal* to perform a task with unnecessarily great effort
WORD ORIGIN Old English *mǣl* measure, set time, meal

meal² *n* **1** the edible part of a grain or bean pulse (excluding wheat) ground to a coarse powder **2** *Scot* oatmeal **3** *chiefly US* maize flour **mealy** *adj*
WORD ORIGIN Old English *melu*

mealie *or***mielie** *n* (often pl) S African same as **maize**
WORD ORIGIN Afrikaans, from Latin *milium* millet

meals-on-wheels *n* a service taking hot meals to the elderly or infirm in their own homes

meal ticket *n slang* a person or situation providing a source of livelihood or income
WORD ORIGIN from original US sense of ticket entitling holder to a meal

mealy-mouthed *adj* unwilling or afraid to speak plainly

mean¹ *vb* **meaning, meant 1** to intend to convey or express: *what do you mean by that?* **2** to denote, represent, or signify: *a red light means 'stop!'; 'gravid' is a technical term meaning 'pregnant'* **3** to intend: *I meant to phone you earlier, but didn't have time* **4** to say or do in all seriousness: *the boss means what she says* **5** to have the importance specified: *music means everything to him* **6** to destine or design for a certain person or purpose: *those sweets weren't meant for you* **7** to produce, cause, or result in: *major road works will mean long traffic delays* **8** to foretell: *those black clouds mean rain* **9 mean well** to have good intentions
WORD ORIGIN Old English *mǣnan*

USAGE
In standard English *mean* should not be followed by *for* when expressing intention: *I didn't mean this to happen* (not *I didn't mean for this to happen*).

mean² *adj* **1** not willing to give or use much of something, esp. money: *she was noticeably mean; don't be mean with the butter* **2** unkind or spiteful: *a mean trick* **3** *informal* ashamed: *she felt mean about not letting the children stay out late* **4** *informal chiefly US, Canad, & Austral* bad-tempered or vicious **5** shabby and poor: *a mean little room* **6** *slang* excellent or skilful: *he plays a mean trumpet* **7 no mean a** of high quality: *no mean player* **b** difficult: *no mean feat* **meanly** *adv* **meanness** *n*
WORD ORIGIN Old English *gemǣne* common

mean³ *n* **1** the middle point, state, or course between limits or extremes **2** *maths* **a** the mid-point between the highest and lowest number in a set **b** the average ▷ *adj* **3** intermediate in size or quantity **4** occurring halfway between extremes or limits; average
WORD ORIGIN Late Latin *medianus* median

meander (mee-**and**-er) *vb* **1** (of a river, road, etc.) to follow a winding course **2** to wander without definite aim or direction ▷ *n* **3** a curve or bend, as in a river **4** a winding course or movement
WORD ORIGIN Greek *Maiandros* the River Maeander

mean deviation *n statistics* the difference between an observed value of a variable and its mean

meanie *or***meany** *n informal* **1** *chiefly Brit* a miserly person **2** *chiefly US* a nasty ill-tempered person

meaning *n* **1** the sense or significance of a word, sentence, or symbol **2** the inner, symbolic, or true interpretation or message: *the meaning of the New Testament*

meaningful *adj* **1** serious and important: *a meaningful relationship* **2** intended to express a feeling or opinion: *a meaningful pause*

meaningless *adj* having no meaning or purpose; futile

means *n* **1** the medium, method, or instrument used to obtain a result or achieve an end: *a means of transport* ▷ *pl n* **2** income: *a man of means* **3 by all means** without hesitation or doubt; certainly **4 by means of** with the use or help of **5 by no** *or***not by any means** on no account; in no way

means test *n* the checking of a person's income to determine whether he or she qualifies for financial aid **means-tested** *adj*

meant *vb* the past of **mean¹**

meantime *n* **1** the intervening period: *in the meantime* ▷ *adv* **2** same as **meanwhile**

mean time *or***mean solar time** *n* the times, at a particular place, measured so as to give 24-hour days (mean solar days) throughout a year

meanwhile *adv* **1** during the intervening period **2** at the same time, esp. in another place

meany *n, pl* **meanies** same as **meanie**

measles *n* a highly contagious viral disease common in children, characterized by fever and a rash of small red spots ▶ See also **German measles**
WORD ORIGIN Low German *masele* spot on the skin

measly *adj* **-slier, -sliest 1** *informal* too small in quantity or value **2** having or relating to measles

measure *n* **1** the size, quantity, or degree of something, as discovered by measurement or calculation **2** a device for measuring distance, volume, etc. such as a graduated scale or container **3** a system or unit of measurement: *the joule is a measure of energy* **4** an amount of alcoholic drink, esp. that served as standard in a bar **5** degree or extent: *a measure of success* **6** a particular action intended to achieve an effect: *radical measures are needed to cut unemployment* **7** a legislative bill, act, or resolution **8** *music* same as **bar¹** (sense 9) **9** *prosody* poetic rhythm or metre **10** *prosody* a metrical foot **11** *old-fashioned* a dance **12 for good measure** as an extra precaution or beyond requirements ▷ *vb* **-suring, -sured 13** to determine the size, amount, etc. of by measurement: *he measured the room for a new carpet* **14** to indicate or record the size, speed, force, etc. of: *this dial measures the pressure in the pipe* **15** to have the size, quantity, etc. specified: *the room measures six feet* **16** to estimate or assess: *you cannot measure intelligence purely by exam results* **17** to function as a measurement of: *the ohm measures electrical resistance* **18** to bring into competition or conflict with: *he measured his strength against that of his opponent* ▶ See also **measure out, measures, measure up**
▷**measurable** *adj*
WORD ORIGIN Latin *mensura*

measured *adj* **1** slow or stately **2** carefully considered; deliberate

measurement *n* **1** the act or process of measuring **2** an amount, extent, or size determined by measuring **3** a system or unit used for measuring: *the kilometre is the standard measurement of distance in most countries* **4 measurements** the size of a person's waist, chest, hips, etc. used when buying clothes

measure out *vb* to carefully pour or put the required amount of (something) into a container: *she measured out a large whisky*

measures *pl n* rock strata that contain a particular type of deposit: *coal measures*

measure up *vb* **1** to take the measurement of (an area): *we went round and measured up for curtains* **2 measure up to** to fulfil (expectations or standards)

measuring *adj* used to measure quantities, esp. in cooking: *a measuring jug*

meat *n* **1** the flesh of animals used as food **2** the essence or gist: *get to the meat of your lecture as quickly as possible* **meatless** *adj*
WORD ORIGIN Old English *mete*

meatball *n* minced beef, shaped into a ball before cooking

meaty *adj* **meatier, meatiest 1** of, like, or full of meat **2** heavily built; fleshy or

Word Trivia

The precise number of words in the English language is a matter for debate. In 2009 an organization called the Global Language Monitor declared that English had acquired its millionth word. However, methods of counting can vary, depending on whether you include things such as proper names, hyphenated and multi-word forms, inflected forms, and derived words, and whether you count each sense of a word as a separate word.

The official list of allowable words for Scrabble is well over 260,000. The list contains only words of 2 to 15 letters, but includes inflected forms. There are 124 two-letter words on the list.

The number of words listed in the unabridged edition of *Collins English Dictionary* is 144,040. The figure does not include inflected forms of words and does not count separate senses as words. (The facts and figures that follow include only words listed in the above-named dictionary.)

More words begin with the letter 's' than with any other letter, while 'x' appears at the start of fewer words than any other letter.

About 65% of the words in the dictionary are nouns, 17% are adjectives, and 13% are verbs. Adverbs, prepositions, pronouns, conjunctions, interjections, and determiners make up the rest of the words in the dictionary.

The longest word in the unabridged edition of *Collins English Dictionary* is *dichlorodiphenyltrichloroethane*, which is the full name of the chemical DDT. It has 31 letters.

The longest word not containing the letter 'e' is *psychopharmacological* (21 letters).

There are 32 words containing four consecutive vowels, including *queue*, *sequoia*, and *obsequious*. But no word contains five consecutive vowels.

The words *sightscreen* and *watchstrap* both contain six consecutive consonants, as do the less familiar words *bergschrund*, *eschscholtzia*, *festschrift*, and *latchstring*.

There are four six-letter words with no vowel except 'y': *rhythm*, *spryly*, *sylphy*, and *syzygy*. *Rhythm* can have an 's' added in the plural to make a seven-letter word without a vowel.

The longest words that contain no vowel including 'y' are *crwth* (a Celtic stringed instrument) and *cwtch* (a shed, cuddle, or hiding place). Both of these words are of Welsh origin and treat the letter 'w' as a vowel.

The longest word composed entirely of letters from the first half of the alphabet is *fiddledeedee* (12 letters).

The longest word composed entirely of letters from the second half of the alphabet is *zoosporous* (10 letters).

The common ten-letter words *perpetuity*, *proprietor*, *repertoire*, and *typewriter* can all be typed using only the top row of a QWERTY keyboard.

Two seven-letter words, *alfalfa* and *shahada* (the Islamic declaration of faith) can be typed using only the middle row of a QWERTY keyboard.

The words *abstemious* and *facetious* are the only ones in which the five vowels 'a', 'e', 'i', 'o', and 'u' occur once each in their alphabetical order.

The words *oxygenize* and *deoxygenize* are the only ones in which the letters 'x', 'y', and 'z' occur once each in their alphabetical order.

The only words containing a double 'j' are *hajj* (the pilgrimage to Mecca) and the related words *hajji* and *hajjah*.

The most grammatically flexible words in English are *out*, *right*, and *so*. Each of these can be used as six different parts of speech.

The word with the most different meanings is *run*, which has 97 separate definitions, not including its use in phrasal verbs.

brawny **3** full of import or interest: *a meaty historical drama*

Mecca *n* **1** the holy city of Islam **2** a place that attracts many visitors

mech. **1** mechanical **2** mechanics

mechanic *n* a person skilled in maintaining or operating machinery or motors
WORD ORIGIN Greek *mēkhanē* machine

mechanical *adj* **1** made, performed, or operated by machinery **2** able to understand how machines work and how to repair or maintain them **3 a** (of an action) done without thought or feeling **b** (of a task) not requiring any thought; routine or repetitive **4** of or involving the science of mechanics **mechanically** *adv*

mechanical drawing *n* a drawing to scale of a machine or architectural plan from which dimensions can be taken

mechanical engineering *n* the branch of engineering concerned with the design, construction, and operation of machines

mechanics *n* **1** the scientific study of motion and force **2** the science of designing, constructing, and operating machines ▷ *pl n* **3** the technical aspects of something

mechanism *n* **1** a system of moving parts that performs some function, esp. in a machine **2** any mechanical device or part of such a device **3** a process or technique: *the body's defence mechanisms* **mechanistic** *adj*

mechanize *or*-**nise** *vb* -**nizing**, -**nized** *or* -**nising**, -**nised** **1** to equip a factory or industry with machinery **2** to make mechanical or automatic **3** *mil* to equip an army with armoured vehicles **mechanization** *or*-**nisation** *n*

MEd Master of Education

med. **1** medical **2** medicine **3** medieval **4** medium

medal *n* a small flat piece of metal bearing an inscription or image, given as an award or in commemoration of some outstanding event
WORD ORIGIN French *médaille*

medallion *n* **1** a disc-shaped ornament worn on a chain round the neck **2** a large medal **3** a circular decorative device used in architecture
WORD ORIGIN Italian *medaglia* medal

medallist *or US* **medalist** *n chiefly sport* a winner of a medal or medals

meddle *vb* -**dling**, -**dled** to interfere annoyingly **meddler** *n* **meddlesome** *adj*
WORD ORIGIN Old French *medler*

media *n* **1** a plural of **medium** **2 the media** the mass media collectively ▷ *adj* **3** of or relating to the mass media: *media hype*
≡ **USAGE**
≡ When *media* refers to the mass media, ≡ it is sometimes treated as a singular ≡ form, as in: *the media has shown great* ≡ *interest in these events*. Many people ≡ think this use is incorrect and that ≡ *media* should always be treated as a ≡ plural form: *the media have shown great* ≡ *interest in these events*.

mediaeval (med-ee-**eve**-al) *adj* same as **medieval**

media event *n* an event that is staged for or exploited by the mass media

medial (**mee**-dee-al) *adj* of or situated in the middle **medially** *adv*
WORD ORIGIN Latin *medius* middle

median *n* **1** a middle point, plane, or part **2** *geom* a straight line joining one corner of a triangle to the midpoint of the opposite side **3** *statistics* the middle value in a frequency distribution, below and above which lie values with equal total frequencies
WORD ORIGIN Latin *medius* middle

median strip *n US, Canad, & NZ* the strip that separates the two sides of a motorway or dual carriageway

mediate (**mee**-dee-ate) *vb* -**ating**, -**ated** **1** to intervene between people or in a dispute in order to bring about agreement **2** to resolve differences by mediation **3** to be changed slightly by (an experience or event): *clients' attitudes to social workers have often been mediated by their past experiences* **mediation** *n* **mediator** *n*
WORD ORIGIN Late Latin *mediare* to be in the middle

medic *n informal* a doctor, medical orderly, or medical student
WORD ORIGIN from MEDICAL

medical *adj* **1** of or relating to the science of medicine or to the treatment of patients without surgery ▷ *n* **2** *informal* a medical examination **medically** *adv*
WORD ORIGIN Latin *medicus* physician

medical certificate *n* **1** a doctor's certificate giving evidence of a person's unfitness for work **2** a document stating the result of a satisfactory medical examination

medicament (mid-**dik**-a-ment) *n* a medicine

medicate *vb* -**cating**, -**cated** **1** to treat a patient with a medicine **2** to add a medication to a bandage, shampoo, etc. **medicative** *adj*
WORD ORIGIN Latin *medicare* to heal

medication *n* **1** treatment with drugs or remedies **2** a drug or remedy

medicinal (mid-**diss**-in-al) *adj* relating to or having therapeutic properties **medicinally** *adv*

medicine *n* **1** any substance used in treating or alleviating the symptoms of disease **2** the science of preventing, diagnosing, or curing disease **3** any nonsurgical branch of medical science **4 take one's medicine** to accept a deserved punishment
WORD ORIGIN Latin *medicina (ars)* (art) of healing

medicine man *n* (among certain peoples) a person believed to have supernatural powers of healing

medico *n, pl* -**cos** *informal* a doctor or medical student

medieval *or* **mediaeval** (med-ee-**eve**-al) *adj* **1** of, relating to, or in the style of the Middle Ages **2** *informal* old-fashioned or primitive **medievalist** *or* **mediaevalist** *n*
WORD ORIGIN New Latin *medium aevum* the middle age

Medieval Greek *n* the Greek language from the 7th to 13th century AD

Medieval Latin *n* the Latin language as used throughout Europe in the Middle Ages

mediocre (mee-dee-**oak**-er) *adj* not very high quality; average or second rate **mediocrity** (mee-dee-**ok**-rit-ee) *n*
WORD ORIGIN Latin *mediocris* moderate

meditate *vb* -**tating**, -**tated** **1** to think about something deeply: *he meditated on the problem* **2** to reflect deeply on spiritual matters **3** to plan, consider, or think of doing something **meditative** *adj* **meditator** *n*
WORD ORIGIN Latin *meditari* to reflect upon

meditation *n* **1** the act of meditating; reflection **2** contemplation of spiritual matters, esp. as a religious practice

Mediterranean *adj* of the Mediterranean Sea, lying between S Europe, N Africa, and SW Asia, or the surrounding region
WORD ORIGIN Latin *medius* middle + *terra* land

medium *adj* **1** midway between extremes of size, amount, or degree: *fry over a medium heat; a man of medium height* ▷ *n, pl* -**dia** *or* -**diums** **2** a middle state, degree, or condition: *the happy medium* **3** a substance which has a particular effect or can be used for a particular purpose: *linseed oil is used as a thinning medium for oil paint* **4** a means for communicating information or news to the public **5** a person who can supposedly communicate with the dead **6** the substance or surroundings in which an organism naturally lives or grows **7** *art* the category of a work of art, as determined by its materials: *his works in the photographic medium*
WORD ORIGIN Latin *medius* middle
≡ **USAGE**
≡ See at **media**.

medium wave *n* a radio wave with a wavelength between 100 and 1000 metres

medlar *n* the apple-like fruit of a small Eurasian tree, which is not edible until it has begun to decay
WORD ORIGIN Old French *medlier*

medley *n* **1** a mixture of various elements **2** a musical composition consisting of various tunes arranged as a continuous whole **3** *swimming* a race in which a different stroke is used for each length
WORD ORIGIN Old French, from *medler* to mix, quarrel

medulla (mid-**dull**-la) *n, pl* -**las** *or* -**lae** (-lee) **1** *anat* the innermost part of an organ or structure **2** *anat* the lower stalklike section of the brain **3** *bot* the central pith of a plant stem **medullary** *adj*
WORD ORIGIN Latin: marrow

medusa (mid-**dew**-za) *n, pl* -**sas** *or* -**sae** (-zee) jellyfish
WORD ORIGIN *Medusa*, in Greek mythology, who had snakes for hair

meek *adj* quiet, and ready to do what other people say **meekly** *adv*
WORD ORIGIN related to Old Norse *mjūkr* amenable

meerkat *n* a South African mongoose
WORD ORIGIN Dutch: sea-cat

meerschaum (**meer**-shum) *n* **1** a white, heat-resistant, claylike mineral **2** a tobacco pipe with a bowl made of this mineral **WORD ORIGIN** German *Meerschaum*, literally: sea foam

meet¹ *vb* **meeting, met 1** to be in or come to the same place at the same time as, either by arrangement or by accident: *I met him in town* **2** to come into contact with something or each other: *his head met the ground with a crack; the town where the Rhine and the Moselle meet* **3** to come to or be at the place of arrival of: *he met his train at noon* **4** to make the acquaintance of, or be introduced to, someone or each other **5** (of people) to gather together for a purpose: *the board meets once a week* **6** to compete, play, or fight against **7** to cope with effectively; satisfy: *they were unable to meet his demands* **8** to pay for (something): *it is difficult to meet the cost of medical insurance* **9** Also: **meet with** to experience or suffer: *he met his death at the Somme* **10 there is more to this than meets the eye** there is more involved in this than appears ▷ *n* **11** a sports meeting **12** *chiefly Brit* the assembly of hounds and huntsmen prior to a hunt **WORD ORIGIN** Old English *mētan*

meet² *adj archaic* proper, fitting, or correct: *meet and proper* **WORD ORIGIN** Old English *gemǣte*

meeting *n* **1** an act of coming together: *a meeting was fixed for the following day* **2** an assembly or gathering of people: *the meeting voted in favour* **3** a sporting competition, as of athletes, or of horse racing

meg *n computers informal* short for **megabyte**

mega *adj slang* extremely good, great, or successful

mega- *combining form* **1** denoting 10⁶: *megawatt* **2** (in computer technology) denoting 2²⁰ (1 048 576): *megabyte* **3** large or great: *megalith* **4** *informal* very great: *megastar* **WORD ORIGIN** Greek *megas* huge, powerful

megabyte *n computers* 2²⁰ or 1 048 576 bytes

megadeath *n* the death of a million people, esp. in a nuclear war or attack

megahertz *n, pl* **megahertz** one million hertz; one million cycles per second

megajoule *n* one million joules

megalith *n* a very large stone, esp. one forming part of a prehistoric monument **megalithic** *adj*

megalomania *n* **1** a mental illness characterized by delusions of power **2** *informal* a craving for power **megalomaniac** *adj, n* **WORD ORIGIN** Greek *megas* great + *mania* madness

megaphone *n* a funnel-shaped instrument used to make someone's voice sound louder, esp. out of doors

megapixel *n* one million pixels: used to describe the resolution of digital images

megapode *n* any of various ground-living birds of Australia, New Guinea, and adjacent islands. Their eggs incubate in mounds of sand or rotting vegetation **WORD ORIGIN** Greek *megas* great + *-podos* -footed

megaton *n* **1** one million tons **2** an explosive power, esp. of a nuclear weapon, equal to the power of one million tons of TNT

megavolt *n* one million volts

megawatt *n* one million watts

meiosis (my-**oh**-siss) *n, pl* **-ses** (-seez) a type of cell division in which reproductive cells are produced, each containing half the chromosome number of the parent nucleus **WORD ORIGIN** Greek *meiōn* less

meitnerium *n chem* an element artificially produced in small quantities by high-energy ion bombardment. Symbol: Mt **WORD ORIGIN** after Lise *Meitner*, physicist

melaleuca (mel-a-**loo**-ka) *n* an Australian shrub or tree with a white trunk and black branches **WORD ORIGIN** Greek *melas* black + *leukos* white

melamine *n* a colourless crystalline compound used in making synthetic resins **WORD ORIGIN** German *Melamin*

melancholia (mel-an-**kole**-lee-a) *n* an old name for **depression** (sense 1)

melancholy (**mel**-an-kol-lee) *n, pl* **-cholies 1** a tendency to gloominess or depression **2** a sad thoughtful state of mind ▷ *adj* **3** characterized by, causing, or expressing sadness **melancholic** *adj, n* **WORD ORIGIN** Greek *melas* black + *kholē* bile

melange (may-**lahnzh**) *n* a mixture or assortment: *a melange of historical facts and legends* **WORD ORIGIN** French *mêler* to mix

melanin *n* a black pigment present in the hair, skin, and eyes of humans and animals **WORD ORIGIN** Greek *melas* black

melanoma *n, pl* **-mas** *or* **-mata** *pathol* a tumour composed of dark-coloured cells, occurring in some skin cancers **WORD ORIGIN** Greek *melas* black + *-oma*, modelled on *carcinoma*

Melba toast *n* very thin crisp toast **WORD ORIGIN** after Dame Nellie *Melba*, singer

meld *vb* to merge or blend **WORD ORIGIN** blend of *melt* + *weld*

melee (**mel**-lay) *n* a noisy riotous fight or crowd **WORD ORIGIN** French, from *mêler* to mix

mellifluous (mel-**lif**-flew-uss) *adj* (of sound) smooth and sweet **WORD ORIGIN** Latin *mel* honey + *fluere* to flow

mellow *adj* **1** (esp. of colours, light, or sounds) soft or rich: *the mellow stillness of a sunny Sunday morning* **2** kind-hearted, esp. through maturity or old age **3** genial and relaxed, for instance through the effects of alcohol or good food **4** (esp. of fruits) sweet, ripe, and full-flavoured **5** (esp. of wine or cheese) having developed a full smooth flavour as a result of maturing **6** (of soil) soft and loamy ▷ *vb* **7** to make or become mellow **8** (foll. by *out*) to make or become calm and relaxed **WORD ORIGIN** origin unknown

melodeon *n* **1** a small accordion **2** a keyboard instrument like a harmonium **WORD ORIGIN** German *Melodie* melody

melodic (mel-**lod**-ik) *adj* **1** of or relating to melody **2** tuneful and pleasant to the ear; melodious **melodically** *adv*

melodious (mel-**lode**-ee-uss) *adj* **1** pleasant to the ear: *he gave a melodious chuckle* **2** tuneful and melodic **melodiousness** *n*

melodrama *n* **1** a play or film full of extravagant action and emotion **2** overdramatic emotion or behaviour **melodramatic** *adj* **melodramatics** *pl n* **WORD ORIGIN** Greek *melos* song + *drama* drama

melody *n, pl* **-dies 1** *music* a succession of notes forming a distinctive sequence; tune **2** sounds that are pleasant because of their tone or arrangement, esp. words of poetry **WORD ORIGIN** Greek *melōidia*

melon *n* any of various large edible fruits which have a hard rind and juicy flesh **WORD ORIGIN** Greek *mēlon* apple

Melpomene (mel-**pom**-in-nee) *n Greek myth* the Muse of tragedy

melt *vb* **1** to change from a solid into a liquid as a result of the action of heat **2** to dissolve: *these sweets melt in the mouth* **3** Also: **melt away** to diminish and finally disappear; fade away: *he felt his inner doubts melt away* **4** to blend so that it is impossible to tell where one thing ends and another begins: *they melted into the trees until the gamekeeper had passed* **5** to make or become emotional or sentimental; soften: *she melted into tears* **meltingly** *adv* **WORD ORIGIN** Old English *meltan* to digest

meltdown *n* **1** (in a nuclear reactor) the melting of the fuel rods, with the possible escape of radioactivity **2** *informal* a sudden disastrous failure **3** *informal* a process of irreversible decline

melting point *n* the temperature at which a solid turns into a liquid

melting pot *n* a place or situation in which many races, ideas, etc. are mixed

meltwater *n* melted snow or ice

member *n* **1** a person who belongs to a group or organization such as a club or political party **2** any part of a plant or animal, such as a limb or petal **3** a Member of Parliament: *the member for Glasgow Central* ▷ *adj* **4** (of a country or group) belonging to an organization or alliance: *a summit of the member countries' heads of state is due* **WORD ORIGIN** Latin *membrum* limb, part

Member of Parliament *n* a person who has been elected to the House of Commons or the equivalent assembly in another country

membership *n* **1** the members of an organization collectively **2** the number of members **3** the state of being a member

membrane n a thin flexible tissue that covers, lines, or connects plant and animal organs or cells **membranous** adj
WORD ORIGIN Latin *membrana* skin covering a part of the body

memento n, pl **-tos** or **-toes** something that reminds one of past events; a souvenir
WORD ORIGIN Latin, imperative of *meminisse* to remember

memento mori n, pl **memento mori** an object intended to remind people of death
WORD ORIGIN Latin: remember you must die

memo n, pl **memos** short for **memorandum**

memoir (**mem**-wahr) n a biography or historical account based on personal knowledge
WORD ORIGIN Latin *memoria* memory

memoirs pl n **1** a collection of reminiscences about a period or series of events, written from personal experience **2** an autobiography

memorabilia pl n, sing **-rabile** objects connected with famous people or events

memorable adj worth remembering or easily remembered because it is very special or important **memorably** adv
WORD ORIGIN Latin *memorare* to remember

memorandum n, pl **-dums** or **-da 1** a note sent by one person or department to another within a business organization **2** a note of things to be remembered **3** law a short written summary of the terms of a transaction
WORD ORIGIN Latin: (something) to be remembered

memorial n **1** something, such as a statue, built or displayed to preserve the memory of someone or something: *a war memorial* ▷ adj **2** in memory of someone or something: *a memorial service*
WORD ORIGIN Late Latin *memoriale* a reminder

memorize or **-rise** vb **-rizing, -rized** or **-rising, -rised** to commit to memory; learn by heart

memory n, pl **-ries 1** the ability of the mind to store and recall past sensations, thoughts, and knowledge: *she can do it from memory* **2** the sum of everything retained by the mind **3** a particular recollection of an event or person: *he started awake with a sudden memory* **4** the length of time one can remember: *my memory doesn't go that far back* **5** commemoration: *in memory of our leader* **6** a person's reputation after death: *a conductor of fond memory* **7** a part of a computer in which information is stored
WORD ORIGIN Latin *memoria*

memory card n a small removable data storage device, used in mobile phones, digital cameras, etc.

Memory Stick n computers **1** trademark a standard format for memory cards **2** memory stick also: **USB memory stick**. Same as **USB drive**

memsahib n (formerly, in India) a term of respect used for a European married woman

WORD ORIGIN *ma'am* + *sahib*

men n the plural of **man**

menace vb **-acing, -aced 1** to threaten with violence or danger ▷ n **2** a threat; a source of danger **3** informal an annoying person or thing; nuisance **menacing** adj
WORD ORIGIN Latin *minax* threatening

ménage (may-**nahzh**) n a household
WORD ORIGIN French

ménage à trois (ah **trwah**) n, pl **ménages à trois** a sexual arrangement involving a married couple and the lover of one of them
WORD ORIGIN French, literally: household of three

menagerie (min-**naj**-er-ee) n a collection of wild animals kept for exhibition
WORD ORIGIN French

mend vb **1** to repair something broken or not working **2** to heal or recover: *a wound like that will take a while to mend* **3** (esp. of behaviour) to improve; make or become better: *if you don't mend your ways you'll be in serious trouble* ▷ n **4** a mended area, esp. on a garment **5 on the mend** regaining one's health
WORD ORIGIN from *amend*

mendacity n the tendency to be untruthful **mendacious** adj
WORD ORIGIN Latin *mendax* untruthful

mendelevium n chem an artificially produced radioactive element. Symbol: Md
WORD ORIGIN after D. I. *Mendeleyev*, chemist

Mendel's laws pl n the principles of heredity proposed by Gregor Mendel (1822–84), Austrian monk and botanist **Mendelism** n

mendicant adj **1** begging **2** (of a monk, nun, etc.) dependent on charity for food ▷ n **3** a mendicant friar **4** a beggar
WORD ORIGIN Latin *mendicus* beggar

menfolk pl n men collectively, esp. the men of a particular family

menhir (**men**-hear) n a single standing stone, dating from prehistoric times
WORD ORIGIN Breton *men* stone + *hir* long

menial (**mean**-nee-al) adj **1** involving or doing boring work of low status ▷ n **2** a domestic servant
WORD ORIGIN Old French *meinie* household

meninges (min-**in**-jeez) pl n, sing **meninx** (**mean**-inks) the three membranes that surround the brain and spinal cord
WORD ORIGIN Greek, plural of *meninx* membrane

meningitis (men-in-**jite**-iss) n inflammation of the meninges, caused by infection and causing severe headache, fever, and rigidity of the neck muscles

meniscus n, pl **-nisci** or **-niscuses 1** the curved upper surface of a liquid standing in a tube, produced by the surface tension **2** a crescent-shaped lens
WORD ORIGIN Greek *mēniskos* crescent

menopause n the period during which a woman's menstrual cycle ceases, normally at an age of 45 to 50

menopausal adj
WORD ORIGIN Greek *mēn* month + *pausis* halt

menorah (min-**or**-a) n Judaism a seven-branched candelabrum used as an emblem of Judaism
WORD ORIGIN Hebrew: candlestick

menses (**men**-seez) n same as **menstruation**
WORD ORIGIN Latin, plural of *mensis* month

menstrual adj of or relating to menstruation: *the menstrual cycle*

menstruate vb **-ating, -ated** to undergo menstruation
WORD ORIGIN Latin *menstruare*, from *mensis* month

menstruation n the approximately monthly discharge of blood from the womb in women of childbearing age who are not pregnant

mensuration n **1** the study of the measurement of geometric magnitudes such as length **2** the act or process of measuring
WORD ORIGIN Latin *mensura* measure

menswear n clothing for men

mental adj **1** of, done by, or involving the mind: *mental alertness* **2** done in the mind without using speech or writing: *mental arithmetic* **3** affected by mental illness: *a mental patient* **4** concerned with mental illness: *a mental hospital* **5** slang extremely foolish or eccentric **mentally** adv
WORD ORIGIN Latin *mens* mind

mental age n the age which a person is considered to have reached in thinking ability, judged by comparing his or her ability with the average for people of various ages: *a twenty-one-year-old woman with a mental age of only ten*

mental handicap n any intellectual disability resulting from injury to or abnormal development of the brain **mentally handicapped** adj

mental illness n any of various disorders in which a person's thoughts, emotions, or behaviour are so abnormal as to cause suffering to himself, herself, or other people

mentality n, pl **-ties** a particular attitude or way of thinking: *the traditional civil service mentality*

menthol n an organic compound found in peppermint oil and used as an antiseptic, decongestant, and painkiller **mentholated** adj
WORD ORIGIN Latin *mentha* mint

mention vb **1** to refer to or speak about briefly or incidentally **2** to include in a report, list etc. because of high standards or an outstanding achievement: *the hotel is mentioned in all the guidebooks; he was twice mentioned in dispatches during the war* **3 not to mention (something)** to say nothing of (something too obvious to mention) ▷ n **4** a slight reference or allusion **5** a recognition or acknowledgment of high quality or an outstanding achievement
WORD ORIGIN Latin *mentio* a calling to mind

mentor n an adviser or guide
WORD ORIGIN *Mentor*, adviser of Telemachus in Homer's *Odyssey*

John Milton

Milton is a giant of English literature. His life overlapped with Shakespeare's by eight years, and he lived through the English Civil War, the Plague, and the Fire of London. He went blind in his early forties, and had to depend on others to lead him about and to take dictation, but this seems only to have sharpened his poetic vision. He wrote a sonnet about this, which opens, 'When I consider how my light is spent...' and ends, 'They also serve who only stand and wait.' But Milton himself did anything but stand and wait.

Milton was a Republican and worked for Oliver Cromwell as his Latin Secretary. By the time he started to dictate his greatest poem, *Paradise Lost*, the Republic had collapsed and there was a king on the throne of England again. Milton himself was only saved from execution by the intervention of powerful friends, and this reality lies behind a lot of the sympathy that Milton seems to show in his poem for Satan, who failed in his struggle against a God whom Milton does not present in a very good light, for all his protestations to the contrary.

The poem tells the story of Adam and Eve, of how they were tempted by Satan and expelled from the Garden of Eden. The characters and events are drawn from biblical and classical traditions, and Milton's own close observation of those who wield absolute power.

Paradise Lost has influenced poets, novelists, artists, and composers from the moment of its publication: in 1674 the poet Dryden turned it into an opera. The title of Philip Pullman's trilogy *His Dark Materials* is taken from the poem, and Pullman's trilogy itself is loosely based on *Paradise Lost*. Pullman decided that Satan is the real hero of the epic, and that the God of the poem is a tyrant. CS Lewis, on the other hand, entertained no such doubts about the goodness of Milton's God, and considered that Milton achieves his stated aim, which is to 'assert Eternal Providence, and justify the ways of God to men'. Lewis was a fervent admirer of *Paradise Lost*, and draws on it in the Narnia stories in episodes in which the White Witch enacts the role of Satan.

The fact that Pullman and Lewis should have arrived at diametrically opposed positions as regards Milton's poem just underlines how magnificently deep it is.

What Milton was able to do, more than perhaps any other poet except Shakespeare, was to wield English in a way that brings it as close to music as words can get. Here are the last lines of *Paradise Lost*, where Adam and Eve, expelled from Paradise, and mortal now after eating the fruit of the tree of knowledge, set off alone:

> They looking back, all the eastern side beheld
> Of Paradise, so late their happy seat,
> Waved over by that flaming brand; the gate
> With dreadful faces thronged and fiery arms:
> Some natural tears they dropped, but wiped them soon;
> The world was all before them, where to choose
> Their place of rest, and Providence their guide:
> They hand in hand, with wandering steps and slow,
> Through Eden took their solitary way.

Milton's life was filled with tragedy. Two of his closest friends died young. He was married three times, since his first wife died in childbirth, and his second wife also died shortly after giving birth. His Republican ideals were thwarted, and his strong support for the complete separation of church and state came to nothing. Some of the thoughts that go through Satan's head no doubt often went through his, particularly the notion that the mind 'Can make a heaven of hell, a hell of heaven'.

Perhaps without such tragedy and disappointment his writing would not have had the weight it does. And he wrote great prose, as well as poetry. During the time when the Republican government was still struggling with the Royalists and trying to suppress dissent, Milton published a defence of freedom of speech called *Areopagitica*. Two of its lines in particular are often quoted:

> A good book is the precious life-blood of a master spirit, embalmed and treasured up on purpose to a life beyond life.

Milton's work has certainly ensured him a life beyond life.

menu *n* **1** a list of dishes served at a meal or that can be ordered in a restaurant **2** a list of options displayed on a visual display unit from which the operator can choose
WORD ORIGIN French: small, detailed (list)

meow *or* **miaow** (mee-**ow**) *n* **1** the characteristic high-pitched cry of a cat; mew ▷ *vb* **2** to make such a sound

MEP (in Britain) Member of the European Parliament

Mephistopheles (mef-iss-**stoff**-ill-eez) *n* a devil in medieval mythology to whom Faust sold his soul **Mephistophelean** *adj*

mercantile *adj* of trade or traders; commercial
WORD ORIGIN Italian *mercante* merchant

Mercator projection (mer-**kate**-er) *n* a way of drawing maps in which latitude and longitude form a rectangular grid, scale being exaggerated with increasing distance from the equator
WORD ORIGIN after G. *Mercator*, cartographer

mercenary *n, pl* **-naries 1** a soldier who fights for a foreign army for money ▷ *adj* **2** motivated by greed or the desire for gain: *calculating and mercenary businessmen* **3** of or relating to a mercenary or mercenaries
WORD ORIGIN Latin *merces* wages

mercerized *or* **-rised** *adj* (of cotton) treated with an alkali to make it strong and shiny
WORD ORIGIN after John *Mercer*, maker of textiles

merchandise *n* **1** goods for buying, selling, or trading with; commodities ▷ *vb* **-dising, -dised 2** to engage in the commercial purchase and sale of goods or services; trade

merchandising *n* **1** the selection and display of goods in a retail outlet **2** commercial goods, esp. ones issued to exploit the popularity of a pop group, sporting event, etc.

merchant *n* **1** a person who buys and sells goods in large quantities and usually of one type: *a wine merchant* **2** *chiefly Scot, US, & Canad* a person engaged in retail trade; shopkeeper **3** *slang* a person dealing in something undesirable: *a gossip merchant* ▷ *adj* **4** of ships involved in commercial trade or their crews: *a merchant sailor; the British merchant fleet*
WORD ORIGIN Latin *mercari* to trade

merchant bank *n* a financial institution that deals primarily with foreign trade and business finance **merchant banker** *n*

merchantman *n, pl* **-men** a merchant ship

merchant navy *n* the ships or crew engaged in a nation's commercial shipping

merciful *adj* **1** (of an act or event) giving relief from pain or suffering: *after months of illness, death came as a merciful release* **2** showing or giving mercy; compassionate **mercifully** *adv*

merciless *adj* without mercy; pitiless, cruel, or heartless **mercilessly** *adv*

mercurial (mer-**cure**-ee-al) *adj* **1** lively and unpredictable: *a mercurial and temperamental chess player* **2** of or containing mercury
WORD ORIGIN Latin *mercurialis*

mercuric *adj* of or containing mercury in the divalent state

mercurous *adj* of or containing mercury in the monovalent state

mercury *n, pl* **-ries** *chem* a silvery toxic metal, the only element liquid at normal temperatures, used in thermometers, barometers, lamps, and dental amalgams. Symbol: Hg
WORD ORIGIN Latin *Mercurius*, messenger of Jupiter

Mercury *n* **1** *Roman myth* the messenger of the gods **2** the second smallest planet and the one nearest the sun

mercy *n, pl* **-cies 1** compassionate treatment of, or attitude towards, an offender or enemy who is in one's power **2** the power to show mercy: *they threw themselves on the King's mercy* **3** a relieving or welcome occurrence or act: *it was a mercy you turned up when you did* **4** **at the mercy of** in the power of ▷ *adj* **5** done or undertaken in an attempt to relieve suffering or bring help: *a mercy mission*
WORD ORIGIN Latin *merces* recompense

mercy killing *n* same as **euthanasia**

mere¹ *adj* nothing more than: *the election in Slovenia seems a mere formality* **merely** *adv*
WORD ORIGIN Latin *merus* pure

mere² *n* *Brit dialect or archaic* a lake
WORD ORIGIN Old English: sea, lake

meretricious *adj* superficially or garishly attractive but of no real value
WORD ORIGIN Latin *meretrix* prostitute

merganser (mer-**gan**-ser) *n, pl* **-sers** *or* **-ser** a large crested marine diving duck
WORD ORIGIN Latin *mergere* to plunge + *anser* goose

merge *vb* **merging, merged 1** to combine, esp. so as to become part of a larger whole: *the two airlines merged in 1983* **2** to blend gradually, without any sudden change being apparent: *late afternoon merged imperceptibly into early evening*
WORD ORIGIN Latin *mergere* to plunge

merger *n* the act of merging, esp. the combination of two or more companies

meridian *n* **1** one of the imaginary lines joining the north and south poles at right angles to the equator, designated by degrees of longitude from 0° at Greenwich to 180° **2** (in acupuncture etc.) any of various channels through which vital energy is believed to circulate round the body
WORD ORIGIN Latin *meridies* midday

meridional *adj* **1** of or along a meridian **2** of or in the south, esp. the south of Europe

meringue (mer-**rang**) *n* **1** stiffly beaten egg whites mixed with sugar and baked **2** a small cake made from this mixture
WORD ORIGIN French

merino *n, pl* **-nos 1** a sheep with long fine wool, originally reared in Spain **2** the yarn made from this wool
WORD ORIGIN Spanish

merit *n* **1** worth or superior quality; excellence: *the film had two sequels, neither of much merit* **2** an admirable or advantageous quality: *the relative merits of film and video as a medium of communication* **3** **have the merit of** to have a positive feature or advantage that the alternatives do not have: *the first version has the merit of being short* **4** **on its merits** on its intrinsic qualities or virtues ▷ *vb* **-riting, -rited 5** to be worthy of; deserve: *the issue merits much fuller discussion*
WORD ORIGIN Latin *meritum* reward

meritocracy (mer-it-**tok**-rass-ee) *n, pl* **-cies** a social system in which power is held by the most talented or intelligent people **meritocrat** *n* **meritocratic** *adj*

meritorious *adj* deserving praise for being good or worthwhile
WORD ORIGIN Latin *meritorius* earning money

merlin *n* a small falcon with dark plumage
WORD ORIGIN Old French *esmerillon*

mermaid *n* an imaginary sea creature with a woman's head and upper body and a fish's tail **merman** *masc n*
WORD ORIGIN *mere* sea + *maid*

merry *adj* **-rier, -riest 1** cheerful and jolly **2** *Austral & Brit informal* slightly drunk **3** **make merry** to take part in noisy cheerful celebrations or fun **merrily** *adv* **merriment** *n*
WORD ORIGIN Old English *merige* agreeable

merry-go-round *n* **1** a fairground roundabout **2** a whirl of activity

merrymaking *n* noisy cheerful celebrations or fun **merrymaker** *n*

mesa *n* a flat-topped hill found in arid regions
WORD ORIGIN Spanish: table

mésalliance (mez-zal-ee-anss) *n* a marriage with a person of lower social status
WORD ORIGIN French

mescal (mess-**kal**) *n* **1** a globe-shaped cactus without spines found in Mexico and the southwestern US **2** a Mexican alcoholic spirit similar to tequila
WORD ORIGIN Mexican Indian *mexcalli*

mescaline *n* a hallucinogenic drug derived from the button-like top of the mescal cactus

mesdames (may-**dam**) *n* the plural of **madame** or **madam** (sense 1)

mesdemoiselles (maid-mwah-**zel**) *n* the plural of **mademoiselle**

mesembryanthemum *n* a low-growing plant with fleshy leaves and bright daisy-like flowers
WORD ORIGIN Greek *mesēmbria* noon + *anthemon* flower

mesh *n* **1** a material resembling a net made from intersecting strands with a space between each strand **2** an open space between the strands of a net or network: *the minimum permitted size of fishing net mesh* **3** (*often pl*) the strands surrounding these spaces **4** anything that ensnares or holds like a net ▷ *adj* **5** made from mesh: *a wire mesh fence* ▷ *vb* **6** to entangle or become entangled **7** (of gear teeth) to engage or interlock **8** to fit together closely or work in

harmony: *she schedules her holidays to mesh with theirs*
WORD ORIGIN probably Dutch *maesche*

mesmerize or **-rise** *vb* **-rizing, -rized** or **-rising, -rised** **1** to fascinate and hold spellbound: *his voice had the entire audience mesmerized* **2** *archaic* to hypnotize **mesmerism** *n* **mesmerizing** *adj*

Mesolithic (mess-oh-**lith**-ik) *adj* of the middle period of the Stone Age, in Europe from about 12 000 to 3000 BC
WORD ORIGIN Greek *misos* middle + *lithos* stone

mesomorph *n physiol* a person with a muscular body build. See also **ectomorph, endomorph**
> **mesomorphic** *adj*
WORD ORIGIN Greek *misos* middle + *morphē* shape

meson (**mee**-zon) *n physics* any of a group of elementary particles that has a mass between those of an electron and a proton
WORD ORIGIN Greek *misos* middle + *-on*, indicating an elementary particle

mesosphere (**mess**-oh-sfeer) *n* the atmospheric layer above the stratosphere

Mesozoic (mess-oh-**zoh**-ik) *adj geol* of the geological era that began 225 million years ago and lasted about 155 million years, during which the dinosaurs emerged, flourished, then became extinct
WORD ORIGIN Greek *misos* middle + *zōion* animal

mess *n* **1** a state of untidiness or confusion, esp. a dirty or unpleasant one: *the house was in a mess* **2** a confused and difficult situation; muddle: *the firm is in a terrible financial mess* **3** *informal* a dirty or untidy person or thing: *there was a nasty burnt mess in the saucepan* **4** a building providing catering, and sometimes recreation, facilities for service personnel **5** a group of service personnel who regularly eat together **6** *old-fashioned* a portion of soft or runny food: *a mess of pottage* ▷ *vb* **7** (of service personnel) to eat in a group ▸ See also **mess about, mess up, mess with**
WORD ORIGIN Old French *mes* dish of food

mess about or **around** *vb* **1** to pass the time doing trivial or silly things without any particular purpose or plan: *messing about in boats* **2** to interfere or meddle: *you have no business messing around here* **3** *chiefly US* to engage in adultery

message *n* **1** a communication from one person or group to another **2** an implicit meaning or moral, as in a work of art **3** a religious or political belief that someone attempts to communicate to others: *paintings with a fierce feminist message* **4 get the message** *informal* to understand
WORD ORIGIN Old French, from Latin *mittere* to send

message board *n* an internet discussion forum

messages *pl n Scot & NE English dialect* household shopping

messaging *n* the sending of a message by any form of electronic communication: *text messaging*

messenger *n* a person who takes messages from one person or group to another
WORD ORIGIN Old French *messagier*

Messiah *n* **1** *Judaism* the awaited king of the Jews, who will be sent by God to free them **2** *Christianity* Jesus Christ, when regarded in this role **3** a liberator of a country or people
WORD ORIGIN Hebrew *māshīach* anointed

Messianic *adj* **1** of or relating to a Messiah, or the arrival on Earth of a Messiah **2 messianic** of or relating to the belief that someone or something will bring about a complete transformation of the existing social order: *a messianic zeal for the free market*

messieurs (may-**syuh**) *n* the plural of **monsieur**

mess jacket *n* a waist-length jacket, worn by officers in the mess for formal dinners

mess kit *n* a soldier's eating utensils for use in the field

Messrs (**mess**-erz) *n* the plural of **Mr**

mess up *vb informal* **1** to make untidy or dirty **2** to spoil something, or do something badly: *he messed up his driving test*

mess with *vb informal chiefly US* to interfere in, or become involved with, a dangerous person, thing, or situation: *he had started messing with drugs*

messy *adj* **messier, messiest** **1** untidy **2** dirty **3** unpleasantly confused or complicated: *the messy, uncontrollable world of real life* **messily** *adv* **messiness** *n*

met *vb* the past of **meet¹**

Met *adj* **1** Meteorological: *the Met Office* ▷ *n* **2 the Met** the Metropolitan Police, who operate in London

metabolic syndrome *n* a condition associated with obesity, which increases the risk of cardiovascular disease and diabetes

metabolism (met-**tab**-ol-liz-zum) *n* the chemical processes that occur in living organisms, resulting in growth, production of energy, and elimination of waste **metabolic** *adj*
WORD ORIGIN Greek *metaballein* to change

metabolize or **-lise** *vb* **-lizing, -lized** or **-lising, -lised** to produce or be produced by metabolism

metacarpus *n, pl* **-pi** the set of five long bones in the hand between the wrist and the fingers **metacarpal** *adj, n*
WORD ORIGIN Greek *meta* after + *karpos* wrist

metal *n* **1 a** *chem* a chemical element, such as iron or copper, that reflects light and can be shaped, forms positive ions, and is a good conductor of heat and electricity **b** an alloy, such as brass or steel, containing one or more of these elements **2** short for **road metal** **3** *informal* short for **heavy metal** **4 metals** the rails of a railway ▷ *adj* **5** made of metal
WORD ORIGIN Greek *metallon* mine

metalanguage *n* the language or system of symbols used to discuss another language or system

metalled or US **metaled** *adj* (of a road) surfaced with crushed rock or small stones: *a metalled driveway*

metallic *adj* **1** of or consisting of metal **2** sounding like two pieces of metal hitting each other: *a metallic click* **3** (of a voice) harsh, unpleasant, and unemotional **4** shining like metal: *metallic paint* **5** (of a taste) unpleasantly harsh and bitter

metalliferous *adj* containing a metallic element
WORD ORIGIN Latin *metallum* metal + *ferre* to bear

metallography *n* the study of the composition and structure of metals

metalloid *n chem* a nonmetallic element, such as arsenic or silicon, that has some of the properties of a metal

metallurgy *n* the scientific study of the structure, properties, extraction, and refining of metals **metallurgical** *adj* **metallurgist** *n*
WORD ORIGIN *metal* + Greek *-urgia*, from *ergon* work

metal road *n* NZ an unsealed road covered in gravel

metalwork *n* **1** the craft of making articles from metal **2** articles made from metal **3** the metal part of something **metalworker** *n*

metamorphic *adj* **1** (of rocks) altered considerably from the original structure and composition by pressure and heat **2** of metamorphosis or metamorphism

metamorphism *n* the process by which metamorphic rocks are formed

metamorphose *vb* **-phosing, -phosed** to change from one state or thing into something different: *the media personality metamorphosed into society hostess*

metamorphosis (met-a-**more**-foss-is) *n, pl* **-ses** (-seez) **1** a complete change of physical form or substance **2** a complete change of character or appearance **3** *zool* the change of form that accompanies transformation into an adult in certain animals, for example the butterfly or frog
WORD ORIGIN Greek: transformation, from *meta* after + *morphē* form

metaphor *n* a figure of speech in which a word or phrase is applied to an object or action that it does not literally apply to in order to imply a resemblance, for example *he is a lion in battle* **metaphorical** *adj* **metaphorically** *adv*
WORD ORIGIN Greek *metapherein* to transfer

metaphysical *adj* **1** of metaphysics **2** abstract, abstruse, or unduly theoretical

Metaphysical *adj* denoting certain 17th-century poets who combined intense feeling with elaborate imagery

metaphysics *n* **1** the philosophical study of the nature of reality **2** abstract or subtle discussion or reasoning
WORD ORIGIN Greek *ta meta ta phusika* the things after the physics, from the arrangement of subjects treated in the works of Aristotle

metastasis (mit-**tass**-tiss-iss) *n, pl* **-ses** (-seez) **1** *pathol* the spreading of a

disease, esp. cancer, from one part of the body to another **2** the spreading of a problem into new areas **metastasize** or **-sise** vb
WORD ORIGIN Greek: transition

metatarsus n, pl **-si** the set of five long bones in the foot between the toes and the ankle **metatarsal** adj, n
WORD ORIGIN Greek meta after + tarsos instep

metathesis (mit-**tath**-iss-iss) n, pl **-ses** (-seez) the transposition of two sounds or letters in a word
WORD ORIGIN Greek metatithenai to transpose

metazoan (met-a-**zoh**-an) n **1** any animal having a body composed of many cells: includes all animals except sponges and protozoans ▷ adj **2** of the metazoans
WORD ORIGIN New Latin Metazoa

meteor n **1** a small piece of rock or metal that has entered the earth's atmosphere from space **2** Also: **shooting star** the bright streak of light appearing in the sky due to a piece of rock or metal burning up because of friction as it falls through the atmosphere
WORD ORIGIN Greek meteōros lofty

meteoric (meet-ee-**or**-rik) adj **1** of or relating to meteors **2** brilliant and very rapid: his meteoric rise to power **meteorically** adv

meteorite n the rocklike remains of a meteoroid that has collided with the earth

meteoroid n any of the small celestial bodies that are thought to orbit the sun. When they enter the earth's atmosphere, they become visible as meteors

meteorol. or **meteor.** **1** meteorological **2** meteorology

meteorology n the study of the earth's atmosphere and weather-forming processes, esp. for weather forecasting **meteorological** adj **meteorologist** n

mete out vb **meting**, **meted** to impose or deal out something, usually something unpleasant: the sentence meted out to him has proved controversial
WORD ORIGIN Old English metan to measure

meter¹ n **1** any device that measures and records the quantity or number of units of something that was used during a specified period or is being used at that moment: a gas meter **2** short for **parking meter 3** short for **taximeter** ▷ vb **4** to measure the amount of something used, or a rate of flow, with a meter
WORD ORIGIN Old English metan to measure

meter² n US same as **metre¹** or **metre²**

-meter n combining form **1** indicating an instrument for measuring: barometer **2** prosody indicating a verse having a specified number of feet: pentameter
WORD ORIGIN Greek metron measure

methadone n a drug similar to morphine, sometimes prescribed as a heroin substitute
WORD ORIGIN (di)meth(yl) + a(mino) + d(iphenyl) + -one, indicating a ketone

methamphetamine n a variety of amphetamine used for its stimulant action

methanal n same as **formaldehyde**

methane n a colourless odourless flammable gas, the main constituent of natural gas
WORD ORIGIN meth(yl) + -ane, indicating an alkane

methane series n a series of saturated hydrocarbons with the general formula C_nH_{2n+2}

methanol n a colourless poisonous liquid used as a solvent and fuel. Also: **methyl alcohol**
WORD ORIGIN methane + -ol, indicating alcohol

methicillin n a semisynthetic penicillin used to treat various infections

methinks vb, past **methought** archaic it seems to me that

method n **1** a way of doing something, esp. a systematic or regular one **2** orderliness of thought or action **3** the techniques of a particular field or subject
WORD ORIGIN Greek methodos, literally: a going after

Method n an acting technique in which the actor bases his or her role on the inner motivation of the character played

methodical adj careful, well-organized, and systematic **methodically** adv

Methodist n **1** a member of any of the Christian Nonconformist denominations that derive from the beliefs and practices of John Wesley and his followers ▷ adj **2** of or relating to Methodists or their Church **Methodism** n

methodology n, pl **-gies 1** the system of methods and principles used in a particular discipline **2** the philosophical study of method **methodological** adj

methought vb archaic the past tense of **methinks**

meths n Brit, Austral, & NZ informal methylated spirits

methyl adj of or containing the monovalent saturated hydrocarbon group of atoms CH_3-: methyl mercury
WORD ORIGIN from methylene

methyl alcohol n same as **methanol**

methylate vb **-ating**, **-ated** to mix with methanol

methylated spirits n alcohol that has been rendered undrinkable by the addition of methanol and a violet dye, used as a solvent or as a fuel for small lamps or heaters. Also: **methylated spirit**

methylene adj of, consisting of, or containing the divalent group of atoms $-CH_2$-: a methylene group or radical
WORD ORIGIN Greek methu wine + hulē wood + -ene, indicating a double bond

meticulous adj very precise about details; careful and thorough **meticulously** adv **meticulousness** n
WORD ORIGIN Latin meticulosus fearful

métier (met-ee-ay) n **1** a profession or trade **2** a person's strong point or speciality
WORD ORIGIN French

Métis (met-**teess**) n, pl **-tis** (-teess, -teez) a person of mixed parentage, esp. the offspring of a Native American and a French Canadian **Métisse** fem n
WORD ORIGIN French

metonymy (mit-**on**-im-ee) n, pl **-mies** a figure of speech in which one thing is replaced by another associated with it, for instance the use of Downing Street to mean the British government
WORD ORIGIN Greek meta-, indicating change + onoma name

metre¹ or US **meter** n the basic SI unit of length, equal to 100 centimetres (39.37 inches): the majority of people are between one and a half and two metres tall
WORD ORIGIN same as METRE²

metre² or US **meter** n **1** prosody the rhythmic arrangement of syllables in verse, usually according to the number and kind of feet in a line **2** music chiefly US the rhythmic arrangement of the beat in a piece of music
WORD ORIGIN Greek metron measure

metre-kilogram-second n see **mks units**

metric adj of or relating to the metre or metric system: use either all metric or all imperial measurements

metrical or **metric** adj **1** of or relating to measurement **2** of or in poetic metre **metrically** adv

metricate vb **-cating**, **-cated** to convert a measuring system or instrument to metric units **metrication** n

metric system n any decimal system of units based on the metre. For scientific purposes SI units are used

metric ton n (not in technical use) a tonne

metro n, pl **-ros** an urban, usually underground, railway system in certain cities, such as Paris
WORD ORIGIN French, from chemin de fer métropolitain metropolitan railway

metronome n a device which indicates the speed music should be played at by producing a clicking sound from a pendulum with an adjustable period of swing
WORD ORIGIN Greek metron measure + nomos law

metropolis (mit-**trop**-oh-liss) n the main city of a country or region
WORD ORIGIN Greek mētēr mother + polis city

metropolitan adj **1** of or characteristic of a metropolis **2** of or consisting of a city and its suburbs: the Tokyo metropolitan region **3** of or belonging to the home territories of a country, as opposed to overseas territories: metropolitan France ▷ n **4** Christianity the senior clergyman, esp. an archbishop, in charge of an ecclesiastical province **5** an inhabitant of a large city

-metry n combining form indicating the process or science of measuring: geometry **-metric** adj combining form
WORD ORIGIN Greek metron measure

mettle n **1** courage or spirit: the lack of mettle evident among British politicians **2** character or abilities: the mettle saints are made of **3 on one's mettle** roused to

Hawaiian Words in English

The islands now known as Hawaii were first encountered by English speakers when Captain James Cook arrived there in 1778 and named them 'the Sandwich Islands' in honour of the 4th Earl of Sandwich, who was at the time the First Lord of the Admiralty (although he is better known for popularizing the snack that bears his name).

Cook was killed on the islands in the following year. His name for the islands outlived him, but not for long. By 1819 the islands had been united as a kingdom and reverted to the local name of 'Hawaii' (perhaps meaning 'small homeland'). In 1898 the Hawaiian Islands were annexed as a possession of the United States, and in 1959 they became America's fiftieth state with the nickname of 'The Aloha State'.

The word *aloha* is just one example of a Hawaiian word that has been adopted into the English language. Traditionally used as both a greeting and parting wish, it connotes not only 'Hello' and 'Goodbye', but more frequently 'Welcome to Paradise', conjuring up images of a sun-bathed tropical haven where the warmth extended to travellers is symbolized by the presentation of a garland of flowers or *lei*. Indeed, it is related to the Māori word *aroha*, which means 'love'.

Words such as *aloha* and *lei* exhibit some of the characteristic features of the Hawaiian language. Like other Polynesian languages, it is notable for having a paucity of consonants in comparison with Indo-European languages. Hawaiian words draw on only seven consonants, and a consonant is always followed immediately by a vowel.

The vowel-heavy nature of the language allows it to produce words such as *aa*, a volcanic rock that hurtles unashamedly onto the opening page of the English dictionary. Volcanoes are the most significant geographical feature of the islands, and the Hawaiian goddess of volcanoes is commemorated in another geological term, *Pele's hair*, which describes fine threads of volcanic glass.

However, the Hawaiian words which are most familiar in English tend to be associated with leisure. Among these is *hula*, the popular dance of the islands, which has spun off two further words into the English language. The *Hula Hoop* is the name given to a ring that dancers attempt to keep in the air by gyrating the hips (and is also the brand name adopted for a popular ring-shaped potato snack), while a *hula skirt* is the name given to a grass skirt like the ones traditionally worn by hula dancers.

Another successful Hawaiian cultural export is the *ukulele*, the small stringed instrument whose name comes from the Hawaiian for 'jumping flea' (supposedly a reference to the movement of the player's fingers over the fretboard).

Hawaiian is also the source of the *lanai* (a room or porch built onto the side of a house), and the brightly coloured loose garment known as the *muu-muu*. *Noni* is a tropical fruit whose juice has been marketed as a health food, while the Hawaiian word *ahi* may be familiar to food enthusiasts as a name for the yellowfin tuna.

Several Hawaiian words feature the pattern known as 'reduplication', where a group of letters is repeated. In Hawaiian, reduplication acts to intensify the meaning of words. Thus *mahi-mahi*, the Hawaiian name for the dolphin, literally means 'strong-strong', and so has the force of 'very strong'.

One of the most recent borrowings from the Hawaiian language has been the word *wiki*, which has come in English to refer to an application that allows anyone who visits a website to edit its content (and is best known as being the basis of the collaborative online encyclopedia called *Wikipedia*). The developer of the wiki was an American computer scientist called Ward Cunningham, who had visited Hawaii and was inspired by the name of the 'wiki wiki bus' that shuttled passengers between terminals at Honolulu airport. Learning that *wiki wiki* was the Hawaiian word for 'very quick', Cunningham thought that 'wiki wiki web' would make a more interesting name for the software he was developing than the more prosaic 'quick web'. The usefulness of the application guaranteed that the name would become widely known, although it soon became shortened to simply 'wiki'.

making one's best efforts
WORD ORIGIN variant of *metal*

MeV million electronvolts (10^6 electronvolts)

mew[1] *n* **1** the characteristic high-pitched cry of a cat; meow ▷ *vb* **2** to make such a sound
WORD ORIGIN imitative

mew[2] *n* a seagull
WORD ORIGIN Old English *mǣw*

mewl *vb* **1** (esp. of a baby) to cry weakly; whimper ▷ *n* **2** a weak or whimpering cry
WORD ORIGIN imitative

mews *n chiefly Brit* **1** a yard or street lined by buildings originally used as stables but now often converted into dwellings ▷ *adj* **2** (of a flat or house) located in a mews: *a mews cottage*
WORD ORIGIN plural of *mew*, originally referring to royal stables built on the site of hawks' mews (cages)

Mex. **1** Mexican **2** Mexico

Mexican *adj* **1** of Mexico ▷ *n* **2** a person from Mexico

Mexican wave *n* the rippling effect produced when the spectators in successive sections of a sports stadium stand up while raising their arms and then sit down
WORD ORIGIN first seen at the World Cup finals in *Mexico* in 1986

mezzanine (**mez**-zan-een) *n* an intermediate storey, esp. one between the ground and first floor
WORD ORIGIN Italian *mezzano* middle

mezzo (**met**-so) *adv* **1** *music* moderately; quite: *mezzo-forte* ▷ *n, pl* **-zos** **2** short for **mezzo-soprano**
WORD ORIGIN Italian: half

mezzo-soprano *n, pl* **-nos** **1** a female voice lower than soprano but higher than contralto **2** a singer with such a voice

mezzotint (**met**-so-tint) *n* **1** a method of engraving done by scraping and burnishing the roughened surface of a copper plate **2** a print made from a plate so treated
WORD ORIGIN Italian *mezzotinto* half tint

mg milligram

Mg *chem* magnesium

M. Glam Mid Glamorgan

Mgr **1** manager **2** monseigneur **3** monsignor

MHz megahertz

mi *n music* same as **me**[2]

MI Michigan

MI5 Military Intelligence, section five; the part of the British security services which combats spying and subversion in Britain

MI6 Military Intelligence, section six; the part of the British security services which spies on other countries. Also called: **SIS**

miasma (mee-**azz**-ma) *n, pl* **-mata** or **-mas** an unwholesome or foreboding atmosphere
WORD ORIGIN Greek: defilement

mica (**my**-ka) *n* any of a group of minerals consisting of flakelike crystals of aluminium or potassium silicates. They have a high resistance to electricity and heat
WORD ORIGIN Latin: crumb

mice *n* the plural of **mouse**

Michaelmas (**mik**-kl-mass) *n* Sept 29, the feast of St Michael the archangel: one of the four quarter days in England, Ireland, and Wales

Michaelmas daisy *n Brit* a garden plant with small daisy-shaped purple, pink, or white flowers in autumn

Mick *n offensive slang* an Irishman
WORD ORIGIN nickname for *Michael*

mickey *n* **take the mickey (out of)** *informal* to tease (someone)
WORD ORIGIN origin unknown

Mickey Finn *n slang* a drink containing a drug to make the drinker unconscious
WORD ORIGIN origin unknown

Mickey Mouse *adj slang* trivial, insignificant, or amateurish: *a Mickey Mouse survey*
WORD ORIGIN after the cartoon character created by Walt Disney

mickle or **muckle** *archaic or Scot & N English dialect adj* **1** large or abundant ▷ *adv* **2** much; greatly ▷ *n* **3** a great amount
WORD ORIGIN Old Norse *mikell*

micro *n, pl* **micros** short for **microcomputer** or **microprocessor**

micro- or **micr-** *combining form* **1** small or minute: *microdot* **2** involving the use of a microscope: *microscopy* **3** denoting 10^{-6}: *microsecond*
WORD ORIGIN Greek *mikros* small

microbe *n* any microscopic organism, esp. a disease-causing bacterium **microbial** or **microbic** *adj*
WORD ORIGIN MICRO- + Greek *bios* life

microbiology *n* the branch of biology involving the study of microorganisms

microblog *n* a blog in which there is a limitation on the length of individual postings **microblogger** *n* **microblogging** *n*

microchemistry *n* chemical experimentation with minute quantities of material

microchip *n* a tiny wafer of semiconductor material, such as silicon, containing an integrated circuit. Often shortened to: **chip**

microcircuit *n* a miniature electronic circuit in which a number of permanently connected components are contained in one small chip of semiconducting material

microcomputer *n* a compact computer in which the central processing unit is contained in one or more silicon chips

microcosm *n* **1** a miniature representation of something: *this area is a microcosm of France as a whole* **2** man regarded as epitomizing the universe **3 in microcosm** on a small scale **microcosmic** *adj*
WORD ORIGIN Greek *mikros kosmos* little world

microdot *n* a greatly reduced photographic copy (about the size of a pinhead) of a document

microeconomics *n* the branch of economics concerned with particular commodities, firms, or individuals and the relationships between them

microelectronics *n* the branch of electronics concerned with microcircuits

microfiche (**my**-kroh-feesh) *n* same as **fiche**
WORD ORIGIN French, from MICRO- + *fiche* small card

microfilm *n* **1** a strip of film on which books or documents can be recorded in miniaturized form ▷ *vb* **2** to photograph a page or document on microfilm

microlight or **microlite** *n* a very small private aircraft with large wings

micrometer (my-**krom**-it-er) *n* an instrument for the accurate measurement of small distances or angles

microminiaturization or **-risation** *n* the production and use of very small electronic components

micron (**my**-kron) *n* a unit of length equal to one millionth of a metre
WORD ORIGIN Greek *mikros* small

microorganism *n* any organism of microscopic size, such as a virus or bacterium

microphone *n* a device for converting sound into electrical energy

microprocessor *n computers* a single integrated circuit which acts as the central processing unit in a small computer

microscope *n* **1** an optical instrument that uses a lens or combination of lenses to produce a greatly magnified image of a small close object **2** any instrument, such as the electron microscope, for producing a greatly magnified visual image of a small object

microscopic *adj* **1** too small to be seen except with a microscope **2** very small; minute **3** of or using a microscope **microscopically** *adv*

microscopy *n* the use of microscopes

microsecond *n* one millionth of a second

microstructure *n* a structure on a microscopic scale, such as that of a metal or a cell

microsurgery *n* intricate surgery performed using a special microscope and miniature precision instruments

microwave *n* **1** an electromagnetic wave with a wavelength of between 0.3 and 0.001 metres: used in radar and cooking **2** short for **microwave oven** ▷ *vb* **-waving, -waved** **3** to cook in a microwave oven

microwave detector *n* a device used by police for recording the speed of a motorist

microwave oven *n* a type of cooker which uses microwaves to cook food quickly

micturate *vb* **-rating, -rated** to urinate **micturition** *n*
WORD ORIGIN Latin *micturire* to desire to urinate

mid[1] *n archaic* the middle
WORD ORIGIN Old English

mid[2] or **'mid** *prep poetic* amid

mid- *combining form* indicating a middle part, point, time, or position: *midday; mid-June; mid-Victorian*

midair *n* some point above ground level, in the air

midday *n* **1** twelve o'clock in the day; noon **2** the middle part of the day, from late morning to early afternoon: *the midday sun*

midden *n Austral & Brit* a dunghill or pile of refuse
WORD ORIGIN from Old Norse

middle *n* **1** an area or point equal in distance from the ends or edges of a place: *a hotel in the middle of town* **2** the time between the first part and last part of an event or period of time: *the middle of June; the film got a bit boring in the middle* **3** the part of the body around the stomach; waist **4 in the middle of** busy doing something: *I'm in the middle of washing the dishes* ▷ *adj* **5** equally distant from the ends or outer edges of something; central: *the middle finger* **6** having an equal number of elder and younger brothers and sisters: *he was the middle child of three* **7** intermediate in status or situation: *middle management* **8** avoiding extremes; moderate: *we must find a middle course between authoritarianism and anarchy*
WORD ORIGIN Old English *middel*

middle age *n* the period of life between youth and old age, usually considered to occur between the ages of 40 and 60 **middle-aged** *adj*

Middle Ages *n European history* **1** (broadly) the period from the fall of the W Roman Empire in 476 AD to the Italian Renaissance **2** (narrowly) the period from about 1000 AD to the 15th century

middle-age spread *or* **middle-aged spread** *n* the fat that appears round many people's waists when they become middle-aged

Middle America *n* the US middle class, esp. those groups that are politically conservative

middlebrow *disparaging n* **1** a person with conventional tastes and limited cultural appreciation ▷ *adj* **2** of or appealing to middlebrows

middle C *n music* the note written on the first ledger line below the treble staff or the first ledger line above the bass staff. On a piano it is near the middle of the keyboard

middle class *n* **1** the social class between the working and upper classes. It consists of business and professional people ▷ *adj* **middle-class 2** of or characteristic of the middle class

middle-distance *adj* **1** *athletics* of or being a race of a length between the sprints and the distance events, esp. the 800 or 1500 metres: *a middle-distance runner* ▷ *n* **middle distance 2** the part of a painting between the foreground and the far distance

middle ear *n* the sound-conducting part of the ear immediately inside the eardrum

Middle East *n* the area around the E Mediterranean, esp. Israel and the Arab countries from Turkey to North Africa and eastwards to Iran **Middle Eastern** *adj*

Middle England *n* a characterization of a predominantly middle-class, middle-income section of British society, living mainly in suburban and rural England

Middle English *n* the English language from about 1100 to about 1450

Middle High German *n* High German from about 1200 to about 1500

Middle Low German *n* Low German from about 1200 to about 1500

middleman *n, pl* -men **1** a trader who buys from the producer and sells to the consumer **2** an intermediary or go-between

middle name *n* **1** a name between a person's first name and surname **2** a characteristic quality for which a person is known: *danger is my middle name*

middle-of-the-road *adj* **1** not extreme, esp. in political views; moderate **2** of or denoting popular music of wide general appeal

middle school *n* (in England and Wales) a school for children aged between 8 or 9 and 12 or 13

middleweight *n* a professional boxer weighing up to 160 pounds (72.5 kg) or an amateur weighing up to 75 kg

middling *adj* **1** neither very good nor very bad **2** moderate in size **3 fair to middling** neither good nor bad, esp. in health ▷ *adv* **4** *informal* moderately: *middling well*

Middx Middlesex

midfield *n soccer* the area between the two opposing defences

midge *n* a small mosquito-like biting insect occurring in dancing swarms, esp. near water
WORD ORIGIN Old English *mycge*

midget *n* **1** a dwarf whose skeleton and features are of normal proportions ▷ *adj* **2** much smaller than normal: *a midget submarine*
WORD ORIGIN *midge* + *-et* small

MIDI *n* a system for transmitting information to electronic musical instruments
WORD ORIGIN *m*(*usical*) *i*(*nstrument*) *d*(*igital*) *i*(*nterface*)

midi- *combining form* of medium or middle size or length: *a midi-skirt*

midi system *n* a complete set of compact hi-fi sound equipment designed as a single unit

midland *n* the central or inland part of a country

Midlands *n* **1 the Midlands** the central counties of England ▷ *adj* **2** of, in, or from the central counties of England: *a Midlands engineering firm*

midmost *adj, adv* in the middle or midst

midnight *n* **1** the middle of the night; 12 o'clock at night ▷ *adj* **2** happening or apparent at midnight or in the middle of the night: *midnight Mass* **3 burn the midnight oil** to work or study late into the night

midnight sun *n* the sun visible at midnight during the summer inside the Arctic and Antarctic circles

mid-off *n cricket* the fielding position on the off side closest to the bowler

mid-on *n cricket* the fielding position on the on side closest to the bowler

midpoint *n* **1** the point on a line equally distant from either end **2** a point in time halfway between the beginning and end of an event

midriff *n* **1** the middle part of the human body between waist and chest **2** *anat* same as **diaphragm** (sense 1)
WORD ORIGIN Old English *midhrif* mid belly

midshipman *n, pl* -men a naval officer of the lowest commissioned rank

midships *adv, adj naut* see **amidships**

midst *n* **1 in our midst** among us **2 in the midst of a** surrounded by **b** at a point during

midsummer *n* **1** the middle or height of summer **2** same as **summer solstice**

Midsummer's Day *or* **Midsummer Day** *n* June 24, the feast of St John the Baptist: one of the four quarter days in England, Ireland, and Wales

midtown *n US & Canad* the centre of a town

midway *adj* **1** in or at the middle of the distance; halfway: *the midway point* ▷ *adv* **2** to the middle of the distance

midweek *n* the middle of the week

Midwest *n* the N central part of the US **Midwestern** *adj*

mid-wicket *n cricket* the fielding position on the on side, roughly the same distance from both wickets, and halfway towards the boundary

midwife *n, pl* -wives a person qualified to deliver babies and to care for women before, during, and after childbirth **midwifery** (mid-**wiff**-fer-ree) *n*
WORD ORIGIN Old English *mid* with + *wīf* woman

midwinter *n* **1** the middle or depth of winter **2** same as **winter solstice**

mien (**mean**) *n literary* a person's manner, bearing, or appearance
WORD ORIGIN probably from obsolete *demean* appearance

mifepristone (mi-**fep**-riss-tone) *n* a technical name for **abortion pill**

miffed *adj informal* offended or upset
WORD ORIGIN perhaps imitative of bad temper

might[1] *vb* **1** the past tense or subjunctive mood of **may**[1]: *he might have come* **2** (used as an auxiliary) expressing possibility: *he might well have gone already*. See **may**[1] (sense 2)
WORD ORIGIN Old English *mihte*
≡ USAGE
≡ See at **may**.

might[2] *n* **1** great power, strength, or vigour **2 with all one's might** using all one's strength and energy **3 (with) might and main** see **main**
WORD ORIGIN Old English *miht*

mighty *adj* mightier, mightiest **1** powerful or strong **2** very great in extent or importance ▷ *adv* **3** *informal chiefly US, Canad, & Austral* very: *mighty hungry* **mightily** *adv* **mightiness** *n*

mignonette (min-yon-**net**) *n* a plant with spikes of small fragrant greenish-white flowers **WORD ORIGIN** French, diminutive of *mignon* dainty

migraine (**mee**-grain) *n* a throbbing headache usually affecting only one side of the head and commonly accompanied by nausea and visual disturbances **WORD ORIGIN** French, from Greek *hemi* half + *kranion* skull

migrant *n* **1** a person or animal that moves from one place to another ▷ *adj* **2** moving from one place to another: *migrant farm labourers*

migrate *vb* **-grating, -grated 1** to go from one place to settle in another, esp. in a foreign country **2** (of living creatures, esp. birds) to journey between different habitats at specific times of the year **migration** *n* **migratory** *adj* **WORD ORIGIN** Latin *migrare* to change one's abode

mikado *n, pl* **-dos** *archaic* the Japanese emperor **WORD ORIGIN** Japanese

mike *n informal* a microphone

mil *n photog* short for **millimetre**: *35-mil film* **WORD ORIGIN** Latin *millesimus* thousandth

milady *n, pl* **-dies** (formerly) a continental title for an English gentlewoman

milch (**miltch**) *adj chiefly Brit* (esp. of cattle) kept for milk **WORD ORIGIN** Old English *-milce* (in compounds)

mild *adj* **1** (of a taste or sensation) not strong; bland **2** gentle or temperate in character, climate, or behaviour **3** not extreme; moderate: *mild criticism of senior officers* **4** feeble; unassertive: *a mild protest* ▷ *n* **5** *Brit* a dark beer flavoured with fewer hops than bitter **WORD ORIGIN** Old English *milde*

mildew *n* **1** a disease of plants caused by a parasitic fungus **2** same as **mould**² ▷ *vb* **3** to affect or become affected with mildew **mildewy** *adj* **WORD ORIGIN** Old English *mildēaw* honey dew

mild steel *n* strong tough steel containing a small quantity of carbon

mile *n* **1** Also: **statute mile** a unit of length used in the UK, the US and certain other countries, equal to 1760 yards. 1 mile is equivalent to 1.60934 kilometres **2** see **nautical mile 3** Also: **miles** *informal* a great distance; great deal: *he missed by miles* **4** a race extending over a mile ▷ *adv* **5 miles** very much: *it's miles better than their first album* **WORD ORIGIN** Latin *milia (passuum)* a thousand (paces)

mileage *n* **1** a distance expressed in miles **2** the total number of miles that a motor vehicle has travelled **3** the number of miles a motor vehicle will travel on one gallon of fuel **4** *informal* the usefulness or benefit of something: *the opposition is trying to make political mileage out of the issue*

mileometer *or* **milometer** (mile-**om**-it-er) *n Brit* a device that records the number of miles that a vehicle has travelled

milepost *n chiefly US & Canad* a signpost that shows the distance in miles to or from a place

miler *n* an athlete, horse, etc. that specializes in races of one mile

milestone *n* **1** a stone pillar that shows the distance in miles to or from a place **2** a significant event in a life or history: *a milestone in Turkish-Bulgarian relations*

milfoil *n* same as **yarrow** **WORD ORIGIN** Latin *mille* thousand + *folium* leaf

milieu (**meal**-yuh) *n, pl* **milieux** *or* **milieus** (**meal**-yuhz) the social and cultural environment in which a person or thing exists: *the film takes for its milieu an apparently wholesome small town* **WORD ORIGIN** French

militant *adj* **1** very active or aggressive in the support of a cause **2** *formal* warring; engaged in warfare ▷ *n* **3** a militant person **militancy** *n* **militantly** *adv* **WORD ORIGIN** Latin *militare* to be a soldier

militarism *n* the pursuit of policies intended to create and maintain aggressive and influential armed forces **militarist** *n, adj* **militaristic** *adj*

militarized *or* **-rised** *adj* occupied by armed forces: *one of the most heavily militarized borders in the world* **militarization** *or* **-risation** *n*

military *adj* **1** of or relating to the armed forces or war **2** of or characteristic of soldiers ▷ *n* **3 the military** the armed services, esp. the army **militarily** *adv* **WORD ORIGIN** Latin *miles* soldier

military police *n* a corps within an army that performs police duties

militate *vb* **-tating, -tated** (of facts or events) to have a strong influence or effect: *our position militated against counter-attacks* ⹝USAGE ⹝ See at **mitigate**.

militia (mill-**ish**-a) *n* a military force of trained civilians enlisted for use in emergency only **militiaman** *n* **WORD ORIGIN** Latin: soldiery

milk *n* **1 a** a whitish fluid secreted by the mammary glands of mature female mammals and used for feeding their young **b** the milk of cows, goats, etc. used by humans as a food and to make cheese, butter, and yogurt **2** any similar fluid, such as the juice of a coconut ▷ *vb* **3** to draw milk from the udder of a cow or other animal **4** to extract as much money, help, or value as possible from: *he was accused of milking the situation for his own ends* **milker** *n* **milkiness** *n* **milky** *adj* **WORD ORIGIN** Old English *milc*

milk-and-water *adj* weak, feeble, or insipid

milk bar *n* (formerly) a snack bar at which milk drinks and light refreshments are served

milk chocolate *n* chocolate that has been made with milk, having a creamy taste

milk float *n Brit* a small electrically powered vehicle used to deliver milk to houses

milkmaid *n* a girl or woman who milks cows

milkman *n, pl* **-men** *Brit, Austral, & NZ* a man who delivers milk to people's houses

milk of magnesia *n* a suspension of magnesium hydroxide in water, used as an antacid and laxative

milk pudding *n* a pudding made by cooking milk with a grain, esp. rice

milk round *n* **1** *Brit & NZ* a route along which a milkman regularly delivers milk **2** *Brit* a regular series of visits made by recruitment officers from industry to colleges

milk shake *n* a cold frothy drink made of milk, flavouring, and sometimes ice cream, whisked or beaten together

milksop *n* a feeble or ineffectual man or youth

milk tooth *n* any of the first set of teeth in young children

Milky Way *n* **1** the diffuse band of light stretching across the night sky that consists of millions of distant stars in our galaxy **2** the galaxy in which the Earth is situated **WORD ORIGIN** translation of Latin *via lactea*

mill *n* **1** a building where grain is crushed and ground to make flour **2** a factory, esp. one which processes raw materials: *a steel mill* **3** any of various processing or manufacturing machines, esp. one that grinds, presses, or rolls **4** a small device for grinding solids: *a pepper mill* **5 go** *or* **be put through the mill** to have an unpleasant experience or ordeal ▷ *vb* **6** to grind, press, or process in or as if in a mill **7** to groove or flute the edge of a coin **8** to move about in a confused manner: *the corridor was full of people milling about* **WORD ORIGIN** Latin *molere* to grind

milled *adj* **1** crushed or ground in a mill: *freshly milled black pepper* **2** (of a coin) having a grooved and often raised edge

millennium (mill-**en**-nee-um) *n, pl* **-nia** (-nee-a) *or* **-niums 1** a period of one thousand years **2 the Millennium** *Christianity* the period of a thousand years of Christ's awaited reign upon earth **3** a future period of peace and happiness **millennial** *adj* **WORD ORIGIN** Latin *mille* thousand + *annus* year

millennium bug *n computers* any software problem arising from the change in date at the start of the 21st century

millepede *n* same as **millipede**

miller *n history* a person who owns or operates a mill, esp. a corn mill

miller's thumb *n* a small freshwater European fish with a flattened body **WORD ORIGIN** from the alleged likeness of the fish's head to a thumb

millesimal (mill-**less**-im-al) *adj* **1** denoting or consisting of a thousandth ▷ *n* **2** a thousandth part of something **WORD ORIGIN** Latin *millesimus*

millet *n* a cereal grass cultivated for its edible grain and as animal fodder **WORD ORIGIN** Latin *milium*

The Influence of Italian on English

The first English dictionary was Italian. John Florio's *Worlde of Wordes* was published in 1598, six years before the one usually credited as the first, Robert Cawdrey's *A Table Alphabeticall*. Florio's dictionary was bilingual, with Italian headwords. But the English synonyms that Florio gave as definitions were so copious they practically amounted to a dictionary on their own.

Florio, a multilingual courtier and tutor to the nobility, had come to England with his Protestant parents, refugees from religious persecution in Italy, and had already augmented the English vocabulary with his free translation of Montaigne's *Essays,* in which he introduced *conscientious, tarnish, facilitate,* and *regret.* He knew Ben Jonson well, and may have befriended Shakespeare. In fact, it's been speculated that he *was* Shakespeare.

Certainly, Shakespeare was no stranger to Italy in literature and drama, since he used it as a setting for *Romeo and Juliet, The Merchant of Venice,* and *The Taming of the Shrew,* not to mention the Rome of *Julius Caesar.* This alone shows the huge impact the Italian Renaissance had on the English *literati.* In the revival of classical learning, Italian was the ideal partner since, among Romance languages, it was the one closest to Latin. The language was formalized by Dante Alighieri in *The Divine Comedy,* and the first sonnets were written in it. Adapted from the *model* of Petrarch (Francesco Petrarca), the sonnet became a mainstay of English poetry. The original was *sonetto,* a 'little song'; there were also Italian originals for *stanza, scenario,* and *novel.*

Since Roman times the Italian primacy in the arts left an impressive linguistic legacy.

Whether one was a *dilettante* or belonged to the *cognoscenti,* there was much to admire, and words to express the admiration, not only of the many *bambinos* and *madonnas* in Italian paintings. There were colours, such as *umber, sienna, sepia, indigo, magenta,* and *pastel* shades. There were the *caricature, cartoon,* and *sketch*; there were the materials of pottery, sculpture, and building such as *porcelain, terra cotta, bronze, granite,* and *stucco.* If Italian did not exist, we would have had to find other words for *arcade, balcony, corridor, dome, cupola, mezzanine, façade, portico, rotunda, studio,* and *villa.*

Over time, Italian became the *lingua franca* of classical music. It designated tempo (*allegro, rondo, presto*), singing voice (*alto, soprano*), and musical forms (*cantata, madrigal, serenade, fugue, oratorio*). At a *concert,* or listening to an *orchestra* led by a *maestro,* we hear such instruments as the *piano, bassoon, cello, oboe, piccolo, trombone, tuba, viola,* and *violin,* though perhaps not the *mandolin.* After the *finale,* the audience shouts '*Bravo!*'

Given the precedent of Machiavelli, who gave us *Machiavellian,* it's not surprising that Italian loanwords, like *ballot, partisan, manifesto, politico, policy, propaganda,* and *fascism,* often relate to politics. Some are connected to crime, like *bandit, bomb, mafia,* and *mafiosa,* or to gambling, like *casino, lotto,* or *lottery.* During the twentieth century, Italian food terms spread globally in the multiple varieties of *pizza* and *pasta,* the latter sometimes sprinkled with *parmesan,* preferably cooked *al dente,* and by the consumption of *coffee* as *espresso* and *cappuccino.* Non-Italians began to drink *chianti* and *grappa.* If they liked seafood, they ate *calamari* and *scampi.* Kitchens and gardens began to speak Italian: the *prosciutto, salami,* and *bologna* (corrupted to *baloney*) in *antipasto* and, to add vitamin content, *artichoke, arugula, broccoli, cauliflower, radicchio,* and *zucchini.*

In the twentieth century, *Ciao!* became a friendly way to say goodbye. An old word, the music verb *segue,* gained wider application to mean any uninterrupted transition. Then, in the 1970s, we began to hear *gonzo,* referring to an overheated style of journalism. *Gonzo* may also derive from Spanish. Not so with *diva,* which in the early twenty-first century appeared in contexts far removed from the *operatic* stage (*Oprah Winfrey, the* diva *of daytime TV*).

Only the etymological *illuminati* know that *pants* derives from *Pantaloon,* a baggy-trousered character in *commedia dell'arte,* or that *jeans* derives from a cloth originally made in Genoa. One oddity of Italian loans is that they often become plural in English, as in *graffiti,* not *graffito,* and *paparazzi,* not *paparazzo.* Some people scatter *confetti* after weddings. Neither Italians nor the rest of the world are bothered by the fact that *vermicelli* means 'little worms'.

milli- *combining form* denoting 10^{-3}: *millimetre*
WORD ORIGIN Latin *mille* thousand

milliard *n* Brit (no longer in technical use) a thousand million
WORD ORIGIN French

millibar *n* a unit of atmospheric pressure equal to 100 newtons per square metre

milligram *or* **milligramme** *n* one thousandth of a gram
WORD ORIGIN French

millilitre *or US* **milliliter** *n* a measure of volume equivalent to one thousandth of a litre

millimetre *or US* **millimeter** *n* a unit of length equal to one thousandth of a metre

milliner *n* a person who makes or sells women's hats **millinery** *n*
WORD ORIGIN originally *Milaner* a native of *Milan*, once famous for its fancy goods

million *n, pl* **-lions** *or* **-lion 1** the number equal to one thousand thousands: 1 000 000 or 10^6 **2** (*often pl*) *informal* an extremely large but unspecified number: *I've got a million things to do today* **millionth** *n, adj*
WORD ORIGIN early Italian *millione*

millionaire *n* a person who has money or property worth at least a million pounds, dollars, etc. **millionairess** *fem n*

millipede *or* **millepede** *n* a small crawling animal with a cylindrical many-segmented body, each segment of which bears two pairs of legs
WORD ORIGIN Latin *mille* thousand + *pes* foot

millisecond *n* one thousandth of a second

millpond *n* a pool which provides water to turn a millwheel

millrace *n* the current of water that turns a millwheel

millstone *n* **1** one of a pair of heavy flat stones that are rotated one against the other to grind grain **2** a heavy burden of responsibility or obligation: *the debt had become a millstone round his neck*

millstream *n* a stream of water used to turn a millwheel

millwheel *n* a water wheel that drives a mill

milometer (mile-**om**-it-er) *n* same as **mileometer**

milord *n* (formerly) a continental title used for an English gentleman
WORD ORIGIN from *my lord*

milt *n* the male reproductive gland, sperm, or semen of a fish
WORD ORIGIN Old English *milte* spleen

mime *n* **1** a style of acting using only gesture and bodily movement and not words **2** a performer specializing in this **3** a performance in this style ▷ *vb* **miming, mimed 4** to express or describe something in actions or gestures without using speech **5** (of musicians) to pretend to be singing or playing music that is actually prerecorded **mimer** *n*
WORD ORIGIN Greek *mimos* imitator

Mimeograph (mim-ee-oh-grahf) *n* **1** *trademark* an office machine for printing multiple copies from a stencil ▷ *vb* **2** to print copies using this machine

mimetic (mim-**met**-ik) *adj* **1** imitating or representing something: *most photographs are mimetic representations of the real world* **2** *biol* of or showing mimicry
WORD ORIGIN Greek *mimeisthai* to imitate

mimic *vb* **-icking, -icked 1** to imitate a person or a way of acting or speaking, esp. to entertain or make fun of **2** to take on the appearance of: *certain flies mimic wasps* **3** to copy closely or in a servile manner: *social climbers in the colonies began to mimic their conquerors* ▷ *n* **4** a person or an animal, such as a parrot, that is clever at mimicking
WORD ORIGIN Greek *mimikos*

mimicry *n, pl* **-ries 1** the act or art of copying or imitating closely **2** *biol* the resemblance shown by one animal species to another dangerous or inedible one, which protects it from predators

mimosa *n* a tropical shrub with ball-like clusters of yellow flowers and leaves sensitive to touch and light
WORD ORIGIN Latin *mimus* mime, because the plant's sensitivity to touch imitates the similar reaction of animals

min. 1 minimum **2** minute *or* minutes

Min. 1 Minister **2** Ministry

minaret *n* a slender tower of a mosque with one or more balconies
WORD ORIGIN Arabic *manārat* lamp

minatory *adj* threatening or menacing
WORD ORIGIN Latin *minari* to threaten

mince *vb* **mincing, minced 1** to chop, grind, or cut into very small pieces **2** to walk or speak in an affected dainty manner **3 not mince one's words** to be direct and to the point rather than making an effort to avoid upsetting people ▷ *n* **4** *chiefly Brit & NZ* minced meat **minced** *adj* **mincer** *n*
WORD ORIGIN Old French *mincier*, from Late Latin *minutia* smallness

mincemeat *n* **1** a mixture of dried fruit and spices used for filling pies **2 make mincemeat of** *informal* to defeat completely

mince pie *n* a small round pastry tart filled with mincemeat

mincing *adj* (of a person or their style of walking or speaking) affectedly elegant

mind *n* **1** the part of a person responsible for thought, feelings, and intention
▶ Related adjective: **mental**
2 intelligence as opposed to feelings or wishes **3** memory or recollection: *his name didn't spring to mind immediately* **4** a person considered as an intellectual being: *one of Europe's greatest minds* **5** the condition or state of a person's feelings or thoughts: *a confused state of mind* **6** an intention or desire: *I have a mind to go* **7** attention or thoughts: *keep your mind on the job* **8** a sound mental state; sanity: *he's out of his mind* **9 change one's mind** to alter one's decision or opinion **10 give someone a piece of one's mind** to scold someone severely **11 in two minds** undecided or wavering **12 make up one's mind** to reach a decision **13 on one's mind** in one's thoughts **14 to my mind** in my opinion ▷ *vb* **15** to take offence at: *do you mind if I open a window?* **16** to pay attention to: *to mind one's own business* **17** to make certain; ensure: *mind you tell him* **18** to take care of: *mind the shop* **19** to be cautious or careful about: *mind how you go* **20** *dialect* to remember ▶ See also **mind out**
WORD ORIGIN Old English *gemynd*

mind-boggling *adj* so large, complicated, or surprising that it causes surprise and shock: *mind-boggling wealth*

minded *adj* having a mind or inclination as specified: *commercially minded*

minder *n* **1** *slang* an aide or assistant, esp. one employed as a bodyguard or public relations officer for someone **2** short for **child minder**

mindful *adj* **mindful of** being aware of and taking into account: *the company is ever mindful of the need to find new markets*

mindless *adj* **1** stupid or careless **2** requiring little or no intellectual effort **3** heedless: *mindless of the risks involved* **mindlessly** *adv* **mindlessness** *n*

Mind Map *n trademark* a method of representing ideas in a diagram, with related concepts arranged around a core concept

mind out *vb* to be careful or pay attention

mind-reader *n* a person seemingly able to make out the thoughts of another

mind's eye *n* **in one's mind's eye** in one's imagination

mine[1] *pron* **1** something or someone belonging to or associated with me: *it's a great favourite of mine* **2 of mine** belonging to or associated with me ▷ *adj* **3** *archaic* same as **my**: *mine eyes; mine host*
WORD ORIGIN Old English *mīn*

mine[2] *n* **1** a place where minerals, esp. coal, ores, or precious stones, are dug from the ground **2** a type of bomb placed in water or under the ground, and designed to destroy ships, vehicles, or people passing over or near it **3** a profitable source or abundant supply: *a mine of information* ▷ *vb* **mining, mined 4** to dig minerals from the ground: *lead has been mined here for over three centuries* **5** to dig a hole or tunnel, esp. in order to obtain minerals **6** to place explosive mines in or on: *the retreating troops had mined the bridge*
WORD ORIGIN Old French

mine dump *n S African* a large mound of waste material from gold-mining operations

minefield *n* **1** an area of ground or water containing explosive mines **2** a subject or situation full of hidden problems

minelayer *n* a warship or aircraft for carrying and laying mines

miner *n* a person who works in a mine, esp. a coal mine

mineral *n* **1** a naturally occurring solid inorganic substance with a characteristic chemical composition and structure **2** any inorganic matter **3** any substance obtained by mining, esp. a metal ore **4** *Brit* a soft drink containing carbonated water and flavourings ▷ *adj* **5** of, containing,

or resembling minerals
WORD ORIGIN Medieval Latin *minera* mine, ore

mineralogy (min-er-**al**-a-jee) *n* the scientific study of minerals **mineralogical** *adj* **mineralogist** *n*

mineral water *n* water containing dissolved mineral salts or gases

Minerva *n* the Roman goddess of wisdom

minestrone (min-ness-**strone**-ee) *n* a soup made from a variety of vegetables and pasta
WORD ORIGIN Italian, from *minestrare* to serve

minesweeper *n* a naval vessel equipped to clear mines

Ming *adj* of or relating to Chinese porcelain from the time of the Ming dynasty, which ruled China from 1368 to 1644

minger *n* Brit informal unattractive person

minging *n* Brit informal unattractive or unpleasant

mingle *vb* -gling, -gled 1 to mix or blend 2 to associate or mix with a group of people: *the performers mingled with the audience after the show*
WORD ORIGIN Old English *mengan* to mix

mingy *adj* -gier, -giest Brit & NZ informal mean or miserly
WORD ORIGIN probably a blend of *mean* + *stingy*

mini *adj* 1 small; miniature 2 (of a skirt or dress) very short ▷ *n, pl* **minis** 3 something very small of its kind, esp. a miniskirt

mini- *combining form* smaller or shorter than the standard size: *minibus; miniseries*
WORD ORIGIN from *miniature* + *minimum*

miniature *n* 1 a model or representation on a very small scale 2 a very small painting, esp. a portrait 3 a very small bottle of whisky or other spirits, which can hold 50 millilitres 4 **in miniature** on a small scale ▷ *adj* 5 much smaller than usual; small-scale **miniaturist** *n*
WORD ORIGIN Medieval Latin *miniare* to paint red (in illuminating manuscripts), from *minium* red lead

miniaturize *or* -rise *vb* -rizing, -rized *or* -rising, -rised to make a very small version of something, esp. electronic components **miniaturization** *or* -risation *n*

minibus *n* a small bus

minicab *n* Brit an ordinary car used as a taxi

minicomputer *n* a small digital computer which is more powerful than a microcomputer

minidisc *n* a small recordable compact disc

minim *n* 1 a unit of fluid measure equal to one sixtieth of a drachm 2 *music* a note with the time value of half a semibreve
WORD ORIGIN Latin *minimus* smallest

minimal *adj* of the least possible quantity or degree

minimalism *n* 1 a type of music based on the repetition of simple elements 2 a design or style using the simplest

and fewest elements to create the maximum effect **minimalist** *adj, n*

minimize *or* -**mise** *vb* -mizing, -mized *or* -mising, -mised 1 to reduce to the lowest possible degree or amount: *these measures should help minimize our costs* 2 to regard or treat as less important than it really is; belittle: *I don't want to minimize the importance of her contribution*

minimum *n, pl* -mums *or* -ma 1 the least possible amount, degree, or quantity: *fry the burgers in the minimum of oil* 2 the least amount recorded, allowed, or reached: *soak the beans for a minimum of eight hours* ▷ *adj* 3 of, being, or showing a minimum or minimums: *the minimum age*
WORD ORIGIN Latin *minimus* least

minimum lending rate *n* (formerly) the minimum rate at which the Bank of England would lend money: replaced in 1981 by the base rate

minimum wage *n* the lowest wage that an employer is permitted to pay by law or union contract

mining *n* 1 the act, process, or industry of extracting coal or ores from the earth 2 *mil* the process of laying mines

minion *n* a servile assistant
WORD ORIGIN French *mignon* darling

miniseries *n, pl* -series a television programme in several parts that is shown on consecutive days over a short period

miniskirt *n* a very short skirt

minister *n* 1 (esp. in Presbyterian and some Nonconformist Churches) a member of the clergy 2 a head of a government department 3 a diplomat with a lower rank than an ambassador ▷ *vb* 4 **minister to** to attend to the needs of **ministerial** *adj*
WORD ORIGIN Latin: servant

minister of state *n* (in the British Parliament) a minister, usually below cabinet rank, appointed to assist a senior minister

Minister of the Crown *n* Brit any Government minister of cabinet rank

ministrations *pl n* the giving of help or service: *the ministrations of the chaplain*
WORD ORIGIN Latin *ministrare* to wait upon

ministry *n, pl* -tries 1 the profession or duties of a minister of religion 2 ministers considered as a group 3 a a government department headed by a minister b the buildings of such a department

mink *n, pl* mink *or* minks 1 a mammal of Europe, Asia, and North America, resembling a large stoat 2 its highly valued fur 3 a garment made of this, esp. a woman's coat or stole
WORD ORIGIN Scandinavian

minneola *n* a juicy citrus fruit that is a cross between a tangerine and a grapefruit

minnow *n, pl* -nows *or* -now a small slender European freshwater fish
WORD ORIGIN Old English *myne*

Minoan (min-**no**-an) *adj* of or denoting the Bronze Age culture of Crete from about 3000 BC to about 1100 BC
WORD ORIGIN *Minos*, in Greek mythology, king of Crete

minor *adj* 1 lesser or secondary in size, frequency, or importance than others of the same kind: *a minor poet* 2 not very serious or significant: *minor injuries* 3 *music* a (of a scale) having a semitone between the second and third and fifth and sixth notes (**natural minor**) b of or based on the minor scale: *his quintet in C minor; a minor third* ▷ *n* 4 a person below the age of legal majority 5 *US, Canad, & Austral education* a subsidiary subject 6 *music* a minor key, chord, mode, or scale ▷ *vb* 7 **minor in** *US education* to study as a subsidiary subject: *to minor in politics*
WORD ORIGIN Latin: less, smaller

minority *n, pl* -ties 1 the smaller of two parts, factions, or groups 2 a group that is different, racially or politically, from a larger group of which it is a part 3 **in the minority** forming or part of the group of people or things made up of less than half of a larger group ▷ *adj* 4 relating to or being a minority: *a minority sport*

Minotaur *n* Greek myth a monster with the head of a bull and the body of a man
WORD ORIGIN Greek *Minōtauros*

minster *n* Brit any of certain cathedrals and large churches, usually originally connected to a monastery
WORD ORIGIN Church Latin *monasterium* monastery

minstrel *n* 1 a medieval singer and musician 2 a performer in a minstrel show
WORD ORIGIN Old French *menestral*

minstrel show *n* a theatrical entertainment consisting of songs and dances performed by actors wearing black face make-up

mint¹ *n* 1 any of various plants with aromatic leaves used for seasoning and flavouring 2 a sweet flavoured with mint **minty** *adj*
WORD ORIGIN Greek *minthē*

mint² *n* 1 a factory where the official coins of a country are made 2 a very large amount of money ▷ *adj* 3 **in mint condition** in perfect condition; as if new ▷ *vb* 4 to make coins by stamping metal 5 to invent or create: *no-one knows who first minted the term 'yuppie'*
WORD ORIGIN Latin *moneta* money, mint

minuet (min-new-**wet**) *n* 1 a stately court dance of the 17th and 18th centuries in triple time 2 music for this dance
WORD ORIGIN French *menuet* dainty

minus *prep* 1 reduced by the subtraction of: *six minus two equals four* 2 informal without or lacking: *he returned minus his jacket* ▷ *adj* 3 indicating or involving subtraction: *a minus sign* 4 Also: **negative** less than zero: *it's minus eight degrees in Montreal today* 5 *education* slightly below the standard of a particular grade: *a C minus for maths* ▷ *n* 6 short for **minus sign** 7 a negative quantity 8 *informal* something detrimental or negative
WORD ORIGIN Latin, neuter of *minor* less

minuscule (**min**-niss-skyool) *adj* very small
WORD ORIGIN Latin *(littera) minuscula* very small (letter)

m

minus sign *n* the symbol –, indicating subtraction, a negative quantity, or a negative electrical charge

minute¹ *n* **1** 60 seconds; one sixtieth of an hour **2** any very short period of time; moment: *I'll be with you in a minute* **3** the distance that can be travelled in a minute: *it's about ten minutes away* **4** a measure of angle equal to one sixtieth of a degree **5** up to the minute the very latest or newest ▷ *vb* **-nuting**, **-nuted 6** to record in minutes: *the decision was minuted in 1990* ► See also **minutes**
WORD ORIGIN Medieval Latin *minuta*, noun use of Latin *minutus* minute (small)

minute² *adj* **1** very small; tiny **2** precise or detailed: *a minute examination* **minutely** *adv*
WORD ORIGIN Latin *minutus*, past participle of *minuere* to diminish

minutes *pl n* an official record of the proceedings of a meeting or conference

minute steak *n* a small piece of steak that can be cooked quickly

minutiae (my-**new**-shee-eye) *pl n*, *sing* **-tia** trifling or precise details
WORD ORIGIN Late Latin, plural of *minutia* smallness

minx *n* a bold or flirtatious girl
WORD ORIGIN origin unknown

Miocene (**my**-oh-seen) *adj geol* of the epoch of geological time about 25 million years ago
WORD ORIGIN Greek *meiōn* less + *kainos* new

miracle *n* **1** an event contrary to the laws of nature and attributed to a supernatural cause **2** any amazing and fortunate event: *it's a miracle that no-one was killed in the accident* **3** a marvellous example of something: *a miracle of organization*
WORD ORIGIN Latin *mirari* to wonder at

miracle play *n* a medieval play based on a biblical story or the life of a saint

miraculous *adj* **1** like a miracle **2** surprising or remarkable

mirage (mir-**rahzh**) *n* **1** an image of a distant object or sheet of water, often inverted or distorted, caused by atmospheric refraction by hot air **2** something illusory: *the mirage of economic recovery*
WORD ORIGIN French, from (*se*) *mirer* to be reflected

mire *n* **1** a boggy or marshy area **2** mud, muck, or dirt **3** an unpleasant or difficult situation that is difficult to get out of: *the country sank deeper into the economic mire* ▷ *vb* **miring, mired 4** to sink or be stuck in a mire: *the company has been mired in financial scandal*
WORD ORIGIN Old Norse *mȳrr*

mirror *n* **1** a sheet of glass with a metal coating on its back, that reflects an image of an object placed in front of it **2** a thing that reflects or depicts something else ▷ *vb* **3** to reflect or represent faithfully: *the book inevitably mirrors my own interests*
WORD ORIGIN Latin *mirari* to wonder at

mirror ball *n* a large revolving ball covered with small pieces of mirror glass so that it reflects light in changing patterns: used in discos and ballrooms

mirror image *n* an image or object that has left and right reversed as if seen in a mirror

mirth *n* laughter, gaiety, or merriment **mirthful** *adj* **mirthless** *adj*
WORD ORIGIN Old English *myrgth*

MIRV multiple independently targeted re-entry vehicle: a missile that has several warheads, each one being aimed at a different target

mis- *prefix* **1** wrong or bad; wrongly or badly: *misunderstanding; mislead* **2** lack of; not: *mistrust*
WORD ORIGIN Old English *mis(se)*-

misadventure *n* **1** an unlucky event; misfortune **2** *law* accidental death not due to crime or negligence

misaligned *adj* not properly aligned; out of true **misalignment** *n*

misalliance *n* an unsuitable alliance or marriage

misanthrope (**miz**-zan-thrope) *or* **misanthropist** (miz-**zan**-throp-ist) *n* a person who dislikes or distrusts people in general **misanthropic** (miz-zan-**throp**-ik) *adj* **misanthropy** (miz-**zan**-throp-ee) *n*
WORD ORIGIN Greek *misos* hatred + *anthrōpos* man

misapply *vb* **-plies, -plying, -plied** to use something for a purpose for which it is not intended or is not suited **misapplication** *n*

misapprehend *vb* to misunderstand **misapprehension** *n*

misappropriate *vb* **-ating, -ated** to take and use money dishonestly **misappropriation** *n*

misbegotten *adj* **1** planned or designed badly or with dishonourable motives or aims **2** *literary or dialect* illegitimate; bastard

misbehave *vb* **-having, -haved** to behave badly **misbehaviour** *or US* **misbehavior** *n*

miscalculate *vb* **-lating, -lated** to calculate or judge wrongly: *we miscalculated the strength of the opposition* **miscalculation** *n*

miscall *vb* to call by the wrong name

miscarriage *n* **1** spontaneous premature expulsion of a fetus from the womb, esp. before the 20th week of pregnancy **2** an act of mismanagement or failure: *a miscarriage of justice*

miscarry *vb* **-ries, -rying, -ried 1** to expel a fetus prematurely from the womb **2** to fail

miscast *vb* **-casting, -cast** to cast a role or an actor in a play or film inappropriately: *the role of the avaricious boss was miscast; she was miscast as Cassandra*

miscegenation (miss-ij-in-**nay**-shun) *n* interbreeding of races, esp. where differences of colour are involved
WORD ORIGIN Latin *miscere* to mingle + *genus* race

miscellaneous (miss-sel-**lane**-ee-uss) *adj* composed of or containing a variety of things; mixed or assorted
WORD ORIGIN Latin *miscere* to mix

miscellany (miss-**sell**-a-nee) *n, pl* **-nies** a mixed assortment of items

mischance *n* **1** bad luck **2** an unlucky event or accident

mischief *n* **1** annoying but not malicious behaviour that causes trouble or irritation **2** an inclination to tease **3** injury or harm caused by a person or thing
WORD ORIGIN Old French *meschief*, from *mes-* mis- + *chef* end

mischief-maker *n* someone who deliberately causes trouble **mischief-making** *n*

mischievous (**miss**-chiv-uss) *adj* **1** full of mischief **2** teasing; slightly malicious **3** intended to cause harm: *a purveyor of mischievous disinformation* **mischievously** *adv*

miscible (**miss**-sib-bl) *adj* able to be mixed: *miscible with water* **miscibility** *n*
WORD ORIGIN Latin *miscere* to mix

misconceived *adj* false, mistaken, or badly thought-out: *a misconceived conception of loyalty*

misconception *n* a false or mistaken view, idea, or belief

misconduct *n* behaviour, such as adultery or professional negligence, that is regarded as immoral or unethical

misconstrue *vb* **-struing, -strued** to interpret mistakenly **misconstruction** *n*

miscreant (**miss**-kree-ant) *n* a wrongdoer or villain
WORD ORIGIN Old French *mescreant* unbelieving

misdeal *vb* **-dealing, -dealt 1** to deal out cards incorrectly ▷ *n* **2** a faulty deal

misdeed *n* an evil or illegal action

misdemeanour *or US* **misdemeanor** *n* **1** a minor wrongdoing **2** *criminal law* (formerly) an offence less serious than a felony

misdirect *vb* to give someone wrong directions or instructions **misdirection** *n*

mise en scène (**meez** on **sane**) *n* **1** the stage setting and scenery in a play **2** the environment of an event
WORD ORIGIN French

miser *n* a person who hoards money and hates spending it: *I'm married to a miser* **miserly** *adj*
WORD ORIGIN Latin: wretched

miserable *adj* **1** unhappy or depressed; wretched **2** causing misery or discomfort: *a miserable existence* **3** sordid or squalid: *miserable living conditions* **4** mean or ungenerous: *a miserable pension* **miserableness** *n* **miserably** *adv*
WORD ORIGIN Latin *miserabilis*

misericord *n* a ledge projecting from the underside of the hinged seat of a choir stall in a church, which the occupant can rest against while standing
WORD ORIGIN Latin *miserere* to pity + *cor* heart

misery *n, pl* **-eries 1** intense unhappiness or suffering **2** something which causes such unhappiness **3** squalid or poverty-stricken conditions **4** *Brit informal* a person who is habitually depressed: *he is such a misery*
WORD ORIGIN Latin *miser* wretched

m

The Use of 'Eh'

I n formal English, the focus is often on long words. However, in terms of sheer frequency, short words dominate English usage. *The* and *a* are actually the most commonly used words in English, owing to the grammar of the language (it's nearly impossible to refer to anything without either the definite or the indefinite article). Then of course we have prepositions like *of*, *to*, and *by*, conjunctions like *and*, *but*, and *not*, the positive and negative responses *yes* and *no*, and even some verbs like *do* and *be*.

However, the most overlooked short words are the ones that are hardly considered words at all: interjections like *um*, *uh*, *huh*, and of course *eh*. Most people would not consider these 'sounds' part of English at all, and may even be shocked to find them defined in a dictionary (if they ever thought to look them up). And yet they do carry meaning. *Um* and *uh* (or *er* in Britain) are the traditional sounds of hesitation, made when the speaker doesn't know the answer to something or quite what to say (*um* is slightly more deliberate, as it includes a consonant sound; *uh*, which is just a vowel, is more, a pure ploy to gain time to get one's thoughts together). *Huh* is, of course, the utterance of bewilderment or inquiry, as when one receives surprising news or didn't quite hear what the other person has said. But perhaps most important of all, at least in Canada, is the word *eh*.

For such a tiny word, the use of *eh*, an interjection, plays a disproportionate role in identifying the Canadian national character. *Eh* is widely used in speech in other English-speaking countries, though more commonly in the United Kingdom than in the United States. Though sometimes its use elicits agreement with the speaker, especially about something obvious (*It's a hot day, eh?*), typically it requests that something be repeated or explained (*Eh? What's that you say?*).

What's been taken as a tic of Canadian speech, however, is the use of *eh* not just to elicit agreement, but to confirm the continuing comprehension or interest of a listener. Such a use can become ludicrous when the word is parachuted almost anywhere into a sentence. (*I'm broke, eh, so I can hardly pay her back, eh?*) In some regards it thus resembles the interjectional use among Canadians and many other English-speakers of another versatile little word, *right*. Like *eh*, *right* may indicate agreement or acknowledgement. However, the most striking parallel with *eh* is as a filler word to confirm that a listener is paying attention to what is being said. In the sentence *I didn't think of it at the time, right, but it was pretty obvious*, a Canadian could easily replace *right* with *eh*.

Americans often use *eh* for the purpose of parodying Canadians, as do Canadians themselves. A sketch contrived by the Canadian actors and comedians Rick Moranis and Dave Thomas exploits several stereotypes. They play the fictive brothers Bob and Doug McKenzie, who are beer-swilling, toque-wearing bumpkins or *hosers* (to cite another Canadianism). The brothers help illustrate that, in the Canadian context, *eh* is a class marker, since it is seldom used by the highly educated, except occasionally for comic effect. At the same time, the brothers' reflexive use of *eh* implies something about how Canadians think of themselves. The compulsive need to repeatedly confirm that a listener understands and closely follows a statement suggests that the speaker, usually male, cannot be sure that he will be believed. This in turn points to the perennial doubts many Canadians have had about the status and authenticity of their own national identity, and the right or power they possess to speak for themselves, especially compared to citizens of the United States. The peculiar use of *eh* thus asserts an excessive diffidence or modesty yet, by its very use, provides a way for the Canadian to distinguish himself from another English-speaker.

It's been suggested that the use of *eh* in Canadian popular speech has declined in recent decades, though only a comparative survey could determine whether this is the case. Even if Canadians no longer use *eh* as much as they used to as an all-purpose interrogative-affirmative-confirmative, the word at least lives on as a potent stereotype or shibboleth.

misfire vb **-firing, -fired 1** (of a firearm) to fail to fire as expected **2** (of a motor engine or vehicle) to fail to fire at the appropriate time **3** to fail to have the intended result; go wrong: *he was injured when a practical joke misfired* ▷ n **4** the act or an instance of misfiring

misfit n a person who is not suited to the role, social group, etc. he or she finds himself or herself in

misfortune n **1** bad luck **2** an unfortunate event

misgivings pl n feelings of uncertainty, fear, or doubt

misgovern vb to govern badly **misgovernment** n

misguided adj mistaken or unwise

mishandle vb **-dling, -dled** to handle or treat badly or inefficiently

mishap n a minor accident

mishear vb **-hearing, -heard** to fail to hear what someone says correctly

mishit sport n **1** a faulty shot, kick, or stroke ▷ vb **-hitting, -hit 2** to hit or kick a ball with a faulty stroke

mishmash n a confused collection or mixture **WORD ORIGIN** reduplication of *mash*

misinform vb to give incorrect information to **misinformation** n

misinterpret vb to understand or represent something wrongly: *the press misinterpreted the President's remarks* **misinterpretation** n

misjudge vb **-judging, -judged** to judge wrongly or unfairly **misjudgment** or **misjudgement** n

mislay vb **-lays, -laying, -laid** to lose something temporarily, esp. by forgetting where it is

mislead vb **-leading, -led** to give false or confusing information to

misleading adj giving a false or confusing impression: *misleading use of statistical data*

mismanage vb **-naging, -naged** to organize or run something badly **mismanagement** n

mismatch vb **1** to form an unsuitable partner, opponent, or set ▷ n **2** an unsuitable match **mismatched** adj

misnamed adj having an inappropriate or misleading name: *the grotesquely misnamed Freedom Party*

misnomer (miss-**no**-mer) n **1** an incorrect or unsuitable name for a person or thing **2** the use of the wrong name **WORD ORIGIN** Old French *mesnommer* to misname

misogyny (miss-**oj**-in-ee) n hatred of women **misogynist** n **misogynous** adj **WORD ORIGIN** Greek *misos* hatred + *gunē* woman

misplace vb **-placing, -placed 1** to lose something temporarily by forgetting where it was placed **2** to put something in the wrong place

misplaced adj **1** (of an emotion or action) directed towards a person or thing that does not deserve it: *misplaced optimism* **2** put in the wrong place: *a scrappy game dominated by misplaced kicking*

misprint n **1** an error in printing ▷ vb **2** to print a letter incorrectly

misprision n law the concealment of the commission of a felony or an act of treason **WORD ORIGIN** Old French *mesprision* error

mispronounce vb **-nouncing, -nounced** to pronounce a word or name wrongly **mispronunciation** n

misquote vb **-quoting, -quoted** to quote inaccurately **misquotation** n

misread vb **-reading, -read 1** to misinterpret or misunderstand: *he misread her politeness as approval* **2** to read incorrectly

misrepresent vb to represent wrongly or inaccurately **misrepresentation** n

misrule vb **-ruling, -ruled 1** to govern inefficiently or without justice ▷ n **2** inefficient or unjust government **3** disorder or lawlessness

miss¹ vb **1** to fail to notice, see, or hear: *it's right at the top of the hill, so you can't miss it; I missed what he said because I was talking at the time* **2** to fail to hit something aimed at: *he threw a stone at the dog but missed* **3** to fail to achieve or reach: *they narrowly missed promotion last season* **4** to fail to take advantage of: *he never missed a chance to make money* **5** to fail or be unable to be present: *he had missed the last three meetings* **6** to be too late for: *we missed the bus and had to walk* **7** to discover or regret the loss or absence of: *the boys miss their father when he's away on business* **8** to escape or avoid narrowly: *it missed the helicopter's rotors by inches* ▷ n **9** a failure to hit, reach, etc.: *an easy miss in the second frame gave his opponent the advantage* **10** give something a miss to decide not to do, go to, or take part in something: *I'll give the pub a miss and have a quiet night in* ▶ See also **miss out** **WORD ORIGIN** Old English *missan*

miss² n informal an unmarried woman or girl **WORD ORIGIN** from *mistress*

Miss n a title of a girl or unmarried woman, usually used before the surname: *Miss Brown to you*

missal n RC Church a book containing the prayers and rites of the Masses for a complete year **WORD ORIGIN** Church Latin *missale*, from *missa* Mass

misshapen adj badly shaped; deformed

missile n **1** a rocket with an exploding warhead, used as a weapon **2** an object or weapon that is thrown, launched, or fired at a target **WORD ORIGIN** Latin *mittere* to send

missing adj **1** not in its proper or usual place and unable to be found **2** not able to be traced and not known to be dead: *seven men were reported missing after the raid* **3** not included in something although it perhaps should have been: *two things are missing from the report*

missing link n **1** any missing section or part in a series **2** the missing link a hypothetical extinct animal, formerly thought to be intermediate between the apes and man

mission n **1** a specific task or duty assigned to a person or group of people **2** a task or duty that a person believes

he or she must achieve; vocation: *he felt it was his mission to pass on his knowledge to other people* **3** a group of people representing or working for a particular country or organization in a foreign country: *the UN peacekeeping mission* **4** a group of people sent by a church to a foreign country to do religious and social work **5** the place in which a church or government mission is based **6** the dispatch of aircraft or spacecraft to achieve a particular task **7** a charitable centre that offers shelter or aid to the poor or needy **8** S African a long and difficult process **WORD ORIGIN** Latin *mittere* to send

missionary n, pl **-naries 1** a person sent abroad by a church to do religious and social work ▷ adj **2** of or relating to missionaries: *missionary work* **3** resulting from a desire to convert people to one's own beliefs: *missionary zeal*

mission statement n an official statement of the aims and objectives of a business or other organization

missive n a formal or official letter **WORD ORIGIN** Latin *mittere* to send

miss out vb **1** to leave out or overlook **2** miss out on to fail to take part in (something enjoyable or beneficial): *she'd missed out on going to university*

misspell vb **-spelling, -spelt** or **-spelled** to spell a word wrongly **misspelling** n

misspend vb **-spending, -spent** to waste or spend unwisely **misspent** adj

missus or **missis** n **1** Brit, Austral, & NZ informal one's wife or the wife of the person addressed or referred to: *the missus is a fabulous cook* **2** an informal term of address for a woman **WORD ORIGIN** spoken version of *mistress*

missy n, pl **missies** informal an affectionate or disparaging form of address to a girl

mist n **1** a thin fog **2** a fine spray of liquid, such as that produced by an aerosol container **3** condensed water vapour on a surface **4** something that causes haziness or lack of clarity, such as a film of tears ▷ vb **5** to cover or be covered with mist: *the windscreen has misted up again; his eyes misted over and he shook with rage* **misty** adj **mistiness** n **WORD ORIGIN** Old English

mistake n **1** an error or blunder **2** a misconception or misunderstanding ▷ vb **-taking, -took, -taken 3** to misunderstand or misinterpret: *the chaplain quite mistook her meaning* **4** to confuse a person or thing with another: *they saw the HMS Sheffield and mistook her for the Bismarck* **5** to choose badly or incorrectly: *he mistook his path* **WORD ORIGIN** Old Norse *mistaka* to take erroneously

mistaken adj **1** wrong in opinion or judgment **2** arising from error in opinion or judgment: *a mistaken viewpoint*

mister n an informal form of address for a man **WORD ORIGIN** variant of *master*

Mister n the full form of **Mr**

mistime vb **-timing, -timed** to do or say at the wrong time

mistle thrush or **missel thrush** n a large European thrush with a brown

back and spotted breast
WORD ORIGIN Old English *mistel* mistletoe

mistletoe *n* a Eurasian evergreen shrub with waxy white berries, which grows as a parasite on various trees
WORD ORIGIN Old English *misteltān*, from *mistel* mistletoe + *tān* twig

mistook *vb* the past tense of **mistake**

mistral *n* a strong cold dry northerly wind of S France
WORD ORIGIN Provençal, from Latin *magistralis* masterful

mistreat *vb* to treat badly **mistreatment** *n*

mistress *n* **1** a woman who has a continuing sexual relationship with a man who is usually married to somebody else **2** a woman in a position of authority, ownership, or control **3** a woman having control over something specified: *she is a mistress of disguise* **4** *chiefly Brit* a female teacher
WORD ORIGIN Old French *maistresse*

mistrial *n* *law* a trial which is invalid because of some error

mistrust *vb* **1** to have doubts or suspicions about ▷ *n* **2** lack of trust **mistrustful** *adj* **mistrustfully** *adv*

misunderstand *vb* **-standing, -stood** to fail to understand properly

misunderstanding *n* **1** a failure to understand properly **2** a disagreement

misunderstood *adj* not properly or sympathetically understood: *a misunderstood adolescent*

misuse *n* **1** incorrect, improper, or careless use: *misuse of drugs* **2** cruel or inhumane treatment ▷ *vb* **-using, -used 3** to use wrongly **4** to treat badly or harshly

mite¹ *n* any of numerous very small creatures of the spider family, some of which live as parasites
WORD ORIGIN Old English *mīte*

mite² *n* **1** a very small creature or thing **2** a very small sum of money **3 a mite** *informal* somewhat: *the main course was a mite bland*
WORD ORIGIN Middle Dutch *mīte*

mitigate *vb* **-gating, -gated** to make less severe or harsh **mitigating** *adj* **mitigation** *n*
WORD ORIGIN Latin *mitis* mild + *agere* to make

≣ **USAGE**
≣ *Mitigate* is sometimes wrongly used
≣ where *militate* is meant: *his behaviour*
≣ *militates* (not *mitigates*) *against his chances*
≣ *of promotion.*

mitochondrion *n, pl* **-dria** *biol* a small spherical or rodlike body found in the cytoplasm of most cells
WORD ORIGIN Greek *mitos* thread + *khondrion* grain

mitosis *n* a type of cell division in which the nucleus divides into two nuclei each containing the same number of chromosomes as the parent nucleus
WORD ORIGIN Greek *mitos* thread

mitre *or US* **miter** (**my**-ter) *n* **1** *Christianity* the headdress of a bishop or abbot, consisting of a tall pointed cleft cap **2** Also: **mitre joint** a corner joint formed by cutting bevels of equal angles at the ends of each piece of material ▷ *vb* **-tring, -tred** *or* **-tering, -tered 3** to join with a mitre joint
WORD ORIGIN Greek *mitra* turban

mitt *n* **1** a glovelike hand covering that does not cover the fingers **2** short for **mitten 3** *slang* a hand **4** a baseball glove
WORD ORIGIN from *mitten*

mitten *n* a glove with one section for the thumb and a single section for the fingers
WORD ORIGIN Old French *mitaine*

mix *vb* **1** to combine or blend into one mass or substance: *mix the water, yeast, and flour into a smooth dough* **2** to be able to combine into one substance: *oil and water do not mix* **3** to form by combining different substances: *to mix cement* **4** to do at the same time: *to mix business and pleasure* **5** to be outgoing in social situations: *he mixed well* **6** *music* to balance and adjust individual performers' parts to make an overall sound by electronic means ▷ *n* **7** something produced by mixing; mixture **8** a mixture of ingredients, esp. one commercially prepared for making a cake **9** *music* the sound produced by mixing ▸ See also **mix-up** > **mixed** *adj*
WORD ORIGIN Latin *miscere*

mixed bag *n* *informal* something made up of different elements, characteristics, or people

mixed blessing *n* an event or situation with both advantages and disadvantages

mixed doubles *pl n* *tennis, badminton* a doubles game with a man and a woman as partners on each side

mixed economy *n* an economy in which some companies are privately owned and others are owned by the government

mixed farming *n* farming involving both the growing of crops and the keeping of livestock **mixed farm** *n*

mixed grill *n* a dish of several kinds of grilled meat, tomatoes, and mushrooms

mixed marriage *n* a marriage between people of different races or religions

mixed metaphor *n* a combination of incongruous metaphors, such as *when the Nazi jackboots sing their swan song*

mixed-up *adj* in a state of mental confusion

mixer *n* **1** a kitchen appliance, usually electrical, used for mixing foods **2** any of various other devices or machines used for mixing things: *a cement mixer* **3** a nonalcoholic drink such as tonic water or ginger ale that is mixed with an alcoholic drink **4** *informal* a person considered in relation to his or her ability to mix socially: *he's not a good mixer*

mixture *n* **1** something produced by blending or combining other things: *top with the cheese and breadcrumb mixture* **2** a combination of different things, such as feelings: *he speaks of her with a mixture of loyalty and regret* **3** *chem* a substance consisting of two or more substances mixed together without any chemical bonding between them

mix-up *n* **1** a confused condition or situation ▷ *vb* **mix up 2** to make into a mixture **3** to confuse: *he mixes Ryan up with Lee* **4 mixed up in** involved in (an activity or group, esp. one that is illegal): *she's mixed up in a drugs racket*

mizzenmast *n* *naut* (on a vessel with three or more masts) the third mast from the bow
WORD ORIGIN Italian *mezzano* middle + MAST

MJ megajoule

Mk (in trade names) mark

mks units *pl n* a metric system of units based on the metre, kilogram, and second: it forms the basis of the SI units

ml 1 millilitre(s) **2** mile(s)

ML Medieval Latin

MLitt Master of Letters
WORD ORIGIN Latin *Magister Litterarum*

Mlle *or* **Mlle.** *pl* **Mlles** *or* **Mlles.** the French equivalent of *Miss*
WORD ORIGIN from *Mademoiselle*

MLR minimum lending rate

mm millimetre(s)

Mme *pl* **Mmes** the French equivalent of *Mrs*
WORD ORIGIN from *Madame, Mesdames*

MMORPG (**more**-peg) massive(ly) multi-player online role-playing game: an internet-based computer game set in a virtual world, where many people can play at the same time and interact with each other

MMR a combined vaccine against measles, mumps, and rubella, given to very young children

MMus Master of Music

Mn *chem* manganese

MN Minnesota

mnemonic (nim-**on**-ik) *n* **1** something, for instance a verse, intended to help the memory ▷ *adj* **2** aiding or meant to aid one's memory **mnemonically** *adv*
WORD ORIGIN Greek *mnēmōn* mindful

mo *n* *informal chiefly Brit* short for **moment** (sense 1)

Mo *chem* molybdenum

MO 1 Medical Officer **2** Missouri

m.o. *or* **MO 1** mail order **2** money order

moa *n* a recently extinct large flightless bird of New Zealand that resembled the ostrich
WORD ORIGIN Māori

moan *n* **1** a low prolonged cry of pain or suffering **2** any similar sound, esp. that made by the wind **3** *informal* a grumble or complaint ▷ *vb* **4** to make a low cry of, or talk in a way suggesting, pain or suffering: *he moaned in pain* **5** to make a sound like a moan: *the wind moaned through the trees* **6** *informal* to grumble or complain **moaner** *n*
WORD ORIGIN Old English *mǣnan* to grieve over

moat *n* a wide ditch, originally filled with water, surrounding a fortified place such as a castle
WORD ORIGIN Old French *motte* mound

mob *n* **1** a riotous or disorderly crowd of people **2** *informal* any group of people **3** the masses **4** *slang* a gang of criminals ▷ *vb* **mobbing, mobbed 5** to attack in a group resembling a mob

6 to surround in a crowd to acclaim or attack: *she was mobbed by her fans when she left the theatre* **WORD ORIGIN** shortened from Latin *mobile vulgus* the fickle populace

mobcap *n* a woman's 18th-century cotton cap with a pouched crown **WORD ORIGIN** obsolete *mob* woman, esp. loose-living + CAP

mobile *adj* **1** able to move or be moved: *mobile toilets* **2** changing quickly in expression: *a mobile face* **3** *sociol* (of individuals or social groups) moving within and between classes, occupations, and localities ▷ *n* **4** a light structure suspended in midair with delicately balanced parts that are set in motion by air currents **5** short for **mobile phone** > **mobility** *n* **WORD ORIGIN** Latin *mobilis*

mobile home *n* a large caravan, usually staying in one place, which people live in permanently

mobile phone *n* a portable telephone powered by batteries

mobilize *or* **-lise** *vb* **-lizing, -lized** *or* **-lising, -lised** **1** to prepare for war or another emergency by organizing resources and the armed services **2** to organize for a purpose: *we must mobilize local residents behind our campaign* **mobilization** *or* **-lisation** *n*

mobster *n US* a member of a criminal organization; gangster

moccasin *n* **1** a type of soft leather shoe traditionally worn by some Native American peoples **2** a soft leather shoe with a raised seam at the front above the toe **WORD ORIGIN** American Indian

mocha (**mock**-a) *n* **1** a dark brown coffee originally imported from the port of Mocha in Arabia **2** a flavouring made from coffee and chocolate

mock *vb* **1** to behave with scorn or contempt towards a person or thing: *her husband mocked her attempts to educate herself* **2** to imitate or mimic, esp. in fun **3** to defy or frustrate: *the team mocked the visitors' attempts to score* ▷ *n* **4 mocks** *informal* (in England and Wales) school examinations taken as practice before public exams ▷ *adj* **5** sham or imitation: *mock Georgian windows* **6** serving as an imitation or substitute, esp. for practice purposes: *a mock battle* ▶ See also **mock-up** > **mocking** *n, adj* **WORD ORIGIN** Old French *mocquer*

mockers *pl n* **put the mockers on** Brit, Austral, & NZ *informal* to ruin the chances of success of **WORD ORIGIN** perhaps from *mock*

mockery *n, pl* **-eries** **1** ridicule, contempt, or derision **2** a person, thing, or action that is so worthless that it seems like a parody: *the interview was a mockery from start to finish* **3 make a mockery of something** to make something appear worthless or foolish: *the judge's decision makes a mockery of the law*

mock-heroic *adj* (of a literary work, esp. a poem) imitating the style of heroic poetry in order to satirize an unheroic subject

mockingbird *n* an American songbird which can mimic the song of other birds

mock orange *n* a shrub with white fragrant flowers like those of the orange

mock turtle soup *n* an imitation turtle soup made from a calf's head

mock-up *n* a working full-scale model of a machine or apparatus for test or research purposes

mod[1] *n Brit* a member of a group of teenagers, originally in the mid-1960s, who were very clothes-conscious and rode motor scooters **WORD ORIGIN** from *modernist*

mod[2] *n* an annual Highland Gaelic meeting with musical and literary competitions **WORD ORIGIN** Gaelic *mòd* assembly

MOD (in Britain) Ministry of Defence

mod. **1** moderate **2** modern

modal (**mode**-al) *adj* **1** of or relating to mode or manner **2** *grammar* (of a verb form or auxiliary verb) expressing possibility, intention, or necessity rather than actuality: 'can', 'might', and 'will' are examples of modal verbs in English **3** *music* of or relating to a mode **modality** *n*

mod cons *pl n informal* modern conveniences, such as hot water and heating

mode *n* **1** a manner or way of doing, acting, or existing **2** a particular fashion or style **3** *music* any of the various scales of notes within one octave **4** *maths* the most frequently occurring of a range of values **WORD ORIGIN** Latin *modus* manner

model *n* **1** a three-dimensional representation, usually on a smaller scale, of a device or structure: *an architect's model of the proposed new housing estate* **2** an example or pattern that people might want to follow: *her success makes her an excellent role model for other young Black women* **3** an outstanding example of its kind: *the report is a model of clarity* **4** a person who poses for a sculptor, painter, or photographer **5** a person who wears clothes to display them to prospective buyers; mannequin **6** a design or style of a particular product: *the cheapest model of this car has a 1300cc engine* **7** a theoretical description of the way a system or process works: *a working model of the human immune system* ▷ *adj* **8** excellent or perfect: *a model husband* **9** being a small-scale representation of: *a model aeroplane* ▷ *vb* **-elling, -elled** *or US* **-eling, -eled** **10** to make a model of: *he modelled a plane out of balsa wood* **11** to plan or create according to a model or models: *it had a constitution modelled on that of the United States* **12** to display (clothing and accessories) as a mannequin **13** to pose for a sculptor, painter, or photographer **WORD ORIGIN** Latin *modulus*, diminutive of *modus* mode

modem (**mode**-em) *n computers* a device for transmitting information between two computers by a telephone line, consisting of a modulator that converts computer signals into audio signals and a corresponding demodulator **WORD ORIGIN** from *mo(dulator)* *dem(odulator)*

moderate *adj* **1** not extreme or excessive: *a man of moderate views; moderate consumption of alcohol* **2** (of a size, rate, intensity, etc.) towards the middle of the range of possible values: *a moderate-sized garden; a moderate breeze* **3** of average quality or extent: *moderate success* ▷ *n* **4** a person who holds moderate views, esp. in politics ▷ *vb* **-rating, -rated** **5** to make or become less extreme or violent: *he has moderated his opinions since then* **6** to preside over a meeting, discussion, etc. **moderately** *adv* **WORD ORIGIN** Latin *moderari* to restrain

moderation *n* **1** the quality of being moderate **2** the act of moderating **3 in moderation** within moderate or reasonable limits

moderato (mod-er-**ah**-toe) *adv music* **1** at a moderate speed **2** with restraint: *allegro moderato* **WORD ORIGIN** Italian

moderator *n* **1** *Presbyterian Church* a minister appointed to preside over a Church court, synod, or general assembly **2** a person who presides over a public or legislative assembly **3** a material, such as heavy water, used for slowing down neutrons in nuclear reactors

modern *adj* **1** of the present or a recent time; contemporary: *there have been very few outbreaks of the disease in modern times* **2** using the latest techniques, equipment, etc.; up-to-date: *modern and efficient railways* **3** of contemporary styles or schools of art, literature, and music, esp. those of an experimental kind ▷ *n* **4** a contemporary person **modernity** *n* **WORD ORIGIN** Late Latin *modernus*, from *modus* mode

Modern English *n* the English language since about 1450

modernism *n* an early- and mid-twentieth century movement in art, literature, and music that rejected traditional styles and techniques **modernist** *n, adj*

modernize *or* **-nise** *vb* **-nizing, -nized** *or* **-nising, -nised** **1** to make modern in style, methods, or equipment: *a commitment to modernizing industry* **2** to adopt modern ways or ideas **modernization** *or* **-nisation** *n*

modern languages *n* the languages spoken in present-day Europe, with the exception of English

modern pentathlon *n* an athletic contest consisting of five different events: horse riding with jumps, fencing with electric épée, freestyle swimming, pistol shooting, and cross-country running

modest *adj* **1** having a humble opinion of oneself or one's accomplishments **2** not extreme or excessive: *a modest increase in inflation* **3** not ostentatious or pretentious: *a modest flat in the suburbs* **4** shy or easily embarrassed **5** old-fashioned (esp. of clothes) not revealing much of the body: *a modest dress* **modestly** *adv* **modesty** *n* **WORD ORIGIN** Latin *modestus* moderate

Walt Whitman – Father of American Poetry

I n 1844 the philosopher Ralph Waldo Emerson published an essay entitled 'The Poet', in which he called for the emergence of a uniquely American poet to sing about life in the emerging nation that was and is the United States. Walt Whitman answered that call.

Whitman was born in Huntington, Long Island, New York, in 1819. His earliest literary offerings showed little promise of his future greatness, and until he began work on *Leaves of Grass*, his poetry followed the popular literary conventions of his time. In the second canto of 'Song of Myself', the speaker intones:

Houses and rooms are full of perfumes, the shelves are
crowded with perfumes,
I breathe the fragrance myself and know it and like it,
The distillation would intoxicate me also, but I shall
not let it

As an educated man and former school teacher, Whitman would have been aware that that *stanza* was Italian for 'room'. As the above passage indicates, Whitman would eventually reject traditional stanzaic verse structure – refusing to let its tempting fragrance 'intoxicate' him – and his best poetry is free verse organized into numbered cantos of varying length, many of which consist of one long 'stanza'. And yet, also shown in this passage, Whitman still has respect for the old forms and the pleasure and knowledge they afford, for he 'breathe[s] the fragrance [him]self and know[s] it and like[s] it'.

This theme of respecting the old traditions without surrendering to them is echoed elsewhere in Whitman's verse, particularly in the fifth canto of 'Starting from Paumanok':

Dead poets, philosophs, priests,
Martyrs, artists, inventors, governments long since,
Language-shapers on other shores,
Nations once powerful, now reduced, withdrawn, or
desolate,
I dare not proceed till I respectfully credit what you
have left wafted hither,
I have perused it, own it is admirable, (moving awhile
among it,)
Think nothing can ever be greater, nothing can ever
deserve more than it deserves,

Regarding it all intently a long while, then dismissing
it,
I stand in my place with my own day here.

Past masters are 'admirable', but the time has arrived for Whitman to stand 'in [his] place with [his] own day here'.

Whitman's day, however, was America's day as well, and part of his purpose in finding his own poetic voice was to give his native country a voice with which to greet the world. In 'To Foreign Lands', an inscription of only three lines, he writes:

I heard that you ask'd for something to prove this
puzzle the New World,
And to define America, her athletic Democracy,
Therefore I send you my poems that you behold in
them what you wanted.

Whitman was well placed to serve as America's national poet: his major work, *Leaves of Grass*, was written in the 1850s and continuously revised until Whitman's death in 1892, embracing both the antebellum and postbellum periods of 19th-century American Literature. It encompasses the Transcendental and Romantic movements, and yet has passages of gravitas and authentic description more in line with Realism. Whitman served as a nurse in the Civil War, aiding soldiers on both sides, an experience which inspired the 'Drum-Taps' section of *Leaves of Grass*. He also composed a series of poems to Abraham Lincoln, most notably 'When Lilacs Last in the Dooryard Bloom'd', his great elegy to the assassinated president.

Yet Whitman remained the poet of the individual, as evidenced by the core work of *Leaves of Grass*, 'Song of Myself', which begins:

I celebrate myself, and sing myself,
And what I assume you shall assume
For every atom belonging to me as good belongs to
you.

Thus Whitman negotiates the paradox of individuality and universalism: by singing of himself, he simultaneously sings of every American and, ultimately, every human, past, present, and future.

modicum *n* a small amount
WORD ORIGIN Latin: a little way

modifier *n grammar* a word or phrase that makes the sense of another word more specific: for example, the noun *garage* is a modifier of *door* in *garage door*

modify *vb* **-fies, -fying, -fied 1** to change or alter slightly **2** to make less extreme or uncompromising **3** *grammar* (of a word or phrase) to act as a modifier to another word or phrase **modification** *n*
WORD ORIGIN Latin *modus* measure + *facere* to make

modish (**mode**-ish) *adj* in the current fashion or style **modishly** *adv*

modiste (mode-**east**) *n* a fashionable dressmaker or milliner
WORD ORIGIN French

modulate *vb* **-lating, -lated 1** to change the tone, pitch, or volume of (one's voice) **2** to adjust or regulate the degree of: *the hormone which modulates the development of the sexual organs* **3** *music* to change from one key to another **4** *physics, electronics* to superimpose the amplitude, frequency, or phase of a wave or signal onto another wave or signal **modulation** *n* **modulator** *n*
WORD ORIGIN Latin *modulari* to modulate

module *n* **1** a standard self-contained unit, such as an assembly of electronic components or a standardized piece of furniture, that can be used in combination with other units **2** *astronautics* a self-contained separable unit making up a spacecraft **3** *education* a short course of study that together with other such courses counts towards a qualification **modular** *adj*
WORD ORIGIN Latin *modulus*, diminutive of *modus* mode

modulus *n, pl* **-li** *physics* a coefficient expressing a specified property, for instance elasticity, of a specified substance
WORD ORIGIN Latin

modus operandi (**mode**-uss op-er-**an**-die) *n, pl* **modi operandi** (**mode**-eye) method of operating
WORD ORIGIN Latin

modus vivendi (**mode**-uss viv-**venn**-die) *n, pl* **modi vivendi** (**mode**-eye) a working arrangement between conflicting interests
WORD ORIGIN Latin: way of living

moggy *or* **mog** *n, pl* **moggies** *or* **mogs** *Brit, Austral, & NZ slang* a cat
WORD ORIGIN dialect *mog*, originally a pet name for a cow

mogul (**moh**-gl) *n* an important or powerful person

Mogul *adj* of or relating to a Muslim dynasty of Indian emperors established in 1526
WORD ORIGIN Persian *mughul* Mongolian

MOH (in Britain) Medical Officer of Health

mohair *n* **1** the long soft silky hair of the Angora goat **2** a fabric made from yarn of this hair and cotton or wool
WORD ORIGIN Arabic *mukhayyar*, literally: choice

Mohammed *or* **Muhammad** *n* the prophet who founded Islam

Mohawk *n* **1** a member of a N American Indian people formerly living along the Mohawk river **2** the language of this people

mohican *n* a punk hairstyle in which the head is shaved at the sides and the remaining strip of hair is worn stiffly erect and often brightly coloured
WORD ORIGIN after the *Mohicans*, a Native American people

Mohican *n* **1** *pl* **-cans** *or* **-can** a member of a N American Indian people formerly living along the Hudson river **2** the language of this people

moiety (**moy**-it-ee) *n, pl* **-ties** *archaic* **1** a half **2** one of two parts or divisions of something
WORD ORIGIN Old French *moitié*

moire (**mwahr**) *n* a fabric, usually silk, with a watered effect
WORD ORIGIN French

moiré (**mwahr**-ray) *adj* **1** having a watered or wavelike pattern ▷ *n* **2** such a pattern, impressed on fabrics **3** a fabric, usually silk, with such a pattern **4** Also: **moiré pattern** a pattern seen when two geometrical patterns, such as grids, are visually superimposed
WORD ORIGIN French

moist *adj* slightly damp or wet
WORD ORIGIN Old French

moisten *vb* to make or become moist

moisture *n* water diffused as vapour or condensed on or in objects

moisturize *or* **-rise** *vb* **-rizing, -rized** *or* **-rising, -rised** to add moisture to the air or the skin **moisturizer** *or* **-riser** *n*

mojo *n, pl* **mojos** *or* **mojoes** *US slang* **1** a charm or magic spell **2** the art of casting magic spells **3** uncanny personal power or influence, esp. the power to attract sexually
WORD ORIGIN from West African

moke *n* **1** *Brit slang* a donkey **2** *Austral & NZ* a horse of inferior quality
WORD ORIGIN origin unknown

mol *chem* mole

mol. **1** molecular **2** molecule

molar *n* **1** a large back tooth specialized for crushing and chewing food ▷ *adj* **2** of any of these teeth
WORD ORIGIN Latin *mola* millstone

molasses *n* **1** the thick brown bitter syrup obtained from sugar during refining **2** *US & Canad* same as **treacle**
WORD ORIGIN Portuguese *melaço*

mold *n, vb US* same as **mould**

mole[1] *n* a small dark raised spot on the skin

mole[2] *n* **1** a small burrowing mammal with velvety dark fur and forelimbs specialized for digging **2** *informal* a spy who has infiltrated an organization and become a trusted member of it
WORD ORIGIN Middle Dutch *mol*

mole[3] *n chem* the basic SI unit of amount of substance: the amount that contains as many elementary entities as there are atoms in 0.012 kilogram of carbon-12
WORD ORIGIN German *Mol*, short for *Molekül* molecule

mole[4] *n* **1** a breakwater **2** a harbour protected by a breakwater
WORD ORIGIN Latin *moles* mass

molecular (mol-**lek**-yew-lar) *adj* of or relating to molecules

molecular formula *n chem* a chemical formula indicating the number and type of atoms in a molecule, but not its structure: NH_3 *is the molecular formula of ammonia*

molecular weight *n chem* the sum of all the atomic weights of the atoms in a molecule

molecule (**mol**-lik-kyool) *n* **1** the simplest unit of a chemical compound that can exist, consisting of two or more atoms held together by chemical bonds **2** a very small particle
WORD ORIGIN New Latin *molecula*, diminutive of Latin *moles* mass

molehill *n* **1** the small mound of earth thrown up by a burrowing mole **2 make a mountain out of a molehill** to exaggerate an unimportant matter out of all proportion

molest *vb* **1** to accost or attack someone, esp. a woman or child, with the intention of assaulting her or him sexually **2** to disturb or injure, esp. by using or threatening violence: *killing, capturing, or molesting the local wildlife was strictly forbidden* **molestation** *n* **molester** *n*
WORD ORIGIN Latin *molestare* to annoy

moll *n slang* a gangster's female accomplice or girlfriend
WORD ORIGIN from *Moll*, familiar form of *Mary*

mollify *vb* **-fies, -fying, -fied** to make someone less angry or upset; soothe: *he sought to mollify his critics* **mollification** *n*
WORD ORIGIN Latin *mollis* soft + *facere* to make

mollusc *or US* **mollusk** *n* an invertebrate with a soft unsegmented body and often a shell, such as a snail, mussel, or octopus
WORD ORIGIN Latin *molluscus*

mollycoddle *vb* **-coddling, -coddled** to give an excessive amount of care and protection to
WORD ORIGIN from *Molly*, girl's name + *coddle*

Molotov cocktail *n* a simple bomb made from a bottle filled with petrol and a cloth wick; petrol bomb
WORD ORIGIN after V. M. *Molotov*, Soviet statesman

molt *vb, n US* same as **moult**

molten *adj* so hot that it has melted and formed a liquid: *molten metal*

molto *adv music* very: *allegro molto; molto adagio*
WORD ORIGIN Italian

molybdenum (mol-**lib**-din-um) *n chem* a very hard silvery-white metallic element used in alloys, esp. to harden and strengthen steels. Symbol: Mo
WORD ORIGIN Greek *molubdos* lead

mom *n informal chiefly US, Canad, & S African* same as **mother**

moment *n* **1** a short period of time **2** a specific instant or point in time: *at that moment the phone rang* **3 the moment** the present point of time: *for the moment he is out of prison* **4** importance, significance, or value: *a matter of greatest moment* **5** *physics* **a** a tendency to produce motion, esp. rotation about a point or axis **b** the product of a physical quantity, such as force or mass, and its distance from a fixed reference point **WORD ORIGIN** Latin *momentum* movement

momentary *adj* lasting for only a moment; temporary **momentarily** *adv*

moment of truth *n* a moment when a person or thing is put to the test

momentous (moh-**men**-tuss) *adj* of great significance **momentousness** *n*

momentum (moh-**men**-tum) *n* **1** the impetus to go forward, develop, or get stronger: *the campaign steadily gathered support and momentum* **2** the impetus of a moving body: *the sledge gathered momentum as it slid ever faster down the slope* **3** *physics* the product of a body's mass and its velocity **WORD ORIGIN** Latin: movement

momma *n chiefly US* an informal or childish word for **mother**

Mon. Monday

mon- *combining form* see **mono-**

monad *n* **1** *philosophy* any fundamental singular metaphysical entity **2** a single-celled organism **3** an atom, ion, or radical with a valency of one **WORD ORIGIN** Greek *monas* unit

monandrous *adj* **1** *biol* having only one stamen in each flower **2** having only one male sexual partner over a period of time **WORD ORIGIN** Greek *monos* sole + *anēr* man

monarch *n* a sovereign head of state, esp. a king, queen, or emperor, who rules by hereditary right **monarchical** *or* **monarchic** *adj* **WORD ORIGIN** Greek *monos* sole + *arkhos* ruler

monarchism *n* the belief that a country should have a hereditary ruler, such as a king, rather than an elected one **monarchist** *n, adj*

monarchy *n, pl* **-chies 1** a form of government in which supreme authority is held by a single hereditary ruler, such as a king **2** a country reigned over by a monarch

monastery *n, pl* **-teries** the building or group of buildings where a community of monks lives **WORD ORIGIN** Greek *monazein* to live alone

monastic *adj* **1** of or relating to monasteries, monks, or nuns **2** (of a way of life) simple and austere; ascetic **monasticism** *n*

monatomic *adj chem* **1** (of an element) consisting of single atoms **2** (of a compound or molecule) having only one atom or group that can be replaced in a reaction

Monday *n* the second day of the week, and the first day of the working week **WORD ORIGIN** Old English *mōnandæg* moon's day

monetarism *n* **1** the theory that inflation is caused by an excess quantity of money in an economy **2** an economic policy based on this theory and a belief in the efficiency of free market forces **monetarist** *n, adj*

monetary *adj* of money or currency **WORD ORIGIN** Latin *moneta* money

money *n* **1** a means of payment and measure of value: *some cultures used to use shells as money* **2** the official currency, in the form of banknotes or coins, issued by a government **3** *moneys or monies law old-fashioned* a financial sum or income **4** an unspecified amount of wealth: *money to lend* **5** *informal* a rich person or rich people: *he married money* **6** **for my money** in my opinion **7** **one's money's worth** full value for the money one has paid for something **8** **put money on** to place a bet on ▸ Related adjective: **pecuniary** **WORD ORIGIN** Latin *moneta*

moneybags *n informal* a very rich person

moneychanger *n* a person engaged in the business of exchanging currencies or money

moneyed *or* **monied** *adj* having a great deal of money; rich

money-grubbing *adj informal* seeking greedily to obtain money **money-grubber** *n*

moneylender *n* a person who lends money at interest as a living

moneymaker *n* **1** a person whose chief concern is to make money **2** a person or thing that is or might be profitable **moneymaking** *adj, n*

money-spinner *n informal* an enterprise, idea, or thing that is a source of wealth

-monger *n combining form* **1** indicating a trader or dealer: *an ironmonger* **2** indicating a promoter of something: *a warmonger* **WORD ORIGIN** Old English *mangere*

mongol *n offensive* (not in technical use) a person affected by Down's syndrome **mongoloid** *n, adj*

Mongolian *adj* **1** of Mongolia ▸*n* **2** a person from Mongolia **3** the language of Mongolia

mongolism *n offensive* a former name (not in technical use) for **Down's syndrome** **WORD ORIGIN** the condition produces facial features similar to those of the Mongoloid peoples

Mongoloid *adj* of a major racial group of mankind, characterized by yellowish skin, straight black hair, and slanting eyes: includes most of the people of SE Asia, E Asia, and the Arctic area of N America

mongoose *n, pl* **-gooses** a small long-tailed predatory mammal of Asia and Africa that kills snakes **WORD ORIGIN** from Marathi (a language of India) *mangūs*

mongrel *n* **1** a dog of mixed breeding **2** something made up of things from a variety of sources: *despite using components from three other cars, this new model is no mongrel* ▸*adj* **3** of mixed breeding or origin: *a mongrel race* **WORD ORIGIN** from obsolete *mong* mixture

monied *adj* same as **moneyed**

monies *n law old-fashioned* a plural of **money**

moniker *or* **monicker** *n slang* a person's name or nickname **WORD ORIGIN** Shelta *munnik*, altered from Irish Gaelic *ainm* name

monism *n philosophy* the doctrine that reality consists of only one basic substance or element, such as mind or matter **monist** *n, adj* **WORD ORIGIN** Greek *monos* sole

monition *n* a warning or caution **WORD ORIGIN** Latin *monere* to warn

monitor *n* **1** a person or device that warns, checks, controls, or keeps a continuous record of something **2** *Brit, Austral, & NZ* a pupil assisting a teacher with various duties **3** a screen used to display certain kinds of information, for example in airports or television studios **4** a large predatory lizard inhabiting warm regions of Africa, Asia, and Australia ▸*vb* **5** to act as a monitor of **6** to observe or record the condition or performance of a person or thing **7** to check a broadcast for acceptable quality or content **monitorial** *adj* **WORD ORIGIN** Latin *monere* to advise

monitory *adj* acting as or giving a warning

monk *n* a male member of a religious community bound by vows of poverty, chastity, and obedience ▸ Related adjective: **monastic** **monkish** *adj* **WORD ORIGIN** Greek *monos* alone

monkey *n* **1** any long-tailed primate that is not a lemur or tarsier **2** (loosely) any primate that is not a human **3** a naughty or mischievous child **4** *slang* £500 or $500 **5** **give a monkey's** *Brit slang* to care about or regard as important: *who gives a monkey's what he thinks?* ▸*vb* **6** **monkey around** *or* **about with** to meddle or tinker with **WORD ORIGIN** origin unknown

monkey business *n informal* mischievous or dishonest behaviour or acts

monkey nut *n Brit* a peanut

monkey puzzle *n* a South American coniferous tree with branches shaped like a candelabrum and stiff sharp leaves

monkey tricks *or US* **monkey shines** *pl n informal* mischievous behaviour or acts

monkey wrench *n chiefly Brit* a wrench with adjustable jaws

monkshood *n* a poisonous plant with hooded blue-purple flowers

mono *adj* **1** short for **monophonic** ▸*n* **2** monophonic sound

mono- *or before a vowel* **mon-** *combining form* **1** one; single: *monorail; monolingual* **2** *chem* indicating that a chemical compound contains a single specified atom or group: *monoxide* **WORD ORIGIN** Greek *monos* alone

monobasic *adj chem* (of an acid, such as hydrogen chloride) having only one replaceable hydrogen atom per molecule

monochromatic *adj* (of light or other electromagnetic radiation) having only one wavelength

m

monochrome adj **1** photog, television black-and-white ▷n **2** a painting or drawing done in a range of tones of a single colour **WORD ORIGIN** Greek monokhrōmos of one colour

monocle (**mon**-a-kl) n (formerly) a lens worn for correcting defective sight in one eye only, held in position by the facial muscles **monocled** adj **WORD ORIGIN** MONO- + Latin oculus eye

monocline n a fold in stratified rocks in which the strata are inclined in the same direction from the horizontal **monoclinal** adj, n **WORD ORIGIN** MONO- + Greek klinein to lean

monoclinic adj crystallog of the crystal system characterized by three unequal axes, one pair of which are not at right angles to each other

monoclonal antibody n an antibody produced from a single clone of cells grown in a culture

monocoque (**mon**-a-cock) n a vehicle body moulded from a single piece of material with no separate load-bearing parts **WORD ORIGIN** French

monocotyledon (mon-no-kot-ill-**leed**-on) n any flowering plant with a single embryonic seed leaf, such as the grasses, lilies, palms, and orchids

monocular adj having or intended for the use of only one eye **WORD ORIGIN** Late Latin monoculus one-eyed

monoculture n the continuous growing of one type of crop

monody n, pl **-dies 1** (in Greek tragedy) an ode sung by a single actor **2** music a style of composition consisting of a single vocal part, usually with accompaniment **monodist** n **WORD ORIGIN** MONO- + Greek aeidein to sing

monoecious (mon-**ee**-shuss) adj **1** (of some flowering plants) having the male and female reproductive organs in separate flowers on the same plant **2** (of some animals and lower plants) hermaphrodite **WORD ORIGIN** MONO- + Greek oikos house

monogamy n the state or practice of having only one husband or wife at a time **monogamous** adj **WORD ORIGIN** MONO- + Greek gamos marriage

monogram n a design of one or more letters, esp. initials, on clothing, stationery, etc. **WORD ORIGIN** Greek monogrammatos consisting of one letter

monograph n a paper, book, or other work concerned with a single subject or aspect of a subject

monolingual adj knowing or expressed in only one language

monolith n **1** a large block of stone **2** a statue, obelisk, or column cut from one block of stone **3** something which can be regarded as forming one large, single, whole: the Christian religion should not be thought of as a monolith **monolithic** adj

WORD ORIGIN Greek monolithos made from a single stone

monologue n **1** a long speech made by one actor in a play or film; soliloquy **2** a dramatic piece for a single performer **3** any long speech by one person, esp. one which prevents other people talking or expressing their views **WORD ORIGIN** Greek monologos speaking alone

USAGE
See at **soliloquy**.

monomania n an obsession with one thing or idea **monomaniac** n, adj

monomer n chem a compound whose molecules can join together to form a polymer

monomial n maths an expression consisting of a single term, such as 5ax **WORD ORIGIN** MONO- + (BIN)OMIAL

mononucleosis (mon-oh-new-klee-oh-siss) n **infectious mononucleosis** same as **glandular fever**

monophonic adj (of a system of broadcasting, recording, or reproducing sound) using only one channel between source and loudspeaker. Short form: **mono**

monoplane n an aeroplane with only one pair of wings

monopolize or **-lise** vb **-lizing, -lized** or **-lising, -lised 1** to have full control or use of, to the exclusion of others **2** to hold exclusive control of a market or supply

monopoly n, pl **-lies 1** exclusive control of the market supply of a product or service **2 a** an enterprise exercising this control **b** the product or service so controlled **3** law the exclusive right granted to a person or company by the state to trade in a specified commodity or area **4** exclusive control, possession, or use of something **monopolist** n **monopolistic** adj **WORD ORIGIN** MONO- + Greek pōlein to sell

Monopoly n trademark a board game for two to six players who deal in 'property' as they move tokens around the board

monorail n a single-rail railway

monosaccharide n a simple sugar, such as glucose, that cannot be broken down into other sugars

monosodium glutamate n a substance which enhances protein flavours: used as a food additive

monosyllable n a word of one syllable **monosyllabic** adj

monotheism n the belief or doctrine that there is only one God **monotheist** n, adj **monotheistic** adj

monotone n **1** a single unvaried pitch level in speech or sound **2** a way of speaking which lacks variety of pitch or expression: he rambled on in a dull monotone **3** lack of variety in style or expression ▷adj **4** unvarying

monotonous adj tedious because of lack of variety **monotonously** adv

monotony n, pl **-nies 1** wearisome routine; dullness **2** lack of variety in pitch or tone

monounsaturated adj of a group of vegetable oils, such as olive oil, that

have a neutral effect on cholesterol in the body

monovalent adj chem **1** having a valency of one **2** having only one valency **monovalence** or **monovalency** n

monoxide n an oxide that contains one oxygen atom per molecule

Monseigneur (mon-sen-**nyur**) n, pl **Messeigneurs** (may-sen-**nyur**) a title given to French prelates and princes **WORD ORIGIN** French, literally: my lord

monsieur (muss-**syuh**) n, pl **messieurs** (may-**syuh**) a French form of address equivalent to sir or Mr **WORD ORIGIN** French, literally: my lord

Monsignor n, pl **Monsignors** or **Monsignori** RC Church a title given to certain senior clergymen **WORD ORIGIN** Italian

monsoon n **1** a seasonal wind of S Asia which blows from the southwest in summer and from the northeast in winter **2** the rainy season when the SW monsoon blows, from about April to October **WORD ORIGIN** Arabic mawsim season

monsoon bucket n NZ a large container for water carried by helicopter and used to extinguish bush and scrub fires

mons pubis (monz **pew**-biss) n, pl **montes pubis** (**mon**-teez) the fatty flesh in human males over the junction of the pubic bones **WORD ORIGIN** New Latin: hill of the pubes

monster n **1** an imaginary beast, usually frightening in appearance **2** a very large person, animal, or thing **3** an exceptionally cruel or wicked person **4** a person, animal, or plant with a marked deformity **WORD ORIGIN** Latin monstrum portent

monstrance n RC Church a vessel in which the consecrated Host is exposed for adoration **WORD ORIGIN** Latin monstrare to show

monstrosity n, pl **-ties 1** an outrageous or ugly person or thing **2** the state or quality of being monstrous

monstrous adj **1** hideous or unnatural in size or character **2** atrocious, unjust, or shocking: the President described the invasion as monstrous **3** huge **4** of or like a monster **5** (of plants and animals) abnormal in structure **monstrously** adv

mons veneris (monz **ven**-er-iss) n, pl **montes veneris** (**mon**-teez) the fatty flesh in human females over the junction of the pubic bones **WORD ORIGIN** New Latin: hill of Venus

montage (**mon**-tahzh) n **1** a picture made by combining material from various sources, such as other pictures or photographs **2** the technique of producing pictures in this way **3** a method of film editing by juxtaposition or partial superimposition of several shots to form a single image **4** a film sequence of this kind **WORD ORIGIN** French

month n **1** one of the twelve divisions (**calendar months**) of the calendar year **2** a period of time extending from one date to a corresponding date in the next

Noah Webster's Spelling Reforms

Noah Webster's reputation as a lexicographer was secured by his contribution to the Merriam-Webster line of dictionaries that are still published today. His much more obvious influence on English, however, is evident to every person who reads or writes American English: Webster is primarily responsible for the spelling reforms in American English that for most people distinguish it from British English. This is why Americans dream in *color,* not in *colour*; why they wear *jewelry* rather than *jewellery*, even on *meager* rather than *meagre* incomes, and drive vehicles after they have obtained a *license*, not a *licence*.

In fact Noah Webster was far more radical in his aims for English spelling reform than is suggested by the differences that exist between British and American today: if he'd had his way, we would write *hav* instead of *have*, *greev* instead of *grieve*, and *spunge* instead of *sponge*.

The English-speaking settlers of North America, starting in the seventeenth century, brought British spelling to the New World more or less intact. However, it must be remembered that spelling was by no means a settled affair before the advent of authoritative dictionaries. The notion we have today of there being a correct spelling for every word was much more fluid in the eighteenth century, and numerous spelling variants for words that we now think of as having a single spelling could be found in print. The idea of an authoritative source for correct spelling did not exist at the time when English-speaking North America was first settled.

It was part of Webster's genius to have decided that the morass of English spelling was a state of affairs that needed addressing. In 1789 – the very year in which the newly formed government of the United States began operations – Webster published an essay with the long-winded but extremely lucid title, 'An Essay on the Necessity, Advantages, and Practicality of Reforming the Mode of Spelling and of Rendering the Orthography of Words Correspondent to Pronunciation'. In it, he argued for the regularization of various spelling patterns that are still associated with him today.

Unlike many people who might write on this topic, Webster was in a good position to promote the reforms that he proposed. This he did chiefly not through his dictionaries, but through his spelling books. The book that eventually came to be called *Webster's Blue-backed Speller* was first published as part of a publication called the *Grammatical Institute*, a textbook for use in American schools. Webster started out conservatively: the spellings that appear in the earliest editions of the book used the most accepted spellings of the time: spellings that we think of as British spellings today. His first such publication was in 1783 – a time when, it must be remembered, the United States had existed for less than a decade. This was also a time when the term 'American English' had not yet been seen in print, and when most Americans gave no thought to the notion that their language might constitute a dialect largely distinct from the mother tongue.

Webster's spelling lessons were a roaring success, partly because he had very little competition, but also partly because he wrote clearly, authoritatively, and with a real instinct for breaking the difficulties of learning into simple steps that children could understand. His *Speller* went on to become the first American publishing success story, being continuously in print throughout much of the nineteenth century, and responsible for teaching generations of American children how to spell. Webster had an opportunity to revisit his own work with each new edition of the book, and he continuously regularized and simplified his spellings. When he published his monumental dictionary in 1828, *An American Dictionary of the English Language*, he used the spellings that distinguish American from British spelling today.

Despite Webster's efforts, there were many American scholars of an Anglophile bent who still looked to England as the authority for the mother tongue, and older spellings continued to appear in scholarly books and journals. Only in the latter half of the nineteenth century, when the American government printing office made the official decision to follow Webster's dictionaries for spelling, did his vision get an official imprimatur.

calendar month **3** a period of four weeks or of 30 days
WORD ORIGIN Old English *mōnath*

monthly *adj* **1** happening or payable once every month: *a monthly magazine* **2** lasting or valid for a month: *a monthly travel pass* ▷ *adv* **3** once a month ▷ *n, pl* **-lies 4** a magazine published once a month

monument *n* **1** something, such as a statue or building, erected in commemoration of a person or event **2** an ancient building which is regarded as an important part of a country's history **3** an exceptional example of the results of something: *the whole town is a monument to bad sixties' architecture*
WORD ORIGIN Latin *monumentum*

monumental *adj* **1** large, impressive, or likely to last or be remembered for a long time: *a monumental three-volume biography* **2** of or being a monument **3** *informal* extreme: *a monumental gamble*

moo *n* **1** the characteristic deep long sound made by a cow ▷ *vb* **2** to make this sound; low

mooch *vb slang* **1** to loiter or walk aimlessly **2** to cadge or scrounge
WORD ORIGIN perhaps Old French *muchier* to skulk

mood¹ *n* **1** a temporary state of mind or temper: *a happy mood* **2** a sullen or gloomy state of mind, esp. when temporary: *she's in a mood* **3** a prevailing atmosphere or feeling: *the current mood of disenchantment with politics* **4 in the mood** inclined to do or have (something)
WORD ORIGIN Old English *mōd* mind, feeling

mood² *n grammar* a form of a verb indicating whether the verb expresses a fact (indicative mood), a wish or supposition (subjunctive mood), or a command (imperative mood)
WORD ORIGIN same as MOOD¹

moody *adj* **moodier, moodiest 1** sullen, sulky, or gloomy **2** temperamental or changeable **moodily** *adv* **moodiness** *n*

Moog *n music trademark* a type of synthesizer
WORD ORIGIN after Robert *Moog*, engineer

mooi *adj S African slang* pleasing or nice
WORD ORIGIN Afrikaans

mooli *n* a type of large white radish
WORD ORIGIN E African native name

moon *n* **1** the natural satellite of the earth ▸ Related adjective: **lunar 2** this satellite as it is seen during its revolution around the earth, esp. at one of its phases: *new moon; full moon* **3** any natural satellite of a planet **4** a month **5 over the moon** *informal* extremely happy; ecstatic ▷ *vb* **6 moon about** *or* **around** to be idle in a listless or dreamy way **moonless** *adj*
WORD ORIGIN Old English *mōna*

moonbeam *n* a ray of moonlight

moon-faced *adj* having a round face

moonlight *n* **1** light from the sun received on earth after reflection by the moon ▷ *adj* **2** illuminated by the moon: *a moonlight walk* ▷ *vb* **-lighting, -lighted 3** *informal* to work at a secondary job, esp. illegally **moonlighter** *n*

moonlight flit *n Austral & Brit informal* a hurried departure at night to avoid paying rent

moonlit *adj* illuminated by the moon

moonscape *n* the surface of the moon or a picture or model of it

moonshine *n* **1** *US & Canad* illegally distilled or smuggled whisky **2** foolish or nonsensical talk or thought

moonshot *n* the launching of a spacecraft to the moon

moonstone *n* a white translucent form of feldspar, used as a gem

moonstruck *adj* slightly mad or odd, as if affected by the moon

moony *adj* **moonier, mooniest** *Brit, Austral, & NZ informal* dreamy or listless

moor¹ *n Brit* an expanse of open uncultivated ground covered with heather, coarse grass, and bracken
WORD ORIGIN Old English *mōr*

moor² *vb* to secure a ship or boat with cables, ropes, or anchors so that it remains in one place **moorage** *n*
WORD ORIGIN Germanic

Moor *n* a member of a Muslim people of North Africa who ruled Spain between the 8th and 15th centuries
WORD ORIGIN Greek *Mauros*

moorhen *n* a waterfowl with black plumage and a red bill

mooring *n* a place where a ship or boat can be tied up or anchored

moorings *pl n naut* the ropes and anchors used in mooring a vessel

Moorish *adj* **1** of or relating to the Moors **2** of a style of architecture used in Spain from the 13th to the 16th century, characterized by the horseshoe arch

moorland *n Brit* an area of moor

moose *n, pl* **moose** a large North American deer with large flattened antlers; the American elk
WORD ORIGIN from a Native American language

moot *adj* **1** subject or open to debate: *a moot point* ▷ *vb* **2** to suggest or bring up for debate: *a compromise proposal, involving building fewer flats, was mooted* ▷ *n* **3** (in Anglo-Saxon England) a local administrative assembly
WORD ORIGIN Old English *gemōt*

mop *n* **1** a tool with a head made of twists of cotton or sponge and a long handle used for washing or polishing floors **2** a similar tool, except smaller and without a long handle, used to wash dishes **3** a thick untidy mass of hair ▷ *vb* **mopping, mopped 4** to clean or soak up with or as if with a mop: *she mopped her brow with a handkerchief* ▸ See also **mop up**
WORD ORIGIN Latin *mappa* napkin

mope *vb* **moping, moped 1** to be gloomy or apathetic **2** to walk around in a gloomy and aimless manner
WORD ORIGIN perhaps from obsolete *mope* fool

moped *n* a light motorcycle not over 50cc
WORD ORIGIN motor + pedal

mopes *pl n* **the mopes** low spirits

mopoke *n* **1** a small spotted owl of Australia and New Zealand **2** *Austral*

slang a slow or lugubrious person
WORD ORIGIN imitative of the bird's cry

moppet *n* same as **poppet**
WORD ORIGIN obsolete *mop* rag doll

mop up *vb* **1** to clean with a mop **2** *informal* to complete the last remaining stages of a job **3** *mil* to clear remaining enemy forces after a battle, by killing them or taking them prisoner

moquette *n* a thick velvety fabric used for carpets and upholstery
WORD ORIGIN French

moraine *n* a ridge or mound formed from debris deposited by a glacier
WORD ORIGIN French

moral *adj* **1** concerned with or relating to the distinction between good and bad or right and wrong behaviour: *moral sense* **2** based on a sense of right and wrong according to conscience: *moral duty* **3** displaying a sense of right and wrong; (of support or a victory) psychological rather than practical ▷ *n* **4** a lesson about right or wrong behaviour that is shown in a fable or event **5 morals** principles of behaviour in accordance with standards of right and wrong **morally** *adv*
WORD ORIGIN Latin *moralis* relating to morals or customs

morale (mor-**rahl**) *n* the degree of confidence or optimism of a person or group
WORD ORIGIN French

moralist *n* **1** a person who has a strong sense of right and wrong **2** someone who criticizes other people for not doing what he or she thinks is morally correct **moralistic** *adj*

morality *n, pl* **-ties 1** good moral conduct **2** the degree to which something is morally acceptable: *we discussed the morality of fox-hunting* **3** a system of moral principles

morality play *n* a medieval type of drama concerned with the conflict between personified virtues and vices

moralize *or* **-lise** *vb* **-lizing, -lized** *or* **-lising, -lised 1** to discuss or consider something in the light of one's own moral beliefs, esp. with disapproval **2** to interpret or explain in a moral sense **3** to improve the morals of

moral philosophy *n* the branch of philosophy dealing with ethics

morass *n* **1** a tract of swampy low-lying land **2** a disordered, confusing, or muddled state of affairs
WORD ORIGIN Old French *marais* marsh

moratorium *n, pl* **-ria** *or* **-riums 1** a legally authorized postponement of the payment of a debt **2** an agreed suspension of activity
WORD ORIGIN Latin *mora* delay

moray *n* a large marine eel marked with brilliant colours
WORD ORIGIN Greek *muraina*

morbid *adj* **1** having an unusual interest in death or unpleasant events **2** *med* relating to or characterized by disease **morbidity** *n* **morbidly** *adv*
WORD ORIGIN Latin *morbus* illness

mordant *adj* **1** sarcastic or caustic: *mordant wit* ▷ *n* **2** a substance used in dyeing to fix colours **3** an acid or other corrosive fluid used to etch lines on a printing plate **WORD ORIGIN** Latin *mordere* to bite

more *adj* **1** the comparative of **much** or **many**: *more joy than you know; even more are leaving the country* **2** additional or further: *no more apples* **3** **more of** to a greater extent or degree: *more of a nuisance* ▷ *adv* **4** used to form the comparative of some adjectives and adverbs: *more quickly* **5** the comparative of **much**: *people listen to the radio more now* **6** **more or less a** as an estimate; approximately **b** to an unspecified extent or degree: *the film was a disaster, more or less* **WORD ORIGIN** Old English *māra*
≡USAGE
≡ See at **most**.

moreish *or* **morish** *adj informal* (of food) causing a desire for more

morel *n* an edible mushroom with a pitted cap **WORD ORIGIN** French *morille*

morello *n, pl* **-los** a variety of small very dark sour cherry **WORD ORIGIN** Italian: blackish

moreover *adv* in addition to what has already been said

morepork *n chiefly NZ* same as **mopoke**

mores (**more**-rayz) *pl n* the customs and conventions embodying the fundamental values of a community **WORD ORIGIN** Latin: customs

Moreton Bay bug *n* an Australian flattish edible shellfish

morganatic *adj* of or designating a marriage between a person of high rank and a person of low rank, by which the latter is not elevated to the higher rank and any children have no rights to inherit the higher party's titles or property **WORD ORIGIN** Medieval Latin *morganaticum* morning-gift after consummation representing the husband's only liability

morgue *n* **1** a mortuary **2** *informal* a store of clippings and back numbers used for reference in a newspaper **WORD ORIGIN** French

moribund *adj* **1** near death **2** no longer performing effectively or usefully: *Romania's moribund economy* **WORD ORIGIN** Latin *mori* to die

morish *adj* same as **moreish**

Mormon *n* **1** a member of the Church of Jesus Christ of Latter-day Saints, founded in 1830 in New York by Joseph Smith ▷ *adj* **2** of the Mormons, their Church, or their beliefs **Mormonism** *n*

morn *n poetic* morning **WORD ORIGIN** Old English *morgen*

mornay *adj* served with a cheese sauce: *haddock mornay* **WORD ORIGIN** after Philippe de *Mornay*, Huguenot leader

morning *n* **1** the first part of the day, ending at noon **2** daybreak; dawn **3** **the morning after** *informal* the aftereffects of excess, esp. a hangover ▷ *adj* **4** of or in the morning: *morning coffee* **WORD ORIGIN** from *morn*, on the model of *evening*

morning dress *n* formal daytime dress for men, consisting of a frock coat with the front cut away (**morning coat**), usually with grey trousers and top hat

morning-glory *n, pl* **-ries** a tropical climbing plant with trumpet-shaped blue, pink, or white flowers, which close in late afternoon

mornings *adv informal* in the morning, esp. regularly, or during every morning

morning sickness *n* nausea occurring shortly after rising in early pregnancy

morning star *n* a planet, usually Venus, seen just before sunrise

Moroccan *adj* **1** of Morocco ▷ *n* **2** a person from Morocco

morocco *n* a fine soft leather made from goatskins **WORD ORIGIN** after *Morocco*, where it was originally made

moron *n* **1** *informal, derogatory* a foolish or stupid person **2** (formerly) a person having an intelligence quotient of between 50 and 70 **moronic** *adj* **WORD ORIGIN** Greek *mōros* foolish

morose (mor-**rohss**) *adj* ill-tempered, sullen, and unwilling to talk very much **morosely** *adv* **WORD ORIGIN** Latin *morosus* peevish

morpheme *n linguistics* a speech element having a meaning or grammatical function that cannot be subdivided into further such elements

morphine *or* **morphia** *n* a drug extracted from opium: used in medicine as an anaesthetic and sedative **WORD ORIGIN** *Morpheus*, in Greek mythology, the god of sleep and dreams

morphing *n* a computer technique used for graphics and in films, in which one image is gradually transformed into another image without individual changes being noticeable in the process **WORD ORIGIN** from METAMORPHOSIS

morphology *n* the science of forms and structures of organisms or words **morphological** *adj*

morris dance *n* an old English folk dance performed by men (**morris men**) who wear a traditional costume decorated with bells **WORD ORIGIN** Middle English *moreys daunce* Moorish dance

morrow *n* **the morrow** *old-fashioned or poetic* **1** the next day **2** the morning **WORD ORIGIN** Old English *morgen* morning

Morse code *n* a code formerly used internationally for transmitting messages, in which letters and numbers are represented by groups of dots and dashes, or by shorter and longer sounds **WORD ORIGIN** after Samuel *Morse*, inventor

morsel *n* a small piece of something, esp. of food **WORD ORIGIN** Old French *mors* a bite

mortal *adj* **1** (of living beings, esp. humans) destined to die sometime rather than living forever **2** causing death; fatal: *a mortal wound* **3** deadly or unrelenting: *he is my mortal enemy* **4** of or resulting from the fear of death:

mortal terror **5** of or involving life or the world: *the hangman's noose ended his mortal existence* **6** great or very intense: *mortal pain* **7** *informal* conceivable or possible: *there was no mortal reason to leave* **8** *slang* long and tedious: *for three mortal hours* ▷ *n* **9** a human being **mortally** *adv* **WORD ORIGIN** Latin *mors* death

mortality *n, pl* **-ties 1** the condition of being mortal **2** great loss of life, as in war or disaster **3** the number of deaths in a given period

mortal sin *n Christianity* a sin that will lead to damnation unless repented of

mortar *n* **1** a small cannon that fires shells in high arcs **2** a mixture of cement or lime or both with sand and water, used to hold bricks or stones together **3** a vessel, usually bowl-shaped, in which substances are crushed with a pestle ▷ *vb* **4** to fire on with mortars **5** to join bricks or stones with mortar **WORD ORIGIN** Latin *mortarium* basin in which mortar is mixed

mortarboard *n* **1** a black tasselled academic cap with a flat square top **2** a small square board with a handle on the underside for carrying mortar

mortgage *n* **1** an agreement under which a person borrows money to buy property, esp. a house, and the lender can take possession of the property if the borrower fails to repay the money **2** a loan obtained under such an agreement: *a mortgage of three times one's income* **3** a regular repayment of money borrowed under such an agreement: *the monthly mortgage on the building* ▷ *vb* **-gaging, -gaged 4** to pledge a house or other property as security for the repayment of a loan ▷ *adj* **5** of or relating to a mortgage: *a mortgage payment* **WORD ORIGIN** Old French, literally: dead pledge

mortgagee *n* the person or organization who lends money in a mortgage agreement

mortgagor *or* **-ger** *n* the person who borrows money in a mortgage agreement

mortice *or* **mortise** (**more**-tiss) *n* **1** a slot or recess cut into a piece of wood or stone to receive a matching projection (tenon) on another piece, or a mortice lock ▷ *vb* **-ticing, -ticed** *or* **-tising, -tised 2** to cut a slot or recess in a piece of wood or stone **3** to join two pieces of wood or stone by means of a mortice and tenon **WORD ORIGIN** Old French *mortoise*

mortice lock *n* a lock set into the edge of a door so that the mechanism of the lock is enclosed by the door

mortician *n chiefly US* same as **undertaker**

mortify *vb* **-fies, -fying, -fied 1** to make someone feel ashamed or embarrassed **2** *Christianity* to subdue one's emotions, the body, etc. by self-denial **3** (of flesh) to become gangrenous **mortification** *n* **mortifying** *adj* **WORD ORIGIN** Latin *mors* death + *facere* to do

m

mortuary *n, pl* **-aries** a building or room where dead bodies are kept before cremation or burial
WORD ORIGIN Latin *mortuarius* of the dead

mosaic (moh-**zay**-ik) *n* a design or decoration made up of small pieces of coloured glass or stone
WORD ORIGIN Greek *mouseios* of the Muses

Mosaic *adj* of or relating to Moses or the laws and traditions ascribed to him

moselle *n* a German white wine from the valley of the river Moselle

mosey *vb* **mosey along** *or* **on** *informal* to walk slowly and casually; amble
WORD ORIGIN origin unknown

Moslem *n, pl* **-lems** *or* **-lem** *adj* same as **Muslim**

mosque *n* a Muslim place of worship
WORD ORIGIN Arabic *masjid* temple

mosquito *n, pl* **-toes** *or* **-tos** a two-winged insect, the females of which pierce the skin of humans and animals to suck their blood
WORD ORIGIN Spanish, diminutive of *mosca* fly

mosquito net *n* a fine curtain or net to keep mosquitoes away, esp. hung over a bed

moss *n* **1** a very small flowerless plant typically growing in dense mats on trees, rocks, or moist ground **2** *Scot & N English* a peat bog or marsh **mossy** *adj*
WORD ORIGIN Old English *mos* swamp

mossie *n* *S African* the common sparrow
WORD ORIGIN Afrikaans

moss rose *n* a variety of rose that has a mossy stem and fragrant pink flowers

most *n* **1** the greatest number or degree: *the most I can ever remember being paid* **2** the majority: *most of his records are dreadful* **3** **at (the) most** at the maximum: *she is fifteen at the most* **4** **make the most of** to use to the best advantage: *they made the most of their chances* ▷ *adj* **5** of or being the majority of a group of things or people or the largest part of something: *most people don't share your views* **6** **the most** the superlative of **many** or **much**: *he has the most talent* ▷ *adv* **7** **the most** used to form the superlative of some adjectives and adverbs: *the most beautiful women in the world* **8** the superlative of **much**: *what do you like most about your job?* **9** very; exceedingly: *a most unfortunate accident*
WORD ORIGIN Old English *māst* or *mǣst*

≡ **USAGE**
≡ *More* and *most* should be distinguished
≡ when used in comparisons. *More*
≡ applies to cases involving two people,
≡ objects, etc., *most* to cases involving
≡ three or more: *John is the more intelligent*
≡ *of the two; he is the most intelligent of the*
≡ *students.*

mostly *adv* **1** almost entirely; generally: *the men at the party were mostly young* **2** on many or most occasions; usually: *rattlesnakes mostly hunt at night*

Most Reverend *n* (in Britain) a courtesy title applied to archbishops

mot (moh) *n* short for **bon mot**
WORD ORIGIN French: word

MOT 1 *Brit* short for **MOT test 2** *Brit* the certificate showing that a vehicle has passed its MOT test **3** *NZ* Ministry of Transport

mote *n* a tiny speck
WORD ORIGIN Old English *mot*

motel *n* a roadside hotel for motorists
WORD ORIGIN mo(tor) + (ho)tel

motet (moh-**tet**) *n* a religious song for a choir in which several voices, usually unaccompanied, sing contrasting parts simultaneously
WORD ORIGIN Old French, diminutive of *mot* word

moth *n* any of numerous chiefly nocturnal insects resembling butterflies, that typically have stout bodies and do not have club-shaped antennae
WORD ORIGIN Old English *moththe*

mothball *n* **1** a small ball of camphor or naphthalene placed in stored clothing to repel clothes moths **2** **put in mothballs** to postpone work on ▷ *vb* **3** to take something out of operation but maintain it for future use **4** to postpone work on

moth-eaten *adj* **1** decayed or scruffy **2** eaten away by or as if by moths: *a moth-eaten suit*

mother *n* **1** a female who has given birth to offspring **2** a person's own mother **3** a title given to certain members of female religious orders **4** motherly qualities, such as maternal affection: *it appealed to the mother in her* **5** **the mother of** a female or thing that creates, founds, or protects something: *the mother of modern feminism; necessity is the mother of invention* **6** **the mother of all** *informal* the greatest example of its kind: *the mother of all parties* ▷ *adj* **7** of or relating to a female or thing that creates, founds, or protects something: *our mother company is in New York* **8** native or innate: *mother wit* ▷ *vb* **9** to give birth to or produce **10** to nurture or protect **motherless** *adj* **motherly** *adj*
WORD ORIGIN Old English *mōdor*

Mother Carey's chicken *n* same as **stormy petrel**
WORD ORIGIN origin unknown

mother country *n* **1** the original country of colonists or settlers **2** a person's native country

motherhood *n* the state of being a mother

Mothering Sunday *n* **1** (in Britain and S Africa) the fourth Sunday in Lent, when mothers traditionally receive presents from their children **2** (in Australia) the second Sunday in May, when mothers traditionally receive presents from their children. Also called: **Mother's Day**

mother-in-law *n, pl* **mothers-in-law** the mother of one's wife or husband

motherland *n* a person's native country

mother-of-pearl *n* a hard iridescent substance that forms the inner layer of the shells of certain molluscs, such as the oyster

Mother's Day *n* **1** see **Mothering Sunday 2** *US & Canad* the second Sunday in May, observed as a day in honour of mothers

mother superior *n, pl* **mother superiors** *or* **mothers superior** the head of a community of nuns

mother tongue *n* the language first learned by a child

mothproof *adj* **1** (esp. of clothes) chemically treated so as to repel clothes moths ▷ *vb* **2** to make mothproof

motif (moh-**teef**) *n* **1** a distinctive idea, esp. a theme elaborated on in a piece of music or literature **2** a recurring shape in a design **3** a single decoration, such as a symbol or name on a piece of clothing
WORD ORIGIN French

motile *adj* capable of independent movement **motility** *n*
WORD ORIGIN Latin *movere* to move

motion *n* **1** the process of continual change in the position of an object; movement: *the motion of the earth round the sun* ▶ Related adjective: **kinetic 2** a movement or gesture: *he made stabbing motions with the spear* **3** a way or style of moving: *massage the back with steady circular motions* **4** a formal proposal to be discussed and voted on in a debate or meeting **5** *Brit* **a** the evacuation of the bowels **b** excrement **6** **go through the motions** to do something mechanically or without sincerity **7** **set in motion** to make operational or start functioning ▷ *vb* **8** to signal or direct a person by a movement or gesture: *she motioned to me to sit down* **motionless** *adj*
WORD ORIGIN Latin *movere* to move

motion picture *n* *US & Canad* a film; movie

motivate *vb* **-vating, -vated 1** to give a reason or inspiration for a course of action to someone: *he was motivated purely by greed* **2** to inspire and encourage someone to do something: *a good teacher must motivate her pupils* **motivation** *n*

motive *n* **1** the reason, whether conscious or unconscious, for a certain course of action **2** same as **motif** (sense 2) ▷ *adj* **3** of or causing motion: *a motive force*
WORD ORIGIN Late Latin *motivus* moving

motive power *n* **1** any source of energy used to produce motion **2** the means of supplying power to an engine or vehicle

mot juste (moh **zhoost**) *n, pl* **mots justes** the appropriate word or expression
WORD ORIGIN French

motley *adj* **1** made up of people or things of different types: *a motley assortment of mules, donkeys, and camels* **2** multicoloured ▷ *n* **3** *history* the costume of a jester
WORD ORIGIN perhaps Old English *mot* speck

motocross *n* the sport of motorcycle racing across rough ground
WORD ORIGIN moto(r) + cross(-country)

motor *n* **1** the engine, esp. an internal-combustion engine, of a vehicle **2** a machine that converts energy, esp. electrical energy, into mechanical energy **3** *chiefly Brit informal* a car ▷ *adj* **4** *chiefly Brit* of or relating to cars and other vehicles powered by petrol or diesel engines: *the motor industry* **5** powered by or relating to a motor:

Inkhorn Terms

In the days before ballpoint pens, anyone who wanted to write something in a permanent form had to apply ink to a pen as a prelude to the act of putting the pen to paper. The receptacles that scribes and scholars used to hold their ink were traditionally made of horn. So an 'inkhorn' was literally a container for ink. But the word also became an adjective, conjuring up the stereotypical medieval scholar: full of obscure classical learning and obsessed with minute distinctions that had no importance in the real world.

This is the image that people seek to evoke when they dismiss a word as an 'inkhorn term'. Inkhorn terms occur when a writer uses his or her knowledge of another language – usually Greek or Latin – to produce a word or phrase whose meaning is obscure to the general reader. Readers may be impressed with how clever the writer is, but they are also likely to be irritated by the affectation.

The expression is especially associated with the sixteenth and seventeenth centuries, when the classical languages were exerting a strong influence on English vocabulary. Some writers looked to classical roots to provide elegant alternatives to the Anglo-Saxon words that formed much of the English lexicon. However, coining English words based on Latin or Greek originals often had the effect of rendering language obscure. This led influential scholars such as Sir John Cheke, Thomas Wilson, and Roger Ascham to crusade against the excessive use of Latinate words in English. Cheke even went so far as to produce a translation of Saint Matthew's Gospel that replaced established words of Latin origin, such as *centurion*, *crucify*, and *resurrection*, with Anglo-Saxon alternatives: *hundreder*, *cross*, and *gainrising*.

This countermovement may not have succeeded in eradicating all traces of Latin from English, but many of the new Latinate terms withered away of their own accord. There was no enthusiasm for adopting *ingent* in place of *huge* or *rigescent* as an alternative for *stiffening*. Yet hundreds of words that might have been condemned as inkhorn terms have gone on to have a useful life as part of the fabric of the language. Among the many words that entered English in the sixteenth century as borrowings from Latin are *area*, *bulb*, *chart*, *decent*, *design*, *event*, *exhaust*, *fact*, *gravity*, *index*, *motor*, *normal*, *section*, *social*, and *various*. It is hard now to imagine English without them.

The debate about the desirability of inkhorn terms can be seen as part of a wider (and still unresolved) debate about the desirability of innovation in language. Conservatives have always sought to curb excessive change, but there will always be writers who seek to exploit the glitter of new and unfamiliar words. Some of the finest exponents of English, including Henry James and Vladimir Nabokov, have delighted in challenging the reader with recherché vocabulary, while other great writers – Jane Austen, for example – have preferred to restrict themselves to words that are in common parlance.

One notable attempt to fix English in a permanent form was made by Samuel Johnson. He envisaged that his *Dictionary of the English Language* (published in 1755) would establish correct usage for all time, but before he had completed his work he was forced to concede that he could only describe and not prescribe how words are used. Language would go on changing.

The idea of peppering one's prose with obscure words of classical origin may seem an unattractive one in an age when familiarity with Greek and Latin can no longer be taken for granted even by the highbrow reader. But some writers of fiction still find a reason to include a smattering of unusual and exotic words in their books. The historical novelist Patrick O'Brian, for example, has used archaic vocabulary to conjure up a sense of the past in naval adventure stories such as *Master and Commander*, while in *Brick Lane* Monica Ali helps to bring to life the experience of Bangladeshi immigrants in London by inserting Bengali words into her English narrative. In both cases, not all of their readers will have understood all of the words immediately, but this has not prevented the books from being widely enjoyed.

a new synthetic motor oil **6** *physiol* producing or causing motion ▷ *vb* **7** to travel by car **8** *informal* to move fast **motorized** *or* **-ised** *adj*
WORD ORIGIN Latin *movere* to move

motorbicycle *n* **1** a motorcycle **2** a moped

motorbike *n informal* a motorcycle

motorboat *n* any boat powered by a motor

motorcade *n* a procession of cars carrying an important person or people
WORD ORIGIN *motor + (caval)cade*

motorcar *n* a more formal word for **car**

motorcycle *n* a two-wheeled vehicle driven by an engine **motorcyclist** *n*

motorist *n* a driver of a car

motorman *n, pl* **-men** *Brit, Austral, & NZ* the driver of an electric train

motor scooter *n* a light motorcycle with small wheels and an enclosed engine

motor vehicle *n* a road vehicle driven by an engine

motorway *n Brit, Austral, & NZ* a dual carriageway for fast-moving traffic, with no stopping permitted and no crossroads

Motown *n trademark* music combining rhythm and blues and pop
WORD ORIGIN *Mo(tor) Town*, nickname for Detroit

motte *n history* a mound on which a castle was built
WORD ORIGIN Old French

MOT test *n* (in Britain) a compulsory annual test of the roadworthiness of motor vehicles over 3 years old

mottled *adj* coloured with streaks or blotches of different shades **mottling** *n*
WORD ORIGIN from *motley*

motto *n, pl* **-toes** *or* **-tos** **1** a short saying expressing the guiding maxim or ideal of a family or organization, esp. when part of a coat of arms **2** a verse or maxim contained in a paper cracker **3** a quotation prefacing a book or chapter of a book
WORD ORIGIN Italian

mould¹ *or US* **mold** *n* **1** a shaped hollow container into which a liquid material is poured so that it can set in a particular shape: *pour the mixture into a buttered mould, cover, and steam for two hours* **2** a shape, nature, or type: *an orthodox Communist in the Stalinist mould* **3** a framework around which something is constructed or shaped: *the heated glass is shaped round a mould inside a kiln* **4** something, esp. a food, made in or on a mould: *salmon mould* ▷ *vb* **5** to make in a mould **6** to shape or form: *a figure moulded out of clay* **7** to influence or direct: *cultural factors moulding our everyday life*
WORD ORIGIN Latin *modulus* a small measure

mould² *or US* **mold** *n* a coating or discoloration caused by various fungi that develop in a damp atmosphere on food, fabrics, and walls
WORD ORIGIN Northern English dialect *mowlde* mouldy

mould³ *or US* **mold** *n* loose soil, esp. when rich in organic matter: *leaf mould*

WORD ORIGIN Old English *molde*

mouldboard *or US* **moldboard** *n* the curved blade of a plough, which turns over the furrow

moulder *or US* **molder** *vb* to crumble or cause to crumble, as through decay: *John Brown's body lies mouldering in the grave*
WORD ORIGIN from MOULD³

moulding *or US* **molding** *n* a shaped ornamental edging

mouldy *or US* **moldy** *adj* **-dier, -diest** **1** covered with mould **2** stale or musty, esp. from age or lack of use **3** *slang* dull or boring

moult *or US* **molt** *vb* **1** (of birds and animals) to shed feathers, hair, or skin so that they can be replaced by a new growth ▷ *n* **2** the periodic process of moulting
WORD ORIGIN Latin *mutare* to change

mound *n* **1** a heap of earth, debris, etc. **2** any heap or pile **3** a small natural hill
WORD ORIGIN origin unknown

mount¹ *vb* **1** to climb or ascend: *he mounted the stairs to his flat* **2** to get up on a horse, a platform, etc. **3** Also: **mount up** to increase or accumulate: *costs do mount up; the tension mounted* **4** to fix onto a backing, setting, or support: *sensors mounted on motorway bridges* **5** to organize and stage a campaign, play, etc.: *the Allies mounted a counter attack on the eastern front* ▷ *n* **6** a backing, setting, or support onto which something is fixed: *a diamond set in a gold mount* **7** a horse for riding: *none of his mounts at yesterday's race meeting finished better than third*
WORD ORIGIN same as MOUNT²

mount² *n* a mountain or hill: used in literature and (when cap.) in proper names: *Mount Etna*
WORD ORIGIN Latin *mons* mountain

mountain *n* **1** a very large, high, and steep hill: *the highest mountain in the Alps* **2** a huge heap or mass: *a mountain of papers* **3** a surplus of a commodity, esp. in the European Union: *a butter mountain* ▷ *adj* **4** of, found on, or for use on a mountain or mountains: *a mountain village*
WORD ORIGIN Latin *mons*

mountain ash *n* a tree with clusters of small white flowers and bright red berries; rowan

mountain bike *n* a type of bicycle with straight handlebars and heavy-duty tyres, originally designed for use over rough hilly ground

mountain cat *n* any of various wild animals of the cat family, such as the bobcat, lynx, or puma

mountaineer *n* **1** a person who climbs mountains ▷ *vb* **2** to climb mountains **mountaineering** *n*

mountain goat *n* a wild goat inhabiting mountainous regions

mountain lion *n* a puma

mountainous *adj* **1** having many mountains: *a mountainous region* **2** like a mountain or mountains, esp. in size: *mountainous waves*

mountain oyster *n NZ informal* a sheep's testicle eaten as food

mountain sickness *n* nausea, headache, and shortness of breath caused by climbing to high altitudes

mountebank *n* **1** (formerly) a person who sold quack medicines in public places **2** a charlatan or fake
WORD ORIGIN Italian *montambanco* a climber on a bench

mounted *adj* riding horses: *mounted police*

Mountie *or* **Mounty** *n, pl* **Mounties** *informal* a member of the Royal Canadian Mounted Police
WORD ORIGIN from *mounted*

mounting *n* same as **mount¹** (sense 6)

mourn *vb* to feel or express sadness for the death or loss of someone or something **mourner** *n*
WORD ORIGIN Old English *murnan*

mournful *adj* **1** feeling or expressing grief and sadness: *he stood by, a mournful expression on his face* **2** (of a sound) suggestive or reminiscent of grief or sadness: *the locomotive gave a mournful bellow* **mournfully** *adv*

mourning *n* **1** sorrow or grief, esp. over a death **2** the conventional symbols of grief for a death, such as the wearing of black **3** the period of time during which a death is officially mourned ▷ *adj* **4** of or relating to mourning

mouse *n, pl* **mice** **1** a small long-tailed rodent similar to but smaller than a rat **2** a quiet, timid, or cowardly person **3** *computers* a hand-held device used to control cursor movements and computing functions without keying ▷ *vb* **mousing, moused** **4** *rare* to stalk and catch mice
WORD ORIGIN Old English *mūs*

mouser *n* a cat or other animal that is used to catch mice

mousetrap *n* **1** a spring-loaded trap for killing mice **2** *Brit informal* cheese of mediocre quality

moussaka *n* a dish originating in the Balkan States, consisting of meat, aubergines, and tomatoes, topped with cheese sauce
WORD ORIGIN Modern Greek

mousse *n* **1** a light creamy dessert made with eggs, cream, and fruit set with gelatine **2** a similar dish made from fish or meat **3** short for **styling mousse**
WORD ORIGIN French: froth

moustache *or US* **mustache** *n* unshaved hair growing on the upper lip
WORD ORIGIN French, from Italian *mostaccio*

mousy *or* **mousey** *adj* **mousier, mousiest** **1** (of hair) dull light brown in colour **2** shy or ineffectual **mousiness** *n*

mouth *n, pl* **mouths** **1** the opening through which many animals take in food and issue sounds **2** the visible part of the mouth; lips **3** a person regarded as a consumer of food: *three mouths to feed* **4** a particular manner of speaking: *a foul mouth* **5** *informal* boastful, rude, or excessive talk: *she is all mouth* **6** the point where a river issues into a sea or lake **7** an opening, such as that of a bottle, tunnel, or gun **8** **down in the mouth** in low spirits ▷ *vb* **9** to form words with movements of the lips but without speaking **10** to speak or say something insincerely, esp. in public: *ministers mouthing platitudes*
WORD ORIGIN Old English *mūth*

mouthful *n, pl* **-fuls 1** the amount of food or drink put into the mouth at any one time when eating or drinking **2** a long word, phrase, or name that is difficult to say **3** *Brit informal* an abusive response: *I asked him to move and he just gave me a mouthful*

mouth organ *n* same as **harmonica**

mouthpiece *n* **1** the part of a wind instrument into which the player blows **2** the part of a telephone receiver into which a person speaks **3** a person or publication expressing the views of an organization

mouthwash *n* a medicated solution for gargling and cleansing the mouth

mouthwatering *adj* (of food) making one want to eat it, because it looks or smells delicious

movable *or* **moveable** *adj* **1** able to be moved; not fixed **2** (of a festival, esp. Easter) varying in date from year to year ▷ *n* **3 movables** movable articles, esp. furniture

move *vb* **moving, moved 1** to go or take from one place to another; change in position: *I moved your books off the table* **2** to start to live or work in a different place: *I moved to Brighton from Bristol last year* **3** to be or cause to be in motion: *the trees were moving in the wind; the car moved slowly down the road* **4** to act or begin to act: *the government plans to move to reduce crime* **5** to cause or prompt to do something: *public opinion moved the President to act* **6** to change the time when something is scheduled to happen: *can I move the appointment to Friday afternoon, please?* **7** to arouse affection, pity, or compassion in; touch: *her story moved me to tears* **8** to change, progress, or develop in a specified way: *the conversation moved to more personal matters* **9** to suggest a proposal formally, as in a debate: *to move a motion* **10** to spend most of one's time with a specified social group: *they both move in theatrical, arty circles* **11** (in board games) to change the position of a piece **12** (of machines) to work or operate **13 a** (of the bowels) to excrete waste **b** to cause the bowels to excrete waste **14** (of merchandise) to be disposed of by being bought **15** to travel quickly: *this car can really move* **16 move heaven and earth** to do everything possible to achieve a result ▷ *n* **17** the act of moving; movement **18** one of a sequence of actions, usually part of a plan: *the first real move towards disarmament* **19** the act of moving one's home or place of business **20 a** (in a boardgame) a player's turn to move his piece **b** (in a boardgame) a manoeuvre of a piece **21 get a move on** *informal* to hurry up **22 make a move** *informal* **a** to prepare or begin to leave a place to go somewhere else: *we'd better make a move if we want to be home before dark* **b** to do something which will produce a response: *neither of us wanted to make the first move* **23 on the move** travelling from place to place

WORD ORIGIN Latin *movere*

move in *vb* **1** Also: **move into** to start to live in a different house or flat **2** to start to live in the same house or flat as: *he moved in with his girlfriend* **3** to attack a person or place, or try to gain influence or control over a person or activity: *the police moved in to break up the demonstration*

movement *n* **1** the act, process, or an instance of moving **2** the manner of moving: *their movement is jerky* **3 a** a group of people with a common ideology **b** the organized action and campaigning of such a group: *a successful movement to abolish child labour* **4** a trend or tendency: *a movement towards shorter working hours* **5** *finance* a change in the price or value of shares, a currency, etc.: *adverse currency movements* **6** *music* a principal self-contained section of a large-scale work, such as a symphony **7** **movements** a person's location and activities during a specific time: *police were trying to piece together the recent movements of the two men* **8 a** the evacuation of the bowels **b** the matter evacuated **9** the mechanism which drives and regulates a watch or clock

move on *vb* **1** to leave one place in order to go elsewhere: *we spent three days in Perth before moving on towards Inverness* **2** to order (someone) to leave and go elsewhere: *we were moved on by the police* **3** to finish one thing and turn one's attention to something else: *can we move on to the next question?*

move over *vb* **1** to change one's position in order to make room for someone else: *if you moved over there'd be room for us both on the couch* **2** to leave one's job so that someone else can have it: *she decided to move over to let someone younger onto the board*

mover *n* **1** a person or animal that moves in a particular way: *a slow mover* **2** the person who first puts forward a proposal **3** *US & Canad* a removal firm or a person who works for one

movie *n* **1** *informal* a cinema film **2 the movies** the cinema: *I want to go to the movies tonight*

moving *adj* **1** arousing or touching the emotions: *a moving account of her son's death* **2** changing or capable of changing position: *a moving target* **movingly** *adv*

moving staircase *or* **stairway** *n* an escalator

mow *vb* **mowing, mowed, mowed** *or* **mown 1** to cut down grass or crops: *a tractor chugged along, mowing hay* **2** to cut the growing vegetation of a field or lawn: *to mow a meadow* **mower** *n*

WORD ORIGIN Old English *māwan*

mow down *vb* to kill in large numbers, esp. by gunfire

mown *vb* the past participle of **mow**

mozzarella (mot-sa-**rel**-la) *n* a moist white curd cheese originally made in Italy from buffalo milk

WORD ORIGIN Italian

MP 1 Member of Parliament **2** Military Police **3** Mounted Police

MP3 *n computers* an audio or video file created using MPEG-1 Audio Layer-3, trade name of a file compression system

MPEG (**em**-peg) *n computers* **a** a standard compressed file format used for audio and video files **b** a file in this format

WORD ORIGIN from *Motion Picture Experts Group*

mpg miles per gallon

mph miles per hour

MPhil Master of Philosophy

MPV multipurpose vehicle

Mr *n, pl* **Messrs** a title used before a man's name or before some office that he holds: *Mr Pickwick; Mr President*

WORD ORIGIN from *mister*

MRI *med* magnetic resonance imaging: a diagnostic scanning technique which gives detailed images of internal tissue by analysing its response to being bombarded with high-frequency radio waves within a strong magnetic field

Mrs *n, pl* **Mrs** *or* **Mesdames** a title used before the name of a married woman

WORD ORIGIN from *mistress*

ms millisecond(s)

Ms (**mizz**) *n* a title used before the name of a woman to avoid indicating whether she is married or not

MS 1 Mississippi **2** multiple sclerosis

MS. *or* **ms.** *pl* **MSS** *or* **mss** manuscript

MSc Master of Science

MSF Manufacturing, Science, and Finance (Union)

MSG monosodium glutamate

MSM mainstream media

MSP (in Britain) Member of the Scottish Parliament

MST Mountain Standard Time

mt megaton

Mt¹ Mount: *Mt Everest*

Mt² *chem* meitnerium

MT Montana

mt. megaton

MTech (in the US) Master of Technology

much *adj* **more, most 1** a large amount or degree of: *there isn't much wine left* ▷ *n* **2** a large amount or degree **3 a bit much** *informal* rather excessive **4 make much of a** to make sense of: *he couldn't make much of her letter* **b** to give importance to: *the press made much of the story* **5 not much of** not to any appreciable degree or extent: *he's not much of a cook* **6 not up to much** *informal* of a low standard: *this beer is not up to much* ▷ *adv* **7** considerably: *I'm much better now* **8** practically or nearly: *it's much the same* **9** often or a great deal: *that doesn't happen much these days* **10 (as) much as** even though; although: *much as I'd like to, I can't come* ▶ See also **more, most**

WORD ORIGIN Old English *mycel*

muchness *n* **much of a muchness** *Brit & NZ* very similar

mucilage (mew-**sill**-ij) *n* **1** a sticky substance used as an adhesive, such as gum or glue **2** a glutinous substance secreted by certain plants **mucilaginous** *adj*

WORD ORIGIN Late Latin *mucilago* mouldy juice

muck *n* **1** dirt or filth **2** farmyard dung or decaying vegetable matter **3** *slang chiefly Brit & NZ* something of poor quality; rubbish: *I don't want to eat this muck* **4 make a muck of** *slang chiefly Brit & NZ* to ruin or spoil ▷ *vb* **5** to spread manure upon ▶ See also **muck about, muck in**, etc.

WORD ORIGIN probably Old Norse

muck about or **around** vb slang **1** to waste time by misbehaving or being silly **2 muck about with** to interfere with, annoy, or waste the time of

muck in vb Brit & NZ slang to share duties or work with other people

muck out vb to clean (a barn, stable, etc.)

muckraking n seeking out and exposing scandal relating to well-known people **muckraker** n

mucksweat n Brit informal profuse sweat

muck up vb informal to ruin, spoil, or do very badly: I mucked up my driving test

mucky adj **1** dirty or muddy: don't come in here with your mucky boots on! **2** sexually explicit; obscene: a mucky book

mucosa n same as **mucous membrane** > **mucosal** adj
WORD ORIGIN Latin mucosus slimy

mucous membrane n a mucus-secreting tissue that lines body cavities or passages

mucus (mew-kuss) n the slimy protective secretion of the mucous membranes **mucosity** n **mucous** adj
WORD ORIGIN Latin: nasal secretions

mud n **1** soft wet earth, as found on the ground after rain or at the bottom of ponds **2** (someone's) name is mud informal (someone) is disgraced **3 throw mud at** informal to slander or vilify ▷ adj **4** made from mud or dried mud: a mud hut
WORD ORIGIN probably Low German mudde

mud bath n **1** a medicinal bath in heated mud **2** a dirty or muddy place, occasion, or state: heavy rain turned the pitch into a mud bath

muddle n **1** a state of untidiness or confusion: the files are in a terrible muddle **2** a state of mental confusion or uncertainty: the government are in a muddle over the economy ▷ vb **-dling, -dled 3** Also: **muddle up** to mix up or confuse (objects or items): you've got your books all muddled up with mine **4** to make (someone) confused: don't muddle her with too many suggestions **muddled** adj
WORD ORIGIN perhaps Middle Dutch moddelen to make muddy

muddleheaded adj mentally confused or vague

muddle through vb to succeed in spite of lack of organization

muddy adj **-dier, -diest 1** covered or filled with mud **2** not clear or bright: muddy colours **3** cloudy: a muddy liquid **4** (esp. of thoughts) confused or vague ▷ vb **-dies, -dying, -died 5** to make muddy **6** to make a situation or issue less clear: the allegations of sexual misconduct only serve to muddy the issue **muddily** adv

mud flat n an area of low muddy land that is covered at high tide but not at low tide

mud flow n the rapid downhill movement of a mass of mud, typically in the shape of a tongue

mudguard n a curved part of a bicycle or other vehicle attached above the wheels to reduce the amount of water or mud thrown up by them

mudpack n a cosmetic paste applied to the face to improve the complexion

mudpie n a mass of mud moulded into a pielike shape by a child

mudslinging n the making of malicious personal attacks on an opponent, esp. in politics **mudslinger** n

muesli (mewz-lee) n a mixture of rolled oats, nuts, and dried fruit, usually eaten with milk
WORD ORIGIN Swiss German

muezzin (moo-ezz-in) n Islam the official of a mosque who calls the faithful to prayer from the minaret
WORD ORIGIN Arabic mu'adhdhin

muff¹ n a tube of fur or cloth into which the hands are placed for warmth
WORD ORIGIN probably Dutch mof

muff² vb **1** to do (something) badly: I muffed my chance to make a good impression **2** to bungle (a shot or catch)
WORD ORIGIN origin unknown

muffin n **1** a small cup-shaped sweet bread roll, usually eaten hot with butter **2** a thick round baked yeast roll, usually toasted and served with butter
WORD ORIGIN origin unknown

muffle vb **-fling, -fled 1** to deaden (a sound or noise), esp. by wrapping the source of it in something: the sound was muffled by the double glazing **2** to wrap up in a scarf or coat for warmth **3** to censor or restrict: an attempt to muffle criticism **muffled** adj
WORD ORIGIN probably Old French moufle mitten

muffler n **1** Brit a thick scarf worn for warmth **2** a device to deaden sound, esp. one on a car exhaust; silencer

mufti n civilian clothes worn by a person who normally wears a military uniform
WORD ORIGIN from Mufti, Muslim religious leader

mug¹ n **1** a large drinking cup with a handle **2** the quantity held by a mug or its contents: a mug of coffee
WORD ORIGIN probably Scandinavian

mug² n **1** slang a person's face or mouth: keep your ugly mug out of this **2** slang a gullible person, esp. one who is swindled easily **3 a mug's game** a worthless activity
WORD ORIGIN perhaps same as MUG¹

mug³ vb **mugging, mugged** to attack someone in order to rob them **mugger** n **mugging** n

muggins n slang **a** a stupid or gullible person **b** a title used humorously to refer to oneself
WORD ORIGIN probably from surname Muggins

muggy adj **-gier, -giest** (of weather or air) unpleasantly warm and humid **mugginess** n
WORD ORIGIN dialect mug drizzle

mug shot n informal a photograph of a person's face, esp. one resembling a police-file picture

mug up vb Brit slang to study a subject hard, esp. for an exam
WORD ORIGIN origin unknown

Muhammad n same as **Mohammed**

mujaheddin or **mujahedeen** (moo-ja-hed-deen) pl n fundamentalist Muslim guerrillas

WORD ORIGIN Arabic mujāhidīn fighters

mukluk n a soft boot, usually of sealskin, worn in the American Arctic
WORD ORIGIN Yupik (native language of Siberia and Alaska) muklok large seal

mulatto (mew-lat-toe) n, pl **-tos** or **-toes** a person with one Black and one White parent
WORD ORIGIN Spanish mulato young mule

mulberry n, pl **-ries 1** a tree with edible blackberry-like fruit, the leaves of which are used to feed silkworms **2** the fruit of any of these trees ▷ adj **3** dark purple
WORD ORIGIN Latin morum

mulch n **1** a mixture of half-rotten vegetable matter and peat used to protect the roots of plants or enrich the soil ▷ vb **2** to cover soil with mulch
WORD ORIGIN obsolete mulch soft

mule¹ n **1** the sterile offspring of a male donkey and a female horse **2** a machine that spins cotton into yarn
WORD ORIGIN Latin mulus

mule² n a backless shoe or slipper
WORD ORIGIN Latin mulleus a magistrate's shoe

muleteer n a person who drives mules

mulga n **1** an Australian acacia shrub growing in desert regions **2** Austral the outback
WORD ORIGIN Aboriginal

mulish adj stubborn; obstinate

mull n Scot a promontory or headland: the Mull of Galloway
WORD ORIGIN probably Gaelic maol

mullah n (formerly) a Muslim scholar, teacher, or religious leader
WORD ORIGIN Arabic mawlā master

mulled adj (of wine or ale) flavoured with sugar and spices and served hot
WORD ORIGIN origin unknown

mullet n, pl **mullets** or **mullet** any of various marine food fishes
WORD ORIGIN Greek mullos

mulligatawny n a curry-flavoured soup of Anglo-Indian origin
WORD ORIGIN Tamil milakutanni pepper water

mullion n a slender vertical bar between the casements or panes of a window **mullioned** adj
WORD ORIGIN Old French moinel

mull over vb to study or ponder: he mulled over the arrangements
WORD ORIGIN probably from muddle

mulloway n a large Australian sea fish, valued for sport and food

multi- combining form **1** many or much: multimillion **2** more than one: multistorey
WORD ORIGIN Latin multus much, many

multicoloured adj having many colours: multicoloured balls of wool

multicultural adj of or for the cultures of several different races

multifarious (mull-tee-fare-ee-uss) adj many and varied: multifarious religious movements and political divisions sprang up around this time
WORD ORIGIN Late Latin multifarius manifold

multiflora rose n a climbing rose with clusters of small fragrant flowers

Sir Walter Scott

Sir Walter Scott, as well as being one of Scotland's greatest writers, is acknowledged as the inventor of the modern historical novel. It is somewhat surprising, then, that he achieved recognition in his own lifetime primarily as a poet.

Scott was born in Edinburgh in 1771. As a boy, he contracted polio and was sent to his grandfather's farm in the Scottish Borders to recuperate. His explorations in the Border country gave him a keen interest in old Border tales and ballads that was to stay with him for the rest of his life. After leaving university, he entered his lawyer father's office as a clerk, rising to be called to the Bar in 1792.

Scott's first major literary works, collections of Border ballads called *Minstrelsy of the Scottish Border*, appeared in 1802 and 1803, and it was a ballad originally composed for the third volume of this publication, *The Lay of the Last Minstrel*, that brought him widespread recognition and huge popularity after its publication in 1805.

His fame was further enhanced by the publication of two further romances. *Marmion* (1808) was a poem of six cantos, written in tetrameter, about the Battle of Flodden Field. It was in this poem that Scott wrote the now famous proverbial words, 'Oh what a tangled web we weave,/When first we practise to deceive!' But it was his next narrative poem, *The Lady of the Lake* (1810), that marked the pinnacle of his fame as a poet. It dramatized the struggle between James V, a sixteenth-century king of Scotland, and the powerful clan Douglas. Scott's aim had been to depict convincing characters in a historical context, and critics praised the poem's portrayal of 'real manners'. The volume sold more than any poetical work previously published. However, later poems did not achieve the success of these earlier works.

It was the huge success of *Waverley*, published in 1814, that helped convince Scott that his future lay in prose composition. Set in Scotland during the Jacobite Rebellion of 1745, the novel tells the story of Edward Waverley, a young Englishman who begins to sympathize with the Jacobite cause. Scott did not name himself as the author, knowing his reputation lay in his poetry, and continued to publish much of his prose either anonymously or with the attribution 'by the author of Waverley' (giving rise to the umbrella term 'the Waverley novels'). He did not acknowledge that he was 'the author of Waverley' until 1827.

Despite the considerable sales of *Waverley*, Scott's finances were often precarious. A publishing company he had set up with John Ballantyne, printer of *Minstrelsy of the Scottish Border*, was on the verge of collapse by 1813. This was a spur to produce more works, and over the next few years, Scott wrote further stories set in seventeenth- and eighteenth-century Scotland, with themes of religious dissension and conflict between English and Scottish, and Highland and Lowland cultures. These included *Guy Mannering* (1815), *The Antiquary* (1816), *Rob Roy* (1817), *The Heart of Midlothian* (1818), and *The Bride of Lammermoor* (1819). In 1819, Scott moved his focus to medieval England in *Ivanhoe*, the story of Cedric, a Saxon nobleman.

In his later years, Scott continued to write, often in an attempt to counter financial difficulties. Acclaimed titles from his last period include *Woodstock* (1826), set during the English Civil War, and *The Fair Maid of Perth* (1828), which tells the story of the fourteenth-century Duke of Rothsay's attempts to abduct Catharine Glover.

Scott suffered from ill health in his final years and died at Abbotsford, his home in the Scottish Borders, in 1832. However, his legacy lives on in the English language: among the words and phrases introduced, if not invented, by Scott are *red-handed*, which he adapted from an old Scots law term *red hand* ('in the act of doing something') and used in *Ivanhoe*, and *strain at the leash*, which appeared in his 1825 novel *The Talisman*. Scott is also credited with bringing the word *glamour* into literary language, extending its sense of 'witchcraft' to mean 'allure'. And his influence remains very visible in the city of his birth: Edinburgh's central railway station takes its name, Waverley, from the novels so named, and the Scott Monument, an imposing Gothic-style construction in Edinburgh's Princes Street, is the tallest monument dedicated to a writer anywhere in the world.

multiform *adj* having many shapes or forms

multilateral *adj* of or involving more than two nations or parties: *multilateral trade negotiations*

multilingual *adj* **1** able to speak more than two languages **2** written or expressed in more than two languages: *a multilingual leaflet*

multimedia *pl n* **1** the combined use of media such as television and slides **2** *computers* of or relating to systems that can manipulate data in a variety of forms, such as sound, graphics, or text

multimillionaire *n* a person who has money or property worth several million pounds, dollars, etc.

multinational *adj* **1** (of a large business company) operating in several countries **2** involving people from several countries: *a multinational peacekeeping force* ▷ *n* **3** a large company operating in several countries

multiparous (mull-**tip**-a-russ) *adj* producing many offspring at one birth **WORD ORIGIN** New Latin *multiparus*

multiple *adj* **1** having or involving more than one part, individual, or element ▷ *n* **2** a number or polynomial which can be divided by another specified one an exact number of times: *6 is a multiple of 2* **multiply** *adv* **WORD ORIGIN** Latin *multiplus*

multiple-choice *adj* (of a test or question) giving a number of possible answers out of which the correct one must be chosen

multiple sclerosis *n* a chronic progressive disease of the central nervous system, resulting in speech and visual disorders, tremor, muscular incoordination, and partial paralysis

multiplex *n, pl* **-plexes 1** a purpose-built complex containing several cinemas and usually restaurants and bars ▷ *adj* **2** having many elements; complex **WORD ORIGIN** Latin: having many folds

multiplicand *n* a number to be multiplied by another number (the **multiplier**)

multiplication *n* **1** a mathematical operation, equivalent to adding a number to itself a specified number of times. For instance, 4 multiplied by 3 equals 12 (i.e. 4+4+4) **2** the act of multiplying or state of being multiplied

multiplication sign *n* the symbol ×, placed between numbers to be multiplied

multiplication table *n* a table giving the results of multiplying two numbers together

multiplicity *n, pl* **-ties 1** a large number or great variety **2** the state of being multiple

multiplier *n* a number by which another number (the **multiplicand**) is multiplied

multiply *vb* **-plies, -plying, -plied 1** to increase or cause to increase in number, quantity, or degree **2** to combine numbers or quantities by multiplication **3** to increase in number by reproduction **WORD ORIGIN** Latin *multiplicare*

multipurpose *adj* having many uses: *a giant multipurpose enterprise*

multipurpose vehicle *n* a large car, similar to a van, designed to carry up to eight passengers

multiracial *adj* consisting of or involving people of many races: *a multiracial society* **multiracialism** *n*

multistage *adj* (of a rocket or missile) having several stages, each of which can be jettisoned after it has burnt out

multistorey *adj* (of a building) having many storeys

multitrack *adj* (in sound recording) using tape containing two or more tracks

multitude *n* **1** a large number of people or things: *a multitude of different pressure groups* **2 the multitude** the common people **multitudinous** *adj* **WORD ORIGIN** Latin *multitudo*

multi-user *adj* (of a computer) capable of being used by several people at once

mum[1] *n chiefly Brit informal* same as **mother** **WORD ORIGIN** a child's word

mum[2] *adj* **1 keep mum** remain silent **2 mum's the word** keep quiet (about something) **WORD ORIGIN** suggestive of closed lips

mumble *vb* **-bling, -bled 1** to speak or say something indistinctly, with the mouth partly closed: *I could hear him mumbling under his breath* ▷ *n* **2** an indistinct or low utterance or sound **WORD ORIGIN** Middle English *momelen*, from MUM[2]

mumbo jumbo *n* **1** meaningless language; nonsense or gibberish **2** foolish religious ritual or incantation **WORD ORIGIN** probably from West African *mama dyumbo*, name of a tribal god

mummer *n* one of a group of masked performers in a folk play or mime **WORD ORIGIN** Old French *momer* to mime

mummery *n, pl* **-meries 1** a performance by mummers **2** hypocritical or ostentatious ceremony

mummified *adj* (of a body) preserved as a mummy **mummification** *n*

mummy[1] *n, pl* **-mies** *chiefly Brit* an embalmed body as prepared for burial in ancient Egypt **WORD ORIGIN** Persian *mūm* wax

mummy[2] *n, pl* **-mies** a child's word for **mother** **WORD ORIGIN** variant of MUM[1]

mumps *n* an infectious viral disease in which the glands below the ear become swollen and painful **WORD ORIGIN** obsolete *mump* to grimace

munch *vb* to chew noisily and steadily **WORD ORIGIN** imitative

mundane *adj* **1** everyday, ordinary, and therefore not very interesting **2** relating to the world or worldly matters **WORD ORIGIN** Latin *mundus* world

mung bean *n* an E Asian bean plant grown for its edible seeds which are used as a source of bean sprouts **WORD ORIGIN** Tamil *mūngu*

municipal *adj* of or relating to a town or city or its local government **WORD ORIGIN** Latin *municipium* a free town

municipality *n, pl* **-ties 1** a city, town, or district enjoying local self-government **2** the governing body of such a unit

munificent (mew-**niff**-fiss-sent) *adj* very generous **munificence** *n* **WORD ORIGIN** Latin *munus* gift + *facere* to make

muniments (**mew**-nim-ments) *pl n law* the title deeds and other documentary evidence relating to the title to land **WORD ORIGIN** Latin *munire* to defend

munitions (mew-**nish**-unz) *pl n* military equipment and stores, esp. ammunition

munted *adj NZ slang* **1** destroyed or ruined **2** abnormal or peculiar

muon (**mew**-on) *n* a positive or negative elementary particle with a mass 207 times that of an electron **WORD ORIGIN** short for *mu meson*

mural (**myoor**-al) *n* **1** a large painting on a wall ▷ *adj* **2** of or relating to a wall **muralist** *n* **WORD ORIGIN** Latin *murus* wall

murder *n* **1** the unlawful intentional killing of one human being by another **2** *informal* something dangerous, difficult, or unpleasant: *shopping on Christmas Eve is murder* **3 cry blue murder** *informal* to make an outcry **4 get away with murder** *informal* to do as one pleases without ever being punished ▷ *vb* **5** to kill someone intentionally and unlawfully **6** *informal* to ruin a piece of music or drama by performing it very badly: *he absolutely murdered that song* **7** *informal* to beat decisively **murderer** *n* **murderess** *fem n* **murderous** *adj* **WORD ORIGIN** Old English *morthor*

murk *n* thick gloomy darkness **WORD ORIGIN** Old Norse *myrkr* darkness

murky *adj* **murkier, murkiest 1** gloomy or dark **2** cloudy or hard to see through: *a murky stagnant pond* **3** obscure and suspicious; shady: *murky goings-on; his murky past* **murkily** *adv* **murkiness** *n*

murmur *vb* **1** to speak or say in a quiet indistinct way **2** to complain ▷ *n* **3** a continuous low indistinct sound, such as that of a distant conversation **4** an indistinct utterance: *a murmur of protest* **5** a complaint or grumble: *he left without a murmur* **6** *med* any abnormal soft blowing sound heard usually over the chest: *a heart murmur* **murmuring** *n, adj* **murmurous** *adj* **WORD ORIGIN** Latin *murmurare* to rumble

Murphy's Law *n* same as **Sod's Law**

murrain (**murr**-rin) *n* any plaguelike disease in cattle **WORD ORIGIN** Old French *morir* to die

mus. 1 museum **2** music **3** musical

MusB or **MusBac** Bachelor of Music

muscle *n* **1** a tissue in the body composed of bundles of elongated cells which produce movement in an organ or part by contracting or relaxing **2** an organ composed of muscle tissue: *the heart is essentially just another muscle* **3** strength or force: *we do not have the political muscle to force through these reforms*

▷ *vb* -**cling**, -**cled** **4 muscle in** to force one's way into a situation; intrude: *I don't like the way he's trying to muscle in here* **WORD ORIGIN** Medical Latin *musculus* little mouse

muscle-bound *adj* having overdeveloped and inelastic muscles

muscleman *n, pl* -**men 1** a man with highly developed muscles **2** a henchman employed to intimidate or use violence upon victims

Muscovite *adj* **1** of Moscow, a city in Russia ▷ *n* **2** a person from Moscow

muscular *adj* **1** having well-developed muscles; brawny **2** of or consisting of muscle: *great muscular effort is needed* **3** forceful or powerful: *a muscular account of Schumann's Fourth Symphony* **muscularity** *n*

muscular dystrophy *n* a hereditary disease in which the muscles gradually weaken and waste away

musculature *n* the arrangement of muscles in an organ, part, or organism

musculoskeletal *adj* of or relating to the skeleton and musculature taken together

MusD *or* **MusDoc** Doctor of Music

muse¹ *vb* **musing, mused** to think deeply and at length about: *she mused unhappily on how right her sister had been* **WORD ORIGIN** Old French *muser*

muse² *n* **the muse** a force or person, esp. a woman, that inspires a creative artist **WORD ORIGIN** Greek *Mousa* a Muse

Muses *pl n Greek myth* the nine sister goddesses, each of whom was the protector of a different art or science

museum *n* a building where objects of historical, artistic, or scientific interest are exhibited and preserved **WORD ORIGIN** Greek *Mouseion* home of the Muses

museum piece *n informal* a very old or old-fashioned object or building

mush¹ *n* **1** a soft pulpy mass **2** *informal* cloying sentimentality **WORD ORIGIN** obsolete *moose* porridge

mush² *Canad interj* **1** an order to dogs in a sled team to start up or go faster ▷ *vb* **2** to travel by or drive a dogsled **WORD ORIGIN** perhaps from imperative of French *marcher* to advance

mushroom *n* **1** an edible fungus consisting of a cap at the end of a stem **2** something resembling a mushroom in shape or rapid growth ▷ *vb* **3** to grow rapidly: *consumer debt mushroomed rapidly in 1989* **WORD ORIGIN** Late Latin *mussirio*

mushroom cloud *n* the large mushroom-shaped cloud produced by a nuclear explosion

mushy *adj* **mushier, mushiest 1** soft and pulpy **2** *informal* excessively sentimental

music *n* **1** an art form consisting of sequences of sounds organized melodically, harmonically, and rhythmically **2** such sounds, esp. when produced by singing or musical instruments **3** any written or printed representation of musical sounds: *I can't read music* **4** any sequence of sounds perceived as pleasing or harmonious

5 face the music *informal* to confront the consequences of one's actions **6 music to one's ears** something, such as a piece of news, that one is pleased to hear **WORD ORIGIN** Greek *mousikē (tekhnē)* (art) in the protection of the Muses

musical *adj* **1** of or used in music **2** talented in or fond of music **3** pleasant-sounding; harmonious: *musical laughter* **4** involving or set to music: *a musical biography of Judy Garland* ▷ *n* **5** a play or film that has dialogue interspersed with songs and dances **musicality** *n* **musically** *adv*

musical box *n* a box containing a mechanical instrument that plays tunes when the box is opened

musical chairs *n* **1** a game in which the players run round a row of chairs while music plays. There is one more player than there are chairs, and when the music stops the player who cannot find a chair to sit on is out **2** any situation involving a number of people in a series of interrelated changes: *the dismissal of the Chancellor started a game of musical chairs in the Cabinet*

music centre *n Brit* a single hi-fi unit containing a turntable, radio, compact disc player, and cassette player

music hall *n chiefly Brit* **1** (formerly) a variety entertainment consisting of songs and comic turns **2** a theatre at which such entertainments were staged

musician *n* a person who plays or composes music, esp. as a profession

musicianship *n* the technical and interpretive skills involved in singing or playing music: *the piano part is simple but performed with great musicianship*

musicology *n* the scholarly study of music **musicologist** *n*

musk *n* **1** a strong-smelling glandular secretion of the male musk deer, used in perfumery **2** any similar substance produced by animals or plants, or manufactured synthetically **WORD ORIGIN** Persian *mushk*

musk deer *n* a small central Asian mountain deer

muskeg *n chiefly Canad* an area of undrained boggy land **WORD ORIGIN** Native American: grassy swamp

musket *n* a long-barrelled muzzle-loading gun fired from the shoulder, a forerunner of the rifle **musketeer** *n* **WORD ORIGIN** Italian *moschetto* arrow, earlier: sparrow hawk

muskmelon *n* any of several varieties of melon, such as the cantaloupe and honeydew

musk ox *n* a large ox, which has a dark shaggy coat, downward-curving horns, and emits a musky smell

muskrat *n, pl* -**rats** *or* -**rat 1** a North American beaver-like amphibious rodent **2** the brown fur of this animal

musk rose *n* a Mediterranean rose, cultivated for its white musk-scented flowers

musky *adj* **muskier, muskiest** having a heady sweet smell **muskiness** *n*

Muslim *or* **Moslem** *n, pl* -**lims** *or* -**lim 1** a follower of the religion of Islam ▷ *adj* **2** of or relating to Islam **WORD ORIGIN** Arabic, literally: one who surrenders

muslin *n* a very fine plain-weave cotton fabric **WORD ORIGIN** French *mousseline*

musquash *n* muskrat fur **WORD ORIGIN** from a Native American language

muss *vb US & Canad informal* to make untidy; rumple: *watch you don't muss up my hair!* **WORD ORIGIN** probably a blend of *mess* + *fuss*

mussel *n* an edible shellfish, with a dark slightly elongated hinged shell, which lives attached to rocks **WORD ORIGIN** Latin *musculus*, diminutive of *mus* mouse

must¹ *vb* **1** used as an auxiliary to express or indicate the need or necessity to do something: *I must go to the shops* **2** used as an auxiliary to express or indicate obligation or requirement: *you must not smoke in here* **3** used as an auxiliary to express or indicate the probable correctness of a statement: *he must be finished by now* **4** used as an auxiliary to express or indicate inevitability: *all good things must come to an end* **5** used as an auxiliary to express or indicate determination: *I must try and finish this* **6** used as an auxiliary to express or indicate conviction or certainty on the part of the speaker: *you must be kidding!* ▷ *n* **7** an essential or necessary thing: *strong boots are a must for hill walking* **WORD ORIGIN** Old English *mōste*, past tense of *mōtan* to be allowed or obliged

must² *n* the pressed juice of grapes or other fruit ready for fermentation **WORD ORIGIN** Latin *mustum* new wine

mustache *n US* same as **moustache**

mustachio *n, pl* -**chios** *often humorous* a moustache, esp. a bushy or elaborate one **mustachioed** *adj* **WORD ORIGIN** Italian *mostaccio*

mustang *n* a small breed of horse, often wild or half wild, found in the southwestern US **WORD ORIGIN** Mexican Spanish *mestengo*

mustard *n* **1** a hot, spicy paste made from the powdered seeds of any of a family of plants **2** any of these plants, which have yellow flowers and slender pods ▷ *adj* **3** brownish-yellow **WORD ORIGIN** Old French *moustarde*

mustard and cress *n* seedlings of white mustard and garden cress, used in salads and as a garnish

mustard gas *n* an oily liquid with poisonous vapour used in chemical warfare, esp. in World War I, which can cause blindness, burns, and sometimes death

mustard plaster *n med* a mixture of powdered black mustard seeds applied to the skin

muster *vb* **1** to summon or gather: *I put as much disbelief in my expression as I could muster* **2** to call or be called together for duty or inspection: *the battalion mustered on the bank of the river* ▷ *n* **3** an assembly of

m

military personnel for duty or inspection **4** a collection, assembly, or gathering **5 pass muster** to be acceptable
WORD ORIGIN Latin *monstrare* to show

musty *adj* **-tier, -tiest 1** smelling or tasting old, stale, or mouldy **2** old-fashioned, dull, or hackneyed: *musty ideas* **mustily** *adv* **mustiness** *n*
WORD ORIGIN perhaps variant of obsolete *moisty*

mutable (**mew**-tab-bl) *adj* able to or tending to change **mutability** *n*
WORD ORIGIN Latin *mutare* to change

mutagen (**mew**-ta-jen) *n* any substance that can induce genetic mutation **mutagenic** *adj*
WORD ORIGIN MUTATION + *-gen* (suffix) producing

mutagenesis (mew-ta-jen-**iss**-iss) *n* the origin and development of a genetic mutation
WORD ORIGIN MUTATION + GENESIS

mutant (**mew**-tant) *n* **1** an animal, organism, or gene that has undergone mutation ▷ *adj* **2** of or resulting from mutation

mutate (mew-**tate**) *vb* **-tating, -tated** to undergo or cause to undergo mutation
WORD ORIGIN Latin *mutare* to change

mutation (mew-**tay**-shun) *n* **1** a change or alteration **2** a change in the chromosomes or genes of a cell which may affect the structure and development of the resultant offspring **3** a physical characteristic in an organism resulting from this type of chromosomal change

mute *adj* **1** not giving out sound or speech; silent **2** unable to speak; dumb **3** unspoken or unexpressed: *she shot him a look of mute entreaty* **4** (of a letter in a word) silent: *the 'k' in 'know' is mute* ▷ *n* **5** a person who is unable to speak **6** any of various devices used to soften the tone of stringed or brass instruments ▷ *vb* **muting, muted 7** to reduce the volume or soften the tone of a musical instrument by means of a mute or soft pedal **8** to reduce the volume of a sound: *the double glazing muted the noise* **mutely** *adv* **muteness** *n*
WORD ORIGIN Latin *mutus* silent

muted *adj* **1** (of a sound or colour) softened: *a muted pink shirt* **2** (of an emotion or action) subdued or restrained: *his response was muted* **3** (of a musical instrument) being played while fitted with a mute: *muted trumpet*

mute swan *n* the swan most commonly seen in Britain, which has a pure white plumage and an orange-red bill

muti (**moo**-tee) *n* S *African* medicine, esp. herbal
WORD ORIGIN Zulu

mutilate (**mew**-till-ate) *vb* **-lating, -lated 1** to injure by tearing or cutting off a limb or essential part; maim **2** to damage a book or text so as to render it unintelligible **3** to spoil or damage severely: *why did he mutilate his favourite tapes and leave ours alone?* **mutilated** *adj* **mutilation** *n* **mutilator** *n*
WORD ORIGIN Latin *mutilare* to cut off

mutineer *n* a person who mutinies

mutinous *adj* **1** openly rebellious **2** characteristic or indicative of mutiny

mutiny (**mew**-tin-ee) *n, pl* **-nies 1** open rebellion against authority, esp. by sailors or soldiers against their officers ▷ *vb* **-nies, -nying, -nied 2** to engage in mutiny: *soldiers who had mutinied and taken control*
WORD ORIGIN Old French *mutin* rebellious

mutt *n slang* **1** a foolish or stupid person **2** a mongrel dog
WORD ORIGIN from *muttonhead*

mutter *vb* **1** to say something or speak in a low and indistinct tone: *he muttered an excuse* **2** to grumble ▷ *n* **3** a muttered sound or complaint **muttering** *n, adj*
WORD ORIGIN Middle English *moteren*

mutton *n* **1** the flesh of mature sheep, used as food **2 mutton dressed as lamb** an older woman dressed up to look young
WORD ORIGIN Medieval Latin *multo* sheep

mutton bird *n* **1** *Austral* a migratory sea bird with dark plumage **2** NZ any of a number of migratory sea birds, the young of which are a Māori delicacy

muttonchops *pl n* side whiskers trimmed in the shape of chops

mutual (**mew**-chew-al) *adj* **1** experienced or expressed by each of two or more people about the other; reciprocal: *mutual respect* **2** common to or shared by two or more people: *a mutual friend* **3** denoting an organization, such as an insurance company, in which the policyholders or investors share the profits and expenses and there are no shareholders **mutuality** *n* **mutually** *adv*
WORD ORIGIN Latin *mutuus* reciprocal

≡ **USAGE**
≡ The use of *mutual* to mean *common to or*
≡ *shared by two or more people* was formerly
≡ considered incorrect, but is now
≡ acceptable. Tautologous use of *mutual*
≡ should be avoided: *cooperation (not*
≡ *mutual cooperation) between the two*
≡ *countries.*

mutual fund *n* US & Canad an investment trust that issues units for public sale and invests the money in many different businesses

Muzak *n trademark* recorded light music played in places such as restaurants and shops

muzzle *n* **1** the projecting part of an animal's face, usually the jaws and nose **2** a guard, made of plastic or strap of strong material, fitted over an animal's nose and jaws to prevent it biting or eating **3** the front end of a gun barrel ▷ *vb* **-zling, -zled 4** to prevent from being heard or noticed: *an attempt to muzzle the press* **5** to put a muzzle on an animal
WORD ORIGIN Old French *muse* snout

muzzy *adj* **-zier, -ziest 1** confused and groggy: *he felt muzzy and hung over* **2** blurred or hazy: *the picture was muzzy and out of focus* **muzzily** *adv* **muzziness** *n*
WORD ORIGIN origin unknown

MV megavolt

MW 1 megawatt **2** *radio* medium wave

mwah *interj* a representation of the sound of a kiss

Mx *physics* maxwell

my *adj* **1** of, belonging to, or associated with the speaker or writer (me): *my own way of doing things* **2** used in various forms of address: *my lord* ▷ *interj* **3** an exclamation of surprise or awe: *my, how you've grown!*
WORD ORIGIN variant of Old English *mīn*

≡ **USAGE**
≡ See at **me**.

myall *n* an Australian acacia with hard scented wood
WORD ORIGIN Aboriginal

mycelium (mice-**eel**-lee-um) *n, pl* **-lia** (-lee-a) the mass forming the body of a fungus
WORD ORIGIN Greek *mukēs* mushroom + *hēlos* nail

Mycenaean (mice-in-**ee**-an) *adj* of or relating to the Aegean civilization of Mycenae, a city in S Greece (1400–1100 BC)

mycology *n* the study of fungi
WORD ORIGIN Greek *mukēs* mushroom + -LOGY

myelin (**my**-ill-in) *n* a white tissue forming an insulating sheath around certain nerve fibres
WORD ORIGIN Greek *muelos* marrow

myeloma (my-ill-**oh**-ma) *n, pl* **-mas** or **-mata** (-ma-ta) a tumour of the bone marrow
WORD ORIGIN Greek *muelos* marrow + *-oma*, modelled on *carcinoma*

mynah or **myna** *n* a tropical Asian starling which can mimic human speech
WORD ORIGIN Hindi *mainā*

Mynheer (min-**near**) *n* a Dutch title of address equivalent to *Sir* or *Mr*
WORD ORIGIN Dutch *mijnheer* my lord

myocardium *n, pl* **-dia** the muscular tissue of the heart **myocardial** *adj*
WORD ORIGIN Greek *mus* muscle + *kardia* heart

myopia (my-**oh**-pee-a) *n* inability to see distant objects clearly because the images are focused in front of the retina; short-sightedness **myopic** (my-**op**-ik) *adj*
WORD ORIGIN Greek *muōps* short-sighted

myriad (**mir**-ree-ad) *adj* **1** innumerable: *the myriad demands of the modern world* ▷ *n* **2** a large indefinite number: *myriads of tiny yellow flowers*
WORD ORIGIN Greek *murias* ten thousand

myriapod *n* an invertebrate with a long segmented body and many legs, such as a centipede
WORD ORIGIN Greek *murias* ten thousand + *pous* foot

myrmidon *n* a follower or henchman
WORD ORIGIN after the followers of Achilles in Greek myth

myrrh (**mur**) *n* the aromatic resin of an African or Asian shrub or tree, used in perfume, incense, and medicine
WORD ORIGIN Greek *murrha*

myrtle (**mur**-tl) *n* an evergreen shrub with pink or white flowers and aromatic blue-black berries
WORD ORIGIN Greek *murtos*

myself *pron* **1** the reflexive form of *I* or *me*: *I really enjoyed myself at the party* **2** *I* or *me* in person, as distinct from anyone else: *I myself know of no answer* **3** my usual self: *I'm not myself today*

The Origin of the Spelling Bee

In the world of lexicography, the term *spelling bee* belongs in the most frustrating category: words and phrases that are commonly used, but whose origins remain unknown.

There are some certainties regarding the history of this phrase, few though they may be. Firstly, the word seems to be of American origin; at least, all the earliest citations come from the United States. Secondly, the spelling variety was not the original 'bee'. Rather, a *spinning bee* is the earliest recorded example. A *bee* in this sense was originally a way of helping one person accomplish a necessary task which could not be completed single-handedly. For example, an *apple-bee* was a gathering of neighbours to assist one of their number in bringing in the apple harvest. There would be several apple-bees in succession, until everyone's apples were harvested. Later the purpose of the bee changed to one of instruction: the *quilting bee*, for instance, was an opportunity for an older generation to instruct the younger one in the practice of quilting. From here the word *bee* developed to mean any social gathering for a specific purpose.

What remains uncertain is where this sense of *bee* actually comes from. It has been widely assumed – even by some prominent dictionaries – that the word refers to the insect. It would seem to make sense: people engaged in *bees* are certainly 'busy as bees', and the social nature of the bee is widely known. However, a competing theory has recently been advanced, suggesting that this *bee* is a shortening of the English dialect word *bean* or *been* (ultimately from the Old English *ben*, the root of the Modern English word *boon*), meaning 'neighbourly help'. This would account for the original purpose of the *bee*. However, it does not account for the word's apparent American origin.

Wherever it comes from, the phrase *spelling bee* – now the most common type of *bee* – first appears in print in 1875, although spelling bees were probably held before then in schools.

In 1925, the *Courier-Journal* newspaper of Louisville, Kentucky conducted a state-wide spelling bee and then invited other newspapers to send school-age spellers of their choice to a national competition in Washington, DC. There were a mere nine contestants.

In 1941, the EW Scripps Company began sponsoring the competition, and the official title was changed to the *Scripps National Spelling Bee*. Participation in the contest has grown steadily ever since.

The *Scripps National Spelling Bee* is open to any winner of a regional spelling bee who has neither completed the eighth grade, reached fifteen years of age, or won a previous National Spelling Bee. Participants from outside the United States are eligible, provided they have also won a regional spelling bee and are of the appropriate age. Since 1994 the national finals have been aired live on the sports channel *ESPN*, and since 2006 they have also been broadcast live on the terrestrial station *ABC*.

The final spelling authority for the *Scripps National Spelling Bee* is *Webster's Third New International Dictionary, Unabridged*, published by Merriam-Webster, although that firm has no official involvement in creating the wordlist. They do, however, produce the spelling study guide *Spell It!*, which is available free to all contestants.

The first round of the National Spelling Bee is conducted via computer; all subsequent rounds are oral. Each speller steps up to the microphone and is given a word to spell. Contestants have two minutes in which they may ask for the word's definition, part of speech, alternative pronunciations (if any), and language of origin. They may also ask to hear the word used in a sentence and they may give the word's root and ask if it is correct. When these two minutes are up, the contestants have a further thirty seconds to spell the word.

From the fourth round onwards any speller who misspells a word is eliminated. The drama of this situation was captured in the 2002 documentary film *Spellbound*. The pressure that these contestants face is intense, and yet the *Scripps National Spelling Bee* remains one of America's most eagerly anticipated educational competitions, and the general concept of the spelling bee is a veritable hallmark of American culture.

mysterious *adj* **1** of unknown cause or nature: *a mysterious illness* **2** creating a feeling of strangeness, curiosity, or wonder: *a fascinating and mysterious old woman* **mysteriously** *adv*

mystery *n, pl* **-teries 1** an unexplained or inexplicable event or phenomenon **2** a person or thing that arouses curiosity or suspense because of an unknown, obscure, or enigmatic quality **3** a story or film which arouses suspense and curiosity because of facts concealed **4** a religious rite, such as the Eucharist in Christianity **WORD ORIGIN** Greek *mustērion* secret rites

mystery play *n* (in the Middle Ages) a type of drama based on the life of Christ

mystery tour *n* an excursion to an unspecified destination

mystic *n* **1** a person who achieves mystical experience ▷ *adj* **2** same as **mystical WORD ORIGIN** Greek *mustēs* one who has been initiated

mystical *adj* **1** relating to or characteristic of mysticism **2** *Christianity* having a sacred significance that is beyond human understanding **3** having occult or metaphysical significance **mystically** *adv*

mysticism *n* **1** belief in or experience of a reality beyond normal human understanding or experience **2** the use of prayer and meditation in an attempt to achieve direct intuitive experience of the divine

mystify *vb* **-fies, -fying, -fied 1** to confuse, bewilder, or puzzle: *his success mystifies many in the fashion industry* **2** to make obscure: *it is important for us not to mystify the function of the scientist* **mystification** *n* **mystifying** *adj*

mystique (miss-**steek**) *n* an aura of mystery, power, and awe that surrounds a person or thing

myth *n* **1 a** a story about superhuman beings of an earlier age, usually of how natural phenomena or social customs came into existence **b** same as **mythology** (senses 1, 2) **2 a** an idea or explanation which is widely held but untrue or unproven: *the myth that the USA is a classless society* **b** a person or thing whose existence is fictional or unproven: *the Loch Ness Monster is a myth* **WORD ORIGIN** Greek *muthos* fable

myth. 1 mythological **2** mythology

mythical *or* **mythic** *adj* **1** of or relating to myth **2** imaginary or fictitious **mythically** *adv*

mythology *n, pl* **-gies 1** myths collectively, esp. those associated with a particular culture or person **2** a body of stories about a person, institution, etc. **3** the study of myths **mythological** *adj*

myxoedema *or US* **myxedema** (mix-id-**deem**-a) *n* a disease caused by an underactive thyroid gland, characterized by puffy eyes, face, and hands, and mental sluggishness **WORD ORIGIN** Greek *muxa* mucus + *oidēma* swelling

myxomatosis (mix-a-mat-**oh**-siss) *n* an infectious and usually fatal viral disease of rabbits causing swellings and tumours **WORD ORIGIN** Greek *muxa* mucus + *-ōma* denoting tumour + *-osis* denoting disease

m

Nn

The letter N is the fourteenth letter of the English alphabet, and starts the second half of the sequence. It comes from the Greek letter *nu* (N,ν), which itself was derived from a letter called *nun* that appears in Semitic alphabets and literally means 'fish'.

The lower-case form of the letter is the standard letter-width, and has no ascending or descending lines. This regularity of form led printers to use the name 'en' for the width of a standard letter, calculating this as half of an 'em' (the longest possible letter-width).

N is unfortunate in having largely negative connotations. Many words that express negatives originally had the Anglo-Saxon word *ne* (meaning 'not') as their first element, and so their modern forms begin with N. This explains why the likes of 'none', 'nowhere', 'never', and 'nothing' all begin with this letter. In a double whammy, the Latin prefix *ne-* also indicates a negative, and words such as 'null' and 'neuter' came into English from that source.

Some words beginning with N have lost their originally negative connotations. For example, the word 'nice' originally meant 'not knowing', but then acquired a range of further meanings (including 'shy' and 'subtle') before eventually coming to signify something that is pleasant and agreeable.

N is also used by mathematicians to stand for any unspecified number, and this meaning has spilled over into mainstream usage. We might complain of saying something 'for the nth time' or of something being done 'to the nth degree' when we want to give the impression that something has been repeated so often that is impossible to keep count of the exact number.

Chess players take the liberty of using N to mean a knight. This is not a sign of illiteracy, but the letter K is already spoken for as the abbreviation for the king, which is regarded as the more important piece of the two. Earlier forms of chess notation used the abbreviation 'Kt' for the knight, but players preferred not to use two letters where one would do, and so 'Kt' was abandoned in favour of the simple but orthographically dubious N.

---

n¹ 1 nano- **2** neutron

n² 1 *maths* a number whose value is not stated: *two to the power n* ▷ *adj* **2** an indefinite number of: *there are n objects in the box* **nth** *adj*

N 1 *chess* knight **2** *chem* nitrogen **3** *physics* newton(s) **4** North(ern) **5** nuclear: *N plant*

n. 1 neuter **2** noun **3** number

N. 1 National(ist) **2** Navy **3** New **4** Norse

Na *chem* sodium
  WORD ORIGIN Latin *natrium*

NA North America

n/a not applicable: used to indicate that a question on a form is not relevant to the person filling it in

Naafi *n* **1** *Brit* Navy, Army, and Air Force Institutes **2** a canteen or shop run by this organization, esp. for military personnel

naan *n* same as **nan bread**

naartjie (**nahr**-chee) *n* *S African* a tangerine
  WORD ORIGIN Afrikaans

nab *vb* **nabbing, nabbed** *informal* **1** to arrest (someone) **2** to catch (someone) doing something wrong
  WORD ORIGIN perhaps Scandinavian

nabob (**nay**-bob) *n* *informal* a rich or important person
  WORD ORIGIN Hindi *nawwāb*; see NAWAB

nacelle (nah-**sell**) *n* a streamlined enclosure on an aircraft, esp. one housing an engine
  WORD ORIGIN French: small boat

nacho *n, pl* **nachos** *Mexican cookery* a snack of a piece of tortilla topped with cheese, peppers, etc.

nacre (**nay**-ker) *n* mother-of-pearl **nacreous** *adj*
  WORD ORIGIN Arabic *naqqārah* shell, drum

nadir *n* **1** the point in the sky directly below an observer and opposite the zenith **2** the lowest or worst point of anything: *I had touched the very nadir of despair*
  WORD ORIGIN Arabic *nazīr as-samt*, literally: opposite the zenith

naevus *or US* **nevus** (**nee**-vuss) *n, pl* **-vi** a birthmark or mole
  WORD ORIGIN Latin

naff *adj* *Brit slang* in poor taste: *naff frocks and trouser suits* **naffness** *n*
  WORD ORIGIN perhaps back slang from *fan*, short for FANNY

nag¹ *vb* **nagging, nagged** **1** to scold or find fault constantly **2 nag at** to be a constant source of discomfort or worry to ▷ *n* **3** a person who nags **nagging** *adj, n*
  WORD ORIGIN Scandinavian

nag² *n* **1** *often disparaging* an old horse **2** a small riding horse
  WORD ORIGIN Germanic

naiad (**nye**-ad) *n, pl* **naiads** *or* **naiades** (**nye**-ad-deez) *Greek myth* a water nymph
  WORD ORIGIN Greek *nāias*

nail *n* **1** a piece of metal with a point at one end and a head at the other, hit with a hammer to join two objects together **2** the hard covering of the upper tips of the fingers and toes **3 hit the nail on the head** to say something exactly correct or accurate **4 on the nail** at once: *he paid always in cash, always on the nail* ▷ *vb* **5** to attach (something) with nails **6** *informal* to arrest or catch (someone)
  WORD ORIGIN Old English *nǣgl*

nail down *vb* **1** to secure or fasten down with nails or as if with nails **2** to force an agreement from **3** to settle in a definite way: *a compromise was agreed in principle but has not yet been nailed down*

nailfile *n* a small metal file used to shape and smooth the nails

nail varnish *or* **polish** *n* a thick liquid applied to the nails as a cosmetic

naive *or* **naïve** (nye-**eev**) *adj* **1** innocent and gullible **2** simple and lacking sophistication: *naive art* **naively** *adv*
  WORD ORIGIN French, from Latin *nativus* native

naivety (nye-**eev**-tee) *or* **naïveté** *n* the state or quality of being naive

naked *adj* **1** without clothes **2** not concealed: *naked aggression* **3** without

any covering: *it was dimly lit by naked bulbs* **4 the naked eye** the eye unassisted by any optical instrument: *difficult to spot with the naked eye* **nakedly** *adv* **nakedness** *n*
WORD ORIGIN Old English *nacod*

namby-pamby *adj Brit, Austral, & NZ* excessively sentimental or prim
WORD ORIGIN nickname of Ambrose Phillips, 18th-century pastoral poet

name *n* **1** a word or term by which a person or thing is known ▸ Related adjective: **nominal 2** reputation, esp. a good one: *he was making a name for himself* **3** a famous person: *she's a big name now* **4 call someone names** *or* **a name** to insult someone by using rude words to describe him or her **5 in name only** not possessing the powers or status implied by one's title: *a leadership in name only* **6 in the name of a** for the sake of: *in the name of decency* **b** by the authority of: *in the name of the law* **7 name of the game** the most significant or important aspect of something: *survival is the name of the game in wartime* **8 to one's name** in one's possession: *she hasn't a penny to her name* ▸ *vb* **naming, named 9** to give a name to **10** to refer to by name: *he refused to name his source* **11** to fix or specify: *he named a time for the meeting* **12** to appoint: *she was named Journalist of the Year* **13** to ban (an MP) from the House of Commons by mentioning him or her formally by name as being guilty of disorderly conduct **14 name names** to cite people in order to blame or accuse them
WORD ORIGIN Old English *nama*

namecheck *vb* **1** to mention (someone) by name ▸ *n* **2** a mention of someone's name, for example on a radio programme

name day *n RC Church* the feast day of a saint whose name one bears

name-dropping *n informal* the practice of referring to famous people as though they were friends, in order to impress others

nameless *adj* **1** without a name **2** unspecified: *the individual concerned had better remain nameless* **3** too horrible to speak about: *the nameless dread*

namely *adv* that is to say

nameplate *n* a small sign on or next to a door giving the occupant's name and, sometimes, profession

namesake *n* a person or thing with the same name as another
WORD ORIGIN probably originally *for the name's sake*

nan bread *or* **naan** *n* a slightly leavened Indian bread in a large flat leaf shape
WORD ORIGIN Hindi

nancy *n, pl* **-cies** *Brit, Austral, & NZ offensive slang* an effeminate or homosexual boy or man. Also called: **nancy boy**
WORD ORIGIN from the girl's name

nanny *n, pl* **-nies 1** a woman whose job is looking after young children ▸ *vb* **nannies, nannying, nannied 2** to nurse or look after someone else's children **3** to be too protective towards (someone)
WORD ORIGIN child's name for a nurse

nanny goat *n* a female goat

nano- *combining form* denoting one thousand millionth (10⁻⁹): *nanosecond*
WORD ORIGIN Latin *nanus* dwarf

nanometre *n* one thousand-millionth of a metre. Symbol: **nm**

nanotechnology *n* a branch of technology dealing with the manufacture of objects with dimensions of less than 100 nanometres and the manipulation of individual molecules and atoms

nap¹ *n* **1** a short sleep ▸ *vb* **napping, napped 2** to have a short sleep **3 catch someone napping** to catch someone unprepared: *they don't want to be caught napping when the army moves again*
WORD ORIGIN Old English *hnappian*

nap² *n* the raised fibres of velvet or similar cloth
WORD ORIGIN probably Middle Dutch *noppe*

nap³ *n* **1** a card game similar to whist **2** *horse racing* a tipster's choice for a certain winner ▸ *vb* **napping, napped 3** *horse racing* to name (a horse) as a likely winner
WORD ORIGIN shortened from *Napoleon*

napalm *n* **1** a highly inflammable jellied petrol, used in firebombs and flame-throwers ▸ *vb* **2** to attack (people or places) with napalm
WORD ORIGIN *na(phthene)* + *palm(itate)* salt of palmitic acid

nape *n* the back of the neck
WORD ORIGIN origin unknown

naphtha *n chem* a liquid mixture distilled from coal tar or petroleum: used as a solvent and in petrol
WORD ORIGIN Greek

naphthalene *n chem* a white crystalline substance distilled from coal tar or petroleum, used in mothballs, dyes, and explosives
WORD ORIGIN *naphtha* + *al(cohol)* + *-ene*

napkin *n* **1** a piece of cloth or paper for wiping the mouth or protecting the clothes while eating **2** same as **sanitary towel**
WORD ORIGIN Latin *mappa* cloth

nappy *n, pl* **-pies** *Brit & NZ* a piece of soft absorbent material, usually disposable, wrapped around the waist and between the legs of a baby to absorb its urine and excrement
WORD ORIGIN from *napkin*

narcissism *n* an exceptional interest in or admiration for oneself **narcissistic** *adj*
WORD ORIGIN after *Narcissus*, a youth in Greek mythology, who fell in love with his reflection

narcissus (nahr-**siss**-uss) *n, pl* **-cissi** (-**siss**-eye) a yellow, orange, or white flower related to the daffodil
WORD ORIGIN Greek *narkissos*, perhaps from *narkē* numbness, because of narcotic properties attributed to the plant

narcosis *n* unconsciousness caused by a narcotic or general anaesthetic
WORD ORIGIN Greek *narkē* numbness

narcotic *n* **1** a drug, such as opium or morphine, that produces numbness and drowsiness, used medicinally but

addictive ▸ *adj* **2** of narcotics or narcosis
WORD ORIGIN Greek *narkē* numbness

nark *slang vb* **1** to annoy ▸ *n* **2** an informer or spy: *copper's nark* **3** *Brit* someone who complains in an irritating or whining manner
WORD ORIGIN probably from Romany *nāk* nose

narky *adj* **narkier, narkiest** *slang* irritable, complaining, or sarcastic

narrate *vb* **-rating, -rated 1** to tell (a story); relate **2** to speak the words accompanying and telling what is happening in a film or TV programme **narrator** *n*
WORD ORIGIN Latin *narrare* to recount

narration *n* **1** a narrating **2** a narrated account or story

narrative *n* **1** an account of events **2** the part of a literary work that relates events ▸ *adj* **3** telling a story: *a narrative account of the main events* **4** of narration: *narrative clarity*

narrow *adj* **1** small in breadth in comparison to length **2** limited in range, extent, or outlook: *a narrow circle of academics* **3** with little margin: *a narrow advantage* ▸ *vb* **4** to make or become narrow **5 narrow down** to restrict or limit: *the search can be narrowed down to a single room* ▸ See also **narrows**
▸ **narrowly** *adv* **narrowness** *n*
WORD ORIGIN Old English *nearu*

narrow boat *n Brit* a long bargelike canal boat

narrow gauge *n* **1** a railway track with less than 56½ inches (1.435 metres) between the lines ▸ *adj* **narrow-gauge 2** denoting a railway with a narrow gauge

narrow-minded *adj* bigoted, intolerant, or prejudiced **narrow-mindedness** *n*

narrows *pl n* a narrow part of a strait, river, or current

narwhal *n* an arctic whale with a long spiral tusk
WORD ORIGIN Old Norse *nāhvalr*, from *nār* corpse + *hvalr* whale

NASA (in the US) National Aeronautics and Space Administration

nasal *adj* **1** of the nose **2** (of a sound) pronounced with air passing through the nose **3** (of a voice) characterized by nasal sounds **nasally** *adv*
WORD ORIGIN Latin *nasus* nose

nascent *adj formal* starting to grow or develop
WORD ORIGIN Latin *nasci* to be born

NASDAQ *US* National Association of Securities Dealers Automated Quotations (System)

nasturtium *n* a plant with yellow, red, or orange trumpet-shaped flowers
WORD ORIGIN Latin: kind of cress

nasty *adj* **-tier, -tiest 1** unpleasant: *a nasty odour* **2** dangerous or painful: *a nasty burn* **3** (of a person) spiteful or ill-natured ▸ *n, pl* **-ties 4** something unpleasant: *video nasties* **nastily** *adv* **nastiness** *n*
WORD ORIGIN probably related to Dutch *nestig* dirty

nat. 1 national **2** nationalist

natal (**nay**-tl) *adj* of or relating to birth
WORD ORIGIN Latin *natalis* of one's birth

The Times UK Spelling Bee

Just as the Scripps National Spelling Bee in the United States began with a newspaper, so the United Kingdom's first national spelling bee began with *The Times*. In 2008 *The Times* proposed a nation-wide competition as a means of getting British school-children interested in spelling. English spelling is notoriously difficult, and many educators – up to and including university level – complain that spelling errors in written work are on the rise. A good grasp of English spelling rules is a hallmark of literacy, and is essential in written communication in formal contexts. As one of Britain's leading national newspapers, and one with a long commitment to issues of education, *The Times* was uniquely placed to launch this massive undertaking.

However, The Times UK National Spelling Bee is no mere copy of the American contest. In the USA, children compete individually. Each contestant takes a turn standing at the microphone before a panel of judges and has a total of two and a half minutes to spell a word. At the first mistaken letter, a bell rings and the child is eliminated from the contest.

The UK Spelling Bee takes a different approach: one designed to make spelling exciting and entertaining, as well as challenging. The competition takes the form of a game show – a kind of *University Challenge* meets *Countdown*. Contestants compete in teams of three players, representing their school, and the game itself is divided into two challenges.

In the first challenge, the Spelling Play-Off, all teams take the stage, each standing behind its own podium, and the 'Spellmaster' asks each contestant in turn to spell a word. They have 30 seconds in which to spell the word, and they may ask for a definition, the word's part of speech, or for the word to be repeated. In the first round, contestants remain in the game even if they misspell their word, but from the second round onwards they are eliminated from the Spelling Play-Off if they misspell. The words increase in difficulty as the game goes on, so a player may have to spell *bubble* in round two and *beneficiary* in round six. The Spelling Play-Off continues, with each correctly spelled word scoring points for the team, until only one player has correctly spelled their word in a round. That speller is the Last Player Standing.

The second half of the game is the Quickfire Challenge, in which teams have two minutes to spell as many words as they can. The teams can choose from Easy Words, which are worth one point each, Medium Words, worth two points each, or Hard Words, worth three points. Contestants can still ask for a definition or a part of speech, but they may also pass on a word they don't know and move on to the next one. The winner of the game is the team with the highest combined score from both challenges.

Just as America's national spelling bee uses *Webster's Third New International Dictionary* as the source for all words used in the competition, The Times UK Spelling Bee uses *Collins English Dictionary* as its official source. Collins supplies more than 6,000 words for use in the UK Spelling Bee, along with the relevant part of speech and a full-sentence definition. Collins also organizes the list into increasing difficulty using sophisticated linguistic criteria and corpus research. This scientific approach to spelling difficulty is an innovation unique to the Times UK Spelling Bee, and is essential to the competition's game-show aspect.

The first Times UK Spelling Bee was held in 2009, with 750 schools participating (quite an improvement on the 9 contestants who took part in the first American National Spelling Bee). In the competition's second year, participation increased to 1,000 schools, with half of the schools which took part in the first year signing up to compete again. The response from contestants, teachers, and spectators alike has been overwhelmingly positive, and the Times UK National Spelling Bee is set to become an eagerly anticipated annual event, uncovering Britain's extraordinary and heretofore uncelebrated spelling talent.

nation *n* a large body of people of one or more cultures or races, organized into a single state: *a major industrialized nation* **WORD ORIGIN** Latin *natio* birth, tribe

national *adj* **1** of or serving a nation as a whole **2** characteristic of a particular nation: *the national character* ▷ *n* **3** a citizen of a particular country: *Belgian nationals* **4** a national newspaper **nationally** *adv*

national anthem *n* a patriotic song adopted by a nation for use on public occasions

National Curriculum *n* (in England and Wales) the curriculum of subjects taught in state schools since 1989

national debt *n* the total outstanding borrowings of a nation's central government

national grid *n* Brit & NZ **1** a network of high-voltage power lines linking major electric power stations **2** the arrangement of vertical and horizontal lines on an ordnance survey map

National Health Service *n* (in Britain) the system of national medical services financed mainly by taxation

national hunt *n* Brit (often cap) horse racing over courses with fences

national insurance *n* (in Britain) state insurance based on contributions from employees and employers, providing payments to the unemployed, the sick, and the retired

nationalism *n* **1** a policy of national independence **2** patriotism, sometimes to an excessive degree **nationalist** *n, adj* **nationalistic** *adj*

nationality *n, pl* **-ties** **1** the fact of being a citizen of a particular nation **2** a group of people of the same race: *young men of all nationalities*

nationalize *or* **-lise** *vb* **-lizing, -lized** *or* **-lising, -lised** to put (an industry or a company) under state control **nationalization** *or* **-lisation** *n*

national park *n* an area of countryside protected by a national government for its scenic or environmental importance and visited by the public

national service *n* chiefly Brit compulsory military service

National Socialism *n* German history the doctrines and practices of the Nazis, involving the supremacy of Hitler, anti-Semitism, state control of the economy, and national expansion **National Socialist** *n, adj*

national superannuation *n* NZ a government pension paid to people of 65 years and over; retirement pension

National Trust *n* (in Britain) an organization concerned with the preservation of historic buildings and areas of natural beauty

nationwide *adj* covering or available to the whole of a nation

native *adj* **1** relating to a place where a person was born: *native land* **2** born in a specified place: *a native New Yorker* **3** native to originating in: *a plant native to alpine regions* **4** natural or inborn: *native genius* **5** relating to the original inhabitants of a country: *archaeology may uncover magnificent native artefacts* **6** go

native (of a settler) to adopt the lifestyle of the local population ▷ *n* **7** a person born in a specified place: *a native of Palermo* **8** an indigenous animal or plant: *the saffron crocus is a native of Asia Minor* **9** a member of the original race of a country, as opposed to colonial immigrants **WORD ORIGIN** Latin *nativus* innate, natural, from *nasci* to be born

Native American *n* same as **American Indian**

native bear *n* Austral same as **koala**

native companion *n* Austral same as **brolga**

native dog *n* Austral same as **dingo**

nativity *n, pl* **-ties** birth or origin **WORD ORIGIN** Late Latin *nativitas* birth

Nativity *n* Christianity **1** the birth of Jesus Christ **2** the feast of Christmas celebrating this

NATO *or* **Nato** North Atlantic Treaty Organization: an international organization established for purposes of collective security

natter Brit & NZ informal *vb* **1** to talk idly and at length ▷ *n* **2** a long idle chat **WORD ORIGIN** dialect *gnatter* to grumble, imitative

natterjack *n* a greyish-brown toad with reddish warty lumps **WORD ORIGIN** origin unknown

natty *adj* **-tier, -tiest** informal smart and spruce **nattily** *adv* **WORD ORIGIN** dialect *net* neat

natural *adj* **1** as is normal or to be expected: *the natural consequence* **2** genuine or spontaneous: *talking in a relaxed, natural manner* **3** of, according to, existing in, or produced by nature: *natural disasters* **4** not acquired; inborn: *their natural enthusiasm* **5** not created by human beings **6** not synthetic: *natural fibres such as wool* **7** (of a parent) not adoptive **8** (of a child) illegitimate **9** music not sharp or flat: F *natural* ▷ *n* **10** informal a person with an inborn talent or skill: *she's a natural at bridge* **11** music a note that is neither sharp nor flat **naturalness** *n*

natural gas *n* a gaseous mixture, consisting mainly of methane, found below ground; used widely as a fuel

natural history *n* the study of animals and plants in the wild

naturalism *n* a movement in art and literature advocating detailed realism **naturalistic** *adj*

naturalist *n* **1** a student of natural history **2** a person who advocates or practises naturalism

naturalize *or* **-lise** *vb* **-lizing, -lized** *or* **-lising, -lised** **1** to give citizenship to (a person born in another country) **2** to introduce (a plant or animal) into another region **3** to cause (a foreign word or custom) to be adopted **naturalization** *or* **-lisation** *n*

natural logarithm *n* a logarithm which has the irrational number *e* as a base

naturally *adv* **1** of course; surely **2** in a natural or normal way **3** instinctively

natural number *n* a positive integer, such as 1, 2, 3, 4 etc.

natural philosophy *n* old-fashioned physics

natural resources *pl n* naturally occurring materials such as coal, oil, and minerals

natural science *n* any of the sciences dealing with the study of the physical world, such as biology, physics, chemistry, and geology

natural selection *n* a process by which only those creatures and plants well adapted to their environment survive

natural wastage *n* chiefly Brit a reduction in the number of employees through not replacing those who leave, rather than by dismissing employees or making them redundant

nature *n* **1** the whole system of the existence, forces, and events of the physical world that are not controlled by human beings **2** fundamental or essential qualities: *the theory and nature of science* **3** kind or sort: *problems of a financial nature* **4** temperament or personality: *an amiable and pleasant nature* **5** by nature essentially: *he was by nature a cautious man* **6** in the nature of essentially; by way of: *it was in the nature of a debate rather than an argument* **WORD ORIGIN** Latin *natura*, from *nasci* to be born

nature reserve *n* an area of land that is preserved and managed in order to protect its animal and plant life

nature study *n* the study of animals and plants by direct observation

nature trail *n* a path through countryside, signposted to draw attention to natural features of interest

naturism *n* same as **nudism** ▷ **naturist** *n, adj*

naught *n* **1** archaic or literary nothing **2** chiefly US the figure 0 ▷ *adv* **3** archaic or literary not at all: *I care naught* **WORD ORIGIN** Old English *nāwiht*

naughty *adj* **-tier, -tiest** **1** (of children) mischievous or disobedient **2** mildly indecent: *naughty lingerie* **naughtily** *adv* **naughtiness** *n* **WORD ORIGIN** (originally: needy, poor) from *naught*

nausea (**naw-zee-a**) *n* **1** the feeling of being about to vomit **2** disgust **WORD ORIGIN** Greek: seasickness, from *naus* ship

nauseate *vb* **-ating, -ated** **1** to cause (someone) to feel sick **2** to arouse feelings of disgust in (someone) **nauseating** *adj*

nauseous *adj* **1** as if about to be sick: *he felt nauseous* **2** sickening

nautical *adj* of the sea, ships, or navigation **WORD ORIGIN** Greek *nautikos*, from *naus* ship

nautical mile *n* a unit of length, used in navigation, standardized as 6080 feet

nautilus *n, pl* **-luses** *or* **-li** a sea creature with a shell and tentacles **WORD ORIGIN** Greek *nautilos* sailor

naval *adj* of or relating to a navy or ships **WORD ORIGIN** Latin *navis* ship

nave¹ *n* the long central part of a church **WORD ORIGIN** Latin *navis* ship, from the similarity in shape

nave² n the hub of a wheel
WORD ORIGIN Old English *nafu, nafa*

navel n the slight hollow in the centre of the abdomen, where the umbilical cord was attached
WORD ORIGIN Old English *nafela*

navel orange n a sweet orange that has a navel-like hollow at the top

navigable adj 1 wide, deep, or safe enough to be sailed through: *the navigable portion of the Nile* 2 able to be steered: *the boat has to be watertight and navigable*

navigate vb -gating, -gated 1 to direct or plot the course or position of a ship or aircraft 2 to travel over or through safely: *your cousin, who's just navigated the Amazon* 3 *informal* to direct (oneself) carefully or safely: *he navigated his unsteady way to the bar* 4 (of a passenger in a vehicle) to read the map and give directions to the driver **navigation** n **navigational** adj **navigator** n
WORD ORIGIN Latin *navis* ship + *agere* to drive

navvy n, pl -vies *Austral & Brit informal* a labourer on a building site or road
WORD ORIGIN from *navigator* builder of a *navigation* (in the sense: canal)

navy n, pl -vies 1 the branch of a country's armed services comprising warships with their crews, and all their supporting services 2 the warships of a nation ▷ adj 3 short for **navy-blue**
WORD ORIGIN Latin *navis* ship

navy-blue adj very dark blue
WORD ORIGIN from the colour of the British naval uniform

nawab (na-**wahb**) n (formerly) a Muslim ruler or powerful landowner in India
WORD ORIGIN Hindi *nawwāb*, from Arabic *nuwwāb*, plural of *na'ib* viceroy

nay interj 1 *old-fashioned* no ▷ n 2 a person who votes against a motion ▷ adv 3 used for emphasis: *I want, nay, need to know*
WORD ORIGIN Old Norse *nei*

Nazarene n 1 **the Nazarene** Jesus Christ 2 *old-fashioned* a Christian 3 a person from Nazareth, a town in N Israel ▷ adj 4 of Nazareth

Nazi n, pl -zis 1 a member of the fascist National Socialist German Workers' Party, which came to power in Germany in 1933 under Adolf Hitler ▷ adj 2 of or relating to the Nazis **Nazism** n
WORD ORIGIN German, phonetic spelling of the first two syllables of *Nationalsozialist* National Socialist

nb *cricket* no-ball

Nb *chem* niobium

NB 1 New Brunswick 2 note well
WORD ORIGIN sense 2 from Latin *nota bene*

NC 1 North Carolina 2 *Brit education* National Curriculum

NCO noncommissioned officer

Nd *chem* neodymium

ND North Dakota

NDT Newfoundland Daylight Time

Ne *chem* neon

NE 1 Nebraska 2 northeast(ern)

ne- *combining form*: *Nearctic*. Same as **neo-**

Neanderthal (nee-**ann**-der-tahl) adj 1 of a type of primitive man that lived in Europe before 12 000 BC 2 *informal* with excessively conservative views: *his notoriously Neanderthal attitude to women*
WORD ORIGIN after *Neandertal*, a valley in Germany

neap n short for **neap tide**
WORD ORIGIN Old English, as in *nēpflōd* neap tide

Neapolitan adj 1 of Naples, a city in SW Italy ▷ n 2 a person from Naples
WORD ORIGIN Greek *Neapolis* new town

neap tide n a tide that occurs at the first and last quarter of the moon when there is the smallest rise and fall in tidal level

near prep 1 at or to a place or time not far away from ▷ adv 2 at or to a place or time not far away 3 short for **nearly**: *the pain damn near crippled him* ▷ adj 4 at or in a place or time not far away: *in the near future* 5 closely connected or intimate: *a near relation* 6 almost being the thing specified: *a mood of near rebellion* ▷ vb 7 to draw close (to): *the participants are nearing agreement* ▷ n 8 the left side of a horse or vehicle **nearness** n
WORD ORIGIN Old English *nēar*, comparative of *nēah* close

nearby adj 1 not far away: *a nearby village* ▷ adv 2 close at hand: *I live nearby*

Near East n same as **Middle East**

nearly adv 1 almost 2 **not nearly** nowhere near: *it's not nearly as easy as it looks*

near miss n 1 any attempt that just fails to succeed 2 an incident in which two aircraft or vehicles narrowly avoid collision 3 a bomb or shot that does not quite hit the target

nearside n 1 *chiefly Brit* the side of a vehicle that is nearer the kerb 2 the left side of an animal

near-sighted adj same as **short-sighted**

near thing n *informal* an event whose outcome is nearly a failure or a disaster, or only just a success

neat adj 1 clean and tidy 2 smoothly or competently done: *a neat answer* 3 (of alcoholic drinks) undiluted 4 *slang chiefly US & Canad* admirable; excellent **neatly** adv **neatness** n
WORD ORIGIN Latin *nitidus* clean

neaten vb to make neat

neath prep *archaic* short for **beneath**

neb n *archaic or dialect* the beak of a bird or the nose of an animal
WORD ORIGIN Old English *nebb*

nebula (**neb**-yew-la) n, pl -lae (-lee) *astron* a hazy cloud of particles and gases **nebular** adj
WORD ORIGIN Latin: mist, cloud

nebulize or -lise vb -lizing, -lized or -lising, -lised to turn (a liquid) into a fine spray

nebulizer or -liser n a device which turns a drug from a liquid into a fine spray which can be inhaled

nebulous adj vague and unclear: *a nebulous concept*

NEC (in Britain) National Executive Committee

necessaries pl n essential items: *the necessaries and comforts of life*

necessarily adv 1 as a certainty: *the factors were not necessarily connected with one another* 2 inevitably: *tourism is an industry that has a necessarily close connection with governments*

necessary adj 1 needed in order to obtain the desired result: *the necessary skills* 2 certain or unavoidable: *the necessary consequences* ▷ n 3 **do the necessary** *informal* to do something that is necessary in a particular situation 4 **the necessary** *informal* the money required for a particular purpose ▷ See also **necessaries**
WORD ORIGIN Latin *necessarius* indispensable

necessitate vb -tating, -tated to compel or require

necessitous adj *literary* very needy

necessity n, pl -ties 1 a set of circumstances that inevitably requires a certain result: *the necessity to maintain safety standards* 2 something needed: *the daily necessities* 3 great poverty 4 **of necessity** inevitably

neck n 1 the part of the body connecting the head with the rest of the body 2 the part of a garment around the neck 3 the long narrow part of a bottle or violin 4 the length of a horse's head and neck taken as the distance by which one horse beats another in a race: *to win by a neck* 5 *informal* impudence 6 **by a neck** by a very small margin: *beaten only by a neck* 7 **get it in the neck** *informal* to be reprimanded or punished severely 8 **neck and neck** absolutely level in a race or competition 9 **neck of the woods** *informal* a particular area: *how did they get to this neck of the woods?* 10 **stick one's neck out** *informal* to risk criticism or ridicule by speaking one's mind 11 **up to one's neck in** *informal* to be deeply involved in: *he was up to his neck in the scandal* ▷ vb 12 *informal* (of two people) to kiss each other passionately
WORD ORIGIN Old English *hnecca*

neckband n a band around the neck of a garment

neckerchief n a piece of cloth worn tied round the neck
WORD ORIGIN neck + kerchief

necklace n 1 a decorative piece of jewellery worn round the neck 2 (in South Africa) a tyre soaked in petrol, placed round a person's neck, and set on fire in order to burn the person to death

neckline n the shape or position of the upper edge of a dress or top

necktie n US same as **tie** (sense 5)

necromancy (**neck**-rome-man-see) n 1 communication with the dead 2 sorcery **necromancer** n
WORD ORIGIN Greek *nekros* corpse + *mantis* prophet

necrophilia n sexual attraction for or sexual intercourse with dead bodies
WORD ORIGIN Greek *nekros* corpse + *philos* loving

necropolis (neck-**rop**-pol-liss) n a cemetery
WORD ORIGIN Greek *nekros* dead + *polis* city

necrosis n 1 *biol, med* the death of cells in the body, as from an interruption of

n

the blood supply **2** *bot* death of plant tissue due to disease or frost **necrotic** *adj*
WORD ORIGIN Greek *nekros* corpse

nectar *n* **1** a sugary fluid produced by flowers and collected by bees **2** *classical myth* the drink of the gods **3** any delicious drink
WORD ORIGIN Greek *nektar*

nectarine *n* a smooth-skinned variety of peach
WORD ORIGIN apparently from *nectar*

ned *n Scot slang* a hooligan
WORD ORIGIN origin unknown

NEDC (formerly) National Economic Development Council. Also (informal): **Neddy**

née *prep* indicating the maiden name of a married woman: *Jane Gray (née Blandish)*
WORD ORIGIN French, past participle (feminine) of *naître* to be born

need *vb* **1** to require or be in want of: *they desperately need success* **2** to be obliged: *the government may need to impose a statutory levy* **3** used to express necessity or obligation and does not add -s when used with singular nouns or pronouns: *need he go?* ▷ *n* **4** the condition of lacking something: *he has need of a new coat* **5** a requirement: *the need for closer economic co-operation* **6** necessity: *there was no need for an explanation* **7** poverty or destitution: *the money will go to those areas where need is greatest* **8** distress: *help has been given to those in need* ▶ See also **needs**
WORD ORIGIN Old English *nēad, nied*

needful *adj* **1** necessary or required ▷ *n* **2** the needful *informal* what is necessary, usually money

needle *n* **1** a pointed slender piece of metal with a hole in it through which thread is passed for sewing **2** a long pointed rod used in knitting **3** same as **stylus** **4** *med* the long hollow pointed part of a hypodermic syringe, which is inserted into the body **5** a pointer on the scale of a measuring instrument **6** a long narrow stiff leaf: *pine needles* **7** *Brit informal* intense rivalry or ill-feeling in a sports match **8** short for **magnetic needle 9 have** or **get the needle** *Brit informal* to be annoyed ▷ *vb* **-dling, -dled 10** *informal* to goad or provoke
WORD ORIGIN Old English *nēdl*

needlecord *n* a fine-ribbed corduroy fabric

needlepoint *n* **1** embroidery done on canvas **2** lace made by needles on a paper pattern

needless *adj* not required; unnecessary **needlessly** *adv*

needlewoman *n, pl* **-women** a woman who does needlework

needlework *n* sewing and embroidery

needs *adv* **1** necessarily: *they must needs be admired* ▷ *pl n* **2** what is required: *he provides them with their needs*

needy *adj* **needier, neediest** in need of financial support

ne'er *adv poetic* never

ne'er-do-well *n* **1** an irresponsible or lazy person ▷ *adj* **2** useless; worthless: *his ne'er-do-well brother*

nefarious (nif-**fair**-ee-uss) *adj literary* evil; wicked
WORD ORIGIN Latin *ne* not + *fas* divine law

neg. negative

negate *vb* **-gating, -gated 1** to cause to have no value or effect: *his prejudices largely negate his accomplishments* **2** to deny the existence of
WORD ORIGIN Latin *negare*

negation *n* **1** the opposite or absence of something **2** a negative thing or condition **3** a negating

negative *adj* **1** expressing a refusal or denial: *a negative response* **2** lacking positive qualities, such as enthusiasm or optimism **3** *med* indicating absence of the condition for which a test was made **4** *physics* **a** (of an electric charge) having the same electrical charge as an electron **b** (of a body or system) having a negative electric charge; having an excess of electrons **5** same as **minus** (sense 4) **6** measured in a direction opposite to that regarded as positive **7** short for **electronegative 8** of a photographic negative ▷ *n* **9** a statement or act of denial or refusal **10** *photog* a piece of photographic film, exposed and developed, bearing an image with a reversal of tones or colours, from which positive prints are made **11** a word or expression with a negative meaning, such as *not* **12** a quantity less than zero **13 in the negative** indicating denial or refusal **negatively** *adv*

negative equity *n* the holding of a property of fallen value which is worth less than the amount of mortgage still unpaid

negativism *n* a tendency to be unconstructively critical **negativist** *n, adj*

neglect *vb* **1** to fail to give due care or attention to: *she had neglected her child* **2** to fail (to do something) through carelessness: *he neglected to greet his guests* **3** to disregard: *he neglected his duty* ▷ *n* **4** lack of due care or attention: *the city had a look of shabbiness and neglect* **5** the state of being neglected
WORD ORIGIN Latin *neglegere*

neglectful *adj* not paying enough care or attention: *abusive and neglectful parents*

negligee (**neg**-lee-zhay) *n* a woman's light, usually lace-trimmed dressing gown
WORD ORIGIN French

negligence *n* neglect or carelessness **negligent** *adj* **negligently** *adv*

negligible *adj* so small or unimportant as to be not worth considering

negotiable *adj* **1** able to be changed or agreed by discussion: *the prices were negotiable* **2** (of a bill of exchange or promissory note) legally transferable

negotiate *vb* **-ating, -ated 1** to talk with others in order to reach (an agreement) **2** to succeed in passing round or over (a place or a problem) **negotiation** *n* **negotiator** *n*
WORD ORIGIN Latin *negotium* business, from *nec* not + *otium* leisure

Negro *old-fashioned n, pl* **-groes 1** a member of any of the Black peoples originating in Africa ▷ *adj* **2** of Negroes
WORD ORIGIN Latin *niger* black

Negroid *adj* of or relating to the Negro race

neigh *n* **1** the high-pitched sound made by a horse ▷ *vb* **2** to make this sound
WORD ORIGIN Old English *hnēgan*

neighbour *or US* **neighbor** *n* **1** a person who lives near or next to another **2** a person, thing, or country near or next to another
WORD ORIGIN Old English *nēah* near + *būr, gebūr* dweller

neighbourhood *or US* **neighborhood** *n* **1** a district where people live **2** the immediate environment; surroundings **3** the people in a district **4 in the neighbourhood of** approximately ▷ *adj* **5** in and for a district: *our neighbourhood cinema*

neighbouring *or US* **neighboring** *adj* situated nearby: *the neighbouring island*

neighbourly *or US* **neighborly** *adj* kind, friendly, and helpful

neither *adj* **1** not one nor the other (of two): *neither enterprise went well* ▷ *pron* **2** not one nor the other (of two): *neither completed the full term* ▷ *conj* **3 a** used preceding alternatives joined by *nor*; not: *sparing neither strength nor courage* **b** same as **nor** (sense 2) ▷ *adv* **4** *not standard* same as **either** (sense 4)
WORD ORIGIN Old English *nāwther*

▤ **USAGE**
A verb following a compound subject that uses *neither ... (nor)* should be in the singular if both subjects are in the singular: *neither Jack nor John has done the work.*

nelson *n* a wrestling hold in which a wrestler places his arm or arms under his opponent's arm or arms from behind and exerts pressure with his palms on the back of his opponent's neck
WORD ORIGIN from a proper name

nematode *n* a slender unsegmented cylindrical worm
WORD ORIGIN Greek *nēma* thread + *eidos* shape

nemesis (**nem**-miss-iss) *n, pl* **-ses** (-seez) a means of retribution or vengeance
WORD ORIGIN Greek *nemein* to distribute what is due

neo- *combining form* new, recent, or a modern form of: *neoclassicism; neo-Nazi*
WORD ORIGIN Greek *neos* new

neoclassicism *n* a late 18th- and early 19th-century style of art and architecture, based on ancient Roman and Greek models **neoclassical** *adj*

neocolonialism *n* political control wielded by one country over another through control of its economy **neocolonial** *adj*

neocon *n, adj chiefly US* short for **neoconservative**

neoconservative *adj* **1** favouring a return to a set of established (esp. political) conservative values which have been updated to suit current conditions ▷ *n* **2** a person subscribing to neoconservative philosophy

neodymium *n chem* a toxic silvery-white metallic element of the lanthanide series. Symbol: Nd

CS Lewis

C S Lewis ranks as one of the most influential children's writers in English literature, having delighted successive generations with his tales of a magical land visited by children from our world.

He was born Clive Staples Lewis in Belfast in 1898, although from an early age he was known to friends not as 'Clive', or even 'CS', but as 'Jack'. An idyllic early childhood was brought to a sudden end with the illness and death of his mother when he was nine, after which he became an increasingly distant and bookish child. He served in the trenches during World War I before embarking on a successful academic career, specializing in medieval literature.

Most of his working life was spent teaching at Oxford University, where he was a leading figure in a circle of writers who called themselves 'the inklings'. This group included JRR Tolkien, another notable creator of magical worlds.

The most profound event of Lewis's adult life was his conversion from atheism to Christianity in 1929, and his religious faith is borne out in much of his literary output. Nowhere is this done more successfully than in *The Screwtape Letters* (1940), a collection of letters from older devil to a hapless pupil, counselling him on the best ways of placing temptation before humans.

Lewis was a prolific writer, publishing literary criticism (including *The Allegory of Love*, a seminal work on medieval romance), theological works, poetry, and even science fiction. However, his enduring popularity rests on the seven children's books known as *The Chronicles of Narnia*, which were published between 1950 and 1956.

The first and best-known book of the series is *The Lion, the Witch and the Wardrobe*. In it a group of children hiding in a wardrobe find themselves transported into a magical land called Narnia, where animals can talk and where the reign of a cruel witch is brought to an end by the forces of good, led by the lion Aslan. The climax of the adventure, in which Aslan gives himself up to be killed and subsequently comes back to life, is clearly modelled on Christ's crucifixion and resurrection, and it is not hard to see elements of Christian allegory throughout the Narnian chronicles. *The Magician's Nephew* deals with the creation of the world and the entry of evil into it in a way that recalls the story of the Garden of Eden, while *The Last Battle* invites parallels with the Book of Revelation, describing the final destruction of Narnia and the last judgment being passed on its inhabitants.

However, the biblical imagery rarely interferes with the reader's enjoyment of the adventures, and Lewis also draws on non-Christian mythology for inspiration. The action of *Prince Caspian*, with its military campaigns, parleys, and single combat, contains elements of Homer's *Iliad*, while *The Voyage of the Dawn Treader*, with its maritime quest, is reminiscent of the *Odyssey*. Lewis also uses creatures from classical mythology – centaurs, fauns, satyrs, dryads, and hamadryads – to populate the landscape of Narnia and imbue the place with a thrilling strangeness. But his mythology is not precisely regimented in the way that Tolkien's Middle Earth is. Besides characters from classical mythology, readers of *The Lion, the Witch and the Wardrobe* also encounter Father Christmas, while Old Father Time is seen in *The Silver Chair*.

Lewis is not especially remarkable as a shaper of language, although he may be given credit for one of the 20th century's more memorable political slogans. In *The Magician's Nephew*, the children Polly and Digory witness the creation of the world of Narnia. There is nothing but darkness when suddenly 'a thousand, thousand points of light leaped out'. The phrase 'a thousand points of light' was picked up by Peggy Noonan, a speechwriter for George Bush Senior, who used it as a metaphor for the many community groups who were active in strengthening American society. After its use in the president's inaugural address in January 1989, the notion of 'a thousand points of light' came to symbolize the ambitions of the Bush presidency. Just what Lewis would have made of this is hard to say.

WORD ORIGIN NEO- + *didymium*, a compound originally thought to be an element

Neolithic *adj* of the period that lasted in Europe from about 4000 to 2400 BC, characterized by primitive farming and the use of polished stone and flint tools and weapons
WORD ORIGIN NEO- + Greek *lithos* stone

neologism (nee-**ol**-a-jiz-zum) *n* a newly coined word, or an established word used in a new sense
WORD ORIGIN NEO- + Greek *logos* word

neon *n* 1 *chem* a colourless odourless rare gas, used in illuminated signs and lights. Symbol: Ne ▷ *adj* 2 of or illuminated by neon: *a flashing neon sign*
WORD ORIGIN Greek: new

neonatal *adj* relating to the first few weeks of a baby's life **neonate** *n*

neon light *n* a glass tube containing neon, which gives a pink or red glow when a voltage is applied

neophyte *n* 1 *formal* a beginner 2 a person newly converted to a religious faith 3 a novice in a religious order
WORD ORIGIN Greek *neos* new + *phuton* a plant

Nepali (nip-**paw**-lee) or **Nepalese** (nep-pal-**leez**) *adj* 1 of Nepal ▷ *n* 2 *pl* -pali, -palis or -palese a person from Nepal 3 the language of Nepal

nephew *n* a son of one's sister or brother
WORD ORIGIN Latin *nepos*

nephritis (nif-**frite**-tiss) *n* inflammation of the kidney
WORD ORIGIN Greek *nephros* kidney

nepotism (**nep**-a-tiz-zum) *n* favouritism shown to relatives and friends by those with power
WORD ORIGIN Italian *nepote* nephew

Neptune *n* 1 the Roman god of the sea 2 the eighth planet from the sun

neptunium *n chem* a silvery metallic element synthesized in the production of plutonium. Symbol: Np
WORD ORIGIN after *Neptune*, the planet

nerd or **nurd** *n slang* 1 a boring or unpopular person, esp. one who is obsessed with a particular subject: *a computer nerd* 2 a stupid and feeble person **nerdish** or **nurdish** *adj*
WORD ORIGIN origin unknown

nervate *adj* (of leaves) with veins

nerve *n* 1 a cordlike bundle of fibres that conducts impulses between the brain and other parts of the body 2 bravery and determination 3 *informal* impudence: *you've got a nerve!* 4 **lose one's nerve** to lose self-confidence and become afraid about what one is doing 5 **strain every nerve** to make every effort (to do something) ▷ *vb* **nerving, nerved** 6 **nerve oneself** to prepare oneself (to do something difficult or unpleasant) ▶ See also **nerves**
WORD ORIGIN Latin *nervus*

nerve cell *n* same as **neuron**

nerve centre *n* 1 a place from which a system or organization is controlled: *an underground nerve centre of intelligence* 2 a group of nerve cells associated with a specific function

nerve gas *n* a poisonous gas which affects the nervous system

nerveless *adj* 1 (of fingers or hands) without feeling; numb 2 (of a person) fearless

nerve-racking or **nerve-wracking** *adj* very distressing or harrowing

nerves *pl n informal* 1 anxiety or tension: *nerves can often be the cause of wedding-day hitches* 2 the ability or inability to remain calm in a difficult situation: *his nerves are in a shocking state* 3 **get on someone's nerves** to irritate someone

nervous *adj* 1 apprehensive or worried 2 excitable; highly strung 3 of or relating to the nerves: *the nervous system* **nervously** *adv* **nervousness** *n*

nervous breakdown *n* a mental illness in which the sufferer ceases to function properly, and experiences symptoms including tiredness, anxiety, and deep depression

nervous system *n* the brain, spinal column, and nerves, which together control thought, feeling, and movement. See **neuron**

nervy *adj* **nervier, nerviest** *Austral & Brit informal* excitable or nervous

ness *n Brit* a headland or cape
WORD ORIGIN Old English *næs*

-ness *suffix* indicating state, condition, or quality: *greatness; selfishness*
WORD ORIGIN Old English *-nes*

nest *n* 1 a place or structure in which birds or other animals lay eggs or give birth to young 2 a cosy or secluded place 3 a set of things of graduated sizes designed to fit together: *a nest of tables* ▷ *vb* 4 to make or inhabit a nest 5 (of a set of objects) to fit one inside another 6 *computers* to position (data) within other data at different ranks or levels
WORD ORIGIN Old English

nest egg *n* a fund of money kept in reserve

nestle *vb* -tling, -tled 1 to snuggle or cuddle closely 2 to be in a sheltered position: *honey-coloured stone villages nestling in wooded valleys*
WORD ORIGIN Old English *nestlian*

nestling *n* a young bird not yet able to fly

net[1] *n* 1 a very fine fabric made from intersecting strands of material with a space between each strand 2 a piece of net, used to protect or hold things or to trap animals 3 (in certain sports) a strip of net over which the ball or shuttlecock must be hit 4 the goal in soccer or hockey 5 a strategy intended to trap people: *innocent fans were caught in the police net* 6 *informal* short for **internet** ▷ *vb* **netting, netted** 7 to catch (a fish or other animal) in a net
WORD ORIGIN Old English *net(t)*

net[2] or **nett** *adj* 1 remaining after all deductions, as for taxes and expenses: *net income* 2 (of weight) excluding the weight of wrapping or container 3 final or conclusive: *the net effect* ▷ *vb* **netting, netted** 4 to yield or earn as a clear profit
WORD ORIGIN French: neat

netball *n* a team game, usually played by women, in which a ball has to be thrown through a net hanging from a ring at the top of a pole

nether *adj old-fashioned* lower or under: *nether regions*
WORD ORIGIN Old English *nithera*, literally: further down

nethermost *adj* lowest

nether world *n* 1 the underworld 2 hell. Also called: **nether regions**

net profit *n* gross profit minus all operating expenses such as wages and overheads

nett *adj, vb* same as **net**[2]

netting *n* a fabric or structure made of net

nettle *n* 1 a plant with stinging hairs on the leaves 2 **grasp the nettle** to attempt something unpleasant with boldness and courage
WORD ORIGIN Old English *netele*

nettled *adj* irritated or annoyed

nettle rash *n* a skin condition, usually caused by an allergy, in which itchy red or white raised patches appear

network *n* 1 a system of intersecting lines, roads, veins, etc. 2 an interconnecting group or system: *a network of sympathizers and safe-houses* 3 *radio, television* a group of broadcasting stations that all transmit the same programme at the same time 4 *electronics, computers* a system of interconnected components or circuits ▷ *vb* 5 *radio, television* to broadcast (a programme) over a network

neural *adj* of a nerve or the nervous system

neuralgia *n* severe pain along a nerve **neuralgic** *adj*

neuritis (nyoor-**rite**-tiss) *n* inflammation of a nerve or nerves, often causing pain and loss of function in the affected part

neurology *n med* the scientific study of the nervous system **neurological** *adj* **neurologist** *n*

neuron or **neurone** *n* a cell specialized to conduct nerve impulses
WORD ORIGIN Greek

neurosis (nyoor-**oh**-siss) *n, pl* -ses (-seez) a mental disorder producing hysteria, anxiety, depression, or obsessive behaviour

neurosurgery *n med* the branch of surgery concerned with the nervous system **neurosurgeon** *n* **neurosurgical** *adj*

neurotic *adj* 1 tending to be emotionally unstable 2 afflicted by neurosis ▷ *n* 3 a person afflicted with a neurosis or tending to be emotionally unstable

neurotransmitter *n biochem* a chemical by which a nerve cell communicates with another nerve cell or with a muscle

neuter *adj* 1 *grammar* denoting a gender of nouns which are neither male nor female 2 (of animals and plants) sexually underdeveloped ▷ *n* 3 *grammar* **a** the neuter gender **b** a neuter noun 4 a sexually underdeveloped female insect, such as a worker bee 5 a castrated animal ▷ *vb* 6 to castrate (an animal)
WORD ORIGIN Latin *ne* not + *uter* either (of two)

neutral *adj* **1** not taking any side in a war or dispute **2** of or belonging to a neutral party or country **3** not displaying any emotions or opinions **4** (of a colour) not definite or striking **5** *chem* neither acidic nor alkaline **6** *physics* having zero charge or potential ▷ *n* **7** a neutral person or nation **8** the position of the controls of a gearbox that leaves the gears unconnected to the engine **neutrality** *n*
WORD ORIGIN Latin *neutralis* of neuter gender

neutralize *or* -**lise** *vb* -**lizing**, -**lized** *or* -**lising**, -**lised** **1** to make electrically or chemically neutral **2** to make ineffective by counteracting **3** to make (a country) neutral by international agreement: *the great powers neutralized Belgium in the 19th century* **neutralization** *or* -**lisation** *n*

neutrino (new-**tree**-no) *n, pl* -**nos** *physics* an elementary particle with no mass or electrical charge
WORD ORIGIN Italian diminutive of *neutrone* neutron

neutron *n physics* a neutral elementary particle of about the same mass as a proton
WORD ORIGIN from *neutral*, on the model of *electron*

neutron bomb *n* a nuclear weapon designed to kill people and animals while leaving buildings virtually undamaged

never *adv* **1** at no time; not ever **2** certainly not; not at all **3** Also: **well I never!** surely not!
WORD ORIGIN Old English *nǣfre*

≡ **USAGE**
≡ In informal speech and writing, *never*
≡ can be used instead of *not* with the
≡ simple past tenses of certain verbs, for
≡ emphasis (*I never said that; I never realized*
≡ *how clever he was*), but this usage should
≡ be avoided in serious writing.

never-ending *adj* long and boring
nevermore *adv literary* never again
never-never *n* **the never-never** *informal* hire-purchase: *they are buying it on the never-never*

never-never land *n* an imaginary idyllic place

nevertheless *adv* in spite of that

new *adj* **1** recently made, brought into being, or acquired: *a new car* **2** of a kind never before existing; novel: *a new approach to monetary policy* **3** recently discovered: *testing new drugs* **4** recently introduced to or inexperienced in a place or situation: *new to this game* **5** fresh; additional: *you can acquire new skills* **6** unknown: *this is new to me* **7** (of a cycle) beginning again: *a new era* **8** (of crops) harvested early: *new potatoes* **9** changed for the better: *she returned a new woman* ▷ *adv* **10** recently, newly: *new-laid eggs* ▶ See also **news** ▷ **newish** *adj* **newness** *n*
WORD ORIGIN Old English *nīowe*

New Age *n* **1** a philosophy, originating in the late 1980s, characterized by a belief in alternative medicine, astrology, and spiritualism ▷ *adj* **2** of the New Age: *New Age therapies* **New Ager** *n*

New Age Music *n* a type of gentle melodic largely instrumental popular music originating in the USA in the late 1980s

New Australian *n Austral* an Australian name for a recent immigrant, esp. one from Europe

newbie *n informal* a person new to a job, club, etc.

newborn *adj* recently or just born

New Canadian *n Canad* a recent immigrant to Canada

new chum *n Austral & NZ, archaic informal* a recent British immigrant

newcomer *n* a recent arrival or participant

newel *n* **1** Also called: **newel post** the post at the top or bottom of a flight of stairs that supports the handrail **2** the central pillar of a winding staircase
WORD ORIGIN Old French *nouel* knob

newfangled *adj* objectionably or unnecessarily modern
WORD ORIGIN Middle English *newefangel* liking new things

new-found *adj* newly or recently discovered: *new-found confidence*

New Jerusalem *n Christianity* heaven

New Latin *n* the form of Latin used since the Renaissance, mainly for scientific names

newly *adv* **1** recently **2** again; anew: *newly interpreted*

newlyweds *pl n* a recently married couple

New Man *n* **the New Man** *chiefly Brit* a type of modern man who allows the caring side of his nature to show by being supportive and by sharing childcare and housework

new maths *n Brit* an approach to mathematics in which basic set theory is introduced at an elementary level

new moon *n* the moon when it appears as a narrow crescent at the beginning of its cycle

news *n* **1** important or interesting new happenings **2** information about such events, reported in the mass media **3** **the news** a television or radio programme presenting such information **4** interesting or important new information: *it's news to me* **5** a person or thing widely reported in the mass media: *reggae is suddenly big news again*

news agency *n* an organization that collects news reports and sells them to newspapers, magazines, and TV and radio stations

newsagent *n Brit* a shopkeeper who sells newspapers and magazines

newscast *n* a radio or television broadcast of the news **newscaster** *n*
WORD ORIGIN news + (broad)cast

news conference *n* same as **press conference**

newsflash *n* a brief item of important news, which interrupts a radio or television programme

newsgroup *n computers* a forum where subscribers exchange information about a specific subject by e-mail

newsletter *n* a periodical bulletin issued to members of a group

newspaper *n* a weekly or daily publication consisting of folded sheets and containing news, features, and advertisements

newspeak *n* the language of politicians and officials regarded as deliberately ambiguous and misleading
WORD ORIGIN from the novel *1984* by George Orwell

newsprint *n* an inexpensive wood-pulp paper used for newspapers

newsreader *n* a news announcer on radio or television

newsreel *n* a short film with a commentary which presents current events

newsroom *n* a room in a newspaper office or radio or television station where news is received and prepared for publication or broadcasting: *a journalist who was in the newsroom at the time*

newsstand *n* a portable stand from which newspapers are sold

New Style *n* the present method of reckoning dates using the Gregorian calendar

newsworthy *adj* sufficiently interesting to be reported as news

newsy *adj* **newsier**, **newsiest** (of a letter) full of news

newt *n* a small amphibious creature with a long slender body and tail and short legs
WORD ORIGIN mistaken division of *an ewt; ewt* from Old English *efeta*

New Testament *n* the second part of the Christian Bible, dealing with the life and teachings of Christ and his followers

newton *n* the SI unit of force that gives an acceleration of 1 metre per second per second to a mass of 1 kilogram
WORD ORIGIN after Sir Isaac *Newton*, scientist

new town *n* (in Britain) a town planned as a complete unit and built with government sponsorship

new wave *n* a movement in politics, the arts, or music that consciously breaks with traditional values

New World *n* **the New World** the western hemisphere of the world, esp. the Americas

New Year *n* the first day or days of the year in various calendars, usually a holiday

New Year's Day *n* January 1, celebrated as a holiday in many countries

New Year's Eve *n* December 31

New Zealander *n* a person from New Zealand

next *adj* **1** immediately following: *the next generation* **2** immediately adjoining: *in the next room* **3** closest to in degree: *the next-best thing* ▷ *adv* **4** at a time immediately to follow: *the patient to be examined next* **5** **next to a** adjacent to: *the house next to ours* **b** following in degree: *next to my wife, I love you most* **c** almost: *the evidence is next to totally useless*
WORD ORIGIN Old English *nēhst*, superlative of *nēah* near

n

next door – nine | 548

next door *adj, adv* in, at, or to the adjacent house or flat: *the Cabinet retired next door; the people next door*

next of kin *n* a person's closest relative

nexus *n, pl* **nexus** **1** a connection or link **2** a connected group or series **WORD ORIGIN** Latin, from *nectere* to bind

NF Newfoundland

Nfld. Newfoundland

ngati (**nah-tee**) *n, pl* **ngati** NZ (occurring as part of the tribe name) a tribe or clan **WORD ORIGIN** Māori

NH New Hampshire

NHS (in Britain) National Health Service

Ni *chem* nickel

NI 1 (in Britain) National Insurance **2** Northern Ireland

niacin *n* a vitamin of the B complex that occurs in milk, liver, and yeast. Also called: **nicotinic acid** **WORD ORIGIN** from *ni(cotinic) ac(id)* + *-in* denoting a chemical substance

nib *n* the writing point of a pen **WORD ORIGIN** origin unknown

nibble *vb* **-bling, -bled 1** to take little bites (of) **2** to bite gently: *she nibbled at her lower lip* ▷ *n* **3** a little bite **4** a light hurried meal **WORD ORIGIN** related to Low German *nibbelen*

nibs *n* **his** or **her nibs** *slang* a mock title used of an important or self-important person **WORD ORIGIN** origin unknown

NICAM near-instantaneous companding system: a technique for coding audio signals into digital form

nice *adj* **1** pleasant **2** kind: *it's really nice of you to worry about me* **3** good or satisfactory: *a nice clean operation* **4** subtle: *a nice distinction* **nicely** *adv* **niceness** *n* **WORD ORIGIN** Latin *nescius* ignorant

nicety *n, pl* **-ties 1** a subtle point: *the niceties of our arguments* **2** a refinement or delicacy: *social niceties* **3 to a nicety** precisely

niche (**neesh**) *n* **1** a recess in a wall for a statue or ornament **2** a position exactly suitable for the person occupying it: *perhaps I will find my niche in a desk job* ▷ *adj* **3** of or aimed at a specialist group or market: *niche retailing ventures* **WORD ORIGIN** Old French *nichier* to nest

nick *vb* **1** to make a small cut in **2** *chiefly Brit slang* to steal **3** *chiefly Brit slang* to arrest ▷ *n* **4** a small notch or cut **5** *slang* a prison or police station **6** *informal* condition: *in good nick* **7 in the nick of time** just in time **WORD ORIGIN** perhaps Middle English *nocke* nock

nickel *n* **1** *chem* a silvery-white metallic element that is often used in alloys. Symbol: Ni **2** a US or Canadian coin worth five cents **WORD ORIGIN** German *Kupfernickel* nickel ore, literally: copper demon; it was mistakenly thought to contain copper

nickelodeon *n* US an early type of jukebox **WORD ORIGIN** *nickel* + *(mel)odeon*

nickel silver *n* an alloy containing copper, zinc, and nickel

nicker *n, pl* **nicker** *Brit slang* a pound sterling **WORD ORIGIN** origin unknown

nick-nack *n* same as **knick-knack**

nickname *n* **1** a familiar, pet, or derisory name given to a person or place ▷ *vb* **-naming, -named 2** to call (a person or place) by a nickname: *Gaius Caesar Augustus Germanicus, nicknamed Caligula* **WORD ORIGIN** mistaken division of *an ekename* an additional name

nicotine *n* a poisonous alkaloid found in tobacco **nicotinic** *adj* **WORD ORIGIN** after J. Nicot, who introduced tobacco into France

nictitating membrane *n* (in reptiles, birds, and some mammals) a thin fold of skin under the eyelid that can be drawn across the eye

niece *n* a daughter of one's sister or brother **WORD ORIGIN** Latin *neptis* granddaughter

niff *Brit slang n* **1** a stink ▷ *vb* **2** to stink **niffy** *adj* **WORD ORIGIN** perhaps from *sniff*

nifty *adj* **-tier, -tiest** *informal* neat or smart **WORD ORIGIN** origin unknown

Nigerian *adj* **1** of Nigeria ▷ *n* **2** a person from Nigeria

niggard *n* a stingy person **WORD ORIGIN** perhaps from Old Norse

niggardly *adj* not generous: *it pays its staff on a niggardly scale* **niggardliness** *n*

nigger *n* *offensive* a Black person **WORD ORIGIN** Spanish *negro*

niggle *vb* **-gling, -gled 1** to worry slightly **2** to find fault continually ▷ *n* **3** a small worry or doubt **4** a trivial objection or complaint **niggling** *adj* **WORD ORIGIN** Scandinavian

nigh *archaic, poetic adv* **1** nearly ▷ *adj* **2** near ▷ *prep* **3** close to **WORD ORIGIN** Old English *nēah, nēh*

night *n* **1** the period of darkness that occurs each 24 hours, between sunset and sunrise ▶ Related adjective: **nocturnal 2** the period between sunset and bedtime; evening **3** the time between bedtime and morning **4** nightfall or dusk **5** an evening designated for a specific activity: *opening night* **6 make a night of it** to celebrate the whole evening *adj* **7** of, occurring, or working at night: *the night sky* ▶ See also **nights** **WORD ORIGIN** Old English *niht*

nightcap *n* **1** a drink taken just before bedtime **2** a soft cap formerly worn in bed

nightclub *n* a place of entertainment open until late at night, usually offering drink, a floor show, and dancing

nightdress *n* a loose dress worn in bed by women or girls

nightfall *n* the approach of darkness; dusk

nightgown *n* same as **nightdress**

nightie *n* *informal* short for **nightdress**

nightingale *n* a small bird with a musical song, usually heard at night **WORD ORIGIN** Old English *nihtegale*, literally: night singer

nightjar *n* a nocturnal bird with a harsh cry **WORD ORIGIN** *night* + JAR² (so called from its discordant cry)

nightlife *n* the entertainment and social activities available at night in a town or city: *New York nightlife*

night-light *n* a dim light left on overnight

nightlong *adj, adv* throughout the night

nightly *adj* **1** happening each night ▷ *adv* **2** each night

nightmare *n* **1** a terrifying or deeply distressing dream **2** a terrifying or unpleasant experience **3** a thing that is feared: *wheels and loose straps are a baggage handler's nightmare* **nightmarish** *adj* **WORD ORIGIN** *night* + Old English *mare, mære* evil spirit

nights *adv* *informal* at night or on most nights: *he works nights*

night safe *n* a safe built into the outside wall of a bank, in which customers can deposit money when the bank is closed

night school *n* an educational institution that holds classes in the evening

nightshade *n* a plant which produces poisonous berries with bell-shaped flowers **WORD ORIGIN** Old English *nihtscada*

nightshirt *n* a long loose shirtlike garment worn in bed

night soil *n* *archaic* human excrement collected at night from cesspools or privies

nightspot *n* *informal* a nightclub

night-time *n* the time from sunset to sunrise

night watch *n* **1** a watch or guard kept at night for security **2** the period of time this watch is kept

night watchman *n* a person who keeps guard at night on a factory or other building

nihilism (**nye-ill-liz-zum**) *n* a total rejection of all established authority and institutions **nihilist** *n, adj* **nihilistic** *adj* **WORD ORIGIN** Latin *nihil* nothing

-nik *suffix forming nouns* indicating a person associated with a particular state or quality: *refusenik* **WORD ORIGIN** Russian

nil *n* nothing: esp. as a score in games **WORD ORIGIN** Latin

nimble *adj* **1** agile and quick in movement **2** mentally alert or acute **nimbly** *adv* **WORD ORIGIN** Old English *nǣmel* quick to grasp + *numol* quick at seizing

nimbus *n, pl* **-bi** or **-buses 1** a dark grey rain cloud **2** a halo **WORD ORIGIN** Latin: cloud

NIMBY not in my back yard: used of people who are opposed to any building or changes that will affect them directly

nincompoop *n* *informal* a stupid person **WORD ORIGIN** origin unknown

nine *n* **1** the cardinal number that is the sum of one and eight **2** a numeral,

Words from Literature
part 18

navigator *n* a navigator was originally someone employed to dig canals. It is the origin of the word 'navvy' meaning a labourer
> She ascertained from me in a few words what it was all about, comforted Dora, and gradually convinced her that I was not a labourer – from my manner of stating the case I believe Dora concluded that I was a navigator, and went balancing myself up and down a plank all day with a wheelbarrow – and so brought us together in peace.
> *David Copperfield* Charles Dickens

necromancy *n* a kind of magic where the magician speaks to spirits or ghosts to find out what will happen in the future
> He surfeits upon cursed necromancy
> *Doctor Faustus* chorus Christopher Marlowe

negus *n* a hot drink made from sweetened wine and water
> He sat placidly perusing the newspaper, with his little head on one side, and a glass of warm sherry negus at his elbow.
> *David Copperfield* Charles Dickens

nice *adj* discriminating; able to make good judgements or choices
> consequently a claim to be nice
> *Emma* Jane Austen

nigh *adv* nigh means near
> He'll never know how nigh he come to getting lynched
> *The Adventures of Huckleberry Finn* Mark Twain

nimbleness *n* nimbleness means being able to move very quickly or skilfully
> and with incredible accuracy and nimbleness
> *Treasure Island* Robert Louis Stevenson

noggin *n* a noggin is a small mug or a wooden cup
> you'll bring me one noggin of rum
> *Treasure Island* Robert Louis Stevenson

none *adj* neither
> none can die
> *The Good-Morrow* John Donne

notice *n* an observation
> Arch are his notices
> *The Prelude* William Wordsworth

occiput *n* occiput means the back of the head
> saw off the occiput of each couple
> *Gulliver's Travels* Jonathan Swift

officiously *adj* kindly
> the governess who attended Glumdalclitch very officiously lifted me up
> *Gulliver's Travels* Jonathan Swift

old salt *phrase* old salt is a slang term for an experienced sailor
> a 'true sea-dog,' and a 'real old salt,'
> *Treasure Island* Robert Louis Stevenson

or ere *phrase* before
> or ere the Hall was built
> *The Prelude* William Wordsworth

ostler *n* someone who looks after horses at an inn
> The bill paid, and the waiter remembered, and the ostler not forgotten, and the chambermaid taken into consideration
> *Great Expectations* Charles Dickens

ostry *n* an ostry is an old word for a pub or hotel
> lest I send you into the ostry with a vengeance
> *Doctor Faustus* 2.2 Christopher Marlowe

outrunning the constable *phrase* outrunning the constable meant spending more than you earn
> but I shall by this means be able to check your bills and to pull you up if I find you outrunning the constable.
> *Great Expectations* Charles Dickens

over *adj* across
> It is in length six yards, and in the thickest part at least three yards over
> *Gulliver's Travels* Jonathan Swift

9 or IX, representing this number **3** something representing or consisting of nine units **4 dressed up to the nines** *informal* elaborately dressed **5 999** (in Britain) the telephone number of the emergency services ▷ *adj* **6** amounting to nine: *nine men* **ninth** *adj, n*
WORD ORIGIN Old English *nigon*

nine-days wonder *n* something that arouses great interest, but only for a short period

nine-eleven, 9-11, or **9/11** *n* the 11th of September 2001, the day on which the twin towers of the World Trade Center in New York were flown into and destroyed by aeroplanes hijacked by Islamic fundamentalists. Also called: **September eleven**
WORD ORIGIN from the US custom of expressing dates in figures, the day of the month following the number of the month

ninefold *adj* **1** having nine times as many or as much **2** having nine parts ▷ *adv* **3** by nine times as much or as many

ninepins *n* the game of skittles

nineteen *n* **1** the cardinal number that is the sum of ten and nine **2** a numeral, 19 or XIX, representing this number **3** something representing or consisting of nineteen units **4 talk nineteen to the dozen** to talk very fast ▷ *adj* **5** amounting to nineteen: *nineteen years* **nineteenth** *adj, n*

nineteenth hole *n golf slang* the bar in a golf clubhouse
WORD ORIGIN from its being the next objective after a standard 18-hole round

ninety *n, pl* **-ties 1** the cardinal number that is the product of ten and nine **2** a numeral, 90 or XC, representing this number **3** something representing or consisting of ninety units **4 nineties** the numbers 90 to 99, esp. when used to refer to a year of someone's life or of a century ▷ *adj* **5** amounting to ninety: *ninety degrees* **ninetieth** *adj, n*

ninja *n, pl* **-ja** or **-jas** a person skilled in ninjutsu, a Japanese martial art characterized by stealthy movement and camouflage
WORD ORIGIN Japanese

ninny *n, pl* **-nies** a stupid person
WORD ORIGIN perhaps from *an innocent*

niobium *n chem* a white superconductive metallic element. Symbol: Nb
WORD ORIGIN Latin after *Niobe* (daughter of Tantalus); because it occurred in tantalite

nip¹ *vb* **nipping, nipped 1** *informal* to hurry **2** to pinch or squeeze **3** to bite lightly **4** (of the cold) to affect (someone) with a stinging sensation **5** to check the growth of (something): *a trite script nips all hope in the bud* ▷ *n* **6** a pinch or light bite **7** sharp coldness: *a nip in the air*
WORD ORIGIN perhaps from Old Norse

nip² *n* a small drink of spirits
WORD ORIGIN from *nipperkin* a vessel holding a half-pint or less

nipper *n Brit, Austral, & NZ informal* a small child

nipple *n* **1** the small projection in the centre of each breast, which in females contains the outlet of the milk ducts **2** a small projection through which oil or grease can be put into a machine or component
WORD ORIGIN perhaps from *neb* peak, tip

nippy *adj* **-pier, -piest 1** (of weather) frosty or chilly **2** *informal* quick or nimble **3** (of a motor vehicle) small and relatively powerful

nirvana (near-**vah**-na) *n Buddhism, Hinduism* the ultimate state of spiritual enlightenment and bliss attained by extinction of all desires and individual existence
WORD ORIGIN Sanskrit: extinction

nisi (nye-sigh) *adj* see **decree nisi**

Nissen hut *n chiefly Brit* a tunnel-shaped military shelter made of corrugated steel
WORD ORIGIN after Lt Col. Peter *Nissen*, mining engineer

nit¹ *n* the egg or larva of a louse
WORD ORIGIN Old English *hnitu*

nit² *n informal* short for **nitwit**

nit-picking *informal n* **1** a concern with insignificant details, usually with the intention of finding fault ▷ *adj* **2** showing such concern

nitrate *chem n* **1** a salt or ester of nitric acid **2** a fertilizer containing nitrate salts ▷ *vb* **-trating, -trated 3** to treat with nitric acid or a nitrate **4** to convert or be converted into a nitrate **nitration** *n*

nitre or US **niter** *n chem* same as **potassium nitrate**
WORD ORIGIN Latin *nitrum*

nitric *adj chem* of or containing nitrogen

nitric acid *n chem* a colourless corrosive liquid widely used in industry

nitride *n chem* a compound of nitrogen with a more electropositive element

nitrify *vb* **-fies, -fying, -fied** *chem* **1** to treat (a substance) or cause (a substance) to react with nitrogen **2** to treat (soil) with nitrates **3** to convert (ammonium compounds) into nitrates by oxidation **nitrification** *n*

nitrite *n chem* a salt or ester of nitrous acid

nitro- or before a vowel **nitr-** *combining form* **1** indicating that a chemical compound contains the univalent group, -NO₂: *nitrobenzene* **2** indicating that a chemical compound is a nitrate ester: *nitrocellulose*
WORD ORIGIN Greek *nitron* nitre

nitrogen (**nite**-roj-jen) *n chem* a colourless odourless gas that forms four-fifths of the air and is an essential part of all animal and plant life. Symbol: N **nitrogenous** *adj*

nitrogen cycle *n* the natural cycle by which nitrates in the soil, derived from dead organic matter, are absorbed by plants and reduced to nitrates again when the plants and the animals feeding on them die and decay

nitrogen fixation *n* the conversion of atmospheric nitrogen into nitrogen compounds by soil bacteria

nitroglycerine or **nitroglycerin** *n chem* a thick pale yellow explosive

liquid made from glycerol and nitric and sulphuric acids

nitrous *adj chem* derived from or containing nitrogen in a low valency state

nitrous acid *n chem* a weak acid known only in solution and in the form of nitrite salts

nitrous oxide *n chem* a colourless gas used as an anaesthetic

nitty-gritty *n* **the nitty-gritty** *informal* the basic facts of a matter or situation
WORD ORIGIN perhaps rhyming compound from *grit*

nitwit *n informal* a stupid person
WORD ORIGIN perhaps NIT¹ + WIT¹

NJ New Jersey

nkosi (ing-**koss**-ee) *n S African* a term of address to a superior; master; chief
WORD ORIGIN Nguni (language group of southern Africa) *inkosi* chief, lord

nm nanometre

NM New Mexico

no¹ *interj* **1** used to express denial, disagreement, or refusal ▷ *n, pl* **noes** or **nos 2** an answer or vote of no **3** a person who answers or votes no
WORD ORIGIN Old English *nā*

no² *adj* **1** not any, not a, or not one: *I have no money; no comment* **2** not at all: *he's no exception* **3** not: *no taller than a child* **4 no way!** an expression of emphatic refusal or denial
WORD ORIGIN Old English *nān* none

No¹ or **Noh** *n, pl* **No** or **Noh** the stylized classical drama of Japan, using music and dancing
WORD ORIGIN Japanese *nō* talent

No² *chem* nobelium

No. or **no.** *pl* **Nos.** or **nos.** number
WORD ORIGIN French *numéro*

n.o. *cricket* not out

nob *n chiefly Brit slang* a person of wealth or social distinction
WORD ORIGIN origin unknown

no-ball *n cricket* an improperly bowled ball, for which the batting side scores a run. Abbrev: **nb**

nobble *vb* **-bling, -bled** *chiefly Brit, Austral, & NZ slang* **1** to bribe or threaten **2** to disable (a racehorse) to stop it from winning **3** to steal
WORD ORIGIN *a nobbler*, a false division of *an hobbler* one who hobbles horses

nobelium *n chem* a radioactive element produced artificially from curium. Symbol: No
WORD ORIGIN after *Nobel* Institute, Stockholm, where it was discovered

Nobel prize (no-**bell**) *n* a prize for outstanding contributions to chemistry, physics, physiology and medicine, literature, economics, and peace that may be awarded annually
WORD ORIGIN after Alfred *Nobel*, chemist & philanthropist

nobility *n* **1** the quality of being noble; dignity **2** the class of people who hold titles and high social rank

noble *adj* **1** having or showing high moral qualities: *a noble cause* **2** belonging to a class of people who hold titles and high social rank **3** impressive and magnificent: *a noble*

beast **4** *chem* (of certain metals) resisting oxidation ▷ *n* **5** a person who holds a title and high social rank **nobly** *adv*
WORD ORIGIN Latin *nobilis*, originally capable of being known, hence well-known

noble gas *n* any of the unreactive gases helium, neon, argon, krypton, xenon, and radon

nobleman *or fem* **noblewoman** *n, pl* **-men** *or* **-women** a person of noble rank

noblesse oblige (no-**bless** oh-**bleezh**) *n often ironic* the supposed obligation of the nobility to be honourable and generous
WORD ORIGIN French, lit: nobility obliges

nobody *pron* **1** no person; no-one ▷ *n, pl* **-bodies 2** a person of no importance
≡ **USAGE**
≡ See at **everyone**.

no-brainer *n slang* something that requires little or no mental effort

nock *n* **1** a notch on an arrow that fits on the bowstring **2** a groove at either end of a bow that holds the bowstring
WORD ORIGIN related to Swedish *nock* tip

no-claims bonus *or* **no-claim bonus** *n* a reduction in the cost of an insurance policy made if no claims have been made in a specified period

nocturnal *adj* **1** of the night **2** (of animals) active at night
WORD ORIGIN Latin *nox* night

nocturne *n* a short dreamy piece of music

nod *vb* **nodding, nodded 1** to lower and raise (one's head) briefly, to express agreement or greeting **2** to express by nodding: *he nodded his approval* **3** to sway or bend forwards and back **4** to let one's head fall forward with sleep **5 nodding acquaintance** a slight knowledge (of a subject or person) ▷ *n* **6** a quick down-and-up movement of the head, in agreement **7 land of Nod** an imaginary land of sleep
WORD ORIGIN origin unknown

noddle *n chiefly Brit informal* the head or brains
WORD ORIGIN origin unknown

noddy *n, pl* **-dies 1** a tropical tern with a dark plumage **2** a fool
WORD ORIGIN perhaps from obsolete *noddy* foolish, drowsy

node *n* **1** *bot* the point on a plant stem from which the leaves grow **2** *maths* a point at which a curve crosses itself **3** a knot or knob **4** *physics* a point in a vibrating body at which there is practically no vibration **5** *anat* any natural bulge or swelling: *lymph node* **6** *astron* either of the two points at which the orbit of a body intersects the path of the sun or the orbit of another body **nodal** *adj*
WORD ORIGIN Latin *nodus* knot

nod off *vb informal* to fall asleep

nodule *n* **1** a small rounded lump, knot, or node **2** a rounded mineral growth on the root of a plant such as clover **nodular** *adj*
WORD ORIGIN Latin *nodulus*

Noel *or* **Noël** *n* same as **Christmas**
WORD ORIGIN French, from Latin *natalis* a birthday

nog *n* an alcoholic drink containing beaten egg
WORD ORIGIN origin unknown

noggin *n* **1** *informal* the head **2** a small quantity of spirits
WORD ORIGIN origin unknown

no-go area *n* a district that is barricaded off so that the police or army can enter only by force

noise *n* **1** a sound, usually a loud or disturbing one **2** loud shouting; din **3** an undesired electrical disturbance in a signal **4** unwanted or irrelevant elements in a visual image: *removing noise from pictures* **5 noises** conventional utterances conveying a reaction: *he made the appropriate noises* ▷ *vb* **noising, noised 6 be noised abroad** (of news or gossip) to be spread
WORD ORIGIN Latin *nausea* seasickness

noiseless *adj* making little or no sound **noiselessly** *adv*

noise pollution *n* annoying or harmful noise in an environment

noisette (nwah-**zett**) *n* a hazelnut chocolate
WORD ORIGIN French

noisome *adj formal* **1** (of smells) offensive **2** extremely unpleasant
WORD ORIGIN obsolete *noy*, variant of *annoy*

noisy *adj* **noisier, noisiest 1** making a lot of noise **2** (of a place) full of noise **noisily** *adv*

nomad *n* **1** a member of a tribe who move from place to place to find pasture and food **2** a wanderer **nomadic** *adj*
WORD ORIGIN Greek *nomas* wandering for pasture

no-man's-land *n* land between boundaries, esp. an unoccupied zone between opposing forces

nom de plume *n, pl* **noms de plume** same as **pen name**
WORD ORIGIN French

nomenclature (no-**men**-klatch-er) *n formal* the system of names used in a particular subject
WORD ORIGIN Latin *nomenclatura* list of names

nominal *adj* **1** in name only: *nominal independence* **2** very small in comparison with real worth: *a nominal amount of aid* **nominally** *adv*
WORD ORIGIN Latin *nomen* name

nominalism *n* the philosophical theory that a general name, such as *dog*, is merely a name and does not denote a real object **nominalist** *n*

nominal value *n* same as **par value**

nominate *vb* **-nating, -nated 1** to propose (someone) as a candidate **2** to appoint (someone) to an office or position **nomination** *n*
WORD ORIGIN Latin *nomen* name

nominative *n grammar* a grammatical case in some languages that identifies the subject of a verb
WORD ORIGIN Latin *nominativus* belonging to naming

nominee *n* a person who is nominated to an office or as a candidate

non- *prefix* **1** indicating negation: *nonexistent* **2** indicating refusal or failure: *noncooperation* **3** indicating exclusion from a specified class: *nonfiction* **4** indicating lack or absence: *nonevent*
WORD ORIGIN Latin *non* not

nonaddictive *adj* not causing addiction

nonage *n* **1** *law* the state of being under full legal age for various actions **2** a period of immaturity

nonagenarian *n* a person who is from 90 to 99 years old
WORD ORIGIN Latin *nonaginta* ninety

nonaggression *n* the policy of not attacking other countries

nonagon *n geom* a figure with nine sides **nonagonal** *adj*

nonalcoholic *adj* containing no alcohol

nonaligned *adj* (of a country) not part of a major alliance or power bloc **nonalignment** *n*

nonbeliever *n* a person who does not follow a particular religious movement

nonbelligerent *adj* (of a country) not taking part in a war

nonce *n* **for the nonce** for the present
WORD ORIGIN a mistaken division of *for then anes*, for the once

nonce word *n* a word coined for a single occasion

nonchalant (**non**-shall-ant) *adj* casually unconcerned or indifferent **nonchalance** *n* **nonchalantly** *adv*
WORD ORIGIN French, from *nonchaloir* to lack warmth

non-com *n* short for **noncommissioned officer**

noncombatant *n* a member of the armed forces whose duties do not include fighting, such as a chaplain or surgeon

noncombustible *adj* not capable of igniting and burning

noncommissioned officer *n* (in the armed forces) a person who is appointed as a subordinate officer, from the lower ranks, rather than by a commission

noncommittal *adj* not committing oneself to any particular opinion

noncompliance *n* failure or refusal to do as requested

non compos mentis *adj* of unsound mind
WORD ORIGIN Latin: not in control of one's mind

nonconductor *n* a substance that is a poor conductor of heat, electricity, or sound

nonconformist *n* **1** a person who does not conform to generally accepted patterns of behaviour or thought ▷ *adj* **2** (of behaviour or ideas) not conforming to accepted patterns: *men who pride themselves on their nonconformist past* **nonconformity** *n*

Nonconformist *n* **1** a member of a Protestant group separated from the Church of England ▷ *adj* **2** of or relating to Nonconformists

noncontributory *adj Brit* denoting a pension scheme for employees, the premiums of which are paid entirely by the employer

n

non-cooperation *n* the refusal to do more than is legally or contractually required of one

noncustodial *adj* not involving imprisonment: *a noncustodial sentence*

nondescript *adj* lacking outstanding features
WORD ORIGIN NON- + Latin *descriptus*, past participle of *describere* to copy

non-domicile *n Brit* a UK resident who claims another country as his or her permanent home, esp. to escape certain taxes. Also shortened to: **non-dom**

non-domiciled *adj Brit* of or denoting a person who is resident in the UK but who claims domicile in another country

nondrinker *n* a person who does not drink alcohol

none *pron* **1** not any: *none of the men was represented by a lawyer; none of it meant anything to him* **2** no-one; nobody: *none could deny it* **3** none the in no degree: *her parents were none the wiser*
WORD ORIGIN Old English *nān*, literally: not one
⋮ **USAGE**
⋮ None is a singular pronoun and should
⋮ be used with a singular form of a verb:
⋮ *none of the students has* (not *have*) *a car.*

nonentity (non-**enn**-tit-tee) *n, pl* **-ties** an insignificant person or thing

non-essential *adj* not absolutely necessary

nonetheless *adv* despite that; however

nonevent *n* a disappointing or insignificant occurrence which was expected to be important

nonexistent *adj* not existing in a particular place **nonexistence** *n*

nonferrous *adj* **1** denoting a metal other than iron **2** not containing iron

nonfiction *n* writing that deals with facts or real events

nonflammable *adj* not easily set on fire

nonfunctional *adj* having no practical function

nonintervention *n* refusal to intervene in the affairs of others

noniron *adj* not requiring ironing

nonmember *n* a person who is not a member of a particular club or organization

nonmetal *n chem* a chemical element that forms acidic oxides and is a poor conductor of heat and electricity **nonmetallic** *adj*

nonmoral *adj* not involving morality; neither moral nor immoral

non-native *adj* not originating in a particular place

non-nuclear *adj* not involving or using nuclear power or weapons

no-nonsense *adj* sensible, practical, and straightforward: *a no-nonsense approach to crime*

nonpareil (non-par-**rail**) *n* a person or thing that is unsurpassed
WORD ORIGIN French, from NON- + *pareil* similar

non-partisan *adj* not supporting any single political party

non-payment *n* failure to pay money owed

nonplussed *or US* **nonplused** *adj* perplexed
WORD ORIGIN Latin *non plus* no further

nonprofessional *adj* not earning a living at a specified occupation: *nonprofessional investors*

non-profit-making *adj* not intended to make a profit

nonproliferation *n* limitation of the production or spread of something such as nuclear or chemical weapons

nonrepresentational *adj art* same as **abstract**

nonresident *n* a person who does not live in a particular country or place

nonsectarian *adj* not confined to any specific subdivision of a religious group

nonsense *n* **1** something that has or makes no sense **2** unintelligible language **3** foolish behaviour: *she'll stand no nonsense* **nonsensical** *adj*

non sequitur (**sek**-wit-tur) *n* a statement having little or no relation to what preceded it
WORD ORIGIN Latin: it does not follow

nonslip *adj* designed to prevent slipping: *a nonslip mat*

nonsmoker *n* **1** a person who does not smoke **2** a train carriage or compartment in which smoking is forbidden

nonsmoking *or* **no-smoking** *adj* denoting an area in which smoking is forbidden

nonstandard *adj* denoting words, expressions, or pronunciations that are not regarded as correct by educated native speakers of a language

nonstarter *n* a person or an idea that has little chance of success

nonstick *adj* (of cooking utensils) coated with a substance that food will not stick to when cooked

nonstop *adj* **1** without a stop: *two weeks of nonstop rain* ▷ *adv* **2** without a stop: *most days his phone rings nonstop*

nontoxic *adj* not poisonous

non-U *adj Brit informal* (of language or behaviour) not characteristic of the upper classes

nonunion *adj* **1** (of a company) not employing trade union members: *a nonunion shop* **2** (of a person) not belonging to a trade union

nonverbal *adj* not involving the use of language

non-violent *adj* using peaceful methods to bring about change **nonviolence** *n*

nonvoting *adj finance* (of shares in a company) not entitling the holder to vote at company meetings

non-White *adj* **1** belonging to a race of people not European in origin ▷ *n* **2** a member of one of these races

noodle *n* a simpleton
WORD ORIGIN a blend of *noddle* + *noodles*

noodles *pl n* ribbon-like strips of pasta
WORD ORIGIN German *Nudeln*

nook *n* **1** a corner or recess **2** a secluded or sheltered place
WORD ORIGIN origin unknown

noon *n* the middle of the day; 12 o'clock
WORD ORIGIN Latin *nona (hora)* ninth hour (originally 3 pm, the ninth hour from sunrise)

noonday *adj* happening or appearing at noon

no-one *or* **no one** *pron* no person; nobody
⋮ **USAGE**
⋮ See at **everyone**.

noose *n* a loop in the end of a rope, tied with a slipknot, such as one used to hang people
WORD ORIGIN Latin *nodus* knot

nope *interj informal* no

nor *conj* **1** used to join alternatives, the first of which is preceded by *neither*; and not: *neither willing nor able* **2** and not ... either: *he had not arrived yet, nor had any of the models*
WORD ORIGIN contraction of Old English *nōther*

nordic *adj skiing* of competitions in cross-country racing and ski-jumping

Nordic *adj* of Scandinavia or its typically tall, blond, and blue-eyed people
WORD ORIGIN French *nordique* of the north

norm *n* a standard that is required or regarded as normal
WORD ORIGIN Latin *norma* carpenter's square

normal *adj* **1** usual, regular, or typical: *the study of normal behaviour* **2** free from mental or physical disorder **3** *geom* same as **perpendicular** (sense 1) ▷ *n* **4** the usual, regular, or typical state, degree, or form **5** *geom* a perpendicular line or plane **normality** *or esp. US* **normalcy** *n*
WORD ORIGIN Latin *normalis* conforming to the carpenter's square

normalize *or* **-lise** *vb* **-lizing, -lized** *or* **-lising, -lised 1** to make or become normal **2** to bring into conformity with a standard **normalization** *or* **-lisation** *n*

normally *adv* **1** as a rule; usually **2** in a normal manner

Norman *n* **1** a person from Normandy in N France, esp. one of the people who conquered England in 1066 **2** same as **Norman French** ▷ *adj* **3** of the Normans or their dialect of French **4** of Normandy **5** of a style of architecture used in Britain from the Norman Conquest until the 12th century, with rounded arches and massive masonry walls

Norman French *n* the medieval Norman and English dialect of Old French

normative *adj* of or establishing a norm or standard: *a normative model*

Norn *n Norse myth* any of the three virgin goddesses of fate
WORD ORIGIN Old Norse

Norse *adj* **1** of ancient and medieval Scandinavia **2** of Norway ▷ *n* **3 a** the N group of Germanic languages spoken in Scandinavia **b** any one of these languages, esp. in their ancient or medieval forms

Norseman *n, pl* **-men** same as **Viking**

north *n* **1** one of the four cardinal points of the compass, at 0° or 360° **2** the

SCRABBLE
Three-Letter Words, part 6
NAG–PIS

NAG scold constantly
NAH no
NAM distraint
NAN word for grandmother
NAP short sleep
NAS has not or was not
NAT supporter of nationalism
NAW no
NAY no
NEB beak of a bird
NED derogatory Scots word for a young working-class male
NEE born
NEF church nave
NEG photographic negative
NEK mountain pass
NEP catmint
NET meshed fabric
NEW recently made
NIB writing point of a pen
NID pheasant's nest
NIE archaic spelling of nigh
NIL nothing
NIM game with matchsticks
NIP pinch
NIS friendly goblin
NIT egg or larva of a louse
NIX be careful!
NOB person of social standing
NOD lower and raise (one's head)
NOG alcoholic drink
NOH drama of Japan
NOM name
NON not
NOO Japanese musical drama
NOR and not
NOS plural form of no
NOT expressing negation
NOW at or for the present time
NOX nitrogen oxide

NOY harass
NTH of an unspecified number
NUB point or gist
NUN female member of a religious order
NUR knot of wood
NUS plural form of nu
NUT fruit
NYE flock of pheasants
NYS plural form of ny
OAF stupid person
OAK tree
OAR pole with a broad blade
OAT grass grown for its edible seed
OBA Yoruba chief or ruler
OBE ancient village
OBI Japanese sash
OBO ship carrying oil and ore
OBS plural form of ob
OCA South American herbaceous plant
OCH expression of surprise
ODA room in a harem
ODD unusual, peculiar
ODE lyric poem
ODS plural form of od
OES plural form of oe
OFF not on; away
OFT often
OHM unit of electrical resistance
OHO exclamation of surprise or derision
OHS plural form of oh
OIK person regarded as inferior
OIL viscous liquid
OKA unit of weight
OKE unit of weight
OLD having lived for a long time
OLE exclamation of approval

OLM salamander
OMS plural form of om
ONE single
ONO Hawaiian fish
ONS plural form of on
ONY Scots word for any
OOF money
OOH exclamation of surprise
OOM title of respect
OON Scots word for oven
OOP Scots word for bind
OOR Scots word for our
OOS plural form of oo
OOT Scots word for out
OPE archaic word for open
OPS plural form of op
OPT show a preference
ORA plural form of os
ORB decorated sphere
ORC whale
ORD point of a weapon
ORE mineral
ORF disease of sheep
ORS plural form of or
ORT fragment
OSE long winding ridge of gravel, sand, etc
OUD musical instrument
OUK Scots word for week
OUP Scots word for bind
OUR belonging to us
OUS plural form of ou
OUT outside
OVA plural of ovum
OWE be obliged to pay money
OWL bird of prey
OWN used to indicate possession
OWT dialect word for anything
OXO (as in oxo acid) acid that contains oxygen
OXY oxygen
OYE grandchild
OYS plural form of oy

PAC soft shoe
PAD material for protection
PAH exclamation of disgust, disbelief, etc
PAL friend
PAM knave of clubs
PAN metal container for cooking
PAP soft food, mash
PAR usual or average condition
PAS dance step
PAT tap lightly
PAV short for pavlova
PAW animal's foot
PAX kiss of peace
PAY give money for goods
PEA plant, vegetable
PEC pectoral muscle
PED pannier
PEE urinate
PEG pin or clip
PEH letter of the Hebrew alphabet
PEN instrument for writing in ink
PEP high spirits
PER for each
PES technical name for foot
PET animal kept for companionship
PEW seat in a church
PHI 21st letter of the Greek alphabet
PHO noodle soup
PHT expression of irritation or reluctance
PIA pious
PIC photograph, picture
PIE pastry dish
PIG animal
PIN piece of stiff wire for fastening
PIP small seed in a fruit
PIR Sufi master
PIS plural form of pi

direction along a meridian towards the North Pole **3** the direction in which a compass needle points; magnetic north **4 the north** any area lying in or towards the north ▷ *adj* **5** in or towards the north **6** (esp. of the wind) from the north ▷ *adv* **7** in, to, or towards the north

WORD ORIGIN Old English

North *n* **1 the North a** the northern part of England, generally regarded as reaching the southern boundaries of Yorkshire, Derbyshire, and Cheshire **b** (in the US) the states north of the Mason-Dixon Line that were known as the Free States during the Civil War **c** the economically and technically advanced countries of the world ▷ *adj* **2** of or denoting the northern part of a country or area

Northants Northamptonshire

northbound *adj* going towards the north

North Country *n* **the North Country** same as **North** (sense 1a)

northeast *n* **1** the direction midway between north and east **2 the northeast** any area lying in or towards the northeast ▷ *adj also* **northeastern 3** (*sometimes cap*) of or denoting that part of a country or area which lies in the northeast **4** situated in, moving towards, or facing the northeast **5** (esp. of the wind) from the northeast ▷ *adv* **6** in, to, or towards the northeast **northeasterly** *adj, adv, n*

Northeast *n* **the Northeast** the northeastern part of England, esp. Northumberland and Durham

northeaster *n* a strong wind or storm from the northeast

northerly *adj* **1** of or in the north ▷ *adv, adj* **2** towards the north **3** from the north: *a cold northerly wind*

northern *adj* **1** situated in or towards the north **2** facing or moving towards the north **3** (*sometimes cap*) of or characteristic of the north or North **northernmost** *adj*

Northerner *n* a person from the north of a country or area, esp. England

northern hemisphere *n* that half of the globe lying north of the equator

northern lights *pl n* same as **aurora borealis**

northings *pl n* a series of numbers in a grid reference indicating the distance northwards from a given latitude

Northman *n, pl* **-men** same as **Viking**

North Pole *n* the northernmost point on the earth's axis, at a latitude of 90°N, which has very low temperatures

North Star *n* **the North Star** same as **Pole Star**

Northumb. Northumberland

northward *adj, adv also* **northwards 1** towards the north ▷ *n* **2** the northward part or direction

northwest *n* **1** the direction midway between north and west **2 the northwest** any area lying in or towards the northwest ▷ *adj also* **northwestern 3** (*sometimes cap*) of or denoting that part of a country or area which lies in the northwest **4** situated

in, moving towards, or facing the northwest **5** (esp. of the wind) from the northwest ▷ *adv* **6** in, to, or towards the northwest **northwesterly** *adj, adv, n*

Northwest *n* **the Northwest** the northwestern part of England, esp. Lancashire and the Lake District

northwester *n* a strong wind or storm from the northwest

Norwegian *adj* **1** of Norway ▷ *n* **2** a person from Norway **3** the language of Norway

nor'wester *n* NZ a hot dry wind

Nos. *or* **nos.** numbers

nose *n* **1** the organ situated above the mouth, used for smelling and breathing **2** the sense of smell **3** the front part of a vehicle **4** the distinctive smell of a wine or perfume **5** instinctive skill in finding something: *he had a nose for media events* **6 get up someone's nose** *informal* to annoy someone **7 keep one's nose clean** to stay out of trouble **8 look down one's nose at** *informal* to be haughty towards **9 pay through the nose** *informal* to pay a high price **10 put someone's nose out of joint** *informal* to make someone envious by doing what he would have liked to do or had expected to do **11 rub someone's nose in it** *informal* to remind someone unkindly of a failing or error **12 turn up one's nose at** *informal* to show contempt for **13 win by a nose** to win by a narrow margin ▷ *vb* **nosing, nosed 14** to move forward slowly and carefully: *a motorboat nosed out of the mist* **15** to pry or snoop **16 nose out** to discover by searching or prying

WORD ORIGIN Old English *nosu*

nosebag *n* a bag containing feed, fastened around the head of a horse

noseband *n* the part of a horse's bridle that goes around the nose

nosebleed *n* bleeding from the nose

nose cone *n* the cone-shaped front section of a missile or spacecraft

nose dive *n* **1** (of an aircraft) a sudden plunge with the nose pointing downwards **2** *informal* a sudden drop: *when we fail our self-confidence takes a nose dive* ▷ *vb* **nose-dive, -diving, -dived 3** to take a nose dive

nosegay *n* a small bunch of flowers

WORD ORIGIN nose + *gay* (archaic) toy

nosey *or* **nosy** *adj* **nosier, nosiest** *informal* prying or inquisitive **nosiness** *n*

nosey parker *n* *Brit & S African informal* a prying person

WORD ORIGIN arbitrary use of surname *Parker*

nosh *Brit, Austral, & NZ slang n* **1** food ▷ *vb* **2** to eat

WORD ORIGIN Yiddish

nosh-up *n* *Brit slang* a large meal

nostalgia *n* **1** a sentimental yearning for the past **2** homesickness **nostalgic** *adj* **nostalgically** *adv*

WORD ORIGIN Greek *nostos* a return home + *algios* pain

nostril *n* either of the two openings at the end of the nose

WORD ORIGIN Old English *nosu* nose + *thyrel* hole

nostrum *n* **1** a quack medicine **2** a favourite remedy

WORD ORIGIN Latin: our own (make)

nosy *adj* **nosier, nosiest** same as **nosey**

not *adv* **1** used to negate the sentence, phrase, or word that it modifies: *I will not stand for it* **2 not that** which is not to say that: *not that I've ever heard him complain*

WORD ORIGIN Old English *nāwiht*, from *nā* no + *wiht* creature, thing

nota bene (**note**-a **ben**-nay) note well; take note

WORD ORIGIN Latin

notable (**note**-a-bl) *adj* **1** worthy of being noted; remarkable ▷ *n* **2** a person of distinction **notability** *n* **notably** *adv*

WORD ORIGIN Latin *notare* to note

notary *or* **notary public** (**note**-a-ree) *n, pl* **notaries** *or* **notaries public** a public official, usually a solicitor, who is legally authorized to attest and certify documents

WORD ORIGIN Latin *notarius* one who makes notes, a clerk

notation (no-**tay**-shun) *n* **1** representation of numbers or quantities in a system by a series of symbols **2** a set of such symbols

WORD ORIGIN Latin *notare* to note

notch *n* **1** a V-shaped cut **2** *informal* a step or level: *the economy moved up another notch* ▷ *vb* **3** to cut a notch in **4 notch up** *informal* to score or achieve: *he notched up a hat trick of wins*

WORD ORIGIN mistaken division of *an otch*, from Old French *oche* notch

note *n* **1** a brief informal letter **2** a brief record in writing for future reference **3** a critical comment or explanation in a book **4** an official written communication, as from a government or from a doctor **5** short for **banknote 6** Brit & NZ a musical sound of a particular pitch **7** a written symbol representing the pitch and duration of a musical sound **8** chiefly Brit a key on a piano, organ, or other keyboard instrument **9** a particular feeling or atmosphere: *an optimistic note* **10** a distinctive vocal sound, as of a type of animal **11** a sound used as a signal or warning: *the note to retreat was sounded* **12** short for **promissory note 13 of note a** distinguished or famous **b** important: *nothing of note* **14 strike the right note** to behave appropriately **15 take note of** to pay attention to ▷ *vb* **noting, noted 16** to notice; pay attention to: *such criticism should be noted* **17** to make a written note of: *he noted it in his diary* **18** to remark upon: *I note that you do not wear shoes*

WORD ORIGIN Latin *nota* sign

notebook *n* a book for writing in

notebook computer *n* a portable computer approximately the size of a sheet of A4 paper

notecase *n* same as **wallet**

noted *adj* well-known: *a noted scholar*

notelet *n* a folded card with a printed design on the front, for writing informal letters

notepad *n* a number of sheets of paper fastened together along one edge, used for writing notes or letters on

notepaper *n* paper used for writing letters

noteworthy *adj* worth noting; remarkable

nothing *pron* 1 not anything: *I felt nothing* 2 a matter of no importance: *don't worry, it's nothing* 3 absence of meaning, value, or worth: *the industry shrank to almost nothing* 4 the figure 0 5 **have** or **be nothing to do with** to have no connection with 6 **nothing but** not something other than; only 7 **nothing doing** *informal* an expression of dismissal or refusal 8 **nothing less than** downright: *nothing less than complete withdrawal* 9 **think nothing of something** to regard something as easy or natural ▷ *adv* 10 not at all: *he looked nothing like his brother* ▷ *n* 11 *informal* a person or thing of no importance or significance **WORD ORIGIN** Old English *nāthing, nān thing*

≣ **USAGE**
≣ *Nothing* normally takes a singular
≣ verb, but when *nothing* but is followed
≣ by a plural form of a noun, a plural
≣ verb is usually used: *it was a large room*
≣ *where nothing but souvenirs were sold.*

nothingness *n* 1 nonexistence 2 total insignificance

notice *n* 1 observation or attention: *to attract notice* 2 a displayed placard or announcement giving information 3 advance notification of something such as intention to end a contract of employment: *she handed in her notice* 4 a theatrical or literary review: *the film reaped ecstatic notices* 5 **at short notice** with very little notification 6 **take no notice of** to ignore or disregard 7 **take notice** to pay attention ▷ *vb* **-ticing, -ticed** 8 to become aware (of) 9 to point out or remark upon **WORD ORIGIN** Latin *notus* known

noticeable *adj* easily seen or detected **noticeably** *adv*

notice board *n* a board on which notices are displayed

notifiable *adj* having to be reported to the authorities: *a notifiable disease*

notification *n* 1 the act of notifying someone of something 2 a formal announcement

notify *vb* **-fies, -fying, -fied** to inform: *notify gas and electricity companies of your moving date* **WORD ORIGIN** Latin *notus* known + *facere* to make

notion *n* 1 an idea or opinion 2 a whim **WORD ORIGIN** Latin *notio* a becoming acquainted (with)

notional *adj* hypothetical, imaginary, or unreal: *a notional dividend payment*

notorious *adj* well known for some bad reason **notoriety** *n* **notoriously** *adv* **WORD ORIGIN** Medieval Latin *notorius* well-known

not proven *adj* a verdict in Scottish courts, given when there is insufficient evidence to convict the accused

no-trump *cards n* 1 a bid or hand without trumps ▷ *adj* 2 (of a hand) suitable for playing without trumps

Notts Nottinghamshire

notwithstanding *prep* 1 in spite of ▷ *adv* 2 nevertheless

nougat *n* a hard chewy pink or white sweet containing chopped nuts **WORD ORIGIN** French, from Latin *nux* nut

nought *n* 1 the figure 0 ▷ *n, adv* 2 same as **naught** **WORD ORIGIN** Old English *nōwiht*, from *ne* not, no + *ōwiht* something

noughties *pl n informal* the decade from 2000 to 2009

noughts and crosses *n Brit* a game in which two players, one using a nought, the other a cross, alternately mark squares formed by two pairs of crossed lines, the winner being the first to get three of his or her symbols in a row

noun *n* a word that refers to a person, place, or thing **WORD ORIGIN** Latin *nomen* name

nourish *vb* 1 to provide with the food necessary for life and growth 2 to encourage or foster (an idea or feeling) **nourishing** *adj* **WORD ORIGIN** Latin *nutrire* to feed

nourishment *n* the food needed to nourish the body

nous *n old-fashioned, slang* common sense **WORD ORIGIN** Greek: mind

nouveau riche (**noo**-voh **reesh**) *n, pl* **nouveaux riches** (**noo**-voh **reesh**) a person who has become wealthy recently and is regarded as vulgar **WORD ORIGIN** French: new rich

nouvelle cuisine (**noo**-vell kwee-**zeen**) *n* a style of preparing and presenting food with light sauces and unusual combinations of flavours **WORD ORIGIN** French: new cooking

Nov. November

nova *n, pl* **-vae** or **-vas** a star that undergoes an explosion and fast increase of brightness, then gradually decreases to its original brightness **WORD ORIGIN** New Latin *nova (stella)* new (star)

novel¹ *n* a long fictional story in book form **WORD ORIGIN** Latin *novella (narratio)* new (story)

novel² *adj* fresh, new, or original: *a novel approach* **WORD ORIGIN** Latin *novus* new

novelette *n* a short novel, usually one regarded as trivial or sentimental

novelist *n* a writer of novels

novella *n, pl* **-las** a short narrative tale or short novel **WORD ORIGIN** Italian

novelty *n, pl* **-ties** 1 the quality of being new and interesting 2 a new or unusual experience or thing 3 a small cheap toy or trinket

November *n* the eleventh month of the year **WORD ORIGIN** Latin: ninth month

novena (no-**vee**-na) *n, pl* **-nas** or **-nae** (-nee) *RC Church* a set of prayers or services on nine consecutive days **WORD ORIGIN** Latin *novem* nine

novice (**nov**-viss) *n* 1 a beginner 2 a person who has entered a religious order but has not yet taken vows **WORD ORIGIN** Latin *novus* new

novitiate or **noviciate** *n* 1 the period of being a novice 2 the part of a monastery or convent where the novices live

now *adv* 1 at or for the present time 2 immediately: *bring it now* 3 in these times; nowadays 4 given the present circumstances: *now do you understand why?* 5 **a** used as a hesitation word: *now, I can't really say* **b** used for emphasis: *now listen to this* **c** used at the end of a command: *run along now* 6 **just now a** very recently: *he left just now* **b** very soon: *I'm going just now* 7 **now and again** or **then** occasionally 8 **now now!** an exclamation used to tell someone off or to calm someone ▷ *conj* 9 Also: **now that** seeing that: *now you're here, you can help me* ▷ *n* 10 the present time: *now is the time to go* **WORD ORIGIN** Old English *nū*

nowadays *adv* in these times: *nowadays his work is regarded as out-of-date*

Nowell *n* same as **Noel**

nowhere *adv* 1 in, at, or to no place 2 **getting nowhere** *informal* making no progress 3 **nowhere near** far from: *the stadium is nowhere near completion* ▷ *n* 4 **in the middle of nowhere** (of a place) completely isolated

no-win *adj* with no possibility of a favourable outcome: *a no-win situation*

nowt *n N English dialect* nothing **WORD ORIGIN** from *naught*

noxious *adj* 1 poisonous or harmful 2 extremely unpleasant **WORD ORIGIN** Latin *noxius* harmful

nozzle *n* a projecting spout from which fluid is discharged **WORD ORIGIN** diminutive of *nose*

Np *chem* neptunium

nr near

NS 1 New Style (method of reckoning dates) 2 Nova Scotia

NSPCC (in Britain) National Society for the Prevention of Cruelty to Children

NST Newfoundland Standard Time

NSW New South Wales

NT 1 (in Britain) National Trust 2 New Testament 3 Northern Territory 4 Nunavut

-n't not: added to *be* or *have*, or auxiliary verbs: *can't; don't; isn't*

nth *adj* see **n²**

nuance (**new**-ahnss) *n* a subtle difference, as in colour, meaning, or tone **WORD ORIGIN** French

nub *n* the point or gist: *this is the nub of his theory* **WORD ORIGIN** Middle Low German *knubbe* knob

nubble *n* a small lump **nubbly** *adj* **WORD ORIGIN** from *nub*

nubile (**new**-bile) *adj* 1 (of a young woman) sexually attractive 2 (of a young woman) old enough or mature enough for marriage **WORD ORIGIN** Latin *nubere* to marry

nubuck (**new**-buk) *n* (sometimes cap) leather that has been rubbed on the flesh side of the skin to give it a fine, velvet-like finish

nuclear *adj* 1 of nuclear weapons or energy 2 of an atomic nucleus: *nuclear fission*

n

nuclear bomb n a bomb whose force is due to uncontrolled nuclear fusion or fission

nuclear energy n energy released during a nuclear reaction as a result of fission or fusion

nuclear family n sociol, anthropol a family consisting only of parents and their offspring

nuclear fission n nuclear physics the splitting of an atomic nucleus, either spontaneously or by bombardment by a neutron: used in atomic bombs and nuclear power plants

nuclear-free adj (of an area) barred, esp. by local authorities, from being supplied with nuclear-generated electricity and from storing nuclear waste or weapons

nuclear fusion n nuclear physics the combination of two nuclei to form a heavier nucleus with the release of energy: used in hydrogen bombs

nuclear physics n the branch of physics concerned with the structure of the nucleus and the behaviour of its particles

nuclear power n power produced by a nuclear reactor

nuclear reaction n physics a process in which the structure and energy content of an atomic nucleus is changed by interaction with another nucleus or particle

nuclear reactor n nuclear physics a device in which a nuclear reaction is maintained and controlled to produce nuclear energy

nuclear winter n a theoretical period of low temperatures and little light that has been suggested would occur after a nuclear war

nucleate adj 1 having a nucleus ▷ vb -ating, -ated 2 to form a nucleus

nuclei (new-klee-eye) n the plural of **nucleus**

nucleic acid n biochem a complex compound, such as DNA or RNA, found in all living cells

nucleon n physics a proton or neutron

nucleonics n the branch of physics concerned with the applications of nuclear energy **nucleonic** adj

nucleus n, pl -clei 1 physics the positively charged centre of an atom, made of protons and neutrons, about which electrons orbit 2 a central thing around which others are grouped 3 a centre of growth or development: the nucleus of a new relationship 4 biol the part of a cell that contains the chromosomes and associated molecules that control the characteristics and growth of the cell 5 chem a fundamental group of atoms in a molecule serving as the base structure for related compounds **WORD ORIGIN** Latin: kernel

nude adj 1 completely undressed ▷ n 2 a naked figure in painting, sculpture, or photography 3 **in the nude** naked **nudity** n **WORD ORIGIN** Latin nudus

nudge vb nudging, nudged 1 to push (someone) gently with the elbow to get attention 2 to push (something or

someone) lightly: the dog nudged the stick with its nose 3 to persuade (someone) gently ▷ n 4 a gentle poke or push **WORD ORIGIN** origin unknown

nudism n the practice of not wearing clothes, for reasons of health **nudist** n, adj

nugatory (new-gat-tree) adj formal 1 of little value 2 not valid: their rejection rendered the treaty nugatory **WORD ORIGIN** Latin nugae trifling things

nugget n 1 a small lump of gold in its natural state 2 something small but valuable: a nugget of useful knowledge ▷ vb 3 NZ & S African to polish footwear **WORD ORIGIN** origin unknown

nuisance n 1 a person or thing that causes annoyance or bother ▷ adj 2 causing annoyance or bother: nuisance calls **WORD ORIGIN** Old French nuire to injure

NUJ (in Britain) National Union of Journalists

nuke slang vb nuking, nuked 1 to attack with nuclear weapons ▷ n 2 a nuclear bomb

null adj 1 **null and void** not legally valid 2 **null set** maths a set with no members **nullity** n **WORD ORIGIN** Latin nullus none

nulla-nulla n a wooden club used by Australian Aborigines

nullify vb -fies, -fying, -fied 1 to make (something) ineffective 2 to make (something) legally void **nullification** n **WORD ORIGIN** Latin nullus of no account + facere to make

NUM (in Britain & S Africa) National Union of Mineworkers

numb adj 1 deprived of feeling through cold, shock, or fear 2 unable to move; paralysed ▷ vb 3 to make numb **numbly** adv **numbness** n **WORD ORIGIN** Middle English nomen, literally: taken (with paralysis)

numbat n a small Australian marsupial with a long snout and tongue

number n 1 a concept of quantity that is or can be derived from a single unit, a sum of units, or zero 2 the word or symbol used to represent a number 3 a numeral or string of numerals used to identify a person or thing: an account number 4 the person or thing so identified: he was seeded number two 5 sum or quantity: a very large number of people have telephoned 6 one of a series, as of a magazine 7 a self-contained piece of pop or jazz music 8 a group of people: one of their number might be willing 9 informal an admired article: that little number is by Dior 10 grammar classification of words depending on how many people or things are referred to 11 **any number of** many 12 **beyond or without number** innumerable 13 **have someone's number** informal to have discovered someone's true character or intentions 14 **one's number is up** Austral & Brit informal one is about to die ▷ vb 15 to count 16 to assign a number to: numbered seats 17 to add up to: the illustrations numbered well over fifty 18 to include in a group: he numbered several Americans among his friends 19 **one's days are numbered** something unpleasant,

such as death, is likely to happen to one soon **WORD ORIGIN** Latin numerus

number crunching n computers the large-scale processing of numerical data

numberless adj too many to be counted

number one n 1 informal oneself: he looks after number one 2 informal the bestselling pop record in any one week ▷ adj 3 first in importance, urgency, or quality: he's their number one suspect

numberplate n a plate on a motor vehicle showing the registration number

Number Ten n 10 Downing Street, the British prime minister's official London residence

numbskull or **numskull** n a stupid person

numeral n a word or symbol used to express a sum or quantity **WORD ORIGIN** Latin numerus number

numerate adj able to do basic arithmetic **numeracy** n

numeration n 1 the act or process of numbering or counting 2 a system of numbering

numerator n maths the number above the line in a fraction

numerical or **numeric** adj measured or expressed in numbers: record the severity of your symptoms in numerical form **numerically** adv

numerology n the study of numbers and of their supposed influence on human affairs

numerous adj 1 many: they carried out numerous bombings 2 consisting of a large number of people or things: the cast is not as numerous as one might suppose

numinous adj formal 1 arousing spiritual or religious emotions 2 mysterious or awe-inspiring **WORD ORIGIN** Latin numen divine will

numismatics n the study or collection of coins or medals **numismatist** n **WORD ORIGIN** Greek nomisma piece of currency

numskull n same as **numbskull**

nun n a female member of a religious order **WORD ORIGIN** Late Latin nonna

nuncio n, pl -cios RC Church a papal ambassador **WORD ORIGIN** Latin nuntius messenger

nunnery n, pl -neries a convent

nunny bag n Canad (in Newfoundland) a small sealskin knapsack **WORD ORIGIN** probably from Scots dialect noony lunch

nuptial adj relating to marriage: a nuptial blessing **WORD ORIGIN** Latin nuptiae marriage

nuptials pl n a wedding

nurd n slang same as **nerd**

nurse n 1 a person trained to look after sick people, usually in a hospital 2 short for **nursemaid** ▷ vb nursing, nursed 3 to look after (a sick person) 4 to breast-feed (a baby) 5 (of a baby) to feed at its mother's breast 6 to try to cure (an ailment) 7 to harbour or foster (a feeling) 8 to clasp fondly:

Edward Lear

E dward Lear (1812–88) was a gifted artist and travel writer, but it is as the author of nonsense verse that he is best remembered. He was born in London, into a family that could already boast twenty children. This was extravagant, even by nineteenth-century standards, and more than his parents could financially support. Consequently, Lear from an early age lived with his sister, twenty years his senior, and was largely educated by her.

He made his name with illustrations of animals and plants, and at one time gave drawing lessons to Queen Victoria. His travels in Europe and India not only allowed him to paint and sketch exotic landscapes but to publish self-illustrated accounts such as *Journal of a Landscape Painter in Corsica* (1870).

Lear suffered from epilepsy and depression and it seems that his nonsense writings were partly derived from his need to escape into a fantasy world. In more immediate terms, he began writing nonsense verse for the entertainment of the children of the Earl of Derby, an early patron, and when these pieces were collected and published as *A Book of Nonsense* in 1846 it was an instant success. He followed this up with several more volumes of the same. He was one of the first popularizers of the limerick and he produced many, although without the bawdiness or *double-entendres* that are usually associated with the form. He liked to make up impressive-sounding words, such as *ombliferous* in the limerick below:

There was a Young Person of Crete,
Whose toilette was far from complete;
She dressed in a sack
Spickle-speckled with black,
That ombliferous Person of Crete.

Like many of his other neologisms, such as *flumpetty* or *slobaciously*, the word is intended to be utter nonsense, but it contains just enough elements of recognizable real words and meanings to give the impression that it might mean *something*.

Less grounded in reality were some of the names of imagined places and beings that Lear dreamed up, such as *The Dong with the Luminous Nose*, *The Pobble Who Has No Toes*, and *The Yonghy-Bonghy-Bo*. As a poet, Lear had a good ear for the sounds of words, and he tended to invent names that were at once fantastical yet pleasant in some way, as if to reassure his young readers that nothing very horrible was being described. The beauty of his nonsense names is that everyone is given the freedom to imagine what kind of person or place that they apply to:

Far and few, far and few,
Are the lands where the Jumblies live;
Their heads are green, and their hands are blue,
And they went to sea in a sieve.

Lear's nonsense was not only popular with his contemporaries but had an enduring influence on the humour of later generations, ranging from the nonsense writings of Spike Milligan and John Lennon (including several Beatles lyrics), through the children's books of Dr Seuss, to the surreal comedy of *Monty Python's Flying Circus* and *The Mighty Boosh*. His neologisms, on the other hand, have not found a permanent place in the English language, with the notable exception of one term: *runcible*.

In *Collins English Dictionary*, a *runcible spoon* is defined thus: 'a forklike utensil with two broad prongs and one sharp curved prong'. The first appearance of the word was in Lear's poem 'The Owl and the Pussycat', in which the eponymous creatures 'dined on mince, and slices of quince, /Which they ate with a runcible spoon'.

No-one can tell exactly what Lear intended a runcible spoon to look like, and indeed he uses the term *runcible* in another nonsense verse where the meaning is equally vague but obviously different. However, the inventor of the actual piece of cutlery undoubtedly was trying to imagine an implement that would be equally handy for consuming both mince and quince, and it is this liberation of the imagination that is Lear's greatest legacy.

she nursed her drink **nursing** *n, adj*
WORD ORIGIN Latin *nutrire* to nourish

nursemaid *or* **nurserymaid** *n* a woman employed to look after children

nursery *n, pl* **-ries 1** a room in a house where children sleep or play **2** a place where children are taken care of when their parents are at work **3** a place where plants and young trees are grown for sale

nurseryman *n, pl* **-men** a person who raises plants and trees for sale

nursery nurse *n* a person trained to look after children of pre-school age

nursery rhyme *n* a short traditional verse or song for children

nursery school *n* a school for young children from three to five years old

nursery slopes *pl n* gentle slopes used by beginners in skiing

nursery stakes *pl n* a race for two-year-old horses

nursing home *n* a private hospital or home for people who are old or ill

nursing officer *n* (in Britain) the administrative head of the nursing staff of a hospital

nurture *n* **1** the act or process of promoting the development of a child or young plant ▷ *vb* **-turing, -tured 2** to promote or encourage the development of
WORD ORIGIN Latin *nutrire* to nourish

nut *n* **1** a dry one-seeded fruit that grows inside a hard shell **2** the edible inner part of such a fruit **3** a small piece of metal with a hole in it, that screws on to a bolt **4** *slang* an eccentric or insane person **5** *slang* the head **6** *slang* an enthusiast: *a health nut* **7** *Brit* a small piece of coal **8 a hard** *or* **tough nut to crack** a person or thing that presents difficulties **9 do one's nut** *Austral & Brit slang* to be very angry ▸ See also **nuts**

WORD ORIGIN Old English *hnutu*

NUT (in Britain & S Africa) National Union of Teachers

nutcase *n slang* an insane person

nutcracker *n* a device for cracking the shells of nuts. Also: **nutcrackers**

nuthatch *n* a songbird that feeds on insects, seeds, and nuts
WORD ORIGIN Middle English *notehache* nut hatchet, from its habit of splitting nuts

nutmeg *n* a spice made from the seed of a tropical tree
WORD ORIGIN Old French *nois muguede* musk-scented nut

nutraceutical *n* see **functional food**

nutria (**new**-tree-a) *n* the fur of the coypu
WORD ORIGIN Latin *lutra* otter

nutrient (**new**-tree-ent) *n* **1** a substance that provides nourishment: *their only source of nutrient* ▷ *adj* **2** providing nourishment
WORD ORIGIN Latin *nutrire* to nourish

nutriment (**new**-tree-ment) *n* the food or nourishment required by all living things to grow and stay healthy
WORD ORIGIN Latin *nutrimentum*

nutrition (**new**-**trish**-un) *n* **1** the process of taking in and absorbing nutrients **2** the process of being nourished **3** the study of nutrition **nutritional** *adj* **nutritionist** *n*
WORD ORIGIN Latin *nutrire* to nourish

nutritious *adj* providing nourishment
WORD ORIGIN Latin *nutrix* nurse

nutritive *adj* of nutrition; nutritious

nuts *adj slang* **1** insane **2 nuts about** very fond of or enthusiastic about

nuts and bolts *pl n informal* the essential or practical details: *the nuts and bolts of photography*

nutshell *n* **in a nutshell** in essence; briefly

nutter *n Brit & NZ slang* an insane person

nutty *adj* **-tier, -tiest 1** containing or resembling nuts **2** *slang* insane or eccentric **nuttiness** *n*

nux vomica *n* the seed of a tree, containing strychnine
WORD ORIGIN Medieval Latin: vomiting nut

nuzzle *vb* **-zling, -zled** to push or rub gently with the nose or snout
WORD ORIGIN from *nose*

NV Nevada

nvCJD new-variant Creutzfeldt-Jakob disease

NW northwest(ern)

NWT Northwest Territories (of Canada)

NY *or* **N.Y.** New York

NYC New York City

nylon *n* a synthetic material used for clothing and many other products
WORD ORIGIN originally a trademark

nylons *pl n* stockings made of nylon

nymph *n* **1** *myth* a spirit of nature, represented as a beautiful young woman **2** the larva of certain insects, resembling the adult form **3** *chiefly poetic* a beautiful young woman
WORD ORIGIN Greek *numphē*

nymphet *n* a girl who is sexually precocious and desirable

nympho *n, pl* **-phos** *informal* short for **nymphomaniac**

nymphomaniac *n* a woman with an abnormally intense sexual desire **nymphomania** *n*
WORD ORIGIN Greek *numphē* nymph + *mania* madness

NZ, N.Z. New Zealand

NZE New Zealand English

NZRFU New Zealand Rugby Football Union

NZSE40 Index New Zealand Stock Exchange 40 Index

Oo

The letter O is the fifteenth letter of the English alphabet. A similarly shaped letter is found in the Semitic alphabets, where it is called *ayin*, meaning 'eye'. The Greeks applied this shape to a vowel sound and called it *omicron* (O,o).

In fact, the Greek alphabet has two letters that represent O: *omicron* is literally 'small O', and represents the shorter sound used in 'dot', while the final letter of the Greek alphabet is *omega* (Ω,ω) – literally 'large O' – which represents the longer sound used in 'note'. In the Roman alphabet only one of the letters was deemed necessary, and the simple circular shape was the one that found favour.

A similarly shaped symbol was independently developed in India to represent the mathematical concept of zero. This was adopted by Arab mathematicians, and reached Europe in the Middle Ages. Since then the circular letter and the similarly shaped number have become inextricably linked. People often use the name of the letter O when they are talking about the number, although there is no reciprocal arrangement: you don't use 'zero' to refer to the letter.

When it occurs at the start of a surname, the letter O suggests an Irish origin. In names such as O'Neill and O'Driscoll, it comes from an Irish word meaning 'descendant', and performs a similar function to the Scottish 'Mac'.

As an abbreviation, O frequently means 'old' or 'ordinary', but the connotations are not necessarily unfavourable. 'O levels' were the ordinary examinations of the General Certificate of Education, as opposed to the more advanced A levels. These examinations have been superseded by GCSEs in England, Wales and Northern Ireland, but are still set in some countries. A comparable examination in Scottish schools was called an 'O grade', but this too has been phased out in the course of educational reform.

The Story of O was a notorious erotic novel by French writer Pauline Réage. Perhaps the round shape of the letter was considered suggestive by the author, but the letter has not always been associated with carnal things. Many of the Christian Church's Latin hymns and prayers begin with the exclamation 'O'. The 'fifteen O's' are prayers composed by Saint Bridget, which meditate on the sufferings of Christ, and the 'seven O's of Advent' are hymns that similarly begin with the word 'O', and which were traditionally sung in the period before Christmas.

O¹ 1 *chem* oxygen **2** Old **3** same as **nought**

O² interj same as **oh**

o. *or* **O.** old

o' *prep informal or old-fashioned* of: *a cup o' tea*

OA Order of Australia

oaf *n* a stupid or clumsy person **oafish** *adj*
WORD ORIGIN variant of Old English *ælf* elf

oak *n* **1** a large forest tree with hard wood, acorns as fruits, and leaves with rounded projections **2** the wood of this tree, used as building timber and for making furniture **oaken** *adj*
WORD ORIGIN Old English *āc*

oak apple *or* **gall** *n* a brownish round lump or ball produced on oak trees by certain wasps

Oaks *n* **the Oaks** an annual horse race for three-year-old fillies, run at Epsom
WORD ORIGIN named after an estate near Epsom

oakum *n* loose fibre obtained by unravelling old rope, used for filling cracks in wooden ships

WORD ORIGIN Old English *ācumba*, literally: off-combings

OAM Medal of the Order of Australia

OAP (in Britain) old age pensioner

oar *n* **1** a long pole with a broad blade, used for rowing a boat **2** **put** *or* **stick one's oar in** to interfere or interrupt
WORD ORIGIN Old English *ār*

oarsman *or fem* **oarswoman** *n, pl* **-men** *or* **-women** a person who rows **oarsmanship** *n*

oasis *n, pl* **-ses 1** a fertile patch in a desert **2** a place or situation offering relief in the midst of difficulty
WORD ORIGIN Greek

oast *n chiefly Brit* an oven for drying hops
WORD ORIGIN Old English *āst*

oast house *n chiefly Brit* a building containing ovens for drying hops

oat *n* **1** a hard cereal grown as food **2 oats** the edible grain of this cereal **3 sow one's wild oats** to have casual sexual relationships while young **oaten** *adj*
WORD ORIGIN Old English *āte*

oatcake *n* a thin unsweetened biscuit made of oatmeal

oath *n, pl* **oaths 1** a solemn promise, esp. to tell the truth in a court of law **2** an offensive or blasphemous expression; a swearword **3 on** *or* **under oath** having made a solemn promise to tell the truth, esp. in a court of law
WORD ORIGIN Old English *āth*

oatmeal *n* **1** a coarse flour made by grinding oats ▷ *adj* **2** greyish-yellow

ob. (on tombstones) he *or* she died
WORD ORIGIN Latin *obiit*

obbligato (ob-lig-**gah**-toe) *music adj* **1** not to be omitted in performance ▷ *n, pl* **-tos 2** an essential part or accompaniment: *an aria with bassoon obbligato*
WORD ORIGIN Italian

obdurate *adj* not to be persuaded; hardhearted or obstinate **obduracy** *n*
WORD ORIGIN Latin *obdurare* to make hard

OBE (in Britain) Officer of the Order of the British Empire

obedient *adj* obeying or willing to obey **obedience** *n* **obediently** *adv*
WORD ORIGIN Latin *oboediens*

obeisance (oh-**bay**-sanss) *n formal* **1** an attitude of respect or humble obedience

2 a bow or curtsy showing this attitude **obeisant** *adj*
WORD ORIGIN Old French *obéissant* obeying

obelisk (**ob**-bill-isk) *n* **1** a four-sided stone pillar that tapers to a pyramid at the top **2** *printing* same as **dagger** (sense 2)
WORD ORIGIN Greek *obeliskos* a little spit

obese (oh-**beess**) *adj* very fat **obesity** *n*
WORD ORIGIN Latin *obesus*

obey *vb* **1** to carry out instructions or orders; be obedient **2** to act in accordance with one's feelings, an impulse, etc.: *I had obeyed the impulse to open the gate and had walked up the drive*
WORD ORIGIN Latin *oboedire*

obfuscate *vb* **-cating, -cated** *formal* to make something unnecessarily difficult to understand **obfuscation** *n* **obfuscatory** *adj*
WORD ORIGIN Latin *ob-* (intensive) + *fuscare* to blacken

obituary *n, pl* **-aries** a published announcement of a death, usually with a short biography of the dead person **obituarist** *n*
WORD ORIGIN Latin *obitus* death

obj. 1 objection **2** *grammar* object(ive)

object[1] *n* **1** a thing that can be touched or seen **2** a person or thing seen as a focus for feelings, actions, or thought: *she had become for him an object of compassion* **3** an aim or purpose: *the main object of the exercise* **4** *philosophy* that which can be perceived by the mind, as contrasted with the thinking subject **5** *grammar* a noun, pronoun, or noun phrase that receives the action of a verb or is governed by a preposition, such as *the bottle* in *she threw the bottle* **6** **no object** not a hindrance or obstacle: *money's no object*
WORD ORIGIN Late Latin *objectus* something thrown before (the mind)

object[2] *vb* **1** to express disapproval or opposition: *my colleagues objected strongly to further delays* **2** to state as one's reason for opposing: *he objected that his small staff would be unable to handle the added work* **objector** *n*
WORD ORIGIN Latin *ob-* against + *jacere* to throw

objection *n* **1** an expression or feeling of opposition or disapproval **2** a reason for opposing something: *the planning officer had raised no objection to the proposals*

objectionable *adj* offensive or unacceptable

objective *n* **1** an aim or purpose: *the objective is to highlight the environmental threat to the planet* **2** *grammar* a grammatical case in some languages that identifies the direct object of a verb or preposition **3** *optics* the lens nearest to the object observed in an optical instrument ▷ *adj* **4** not distorted by personal feelings or bias: *I have tried to be as objective as possible in my presentation* **5** of or relating to actual facts as opposed to thoughts or feelings: *stand back and try to take a more objective view of your life as a whole* **6** existing independently of the mind; real **objectival** *adj* **objectively** *adv* **objectivity** *n*

object lesson *n* a practical demonstration of some principle or ideal

objet d'art (**ob**-zhay **dahr**) *n, pl* **objets d'art** (**ob**-zhay **dahr**) a small object considered to be of artistic worth
WORD ORIGIN French: object of art

oblate *adj geom* (of a sphere) flattened at the poles: *the oblate spheroid of the earth*
WORD ORIGIN New Latin *oblatus* lengthened

oblation *n* **1** *Christianity* the offering of bread and wine to God at Communion **2** any offering made for religious purposes **oblational** *adj*
WORD ORIGIN Medieval Latin *oblatus* offered

obligated *adj* being morally or legally bound to do something: *they are obligated to provide temporary accommodation* **obligative** *adj*

obligation *n* **1** a moral or legal duty **2** the binding power of such a duty: *I feel under some obligation to help you with your education* **3** a sense of being in debt because of a service or favour: *I don't want him marrying me out of obligation*

obligatory *adj* required or compulsory because of custom or law

oblige *vb* **obliging, obliged 1** to compel someone by legal, moral, or physical means to do something **2** to make (someone) indebted or grateful for a favour: *I am obliged to you for your help* **3** to do a favour to someone: *she obliged the guests with a song*
WORD ORIGIN Latin *ob-* towards + *ligare* to bind

obliging *adj* willing to be helpful **obligingly** *adv*

oblique (oh-**bleak**) *adj* **1** at an angle; slanting **2** *geom* (of lines or planes) neither perpendicular nor parallel to one another **3** indirect or evasive: *only oblique references have been made to the anti-government unrest* ▷ *n* **4** same as **solidus** > **obliquely** *adv* **obliqueness** *n*
WORD ORIGIN Latin *obliquus*

oblique angle *n* an angle that is not a right angle or any multiple of a right angle

obliterate *vb* **-rating, -rated** to destroy every trace of; wipe out completely **obliteration** *n*
WORD ORIGIN Latin *oblitterare* to erase

oblivion *n* **1** the condition of being forgotten or disregarded: *the Marxist-Leninist wing of the party looks set to sink into oblivion* **2** the state of being unaware or unconscious: *guests seemed to feel a social obligation to drink themselves into oblivion*
WORD ORIGIN Latin *oblivio* forgetfulness

oblivious *adj* unaware or unconscious: *oblivious of her soaking clothes; I was oblivious to the beauty* **obliviousness** *n*

oblong *adj* **1** having an elongated, rectangular shape ▷ *n* **2** a figure or object having this shape
WORD ORIGIN Latin *oblongus*

obloquy (**ob**-lock-wee) *n, pl* **-quies** *formal* **1** abusive statements or blame: *the British press was held up to moral obloquy* **2** disgrace brought about by this: *the punishment of lifelong public obloquy and private embarrassment*
WORD ORIGIN Latin *obloquium* contradiction

obnoxious *adj* extremely unpleasant **obnoxiousness** *n*
WORD ORIGIN Latin *obnoxius*

oboe *n* a double-reeded woodwind instrument with a penetrating nasal tone **oboist** *n*
WORD ORIGIN French *haut bois*, literally: high wood (referring to its pitch)

obs. obsolete

obscene *adj* **1** offensive to accepted standards of decency or modesty **2** *law* tending to deprave or corrupt: *an obscene publication* **3** disgusting: *a great dark obscene pool of blood* **obscenity** *n*
WORD ORIGIN Latin *obscenus* inauspicious

obscure *adj* **1** not well-known: *the concerts feature several obscure artists* **2** not easily understood: *the contracts are written in obscure language* **3** unclear or indistinct ▷ *vb* **-scuring, -scured 4** to make unclear or vague; hide: *no amount of bluster could obscure the fact that the prime minister had run out of excuses* **5** to cover or cloud over **obscuration** *n* **obscurity** *n*
WORD ORIGIN Latin *obscurus* dark

obsequies (**ob**-sick-weez) *pl n, sing* **-quy** *formal* funeral rites
WORD ORIGIN Medieval Latin *obsequiae*

obsequious (ob-**seek**-wee-uss) *adj* being overattentive in order to gain favour **obsequiousness** *n*
WORD ORIGIN Latin *obsequiosus* compliant

observance *n* **1** the observing of a law or custom **2** a ritual, ceremony, or practice, esp. of a religion

observant *adj* quick to notice details around one; sharp-eyed

observation *n* **1** the act of watching or the state of being watched **2** a comment or remark **3** detailed examination of something before analysis, diagnosis, or interpretation: *you may be admitted to hospital for observation and rest* **4** the facts learned from observing **5** the ability to notice things: *she has good powers of observation* **observational** *adj*

observatory *n, pl* **-ries** a building specially designed and equipped for studying the weather and the stars

observe *vb* **-serving, -served 1** to see or notice: *after some hours I observed a change in the animal's behaviour* **2** to watch (something) carefully **3** to make scientific examinations of **4** to remark: *the speaker observed that times had changed* **5** to keep (a law or custom) **observable** *adj* **observer** *n*
WORD ORIGIN Latin *observare*

obsessed *adj* thinking about someone or something all the time: *he had become obsessed with her* **obsessive** *adj, n*
WORD ORIGIN Latin *obsessus* besieged

obsession *n* **1** something that preoccupies a person to the exclusion of other things: *his principal obsession was with trying to economize* **2** *psychiatry* a persistent idea or impulse, often associated with anxiety and mental illness **obsessional** *adj*

obsidian *n* a dark glassy volcanic rock
WORD ORIGIN after *Obsius*, the discoverer of a stone resembling obsidian

Printing and the English Language

The printed word has been part of Western Culture for more than 500 years. We live in a post-print age, where printing itself seems 'old-fashioned', part of the distant past; indeed we take printing for granted. But it has not always been with us, and its arrival influenced the development of the English language.

Printing was invented not once but twice. The Chinese had developed a method of printing using carved wooden blocks as early as the seventh century. These blocks held entire passages of writing, carved in relief (meaning the characters stood out from a flat surface). The blocks were inked and pressed to paper. This was more efficient, in the long run, than copying the same words again and again by hand, but unfortunately each block could be used only for one passage of one text. By the 15th century, the Chinese had developed smaller wooden blocks containing single characters, which were more versatile.

At about this time, in Europe, Johannes Gutenberg invented the printing press, apparently without any knowledge of printing in China. Gutenberg's invention was inspired by the wine press. He used individual pieces of movable type (small metal blocks depicting a single letter or punctuation mark in relief) arranged in a *forme* (a metal frame), which was pressed by a hand-operated machine onto paper or vellum. The movable type pieces could be used to create virtually any text.

Printing allowed books to be produced and disseminated more rapidly and cheaply than ever before. The painstakingly slow process of scribal book production had made books and manuscripts rare and expensive. Also, scribal book production was particularly prone to errors and variation: no two manuscripts of a given text were identical, even when copied by the same scribe. Printing meant that all copies of a given edition of a book were exactly alike.

Printing was developed to fill a niche in the market. Increasing literacy during the Renaissance led to greater demand for books, so the book industry needed a way to produce books more quickly and in larger quantities. This expanding market attracted ambitious entrepreneurs, such as the man who introduced printing to Britain.

William Caxton was a 15th-century English merchant. He travelled widely during his life, and having observed German printing first-hand in Cologne, resolved to set up his own printing press. In 1475 he produced *The Recuyell of the Historyes of Troye*, which was the first book ever to be printed in English.

Though Caxton is well known among language historians for his comments on the spoken English of his time, he himself was no linguist. His interest in language was that of a businessman, and his approach to it was pragmatic. No standardized English existed in Caxton's day: neither spelling, grammar, nor pronunciation was fixed in one authoritative, nationally accepted variety. And yet Caxton's English books were to be distributed more widely than any manuscript had ever been. Caxton therefore had to print in an English that could be understood by the widest possible audience.

Caxton's influence on the English language is seen in the form of the word *egg*. The original Anglo-Saxon word was æȝ (pronounced like 'eye'), which became *ey* in Middle English (plural *eyren*). The form *egg* came from Old Norse, and was originally Northern English. Caxton famously asks 'what sholde a man in thyse dayes now wryte, egges or eyren, certaynly it is harde to playse every man'. And yet it was the dialect form that Caxton and his followers printed, eventually becoming the standard word.

Caxton's choice, however, was not informed by any linguistic or historical considerations. He would not have cared which form was 'correct', or even which was most familiar to him (he came from Kent, where *ey* was used). The form *egg* makes more printing sense, as it is not confusable with *eye*, which could also be spelled *ey*.

Caxton's books are not without variation (he prints *asked* both as *axed* and *axyd* on the same page). But when Caxton made a decision about how to spell a word, it was replicated and spread throughout Britain, giving him more influence on the language than any scribe could have hoped for.

obsolescent *adj* becoming obsolete or out of date **obsolescence** *n*

obsolete *adj* no longer used; out of date
WORD ORIGIN Latin *obsoletus* worn out

≡ USAGE
≡ The word *obsoleteness* is hardly ever
≡ used, *obsolescence* standing as the noun
≡ form for both *obsolete* and *obsolescent*.

obstacle *n* **1** a situation or event that prevents something being done: *there are obstacles which could slow the development of a vaccine* **2** a person or thing that hinders movement
WORD ORIGIN Latin *obstaculum*, from *ob-* against + *stare* to stand

obstetrician *n* a doctor who specializes in obstetrics

obstetrics *n* the branch of medicine concerned with pregnancy and childbirth **obstetric** *adj*
WORD ORIGIN Latin *obstetrix* a midwife

obstinate *adj* **1** keeping stubbornly to a particular opinion or course of action **2** difficult to treat or deal with: *obstinate weeds* **obstinacy** *n* **obstinately** *adv*
WORD ORIGIN Latin *obstinatus*

obstreperous *adj* noisy and difficult to control: *her obstreperous teenage son*
WORD ORIGIN Latin *ob-* against + *strepere* to roar

obstruct *vb* **1** to block a way with an obstacle **2** to make progress or activity difficult: *this government will never obstruct the course of justice* **3** to block a clear view of
WORD ORIGIN Latin *obstructus* built against

obstruction *n* **1** a person or thing that obstructs **2** the act of obstructing or being obstructed **3** *sport* the act of unfairly impeding an opposing player

obstructionist *n* a person who deliberately obstructs legal or parliamentary business **obstructionism** *n*

obstructive *adj* deliberately causing difficulties or delays **obstructively** *adv* **obstructiveness** *n*

obtain *vb* **1** to gain possession of; get **2** *formal* to be customary or accepted: *silence obtains from eight in the evening* **obtainable** *adj*
WORD ORIGIN Latin *obtinere* to take hold of

obtrude *vb* **-truding, -truded 1** to push oneself or one's opinions on others in an unwelcome way **2** to be or make unpleasantly noticeable **obtrusion** *n*
WORD ORIGIN Latin *obtrudere*

obtrusive *adj* unpleasantly noticeable: *the music should fit your mood, it shouldn't be too obtrusive* **obtrusiveness** *n*

obtuse *adj* **1** mentally slow or emotionally insensitive **2** *maths* (of an angle) between 90° and 180° **3** not sharp or pointed; blunt **obtuseness** *n*
WORD ORIGIN Latin *obtusus* dulled

obverse *n* **1** a counterpart or opposite: *his true personality being the obverse of his outer image* **2** the side of a coin that bears the main design **3** the front, top, or main surface of anything
WORD ORIGIN Latin *obversus* turned towards

obviate *vb* **-ating, -ated** *formal* to avoid or prevent (a need or difficulty): *a*
mediator will obviate the need for independent legal advice
WORD ORIGIN Latin *obviare*

≡ USAGE
≡ Only things which have not yet
≡ occurred can be *obviated*. For example,
≡ one can *obviate* a possible future
≡ difficulty, but not one which already
≡ exists.

obvious *adj* **1** easy to see or understand ▷ *n* **2 state the obvious** to say something that is unnecessary or already known: *he is prone to stating the obvious* **obviously** *adv* **obviousness** *n*
WORD ORIGIN Latin *obvius*

ocarina *n* a small egg-shaped wind instrument with a mouthpiece and finger holes
WORD ORIGIN Italian: little goose

occasion *n* **1** a particular event or the time at which it happens **2** a need or reason to do or be something: *we barely knew him and never had occasion to speak of him* **3** a suitable time or opportunity to do something **4** a special event, time, or celebration: *a wedding day is a truly special occasion* **5 on occasion** every so often **6 rise to the occasion** to meet the special demands of a situation ▷ *vb* **7** *formal* to cause, esp. incidentally
WORD ORIGIN Latin *occasio* a falling down

occasional *adj* happening from time to time; not frequent or regular **occasionally** *adv*

occasional table *n* a small table with no regular use

Occident *n* the western hemisphere, esp. Europe and America **Occidental** *adj*
WORD ORIGIN Latin *occidere* to fall (with reference to the setting sun)

occiput (**ox**-sip-putt) *n anat* the back of the head or skull **occipital** *adj*
WORD ORIGIN Latin *ob-* at the back of + *caput* head

occlude *vb* **-cluding, -cluded** *formal* **1** to block or stop up a passage or opening: *the arteries are occluded by deposits of plaque* **2** to shut in or out: *slowly occluding him from Nash's vision* **3** *chem* (of a solid) to absorb and retain a gas or other substance **occlusion** *n*
WORD ORIGIN Latin *occludere*

occluded front *n meteorol* the front formed when the cold front of a depression overtakes a warm front, raising the warm air from ground level

occult *adj* **1** involving mystical or supernatural phenomena or powers **2** beyond ordinary human understanding **3** secret or mysterious ▷ *n* **4 the occult** the knowledge and study of occult phenomena and powers
WORD ORIGIN Latin *occultus* hidden, secret

occupancy *n, pl* **-cies 1** the act of occupying a property **2** the period of time during which one is an occupant of a property

occupant *n* a person occupying a property, position, or place

occupation *n* **1** a person's job or profession **2** any activity on which someone's time is spent: *a pleasant and rewarding occupation* **3** the control of a country by a foreign military power
4 the act of occupying or the state of being occupied: *the occupation of Kuwait* **occupational** *adj*

occupational hazard *n* something unpleasant that occurs due to your job: *frequent colds are an occupational hazard in teaching*

occupational therapy *n* treatment of people with physical, emotional, or social problems using purposeful activity to help them overcome or learn to accept their problems

occupier *n Brit* the person who lives in a particular house, whether as owner or tenant

occupy *vb* **-pies, -pying, -pied 1** to live, stay, or work in (a house, flat, or office) **2** to keep (someone or someone's mind) busy **3** to take up (time or space) **4** to move in and take control of (a country or other place): *soldiers have occupied the country's television station* **5** to fill or hold (a position or office)
WORD ORIGIN Latin *occupare* to seize hold of

occur *vb* **-curring, -curred 1** to happen **2** to be found or be present; exist **3 occur to** to come into the mind of
WORD ORIGIN Latin *occurrere* to run up to

≡ USAGE
≡ It is usually regarded as incorrect to
≡ talk of pre-arranged events *occurring* or
≡ *happening*: the wedding took place (not
≡ *occurred* or happened) in the afternoon.

occurrence *n* **1** something that happens **2** the fact of occurring: *the likelihood of its occurrence increases with age*

ocean *n* **1** the vast area of salt water covering about 70 per cent of the earth's surface **2** one of the five principal divisions of this: the Atlantic, Pacific, Indian, Arctic, and Antarctic **3** *informal* a huge quantity or expanse: *oceans of replies* **4** *literary* the sea **oceanic** *adj*
WORD ORIGIN from *Oceanus*, Greek god of the stream believed to flow round the earth

ocean-going *adj* (of a ship or boat) suited for travel on the open ocean

oceanography *n* the study of oceans and their environment **oceanographer** *n* **oceanographic** *adj*

ocelot (**oss**-ill-lot) *n* a large cat of Central and South America with a dark-spotted yellow-grey coat
WORD ORIGIN Mexican Indian *ocelotl* jaguar

och *interj Scot & Irish* an expression of surprise, annoyance, or disagreement

oche (**ok**-kee) *n darts* a mark on the floor behind which a player must stand when throwing a dart
WORD ORIGIN origin unknown

ochre *or US* **ocher** (**oak**-er) *n* **1** a yellow or reddish-brown earth used in paints or dyes ▷ *adj* **2** moderate yellow-orange to orange
WORD ORIGIN Greek *ōkhros* pale yellow

o'clock *adv* used after a number between one and twelve to specify an hour: *five o'clock in the morning*

OCR optical character recognition: the ability (through a computer device) for letters and numbers to be optically scanned and input to a storage device

Oct. October

octagon *n* a geometric figure with eight sides **octagonal** *adj*
WORD ORIGIN Greek *oktagōnos* having eight angles

octahedron (ok-ta-**heed**-ron) *n, pl* **-drons** *or* **-dra** a solid figure with eight plane faces

octane *n* a liquid hydrocarbon found in petroleum

octane number *or* **rating** *n* a number indicating the quality of a petrol

octave *n* **1 a** the musical interval between the first note and the eighth note of a major or minor scale **b** the higher of these two notes **c** the series of notes filling this interval **2** *prosody* a rhythmic group of eight lines of verse
WORD ORIGIN Latin *octo* eight

octavo *n, pl* **-vos 1** a book size resulting from folding a sheet of paper of a standard size to form eight leaves **2** a book or sheet of this size
WORD ORIGIN New Latin *in octavo* in an eighth (of a sheet)

octet *n* **1** a group of eight instrumentalists or singers **2** a piece of music for eight performers
WORD ORIGIN Latin *octo* eight

October *n* the tenth month of the year
WORD ORIGIN Latin *octo* eight, since it was originally the eighth month in Roman reckoning

octogenarian *n* **1** a person between 80 and 89 years old ▷ *adj* **2** between 80 and 89 years old
WORD ORIGIN Latin *octogenarius* containing eighty

octopus *n, pl* **-puses** a sea creature with a soft oval body and eight long tentacles with suckers
WORD ORIGIN Greek *oktōpous* having eight feet

ocular *adj* of or relating to the eyes or sight
WORD ORIGIN Latin *oculus* eye

oculist *n* old-fashioned an ophthalmologist

OD *informal n* **1** an overdose of a drug ▷ *vb* **OD'ing, OD'd 2** to take an overdose of a drug

odalisque (**ode**-a-lisk) *n* a female slave in a harem
WORD ORIGIN Turkish *ōdalik*

odd *adj* **1** unusual or peculiar: *his increasingly odd behaviour* **2** occasional or incidental: *the odd letter from a friend abroad, the occasional postcard from a chum* **3** leftover or additional: *we use up odd pieces of fabric to make up jerseys in wild designs* **4** (of a number) not divisible by two **5** being part of a pair or set when the other or others are missing: *the drawer was full of odd socks* **6** somewhat more than the round numbers specified: *I had known him for the past twenty-odd years* **7 odd man** *or* **one out** a person or thing excluded from others forming a group or unit
▷ See also **odds** ▷ **oddly** *adv* **oddness** *n*
WORD ORIGIN Old Norse *oddi* angle, point, third or odd number

oddball *n* informal a strange or eccentric person

oddity *n, pl* **-ties 1** an odd person or thing **2** a peculiar characteristic **3** the quality of being or appearing unusual or strange

odd-man rush *n* ice hockey an attacking move when the defence is outnumbered by the opposing team

oddments *pl n* odd pieces or things; leftovers: *oddments of wool*

odds *pl n* **1** the probability, expressed as a ratio, that something will or will not happen: *the odds against an acquittal had stabilized at six to four* **2** the difference, expressed as a ratio, between the money placed on a bet and the amount that would be received as winning payment: *the current odds are ten to one* **3** the likelihood that a certain state of affairs will be so: *the odds are that you are going to fail* **4** the advantage that one contender is judged to have over another: *the odds are in his favour* **5 it makes no odds** *Austral & Brit* it does not matter **6 at odds** on bad terms **7** at variance **8 over the odds** more than is expected or necessary

odds and ends *pl n* small, usually unimportant, objects, jobs to be done, etc.: *I have brought a few odds and ends with me*

odds-on *adj* having a better than even chance of winning

ode *n* a lyric poem, usually addressed to a particular subject, with lines of varying lengths and metres
WORD ORIGIN Greek *ōidē* song

Odin *n* the chief god in Norse mythology

odious *adj* offensive or hateful: *I steeled myself for the odious task* **odiousness** *n*
WORD ORIGIN see ODIUM

odium (**oh**-dee-um) *n* formal widespread dislike or disapproval of a person or action
WORD ORIGIN Latin

odometer (**odd-om**-it-er) *n US & Canad* same as **mileometer**
WORD ORIGIN Greek *hodos* way + -METER

odoriferous *adj* formal having or giving off a pleasant smell

odour *or US* **odor** *n* a particular and distinctive scent or smell **odorous** *adj* **odourless** *adj*
WORD ORIGIN Latin *odor*

odyssey (**odd**-iss-ee) *n* a long eventful journey

OE *NZ informal* overseas experience: *he's away on his OE*

OECD Organization for Economic Cooperation and Development

oedema *or* **edema** (id-**deem**-a) *n, pl* **-mata** *pathol* an abnormal accumulation of fluid in the tissues of the body, causing swelling
WORD ORIGIN Greek *oidēma* swelling

Oedipus complex (**ee**-dip-puss) *n psychoanal* the usually unconscious sexual desire of a child, esp. a male child, for the parent of the opposite sex **oedipal** *adj*

o'er *prep, adv poetic* over

oesophagus (ee-**soff**-a-guss) *n, pl* **-gi** (-guy) the tube through which food travels from the throat to the stomach; gullet **oesophageal** *adj*
WORD ORIGIN Greek *oisophagos*

oestrogen (**ee**-stra-jen) *n* a female sex hormone that controls the reproductive cycle, and prepares the body for pregnancy

WORD ORIGIN from *oestrus* + -*gen* (suffix) producing

oestrus (**ee**-struss) *n* a regularly occurring period of fertility and sexual receptivity in the reproductive cycle of most female mammals, except humans; heat
WORD ORIGIN Greek *oistros* gadfly, hence frenzy

of *prep* **1** belonging to; situated in or coming from; because of: *the inhabitants of former East Germany; I saw five people die of chronic hepatitis* **2** used after words or phrases expressing quantities: *a pint of milk* **3** specifying an amount or value: *we had to release the bombs at a height of 400 metres* **4** made up of, containing, or characterized by: *a length of rope; she is a woman of enviable beauty* **5** used to link a verbal noun with a following noun or noun phrase that is either the subject or the object of the verb: *the sudden slipping of the plates of the Earth's crust; the bombing of civilian targets* **6** at a given distance or space of time from: *you can still find wood within a mile of the village; he had been within hours of leaving for Romania* **7** used to specify or give more information about: *the city of Glasgow; a meeting on the subject of regional security* **8** about or concerning: *speaking of boycotts* **9** *US* before the hour of: *about quarter of eight in the evening*
WORD ORIGIN Old English

☰USAGE
☰See at **off**.

Ofcom *n* (in Britain) Office of Communications: a government body regulating the telecommunications industries

off *prep* **1** so as to be no longer in contact with: *take the wok off the heat* **2** so as to be no longer attached to or associated with: *making use of benefit disqualification to terrorize the unemployed off the register* **3** away from: *he was driven off the road* **4** situated near to or leading away from: *they were laying out a bombing range off the coast* **5** no longer having a liking for: *she's gone off you lately* **6** no longer using: *he was off heroin for a year* ▷ *adv* **7** so as to deactivate or disengage: *turn off the gas supply* **8 a** so as to get rid of: *he was flying at midnight so he had to sleep off his hangover* **b** as a reduction in price: *she took 20% off* **9** spent away from work or other duties: *it was the assistant manager's day off* **10** away; at a distance: *the men dashed back to their car and sped off* **11** away in the future: *the date was six weeks off* **12** so as to be no longer taking place: *the investigation was hastily called off* **13** removed from contact with something: *he took the jacket off* **14 off and on** occasionally; not regularly or continuously: *we lived together off and on* ▷ *adj* **15** not on; no longer operating: *her bedroom light was off* **16** cancelled or postponed: *the deal is off and your deposit will be returned in full* **17** in a specified condition, esp. regarding money or provisions: *a married man with four children is better off on the dole; how are you off for money?* **18** not up to the usual standard: *an off year for good wine* **19** no longer on the menu: *haddock is off* **20** (of food or drink) having gone bad or sour: *this milk is off* ▷ *n* **21** *cricket* the side of the field to the right of a right-handed batsman when he is facing the bowler

WORD ORIGIN variant of *of*

USAGE
In standard English, *off* is not followed by *of*: *he stepped off* (not *off of*) *the platform.*

offal *n* the edible internal parts of an animal, such as the heart or liver
WORD ORIGIN *off* + *fall*, referring to parts cut off

offal pit *or* **hole** *n* NZ a place on a farm for the disposal of animal offal

offbeat *adj* unusual, unconventional, or eccentric

off-break *n* cricket a bowled ball that spins from off to leg on pitching

off colour *adj* 1 slightly ill; unwell 2 slightly indecent: *an off-colour joke*

offcut *n* a piece of paper, wood, or fabric remaining after the main pieces have been cut; remnant

offence *or* US **offense** *n* 1 a breaking of a law or rule; crime 2 annoyance or anger 3 a cause of annoyance or anger 4 **give offence** to cause to feel upset or angry 5 **take offence** to feel hurt or offended

offend *vb* 1 to hurt the feelings of (a person); insult 2 to be disagreeable to; disgust: *the lady was offended by what she saw* 3 to commit a crime **offender** *n* **offending** *adj*
WORD ORIGIN Latin *offendere*

offensive *adj* 1 unpleasant or disgusting to the senses: *there was an offensive smell of beer* 2 causing annoyance or anger; insulting 3 for the purpose of attack rather than defence ▷ *n* 4 an attitude or position of aggression: *to go on the offensive* 5 an attack or hostile action: *troops had launched a major offensive against the rebel forces* **offensively** *adv*

offer *vb* 1 to present for acceptance or rejection: *I offered her a lift* 2 to provide: *this department offers a wide range of courses* 3 to present itself: *if an opportunity should offer* 4 to be willing (to do something): *his father offered to pay his tuition* 5 to put forward (a proposal, information, or opinion) for consideration: *may I offer a different view?* 6 to present for sale 7 to propose as payment; bid 8 to present (a prayer or sacrifice) as an act of worship 9 to show readiness for: *to offer resistance* ▷ *n* 10 something that is offered 11 the act of offering
WORD ORIGIN Latin *offerre* to present

offering *n* 1 something that is offered 2 a contribution to the funds of a religious organization 3 a sacrifice to a god

offertory *n, pl* **-tories** Christianity 1 the part of a church service when the bread and wine for communion are offered for consecration 2 the collection of money at this service 3 the prayers said or sung while the worshippers' offerings are being brought to the altar

off-grid *adj* not involving or requiring the use of mainstream sources of energy

offhand *adj also* **offhanded** 1 curt or casual in manner: *I felt calm enough to adopt a casual offhand manner* ▷ *adv* 2 without preparation: *I don't know*

offhand why that should be so **offhandedly** *adv* **offhandedness** *n*

office *n* 1 a room, set of rooms, or building in which business, professional duties, or clerical work are carried out 2 a department of an organization dealing with particular business: *cheque books were sent from the printer to the bank's sorting office* 3 the group of people working in an office: *she assured him that the office was running smoothly* 4 a government department or agency: *Office of Fair Trading* 5 a position of trust or authority, as in a government: *he would not seek a second term of office* 6 a place where tickets, information, or some service can be obtained: *why don't you give the ticket office a ring?* 7 Christianity a religious ceremony or service 8 **good offices** the help given by someone to someone else: *Syria's good offices finally led to the release of two Western hostages* 9 **in** *or* **out of office** (of a government) in *or* out of power
WORD ORIGIN Latin *officium* service, duty

officer *n* 1 a person in the armed services, or on a non-naval ship, who holds a position of authority 2 a policeman or policewoman 3 a person holding a position of authority in a government or organization

official *adj* 1 of an office or position of authority: *I'm not here in any official capacity* 2 approved by or derived from authority: *there has been no official announcement* 3 formal or ceremonial: *he was speaking at an official dinner in Warsaw* ▷ *n* 4 a person holding a position of authority **officially** *adv*

officialdom *n* officials or bureaucrats collectively

officialese *n* language typical of official documents, esp. when wordy or pompous

Official Receiver *n* Brit an officer appointed by the government to deal with the affairs of a bankrupt person or company

officiate *vb* **-ating, -ated** 1 to perform the duties of an office; act in an official capacity: *the referee will officiate at the match* 2 to conduct a religious or other ceremony: *the priest officiated at the wedding* **officiation** *n* **officiator** *n*

officious *adj* offering unwanted advice or services; interfering **officiousness** *n*
WORD ORIGIN Latin *officiosus* kindly

offing *n* 1 the part of the sea that can be seen from the shore 2 **in the offing** Brit, Austral, & NZ not far off; likely to occur soon

off key *adj* music 1 out of tune: *an off-key rendition* ▷ *adv* 2 out of tune: *he sings off key*

off-licence *n* Brit a shop or a counter in a shop where alcoholic drink is sold for drinking elsewhere

off-line *adj* (of computer equipment) not directly connected to or controlled by the central processing unit of a computer

off-load *vb* to get rid of (something unpleasant), usually by giving it to someone else: *you take all the credit and off-load all the blame*

off-peak *adj* (of services) used at times

other than those of greatest demand

off-putting *adj* informal rather unpleasant or disturbing: *it can be very off-putting when you first visit a social security office*

off-road *adj* (of a motor vehicle) designed for use away from public roads

off-roader *n* a motor vehicle designed for use away from public roads

offset *vb* **-setting, -set** 1 to cancel out or compensate for 2 to print (something) using the offset process ▷ *n* 3 a printing method in which the impression is made onto a surface, such as a rubber roller, which transfers it to the paper 4 bot a short runner in certain plants that produces roots and shoots at the tip

offshoot *n* 1 a shoot growing from the main stem of a plant 2 something that has developed from something else

offshore *adj, adv* 1 away from or at some distance from the shore ▷ *adj* 2 sited or conducted at sea: *he reversed his position on offshore drilling*

offside *adj, adv* 1 sport (of a player) in a position illegally ahead of the ball when it is played ▷ *n* 2 chiefly Brit the side of a vehicle nearest the centre of the road

off spin *n* cricket a method of spin bowling delivery in which the ball spins from off to leg after bouncing **off-spinner** *n*

offspring *n* 1 the immediate descendant or descendants of a person or animal 2 a product, outcome, or result: *the women's liberation movement was the offspring of the 1960s*

off-the-peg *adj* (of clothing) ready to wear; not produced especially for the person buying

Ofgem *n* (in Britain) Office of Gas and Electricity Markets: the body which regulates the power supply industries

Oflot *n* (in Britain) Office of the National Lottery: the body which oversees the running of the National Lottery

Ofsted *n* (in Britain) Office for Standards in Education: the body which assesses the educational standards of schools in England and Wales

oft *adv* old-fashioned or poetic short for **often**
WORD ORIGIN Old English

often *adv* 1 frequently; much of the time 2 **as often as not** quite frequently 3 **every so often** occasionally 4 **more often than not** in more than half the instances
WORD ORIGIN Middle English variant of *oft*

Ofwat *n* (in Britain) Office of Water Services: the body which regulates the activities of the water companies in England and Wales

ogee arch (**oh**-jee) *n* a pointed arch made with an S-shaped curve on each side
WORD ORIGIN probably from Old French

ogle *vb* **ogling, ogled** to stare at (someone) lustfully
WORD ORIGIN probably from Low German *oegeln*

Word Histories
part 9

Oboe comes from French *haut bois*, meaning 'high wood', a reference to the instrument's relatively high pitch compared to other instruments of the woodwind family.

Odyssey: 'The Odyssey' is one of the two great poems attributed to the Greek poet Homer. It describes the ten-year homeward journey of the Greek hero Odysseus, king of Ithaca, after the Trojan War.

Ogre: A plausible explanation of 'ogre' is that it derives either from the Ogurs, a Turkic nomad people of the Central Asian Steppe, or the Magyars (On-Ogurs, Hongres, Hungarians), who may have had some links to the Ogurs. The Magyars certainly earned a ferocious reputation with their attacks on Western Europe in the 10th century, but the term does not appear in print until long after they had settled down. Charles Perrault, the French writer of fairy tales, is the first to use it, in 1697, and probably borrowed it from the Italian *orco*, meaning a demon or monster. *Orco* ultimately derives from *Orcus*, a Latin name for the Roman god of the Underworld.

Pandemonium: *Pandemonium* is the capital of Hell in John Milton's poem 'Paradise Lost'. The word 'pandemonium' comes from Greek *pan*, meaning 'all', and *daimon*, meaning 'demon' or 'spirit'.

Paraphernalia: In Latin a married woman's *parapherna* or *paraphernalia* was her personal property, what she herself owned as opposed to her dowry. The words come from Greek *para*, meaning 'beside', and *phernē*, meaning 'dowry'.

Parasite comes from Greek *parasitos*, meaning 'someone who eats at someone else's table'.

While **Pickaxe** seems an entirely self-explanatory word, it is actually a good example of folk etymology. The word entered English as the Old French word *picois*, 'pick' – the 'axe' element represents an attempt to explain the second syllable.

Platonic comes from the name of the Greek philosopher Plato (428–347 BC).

Pommy, the derogatory Australian term for a British person, purportedly derives from the initials emblazoned on the clothes of newly arrived convicts when Australia was still a penal colony: POME Prisoner Of Mother England or, alternatively, POHM Prisoner Of His Majesty. Like most 'backronyms', these are highly suspect; there is no evidence of convicts wearing either set of initials. A more plausible theory is that 'pommy' is a 19th- or early 20th-century contraction of 'pomegranate', either in reference to the sunburned faces of Britons in hot climates such as Australia, or as rough rhyming slang for 'immigrant'. An Afrikaans equivalent to 'pommy', *rooinek*, 'redneck', alludes to the propensity of Britons to turn red in the sun, so it may well be that the origins of 'pommy' lie in an unflattering comparison to the rubicund fruit.

Posh: A persistent explanation for 'posh' is that it is an acronym of Port Out, Starboard Home. This was supposedly printed on the tickets of passengers who had paid for the most expensive cabins on voyages to India, and which were on the shady side of the deck on both the outward and return voyages. Sadly, no-one has been able to produce such a ticket, nor are there any records of tickets being printed thus in the records of the companies that provided sailings to India. Most likely, the word comes from the Romany *posh*, meaning 'half'. This was used in several phrases related to money, eg *posh-kooroona*, 'half-crown'; the association with money seems to have led to the term being used for expensive items and then for the expensively dressed, or dandies, from where the current meaning derives.

Pyjamas comes from Persian *pāy jāma*, meaning 'leg clothing'.

Rhinoceros came into English via Latin from Greek *rhinokerōs*, from *rhino-*, meaning 'of the nose', and *keras*, meaning 'horn'.

O grade *n* **1** (formerly) the basic level of the Scottish Certificate of Education **2** a pass in a particular subject at O grade: *she has eight O grades*

ogre *n* **1** (in folklore) a man-eating giant **2** any monstrous or cruel person **ogreish** *adj* **ogress** *fem n* **WORD ORIGIN** French

oh *interj* an exclamation of surprise, pain, pleasure, fear, or annoyance

OH Ohio

ohm *n* the SI unit of electrical resistance **WORD ORIGIN** after Georg Simon *Ohm*, physicist

OHMS (in Britain and the Commonwealth) On Her (*or* His) Majesty's Service

oil *n* **1** any of a number of viscous liquids with a smooth sticky feel, which are usually flammable, insoluble in water, and are obtained from plants, animals, or mineral deposits by synthesis **2** same as **petroleum 3** a substance derived from petroleum and used for lubrication **4** *Brit* paraffin as a domestic fuel **5** oil colour or paint **6** an oil painting ▷ *vb* **7** to lubricate with oil or apply oil to **8 oil the wheels** to make things run smoothly **WORD ORIGIN** Latin *oleum* (olive) oil

oilcloth *n* a cotton fabric treated with oil or a synthetic resin to make it waterproof, formerly used esp. for tablecloths

oilfield *n* an area containing reserves of oil

oilfired *adj* using oil as fuel

oil paint *n* a thick paint made of pigment ground in linseed oil

oil painting *n* **1** a picture painted with oil paints **2** the art of painting with oil paints

oil rig *n* a structure used as a base when drilling an oil well

oil-seed rape *n* same as **rape²**

oilskin *n* **1** a thick cotton fabric treated with oil to make it waterproof **2** a protective outer garment made of this fabric

oil slick *n* a mass of floating oil covering an area of water

oil well *n* a well bored into the earth or sea bed to a supply of oil

oily *adj* **oilier, oiliest 1** soaked or covered with oil **2** of, containing, or like oil **3** attempting to gain favour by insincere behaviour and flattery **oiliness** *n*

oink *n* the grunt of a pig or an imitation of this

ointment *n* a smooth greasy substance applied to the skin to heal or protect, or as a cosmetic: *home-made creams and ointments* **WORD ORIGIN** Latin *unguentum* unguent

OK Oklahoma

O.K. *informal interj* **1** an expression of approval or agreement ▷ *adj* **2** in good or satisfactory condition ▷ *adv* **3** reasonably well or in a satisfactory manner ▷ *vb* **O.K.ing, O.K.ed 4** to approve or endorse ▷ *n, pl* **O.K.s 5** approval or agreement **WORD ORIGIN** perhaps from *o(ll) k(orrect)*, jocular alteration of *all correct*

okapi (oh-**kah**-pee) *n, pl* **-pis** *or* **-pi** an African mammal related to the giraffe, but with a shorter neck, a reddish coat, and white stripes on the legs **WORD ORIGIN** from a Central African word

okay *interj, adj, adv, vb, n* same as **O.K.**

okra *n* a tall plant with long green pods that are used as food **WORD ORIGIN** West African

old *adj* **1** having lived or existed for a long time: *the old woman; burning witches is one old custom I've no desire to see revived* **2** of or relating to advanced years or a long life: *I twisted my knee as I tried to squat and cursed old age* **3** worn with age or use: *the old bathroom fittings* **4** having lived or existed for a specified period: *he is 60 years old* **5** the earlier or earliest of two or more things with the same name: *the old edition; the Old Testament* **6** designating the form of a language in which the earliest known records are written: *Old English* **7** familiar through long acquaintance or repetition: *an old acquaintance; the legalization argument is an old and familiar one* **8** dear: used as a term of affection or familiarity: *always rely on old Tom to turn out* **9** out of date; unfashionable **10** former or previous: *my old housekeeper lent me some money* **11** of long standing: *he's an old and respected member of staff* **12 good old days** an earlier period of time regarded as better than the present ▷ *n* **13** an earlier or past time: *in days of old* **oldish** *adj* **WORD ORIGIN** Old English *eald*

old age pension *n* a former name for **retirement pension** ▷ **old age pensioner** *n*

Old Bailey *n* the Central Criminal Court of England

old boy *n* **1** a male ex-pupil of a school **2** *informal chiefly Brit* **a** a familiar form of address used to refer to a man **b** an old man

old country *n* the country of origin of an immigrant or an immigrant's ancestors

olde *adj facetious* quaint **WORD ORIGIN** from the former spelling of old

olden *adj archaic or poetic* old: *in the olden days the girls were married young*

Old English *n* the English language of the Anglo-Saxons, spoken from the fifth century AD to about 1100. Also called: **Anglo-Saxon**

Old English sheepdog *n* a large sheepdog with thick shaggy hair

old-fashioned *adj* **1** in the style of a previous period; outdated: *she wore her hair in a strangely old-fashioned tight hairdo* **2** favouring or denoting the styles or ideas of a former time: *old-fashioned values*

old flame *n informal, old-fashioned* a person with whom one once had a romantic relationship

Old French *n* the French language in its earliest forms, from about the 9th century up to about 1400

old girl *n* **1** a female ex-pupil of a school **2** *informal chiefly Brit* **a** a familiar form of address used to refer to a woman **b** an old woman

old guard *n* a group of people in an organization who have traditional values: *the company's old guard is making way for a new, more youthful team* **WORD ORIGIN** after Napoleon's imperial guard

old hand *n* a skilled or experienced person

old hat *adj* old-fashioned or dull

Old High German *n* a group of West Germanic dialects that developed into modern German; High German up to about 1200

old identity *n* NZ a well-known local person who has lived in an area for a long time

oldie *n informal* an old song, film, or person

old lady *n informal* one's mother or wife

old maid *n* **1** a woman regarded as unlikely ever to marry; spinster **2** *informal* a prim, fussy, or excessively cautious person

old man *n* **1** *informal* one's father **2** one's husband **3** an affectionate form of address used to a man

old master *n* **1** one of the great European painters of the period 1500 to 1800 **2** a painting by one of these

old moon *n* a phase of the moon between last quarter and new moon, when it appears as a waning crescent

Old Nick *n informal* Satan

old school *n* a group of people favouring traditional or conservative ideas or practices

old school tie *n* the system of mutual help supposed to operate among the former pupils of independent schools

Old Style *n* the former method of reckoning dates using the Julian calendar

Old Testament *n* the first part of the Christian Bible, containing the sacred Scriptures of the Hebrews

old-time *adj* of or relating to a former time; old-fashioned: *an old-time waltz*

old wives' tale *n* a belief, usually superstitious or foolish, passed on by word of mouth as a piece of traditional wisdom

old woman *n* **1** *informal* one's mother or wife **2** a timid, fussy, or cautious person **old-womanish** *adj*

Old World *n* that part of the world that was known to Europeans before the discovery of the Americas; the eastern hemisphere

old-world *adj* of or characteristic of former times; quaint or traditional

oleaginous (oh-lee-**aj**-in-uss) *adj* like or producing oil; oily **WORD ORIGIN** Latin *oleaginus*

oleander (oh-lee-**ann**-der) *n* an evergreen Mediterranean shrub with fragrant white, pink, or purple flowers **WORD ORIGIN** Medieval Latin

O level *n* **1** (formerly, in Britain) the basic level of the General Certificate of Education **2** a pass in a particular subject at O level: *a very intelligent young woman with ten O levels*

olfactory *adj* of the sense of smell **WORD ORIGIN** Latin *olere* to smell + *facere* to make

oligarchy (ol-lee-gark-ee) *n, pl* **-chies 1** government by a small group of people **2** a state governed this way **3** a small group of people governing such a state **oligarchic** *or* **oligarchical** *adj*
WORD ORIGIN Greek *oligos* few + *arkhein* to rule

Oligocene (ol-lig-go-seen) *adj geol* of the epoch of geological time about 35 million years ago
WORD ORIGIN Greek *oligos* little + *kainos* new

oligopoly *n, pl* **-lies** *econ* a market situation in which control over the supply of a commodity is held by a small number of producers
WORD ORIGIN Greek *oligos* few + *pōlein* to sell

olive *n* **1** an evergreen Mediterranean tree **2** the small green or black fruit of this tree ▷ *adj* **3** short for **olive-green**
WORD ORIGIN Latin *oliva*

olive branch *n* a peace offering: *I should offer some kind of olive branch and get in touch with them*

olive-green *adj* deep yellowish-green

olive oil *n* a yellowish-green oil pressed from ripe olives and used in cooking and medicines

oloroso (ol-ler-**roh**-so) *n* a golden-coloured sweet sherry
WORD ORIGIN Spanish: fragrant

Olympiad *n* **1** a staging of the modern Olympic Games **2** an international contest in chess or other games

Olympian *adj* **1** of Mount Olympus or the classical Greek gods **2** majestic or godlike ▷ *n* **3** a competitor in the Olympic Games **4** a god of Mount Olympus

Olympic *adj* of the Olympic Games

Olympic Games *n* **1** an ancient Greek festival, held every fourth year in honour of Zeus, consisting of games and festivities **2** Also called: **the Olympics** the modern revival of these games, consisting of international athletic and sporting contests held every four years in a selected country

OM Order of Merit (a Brit. title)

ombudsman *n, pl* **-men** an official who investigates citizens' complaints against the government or its servants
WORD ORIGIN Swedish: commissioner

omega *n* **1** the 24th and last letter of the Greek alphabet (Ω, ω) **2** the ending or last of a series

omega-3 *n* an unsaturated fatty acid that occurs naturally in fish oil, valuable in reducing blood cholesterol

omelette *or esp. US* **omelet** *n* a dish of beaten eggs cooked in a flat pan and often folded round a savoury filling
WORD ORIGIN French

omen *n* **1** a thing or occurrence regarded as a sign of future happiness or disaster **2** prophetic significance: *birds of ill omen*
WORD ORIGIN Latin

OMG Oh my God!: used esp. in emails, text messages, etc.

ominous *adj* warning of evil
ominously *adv*
WORD ORIGIN Latin *ominosus*

omission *n* **1** something that has been left out or passed over **2** an act of missing out or failing to do something: *we regret the omission of these and the names of the other fine artists*

omit *vb* **omitting, omitted 1** to fail to include; leave out **2** to fail (to do something)
WORD ORIGIN Latin *omittere*

omnibus *n, pl* **-buses 1** a collection of works by one author or several works on a similar topic, reprinted in one volume **2** Also called: **omnibus edition** a television or radio programme consisting of two or more episodes of a serial broadcast earlier in the week **3** *old-fashioned* a bus ▷ *adj* **4** consisting of or dealing with several different things at once: *this year's version of an omnibus crime bill*
WORD ORIGIN Latin, literally: for all

omnipotent (om-**nip**-a-tent) *adj* having very great or unlimited power
omnipotence *n*
WORD ORIGIN Latin *omnipotens* all-powerful

omnipresent *adj* (esp. of a god) present in all places at the same time
omnipresence *n*
WORD ORIGIN Latin *omnis* all + *praesens* present

omniscient (om-**niss**-ee-ent) *adj formal* knowing or seeming to know everything **omniscience** *n*
WORD ORIGIN Latin *omnis* all + *scire* to know

omnivore (**om**-niv-vore) *n* an animal that eats any type of food

omnivorous (om-**niv**-or-uss) *adj*
1 eating any type of food **2** taking in everything indiscriminately: *his omnivorous sociability has meant constant hard work for his wife*
WORD ORIGIN Latin *omnivorus* all-devouring

on *prep* **1** in contact with or at the surface of: *let the cakes stand in the tins on a wire rack; she had dirt on her dress* **2** attached to: *a piece of paper on a clipboard* **3** carried with: *the message found on her* **4** near to or along the side of: *the hotel is on the coast* **5** within the time limits of (a day or date): *they returned to Moscow on 22nd September* **6** being performed upon or relayed through the medium of: *a construction of refined sounds played on special musical instruments; what's on television?* **7** at the occasion of: *she had received numerous letters congratulating her on her election* **8** immediately after or at the same time as: *check with the tourist office on arrival* **9** through the use of: *an extraordinarily vigorous man who thrives on physical activity; the program runs on the Unix operating system* **10** regularly taking (a drug): *she's on the pill* **11** by means of (a mode of transport): *his only way up the hill had to be on foot; they get around on bicycles* **12** in the process or course of: *he is away on a climbing expedition; coal miners have been on strike for six weeks* **13** concerned with or relating to: *ten million viewers watched the recent series on homelessness* **14** (of a statement or action) having as basis or grounds: *I have it on good authority* **15** charged to: *all drinks are on the house for the rest of the evening* **16** staked as a bet: *I'll have a bet on the favourite* ▷ *adv* **17** in operation; functioning: *the lights had been left on all night* **18** attached to, surrounding, or placed in contact with something: *they escaped with nothing on except sleeveless shirts and shorts* **19** taking place: *what do you have on tonight?* **20** continuously or persistently: *the crisis must not be allowed to drag on indefinitely* **21** forwards or further: *they trudged on* **22** **on and off** occasionally; not regularly or continuously **23** **on and on** without ceasing; continually ▷ *adj* **24** *informal* performing: *who's on next?* **25** *informal* definitely taking place: *is the party still on?* **26** *informal* tolerable, practicable, or acceptable: *that's just not on* **27** **on at** *informal* nagging: *he was always on at her to stop smoking* ▷ *n* **28** *cricket* the side of the field to the left of a right-handed batsman when he is facing the bowler
WORD ORIGIN Old English *an, on*

ON Ontario

onager *n, pl* **-gri** *or* **-gers** a wild ass of Persia
WORD ORIGIN Greek *onagros*

onanism *n* **1** withdrawal in sexual intercourse before ejaculation **2** masturbation
WORD ORIGIN after *Onan*: see Genesis 38:9

ONC (in Britain) Ordinary National Certificate

once *adv* **1** one time; on one occasion only **2** at some past time, but no longer: *I was in love once* **3** by one degree (of relationship): *he was Deirdre's cousin once removed* **4** **once and for all** conclusively; for the last time **5** **once in a while** occasionally; now and then **6** **once or twice** a few times **7** **once upon a time** used to begin fairy tales and children's stories ▷ *conj* **8** as soon as: *once you have learned good grammar you can leave it to nature and forget it* ▷ *n* **9** one occasion or case: *once is enough* **10** **all at once a** suddenly **b** simultaneously **11** **at once a** immediately **b** simultaneously **12** **for once** this time, even if at no other time
WORD ORIGIN Middle English *ones, anes*

once-over *n informal* a quick examination or appraisal

oncogene (**ong**-koh-jean) *n* a gene present in all cells, that when abnormally activated can cause cancer
WORD ORIGIN Greek *onkos* tumour + *-gen* (suffix) producing

oncoming *adj* coming nearer in space or time; approaching: *oncoming traffic*

OND (in Britain) Ordinary National Diploma

one *adj, n* **1** single or lone (person or thing); not two or more: *one civilian has died and thirty-three have been injured* **2** only or unique (person or thing): *he is the one to make correct judgments and influence the public; she was unique, inimitable, one of a kind* **3** a specified (person or thing) as distinct from another or others of its kind: *place one hand under the knee and the other under the ankle; which one is correct?* **4** **one or two** a few ▷ *adj* **5** a certain, indefinite, or unspecified (time): *one day he would learn the truth about her* **6** *informal*, emphatic **a**: *we're on to one hell of a story* ▷ *pron* **7** an indefinite person regarded as typical of every person: *one can always hope that there won't be an accident* **8** any indefinite person: *one can catch fine trout in this stream* **9** I or me: *one only wonders what he has against the dogs* ▷ *n* **10** the smallest natural number and first cardinal number **11** a numeral, 1 or I, representing this number **12** something representing or consisting of one unit **13** *informal* a joke or story: *have you heard the one about the actress and the bishop?* **14 (all) in one** combined or united **15 all one** of no consequence: *leave if you want to, it's all one to me* **16 at one with** in agreement or harmony with **17 one and all** everyone, without exception **18 one by one** one at a time; individually

WORD ORIGIN Old English *ān*

one another *pron* each other: *they seem to genuinely care for one another*

one-armed bandit *n informal* a fruit machine operated by pulling down a lever at one side

one-dimensional *adj* **1** having one dimension **2** completely lacking in depth or complexity: *the production staging is one-dimensional and the direction rigid*

one-horse *adj informal* small or insignificant: *a dusty one-horse town in the foothills of the Karakoram mountain range*

one-liner *n informal* a short joke or witty remark

oneness *n* **1** agreement **2** uniqueness **3** sameness

one-night stand *n* **1** *informal* a sexual encounter lasting only one evening or night **2** a performance given only once at any one place

one-off *n* something that happens or is made only once

onerous (**own**-er-uss) *adj* (of a task) difficult to carry out **onerousness** *n*

WORD ORIGIN Latin *onus* load

oneself *pron* **1** the reflexive form of *one* **2** one's normal or usual self: *one doesn't feel oneself after such an experience*

one-sided *adj* **1** considering or favouring only one side of a matter: *a one-sided version of events* **2** having all the advantage on one side: *it was a one-sided match with Brazil missing a succession of chances*

one-stop *adj* having or providing a range of services or goods in one place: *one-stop shopping*

One Thousand Guineas *n* **the One Thousand Guineas** an annual horse race for three-year-old fillies, run at Newmarket

one-time *adj* at some time in the past; former

one-to-one *adj* **1** (of two or more things) corresponding exactly **2** denoting a relationship or encounter in which someone is involved with only one other person: *one-to-one meetings* **3** *maths* involving the pairing of each member of one set with only one member of another set, without remainder

one-track *adj informal* obsessed with one idea or subject: *she's got a one-track mind*

one-up *adj informal* having an advantage or lead over someone else **one-upmanship** *n*

one-way *adj* **1** moving or allowing travel in one direction only: *the town centre has a baffling one-way system* **2** involving no reciprocal obligation or action: *he does not get anything back out of the one-way relationship*

ongoing *adj* in progress; continuing: *there are still ongoing discussions about the future role of NATO*

onion *n* **1** a vegetable with an edible bulb with a strong smell and taste **2 know one's onions** *Brit & NZ slang* to be fully acquainted with a subject **oniony** *adj*

WORD ORIGIN Latin *unio*

on-line *or* **online** *adj* **1** (of computer equipment) directly connected to and controlled by the central processing unit of a computer **2** of or relating to the internet: *online shopping*

onlooker *n* a person who observes without taking part **onlooking** *adj*

only *adj* **1** alone of its or their kind: *I will be talking to the only journalist to have been inside the prison* **2** (of a child) having no brothers or sisters **3** unique by virtue of superiority; best: *first class is the only way to travel* **4 one and only** incomparable: *the one and only Diana Ross* ▷ *adv* **5** without anyone or anything else being included; alone: *only you can decide if you can abide by this compromise* **6** merely or just: *it's only Henry* **7** no more or no greater than: *I was talking to a priest only a minute ago* **8** merely: *they had only to turn up to win the competition* **9** not earlier than; not until: *I've only found out today why you wouldn't come* **10 if only** *or* **if ... only** used to introduce a wish or hope **11 only too** extremely: *they were only too willing to do anything to help* ▷ *conj* **12** but or however: *those countries are going through the same cycle, only a little later than us*

WORD ORIGIN Old English *ānlīc*

▤ **USAGE**
▤ In informal English, *only* is often used
▤ as a sentence connector: *I would have
▤ phoned you, only I didn't know your number.*
▤ This should be avoided in formal
▤ writing: *I would have phoned you if I'd known
▤ your number.* In formal speech and
▤ writing, *only* is placed directly before
▤ the word or words that it modifies: *she
▤ could interview only three applicants in the
▤ morning.* In all but the most formal
▤ contexts, however, it is generally
▤ regarded as acceptable to put *only*
▤ before the verb: *she could only interview
▤ three applicants in the morning.* Care must
▤ be taken not to create ambiguity, esp.
▤ in written English, in which
▤ intonation will not, as it does in
▤ speech, help to show to which item in
▤ the sentence *only* applies. A sentence
▤ such as *she only drinks tea in the afternoon*
▤ is capable of two interpretations and
▤ is therefore better rephrased either as
▤ *she drinks only tea in the afternoon* (i.e. no
▤ other drink) or *she drinks tea only in the
▤ afternoon* (i.e. at no other time).

o.n.o. *or* near(est) offer

onomatopoeia (on-a-mat-a-**pee**-a) *n* use of a word which imitates the sound it represents, such as *hiss* **onomatopoeic** *or* **onomatopoetic** *adj*

WORD ORIGIN Greek *onoma* name + *poiein* to make

onrush *n* a forceful forward rush or flow; surge

onset *n* a start; beginning

onshore *adj, adv* **1** towards the land: *a stiff onshore wind* **2** on land; not at sea

onside *adj, adv sport* (of a player) in a legal position, for example, behind the ball or with a required number of opponents between oneself and the opposing team's goal line

onslaught *n* a violent attack

WORD ORIGIN Middle Dutch *aenslag*

Ont. Ontario

onto *or* **on to** *prep* **1** to a position that is on: *step onto the train* **2** having discovered or become aware of: *the police are onto us* **3** into contact with: *get onto the factory*

▤ **USAGE**
▤ *Onto* is now generally accepted as a
▤ word in its own right. *On to* is still
▤ used, however, where *on* is considered
▤ to be part of the verb: *he moved on to a
▤ different town* as contrasted with *he
▤ jumped onto the stage.*

ontology *n philosophy* the study of the nature of being **ontological** *adj*

WORD ORIGIN Greek *ōn* being + -LOGY

onus (**own**-uss) *n, pl* **onuses** a responsibility, task, or burden: *the courts put the onus on parents*

WORD ORIGIN Latin: burden

onward *adj* **1** directed or moving forward ▷ *adv also* **onwards** **2** continuing; progressing

onyx *n* a kind of quartz with alternating coloured layers, used as a gemstone

WORD ORIGIN Greek: fingernail (so called from its veined appearance)

oodles *pl n informal* great quantities: *he has shown he can raise oodles of cash*

WORD ORIGIN origin unknown

oolite (**oh**-a-lite) *n* a limestone made up of tiny grains of calcium carbonate **oolitic** *adj*

WORD ORIGIN New Latin *oolites*, literally: egg stone

oom *n S African* a title of respect used to refer to an elderly man

WORD ORIGIN Afrikaans, literally: uncle

oomiak *or* **oomiac** *n* same as **umiak**

oompah *n* a representation of the sound made by a deep brass instrument, esp. in brass band music

oomph *n informal* enthusiasm, vigour, or energy

WORD ORIGIN origin unknown

oops *interj* an exclamation of surprise or of apology when someone has a slight accident or makes a mistake

OOS occupational overuse syndrome: pain caused by repeated awkward movements while at work

ooze[1] *vb* **oozing, oozed** **1** to flow or leak out slowly; seep **2** (of a substance) to discharge moisture **3** to overflow with (a feeling or quality): *he oozes confidence* ▷ *n* **4** a slow flowing or leaking **oozy** *adj*

WORD ORIGIN Old English *wōs* juice

ooze[2] *n* a soft thin mud, such as that found at the bottom of a lake, river, or sea

WORD ORIGIN Old English *wāse* mud

op. opus

William S Burroughs

William Seward Burroughs II was born in 1914 in St Louis, Missouri. He began writing in the 1930s, but did not achieve notoriety until the publication of his most famous novel *Naked Lunch*. Originally published in France in 1959 as **The** *Naked Lunch* (it eventually lost its definite article), the book exists as a series of cut-together vignettes and takes place for the most part in the fictional Interzone (based on Tangier in the 1950s). The dominant themes are addiction and homosexuality, with addiction laid out as an extension of humanity's basic urges (or 'insect need'). This depiction of what he called 'the algebra of need' was a constant strand throughout Burroughs's work.

The book was written in a revolutionary non-linear 'cut-up' style and was assembled with the aid of totemic Beat figures Allen Ginsberg and Jack Kerouac. Burroughs credited Kerouac with the title, which he explained thus: 'The title means exactly what the words say: NAKED Lunch – a frozen moment when everyone sees what is on the end of every fork'. This unflinching perspective is shared with J G Ballard, who described Burroughs's approach to language: 'He was always trying to go through the screen of language to find some sort of truth that lay on the other side. I think his whole cut-up approach was an attempt to cut through the apparent manifest content of language to what he hoped might be some sort of more truthful world'.

Ballard adopted the cut-up style for his novel *Atrocity Exhibition*, and there is a clear link from Burroughs to contemporary authors such as Will Self and Irvine Welsh in terms of style, theme, and subject matter. Norman Mailer famously described Burroughs as 'The only American novelist ... who may conceivably be possessed by genius'. Burroughs's influence on culture outside the literary world has been equally huge. He is credited with coining the term *heavy metal* in his novel *The Soft Machine*, and with popularizing drug-use shibboleths such as 'waiting for the man' and 'The Fear' (drug-induced paranoia).

Burroughs's work features its own rich vocabulary. He is particularly associated with the words *junky* and *queer* (the titles of two of his books), but other examples are from now anachronistic 'jive-talk', such as *croaker* (a doctor, especially one willing to supply drugs), *lush-worker* (a robber of subway drunks), and *sawski* (a $10 bill). Another word he used frequently is *mugwump*. This was originally a US term for a neutral or independent person, especially in politics. It stems from the Algonquian word for 'chief', and was popularized in 19th century US English as a sarcastic reference to someone in power, changing its use in the 1884 Presidential election to mean 'dissident' or 'political independent'. In Burroughs's Interzone, however, *mugwumps* are tall, gaunt, semi-reptilian, sexually predacious creatures. Words linked to sexuality and sickness are also a recurring feature, including *orgone* (a hypothetical form of energy that is a manifestation of the human libido), *latah* (a psychological condition observed particularly in Malaysia in which an individual may become suggestible following a shock), and *bang-utot*, an invented condition, but one which is a portmanteau word combining *bangungot* (a Filipino word for Sudden Infant Death Syndrome), and *koro* (the irrational fear that one's sexual organs are retracting into one's body and disappearing).

Burroughs's writings were ferociously critical of any system of control, whether the media ('Let them see what is on the long end of that newspaper spoon'), the state (Burroughs claimed certain scenes in *Naked Lunch* were a protest against capital punishment in the same satirical tradition as Jonathan Swift's 18th Century *A Modest Proposal*), or indeed any institution or organization. Drugs were a form of control ('Junk is the ideal product...the ultimate merchandise') and so was language, which Burroughs described as 'a virus from outer space'. His theory of communication was that 'The written word was actually a virus ... that made the spoken word possible. The word has not been recognized as a virus because it has achieved a state of stable symbiosis with the host...' (from *The Job*, 1974, a collection of interviews).

He notes when describing *Naked Lunch*: 'Because there are many forms of addiction I think that they all obey basic laws. In the words of Heisenberg: "This may not be the best of all possible universes but it may well prove to be one of the simplest." If man can *see*.'

opacity (ohp-**ass**-it-tee) *n, pl* **-ties 1** the state or quality of being opaque **2** the quality of being difficult to understand; unintelligibility

opal *n* a precious stone, usually milky or bluish in colour, with shimmering changing reflections
WORD ORIGIN Greek *opallios*

opalescent *adj* having shimmering changing reflections, like opal **opalescence** *n*

opaque *adj* **1** not able to be seen through; not transparent or translucent **2** hard to understand; unintelligible
WORD ORIGIN Latin *opacus* shady

op. cit. (op sit) (in textual annotations) in the work cited
WORD ORIGIN Latin *opere citato*

OPEC Organization of Petroleum-Exporting Countries

open *adj* **1** not closed, fastened, or blocked up: *the doctor's office was open* **2** not enclosed, covered, or wrapped: *the parcel was open* **3** extended, expanded, or unfolded: *an open flower* **4** ready for business: *some of the crafts rooms and photography shops are open all night* **5** (of a job) available: *all the positions on the council should be open to females* **6** unobstructed by buildings or trees: *we lived in a small market town surrounded by open countryside* **7** free to all to join in, enter, or use: *there was an open competition and I was appointed* **8** (of a season or period) not restricted for purposes of hunting game of various kinds **9** not decided or finalized: *the legality of these sales is still an open question* **10** ready to consider new ideas: *I was able to approach their problem with an open mind* **11** honest and frank **12** generous: *she has given me love and the open hand* **13** exposed to view; blatant: *there has never been such sustained and open criticism of the President* **14** unprotected; susceptible: *a change of policy which would leave vulnerable youths open to exploitation* **15** having spaces or gaps: *open ranks; an open texture* **16** *computers* designed to an internationally agreed standard to allow communication between computers irrespective of size or manufacturer **17** *music* **a** (of a string) not stopped with the finger **b** (of a note) played on such a string **18** *sport* (of a goal or court) unguarded or relatively unprotected **19** (of a wound) exposed to the air ▷ *vb* **20** to make or become open: *it was easy to open the back door and to slip noiselessly outside; she knelt and tried to open the drawer* **21** to set or be set in action; start: *the US will have to open talks on Palestinian rights; I want to open a dress shop* **22** to arrange for (a bank account), usually by making an initial deposit **23** to declare open ceremonially or officially ▷ *n* **24** *sport* a competition which anyone may enter **25 the open** any wide or unobstructed area **opener** *n* **openly** *adv* **openness** *n*
WORD ORIGIN Old English

open air *n* the place or space where the air is unenclosed; outdoors

open-and-shut *adj* easily decided or solved; obvious: *an open-and-shut case*

opencast mining *n* mining by excavating from the surface
WORD ORIGIN *open* + archaic *cast* ditch, cutting

open day *n* a special occasion on which a school, university, or other institution is open for the public to visit

open-ended *adj* **1** without definite limits; unrestricted: *the schedule is open-ended* **2** (of an activity) done without the aim of attaining a particular result or decision: *the dangers of open-ended military involvement*

open-eyed *adj* **1** with the eyes wide open, as in amazement **2** watchful; alert

open-handed *adj* generous

open-hearted *adj* **1** kind or generous **2** willing to speak one's mind; candid

open-heart surgery *n* surgical repair of the heart during which the heart is exposed and the blood circulation is maintained mechanically

open house *n* a situation in which people allow friends or visitors to come to their house whenever they want to

opening *n* **1** the beginning or first part of something **2** the first performance of a theatrical production **3** a chance or opportunity: *an opening into show business* **4** a hole or gap

opening time *n* *Austral & Brit* the time at which public houses can legally open for business

open letter *n* a letter, esp. one of protest, addressed to an individual but published in a newspaper or magazine for all to read

open market *n* a process by which prices are decided by supply and demand and goods are sold anywhere

open-minded *adj* willing to consider new ideas; unprejudiced

open-mouthed *adj* gaping in surprise

open-plan *adj* having no or few dividing walls between areas: *the house includes an open-plan living room and dining area*

open prison *n* a prison in which the prisoners are not locked up, thus extending the range of work they can do

open secret *n* something that is supposed to be secret but is widely known

open source *n* **1** intellectual property, esp. computer source code, made freely available to the public by its creators ▷ *adj* **2** relating to this code: *open-source software*

open-standard *adj* (of computer programs, codes, etc.) freely available to all users

Open University *n* (in Britain) a university teaching by means of television and radio lectures, correspondence courses, and summer schools

open up *vb* **1** to make or become accessible: *the Berlin Wall came down and opened up new territory for dramatists* **2** to speak freely or without self-restraint **3** to start firing a gun or guns **4** *informal* to increase the speed of (a vehicle)

open verdict *n* a finding by a coroner's jury of death, without stating the cause

opera¹ *n* a dramatic work in which most or all of the text is sung to orchestral accompaniment **2** the branch of music or drama relating to operas **3** a group that produces or performs operas **4** a theatre where opera is performed
WORD ORIGIN Latin: work

opera² *n* a plural of **opus**

operable *adj* **1** capable of being treated by a surgical operation **2** capable of being operated or put into practice **operability** *n*

opera glasses *pl n* small low-powered binoculars used by audiences in theatres

opera house *n* a theatre specially designed for the performance of operas

operand *n* *maths* a quantity, variable, or function upon which an operation is performed

operate *vb* **-ating, -ated 1** to work **2** to control the working of (a machine) **3** to manage, direct, or run (a business or system) **4** to perform a surgical operation (upon a person or animal) **5** to conduct military or naval operations
WORD ORIGIN Latin *operari* to work

operatic *adj* **1** of or relating to opera **2** overdramatic or exaggerated: *he was about to go out with his operatic strut*

operating system *n* the software controlling a computer

operating theatre *or US* **room** *n* a room in which surgical operations are performed

operation *n* **1** the act or method of operating **2** the condition of being in action: *there are 20 teleworking centres in operation around the country* **3** an action or series of actions done to produce a particular result: *a large-scale police operation has been in place to manage the heavy traffic* **4** *surgery* a surgical procedure carried out to remove, replace, or repair a diseased or damaged part of the body **5** a military or naval manoeuvre **6** *maths* any procedure, such as addition, in which a number is derived from another number or numbers by applying specific rules

operational *adj* **1** in working order and ready for use **2** of or relating to an action done to produce a particular result

operations research *n* the analysis of problems in business and industry. Also called: **operational research**

operative (**op**-rat-tiv) *adj* **1** in force, effect, or operation: *these pension provisions became operative from 1978* **2** (of a word) particularly relevant or significant: *'if' is the operative word* **3** of or relating to a surgical operation ▷ *n* **4** a worker with a special skill

operator *n* **1** a person who operates a machine or instrument, esp. a telephone switchboard **2** a person who runs a business: *your tour operator will arrange a visa for you* **3** *informal* a person who manipulates affairs and other people: *she considered him a shrewd operator who only liked to appear to be simple* **4** *maths* any symbol, term, or letter used to indicate or express a specific operation or process

operculum (oh-**perk**-yew-lum) *n, pl* **-la** (-la) *or* **-lums** a covering flap or lidlike structure in animals or plants **WORD ORIGIN** Latin: lid

operetta *n* a type of comic or light-hearted opera

ophthalmia *n* inflammation of the eyeball or conjunctiva **WORD ORIGIN** Greek *ophthalmos* eye

ophthalmic *adj* of or relating to the eye

ophthalmic optician *n* see **optician** (sense 1)

ophthalmology *n* the branch of medicine concerned with the eye and its diseases **ophthalmologist** *n*

ophthalmoscope *n* an instrument for examining the interior of the eye

opiate (oh-pee-ate) *n* 1 a narcotic or sedative drug containing opium 2 something that causes mental dullness or inactivity

opine *vb* **opining, opined** *formal* to hold or express an opinion: *he opined that the navy would have to start again from the beginning* **WORD ORIGIN** Latin *opinari*

opinion *n* 1 belief not founded on certainty or proof but on what seems probable 2 evaluation or estimation of a person or thing: *they seemed to share my high opinion of her* 3 a judgment given by an expert: *medical opinion* 4 **a matter of opinion** a point open to question **WORD ORIGIN** Latin *opinio* belief

opinionated *adj* holding very strong opinions which one is convinced are right

opinion poll *n* same as **poll** (sense 1)

opium (oh-pee-um) *n* an addictive narcotic drug made from the seed capsules of the opium poppy and used in medicine as a painkiller and sedative **WORD ORIGIN** Latin: poppy juice

opossum *n, pl* **-sums** *or* **-sum** 1 a thick-furred American marsupial, with a long snout and a hairless prehensile tail 2 *Austral & NZ* a similar Australian animal, such as a phalanger **WORD ORIGIN** Native American *aposoum*

opponent *n* a person who opposes another in a contest, battle, or argument **WORD ORIGIN** Latin *opponere* to oppose

opportune *adj formal* 1 happening at a time that is suitable or advantageous: *there was an opportune knock at the door* 2 (of time) suitable for a particular purpose: *I have arrived at a very opportune moment* **WORD ORIGIN** Latin *opportunus*, from *ob-* to + *portus* harbour (originally: coming to the harbour, obtaining timely protection)

opportunist *n* 1 a person who adapts his or her actions to take advantage of opportunities and circumstances without regard for principles ▷ *adj* 2 taking advantage of opportunities and circumstances in this way **opportunism** *n* **opportunistic** *adj*

opportunity *n, pl* **-ties** 1 a favourable combination of circumstances or a good chance or prospect

opportunity shop *n* *Austral & NZ* a shop selling second-hand clothes, sometimes for charity. Sometimes shortened to: **op-shop**

opposable *adj zool* (of the thumb) capable of touching the tip of all the other fingers

oppose *vb* **-posing, -posed** 1 Also: **be opposed to** to be against (something or someone) in speech or action 2 **as opposed to** in strong contrast with: *I'm a realist as opposed to a theorist* **opposing** *adj* **WORD ORIGIN** Latin *opponere*

opposite *adj* 1 situated on the other or further side 2 facing or going in contrary directions: *he saw another small craft heading the opposite way* 3 completely different: *I have a different, in fact, opposite view on this subject* 4 *maths* (of a side in a triangle) facing a specified angle ▷ *n* 5 a person or thing that is opposite; antithesis ▷ *prep* 6 facing; across from ▷ *adv* 7 in an opposite position: *fragments smashed through the windows of the house opposite*

opposite number *n* a person holding an equivalent position in another group or organization: *a ritual exchange of insults with an opposite number*

opposition *n* 1 the act of opposing or being opposed 2 hostility, resistance, or disagreement 3 a person or group antagonistic or opposed to another 4 a political party or group opposed to the ruling party or government 5 *astrol* a diametrically opposite position of two heavenly bodies

oppress *vb* 1 to put down or control by cruelty or force 2 to make anxious or uncomfortable **oppression** *n* **oppressor** *n* **WORD ORIGIN** Latin *ob-* against + *premere* to press

oppressive *adj* 1 cruel, harsh, or tyrannical 2 uncomfortable or depressing: *a small flat can become rather oppressive* 3 (of weather) hot and humid **oppressiveness** *n*

opprobrium (op-**probe**-ree-um) *n formal* 1 the state of being abused or scornfully criticized 2 a cause of disgrace or shame **opprobrious** *adj* **WORD ORIGIN** Latin *ob-* against + *probrum* a shameful act

oppugn (op-**pewn**) *vb formal* to call into question; dispute **WORD ORIGIN** Latin *ob-* against + *pugnare* to fight

op-shop *n* *Austral & NZ* short for **opportunity shop**

opt *vb* to show preference (for) or choose (to do something) **WORD ORIGIN** Latin *optare* to choose

optic *adj* of the eye or vision **WORD ORIGIN** Greek *optos* visible

optical *adj* 1 of or involving light or optics 2 of the eye or the sense of sight; optic 3 (of a lens) helping vision

optical fibre *n* a thin flexible glass fibre used in fibre optics to transmit information

optician *n* 1 Also called: **ophthalmic optician** a person who is qualified to examine the eyes and prescribe and supply spectacles and contact lenses 2 Also called: **dispensing optician** a person who supplies and fits spectacle frames and lenses, but is not qualified to prescribe lenses

optic nerve *n* a cranial nerve of vertebrates that conducts nerve impulses from the retina of the eye to the brain

optics *n* the science dealing with light and vision

optimal *adj* best or most favourable

optimism *n* 1 the tendency to take the most hopeful view in all matters 2 *philosophy* the doctrine of the ultimate triumph of good over evil **optimist** *n* **optimistic** *adj* **optimistically** *adv* **WORD ORIGIN** Latin *optimus* best

optimize *or* **-mise** *vb* **-mizing, -mized** *or* **-mising, -mised** to make the most of

optimum *n, pl* **-ma** *or* **-mums** 1 the most favourable conditions or best compromise possible ▷ *adj* 2 most favourable or advantageous; best: *balance is a critical part of an optimum diet* **WORD ORIGIN** Latin: the best (thing)

option *n* 1 the power or liberty to choose: *we have no option other than to fully comply* 2 something that is or may be chosen: *the menu includes a vegetarian option* 3 an exclusive right, usually for a limited period, to buy or sell something at a future date: *a producer could extend his option on the material for another six months* 4 **keep** *or* **leave one's options open** not to commit oneself 5 **soft option** an easy alternative ▷ *vb* 6 to obtain or grant an option on: *the film rights are optioned by an international film director* **WORD ORIGIN** Latin *optare* to choose

optional *adj* possible but not compulsory; open to choice

optometrist (op-**tom**-met-trist) *n* a person qualified to examine the eyes and prescribe and supply spectacles and contact lenses **optometry** *n*

opt out *vb* 1 (often foll. by *of*) to choose not to be involved (in) or part (of), used esp. of schools and hospitals that leave the public sector ▷ *n* **opt-out** 2 the act of opting out, esp. of a local authority administration

opulent (op-pew-lent) *adj* 1 having or indicating wealth 2 abundant or plentiful **opulence** *n* **WORD ORIGIN** Latin *opulens*

opus (oh-puss) *n, pl* **opuses** *or* **opera** an artistic creation, esp. a musical work by a particular composer, numbered in order of publication: *Beethoven's opus 61* **WORD ORIGIN** Latin: a work

or *conj* 1 used to join alternatives: *do you want to go out or stay at home?* 2 used to join rephrasings of the same thing: *twelve, or a dozen* **WORD ORIGIN** Middle English contraction of *other*

OR Oregon

oracle *n* 1 a shrine in ancient Greece or Rome at which gods were consulted through the medium of a priest or priestess for advice or prophecy 2 a prophecy or statement made by an oracle 3 any person believed to indicate future action with infallible authority **WORD ORIGIN** Latin *oraculum*

oracular *adj* 1 of or like an oracle 2 wise and prophetic 3 mysterious or ambiguous

oral *adj* **1** spoken or verbal; using spoken words **2** of or for use in the mouth: *an oral thermometer* **3** (of a drug) to be taken by mouth: *an oral contraceptive* ▷ *n* **4** an examination in which the questions and answers are spoken rather than written **orally** *adv*
WORD ORIGIN Latin *os, oris* mouth

orange *n* **1** a round reddish-yellow juicy citrus fruit **2** the evergreen tree on which it grows **3** a colour between red and yellow; the colour of an orange ▷ *adj* **4** of a colour between red and yellow
WORD ORIGIN Arabic *nāranj*

orangeade *n* *Brit* a usually fizzy orange-flavoured drink

orange blossom *n* the flowers of the orange tree, traditionally worn by brides

Orangeman *n, pl* **-men** a member of a political society founded in Ireland in 1795 to uphold Protestantism
WORD ORIGIN after William, prince of *Orange*, later William III

orangery *n, pl* **-eries** a conservatory or greenhouse in which orange trees are grown in cooler climates

orangey *adj* slightly orange

orang-utan *or* **orang-utang** *n* a large ape of the forests of Sumatra and Borneo, with shaggy reddish-brown hair and long arms
WORD ORIGIN Malay *ōrang* man + *hūtan* forest

oration *n* a formal or ceremonial public speech
WORD ORIGIN Latin *oratio*

orator (or-rat-tor) *n* a person who gives an oration, esp. one skilled in persuasive public speaking

oratorio (or-rat-**tor**-ee-oh) *n, pl* **-rios** a musical composition for soloists, chorus, and orchestra, based on a religious theme
WORD ORIGIN Italian

oratory¹ (or-rat-tree) *n* the art or skill of public speaking
WORD ORIGIN Latin *(ars) oratoria* (the art of) public speaking

oratory² *n, pl* **-ries** a small room or building set apart for private prayer
WORD ORIGIN Latin *orare* to pray

orb *n* **1** an ornamental sphere with a cross on top, carried by a king or queen in important ceremonies **2** a sphere; globe **3** *poetic* the eye **4** *obsolete or poetic* a heavenly body, such as the sun
WORD ORIGIN Latin *orbis* circle, disc

orbit *n* **1** the curved path followed by something, such as a heavenly body or spacecraft, in its motion around another body **2** a range or sphere of action or influence **3** *anat* the eye socket ▷ *vb* **-biting, -bited** **4** to move around (a heavenly body) in an orbit **5** to send (a satellite or spacecraft) into orbit **orbital** *adj*
WORD ORIGIN Latin *orbis* circle

Orcadian *n* **1** a person from Orkney ▷ *adj* **2** of Orkney
WORD ORIGIN Latin *Orcades* the Orkney Islands

orchard *n* an area of land on which fruit trees are grown
WORD ORIGIN Old English *orceard*

orchestra *n* **1** a large group of musicians whose members play a variety of different instruments **2** Also called: **orchestra pit** the space, in front of or under the stage, reserved for musicians in a theatre **orchestral** *adj*
WORD ORIGIN Greek: the space in the theatre for the chorus

orchestrate *vb* **-trating, -trated** **1** to score or arrange (a piece of music) for orchestra **2** to arrange (something) in order to produce a particular result: *he had orchestrated today's meeting* **orchestration** *n*

orchid *n* a plant having flowers of unusual shapes and beautiful colours, usually with one lip-shaped petal which is larger than the other two
WORD ORIGIN Greek *orkhis* testicle, because of the shape of its roots

ordain *vb* **1** to make (someone) a member of the clergy **2** *formal* to decree or order with authority **ordainment** *n*
WORD ORIGIN Late Latin *ordinare*

ordeal *n* **1** a severe or trying experience **2** *history* a method of trial in which the accused person was subjected to physical danger
WORD ORIGIN Old English *ordāl, ordēl* verdict

order *n* **1** an instruction that must be obeyed; command **2** a state in which everything is arranged logically, comprehensibly, or naturally: *she strove to keep more order in the house* **3** an arrangement of things in succession; sequence: *group them by letter and then put them in numerical order* **4** an established or customary system of society: *there is an opportunity here for a new world order* **5** a peaceful or harmonious condition of society: *riot police were called in to restore order* **6 a** an instruction to supply something in return for payment: *the waitress came to take their order* **b** the thing or things supplied **7** a written instruction to pay money: *post the coupon below with a cheque or postal order* **8** a social class: *the result will be harmful to society as a whole and to the lower orders in particular* **9** *biol* one of the groups into which a class is divided, containing one or more families **10** kind or sort: *the orchestra played superbly and the singing was of the highest order* **11** Also called: **religious order** a religious community of monks or nuns **12** a group of people who have been awarded a particular honour: *the Order of the Garter* **13** the office or rank of a Christian minister: *he studied for the priesthood as a young man, but never took Holy Orders* **14** the procedure and rules followed by an assembly or meeting: *a point of order* **15** one of the five major classical styles of architecture, classified by the type of columns used **16 a tall order** something difficult or demanding **17 in order a** in sequence **b** properly arranged: *everything is in order for your trip* **c** appropriate or fitting **18 in order that** so that **19 in order to** so that it is possible to: *a healthy diet is necessary in order to keep fit* **20 in** *or* **of the order of** amounting approximately to: *summer temperatures are usually in the order of 35°* **21 keep order** to ensure that people obey the law or behave in an acceptable manner **22 on order** having been ordered but not yet delivered **23 out of order a** not in sequence **b** not working: *the lift was out of order, so we had to use the stairs* **c** not following the rules or customary procedure: *the chairperson ruled the motion out of order* **24 to order** according to a buyer's specifications ▷ *vb* **25** to command or instruct (to do something): *she ordered her son to wash the dishes; the police ordered her into the house* **26** to request (something) to be supplied in return for payment: *I ordered a new car three weeks ago, but it hasn't been delivered yet* **27** to arrange (things) methodically or in their proper places ▷ *interj* **28** an exclamation demanding that orderly behaviour be restored
WORD ORIGIN Latin *ordo*

order around *or* **about** *vb* to repeatedly tell (someone) what to do in a bossy or unsympathetic way: *it was intolerable that those two fat slobs could order her around*

orderly *adj* **1** tidy or well-organized: *they evacuated the building in an orderly manner* **2** well-behaved; law-abiding ▷ *n, pl* **-lies** **3** *med* a male hospital attendant **4** *mil* a soldier whose duty is to carry out orders or perform minor tasks for a more senior officer **orderliness** *n*

Order of Merit *n* *Brit* an order awarded for outstanding achievement in any field

order paper *n* a list indicating the order of business, esp. in Parliament

ordinal number *n* a number indicating position in a sequence, such as *first, second, third*

ordinance *n* an official rule or order
WORD ORIGIN Latin *ordinare* to set in order

ordinarily *adv* in ordinary or usual practice; usually; normally

ordinary *adj* **1** usual or normal: *it was an ordinary working day for them* **2** not special or different in any way: *what do ordinary Germans feel about reunification?* **3** dull or unexciting: *the restaurant charged very high prices for very ordinary cooking* ▷ *n, pl* **-naries** **4** *RC Church* the parts of the Mass that do not vary from day to day **5 out of the ordinary** unusual
WORD ORIGIN Latin *ordinarius* orderly

Ordinary level *n* (in Britain) the formal name for **O level**

ordinary rating *n* a rank in the Royal Navy equivalent to that of a private in the army

ordinary seaman *n* *Brit, Austral, & NZ* a seaman of the lowest rank

ordinary shares *pl n* *Austral & Brit* shares issued by a company entitling their holders to a dividend according to the profits of the company and to a claim on net assets

ordinate *n* *maths* the vertical coordinate of a point in a two-dimensional system of coordinates
WORD ORIGIN Latin *ordinare* to arrange in order

ordination *n* the act or ceremony of making someone a member of the clergy

ordnance *n* **1** weapons and other military supplies **2 the ordnance** a government department dealing with military supplies

Nautical English

How a small population on a smattering of offshore islands created a world empire is one of the most astonishing phenomena in history. The British Empire would not have been possible without ships. Those who sailed them spoke English. It follows that our language is drenched with the words used by explorers and exploiters, and the navy that backed them both.

Even during the period of Middle English, a vast vocabulary of nautical terms existed. Often derived from Old Norse, some of these terms survive today, as in *bow*, *keel*, and *stern*. Specialized words and phrases made *headway* into common speech. Each succeeding century carried a *ballast* of them, beginning in the 1500s and 1600s. Crews *battened down the hatches* or let *rigging* and *spars* – a last resort – *go by the board* lest vessels *founder* and *come to a bitter end*. Those on *first-rate* ships *by and large* survived their epic voyages. Their ships waited *in the offing*, offshore, then, once they *embarked*, sought *leeway*. As first steam, then diesel, replaced sail power, the linguistic spillover from sea to land persisted. During these times, what emerged were *taken aback, back and fill, see how the land lies, cut and run, close quarters, forge ahead, run afoul, high and dry, chock-a-block*, and *hard and fast*.

The crews in any ship are ordered in a rigid hierarchy, especially on a fighting ship in the sailing era such as a *privateer* or *man of war*. With the force of rank came punishment, beginning with a verbal *dressing down* in which the crew was expected to stand at attention and *toe the line*, sometimes to watch one of their mates being flogged *over the barrel*. Sometimes the *deck* was so crowded there was *no room to swing a cat* (the cat being the *cat o' nine tails*, a reference to the whip's knotted cords). Like these phrases, many nautical terms washed up far from their original context, as in the case of *fenders, overhaul, mainstay, tide over*, and *clean bill of health*. The first *rummage sale* was of damaged cargo. *Aloof* originally meant *upwind* of other vessels, *scuttlebutt* was not gossip but a cask of drinking water (the precursor of the modern-day water-cooler),

and a *galoot* was not an oaf in the Old West, but a soldier or marine.

The *seacocks* of word coinage and usage were opened for the names of knots and flags, and the many terms for varieties of wind, weather, and water. But the flow of nautical traffic was not one-way. Over the centuries, ships bore codfish, beaver hides, seal pelts, timber, iron ore, and grain from North America to Europe. A multitude of regional terms emerged from the fisheries of Atlantic Canada, the shipbuilding and whaling industries of New England, and inland shipping on the five Great Lakes. Specialized parlance stretched into the twentieth century with the advent of long-distance yachts, ocean liners, and cruise ships. Nautical terms were transferred wholesale into new technology, both below water in *submarines*, and above it, in aircraft. As we cruise above the clouds, we hear a voice issuing from the *flight deck*: 'This is your captain speaking.'

One does not have to go far through a dictionary to find nautical terms, many prefixed with *a-*: *aback, abaft, abeam, aboard, adrift, afloat*, and *aground*. Nautical slang, overwhelmingly male, is especially salty, most probably because there are few confined spaces where more things can go wrong than aboard a ship. Also of linguistic interest is the fact that the etymology of nautical words is more disputed than any other. Take *posh*, a word that may originate in slang, but emphatically is not an acronym for *Port Out, Starboard Home*, supposedly indicating the comfy, shady side of a transoceanic passenger ship – unlike conditions during the *Age of Sail*.

In those days, pirates were not especially amusing people to meet, but today many find that imitating how they spoke, largely based on fiction, films, and TV shows, all too expressively funny. There is even an International Talk Like a Pirate Day (September 19), in which office workers are encouraged to relieve tedium by saying to each other such things as 'Ahoy, me hearty!', 'Smartly, me lass', and 'Avast, ye scurvy bilge rat, arrr!' It's one way to pass the time.

WORD ORIGIN variant of *ordinance*

Ordnance Survey *n* the British government organization that produces detailed maps of Britain and Ireland

Ordovician (or-doe-**vish**-ee-an) *adj geol* of the period of geological time about 500 million years ago
WORD ORIGIN Latin *Ordovices*, ancient Celtic tribe in N Wales

ordure *n* excrement; dung
WORD ORIGIN Old French *ord* dirty

ore *n* rock or mineral from which valuable substances such as metals can be extracted
WORD ORIGIN Old English *ār*, *ōra*

oregano (or-rig-**gah**-no) *n* a sweet-smelling herb used as seasoning
WORD ORIGIN Greek *origanon* an aromatic herb

organ *n* **1** a part in animals and plants that is adapted to perform a particular function, for example the heart or lungs **2 a** a musical keyboard instrument which produces sound by forcing air through pipes of a variety of lengths **b** Also called: **electric organ** a keyboard instrument which produces similar sounds electronically **3** a means of communication, such as a newspaper issued by a specialist group or party **4** *euphemistic* a penis
WORD ORIGIN Greek *organon* tool

organdie *n* a fine, slightly stiff cotton fabric
WORD ORIGIN French *organdi*

organ-grinder *n* (formerly) an entertainer who played a barrel organ in the streets

organic *adj* **1** of, produced by, or found in plants or animals: *the rocks were carefully searched for organic remains* **2** not using, or grown without, artificial fertilizers or pesticides: *organic vegetables; an organic farm* **3** *chem* of or belonging to the class of chemical compounds that are formed from carbon **4** (of change or development) gradual and natural rather than sudden or forced **5** made up of many different parts which contribute to the way in which the whole society or structure works: *an organic whole* **organically** *adv*

organic chemistry *n chem* the branch of chemistry dealing with carbon compounds

organism *n* **1** an animal or plant **2** anything resembling a living creature in structure, behaviour, or complexity: *cities are more complicated organisms than farming villages*

organist *n* a person who plays the organ

organization *or* **-nisation** *n* **1** an organized group of people, such as a club, society, union, or business **2** the act of organizing: *setting up the European tour took a lot of organization* **3** the structure and arrangement of the different parts of something: *the report recommended radical changes in the organization of the social services department* **4** the state of being organized: *the material in this essay lacks any sort of organization* **organizational** *or* **-nisational** *adj*

organize *or* **-nise** *vb* **-nizing, -nized** *or* **-nising, -nised 1** to plan and arrange (something): *we organized a protest meeting in the village hall* **2** to arrange systematically: *the files are organized in alphabetical order and by date* **3** to form, join, or recruit (people) into a trade union: *the seasonal nature of tourism makes it difficult for hotel workers to organize* **organizer** *or* **-niser** *n*
WORD ORIGIN Medieval Latin *organizare*

organized *or* **-nised** *adj* **1** planned and controlled on a large scale and involving many people: *organized crime* **2** orderly and efficient: *a highly organized campaign* **3** (of the workers in a factory or office) belonging to a trade union: *socialism is especially popular among organized labour*

organza *n* a thin stiff fabric of silk, cotton, or synthetic fibre
WORD ORIGIN origin unknown

orgasm *n* the most intense point of pleasure and excitement during sexual activity **orgasmic** *adj*
WORD ORIGIN Greek *orgasmos*

orgy *n, pl* **-gies 1** a wild party involving promiscuous sexual activity and excessive drinking **2** an act of immoderate or frenzied indulgence: *the rioters were engaged in an orgy of destruction* **orgiastic** *adj*
WORD ORIGIN Greek *orgia* secret rites

oriel window *or* **oriel** *n* a window built out from the wall of a house at an upper level
WORD ORIGIN Old French *oriol* gallery

orient *vb* **1 2** to position or set (for example a map or chart) with relation to the points of the compass or other specific directions **3 orient oneself** to adjust or align oneself or one's ideas according to new surroundings or circumstances: *new employees can take some time to orient themselves to the company's procedures* **4 be oriented to** *or* **towards** to work or act with a particular aim, idea, or person in mind: *many people feel that Britain is too much oriented to the Americans* ▷ *n* **5** *poetic* the east
WORD ORIGIN Latin *oriens* rising (sun)

Orient *n* **the Orient** East Asia

oriental *adj* eastern

Oriental *adj* **1** of the Orient ▷ *n* **2** a person from the Orient

orientate *vb* **-tating, -tated** same as **orient**

-orientated *or* **-oriented** *adj combining form* interested in or directed towards the thing specified: *career-orientated women*

orientation *n* **1** the activities and aims that a person or organization is interested in: *the course has a practical rather than theoretical orientation* **2** the position of an object with relation to the points of the compass or other specific directions: *the room's southerly orientation means that it receives a lot of light* ▷ *adj* **3** of or providing information or training needed to understand a new situation or environment: *nearly every college has an orientation programme*

orienteering *n* a sport in which contestants race on foot over a cross-country course consisting of checkpoints found with the aid of a map and compass
WORD ORIGIN Swedish *orientering*

orifice (or-rif-fiss) *n* an opening or hole through which something can pass, esp. one in the body such as the mouth or anus
WORD ORIGIN Latin *os* mouth + *facere* to make

orig. 1 origin **2** original(ly)

origami (or-rig-**gah**-mee) *n* the art, originally Japanese, of folding paper intricately into decorative shapes
WORD ORIGIN Japanese *ori* a fold + *kami* paper

origin *n* **1** the point, source, or event from which something develops: *the origin of the term 'jazz' is obscure; the war had its origin in the clash between rival nationalists* **2** the country, race, or social class of a person's parents or ancestors: *an Australian of Greek origin; he was proud of his working-class origins* **3** *maths* the point at which the horizontal and vertical axes intersect
WORD ORIGIN Latin *origo* beginning

original *adj* **1** first or earliest: *the dining room also has attractive original beams* **2** fresh and unusual; not copied from or based on something else: *the composer's work has created some original and attractive choreography* **3** able to think of or carry out new ideas or concepts: *he is an excitingly original writer* **4** being the first and genuine form of something, from which a copy or translation is made: *all French recipes were translated from the original abridged versions* ▷ *n* **5** the first and genuine form of something, from which others are copied or translated: *the original is in the British Museum* **6** a person or thing used as a model in art or literature: *she claimed to be the original on whom Lawrence based Lady Chatterley* **originality** *n* **originally** *adv*

original sin *n* a state of sin believed by some Christians to be inborn in all human beings as a result of Adam's disobedience

originate *vb* **-nating, -nated** to come or bring (something) into existence: *humans probably originated in East Africa* **origination** *n* **originator** *n*

oriole *n* a songbird with a long pointed bill and a mostly yellow-and-black plumage
WORD ORIGIN Latin *aureolus* golden

ormolu *n* a gold-coloured alloy of copper, tin, or zinc, used to decorate furniture and other articles
WORD ORIGIN French *or moulu* ground gold

ornament *n* **1** anything that adorns someone or something; decoration: *the room's only ornament was a dim, oily picture of the Holy Family* **2** decorations collectively: *he had no watch, nor ornament of any kind* **3** a small decorative object: *I hit a garden ornament while parking* **4** a person whose character or talent makes them an asset to society or the group to which they belong: *an ornament of the firm* **5** *music* a note or group of notes which embellishes the melody but is not an integral part of it, for instance a trill ▷ *vb* **6** to decorate or adorn: *the hall had a high ceiling, ornamented with plaster fruits and flowers* **ornamental** *adj* **ornamentation** *n* **ornamented** *adj*
WORD ORIGIN Latin *ornamentum*

ornate *adj* **1** heavily or elaborately decorated: *an ornate ceiling painted with allegorical figures* **2** (of style in writing) overelaborate; using many literary expressions **ornately** *adv*
WORD ORIGIN Latin *ornare* to decorate

ornithology *n* the study of birds **ornithological** *adj* **ornithologist** *n*
WORD ORIGIN Greek *ornis* bird

orotund *adj* **1** (of the voice) resonant and booming **2** (of speech or writing) pompous; containing many long or formal words
WORD ORIGIN Latin *ore rotundo* with rounded mouth

orphan *n* **1** a child whose parents are dead ▷ *vb* **2** to cause (someone) to become an orphan: *she was orphaned at 16 when her parents died in a car crash*
WORD ORIGIN Greek *orphanos*

orphanage *n* a children's home for orphans and abandoned children

orphaned *adj* having no living parents

orrery *n, pl* **-ries** a mechanical model of the solar system in which the planets can be moved around the sun
WORD ORIGIN originally made for the Earl of *Orrery*

orris *n* **1** a kind of iris that has fragrant roots **2** Also: **orrisroot** the root of this plant prepared and used as perfume
WORD ORIGIN variant of *iris*

orthodontics *n* the branch of dentistry concerned with correcting irregularities of the teeth **orthodontic** *adj* **orthodontist** *n*
WORD ORIGIN Greek *orthos* straight + *odōn* tooth

orthodox *adj* conforming to traditional or established standards in religion, behaviour, or attitudes: *orthodox medicine; the concerto has a more orthodox structure than is usual for this composer* **orthodoxy** *n*
WORD ORIGIN Greek *orthos* correct + *doxa* belief

Orthodox *adj* **1** of the Orthodox Church of Eastern Europe **2** of or being the form of Judaism characterized by traditional interpretation of and strict adherence to Mosaic Law: *an Orthodox Jew*

Orthodox Church *n* the Christian Church dominant in Eastern Europe, which has the Greek Patriarch of Constantinople as its head

orthography *n* **1** spelling considered to be correct: *British and American orthography is different in many cases* **2** the study of spelling **orthographic** *adj*
WORD ORIGIN Greek *orthos* correct + *graphein* to write

orthopaedics *or US* **orthopedics** *n* the branch of surgery concerned with disorders of the bones and joints **orthopaedic** *or US* **orthopedic** *adj* **orthopaedist** *or US* **orthopedist** *n*
WORD ORIGIN Greek *orthos* straight + *pais* child

ortolan *n* a small European songbird eaten as a delicacy
WORD ORIGIN Latin *hortulus* a little garden

oryx *n* any of various large straight-horned African antelopes

Os *chem* osmium

OS 1 (in Britain) Ordnance Survey **2** outsize(d)

Oscar *n* an award in the form of a small gold statuette awarded annually in the US for outstanding achievements in various aspects of the film industry: *he won an Oscar for Best Supporting Actor in 1974*
WORD ORIGIN said to have been named after a remark made by an official that it reminded her of her uncle Oscar

oscillate (**oss**-ill-late) *vb* **-lating, -lated 1** to swing repeatedly back and forth: *its wings oscillate up and down many times a second* **2** to waver between two extremes of opinion, attitude, or behaviour: *the government oscillates between a desire for reform and a desire to keep its powers intact* **3** *physics* (of an electric current) to vary between minimum and maximum values **oscillation** *n* **oscillator** *n*
WORD ORIGIN Latin *oscillare* to swing

oscilloscope (oss-**sill**-oh-scope) *n* an instrument that produces a visual representation of an oscillating electric current on the screen of a cathode-ray tube

osier (**oh**-zee-er) *n* **1** a willow tree whose flexible branches or twigs are used for making baskets and furniture **2** a twig or branch from this tree
WORD ORIGIN Old French

Osiris *n* an Egyptian god of the underworld

osmium *n* *chem* a very hard brittle bluish-white metal, the heaviest known element. Symbol: Os
WORD ORIGIN Greek *osmē* smell, from its penetrating odour

osmoregulation *n* *zool* the adjustment of the osmotic pressure of a cell or organism in relation to the surrounding fluid

osmosis *n* **1** the diffusion of liquids through a membrane until they are mixed **2** the process by which people or ideas influence each other gradually and subtly **osmotic** *adj*
WORD ORIGIN Greek *ōsmos* push

osprey *n* a large fish-eating bird of prey, with a dark back and whitish head and underparts
WORD ORIGIN Old French *ospres*, apparently from Latin *ossifraga*, literally: bone-breaker

osseous *adj* consisting of or like bone
WORD ORIGIN Latin *os* bone

ossify *vb* **-fies, -fying, -fied 1** to change into bone; harden **2** to become rigid, inflexible, or unprogressive: *ossified traditions* **ossification** *n*
WORD ORIGIN Latin *os* bone + *facere* to make

ostensible *adj* apparent or seeming; alleged: *our ostensible common interest is boats* **ostensibly** *adv*
WORD ORIGIN Latin *ostendere* to show

ostensive *adj* directly showing or pointing out: *he gave ostensive definitions to things*
WORD ORIGIN Latin *ostendere* to show

ostentation *n* pretentious, showy, or vulgar display: *she felt the gold taps in the bathroom were tasteless ostentation* **ostentatious** *adj* **ostentatiously** *adv*

osteoarthritis (ost-ee-oh-arth-**rite**-iss) *n* chronic inflammation of the joints, causing pain and stiffness **osteoarthritic** *adj*

WORD ORIGIN Greek *osteon* bone + ARTHRITIS

osteopathy *n* a system of healing based on the manipulation of bones or muscle **osteopath** *n*
WORD ORIGIN Greek *osteon* bone + *patheia* suffering

osteoporosis (ost-ee-oh-pore-**oh**-siss) *n* brittleness of the bones, caused by lack of calcium
WORD ORIGIN Greek *osteon* bone + *poros* passage

ostinato *n, pl* **-tos** *music* a persistently repeated phrase or rhythm
WORD ORIGIN Italian, from Latin *obstinatus* obstinate

ostler *n* (formerly) a stableman at an inn
WORD ORIGIN variant of *hostler*, from *hostel*

ostracize *or* **-cise** *vb* **-cizing, -cized** *or* **-cising, -cised** to exclude or banish (a person) from a particular group or from society: *he was ostracized from his family when his affair became known* **ostracism** *n*
WORD ORIGIN Greek *ostrakizein* to select someone for banishment by voting on potsherds

ostrich *n* **1** a large African bird which runs fast but cannot fly, and has a long neck, long legs, and soft dark feathers **2** a person who refuses to recognize an unpleasant truth: *he accused the Minister of being 'an ostrich with its head stuck in the sand, while all around him unemployment soars'*
WORD ORIGIN Greek *strouthion*

OT Old Testament

OTC (in Britain) Officers' Training Corps

OTE *chiefly Brit* (esp. in job adverts) on target earnings: the minimum amount of money a salesman is expected to make

other *adj* **1** remaining (one or ones) in a group of which one or some have been specified: *she wasn't getting on with the other children* **2** being a different one or ones from the one or ones already specified or understood: *other people might not be so tolerant of your behaviour; are you sure it's not in your other pocket?* **3** refers to a place or time which is not the one the speaker or writer is in: *results in other countries have been most encouraging* **4** additional; further: *there is one other thing for the government to do* **5** **every other** every alternate: *the doctor sees me every other week* **6** **other than a** apart from: *he knew little of the country other than it was Muslim* **b** different from: *treatment other than a hearing aid will be possible for those with inner ear deafness* **7** **or other** used to add vagueness to the preceding word or phrase: *he could take some evening course or other which could lead to an extra qualification; he was called away from the house on some pretext or other* **8** **the other day** a few days ago ▷ *n* **9** an additional person or thing: *show me one other* **10** **others** people apart from the person who is being spoken or written about: *she devoted her entire life to helping others* **11** **the others** the people or things remaining in a group of which one or some have been specified: *I can't speak for the others* ▷ *adv* **12** otherwise; differently: *they couldn't behave other than they do* **otherness** *n*
WORD ORIGIN Old English *ōther*

O

≡ **USAGE**
≡ See at **otherwise**.

other ranks *pl n Austral & Brit* (in the armed forces) all those who do not hold a commissioned rank

otherwise *conj* **1** or else; if not, then: *I was 50 but said I was 40, otherwise I'd never have got a job* ▷ *adv* **2** differently: *it was fruitless to pretend or to hope otherwise* **3** in other respects: *shrewd psychological twists perk up an otherwise predictable story line* ▷ *adj* **4** different: *circumstances beyond our control dictated that it should be otherwise* ▷ *pron* **5** or otherwise or not; or the opposite: *he didn't want company, talkative or otherwise*

≡ **USAGE**
≡ The expression *otherwise than* means *in*
≡ *any other way than* and should not be
≡ followed by an adjective: *no-one taught*
≡ *by this method can be other than* (not
≡ *otherwise than*) *successful; you are not*
≡ *allowed to use the building otherwise than as*
≡ *a private dwelling.*

otherworldly *adj* **1** concerned with spiritual rather than practical matters: *his otherworldly manner concealed a ruthless business mind* **2** mystical or supernatural: *this part of Italy has an otherworldly beauty*

otiose (**oh**-tee-oze) *adj* serving no useful purpose: *such a strike is almost otiose* **WORD ORIGIN** Latin *otiosus* leisured

OTT *slang* over the top

otter *n* a small freshwater fish-eating animal with smooth brown fur, a streamlined body, and webbed feet **WORD ORIGIN** Old English *otor*

ottoman *n, pl* **-mans** a storage chest with a padded lid for use as a seat **WORD ORIGIN** French *ottomane*, feminine of *Ottoman*

Ottoman *adj* **1** *history* of the Ottomans or the Ottoman Empire, the Turkish empire which lasted from the late 13th century until the end of World War I, and at its height included the Balkans and much of N Africa ▷ *n, pl* **-mans** **2** a member of a Turkish people who formed the basis of this empire **WORD ORIGIN** Arabic *Othmāni*

ou (oh) *n S African slang* a man, bloke, or chap **WORD ORIGIN** Afrikaans

OU **1** the Open University **2** Oxford University

oubaas (oh-bahss) *n S African* a man in authority **WORD ORIGIN** Afrikaans *ou* man + *baas* boss

oubliette (oo-blee-**ett**) *n history* a dungeon, the only entrance to which is a trap door in the ceiling **WORD ORIGIN** French *oublier* to forget

ouch *interj* an exclamation of sharp sudden pain

ought *vb* **1** used to express duty or obligation: *she ought to tell this to the police* **2** used to express advisability: *we ought to get the roof repaired before the attics get any damper* **3** used to express probability or expectation: *a good lawyer ought to be able to fix it for you* **4** used to express a desire on the part of the speaker: *you ought to have a good breakfast before you hit the road* **WORD ORIGIN** Old English *āhte*, past tense of *āgan* to owe

≡ **USAGE**
≡ In correct English, *ought* is not used
≡ with *did* or *had*. I ought not to do it, not I
≡ *didn't ought to do it*; *I ought not to have done*
≡ *it*, not *I hadn't ought to have done it.*

oughtn't ought not

Ouija board *or* **Ouija** (**weej**-a) *n trademark* a board on which are marked the letters of the alphabet. Answers to questions are spelt out by a pointer, which is supposedly guided by spirits **WORD ORIGIN** French *oui* yes + German *ja* yes

ouma (oh-mah) *n S African* **1** grandmother, often as a title with a surname **2** *slang* any elderly woman **WORD ORIGIN** Afrikaans

ounce *n* **1** a unit of weight equal to one sixteenth of a pound or 28.4 grams **2** short for **fluid ounce** **3** a small amount: *you haven't got one ounce of control over her* **WORD ORIGIN** Latin *uncia* a twelfth

OUP (in Northern Ireland) Official Unionist Party

oupa (oh-pah) *n S African* **1** grandfather, often as a title with a surname **2** *slang* any elderly man **WORD ORIGIN** Afrikaans

our *adj* **1** of, belonging to, or associated with us: *our daughter* **2** a formal word for *my* used by monarchs **WORD ORIGIN** Old English *ūre*

Our Father *n* same as the **Lord's Prayer**

ours *pron* **1** something belonging to us: *ours are smaller guns than those; the money is ours* **2** of ours belonging to or associated with us: *my wife and a friend of ours had both deserted me*

ourself *pron archaic* a formal word for *myself* used by monarchs

ourselves *pron* **1 a** the reflexive form of *we* or *us*: *we humiliated ourselves* **b** used for emphasis: *we ourselves will finish it* **2** our usual selves: *we've not been feeling quite ourselves since the accident* **3** *not standard* used instead of *we* or *us* in compound noun phrases: *other people and ourselves*

ousel *n* same as **ouzel**

oust *vb* to force (someone) out of a position; expel: *the coup which ousted the President* **WORD ORIGIN** Anglo-Norman *ouster*

ouster *n US* an act or instance of forcing someone out of a position: *the demonstrators called for the ouster of the police chief*

out *adv, adj* **1** away from the inside of a place: *she took her purse out; inspection of the eggs should be done when the hen is out of the nest* **2** away from one's home or place of work for a short time: *I called earlier but you were out; a search party is out looking for survivors* **3** no longer burning, shining, or functioning: *he switched the light out; the living-room fire went out while we were next door eating* **4** used up; not having any more of: *their supplies ran out after two weeks; we're out of milk* **5** public; revealed: *our dirty little secret is out* **6** available to the public: *her biography will be out in December* **7** (of the sun, stars, or moon) visible **8** in bloom: *the roses are out early this year* **9** not in fashion or current usage: *trying to be trendy is out* **10** excluded from consideration: *cost cutting is out of the*

question **11** not allowed: *smoking on duty is out* **12** out for *or* to wanting or intent on (something or doing something): *the young soldiers were out for revenge; they're out to get me* **13** *sport* (of a player in a sport like cricket or baseball) no longer batting because he or she has been dismissed by being caught, bowled, etc. **14** on strike **15** in or into a state of unconsciousness: *he went outside and passed out in an alley* **16** used to indicate a burst of activity as indicated by a verb: *war broke out in the Gulf* **17** out of existence: *the mistakes were scored out* **18** to the fullest extent: *spread out* **19** loudly; clearly: *he cried out in shock and pain* **20** to a conclusion; completely: *she'd worked it out for herself* **21** existing: *the friendliest dog out* **22** inaccurate or incorrect: *the estimate was out by £60* **23** not in office or authority: *she was finally voted out as party leader* **24** (of a period of time) completed: *before the year is out* **25** openly homosexual: *I came out as a lesbian when I was still in my teens* **26** old-fashioned (of a young woman) in or into upper-class society life: *Lucinda had a large party when she came out* **27** out of **a** at or to a point outside: *the train pulled out of the station* **b** away from; not in: *they're out of touch with reality; out of focus* **c** because of; motivated by: *out of jealousy* **d** from (a material or source): *made out of plastic* **e** no longer in a specified state or condition: *out of work; out of practice* ▷ *adj* **28** *informal* not concealing one's homosexuality ▷ *prep* **29** *US or not standard* out of; out through: *he ran out the door* ▷ *interj* **30 a** an exclamation of dismissal **b** (in signalling and radio) an expression used to signal that the speaker is signing off: *over and out!* ▷ *vb* **31** *informal* (of homosexuals) to expose (a public figure) as being a fellow homosexual **32** *informal* to reveal something embarrassing or unknown about (a person): *he was outed as a talented goal scorer* **WORD ORIGIN** Old English *ūt*

≡ **USAGE**
≡ The use of *out* as a preposition, though
≡ common in American English, is
≡ regarded as incorrect in standard
≡ British English: *he climbed out of* (not
≡ *out*) *a window; he went out through* (not *out*)
≡ *the door.*

out- *prefix* **1** excelling or surpassing in a particular action: *outlast; outlive* **2** at or from a point away, outside: *outpost; outpatient* **3** going away, outward: *outcrop; outgrowth*

outage *n* a period of power failure

out and about *adj* regularly going out of the house to work, take part in social activity, etc. esp. after an illness

out-and-out *adj* absolute; thorough: *it's an out-and-out lie*

outback *n* the remote bush country of Australia

outbid *vb* **-bidding, -bidded** *or* **-bid** to offer a higher price than (another person)

outboard motor *n* a portable petrol engine that can be attached externally to the stern of a boat to propel it

outbox *n computers* a folder in which outgoing messages are stored

Words from Literature
part 19

over the broomstick *phrase* this is a phrase meaning getting married without a formal ceremony
> They both led tramping lives, and this woman in Gerrard-street here, had been married very young, over the broomstick (as we say), to a tramping man, and was a perfect fury in point of jealousy.
> *Great Expectations* Charles Dickens

own *v* own means to admit or to acknowledge
> It's my old girl that advises. She has the head. But I never own to it before her. Discipline must be maintained
> *Bleak House* Charles Dickens

page *n* a boy employed to run errands
> not my feigned page
> *On His Mistress* John Donne

paid pretty dear *phrase* paid a high price or suffered a lot
> I paid pretty dear for my monthly fourpenny piece
> *Treasure Island* Robert Louis Stevenson

pannikin *n* a small tin cup
> of lifting light glasses and cups to his lips, as if they were clumsy pannikins
> *Great Expectations* Charles Dickens

pard *n* a pard is a leopard
> Not charioted by Bacchus and his pards
> *Ode to a Nightingale* John Keats

parlour boarder *n* a pupil who lived with a family
> and somebody had lately raised her from the condition of scholar to parlour boarder
> *Emma* Jane Austen

particular, a London *phrase* London in Victorian times and up to the 1950s was famous for having very dense fog, which was a combination of real fog and the smog of pollution from factories
> "This is a London particular ... A fog, miss"
> *Bleak House* Charles Dickens

patten *n* pattens were wooden soles which were fixed to shoes to protect the shoes in wet weather
> carrying a basket like the Great Seal of England in plaited straw, a pair of pattens, a spare shawl, and an umbrella, though it was a fine bright day
> *Great Expectations* Charles Dickens

paviour *n* a paviour was a labourer who worked on the street pavement
> the paviour his pickaxe
> *Oliver Twist* Charles Dickens

peccant *adj* peccant means unhealthy
> other peccant humours
> *Gulliver's Travels* Jonathan Swift

penetralium *n* penetralium is a word used to describe the inner rooms of the house
> and I had no desire to aggravate his impatience previous to inspecting the penetralium
> *Wuthering Heights* Emily Brontë

pensive *adv* pensive means deep in thought or thinking seriously about something
> and she was leaning pensive on a tomb-stone on her right elbow
> *The Adventures of Huckleberry Finn* Mark Twain

penury *n* penury is the state of being extremely poor
> Distress, if not penury, loomed in the distance
> *Tess of the D'Urbervilles* Thomas Hardy

perspective *n* telescope
> a pocket perspective
> *Gulliver's Travels* Jonathan Swift

phaeton *n* an open carriage for four people
> often condescends to drive by my humble abode in her little phaeton and ponies
> *Pride and Prejudice* Jane Austen

phantasm *n* an illusion, something that is not real. It is sometimes used to mean ghost
> Experience had bred no fancies in him that could raise the phantasm of appetite
> *Silas Marner* George Eliot

outbreak *n* a sudden occurrence of disease or war

outbuilding *n* same as **outhouse**

outburst *n* 1 a sudden strong expression of emotion, esp. of anger: *such emotional outbursts do nothing to help calm discussion of the matter* 2 a sudden period of violent activity: *this sudden outburst of violence has come as a shock*

outcast *n* a person who is rejected or excluded from a particular group or from society

outclass *vb* to surpass (someone) in performance or quality

outcome *n* the result or consequence of something

outcrop *n* part of a rock formation that sticks out of the earth

outcry *n, pl* **-cries** a widespread or vehement protest: *there was great popular outcry against the plan for a dual carriageway*

outdated *adj* old-fashioned or obsolete

outdistance *vb* **-tancing, -tanced** 1 to surpass (someone) in a particular activity 2 to leave (other competitors) behind in a race

outdo *vb* **-does, -doing, -did, -done** to be more successful or better than (someone or something) in performance: *this car easily outdoes its rivals when it comes to comfort*

outdoor *adj* 1 taking place, existing, or intended for use in the open air: *have a swim at the beach or outdoor pool; she was just taking off her outdoor clothing* 2 fond of the outdoors: *Paul was a butch outdoor type*

outdoors *adv* 1 in the open air; outside: *he hardly ever went outdoors* ▷ *n* 2 the world outside or far away from buildings; the open air: *he'd forgotten his fear of the outdoors*

outer *adj* 1 on the outside; external: *the building's outer walls were painted pale pink* 2 further from the middle: *the outer suburbs* ▷ *n* 3 *archery* **a** the white outermost ring on a target **b** a shot that hits this ring

outermost *adj* furthest from the centre or middle

outer space *n* space beyond the atmosphere of the earth

outface *vb* **-facing, -faced** to subdue or disconcert (someone) by staring

outfall *n* *Brit, Austral, & NZ* the mouth of a river, drain, or pipe: *the survey measured pollution levels near sewer outfalls*

outfield *n* 1 *cricket* the area of the field far from the pitch 2 *baseball* the area of the playing field beyond the lines connecting first, second, and third bases **outfielder** *n*

outfit *n* 1 a set of clothes worn together 2 *informal* a group of people working together as a unit 3 a set of equipment for a particular task; kit: *a complete anti-snakebite outfit*

outfitter *n* *old-fashioned* a shop or person that sells men's clothes

outflank *vb* 1 to go around and beyond the side of (an enemy army) 2 to get the better of (someone)

outflow *n* 1 anything that flows out, such as liquid or money 2 the amount that flows out

outfox *vb* to defeat or foil (someone) by being more cunning; outsmart

outgoing *adj* 1 leaving: *some members of the outgoing government continued to attend the peace talks* 2 friendly and sociable

outgoings *pl n* expenses

outgrow *vb* **-growing, -grew, -grown** 1 to grow too large for (clothes or shoes): *it's amazing how quickly children outgrow their clothes* 2 to lose (a way of behaving or thinking) in the course of becoming more mature: *most teenagers outgrow their moodiness as they near adulthood* 3 to grow larger or faster than (someone or something): *the weeds threatened to outgrow and choke the rice plants*

outgrowth *n* 1 a natural development or consequence: *he argued that religion was an outgrowth of magic* 2 a thing growing out of a main body; offshoot

outhouse *n* a building near to, but separate from, a main building

outing *n* 1 a trip or excursion 2 *informal* the naming by homosexuals of other prominent homosexuals, often against their will

outlandish *adj* extremely unconventional; bizarre

outlast *vb* to last longer than

outlaw *n* 1 *history* a criminal who has been deprived of legal protection and rights ▷ *vb* 2 to make (something) illegal: *racial discrimination was formally outlawed* 3 *history* to make (someone) an outlaw **outlawed** *adj*

outlay *n* the money, effort, or time spent on something

outlet *n* 1 a means of expressing one's feelings: *the shock would give her an outlet for her own grief* 2 **a** a market for a product: *there is a huge sales outlet for personal computers* **b** a shop or organization selling the goods of a particular producer or wholesaler or manufacturer: *her own brand is now sold to outlets throughout the world* 3 an opening permitting escape or release: *make sure the exhaust outlet is not blocked*

outline *n* 1 a general explanation or description of something, which does not give all the details: *the course gave a brief outline of twentieth-century music* 2 **outlines** the important features of something: *the outlines of his theory are correct, we just need to fill in the details* 3 the general shape of something, esp. when only the profile and not the details are visible: *it was still light enough to see the outline of the distant mountains* 4 a drawing showing only the external lines of an object ▷ *vb* **-lining, -lined** 5 to give the main features or general idea of (something): *I outlined what we had done and what we had still to do* 6 to show the general shape of an object but not its details, as light does coming from behind an object: *we could see the towers of the city outlined against the night sky*

outlive *vb* **-living, -lived** 1 to live longer than (someone): *she only outlived her husband by a few months* 2 to live beyond (a date or period): *the sparrow outlived the winter* 3 **outlive its usefulness** to be no longer useful or necessary: *some argued that the organization had outlived its usefulness*

outlook *n* 1 a general attitude to life: *my whole outlook on life had changed* 2 the probable condition or outcome of something: *the economic outlook is not good* 3 the weather forecast for the next few days: *the outlook for the weekend* 4 the view from a place: *a dreary outlook of chimneys and smoke*

outlying *adj* far away from the main area

outmanoeuvre *or US* **outmaneuver** *vb* **-vring, -vred** *or* **-vering, -vered** to gain an advantage over (someone) by skilful dealing: *the management outmanoeuvred us into accepting redundancies*

outmatch *vb* to surpass or outdo (someone)

outmoded *adj* no longer fashionable or accepted

outnumber *vb* to exceed in number: *they were outnumbered by fifty to one*

out of bounds *adj, adv* 1 (often foll. by *to*) not to be entered (by): *the area has been out of bounds to foreign journalists and closed to tourists* 2 (in a sport such as golf) outside the boundaries of the course or playing area

out-of-date *adj, adv* old-fashioned; outmoded

out of doors *adv* in the open air; outside

out of pocket *adj* having lost or spent money: *I was £10 out of pocket after paying for their drinks*

out-of-the-way *adj* remote and isolated: *an out-of-the-way village in the Bavarian Forest*

out-of-work *adj* unemployed: *an out-of-work engineer*

outpace *vb* **-pacing, -paced** 1 to go faster than (someone) 2 to surpass or outdo (someone or something) in growth, development, etc.: *the increase in the number of households is outpacing the number of houses being built*

outpatient *n* a patient who visits a hospital for treatment but does not stay there overnight

outport *n* *Canad* an isolated fishing village, esp. in Newfoundland

outpost *n* a small settlement in a distant part of the country or in a foreign country, which is used for military or trading purposes

outpouring *n* 1 a great amount of something that is produced very rapidly: *a prolific outpouring of ideas and energy* 2 a passionate outburst: *the hysterical outpourings of fanatics*

output *n* 1 the amount of something that is made or produced: *our weekly output has increased by 240 tonnes* 2 *electronics* the power, voltage, or current delivered by a circuit or component 3 *computers* the information produced by a computer ▷ *vb* **-putting, -putted** *or* **-put** 4 *computers* to produce (data) at the end of a process

outrage *n* 1 deep indignation, anger, or resentment: *she felt a sense of outrage that he should abandon her like that* 2 an extremely vicious or cruel act; gross violation of decency, morality, or honour: *there have been reports of another bombing outrage in the capital* ▷ *vb* **-raging,**

-raged 3 to cause deep indignation, anger, or resentment in (someone): *they were outraged by the news of the assassination*
WORD ORIGIN French *outré* beyond

outrageous *adj* **1** unusual and shocking: *his sense of humour made him say and do the most outrageous things* **2** shocking and socially or morally unacceptable: *I will fight these outrageous accusations of corruption in the courts if necessary* **outrageously** *adv*

outrank *vb* to be of higher rank than (someone)

outré (oo-**tray**) *adj* eccentric and rather shocking
WORD ORIGIN French: having gone beyond

outrider *n* a person who rides a motorcycle or horse in front of or beside an official vehicle as an attendant or guard

outrigger *n* **1** a stabilizing framework projecting from the side of a boat or canoe **2** a boat or canoe equipped with such a framework

outright *adj* **1** complete; total: *he is close to an outright victory* **2** straightforward and direct: *outright hostility* ▷ *adv* **3** completely: *the film was banned outright* **4** instantly: *my driver was killed outright* **5** openly: *ask her outright why she treated you as she did*

outrun *vb* **-running, -ran, -run 1** to run faster or further than (someone) **2** to develop faster than (something): *the population of the city is in danger of outrunning the supply of houses*

outsell *vb* **-selling, -sold** to be sold in greater quantities than: *CDs are now outselling cassettes*

outset *n* a start; beginning: *we never really hit it off from the outset*

outshine *vb* **-shining, -shone** to be better than (someone) at something: *by university she had begun to outshine me in sports*

outside *prep* **1** on or to the exterior of: *a crowd gathered outside the court* **2** beyond the limits of: *it was outside my experience and beyond my ability* **3** apart from; other than: *no-one knows outside us* ▷ *adj* **4** on or of the outside: *an outside light is also a good idea* **5** remote; unlikely: *I still had an outside chance of the title* **6** coming from outside a particular group or organization: *the patient had been subjected to outside influences* **7** of or being the lane in a road which is further from the side than other lanes going in the same direction: *he was doing 120 in the outside lane* ▷ *adv* **8** outside a specified thing or place; out of doors: *we went outside to get some fresh air* **9** *slang* not in prison ▷ *n* **10** the external side or surface of something **11** at the outside *informal* at the very most: *I'll be away four days at the outside*

USAGE
The use of *outside of* and *inside of*, although fairly common, is generally thought to be incorrect or non-standard: *she waits outside (not outside of) the school.*

outside broadcast *n radio, television* a broadcast not made from a studio

outsider *n* **1** a person excluded from a group **2** a contestant thought unlikely to win

outsize *adj* **1** Also: **outsized** very large or larger than normal ▷ *n* **2** an outsize garment

outskirts *pl n* the parts of a town or city that are furthest from the centre: *an office in the northernmost outskirts of Glasgow*

outsmart *vb informal* same as **outwit**

outsource *vb* **1** to subcontract (work) to another company **2** to buy (components for a product) rather than manufacture them

outspan *S African n* **1** an area on a farm kept available for travellers to rest and refresh their animals ▷ *vb* **-spanning, -spanned 2** to unharness or unyoke (animals) **3** to relax
WORD ORIGIN Afrikaans *uit* out + *spannen* to stretch

outspoken *adj* **1** saying exactly what one thinks: *an outspoken critic of human rights abuses* **2** spoken candidly: *she is known for her outspoken views* **outspokenness** *n*

outspread *adj* spread or stretched out as far as possible: *a gull glided by with outspread wings*

outstanding *adj* **1** very good; excellent: *an outstanding performance* **2** still to be dealt with or paid: *outstanding bills; a few outstanding problems have to be put right* **3** very obvious or important: *there are significant exceptions, of which oil is the outstanding example* **outstandingly** *adv*

outstation *n* a station or post in a remote region

outstay *vb* same as **overstay**

outstretched *adj* extended or stretched out as far as possible: *he pushed a wad of drachma notes into the young man's outstretched hand*

outstrip *vb* **-stripping, -stripped 1** to surpass (someone) in a particular activity: *his newspapers outstrip all others in vulgarity* **2** to go faster than (someone)

outtake *n* an unreleased take from a recording session, film, or television programme

out there *adj slang* unconventional or eccentric

out-tray *n* a shallow basket in an office for collecting letters and documents that are to be sent out

outvote *vb* **-voting, -voted** to defeat (someone) by getting more votes than him or her

outward *adj* **1** apparent or superficial: *to outward appearances the house is largely unchanged today* **2** of or relating to the outside: *outward shape* **3** (of a journey) away from a place to which one intends to return ▷ *adv also* **outwards 4** in an outward direction; towards the outside **outwardly** *adv*

outweigh *vb* **1** to be more important, significant, or influential than: *these niggles are outweighed by the excellent cooking and service* **2** to be heavier than

outwit *vb* **-witting, -witted** to gain an advantage over (someone) by cunning or ingenuity

outworks *pl n mil* defences which lie outside the main fortifications of a fort etc.

outworn *adj* (of a belief or custom) old-fashioned and no longer of any use or relevance: *there is no point in pandering to outworn superstition*

ouzel or **ousel** (**ooze**-el) *n* same as **dipper** (sense 2)
WORD ORIGIN Old English *ōsle*

ouzo (**ooze**-oh) *n, pl* **ouzos** a strong aniseed-flavoured alcoholic drink from Greece
WORD ORIGIN Modern Greek *ouzon*

ova *n* the plural of **ovum**

oval *adj* **1** egg-shaped ▷ *n* **2** anything that is oval in shape, such as a sports ground
WORD ORIGIN Latin *ovum* egg

ovary *n, pl* **-ries 1** a reproductive organ in women and female animals in which eggs are produced **2** *bot* the lower part of a pistil, containing the ovules **ovarian** *adj*
WORD ORIGIN Latin *ovum* egg

ovate *adj* shaped like an egg: *the tree has bluish-green, ovate leaves*
WORD ORIGIN Latin *ovatus* egg-shaped

ovation *n* an enthusiastic round of applause
WORD ORIGIN Latin *ovatio* rejoicing

oven *n* **1** an enclosed heated compartment or container for baking or roasting food, or for drying or firing ceramics ▷ *vb* **2** to cook in an oven
WORD ORIGIN Old English *ofen*

over *prep* **1** directly above; across the top or upper surface of: *set the frying pan over a low heat* **2** on or to the other side of: *the pilot flew over the Channel* **3** during or throughout (a period of time): *over the next few months it became clear what was happening* **4** throughout the whole extent of: *the effects are being felt all over the country now* **5** by means of (an instrument of telecommunication): *there was an announcement over the Tannoy system* **6** more than: *she had met him over a year ago* **7** concerning; about: *there has been much argument over these figures* **8** while occupied in: *I'll tell you over dinner tonight* **9** having recovered from the effects of: *he appeared to be over his niggling injury problems* **10** all over someone *informal* extremely affectionate or attentive towards someone **11** over and above added to; in addition to ▷ *adv* **12** in a state, condition, or position over something: *to climb over* **13** onto its side: *the jug toppled over* **14** at or to a point across an intervening space: *she carried him over to the other side of the river* **15** covering the whole area: *there's poverty the world over* **16** from beginning to end: *to read a document over* **17** all over **a** finished **b** over one's entire body **c** typically: *that's him all over* **18** over again once more **19** over and over (again) repeatedly ▷ *interj* **20** (in signalling and radio) it is now your turn to speak ▷ *adj* **21** finished; no longer in progress: *the second round of voting is over* ▷ *adv* **22** remaining: *there wasn't any money left over* ▷ *adj* **23** surplus ▷ *n* **24** *cricket* **a** a series of six balls bowled by a bowler from the same end of the pitch **b** the play during this
WORD ORIGIN Old English *ofer*

O

over- *prefix* **1** excessive or excessively: *overcharge; overdue* **2** superior in rank: *overlord* **3** indicating location or movement above: *overhang* **4** indicating movement downwards: *overthrow*

overabundance *n* more than is really needed; excess

overact *vb* to act in an exaggerated way

overactive *adj* more active than is normal or desirable: *an overactive thyroid gland*

overall *adj* **1** from one end to the other: *the overall length* **2** including everything; total: *the overall cost* ▷ *adv* **3** in general; on the whole: *overall, I think this is the better car* ▷ *n* **4** Brit & NZ a coat-shaped work garment worn over ordinary clothes as a protection against dirt **5** **overalls** work trousers with a bib and braces or jacket attached, worn over ordinary clothes as a protection against dirt and wear

overambitious *adj* attempting more than one has the ability to do well: *good plain cookery marred by overambitious sauces*

overarching *adj* overall or all-encompassing: *an overarching concept*

overarm *sport adj* **1** bowled, thrown, or performed with the arm raised above the shoulder ▷ *adv* **2** with the arm raised above the shoulder

overawe *vb* **-awing, -awed** to affect (someone) with an overpowering sense of awe: *he was overawed by the prospect of meeting the Prime Minister*

overbalance *vb* **-lancing, -lanced** to lose one's balance

overbearing *adj* **1** imposing one's views in an unpleasant or forceful manner **2** of particular or overriding importance: *an overbearing need*

overblown *adj* inflated or excessive: *humiliation comes from having overblown expectations for yourself*

overboard *adv* **1** from a boat or ship into the water: *many passengers drowned when they jumped overboard to escape the flames* **2** **go overboard** *informal* **a** to be extremely enthusiastic **b** to go to extremes **3** **throw overboard** to reject or abandon (an idea or a plan)

overburden *vb* to have more of something than it is possible to cope with: *the city's streets are already overburdened by rush-hour motorists*

overcast *adj* (of the sky or weather) cloudy

overcharge *vb* **-charging, -charged** to charge too high a price

overcoat *n* a warm heavy coat worn in cold weather

overcome *vb* **-coming, -came, -come** **1** to deal successfully with or control (a problem or feeling): *once I'd overcome my initial nerves I discovered hang-gliding was great fun* **2** (of an emotion or a feeling) to affect (someone) strongly or make (someone) powerless: *he was overcome by a sudden surge of jealousy* **3** to defeat (someone) in a conflict

overcompensate *vb* **-sating, -sated** to attempt to make up for or cancel out (something) to an unnecessary degree: *when bookings dropped slightly, the company overcompensated by slashing the price of its holidays by 50%*

overconfident *adj* having more belief in one's abilities than is justified

overcook *vb* to spoil food by cooking it for too long

overcrowded *adj* containing more people or things than is desirable: *overcrowded commuter trains*

overcrowding *n* the cramming of too many people into too small a space: *prison overcrowding and poor conditions*

overdo *vb* **-does, -doing, -did, -done** **1** to do (something) to excess **2** to exaggerate (something) **3** to cook (something) too long **4** **overdo it** or **things** to do something to a greater degree than is advisable or healthy

overdose *n* **1** a larger dose of a drug than is safe: *she tried to kill herself with an overdose of alcohol and drugs* ▷ *vb* **-dosing, -dosed** **2** to take more of a drug than is safe, either accidentally or deliberately: *this drug is rarely prescribed because it is easy to overdose fatally on it*

overdraft *n* **1** the withdrawal of more money from a bank account than there is in it **2** the amount of money withdrawn thus

overdraw *vb* **-drawing, -drew, -drawn** to withdraw more money from a bank account than is in it

overdrawn *adj* **1** having overdrawn one's bank account **2** (of an account) in debit

overdressed *adj* wearing clothes which are too elaborate or formal for the occasion

overdrive *n* **1** a very high gear in a motor vehicle, used at high speeds to reduce wear **2** a state of great activity or excitement: *the government propaganda machine went into overdrive to try to play down the Minister's comments*

overdub *vb* **-dubbing, -dubbed** **1** to add (new sounds) to a tape in such a way that the old and the new sounds can be heard ▷ *n* **2** a sound or series of sounds added by this method

overdue *adj* **1** not having arrived or happened by the time expected or desired: *a reassessment of policy on this issue is long overdue* **2** (of money) not having been paid by the required date: *by this time his rent was three weeks overdue* **3** (of a library book) not having been returned to the library by the required date

overeat *vb* **-eating, -ate, -eaten** to eat more than is necessary or healthy

overemphasize or **-sise** *vb* **-sizing, -sized** or **-sising, -sised** to give (something) more importance than is necessary or appropriate

overestimate *vb* **-mating, -mated** to believe something or someone to be bigger, more important, or better than is the case **overestimation** *n*

overexcited *adj* excessively enthusiastic or agitated

overexert *vb* to exhaust or injure oneself by doing too much **overexertion** *n*

overexposed *adj* (of a photograph) too light in colour because the film has been exposed to light for too long

overfeed *vb* **-feeding, -fed** to give (a person, plant, or animal) more food than is necessary or healthy

overfill *vb* to put more into (something) than there is room for

overflow *vb* **-flowing, -flowed** or formerly **-flown 1** to flow over (a brim) **2** to be filled beyond capacity so as to spill over **3** **overflow with** to be filled with (an emotion): *a letter overflowing with passion and ardour* ▷ *n* **4** something that overflows, usually a liquid **5** an outlet that enables surplus liquid to be drained off **6** the amount by which a limit or capacity is exceeded ▷ *adj* **7** of or being a subsidiary thing for use when there is no room left in the main one: *an overflow car park*

overgraze *vb* **-grazing, -grazed** to graze (land) too intensively so that it is damaged and no longer provides nourishment

overgrown *adj* covered over with plants or weeds: *they headed up the overgrown and winding trail*

overhang *vb* **-hanging, -hung 1** to project or hang over beyond (something) ▷ *n* **2** an overhanging part or object

overhaul *vb* **1** to examine (a system or an idea) carefully for faults **2** to make repairs or adjustments to (a vehicle or machine) **3** to overtake (a vehicle or person) ▷ *n* **4** a thorough examination and repair

overhead *adj* **1** situated or operating above head height: *overhead compartments* ▷ *adv* **2** over or above head height: *the missile streaked overhead*

overhead projector *n* a projector that throws an enlarged image of a transparency onto a surface above and behind the person using it

overheads *pl n* the general costs of running a business, such as rent, electricity, and stationery

overhear *vb* **-hearing, -heard** to hear (a speaker or remark) unintentionally or without the knowledge of the speaker

overheat *vb* **1** to make or become too hot **2** to cause (an economy) to tend towards inflation **3** **become overheated** (of a person, discussion, etc.) to become angry or agitated: *the Colonel becomes overheated if he sees the term 'Ms' in the newspaper*

overindulge *vb* **-dulging, -dulged** to do too much of something pleasant, such as eating or drinking: *nobody ever wants a hangover, but we all overindulge occasionally* **overindulgence** *n*

overjoyed *adj* extremely pleased

overkill *n* any treatment that is greater than that required: *the overkill in negative propaganda resulted in this upsurge*

overlap *vb* **-lapping, -lapped 1** (of two things) to share part of the same space as or lie partly over (each other): *slice the meat and lay it in overlapping slices in a serving dish* **2** to coincide partly in time or subject: *their careers have overlapped for the last ten years* ▷ *n* **3** a part that overlaps **4** the amount or length of something overlapping

overlay *vb* **-laying, -laid 1** to cover (a surface) with an applied decoration: *a woollen cloth overlaid with gold and silver embroidery* ▷ *n* **2** something that is laid over something else; a covering **3** an

Please Reveal Today's Countdown Conundrum...

Some time in early 1982, somebody decided it would be a good idea to open a new television station with a remit to attract the under-35s by showing a game show based on words and numbers.

It was a decision that led some people to think the programme controllers at Channel 4 had taken leave of their senses, but from that first day, *Countdown* was one of the channel's most-watched programmes, and its popularity has hardly wavered in the thirty years or so since.

Countdown is a national institution. Can there be anyone in the country who has never settled down with a cup of tea to lose themselves in the comforting rhythm of letters games, numbers games, and conundrums, all set off by the familiar giant clock and the tickety-tockety tune?

The face most people still associate with *Countdown* is that of Richard Whiteley, the rather bumbly, pun-addicted presenter who was the programme's front man from the first edition until his death in 2005 at the age of 61. *Countdown* took this modest man from being an obscure local news reporter in Yorkshire to national fame, thanks to his warmth, his empathy with the viewers, and his cunning pretence of being not quite as bright as the contestants. And if it wasn't a pretence, well, it worked, and he was bright enough not to try and change it.

Countdown struggled for a while to fill the gap Richard left, with the next two presenters, both successful TV veterans, not quite fitting the bill. The punster in Richard would have enjoyed the fact that the French programme on which *Countdown* is based was called *Des Chiffres et Des Lettres*, and the British version has now had Des Lynam and Des O'Connor.

The programme has now found its feet again with Jeff Stelling as presenter, assisted by Rachel Riley, but our run-through the faces of *Countdown* would be incomplete without mentioning the woman who advanced to fame in tandem with Richard Whiteley. Carol Vorderman had never appeared on television before, but she exactly fitted the programme's need for a telegenic woman who could do maths – not a category in which most showbusiness agents' files are full to bursting. Carol's journey to megastardom on the basis of good looks and the ability to multiply 64 by seven has been a TV phenomenon. A natural performer who enjoyed warming up the elderly *Countdown* audience with a dirty joke, she is now a veteran of everything from laddish panel shows to the World Chess Championship.

The presenting team has always been backed up by two very important people, the occupiers of the rather tweely-named Dictionary Corner. One celebrity and one lexicographer search out the longest words and try to beat the contestants, a unique game-show twist. After various lexicographers were tried through the years, Susie Dent has now made the role her own, and has branched out into writing her own books on words.

Although contestants need to possess both linguistic and numerical skills to excel on *Countdown*, the rounds with letters are the ones most likely to appeal to word-lovers. Each letters round is played with a set of nine letters containing at least three vowels and four consonants. Contestants search their brains for the longest word out of this letter set, using each letter only once. As in the board game Scrabble, the frequency of each letter in the pile is determined by its frequency in the English language, so that S and T are common letters, but Q and Z are not. The Conundrum round is based on a nine-letter anagram which is often deliberately displayed as a fake compound word to mislead the contestants, eg *thinebear*. If the conundrum has more than one possible answer, then any of them are accepted, eg *hibernate* or *inbreathe*.

Of course, it would be wrong to talk only about the presenters and rules of this game show, for *Countdown* is really all about the contestants. The programme is only as good as those who play it, and it is they more than anyone who will carry it forward, anagramming and calculating on our digital plasma screens in the decades to come.

applied decoration or layer, for example of gold leaf

overleaf *adv* on the other side of the page

overlie *vb* **-lying, -lay, -lain** to lie on or cover (something or someone): *a thin layer of black dust overlay everything*

overload *vb* **1** to put too large a load on or in (something): *the aircraft was dangerously overloaded* **2** to cause (a transport system) to be unable to function properly because too many people or vehicles are using it: *Heathrow Airport was already overloaded by 1972* **3** to try to put more electricity through a system than the system can cope with ▷ *n* **4** an excessive load

overlook *vb* **1** to fail to notice (something) **2** to disregard or ignore (misbehaviour or a fault): *I'm prepared to overlook your failure, but don't do it again* **3** to give a view of (something) from above: *a cliff overlooking the Atlantic*

overlord *n* a supreme lord or master

overly *adv* too; excessively

overman *vb* **-manning, -manned** to provide with too many staff: *the company is not overmanned overall, but it has too many managers and not enough productive workers* **overmanned** *adj* **overmanning** *n*

overmuch *adv, adj* too much; very much

overnight *adv* **1** during the night **2** in or as if in the course of one night; suddenly: *we are not saying that a change like this would happen overnight* ▷ *adj* **3** done in, occurring in, or lasting the night: *the army has ordered an overnight curfew* **4** staying for one night: *overnight guests* **5** for use during a single night: *should I pack an overnight case?* **6** happening very quickly; sudden: *he doesn't expect the programme to be an overnight success*

overpaid *adj* earning more money than one deserves

overpass *n* same as **flyover**

overplay *vb* **1** to overemphasize (something) **2 overplay one's hand** to overestimate the worth or strength of one's position

overpopulated *adj* (of a town or country) having more people living in it than it can support

overpopulation *n* the state of being overpopulated

overpower *vb* **1** to conquer or subdue (someone) by superior force **2** to have such a strong effect on (someone) as to make him or her helpless or ineffective: *I was so appalled, so overpowered by my guilt and my shame that I was unable to speak* **overpowering** *adj*

overpriced *adj* costing more than it is thought to be worth

overprint *vb* **1** to print (additional matter or another colour) onto (something already printed) ▷ *n* **2** additional matter or another colour printed onto something already printed

overqualified *adj* having more professional or academic qualifications than are required for a job

overrate *vb* to have too high an opinion of: *the director's role was seriously overrated*

overreach *vb* **overreach oneself** to fail by trying to be too clever or achieve too

much: *he built up a successful media empire before he overreached himself and lost much of his fortune*

overreact *vb* to react more strongly or forcefully than is necessary: *allergies happen when the body overreacts to a harmless substance* **overreaction** *n*

override *vb* **-riding, -rode, -ridden 1** to set aside or disregard (a person or a person's decisions) by having superior authority or power: *the managing director can override any decision he doesn't like* **2** to be more important than or replace (something): *unsurprisingly the day-to-day struggle for survival overrode all moral considerations* **overriding** *adj*

overripe *adj* (of a fruit or vegetable) so ripe that it has started to decay or go soft

overrule *vb* **-ruling, -ruled 1** to reverse the decision of (a person or organization with less power): *the President overruled the hardliners in the party who wanted to use force* **2** to rule or decide against (an argument or decision): *the initial judgment was overruled by the Supreme Court*

overrun *vb* **-running, -ran, -run 1** to conquer (territory) rapidly by force of number **2** to spread over (a place) rapidly: *dirty tenements, overrun by lice, rats, and roaches* **3** to extend or run beyond a set limit: *Tuesday's lunch overran by three-quarters of an hour*

overseas *adv* **1** across the sea; abroad ▷ *adj* **2** of, to, from, or in a distant country or countries ▷ *n* **3** *informal* a foreign country or foreign countries collectively

oversee *vb* **-seeing, -saw, -seen** to watch over and direct (someone or something); supervise **overseer** *n*

oversell *vb* **-selling, -sold** to exaggerate the merits or abilities of

oversew *vb* **-sewing, -sewed, -sewn** or **-sewed** to sew (two edges) with stitches that pass over them both

oversexed *adj* more interested in sex than is thought decent

overshadow *vb* **1** to make (someone or something) seem insignificant or less important by comparison **2** to sadden the atmosphere of: *news of their team-mate's injury overshadowed the victory celebrations*

overshoe *n* a protective shoe worn over an ordinary shoe

overshoot *vb* **-shooting, -shot** to go beyond (a mark or target): *the plane overshot the main runway*

overshot *adj* (of a water wheel) driven by a flow of water that passes over the wheel

oversight *n* a mistake caused by not noticing something

oversimplify *vb* **-fies, -fying, -fied** to make something seem simpler than it really is: *the Nationalists' analysis oversimplifies the problems facing the country today*

oversized *adj* much larger than the usual size

oversleep *vb* **-sleeping, -slept** to sleep beyond the intended time for getting up

overspend *vb* **-spending, -spent** to spend more than one can afford

overspill *n* *Brit* the rehousing of people from crowded cities in smaller towns

overstate *vb* **-stating, -stated** to state (something) too strongly; overemphasize **overstatement** *n*

overstay *vb* **overstay one's welcome** to stay as a guest longer than one's host or hostess would like

overstayer *n* *NZ* a person who remains in New Zealand after their permit has expired

overstep *vb* **-stepping, -stepped 1** to go beyond the limits of what is thought acceptable: *he had overstepped his authority by acting without consulting his superiors* **2 overstep the mark** to go too far and behave in an unacceptable way

overstretch *vb* **1** to attempt to do more than there is time or capability for: *for the first time in her career she may have overstretched her talents* **2** to damage (something) by stretching it further than it can safely go: *he overstretched his Achilles tendon* **overstretched** *adj*

overstrung *adj* too highly strung; tense

overt *adj* done or shown in an open and obvious way: *jurors were now looking at the defendant with overt hostility* **overtly** *adv*

WORD ORIGIN Old French

overtake *vb* **-taking, -took, -taken 1** *chiefly Brit* to move past (another vehicle or person) travelling in the same direction **2** to do better than (someone) after catching up with him or her **3** to come upon (someone) suddenly or unexpectedly: *a mortal tiredness overtook him*

overtax *vb* **1** to impose too great a strain on: *a singer who had overtaxed her voice* **2** to tax (people) too heavily

over-the-top *adj* *slang* excessive; beyond the usual or acceptable bounds of behaviour

overthrow *vb* **-throwing, -threw, -thrown 1** to defeat and replace (a ruler or government) by force **2** to replace (standards or values) ▷ *n* **3** downfall or destruction: *the overthrow of the US-backed dictatorship*

overtime *n* **1** work at a regular job done in addition to regular working hours **2** pay for such work ▷ *adv* **3** in addition to one's regular working hours: *she had been working overtime and she fell asleep at the wheel*

overtone *n* **1** an additional meaning or hint: *I don't want to deny that from time to time there are political overtones* **2** *music, acoustics* any of the tones, with the exception of the principal or lowest one, that make up a musical sound

overture *n* **1** *music* **a** a piece of orchestral music played at the beginning of an opera, oratorio, ballet, musical comedy, or film, often containing the main musical themes of the work **b** a one-movement orchestral piece, usually having a descriptive or evocative title: *the 1812 Overture* **2 overtures** opening moves towards a new relationship or agreement: *the German government made a variety of friendly overtures towards the French*

WORD ORIGIN Late Latin *apertura* opening

overturn vb 1 to turn over or upside down 2 to overrule or reverse (a legal decision) 3 to overthrow or destroy (a government)

overuse vb 1 to use excessively ▷ n 2 excessive use

overvalue vb -valuing, -valued to regard (someone or something) as much more important or valuable than is the case: his approach overvalues hard work and undervalues true skill **overvalued** adj

overview n a general survey

overweening adj (of opinions or qualities) excessive or immoderate: your modesty is a cover for your overweening conceit **WORD ORIGIN** obsolete ween to think

overweight adj 1 (of a person) weighing more than is healthy 2 weighing more than is usual or permitted

overwhelm vb 1 to overpower the thoughts, emotions, or senses of (someone): we were overwhelmed with grief 2 to overcome (people) with irresistible force: gang violence has overwhelmed an ailing police force **overwhelming** adj **overwhelmingly** adv

overwork vb 1 to work too hard or too long 2 to use (something) too much: anti-communism was already being overworked by others ▷ n 3 excessive work

overwrite vb -writing, -wrote, -written 1 to record on a storage medium, such as a magnetic disk, thus destroying what was originally recorded there 2 to write (something) in an excessively ornate style

overwrought adj tense, nervous, and agitated

oviduct n anat the tube through which eggs are conveyed from an ovary **WORD ORIGIN** Latin ovum egg + ducere to lead

oviform adj biol shaped like an egg **WORD ORIGIN** Latin ovum egg + forma shape

ovine adj of or like a sheep **WORD ORIGIN** Latin ovis sheep

oviparous (oh-**vip**-par-uss) adj zool producing eggs that hatch outside the body of the mother **WORD ORIGIN** Latin ovum egg + -parus bearing

ovoid (**oh**-void) adj egg-shaped

ovulate (**ov**-yew-late) vb -lating, -lated biol to produce or release eggs from an ovary **ovulation** n

ovule n 1 bot the part of a plant that contains the egg cell and develops into the seed after fertilization 2 zool an immature ovum **WORD ORIGIN** Latin ovum egg

ovum (**oh**-vum) n, pl **ova** an unfertilized female egg cell **WORD ORIGIN** Latin: egg

owe vb owing, owed 1 to be under an obligation to pay an amount of money to (someone): he owes me a lot of money 2 to feel an obligation to do or give: I think I owe you an apology 3 **owe something to** to have something as a result of: many serving officers owe their present position to the former president **WORD ORIGIN** Old English āgan to have

owing adj 1 not yet paid; due: the bailiffs seized goods worth far more than the amount owing 2 **owing to** because of; as a result of: the flight was delayed owing to fog

owl n a bird of prey which has a flat face, large eyes, and a small hooked beak, and which is active at night **owlish** adj **WORD ORIGIN** Old English ūle

own adj (preceded by a possessive) 1 used to emphasize that something belongs to a particular person: rely on your own instincts ▷ pron (preceded by a possessive) 2 the one or ones belonging to a particular person: I had one of my own 3 the people that someone feels loyalty to, esp. relations: we all look after our own around here 4 **come into one's own** to fulfil one's potential 5 **hold one's own** to have the necessary ability to deal successfully with a situation: he chose a partner who could hold her own with the best 6 **on one's own** a without help: you'll never manage to lift that on your own b by oneself; alone: he lives on his own in a flat in town ▷ vb 7 to have (something) as one's possession: he owns homes in four countries 8 Also: **own up to** to confess or admit: I own I could not bear to think of it; I thought she was going to own up to an affair **owner** n **ownership** n **WORD ORIGIN** Old English āgen

owner-occupier n someone who owns the house in which he or she lives

ownership flat n NZ a flat owned by the occupier

own goal n 1 soccer a goal scored by a player accidentally playing the ball into his or her own team's net 2 informal any action that results in disadvantage to the person who took it or to his or her associates: the minister's admission was the latest in a series of own goals by the government

ox n, pl **oxen** a castrated bull used for pulling heavy loads and for meat **WORD ORIGIN** Old English oxa

oxalic acid n a colourless poisonous acid found in many plants **WORD ORIGIN** Latin oxalis garden sorrel

oxbow lake n a crescent-shaped lake on the flood plain of a river and constituting the remnant of a former meander

Oxbridge n Brit the British universities of Oxford and Cambridge considered together

oxen n the plural of **ox**

Oxfam Oxford Committee for Famine Relief

oxidation n the act or process of oxidizing

oxide n chem a compound of oxygen with another element **WORD ORIGIN** French

oxidize or **-dise** vb -dizing, -dized or -dising, -dised to react chemically with oxygen, as in burning or rusting **oxidization** or **-disation** n

Oxon Oxfordshire

Oxon. (in degree titles) of Oxford University **WORD ORIGIN** Latin Oxoniensis

oxtail n the tail of an ox, used in soups and stews

oxyacetylene n a mixture of oxygen and acetylene, used in blowlamps for cutting or welding metals at high temperatures

oxygen n chem a colourless, odourless gaseous element essential to life processes and to combustion. Symbol: O **WORD ORIGIN** Greek oxus sharp + -genēs producing: from former belief that all acids contained oxygen

oxygenate vb -nating, -nated to add oxygen to: to oxygenate blood

oxygen mask n a small bowl-shaped object which is connected via a pipe to a cylinder of oxygen and can be placed over a person's nose and mouth to help him or her breathe

oxygen tent n med a transparent enclosure covering a bedridden patient, into which oxygen is released to aid breathing

oxymoron (ox-see-**more**-on) n a figure of speech that combines two apparently contradictory terms, for example cruel kindness **WORD ORIGIN** Greek oxus sharp + mōros stupid

oyez or **oyes** interj a cry usually uttered three times by a public crier or court official calling for silence and attention **WORD ORIGIN** Old French oiez! hear!

oyster n 1 an edible shellfish, some types of which produce pearls 2 **the world is your oyster** you are in a position where there is every possible chance of personal advancement and satisfaction ▷ adj 3 greyish-white **WORD ORIGIN** Greek ostreon

oystercatcher n a wading bird with black-and-white plumage and a long stout red bill

oz or **oz.** ounce **WORD ORIGIN** Italian onza

Oz n slang Australia

ozone n 1 a form of oxygen with a strong odour, formed by an electric discharge in the atmosphere 2 informal clean bracing air, as found at the seaside **WORD ORIGIN** Greek ozein to smell

ozone layer n a layer of ozone in the upper atmosphere that absorbs harmful ultraviolet rays from the sun

O

Pp

The letter P is the sixteenth letter of the English alphabet. The Greek equivalent of this letter is *pi* (Π,π), which was derived from the Hebrew and Phoenician letter called *peh*, meaning literally 'mouth'.

The Greeks found it easy to enunciate this letter before the consonants S and T. This is less natural for speakers of English, and so the P is treated as a silent letter in some words derived from the Greek, such as 'pterodactyl' and 'psychology'.

The Roman alphabet eschewed the shape of the Greek *pi*, and took its letter P instead from the Etruscan alphabet, which had used an alternative, more rounded, form of the Phoenician letter *peh* to represent the /p/ sound. In its original form, the loop at the top of the stem faced to the left, but the Romans turned the letter around to give the familiar modern form of P.

In its lower-case form, P has a descending line and is almost a mirror image of the lower-case form of Q. The potential for confusing these letters may have been the original reason why people are cautioned about their behaviour by being advised to 'mind their p's and q's'.

The letter P is a distinctive feature in certain Celtic languages, such as Welsh and Breton, occurring in places where the other languages of the family characteristically use a Q or C. Hence languages such as Welsh are referred to by linguists as 'P-Celtic', while the languages which do not exhibit this feature are called 'Q-Celtic'.

On road signs, a white letter P on a blue background has become an iconic symbol for a parking area. This sign is likely to be more welcome to drivers than a green letter P on a white background, as displayed by recently qualified drivers in some countries (the letter P here standing for 'probationary').

British taxpayers associate the letter P with certain forms issued by the Inland Revenue as part of its Pay-As-You-Earn system. The notorious P45 form is given to workers who leave their employment before the end of the tax year, so that 'getting your P45' is a roundabout way of talking about getting the sack. For anyone who manages to get to the end of a tax year without incurring this misfortune, the reward is a different form called a P60.

---

p *or* **P** *n, pl* **p's, P's** *or* **Ps 1** the 16th letter of the English alphabet **2 mind one's p's and q's** to be careful to behave correctly and use polite language

p 1 *Brit, Austral, & NZ* penny **2** *Brit* pence

P 1 *chem* phosphorus **2** (on road signs) parking **3** *chess* pawn

p. 1 *pl* **pp.** page **2** per

pa¹ *n informal* father

pa² *n NZ* (formerly) a fortified Māori settlement

Pa 1 *chem* protactinium **2** *physics* pascal

PA 1 Pennsylvania **2** personal assistant **3** public-address system

p.a. yearly
> **WORD ORIGIN** Latin *per annum*

pace¹ *n* **1 a** a single step in walking **b** the length of a step **2** speed of walking or running **3** speed of doing some other activity: *efforts to accelerate the pace of change are unlikely to succeed* **4** manner of walking **5 keep pace with** to advance at the same speed as **6 put someone through his** *or* **her paces** to test someone's ability **7 set the pace** to determine the speed at which a group advances ▷ *vb* **pacing, paced 8** to walk with regular steps, often in anxiety or impatience: *he paced up and down the foyer*

impatiently **9** to set the speed for (the competitors) in a race **10 pace out** to measure by paces
> **WORD ORIGIN** Latin *passus* step

pace² *prep* with due respect to: used to express polite disagreement
> **WORD ORIGIN** Latin, from *pax* peace

pacemaker *n* **1** an electronic device positioned in the body, next to the heart, to regulate the heartbeat **2** a competitor who, by leading a race, causes it to be run at a particular speed

pachyderm (**pak-**ee-durm) *n* a large thick-skinned mammal, such as an elephant or rhinoceros
> **WORD ORIGIN** Greek *pakhus* thick + *derma* skin

pacific *adj formal* tending to bring peace; non-aggressive; peaceful
> **WORD ORIGIN** Latin *pax* peace + *facere* to make

Pacific *adj* of the Pacific Ocean, the world's largest and deepest ocean, lying between Asia and Australia and America, or its islands

pacifier *n US & Canad* a baby's dummy

pacifist *n* a person who is totally opposed to violence and refuses to take part in war **pacifism** *n*

pacify *vb* **-fies, -fying, -fied** to soothe or calm **pacification** *n*
> **WORD ORIGIN** Old French *pacifier*; see PACIFIC

pack¹ *n* **1** a bundle or load carried on the back **2** *Brit & NZ* a complete set of playing cards **3** a group of animals that hunt together: *a pack of hounds* **4** *rugby* the forwards of a team **5** any collection of people or things: *a pack of lies* **6** *chiefly US & Canad* same as **packet** (sense 1) **7** an organized group of Cub Scouts or Brownie Guides **8** same as **rucksack** or **backpack 9** Also called: **face pack** a cream treatment that cleanses and tones the skin ▷ *vb* **10** to put (articles) in a case or container for moving **11** to roll (articles) up into a bundle **12** to press tightly together; cram: *thousands of people packed into the city's main square* **13** (foll. by *off*) to send away hastily: *their young son came in to say good night and was packed off to bed* **14** *slang* to be able to deliver a specified amount of unexpected or violent force or power: *the film's unexpected ending packs quite a punch* **15** *US informal* to carry (a gun) habitually **16 send someone packing** *informal* to dismiss someone abruptly ▸ See also **pack in, pack up**
> **WORD ORIGIN** origin unknown

James Ellroy

James Ellroy, born Lee Earle Ellroy in Los Angeles in 1948, is best known for his crime writing as an obsessive chronicler of 'white men doing bad things in the name of authority'. His novels use multiple perspectives from intersecting characters on both sides of the law, most of whom are driven by trauma and all of whom wrestle with their own weaknesses, vices, and psychoses.

Ellroy's ascent to his current status as self-described 'Demon Dog of American Literature' began with contemporary crime fiction (his first novel *Brown's Requiem*, and the Lloyd Hopkins trilogy) and continued through his celebrated and bestselling 'LA Quartet' (*The Black Dahlia*, *The Big Nowhere*, *LA Confidential*, and *White Jazz* – all set in 1940s and 1950s Los Angeles). He has more recently moved from crime fiction to the historical novel with the 'Underworld USA' trilogy – comprising *American Tabloid*, *The Cold Six Thousand*, and *Blood's A Rover*. His crime fiction is complemented by true crime writings. The most significant of these are biographical and focus on his mother's own murder when he was ten years old. This event informed his life and writing and fed his fixation with crime. The circumstances mirrored the infamous Black Dahlia case, an unsolved murder which formed the basis of his first novel in his fictional LA Quartet (Ellroy also wrote an account of the reopening of the investigation into his mother's death as *My Dark Places*).

The most distinctive feature of Ellroy's writing is his 'telegraphic' style, using short, declarative sentences with little or no expository language. And no compound sentences. Ellroy also peppers his prose with a dizzying blend of outdated underworld cant, hepcat jazz slang, and brutal bullet-point police procedural jargon. The telegraphic approach had a practical basis: Ellroy's agent had asked him to drastically cut down a draft of *LA Confidential*, and his harsh pruning gave the book a phonetic feel.

Ellroy's inside knowledge of criminal vocabulary was developed during a period of delinquency in his youth, which led to several short periods of incarceration. His writing features numerous examples, some of which are familiar pulp staples such as *blue* or *bull* meaning 'police officer', *brace* meaning 'interrogate', and *hinky* as 'suspicious'. Yiddish is a source of other terms, for instance *ganef* (thief) and *gunsel* (armed criminal), while *glom* (meaning to perceive or pick up an idea, differing from its original meaning of to steal or grab) is most likely from the Scots word *glam*, to snatch at. Despite *glom*'s change in meaning, Ellroy's works still feature a vast array of synonyms for 'steal' (as befits any criminal slang, its purpose being to disguise the intention of the speaker) including *boost*, *filch*, and *kipe* (from Old Norse *kippa* via now-obsolete 13th-century English *kip*).

To fully formulate his stylistic approach, Ellroy combined his staccato prose and underworld lexicon with the alliterative, innuendo-strewn language of Hollywood gossip magazines from the 1940s and 1950s, the most (in)famous of which was *Confidential*.

Most of his works address the public hunger for an insight into the minutiae of celebrity lives and (especially) their sexual peccadilloes. This perverse intrigue is tempered by his own moral outrage and unflinching self-analysis, exhibited in *My Dark Places*, *Crime Wave*, and his essay on his pre-sobriety self *My Life As A Creep*.

Ellroy's early literary influences were from diverse sources, comprising tabloid magazines and the Bible. He at first read Raymond Chandler, but gradually came to identify more with Dashiell Hammett's protagonists: morally compromised men who operated in corrupt systems ('Chandler wrote the kind of man he wanted to be, and Hammett wrote the kind of man he was afraid he was'). Joseph Wambaugh also had a major impact: 'He made me ashamed of my life. Not enough to change it.'

Ellroy attempts to strip down the sentence to its bare essentials. This makes him a formidable experimental writer. His style continues to develop into even more extreme forms of sentence compression, and in his most recent collection of essays *Destination: Morgue!* alliteration becomes art form. He states his future ambitions thus: 'I want to write Great American Novels. Plural.'

pack² *vb* to fill (a committee, jury, or audience) with one's own supporters **WORD ORIGIN** perhaps from *pact*

package *n* **1** a small parcel **2** Also: **package deal** a deal in which separate items are presented together as a unit **3** *US & Canad* same as **packet** (sense 1) ▷ *vb* **-aging, -aged 4** to put (something) into a package **packaging** *n*

package holiday *n* a holiday in which everything is arranged by one company for a fixed price

packet *n* **1** a container, together with its contents: *a packet of crisps* **2** a small parcel **3** Also: **packet boat** a boat that transports mail, passengers, or goods on a fixed short route **4** *slang* a large sum of money: *she was paid a packet* **5** *computers* a unit into which a larger piece of data is broken down for more efficient transmission **WORD ORIGIN** Old French *pacquet*

packhorse *n* a horse used to carry goods

pack ice *n* a large area of floating ice, consisting of pieces that have become massed together

pack in *vb informal* to stop doing (something): *I'm going to pack it in and resign*

packing *n* material, such as paper or plastic, used to protect packed goods

packsack *n* the US and Canadian word for **haversack**

packthread *n* a strong thread for sewing or tying up packages

pack up *vb* **1** to put (articles) in a bag or case before leaving **2** *informal* to stop doing (something) **3** (of a machine) to break down

pact *n* a formal agreement between two or more parties **WORD ORIGIN** Latin *pactum*

pad¹ *n* **1** a thick piece of soft material used for comfort, shape, protection, or absorption **2** a number of sheets of paper fastened together along one edge **3** the fleshy cushioned underpart of an animal's paw **4** a level area or flat-topped structure, from which rockets are launched or helicopters take off **5** the floating leaf of the water lily **6** *slang* a person's residence ▷ *vb* **padding, padded 7** to fill (something) out with soft material for comfort, shape, or protection **8 pad out** to lengthen (a speech or piece of writing) with unnecessary words or pieces of information **WORD ORIGIN** origin unknown

pad² *vb* **padding, padded 1** to walk with a soft or muffled step **2** to travel (a route) on foot: *men padding the streets in cheap sneakers* **WORD ORIGIN** Middle Dutch *pad* path

padded cell *n* a room with padded walls in a psychiatric hospital, in which patients who are likely to injure themselves are placed

padding *n* **1** any soft material used to pad something **2** unnecessary information put into a speech or written work to make it longer

paddle¹ *n* **1** a short light oar with a flat blade at one or both ends **2** a paddle wheel used to move a boat **3** a blade of

a water wheel or paddle wheel ▷ *vb* **-dling, -dled 1** to move (a boat) with a paddle **5** to swim with short rapid strokes, like a dog **6** *US & Canad informal* to spank **WORD ORIGIN** origin unknown

paddle² *vb* **-dling, -dled 1** to walk barefoot in shallow water **2** to dabble (one's fingers, hands, or feet) in water ▷ *n* **3** the act of paddling in water **WORD ORIGIN** origin unknown

paddle steamer *n* a ship propelled by paddle wheels turned by a steam engine

paddle wheel *n* a large wheel fitted with paddles, turned by an engine to propel a ship

paddock *n* **1** a small enclosed field for horses **2** (in horse racing) the enclosure in which horses are paraded and mounted before a race **3** *Austral & NZ* any area of fenced land **WORD ORIGIN** Old English *pearruc* enclosure

paddy¹ *n, pl* **-dies 1** Also: **paddy field** a field planted with rice **2** rice as a growing crop or when harvested but not yet milled **WORD ORIGIN** Malay *pādī*

paddy² *n, pl* **-dies** *Brit & NZ informal* a fit of temper **WORD ORIGIN** from *Paddy*, informal name for an Irishman

pademelon, paddymelon (**pad**-ee-mel-an) *n* a small Australian wallaby

padkos (**pudd**-koss) *n S African* snacks and provisions for a journey **WORD ORIGIN** Afrikaans, literally: road food

padlock *n* **1** a detachable lock with a hinged hoop fastened through a ring on the object to be secured ▷ *vb* **2** to fasten (something) with a padlock **WORD ORIGIN** origin unknown

padre (**pah**-dray) *n informal* a chaplain to the armed forces **WORD ORIGIN** via Spanish or Italian from Latin *pater* father

paean (**pee**-an) *n literary* an expression of praise or joy **WORD ORIGIN** Greek *paian* hymn to Apollo

paediatrician *or US* **pediatrician** *n* a doctor who specializes in children's diseases

paediatrics *or US* **pediatrics** *n* the branch of medicine concerned with children and their diseases **paediatric** *or US* **pediatric** *adj* **WORD ORIGIN** Greek *pais*, *paid-* child + *iatros* physician

paedophile *or US* **pedophile** *n* a person who is sexually attracted to children

paedophilia *or US* **pedophilia** *n* the condition of being sexually attracted to children **WORD ORIGIN** Greek *pais*, *paid-* child + *philos* loving

paella (pie-**ell**-a) *n* a Spanish dish made from rice, shellfish, chicken, and vegetables **WORD ORIGIN** Catalan

pagan *adj* **1** having, being, or relating to religious beliefs, esp. ancient ones,

which are not part of any of the world's major religions: *this was the site of a pagan temple to the sun* **2** irreligious ▷ *n* **3** a person who does not belong to any of the world's major religions **4** a person without any religion **paganism** *n* **WORD ORIGIN** Church Latin *paganus* civilian (hence not a soldier of Christ)

page¹ *n* **1** one side of one of the leaves of a book, newspaper, or magazine **2** one of the leaves of a book, newspaper, or magazine **3** *literary* a period or event: *a new page in the country's political history* **4** a screenful of information from a website or teletext service **WORD ORIGIN** Latin *pagina*

page² *n* **1** a small boy who attends a bride at her wedding **2** a youth employed to run errands for the guests in a hotel or club **3** *medieval history* a boy in training for knighthood ▷ *vb* **paging, paged 4** to summon (a person), by bleeper or loudspeaker, in order to pass on a message **WORD ORIGIN** Greek *pais* child

pageant *n* **1** an outdoor show portraying scenes from history **2** any magnificent display or procession **WORD ORIGIN** perhaps from Latin *pagina* scene of a play

pageantry *n* spectacular display or ceremony

pageboy *n* **1** a hairstyle in which the hair is smooth and the same medium length with the ends curled under **2** same as **page²** (senses 1, 2)

pagination *n* the numbering in sequence of the pages of a book or manuscript **paginate** *vb*

pagoda *n* a pyramid-shaped Asian temple or tower **WORD ORIGIN** Portuguese *pagode*

paid *vb* **1** past of **pay 2 put paid to** to end or destroy: *a knee injury put paid to his promising sporting career*

pail *n* **1** a bucket **2** Also called: **pailful** the amount contained in a pail: *a pail of water* **WORD ORIGIN** Old English *pægel*

pain *n* **1** physical hurt or discomfort caused by injury or illness **2** emotional suffering **3** Also called: **pain in the neck** *informal* a person or thing that is annoying or irritating **4 on pain of** subject to the penalty of: *orders which their soldiers were bound to follow on pain of death* ▷ *vb* **5** to cause (a person) physical or mental suffering **6** *informal* to annoy; irritate ▸ See also **pains** ▷ **painless** *adj* **WORD ORIGIN** Latin *poena* punishment

pained *adj* having or suggesting pain or distress: *a pained look*

painful *adj* **1** causing pain or distress: *painful inflammation of the joints; he began the painful task of making funeral arrangements* **2** affected with pain: *the symptoms include fever and painful joints* **3** tedious or difficult: *the hours passed with painful slowness* **4** *informal* extremely bad: *a painful so-called comedy* **painfully** *adv*

painkiller *n* a drug that relieves pain

pains *pl n* care or trouble: *they are at great pains to appear realistic and responsible*

painstaking *adj* extremely careful and thorough **painstakingly** *adv*

paint *n* **1** a coloured substance, spread on a surface with a brush or a roller, that forms a hard coating **2** a dry film of paint on a surface **3** *informal* face make-up ▷ *vb* **4** to apply paint to paper or canvas to make a picture of **5** to coat (a surface) with paint **6** to describe vividly in words: *the survey paints a dismal picture of growing hunger and disease* **7** to apply make-up to (the face) **8** to apply (liquid) to (a surface): *paint the varnish on and leave it to dry for at least four hours* **9 paint the town red** *informal* to celebrate in a lively way
WORD ORIGIN Latin *pingere* to paint

paintbrush *n* a brush used to apply paint

painted lady *n* a butterfly with pale brownish-red mottled wings

painter¹ *n* **1** an artist who paints pictures **2** a person who paints surfaces of buildings as a trade

painter² *n* a rope attached to the bow of a boat for tying it up
WORD ORIGIN probably from Old French *penteur* strong rope

painting *n* **1** a picture produced by using paint **2** the art of producing pictures by applying paints to paper or canvas **3** the act of applying paint to a surface

paintwork *n* the covering of paint on parts of a vehicle, building, etc.: *someone had damaged the Porsche by scraping a key along its paintwork*

pair *n* **1** two identical or similar things matched for use together: *a pair of shoes* **2** two people, animals, or things used or grouped together: *a pair of tickets* **3** an object consisting of two identical or similar parts joined together: *a pair of jeans* **4** a male and a female animal of the same species kept for breeding purposes **5** *parliament* two opposed members who both agree not to vote on a specified motion **6** two playing cards of the same denomination **7** one member of a matching pair: *I can't find the pair to this glove* ▷ *vb* **8** to group (people or things) in twos **9 pair off** to separate into groups of two
WORD ORIGIN Latin *par* equal
≡ **USAGE**
≡ Like other collective nouns, *pair* takes
≡ a singular or a plural verb according
≡ to whether it is seen as a unit or as a
≡ collection of two things: *the pair are said*
≡ *to dislike each other; a pair of good shoes is*
≡ *essential.*

paisley pattern *or* **paisley** *n* a detailed pattern of small curving shapes, used in fabric
WORD ORIGIN after *Paisley*, town in Scotland

pajamas *pl n* US pyjamas

pakeha (**pah**-kee-hah) *n, pl* **pakeha** *or* **pakehas** NZ a person of European descent, as distinct from a Māori
WORD ORIGIN Māori

Paki *Brit slang, offensive n* **1** a Pakistani or person of Pakistani descent ▷ *adj* **2** Pakistani or of Pakistani descent

Pakistani *adj* **1** of Pakistan ▷ *n* **2** a person from Pakistan

pal *informal n* **1** a close friend ▷ *vb* **palling, palled 2 pal up with** to become friends with
WORD ORIGIN Romany: brother

palace *n* **1** the official residence of a king, queen, president, or archbishop **2** a large and richly furnished building
WORD ORIGIN Latin *Palatium* Palatine, the site of the palace of the emperors in Rome

paladin *n* **1** one of the legendary twelve peers of Charlemagne's court **2** (formerly) a knight who did battle for a king or queen
WORD ORIGIN Italian *paladino*

palaeo- *or US* **paleo-** *combining form* old, ancient, or prehistoric: *palaeobotany*

Palaeocene *or US* **Paleocene** (**pal**-ee-oh-seen) *adj geol* of the epoch of geological time about 65 million years ago
WORD ORIGIN Greek *palaeo-* ancient + *kainos* new

palaeography *or US* **paleography** (pal-ee-**og**-ra-fee) *n* the study of ancient handwriting
WORD ORIGIN Greek *palaeo-* ancient + -GRAPHY

Palaeolithic *or US* **Paleolithic** (pal-ee-oh-**lith**-ik) *adj* of the period from about 2.5 to 3 million years ago until about 12 000 BC, during which primitive man emerged and unpolished chipped stone tools were made
WORD ORIGIN Greek *palaeo-* ancient + *lithos* stone

palaeontology *or US* **paleontology** (pal-ee-on-**tol**-a-jee) *n* the study of past geological periods and fossils **palaeontologist** *or US* **paleontologist** *n*
WORD ORIGIN Greek *palaeo-* ancient + *ōn, ont-* being + -LOGY

Palaeozoic *or US* **Paleozoic** (pal-ee-oh-**zoh**-ik) *adj geol* of the geological era that lasted from about 600 million years ago to 230 million years ago
WORD ORIGIN Greek *palaeo-* ancient + *zōion* animal

Palagi (pa-**lang**-gee) *n, pl* **-gis** NZ the Samoan name for a Pakeha

palanquin (pal-an-**keen**) *n* (formerly, in the Orient) a covered bed in which someone could be carried on the shoulders of four men
WORD ORIGIN Portuguese *palanquim*

palatable *adj* **1** (of food or drink) pleasant to taste **2** (of an experience or idea) acceptable or satisfactory

palate *n* **1** the roof of the mouth **2** the sense of taste: *a range of dishes to tempt every palate*
WORD ORIGIN Latin *palatum*
≡ **USAGE**
≡ Avoid confusion with **palette** or
≡ **pallet.**

palatial *adj* like a palace; magnificent: *his palatial home*

palatinate *n* a territory ruled by a palatine prince or noble or a count palatine

palatine *adj* possessing royal prerogatives: *a count palatine*
WORD ORIGIN Latin *palatium* palace

palaver (pal-**lah**-ver) *n* time-consuming fuss: *all the palaver involved in obtaining a visa*
WORD ORIGIN Portuguese *palavra* talk

palazzo pants *pl n* women's trousers with very wide legs
WORD ORIGIN Italian *palazzo* palace

pale¹ *adj* **1** (of a colour) whitish and not very strong: *pale yellow* **2** (of a complexion) having a whitish appearance, usually because of illness, shock, or fear **3** lacking brightness or colour: *the pale, chill light of an October afternoon* ▷ *vb* **paling, paled 4** to become pale or paler: *the girl paled at the news* **paleness** *n*
WORD ORIGIN Latin *pallidus*

pale² *n* **1** a wooden post used in fences **2 a** a fence made of pales **b** a boundary **3 beyond the pale** outside the limits of social convention: *the destruction of forests is beyond the pale*
WORD ORIGIN Latin *palus* stake

paleface *n* an offensive term for a White person, said to have been used by Native Americans of N America

Palestinian *adj* **1** of Palestine, an area in the Middle East between the Jordan River and the Mediterranean ▷ *n* **2** an Arab from this area, esp. one living in Israel or Israeli-occupied territory or as a refugee

palette *n* **1** a flat board used by artists to mix paints **2** the range of colours characteristic of a particular artist or school of painting: *he uses a cool palette with no strong red* **3** the range of colours or patterns that can be displayed on the visual display unit of a computer
WORD ORIGIN French
≡ **USAGE**
≡ Avoid confusion with **palate** or **pallet.**

palette knife *n* a spatula with a thin flexible blade used in painting or cookery

palindrome *n* a word or phrase that reads the same backwards or forwards, such as *able was I ere I saw Elba*
WORD ORIGIN Greek *palindromos* running back again

paling *n* **1** a fence made of pales **2** pales collectively **3** a single pale

palisade *n* **1** a fence made of stakes driven into the ground **2** one of the stakes used in such a fence
WORD ORIGIN Latin *palus* stake

pall¹ *n* **1** a cloth spread over a coffin **2** a coffin at a funeral ceremony **3** a dark heavy covering: *a pall of smoke and dust hung in the air* **4** a depressing atmosphere: *a pall hung on them all after his death*
WORD ORIGIN Latin *pallium* cloak

pall² *vb* to become boring or uninteresting, esp. by continuing for too long: *any pleasure had palled long before the two-hour programme was over*
WORD ORIGIN variant of *appal*

Palladian *adj* of a style of architecture characterized by symmetry and the revival and development of ancient Roman styles
WORD ORIGIN after Andrea *Palladio*, Italian architect

palladium *n chem* a rare silvery-white element of the platinum metal group, used in jewellery. Symbol: Pd
WORD ORIGIN after the asteroid *Pallas*

pallbearer *n* a person who helps to carry or who escorts the coffin at a funeral

pallet[1] *n* a straw-filled mattress or bed
WORD ORIGIN Latin *palea* straw

pallet[2] *n* **1** a tool with a flat, sometimes flexible, blade used for shaping pottery **2** a portable platform for storing and moving goods
WORD ORIGIN Latin *pala* spade

≡ USAGE
≡ Avoid confusion with **palate** or **palette**.

palliasse *n* a straw-filled mattress; pallet
WORD ORIGIN French *paillasse*

palliate *vb* -ating, -ated **1** to lessen the severity of (pain or disease) without curing it **2** to cause (an offence) to seem less serious
WORD ORIGIN Latin *pallium* a cloak

palliative *adj* **1** relieving without curing ▷ *n* **2** something that palliates, such as a sedative drug **3** something that alleviates or lessens a problem: *equal pay was a palliative for the growing unrest among women*

pallid *adj* **1** lacking colour, brightness, or vigour: *a pallid autumn sun* **2** lacking energy or vitality; insipid: *many militants find the party's socialism too pallid*
WORD ORIGIN Latin *pallidus*

pallor *n* paleness of complexion, usually because of illness, shock, or fear
WORD ORIGIN Latin: whiteness

pally *adj* -lier, -liest *informal* on friendly terms

palm[1] *n* **1** the inner surface of the hand from the wrist to the base of the fingers **2** the part of a glove that covers the palm **3 in the palm of one's hand** at one's mercy or command: *he had the jury in the palm of his hand* ▷ *vb* **4** to hide (something) in the hand: *he palmed the key* ▶ See also **palm off**
WORD ORIGIN Latin *palma*

palm[2] *or* **palm tree** *n* a tropical or subtropical tree with a straight unbranched trunk crowned with long pointed leaves
WORD ORIGIN Latin *palma*, from the likeness of its spreading fronds to a hand

palmate *adj* shaped like an open hand: *palmate leaves*

palmetto *n, pl* -tos a small palm tree with fan-shaped leaves
WORD ORIGIN Spanish *palmito* a little palm

palmistry *n* fortune-telling by examining the lines and bumps of the hand **palmist** *n*

palm off *vb* **1** to get rid of (someone or something) by passing it on to another: *the risk has to be shared with subcontractors, not simply palmed off on them* **2** to divert (someone) by a lie or excuse: *Mark was palmed off with a series of excuses*

palm oil *n* an oil obtained from the fruit of certain palm trees, used as an edible fat and in soap

Palm Sunday *n* the Sunday before Easter

palmtop *adj* (of a computer) small enough to be held in the hand

palmy *adj* palmier, palmiest **1** successful, prosperous and happy: *the palmy days of youth* **2** covered with palm trees: *palmy beaches*

palomino *n, pl* -nos a golden or cream horse with a white mane and tail
WORD ORIGIN Spanish: dovelike

palpable *adj* **1** obvious: *palpable nonsense* **2** (of a feeling or an atmosphere) so intense that it seems capable of being touched: *an air of palpable gloom hung over him* **palpably** *adv*
WORD ORIGIN Latin *palpare* to touch

palpate *vb* -pating, -pated *med* to examine (an area of the body) by touching **palpation** *n*
WORD ORIGIN Latin *palpare* to stroke

palpitate *vb* -tating, -tated **1** (of the heart) to beat rapidly **2** to flutter or tremble **palpitation** *n*
WORD ORIGIN Latin *palpitare*

palsy (**pawl**-zee) *n pathol* paralysis of a specified type: *cerebral palsy* **palsied** *adj*
WORD ORIGIN Old French *paralisie*

paltry *adj* -trier, -triest insignificant
WORD ORIGIN Low Germanic *palter*, *paltrig* ragged

pampas *n* the extensive grassy plains of South America
WORD ORIGIN Native American *bamba* plain

pampas grass *n* a South American grass with large feathery silver-coloured flower branches

pamper *vb* to treat (someone) with excessive indulgence or care; spoil
WORD ORIGIN Germanic

pamphlet *n* a thin paper-covered booklet, often on a subject of current interest
WORD ORIGIN Medieval Latin *Pamphilus*, title of a poem

pamphleteer *n* a person who writes or issues pamphlets

pan[1] *n* **1** a wide long-handled metal container used in cooking **2** any of various similar containers used in industry, etc. **3** either of the two dishes on a set of scales **4** *Brit* the bowl of a lavatory **5** a natural or artificial hollow in the ground: *a saltpan* ▷ *vb* **panning**, **panned 6** to sift gold from (a river) in a shallow pan **7** *informal* to criticize harshly: *his first film was panned by the critics* ▶ See also **pan out**
WORD ORIGIN Old English *panne*

pan[2] *vb* panning, panned **1** to move (a film camera) or (of a film camera) to be moved to follow a moving object or to take in a whole scene ▷ *n* **2** the act of panning
WORD ORIGIN from *panoramic*

pan- *combining form* including or relating to all parts or members: *Pan-American*
WORD ORIGIN Greek

panacea (pan-a-**see**-a) *n* a remedy for all diseases or problems
WORD ORIGIN Greek *pan-* all + *akēs* remedy

panache (pan-**ash**) *n* a confident and stylish manner: *the orchestra played with great panache*
WORD ORIGIN Old Italian *pennacchio* feather

panama hat *or* **panama** *n* a straw hat with a rounded crown and a wide brim

Pan-American *adj* of North, South, and Central America collectively

panatella *n* a long slender cigar

WORD ORIGIN American Spanish *panetela* long thin biscuit

pancake *n* **1** a thin flat circle of fried batter **2** Also called: **pancake landing** an aircraft landing made by levelling out a few feet from the ground and then dropping onto it

Pancake Day *n* Shrove Tuesday, when people traditionally eat pancakes

panchromatic *adj photog* (of an emulsion or film) sensitive to light of all colours

pancreas (**pang**-kree-ass) *n* a large gland behind the stomach, that produces insulin and aids digestion **pancreatic** *adj*
WORD ORIGIN Greek *pan-* all + *kreas* flesh

panda *n* **1** Also called: **giant panda** a large black-and-white bearlike animal from the high mountain bamboo forests of China **2** Also called: **lesser panda**, **red panda** a raccoon-like animal of the mountain forests of S Asia, with a reddish-brown coat and ringed tail
WORD ORIGIN Nepalese

panda car *n Brit* a police patrol car

pandemic *adj* (of a disease) occurring over a wide geographical area
WORD ORIGIN Greek *pandēmos* general

pandemonium *n* wild confusion; uproar
WORD ORIGIN Greek *pan-* all + *daimōn* demon

pander *vb* **1** (foll. by *to*) to indulge (a person or his or her desires): *he pandered to popular fears* ▷ *n* **2** *chiefly archaic* a person who procures a sexual partner for someone
WORD ORIGIN after *Pandarus*, in legend, the procurer of Cressida for Troilus

pandit *n Hinduism* same as **pundit** (sense 2)

Pandora's box *n* a source of many unforeseen difficulties
WORD ORIGIN a box, in Greek myth, from which all human problems were released

p & p *Brit* postage and packing

pane *n* a sheet of glass in a window or door
WORD ORIGIN Latin *pannus* rag

panegyric (pan-ee-**jirr**-rik) *n* a formal speech or piece of writing that praises a person or event
WORD ORIGIN Greek *panēguris* public gathering

panel *n* **1** a distinct section of a larger surface area, such as that in a door **2** any distinct section of something formed from a sheet of material, such as part of a car body **3** a piece of material inserted in a garment **4** a group of people acting as a team, such as in a quiz or a discussion before an audience **5** *law* **a** a list of jurors **b** the people on a jury **6** short for **instrument panel** ▷ *adj* **7** of a group acting as a panel: *a panel game* ▷ *vb* -elling, -elled *or US* -eling, -eled **8** to cover or decorate with panels
WORD ORIGIN Old French: portion

panel beater *n* a person who repairs damage to car bodies

panelling *or US* **paneling** *n* panels collectively, such as on a wall or ceiling

Braille

Braille is the most widely used system of creating texts for blind people. It uses different combinations of raised dots in cells of six paired spaces, arranged in rectangles containing three columns of three dots each, to represent letters, numbers, and other symbols such as those used in musical notation. The reader uses tactile perception to identify the characters, running a finger or fingers along the rows of cells. As in visible printed text, a line space separates each horizontal row of text from the ones above and below.

To facilitate description of the cells, the dots are numbered 1-2-3 down the left, and 4-5-6 down the right. For example, the letter 'a' is represented by a raised dot in space 1, at the top left-hand of the cell; raised dots in positions 2-3-4 – at the middle and bottom in the left column and on top of the right column – is the equivalent of letter 's'. Punctuation is represented by its own unique set of characters: a dot in position 2 represents a comma, dots in positions 3 and 6 a hyphen.

In Braille adapted for languages that do not use Latin alphabets, the cells are generally assigned according to how the sound represented by the character is transliterated into a Latin character. Thus, for example, the Arabic character *fa* is mapped onto the cell for Latin 'f', although it does not appear in this position in the Arabic alphabet. There are extensions for letters with diacritics: ç, for example, is the cell 3-5-6 (the *cedilla* symbol) immediately followed by 1-4 (letter 'c'), with no space between.

Grade 1 Braille involves simply substituting the equivalent Braille character for its printed equivalent, but this method takes up a lot of space and can be slow to read. Therefore, almost all Braille publications are transcribed in what is called *Grade 2 Braille*, in which cells are used individually or in combination with others to form a variety of contracted forms, whole words, or parts of words. Many of the most commonly used words are contracted to single characters; *but* is contracted to the single letter 'b', and *do* is contracted to 'd'. Parts of words may also be contracted. For example, the combination *ch* is the character with dots 1 and 6.

The word *him* is contracted to the two letters 'h' and 'm'.

Braille script can be produced in several ways. A pointed stylus can be used to punch dots into paper using a Braille template with rows of six-dot cells in it as a guide. Braille texts may also be produced by a machine similar to a typewriter, known as a Braillewriter. Software programs are available that can reproduce information on a computer screen on a special Braille display, and Braille printers can produce embossed hard copy. For these electronic displays and embossers, Braille has been extended to an 8-dot code, which means the case of a letter can be directly coded in the cell with the letter, and all the printable ASCII characters can be represented in a single cell.

The inventor of the system, Louis Braille (1809–52), was blind from the age of five. In 1819, he was sent to the *Institut des Jeunes Aveugles* in Paris, the first educational establishment in the world for students who were blind. It was here that he was introduced to a previous experiment in communication called 'nightwriting'. Devised by French army commander Charles Barbier as a communication system to be used by the military silently at night, it utilized twelve-dot grids that could be read by touch. Over the next few years, the teenage Louis Braille adapted this into the now familiar six-point cell system which could be more easily learned and read, and extended it to include punctuation, capitalization, and musical and mathematical symbols. It was not until 1854 that Braille became officially recognized for use in France. In 1932, representatives from the United States and Great Britain met to agree Standard English Braille, a universal Braille code for English speakers.

Today, the learning and use of Braille is apparently in decline, and there is still some controversy over its value, with some people holding the view that using a substantially different communication system can lead to the further exclusion of blind people from sighted society. Nevertheless, Braille remains a common method of making information accessible to blind people, not just in books and leaflets but also on lift buttons, public maps, and other displays.

panellist or US **panelist** n a member of a panel, usually on radio or television

panel van n Austral & NZ a small van

pang n a sudden sharp feeling of pain or sadness
WORD ORIGIN Germanic

pangolin n an animal of tropical countries with a scaly body and a long snout for feeding on ants and termites. Also called: **scaly anteater**
WORD ORIGIN Malay peng-gōling

panic n 1 a sudden overwhelming feeling of terror or anxiety, sometimes affecting a whole group of people ▷ adj 2 of or resulting from such terror: panic measures ▷ vb **-nicking, -nicked** 3 to feel or cause to feel panic **panicky** adj
WORD ORIGIN Greek panikos emanating from Pan, god of the fields

panicle n bot a loose, irregularly branched cluster of flowers, such as in the oat
WORD ORIGIN Latin panicula tuft

panic-stricken adj affected by panic

panini n, pl **-ni** or **-nis** a type of Italian bread usually served grilled with a variety of fillings

panjandrum n a pompous self-important official
WORD ORIGIN after a character in a nonsense work

pannier n 1 one of a pair of bags fixed on either side of the back wheel of a bicycle or motorcycle 2 one of a pair of large baskets slung over a beast of burden
WORD ORIGIN Old French panier

panoply (**pan**-a-plee) n a magnificent array: ambassadors equipped with the full panoply of diplomatic bags, codes and cyphers
WORD ORIGIN Greek pan- all + hopla armour

panorama n 1 a wide unbroken view in all directions: the beautiful panorama of the Cornish coast 2 a wide or comprehensive survey of a subject: the panorama of American life 3 a picture of a scene unrolled before spectators a part at a time so as to appear continuous **panoramic** adj
WORD ORIGIN Greek pan- all + horama view

pan out vb 1 informal to work out; result: Parker's research did not pan out too well 2 (of gravel) to yield gold by panning

panpipes pl n a musical wind instrument made of tubes of decreasing lengths joined together

pansy n, pl **-sies** 1 a garden plant whose flowers have rounded white, yellow, or purple velvety petals 2 offensive slang an effeminate or homosexual man or boy
WORD ORIGIN Old French pensée thought

pant vb 1 to breathe with noisy gasps after exertion 2 to say (something) while breathing in this way 3 (foll. by for) to have a frantic desire for ▷ n 4 the act of panting
WORD ORIGIN Greek phantasioun to have visions

pantaloons pl n baggy trousers gathered at the ankles
WORD ORIGIN French pantalon trousers

pantechnicon n Brit a large van used for furniture removals
WORD ORIGIN Greek pan- all + tekhnē art; originally a London bazaar later used as a furniture warehouse

pantheism n 1 the belief that God is present in everything 2 readiness to worship all gods **pantheist** n **pantheistic** adj

pantheon n 1 (in ancient Greece or Rome) a temple built to honour all the gods 2 all the gods of a particular creed: the Celtic pantheon of horse gods 3 a group of very important people: he deserves a place in the pantheon of social reformers
WORD ORIGIN Greek pan- all + theos god

panther n a leopard, usually a black one
WORD ORIGIN Greek

panties pl n women's or children's underpants

pantihose pl n US & Austral women's tights

pantile n a roofing tile, with an S-shaped cross section
WORD ORIGIN PAN¹ + tile

panto n, pl **-tos** Brit informal short for **pantomime** (sense 1)

pantograph n 1 an instrument for copying drawings or maps to any scale 2 a device on the roof of an electric train to carry the current from an overhead wire
WORD ORIGIN Greek pant- all + graphein to write

pantomime n 1 (in Britain) a play based on a fairy tale and performed at Christmas time 2 a theatrical entertainment in which words are replaced by gestures and bodily actions 3 informal chiefly Brit a confused or farcical situation
WORD ORIGIN Greek pantomīmos

pantry n, pl **-tries** a small room or large cupboard in which food is kept
WORD ORIGIN Latin panis bread

pants pl n 1 Brit an undergarment with two leg holes, covering the body from the waist or hips to the thighs 2 US, Canad, Austral, & NZ trousers or shorts 3 **bore** or **scare the pants off someone** informal to bore or scare someone very much
WORD ORIGIN shortened from pantaloons

pantyhose pl n Austral & NZ women's tights

pap¹ n 1 a soft food for babies or invalids 2 worthless or oversimplified entertainment or information 3 S African maize porridge
WORD ORIGIN Latin pappare to eat

pap² n old-fashioned Scot & N English dialect a nipple or teat
WORD ORIGIN from Old Norse

papa (pap-**pah**) n old-fashioned, informal father
WORD ORIGIN French

papacy (**pay**-pa-see) n, pl **-cies** 1 the office or term of office of a pope 2 the system of government in the Roman Catholic Church that has the pope as its head
WORD ORIGIN Medieval Latin papa pope

papal adj of the pope or the papacy

paparazzo (pap-a-**rat**-so) n, pl **-razzi** (-**rat**-see) a freelance photographer who specializes in taking shots of famous people without their knowledge or consent
WORD ORIGIN Italian

papaya (pap-**pie**-a) n a large green fruit with a sweet yellow flesh, that grows in the West Indies
WORD ORIGIN Spanish

paper n 1 a flexible material made in sheets from wood pulp or other fibres and used for writing on, decorating walls, or wrapping parcels 2 short for **newspaper** or **wallpaper** 3 **papers** documents, such as a passport, which can identify the bearer 4 a set of examination questions 5 **papers** the collected diaries or letters of someone's private or public life 6 a lecture or an essay on a specific subject 7 **on paper** in theory, as opposed to fact: countless ideas which look good on paper just don't work in practice ▷ adj 8 made of paper: paper towels; a paper bag 9 recorded on paper but not yet existing in practice: a paper profit of more than $50 million ▷ vb 10 to cover (walls) with wallpaper ▸ See also **paper over** ▷ **papery** adj
WORD ORIGIN Latin papyrus

paperback n 1 a book with covers made of flexible card ▷ adj 2 of a paperback or publication of paperbacks: a paperback novel

paperboy or **papergirl** n a boy or girl employed to deliver newspapers to people's homes

paper chase n a former type of cross-country run in which a runner lays a trail of paper for others to follow

paperclip n a bent wire clip for holding sheets of paper together

paperhanger n a person who hangs wallpaper as an occupation

paperknife n, pl **-knives** a knife-shaped object with a blunt blade for opening sealed envelopes

paper money n banknotes, rather than coins

paper over vb to conceal (something unpleasant or difficult)

paperweight n a small heavy object placed on top of loose papers to prevent them from scattering

paperwork n clerical work, such as the writing of reports or letters

papier-mâché (**pap**-yay **mash**-ay) n 1 a hard substance made of layers of paper mixed with paste and moulded when moist ▷ adj 2 made of papier-mâché
WORD ORIGIN French, literally: chewed paper

papilla (pap-**pill**-a) n, pl **-lae** (-lee) biol a small projection of tissue at the base of a hair, tooth, or feather **papillary** adj
WORD ORIGIN Latin: nipple

papist n, adj usually offensive same as **Roman Catholic**
WORD ORIGIN Church Latin papa pope

papoose n a Native American baby
WORD ORIGIN Native American papoos

paprika n a mild powdered seasoning made from red peppers
WORD ORIGIN Hungarian

Pap test or **smear** n med same as **cervical smear**
WORD ORIGIN after George Papanicolaou, anatomist

papyrus (pap-**ire**-uss) n, pl **-ri** (-rye) or **-ruses** 1 a tall water plant of Africa 2 a kind of paper made from the stem of

this plant, used by the ancient Egyptians, Greeks, and Romans **3** an ancient document written on this paper
WORD ORIGIN Greek *papuros* reed

par *n* **1** the usual or average condition: *I feel slightly below par most of the time* **2** golf a standard score for a hole or course that a good player should make: *four under par with two holes to play* **3** finance the established value of the unit of one national currency in terms of the unit of another **4** commerce short for **par value 5 on a par with** equal or equivalent to: *an environmental disaster on a par with Chernobyl* **6 par for the course** to be expected: *random acts of violence were par for the course in the capital*
WORD ORIGIN Latin: equal

par. **1** paragraph **2** parenthesis

para *n informal* **1** a paratrooper **2** a paragraph

para- *or before a vowel* **par-** *prefix* **1** beside or near: *parameter* **2** beyond: *parapsychology* **3** resembling: *paratyphoid fever*
WORD ORIGIN Greek

parable *n* a short story that uses familiar situations to illustrate a religious or moral point
WORD ORIGIN Greek *parabolē* analogy

parabola (par-**ab**-bol-a) *n geom* an open plane curve formed by the intersection of a cone by a plane parallel to its side **parabolic** *adj*
WORD ORIGIN Greek *parabolē* a setting alongside

paracetamol *n* a mild pain-relieving drug
WORD ORIGIN from *para-acetamidophenol*

parachute *n* **1** a large fabric canopy connected by a harness, that slows the descent of a person or package from an aircraft ▷ *vb* **-chuting, -chuted 2** to land or to drop (supplies or troops) by parachute from an aircraft **parachutist** *n*
WORD ORIGIN French

parade *n* **1** an ordered march or procession **2** a public promenade or street of shops **3** a blatant but sometimes insincere display: *a man who made a parade of liking his own company best* ▷ *vb* **-rading, -raded 4** to exhibit or flaunt: *he neither paraded nor disguised his devout faith* **5** to walk or march, esp. in a procession
WORD ORIGIN French: a making ready

parade ground *n* a place where soldiers assemble regularly for inspection or display

paradigm (**par**-a-dime) *n* a model or example: *his experience is a paradigm for the young artist*
WORD ORIGIN Greek *paradeigma* pattern

paradise *n* **1** heaven; where the good go after death **2** the Garden of Eden **3** any place or condition that fulfils a person's desires
WORD ORIGIN Greek *paradeisos* garden

paradise duck *n* a New Zealand duck with bright feathers

paradox *n* **1** a statement that seems self-contradictory but may be true: *it's a strange paradox that a musician must practise improvising to become a good improviser* **2** a

self-contradictory proposition, such as *I always tell lies* **3** a person or thing that is made up of contradictory elements **paradoxical** *adj* **paradoxically** *adv*
WORD ORIGIN Greek *paradoxos* opposed to existing notions

paraffin *n* **1** *Brit* a liquid mixture distilled from petroleum or shale and used as a fuel or solvent **2** *chem* the former name for **alkane**
WORD ORIGIN Latin *parum* too little + *affinis* adjacent; so called from its chemical inertia

paraffin wax *n* a white waxlike substance distilled from petroleum and used to make candles and as a sealing agent

paragon *n* a model of perfection: *a paragon of female integrity and determination*
WORD ORIGIN Old Italian *paragone* comparison

paragraph *n* **1** a section of a piece of writing, usually devoted to one idea, which begins on a new line and is often indented **2** *printing* the character ¶, used to indicate the beginning of a new paragraph ▷ *vb* **3** to put (a piece of writing) into paragraphs
WORD ORIGIN Greek *paragraphos* line drawing attention to part of a text

parakeet *n* a small colourful parrot with a long tail
WORD ORIGIN Spanish *periquito* parrot

paralegal *n* a person trained to assist lawyers but not qualified to practise law

parallax *n* an apparent change in an object's position due to a change in the observer's position
WORD ORIGIN Greek *parallaxis* change

parallel *adj* **1** separated by an equal distance at every point: *parallel lines; a path parallel to the main road* **2** precisely corresponding: *we decide our salaries by comparison with parallel jobs in other charities* **3** *computers* operating on several items of information or instructions at the same time ▷ *n* **4** *maths* one of a set of parallel lines or planes **5** something with similar features to another **6** a comparison; similarity between two things: *she attempted to excuse herself by drawing a parallel between her behaviour and ours* **7** Also called: **parallel of latitude** any of the imaginary lines around the earth parallel to the equator, marking degrees of latitude **8** *printing* the character ‖, used as a reference mark ▷ *vb* **9** to correspond to: *the increase in smoking is paralleled by an increase in lung cancer*
WORD ORIGIN Greek *parallēlos* alongside one another

parallel bars *pl n gymnastics* a pair of wooden bars on upright posts used for various exercises

parallelepiped (par-a-lel-ee-**pipe**-ed) *n geom* a solid shape whose six faces are parallelograms
WORD ORIGIN Greek *parallēlos* parallel + *epipedon* plane surface

parallelism *n* **1** the state of being parallel **2** a close likeness

parallelogram *n geom* a plane figure whose opposite sides are parallel and equal in length

WORD ORIGIN Greek *parallēlos* parallel + *grammē* line

paralyse *or US* **-lyze** *vb* **-lysing, -lysed** *or* **-lyzing, -lyzed 1** *pathol* to affect with paralysis **2** to make immobile: *he was paralysed by fear*
WORD ORIGIN French *paralyser*

paralysis *n* **1** *pathol* inability to move all or part of the body due to damage to the nervous system **2** a state of inactivity: *the economic chaos and political paralysis into which the country has sunk*
WORD ORIGIN Greek *paralusis*, from *para-* beyond + *lusis* a loosening

paralytic *adj* **1** of or relating to paralysis **2** *Brit informal* very drunk ▷ *n* **3** a person who is paralysed

paramecium (par-a-**mee**-see-um) *n, pl* **-cia** (-see-a) a single-celled animal which lives in ponds, puddles, and sewage filters and swims by means of cilia

paramedic *n* a person, such as a member of an ambulance crew, whose work supplements that of the medical profession **paramedical** *adj*

parameter (par-**am**-it-er) *n* **1** *maths* an arbitrary constant that determines the specific form of a mathematical expression, such as *a* and *b* in $y = ax^2 + b$ **2** *informal* any limiting factor: *exchange rates are allowed to fluctuate only within designated parameters*
WORD ORIGIN Greek *para* beside + *metron* measure

paramilitary *adj* denoting a group of people organized on military lines

paramount *adj* of the greatest importance
WORD ORIGIN Old French *par* by + *-amont* above

paramour *n old-fashioned* an adulterous lover
WORD ORIGIN Old French, literally: through love

paranoia *n* **1** a mental disorder which causes delusions of grandeur or of persecution **2** *informal* intense fear or suspicion, usually unfounded **paranoid** *or* **paranoiac** *adj, n*
WORD ORIGIN Greek *para-* beyond + *noos* mind

paranormal *adj* **1** beyond normal scientific explanation ▷ *n* **2 the paranormal** paranormal happenings or matters generally

parapet *n* **1** a low wall or railing along the edge of a balcony or roof **2** *mil* a mound of sandbags in front of a trench to conceal and protect troops from fire
WORD ORIGIN Italian *parapetto*

paraphernalia *n* various articles or bits of equipment
WORD ORIGIN Greek *para-* beyond + *phernē* dowry

paraphrase *n* **1** an expression of a statement or text in other words ▷ *vb* **-phrasing, -phrased 2** to put (a statement or text) into other words
WORD ORIGIN Greek *paraphrazein* to recount

paraplegia (par-a-**pleej**-ya) *n pathol* paralysis of the lower half of the body **paraplegic** *adj, n*
WORD ORIGIN Greek: a blow on one side

P

parapsychology n the study of mental phenomena such as telepathy

Paraquat n trademark an extremely poisonous weedkiller

parasite n 1 an animal or plant that lives in or on another from which it obtains nourishment 2 a person who habitually lives at the expense of others; sponger **parasitic** adj
WORD ORIGIN Greek para- beside + sitos grain

parasol n an umbrella-like sunshade
WORD ORIGIN French

paratrooper n a member of the paratroops

paratroops pl n troops trained to be dropped by parachute into a battle area

paratyphoid fever n a disease resembling but less severe than typhoid fever

parboil vb to boil (food) until partially cooked
WORD ORIGIN Late Latin perbullire to boil thoroughly; modern meaning due to confusion of par- with part

parcel n 1 something wrapped up; a package 2 a group of people or things sharing something in common: a parcel of fools 3 a distinct portion of land: he was the recipient of a substantial parcel of land ▷ vb -celling, -celled or US -celing, -celed 4 (often foll. by up) to wrap (something) up into a parcel 5 (foll. by out) to divide (something) into portions: the children were parcelled out to relatives
WORD ORIGIN Old French parcelle

parch vb 1 to deprive (something) of water; dry up: the summer sun parched the hills 2 to make (someone) very thirsty: I'm parched. Have we got any lemonade?
WORD ORIGIN origin unknown

parchment n 1 a thick smooth material made from animal skin and used for writing on 2 a manuscript made of this material 3 a stiff yellowish paper resembling parchment
WORD ORIGIN Greek pergamēnē, from Pergamēnos of Pergamum (where parchment was made)

pardon vb 1 to forgive or excuse (a person) for (an offence, mistake etc.): I hope you'll pardon the wait; to pardon someone ▷ n 2 forgiveness 3 official release from punishment for a crime ▷ interj 4 Also: pardon me, I beg your pardon **a** sorry; excuse me **b** what did you say? **pardonable** adj
WORD ORIGIN Medieval Latin perdonare to forgive freely

pare vb **paring, pared** 1 to peel (the outer layer) from (something): thinly pare the rind from the grapefruit 2 to trim or cut the edge of 3 to decrease bit by bit: the government is prepared to pare down the armed forces
WORD ORIGIN Latin parare to make ready

parent n 1 a father or mother 2 a person acting as a father or mother; guardian 3 a plant or animal that has produced one or more plants or animals **parental** adj **parenthood** n
WORD ORIGIN Latin parens, from parere to bring forth

parentage n ancestry or family

parent company n a company that owns a number of smaller companies

parenthesis (par-en-thiss-iss) n, pl -ses (-seez) 1 a word or phrase inserted into a passage, and marked off by brackets or dashes 2 Also called: **bracket** either of a pair of characters ( ), used to enclose such a phrase **parenthetical** adj **parenthetically** adv
WORD ORIGIN Greek: something placed in besides

parenting n the activity of bringing up children

parent teacher association n an organization consisting of the parents and teachers of school pupils formed to organize activities on behalf of the school

par excellence adv beyond comparison: this book justifies its claim to be a reference work par excellence
WORD ORIGIN French

parfait (par-fay) n a dessert consisting of layers of ice cream, fruit, and sauce, topped with whipped cream, and served in a tall glass: a blackberry and apricot parfait
WORD ORIGIN French: perfect

pariah (par-rye-a) n a social outcast: the man they regard as a pariah
WORD ORIGIN Tamil paraiyan drummer

parietal (par-rye-it-al) adj anat, biol of or forming the walls of a body cavity: the parietal bones of the skull
WORD ORIGIN Latin paries wall

paring n something that has been cut off something

parish n 1 an area that has its own church and a priest or pastor ▸ Related adjective: **parochial** 2 the people who live in a parish 3 (in England and, formerly, Wales) the smallest unit of local government
WORD ORIGIN Greek paroikos neighbour

parish clerk n an official who performs various (esp. administrative) duties for a church or civil parish

parish council n (in England and, formerly, Wales) the administrative body of a parish. See **parish** (sense 3)

parishioner n a person who lives in a particular parish

parish register n a book in which the births, baptisms, marriages, and deaths in a parish are recorded

parity n 1 equality, for example of rank or pay 2 close or exact equivalence: the company maintained parity with the competition 3 finance equivalence between the units of currency of two countries
WORD ORIGIN Latin par equal

park n 1 a large area of open land for recreational use by the public 2 a piece of open land for public recreation in a town 3 Brit a large area of private land surrounding a country house 4 an area designed to accommodate a number of related enterprises: a science park 5 US & Canad a playing field or sports stadium 6 the park Brit informal the pitch in soccer ▷ vb 7 to stop and leave (a vehicle) temporarily: I parked between the two cars already outside; police vans were parked on every street corner 8 informal to leave or put (someone or something) somewhere: she parked herself on the sofa and stayed there all evening **parking** n
WORD ORIGIN Germanic

parka n a long jacket with a quilted lining and a fur-trimmed hood
WORD ORIGIN from Aleutian (language of Aleutian Islands, off Alaska): skin

parkade n Canad a building used as a car park

park and ride n a transportation scheme in which drivers park some distance away from a city centre, tourist attraction, etc. and complete their journey by public transport

parkette n Canad a small public car park

parkin n Brit a moist spicy ginger cake usually containing oatmeal
WORD ORIGIN origin unknown

parking lot n US & Canad area or building where vehicles may be left for a time

parking meter n a coin-operated device beside a parking space that indicates how long a vehicle may be left parked

parking ticket n the notice of a fine served on a motorist for a parking offence

Parkinson's disease or **Parkinsonism** n a progressive disorder of the central nervous system which causes tremor, rigidity, and impaired muscular coordination
WORD ORIGIN after J. Parkinson, surgeon

Parkinson's law n the notion that work expands to fill the time available for its completion
WORD ORIGIN after C. N. Parkinson, historian and writer

parkland n grassland with scattered trees

parky adj **parkier, parkiest** Brit informal (of the weather) chilly
WORD ORIGIN origin unknown

parlance n the manner of speaking associated with a particular group or subject: he had, in Marxist parlance, a 'petit bourgeois' mentality
WORD ORIGIN French parler to talk

parley old-fashioned n 1 a discussion between members of opposing sides to decide terms of agreement ▷ vb 2 to have a parley
WORD ORIGIN French parler to talk

parliament n a law-making assembly of a country
WORD ORIGIN Old French parlement, from parler to speak

Parliament n 1 the highest law-making authority in Britain, consisting of the House of Commons, the House of Lords, and the sovereign 2 the equivalent law-making authority in another country

parliamentarian n an expert in parliamentary procedures

parliamentary adj 1 of or from a parliament: parliamentary elections 2 conforming to the procedures of a parliament: parliamentary language

parlour or US **parlor** n 1 old-fashioned a living room for receiving visitors 2 a room or shop equipped as a place of business: an ice-cream parlour
WORD ORIGIN Old French parler to speak

parlous adj archaic or humorous dangerously bad; dire: the parlous state of the economy
WORD ORIGIN variant of perilous

Words from Shakespeare
part 14

place *n* a person's position or rank
Sons, kinsmen, thanes,
And you whose places are the nearest
Macbeth 1.4

post *n* a messenger
there are twenty weak and wearied posts
Come from the north *Henry IV* part II 2.4

pox *n* any disease during which the victim had blisters on the skin. It was also a curse, a swear word
The pox of such antic, lisping, affecting phantasims
Romeo and Juliet 2.4

prate *v* to chatter
if thou prate of mountains *Hamlet* 5.1

prattle *v* to chatter or talk without purpose
I prattle out of fashion, and I dote In mine own comforts *Othello* 2.1

precept *n* an order or command
and my father's precepts I therein do forget.
The Tempest 3.1

present *adj* immediate
We'll put the matter to the present push
Hamlet 5.1

prithee *int* please or may I ask – a polite request
I prithee, and I'll pay thee bounteously
Twelfth Night 1.2

prodigal *n* someone who wastes or squanders money
he's a very fool, and a prodigal *Twelfth Night* 1.3

purpose *n* intention
understand my purposes aright *King Lear* 1.4

quaff *v* to drink heavily or take a big drink
That quaffing and drinking will undo you
Twelfth Night 1.3

quaint *adj* clever, ingenious
with a quaint device *The Tempest* 3.3

quaint *adj* cunning
I'll ... tell quaint lies *Merchant of Venice* 3.4

quaint *adj* pretty, attractive
The clamorous owl, that nightly hoots and wonders
At our quaint spirit *A Midsummer Night's Dream* 2.2

quoth *v* to say
'Tis dinner time.' quoth I *The Comedy of Errors* 2.1

rack *n* a cloud or a cloud formation
And, like this insubstantial pageant faded,
Leave not a rack behind *The Tempest* 4.1

rail *v* to rant or swear at. It is still used occasionally today
Why do I rail on thee *Richard II* 5.5

rate *n* estimate, opinion
My son is lost, and, in my rate, she too
The Tempest 2.1

recreant *n* a coward
Come, recreant, come, thou child
A Midsummer Night's Dream 3.2

remembrance *n* memory or recollection
our remembrances of days foregone
All's Well That Ends Well 1.3

resolute *adj* firm or not going to change your mind
You are resolute, then? *Twelfth Night* 1.5

revels *n* celebrations or a party
Our revels now are ended *The Tempest* 4.1

rough-cast *n* a mixture of lime and gravel (sometimes shells too) for use on an outer wall
and let him have some plaster, or some loam, or some rough-cast about him, to signify wall
A Midsummer Night's Dream 3.1

sack *n* dry white wine
My man-monster hath drowned his tongue in sack. *The Tempest* 3.2

sad *adj* serious, grave
comes me the Prince and Claudio... in sad conference *Much Ado About Nothing* 1.3

Parmesan (**par**-miz-zan) *n* a hard strong-flavoured cheese used grated on pasta dishes and soups **WORD ORIGIN** Italian *parmegiano* of Parma, Italy

parochial *adj* **1** narrow in outlook; provincial **2** of or relating to a parish **parochialism** *n* **WORD ORIGIN** see PARISH

parody *n, pl* **-dies 1** a piece of music or literature that mimics the style of another composer or author in a humorous way **2** something done so badly that it seems like an intentional mockery ▷ *vb* **-dies, -dying, -died 3** to make a parody of **parodist** *n* **WORD ORIGIN** Greek *paroidia* satirical poem

parole *n* **1** the freeing of a prisoner before his or her sentence has run out, on condition that he or she behaves well **2** a promise given by a prisoner to behave well if granted liberty or partial liberty **3 on parole** conditionally released from prison ▷ *vb* **-roling, -roled 4** to place (a person) on parole **WORD ORIGIN** Old French *parole d'honneur* word of honour

parotid gland *n anat* either of a pair of salivary glands in front of and below the ears **WORD ORIGIN** Greek *para-* near + *ous* ear

paroxysm *n* **1** an uncontrollable outburst of emotion: *a paroxysm of grief* **2** *pathol* **a** a sudden attack or recurrence of a disease **b** a fit or convulsion **paroxysmal** *adj* **WORD ORIGIN** Greek *paroxunein* to goad

parquet (**par**-kay) *n* **1** a floor covering made of blocks of wood ▷ *vb* **2** to cover (a floor) with parquetry **WORD ORIGIN** Old French: small enclosure

parquetry (**par**-kit-tree) *n* pieces of wood arranged in a geometric pattern, used to cover floors

parr *n* a salmon up to two years of age **WORD ORIGIN** origin unknown

parricide *n* **1** a person who kills one of his or her parents **2** the act of killing either of one's parents **parricidal** *adj* **WORD ORIGIN** Latin *parricidium* murder of a parent or relative

parrot *n* **1** a tropical bird with a short hooked beak, bright plumage, and an ability to mimic human speech **2** a person who repeats or imitates someone else's words **3 sick as a parrot** *usually facetious* extremely disappointed ▷ *vb* **-roting, -roted 4** to repeat or imitate (someone else's words) without understanding them **WORD ORIGIN** probably from French *paroquet*

parrot fever *n* same as **psittacosis**

parrotfish *n* a brightly coloured sea fish

parry *vb* **-ries, -rying, -ried 1** to ward off (an attack) **2** to avoid answering (questions) in a clever way ▷ *n, pl* **-ries 3** an instance of parrying **4** a skilful evasion of a question **WORD ORIGIN** French *parer* to ward off

parse (**parz**) *vb* **parsing, parsed** to analyse (a sentence or the words in a sentence) grammatically **WORD ORIGIN** Latin *pars (orationis)* part (of speech)

parsec *n* a unit of astronomical distance equivalent to 3.0857×10^{16} metres or 3.262 light years **WORD ORIGIN** *parallax* + *second* (of time)

parsimony *n formal* extreme caution in spending **parsimonious** *adj* **WORD ORIGIN** Latin *parcimonia*

parsley *n* a herb with curled pleasant-smelling leaves, used for seasoning and decorating food **WORD ORIGIN** Middle English *persely*

parsnip *n* a long tapering cream-coloured root vegetable **WORD ORIGIN** Latin *pastinaca*

parson *n* **1** a parish priest in the Church of England **2** any clergyman **3** NZ a nonconformist minister **WORD ORIGIN** Latin *persona* personage

parsonage *n* the residence of a parson, provided by the parish

parson's nose *n* the rump of a fowl when cooked

part *n* **1** a piece or portion **2** one of several equal divisions: *a salad dressing made with two parts oil to one part vinegar* **3** an actor's role in a play **4** a person's duty: *his ancestors had done their part nobly and well at Bannockburn* **5** an involvement in or contribution to something: *he was jailed for his part in the fraud* **6** a region or area: *he's well known in these parts; the weather in this part of the country is extreme* **7** *anat* an area of the body **8** a component that can be replaced in a vehicle or machine **9** *US, Canad, & Austral* same as **parting** (sense 2) **10** *music* a melodic line assigned to one or more instrumentalists or singers **11 for my part** as far as I am concerned **12 for the most part** generally **13 in part** to some degree; partly **14 on the part of** on behalf of **15 part and parcel of** an essential ingredient of **16 play a part a** to pretend to be what one is not **b** (foll. by *in*) to have something to do with: *examinations play a large part in education and in schools* **17 take part in** to participate in **18 take someone's part** to support someone, for example in an argument **19 take something in good part** to respond to (teasing or criticism) with good humour ▷ *vb* **20** to divide or separate from one another: *her lips parted in laughter; the cord parted with a pop* **21** to go away from one another: *we parted with handshakes all round* **22** to split: *the path parts here* **23** to arrange (the hair) in such a way that a line of scalp is left showing ▷ *adv* **24** to some extent; partly: *this book is part history, part travelogue* **25 part from** to cause (someone) to give up: *I was astonished at the way Henry parted his audience from their money* **26 part with** to give up: *check carefully before you part with your cash* ▶ See also **parts** **WORD ORIGIN** Latin *pars* a part

partake *vb* **-taking, -took, -taken 1** partake in to take part in **2** partake of to take (food or drink) **WORD ORIGIN** from earlier *part taker*

USAGE
Partake of is sometimes wrongly used as if it were a synonym of *eat* or *drink*. Correctly, one can only *partake of* food or drink which is available for several people to share.

parterre *n* **1** a formally patterned flower garden **2** the pit of a theatre **WORD ORIGIN** French

Parthian shot *n* a hostile remark or gesture delivered while departing **WORD ORIGIN** from the custom of archers from Parthia, an ancient Asian empire, who shot their arrows backwards while retreating

partial *adj* **1** relating to only a part; not complete: *partial deafness* **2** biased: *religious programmes can be as partial as they like* **3 be partial to** to have a particular liking for **partiality** *n* **partially** *adv* **WORD ORIGIN** Latin *pars* part

USAGE
See at **partly**.

participate *vb* **-pating, -pated** ● participate in to become actively involved in **participant** *n* **participation** *n* **participatory** *adj* **WORD ORIGIN** Latin *pars* part + *capere* to take

participle *n grammar* a form of a verb that is used in compound tenses or as an adjective. See also **present participle, past participle** ▷ **participial** *adj* **WORD ORIGIN** Latin *pars* part + *capere* to take

particle *n* **1** an extremely small piece or amount: *clean thoroughly to remove all particles of dirt* **2** *grammar* an uninflected part of speech, such as an interjection or preposition **3** *physics* a minute piece of matter, such as an electron or proton **WORD ORIGIN** Latin *pars* part

parti-coloured *or US* **particolored** *adj* having different colours in different parts **WORD ORIGIN** from obsolete *party* of more than one colour

particular *adj* **1** of, belonging to, or being one person or thing; specific: *the particular type of tuition on offer* **2** exceptional or special: *the report voices particular concern over the state of the country's manufacturing industry* **3** providing specific details or circumstances: *a particular account* **4** difficult to please; fussy ▷ *n* **5** a separate distinct item as opposed to a generalization: *moving from the general to the particular* **6** an item of information; detail: *she refused to go into particulars* **7 in particular** especially or exactly: *three painters in particular were responsible for these developments* **particularly** *adv* **WORD ORIGIN** Latin *particula* a small part

particularity *n, pl* **-ties 1** great attentiveness to detail **2** the state of being particular as opposed to general; individuality

particularize *or* **-rise** *vb* **-rizing, -rized** *or* **-rising, -rised** to give details about (something) **particularization** *or* **-risation** *n*

parting *n* **1** a departure or leave-taking **2** *Brit & NZ* the line of scalp showing when sections of hair are combed in opposite directions **3** the act of dividing (something): *the parting of the Red Sea*

parting shot *n* a hostile remark or gesture delivered while departing

partisan *n* **1** a person who supports a particular cause or party **2** a member of an armed resistance group within occupied territory ▷ *adj* **3** prejudiced or one-sided **partisanship** *n*
WORD ORIGIN Old Italian *partigiano*

partition *n* **1** a large screen or thin wall that divides a room **2** the division of a country into two or more independent countries ▷ *vb* **3** to separate (a room) into sections: *the shower is partitioned off from the rest of the bathroom* **4** to divide (a country) into separate self-governing parts: *the subcontinent was partitioned into India and Pakistan*
WORD ORIGIN Latin *partire* to divide

partitive *grammar adj* **1** (of a noun) referring to part of something. The phrase *some of the butter* is a partitive construction ▷ *n* **2** a partitive word, such as *some* or *any*
WORD ORIGIN Latin *partire* to divide

partly *adv* not completely

≡ **USAGE**
≡ Partly and *partially* are to some extent
≡ interchangeable, but *partly* should be
≡ used when referring to a part or parts
≡ of something: *the building is partly* (not
≡ *partially*) *of stone*, while *partially* is
≡ preferred for the meaning *to some*
≡ *extent*: *his mother is partially* (not *partly*)
≡ *sighted*.

partner *n* **1** either member of a couple in a relationship **2** a member of a business partnership **3** one of a pair of dancers or of players on the same side in a game: *her bridge partner* **4** an ally or companion: *the country's main European trading partner* ▷ *vb* **5** to be the partner of (someone)
WORD ORIGIN Middle English *parcener* joint inheritor

partnership *n* **1** a relationship in which two or more people or organizations work together in a business venture **2** the condition of being a partner

part of speech *n grammar* a class of words, such as a noun, verb, or adjective, sharing important syntactic or semantic features

partook *vb* the past tense of **partake**

partridge *n, pl* **-tridges** *or* **-tridge** a game bird with an orange-brown head, greyish neck, and a short rust-coloured tail
WORD ORIGIN Latin *perdix*

parts *pl n literary* abilities or talents: *a man of many parts*

part song *n* a song composed in harmonized parts

part-time *adj* **1** for less than the normal full working time: *a part-time job* ▷ *adv* **part time 2** on a part-time basis: *he works part time* **part-timer** *n*

parturient *adj formal* giving birth
WORD ORIGIN Latin *parturire* to be in labour

parturition *n* the process of giving birth
WORD ORIGIN Latin *parturire* to be in labour

party *n, pl* **-ties 1** a social gathering for pleasure **2** a group of people involved in the same activity: *a search party* **3** a group of people sharing a common political aim **4** the person or people who take part in or are involved in something, esp. a legal action or dispute: *a judge will decide who the guilty party is* **5** *informal, humorous* a person: *he's an odd old party* ▷ *vb* **-ties, -tying, -tied 6** *informal* to celebrate; have a good time
WORD ORIGIN Old French *partie* part

party line *n* **1** the policies of a political party **2** a telephone line shared by two or more subscribers

party wall *n property law* a common wall separating two properties

par value *n* the value printed on a share certificate or bond at the time of its issue

parvenu *orfem* **parvenue** (**par**-ven-new) *n* a person newly risen to a position of power or wealth who is considered to lack culture or education
WORD ORIGIN French

pascal *n* the SI unit of pressure; the pressure exerted on an area of 1 square metre by a force of 1 newton
WORD ORIGIN after B. *Pascal*, mathematician and scientist

Pascal *n* a high-level computer programming language developed as a teaching language
WORD ORIGIN after B. *Pascal*, mathematician and scientist

paschal (**pask**-l) *adj* **1** of or relating to the Passover **2** of or relating to Easter
WORD ORIGIN Hebrew *pesah* Passover

pas de deux (pah de **duh**) *n, pl* **pas de deux** *ballet* a dance for two people
WORD ORIGIN French: step for two

pasha *n* (formerly) a high official of the Ottoman Empire: placed after a name when used as a title
WORD ORIGIN Turkish *paşa*

pashmina (pash-**mee**-na) *n* a type of cashmere scarf or shawl made from the underfur of Tibetan goats
WORD ORIGIN Persian *pashm* wool

paso doble (**pass**-so **dobe**-lay) *n* **1** a modern ballroom dance in fast duple time **2** music for this dance
WORD ORIGIN Spanish: double step

pas op (**pass** op) *interj S African* beware
WORD ORIGIN Afrikaans

paspalum (pass-**pale**-um) *n Austral & NZ* a type of grass with wide leaves

pasqueflower *n* a small purple-flowered plant of Europe and Asia
WORD ORIGIN French *passefleur*, changed to *pasqueflower* Easter flower, because it blooms at Easter

pass *vb* **1** to go by or past (a person or thing) **2** to continue or extend in a particular direction: *the road to Camerino passes through some fine scenery* **3** to go through or cause (something) to go through (an obstacle or barrier): *the bullet passed through his head* **4** to be successful in (a test or examination) **5** to spend (time) or (of time) go by: *the time passed surprisingly quickly* **6** to hand over or be handed over: *she passed me her glass* **7** to be inherited by: *his mother's small estate had passed to him after her death* **8** *sport* to hit, kick, or throw (the ball) to another player **9** (of a law-making body) to agree to (a law or proposal): *the bill was passed by parliament last week* **10** to pronounce (judgment): *the court is expected to pass sentence later today* **11** to move onwards or over: *a flicker of amusement passed over his face* **12** to exceed: *Australia's population has just passed the 17 million mark* **13** to go without comment: *the insult passed unnoticed* **14** to choose not to answer a question or not to make a bid or a play in card games **15** to discharge (urine etc.) from the body **16** to come to an end or disappear: *the madness will soon pass* **17** (foll. by *for* or *as*) to be likely to be mistaken for (someone or something else): *the few sunny days that pass for summer in this country* **18** *old-fashioned* to take place: *what passed at the meeting?* **19 pass away** *or* **on** *euphemistic* to die ▷ *n* **20** a successful result in an examination or test **21** *sport* the transfer of a ball from one player to another **22** a route through a range of mountains where there is a gap between peaks **23** a permit or licence **24** *mil* a document authorizing leave of absence **25** *bridge, etc.* an instance of choosing not to answer a question or not to make a bid or a play in card games **26 a pretty pass** a bad state of affairs **27 make a pass at** *informal* to try to persuade (someone) to have sex: *he made a pass at his secretary* ▶ See also **pass off, pass out**, etc.
WORD ORIGIN Latin *passus* step

≡ **USAGE**
≡ The past participle of *pass* is
≡ sometimes wrongly spelt *past*: *the time*
≡ *for recriminations has passed* (not *past*).

pass. passive

passable *adj* **1** adequate or acceptable: *passable if hardly faultless German* **2** (of a road, path, etc.) capable of being travelled along: *most main roads are passable with care despite the snow* **passably** *adv*

passage *n* **1** a channel or opening providing a way through **2** a hall or corridor **3** a section of a written work, speech, or piece of music **4** a journey by ship **5** the act of passing from one place or condition to another: *Ireland faced a tough passage to qualify for the World Cup finals* **6** the right or freedom to pass: *the aid convoys were guaranteed safe passage through rebel-held areas* **7** the establishing of a law by a law-making body
WORD ORIGIN Old French *passer* to pass

passageway *n* corridor or passage

passbook *n* **1** a book issued by a bank or building society for recording deposits and withdrawals **2** *S African* formerly, an official identity document

passé (**pas**-say) *adj* out-of-date: *smoking is a bit passé these days*
WORD ORIGIN French

passenger *n* **1** a person travelling in a vehicle driven by someone else **2** *Brit & NZ* a member of a team who does not take an equal share of the work: *you'll have to pull your weight – we can't afford passengers*
WORD ORIGIN Old French *passager* passing

passer-by *n, pl* **passers-by** a person who is walking past someone or something

passerine *adj* **1** belonging to an order of perching birds that includes the larks,

finches, and starlings ▷ *n* **2** any bird of this order
WORD ORIGIN Latin *passer* sparrow

passim *adv* throughout: used to indicate that what is referred to occurs frequently in a particular piece of writing
WORD ORIGIN Latin

passing *adj* **1** momentary or short-lived: *a passing fad* **2** casual or superficial: *a passing resemblance* ▷ *n* **3** *euphemistic* death **4** the ending of something: *the passing of the old order in Eastern Europe* **5 in passing** briefly and without going into detail; incidentally: *this fact is only noted in passing*

passion *n* **1** intense sexual love **2** any strongly felt emotion **3** a strong enthusiasm for something: *a passion for football* **4** the object of an intense desire or enthusiasm: *flying is his abiding passion* **passionless** *adj*
WORD ORIGIN Latin *pati* to suffer

Passion *n* the sufferings of Christ from the Last Supper to his death on the cross

passionate *adj* **1** showing intense sexual desire **2** capable of or revealing intense emotion: *a passionate speech* **passionately** *adv*

passionflower *n* a tropical plant with brightly coloured showy flowers
WORD ORIGIN parts of the flowers are said to resemble the instruments of the Crucifixion

passion fruit *n* the edible egg-shaped fruit of the passionflower

Passion play *n* a play about the Passion of Christ

passive *adj* **1** not taking an active part **2** submissive and receptive to outside forces **3** *grammar* denoting a form of verbs used to indicate that the subject is the recipient of the action, as *was broken* in *The glass was broken by that boy over there* **4** *chem* (of a substance) chemically unreactive ▷ *n* **5** *grammar* the passive form of a verb **passively** *adv* **passivity** *n*
WORD ORIGIN Latin *passivus* capable of suffering

passive resistance *n* resistance to a government or the law by nonviolent acts such as fasting, peaceful demonstrations, or refusing to cooperate

passive smoking *n* the unwilling inhalation of smoke from other people's cigarettes by a nonsmoker

passkey *n* **1** a private key **2** same as **master key** or **skeleton key**

pass law *n* (formerly in South Africa) a law restricting the movement of Black Africans

pass off *vb* **1** to present (something or oneself) under false pretences: *women who passed themselves off effectively as men* **2** to come to a gradual end: *the effects of the gas passed off relatively peacefully* **3** to take place: *the main demonstration passed off peacefully*

pass out *vb* **1** *informal* to become unconscious; faint **2** *Brit* (of an officer cadet) to qualify for a military commission

pass over *vb* **1** to take no notice of; disregard: *she claims she had been passed over for promotion because she is a woman* **2** to

ignore or not discuss: *this disaster cannot be passed over lightly*

Passover *n* an eight-day Jewish festival commemorating the sparing of the Israelites in Egypt
WORD ORIGIN *pass over*, translation of Hebrew *pesah*

passport *n* **1** an official document issued by a government, which identifies the holder and grants him or her permission to travel abroad **2** an asset that gains a person admission or acceptance: *good qualifications are no automatic passport to a job*
WORD ORIGIN French *passer* to pass + *port* port

pass up *vb* *informal* to let (something) go by; disregard: *am I passing up my one chance to be really happy?*

password *n* a secret word or phrase that ensures admission by proving identity or membership

past *adj* **1** of the time before the present: *the past history of the world* **2** no longer in existence: *past happiness* **3** immediately previous: *the past year* **4** former: *a past president* **5** *grammar* indicating a tense of verbs used to describe actions that have been begun or completed at the time of speaking ▷ *n* **6 the past** the period of time before the present: *a familiar face from the past* **7** the history of a person or nation **8** an earlier disreputable period of someone's life: *a woman with a bit of a past* **9** *grammar* **a** the past tense **b** a verb in the past tense ▷ *adv* **10** on or onwards: *I called but he just walked past* **11** at a time before the present; ago: *three years past* ▷ *prep* **12** beyond in time: *it's past midnight* **13** beyond in place: *a procession of mourners filed past the coffin* **14** beyond the limit of: *riches past his wildest dreams* **15 not put it past someone** to consider someone capable of (a particular action): *I wouldn't put it past him to double-cross us* **16 past it** *informal* unable to do the things one could do when younger
WORD ORIGIN from *pass*

pasta *n* a type of food, such as spaghetti, that is made from a dough of flour and water and formed into different shapes
WORD ORIGIN Italian

paste *n* **1** a soft moist mixture, such as toothpaste **2** an adhesive made from water and flour or starch, for use with paper **3** a smooth creamy preparation of fish, meat, or vegetables for spreading on bread: *sausage paste* **4** *Brit & NZ* dough for making pastry **5** a hard shiny glass used to make imitation gems ▷ *vb* **pasting, pasted 6** to attach by paste: *she bought a scrapbook and carefully pasted in it all her clippings* **7** *slang* to beat or defeat (someone)
WORD ORIGIN Greek *pastē* barley porridge

pasteboard *n* a stiff board made by pasting layers of paper together

pastel *n* **1 a** a crayon made of ground pigment bound with gum **b** a picture drawn with such crayons **2** a pale delicate colour ▷ *adj* **3** (of a colour) pale and delicate: *pastel pink*
WORD ORIGIN Latin *pasta* paste

pastern *n* the part of a horse's foot between the fetlock and the hoof

WORD ORIGIN Old French *pasture* a tether

paste-up *n printing* a sheet of paper or board with artwork and proofs pasted on it, which is photographed prior to making a plate

pasteurize *or* **-rise** *vb* **-rizing, -rized** *or* **-rising, -rised** to destroy bacteria (in beverages or solid foods) by a special heating process **pasteurization** *or* **-risation** *n*
WORD ORIGIN after Louis *Pasteur*, chemist

pastiche (past-**eesh**) *n* a work of art that mixes styles or copies the style of another artist
WORD ORIGIN French

pastille *n* a small fruit-flavoured and sometimes medicated sweet
WORD ORIGIN Latin *pastillus* small loaf

pastime *n* an activity which makes time pass pleasantly

pasting *n* **1** *slang* a thrashing or heavy defeat **2** *informal* strong criticism

past master *n* a person with a talent for or experience in a particular activity: *a past master at manipulating the media*

pastor *n* a member of the clergy in charge of a congregation
WORD ORIGIN Latin: shepherd

pastoral *adj* **1** of or depicting country life or scenery **2** (of land) used for pasture **3** of or relating to a member of the clergy or his or her duties **4** of or relating to shepherds or their work ▷ *n* **5** a literary work, picture, or piece of music portraying country life **6** a letter from a bishop to the clergy or people of his diocese
WORD ORIGIN Latin *pastor* shepherd

pastorale (past-or-**ahl**) *n*, *pl* **-rales** a musical composition that suggests country life
WORD ORIGIN Italian

pastoralism *n* a system of agriculture in dry grassland regions based on raising stock such as cattle, sheep, or goats **pastoralist** *n*

past participle *n grammar* a form of verb used to form compound past tenses and passive forms of the verb and to modify nouns: *spoken is the past participle of speak*

pastrami *n* highly seasoned smoked beef
WORD ORIGIN Yiddish

pastry *n* **1** a dough of flour, water, and fat **2** *pl* **-tries** an individual cake or pie **3** baked foods, such as tarts, made with this dough
WORD ORIGIN from *paste*

pasturage *n* **1** the business of grazing cattle **2** same as **pasture**

pasture *n* **1** land covered with grass, suitable for grazing by farm animals **2** the grass growing on this land
WORD ORIGIN Latin *pascere* to feed

pasty¹ (**pay**-stee) *adj* **pastier, pastiest** (of the complexion) pale and unhealthy-looking

pasty² (**past**-ee) *n*, *pl* **pasties** a round of pastry folded over a filling of meat and vegetables
WORD ORIGIN Old French *pastée*

Words from Literature
part 20

physic *n* medicine
> there I studied physic two years and seven
> months
> *Gulliver's Travels* Jonathan Swift

pinion *v* to pinion is to hold both arms so that a person cannot move them
> But the relentless Ghost pinioned him in both
> his arms, and forced him to observe what
> happened next.
> *A Christmas Carol* Charles Dickens

piquet *n* a popular card game in the 18th century
> Mr Hurst and Mr Bingley were at piquet
> *Pride and Prejudice* Jane Austen

plaister *n* a piece of cloth on which an apothecary (or pharmacist) would spread ointment. The cloth is then applied to wounds or bruises to treat them
> Then, she gave the knife a final smart wipe on
> the edge of the plaister, and then sawed a very
> thick round off the loaf: which she finally, before
> separating from the loaf, hewed into two halves,
> of which Joe got one, and I the other.
> *Great Expectations* Charles Dickens

plantation *n* plantations are colonies, ie countries controlled by a more powerful country
> besides our plantations in America
> *Gulliver's Travels* Jonathan Swift

plastic *adj* an old term meaning having the power to form or influence
> A plastic power abode with me
> *The Prelude* William Wordsworth

player *n* an actor
> of players which upon the world's stage be
> *On His Mistress* John Donne

plump *adv* all at once, suddenly
> But it took a bit of time to get it well round, the
> change come so uncommon plump, didn't it?
> *Great Expectations* Charles Dickens

plunder *v* to plunder is to rob or steal from
> These crosses stand for the names of ships
> or towns that they sank or plundered
> *Treasure Island* Robert Louis Stevenson

pommel *v* to pommel someone is to hit them repeatedly with your fist
> shug him round the neck, pommel his back,
> and kick his legs in irrepressible affection!
> *A Christmas Carol* Charles Dickens

poor's rates *n* property taxes which were used to support the poor
> "Oh!" replied the undertaker; "why, you know,
> Mr. Bumble, I pay a good deal towards the poor's
> rates."
> *Oliver Twist* Charles Dickens

popular *adj* ruled by the people, or Republican, rather than ruled by a monarch
> With those of Greece compared and popular Rome
> *The Prelude* William Wordsworth

porringer *n* a porringer is a small bowl
> Of this festive composition each boy had one
> porringer, and no more
> *Oliver Twist* Charles Dickens

postboy *n* a postboy was the driver of a horse-drawn carriage
> He spoke to a postboy who was dozing under the
> gateway
> *Oliver Twist* Charles Dickens

post-chaise *n* a fast carriage for two or four passengers
> Looking round, he saw that it was a post-chaise,
> driven at great speed
> *Oliver Twist* Charles Dickens

postern *n* a small gate usually at the back of a building
> The little servant happening to be entering the
> fortress with two hot rolls, I passed through
> the postern and crossed the drawbridge, in her
> company
> *Great Expectations* Charles Dickens

pat[1] *vb* **patting, patted 1** to tap (someone or something) lightly with the hand **2** to shape (something) with a flat instrument or the palm of the hand **3 pat someone on the back** *informal* to congratulate someone ▷ *n* **4** a gentle tap or stroke **5** a small shaped lump of something soft, such as butter **6 pat on the back** *informal* an indication of approval **WORD ORIGIN** probably imitative

pat[2] *adv* **1 Also: off pat** thoroughly learned: *he had all his answers off pat* **2 stand pat** *chiefly US & Canad* to stick firmly to a belief or decision ▷ *adj* **3** quick, ready, or glib: *a pat generalization* **WORD ORIGIN** perhaps adverbial use ('with a light stroke') OF PAT[1]

patch *n* **1** a piece of material used to cover a hole in a garment **2** a small contrasting section: *there was a bald patch on the top of his head* **3** a small plot of land **4** *med* a protective covering for an injured eye **5** a scrap or remnant **6** the area under someone's supervision, such as a policeman or social worker **7 a bad patch** a difficult time **8 not a patch on** not nearly as good as ▷ *vb* **9** to mend (a garment) with a patch **10 patch together** to produce (something) by piecing parts together hurriedly or carelessly **11 patch up a** to mend (something) hurriedly or carelessly **b** to make up (a quarrel) **WORD ORIGIN** perhaps from French *pieche* piece

patchwork *n* **1** needlework done by sewing together pieces of different materials **2** something made up of various parts

patchy *adj* **patchier, patchiest 1** of uneven quality or intensity: *since then her career has been patchy* **2** having or forming patches

pate *n* *old-fashioned or humorous* the head or the crown of the head **WORD ORIGIN** origin unknown

pâté (**pat**-ay) *n* a spread of finely minced meat, fish, or vegetables often served as a starter **WORD ORIGIN** French

pâté de foie gras (de fwah **grah**) *n* a smooth rich paste made from the liver of specially fattened geese **WORD ORIGIN** French: pâté of fat liver

patella (pat-**tell**-a) *n, pl* **-lae** (-lee) *anat* kneecap **patellar** *adj* **WORD ORIGIN** Latin

paten (**pat**-in) *n* a plate, usually made of silver or gold, used for the bread at Communion **WORD ORIGIN** Latin *patina* pan

patent *n* **1 a** an official document granting the exclusive right to make, use, and sell an invention for a limited period **b** the right granted by such a document **2** an invention protected by a patent ▷ *adj* **3** open or available for inspection: *letters patent* **4** obvious: *their scorn was patent to everyone* **5** concerning protection of or appointment of a patent **6** (of food, drugs, etc.) made or held under a patent ▷ *vb* **7** to obtain a patent for (an invention) **WORD ORIGIN** Latin *patere* to lie open

USAGE
The pronunciation **pat**-tunt is heard in *letters patent* and *Patent Office* and is the usual US pronunciation for all senses. In Britain **pat**-tunt is sometimes heard for senses 1, 2 and 3, but **pay**-tunt is commoner and is regularly used in collocations like *patent leather*.

patent leather *n* leather processed with lacquer to give a hard glossy surface

patently *adv* clearly and obviously: *an outdated and patently absurd promise*

patent medicine *n* a medicine with a patent, available without a prescription

Patent Office *n* a government department that issues patents

pater *n* *Brit, humorous* father **WORD ORIGIN** Latin

paternal *adj* **1** fatherly: *paternal authority* **2** related through one's father: *his paternal grandmother* **paternally** *adv* **WORD ORIGIN** Latin *pater* father

paternalism *n* authority exercised in a way that limits individual responsibility **paternalistic** *adj* **WORD ORIGIN** Latin *pater* father

paternity *n* **1** the fact or state of being a father **2** descent or derivation from a father

paternity suit *n* legal proceedings, usually brought by an unmarried mother, in order to gain legal recognition that a particular man is the father of her child

Paternoster *n* *RC Church* the Lord's Prayer **WORD ORIGIN** Latin *pater noster* our father

path *n, pl* **paths 1** a road or way, often a narrow trodden track **2** a surfaced walk, such as through a garden **3** the course or direction in which something moves: *his car skidded into the path of an oncoming lorry* **4** a course of conduct: *the path of reconciliation and forgiveness* **WORD ORIGIN** Old English *pæth*

pathetic *adj* **1** arousing pity or sympathy **2** distressingly inadequate: *his pathetic attempt to maintain a stiff upper lip failed* **pathetically** *adv* **WORD ORIGIN** Greek *pathos* suffering

pathetic fallacy *n* (in literature) the presentation of inanimate objects in nature as possessing human feelings

pathname *n* *computers* the name of a file or directory together with its position in relation to other directories

pathogen *n* any agent, such as a bacterium, that can cause disease **pathogenic** *adj* **WORD ORIGIN** Greek *pathos* suffering + *-gen* (suffix) producing

pathological *adj* **1** of or relating to pathology **2** *informal* compulsively motivated: *pathological jealousy*

pathology *n* the branch of medicine that studies diseases **pathologist** *n* **WORD ORIGIN** Greek *pathos* suffering + -LOGY

pathos *n* the power, for example in literature, of arousing feelings of pity or sorrow **WORD ORIGIN** Greek: suffering

pathway *n* a path

patience *n* **1** the capacity for calmly enduring difficult situations: *the endless patience of the nurses* **2** the ability to wait calmly for something to happen without complaining or giving up: *he urged the international community to have patience to allow sanctions to work* **3** *Brit & NZ* a card game for one player only **WORD ORIGIN** Latin *pati* to suffer

patient *adj* **1** enduring difficult situations with an even temper **2** persevering or diligent: *his years of patient work may finally pay off* ▷ *n* **3** a person who is receiving medical care **patiently** *adv*

patina *n* **1** a film formed on the surface of a metal **2** the sheen on the surface of an old object, caused by age and much handling **WORD ORIGIN** Italian: coating

patio *n, pl* **-tios 1** a paved area adjoining a house: *a barbecue on the patio* **2** an open inner courtyard in a Spanish or Spanish-American house **WORD ORIGIN** Spanish: courtyard

patisserie (pat-**eess**-er-ee) *n* **1** a shop where fancy pastries are sold **2** such pastries **WORD ORIGIN** French

patois (**pat**-wah) *n, pl* **patois** (**pat**-wahz) **1** a regional dialect of a language **2** the jargon of a particular group **WORD ORIGIN** Old French: rustic speech

patrial *n* (in Britain, formerly) a person with a right by statute to live in the United Kingdom, and so not subject to immigration control **WORD ORIGIN** Latin *patria* native land

patriarch *n* **1** the male head of a tribe or family **2** *Bible* any of the men regarded as the fathers of the human race or of the Hebrew people **3 a** *RC Church* the pope **b** *Eastern Orthodox Church* a highest-ranking bishop **4** an old man who is respected **patriarchal** *adj* **WORD ORIGIN** Church Latin *patriarcha*

patriarchate *n* the office, jurisdiction, or residence of a patriarch

patriarchy *n* **1** a form of social organization in which males hold most of the power **2** *pl* **-chies** a society governed by such a system

patrician *n* **1** a member of the nobility of ancient Rome **2** an aristocrat **3** a person of refined conduct and tastes ▷ *adj* **4** (in ancient Rome) of or relating to patricians **5** aristocratic **WORD ORIGIN** Latin *patricius* noble

patricide *n* **1** the act of killing one's father **2** a person who kills his or her father **patricidal** *adj* **WORD ORIGIN** Latin *pater* father + *caedere* to kill

patrimony *n, pl* **-nies** an inheritance from one's father or other ancestor **WORD ORIGIN** Latin *patrimonium* paternal inheritance

patriot *n* a person who loves his or her country and passionately supports its interests **patriotic** *adj* **patriotically** *adv* **patriotism** *n* **WORD ORIGIN** Greek *patris* native land

patrol *n* **1** the action of going round an area or building at regular intervals for purposes of security or observation

2 a person or group that carries out such an action **3** a group of soldiers or ships involved in patrolling a particular area **4** a division of a troop of Scouts or Guides ▷ *vb* **-trolling, -trolled 5** to engage in a patrol of (a place): *peacekeepers patrolled several areas of the city* **WORD ORIGIN** French *patrouiller*

patrol car *n* a police car used for patrolling streets

patron *n* **1** a person who financially supports artists, writers, musicians, or charities **2** a regular customer of a shop, hotel, etc. **WORD ORIGIN** Latin *patronus* protector

patronage *n* **1** the support or custom given by a patron **2** (in politics) the ability or power to appoint people to jobs **3** a condescending manner

patronize *or*-**nise** *vb* **-nizing, -nized** *or* **-nising, -nised 1** to treat (someone) in a condescending way **2** to be a patron of **patronizing** *or*-**nising** *adj* **patronizingly** *or*-**nisingly** *adv*

patron saint *n* a saint regarded as the particular guardian of a country or a group of people

patronymic *n* a name derived from one's father's or a male ancestor **WORD ORIGIN** Greek *patēr* father + *onoma* name

patter¹ *vb* **1** to make repeated light tapping sounds **2** to walk with quick soft steps ▷ *n* **3** a quick succession of light tapping sounds, such as by feet: *the steady patter of rain against the window* **WORD ORIGIN** from PAT¹

patter² *n* **1** the glib rapid speech of comedians or salesmen **2** chatter **3** the jargon of a particular group ▷ *vb* **4** to speak glibly and rapidly **WORD ORIGIN** Latin *pater* in *Pater Noster* Our Father

pattern *n* **1** an arrangement of repeated parts or decorative designs **2** a regular recognizable way that something is done: *I followed a normal eating pattern* **3** a plan or diagram used as a guide to making something: *a knitting pattern* **4** a model worthy of imitation: *a pattern of kindness* **5** a representative sample ▷ *vb* **6** (foll. by *after* or *on*) to model: *an orchestra patterned after Count Basie's* **WORD ORIGIN** Medieval Latin *patronus* example

patterned *n* having a decorative pattern on it: *a selection of plain and patterned fabrics*

patty *n, pl* **-ties** a small round pie filled with meat or vegetables **WORD ORIGIN** French *pâté*

paua (**pah**-ooh-uh) *n* an edible shellfish of New Zealand, which has a pearly shell used for jewellery **WORD ORIGIN** Māori

paucity *n formal* **1** scarcity **2** smallness of amount or number **WORD ORIGIN** Latin *paucus* few

paunch *n* a protruding belly or abdomen **paunchy** *adj* **WORD ORIGIN** Latin *pantices* bowels

pauper *n old-fashioned* **1** a person who is extremely poor **2** (formerly) a person supported by public charity **WORD ORIGIN** Latin: poor

pause *vb* **pausing, paused 1** to stop doing (something) for a short time **2** to hesitate: *she answered him without pausing* ▷ *n* **3** a temporary stop or rest in speech or action **4** *music* a continuation of a note or rest beyond its normal length **5** **give someone pause** to cause someone to hesitate: *it gave him pause for reflection* **WORD ORIGIN** Greek *pausis*

pavane (pav-**van**) *n* **1** a slow and stately dance of the 16th and 17th centuries **2** music for this dance **WORD ORIGIN** Spanish *pavana*

pave *vb* **paving, paved 1** to cover (a road or area of ground) with a firm surface to make it suitable for walking or travelling on **2** **pave the way for** to prepare or make easier: *the arrests paved the way for the biggest-ever Mafia trial* **WORD ORIGIN** Old French *paver*

pavement *n* **1** a hard-surfaced path for pedestrians, alongside and a little higher than a road **2** the material used in paving **3** US the surface of a road **WORD ORIGIN** Latin *pavimentum* hard floor

pavilion *n* **1** a building at a sports ground, esp. a cricket pitch, in which players can wash and change **2** an open building or temporary structure used for exhibitions **3** a summerhouse or other decorative shelter **4** a large ornate tent **WORD ORIGIN** Latin *papilio* butterfly, tent

paving *n* **1** a paved surface **2** material used for a pavement

pavlova *n* a meringue cake topped with whipped cream and fruit **WORD ORIGIN** after Anna *Pavlova*, ballerina

paw *n* **1** a four-legged mammal's foot with claws and pads **2** *informal* a hand ▷ *vb* **3** to scrape or hit with the paws **4** *informal* to touch or caress (someone) in a rough or overfamiliar manner **WORD ORIGIN** Germanic

pawl *n* a pivoted lever shaped to engage with a ratchet to prevent motion in a particular direction **WORD ORIGIN** Dutch *pal*

pawn¹ *vb* **1** to deposit (an article) as security for money borrowed **2** to stake or risk: *I will pawn my honour on this matter* ▷ *n* **3** an article deposited as security **4** the condition of being so deposited: *in pawn* **WORD ORIGIN** Old French *pan* security

pawn² *n* **1** a chessman of the lowest value, usually able to move only one square forward at a time **2** a person or thing manipulated by someone else: *our city is just a pawn in their power games* **WORD ORIGIN** Anglo-Norman *poun*, from Medieval Latin *pedo* infantryman

pawnbroker *n* a person licensed to lend money on goods deposited **pawnbroking** *n*

Pawnee *n, pl* **Pawnees** *or* **Pawnee 1** a member of a group of Native American peoples, formerly living in Nebraska and Kansas, now chiefly in Oklahoma **2** the language of these peoples

pawnshop *n* the premises of a pawnbroker

pawpaw (**paw**-paw) *n* same as **papaya**

pax *n* **1** *chiefly RC Church* the kiss of peace ▷ *interj* **2** *Brit school slang* a call signalling a desire to end hostilities **WORD ORIGIN** Latin: peace

pay *vb* **pays, paying, paid 1** to give (money) in return for goods or services: *Willie paid for the drinks; nurses are not very well paid* **2** to settle (a debt or obligation) by giving or doing something: *he has paid his debt to society* **3** to suffer: *she paid dearly for her mistake* **4** to give (a compliment, regards, attention, etc.) **5** to profit or benefit (someone): *it doesn't always pay to be honest* **6** to make (a visit or call) **7** to yield a return of: *the account pays 5% interest* **8** **pay one's way a** to contribute one's share of expenses **b** to remain solvent without outside help ▷ *n* **9** money given in return for work or services; a salary or wage **10** **in the pay of** employed by ▷ See also **pay back, pay for**, etc. **WORD ORIGIN** Latin *pacare* to appease

payable *adj* **1** (often foll. by *on*) due to be paid: *the instalments are payable on the third of each month* **2** that is capable of being paid: *pensions are payable to those disabled during the wars*

pay back *vb* **1** to repay (a loan) **2** to make (someone) suffer for a wrong he or she has done you: *I want to pay him back for all the suffering he's caused me*

PAYE (in Britain, Australia and New Zealand) pay as you earn; a system by which income tax is deducted by employers and paid directly to the government

payee *n* the person to whom a cheque or money order is made out

pay for *vb* **1** to make payment for **2** to suffer or be punished for (a mistake)

paying guest *n euphemistic* a lodger

payload *n* **1** the amount of passengers, cargo, or bombs which an aircraft can carry **2** the part of a cargo which earns revenue **3** the explosive power of a warhead or bomb carried by a missile or aircraft

paymaster *n* an official responsible for the payment of wages and salaries

payment *n* **1** the act of paying **2** a sum of money paid **3** something given in return; punishment or reward

pay off *vb* **1** to pay the complete amount of (a debt) **2** to pay (someone) all that is due in wages and dismiss him or her from employment **3** to turn out successfully: *her persistence finally paid off* **4** *informal* to give a bribe to ▷ *n* **payoff 5** *informal* the climax or outcome of events **6** *informal* a bribe **7** the final payment of a debt **8** the final settlement, esp. in retribution: *the payoff came when the gang besieged the squealer's house*

payola *n informal* a bribe to secure special treatment, esp. to promote a commercial product

pay out *vb* **1** to spend (money) on a particular thing **2** to release (a rope) gradually, bit by bit ▷ *n* **payout 3** a sum of money paid out

pay-per-view *n* a television broadcasting system where a charge is made for receiving a specific programme

payphone *n* a coin-operated telephone

payroll *n* a list of employees, giving the salary or wage of each

payslip *n* a note given to an employee stating his or her salary or wage and detailing the deductions

pay up *vb* to pay (money) promptly or in full

Pb *chem* lead

WORD ORIGIN New Latin *plumbum*

pc 1 per cent **2** postcard

PC 1 personal computer **2** (in Britain) Police Constable **3** *informal* short for **politically correct 4** (in Britain) Privy Council *or* Counsellor **5** (in Canada) Progressive Conservative

PCOS polycystic ovary syndrome

PCV (in Britain) passenger carrying vehicle

pd paid

Pd *chem* palladium

PDA personal digital assistant

PDF portable document format: a format in which documents may be viewed

PDSA (in Britain) People's Dispensary for Sick Animals

PDT Pacific Daylight Time

PE 1 physical education **2** Prince Edward Island

pea *n* **1** an annual climbing plant with green pods containing green seeds **2** the seed of this plant, eaten as a vegetable

WORD ORIGIN from *pease* (incorrectly assumed to be a plural)

peace *n* **1** stillness or silence **2** absence of mental anxiety: *peace of mind* **3** absence of war **4** harmony between people or groups **5** a treaty marking the end of a war **6** law and order within a state: *a breach of the peace* **7** **at peace a** dead: *the old lady is at peace now* **b** in a state of harmony or serenity **8** **hold** *or* **keep one's peace** to keep silent **9** **keep the peace** to maintain law and order

WORD ORIGIN Latin *pax*

peaceable *adj* **1** inclined towards peace **2** tranquil or calm

peace dividend *n* additional money available to a government from cuts in defence expenditure because of the end of a period of hostilities

peaceful *adj* **1** not in a state of war or disagreement **2** calm or tranquil **peacefully** *adv*

peacemaker *n* a person who brings about peace, esp. between others

peace offering *n* something given or said in order to restore peace: *I bought Mum some flowers as a peace offering*

peace pipe *n* a long decorated pipe smoked by Native Americans, esp. as a token of peace

peacetime *n* a period without war

peach *n* **1** a soft juicy fruit with a downy skin, yellowish-orange sweet flesh, and a single stone **2** *informal* a person or thing that is especially pleasing: *a peach of a goal* ▷ *adj* **3** pale pinkish-orange

WORD ORIGIN Latin *Persicum malum* Persian apple

peach melba *n* a dessert made of halved peaches, vanilla ice cream, and raspberries

WORD ORIGIN after Dame Nellie *Melba*, singer

peachy *adj* **peachier, peachiest** of or like a peach, esp. in colour or texture

peacock *n*, *pl* **-cocks** *or* **-cock 1** a large male bird of the pheasant family with a crested head and a very large fanlike tail with blue and green eyelike spots **2** a vain strutting person **peahen** *fem n*

WORD ORIGIN Latin *pavo* peacock + COCK

peafowl *n* a peacock or peahen

peak *n* **1** a pointed tip or projection: *the peak of the roof* **2** **a** the pointed summit of a mountain **b** a mountain with a pointed summit **3** the point of greatest success or achievement: *the peak of his career* **4** a projecting piece on the front of some caps ▷ *vb* **5** to form or reach a peak ▷ *adj* **6** of or relating to a period of greatest demand: *hotels are generally dearer in peak season*

WORD ORIGIN perhaps from *pike* (the weapon)

peaked *adj* having a peak

peak load *n* the maximum load on an electrical power-supply system

peaky *adj* **peakier, peakiest** pale and sickly

WORD ORIGIN origin unknown

peal *n* **1** a long loud echoing sound, such as of bells or thunder ▷ *vb* **2** to sound with a peal or peals

WORD ORIGIN Middle English *pele*

peanut *n* a plant with edible nutlike seeds which ripen underground. See also **peanuts**

peanut butter *n* a brownish oily paste made from peanuts

peanuts *n* *slang* a trifling amount of money

pear *n* **1** a sweet juicy fruit with a narrow top and a rounded base **2** **go pear-shaped** *informal* to go wrong: *the plan started to go pear-shaped*

WORD ORIGIN Latin *pirum*

pearl *n* **1** a hard smooth greyish-white rounded object found inside the shell of a clam or oyster and much valued as a gem **2** see **mother-of-pearl 3** a person or thing that is like a pearl in beauty or value ▷ *adj* **4** of, made of, or set with pearl or mother-of-pearl ▷ *vb* **5** to set with or as if with pearls **6** to shape into or assume a pearl-like form or colour **7** to dive for pearls

WORD ORIGIN Latin *perna* sea mussel

pearl barley *n* barley ground into small round grains, used in soups and stews

pearly *adj* **pearlier, pearliest 1** resembling a pearl, esp. in lustre **2** decorated with pearls or mother-of-pearl

Pearly Gates *pl n* *informal* the entrance to heaven

pearly king *or fem* **pearly queen** *n* the London barrow vendor whose ceremonial clothes display the most lavish collection of pearl buttons

peasant *n* **1** a member of a low social class employed in agricultural labour **2** *informal* an uncouth or uncultured person

WORD ORIGIN Old French *païsant*

peasantry *n* peasants as a class

pease *n*, *pl* **pease** *archaic or dialect* same as **pea**

WORD ORIGIN Old English *pise, peose*

pease pudding *n* (esp. in Britain) a dish of split peas that have been soaked and boiled

peasouper *n* *informal chiefly Brit* thick dirty yellowish fog

peat *n* decaying vegetable matter found in uplands and bogs and used as a fuel (when dried) and as a fertilizer

WORD ORIGIN perhaps Celtic

pebble *n* **1** a small smooth rounded stone, esp. one worn by the action of water ▷ *vb* **-bling, -bled 2** to cover with pebbles **pebbly** *adj*

WORD ORIGIN Old English *papolstān* pebble stone

pebble dash *n* *Austral & Brit* a finish for external walls consisting of small stones set in plaster

pec *n* *informal* a pectoral muscle: *a gigolo with flowing blond locks and rippling pecs*

pecan (**pee**-kan) *n* a smooth oval nut with a sweet oily kernel that grows on hickory trees in the Southern US

WORD ORIGIN Native American *paccan*

peccadillo *n*, *pl* **-loes** *or* **-los** a trivial misdeed

WORD ORIGIN Spanish *pecadillo*, from Latin *peccare* to sin

peccary *n*, *pl* **-ries** *or* **-ry** a piglike animal native to American forests

WORD ORIGIN Carib

peck¹ *vb* **1** to strike or pick up with the beak **2** *informal* to kiss (a person) quickly and lightly **3** **peck at** to eat slowly and reluctantly: *pecking away at your lunch* ▷ *n* **4** a quick light blow from a bird's beak **5** a mark made by such a blow **6** *informal* a quick light kiss

WORD ORIGIN origin unknown

peck² *n* an obsolete unit of liquid measure equal to one quarter of a bushel or 2 gallons (9.1 litres)

WORD ORIGIN Anglo-Norman

pecker *n* **keep one's pecker up** *Brit & NZ slang* to remain cheerful

pecking order *n* the order of seniority or power in a group: *she came from a family low in the social pecking order*

peckish *adj* *informal* feeling slightly hungry

pectin *n* *biochem* a water-soluble carbohydrate that occurs in ripe fruit: used in the manufacture of jams because of its ability to gel

WORD ORIGIN Greek *pēktos* congealed

pectoral *adj* **1** of or relating to the chest, breast, or thorax: *pectoral fins* **2** worn on the breast or chest: *a pectoral cross* ▷ *n* **3** a pectoral organ or part, esp. a muscle or fin

WORD ORIGIN Latin *pectus* breast

pectoral fin *n* a fin, just behind the head in fishes, that helps to control the direction of movement

peculate *vb* **-lating, -lated** *literary* to embezzle (public money) **peculation** *n*

WORD ORIGIN Latin *peculari*

peculiar *adj* **1** strange or odd: *a peculiar idea* **2** distinct or special **3** (foll. by *to*) belonging exclusively (to): *a fish peculiar to these waters*

WORD ORIGIN Latin *peculiaris* concerning private property

James Joyce

His books are practically worshipped by his supporters (usually academics), and consistently ignored by almost everybody else. Among those who have heard of him, he is most famous for writing books which are difficult to read and impossible to understand. He was once chiefly associated with the *stream of consciousness* technique and (unfairly, as he only did this in one chapter of one book) with forgoing all punctuation. And yet for all that, he has made an indelible mark on English literary style and the language itself.

In literary terms, Joyce belongs to the school of High Modernism: highly educated, often elitist authors who came to prominence in the years between the first and second world wars. He was a contemporary of Virginia Woolf and Ernest Hemingway, and an acquaintance (though not necessarily an admirer) of Gertrude Stein, a friend of T S Eliot, and a mentor to Samuel Beckett. In his native Ireland he solicited the company of great poets like Æ (George Russell) and WB Yeats; in his life abroad, he benefited from the kindness of Ezra Pound (who bought Joyce a pair of shoes when he could not afford to buy his own); and during his time in Trieste, he encouraged the work of Italo Svevo (Emilio Schmitz), who went on to become one of Italy's most respected authors, and served as a model for Joyce's own character Leopold Bloom.

Joyce has also exerted a tremendous influence on some of the most renowned authors in the English language. William Faulkner wrote *The Sound and the Fury* in a rich, evocative internal-monologue style after being inspired by Joyce's *A Portrait of the Artist as a Young Man*. Anthony Burgess took a copy of *Finnegans Wake* to the front in World War II, and remained a lifelong aficionado of Joyce, and one of his most vocal supporters. Burgess's own experiments with English style, including the portmanteau Nadsat language of *A Clockwork Orange* are certainly indebted to Joyce, and Burgess made Joyce a character in his novel *Earthly Powers*. The American science-fiction writer Philip K Dick – who enjoys his own cult following – was a great admirer of Joyce, and quotes a passage from *Finnegans Wake* in his novel *The Divine Invasion* (though he seems to believe that Joyce was channelling messages from outer space). Tom Robbins is an admitted Joyce fan, and recounts an incident where Buddhist monks resort to a Japanese translation of *Finnegans Wake* in order to perform Christian funeral rites for an Allied pilot who crash-landed near their monastery. Even Salman Rushdie's depiction of the multilingual environment of India has drawn comparisons to Joyce's famous word-play.

Joyce's influence reaches beyond these (and other) writers – and high-flown literary style – to the language English speakers use every day. One of Joyce's more lasting effects on English is the concept of *Bloomsday*, an annual 'holiday' of sorts celebrated every 16 June in Dublin and other cities around the world in honour of Joyce and in particular the novel *Ulysses*, his acknowledged masterpiece. All the events of *Ulysses* take place during eighteen hours of 16 June 1904 (which was Joyce's first date with Nora Barnacle, the woman who would – eventually – become his wife). A more common word coined by Joyce is *quark*, which first appears in *Finnegans Wake*: 'Three quarks for Muster Mark'. The previously undefined word was later chosen by Murray Gell-Mann for the elementary particle he hypothesized in 1964. But the most common word associated with Joyce is *loo*. While we can hypothesize the etymology from the French *lieux d'aisance*, the fact is this word, though common enough now, first appears in print in Joyce's *Ulysses*: the character Stephen Dedalus (Joyce's alter ego) is meditating on the battle of Waterloo and puns *Waterloo* with *water-closet*. Whether this indicates that *loo* was already used to mean 'toilet'' or whether this usage originates from Joyce is impossible to determine from existing evidence ... though the language of the lavatory was a favourite theme in Joyce.

peculiarity n, pl **-ties 1** a strange or unusual habit; eccentricity **2** a distinguishing trait **3** the state or quality of being peculiar

pecuniary adj **1** of or relating to money **2** law (of an offence) involving a monetary penalty
WORD ORIGIN Latin pecunia money

pedagogue or US sometimes **pedagog** n a teacher, esp. a pedantic one
pedagogic adj
WORD ORIGIN Greek pais boy + agōgos leader

pedagogy (**ped**-a-goj-ee) n the principles, practice, or profession of teaching

pedal¹ n **1** a foot-operated lever used to control a vehicle or machine, or to modify the tone of a musical instrument ▷ vb **-dalling, -dalled** or US **-daling, -daled 2** to propel (a bicycle) by operating the pedals **3** to operate the pedals of an organ or piano
WORD ORIGIN Latin pedalis, from pes foot

pedal² adj of or relating to the foot or the feet
WORD ORIGIN Latin pedalis, from pes foot

pedant n a person who is concerned chiefly with insignificant detail or who relies too much on academic learning
pedantic adj **pedantically** adv
WORD ORIGIN Italian pedante teacher

pedantry n, pl **-ries** the practice of being a pedant, esp. in the minute observance of petty rules or details

peddle vb **-dling, -dled 1** to sell (goods) from place to place **2** to sell illegal drugs **3** to advocate (an idea or information) persistently: the version of events being peddled by his opponents
WORD ORIGIN from pedlar

pederast or **paederast** n a man who has homosexual relations with boys
pederasty or **paederasty** n
WORD ORIGIN Greek pais boy + erastēs lover

pedestal n **1** a base that supports something, such as a statue **2 put someone on a pedestal** to admire someone very much
WORD ORIGIN Old Italian piedestallo

pedestrian n **1** a person who travels on foot ▷ adj **2** dull or commonplace: a pedestrian performance
WORD ORIGIN Latin pes foot

pedestrian crossing n Austral & Brit a path across a road marked as a crossing for pedestrians

pedestrianize or **-nise** vb **-nizing, -nized** or **-nising, -nised** to convert (a street or shopping area) into an area for pedestrians only

pedestrian precinct n Brit an area of a town for pedestrians only, esp. an area of shops

pedicure n medical or cosmetic treatment of the feet
WORD ORIGIN Latin pes foot + curare to care for

pedigree n **1** the line of descent of a purebred animal **2** a document recording this **3** a genealogical table, esp. one indicating pure ancestry
WORD ORIGIN Old French pie de grue crane's foot, alluding to the spreading

lines used in a genealogical chart

pediment n a triangular part over a door, as used in classical architecture
WORD ORIGIN obsolete periment, perhaps workman's corruption of pyramid

pedlar or esp. US **peddler** n a person who peddles
WORD ORIGIN Middle English ped basket

pedometer (pid-**dom**-it-er) n a device that measures the distance walked by recording the number of steps taken
WORD ORIGIN Latin pes foot + METER

peduncle n **1** bot a plant stalk bearing a flower cluster or solitary flower **2** anat, pathol any stalklike structure
peduncular adj
WORD ORIGIN Latin pediculus little foot

pee informal vb **peeing, peed 1** to urinate ▷ n **2** urine **3** the act of urinating
WORD ORIGIN euphemistic for piss

peek vb **1** to glance quickly or secretly ▷ n **2** such a glance
WORD ORIGIN Middle English pike

peel vb **1** to remove the skin or rind of (a fruit or vegetable) **2** to come off in flakes **3** (of a person or part of the body) to shed skin in flakes as a result of sunburn ▷ n **4** the skin or rind of a fruit, etc. See also **peel off**
WORD ORIGIN Latin pilare to make bald

peelings pl n strips of skin or rind that have been peeled off: potato peelings

peel off vb **1** to remove or be removed by peeling: this softens the paint, which can then be peeled off **2** slang to take off one's clothes or a piece of clothing **3** to leave a group of moving people, vehicles, etc. by taking a course that curves away to one side: two aircraft peeled off to attack the enemy bombers

peen n the end of a hammer head opposite the striking face, often rounded or wedge-shaped
WORD ORIGIN origin unknown

peep¹ vb **1** to look slyly or quickly, such as through a small opening or from a hidden place **2** to appear partially or briefly: the sun peeped through the clouds ▷ n **3** a quick or sly look **4** the first appearance: the peep of dawn
WORD ORIGIN variant of peek

peep² vb **1** (esp. of young birds) to make small shrill noises ▷ n **2** a peeping sound
WORD ORIGIN imitative

Peeping Tom n a man who furtively observes women undressing
WORD ORIGIN after the tailor who, according to legend, peeped at Lady Godiva when she rode naked through Coventry

peepshow n a box containing a series of pictures that can be seen through a small hole

peer¹ n **1** a member of a nobility **2** a person who holds any of the five grades of the British nobility: duke, marquess, earl, viscount, and baron **3** a person of equal social standing, rank, age, etc.: he is greatly respected by his peers in the arts world
WORD ORIGIN Latin par equal

peer² vb **1** to look intently or as if with difficulty: Walter peered anxiously at his father's face **2** to appear dimly: the sun peered through the fog

WORD ORIGIN Flemish pieren to look with narrowed eyes

peerage Brit n **1** the whole body of peers; aristocracy **2** the position, rank, or title of a peer

peeress n **1** (in Britain) a woman holding the rank of a peer **2** the wife or widow of a peer

peer group n a social group composed of people of similar age and status

peerless adj having no equals; unsurpassed

peer pressure n influence from one's peer group

peeve informal vb **peeving, peeved 1** to irritate or annoy: the way he looked at her peeved her ▷ n **2** something that irritates: my pet peeve **peeved** adj
WORD ORIGIN from peevish

peevish adj fretful or irritable
peevishly adv
WORD ORIGIN origin unknown

peewee n a black-and-white Australian bird

peewit or **pewit** n same as **lapwing**
WORD ORIGIN imitative of its call

peg n **1** a small pin or bolt used to join two parts together, to fasten, or to mark **2** a hook or knob for hanging things on **3** music a pin on a stringed instrument which can be turned to tune the string wound around it **4** Also called: **clothes peg** a split or hinged pin for fastening wet clothes to a line to dry **5** Brit a small drink of spirits **6** an opportunity or pretext for doing something: the play's subject matter provides a perfect peg for a discussion of issues like morality and faith **7 bring** or **take (someone) down a peg** to lower the pride of (someone) **8 off the peg** Brit & NZ (of clothes) ready-to-wear, as opposed to tailor-made ▷ vb **pegging, pegged 9** to insert a peg into **10** to secure with pegs: the balloon was pegged down to stop it drifting away **11** to mark (a score) with pegs, as in some card games **12** chiefly Brit to work steadily: he pegged away at his job for years **13** to fix or maintain something, such as prices, at a particular level or value: a fixed-rate mortgage, pegged at 9.6 per cent. See also **peg out**
WORD ORIGIN Low Germanic pegge

pegboard n **1** a board with a pattern of holes into which small pegs can be fitted, used for playing certain games or keeping a score **2** hardboard with rows of holes from which articles may be hung for display

peggy square n NZ a small hand-knitted square

peg leg n informal **1** an artificial leg **2** a person with an artificial leg

peg out vb **1** informal to collapse or die **2** to mark or secure with pegs: the scientists pegged out a hectare of land in order to study every plant in it

PEI Prince Edward Island

peignoir (**pay**-nwahr) n a woman's light dressing gown
WORD ORIGIN French

pejorative (pij-**jor**-a-tiv) adj **1** (of a word or expression) having an insulting or critical sense ▷ n **2** a pejorative word or expression

WORD ORIGIN Late Latin *pejorare* to make worse

peke *n informal* a Pekingese dog

Pekingese or **Pekinese** *n* **1** *pl* **-ese** a small dog with a long straight coat, curled plumed tail, and short wrinkled muzzle **2** the dialect of Mandarin Chinese spoken in Beijing

pelargonium *n* a plant with circular leaves and red, pink, or white flowers: includes many cultivated geraniums
WORD ORIGIN Greek *pelargos* stork

pelf *n contemptuous* money or wealth
WORD ORIGIN Old French *pelfre* booty

pelican *n* a large water bird with a pouch beneath its long bill for holding fish
WORD ORIGIN Greek *pelekan*

pelican crossing *n* (in Britain) a type of road crossing with a pedestrian-operated traffic-light system
WORD ORIGIN from *pe(destrian) li(ght) con(trolled) crossing*, with *-con* adapted to *-can* of *pelican*

pelisse (pel-**leess**) *n* a cloak or loose coat which is usually fur-trimmed
WORD ORIGIN Old French, from Latin *pellis* skin

pellagra *n pathol* a disease caused by a diet lacking in vitamin B, which results in scaling of the skin, diarrhoea and mental disorder
WORD ORIGIN Italian, from *pelle* skin + Greek *agra* paroxysm

pellet *n* **1** a small round ball, esp. of compressed matter **2 a** an imitation bullet used in toy guns **b** a piece of small shot **3** a small pill
WORD ORIGIN Latin *pila* ball

pell-mell *adv* **1** in a confused headlong rush: *the hounds ran pell-mell into the yard* **2** in a disorderly manner: *the things were piled pell-mell in the room*
WORD ORIGIN Old French *pesle-mesle*

pellucid *adj literary* **1** transparent or translucent **2** extremely clear in style and meaning
WORD ORIGIN Latin *pellucidus*

pelmet *n* a board or piece of fabric used to conceal the curtain rail
WORD ORIGIN probably from French *palmette* palm-leaf decoration on cornice moulding

pelota *n* a game played by two players who use a basket strapped to their wrists or a wooden racket to propel a ball against a specially marked wall
WORD ORIGIN Spanish: ball

pelt¹ *vb* **1** to throw (missiles) at **2** (foll. by *along* etc.) to hurry **3** to rain heavily ▷ *n* **4** a blow **5 at full pelt** very quickly: *she ran down the street at full pelt*
WORD ORIGIN origin unknown

pelt² *n* the skin or fur of an animal, esp. as material for clothing or rugs: *the lucrative international trade in beaver pelts*
WORD ORIGIN probably from Latin *pellis* skin

pelvis *n, pl* **-vises** or **-ves 1** the framework of bones at the base of the spine, to which the hips are attached **2** the bones that form this structure **pelvic** *adj*
WORD ORIGIN Latin: basin

pen¹ *n* **1** an instrument for writing or drawing using ink. See also **ballpoint, fountain pen 2 the pen** writing as an occupation ▷ *vb* **penning, penned 3** to write or compose
WORD ORIGIN Latin *penna* feather

pen² *n* **1** an enclosure in which domestic animals are kept **2** any place of confinement ▷ *vb* **penning, penned** or **pent 3** to enclose (animals) in a pen **4 penned in** being or feeling trapped or confined: *she stood penned in by bodies at the front of the crowd*
WORD ORIGIN Old English *penn*

pen³ *n US & Canad informal* short for **penitentiary** (sense 1)

pen⁴ *n* a female swan
WORD ORIGIN origin unknown

Pen. Peninsula

penal (**pee**-nal) *adj* **1** of or relating to punishment **2** used as a place of punishment: *a penal colony* **penally** *adv*
WORD ORIGIN Latin *poena* penalty

penal code *n* the body of laws relating to crime and punishment

penalize or **-lise** *vb* **-lizing, -lized** or **-lising, -lised 1** to impose a penalty on (someone) for breaking a law or rule **2** to inflict a disadvantage on: *why should I be penalized just because I'm a woman?* **penalization** or **-lisation** *n*

penalty *n, pl* **-ties 1** a legal punishment for a crime or offence **2** loss or suffering as a result of one's own action: *we are now paying the penalty for neglecting to keep our equipment up to date* **3** *sport, games, etc.* a handicap awarded against a player or team for illegal play, such as a free shot at goal by the opposing team
WORD ORIGIN Latin *poena*

penalty box *n* **1** Also called: **penalty area** *soccer* a rectangular area in front of the goal, within which a penalty is awarded for a serious foul by the defending team **2** *ice hockey* a bench for players serving time penalties

penalty corner *n hockey* a free hit from the goal line taken by the attacking side

penalty shoot-out *n sport* a method of deciding the winner of a drawn match, in which players from each team attempt to score with a penalty shot

penance *n* **1** voluntary self-punishment to make amends for a sin **2** *RC Church* a sacrament in which repentant sinners are forgiven provided they confess their sins to a priest and perform a penance
WORD ORIGIN Latin *paenitentia* repentance

pence *n* a plural of **penny**

≡ **USAGE**
≡ Since the decimalization of British
≡ currency and the introduction of the
≡ abbreviation *p*, as in 10*p*, 85*p*, etc. the
≡ abbreviation has tended to replace
≡ *pence* in speech, as in 4*p*, 12*p*, etc.

penchant (**pon**-shon) *n* strong inclination or liking: *a stylish woman with a penchant for dark glasses*
WORD ORIGIN French

pencil *n* **1** a rod of graphite encased in wood which is used for writing or drawing ▷ *vb* **-cilling, -cilled** or *US* **-ciling, -ciled 2** to draw, colour, write, or mark with a pencil **3 pencil in** to note, arrange, or include provisionally or tentatively
WORD ORIGIN Latin *penicillus* painter's brush

pendant *n* **a** an ornament worn on a chain round the neck: *a beautiful pearl pendant* **b** an ornament that hangs from a piece of jewellery
WORD ORIGIN Latin *pendere* to hang down

pendent *adj literary* **1** dangling **2** jutting
WORD ORIGIN see PENDANT

pending *prep* **1** while waiting for ▷ *adj* **2** not yet decided or settled **3** imminent: *these developments have been pending for some time*

pendulous *adj literary* hanging downwards and swinging freely
WORD ORIGIN Latin *pendere* to hang down

pendulum *n* **1** a weight suspended so it swings freely under the influence of gravity **2** such a device used to regulate a clock mechanism **3** a movement from one attitude or belief towards its opposite: *the pendulum has swung back to more punitive measures*

penetrate *vb* **-trating, -trated 1** to find or force a way into or through **2** to diffuse through; permeate: *the smell of cooking penetrated through to the sitting room* **3** to see through: *the sunlight did not penetrate the thick canopy of leaves* **4** (of a man) to insert the penis into the vagina of (a woman) **5** to grasp the meaning of (a principle, etc.) **penetrable** *adj* **penetrative** *adj*
WORD ORIGIN Latin *penetrare*

penetrating *adj* tending to or able to penetrate: *a penetrating mind; a penetrating voice*

penetration *n* **1** the act or an instance of penetrating **2** the ability or power to penetrate **3** keen insight or perception

pen friend *n* a person with whom one exchanges letters, often a person in another country whom one has not met

penguin *n* a flightless black-and-white sea bird with webbed feet and wings modified as flippers for swimming
WORD ORIGIN origin unknown

penicillin *n* an antibiotic used to treat diseases caused by bacteria
WORD ORIGIN Latin *pencillus* tuft of hairs

peninsula *n* a narrow strip of land projecting from the mainland into a sea or lake **peninsular** *adj*
WORD ORIGIN Latin, literally: almost an island

≡ **USAGE**
≡ The noun *peninsula* is sometimes
≡ confused with the adjective *peninsular*:
≡ *the Iberian peninsula* (not *peninsular*).

penis *n, pl* **-nises** or **-nes** the organ of copulation in higher vertebrates, also used for urinating in many mammals **penile** *adj*
WORD ORIGIN Latin

penitent *adj* **1** feeling regret for one's sins; repentant ▷ *n* **2** a person who is penitent **penitence** *n*
WORD ORIGIN Church Latin *paenitens* regretting

P

penitential adj of, showing, or as a penance

penitentiary n, pl -ries **1** (in the US and Canada) a state or federal prison ▷ adj **2** of or for penance **3** used for punishment and reformation: *the penitentiary system*
WORD ORIGIN Latin *paenitens* penitent

penknife n, pl -knives a small knife with one or more blades that fold into the handle

penmanship n formal style or technique of writing by hand

pen name n a name used by a writer instead of his or her real name; nom de plume

pennant n **1** a long narrow flag, esp. one used by ships as identification or for signalling **2** chiefly US, Canad, & Austral a flag indicating the winning of a championship in certain sports
WORD ORIGIN probably a blend of *pendant + pennon*

penniless adj very poor

pennon n **1** a long flag, often tapering and divided at the end, originally a knight's personal flag **2** a small tapering or triangular flag flown by a ship or boat
WORD ORIGIN Latin *penna* feather

penny n, pl **pennies** or **pence** **1** a British bronze coin worth one hundredth of a pound **2** a former British and Australian coin worth one twelfth of a shilling **3** pl **pennies** US & Canad a cent **4** informal chiefly Brit the least amount of money: *I don't have a penny* **5** a pretty penny informal a considerable sum of money **6** spend a penny Brit & NZ informal to urinate **7** the penny dropped informal the explanation of something was finally understood
WORD ORIGIN Old English *penig, pening*

Penny Black n the first adhesive postage stamp, issued in Britain in 1840

penny-dreadful n, pl -fuls Brit informal a cheap, often lurid book or magazine

penny-farthing n Brit an early type of bicycle with a large front wheel and a small rear wheel

penny-pinching adj **1** excessively careful with money; miserly ▷ n **2** miserliness **penny-pincher** n

pennyroyal n a Eurasian plant with hairy leaves and small mauve flowers, which provides an aromatic oil used in medicine
WORD ORIGIN Old French *pouliol* pennyroyal + *real* royal

penny-wise adj penny-wise and pound-foolish careful or thrifty in small matters but wasteful in large ventures

pennywort n a Eurasian rock plant with whitish-green tubular flowers and rounded leaves

pennyworth n **1** the amount that can be bought for a penny **2** a small or insignificant amount of something: *they'd thrown in their pennyworth of opinion*

penology (pee-**nol**-a-jee) n the study of the punishment of criminals and of prison management
WORD ORIGIN Greek *poinē* punishment

pen pal n informal same as **pen friend**

penpusher n a person whose work involves a lot of boring paperwork **penpushing** adj, n

pension¹ n **1** a regular payment made by the state or a former employer to a person who has retired or to a widowed or disabled person ▷ vb **2** to grant a pension to. See also **pension off** ▷ **pensionable** adj **pensioner** n
WORD ORIGIN Latin *pensio* a payment

pension² (pon-syon) n (in France and some other countries) a relatively cheap boarding house
WORD ORIGIN French: extended meaning of *pension* grant

pension off vb to cause (someone) to retire from a job and pay him or her a pension

pensive adj deeply thoughtful, often with a tinge of sadness **pensively** adv
WORD ORIGIN Latin *pensare* to consider

pent vb a past of **pen²**

penta- combining form five: *pentagon; pentameter*
WORD ORIGIN Greek *pente*

pentacle n same as **pentagram**
WORD ORIGIN Italian *pentacolo* something having five corners

pentagon n geom a figure with five sides **pentagonal** adj

Pentagon n a five-sided building that houses the headquarters of the US Department of Defense

pentagram n a star-shaped figure with five points

pentameter (pen-**tam**-it-er) n a line of poetry consisting of five metrical feet

Pentateuch (**pent**-a-tyuke) n the first five books of the Old Testament **Pentateuchal** adj
WORD ORIGIN Greek *pente* five + *teukhos* scroll case

pentathlon n an athletic contest consisting of five different events. See also **modern pentathlon**
WORD ORIGIN Greek *pente* five + *athlon* contest

pentatonic scale n music a scale consisting of five notes

pentavalent adj chem having a valency of five

Pentecost n a Christian festival occurring on Whit Sunday celebrating the descent of the Holy Ghost to the apostles
WORD ORIGIN Greek *pentēkostē* fiftieth (day after the Resurrection)

Pentecostal adj relating to any of the Christian groups that have a charismatic and fundamentalist approach to Christianity

penthouse n a luxurious flat built on the top floor or roof of a building
WORD ORIGIN Middle English *pentis*, later *penthouse*, from Latin *appendere* to hang from

pent-up adj not released; repressed: *full of pent-up emotional violence*

penultimate adj second last

penumbra n, pl -brae or -bras **1** the partially shadowed region which surrounds the full shadow in an eclipse **2** literary a partial shadow **penumbral** adj

WORD ORIGIN Latin *paene* almost + *umbra* shadow

penurious adj formal **1** niggardly with money **2** lacking money or means

penury n formal **1** extreme poverty **2** extreme scarcity
WORD ORIGIN Latin *penuria*

peon n a Spanish-American farm labourer or unskilled worker
WORD ORIGIN Spanish

peony n, pl -nies a garden plant with showy pink, red, white, or yellow flowers
WORD ORIGIN Greek *paiōnia*

people pl n **1** persons collectively or in general **2** a group of persons considered together: *old people suffer from anaemia more often than younger people do* **3** pl -ples the persons living in a particular country: *the American people* **4** one's family or ancestors: *her people originally came from Skye* **5** the people **a** the mass of ordinary persons without rank or privileges **b** the body of persons in a country who are entitled to vote ▷ vb -pling, -pled **6** to provide with inhabitants: *the centre of the continent is sparsely peopled*
WORD ORIGIN Latin *populus*

⟨USAGE
⟨See at person.

people carrier n same as **multipurpose vehicle**

people mover n Brit, Austral, & NZ same as **multipurpose vehicle**

pep n **1** high spirits, energy, or vitality ▷ vb **pepping, pepped 2** pep up to make more lively or interesting: *the company has spent thousands trying to pep up its image*
WORD ORIGIN short for *pepper*

peplum n, pl -lums or -la a flared ruffle attached to the waist of a garment
WORD ORIGIN Greek *peplos* shawl

pepper n **1** a sharp hot condiment obtained from the fruit of an East Indian climbing plant **2** Also called: **capsicum** a colourful tropical fruit used as a vegetable and a condiment ▷ vb **3** to season with pepper **4** to sprinkle liberally: *his speech is heavily peppered with Americanisms* **5** to pelt with small missiles
WORD ORIGIN Greek *peperi*

pepper-and-salt adj **1** (of a fabric) marked with a fine mixture of black and white **2** (of hair) streaked with grey

peppercorn n the small dried berry of the pepper plant

peppercorn rent n Brit a rent that is very low or nominal

pepper mill n a small hand mill used to grind peppercorns

peppermint n **1** a mint plant which produces a pungent oil, used as a flavouring **2** a sweet flavoured with peppermint

pepperoni n a dry sausage of pork and beef spiced with pepper
WORD ORIGIN Italian *peperoni* peppers

pepper spray n a defence spray agent derived from hot cayenne peppers, which causes temporary blindness and breathing difficulty

peppery adj **1** tasting of pepper **2** irritable

Less or Fewer?

In September 2008 a leading British supermarket chain announced that it was changing the wording above its fast-track checkouts from '10 items or less' to 'up to 10 items'. Why did it decide to go all this trouble? It had finally tired of the number of complaints it received complaining that the phrase '10 items or less' is contrary to the rules of grammar.

The case of the supermarket sign is just one example of the confusion that exists in the mind of many English-speakers around the words *less* and *fewer*. The basis of this confusion is that both words are used in comparisons. People who take an interest in such matters are inclined to point out that *less* is the comparative form of *little* or *a little*, and so it means 'smaller in quantity', while *fewer* is the comparative form of *few* or *a few*, and so it means 'smaller in number'.

The phrase *a little* is used when we refer to things that can't be counted in terms of numbers – what is technically called an 'uncountable' noun. You can be offered *a little water*, *a little cheese*, or *a little money*. Abstract nouns are especially likely to fall into this category: you can have *a little hope*, *a little luck*, or *a little sympathy*. When we are comparing one amount of any of these things with another amount, we can therefore talk about having *less* of it: *less cheese*, *less money*, *less hope*, *less sympathy*.

On the other side of the equation are things that can be counted in terms of numbers – what are technically called 'countable' nouns. You can have one cup, two cups, or any number of cups. (A key distinction is that countable nouns have both singular and plural forms, whereas uncountable nouns are only talked about in the singular.) When we talk about a small number of things, we may talk about *a few cups*. Similarly, we may talk about *a few people* or *a few shops*. It follows that when we are comparing one number with another we should talk about the smaller number being *fewer*: *fewer cups*, *fewer people*, *fewer shops*.

Some items, of course, can be counted in some contexts but not in others. We tend to think of coffee as an uncountable mass, and we might be told by doctors to drink *less* coffee. But we can also think of a cup of coffee as 'a coffee', and talk about drinking one, two or three coffees a day. A grammatically careful doctor advising a patient to cut down from three cups a day to one would therefore urge the patient to drink *fewer* coffees. Notice that *fewer* is always used with a plural noun, while *less* is always followed by a singular.

We don't usually have much trouble working out whether to say *few* or *little* when we speak. We are seldom tempted to refer to *a few money* or *a little shops*. However, when it comes to the comparative forms the word *less* is a much, much more common word in English than its counterpart *fewer*. It occurs about ten times as often, and is familiar from phrases such as *no less* and *much less*. It is surely this familiarity that calls the word *less* to mind when people are making comparisons and causes them to refer to *less books*, *less trees*, and *less calories*.

But does it really matter which form we use? Latitudinarians will say that whether one says that a food contains *less calories* or *fewer calories*, there can be no possible confusion as to what is meant, and the effect on your waistline will be the same. Customers of the supermarket chain that had a sign about '10 items or less' were not misled about whether or not they qualified to use the quick checkout service. If people who read articles about grammar didn't insist on pointing out the correct form, we could happily use *less* all the time and no-one would lose any sleep about it. For sticklers who take a pride in being grammatically correct, however, there is no question of losing the distinction between the two words. The two sides are doomed never to agree.

pep pill *n informal* a tablet containing a stimulant drug

pepsin *n* an enzyme produced in the stomach, which, when activated by acid, breaks down proteins
WORD ORIGIN Greek *peptein* to digest

pep talk *n informal* a talk designed to increase confidence and enthusiasm

peptic *adj* **1** of or relating to digestion **2** of or caused by pepsin or the action of the digestive juices: *a peptic ulcer*
WORD ORIGIN Greek *peptein* to digest

peptic ulcer *n* an ulcer in the stomach or duodenum

peptide *n chem* a compound consisting of two or more amino acids linked by chemical bonding between the amino group of one and the carboxyl group of another

per *prep* **1** for every: *three pence per pound; 30 pounds per week* **2** by; through **3** as per according to: *proceed as per the instructions* **4** as per usual *or* as per normal *informal* as usual
WORD ORIGIN Latin: by, for each

peradventure *archaic adv* **1** by chance; perhaps ▷ *n* **2** chance or doubt
WORD ORIGIN Old French *par aventure* by chance

perambulate *vb* **-lating, -lated** *formal* to walk about (a place) **perambulation** *n*
WORD ORIGIN Latin *per-* through + *ambulare* to walk

perambulator *n formal* same as **pram**

per annum *adv* in each year
WORD ORIGIN Latin

per capita *adj, adv* of or for each person: *the average per capita wage has increased*
WORD ORIGIN Latin, literally: according to heads

perceive *vb* **-ceiving, -ceived** **1** to become aware of (something) through the senses **2** to understand or grasp **perceivable** *adj*
WORD ORIGIN Latin *percipere* to seize entirely

per cent *adv* **1** in each hundred. Symbol: % ▷ *n also* **percent** **2** a percentage or proportion
WORD ORIGIN Medieval Latin *per centum* out of every hundred

percentage *n* **1** proportion or rate per hundred parts **2** any proportion in relation to the whole: *a small percentage of the population* **3** *informal* profit or advantage

percentile *n* one of 99 actual or notional values of a variable dividing its distribution into 100 groups with equal frequencies

perceptible *adj* able to be perceived; recognizable **perceptibly** *adv*

perception *n* **1** the act of perceiving **2** insight or intuition: *his acute perception of other people's emotions* **3** the ability to perceive **4** way of viewing: *advertising affects the customer's perception of a product* **perceptual** *adj*
WORD ORIGIN Latin *perceptio* comprehension

perceptive *adj* **1** observant **2** able to perceive **perceptively** *adv* **perceptiveness** *n*

perch¹ *n* **1** a branch or other resting place above ground for a bird **2** any

raised resting place: *from his perch on the bar stool* ▷ *vb* **3** (of birds) to alight or rest on a perch: *it fluttered to the branch and perched there for a moment* **4** to place or position precariously: *he was perched uneasily on the edge of his chair*
WORD ORIGIN Latin *pertica* long staff

perch² *n, pl* **perch** *or* **perches** **1** a spiny-finned edible freshwater fish of Europe and North America **2** any of various similar or related fishes
WORD ORIGIN Greek *perkē*

perchance *adv archaic or poetic* **1** perhaps **2** by chance
WORD ORIGIN Anglo-French *par chance*

percipient *adj formal* quick at perceiving; observant **percipience** *n*
WORD ORIGIN Latin *percipiens* observing

percolate *vb* **-lating, -lated** **1** to pass or filter through very small holes: *the light percolating through the stained-glass windows cast coloured patterns on the floor* **2** to spread gradually: *his theories percolated through the academic community* **3** to make (coffee) or (of coffee) to be made in a percolator **percolation** *n*
WORD ORIGIN Latin *per-* through + *colare* to strain

percolator *n* a coffeepot in which boiling water is forced up through a tube and filters down through the coffee grounds into a container

percussion *n* **1** the striking of one thing against another **2** *music* percussion instruments collectively **percussive** *adj*
WORD ORIGIN Latin *percutere* to hit

percussion cap *n* a detonator which contains material that explodes when struck

percussion instrument *n* a musical instrument, such as the drums, that produces a sound when struck directly

percussionist *n music* a person who plays percussion instruments

perdition *n* **1** *Christianity* final and unalterable spiritual ruin; damnation **2** same as **hell**
WORD ORIGIN Late Latin *perditio* ruin

peregrinate *vb* **-nating, -nated** *formal* to travel or wander about from place to place **peregrination** *n*
WORD ORIGIN Latin *peregrinari* to travel

peregrine falcon *n* a European falcon with dark plumage on the back and wings and lighter underparts
WORD ORIGIN Latin *peregrinus* foreign

peremptory *adj* **1** urgent or commanding: *a peremptory knock on the door* **2** expecting immediate obedience without any discussion: *he gave peremptory instructions to his son* **3** dogmatic **peremptorily** *adv*
WORD ORIGIN Latin *peremptorius* decisive

perennial *adj* **1** lasting throughout the year or through many years ▷ *n* **2** a plant that continues its growth for at least three years
WORD ORIGIN Latin *per-* through + *annus* year

perestroika *n* (in the late 1980s) the policy of restructuring the Soviet economy and political system
WORD ORIGIN Russian: reconstruction

perfect *adj* **1** having all essential elements **2** faultless: *a perfect circle* **3** correct or

precise: *perfect timing* **4** utter or absolute: *a perfect stranger* **5** excellent in all respects: *a perfect day* **6** *maths* exactly divisible into equal integral or polynomial roots: *36 is a perfect square* **7** *grammar* denoting a tense of verbs used to describe a completed action ▷ *n* **8** *grammar* the perfect tense ▷ *vb* **9** to improve to one's satisfaction: *he is in Paris to perfect his French* **10** to make fully accomplished: *he perfected the system* **perfectly** *adv*
WORD ORIGIN Latin *perficere* to complete

USAGE
For most of its meanings, the adjective *perfect* describes an absolute state, i.e. one that cannot be qualified; thus something is either *perfect* or not *perfect*, and cannot be *more perfect* or *less perfect*. However when *perfect* means excellent in all respects, a comparative can be used with it without absurdity: *the next day the weather was even more perfect.*

perfectible *adj* capable of becoming or being made perfect **perfectibility** *n*

perfection *n* the state or quality of being perfect
WORD ORIGIN Latin *perfectio* a completing

perfectionism *n* the demand for the highest standard of excellence **perfectionist** *n, adj*

perfect pitch *n* same as **absolute pitch**

perfidious *adj literary* treacherous or deceitful **perfidy** *n*
WORD ORIGIN Latin *perfidus*

perforate *vb* **-rating, -rated** **1** to make a hole or holes in **2** to punch rows of holes between (stamps) for ease of separation **perforable** *adj* **perforator** *n*
WORD ORIGIN Latin *per-* through + *forare* to pierce

perforation *n* **1** a hole or holes made in something **2** a series of punched holes, such as that between individual stamps

perforce *adv formal* of necessity
WORD ORIGIN Old French *par force*

perform *vb* **1** to carry out (an action): *the hospital performs more than a hundred such operations each year* **2** to present (a play or concert): *he performed a couple of songs from his new album* **3** to fulfil: *you have performed the first of two conditions* **performable** *adj* **performer** *n*
WORD ORIGIN Old French *parfournir*

performance *n* **1** the act or process of performing **2** an artistic or dramatic production: *the concert includes the first performance of a new trumpet concerto* **3** manner or quality of functioning: *the car's overall performance is excellent* **4** *informal* conduct or behaviour, esp. when distasteful: *what did you mean by that performance at the restaurant?*

perfume *n* **1** a liquid cosmetic worn for its pleasant smell **2** a fragrant smell ▷ *vb* **-fuming, -fumed** **3** to impart a perfume to **perfumed** *adj*
WORD ORIGIN French *parfum*, from Latin *per* through + *fumare* to smoke

perfumer *n* a person who makes or sells perfume **perfumery** *n*

perfunctory *adj formal* done only as a matter of routine: *he gave his wife a perfunctory kiss* **perfunctorily** *adv* **perfunctoriness** *n*

WORD ORIGIN Late Latin *perfunctorius* negligent

perfuse *vb* **-fusing, -fused 1** to permeate (a liquid, colour, etc.) through or over (something) **2** *surgery* to pass (a fluid) through tissue

pergola *n* an arched trellis or framework that supports climbing plants
WORD ORIGIN Italian

perhaps *adv* **1** possibly; maybe **2** approximately; roughly: *it would have taken perhaps three or four minutes*
WORD ORIGIN earlier *perhappes*, from *per* by + *happes* chance

perianth *n bot* the outer part of a flower
WORD ORIGIN Greek *peri-* around + *anthos* flower

pericardium *n, pl* **-dia** the membranous sac enclosing the heart **pericardial** *adj*
WORD ORIGIN Greek *peri-* around + *kardia* heart

pericarp *n bot* the part of a fruit enclosing the seed that develops from the wall of the ovary
WORD ORIGIN Greek *peri-* around + *karpos* fruit

perigee *n astron* the point in its orbit around the earth when the moon or a satellite is nearest the earth
WORD ORIGIN Greek *peri-* near + *gea* earth

perihelion *n, pl* **-lia** *astron* the point in its orbit around the sun when a planet or comet is nearest the sun
WORD ORIGIN Greek *peri-* near + *hēlios* sun

peril *n* great danger or jeopardy
perilous *adj*
WORD ORIGIN Latin *periculum*

perimeter (per-**rim**-it-er) *n* **1** *maths* **a** the curve or line enclosing a plane area **b** the length of this curve or line **2** any boundary around something
WORD ORIGIN Latin *perimetros*

perinatal *adj* of or occurring in the period from about three months before to one month after birth
WORD ORIGIN Greek *peri-* around + Latin *natus* born

perineum (per-rin-**nee**-um) *n, pl* **-nea** (-**nee**-a) *anat* the region of the body between the anus and the genitals
perineal *adj*
WORD ORIGIN Greek *perinaion*

period *n* **1** a portion of time: *six inches of rain fell in a 24-hour period* **2** a portion of time specified in some way: *the President's first period of office* **3** an occurrence of menstruation **4** *geol* a unit of geological time during which a system of rocks is formed: *the Jurassic period* **5** a division of time at school, college, or university when a particular subject is taught **6** *physics, maths* the time taken to complete one cycle of a regularly recurring phenomenon **7** *chem* one of the horizontal rows of elements in the periodic table **8** *chiefly US & Canad* same as **full stop** ▷ *adj* **9** dating from or in the style of an earlier time: *a performance on period instruments*
WORD ORIGIN Greek *periodos* circuit

periodic *adj* recurring at intervals
periodically *adv* **periodicity** *n*

periodical *n* **1** a publication issued at regular intervals, usually monthly or weekly ▷ *adj* **2** of or relating to such publications **3** periodic or occasional

periodic law *n chem* the principle that the chemical properties of the elements are periodic functions of their atomic numbers

periodic table *n chem* a table of the elements, arranged in order of increasing atomic number, based on the periodic law

peripatetic (per-rip-a-**tet**-ik) *adj* **1** travelling from place to place **2** *Brit* employed in two or more educational establishments and travelling from one to another: *a peripatetic violin teacher* ▷ *n* **3** a peripatetic person
WORD ORIGIN Greek *peripatein* to pace to and fro

peripheral (per-**if**-er-al) *adj* **1** not relating to the most important part of something; incidental **2** of or relating to a periphery ▷ *n* **3** *computers* any device, such as a disk or modem, concerned with input/output or storage

periphery (per-**if**-er-ee) *n, pl* **-eries 1** the boundary or edge of an area or group: *slums sprouted up on the periphery of the city* **2** fringes of a field of activity: *less developed countries on the periphery of the capitalist system*
WORD ORIGIN Greek *peri-* around + *pherein* to bear

periphrasis (per-**if**-ra-siss) *n, pl* **-rases** (-ra-seez) a roundabout way of expressing something; circumlocution
WORD ORIGIN Greek *peri-* around + *phrazein* to declare

periscope *n* an optical instrument used, esp. in submarines, to give a view of objects on a different level
WORD ORIGIN Greek *periskopein* to look around

perish *vb* **1** to be destroyed or die **2** to cause to suffer: *we were perished with cold* **3** to rot or cause to rot: *to prevent your swimsuit from perishing, rinse it in clean water before it dries*
WORD ORIGIN Latin *perire* to pass away entirely

perishable *adj* **1** liable to rot ▷ *n* **2** (often *pl*) a perishable article, esp. food

perishing *adj* **1** *informal* (of weather) extremely cold **2** *slang* confounded or blasted: *get rid of the perishing lot!*

peristalsis (per-riss-**tal**-siss) *n, pl* **-ses** (-seez) *physiol* the wavelike involuntary muscular contractions of the walls of the digestive tract **peristaltic** *adj*
WORD ORIGIN Greek *peri-* around + *stalsis* compression

peritoneum (per-rit-toe-**nee**-um) *n, pl* **-nea** (-**nee**-a) *or* **-neums** a serous sac that lines the walls of the abdominal cavity and covers the abdominal organs
peritoneal *adj*
WORD ORIGIN Greek *peritonos* stretched around

peritonitis (per-rit-tone-**ite**-iss) *n* inflammation of the peritoneum, causing severe abdominal pain

periwig *n historical* a wig formerly worn by men
WORD ORIGIN French *perruque*

periwinkle¹ *n* same as **winkle** (sense 1)

WORD ORIGIN origin unknown

periwinkle² *n* a Eurasian evergreen plant with trailing stems and blue flowers
WORD ORIGIN Old English *perwince*

perjure *vb* **-juring, -jured** ● **perjure oneself** *criminal law* to deliberately give false evidence while under oath **perjurer** *n*
WORD ORIGIN Latin *perjurare*

perjury (**per**-jer-ee) *n, pl* **-juries** *criminal law* the act of deliberately giving false evidence while under oath
WORD ORIGIN Latin *perjurium* a false oath

perk¹ *n informal* an incidental benefit gained from a job, such as a company car
WORD ORIGIN short for *perquisite*

perk² *vb informal* short for **percolate** (sense 3)

perk up *vb* **1** to make or become more cheerful **2** to rise or cause to rise briskly: *the dog's ears perked up suddenly*
WORD ORIGIN origin unknown

perky *adj* **perkier, perkiest 1** jaunty or lively **2** confident or spirited

Perl *n* a computer programming language that is used for text manipulation, esp. on the World Wide Web
WORD ORIGIN practical extraction and report language

perlemoen (per-la-**moon**) *n S African* same as **abalone**
WORD ORIGIN Afrikaans, from Dutch

perm¹ *n* **1** a hairstyle with long-lasting waves or curls produced by treating the hair with chemicals ▷ *vb* **2** to give a perm to (hair)

perm² *n informal* short for **permutation** (sense 4)

permafrost *n* ground that is permanently frozen
WORD ORIGIN *perma(nent)* + *frost*

permanent *adj* **1** existing or intended to exist forever: *a permanent solution* **2** not expected to change: *a permanent condition* **permanence** *n* **permanently** *adv*
WORD ORIGIN Latin *permanens* continuing

permanent wave *n* same as **perm¹** (sense 1)

permanent way *n chiefly Brit* the track of a railway, including the sleepers and rails

permanganate *n* a salt of an acid containing manganese, used as a disinfectant

permeable *adj* capable of being permeated, esp. by liquids
permeability *n*

permeate *vb* **-ating, -ated 1** to penetrate or spread throughout (something): *his mystical philosophy permeates everything he creates* **2** to pass through or cause to pass through by osmosis or diffusion: *the rain permeated her anorak* **permeation** *n*
WORD ORIGIN Latin *permeare*

Permian *adj geol* of the period of geological time about 280 million years ago
WORD ORIGIN after Perm, Russian port

permissible *adj* permitted or allowable
permissibility *n*

permission *n* authorization to do something

permissive *adj* tolerant or lenient, esp. in sexual matters: *the so-called permissive society* **permissiveness** *n*

permit *vb* **-mitting, -mitted 1** to allow (something) to be done or to happen: *smoking is not permitted in the office* **2** to allow (someone) to do something: *her father does not permit her to eat sweets* **3** to allow the possibility (of): *they saw each other as often as time and circumstances permitted* ▷ *n* **4** an official document granting permission to do something **WORD ORIGIN** Latin *permittere*

permutate *vb* **-tating, -tated** to alter the sequence or arrangement (of): *endlessly permutating three basic designs*

permutation *n* **1** *maths* an ordered arrangement of the numbers or terms of a set into specified groups: *the permutations of a, b, and c, taken two at a time, are ab, ba, ac, ca, bc, cb* **2** a combination of items made by reordering **3** a transformation **4** a fixed combination for selections of results on football pools **WORD ORIGIN** Latin *permutare* to change thoroughly

pernicious *adj formal* **1** wicked or malicious: *pernicious lies* **2** causing grave harm; deadly **WORD ORIGIN** Latin *pernicies* ruin

pernicious anaemia *n* a severe form of anaemia resulting in a reduction of the red blood cells, weakness, and a sore tongue

pernickety *adj informal* **1** excessively fussy about details **2** (of a task) requiring close attention **WORD ORIGIN** origin unknown

peroration *n formal* the concluding part of a speech which sums up the points made previously **WORD ORIGIN** Latin *peroratio*

peroxide *n* **1** hydrogen peroxide used as a hair bleach **2** any of a class of metallic oxides, such as sodium peroxide, Na_2O_2 ▷ *adj* **3** bleached with or resembling peroxide: *a peroxide blonde* ▷ *vb* **-iding, -ided 4** to bleach (the hair) with peroxide

perp *n US & Canad informal* a person who has committed a crime **WORD ORIGIN** short for *perpetrator*

perpendicular *adj* **1** at right angles to a given line or surface **2** upright; vertical **3** denoting a style of English Gothic architecture characterized by vertical lines ▷ *n* **4** *geom* a line or plane perpendicular to another **perpendicularity** *n* **WORD ORIGIN** Latin *perpendiculum* a plumb line

perpetrate *vb* **-trating, -trated** to perform or be responsible for (a deception or crime) **perpetration** *n* **perpetrator** *n* **WORD ORIGIN** Latin *perpetrare*

≡ USAGE
≡ Perpetrate and perpetuate are sometimes
≡ confused: *he must answer for the crimes he*
≡ *has perpetrated* (not *perpetuated*); *the book*
≡ *helped to perpetuate* (not *perpetrate*) *some of*
≡ *the myths surrounding his early life.*

perpetual *adj* **1** never ending or never changing: *Mexico's colourful scenery and nearly perpetual sunshine* **2** continually repeated: *his mother's perpetual worries about his health* **perpetually** *adv* **WORD ORIGIN** Latin *perpetualis*

perpetual motion *n* motion of a hypothetical mechanism that continues indefinitely without any external source of energy

perpetuate *vb* **-ating, -ated** to cause to continue: *images that perpetuate stereotypes of Black people as illiterate, happy-go-lucky entertainers* **perpetuation** *n* **WORD ORIGIN** Latin *perpetuare* to continue without interruption

≡ USAGE
≡ See at **perpetrate**.

perpetuity *n, pl* **-ties 1** eternity **2** the state of being perpetual **3** something perpetual, such as a pension that is payable indefinitely **4 in perpetuity** forever **WORD ORIGIN** Latin *perpetuitas* continuity

perplex *vb* **1** to puzzle or bewilder **2** to complicate: *this merely perplexes the issue* **perplexing** *adj* **WORD ORIGIN** Latin *perplexus* entangled

perplexity *n, pl* **-ties 1** the state of being perplexed **2** something that perplexes

perquisite *n formal* same as **perk¹** **WORD ORIGIN** Latin *perquirere* to seek earnestly for something

perry *n, pl* **-ries** an alcoholic drink made from fermented pear juice **WORD ORIGIN** Old French *peré*

per se (per **say**) *adv* in itself **WORD ORIGIN** Latin

persecute *vb* **-cuting, -cuted 1** to oppress or maltreat (someone), because of race or religion **2** to harass (someone) persistently **persecution** *n* **persecutor** *n* **WORD ORIGIN** Latin *persequi* to take vengeance upon

perseverance *n* continued steady belief or efforts; persistence

persevere *vb* **-severing, -severed** (often foll. by *with* or *in*) to continue to make an effort despite difficulties **WORD ORIGIN** Latin *perseverus* very strict

Persian *adj* **1** of ancient Persia or modern Iran ▷ *n* **2** a person from Persia (now Iran) **3** the language of Iran or of Persia

Persian carpet *n* a hand-made carpet or rug with flowing or geometric designs in rich colours

Persian cat *n* a long-haired variety of domestic cat

Persian lamb *n* **1** a black loosely curled fur from the karakul lamb **2** a karakul lamb

persiflage (per-sif-**flahzh**) *n literary* light frivolous conversation or writing **WORD ORIGIN** French

persimmon *n* a sweet red tropical fruit **WORD ORIGIN** from a Native American language

persist *vb* **1** to continue without interruption: *if the symptoms persist, see your doctor* **2** (often foll. by *in* or *with*) to continue obstinately despite opposition: *she persisted in using these controversial methods* **WORD ORIGIN** Latin *persistere*

persistent *adj* **1** unrelenting: *persistent rain* **2** showing persistence: *she was a persistent woman* **persistence** *n* **persistently** *adv*

persistent vegetative state *n med* an irreversible condition, resulting from brain damage, characterized by lack of consciousness, thought, and feeling, although reflex activities continue

person *n, pl* **people** *or* **persons 1** an individual human being **2** the body of a human being: *he was found to have a knife concealed about his person* **3** *grammar* a category into which pronouns and forms of verbs are subdivided to show whether they refer to the speaker, the person addressed, or some other individual or thing **4 in person** actually doing something or being somewhere oneself: *I had the chance to hear her speak in person* **WORD ORIGIN** Latin *persona* mask

≡ USAGE
≡ People is the word usually used to refer
≡ to more than one individual: *there were*
≡ *a hundred people at the reception.* Persons is
≡ rarely used, except in official English:
≡ *several persons were interviewed.*

-person *n combining form* sometimes used instead of *man* and *woman* or *lady*: *chairperson*

≡ USAGE
≡ See at **man**.

persona (per-**soh**-na) *n, pl* **-nae** (-nee) the personality that a person adopts and presents to other people **WORD ORIGIN** Latin: mask

personable *adj* pleasant in appearance and personality

personage *n* **1** an important or distinguished person **2** any person

personal *adj* **1** of the private aspects of a person's life: *redundancy can put an enormous strain on personal relationships* **2** of a person's body: *personal hygiene* **3** belonging to, or for the sole use of, a particular individual: *he disappeared, leaving his passport, diary and other personal belongings in his flat* **4** undertaken by an individual: *the sponsorship deal requires him to make a number of personal appearances for publicity purposes* **5** offensive in respect of an individual's personality or intimate affairs: *he has suffered a lifetime of personal remarks about his weight* **6** having the attributes of an individual conscious being: *a personal God* **7** *grammar* of person **8** *law* of movable property, such as money

personal assistant *n* a person who is employed to help someone with his or her work, esp. the secretarial and administrative aspects of it

personal column *n* a newspaper column containing personal messages and advertisements

personal computer *n* a small computer used for word processing or computer games

personality *n, pl* **-ties 1** *psychol* the distinctive characteristics which make an individual unique **2** the distinctive character of a person which makes him or her socially attractive: *some people find him lacking in personality and a bit colourless*

Lancashire Dialect

As far as the English language is concerned, the historic county of Lancashire contains two rather separate traditions. Most of the county speaks with some version of the accent made familiar by noted Lancastrians such as Fred Dibnah (a native of Bolton), Gracie Fields (from Rochdale), and George Formby (born in Wigan). However, the area around the port city of Liverpool has a quite different dialect, known as 'Scouse', which is discussed elsewhere in this book.

Even leaving the complication of Scouse aside, it would be dangerous to consider Lancastrian as being a single dialect. It is said that differences in dialect can be detected every ten miles in Lancashire, and certainly the speech of urban Manchester manifests different features to that encountered in mill towns and rural areas in the north of the county.

Moreover, the Lancashire dialect has some features in common with Yorkshire speech, so that the two are often combined as 'Northern' in the minds of people from the South and Midlands. In both counties the archaic forms *thee* and *thou* are used as alternatives for *you*, and expressions such as 'us books' or 'us boots' are used when Standard English would require the possessive adjective *our*. Northerners of all descriptions might call a person who behaves foolishly a 'daft a'peth' (an *a'peth* being a halfpenny's worth of something), claim to be 'spitting feathers' when they feel thirsty, or look at threatening clouds in the distance and pronounce it to be 'black over Bill's mother's'.

There are, however, some features that distinguish the Lancashire dialect. Lancastrian speech is typically 'rhotic', sounding the letter 'r' after a vowel in words such as *board* and *start*, while other Northern accents would generally leave it silent. Lancastrians also have some idiosyncratic vowels. The vowel sound in words such as *book* and *look* is typically lengthened so that these words rhyme with *fluke*, while words such as *air* and *care* are pronounced so that they rhyme with *fur*.

Lancastrians who set foot outside the county will be met with blank stares if they refer to string as *bant* or ask for a *barm cake* when they want to buy a soft bread roll. Other dialect words used in the county include *flash* ('a pond that has been created as a consequence of subsidence'), *bobbins* ('bad' or 'worthless'), *speel* ('a splinter of wood'), and *wickthing* ('a creepy-crawly').

The traditional stereotype of Lancashire was a place of smoking factories, where workers wore clogs and flat caps, ate black puddings, and exclaimed 'Ee, bah gum!', 'By 'eck!', and 'Ecky thump!' while discussing 'trouble at mill'. Comedians have had plenty of fun with this image. In the 1970s, the Goodies satirized the contemporary craze for kung fu by imagining 'Ecky thump' to be a traditional Lancashire martial art in which black puddings were hurled as weapons (an episode so funny that one unfortunate viewer literally died laughing). In the following decade, the comedy drama *Brass* created a gloriously over-the-top caricature of a pathologically callous mill owner lording it over forelock-tugging workers.

You won't see too many people wearing clogs in Lancashire these days. In the late 1980s, Manchester was rechristened 'Madchester' as it found itself at the centre of Britain's electronic music scene. The redevelopment of central Manchester in the 1990s cemented its status as a vibrant modern city. The changes undergone by the region have even been reflected in the long-running soap opera *Coronation Street*, set in the fictional suburb of Weatherfield. Regular viewers gain a picture not only of the way the people of Lancashire live but also of how they speak. They soon become accustomed to characters greeting each other as 'chuck' and exclaiming 'Ee!' whenever they are taken aback. After a while they may even cease to be perplexed when they hear someone who feels abandoned and neglected complain of being left 'like piffy on a rock bun'.

3 a well-known person in a certain field; celebrity **4** a remarkable person: *she is a personality to be reckoned with* **5** (*often pl*) an offensive personal remark: *the argument never degenerated into personalities*

personalize *or* **-lise** *vb* **-lizing, -lized** *or* **-lising, -lised 1** to base (an argument or discussion) around people's characters rather than on abstract arguments **2** to mark (stationery or clothing) with a person's initials or name **3** same as **personify**

personally *adv* **1** without the help of others: *she had seen to it personally that permission was granted* **2** in one's own opinion: *personally, I think it's overrated* **3** as if referring to oneself: *yes, he was rather rude but it's not worth taking it personally* **4** as a person: *I don't like him personally, but he's fine to work with*

personal organizer *n* **1** a diary for storing personal records, appointments, etc. **2** a pocket-sized electronic device that performs the same functions

personal pronoun *n* a pronoun such as *I, you, he, she, it, we,* and *they* that represents a definite person or thing

personal stereo *n chiefly Brit* a small portable audio cassette player used with lightweight headphones

persona non grata (non **grah**-ta) *n, pl* **personae non gratae** (**grah**-tee) an unacceptable person
WORD ORIGIN Latin

personate *vb* **-ating, -ated** *criminal law* to assume the identity of (another person) with intent to deceive **personation** *n*

personify *vb* **-fies, -fying, -fied 1** to give human characteristics to (a thing or abstraction) **2** to represent (an abstract quality) in human or animal form **3** (of a person or thing) to represent (an abstract quality), as in art **4** to be the embodiment of: *she can be charm personified* **personification** *n*

personnel *n* **1** the people employed in an organization or for a service **2** the department in an organization that appoints or keeps records of employees **3** (in the armed forces) people, as opposed to machinery or equipment
WORD ORIGIN French

perspective *n* **1** a way of regarding situations or facts and judging their relative importance: *the female perspective on sex and love* **2** objectivity: *Kay's problems helped me put my minor worries into perspective* **3** a method of drawing that gives the effect of solidity and relative distances and sizes **4** the appearance of objects or buildings relative to each other, determined by their distance from the viewer
WORD ORIGIN Latin *perspicere* to inspect carefully

Perspex *n trademark* a clear acrylic resin used as a substitute for glass

perspicacious *adj formal* acutely perceptive or discerning **perspicacity** *n*
WORD ORIGIN Latin *perspicax*

perspicuous *adj literary* (of speech or writing) easily understood; lucid **perspicuity** *n*
WORD ORIGIN Latin *perspicuus* transparent

perspiration *n* **1** the salty fluid secreted by the sweat glands of the skin; sweat **2** the act of sweating

perspire *vb* **-spiring, -spired** to sweat
WORD ORIGIN Latin *per-* through + *spirare* to breathe

persuade *vb* **-suading, -suaded 1** to make (someone) do something by reason or charm: *we tried to persuade him not to come up the mountain with us* **2** to cause to believe; convince: *persuading people of the need for enforced environmental protection may be difficult* **persuadable** *adj*
WORD ORIGIN Latin *persuadere*

persuasion *n* **1** the act of persuading **2** the power to persuade **3** a set of beliefs; creed: *the Roman Catholic persuasion; literary intellectuals of the modernist persuasion*

persuasive *adj* able to persuade: *a persuasive argument* **persuasively** *adv*

pert *adj* **1** saucy or impudent **2** attractive in a neat way: *pert buttocks*
WORD ORIGIN Latin *apertus* open

pertain *vb* (*often foll. by to*) **1** to have reference or relevance: *the notes pertaining to the case* **2** to be appropriate: *the product pertains to real user needs* **3** to belong (to) or be a part (of)
WORD ORIGIN Latin *pertinere*

pertinacious *adj* **1** doggedly resolute in purpose or belief **2** stubbornly persistent **pertinacity** *n*
WORD ORIGIN Latin *per-* (intensive) + *tenax* clinging

pertinent *adj* relating to the matter at hand; relevant **pertinence** *n*
WORD ORIGIN Latin *pertinens*

perturb *vb* **1** to disturb the composure of **2** to throw into disorder
WORD ORIGIN Latin *perturbare* to confuse

perturbation *n literary* anxiety or worry

peruke *n historical* a wig for men worn in the 17th and 18th centuries
WORD ORIGIN French *perruque*

peruse *vb* **-rusing, -rused 1** to read or examine with care **2** to browse or read in a leisurely way **perusal** *n*
WORD ORIGIN *per-* (intensive) + *use*

pervade *vb* **-vading, -vaded** to spread through or throughout (something) **pervasion** *n* **pervasive** *adj*
WORD ORIGIN Latin *per-* through + *vadere* to go

perverse *adj* **1** deliberately acting in a way different from what is regarded as normal or proper **2** wayward or contrary; obstinate **perversely** *adv* **perversity** *n*
WORD ORIGIN Latin *perversus* turned the wrong way

perversion *n* **1** any abnormal means of obtaining sexual satisfaction **2** the act of perverting

pervert *vb* **1** to use wrongly or badly **2** to interpret wrongly or badly; distort **3** to lead (someone) into abnormal behaviour, esp. sexually; corrupt **4** to debase ▷ *n* **5** a person who practises sexual perversion **perverted** *adj*
WORD ORIGIN Latin *pervertere* to turn the wrong way

pervious *adj* **1** able to be penetrated; permeable: *the thin walls were pervious to the*

slightest sound **2** receptive to new ideas; open-minded
WORD ORIGIN Latin *per-* through + *via* a way

Pesach *or* **Pesah** (**pay**-sahk) *n* same as **Passover**

peseta (pess-**say**-ta) *n* a former monetary unit of Spain
WORD ORIGIN Spanish

pesky *adj* **peskier, peskiest** *informal chiefly US & Canad* troublesome
WORD ORIGIN probably changed from *pesty*

peso (**pay**-so) *n, pl* **-sos** the standard monetary unit of Chile, Colombia, Cuba, the Dominican Republic, Mexico, the Philippines, and Uruguay
WORD ORIGIN Spanish: weight

pessary *n, pl* **-ries** *med* **1** a device worn in the vagina, either as a support for the uterus or as a contraceptive **2** a vaginal suppository
WORD ORIGIN Greek *pessos* plug

pessimism *n* **1** the tendency to expect the worst in all things **2** the doctrine of the ultimate triumph of evil over good **pessimist** *n* **pessimistic** *adj* **pessimistically** *adv*
WORD ORIGIN Latin *pessimus* worst

pest *n* **1** an annoying person or thing; nuisance **2** any organism that damages crops, or injures or irritates livestock or man
WORD ORIGIN Latin *pestis* plague

pester *vb* to annoy or nag continually
WORD ORIGIN Old French *empestrer* to hobble (a horse)

pesticide *n* a chemical used to destroy pests, esp. insects
WORD ORIGIN *pest* + Latin *caedere* to kill

pestilence *n literary* any deadly epidemic disease, such as the plague

pestilent *adj* **1** annoying or irritating **2** highly destructive morally or physically **3** likely to cause infectious disease **pestilential** *adj*
WORD ORIGIN Latin *pestis* plague

pestle *n* a club-shaped instrument for grinding or pounding substances in a mortar
WORD ORIGIN Old French *pestel*

pet¹ *n* **1** a tame animal kept for companionship or pleasure **2** a person who is favoured or indulged: *teacher's pet* ▷ *adj* **3** kept as a pet: *a pet hamster* **4** of or for pet animals: *pet food* **5** strongly felt or particularly cherished: *a pet hatred; he would not stand by and let his pet project be abandoned* ▷ *vb* **petting, petted 6** to treat as a pet; pamper **7** to pat or stroke affectionately **8** *informal* (of two people) to caress each other in an erotic manner
WORD ORIGIN origin unknown

pet² *n* a fit of sulkiness
WORD ORIGIN origin unknown

petal *n* any of the brightly coloured leaflike parts which head of a flower **petalled** *adj*
WORD ORIGIN Greek *petalon* leaf

petard *n* **1** (formerly) a device containing explosives used to break through a wall or door **2** hoist with one's own petard being the victim of one's own schemes
WORD ORIGIN French: firework

peter out *vb* to come gradually to an end: *the road petered out into a rutted track* **WORD ORIGIN** origin unknown

Peter Pan *n* a youthful or immature man **WORD ORIGIN** after the main character in *Peter Pan*, a play

pethidine (**peth**-id-een) *n* a white crystalline water-soluble drug used to relieve pain **WORD ORIGIN** perhaps a blend of *piperidine + ethyl*

petiole *n bot* the stalk which attaches a leaf to a plant **WORD ORIGIN** Latin *petiolus* little foot

petit bourgeois (**pet**-ee boor-zhwah) *n, pl* **petits bourgeois** (**pet**-ee boor-zhwah**z**) the lower middle class **WORD ORIGIN** French

petite (pit-**eat**) *adj* (of a woman) small and dainty **WORD ORIGIN** French

petit four (**pet**-ee four) *n, pl* **petits fours** (**pet**-ee **fours**) a very small fancy cake or biscuit **WORD ORIGIN** French, literally: little oven

petition *n* **1** a written document signed by a large number of people demanding some form of action from a government or other authority **2** any formal request to a higher authority **3** *law* a formal application in writing made to a court asking for some specific judicial action: *she filed a petition for divorce* ▷ *vb* **4** to address or present a petition to (a government or to someone in authority): *he petitioned the Crown for mercy* **5** (foll. by *for*) to seek by petition: *the firm's creditors petitioned for liquidation* **petitioner** *n* **WORD ORIGIN** Latin *petere* to seek

petit mal (**pet**-ee **mal**) *n* a mild form of epilepsy in which there are periods of loss of consciousness for up to 30 seconds **WORD ORIGIN** French: little illness

petit point (**pet**-ee **point**) *n* **1** a small diagonal needlepoint stitch used for fine detail **2** work done with such stitches **WORD ORIGIN** French: small point

pet name *n* an affectionate nickname for a close friend or family member

petrel *n* a sea bird with a hooked bill and tubular nostrils, such as the albatross, storm petrel, or shearwater **WORD ORIGIN** variant of earlier *pitteral*

Petri dish (**pet**-ree) *n* a shallow dish used in laboratories, esp. for producing cultures of bacteria **WORD ORIGIN** after J. R. Petri, bacteriologist

petrify *vb* **-fies, -fying, -fied** **1** to stun or daze with fear: *he was petrified of going to jail* **2** (of organic material) to turn to stone **3** to make or become unable to change or develop: *a society petrified by outmoded conventions* **petrification** *n* **WORD ORIGIN** Greek *petra* stone

petrochemical *n* a substance, such as acetone, obtained from petroleum **petrochemistry** *n*

petrodollar *n* money earned by a country by exporting petroleum

petrol *n* a volatile flammable liquid obtained from petroleum and used as a fuel for internal-combustion engines **WORD ORIGIN** see PETROLEUM

petrolatum (pet-rol-**late**-um) *n* a translucent jelly-like substance obtained from petroleum: used as a lubricant and in medicine as an ointment base

petrol bomb *n* a simple grenade consisting of a bottle filled with petrol. A piece of cloth is put in the neck of the bottle and set alight just before the bomb is thrown

petroleum *n* a dark-coloured thick flammable crude oil occurring in sedimentary rocks, consisting mainly of hydrocarbons: the source of petrol and paraffin **WORD ORIGIN** Latin *petra* stone + *oleum* oil

petroleum jelly *n* same as **petrolatum**

petrol station *n Brit* same as **filling station**

petticoat *n* a woman's underskirt **WORD ORIGIN** from *petty + coat*

pettifogging *adj* excessively concerned with unimportant detail **pettifogger** *n* **WORD ORIGIN** origin unknown

pettish *adj* peevish or fretful **pettishness** *n* **WORD ORIGIN** from PET²

petty *adj* **-tier, -tiest** **1** trivial or unimportant: *petty details* **2** small-minded: *petty spite* **3** low in importance: *petty criminals* **pettily** *adv* **pettiness** *n* **WORD ORIGIN** French *petit* little

petty cash *n* a small cash fund for minor incidental expenses

petty officer *n* a noncommissioned officer in the navy

petulant *adj* unreasonably irritable or peevish **petulance** *n* **petulantly** *adv* **WORD ORIGIN** Latin *petulans* bold

petunia *n* a tropical American plant with pink, white, or purple funnel-shaped flowers **WORD ORIGIN** obsolete French *petun* variety of tobacco

pew *n* **1 a** (in a church) a long benchlike seat with a back, used by the congregation **b** (in a church) an enclosed compartment reserved for the use of a family or group **2 take a pew** take a seat **WORD ORIGIN** Greek *pous* foot

pewter *n* **1** an alloy containing tin, lead, and sometimes copper and antimony **2** dishes or kitchen utensils made from pewter **WORD ORIGIN** Old French *peaultre*

pfennig (**fen**-ig) *n* a former German monetary unit worth one hundredth of a mark **WORD ORIGIN** German: penny

PG indicating that a film certified for viewing by anyone, but which contains scenes that may be unsuitable for children, for whom parental guidance is necessary

pH *n* potential of hydrogen; a measure of the acidity or alkalinity of a solution

phaeton (**fate**-on) *n* a light four-wheeled horse-drawn carriage with or without a top **WORD ORIGIN** from French, after *Phaëthon*, character in Greek myth

phagocyte (**fag**-go-site) *n* a cell or protozoan that engulfs particles, such as microorganisms **WORD ORIGIN** Greek *phagein* to eat + *kutos* vessel

phalanger *n* an Australian marsupial with dense fur and a long tail **WORD ORIGIN** Greek *phalaggion* spider's web, referring to its webbed hind toes

phalanx (**fal**-lanks) *n, pl* **phalanxes** or **phalanges** (fal-**lan**-jeez) **1** any closely grouped mass of people: *a solid phalanx of reporters and photographers* **2** a number of people united for a common purpose **3** an ancient Greek battle formation of infantry in close ranks **WORD ORIGIN** Greek

phallic *adj* of or resembling a phallus: *a phallic symbol*

phallus (**fal**-luss) *n, pl* **-luses** or **-li** (-lie) **1** same as **penis** **2** an image of the penis as a symbol of reproductive power **WORD ORIGIN** Greek *phallos*

phantasm *n* **1** a phantom **2** an unreal vision; illusion **phantasmal** *adj* **WORD ORIGIN** Greek *phantasma*

phantasmagoria *n* a shifting medley of dreamlike figures **phantasmagoric** *adj* **WORD ORIGIN** probably from French *fantasmagorie* production of phantoms

phantasy *n, pl* **-sies** *archaic* same as **fantasy**

phantom *n* **1** an apparition or spectre **2** the visible representation of something abstract, such as in a dream or hallucination: *the phantom of liberty* ▷ *adj* **3** deceptive or unreal: *she regularly took days off for what her bosses considered phantom illnesses* **WORD ORIGIN** Latin *phantasma*

Pharaoh (**fare**-oh) *n* the title of the ancient Egyptian kings **WORD ORIGIN** Egyptian *pr-'o* great house

Pharisee *n* **1** a member of an ancient Jewish sect teaching strict observance of Jewish traditions **2** (often not cap) a self-righteous or hypocritical person **Pharisaic** *adj* **WORD ORIGIN** Hebrew *pārūsh* separated

pharmaceutical *adj* of or relating to drugs or pharmacy

pharmaceutics *n* same as **pharmacy** (sense 1)

pharmacist *n* a person qualified to prepare and dispense drugs

pharmacology *n* the science or study of drugs **pharmacological** *adj* **pharmacologist** *n*

pharmacopoeia (far-ma-koh-**pee**-a) *n* an authoritative book containing a list of medicinal drugs along with their uses, preparation and dosages **WORD ORIGIN** Greek *pharmakopoiia* art of preparing drugs

pharmacy *n* **1** the preparation and dispensing of drugs **2** *pl* **-cies** a dispensary **WORD ORIGIN** Greek *pharmakon* drug

pharyngitis (far-rin-**jite**-iss) *n* inflammation of the pharynx, causing a sore throat

pharynx (**far**-rinks) *n, pl* **pharynges** (far-**rin**-jeez) or **pharynxes** the part of the alimentary canal between the mouth and the oesophagus **pharyngeal** *adj* **WORD ORIGIN** Greek *pharunx* throat

p

phase *n* **1** any distinct or characteristic stage in a sequence of events: *these two CDs sum up two distinct phases in the singer's career* **2** *astron* one of the recurring shapes of the portion of the moon, Mercury, or Venus illuminated by the sun **3** *physics* a particular stage in a periodic process or phenomenon **4** *physics* **in** or **out of phase** (of two waves or signals) reaching or not reaching corresponding phases at the same time ▷ *vb* **phasing, phased 5** to do or introduce gradually: *the redundancies will be phased over two years*. See also **phase in, phase out**
WORD ORIGIN Greek *phasis* aspect

phase in *vb* to introduce in a gradual or cautious manner: *the scheme was phased in over seven years*

phase out *vb* to discontinue gradually: *rent subsidies are being phased out*

PhD Doctor of Philosophy

pheasant *n* a long-tailed bird with a brightly coloured plumage in the male: native to Asia but introduced elsewhere
WORD ORIGIN Latin *phasianus*

phenobarbitone or **phenobarbital** *n* a sedative used to treat insomnia and epilepsy

phenol *n* a white crystalline derivative of benzene, used as an antiseptic and disinfectant and in the manufacture of resins, explosives, and pharmaceutical substances
WORD ORIGIN Greek *phaino*- shining; because originally prepared from illuminating gas

phenomena *n* a plural of **phenomenon**

phenomenal *adj* **1** extraordinary or outstanding: *a phenomenal success* **2** of or relating to a phenomenon **phenomenally** *adv*

phenomenalism *n* *philosophy* the doctrine that all knowledge comes from sense perception **phenomenalist** *n, adj*

phenomenon *n, pl* **-ena** or **-enons 1** anything that can be perceived as an occurrence or fact **2** any remarkable occurrence or person
WORD ORIGIN Greek *phainomenon*, from *phainesthai* to appear

⣿ **USAGE**
⣿ Although *phenomena* is often treated as
⣿ if it were singular, correct usage is to
⣿ employ *phenomenon* with a singular
⣿ construction and *phenomena* with a
⣿ plural: *that is an interesting phenomenon*
⣿ (not *phenomena*); *several new phenomena*
⣿ *were recorded in his notes.*

phenotype *n* the physical form of an organism as determined by the interaction of its genetic make-up and its environment

phenyl (**fee**-nile) *adj* of, containing, or consisting of the monovalent group C_6H_5, derived from benzene: *a phenyl group*

phew *interj* an exclamation of relief, surprise, disbelief, or weariness

phial *n* a small bottle for liquid medicine
WORD ORIGIN Greek *phialē* wide shallow vessel

phil. 1 philharmonic **2** philosophy

philadelphus *n* a shrub grown for its strongly scented showy flowers

WORD ORIGIN Greek *philadelphon*, literally: loving one's brother

philander *vb* (of a man) to flirt or have many casual love affairs with women **philanderer** *n* **philandering** *adj, n*
WORD ORIGIN Greek *philandros* fond of men, used as a name for a lover in literary works

philanthropy *n, pl* **-pies 1** the practice of helping people less well-off than oneself **2** love of mankind in general **philanthropic** *adj* **philanthropist** *n*
WORD ORIGIN Greek *philanthrōpia* love of mankind

philately (fill-**lat**-a-lee) *n* the collection and study of postage stamps **philatelist** *n*
WORD ORIGIN Greek *philos* loving + *ateleia* exemption from tax

philharmonic *adj* **1** fond of music ▷ *n* **2** a specific choir, orchestra, or musical society: *the Vienna Philharmonic*
WORD ORIGIN French *philharmonique*

philippic *n* a bitter verbal attack
WORD ORIGIN after the orations of Demosthenes against Philip of Macedon

Philippine *adj, n* same as **Filipino**

philistine *n* **1** a person who is hostile towards culture and the arts ▷ *adj* **2** boorishly uncultured **philistinism** *n*

Philistine *n* a member of the non-Semitic people who inhabited ancient Palestine

philology *n* the science of the structure and development of languages **philological** *adj* **philologist** *n*
WORD ORIGIN Greek *philologia* love of language

philosopher *n* **1** a person who studies philosophy **2** a person who remains calm and stoical in the face of difficulties or disappointments

philosopher's stone *n* a substance thought by alchemists to be capable of changing base metals into gold

philosophical or **philosophic** *adj* **1** of or relating to philosophy or philosophers **2** calm and stoical in the face of difficulties or disappointments **philosophically** *adv*

philosophize or **-phise** *vb* **-phizing, -phized** or **-phising, -phised** to discuss in a philosophical manner **philosophizer** or **-phiser** *n*

philosophy *n, pl* **-phies 1** the academic study of knowledge, thought, and the meaning of life **2** the particular doctrines of a specific individual or school relating to these issues: *the philosophy of John Locke* **3** any system of beliefs or values **4** a personal outlook or viewpoint
WORD ORIGIN Greek *philosophia* love of wisdom

philtre or *US* **philter** *n* a drink supposed to arouse desire
WORD ORIGIN Greek *philtron* love potion

phishing *n* the practice of using fraudulent e-mails and copies of legitimate websites to extract financial data from computer users for criminal purposes

phlebitis (fleb-**bite**-iss) *n* inflammation of a vein, usually in the legs **phlebitic** *adj*
WORD ORIGIN Greek *phleps* vein

phlegm (**flem**) *n* **1** the thick yellowish substance secreted by the walls of the respiratory tract **2** apathy or stolidity **3** calmness **phlegmy** *adj*
WORD ORIGIN Greek *phlegma*

phlegmatic (fleg-**mat**-ik) *adj* having an unemotional disposition

phloem (**flow**-em) *n* *bot* the plant tissue that acts as a path for the distribution of food substances to all parts of the plant
WORD ORIGIN Greek *phloos* bark

phlox *n, pl* **phlox** or **phloxes** a plant with clusters of white, red, or purple flowers
WORD ORIGIN Greek, literally: flame

phobia *n* *psychiatry* an intense and irrational fear of a given situation or thing **phobic** *adj, n*
WORD ORIGIN Greek *phobos* fear

Phoenician (fon-**nee**-shun) *adj* **1** of Phoenicia, an ancient E Mediterranean country ▷ *n* **2** a person from Phoenicia

phoenix *n* a legendary Arabian bird said to set fire to itself and rise anew from the ashes every 500 years
WORD ORIGIN Greek *phoinix*

phone *n, vb* **phoning, phoned** short for **telephone**

phonecard *n* a card used instead of coins to operate certain public telephones

phone-in *n* a radio or television programme in which telephone questions or comments from the public are broadcast live as part of a discussion

phoneme *n* *linguistics* one of the set of speech sounds in any given language that serve to distinguish one word from another **phonemic** *adj*
WORD ORIGIN Greek *phōnēma* sound, speech

phonemics *n* the classification and analysis of the phonemes of a language

phonetic *adj* **1** of phonetics **2** denoting any perceptible distinction between one speech sound and another **3** conforming to pronunciation: *phonetic spelling* **phonetically** *adv*
WORD ORIGIN Greek *phōnein* to make sounds, speak

phonetics *n* the study of speech processes, including the production, perception, and analysis of speech sounds

phoney or *esp. US* **phony** *informal adj* **-nier, -niest 1** not genuine: *a phoney Belgian 50-franc coin* **2** (of a person) insincere or pretentious ▷ *n, pl* **-neys** or *esp. US* **-nies 3** an insincere or pretentious person **4** something that is not genuine
WORD ORIGIN origin unknown

phonograph *n* **1** an early form of record player capable of recording and reproducing sound on wax cylinders **2** *US & Canad* a record player
WORD ORIGIN Greek *phonē* sound + *graphein* to write

phonology *n, pl* **-gies 1** the study of the sound system in a language **2** such a sound system **phonological** *adj*
WORD ORIGIN Greek *phonē* sound, voice + -LOGY

phooey *interj informal* an exclamation of scorn or contempt
WORD ORIGIN probably variant of *phew*

Jafaikan

If you live in inner London you will know that young people of all ethnic backgrounds speak with an accent that sounds more Jamaican than anything else. And you may be familiar with the corresponding vocabulary, which includes *nang* (good), *deep* (bad), and *safe* (hello). Of course, there is nothing new about teenagers coining jargon and applying existing words to different meanings to signal their shared identity and distinctness from other age-groups. But Jafaikan is different. It has a systematic grammar and phonology, as well as a substantial vocabulary. And, unusually, it crosses ethnic boundaries, with white indigenous youths, as well as those of Afro-Caribbean, Arab, and Bengali descent, all using the same dialect.

The term 'Jafaikan' or 'Jafaican' is a blend of 'Jamaican' and 'African', reflecting the fact that the dialect is most obviously influenced by the speech of the Afro-Caribbean migrants who began coming to London in the 1940s. Additionally, and probably falsely, 'fake' is understood to be part of the etymology, reinforcing perceptions that the dialect is a conscious imitation of black youths by white youths, seeking the prestige they associate with Black culture (behaviour famously satirized in the character of Ali G, played by a white comedian with the catch-phrase 'Is it cos I is black?'). The dialect's popularity across the range of ethnic groups is seen by some as proof that it is nothing more than an affectation. The reality is more complex.

Linguists conducting the first major research into Jafaikan argue that its white speakers cannot simply be understood as 'talking like black kids' and point instead to the shared linguistic environment of multicultural London. Inner London is one of the world's most ethnically diverse areas and children growing up there are exposed to a rich mixture of English that includes elements imported from second languages and other English dialects as well as local London English. Out of this environment the new variety emerged, heavily influenced by the Caribbean English passed down through the generations by the original migrants, but not limited to the Afro-Caribbean or any other ethnic group. The researchers prefer the term Multicultural London English (MLE).

Unsurprisingly, MLE vocabulary privileges typical teenage concerns such as fashion and relationships, with *bustin* (wearing), *chops* (jewellery), *creps* (trainers), *blud* (friend), and *choong* (attractive). Many words are Jamaican in origin but some come directly from African languages. The influence of popular music genres, particularly rap, hip-hop, and grime, is also evident. *Ish*, a reversal of 'shit' (in the sense 'stuff'), stems from the altering of offensive words in rap songs that enables them to receive airplay.

The most significant developments have taken place in pronunciation. In the vowel system, the long vowels of London English have shortened, so that 'face' sounds like 'fehs', resembling Northern English but also matching Caribbean pronunciation. The glottal stop as a variant for /t/, which has achieved near-respectability in the Estuary English of South East England (*there's a lo' of i' abou'*), is apparently receding under the influence of Jafaikan.

Notable grammatical features include the regularizing of the verb 'to be' in the past tense as *was* across the singular and plural conjugations (*I was, we was*) and *weren't* in the negative (*I weren't, we weren't*), although researchers note that this is less marked in ethnic-minority speakers. And tag questions ('Nice day, isn't it?', 'He lives in Hackney, doesn't he?') are limited to *isn't it?* (realized as *innit?*), giving 'He lives in Hackney, innit?'

The future of Jafaikan will depend on whether its current speakers continue to use it into adulthood. The researchers note that its rise coincides with a general process of dialect-levelling across the United Kingdom, resulting in people in different areas sounding more and more like each other. Speakers may lose the dialect if they move to different areas or into jobs where they are expected to speak Standard English. However, there is evidence that it is spreading to other multicultural cities as a result both of population movement and the influence of popular MLE-speaking music artists such as Dizzee Rascal. The lead researcher, Professor Paul Kerswill, observes, 'It'll become more mainstream through force of numbers and continued migration, and because it's considered cool.'

phosgene (foz-jean) *n* a poisonous gas used in warfare
WORD ORIGIN Greek *phōs* light + *-genēs* born

phosphate *n* **1** any salt or ester of any phosphoric acid **2** (*often pl*) chemical fertilizer containing phosphorous compounds **phosphatic** *adj*

phosphor *n* a substance capable of emitting light when irradiated with particles of electromagnetic radiation
WORD ORIGIN Greek *phōsphoros* phosphorus

phosphoresce *vb* **-rescing, -resced** to exhibit phosphorescence

phosphorescence *n* **1** *physics* a fluorescence that persists after the bombarding radiation producing it has stopped **2** the light emitted in phosphorescence **phosphorescent** *adj*

phosphoric *adj* of or containing phosphorus in the pentavalent state

phosphorous *adj* of or containing phosphorus in the trivalent state

phosphorus *n chem* a toxic flammable nonmetallic element which appears luminous in the dark. It exists in two forms, white and red. Symbol: P
WORD ORIGIN Greek *phōsphoros* light-bringing

photo *n, pl* **-tos** short for **photograph**

photo- *combining form* **1** of or produced by light: *photosynthesis* **2** indicating a photographic process: *photolithography*
WORD ORIGIN Greek *phōs, phōt-* light

photocell *n* a cell which produces a current or voltage when exposed to light or other electromagnetic radiation

photocopier *n* a machine using light-sensitive photographic materials to reproduce written, printed, or graphic work

photocopy *n, pl* **-copies 1** a photographic reproduction of written, printed, or graphic work ▷ *vb* **-copies, -copying, -copied 2** to reproduce on photographic material

photoelectric *adj* of or concerned with electric or electronic effects caused by light or other electromagnetic radiation **photoelectricity** *n*

photoengraving *n* **1** a photomechanical process for producing letterpress printing plates **2** a print made from such a plate **photoengrave** *vb*

photo finish *n* a finish of a race in which contestants are so close that a photograph is needed to decide the result

Photofit *n trademark* a picture of someone wanted by the police which has been made by combining photographs of different facial features resembling those of the wanted person

photoflash *n* same as **flashbulb**

photoflood *n* a highly incandescent electric lamp used for indoor photography and television

photogenic *adj* **1** (esp. of a person) always looking attractive in photographs **2** *biol* producing or emitting light

photograph *n* **1** a picture made by the chemical action of light on sensitive film ▷ *vb* **2** to take a photograph of

photographic *adj* **1** of or like photography or a photograph **2** (of a person's memory) able to retain facts or appearances in precise detail **photographically** *adv*

photography *n* **1** the process of recording images on sensitized material by the action of light **2** the practice of taking photographs **photographer** *n*

photogravure *n* a process in which an etched metal plate for printing is produced by photography
WORD ORIGIN PHOTO- + French *gravure* engraving

photolithography *n* a lithographic printing process using photographically made plates **photolithographer** *n*

photometer (foe-**tom**-it-er) *n* an instrument used to measure the intensity of light

photometry (foe-**tom**-it-tree) *n* the branch of physics concerned with the measurement of the intensity of light **photometrist** *n*

photomontage (foe-toe-mon-**tahzh**) *n* **1** the combination of several photographs to produce one picture **2** a picture produced in this way

photon *n physics* a quantum of electromagnetic radiation energy, such as light, having both particle and wave behaviour

photosensitive *adj* sensitive to electromagnetic radiation, esp. light

Photoshop *n* **1** *trademark* a software application for managing and editing digital images ▷ *vb* **2** *informal* to alter (a digital image) using Photoshop or a similar application

photostat *n* **1** a type of photocopying machine or process **2** any copy made by such a machine ▷ *vb* **-statting, -statted** *or* **-stating, -stated 3** to make a photostat copy (of)

photosynthesis *n* (in plants) the process by which a green plant uses sunlight to build up carbohydrate reserves **photosynthesize** *or* **-sise** *vb* **photosynthetic** *adj*

phototropism (foe-toe-**trope**-iz-zum) *n* the growth of plants towards a source of light **phototropic** *adj*
WORD ORIGIN PHOTO- + Greek *tropos* turn

phrasal verb *n* a phrase that consists of a verb plus an adverb or preposition, esp. one whose meaning cannot be deduced from its parts, such as *take in* meaning *deceive*

phrase *n* **1** a group of words forming a unit of meaning in a sentence **2** an idiomatic or original expression **3** *music* a small group of notes forming a coherent unit of melody ▷ *vb* **phrasing, phrased 4** to express orally or in a phrase: *I could have phrased that better* **5** *music* to divide (a melodic line or part) into musical phrases, esp. in performance **phrasal** *adj*
WORD ORIGIN Greek *phrasis* speech

phrase book *n* a book containing frequently used expressions and their equivalent in a foreign language

phraseology *n, pl* **-gies** the manner in which words or phrases are used

phrasing *n* **1** the exact words used to say or write something **2** the way in which someone who is performing a piece of music or reading aloud divides up the work being performed by pausing slightly in appropriate places

phrenology *n* (formerly) the study of the shape and size of the skull as a means of finding out a person's character and mental ability **phrenological** *adj* **phrenologist** *n*
WORD ORIGIN Greek *phrēn* mind + -LOGY

phut *informal n* **1** a representation of a muffled explosive sound ▷ *adv* **2 go phut** to break down or collapse
WORD ORIGIN imitative

phylactery *n, pl* **-teries** *Judaism* either of the pair of square cases containing biblical passages, worn by Jewish men on the left arm and head during weekday morning prayers
WORD ORIGIN Greek *phulaktērion* safeguard

phylum *n, pl* **-la** *biol* one of the major groups into which the animal and plant kingdoms are divided, containing one or more classes
WORD ORIGIN Greek *phulon* race

physical *adj* **1** of the body, as distinguished from the mind or spirit **2** of material things or nature: *the physical world* **3** of or concerned with matter and energy **4** of or relating to physics **physically** *adv*

physical education *n* training and practice in sports and gymnastics

physical geography *n* the branch of geography that deals with the natural features of the earth's surface

physical jerks *pl n Austral & Brit informal* repetitive keep-fit exercises

physical science *n* any of the sciences concerned with nonliving matter, such as physics, chemistry, astronomy, and geology

physician *n* **1** a medical doctor **2** *archaic* a healer
WORD ORIGIN Greek *phusis* nature

physicist *n* a person versed in or studying physics

physics *n* **1** the branch of science concerned with the properties of matter and energy and the relationships between them **2** physical properties of behaviour: *the physics of the electron*
WORD ORIGIN translation of Greek *ta phusika* natural things

physio *n* **1** short for **physiotherapy** **2** *pl* **physios** short for **physiotherapist**

physiognomy (fiz-ee-**on**-om-ee) *n* **1** a person's face considered as an indication of personality **2** the outward appearance of something: *the changed physiognomy of the forests*
WORD ORIGIN Greek *phusis* nature + *gnōmōn* judge

physiography *n* same as **physical geography**
WORD ORIGIN Greek *phusis* nature + -GRAPHY

physiology *n* **1** the branch of science concerned with the functioning of organisms **2** the processes and

functions of all or part of an organism **physiologist** *n* **physiological** *adj*
WORD ORIGIN Greek *phusis* nature + -LOGY

physiotherapy *n* the treatment of disease or injury by physical means, such as massage or exercises, rather than by drugs **physiotherapist** *n*
WORD ORIGIN *physio-* (prefix) physical + *therapy*

physique *n* person's bodily build and muscular development
WORD ORIGIN French

pi *n, pl* **pis 1** the 16th letter in the Greek alphabet (Π, π) **2** *maths* a number that is the ratio of the circumference of a circle to its diameter; approximate value: 3.141 592... Symbol: π

pianissimo *adj, adv music* to be performed very quietly
WORD ORIGIN Italian

pianist *n* a person who plays the piano

piano¹ *n, pl* **-anos** a musical instrument played by depressing keys that cause hammers to strike strings and produce audible vibrations
WORD ORIGIN short for *pianoforte*

piano² *adj, adv music* to be performed softly
WORD ORIGIN Italian

piano accordion *n* an accordion in which the right hand plays a piano-like keyboard **piano accordionist** *n*

pianoforte (pee-ann-oh-**for**-tee) *n* the full name for **piano¹**
WORD ORIGIN Italian *piano e forte* soft and loud

Pianola (pee-an-oh-la) *n trademark* a type of mechanical piano, the music for which is encoded in perforations in a paper roll

piazza *n* **1** a large open square in an Italian town **2** *chiefly Brit* a covered passageway or gallery
WORD ORIGIN Italian: marketplace

pibroch (**pee**-brok) *n* a form of music for Scottish bagpipes, consisting of a theme and variations
WORD ORIGIN Gaelic *piobaireachd*

pic *n, pl* **pics** or **pix** *informal* a photograph or illustration

pica (**pie**-ka) *n* **1** a size of printer's type giving six lines to the inch **2** a size of typewriter type that has ten characters to the inch
WORD ORIGIN Latin *pica* magpie; sense connection obscure

picador *n bullfighting* a horseman who wounds the bull with a lance to weaken it
WORD ORIGIN Spanish

picaresque *adj* of or relating to a type of fiction in which the hero, a rogue, goes through a series of episodic adventures
WORD ORIGIN Spanish *pícaro* a rogue

picayune (pick-a-**yoon**) *US & Canad informal adj* **1** of small value or importance **2** mean or petty ▷ *n* **3** any coin of little value, such as a five-cent piece **4** an unimportant person or thing
WORD ORIGIN French *picaillon* coin from Piedmont

piccalilli *n* a pickle of mixed vegetables in a mustard sauce
WORD ORIGIN origin unknown

piccanin *n S African, offensive* a Black African child
WORD ORIGIN variant of *piccaninny*

piccaninny or *esp. US* **pickaninny** *n, pl* **-nies** *offensive* a small Black or Aboriginal child
WORD ORIGIN perhaps from Portuguese *pequenino* tiny one

piccolo *n, pl* **-los** a woodwind instrument an octave higher than the flute
WORD ORIGIN Italian: small

pick¹ *vb* **1** to choose or select **2** to gather (fruit, berries, or crops) from (a tree, bush, or field) **3** to remove loose particles from: *she picked some bits of fluff off her sleeve* **4** (foll. by *at*) to nibble (at) without appetite **5** to provoke (an argument or fight) deliberately **6** to separate (strands or fibres), as in weaving **7** to steal from (someone's pocket) **8** to open (a lock) with an instrument other than a key **9** to make (one's way) carefully on foot: *they picked their way through the rubble* **10 pick and choose** to select fastidiously or fussily ▷ *n* **11** choice: *take your pick* **12** the best: *the pick of the country's young cricketers* ▶ See also **pick off**, **pick on**, etc.
WORD ORIGIN Middle English *piken*

pick² *n* **1** a tool with a handle and a long curved steel head, used for loosening soil or breaking rocks **2** any tool used for picking, such as an ice pick or toothpick **3** a plectrum ▷ *vb* **4** to pierce or break up (a hard surface) with a pick
WORD ORIGIN perhaps a variant of PIKE²

pickaback *n, adv* same as **piggyback**

pickaxe or *US* **pickax** *n* a large pick

picket *n* **1** a person or group standing outside a workplace to dissuade strikebreakers from entering **2** a small unit of troops posted to give early warning of attack **3** a pointed stake that is driven into the ground to support a fence ▷ *vb* **-eting, -eted 4** to act as pickets outside (a workplace)
WORD ORIGIN Old French *piquer* to prick

picket fence *n* a fence consisting of pickets driven into the ground

picket line *n* a line of people acting as pickets

pickings *pl n* money or profits acquired easily

pickle *n* **1** (*often pl*) food, esp. vegetables preserved in vinegar or brine **2** a liquid or marinade, such as spiced vinegar, for preserving vegetables, meat, or fish **3** *informal* an awkward or difficult situation: *to be in a pickle; they are in a pickle over what to do with toxic waste* ▷ *vb* **-ling, -led 4** to preserve or treat in a pickling liquid
WORD ORIGIN probably Middle Dutch *pekel*

pickled *adj* **1** (of food) preserved in a pickling liquid **2** *informal* drunk

pick-me-up *n informal* a tonic, esp. a special drink taken as a stimulant

pick off *vb* to aim at and shoot (people or things) one by one

pick on *vb* to continually treat someone unfairly

pick out *vb* **1** to select for use or special consideration: *she picked out a wide gold*

wedding ring **2** to distinguish (an object from its surroundings), such as in painting: *the wall panels are light brown, with their edges picked out in gold* **3** to recognize (a person or thing): *the culprit was picked out at a police identification parade* **4** to play (a tune) tentatively, as by ear

pickpocket *n* a person who steals from the pockets of others in public places

pick up *vb* **1** to lift or raise: *he picked up his glass* **2** to obtain or purchase: *a couple of pictures she had picked up in a flea market in Paris* **3** to improve in health or condition: *the tourist trade has picked up after the slump caused by the Gulf War* **4** to learn as one goes along: *she had a good ear and picked up languages quickly* **5** to raise (oneself) after a fall or setback: *she picked herself up and got on with her life* **6** to resume; return to **7** to accept the responsibility for paying (a bill) **8** to collect or give a lift to (passengers or goods) **9** *informal* to become acquainted with for a sexual purpose **10** *informal* to arrest **11** to receive (sounds or signals)

pick-up *n* **1** a small truck with an open body used for light deliveries **2** *informal* a casual acquaintance made for a sexual purpose **3** *informal* **a** a stop to collect passengers or goods **b** the people or things collected **4** a device which converts vibrations into electrical signals, such as that to which a record player stylus is attached

picky *adj* **pickier, pickiest** *Brit, Austral, & NZ informal* fussy; finicky

picnic *n* **1** an excursion on which people bring food to be eaten in the open air **2** an informal meal eaten out-of-doors **3 no picnic** *informal* a hard or disagreeable task ▷ *vb* **-nicking, -nicked 4** to eat or take part in a picnic **picnicker** *n*
WORD ORIGIN French *piquenique*

pico- *combining form* denoting 10⁻¹²: *picofarad*
WORD ORIGIN Spanish *pico* small quantity

picot (**peek**-oh) *n* any of a pattern of small loops, for example on lace

Pict *n* a member of any of the peoples who lived in N Britain in the first to the fourth centuries AD **Pictish** *adj*
WORD ORIGIN Late Latin *Picti* painted men

pictograph *n* **1** a picture or symbol standing for a word or group of words, as in written Chinese **2** Also called: **pictogram** a chart on which symbols are used to represent values **pictographic** *adj*
WORD ORIGIN Latin *pingere* to paint

pictorial *adj* **1** relating to or expressed by pictures ▷ *n* **2** a periodical containing many pictures
WORD ORIGIN Latin *pingere* to paint

picture *n* **1** a visual representation produced on a surface, such as in a photograph or painting **2** a mental image: *neither had any clear picture of whom they were looking for* **3** a description or account of a situation considered as an observable scene: *the reports do not provide an accurate picture of the spread of AIDS* **4** a person or thing resembling another: *he is the picture of a perfect host* **5** a person

p

or scene typifying a particular state: *his face was a picture of dejection* **6** the image on a television screen **7** a cinema film **8 in the picture** informed about a situation **9 the pictures** a cinema or film show ▷ *vb* **-turing, -tured 10** to visualize or imagine **11** to describe or depict vividly: *a documentary that had pictured the police as good-natured dolts* **12** to put in a picture or make a picture of: *the women pictured above are all the same age* **WORD ORIGIN** Latin *pingere* to paint

picture rail *n* the rail near the top of a wall from which pictures are hung

picturesque *adj* **1** visually pleasing, as in being striking or quaint: *a small picturesque harbour* **2** (of language) graphic or vivid **WORD ORIGIN** French *pittoresque*

picture window *n* a large window with a single pane of glass, usually facing a view

piddle *vb* **-dling, -dled 1** *informal* to urinate **2 piddle about** *or* **around** *or* **away** to spend (one's time) aimlessly: *we have been piddling around for seven months* **WORD ORIGIN** origin unknown

piddling *adj informal* petty or trivial: *piddling amounts of money*

pidgin *n* a language made up of elements of two or more languages and used between the speakers of the languages involved **WORD ORIGIN** supposed Chinese pronunciation of *business*

pidgin English *n* a pidgin in which one of the languages involved is English

pie *n* **1** a sweet or savoury filling baked in pastry **2 pie in the sky** illusory hope or promise of some future good **WORD ORIGIN** origin unknown

piebald *adj* **1** marked in two colours, esp. black and white ▷ *n* **2** a black-and-white horse **WORD ORIGIN** dialect *pie* magpie + BALD

piece *n* **1** a separate bit or part **2** an instance or occurrence: *a piece of luck* **3** an example or specimen of a style or type: *each piece of furniture is crafted from native red pine by traditional methods* **4** a literary, musical, or artistic composition **5** a coin: *a fifty-pence piece* **6** a firearm or cannon **7** a small object used in playing various games: *a chess piece* **8 go to pieces** (of a person) to lose control of oneself; have a breakdown ▷ *vb* **piecing, pieced 9** (often foll. by *together*) to fit or assemble bit by bit **10** (often foll. by *up*) to patch or make up (a garment) by adding pieces **WORD ORIGIN** Middle English *pece*

pièce de résistance (**pyess** de ray-**zeest**-onss) *n* the most outstanding item in a series **WORD ORIGIN** French

piece goods *pl n* goods, esp. fabrics, made in standard widths and lengths

piecemeal *adv* **1** bit by bit; gradually ▷ *adj* **2** fragmentary or unsystematic: *a piecemeal approach* **WORD ORIGIN** Middle English *pece* piece + *-mele* a measure

piece of eight *n, pl* **pieces of eight** a former Spanish coin worth eight reals

piecework *n* work paid for according to the quantity produced

pie chart *n* a circular graph divided into sectors proportional to the sizes of the quantities represented

pied *adj* having markings of two or more colours **WORD ORIGIN** dialect *pie* magpie

pied-à-terre (**pyay**-da-**tair**) *n, pl* **pieds-à-terre** (**pyay**-da-**tair**) a flat or other lodging for occasional use **WORD ORIGIN** French, literally: foot on (the) ground

pie-eyed *adj slang* drunk

pier *n* **1** a structure with a deck that is built out over water and used as a landing place or promenade **2** a pillar or support that bears heavy loads **3** the part of a wall between two adjacent openings **WORD ORIGIN** Middle English *per*

pierce *vb* **piercing, pierced 1** to make a hole in (something) with a sharp point **2** to force (a way) through (something) **3** (of light) to shine through (darkness) **4** (of sounds or cries) to sound sharply through (the silence) **5** to penetrate: *the cold pierced the air* **piercing** *adj* **WORD ORIGIN** Old French *percer*

pier glass *n* a tall narrow mirror, designed to hang on the wall between windows

Pierrot (**pier**-roe) *n* a male character from French pantomime with a whitened face, white costume, and pointed hat

pietism *n* exaggerated piety

piety *n, pl* **-ties 1** dutiful devotion to God and observance of religious principles **2** the quality of being pious **3** a pious action or saying **WORD ORIGIN** Latin *pietas*

piezoelectric effect (pie-eez-oh-ill-**ek**-trik) *or* **piezoelectricity** *n physics* **a** the production of electricity by applying a mechanical stress to certain crystals **b** the converse effect in which stress is produced in a crystal as a result of an applied voltage **WORD ORIGIN** Greek *piezein* to press

piffle *n informal* nonsense **WORD ORIGIN** origin unknown

piffling *adj informal* worthless; trivial

pig *n* **1** a mammal with a long head, a snout, and bristle-covered skin, which is kept and killed for pork, ham, and bacon ▸ Related adjective: **porcine 2** *informal* a dirty, greedy, or bad-mannered person **3** *offensive slang* a policeman **4** a mass of metal cast into a simple shape **5** *Brit informal* something that is difficult or unpleasant: *the coast is a pig for little boats* **6 a pig in a poke** something bought or received without previous sight or knowledge **7 make a pig of oneself** *informal* to overeat ▷ *vb* **pigging, pigged 8** (of a sow) to give birth **9** (often foll. by *out*) *slang* to eat greedily or to excess: *she had pigged out on pizza before the show* **WORD ORIGIN** Middle English *pigge*

pigeon[1] *n* **1** a bird which has a heavy body, small head, and short legs, and is usually grey in colour **2** *slang* a victim or dupe **WORD ORIGIN** Old French *pijon* young dove

pigeon[2] *n informal* concern or responsibility: *this is our pigeon – there's nothing to keep you* **WORD ORIGIN** from *pidgin*

pigeonhole *n* **1** a small compartment, such as in a bureau, for filing papers ▷ *vb* **-holing, -holed 2** to classify or categorize **3** to put aside

pigeon-toed *adj* with the toes or feet turned inwards

piggery *n, pl* **-geries** a place where pigs are kept

piggish *adj* **1** like a pig in appetite or manners **2** stubborn **piggishness** *n*

piggy *n, pl* **-gies 1** a child's word for a **pig** ▷ *adj* **-gier, -giest 2** same as **piggish**

piggyback *or* **pickaback** *n* **1** a ride on the back and shoulders of another person ▷ *adv, adj* **2** on the back and shoulders of another person

piggy bank *n* a child's bank shaped like a pig with a slot for coins

pig-headed *adj* stupidly stubborn

pig iron *n* crude iron produced in a blast furnace and poured into moulds

piglet *n* a young pig

pigment *n* **1** any substance which gives colour to paint or dye **2** a substance which occurs in plant or animal tissue and produces a characteristic colour **pigmentary** *adj* **WORD ORIGIN** Latin *pigmentum*

pigmentation *n* colouring in plants, animals, or humans, caused by the presence of pigments

Pigmy *n, pl* **-mies** same as **Pygmy**

pigskin *n* **1** the skin of the domestic pig **2** leather made of this skin **3** *US & Canad informal* a football

pigsty *or US & Canad* **pigpen** *n, pl* **-sties 1** a pen for pigs **2** an untidy place

pigswill *n* waste food or other edible matter fed to pigs

pigtail *n* a plait of hair or one of two plaits on either side of the face

pike[1] *n, pl* **pike** *or* **pikes** a large predatory freshwater fish with a broad flat snout, strong teeth, and a long body covered with small scales **WORD ORIGIN** Old English *pīc* point, from the shape of its jaw

pike[2] *n* a medieval weapon consisting of a metal spearhead on a long pole **pikeman** *n* **WORD ORIGIN** Old English *pīc* point

pikelet *n Austral & NZ* a small thick pancake

piker *n Austral & NZ slang* shirker

pikestaff *n* **1** the wooden handle of a pike **2 plain as a pikestaff** very obvious or noticeable

pikey *n Brit slang, derogatory* **1** a gypsy or vagrant **2** a member of the underclass

pilaster *n* a shallow rectangular column attached to the face of a wall **pilastered** *adj* **WORD ORIGIN** Latin *pila* pillar

pilau *or* **pilaf** *n* a Middle Eastern dish, consisting of rice flavoured with spices and cooked in stock, to which meat, poultry, or fish may be added **WORD ORIGIN** Turkish *pilāw*

pilchard *n* a small edible sea fish of the herring family, with a rounded body

EE Cummings

In some respects, EE Cummings ('e. e. cummings' as the poet usually spelled his name in books) was the most traditional of lyricists. He dealt, often in disguised irregular sonnets, with the immemorial tropes of love and death and their natural analogues of weather, flowers, and the seasons. Yet, a much-exhibited visual artist as well as a poet, he wrenched syntax and invented a personal notation of spelling, punctuation, and spacing that, often termed 'eccentric', was in fact calculated and systematic from his first book *Tulips and Chimneys* (1923) to the end of his working life.

Cumming's idiosyncrasies, together with an unabashed romanticism that was interspersed here and there with declared religious faith, explicit eroticism, and barbed satire, set him apart from other American poets. Although he received honours and accolades in his lifetime, he sometimes had to self-publish his books and one of them, *No Thanks,* has a dedicatory poem shaped like a funerary urn, listing all the publishers that had rejected him. Critics have been equivocal about his work, the consensus perhaps being that he is a 'major minor poet'. Unlike many of his fellow poets, he was prolific, quotable, and popular, styled 'the lower-case poet' for his intermittent practice of spelling 'I' as 'i'.

The son of supportive parents, his father a Unitarian minister who had been a Harvard professor, Cummings was classically educated, graduating from Harvard in Greek and Latin. During World War One, he went to France in 1917 to join an ambulance corps. Due to a mix-up, he was left stranded in Paris then, suspected of treason, spent several months in an internment camp, the source for his highly autobiographical novel *The Enormous Room.* He was returned to America, and served briefly in the army. After spending two years in Paris, he mainly lived in New York and New Hampshire for the rest of his life, apart from extended travels, notably to the Soviet Union in 1931, which was the basis of his nonfiction work *Eimi,* unusual for the time in its jaundiced view of the Marxist work-in-progress: he called the new state an 'uncircus of noncreatures'. A supreme individualist, he despised anything smacking of the collective. For him, feeling and emotion always trumped science and reason.

In a personal life of fraught complexity, he was married three times, and his romantic partners often figure in his poetry. Apart from early work as a magazine essayist and portrait artist, Cummings had only one true vocation: poetry. At first influenced by Gertrude Stein and Amy Lowell, he soon became uniquely himself. His work is often like a cognitive experiment in how far language can be stretched and still make sense. He fragmented words ('d is app ea r in gly'), spelled phonetically ('Jimmie's got a goil'), rearranged punctuation (struggling souls are 'like caught.brave:flies'), invented portmanteau compounds ('make me a child, stout hurdysturdygurdyman'), turned nouns into verbs and adjectives and conjunctions into nouns, and made pictures of words ('mOOn Over tOwns mOOn'). Playing with catchwords and clichés, his register veered from slang to dialect ('why are these pipples taking their hets off?') to the formal or archaic ('ere with the dirt death shall him vastly gird'). But he was never experimental for its own sake; his innovations served an aesthetic end.

In *she being Brand* driving a car becomes a virtuoso extended metaphor for sex: Cummings does it comically ('I went right to it flooded-the-curburetor cranked her'), yet somehow manages to avoid turning the process into a crude joke. In his work, love and death permanently interrogate each other, and the result, he consistently maintains, is a process, not a product. In the Introduction to one of his books, he says, 'Never the murdered finalities of wherewhen and yesno, impotentnongamesofwrongrightandrightwrong;never to gain or pause, never the soft adventure of undoom,greedy anguishes and cringing ecstacies of inexistence;never to rest and never to have:only to grow.' He concludes, 'Always the beautiful answer who asks a more beautiful question.' Cummings found his answers. In *somewhere i have never travelled,gladly beyond* he gave English one of its greatest love poems and one of the loveliest lines in all poetry: 'nobody, not even the rain,has such small hands.'

covered with large scales
WORD ORIGIN origin unknown

pile¹ *n* **1** a collection of objects laid on top of one another **2** *informal* a large amount: *boxing has made him a pile of money; I've got piles of work to do* **3** same as **pyre** **4** a large building or group of buildings **5** *physics* a nuclear reactor ▷ *vb* **piling, piled 6** (often foll. by *up*) to collect or be collected into a pile: *snow piled up in the drive* **7** (foll. by *in, into, off* or *out* etc.) to move in a group, often in a hurried manner: *the crew piled into the van* **8 pile it on** *informal* to exaggerate ▶ See also **pile up**
WORD ORIGIN Latin *pila* stone pier

pile² *n* a long heavy beam driven into the ground as a foundation for a structure
WORD ORIGIN Latin *pilum*

pile³ *n* the fibres in a fabric that stand up or out from the weave, such as in carpeting or velvet
WORD ORIGIN Latin *pilus* hair

pile-driver *n* a machine that drives piles into the ground

piles *pl n* swollen veins in the rectum; haemorrhoids
WORD ORIGIN Latin *pilae* balls

pile up *vb* **1** to gather or be gathered in a pile ▷ *n* **pile-up 2** *informal* a traffic accident involving several vehicles

pilfer *vb* to steal (minor items) in small quantities
WORD ORIGIN Old French *pelfre* booty

pilgrim *n* **1** a person who journeys to a holy place **2** any wayfarer
WORD ORIGIN Latin *peregrinus* foreign

pilgrimage *n* **1** a journey to a shrine or other holy place **2** a journey or long search made for sentimental reasons: *a sentimental pilgrimage to the poet's birthplace*

Pilgrim Fathers *pl n* the English Puritans who founded Plymouth Colony in SE Massachusetts (1620)

pill *n* **1** a small mass of medicine intended to be swallowed whole **2 the pill** *informal* an oral contraceptive taken by a woman **3** something unpleasant that must be endured: *her reinstatement was a bitter pill to swallow; the pill was sweetened by a reduction in interest*
WORD ORIGIN Latin *pilula* a little ball

pillage *vb* **-laging, -laged 1** to steal property violently, often in war ▷ *n* **2** the act of pillaging **3** something obtained by pillaging; booty
WORD ORIGIN Old French *piller* to despoil

pillar *n* **1** an upright support of stone, brick, or metal; column **2** something resembling this: *a pillar of smoke* **3** a prominent supporter or member: *a pillar of society* **4 from pillar to post** from one place to another
WORD ORIGIN Latin *pila*

pillar box *n* (in Britain) a red pillar-shaped public letter box situated in the street

pillbox *n* **1** a box for pills **2** a small enclosed fort of reinforced concrete **3** a small round hat

pillion *n* **1** a seat for a passenger behind the rider of a motorcycle or horse ▷ *adv* **2** on a pillion: *the motorbike on which he was riding pillion*
WORD ORIGIN from Gaelic

pillock *n* *slang* a stupid or annoying person
WORD ORIGIN Scandinavian dialect *pillicock* penis

pillory *n, pl* **-ries 1** *historical* a wooden frame in which offenders were locked by the neck and wrists and exposed to public abuse and ridicule ▷ *vb* **-ries, -rying, -ried 2** to expose to public ridicule **3** to punish by putting in a pillory
WORD ORIGIN Old French *pilori*

pillow *n* **1** a cloth bag stuffed with feathers, polyester fibre, or pieces of foam rubber used to support the head in bed ▷ *vb* **2** to rest (one's head) on or as if on a pillow: *he pillowed his head in her lap*
WORD ORIGIN Old English *pylwe*

pillowcase *or* **pillowslip** *n* a removable washable cover for a pillow

pilot *n* **1** a person who is qualified to fly an aircraft or spacecraft **2** a person employed to steer a ship into or out of a port **3** a person who acts as a guide ▷ *adj* **4** serving as a test or trial: *a pilot scheme* **5** serving as a guide: *a pilot beacon* ▷ *vb* **-loting, -loted 6** to act as pilot of **7** to guide or lead (a project or people): *the legislation was piloted through its committee stage*
WORD ORIGIN French *pilote*

pilot light *n* a small flame that lights the main burner of a gas appliance

pilot officer *n* the most junior commissioned rank in certain air forces

pimento *n, pl* **-tos** same as **allspice** or **pimiento**
WORD ORIGIN Spanish *pimiento* pepper plant

pimiento (pim-**yen**-toe) *n, pl* **-tos** a Spanish pepper with a red fruit used as a vegetable
WORD ORIGIN variant of PIMENTO

pimp *n* **1** a man who obtains customers for a prostitute, in return for a share of his or her earnings ▷ *vb* **2** to act as a pimp
WORD ORIGIN origin unknown

pimpernel *n* a plant, such as the scarlet pimpernel, typically having small star-shaped flowers
WORD ORIGIN Old French *pimpernelle*

pimple *n* a small swollen infected spot on the skin **pimpled** *adj* **pimply** *adj*
WORD ORIGIN Middle English

pimp up, pimp out *vb* to make (someone or something, esp. a car) more extravagantly decorated, as with flashy accessories, etc. **pimped-up** *or* **pimped-out** *adj*

pin *n* **1** a short stiff straight piece of wire with a pointed end and a rounded head: used mainly for fastening **2** short for **cotter pin, hairpin, rolling pin** or **safety pin 3** a wooden or metal peg **4** a pin-shaped brooch **5** (in various bowling games) a club-shaped wooden object set up in groups as a target **6** a clip that prevents a hand grenade from exploding until it is removed or released **7** *golf* the flagpole marking the hole on a green **8** *informal* a leg ▷ *vb* **pinning, pinned 9** to fasten with a pin or pins **10** to seize and hold fast: *they pinned his arms behind his back* **11 pin something on someone** *informal* to

place the blame for something on someone: *corruption charges are the easiest to pin on former dictators* ▶ See also **pin down**
WORD ORIGIN Old English *pinn*

PIN Personal Identity Number: a code number used in conjunction with a bank card to enable an account holder to use certain computerized systems, such as cash dispensers

pinafore *n* **1** *chiefly Brit* an apron with a bib **2** a dress with a sleeveless bodice or bib top, worn over a jumper or blouse
WORD ORIGIN pin + afore in front

pinball *n* an electrically operated table game in which the player shoots a small ball through several hazards

pince-nez (panss-**nay**) *n, pl* pince-nez glasses that are held in place only by means of a clip over the bridge of the nose
WORD ORIGIN French, literally: pinch-nose

pincers *pl n* **1** a gripping tool consisting of two hinged arms and curved jaws **2** the jointed grasping arms of crabs and lobsters
WORD ORIGIN Old French *pincier* to pinch

pinch *vb* **1** to squeeze (something, esp. flesh) between a finger and thumb **2** to squeeze by being too tight: *shoes that pinch* **3** to cause stinging pain to: *the cold pinched his face* **4** to make thin or drawn-looking, such as from grief or cold **5** *informal* to steal **6** *informal* to arrest **7** (usually foll. by *out* or *back*) to remove the tips of (a plant shoot) to correct or encourage growth ▷ *n* **8** a squeeze or sustained nip **9** the quantity that can be taken up between a thumb and finger: *a pinch of ground ginger* **10** extreme stress or need: *most companies are feeling the pinch of recession* **11 at a pinch** if absolutely necessary **12 feel the pinch** to be forced to economize
WORD ORIGIN probably from Old French

pinchbeck *n* **1** an alloy of copper and zinc, used as imitation gold ▷ *adj* **2** sham or cheap
WORD ORIGIN after C. Pinchbeck, watchmaker who invented the alloy

pincushion *n* a small cushion in which pins are stuck ready for use

pin down *vb* **1** to force (someone) to make a decision or carry out a promise **2** to define clearly: *the courts have found it difficult to pin down what exactly obscenity is*

pine¹ *n* **1** an evergreen tree with long needle-shaped leaves and brown cones **2** the light-coloured wood of this tree
WORD ORIGIN Latin *pinus*

pine² *vb* **pining, pined 1** (often foll. by *for*) to feel great longing (for) **2** (often foll. by *away*) to become ill or thin through grief or longing
WORD ORIGIN Old English *pīnian* to torture

pineal gland *or* **body** (pin-ee-al) *n* a small cone-shaped gland at the base of the brain
WORD ORIGIN Latin *pinea* pine cone

pineapple *n* a large tropical fruit with juicy flesh and a thick hard skin
WORD ORIGIN Middle English *pinappel* pine cone

pine cone *n* the woody seed case of a pine tree

p

pine marten n a mammal of N European and Asian coniferous woods, with dark brown fur and a creamy-yellow patch on the throat

ping n 1 a short high-pitched sound, such as of a bullet striking metal ▷ vb 2 to make such a noise **WORD ORIGIN** imitative

pinger n a device that makes a pinging sound, esp. a timer

Ping-Pong n trademark same as **table tennis**

pinhead n 1 the head of a pin 2 informal a stupid person **pinheaded** adj

pinhole n a small hole made with or as if with a pin

pinion[1] n 1 chiefly poetic a bird's wing 2 the outer part of a bird's wing including the flight feathers ▷ vb 3 to immobilize (someone) by holding or tying his or her arms 4 to confine **WORD ORIGIN** Latin pinna wing

pinion[2] n a cogwheel that engages with a larger wheel or rack **WORD ORIGIN** French pignon

pink[1] n 1 a colour between red and white 2 anything pink, such as pink paint or pink clothing: packaged in pink 3 a garden plant with pink, red, or white fragrant flowers ▷ adj 5 of a colour between red and white 6 informal having mild left-wing sympathies 7 informal relating to homosexuals or homosexuality: the pink vote ▷ vb 8 same as **knock** (sense 7) > **pinkish** or **pinky** adj **WORD ORIGIN** origin unknown

pink[2] vb to cut with pinking shears **WORD ORIGIN** perhaps from Low German

pinkie or **pinky** n, pl -ies Scot, US, Canad, & NZ the little finger **WORD ORIGIN** Dutch pinkje

pinking shears pl n scissors with a serrated edge that give a wavy edge to material cut and so prevent fraying

pin money n a small amount of extra money earned to buy small luxuries

pinna n anat the external part of the ear

pinnace n a ship's boat **WORD ORIGIN** French pinace

pinnacle n 1 the highest point of fame or success 2 a towering peak of a mountain 3 a slender spire **WORD ORIGIN** Latin pinna wing

pinnate adj bot (of compound leaves) having leaflets growing opposite each other in pairs **WORD ORIGIN** Latin pinna feather

pinny n, pl -nies an informal or child's name for **pinafore** (sense 1)

pinotage (**pin**-oh-tazh) n a red wine blended from the Pinot Noir and Hermitage grapes that is unique to South Africa

pinpoint vb 1 to locate or identify exactly: we've pinpointed the fault ▷ adj 2 exact: pinpoint accuracy

pinprick n a small irritation or annoyance

pins and needles n informal a tingling sensation in a part of the body

pinstripe n (in textiles) a very narrow stripe in fabric or the fabric itself

pint n 1 Brit a unit of liquid measure equal to one eighth of an imperial gallon (0.568 litre) 2 US a unit of liquid measure equal to one eighth of a US gallon (0.473 litre) 3 Brit informal a pint of beer **WORD ORIGIN** Old French pinte

pinta n Brit informal a pint of milk **WORD ORIGIN** phonetic rendering of pint of

pintail n, pl -tails or -tail a greyish-brown duck with a pointed tail

pintle n a pin or bolt forming the pivot of a hinge **WORD ORIGIN** Old English pintel penis

pinto US & Canad adj 1 marked with patches of white; piebald ▷ n, pl -tos 2 a pinto horse **WORD ORIGIN** American Spanish

pint-size or **pint-sized** adj informal very small

pin tuck n a narrow, ornamental fold used on shirt fronts and dress bodices

pin-up n 1 informal a picture of a sexually attractive person, often partially or totally undressed 2 slang a person who has appeared in such a picture: your favourite pin-up 3 a photograph of a famous personality

pinwheel n same as **Catherine wheel**

Pinyin n a system of spelling used to represent Chinese in Roman letters

pion or **pi meson** n physics any of three subatomic particles which are classified as mesons

pioneer n 1 an explorer or settler of a new land or region 2 an originator or developer of something new ▷ vb 3 to be a pioneer (in or of) 4 to initiate or develop: the new technique was pioneered in France **WORD ORIGIN** Old French paonier infantryman

pious adj 1 religious or devout 2 insincerely reverent; sanctimonious **piousness** n **WORD ORIGIN** Latin pius

pip[1] n the seed of a fleshy fruit, such as an apple or pear **WORD ORIGIN** short for pippin

pip[2] n 1 a short high-pitched sound used as a time signal on radio 2 any of the spots on a playing card, dice, or domino 3 informal the emblem worn on the shoulder by junior officers in the British Army, indicating their rank **WORD ORIGIN** imitative

pip[3] n 1 a contagious disease of poultry 2 facetious slang a minor human ailment 3 **get** or **have the pip** NZ slang to sulk 4 **give someone the pip** Brit, NZ, & S African slang to annoy someone: it really gives me the pip **WORD ORIGIN** Middle Dutch pippe

pip[4] vb pipping, pipped • **pip someone at the post** Brit & NZ slang to defeat someone whose success seems certain **WORD ORIGIN** probably from PIP[2]

pipe n 1 a long tube for conveying water, oil, or gas 2 **a** a tube with a small bowl at the end for smoking tobacco **b** the amount of tobacco that fills the bowl of a pipe 3 zool, bot any of various hollow organs, such as the respiratory passage of certain animals 4 **a** a tubular instrument in which air vibrates and produces a

musical sound **b** any of the tubular devices on an organ 5 a boatswain's whistle 6 **put that in your pipe and smoke it** informal accept that fact if you can 7 **the pipes** see **bagpipes** ▷ vb piping, piped 8 to play (music) on a pipe 9 to summon or lead by a pipe: to pipe in the haggis 10 **a** to signal orders to (the crew) by a boatswain's pipe **b** to signal the arrival or departure of: he piped his entire ship's company on deck 11 to utter in a shrill tone 12 to convey (water, oil, or gas) by pipe 13 to force cream or icing through a shaped nozzle to decorate food ▶ See also **pipe down**, **pipe up** **WORD ORIGIN** Old English pīpe

pipeclay n a fine white pure clay, used in tobacco pipes and pottery and to whiten leather and similar materials

pipe cleaner n a short length of wire covered with tiny tufts of yarn: used to clean the stem of a tobacco pipe

piped music n light music played as background music in public places

pipe down vb informal to stop talking or making noise

pipe dream n a fanciful or impossible plan or hope **WORD ORIGIN** alluding to dreams produced by smoking an opium pipe

pipeline n 1 a long pipe for transporting oil, water, or gas 2 a means of communication 3 **in the pipeline** in preparation

pipe organ n same as **organ** (sense 2a)

piper n a person who plays a pipe or bagpipes

pipette n a slender glass tube for transferring or measuring out liquids **WORD ORIGIN** French: little pipe

pipe up vb to speak up unexpectedly

pipi n, pl pipi or pipis Austral & NZ an edible mollusc of Australia and New Zealand **WORD ORIGIN** Māori

piping n 1 a system of pipes 2 a string of icing or cream used to decorate cakes and desserts 3 a thin strip of covered cord or material, used to edge hems or cushions 4 the sound of a pipe or bagpipes 5 a shrill voice or whistling sound: a dove's cool piping ▷ adj 6 making a shrill sound ▷ adv 7 **piping hot** extremely hot

pipistrelle n a type of small brownish bat found throughout the world **WORD ORIGIN** Italian pipistrello

pipit n a small songbird with a brownish speckled plumage and a long tail **WORD ORIGIN** probably imitative

pippin n a type of eating apple **WORD ORIGIN** Old French pepin

pipsqueak n informal an insignificant or contemptible person

piquant (**pee**-kant) adj 1 having a spicy taste 2 stimulating to the mind: love was a forbidden piquant secret **piquancy** n **WORD ORIGIN** French, literally: prickling

pique (**peek**) n 1 a feeling of resentment or irritation, such as from hurt pride ▷ vb piquing, piqued 2 to hurt (someone's) pride 3 to excite (curiosity or interest) **WORD ORIGIN** French piquer to prick

p

piqué (**pee**-kay) *n* a stiff ribbed fabric of cotton, silk, or spun rayon **WORD ORIGIN** French: pricked

piquet (pik-**ket**) *n* a card game for two people played with a reduced pack **WORD ORIGIN** French

piracy *n*, *pl* **-cies 1** *Brit & NZ* robbery on the seas **2** a crime, such as hijacking, committed aboard a ship or aircraft **3** the unauthorized use of patented or copyrighted material

piranha *n* a small fierce freshwater fish of tropical America, with strong jaws and sharp teeth **WORD ORIGIN** S American Indian: fish with teeth

pirate *n* **1** a person who commits piracy **2** a vessel used by pirates **3** a person who illegally sells or publishes someone else's literary or artistic work **4** a person or group of people who broadcast illegally ▷ *vb* **-rating, -rated 5** to sell or reproduce (artistic work, ideas, etc.) illegally **piratical** *adj* **WORD ORIGIN** Greek *peira* an attack

piri-piri *n* a hot sauce, of Portuguese colonial origin, made from red chilli peppers **WORD ORIGIN** from a Bantu language: pepper

pirouette *n* **1** a body spin performed on the toes or the ball of the foot ▷ *vb* **-etting, -etted 2** to perform a pirouette **WORD ORIGIN** French

piscatorial *adj formal* of or relating to fish, fishing, or fishermen **WORD ORIGIN** Latin *piscatorius*

Pisces *n astrol* the twelfth sign of the zodiac; the Fishes **WORD ORIGIN** Latin

pisciculture (**piss**-ee-cult-cher) *n formal* the rearing and breeding of fish under controlled conditions **WORD ORIGIN** Latin *piscis* fish

piscine (**piss**-sign) *adj* of or resembling a fish **WORD ORIGIN** Latin *piscis* fish

piss *taboo vb* **1** to urinate **2** to discharge as or in one's urine: *to piss blood* ▷ *n* **3** an act of urinating **4** urine **5** **take the piss** to make fun of or mock someone. See also **piss down, piss off WORD ORIGIN** probably imitative

pissant *US*, *derogatory slang n* **1** an insignificant or contemptible person ▷ *adj* **2** insignificant or contemptible **WORD ORIGIN** from PISS + ANT

piss down *vb taboo slang* to rain heavily

pissed *adj slang* **1** *Brit, Austral, S Africa, & NZ* drunk **2** *US & Canad* angry

piss off *vb taboo slang* **1** to annoy or disappoint **2** to go away: often used to dismiss a person

pistachio *n*, *pl* **-chios** a Mediterranean nut with a hard shell and an edible green kernel **WORD ORIGIN** Persian *pistah*

piste (**peest**) *n* a slope or course for skiing **WORD ORIGIN** French

pistil *n* the seed-bearing part of a flower **WORD ORIGIN** Latin *pistillum* pestle

pistillate *adj bot* (of plants) having pistils

pistol *n* a short-barrelled handgun **WORD ORIGIN** Czech *pišt'ala*

pistol-whip *vb* **-whipping, -whipped** *US* to beat or strike with a pistol barrel

piston *n* a cylindrical part that slides to and fro in a hollow cylinder: in an engine it is attached by a rod to other parts, thus its movement causes the other parts to move **WORD ORIGIN** Old Italian *pistone*

pit¹ *n* **1** a large deep opening in the ground **2** a coal mine **3** *anat* **a** a small natural depression on the surface of a body or organ **b** the floor of any natural bodily cavity: *the pit of the stomach* **4** *pathol* a pockmark **5** a concealed danger or difficulty **6** an area at the side of a motor-racing track for servicing or refuelling vehicles **7** the area occupied by the orchestra in a theatre **8** an enclosure for fighting animals or birds **9** the back of the ground floor of a theatre **10** same as **pitfall** (sense 2) **11** **the pit** hell ▷ *vb* **pitting, pitted 12** (often foll. by *against*) to match in opposition, esp. as antagonists: *sister pitted against sister* **13** to mark with small dents or scars **14** to place or bury in a pit **15** **pit one's wits against** to compete against in a test or contest ▷ See also **pits WORD ORIGIN** Old English *pytt*

pit² *chiefly US & Canad n* **1** the stone of various fruits ▷ *vb* **pitting, pitted 2** to remove the stone from (a fruit) **WORD ORIGIN** Dutch: kernel

pitapat *adv* **1** with quick light taps ▷ *n* **2** such taps **WORD ORIGIN** imitative

pit bull terrier *n* a strong muscular terrier with a short coat

pitch¹ *vb* **1** to hurl or throw **2** to set up (a tent or camp) **3** to slope or fall forwards or downwards: *she pitched forwards like a diver* **4** (of a ship or plane) to dip and raise its back and front alternately **5** to set the level or tone of: *his ambitions were pitched too high* **6** to aim to sell (a product) to a specified market or on a specified basis **7** *music* to sing or play (a note or interval) accurately ▷ *n* **8** *chiefly Brit* (in many sports) the field of play **9** a level of emotion: *children can wind their parents up to a pitch of anger and guilt* **10** the degree or angle of slope **11** the distance between corresponding points on adjacent threads on a screw thread **12** the pitching motion of a ship or plane **13** *music* the highness or lowness of a note in relation to other notes: *low pitch* **14** the act or manner of pitching a ball **15** *chiefly Brit* the place where a street or market trader regularly sells **16** *slang* a persuasive sales talk, esp. one routinely repeated ▷ See also **pitch in, pitch into WORD ORIGIN** Middle English *picchen*

pitch² *n* **1** a thick sticky substance formed from coal tar and used for paving or waterproofing **2** any similar substance, such as asphalt, occurring as a natural deposit ▷ *vb* **3** to apply pitch to **WORD ORIGIN** Old English *pic*

pitch-black *adj* extremely dark; unlit: *it was a wild night, pitch-black, with howling gales*

pitchblende *n* a blackish mineral which is the principal source of uranium and radium **WORD ORIGIN** German *Pechblende*

pitch-dark *adj* extremely or completely dark

pitched battle *n* a fierce fight

pitcher¹ *n* a large jug, usually rounded with a narrow neck **WORD ORIGIN** Old French *pichier*

pitcher² *n* baseball the player on the fielding team who throws the ball to the batter

pitcher plant *n* a plant with pitcher-like leaves that attract and trap insects, which are then digested

pitchfork *n* **1** a long-handled fork with two or three long curved prongs for tossing hay ▷ *vb* **2** to use a pitchfork on (something)

pitch in *vb* to cooperate or contribute

pitch into *vb informal* to attack (someone) physically or verbally

pitch pine *n* a pine tree of North America: a source of turpentine and pitch

pitch pipe *n* a small pipe that sounds a note to establish the correct starting note for unaccompanied singing

piteous *adj* arousing or deserving pity: *the piteous mewing of an injured kitten* **piteousness** *n*

pitfall *n* **1** an unsuspected difficulty or danger **2** a trap in the form of a concealed pit, designed to catch men or wild animals **WORD ORIGIN** Old English *pytt* pit + *fealle* trap

pith *n* **1** the soft white lining inside the rind of fruits such as the orange **2** the essential part: *policy, though, isn't the pith of what happened yesterday* **3** the soft spongy tissue in the centre of the stem of certain plants **WORD ORIGIN** Old English *pitha*

pithead *n* the top of a mine shaft and the buildings and hoisting gear around it

pith helmet *n* a lightweight hat made of the pith of the sola, an E Indian swamp plant, that is worn for protection from the sun

pithy *adj* **pithier, pithiest 1** terse and full of meaning **2** of, resembling, or full of pith **pithiness** *n*

pitiable *adj* arousing or deserving pity or contempt **pitiableness** *n*

pitiful *adj* arousing or deserving great pity or contempt **pitifully** *adv* **pitifulness** *n*

pitiless *adj* feeling no pity or mercy **pitilessly** *adv*

piton (**peet**-on) *n* mountaineering a metal spike that may be driven into a crack and used to secure a rope **WORD ORIGIN** French

pits *pl n* **the pits** *slang* the worst possible person, place, or thing **WORD ORIGIN** perhaps from *armpits*

pitta bread *or* **pitta** *n* a flat rounded slightly leavened bread, originally from the Middle East **WORD ORIGIN** Modern Greek *pitta* a cake

Words from Literature
part 21

pottle *n* a pottle was a small basket
   He had a paper-bag under each arm and a pottle
   of strawberries in one hand...
   Great Expectations Charles Dickens

pounce *n* a fine powder used to prevent ink spreading
on untreated paper
   in that grim atmosphere of pounce and parchment,
   red-tape, dusty wafers, ink-jars, brief and draft
   paper, law reports, writs, declarations, and bills
   of costs
   David Copperfield Charles Dickens

pox *n* sexually transmitted diseases like syphilis
   how the pox in all its consequences and
   denominations
   Gulliver's Travels Jonathan Swift

prelibation *n* a foretaste of or an example of
something to come
   A prelibation to the mower's scythe
   The Prelude William Wordsworth

prentice *n* an apprentice
   and Joe, sitting on an old gun, had told me that
   when I was 'prentice to him regularly bound,
   we would have such Larks there!
   Great Expectations Charles Dickens

presently *adv* immediately
   I presently knew what they meant
   Gulliver's Travels Jonathan Swift

pumpion *n* pumpkin
   for it was almost as large as a small pumpion
   Gulliver's Travels Jonathan Swift

punctual *adj* kept in one place
   was not a punctual presence, but a spirit
   The Prelude William Wordsworth

quadrille *n* a dance invented in France which is
usually performed by four couples
   However, Mr Swiveller had Miss Sophy's hand
   for the first quadrille (country-dances being low,
   were utterly proscribed)
   The Old Curiosity Shop Charles Dickens

quadrille *n* a card game for four people
   to make up her pool of quadrille in the evening
   Pride and Prejudice Jane Austen

quality *n* gentry or upper-class people
   if you are with the quality
   The Adventures of Huckleberry Finn Mark Twain

quid *n* a quid is something chewed or kept in the
mouth, like a piece of tobacco
   rolling his quid
   Treasure Island Robert Louis Stevenson

quit *v* to avenge or to make even
   But Faustus's death shall quit my infamy
   Doctor Faustus 4.3 Christopher Marlowe

rag *n* rags are divisions
   Nor hours, days, months, which are the rags
   of time
   The Sun Rising John Donne

raiment *n* clothing
   the mountain shook off turf and flower, had only
   heath for raiment and crag for gem
   Jane Eyre Charlotte Brontë

rain cats and dogs *phrase* an expression meaning
rain heavily. The origin of the expression is unclear
   But it'll perhaps rain cats and dogs to-morrow
   Silas Marner George Eliot

raise Cain *phrase* to raise Cain means to cause a lot of
trouble. Cain is a character in the Bible who killed his
brother Abel
   and every time he got drunk he raised Cain
   around town
   The Adventures of Huckleberry Finn Mark Twain

rambling *adj* rambling means confused and not
very clear
   my head began to be filled very early with
   rambling thoughts
   Robinson Crusoe Daniel Defoe

pittance n a very small amount of money
WORD ORIGIN Old French *pietance* ration

pitter-patter n 1 the sound of light rapid taps or pats, such as of rain drops ▷ vb 2 to make such a sound

pituitary or **pituitary gland** n the gland at the base of the brain which secretes hormones that affect skeletal growth, development of the sex glands, and other functions of the body
WORD ORIGIN Late Latin *pituitarius* slimy

pity n, pl **pities** 1 sorrow felt for the sufferings of others 2 a cause of regret: *it's a great pity he did not live longer* 3 **have** or **take pity on** to have sympathy or show mercy for ▷ vb **pities, pitying, pitied** 4 to feel pity for **pitying** adj
WORD ORIGIN Latin *pietas* duty

pivot n 1 a central shaft around which something turns 2 the central person or thing necessary for progress or success ▷ vb **-oting, -oted** 3 to turn on or provide with a pivot
WORD ORIGIN Old French

pivotal adj 1 of crucial importance 2 of or acting as a pivot

pix n informal a plural of **pic**

pixel n the smallest constituent unit of an image, as on a visual display unit
WORD ORIGIN from *pix* pictures + *el(ement)*

pixie or **pixy** n, pl **pixies** (in folklore) a fairy or elf

pizza n a dish of Italian origin consisting of a baked disc of dough covered with a wide variety of savoury toppings
WORD ORIGIN Italian

pizzazz or **pizazz** n informal an attractive combination of energy and style
WORD ORIGIN origin obscure

pizzicato (pit-see-**kah**-toe) adj, adv music (in music for the violin family) to be plucked with the finger
WORD ORIGIN Italian: pinched

Pl. (in street names) Place

plaas n S African a farm
WORD ORIGIN Afrikaans

placard n 1 a notice that is paraded in public ▷ vb 2 to attach placards to
WORD ORIGIN Old French *plaquart*

placate vb **-cating, -cated** to calm (someone) to stop him or her feeling angry or upset **placatory** adj
WORD ORIGIN Latin *placare*

place n 1 a particular part of a space or of a surface 2 a geographical point, such as a town or city 3 a position or rank in a sequence or order 4 an open square lined with houses in a city or town 5 space or room 6 a house or living quarters: *he's buying his own place* 7 any building or area set aside for a specific purpose 8 the point reached in reading or speaking: *her finger was pressed to the page as if marking her place* 9 right or duty: *it's not my place to do their job for them* 10 appointment, position, or job: *she won a place at university* 11 position, condition, or state: *you know what your place in the world is* 12 a space or seat, as at a dining table 13 maths the relative position of a digit in a number

14 **all over the place** in disorder or disarray 15 **go places** informal to become successful 16 **in** or **out of place** in or out of the proper or customary position 17 **in place of a** instead of: *leeks can be used in place of the broccoli* **b** in exchange for: *he gave her it in place of her ring* 18 **know one's place** to be aware of one's inferior position 19 **put someone in his** or **her place** to humble someone who is arrogant, conceited, etc. 20 **take place** to happen or occur 21 **take the place of** to be a substitute for ▷ vb **placing, placed** 22 to put in a particular or appropriate place 23 to find or indicate the place of: *I bet you the media couldn't have placed Neath on the map before the by-election* 24 to identify or classify by linking with an appropriate context: *I felt I should know him, but could not quite place him* 25 to make (an order or bet) 26 to find a home or job for (someone) 27 (often foll. by with) to put under the care (of) 28 (of a racehorse, greyhound, athlete, etc.) to arrive in first, second, third, or sometimes fourth place
WORD ORIGIN Latin *platea* courtyard

placebo (plas-**see**-bo) n, pl **-bos** or **-boes** med an inactive substance given to a patient usually to compare its effects with those of a real drug but sometimes for the psychological benefit gained by the patient through believing that he or she is receiving treatment
WORD ORIGIN Latin: I shall please

place kick n rugby, American football, etc. a kick in which the ball is placed in position before it is kicked

placement n 1 arrangement or position 2 a temporary job which someone is given as part of a training course: *many pupils have been on work placements with local businesses* 3 the act or an instance of finding someone a job or a home: *the main task of the adoption agency is to find the best family placement for each child*

placenta (plass-**ent**-a) n, pl **-tas** or **-tae** the organ formed in the womb of most mammals during pregnancy, providing oxygen and nutrients for the fetus **placental** adj
WORD ORIGIN Latin, from Greek *plakoeis* flat cake

place setting n the cutlery, crockery, and glassware laid for one person at a dining table

placid adj having a calm appearance or nature: *placid waters; a placid temperament* **placidity** or **placidness** n **placidly** adv
WORD ORIGIN Latin *placidus* peaceful

placket n dressmaking an opening at the waist of a dress or skirt for buttons or zips or for access to a pocket
WORD ORIGIN perhaps from Medieval Dutch *plackaet* breastplate

plagiarize or **-rise** (**play**-jer-ize) vb **-rizing, -rized** or **-rising, -rised** to steal ideas or passages from (another's work) and present them as one's own **plagiarism** n **plagiarizer** or **-riser** n
WORD ORIGIN Latin *plagium* kidnapping

plague n 1 any widespread and usually highly contagious disease with a high fatality rate 2 an infectious disease of rodents transmitted to man by the bite of the rat flea; bubonic plague 3 something that afflicts or harasses:

a plague of locusts 4 informal a nuisance ▷ vb **plaguing, plagued** 5 to afflict or harass: *a playing career plagued by injury* 6 informal to annoy or pester
WORD ORIGIN Latin *plaga* a blow

plaice n, pl **plaice** or **plaices** an edible European flatfish with a brown body marked with red or orange spots
WORD ORIGIN Greek *platus* flat

plaid n 1 a long piece of tartan cloth worn over the shoulder as part of Highland costume 2 a crisscross weave or cloth
WORD ORIGIN Scottish Gaelic *plaide*

Plaid Cymru (plide **kumm**-ree) n the Welsh nationalist party
WORD ORIGIN Welsh

plain adj 1 flat or smooth 2 easily understood: *he made it plain what he wanted from me* 3 honest or blunt: *the plain fact is that my mother has no time for me* 4 without adornment: *a plain brown envelope* 5 not good-looking 6 (of fabric) without pattern or of simple weave 7 lowly, esp. in social rank or education: *the plain people of Ireland* 8 knitting of or done in plain stitch ▷ n 9 a level stretch of country 10 a simple stitch in knitting made by passing the wool round the front of the needle ▷ adv 11 clearly or simply: *that's just plain stupid!* **plainly** adv **plainness** n
WORD ORIGIN Latin *planus* level, clear

plainchant n same as **plainsong**

plain chocolate n Brit chocolate with a slightly bitter flavour and dark colour

plain clothes pl n ordinary clothes, as opposed to uniform, worn by a detective on duty

plain flour n flour to which no raising agent has been added

plain sailing n 1 informal smooth or easy progress 2 naut sailing in a body of water that is unobstructed; clear sailing

plainsong n the style of unaccompanied choral music used in the medieval Church, esp. in Gregorian chant
WORD ORIGIN translation of Medieval Latin *cantus planus*

plain speaking n saying exactly what one thinks **plain-spoken** adj

plaint n 1 archaic a complaint or lamentation 2 law a statement in writing of grounds of complaint made to a court of law
WORD ORIGIN Old French *plainte*

plaintiff n a person who sues in a court of law
WORD ORIGIN Old French *plaintif* complaining

plaintive adj sad and mournful **plaintively** adv
WORD ORIGIN Old French *plaintif* grieving

plait (platt) n 1 a length of hair that has been plaited ▷ vb 2 to intertwine (strands or strips) in a pattern
WORD ORIGIN Latin *plicare* to fold

plan n 1 a method thought out for doing or achieving something 2 a detailed drawing to scale of a horizontal section through a building 3 an outline or sketch ▷ vb **planning, planned**

4 to form a plan (for) **5** to make a plan of (a building) **6** to intend
WORD ORIGIN Latin *planus* flat

planchette *n* a device on which messages are written under supposed spirit guidance
WORD ORIGIN French: little board

plane¹ *n* **1** an aeroplane **2** *maths* a flat surface in which a straight line joining any two of its points lies entirely on that surface **3** a level surface: *an inclined plane* **4** a level of existence or attainment: *her ambition was set on a higher plane than pulling pints in a pub* ▷ *adj* **5** level or flat **6** *maths* lying entirely in one plane ▷ *vb* **planing, planed 7** to glide or skim: *they planed over the ice*
WORD ORIGIN Latin *planum* level surface

plane² *n* **1** a tool with a steel blade for smoothing timber ▷ *vb* **planing, planed 2** to smooth (timber) using a plane **3** (often foll. by *away* or *off*) to remove using a plane
WORD ORIGIN Latin *planare* to level

planet *n* any of the nine celestial bodies, Mercury, Venus, Earth, Mars, Jupiter, Saturn, Uranus, Neptune, or Pluto, that revolve around the sun in oval-shaped orbits **planetary** *adj*
WORD ORIGIN Greek *planaein* to wander

planetarium *n, pl* **-riums** *or* **-ria 1** an instrument for projecting images of the sun, moon, stars, and planets onto a domed ceiling **2** a building in which such an instrument is housed

planetoid (plan-it-oid) *n* see **asteroid**

plane tree *or* **plane** *n* a tree with rounded heads of fruit and leaves with pointed lobes
WORD ORIGIN Greek *platos* wide (because of its broad leaves)

plangent (plan-jent) *adj* (of sounds) mournful and resounding

plank *n* **1** a long flat piece of sawn timber **2** one of the policies in a political party's programme **3 walk the plank** to be forced by sailors to walk to one's death off the end of a plank jutting out from the side of a ship
WORD ORIGIN Late Latin *planca* board

planking *n* a number of planks

plankton *n* the small drifting plants and animals on the surface layer of a sea or lake
WORD ORIGIN Greek *planktos* wandering

planner *n* **1** a person who makes plans, esp. for the development of a town, building, etc. **2** a chart for recording future appointments, etc.

planning permission *n* formal permission granted by a local authority for the construction, alteration, or change of use of a building

plant *n* **1** a living organism that grows in the ground and lacks the power of movement **2** the land, building, and equipment used in an industry or business **3** a factory or workshop **4** mobile mechanical equipment for construction or road-making **5** *informal* a thing positioned secretly for discovery by someone else, often in order to incriminate an innocent person ▷ *vb* **6** to set (seeds or crops) into the ground to grow: *it's the wrong time of year for planting roses* **7** to place firmly in position:

I planted my chair beside hers **8** to introduce into someone's mind: *once Wendy had planted the idea in the minds of the owners, they quite fancied selling* **9** *slang* to deliver (a blow or kiss) **10** *informal* to position or hide (someone) in order to deceive or observe **11** *informal* to hide or secrete (something), usually for some illegal purpose or in order to incriminate someone
WORD ORIGIN Old English

plantain¹ *n* a plant with a rosette of broad leaves and a slender spike of small greenish flowers
WORD ORIGIN Latin *planta* sole of the foot

plantain² *n* **1** a large tropical fruit like a green-skinned banana **2** the tree on which this fruit grows
WORD ORIGIN Spanish *platano*

plantation *n* **1** an estate, esp. in tropical countries, where cash crops such as rubber or coffee are grown on a large scale **2** a group of cultivated trees or plants **3** (formerly) a colony of settlers

planter *n* **1** the owner or manager of a plantation **2** a decorative pot for house plants

plantigrade *adj* walking on the entire sole of the foot, as humans and bears do
WORD ORIGIN Latin *planta* sole of the foot + *gradus* a step

plaque *n* **1** a commemorative inscribed stone or metal plate **2** Also called: **dental plaque** a filmy deposit on teeth consisting of mucus, bacteria, and food, that causes decay
WORD ORIGIN French

plasma *n* **1** the clear yellowish fluid portion of blood which contains the corpuscles and cells **2** a sterilized preparation of such fluid, taken from the blood, for use in transfusions **3** a former name for **protoplasm 4** *physics* a hot ionized gas containing positive ions and free electrons
WORD ORIGIN Greek: something moulded

plasma screen *n* a type of flat screen on a television or a visual display unit in which the image is created by electric current passing through many gas-filled cells

plaster *n* **1** a mixture of lime, sand, and water that is applied to a wall or ceiling as a soft paste and dries as a hard coating **2** *Brit, Austral, & NZ* an adhesive strip of material for dressing a cut or wound **3** short for **mustard plaster** or **plaster of Paris** ▷ *vb* **4** to coat (a wall or ceiling) with plaster **5** to apply like plaster: *he plastered his face with shaving cream* **6** to cause to lie flat or to adhere: *his hair was plastered to his forehead* **plasterer** *n*
WORD ORIGIN Greek *emplastron* healing dressing

plasterboard *n* a thin rigid board, made of plaster compressed between two layers of fibreboard, used to form or cover interior walls

plastered *adj slang* drunk

plaster of Paris *n* a white powder that sets to a hard solid when mixed with water, used for making sculptures and casts for setting broken limbs

plastic *n* **1** any of a large number of synthetic materials that can be moulded when soft and then set **2** *informal* Also called: **plastic money** credit cards etc. as opposed to cash ▷ *adj* **3** made of plastic **4** easily influenced **5** capable of being moulded or formed **6** of moulding or modelling: *the plastic arts* **7** *slang* superficially attractive yet artificial or false: *glamorous models with plastic smiles* **plasticity** *n*
WORD ORIGIN Greek *plastikos* mouldable

plastic bullet *n* a solid PVC cylinder fired by the police in riot control

plastic explosive *n* an adhesive jelly-like explosive substance

Plasticine *n trademark* a soft coloured material used, esp. by children, for modelling

plasticize *or* **-cise** *vb* **-cizing, -cized** *or* **-cising, -cised** to make or become plastic

plasticizer *or* **-ciser** *n* a substance added to a plastic material to soften it and improve flexibility

plastic surgery *n* the branch of surgery concerned with the repair or reconstruction of missing, injured, or malformed tissues or parts **plastic surgeon** *n*

plate *n* **1** a shallow dish made of porcelain, earthenware, glass, etc. on which food is served **2** Also called: **plateful** the contents of a plate **3** a shallow dish for receiving a collection in church **4** flat metal of even thickness obtained by rolling **5** a thin coating of metal usually on another metal **6** dishes or cutlery made of gold or silver **7** a sheet of metal, plastic, or rubber having a printing surface produced by a process such as stereotyping **8** a print taken from such a sheet or from a woodcut **9** a thin flat sheet of a substance, such as glass **10** a small piece of metal or plastic with an inscription, fixed to another surface: *a brass name plate* **11** *photog* a sheet of glass coated with photographic emulsion on which an image can be formed by exposure to light **12** *informal* same as **denture 13** *anat* any flat platelike structure **14** a cup awarded to the winner of a sporting contest, esp. a horse race **15** any of the rigid layers of the earth's crust **16 have a lot on one's plate** to have many pressing things to deal with **17 on a plate** acquired without trouble: *he got the job handed to him on a plate* ▷ *vb* **plating, plated 18** to coat (a metal surface) with a thin layer of another metal **19** to cover with metal plates, usually for protection **20** to form (metal) into plate, usually by rolling
WORD ORIGIN Old French: something flat

plateau (plat-oh) *n, pl* **-teaus** *or* **-teaux** (-ohs) **1** a wide level area of high land **2** a relatively long period of stability: *the body temperature rises to a plateau that it keeps until shortly before bedtime* ▷ *vb* **3** to remain stable for a long period
WORD ORIGIN French

plated *adj* coated with a layer of metal

plate glass *n* glass produced in thin sheets, used for windows and mirrors

platelayer *n Brit* a workman who lays and maintains railway track

platelet *n* a minute particle occurring in the blood of vertebrates and involved in the clotting of the blood

platen *n* **1** the roller on a typewriter, against which the keys strike **2** a flat plate in a printing press that presses the paper against the type **WORD ORIGIN** Old French *platine*

platform *n* **1** a raised floor **2** a raised area at a railway station where passengers get on or off the trains **3** see **drilling platform 4** the declared aims of a political party **5** the thick raised sole of some shoes **6** a type of computer hardware or operating system **WORD ORIGIN** French *plat* flat + *forme* layout

platform game *n* a type of computer game that is played by moving a figure on the screen through a series of obstacles

platform ticket *n* a ticket for admission to railway platforms but not for travel

plating *n* **1** a coating of metal **2** a layer or covering of metal plates

platinum *n* a silvery-white metallic element, very resistant to heat and chemicals: used in jewellery, laboratory apparatus, electrical contacts, dentistry, electroplating, and as a catalyst. Symbol: Pt **WORD ORIGIN** Spanish *platina* silvery element

platinum blonde *n* a girl or woman with silvery-blonde hair

platitude *n* a trite or unoriginal remark: *it's a platitude, but people need people* **platitudinous** *adj* **WORD ORIGIN** French: flatness

platonic *adj* friendly or affectionate but without physical desire: *platonic love*

Platonic *adj* of the philosopher Plato or his teachings

Platonism (**plate**-on-iz-zum) *n* the teachings of Plato (?427–?347 BC), Greek philosopher, and his followers **Platonist** *n*

platoon *n mil* a subunit of a company, usually comprising three sections of ten to twelve men **WORD ORIGIN** French *peloton* little ball, group of men

platteland *n* **the platteland** (in South Africa) the country districts or rural areas **WORD ORIGIN** Afrikaans

platter *n* a large shallow, usually oval, dish **WORD ORIGIN** Anglo-Norman *plater*

platypus *or* **duck-billed platypus** *n, pl* -**puses** an Australian egg-laying amphibious mammal, with dense fur, webbed feet, and a ducklike bill **WORD ORIGIN** Greek *platus* flat + *pous* foot

plaudit *n* (*usually pl*) an expression of enthusiastic approval **WORD ORIGIN** Latin *plaudite* applaud!

plausible *adj* **1** apparently reasonable or true: *a plausible excuse* **2** apparently trustworthy or believable: *he is an extraordinarily plausible liar* **plausibility** *n* **plausibly** *adv*

WORD ORIGIN Latin *plausibilis* worthy of applause

play *vb* **1** to occupy oneself in (a sport or recreation) **2** to compete against (someone) in a sport or game: *I saw Brazil play Argentina recently* **3** to fulfil (a particular role) in a team game: *he usually plays in midfield* **4** (often foll. by *about* or *around*) to behave carelessly: *he's only playing with your affections, you know* **5** to act the part (of) in a dramatic piece: *he has played Hamlet to packed Broadway houses* **6** to perform (a dramatic piece) **7 a** to perform (music) on an instrument **b** to be able to perform on (a musical instrument): *she plays the bassoon* **8** to send out (water) or cause to send out (water): *they played a hose across the wrecked building* **9** to cause (a radio etc.) to emit sound **10** to move freely or quickly: *the light played across the water* **11** *stock exchange* to speculate for gain in (a market) **12** *angling* to tire (a hooked fish) by alternately letting out and reeling in the line **13** to put (a card) into play **14** to gamble **15 play fair** *or* **false with** to act fairly *or* unfairly with **16 play for time** to gain time to one's advantage by the use of delaying tactics **17 play into the hands of** to act unwittingly to the advantage of (an opponent) **18 play politics a** to negotiate politically **b** to exploit an important issue merely for political gain **c** to make something into a political issue ▷ *n* **19 a a** dramatic piece written for performance by actors **b** the performance of such a piece **20** games or other activity undertaken for pleasure **21** the playing of a game or the time during which a game is in progress: *rain stopped play* **22** conduct: *fair play* **23** gambling **24** activity or operation: *radio allows full play to your imagination* **25** scope for freedom of movement: *there was a lot of play in the rope* **26** free or rapidly shifting motion: *the play of light on the water* **27** fun or jest: *I used to throw cushions at her in play* **28 in** *or* **out of play** (of a ball in a game) in *or* not in a position for continuing play according to the rules **29 make a play for** *informal* to make an obvious attempt to gain (something) ▸ See also **play along, playback,** etc. **playable** *adj* **WORD ORIGIN** Old English *plega, plegan*

play along *vb* to cooperate (with) temporarily: *I'll play along with them for the moment*

playback *n* **1** the playing of a recording on magnetic tape ▷ *vb* **play back 2** to listen to or watch (something recorded)

playbill *n* a poster or bill advertising a play

playboy *n* a rich man who devotes himself to such pleasures as nightclubs and female company

playcentre *n NZ* a centre for preschool children run by parents

play down *vb* to minimize the importance of: *she played down the problems of the company*

player *n* **1** a person who takes part in a game or sport **2** a person who plays a musical instrument **3** *informal* a leading participant in a particular field or activity: *one of the key players in Chinese politics* **4** an actor

player piano *n* a mechanical piano; Pianola

playful *adj* **1** good-natured and humorous: *a playful remark* **2** full of high spirits and fun: *a playful child* **playfully** *adv*

playgoer *n* a person who goes often to the theatre

playground *n* **1** an outdoor area for children's play, either with swings and slides, or adjoining a school **2** a place or activity enjoyed by a specified person or group: *they oppose turning the island into a tourist playground*

playgroup *n* a regular meeting of infants for supervised creative play

playhouse *n* a theatre

playing field *n* (*sometimes pl*) *Brit & NZ* a field or open space used for sport

playlist *n* a list of records chosen for playing, such as on a radio station

play-lunch *n Austral & NZ* a child's mid-morning snack at school

playmaker *n sport* a player who creates scoring opportunities for his or her team-mates

playmate *n* a companion in play

play off *vb* **1** to set (two people) against each other for one's own ends: *she delighted in playing one parent off against the other* **2** to take part in a play-off ▷ *n* **play-off 3** *sport* an extra contest to decide the winner when there is a tie **4** *chiefly US & Canad* a contest or series of games to determine a championship

play on *vb* to exploit (the feelings or weakness of another): *he played on my sympathy*

play on words *n* same as **pun**

playpen *n* a small portable enclosure in which a young child can safely be left to play

playschool *n* a nursery group for preschool children

PlayStation *n trademark* a video games console

plaything *n* **1** a toy **2** a person regarded or treated as a toy

playtime *n* a time for play or recreation, such as a school break

play up *vb* **1** to highlight: *the temptation is to play up the sensational aspects of the story* **2** *Austral & Brit informal* to behave in an unruly way **3** to give (one) trouble or not be working properly: *my back's playing me up again; the photocopier's started to play up* **4 play up to** to try to please by flattery

playwright *n* a person who writes plays

plaza *n* **1** an open public square, usually in Spain **2** *chiefly US & Canad* a modern shopping complex **WORD ORIGIN** Spanish

PLC *or* **plc** (in Britain) Public Limited Company

plea *n* **1** an emotional appeal **2** *law* a statement by or on behalf of a defendant **3** an excuse: *his plea of poverty rings a little hollow* **WORD ORIGIN** Anglo-Norman *plai*

plead *vb* **pleading, pleaded, plead** *or esp. Scot & US* **pled 1** (sometimes foll. by *with*) to ask with deep feeling **2** to give as an excuse: *whenever she invites him to dinner, he*

Sign Language

Sign language is a system of manual communication used by deaf people. There are two types of system: *concept-based*, where gestures, facial expressions, and body language are used to reconstruct a concept, and *language-based*, where signs are used to 'spell out' the words in the language.

The the leading sign languages from English-speaking communities, British Sign Language (BSL) and American Sign Language (ASL), are concept-based systems but, perhaps surprisingly, they are largely mutually unintelligible. Australian Sign Language (Auslan) and New Zealand Sign Language have developed from BSL, although they also borrow from ASL and other sign languages. Ireland has its own languages, Irish Sign Language (ISL) and Northern Ireland Sign Language (NISL). Each sign language can form its own varieties that reflect the influence of a particular community, so there can be significant variations even between different areas of the same country.

In concept-based systems, signs are used to express all the meanings and subtleties that can be conveyed in spoken or written language. In any of these systems there can be thousands of signs, and there are rules governing how they are formed and combined. Objects are often placed first, so the spoken sentence 'Jane bought a car' would be interpreted by first signing 'a car' then commenting on who bought it (Jane). Signers will set up the placement of a particular object in space by signing the object then physically 'placing' the object somewhere in front of the addressee. The signer can then use gaze and signs for directional verbs to refer to this object. Time relationships can be expressed in a similar way, with the signer dividing the space in front of them into zones, with future time indicated in a zone further forward in front of the body. The repetition of signs can indicate plurality or emphasis, while facial expressions can be used to indicate not just emotions but also, for example, grammatical information such as questions (which can be signalled with a raised eyebrow).

There are other systems which are more closely related to spoken or written English, such as *fingerspelling*, a method of spelling words using hand signs. Most alphabets use a unique hand sign to represent an individual letter, often with a hand shape based on a representation of the shape of the letter as it is written, but the signs might also incorporate palm orientation, and sometimes movement, location, and mouth pattern. Fingerspelling can be used in its own right, but it can also be used in concept-based systems to spell out names which have no sign or for which the signer does not know the sign, or to clarify a sign for the addressee. It can also be incorporated into fixed signs: the sign for 'gold', for example, is the letter 'g' and then movement of the hands in a 'shimmering' motion. Also used in Britain is Sign Supported English (SSE), which uses the same signs as BSL but in the same order as spoken English rather than following the formal syntax of BSL. SSE is used to support the learning of spoken English grammar alongside sign language. Makaton is a largely pictorial, simplified form of sign language used primarily with children. The signs are used while speaking to support the spoken words, with the aim that speech takes over after the link is made between the sign and the spoken word.

The origins of modern sign languages can be traced to France where, in 1771, the Abbé Charles-Michel de l'Épée established the first educational institution for deaf people. He created a series of signs for French grammatical markers to teach to his students, and a combination of these grammatical signs and an already extant language, Old French Sign Language, evolved into French Sign Language (LSF). An American clergyman called Thomas Gallaudet, who had visited Paris, then brought French Sign Language to a school for deaf people he founded in Connecticut in 1817. The combination of French and local signs taught in the school would develop into American Sign Language.

In the nineteenth century, BSL was used in British schools, but the twentieth century saw a change in attitudes, with educators maintaining that deaf people should instead be taught to speak and lip-read. However, sign language is widely used to interpret for deaf people on television, at theatres, and in conferences, and with an estimated 50,000 people in the United Kingdom using BSL, it was recognized as an official minority language in 2003.

pleads a prior engagement **3** *law* to declare oneself to be (guilty or not guilty) of the charge made against one **4** *law* to present (a case) in a court of law
WORD ORIGIN Latin *placere* to please

pleadings *pl n law* the formal written statements presented by the plaintiff and defendant in a lawsuit

pleasant *adj* **1** pleasing or enjoyable: *what a pleasant surprise* **2** having pleasing manners or appearance: *he was a pleasant boy* **pleasantly** *adv*
WORD ORIGIN Old French *plaisant*

pleasantry *n, pl* **-ries 1** (often *pl*) a polite or jocular remark: *we exchanged pleasantries about the weather* **2** agreeable jocularity
WORD ORIGIN French *plaisanterie*

please *vb* **pleasing, pleased 1** to give pleasure or satisfaction to (a person) **2** to regard as suitable or satisfying: *he can get almost anyone he pleases to work with him* **3** if you wish, sometimes used in ironic exclamation **4 pleased with** happy because of **5 please oneself** to do as one likes ▷ *adv* **6** used in making polite requests or pleading: *please sit down* **7 yes please** a polite phrase used to accept an offer or invitation **pleased** *adj*
WORD ORIGIN Latin *placere*

pleasing *adj* giving pleasure

pleasurable *adj* enjoyable or agreeable **pleasurably** *adv*

pleasure *n* **1** a feeling of happiness and contentment: *the pleasure of hearing good music* **2** something that gives enjoyment: *his garden was his only pleasure* **3** the activity of enjoying oneself: *business before pleasure* **4** *euphemistic* sexual gratification: *he took his pleasure of her* **5** a person's preference
WORD ORIGIN Old French *plaisir*

pleat *n* **1** a fold formed by doubling back fabric and pressing or stitching into place ▷ *vb* **2** to arrange (material) in pleats
WORD ORIGIN variant of *plait*

pleb *n Brit informal, often offensive* a common vulgar person

plebeian (pleb-**ee**-an) *adj* **1** of the lower social classes **2** unrefined: *plebeian tastes* ▷ *n* **3** one of the common people, usually of ancient Rome **4** a coarse or unrefined person
WORD ORIGIN Latin *plebs* the common people of ancient Rome

plebiscite (**pleb**-iss-ite) *n* a direct vote by all the electorate on an issue of national importance
WORD ORIGIN Latin *plebiscitum* decree of the people

plectrum *n, pl* **-trums** or **-tra** an implement for plucking the strings of a guitar or similar instrument
WORD ORIGIN Greek *plektron*

pled *vb US & Scot* a past (esp. in legal usage) of **plead**

pledge *n* **1** a solemn promise **2 a** something valuable given as a guarantee that a promise will be kept or a debt paid **b** the condition of being used as security: *in pledge* **3** a token: *a pledge of good faith* **4** an assurance of support or goodwill, given by drinking a toast: *we drank a pledge to their success*

5 take or **sign the pledge** to vow not to drink alcohol ▷ *vb* **pledging, pledged 6** to promise solemnly **7** to promise to give (money to charity, etc.) **8** to bind by or as if by a pledge: *I was pledged to secrecy* **9** to give (one's word or property) as a guarantee **10** to drink a toast to (a person or cause)
WORD ORIGIN Old French *plege*

Pleiocene *adj, n* same as **Pliocene**

Pleistocene (**ply**-stow-seen) *adj geol* of the epoch of geological time from about 1.6 million to 10 000 years ago
WORD ORIGIN Greek *pleistos* most + *kainos* recent

plenary *adj* **1** (of an assembly) attended by all the members **2** full or complete: *plenary powers*
WORD ORIGIN Latin *plenus* full

plenipotentiary *adj* **1** (usually of a diplomat) invested with full authority ▷ *n, pl* **-aries 2** a diplomat or representative who has full authority to transact business
WORD ORIGIN Latin *plenus* full + *potentia* power

plenitude *n literary* **1** abundance **2** fullness or completeness
WORD ORIGIN Latin *plenus* full

plenteous *adj literary* **1** abundant: *a plenteous supply* **2** producing abundantly: *a plenteous harvest*

plentiful *adj* existing in large amounts or numbers **plentifully** *adv*

plenty *n, pl* **-ties 1** (often foll. by *of*) a great number or amount: *plenty of time* **2** abundance: *an age of plenty* ▷ *adj* **3** very many: *there's plenty more fish in the sea* ▷ *adv* **4** *informal* more than adequately: *that's plenty fast enough for me*
WORD ORIGIN Latin *plenus* full

pleonasm *n rhetoric* **1** the use of more words than necessary, such as *a tiny little child* **2** an unnecessary word or phrase **pleonastic** *adj*
WORD ORIGIN Greek *pleonasmos* excess

plethora *n* an excess
WORD ORIGIN Greek *plēthōrē* fullness

pleura (**ploor**-a) *n, pl* **pleurae** (**ploor**-ee) *anat* the thin transparent membrane enveloping the lungs **pleural** *adj*
WORD ORIGIN Greek: side, rib

pleurisy *n* inflammation of the pleura, making breathing painful **pleuritic** *adj, n*

plexus *n, pl* **-uses** or **-us** a complex network of nerves or blood vessels
WORD ORIGIN Latin *plectere* to braid

pliable *adj* **1** easily bent: *pliable branches* **2** easily influenced: *his easy and pliable nature* **pliability** *n*

pliant *adj* **1** easily bent; supple: *pliant young willow and hazel twigs* **2** easily influenced: *he was a far more pliant subordinate than his predecessor* **pliancy** *n*
WORD ORIGIN Old French *plier* to fold

pliers *pl n* a gripping tool consisting of two hinged arms usually with serrated jaws
WORD ORIGIN from PLY¹

plight¹ *n* a dangerous or difficult situation: *the plight of the British hostages*
WORD ORIGIN Old French *pleit* fold, and probably influenced by Old English *pliht* peril

plight² *vb* **plight one's troth** *old-fashioned* to make a promise to marry
WORD ORIGIN Old English *pliht* peril

Plimsoll line *n* a line on the hull of a ship showing the level that the water should reach if the ship is properly loaded
WORD ORIGIN after Samuel *Plimsoll*, who advocated its adoption

plimsolls *pl n Brit* light rubber-soled canvas sports shoes
WORD ORIGIN from the resemblance of the sole to a Plimsoll line

plinth *n* **1** a base on which a statue stands **2** the slab that forms the base of a column or pedestal
WORD ORIGIN Greek *plinthos* brick

Pliocene or **Pleiocene** (**ply**-oh-seen) *adj geol* of the epoch of geological time about 10 million years ago
WORD ORIGIN Greek *pleiōn* more + *kainos* recent

PLO Palestine Liberation Organization

plod *vb* **plodding, plodded 1** to walk with heavy slow steps **2** to work slowly and steadily ▷ *n* **3** the act of plodding **4** *Brit slang* a policeman **plodder** *n*
WORD ORIGIN imitative

plonk¹ *vb* **1** to put down heavily and carelessly: *he plonked himself down on the sofa* ▷ *n* **2** the act or sound of plonking
WORD ORIGIN variant of *plunk*

plonk² *n informal* cheap inferior wine
WORD ORIGIN origin unknown

plonker *n Brit slang* a stupid person
WORD ORIGIN origin unknown

plop *n* **1** the sound made by an object dropping into water without a splash ▷ *vb* **plopping, plopped 2** to drop with such a sound: *a tear rolled down his cheek and plopped into his soup* **3** to fall or be placed heavily or carelessly: *we plopped down on the bed and went straight to sleep*
WORD ORIGIN imitative

plosive *phonetics adj* **1** pronounced with a sudden release of breath ▷ *n* **2** a plosive consonant
WORD ORIGIN French *explosif* explosive

plot¹ *n* **1** a secret plan for an illegal purpose **2** the story of a play, novel, or film ▷ *vb* **plotting, plotted 3** to plan secretly; conspire **4** to mark (a course) on a map **5** to make a plan or map of **6 a** to locate (points) on a graph by means of coordinates **b** to draw (a curve) through these points **7** to construct the plot of (a play, novel, or film) **plotter** *n*
WORD ORIGIN from PLOT², influenced by obsolete *complot* conspiracy

plot² *n* a small piece of land: *there was a small vegetable plot in the garden*
WORD ORIGIN Old English

plough or esp. US **plow** *n* **1** an agricultural tool for cutting or turning over the earth **2** a similar tool used for clearing snow ▷ *vb* **3** to turn over (the soil) with a plough **4** to make (furrows or grooves) in (something) with or as if with a plough **5** (sometimes foll. by *through*) to move (through something) in the manner of a plough: *the ship ploughed through the water* **6** (foll. by *through*) to work at slowly or perseveringly **7** to invest (money): *he ploughed the profits back into the business*

8 plough into (of a vehicle, plane, etc.) to run uncontrollably into (something): *the aircraft ploughed into a motorway embankment* **WORD ORIGIN** Old English *plōg* plough land

Plough *n* **the Plough** the group of the seven brightest stars in the constellation Ursa Major

ploughman *or esp. US* **plowman** *n, pl* **-men** a man who ploughs

ploughman's lunch *n* a snack lunch consisting of bread and cheese with pickle

ploughshare *or esp. US* **plowshare** *n* the cutting blade of a plough

plover *n* a shore bird with a round head, straight bill, and long pointed wings **WORD ORIGIN** Old French *plovier* rainbird

plow *n, vb US* same as **plough**

ploy *n* a manoeuvre designed to gain an advantage in a situation: *a cheap political ploy* **WORD ORIGIN** from obsolete noun sense of *employ*, meaning an occupation

pluck *vb* **1** to pull or pick off **2** to pull out the feathers of (a bird for cooking) **3** (foll. by *off* or *away* etc.) *archaic* to pull (something) forcibly or violently (from something or someone) **4** to sound the strings of (a musical instrument) with the fingers or a plectrum **5** *slang* to swindle ▷ *n* **6** courage **7** a pull or tug **8** the heart, liver, and lungs of an animal used for food ▸ See also **pluck up** **WORD ORIGIN** Old English *pluccian*

pluck up *vb* to summon up (courage)

plucky *adj* **pluckier, pluckiest** courageous **pluckily** *adv* **pluckiness** *n*

plug *n* **1** an object used to block up holes or waste pipes **2** a device with one or more pins which connects an appliance to an electricity supply **3** *informal* a favourable mention of a product etc. for example on television, to encourage people to buy it **4** see **spark plug** **5** a piece of tobacco for chewing ▷ *vb* **plugging, plugged 6** to block or seal (a hole or gap) with a plug **7** *informal* to make frequent favourable mentions of (a product etc.), for example on television **8** *slang* to shoot: *he lifted the rifle and plugged the deer* **9** *slang* to punch **10** (foll. by *along* or *away* etc.) *informal* to work steadily ▸ See also **plug in** **WORD ORIGIN** Middle Dutch *plugge*

plug in *vb* to connect (an electrical appliance) to a power source by pushing a plug into a socket

plum *n* **1** an oval dark red or yellow fruit with a stone in the middle, that grows on a small tree **2** a raisin, as used in a cake or pudding **3** *informal* something of a superior or desirable kind ▷ *adj* **4** made from plums: *plum cake* **5** dark reddish-purple **6** very desirable: *plum targets for attack* **WORD ORIGIN** Old English *plūme*

plumage *n* the feathers of a bird **WORD ORIGIN** Old French *plume* feather

plumb *vb* **1** to understand (something obscure): *to plumb a mystery* **2** to test the alignment of or make vertical with a plumb line **3** (foll. by *in* or *into*) to connect (an appliance or fixture) to a water pipe or drainage system: *the shower should be plumbed in professionally* **4 plumb the depths** (usually foll. by *of*) to experience the worst extremes (of something): *to plumb the depths of despair* ▷ *n* **5** a lead weight hanging at the end of a string and used to test the depth of water or to test whether something is vertical **6 out of plumb** not vertical ▷ *adv* **7** vertical or perpendicular **8** *informal chiefly US* utterly: *plumb stupid* **9** *informal* exactly: *plumb in the centre* **WORD ORIGIN** Latin *plumbum* lead

plumber *n* a person who fits and repairs pipes and fixtures for water, drainage, or gas systems **WORD ORIGIN** Old French *plommier* worker in lead

plumbing *n* **1** the pipes and fixtures used in a water, drainage, or gas system **2** the trade or work of a plumber

plumb line *n* a string with a metal weight at one end, used to test the depth of water or to test whether something is vertical

plume *n* **1** a large ornamental feather **2** a group of feathers worn as a badge or ornament on a hat **3** something like a plume: *a plume of smoke* ▷ *vb* **pluming, plumed 4** to adorn with plumes **5** (of a bird) to preen (its feathers) **6 plume oneself** (foll. by *on* or *upon*) to be proud of oneself or one's achievements, esp. unjustifiably: *she was pluming herself on her figure* **WORD ORIGIN** Old French

plummet *vb* **-meting, -meted 1** to drop down; plunge ▷ *n* **2** the weight on a plumb line or fishing line **WORD ORIGIN** Old French *plommet* ball of lead

plummy *adj* **-mier, -miest 1** of, full of, or like plums: *a red wine full of ripe plummy fruit* **2** *Brit informal* (of a voice) deep, rich, and usually upper-class in manner: *his plummy condescending voice* **3** *Brit informal* desirable: *they lived plummy lives in the hills of Tuscany*

plump¹ *adj* **1** full or rounded: *until puberty I was really quite plump* ▷ *vb* **2** (often foll. by *up* or *out*) to make (something) fuller or rounded: *she plumped up the cushions on the couch* **plumpness** *n* **WORD ORIGIN** Middle Dutch *plomp* blunt

plump² *vb* **1** (often foll. by *down* or *into* etc.) to drop or sit suddenly and heavily: *he plumped down on the seat* **2 plump for** to choose one from a selection ▷ *n* **3** a heavy abrupt fall or the sound of this ▷ *adv* **4** suddenly or heavily **5** directly: *the plane landed plump in the middle of the field* **6** in a blunt, direct, or decisive manner **WORD ORIGIN** probably imitative

plum pudding *n* a boiled or steamed pudding made with flour, suet, and dried fruit

plumy *adj* **plumier, plumiest 1** like a feather **2** covered or adorned with feathers

plunder *vb* **1** to seize (valuables or goods) from (a place) by force, usually in wartime; loot ▷ *n* **2** anything plundered; booty **3** the act of plundering; pillage **WORD ORIGIN** probably from Dutch *plunderen*

plunge *vb* **plunging, plunged 1** (usually foll. by *into*) to thrust or throw (something or oneself) forcibly or suddenly: *they plunged into the sea; he plunged the knife in to the hilt* **2** to throw or be thrown into a certain condition: *the room was plunged into darkness* **3** (usually foll. by *into*) to involve or become involved deeply (in) **4** to move swiftly or impetuously **5** to descend very suddenly or steeply: *temperatures were plunging* **6** *informal* to gamble recklessly ▷ *n* **7** a leap or dive **8** *informal* a swim **9** a pitching motion **10 take the plunge** *informal* to make a risky decision which cannot be reversed later **WORD ORIGIN** Old French *plongier*

plunger *n* **1** a rubber suction cup used to clear blocked drains **2** a device with a plunging motion; piston

plunk *vb* **1** to pluck the strings of (an instrument) to produce a twanging sound **2** (often foll. by *down*) to drop or be dropped heavily ▷ *n* **3** the act or sound of plunking **WORD ORIGIN** imitative

Plunket baby *n NZ* a baby brought up according to the principles of the Plunket Society

Plunket nurse *n NZ* a nurse working for the Plunket Society

Plunket Society *n NZ* an organization for the care of mothers and babies

pluperfect *grammar adj* **1** denoting a tense of verbs used to describe an action completed before a past time. In English this is a compound tense formed with *had* plus the past participle ▷ *n* **2** the pluperfect tense **WORD ORIGIN** Latin *plus quam perfectum* more than perfect

plural *adj* **1** of or consisting of more than one **2** *grammar* denoting a word indicating more than one ▷ *n* **3** *grammar* **a** the plural number **b** a plural form **WORD ORIGIN** Latin *plus* more

pluralism *n* **1** the existence and toleration in a society of a variety of groups of different ethnic origins, cultures, or religions **2** the holding of more than one office by a person **pluralist** *n, adj* **pluralistic** *adj*

plurality *n, pl* **-ties 1** the state of being plural **2** *maths* a number greater than one **3** a large number **4** a majority

pluralize *or* **-lise** *vb* **-lizing, -lized** *or* **-lising, -lised** to make or become plural

plus *prep* **1** increased by the addition of: *four plus two* **2** with the addition of: *a good salary, plus a company car* ▷ *adj* **3** indicating addition: *a plus sign* **4** *maths* same as **positive** (sense 7) **5** on the positive part of a scale **6** indicating the positive side of an electrical circuit **7** involving advantage: *a plus factor* **8** *informal* having a value above the value stated: *it must be worth a thousand pounds plus* **9** slightly above a specified standard: *he received a B plus for his essay* ▷ *n* **10** a plus sign (+), indicating addition **11** a positive quantity **12** *informal* something positive or an advantage **13** a gain, surplus, or advantage **WORD ORIGIN** Latin: more

p

Plus, together with, and *along with* do not create compound subjects in the way that *and* does: the number of the verb depends on that of the subject to which *plus, together with,* or *along with* is added: *this task, plus all the others, was* (not *were*) *undertaken by the government; the doctor, together with the nurses, was* (not *were*) *waiting for the patient.*

plus fours *pl n* men's baggy knickerbockers gathered in at the knee, now only worn for hunting or golf **WORD ORIGIN** because made with four inches of material to hang over at the knee

plush *n* **1** a velvety fabric with a long soft pile, used for furniture coverings ▷ *adj* **2** Also: **plushy** *informal* luxurious **WORD ORIGIN** French *pluche*

plus-one *n informal* someone who accompanies an invited person to a social function

Pluto *n* **1** *classical myth* the god of the underworld **2** the smallest planet and the one farthest from the sun

plutocracy *n, pl* **-cies 1** government by the wealthy **2** a state ruled by the wealthy **3** a group that exercises power on account of its wealth **plutocratic** *adj* **WORD ORIGIN** Greek *ploutos* wealth + *-kratia* rule

plutocrat *n* a person who is powerful because of being very rich

plutonic *adj* (of igneous rocks) formed from molten rock that has cooled and solidified below the earth's surface **WORD ORIGIN** after the Greek god *Pluto*

plutonium *n chem* a toxic radioactive metallic element, used in nuclear reactors and weapons. Symbol: Pu **WORD ORIGIN** after *Pluto*, because Pluto lies beyond Neptune and plutonium was discovered soon after neptunium

pluvial *adj geog, geol* of or due to the action of rain **WORD ORIGIN** Latin *pluvia* rain

ply¹ *vb* **plies, plying, plied 1** to work at (a job or trade) **2** to use (a tool) **3** (usually foll. by *with*) to provide (with) or subject (to) persistently: *he plied us with drink; he plied me with questions* **4** to work steadily **5** (of a ship) to travel regularly along (a route): *to ply the trade routes* **WORD ORIGIN** Middle English *plye*, short for *aplye* to apply

ply² *n, pl* **plies 1** a layer or thickness, such as of fabric or wood **2** one of the strands twisted together to make rope or yarn **WORD ORIGIN** Old French *pli* fold

Plymouth Brethren *pl n* a Puritanical religious sect with no organized ministry

plywood *n* a board made of thin layers of wood glued together under pressure, with the grain of one layer at right angles to the grain of the next

Pm *chem* promethium

PM 1 Prime Minister **2** Postmaster **3** Paymaster

p.m. 1 after noon **WORD ORIGIN** Latin *post meridiem* **2** postmortem (examination)

PMG 1 Postmaster General **2** Paymaster General

PMS premenstrual syndrome

PMT premenstrual tension

pneumatic *adj* **1** operated by compressed air: *pneumatic drill* **2** containing compressed air: *a pneumatic tyre* **3** of or concerned with air, gases, or wind **WORD ORIGIN** Greek *pneuma* breath, wind

pneumatics *n* the branch of physics concerned with the mechanical properties of air and other gases

pneumonia *n* inflammation of one or both lungs **WORD ORIGIN** Greek *pneumōn* lung

po *n, pl* **pos** *Brit, old-fashioned informal* a chamber pot **WORD ORIGIN** from POT¹

Po *chem* polonium

PO 1 Also: **p.o.** *Brit* postal order **2** Post Office **3** petty officer **4** Pilot Officer

poach¹ *vb* **1** to catch (game or fish) illegally on someone else's land **2 a** to encroach on (someone's rights or duties) **b** to steal (an idea, employee, or player) **poacher** *n* **WORD ORIGIN** Old French *pocher*

poach² *vb* to simmer (food) very gently in liquid **WORD ORIGIN** Old French *pochier* to enclose in a bag

pock *n* **1** a pus-filled blister resulting from smallpox **2** a pockmark **WORD ORIGIN** Old English *pocc*

pocket *n* **1** a small pouch sewn into clothing for carrying small articles **2** any pouchlike container, esp. for catching balls at the edge of a snooker table **3** a small isolated area or group: *a pocket of resistance* **4** a cavity in the earth, such as one containing ore **5 in one's pocket** under one's control **6 out of pocket** having made a loss ▷ *vb* **-eting, -eted 7** to put into one's pocket **8** to take secretly or dishonestly **9** *billiards, etc.* to drive (a ball) into a pocket **10** to conceal or suppress: *he pocketed his pride and asked for help* ▷ *adj* **11** small: *a pocket edition* **WORD ORIGIN** Anglo-Norman *poket* a little bag

pocketbook *n chiefly US* a small case for money and papers

pocket borough *n* (before the Reform Act of 1832) an English borough constituency controlled by one person or family

pocketful *n, pl* **-fuls** as much as a pocket will hold

pocketknife *n, pl* **-knives** a small knife with one or more blades that fold into the handle; penknife

pocket money *n* **1** a small weekly sum of money given to children by parents **2** money for small personal expenses

pockmarked *adj* **1** (of the skin) marked with pitted scars after the healing of smallpox **2** (of a surface) covered in many small hollows: *the building is pockmarked with bullet holes* **pockmark** *n*

pod *n* **1 a** a long narrow seedcase containing peas, beans, etc. **b** the seedcase as distinct from the seeds ▷ *vb* **podding, podded 2** to remove the pod from **WORD ORIGIN** origin unknown

podcast *n* **1** an audio file similar to a radio broadcast, which can be downloaded and listened to on a computer, iPod™, etc. ▷ *vb* **-casts, -casting, -cast** or **-casted 2** to create such files and make them available for downloading **3** to make (music, interviews, etc.) available using this format **podcaster** *n* **podcasting** *n*

podgy *adj* **podgier, podgiest** short and fat **podginess** *n* **WORD ORIGIN** from *podge* a short plump person

podiatry (pod-**eye**-a-tree) *n* another word for **chiropody** ▷ **podiatrist** *n*

podium *n, pl* **-diums** or **-dia 1** a small raised platform used by conductors or speakers **2** a plinth that supports a colonnade or wall **WORD ORIGIN** Latin: platform

poem *n* **1** a literary work, often in verse, usually dealing with emotional or descriptive themes in a rhythmic form **2** a literary work that is not in verse but deals with emotional or descriptive themes in a rhythmic form: *a prose poem* **3** anything like a poem in beauty or effect: *his painting is a poem on creation* **WORD ORIGIN** Greek *poiēma* something created

poep (**poop**) *n S African, taboo* **1** an emission of intestinal gas from the anus **2** a mean or despicable person **WORD ORIGIN** Afrikaans

poesy *n archaic* poetry

poet *n* **1** a writer of poetry **2** a person with great imagination and creativity **WORD ORIGIN** Greek *poiētēs* maker, poet

poetaster *n* a writer of inferior verse

poetic or **poetical** *adj* **1** like poetry, by being expressive or imaginative **2** of poetry or poets **3** recounted in verse

poetic justice *n* an appropriate punishment or reward for previous actions

poetic licence *n* freedom from the normal rules of language or truth, as in poetry

poet laureate *n, pl* **poets laureate** *Brit* the poet selected by the British sovereign to write poems on important occasions

poetry *n* **1** poems in general **2** the art or craft of writing poems **3** a poetic quality that prompts an emotional response: *her acting was full of poetry* **WORD ORIGIN** Latin *poeta* poet

po-faced *adj* wearing a disapproving stern expression **WORD ORIGIN** perhaps from PO + POKER-FACED

pogey or **pogy** (**pohg**-ee) *n, pl* **pogeys** or **pogies** *Canad slang* **1** financial or other relief given to the unemployed by the government; dole **2** unemployment insurance **WORD ORIGIN** from earlier *pogie* workhouse

pogo stick *n* a pole with steps for the feet and a spring at the bottom, so that the user can bounce up, down, and along on it **WORD ORIGIN** origin unknown

pogrom *n* an organized persecution and massacre **WORD ORIGIN** Russian: destruction

The NATO Alphabet

When Andy McNab chose *Bravo Two Zero* as the title of his 1993 book about an SAS patrol in Iraq, he was relying on the word *Bravo* to conjure up the sense of danger that attaches to a military expedition. *Bravo* owes this connotation in part to its inclusion in what is known as 'the NATO alphabet'.

The NATO alphabet was developed for the accurate transmission of messages in radio and telephone communication. Because many of the letters in the English alphabet have similar sounds (think of how easy it is to mishear 'b' as 'p' or 'n' as 'm'), it helps to ensure that a message is received correctly if words are used to represent each letter of the message. Each of the words used in the NATO alphabet is a common word and begins with the letter it represents. The idea is that a person hearing the word cannot then be mistaken about the letter for which it stands. The words used are as follows:

A	Alpha
B	Bravo
C	Charlie
D	Delta
E	Echo
F	Foxtrot
G	Golf
H	Hotel
I	India
J	Juliet
K	Kilo
L	Lima
M	Mike
N	November
O	Oscar
P	Papa
Q	Quebec
R	Romeo
S	Sierra
T	Tango
U	Uniform
V	Victor
W	Whisky
X	X-ray
Y	Yankee
Z	Zulu

The name 'NATO' may suggest that the alphabet was specifically designed for military communications, but in fact NATO only embraced and gave its name to a system proposed for civilian use by the International Air Transport Association (IATA) in the 1950s. This was an attempt to impose a single system in place of several different alphabets that had been used during World War II, including one which had *Apple, Beer,* and *Charlie* as the first three letters and another which used *Able, Baker,* and *Charlie.*

A standard international version was finally adopted by IATA in 1951. After a few teething troubles, which saw *Coca, Metro, Nectar, Union,* and *eXtra* (the latter representing the letter 'x') discarded, the alphabet achieved its current form in 1956.

The hallmark of the system is that the words must all be clearly distinguishable from each other. Moreover, all of the words should be easy to pronounce and recognize for all users of the system – not just those who have English as their first language.

The alphabet has also been extended to accommodate letters that are not used in English words. *Ñoño* is used to represent the letter 'ñ', which occurs in certain Spanish words, while *Ärger, Ökonom,* and *Übermut* are used to represent the various letters written with umlauts that occur in German.

As the words used in the basic alphabet were widely used in both military and civilian communication, some of them became culturally significant in the second half of the 20th century. During the Vietnam War, American and Australian forces referred to the Viet Cong as 'Victor Charlie', which gave rise to the use of 'Charlie' as a shorthand for the enemy. Meanwhile Checkpoint 'C' on the border between East and West Berlin became known as 'Checkpoint Charlie', a place and name which became symbolic of the Cold-War tension between NATO and the Warsaw Pact. On a more mundane level, *Juliet Bravo* was the title of a British television drama series of the 1980s which portrayed the plight of a female police inspector whose struggles to foil the criminal fraternity were matched by her struggles to establish herself as a woman in a traditionally male profession.

poi *n* NZ a ball of woven flax swung rhythmically by Māori women during poi dances
WORD ORIGIN Māori

poi dance *n* NZ a women's formation dance that involves singing and twirling a poi

poignant *adj* 1 sharply painful to the feelings: *a poignant reminder* 2 cutting: *poignant wit* 3 pertinent in mental appeal: *a poignant subject* **poignancy** *n*
WORD ORIGIN Latin *pungens* pricking

poinsettia *n* a shrub of Mexico and Central America, widely grown for its showy scarlet bracts, which resemble petals
WORD ORIGIN after J. P. Poinsett, US Minister to Mexico

point *n* 1 the essential idea in an argument or discussion: *I agreed with the point he made* 2 a reason or aim: *what is the point of this exercise?* 3 a detail or item 4 a characteristic: *he has his good points* 5 a location or position 6 a dot or tiny mark 7 a dot used as a decimal point or a full stop 8 the sharp tip of anything: *the point of the spear* 9 a headland: *the soaring cliffs at Dwerja Point in the southwest of the island* 10 *maths* a geometric element having a position located by coordinates, but no magnitude 11 a specific condition or degree: *freezing point* 12 a moment: *at that point he left* 13 (*often pl*) any of the extremities, such as the tail, ears, or feet, of a domestic animal 14 (*often pl*) *ballet* the tip of the toes 15 a single unit for measuring something such as value, or of scoring in a game 16 *printing* a unit of measurement equal to one twelfth of a pica 17 *navigation* one of the 32 direction marks on the compass 18 *cricket* a fielding position at right angles to the batsman on the off side 19 either of the two electrical contacts that make or break the circuit in the distributor of a motor vehicle 20 *Brit, Austral, & NZ* (*often pl*) a movable section of railway track used to direct a train from one line to another 21 *Brit* short for **power point** 22 *boxing* a mark awarded for a scoring blow or knockdown 23 **beside the point** irrelevant 24 **make a point of a** to make a habit of (something) **b** to do (something) because one thinks it important 25 **on** *or* **at the point of** about to; on the verge of: *on the point of leaving* 26 **to the point** relevant 27 **up to a point** not completely ▷ *vb* 28 (usually foll. by *at* or *to*) to show the position or direction of something by extending a finger or other pointed object towards it 29 (usually foll. by *at* or *to*) to single out one person or thing from among several: *all the symptoms pointed to epilepsy* 30 to direct or face in a specific direction: *point me in the right direction* 31 to finish or repair the joints in brickwork with mortar or cement 32 (of gun dogs) to show where game is lying by standing rigidly with the muzzle turned towards it ▷ See also **point out**
WORD ORIGIN Latin *pungere* to pierce

point-blank *adj* 1 fired at a very close target 2 plain or blunt: *a point-blank refusal to discuss the matter* ▷ *adv* 3 directly or bluntly: *the Minister was asked point-blank if he intended to resign*
WORD ORIGIN point + blank (centre spot of an archery target)

point duty *n* the control of traffic by a policeman at a road junction

pointed *adj* 1 having a sharp tip 2 cutting or incisive: *pointed wit* 3 obviously directed at a particular person: *a pointed remark* 4 emphasized or obvious: *pointed ignorance* **pointedly** *adv*

pointer *n* 1 something that is a helpful indicator of how a situation has arisen or may turn out: *a significant pointer to the likely resumption of talks* 2 an indicator on a measuring instrument 3 a long stick used by teachers, to point out particular features on a map, chart, etc. 4 a large smooth-coated gun dog

pointillism (**pwan**-till-iz-zum) *n* a technique used by some impressionist painters, in which dots of colour are placed side by side so that they merge when seen from a distance **pointillist** *n, adj*
WORD ORIGIN French

pointing *n* the insertion of mortar between the joints in brickwork

pointless *adj* without meaning or purpose

point of no return *n* a point at which one is committed to continuing with an action

point of order *n, pl* **points of order** an objection in a meeting to the departure from the proper procedure

point of view *n, pl* **points of view** 1 a mental viewpoint or attitude: *she refuses to see the other person's point of view* 2 a way of considering something: *a scientific point of view*

point out *vb* to draw someone's attention to

point-to-point *n Brit* a steeplechase organized by a hunt

poise *n* 1 dignified manner 2 physical balance: *the poise of a natural model* 3 mental balance: *he recovered his poise* ▷ *vb* **poising, poised** 4 to be balanced or suspended 5 to be held in readiness: *the cats were poised to spring on her*
WORD ORIGIN Old French *pois* weight

poised *adj* 1 absolutely ready 2 behaving with or showing poise

poison *n* 1 a substance that causes death or injury when swallowed or absorbed 2 something that destroys or corrupts: *the poison of Nazism* ▷ *vb* 3 to give poison to someone 4 to add poison to something 5 to have a harmful or evil effect on 6 (foll. by *against*) to turn (a person's mind) against: *he poisoned her mind against me* **poisoner** *n*
WORD ORIGIN Latin *potio* a drink, esp. a poisonous one

poison ivy *n* a North American climbing plant that causes an itching rash if it touches the skin

poisonous *adj* 1 of or like a poison 2 malicious

poison-pen letter *n* a malicious anonymous letter

poke¹ *vb* **poking, poked** 1 to jab or prod with an elbow, finger, etc. 2 to make a hole by poking 3 (sometimes foll. by *at*) to thrust (at): *she poked at the food with her fork* 4 (usually foll. by *in* or *through* etc.) to thrust forward or out: *yellow hair poked from beneath his cap* 5 to stir (a fire) by poking 6 (often foll. by *about* or *around*) to search or pry 7 **poke one's nose into** to meddle in ▷ *n* 8 a jab or prod
WORD ORIGIN Low German & Middle Dutch *poken*

poke² *n* 1 *dialect* a pocket or bag 2 **a pig in a poke** see **pig**
WORD ORIGIN Old French *poque*

poker¹ *n* a metal rod with a handle for stirring a fire

poker² *n* a card game of bluff and skill in which players bet on the hands dealt
WORD ORIGIN origin unknown

poker face *n informal* an expressionless face, such as that of a poker player trying to hide the value of his or her cards **poker-faced** *adj*

pokerwork *n* the art of producing pictures or designs on wood by burning it with a heated metal point

poky *adj* **pokier, pokiest** (of a room) small and cramped **pokiness** *n*

pol. 1 political 2 politics

polar *adj* 1 of or near either of the earth's poles or the area inside the Arctic or Antarctic Circles 2 of or having a pole or polarity 3 directly opposite in tendency or nature: *polar opposites*

polar bear *n* a white bear of coastal regions of the North Pole

polar circle *n* the Arctic or Antarctic Circle

polarity *n, pl* **-ties** 1 the state of having two directly opposite tendencies or opinions 2 the condition of a body which has opposing physical properties, usually magnetic poles or electric charge 3 the particular state of a part with polarity: *an electrode with positive polarity*

polarization *or* **-risation** *n* 1 the condition of having or giving polarity 2 *physics* the condition in which waves of light or other radiation are restricted to certain directions of vibration

polarize *or* **-rise** *vb* **-rizing, -rized** *or* **-rising, -rised** 1 to cause people to adopt directly opposite opinions: *political opinion had polarized since the restoration of democracy* 2 to have or give polarity or polarization

Polaroid *n trademark* 1 a type of plastic that polarizes light: used in sunglasses to eliminate glare 2 **Polaroid camera** a camera that produces a finished print by developing and processing it inside the camera within a few seconds 3 **Polaroids** sunglasses with Polaroid plastic lenses

polder *n* a stretch of land reclaimed from the sea
WORD ORIGIN Middle Dutch *polre*

pole¹ *n* 1 a long slender rounded piece of wood, metal, or other material 2 **up the pole** *Brit, Austral, & NZ informal* **a** slightly mad **b** in a predicament
WORD ORIGIN Latin *palus* a stake

pole² *n* 1 either end of the earth's axis of rotation. See also **North Pole, South Pole** 2 *physics* **a** either of the opposite forces of a magnet **b** either of two points at which there are opposite electric charges **3** either of two directly opposite tendencies or opinions **4 poles apart** having widely divergent opinions or tastes **WORD ORIGIN** Greek *polos* pivot

Pole *n* a person from Poland

poleaxe *or US* **poleax** *vb* **-axing, -axed 1** to hit or stun with a heavy blow ▷ *n* **2** an axe formerly used in battle or used by a butcher **WORD ORIGIN** Middle English *pollax* battle-axe

polecat *n, pl* **-cats** *or* **-cat 1** a dark brown mammal like a weasel that gives off a foul smell **2** *US* a skunk **WORD ORIGIN** origin unknown

pole dancing *n* a form of entertainment in which a scantily dressed woman dances erotically, turning on and posing against a vertically fixed pole on stage **pole dancer** *n*

polemic (pol-em-ik) *n* **1** a fierce attack on or defence of a particular opinion, belief, etc.: *anti-capitalist polemic* ▷ *adj also* **polemical 2** of or involving dispute or controversy **polemicist** *n* **WORD ORIGIN** Greek *polemos* war

polemics *n* the art of dispute

pole position *n* **1** (in motor racing) the starting position on the inside of the front row, generally considered the best one **2** an advantageous starting position

pole star *n* a guiding principle or rule

Pole Star *n* **the Pole Star** the star closest to the northern celestial pole

pole vault *n* **1 the pole vault** a field event in which competitors try to clear a high bar with the aid of a very flexible long pole ▷ *vb* **pole-vault 2** to perform or compete in the pole vault **pole-vaulter** *n*

police *n* **1** (often preceded by *the*) the organized civil force in a state which keeps law and order **2** the men and women who are members of such a force **3** an organized body with a similar function: *security police* ▷ *vb* **-licing, -liced 4** to maintain order or control by means of a police force or similar body **WORD ORIGIN** French, from Latin *politia* administration

police dog *n* a dog trained to help the police

policeman *or fem* **policewoman** *n, pl* **-men** *or fem* **-women** a member of a police force

police procedural *n* a novel, film, or television drama that deals with police work

police state *n* a state in which a government controls people's freedom through the police

police station *n* the office of the police force of a district

policy¹ *n, pl* **-cies 1** a plan of action adopted by a person, group, or government **2** *archaic* wisdom or prudence **WORD ORIGIN** Old French *policie*, from Latin *politia* administration

policy² *n, pl* **-cies** a document containing an insurance contract **policyholder** *n*

WORD ORIGIN Old French *police* certificate

polio *n* short for **poliomyelitis**

poliomyelitis (pole-ee-oh-my-el-**lite**-iss) *n* a viral disease which affects the brain and spinal cord, often causing paralysis **WORD ORIGIN** Greek *polios* grey + *muelos* marrow

polish *vb* **1** to make smooth and shiny by rubbing **2** to perfect or complete: *media experts he had hired to polish his image* **3** to make or become elegant or refined: *not having polished his south London accent didn't help his career* ▷ *n* **4** a substance used for polishing **5** a shine or gloss **6** elegance or refinement. See also **polish off, polish up** **WORD ORIGIN** Latin *polire* to polish

Polish *adj* **1** of Poland ▷ *n* **2** the language of Poland

polished *adj* **1** accomplished: *a polished actor* **2** done or performed well or professionally: *a polished performance*

polish off *vb informal* **1** to finish completely **2** to dispose of or kill

polish up *vb* **1** to make smooth and shiny by polishing **2** to improve (a skill or ability) by working at it: *I'm going to evening classes to polish up my German*

Politburo *n* formerly, the chief decision-making committee of a Communist country **WORD ORIGIN** Russian

polite *adj* **1** having good manners; courteous **2** cultivated or refined: *polite society* **3** socially correct but insincere: *he smiled a polite response and stifled an urge to scream* **politely** *adv* **politeness** *n* **WORD ORIGIN** Latin *politus* polished

politic *adj* **1** wise or possibly advantageous: *I didn't feel it was politic to mention it* **2** artful or shrewd: *a politic manager* **3** crafty; cunning: *a politic old scoundrel* **4** *archaic* political. See also **body politic** **WORD ORIGIN** Old French *politique*, from Greek *polis* city

political *adj* **1** of the state, government, or public administration **2** relating to or interested in politics: *she was always a very political person* **3** of the parties and the partisan aspects of politics: *the government blames political opponents for fanning the unrest* **politically** *adv*

politically correct *adj* displaying progressive attitudes, esp. in using vocabulary which is intended to avoid any implied prejudice

political prisoner *n* a person imprisoned for holding particular political beliefs

political science *n* the study of the state, government, and politics **political scientist** *n*

politician *n* a person actively engaged in politics, esp. a member of parliament

politicize *or* **-cise** *vb* **-cizing, -cized** *or* **-cising, -cised 1** to make political or politically aware **2** to take part in political discussion or activity **politicization** *or* **-cisation** *n*

politics *n* **1** (*functioning as sing*) the art and science of government **2** (*functioning as pl*) political opinions or sympathies: *his conservative politics* **3** (*functioning as pl*)

political activities or affairs: *party politics* **4** (*functioning as sing*) the business or profession of politics **5** (*functioning as sing or pl*) any activity concerned with the acquisition of power: *company politics are often vicious*

polity *n, pl* **-ties** *formal* **1** a politically organized state, church, or society **2** a form of government of a state, church, or society **WORD ORIGIN** Greek *politeia* citizenship, from *polis* city

polka *n* **1** a lively 19th-century dance **2** music for this dance ▷ *vb* **-kaing, -kaed 3** to dance a polka **WORD ORIGIN** Czech *pulka* half-step

polka dots *pl n* a regular pattern of small bold spots on a fabric

poll *n* **1** Also called: **opinion poll** the questioning of a random sample of people to find out the general opinion **2** the casting, recording, or counting of votes in an election **3** the result of such a voting: *a marginal poll* **4** the head ▷ *vb* **5** to receive (a certain number of votes) **6** to record the votes of: *he polled the whole town* **7** to question (a person, etc.) as part of an opinion poll **8** to vote in an election **9** to clip or shear **10** to remove or cut short the horns of (cattle) **WORD ORIGIN** Middle Low German *polle* hair, head, top of a tree

pollack *or* **pollock** *n, pl* **-lacks, -lack** *or* **-locks, -lock** a food fish related to the cod, found in northern seas **WORD ORIGIN** origin unknown

pollard *n* **1** an animal that has shed its horns or has had them removed **2** a tree with its top cut off to encourage a more bushy growth ▷ *vb* **3** to cut off the top of (a tree) to make it grow bushy **pollarded** *adj* **WORD ORIGIN** see POLL

pollen *n* a fine powder produced by flowers to fertilize other flowers of the same species **WORD ORIGIN** Latin: powder

pollen count *n* a measure of the amount of pollen in the air over a 24-hour period, often published as a warning to hay fever sufferers

pollinate *vb* **-nating, -nated** to fertilize by the transfer of pollen **pollination** *n*

polling booth *n* a compartment in which a voter can mark his or her ballot paper in private during an election

polling station *n* a building where voters go during an election to cast their votes

pollock *n* same as **pollack**

pollster *n* a person who conducts opinion polls

poll tax *n* any tax levied per head of adult population, esp. the tax which replaced domestic rates (in Scotland from 1989 and England and Wales from 1990, until 1993)

pollutant *n* a substance that pollutes, usually the chemical waste of an industrial process

pollute *vb* **-luting, -luted 1** to contaminate with poisonous or harmful substances **2** to corrupt morally **pollution** *n* **WORD ORIGIN** Latin *polluere* to defile

P

polo n **1** a game like hockey played on horseback with long-handled mallets and a wooden ball **2** short for **water polo**
WORD ORIGIN Tibetan *pulu* ball

polonaise n **1** a stately Polish dance **2** music for this dance
WORD ORIGIN French *danse polonaise* Polish dance

polo neck n a sweater with a high tight turned-over collar

polonium n *chem* a rare radioactive element found in trace amounts in uranium ores. Symbol: Po
WORD ORIGIN Medieval Latin *Polonia* Poland; in honour of the nationality of its discoverer, Marie Curie

polo shirt n a cotton short-sleeved shirt with a collar and three-button opening at the neck

poltergeist n a spirit believed to be responsible for noises and acts of mischief, such as throwing objects about
WORD ORIGIN German *poltern* to be noisy + *Geist* ghost

poltroon n *obsolete* a complete coward
WORD ORIGIN Old Italian *poltrone* lazy good-for-nothing

poly n, pl **polys** *informal* short for **polytechnic**

poly- *combining form* many or much: *polyhedron; polysyllabic*
WORD ORIGIN Greek *polus*

polyandry n the practice of having more than one husband at the same time **polyandrous** adj
WORD ORIGIN Greek *polus* many + *anēr* man

polyanthus n, pl **-thuses** a hybrid garden primrose with brightly coloured flowers
WORD ORIGIN Greek: having many flowers

polychromatic adj **1** having many colours **2** (of radiation) containing more than one wavelength

polycystic ovary syndrome n a hormonal disorder preventing ovulation, leading to reduced fertility, hirsutism, and weight gain. Abbreviation: **PCOS**

polyester n a synthetic material used to make plastics and textile fibres

polyethylene n same as **polythene**

polygamy (pol-**ig**-a-mee) n the practice of having more than one wife or husband at the same time **polygamist** n **polygamous** adj
WORD ORIGIN Greek *polus* many + *gamos* marriage

polyglot adj **1** able to speak many languages **2** written in or using many languages ▷ n **3** a person who can speak many languages
WORD ORIGIN Greek *poluglōttos* many-tongued

polygon n a geometrical figure with three or more sides and angles **polygonal** adj
WORD ORIGIN Greek *polugōnon* figure with many angles

polygraph n an instrument for recording pulse rate and perspiration, often used as a lie detector

WORD ORIGIN Greek *polugraphos* writing copiously

polygyny n the practice of having more than one wife at the same time **polygynous** adj
WORD ORIGIN Greek *polus* many + *gunē* woman

polyhedron n, pl **-drons** or **-dra** a solid figure with four or more sides **polyhedral** adj
WORD ORIGIN Greek *polus* many + *hedron* side

Polyhymnia n *Greek myth* the muse of singing, mime, and sacred dance

polymath n a person of great and varied learning
WORD ORIGIN Greek *polumathēs* having much knowledge

polymer n a natural or synthetic compound with large molecules made up of simple molecules of the same kind

polymeric adj of or being a polymer: *polymeric materials such as PVC*
WORD ORIGIN Greek *polumerēs* having many parts

polymerization or **-isation** n the process of forming a polymer **polymerize** or **-ise** vb

polymorphous or **polymorphic** adj having, or passing through many different forms or stages
WORD ORIGIN Greek *polus* many + *morphē* form

Polynesian adj **1** of Polynesia ▷ n **2** a person from Polynesia **3** any of the languages of Polynesia

polynomial *maths* adj **1** consisting of two or more terms ▷ n **2** an algebraic expression consisting of the sum of a number of terms

polyp n **1** *zool* a small sea creature that has a hollow cylindrical body with a ring of tentacles around the mouth **2** *pathol* a small growth on the surface of a mucous membrane
WORD ORIGIN Greek *polupous* having many feet

polyphonic adj *music* consisting of several melodies played together

polyphony (pol-**if**-on-ee) n, pl **-nies** polyphonic style of composition or a piece of music using it
WORD ORIGIN Greek *poluphōnia* diversity of tones

polysaccharide n a carbohydrate which consists of a number of linked sugar molecules, such as starch or cellulose

polystyrene n a synthetic material used esp. as white rigid foam for insulating and packing

polysyllable n a word having more than two syllables **polysyllabic** adj

polytechnic n **1** *Brit* (in New Zealand and formerly in Britain) college offering courses in many subjects at and below degree level ▷ adj **2** of or relating to technical instruction
WORD ORIGIN Greek *polutekhnos* skilled in many arts

polytheism n belief in more than one god **polytheistic** adj **polytheist** n

polythene n a light plastic material made from ethylene, usually made into thin sheets or bags

polyunsaturated adj of a group of fats that are less likely to contribute to the build-up of cholesterol in the body

polyurethane n a synthetic material used esp. in paints

polyvinyl chloride n see **PVC**

pom n *Austral & NZ slang* person from England. See also: **pommy**

pomace (**pumm**-iss) n apple pulp left after pressing for juice
WORD ORIGIN Latin *pomum* apple

pomade n a perfumed oil put on the hair to make it smooth and shiny, esp. formerly
WORD ORIGIN French *pommade*

pomander n **1** a mixture of sweet-smelling substances in a container, used to perfume drawers or cupboards **2** a container for such a mixture
WORD ORIGIN Medieval Latin *pomum ambrae* apple of amber

pomegranate n a round tropical fruit with a tough reddish rind containing many seeds in a juicy red pulp
WORD ORIGIN Latin *pomum* apple + *granatus* full of seeds

pomelo (**pom**-ill-oh) n, pl **-los** the edible yellow fruit, like a grapefruit, of a tropical tree
WORD ORIGIN Dutch *pompelmoes*

Pomeranian n a toy dog with a long straight silky coat
WORD ORIGIN after *Pomerania*, region of N central Europe

pomfret (**pum**-frit) or **pomfret-cake** n a small black rounded liquorice sweet
WORD ORIGIN from *Pomfret*, earlier form of *Pontefract*, Yorks., where originally made

pommel n **1** the raised part on the front of a saddle **2** a knob at the top of a sword handle ▷ vb **-melling, -melled** or US **-meling, -meled** **3** same as **pummel**
WORD ORIGIN Old French *pomel* knob

pommy n, pl **-mies** (*sometimes cap*) *slang* a word used by Australians and New Zealanders for a British person. Sometimes shortened to: **pom**
WORD ORIGIN origin unknown

pomp n **1** stately display or ceremony **2** ostentatious display
WORD ORIGIN Greek *pompē* procession

pompom n **1** a decorative ball of tufted silk or wool **2** the small round flower head of some dahlias and chrysanthemums
WORD ORIGIN French

pom-pom n an automatic rapid-firing gun
WORD ORIGIN imitative

pompous adj **1** foolishly dignified or self-important **2** foolishly grand in style: *a pompous speech* **pomposity** n **pompously** adv

ponce *offensive slang chiefly Brit* n **1** an effeminate man **2** same as **pimp** ▷ vb **poncing, ponced 3** (often foll. by *around* or *about*) *Austral & Brit* to act stupidly or waste time
WORD ORIGIN from *Polari*, an English slang derived from the lingua franca of the Mediterranean ports

poncho n, pl **-chos** a type of cloak made of a piece of cloth with a hole in the middle for the head
WORD ORIGIN American Spanish

Southern American English

Speaking English with a 'Southern accent' is a time-honoured distinction in the United States, and one that is immediately recognized, owing to the many prominent Southerners whose voices have left a mark on history or popular culture – Presidents Lyndon B Johnson, Jimmy Carter, and Bill Clinton, for example, or Dolly Parton, Loretta Lynn, and Tommy Lee Jones. 'Southern accent' can be a misleading generalization, however, because in fact Southern American English is a group of dialects. A German or an untravelled Minnesotan may not distinguish between the speech of a Georgian and a Texan, but a Georgian and a Texan, after an exchange of a few words, will probably recognize that they are from opposite ends of the South.

Despite the dialectal differences, English in the Southern United States (or *Dixie*, as the area is often affectionately called by its natives) has many common features that make it easy for most listeners to pick out. Perhaps most prominent are the features that contribute to the 'Southern Drawl'. It's not only a tendency to speak more slowly than their northern counterparts: there's solid phonetic evidence that Southerners diphthongize simple vowels – or in other words, convert single vowel sounds into two-part vowels, in which they gently slide from one sound to the other. This might be heard in pronunciations such as *piyit* for *pit* and *dyens* for *dance*. On the other hand, the usual diphthong in words like *nice* and *rice* may be shortened so that the words come out more like *nas* and *ras*.

Those wishing to parody or imitate a general Southern accent usually start with the features that mark the drawl. Another feature common to dialects across the South that imitators easily grasp is to leave the *g* sound off the end of participles and gerunds ending in *-ing* ('How ya doin'?'). While you're at it, you can nearly always drop the verb *be* in the second and third person when its only job is to link the subject to the predicate (which is why it's 'How ya doin'?', not 'How are you doin'?'). And, if you're addressing your greeting to more than one person (or for some speakers, even if you're not), the standard form for plural *you* is *y'all* – another hallmark of Southern speech. So: 'How y'all doin'?'

Southerners have a couple of twists on common verb modalities that set their dialects apart from all others. One is the colloquial use of the participle *done* to form a makeshift perfect tense that standard English speakers would form with *have*: 'She done left him again' for 'She has left him again.' Another is the use of *fixin' to* in place of *about to* for incipient or planned actions: 'She's fixin' to leave him again.'

Many Southern dialects have other features that readily set them apart from dialects elsewhere in the United States, while at the same time giving clues to the origins of Southern English across the sea. One is the circumfix *a-...-in'* around a verb, to produce a sentence along the lines of 'It was a-rainin' all week' as opposed to 'It rained all week.' While this construction has a Southern ring today, consider the lines of the 17th-century English poet Robert Herrick: 'Gather ye rosebuds while ye may,/Old time is still a-flying.' Another charming feature of Southern English with transatlantic precedent is the persistence of *yonder* as a determiner. This use is frequent in both Shakespeare and the King James Bible, but seldom found in modern English dialects outside of the South, where you can still 'have a picnic under yonder tree'.

A southerner is likely to answer a yes/no question with a tag rather than the words 'yes' or 'no'. Thus, in response to 'Does Miss Smith live here?' you may get back 'She does.' There is speculation that this speech habit has its roots in Gaelic languages that have no words for 'yes' and 'no'; the heavy influx of Scots and Irish into the South from the 17th century onwards is cited in support of this.

Perhaps the richest contribution of Southern English to the mainstream is its rich vocabulary of colourful phrases that seem to carry with them a reminder of gentler, pastoral days gone by: 'Hold your horses!' a peremptory but not unkind way of saying 'be patient'; 'go hog wild' for 'become extremely enthusiastic'; and 'play possum' for 'pretend to be sleeping'. A grateful Southerner is likely to say that he or she is 'much obliged' in place of saying 'thank you' – confirming the place that the rich web of social reciprocation, always a feature of life in the South, is still alive today.

pond n a pool of still water
WORD ORIGIN Middle English *ponde* enclosure

ponder vb (sometimes foll. by *on* or *over*) to consider thoroughly or deeply
ponderable adj
WORD ORIGIN Latin *ponderare* to weigh, consider

ponderous adj **1** serious and dull: *much of the film is ponderous and pretentious* **2** heavy or huge **3** (of movement) slow and clumsy
WORD ORIGIN Latin *ponderosus* of great weight

pondok or **pondokkie** n (in southern Africa) a crudely made house or shack
WORD ORIGIN Malay *pondók* leaf house

pondweed n a plant which grows in ponds and slow streams

pong Austral & Brit informal n **1** a strong unpleasant smell ▷ vb **2** to give off a strong unpleasant smell **pongy** adj
WORD ORIGIN origin unknown

ponga (**pong**-a) n a tall New Zealand tree fern with large leathery leaves
WORD ORIGIN Māori

poniard (**pon**-yerd) n a small slender dagger
WORD ORIGIN Old French *poignard*

pontiff n the Pope
WORD ORIGIN Latin *pontifex* high priest

pontifical adj **1** of a pontiff **2** pompous or dogmatic in manner

pontificate vb -cating, -cated **1** to speak in a dogmatic manner **2** to officiate as a pontiff ▷ n **3** the term of office of a Pope

pontoon[1] n a floating platform used to support a bridge
WORD ORIGIN Latin *ponto* punt

pontoon[2] n a card game in which players try to obtain sets of cards worth 21 points
WORD ORIGIN probably an alteration of French *vingt-et-un* twenty-one

pony n, pl -nies a breed of small horse
WORD ORIGIN Scots *powney*, perhaps from Latin *pullus* young animal, foal

ponytail n a hairstyle in which the hair is tied in a bunch at the back of the head and hangs down like a tail

pony trekking n the pastime of riding ponies cross-country

poodle n a dog with curly hair, which is sometimes clipped
WORD ORIGIN German *Pudel*

poof n Brit, Austral, & NZ offensive slang a male homosexual **poofy** adj
WORD ORIGIN French *pouffe* puff

pooh interj an exclamation of disdain, scorn, or disgust

pooh-pooh vb to express disdain or scorn for

pool[1] n **1** a small body of still water **2** a small body of spilt liquid: *a pool of blood* **3** see **swimming pool** **4** a deep part of a stream or river
WORD ORIGIN Old English *pōl*

pool[2] n **1** a shared fund of resources or workers: *a typing pool* **2** a billiard game in which all the balls are potted with the cue ball **3** the combined stakes of those betting in many gambling games **4** commerce a group of producers who agree to maintain output levels and high prices ▷ vb **5** to put into a common fund
WORD ORIGIN French *poule*, literally: hen used to signify stakes in a card game

pools pl n **the pools** chiefly Brit a nationwide mainly postal form of gambling which bets on the results of football matches

poop n naut a raised part at the back of a sailing ship
WORD ORIGIN Latin *puppis*

pooped adj US, Canad, Austral, & NZ slang exhausted or tired: *if I wasn't so pooped I'd run and have a look at it*
WORD ORIGIN Middle English *poupen* to blow

poor adj **1** having little money and few possessions **2** less than is necessary or expected: *it was a poor reward for all his effort* **3** (sometimes foll. by *in*) lacking in (something): *a food which is rich in energy but poor in vitamins* **4** inferior: *poor quality* **5** disappointing or disagreeable: *a poor play* **6** pitiable; unlucky: *poor John is ill* **7** poor man's (something) a cheaper substitute for (something): *pewter, sometimes known as poor man's silver*
WORD ORIGIN Latin *pauper*

poorhouse n same as **workhouse**

poor law n English history a law providing for support of the poor from parish funds

poorly adv **1** badly ▷ adj **2** informal rather ill

poor White n often offensive a poverty-stricken White person, usually in the southern US or South Africa

pop[1] vb popping, popped **1** to make or cause to make a small explosive sound **2** (often foll. by *in* or *out* etc.) informal to enter or leave briefly or suddenly: *his mother popped out to buy him an ice cream* **3** to place suddenly or unexpectedly: *Benny popped a sweet into his mouth* **4** to burst with a small explosive sound **5** (of the eyes) to protrude **6** informal to pawn **7** pop the question informal to propose marriage ▷ n **8** a light sharp explosive sound **9** Brit informal a nonalcoholic fizzy drink ▷ adv **10** with a pop ▸ See also **pop off**
WORD ORIGIN imitative

pop[2] n **1** music of general appeal, esp. to young people, that usually has a strong rhythm and uses electrical amplification ▷ adj **2** relating to pop music: *a pop concert* **3** informal short for **popular**

pop[3] n informal **1** father **2** an old man

POP **1** point of presence: a device that enables access to the internet **2** post office protocol: a protocol which brings e-mail to and from a mail server

pop. **1** population **2** popular(ly)

pop art n a movement in modern art that uses the methods, styles, and themes of popular culture and mass media

popcorn n grains of maize heated until they puff up and burst

Pope n the bishop of Rome as head of the Roman Catholic Church
WORD ORIGIN Greek *pappas* father

popery (**pope**-er-ee) n offensive Roman Catholicism

popeyed adj **1** staring in astonishment **2** having bulging eyes

popgun n a toy gun that fires a pellet or cork by means of compressed air

popinjay n a conceited, foppish, or overly talkative person
WORD ORIGIN Arabic *babaghā* parrot

popish (**pope**-ish) adj offensive relating to Roman Catholicism

poplar n a tall slender tree with light soft wood, triangular leaves, and catkins
WORD ORIGIN Latin *populus*

poplin n a strong plain-woven fabric, usually of cotton, with fine ribbing
WORD ORIGIN French *papeline*

pop off vb informal **1** to depart suddenly **2** to die suddenly

poppadom or **poppadum** n a thin round crisp fried Indian bread
WORD ORIGIN Hindi

popper n Brit informal a press stud

poppet n a term of affection for a small child or sweetheart
WORD ORIGIN variant of *puppet*

popping crease n cricket a line in front of and parallel with the wicket where the batsman stands
WORD ORIGIN from obsolete *pop* to hit

poppy n, pl -pies **1** a plant with showy red, orange, or white flowers **2** a drug, such as opium, obtained from these plants **3** an artificial red poppy worn to mark Remembrance Sunday and in New Zealand to mark Anzac Day ▷ adj **4** reddish-orange
WORD ORIGIN Old English *popæg*

poppycock n informal nonsense
WORD ORIGIN Dutch dialect *pappekak*, literally: soft excrement

Poppy Day n informal Remembrance Sunday

Popsicle n trademark the US and Canadian term for **ice lolly**

populace n the common people; masses
WORD ORIGIN Latin *populus*

popular adj **1** widely liked or admired **2** (often foll. by *with*) liked by a particular person or group: *the bay is popular with windsurfers and water-skiers* **3** common among the general public: *the groundswell of popular feeling* **4** designed to appeal to a mass audience: *an attack on him in the popular press* **popularity** n **popularly** adv
WORD ORIGIN Latin *popularis* of the people

popular front n a left-wing group or party opposed to fascism

popularize or **-rise** vb -rizing, -rized or -rising, -rised **1** to make popular **2** to make easily understandable **popularization** or **-risation** n

populate vb -lating, -lated **1** (often passive) to live in: *a mountainous region populated mainly by Armenians* **2** to provide with inhabitants **populated** adj
WORD ORIGIN Latin *populus* people

population n **1** all the inhabitants of a place **2** the number of such inhabitants **3** all the people of a particular class in a place: *the bulk of the rural population lives in*

poverty 4 *ecology* a group of individuals of the same species inhabiting a given area: *a population of grey seals*

populism *n* a political strategy based on a calculated appeal to the interests or prejudices of ordinary people: *the Islamic radicals preach a heady message of populism and religion* **populist** *adj, n*

populous *adj* containing many inhabitants

pop-up *adj* **1** (of an appliance) characterized by or having a mechanism that pops up **2** (of a book) having pages that rise when opened, to simulate a three-dimensional form **3** *computers* (of a menu on a computer screen, etc.) suddenly appearing when an option is selected ▷ *n computers* **4** something that appears over or above the open window on a computer screen

porangi (**pore**-ang-ee) *adj NZ informal* crazy; mad
WORD ORIGIN Māori

porbeagle *n* a kind of shark

porcelain *n* **1** a delicate type of china **2** an object or objects made of this
WORD ORIGIN French *porcelaine*, from Italian *porcellana* cowrie shell

porch *n* a covered approach to the entrance of a building
WORD ORIGIN French *porche*

porcine *adj* of or like a pig
WORD ORIGIN Latin *porcus* a pig

porcupine *n* a large rodent covered with long pointed quills
WORD ORIGIN Middle English *porc despyne* pig with spines

pore¹ *vb* **poring, pored** ● **pore over** to examine or study intently: *a wife who pored over account books and ledgers all day*
WORD ORIGIN Middle English *pouren*
☰ USAGE
☰ See at **pour**.

pore² *n* **1** a small opening in the skin or surface of an animal or plant **2** any small hole, such as a tiny gap in a rock
WORD ORIGIN Greek *poros* passage, pore

poriferan (por-**riff**-er-an) *n biol* a sponge
WORD ORIGIN from New Latin *porifer* bearing pores

pork *n* the flesh of pigs used as food
WORD ORIGIN Latin *porcus* pig

porker *n* a pig fattened for food

pork pie *n* a pie with a minced pork filling

porky *adj* **porkier, porkiest 1** of or like pork **2** *informal* fat or obese

porn *or* **porno** *n, adj informal* short for **pornography** or **pornographic**

pornography *n* writings, pictures, or films designed to be sexually exciting **pornographer** *n* **pornographic** *adj*
WORD ORIGIN Greek *pornographos* writing of prostitutes

porous *adj* **1** allowing air and liquids to be absorbed **2** *biol, geol* having pores **porosity** *n*
WORD ORIGIN Late Latin *porus* passage, pore

porphyry (**por**-fir-ee) *n, pl* -ries a reddish-purple rock with large crystals of feldspar in it **porphyritic** *adj*
WORD ORIGIN Greek *porphuros* purple

porpoise *n, pl* -poises *or* -poise a small mammal of the whale family with a blunt snout
WORD ORIGIN Latin *porcus* pig + *piscis* fish

porridge *n* **1** a dish made of oatmeal or other cereal, cooked in water or milk **2** *chiefly Brit slang* a term of imprisonment
WORD ORIGIN variant of *pottage*

porringer *n* a small dish, often with a handle, used esp. formerly for soup or porridge
WORD ORIGIN Middle English *potinger*

port¹ *n* a town with a harbour where ships can load and unload
WORD ORIGIN Latin *portus*

port² *n* **1** the left side of an aircraft or ship when facing the front of it ▷ *vb* **2** to turn or be turned towards the port
WORD ORIGIN origin unknown

port³ *n* a strong sweet fortified wine, usually dark red
WORD ORIGIN after *Oporto*, Portugal, from where it came originally

port⁴ *n* **1** *naut* **a** an opening with a watertight door in the side of a ship, used for loading, etc. **b** see **porthole 2** *electronics* a logical circuit for the input and output of data
WORD ORIGIN Latin *porta* gate

port⁵ *vb computers* to change (programs) from one system to another
WORD ORIGIN probably from PORT⁴

portable *adj* **1** easily carried ▷ *n* **2** an article designed to be easily carried, such as a television or typewriter **portability** *n*
WORD ORIGIN Latin *portare* to carry

portage *n* **1** the transporting of boats and supplies overland between navigable waterways **2** the route used for such transport ▷ *vb* -taging, -taged **3** to transport (boats and supplies) in this way
WORD ORIGIN French

portal *n* **1** *literary* a large and impressive gateway or doorway **2** *computers* an internet site providing links to other sites
WORD ORIGIN Latin *porta* gate

portcullis *n* an iron grating suspended in a castle gateway, that can be lowered to bar the entrance
WORD ORIGIN Old French *porte coleïce* sliding gate

portend *vb* to be an omen of: *the 0.5% increase certainly portends higher inflation ahead*
WORD ORIGIN Latin *portendere* to indicate

portent *n* **1** a sign of a future event **2** great or ominous significance: *matters of great portent* **3** a marvel
WORD ORIGIN Latin *portentum* sign

portentous *adj* **1** of great or ominous significance **2** self-important or pompous: *there was nothing portentous or solemn about him*

porter¹ *n* **1** a man employed to carry luggage at a railway station or hotel **2** a hospital worker who transfers patients between rooms **porterage** *n*
WORD ORIGIN Latin *portare* to carry

porter² *n chiefly Brit* a doorman or gatekeeper of a building
WORD ORIGIN Latin *porta* door

porter³ *n Brit* a dark sweet ale brewed from black malt
WORD ORIGIN short for *porter's ale*

porterhouse *n* a thick, choice beef steak. Also called: **porterhouse steak**
WORD ORIGIN formerly, a place that served porter, beer, and sometimes meals

portfolio *n, pl* -os **1** a flat case for carrying maps, drawings, or papers **2** selected examples, such as drawings or photographs, that show an artist's recent work **3** the area of responsibility of the head of a government department: *the defence portfolio* **4** a list of investments held by an investor **5 Minister without portfolio** a cabinet minister without responsibility for a government department
WORD ORIGIN Italian *portafoglio*

porthole *n* a small round window in a ship or aircraft

portico *n, pl* -coes *or* -cos a porch or covered walkway with columns supporting the roof
WORD ORIGIN Italian, from Latin *porticus*

portion *n* **1** a part of a whole **2** a part belonging to a person or group **3** a helping of food served to one person **4** *law* a dowry **5** *literary* someone's fate or destiny: *utter disaster was my portion* ▷ *vb* **6** to divide (something) into shares **portion out**
WORD ORIGIN Latin *portio*

portion out *vb* to distribute or share (something) among a group of people: *the British portioned out the oil-rich lands to various sheikhs*

portly *adj* -lier, -liest stout or rather fat
WORD ORIGIN from *port* (in the sense: deportment)

portmanteau *n, pl* -teaus *or* -teaux *old-fashioned* a large suitcase made of stiff leather that opens out into two compartments
WORD ORIGIN French: cloak carrier

portmanteau word *n* a word made by joining together the beginning and end of two other words, such as *brunch*. Also called: **blend**

portrait *n* **1** a painting, drawing, or photograph of a person, often only of the face **2** a description **portraitist** *n*
WORD ORIGIN French

portraiture *n* **1** the art of making portraits **2** a description **3 a** a portrait **b** portraits collectively

portray *vb* to describe or represent (someone) by artistic means, such as in writing or on film **portrayal** *n*
WORD ORIGIN Old French *portraire* to depict

Portuguese *adj* **1** of Portugal ▷ *n* **2** *pl* -guese a person from Portugal **3** the language of Portugal and Brazil

Portuguese man-of-war *n* a large sea creature like a jellyfish, with long stinging tentacles

pose *vb* **posing, posed 1** to take up a particular position to be photographed or drawn **2** to behave in an affected way in order to impress others **3** (often foll. by *as*) to pretend to be (someone one is not) **4** to create or be (a problem, threat, etc.): *dressing complicated wounds has always posed a problem for doctors* **5** to put forward or ask: *the question you posed earlier* ▷ *n* **6** a position taken up for an artist or photographer **7** behaviour adopted for effect

WORD ORIGIN Old French *poser* to set in place

Poseidon *n* Greek myth the god of the sea

poser¹ *n* **1** Brit, Austral, & NZ informal a person who likes to be seen in trendy clothes in fashionable places **2** a person who poses

poser² *n* a baffling question

poseur *n* a person who behaves in an affected way in order to impress others

WORD ORIGIN French

posh *adj informal chiefly Brit* **1** smart or elegant **2** upper-class

WORD ORIGIN probably from obsolete slang *posh* a dandy

posit (**pozz**-it) *vb* **-iting, -ited** to lay down as a basis for argument: *the archetypes posited by modern psychology*

WORD ORIGIN Latin *ponere* to place

position *n* **1** place or location: *the hotel is in an elevated position above the River Wye* **2** the proper or usual place **3** the way in which a person or thing is placed or arranged: *an upright position* **4** point of view; attitude: *the Catholic Church's position on contraception* **5** social status, esp. high social standing **6** a job; appointment **7** sport a player's allotted role or place in the playing area **8** mil a place occupied for tactical reasons **9 in a position to** able to: *you were not in a position to repay the money* ▷ *vb* **10** to put in the proper or usual place; locate **positional** *adj*

WORD ORIGIN Latin *ponere* to place

positive *adj* **1** expressing certainty: *a positive answer* **2** definite or certain: *are you absolutely positive about the date?* **3** tending to emphasize what is good; constructive: *positive thinking* **4** tending towards progress or improvement: *investment that could have a positive impact on the company's fortunes* **5** philosophy constructive rather than sceptical **6** informal complete; downright: *a positive delight* **7** maths having a value greater than zero: *a positive number* **8** grammar denoting the unmodified form of an adjective as opposed to its comparative or superlative form **9** physics (of an electric charge) having an opposite charge to that of an electron **10** physics short for **electropositive 11** med (of the result of an examination or test) indicating the presence of a suspected condition or organism ▷ *n* **12** something positive **13** maths a quantity greater than zero **14** photog a print showing an image whose colours and tones correspond to those of the original subject **15** grammar the positive degree of an adjective or adverb **16** a positive object, such as a terminal in a cell **positively** *adv* **positiveness** *or* **positivity** *n*

WORD ORIGIN Late Latin *positivus*

positive discrimination *n* the provision of special opportunities for a disadvantaged group

positive vetting *n* Brit the thorough checking of all aspects of a person's life to ensure his or her suitability for a position that may involve national security

positivism *n* a system of philosophy that accepts only things that can be seen or proved **positivist** *n*, *adj*

positron *n* physics the antiparticle of the electron, having the same mass but an equal and opposite charge

WORD ORIGIN *posi(tive)* + *(elec)tron*

poss. **1** possible **2** possession **3** possessive **4** possibly

posse (**poss**-ee) *n* **1** US a selected group of men on whom the sheriff may call for assistance **2** informal a group of friends or associates: *a posse of reporters* **3** (in W Canada) a troop of horses and riders who perform at rodeos

WORD ORIGIN Latin: to be able

possess *vb* **1** to have as one's property; own **2** to have as a quality or attribute: *he possessed an innate elegance, authority, and wit on screen* **3** to gain control over or dominate: *absolute terror possessed her* **possessor** *n*

WORD ORIGIN Latin *possidere*

possessed *adj* **1** (foll. by *of*) owning or having: *he is possessed of a calm maturity far beyond his years* **2** under the influence of a powerful force, such as a spirit or strong emotion: *possessed by the devil; she was possessed by a frenzied urge to get out of Moscow*

possession *n* **1** the state of possessing; ownership: *how had this compromising picture come into the possession of the press?* **2** anything that is possessed **3 possessions** wealth or property **4** the state of being controlled by or as if by evil spirits **5** the occupancy of land or property: *troops had taken possession of the airport* **6** a territory subject to a foreign state **7** the criminal offence of having something illegal on one's person: *arrested for drug dealing and possession* **8** sport control of the ball by a team or player: *City had most of the possession, but couldn't score*

possessive *adj* **1** of possession **2** desiring excessively to possess or dominate: *a possessive husband* **3** grammar denoting a form of a noun or pronoun used to convey possession, as *my* or *Harry's*: *a possessive pronoun* ▷ *n* **4** grammar **a** the possessive case **b** a word in the possessive case **possessiveness** *n*

possibility *n, pl* **-ties 1** the state of being possible **2** anything that is possible **3** a competitor or candidate with a chance of success **4** a future prospect or potential: *all sorts of possibilities began to open up*

possible *adj* **1** capable of existing, happening, or proving true: *the earliest possible moment* **2** capable of being done: *I am grateful to the library staff for making this work possible* **3** having potential: *a possible buyer* **4** feasible but less than probable: *it's possible that's what he meant, but I doubt it* ▷ *n* **5** same as **possibility** (sense 3)

WORD ORIGIN Latin *possibilis*

≡ **USAGE**
≡ Although it is very common to talk
≡ about something being *very possible* or
≡ *more possible*, these uses are generally
≡ thought to be incorrect, since *possible*
≡ describes an absolute state, and
≡ therefore something can only be
≡ *possible* or *not possible: it is very likely*

≡ (not *very possible*) *that he will resign; it has*
≡ *now become easier* (not *more possible*) *to*
≡ *obtain an entry visa.*

possibly *adv* **1** perhaps or maybe **2** by any means; at all: *he can't possibly come*

possum *n* **1** informal an opossum **2** Austral & NZ a phalanger **3 play possum** to pretend to be dead, ignorant, or asleep in order to deceive an opponent

post¹ *n* **1** an official system of mail delivery **2** letters or packages that are transported and delivered by the Post Office; mail **3** a single collection or delivery of mail **4** a postbox or post office: *take this to the post* **5** computers an item of e-mail made publicly available ▷ *vb* **6** to send by post **7** computers to make (e-mail) publicly available **8** book-keeping **a** to enter (an item) in a ledger **b** (often foll. by *up*) to enter all paper items in (a ledger) **9 keep someone posted** to inform someone regularly of the latest news

WORD ORIGIN Latin *posita* something placed

post² *n* **1** a length of wood, metal, or concrete fixed upright to support or mark something **2** horse racing **a** either of two upright poles marking the beginning and end of a racecourse **b** the finish of a horse race ▷ *vb* **3** (sometimes foll. by *up*) to put up (a notice) in a public place **4** to publish (a name) on a list

WORD ORIGIN Latin *postis*

post³ *n* **1** a position to which a person is appointed; job **2** a position to which a soldier or guard is assigned for duty **3** a permanent military establishment **4** Brit either of two military bugle calls (**first post** and **last post**) giving notice of the time to retire for the night ▷ *vb* **5** Austral & Brit to send (someone) to a new place to work **6** to assign to or station at a particular place or position: *guards were posted at the doors*

WORD ORIGIN French *poste*, from Latin *ponere* to place

post- *prefix* **1** after in time: *postgraduate* **2** behind: *postdated*

WORD ORIGIN Latin

postage *n* the charge for sending a piece of mail by post

postage stamp *n* same as **stamp** (sense 1)

postal *adj* of a post office or the mail-delivery service

postal order *n* a written money order sent by post and cashed at a post office by the person who receives it

postbag *n* **1** chiefly Brit a mailbag **2** the mail received by a magazine, radio programme, or public figure

postbox *n* same as **letter box** (sense 2)

postcard *n* a card, often with a picture on one side, for sending a message by post without an envelope

post chaise (**shaze**) *n* old-fashioned a four-wheeled horse-drawn coach formerly used as a rapid means of carrying mail and passengers

postcode *n* a system of letters and numbers used to aid the sorting of mail

A History of English –
Early Modern English

Assigning the historical boundaries for language change is a hazy and arbitrary business. Yet plainly a language goes through phases. To the reader of today, Old English looks less familiar than Albanian, but Middle English merely looks comprehensively misspelled. Chaucer's *Canterbury Tales* is not fully intelligible without a glossary; Shakespeare's *Hamlet* only needs the occasional note. We speak Modern English, yet the present is a moving point and quickly becomes the past.

Most linguists assign Early Modern English to the period between the beginnings of the sixteenth and eighteenth centuries or, measuring the period in poets, from Sir Thomas Wyatt (1503-42) to John Dryden (1631-1700). We can take as one starting point the death in 1499 of William Caxton, who had produced the first English printed book only about two decades after Johannes Gutenberg's Bible appeared. Gutenberg had been the first to combine movable type, oil-based ink, and a wooden press into a workable system for printing books.

The early printers in English established conventions that sometimes makes reading their books a puzzle. The *u* and *v* seem interchangeable, but there was a method: the first letter of a word was *v*, and in other positions was *u*. Except as an initial capital or as a final letter, the *s* was rendered ſ, like an *f* without the cross-bar, and the doubled *ss* as ff or ſs. The letter *i* often represented both the vowel *i* and the consonant *j* (*ioy* for *joy*). *And* was often given as &, the ampersand. Often, printers just composed words to fit a typeset line of text, or set them the way they thought they should sound. A silent *e* was appended to words, and consonants preceding it were sometimes doubled (*manne* for *man*, *runne* for *run*). Classical Latin and Greek affected the language: the Middle English *dette* became *debt*, after the Latin *debitum*. Ever since, silent letters such as *b* have bedeviled English-language learners.

Since tape recorders weren't about in the sixteenth century, and speakers of Early Modern English aren't around today, we can only approximate how people pronounced their words. Scholars do it by noting that different spellings must have reflected different pro-nunciations, and by examining patterns of rhymes. However, our understanding of how people spoke is mainly confined to works from the highly educated, because they, not illiterate agricultural labourers or kitchen maids, were the ones who left the texts.

In relating how spoken language changed in Early Modern English, linguists invariably cite the portentous-sounding Great Vowel Shift of the fifteenth and sixteenth centuries, whereby long vowels were pronounced differently: *house* rhymed with *goose* in Middle English; by the sixteenth century it rhymed with *dose*. Words like *cook* and *book* had a long-*u* sound, making them sound somewhat like *coo* and *boo*. Exactly why these widespread changes occurred is much debated, but unquestionably they became pervasive.

Reverting to the beginnings of Early Modern English, the language of the King James Bible used two main forms of *you*: the informal singular pronoun *thou*, and *ye* for both plural and formal singular pronouns. *Thou* as a grammatical object was *thee*, its possessive forms were *thy* and *thine*, and its reflexive form was *thyself*. The objective form of *ye* was *you*, its possessive forms were *your* and *yours*, and its reflexive forms were *yourself* and *yourselves*. Before a vowel, *my* became *mine* (*thine* or *mine eyes*). The verbs that followed *thou* ended in *-est* or *-st* (*thou takest*), and third-person singular conjugations ended in *-eth* or *-th* (*she taketh*).

The King James Bible also reminds us that a few words had different meanings then: *suffer* as in 'Suffer the little children' meant 'permit' – a meaning which survives in the phrase 'He does not suffer fools gladly'. The wordstock of Early Modern English was enlarged by the continuing influence of French, and the fact that Latin was the language of scholarship and diplomacy. The prestige of Latin led the poet laureate John Skelton (1460-1529) to introduce some 1,500 new Latinate words into the language, among them the enduring *accumulate*, *celebrate*, *imitation*, and *variety*. More extreme neologists tried to replace Anglo-Saxon's little words of house and home with tortured, erudite *inkhorn* words, such as *exsiccate* for *to dry*.

English was sorting itself out.

post-consumer *adj* (of a consumer item) discarded for disposal or recovery having been recycled: ... *made from 75% post-consumer waste*

postdate *vb* **-dating, -dated 1** to write a future date on (a cheque or document) **2** to occur at a later date than **3** to assign a date to (an event or period) that is later than its previously assigned date

poster *n* **1** a large notice displayed in a public place as an advertisement **2** a large printed picture

poste restante *n* a post-office department where mail is kept until it is called for
WORD ORIGIN French, literally: mail remaining

posterior *n* **1** *formal or humorous* the buttocks ▷ *adj* **2** at the back of or behind something: *posterior leg muscles* **3** coming after in a series or time
WORD ORIGIN Latin: latter

posterity *n* **1** future generations **2** all of one's descendants
WORD ORIGIN Latin *posterus* coming after

postern *n* a small back door or gate
WORD ORIGIN Old French *posterne*

post-free *adv, adj* **1** *Austral & Brit* with the postage prepaid **2** free of postal charge

postgraduate *n* **1** a person who is studying for a more advanced qualification after obtaining a degree ▷ *adj* **2** of or for postgraduates

posthaste *adv* with great speed

posthumous (**poss**-tume-uss) *adj* **1** happening after one's death **2** born after the death of one's father **3** (of a book) published after the author's death **posthumously** *adv*
WORD ORIGIN Latin *postumus* the last

postie *n* *Scot, Austral, & NZ informal* a postman

postilion *or* **postillion** *n* (esp. formerly) a person who rides one of a pair of horses drawing a coach
WORD ORIGIN French *postillon*

postimpressionism *n* a movement in painting in France at the end of the 19th century which rejected Impressionism but adapted its use of pure colour to paint with greater subjective emotion **postimpressionist** *n, adj*

posting *n* **1** a job to which someone is assigned by his or her employer, which involves moving to a particular town or country: *Bonn was his third posting overseas* **2** *computers* an e-mail message that is publicly available

postman *or fem* **postwoman** *n, pl* **-men** *or fem* **-women** a person who collects and delivers mail as a profession

postmark *n* **1** an official mark stamped on mail, showing the place and date of posting ▷ *vb* **2** to put such a mark on (mail)

postmaster *n* **1** Also (fem): **postmistress** an official in charge of a post office **2** the person who manages the e-mail at a site

postmaster general *n, pl* **postmasters general** the executive head of the postal service

postmeridian *adj* occurring after noon
WORD ORIGIN Latin *postmeridianus*

postmortem *n* **1** In full: **postmortem examination** medical examination of a dead body to discover the cause of death **2** analysis of a recent event: *a postmortem on the party's recent appalling by-election results* ▷ *adj* **3** occurring after death
WORD ORIGIN Latin, literally: after death

postnatal *adj* occurring after childbirth: *postnatal depression*

post office *n* **1** a building where stamps are sold and postal business is conducted

Post Office *n* a government department responsible for postal services

postoperative *adj* of or occurring in the period after a surgical operation

postpaid *adv, adj* with the postage prepaid

postpone *vb* **-poning, -poned** to put off until a future time **postponement** *n*
WORD ORIGIN Latin *postponere* to put after

postpositive *adj* *grammar* (of an adjective) placed after the word it modifies

postprandial *adj* *formal* after dinner
WORD ORIGIN Latin *post-* after + *prandium* midday meal

postscript *n* a message added at the end of a letter, after the signature
WORD ORIGIN Late Latin *postscribere* to write after

post-traumatic stress disorder *n* a psychological condition, characterized by anxiety, withdrawal, and a proneness to physical illness, that may follow a traumatic experience

postulant *n* an applicant for admission to a religious order
WORD ORIGIN Latin *postulare* to ask

postulate *formal vb* **-lating, -lated 1** to assume to be true as the basis of an argument or theory **2** to ask, demand, or claim ▷ *n* **3** something postulated **postulation** *n*
WORD ORIGIN Latin *postulare* to ask for

posture *n* **1** a position or way in which a person stands, walks, etc.: *good posture* **2** a mental attitude: *a cooperative posture* **3** an affected attitude: *an intellectual posture* ▷ *vb* **-turing, -tured 4** to behave in an exaggerated way to attract attention **5** to assume an affected attitude **postural** *adj*
WORD ORIGIN Latin *positura*

postviral fatigue syndrome *or* **postviral syndrome** *n* same as **chronic fatigue syndrome**

postwar *adj* occurring or existing after a war

posy *n, pl* **-sies** a small bunch of flowers
WORD ORIGIN variant of *poesy*

pot¹ *n* **1** a round deep container, often with a lid, used for cooking **2** the amount that a pot will hold **3** short for **flowerpot** or **teapot 4** a handmade piece of pottery **5** *billiards, etc.* a shot by which a ball is pocketed **6** a chamber pot **7** the money in the pool in gambling games **8** (often *pl*) *informal* a large sum of money **9** *informal*

a cup or other trophy **10** see **potbelly 11 go to pot** to go to ruin ▷ *vb* **potting, potted 12** to put (a plant) in soil in a flowerpot **13** *billiards, etc.* to pocket (a ball) **14** to preserve (food) in a pot **15** to shoot (game) for food rather than for sport **16** to shoot casually or without careful aim **17** *informal* to capture or win
WORD ORIGIN Old English *pott*

pot² *n* *slang* cannabis
WORD ORIGIN perhaps from Mexican Indian *potiguaya*

potable (**pote**-a-bl) *adj* *formal* drinkable
WORD ORIGIN Latin *potare* to drink

potage (po-**tahzh**) *n* thick soup
WORD ORIGIN French

potash *n* **1** potassium carbonate, used as fertilizer **2** a compound containing potassium: *permanganate of potash*
WORD ORIGIN from *pot ashes*, because originally obtained by evaporating the lye of wood ashes in pots

potassium *n* *chem* a light silvery element of the alkali metal group. Symbol: K
WORD ORIGIN New Latin *potassa* potash

potassium nitrate *n* a crystalline compound used in gunpowders, fertilizers, and as a preservative for foods (E252)

potation *n* *formal* **1** the act of drinking **2** a drink, usually alcoholic
WORD ORIGIN Latin *potare* to drink

potato *n, pl* **-toes 1** a starchy vegetable that grows underground **2** the plant from which this vegetable is obtained
WORD ORIGIN Spanish *patata*, from a Native American language

potato beetle *n* same as **Colorado beetle**

potato chip *n* the US and Canadian term for **crisp** (sense 7)

potato crisp *n* same as **crisp** (sense 7)

potbelly *n, pl* **-lies 1** a bulging belly **2** a person with such a belly

potboiler *n* *informal* an inferior work of art produced quickly to make money

pot-bound *adj* (of a pot plant) having roots too big for its pot, so that it is unable to grow further

poteen *or* **poitín** *n* (in Ireland) illegally made alcoholic drink
WORD ORIGIN Irish *poitín* little pot

potent *adj* **1** having great power or influence **2** (of arguments) persuasive or forceful **3** highly effective: *a potent poison* **4** (of a male) capable of having sexual intercourse **potency** *n*
WORD ORIGIN Latin *potens* able

potentate *n* a ruler or monarch
WORD ORIGIN Latin *potens* powerful

potential *adj* **1 a** possible but not yet actual: *potential buyers* **b** capable of being or becoming; latent: *potential danger* ▷ *n* **2** ability or talent not yet in full use: *she has great potential as a painter* **3** In full: **electric potential** the work required to transfer a unit positive electric charge from an infinite distance to a given point **potentially** *adv*
WORD ORIGIN Latin *potentia* power

potential difference *n* the difference in electric potential between two points in an electric field, measured in volts

potential energy *n* the energy which an object has stored up because of its position

potentiality *n, pl* **-ties** latent capacity for becoming or developing

pother (rhymes with **bother**) *n literary* a fuss or commotion
WORD ORIGIN origin unknown

potherb *n* a plant whose leaves, flowers, or stems are used in cooking

pothole *n* **1** a hole in the surface of a road **2** a deep hole in a limestone area

potholing *n* the sport of exploring underground caves **potholer** *n*

pothook *n* **1** an S-shaped hook for suspending a pot over a fire **2** an S-shaped mark in handwriting

potion *n* a drink of medicine, poison, or some supposedly magic liquid
WORD ORIGIN Latin *potio* a drink, esp. a poisonous one

pot luck *n* **take pot luck** *informal* to accept whatever happens to be available: *we'll take pot luck at whatever restaurant might still be open*

potoroo *n, pl* **-roos** an Australian leaping rodent

potpourri (po-**poor**-ee) *n, pl* **-ris** **1** a fragrant mixture of dried flower petals **2** an assortment or medley
WORD ORIGIN French, literally: rotten pot

pot roast *n* meat cooked slowly in a covered pot with very little liquid

potsherd *n* a broken piece of pottery
WORD ORIGIN *pot* + *schoord* piece of broken crockery

pot shot *n* **1** a shot taken without careful aim **2** a shot fired at an animal within easy range

pottage *n* a thick soup or stew
WORD ORIGIN Old French *potage* contents of a pot

potted *adj* **1** grown in a pot: *potted plant* **2** cooked or preserved in a pot: *potted shrimps* **3** *informal* shortened or abridged: *a potted history*

potter[1] *n* a person who makes pottery

potter[2] *or esp. US & Canad* **putter** *vb* **1** to move with little energy or direction: *I saw him pottering off to see his canaries* **2** *potter about or around or away* to be busy in a pleasant but aimless way: *he potters away doing God knows what all day*
WORD ORIGIN Old English *potian* to thrust

Potteries *n* **the Potteries** a region of W central England, in Staffordshire, where many china industries are situated

potter's wheel *n* a flat spinning disc on which clay is shaped by hand

pottery *n, pl* **-teries** **1** articles made from baked clay **2** a place where such articles are made **3** the craft of making such articles

potting shed *n* a garden hut in which plants are put in flowerpots and potting materials are stored

potty[1] *adj* **-tier, -tiest** *informal* **1** slightly crazy **2** trivial or insignificant **3** (foll. by *about*) very keen (on) **pottiness** *n*
WORD ORIGIN origin unknown

potty[2] *n, pl* **-ties** a bowl used as a toilet by a small child

pouch *n* **1** a small bag **2** a baglike pocket in various animals, such as the cheek fold in hamsters ▷ *vb* **3** to place in or as if in a pouch **4** to make or be made into a pouch
WORD ORIGIN Old French *poche* bag

pouf *or* **pouffe** (**poof**) *n* a large solid cushion used as a seat
WORD ORIGIN French

poulterer *n Brit* a person who sells poultry

poultice (**pole**-tiss) *n med* a moist dressing, often heated, applied to painful and swollen parts of the body
WORD ORIGIN Latin *puls* a thick porridge

poultry *n* domestic fowls
WORD ORIGIN Old French *pouletrie*

pounce *vb* **pouncing, pounced** **1** (often foll. by *on* or *upon*) to spring upon suddenly to attack or capture ▷ *n* **2** the act of pouncing; a spring or swoop
WORD ORIGIN origin unknown

pound[1] *n* **1** the standard monetary unit of the United Kingdom and some other countries, made up of 100 pence. Official name: **pound sterling** **2** the standard monetary unit of various other countries, such as Cyprus and Malta **3** a unit of weight made up of 16 ounces and equal to 0.454 kilograms
WORD ORIGIN Old English *pund*

pound[2] *vb* **1** (sometimes foll. by *on* or *at*) to hit heavily and repeatedly **2** to crush to pieces or to powder **3** (foll. by *out*) to produce, by typing heavily **4** (of the heart) to throb heavily **5** to run with heavy steps
WORD ORIGIN Old English *pūnian*

pound[3] *n* an enclosure for stray dogs or officially removed vehicles
WORD ORIGIN Old English *pund-*

poundage *n* **1** a charge of so much per pound of weight **2** a charge of so much per pound sterling

-pounder *n combining form* **1** something weighing a specified number of pounds: *a 200-pounder* **2** something worth a specified number of pounds: *a ten-pounder* **3** a gun that discharges a shell weighing a specified number of pounds: *a two-pounder*

pour *vb* **1** to flow or cause to flow out in a stream **2** to rain heavily **3** to be given or obtained in large amounts: *foreign aid is pouring into Iran* **4** to move together in large numbers: *the fans poured onto the pitch*
WORD ORIGIN origin unknown

USAGE
The verbs *pour* and *pore* are sometimes confused: *she poured cream over her strudel; she pored* (not *poured*) *over the manuscript.*

pourboire (**poor**-bwahr) *n* a tip or gratuity
WORD ORIGIN French, literally: for drinking

pout *vb* **1** to thrust out (the lips) sullenly or provocatively **2** to swell out; protrude ▷ *n* **3** a pouting
WORD ORIGIN origin unknown

pouter *n* a breed of domestic pigeon that can puff out its crop

poutine (poo-**teen**) *n Canad* a dish of chipped potatoes topped with curd cheese and a tomato-based sauce

poverty *n* **1** the state of lacking adequate food or money **2** lack or scarcity: *a poverty of information* **3** inferior quality or inadequacy: *the poverty of political debate in this country*
WORD ORIGIN Old French *poverté*

poverty-stricken *adj* extremely poor

poverty trap *n* the situation of being unable to raise one's living standard because any extra income would result in state benefits being reduced or withdrawn

pow *interj* an exclamation to indicate that a collision or explosion has taken place

POW prisoner of war

powder *n* **1** a substance in the form of tiny loose particles **2** a medicine or cosmetic in this form ▷ *vb* **3** to cover or sprinkle with powder **powdery** *adj*
WORD ORIGIN Old French *poldre*, from Latin *pulvis* dust

powdered *adj* **1** sold in the form of a powder, esp. one which has been formed by grinding or drying the original material: *powdered milk* **2** covered or made up with a cosmetic in the form of a powder: *liveried footmen in powdered wigs*

powder keg *n* **1** a potential source of violence or disaster: *a political powder keg* **2** a small barrel for holding gunpowder

powder puff *n* a soft pad used to apply cosmetic powder to the skin

powder room *n* a ladies' cloakroom or toilet

power *n* **1** ability to do something **2** (*often pl*) a specific ability or faculty **3** political, financial, or social force or authority: *men's use of power over women in a subordinate position in the workforce; economic power is the bedrock of political power* **4** a position of control, esp. over the running of a country: *he seized power in a coup in 1966* **5** a state with political, industrial, or military strength **6** a person or group having authority **7** a prerogative or privilege: *the power of veto* **8** official or legal authority **9** *maths* the value of a number or quantity raised to some exponent **10** *physics, engineering* a measure of the rate of doing work expressed as the work done per unit of time **11** the rate at which electrical energy is fed into or taken from a device or system, measured in watts **12** mechanical energy as opposed to manual labour **13** a particular form of energy: *nuclear power* **14** the magnifying capacity of a lens or optical system **15** *informal* a great deal: *a power of good* **16** **the powers that be** established authority ▷ *vb* **17** to supply with power ▷ *adj* **18** producing or using electrical energy: *a large selection of power tools*
WORD ORIGIN Anglo-Norman *poer*

powerboat *n* a fast powerful motorboat

power cut *n* a temporary interruption in the supply of electricity

powerful *adj* **1** having great power or influence **2** having great physical strength **3** extremely effective: *a powerful drug* **powerfully** *adv* **powerfulness** *n*

powerhouse *n* **1** *informal* a forceful person or thing **2** an electrical generating station

powerless adj without power or authority; unable to act **powerlessly** adv **powerlessness** n

power of attorney n **1** legal authority to act for another person **2** the document conferring such authority

power play n **1** behaviour or tactics intended to magnify a person's influence or power **2** the use of brute strength or force of numbers in order to achieve an objective

power point n an electrical socket fitted into a wall for plugging in electrical appliances

power pole n Austral & NZ a pole carrying an overhead power line

power-sharing n a political arrangement in which opposing groups in a society participate in government

power station n an installation for generating and distributing electricity

power steering n a type of steering in vehicles in which the turning of the steering wheel is assisted by power from the engine

powwow n **1** a talk or meeting **2** a meeting of Native Americans of N America ▷ vb **3** to hold a powwow **WORD ORIGIN** from a Native American language

pox n **1** a disease in which pus-filled blisters or pimples form on the skin **2** the pox informal syphilis **WORD ORIGIN** changed from pocks, plural of pock

pp 1 past participle **2** (in signing documents on behalf of someone else) by delegation to **WORD ORIGIN** Latin per procurationem

≡ USAGE
≡ In formal correspondence, when
≡ Brenda Smith is signing on behalf of
≡ Peter Jones, she should write Peter Jones
≡ pp (or per pro) Brenda Smith, not the other
≡ way about.

pp. pages

PPS 1 parliamentary private secretary **2** additional postscript **WORD ORIGIN** Latin post postscriptum

PPTA (in New Zealand) Post Primary Teachers Association

PQ 1 Province of Quebec **2** (in Canada) Parti Québecois

PQE, Pqe post-qualification experience

pr pl **prs** pair

Pr chem praseodymium

PR 1 proportional representation **2** public relations

pr. 1 price **2** pronoun

practicable adj **1** capable of being done **2** usable **practicability** n **WORD ORIGIN** French praticable

≡ USAGE
≡ See at **practical**.

practical adj **1** involving experience or actual use rather than theory **2** concerned with everyday matters: the kind of practical and emotional upheaval that divorce can bring **3** sensible, useful, and effective rather than fashionable or attractive: it's a marvellous design, because it's comfortable, it's practical, and it actually looks good **4** involving the simple basics: practical skills **5** being very close to

(a state); virtual: it's a practical certainty ▷ n **6** an examination or lesson in which something has to be made or done **practicality** n **practically** adv **WORD ORIGIN** Greek praktikos, from prassein to experience

≡ USAGE
≡ A distinction is usually made between
≡ practical and practicable. Practical refers
≡ to a person, idea, project, etc. as being
≡ more concerned with or relevant to
≡ practice than theory: he is a very practical
≡ person; the idea had no practical application.
≡ Practicable refers to a project or idea as
≡ being capable of being done or put
≡ into effect: the plan was expensive, yet
≡ practicable.

practical joke n a trick intended to make someone look foolish **practical joker** n

practice n **1** something done regularly or repeatedly **2** repetition of an activity in order to gain skill: regular practice is essential if you want to play an instrument well **3** the business or surgery of a doctor or lawyer **4** the act of doing something: I'm not sure how effective these methods will be when put into practice **5** in practice **a** what actually happens as distinct from what is supposed to happen: many ideas which look good on paper just don't work in practice **b** skilled in something through having had a lot of regular recent experience at it: I still go shooting, just to keep in practice **6** out of practice not having had much regular recent experience at an activity: although out of practice, I still love playing my violin **WORD ORIGIN** Greek praktikē practical work

practise or US **practice** vb **-tising, -tised** or **-ticing, -ticed 1** to do repeatedly in order to gain skill **2** to take part in or follow (a religion etc.): none of them practise Islam **3** to work at (a profession): he originally intended to practise medicine **4** to do regularly: they practise meditation **WORD ORIGIN** Greek prattein to do

practised adj expert or skilled because of long experience in a skill or field: the doctor answered with a practised smoothness

practising adj taking part in an activity or career on a regular basis: a practising barrister

practitioner n a person who practises a profession

praetor (**pree**-tor) n (in ancient Rome) a senior magistrate ranking just below the consuls **praetorian** adj, n **WORD ORIGIN** Latin

pragmatic adj **1** concerned with practical consequences rather than theory **2** philosophy of pragmatism **pragmatically** adv **WORD ORIGIN** Greek pragmatikos

pragmatism n **1** policy dictated by practical consequences rather than by theory **2** philosophy the doctrine that the content of a concept consists only in its practical applicability **pragmatist** n, adj

prairie n (often pl) a large treeless area of grassland of North America **WORD ORIGIN** French, from Latin pratum meadow

prairie dog n a rodent that lives in burrows in the N American prairies

praise vb **praising, praised 1** to express admiration or approval for **2** to express thanks and worship to (one's God) ▷ n **3** the expression of admiration or approval **4 sing someone's praises** to praise someone highly **WORD ORIGIN** Latin pretium prize

praiseworthy adj deserving praise; commendable

praline (**prah**-leen) n a sweet made of nuts with caramelized sugar **WORD ORIGIN** French

pram n a four-wheeled carriage for a baby, pushed by a person on foot **WORD ORIGIN** altered from perambulator

prance vb **prancing, pranced 1** to walk with exaggerated movements **2** (of an animal) to move with high springing steps ▷ n **3** the act of prancing **WORD ORIGIN** origin unknown

prang old-fashioned slang n **1** a crash in an aircraft or car ▷ vb **2** to crash or damage (an aircraft or car) **WORD ORIGIN** perhaps imitative

prank n a mischievous trick **prankster** n **WORD ORIGIN** origin unknown

praseodymium (pray-zee-oh-**dim**-ee-um) n chem a silvery-white element of the lanthanide series of metals. Symbol: Pr **WORD ORIGIN** New Latin

prat n Brit, Austral, & NZ slang an incompetent or ineffectual person **WORD ORIGIN** probably special use of earlier prat buttocks, origin unknown

prate vb **prating, prated 1** to talk idly and at length ▷ n **2** chatter **WORD ORIGIN** Germanic

prattle vb **-tling, -tled 1** to chatter in a foolish or childish way ▷ n **2** foolish or childish talk **WORD ORIGIN** Middle Low German pratelen to chatter

prawn n a small edible shellfish **WORD ORIGIN** origin unknown

praxis n **1** practice as opposed to the theory **2** accepted practice or custom **WORD ORIGIN** Greek: deed, action

pray vb **1** to say prayers (to one's God) **2** to ask earnestly; beg ▷ adv **3** archaic I beg you; please: pray, leave us alone **WORD ORIGIN** Latin precari to implore

prayer[1] n **1** a thanksgiving or an appeal spoken to one's God **2** a set form of words used in praying: the Lord's Prayer **3** an earnest request **4** the practice of praying: call the faithful to prayer **5** (often pl) a form of devotion spent mainly praying: morning prayers **6** something prayed for

prayer[2] n a person who prays

prayer book n a book of prayers used in church or at home

prayer mat or **prayer rug** n the small carpet on which a Muslim performs his or her daily prayers

prayer wheel n Buddhism (in Tibet) a cylinder inscribed with prayers, each turning of which is counted as an uttered prayer

praying mantis n same as **mantis**

The Influence of Latin on English

Latin, the language spoken by the ancient Romans, has exerted a greater influence on English vocabulary than any other language. It has been estimated that nearly 30% of the words in English come directly from Latin, and a further 30% come from French. Since the French language itself developed out of Latin, it can reasonably be said that over half of the words in English can ultimately be traced back to the Latin language.

Britain had its first major brush with Latin as a province of the Roman Empire between 43 and 400 AD. The Romans eventually abandoned Britain, however, and a wave of Saxon invaders brought with them a new language that would eventually become English.

Latin made its first impression on this Anglo-Saxon tongue as the language of the Roman Catholic Church, especially after Saint Augustine arrived in Britain in 597 to convert the Anglo-Saxons to Christianity. In spite of the best efforts of the Church, however, the English language remained essentially a Germanic tongue until 1066.

The Norman invasion changed everything. The language of the new rulers, which was descended from Latin, existed alongside the native Anglo-Saxon. As the Norman and Saxon populations became gradually intermingled, Latinate words from the Norman settlers became part of the English language.

The co-existence of a substantial body of Latinate words alongside Anglo-Saxon words is a defining feature of English. Thanks to this phenomenon, speakers of English invariably have options when they speak: they can 'stay' somewhere or they can 'remain'; they can 'stop' or they can 'desist'. As a rule, words that derive from Latin (such as 'remain' and 'desist') are more formal than their Anglo-Saxon counterparts. Sometimes parallel words from the two source languages came to be used in different ways: the Latinate 'solar', for example, having a different usage to the Anglo-Saxon 'sunny'.

In later years Latin continued to enjoy an exalted status as the language of the Church and of scholarship. Writers such as Spenser, Shakespeare, and Milton plundered Latin to come up with new poetic vocabulary. Lawyers, doctors, and scientists used Latin, and through them Latin words filtered into everyday English. It was also natural for scholars to turn to Latin to supply new words when these were required to describe scientific and technical innovations.

Most Latin words that have reached English have changed their form in the process. The Latin word *dignitas* comes into English as 'dignity', while *multitudo* becomes 'multitude'. Yet words such as *quasi*, *via*, *gravitas*, and *verbatim* have survived in a form that would have been familiar to Livy and Cicero. However, the Romans would have been surprised at the changes in meaning that some of their words have acquired in English. For example, in classical Latin *matrix* means 'womb' and *ratio* means 'reason', while *omnibus* means 'for everyone'.

A single Latin word can be at the root of numerous English words. Thus the verb *vorare*, meaning 'to eat', emerges in words such as 'devour', 'voracious', 'carnivore', and any number of other words ending in the suffix '-vore'. Any word with the letters 'capt' or 'cept' (including 'capture', 'accept', and 'concept') is likely to be derived from *capere*, meaning 'to take'. Words that have the letters 'fact' ('factory', 'manufacture', 'satisfaction') are likely to come from *facere*, meaning 'to do' or 'to make'. Moreover, as these root forms became an established part of English, they have gone on to generate further new words.

Latin is also the source of many phrases that have found their way into English, often as a result of their use in legal and ecclesiastical terminology. Such was the familiarity of educated English speakers with Latin, that it was never considered necessary to render these into English. Thus we talk of *non sequiturs* and *quid pro quos*, of doing something *ad nauseam* or being *in situ*. Latin phrases have also been the source of common abbreviations, which are often used without a thought to their origin. How many of us are really aware when use AD (*anno Domini*), eg (*exempli gratia*), i.e. (*id est*), or PS (*post scriptum*), that we are using the language of the ancient Romans?

pre- *prefix* before in time or position: *predate; pre-eminent*
WORD ORIGIN Latin *prae*

preach *vb* **1** to talk on a religious theme as part of a church service **2** to speak in support of (something) in a moralizing way
WORD ORIGIN Latin *praedicare* to proclaim

preacher *n* a person who preaches

preamble *n* an introduction that comes before something spoken or written
WORD ORIGIN Latin *prae* before + *ambulare* to walk

prearranged *adj* arranged beforehand **prearrangement** *n*

prebend *n* **1** the allowance paid by a cathedral or collegiate church to a canon or member of the chapter **2** the land or tithe from which this is paid **prebendal** *adj*
WORD ORIGIN Old French *prébende*

prebendary *n, pl* **-daries** a clergyman who is a member of the chapter of a cathedral

Precambrian *or* **Pre-Cambrian** *adj geol* of the earliest geological era, lasting from about 4500 million years ago to 600 million years ago

precancerous *adj* relating to cells that show signs that they may develop cancer

precarious *adj* (of a position or situation) dangerous or insecure **precariously** *adv*
WORD ORIGIN Latin *precarius* obtained by begging

precaution *n* an action taken in advance to prevent an undesirable event **precautionary** *adj*
WORD ORIGIN Latin *prae* before + *cavere* to beware

precede *vb* **-ceding, -ceded** to go or be before (someone or something) in time, place, or rank
WORD ORIGIN Latin *praecedere*

precedence (**press**-i-denss) *n* formal order of rank or position

precedent *n* **1** a previous occurrence used to justify taking the same action in later similar situations **2** *law* a judicial decision that serves as an authority for deciding a later case ▷ *adj* **3** preceding

precentor *n* a person who leads the singing in church services
WORD ORIGIN Latin *prae* before + *canere* to sing

precept *n* **1** a rule of conduct **2** a rule for morals **3** *law* a writ or warrant **preceptive** *adj*
WORD ORIGIN Latin *praeceptum*

preceptor *n rare* an instructor **preceptorial** *adj*

precession *n* **1** the act of preceding **2** the motion of a spinning body, in which the axis of rotation sweeps out a cone **3** **precession of the equinoxes** the slightly earlier occurrence of the equinoxes each year
WORD ORIGIN Latin *praecedere* to precede

precinct *n* **1** *Brit, Austral, & S African* an area in a town closed to traffic: *a shopping precinct* **2** *Brit, Austral, & S African* an enclosed area around a building **3** *US*

an administrative area of a city
WORD ORIGIN Latin *praecingere* to surround

precincts *pl n* the surrounding region

preciosity (presh-ee-**oss**-it-ee) *n, pl* **-ties** affectation

precious *adj* **1** very costly or valuable: *precious jewellery* **2** loved and treasured **3** very affected in speech, manners, or behaviour **4** *informal* worthless: *nothing is too good for his precious dog* ▷ *adv* **5** *informal* very: *there's precious little to do in this town*
WORD ORIGIN Latin *pretiosus* valuable

precious metal *n* gold, silver, or platinum

precious stone *n* a rare mineral, such as diamond, ruby, or opal, that is highly valued as a gem

precipice *n* the very steep face of a cliff
WORD ORIGIN Latin *praecipitium* steep place

precipitant *adj* **1** hasty or rash **2** rushing or falling rapidly ▷ *n* **3** something which helps bring about an event or condition: *stressful events are often the precipitant for a manic attack*

precipitate *vb* **-tating, -tated** **1** to cause to happen earlier than expected: *the scandal could bring the government down, precipitating a general election* **2** to condense or cause to condense and fall as snow or rain **3** *chem* to cause to be deposited in solid form from a solution **4** to throw from a height: *the encircled soldiers chose to precipitate themselves into the ocean* ▷ *adj* **5** done rashly or hastily **6** rushing ahead ▷ *n* **7** *chem* a precipitated solid
WORD ORIGIN Latin *praecipitare* to throw down headlong

precipitation *n* **1** the formation of a chemical precipitate **2** *meteorol* **a** rain, hail, snow, or sleet formed by condensation of water vapour in the atmosphere **b** the falling of these **3** rash haste: *they decamped with the utmost precipitation*

precipitous *adj* **1** very steep: *precipitous cliffs* **2** very quick and severe: *a precipitous decline* **3** rapid and unplanned; hasty: *European governments urged the Americans not to make a precipitous decision*
USAGE
The use of *precipitous* to mean *hasty* is thought by some people to be incorrect.

précis (**pray**-see) *n, pl* **précis** **1** a short summary of a longer text ▷ *vb* **2** to make a précis of
WORD ORIGIN French

precise *adj* **1** particular or exact: *this precise moment* **2** strictly correct in amount or value: *precise measurements* **3** working with total accuracy: *precise instruments* **4** strict in observing rules or standards **precisely** *adv*
WORD ORIGIN Latin *prae* before + *caedere* to cut

precision *n* **1** the quality of being precise ▷ *adj* **2** accurate: *precision engineering*

preclude *vb* **-cluding, -cluded** *formal* to make impossible to happen
WORD ORIGIN Latin *prae* before + *claudere* to close

precocious *adj* having developed or matured early or too soon **precocity** *n*
WORD ORIGIN Latin *prae* early + *coquere* to ripen

precognition *n psychol* the alleged ability to foresee future events
WORD ORIGIN Latin *praecognoscere* to foresee

preconceived *adj* (of ideas etc.) formed without real experience or reliable information **preconception** *n*

precondition *n* something that is necessary before something else can come about

precursor *n* **1** something that comes before and signals something to follow; a forerunner **2** a predecessor
WORD ORIGIN Latin *praecursor* one who runs in front

pred. predicate

predacious *adj* (of animals) habitually hunting and killing other animals for food
WORD ORIGIN Latin *praeda* plunder

predate *vb* **-dating, -dated** **1** to occur at an earlier date than **2** to write a date on (a document) that is earlier than the actual date

predator *n* an animal that kills and eats other animals

predatory (**pred**-a-tree) *adj* **1** (of animals) habitually hunting and killing other animals for food **2** eager to gain at the expense of others
WORD ORIGIN Latin *praedari* to pillage

predecease *vb* **-ceasing, -ceased** to die before (someone else)

predecessor *n* **1** a person who precedes another in an office or position **2** an ancestor **3** something that precedes something else: *the library will be more extravagant than its predecessors*
WORD ORIGIN Latin *prae* before + *decedere* to go away

predestination *n Christian theol* the belief that future events have already been decided by God

predestined *adj Christian theol* determined in advance by God
WORD ORIGIN Latin *praedestinare* to resolve beforehand

predetermine *vb* **-mining, -mined** **1** to determine beforehand **2** to influence or bias **predetermined** *adj*

predicable *adj* capable of being predicated

predicament *n* an embarrassing or difficult situation
WORD ORIGIN see PREDICATE

predicant (**pred**-ik-ant) *adj* **1** of preaching ▷ *n* **2** a member of a religious order founded for preaching, usually a Dominican
WORD ORIGIN Latin *praedicans* preaching

predicate *n* **1** *grammar* the part of a sentence in which something is said about the subject **2** *logic* something that is asserted about the subject of a proposition ▷ *vb* **-cating, -cated** **3** to base or found: *political aims which are predicated upon a feminist view of women's oppression* **4** to declare or assert: *it has been predicated that if we continue with our current sexual behaviour every family will have an AIDS victim* **5** *logic* to assert (something)

about the subject of a proposition **predication** n **predicative** adj
WORD ORIGIN Latin *praedicare* to assert publicly

predict vb to tell about in advance; prophesy **predictable** adj **predictably** adv **predictor** n
WORD ORIGIN Latin *praedicere*

prediction n **1** the act of forecasting in advance **2** something that is forecast in advance

predictive adj **1** relating to or able to make predictions **2** (of a word processor) able to complete words after only part of a word has been keyed

predikant (pred-ik-**ant**) n a minister in the Dutch Reformed Church in South Africa
WORD ORIGIN Dutch

predilection n formal a preference or liking
WORD ORIGIN French *prédilection*

predispose vb **-posing, -posed** (often foll. by *to*) **1** to influence (someone) in favour of something: *some scientists' social class background predisposes them to view the natural world in a certain way* **2** to make (someone) susceptible to something: *a high-fat diet appears to predispose men towards heart disease* **predisposition** n

predominant adj being more important or noticeable than others: *improved living conditions probably played the predominant role in reducing disease in the nineteenth century* **predominance** n **predominantly** adv

predominate vb **-nating, -nated** **1** to be the most important or controlling aspect or part: *the image of brutal repression that has tended to predominate since the protests were crushed* **2** to form the greatest part or be most common: *women predominate in this gathering*
WORD ORIGIN Latin *prae* before + *dominari* to rule

pre-eminent adj outstanding **pre-eminence** n

pre-empt vb to prevent an action by doing something which makes it pointless or impossible: *he pre-empted his expulsion from the party by resigning*

pre-emption n law the purchase of or right to buy property in advance of others
WORD ORIGIN Medieval Latin *praeemere* to buy beforehand

pre-emptive adj mil designed to damage or destroy an enemy's attacking strength before it can be used: *a pre-emptive strike*

preen vb **1** (of birds) to clean or trim (feathers) with the beak **2** to smarten (oneself) carefully **3** **preen oneself** (often foll. by *on*) to be self-satisfied
WORD ORIGIN Middle English *preinen*

pref. **1** preface **2** prefatory **3** preference **4** preferred **5** prefix

prefab n a prefabricated house

prefabricated adj (of a building) made in shaped sections for quick assembly

preface (**pref**-iss) n **1** an introduction to a book, usually explaining its intention or content **2** anything introductory ▷ vb **-facing, -faced 3** to say or do

something before proceeding to the main part **4** to act as a preface to
WORD ORIGIN Latin *praefari* to say in advance

prefatory adj concerning a preface
WORD ORIGIN Latin *praefari* to say in advance

prefect n **1** Brit, Austral, & NZ a senior pupil in a school with limited power over the behaviour of other pupils **2** (in some countries) the chief administrative officer in a department
WORD ORIGIN Latin *praefectus* one put in charge

prefecture n the office or area of authority of a prefect

prefer vb **-ferring, -ferred 1** to like better: *most people prefer television to reading books* **2** law to put (charges) before a court for judgment **3** (often passive) to promote over another or others
WORD ORIGIN Latin *praeferre* to carry in front, prefer

≡ **USAGE**
≡ Normally, *to* is used after *prefer* and ≡ *preferable*, not *than*: *I prefer Brahms to* ≡ *Tchaikovsky; a small income is preferable to* ≡ *no income at all*, but *than* or *rather than* ≡ should be used to link infinitives: ≡ *I prefer to walk than/rather than to catch* ≡ *the train.*

preferable adj more desirable or suitable **preferably** adv

≡ **USAGE**
≡ Since *preferable* already means *more* ≡ *desirable*, you should not say ≡ something is *more preferable* or *most* ≡ *preferable*. See also at **prefer**.

preference n **1** a liking for one thing above the rest **2** a person or thing preferred

preference shares pl n shares issued by a company which give their holders a priority over ordinary shareholders to payment of dividend

preferential adj **1** showing preference: *preferential treatment* **2** indicating a special favourable status in business affairs: *the President is to renew China's preferential trading status* **3** indicating a voting system which allows voters to rank candidates in order of preference: *a multi-option referendum with preferential voting*

preferment n promotion to a higher position

prefigure vb **-guring, -gured 1** to represent or suggest in advance **2** to imagine beforehand

prefix n **1** grammar a letter or group of letters put at the beginning of a word to make a new word, such as *un-* in *unhappy* **2** a title put before a name, such as *Mr* ▷ vb **3** grammar to add (a letter or group of letters) as a prefix to the beginning of a word **4** to put before

pregnant adj **1** carrying a fetus or fetuses within the womb **2** full of meaning or significance: *a pregnant pause* **pregnancy** n
WORD ORIGIN Latin *praegnans*

prehensile adj capable of curling round objects and grasping them: *a prehensile tail*
WORD ORIGIN Latin *prehendere* to grasp

prehistoric adj of man's development before the appearance of the written word **prehistory** n

preindustrial adj of a time before the mechanization of industry

prejudge vb **-judging, -judged** to judge before knowing all the facts

prejudice n **1** an unreasonable or unfair dislike or preference **2** intolerance of or dislike for people because they belong to a specific race, religion, or group: *class prejudice* **3** the act or condition of holding such opinions **4** harm or detriment: *conduct to the prejudice of good order and military discipline* **5** **without prejudice** law without harm to an existing right or claim ▷ vb **-dicing, -diced 6** to cause (someone) to have a prejudice **7** to harm: *the incident prejudiced his campaign*
WORD ORIGIN Latin *prae* before + *judicium* sentence

prejudicial adj harmful; damaging

prelacy n, pl **-cies 1 a** the office or status of a prelate **b** prelates collectively **2** often offensive government of the Church by prelates

prelate (**prel**-it) n a clergyman of high rank, such as a bishop
WORD ORIGIN Church Latin *praelatus*, from Latin *praeferre* to hold in special esteem

preliminaries pl n same as **prelims**

preliminary adj **1** occurring before or in preparation; introductory ▷ n, pl **-naries 2** an action or event occurring before or in preparation for an activity: *the discussions are a preliminary to the main negotiations* **3** a qualifying contest held before a main competition
WORD ORIGIN Latin *prae* before + *limen* threshold

prelims pl n **1** the pages of a book, such as the title page and contents, which come before the main text **2** the first public examinations in some universities
WORD ORIGIN a contraction of *preliminaries*

prelude (**prel**-yewd) n **1 a** an introductory movement in music **b** a short piece of music for piano or organ **2** an event introducing or preceding the main event ▷ vb **-luding, -luded 3** to act as a prelude to (something) **4** to introduce by a prelude
WORD ORIGIN Latin *prae* before + *ludere* to play

premarital adj occurring before marriage: *premarital sex*

premature adj **1** happening or done before the normal or expected time: *premature ageing* **2** impulsive or hasty: *a premature judgment* **3** (of a baby) born weeks before the date when it was due to be born **prematurely** adv
WORD ORIGIN Latin *prae* in advance + *maturus* ripe

premedication n surgery any drugs given to prepare a patient for a general anaesthetic

premeditated adj planned in advance **premeditation** n

premenstrual adj occurring or experienced before a menstrual period

p

premenstrual syndrome *or* **tension** *n* symptoms, such as nervous tension, that may be experienced because of hormonal changes in the days before a menstrual period starts

premier *n* **1** a prime minister **2** a head of government of a Canadian province or Australian state ▷ *adj* **3** first in importance or rank: *Torbay, Devon's premier resort* **4** first in occurrence **premiership** *n*
WORD ORIGIN Latin *primus* first

premiere *n* **1** the first public performance of a film, play, or opera ▷ *vb* **-ering, -ered** **2** to give, or (of a film, play, or opera) be, a premiere: *the play was premiered last year in Johannesburg; the movie premieres tomorrow*
WORD ORIGIN French, feminine of *premier* first

premise *or* **premiss** *n* *logic* a statement that is assumed to be true and is used as a basis for an argument
WORD ORIGIN Medieval Latin *praemissa* sent on before

premises *pl n* **1** a piece of land together with its buildings **2** *law* (in a deed) the matters referred to previously

premium *n* **1** an extra sum of money added to a standard rate, price, or wage: *the superior taste persuades me to pay the premium for bottled water* **2** the (regular) amount paid for an insurance policy **3** the amount above the usual value at which something sells: *some even pay a premium of up to 15% for the privilege* **4** great value or regard: *we do put a very high premium on common sense* **5** **at a premium a** in great demand, usually because of scarcity **b** at a higher price than usual
WORD ORIGIN Latin *praemium* prize

Premium Savings Bonds *pl n* (in Britain) savings certificates issued by the government, on which no interest is paid, but there is a monthly draw for cash prizes. Also called: **premium bonds**

premolar *n* a tooth between the canine and first molar in adult humans

premonition *n* a feeling that something unpleasant is going to happen; foreboding **premonitory** *adj*
WORD ORIGIN Latin *prae* before + *monere* to warn

prenatal *adj* before birth; during pregnancy

preoccupy *vb* **-pies, -pying, -pied** to fill the thoughts or mind of (someone) to the exclusion of other things **preoccupation** *n*
WORD ORIGIN Latin *praeoccupare* to capture in advance

preordained *adj* decreed or determined in advance

preowned *adj euphemistic* already used; second-hand

prep *n Brit informal* short for **preparation** (sense 4)

prep. **1** preparation **2** preparatory **3** preposition

prepacked *adj* (of goods) sold already wrapped

prepaid *adj* paid for in advance

preparation *n* **1** the act of preparing or being prepared **2** (*often pl*) something done in order to prepare for something else: *to make preparations for a wedding* **3** something that is prepared, such as a medicine **4** *Brit, old-fashioned* **a** homework **b** the period reserved for this

preparatory (prip-**par**-a-tree) *adj* **1** preparing for: *a preparatory meeting to organize the negotiations* **2** introductory **3** **preparatory to** before: *Jack cleared his throat preparatory to speaking*

preparatory school *n* **1** *Brit & S African* a private school for children between the ages of 6 and 13, generally preparing pupils for public school **2** (in the US) a private secondary school preparing pupils for college

prepare *vb* **-paring, -pared** **1** to make or get ready: *the army prepared for battle* **2** to put together using parts or ingredients: *he had spent most of the afternoon preparing the meal* **3** to equip or outfit, as for an expedition **4** **be prepared to** to be willing and able to: *I'm not prepared to say*
WORD ORIGIN Latin *prae* before + *parare* to make ready

prepay *vb* **-paying, -paid** to pay for in advance **prepayment** *n*

preponderant *adj* greater in amount, force, or influence **preponderance** *n*

preponderate *vb* **-ating, -ated** to be more powerful, important, or numerous (than): *the good preponderate over the bad*
WORD ORIGIN Late Latin *praeponderare* to be of greater weight

preposition *n* a word used before a noun or pronoun to relate it to the other words, for example in *in* in *he is in the car* **prepositional** *adj*
WORD ORIGIN Latin *praepositio* a putting before

USAGE
The practice of ending a sentence with a preposition (*Venice is a place I should like to go to*) was formerly regarded as incorrect, but is now acceptable and is the preferred form in many contexts.

prepossess *vb* **1** to make a favourable impression in advance **2** to preoccupy or engross mentally **prepossession** *n*

prepossessing *adj* making a favourable impression; attractive

preposterous *adj* utterly absurd
WORD ORIGIN Latin *praeposterus* reversed

prep school *n informal* see **preparatory school**

prepuce (**pree**-pyewss) *n* **1** the retractable fold of skin covering the tip of the penis; foreskin **2** the retractable fold of skin covering the tip of the clitoris
WORD ORIGIN Latin *praeputium*

Pre-Raphaelite (pree-**raff**-a-lite) *n* **1** a member of a group of painters in the nineteenth century who revived the style considered typical of Italian painting before Raphael ▷ *adj* **2** of or in the manner of Pre-Raphaelite painting and painters

prerecord *vb* to record (music or a programme) in advance so that it can be played or broadcast later **prerecorded** *adj*

prerequisite *n* **1** something that is required before something else is possible ▷ *adj* **2** required before something else is possible

prerogative *n* a special privilege or right
WORD ORIGIN Latin *praerogativa* privilege

pres. **1** present (time) **2** presidential
Pres. President

presage (**press**-ij) *vb* **-aging, -aged** **1** to be a warning or sign of something about to happen: *the windless air presaged disaster* ▷ *n* **2** an omen **3** a misgiving
WORD ORIGIN Latin *praesagire* to perceive beforehand

presbyopia *n med* a gradual inability of the eye to focus on nearby objects
WORD ORIGIN Greek *presbus* old man + *ōps* eye

presbyter *n* **1** (in some episcopal Churches) an official with administrative and priestly duties **2** (in the Presbyterian Church) an elder **presbyterial** *adj*
WORD ORIGIN Greek *presbuteros* an older man

presbyterian *adj* **1** of or designating Church government by lay elders ▷ *n* **2** someone who supports this type of Church government **presbyterianism** *n*

Presbyterian *adj* **1** of any of the Protestant Churches governed by lay elders ▷ *n* **2** a member of a Presbyterian Church **Presbyterianism** *n*

presbytery *n, pl* **-teries** **1** *Presbyterian Church* a local Church court **2** *RC Church* the residence of a parish priest **3** elders collectively **4** the part of a church east of the choir; a sanctuary
WORD ORIGIN see PRESBYTER

preschool *adj* of or for children below the age of five: *a preschool playgroup*

prescience (**press**-ee-enss) *n formal* knowledge of events before they happen **prescient** *adj*
WORD ORIGIN Latin *praescire* to know beforehand

prescribe *vb* **-scribing, -scribed** **1** *med* to recommend the use of (a medicine or other remedy) **2** to lay down as a rule
WORD ORIGIN Latin *praescribere* to write previously

prescript *n* something laid down or prescribed

prescription *n* **1 a** written instructions from a doctor for the preparation and use of a medicine **b** the medicine prescribed **2** written instructions from an optician specifying the lenses needed to correct bad eyesight **3** a prescribing
WORD ORIGIN Legal Latin *praescriptio* an order

prescriptive *adj* **1** laying down rules **2** based on tradition

presence *n* **1** the fact of being in a specified place: *the test detects the presence of sugar in the urine* **2** impressive personal appearance or bearing: *a person of dignified and commanding presence* **3** the company or nearness of a person: *she seemed completely unaware of my presence* **4** *mil* a force stationed in another country: *the American-led military presence in the Gulf*

Canadian English Pronunciation

It is Canadians' fate to sometimes be mistaken by the British for Americans, and by Americans for Scots.

The first confusion arises because the urban middle-class Canadian sounds much like, say, an American television newscast anchor on a national network. Except in St. John's, Newfoundland, that accent is amazingly consistent in larger Canadian cities coast to coast from Halifax to Vancouver. The consistency is surprising, though job mobility and urbanization will both tend to blend the accents of newcomers. Definitely unsurprising is a resemblance to general American speech, since the original North American settlers had similar origins in the British Isles, and a majority of Canadians live within 300 kilometres of the US border.

A second, lesser, confusion arises from the tendency of some American ears to hear the Canadian pronunciation of, for example, *about* as *aboot* or *aboat*. This involves how people pronounce diphthongs, the combination of two vowels in a single syllable in which a vowel begins as one sound and moves toward becoming another. *Canadian raising*, a term coined by the linguist JK Chambers, relates to the phenomenon by which the tongue is raised to produce the diphthong in a word like *knife* but remains low in *knives*. Similarly, it is raised for the vowel sound in *clout* but low in *cloud*. Such raised vowels are unusual in most of the United States.

Some commentators have attributed the prevailing Canadian accent historically to the influence of Scottish immigrants and of the United Empire Loyalists who fled north to Eastern Canada following the American Revolution. Canadians generally pronounce *caller* with the same vowel sound as *collar*, that is, pronounce the *a* and *o* as in *pot* and *car*, whereas most US accents have different vowel sounds in these two words, and in many others, such as *cot* and *caught*, or *knotty* and *naughty*.

Especially in informal speech, Canadians typically employ the phonetic feature that linguists charmingly call *T-flapping*, by which the *t* is pronounced *d* between vowels and after *r*, so that *metal* sounds like *medal*, and *butter* sounds like *budder*. They also tend to omit the *h* sound in *which*, giving the word the identical pronunciation as *witch*. Unlike most Americans, they pronounce the *e* long in *lever*.

But any generalization must confront the fact that not everyone lives in cities and dialectal pockets exist, conspicuously throughout Newfoundland, but also in places like Lunenburg and Cape Breton in Nova Scotia, and the Ottawa Valley in Ontario with its characteristic twang. A rural Nova Scotian, for example, may say *worsh* for *wash*, and shorten the *oo* sound in *food*. As well, an English-speaking Quebecker may inject French words into everyday discourse, and in doing so approximate French pronunciations. In general, the longer the history of a place, the more likely the accent of its people will be distinct from those whose forbears arrived more recently.

Aboriginals who migrate to cities, and the immigrants who come from all parts of the world, naturally speak differently from the majority of urban dwellers, at least in the first generation. The variety of foreign accents, from Chinese to Pakistani to Somali, is in fact one of the delights of living in a big city. The effects of official multiculturalism, which encourages immigrants to retain their first language, has an effect. As well, the varied forms of ESL (English as a Second Language) instruction influences how English will be spoken. Notwithstanding, the children of immigrants normally grow up sounding like their playmates and classmates. In any event, local, rural, class-related, or ethnically-based accents will continue to exist: one proof is that, after long North American residence, some Jews still speak with a vocabulary and syntax that hearken back to Yiddish.

Some Canadians deplore the resemblance of their English to standard American speech, regarding the latter as part of a general cultural bombardment from the United States and a threat to their national identity. But it's a happy fact that accents flow back and forth across borders, and it would be as logical for residents of upper New York state or Denver, Colorado to deplore the rampant Canadianization of their speech.

5 an invisible spirit felt to be nearby: *I felt a presence in the room* **WORD ORIGIN** Latin *praesentia* a being before

presence of mind *n* the ability to stay calm and act sensibly in a crisis

present¹ *adj* **1** being in a specified place: *he had been present at the birth of his son* **2** existing or happening now **3** current: *the present exchange rate* **4** *grammar* of a verb tense used when the action described is happening now ▷ *n* **5** *grammar* the present tense **6 at present** now **7 for the present** for now; temporarily **8 the present** the time being; now ▸ See also **presents** **WORD ORIGIN** Latin *praesens*

present² *n* (prez-int) **1** a gift ▷ *vb* (pri-**zent**) **2** to introduce (a person) formally to another **3** to introduce to the public: *the Museum of Modern Art is presenting a retrospective of his work* **4** to introduce and compere (a radio or television show) **5** to show or exhibit: *they took advantage of every tax dodge that presented itself* **6** to bring about: *the case presented a large number of legal difficulties* **7** to put forward or submit: *they presented a petition to the Prime Minister* **8** to give or offer formally: *he was presented with a watch to celebrate his twenty-five years with the company* **9** to hand over for action or payment: *to present a bill* **10** to portray in a particular way: *her lawyer presented her as a naive woman who had got into bad company* **11** to aim (a weapon) **12 present arms** to salute with one's weapon **WORD ORIGIN** Latin *praesentare* to exhibit

presentable *adj* **1** fit to be seen by or introduced to other people **2** acceptable: *the team reached a presentable total* **presentability** *n*

presentation *n* **1** the act of presenting or being presented **2** the manner of presenting **3** a talk or lecture; the manner of presenting **4** a formal ceremony in which an award is made **5** a public performance, such as a play or a ballet

present-day *adj* of the modern day; current: *even by present-day standards these were large aircraft*

presenter *n* a person who introduces a radio or television show and links the items in it

presentiment (priz-**zen**-tim-ent) *n* a sense that something unpleasant is about to happen; premonition **WORD ORIGIN** obsolete French *pressentir* to sense beforehand

presently *adv* **1** soon: *you will understand presently* **2** chiefly *Scot, US, & Canad* at the moment: *these methods are presently being developed*

present participle *n grammar* a form of verb, ending in *-ing*, which is used to describe action that is happening at the same time as that of the main verb

present perfect *adj, n grammar* same as **perfect** (senses 7, 8)

presents *pl n law* used in a deed or document to refer to itself: *know all men by these presents*

preservative *n* **1** a chemical added to foods to prevent decay ▷ *adj* **2** preventing decay

preserve *vb* **-serving, -served 1** to keep safe from change or extinction; protect: *we are interested in preserving world peace* **2** to protect from decay or damage: *the carefully preserved village of Cregneish* **3** to treat (food) in order to prevent it from decaying **4** to maintain; keep up: *the 1.2% increase in earnings needed to preserve living standards* ▷ *n* **5** an area of interest restricted to a particular person or group: *working-class preserves such as pigeon racing* **6** (*usually pl*) fruit preserved by cooking in sugar **7** an area where game is kept for private hunting or fishing **preservation** *n* **WORD ORIGIN** Latin *prae* before + *servare* to keep safe

preset *vb* **-setting, -set 1** to set the timer on a piece of equipment so that it starts to work at a specific time ▷ *adj* **2** (of equipment) with the controls set in advance

preshrunk *adj* (of fabric or a garment) having been shrunk during manufacture so that further shrinkage will not occur when washed

preside *vb* **-siding, -sided 1** to chair a meeting **2** to exercise authority: *he presided over the burning of the books* **WORD ORIGIN** Latin *praesidere* to superintend

presidency *n, pl* **-cies** the office or term of a president

president *n* **1** the head of state of a republic, esp. of the US **2** the head of a company, society, or institution **3** a person who presides over a meeting **4** the head of certain establishments of higher education **presidential** *adj* **WORD ORIGIN** Late Latin *praesidens* ruler

presidium *n* (in Communist countries) a permanent administrative committee **WORD ORIGIN** Russian *prezidium*

press¹ *vb* **1** to apply weight or force to: *he pressed the button on the camera* **2** to squeeze: *she pressed his hand* **3** to compress to alter in shape **4** to smooth out creases by applying pressure or heat **5** to make (objects) from soft material by pressing with a mould **6** to crush to force out (juice) **7** to urge (someone) insistently: *they pressed for an answer* **8** to force or compel: *I was pressed into playing rugby at school* **9** to plead or put forward strongly: *they intend to press their claim for damages in the courts* **10** to be urgent: *time presses* **11** (sometimes foll. by *on* or *forward*) to continue in a determined way: *they pressed on with their journey* **12** to crowd; push: *shoppers press along the pavements* **13 pressed for** short of: *pressed for time* ▷ *n* **14** any machine that exerts pressure to form or cut materials or to extract liquids or compress solids **15** see **printing press 16** the art or process of printing **17** the opinions and reviews in the newspapers: *the government is not receiving a good press at the moment* **18** the act of pressing or state of being pressed: *at the press of a button* **19** a crowd: *a press of people at the exit* **20** a cupboard for storing clothes or linen **21 go to press** to go to be printed: *when is this book going to press?* **22 the press a** news media collectively, esp. newspapers **b** journalists collectively **WORD ORIGIN** Old French *presser*

press² *vb* **1** to recruit (men) forcibly for military service **2** to use for a purpose other than intended: *press into service* **WORD ORIGIN** from *prest* to recruit soldiers

press agent *n* a person employed to obtain favourable publicity for an individual or organization

press box *n* a room at a sports ground reserved for reporters

press conference *n* an interview for reporters given by a famous person

press gallery *n* an area for newspaper reporters, esp. in a parliament

press gang *n* **1** (formerly) a group of men used to capture men and boys and force them to join the navy ▷ *vb* **press-gang 2** to force (a person) to join the navy by a press gang **3** to persuade (someone) to do something that he or she does not want to do: *he was press-ganged into joining the family business*

pressing *adj* **1** demanding immediate attention ▷ *n* **2** a large number of gramophone records produced at one time

press stud *n Brit* a fastener in which one part with a projecting knob snaps into a hole on another part

press-up *n* an exercise in which the body is raised from and lowered to the floor by straightening and bending the arms

pressure *n* **1** the state of pressing or being pressed **2** the application of force by one body on the surface of another **3** urgent claims or demands: *to work under pressure* **4** a condition that is hard to bear: *the pressure of grief* **5** *physics* the force applied to a unit area of a surface **6 bring pressure to bear on** to use influence or authority to persuade ▷ *vb* **-suring, -sured 7** to persuade forcefully: *he was pressured into resignation* **WORD ORIGIN** Late Latin *pressura* a pressing, from Latin *premere* to press

pressure cooker *n* an airtight pot which cooks food quickly by steam under pressure **pressure-cook** *vb*

pressure group *n* a group that tries to influence policies or public opinion

pressurize *or* **-rise** *vb* **-rizing, -rized** *or* **-rising, -rised 1** to increase the pressure in (an aircraft cabin, etc.) in order to maintain approximately atmospheric pressure when the external pressure is low **2** to make insistent demands of (someone): *do not be pressurized into making a decision* **pressurization** *or* **-risation** *n*

prestidigitation *n formal* same as **sleight of hand** > **prestidigitator** *n* **WORD ORIGIN** French

prestige *n* **1** high status or respect resulting from success or achievements: *a symbol of French power and prestige* **2** the power to impress: *a humdrum family car with no prestige* **prestigious** *adj* **WORD ORIGIN** Latin *praestigiae* tricks

presto *music adv* **1** very fast ▷ *n, pl* **-tos 2** a passage to be played very quickly **WORD ORIGIN** Italian

presumably *adv* one supposes or guesses; probably: *he emerged from what was presumably the kitchen carrying a tray*

presume *vb* **-suming, -sumed 1** to take (something) for granted: *I presume he's dead* **2** to dare (to): *I would not presume to lecture you on medical matters, Dr Jacobs* **3** (foll. by *on* or *upon*) to rely or depend: *don't presume on his agreement* **4** (foll. by *on* or *upon*) to take advantage (of): *I'm afraid I presumed on Aunt Ginny's generosity* **presumedly** *adv* **presuming** *adj*
WORD ORIGIN Latin *praesumere* to take in advance

presumption *n* **1** the act of presuming **2** a basis on which an assumption is made **3** bold insolent behaviour **4** a belief or assumption based on reasonable evidence **presumptive** *adj*

presumptuous *adj* bold and insolent

presuppose *vb* **-posing, -posed 1** to require as a previous condition in order to be true: *the idea of integration presupposes a disintegrated state* **2** to take for granted **presupposition** *n*

preteen *n* a boy or girl approaching his or her teens

pretence *or US* **pretense** *n* **1** an action or claim that could mislead people into believing something which is not true: *Daniel made a pretence of carefully reading it; the pretence that many of the unemployed are on 'training schemes'* **2** a false display; affectation: *she abandoned all pretence of work and watched me* **3** a claim, esp. a false one, to a right, title, or distinction **4** make-believe **5** a pretext: *they were placed in a ghetto on the pretence that they would be safe there*

pretend *vb* **1** to claim or give the appearance of (something untrue): *he pretended to be asleep* **2** to make believe: *one of the actresses pretended to urinate into a bucket* **3** (foll. by *to*) to present a claim, esp. a doubtful one: *to pretend to the throne*
WORD ORIGIN Latin *praetendere* to stretch forth, feign

pretender *n* a person who makes a false or disputed claim to a throne or title

pretension *n* **1** (*often pl*) a false claim to merit or importance **2** the quality of being pretentious

pretentious *adj* **1** making (unjustified) claims to special merit or importance: *many critics thought her work and ideas pretentious and empty* **2** vulgarly showy; ostentatious: *a family restaurant with no pretentious furnishing*

preterite *or esp. US* **preterit** (**pret**-er-it) *grammar n* **1** a past tense of verbs, such as *jumped, swam* **2** a verb in this tense ▷ *adj* **3** expressing such a past tense
WORD ORIGIN Late Latin *praeteritum* (*tempus*) past (time)

preternatural *adj* beyond what is natural; supernatural
WORD ORIGIN Latin *praeter naturam* beyond the scope of nature

pretext *n* a false reason given to hide the real one: *delivering the book had been a good pretext for seeing her again*
WORD ORIGIN Latin *praetextum* disguise, from *praetexere* to weave in front

prettify *vb* **-fies, -fying, -fied** to make pretty

pretty *adj* **-tier, -tiest 1** attractive in a delicate or graceful way **2** pleasant to look at **3** *informal, often ironic* excellent or fine: *well, this is a pretty state of affairs to have*

got into ▷ *adv* **4** *informal* fairly: *I think he and Nicholas got on pretty well* **5** **sitting pretty** *informal* in a favourable state **prettily** *adv* **prettiness** *n*
WORD ORIGIN Old English *prættig* clever

pretty-pretty *adj informal* excessively pretty

pretzel *n* a brittle salted biscuit in the shape of a knot
WORD ORIGIN from German

prevail *vb* **1** (often foll. by *over* or *against*) to prove superior; gain mastery: *moderate nationalists have until now prevailed over the radicals* **2** to be the most important feature: *a casual good-natured mood prevailed* **3** to be generally established: *this attitude has prevailed for many years* **4** **prevail on** or **upon** to succeed in persuading: *he had easily been prevailed upon to accept a lift*
WORD ORIGIN Latin *praevalere* to be superior in strength

prevailing *adj* **1** widespread: *the prevailing mood* **2** most usual: *the prevailing wind is from the west*

prevalent *adj* widespread or common **prevalence** *n*

prevaricate *vb* **-cating, -cated** to avoid giving a direct or truthful answer **prevarication** *n* **prevaricator** *n*
WORD ORIGIN Latin *praevaricari* to walk crookedly

prevent *vb* **1** to keep from happening: *vitamin C prevented scurvy* **2** (often foll. by *from*) to keep (someone from doing something): *circumstances prevented her from coming* **preventable** *adj* **prevention** *n*
WORD ORIGIN Latin *praevenire*

preventive *adj* **1** intended to prevent or hinder **2** *med* tending to prevent disease ▷ *n* **3** something that serves to prevent **4** *med* any drug or agent that tends to prevent disease. Also: **preventative**

preview *n* **1** an opportunity to see a film, exhibition, or play before it is shown to the public ▷ *vb* **2** to view in advance

previous *adj* **1** coming or happening before **2** *informal* happening too soon; premature: *such criticism is a bit previous because no definite decision has yet been taken* **3** **previous to** before **previously** *adv*
WORD ORIGIN Latin *praevius* leading the way

prewar *adj* relating to the period before a war, esp. before World War I or II

prey *n* **1** an animal hunted and killed for food by another animal **2** the victim of a hostile person, influence, emotion, or illness: *children are falling prey to the disease* **3** **bird** *or* **beast of prey** a bird *or* animal that kills and eats other birds or animals ▷ *vb* (often foll. by *on* or *upon*) **4** to hunt and kill for food **5** to worry or obsess: *it preyed on his conscience* **6** to make a victim (of others), by profiting at their expense
WORD ORIGIN Old French *preie*

price *n* **1** the amount of money for which a thing is bought or sold **2** the cost at which something is obtained: *the price of making the wrong decision* **3** **at any price** whatever the price or cost **4** **at a price** at a high price **5** *gambling* odds **6** **what price (something)?** what are the chances of (something) happening

now? ▷ *vb* **pricing, priced 7** to fix the price of **8** to discover the price of
WORD ORIGIN Latin *pretium*

price-fixing *n* the setting of prices by agreement among producers and distributors

priceless *adj* **1** extremely valuable **2** *informal* extremely amusing

pricey *adj* **pricier, priciest** *informal* expensive

prick *vb* **1** to pierce lightly with a sharp point **2** to cause a piercing sensation (in): *a needle pricked her finger* **3** to cause a sharp emotional pain (in): *the film pricked our consciences about the plight of the Afghan refugees* **4** **prick up one's ears a** (of a dog) to make the ears stand erect **b** (of a person) to listen attentively ▷ *n* **5** a sudden sharp pain caused by pricking **6** a mark made by a sharp point **7** a sharp emotional pain: *a prick of conscience* **8** *slang taboo* a penis **9** *slang offensive* a man who provokes contempt
WORD ORIGIN Old English *prica* point, puncture

prickle *n* **1** *bot* a thorn or spike on a plant **2** a pricking or stinging sensation ▷ *vb* **-ling, -led 3** to feel a stinging sensation
WORD ORIGIN Old English *pricel*

prickly *adj* **-lier, -liest 1** having prickles **2** tingling or stinging: *he had a prickly feeling down his back* **3** touchy or irritable: *Canadians are notoriously prickly about being taken for Americans*

prickly heat *n* an itchy rash that occurs in very hot moist weather

prickly pear *n* **1** a tropical cactus with edible oval fruit **2** the fruit of this plant

pride *n* **1** satisfaction in one's own or another's success or achievements: *his obvious pride in his son's achievements* **2** an excessively high opinion of oneself **3** a sense of dignity and self-respect: *he must swallow his pride and ally himself with his political enemies* **4** one of the better or most admirable parts of something: *the pride of the main courses is the Japanese fish and vegetable tempura* **5** a group of lions **6** **pride and joy** the main source of pride: *the car was his pride and joy* **7** **pride of place** the most important position ▷ *vb* **priding, prided 8** (foll. by *on* or *upon*) to take pride in (oneself) for
WORD ORIGIN Old English *prȳde*

prie-dieu (pree-**dyuh**) *n* an upright frame with a ledge for kneeling upon, for use when praying
WORD ORIGIN French *prier* to pray + *Dieu* God

priest *n* **1** (in the Christian Church) a person ordained to administer the sacraments and preach **2** a minister of any religion **3** an official who performs religious ceremonies **priestess** *fem n* **priesthood** *n* **priestly** *adj*
WORD ORIGIN Old English *prēost*, apparently from *presbyter*

prig *n* a person who is smugly self-righteous and narrow-minded **priggish** *adj* **priggishness** *n*
WORD ORIGIN origin unknown

prim *adj* **primmer, primmest** affectedly proper, or formal, and rather prudish **primly** *adv*
WORD ORIGIN origin unknown

prima ballerina *n* a leading female ballet dancer

WORD ORIGIN Italian: first ballerina

primacy *n, pl* **-cies 1** the state of being first in rank, grade, or order **2** *Christianity* the office of an archbishop

prima donna *n, pl* **prima donnas 1** a leading female opera singer **2** *informal* a temperamental person

WORD ORIGIN Italian: first lady

primaeval *adj* same as **primeval**

prima facie (**prime**-a fay-shee) *adv* as it seems at first

WORD ORIGIN Latin

primal *adj* **1** of basic causes or origins **2** chief or most important

WORD ORIGIN Latin *primus* first

primarily *adv* **1** chiefly or mainly **2** originally

primary *adj* **1** first in importance **2** first in position or time, as in a series: *he argued that the country was only in the primary stage of socialism* **3** fundamental or basic: *the new policy will put the emphasis on primary health care rather than hospital care* **4** being the first stage; elementary: *all new recruits participated in the same primary training courses* **5** relating to the education of children up to the age of 11 or 12 **6** (of an industry) involving the obtaining of raw materials **7** (of the flight feathers of a bird's wing) outer and longest **8** being the part of an electric circuit in which a changing current causes a current in a neighbouring circuit: *a primary coil* ▷ *n, pl* **-ries 9** a person or thing that is first in position, time, or importance **10** (in the US) an election in which the voters of a state choose a candidate for office. Full name: **primary election 11** a primary school **12** a primary colour **13** any of the outer and longest flight feathers of a bird's wing **14** a primary part of an electric circuit

WORD ORIGIN Latin *primarius* principal

primary accent *or* **stress** *n linguistics* the strongest accent in a word

primary colours *pl n* **1** *physics* the colours red, green, and blue from which all other colours can be obtained by mixing **2** *art* the colours red, yellow, and blue from which all other colours can be obtained by mixing

primary school *n* **1** (in England and Wales) a school for children between the ages of 5 and 11 **2** (in Scotland, Australia and New Zealand) a school for children between the ages of 5 and 12 **3** (in the US and Canada) a school equivalent to the first three or four grades of elementary school

primate¹ *n* a mammal with flexible hands and feet and a highly developed brain, such as a monkey, an ape, or a human being

primate² *n* an archbishop

WORD ORIGIN Latin *primas* principal

prime *adj* **1** first in importance: *the prime aim* **2** of the highest quality: *prime beef* **3** typical: *a prime example* ▷ *n* **4** the time when a thing is at its best **5** a period of power, vigour, and activity: *he was in the prime of life* **6** *maths* short for **prime number** ▷ *vb* **priming, primed 7** to give (someone) information in advance to

prepare him or her **8** to prepare (a surface) for painting **9** to prepare (a gun or mine) before detonating or firing **10** to fill (a pump) with its working fluid, to expel air from it before starting **11** to prepare (something)

WORD ORIGIN Latin *primus* first

prime meridian *n* the 0° meridian from which the other meridians are worked out, usually taken to pass through Greenwich

Prime Minister *n* the leader of a government

prime mover *n* a person or thing which was important in helping create an idea, situation, etc.: *he was the prime mover behind the coup*

prime number *n* an integer that cannot be divided into other integers but is only divisible by itself or 1, such as 2, 3, 5, 7, and 11

primer¹ *n* **1** a substance applied to a surface as a base coat or sealer **2** a device for detonating the main charge in a gun or mine

WORD ORIGIN see PRIME (verb)

primer² *n* an introductory text, such as a school textbook

WORD ORIGIN Medieval Latin *primarius (liber)* a first (book)

prime stock *n* NZ livestock in peak condition and ready for killing

primeval (prime-ee-val) *adj* of the earliest age of the world

WORD ORIGIN Latin *primus* first + *aevum* age

primitive *adj* **1** of or belonging to the beginning **2** *biol* of an early stage in development: *primitive amphibians* **3** characteristic of an early simple state, esp. in being crude or basic: *a primitive dwelling* ▷ *n* **4** a primitive person or thing **5** a painter of any era whose work appears childlike or untrained **6** a work by such an artist

WORD ORIGIN Latin *primitivus* earliest of its kind

primogeniture *n* **1** *formal* the state of being the first-born child **2** *law* the right of an eldest son to inherit all the property of his parents

WORD ORIGIN Medieval Latin *primogenitura* birth of a first child

primordial *adj formal* existing at or from the beginning

WORD ORIGIN Late Latin *primordialis* original

primp *vb* to tidy (one's hair or clothes) fussily

WORD ORIGIN probably from *prim*

primrose *n* **1** a wild plant which has pale yellow flowers in spring ▷ *adj* **2** Also: **primrose yellow** pale yellow **3** of primroses

WORD ORIGIN Medieval Latin *prima rosa* first rose

primrose path *n* (often preceded by *the*) a pleasurable way of life

primula *n* a type of primrose with brightly coloured funnel-shaped flowers

WORD ORIGIN Medieval Latin *primula (veris)* little first one (of the spring)

Primus *n trademark* a portable paraffin cooking stove, used esp. by campers

prince *n* **1** a male member of a royal family, esp. the son of the king or queen **2** the male ruler of a small country **3** an outstanding member of a specified group: *Dryden, that prince of poets*

WORD ORIGIN Latin *princeps* first man, ruler

prince consort *n* the husband of a queen, who is himself a prince

princely *adj* **-lier, -liest 1** of or characteristic of a prince **2** generous or lavish

Prince of Wales *n* the eldest son of the British sovereign

princess *n* **1** a female member of a royal family, esp. the daughter of the king or queen **2** the wife of a prince

Princess Royal *n* a title sometimes given to the eldest daughter of the British sovereign

principal *adj* **1** first in importance, rank, or value: *salt is the principal source of sodium in our diets; the Republic's two principal parties* ▷ *n* **2** the head of a school or other educational institution **3** a person who holds one of the most important positions in an organization: *she became a principal in the home finance department* **4** the leading actor in a play **5** *law* **a** a person who engages another to act as his or her agent **b** a person who takes an active part in a crime **c** the person held responsible for fulfilling an obligation **6** *finance* **a** capital or property, as contrasted with income **b** the original amount of a debt on which interest is calculated **principally** *adv*

WORD ORIGIN Latin *principalis* chief

≡ **USAGE**
≡ See at **principle**.

principal boy *n* Brit the leading male role in a pantomime, traditionally played by a woman

principality *n, pl* **-ties** a territory ruled by a prince

principal parts *pl n grammar* the main verb forms, from which all other verb forms may be deduced

principle *n* **1** a moral rule guiding personal conduct: *he'd stoop to anything – he has no principles* **2** a set of such moral rules: *a man of principle* **3** a basic or general truth: *the principle of freedom of expression* **4** a basic law or rule underlying a particular theory or philosophy: *the government has been deceitful and has violated basic principles of democracy* **5** a general law in science: *the principle of the conservation of mass* **6** *chem* a constituent of a substance that determines its characteristics **7** in principle in theory though not always in practice **8** on principle because of one's beliefs

WORD ORIGIN Latin *principium* beginning, basic tenet

≡ **USAGE**
≡ *Principle* and *principal* are often
≡ confused: *the principal (not principle)*
≡ *reason for his departure; the plan was*
≡ *approved in principle (not in principal)*.

principled *adj* (of a person or action) guided by moral rules: *principled opposition to the war*

prink *vb* **1** to dress (oneself) finely **2** to preen oneself

Graham Greene

Born into an educated, well-connected family, a headmaster's son, an Oxford graduate, Graham Greene excelled at practically every genre except verse: novels and short stories of course, but also autobiography and biography, the essay, the book review, travel writing, the play, and the screenplay. A sense of indignation or comedy in his journalism at least twice led him to be the losing defendant in libel suits. Like his friend Evelyn Waugh a Roman Catholic convert, he was the most contrarian of Catholics. A sometime spy agency employee or informant, he was allergic to American foreign policy, indeed to most things American. He sympathized with dictators and traitors, though the sympathy served a complex moral vision. Although the French may have pronounced his name 'Grim Grin', he was inordinately fond of hoaxes, impersonations, and practical jokes. A philanderer, the most unfaithful of spouses, he never ceased mulling over questions of fidelity and betrayal. Mexico, Cuba, Haiti, Argentina, West Africa, and Vietnam were points of his traveller's compass; toward the end of his life he lived for long periods in France and Switzerland. He was one of those English writers who could not stay put.

The country called *Greeneland* is a seedy, sometimes exotic, territory in which a troubled protagonist reacts to equivocal people and inexorable circumstances, posing conflicting questions to himself about human and divine justice. Intrinsic to Greene's fiction is an atmosphere that he made his own, at one with a clear, swift, uncluttered style. Take the opening sentence of his essay, 'George Moore and Others', which might almost describe a typical Greene setting: 'A sunk railway track and gin distillery flank the gritty street.' Dialogue is given with a dramatist's economy; action seen through a cinematographer's eye. The scene is instantly set, as in the opening to *Brighton Rock:* 'Hale knew, before he had been in Brighton three hours, that they meant to murder him.' It was no accident that many of his novels were filmed, and that he wrote the screenplay for the classic film *The Third Man.* Melodrama he regarded as one of his tools.

Greene was intensely self-aware, not least of his shifty persona. Introducing his novel *The Comedians*, he says, 'Many readers assume – I know it from experience – that an "I" is always the author. So in my time I have been considered the murderer of a friend, the jealous lover of a civil-servant's wife, and an obsessive player at roulette.'

A compulsive balancer of Manichaean dualities, an expert timer of the moment when peaceful dreams become waking nightmares, he is an anatomist of good intentions gone astray and of redemptive suicides. He once told an interviewer, "... redemption is not the exact word. We must be careful of our language. They have all understood in the end. This is perhaps the religious sense." In *The End of the Affair*, a man wages war with God over possession of a woman's body and soul, at one point addressing Him: '... she wasn't deceiving me with You when she lay here with me, on this bed, with this pillow under her back. When she slept, I was with her, not You. It was I who penetrated her, not You.'

With an almost Freudian conviction, he held that childhood rehearses adulthood. He was a master of tragic regrets: the alcoholic priest in *The Power and the Glory* 'felt like someone who had missed happiness by seconds at an appointed place'. In his prologue to *Collected Essays*, he quotes the poet Æ: 'In the lost boyhood of Judas / Christ was betrayed.' But the sombre beginning yields at the end of this volume to essayistic hilarity, as when he writes about Beatrix Potter as if she were Shakespeare: '...in 1904, with the publication of *Two Bad Mice*, Miss Potter opened the series of her great comedies.' Or, in 'Great Dog of Weimar', he writes, 'I have always suspected dogs: solid, well-meaning, reliable, they seem to possess all the least attractive human virtues.'

In his best novels, the tormented or quixotic events of his characters' lives are informed by a divine reality. Greene had a unique gift for concretizing metaphysical abstractions and emotions. Although other writers might have used an expression like 'Hope flickered like a candle', for Greene a candle flickered like hope.

WORD ORIGIN probably changed from *prank* to adorn

print *vb* **1** to reproduce (a newspaper, book, etc.) in large quantities by mechanical or electronic means **2** to reproduce (text or pictures) by applying ink to paper **3** to write in letters that are not joined up **4** to stamp (fabric) with a design **5** to produce (a photograph) from a negative **6** to fix in the mind or memory ▷ *n* **7** printed content, such as newsprint **8** a printed publication, such as a book **9** a picture printed from an engraved plate or wood block **10** printed text, with regard to the typeface: *italic print* **11** a photograph produced from a negative **12** a fabric with a printed design **13** a mark made by pressing something onto a surface **14** see **fingerprint 15 in print a** in printed or published form **b** (of a book) available from a publisher **16 out of print** no longer available from a publisher ▸ See also **print out**
WORD ORIGIN Old French *preindre* to make an impression

printed circuit *n* an electronic circuit in which the wiring is a metallic coating printed on a thin insulating board

printer *n* **1** a person or business engaged in printing **2** a machine that prints **3** *computers* a machine that prints out results on paper

printing *n* **1** the process of producing printed matter **2** printed text **3** all the copies of a book printed at one time **4** a form of writing in which the letters are not joined together

printing press *n* a machine used for printing

print out *vb* **1** *computers* to produce (printed information) ▷ *n* **print-out, printout 2** printed information from a computer

prior¹ *adj* **1** previous: *prior knowledge* **2 prior to** before
WORD ORIGIN Latin: previous

prior² *n* **1** the head monk in a priory **2** the abbot's deputy in a monastery **prioress** *fem n*
WORD ORIGIN Late Latin: head

priority *n, pl* **-ties 1** the most important thing that must be dealt with first **2** the right to be or go before others

priory *n, pl* **-ories** a religious house where certain orders of monks or nuns live

prise *or* **prize** *vb* **prising, prised** *or* **prizing, prized** to force open or out by levering
WORD ORIGIN Old French *prise* a taking

prism *n* **1** a transparent block, often with triangular ends and rectangular sides, used to disperse light into a spectrum or refract it in optical instruments **2** *maths* a polyhedron with parallel bases and sides that are parallelograms
WORD ORIGIN Greek *prisma* something shaped by sawing

prismatic *adj* **1** of or shaped like a prism **2** exhibiting bright spectral colours; rainbow-like: *prismatic light*

prison *n* **1** a public building used to hold convicted criminals and accused people

awaiting trial **2** any place of confinement
WORD ORIGIN Old French *prisun*, from Latin *prensio* a capturing

prisoner *n* **1** a person kept in prison as a punishment for a crime, or while awaiting trial **2** a person confined by any restraints: *he's a prisoner of his own past* **3 take (someone) prisoner** to capture and hold (someone) as a prisoner

prisoner of war *n* a serviceman captured by an enemy in wartime

prissy *adj* **-sier, -siest** prim and prudish **prissily** *adv*
WORD ORIGIN probably from *prim* + *sissy*

pristine *adj* **1** completely new, clean, and pure: *pristine white plates* **2** of or involving the original, unchanged, and unspoilt period or state: *the viewing of wild game in its pristine natural state*
WORD ORIGIN Latin *pristinus* primitive

privacy *n* **1** the condition of being private **2** secrecy

private *adj* **1** not for general or public use: *a private bathroom* **2** confidential or secret: *a private conversation* **3** involving someone's domestic and personal life rather than his or her work or business: *what I do in my private life is none of your business* **4** owned or paid for by individuals rather than by the government: *private enterprise* **5** not publicly known: *they had private reasons for the decision* **6** having no public office, rank, or position: *the Red Cross received donations from private citizens* **7** (of a place) quiet and secluded: *the garden is completely private* **8** (of a person) quiet and retiring: *she was private – her life was her own* ▷ *n* **9** a soldier of the lowest rank in the army **10 in private** in secret **privately** *adv*
WORD ORIGIN Latin *privatus* belonging to one individual, withdrawn from public life

private bill *n* a bill presented to Parliament on behalf of a private individual or corporation

private company *n* a limited company that does not issue shares for public subscription

private detective *n* a person hired by a client to do detective work

privateer *n* **1** a privately owned armed vessel authorized by the government to take part in a war **2** a captain of such a ship

private eye *n informal* a private detective

private income *n* income from sources other than employment, such as investment

private member *n* a Member of Parliament who is not a government minister

private member's bill *n* a law proposed by a Member of Parliament who is not a government minister

private parts *or* **privates** *pl n euphemistic* the genitals

private school *n* a school controlled by a private body, accepting mostly fee-paying pupils

private sector *n* the part of a country's economy that consists of privately owned enterprises

privation *n formal* loss or lack of the necessities of life
WORD ORIGIN Latin *privatio* deprivation

privative (priv-a-tiv) *adj* **1** causing privation **2** *grammar* expressing lack or absence, for example *-less* and *un-*

privatize *or* **-tise** *vb* **-tizing, -tized** *or* **-tising, -tised** to sell (a state-owned company) to individuals or a private company **privatization** *or* **-tisation** *n*

privet *n* a bushy evergreen shrub used for hedges
WORD ORIGIN origin unknown

privilege *n* **1** a benefit or advantage granted only to certain people: *a privilege of rank* **2** the opportunity to do something which gives you great satisfaction and which most people never have the chance to do: *I had the privilege of meeting the Queen when she visited our school* **3** the power and advantages that come with great wealth or high social class: *the use of violence to protect class privilege and thwart popular democracy*
WORD ORIGIN Latin *privilegium* law relevant to rights of an individual

privileged *adj* enjoying a special right or immunity

privy *adj* **privier, priviest 1** *archaic* secret **2 privy to** sharing in the knowledge of something secret ▷ *n, pl* **privies 3** *obsolete* a toilet, esp. an outside one
WORD ORIGIN Old French *privé* something private

Privy Council *n* **1** the private council of the British king or queen **2** (in Canada) a formal body of advisers of the governor general **Privy Counsellor** *n*

privy purse *n* an allowance voted by Parliament for the private expenses of the king or queen

privy seal *n* (in Britain) a seal affixed to certain documents of state

prize¹ *n* **1** something of value, such as a trophy, given to the winner of a contest or game **2** something given to the winner of any game of chance, lottery, etc. **3** something striven for ▷ *adj* **4** winning or likely to win a prize: *a prize bull*
WORD ORIGIN Old French *prise* a capture

prize² *vb* **prizing, prized** to value highly
WORD ORIGIN Old French *preisier* to praise

prizefight *n* a boxing match for a prize or purse **prizefighter** *n*

pro¹ *adv* **1** in favour of a motion etc. ▷ *prep* **2** in favour of ▷ *n, pl* **pros 3** (*usually pl*) an argument or vote in favour of a proposal or motion ▸ See also **pros and cons**
WORD ORIGIN Latin: in favour of

pro² *n, pl* **pros,** *adj informal* **1** short for **professional 2** a prostitute

PRO public relations officer

pro-¹ *prefix* **1** in favour of; supporting: *pro-Chinese* **2** acting as a substitute for: *pronoun*
WORD ORIGIN Latin

pro-² *prefix* before in time or position: *proboscis*
WORD ORIGIN Greek

proactive *adj* tending to initiate change rather than reacting to events

probability *n, pl* **-ties 1** the condition of being probable **2** an event or other thing that is likely to happen or be true **3** *statistics* a measure of the likelihood of an event happening

probable *adj* **1** likely to happen or be true **2** most likely: *the probable cause of the accident* ▷ *n* **3** a person who is likely to be chosen for a team, event, etc. **WORD ORIGIN** Latin *probabilis* that may be proved

probably *adv* in all likelihood or probability: *the wedding's probably going to be in late August*

probate *n* **1** the process of officially proving the validity of a will **2** the official certificate stating that a will is genuine **WORD ORIGIN** Latin *probare* to inspect

probation *n* **1** a system of dealing with offenders, esp. juvenile ones, by placing them under supervision **2 on probation a** under the supervision of a probation officer **b** undergoing a test or trial period, such as at the start of a new job **probationary** *adj* **WORD ORIGIN** Latin *probare* to test

probationer *n* **1** a person on a trial period in a job **2** a person under the supervision of a probation officer

probation officer *n* an officer of a court who supervises offenders placed on probation

probe *vb* **probing, probed 1** to investigate, or look into, closely **2** to poke or examine (something) with or as if with a probe: *he probed carefully with his fingertips* ▷ *n* **3** *surgery* a slender instrument for exploring a wound etc. **4** a thorough inquiry, such as one into corrupt practices **5** see **space probe WORD ORIGIN** Latin *probare* to test

probiotic *n* **1** a bacterium that protects the body from harmful bacteria ▷ *adj* **2** of or relating to probiotics: *probiotic yogurts*

probity *n formal* honesty; integrity **WORD ORIGIN** Latin *probitas* honesty

problem *n* **1** something or someone that is difficult to deal with **2** a puzzle or question set for solving **3** *maths* a statement requiring a solution usually by means of several operations ▷ *adj* **4** of a literary work that deals with difficult moral questions: *a problem play* **5** difficult to deal with or creating difficulties for others: *a problem child* **WORD ORIGIN** Greek *problēma* something put forward

problematic *or* **problematical** *adj* difficult to solve or deal with

proboscis (pro-**boss**-iss) *n* **1** a long flexible trunk or snout, such as an elephant's **2** the elongated mouth part of certain insects **WORD ORIGIN** Greek *proboskis* trunk of an elephant

procedure *n* **1** a way of doing something, esp. an established method **2** the established form of conducting the business of a legislature **procedural** *adj*

proceed *vb* **1** to advance or carry on, esp. after stopping **2** (often foll. by *with*) to start or continue doing: *he proceeded to pour himself a large whisky* **3** *formal* to walk or go **4** (often foll. by *against*) to start a legal action **5** *formal* to arise (from): *their mutual dislike proceeded from differences of political opinion* **WORD ORIGIN** Latin *procedere* to advance

proceeding *n* **1** an act or course of action **2 proceedings** the events of an occasion: *millions watched the proceedings on television* **3 proceedings** the minutes of the meetings of a society **4 proceedings** legal action

proceeds *pl n* the amount of money obtained from an event or activity

process¹ *n* **1** a series of actions or changes: *a process of genuine national reconciliation* **2** a series of natural developments which result in an overall change: *the ageing process* **3** a method of doing or producing something: *the various production processes use up huge amounts of water* **4 a** a summons to appear in court **b** an action at law **5** a natural outgrowth or projection of a part or organism **6 in the process of** during or in the course of ▷ *vb* **7** to handle or prepare by a special method of manufacture **8** *computers* to perform operations on (data) in order to obtain the required information **WORD ORIGIN** Latin *processus* an advancing

process² *vb* to move in an orderly or ceremonial group: *the cult members processed through the streets to the music of tambourines*

processed *adj* (of food) treated by adding colouring, preservatives, etc. to improve its appearance or the period it will stay edible: *processed cheese*

procession *n* **1** a line of people or vehicles moving forwards in an orderly or ceremonial manner **2** the act of proceeding in a regular formation **WORD ORIGIN** Latin *processio* a marching forwards

processional *adj* **1** of or suitable for a procession: *the processional route* ▷ *n* **2** *Christianity* a hymn sung as the clergy enter church

processor *n* **1** *computers* same as **central processing unit 2** a person or thing that carries out a process

proclaim *vb* **1** to announce publicly; declare: *Greece was proclaimed an independent kingdom in 1832* **2** to indicate plainly: *the sharp hard glint in the eye proclaimed her determination* **proclamation** *n* **WORD ORIGIN** Latin *proclamare* to shout aloud

proclivity *n, pl* **-ties** *formal* a tendency or inclination **WORD ORIGIN** Latin *proclivitas*

procrastinate *vb* **-nating, -nated** to put off (an action) until later; delay **procrastination** *n* **procrastinator** *n* **WORD ORIGIN** Latin *procrastinare* to postpone until tomorrow

procreate *vb* **-ating, -ated** *formal* to produce (offspring) **procreative** *adj* **procreation** *n* **WORD ORIGIN** Latin *procreare*

Procrustean *adj* ruthlessly enforcing uniformity **WORD ORIGIN** after *Procrustes*, robber in Greek myth who fitted travellers into

his bed by stretching or lopping off their limbs

proctor *n* a member of the staff of certain universities having duties including the enforcement of discipline **proctorial** *adj* **WORD ORIGIN** syncopated variant of *procurator*

procurator fiscal *n* (in Scotland) a legal officer who acts as public prosecutor and coroner

procure *vb* **-curing, -cured 1** to get or provide: *it remained very difficult to procure food and fuel* **2** to obtain (people) to act as prostitutes **procurement** *n* **WORD ORIGIN** Latin *procurare* to look after

procurer *n* a person who obtains people to act as prostitutes

prod *vb* **prodding, prodded 1** to poke with a pointed object **2** to rouse (someone) to action ▷ *n* **3** the act of prodding **4** a reminder **WORD ORIGIN** origin unknown

prodigal *adj* **1** recklessly wasteful or extravagant **2 prodigal of** lavish with: *you are prodigal of both your toil and your talent* ▷ *n* **3** a person who squanders money **prodigality** *n* **WORD ORIGIN** Latin *prodigere* to squander

prodigious *adj* **1** very large or immense **2** wonderful or amazing **WORD ORIGIN** Latin *prodigiosus* marvellous

prodigy *n, pl* **-gies 1** a person, esp. a child, with marvellous talent **2** anything that is a cause of wonder **WORD ORIGIN** Latin *prodigium* an unnatural happening

produce *vb* **-ducing, -duced 1** to bring (something) into existence **2** to present to view: *he produced his passport* **3** to make: *this area produces much of Spain's best wine* **4** to give birth to **5** to present on stage, film, or television: *the girls and boys write and produce their own plays* **6** to act as producer of ▷ *n* **7** food grown for sale: *farm produce* **8** something produced **producible** *adj* **WORD ORIGIN** Latin *producere* to bring forward

producer *n* **1** a person with the financial and administrative responsibility for a film or television programme **2** a person responsible for the artistic direction of a play **3** a person who supervises the arrangement, performance, and mixing of a recording **4** a person or thing that produces

product *n* **1** something produced **2** a consequence: *their skill was the product of hours of training* **3** *maths* the result achieved by multiplication

production *n* **1** the act of producing **2** anything that is produced **3** the amount produced or the rate at which it is produced **4** *econ* the creation or manufacture of goods and services **5** any work created as a result of literary or artistic effort **6** the presentation of a play, opera, etc. **7** the artistic direction of a play **8** the overall sound of a recording

production line *n* a system in a factory in which an item being manufactured is moved from machine to machine by conveyor belt, and each machine carries out one step in the manufacture of the item

productive *adj* 1 producing or having the power to produce 2 yielding favourable results 3 *econ* producing goods and services that have exchange value: *the country's productive capacity* 4 (foll. by *of*) resulting in: *a period highly productive of books and ideas* **productivity** *n*

product placement *n* the practice of a company of paying for its product to appear prominently in a film or television programme

proem (**pro**-em) *n formal* an introduction or preface **WORD ORIGIN** Greek *pro*- before + *hoimē* song

Prof. Professor

profane *adj* 1 showing disrespect for religion or something sacred 2 secular 3 coarse or blasphemous: *profane language* ▷ *vb* **-faning, -faned** 4 to treat (something sacred) with irreverence 5 to put to an unworthy use **profanation** *n* **WORD ORIGIN** Latin *profanus* outside the temple

profanity *n, pl* **-ties** 1 the quality of being profane 2 coarse or blasphemous action or speech

profess *vb* 1 to claim (something as true), often falsely: *he professes not to want the job of prime minister* 2 to acknowledge openly: *he professed great relief at getting some rest* 3 to have as one's belief or religion: *most Indonesians profess the Islamic faith* **professed** *adj* **WORD ORIGIN** Latin *profiteri* to confess openly

profession *n* 1 a type of work that requires special training, such as in law or medicine 2 the people employed in such an occupation 3 a declaration of a belief or feeling: *a profession of faith* **WORD ORIGIN** Latin *professio* public acknowledgment

professional *adj* 1 of a profession 2 taking part in an activity, such as sport or music, as a means of livelihood 3 displaying a high level of competence or skill: *a professional and polished performance* 4 undertaken or performed by people who are paid: *professional golf* ▷ *n* 5 a professional person **professionalism** *n* **professionally** *adv*

professor *n* 1 the highest rank of teacher in a university 2 *chiefly US & Canad* any teacher in a university or college 3 *rare* a person who professes his or her opinions or beliefs **professorial** *adj* **professorship** *n* **WORD ORIGIN** Latin: a public teacher

proffer *vb formal* to offer for acceptance **WORD ORIGIN** Old French *proffrir*

proficient *adj* skilled; expert **proficiency** *n* **WORD ORIGIN** Latin *proficere* to make progress

profile *n* 1 an outline, esp. of the human face, as seen from the side 2 a short biographical sketch **WORD ORIGIN** Italian *profilo*

profiling *n* the practice of categorizing people and predicting their behaviour according to particular characteristics such as race or age

profit *n* 1 (*often pl*) money gained in business or trade 2 a benefit or advantage ▷ *vb* **-iting, -ited** 3 to gain a profit or advantage: *we do not want to profit from someone else's problems* **WORD ORIGIN** Latin *proficere* to make progress

profitable *adj* making money or gaining an advantage or benefit **profitability** *n* **profitably** *adv*

profit and loss *n book-keeping* an account showing the year's income and expense items and indicating gross and net profit or loss

profiteer *n* 1 a person who makes excessive profits at the expense of the public ▷ *vb* 2 to make excessive profits **profiteering** *n*

profit-sharing *n* a system in which a portion of the net profit of a business is shared among its employees

profligate *adj* 1 recklessly extravagant 2 shamelessly immoral ▷ *n* 3 a profligate person **profligacy** *n* **WORD ORIGIN** Latin *profligatus* corrupt

pro forma *adj* 1 laying down a set form ▷ *adv* 2 performed in a set manner **WORD ORIGIN** Latin: for form's sake

profound *adj* 1 showing or needing great knowledge: *a profound knowledge of Greek literature* 2 strongly felt; intense: *profound relief* 3 extensive: *profound changes* 4 situated at or having a great depth **profoundly** *adv* **profundity** *n* **WORD ORIGIN** Latin *profundus* deep

profuse *adj* 1 plentiful or abundant: *he broke out in a profuse sweat* 2 (often foll. by *in*) generous in the giving (of): *he was profuse in his apologies* **profusely** *adv* **profusion** *n* **WORD ORIGIN** Latin *profundere* to pour lavishly

progenitor (pro-**jen**-it-er) *n* 1 a direct ancestor 2 an originator or founder **WORD ORIGIN** Latin: ancestor

progeny (**proj**-in-ee) *n, pl* **-nies** 1 offspring; descendants 2 an outcome **WORD ORIGIN** Latin *progenies* lineage

progesterone *n* a hormone, produced in the ovary, that prepares the womb for pregnancy and prevents further ovulation **WORD ORIGIN** PRO-[1] + *ge*(station) + *ster*(ol) + -*one*

prognathous *adj* having a projecting lower jaw

prognosis *n, pl* **-noses** 1 *med* a forecast about the course or outcome of an illness 2 any forecast **WORD ORIGIN** Greek: knowledge beforehand

prognosticate *vb* **-cating, -cated** 1 to foretell (future events) 2 to indicate or suggest beforehand **prognostication** *n* **prognosticator** *n* **WORD ORIGIN** Medieval Latin *prognosticare* to predict

program *n* 1 a sequence of coded instructions which enables a computer to perform various tasks ▷ *vb* **-gramming, -grammed** 2 to arrange (data) so that it can be processed by a computer 3 to feed a program into (a computer) **programmer** *n*

programmable *or* **programable** *adj* capable of being programmed for computer processing

programme *or US* **program** *n* 1 a planned series of events 2 a broadcast on radio or television 3 a printed list of items or performers in an entertainment ▷ *vb* **-gramming, -grammed** *or US* **-graming, -gramed** 4 to schedule (something) as a programme **programmatic** *adj* **WORD ORIGIN** Greek *programma* written public notice

programming language *n* a language system by which instructions to a computer are coded, that is understood by both user and computer

progress *n* 1 improvement or development 2 movement forward or advance 3 **in progress** taking place ▷ *vb* 4 to become more advanced or skilful 5 to move forward **WORD ORIGIN** Latin *progressus* a going forwards

progression *n* 1 the act of progressing; advancement 2 the act or an instance of moving from one thing in a sequence to the next 3 *maths* a sequence of numbers in which each term differs from the succeeding term by a fixed ratio

progressive *adj* 1 favouring political or social reform 2 happening gradually: *a progressive illness* 3 (of a dance, card game, etc.) involving a regular change of partners ▷ *n* 4 a person who favours political or social reform **progressively** *adv*

prohibit *vb* **-biting, -bited** 1 to forbid by law or other authority 2 to hinder or prevent: *the paucity of information prohibits us from drawing reliable conclusions* **prohibitor** *n* **WORD ORIGIN** Latin *prohibere* to prevent

prohibition *n* 1 the act of forbidding 2 a legal ban on the sale or drinking of alcohol 3 an order or decree that forbids **prohibitionist** *n*

Prohibition *n* the period (1920–33) when making, selling, and transporting alcohol was banned in the US **Prohibitionist** *n*

prohibitive *adj* 1 (esp. of prices) too high to be affordable 2 prohibiting or tending to prohibit: *a prohibitive distance*

project *n* 1 a proposal or plan 2 a detailed study of a particular subject ▷ *vb* 3 to make a prediction based on known data and observations 4 to cause (an image) to appear on a surface 5 to communicate (an impression): *he wants to project an image of a deep-thinking articulate gentleman* 6 to jut out 7 to cause (one's voice) to be heard clearly at a distance 8 to transport in the imagination: *it's hard to project oneself into his situation* **WORD ORIGIN** Latin *proicere* to throw down

projectile *n* 1 an object thrown as a weapon or fired from a gun ▷ *adj* 2 designed to be thrown forwards 3 projecting forwards **WORD ORIGIN** New Latin *projectilis* jutting forwards

projection *n* 1 a part that juts out 2 a forecast based on known data

Corpus Lexicography

For centuries, dictionaries have been based to some extent on the analysis of texts. In preparation for his *A Dictionary of the English Language*, published in 1755, Samuel Johnson spent several years reading and annotating books (mostly by literary authors such as Shakespeare, Milton, and Dryden) to find examples of words in use which would help determine his word-list and provide illustrative quotations. Thus Johnson used a 'corpus' in the sense 'a body of writings', if a very selective one.

In modern linguistics, the term 'corpus' is used in the more specific sense of a machine-readable collection of texts which is representative of the language it is being used to analyse. A corpus on which a general English dictionary is based must contain representative samples from a range of text-types (such as spoken English, newspapers, magazines, books, and reports) covering a range of genres (such as fiction, business, politics, sport, religion, and science) from a range of English-speaking countries.

The first corpus of this kind which was designed specifically for lexicographical use was Collins' *COBUILD*, established in 1980 at the University of Birmingham. By 1982 the corpus had reached 7.3 million words, which at that time was a considerable amount of data. Over the last few decades, the amount of data that can be processed by computer has increased enormously, and Collins' corpus holdings now stand at over 4 billion words.

Corpora are accessed using concordance programmes, allowing the lexicographer to search for a word (or a *lemma*; that is, the word with all its inflections) and retrieve a list of citations. Thus, a search for *quality* in Collins' corpus, the *Bank of English*, yields citations such as the following:

rate the most important < qualities > in an ideal lover

I had leadership < qualities > and was prepared to listen

a billion pound programme to improve water < quality >

Their flying was inconsiderate of residents' < quality > of life

The more that we support < quality > butchers and producers

Even these few lines (and a search for *quality* yields thousands) indicate some of its senses. As a countable noun (in *important qualities* and *leadership qualities*) it can mean 'characteristic'; as an uncountable noun (*water quality, quality of life*) it tends to mean 'standard of excellence'; and as a noun modifier (*quality butchers*) it means 'excellent'. Concordances can also be sorted by the word to the left or right, so that, for example, all the instances of *quality of life* could be seen together. The lexicographer can click on any citation and find the source text, which can provide useful information about whether a particular sense tends to be used in, for example, spoken English or newspaper English. Citations can also be used as authentic examples of a word; Collins' *COBUILD* was the first English dictionary to consistently use genuine rather than invented examples to illustrate the meanings of words.

In recent years, the software that is used to extract data from corpora has become increasingly sophisticated. One important development has been the *sketch engine* created by Lexical Computing Ltd. This is an interface with various features including *word sketch*. A word sketch is a lexical profile which shows the most significant patterns and collocations of a given word. This is particularly useful for highly frequent words with many meanings, such as *make*, of which there are over 2 million occurrences in the *Bank of English*. A word sketch for *make* shows that it is most frequently found in the pattern 'verb + noun', and that the most salient noun collocates are *decision, sense, mistake* and *difference*. *Make* is also frequently followed by an adjective, especially in the phrases *make sure* and *make clear*, and by 'noun + adjective', especially in *make something easy/difficult*. The most frequent phrasal verb with *make* is *make up*, particularly in the sense 'invent' (as in *make up a story*) and 'supply what is lacking' (as in *make up the shortfall*).

A corpus is an invaluable tool in showing real usage and highlighting the most frequent senses of a word. As Sidney Landau wrote in his lexicographers' bible, *Dictionaries*, 'Humans are still writing dictionaries... But the corpus is a tool which has breathed new life into the art of lexicography.'

3 the process of showing film on a screen **4** the representation on a flat surface of a three-dimensional figure or curved line

projectionist *n* a person who operates a film projector

projector *n* an apparatus for projecting photographic images, film, or slides onto a screen

prolapse *pathol n* **1** Also: **prolapsus** the slipping down of an internal organ of the body from its normal position ▷ *vb* **-lapsing, -lapsed 2** (of an internal organ) to slip from its normal position **WORD ORIGIN** Latin *prolabi* to slide along

prolapsed *adj pathol* (of an internal organ) having slipped from its normal position

prolate *adj geom* having a polar diameter which is longer than the equatorial diameter **WORD ORIGIN** Latin *prolatus* enlarged

prole *n chiefly Brit offensive slang* a proletarian

proletarian (pro-lit-**air**-ee-an) *adj* **1** of the proletariat ▷ *n* **2** a member of the proletariat

proletariat (pro-lit-**air**-ee-at) *n* the working class **WORD ORIGIN** Latin *proletarius* one whose only contribution to the state was his offspring

proliferate *vb* **-rating, -rated 1** to increase rapidly in numbers **2** to grow or reproduce (new parts, such as cells) rapidly **proliferation** *n* **WORD ORIGIN** Latin *proles* offspring + *ferre* to bear

prolific *adj* **1** producing a constant creative output: *a prolific author* **2** producing fruit or offspring in abundance **3** (often foll. by *in* or *of*) rich or fruitful **prolifically** *adv* **WORD ORIGIN** Latin *proles* offspring

prolix *adj* (of a speech or piece of writing) overlong and boring **prolixity** *n* **WORD ORIGIN** Latin *prolixus* stretched out widely

prologue *or US often* **prolog** *n* **1** an introduction to a play or book **2** an event that comes before another: *this success was a happy prologue to their transatlantic tour* **WORD ORIGIN** Greek *pro-* before + *logos* discourse

prolong *vb* to make (something) last longer **prolongation** *n* **WORD ORIGIN** Late Latin *prolongare*

prom *n* **1** *Brit* short for **promenade** (sense 1) or **promenade concert 2** *US & Canad informal* a formal dance held at a high school or college

PROM *n computers* Programmable Read Only Memory

promenade *n* **1** *chiefly Brit* a paved walkway along the seafront at a holiday resort **2** *old-fashioned* a leisurely walk for pleasure or display ▷ *vb* **-nading, -naded 3** *old-fashioned* to take a leisurely walk **WORD ORIGIN** French

promenade concert *n* a concert at which some of the audience stand rather than sit

promethium (pro-**meeth**-ee-um) *n chem* an artificial radioactive element

of the lanthanide series. Symbol: Pm **WORD ORIGIN** from *Prometheus*, in Greek mythology, the Titan who gave fire to mankind

prominent *adj* **1** standing out from the surroundings; noticeable **2** widely known; famous **3** jutting or projecting outwards: *prominent eyes* **prominence** *n* **prominently** *adv* **WORD ORIGIN** Latin *prominere* to jut out

promiscuous *adj* **1** taking part in many casual sexual relationships **2** *formal* consisting of different elements mingled indiscriminately **promiscuity** *n* **WORD ORIGIN** Latin *promiscuus* indiscriminate

promise *vb* **-mising, -mised 1** to say that one will definitely do or not do something: *I promise I'll have it finished by the end of the week* **2** to undertake to give (something to someone): *he promised me a car for my birthday* **3** to show signs of; seem likely: *she promises to be a fine singer* **4** to assure (someone) of the certainty of something: *everything's fine, I promise you* ▷ *n* **5** an undertaking to do or not do something **6** indication of future success: *a young player who shows great promise* **WORD ORIGIN** Latin *promissum* a promise

Promised Land *n* **1** *Bible* the land of Canaan **2** any longed-for place where one expects to find greater happiness

promising *adj* likely to succeed or turn out well

promissory note *n commerce chiefly US* a written promise to pay a stated sum of money to a particular person on a certain date or on demand

promo *n, pl* **-mos** *informal* an item produced to promote a product, esp. a video used to promote a pop record

promontory *n, pl* **-ries** a point of high land that juts out into the sea **WORD ORIGIN** Latin *promunturium* headland

promote *vb* **-moting, -moted 1** to encourage the progress or success of: *all attempts to promote a lasting ceasefire have failed* **2** to raise to a higher rank or position **3** to encourage the sale of (a product) by advertising **4** to work for: *he actively promoted reform* **promotion** *n* **promotional** *adj* **WORD ORIGIN** Latin *promovere* to push onwards

promoter *n* **1** a person who helps to organize and finance an event, esp. a sports one **2** a person or thing that encourages the progress or success of: *a promoter of terrorism*

prompt *vb* **1** to cause (an action); bring about: *the killings prompted an anti-Mafia crackdown* **2** to motivate or cause someone to do something: *I still don't know what prompted me to go* **3** to remind (an actor) of lines forgotten during a performance **4** to refresh the memory of ▷ *adj* **5** done without delay **6** quick to act ▷ *adv* **7** *informal* punctually: *at 8 o'clock prompt* ▷ *n* **8** anything that serves to remind **promptly** *adv* **promptness** *n* **WORD ORIGIN** Latin *promptus* evident

prompter *n* **a** a person offstage who reminds the actors of forgotten lines

b a device which performs a similar function for public speakers, TV presenters, etc.

promulgate *vb* **-gating, -gated 1** to put (a law or decree) into effect by announcing it officially **2** to make widely known **promulgation** *n* **promulgator** *n* **WORD ORIGIN** Latin *promulgare*

pron. 1 pronoun **2** pronunciation

prone *adj* **1** having a tendency to be affected by or do something: *I am prone to indigestion* **2** lying face downwards; prostrate **WORD ORIGIN** Latin *pronus* bent forward

prong *n* a long pointed projection from an instrument or tool such as a fork **WORD ORIGIN** Middle English

pronominal *adj grammar* relating to or playing the part of a pronoun

pronoun *n* a word, such as *she* or *it*, that replaces a noun or noun phrase that has already been or is about to be mentioned **WORD ORIGIN** Latin *pronomen*

pronounce *vb* **-nouncing, -nounced 1** to speak (a sound or sounds), esp. clearly or in a certain way **2** to announce or declare officially: *I now pronounce you man and wife* **3** to declare as one's judgment: *he pronounced the wine drinkable* **pronounceable** *adj* **WORD ORIGIN** Latin *pronuntiare* to announce

pronounced *adj* very noticeable: *he speaks with a pronounced lisp*

pronouncement *n* a formal announcement

pronto *adv informal* at once **WORD ORIGIN** Spanish: quick

pronunciation *n* **1** the recognized way to pronounce sounds in a given language **2** the way in which someone pronounces words

proof *n* **1** any evidence that confirms that something is true or exists **2** *law* the total evidence upon which a court bases its verdict **3** *maths, logic* a sequence of steps or statements that establishes the truth of a proposition **4** the act of testing the truth of something **5** an early copy of printed matter for checking before final production **6** *photog* a trial print from a negative **7** (esp. formerly) a defined level of alcoholic content used as a standard measure for comparing the alcoholic strength of other liquids: *Moldavian ruby port, 17° proof* ▷ *adj* **8** (foll. by *against*) able to withstand: *proof against tears* **9** (esp. formerly) having a level of alcoholic content used as a standard measure for comparing the alcoholic strength of other liquids ▷ *vb* **10** to take a proof from (type matter) **11** to render (something) proof, esp. to waterproof **WORD ORIGIN** Old French *preuve* a test

proofread *vb* **-reading, -read** to read and correct (printer's proofs) **proofreader** *n*

proof spirit *n* (in Britain) an alcoholic beverage that contains a standard percentage of alcohol

prop[1] *vb* **propping, propped** (often foll. by *up*) **1** to support (something or someone) in an upright position: *she was* *propped up by pillows* **2** to sustain or support: *the type of measures necessary to prop up the sagging US economy* **3** (often foll. by *against*) to place or lean ▷ *n* **4** something that gives rigid support, such as a pole **5** a person or thing giving moral support **WORD ORIGIN** perhaps from Middle Dutch *proppe*

prop² *n* a movable object used on the set of a film or play

prop³ *n informal* a propeller

prop. **1** proper(ly) **2** property **3** proposition **4** proprietor

propaganda *n* **1** the organized promotion of information to assist or damage the cause of a government or movement **2** such information **propagandist** *n, adj* **WORD ORIGIN** Italian

propagate *vb* **-gating, -gated 1** to spread (information or ideas) **2** *biol* to reproduce or breed **3** *horticulture* to produce (plants) **4** *physics* to transmit, esp. in the form of a wave: *the electrical signal is propagated through a specialized group of conducting fibres* **propagation** *n* **propagator** *n* **WORD ORIGIN** Latin *propagare* to increase (plants) by cuttings

propane *n* a flammable gas found in petroleum and used as a fuel **WORD ORIGIN** from *propionic (acid)*

propel *vb* **-pelling, -pelled** to cause to move forwards **propellant** *n, adj* **WORD ORIGIN** Latin *propellere*

propeller *n* a revolving shaft with blades to drive a ship or aircraft

propene *n* same as **propylene**

propensity *n, pl* **-ties** *formal* a natural tendency: *his problem had always been a propensity to live beyond his means* **WORD ORIGIN** Latin *propensus* inclined to

proper *adj* **1** real or genuine: *a proper home* **2** appropriate or usual: *good wine must have the proper balance of sugar and acid* **3** suited to a particular purpose: *they set out without any proper climbing gear* **4** correct in behaviour: *in many societies it is not considered proper for a woman to show her legs* **5** excessively moral: *she was very strait-laced and proper* **6** being or forming the main or central part of something: *a suburb some miles west of the city proper* **7** *Brit, Austral, & NZ informal* complete: *you made him look a proper fool* **properly** *adv* **WORD ORIGIN** Latin *proprius* special

proper fraction *n* a fraction in which the numerator has a lower absolute value than the denominator, for example ½

proper noun *or* **name** *n* the name of a person or place, for example *Iceland* or *Patrick*

property *n, pl* **-ties 1** something owned **2** *law* the right to possess, use, and dispose of anything **3** possessions collectively **4** land or buildings owned by someone **5** a quality or attribute: *the oils have healing properties* **6** same as **prop²** **WORD ORIGIN** Latin *proprius* one's own

prophecy *n, pl* **-cies 1** a prediction **2 a** a message revealing God's will **b** the act of uttering such a message **3** the function or activity of a prophet

prophesy *vb* **-sies, -sying, -sied** to foretell

prophet *n* **1** a person supposedly chosen by God to pass on His message **2** a person who predicts the future: *a prophet of doom* **3** a spokesman for, or advocate of, some cause: *a prophet of revolution* **prophetess** *fem n* **WORD ORIGIN** Greek *prophētēs* one who declares the divine will

Prophet *n* **the** the main name used of Mohammed, the founder of Islam

prophetic *adj* **1** foretelling what will happen **2** of the nature of a prophecy **prophetically** *adv*

prophylactic *adj* **1** preventing disease ▷ *n* **2** a drug or device that prevents disease **3** *chiefly US* a condom **WORD ORIGIN** Greek *prophulassein* to guard by taking advance measures

propinquity *n formal* nearness in time, place, or relationship **WORD ORIGIN** Latin *propinquus* near

propitiate *vb* **-ating, -ated** to appease (someone, esp. a god or spirit); make well disposed **propitiable** *adj* **propitiation** *n* **propitiator** *n* **propitiatory** *adj* **WORD ORIGIN** Latin *propitiare*

propitious *adj* **1** favourable or auspicious: *a propitious moment* **2** likely to prove favourable; advantageous: *his origins were not propitious for a literary career* **WORD ORIGIN** Latin *propitius* well disposed

proponent *n* a person who argues in favour of something **WORD ORIGIN** Latin *proponere* to propose

proportion *n* **1** relative size or extent: *a large proportion of our revenue comes from advertisements* **2** correct relationship between parts **3** a part considered with respect to the whole: *the proportion of women in the total workforce* **4 proportions** dimensions or size: *a building of vast proportions* **5** *maths* a relationship between four numbers in which the ratio of the first pair equals the ratio of the second pair **6 in proportion a** comparable in size, rate of increase, etc. **b** without exaggerating ▷ *vb* **7** to adjust in relative amount or size: *the size of the crops are very rarely proportioned to the wants of the inhabitants* **8** to cause to be harmonious in relationship of parts **WORD ORIGIN** Latin *pro portione*, literally: for (its, one's) portion

proportional *adj* **1** being in proportion ▷ *n* **2** *maths* an unknown term in a proportion, for example in *a/b = c/x, x* is the fourth proportional **proportionally** *adv*

proportional representation *n* the representation of political parties in parliament in proportion to the votes they win

proportionate *adj* being in proper proportion **proportionately** *adv*

proposal *n* **1** the act of proposing **2** a suggestion put forward for consideration **3** an offer of marriage

propose *vb* **-posing, -posed 1** to put forward (a plan) for consideration **2** to nominate (someone) for a position **3** to intend (to do something): *I don't propose to waste any more time discussing it* **4** to ask

people to drink a toast **5** (often foll. by *to*) to make an offer of marriage **WORD ORIGIN** Old French *proposer*, from Latin *proponere* to display

proposition *n* **1** a proposal or offer **2** *logic* a statement that affirms or denies something and is capable of being true or false **3** *maths* a statement or theorem, usually containing its proof **4** *informal* a person or matter to be dealt with: *even among experienced climbers the mountain is considered a tough proposition* **5** *informal* an invitation to engage in sexual intercourse ▷ *vb* **6** to invite (someone) to engage in sexual intercourse **WORD ORIGIN** Latin *propositio* a setting forth

propound *vb* to put forward for consideration **WORD ORIGIN** Latin *proponere* to set forth

proprietary *adj* **1** denoting a product manufactured and distributed under a trade name **2** possessive: *she watched them with a proprietary eye* **3** privately owned and controlled **WORD ORIGIN** Late Latin *proprietarius* an owner

proprietor *n* an owner of a business establishment **proprietress** *fem n* **proprietorial** *adj*

propriety *n, pl* **-ties 1** the quality or state of being appropriate or fitting **2** correct conduct **3 the proprieties** the standards of behaviour considered correct by polite society **WORD ORIGIN** Old French *propriété*, from Latin *proprius* one's own

propulsion *n* **1** a force that moves (something) forward **2** the act of propelling or the state of being propelled **propulsive** *adj* **WORD ORIGIN** Latin *propellere* to propel

propylene *or* **propene** *n* a gas found in petroleum and used to produce many organic compounds **WORD ORIGIN** from *propionic (acid)*

pro rata *adv, adj* in proportion **WORD ORIGIN** Medieval Latin

prorogue *vb* **-roguing, -rogued** to suspend (Parliament) without dissolving it **prorogation** *n* **WORD ORIGIN** Latin *prorogare*, literally: to ask publicly

prosaic (pro-**zay**-ik) *adj* **1** lacking imagination; dull **2** having the characteristics of prose **prosaically** *adv*

pros and cons *pl n* the advantages and disadvantages of a situation **WORD ORIGIN** Latin *pro* for + *con(tra)* against

proscenium *n, pl* **-nia** or **-niums** the arch in a theatre separating the stage from the auditorium **WORD ORIGIN** Greek *pro* before + *skēnē* scene

proscribe *vb* **-scribing, -scribed 1** to prohibit (something) **2** to condemn (something); to outlaw or banish **proscription** *n* **proscriptive** *adj* **WORD ORIGIN** Latin *proscribere* to put up a public notice

prose *n* **1** ordinary spoken or written language in contrast to poetry **2** a passage set for translation into a foreign language **3** commonplace or

p

dull talk ▷ vb **prosing, prosed 4** to speak or write in a tedious style **WORD ORIGIN** Latin *prosa oratio* straightforward speech

prosecute vb **-cuting, -cuted 1** to bring a criminal charge against (someone) **2** to continue to do (something): *the business of prosecuting a cold war through propaganda* **3 a** to seek redress by legal proceedings **b** to institute or conduct a prosecution **prosecutor** n **WORD ORIGIN** Latin *prosequi* to follow

prosecution n **1** the act of bringing criminal charges against someone **2** the institution and conduct of legal proceedings against a person **3** the lawyers acting for the Crown to put the case against a person **4** the carrying out of something begun

proselyte (**pross**-ill-ite) n a recent convert **proselytism** n **WORD ORIGIN** Greek *prosēlutos* recent arrival, convert

proselytize or **-tise** (**pross**-ill-it-ize) vb **-tizing, -tized** or **-tising, -tised** to attempt to convert (someone)

prosody (**pross**-a-dee) n **1** the study of poetic metre and techniques **2** the vocal patterns in a language **prosodic** adj **prosodist** n **WORD ORIGIN** Greek *prosōidia* song set to music

prospect n **1** (pl) chances or opportunities for future success: *a job with impossible workloads and poor career prospects* **2** expectation, or something anticipated: *she was terrified at the prospect of bringing up two babies on her own* **3** old-fashioned a view or scene: *a prospect of spires, domes, and towers* ▷ vb **4** (sometimes foll. by for) to search for gold or other valuable minerals **WORD ORIGIN** Latin *prospectus* distant view

prospective adj **1** future: *prospective customers* **2** expected or likely: *the prospective loss* **prospectively** adv

prospector n a person who searches for gold or other valuable minerals

prospectus n, pl **-tuses** a booklet produced by a university, company, etc. giving details about it and its activities

prosper vb to be successful **WORD ORIGIN** Latin *prosperare* to succeed

prosperity n success and wealth

prosperous adj wealthy and successful

prostate n a gland in male mammals that surrounds the neck of the bladder. Also called: **prostate gland** **WORD ORIGIN** Greek *prostatēs* something standing in front (of the bladder)

prosthesis (pross-**theess**-iss) n, pl **-ses** (-seez) surgery **a** the replacement of a missing body part with an artificial substitute **b** an artificial body part such as a limb, eye, or tooth **prosthetic** adj **WORD ORIGIN** Greek: an addition

prostitute n **1** a person who offers sexual intercourse in return for payment ▷ vb **-tuting, -tuted 2** to offer (oneself or another) in sexual intercourse for money **3** to offer (oneself or one's talent) for unworthy purposes **prostitution** n **WORD ORIGIN** Latin *pro-* in public + *statuere* to cause to stand

prostrate adj **1** lying face downwards **2** physically or emotionally exhausted ▷ vb **-trating, -trated 3** prostrate oneself to cast (oneself) face downwards, as in submission **4** to exhaust physically or emotionally **prostration** n **WORD ORIGIN** Latin *prosternere* to throw to the ground

prosy adj **prosier, prosiest** dull and long-winded **prosily** adv

Prot. 1 Protectorate **2** Protestant

protactinium n chem a toxic radioactive metallic element. Symbol: Pa

protagonist n **1** a supporter of a cause: *a great protagonist of the ideas and principles of mutuality* **2** the leading character in a play or story **WORD ORIGIN** Greek *prōtos* first + *agōnistēs* actor

protea (**pro**-tee-a) n an African shrub with showy heads of flowers **WORD ORIGIN** after *Proteus*, a sea god who could take many shapes

protean (pro-**tee**-an) adj capable of constantly changing shape or form: *he is a protean stylist who can move from blues to ballads with consummate ease* **WORD ORIGIN** after *Proteus*; see PROTEA

protect vb **1** to defend from trouble, harm, or loss **2** econ to assist (domestic industries) by taxing imports **WORD ORIGIN** Latin *protegere* to cover before

protection n **1** the act of protecting or the condition of being protected **2** something that keeps (one) safe **3 a** the charging of taxes on imports, to protect domestic industries **b** Also called: **protectionism** the policy of such taxation **4** informal Also called: **protection money** money paid to gangsters to avoid attack or damage **protectionism** n **protectionist** n, adj

protective adj **1** giving protection: *protective clothing* **2** tending or wishing to protect someone **protectively** adv **protectiveness** n

protector n **1** a person or thing that protects **2** history a person who acts for the king or queen during his or her childhood, absence, or incapacity **protectress** fem n

protectorate n **1** a territory largely controlled by a stronger state **2** the office or term of office of a protector

protégé or fem **protégée** (**pro**-tizh-ay) n a person who is protected and helped by another **WORD ORIGIN** French *protéger* to protect

protein n any of a large group of nitrogenous compounds that are essential for life **WORD ORIGIN** Greek *prōteios* primary

pro tempore adv, adj for the time being. Often shortened to: **pro tem**

protest n **1** public, often organized, demonstration of objection **2** a strong objection **3** a formal statement declaring that a debtor has dishonoured a bill **4** the act of protesting ▷ vb **5** to take part in a public demonstration to express one's support for or disapproval of an action, proposal, etc.: *the workers marched through the city to protest against the closure of their factory* **6** to disagree or object: *'I'm OK,' she protested* **7** to assert in a formal or solemn manner: *all three repeatedly protested their innocence* **8** US & NZ to object forcefully to: *students and teachers have protested the budget reductions* **protestant** adj, n **protester** n **WORD ORIGIN** Latin *protestari* to make a formal declaration

Protestant n **1** a follower of any of the Christian Churches that separated from the Roman Catholic Church in the 16th century ▷ adj **2** of or relating to any of these Churches or their followers **Protestantism** n

protestation n formal a strong declaration

protium n the most common isotope of hydrogen, with a mass number of 1 **WORD ORIGIN** from Greek *prōtos* first

proto- or sometimes before a vowel **prot-** combining form **1** first: *protomartyr* **2** original: *prototype* **WORD ORIGIN** Greek *prōtos* first

protocol n **1** the rules of behaviour for formal occasions **2** a record of an agreement in international negotiations **3** computers a standardized format for exchanging data, esp. between different computer systems **WORD ORIGIN** Late Greek *prōtokollon* sheet glued to the front of a manuscript

proton (**pro**-ton) n a positively charged elementary particle, found in the nucleus of an atom **WORD ORIGIN** Greek *prōtos* first

protoplasm n biol a complex colourless substance forming the living contents of a cell **protoplasmic** adj **WORD ORIGIN** Greek *prōtos* first + *plasma* form

prototype n **1** an early model of a product, which is tested so that the design can be changed if necessary **2** a person or thing that serves as an example of a type

protozoan (pro-toe-**zoe**-an) n, pl **-zoa** a very tiny single-celled invertebrate, such as an amoeba. Also: **protozoon** **WORD ORIGIN** Greek *prōtos* first + *zoion* animal

protract vb to lengthen or extend (a situation etc.) **protracted** adj **protraction** n **WORD ORIGIN** Latin *protrahere* to prolong

protractor n an instrument for measuring angles, usually a flat semicircular piece of plastic

protrude vb **-truding, -truded** to stick out or project **protrusion** n **protrusive** adj **WORD ORIGIN** PRO-² + Latin *trudere* to thrust

protuberant adj swelling out; bulging **protuberance** n **WORD ORIGIN** Late Latin *protuberare* to swell

proud adj **1** feeling pleasure or satisfaction: *she was proud of her daughter's success* **2** feeling honoured **3** haughty or arrogant **4** causing pride: *the city's proud history* **5** dignified: *too proud to accept charity* **6** (of a surface or edge) projecting or protruding ▷ adv **7** do someone proud to entertain someone on a grand scale: *Mum did us all proud last Christmas* **proudly** adv **WORD ORIGIN** Old French *prud, prod* brave

The Terminology of Music in English

Responding to a piece of writing is mainly rational; responding to a piece of music is mainly intuitive. If that were not so, studies would not have determined that cows give more milk after listening to Mozart. The same point would hold true if cows gave less milk after listening to Schoenberg.

Describing music's nature and effects, like that of the visual arts, is difficult. The Paleolithic origins of music, like that of language, are mysterious. Even to transcribe it requires the *staff notation* of symbols to indicate *pitch*, *rhythm*, and *tempo* in a *score* or *sheet music*. In Western antiquity, the Greek 'art of the Muses' was bound up with religion and theatre as a social activity; the harp and the pipe are honoured in the Old Testament. Unlike the oral transmission of *traditional music*, the written score, a record of compositional intentions, passed along *classical* or *art music* through generations, including the vocal music of the *choir*, the *opera* and, much later, the *art song*. Evolving from Christian liturgical practice, Western music became played by *orchestral* instruments in the *brass*, *string*, *wind*, *woodwind*, *horn*, and *percussion* groups, or by solo *keyboard* instruments such as the *organ*, *harpsichord*, and *piano*.

In retrospect, we can define, at least hazily, artistic periods: the *Medieval*, *Renaissance*, *Baroque*, *Classical*, *Romantic*, *Modern*, and *Postmodern*, each associated with a cluster of great composers and, in the past two centuries, with conductors or performers. The Classical, Modern, and Postmodern are confusingly named. The last two categories have perplexing subdivisions such as *impressionist*, *expressionist*, *serial*, *aleatory*, or *minimalist*. Making verbal sense of classical music requires not just the acquisition of technical vocabulary but at least a smattering of foreign languages. The language of this music is Italian (*cadenza*, *bel canto*, *forte*), augmented by terms from German (*waltz*, *lied*) and French (*ensemble*, *nocturne*). Varieties of English can differ in their choice of terminology: the American *whole note*, *English horn*, and *flutist* are the British *semibreve*, *cor anglais*, and *flautist*.

Classical music sometimes overlaps with folk or popular forms, and those who favour it do not necessarily belong to high society or the wealthy. The American musical genus is populist. First came the hybrid form *jazz*, improvised, or later played by a *big band*, and the orally transmitted *blues*. Both forms originated in the African-American South. *Folk* and *country and western* music built on the British ballad tradition. The Broadway *musical* partly derived from the European *operetta*. In the middle of the twentieth century came the explosive power of *rock* or *rock 'n' roll*. Each of these developments spawned spin-offs and fusions. Dance was allied with a thudding, repetitive beat in discothèques, and in such Black urban forms as *rap* and *hip-hop*. Music emotionally punctuated movies, and poignant or syrupy songs dominated *MOR* (*Middle of the Road*) radio heard by the middle class; it was ambient in elevators and shopping malls as nebulous *Muzak*. The rhythms and harmonies of Asian and African peoples, born of age-old, sophisticated traditions of their own, arrived in the West as *world music*.

Burgeoning technology in the production and distribution of *pop music* introduced many new terms. Successively, *singles* and *LPs* were played on *phonographs*, *cassettes* in *tape decks*, *CDs* on *disk drives*, and tracks *downloaded* from the internet. Playing the *acoustic guitar* became a mass pastime in the twentieth century, then the guitars became electric in the *rock bands* that held *jam sessions* in countless suburban garages. Parallel to the exponential spread of personal computers, electronics revolutionized the recording, storage, play, and transmission of music. Words such as *reverb* and *amp* were succeeded by *synthesizer* and *sampling*. In this shift from the *analogue* to the *digital*, the computer became itself a musical instrument.

Music-based idioms are everywhere. We grimly *face the music*; good news is *music to our ears*. Braggarts *blow their own trumpet* and bluffers go into *a song and dance*, unless they *change their tune*. If we do everything we can, we *pull out all the stops*. If we hear something we think we heard before, it *rings a bell*. If you decide to act according to circumstances, you *play it by ear*. Music may transcend language but it also plays a part in its creation.

proud flesh *n* a mass of tissue formed around a healing wound

prove *vb* **proving, proved; proved** or **proven 1** to establish the truth or validity of: *such a claim is difficult to prove scientifically* **2** *law* to establish the genuineness of (a will) **3** to show (oneself) to be: *he proved equal to the task* **4** to be found to be: *it proved to be a trap* **5** (of dough) to rise in a warm place before baking **provable** *adj* **WORD ORIGIN** Latin *probare* to test

proven *vb* **1** a past participle of **prove 2** see **not proven** ▷ *adj* **3** known from experience to work: *a proven ability to make money*

provenance (**prov**-in-anss) *n* a place of origin **WORD ORIGIN** French

Provençal (prov-on-**sahl**) *adj* **1** of Provence, in SE France ▷ *n* **2** a language of Provence **3** a person from Provence

provender *n* *old-fashioned* fodder for livestock **WORD ORIGIN** Old French *provendre*

proverb *n* a short memorable saying that expresses a truth or gives a warning, for example is *half a loaf is better than no bread* **WORD ORIGIN** Latin *proverbium*

proverbial *adj* **1** well-known because commonly or traditionally referred to **2** of a proverb **proverbially** *adv*

provide *vb* **-viding, -vided 1** to make available **2** to afford; yield: *social activities providing the opportunity to meet new people* **3** (often foll. by *for* or *against*) to take careful precautions: *we provide for the possibility of illness in the examination regulations* **4** (foll. by *for*) to support financially: *both parents should be expected to provide for their children* **5** *formal* **provide for** (of a law, treaty, etc.) to make possible: *a bill providing for stiffer penalties for racial discrimination* **provider** *n* **WORD ORIGIN** Latin *providere* to provide for

providence *n* **1** God or nature seen as a protective force that oversees people's lives **2** the foresight shown by a person in the management of his or her affairs

Providence *n* *Christianity* God, esp. as showing foreseeing care of his creatures

provident *adj* **1** thrifty **2** showing foresight **WORD ORIGIN** Latin *providens* foreseeing

providential *adj* fortunate, as if through divine involvement

provident society *n* same as **friendly society**

providing or **provided** *conj* on condition (that): *the deal is on, providing he passes his medical*

province *n* **1** a territory governed as a unit of a country or empire **2** an area of learning, activity, etc. **3 the provinces** those parts of a country lying outside the capital **WORD ORIGIN** Latin *provincia* conquered territory

provincewide *Canad adj* **1** relating to the whole of a province: *a provincewide referendum* ▷ *adv* **2** throughout a province: *an advertising campaign to go provincewide*

provincial *adj* **1** of a province **2** unsophisticated or narrow-minded **3** NZ denoting a football team representing a province ▷ *n* **4** an unsophisticated person **5** a person from a province or the provinces **provincialism** *n*

provision *n* **1** the act of supplying something **2** something supplied **3 provisions** food and other necessities **4** a condition incorporated in a document **5 make provision for** to make arrangements for beforehand: *many restaurants still make no provision for non-smokers* ▷ *vb* **6** to supply with provisions **WORD ORIGIN** Latin *provisio* a providing

provisional *adj* temporary or conditional: *a provisional diagnosis* **provisionally** *adv*

Provisional *n* a member of the Provisional IRA or Sinn Féin

proviso (pro-**vize**-oh) *n, pl* **-sos** or **-soes** a condition or stipulation **provisory** *adj* **WORD ORIGIN** Medieval Latin *proviso quod* it being provided that

provocation *n* **1** the act of provoking or inciting **2** something that causes indignation or anger

provocative *adj* provoking or inciting, esp. to anger or sexual desire: *a provocative remark* **provocatively** *adv*

provoke *vb* **-voking, -voked 1** to deliberately act in a way intended to anger someone: *waving a red cape, Delgado provoked the animal into charging* **2** to incite or stimulate: *the army seems to have provoked this latest confrontation* **3** (often foll. by *into*) to cause a person to react in a particular, often angry, way: *keeping your true motives hidden may provoke others into being just as two-faced with you* **4** to bring about: *the case has provoked furious public debate* **provoking** *adj* **WORD ORIGIN** Latin *provocare* to call forth

provost *n* **1** the head of certain university colleges or schools **2** the chief councillor of a Scottish town **WORD ORIGIN** Old English *profost*

provost marshal *n* the officer in charge of military police in a camp or city

prow *n* the bow of a vessel **WORD ORIGIN** Greek *prōra*

prowess *n* **1** superior skill or ability **2** bravery or fearlessness **WORD ORIGIN** Old French *proesce*

prowl *vb* **1** (sometimes foll. by *around* or *about*) to move stealthily around (a place) as if in search of prey or plunder ▷ *n* **2** the act of prowling **3 on the prowl** moving around stealthily **prowler** *n* **WORD ORIGIN** origin unknown

prox. proximo (next month)

proximate *adj* **1** next or nearest in space or time **2** very near **3** immediately coming before or following in a series **4** approximate **WORD ORIGIN** Latin *proximus* next

proximity *n* **1** nearness in space or time **2** nearness or closeness in a series **WORD ORIGIN** Latin *proximitas* closeness

proxy *n, pl* **proxies 1** a person authorized to act on behalf of someone else: *the firm's creditors can vote either in person or by*

proxy 2 the authority to act on behalf of someone else **WORD ORIGIN** Latin *procuratio* procuration

proxy server *n* *computers* a computer that acts as an intermediary between a client machine and a server, caching information to save access time

Prozac *n trademark* an antidepressant drug

prude *n* a person who is excessively modest or prim, esp. regarding sex **prudery** *n* **prudish** *adj* **WORD ORIGIN** Old French *prode femme* respectable woman

prudent *adj* **1** sensible and careful **2** discreet or cautious **3** exercising good judgment **prudence** *n* **prudently** *adv* **WORD ORIGIN** Latin *prudens* far-sighted

prudential *adj old-fashioned* showing prudence: *prudential reasons* **prudentially** *adv*

prune[1] *n* a purplish-black partially dried plum **WORD ORIGIN** Latin *prunum* plum

prune[2] *vb* **pruning, pruned 1** to cut off dead or surplus branches of (a tree or shrub) **2** to shorten or reduce **WORD ORIGIN** Old French *proignier* to clip

prurient *adj* **1** excessively interested in sexual matters **2** exciting lustfulness **prurience** *n* **WORD ORIGIN** Latin *prurire* to lust after, itch

Prussian *adj* **1** of Prussia, a former German state ▷ *n* **2** a person from Prussia

prussic acid *n* the extremely poisonous solution of hydrogen cyanide **WORD ORIGIN** French *acide prussique* Prussian acid

pry *vb* **pries, prying, pried** (often foll. by *into*) to make an impertinent or uninvited inquiry (about a private matter) **WORD ORIGIN** origin unknown

PS 1 Also: **ps** postscript **2** private secretary

PSA (in New Zealand) Public Service Association

psalm *n* (*often cap*) any of the sacred songs that make up a book (Psalms) of the Old Testament **WORD ORIGIN** Greek *psalmos* song accompanied on the harp

psalmist *n* a writer of psalms

psalmody *n, pl* **-dies** the singing of sacred music

Psalter *n* **1** the Book of Psalms **2** a book containing a version of Psalms **WORD ORIGIN** Greek *psaltērion* stringed instrument

psaltery *n, pl* **-teries** an ancient musical instrument played by plucking strings

PSBR (in Britain) public sector borrowing requirement: the money needed by the public sector of the economy for items not paid for by income

psephology (sef-**fol**-a-jee) *n* the statistical and sociological study of elections **psephologist** *n* **WORD ORIGIN** Greek *psephos* pebble, vote + -LOGY

pseud *n informal* a pretentious person

pseudo *adj informal* not genuine

pseudo- *or sometimes before a vowel*
pseud- *combining form* false, pretending, or unauthentic: *pseudo-intellectual*
WORD ORIGIN Greek *pseudēs* false

pseudonym *n* a fictitious name adopted, esp. by an author **pseudonymity** *n* **pseudonymous** *adj*
WORD ORIGIN Greek *pseudēs* false + *onoma* name

psittacosis *n* a viral disease of parrots that can be passed on to humans
WORD ORIGIN Greek *psittakos* a parrot

psoriasis (so-**rye**-a-siss) *n* a skin disease with reddish spots and patches covered with silvery scales
WORD ORIGIN Greek: itching disease

psst *interj* a sound made to attract someone's attention, esp. without others noticing

PST Pacific Standard Time

PSV (in Britain, formerly) public service vehicle

psyche *n* the human mind or soul
WORD ORIGIN Greek *psukhē* breath, soul

psychedelic *adj* **1** denoting a drug that causes hallucinations **2** *informal* having vivid colours and complex patterns similar to those experienced during hallucinations
WORD ORIGIN Greek *psukhē* mind + *delos* visible

psychiatry *n* the branch of medicine concerned with the study and treatment of mental disorders **psychiatric** *adj* **psychiatrist** *n*

psychic *adj* **1** relating to or having powers (especially mental powers) which cannot be explained by natural laws **2** relating to the mind ▷ *n* **3** a person who has psychic powers **psychical** *adj*

psycho *informal n, pl* **-chos 1** same as **psychopath** ▷ *adj* **2** same as **psychopathic**

psycho- *or sometimes before a vowel*
psych- *combining form* indicating the mind or mental processes: *psychology; psychosomatic*
WORD ORIGIN Greek *psukhē* spirit, breath

psychoactive *adj* capable of affecting mental activity: *a psychoactive drug*

psychoanalyse *or esp. US* **-lyze** *vb* **-lysing, -lysed** *or* **-lyzing, -lyzed** to examine or treat (a person) by psychoanalysis

psychoanalysis *n* a method of treating mental and emotional disorders by discussion and analysis of the patient's thoughts and feelings **psychoanalyst** *n* **psychoanalytical** *or* **psychoanalytic** *adj*

psychogenic *adj psychol* (esp. of disorders or symptoms) of mental, rather than organic, origin

psychological *adj* **1** relating to the mind or mental activity **2** relating to psychology **3** having its origin in the mind: *his backaches are purely psychological* **psychologically** *adv*

psychological moment *n* the best time for achieving the desired response or effect

psychological warfare *n* the military application of psychology, esp. to influence morale in time of war

psychology *n, pl* **-gies 1** the scientific study of all forms of human and animal behaviour **2** *informal* the mental make-up of a person **psychologist** *n*

psychopath *n* a person afflicted with a personality disorder which causes him or her to commit antisocial and sometimes violent acts **psychopathic** *adj*

psychopathology *n* the scientific study of mental disorders

psychopathy (sike-**op**-ath-ee) *n* any mental disorder or disease

psychosis (sike-**oh**-siss) *n, pl* **-ses** (-seez) a severe mental disorder in which the sufferer's contact with reality becomes highly distorted: *a classic case of psychosis* **psychotic** *adj*

psychosomatic *adj* (of a physical disorder) thought to have psychological causes, such as stress

psychotherapy *n* the treatment of nervous disorders by psychological methods **psychotherapeutic** *adj* **psychotherapist** *n*

psych up *vb* to prepare (oneself or another) mentally for a contest or task

pt 1 part **2** past tense **3** point **4** port **5** pro tempore

Pt *chem* platinum

PT *old-fashioned* physical training

pt. pint

PTA Parent Teacher Association

ptarmigan (**tar**-mig-an) *n* a bird of the grouse family that turns white in winter

Pte. *mil* private

pterodactyl (terr-roe-**dak**-til) *n* an extinct flying reptile with batlike wings
WORD ORIGIN Greek *pteron* wing + *daktulos* finger

PTO *or* **pto** please turn over

Ptolemaic (tol-lim-**may**-ik) *adj* relating to Ptolemy, the 2nd-century AD Greek astronomer, or to his belief that the earth was in the centre of the universe

ptomaine *or* **ptomain** (**toe**-main) *n* any of a group of poisonous alkaloids found in decaying matter
WORD ORIGIN Greek *ptoma* corpse

PTSD post-traumatic stress disorder

Pty *Austral & S African* Proprietary

Pu *chem* plutonium

pub *n* **1** *chiefly Brit* a building with a licensed bar where alcoholic drinks may be bought and drunk **2** *Austral & NZ* a hotel

pub. 1 public **2** publication **3** published **4** publisher **5** publishing

pub-crawl *n informal* a drinking tour of a number of pubs

puberty (**pew**-ber-tee) *n* the beginning of sexual maturity **pubertal** *adj*
WORD ORIGIN Latin *pubertas* maturity

pubes *n, pl* **pubes 1** the region above the genitals **2** pubic hair **3** the plural of **pubis**
WORD ORIGIN Latin

pubescent *adj* **1** arriving or arrived at puberty **2** covered with down, as some plants and animals **pubescence** *n*
WORD ORIGIN Latin *pubescere* to reach manhood

pubic (**pew**-bik) *adj* of or relating to the pubes or pubis: *pubic hair*

pubis *n, pl* **-bes** one of the three sections of the hipbone that forms part of the pelvis
WORD ORIGIN New Latin *os pubis* bone of the pubes

public *adj* **1** relating to the people as a whole **2** provided by the government: *public service* **3** open to all: *public gardens* **4** well-known: *a public figure* **5** performed or made openly: *public proclamation* **6** maintained by and for the community: *a public library* **7** open, acknowledged, or notorious: *a public scandal* **8 go public a** (of a private company) to offer shares for sale to the public: *few German firms have gone public in recent years* **b** to make information, plans, etc. known: *the group would not have gone public with its suspicions unless it was fully convinced of them* ▷ *n* **9** the community or people in general **10** a particular section of the community: *the racing public* **publicly** *adv*
WORD ORIGIN Latin *publicus*

public-address system *n* a system of microphones, amplifiers, and loudspeakers for increasing the sound level of speech or music at public gatherings

publican *n Brit, Austral, & NZ* a person who owns or runs a public house

publication *n* **1** the publishing of a printed work **2** any printed work offered for sale **3** the act of making information known to the public

public bar *n* a bar in a hotel or pub which is cheaper and more basically furnished than the lounge or saloon bar

public company *or* **public limited company** *n* a limited company whose shares may be purchased by the public

public convenience *n* a public toilet

public enemy *n* a notorious person who is considered a danger to the public

public house *n* **1** *Brit* a pub **2** *US & Canad* an inn or small hotel

publicist *n* a person, such as a press agent or journalist, who publicizes something

publicity *n* **1** the process or information used to arouse public attention **2** the public interest so aroused

publicize *or* **-cise** *vb* **-cizing, -cized** *or* **-cising, -cised** to bring to public attention

public lending right *n* the right of authors to receive payment when their books are borrowed from public libraries

public prosecutor *n law* an official in charge of prosecuting important cases

public relations *n* the practice of gaining the public's goodwill and approval for an organization

public school *n* **1** (in England and Wales) a private independent fee-paying secondary school **2** (in certain Canadian provinces) a public elementary school as distinguished from a separate school **3** (in the US) any school that is part of a free local educational system

P

public sector *n* the part of a country's economy that consists of state-owned industries and services

public servant *n* **1** an elected or appointed holder of a public office **2** *Austral & NZ* a civil servant

public service *n* *Austral & NZ* the civil service

public-spirited *adj* having or showing an active interest in the good of the community

public utility *n* an organization that supplies water, gas, or electricity to the public

publish *vb* **1** to produce and issue (printed matter) for sale **2** to have one's written work issued for publication **3** to announce formally or in public **publishing** *n*
WORD ORIGIN Latin *publicare* to make public

publisher *n* **1** a company or person that publishes books, periodicals, music, etc. **2** *US & Canad* the proprietor of a newspaper

puce *adj* dark brownish-purple: *his face suddenly turned puce with futile rage*
WORD ORIGIN French *couleur puce* flea colour

puck¹ *n* a small disc of hard rubber used in ice hockey
WORD ORIGIN origin unknown

puck² *n* a mischievous or evil spirit **puckish** *adj*
WORD ORIGIN Old English *pūca*

pucker *vb* **1** to gather into wrinkles ▷ *n* **2** a wrinkle or crease
WORD ORIGIN origin unknown

pudding *n* **1** a dessert, esp. a cooked one served hot **2** a savoury dish with pastry or batter: *steak-and-kidney pudding* **3** a sausage-like mass of meat: *black pudding*
WORD ORIGIN Middle English *poding*

puddle *n* **1** a small pool of water, esp. of rain **2** a worked mixture of wet clay and sand that is impervious to water ▷ *vb* **-dling, -dled** **3** to make (clay etc.) into puddle **4** to subject (iron) to puddling **puddly** *adj*
WORD ORIGIN Middle English *podel*

pudenda *pl n* the human genitals, esp. of a female
WORD ORIGIN Latin: the shameful (parts)

pudgy *adj* **pudgier, pudgiest** *chiefly US* podgy **pudginess** *n*
WORD ORIGIN origin unknown

puerile *adj* silly and childish **puerility** *n*
WORD ORIGIN Latin *puer* a boy

puerperal (pew-**er**-per-al) *adj* concerning the period following childbirth
WORD ORIGIN Latin *puerperium* childbirth

puerperal fever *n* a serious, formerly widespread, form of blood poisoning caused by infection during childbirth

puerperium (pure-**peer**-ee-um) *n* the period after childbirth

puff *n* **1** a short quick blast of breath, wind, or smoke **2** the amount of wind or smoke released in a puff **3** the sound made by a puff **4** an act of inhaling and expelling cigarette smoke **5** a light pastry usually filled with cream and

jam **6** **out of puff** out of breath: *by the third flight of stairs she was out of puff* ▷ *vb* **7** to blow or breathe in short quick blasts **8** (often foll. by *out*) to cause to be out of breath **9** to take draws at (a cigarette) **10** to move with or by the emission of puffs: *the steam train puffed up the incline* **11** (often foll. by *up* or *out*) to swell **puffy** *adj*
WORD ORIGIN Old English *pyffan*

puff adder *n* a large venomous African viper whose body swells when alarmed

puffball *n* a ball-shaped fungus that sends out a cloud of brown spores when mature

puffin *n* a black-and-white sea bird with a brightly coloured beak
WORD ORIGIN origin unknown

puff pastry *or US* **puff paste** *n* a light flaky pastry

pug *n* a small dog with a smooth coat, lightly curled tail, and a short wrinkled nose
WORD ORIGIN origin unknown

pugilist (**pew**-jil-ist) *n* a boxer **pugilism** *n* **pugilistic** *adj*
WORD ORIGIN Latin *pugil* a boxer

pugnacious *adj* ready and eager to fight **pugnacity** *n*
WORD ORIGIN Latin *pugnax*

pug nose *n* a short stubby upturned nose **pug-nosed** *adj*
WORD ORIGIN from *pug* (the dog)

puissance *n* a showjumping competition that tests a horse's ability to jump large obstacles
WORD ORIGIN see PUISSANT

puissant (**pew**-iss-sant) *adj archaic or poetic* powerful
WORD ORIGIN Old French, from Latin *potens* mighty

puke *slang vb* **puking, puked** **1** to vomit ▷ *n* **2** the act of vomiting **3** the matter vomited
WORD ORIGIN probably imitative

pukeko (**poo**-kek-oh) *n, pl* **-kos** a brightly coloured New Zealand wading bird
WORD ORIGIN Māori

pukka *adj* **1** properly done, constructed, etc. **2** genuine or real
WORD ORIGIN Hindi *pakkā* firm

pulchritude *n formal or literary* physical beauty **pulchritudinous** *adj*
WORD ORIGIN Latin *pulchritudo*

pule *vb* **puling, puled** *literary* to whine or whimper
WORD ORIGIN imitative

pull *vb* **1** to exert force on (an object) to draw it towards the source of the force **2** to strain or stretch **3** to remove or extract: *he pulled a crumpled tenner from his pocket* **4** *informal* to draw out (a weapon) for use: *he pulled a knife on his attacker* **5** *informal* to attract: *the game is expected to pull a large crowd* **6** *slang* to attract a sexual partner **7** (usually foll. by *on* or *at*) to drink or inhale deeply: *he pulled on his pipe* **8** to possess or exercise the power to move: *this car doesn't pull well on hills* **9** to withdraw or remove: *the board pulled their support* **10** *printing* to take (a proof) from type **11** *golf, baseball, etc.* to hit (a ball) away from the direction in which the player intended to hit it

12 *cricket* to hit (a ball) to the leg side **13** to row (a boat) or take a stroke of (an oar) in rowing **14** **pull a face** to make a grimace **15** **pull a fast one** *slang* (often foll. by *on*) to play a sly trick **16** **pull apart** *or* **to pieces** to criticize harshly **17** **pull (one's) punches** to limit the force of one's criticisms or blows ▷ *n* **18** the act of pulling **19** the force used in pulling: *the pull of the moon affects the tides* **20** the act of taking in drink or smoke **21** *printing* a proof taken from type **22** something used for pulling, such as a handle **23** *informal* power or influence: *his uncle is chairman of the company, so he has quite a lot of pull* **24** *informal* the power to attract attention or support **25** a single stroke of an oar in rowing **26** the act of pulling the ball in golf, cricket, etc. ▷ See also **pull down, pull in,** etc.
WORD ORIGIN Old English *pullian*

pull down *vb* to destroy or demolish: *the old houses were pulled down*

pullet *n* a hen less than one year old
WORD ORIGIN Old French *poulet* chicken

pulley *n* a wheel with a grooved rim in which a belt, chain, or piece of rope runs in order to lift weights by a downward pull
WORD ORIGIN Old French *polie*

pull in *vb* **1** Also: **pull over** (of a motor vehicle) to draw in to the side of the road **2** (often foll. by *to*) to reach a destination: *the train pulled in to the station* **3** to attract: *his appearance will pull in the crowds* **4** *Brit, Austral, & NZ slang* to arrest **5** to earn (money): *he pulls in at least thirty thousand a year*

Pullman *n, pl* **-mans** *chiefly Brit* a luxurious railway coach
WORD ORIGIN after G. M. *Pullman*, its inventor

pull off *vb informal* to succeed in accomplishing (something difficult): *super-heroes who pull off the impossible*

pull out *vb* **1 a** (of a motor vehicle) to draw away from the side of the road **b** (of a motor vehicle) to move out from behind another vehicle to overtake **2** to depart: *the train pulled out of the station* **3** to withdraw: *several companies have pulled out of the student market* **4** to remove by pulling **5** to abandon a situation

pullover *n* a sweater that is pulled on over the head

pull through *vb* to survive or recover, esp. after a serious illness

pull together *vb* **1** to cooperate or work in harmony **2** **pull oneself together** *informal* to regain one's self-control

pull up *vb* **1** (of a motor vehicle) to stop **2** to remove by the roots **3** to rebuke

pulmonary *adj* **1** of or affecting the lungs **2** having lungs or lunglike organs
WORD ORIGIN Latin *pulmo* a lung

pulp *n* **1** a soft wet substance made from matter which has been crushed or beaten: *mash the strawberries to a pulp* **2** the soft fleshy part of a fruit or vegetable: *halve the tomatoes then scoop the seeds and pulp into a bowl* **3** printed or recorded material with little depth or designed to shock: *pulp fiction; a tape player churned out disco pulp* ▷ *vb* **4** to reduce

Geoffrey Chaucer

Geoffrey Chaucer was born around 1340 into a family of London vintners. Little is known of his early life. His adult years, however, have been more fully documented, as Chaucer was a prominent figure in fourteenth-century England. He was, at various points in his life, a soldier, a member of the royal household, a diplomat, a controller of customs, and a clerk of the King's works in charge of several royal buildings. He married Philippa Roet, whose sister later married John of Gaunt, Chaucer's patron. Chaucer was well-connected and well-travelled; he made at least two diplomatic trips to Italy where he may have met the great Italian poets Boccaccio and Petrarch. He died in 1400 – the date of death given on his tomb is 25th October – and is buried in Westminster Abbey.

Chaucer's first major work was *The Book of the Duchess*, a dream-vision which he wrote to commemorate the death of his patron's first wife, Blanche. The narrator of the poem describes how he fell asleep while reading, and woke in a chamber surrounded by stained-glass windows depicting scenes from the *Romaunt de la Rose* (a French allegorical poem which Chaucer may have partially translated into English). The dreamer-narrator leaves the chamber and meets a knight who is playing a game of chess. The knight speaks of the woman he loved, who died and left him full of grief. The poem ends with the dreamer-narrator waking up and deciding that the dream was so 'queynte' (curious, remarkable) that he will put it into rhyme. Several more of Chaucer's works use the literary convention of the dream-vision: *The Legend of Good Women*, *The House of Fame*, and *The Parliament of Fowls*. This genre allowed Chaucer to layer his narratives and present related scenes (often with an authentic dreamlike quality) while letting the reader link and interpret them.

Troilus and Criseyde is perhaps the best of his completed works. It is based on Boccaccio's *Il Filostrato* (which was itself based on an earlier French poem). The story is of a young prince of Troy, Troilus, who falls in love with a young lady, Criseyde. However, tragedy ensues: the couple are separated, and Criseyde betrays Troilus by falling in love with a Greek warrior. When Troilus learns of this he throws himself into battle and is killed; in heaven, he gains perspective on the folly and transience of earthly love. While Chaucer did not substantially alter the plot of his source material, he added depth and subtlety: in particular, his treatment of Criseyde is sympathetic, and presents her betrayal in the light of her fear and confusion. The poem also contains the humour that suffuses many of Chaucer's works.

However, it is *The Canterbury Tales*, written at the end of Chaucer's life and never completed, which is generally agreed to be his masterpiece. *The Canterbury Tales* is a diverse collection of poems, linked by the narrative device of a pilgrimage to Canterbury where each pilgrim is asked to tell a story. The tales are based on a variety of genres: for example, *The Knight's Tale* is a romance which reflects on the ideals of courtly love; *The Miller's Tale* is a 'fabliau', a comic bawdy tale using stock themes of cuckoldry and deception; while *The Wife of Bath's Tale* uses the literary convention of the 'loathly lady', an old hag who transforms into a beautiful woman on being kissed by a man. The linking of the poems is masterly, and each tale can be interpreted in relation to its teller. Perhaps the most celebrated quality of the *Tales* is its lifelike quality. Although all the pilgrims are to some extent conventional characters, such as the hypocritical monk and the untrustworthy miller, they are brought to life by Chaucer's eye and ear for authenticating detail.

Chaucer was the first English poet to use heroic couplets – rhymed pairs of lines in iambic pentameter – and this earned him the title 'the father of English poetry'. He is equally remembered for his portrayal of human nature in all its forms: in the words of William Blake, 'as Newton numbered the stars, and as Linnaeus numbered the plants, so Chaucer numbered the classes of men'.

a material to pulp: *he began to pulp the orange in his fingers* **pulpy** *adj*
WORD ORIGIN Latin *pulpa*

pulpit *n* **1** a raised platform in churches used for preaching **2** (usually preceded by *the*) preaching or the clergy
WORD ORIGIN Latin *pulpitum* a platform

pulpwood *n* pine, spruce, or any other soft wood used to make paper

pulsar *n* a very small star which emits regular pulses of radio waves
WORD ORIGIN from *puls(ating st)ar*

pulsate *vb* **-sating, -sated** **1** to expand and contract rhythmically, like a heartbeat **2** to quiver or vibrate: *the images pulsate with energy and light* **3** *physics* to vary in intensity or magnitude **pulsation** *n*
WORD ORIGIN Latin *pulsare* to push

pulse¹ *n* **1** *physiol* **a** the regular beating of blood through the arteries at each heartbeat **b** a single such beat **2** *physics, electronics* a sudden change in a quantity, such as a voltage, that is normally constant in a system **3** a regular beat or vibration **4** bustle or excitement: *the lively pulse of a city* **5** the feelings or thoughts of a group as they can be measured: *the political pulse of the capital* ▷ *vb* **pulsing, pulsed 6** to beat, throb, or vibrate
WORD ORIGIN Latin *pulsus* a beating

pulse² *n* the edible seeds of pod-bearing plants, such as peas, beans, and lentils
WORD ORIGIN Latin *puls* pottage of pulse

pulverize *or*-**rise** *vb* **-rizing, -rized** *or* **-rising, -rised** **1** to reduce to fine particles by crushing or grinding **2** to destroy completely **pulverization** *or*-**risation** *n*
WORD ORIGIN Latin *pulvis* dust

puma *n* a large American wild cat with a plain greyish-brown coat and a long tail
WORD ORIGIN S American Indian

pumice (**pumm**-iss) *n* a light porous stone used for scouring and for removing hard skin. Also called: **pumice stone**
WORD ORIGIN Old French *pomis*

pummel *vb* **-melling, -melled** *or US* **-meling, -meled** to strike repeatedly with the fists
WORD ORIGIN see POMMEL

pump¹ *n* **1** a device to force a gas or liquid to move in a particular direction ▷ *vb* **2** (sometimes foll. by *from* or *out* etc.) to raise or drive (air, liquid, etc.) with a pump, esp. into or from something **3** (usually foll. by *in* or *into*) to supply in large amounts: *pumping money into the economy* **4** to operate (a handle etc.) in the manner of a pump: *he was warmly applauded, and his hand was pumped by well-wishers* **5** to obtain information from (someone) by persistent questioning **6 pump iron** *slang* to exercise with weights; do body-building exercises
WORD ORIGIN Middle Dutch *pumpe* pipe

pump² *n* **1** *chiefly Brit* a shoe with a rubber sole, used in games such as tennis; plimsoll **2** *chiefly Brit* a low-cut low-heeled shoe, worn for dancing
WORD ORIGIN origin unknown

pumpernickel *n* a slightly sour black bread made of coarse rye flour
WORD ORIGIN from German

pumpkin *n* **1** a large round fruit with a thick orange rind, pulpy flesh, and many seeds **2** the creeping plant that bears this fruit
WORD ORIGIN Greek *pepōn* ripe

pun *n* **1** the use of words to exploit double meanings for humorous effect, for example *my dog's a champion boxer* ▷ *vb* **punning, punned 2** to make puns
WORD ORIGIN origin unknown

punch¹ *vb* **1** to strike at with a clenched fist ▷ *n* **2** a blow with the fist **3** *informal* point or vigour: *the jokes are mildly amusing but lack any real punch*
WORD ORIGIN probably variant of *pounce* to stamp

punch² *n* **1** a tool or machine for shaping, piercing, or engraving **2** *computers* a device for making holes in a card or paper tape ▷ *vb* **3** to pierce, cut, stamp, shape, or drive with a punch
WORD ORIGIN Latin *pungere* to prick

punch³ *n* a mixed drink containing fruit juice and, usually, alcoholic liquor, generally hot and spiced
WORD ORIGIN origin unknown

Punch *n* the main character in the children's puppet show, Punch and Judy

punchbag *n* a stuffed or inflated bag suspended by a flexible rod, that is punched for exercise, esp. boxing training

punchball *n* a stuffed or inflated ball supported by a flexible rod, that is punched for exercise, esp. boxing training

punchbowl *n* a large bowl for serving punch

punch-drunk *adj* dazed and confused through suffering repeated blows to the head

punched card *or esp. US* **punch card** *n computers* a card on which data can be coded in the form of punched holes

Punchinello *n, pl* **-los** *or*-**loes** a clown from Italian puppet shows, the origin of Punch
WORD ORIGIN Italian *Polecenella*

punch line *n* the last line of a joke or funny story that gives it its point

punch-up *n informal* a fight or brawl

punchy *adj* **punchier, punchiest** *informal* effective or forceful: *learn to compose short concise punchy letters*

punctilious *adj formal* **1** paying careful attention to correct social behaviour **2** attentive to detail **punctiliously** *adv*
WORD ORIGIN Latin *punctum* a point

punctual *adj* **1** arriving or taking place at an arranged time **2** (of a person) always keeping exactly to arranged times **punctuality** *n* **punctually** *adv*
WORD ORIGIN Medieval Latin *punctualis* concerning detail

punctuate *vb* **-ating, -ated** **1** to insert punctuation marks into (a written text) **2** to interrupt at frequent intervals: *the meeting was punctuated by heckling* **3** to emphasize: *he punctuated the question by pressing the muzzle into the pilot's neck*
WORD ORIGIN Latin *pungere* to puncture

punctuation *n* **1** the use of symbols, such as commas, to indicate speech patterns and meaning not otherwise shown by the written language **2** the

symbols used for this purpose

punctuation mark *n* any of the signs used in punctuation, such as a comma

puncture *n* **1** a small hole made by a sharp object **2** a tear and loss of pressure in a tyre **3** the act of puncturing or perforating ▷ *vb* **-turing, -tured** **4** to pierce a hole in (something) with a sharp object **5** to cause (a tyre etc.) to lose pressure by piercing
WORD ORIGIN Latin *pungere* to prick

pundit *n* **1** an expert on a subject who often speaks or writes about it for a non-specialist audience: *Spain's leading sports pundit, who hosts two TV programmes* **2** a Hindu scholar learned in Sanskrit, religion, philosophy, or law
WORD ORIGIN Hindi *pandit*

pungent *adj* **1** having a strong sharp bitter smell or taste **2** (of speech or writing) biting; critical **pungency** *n*
WORD ORIGIN Latin *pungens* piercing

punish *vb* **1** to force (someone) to undergo a penalty for some crime or misbehaviour **2** to inflict punishment for (some crime or misbehaviour) **3** to treat harshly, esp. by overexertion: *he continued to punish himself in the gym* **punishable** *adj* **punishing** *adj*
WORD ORIGIN Latin *punire*

punishment *n* **1** a penalty for a crime or offence **2** the act of punishing or state of being punished **3** *informal* rough physical treatment: *the boxer's face could not withstand further punishment*

punitive (**pew**-nit-tiv) *adj* relating to punishment: *punitive measures*

punk *n* **1** a worthless person **2** a youth movement of the late 1970s, characterized by anti-Establishment slogans, short spiky hair, and the wearing of worthless articles such as safety pins for decoration **3** short for **punk rock 4** a follower of the punk movement or of punk rock ▷ *adj* **5** relating to the punk youth movement of the late 1970s: *a punk band* **6** worthless or insignificant
WORD ORIGIN origin unknown

punkah *or* **punka** *n* (in India) a ceiling fan made of a cloth stretched over a rectangular frame
WORD ORIGIN Hindi *pankhā*

punk rock *n* rock music of the punk youth movement of the late 1970s, characterized by energy and aggressive lyrics and performance **punk rocker** *n*

punnet *n* a small basket for fruit
WORD ORIGIN origin unknown

punster *n* a person who is fond of making puns

punt¹ *n* **1** an open flat-bottomed boat, propelled by a pole ▷ *vb* **2** to propel (a punt) by pushing with a pole on the bottom of a river
WORD ORIGIN Latin *ponto*

punt² *n* **1** a kick in certain sports, such as rugby, in which the ball is dropped and kicked before it hits the ground ▷ *vb* **2** to kick (a ball) using a punt
WORD ORIGIN origin unknown

punt³ *chiefly Brit vb* **1** to gamble or bet ▷ *n* **2** a gamble or bet, esp. against the bank, such as in roulette **3 take a punt at** *Austral & NZ* to make an attempt at
WORD ORIGIN French *ponter*

P

punt[4] *n* a former monetary unit of the Republic of Ireland

punter *n* **1** a person who places a bet **2** *Brit, Austral, & NZ informal* any member of the public, esp. when a customer: *the punters are flocking into the sales*

puny *adj* **-nier, -niest** small and weakly **WORD ORIGIN** Old French *puisné* born later

pup *n* **1 a** a young dog; puppy **b** the young of various other animals, such as the seal ▷ *vb* **pupping, pupped 2** (of dogs, seals, etc.) to give birth to pups

pupa (**pew**-pa) *n, pl* **-pae** (-pee) *or* **-pas** an insect at the stage of development between larva and adult **pupal** *adj* **WORD ORIGIN** Latin: a doll

pupil[1] *n* a student who is taught by a teacher **WORD ORIGIN** Latin *pupus* a child

pupil[2] *n* the dark circular opening at the centre of the iris of the eye **WORD ORIGIN** Latin *pupilla*, diminutive of *pupa* doll; from the tiny reflections in the eye

puppet *n* **1** a small doll or figure moved by strings attached to its limbs or by the hand inserted in its cloth body **2** a person or state that appears independent but is controlled by another: *the former cabinet ministers have denied that they are puppets of a foreign government* **WORD ORIGIN** Latin *pupa* doll

puppeteer *n* a person who operates puppets

puppy *n, pl* **-pies 1** a young dog **2** *informal, contemptuous* a brash or conceited young man **puppyish** *adj* **WORD ORIGIN** Old French *popée* doll

puppy fat *n* fatty tissue that develops in childhood or adolescence and usually disappears with maturity

purblind *adj* **1** partly or nearly blind **2** lacking in understanding **WORD ORIGIN** *pure* (that is, utterly) *blind*

purchase *vb* **-chasing, -chased 1** to obtain (goods) by payment **2** to obtain by effort or sacrifice: *he had purchased his freedom at the expense of his principles* ▷ *n* **3** something that is bought **4** the act of buying **5** the mechanical advantage achieved by a lever **6** a firm leverage or grip **purchaser** *n* **WORD ORIGIN** Old French *porchacier* to strive to obtain

purdah *n* the custom in some Muslim and Hindu communities of keeping women in seclusion, with clothing that conceals them completely when they go out **WORD ORIGIN** Hindi *parda* veil

pure *adj* **1** not mixed with any other materials or elements: *pure wool* **2** free from tainting or polluting matter: *pure water* **3** innocent: *pure love* **4** complete: *Pamela's presence on that particular flight was pure chance* **5** (of a subject) studied in its theoretical aspects rather than for its practical applications: *pure mathematics* **6** of unmixed descent **purely** *adv* **pureness** *n* **WORD ORIGIN** Latin *purus* unstained

purebred *adj* denoting a pure strain obtained through many generations of controlled breeding

puree (**pure**-ray) *n* **1** a smooth thick pulp of sieved fruit, vegetables, meat, or fish ▷ *vb* **-reeing, -reed 2** to make (foods) into a puree **WORD ORIGIN** French

purgative *med n* **1** a medicine for emptying the bowels ▷ *adj* **2** causing emptying of the bowels

purgatory *n* **1** *chiefly RC Church* a place in which the souls of those who have died undergo limited suffering for their sins on earth before they go to heaven **2** a situation of temporary suffering or torment: *it was purgatory living in the same house as him* **purgatorial** *adj* **WORD ORIGIN** Latin *purgare* to purify

purge *vb* **purging, purged 1** to rid (something) of undesirable qualities **2** to rid (an organization etc.) of undesirable people: *the party was purged* **3 a** to empty (the bowels) **b** to cause (a person) to empty his or her bowels **4 a** *law* to clear (a person) of a charge **b** to free (oneself) of guilt by showing repentance **5** to be purified ▷ *n* **6** the act or process of purging **7** the removal of undesirables from a state, organization, or political party **8** a medicine that empties the bowels **WORD ORIGIN** Latin *purgare* to purify

purify *vb* **-fies, -fying, -fied 1** to free (something) of harmful or inferior matter **2** to free (a person) from sin or guilt **3** to make clean, for example in a religious ceremony **purification** *n* **WORD ORIGIN** Latin *purus* pure + *facere* to make

purism *n* strict insistence on the correct usage or style, such as in grammar or art **purist** *adj, n* **puristic** *adj*

puritan *n* **1** a person who follows strict moral or religious principles ▷ *adj* **2** of or like a puritan: *he maintained a streak of puritan self-denial* **puritanism** *n* **WORD ORIGIN** Late Latin *puritas* purity

Puritan *history n* **1** a member of the extreme English Protestants who wished to strip the Church of England of most of its rituals ▷ *adj* **2** of or relating to the Puritans **Puritanism** *n*

puritanical *adj* **1** *usually disparaging* strict in moral or religious outlook **2** (*sometimes cap*) of or relating to a puritan or the Puritans **puritanically** *adv*

purity *n* the state or quality of being pure

purl[1] *n* **1** a knitting stitch made by doing a plain stitch backwards **2** a decorative border, such as of lace ▷ *vb* **3** to knit in purl stitch **WORD ORIGIN** dialect *pirl* to twist into a cord

purl[2] *vb literary* (of a stream) to flow with a gentle movement and a murmuring sound **WORD ORIGIN** probably imitative

purlieu (**per**-lyoo) *n* **1** *English history* land on the edge of a royal forest **2** (*usually pl*) *literary* a neighbouring area; outskirts **3** (*often pl*) *literary* a place one frequents: *the committee was the purlieu of civil servants* **WORD ORIGIN** Anglo-French *puralé* a going through

purlin *or* **purline** *n* a horizontal beam that supports the rafters of a roof **WORD ORIGIN** origin unknown

purloin *vb formal* to steal **WORD ORIGIN** Old French *porloigner* to put at a distance

purple *n* **1** a colour between red and blue **2** cloth of this colour, often used to symbolize royalty or nobility **3** the official robe of a cardinal **4** anything purple, such as purple paint or purple clothing: *a large lady, unwisely dressed in purple* ▷ *adj* **5** of a colour between red and blue **6** (of writing) excessively elaborate: *purple prose* **purplish** *adj* **WORD ORIGIN** Greek *porphura* the purple fish (murex)

purple heart *n informal chiefly Brit* a heart-shaped purple tablet consisting mainly of amphetamine

Purple Heart *n* a decoration awarded to members of the US Armed Forces wounded in action

purport *vb* **1** to claim to be or do something, esp. falsely: *painkillers may actually cause the headaches they purport to cure* **2** (of speech or writing) to signify or imply ▷ *n* **3** meaning or significance **WORD ORIGIN** Old French *porporter* to convey

purpose *n* **1** the reason for which anything is done, created, or exists **2** a fixed design or idea that is the object of an action **3** determination: *his easy manner only lightly conceals a clear sense of purpose* **4** practical advantage or use: *we debated senseless points of dogma for hours to no fruitful purpose* **5** **on purpose** intentionally ▷ *vb* **-posing, -posed 6** to intend or determine to do (something) **WORD ORIGIN** Old French *porposer* to plan

purpose-built *adj* made to serve a specific purpose

purposeful *adj* with a fixed and definite purpose; determined **purposefully** *adv*
⟐ USAGE
⟐ *Purposefully* is sometimes wrongly used where *purposely* is meant: *he had purposely (not purposefully) left the door unlocked.*

purposely *adv* on purpose
⟐ USAGE
⟐ See at **purposeful**.

purposive *adj formal* **1** having or showing a definite intention: *the establishment of the camps lacks a purposive trend towards a solution* **2** useful

purr *vb* **1** (esp. of cats) to make a low vibrant sound, usually considered as expressing pleasure **2** to express (pleasure) by this sound or by a sound suggestive of purring ▷ *n* **3** a purring sound **WORD ORIGIN** imitative

purse *n* **1** a small pouch for carrying money **2** *US, Canad, Austral, & NZ* a woman's handbag **3** wealth or resources: *the public purse appeared bottomless* **4** a sum of money that is offered as a prize ▷ *vb* **pursing, pursed 5** to pull (the lips) into a small rounded shape **WORD ORIGIN** Old English *purs*

purser *n* an officer aboard a ship who keeps the accounts

purse strings *pl n* **hold the purse strings** to control the spending of a particular family, group, etc.

P

pursuance *n formal* the carrying out of an action or plan: *the pursuance of duty had taken him abroad*

pursue *vb* **-suing, -sued 1** to follow (a person, vehicle, or animal) in order to capture or overtake **2** to try hard to achieve (some desire or aim) **3** to follow the guidelines of (a plan or policy) **4** to apply oneself to (studies or interests) **5** to follow persistently or seek to become acquainted with: *was his desire to pursue and marry Carol based purely on her looks?* **6** to continue to discuss or argue (a point or subject) **pursuer** *n*
WORD ORIGIN Old French *poursivre*

pursuit *n* **1** the act of pursuing **2** an occupation or pastime

pursuivant (**purse**-iv-ant) *n* the lowest rank of heraldic officer
WORD ORIGIN Old French

purulent (**pure**-yew-lent) *adj* of, relating to, or containing pus **purulence** *n*
WORD ORIGIN Latin *purulentus*

purvey *vb* **1** to sell or provide (foodstuffs) **2** to provide or make available: *the foreign ministry used him to purvey sensitive items of diplomatic news* **purveyor** *n*
WORD ORIGIN Old French *porveeir* to provide

purview *n* **1** scope of operation: *each designation falls under the purview of a different ministry* **2** breadth or range of outlook: *he hopes that the purview of science will be widened*
WORD ORIGIN Anglo-Norman *purveu*

pus *n* the yellowish fluid that comes from inflamed or infected tissue
WORD ORIGIN Latin

push *vb* **1** (sometimes foll. by *off* or *away* etc.) to apply steady force to in order to move **2** to thrust (one's way) through something, such as a crowd **3** (sometimes foll. by *for*) to be an advocate or promoter (of): *there are many groups you can join to push for change* **4** to spur or drive (oneself or another person) in order to achieve more effort or better results: *you must be careful not to push your children too hard* **5** *informal* to sell (narcotic drugs) illegally ▷ *n* **6** the act of pushing; thrust **7** *informal* drive or determination: *everything depends on him having the push to obtain the money* **8** *informal* a special effort to achieve something: *when this push spent itself it was obvious the bid had failed* **9** **the push** *Brit & NZ informal* dismissal from employment ▸ See also **push about, push off,** etc.
WORD ORIGIN Latin *pulsare*

push about *or* **around** *vb informal* to bully: *don't let them push you around*

push-bike *n Brit, Austral, & NZ informal* a bicycle

push button *n* **1** an electrical switch operated by pressing a button ▷ *adj* **push-button 2** operated by a push button: *a push-button radio*

pushchair *n Brit* a small folding chair on wheels in which a small child can be wheeled around: *escalators are difficult with pushchairs*

pushed *adj* (often foll. by *for*) *informal* short of: *pushed for time*

pusher *n informal* a person who sells illegal drugs

pushing *prep* **1** almost or nearly (a certain age, speed, etc.): *pushing fifty* ▷ *adj* **2** aggressively ambitious

push off *vb informal* to go away; leave

pushover *n informal* **1** something that is easily achieved **2** a person, team, etc. that is easily taken advantage of or defeated

push-start *vb* **1** to start (a motor vehicle) by pushing it, thus turning the engine ▷ *n* **2** this process

push through *vb* to force to accept: *the President wants to push through his economic package*

pushy *adj* **pushier, pushiest** *informal* offensively assertive or ambitious

pusillanimous *adj formal* timid and cowardly: *pusillanimous behaviour* **pusillanimity** *n*
WORD ORIGIN Latin *pusillus* weak + *animus* courage

puss *n* **1** *informal* a cat **2** *slang* a girl or woman
WORD ORIGIN probably Low German

pussy[1] *n, pl* **pussies 1** Also called: **pussycat** *informal* a cat **2** *taboo slang* the female genitals
WORD ORIGIN from *puss*

pussy[2] *adj* **-sier, -siest** containing or full of pus

pussyfoot *vb informal* **1** to move about stealthily **2** to avoid committing oneself: *don't let's pussyfoot about naming the hit man*

pussy willow *n* a willow tree with silvery silky catkins

pustulate *vb* **-lating, -lated** to form into pustules

pustule *n* a small inflamed raised area of skin containing pus **pustular** *adj*
WORD ORIGIN Latin *pustula* a blister

put *vb* **putting, put 1** to cause to be (in a position or place): *he put the book on the table* **2** to cause to be (in a state or condition): *what can be done to put things right?* **3** to lay (blame, emphasis, etc.) on a person or thing: *don't try to put the blame on someone else!* **4** to set or commit (to an action, task, or duty), esp. by force: *she put him to work weeding the garden* **5** to estimate or judge: *I wouldn't put him in the same class as Verdi as a composer* **6** (foll. by *to*) to utilize: *he put his culinary skills to good use when he opened a restaurant* **7** to express: *he didn't put it quite as crudely as that* **8** to make (an end or limit): *opponents claim the scheme will put an end to much of the sailing and boating in the area* **9** to present for consideration; propose: *he put the question to the committee* **10** to invest (money) in or expend (time or energy) on: *they put a lot of money into the sport* **11** to throw or cast: *put the shot* ▷ *n* **12** a throw, esp. in putting the shot
▸ See also **put about, put across,** etc.
WORD ORIGIN Middle English *puten* to push

put about *vb* **1** to make widely known: *a rumour was put about that he had been drunk* **2** *naut* to change course

put across *vb* to communicate successfully: *he's not very good at putting his ideas across*

put aside *vb* **1** to save: *try to put some money aside in case of emergencies* **2** to

disregard: *put aside adolescent fantasies of romance*

putative (**pew**-tat-iv) *adj formal* **1** commonly regarded as being: *the desire of the putative father to establish his possible paternity* **2** considered to exist or have existed; inferred: *a putative earlier form*
WORD ORIGIN Latin *putare* to consider

put away *vb* **1** to save: *it takes a lot of discipline to put away something for your old age* **2** *informal* to lock up in a prison, mental institution, etc.: *we have enough evidence to put him away for life* **3** *informal* to eat or drink in large amounts: *he put away three beers and three huge shots of brandy*

put back *vb* **1** to return to its former place **2** to move to a later time: *the finals could be put back until Monday*

put down *vb* **1** to make a written record of **2** to repress: *the rising was put down with revolting cruelty* **3** to consider: *I'd put him down as a complete fool* **4** to attribute: *the government's defeat in the election can be put down to a general desire for change* **5** to put (an animal) to death **6** *slang* to belittle or humiliate ▷ *n* **put-down 7** *informal* a cruelly crushing remark

put forward *vb* **1** to propose or suggest **2** to offer the name of; nominate

put in *vb* **1** to devote (time or effort): *the competitors who did best were the ones who had put in some practice* **2** (often foll. by *for*) to apply (for a job) **3** to submit: *they have put in an official complaint* **4** *naut* to bring a vessel into port

put off *vb* **1** to postpone: *ministers have put off making a decision until next month* **2** to evade (a person) by delay: *they tried to put him off, but he came anyway* **3** to cause dislike in: *he was put off by her appearance* **4** to cause to lose interest in: *the accident put him off sailing* **5** to distract: *a swerving cyclist may have put off the driver*

put on *vb* **1** to dress oneself in **2** to adopt (an attitude or feeling) insincerely: *I don't see why you have to put on that fake American accent* **3** to present (a play or show) **4** to add: *I've put on nearly a stone since September* **5** to cause (an electrical device) to function: *he put on the light* **6** to bet (money) on a horse race or game **7** to impose: *the government has put a tax on gas*

put out *vb* **1 a** to annoy or anger **b** to disturb or confuse **2** to extinguish (a fire, light, etc.) **3** to inconvenience (someone): *I hope I'm not putting you out* **4** to select or lay out for use: *she put out two clean cloths in the kitchen* **5** to publish or broadcast: *she put out a statement denying the rumours* **6** to dislocate: *he put his back out digging the garden*

put over *vb informal* to communicate (facts or information)

putrefy *vb* **-fies, -fying, -fied** *formal* (of organic matter) to rot and produce an offensive smell **putrefaction** *n*
WORD ORIGIN Latin *putrefacere*

putrescent *adj formal* becoming putrid; rotting: *putrescent toadstools* **putrescence** *n*
WORD ORIGIN Latin *putrescere* to become rotten

putrid *adj* **1** (of organic matter) rotting: *putrid meat* **2** sickening or foul: *a putrid stench* **3** *informal* deficient in quality or value: *a penchant for putrid puns* **4** morally

Hunter S Thompson

Hunter Stockton Thompson is best known as the inventor and pioneer of *gonzo journalism*, a hugely influential form of The New Journalism that had developed in the 1960s. The New Journalism (a term coined by Tom Wolfe) was characterized by a move away from more traditional objective reporting. Gonzo journalism took this approach several steps further by incorporating black humour, raving rhetoric, drug and alcohol misuse, hallucinatory imagery, and the blurring of fact and fiction into its wildly subjective first-person style. *Gonzo* is defined by *Collins English Dictionary* as: (in the journalistic sense) 'explicitly including the writer's feelings at the time of witnessing the events or undergoing the experiences written about'. Thompson himself coined the phrase, but it may have roots in the Spanish *ganso*, meaning 'idiot' or 'bumpkin' (the literal translation is 'goose').

Thompson's early works (notably as a sports journalist) were, by necessity, more conventional before the Gonzo style was debuted in his article *The Kentucky Derby is Decadent and Depraved* (accompanied by warped illustrations from Ralph Steadman, who would become a long-term collaborator). The article focussed not on the race itself, but on the drunken behaviour of the spectators ('We had come there to watch the real beasts perform.'). This included Thompson and Steadman who, in their attempt to better understand the event, became the story themselves. Thompson's own description of Gonzo journalism is: 'a style of "reporting" based on William Faulkner's idea that the best fiction is far more true than any kind of journalism – and the best journalists have always known this.' His opinion of objective journalism was uncompromising: 'The phrase itself is a pompous contradiction in terms.'

Thompson was born in Kentucky in 1937 and is known historically as a Doctor of Journalism, although his doctorate was actually in Divinity, and came via mail order. His main literary influences were heavyweights: Hemingway, Joseph Conrad, F Scott Fitzgerald, and Mark Twain. He also invoked (sarcastically) Horatio Alger's morally simplistic tales of righteous men. He was influenced by writings about men on mythic journeys, and he treated his writing as the same: his unifying theme was a search for the American Dream, and his quest was no less serious for all its humour and madness. Having spent much of his working life typing copy in hotel rooms, Thompson also claimed to have 'stolen more quotes and thoughts and purely elegant starbursts of writing from the book of Revelation than anything else in the English language' as there would always be a Bible to read for inspiration.

His earliest major success was with his investigative sociological memoir of riding with motorcycle gangs *Hell's Angels* (1965) but his most famous title is undoubtedly *Fear and Loathing in Las Vegas: A Savage Journey to the Heart of the American Dream* (1972). The work was originally intended as an article covering the Mint 400 motorcycle race for *Sports Illustrated* magazine. What resulted was an account of the weekend's drug-fuelled experiences. The article was eventually published by *Rolling Stone* magazine, and later as a book. Its opening sentence is as iconic as anything in American literature ('We were somewhere around Barstow on the edge of the desert when the drugs began to take hold...') and it features in its celebrated passage on 'the wave' Thompson's most concentrated critique of the counter-culture and its failure to acknowledge the 'grim meat-hook realities' of existence.

Thompson's use of language is distinctive and hyperbolic, with the use of certain modifiers and intensifiers as motif. *Savage*, *atavistic*, and *outlaw* are prevalent, along with *frenzy*, *swine*, *rotten*, and *craziness*. His writing style is highly charged and emotive, combining the adrenaline of New Journalism with the man-on-an-obsessive-personal-quest voice of Hemingway or Conrad. Thompson opens his most celebrated work *Fear And Loathing In Las Vegas* with a quote from Dr Johnson ('He who makes a beast of himself gets rid of the pain of being a man') and closes *Hell's Angels* with a quote from *Heart of Darkness*: 'I wanted something original, but there was no escaping the echo of Mistah Kurtz's final words from the heart of darkness: "The horror! The horror! ... Exterminate all the brutes!"'

Thompson committed suicide in 2005. His remains were blasted into the sky by cannon, as per his request.

corrupt **putridity** n
WORD ORIGIN Latin *putrere* to be rotten

putsch n a violent and sudden political revolt: *an attempted putsch against the general*
WORD ORIGIN from German

putt *golf* n **1** a stroke on the green with a putter to roll the ball into or near the hole ▷ vb **2** to strike (the ball) in this way
WORD ORIGIN Scot

puttee n (*usually pl*) (esp. as part of a military uniform) a strip of cloth worn wound around the leg from the ankle to the knee
WORD ORIGIN Hindi *pattī*

putter n *golf* a club, usually with a short shaft, for putting

put through vb **1** to connect by telephone: *I'm sorry, you've been put through to the wrong extension* **2** to carry out to a conclusion

putting green n (on a golf course) the area of closely mown grass around the hole

putty n, pl **-ties 1** a stiff paste used to fix glass into frames and fill cracks in woodwork ▷ vb **-ties, -tying, -tied 2** to fix or fill with putty
WORD ORIGIN French *potée* a potful

put up vb **1** to build or erect: *I want to put up a fence round the garden* **2** to display (a poster, sign, etc.) **3** to accommodate or be accommodated at: *can you put me up for tonight?* **4** to increase (prices) **5** to submit (a plan, case, etc.) **6** to offer: *the factory is being put up for sale* **7** to give: *they put up a good fight* **8** to provide (money) for: *they put up 35% of the film's budget* **9** to nominate or be nominated as a candidate: *the party have yet to decide whether to put up a candidate* **10 put up to** to incite to: *I wonder who put them up to it?* **11 put up with** *informal* to endure or tolerate ▷ adj **put-up 12** *informal* dishonestly or craftily prearranged: *a put-up job*

put upon vb to take advantage of (someone): *he's always being put upon*

putz n *US slang* a despicable or stupid person
WORD ORIGIN Yiddish *puts* ornament

puzzle vb **-zling, -zled 1** to baffle or bewilder **2 puzzle out** to solve (a problem) by mental effort **3 puzzle over** to think deeply about in an attempt to understand: *he puzzled over the squiggles and curves on the paper* ▷ n **4** a

problem that cannot be easily solved **5** a toy, game, or question presenting a problem that requires skill or ingenuity for its solution **puzzlement** n **puzzled** adj **puzzler** n **puzzling** adj
WORD ORIGIN origin unknown

PVC polyvinyl chloride

PVS persistent vegetative state

PW policewoman

PWR pressurized-water reactor

pyaemia or **pyemia** n *med* blood poisoning with pus-forming microorganisms in the blood
WORD ORIGIN Greek *puon* pus + *haima* blood

pye-dog or **pi-dog** n a half-wild Asian dog with no owner
WORD ORIGIN Hindi *pāhī* outsider

pygmy n, pl **-mies 1** something that is a very small example of its type **2** an abnormally undersized person **3** a person of little importance or significance ▷ adj **4** very small: *the pygmy anteater*
WORD ORIGIN Greek *pugmaios* undersized

Pygmy n, pl **-mies** a member of one of the very short peoples of Equatorial Africa

pyjamas or US **pajamas** pl n a loose-fitting jacket or top and trousers worn to sleep in
WORD ORIGIN Persian *pai* leg + *jāma* garment

pylon n **1** chiefly *Brit* a large vertical steel tower-like structure supporting high-tension electrical cables **2** *US & Canad* a plastic cone used to demarcate areas, esp. on public roads
WORD ORIGIN Greek *pulōn* a gateway

pyorrhoea or esp. US **pyorrhea** (pire-**ree**-a) n *med* a discharge of pus, esp. in diseases of the gums or tooth sockets
WORD ORIGIN Greek *puon* pus + *rhein* to flow

pyramid n **1** a huge stone building with a square base and four sloping triangular sides meeting in a point, such as the royal tombs built by the ancient Egyptians **2** *maths* a solid figure with a polygonal base and triangular sides that meet in a common vertex **pyramidal** adj
WORD ORIGIN Greek *puramis*

pyramid selling n the practice of selling distributors batches of goods which they then subdivide and sell to

other distributors, this process continuing until the final distributors are left with a stock that is unsaleable except at a loss

pyre n a pile of wood for cremating a corpse
WORD ORIGIN Greek *pur* fire

pyrethrum (pie-**reeth**-rum) n **1** a Eurasian chrysanthemum with white, pink, red, or purple flowers **2** an insecticide prepared from dried pyrethrum flowers
WORD ORIGIN Greek *purethron*

pyretic (pie-**ret**-ik) adj *pathol* of, relating to, or characterized by fever
WORD ORIGIN Greek *puretos* fever

Pyrex n *trademark* a variety of heat-resistant glassware used in cookery and chemical apparatus

pyrite (**pie**-rite) n a yellow mineral consisting of iron sulphide in cubic crystalline form. Formula: FeS_2
WORD ORIGIN Latin *pyrites* flint

pyrites (pie-**rite**-eez) n, pl **-tes 1** same as **pyrite 2** a disulphide of a metal, esp. of copper and tin

pyromania n *psychiatry* the uncontrollable impulse and practice of setting things on fire **pyromaniac** n, adj
WORD ORIGIN Greek *pur* fire + *mania* madness

pyrotechnics n **1** the art of making fireworks **2** a firework display **3** a brilliant display of skill: *all those courtroom pyrotechnics* **pyrotechnic** adj
WORD ORIGIN Greek *pur* fire + *tekhnē* art

Pyrrhic victory (**pir**-ik) n a victory in which the victor's losses are as great as those of the defeated
WORD ORIGIN after *Pyrrhus*, who defeated the Romans in 279 BC but suffered heavy losses

Pythagoras' theorem (pie-**thag**-or-ass) n the theorem that in a right-angled triangle the square of the length of the hypotenuse equals the sum of the squares of the other two sides
WORD ORIGIN after *Pythagoras*, Greek philosopher and mathematician

python n a large nonpoisonous snake of Australia, Africa, and S Asia which kills its prey by crushing it with its body
WORD ORIGIN after *Python*, a dragon killed by Apollo

pyx n *Christianity* any receptacle in which the bread used in Holy Communion is kept
WORD ORIGIN Latin *pyxis* small box

P

Qq

The letter Q is the seventeenth letter of the English alphabet. It has no equivalent in the standard Greek alphabet, although the early Greek alphabet had a letter called *koppa*, which had a similar shape to Q, but a vertical rather than a curved tail. This was derived from a Phoenician letter called *qoph*, which literally meant 'monkey'. (The characteristic 'tail' of the Q may therefore have started out as a representation of a monkey's tail.) In Classical Greek, the *koppa* had been discarded from the alphabet, its sound being too similar to that of *kappa*, although it continued to be used as a numeral.

However, the letter was preserved in the writing of the Etruscans, and from there it found its way into the Roman alphabet. In the Roman alphabet the letter had a /k/ sound, but was differentiated from C and K by being used in front of the consonant V, which was sounded like a W and regarded as identical with the letter U. Thus Q acquired both its distinctive /kw/ sound and also the characteristic of being always followed by U.

The fact that a Q cannot (except in a few words loaned from languages such as Arabic) be used without a U makes it an unwelcome letter for players of Scrabble. The opportunities to play the letter are scarce, but it does score a premium of 10 points.

Only a small number of English words begin with the letter Q, but these include 'quiz', 'question', and 'query', all of which give the letter associations with mystery and interrogation.

The use of Q to mean 'query' is observed in the name 'Q-boat', a military vessel with concealed guns that was used to combat the threat posed by submarines during both World Wars. Similarly, an acute disease of unknown origin was called 'Q-fever', and kept this name even after its source was identified by scientists.

These associations would seem to make Q a natural code-letter for the secret-service boffin (played on screen by Desmond Llewelyn and latterly by John Cleese) who devises all manner of fiendish gadgets for agents in the James Bond stories. In fact, however, Ian Fleming alighted on this initial because of the character's role as a supervisor of equipment or 'quartermaster'.

Q 1 *chess* queen **2** question

q. 1 quart **2** quarter **3** question **4** quire

Q. 1 Queen **2** question

QC 1 Queen's Counsel **2** Quebec

QED which was to be shown or proved **WORD ORIGIN** Latin *quod erat demonstrandum*

QLD *or* **Qld** Queensland

QM Quartermaster

qr. *pl* **qrs 1** quarter **2** quire

qt *pl* **qt** *or* **qts** quart

q.t. *n* **on the q.t.** *informal* secretly

qua (kwah) *prep* in the capacity of; by virtue of being **WORD ORIGIN** Latin

quack¹ *vb* **1** (of a duck) to utter a harsh guttural sound **2** to make a noise like a duck ▷ *n* **3** the sound made by a duck **WORD ORIGIN** imitative

quack² *n* **1** an unqualified person who claims medical knowledge **2** *Brit, Austral, & NZ informal* a doctor **quackery** *n* **WORD ORIGIN** short for *quacksalver*, from Dutch

quad¹ *n* short for **quadrangle** (sense 1)

quad² *n informal* a quadruplet

quad³ *n* **1** quadraphonics ▷ *adj* **2** quadraphonic

quad bike *or* **quad** *n* a vehicle like a small motorcycle, with four large wheels, designed for agricultural and sporting uses

quadrangle *n* **1** a rectangular courtyard with buildings on all four sides **2** *geom* a figure consisting of four points connected by four lines **quadrangular** *adj* **WORD ORIGIN** Late Latin *quadrangulum*

quadrant *n* **1** *geom* **a** a quarter of the circumference of a circle **b** the area enclosed by two perpendicular radii of a circle **2** a piece of a mechanism in the form of a quarter circle **3** an instrument formerly used in astronomy and navigation for measuring the altitudes of stars **WORD ORIGIN** Latin *quadrans* a quarter

quadraphonic *adj* using four independent channels to reproduce or record sound **quadraphonics** *n*

quadrate *n* **1** a cube or square, or a square or cubelike object ▷ *vb* **-rating, -rated 2** to make square or rectangular **WORD ORIGIN** Latin *quadrare* to make square

quadratic *maths n* **1** Also called: **quadratic equation** an equation in which the variable is raised to the power of two, but nowhere raised to a higher power: *solve the quadratic equation* $2x^2-3x-6=3$ ▷ *adj* **2** of or relating to the second power

quadrennial *adj* **1** occurring every four years **2** lasting four years

quadri- *or before a vowel* **quadr-** *combining form* four: *quadrilateral* **WORD ORIGIN** Latin

quadriceps *n anat* a muscle at the front of the thigh **WORD ORIGIN** New Latin

quadrilateral *adj* **1** having four sides ▷ *n* **2** a polygon with four sides

quadrille *n* **1** a square dance for four couples **2** music for this dance **WORD ORIGIN** Spanish *cuadrilla*

quadrillion *n, pl* **-lions** *or* **-lion 1** (in Britain, France, and Germany) the number represented as one followed by 24 zeros (10^{24}) **2** (in the US and Canada) the number represented as one followed by 15 zeros (10^{15}) **WORD ORIGIN** French *quadrillon*

quadriplegia *n* paralysis of all four limbs **quadriplegic** *adj, n* **WORD ORIGIN** QUADRI- + Greek *plēssein* to strike

quadruped (kwod-roo-ped) *n* an animal, esp. a mammal, that has four legs

WORD ORIGIN Latin *quadru-* four + *pes* foot

quadruple *vb* **-pling, -pled 1** to multiply by four ▷ *adj* **2** four times as much or as many **3** consisting of four parts **4** *music* having four beats in each bar ▷ *n* **5** a quantity or number four times as great as another
WORD ORIGIN Latin *quadru-* four + *-plus* -fold

quadruplet *n* one of four children born at one birth

quadruplicate *adj* **1** fourfold or quadruple ▷ *vb* **-cating, -cated 2** to multiply or be multiplied by four
WORD ORIGIN Latin *quadruplicare* to increase fourfold

quaff (**kwoff**) *vb old-fashioned* to drink heartily or in one draught
WORD ORIGIN perhaps imitative

quagga *n, pl* **-gas** *or* **-ga** a recently extinct zebra, striped only on the head and shoulders
WORD ORIGIN Hottentot *qŭagga*

quagmire (**kwog**-mire) *n* a soft wet area of land that gives way under the feet; bog
WORD ORIGIN from *quag* bog + *mire*

quail¹ *n, pl* **quails** *or* **quail** a small game bird of the partridge family
WORD ORIGIN Old French *quaille*

quail² *vb* to shrink back with fear; cower
WORD ORIGIN origin unknown

quaint *adj* attractively unusual, esp. in an old-fashioned style
WORD ORIGIN Old French *cointe*, from Latin *cognitus* known

quake *vb* **quaking, quaked 1** to shake or tremble with or as if with fear **2** to shudder because of instability ▷ *n* **3** *informal* an earthquake
WORD ORIGIN Old English *cwacian*

Quaker *n* a member of a Christian sect, the Religious Society of Friends **Quakerism** *n*
WORD ORIGIN originally an offensive nickname

qualification *n* **1** an official record of achievement awarded on the successful completion of a course of training or passing of an examination **2** an ability, quality, or attribute, esp. one that fits a person to perform a particular job or task **3** a condition that modifies or limits; restriction **4** the act of qualifying or being qualified

qualified *adj* **1** having successfully completed a training course or passed the exams necessary in order to be entitled to work in a particular profession: *a qualified lawyer* **2** having the abilities, qualities, or attributes necessary to perform a particular job or task **3** having completed a training or degree course and gained the relevant certificates **4** limited or restricted; not wholehearted: *the mission was only a qualified success*

qualify *vb* **-fies, -fying, -fied 1** to have the abilities or attributes required in order to do or have something, such as a job: *he qualified as a teacher; she did not qualify for a State pension at that time* **2** to moderate or restrict (a statement one has made) **3** to describe or be described as having a particular quality: *it was neither witty nor subtle enough to qualify as*

a spoof **4** to be successful in one stage of a competition and as a result progress to the next stage: *Lewis failed to qualify for the 100 metres* **5** *grammar* to modify the sense of (a word) **qualifier** *n*
WORD ORIGIN Latin *qualis* of what kind + *facere* to make

qualitative *adj* involving or relating to distinctions based on quality

qualitative analysis *n chem* analysis of a substance to determine its constituents

quality *n, pl* **-ties 1** degree or standard of excellence **2** a distinguishing characteristic or attribute **3** the basic character or nature of something **4** a feature of personality **5** (formerly) high social status ▷ *adj* **6** excellent or superior: *a quality product*
WORD ORIGIN Latin *qualis* of what sort

quality assurance *n commerce* the process of verifying that a product conforms to required standards, often performed by an independent assessor

quality control *n* checking of the relative quality of a manufactured product, usually by testing samples

qualm (**kwahm**) *n* **1** a pang of conscience; scruple **2** a sudden sensation of misgiving **3** a sudden feeling of sickness or nausea
WORD ORIGIN Old English *cwealm* death or plague

quandary *n, pl* **-ries** a situation in which it is difficult to decide what to do; predicament; dilemma
WORD ORIGIN origin unknown

quandong (**kwon**-dong) *n* **1** a small Australian tree with edible fruit and nuts used in preserves **2** an Australian tree with pale timber

quango *n, pl* **-gos** a semipublic government-financed administrative body whose members are appointed by the government
WORD ORIGIN *qu(asi-)a(utonomous) n(on) g(overnmental) o(rganization)*

quantify *vb* **-fies, -fying, -fied** to discover or express the quantity of **quantifiable** *adj* **quantification** *n*
WORD ORIGIN Latin *quantus* how much + *facere* to make

quantitative *adj* **1** involving considerations of amount or size **2** capable of being measured

quantitative analysis *n chem* analysis of a substance to determine the proportions of its constituents

quantitative easing *or* **quantitive easing** *n* the practice of increasing the supply of money in order to stimulate economic activity

quantity *n, pl* **-ties 1** a specified or definite amount or number **2** the aspect of anything that can be measured, weighed, or counted **3** a large amount **4** *maths* an entity having a magnitude that may be denoted by a numerical expression
WORD ORIGIN Latin *quantus* how much

USAGE
The use of a plural noun after *quantity of* as in *a large quantity of bananas* was formerly considered incorrect, but is now acceptable.

quantity surveyor *n* a person who estimates the cost of the materials and labour necessary for a construction job

quantum *n, pl* **-ta 1** an amount or quantity, esp. a specific amount **2** *physics* the smallest quantity of some physical property that a system can possess ▷ *adj* **3** of or designating a major breakthrough or sudden advance: *a quantum leap in business computing*
WORD ORIGIN Latin *quantus* how much

quantum theory *n* a theory concerning the behaviour of physical systems based on the idea that they can only possess certain properties, such as energy and angular momentum, in discrete amounts (quanta)

quarantine *n* **1** a period of isolation, esp. of people or animals arriving from abroad, to prevent the spread of disease ▷ *vb* **-tining, -tined 2** to isolate in or as if in quarantine
WORD ORIGIN Italian *quarantina* period of forty days

quark *n physics* the hypothetical elementary particle supposed to be a fundamental unit of all baryons and mesons
WORD ORIGIN special use of a word coined by James Joyce in the novel *Finnegans Wake*

quarrel *n* **1** an angry disagreement; argument **2** a cause of dispute; grievance ▷ *vb* **-relling, -relled** *or US* **-reling, -reled** (often foll. by *with*) **3** to engage in a disagreement or dispute; argue **4** to find fault; complain
WORD ORIGIN Latin *querella* complaint

quarrelsome *adj* inclined to quarrel or disagree

quarry¹ *n, pl* **-ries 1** a place where stone is dug from the surface of the earth ▷ *vb* **-ries, -rying, -ried 2** to extract (stone) from a quarry
WORD ORIGIN Old French *quarriere*

quarry² *n, pl* **-ries 1** an animal that is being hunted; prey **2** anything pursued
WORD ORIGIN Middle English *quirre* entrails offered to the hounds

quarry tile *n* an unglazed floor tile

quart *n* a unit of liquid measure equal to one quarter of a gallon or two pints (1.136 litres)
WORD ORIGIN Latin *quartus* fourth

quarter *n* **1** one of four equal parts of something such as an object or quantity **2** the fraction equal to one divided by four (¼) **3** a fourth part of a year; three months **4** *Brit informal* a unit of weight equal to four ounces (113.4 grams) **5** a region or district of a town or city: *the French quarter of New Orleans* **6** a region, direction, or point of the compass **7** *US & Canad* a coin worth 25 cents **8** short for **quarter-hour 9** *astron* **a** one fourth of the moon's period of revolution around the earth **b** either of two phases of the moon when half of the lighted surface is visible **10** (*sometimes pl*) an unspecified person or group of people: *it met stiff opposition in some quarters* **11** mercy or pity shown to a defeated opponent: *no quarter was asked or given* **12** any of the four limbs of a quadruped ▷ *vb* **13** to divide into four equal parts **14** (formerly) to

The History of the Crossword

The crossword as we know it is only about 100 years old. The first crossword appeared in the New York Sunday newspaper *World* in 1913. A journalist, Arthur Wynne, had been asked to create a new game for the 'fun' section of the paper and, recalling acrostic puzzles from his childhood, devised a diamond-shaped grid with clues for the words. He called this a 'Word Cross'. This later became known as a 'cross-word'. When the hyphen disappeared, the crossword had arrived.

The first British crossword was a 'quick' crossword, appearing in 1923. A setter with the awe-inspiring pseudonym of Torquemada (Edward Powys Mathers) championed the cryptic element of crosswords from the mid-1920s. The first *Times* crossword was published in 1930; by then most British newspapers were carrying a crossword puzzle. A crossword-solving craze had begun which endures to this day, boosting daily sales of national newspapers and giving a focus to tea breaks across the land.

Cryptic crosswords are a phenomenon enjoyed mainly in the United Kingdom, Ireland, and the English-speaking Commonwealth countries. American crosswords tend to be of the quick variety and rely on every letter being 'checked', ie crossed by another letter on the grid. Cryptic crosswords are known in the United States as 'British crosswords'.

Cryptic and quick crosswords differ in that the surface meaning of a quick crossword clue corresponds to the solution, eg 'nimble' (5) has the solution AGILE. Quick crosswords tend to make use of synonyms (as above) or hyponyms, where the solution is a more specific type of the clue word, eg 'dress' (4) has the solution SARI. The challenge of quick crosswords is that the solver doesn't know whether their solution is the correct one: 'nimble' could be LIGHT; 'dress' could be TOGA. Solvers build up confidence in their solutions using the checked letters of the unfolding grid. The beauty of cryptic crosswords, on the other hand, is that solvers can immediately be certain that their solutions are correct. This is because there are always two ways to solve a cryptic clue. One aspect of a cryptic clue is the definition: a word or phrase which is a synonym or hypernym (a superordinate word of which other words are 'types') of the solution. The other aspect is the wordplay: a device such as an anagram, reversal, or charade which employs specific letters from the clue. The clue as a whole is written so that the surface meaning distracts or actively misdirects the solver from the solution, eg

The flower of Glasgow? (5)

The solver expects the solution to be a flower, not a flow-er, ie the river CLYDE.

The cryptic crossword grid is now standardized with 15 squares across and 15 squares down. Many setters and solvers also find half-turn rotational symmetry appealing, ie the grid looks the same upside-down as the right way up. Many crossword editors abide by the rules of clueing fairness set down by the pioneering *Observer* setter Ximenes (DS Macnutt). Ximenes is succeeded at *The Observer* in modern times by Azed (Jonathan Crowther), who believes that a good cryptic clue contains three elements: a precise definition; a fair subsidiary indication (wordplay); nothing else.

The opposing school of crossword clueing (non-Ximenean) is practised by Araucaria (John Graham), whose unique jigsaw puzzles in *The Guardian* have attracted a cult following for their ingenuity, wit, and occasional flouting of fair play.

Another 'cryptic' element of the crossword puzzle is the setter's pseudonym. Crossword setters have long concealed their identities with an allusive nom de plume. A good few refer to the Spanish Inquisition – Torquemada, Ximenes, Azed (Deza backwards) – but most make reference to the setter's real name or interests (eg some of Don Manley's pseudonyms are types of 'don' – Quixote, Giovanni, Pasquale).

In recent years, the rise of the numerical puzzle in the west may have temporarily challenged the supremacy of the crossword puzzle, but its popularity still continues, albeit alongside Sudoku and its ilk. Both puzzles are thought to give our little grey cells a good work-out, keeping our brains healthy into old age, so the cryptic crossword looks likely to endure for another 100 years and more.

dismember (a human body) **15** to billet or be billeted in lodgings **16** *heraldry* to divide (a shield) into four separate bearings ▷ *adj* **17** being or consisting of one of four equal parts ▸ See also **quarters**
WORD ORIGIN Latin *quartus* fourth

quarterback *n* a player in American football who directs attacking play

quarter day *n* *Brit* any of four days in the year when certain payments become due

quarterdeck *n* *naut* the rear part of the upper deck of a ship, traditionally for official or ceremonial use

quarterfinal *n* the round before the semifinal in a competition

quarter-hour *n* **1** a period of 15 minutes **2** either of the points of time 15 minutes before or after the hour

quarterlight *n* *Brit* a small pivoted window in the door of a car for ventilation

quarterly *adj* **1** occurring, done, due, or issued at intervals of three months ▷ *n, pl* **-lies 2** a periodical issued every three months ▷ *adv* **3** once every three months

quartermaster *n* **1** a military officer responsible for accommodation, food, and equipment **2** a naval officer responsible for navigation

quarters *pl n* accommodation, esp. as provided for military personnel

quarter sessions *n* (formerly) a court with limited jurisdiction, held four times a year

quarterstaff *n, pl* **-staves** a stout iron-tipped wooden staff about 6ft long, formerly used as a weapon
WORD ORIGIN origin unknown

quartet *n* **1** a group of four singers or instrumentalists **2** a piece of music for four performers **3** any group of four
WORD ORIGIN Italian *quarto* fourth

quartile *n* **1** one of three values of a variable dividing its distribution into four groups with equal frequencies ▷ *adj* **2** of a quartile

quarto *n, pl* **-tos** a book size resulting from folding a sheet of paper into four leaves or eight pages
WORD ORIGIN New Latin *in quarto* in quarter

quartz *n* a hard glossy mineral consisting of crystalline silicon dioxide
WORD ORIGIN German *Quarz*

quartz clock *or* **watch** *n* a very accurate clock or watch that is operated by a vibrating quartz crystal

quartz crystal *n* a thin plate or rod cut from a piece of quartz and ground so that it vibrates at a particular frequency

quasar (**kway**-zar) *n* any of a class of extremely distant starlike objects that are powerful sources of radio waves and other forms of energy
WORD ORIGIN *quas(i-stell)ar (radio source)*

quash *vb* **1** to officially reject (something, such as a judgment or decision) as invalid **2** to defeat or suppress forcefully and completely
WORD ORIGIN Latin *quassare* to shake

quasi- (**kway**-zie) *combining form* **1** almost but not really; seemingly: *a quasi-religious*

cult **2** resembling but not actually being; so-called: *a quasi-scholar*
WORD ORIGIN Latin: as if

quassia (**kwosh**-a) *n* **1** a tropical American tree with bitter bark and wood **2** the wood of this tree or a bitter compound extracted from it, used in insecticides
WORD ORIGIN after Graman *Quassi*, who discovered its medicinal value

quaternary *adj* consisting of four parts
WORD ORIGIN Latin *quaterni* by fours

Quaternary *adj* *geol* of the most recent period of geological time, which started about one million years ago

quatrain *n* a stanza or poem of four lines
WORD ORIGIN French, from Latin *quattuor* four

quatrefoil *n* **1** a leaf composed of four leaflets **2** *archit* a carved ornament of four arcs about a common centre
WORD ORIGIN Old French *quatre* four + *-foil* leaflet

quattrocento (kwat-roe-**chen**-toe) *n* the 15th century, esp. in reference to Renaissance Italian art
WORD ORIGIN Italian: four hundred (short for fourteen hundred)

quaver *vb* **1** (esp. of the voice) to quiver or tremble **2** to say or sing (something) with a trembling voice ▷ *n* **3** *music* a note having the time value of an eighth of a semibreve **4** a tremulous sound or note **quavering** *adj*
WORD ORIGIN Germanic

quay (**kee**) *n* a wharf built parallel to the shoreline
WORD ORIGIN Old French *kai*

Que. Quebec

queasy *adj* **-sier, -siest 1** having the feeling that one is about to vomit; nauseous **2** feeling or causing uneasiness **queasily** *adv* **queasiness** *n*
WORD ORIGIN origin unknown

queen *n* **1** a female sovereign who is the official ruler or head of state **2** the wife of a king **3** a woman, thing, or place considered the best or most important of her or its kind: *the rose is considered the queen of garden flowers* **4** *slang* an effeminate male homosexual **5** the only fertile female in a colony of bees, wasps, or ants **6** a playing card with a picture of a queen on it **7** a chessman, able to move in a straight line in any direction ▷ *vb* **8** *chess* to promote (a pawn) to a queen when it reaches the eighth rank **9 queen it** *informal* to behave in an overbearing manner: *she is more beautiful than ever and still queening it over everybody* **queenly** *adj*
WORD ORIGIN Old English *cwēn*

Queen Anne *adj* **1** of or in an 18th-century style of furniture characterized by the use of curves **2** of or in an early 18th-century English architectural style characterized by the use of red bricks and classical ornamentation

queen consort *n* the wife of a reigning king

queen mother *n* the widow of a former king who is also the mother of the reigning sovereign

queen post *n* *building* one of a pair of vertical posts that connect the tie

beam of a truss to the principal rafters of a roof

Queen's Bench *n* (in Britain) one of the divisions of the High Court of Justice

Queensberry rules *pl n* **1** the code of rules followed in modern boxing **2** *informal* gentlemanly conduct, esp. in a dispute
WORD ORIGIN after the ninth Marquess of *Queensberry*, who originated the rules

Queen's Counsel *n* **1** (in Britain, Australia and New Zealand) a barrister or advocate appointed Counsel to the Crown **2** (in Canada and New Zealand) an honorary title bestowed on lawyers with long experience

Queen's English *n* correctly spoken and written British English

queen's evidence *n* *English law* evidence given for the Crown against former associates in crime by an accomplice

Queen's Guide *or* **Scout** *n* a Guide or Scout who has passed the highest tests of proficiency

queen's highway *n* **1** (in Britain) any public road or right of way **2** (in Canada) a main road maintained by the provincial government

queer *adj* **1** not normal or usual; odd or strange **2** *informal* dubious; shady **3** *Brit* faint, giddy, or queasy **4** *informal, usually offensive* homosexual **5** *informal* eccentric or slightly mad ▷ *n* **6** *informal, usually offensive* a homosexual ▷ *vb* **7 queer someone's pitch** *informal* to spoil or thwart someone's chances of something
WORD ORIGIN origin unknown

USAGE
Although the term *queer* meaning homosexual is still considered derogatory when used by non-homosexuals, it is now being used by homosexuals of themselves as a positive term, as in *queer politics, queer cinema*.

queer street *n* **in queer street** *informal* in a difficult financial situation, esp. debt or bankruptcy

quell *vb* **1** to suppress (rebellion or unrest); subdue **2** to overcome or allay
WORD ORIGIN Old English *cwellan* to kill

quench *vb* **1** to satisfy (one's thirst) **2** to put out; extinguish **3** to suppress or subdue **4** *metallurgy* to cool (hot metal) by plunging it into cold water
WORD ORIGIN Old English *ācwencan* to extinguish

quern *n* a stone hand mill for grinding corn
WORD ORIGIN Old English *cweorn*

querulous (**kwer**-yew-luss) *adj* complaining; whining or peevish **querulously** *adv*
WORD ORIGIN Latin *queri* to complain

query *n, pl* **-ries 1** a question, esp. one expressing doubt **2** a question mark ▷ *vb* **-ries, -rying, -ried 3** to express uncertainty, doubt, or an objection concerning (something) **4** to express as a query; ask
WORD ORIGIN Latin *quaere* ask!

quesadilla *n* *Mexican cookery* a toasted tortilla filled with cheese and sometimes other ingredients **WORD ORIGIN** Spanish, diminutive of *queso* cheese

quest *n* **1** a looking for or seeking; search **2** the object of a search; a goal or target ▷ *vb* **3** **quest for** to go in search of **4** (of dogs) to search for game **WORD ORIGIN** Old French *queste*

question *n* **1** a form of words addressed to a person in order to obtain an answer; interrogative sentence **2** a point at issue: *they were silent on the question of social justice* **3** a difficulty or uncertainty **4 a** an act of asking **b** an investigation into some problem **5** a motion presented for debate **6 beyond (all) question** beyond (any) doubt **7 call something into question a** to make something the subject of disagreement **b** to cast doubt upon the validity or truth of something **8 in question** under discussion: *the area in question was not contaminated* **9 out of the question** beyond consideration; impossible ▷ *vb* **10** to put a question or questions to (a person); interrogate **11** to make (something) the subject of dispute **12** to express uncertainty; doubt **WORD ORIGIN** Latin *quaestio*

USAGE
The *question whether* should be used rather than the *question of whether* or the *question as to whether*: this leaves open the *question whether he acted correctly*.

questionable *adj* **1** (esp. of a person's morality or honesty) doubtful **2** of disputable value or authority **questionably** *adv*

questioner *n* a person who asks a question

questioning *adj* **1** proceeding from or characterized by doubt or uncertainty **2** intellectually inquisitive: *a questioning mind* ▷ *n* **3** interrogation

question mark *n* **1** the punctuation mark (?), used at the end of questions **2** a doubt or uncertainty: *a question mark still hangs over their success*

question master *n* Brit the person chairing a radio or television quiz or panel game

questionnaire *n* a set of questions on a form, used to collect statistical information or opinions from people

question time *n* (in parliamentary bodies of the British type) the time set aside each day for questions to government ministers

queue *n* **1** a line of people or vehicles waiting for something ▷ *vb* **queuing** or **queueing**, **queued 2** (often foll. by *up*) to form or remain in a line while waiting **WORD ORIGIN** Latin *cauda* tail

quibble *vb* **-bling**, **-bled 1** to make trivial objections ▷ *n* **2** a trivial objection or equivocation, esp. one used to avoid an issue **3** archaic a pun **WORD ORIGIN** origin unknown

quiche (**keesh**) *n* a savoury flan with an egg custard filling to which cheese, bacon, or vegetables are added **WORD ORIGIN** French

quick *adj* **1** characterized by rapidity of movement or action; fast **2** lasting or taking a short time **3** immediate or prompt: *her quick action minimized the damage* **4** eager or ready to perform (an action): *quick to condemn* **5** responsive to stimulation; alert; lively: *they were impressed by his quick mind* **6** easily excited or aroused: *he is impulsive and has a quick temper* **7** nimble in one's movements or actions; deft: *she has quick hands* ▷ *n* **8** any area of sensitive flesh, esp. that under a nail **9 cut someone to the quick** to hurt someone's feelings deeply **10 the quick** archaic living people ▷ *adv* **11** in a rapid manner; swiftly **quickly** *adv* **quickness** *n* **WORD ORIGIN** Old English *cwicu* living

quick-change artist *n* an actor or entertainer who undertakes several rapid changes of costume during a performance

quicken *vb* **1** to make or become faster; accelerate **2** to impart to or receive vigour or enthusiasm: *science quickens the imagination* **3 a** (of a fetus) to begin to show signs of life **b** (of a pregnant woman) to reach the stage of pregnancy at which movements of the fetus can be felt

quick-freeze *vb* **-freezing**, **-froze**, **-frozen** to preserve (food) by subjecting it to rapid refrigeration

quickie *informal n* **1** anything made or done rapidly ▷ *adj* **2** made or done rapidly: *a quickie divorce*

quicklime *n* a white caustic solid, mainly composed of calcium oxide, used in the manufacture of glass and steel

quicksand *n* a deep mass of loose wet sand that submerges anything on top of it

quickset *chiefly Brit adj* **1** (of plants or cuttings) planted so as to form a hedge ▷ *n* **2** a hedge composed of such plants

quicksilver *n* the metal mercury

quickstep *n* **1** a modern ballroom dance in rapid quadruple time **2** music for this dance

quick-tempered *adj* easy to anger

quick-witted *adj* having a keenly alert mind **quick-wittedness** *n*

quid[1] *n, pl* **quid** Brit slang **1** a pound (sterling) **2 be quids in** to be in a very favourable or advantageous position **WORD ORIGIN** origin unknown

quid[2] *n* a piece of tobacco for chewing **WORD ORIGIN** Old English *cwidu* chewing resin

quiddity *n, pl* **-ties 1** the essential nature of something **2** a petty or trifling distinction **WORD ORIGIN** Latin *quid* what

quid pro quo *n, pl* **quid pro quos** one thing, esp. an advantage or object, given in exchange for another **WORD ORIGIN** Latin: something for something

quiescent (kwee-**ess**-ent) *adj formal* quiet, inactive, or dormant **quiescence** *n* **WORD ORIGIN** Latin *quiescere* to rest

quiet *adj* **1** characterized by an absence of noise **2** calm or tranquil: *the sea is quiet today* **3** untroubled: *a quiet life* **4** not busy: *business is quiet this morning* **5** private or secret: *I had a quiet word with her* **6** free from anger, impatience, or other extreme emotion **7** not showy: *quiet colours; a quiet wedding* **8** modest or reserved: *quiet humour* ▷ *n* **9** the state of being silent, peaceful, or untroubled **10 on the quiet** without other people knowing ▷ *vb* **11** to make or become calm or silent **quietly** *adv* **quietness** *n* **WORD ORIGIN** Latin *quies* repose

quieten *vb* Brit & NZ **1** (often foll. by *down*) to make or become calm or silent **2** to allay (fear or doubts)

quietism *n formal* passivity and calmness of mind towards external events **quietist** *n, adj*

quietude *n formal* quietness, peace, or tranquillity

quietus *n, pl* **-tuses 1** literary a release from life; death **2** the discharge or settlement of debts or duties **WORD ORIGIN** Latin *quietus est*, literally: he is at rest

quiff *n* Brit a tuft of hair brushed up above the forehead **WORD ORIGIN** origin unknown

quill *n* **1** Also called: **quill pen** a feather made into a pen **2 a** any of the large stiff feathers of the wing or tail of a bird **b** the hollow stem of a feather **3** any of the stiff hollow spines of a porcupine or hedgehog **WORD ORIGIN** origin unknown

quilling *n* a decorative craftwork in which material such as glass, fabric or paper is formed into small bands or rolls that form the basis of a design

quilt *n* **1** a cover for a bed, consisting of a soft filling sewn between two layers of material, usually with crisscross seams **2** a continental quilt; duvet ▷ *vb* **3** to stitch together two layers of (fabric) with padding between them **quilted** *adj* **WORD ORIGIN** Old French *coilte* mattress

quin *n* a quintuplet

quince *n* the acid-tasting pear-shaped fruit of an Asian tree, used in preserves **WORD ORIGIN** Greek *kudōnion*

quincunx *n* a group of five objects arranged in the shape of a rectangle with one at each corner and the fifth in the centre **WORD ORIGIN** Latin: five twelfths; in ancient Rome, this was a coin marked with five spots

quinine *n* a bitter drug extracted from cinchona bark, used as a tonic and formerly in malaria therapy **WORD ORIGIN** Spanish *quina* cinchona bark

quinquennial *adj* occurring once every five years or over a period of five years

quinquereme *n* an ancient Roman galley with five banks of oars **WORD ORIGIN** Latin *quinque* five + *remus* oar

quinsy *n* inflammation of the tonsils and throat, with abscesses **WORD ORIGIN** Greek *kuōn* dog + *ankhein* to strangle

quint *n* US & Canad a quintuplet

quintal *n* **1** a unit of weight equal to (esp. in Britain) 112 pounds (50.85 kg) or (esp. in US) 100 pounds (45.36 kg) **2** a unit of weight equal to 100 kilograms **WORD ORIGIN** Arabic *qintār*

q

quintessence *n* **1** the perfect representation of a quality or state **2** an extract of a substance containing its central nature in its most concentrated form **quintessential** *adj*
WORD ORIGIN Medieval Latin *quinta essentia* the fifth essence

quintet *n* **1** a group of five singers or instrumentalists **2** a piece of music for five performers **3** any group of five
WORD ORIGIN Italian *quintetto*

quintillion *n, pl* **-lions** *or* **-lion 1** (in Britain, France, and Germany) the number represented as one followed by 30 zeros (10^{30}) **2** (in the US and Canada) the number represented as one followed by 18 zeros (10^{18})
WORD ORIGIN Latin *quintus* fifth

quintuple *vb* **-pling, -pled 1** to multiply by five ▷ *adj* **2** five times as much or as many **3** consisting of five parts ▷ *n* **4** a quantity or number five times as great as another
WORD ORIGIN Latin *quintus* fifth + *-plus* -fold

quintuplet *n* one of five children born at one birth

quip *n* **1** a witty saying ▷ *vb* **quipping, quipped 2** to make a quip
WORD ORIGIN probably from Latin *quippe* indeed, to be sure

quire *n* a set of 24 or 25 sheets of paper
WORD ORIGIN Old French *quaier*

quirk *n* **1** a peculiarity of character; mannerism or foible **2** an unexpected twist or turn: *a strange quirk of fate* **quirky** *adj*
WORD ORIGIN origin unknown

quisling *n* a traitor who aids an occupying enemy force; collaborator
WORD ORIGIN after Vidkun *Quisling*, Norwegian collaborator with the Nazis

quit *vb* **quitting, quit 1** to stop (doing something) **2** to resign (from): *the Prime Minister's decision to quit; he quit his job as a salesman* **3** to leave (a place) **quitter** *n*
WORD ORIGIN Old French *quitter*

quitch *or* **quitch grass** *n* same as **couch grass**

quite *adv* **1** (*not used with a negative*) to a greater than average extent; somewhat: *he found her quite attractive* **2** absolutely: *you're quite right* **3** in actuality; truly **4 quite a** *or* **an** of an exceptional kind: *she is quite a girl* **5 quite something** a

remarkable thing or person ▷ *interj* **6** an expression used to indicate agreement
WORD ORIGIN adverbial use of *quite* (adjective) quit, free of

≡ **USAGE**
≡ See at **very**.

quits *adj informal* **1** on an equal footing **2 call it quits** to end a dispute or contest, agreeing that honours are even

quittance *n* **1** release from debt or other obligation **2** a document certifying this
WORD ORIGIN Old French *quitter* to release from obligation

quiver¹ *vb* **1** to shake with a tremulous movement; tremble ▷ *n* **2** a shaking or trembling **quivering** *adj*
WORD ORIGIN obsolete *cwiver* quick, nimble

quiver² *n* a case for holding or carrying arrows
WORD ORIGIN Old French *cuivre*

quixotic (kwik-**sot**-ik) *adj* unrealistically optimistic or chivalrous **quixotically** *adv*
WORD ORIGIN after Don *Quixote* in Cervantes' romance

quiz *n, pl* **quizzes 1** an entertainment in which the knowledge of the players is tested by a series of questions **2** any set of quick questions designed to test knowledge **3** an investigation by close questioning ▷ *vb* **quizzing, quizzed 4** to investigate by close questioning; interrogate
WORD ORIGIN origin unknown

quizzical *adj* questioning and mocking or supercilious: *the question elicits a quizzical expression* **quizzically** *adv*

quod *n Brit slang* a jail
WORD ORIGIN origin unknown

quoin *n* **1** an external corner of a wall **2** the stone forming the outer corner of a wall; a cornerstone **3** a wedge
WORD ORIGIN variant of *coin* (in former sense of corner)

quoit *n* a large ring used in the game of quoits
WORD ORIGIN origin unknown

quoits *n* a game in which quoits are tossed at a stake in the ground in attempts to encircle it

quokka *n* a small Australian wallaby

quondam *adj formal* of an earlier time; former: *her quondam employers*
WORD ORIGIN Latin

quorate *adj* having or being a quorum: *the meeting is now quorate*

Quorn *n trademark* a vegetable protein used as a meat substitute

quorum *n* the minimum number of members required to be present in a meeting or assembly before any business can be transacted
WORD ORIGIN Latin, literally: of whom

quota *n* **1** the share that is due from, due to, or allocated to a person or group **2** the prescribed number or quantity allowed, required, or admitted
WORD ORIGIN Latin *quotus* of what number

quotation *n* **1** a written or spoken passage repeated exactly in a later work, speech, or conversation, usually with an acknowledgment of its source **2** the act of quoting **3** an estimate of costs submitted by a contractor to a prospective client

quotation marks *pl n* the punctuation marks used to begin and end a quotation, either " and " or ' and '

quote *vb* **quoting, quoted 1** to repeat (words) exactly from (an earlier work, speech, or conversation), usually with an acknowledgment of their source **2** to state a price for goods or a job of work **3** to put quotation marks round (words) ▷ *n* **4** *informal* a quotation **5 quotes** *informal* quotation marks ▷ *interj* **6** an expression used to indicate that the words that follow are a quotation **quotable** *adj*
WORD ORIGIN Medieval Latin *quotare* to assign reference numbers to passages

quoth *vb archaic* (foll. by *I, he* or *she*) said
WORD ORIGIN Old English *cwæth*

quotidian *adj* **1** daily **2** *literary* commonplace **3** (esp. of fever) recurring daily
WORD ORIGIN Latin *quotidianus*

quotient *n* the result of the division of one number or quantity by another
WORD ORIGIN Latin *quotiens* how often

Quran (koo-**rahn**) *n* same as **Koran**

q.v. (denoting a cross-reference) which (word, item, etc.) see
WORD ORIGIN New Latin *quod vide*

qwerty *or* **QWERTY keyboard** *n* the standard English language typewriter or computer keyboard with the characters q, w, e, r, t, and y at the top left of the keyboard

q

Vladimir Nabokov

Vladimir Nabokov was born in Saint Petersburg in 1899. By the age of five, he could speak English and French as well as his parents' native language of Russian. Many young children acquire language easily, but no writer, not even Joseph Conrad, wrote so fluently in a second language.

The affluent family of Vladimir Nabokov (pronounced, he advised, 'vla-DEE-mir, to rhyme with redeemer, na-BOAK-off') fled Saint Petersburg from the Bolsheviks in 1917, ending up in Berlin. Nabokov attended Cambridge University and, while enduring émigré poverty, wrote nine novels in Russian under a pseudonym. In 1940, he fled again, this time from the Nazis in France. In the United States, friends got him teaching jobs at Wellesley College and later Cornell University, where he began to write lectures, novels, and stories in English; he became an American citizen in 1948. In 1959, financed by the overnight success of his novel *Lolita*, he and his devoted wife Vera began living in a palatial hotel in Montreux, Switzerland, where he spent the rest of his life.

A self-trained lepidopterist, Nabokov insatiably hunted and discovered genera of butterflies for many years, and also devised and published chess problems. The qualities of precise descriptiveness and puzzle-making informed his fiction, as did his synaesthesia, the perception of letters of the alphabet in colour. Fiction was a serious game in which an intricate world was painstakingly constructed according to rules only tangentially related to the one in which the author lived. This process did not prevent him from teasingly interposing elements of his own past, such as the Berlin assassination in 1922 of his father, a prominent social-democrat politician.

Nabokov's mandarin style is saturated with supercharged puns, multilingual allusions, and startling visual and auditory effects. Anthropomorphism often figures. In the short story 'Cloud, Castle, Lake', he writes, 'The locomotive, working rapidly with its elbows, hurried through a pine forest, then – with relief – among fields.' Structurally, too, he was audacious. *Pale Fire* consists of a character's 999-line poem in couplets, complete with a Foreword, Commentary, and Index by a dementedly self-obsessed annotator. In it, 'Hurricane Lolita' is mentioned. The notoriety of *Lolita*, dealing with the obsession of a middle-aged man with a 12-year-old girl, forced him to reiterate, 'My knowledge of nymphets is purely scholarly.' He told an interviewer, 'Lolita is famous, not I. I am an obscure, doubly obscure, novelist with an unpronounceable name.'

He often translated from English to Russian and back again. His old friend and benefactor Edmund Wilson said he attempted to 'correlate his English and his Russian sides' which continued to 'elude one another'. Wilson said this in a long review of Nabokov's four-volume translation with commentary of Pushkin's *Eugene Onegin*, in which he criticized the author (for whom he felt 'a warm affection sometimes chilled by exasperation') for pedantic longueurs, lame verse rendering, and – taking his life in his hands – mistakes in Russian. Nabokov responded in kind: 'A patient confidant of his long and hopeless infatuation with the Russian language, I have always done my best to explain to him his mistakes of pronunciation, grammar and interpretation.'

In his nonfiction work *Strong Opinions*, Nabokov wrote, 'Do you know how poetry started? I always think that it started when a cave boy came running back to the cave, through the tall grass, shouting as he ran, "Wolf, wolf," and there was no wolf. His baboon-like parents, great sticklers for the truth, gave him a hiding, no doubt, but poetry had been born – the tall story had been born in the tall grass.' He also noted in a lecture that 'The good reader is one who has imagination, memory, a dictionary, and some artistic sense – which sense I propose to develop in myself and in others whenever I have the chance.' He attempted to loan a Russian word to English: *poshlost* (pronounced 'PUSH-lost') by which he meant 'corny trash, vulgar clichés, Philistinism in all its phases, imitations of imitations, bogus profundities, crude, moronic and dishonest pseudoliterature'. To these bugbears he added Freudian psychoanalysis, biographical criticism, and 'great ideas' – which were 'hogwash'. He wanted new worlds made, and made them in his fiction.

Rr

The letter R is the eighteenth letter of the English alphabet. In Semitic alphabets, there was a letter called *resh*, which literally means 'head', and resembled the profile of a human form facing to the left. The Greeks reversed the direction of this letter and the result was their letter *rho* (P,ρ).

The Greek name of the letter is preserved in some English words concerned with the letter R. The excessive or idiosyncratic pronunciation of this letter is called 'rhotacism'. (And R is certainly a letter that is prone to idiosyncratic pronunciation. In Scottish, Irish and most North American accents, the letter is pronounced wherever it occurs in spelling, whereas English accents do not sound the letter in words such as 'cart' and 'bird'.)

The Etruscans adopted the Greek *rho* but found that its shape was similar to the way they wrote the letter P, and so they added a short stroke to make the two letters more easily distinguishable. In the Roman alphabet, this stroke was lengthened downwards to give the modern form of the letter. The Romans pronounced this letter in a rolling way which suggested growling, and so they gave it the nickname of 'the dog letter'.

Dogs are not the only animals to be associated with this letter. For gastronomes, the letter is likely to bring to mind oysters, and the saying these shellfish should be eaten only when there is an R in the month. This saying is based on the fact that the cooler months (at least in the Northern Hemisphere) from September to April all contain the letter R. In the warm months from May to August there is more chance of food spoiling in the heat, and none of these months is spelt with an R. Moreover, oysters spawn in the summer months, which is said to impair the texture and flavour.

In education, 'the three R's' were the elementary skills of reading, writing, and arithmetic, which were once placed at the heart of the curriculum. Ironically, of course, only one of these words is actually spelt with an initial R, but the prominent /r/ sounds at the front of these words proved more powerful than the niceties of spelling when it came to devising a memorable slogan.

---

r 1 radius 2 ratio 3 right 4 *cricket* run(s)

R 1 *chem* radical 2 Regina 3 Registered Trademark 4 *physics, electronics* resistance 5 Rex 6 River 7 *chess* rook

Ra *chem* radium

RA 1 rear admiral 2 (in Britain) Royal Academy 3 (in Britain) Royal Artillery

RAAF Royal Australian Air Force

rabbi (**rab**-bye) *n, pl* **-bis** 1 the spiritual leader of a Jewish congregation 2 an expert in or teacher of Jewish Law **rabbinical** *adj*
  WORD ORIGIN Hebrew: my master

rabbit *n, pl* **-bits** *or* **-bit** 1 a common burrowing mammal with long ears and a short fluffy tail ▷ *vb* **-biting, -bited** 2 *informal* to talk too much: *he keeps rabbiting on about interrogation*
  WORD ORIGIN origin unknown

rabbit ears *pl n* Austral & NZ an indoor television aerial

rabbit fence *n* a fence to prevent the spread of rabbits

rabbiting *n* **go rabbiting** to hunt rabbits

rabbit punch *n* a short sharp blow to the back of the neck

rabble *n* 1 a disorderly crowd of noisy people 2 **the rabble** *contemptuous* the common people
  WORD ORIGIN origin unknown

rabble-rouser *n* a person who stirs up the feelings of the mob **rabble-rousing** *adj, n*

Rabelaisian *adj* characterized by broad, often bawdy humour and sharp satire
  WORD ORIGIN after the work of the French writer, François *Rabelais*

rabid *adj* 1 fanatical: *a rabid separatist* 2 having rabies **rabidity** *n*
  WORD ORIGIN Latin *rabidus* frenzied

rabies (**ray**-beez) *n pathol* a fatal infectious viral disease of the nervous system transmitted by dogs and certain other animals
  WORD ORIGIN Latin: madness

RAC (in Britain) Royal Automobile Club

raccoon *or* **racoon** *n, pl* **-coons** *or* **-coon** a small American mammal with a long striped tail
  WORD ORIGIN from a Native American language

race¹ *n* 1 a contest of speed 2 any competition or rivalry: *the arms race* 3 a rapid current of water 4 a channel of a stream: *a mill race* 5 *Austral & NZ* a narrow passage through which sheep pass individually, as to a sheep dip ▷ *vb* **racing, raced** 6 to take part in a contest of speed with (someone) 7 to enter (an animal or vehicle) in a race: *to race greyhounds* 8 to travel as fast as possible 9 (of an engine) to run faster than normal 10 (of the heart) to beat faster than normal ▶ See also **races** > **racer** *n* **racing** *adj, n*
  WORD ORIGIN Old Norse *rās* running

race² *n* 1 a group of people of common ancestry with distinguishing physical features, such as skin colour or build 2 **the human race** human beings collectively 3 a group of animals or plants having common characteristics that distinguish them from other members of the same species
  WORD ORIGIN Italian *razza*

race caller *n* a professional horse-racing commentator

racecourse *n* a long broad track on which horses are raced

racehorse *n* a horse specially bred for racing

raceme (**rass**-eem) *n bot* a cluster of flowers along a central stem, as in the foxglove
  WORD ORIGIN Latin *racemus* bunch of grapes

race meeting *n* a series of horse or greyhound races held at the same place

race relations *pl n* the relations between members of two or more races within a single community

race riot *n* a riot involving violence between people of different races

races *pl n* **the races** a series of contests of speed between horses or greyhounds over a fixed course

racetrack *n* **1** a circuit used for races between cars, bicycles, or runners **2** *US & Canad* a racecourse

racial *adj* **1** relating to the division of the human species into races **2** typically associated with any such group **racially** *adv*

racism *or* **racialism** *n* **1** hostile or oppressive behaviour towards people because they belong to a different race **2** the belief that some races are innately superior to others because of hereditary characteristics **racist** *or* **racialist** *n, adj*

rack¹ *n* **1** a framework for holding particular articles, such as coats or luggage **2** a straight bar with teeth on its edge, to work with a cogwheel **3** **the rack** *history* an instrument of torture that stretched the body of the victim ▷ *vb* **4** to cause great suffering to: *Germany was racked by food riots* **5** **rack one's brains** to try very hard to think of something **WORD ORIGIN** probably from Middle Dutch *rec* framework
≡ **USAGE**
≡ See at **wrack¹**.

rack² *n* **go to rack and ruin** to be destroyed through neglect **WORD ORIGIN** variant of WRACK¹

rack³ *vb* to clear (wine or beer) by siphoning it off from the dregs

rack⁴ *n* the neck or rib part of a joint of meat

rack-and-pinion *n* a device for converting rotary into linear motion and vice versa, in which a gearwheel (the pinion) engages with a flat toothed bar (the rack)

racket¹ *n* **1** a noisy disturbance **2** an illegal activity done to make money **3** *slang* a business or occupation: *I've been in the racket since I was sixteen* ▷ *vb* **-eting, -eted 4** to make a commotion **rackety** *adj* **WORD ORIGIN** probably imitative

racket² *or* **racquet** *n* a bat consisting of an oval frame surrounding a mesh of strings, with a handle, used in tennis, badminton, and squash ▶ See also **rackets** **WORD ORIGIN** French *raquette*

racketeer *n* a person who makes money from illegal activities **racketeering** *n*

rackets *n* a game similar to squash, played by two or four people

rack-rent *n* an extortionate rent

raclette *n* a Swiss dish of melted cheese, usually served on boiled potatoes **WORD ORIGIN** French

raconteur (rak-on-**tur**) *n* a person skilled in telling stories **WORD ORIGIN** French

racoon *n, pl* **-coons** *or* **-coon** same as **raccoon**

racquet *n* same as **racket²**

racy *adj* **racier, raciest 1** slightly shocking: *a racy comedy* **2** spirited or lively: *a racy literary style* **racily** *adv* **raciness** *n*

rad radian

RADA (in Britain) Royal Academy of Dramatic Art

radar *n* **1** a method of detecting the position and velocity of a distant object by bouncing a narrow beam of extremely high-frequency radio pulses off it **2** the equipment used in this **WORD ORIGIN** *ra(dio) d(etecting) a(nd) r(anging)*

radar trap *n* a device which uses radar to detect motorists who break the speed limit

raddle *vb Austral & NZ* to mark sheep for identification

raddled *adj* (of a person) untidy or rundown in appearance **WORD ORIGIN** from *rud* red ochre

radial *adj* **1** spreading out from a common central point **2** of a radius or ray **3** short for **radial-ply** ▷ *n* **4** a radial-ply tyre **radially** *adv*

radial-ply *adj* (of a tyre) having the fabric cords in the outer casing running radially to enable the sidewalls to be flexible

radian *n* an SI unit of plane angle; the angle between two radii of a circle that cut off on the circumference an arc equal in length to the radius

radiant *adj* **1** characterized by health and happiness: *radiant good looks* **2** shining **3** emitted as radiation: *radiant heat* **4** sending out heat by radiation: *radiant heaters* **radiance** *n* **WORD ORIGIN** Latin *radiare* to shine

radiant energy *n* energy that is emitted or propagated in the form of particles or electromagnetic radiation

radiate *vb* **-ating, -ated 1** to spread out from a central point **2** to show (an emotion or quality) to a great degree: *she radiated competence and composure* **3** to emit or be emitted as radiation ▷ *adj* **4** having rays or a radial structure **WORD ORIGIN** Latin *radiare* to emit rays

radiation *n* **1** *physics* **a** the emission of energy as particles, electromagnetic waves or sound **b** the particles or waves emitted **2** the process of radiating

radiation sickness *n* illness caused by overexposure to radioactive material or X-rays

radiator *n* **1** *Brit* a device for heating a room or building, consisting of a series of pipes containing hot water **2** a device for cooling an internal-combustion engine, consisting of thin-walled tubes containing water **3** *Austral & NZ* an electric fire

radical *adj* **1** favouring fundamental change in political or social conditions: *a radical student movement* **2** of the essential nature of a person or thing; fundamental: *a radical fault* **3** searching or thorough: *a radical interpretation* **4** *maths* of or containing roots of numbers or quantities ▷ *n* **5** a person who favours fundamental change in existing institutions or in political, social, or economic conditions **6** *maths* a root of a number or quantity, such as $\sqrt[3]{5}$, $\sqrt{x}$ **7** *chem* an atom or group of atoms that acts as a unit during

chemical reactions **radicalism** *n* **radically** *adv* **WORD ORIGIN** Latin *radix* a root

radicalize *or* **-lise** *vb* **-lizing, -lized** *or* **-lising, -lised** to make (a person, group, or situation) radical or more radical: *the feelings of its own radicalized population*

radical sign *n* the symbol $\sqrt{}$ placed before a number or quantity to indicate the extraction of a root, esp. a square root. The value of a higher root is indicated by a raised digit in front of the symbol, as in $\sqrt[3]{}$

radicchio (rad-**deek**-ee-oh) *n, pl* **-chios** an Italian variety of chicory, with purple leaves streaked with white that are eaten raw in salads

radicle *n bot* **a** the part of the embryo of seed-bearing plants that develops into the main root **b** a very small root or rootlike part **WORD ORIGIN** Latin *radix* root

radii *n* a plural of **radius**

radio *n, pl* **-dios 1** the use of electromagnetic waves for broadcasting or two-way communication without the use of linking wires **2** an electronic device for converting radio signals into sounds **3** a communications device for sending and receiving messages using radio waves **4** sound broadcasting ▷ *vb* **5** to transmit (a message) by radio ▷ *adj* **6** of, relating to, or using radio broadcasting or radio signals: *a radio interview* **7** using or producing electromagnetic waves in the range used for radio signals: *radio astronomy* **WORD ORIGIN** Latin *radius* ray

radio- *combining form* **1** (denoting) radio **2** (denoting) radioactivity or radiation: *radiocarbon*

radioactive *adj* showing or using radioactivity

radioactivity *n* the spontaneous emission of radiation from atomic nuclei. The radiation can consist of alpha or beta particles, or gamma rays

radio astronomy *n* astronomy using a radio telescope to analyse signals received from radio sources in space

radiocarbon *n* a radioactive isotope of carbon, esp. carbon-14

radiocarbon dating *n* same as **carbon dating**

radiochemistry *n* the chemistry of radioactive substances

radio-controlled *adj* controlled by signals sent by radio

radio frequency *n* any electromagnetic frequency that lies in the range 10 kilohertz to 300 000 megahertz and can be used for broadcasting

radiogram *n Brit* an old-fashioned combined radio and record player

radiograph *n* an image produced on a special photographic film or plate by radiation, usually by X-rays

radiography (ray-dee-**og**-ra-fee) *n* the production of radiographs for use in medicine or industry **radiographer** *n*

radioisotope *n* a radioactive isotope

radiology (ray-dee-**ol**-a-jee) *n* the use of X-rays and radioactive substances in the diagnosis and treatment of disease **radiologist** *n*

r

radioscopy (ray-dee-**oss**-kop-ee) *n* examination of a person or object by means of a fluorescent screen and an X-ray source

radiosonde *n* an airborne instrument to send meteorological information back to earth by radio **WORD ORIGIN** RADIO- + French *sonde* sounding line

radiotelegraphy *n* telegraphy in which messages are transmitted by radio waves

radiotelephone *n* a telephone which sends and receives messages using radio waves rather than wires **radiotelephony** *n*

radio telescope *n* an instrument used in radio astronomy to pick up and analyse radio waves from space

radiotherapy *n* the treatment of disease, esp. cancer, by radiation

radio wave *n* an electromagnetic wave of radio frequency

radish *n* a small hot-flavoured red root vegetable eaten raw in salads **WORD ORIGIN** Latin *radix* root

radium *n chem* a highly radioactive luminescent metallic element, found in pitchblende. Symbol: Ra **WORD ORIGIN** Latin *radius* ray

radius (**ray**-dee-uss) *n, pl* -**dii** (-dee-eye) *or* -**diuses 1** a straight line joining the centre of a circle to any point on the circumference **2** the length of this line **3** *anat* the outer, slightly shorter of the two bones of the forearm **4** a circular area of a specified size round a central point: *within a seven-mile radius of the club* **WORD ORIGIN** Latin: ray, spoke

radon (**ray**-don) *n chem* a colourless radioactive element of the noble gas group. Symbol: Rn **WORD ORIGIN** from *radium*

RAF (in Britain) Royal Air Force

Rafferty *or* **Rafferty's rules** *pl n* *Austral & NZ slang* no rules at all **WORD ORIGIN** origin unknown

raffia *n* a fibre obtained from the leaves of a palm tree, used for weaving **WORD ORIGIN** Malagasy

raffish *adj* unconventional or slightly disreputable **WORD ORIGIN** obsolete *raff* rubbish

raffle *n* **1** a lottery, often to raise money for charity, in which the prizes are goods rather than money ▷ *vb* -**fling**, -**fled 2** to offer as a prize in a raffle **WORD ORIGIN** Old French

raft *n* a floating platform of logs or planks tied together **WORD ORIGIN** Old Norse *raptr* rafter

rafter *n* any of the parallel sloping beams that form the framework of a roof **WORD ORIGIN** Old English

rag¹ *n* **1** a small piece of cloth **2** *Brit, Austral, & NZ informal* a newspaper **3** **rags** old tattered clothing **4** **from rags to riches** from being extremely poor to being extremely wealthy **WORD ORIGIN** probably formed from *ragged*, from Old English *raggig*

rag² *Brit vb* **ragging, ragged 1** to tease **2** to play rough practical jokes on ▷ *n*

3 a boisterous practical joke ▷ *adj* **4** (in British universities and colleges) of various events organized to raise money for charity: *a rag week* **WORD ORIGIN** origin unknown

rag³ *n* a piece of ragtime music

ragamuffin *n* **1** a ragged dirty child **2** same as **ragga** **WORD ORIGIN** probably from RAG¹

rag-and-bone man *n Brit* a man who goes from street to street buying old clothes and furniture

ragbag *n* a confused mixture: *the traditional ragbag of art traders*

rage *n* **1** intense anger or passion **2** a fashion or craze: *the dance was the rage of Europe* **3** aggressive behaviour associated with a specified activity or environment: *road rage; school rage* **4** **all the rage** *informal* very popular **5** *Austral & NZ informal* a dance or party ▷ *vb* **raging, raged 6** to feel or show intense anger **7** to proceed violently and without restraint: *the argument was still raging* **WORD ORIGIN** Latin *rabies* madness

ragga *n* a dance-oriented style of reggae **WORD ORIGIN** from RAGAMUFFIN

ragged (**rag**-gid) *adj* **1** dressed in shabby or torn clothes **2** (of clothes) tattered and torn **3** having a rough or uneven surface or edge **4** neglected or untidy: *the ragged stone-built village*

ragged robin *n* a plant that has pink or white flowers with ragged petals

raglan *adj* **1** (of a sleeve) joined to the garment by diagonal seams from the collar to the underarm **2** (of a garment) with this style of sleeve **WORD ORIGIN** after Lord *Raglan*

ragout (**rag**-goo) *n* a richly seasoned stew of meat and vegetables **WORD ORIGIN** French

ragtag *n* **ragtag and bobtail** the common people

ragtime *n* a style of jazz piano music with a syncopated melody **WORD ORIGIN** probably *ragged time*

rag trade *n informal* the clothing business

ragwort *n* a plant with ragged leaves and yellow flowers

raid *n* **1** a sudden surprise attack: *a bombing raid* **2** a surprise visit by police searching for people or goods: *a drugs raid* ▷ *vb* **3** to make a raid on **4** to sneak into (a place) in order to steal **raider** *n* **WORD ORIGIN** Old English *rād* military expedition

rail¹ *n* **1** a horizontal bar supported by vertical posts, used as a fence or barrier **2** a horizontal bar on which to hang things: *a curtain rail* **3** one of a pair of parallel bars that serve as a running surface for the wheels of a train **4** railway: *by car or by rail* **5** **go off the rails** to start behaving improperly or eccentrically ▷ *vb* **6** to fence (an area) with rails **WORD ORIGIN** Old French *raille* rod

rail² *vb* **rail against** *or* **at** to complain bitterly or loudly about **WORD ORIGIN** Old French *railler* to mock

rail³ *n* a small wading marsh bird **WORD ORIGIN** Old French *raale*

railcard *n Brit* an identity card, which pensioners or young people can buy, entitling them to cheaper rail travel

railhead *n* **1** a terminal of a railway **2** the farthest point reached by completed track on an unfinished railway

railing *n* a fence made of rails supported by posts

raillery *n, pl* -**leries** good-natured teasing **WORD ORIGIN** French *railler* to tease

railroad *n* **1** *US* a railway ▷ *vb* **2** *informal* to force (a person) into an action with haste or by unfair means

railway *n* **1** a track composed of a line of parallel metal rails fixed to sleepers, on which trains run **2** any track on which the wheels of a vehicle may run: *a cable railway* **3** the rolling stock, buildings, and tracks used in such a transport system **4** the organization responsible for operating a railway network

raiment *n archaic or poetic* clothing **WORD ORIGIN** from *arrayment*

rain *n* **1 a** water falling from the sky in drops formed by the condensation of water vapour in the atmosphere **b** a fall of rain ▶ Related adjective: **pluvial** **2** a large quantity of anything falling rapidly: *a rain of stones descended on the police* **3** (**come**) **rain or shine** regardless of circumstances **4** **right as rain** *informal* perfectly all right ▷ *vb* **5** to fall as rain: *it's raining back home* **6** to fall rapidly and in large quantities: *steel rungs and sawdust raining down* **7** **rained off** cancelled or postponed because of rain. US and Canad term: **rained out** ▶ See also **rains** ▷ **rainy** *adj* **WORD ORIGIN** Old English *regn*

rainbird *n S African* a common name for **Burchell's coucal**, a bird whose call is believed to be a sign of impending rain

rainbow *n* an arched display in the sky of the colours of the spectrum, caused by the refraction and reflection of the sun's rays through rain

rainbow nation *n* the South African nation

rainbow trout *n* a freshwater trout with black spots and two red stripes

rain check *n* **take a rain check** *informal* to request or accept the postponement of an offer

raincoat *n* a coat made of a waterproof material

rainfall *n* the amount of rain, hail, or snow in a specified place and time

rainforest *n* dense forest found in tropical areas of heavy rainfall

rains *pl n* **the rains** the season in the tropics when there is a lot of rain

rainstorm *n* a storm with heavy rain

rainwater *n* water from rain

rainy day *n* a future time of need, esp. financial need

raise *vb* **raising, raised 1** to lift to a higher position or level **2** to place in an upright position **3** to increase in amount, quality, or intensity: *to raise interest rates* **4** to collect or gather together: *to raise additional capital; to raise an army* **5** to cause to be expressed: *to raise a smile* **6** to stir up **7** to bring up:

Word Histories
part 10

The word **robot** was first used by the Czech writer Karel Capek (1890–1938) in his play *R.U.R.*, published in 1920. In the play, people create manlike machines called robots. The word 'robot' comes from Czech *robota*, meaning 'work'.

Rule of thumb: A recurrent claim, widely circulated on the internet, is that 'rule of thumb' refers to an ancient law that allowed a man to beat his wife with a rod, so long as the rod in question was no thicker than his thumb. There are a few references to such a law in the 18th- and 19th-centuries, though these seem be drawing on folklore rather than fact, and none of them connect this law to the phrase 'rule of thumb'. That association seems to have come about in 1976 when an article described the supposed wife-beating principle as 'a rule of thumb, so to speak'. The true origins of 'rule of thumb' seem to lie in the sense of 'rule' as a device for measuring: a ruler. The first joint of the thumb tends to be about an inch long, and thus represents a practical means of obtaining rough measurements.

Sadism: The sexual debauchery and scandalous erotic novels of the French writer and soldier the Marquis de Sade (1740–1814) gave rise to this word. The Marquis suffered long periods of imprisonment as punishment for his behaviour and was an infamous figure of his day.

Sandwich: Sandwiches are named after John Montagu (1718–1792), the 4th Earl of Sandwich, who was in the habit of spending whole days at gambling tables. Since he did not want to leave the tables to eat, he asked waiters to bring him meals in the form of meat placed between two slices of bread.

Saxophone: The saxophone is named after its inventor, Adolphe Sax (1814–1894), a French musical-instrument maker. Sax invented a number of other musical instruments, including the saxhorn, the sax-tromba, and the saxtuba.

Sceptic: The Sceptics were a school of philosophers in ancient Greece who believed that nothing could be known for certain. The word 'sceptic' comes from the Greek word *skeptikos*, meaning 'someone who considers', from the verb *skeptesthai*, meaning 'to consider'.

Shamefaced: The etymology of 'shamefaced' seems obvious; a person's feeling of shame often shows on their face. But the word was originally 'shamefast', and comes from the Old English *sceamfaest*: literally 'bound by shame'. The 'faced' element in the modern word represents a rationalization of the word that happily – and unlike most folk etymologies – makes perfect sense.

Shampoo: A shampoo was originally a massage rather than a wash. The word 'shampoo' is derived from the Hindi verb *chāmpnā*, meaning 'to press, knead, or massage'.

Sherry is named after the town of *Jerez de la Frontera* in southwestern Spain, where it was first made.

Shrapnel is named after Henry *Shrapnel* (1761–1842), the English artillery officer who invented it.

Sideburns are named after a 19th-century American general, Ambrose *Burnside* (1824–1881), who wore whiskers like this. Such whiskers were first known as 'burnsides', and then as 'sideburns'.

Sinister: In Latin *sinister* means 'left' or 'on the left-hand side'. The word came to have its 'sinister' meaning because the left side was considered unlucky.

Siren: The Sirens in Greek mythology were sea nymphs with beautiful voices who sang to lure sailors to their deaths on the rocks where the nymphs lived.

Sirloin: According to folklore, 'sirloin' owes its 'sir' to a knighting by an English king, as a reward for its excellence on the plate. There are conflicting accounts as to the king this was: Henry VIII, James VI and I, and Charles II have all been credited with the deed at various times. In fact, the 'sir' is a corruption of French *sur*, above, so the cut simply means 'above the loin' or 'the upper loin'.

to raise a family **8** to grow: *to raise a crop* **9** to put forward for consideration: *they raised controversial issues* **10** to arouse from sleep or death **11** to build: *to raise a barn* **12** to bring to an end: *to raise a siege* **13** to establish radio communications with: *we raised Moscow last night* **14** to advance in rank; promote **15** *maths* to multiply (a number) by itself a specified number of times: *8 is 2 raised to the power 3* **16** to cause (dough) to rise, as by the addition of yeast **17** *cards* to bet more than the previous player **18 raise Cain a** to create a disturbance **b** to protest vehemently ▷ *n* **19** *US, Canad, & NZ* an increase in pay **WORD ORIGIN** Old Norse *reisa*

raised *adj* higher than the surrounding area: *a small raised platform*

raisin *n* a dried grape **WORD ORIGIN** Old French: grape

raison d'être (**ray**-zon **det**-ra) *n, pl* **raisons d'être** (**ray**-zon **det**-ra) reason or justification for existence **WORD ORIGIN** French

raita (**rye**-ta) *n* an Indian dish of chopped cucumber, mint, etc. in yogurt, served with curry **WORD ORIGIN** Hindi

Raj *n* **the Raj** the British government in India before 1947 **WORD ORIGIN** Hindi

raja or **rajah** *n history* an Indian prince or ruler **WORD ORIGIN** Hindi

rake¹ *n* **1** a farm or garden tool consisting of a row of teeth set in a headpiece attached to a long shaft and used for gathering leaves or straw, or for smoothing loose earth **2** any of various implements similar in shape or function ▷ *vb* **raking, raked 3** to scrape or gather with a rake **4** to smooth (a surface) with a rake **5** Also: **rake out** to clear (ashes) from (a fire) **6 rake together** or **up** to gather (items or people) with difficulty, as from a limited supply **7** to search or examine carefully: *raking over the past is not always popular* **8** to direct (gunfire) along the length of (a target): *the machine guns raked up and down their line* **9** to scrape or graze: *he raked the tip of his shoe across the pavement* ▸ See also **rake in, rake-off**, etc. **WORD ORIGIN** Old English *raca*

rake² *n* an immoral man **WORD ORIGIN** short for *rakehell*

rake³ *n* **1** the degree to which an object slopes ▷ *vb* **raking, raked 2** to slope from the vertical, esp. (of a ship's mast) towards the stern **3** to construct with a backward slope **WORD ORIGIN** origin unknown

raked *adj* (of a surface) sloping so that it is higher at the back than at the front

rake in *vb informal* to acquire (money) in large amounts

rake-off *n slang* a share of profits, esp. an illegal one

rake up *vb* to bring back memories of (a forgotten unpleasant event): *she doesn't want to rake up the past*

rakish¹ (**ray**-kish) *adj* dashing or jaunty: *a hat which he wore at a rakish angle* **WORD ORIGIN** probably from RAKE³

rakish² *adj* immoral: *a rakish life of drinking and womanizing* **rakishly** *adv* **WORD ORIGIN** from RAKE²

rallentando *music adj, adv* **1** becoming slower ▷ *n* **2** a passage in which the music becomes slower **WORD ORIGIN** Italian

rally¹ *n, pl* **-lies 1** a large gathering of people for a meeting **2** a marked recovery of strength, as during illness **3** *stock exchange* a sharp increase in price or trading activity after a decline **4** *tennis, squash, etc.* an exchange of several shots before one player wins the point **5** a car-driving competition on public roads ▷ *vb* **-lies, -lying, -lied 6** to bring or come together after being dispersed **7** to bring or come together for a common cause **8** to summon up (one's strength or spirits) **9** to recover (sometimes only temporarily) from an illness **10** *stock exchange* to increase sharply after a decline **WORD ORIGIN** Old French *rallier*

rally² *vb* **-lies, -lying, -lied** to mock or tease (someone) in a good-natured way **WORD ORIGIN** Old French *railler* to tease

rally round *vb* to group together to help someone

ram *n* **1** an uncastrated adult male sheep **2** a hydraulically or pneumatically driven piston **3** the falling weight of a pile driver **4** short for **battering ram** ▷ *vb* **ramming, rammed 5** to strike against with force **6** to force or drive: *he rammed his sword into the man's belly* **7** to stuff or cram **8 ram something home** to make something clear or obvious: *to ram home the message* **9 ram something down someone's throat** to put forward or emphasize an argument or idea with excessive force **WORD ORIGIN** Old English *ramm*

RAM *computers* random access memory: a temporary storage space which loses its contents when the computer is switched off

Rama *n* a Hindu god, the incarnation of Vishnu

Ramadan *n* **1** the ninth month of the Muslim year, 30 days long, during which strict fasting is observed from sunrise to sunset **2** the fast itself

ramble *vb* **-bling, -bled 1** to walk for relaxation, sometimes with no particular direction **2** to speak or write in a confused style **3** to grow or develop in a random fashion ▷ *n* **4** a walk, esp. in the countryside **WORD ORIGIN** Middle English *romblen*

rambler *n* **1** a person who takes country walks **2** a climbing rose

rambling *adj* **1** long and irregularly shaped: *a rambling fourteenth-century church* **2** (of speech or writing) confused and long-winded ▷ *n* **3** the activity of going for long walks in the country

RAMC Royal Army Medical Corps

ramekin (**ram**-ik-in) *n* a small container for baking and serving one portion of food **WORD ORIGIN** French *ramequin*

ramification *n* **1 ramifications** the consequences or complications resulting from an action **2** a structure of branching parts

ramify *vb* **-fies, -fying, -fied 1** to become complex **2** to spread in branches; subdivide **WORD ORIGIN** French *ramifier*

ramjet *n* **a** a type of jet engine in which fuel is burned in a duct using air compressed by the forward speed of the aircraft **b** an aircraft powered by such an engine

ramp *n* **1** a slope that joins two surfaces at different levels **2** a place where the level of a road surface changes because of roadworks **3** a movable stairway by which passengers enter and leave an aircraft **4** *Brit* a small hump on a road to make traffic slow down **WORD ORIGIN** Old French *ramper* to crawl, rear

rampage *vb* **-paging, -paged 1** to rush about violently ▷ *n* **2 on the rampage** behaving violently or destructively **WORD ORIGIN** Scots

rampant *adj* **1** growing or spreading uncontrollably **2** *heraldry* (of a beast) standing on the hind legs, the right foreleg raised above the left: *a lion rampant* **WORD ORIGIN** Old French *ramper* to crawl, rear

rampart *n* a mound of earth or a wall built to protect a fort or city **WORD ORIGIN** Old French

rampike *n Canad* a tall tree that has been burned bare of branches

ramp up *vb* **1** to increase or cause to increase **2** to increase the effort involved in a process

ram raid *n informal* a raid on a shop in which a stolen car is driven into the window **ram raider** *n*

ramrod *n* **1** a long thin rod for cleaning the barrel of a gun or forcing gunpowder into an old-fashioned gun ▷ *adj* **2** (of someone's posture) very straight and upright

ramshackle *adj* badly made or cared for: *a curious ramshackle building* **WORD ORIGIN** obsolete *ransackle* to ransack

ran *vb* the past tense of **run**

RAN Royal Australian Navy

ranch *n* **1** a large cattle farm in the American West **2** *chiefly US & Canad* a large farm for the rearing of a particular kind of livestock or crop: *he owned a yak ranch in Tibet* ▷ *vb* **3** to run a ranch **rancher** *n* **WORD ORIGIN** Mexican Spanish *rancho* small farm

ranchslider *n NZ* a glazed sliding door usually opening onto an outside terrace

rancid *adj* (of fatty foods) stale and having an offensive smell **rancidity** *n* **WORD ORIGIN** Latin *rancidus*

rancour or *US* **rancor** *n* deep bitter hate **rancorous** *adj* **WORD ORIGIN** Old French

rand *n* the standard monetary unit of the Republic of South Africa **WORD ORIGIN** from *Witwatersrand*, S Transvaal, referring to the gold-mining there

R & B rhythm and blues

R & D research and development

random *adj* **1** lacking any definite plan or prearranged order: *a random sample* ▷ *n* **2 at random** not following any prearranged order **randomly** *adv* **randomness** *n*
WORD ORIGIN Old French *randir* to gallop

random access *n* a method of reading data from a computer file without having to read through the file from the beginning

randy *adj* **randier, randiest** *informal* sexually aroused **randily** *adv* **randiness** *n*
WORD ORIGIN probably from obsolete *rand* to rant

ranee *n* same as **rani**

rang *vb* the past tense of **ring¹**
☰ USAGE
☰ See at **ring¹**.

rangatira (rung-a-**teer**-a) *n* NZ a Māori chief of either sex
WORD ORIGIN Māori

range *n* **1** the limits within which a person or thing can function effectively: *academic ability range* **2 a** the maximum effective distance of a projectile fired from a weapon **b** the distance between a target and a weapon **3** the total distance which a ship, aircraft, or vehicle can travel without taking on fresh fuel **4** the difference in pitch between the highest and lowest note of a voice or musical instrument **5** a whole set of related things: *a range of treatments was available* **6** the total products of a manufacturer, designer, or stockist: *the latest skin-care range* **7** the limits within which something can lie: *a range of prices* **8** *US & Canad* an extensive tract of open land on which livestock can graze **9** a chain of mountains **10** an area set aside for shooting practice or rocket testing **11** a large cooking stove with one or more ovens **12** *maths* the set of values that a function or variable can take ▷ *vb* **ranging, ranged 13** to vary between one point and another **14** to cover a specified period or specified things: *attitudes ranged from sympathy to indifference* **15** to roam (over) **16** to establish or be situated in a line or series **17** to put into a specific category: *they ranged themselves with the opposition*
WORD ORIGIN Old French: row

rangefinder *n* an instrument for finding how far away an object is

ranger *n* **1** an official in charge of a park or nature reserve **2** *US* an armed trooper employed to police a State or district: *a Texas ranger*

Ranger *or* **Ranger Guide** *n* *Austral & Brit* a member of the senior branch of the Guides

rangy (**rain**-jee) *adj* **rangier, rangiest** having long slender limbs

rani *or* **ranee** *n* the wife or widow of a raja
WORD ORIGIN Hindi

rank¹ *n* **1** a position within a social organization: *the rank of superintendent* **2** high social or other standing: *accusations were made against people of high rank* **3** a person's social class: *it was too grand for someone of his lowly rank* **4** the position of an item in any ordering or sequence **5** a line or row of people or things **6** a place where taxis wait to be hired **7** a line of people, esp. soldiers, positioned one beside the other **8** any of the eight horizontal rows of squares on a chessboard **9 close ranks** to maintain solidarity **10 pull rank** to get one's own way by virtue of one's superior position **11 rank and file** the ordinary people or members of a group **12 the ranks** the common soldiers ▷ *vb* **13** to give or hold a specific position in an organization or group **14** to arrange in rows or lines **15** to arrange in sequence: *to rank students according to their grades* **16** to be important: *the legendary coronation stone ranks high in the hearts of patriots*
WORD ORIGIN Old French *ranc*

rank² *adj* **1** complete or absolute: *rank incompetence* **2** smelling offensively strong **3** growing too quickly: *rank weeds*
WORD ORIGIN Old English *ranc* straight, proud

rankle *vb* **-kling, -kled** to continue to cause resentment or bitterness
WORD ORIGIN Old French *draoncle* ulcer

ransack *vb* **1** to search through every part of (a place or thing) **2** to plunder or pillage
WORD ORIGIN Old Norse *rann* house + *saka* to search

ransom *n* **1** the money demanded in return for the release of someone who has been kidnapped **2 hold to ransom a** to keep (a prisoner) in confinement until payment is received **b** to attempt to force (a person) to do something ▷ *vb* **3** to pay money to obtain the release of (a prisoner) **4** to set free (a prisoner) in return for money **ransomer** *n*
WORD ORIGIN Old French *ransoun*

rant *vb* **1** to talk in a loud and excited way ▷ *n* **2** loud excited speech **ranting** *adj, n*
WORD ORIGIN Dutch *ranten* to rave

ranunculus *n, pl* **-luses** *or* **-li** a genus of plants including the buttercup
WORD ORIGIN Latin *rana* frog

RAOC Royal Army Ordnance Corps

rap¹ *vb* **rapping, rapped 1** to hit with a sharp quick blow **2** to knock loudly and sharply **3 rap out** to utter in sharp rapid speech: *he rapped out his address* **4** to perform a rhythmic monologue with musical backing **5** *slang* to talk in a relaxed and friendly way **6** to rebuke or criticize sharply **7 rap over the knuckles** to reprimand ▷ *n* **8** a sharp quick blow or the sound produced by it **9** a fast rhythmic monologue over a musical backing **10** a sharp rebuke or criticism **11** *slang* a legal charge: *a murder rap* **12 take the rap** *slang* to suffer the punishment for a crime, whether guilty or not **rapper** *n*
WORD ORIGIN probably from Old Norse

rap² *n* **not care a rap** to not care in the least: *she didn't care a rap for us*
WORD ORIGIN probably from *ropaire*, counterfeit coin formerly current in Ireland

rapacious *adj* **1** greedy or grasping **2** (of animals or birds) living by catching prey **rapacity** *n*
WORD ORIGIN Latin *rapax*

rape¹ *vb* **raping, raped 1** to force (someone) to submit to sexual intercourse ▷ *n* **2** the act of raping **3** any violation or abuse: *the rape of the country's natural resources* **rapist** *n*
WORD ORIGIN Latin *rapere* to seize

rape² *n* a yellow-flowered plant cultivated for its seeds, **rapeseed,** which yield a useful oil, **rape oil,** and as a fodder plant
WORD ORIGIN Latin *rapum* turnip

rapid *adj* **1** (of an action) taking or lasting a short time **2** acting or moving quickly: *a rapid advance* **rapidly** *adv* **rapidity** *n*
WORD ORIGIN Latin *rapidus*

rapid eye movement *n* the movement of the eyeballs while a person is dreaming

rapids *pl n* part of a river where the water is very fast and turbulent

rapier (**ray**-pyer) *n* a long narrow two-edged sword
WORD ORIGIN Old French *espee rapiere* rasping sword

rapine (**rap**-pine) *n* pillage or plundering
WORD ORIGIN Latin *rapina*

rapport (rap-**pore**) *n* a sympathetic relationship or understanding
WORD ORIGIN French

rapprochement (rap-**prosh**-mong) *n* a re-establishment of friendly relations: *the policy of rapprochement with Eastern Europe*
WORD ORIGIN French

rapscallion *n* *old-fashioned* a rascal or rogue
WORD ORIGIN earlier *rascallion*

rap sheet *n* *chiefly US & Canad informal* a police record of an individual's criminal history

rapt *adj* **1** totally engrossed: *rapt attention* **2** arising from or showing rapture: *with a rapt look on his face*
WORD ORIGIN Latin *raptus* carried away

raptor *n* any bird of prey **raptorial** *adj*
WORD ORIGIN Latin: robber

rapture *n* **1** extreme happiness or delight **2 raptures** ecstatic joy: *they will be in raptures over the rugged scenery* **rapturous** *adj*
WORD ORIGIN Latin *raptus* carried away

rare¹ *adj* **1** uncommon or unusual: *a rare plant* **2** not happening or done very often: *a rare appearance in London* **3** of uncommonly high quality: *a rare beauty* **4** (of air at high altitudes) having low density; thin
WORD ORIGIN Latin *rarus* sparse

rare² *adj* (of meat) very lightly cooked
WORD ORIGIN Old English *hrēr*

rarebit *n* short for **Welsh rarebit**

rare earth *n* *chem* **1** any oxide of a lanthanide **2** Also called: **rare-earth element** any element of the lanthanide series

rarefied (**rare**-if-ide) *adj* **1** highly specialized: *the rarefied world of classical ballet* **2** (of air) thin **3** exalted in character: *the rarefied heights of academic excellence*

rarely *adv* **1** hardly ever **2** to an unusual degree; exceptionally

raring *adj* **raring to do something** keen and willing to do something
WORD ORIGIN *rare*, variant of REAR²

rarity *n, pl* **-ties 1** something that is valuable because it is unusual **2** the state of being rare

rascal *n* **1** a scoundrel or rogue **2** a mischievous child **rascally** *adj*
WORD ORIGIN Old French *rascaille* rabble

rase *vb* **rasing, rased** same as **raze**

rash¹ *adj* acting or done without proper thought or consideration; hasty: *rash actions* **rashly** *adv* **rashness** *n*
WORD ORIGIN Old High German *rasc* hurried, clever

rash² *n* **1** an outbreak of spots or patches on the skin, caused by illness or allergy **2** an outbreak of occurrences: *a rash of censorship trials*
WORD ORIGIN Old French *rasche*

rasher *n* a thin slice of bacon
WORD ORIGIN origin unknown

rasp *n* **1** a harsh grating noise **2** a coarse file with rows of raised teeth ▷ *vb* **3** to say or speak in a grating voice **4** to make a harsh grating noise **5** to scrape or rub (something) roughly **6** to irritate (one's nerves)
WORD ORIGIN Old French *raspe*

raspberry *n, pl* **-ries 1** the red fruit of a prickly shrub of Europe and North America **2** *informal* a spluttering noise made with the tongue and lips to express contempt: *she blew a loud raspberry*
WORD ORIGIN origin unknown

Rastafarian *or* **Rasta** *n* **1** a believer in a religion of Jamaican origin that regards Ras Tafari, the former emperor of Ethiopia, Haile Selassie, as God ▷ *adj* **2** of Rastafarians

raster *n* **1** an image consisting of rows of pixel information, such as a JPEG, GIF etc. **2** a pattern of horizontal scanning lines traced by an electron beam, esp. on a television screen
WORD ORIGIN from German *Raster* screen

rasterize *vb* to convert (a digitized image) into a form that can be printed or represented on a VDU

rat *n* **1** a long-tailed rodent, similar to but larger than a mouse **2** *informal* someone who is disloyal or treacherous **3** **smell a rat** to detect something suspicious ▷ *vb* **ratting, ratted 4 rat on a** to betray (someone): *good friends don't rat on each other* **b** to go back on (an agreement): *his ex-wife claims he ratted on their divorce settlement* **5** to hunt and kill rats
WORD ORIGIN Old English *ræt*

ratafia (rat-a-**fee**-a) *n* **1** a liqueur made from fruit **2** an almond-flavoured biscuit
WORD ORIGIN West Indian Creole French

rat-arsed *adj* *Austral & Brit slang* drunk

rat-a-tat *or* **rat-a-tat-tat** *n* a repeated knocking or tapping sound

ratatouille (rat-a-**twee**) *n* a vegetable casserole made of stewed tomatoes, aubergines, etc.
WORD ORIGIN French

ratbag *n* *slang* an eccentric, stupid, or unreliable person

ratbaggery *n* *Austral slang* nonsense, eccentricity, or stupidity

ratchet *n* **1** a device in which a toothed rack or wheel is engaged by a pivoted lever which permits motion in one direction only **2** the toothed rack or wheel in such a device **3** to operate using a ratchet **4** (usually foll. by *up* or *down*) to increase or decrease, esp. irreversibly: *Hitchcock ratchets up the tension once again*
WORD ORIGIN French *rochet*

rate¹ *n* **1** a quantity or amount considered in relation to or measured against another quantity or amount: *he was publishing at the rate of about 10 books a year* **2** a price or charge with reference to a standard or scale: *an exchange rate* **3** the speed of progress or change: *crime is increasing at an alarming rate* **4** a charge made per unit for a commodity or service **5** see **rates 6** relative quality: *a third-rate power* **7 at any rate** in any case ▷ *vb* **rating, rated 8** to assign a position on a scale of relative values: *he is rated as one of the top caterers in the country* **9** to estimate the value of: *we rate your services highly* **10** to consider or regard: *it could hardly be rated a success* **11** to be worthy of: *it barely rates a mention* **12** *informal* to have a high opinion of: *the cognoscenti have always rated his political skills*
WORD ORIGIN Medieval Latin *rata*

rate² *vb* **rating, rated** to scold or criticize severely
WORD ORIGIN perhaps related to Swedish *rata*

rateable *adj* **1** able to be rated or evaluated **2** liable to payment of rates

rateable value *n* (in Britain) a fixed value assigned to a property, used to assess the rates due on it

rate-cap *vb* **-capping, -capped** (formerly in Britain) to put an upper limit on the rates charged by a local council **rate-capping** *n*

ratepayer *n* a person who pays local rates on a building

rates *pl n* (in some countries) a tax on property levied by a local authority

rather *adv* **1** fairly: *that was a rather narrow escape* **2** to a limited extent: *I rather thought that was the case* **3** more truly or appropriately: *they tend to be cat rather than dog people* **4** more willingly: *I would rather go straight home* ▷ *interj* **5** an expression of strong affirmation: *Is it worth seeing? — Rather!*
WORD ORIGIN Old English *hrathor*, comparative of *hrathe* ready, quick

USAGE
Both *would* and *had* are used with *rather* in sentences such as I would rather (or had rather) go to the film than to the play. *Had rather* is less common and now widely regarded as slightly old-fashioned.

ratify *vb* **-fies, -fying, -fied** to give formal approval or consent to: *they ratified the treaty* **ratification** *n*
WORD ORIGIN Latin *ratus* fixed + *facere* to make

rating *n* **1** a valuation or assessment **2** a classification according to order or grade **3** a noncommissioned sailor **4 ratings** the size of the audience for a TV or radio programme

ratio *n, pl* **-tios 1** the relationship between two numbers or amounts expressed as a proportion: *a ratio of one instructor to every five pupils* **2** *maths* a quotient of two numbers or quantities
WORD ORIGIN Latin: a reckoning

ration *n* **1** a fixed allowance of something that is scarce, such as food or petrol in wartime **2 rations** a fixed daily allowance of food, such as that given to a soldier ▷ *vb* **3** to restrict the distribution of (something): *the government has rationed petrol* **4** to distribute a fixed amount of something to each person in a group **rationing** *n*
WORD ORIGIN Latin *ratio* reckoning

rational *adj* **1** reasonable or sensible **2** using reason or logic in thinking out a problem **3** capable of reasoning: *man is a rational being* **4** sane: *rational behaviour* **5** *maths* able to be expressed as a ratio of two integers: *a rational number* **rationality** *n* **rationally** *adv*
WORD ORIGIN Latin *rationalis*

rationale (rash-a-**nahl**) *n* the reason for an action or belief

rationalism *n* the philosophy that regards reason as the only basis for beliefs or actions **rationalist** *n* **rationalistic** *adj*

rationalize *or* **-lise** *vb* **-lizing, -lized** *or* **-lising, -lised 1** to find reasons to justify or explain (one's actions) **2** to apply logic or reason to (something) **3** to get rid of unnecessary equipment or staff to make (a business) more efficient **rationalization** *or* **-lisation** *n*

rational number *n* any real number that can be expressed in the form *a/b*, where *a* and *b* are integers and *b* is not zero, as 7 or 7/3

ratpack *n* *slang* the members of the press who pursue celebrities and give wide coverage of their private lives: *the royal ratpack*

rat race *n* a continual routine of hectic competitive activity: *get out of the rat race for a while*

rattan *n* a climbing palm with tough stems used for wickerwork and canes
WORD ORIGIN Malay *rōtan*

ratter *n* a dog or cat that catches and kills rats

rattle *vb* **-tling, -tled 1** to make a rapid succession of short sharp sounds, such as when loose pellets are shaken in a container **2** to send, move, or drive with such a sound: *rain rattled against the window* **3** to shake briskly causing sharp sounds **4** *informal* to frighten or confuse **5 rattle off** *or* **out** to recite perfunctorily or rapidly **6 rattle on** *or* **away** to talk quickly and at length about something unimportant **7 rattle through** to do (something) very quickly: *she rattled through a translation* ▷ *n* **8** a rapid succession of short sharp sounds **9** a baby's toy filled with small pellets that rattle when shaken **rattly** *adj*
WORD ORIGIN Middle Dutch *ratelen*

rattlesnake *n* a poisonous snake with loose horny segments on the tail that make a rattling sound

Collins Bank of English and Wordbanks Online

n 1980 COBUILD (Collins Birmingham University International Language Database) pioneered the use of corpora in the dictionary creation process. By 1982 the COBUILD corpus had reached 7.3 million words, which at that time was a considerable amount of data. Over the last few decades, the amount of data that can be processed by computer has increased enormously, and Collins' corpus holdings now stand at over 4 billion words and grow daily. The English corpus is known as the 'Bank of English'.

This huge collection is composed of a wide range of different types of writing and speech containing samples of the English language from hundreds of different sources. Written texts come from newspapers, magazines, fiction and non-fiction, brochures, leaflets, reports, letters, and so on. The spoken word is represented by 20 million words of transcriptions of everyday casual conversation, radio broadcasts, meetings, interviews, discussions, etc. The material is up to date, with the majority of texts originating after 1990. Taken together, the Bank of English provides objective evidence and essential information about the English which most people read, write, speak, and hear every day of their lives.

As the Bank of English is updated regularly we use it to add in all the most important new words and meanings as they enter the English language. This evolving nature marks the Bank of English out from static corpora, which rapidly date and reflect a snapshot of English from many years ago. It is much easier to decide which words and phrases to include, and which to omit, when we have accurate figures from such a large collection of language. Most recently Collins have developed innovative 'Monitor Corpus' software which tracks word statistics and usage over time and flags up new coinages monthly which our lexicographers routinely analyse and use as a source for new words and meanings.

It has now become relatively easy to gather large quantities of spoken and written English. Publishers of books, magazines, and newspapers routinely use electronic media as well as print. Nowadays the problem is not finding the language, but managing and controlling it, and making sensible and balanced selections. In designing the present shape of the Bank of English we balanced a number of factors: spoken and written, British and American English and other regional varieties from native speaker communities, books and magazines, and other classifications within those.

The use of corpora in word analysis for academic research and in classrooms has grown in recent years. In an effort to give researchers and teachers access to corpus resources Collins decided to launch the 'Wordbanks Online' service. This is a corpus service offering everyone the chance to tap into the unique resources of the 'Collins Word Web', on which the highly successful range of Collins dictionaries is based.

By using this service you can access authentic examples of vocabulary, word usage, and grammar and carry out in-depth linguistic analyses for your research thesis or dissertation. In the classroom environment you can work interactively with corpora and it allows you to prepare worksheets and study materials based on real data.

The Wordbanks Online corpus contains 550 million words from a wide range of texts and sources, both written and spoken, and accounts for no less than eight varieties of English. The majority of sources in the corpus date from between 2001 and 2005 and, consequently, it is one of the most current corpora available for subscription.

To access the service visit the website collinslanguage.com/wordbanks. The service uses software known as the 'Sketch Engine', developed by Lexicom Ltd. Further details about the types of analysis possible are found in the essay on Corpus Lexicography.

rattletrap *n informal* a broken-down old vehicle

rattling *adv informal, old-fashioned* very: *a rattling good yarn*

ratty *adj* **-tier, -tiest** *informal* **1** cross and irritable **2** (of the hair) straggly and greasy **rattily** *adv* **rattiness** *n*

raucous *adj* loud and harsh
WORD ORIGIN Latin *raucus*

raunchy *adj* **-chier, -chiest** *slang* sexy or earthy
WORD ORIGIN origin unknown

ravage *vb* **-vaging, -vaged** **1** to cause extensive damage to ▷ *n* **2 ravages** the damaging effects: *the ravages of weather and pollution*
WORD ORIGIN Old French *ravir* to snatch away

rave *vb* **raving, raved** **1** to talk in a wild or incoherent manner **2** *informal* to write or speak (about) with great enthusiasm ▷ *n* **3** *informal* an enthusiastically favourable review **4** *slang* a professionally organized large-scale party with electronic dance music **5** a name given to various types of dance music, such as techno, that feature a fast electronic rhythm
WORD ORIGIN probably from Old French *resver* to wander

ravel *vb* **-velling, -velled** *or US* **-veling, -veled** **1** to tangle or become entangled **2** (of a fabric) to fray out in loose ends; unravel
WORD ORIGIN Middle Dutch *ravelen*

raven *n* **1** a large bird of the crow family with shiny black feathers ▷ *adj* **2** (of hair) shiny black
WORD ORIGIN Old English *hræfn*

ravening *adj* (of animals) hungrily searching for prey

ravenous *adj* **1** very hungry **2** ravening **ravenously** *adv*
WORD ORIGIN Old French *ravineux*

raver *n slang* **1** *Brit, Austral, & S African* a person who leads a wild or uninhibited social life **2** a person who enjoys rave music and goes to raves

ravine (rav-**veen**) *n* a deep narrow steep-sided valley worn by a stream
WORD ORIGIN Old French: torrent

raving *adj* **1** delirious **2** *informal* great or exceptional: *a raving beauty* ▷ *adv* **3** to an excessive degree: *raving mad* ▷ *n* **4 ravings** frenzied or wildly extravagant talk

ravioli *pl n* small squares of pasta with a savoury filling, such as meat or cheese
WORD ORIGIN Italian

ravish *vb* **1** to enrapture or delight: *tourists ravished by our brilliant costumes* **2** *literary* to rape **ravishment** *n*
WORD ORIGIN Latin *rapere* to seize

ravishing *adj* lovely or delightful **ravishingly** *adv*

raw *adj* **1** (of food) not cooked **2** in an unfinished or unrefined state: *raw sewage* **3** not selected or modified: *raw data* **4** (of the skin or a wound) painful, with the surface scraped away **5** untrained or inexperienced: *a raw recruit* **6** (of the weather) harshly cold and damp **7** frank or realistic: *a raw reality* **8 raw deal** *informal* unfair or dishonest treatment ▷ *n* **9 in the raw a** *informal* naked **b** in a natural and uncivilized state: *to see life in the raw* **10 on the raw** *Brit informal* sensitive to upset: *my nerves are on the raw today*
WORD ORIGIN Old English *hrēaw*

rawboned *adj* having a lean bony physique

rawhide *n* **1** untanned hide **2** a whip or rope made of strips of this

Rawlplug *n trademark* a short fibre or plastic tube used to provide a fixing in a wall for a screw

ray¹ *n* **1** a narrow beam of light **2** any of a set of lines spreading from a central point **3** a slight indication: *a ray of hope* **4** *maths* a straight line extending from a point **5** a thin beam of electromagnetic radiation or particles **6** any of the spines that support the fin of of a fish
WORD ORIGIN Old French *rai*

ray² *n* a sea fish related to the sharks, with a flattened body and a long whiplike tail
WORD ORIGIN Old French *raie*

ray³ *n music* (in tonic sol-fa) the second note of any ascending major scale

rayon *n* a textile fibre or fabric made from cellulose
WORD ORIGIN French

raze *or* **rase** *vb* **razing, razed** *or* **rasing, rased** to destroy (buildings or a town) completely
WORD ORIGIN Old French *raser*

razoo *n, pl* **-zoos** *Austral & NZ informal* an imaginary coin: *we haven't got a brass razoo*
WORD ORIGIN origin unknown

razor *n* an implement with a sharp blade, used for shaving
WORD ORIGIN Old French *raseor*

razorbill *n* a black-and-white sea bird with a stout sideways flattened bill

razor shell *n* **1** a burrowing shellfish with a long narrow shell **2** this shell

razor wire *n* strong wire with pieces of sharp metal set across it at intervals

razzle-dazzle *or* **razzmatazz** *n slang* **1** noisy or showy fuss or activity **2** a spree or frolic
WORD ORIGIN rhyming compound from *dazzle*

Rb *chem* rubidium

RC 1 Red Cross **2** Roman Catholic

Rd road

re¹ *prep* with reference to
WORD ORIGIN Latin *res* thing

re² *n music* same as **ray³**

Re *chem* rhenium

RE 1 (in Britain) Religious Education **2** Royal Engineers

re- *prefix* **1** (used with many main words to mean) repetition of an action: *remarry* **2** (used with many main words to mean) return to a previous condition: *renew*
WORD ORIGIN Latin

reach *vb* **1** to arrive at or get to (a place) **2** to make a movement (towards), as if to grasp or touch: *she reached for her bag* **3** to succeed in touching: *I can't reach that shelf unless I stand on a chair* **4** to make contact or communication with: *to reach a wider audience* **5** to extend as far as (a point or place): *to reach the ceiling* **6** to come to (a certain condition or situation): *to reach a compromise* **7** to arrive at or amount to (an amount or value): *temperatures in Greece reached 35° yesterday* **8** *informal* to give (something to a person) with the outstretched hand ▷ *n* **9** the extent or distance of reaching: *within easy reach* **10** the range of influence or power: *it symbolized America's global reach* **11 reaches** a section of river, land, or sky: *the quieter reaches of the upper Thames* **reachable** *adj*
WORD ORIGIN Old English *rǣcan*

reach-me-down *adj Brit informal* cheap and ready-made or second-hand: *a reach-me-down suit*

reacquaint *vb* **reacquaint oneself with** *or* **become reacquainted with** to get to know (someone) again

react *vb* **1** (of a person or thing) to act in response to another person, a stimulus, or a situation **2 react against** to act in an opposing or contrary manner **3** *chem* to undergo a chemical reaction **4** *physics* to exert an equal force in the opposite direction to an acting force
WORD ORIGIN Late Latin *reagere*

reactance *n electronics* the resistance to the flow of an alternating current caused by the inductance or capacitance of the circuit

reactant *n* a substance that participates in a chemical reaction

reaction *n* **1** a physical or emotional response to a stimulus **2** any action resisting another **3** opposition to change **4** *med* any effect produced by a drug or by a substance (allergen) to which a person is allergic **5** *chem* a process that involves changes in the structure and energy content of atoms, molecules, or ions **6** the equal and opposite force that acts on a body whenever it exerts a force on another body **7 reactions** someone's ability to act in response to something that happens

USAGE
Reaction is used to refer both to an instant response (*her reaction was one of amazement*) and to a considered response in the form of a statement (*the Minister gave his reaction to the court's decision*). Some people think this second use is incorrect.

reactionary *adj* **1** opposed to political or social change ▷ *n, pl* **-aries 2** a person opposed to radical change

reactivate *vb* **-vating, -vated** to make (something) active again **reactivation** *n*

reactive *adj* **1** readily taking part in chemical reactions: *ozone is a highly reactive form of oxygen gas* **2** of or having a reactance **3** responsive to stimulus **reactively** *adv* **reactivity** *n*

reactor *n* short for **nuclear reactor**

read *vb* **reading, read** **1** to look at and understand or take in (written or printed matter) **2** to look at and say aloud **3** to have a certain wording: *the memorandum read as follows* **4** to interpret in a specified way: *it can be read as satire* **5** to interpret the significance or meaning of: *an astrologer who reads Tarot* **6** to register or show: *the meter reads 100*

7 to make out the true nature or mood of: *she had read his thoughts* **8** to interpret (signs, characters, etc.) other than by visual means: *to read Braille* **9** to have sufficient knowledge of (a language) to understand the written word **10** to undertake a course of study in (a subject): *to read economics* **11** to gain knowledge by reading: *he read about the war* **12** to hear and understand, esp. when using a two-way radio: *we are reading you loud and clear* **13** *computers* to obtain (data) from a storage device, such as magnetic tape ▷ *n* **14** matter suitable for reading: *this book is a very good read* **15** a spell of reading ▸ See also **read into, read out**, etc. **WORD ORIGIN** Old English *rǣdan* to advise, explain

readable *adj* **1** enjoyable to read **2** (of handwriting or print) legible

reader *n* **1** a person who reads **2** a person who reads aloud in public **3** a person who reads and judges manuscripts sent to a publisher **4** a book of texts for those learning a foreign language **5** *Brit* a member of staff below a professor but above a senior lecturer at a university **6** a proofreader **7** short for **lay reader**

readership *n* all the readers collectively of a publication or author: *a new format would alienate its readership*

reading *n* **1** the act of reading **2** ability to read: *disputes over methods of teaching reading* **3** material for reading **4** a public recital of a literary work **5** a measurement indicated by a gauge or dial **6** *parliamentary procedure* one of the three stages in the passage of a bill through a legislative assembly **7** the form of a particular word or passage in a given text **8** an interpretation of a situation or something said ▷ *adj* **9** of or for reading: *reading glasses*

read into *vb* to discover in a statement (meanings not intended by the speaker or writer): *one of the implications we must read into the work*

readjust *vb* to adapt to a new situation **readjustment** *n*

readmit *vb* **-mitting, -mitted** to let (a person or country) back into a place or organization **readmission** *n*

read out *vb* **1** to read (something) aloud **2** to retrieve information from a computer memory ▷ *n* **read-out 3** the information retrieved from a computer memory

read up *vb* to read intensively about (a subject) in order to get information: *he had read up on the cases*

read-write head *n computers* an electromagnet that can both read and write information on a magnetic tape or disk

ready *adj* **readier, readiest 1** prepared for use or action **2** prompt or eager: *the ready use of corporal punishment* **3** quick or intelligent: *a ready wit* **4 ready to** on the point of or liable to: *ready to pounce* **5** easily available: *his ready tears* ▷ *n* **6** *informal* same as **ready money 7 at the ready** poised for use: *with pen at the ready* ▷ *vb* **readies, readying, readied 8** to make ready; prepare

readily *adv* **readiness** *n* **WORD ORIGIN** Old English *(ge)rǣde*

ready-made *adj* **1** for immediate use by any customer **2** extremely convenient or ideally suited: *a ready-made audience*

ready money *n* cash for immediate use. Also: **the ready, the readies**

reaffirm *vb* to state again **reaffirmation** *n*

reafforest *vb* to plant new trees in (an area that was formerly forested) **reafforestation** *n*

reagent (ree-**age**-ent) *n* a chemical substance that reacts with another, used to detect the presence of the other

real¹ *adj* **1** existing or occurring in the physical world **2** actual: *the real agenda* **3** important or serious: *the real challenge* **4** rightly so called: *a real friend* **5** genuine: *the council has no real authority* **6** (of food or drink) made in a traditional way to ensure the best flavour **7** *maths* involving or containing real numbers alone **8** relating to immovable property such as land or buildings: *real estate* **9** *econ* (of prices or incomes) considered in terms of purchasing power rather than nominal currency value **10 the real thing** the genuine article, not a substitute or imitation **WORD ORIGIN** Latin *res* thing

real² *n* a former small Spanish or Spanish-American silver coin **WORD ORIGIN** Spanish, literally: royal

real ale *n chiefly Brit* beer that has fermented in the barrel

real estate *n* immovable property, esp. land and houses

realignment (ree-a-**line**-ment) *n* a new arrangement or organization: *there will be a realignment of party allegiances*

realism *n* **1** awareness or acceptance of things as they are, as opposed to the abstract or ideal **2** a style in art or literature that attempts to show the world as it really is **3** *philosophy* the theory that physical objects continue to exist whether they are perceived or not **realist** *n* **realistic** *adj* **realistically** *adv*

reality *n, pl* **-ties 1** the state of things as they are or appear to be, rather than as one might wish them to be **2** something that is real **3** the state of being real **4 in reality** in fact

reality TV *n* television programmes focusing on members of the public living in conditions created especially by the programme makers

realize or **-lise** *vb* **-lizing, -lized** or **-lising, -lised 1** to be aware of or grasp the significance of **2** to achieve (a plan or ambition) **3** to convert (property or goods) into cash **4** (of goods or property) to sell for (a certain sum): *this table realized a large sum at auction* **5** to produce a complete work of art from an idea or draft **realizable** or **-lisable** *adj* **realization** or **-lisation** *n*

really *adv* **1** truly: *really boring* **2** in reality: *it's really quite harmless* ▷ *interj* **3** an exclamation of dismay, doubt, or surprise

☰USAGE
☰See at **very**.

realm *n* **1** a kingdom **2** a field of interest or study: *the realm of science* **WORD ORIGIN** Old French *reialme*

real number *n* any rational or irrational number

real tennis *n* an ancient form of tennis played in a four-walled indoor court

real-time *adj* (of a computer system) processing data as it is received

realtor *n US & Canad* an estate agent **WORD ORIGIN** from a trademark

realty *n* same as **real estate**

ream *n* **1** a number of sheets of paper, now equal to 500 or 516 sheets (20 quires) **2 reams** *informal* a large quantity (of written material): *reams of verse* **WORD ORIGIN** Arabic *rizmah* bale

reap *vb* **1** to cut and gather (a harvest) **2** to receive as the result of a previous activity: *reap the benefits of our efforts* **WORD ORIGIN** Old English *riopan*

reaper *n* **1** a person who reaps or a machine for reaping **2 the grim reaper** death

reappear *vb* to come back into view **reappearance** *n*

reappraise *vb* **-praising, -praised** to consider or review (something) to see if changes are needed **reappraisal** *n*

rear¹ *n* **1** the back part **2** the area or position that lies at the back **3** *informal* the buttocks **4 bring up the rear** to come last ▷ *adj* **5** of or in the rear: *the rear carriage* **WORD ORIGIN** Old French *rer*

rear² *vb* **1** to care for and educate (children) until maturity **2** to breed (animals) or grow (plants) **3** (of a horse) to lift the front legs in the air and stand nearly upright **4** to place or lift (something) upright **WORD ORIGIN** Old English *rǣran*

rear admiral *n* a high-ranking naval officer

rearguard *n* **1** the troops who protect the rear of a military formation ▷ *adj* **2 rearguard action** an effort to prevent or postpone something that is unavoidable

rear light or **rear lamp** *n* a red light, usually one of a pair, attached to the rear of a vehicle. Also called: **tail-light, tail lamp**

rearm *vb* **1** to arm again **2** to equip with better weapons **rearmament** *n*

rearmost *adj* nearest the back

rearrange *vb* **-ranging, -ranged** to organize differently **rearrangement** *n*

rear-view mirror *n* a mirror on a motor vehicle enabling the driver to see the traffic behind

rearward *adj* **1** in the rear ▷ *adv* also **rearwards 2** towards the rear

reason *n* **1** a cause or motive for a belief or action: *he had two reasons for his dark mood* **2** the ability to think or argue rationally **3** an argument in favour of or a justification for something: *there is every reason to encourage people to keep fit* **4** sanity **5 by reason of** because of **6 within reason** within moderate or justifiable bounds **7 it stands to reason** it is logical or obvious ▷ *vb* **8** to think

logically in forming conclusions
9 reason with to persuade by logical arguments into doing something
10 reason out to work out (a problem) by reasoning
WORD ORIGIN Latin *reri* to think

≡ USAGE
≡ The expression *the reason is because...* should be avoided. Instead one should
≡ say either *this is because...* or *the reason is*
≡ *that...*

reasonable *adj* **1** sensible **2** not making unfair demands **3** logical: *a reasonable explanation* **4** moderate in price **5** average: *a reasonable amount of luck* **reasonably** *adv* **reasonableness** *n*

reasoned *adj* well thought out or well presented: *a reasoned explanation*

reasoning *n* **1** the process of drawing conclusions from facts or evidence **2** the conclusions reached in this way

reassemble *vb* **-bling, -bled** to put back together again

reassert *vb* **1** to state or declare again **2 reassert oneself** to become significant or noticeable again: *reality had reasserted itself*

reassess *vb* to reconsider the value or importance of **reassessment** *n*

reassure *vb* **-assuring, -assured** to relieve (someone) of anxieties **reassurance** *n* **reassuring** *adj*

rebate¹ *n* a refund or discount **WORD ORIGIN** Old French *rabattre* to beat down

rebate² *or* **rabbet** *n* **1** a groove cut into a piece of timber into which another piece fits ▷ *vb* **-bating, -bated** *or* **-beting, -beted** **2** to cut a rebate in **3** to join (pieces of timber) with a rebate **WORD ORIGIN** Old French *rabattre* to beat down

rebel *vb* **-belling, -belled** **1** to fight against the ruling power **2** to reject accepted conventions of behaviour ▷ *n* **3** a person who rebels **4** a person who rejects accepted conventions of behaviour ▷ *adj* **5** rebelling: *rebel councillors* **WORD ORIGIN** Latin *re-* again + *bellum* war

rebellion *n* **1** organized opposition to a government or other authority involving the use of violence **2** nonviolent opposition to a government or other authority: *a Tory backbenchers' rebellion* **3** rejection of accepted conventions of behaviour **WORD ORIGIN** Latin *rebellio*

rebellious *adj* rebelling or showing a tendency towards rebellion **rebelliously** *adv*

rebirth *n* a revival or renaissance: *the rebirth of their nation*

reboot *vb* to shut down and then restart (a computer system)

rebore *or* **reboring** *n* the boring of a cylinder to restore its true shape

reborn *adj* active again after a period of inactivity

rebound *vb* **1** to spring back from a sudden impact **2** (of a plan or action) to misfire so as to hurt the person responsible ▷ *n* **3** the act of rebounding **4 on the rebound** *informal* while

recovering from rejection: *she married him on the rebound*

rebrand *vb* to change or update the image of (an organization or product)

rebuff *vb* **1** to snub and reject an offer or suggestion ▷ *n* **2** a blunt refusal; snub **WORD ORIGIN** Old French *rebuffer*

rebuild *vb* **-building, -built** **1** to build (a building or town) again, after severe damage **2** to develop (something such as a business or relationship) again after destruction or damage

rebuke *vb* **-buking, -buked** **1** to scold sternly ▷ *n* **2** a stern scolding **WORD ORIGIN** Old French *rebuker*

rebus (**ree**-buss) *n, pl* **-buses** a puzzle consisting of pictures and symbols representing syllables and words **WORD ORIGIN** Latin: by things

rebut *vb* **-butting, -butted** to prove that (a claim) is untrue **rebuttal** *n* **WORD ORIGIN** Old French *reboter*

rec *n* short for **recreation**

recalcitrant *adj* wilfully disobedient **recalcitrance** *n* **WORD ORIGIN** Latin *re-* again + *calcitrare* to kick

recall *vb* **1** to bring back to mind **2** to order to return **3** to annul or cancel ▷ *n* **4** the ability to remember things **5** an order to return

recant *vb* to take back (a former belief or statement) publicly **recantation** *n* **WORD ORIGIN** Latin *re-* again + *cantare* to sing

recap *informal vb* **-capping, -capped** **1** to recapitulate ▷ *n* **2** a recapitulation

recapitulate *vb* **-lating, -lated** to restate the main points of (an argument or speech) **WORD ORIGIN** Late Latin *recapitulare*, literally: to put back under headings

recapitulation *n* **1** the act of recapitulating **2** *music* the repeating of earlier themes, esp. in the final section of a movement

recapture *vb* **-turing, -tured** **1** to relive vividly (a former experience or sensation): *recaptured some of those first feelings* **2** to capture again ▷ *n* **3** the act of recapturing

recast *vb* **-casting, -cast** **1** to give a new form or shape to: *he found the organization wholly recast* **2** to change the actors or singers in (a play, musical, or opera) **3** to rework (a piece of writing or music): *she has recast most of my book*

recce *chiefly Brit slang vb* **-ceing, -ced** *or* **-ceed** **1** to reconnoitre ▷ *n* **2** reconnaissance

recede *vb* **-ceding, -ceded** **1** to withdraw from a point or limit: *the tide had receded* **2** to become more distant: *the threat of intervention had receded* **3** (of a man's hair) to stop growing at the temples and above the forehead **4** to slope backwards: *a receding chin* **WORD ORIGIN** Latin *recedere* to go back

receipt *n* **1** a written acknowledgment that money or goods have been received **2** the act of receiving **3 receipts** money taken in over a particular period by a shop or business **WORD ORIGIN** Old French *receite*

receive *vb* **-ceiving, -ceived** **1** to get (something offered or sent to one) **2** to experience: *he received a knife wound* **3** to greet (guests) **4** to have (an honour) bestowed: *he received the Order of the Garter* **5** to admit (a person) to a society or condition: *he was received into the Church* **6** to convert (incoming radio or television signals) into sounds or pictures **7** to be informed of (news) **8** to react to: *the article was well received* **9** to support or sustain (the weight of something) **10** *tennis, etc.* to play at the other end from the server **11** *Brit & NZ* to buy and sell stolen goods **WORD ORIGIN** Latin *recipere*

received *adj* generally accepted or believed: *contrary to received wisdom*

Received Pronunciation *n* the accent of standard Southern British English

receiver *n* **1** the detachable part of a telephone that is held to the ear **2** the equipment in a telephone, radio, or television that converts the incoming signals into sound or pictures **3** a person appointed by a court to manage property of a bankrupt **4** a person who receives stolen goods knowing they have been stolen

receivership *n law* the state of being administered by a receiver: *the company went into receivership*

recent *adj* **1** having happened lately **2** new **recently** *adv* **WORD ORIGIN** Latin *recens* fresh

Recent *adj* same as **Holocene**

receptacle *n* **1** an object used to contain something **2** *bot* the enlarged or modified tip of the flower stalk that bears the flower **WORD ORIGIN** Latin *receptaculum* store-place

reception *n* **1** an area in an office, hotel, etc. where visitors are received or reservations dealt with **2** a formal party for guests, esp. after a wedding **3** the manner in which something is received: *an enthusiastic reception* **4** the act of formally welcoming **5** *radio, television* the quality of a received broadcast: *the reception was poor*

receptionist *n* a person employed to receive guests or clients and deal with reservations and appointments

reception room *n* a room in a private house suitable for entertaining guests

receptive *adj* willing to consider and accept new ideas or suggestions **receptivity** *or* **receptiveness** *n*

receptor *n physiol* a sensory nerve ending that changes specific stimuli into nerve impulses

recess *n* **1** a space, such as an alcove, set back in a wall **2** a holiday between sessions of work **3 recesses** secret hidden places: *the recesses of her brain* **4** *US & Canad* a break between classes at a school **WORD ORIGIN** Latin *recessus* a retreat

recessed *adj* hidden or placed in a recess

recession *n* **1** a period of economic difficulty when little is being bought or sold **2** the act of receding

recessional *n* a hymn sung as the clergy and choir withdraw after a church service

Words from Literature
part 22

raree-show *n* an old term for a peep-show or a fairground entertainment
> A raree-show is here, with children gathered round
> *The Prelude* William Wordsworth

recusant *n* recusants are people who resisted authority
> hardy recusants
> *The Prelude* William Wordsworth

redounding *v* eddying. An eddy is a movement in water or air which goes round and round instead of flowing in one direction
> mists and steam-like fogs redounding everywhere
> *The Prelude* William Wordsworth

redundant *adj* here redundant means overflowing but Wordsworth also uses it to mean excessively large or too big
> A tempest, a redundant energy
> *The Prelude* William Wordsworth

reflex *n* reflex is a shortened version of reflexion, which is an alternative spelling of reflection
> To cut across the reflex of a star
> *The Prelude* William Wordsworth

reformatory *n* a prison for young offenders or criminals
> Even when I was taken to have a new suit of clothes, the tailor had orders to make them like a kind of Reformatory, and on no account to let me have the free use of my limbs.
> *Great Expectations* Charles Dickens

remorse *n* pity or compassion
> by that remorse
> *On His Mistress* John Donne

render *v* in this context render means give
> and Sarah could render no reason that would be sanctioned by the feeling of the community.
> *Silas Marner* George Eliot

repeater *n* a repeater was a watch that chimed the last hour when a spring was pressed, as a result it was useful in the dark
> And his watch is a gold repeater, and worth a hundred pound if it's worth a penny.
> *Great Expectations* Charles Dickens

repugnance *n* a strong dislike of something or someone
> overcoming a strong repugnance
> *Treasure Island* Robert Louis Stevenson

reverence *n* reverence means a bow
> made my reverence
> *Gulliver's Travels* Jonathan Swift

reverie *n* a reverie is a day dream
> I can guess the subject of your reverie
> *Pride and Prejudice* Jane Austen

revival *n* a religious meeting held in public
> well I'd ben a-runnin' a little temperance revival thar' bout a week
> *The Adventures of Huckleberry Finn* Mark Twain

revolt *v* to turn back or stop your present course of action and go back to what you were doing before
> Revolt, or I'll in piecemeal tear thy flesh
> *Doctor Faustus* 5.1 Christopher Marlowe

rheumatics or **rheumatism** *n* rheumatics is an illness that makes your joints or muscles stiff and painful
> a new cure for the rheumatics
> *Treasure Island* Robert Louis Stevenson

riddance *n* something that you are pleased has gone or been left behind
> I'd better go into the house, and die and be a riddance
> *David Copperfield* Charles Dickens

rimy *adj* covered in ice or frost
> It was a rimy morning, and very damp
> *Great Expectations* Charles Dickens

riper *adj* more mature or older
> At riper years to Wittenberg he went
> *Doctor Faustus* chorus Christopher Marlowe

recessive *adj* **1** tending to recede **2** *genetics* (in a pair of genes) designating a gene that has a characteristic which will only be passed on if the other gene has the same characteristic

recharge *vb* **-charging, -charged** to cause (a battery) to take in and store electricity again **rechargeable** *adj*

recherché (rish-**air**-shay) *adj* **1** studiedly refined or elegant **2** known only to connoisseurs **WORD ORIGIN** French: thoroughly sought after

recidivism *n* habitual relapse into crime **recidivist** *n*, *adj* **WORD ORIGIN** Latin *recidivus* falling back

recipe *n* **1** a list of ingredients and directions for making a particular dish **2** a method for achieving something: *a recipe for industrial chaos* **WORD ORIGIN** Latin, literally: take (it)!

recipient *n* a person who receives something

reciprocal (ris-**sip**-pro-kl) *adj* **1** done or felt by each of two people or groups to or about the other: *a reciprocal agreement* **2** given or done in return: *a reciprocal invitation* **3** *grammar* (of a pronoun) indicating that action is given and received by each subject, for example, *each other* in *they started to shout at each other* ▷ *n* **4** Also called: **inverse** *maths* a number or quantity that when multiplied by a given number or quantity gives a product of one: *the reciprocal of 2 is 0.5* **reciprocally** *adv* **WORD ORIGIN** Latin *reciprocus* alternating

reciprocate *vb* **-cating, -cated 1** to give or feel in return: *not everyone reciprocated his enthusiasm* **2** (of a machine part) to move backwards and forwards **reciprocation** *n*

reciprocity *n* **1** reciprocal action or relation **2** a mutual exchange of commercial or other privileges

recital (ris-**site**-al) *n* **1** a musical performance by a soloist or soloists **2** the act of reciting something learned or prepared **3** a narration or description: *she plagued her with the recital of constant ailments and illnesses*

recitation *n* **1** the act of reciting poetry or prose from memory **2** something recited

recitative (ress-it-a-**teev**) *n* a narrative passage in an opera or oratorio, reflecting the natural rhythms of speech **WORD ORIGIN** Italian *recitativo*

recite *vb* **-citing, -cited 1** to repeat (a poem or passage) aloud from memory before an audience **2** to give a detailed account of **WORD ORIGIN** Latin *recitare*

reckless *adj* having no regard for danger or consequences: *reckless driving* **WORD ORIGIN** Old English *recceleás*

reckon *vb* **1** *informal* to be of the opinion: *she reckoned she could find them* **2** to consider: *he reckoned himself a failure* **3** to calculate or compute **4** to expect **5 reckon with** to take into account: *there is this ancestral hatred to reckon with* **6 reckon without** to fail to take into account **7 reckon on** or **upon** to rely on

or expect: *they can't reckon on your automatic support* **WORD ORIGIN** Old English *(ge)recenian*

recount

reckoning *n* **1** counting or calculating: *by his reckoning, he owed him money* **2** retribution for one's actions: *the moment of reckoning came* **3** settlement of an account or bill

reclaim *vb* **1** to get back possession of: *the club is now trying to reclaim the money from the blockaders* **2** to convert (unusable or submerged land) into land suitable for farming or building on **3** to recover (useful substances) from waste products **reclamation** *n* **WORD ORIGIN** Latin *reclamare* to cry out

recline *vb* **-clining, -clined** to rest in a leaning position **WORD ORIGIN** Latin *reclinare*

reclining *adj* (of a seat) with a back that can be adjusted to slope at various angles

recluse *n* a person who lives alone and avoids people **reclusive** *adj* **WORD ORIGIN** Late Latin *recludere* to shut away

recognition *n* **1** the act of recognizing **2** acceptance or acknowledgment **3** formal acknowledgment of a government or of the independence of a country **4 in recognition of** as a token of thanks for

recognizance *or* **recognisance** (rik-**og**-nizz-anss) *n* *law* **a** an undertaking made before a court or magistrate to do something specified, such as to appear in court on a stated day **b** a sum of money promised as a guarantee of this undertaking **WORD ORIGIN** Old French *reconoissance*

recognize *or* **-nise** *vb* **-nizing, -nized** *or* **-nising, -nised 1** to identify (a person or thing) as someone or something already known **2** to accept or be aware of (a fact or problem): *to recognize change* **3** to acknowledge formally the status or legality of (something or someone): *an organization recognized by the UN* **4** to show approval or appreciation of (something) **5** to make formal acknowledgment of (a claim or duty): *I must ask for her to be recognized as a hostile witness* **recognizable** *or* **-nisable** *adj* **WORD ORIGIN** Latin *re-* again + *cognoscere* to know

recoil *vb* **1** to jerk or spring back **2** to draw back in fear or horror **3** (of an action) to go wrong so as to hurt the person responsible ▷ *n* **4** the backward movement of a gun when fired **5** the act of recoiling **WORD ORIGIN** Old French *reculer*

recollect *vb* to remember **recollection** *n* **WORD ORIGIN** Latin *recolligere* to gather again

recombinant (ree-**kom**-bin-ant) *adj* *genetics* produced by the combining of genetic material from more than one origin

recommend *vb* **1** to advise as the best course or choice **2** to praise or commend: *I would wholeheartedly recommend his books* **3** to make attractive or advisable: *she has everything to recommend her* **recommendation** *n*

WORD ORIGIN Latin *re-* again + *commendare* to commend

recompense *vb* **-pensing, -pensed 1** to pay or reward for work or help **2** to compensate or make up for loss or injury ▷ *n* **3** compensation for loss or injury **4** reward or repayment **WORD ORIGIN** Latin *re-* again + *compensare* to balance

reconcile *vb* **-ciling, -ciled 1** to make (two apparently conflicting things) compatible or consistent with each other: *in many cases science and religion are reconciled* **2** to re-establish friendly relations with (a person or people) or between (people) **3** to accept or cause to accept (an unpleasant situation): *we reconciled ourselves to a change* **WORD ORIGIN** Latin *reconciliare*

reconciliation *n* **1** the state of being reconciled **2** the act of reconciling people or groups **3** *S African* a political term emphasizing the need to acknowledge the wrongs of the past

recondite *adj* *formal* **1** requiring special knowledge **2** dealing with abstruse or profound subjects **WORD ORIGIN** Latin *reconditus* hidden away

recondition *vb* to restore to good condition or working order: *a reconditioned engine* **reconditioned** *adj*

reconnaissance (rik-**kon**-iss-anss) *n* **1** the process of obtaining information about the position and movements of an enemy **2** a preliminary inspection **WORD ORIGIN** French

reconnoitre *or US* **reconnoiter** (rek-a-**noy**-ter) *vb* to make a reconnaissance of **WORD ORIGIN** obsolete French *reconnoître*

reconsider *vb* to think about again, with a view to changing one's policy or course of action **reconsideration** *n*

reconstitute *vb* **-tuting, -tuted 1** to reorganize in a slightly different form **2** to restore (dried food) to its former state by adding water **reconstitution** *n*

reconstruct *vb* **1** to build again **2** to reorganize: *three works proved useful in reconstructing the training routine* **3** to form a picture of (a past event, esp. a crime) by piecing together evidence **reconstruction** *n*

reconvene *vb* to gather together again after an interval: *we reconvene tomorrow*

record *n* (**rek**-ord) **1** a document or other thing that preserves information **2 records** information or data on a subject collected over a long period: *dental records* **3** a thin disc of a plastic material upon which sound has been recorded in a continuous spiral groove on each side **4** the best recorded achievement in some field: *her score set a Games record* **5** the known facts about a person's achievements **6** a list of crimes of which an accused person has previously been convicted **7** anything serving as evidence or as a memorial: *the First World War is a record of human folly* **8** *computers* a group of data or piece of information preserved as a unit in machine-readable form **9 for the record** for the sake of strict factual accuracy **10 go on record** to state one's views publicly **11 have a record** to have previous criminal convictions **12 off the record** not for publication **13 on record a** stated in a public document **b** publicly known ▷ *adj* **14** being the highest or lowest, or best or worst ever achieved: *record losses* ▷ *vb* (rik-**kord**) **15** to put in writing to preserve the true facts: *to record the minutes of a meeting* **16** to preserve (sound, TV programmes, etc.) on plastic disc, magnetic tape, etc. for reproduction on a playback device **17** to show or register **WORD ORIGIN** Latin *recordari* to remember

recorded delivery *n* a postal service by which an official receipt is obtained for the posting and delivery of a letter or parcel

recorder *n* **1** a person or machine that records, esp. a video, cassette, or tape recorder **2** *music* a wind instrument, blown through the end, with finger-holes and a reedlike tone **3** (in England and Wales) a barrister or solicitor appointed to sit as a part-time judge in the crown court

recording *n* **1** something that has been recorded **2** the process of storing sounds or visual signals for later use

record player *n* a device for reproducing the sounds stored on a record

recount *vb* to tell the story or details of **WORD ORIGIN** Old French *reconter*

re-count *vb* **1** to count again ▷ *n* **2** a second or further count, esp. of votes in an election

recoup (rik-**koop**) *vb* **1** to regain or make good (a loss) **2** to reimburse or compensate (someone) for a loss **recoupment** *n* **WORD ORIGIN** Old French *recouper* to cut back

recourse *n* **1 have recourse to** to turn to a source of help or course of action **2** a source of help or course of action that is turned to when in difficulty **WORD ORIGIN** Latin *re-* back + *currere* to run

recover *vb* **1** (of a person) to regain health, spirits, or composure **2** to regain a former and better condition: *real wages have recovered from the recession* **3** to find again or obtain the return of (something lost) **4** to get back or make good (expense or loss) **5** to obtain (useful substances) from waste **6** *law* to gain (something) by the judgment of a court: *it should be possible to recover damages* **recoverable** *adj* **WORD ORIGIN** Latin *recuperare*

recovery *n, pl* **-veries 1** the act of recovering from sickness, a shock, or a setback **2** restoration to a former and better condition **3** the regaining of something lost **4** the extraction of useful substances from waste

recreant *n archaic* a disloyal or cowardly person **WORD ORIGIN** Old French *recroire* to surrender

re-create *vb* **-creating, -created** to make happen or exist again **re-creation** *n*

recreation *n* an activity done for pleasure or relaxation **recreational** *adj* **WORD ORIGIN** Latin *recreare* to refresh

recreation ground *n* an area of publicly owned land where sports and games may be played

recrimination *n* accusations made by two people or groups about each other: *bitter recrimination* **recriminatory** *adj* **WORD ORIGIN** Latin *re-* back + *criminari* to accuse

recrudescence *n literary* an outbreak of trouble or a disease after a period of quiet **WORD ORIGIN** Latin *re-* again + *crudus* bloody, raw

recruit *vb* **1** to enlist (people) for military service **2** to enrol or obtain (members or support) ▷ *n* **3** a newly joined member of a military service **4** a new member or supporter **recruitment** *n* **WORD ORIGIN** French *recrute* new growth

rectal *adj* of the rectum

rectangle *n* an oblong shape with four straight sides and four right angles **rectangular** *adj* **WORD ORIGIN** Latin *rectus* straight + *angulus* angle

rectify *vb* **-fies, -fying, -fied 1** to put right; correct **2** *chem* to separate (a substance) from a mixture by distillation **3** *electronics* to convert (alternating current) into direct current **rectification** *n* **rectifier** *n* **WORD ORIGIN** Latin *rectus* straight + *facere* to make

rectilinear (rek-tee-**lin**-ee-er) *adj formal* **1** in a straight line **2** bounded by or formed of straight lines

rectitude *n* moral or religious correctness: *a model of rectitude* **WORD ORIGIN** Latin *rectus* right

recto *n, pl* **-tos 1** the right-hand page of a book **2** the front of a sheet of printed paper **WORD ORIGIN** Latin: on the right

rector *n* **1** *Church of England* a clergyman in charge of a parish **2** *RC Church* a cleric in charge of a college or congregation **3** *chiefly Brit* the head of certain academic institutions **4** (in Scotland) a high-ranking official in a university, elected by the students **rectorship** *n* **WORD ORIGIN** Latin: director

rectory *n, pl* **-ries** the house of a rector

rectum *n, pl* **-tums** *or* **-ta** the lower part of the alimentary canal, ending in the anus **WORD ORIGIN** Latin: straight

recumbent *adj* lying down **WORD ORIGIN** Latin *recumbere* to lie back

recuperate *vb* **-rating, -rated** to recover from illness or exhaustion **recuperation** *n* **recuperative** *adj* **WORD ORIGIN** Latin *recuperare*

recur *vb* **-curring, -curred 1** to happen or occur again **2** (of a thought or feeling) to come back to the mind **recurrence** *n* **recurrent** *adj* **recurring** *adj* **WORD ORIGIN** Latin *re-* again + *currere* to run

recurring decimal *n* a rational number that contains a pattern of digits repeated indefinitely after the decimal point: *1 divided by 11 gives the recurring decimal 0.09090909...*

recusant (**rek**-yew-zant) *n* **1** *history* a Roman Catholic who did not attend the services of the Church of England **2** a person who refuses to obey authority **recusancy** *n* **WORD ORIGIN** Latin *recusans* refusing

recycle *vb* **-cling, -cled 1** to reprocess (something already used) for further use: *public demand for recycled paper* **2** to pass (a substance) through a system again for further use **recyclable** *adj*

red *adj* **redder, reddest 1** of a colour varying from crimson to orange; of the colour of blood **2** reddish in colour or having parts or marks that are reddish: *red deer* **3** flushed in the face from anger or shame **4** (of the eyes) bloodshot **5** (of wine) made from black grapes and coloured by their skins ▷ *n* **6** the colour red; the colour of blood **7** anything red, such as red clothing or red paint: *she had dressed in red* **8 in the red** *informal* in debt **9 see red** *informal* to become very angry **redness** *n* **reddish** *adj* **WORD ORIGIN** Old English *rēad*

Red *informal n* **1** a Communist or socialist ▷ *adj* **2** Communist or socialist

red admiral *n* a butterfly with black wings with red and white markings

redback spider *n* a small venomous Australian spider with a red stripe on the back of the abdomen

red blood cell *n* same as **erythrocyte**

red-blooded *adj informal* vigorous or virile

redbreast *n* a robin

redbrick *adj* (of a British university) founded in the late 19th or early 20th century

red card *soccer n* **1** a piece of red pasteboard raised by a referee to indicate that a player has been sent off ▷ *vb* **red-card 2** to send off (a player)

red carpet *n* very special treatment given to an important guest

redcoat *n* **1** *history* a British soldier **2** *Canad informal* a Mountie

Red Crescent *n* the name and symbol used by the Red Cross in Muslim countries

Red Cross *n* an international organization (**Red Cross Society**) which helps victims of war or natural disaster

redcurrant *n* a very small red edible fruit that grows in bunches on a bush

red deer *n* a large deer of Europe and Asia, which has a reddish-brown coat and a short tail

redden *vb* **1** to make or become red or redder **2** to blush

redecorate *vb* to paint or wallpaper (a room) again **redecoration** *n*

redeem *vb* **1** to make up for **2** to reinstate (oneself) in someone's good opinion: *he missed a penalty but redeemed himself by setting up the winning goal* **3** *Christianity* (of Christ as Saviour) to free (humanity) from sin by death on the Cross **4** to buy back: *she didn't have the money to redeem it* **5** to pay off (a loan or debt) **6** to convert (bonds or shares) into cash **7** to exchange (coupons) for goods **8** to fulfil (a promise): *I vowed to abide by the bill and have redeemed my pledge* **redeemable** *adj* **redeemer** *n*

WORD ORIGIN Latin *re-* back + *emere* to buy

Redeemer *n* the Redeemer *Christianity* Jesus Christ

redeeming *adj* making up for faults or deficiencies: *the soundtrack is the film's only redeeming feature*

redemption *n* **1** the act of redeeming **2** the state of being redeemed **3** *Christianity* deliverance from sin through the incarnation and death of Christ **redemptive** *adj*

redeploy *vb* to assign (people) to new positions or tasks **redeployment** *n*

redevelop *vb* to rebuild or renovate (an area or building) **redeveloper** *n* **redevelopment** *n*

redfish *n, pl* **-fish** *or* **-fishes** *Canad* same as **kokanee**

red flag *n* **1** a symbol of revolution **2** a warning of danger

red-handed *adj* **catch someone red-handed** to catch someone in the act of doing something wrong or illegal

red hat *n* the broad-brimmed crimson hat given to cardinals as the symbol of their rank

redhead *n* a person with reddish hair **redheaded** *adj*

red herring *n* something which diverts attention from the main issue

red-hot *adj* **1** (of metal) glowing hot **2** extremely hot **3** very keen or excited **4** furious: *one of those red-hot blazes of temper* **5** very recent or topical: *red-hot information*

red-hot poker *n* a garden plant with spikes of red or yellow flowers

Red Indian *n, adj offensive* Native American

redirect *vb* **1** to send in a new direction or course **2** to send (mail) to a different address

redistribute *vb* **-uting, -uted** to share out in a different way: *to redistribute the world's wealth*

redistribution *n* **1** the act of redistributing **2** a revision of the number of seats that each province has in the Canadian House of Commons, made every ten years

red lead *n* a bright-red poisonous insoluble oxide of lead

red-letter day *n* a memorably important or happy occasion **WORD ORIGIN** from the red letters in ecclesiastical calendars to indicate saints' days

red light *n* **1** a traffic signal to stop **2** a danger signal

red-light district *n* an area where many prostitutes work

red meat *n* meat, such as beef or lamb, that is dark brown when cooked

redo *vb* **-doing, -did, -done 1** to do over again in order to improve **2** *informal* to redecorate: *we should consider redoing some of the rooms*

redolent *adj* **redolent of** *or* **with 1** reminiscent or suggestive of: *a castle redolent of historical novels* **2** smelling of: *the warm heavy air was redolent of sea and flowers* **redolence** *n* **WORD ORIGIN** Latin *redolens*

redouble *vb* **-bling, -bled 1** to make or become much greater: *the party will have to redouble its efforts* **2** *bridge* to double (an opponent's double)

redoubt *n* **1** a small fort defending a hill top or pass **2** a stronghold **WORD ORIGIN** French *redoute*

redoubtable *adj* to be feared and respected: *the redoubtable Mr Brooks* **redoubtably** *adv* **WORD ORIGIN** Old French *redouter* to dread

redound *vb* **1 redound to** to have an advantageous or disadvantageous effect on: *individual rights redound to the common good* **2 redound on** *or* **upon** to recoil or rebound on **WORD ORIGIN** Latin *redundare* to stream over

redox *n* a chemical reaction between two substances, in which one is oxidized and the other reduced

red pepper *n* **1** the red ripe fruit of the sweet pepper, eaten as a vegetable **2** same as **cayenne pepper**

redraft *vb* to write a second copy of (a letter, proposal, essay, etc.)

red rag *n* something that infuriates or provokes: *a red rag to businessmen* **WORD ORIGIN** so called because red objects supposedly infuriate bulls

redress *vb* **1** to make amends for **2** to adjust in order to make fair or equal: *to redress the balance* ▷ *n* **3** compensation or reparation **4** the setting right of a wrong **WORD ORIGIN** Old French *redrecier* to set up again

red salmon *n* a salmon with reddish flesh

redshank *n* a large common European sandpiper with red legs

red shift *n* the appearance of lines in the spectrum of distant stars nearer the red end of the spectrum than on earth: used to calculate the velocity of objects in relation to the earth

redskin *n* *informal, offensive* a Native American **WORD ORIGIN** so called because one now extinct tribe painted themselves with red ochre

red squirrel *n* a reddish-brown squirrel of Europe and Asia

redstart *n* **1** a European songbird of the thrush family, the male of which has an orange-brown tail and breast **2** a North American warbler **WORD ORIGIN** Old English *rēad* red + *steort* tail

red tape *n* time-consuming official rules or procedure **WORD ORIGIN** from the red tape used to bind official government documents

reduce *vb* **-ducing, -duced 1** to bring down or lower: *monitoring could reduce the number of perinatal deaths* **2** to weaken or lessen: *vegetarian diets reduce cancer risk* **3** to bring by force or necessity to some state or action: *it reduced her to helpless laughter* **4** to slim **5** to set out systematically as an aid to understanding: *reducing the problem to three main issues* **6** *cookery* to thicken (a sauce) by boiling away some of its

liquid **7** to impoverish: *to be in reduced circumstances* **8** *chem* **a** to undergo a chemical reaction with hydrogen **b** to lose oxygen atoms **c** to increase the number of electrons **9** *maths* to simplify the form of (an expression or equation), esp. by substitution of one term by another **reducible** *adj* **WORD ORIGIN** Latin *reducere* to bring back

reduction *n* **1** the act of reducing **2** the amount by which something is reduced **3** a reduced form of an original, such as a copy of a document on a smaller scale **reductive** *adj*

redundant *adj* **1** deprived of one's job because it is no longer necessary or sufficiently profitable **2** surplus to requirements **redundancy** *n* **WORD ORIGIN** Latin *redundans* overflowing

reduplicate *vb* **-cating, -cated** to make double; repeat

redwood *n* a giant Californian conifer with reddish bark

re-echo *vb* **-oing, -oed** to echo over and over again

reed *n* **1** a tall grass that grows in swamps and shallow water **2** a straight hollow stem of this plant **3** *music* **a a** thin piece of cane or metal in certain wind instruments, which vibrates producing a musical note when the instrument is blown **b** a wind instrument or organ pipe that sounds by means of a reed **WORD ORIGIN** Old English *hrēod*

reedy *adj* **reedier, reediest 1** harsh or thin in tone: *his reedy, hesitant voice* **2** (of a place) full of reeds **reedily** *adv* **reediness** *n*

reef¹ *n* **1** a ridge of rock, sand, or coral, lying just beneath the surface of the sea: *a coral reef* **2** a vein of ore **WORD ORIGIN** Middle Dutch *ref*

reef² *naut n* **1** the part of a sail which can be rolled up to reduce its area ▷ *vb* **2** to reduce the area of (sail) by taking in a reef **WORD ORIGIN** Middle Dutch *rif*

reefer *n* **1** Also called: **reefer jacket** a man's short heavy double-breasted woollen jacket **2** *old-fashioned, slang* a hand-rolled cigarette containing cannabis **WORD ORIGIN** from the cigarette's resemblance to the rolled reef of a sail

reef knot *n* a knot consisting of two overhand knots turned opposite ways

reek *vb* **1** to give off a strong unpleasant smell **2 reek of** to give a strong suggestion of: *the scene had reeked of insincerity* **3** *dialect* to give off smoke or fumes ▷ *n* **4** a strong unpleasant smell **5** *dialect* smoke or steam **WORD ORIGIN** Old English *rēocan*

reel¹ *n* **1** a cylindrical object or frame that turns on an axis and onto which film, tape, wire, or thread is wound **2** a winding device attached to a fishing rod, used for casting and winding in the line **3** a roll of film for projection ▷ *vb* **4 reel in** to wind or draw in on a reel **WORD ORIGIN** Old English *hrēol*

reel² *vb* **1** to move unsteadily or spin round, as if about to fall **2** to be in a

Gertrude Stein

Gertrude Stein was born in 1874, the youngest child in a wealthy German Jewish family of Oakland, California. Until she moved to Paris in 1903 at the age of 29, the most famous unread writer of the twentieth century seemed unformed. Intellectually brilliant, she had studied psychology under William James at Radcliffe College and medicine at Johns Hopkins University. But it was only when she set up house in Paris with her art-collecting brother Leo that her legend began. She became a patron of virtually every significant French painter of the time. Later, she maintained a salon on the Rue de Fleurus to which expatriate American writers gravitated. She named them 'the Lost Generation'. She became the emblem of literary experiment and unshakeable personal authority. As if creating a motto for the avant-garde, she said, 'If it can be done, why do it?' Before she and her brother bitterly parted in 1912, Stein and Alice B. Toklas formed a *ménage* that endured until Stein's death. During World War I, they acquired a Ford and drove supplies to French hospitals. 'America is my country, but Paris is my hometown,' she said. With no false modesty, she also declared, 'Paris was the place that suited those of us that were to create the twentieth-century art and literature...'

In a flat festooned with paintings by Cézanne, Picasso, and Matisse, she wrote daily in half-hour bursts; Toklas faithfully typed the output. Since she seldom revised anything she wrote, a vast quantity of stories, novels, plays, and vignettes piled up, which at first found only a tiny readership. Only after her oracular legend had grown and she published the charming *Autobiography of Alice B. Toklas* (which was actually an autobiography of Stein herself), did she become a household name in the United States. With her rhomboidal figure, close-cropped Roman Emperor's head, and homespun-looking clothes, she was good newspaper copy, as were her gnomic aphorisms such as 'Rose is a rose is a rose' (often misquoted as 'A rose is...') and 'Pigeons on the grass, alas'. She said of Oakland, 'There is no there there,' and of Ezra Pound

that he was 'a village explainer, excellent if you were a village, but if you were not, not'. Even when her work was parodied, her conviction that she was the greatest writer of her age never wavered. She brooked no criticism; anything less than adulation would not do. She carefully fashioned her own monument; the fact that, as a Jew, she survived World War II thanks to the protection of a Nazi collaborator only became known decades after her death.

Stein's celebrity was well-founded, if only because of the impact she made on other writers: on the prose of Ernest Hemingway, whose sentences sometimes borrowed her rhythms and repetitions, and on the poetry of e e cummings and John Ashbery. Virgil Thomson turned her words into the operas *Four Saints in Three Acts* and *The Mother of Us All*. Currently, her work has a special appeal to academics involved in gender studies. What is most attractive to some is that her work is more process than product, and that, like a painting, figures dissolve into ground. Although she attempted to emulate the disciplined severity of Cézanne and the Cubists, her work is all texture and no structure. This is especially true of her 900-page novel *The Making of Americans*, which lacks both dialogue and linear action. As she commented, 'I was making a continuous present a continuous beginning again and again'. Although her work is rife with free-floating wordplay ('Chicken. Alas a dirty word, alas a dirty third, alas a dirty bird'), she rejects simile, metaphor, and allusiveness. For her, each phrase or sentence equals the other. Her nouns tend to be Anglo-Saxon, not Latinate, and her verbs use the -*ing* endings of the present progressive or continuous tense. Oddly in someone who was so visually oriented, sense surrenders to sound.

Perhaps the last word may be left to her friend Sherwood Anderson, who said in a letter to his brother, 'I do not think her too important. I do think she had an important thing to do, not for the public, but for the artist who happens to work with words as his material.' He would never have dared say it to her face.

state of confusion or stress: *my mind was still reeling*

WORD ORIGIN probably from REEL¹

reel³ *n* **1** a lively Scottish dance **2** music for this dance

WORD ORIGIN from REEL²

re-elect *vb* to vote for (someone) to retain his or her position, for example as a Member of Parliament **re-election** *n*

reel off *vb* to recite or write fluently or quickly

re-enact *vb* to act out (a previous event) again **re-enactment** *n*

re-enter *vb* **1** to come back into (a place, esp. a country) **2** (of a spacecraft) to return into (the earth's atmosphere) **re-entry** *n*

re-equip *vb* **-equipping, -equipped** to provide with fresh supplies, components, etc.

re-establish *vb* to create or set up (an organization, link, etc.) again **re-establishment** *n*

reeve *n* **1** *English history* the local representative of the king in a shire until the early 11th century **2** (in medieval England) a steward who supervised the daily affairs of a manor **3** *Canad government* (in some provinces) a president of a local council

WORD ORIGIN Old English *gerēfa*

re-examine *vb* **-examining, -examined** to inspect or investigate again **re-examination** *n*

ref *n informal* the referee in a sport

refectory *n, pl* **-ries** a dining hall in a religious or academic institution

WORD ORIGIN Latin *refectus* refreshed

refectory table *n* a long narrow dining table supported by two trestles

refer *vb* **-ferring, -ferred** ● **refer to 1** to mention or allude to **2** to be relevant or relate (to): *the word cancer refers to many quite specific different diseases* **3** to seek information (from): *he referred to his notes* **4** to direct the attention of (someone) for information: *the reader is referred to the introduction* **5** to direct (a patient or client) to another doctor or agency: *her GP referred her to a specialist* **6** to hand over for consideration or decision: *to refer a complaint to another department* **referable** or **referrable** *adj* **referral** *n*

WORD ORIGIN Latin *re-* back + *ferre* to carry

USAGE

The common practice of adding *back* to *refer* is tautologous, since this meaning is already contained in the *re-* of *refer*: this refers to (not *back to*) what has already been said. However, when *refer* is used in the sense of passing a document or question for further consideration to the person from whom it was received, it may be appropriate to say *he referred the matter back*.

referee *n* **1** the umpire in various sports, such as football and boxing **2** a person who is willing to provide a reference for someone for a job **3** a person referred to for a decision or opinion in a dispute ▷ *vb* **-reeing, -reed 4** to act as a referee

reference *n* **1** the act of referring **2** a mention: *this book contains several references to the Civil War* **3** direction to a passage elsewhere in a book or to another book **4** a book or passage referred to **5** a written testimonial regarding one's character or capabilities **6** a person referred to for such a testimonial **7** relation or restriction, esp. to or by membership of a specific group: *without reference to sex or age* **8 with reference to** concerning ▷ *adj* **9** containing information or facts: *reference books* **referential** *adj*

referendum *n, pl* **-dums** or **-da** a direct vote of the electorate on a question of importance

WORD ORIGIN Latin: something to be carried back

refill *vb* **1** to fill (something) again ▷ *n* **2** a second or subsequent filling: *I held out my glass for a refill* **3** a replacement supply of something in a permanent container **refillable** *adj*

refine *vb* **-fining, -fined 1** to make free from impurities; purify **2** to improve: *surgical techniques are constantly being refined* **3** to separate (a mixture) into pure constituents: *molasses is a residual syrup obtained during sugar refining*

refined *adj* **1** cultured or polite **2** freed from impurities **3** highly developed and effective: *refined intelligence tests*

refinement *n* **1** an improvement to something, such as a piece of equipment **2** fineness of taste or manners **3** a subtle point or distinction **4** the act of refining

refinery *n, pl* **-neries** a factory for purifying a raw material, such as sugar or oil

refit *vb* **-fitting, -fitted 1** to make (a ship) ready for use again by repairing or re-equipping ▷ *n* **2** a repair or re-equipping for further use

reflation *n* an increase in the supply of money and credit designed to encourage economic activity **reflate** *vb* **reflationary** *adj*

WORD ORIGIN RE- + *-flation*, as in *inflation*

reflect *vb* **1** (of a surface or object) to throw back (light, heat, or sound) **2** (of a mirror) to form an image of (something) by reflection **3** to show: *many of her books reflect her obsession with fine art* **4** to consider carefully **5 reflect on** or **upon** to cause to be regarded in a specified way: *the incident reflects very badly on me* **6** to bring as a consequence: *the programme reflected great credit on the technicians*

WORD ORIGIN Latin *re-* back + *flectere* to bend

reflecting telescope *n* a telescope in which the initial image is formed by a concave mirror

reflection *n* **1** the act of reflecting **2** the return of rays of light, heat, or sound **3** an image of an object given back in a mirror **4** careful or long consideration **5 on reflection** after careful consideration or reconsideration **6** discredit or blame: *it's a sad reflection on modern morality* **7** *maths* a transformation of a shape in which right and left, or top and bottom, are reversed

reflective *adj* **1** characterized by quiet thought or contemplation **2** capable of reflecting: *a reflective coating*

reflector *n* **1** a polished surface for reflecting light **2** a reflecting telescope

reflex *n* **1** an immediate involuntary response to a given stimulus **2** a mechanical response to a particular situation, involving no conscious decision **3** an image produced by reflection ▷ *adj* **4** of or caused by a reflex: *a reflex action* **5** reflected **6** *maths* (of an angle) between 180° and 360°

WORD ORIGIN Latin *reflexus* bent back

reflex camera *n* a camera which uses a mirror to channel light from a lens to the viewfinder, so that the image seen is the same as the image photographed

reflexive *adj* **1** *grammar* denoting a pronoun that refers back to the subject of a sentence or clause. Thus, in *that man thinks a great deal of himself*, the pronoun *himself* is reflexive **2** *grammar* denoting a verb used with a reflexive pronoun as its direct object, as in *to dress oneself* **3** *physiol* of or relating to a reflex ▷ *n* **4** a reflexive pronoun or verb

reflexology *n* foot massage as a therapy in alternative medicine **reflexologist** *n*

reform *n* **1** correction of abuses or malpractices: *a programme of economic reforms* **2** improvement of morals or behaviour ▷ *vb* **3** to improve (a law or institution) by correcting abuses **4** to give up or cause to give up a bad habit or way of life **reformative** *adj* **reformer** *n*

WORD ORIGIN Latin *reformare* to form again

reformation (ref-fer-**may**-shun) *n* **1** a reforming **2 the Reformation** a religious movement in 16th-century Europe that began as an attempt to reform the Roman Catholic Church and resulted in the establishment of the Protestant Churches

reformatory *n, pl* **-ries** (formerly) a place where young offenders were sent to be reformed

Reformed *adj* of a Protestant Church, esp. a Calvinist one

reformist *adj* **1** advocating reform rather than abolition, esp. of a religion or a political movement ▷ *n* **2** a person advocating reform

refract *vb* to cause light, heat, or sound to undergo refraction **refractive** *adj* **refractor** *n*

WORD ORIGIN Latin *re-* back + *frangere* to break

refracting telescope *n* a type of telescope in which the image is formed by a set of lenses. Also called: **refractor**

refraction *n* *physics* **1** the change in direction of a wave, such as light or sound, in passing from one medium to another in which it has a different velocity **2** the amount by which a wave is refracted

refractory *adj* **1** *formal* stubborn or rebellious **2** *med* not responding to treatment **3** (of a material) able to withstand high temperatures without fusion or decomposition

refrain¹ *vb* **refrain from** to keep oneself from doing

WORD ORIGIN Latin *refrenare* to check with a bridle

refrain² *n* **1** a frequently repeated part of a song **2** a much repeated saying or idea
WORD ORIGIN Latin *refringere* to break into pieces

refrangible *adj* capable of being refracted

refresh *vb* **1** to revive or reinvigorate, for example through rest, drink, or food **2** to stimulate (the memory) **refresher** *n*
WORD ORIGIN Old French *refreschir*

refresher course *n* a course designed to improve or update a person's knowledge of a subject

refreshing *adj* **1** having a reviving effect **2** pleasantly different or new: *refreshing candour*

refreshment *n* **1** the act of refreshing **2** **refreshments** snacks and drinks served as a light meal

refrigerant *n* **1** a fluid capable of vaporizing at low temperatures, used in refrigerators ▷ *adj* **2** causing cooling or freezing

refrigerate *vb* **-rating, -rated** to chill or freeze in order to preserve **refrigeration** *n*
WORD ORIGIN Latin *refrigerare* to make cold

refrigerator *n* the full name for **fridge**

refuel *vb* **-elling, -elled** *or US* **-eling, -eled** to supply or be supplied with fresh fuel

refuge *n* **1** shelter or protection from danger or hardship **2** a place, person, or thing that offers protection or help
WORD ORIGIN Latin *re-* back + *fugere* to escape

refugee *n* a person who has fled from some danger, such as war or political persecution

refulgent *adj literary* shining brightly **refulgence** *n*
WORD ORIGIN Latin *refulgere* to reflect

refund *vb* **1** to give back (money) **2** to pay back (a person) ▷ *n* **3** return of money to a purchaser or the amount returned **refundable** *adj*
WORD ORIGIN Latin *re-* back + *fundere* to pour

refurbish *vb* to renovate and brighten up **refurbishment** *n*

refusal *n* **1** the act of refusing **2** the opportunity to reject or accept: *he was given first refusal on all three scripts*

refuse¹ *vb* **-fusing, -fused** **1** to be determined not (to do something): *he refuses to consider it* **2** to decline to give or allow (something) to (someone): *if the judge refuses bail, he'll appeal* **3** to decline to accept (something offered): *he refused the captaincy* **4** (of a horse) to be unwilling to jump a fence
WORD ORIGIN Latin *refundere* to pour back

refuse² *n* anything thrown away; rubbish
WORD ORIGIN Old French *refuser* to refuse

refusenik *n* **1** (formerly) a Jew in the USSR who was refused permission to emigrate **2** a person who refuses to obey a law or cooperate with the government because of strong beliefs

refute *vb* **-futing, -futed** to prove (a statement or theory) to be false or incorrect **refutation** *n*
WORD ORIGIN Latin *refutare*

≡ USAGE
≡ The use of *refute* to mean *deny* is
≡ thought by many people to be
≡ incorrect.

regain *vb* **1** to get back or recover **2** to reach again: *to regain the shore*

regal *adj* **1** of or fit for a king or queen **2** splendid and dignified; magnificent: *a luxury cruise liner on her serene and regal way around the better ports* **regality** *n* **regally** *adv*
WORD ORIGIN Latin *regalis*

regale *vb* **-galing, -galed** **1** to give delight or amusement to: *she would regale her friends with stories* **2** to provide with abundant food or drink
WORD ORIGIN French *régaler*

regalia *n* the ceremonial emblems or robes of royalty or high office
WORD ORIGIN Medieval Latin: royal privileges

regard *vb* **1** to look upon or think of in a specified way: *angina can therefore be regarded as heart cramp* **2** to look closely or attentively at (something or someone) **3** to take notice of: *he has never regarded the conventions* **4** **as regards** on the subject of ▷ *n* **5** respect or affection: *you haven't a high regard for her opinion* **6** attention: *he eats what he wants with no regard to health* **7** a gaze or look **8** reference or connection: *with regard to my complaint* **9** **regards** an expression of goodwill: *give her my regards*
WORD ORIGIN Old French *regarder* to look at, care about

regardful *adj* **regardful of** paying attention to

regarding *prep* on the subject of; relating to

regardless *adj* **1** **regardless of** taking no notice of: *the illness can affect anyone regardless of their social class* ▷ *adv* **2** in spite of everything: *I carried on regardless*

regatta *n* a series of races of boats or yachts
WORD ORIGIN obsolete Italian *rigatta* contest

regency *n, pl* **-cies** **1** government by a regent **2** the status of a regent **3** a period when a regent is in power
WORD ORIGIN Latin *regere* to rule

Regency *adj* of the regency (1811–20) of the Prince of Wales (later George IV) or the styles of architecture or furniture produced during it

regenerate *vb* (ri-**jen**-er-ate), **-rating, -rated** **1** to undergo or cause to undergo physical, economic, or spiritual renewal **2** to come or bring into existence once again **3** to replace (lost or damaged tissues or organs) by new growth ▷ *adj* (ri-**jen**-er-it) **4** physically, economically, or spiritually renewed **regeneration** *n* **regenerative** *adj*

regent *n* **1** the ruler of a country during the childhood, absence, or illness of its monarch **2** *US & Canad* a member of the governing board of certain schools and colleges ▷ *adj* **3** acting as a regent: *the Prince Regent*
WORD ORIGIN Latin *regere* to rule

reggae *n* a type of popular music of Jamaican origin with a strong beat
WORD ORIGIN West Indian

regicide *n* **1** the killing of a king **2** a person who kills a king
WORD ORIGIN Latin *rex* king + *caedere* to kill

regifting *n* the practice of giving an unwanted gift to another person

regime (ray-**zheem**) *n* **1** a system of government **2** a particular administration: *the corrupt regime* **3** *med* a regimen
WORD ORIGIN French

regimen *n* a prescribed system of diet and exercise
WORD ORIGIN Latin: guidance

regiment *n* **1** an organized body of troops as a unit in the army **2** a large number or group **regimental** *adj*
WORD ORIGIN Late Latin *regimentum* government

regimentals *pl n* **1** the uniform and insignia of a regiment **2** military uniform

regimental sergeant major *n mil* the senior warrant officer in a regiment or battalion

regimented *adj* very strictly controlled: *the regimented confines of the school* **regimentation** *n*

Regina *n* queen: now used chiefly in documents and inscriptions
WORD ORIGIN Latin

region *n* **1** an administrative division of a country **2** an area considered as a unit for geographical or social reasons **3** a sphere of activity or interest **4** a part of the body: *the lumbar region* **5** **in the region of** approximately: *in the region of 100 000 troops* **6** **the regions** the parts of a country away from the capital: *discord between Moscow and the regions* **regional** *adj*
WORD ORIGIN Latin *regio*

regionalism *n* **1** the division of a country or organization into geographical regions each having some autonomy **2** loyalty to one's home region

register *n* **1** an official list recording names, events, or transactions **2** the book in which such a list is written **3** a device that records data, totals sums of money, etc.: *a cash register* **4** a style of speaking or writing, such as slang, used in particular circumstances or social situations **5** *music* **a** the timbre characteristic of a certain manner of voice production **b** any of the stops on an organ in respect of its tonal quality: *the flute register* ▷ *vb* **6** to enter (an event, person's name, ownership, etc.) in a register **7** to show on a scale or other measuring instrument **8** to show in a person's face or bearing: *his face registered surprise* **9** *informal* to have an effect or make an impression: *the news did not register at first* **10** to have a letter or parcel insured against loss by the Post Office: *registered mail* **registration** *n*
WORD ORIGIN Medieval Latin *registrum*

register office *n Brit* a government office where civil marriages are performed and births, marriages, and deaths are recorded

registrar n **1** a person who keeps official records **2** an official responsible for student records and enrolment in a college **3** a hospital doctor senior to a houseman but junior to a consultant

registration document n Austral & Brit a document giving identification details of a vehicle, including its owner's name

registration number n a sequence of letters and numbers given to a motor vehicle when it is registered, displayed on numberplates at the front and rear

registry n, pl **-tries 1** a place where official records are kept **2** the registration of a ship's country of origin: a ship of Liberian registry

registry office n Brit & NZ same as **register office**

Regius professor (reej-yuss) n Brit a person appointed by the Crown to a university chair founded by a royal patron **WORD ORIGIN** Latin regius royal

regress vb **1** to return to a former and worse condition ▷ n **2** return to a former and worse condition **regressive** adj **WORD ORIGIN** Latin regredi to go back

regression n **1** the act of regressing **2** psychol the use by an adult of behaviour more appropriate to a child

regret vb **-gretting, -gretted 1** to feel sorry or upset about **2** to express apology or distress: we regret any misunderstanding caused ▷ n **3** a feeling of repentance, guilt, or sorrow **4 regrets** a polite expression of refusal: she had sent her regrets **regretful** adj **regretfully** adv **regrettable** adj **regrettably** adv **WORD ORIGIN** Old French regreter

USAGE
Regretful and regretfully are sometimes wrongly used where regrettable and regrettably are meant: he gave a regretful smile; he smiled regretfully; this is a regrettable (not regretful) mistake; regrettably (not regretfully), I shall be unable to attend.

regroup vb **1** to reorganize (military forces) after an attack or a defeat **2** to rearrange into a new grouping

regular adj **1** normal, customary, or usual **2** symmetrical or even: regular features **3** according to a uniform principle, arrangement, or order **4** occurring at fixed or prearranged intervals: we run regular advertisements in the press **5** following a set rule or normal practice **6** grammar following the usual pattern of formation in a language: regular verbs **7** of or serving in the permanent military services: the regular armed forces **8** maths (of a polygon) having all its sides and angles the same **9** officially qualified or recognized: he's not a regular doctor **10** informal not constipated: eating fresh vegetables helps keep you regular **11** US & Canad informal likeable: a regular guy **12** complete or utter: a regular fool **13** subject to the rule of an established religious community: canons regular ▷ n **14** a professional long-term serviceman in a military unit **15** informal a frequent customer or visitor **regularity** n

regularize or **-rise** vb **regularly** adv **WORD ORIGIN** Latin regula ruler, model

regulate vb **-lating, -lated 1** to control by means of rules: a code of practice to regulate advertising by schools **2** to adjust slightly: he had to take drugs to regulate his heartbeat **regulatory** adj **WORD ORIGIN** Late Latin regulare to control

regulation n **1** a rule that governs procedure or behaviour **2** the act of regulating ▷ adj **3** in accordance with rules or conventions: dressed in the orchestra's regulation black tie

regulator n **1** a mechanism that automatically controls pressure, temperature, etc. **2** the mechanism by which the speed of a clock is regulated

regurgitate vb **-tating, -tated 1** to vomit **2** (of some birds and animals) to bring back (partly digested food) to the mouth to feed the young **3** to reproduce (ideas or facts) without understanding them **regurgitation** n **WORD ORIGIN** Medieval Latin re- back + gurgitare to flood

rehabilitate vb **-tating, -tated 1** to help (a person) to readapt to society after illness or imprisonment **2** to restore to a former position or rank **3** to restore the good reputation of **rehabilitation** n **WORD ORIGIN** Medieval Latin rehabilitare to restore

rehash vb **1** to use (old or already used ideas) in a slightly different form without real improvement ▷ n **2** old ideas presented in a new form **WORD ORIGIN** re- again + hash to chop into pieces

rehearse vb **-hearsing, -hearsed 1** to practise (a play, concert, etc.) for public performance **2** to repeat aloud: he rehearsed his familiar views on the press **3** to train (a person) for public performance **rehearsal** n **rehearser** n **WORD ORIGIN** Old French rehercier to harrow a second time

rehouse vb **-housing, -housed** to provide with a new and better home

Reich (rike) n the former German state, esp. the Nazi dictatorship in Germany from 1933–45 (**Third Reich**) **WORD ORIGIN** German: kingdom

reign n **1** the period during which a monarch is the official ruler of a country **2** a period during which a person or thing is dominant: a reign of terror ▷ vb **3** to rule (a country) **4** to be supreme: a sense of confusion reigns in the capital **WORD ORIGIN** Old French reigne

USAGE
Reign is sometimes wrongly written for rein in certain phrases: he gave full rein (not reign) to his feelings; it will be necessary to rein in (not reign in) public spending.

reigning adj currently holding a title or championship: the reigning world champion

reimburse vb **-bursing, -bursed** to repay (someone) for (expenses or losses) **reimbursement** n **WORD ORIGIN** Medieval Latin imbursare to put in a moneybag

rein n **1 reins a** long narrow straps attached to a bit to control a horse

b narrow straps attached to a harness to control a young child **c** means of control: to take up the reins of government **2 give (a) free rein** to allow a considerable amount of freedom **3 keep a tight rein on** to control carefully: we have to keep a tight rein on expenditure ▷ vb **4** to restrain or halt with reins **5** to control or limit: public spending was reined in ▶ See also **rein in** **WORD ORIGIN** Old French resne

USAGE
See at **reign**.

reincarnate vb **-nating, -nated** to be born again in a different body: souls may be reincarnated in human forms

reincarnation n **1** the belief that after death the soul is reborn in another body **2** an instance of rebirth in another body **3** reappearance in a new form of a principle or idea: he was the reincarnation of the old Republican Party isolationist

reindeer n, pl **-deer** or **-deers** a deer with large branched antlers that lives in the arctic regions **WORD ORIGIN** Old Norse hreindȳri

reinforce vb **-inforcing, -inforced 1** to give added emphasis to (an idea or feeling): his tired face reinforced his own weariness **2** to make physically stronger or harder: the plastic panels were reinforced with carbon fibre **3** to give added support to (a military force) by providing more men or equipment: the army garrison had been reinforced with helicopters **reinforcement** n **WORD ORIGIN** French renforcer

reinforced concrete n concrete with steel bars or mesh embedded in it to strengthen it

rein in vb **1** to stop (a horse) by pulling on the reins **2** to restrict or stop: either prices or wage packets had to be reined in

reinstate vb **-stating, -stated 1** to restore to a former rank or status **2** to cause to exist or be important again: reinstate some semblance of order **reinstatement** n

reinvigorate vb to give renewed energy to; refresh

reissue n **1** a book, CD, etc. that is published or released again after being unavailable for a time ▷ vb **2** to publish or release (a book, CD, etc.) again after a period of unavailability

reiterate vb **-rating, -rated** formal to repeat again and again **reiteration** n **WORD ORIGIN** Latin reiterare

reject vb **1** to refuse to accept, use, or believe **2** to deny to (a person) the feelings hoped for: the boy had been rejected by his mother **3** to pass over or throw out as useless **4** (of an organism) to fail to accept (a tissue graft or organ transplant) ▷ n **5** a person or thing rejected as not up to standard **rejection** n **WORD ORIGIN** Latin reicere to throw back

rejig vb **-jigging, -jigged 1** to re-equip (a factory or plant) **2** informal to rearrange or manipulate, sometimes in an unscrupulous way: the promoter hastily rejigged the running order

rejoice vb **-joicing, -joiced** to feel or express great happiness **rejoicing** n **WORD ORIGIN** Old French resjoir

SCRABBLE
Three-Letter Words, part 7
PIT–SIF

PIT	hole in the ground		Church services	REW	archaic spelling of rue	SAE	Scots word for so
PIU	musical term meaning more	PYX	receptacle for the Eucharistic Host	REX	king	SAG	sink in the middle
PIX	photographs			REZ	reservation	SAI	capuchin monkey
PLU	beaver skin used as a unit of value	QAT	shrub whose leaves have narcotic properties	RHO	17th letter of the Greek alphabet	SAL	salt
						SAM	collect, gather up
PLY	work at (a job or trade)	QIS	plural form of qi	RHY	archaic spelling of rye	SAN	short for sanatorium
POA	type of grass	QUA	in the capacity of	RIA	long narrow inlet of the seacoast	SAP	fluid that circulates in plants
POD	seed case of peas	RAD	former unit of radiation				
POH	exclamation expressing contempt			RIB	bone	SAR	marine fish
		RAG	fragment of cloth	RID	clear or relieve (of)	SAT	part of the verb to sit
POI	ball of woven flax	RAH	US word for cheer	RIF	discharge from military service	SAU	archaic past form of see
POL	short for politician	RAI	type of Algerian pop music				
POM	short for pommy			RIG	arrange in a dishonest way	SAV	saveloy
POO	defecate	RAJ	(in India) government			SAW	hand tool
POP	make a small explosive sound	RAM	male sheep	RIM	edge or border	SAX	saxophone
		RAN	part of the verb to run	RIN	Scots variant of run	SAY	speak or utter
POS	plural form of po	RAP	hit with a sharp quick blow	RIP	tear violently	SAZ	musical instrument
POT	round deep container			RIT	Scots word for cut or slit	SEA	mass of salt water
POW	sound imitative of a collision, explosion, etc	RAS	headland			SEC	short for second
		RAT	long-tailed rodent	RIZ	dialectal past form of rise	SED	old spelling of said
		RAW	uncooked			SEE	perceive with the eyes or mind
POX	disease	RAX	stretch or extend	ROB	steal from		
POZ	short for positive	RAY	single line of light	ROC	mythological bird	SEG	metal stud on shoe sole
PRE	before	REB	soldier in the American Civil War	ROD	slender straight bar		
PRO	in favour of			ROE	mass of eggs in a fish	SEI	type of whale
PRY	make an impertinent inquiry	REC	short for recreation ground	ROK	mythological bird	SEL	Scots word for self
				ROM	male gypsy	SEN	monetary unit
PSI	23rd letter of the Greek alphabet	RED	colour	ROO	kangaroo	SER	unit of weight
		REE	Scots word for walled enclosure	ROT	decompose or decay	SET	put in a specified position or state
PST	sound to attract attention			ROW	straight line of people or things		
		REF	short for referee			SEW	join with thread
PUB	building with a licensed bar	REG	short for registration number	RUB	apply pressure and friction	SEX	state of being male or female
PUD	short for pudding			RUC	mythological bird	SEY	Scots word for part of cow
PUG	small snub-nosed dog	REH	(in India) surface crust on the soil	RUD	redness, flush		
PUH	exclamation expressing contempt			RUE	feel regret for	SEZ	informal spelling of says
		REI	former Portuguese coin	RUG	small carpet		
PUL	Afghan monetary unit			RUM	alcoholic drink	SHA	be quiet
PUN	play on words	REM	dose of ionizing radiation	RUN	move quickly	SHE	female person or animal
PUP	young dog			RUT	furrow made by wheels		
PUR	obsolete form of purr	REN	archaic variant of run			SHH	sound made to ask for silence
PUS	yellowish fluid	REO	language	RYA	Scandinavian rug		
PUT	place in a position	REP	short for representative	RYE	grain	SHY	not at ease in company
PUY	small volcanic cone			SAB	short for saboteur		
PYA	monetary unit of Myanmar	RES	residence	SAC	pouchlike structure in an animal	SIB	blood relative
		RET	moisten or soak flax			SIC	so or thus
PYE	book for finding	REV	revolution (of an engine)	SAD	sorrowful, unhappy	SIF	South African slang for disgusting

rejoin¹ *vb* to come together with (someone or something) again

rejoin² *vb* to reply in a sharp or witty way
WORD ORIGIN Old French *rejoindre*

rejoinder *n* a sharp or witty reply

rejuvenate *vb* **-nating, -nated** to give back youth or vitality to **rejuvenation** *n*
WORD ORIGIN Latin *re-* again + *juvenis* young

rekindle *vb* **-dling, -dled** to arouse (former emotions or interests)

relapse *vb* **-lapsing, -lapsed 1** to fall back into bad habits or illness ▷ *n* **2** the act of relapsing **3** the return of ill health after an apparent or partial recovery
WORD ORIGIN Latin *re-* back + *labi* to slip

relate *vb* **-lating, -lated 1** to establish a relation between **2** to have reference or relation to **3** to have an understanding (of people or ideas): *the inability to relate to others* **4** to tell (a story) or describe (an event)
WORD ORIGIN Latin *relatus* brought back

related *adj* **1** linked by kinship or marriage **2** connected or associated: *salts and related compounds*

relation *n* **1** the connection between things or people **2** a person who is connected by blood or marriage **3** connection by blood or marriage **4** an account or narrative **5 in** *or* **with relation to** with reference to: *an inquiry into export controls in relation to Iraq*

relations *pl n* **1** social or political dealings between individuals or groups **2** family or relatives **3** *euphemistic* sexual intercourse

relationship *n* **1** the dealings and feelings that exist between people or groups **2** an emotional or sexual affair **3** the connection between two things: *the relationship between exercise and mental health* **4** association by blood or marriage

relative *adj* **1** true to a certain degree or extent: *a zone of relative affluence* **2** having significance only in relation to something else: *time is relative* **3 relative to** in proportion to: *it will benefit from high growth in earnings relative to prices* **4** respective: *the relative qualities of speed and accuracy* **5** relevant: *the facts relative to the enquiry* **6** *grammar* of a clause (**relative clause**) that modifies a noun or pronoun occurring earlier in the sentence **7** *grammar* of or belonging to a class of words, such as *who*, *which*, or *that*, which function as conjunctions introducing relative clauses ▷ *n* **8** a person who is related by blood or marriage **relatively** *adv*

relative atomic mass *n* same as **atomic weight**

relativity *n* **1** either of two theories developed by Albert Einstein, the **special theory of relativity**, which requires that the laws of physics shall be the same as seen by any two different observers in uniform relative motion, and the **general theory of relativity**, which considers observers with relative acceleration and leads to a theory of gravitation **2** the state of being relative

relax *vb* **1** to make or become less tense, looser, or less rigid **2** to ease up from effort or attention **3** to make (rules or discipline) less strict **4** to become more friendly **5** to lessen the intensity of: *he relaxed his vigilance in the lulls between attacks* **relaxed** *adj*
WORD ORIGIN Latin *relaxare* to loosen

relaxation *n* **1** rest after work or effort **2** a form of recreation: *his favoured form of relaxation was walking on the local moors* **3** the act of relaxing

relay *n* **1** a fresh set of people or animals relieving others **2** short for **relay race 3** an automatic device that controls a valve or switch, esp. one in which a small change in current or voltage controls the switching on or off of circuits **4** *radio* a combination of a receiver and transmitter designed to receive radio signals and retransmit them ▷ *vb* **5** to pass on (a message) **6** to retransmit (a signal) by means of a relay **7** *Brit* to broadcast (a performance or event) as it happens
WORD ORIGIN Old French *relaier* to leave behind

relay race *n* a race between teams in which each contestant covers a specified portion of the distance

release *vb* **-leasing, -leased 1** to free (a person or animal) from captivity or imprisonment **2** to free (someone) from obligation or duty **3** to free (something) from (one's grip) **4** to allow news or information to be made public or available **5** to allow (something) to move freely: *she released the handbrake* **6** to issue (a CD, film, or book) for sale or public showing: *the CD was originally released six years ago* **7** to give out heat, energy, radiation, etc.: *the explosion released a cloud of toxic gas* ▷ *n* **8** the act of freeing or state of being freed **9** a statement to the press **10** the act of issuing for sale or publication **11** something issued for sale or public showing
WORD ORIGIN Old French *relesser*

relegate *vb* **-gating, -gated 1** to put in a less important position **2** to demote (a sports team) to a lower division: *four clubs were relegated from the first division* **relegation** *n*
WORD ORIGIN Latin *re-* back + *legare* to send

relent *vb* **1** to change one's mind about some decision **2** to become milder or less severe: *the weather relented*
WORD ORIGIN Latin *re-* back + *lentare* to bend

relentless *adj* **1** never stopping or reducing in severity: *relentless deterioration in standards* **2** (of a person) determined and pitiless

relevant *adj* to do with the matter in hand **relevance** *n*
WORD ORIGIN Medieval Latin *relevans*

reliable *adj* able to be trusted **reliability** *n* **reliably** *adv*

reliance *n* the state of relying on or trusting (a person or thing) **reliant** *adj*

relic *n* **1** an object or custom that has survived from the past **2** something valued for its past associations **3** relics remaining parts or traces **4** *RC Church*, *Eastern Church* a body part or possession of a saint, venerated as holy
WORD ORIGIN Latin *reliquiae* remains

relict *n* *archaic* **1** a relic **2** a widow
WORD ORIGIN Latin *relictus* left behind

relief *n* **1** a feeling of cheerfulness that follows the removal of anxiety, pain, or distress **2** a temporary pause in anxiety, pain, or distress **3** money, food, or clothing given to people in special need: *disaster relief* **4** the act of freeing a besieged town or fortress: *the relief of Mafeking* **5** a person who replaces another at some task or duty **6** a bus, plane, etc. that carries additional passengers when a scheduled service is full **7** Also called: **relievo** *sculpture, archit* the projection of a carved design from the surface **8** any vivid effect resulting from contrast: *a welcome relief* **9** the difference between the highest and lowest level: *study the map of relief and the rainfall map* **10 on relief** *US & Canad* (of people) in receipt of government aid because of personal need
WORD ORIGIN Old French *relever* to relieve

relief map *n* a map showing the shape and height of the land surface by contours and shading

relieve *vb* **-lieving, -lieved 1** to lessen (pain, distress, boredom, etc.) **2** to bring assistance to (someone in need): *a plan to relieve those facing hunger* **3** to free (someone) from an obligation: *a further attempt to relieve the taxpayers of their burdens* **4** to take over the duties of (someone): *the night nurse came in to relieve her* **5** to free (a besieged town or fort) **6 relieve oneself** to urinate or defecate **7** to set off by contrast: *painted walls are marginally relieved by some abstract prints* **8** *informal* to take from: *the prince had relieved him of his duties* **relieved** *adj*
WORD ORIGIN Latin *re-* again + *levare* to lighten

religion *n* **1** belief in or worship of a supernatural power or powers considered to be divine or to have control of human destiny **2** any formal expression of such belief: *the Christian religion* **3** *chiefly RC Church* the way of life entered upon by monks and nuns: *to enter religion*
WORD ORIGIN Latin *religio*

religious *adj* **1** of religion **2** pious or devout **3** scrupulous or conscientious: *religious attention to detail* **4** *Christianity* relating to the way of life of monks and nuns ▷ *n* **5** *Christianity* a monk or nun **religiously** *adv*

relinquish *vb* *formal* **1** to give up: *that hope has to be relinquished* **2** to renounce (a claim or right) **3** to release one's hold on **relinquishment** *n*
WORD ORIGIN Latin *relinquere*

reliquary (**rel-lik-wer-ee**) *n, pl* **-quaries** a container for relics of saints

relish *vb* **1** to savour or enjoy (an experience) to the full **2** to anticipate eagerly ▷ *n* **3** liking or enjoyment: *he has an enormous relish for life* **4** pleasurable anticipation: *his early relish for a new challenge* **5** an appetizing or spicy food, such as a pickle, added to a main dish to improve its flavour **6** a zestful quality: *he tells stories with great relish*
WORD ORIGIN earlier *reles* aftertaste

relive vb **-living, -lived** to experience (a sensation or event) again, esp. in the imagination

reload vb to put fresh ammunition into (a firearm)

relocate vb **-cating, -cated** to move or be moved to a new place of work **relocation** n

reluctance n **1** unwillingness to do something **2** physics a measure of the resistance of a closed magnetic circuit to a magnetic flux **WORD ORIGIN** Latin reluctari to resist

reluctant adj unwilling or disinclined **reluctantly** adv

rely vb **-lies, -lying, -lied** ● **rely on** or **upon a** to be dependent on: the organization relies on voluntary contributions **b** to have trust or confidence in: you can rely on his judgment **WORD ORIGIN** Old French relier to fasten together

REM rapid eye movement

remain vb **1** to continue to be: the situation remains alarming **2** to stay behind or in the same place: to remain at home **3** to be left after use or the passage of time **4** to be left to be done, said, etc.: whether this will be a long-term trend remains to be seen **WORD ORIGIN** Latin remanere

remainder n **1** a part or portion that is left after use or the passage of time: we ate some biscuits and the remainder of the jam **2** maths **a** the amount left over when one quantity cannot be exactly divided by another: for 10 ÷ 3, the remainder is 1 **b** the amount left over when one quantity is subtracted from another **3** a number of copies of a book sold cheaply because it has been impossible to sell them at full price ▷ vb **4** to sell (copies of a book) as a remainder

remains pl n **1** parts left over from something after use or the passage of time: the remains of the old Roman fortress **2** a corpse

remake vb **-making, -made 1** to make again in a different way ▷ n **2** a new version of an old film

remand vb **1** law to send (a prisoner or accused person) back into custody or put on bail before trial ▷ n **2** the sending of a person back into custody or putting on bail before trial **3** on remand in custody or on bail awaiting trial **WORD ORIGIN** Latin re- back + mandare to command

remand centre n a place where accused people are detained while awaiting trial

remark vb **1** to pass a casual comment (about) **2** to say **3** to observe or notice ▷ n **4** a brief casually expressed thought or opinion **WORD ORIGIN** Old French remarquer to observe

remarkable adj **1** worthy of note or attention: a remarkable career **2** striking or extraordinary: a thing of remarkable beauty **remarkably** adv

remarry vb **-ries, -rying, -ried** to marry again following a divorce or the death of one's previous spouse **remarriage** n

REME Royal Electrical and Mechanical Engineers

remedial adj **1** providing or intended as a remedy **2** of special teaching for slow learners: remedial classes **remedially** adv

remedy n, pl **-edies 1** a drug or treatment for curing pain or disease **2** a way of solving a problem: every statesman promised a remedy for unemployment ▷ vb **-edies, -edying, -edied 3** to put right or improve **remediable** adj **WORD ORIGIN** Latin remedium a cure

remember vb **1** to become aware of (something forgotten) again **2** to keep (an idea, intention, etc.) in one's mind: remember to write **3** to give money to (someone), as in a will or in tipping **4 remember to** to mention (a person's name) to another person, by way of greeting: remember me to her **5** to commemorate: we are here to remember the dead **WORD ORIGIN** Latin re- again + memor mindful

remembrance n **1** a memory **2** a memento or keepsake **3** the act of honouring some past event or person

Remembrance Day n **1** (in Britain) Remembrance Sunday **2** (in Canada and Australia) a statutory holiday observed on November 11 in memory of the dead of both World Wars

Remembrance Sunday n (in Britain) the Sunday closest to November 11, on which the dead of both World Wars are commemorated

remind vb **1** to cause to remember: remind her that she was on duty **2** to put in mind (of someone or something): you remind me of Alice in Wonderland

reminder n **1** something that recalls the past **2** a note to remind a person of something not done

reminisce vb **-niscing, -nisced** to talk or write about old times or past experiences

reminiscence n **1** the act of recalling or narrating past experiences **2** something remembered from the past **3 reminiscences** stories about a person's life, often presented in a book

reminiscent adj **1 reminiscent of** reminding or suggestive of **2** characterized by reminiscence **WORD ORIGIN** Latin reminisci to call to mind

remiss adj formal careless in attention to duty or responsibility **WORD ORIGIN** Latin remissus

remission n **1** a reduction in the length of a prison term **2** forgiveness for sin **3** easing of intensity of the symptoms of a disease **4** a release from an obligation

remit vb (rim-**mitt**), **-mitting, -mitted 1** to send (money) for goods or services **2** to cancel (a punishment or debt) **3** law to send back (a case) to a lower court for further consideration **4** to slacken or ease off **5** archaic to forgive (crime or sins) ▷ n (**ree**-mitt) **6** area of authority: within the review body's remit **WORD ORIGIN** Latin re- back + mittere to send

remittance n money sent as payment

remittent adj (of a disease) periodically less severe

remix vb **1** to change the relative prominence of each performer's part of (a recording) ▷ n **2** a remixed version of a recording

remnant n **1** a part left over **2** a piece of material from the end of a roll **3** a surviving trace or vestige: the authorities drafted in the military to crush any remnant of protest **WORD ORIGIN** Old French remenant remaining

remodel vb **-delling, -delled** to give a different shape or form to: a renaissance of boutiques and remodelled apartments; the country is planning to remodel its armed forces

remonstrance n formal a strong protest about something

remonstrate vb **-strating, -strated** formal to argue in protest or objection: the player remonstrated loudly with the official **remonstration** n **WORD ORIGIN** Latin re- again + monstrare to show

remorse n a sense of deep regret and guilt for something one did **remorseful** adj **WORD ORIGIN** Medieval Latin remorsus a gnawing

remorseless adj **1** constantly unkind and lacking pity: remorseless fate **2** continually intense: the superintendent's remorseless gaze

remote adj **1** far away **2** far from civilization **3** distant in time **4** not relevant: the issues seem remote from the general population **5** (of a person's manner) aloof or abstracted **6** slight or faint: a remote possibility **7** operated from a distance; remote-controlled: a remote manipulator arm **remotely** adv **WORD ORIGIN** Latin remotus far removed

remote control n control of an apparatus from a distance by radio or electrical signals **remote-controlled** adj

remould vb **1** to change completely: to remould the country **2** Brit to bond a new tread onto the casing of (a worn pneumatic tyre) ▷ n **3** Brit a tyre made by this process

removable adj capable of being removed from a place or released from another object: a farmer's truck with removable wooden sides

removal n **1** the act of removing or state of being removed **2** the process of moving one's possessions from a previous address to a new one

remove vb **-moving, -moved 1** to take away and place elsewhere **2** to take (clothing) off **3** to get rid of **4** to dismiss (someone) from office **5** formal to change the location of one's home or place of business ▷ n **6** the degree of difference: one remove away from complete rebuttal **7** Brit (in certain schools) a class or form designed to prepare pupils for senior classes **WORD ORIGIN** Old French removoir

removed adj **1** very different or distant: madness seemed far removed from the sunny order of things **2** separated by a degree of descent: the child of a person's first cousin is their first cousin once removed

r

remunerate vb **-rating, -rated** formal to reward or pay for work or service **remuneration** n **remunerative** adj
WORD ORIGIN Latin remunerari

renaissance n a renewal of interest or creativity in an area: a complete renaissance in maze building
WORD ORIGIN French

Renaissance n **1 the Renaissance** the great revival of art, literature, and learning in Europe in the 14th, 15th, and 16th centuries ▷ adj **2** of or from the Renaissance

renal (**ree**-nal) adj of the kidneys
WORD ORIGIN Latin renes kidneys

renascent adj literary becoming active or vigorous again: renascent nationalism **renascence** n
WORD ORIGIN Latin renasci to be born again

rend vb **rending, rent** literary **1** to tear violently **2** (of a sound) to break (the silence) with a shrill or piercing tone
WORD ORIGIN Old English rendan

render vb **1** to cause to become: he was rendered unconscious by his wound **2** to give or provide (aid, a service, etc.) **3** formal to present or submit (a bill) **4** to translate **5** to represent in painting, music, or acting **6** to yield or give: he rendered up his soul to God **7** to cover with plaster **8** to melt down (fat) **rendering** n
WORD ORIGIN Old French rendre

rendezvous (**ron**-day-voo) n, pl **-vous** (-vooz) **1** an appointment to meet at a specified time and place **2** a place where people meet ▷ vb **3** to meet at a specified time or place
WORD ORIGIN French

rendition n formal **1** a performance of a piece of music or a dramatic role **2** a translation

renegade n a person who deserts a cause for another
WORD ORIGIN Spanish renegado

renege (rin-**nayg**) vb **-neging, -neged** to go back (on an agreement or promise): the politicians reneged on every promise
WORD ORIGIN Medieval Latin renegare to renounce

renew vb **1** to begin again **2** to take up again after a break: they wanted to renew diplomatic ties **3** to make valid again: we didn't renew the lease **4** to grow again **5** to restore to a new or fresh condition **6** to replace (an old or worn-out part or piece) **7** to restate or reaffirm (a promise) **renewal** n

renewable adj **1** able to be renewed **2** (of energy or an energy source) inexhaustible or capable of being perpetually replenished ▷ pl n **renewables 3** renewable energy sources, such as wind and wave power

rennet n a substance prepared from the stomachs of calves and used for curdling milk to make cheese
WORD ORIGIN Old English gerinnan to curdle

renounce vb **-nouncing, -nounced 1** to give up (a belief or habit) voluntarily **2** to give up formally (a claim or right): he would renounce his rights to the throne
WORD ORIGIN Latin renuntiare

renovate vb **-vating, -vated** to restore to good condition **renovation** n **renovator** n
WORD ORIGIN Latin re- again + novare to make new

renown n widespread good reputation
WORD ORIGIN Old French renom

renowned adj famous

rent¹ vb **1** to give or have use of (land, a building, a machine, etc.) in return for periodic payments ▷ n **2** a payment made periodically for the use of land, a building, a machine, etc.
WORD ORIGIN Old French rente revenue

rent² n **1** a slit made by tearing ▷ vb **2** the past of **rend**

rental n **1** the amount paid or received as rent ▷ adj **2** of or relating to rent

rent boy n a young male prostitute

rentier (**ron**-tee-ay) n a person who lives off unearned income such as rents or interest

renunciation n **1** the act or an instance of renouncing **2** a formal declaration renouncing something

reo n NZ a language
WORD ORIGIN Māori

reopen vb to open again after a period of being closed or suspended: the Supreme Court has agreed to reopen the case

reorder vb to change the order of; organize differently

reorganize or **-nise** vb **-nizing, -nized** or **-nising, -nised** to organize in a new and more efficient way **reorganization** or **-nisation** n

rep¹ n theatre short for **repertory company**

rep² n **1** a sales representative **2** someone elected to represent a group of people: the union rep **3** NZ informal a rugby player selected to represent his district

repair¹ vb **1** to restore (something damaged or broken) to good condition or working order **2** to make up for (a mistake or injury) **3** to heal (a breach or division) in (something): he is attempting to repair his country's relations with America ▷ n **4** the act, task, or process of repairing **5** a part that has been repaired **6** state or condition: many museums may have to close because they are in such bad repair **repairable** adj
WORD ORIGIN Latin re- again + parare to make ready

repair² vb **repair to** to go to (a place)
WORD ORIGIN Latin re- back + patria fatherland

reparable (**rep**-rab-bl) adj able to be repaired or remedied

reparation n **1** the act of making up for loss or injury **2 reparations** compensation paid by a defeated nation after a war for the damage and injuries it caused
WORD ORIGIN Latin reparare to repair

repartee n **1** conversation consisting of witty remarks **2** a sharp witty remark made as a reply
WORD ORIGIN French repartie

repast n literary a meal
WORD ORIGIN Old French repaistre to feed

repatriate vb **-ating, -ated 1** to send back (a person) to the country of his or her birth or citizenship ▷ n **2** a person

who has been repatriated: Algerian repatriates **repatriation** n
WORD ORIGIN Latin re- back + patria fatherland

repay vb **-paying, -paid 1** to refund or reimburse **2** to make a return for (something): to repay hospitality **repayable** adj **repayment** n

repeal vb **1** to cancel (a law) officially ▷ n **2** the act of repealing: the repeal of repressive legislation **repealable** adj
WORD ORIGIN Old French repeler

repeat vb **1** to say, write, or do again **2** to tell to another person (the secrets told to one by someone else) **3** to recite (a poem, etc.) from memory **4** to occur more than once: this pattern repeats itself many times **5** (of food) to be tasted again after eating as the result of belching **6** to say (the words or sounds) uttered by someone else; echo ▷ n **7** the act or an instance of repeating **8** a word, action, pattern, etc. that is repeated **9** radio, television a broadcast of a programme which has been broadcast before **10** music a passage that is an exact restatement of the passage preceding it **repeated** adj **repeatedly** adv **repeatable** adj
WORD ORIGIN Latin repetere to seek again

▤ **USAGE**
▤ Since again is part of the meaning of
▤ repeat, one should not say something
▤ is repeated again.

repeater n **1** a gun capable of firing several shots without reloading **2** a clock or watch which strikes the hour or quarter-hour just past, when a spring is pressed

repel vb **-pelling, -pelled 1** to cause (someone) to feel disgusted **2** to force or drive back (someone or something) **3** to be effective in keeping away or controlling: these buzzers are claimed to repel female mosquitoes **4** to fail to mix with or absorb: water and oil repel each other **5** to reject or spurn: she repelled his advances
WORD ORIGIN Latin re- back + pellere to push

▤ **USAGE**
▤ See at **repulse**.

repellent adj **1** disgusting or distasteful **2** resisting water etc. ▷ n **3** a chemical used to keep insects or other creatures away

repent vb to feel regret for (something bad one has done) **repentance** n **repentant** adj
WORD ORIGIN Old French repentir

repercussion n **1 repercussions** results or consequences of an action or event **2** an echo or reverberation
WORD ORIGIN Latin repercutere to strike back

repertoire n **1** all the works that a company or performer can perform **2** the entire stock of skills or techniques that someone or something, such as a computer, is capable of: a superb repertoire of shots
WORD ORIGIN French

repertory n, pl **-ries 1** same as **repertoire** (sense 2) **2** short for **repertory company**
WORD ORIGIN Late Latin repertorium storehouse

International Phonetic Alphabet

The International Phonetic Alphabet – usually shortened to IPA – is used in dictionaries to represent how words are pronounced. IPA was created by the International Phonetic Association, a representative organization for phoneticians, with the aim of creating a standard set of symbols into which any sound in any language could be transcribed. The first version was developed in the 19th century by Paul Passy, Daniel Jones, AJ Ellis, and Henry Sweet, and there have been occasional revisions since then.

The symbols used in IPA are based largely on the Roman alphabet: /p/ and /b/, for example, correspond to the sounds represented by those letters in English. Some sounds are represented by reversed or inverted Roman letters, eg /ə/, or Greek letters, eg /ʊ/ (upsilon). To convey further subtleties of pronunciation, diacritics might be used with the main characters. All the symbols are displayed on a chart containing consonant sounds, vowel sounds, and other refining symbols.

Consonants are arranged in a table according to where the sound is articulated in the mouth. The consonant sounds produced at the lips, known as bilabial consonants, eg 'p' and 'b', are shown at the far left of the consonant chart. Further back in the chart are palatal consonants, eg the 'ng' sound in 'waiting' where the sound is articulated with the tongue against the hard palate. To the far right are glottal sounds such as 'h', where the sound consists of a flow of air through the vocal cords. Where symbols appear in pairs, the one to the right, eg /b/, represents the voiced labial consonant, ie it is accompanied by vibration of the vocal cords, and the one on the left, eg /p/, is the unvoiced consonant that is not accompanied by this vibration. Consonant sounds that are initiated in the mouth rather than from the lungs – called nonpulmonic – are also represented. Such sounds are not used as phonemes in English but can be found in other languages, such as the clicks heard in some languages of southern Africa, symbolized by eg ʘ or !.

Vowel symbols are placed on a grid representing the shape of the inner mouth, according to the place and manner of articulation – where the tongue is placed when the sound is made (high or low in the mouth), and the position of the lips (open or closed). The 'ee' sound in 'bee', represented by the symbol /i/, is articulated with the tongue at the front of the mouth and the lips only slightly apart, and this appears at the top left of the grid. Where symbols appear in pairs, the one to the right, eg /ɔ/ (as in the sound in 'lot'), represents a rounded vowel, ie it is accompanied by rounding of the lips. On the left is the vowel produced without this rounding of the lips.

Other features of pronunciation are represented, such as stress: this is shown by a short vertical line before the sound, at the top for primary stress and at the bottom for secondary stress, eg /ˈprəʊˌnaʊn/ (pronoun). Intonation can also be conveyed by symbols and diacritics, eg ě shows a rising intonation on the /e/ sound, and ê a falling intonation. A long vowel is indicated by a following triangular colon, eg /pliːz/ (please).

IPA can be used for both phonemic and phonetic transcription of sounds. Phonemic transcription represents phonological units, or phonemes – one of the set of basic speech sounds that is used to distinguish one word from another in any language. Such a transcription largely uses the main symbols of IPA, and is conventionally shown inside slant lines / /. However, there are enough symbols and combining diacritics to convey more subtle variations of articulation that do not change the meaning of a word. Therefore, it can be used to produce a detailed phonetic transcription, which shows the speech sounds in a particular pronunciation. For example, [ē] represents a nasalized vowel, ie one produced with a simultaneous flow of air through the nose, while [dl], with a small 'l' beside it, means the sound is articulated with lateral release, i.e. with air released over the sides of the tongue. This more detailed transcription of speech is conventionally contained within square brackets [ ].

Today, IPA is widely used by linguists, language teachers, translators, lexicographers, and speech pathologists. In 1990, a set of 'Extensions to the IPA' was published to facilitate the transcription of atypical or disordered speech, including symbols for the sounds made, for example, with a cleft palate or in lisping.

repertory company n a permanent theatre company producing a succession of plays

repetition n **1** the act of repeating **2** a thing that is repeated **3** a replica or copy **repetitious** adj **repetitive** adj

rephrase vb -phrasing, -phrased to express in different words **rephrasing** n

repine vb -pining, -pined literary to be worried or discontented **WORD ORIGIN** RE- + PINE²

replace vb -placing, -placed **1** to take the place of **2** to substitute a person or thing for (another): we need to replace that chair **3** to put (something) back in its rightful place

replacement n **1** the act or process of replacing **2** a person or thing that replaces another

replay n **1** a showing again of a sequence of action immediately after it happens **2** a second sports match played because an earlier game was drawn ▷ vb **3** to play (a recording, match, etc.) again

replenish vb to make full or complete again by supplying what has been used up **replenishment** n **WORD ORIGIN** Old French replenir

replete adj **1** pleasantly full of food and drink **2** well supplied: a world replete with true horror **repletion** n **WORD ORIGIN** Latin repletus

replica n an exact copy **WORD ORIGIN** Italian, literally: a reply

replicate vb -cating, -cated to make or be an exact copy of; reproduce **replication** n **WORD ORIGIN** Latin replicatus bent back

reply vb -plies, -plying, -plied **1** to make answer (to) in words or writing or by an action **2** to say (something) in answer: she replied that she did not believe him ▷ n, pl -plies **3** an answer or response **WORD ORIGIN** Old French replier to fold again

report vb **1** to give an account (of) **2** to give an account of the results of an investigation (into): the commission is to report on global warming **3** to make a formal report on (a subject) **4** to make a formal complaint about **5** to present (oneself) at an appointed place or for a specific purpose: report to the manager's office **6** **report to** to be responsible to and under the authority of **7** to act as a reporter ▷ n **8** an account prepared after investigation and published or broadcast **9** an account of the discussions of a committee or other group of people: I have the report of the mining union **10** a story for which there is no absolute proof: according to report, he is not dead **11** Brit & NZ a statement on the progress of a school child **12** a loud bang made by a gun or explosion **13** comment on a person's character or actions: he is of good report here **reportedly** adv **WORD ORIGIN** Latin re- back + portare to carry

reported speech n a report of what someone said that gives the content of the speech without repeating the exact words

reporter n a person who gathers news for a newspaper or broadcasting organization

repose¹ n **1** a state of quiet restfulness **2** calmness or composure **3** sleep ▷ vb -posing, -posed **4** to lie or lay down at rest **5** to lie when dead **WORD ORIGIN** Old French reposer

repose² vb -posing, -posed to put (trust) in a person or thing **WORD ORIGIN** Latin reponere to store up

reposition vb to place in a different position

repository n, pl -ries **1** a place or container in which things can be stored for safety: a repository for national treasures **2** a person to whom a secret is entrusted **WORD ORIGIN** Latin repositorium

repossess vb (of a lender) to take back (property) from a customer who is behind with payments, for example mortgage repayments **repossession** n

reprehend vb to find fault with **WORD ORIGIN** Latin reprehendere

reprehensible adj deserving criticism: Willie's reprehensible behaviour

represent vb **1** to act as the authorized delegate for (a person, country, etc.): she represented her country at the Olympic Games **2** to act as a substitute (for) **3** to stand as an equivalent of **4** to be a means of expressing: the lights are relit to represent resurrection **5** to display the characteristics of: romanticism in music is represented by Liszt **6** to describe as having a specified character or quality: the magical bird was often represented as having two heads **7** to state or explain **8** to present an image of through a picture or sculpture **9** to bring clearly before the mind **WORD ORIGIN** Latin repraesentare to exhibit

representation n **1** the state of being represented **2** anything that represents, such as a pictorial portrait **3 representations** formal statements made to an official body by a person making a complaint **representational** adj

representative n **1** a person chosen to act for or represent a group **2** a person who tries to sell the products or services of a firm **3** a typical example ▷ adj **4** typical of a class or kind **5** representing **6** including examples of all the interests or types in a group **7** acting as deputy for another **8** of a political system in which people choose a person to make decisions on their behalf

repress vb **1** to keep (feelings) under control **2** to restrict the freedom of: he continued to repress his people **3** psychol to banish (unpleasant thoughts) from one's conscious mind **repression** n **repressive** adj **WORD ORIGIN** Latin reprimere to press back

reprieve vb -prieving, -prieved **1** to postpone the execution of (a condemned person) **2** to give temporary relief to ▷ n **3** a postponement or cancellation of a punishment **4** a warrant granting a postponement or cancellation **5** a temporary relief from pain or harm **WORD ORIGIN** Old French repris (something) taken back

reprimand vb **1** to blame (someone) officially for a fault ▷ n **2** an instance of blaming someone officially **WORD ORIGIN** French réprimande

reprint vb **1** to print further copies of (a book) ▷ n **2** a reprinted copy

reprisal n an act of taking revenge: many residents say they are living in fear of reprisals by the army **WORD ORIGIN** Old French reprisaille

reprise (rip-**preez**) music n **1** the repeating of an earlier theme ▷ vb -prising, -prised **2** to repeat an earlier theme

reproach n **1** blame or rebuke **2** a scolding **3 beyond reproach** beyond criticism ▷ vb **4** to express disapproval (of someone's actions) **reproachful** adj **WORD ORIGIN** Old French reprochier

reprobate (**rep**-roh-bate) n **1** an unprincipled bad person ▷ adj **2** morally unprincipled **WORD ORIGIN** Late Latin reprobatus held in disfavour

reprobation n literary disapproval or blame

reproduce vb -ducing, -duced **1** to make a copy or representation of **2** biol to produce offspring **3** to re-create **reproducible** adj

reproduction n **1** biol a process by which an animal or plant produces one or more individuals similar to itself **2** a copy of a work of art **3** the quality of sound from an audio system **4** the act or process of reproducing ▷ adj **5** made in imitation of an earlier style: reproduction furniture **reproductive** adj

reproof n a severe blaming of someone for a fault

reprove vb -proving, -proved to speak severely to (someone) about a fault **reprovingly** adv **WORD ORIGIN** Old French reprover

reptile n **1** a cold-blooded animal, such as a tortoise, snake, or crocodile, that has an outer covering of horny scales or plates and lays eggs **2** a contemptible grovelling person **reptilian** adj **WORD ORIGIN** Late Latin reptilis creeping

republic n **1** a form of government in which the people or their elected representatives possess the supreme power **2** a country in which the head of state is an elected or nominated president **WORD ORIGIN** Latin respublica, literally: the public thing

republican adj **1** of or supporting a republic ▷ n **2** a person who supports or advocates a republic **republicanism** n

Republican adj **1** belonging to the Republican Party, the more conservative of the two main political parties in the US **2** belonging to the Irish Republican Army ▷ n **3** a member or supporter of the Republican Party in the US **4** a member or supporter of the Irish Republican Army **Republicanism** n

repudiate (rip-**pew**-dee-ate) vb -ating, -ated **1** to reject the authority or

validity of **2** to disown (a person) **3** to refuse to acknowledge or pay (a debt) **repudiation** n
WORD ORIGIN Latin *repudium* divorce

repugnant adj offensive or disgusting **repugnance** n
WORD ORIGIN Latin *repugnans* resisting

repulse vb **-pulsing, -pulsed 1** to be disgusting to: *this act of feminist rage repulsed as many as it delighted* **2** to drive (an army) back **3** to reject with coldness or discourtesy: *she repulsed his advances* ▷ n **4** a driving back **5** a cold discourteous rejection or refusal
WORD ORIGIN Latin *repellere*

USAGE
Some people think that the use of *repulse* in sentences such as *he was repulsed by what he saw* is incorrect and that the correct word is *repel*.

repulsion n **1** a feeling of disgust or aversion **2** *physics* a force separating two objects, such as the force between two like electric charges

repulsive adj **1** disgusting or distasteful **2** *physics* of repulsion **repulsively** adv

reputable (**rep-pew-tab-bl**) adj trustworthy or respectable **reputably** adv

reputation n **1** the opinion generally held of a person or thing **2** a high opinion generally held about a person or thing **3** notoriety or fame, esp. for some specified characteristic
WORD ORIGIN Latin *reputatio*

repute n good reputation: *a sculptor of international repute*
WORD ORIGIN Latin *reputare* to think over

reputed adj supposed or rumoured: *the island was reputed to have held a Roman temple; the reputed murderess* **reputedly** adv

request vb **1** to ask for or politely demand: *we requested a formal meeting with the committee* ▷ n **2** the act or an instance of asking for something: *a polite request* **3** something asked for **4** **on request** if asked for: *most companies will send samples on request*
WORD ORIGIN Old French *requeste*

Requiem (**rek-wee-em**) n **1** RC Church a Mass celebrated for the dead **2** a musical setting of this Mass
WORD ORIGIN Latin *requies* rest

require vb **-quiring, -quired 1** to need **2** to be a necessary condition: *the decision requires a logical common-sense approach* **3** to insist upon **4** to order or command: *family doctors are required to produce annual reports*
WORD ORIGIN Latin *requirere* to seek to know

USAGE
The use of *require to* as in *I require to see the manager* or *you require to complete a special form* is thought by many people to be incorrect: *I need to see the manager; you are required to complete a special form*.

requirement n **1** something demanded or imposed as an obligation **2** a specific need or want

requisite (**rek-wizz-it**) adj **1** absolutely essential ▷ n **2** something essential
WORD ORIGIN Latin *requisitus* sought after

requisition vb **1** to demand and take for use, esp. for military or public use ▷ n **2** a formal request or demand for the use of something **3** the act of taking something over, esp. for military or public use **4** a formal written demand

requite vb **-quiting, -quited** to return to someone (the same treatment or feeling as received): *an Australian who requites her love* **requital** n
WORD ORIGIN re- back + obsolete *quite* to repay

reredos (**rear-doss**) n a screen or wall decoration at the back of an altar
WORD ORIGIN Old French *arere* behind + *dos* back

reroute vb **-routing, -routed** to send or direct by a different route

rerun n **1** a film or programme that is broadcast again **2** a race that is run again ▷ vb **-running, -ran, -run 3** to put on (a film or programme) again **4** to run (a race) again

resale n the selling again of something purchased

reschedule vb **-duling, -duled 1** to change the time, date, or schedule of: *the show has been rescheduled for August* **2** to arrange a revised schedule for repayment of (a debt)

rescind vb to annul or repeal **rescission** n
WORD ORIGIN Latin *rescindere* to cut off

rescue vb **-cuing, -cued 1** to bring (someone or something) out of danger or trouble ▷ n **2** the act or an instance of rescuing **rescuer** n
WORD ORIGIN Old French *rescourre*

reseal vb to close or secure tightly again

research n **1** systematic investigation to establish facts or collect information on a subject ▷ vb **2** to carry out investigations into (a subject) **researcher** n
WORD ORIGIN Old French *recercher* to search again

resemble vb **-bling, -bled** to be or look like **resemblance** n
WORD ORIGIN Old French *resembler*

resent vb to feel bitter or indignant about **resentful** adj **resentment** n
WORD ORIGIN French *ressentir*

reservation n **1** a doubt: *his only reservation was, did he have the stamina?* **2** an exception or limitation that prevents one's wholehearted acceptance: *work I admire without reservation* **3** a seat, room, etc. that has been reserved **4** (esp. in the US) an area of land set aside for American Indian peoples: *the Cherokee reservation* **5** Brit short for **central reservation**

reserve vb **-serving, -served 1** to keep back or set aside for future use **2** to obtain by arranging beforehand: *I phoned to reserve two tickets* **3** to keep for oneself: *the association reserves the right to charge a fee* **4** to delay announcing (a legal judgment) ▷ n **5** something kept back or set aside for future use **6** the state or condition of being reserved: *we're keeping these two in reserve* **7** *sport* a substitute **8** an area of publicly owned land used for sport, etc.: *a wildlife reserve* **9** the hiding of one's feelings and personality **10** the part of a nation's

armed services not in active service **11 reserves** *finance* money or assets held by a bank or business to meet future expenses **12** *Canad* an Indian reservation
WORD ORIGIN Latin *reservare* to keep

reserved adj **1** not showing one's feelings **2** set aside for use by a particular person

reserve price n the minimum price acceptable to the owner of property being auctioned or sold

reservist n a member of a nation's military reserve

reservoir n **1** a natural or artificial lake for storing water for community use **2** a large supply of something: *a vast reservoir of youthful enthusiasm*
WORD ORIGIN French *réservoir*

resettle vb **-tling, -tled** to settle to live in a different place **resettlement** n

reshuffle n **1** a reorganization of jobs in a government or company ▷ vb **-fling, -fled 2** to reorganize jobs or duties in a government or company

reside vb **-siding, -sided** *formal* **1** to live permanently (in a place): *my daughter resides in Europe* **2** to be present (in): *desire resides in the unconscious*
WORD ORIGIN Latin *residere* to sit back

residence n **1** a person's home or house **2** a large imposing house **3** the fact of residing in a place **4** a period of residing in a place **5 in residence a** living in a particular place: *the Monarch was not in residence* **b** (of an artist) working for a set period at a college, gallery, etc.: *composer in residence*

resident n **1** a person who lives in a place **2** a bird or animal that does not migrate ▷ adj **3** living in a place **4** living at a place in order to carry out a job: *a resident custodian* **5** employed for one's specialized abilities: *the Museum's resident expert on seventeenth-century Dutch art* **6** (of birds and animals) not in the habit of migrating

residential adj **1** (of a part of a town) consisting mainly of houses **2** providing living accommodation: *residential clubs for homeless boys*

residential school n a government boarding school in N Canada for Indian and Inuit students

residual adj **1** of or being a remainder ▷ n **2** something left over as a residue

residue n **1** what is left over after something has been removed **2** *law* what is left of an estate after the discharge of debts and distribution of specific gifts
WORD ORIGIN Latin *residuus* remaining over

residuum n, pl **-ua** same as **residue**

resign vb **1** to give up office or a job **2** to accept (an unpleasant fact): *he resigned himself to the inevitable* **3** to give up (a right or claim)
WORD ORIGIN Latin *resignare* to unseal, destroy

resignation n **1** the act of resigning **2** a formal document stating one's intention to resign **3** passive endurance of difficulties: *full of quiet resignation*

resigned adj content to endure something unpleasant **resignedly** adv

resilient adj 1 (of a person) recovering easily and quickly from misfortune or illness 2 (of an object) capable of regaining its original shape or position after bending or stretching **resilience** n
WORD ORIGIN Latin resilire to jump back

resin (rezz-in) n 1 a solid or semisolid substance obtained from certain plants: cannabis resin 2 a similar substance produced synthetically **resinous** adj
WORD ORIGIN Latin resina

resist vb 1 to stand firm against or oppose: the party's old guard continue to resist economic reform 2 to refrain from in spite of temptation: I couldn't resist a huge portion of almond cake 3 to refuse to comply with: to resist arrest 4 to be proof against: airport design should be strengthened to help resist explosion **resistible** adj
WORD ORIGIN Latin resistere

resistance n 1 the act of resisting 2 the capacity to withstand something, esp. the body's natural capacity to withstand disease 3 electronics the opposition to a flow of electric current through a circuit, component, or substance 4 any force that slows or hampers movement: wind resistance 5 line of least resistance the easiest, but not necessarily the best, course of action **resistant** adj, n

Resistance n the Resistance an illegal organization fighting for national liberty in a country under enemy occupation

resistor n an electrical component designed to introduce a known value of resistance into a circuit

resit vb -sitting, -sat 1 to sit (an examination) again ▷ n 2 an examination which one must sit again

reskill vb to train (workers) to acquire new skills **reskilling** n

resolute adj firm in purpose or belief **resolutely** adv
WORD ORIGIN Latin resolutus

resolution n 1 firmness or determination 2 a decision to do something 3 a formal expression of opinion by a meeting 4 the act of resolving 5 music the process in harmony whereby a dissonant note or chord is followed by a consonant one 6 the ability of a television to reproduce fine detail 7 physics Also called: **resolving power** the ability of a telescope or microscope to produce separate images of closely placed objects

resolvable or **resoluble** adj able to be resolved or analysed

resolve vb -solving, -solved 1 to decide or determine firmly 2 to express (an opinion) formally by a vote 3 to separate or cause to separate into (constituent parts) 4 to find the answer or solution to 5 to explain away or dispel: to resolve the controversy 6 music to follow (a dissonant note or chord) by one producing a consonance 7 physics to distinguish between (separate parts) of (an image) as in a microscope, telescope, or other optical instrument ▷ n 8 absolute determination: he spoke of

his resolve to deal with the problem of terrorism
WORD ORIGIN Latin resolvere to unfasten, reveal

resolved adj determined

resonance n 1 the condition or quality of being resonant 2 sound produced by a body vibrating in sympathy with a neighbouring source of sound
WORD ORIGIN Latin resonare to resound

resonant adj 1 resounding or re-echoing 2 producing resonance: the resonant cavities of the mouth 3 full of resonance: his voice is a resonant baritone

resonate vb -nating, -nated to resound or cause to resound **resonator** n

resort vb 1 resort to to have recourse (to) for help, use, etc.: some people have resorted to begging for food 2 to go, esp. often or habitually: to resort to the beach ▷ n 3 a place to which many people go for holidays 4 the use of something as a means or aid 5 last resort the last possible course of action open to a person
WORD ORIGIN Old French resortir to come out again

resound (riz-zownd) vb 1 to ring or echo with sound 2 (of sounds) to echo or ring 3 to be widely known: his fame resounded throughout India
WORD ORIGIN Latin resonare to sound again

resounding adj 1 echoing 2 clear and emphatic: he won a resounding victory **resoundingly** adv

resource n 1 resources sources of economic wealth, esp. of a country or business enterprise: mineral resources 2 resources money available for use 3 something resorted to for aid or support: he saw the university as a resource for the community 4 the ability to deal with problems: a man of resource 5 a means of doing something: resistance was their only resource
WORD ORIGIN Old French resourdre to spring up again

resourceful adj capable and full of initiative **resourcefulness** n

respect n 1 consideration: respect for my feelings 2 an attitude of deference or esteem 3 the state of being honoured or esteemed 4 a detail or characteristic: in virtually all respects boys develop more slowly than girls 5 in respect of or with respect to in reference or relation to 6 respects polite greetings: he paid his respects to her and left ▷ vb 7 to have an attitude of esteem towards: she is the person I most respect and wish to emulate 8 to pay proper attention or consideration to: he called on rebel groups to respect a cease-fire **respecter** n
WORD ORIGIN Latin respicere to pay attention to

respectable adj 1 worthy of respect 2 having good social standing or reputation 3 relatively or fairly good: they obtained respectable results 4 fit to be seen by other people **respectability** n **respectably** adv

respectful adj full of or showing respect **respectfully** adv

respecting prep on the subject of

respective adj relating separately to each of several people or things: the culprits will be repatriated to their respective countries

respectively adv (in listing things that refer to another list) separately in the order given: Diotema and Mantinea were tutors to Pythagoras and Socrates respectively

respiration (ress-per-**ray**-shun) n 1 breathing 2 the process in living organisms of taking in oxygen and giving out carbon dioxide 3 the breakdown of complex organic substances that takes place in the cells of animals and plants, producing energy and carbon dioxide **respiratory** adj

respirator n 1 a device worn over the mouth and nose to prevent the breathing in of poisonous fumes 2 an apparatus for providing artificial respiration

respire vb -spiring, -spired 1 to breathe 2 to undergo respiration
WORD ORIGIN Latin respirare to exhale

respite n 1 an interval of rest: I allowed myself a six month respite to enjoy my family 2 a temporary delay
WORD ORIGIN Old French respit

resplendent adj 1 brilliant or splendid in appearance 2 shining **resplendence** n
WORD ORIGIN Latin re- again + splendere to shine

respond vb 1 to state or utter (something) in reply 2 to act in reply: the government must respond accordingly to our recommendations 3 to react favourably: most headaches will respond to the use of relaxants
WORD ORIGIN Old French respondre

respondent n law a person against whom a petition is brought

response n 1 the act of responding 2 a reply or reaction 3 a reaction to stimulation of the nervous system 4 responses Christianity the words recited or sung in reply to the priest at a church service

responsibility n, pl -ties 1 the state of being responsible 2 a person or thing for which one is responsible

responsible adj 1 responsible for having control or authority over 2 being the agent or cause (of some action): only a small number of students were responsible for the disturbances 3 responsible to being accountable for one's actions and decisions to: management should be made more responsible to shareholders 4 rational and accountable for one's own actions 5 (of a position or duty) involving decision and accountability **responsibly** adv
WORD ORIGIN Latin respondere to respond

responsive adj reacting quickly or favourably to something **responsiveness** n

respray n a new coat of paint applied to a vehicle

rest¹ n 1 relaxation from exertion or labour 2 a period of inactivity 3 relief or refreshment 4 calm 5 death regarded as repose: now he has gone to his eternal rest 6 at rest a not moving b calm c dead d asleep 7 a pause or interval 8 a mark in a musical score indicating a pause lasting a specific time 9 a thing or place on which to put something for support or to steady it

Detective Fiction

Detective fiction has a rich and varied history, from the none-more-sophisticated sleuthing of Sir Arthur Conan Doyle's Sherlock Holmes to the lurid pulp investigations of Mickey Spillane's Mike Hammer. The genre can be categorized as a subset of crime fiction and is identified by certain literary devices and conventions. These include a protagonist who usually works outside official channels, and who employs deduction, logic, or other analytical techniques to solve crimes. This central detective character is often accompanied by an associate or sidekick, who may act as narrator or as a 'surrogate reader', asking questions that prompt exposition or advance the plot.

Voltaire's philosophical work *Zadig ou La Destinée* (1747) and Hoffmann's *Das Fräulein von Scuderi* (1818) are often cited as progenitors of the genre. However, it is widely accepted that the first work of detective fiction is Edgar Allan Poe's *The Murders in the Rue Morgue* (1841), in which the character C Auguste Dupin solves a crime that baffles the authorities. Two more tales were written by Poe using Dupin, and the use of a recurring central character has proved to be another of the genre's defining characteristics.

Many of the genre's conventions were most firmly established by the most famous fictional detective: Sherlock Holmes. Holmes was a brilliant and driven detective who first appeared in *A Study in Scarlet* (1887) and was accompanied on his investigations by Dr Watson, who in most cases acts as narrator. Sir Arthur Conan Doyle killed off his wildly successful creation in *The Adventure of the Final Problem* (1893) in a tumble from the Reichenbach Falls with his nemesis, Professor Moriarty. Public demand was, however, too great to allow the character to rest in peace, and Conan Doyle reluctantly resurrected Holmes in *The Adventure of the Empty House* (1903).

The Golden Age of detective fiction from the late 19th to early 20th century was dominated by Agatha Christie with her literary creations Miss Marple and Hercule Poirot. This was the era of the 'manor house murder', which had its roots in the well-publicized real-life case of Constance Kent. *The Mystery of Edwin Drood* (1870) by Charles Dickens was also influenced by the case, and both this work and *Bleak House* (1852) use aspects of detective fiction in their narrative.

The Golden Age was dominated by British authors, often using upper-class gatherings as their setting. However, as the 20th century advanced, contributions to the genre from the United States were far removed from country houses or polite society. The writings of Dashiell Hammett such as *The Maltese Falcon* (1930) and *The Thin Man* (1934) came with a hardboiled edge, black humour, and stylized dialogue. Protagonists were generally private investigators (popularizing the term *private eye*). Raymond Chandler's writings employed first-person narration, which became another genre staple, and his creation Philip Marlowe, who debuted in *The Big Sleep* (1939), was to become an iconic figure of the detective novel, as had Hammett's Sam Spade before him.

Notable authors from the latter half of the 20th century include PD James, who published her first novel featuring Adam Dalgliesh, *Cover Her Face*, in 1962; Ruth Rendell, who published her Inspector Wexford series; Colin Dexter, the creator of Inspector Morse; and Reginald Hill, who has written over 20 novels featuring Yorkshire detectives Dalziel and Pascoe. More recent additions to the genre include Ian Rankin's *Rebus* series and the forensic detective novels of Patricia Cornwell and Kathy Reichs. A recent wave of detective fiction has been led by Scandinavian authors such as Henning Mankell (author of the *Wallander* stories) and Stieg Larsson, whose *The Girl With The Dragon Tattoo* (2005) and its sequels were published posthumously.

10 lay to rest to bury (a dead person) ▷ *vb* **11** to become or make refreshed **12** to position (oneself, etc.) for rest or relaxation **13** to place for support or steadying: *he slumped forward to rest his head on his forearms* **14** to depend or rely: *his presidency rested on the outcome of the crisis* **15** to direct (one's eyes) or (of one's eyes) to be directed: *she rested her gaze on the face of the statue* **16** to be at ease **17** to cease or cause to cease from motion or exertion **18** to remain without further attention or action: *she refused to let the matter rest* **19** *law* to finish the introduction of evidence in (a case) **20** to put (pastry) in a cool place to allow the gluten to contract **WORD ORIGIN** Old English *ræst*, *reste*

rest² *n* **1 the rest a** something left; remainder **b** the others: *the rest of the world* ▷ *vb* **2** to continue to be (as specified): *your conscience can rest easy* **WORD ORIGIN** Old French *rester* to remain

rest area *n Austral & NZ* a motorist's stopping place off a highway, equipped with tables and seats

restart *vb* to commence (something) or set (something) in motion again

restate *vb* to state or affirm (something) again or in a different way **restatement** *n*

restaurant *n* a place where meals are prepared and served to customers **WORD ORIGIN** French

restaurant car *n* a railway coach in which meals are served

restaurateur (rest-er-a-**tur**) *n* a person who owns or runs a restaurant

rest-cure *n* a rest taken as part of a course of medical treatment

restful *adj* relaxing or soothing

restitution *n* **1** the act of giving back something that has been lost or stolen **2** *law* compensation for loss or injury **WORD ORIGIN** Latin *restituere* to rebuild

restive *adj* **1** restless or uneasy **2** impatient of control or authority **WORD ORIGIN** Old French *restif* balky

restless *adj* **1** bored or dissatisfied **2** unable to stay still or quiet **3** not restful: *a restless sleep* **restlessly** *adv* **restlessness** *n*

restoration *n* **1** the act of restoring to a former or original condition, place, etc. **2** the giving back of something lost or stolen **3** something restored, replaced, or reconstructed **4** a model or representation of a ruin or extinct animal **5 the Restoration** *Brit* the re-establishment of the monarchy in 1660 or the reign of Charles II (1660–85)

restorative (rist-**or**-a-tiv) *adj* **1** giving back health or good spirits ▷ *n* **2** a food or medicine that gives back health or good spirits

restore *vb* **-storing, -stored 1** to return (something) to its original or former condition **2** to bring back to health or good spirits **3** to return (something lost or stolen) to its owner **4** to re-enforce or re-establish: *he must restore confidence in himself and his government; they worked to restore the monarchy* **5** to reconstruct (a ruin, extinct animal, etc.) **restorer** *n* **WORD ORIGIN** Latin *restaurare* to rebuild

restrain *vb* **1** to hold (someone) back from some action **2** to limit or restrict: *restrain any tendency to impulse-buy* **3** to deprive (someone) of liberty **WORD ORIGIN** Latin *re-* back + *stringere* to draw

restrained *adj* not displaying emotion

restraint *n* **1** something that restrains **2** the ability to control one's impulses or passions **3** a restraining or being restrained

restrict *vb* to confine or keep within certain limits **restrictive** *adj* **WORD ORIGIN** Latin *restrictus* bound up

restriction *n* a rule or situation that limits or controls something or someone: *operating under severe financial restrictions*

restrictive practice *n* **1** a trading agreement against the public interest **2** a practice of a union or other group tending to limit the freedom of other workers or employers

rest room *n US, Canad, & Austral* a toilet in a public building

restructure *vb* **-turing, -tured** to organize in a different way: *to restructure the world economy*

result *n* **1** the outcome or consequence of an action, policy, etc. **2** the final score of a sporting contest **3** a number or value obtained by solving a mathematical problem **4** a favourable result, esp. a victory or success: *the best chance of a result is at Cheltenham* **5** results the marks or grades obtained in an examination ▷ *vb* **6 result from** to be the outcome or consequence of: *poverty resulting from high unemployment* **7 result in** to end in (a specified way): *negotiations which resulted in the Treaty of Paris* **WORD ORIGIN** Latin *resultare* to spring from

resultant *adj* **1** arising as a result: *the resultant publicity* ▷ *n* **2** *maths, physics* a single vector that is the vector sum of two or more other vectors, such as a force which results from two other forces acting on a single point

resume *vb* **-suming, -sumed 1** to begin again or go on with (something interrupted) **2** to occupy again or recover: *he will resume his party posts today* **WORD ORIGIN** Latin *resumere*

résumé (**rezz**-yew-may) *n* **1** a short descriptive summary **2** *US, Canad, & Austral* a curriculum vitae **WORD ORIGIN** French

resumption *n* the act of resuming or beginning again

resurgence *n* a rising again to vigour: *worldwide religious resurgence* **resurgent** *adj* **WORD ORIGIN** Latin *resurgere* to rise again

resurrect *vb* **1** to bring or be brought back to life from death **2** to bring back into use or activity

resurrection *n* **1** a return to life by a dead person **2** revival or renewal **3 the Resurrection a** *Christian theol* the rising again of Christ from the tomb three days after his death **b** the rising again from the dead of all people at the Last Judgment **WORD ORIGIN** Latin *resurgere* to rise again

resuscitate (ris-**suss**-it-tate) *vb* **-tating, -tated** to restore to consciousness **resuscitation** *n* **WORD ORIGIN** Latin *re-* again + *suscitare* to raise

retail *n* **1** the sale of goods individually or in small quantities to the public ▷ *adj* **2** of or engaged in such selling: *auctioneers have been successful in cornering the retail market* ▷ *adv* **3** in small amounts or at a retail price ▷ *vb* **4** to sell or be sold in small quantities to the public **5** to relate (gossip or scandal) in detail: *he gleefully retailed the story* **retailer** *n* **WORD ORIGIN** Old French *re-* again + *taillier* to cut

retail therapy *n* the action of shopping for clothes, etc. esp. to cheer oneself up

retain *vb* **1** to keep in one's possession **2** to be able to hold or contain: *with this method the salmon retains its flavour and texture* **3** *law* to engage the services of (a barrister) by payment of a preliminary fee **4** (of a person) to be able to remember (something) without difficulty **5** to hold in position **WORD ORIGIN** Latin *retinere* to hold back

retainer *n* **1** a fee paid in advance to engage someone's services **2** *Brit, Austral, & NZ* a reduced rent paid for a room or flat to reserve it for future use **3** a servant who has been with a family for a long time

retaining wall *n* a wall constructed to hold back earth, loose rock, etc.

retake *vb* **-taking, -took, -taken 1** to recapture: *to retake Jerusalem* **2** to take something, such as an examination or vote, again ▷ *n* **3** *films* a rephotographed scene

retaliate *vb* **-ating, -ated 1** to repay some injury or wrong in kind **2** to cast (accusations) back upon a person **retaliation** *n* **retaliatory** *adj* **WORD ORIGIN** Latin *re-* back + *talis* of such kind

retard *vb* to delay or slow down (the progress or development) **retardant** *n*, *adj* **retardation** *n* **WORD ORIGIN** Latin *retardare*

retarded *adj* underdeveloped mentally

retch *vb* **1** to undergo spasms of the stomach as if one is vomiting ▷ *n* **2** an involuntary spasm of the stomach **WORD ORIGIN** Old English *hræcan*

retention *n* **1** the act of retaining or state of being retained **2** the capacity to remember **3** *pathol* the abnormal holding of something within the body, esp. fluid **retentive** *adj*

rethink *vb* **-thinking, -thought 1** to think about (something) again with a view to changing one's tactics ▷ *n* **2** the act or an instance of thinking again

reticent *adj* not willing to say or tell much **reticence** *n* **WORD ORIGIN** Latin *reticere* to keep silent

reticulate *adj* in the form of a network or having a network of parts: *a reticulate leaf* **reticulation** *n* **WORD ORIGIN** Late Latin *reticulatus* like a net

retina *n, pl* **-nas** *or* **-nae** the light-sensitive inner lining of the back of the eyeball **retinal** *adj* **WORD ORIGIN** Medieval Latin

retinopathy n any of various noninflammatory diseases of the retina, which may have serious effects on vision

retinue n a band of attendants accompanying an important person **WORD ORIGIN** Old French *retenue*

retire vb **-tiring, -tired 1** to give up or to cause (a person) to give up work, esp. on reaching pensionable age **2** to go away into seclusion **3** to go to bed **4** to withdraw from a sporting contest, esp. because of injury **5** to pull back (troops) from battle or (of troops) to fall back **retired** adj **retirement** n **WORD ORIGIN** French *retirer*

retirement pension n Brit a regular payment made by the state or a former employee to a retired person over a specified age

retiring adj very shy

retort[1] vb **1** to reply quickly, wittily, or angrily **2** to use (an argument) against its originator ▷ n **3** a sharp, angry, or witty reply **4** an argument used against its originator **WORD ORIGIN** Latin *re-* back + *torquere* to twist, wrench

retort[2] n **1** a glass vessel with a long tapering neck that is bent down, used for distillation **2** a vessel used for heating ores in the production of metals or heating coal to produce gas **WORD ORIGIN** See RETORT[1]

retouch vb to restore or improve (a painting or photograph) with new touches

retrace vb **-tracing, -traced 1** to go back over (one's steps or a route) **2** to go over (a story) from the beginning

retract vb **1** to withdraw (a statement, charge, etc.) as invalid or unjustified **2** to go back on (a promise or agreement) **3** to draw in (a part or appendage): *the rear wheels are retracted for tight spaces* **retraction** n **WORD ORIGIN** Latin *retractare* to withdraw

retractile adj capable of being drawn in: *the retractile claws of a cat*

retrain vb to train to do a new or different job **retraining** n

retread vb **-treading, -treaded 1** to bond a new tread onto (a worn tyre) ▷ n **2** a remoulded tyre

retreat vb **1** mil to withdraw or retire in the face of or from action with an enemy **2** to retire or withdraw to seclusion or shelter **3** to alter one's opinion about something ▷ n **4** the act of retreating or withdrawing **5** mil **a** a withdrawal or retirement in the face of the enemy **b** a bugle call signifying withdrawal or retirement **6** a place to which one may retire, esp. for religious contemplation **7** a period of seclusion, esp. for religious contemplation **8** the act of altering one's opinion about something **WORD ORIGIN** Old French *retret*

retrench vb to reduce expenditure **retrenchment** n **WORD ORIGIN** Old French *re-* off + *trenchier* to cut

retrial n a second trial of a defendant in a court of law

retribution n punishment or vengeance for evil deeds **retributive** adj **WORD ORIGIN** Latin *re-* back + *tribuere* to pay

retrieve vb **-trieving, -trieved 1** to get or fetch back again **2** to bring back to a more satisfactory state: *his attempt to retrieve the situation* **3** to rescue or save **4** to recover (stored information) from a computer system **5** (of dogs) to find and fetch (shot birds and animals) **6** to remember ▷ n **7** the chance of being retrieved: *beyond retrieve* **retrievable** adj **retrieval** n **WORD ORIGIN** Old French *retrover*

retriever n a dog trained to retrieve shot birds and animals

retro adj associated with or revived from the past: *swap sandals for heeled mules to complete the retro look*

retro- prefix **1** back or backwards: *retroactive* **2** located behind: *retrochoir* **WORD ORIGIN** Latin

retroactive adj effective from a date in the past: *justice through retroactive legislation is never justice*

retrograde adj **1** tending towards an earlier worse condition **2** moving or bending backwards **3** (esp. of order) reverse or inverse ▷ vb **-grading, -graded 4** to go backwards or deteriorate **WORD ORIGIN** Latin *retro-* backwards + *gradi* to walk

retrogress vb to go back to an earlier worse condition **retrogression** n **retrogressive** adj **WORD ORIGIN** Latin *retrogressus* having moved backwards

retrorocket n a small rocket on a larger rocket or a spacecraft, that produces thrust in the opposite direction to the direction of flight in order to slow down

retrospect n **in retrospect** when looking back on the past **WORD ORIGIN** Latin *retrospicere* to look back

retrospective adj **1** looking back in time **2** applying from a date in the past: *retrospective legislation* ▷ n **3** an exhibition of an artist's life's work

retroussé (rit-**troo**-say) adj (of a nose) turned upwards **WORD ORIGIN** French

retsina n a Greek wine flavoured with resin **WORD ORIGIN** Modern Greek

return vb **1** to come back to a former place or state **2** to give, put, or send back **3** to repay with something of equivalent value: *she returned the compliment* **4** to hit, throw, or play (a ball) back **5** to recur or reappear: *as he relaxed his appetite returned* **6** to come back or revert in thought or speech: *let's return to what he said* **7** to earn or yield (profit or interest) **8** to answer or reply **9** to vote into office **10** law (of a jury) to deliver (a verdict) ▷ n **11** the act or an instance of coming back **12** the act of being returned **13** replacement or restoration: *the return of law and order* **14** something that is given or sent back **15** sport the act of playing or throwing a ball back **16** a recurrence or reappearance: *the return of tuberculosis* **17** the yield or profit from an investment or venture **18** a statement of one's taxable income (a **tax return**) **19** an answer or reply **20** Brit, Austral, & NZ short for **return ticket 21 in return** in exchange **22 returns** statement of the votes counted at an election **23 by return (of post)** Brit by the next post back to the sender **24 many happy returns (of the day)** a conventional birthday greeting ▷ adj **25** of or being a return: *the team is keen on a return match* **returnable** adj **WORD ORIGIN** Old French *retorner*

returning officer n an official in charge of conducting an election in a constituency

return ticket n a ticket allowing a passenger to travel to a place and back

reunify vb **-fies, -fying, -fied** to bring together again something previously divided **reunification** n

reunion n **1** a gathering of people who have been apart **2** the act of coming together again

reunite vb **-niting, -nited** to bring or come together again after a separation

reuse n **1** the act of using something again ▷ vb **-using, -used 2** to use again **reusable** adj

rev informal n **1** revolution per minute (of an engine) ▷ vb **revving, revved 2** to increase the speed of revolution of (an engine)

rev. 1 revise(d) **2** revision

Rev. Reverend

revalue vb **-valuing, -valued** to adjust the exchange value of (a currency) upwards **revaluation** n

revamp vb to patch up or renovate

Revd. Reverend

reveal vb **1** to disclose or divulge (a secret) **2** to expose to view or show (something concealed) **3** (of God) to disclose (divine truths) **WORD ORIGIN** Latin *revelare* to unveil

revealing adj **1** disclosing information that one did not know: *she made several revealing remarks during the interview* **2** (of clothes) showing more of the body than is usual

reveille (riv-**val**-ee) n a signal given by a bugle or drum to awaken soldiers or sailors in the morning **WORD ORIGIN** French *réveillez!* awake!

revel vb **-velling, -velled** or US **-veling, -veled 1 revel in** to take pleasure or wallow in: *he would revel in his victory* **2** to take part in noisy festivities ▷ n **3 revels** noisy merrymaking **reveller** n **WORD ORIGIN** Old French *reveler*

revelation n **1** the act of making known a truth which was previously secret **2** a fact newly made known **3** a person or experience that proves to be different from expectations: *New York State could prove a revelation to first-time visitors* **4** Christianity God's disclosure of his own nature and his purpose for mankind

Revelation or **Revelations** n informal the last book of the New Testament, containing visionary descriptions of heaven, and of the end of the world

revelry n, pl **-ries** noisy or unrestrained merrymaking

revenge n **1** vengeance for wrongs or injury received **2** something done as a means of vengeance ▷ vb **-venging, -venged 3** to inflict equivalent injury or damage for (injury received) **4** to take vengeance for (oneself or another) **revengeful** adj
WORD ORIGIN Old French *revenger*

revenue n **1** income, esp. that obtained by a government from taxation **2** a government department responsible for collecting taxes
WORD ORIGIN Old French *revenir* to return

reverberate vb **-rating, -rated 1** to resound or re-echo **2** to reflect or be reflected many times **reverberation** n
WORD ORIGIN Latin *re-* again + *verberare* to beat

revere vb **-vering, -vered** to be in awe of and respect deeply
WORD ORIGIN Latin *revereri*

reverence n profound respect **reverential** adj

Reverence n Your or His Reverence a title sometimes used for a Roman Catholic priest

reverend adj **1** worthy of reverence **2** relating to or designating a clergyman ▷ n **3** informal a clergyman

Reverend adj a title of respect for a clergyman

≣ USAGE
≣ *Reverend* with a surname alone
≣ (*Reverend Smith*), as a term of address
≣ (*'Yes, Reverend'*), or in the greeting of
≣ a letter (*Dear Rev. Mr Smith*) are all
≣ generally considered to be wrong
≣ usage. Preferred are (*the*) *Reverend*
≣ *John Smith* or *Reverend Mr Smith* and
≣ *Dear Mr Smith*.

reverent adj feeling or expressing reverence

reverie n absent-minded daydream
WORD ORIGIN Old French *resverie* wildness

revers (riv-**veer**) n, pl **-vers** the turned-back lining of part of a garment, such as the lapel or cuff
WORD ORIGIN French

reverse vb **-versing, -versed 1** to turn or set in an opposite direction, order, or position **2** to change into something different or contrary: *the cabinet intends to reverse the trend of recent polls* **3** to move backwards or in an opposite direction: *as he started to reverse the car, the bomb exploded* **4** to run (machinery) in the opposite direction to normal **5** to turn inside out **6** law to revoke or set aside (a judgment or decree) **7 reverse the charges** to make a telephone call at the recipient's expense ▷ n **8** the opposite or contrary of something **9** the back or rear side of something **10** a change to an opposite position, state, or direction **11** a change for the worse **12** the gear by which a motor vehicle can be made to go backwards **13** the side of a coin bearing a secondary design **14 in reverse** in an opposite or backward direction **15 the reverse of** not at all: *the result was the reverse of his expectations* ▷ adj **16** opposite or contrary in direction, position, etc. **17** denoting the gear by which a motor vehicle can be

made to go backwards **reversal** n
WORD ORIGIN Latin *reversus* turned back

reversible adj **1** capable of being reversed: *the effect of the operation may not be reversible* **2** (of a garment) made so that either side may be used as the outer side

reversing lights pl n a pair of lights on the rear of a motor vehicle that go on when the vehicle is moving backwards

reversion n **1** a return to an earlier condition, practice, or belief **2** biol the return of individuals or organs to a more primitive condition or type **3** the rightful passing of property to the owner or designated heir

revert vb **1** to go back to a former state **2** biol (of individuals or organs) to return to a more primitive, earlier, or simpler condition or type **3** to come back to a subject **4** property law (of an estate) to return to its former owner
WORD ORIGIN Latin *revertere*

≣ USAGE
≣ Since *back* is part of the meaning of
≣ *revert*, one should not say that
≣ someone *reverts back* to a certain type of
≣ behaviour.

review n **1** a critical assessment of a book, film, etc. **2** a publication containing such articles **3** a general survey or report: *the new curriculum is to be set up a year after the conclusions of the review are due* **4** a formal or official inspection **5** the act or an instance of reviewing **6** a second consideration; re-examination **7** a retrospective survey **8** law a re-examination of a case ▷ vb **9** to hold or write a review of **10** to examine again: *the committee will review the ban in the summer* **11** to look back upon (a period of time or sequence of events): *he reviewed his achievements with pride* **12** to inspect formally or officially: *when he reviewed the troops they cheered him* **13** law to re-examine (a decision) judicially
WORD ORIGIN Latin *re-* again + *videre* to see

reviewer n a person who writes reviews of books, films, etc.

revile vb **-viling, -viled** to be abusively scornful of: *his works were reviled and admired in equal measure*
WORD ORIGIN Old French *reviler*

revise vb **-vising, -vised 1** to change or alter: *he grudgingly revised his opinion* **2** to prepare a new edition of (a previously printed work) **3** to read (something) several times in order to learn it in preparation for an examination
WORD ORIGIN Latin *re-* again + *visere* to inspect

Revised Version n a revision of the Authorized Version of the Bible published between 1881 and 1885

revision n **1** the act or process of revising **2** a corrected or new version of a book, article, etc.

revisionism n **1** (in Marxist ideology) any dangerous departure from the true interpretation of Marx's teachings **2** the advocacy of revision of some political theory **revisionist** n, adj

revisory adj of or having the power of revision

revitalize or **-lise** vb **-lizing, -lized** or **-lising, -lised** to make more lively or active

revival n **1** a reviving or being revived **2** a reawakening of religious faith **3** a new production of a play that has not been recently performed **4** a renewed use or interest in: *there has been an Art Deco revival*

revivalism n a movement that seeks to revive religious faith **revivalist** n, adj

revive vb **-viving, -vived 1** to make or become lively or active again **2** to bring or be brought back to life, consciousness, or strength: *revived by a drop of whisky* **3** theatre to put on a new production of (an old play)
WORD ORIGIN Latin *re-* again + *vivere* to live

revivify vb **-fies, -fying, -fied** to give new life to **revivification** n

revoke vb **-voking, -voked 1** to take back or cancel (an agreement, will, etc.) **2** cards to break a rule by failing to follow suit when able to do so ▷ n **3** cards the act of revoking **revocation** n
WORD ORIGIN Latin *revocare* to call back

revolt n **1** a rebellion or uprising against authority **2 in revolt** in the state of rebelling ▷ vb **3** to rise up in rebellion against authority **4** to cause to feel disgust
WORD ORIGIN French *révolter*

revolting adj horrible and disgusting

revolution n **1** the overthrow of a regime or political system by the governed **2** (in Marxist theory) the transition from one system of production in a society to the next **3** a far-reaching and drastic change **4 a** a movement in or as if in a circle **b** one complete turn in a circle: *33 revolutions per minute*
WORD ORIGIN Latin *revolvere* to revolve

revolutionary adj **1** of or like a revolution **2** advocating or engaged in revolution **3** radically new or different: *they have designed revolutionary new materials to build power stations* ▷ n, pl **-naries 4** a person who advocates or engages in revolution

revolutionize or **-nise** vb **-nizing, -nized** or **-nising, -nised** to bring about a radical change in

revolve vb **-volving, -volved 1** to move or cause to move around a centre **2 revolve around** to be centred or focused upon: *the campaign revolves around one man* **3** to occur periodically or in cycles **4** to consider or be considered **revolvable** adj
WORD ORIGIN Latin *revolvere*

revolver n a pistol with a revolving cylinder that allows several shots to be fired without reloading

revolving door n a door with four leaves at right angles to each other, revolving about a vertical axis

revue n a theatrical entertainment with topical sketches and songs
WORD ORIGIN French

revulsion n a violent feeling of disgust
WORD ORIGIN Latin *revulsio*, pulling away, from *re-* back + *vellere* to pull

Ernest Hemingway

Nowhere does the gap between work and writer yawn wider than in the case of Ernest Hemingway. Certainly, he was a man of contradictions. A generous friend who could never forgive anyone who did him a favour. A hypochondriacal, accident-prone adventurer. A Midwestern American who spent most of his adult life outside the United States. A sensitive and compassionate person with nasty streaks of antisemitism and homophobia. A sensuous puritan. A ruthless careerist who tried to effect the transition to the self-defined 'Papa', a Grand Old Man. A big-game hunter who adored animals. A man's man who married four times. A volatile stoic. A shy bully. An impressionable soul yet a sardonic cynic. A son who hated his mother and both pitied and revered his father and, like his father, killed himself. The contradictions only deepen over time: recent biographies have shown him to have been vulnerable, emotionally wounded, and sexually conflicted.

Handed these paradoxes, his admiring or condemnatory readers and critics paid undue attention to the man rather than the work. The imbalance was also partly Hemingway's fault. The chivalric code he devised for himself involved honour and courage enacted while wearing a mask of laconic endurance: it was a code of action, which he sometimes took to the limits of self-parody. Since Hemingway was unusually nomadic and physically active for a writer, unwary observers came to believe in the author's cult of experience: that it was necessary to be a fly fisherman to write about trout, to be a soldier to write about war. Aging brought not wisdom, but mounting insecurities that were linked to his physical decline.

But the writer was also an artist, albeit one with soaring highs and bathetic lows, from the miniature masterpieces of *In Our Time* to the self-pitying leadenness of *Across the River and Into the Trees*. Hemingway was an intent student of great writing; the novels *The Sun Also Rises* and *For Whom the Bell Tolls* take their titles and epigraphs respectively from *Ecclesiastes* and the sermons of John Donne. For this writer, purity of style equated with morality.

Hemingway's style and attitudes derived from several sources, literary and non-literary. From the King James Bible, syntactic parallelism and prepositional noun phrases. From Mark Twain, a savage contempt for the phoney. From his time as a *Toronto Star* foreign correspondent, the virtues of telegraphese. From Sherwood Anderson, a sense of loss, loneliness, and thwarted lives. From Gertrude Stein, the fruitful uses of repetition. From Paul Cézanne, the painter's idea that if an observer looks long and hard at an object he may become one with it. From Ezra Pound, the poet's conviction that every chiselled word counted.

In keeping with Pound's adage, 'Make it new', Hemingway never ceased experimenting with prose effects, as in his attempt to write non-fiction fiction in *Green Hills of Africa*, or his effort in *For Whom the Bell Tolls* to reproduce a peasant woman's Spanish rhythms and idioms. Sometimes he only succeeded in imitating himself, as in *The Old Man and the Sea*, the short novel that convinced a Swedish jury he deserved the Nobel Prize.

Hemingway's style is seemingly simple, though its effects are not: it is capable of great subtlety and symbolic complexity. He is often praised for his understatement, and for his concrete precision. But a famous quotation from *A Farewell to Arms* illustrates other strengths: 'If people bring so much courage to this world the world has to kill them to break them, so of course it kills them. The world breaks every one and afterward many are strong at the broken places. But those that will not break it kills. It kills the very good and the very gentle and the very brave impartially.'

There it is. The slow grave cadence paced by conjunctions, the parallel constructions, the cunning circumlocution ('at the broken places', not 'at the breaks'), the repetition of 'kill', the apparent redundancy and vagueness of a word like 'very' that somehow magically transforms a line and the clinching adverb 'impartially'.

Hemingway's style was dangerously seductive: a single short story, 'The Killers', offered a template for an entire generation of crime-fiction writers. But, despite his enormous influence on modern, especially American, prose, and his legion of imitators, there could be only one Hemingway, and one style.

reward n **1** something given in return for a service **2** a sum of money offered for finding a criminal or missing property **3** something received in return for good or evil: *sacrifice provided its own reward* ▷ vb **4** to give something to (someone) for a service rendered **WORD ORIGIN** Old French *rewarder* to regard

rewarding adj giving personal satisfaction: *my most professionally rewarding experience*

rewarewa (ray-wa-**ray**-wa) n a tall New Zealand tree with reddish wood **WORD ORIGIN** Māori

rewind vb -winding, -wound to run (a tape or film) back to an earlier point in order to replay

rewire vb -wiring, -wired to provide (a house, engine, etc.) with new wiring

reword vb to alter the wording of

rework vb to improve or bring up to date: *they need to rework the system* **reworking** n

rewrite vb -writing, -wrote, -written **1** to write again in a different way ▷ n **2** something rewritten

Rex n king: now used chiefly in documents and inscriptions **WORD ORIGIN** Latin

Rf chem rutherfordium

RFC Rugby Football Club

RGN (in Britain, New Zealand, and Australia) Registered General Nurse

Rh **1** chem rhodium **2** see **Rh factor**

rhapsodize or -**dise** vb -dizing, -dized or -dising, -dised to speak or write with extravagant enthusiasm

rhapsody n, pl -dies **1** music a freely structured and emotional piece of music **2** an expression of ecstatic enthusiasm **rhapsodic** adj **WORD ORIGIN** Greek *rhaptein* to sew together + *ōidē* song

rhea (**ree**-a) n a large fast-running flightless bird of South America, similar to the ostrich **WORD ORIGIN** after *Rhea*, mother of Zeus

rhenium n chem a silvery-white metallic element with a high melting point. Symbol: Re **WORD ORIGIN** Latin *Rhenus* the Rhine

rheostat n a variable resistor in an electrical circuit, such as one used to dim lights **rheostatic** adj **WORD ORIGIN** Greek *rheos* flow + -*statēs* stationary

rhesus factor (**ree**-suss) n see **Rh factor**

rhesus monkey n a small long-tailed monkey of S Asia **WORD ORIGIN** Greek *Rhesos*, mythical Thracian king

rhetoric (**ret**-a-rik) n **1** the art of using speech or writing to persuade or influence **2** artificial or exaggerated language: *there's been no shortage of soaring rhetoric at this summit* **rhetorical** (rit-**tor**-ik-kl) adj **WORD ORIGIN** Greek *rhētorikē (tekhnē)* (art) of rhetoric

rhetorical question n a question to which no answer is required, used for dramatic effect, for example *who knows?*

rheum (**room**) n a watery discharge from the eyes or nose **rheumy** adj **WORD ORIGIN** Greek *rheuma* a flow

rheumatic adj **1** caused by or affected by rheumatism ▷ n **2** a person suffering from rheumatism **rheumatically** adv

rheumatic fever n a disease with inflammation and pain in the joints

rheumatics n informal rheumatism

rheumatism n any painful disorder of joints, muscles, or connective tissue **WORD ORIGIN** Greek *rheuma* a flow

rheumatoid adj (of symptoms) resembling rheumatism

rheumatoid arthritis n a chronic disease causing painful swelling of the joints

Rh factor n an antigen commonly found in human blood: the terms **Rh positive** and **Rh negative** are used to indicate its presence or absence **WORD ORIGIN** after the rhesus monkey, in which it was first discovered

rhinestone n an imitation diamond made of glass **WORD ORIGIN** originally made at Strasbourg, on the Rhine

rhino n, pl -nos or -no a rhinoceros

rhinoceros n, pl -roses or -ros a large plant-eating mammal of SE Asia and Africa with one or two horns on the nose and a very thick skin **WORD ORIGIN** Greek *rhis* nose + *keras* horn

rhinovirus n any of various viruses that occur in the human respiratory tract and cause diseases, such as the common cold

rhizome n a thick horizontal underground stem whose buds develop into new plants **WORD ORIGIN** Greek *rhiza* a root

rhodium n chem a hard silvery-white metallic element, used to harden platinum and palladium. Symbol: Rh **WORD ORIGIN** Greek *rhodon* rose, from the pink colour of its compounds

rhododendron n an evergreen shrub with clusters of showy flowers **WORD ORIGIN** Greek *rhodon* rose + *dendron* tree

rhombohedron (rom-boh-**heed**-ron) n, pl -drons or -dra (-dra) a six-sided prism whose sides are parallelograms **WORD ORIGIN** RHOMBUS + Greek -*edron* -sided

rhomboid n **1** a parallelogram with adjacent sides of unequal length. It resembles a rectangle but does not have 90° angles ▷ adj also **rhomboidal** **2** having such a shape **WORD ORIGIN** Greek *rhomboeidēs* shaped like a rhombus

rhombus (**rom**-buss) n, pl -buses or -bi (-bye) a parallelogram with sides of equal length but no right angles **rhombic** adj **WORD ORIGIN** Greek *rhombos* something that spins

rhubarb n **1** a large-leaved plant with long green and red stalks which can be cooked and eaten **2** a related plant of central Asia, whose root can be dried and used as a laxative or astringent ▷ interj, n **3** the noise made by actors to simulate conversation, esp. by repeating the word *rhubarb* **WORD ORIGIN** Old French *reubarbe*

rhyme n **1** sameness of the final sounds in lines of verse or in words **2** a word that is identical to another in its final sound: *'while' is a rhyme for 'mile'* **3** a piece of poetry with corresponding sounds at the ends of the lines **4** **rhyme or reason** sense or meaning ▷ vb **rhyming**, **rhymed** **5** (of a word) to form a rhyme with another word **6** to compose (verse) in a metrical structure **WORD ORIGIN** Old French *rime*; spelling influenced by *rhythm*

rhymester n a mediocre poet

rhyming slang n slang in which a word is replaced by another word or phrase that rhymes with it, eg *apples and pears* meaning *stairs*

rhythm n **1** any regular movement or beat: *the side-effects can cause changes in the rhythm of the heart beat* **2** any regular pattern that occurs over a period of time: *the seasonal rhythm of the agricultural year* **3** **a** the arrangement of the durations of sound and stress on the notes of a piece of music, usually laid out in regular groups (**bars**) of beats **b** any specific arrangement of such groupings: *waltz rhythm* **4** (in poetry) the arrangement of words to form a regular pattern of stresses **rhythmic** or **rhythmical** adj **rhythmically** adv **WORD ORIGIN** Greek *rhuthmos*

rhythm and blues n a kind of popular music of Black American origin, derived from and influenced by the blues

rhythm method n a method of contraception in which intercourse is avoided at times when conception is most likely

RI Rhode Island

rialto n, pl -tos a market or exchange **WORD ORIGIN** after the *Rialto*, the business centre of medieval Venice

rib[1] n **1** one of the curved bones forming the framework of the upper part of the body and attached to the spinal column **2** a cut of meat including one or more ribs **3** a curved supporting part, such as in the hull of a boat **4** one of a series of raised rows in knitted fabric ▷ vb **ribbing**, **ribbed** **5** to provide or support with ribs **6** to knit to form a rib pattern **ribbed** adj **WORD ORIGIN** Old English *ribb*

rib[2] vb **ribbing**, **ribbed** informal to tease or ridicule **ribbing** n **WORD ORIGIN** short for *rib-tickle*

RIBA Royal Institute of British Architects

ribald adj coarse or obscene in a humorous or mocking way **ribaldry** n **WORD ORIGIN** Old French *ribauld*

riband or **ribband** n a ribbon awarded for some achievement

ribbing n **1** a pattern of ribs in knitted material **2** a framework or structure of ribs

ribbon n **1** a narrow strip of fine material used for trimming, tying, etc. **2** a long narrow strip of inked cloth or plastic used to produce print in a typewriter **3** a small strip of coloured cloth worn as a badge or as a symbol of

an award **4** a long thin strip: *a ribbon of white water* **5 ribbons** ragged strips or shreds: *his clothes were torn to ribbons; his credibility was shot to ribbons*
WORD ORIGIN Old French *riban*

ribbon development *n* the building of houses along a main road

ribbonwood *n* a small evergreen tree of New Zealand

ribcage *n* the bony structure formed by the ribs that encloses the lungs

riboflavin (rye-boe-**flay**-vin) *n* a vitamin of the B complex that occurs in green vegetables, milk, fish, eggs, liver, and kidney: used as a yellow or orange food colouring (**E101**). Also called: **vitamin B**₂
WORD ORIGIN *ribose*, a sugar + Latin *flavus* yellow

ribonucleic acid *n* the full name of **RNA**

rice *n* **1** the edible grain of an erect grass that grows on wet ground in warm climates ▷ *vb* **ricing, riced 2** *US & Canad* to sieve (potatoes or other vegetables) to a coarse mashed consistency
WORD ORIGIN Greek *oruza*

rice paper *n* **1** a thin edible paper made from rice straw **2** a thin Chinese paper made from the rice-paper plant, the pith of which is flattened into sheets

rich *adj* **1** owning a lot of money or property **2** well supplied (with a desirable substance or quality): *a country rich with cultural interest* **3** having an abundance of natural resources, minerals, etc.: *a land rich in unexploited minerals* **4** producing abundantly: *the island is a blend of hilly moorland and rich farmland* **5** luxuriant or prolific: *the meadows rich with corn* **6** (of food) containing much fat or sugar **7** having a full-bodied flavour: *a gloriously rich Cabernet-dominated wine* **8** (of colour) intense or vivid: *her hair had a rich auburn tint* **9** (of sound or a voice) full or resonant **10** very amusing or ridiculous: *a rich joke* **11** (of a fuel-air mixture) containing a relatively high proportion of fuel **richness** *n*
WORD ORIGIN Old English *rīce* (originally of people, with sense: great, mighty)

riches *pl n* valuable possessions or desirable substances: *the unexpected riches of Georgian culture*

richly *adv* **1** in a rich or elaborate manner: *the rooms are richly decorated with a variety of classical motifs* **2** fully and appropriately: *he left the field to a richly deserved standing ovation*

Richter scale *n* a scale for expressing the intensity of an earthquake, ranging from 0 to over 8
WORD ORIGIN after Charles *Richter*, seismologist

rick¹ *n* a large stack of hay or straw
WORD ORIGIN Old English *hrēac*

rick² *vb* **1** to wrench or sprain (a joint) ▷ *n* **2** a wrench or sprain of a joint
WORD ORIGIN variant of *wrick*

rickets *n* a disease of children, caused by a deficiency of vitamin D and characterized by softening of developing bone, and hence bow legs
WORD ORIGIN origin unknown

rickety *adj* **1** likely to collapse or break: *a rickety wooden table* **2** resembling or afflicted with rickets **ricketiness** *n*

rickrack *or* **ricrac** *n* a zigzag braid used for trimming
WORD ORIGIN reduplication of RACK¹

rickshaw *or* **ricksha** *n* **1** a small two-wheeled passenger vehicle pulled by one or two people, used in parts of Asia **2** a similar vehicle with three wheels, propelled by a person pedalling
WORD ORIGIN Japanese *jinrikisha*

ricochet (**rik**-osh-ay) *vb* **-cheting, -cheted** *or* **-chetting, -chetted 1** (of a bullet) to rebound from a surface ▷ *n* **2** the motion or sound of a rebounding bullet
WORD ORIGIN French

ricotta *n* a soft white unsalted Italian cheese made from sheep's milk
WORD ORIGIN Italian

rid *vb* **ridding, rid** *or* **ridded 1 rid of** to relieve (oneself) or make a place free of (something undesirable) **2 get rid of** to relieve or free oneself of (something undesirable)
WORD ORIGIN Old Norse *rythja*

riddance *n* **good riddance** relief at getting rid of someone or something

ridden *vb* **1** the past participle of **ride** ▷ *adj* **2** afflicted or affected by the thing specified: *the police found three bullet-ridden bodies*

riddle¹ *n* **1** a question, puzzle, or verse phrased so that ingenuity is required to find the answer or meaning **2** a puzzling person or thing ▷ *vb* **-dling, -dled 3** to speak in riddles
WORD ORIGIN Old English *rǣdels(e)*

riddle² *vb* **-dling, -dled 1** to pierce with many holes **2** to put through a sieve ▷ *n* **3** a coarse sieve
WORD ORIGIN Old English *hriddel* a sieve

riddled *adj* **riddled with** full of (something undesirable): *riddled with mistakes*

ride *vb* **riding, rode, ridden 1** to sit on and control the movements of (a horse or other animal) **2** to sit on and propel (a bicycle or motorcycle) **3** to travel on or in a vehicle: *he rides around in a chauffeur-driven Rolls-Royce* **4** to travel over: *they rode the countryside in search of shelter* **5** to travel through or be carried across (sea, sky, etc.): *the moon was riding high* **6** *US & Canad* to cause to be carried: *to ride someone out of town* **7** (of a vessel) to lie at anchor **8** to tyrannize over or dominate: *politicians must stop riding roughshod over voters' wishes* **9 be riding on** to be dependent on (something) for success: *a lot is riding on the profits of the film* **10** *informal* to continue undisturbed: *let it ride* **11 riding high** popular and successful ▷ *n* **12** a journey on a bicycle, on horseback, or in a vehicle **13** transport in a vehicle: *most of us have been told not to accept rides from strangers* **14** the type of movement experienced in a vehicle: *a bumpy ride* **15** a path for riding on horseback **16 take for a ride** *informal* to cheat or deceive
WORD ORIGIN Old English *rīdan*

ride out *vb* to survive (a period of difficulty or danger) successfully

rider *n* **1** a person who rides **2** an extra clause or condition added to a document

ride up *vb* (of a garment) to move up from the proper position

ridge *n* **1** a long narrow raised land formation with sloping sides **2** a long narrow raised strip on a flat surface **3** the top of a roof where the two sloping sides meet **4** *meteorol* an elongated area of high pressure **ridged** *adj* **ridgy** *adj*
WORD ORIGIN Old English *hrycg*

ridgepole *n* **1** a timber along the ridge of a roof, to which the rafters are attached **2** the horizontal pole at the apex of a tent

ridicule *n* **1** language or behaviour intended to humiliate or mock ▷ *vb* **-culing, -culed 2** to make fun of or mock
WORD ORIGIN Latin *ridere* to laugh

ridiculous *adj* worthy of or causing ridicule

riding¹ *n* the art or practice of horsemanship

riding² *n* **1 Riding** any of the three former administrative divisions of Yorkshire: North Riding, East Riding, and West Riding **2** *Canad* an electoral constituency
WORD ORIGIN Old English *thriding* a third

riding crop *n* a short whip with a handle at one end for opening gates

riesling *n* a medium-dry white wine
WORD ORIGIN from German

rife *adj* **1** widespread or common **2 rife with** full of: *the media is rife with speculation*
WORD ORIGIN Old English *rīfe*

riff *n* *jazz, rock* a short series of chords
WORD ORIGIN probably from REFRAIN²

riffle *vb* **-fling, -fled 1** to flick through (papers or pages) quickly: *I riffled through the rest of the memos* ▷ *n* **2** *US & Canad* **a** a rapid in a stream **b** a rocky shoal causing a rapid **c** a ripple on water **3** a riffling
WORD ORIGIN probably from *ruffle*

riffraff *n* worthless or disreputable people
WORD ORIGIN Old French *rif et raf*

rifle¹ *n* **1** a firearm having a long barrel with a spirally grooved interior, which gives the bullet a spinning motion and thus greater accuracy over a longer range **2 Rifles** a unit of soldiers equipped with rifles: *the Burma Rifles* ▷ *vb* **-fling, -fled 3** to cut spiral grooves inside the barrel of (a gun) **rifled** *adj*
WORD ORIGIN Old French *rifler* to scratch

rifle² *vb* **-fling, -fled 1** to search (a house or safe) and steal from it **2** to steal and carry off: *he rifled whatever valuables he could lay his hands on*
WORD ORIGIN Old French *rifler* to plunder, scratch

rift *n* **1** a break in friendly relations between people or groups of people **2** a gap or space made by splitting
WORD ORIGIN Old Norse

rift valley *n* a long narrow valley resulting from the subsidence of land between two faults

rig *vb* **rigging, rigged 1** to arrange in a dishonest way, for profit or advantage: *he claimed that the poll was rigged* **2** to set up or prepare (something) hastily ready for use **3** *naut* to equip (a vessel or mast) with (sails or rigging) ▷ *n* **4** an apparatus for drilling for oil and gas **5** *naut* the arrangement of the sails and masts of a vessel **6** apparatus or equipment **7** *informal* an outfit of clothes **8** *US, Canad, & Austral* an articulated lorry ▸ See also **rig out, rig up**
WORD ORIGIN Scandinavian

-rigged *adj* (of a sailing vessel) having a rig of a certain kind: *a square-rigged ship*

rigging *n* the ropes and cables supporting a ship's masts and sails

right *adj* **1** morally or legally acceptable or correct: *his conduct seemed reasonable, even right* **2** correct or true: *the customer is always right* **3** appropriate, suitable, or proper: *there were problems involved in finding the right candidate* **4** most favourable or convenient: *she waited until the right moment to broach the subject* **5** in a satisfactory condition: *things are right again now* **6** accurate: *is that clock right?* **7** correct in opinion or judgment **8** sound in mind or body **9** of or on the side of something or someone that faces east when the front is turned towards the north **10** conservative or reactionary: *it was alleged he was an agent of the right wing* **11** *geom* formed by or containing a line or plane perpendicular to another line or plane: *a right angle* **12** of or on the side of cloth worn or facing outwards **13 in one's right mind** sane **14 she'll be right** *Austral & NZ informal* that's all right; not to worry **15 the right side of a** in favour with: *you'd better stay on the right side of him* **b** younger than: *he's still on the right side of fifty* **16 too right** *informal* an exclamation of agreement ▷ *adv* **17** correctly: *if we change the structure of local government we must do it right* **18** in the appropriate manner: *do it right next time!* **19** straight or directly: *let's go right to bed* **20** in the direction of the east from the point of view of a person or thing facing north **21** all the way: *he drove right up to the gate* **22** without delay: *I'll be right over* **23** exactly or precisely: *right here* **24** fittingly: *it serves him right* **25** to good or favourable advantage: *it all came out right in the end* ▷ *n* **26** a freedom or power that is morally or legally due to a person: *the defendant had an absolute right to a fair trial* **27** anything that accords with the principles of legal or moral justice **28 in the right** the state of being in accordance with reason or truth **29** the right side, direction, or part: *the right of the army* **30 the Right** the supporters or advocates of conservatism or reaction: *the rise of the far Right in France* **31** *boxing* a punch with the right hand **32 rights** *finance* the privilege of a company's shareholders to subscribe for new issues of the company's shares on advantageous terms **33 by right** or **rights** properly: *by rights he should have won* **34 in one's own right** having a claim or title oneself rather than through marriage or other connection **35 to rights** consistent with justice or

orderly arrangement: *he put the matter to rights* ▷ *vb* **36** to bring or come back to a normal or correct state **37** to bring or come back to a vertical position: *he slipped and righted himself at once* **38** to compensate for or redress: *there is a wrong to be righted* **39** to make (something) accord with truth or facts ▷ *interj* **40** an expression of agreement or compliance
WORD ORIGIN Old English *riht*

right angle *n* **1** an angle of 90° or π/2 radians **2 at right angles** perpendicular or perpendicularly **right-angled** *adj*

right-angled triangle *n* a triangle with one angle which is a right angle

right away *adv* without delay

righteous (**rye**-chuss) *adj* **1** moral, just, or virtuous: *the lieutenant was a righteous cop* **2** morally justifiable or right: *her eyes were blazing with righteous indignation* **righteousness** *n*
WORD ORIGIN Old English *rihtwīs*

rightful *adj* **1** in accordance with what is right **2** having a legally or morally just claim: *he is the rightful heir to her fortune* **3** held by virtue of a legal or just claim: *these moves will restore them to their rightful homes* **rightfully** *adv* **rightfulness** *n*

right-hand *adj* **1** of, on, or towards the right: *in the top right-hand corner* **2** for the right hand **3 right-hand man** a person's most valuable assistant

right-handed *adj* **1** more adept with the right hand than with the left **2** made for or by the right hand **3** turning from left to right

rightist *adj* **1** of the political right or its principles ▷ *n* **2** a supporter of the political right **rightism** *n*

rightly *adv* **1** in accordance with the true facts or justice **2** with good reason: *he was rightly praised for his constancy*

right-minded or **right-thinking** *adj* holding opinions or principles considered acceptable by the speaker

right of way *n, pl* **rights of way 1** the right of one vehicle or ship to go before another **2 a** the legal right of someone to pass over someone else's land **b** the path used by this right

right-on *adj informal* trendy and socially aware or relevant: *the judges were fed up with right-on comedy*

Right Reverend *adj* a title of respect for a bishop

rightward *adj* **1** situated on or directed towards the right ▷ *adv also* **rightwards 2** on or towards the right

right whale *n* a large grey or black whalebone whale with a large head
WORD ORIGIN origin unknown

right-wing *adj* **1** conservative or reactionary: *there's a very fast-growing right-wing feeling in our country* **2** belonging to the more conservative part of a political party: *a group of right-wing Labour MPs* ▷ *n* **right wing 3** (often cap) the more conservative or reactionary section, esp. of a political party: *the Right Wing of the Conservative Party* **4** *sport* **a** the right-hand side of the field of play **b** a player positioned in this area in certain games **right-winger** *n*

rigid *adj* **1** inflexible or strict: *the talks will be general without a rigid agenda* **2** physically unyielding or stiff: *use only rigid plastic containers* **rigidity** *n* **rigidly** *adv*
WORD ORIGIN Latin *rigidus*

rigmarole *n* **1** a long complicated procedure **2** a set of incoherent or pointless statements
WORD ORIGIN earlier *ragman roll* a list

rigor mortis *n* the stiffness of joints and muscles of a dead body
WORD ORIGIN Latin: rigidity of death

rigorous *adj* **1** harsh, strict, or severe: *rigorous enforcement of the libel laws* **2** severely accurate: *rigorous scientific testing*

rigour or *US* **rigor** *n* **1** a severe or cruel circumstance: *the rigours of forced labour* **2** strictness in judgment or conduct **3** harsh but just treatment
WORD ORIGIN Latin *rigor*

rig out *vb* **1** to dress: *I was rigged out in my usual green shell suit* **2** to equip: *his car is rigged out with gadgets* ▷ *n* **rigout 3** *informal* a person's clothing or costume

rig up *vb* to set up or build temporarily: *they rigged up a loudspeaker system*

rile *vb* **riling, riled 1** to annoy or anger **2** *US & Canad* to stir up (a liquid)
WORD ORIGIN variant of *roil* to agitate

rill *n* a small stream
WORD ORIGIN Low German *rille*

rim *n* **1** the raised edge of an object **2** the outer part of a wheel to which the tyre is attached **rimless** *adj*
WORD ORIGIN Old English *rima*

rime¹ *literary n* **1** frost formed by the freezing of water droplets in fog onto solid objects ▷ *vb* **riming, rimed 2** to cover with rime or something resembling it **rimy** *adj*
WORD ORIGIN Old English *hrīm*

rime² *n, vb* **riming, rimed** *archaic* same as **rhyme**

rind *n* a hard outer layer on fruits, bacon, or cheese
WORD ORIGIN Old English *rinde*

ring¹ *vb* **ringing, rang, rung 1** to give out a clear resonant sound, like that of a bell **2** to cause (a bell) to give out a ringing sound or (of a bell) to give out such a sound **3** *chiefly Brit & NZ* to call (a person) by telephone **4 ring for** to call by means of a bell: *ring for the maid* **5** (of a building or place) to be filled with sound: *the church rang with singing* **6** (of the ears) to have the sensation of humming or ringing **7** *slang* to change the identity of (a stolen vehicle) by using the licence plate or serial number of another, usually disused, vehicle **8 ring a bell** to bring something to the mind or memory: *the name doesn't ring a bell* **9 ring down the curtain a** to lower the curtain at the end of a theatrical performance **b ring down the curtain on** to put an end to **10 ring true** or **false** to give the impression of being true or false ▷ *n* **11** the act of or a sound made by ringing **12** a sound produced by or sounding like a bell **13** *informal chiefly Brit & NZ* a telephone call **14** an inherent quality: *it has the ring of possibility to it* ▸ See also **ring in, ring off**, etc.
WORD ORIGIN Old English *hringan*

The Letter R in British and American English

In John Guare's play *Six Degrees of Separation*, the wealthy Trent Conway instructs the destitute Paul in upper-class American pronunciation. 'This is the way you must speak,' he says. 'Hear my accent. Hear my voice .... Say bottle of beer.' Paul replies, in his own accent, 'Bodd-ill of bee-ya.' This exchange continues until Paul can say 'bottle of beer', retaining both the hard 't' and the fully-pronounced 'r'. The American pronunciation of 't' as a short 'd' is avoided only by the most careful speakers, and is not widely perceived as an indication of a speaker's education, social status, or region. The same cannot be said for the letter 'r'.

All linguists and students of the English language acknowledge the pronunciation of the letter 'r' as one of the most prominent differences between North American and British varieties of English (usually ranking just behind the 'flat a' or 'broad a' and the placing of accents on words like *research* and *extraordinary*). And yet it would be wrong to assume that there is absolute consistency in how all North American or all British speakers realize this consonant.

The distinction that broadly separates these two international varieties of English is not how the consonant *sounds*; for example, whether it is 'trilled', as in most varieties of Scottish English, or 'retroflex', pronounced by drawing the tongue toward the back of the mouth. Rather, the distinction is whether the consonant is pronounced at all, and in what contexts. In Received Pronunciation or RP, which is still regarded as the 'standard' accent of British English, the letter 'r' is only pronounced when it precedes a vowel, whether at the beginning of a word, as in *row* and *rabbit*, or in the middle, as in *array* and *borrow*. The letter is not pronounced when it is followed by a consonant, as in *start*, or when it comes at the end of a word, as in *colour*. In these contexts, the 'r' becomes part of the vowel sound, or is reduced to the shortest of English vowels, *schwa*. Thus, in RP, *alms* and *arms* are perfect rhymes, as are *lord* and *laud*, while *higher* rhymes with *Maya*.

(There is another British 'r' sound, called *intrusive r* or *linking r*, which occurs when a word which ends with a vowel sound is followed by a word which begins with a vowel sound. This *intrusive r* causes the phrase *law and order* to sound like *Laura Norder*. It is widely heard throughout the UK, but is considered accidental or non-standard.)

The degree to which one pronounces 'r' in all contexts is called *rhoticity* (from the Greek letter *rho*, which is equivalent to 'r'). What makes the difference between British and North American rhoticity fascinating is that they have nearly opposite social connotations. As part of Received Pronunciation, non-rhotic 'r' is considered 'standard', 'correct', even 'upper-class'. In the UK, speakers who use rhotic 'r' betray at least their regional origin (eg West Country, Scotland, Ireland, or certain parts of Northern England).

In the United States, the opposite is true. Though there is no 'standard' American accent comparable to RP, the vast majority of American speakers have a rhotic 'r', the exceptions being certain parts of New England and the American South (in Massachusetts, for example, *Harvard Yard* is pronounced *Hahvud Yahd*). However, even in these regions, particularly in New England, careful speakers will re-introduce rhotic 'r' into their speech to show their education or social status. The exchange in John Guare's play, for example, takes place in Boston, and Trent Conway is a resident of New York City, both cities where non-rhotic 'r' is common. However, in order affect upper-class manners, Paul must learn to pronounce 'r' wherever it is written, even at the end of a word. Later in the play, Trent Conway is referred to as 'the Henry Higgins of our time', comparing him with the elocution-teaching professor of Bernard Shaw's *Pygmalion* who attempts to launch Cockney Eliza Doolittle into polite society. It is appropriate that 'bottle of beer', should, by extension, be the American equivalent of Higgins' practice sentence 'the rain in Spain stays mainly on the plain'. Cockney, after all, is yet another non-rhotic accent.

USAGE
Rang and *sang* are the correct forms of the past tenses of *ring* and *sing*, although *rung* and *sung* are still heard informally and dialectally: *he rung* (*rang*) *the bell*.

ring² *n* **1** a circular band of a precious metal worn on the finger **2** any object or mark that is circular in shape **3** a group of people or things standing or arranged in a circle: *a ring of standing stones* **4** a circular path or course: *crowds of people walking round in a ring* **5** a circular enclosure where circus acts perform or livestock is sold at a market **6** a square raised platform, marked off by ropes, in which contestants box or wrestle **7** a group of people, usually illegal, who control a specified market: *a drugs ring* **8** *chem* a closed loop of atoms in a molecule **9** one of the systems of circular bands orbiting the planets Saturn, Uranus, and Jupiter **10** **the ring** the sport of boxing **11** **throw one's hat in the ring** to announce one's intention to be a candidate or contestant **12** **run rings around** *informal* to outclass completely ▷ *vb* **ringing, ringed 13** to put a ring round **14** to mark (a bird) with a ring or clip for subsequent identification **15** to kill (a tree) by cutting the bark round the trunk **16** to fit a ring in the nose of (a bull, etc.) so that it can be led easily **ringed** *adj*
WORD ORIGIN Old English *hring*

ring binder *n* a loose-leaf binder with metal rings that can be opened to insert perforated paper

ringdove *n* a wood pigeon

ringer *n* **1** Also called: **dead ringer** a person or thing that is almost identical to another **2** *slang* a stolen vehicle the identity of which has been changed by the use of the licence plate or serial number of another, usually disused, vehicle

ring finger *n* the third finger, esp. of the left hand, on which a wedding ring is worn

ring in *vb* to report to someone by telephone

ringleader *n* a person who leads others in illegal or mischievous actions

ringlet *n* a lock of hair hanging down in a spiral curl **ringleted** *adj*

ring main *n* a domestic electrical supply in which outlet sockets are connected to the mains supply through a continuous closed circuit (**ring circuit**)

ringmaster *n* the master of ceremonies in a circus

ring off *vb chiefly Brit & NZ* to end a telephone conversation by replacing the receiver

ring out *vb* to send out a loud resounding noise: *I heard those shots ring out*

ring road *n* a main road that bypasses a town or town centre

ringside *n* **1** the row of seats nearest a boxing or wrestling ring ▷ *adj* **2** providing a close uninterrupted view: *a ringside seat for the election*

ringtail *n Austral* a possum with a curling tail used to grip branches while climbing

ringtone *n* a musical tune played by a mobile phone when it receives a call

ring up *vb* **1** to make a telephone call to **2** to record on a cash register **3** **ring up the curtain a** to begin a theatrical performance **b** **ring up the curtain on** to make a start on

ringworm *n* a fungal infection of the skin producing itchy patches

rink *n* **1** a sheet of ice for skating on, usually indoors **2** an area for roller-skating on **3** a building for ice-skating or roller-skating **4 a** a strip of grass or ice on which a game of bowls or curling is played **b** the players on one side in a game of bowls or curling
WORD ORIGIN Old French *renc* row

rinkhals (**rink**-hals) *n, pl* **-hals** *or* **-halses** a highly venomous snake of Southern Africa capable of spitting its venom accurately at its victim's eyes
WORD ORIGIN Afrikaans

rink rat *n Canad slang* a youth who helps with odd chores at an ice-hockey rink in return for free admission to games

rinse *vb* **rinsing, rinsed 1** to remove soap or shampoo from (clothes, dishes, or hair) by washing it out with clean water **2** to wash lightly, esp. without using soap **3** to cleanse the mouth by swirling water or mouthwash in it and then spitting the liquid out **4** to give a light tint to (hair) ▷ *n* **5** the act or an instance of rinsing **6** *hairdressing* a liquid to tint hair: *a blue rinse*
WORD ORIGIN Old French *rincer*

rioja (ree-**oh**-ha) *n* a red or white Spanish wine with a vanilla bouquet and flavour
WORD ORIGIN *La Rioja*, area in central N Spain

riot *n* **1** a disturbance made by an unruly mob **2** *Brit, Austral, & NZ* an occasion of lively enjoyment **3** a dazzling display: *the pansies provided the essential riot of colour* **4** *slang* a very amusing person or thing **5** **read the riot act** to reprimand severely **6** **run riot a** to behave without restraint **b** (of plants) to grow profusely ▷ *vb* **7** to take part in a riot **rioter** *n* **rioting** *n*
WORD ORIGIN Old French *riote* dispute

riotous *adj* **1** unrestrained and excessive: *riotous decadence* **2** unruly or rebellious **3** characterized by unrestrained merriment: *riotous celebration*

riot shield *n* a large shield used by police controlling crowds

rip *vb* **ripping, ripped 1** to tear or be torn violently or roughly **2** to remove hastily or roughly **3** *informal* to move violently or hurriedly **4** **let rip** to act or speak without restraint ▷ *n* **5** a tear or split ▶ See also **rip off**
WORD ORIGIN origin unknown

RIP may he, she, *or* they rest in peace
WORD ORIGIN Latin *requiescat* or *requiescant in pace*

riparian (rip-**pair**-ee-an) *adj formal* of or on the bank of a river
WORD ORIGIN Latin *ripa* river bank

ripcord *n* a cord pulled to open a parachute from its pack

ripe *adj* **1** mature enough to be eaten or used: *a round ripe apple* **2** fully developed in mind or body **3** suitable: *wait until the time is ripe* **4** **ripe for** ready or eager to (undertake or undergo an action): *China was ripe for revolution* **5** **ripe old age** an elderly but healthy age
WORD ORIGIN Old English *rīpe*

ripen *vb* **1** to make or become ripe **2** to mature

rip off *slang vb* **1** to cheat by overcharging **2** to steal (something) ▷ *n* **rip-off 3** a grossly overpriced article **4** the act of stealing or cheating

riposte (rip-**posst**) *n* **1** a swift clever reply **2** *fencing* a counterattack made immediately after a successful parry ▷ *vb* **-posting, -posted 3** to make a riposte
WORD ORIGIN French

ripple *n* **1** a slight wave on the surface of water **2** a slight ruffling of a surface **3** a sound like water flowing gently in ripples: *a ripple of applause* **4** vanilla ice cream with stripes of another ice cream through it: *raspberry ripple* ▷ *vb* **-pling, -pled 5** to form ripples or flow with a waving motion **6** (of sounds) to rise and fall gently **rippling** *adj*
WORD ORIGIN origin unknown

rip-roaring *adj informal* boisterous and exciting

ripsaw *n* a handsaw for cutting along the grain of timber

rise *vb* **rising, rose, risen 1** to get up from a lying, sitting, or kneeling position **2** to get out of bed, esp. to begin one's day: *she rises at 5 am every day to look after her horse* **3** to move from a lower to a higher position or place **4** to appear above the horizon: *as the sun rises higher the mist disappears* **5** to slope upwards: *the road crossed the valley then rose to a low ridge* **6** to increase in height or level: *the tide rose* **7** to swell up: *dough rises* **8** to increase in strength or degree: *frustration is rising amongst sections of the population* **9** to increase in amount or value: *living costs are rising at an annual rate of nine per cent* **10** *informal* to respond (to a challenge or remark) **11** to revolt: *the people rose against their oppressors* **12** (of a court or parliament) to adjourn **13** to be resurrected **14** to become erect or rigid: *the hairs on his neck rose in fear* **15** to originate: *that river rises in the mountains* **16** *angling* (of fish) to come to the surface of the water ▷ *n* **17** the act or an instance of rising **18** a piece of rising ground **19** an increase in wages **20** an increase in amount, cost, or quantity **21** an increase in height **22** an increase in status or position **23** an increase in degree or intensity **24** the vertical height of a step or of a flight of stairs **25** **get** *or* **take a rise out of** *slang* to provoke an angry reaction from **26** **give rise to** to cause the development of
WORD ORIGIN Old English *rīsan*

riser *n* **1** a person who rises from bed: *an early riser* **2** the vertical part of a step

risible (riz-zib-bl) *adj formal* ridiculous
WORD ORIGIN Latin *ridere* to laugh

rising *n* **1** a rebellion ▷ *adj* **2** increasing in rank or maturity

rising damp *n* seepage of moisture from the ground into the walls of buildings

risk n **1** the possibility of bringing about misfortune or loss **2** a person or thing considered as a potential hazard: *in parts of the world transfusions carry the risk of infection* **3 at risk** in a dangerous situation **4 take** *or* **run a risk** to act without regard to the danger involved ▷ vb **5** to act in spite of the possibility of (injury or loss): *if they clamp down they risk a revolution* **6** to expose to danger or loss **risky** adj **WORD ORIGIN** French *risque*

risk assessment n *business* an analysis of the level of risk attached to a particular activity

risotto n, pl **-tos** a dish of rice cooked in stock with vegetables, meat, etc. **WORD ORIGIN** Italian

risqué (**risk**-ay) adj making slightly rude references to sex: *risqué humour* **WORD ORIGIN** French *risquer* to risk

rissole n a mixture of minced cooked meat coated in egg and breadcrumbs and fried **WORD ORIGIN** French

ritardando adj, adv same as **rallentando** **WORD ORIGIN** Italian

rite n **1** a formal act which forms part of a religious ceremony: *the rite of burial* **2** a custom that is carried out within a particular group: *the barbaric rites of public execution* **3** a particular body of such acts, esp. of a particular Christian Church: *the traditional Anglican rite* **WORD ORIGIN** Latin *ritus*

rite of passage n a ceremony or event that marks an important change in a person's life

ritual n **1** a religious or other ceremony involving a series of fixed actions performed in a certain order **2** these ceremonies collectively: *people need ritual* **3** regular repeated action or behaviour **4** stereotyped activity or behaviour ▷ adj **5** of or like rituals **ritually** adv

ritualism n exaggerated emphasis on the importance of rites and ceremonies **ritualistic** adj **ritualistically** adv

ritzy adj **ritzier, ritziest** slang luxurious or elegant **WORD ORIGIN** after the hotels established by César Ritz

rival n **1** a person or group that competes with another for the same object or in the same field **2** a person or thing that is considered the equal of another: *she is without rival in the field of physics* ▷ adj **3** in the position of a rival ▷ vb **-valling, -valled** *or US* **-valing, -valed 4** to be the equal or near equal of: *his inarticulateness was rivalled only by that of his brother* **5** to try to equal or surpass **WORD ORIGIN** Latin *rivalis*, literally: one who shares the same brook

rivalry n, pl **-ries** active competition between people or groups

riven adj old-fashioned **1** split apart: *the party is riven by factions* **2** torn to shreds **WORD ORIGIN** Old Norse *rifa* to tear, rend

river n **1** a large natural stream of fresh water flowing along a definite course into the sea, a lake, or a larger river ▸ Related adjective: **fluvial 2** an abundant stream or flow: *rivers of blood* **WORD ORIGIN** Old French *riviere*

rivet (**riv**-vit) n **1** a short metal pin for fastening metal plates, with a head at one end, the other end being hammered flat after being put through holes in the plates ▷ vb **-veting, -veted 2** to join by riveting **3** to cause a person's attention to be fixed in fascination or horror: *their eyes riveted on the protesters* **riveter** n **WORD ORIGIN** Old French *river* to fasten

riveting adj very interesting or exciting

rivulet n a small stream **WORD ORIGIN** Latin *rivus* stream

RM 1 Royal Mail **2** Royal Marines **3** (in Canada) Rural Municipality **4** (in Canada) Regional Municipality

RMT (in Britain) (National Union of) Rail, Maritime and Transport (Workers)

Rn *chem* radon

RN 1 (in Canada and New Zealand) Registered Nurse **2** (in Britain) Royal Navy

RNA n *biochem* ribonucleic acid: any of a group of nucleic acids, present in all living cells, that play an essential role in the synthesis of proteins

RNLI (in Britain) Royal National Lifeboat Institution

RNZ Radio New Zealand

RNZAF Royal New Zealand Air Force

RNZN Royal New Zealand Navy

roach¹ n, pl **roaches** or **roach** a European freshwater food fish **WORD ORIGIN** Old French *roche*

roach² n chiefly US & Canad a cockroach

road n **1** a route, usually surfaced, used by travellers and vehicles to get from one place to another **2** a street **3** a way or course: *on the road to recovery* **4** *naut* same as **roadstead 5 one for the road** informal a last alcoholic drink before leaving **6 on the road** travelling about **WORD ORIGIN** Old English *rād*

roadblock n a barrier set up across a road by the police or military, in order to stop and check vehicles

road hog n informal a selfish or aggressive driver

roadholding n the extent to which a vehicle is stable and does not skid on bends or wet roads

roadhouse n a pub or restaurant at the side of a road

roadie n Brit, Austral, & NZ informal a person who transports and sets up equipment for a band

road metal n crushed rock or broken stone used in building roads

road rage n aggressive behaviour by a motorist in response to the actions of another road user

road show n **1** radio a live broadcast from a radio van taking a particular programme on a tour of the country **2** a group of entertainers on tour

roadside n **1** the edge of a road ▷ adj **2** by the edge or side of a road: *a roadside café*

roadstead n naut a partly sheltered anchorage

roadster n an open car with only two seats

road tax n (in Britain) a tax paid on vehicles used on the roads

road test n **1** a test of something, such as a vehicle in actual use ▷ vb **road-test 2** to test (a vehicle etc.) in actual use

roadway n the part of a road that is used by vehicles

roadworks pl n repairs to a road or cable under a road, esp. when they block part of the road

roadworthy adj (of a motor vehicle) mechanically sound **roadworthiness** n

roam vb to walk about with no fixed purpose or direction **WORD ORIGIN** origin unknown

roan adj **1** (of a horse) having a brown or black coat sprinkled with white hairs ▷ n **2** a horse with such a coat **WORD ORIGIN** Spanish *roano*

roar vb **1** (of lions and other animals) to make loud growling cries **2** to shout (something) with a loud deep cry: *'Don't do that!' he roared at me* **3** to make a very loud noise: *the engine roared* **4** to laugh in a loud hearty manner **5** (of a fire) to burn fiercely with a roaring sound ▷ n **6** a roaring noise: *there was a roar as the train came in* **7** a loud deep cry, uttered by a person or crowd, esp. in anger or triumph: *a roar of approval came from the crowd* **WORD ORIGIN** Old English *rārian*

roaring adj **1 a roaring trade** a brisk and profitable business ▷ adv **2 roaring drunk** noisily or boisterously drunk

roast vb **1** to cook (food) by dry heat in an oven or over a fire **2** to brown or dry (coffee or nuts) by exposure to heat **3** informal to make or be extremely hot **4** informal to criticize severely ▷ n **5** a roasted joint of meat ▷ adj **6** cooked by roasting: *roast beef* **roaster** n **WORD ORIGIN** Old French *rostir*

roasting informal adj **1** extremely hot ▷ n **2** severe criticism or scolding

rob vb **robbing, robbed 1** to take something from (a person or place) illegally **2** to deprive, esp. of something deserved: *I can't forgive him for robbing me of an Olympic gold* **robber** n **WORD ORIGIN** Old French *rober*

robbery n, pl **-beries 1** criminal law the stealing of property from a person by using or threatening to use force **2** the act or an instance of robbing

robe n **1** a long loose flowing garment **2** a dressing gown or bathrobe ▷ vb **robing, robed 3** to put a robe on **WORD ORIGIN** Old French

robin n **1** Also called: **robin redbreast** a small Old World songbird with a brown back and an orange-red breast and face **2** a North American thrush similar to but larger than the Old World robin **WORD ORIGIN** arbitrary use of name *Robin*

robot n **1** a machine programmed to perform specific tasks in a human manner, esp. one with a human shape **2** a person of machine-like efficiency **3** S African a set of traffic lights **robotic** adj **WORD ORIGIN** used in R.U.R., a play by a Czech writer, from Czech *robota* work

robotics n the science of designing, building, and using robots

robust adj 1 very strong and healthy 2 sturdily built: *the new generation of robust lasers* 3 requiring or displaying physical strength: *robust tackles*
WORD ORIGIN Latin *robur* an oak, strength

roc n (in Arabian legend) a bird of enormous size and power
WORD ORIGIN Persian *rukh*

rock¹ n 1 geol the mass of mineral matter that makes up part of the earth's crust; stone 2 a large rugged mass of stone 3 *chiefly US, Canad, & Austral* a stone 4 a hard peppermint-flavoured sweet, usually in the shape of a long stick 5 a person or thing on which one can always depend: *your loyalty is a rock* 6 *slang* a precious jewel 7 **on the rocks** a (of a marriage) about to end b (of an alcoholic drink) served with ice
WORD ORIGIN Old French *roche*

rock² vb 1 to move from side to side or backwards and forwards 2 to shake or move (something) violently 3 to feel or cause to feel shock: *key events have rocked both countries* 4 to dance to or play rock music 5 *slang* to be very good ▷ n 6 Also called: **rock music** a style of pop music with a heavy beat 7 a rocking motion ▷ adj 8 of or relating to rock music
WORD ORIGIN Old English *roccian*

rockabilly n a fast style of White rock music which originated in the mid-1950s in the US South
WORD ORIGIN *rock and roll + hillbilly*

rock and roll or **rock'n'roll** n a type of pop music originating in the 1950s as a blend of rhythm and blues and country and western

rock bottom n the lowest possible level

rock cake n a small fruit cake with a rough surface

rock crystal n a pure transparent colourless quartz

rock dove n a common dove from which domestic and wild pigeons are descended

rocker n 1 a rocking chair 2 either of two curved supports on which a rocking chair stands 3 a rock music performer or fan 4 **off one's rocker** *slang* crazy

rockery n, pl **-eries** a garden built of rocks and soil, for growing rock plants

rocket n 1 a self-propelling device, usually cylindrical, which produces thrust by expelling through a nozzle the gases produced by burning fuel, such as one used as a firework or distress signal 2 any vehicle propelled by a rocket engine, as a weapon or carrying a spacecraft 3 *informal* a severe reprimand: *my sister gave me a rocket for writing such dangerous nonsense* ▷ vb **-eting, -eted** 4 to increase rapidly: *within six years their turnover had rocketed* 5 to attack with rockets
WORD ORIGIN Italian *rochetto* little distaff

rocketry n the science and technology of the design and operation of rockets

rock garden n a garden featuring rocks or rockeries

rocking chair n a chair set on curving supports so that the sitter may rock backwards and forwards

rocking horse n a toy horse mounted on a pair of rocking supports on which a child can rock to and fro

rock melon n *US, Austral, & NZ* same as **cantaloupe**

rock pool n a small pool between rocks on the seashore

rock salmon n *Brit* a former term for dogfish when used as a food

rock salt n common salt as a naturally occurring solid mineral

rock tripe n *Canad* any edible lichen that grows on rocks

rocky¹ adj **rockier, rockiest** covered with rocks: *rocky and sandy shores* **rockiness** n

rocky² adj **rockier, rockiest** shaky or unstable: *a rocky relationship* **rockiness** n

rococo (rok-**koe**-koe) adj 1 relating to an 18th-century style of architecture, decoration, and music characterized by elaborate ornamentation 2 excessively elaborate in style
WORD ORIGIN French

rod n 1 a thin straight pole made of wood or metal 2 a cane used to beat people as a punishment 3 short for **fishing rod** 4 a type of cell in the retina, sensitive to dim light **rodlike** adj
WORD ORIGIN Old English *rodd*

rode vb the past tense of **ride**

rodent n a small mammal with teeth specialized for gnawing, such as a rat, mouse, or squirrel **rodent-like** adj
WORD ORIGIN Latin *rodere* to gnaw

rodeo n, pl **-deos** a display of the skills of cowboys, including bareback riding
WORD ORIGIN Spanish

rodomontade n *literary* boastful words or behaviour
WORD ORIGIN French

roe¹ n the ovary and eggs of a female fish, sometimes eaten as food
WORD ORIGIN Middle Dutch *roge*

roe² or **roe deer** n a small graceful deer with short antlers
WORD ORIGIN Old English *rā(ha)*

roentgen (**ront**-gan) n a unit measuring a radiation dose
WORD ORIGIN after the German physicist *Roentgen*, who discovered X-rays

roger interj 1 (used in signalling) message received 2 an expression of agreement
WORD ORIGIN from the name *Roger*, representing R for *received*

rogue n 1 a dishonest or unprincipled person 2 a mischievous person 3 a crop plant which is inferior, diseased, or of a different variety 4 an inferior or defective specimen ▷ adj 5 (of a wild animal) having a savage temper and living apart from the herd: *a rogue elephant* 6 inferior or defective: *rogue heroin* **roguish** adj
WORD ORIGIN origin unknown

roguery n, pl **-gueries** dishonest or immoral behaviour

rogues' gallery n a collection of photographs of known criminals kept by the police for identification purposes

ROI 1 Republic of Ireland 2 *finance* return on investment

roister vb *old-fashioned* to enjoy oneself noisily and boisterously **roisterer** n
WORD ORIGIN Old French *rustre* lout

role n 1 a task or function: *their role in international relations* 2 an actor's part in a production
WORD ORIGIN French

role model n a person regarded by others, esp. younger people, as a good example to follow

roll vb 1 to move along by turning over and over 2 to move along on wheels or rollers 3 to curl or wind into a ball or tube 4 to move along in an undulating movement 5 to rotate wholly or partially: *he would snort in derision, roll his eyes, and heave a deep sigh* 6 to spread out flat or smooth with a roller or rolling pin: *roll the pastry out thinly* 7 (of a ship or aircraft) to turn from side to side around the longitudinal axis 8 to operate or begin to operate: *the cameras continued to roll as she pulled up to the nightclub* 9 to make a continuous deep reverberating sound: *the thunder rolled* 10 to walk in a swaying manner: *the drunks came rolling home* 11 to appear like a series of waves: *mountain ranges rolling away in every direction* 12 to pass or elapse: *watching the time roll away* 13 (of animals) to turn onto the back and kick 14 to trill or cause to be trilled: *she rolled her r's* 15 to throw (dice) ▷ n 16 the act or an instance of rolling 17 anything rolled up into a tube: *a roll of paper towels* 18 a small cake of bread for one person 19 a flat pastry or cake rolled up with a meat, jam, or other filling 20 an official list or register of names: *the electoral roll; the voters' roll* 21 a complete rotation about its longitudinal axis by an aircraft 22 a continuous deep reverberating sound: *the roll of musketry* 23 a swaying or unsteady movement or gait 24 a rounded mass: *rolls of fat* 25 a very rapid beating of the sticks on a drum 26 **on a roll** *slang* experiencing continued good luck or success 27 **strike off the roll** to expel from membership of a professional association ▶ See also **roll in, roll on,** etc.
WORD ORIGIN Old French *roler*

roll call n the reading aloud of an official list of names, to check who is present

rolled gold n a metal, such as brass, coated with a thin layer of gold

roller n 1 a rotating cylinder used for smoothing, supporting a thing to be moved, spreading paint, etc. 2 a small tube around which hair may be wound in order to make it curly 3 a long heavy wave of the sea 4 a cylinder fitted on pivots, used to enable heavy objects to be easily moved

Rollerblade n *trademark* a type of roller skate in which the wheels are set in a single straight line under the boot

roller coaster n (at a funfair) a narrow railway with open carriages, sharp curves and steep slopes

roller skate n 1 a shoe with four small wheels that enable the wearer to glide swiftly over a floor ▷ vb **roller-skate, -skating, -skated** 2 to move on roller skates **roller skater** n

Words from Literature
part 23

rubber *n* a set of games in whist or backgammon
her father was sure of his rubber
Emma Jane Austen

ruffian *n* a person who behaves violently
and when the ruffian had told him
Treasure Island Robert Louis Stevenson

sadness *n* an old term meaning seriousness
But I prithee tell me, in good sadness
Doctor Faustus 2.2 Christopher Marlowe

sail before the mast *phrase* someone who sails
before the mast is a sailor
he had none of the appearance of a man that sailed
before the mast
Treasure Island Robert Louis Stevenson

scabbard *n* the covering for a sword or dagger
Girded round its middle was an antique scabbard;
but no sword was in it, and the ancient sheath was
eaten up with rust
A Christmas Carol Charles Dickens

schooner *n* a fast, medium-sized sailing ship
if schooners, islands, and maroons
Treasure Island Robert Louis Stevenson

science *n* learning or knowledge
Even Science, too, at hand
The Prelude William Wordsworth

scrouge *v* to scrouge means to squeeze or to crowd
to scrouge in and get a sight
The Adventures of Huckleberry Finn Mark Twain

scrutore *n* a scrutore, or escritoire, was a writing
table
set me gently on my feet upon the scrutore
Gulliver's Travels Jonathan Swift

scutcheon or **escutcheon** *n* an escutcheon is a shield
with a coat of arms, or the symbols of a family name,
engraved on it
On the scutcheon we'll have a bend
The Adventures of Huckleberry Finn Mark Twain

sea-dog *phrase* a slang term for an experienced sailor
or pirate
a 'true sea-dog,' and a 'real old salt,'
Treasure Island Robert Louis Stevenson

see the lions *phrase* to see the lions was to go and see
the sights of London. Originally the phrase referred to
the menagerie in the Tower of London and later in
Regent's Park
We will go and see the lions for an hour or two –
it's something to have a fresh fellow like you
to show them to, Copperfield
David Copperfield Charles Dickens

self-conceit *n* your opinion or estimate of yourself
Till swollen with cunning, of a self-conceit
Doctor Faustus chorus Christopher Marlowe

seneschal *n* a steward
where a grey-headed seneschal sings a funny
chorus with a funnier body of vassals
Oliver Twist Charles Dickens

sensible *adj* if you are sensible of something you
are aware or conscious of something
If my children are silly I must hope to be always
sensible of it
Pride and Prejudice Jane Austen

sessions *n* court cases heard at specific times of the year
He lay in prison very ill, during the whole interval
between his committal for trial, and the coming
round of the Sessions.
Great Expectations Charles Dickens

shabby *adj* old and in bad condition
a little bit of a shabby village named Pikesville
The Adventures of Huckleberry Finn Mark Twain

shay-cart *n* a small cart drawn by one horse
"I were at the Bargemen t'other night, Pip;"
whenever he subsided into affection, he called
me Pip, and whenever he relapsed into politeness
he called me Sir; "when there come up in his
shay-cart Pumblechook."
Great Expectations Charles Dickens

roller towel *n* **1** a towel with the two ends sewn together, hung on a roller **2** a towel wound inside a roller enabling a clean section to be pulled out when needed

rollicking *adj* boisterously carefree: *a rollicking read*
WORD ORIGIN origin unknown

roll in *vb* **1** to arrive in large numbers **2 be rolling in** *slang* to have plenty of (money etc.)

rolling *adj* **1** having gentle rising and falling slopes: *rolling hills* **2** (of a walk) slow and swaying **3** subject to regular review and updating: *a 10-year rolling programme* **4** progressing by stages or in succession: *a rolling campaign*

rolling mill *n* **1** a factory where metal ingots are passed between rollers to produce sheets or bars of the required shape **2** a machine with rollers for doing this

rolling pin *n* a cylinder with handles at both ends used for rolling pastry

rolling stock *n* the locomotives and coaches of a railway

rolling stone *n* a restless or wandering person

rollmop *n* a herring fillet rolled around onion slices and pickled
WORD ORIGIN German *rollen* to roll + *Mops* pug dog

rollneck *adj* (of a garment) having a high neck that is worn rolled over

roll of honour *n* a list of those who have died in war for their country

roll on *interj* **1** used to express the wish that an eagerly anticipated event will come quickly: *roll on the next light-hearted romp* ▷ *adj* **roll-on 2** (of a deodorant) applied by means of a revolving ball fitted into the neck of the container

roll-on/roll-off *adj* denoting a ship designed so that vehicles can be driven straight on and straight off

roll over *vb* **1** to overturn **2** to allow (a loan or prize) to continue in force for a further period ▷ *n* **rollover 3** an instance of such a continuance of a loan or prize

roll-top *adj* (of a desk) having a slatted wooden panel that can be pulled down over the writing surface when not in use

roll up *vb* **1** to form into a cylindrical shape: *roll up a length of black material* **2** *informal* to arrive ▷ *n* **roll-up 3** *Brit informal* a cigarette made by the smoker from loose tobacco and cigarette papers

roly-poly *adj* **1** plump or chubby ▷ *n, pl* **-lies 2** *Brit* a strip of suet pastry spread with jam, rolled up, and baked or steamed
WORD ORIGIN probably from *roll*

ROM *n computers* read only memory: a storage device that holds data permanently and cannot be altered by the programmer

roman *adj* **1** in or relating to the vertical style of printing type used for most printed matter ▷ *n* **2** roman type
WORD ORIGIN so called because the style of letters is that used in ancient Roman inscriptions

Roman *adj* **1** of Rome, a city in Italy, or its inhabitants in ancient or modern times **2** of Roman Catholicism or the Roman Catholic Church ▷ *n* **3** a person from ancient or modern Rome

Roman alphabet *n* the alphabet evolved by the ancient Romans for writing Latin, used for writing most of the languages of W Europe, including English

Roman blind *n* a window blind which gathers into horizontal folds from the bottom when drawn up

Roman candle *n* a firework that produces a steady stream of coloured sparks
WORD ORIGIN it originated in Italy

Roman Catholic *adj* **1** of the Roman Catholic Church ▷ *n* **2** a member of this Church **Roman Catholicism** *n*

Roman Catholic Church *n* the Christian Church over which the pope presides

romance *n* **1** a love affair: *a failed romance* **2** love, esp. romantic love idealized for its purity or beauty **3** a spirit of or inclination for adventure or mystery **4** a mysterious or sentimental quality **5** a story or film dealing with love, usually in an idealized way **6** a story or film dealing with events and characters remote from ordinary life **7** an extravagant, absurd, or fantastic account **8** a medieval narrative dealing with adventures of chivalrous heroes ▷ *vb* **-mancing, -manced 9** to tell extravagant or improbable lies
WORD ORIGIN Old French *romans*

Romance *adj* of the languages derived from Latin, such as French, Spanish, and Italian

Romanesque *adj* of or in the style of architecture used in Europe from the 9th to the 12th century, characterized by rounded arches and massive walls

Romanian *adj* **1** of Romania ▷ *n* **2** a person from Romania **3** the language of Romania

Roman nose *n* a nose with a high prominent bridge

Roman numerals *pl n* the letters used as numerals by the Romans, used occasionally today: I (= 1), V (= 5), X (= 10), L (= 50), C (= 100), D (= 500), and M (= 1000). VI = 6 (V + I) but IV = 4 (V – I)

romantic *adj* **1** of or dealing with love **2** idealistic but impractical: *a romantic notion* **3** evoking or given to thoughts and feelings of love: *romantic images* **4 Romantic** relating to a movement in European art, music, and literature in the late 18th and early 19th centuries, characterized by an emphasis on feeling and content rather than order and form ▷ *n* **5** a person who is idealistic or amorous **6** a person who likes or produces artistic works in the style of Romanticism **romantically** *adv*

romanticism *n* **1** idealistic but unrealistic thoughts and feelings **2 Romanticism** the spirit and style of the Romantic art, music, and literature of the late 18th and early 19th centuries **romanticist** *n*

romanticize *or* **-cise** *vb* **-cizing, -cized** *or* **-cising, -cised** to describe or regard (something or someone) in an unrealistic and idealized way: *the Victorian legacy of romanticizing family life*

Romany *n* **1** *pl* **-nies** a Gypsy **2** the language of the Gypsies
WORD ORIGIN Romany *romani* (adjective) Gypsy

Romeo *n, pl* **Romeos** an ardent male lover
WORD ORIGIN after the hero of Shakespeare's *Romeo and Juliet*

romp *vb* **1** to play or run about wildly or joyfully **2 romp home** *or* **in** to win a race or other competition easily **3 romp through** to do (something) quickly and easily ▷ *n* **4** a noisy or boisterous game or prank
WORD ORIGIN probably from Old French *ramper* to crawl, climb

rompers *pl n* Also called: **romper suit** a one-piece baby garment combining trousers and a top

rondavel *n S African* a small circular building with a cone-shaped roof
WORD ORIGIN origin unknown

rondeau (ron-doe) *n, pl* **-deaux** (-doe) a poem consisting of 13 or 10 lines with the opening words of the first line used as a refrain
WORD ORIGIN Old French

rondo *n, pl* **-dos** a piece of music with a leading theme continually returned to: often forms the last movement of a sonata or concerto
WORD ORIGIN Italian

roo *n, pl* **roos** *Austral informal* a kangaroo

rood *n* **1** *Christianity* the Cross **2** a crucifix
WORD ORIGIN Old English *rōd*

rood screen *n* (in a church) a screen separating the nave from the choir

roof *n, pl* **roofs 1** a structure that covers or forms the top of a building **2** the top covering of a vehicle, oven, or other structure **3** the highest part of the mouth or a cave **4 hit** *or* **go through the roof** *informal* to get extremely angry **5 raise the roof** *informal* to be very noisy ▷ *vb* **6** to put a roof on
WORD ORIGIN Old English *hrōf*

roof garden *n* a garden on a flat roof of a building

roofing *n* material used to build a roof

roof rack *n* a rack for carrying luggage attached to the roof of a car

rooftree *n* same as **ridgepole**

rooibos (roy-boss) *n S African* a kind of tea made from the leaves of a South African wild shrub. Also called: **rooibos tea, bush tea**
WORD ORIGIN Afrikaans *rooi* red + *bos* bush

rooinek (roy-neck) *n S African* a contemptuous name for an Englishman
WORD ORIGIN Afrikaans *rooi* red + *nek* neck

rook¹ *n* **1** a large European black bird of the crow family ▷ *vb* **2** *old-fashioned, slang* to cheat or swindle
WORD ORIGIN Old English *hrōc*

rook² *n* a chessman that may move any number of unoccupied squares in a straight line, horizontally or vertically; castle
WORD ORIGIN Arabic *rukhkh*

rookery n, pl **-eries 1** a group of nesting rooks **2** a colony of penguins or seals

rookie n informal a newcomer without much experience **WORD ORIGIN** changed from recruit

room n **1** an area within a building enclosed by a floor, a ceiling, and walls **2** the people present in a room: the whole room was laughing **3** unoccupied or unobstructed space: there wasn't enough room **4** **room for** opportunity or scope for: there was no room for acts of heroism **5** **rooms** lodgings ▷ vb **6** US to occupy or share a rented room: I roomed with him for five years **WORD ORIGIN** Old English rūm

rooming house n US a house with self-contained furnished rooms or flats for renting

roommate n a person with whom one shares a room or apartment

room service n service in a hotel providing food and drinks in guests' rooms

roomy adj **roomier**, **roomiest** with plenty of space inside: a roomy entrance hall **roominess** n

roost n **1** a place where birds rest or sleep ▷ vb **2** to rest or sleep on a roost **3** **come home to roost** to have unfavourable repercussions **4** **rule the roost** to have authority over people in a particular place **WORD ORIGIN** Old English hrōst

rooster n the male of the domestic fowl; a cock

root[1] n **1** the part of a plant that anchors the rest of the plant in the ground and absorbs water and mineral salts from the soil **2** a plant with an edible root, such as a carrot **3** anat the part of a tooth, hair, or nail that is below the skin **4** **roots** a person's sense of belonging in a place, esp. the one in which he or she was brought up **5** source or origin **6** the essential part or nature of something: the root of a problem **7** linguistics the form of a word from which other words and forms are derived **8** maths a quantity that when multiplied by itself a certain number of times equals a given quantity: what is the cube root of a thousand? **9** Also called: **solution** maths a number that when substituted for the variable satisfies a given equation **10** Austral & NZ slang sexual intercourse **11** **root and branch** entirely or utterly ▶ Related adjective: **radical** vb **12** Also: **take root** to establish a root and begin to grow **13** Also: **take root** to become established or embedded **14** Austral & NZ slang to have sexual intercourse (with) ▶ See also **root out**, **roots** **WORD ORIGIN** Old English rōt

root[2] vb **1** Brit to dig up the earth in search of food, using the snout: dogs were rooting in the rushes for bones **2** informal to search vigorously but unsystematically: she was rooting around in her large untidy purse **WORD ORIGIN** Old English wrōtan

root canal n the passage in the root of a tooth through which its nerves and blood vessels enter

root crop n a crop, such as potato or turnip, cultivated for its roots

root for vb informal to give support to (a team or contestant) **WORD ORIGIN** origin unknown

rootle vb **-ling**, **-led** Brit same as **root**[2]

rootless adj having no sense of belonging: a rootless city dweller

root mean square n the square root of the average of the squares of a set of numbers or quantities, for example the root mean square of 1, 2, and 4 is $\sqrt{[(1^2 + 2^2 + 4^2)/3]} = \sqrt{7}$

root out vb to get rid of completely: a major drive to root out corruption

roots adj (of popular music) going back to the origins of a style, esp. in being unpretentious: roots reggae

rootstock n same as **rhizome**

rope n **1** a fairly thick cord made of intertwined fibres or wire **2** a row of objects fastened to form a line: a twenty-inch rope of pearls **3** **know the ropes** to have a thorough understanding of a particular activity **4** **the rope a** a rope noose used for hanging someone **b** death by hanging ▷ vb **roping**, **roped 5** to tie with a rope **6** **rope off** to enclose or divide with a rope **WORD ORIGIN** Old English rāp

rope in vb to persuade to take part in some activity

ropey or **ropy** adj **ropier**, **ropiest** Brit informal **1** poor or unsatisfactory in quality: a ropey performance **2** slightly unwell **ropiness** n

Roquefort n a strong blue-veined cheese made from ewes' milk **WORD ORIGIN** after Roquefort, village in S France

ro-ro adj (of a ferry) roll-on/roll-off

rorqual n a whalebone whale with a fin on the back **WORD ORIGIN** Norwegian rörhval

Rorschach test (**ror**-shahk) n psychol a personality test consisting of a number of unstructured inkblots for interpretation **WORD ORIGIN** after H. Rorschach, psychiatrist

rort Austral informal n **1** a dishonest scheme ▷ vb **2** to take unfair advantage of something

rosaceous adj of or belonging to a family of plants typically having five-petalled flowers, which includes the rose, strawberry, and many fruit trees

rosary n, pl **-saries** RC Church **1** a series of prayers counted on a string of beads **2** a string of beads used to count these prayers as they are recited **WORD ORIGIN** Latin rosarium rose garden

rose[1] n **1** a shrub or climbing plant with prickly stems and fragrant flowers **2** the flower of any of these plants **3** a plant similar to this, such as the Christmas rose **4** a perforated cap fitted to a watering can or hose, causing the water to come out in a spray **5** **bed of roses** a situation of comfort or ease ▷ adj **6** reddish-pink **WORD ORIGIN** Latin rosa

rose[2] vb the past tense of **rise**

rosé (**roe**-zay) n a pink wine **WORD ORIGIN** French

roseate (**roe**-zee-ate) adj **1** of the colour rose or pink **2** excessively optimistic

rosebay willowherb n a widespread perennial plant that has spikes of deep pink flowers

rosebud n a rose that has not yet fully opened

rose-coloured adj **1** reddish-pink **2** **see through rose-coloured** or **rose-tinted glasses** or **spectacles** to view in an unrealistically optimistic light

rosehip n the berry-like fruit of a rose plant

rosella n a type of Australian parrot

rosemary n, pl **-maries** an aromatic European shrub widely cultivated for its grey-green evergreen leaves, which are used in cookery and perfumes **WORD ORIGIN** Latin ros dew + marinus marine

rosette n a rose-shaped decoration, esp. a circular bunch of ribbons

rose-water n scented water made by the distillation of rose petals

rose window n a circular window with spokes branching out from the centre to form a symmetrical roselike pattern

rosewood n a fragrant dark wood used to make furniture

Rosh Hashanah or **Rosh Hashana** n the festival celebrating the Jewish New Year **WORD ORIGIN** Hebrew: beginning of the year

rosin (**rozz**-in) n **1** a translucent brittle substance produced from turpentine and used for treating the bows of stringed instruments ▷ vb **2** to apply rosin to **WORD ORIGIN** variant of resin

ROSPA (in Britain) Royal Society for the Prevention of Accidents

roster n **1** a list showing the order in which people are to perform a duty ▷ vb **2** to place on a roster **WORD ORIGIN** Dutch rooster grating or list

rostrum n, pl **-trums** or **-tra** a platform or stage **WORD ORIGIN** Latin: beak

rosy adj **rosier**, **rosiest 1** of the colour rose or pink: rosy cheeks **2** hopeful or promising: the analysis revealed a far from rosy picture **rosiness** n

rot vb **rotting**, **rotted 1** to decay or cause to decay **2** to deteriorate slowly, mentally and physically: I thought he was either dead or rotting in a Chinese jail ▷ n **3** the process of rotting or the state of being rotten **4** something decomposed **5** short for **dry rot 6** a plant or animal disease which causes decay of the tissues **7** nonsense **WORD ORIGIN** Old English rotian

rota n a list of people who take it in turn to do a particular task **WORD ORIGIN** Latin: a wheel

rotary adj **1** revolving **2** operating by rotation ▷ n, pl **-ries 3** US & Canad a traffic roundabout

Rotary Club n a club that is part of **Rotary International**, an international association of professionals and businesspeople who raise money for charity **Rotarian** n, adj

rotate vb -tating, -tated 1 to turn around a centre or pivot 2 to follow or cause to follow a set sequence 3 to regularly change the type of crop grown on a piece of land in order to preserve the fertility of the soil **rotation** n **rotational** adj
WORD ORIGIN Latin rota wheel

rotator cuff n anat the structure around the shoulder joint consisting of the capsule of the joint along with the tendons of the adjacent muscles

Rotavator n trademark a mechanical cultivator with rotary blades

rote adj 1 done by routine repetition: rote learning ▷ n 2 **by rote** by repetition: we learned by rote
WORD ORIGIN origin unknown

rotgut n chiefly Brit facetious slang alcoholic drink of inferior quality

rotisserie n a rotating spit on which meat and poultry can be cooked
WORD ORIGIN French

rotor n 1 the rotating part of a machine or device, such as the revolving arm of the distributor of an internal-combustion engine 2 a rotating device with blades projecting from a hub which produces thrust to lift a helicopter

rotten adj 1 decomposing or decaying: rotten vegetables 2 breaking up through age or hard use: the window frames are rotten 3 informal very bad: what rotten luck! 4 morally corrupt: this country's politics are rotten and out of date 5 informal miserably unwell: I had glandular fever and spent that year feeling rotten 6 informal distressed and embarrassed: I'm feeling rotten as a matter of fact, rotten and guilty ▷ adv 7 informal extremely; very much: men fancy her rotten
WORD ORIGIN Old Norse rotinn

rotter n chiefly Brit old-fashioned slang a despicable person

Rottweiler (rot-vile-er) n a large sturdy dog with a smooth black-and-tan coat and a docked tail
WORD ORIGIN Rottweil, German city where it was first bred

rotund (roe-tund) adj 1 round and plump 2 (of speech) pompous or grand **rotundity** n **rotundly** adv
WORD ORIGIN Latin rotundus

rotunda n a circular building or room, esp. with a dome
WORD ORIGIN Italian rotonda

rouble or **ruble** (roo-bl) n the standard monetary unit of Russia and Tadzhikistan
WORD ORIGIN Russian rubl

roué (roo-ay) n a man who leads a sensual and immoral life
WORD ORIGIN French

rouge n 1 a red cosmetic for adding colour to the cheeks ▷ vb **rouging**, **rouged** 2 to apply rouge to
WORD ORIGIN French: red

rough adj 1 not smooth; uneven or irregular 2 not using enough care or gentleness 3 difficult or unpleasant: tomorrow will be a rough day 4 approximate: a rough guess 5 violent or stormy 6 troubled by violence or crime: he lived in a rough area 7 incomplete or basic: a rough draft 8 lacking refinement: a rough shelter 9 (of ground) covered with scrub or rubble 10 harsh or grating to the ear 11 harsh or sharp: the rough interrogation of my father 12 unfair; rough luck 13 informal ill: Feeling rough? A good stiff drink will soon fix that! 14 shaggy or hairy: the rough wool of her sweater 15 (of work etc.) requiring physical rather than mental effort: wear gloves for any rough work ▷ vb 16 to make rough 17 **rough it** informal to live without the usual comforts of life ▷ n 18 rough ground 19 a sketch or preliminary piece of artwork 20 informal a violent person 21 **in rough** in an unfinished or crude state 22 **the rough** golf the part of the course beside the fairways where the grass is untrimmed 23 the unpleasant side of something: you have to take the rough with the smooth ▷ adv 24 roughly 25 **sleep rough** to spend the night in the open without shelter ▸ See also **rough out, rough up** ▷ **roughly** adv
WORD ORIGIN Old English rūh

roughage n the coarse indigestible constituents of food, which help digestion

rough-and-ready adj 1 hastily prepared but adequate for the purpose 2 (of a person) without formality or refinement

rough-and-tumble n 1 a playful fight 2 a disorderly situation

roughcast n 1 a mixture of plaster and small stones for outside walls ▷ vb -casting, -cast 2 to put roughcast on (a wall)

rough diamond n 1 an unpolished diamond 2 a kind or trustworthy person whose manners are not good

roughen vb to make or become rough

rough-hewn adj roughly shaped or cut without being properly finished

roughhouse n slang rough or noisy behaviour

roughneck n slang 1 a violent person 2 a worker on an oil rig

rough out vb to prepare (a sketch or report) in preliminary form: he offered to rough out some designs for the sets

roughshod adv **ride roughshod over** to act with complete disregard for

rough up vb informal to beat up

roulette n a gambling game in which a ball is dropped onto a revolving wheel with numbered coloured slots
WORD ORIGIN French

round adj 1 having a flat circular shape, like a hoop 2 having the shape of a ball 3 curved; not angular 4 involving or using circular motion 5 complete 6 maths **a** forming or expressed by a whole number, with no fraction **b** expressed to the nearest ten, hundred, or thousand: in round figures ▷ adv 7 on all or most sides 8 on or outside the circumference or perimeter: ponds which are steeply sided all round 9 in rotation or revolution: she swung round on me 10 by a circuitous route: a four-month cruise round the Mediterranean 11 to all members of a group: handing cigarettes round 12 to a specific place: the boys invited him round 13 **all year round** throughout the year ▷ prep 14 surrounding or encircling: wrap your sash round the wound 15 on all or most sides of: the man turned in a circle, looking all round him 16 on or outside the circumference or perimeter of 17 from place to place in: a trip round the island in an ancient bus 18 reached by making a partial circuit about: just round the corner 19 revolving about: if you have two bodies in orbit, they orbit round their common centre of gravity ▷ vb 20 to move round: as he rounded the last corner, he raised a fist ▷ n 21 a round shape or object 22 a session: a round of talks 23 a series: the petty round of domestic matters 24 a series of calls: a paper round 25 the daily round the usual activities of a person's day 26 a playing of all the holes on a golf course 27 a stage of a competition: the first round of the Portuguese Open 28 one of a number of periods in a boxing or wrestling match 29 a single turn of play by each player in a card game 30 a number of drinks bought at one time for a group of people 31 a bullet or shell for a gun 32 a single discharge by a gun 33 music a part song in which the voices follow each other at equal intervals 34 circular movement 35 **a** a single slice of bread **b** a serving of sandwiches made from two complete slices of bread 36 a general outburst: a round of applause 37 **in the round a** in full detail **b** theatre with the audience all round the stage 38 **go the rounds** (of information or infection) to be passed around from person to person ▸ See also **round down, round off**
WORD ORIGIN Old French ront
≡**USAGE**
≡See at **around**.

roundabout n 1 a road junction in which traffic moves in one direction around a central island 2 a revolving circular platform, often with seats, on which people ride for amusement ▷ adj 3 not straightforward: the roundabout sea route; she thought of asking about it in a roundabout way ▷ adv, prep **round about 4** approximately: round about 1900

round dance n 1 a dance in which the dancers form a circle 2 a ballroom dance, such as the waltz, in which couples revolve

round down vb to lower (a number) to the nearest whole number or ten, hundred, or thousand below it

roundel n 1 a circular identifying mark on military aircraft 2 a small circular object
WORD ORIGIN Old French rondel little circle

roundelay n a song in which a line or phrase is repeated as a refrain
WORD ORIGIN Old French rondelet

rounders n Brit & NZ a bat and ball game in which players run between posts after hitting the ball

Roundhead n English history a supporter of Parliament against Charles I during the Civil War
WORD ORIGIN referring to their short-cut hair

roundhouse n US & Canad a circular building in which railway locomotives are serviced

Esperanto

Esperanto is an artificial language, created by Ludwig Lazarus Zamenhof (1859–1917), a Polish oculist and philologist. He published its first manual in 1887 under a pseudonym, Doktoro Esperanto, before producing the authoritative version, *Fundamento de Esperanto*, in 1905. Zamenhof's intention was to create a language that was easy to learn and suitable for international use. He believed that because it would be derived from several languages, it would be politically neutral, and so its use could help reduce resentment and cultivate peace between nations. *Esperanto*, in Esperanto, means 'the one who hopes' (from Latin *sperare* 'to hope'), thus encapsulating Zamenhof's aspirations for the language he had invented.

Esperanto takes its structure and vocabulary from European languages, and so it can be considered part of the larger Indo-European family to which these languages belong. Most of Esperanto vocabulary is borrowed from Romance languages, eg *amika* (friendly) from Latin *amicus*, with a large proportion taken from Germanic languages including English, eg *jes* from *yes*. The remainder is made up of Greek and Slavonic elements, eg *kaj* ('and') from Greek *kai*. However, individual words can be created from a number of roots, and so may incorporate elements of different languages.

Zamenhof's original manual supplied around 900 root words, with a derivational morphology that allowed the user to create a number of words using roots and affixes, so that fewer individual items had to be learned. Thus, *malgranda* ('small') is derived from *mal-* (negating prefix) and *granda* ('big'), and *memorinda* ('memorable') is formed from *memor* ('memory') and *-inda* ('worthy of'). Compounding is also used in word formation, eg *birdokanto* ('birdsong'). This is not to say that the vocabulary of Esperanto has not been augmented – many new words have been borrowed to refer to new concepts, often technical or scientific. However, the more commonly used terms are usually derived from existing words in Esperanto, eg *komputilo* ('computer'), from Esperanto *komputi* ('to compute').

Grammatically, Esperanto is inflectional, with fixed paradigms: nouns end in *-o*, eg *hundo* ('dog'), adjectives end in *-a*, eg *bona* ('good'). Plurals end in *-j* (*bonaj hundoj*), with the adjective agreeing with the noun, and direct objects end in *-on*. There are six verb inflections, with three tenses and three moods. The infinitive verb ends in *-i*, eg *havi* ('to have'), with the ending *-as* used for the present tense, *-is* for the past, and *-os* for the future; and *-us* for conditional and *-u* for jussive (used for wishes and commands). Verbs are not changed according to the number or person of the subject, so the same verb form is used for singular or plural, or for first, second, or third person.

Grammatical function words in Esperanto include pronouns, such as the personal, eg *vi* ('you') and *mi* ('I'), and the demonstrative, eg *tio* ('that'). Prepositions always come at the beginning of a noun phrase (word order is otherwise fairly free, although in practice sentences usually have the subject-verb-object order typical of English). There is a single definite article, *la*, used in a similar way to English 'the', but no indefinite article corresponding to 'a', with a word such as *hundo* meaning 'dog' or 'a dog' depending on context, eg *hundo estas besto* ('a dog is an animal').

The spelling system of Esperanto is phonetic, using a 28-letter alphabet that does not contain *q, w, x,* or *y,* but does include ĉ, ĝ, ĥ, ĵ, ŝ, representing the sounds found in *chair, germ, loch, déjà vu,* and *ship* respectively. The alphabet also includes ŭ, which is combined with other vowels to form diphthongs. There are only five cardinal vowels in the alphabet, so their pronunciation can vary considerably from speaker to speaker; *e*, for example can range from the sound in *grey* to the sound in *bed*). In spoken Esperanto, stress is put on the second-last syllable of polysyllabic words.

Esperanto has the features of a well established language, with false friends and puns, and contractions such as *sa* for *saluton* ('hello'). It is now the most widely spoken artificial language, with users estimated anywhere between 500,000 and two million worldwide, and its own international organization. Its recognition is such that the word *Esperanto* is sometimes used to refer to any mode of expression that is either artificial or universally understood. On this evidence, Esperanto has been a success, even if has not achieved the status of the world's second language.

roundly *adv* bluntly or thoroughly: *the Church roundly criticized the bill*

round off *vb* to complete agreeably or successfully: *our afternoon was rounded off with coffee and biscuits*

round on *vb* to attack or reply to (someone) with sudden irritation or anger

round robin *n* **1** a petition with the signatures in a circle to disguise the order of signing **2** a tournament in which each player plays against every other player

round-shouldered *adj* denoting poor posture with drooping shoulders and a slight forward bending of the back

round table *n* a meeting of people on equal terms for discussion

Round Table *n* **1** (in Arthurian legend) the table of King Arthur, shaped so that his knights could sit around as equals **2** one of an organization of clubs of young business and professional men who meet in order to further charitable work

round-the-clock *adj* throughout the day and night

round trip *n* a journey to a place and back again

round up *vb* **1** to gather together: *the police had rounded up a circle of drug users* **2** to raise (a number) to the nearest whole number or ten, hundred, or thousand above it ▷ *n* **roundup 3** a summary or discussion of news and information **4** the act of gathering together livestock or people

roundworm *n* a worm that is a common intestinal parasite of man

rouse¹ *vb* **rousing, roused 1** to wake up **2** to provoke or excite: *his temper was roused and he had a gun* **3 rouse oneself** to become energetic
WORD ORIGIN origin unknown

rouse² (rhymes with **mouse**) *vb* (foll. by *on*) *Austral* to scold or rebuke

rouseabout *n Austral & NZ* a labourer in a shearing shed

rousing *adj* lively or vigorous: *a rousing speech*

roustabout *n* **1** an unskilled labourer on an oil rig **2** *Austral & NZ* another word for **rouseabout**

rout¹ *n* **1** an overwhelming defeat **2** a disorderly retreat **3** a noisy rabble ▷ *vb* **4** to defeat and put to flight
WORD ORIGIN Anglo-Norman *rute*

rout² *vb* **1** to find by searching **2** to drive out: *the dissidents had been routed out* **3** to dig (something) up
WORD ORIGIN variant of ROOT²

route *n* **1** the choice of roads taken to get to a place **2** a fixed path followed by buses, trains, etc. between two places **3** a chosen way or method: *the route to prosperity* ▷ *vb* **routeing, routed 4** to send by a particular route
WORD ORIGIN Old French *rute*

≡ **USAGE**
≡ When forming the present participle
≡ or verbal noun from the verb *to route* it
≡ is preferable to retain the *e* in order to
≡ distinguish the word from *routing*, the
≡ present participle or verbal noun from
≡ *rout¹*, to defeat, or *rout²*, to dig,

≡ rummage: *the routeing of buses from the*
≡ *city centre to the suburbs*. The spelling
≡ *routing* in this sense is, however,
≡ sometimes encountered, esp. in
≡ American English.

routemarch *n mil* a long training march

router *n computers* a device that allows data to be moved efficiently between two points on a network

routine *n* **1** a usual or regular method of procedure **2** the boring repetition of tasks: *mindless routine* **3** a set sequence of dance steps **4** *computers* a program or part of a program performing a specific function: *an input routine* ▷ *adj* **5** relating to or characteristic of routine
WORD ORIGIN Old French *route* a customary way

roux (**roo**) *n* a cooked mixture of fat and flour used as a basis for sauces
WORD ORIGIN French: brownish

rove *vb* **roving, roved 1** to wander about (a place) **2** (of the eyes) to look around **rover** *n*
WORD ORIGIN probably from Old Norse

row¹ (rhymes with **know**) *n* **1** an arrangement of people or things in a line: *a row of shops* **2** a line of seats in a cinema or theatre **3** *Brit* a street lined with identical houses **4** *maths* a horizontal line of numbers **5 in a row** in succession: *five championships in a row*
WORD ORIGIN Old English *rāw, rǣw*

row² (rhymes with **know**) *vb* **1** to propel (a boat) by using oars **2** to carry (people or goods) in a rowing boat **3** to take part in the racing of rowing boats as a sport ▷ *n* **4** an act or spell of rowing **5** an excursion in a rowing boat **rowing** *n*
WORD ORIGIN Old English *rōwan*

row³ (rhymes with **cow**) *informal n* **1** a noisy quarrel **2** a controversy or dispute: *the row over Europe* **3** a noisy disturbance: *go to the insurance offices and kick up a row about your money* **4** a reprimand ▷ *vb* **5** to quarrel noisily
WORD ORIGIN origin unknown

rowan *n* a European tree with white flowers and red berries; mountain ash
WORD ORIGIN Scandinavian

rowdy *adj* **-dier, -diest 1** rough, noisy, or disorderly ▷ *n, pl* **-dies 2** a person like this **rowdily** *adv*
WORD ORIGIN origin unknown

rowel (rhymes with **towel**) *n* a small spiked wheel at the end of a spur
WORD ORIGIN Old French *roel* a little wheel

rowing boat *n* a small pleasure boat propelled by oars. Usual US and Canad word: **rowboat**

rowlock (**rol**-luk) *n* a swivelling device attached to the top of the side of a boat that holds an oar in place

royal *adj* **1** of or relating to a king or queen or a member of his or her family: *the royal yacht* **2 Royal** supported by or in the service of royalty: *the Royal Society of Medicine* **3** very grand: *royal treatment* ▷ *n* **4** *informal* a king or queen or a member of his or her family **royally** *adv*
WORD ORIGIN Old French *roial*

Royal Air Force *n* the air force of the United Kingdom

royal-blue *adj* deep blue

royalist *n* **1** a supporter of a monarch or monarchy ▷ *adj* **2** of or relating to royalists **royalism** *n*

royal jelly *n* a substance secreted by worker bees and fed to all larvae when very young and to larvae destined to become queens throughout their growth

Royal Marines *pl n Brit* a corps of soldiers specially trained in amphibious warfare

Royal Navy *n* the navy of the United Kingdom

royalty *n, pl* **-ties 1** royal people **2** the rank or power of a king or queen **3** a percentage of the revenue from the sale of a book, performance of a work, use of a patented invention or of land, paid to the author, inventor, or owner

royal warrant *n* an authorization to a tradesman to supply goods to a royal household

RPI (in Britain) retail price index: a measure of the changes in the average level of retail prices of selected goods

rpm revolutions per minute

RR 1 Right Reverend **2** *US & Canad* rural route

RSA 1 Republic of South Africa **2** (in New Zealand) Returned Services Association **3** Royal Scottish Academy **4** Royal Society of Arts

RSI repetitive strain injury: pain in the arm caused by repeated awkward movements, such as in typing

RSM (in Britain) regimental sergeant major

RSPCA (in Britain) Royal Society for the Prevention of Cruelty to Animals

RSS Rich Site Summary *or* Really Simple Syndication: a way of allowing web users to receive updated information from selected websites on their browser

RSVP please reply
WORD ORIGIN French *répondez s'il vous plaît*

RTA *Brit* road traffic accident

Rt Hon. Right Honourable: a title of respect for a Privy Councillor, certain peers, and the Lord Mayor or Lord Provost of certain cities

Ru *chem* ruthenium

RU486 *n* the technical name for **abortion pill**

rub *vb* **rubbing, rubbed 1** to apply pressure and friction to (something) with a circular or backwards-and-forwards movement **2** to move (something) with pressure along or against (a surface) **3** to clean, polish, or dry by rubbing **4** to spread with pressure, esp. so that it can be absorbed: *rub beeswax into all polishable surfaces* **5** to chafe or fray through rubbing **6** to mix (fat) into flour with the fingertips, as in making pastry **7 rub it in** to emphasize an unpleasant fact **8 rub up the wrong way** to annoy ▷ *n* **9** the act of rubbing **10 the rub** the obstacle or difficulty: *there's the rub* ▸ See also **rub along, rub down**, etc.
WORD ORIGIN origin unknown

rub along *vb* **1** to have a friendly relationship **2** to continue in spite of difficulties

rubato *music n, pl* **-tos 1** flexibility of tempo in performance: *his playing brought much beautifully felt but never sentimental rubato to the music* ▷ *adj, adv* **2** to be played with a flexible tempo
WORD ORIGIN Italian, literally: robbed

rubber[1] *n* **1** an elastic material obtained from the latex of certain plants, such as the rubber tree **2** a similar substance produced synthetically **3** a piece of rubber used for erasing something written **4** *US slang* a condom **5 rubbers** *US* rubber-coated waterproof overshoes ▷ *adj* **6** made of or producing rubber **rubbery** *adj*
WORD ORIGIN the tree was so named because its product was used for rubbing out writing

rubber[2] *n* **1** *bridge, whist* a match of three games **2** a series of matches or games in various sports
WORD ORIGIN origin unknown

rubber band *n* a continuous loop of thin rubber, used to hold papers together

rubberize *or* **-ise** *vb* **-izing, -ized** *or* **-ising, -ised** to coat or treat with rubber

rubberneck *slang vb* **1** to stare in a naive or foolish manner ▷ *n* **2** a person who stares inquisitively **3** a sightseer or tourist

rubber plant *n* **1** a large house plant with glossy leathery leaves **2** same as **rubber tree**

rubber stamp *n* **1** a device used for imprinting dates or signatures on forms or invoices **2** automatic authorization of something **3** a person or body that gives official approval to decisions taken elsewhere but has no real power ▷ *vb* **rubber-stamp 4** *informal* to approve automatically

rubber tree *n* a tropical tree cultivated for its latex, which is the major source of commercial rubber

rubbing *n* an impression taken of an engraved or raised design by laying paper over it and rubbing with wax or charcoal

rubbish *n* **1** discarded or waste matter **2** anything worthless or of poor quality: *the rubbish on television* **3** foolish words or speech ▷ *vb* **4** *informal* to criticize **rubbishy** *adj*
WORD ORIGIN origin unknown

rubble *n* **1** debris from ruined buildings **2** pieces of broken stones or bricks
WORD ORIGIN origin unknown

rub down *vb* **1** to prepare (a surface) for painting by rubbing it with sandpaper **2** to dry or clean (an animal or person) vigorously, esp. after exercise

rubella (roo-**bell**-a) *n* a mild contagious viral disease characterized by cough, sore throat, and skin rash. Also called: **German measles**
WORD ORIGIN Latin *rubellus* reddish

Rubicon (**roo**-bik-on) *n* **cross the Rubicon** to commit oneself to a course of action which cannot be altered
WORD ORIGIN a stream in N Italy: by leading his army across it, Julius Caesar caused civil war in Rome in 49 BC

rubicund (**roo**-bik-kund) *adj* old-fashioned of a reddish colour
WORD ORIGIN Latin *rubicundus*

rubidium (roo-**bid**-ee-um) *n chem* a soft highly reactive radioactive metallic element used in electronic valves, photocells, and special glass. Symbol: Rb
WORD ORIGIN Latin *rubidus* red

ruble *n* same as **rouble**

rub off *vb* **1** to remove or be removed by rubbing: *rub the skins off the hazelnuts* **2** to have an effect through close association: *glamour can rub off on you by association*

rub out *vb* **1** to remove or be removed with a rubber **2** *US slang* to murder

rubric (**roo**-brik) *n* **1** a set of rules of conduct or procedure, esp. one for the conduct of Christian church services **2** a title or heading in a book
WORD ORIGIN Latin *ruber* red

ruby *n, pl* **-bies 1** a deep red transparent precious gemstone ▷ *adj* **2** deep red **3** denoting a fortieth anniversary: *a ruby wedding*
WORD ORIGIN Latin *ruber* red

RUC Royal Ulster Constabulary: a former name for the Police Service of Northern Ireland

ruche *n* a strip of pleated or frilled lace or ribbon used to decorate clothes
WORD ORIGIN French, literally: beehive

ruck[1] *n* **1 the ruck** ordinary people, often in a crowd **2** *rugby* a loose scrum that forms around the ball when it is on the ground
WORD ORIGIN probably from Old Norse

ruck[2] *n* **1** a wrinkle or crease ▷ *vb* **2** to wrinkle or crease: *the toe of his shoe had rucked up one corner of the pale rug*
WORD ORIGIN Scandinavian

rucksack *n Brit, Austral, & S African* a large bag, with two straps, carried on the back
WORD ORIGIN from German

ruction *n informal* **1** an uproar **2 ructions** an unpleasant row
WORD ORIGIN origin unknown

rudder *n* **1** *naut* a vertical hinged piece that projects into the water at the stern, used to steer a boat **2** a vertical control surface attached to the rear of the fin used to steer an aircraft **rudderless** *adj*
WORD ORIGIN Old English *rōther*

ruddy *adj* **-dier, -diest 1** (of the complexion) having a healthy reddish colour **2** red or pink: *a ruddy glow* ▷ *adv, adj* **3** *informal* bloody: *too ruddy slow; I just went through the ruddy ceiling*
WORD ORIGIN Old English *rudig*

rude *adj* **1** insulting or impolite **2** vulgar or obscene: *rude words* **3** unexpected and unpleasant: *we received a rude awakening* **4** roughly or crudely made: *the rude hovels* **5** robust or sturdy: *the very picture of rude health* **6** lacking refinement **rudely** *adv* **rudeness** *n*
WORD ORIGIN Latin *rudis*

rudiment *n* **1 rudiments a** the simplest and most basic stages of a subject: *the rudiments of painting* **b** a partially developed version of something: *the rudiments of a democratic society* **2** *biol* an organ or part that is incompletely developed or no longer functions **rudimentary** *adj*
WORD ORIGIN Latin *rudimentum*

rue[1] *vb* **ruing, rued** *literary* to feel regret for
WORD ORIGIN Old English *hrēowan*

rue[2] *n* an aromatic shrub with bitter evergreen leaves formerly used in medicine
WORD ORIGIN Greek *rhutē*

rueful *adj* feeling or expressing sorrow or regret: *a rueful smile* **ruefully** *adv*

ruff[1] *n* **1** a circular pleated or fluted cloth collar **2** a natural growth of long or coloured hair or feathers around the necks of certain animals or birds **3** a bird of the sandpiper family
WORD ORIGIN from *ruffle*

ruff[2] *n, vb cards* same as **trump**[1] (senses 1, 2)
WORD ORIGIN Old French *roffle*

ruffian *n* a violent lawless person
WORD ORIGIN Old French *rufien*

ruffle *vb* **-fling, -fled 1** to disturb the smoothness of: *the wind was ruffling Dad's hair* **2** to annoy or irritate **3** (of a bird) to erect its feathers in anger or display **4** to flick cards or pages rapidly ▷ *n* **5** a strip of pleated material used as a trim
WORD ORIGIN Germanic

rufous *adj* (of birds or animals) reddish-brown
WORD ORIGIN Latin *rufus*

rug *n* **1** a small carpet **2** a thick woollen blanket **3** *slang* a wig **4 pull the rug out from under** to betray or leave defenceless
WORD ORIGIN Scandinavian

rugby *or* **rugby football** *n* a form of football played with an oval ball in which the handling and carrying of the ball is permitted
WORD ORIGIN after the public school at *Rugby*, where it was first played

rugby league *n* a form of rugby played between teams of 13 players

rugby union *n* a form of rugby played between teams of 15 players

rugged (**rug**-gid) *adj* **1** rocky or steep: *the rugged mountains of Sicily's interior* **2** with an uneven or jagged surface **3** (of the face) strong-featured **4** rough, sturdy, or determined in character **5** (of equipment or machines) designed to withstand rough treatment or use in rough conditions
WORD ORIGIN probably from Old Norse

rugger *n chiefly Brit informal* rugby

rug rat *n informal* a young child not yet walking

ruin *vb* **1** to destroy or spoil completely: *the suit was ruined* **2** to cause (someone) to lose money: *the first war ruined him* ▷ *n* **3** the state of being destroyed or decayed **4** loss of wealth or position **5** a destroyed or decayed building or town **6** something that is severely damaged: *my heart was an aching ruin*
WORD ORIGIN Latin *ruina* a falling down

ruination *n* **1** the act of ruining or the state of being ruined **2** something that causes ruin

ruinous *adj* **1** causing ruin or destruction **2** more expensive than can reasonably be afforded: *ruinous rates of exchange* **ruinously** *adv*

rule *n* **1** a statement of what is allowed, for example in a game or procedure **2** a customary form or procedure: *he has his own rule: be firm, be clear, but never be rude*

r

3 the rule the common order of things: *humanitarian gestures were more the exception than the rule* **4** the exercise of governmental authority or control: *the rule of President Marcos* **5** the period of time in which a monarch or government has power: *four decades of Communist rule* **6** a device with a straight edge for guiding or measuring: *a slide rule* **7** *printing* a long thin line or dash **8** *Christianity* a systematic body of laws and customs followed by members of a religious order **9** *law* an order by a court or judge **10 as a rule** usually ▷ *vb* **ruling, ruled 11** to govern (people or a political unit) **12** to be pre-eminent or superior **13** to be customary or prevalent: *chaos ruled as the scene turned into one of total confusion* **14** to decide authoritatively: *the judges ruled that men could be prosecuted for rape offences against their wives* **15** to mark with straight parallel lines or one straight line **16** to restrain or control **WORD ORIGIN** Old French *riule*

rule of thumb *n* a rough and practical approach, based on experience, rather than theory

rule out *vb* **1** to dismiss from consideration **2** to make impossible

ruler *n* **1** a person who rules or commands **2** a strip of wood, metal, or plastic, with straight edges, used for measuring and drawing straight lines

ruling *adj* **1** controlling or exercising authority **2** predominant ▷ *n* **3** a decision of someone in authority

rum¹ *n* alcoholic drink made from sugar cane **WORD ORIGIN** origin unknown

rum² *adj* **rummer, rummest** *Brit slang* strange or unusual **WORD ORIGIN** origin unknown

Rumanian *adj, n* same as **Romanian**

rumba *n* **1** a rhythmic and syncopated dance of Cuban origin **2** music for this dance **WORD ORIGIN** Spanish

rumble *vb* **-bling, -bled 1** to make or cause to make a deep echoing sound: *thunder rumbled overhead* **2** to move with such a sound: *a slow freight train rumbled past* **3** *Brit slang* to find out about (someone or something): *his real identity was rumbled* ▷ *n* **4** a deep resonant sound **5** *slang* a gang fight **rumbling** *adj, n* **WORD ORIGIN** probably from Middle Dutch *rummelen*

rumbustious *adj* boisterous or unruly **WORD ORIGIN** probably variant of *robustious*

ruminant *n* **1** a mammal that chews the cud, such as cattle, sheep, deer, goats, and camels ▷ *adj* **2** of ruminants **3** meditating or contemplating in a slow quiet way

ruminate *vb* **-nating, -nated 1** (of ruminants) to chew (the cud) **2** to meditate or ponder **rumination** *n* **ruminative** *adj* **WORD ORIGIN** Latin *ruminare* to chew the cud

rummage *vb* **-maging, -maged 1** to search untidily ▷ *n* **2** an untidy search through a collection of things **WORD ORIGIN** Old French *arrumage* to stow cargo

rummage sale *n* *US & Canad* a jumble sale

rummy *n* a card game based on collecting sets and sequences **WORD ORIGIN** origin unknown

rumour or *US* **rumor** *n* **1** information, often a mixture of truth and untruth, told by one person to another **2** gossip or common talk ▷ *vb* **3 be rumoured** to be circulated as a rumour: *he is rumoured to have at least 53 yachts* **WORD ORIGIN** Latin *rumor*

rump *n* **1** a person's buttocks **2** the rear part of an animal's or bird's body **3** Also called: **rump steak** a cut of beef from the rump **4** a small core of members within a group who remain loyal to it: *the rump of the once-influential communist party* **WORD ORIGIN** probably from Old Norse

rumple *vb* **-pling, -pled** to make or become crumpled or dishevelled **WORD ORIGIN** Middle Dutch *rompelen*

rumpus *n, pl* **-puses** a noisy or confused commotion **WORD ORIGIN** origin unknown

rumpy-pumpy *n* *informal* sexual intercourse

run *vb* **running, ran, run 1** to move on foot at a rapid pace **2** to pass over (a distance or route) in running: *being a man isn't about running the fastest mile* **3** to take part in (a race): *I ran a decent race* **4** to carry out as if by running: *he is running errands for his big brother* **5** to flee **6** to travel somewhere in a vehicle **7** to give a lift to (someone) in a vehicle: *one wet day I ran her down to the service* **8** to drive or maintain and operate (a vehicle) **9** to travel regularly between places on a route: *trains running through the night* **10** to move or pass quickly: *he ran his hand across his forehead* **11** to function or cause to function: *run the video tape backwards* **12** to manage: *he ran a small hotel* **13** to continue in a particular direction or for a particular time or distance: *a road running alongside the Nile; a performing arts festival running in the city for six weeks* **14** *law* to have legal force or effect: *the club's lease runs out next May* **15** to be subjected to or affected by: *she ran a high risk of losing her hair* **16** to tend or incline: *he was of medium height and running to fat* **17** to recur persistently or be inherent: *the capacity for infidelity ran in the genes* **18** to flow or cause (liquids) to flow: *sweat ran down her face* **19** to dissolve and spread: *the soles of the shoes peeled off and the colours ran* **20** (of stitches) to unravel **21** to spread or circulate: *rumours ran around quickly* **22** to publish or be published in a newspaper or magazine: *our local newspaper ran a story on the appeal* **23** *chiefly US & Canad* to stand as a candidate for political or other office: *he has formally announced his decision to run for the office of President* **24** to get past or through: *the oil tanker was hit as it tried to run the blockade* **25** to smuggle (goods, esp. arms) **26** (of fish) to migrate upstream from the sea, esp. in order to spawn **27** *cricket* to score (a run or number of runs) by hitting the ball and running between the wickets ▷ *n* **28** the act or an instance of running: *he broke into a run* **29** a distance covered by

running or a period of running: *it's a short run of about 20 kilometres* **30** a trip in a vehicle, esp. for pleasure: *our only treat is a run in the car to Dartmoor* **31** free and unrestricted access: *he had the run of the house* **32 a** a period of time during which a machine or computer operates **b** the amount of work performed in such a period **33** a continuous or sustained period: *a run of seven defeats* **34** a continuous sequence of performances: *the play had a long run* **35** *cards* a sequence of winning cards in one suit: *a run of spades* **36** type, class, or category: *he had nothing in common with the usual run of terrorists* **37** a continuous and urgent demand: *a run on the pound* **38** a series of unravelled stitches, esp. in tights **39** a steeply inclined course, esp. a snow-covered one used for skiing **40** an enclosure for domestic fowls or other animals: *the chicken run* **41** (esp. in Australia and New Zealand) a tract of land for grazing livestock **42** the migration of fish upstream in order to spawn **43** *music* a rapid scalelike passage of notes **44** *cricket* a score of one, normally achieved by both batsmen running from one end of the wicket to the other after one of them has hit the ball **45** *baseball* an instance of a batter touching all four bases safely, thereby scoring **46 a run for one's money** *informal* **a** a close competition **b** pleasure or success from an activity **47 in the long run** as an eventual outcome **48 on the run** escaping from arrest **49 the runs** *slang* diarrhoea ▷ See also **runabout, run across,** etc. **WORD ORIGIN** Old English *runnen*

runabout *n* **1** a small car used for short journeys ▷ *vb* **run about 2** to move busily from place to place

run across *vb* to meet unexpectedly by chance

run along *vb* to go away

run away *vb* **1** to go away **2** to escape **3** (of a horse) to gallop away uncontrollably: *the horse ran away with him* **4 run away with a** to abscond or elope with: *I ran away with David* **b** to escape from the control of: *he let his imagination run away with him* **c** to win easily or be certain of victory in (a competition): *the Spaniards at one stage seemed to be running away with the match* ▷ *n* **runaway 5** a person or animal that runs away ▷ *adj* **runaway 6** no longer under control: *a runaway train* **7** (of a race or victory) easily won

run down *vb* **1** to be rude about: *he is busy running us down and insulting other Europeans* **2** to reduce in number or size: *it should be possible to run down the existing hospitals almost entirely* **3** (of a device such as a clock or battery) to lose power gradually and cease to function **4** to hit and knock to the ground with a moving vehicle **5** to pursue and find or capture: *while I was there, Moscow ran me down, convinced I was ready to defect* ▷ *adj* **rundown 6** tired or ill **7** shabby or dilapidated ▷ *n* **rundown 8** a reduction in number or size **9** a brief review or summary

rune *n* **1** any of the characters of the earliest Germanic alphabet **2** an

American Situation Comedy

Ever since the television set became a household fixture in the 1950s, the situation comedy has offered to the world the smiling face of America. At first, it was overwhelmingly the white, middle-class face of the person who bought the products whose commercials funded the programmes. What this customer saw were recurring characters whose personalities were unchanging but who were embroiled in ever-changing comic interactions and entanglements among family members (*All in the Family*), frequenters of a neighbourhood hang-out (*Cheers*), co-workers (*Taxi*), or a cluster of pals (*Friends*). Such scenarios did not differ much from a long tradition of stage comedy, and the theatrical tradition found an echo in the applause-simulating laugh tracks that punctuated the action. At first, movie comedians such as Bob Hope and Milton Berle, and radio stars such as Jack Benny and the team of George Burns and Gracie Allen, directly transferred themselves to the new medium. Later, stand-up comedians such as Bill Cosby, Bob Newhart, Jerry Seinfeld, and Chris Rock assumed the central roles in eponymous series, addressing a remote, rather than a live, audience.

When they were husbands and fathers, sitcom characters at first tended to be those epitomized in the title *Father Knows Best*, sometimes with madcap or scatty wives, as in *I Love Lucy*. Over time, the women's movement and changing social mores brought forth spikier, more intelligent women, as in *Maude* and *The Mary Tyler Moore Show*. Men became hapless clowns, although the lovable dad resurfaced in *The Cosby Show*: this time, however, the lovable dad was black. Moreover, from the early 1960s onwards, producers saw fit to explore variations on the traditional nuclear family: *The Brady Bunch* involved a blended family, *My Three Sons* a widower and his children, *The Partridge Family* a widow and her children.

Over time, other genres intervened, such as science fiction in the animated *The Jetsons*, unthreatening ghouls and witches in *The Addams Family* and *Bewitched*, fantasy and parody in *Get Smart* and *Soap*, pop music in *The Monkees*. Even the Korean

War took on a humorous cast in *M*A*S*H*. As time passed, nostalgia became operative in sitcoms such as *Happy Days* and *The Wonder Years*. Sexual titillation surfaced in *Three's Company*, and the working class were portrayed in *Roseanne* and *Married with Children*. *All in the Family* and its lead character, the hilariously bigoted 'Archie Bunker', introduced not only raunchier dialogue, but exploded erstwhile taboos.

That was the sociological side of the American sitcom. Linguistically, television did not give children their accents: their peer groups did. In fact, considering its cultural dominance, television added surprisingly few new words to the language besides the passively-viewing *couch potato* and the *remote* that aided *channel-surfing*. What the sitcom, like television in general, mainly brought to everyday speech was a multitude of signature catchphrases: 'Now cut that out!' from *The Jack Benny Program*; 'Say good night, Gracie' from *The Burns & Allen Show*; 'How sweet it is!' from *The Jackie Gleason Show*; 'De plane! De plane!' from *Fantasy Island*; 'No soup for you!' from *Seinfeld* and, from a female character in the same series, 'Yadda yadda yadda' (a version of 'blah blah blah' that maddened her boyfriend because of the vital details it concealed).

Animated sitcoms yielded their own harvest of catchphrases, such as 'Yabba dabba do!' from *The Flintstones* and 'Oh, my God! They killed Kenny!' from *South Park*. Animation, the biggest innovation in sitcom history, summoned a new, sharper edge of implied social comment. In *Family Guy* and *The Simpsons* the endearing dads of early sitcoms became transformed into craven or gluttonous buffoons in the form of Peter Griffin and Homer Simpson. The long-running *The Simpsons* was the apotheosis of the form: Homer often commented 'D'Oh!' and was given to self-betraying reflections such as, 'Ah, sweet pity. Where would my love life have been without it?' When, in 1958, the news broadcaster Edward Murrow observed, 'Television in the main is being used to distract, delude, amuse, and insulate us', he could not have anticipated the satirical bite of *The Simpsons*. But that does not mean that he was entirely wrong.

obscure piece of writing using mysterious symbols **runic** *adj*
WORD ORIGIN Old Norse *rūn* secret

rung[1] *n* **1** one of the bars forming the steps of a ladder **2** a crosspiece between the legs of a chair
WORD ORIGIN Old English *hrung*

rung[2] *vb* the past participle of **ring**[1]

run-holder *n Austral & NZ* the owner or manager of a sheep or cattle station

run in *vb* **1** to run (an engine) gently, usually when it is new **2** *informal* to arrest ▷ *n* **run-in 3** *informal* an argument or quarrel **4** an approach to the end of an event: *the run-in for the championship*

run into *vb* **1** to be beset by: *the mission has run into difficulty* **2** to meet unexpectedly **3** to extend to: *businessmen denied losses running into the thousands* **4** to collide with

runnel *n literary* a small stream
WORD ORIGIN Old English *rynele*

runner *n* **1** a competitor in a race **2** a messenger for a firm **3** a person involved in smuggling **4 a** either of the strips of metal or wood on which a sledge runs **b** the blade of an ice skate **5** *bot* a slender horizontal stem of a plant, such as the strawberry, that grows along the surface of the soil and produces new roots and shoots **6** a long strip of cloth used to decorate a table or as a rug **7** a roller or guide for a sliding component **8 do a runner** *slang* to run away to escape trouble or to avoid paying for something

runner bean *n* the edible pod and seeds of a type of climbing bean plant

runner-up *n, pl* **runners-up** a person who comes second in a competition

running *adj* **1** maintained continuously: *a running battle* **2** without interruption: *for the third day running* **3 a** flowing: *rinse them under cold running water* **b** supplied through a tap: *there is no electricity, no running water, and no telephone* **4** operating: *running costs* **5** discharging pus: *a running sore* **6** accomplished at a run: *a running jump* **7** moving or slipping easily, as a rope or a knot ▷ *n* **8** the act of moving or flowing quickly **9** management or organization: *the running of the farm* **10** the operation or maintenance of a machine **11 in** or **out of the running** having *or* not having a good chance in a competition **12 make the running** to set the pace in a competition or race

running board *n* a board along the side of a vehicle, for help in stepping into it

running head *n printing* a heading printed at the top of every page of a book

running mate *n* **1** *US* a candidate for the lesser of two linked positions, esp. a candidate for the vice-presidency **2** a horse that pairs another in a team

running repairs *pl n* repairs that are done without greatly disrupting operations

runny *adj* **-nier, -niest 1** tending to flow: *a runny egg* **2** producing moisture: *a runny nose*

run off *vb* **1** to leave quickly **2 run off with a** to run away with in order to marry or live with **b** to steal **3** to produce (copies of a document) on a machine **4** to drain (liquid) or (of liquid) to be drained ▷ *n* **run-off 5** an extra race or contest to decide the winner after a tie **6** *NZ* grazing land for cattle

run-of-the-mill *adj* ordinary or average

run on *vb* to continue without interruption

run out *vb* **1** to use up or (of a supply) to be used up: *we soon ran out of gas* **2** to become invalid: *my passport has run out* **3 run out on** *informal* to desert or abandon **4** *cricket* to dismiss (a running batsman) by breaking the wicket with the ball while he is running between the wickets ▷ *n* **run-out 5** *cricket* dismissal of a batsman by running him out

run over *vb* **1** to knock down (a person) with a moving vehicle **2** to overflow **3** to examine hastily

runt *n* **1** the smallest and weakest young animal in a litter **2** an undersized or inferior person
WORD ORIGIN origin unknown

run through *vb* **1** to practise or rehearse **2** to pierce with a sword or other weapon ▷ *n* **run-through 3** a practice or rehearsal

run to *vb* **1** to reach an amount or size: *the testimony ran to a million words* **2** to be or have enough money for: *we do not run to these luxuries, I am afraid*

run up *vb* **1** to amass: *running up massive debts* **2** to make by sewing together quickly **3 run up against** to experience (difficulties) ▷ *n* **run-up 4** the time just before an event: *the run-up to the elections*

runway *n* a hard level roadway where aircraft take off and land

rupee *n* the standard monetary unit of a number of countries including India and Pakistan
WORD ORIGIN Hindi *rupaīyā*

rupture *n* **1** the act of breaking or the state of being broken **2** a breach of peaceful or friendly relations **3** *pathol* a hernia ▷ *vb* **-turing, -tured 4** to break or burst **5** to cause a breach in relations or friendship **6** to affect or be affected with a hernia
WORD ORIGIN Latin *rumpere* to burst forth

rural *adj* in or of the countryside
WORD ORIGIN Latin *ruralis*

rural dean *n chiefly Brit* a clergyman with authority over a group of parishes

rural route *n US & Canad* a mail service or route in a rural area

ruse (**rooz**) *n* an action or plan intended to mislead someone
WORD ORIGIN Old French

rush[1] *vb* **1** to move or do very quickly **2** to force (someone) to act hastily **3** to make a sudden attack upon (a person or place): *scores of pubescent girls rushed the stage* **4** to proceed or approach in a reckless manner **5** to come or flow quickly or suddenly: *the water rushed in, and the next instant the boat was swamped* ▷ *n* **6** a sudden quick or violent movement **7** a sudden demand or need **8** a sudden surge towards someone or something: *the gold rush* **9** a sudden surge of sensation **10** a sudden flow of air or liquid **11 rushes** (in film-making) the initial prints of a scene before editing ▷ *adj* **12** done with speed or urgency: *a rush job*
WORD ORIGIN Old French *ruser* to put to flight

rush[2] *n* a plant which grows in wet places and has a slender pithy stem **rushy** *adj*
WORD ORIGIN Old English *risce, rysce*

rush hour *n* a period at the beginning and end of the working day when large numbers of people are travelling to or from work

rush light *n* an old-fashioned candle made of rushes

rusk *n* a hard brown crisp biscuit, often used for feeding babies
WORD ORIGIN Spanish or Portuguese *rosca* screw, bread shaped in a twist

russet *adj* **1** *literary* reddish-brown: *a disarray of russet curls* ▷ *n* **2** an apple with a rough reddish-brown skin
WORD ORIGIN Latin *russus*

Russian *adj* **1** of Russia ▷ *n* **2** a person from Russia **3** the official language of Russia and, formerly, of the Soviet Union

Russian doll *n* any of a set of hollow wooden figures, each of which splits in half to contain the next smallest figure, down to the smallest

Russian roulette *n* an act of bravado in which a person spins the cylinder of a revolver loaded with only one cartridge and presses the trigger with the barrel against his or her own head

rust *n* **1** a reddish-brown oxide coating formed on iron or steel by the action of oxygen and moisture **2** a fungal disease of plants which produces a reddish-brown discoloration ▷ *adj* **3** reddish-brown ▷ *vb* **4** to become coated with a layer of rust **5** to deteriorate through lack of use: *my brain had rusted up*
WORD ORIGIN Old English *rūst*

rust belt *n* an area where heavy industry is in decline, esp. in the Midwest of the United States

rustic *adj* **1** of or resembling country people **2** of or living in the country **3** crude, awkward, or uncouth **4** made of untrimmed branches: *rustic furniture* ▷ *n* **5** a person from the country **rusticity** *n*
WORD ORIGIN Latin *rusticus*

rusticate *vb* **-cating, -cated 1** *Brit* to send (a student) down from university for a specified time as a punishment **2** to retire to the country **3** to make or become rustic
WORD ORIGIN Latin *rus* the country

rustle[1] *vb* **-tling, -tled 1** to make a low crisp whispering sound: *the leaves rustled in the breeze* ▷ *n* **2** this sound
WORD ORIGIN Old English *hrūxlian*

rustle[2] *vb* **-tling, -tled** *chiefly US & Canad* to steal (livestock) **rustler** *n*
WORD ORIGIN probably from RUSTLE[1] (in the sense: to move with a quiet sound)

rustle up *vb informal* to prepare or find at short notice: *Bob rustled up a meal*

rusty *adj* **rustier, rustiest 1** affected by rust: *a rusty old freighter* **2** reddish-brown

r

3 out of practice in a skill or subject: *your skills may be a little rusty, but your past experience will more than make up for that* **rustily** *adv* **rustiness** *n*

rut¹ *n* **1** a groove or furrow in a soft road, caused by wheels **2** dull settled habits or way of living: *his career was in a rut* **WORD ORIGIN** probably from French *route* road

rut² *n* **1** a recurrent period of sexual excitement in certain male ruminants ▷ *vb* **rutting, rutted 2** (of male ruminants) to be in a period of sexual excitement **WORD ORIGIN** Old French *rut* noise, roar

rutabaga *n* the US and Canadian term for **swede**

ruthenium *n chem* a rare hard brittle white metallic element. Symbol: Ru **WORD ORIGIN** Medieval Latin *Ruthenia* Russia, where it was discovered

rutherfordium *n chem* an artificially produced radioactive element. Symbol: Rf **WORD ORIGIN** after E. *Rutherford*, physicist

ruthless *adj* **1** feeling or showing no mercy **2** thorough and forceful, regardless of effect: *the ruthless pursuit of cost-effectiveness* **ruthlessly** *adv*

ruthlessness *n* **WORD ORIGIN** *ruth* pity

rutted *adj* (of a road) very uneven because of ruts

RV Revised Version (of the Bible)

rye *n* **1** a tall grasslike cereal grown for its light brown grain **2** the grain of this plant **3** Also called: **rye whiskey** whisky distilled from rye **4** US short for **rye bread** **WORD ORIGIN** Old English *ryge*

rye bread *n* bread made entirely or partly from rye flour

rye-grass *n* any of several grasses grown for fodder

Ss

The letter S is the nineteenth letter of the English alphabet. It came into the Roman alphabet from the Greek letter *sigma* (Σ,σ). Before that, the Greeks had adopted it from a letter called *shin*, which featured in Semitic alphabets and literally meant 'teeth'. The Semitic letter had two sharp edges pointing downwards, like a W (and indeed rather like two sharp teeth), but the Greeks rotated the letter through ninety degrees to produce their *sigma*. When the lower-case form of the Greek *sigma* came at the end of a word, it was written with a more rounded shape (ς), and this influenced the Romans to smooth out the sharp edges of the Greek *sigma* and produce the current shape of the letter S.

The idea that S should have a different lower-case form when it occurs at the end of word did not end with the Greeks. The 'long S' was a single stroke with a small curve at each end (∫), which was used at the start and middle of words until the nineteenth century and contrasted with the more familiar 'short s', which was confined to the end of words.

To modern eyes, the long S looks more like a lower-case F, and this may have led to its extinction.

The elegance of the S shape has not gone unrecognized, and an ornate collar composed of 74 connected S-shaped pieces of silver has been used as a symbol of high office since the 14th century. It is currently worn in Britain by the Sergeant at Arms of the House of Commons.

S is an extremely widely used letter in English. There are more English words beginning with S than with any other letter, accounting for well over ten per cent of an English dictionary. However, the letter is even more notable for its capacity to appear at the *end* of words. It can be added to nouns to make a plural and also to verbs to make the third person singular form of the present tense. This means that to Scrabble players an S is manna from heaven. It can be added to the end of most words on the board, allowing a new word to be built at right angles to the first, thus allowing plays that generate very high scores.

---

s second (of time)

S 1 South(ern) **2** *chem* sulphur **3** *physics* siemens

-'s *suffix* **1** forming the possessive singular of nouns and some pronouns: *woman's; one's* **2** forming the possessive plural of nouns whose plurals do not end in -s: *children's* **3** forming the plural of numbers, letters, or symbols: *20's* **4** *informal* contraction of *is* or *has*: *it's over* **5** *informal* contraction of *us* with *let*: *let's go*

SA 1 Salvation Army **2** South Africa **3** South America **4** South Australia

SAA South African Airways

Sabbath *n* **1** Saturday, observed by Jews as the day of worship and rest **2** Sunday, observed by Christians as the day of worship and rest
WORD ORIGIN Hebrew *shābath* to rest

sabbatical *adj* **1** denoting a period of leave granted at intervals to university teachers for rest, study, or travel: *a sabbatical year* ▷ *n* **2** a sabbatical period
WORD ORIGIN see SABBATH

SABC South African Broadcasting Corporation

sable *n, pl* **-bles** *or* **-ble 1** a marten of N Asia, N Europe, and America, with dark brown luxuriant fur **2** the highly valued fur of this animal, used to make coats and hats ▷ *adj* **3** dark brown-to-black
WORD ORIGIN Slavic

sable antelope *n* a large black African antelope with stout backward-curving horns

sabot (**sab**-oh) *n* a heavy wooden or wooden-soled shoe; clog
WORD ORIGIN French

sabotage *n* **1** the deliberate destruction or damage of equipment, for example by enemy agents or dissatisfied employees **2** deliberate obstruction of or damage to a cause or effort ▷ *vb* **-taging, -taged 3** to destroy or disrupt by sabotage
WORD ORIGIN French

saboteur *n* a person who commits sabotage
WORD ORIGIN French

sabre *or* US **saber** *n* **1** a heavy single-edged cavalry sword with a curved blade **2** a light sword used in fencing, with a narrow V-shaped blade
WORD ORIGIN German (dialect) *Sabel*

sac *n* a pouch or pouchlike part in an animal or plant
WORD ORIGIN Latin *saccus*

saccharin *n* an artificial sweetener
WORD ORIGIN Greek *sakkharon* sugar

saccharine *adj* **1** excessively sweet or sentimental: *saccharine ballads* **2** like or containing sugar or saccharine

sacerdotal *adj formal* of priests or the priesthood

WORD ORIGIN Latin *sacerdos* priest

sachet *n* **1** a small sealed usually plastic envelope containing a small portion of a substance such as shampoo **2** a small soft bag of perfumed powder, placed in drawers to scent clothing
WORD ORIGIN French

sack¹ *n* **1** a large bag made of coarse cloth or thick paper and used for carrying or storing goods **2** the amount contained in a sack **3 the sack** *informal* dismissal from employment **4** *slang* bed **5 hit the sack** *slang* to go to bed ▷ *vb* **6** *informal* to dismiss from employment **sacklike** *adj*
WORD ORIGIN Greek *sakkos*

sack² *n* **1** the plundering of a captured town or city by an army or mob ▷ *vb* **2** to plunder and partially destroy (a town or city)
WORD ORIGIN French *mettre à sac* to put (loot) in a sack

sackbut *n* a medieval form of trombone
WORD ORIGIN French *saqueboute*

sackcloth *n* **1** same as **sacking 2** garments made of such cloth, worn formerly to indicate mourning **3 sackcloth and ashes** an exaggerated attempt to apologize or compensate for a mistake or wrongdoing

sacking *n* coarse cloth woven from flax, hemp, or jute, and used to make sacks

sacrament *n* **1** a symbolic religious ceremony in the Christian Church,

Joseph Conrad

If the literary and cultural movement known as Modernism can be said to have anything like a single precursor, it is fitting that it should be Joseph Conrad, whose very biography seems to personify the Modernist perspective.

Modernism is, essentially, a dislodging of what was previously considered stable: time, identity, motivation, even language itself are shown to be fluid, transient, changeable, or illusory. That Conrad should be the prototype of the Modernist author is demonstrable by considering this basic fact: his name is not even Joseph Conrad.

Born Józef Teodor Konrad Korzeniowski in December 1857, Conrad came from a Polish noble family, although his birthplace, Berdyczów, is in present-day Ukraine. During Conrad's life, Poland was part of the Russian Empire: Conrad essentially held a nationality that did not exist. Furthermore, his family were exiled after Conrad's father helped plan the ill-fated January Uprising of 1863. Such a background would give Conrad credentials in exile and dislocation that could trump those of voluntary expat writers such as James Joyce, Gertrude Stein, or Ernest Hemingway.

Conrad was also a linguistic expatriate, writing exclusively in English, even though he did not speak the language with any particular fluency. (Even as an adult, his spoken English was marked with a heavy Polish accent.) Again, this kind of exile would be imitated by later writers – Samuel Beckett, for example, choosing to write in French – but for Conrad it was a necessity: Polish was the language of a non-existent country and, as Conrad became a British subject at the age of 29, English was the natural language to use to reach an audience.

Before becoming a writer, Conrad served in the French and British merchant navies, exposing him to the foreign countries which would serve as settings for his novels and stories, as well as giving him ample experience of travel on the open sea or up rivers, a perennial Modernist theme. For water, with its constantly moving, changing nature, is one of the most important symbols in the Modernist canon.

Conrad's complete bibliography is vast, but like Anthony Burgess, he is primarily remembered for one work, and, again like Burgess, largely due to a loose film adaptation. *Heart of Darkness* tells the story of Marlowe, an Englishman who takes a job on a steamship transporting ivory along the Congo River in Africa, although his main task is to find the elusive ivory trader Kurtz and return him to civilization. Marlowe discovers that Kurtz has set himself up as a god among the local tribe and established a regime of brutality. Kurtz is also painfully emaciated and clearly dying of tuberculosis. Marlowe gets Kurtz aboard his ship, but Kurtz dies en route, uttering the novel's most famous lines 'The horror! The horror!' – apparently a reflection on the violence that has characterized his life.

The novel, first published serially in 1899, is on the cusp of High Modernism (Joyce's *Dubliners*, for instance, although published in 1914, was largely written in 1904). It has many stylistic and structural features that Modernists would later make use of. The main story is told in a 'frame narrative': Marlowe's story about Africa is told in the first person, but reported to the reader by an unnamed first person narrator as he, Marlowe, and others sit aboard a boat on the Thames. Thus the story's main events are mediated by two subjective, first-person perspectives. In addition, *Heart of Darkness* is famous for its unflinching gaze into the psychology of its characters; this 'psychological realism' would survive into the Modernist period, when authors who were otherwise happy to let reality slip, remained honest and accurate regarding the inner workings of the human mind. Finally, Conrad's novel creates a definite sense of place. Later Modernist authors would also excel at authentic re-creations of real places.

In 1979 *Heart of Darkness* was loosely adapted into Francis Ford Coppola's film *Apocalypse Now*. The setting was changed to the Vietnam War; in place of Marlowe, the American Captain Benjamin Willard is dispatched into the jungle to assassinate Colonel Kurtz, an army officer who has gone insane. Kurtz is portrayed by a corpulent Marlon Brando, a sharp contrast to Conrad's consumptive, emaciated Kurtz, but his dying words are retained, fixing them in popular consciousness for generations to come.

such as baptism or communion **2** Holy Communion **3** something regarded as sacred **sacramental** adj
WORD ORIGIN Latin sacrare to consecrate

sacred adj **1** exclusively devoted to a god or gods; holy **2** connected with religion or intended for religious use: sacred music **3** regarded as too important to be changed or interfered with: sacred principles of free speech **4 sacred to** dedicated to: the site is sacred to Vishnu
WORD ORIGIN Latin sacer holy

sacred cow n informal a person, custom, belief, or institution regarded as being beyond criticism
WORD ORIGIN alluding to the Hindu belief that cattle are sacred

sacrifice n **1** a surrender of something of value in order to gain something more desirable or prevent some evil **2** a ritual killing of a person or animal as an offering to a god **3** a symbolic offering of something to a god **4** the person or animal killed or offered ▷ vb **-ficing, -ficed 5** to make a sacrifice (of) **6** chess to permit or force one's opponent to capture (a piece) as a tactical move **sacrificial** adj
WORD ORIGIN Latin sacer holy + facere to make

sacrilege n **1** the misuse of or disrespect shown to something sacred **2** disrespect for a person who is widely admired or a belief that is widely accepted: it is a sacrilege to offend democracy **sacrilegious** adj
WORD ORIGIN Latin sacrilegus temple robber

sacristan n a person in charge of the contents of a church; sexton
WORD ORIGIN Latin sacer holy

sacristy n, pl **-ties** a room attached to a church or chapel where the sacred objects are kept

sacrosanct adj regarded as too important to be criticized or changed: weekend rest days were considered sacrosanct by staff **sacrosanctity** n
WORD ORIGIN Latin sacer holy + sanctus hallowed

sacrum (**say**-krum) n, pl **-cra** anat the large wedge-shaped bone in the lower part of the back
WORD ORIGIN Latin os sacrum holy bone, because it was used in sacrifices

sad adj **sadder, saddest 1** feeling sorrow; unhappy **2** causing, suggesting, or expressing sorrow: a sad story **3** deplorably bad: the garden was in a sad state **4** regrettable: it's rather sad he can't be with us **5** Brit informal ridiculously pathetic: a sad, boring little wimp **6** vb **pack a sad** NZ slang to strongly express sadness or displeasure **sadly** adv **sadness** n
WORD ORIGIN Old English sæd weary

sadden vb to make (someone) sad

saddle n **1** a seat for a rider, usually made of leather, placed on a horse's back and secured under its belly **2** a similar seat on a bicycle, motorcycle, or tractor **3** a cut of meat, esp. mutton, consisting of both loins **4 in the saddle** in a position of control ▷ vb **-dling, -dled 5** to put a saddle on (a horse): we saddled up at dawn **6 saddle with** to

burden with (a responsibility): he was also saddled with debt
WORD ORIGIN Old English sadol, sadul

saddleback n **1** an animal with a marking resembling a saddle on its back **2** a hill with a concave outline at the top **saddle-backed** adj

saddlebag n a pouch or small bag attached to the saddle of a horse, bicycle, or motorcycle

saddle horse n a horse trained for riding only

saddler n a person who makes, deals in, or repairs saddles and other leather equipment for horses

saddlery n, pl **-dleries 1** saddles and harness for horses collectively **2** the work or place of work of a saddler

saddle soap n a soft soap used to preserve and clean leather

saddletree n the frame of a saddle

saddo n Brit informal a pathetic or socially inadequate person

Sadducee (sad-yew-see) n Judaism a member of an ancient Jewish sect that denied the resurrection of the dead and accepted only the traditional written law

sadhu (sah-doo) n a Hindu wandering holy man
WORD ORIGIN Sanskrit

sadism (**say**-diz-zum) n the gaining of pleasure, esp. sexual pleasure, from infliction of suffering on another person **sadist** n **sadistic** adj **sadistically** adv
WORD ORIGIN after the Marquis de Sade, soldier & writer

sadomasochism n **1** the combination of sadistic and masochistic elements in one person, characterized by both submissive and aggressive periods in relationships with others **2** a sexual practice in which one partner adopts a masochistic role and the other a sadistic one **sadomasochist** n **sadomasochistic** adj

s.a.e. Brit, Austral, & NZ stamped addressed envelope

safari n, pl **-ris** an overland expedition for hunting or observing animals, esp. in Africa
WORD ORIGIN Swahili: journey

safari park n an enclosed park in which wild animals are kept uncaged in the open and can be viewed by the public from cars or buses

safe adj **1** giving security or protection from harm: a safe environment **2** free from danger: she doesn't feel safe **3** taking or involving no risks: a safe bet **4** not dangerous: the beef is safe to eat **5 on the safe side** as a precaution ▷ n **6** a strong metal container with a secure lock, for storing money or valuables **safely** adv
WORD ORIGIN Old French salf

safe-conduct n **1** a document giving official permission to travel through a dangerous region, esp. in time of war **2** the protection given by such a document

safe-deposit or **safety-deposit** n a place or building with facilities for the safe storage of money and valuables

safeguard vb **1** to protect (something) from being harmed or destroyed ▷ n **2** a person or thing that ensures protection against danger or harm: safeguards to prevent air collisions

safekeeping n protection from theft or damage: I put my money in a bank for safekeeping

safe sex or **safer sex** n nonpenetrative sex, or intercourse using a condom, intended to prevent the spread of HIV

safety n, pl **-ties 1** the quality or state of being free from danger **2** shelter: they swam to safety

safety belt n same as **seat belt**

safety catch n a mechanism on a gun that prevents it from being fired accidentally

safety curtain n a fireproof curtain that can be lowered to separate the auditorium from the stage in a theatre to prevent the spread of a fire

safety lamp n a miner's oil lamp designed to prevent it from igniting combustible gas

safety match n a match that will light only when struck against a specially prepared surface

safety net n **1** a large net under a trapeze or high wire to catch performers if they fall **2** something that can be relied on for help in the event of difficulties: the social security safety net

safety pin n a pin bent back on itself so that it forms a spring, with the point shielded by a guard when closed

safety razor n a razor with a guard over the blade or blades to protect the skin from deep cuts

safety valve n **1** a valve in a boiler or machine that allows fluid or gases to escape at excess pressure **2** an outlet that allows one to express strong feelings without harming or offending other people: sport acted as a safety valve for his pent-up frustrations

safflower n a thistle-like plant with orange-yellow flowers, which yields a dye and an oil used in paints, medicines, and cooking
WORD ORIGIN Old French saffleur

saffron n **1** a type of crocus with purple or white flowers with orange stigmas **2** the dried orange-coloured stigmas of this plant, used for colouring or flavouring ▷ adj **3** orange-yellow
WORD ORIGIN Arabic za'farān

sag vb **sagging, sagged 1** to sink in the middle, under weight or pressure: the bed sagged nearly to the floor **2** (of courage or spirits) to weaken or tire **3** (of clothes) to hang loosely or unevenly **4** to fall in value: the stock market sagged ▷ n **5** the act or state of sagging **saggy** adj
WORD ORIGIN from Old Norse

saga (**sah**-ga) n **1** a medieval Scandinavian legend telling the adventures of a hero or a family **2** informal a long story or series of events: the long-running saga of the hostage issue
WORD ORIGIN Old Norse

sagacious adj formal wise or sensible **sagaciously** adv **sagacity** n
WORD ORIGIN Latin sagax

sage[1] *n* **1** a person, esp. an old man, regarded as being very wise ▷ *adj* **2** very wise or knowledgeable, esp. as the result of age or experience
WORD ORIGIN Latin *sapere* to be sensible

sage[2] *n* **1** a Mediterranean plant with grey-green leaves which are used in cooking for flavouring **2** short for **sagebrush**
WORD ORIGIN Latin *salvus* in good health (from its curative properties)

sagebrush *n* an aromatic plant of W North America, with silver-green leaves and large clusters of small white flowers

Sagittarius *n astrol* the ninth sign of the zodiac; the Archer
WORD ORIGIN Latin

sago *n* an edible starch from the powdered pith of the sago palm tree, used for puddings and as a thickening agent
WORD ORIGIN Malay *sāgū*

sahib *n* an Indian term of address equivalent to *sir*, formerly used as a mark of respect to a European man
WORD ORIGIN Urdu

said *adj* **1** named or mentioned already: *she had heard that the said lady was also a medium* ▷ *vb* **2** the past of **say**

sail *n* **1** a sheet of canvas or other fabric, spread on rigging to catch the wind and move a ship over water **2** a voyage on such a ship: *a relaxing sail across the lake* **3** a ship or ships with sails: *to travel by sail* **4** one of the revolving arms of a windmill **5 set sail** to begin a voyage by water **6 under sail a** under way **b** with sail hoisted ▷ *vb* **7** to travel in a boat or ship: *to sail around the world* **8** to begin a voyage: *he hoped to sail at eleven* **9** (of a ship) to move over the water **10** to navigate (a ship): *she sailed the schooner up the channel* **11** to sail over: *he had already sailed the Pacific* **12** to move along smoothly **13 sail into** *informal* to make a violent attack on **14 sail through** to progress quickly or effortlessly: *the top seed sailed through to the second round*
WORD ORIGIN Old English *segl*

sailboard *n* a board with a mast and a single sail, used for windsurfing

sailcloth *n* **1** the fabric used for making sails **2** a canvas-like cloth used for clothing

sailfish *n, pl* **-fish** or **-fishes** a large tropical game fish, with a long sail-like fin on its back

sailor *n* **1** any member of a ship's crew, esp. one below the rank of officer **2** a person considered as liable or not liable to seasickness: *a good sailor*

sainfoin (**san**-foin) *n* a Eurasian plant with pink flowers, widely grown as feed for grazing farm animals
WORD ORIGIN Medieval Latin *sanum faenum* wholesome hay

saint *n* **1** a person who after death is formally recognized by a Christian Church as deserving special honour because of having lived a very holy life **2** an exceptionally good person **sainthood** *n* **saintlike** *adj*
WORD ORIGIN Latin *sanctus* holy

Saint Bernard *n* a very large dog with a dense red-and-white coat, formerly used as a mountain-rescue dog

sainted *adj* **1** formally recognized by a Christian Church as a saint **2** having the qualities, such as patience and kindness, of a saint **3** hallowed or holy

Saint John's wort *n* a plant with yellow flowers

Saint Leger *n* an annual horse race for three-year-old horses, run at Doncaster

saintly *adj* behaving in a very good, patient, or holy way **saintliness** *n*

Saint Vitus's dance *n pathol* a nontechnical name for **chorea**

saithe *n Brit* a dark-coloured food fish found in northern seas
WORD ORIGIN Old Norse *seithr* coalfish

sake[1] *n* **1 for someone's** or **one's own sake** for the benefit or interest of someone or oneself **2 for the sake of something** for the purpose of obtaining or achieving something **3 for its own sake** for the enjoyment obtained by doing something **4** used in various exclamations of annoyance, impatience, or urgency: *for God's sake*
WORD ORIGIN Old English *sacu* lawsuit (hence, a cause)

sake[2] or **saki** (**sah**-kee) *n* a Japanese alcoholic drink made from fermented rice
WORD ORIGIN Japanese

salaam (sal-**ahm**) *n* **1** a Muslim greeting consisting of a deep bow with the right palm on the forehead **2** a greeting signifying peace ▷ *vb* **3** to make a salaam (to)
WORD ORIGIN Arabic *salām* peace

salacious *adj* **1** having an excessive interest in sex **2** (of books, films, or jokes) concerned with sex in an unnecessarily detailed way **salaciousness** *n*
WORD ORIGIN Latin *salax* fond of leaping

salad *n* a dish of raw vegetables, often served with a dressing, eaten as a separate course or as part of a main course
WORD ORIGIN Old French *salade*

salad days *pl n* a period of youth and inexperience

salad dressing *n* a sauce for salad, such as oil and vinegar or mayonnaise

salamander *n* **1** a tailed amphibian which looks like a lizard **2** a mythical creature supposed to live in fire
WORD ORIGIN Greek *salamandra*

salami *n* a highly spiced sausage, usually flavoured with garlic
WORD ORIGIN Italian

salaried *adj* earning or providing a salary: *a salaried employee; a salaried position*

salary *n, pl* **-ries** a fixed regular payment made by an employer, usually monthly, for professional or office work
WORD ORIGIN Latin *salarium* the sum given to Roman soldiers to buy salt

sale *n* **1** the exchange of goods or property for an agreed sum of money **2** the amount sold **3** an event at which goods are sold at reduced prices **4** an auction **5 sales** the department dealing with selling its company's products
WORD ORIGIN Old English *sala*

saleable or US **salable** *adj* fit for selling or capable of being sold **saleability** or US **salability** *n*

sale of work *n* a sale of articles, often handmade, the proceeds of which go to a charity

saleroom *n chiefly Brit* a room where objects are displayed for sale by auction

salesgirl *n* a young woman who sells goods in a shop

salesman *n, pl* **-men 1** a man who sells goods in a shop **2** short for **travelling salesman**

salesmanship *n* the technique of or skill in selling

salesperson *n, pl* **-people** or **-persons** a person who sells goods in a shop

sales pitch or **talk** *n* persuasive talk used by a salesperson in persuading a customer to buy something

saleswoman *n, pl* **-women** a woman who sells goods in a shop

saleyard *n Austral & NZ* an area with pens for holding animals before auction

salicylic acid (sal-liss-**ill**-ik) *n* a white crystalline substance used to make aspirin and as a fungicide
WORD ORIGIN Latin *salix* willow

salient (**say**-lee-ent) *adj* **1** (of points or facts) most important: *the salient points of his speech* ▷ *n* **2** *mil* a projection of the forward line of an army into enemy-held territory
WORD ORIGIN Latin *salire* to leap

saline (**say**-line) *adj* **1** of or containing salt: *a saline flavour* **2** *med* of or relating to a saline: *a saline drip* ▷ *n* **3** *med* a solution of sodium chloride and water **salinity** *n*
WORD ORIGIN Latin *sal* salt

salinization or **-nisation** *n* the process by which salts accumulate in undrained land, damaging its potential for plant growth

saliva (sal-**lie**-va) *n* the watery fluid secreted by glands in the mouth, which aids digestion **salivary** *adj*
WORD ORIGIN Latin

salivate *vb* **-vating, -vated** to produce saliva, esp. an excessive amount **salivation** *n*

sallee *n Austral* **1** a SE Australian eucalyptus with a pale grey bark **2** an acacia tree

sallow *adj* (of human skin) of an unhealthy pale or yellowish colour **sallowness** *n*
WORD ORIGIN Old English *salu*

sally *n, pl* **-lies 1** a witty remark **2** a sudden brief attack by troops **3** an excursion ▷ *vb* **-lies, -lying, -lied 4 sally forth a** to set out on a journey **b** to set out in an energetic manner
WORD ORIGIN Latin *salire* to leap

salmon *n, pl* **-mons** or **-mon** a large pink-fleshed fish which is highly valued for food and sport: *salmon live in the sea but return to fresh water to spawn*
WORD ORIGIN Latin *salmo*

salmonella (sal-mon-**ell**-a) *n* a kind of bacteria that can cause food poisoning
WORD ORIGIN after Daniel E. *Salmon*, veterinary surgeon

salmon ladder *n* a series of steps designed to enable salmon to move upstream to their breeding grounds

salon n **1** a commercial establishment in which hairdressers or fashion designers carry on their business **2** an elegant room in a large house in which guests are received **3** an informal gathering, esp. in the 18th, 19th, and early 20th centuries, of major literary, artistic, and political figures in a fashionable household **4** an art exhibition **WORD ORIGIN** French

saloon n **1** a two-door or four-door car with a fixed roof **2** a comfortable but more expensive bar in a pub or hotel **3** a large public room on a passenger ship **4** chiefly US & Canad a place where alcoholic drink is sold and consumed **WORD ORIGIN** from salon

salsa n **1** a lively Puerto Rican dance **2** big-band music accompanying this dance **WORD ORIGIN** Spanish, literally: sauce

salsify n, pl **-fies** a Mediterranean plant with a long white edible root **WORD ORIGIN** Italian sassefrica

salt n **1** sodium chloride, a white crystalline substance, used for seasoning and preserving food **2** chem a crystalline solid compound formed from an acid by replacing its hydrogen with a metal **3** lively wit: his humour added salt to the discussion **4** old salt an experienced sailor **5** rub salt into someone's wounds to make an unpleasant situation even worse for someone **6** salt of the earth a person or people regarded as the finest of their kind **7** take something with a pinch of salt to refuse to believe something is completely true or accurate **8** worth one's salt worthy of one's pay; efficient ▷ vb **9** to season or preserve with salt **10** to scatter salt over (an iced road or path) to melt the ice ▷ adj **11** preserved in or tasting of salt: salt beef ▶ See also **salt away**, **salts** > **salted** adj **WORD ORIGIN** Old English sealt

SALT Strategic Arms Limitation Talks or Treaty

salt away vb to hoard or save (money) for the future

saltbush n a shrub that grow in alkaline

saltcellar n a small container for salt used at the table **WORD ORIGIN** changed from salt saler; saler from Old French saliere container for salt

saltire n **1** heraldry a diagonal cross on a shield **2** the national flag of Scotland, a white diagonal cross on a blue background

salt lick n **1** a place where wild animals go to lick salt deposits **2** a block of salt given to domestic animals to lick

saltpetre or US **saltpeter** n same as **potassium nitrate** **WORD ORIGIN** Latin sal petrae salt of rock

salts pl n **1** med mineral salts used as a medicine **2** like a dose of salts informal very quickly

saltwater adj of or inhabiting salt water, esp. the sea: saltwater fish

salty adj **saltier**, **saltiest** **1** of, tasting of, or containing salt **2** (esp. of humour) sharp and witty **saltiness** n

salubrious adj favourable to health **salubrity** n **WORD ORIGIN** Latin salus health

Saluki n a tall hound with a smooth coat and long fringes on the ears and tail **WORD ORIGIN** from Saluq, ancient Arabian city

salutary adj **1** (of an experience) producing a beneficial result despite being unpleasant: a salutary reminder **2** promoting health **WORD ORIGIN** Latin salutaris wholesome

salutation n formal a greeting by words or actions **WORD ORIGIN** Latin salutare to greet

salute vb **-luting**, **-luted** **1** to greet with friendly words or gestures of respect, such as bowing **2** to acknowledge with praise: the statement salutes the changes of the past year **3** mil to pay formal respect to (someone) by raising the right hand to the forehead ▷ n **4** the act of saluting as a formal military gesture of respect **5** the act of firing guns as a military greeting of honour **WORD ORIGIN** Latin salutare to greet

salvage n **1** the rescue of a ship or its cargo from loss at sea **2** the saving of any goods or property from destruction or waste **3** the goods or property so saved **4** compensation paid for the salvage of a ship or its cargo ▷ vb **-vaging**, **-vaged** **5** to save (goods or property) from shipwreck, destruction, or waste **6** to gain (something beneficial) from a failure: it's too late to salvage anything from the whole dismal display **salvageable** adj **WORD ORIGIN** Latin salvare to save

salvation n **1** the act of preserving someone or something from harm **2** a person or thing that preserves from harm **3** Christianity the fact or state of being saved from the influence or consequences of sin **WORD ORIGIN** Latin salvatus saved

Salvation Army n a Christian body organized on military lines for working among the poor and spreading the Christian faith

salve n **1** an ointment for wounds **2** anything that heals or soothes ▷ vb **salving**, **salved** **3** salve one's conscience to do something in order to feel less guilty **WORD ORIGIN** Old English sealf

salver n a tray, usually a silver one, on which something is presented **WORD ORIGIN** Spanish salva tray from which the king's taster sampled food

salvia n any small plant or shrub of the sage genus **WORD ORIGIN** Latin

salvo n, pl **-vos** or **-voes** **1** a simultaneous discharge of guns in battle or on a ceremonial occasion **2** an outburst of applause or questions **WORD ORIGIN** Italian salva, from Latin salve! greetings!

sal volatile (sal vol-at-ill-ee) n a solution of ammonium carbonate, used as smelling salts **WORD ORIGIN** New Latin: volatile salt

SAM surface-to-air missile

Samaritan n **1** short for **Good Samaritan** **2** a member of a voluntary organization (**the Samaritans**) which offers counselling to people in despair, esp. by telephone

samarium n chem a silvery metallic element of the rare-earth series. Symbol: Sm **WORD ORIGIN** after Col. von Samarski, Russian inspector of mines

samba n, pl **-bas** **1** a lively Brazilian dance **2** music for this dance **WORD ORIGIN** Portuguese

same adj (usually preceded by the) **1** being the very one: she is wearing the same hat **2** being the one previously referred to: it causes problems for the same reason **3** alike in kind or quantity: the same age **4** unchanged in character or nature: his attitude is the same as ever **5** all the same or just the same nevertheless; even so **6** be all the same to be a matter of indifference: it was all the same to me ▷ adv **7** in the same way; similarly: I felt much the same ▷ n **8** the same something that is like something else in kind or quantity: this is basically much more of the same **sameness** n **WORD ORIGIN** Old Norse samr

USAGE
The use of same exemplified in if you send us your order for the materials, we will deliver same tomorrow is common in business and official English. In general English, however, this use of the word is avoided: may I borrow your book? I'll return it (not same) tomorrow.

samizdat n (in the former Soviet Union) a system of secret printing and distribution of banned literature **WORD ORIGIN** Russian

samosa n (in Indian cookery) a small fried triangular spiced meat or vegetable pasty. Also (in S Africa): **samoosa** **WORD ORIGIN** Hindi

samovar n a Russian metal tea urn in which the water is heated by an inner container **WORD ORIGIN** Russian

Samoyed n a dog with a thick white coat and a tightly curled tail **WORD ORIGIN** Russian Samoed

sampan n a small flat-bottomed boat with oars, used esp. in China **WORD ORIGIN** Chinese san three + pan board

samphire n a plant found on rocks by the seashore **WORD ORIGIN** French herbe de Saint Pierre Saint Peter's herb

sample n **1** a small part of anything, taken as being representative of a whole ▷ vb **-pling**, **-pled** **2** to take a sample or samples of **3** music **a** to take a short extract from (one record) and mix it into a different backing track **b** to record (a sound) and feed it into a computerized synthesizer so that it can be reproduced at any pitch **sampling** n **WORD ORIGIN** Latin exemplum

sampler n **1** a piece of embroidery done to show the embroiderer's skill in using many different stitches **2** music a piece of electronic equipment used for sampling

Samson n a man of outstanding physical strength

Military Slang

Any organized group uses its own customized version of the English language. Different trades, sports, professions, or social circles have their own linguistic conventions which they use as shorthand to improve communication, or to restrict knowledge to a limited number of people. For these reasons, it is rare for specific jargon to be used widely or understood in everyday speech. Military slang is an exception to the rule. In the first half of the twentieth century, many words previously confined to military use were introduced to the wider English language. Many of these are now so deeply rooted in contemporary English that it would be hard to imagine their absence.

For example, World War I introduced the trench terminology *Blighty* (a contracted form of the Hindi *bilayati*, which originated in the British army in India), *camouflage* (from the French *camouflet*), *dogfight* (in the sense of an aerial battle), *strafe* (from the German *strafen*, to punish), and *AWOL* into everyday speech. These phrases were popularized by writers such as Siegfried Sassoon and Arthur Guy Empey (whose war memoir *Over the Top* brought that phrase into mass usage).

World War II saw the coinage of many phrases still used today, such as a *Dear John* letter and *Tail End Charlie* (the last in a series of pilots to take off on a bombing raid, or a nickname for a tailgunner). As with World War I, many authors wrote about their experiences and brought this colourful language to more mainstream recognition, although sometimes with concessions to the social mores of the time. (Norman Mailer was persuaded by his publishers to substitute *fug* for the f-word throughout his 1948 novel *The Naked and the Dead*, as the word was still considered taboo.) Also, in the United Kingdom, national service was compulsory until the late 1950s, and the preceding generations had fought in and lived through two world wars, which meant that a huge proportion of the population had direct experience of military life and military language.

In the latter half of the twentieth century (and so far in the twenty-first) it is American military slang that has been predominant. The days when Joseph Heller had to invent a term for military madness (*Catch-22*) were over, as the Vietnam conflict brought forth phrases such as *friendly fire* and *fugazi*. Jargon and slang used in the Vietnam conflict were introduced to the English language via a different set of media. In print, there were many successful memoirs written and published during the war (notably Tim O'Brien's *If I Die in a Combat Zone*, David Maraniss's *They Walked into Sunlight*, Ron Kovic's *Born on the Fourth of July*, and Michael Herr's *Dispatches*). However, with a few notable exceptions, it was not until the mid-1980s when Oliver Stone's *Platoon* won several Academy Awards that direct depictions of the war became widely acceptable in cinema. The harsh language and at-first-impenetrable acronyms of the infantry (or 'grunts') became familiar to many households via the television screen, as the release of Vietnam-set films coincided with the home video boom, and with a loosening of the use of expletives in major Hollywood productions.

In Britain, the Falklands War brought *yomping* (Royal Marine slang for making an arduous trek while carrying full kit) into common use, and the rolling news coverage of Operation Desert Storm produced its own lexicon, such as *jarhead* (meaning a member of the United States Marine Corps – so called because of their distinctive close-cropped haircuts) and the notorious euphemism *collateral damage*. The news media provided a much more immediate exposure to the terminology of war, sidestepping a more gradual acceptance through culture or the arts.

Military operations in Iraq and Afghanistan have provided a new terms, such as *IED* (Improvised Explosive Device). Also, journalists are *embedded* with military units, in order to provide coverage closer to the ground. This symbiotic relationship between the military and the media means that the language of the soldier is increasingly reflected in news reporting. Even in the era of the professional army, military slang finds its way into general use.

WORD ORIGIN from the biblical character who was renowned for his strength

samurai *n, pl* **-rai** a member of the aristocratic warrior caste of feudal Japan
WORD ORIGIN Japanese

sanatorium *or US* **sanitarium** *n, pl* **-riums** *or* **-ria** **1** an institution providing medical treatment and rest for invalids or convalescents **2** *Brit* a room in a boarding school where sick pupils may be treated
WORD ORIGIN Latin *sanare* to heal

sanctify *vb* **-fies, -fying, -fied** **1** to make holy **2** to free from sin **3** to approve (an action or practice) as religiously binding: *she is trying to make amends for her marriage not being sanctified* **sanctification** *n*
WORD ORIGIN Latin *sanctus* holy + *facere* to make

sanctimonious *adj* pretending to be very religious and virtuous
WORD ORIGIN Latin *sanctimonia* sanctity

sanction *n* **1** permission granted by authority: *official sanction* **2** support or approval: *they could not exist without his sanction* **3** something that gives binding force to a law, such as a penalty for breaking it or a reward for obeying it **4 sanctions** coercive measures, such as boycotts and trade embargoes, taken by one or more states against another guilty of violating international law ▷ *vb* **5** to officially approve of or allow: *they do not want to sanction direct payments* **6** to confirm or ratify
WORD ORIGIN Latin *sancire* to decree

sanctity *n* the quality of something considered so holy or important it must be respected totally: *the sanctity of the Sabbath; the sanctity of marriage*

sanctuary *n, pl* **-aries** **1** a holy place, such as a consecrated building or shrine **2** the part of a church nearest the main altar **3** a place of refuge or protection for someone who is being chased or hunted **4** refuge or safety: *the sanctuary of your own home* **5** a place, protected by law, where animals can live and breed without interference
WORD ORIGIN Latin *sanctus* holy

sanctum *n, pl* **-tums** *or* **-ta** **1** a sacred or holy place **2** a room or place of total privacy
WORD ORIGIN Latin

sand *n* **1** a powdery substance consisting of very small rock or mineral grains, found on the seashore and in deserts **2 sands** a large sandy area, esp. on the seashore or in a desert ▷ *vb* **3** to smooth or polish the surface of (something) with sandpaper or a sander **4** to fill with sand: *the channel sanded up*
WORD ORIGIN Old English

sandal *n* a light shoe consisting of a sole held on the foot by thongs or straps **sandalled** *or US* **sandaled** *adj*
WORD ORIGIN Greek *sandalon*

sandalwood *n* **1** the hard light-coloured wood of a S Asian or Australian tree, which is used for carving and for incense, and which yields an aromatic oil used in perfumes **2** a tree yielding this wood
WORD ORIGIN Sanskrit *candana*

sandbag *n* **1** a sack filled with sand used to make a temporary defence against gunfire or flood water ▷ *vb* **-bagging, -bagged** **2** to protect or strengthen with sandbags

sandbank *or* **sand bar** *n* a bank of sand in a sea or river, that may be exposed at low tide

sandblast *n* **1** a jet of sand blown from a nozzle under air or steam pressure ▷ *vb* **2** to clean or decorate (a surface) with a sandblast **sandblaster** *n*

sandboy *n* **happy as a sandboy** very happy

sand castle *n* a model of a castle made from sand

sander *n* a power-driven tool for smoothing surfaces, removing layers of paint from walls, etc.

S & M *informal* sadomasochism

sandman *n, pl* **-men** (in folklore) a magical person supposed to put children to sleep by sprinkling sand in their eyes

sand martin *n* a small brown European songbird which nests in tunnels bored in sand or river banks

sandpaper *n* **1** a strong paper coated with sand or other abrasive material for smoothing or polishing a surface ▷ *vb* **2** to smooth or polish (a surface) with sandpaper

sandpiper *n* a wading shore bird with a long bill and slender legs

sandpit *n* a shallow pit or container holding sand for children to play in

sandshoes *pl n* light canvas shoes with rubber soles

sandstone *n* a sedimentary rock consisting mainly of sand grains, much used in building

sandstorm *n* a strong wind that whips up clouds of sand, esp. in a desert

sandwich *n* **1** two or more slices of bread, usually buttered, with a layer of food between them ▷ *vb* **2** to place between two other things: *shops sandwiched between flats*
WORD ORIGIN after 4th Earl of *Sandwich*, who ate sandwiches rather than leave the gambling table for meals

sandwich board *n* one of two connected boards that are hung over the shoulders in front of and behind a person to display advertisements

sandwich course *n* *Brit* an educational course consisting of alternate periods of study and industrial work

sandy *adj* **sandier, sandiest** **1** resembling, containing, or covered with sand **2** (of hair) reddish-yellow **sandiness** *n*

sane *adj* **1** having a normal healthy mind **2** sensible or well-judged: *sane advice*
WORD ORIGIN Latin *sanus* healthy

sang *vb* the past tense of **sing**
ⱶ **USAGE**
Ⱶ See at **ring**[1].

sang-froid (sahng-**frwah**) *n* composure and calmness in a difficult situation
WORD ORIGIN French, literally: cold blood

sangoma (sang-**go**-ma) *n S African* a witch doctor
WORD ORIGIN Nguni (language group of southern Africa) *isangoma* a diviner

sangria *n* a Spanish drink of red wine, sugar, spices, and fruit
WORD ORIGIN Spanish: a bleeding

sanguinary *adj formal* **1** (of a battle or fight) involving much violence and bloodshed **2** (of a person) eager to see violence and bloodshed **3** of or stained with blood
WORD ORIGIN Latin *sanguinarius*

sanguine *adj* **1** cheerful and confident **2** (of the complexion) ruddy
WORD ORIGIN Latin *sanguineus* bloody

Sanhedrin (**san**-id-rin) *n Judaism* the highest court and supreme council of the ancient Jewish nation

sanitary *adj* **1** promoting health by getting rid of dirt and germs **2** free from dirt or germs; hygienic
WORD ORIGIN Latin *sanitas* health

sanitary towel *or esp. US* **napkin** *n* a pad worn externally by women during menstruation to absorb the flow of blood

sanitation *n* **1** the use of sanitary measures to maintain public health **2** the drainage and disposal of sewage

sanitize *or* **-tise** *vb* **-tizing, -tized** *or* **-tising, -tised** to omit unpleasant details to make (news) more acceptable

sanity *n* **1** the state of having a normal healthy mind **2** good sense or soundness of judgment
WORD ORIGIN Latin *sanitas* health

sank *vb* the past tense of **sink**

sans-culotte (sanz-kew-**lot**) *n* a revolutionary extremist
WORD ORIGIN French, literally: without knee breeches, because during the French Revolution the revolutionaries wore trousers

Sanskrit *n* the classical literary language of India, used since ancient times for religious purposes **Sanskritic** *adj*
WORD ORIGIN Sanskrit *samskrta* perfected

Santa Claus *n* the legendary patron saint of children, who brings presents to children on Christmas Eve, commonly identified with Saint Nicholas

sap[1] *n* **1** a thin liquid that circulates in a plant, carrying food and water **2** *slang* a gullible person ▷ *vb* **sapping, sapped** **3** to drain of sap
WORD ORIGIN Old English *sæp*

sap[2] *vb* **sapping, sapped** **1** to weaken or exhaust the strength or confidence of **2** to undermine (an enemy position) by digging saps ▷ *n* **3** a deep and narrow trench used to approach or undermine an enemy position
WORD ORIGIN Italian *zappa* spade

sapient (**say**-pee-ent) *adj often used ironically* having great wisdom or sound judgment **sapience** *n*
WORD ORIGIN Latin *sapere* to taste, know

sapling *n* a young tree

saponify *vb* **-fies, -fying, -fied** *chem* to convert (a fat) into a soap by treatment with alkali **saponification** *n*
WORD ORIGIN Latin *sapo* soap

sapper n 1 a soldier who digs trenches 2 (in the British Army) a private of the Royal Engineers

sapphire n 1 a transparent blue precious stone ▷ adj 2 deep blue **WORD ORIGIN** Greek sappheiros

sappy adj -pier, -piest (of plants) full of sap

saprophyte n biol any plant, such as a fungus, that lives and feeds on dead organic matter **WORD ORIGIN** Greek sapros rotten + phuton plant

sarabande or **saraband** n 1 a stately slow Spanish dance 2 music for this dance **WORD ORIGIN** Spanish zarabanda

Saracen n 1 an Arab or Muslim who opposed the Crusades ▷ adj 2 of the Saracens **WORD ORIGIN** Late Greek Sarakēnos

sarcasm n 1 mocking or ironic language intended to insult someone 2 the use or tone of such language **WORD ORIGIN** Greek sarkazein to rend the flesh

sarcastic adj 1 full of or showing sarcasm 2 tending to use sarcasm: a sarcastic critic **sarcastically** adv

sarcoma n pathol a malignant tumour beginning in connective tissue **WORD ORIGIN** Greek sarkōma fleshy growth

sarcophagus (sahr-**koff**-a-guss) n, pl -gi (-guy) or -guses a stone or marble coffin or tomb, esp. one bearing sculpture or inscriptions **WORD ORIGIN** Greek sarkophagos flesh-devouring

sardine n, pl -dines or -dine 1 a small fish of the herring family, often preserved in tightly packed tins 2 like sardines very closely crowded together **WORD ORIGIN** Latin sardina

sardonic adj (of behaviour) mocking or scornful **sardonically** adv **WORD ORIGIN** Greek sardonios

sardonyx n a type of gemstone with alternating reddish-brown and white parallel bands **WORD ORIGIN** Greek sardonux

sargassum n a floating brown seaweed with long stringy fronds containing air sacs **WORD ORIGIN** Portuguese sargaço

sarge n informal sergeant

sari or **saree** n, pl -ris or -rees the traditional dress of Hindu women, consisting of a very long piece of cloth swathed around the body with one end over the shoulder **WORD ORIGIN** Hindi

sarking n Scot, N English, Austral, & NZ flat planking supporting the roof cladding of a building **WORD ORIGIN** Scots sark shirt

sarky adj -kier, -kiest informal sarcastic

sarmie n S African children's slang a sandwich

sarnie n S English informal a sandwich

sarong n a garment worn by Malaysian men and women, consisting of a long piece of cloth tucked around the waist or under the armpits **WORD ORIGIN** Malay

SARS 1 severe acute respiratory syndrome; a severe and contagious viral infection of the lungs characterized by high fever, a dry cough, and breathing difficulties 2 South African Revenue Service

sarsaparilla n a nonalcoholic drink prepared from the roots of a tropical American climbing plant **WORD ORIGIN** Spanish zarzaparrilla

sartorial adj formal of men's clothes or tailoring: sartorial elegance **WORD ORIGIN** Latin sartor a tailor

SAS (in Britain) Special Air Service

sash¹ n a long piece of cloth worn around the waist or over one shoulder, usually as a symbol of rank **WORD ORIGIN** Arabic shāsh muslin

sash² n 1 a frame that contains the panes of a window or door 2 a complete frame together with panes of glass **WORD ORIGIN** French châssis a frame

sashay vb informal to move or walk in a casual or a showy manner: the models sashayed down the catwalk **WORD ORIGIN** French chassé a gliding dance step

sash cord n a strong cord connecting a weight to the sliding half of a sash window

sashimi (sah-**shee**-mee) n a Japanese dish of thin fillets of raw fish **WORD ORIGIN** Japanese sashi piercing + mi fish

sash window n a window consisting of two sashes placed one above the other so that the window can be opened by sliding one frame over the front of the other

Sask. Saskatchewan

sassafras n a tree of North America, with aromatic bark used medicinally and as a flavouring **WORD ORIGIN** Spanish sasafras

Sassenach n Scot & occasionally Irish an English person **WORD ORIGIN** Gaelic Sassunach

sat vb the past of **sit**

Sat. Saturday

Satan n the Devil **WORD ORIGIN** Hebrew: plotter

satanic adj 1 of Satan 2 supremely evil or wicked

Satanism n the worship of Satan **Satanist** n, adj

satchel n a small bag, usually with a shoulder strap **WORD ORIGIN** Old French sachel

sate vb sating, sated to satisfy (a desire or appetite) fully **WORD ORIGIN** Old English sadian

satellite n 1 a man-made device orbiting the earth or another planet, used in communications or to collect scientific information 2 a heavenly body orbiting a planet or star: the earth is a satellite of the sun 3 a country controlled by or dependent on a more powerful one ▷ adj 4 of, used in, or relating to the transmission of television signals from a satellite to the home: satellite TV; a satellite dish **WORD ORIGIN** Latin satelles an attendant

satiate (**say**-she-ate) vb -ating, -ated to provide with more than enough, so as to disgust or weary: enough cakes to satiate several children **satiable** adj **satiation** n **WORD ORIGIN** Latin satiare

satiety (sat-**tie**-a-tee) n formal the feeling of having had too much

satin n 1 a fabric, usually made from silk or rayon, closely woven to give a smooth glossy surface on one side ▷ adj 2 like satin in texture: satin polyurethane varnish **satiny** adj **WORD ORIGIN** Arabic zaitūnī

satinwood n 1 a hard wood with a satiny texture, used in fine furniture 2 the East Indian tree yielding this wood

satire n 1 the use of ridicule to expose incompetence, evil, or corruption 2 a play, novel, or poem containing satire **satirical** adj **WORD ORIGIN** Latin satira a mixture

satirist n 1 a writer of satire 2 a person who uses satire

satirize or **-rise** vb -rizing, -rized or -rising, -rised to ridicule (a person or thing) by means of satire **satirization** or **-risation** n

satisfaction n 1 the pleasure obtained from the fulfilment of a desire 2 something that brings fulfilment: craft workers get satisfaction from their work 3 compensation or an apology for a wrong done: consumers unable to get satisfaction from the gas board

satisfactory adj 1 adequate or acceptable 2 giving satisfaction **satisfactorily** adv

satisfy vb -fies, -fying, -fied 1 to fulfil the desires or needs of (a person): his answer didn't satisfy me 2 to provide sufficiently for (a need or desire): to satisfy public demand 3 to convince: that trip did seem to satisfy her that he was dead 4 to fulfil the requirements of: unable to satisfy the conditions set by the commission **satisfiable** adj **satisfying** adj **WORD ORIGIN** Latin satis enough + facere to make

satnav n motoring informal satellite navigation

satrap n (in ancient Persia) a provincial governor or subordinate ruler **WORD ORIGIN** Old Persian khshathrapāvan, literally: protector of the land

SATs Brit standard assessment tasks

satsuma n a small loose-skinned variety of orange with easily separable segments **WORD ORIGIN** Satsuma, former province of Japan

saturate vb -rating, -rated 1 to soak completely 2 to fill so completely that no more can be added: saturating the area with their men 3 chem to combine (a substance) or (of a substance) to be combined with the greatest possible amount of another substance **WORD ORIGIN** Latin saturare

saturation n 1 the process or state that occurs when one substance is filled so full of another substance that no more can be added 2 mil the use of very heavy force, esp. bombing, against an area

saturation point n 1 the point at which the maximum amount of a substance has been absorbed **2** the point at which some capacity is at its fullest; limit: *the market is close to saturation point*

Saturday *n* the seventh day of the week
WORD ORIGIN Latin *Saturni dies* day of Saturn

Saturn *n* **1** the Roman god of agriculture and vegetation **2** the sixth planet from the sun, second largest in the solar system, around which revolve concentric rings

Saturnalia *n, pl* **-lia** *or* **-lias 1** the ancient Roman festival of Saturn, renowned for its unrestrained revelry **2 saturnalia** a wild party or orgy
WORD ORIGIN Latin *Saturnalis* relating to Saturn

saturnine *adj* having a gloomy temperament or appearance
WORD ORIGIN Latin *Saturnus* Saturn, from the gloomy influence attributed to the planet

satyr *n* **1** *Greek myth* a woodland god represented as having a man's body with the ears, horns, tail, and legs of a goat **2** a man who has strong sexual desires
WORD ORIGIN Greek *saturos*

sauce *n* **1** a liquid added to food to enhance its flavour **2** anything that adds interest or zest **3** *chiefly Brit informal* impudent language or behaviour
WORD ORIGIN Latin *salsus* salted

sauce boat *n* a boat-shaped container for serving sauce

saucepan *n* a metal pan with a long handle and often a lid, used for cooking food

saucer *n* **1** a small round dish on which a cup is set **2** something shaped like a saucer **saucerful** *n*
WORD ORIGIN Old French *saussier* container for sauce

saucy *adj* **saucier, sauciest 1** cheeky or slightly rude in an amusing and light-hearted way **2** jaunty and boldly smart: *a saucy hat* **sauciness** *n*

sauerkraut *n* a German dish of finely shredded pickled cabbage
WORD ORIGIN German *sauer* sour + *Kraut* cabbage

sault (**soo**) *n Canad* a waterfall or rapids
WORD ORIGIN French *saut* a leap

sauna *n* **1** a Finnish-style hot steam bath, usually followed by a cold plunge **2** the place in which such a bath is taken
WORD ORIGIN Finnish

saunter *vb* **1** to walk in a leisurely manner; stroll ▷ *n* **2** a leisurely pace or stroll
WORD ORIGIN origin unknown

saurian *adj* of or resembling a lizard
WORD ORIGIN Greek *sauros* lizard

sausage *n* **1** finely minced meat mixed with fat, cereal, and seasonings, in a tube-shaped casing **2** an object shaped like a sausage **3 not a sausage** *informal* nothing at all
WORD ORIGIN Old French *saussiche*

sausage dog *n informal* same as **dachshund**

sausage roll *n* a roll of sausage meat in pastry

sausage sizzle *n Austral & NZ* an event at which sausages are barbecued, often to raise money for a school or other organization

sauté (**so-tay**) *vb* **-téing** *or* **-téeing, -téed 1** to fry (food) quickly in a little fat ▷ *n* **2** a dish of sautéed food ▷ *adj* **3** sautéed until lightly brown: *sauté potatoes*
WORD ORIGIN French: tossed

Sauternes (**so-turn**) *n* a sweet white wine produced in the southern Bordeaux district of France

savage *adj* **1** wild and untamed: *savage tigers* **2** fierce and cruel: *savage cries* **3** (of peoples) uncivilized or primitive: *savage tribes* **4** rude, crude, and violent: *savage behaviour on the terraces* **5** (of terrain) wild and uncultivated ▷ *n* **6** a member of an uncivilized or primitive society **7** a fierce or vicious person ▷ *vb* **-vaging, -vaged 8** to attack ferociously and wound: *savaged by a wild dog* **9** to criticize extremely severely: *savaged by the press for incompetence* **savagely** *adv*
WORD ORIGIN Latin *silvaticus* belonging to a wood

savagery *n, pl* **-ries** viciousness and cruelty

savannah *or* **savanna** *n* open grasslands, usually with scattered bushes or trees, in Africa
WORD ORIGIN Spanish *zavana*

savant *n* a very wise and knowledgeable man **savante** *fem n*
WORD ORIGIN French

save[1] *vb* **saving, saved 1** to rescue or preserve (a person or thing) from danger or harm **2** to avoid the spending, waste, or loss of (something): *an appeal on television for the public to save energy* **3** to set aside or reserve (money or goods) for future use: *I'm saving for a vintage Mercedes* **4** to treat with care so as to preserve **5** to prevent the necessity for: *a chance saved him from having to make up his mind* **6** *sport* to prevent (a goal) by stopping (a ball or puck) **7** *Christianity* to free (someone) from the influence or consequences of sin ▷ *n* **8** *sport* the act of saving a goal **9** *computers* an instruction to write information from the memory onto a tape or disk **savable** *or* **saveable** *adj* **saver** *n*
WORD ORIGIN Old French *salver*

save[2] *old-fashioned prep* **1** (often foll. by *for*) with the exception of: *the stage was empty save for a single chair* ▷ *conj* **2** but
WORD ORIGIN Middle English *sauf*

save as you earn *n* (in Britain) a savings scheme operated by the government, in which regular deposits are made into a savings account from a salary

saveloy *n Brit, Austral, & NZ* a highly seasoned smoked sausage made from salted pork
WORD ORIGIN Italian *cervellato*

saving *n* **1** preservation from destruction or danger **2** a reduction in the amount of time or money used **3 savings** money saved for future use ▷ *adj* **4** tending to rescue or preserve ▷ *prep* **5** with the exception of

saving grace *n* a good quality in a person that prevents him or her from being entirely bad or worthless

saviour *or US* **savior** *n* a person who rescues another person or a thing from danger or harm
WORD ORIGIN Church Latin *Salvator* the Saviour

Saviour *or US* **Savior** *n Christianity* Jesus Christ, regarded as the saviour of people from sin

savoir-faire (**sav-wahr-fair**) *n* the ability to say and do the right thing in any situation
WORD ORIGIN French

savory *n, pl* **-vories** an aromatic plant whose leaves are used in cooking
WORD ORIGIN Latin *satureia*

savour *or US* **savor** *vb* **1** to enjoy and appreciate (food or drink) slowly **2** to enjoy (a pleasure) for as long as possible: *an experience to be savoured* **3 savour of a** to have a suggestion of: *that could savour of ostentation* **b** to possess the taste or smell of: *the vegetables savoured of coriander* ▷ *n* **4** the taste or smell of something **5** a slight but distinctive quality or trace
WORD ORIGIN Latin *sapor* taste

savoury *or US* **savory** *adj* **1** salty or spicy: *savoury foods* **2** attractive to the sense of taste or smell **3** pleasant or acceptable: *one of the book's less savoury characters* ▷ *n, pl* **-ries 4** *chiefly Brit* a savoury dish served before or after a meal **savouriness** *or US* **savoriness** *n*

savoy *n* a cabbage with a compact head and wrinkled leaves
WORD ORIGIN after the *Savoy* region in France

savvy *slang vb* **-vies, -vying, -vied 1** to understand ▷ *n* **2** understanding or common sense ▷ *adj* **3** shrewd
WORD ORIGIN corruption of Spanish *sabe (usted)* (you) know

saw[1] *n* **1** a cutting tool with a toothed metal blade or edge, either operated by hand or powered by electricity ▷ *vb* **sawing, sawed; sawed** *or* **sawn 2** to cut with or as if with a saw **3** to form by sawing **4** to move (an object) from side to side as if moving a saw
WORD ORIGIN Old English *sagu*

saw[2] *vb* the past tense of **see**[1]

saw[3] *n old-fashioned* a wise saying or proverb
WORD ORIGIN Old English *sagu* a saying

saw doctor *n NZ* a sawmill specialist who sharpens and services saw blades

sawdust *n* particles of wood formed by sawing

sawfish *n, pl* **-fish** *or* **-fishes** a sharklike ray with a long toothed snout resembling a saw

sawhorse *n Austral & NZ* a structure for supporting wood that is being sawn

sawmill *n* a factory where timber is sawn into planks

sawn *vb* a past participle of **saw**[1]

sawn-off *or esp. US* **sawed-off** *adj* (of a shotgun) having the barrel cut short to make concealment of the weapon easier

saw-off *n Canad* **1** a deadlock or stalemate **2** a compromise

sawyer *n* a person who saws timber for a living

sax *n informal* short for **saxophone**

Word Histories
part 11

Slave is derived from Latin *Sclavus*, meaning 'a Slav', because the Slavonic races were frequently conquered and enslaved during the Middle Ages.

Sleuth is a shortened form of *sleuthhound*, meaning a 'tracker dog'. It denoted a dog, such as a bloodhound, that can follow trails. The 'sleuth' part of the word comes from Old Norse *sloth*, meaning 'track'.

Slogan is derived from Gaelic *sluagh-ghairm*, which means 'war cry'.

Snob is sometimes held to be a contraction of the Latin *sine nobilitate*, 'without nobility'. This sounds plausible, but sits uncomfortably with the word's earlier meaning – 'a shoemaker'. How a shoemaker came to be a social climber is not entirely clear, but it may well have something to do with the flattery a shoemaker might be expected to give a potential client who was trying on his wares – especially as, in earlier times, only the wealthy would be buying shoes.

Soccer is formed from *Association Football*.

Sofa comes from Arabic *suffah*, meaning 'an upholstered raised platform'.

Spam, the trademark name for the tinned meat, is apparently a contraction of 'spiced ham'. The sense of unwanted e-mail messages is sometimes said to be an acronym of Stupid Pointless Annoying Mail or Shit Posing As Mail. Another widely touted theory is that the term refers to the effects of throwing the contents of a tin of Spam at a wall; though most of it will fall off, some will stick, which is the desired effect of spam e-mail. In fact, the term derives from the cult television show *Monty Python's Flying Circus*. One surreal sketch shows a café in which Spam is part of every dish; the café is filled with Vikings who sing a song endlessly repeating the word 'Spam', thus preventing any normal conversation. This mirrors the irritating ubiquity of junk e-mail and its disruptive effect on internet discussion boards, hence the term.

Spartan means 'belonging to *Sparta*', a city in ancient Greece whose inhabitants were famous for their discipline, military skill, and stern and plain way of life. Compare the word history for **laconic**.

A '**spinster**' was originally a spinner, that is, a person – not necessarily a woman – whose occupation was spinning. It is said that a young woman was not considered fit to be a wife until she had spun a certain amount of household linen. Hence, the word came to designate an unmarried woman.

Spitting image: There are several popular explanations for 'spitting image'. One contends that it was originally 'spit an image', and refers to a magic ritual, in which a person's saliva and a doll in their image were required to create a supernatural double. Another is that the phrase was originally 'splitting image', meaning people who look so alike that they seem to be the same person split into two. A third version is that the phrase is a corruption of 'spirit and image', and refers to someone's body and soul, ie their complete being. The first theory is correct insofar as an earlier form of the phrase was 'spit and image', but the earliest version is simply 'the spit'; the 'image' is a later addition. Clearly, therefore, 'spitting image' is the result of folk etymology transforming 'spit and image', and obviously the 'spit' is the important part of the phrase. Spittle has been traditionally associated with a person's essence, though the reference may be to seminal, rather than oral, ejaculation, especially when a son is described as 'the spit' of his father.

saxifrage *n* an alpine rock plant with small white, yellow, purple, or pink flowers **WORD ORIGIN** Late Latin *saxifraga*, literally: rock breaker

Saxon *n* **1** a member of a West Germanic people who raided and settled parts of Britain in the fifth and sixth centuries AD **2** any of the West Germanic dialects spoken by the ancient Saxons ▷ *adj* **3** of the ancient Saxons or their language **WORD ORIGIN** Late Latin *Saxon-*, *Saxo*

saxophone *n* a brass wind instrument with keys and a curved metal body **saxophonist** *n* **WORD ORIGIN** after Adolphe *Sax*, who invented it

say *vb* **saying, said 1** to speak or utter **2** to express (an idea) in words: *I can't say what I feel* **3** to state (an opinion or fact) positively: *I say you are wrong* **4** to indicate or show: *the clock says ten to nine* **5** to recite: *to say grace* **6** to report or allege: *they say we shall have rain today* **7** to suppose as an example or possibility: *let us say that he is lying* **8** to convey by means of artistic expression: *what does the artist have to say in this picture?* **9** to make a case for: *there is much to be said for it* **10 go without saying** to be so obvious as to need no explanation **11 to say the least** at the very least ▷ *adv* **12** approximately: *there were, say, 20 people present* **13** for example: *choose a number, say, four* ▷ *n* **14** the right or chance to speak: *the opposition has hardly had a say in these affairs* **15** authority, esp. to influence a decision: *he has a lot of say* **WORD ORIGIN** Old English *secgan*

SAYE (in Britain) save as you earn

saying *n* a well-known phrase or sentence expressing a belief or a truth

Sb *chem* antimony **WORD ORIGIN** New Latin *stibium*

Sc *chem* scandium

SC South Carolina

scab *n* **1** the dried crusty surface of a healing skin wound or sore **2** *disparaging* a person who refuses to support a trade union's actions, and continues to work during a strike **3** a contagious disease of sheep, caused by a mite **4** a fungal disease of plants ▷ *vb* **scabbing, scabbed 5** to become covered with a scab **6** *disparaging* to work as a scab **WORD ORIGIN** Old English *sceabb*

scabbard *n* a holder for a sword or dagger **WORD ORIGIN** Middle English *scauberc*

scabby *adj* **-bier, -biest 1** *pathol* covered with scabs **2** *informal* mean or despicable **scabbiness** *n*

scabies (skay-beez) *n* a contagious skin infection caused by a mite, characterized by intense itching **WORD ORIGIN** Latin *scabere* to scratch

scabious (skay-bee-uss) *n* a plant with showy blue, red, or whitish dome-shaped flower heads **WORD ORIGIN** Medieval Latin *scabiosa herba* the scabies plant

scabrous (skay-bruss) *adj* **1** rough and scaly **2** indecent or crude: *scabrous stand-up comedy* **WORD ORIGIN** Latin *scaber* rough

scaffold *n* **1** a temporary framework used to support workmen and materials during the construction or repair of a building **2** a raised wooden platform on which criminals are hanged; gallows **WORD ORIGIN** Old French *eschaffaut*

scaffolding *n* **1** a scaffold or scaffolds **2** the building materials used to make scaffolds

scalar *maths n* **1** a quantity, such as time or temperature, that has magnitude but not direction ▷ *adj* **2** having magnitude but not direction **WORD ORIGIN** Latin *scala* ladder

scald *vb* **1** to burn with hot liquid or steam **2** to sterilize with boiling water **3** to heat (a liquid) almost to boiling point ▷ *n* **4** a burn caused by scalding **WORD ORIGIN** Late Latin *excaldare* to wash in warm water

scale¹ *n* **1** one of the thin flat overlapping plates covering the bodies of fishes and reptiles **2** a thin flat piece or flake **3** a coating which sometimes forms in kettles and hot-water pipes in areas where the water is hard **4** tartar formed on the teeth ▷ *vb* **scaling, scaled 5** to remove the scales or coating from **6** to peel off in flakes or scales **7** to cover or become covered with scales **scaly** *adj* **WORD ORIGIN** Old French *escale*

scale² *n* **1** (*often pl*) a machine or device for weighing **2** one of the pans of a balance **3 tip the scales** to have a decisive influence **4 tip the scales at** to amount in weight to **WORD ORIGIN** Old Norse *skāl* bowl

scale³ *n* **1** a sequence of marks at regular intervals, used as a reference in making measurements **2** a measuring instrument with such a scale **3** the ratio between the size of something real and that of a representation of it: *the map has a scale of 1:10 000* **4** a series of degrees or graded system of things: *the Western wage scale for the same work* **5** a relative degree or extent: *growing flowers on a very small scale* **6** *music* a sequence of notes taken in ascending or descending order, esp. within one octave **7** *maths* the notation of a given number system: *the decimal scale* ▷ *vb* **scaling, scaled 8** to climb to the top of (an object or height): *the men scaled a wall* **9 scale up** or **down** to increase or reduce proportionally in size: *the design can easily be scaled up; after five days the search was scaled down* **WORD ORIGIN** Latin *scala* ladder

scalene *adj maths* (of a triangle) having all sides of unequal length **WORD ORIGIN** Greek *skalēnos*

scallion *n* a spring onion **WORD ORIGIN** Anglo-French *scalun*

scallop *n* **1** an edible marine mollusc with two fluted fan-shaped shells **2** a single shell of this mollusc **3** one of a series of small curves along an edge **scalloping** *n* **WORD ORIGIN** Old French *escalope* shell

scalloped *adj* decorated with small curves along the edge

scallywag *n informal* a badly behaved but likeable person; rascal **WORD ORIGIN** origin unknown

scalp *n* **1** *anat* the skin and hair covering the top of the head **2** (formerly among Native Americans of N America) a part of this removed as a trophy from a slain enemy ▷ *vb* **3** to cut the scalp from **4** *informal chiefly US* to buy and resell so as to make a high or quick profit **WORD ORIGIN** probably from Old Norse *skālpr* sheath

scalpel *n* a small surgical knife with a very sharp thin blade **WORD ORIGIN** Latin *scalper* a knife

scam *n slang* a stratagem for gain; a swindle

scamp *n* a mischievous person, esp. a child **WORD ORIGIN** probably from Middle Dutch *schampen* to decamp

scamper *vb* **1** to run about hurriedly or quickly ▷ *n* **2** the act of scampering **WORD ORIGIN** see SCAMP

scampi *n* large prawns, usually eaten fried in breadcrumbs **WORD ORIGIN** Italian

scan *vb* **scanning, scanned 1** to scrutinize carefully **2** to glance over quickly **3** *prosody* to analyse (verse) by examining its rhythmic structure **4** *prosody* (of a line or verse) to be metrically correct **5** to examine or search (an area) by systematically moving a beam of light or electrons, or a radar or sonar beam over it **6** *med* to obtain an image of (a part of the body) by means of ultrasound or a scanner ▷ *n* **7** an instance of scanning **8** *med* **a** the examination of part of the body by means of a scanner **b** the image produced by a scanner **WORD ORIGIN** Latin *scandere* to climb

scandal *n* **1** a disgraceful action or event: *the chairman resigned after a loans scandal* **2** shame or outrage arising from a disgraceful action or event: *the figures were a national scandal* **3** malicious gossip **scandalous** *adj* **scandalously** *adv* **WORD ORIGIN** Greek *skandalon* a trap

scandalize or **-ise** *vb* **-izing, -ized** or **-ising, -ised** to shock or be shocked by improper behaviour

scandalmonger *n* a person who spreads or enjoys scandal or gossip

Scandinavian *adj* **1** of Scandinavia (Norway, Sweden, Denmark, and often Finland, Iceland, and the Faeroe Islands) ▷ *n* **2** a person from Scandinavia **3** the northern group of Germanic languages, consisting of Swedish, Danish, Norwegian, Icelandic, and Faeroese

scandium *n chem* a rare silvery-white metallic element. Symbol: Sc **WORD ORIGIN** Latin *Scandia* Scandinavia, where discovered

scanner *n* **1** an aerial or similar device designed to transmit or receive signals, esp. radar signals **2** a device used in medical diagnosis to obtain an image of an internal organ or part

scansion *n* the metrical scanning of verse

scant *adj* scarcely sufficient: *some issues will get scant attention* **WORD ORIGIN** Old Norse *skamt* short

scanty *adj* **scantier, scantiest** barely sufficient or not sufficient **scantily** *adv* **scantiness** *n*

scapegoat *n* **1** a person made to bear the blame for others ▷ *vb* **2** to make a scapegoat of
WORD ORIGIN *escape* + *goat*, coined to translate Biblical Hebrew *azāzēl*, probably goat for Azazel, mistakenly thought to mean 'goat that escapes'

scapula (**skap**-pew-la) *n, pl* **-lae** (-lee) the technical name for **shoulder blade**
WORD ORIGIN Late Latin: shoulder

scapular *adj* **1** *anat* of the scapula ▷ *n* **2** a loose sleeveless garment worn by monks over their habits

scar¹ *n* **1** a mark left on the skin following the healing of a wound **2** a permanent effect on a person's character resulting from emotional distress **3** a mark on a plant where a leaf was formerly attached **4** a mark of damage ▷ *vb* **scarring, scarred 5** to mark or become marked with a scar **6** to permanently effect or be permanently affected by mental trauma: *their divorce will scar those kids for life*
WORD ORIGIN Greek *eskhara* scab

scar² *n* a bare craggy rock formation
WORD ORIGIN Old Norse *sker* low reef

scarab *n* **1** the black dung-beetle, regarded by the ancient Egyptians as divine **2** an image or carving of this beetle
WORD ORIGIN Latin *scarabaeus*

scarce *adj* **1** insufficient to meet the demand: *scarce water resources* **2** not common; rarely found **3** make oneself scarce *informal* to go away ▷ *adv* **4** *archaic or literary* scarcely
WORD ORIGIN Old French *scars*

scarcely *adv* **1** hardly at all **2** often used ironically probably or definitely not: *that is scarcely justification for your actions*
≡ **USAGE**
≡ See at **hardly**.

scarcity *n, pl* **-ties** an inadequate supply

scare *vb* **scaring, scared 1** to frighten or be frightened **2 scare away** or **off** to drive away by frightening ▷ *n* **3** a sudden attack of fear or alarm: *you gave me a scare* **4** a period of general fear or alarm: *the latest AIDS scare*
WORD ORIGIN Old Norse *skirra*

scarecrow *n* **1** an object, usually in the shape of a man, made out of sticks and old clothes, to scare birds away from crops **2** *informal* a raggedly dressed person

scaremonger *n* a person who starts or spreads rumours of disaster to frighten people **scaremongering** *n*

scarf¹ *n, pl* **scarves** or **scarfs** a piece of material worn around the head, neck, or shoulders
WORD ORIGIN origin unknown

scarf² *n, pl* **scarfs 1** a joint between two pieces of timber made by notching the ends and strapping or gluing the two pieces together ▷ *vb* **2** to join (two pieces of timber) by means of a scarf
WORD ORIGIN probably from Old Norse

scarify *vb* **-fies, -fying, -fied 1** *surgery* to make slight incisions in (the skin) **2** *agriculture* to break up and loosen (topsoil) **3** to criticize without mercy **scarification** *n*
WORD ORIGIN Latin *scarifare* to scratch open

≡ **USAGE**
≡ *Scarify* is sometimes wrongly thought
≡ to mean the same as *scare*: *a frightening*
≡ (not *scarifying*) film.

scarlatina *n* the technical name for **scarlet fever**
WORD ORIGIN Italian *scarlatto* scarlet

scarlet *adj* bright red
WORD ORIGIN Old French *escarlate* fine cloth

scarlet fever *n* an acute contagious disease characterized by fever, a sore throat, and a red rash on the body

scarp *n* **1** a steep slope or ridge of rock **2** *fortifications* the side of a ditch cut nearest to a rampart
WORD ORIGIN Italian *scarpa*

scarper *vb* *chiefly Brit slang* to run away or escape
WORD ORIGIN origin unknown

Scart or **SCART** *n electronics* a plug-and-socket system which carries pictures and sound, used in home entertainment systems

scarves *n* a plural of **scarf¹**

scary *adj* **scarier, scariest** *informal* quite frightening

scat¹ *vb* **scatting, scatted** *informal* to go away in haste
WORD ORIGIN origin unknown

scat² *n* **1** a type of jazz singing using improvised vocal sounds instead of words ▷ *vb* **scatting, scatted 2** to sing jazz in this way
WORD ORIGIN perhaps imitative

scathing *adj* harshly critical: *there was a scathing review of the play in the paper* **scathingly** *adv*
WORD ORIGIN Old Norse *skathi* harm

scatology *n* preoccupation with obscenity, esp. with references to excrement **scatological** *adj*
WORD ORIGIN Greek *skat-* excrement + -LOGY

scatter *vb* **1** to throw about in various directions: *scatter some oatmeal on top of the cake* **2** to separate and move in various directions; disperse: *the infantry were scattering* ▷ *n* **3** the act of scattering **4** a number of objects scattered about
WORD ORIGIN probably variant of *shatter*

scatterbrain *n* a person who is incapable of serious thought or concentration **scatterbrained** *adj*

scattershot *adj* wide-ranging but indiscriminate: *a scattershot approach to conservation*

scatty *adj* **-tier, -tiest** *informal* rather absent-minded **scattiness** *n*
WORD ORIGIN from *scatterbrained*

scavenge *vb* **-enging, -enged** to search for (anything usable) among discarded material

scavenger *n* **1** a person who collects things discarded by others **2** any animal that feeds on discarded or decaying matter
WORD ORIGIN Old French *escauwer* to scrutinize

SCE (in Scotland) Scottish Certificate of Education

scenario *n, pl* **-narios 1** a summary of the plot and characters of a play or film **2** an imagined sequence of future events: *the likeliest scenario is*

another general election within a year
WORD ORIGIN Italian

scene *n* **1** the place where an action or event, real or imaginary, occurs **2** an incident or situation, real or imaginary, esp. as described or represented **3** a division of an act of a play, in which the setting is fixed and the action is continuous **4** *films* a shot or series of shots that constitutes a unit of the action **5** the backcloths or screens used to represent a location in a play or film set **6** the view of a place or landscape **7** a display of emotion or loss of temper in public: *you do not want to cause a scene* **8** *informal* a particular activity or aspect of life, and all the things associated with it: *the club scene* **9 behind the scenes a** backstage **b** in secret or in private
WORD ORIGIN Greek *skēnē* tent, stage

scenery *n, pl* **-eries 1** the natural features of a landscape **2** *theatre* the painted backcloths or screens used to represent a location in a theatre or studio

scenic *adj* **1** of or having beautiful natural scenery: *untouched scenic areas* **2** of the stage or stage scenery: *scenic artists*

scent *n* **1** a distinctive smell, esp. a pleasant one **2** a smell left in passing, by which a person or animal may be traced **3** a trail or series of clues by which something is followed: *he must have got on to the scent of the story through you* **4** perfume ▷ *vb* **5** to become aware of by smelling **6** to suspect: *he scented the beginnings of irritation in the car* **7** to fill with odour or fragrance **scented** *adj*
WORD ORIGIN Old French *sentir* to sense

sceptic or *US* **skeptic** (**skep**-tik) *n* **1** a person who habitually doubts generally accepted beliefs **2** a person who doubts the truth of a religion **sceptical** or *US* **skeptical** *adj* **sceptically** or *US* **skeptically** *adv* **scepticism** or *US* **skepticism** *n*
WORD ORIGIN Greek *skeptikos* one who reflects upon

sceptre or *US* **scepter** *n* an ornamental rod symbolizing royal power **sceptred** or *US* **sceptered** *adj*
WORD ORIGIN Greek *skeptron* staff

Schadenfreude (**shah**-den-froy-da) *n* one person's delight in another's misfortune
WORD ORIGIN German *Schaden* harm + *Freude* joy

schedule *n* **1** a timed plan of procedure for a project **2** a list of details or items: *the schedule of priorities* **3** a timetable ▷ *vb* **-uling, -uled 4** to plan and arrange (something) to happen at a certain time **5** to make a schedule or include in a schedule
WORD ORIGIN Latin *scheda* sheet of paper

schema *n, pl* **-mata** an outline of a plan or theory
WORD ORIGIN Greek: form

schematic *adj* presented as a diagram or plan **schematically** *adv*

schematize or **-tise** *vb* **-tizing, -tized** or **-tising, -tised** to form into or arrange in a systematic arrangement or plan

scheme *n* **1** a systematic plan for a course of action **2** a systematic

arrangement of parts or features: *colour scheme* **3** a secret plot **4** a chart, diagram, or outline **5** a plan formally adopted by a government or organization: *a pension scheme* ▷ *vb* **scheming, schemed 6** to plan in an underhand manner **schemer** *n* **scheming** *adj, n*
WORD ORIGIN Greek *skhēma* form

scherzo (**skairt**-so) *n, pl* **-zos** a quick lively piece of music, often the second or third movement in a sonata or symphony
WORD ORIGIN Italian: joke

schilling *n* a former monetary unit of Austria
WORD ORIGIN from German: shilling

schism (**skizz**-um) *n* the division of a group, esp. a religious group, into opposing factions, due to differences in doctrine **schismatic** *adj*
WORD ORIGIN Greek *skhizein* to split

schist (**skist**) *n* a crystalline rock which splits into thin layers
WORD ORIGIN Greek *skhizein* to split

schistosomiasis (shiss-ta-so-**my**-a-siss) *n* same as **bilharzia**

schizo (**skit**-so) *offensive adj* **1** schizophrenic ▷ *n, pl* **-os 2** a schizophrenic person

schizoid *adj* **1** *psychol* having a personality disorder characterized by extreme shyness and extreme sensitivity **2** *informal* characterized by conflicting or contradictory ideas or attitudes ▷ *n* **3** a person who has a schizoid personality

schizophrenia *n* **1** a psychotic disorder characterized by withdrawal from reality, hallucinations, or emotional instability **2** *informal* behaviour that seems to be motivated by contradictory or conflicting principles **schizophrenic** *adj, n*
WORD ORIGIN Greek *skhizein* to split + *phrēn* mind

schmaltz *n* excessive sentimentality, esp. in music **schmaltzy** *adj*
WORD ORIGIN Yiddish: melted fat

schnapps *n* a strong dry alcoholic drink distilled from potatoes
WORD ORIGIN German *Schnaps*

schnitzel *n* a thin slice of meat, esp. veal
WORD ORIGIN German: cutlet

scholar *n* **1** a person who studies an academic subject **2** a student who has a scholarship **3** a pupil **scholarly** *adj*
WORD ORIGIN Latin *schola* school

scholarship *n* **1** academic achievement; learning gained by serious study **2** financial aid provided for a scholar because of academic merit

scholastic *adj* **1** of schools, scholars, or education **2** of or relating to scholasticism ▷ *n* **3** a scholarly person **4** a disciple or adherent of scholasticism
WORD ORIGIN Greek *skholastikos* devoted to learning

scholasticism *n* the system of philosophy, theology, and teaching that dominated medieval Europe and was based on the writings of Aristotle

school¹ *n* **1** a place where children are educated **2** the staff and pupils of a

school **3** a regular session of instruction in a school: *we stayed behind after school* **4** a faculty or department specializing in a particular subject: *the dental school* **5** a place or sphere of activity that instructs: *the school of hard knocks* **6** a group of artists, writers, or thinkers, linked by the same style, teachers, or methods **7** *informal* a group assembled for a common purpose, such as gambling: *a card school* ▷ *vb* **8** to educate or train: *she schooled herself to be as ambitious as her sister*
WORD ORIGIN Greek *skholē* leisure spent in the pursuit of knowledge

school² *n* a group of sea-living animals that swim together, such as fish, whales, or dolphins
WORD ORIGIN Old English *scolu* shoal

schoolboy *n* a boy attending school

schooled *adj* **schooled in** trained or educated in: *well schooled in history*

schoolgirl *n* a girl attending school

schoolhouse *n* **1** a building used as a school **2** a house attached to a school

schoolie *n* *Austral informal* a schoolteacher or a high-school student

schoolies week *n* *Austral informal* a week of post-exam celebrations for students who have just completed their final year of high school

schooling *n* the education a person receives at school

schoolmarm *n* *informal* **1** a woman schoolteacher **2** a woman who is old-fashioned and easily shocked by bad language or references to sex

schoolmaster *or fem* **schoolmistress** *n* a person who teaches in or runs a school

schoolteacher *n* a person who teaches in a school

school year *n* **1** a twelve-month period, usually of three terms, during which pupils remain in the same class **2** the time during this period when the school is open

schooner *n* **1** a sailing ship with at least two masts, one at the back and one at the front **2** *Brit* a large glass for sherry **3** *US, Canad, Austral, & NZ* a large glass for beer
WORD ORIGIN origin unknown

schottische *n* **1** a 19th-century German dance resembling a slow polka **2** music for this dance
WORD ORIGIN German *der schottische Tanz* the Scottish dance

schuss (**shooss**) *n* *skiing* a straight high-speed downhill run
WORD ORIGIN from German

sciatic *adj* **1** *anat* of the hip or the hipbone **2** of or afflicted with sciatica: *a sciatic injury*
WORD ORIGIN Greek *iskhia* hip joint

sciatica *n* severe pain in the large nerve in the back of the leg

science *n* **1** the study of the nature and behaviour of the physical universe, based on observation, experiment, and measurement **2** the knowledge obtained by these methods **3** any particular branch of this knowledge: *medical science* **4** any body of knowledge organized in a way resembling that of

the physical sciences but concerned with other subjects: *political science*
WORD ORIGIN Latin *scientia* knowledge

science fiction *n* stories and films that make imaginative use of scientific knowledge or theories

science park *n* an area where scientific research and commercial development are carried on in cooperation

scientific *adj* **1** relating to science or a particular science: *scientific discovery* **2** done in a systematic way, using experiments or tests **scientifically** *adv*

scientist *n* a person who studies or practises a science

sci-fi *n* short for **science fiction**

scimitar *n* a curved oriental sword
WORD ORIGIN probably from Persian *shimshīr*

scintilla (sin-**till**-a) *n* a very small amount; hint or trace
WORD ORIGIN Latin: a spark

scintillate *vb* **-lating, -lated** to give off (sparks); sparkle **scintillation** *n*
WORD ORIGIN Latin *scintilla* a spark

scintillating *adj* (of conversation or humour) very lively and amusing

scion (**sy**-on) *n* **1** a descendant or young member of a family **2** a shoot of a plant for grafting onto another plant
WORD ORIGIN Old French *cion*

scissors *pl n* a cutting instrument held in one hand, with two crossed blades pivoted so that they close together on what is to be cut
WORD ORIGIN Old French *cisoires*

sclera (**skleer**-a) *n* *biol* the tough white substance that forms the outer covering of the eyeball
WORD ORIGIN Greek *sklēros* hard

sclerosis (skleer-**oh**-siss) *n, pl* **-ses** (-seez) *pathol* an abnormal hardening or thickening of body tissues, esp. of the nervous system or the inner wall of arteries
WORD ORIGIN Greek *sklērōsis* a hardening

sclerotic (skleer-**rot**-ik) *adj* **1** of or relating to the sclera **2** of, relating to, or having sclerosis

scoff¹ *vb* **1** (often foll. by *at*) to speak in a scornful and mocking way about (something) ▷ *n* **2** a mocking expression; jeer **scoffing** *adj, n*
WORD ORIGIN probably from Old Norse

scoff² *vb* *informal* to eat (food) fast and greedily
WORD ORIGIN variant of *scaff* food

scold *vb* **1** to find fault with or rebuke (a person) harshly **2** *old-fashioned* to use harsh or abusive language ▷ *n* **3** a person, esp. a woman, who constantly scolds **scolding** *n*
WORD ORIGIN from Old Norse *skáld*

scollop *n, vb* same as **scallop**

sconce *n* a bracket fixed to a wall for holding candles or lights
WORD ORIGIN Late Latin *absconsa* dark lantern

scone *n* a small plain cake baked in an oven or on a griddle
WORD ORIGIN Scots

scoop *n* **1** a spoonlike tool with a deep bowl, used for handling loose or soft materials such as flour or ice cream **2** the deep shovel of a mechanical

Words from Literature
part 24

shilling *n* a shilling is an old unit of currency. There were twenty shillings in every British pound
"Ten shillings too much," said the gentleman in the white waistcoat.
Oliver Twist Charles Dickens

shine *n* shines are tricks or games
well, it would make a cow laugh to see the shines that old idiot cut
The Adventures of Huckleberry Finn Mark Twain

shirking *adj* lazy and trying to avoid work
some of you shirking lubbers
Treasure Island Robert Louis Stevenson

shiver my timbers *phrase* an expression which was used by sailors and pirates to express surprise
why, shiver my timbers, if I hadn't forgotten my score!
Treasure Island Robert Louis Stevenson

shoe-roses *n* roses made from ribbons which were stuck on to shoes as decoration
the very shoe-roses for Netherfield were got by proxy
Pride and Prejudice Jane Austen

singular *adj* very great and remarkable or strange
"Singular dream," he says
The Adventures of Huckleberry Finn Mark Twain

sire *n* an old word which means lord or master or elder
She also defied her sire
Little Women Louisa May Alcott

sixpence *n* a sixpence was half of a shilling
if she had only a shilling in the world, she would be very likely to give away sixpence of it
Emma Jane Austen

slavey *n* the word slavey was used when there was only one servant in a house or boarding-house – so she had to perform all the duties of a larger staff
Two distinct knocks, sir, will produce the slavey at any time
The Old Curiosity Shop Charles Dickens

slender *adj* weak
In slender accents of sweet verse
The Prelude William Wordsworth

slop-shop *n* a shop where cheap ready-made clothes were sold. They mainly sold clothes to sailors
Accordingly, I took the jacket off, that I might learn to do without it; and carrying it under my arm, began a tour of inspection of the various slop-shops.
David Copperfield Charles Dickens

sluggard *n* a lazy person
"Stand up and repeat 'Tis the voice of the sluggard,'" said the Gryphon.
Alice's Adventures in Wonderland Lewis Carroll

smalls *n* short trousers
It is difficult for a large-headed, small-eyed youth, of lumbering make and heavy countenance, to look dignified under any circumstances; but it is more especially so, when superadded to these personal attractions are a red nose and yellow smalls
Oliver Twist Charles Dickens

sneeze-box *n* a box for snuff was called a sneeze-box because sniffing snuff makes the user sneeze
To think of Jack Dawkins – lummy Jack – the Dodger – the Artful Dodger – going abroad for a common twopenny-halfpenny sneeze-box!
Oliver Twist Charles Dickens

snort *v* to sleep
Or snorted we in the Seven Sleepers' den?
The Good-Morrow John Donne

snuff *n* tobacco in powder form which is taken by sniffing
as he thrust his thumb and forefinger into the proffered snuff-box of the undertaker: which was an ingenious little model of a patent coffin.
Oliver Twist Charles Dickens

digger **3** the amount taken up by a scoop **4** the act of scooping or dredging **5** a news story reported in one newspaper before all the others ▷ *vb* **6** (often foll. by *up*) to take up and remove (something) with or as if with a scoop **7 scoop out** to hollow out with or as if with a scoop **8** to beat (rival newspapers) in reporting a news item **9** to win (a prize, a large sum of money, etc.) **WORD ORIGIN** Germanic

scoot *vb* to leave or move quickly **WORD ORIGIN** origin unknown

scooter *n* **1** a child's small cycle which is ridden by pushing the ground with one foot **2** a light motorcycle with a small engine

scope *n* **1** opportunity for using abilities: *ample scope for creative work* **2** range of view or grasp: *that is outside my scope* **3** the area covered by an activity or topic: *the scope of his essay was vast* **WORD ORIGIN** Greek *skopos* target

scorbutic (score-**byewt**-ik) *adj* of or having scurvy **WORD ORIGIN** Medieval Latin *scorbutus*

scorch *vb* **1** to burn or become burnt slightly on the surface **2** to parch or shrivel from heat **3** *informal* to criticize harshly ▷ *n* **4** a slight burn **5** a mark caused by the application of excessive heat **scorching** *adj* **WORD ORIGIN** probably from Old Norse *skorpna* to shrivel up

scorcher *n informal* a very hot day

score *n* **1** the total number of points made by a side or individual in a game **2** the act of scoring a point or points: *there was no score and three minutes remained* **3 the score** *informal* the actual situation: *what's the score on this business?* **4** *old-fashioned* a group or set of twenty: *three score years and ten* **5 scores of** lots of: *we received scores of letters* **6** *music* a written version of a piece of music showing parts for each musician **7 a** the incidental music for a film or play **b** the songs and music for a stage or film musical **8** a mark or scratch **9** a record of money due: *what's the score for the drinks?* **10** an amount recorded as due **11** a reason: *some objections were made on the score of sentiment* **12** a grievance: *a score to settle* **13 over the score** *informal* excessive or unfair ▷ *vb* **scoring, scored** **14** to gain (a point or points) in a game or contest **15** to make a total score of **16** to keep a record of the score (of) **17** to be worth (a certain number of points) in a game: *red aces score twenty* **18** to make cuts or lines in or on **19** *slang* to purchase an illegal drug **20** *slang* to succeed in finding a sexual partner **21** to arrange (a piece of music) for specific instruments or voices **22** to write the music for (a film or play) **23** to achieve (success or an advantage): *your idea scored with the boss* **WORD ORIGIN** Old English *scora*

scoreboard *n sport* a board for displaying the score of a game or match

scorecard *n* **1** a card on which scores are recorded in games such as golf **2** a card identifying the players in a sports match, esp. cricket

score off *vb* to make a clever or insulting reply to what someone has just said: *they spent the evening scoring off each other*

scorer *n* **1** a player of a sport who scores a goal, run, or point: *Ireland's record goal scorer has announced his retirement* **2** a person who keeps note of the score of a match or competition as it is being played

scoria (score-ee-a) *n* **1** *geol* a mass of solidified lava containing many cavities **2** refuse left after ore has been smelted **WORD ORIGIN** Latin: dross

scorn *n* **1** open contempt for a person or thing ▷ *vb* **2** to treat with contempt: *she attacked the government for scorning her profession* **3** to refuse to have or do (something) because it is felt to be undesirable or wrong: *youths who scorn traditional morals* **scornful** *adj* **scornfully** *adv* **WORD ORIGIN** Old French *escharnir*

Scorpio *n astrol* the eighth sign of the zodiac; the Scorpion **WORD ORIGIN** Latin

scorpion *n* a small lobster-shaped animal with a sting at the end of a jointed tail **WORD ORIGIN** Greek *skorpios*

Scot *n* a person from Scotland

Scot. **1** Scotland **2** Scottish

scotch *vb* **1** to put an end to: *she had scotched the idea of bingo in the church* **2** to wound without killing **WORD ORIGIN** origin unknown

Scotch¹ *not standard adj* **1** same as **Scottish** ▷ *pl n* **2 the Scotch** the Scots

≡ **USAGE**
≡ In the north of England and in
≡ Scotland, *Scotch* is not used outside
≡ fixed expressions such as *Scotch whisky*.
≡ The use of *Scotch* for *Scots* or *Scottish* is
≡ otherwise felt to be incorrect, esp.
≡ when applied to people.

Scotch² *n* whisky distilled in Scotland from fermented malted barley

Scotch broth *n Brit* a thick soup made from mutton or beef stock, vegetables, and pearl barley

Scotch egg *n* a hard-boiled egg encased in sausage meat and breadcrumbs, and fried

Scotch mist *n* a heavy wet mist or drizzle

scot-free *adv, adj* without harm or punishment: *the real crooks got off scot-free* **WORD ORIGIN** obsolete *scot* a tax

Scotland Yard *n* the headquarters of the police force of metropolitan London

Scots *adj* **1** of Scotland ▷ *n* **2** any of the English dialects spoken or written in Scotland

Scotsman *or fem* **Scotswoman** *n, pl* **-men** *or* **-women** a person from Scotland

Scots pine *n* **1** a coniferous tree found in Europe and Asia, with needle-like leaves and brown cones **2** the wood of this tree

Scottish *adj* of Scotland

scoundrel *n old-fashioned* a person who cheats and deceives **WORD ORIGIN** origin unknown

scour¹ *vb* **1** to clean or polish (a surface) by rubbing with something rough **2** to clear (a channel) by the force of water ▷ *n* **3** the act of scouring **scourer** *n* **WORD ORIGIN** Old French *escurer*

scour² *vb* **1** to search thoroughly and energetically: *he had scoured auction salerooms* **2** to move quickly over (land) in search or pursuit **WORD ORIGIN** probably from Old Norse *skūr* shower

scourge *n* **1** a person who or thing that causes affliction or suffering **2** a whip formerly used for punishing people ▷ *vb* **scourging, scourged** **3** to cause severe suffering to **4** to whip **WORD ORIGIN** Latin *excoriare* to whip

Scouse *Brit informal n* **1** Also called: **Scouser** a person from Liverpool **2** the Liverpool dialect ▷ *adj* **3** of Liverpool, its people, or their dialect **WORD ORIGIN** from *lobscouse* a sailor's stew

scout *n* **1** *mil* a person sent to find out the position of the enemy **2** same as **talent scout** **3** the act or an instance of scouting ▷ *vb* **4** to examine or observe (something) in order to obtain information **5 scout about** *or* **around** to go in search of something **WORD ORIGIN** Old French *ascouter* to listen to

Scout *or* **scout** *n* a member of the Scout Association, an organization for young people which aims to develop character and promote outdoor activities **Scouting** *n*

scow *n* an unpowered barge used for carrying freight **WORD ORIGIN** Low German *schalde*

scowl *vb* **1** to have an angry or bad-tempered facial expression ▷ *n* **2** an angry or bad-tempered facial expression **WORD ORIGIN** probably from Old Norse

scrabble *vb* **-bling, -bled** **1** to scrape at or grope for something with hands, feet, or claws: *scrabbling with his feet to find a foothold* **2** to move one's hands about in order to find something one cannot see: *scrabbling in her handbag for a comb* **WORD ORIGIN** Middle Dutch *schrabbelen*

Scrabble *n trademark* a board game in which words are formed by placing letter tiles in a pattern similar to a crossword puzzle

scrag *n* **1** the thin end of a neck of veal or mutton **2** a thin or scrawny person or animal **WORD ORIGIN** perhaps variant of *crag*

scraggy *adj* **-gier, -giest** unpleasantly thin and bony **scragginess** *n*

scram¹ *vb* **scramming, scrammed** *informal* to leave very quickly **WORD ORIGIN** from *scramble*

scram² *n* **1** an emergency shutdown of a nuclear reactor ▷ *vb* **scramming, scrammed** **2** (of a nuclear reactor) to shut down or be shut down in an emergency **WORD ORIGIN** perhaps from SCRAM¹

scramble *vb* **-bling, -bled** **1** to climb or crawl hurriedly by using the hands to aid movement **2** to go hurriedly or in a disorderly manner **3** to compete with others in a rough and undignified way:

spectators scrambled for the best seats **4** to jumble together in a haphazard manner **5** to cook (eggs that have been whisked up with milk) in a pan **6** *mil* (of a crew or aircraft) to take off quickly in an emergency **7** to make (transmitted speech) unintelligible by the use of an electronic scrambler ⊳ *n* **8** the act of scrambling **9** a climb or trek over difficult ground **10** a rough and undignified struggle to gain possession of something **11** *mil* an immediate takeoff of crew or aircraft in an emergency **12** *Brit* a motorcycle race across rough open ground

WORD ORIGIN blend of SCRABBLE + RAMP

scrambler *n* an electronic device that makes broadcast or telephone messages unintelligible without a special receiver

scramjet *n* **a** a type of ramjet in which the forward motion of the craft forces oxygen to mix with fuel (usually hydrogen) at supersonic speeds within a duct in the engine **b** an aircraft powered by such an engine

WORD ORIGIN from s(*upersonic*) + c(*ombustion*) + RAMJET

scrap¹ *n* **1** a small piece of something larger; fragment **2** waste material or used articles, often collected and reprocessed **3 scraps** pieces of leftover food ⊳ *vb* **scrapping, scrapped 4** to discard as useless

WORD ORIGIN Old Norse *skrap*

scrap² *informal n* **1** a fight or quarrel ⊳ *vb* **scrapping, scrapped 2** to quarrel or fight

WORD ORIGIN perhaps from *scrape*

scrapbook *n* a book of blank pages in which newspaper cuttings or pictures are stuck

scrape *vb* **scraping, scraped 1** to move (a rough or sharp object) across (a surface) **2** (often foll. by *away* or *off*) to remove (a layer) by rubbing **3** to produce a grating sound by rubbing against (something else) **4** to injure or damage by scraping: *he had scraped his knees* **5 scrimp and scrape** see **scrimp** (sense 2) ⊳ *n* **6** the act or sound of scraping **7** a scraped place: *a scrape on the car door* **8** *informal* an awkward or embarrassing situation **9** *informal* a conflict or struggle **scraper** *n*

WORD ORIGIN Old English *scrapian*

scrape through *vb* to succeed in or survive with difficulty: *both teams had scraped through their semifinals*

scrape together *or* **up** *vb* to collect with difficulty: *he scraped together enough money to travel*

scrapheap *n* **on the scrapheap** (of people or things) no longer required: *I was tossed on the scrapheap at a very early age*

scrappy *adj* **-pier, -piest** badly organized or done: *a scrappy draft of a chapter of my thesis*

scratch *vb* **1** to mark or cut (the surface of something) with a rough or sharp instrument **2** (often foll. by *at* or *out* etc.) to tear or dig with the nails or claws **3** to scrape (the surface of the skin) with the nails to relieve itching **4** to rub against (the skin) causing a slight cut **5** to make or cause to make a grating sound **6** (sometimes foll. by *out*)

to erase or cross out **7** to withdraw from a race or (in the US) an election ⊳ *n* **8** the act of scratching **9** a slight cut on a person's or an animal's body **10** a mark made by scratching **11** a slight grating sound **12 from scratch** *informal* from the very beginning **13 not up to scratch** *informal* not up to standard ⊳ *adj* **14** put together at short notice: *a scratch team* **15** *sport* with no handicap allowed: *a scratch golfer* **scratchy** *adj*

WORD ORIGIN Germanic

scratchcard *n* a ticket that reveals whether or not the holder is eligible for a prize when the surface is removed by scratching

scratching *n* *music* a sound produced when the record groove in contact with the stylus of a record player is moved back and forth by hand

scrawl *vb* **1** to write carelessly or hastily ⊳ *n* **2** careless or scribbled writing **scrawly** *adj*

WORD ORIGIN perhaps blend of SPRAWL + CRAWL

scrawny *adj* **scrawnier, scrawniest** very thin and bony **scrawniness** *n*

WORD ORIGIN dialect *scranny*

scream *vb* **1** to make a sharp piercing cry or sound because of fear or pain **2** (of a machine) to make a high-pitched noise **3** to laugh wildly **4** to utter with a scream: *he screamed abuse up into the sky* **5** to be unpleasantly conspicuous: *bad news screaming out from the headlines* ⊳ *n* **6** a sharp piercing cry or sound, esp. of fear or pain **7** *informal* a very funny person or thing

WORD ORIGIN Germanic

scree *n* a pile of rock fragments at the foot of a cliff or hill, often forming a sloping heap

WORD ORIGIN Old English *scrīthan* to slip

screech¹ *n* **1** a shrill or high-pitched sound or cry ⊳ *vb* **2** to utter a shrill cry **screechy** *adj*

WORD ORIGIN earlier *scritch*, imitative

screech² *n* *Canad* a dark rum

WORD ORIGIN origin unknown

screech owl *n* **1** *Brit* same as **barn owl 2** a small North American barn owl

screed *n* a long tiresome speech or piece of writing

WORD ORIGIN probably from Old English *scrēade* shred

screen *n* **1** the blank surface of a television set, VDU, or radar receiver, on which a visible image is formed **2** the white surface on which films or slides are projected **3 the screen** the film industry or films collectively **4** a light movable frame, panel, or partition used to shelter, divide, or conceal **5** anything that shelters, protects, or conceals: *a screen of leaves blocking out the sun* **6** a frame containing a mesh that is used to keep out insects ⊳ *vb* **7** (sometimes foll. by *off*) to shelter, protect, or conceal with or as if with a screen **8** to test or check (an individual or group) so as to assess suitability for a task or to detect the presence of a disease or weapons: *women screened for breast cancer* **9** to show (a film) in the cinema or show (a programme) on television

WORD ORIGIN Old French *escren*

screenplay *n* the script for a film, including instructions for sets and camera work

screen process *n* a method of printing by forcing ink through a fine mesh of silk or nylon, some parts of which have been treated so as not to let the ink pass

screen saver *n* *computers* software that produces changing images on a monitor when the computer is operating but idle

screenshot *n* an image created by copying part or all of the display on a computer screen at a particular moment

screenwriter *n* a person who writes screenplays

screw *n* **1** a metal pin with a spiral ridge along its length, twisted into materials to fasten them together **2** a threaded cylindrical rod that engages with a similarly threaded cylindrical hole **3** a thread in a cylindrical hole corresponding with the one on the screw with which it is designed to engage **4** anything resembling a screw in shape **5** *slang* a prison guard **6** *taboo slang* an act of or partner in sexual intercourse **7 have a screw loose** *informal* to be insane **8 put the screws on** *slang* to use force on or threatening behaviour against ⊳ *vb* **9** to rotate (a screw or bolt) so as to drive it into or draw it out of a material **10** to twist or turn: *she screwed up the sheet of paper* **11** to attach or fasten with or as if with a screw or screws **12** *informal* to take advantage of, esp. illegally: *screwed by big business* **13** *informal* to distort or contort: *his face was screwed up in pain* **14** (often foll. by *out of*) *informal* to force out of; extort **15** *taboo slang* to have sexual intercourse (with) **16 have one's head screwed on the right way** *informal* to be sensible

▸ See also **screw up**

WORD ORIGIN French *escroe*

screwball *slang chiefly US & Canad n* **1** an odd or eccentric person ⊳ *adj* **2** crazy or eccentric: *a screwball comedy*

screwdriver *n* **1** a tool used for turning screws, consisting of a long thin metal rod with a flattened tip that fits into a slot in the head of the screw **2** a drink consisting of orange juice and vodka

screw top *n* **1** a bottle top that screws onto the bottle, allowing the bottle to be resealed after use **2** a bottle with such a top

screw up *vb* **1** *informal* to mishandle or spoil (something): *that screws up all my arrangements* **2** to twist out of shape or distort **3 screw up one's courage** to force oneself to be brave **screwed-up** *adj*

screwy *adj* **screwier, screwiest** *informal* crazy or eccentric

scribble *vb* **-bling, -bled 1** to write or draw quickly and roughly **2** to make meaningless or illegible marks (on) ⊳ *n* **3** something written or drawn quickly or roughly **4** meaningless or illegible marks **scribbler** *n* **scribbly** *adj*

WORD ORIGIN Latin *scribere* to write

scribe *n* **1** a person who made handwritten copies of manuscripts or documents before the invention of

S

printing **2** *Bible* a recognized scholar and teacher of the Jewish Law
WORD ORIGIN Latin *scriba* clerk

scrimmage *n* **1** a rough or disorderly struggle ▷ *vb* **-maging, -maged 2** to take part in a scrimmage
WORD ORIGIN earlier *scrimish*

scrimp *vb* **1** to be very sparing in the use of something: *they were scrimping by on the last of the potatoes* **2 scrimp and save** or **scrape** to spend as little money as possible
WORD ORIGIN Scots

scrip¹ *n finance* a certificate representing a claim to shares or stocks
WORD ORIGIN short for *subscription receipt*

scrip² or **script** *n informal* a medical prescription
WORD ORIGIN from PRESCRIPTION

script *n* **1** the text of a play, TV programme, or film for the use of performers **2** an alphabet or system of writing: *Cyrillic script* **3** a candidate's answer paper in an examination **4** handwriting **5** a typeface which looks like handwriting ▷ *vb* **6** to write a script for
WORD ORIGIN Latin *scriptum* something written

scripture *n* the sacred writings of a religion **scriptural** *adj*
WORD ORIGIN Latin *scriptura* written material

Scripture *n Christianity* the Old and New Testaments

scriptwriter *n* a person who writes scripts, esp. for a film or TV programme **scriptwriting** *n*

scrofula *n no longer in technical use* tuberculosis of the lymphatic glands **scrofulous** *adj*
WORD ORIGIN Medieval Latin

scroggin *n NZ* a mixture of nuts and dried fruits

scroll *n* **1** a roll of parchment or paper, usually inscribed with writing **2** an ancient book in the form of a roll of parchment, papyrus, or paper **3** a decorative carving or moulding resembling a scroll ▷ *vb* **4** *computers* to move (text) on a screen in order to view a section that cannot be fitted into a single display
WORD ORIGIN Middle English *scrowle*

Scrooge *n* a mean or miserly person
WORD ORIGIN after a character in Dickens' story *A Christmas Carol*

scrotum *n* the pouch of skin containing the testicles in most male mammals
WORD ORIGIN Latin

scrounge *vb* **scrounging, scrounged** *informal* to get (something) by asking for it rather than buying it or working for it **scrounger** *n*
WORD ORIGIN dialect *scrunge* to steal

scrub¹ *vb* **scrubbing, scrubbed 1** to rub (something) hard in order to clean it **2** to remove (dirt) by rubbing with a brush and water **3 scrub up** (of a surgeon) to wash the hands and arms thoroughly before operating **4** *informal* to delete or cancel (an idea or plan) ▷ *n* **5** the act of scrubbing
WORD ORIGIN Middle Low German *schrubben* or Middle Dutch *schrobben*

scrub² *n* **1** vegetation consisting of stunted trees or bushes growing in a dry area **2** an area of dry land covered with such vegetation ▷ *adj* **3** stunted or inferior: *scrub pines*
WORD ORIGIN variant of *shrub*

scrubber *n* **1** *Austral & Brit offensive slang* a woman who has many sexual partners **2** a device that removes pollutants from the gases that are produced when coal is burned industrially

scrubby *adj* **-bier, -biest 1** (of land) rough, dry, and covered with scrub **2** (of plants) stunted **3** *Brit informal* shabby or untidy

scrubs *pl n* the hygienic clothing worn by surgeons and other operating-theatre staff during an operation

scruff¹ *n* the nape of the neck: *the sergeant had him by the scruff of the neck*
WORD ORIGIN perhaps from Old Norse *skoft* hair

scruff² *n informal* a very untidy person

scruffy *adj* **scruffier, scruffiest** dirty and untidy in appearance

scrum *n* **1** *rugby* a formation in which players from each side form a tight pack and push against each other in an attempt to get the ball, which is thrown on the ground between them **2** *informal* a disorderly struggle ▷ *vb* **scrumming, scrummed 3** (usually foll. by *down*) *rugby* to form a scrum
WORD ORIGIN from *scrummage*

scrum half *n rugby* a player who puts in the ball at scrums and tries to regain its possession in order to pass it to his team's backs

scrummage *n, vb* **-maging, -maged 1** *rugby* same as **scrum 2** same as **scrimmage**
WORD ORIGIN variant of *scrimmage*

scrump *vb Brit dialect* to steal (apples) from an orchard or garden
WORD ORIGIN variant of *scrimp*

scrumptious *adj informal* delicious or very attractive
WORD ORIGIN probably changed from *sumptuous*

scrumpy *n Brit* a rough dry cider brewed in the West Country of England
WORD ORIGIN dialect *scrump* withered apples

scrunch *vb* **1** to press or crush noisily or be pressed or crushed noisily ▷ *n* **2** the act or sound of scrunching: *the scrunch of tyres on gravel*
WORD ORIGIN variant of *crunch*

scrunchie *n* a loop of elastic covered loosely with fabric, used to hold the hair in a ponytail

scruple *n* **1** a doubt or hesitation as to what is morally right in a certain situation: *he had no scruples about the drug trade* ▷ *vb* **-pling, -pled 2** to have doubts (about), esp. on moral grounds
WORD ORIGIN Latin *scrupulus* a small weight

scrupulous *adj* **1** taking great care to do what is fair, honest, or morally right **2** very careful or precise: *scrupulous attention to detail* **scrupulously** *adv*
WORD ORIGIN Latin *scrupulosus*

scrutinize or **-nise** *vb* **-nizing, -nized** or **-nising, -nised** to examine carefully or in minute detail

scrutiny *n, pl* **-nies 1** very careful study or observation **2** a searching look
WORD ORIGIN Late Latin *scrutari* to search

scuba (**skew**-ba) *n* an apparatus used in skin diving, consisting of cylinders containing compressed air attached to a breathing apparatus
WORD ORIGIN s(elf-)c(ontained) u(nderwater) b(reathing) a(pparatus)

scud *vb* **scudding, scudded 1** (esp. of clouds) to move along quickly **2** *naut* to run before a gale ▷ *n* **3** the act of scudding **4** spray, rain, or clouds driven by the wind
WORD ORIGIN probably Scandinavian

scuff *vb* **1** to drag (the feet) while walking **2** to scrape (one's shoes) by doing so ▷ *n* **3** a mark caused by scuffing **4** the act or sound of scuffing
WORD ORIGIN probably imitative

scuffle *vb* **-fling, -fled 1** to fight in a disorderly manner ▷ *n* **2** a short disorganized fight **3** a scuffling sound
WORD ORIGIN Scandinavian

scull *n* **1** a single oar moved from side to side over the back of a boat **2** one of a pair of small oars, both of which are pulled by one oarsman **3** a racing boat rowed by one oarsman pulling two oars ▷ *vb* **4** to row (a boat) with a scull **sculler** *n*
WORD ORIGIN origin unknown

scullery *n, pl* **-leries** *chiefly Brit* a small room where washing-up and other kitchen work is done
WORD ORIGIN Anglo-Norman *squillerie*

scullion *n archaic* a servant employed to do the hard work in a kitchen
WORD ORIGIN Old French *escouillon* cleaning cloth

sculpt *vb* same as **sculpture**

sculptor or *fem* **sculptress** *n* a person who makes sculptures

sculpture *n* **1** the art of making figures or designs in wood, plaster, stone, or metal **2** works or a work made in this way ▷ *vb* **-turing, -tured 3** to carve (a material) into figures or designs **4** to represent (a person or thing) in sculpture **5** to form or be formed in the manner of sculpture: *limestone sculptured by fast-flowing streams* **sculptural** *adj*
WORD ORIGIN Latin *sculptura* a carving

scum *n* **1** a layer of impure or waste matter that forms on the surface of a liquid: *the build-up of soap scum* **2** a person or people regarded as worthless or criminal ▷ *vb* **scumming, scummed 3** to remove scum from **4** *rare* to form a layer of or become covered with scum **scummy** *adj*
WORD ORIGIN Germanic

scumbag *n slang* an offensive or despicable person
WORD ORIGIN perhaps from earlier US sense: condom

scungy (**skun**-jee) *adj* **scungier, scungiest** *Austral & NZ slang* miserable, sordid, or dirty
WORD ORIGIN origin unknown

scunner *dialect chiefly Scot vb* **1** to produce a feeling of dislike in ▷ *n* **2 take a**

Words from Shakespeare
part 15

sampler *n* a piece of embroidery, which often showed the family tree
Both on one sampler, sitting on one cushion
A Midsummer Night's Dream 3.2

saucy *adj* rude
I heard you were saucy at my gates *Twelfth Night* 1.5

schooling *n* advice
I have some private schooling for you both.
A Midsummer Night's Dream 1.1

seething *adj* boiling
Lovers and madmen have such seething brains
A Midsummer Night's Dream 5.1

semblative *adj* resembling or looking like
And all is semblative a woman's part.
Twelfth Night 1.4

several *adj* separate or different
twenty several messengers
Anthony and Cleopatra 1.5

shrew *n* an annoying person or someone who makes you cross
Bless you, fair shrew. *Twelfth Night* 1.3

shroud *v* to hide or shelter
I will here, shroud till the dregs of the storm be past *The Tempest* 2.2

sickleman *n* someone who used a sickle to harvest crops
You sunburnt sicklemen, of August weary
The Tempest 4.1

soft *int* wait a moment or stop
But, soft, what nymphs are these
A Midsummer Night's Dream 4.1

something *adv* somewhat or rather
Be something scanter of your maiden presence
Hamlet 1.3

sooth *adv* truly
Yes, sooth; and so do you
A Midsummer Night's Dream 3.2

spleen *n* fury or anger
That, in a spleen, unfolds both heaven and earth
A Midsummer Night's Dream 1.1

sport *n* recreation or entertainment
I see our wars
Will turn unto a peaceful comic sport
Henry VI part 1 2.2

strain *n* a tune or a musical phrase
and so die
That strain again! it had a dying fall.
Twelfth Night 1.1

suffer *v* to perish or die
but an islander that hath lately suffered by a thunderbolt. *The Tempest* 2.2

suit *n* a petition, request or a proposal of marriage
Because she will admit no kind of suit
Twelfth Night 1.2

sup *v* to have supper
Go know of Cassio where he supped tonight
Othello 5.1

surfeit *n* an amount which is too large
If music be the food of love, play on;
Give me excess of it, that, surfeiting,
The appetite may sicken *Twelfth Night* 1.1

swain *n* a suitor or person who wants to marry
take this transformed scalp
From off the head of this Athenian swain
A Midsummer Night's Dream 4.1

thereto *adv* also
If she be black, and thereto have a wit *Othello* 2.1

throstle *n* a name for a song-bird
The throstle with his note so true
A Midsummer Night's Dream 3.1

tidings *n* news
that upon certain tidings now arrived, importing the mere perdition of the Turkish fleet *Othello* 2.2

scunner to to take a strong dislike to **3** a person or thing that is disliked
WORD ORIGIN Scots *skunner*

scupper[1] *n naut* a drain or spout in a ship's side allowing water on the deck to flow overboard
WORD ORIGIN origin unknown

scupper[2] *vb* **1** *Brit & NZ slang* to defeat or ruin: *a deliberate attempt to scupper the peace talks* **2** to sink (one's ship) deliberately
WORD ORIGIN origin unknown

scurf *n* **1** same as **dandruff 2** any flaky or scaly matter sticking to or peeling off a surface **scurfy** *adj*
WORD ORIGIN Old English

scurrilous *adj* untrue or unfair, insulting, and designed to damage a person's reputation: *scurrilous allegations* **scurrility** *n*
WORD ORIGIN Latin *scurra* buffoon

scurry *vb* **-ries, -rying, -ried 1** to run quickly with short steps ▷ *n, pl* **-ries 2** a quick hurrying movement or the sound of this movement **3** a short shower of rain or snow
WORD ORIGIN probably from *hurry-scurry*

scurvy *n* **1** a disease caused by a lack of vitamin C, resulting in weakness, spongy gums, and bleeding beneath the skin ▷ *adj* **-vier, -viest 2** *old-fashioned* deserving contempt **scurviness** *n*
WORD ORIGIN from *scurf*

scut *n* the short tail of animals such as the deer and rabbit
WORD ORIGIN probably from Old Norse

scuttle[1] *n* same as **coal scuttle**
WORD ORIGIN Latin *scutella* bowl

scuttle[2] *vb* **-tling, -tled 1** to run with short quick steps ▷ *n* **2** a hurried pace or run
WORD ORIGIN probably from *scud*

scuttle[3] *vb* **-tling, -tled 1** *naut* to cause (a ship) to sink by making holes in the sides or bottom **2** to ruin (hopes or plans) or have them ruined: *a new policy scuttled by popular resistance* ▷ *n* **3** *naut* a small hatch in a ship's deck or side
WORD ORIGIN Spanish *escotilla* a small opening

Scylla (**sill**-a) *n* **1** (in classical mythology) a sea monster believed to drown sailors navigating the Straits of Messina **2 between Scylla and Charybdis** in an awkward situation in which avoidance of either of two dangers means exposure to the other

scythe *n* **1** a long-handled tool for cutting grass or grain, with a curved sharpened blade that is swung parallel to the ground ▷ *vb* **scything, scythed 2** to cut (grass or grain) with a scythe
WORD ORIGIN Old English *sigthe*

SD South Dakota

SDI Strategic Defense Initiative

SDLP (in Northern Ireland) Social Democratic and Labour Party

Se *chem* selenium

SE southeast(ern)

sea *n* **1 the sea** the mass of salt water that covers three-quarters of the earth's surface **2 a** one of the smaller areas of this: *the Irish Sea* **b** a large inland area of water: *the Caspian Sea* **3** the area on or close to the edge of the sea, esp. as a place where holidays are taken: *a day by the sea* **4** strong and uneven swirling movement of waves: *rough seas* **5** anything resembling the sea in size or movement: *a sea of red and yellow flags* **6 at sea a** on the ocean **b** in a state of confusion or uncertainty **7 go to sea** to become a sailor **8 put out to sea** to start a sea voyage
WORD ORIGIN Old English *sǣ*

sea anchor *n naut* a canvas-covered frame, dragged in the water behind a ship to slow it down or reduce drifting

sea anemone *n* a marine animal with a round body and rings of tentacles which trap food from the water

sea bird *n* a bird that lives on or near the sea

seaboard *n* land bordering on the sea

seaborgium *n chem* a synthetic element. Symbol: Sg
WORD ORIGIN after Glenn *Seaborg*, physicist and chemist

seaborne *adj* **1** carried on or by the sea **2** transported by ship: *seaborne reinforcements*

sea breeze *n* a breeze blowing inland from the sea

sea cow *n* **1** a whalelike mammal such as a dugong or manatee **2** *archaic* a walrus

sea dog *n* an experienced or old sailor

seafarer *n* **1** a traveller who goes by sea **2** a sailor

seafaring *adj* **1** travelling by sea **2** working as a sailor ▷ *n* **3** the act of travelling by sea **4** the work of a sailor

seafood *n* edible saltwater fish or shellfish

seafront *n* a built-up area facing the sea

seagoing *adj* built for travelling on the sea

sea-green *adj* bluish-green

seagull *n* same as **gull**

sea horse *n* a small marine fish with a horselike head, which swims upright

sea kale *n* a European coastal plant with broad fleshy leaves and asparagus-like shoots that can be eaten

seal[1] *n* **1** a special design impressed on a piece of wax, lead, or paper, fixed to a letter or document as a mark of authentication **2** a stamp or signet ring engraved with a design to form such an impression **3** a substance placed over an envelope or container, so that it cannot be opened without the seal being broken **4** something that serves as an official confirmation of approval: *seal of approval* **5** any substance or device used to close an opening tightly **6 set the seal on** to confirm something: *the experience set the seal on their friendship* ▷ *vb* **7** to close or secure with or as if with a seal: *once the manuscripts were sealed up, they were forgotten about* **8 seal off** to enclose or isolate (a place) completely **9** to close tightly so as to make airtight or watertight **10** to inject a compound around the edges of something to make it airtight or watertight **11** to attach a seal to or stamp with a seal **12** to finalize or authorize **13 seal one's fate** to make sure one dies or fails **14 seal one's lips** to promise not to reveal a secret **sealable** *adj*
WORD ORIGIN Latin *signum* a sign

seal[2] *n* **1** a fish-eating mammal with four flippers, which lives in the sea but comes ashore to breed **2** sealskin ▷ *vb* **3** to hunt seals
WORD ORIGIN Old English *seolh*

sealant *n* any substance, such as wax, used for sealing, esp. to make airtight or watertight

sea legs *pl n informal* the ability to maintain one's balance on board ship and to avoid being seasick

sea level *n* the average level of the sea's surface in relation to the land

sealing wax *n* a hard material made of shellac and turpentine, which softens when heated and which is used to make a seal

sea lion *n* a type of large seal found in the Pacific Ocean

Sea Lord *n* (in Britain) a naval officer on the admiralty board of the Ministry of Defence

sealskin *n* the skin or prepared fur of a seal, used to make coats

seam *n* **1** the line along which pieces of fabric are joined by stitching **2** a ridge or line made by joining two edges: *the seam between the old and the new buildings* **3** a long narrow layer of coal, marble, or ore formed between layers of other rocks **4** a mark or line like a seam, such as a wrinkle or scar ▷ *adj* **5** *cricket* of a style of bowling in which the bowler uses the stitched seam round the ball in order to make it swing in flight and after touching the ground: *a seam bowler* ▷ *vb* **6** to join together by or as if by a seam **7** to mark with furrows or wrinkles
WORD ORIGIN Old English *sēam*

seaman *n, pl* **-men 1** a man ranking below an officer in a navy **2** a sailor

seamanship *n* skill in navigating and operating a ship

seamer *or* **seam bowler** *n cricket* a fast bowler who makes the ball bounce on its seam so that it will change direction

seamless *adj* **1** (of a garment) without seams **2** continuous or flowing: *a seamless performance* **seamlessness** *n*

seamstress *n* a woman who sews, esp. professionally

seamy *adj* **seamier, seamiest** involving the sordid and unpleasant aspects of life, such as crime, prostitution, poverty, and violence **seaminess** *n*

seance *or* **séance** (**say**-onss) *n* a meeting at which a spiritualist attempts to communicate with the spirits of the dead
WORD ORIGIN French

seaplane *n* an aircraft that is designed to land on and take off from water

seaport *n* a town or city with a harbour for boats and ships

sear *vb* **1** to scorch or burn the surface of **2** to cause to wither
WORD ORIGIN Old English *sēarian* to become withered

search *vb* **1** to look through (a place) thoroughly in order to find someone or something **2** to examine (a person) for hidden objects **3** to look at or examine (something) closely: *I searched my heart for one good thing she had done* **4 search out** to find by searching **5** to make a search **6 search me** *informal* I don't know ▷ *n* **7** an attempt to find something by looking somewhere **WORD ORIGIN** Old French *cerchier*

search engine *n computers* an internet service enabling users to search for items of interest

Search Engine Optimization *n* the process of improving a website's page ranking in a search engine

searching *adj* keen or thorough: *a searching analysis* **searchingly** *adv*

searchlight *n* **1** a light with a powerful beam that can be shone in any direction **2** the beam of light produced by this device

search warrant *n* a legal document allowing a policeman to enter and search premises

seascape *n* a drawing, painting, or photograph of a scene at sea

Sea Scout *n* a member of the branch of the Scouts which gives training in seamanship

seashell *n* the empty shell of a marine mollusc

seashore *n* land bordering on the sea

seasick *adj* suffering from nausea and dizziness caused by the movement of a ship at sea **seasickness** *n*

seaside *n* an area, esp. a holiday resort, bordering on the sea

season *n* **1** one of the four divisions of the year (spring, summer, autumn, and winter), each of which has characteristic weather conditions **2** a period of the year characterized by particular conditions or activities: *the typhoon season; the football season* **3** the period during which any particular species of animal, bird, or fish is legally permitted to be caught or killed: *the deer season* **4** any definite or indefinite period: *the busy season* **5** any period during which a show or play is performed at one venue: *the show ran for three seasons* **6 in season a** (of game) permitted to be killed **b** (of fresh food) readily available **c** (of animals) ready to mate ▷ *vb* **7** to add herbs, salt, pepper, or spice to (food) in order to enhance the flavour **8** (in the preparation of timber) to dry and harden **9** to make experienced: *old men seasoned by living* **seasoned** *adj* **WORD ORIGIN** Latin *satio* a sowing

seasonable *adj* **1** suitable for the season: *a seasonable Christmas snow scene* **2** coming or happening just at the right time: *seasonable advice*

seasonal *adj* of or depending on a certain season or seasons of the year: *seasonal employment* **seasonally** *adv*

seasoning *n* something that is added to food to enhance the flavour

season ticket *n* a ticket for a series of events or number of journeys, usually bought at a reduced rate

seat *n* **1** a piece of furniture designed for sitting on, such as a chair **2** the part of a chair or other piece of furniture on which one sits **3** a place to sit in a theatre, esp. one that requires a ticket: *there were two empty front-row seats at the*

pageant **4** the buttocks **5** the part of a garment covering the buttocks **6** the part or surface on which an object rests **7** the place or centre in which something is based: *the seat of government* **8** Brit a country mansion **9** a membership or the right to membership of a legislative or administrative body: *a seat on the council* **10** *chiefly Brit* a parliamentary constituency **11** the manner in which a rider sits on a horse ▷ *vb* **12** to bring to or place on a seat **13** to provide seats for: *the dining hall seats 150 people* **14** to set firmly in place **WORD ORIGIN** Old English *gesete*

seat belt *n* a strap attached to a car or aircraft seat, worn across the body to prevent a person being thrown forward in the event of a collision

seating *n* **1** seats which are provided somewhere, esp. in a public place: *the grandstand has seating for 10 000; hard plastic seating* ▷ *adj* **2** of or relating to the provision of places to sit: *the delegation leader complained about the seating arrangements*

sea urchin *n* a small sea animal with a round body enclosed in a spiny shell

seaward *adv also* **seawards 1** towards the sea ▷ *adj* **2** directed or moving towards the sea

seawater *n* salt water from the sea

seaweed *n* any plant growing in the sea or on the seashore

seaworthy *adj* (of a ship) in a fit condition for a sea voyage **seaworthiness** *n*

sebaceous *adj* of, like, or secreting fat **WORD ORIGIN** Latin *sebum* tallow

sebaceous glands *pl n* the small glands in the skin that secrete oil into hair follicles and onto most of the body surface

sebum (**see**-bum) *n* the oily substance secreted by the sebaceous glands **WORD ORIGIN** Latin: tallow

sec¹ *adj* (of wines) dry **WORD ORIGIN** French

sec² *n informal* a second (of time): *hang on a sec*

sec³ secant

sec. **1** second (of time) **2** secondary **3** secretary

secant (**seek**-ant) *n* **1** (in trigonometry) the ratio of the length of the hypotenuse to the length of the adjacent side in a right-angled triangle; the reciprocal of cosine **2** a straight line that intersects a curve **WORD ORIGIN** Latin *secare* to cut

secateurs *pl n* a small pair of gardening shears for pruning **WORD ORIGIN** French

secede *vb* **-ceding, -ceded** to make a formal withdrawal of membership from a political alliance, federation, or group: *it will secede from the federation within six months* **WORD ORIGIN** Latin *se-* apart + *cedere* to go

secession *n* the act of seceding **secessionism** *n* **secessionist** *n, adj*

seclude *vb* **-cluding, -cluded 1** to remove from contact with others **2** to shut off

or screen from view **WORD ORIGIN** Latin *secludere*

secluded *adj* **1** kept apart from the company of others: *a secluded private life* **2** private and sheltered: *a secluded cottage*

seclusion *n* the state of being secluded; privacy: *the seclusion of his winter retreat*

second¹ *adj* **1** coming directly after the first in order **2** rated, graded, or ranked between the first and third levels **3** alternate: *every second Saturday* **4** another of the same kind; additional: *a second chance* **5** resembling or comparable to a person or event from the past: *a second Virgin Mary* **6** of lesser importance or position; inferior **7** denoting the second lowest forward gear in a motor vehicle **8** *music* denoting a musical part, voice, or instrument subordinate to or lower in pitch than another (the first): *the second tenors* **9 at second hand** by hearsay ▷ *n* **10** a person or thing that is second **11** Brit education an honours degree of the second class **12** the second lowest forward gear in a motor vehicle **13** (in boxing or duelling) an attendant who looks after a boxer or duellist **14 seconds a** *informal* a second helping of food or the second course of a meal **b** goods that are sold cheaply because they are slightly faulty ▷ *vb* **15** to give aid or backing to **16** (in boxing or duelling) to act as second to (a boxer or duellist) **17** to express formal support for (a motion proposed in a meeting) ▷ *adv* **18** Also: **secondly** in the second place **WORD ORIGIN** Latin *secundus* next in order

second² *n* **1** the basic SI unit of time, equal to $\frac{1}{60}$ of a minute **2** $\frac{1}{60}$ of a minute of angle **3** a very short period of time **WORD ORIGIN** Latin *pars minuta secunda* the second small part (a minute being the first small part of an hour)

second³ (sik-**kond**) *vb* Brit & NZ to transfer (a person) temporarily to another job **secondment** *n* **WORD ORIGIN** French *en second* in second rank

secondary *adj* **1** below the first in rank or importance: *a secondary consideration* **2** coming next after the first: *secondary cancers* **3** derived from or depending on what is primary or first: *a secondary source* **4** of or relating to the education of people between the ages of 11 and 18 or, in New Zealand, between 13 and 18: *secondary education* **5** (of an industry) involving the manufacture of goods from raw materials ▷ *n, pl* **-aries 6** a person or thing that is secondary

secondary colour *n* a colour formed by mixing two primary colours

secondary picketing *n* the picketing by striking workers of the premises of a firm that supplies or distributes goods to or from their employer

second-best *adj* **1** next to the best ▷ *adv* **second best 2 come off second best** *informal* to fail to win against someone ▷ *n* **second best 3** an inferior alternative

second chamber *n* the upper house of a two-chamber system of government

second childhood *n* the time in an old person's life when he or she starts to suffer from memory loss and confusion; senility

second class *n* **1** the class or grade next in value, rank, or quality to the first ▷ *adj* **second-class 2** of the class or grade next to the best in value, rank, or quality **3** shoddy or inferior **4** denoting the class of accommodation in a hotel or on a train, aircraft, or ship, lower in quality and price than first class **5** (of mail) sent by a cheaper type of postage and taking slightly longer to arrive than first-class mail ▷ *adv* **6** by second-class mail, transport, etc.

Second Coming *n* the prophesied return of Christ to earth at the Last Judgment

second cousin *n* the child of one's parent's first cousin

second-degree burn *n* a burn in which blisters appear on the skin

second fiddle *n* *informal* a person who has a secondary status

second floor *n* the storey of a building immediately above the first and two floors up from the ground

second-hand *adj* **1** previously owned or used **2** not from an original source or one's own experience: *second-hand opinions* **3** dealing in or selling goods that are not new: *second-hand furniture shops* ▷ *adv* **4** from a source of previously owned or used goods: *they preferred to buy second-hand* **5** not directly or from one's own experience: *his knowledge had been gleaned second-hand*

second hand *n* a pointer on the face of a watch or clock that indicates the seconds

second lieutenant *n* an officer holding the lowest commissioned rank in an army or navy

secondly *adv* same as **second**[1] (sense 18)

second nature *n* a habit or characteristic practised for so long that it seems to be part of one's character

second person *n* the form of a pronoun or verb used to refer to the person or people being addressed

second-rate *adj* **1** not of the highest quality; mediocre **2** second in importance or rank: *a second-rate citizen*

second sight *n* the supposed ability to foresee the future or see actions taking place elsewhere

second thoughts *pl n* a revised opinion or idea on a matter already considered

second wind *n* **1** the return of comfortable breathing following difficult or strenuous exercise **2** renewed ability to continue in an effort

secrecy *n, pl* **-cies 1** the state of being secret **2** the ability or tendency to keep things secret

secret *adj* **1** kept hidden or separate from the knowledge of all or all but a few others **2** secretive: *she had become a secret drinker* **3** operating without the knowledge of outsiders: *secret organizations* ▷ *n* **4** something kept or to be kept hidden **5** something unrevealed; a mystery: *the secrets of nature*

6 an underlying explanation or reason: *the secret of great-looking hair* **7** **in secret** without the knowledge of others secretly *adv*

WORD ORIGIN Latin *secretus* concealed

secret agent *n* a person employed by a government to find out the military and political secrets of other governments

secretaire (sek-rit-**air**) *n* same as **escritoire**

secretariat *n* **1 a** an office responsible for the secretarial, clerical, and administrative affairs of a legislative body or international organization **b** the staff of such an office or department **2** the premises of a secretariat

WORD ORIGIN French

secretary *n, pl* **-taries 1** a person who handles correspondence, keeps records, and does general clerical work for an individual or organization **2** the official manager of the day-to-day business of a society, club, or committee **3** (in Britain) a senior civil servant who assists a government minister **4** (in the US) the head of a government administrative department **secretarial** *adj*

WORD ORIGIN Medieval Latin *secretarius* someone entrusted with secrets

secretary bird *n* a large long-legged African bird of prey

secretary-general *n, pl* **secretaries-general** the chief administrative official of a legislative body or international organization

secretary of state *n* **1** (in Britain) the head of a major government department **2** (in the US) the head of the government department in charge of foreign affairs

secrete[1] *vb* **-creting, -creted** (of a cell, organ, or gland) to produce and release (a substance) **secretory** (sik-**reet**-or-ee) *adj*

secrete[2] *vb* **-creting, -creted** to put in a hiding place

WORD ORIGIN variant of obsolete *secret* to hide away

secretion *n* **1** a substance that is released from a cell, organ, or gland **2** the process involved in producing and releasing such a substance

WORD ORIGIN Latin *secretio* a separation

secretive *adj* hiding feelings and intentions **secretively** *adv*

secret police *n* a police force that operates secretly to suppress opposition to the government

secret service *n* a government agency or department that conducts intelligence or counterintelligence operations

sect *n* **1** a subdivision of a larger religious or political group, esp. one regarded as extreme in its beliefs or practices **2** a group of people with a common interest or philosophy

WORD ORIGIN Latin *secta* faction

sectarian *adj* **1** of or belonging to a sect **2** narrow-minded as a result of supporting a particular sect ▷ *n* **3** a member of a sect **sectarianism** *n*

section *n* **1** a part cut off or separated from the main body of something: *a non-smoking section* **2** a part or subdivision of a piece of writing or a book: *the business section* **3** a distinct part of a country or community: *the Arabic section* **4** *surgery* the act or process of cutting or separating by cutting **5** *geom* a plane surface formed by cutting through a solid **6** short for **Caesarean section 7** NZ a plot of land for building on **8** *Austral & NZ* a fare stage on a bus ▷ *vb* **9** to cut or divide into sections **10** to commit (a mentally disturbed person) to a mental hospital

WORD ORIGIN Latin *secare* to cut

sectional *adj* **1** concerned with a particular area or group within a country or community, esp. to the exclusion of others: *narrow sectional interests* **2** made of sections **3** of a section

sector *n* **1** a part or subdivision, esp. of a society or an economy: *the public sector* **2** *geom* either portion of a circle bounded by two radii and the arc cut off by them **3** a portion into which an area is divided for military operations

WORD ORIGIN Latin: a cutter

secular *adj* **1** relating to worldly as opposed to sacred things **2** not connected with religion or the church **3** (of clerics) not bound by religious vows to a monastic or other order

WORD ORIGIN Late Latin *saecularis*

secularism *n* the belief that religion should have no place in civil affairs **secularist** *n, adj*

secularize *or* **-rise** *vb* **-rizing, -rized** *or* **-rising, -rised** to change (something, such as education) so that it is no longer connected with religion or the Church **secularization** *or* **-risation** *n*

secure *adj* **1** free from danger or damage **2** free from fear, doubt, or care **3** tightly locked or well protected **4** fixed or tied firmly in position **5** able to be relied on: *secure profits* ▷ *vb* **-curing, -cured 6** to obtain: *to secure a change in German policy* **7** to make or become free from danger or fear **8** to make safe from loss, theft, or attack **9** to attach; make fast or firm **10** to guarantee (payment of a loan) by giving something as security **securely** *adv*

WORD ORIGIN Latin *securus* free from care

security *n, pl* **-ties 1** precautions taken to ensure against theft, espionage, or other danger **2** the state of being free from danger, damage, or worry **3** assured freedom from poverty: *the security of a weekly pay cheque* **4** a certificate of ownership, such as a share, stock, or bond **5** something given or pledged to guarantee payment of a loan

security risk *n* someone or something thought to be a threat to state security

sedan *n* *US, Canad, Austral, & NZ* a saloon car

WORD ORIGIN origin unknown

sedan chair *n* an enclosed chair for one passenger, carried on poles by two bearers, commonly used in the 17th and 18th centuries

The Influence of Spanish on English

The members of the Spanish Royal Academy, who publish the most authoritative dictionary of Spanish and issue guidance on spelling and grammar, are constantly wringing their hands at the prospect of the imminent disintegration of Spanish. They know that there's little they can do to stop the influx of migrant words, and they're aware that almost every new gadget or fashion or sport (like *el frisbee*) arrives with an English tag on it. But the traffic isn't all one way. There's plenty of Spanish that finds its way into English.

There is no English Academy to 'protect' the language, and English happily absorbs any words that it finds convenient, no matter where they come from. For example, every time a new species or a new disease is identified, people turn to Latin and Greek to coin names for them. This means that English is stuffed full of odd-looking medical and scientific terms which it has been accumulating for the last two or three centuries. Words like *antibiotic* (from *anti* + *bio* + *tic*) just fit right in, and alarm nobody. You could say English was tolerant, or undiscriminating, or maybe promiscuous, but essentially, if it needs somebody else's word, it'll take it. It's this sponge-like quality of English that's one of the reasons that it's such a successful international language; it might already contain quite a lot of words from whatever language it is that you speak.

You get a particularly good start if you speak Spanish. All those Latin words sound familiar straight away, because Spanish has its roots in Latin. Some things on the lunch menu will look familiar, too; the words *tomato* and *potato* were stolen from Spanish at about the same time Sir Francis Drake was capturing galleons (also a Spanish word) full of doubloons. The dessert *chocolate* comes from a Mexican word via Spanish. If you're a Spanish speaker from Mexico, you'll be delighted to see *fajitas*, maybe with *avocado* or *guacamole*, also words imported from Mexico via Spanish. But if you want to indulge in *tobacco* (a *cigar*, perhaps), *amigo*, you'll have to go outside.

Spanish has had an effect on culture which goes beyond words. The word 'Latino' conjures up images of couples dancing flamboyantly together. Flamenco and salsa classes are becoming more and more popular, as people try to share in the carefree life of the Spanish-speaking world. About a quarter of a million British citizens have opted to actually go and live in Spain, and they do their best to learn something of the language and culture, especially where it involves music, dancing and drinking. Corona, Sol, and other well-known brands of Mexican beer are very popular, as is *tequila*.

The millions of migrant Mexican workers in the United States take their language with them, and together with the Cubans, Puerto Ricans, and other Spanish speakers make up more than ten percent of the population of the United States. Signs in California and other states are bilingual, and a significant proportion of the population need never worry about learning to speak English at all. Hollywood and television reflect this, and Spanish has become fashionable right across the world. The hit American television series *The West Wing* imagined a Hispanic presidential candidate. Actor Arnold Schwarzenneger may have been born speaking German in Vienna, but one of his most famous lines is 'Hasta la vista, baby' in his role as the Terminator. Even fake Spanish is popular: 'no problemo' is based on a misunderstanding – the Spanish word is *problema*, and you'd say 'no hay problema'.

The dominant world language is usually the language of the dominant economic power, and the Spanish empire of the 16th and 17th centuries was responsible for hundreds of new words entering English as the New World was opened up. With the decline in Spanish power in the 18th century, the flow of loan words also diminished. But now we are experiencing a new wave of Spanish words and Latino ideas, with a sudden burst of creative activity from writers and directors who are bilingual and bicultural. Suddenly it's sexy to speak Spanish, to travel to Latin-American countries, and to snack on *nachos*.

sedate¹ *adj* **1** quiet, calm, and dignified **2** slow or unhurried: *a sedate walk to the beach* **sedately** *adv*
WORD ORIGIN Latin *sedare* to soothe

sedate² *vb* **-dating, -dated** to calm down or make sleepy by giving a sedative drug to

sedation *n* **1** a state of calm, esp. when brought about by sedatives **2** the administration of a sedative

sedative *adj* **1** having a soothing or calming effect ▷ *n* **2** *med* a sedative drug or agent that makes people sleep or calm down
WORD ORIGIN Latin *sedatus* assuaged

sedentary (**sed**-en-tree) *adj* **1** done sitting down and involving very little exercise: *a sedentary job* **2** tending to sit about without taking much exercise
WORD ORIGIN Latin *sedere* to sit

sedge *n* a coarse grasslike plant growing on wet ground **sedgy** *adj*
WORD ORIGIN Old English *secg*

sedge warbler *n* a European songbird living in marshy areas

sediment *n* **1** matter that settles to the bottom of a liquid **2** material that has been deposited by water, ice, or wind **sedimentary** *adj*
WORD ORIGIN Latin *sedimentum* a settling

sedition *n* speech, writing, or behaviour intended to encourage rebellion or resistance against the government **seditionary** *n, adj* **seditious** *adj*
WORD ORIGIN Latin *seditio* discord

seduce *vb* **-ducing, -duced** **1** to persuade to have sexual intercourse **2** to tempt into wrongdoing **seduction** *n*
WORD ORIGIN Latin *seducere* to lead apart

seductive *adj* **1** (of a woman) sexually attractive **2** very attractive or tempting: *a seductive argument* **seductively** *adv* **seductiveness** *n*

sedulous *adj* diligent or painstaking: *a sedulous concern with the achievements of western thought* **sedulously** *adv*
WORD ORIGIN Latin *sedulus*

sedum *n* a rock plant with thick clusters of white, yellow, or pink flowers
WORD ORIGIN Latin

see¹ *vb* **seeing, saw, seen** **1** to look at or recognize with the eyes **2** to understand: *I explained the problem but he could not see it* **3** to perceive or be aware of: *she had never seen him so angry* **4** to view, watch, or attend: *we had barely seen a dozen movies in our lives* **5** to foresee: *they could see what their fate was to be* **6** to find out (a fact): *I was ringing to see whether you'd got it* **7** to make sure (of something) or take care (of something): *see that he is never in a position to do these things again; you must see to it* **8** to consider or decide: *see if you can come next week* **9** to have experience of: *he had seen active service in the revolution* **10** to meet or pay a visit to: *I see my specialist every three months* **11** to receive: *the Prime Minister will see the deputation now* **12** to frequent the company of: *we've been seeing each other since then* **13** to accompany: *she saw him to the door* **14** to refer to or look up: *see page 35* **15** (in gambling, esp. in poker) to match (another player's bet) or match the bet of (another player) by staking an equal

sum **16** **see fit** to consider it proper (to do something): *I did not see fit to send them home* **17** **see you** or **see you later** or **be seeing you** an expression of farewell
▶ See also **see about**, **see into**, etc.
WORD ORIGIN Old English *sēon*

see² *n* the diocese of a bishop or the place within it where his cathedral is situated
WORD ORIGIN Latin *sedes* a seat

see about *vb* **1** to take care of: *I'll see about some coffee* **2** to investigate: *to see about a new car*

seed *n* **1** *bot* the mature fertilized grain of a plant, containing an embryo ready for germination ▶ Related adjective: **seminal** **2** such seeds used for sowing **3** the source, beginning, or origin of anything: *the seeds of dissent* **4** *chiefly Bible* descendants; offspring: *the seed of David* **5** *sport* a player ranked according to his or her ability **6** **go** or **run to seed a** (of plants) to produce and shed seeds after flowering **b** to lose strength or usefulness ▷ *vb* **7** to plant (seeds) in (soil) **8** (of plants) to produce or shed seeds **9** to remove the seeds from (fruit or plants) **10** to scatter silver iodide in (clouds) in order to cause rain **11** to arrange (the draw of a tournament) so that outstanding teams or players will not meet in the early rounds **seedless** *adj*
WORD ORIGIN Old English *sēd*

seedbed *n* **1** an area of soil prepared for the growing of seedlings before they are transplanted **2** the place where something develops: *a seedbed of immorality*

seedling *n* a plant produced from a seed, esp. a very young plant

seed pearl *n* a very small pearl

seed pod *n* *bot* a carpel or pistil enclosing the seeds of a plant, esp. a flowering plant

seedy *adj* **seedier, seediest** **1** shabby in appearance: *a seedy cinema* **2** *informal* physically unwell **3** (of a plant) at the stage of producing seeds **seediness** *n*

seeing *n* **1** the sense or faculty of sight ▷ *conj* **2** (often foll. by *that* or *as*) in light of the fact (that)
≡USAGE
≡The use of *seeing as how* as in *seeing as (how) the bus is always late, I don't see any reason to hurry* is generally thought to be incorrect or non-standard.

see into *vb* to discover the true nature of: *he could see into my intentions*

seek *vb* **seeking, sought** **1** to try to find by searching: *to seek employment* **2** to try to obtain: *to seek a diplomatic solution* **3** to try (to do something): *we seek to establish a stable relationship*
WORD ORIGIN Old English *sēcan*

seek out *vb* to search hard for and find (a specific person or thing): *you should seek out healthy role models*

seem *vb* **1** to appear to the mind or eye; give the impression of: *the car seems to be running well* **2** to appear to be: *there seems no need for all this nonsense* **3** to have the impression: *I seem to remember you were there too*
WORD ORIGIN Old Norse *sōma* to be suitable

≡USAGE
≡See at **like**.

seeming *adj* apparent but not real: *his seeming willingness to participate* **seemingly** *adv*

seemly *adj* **-lier, -liest** *formal* proper or fitting

seen *vb* the past participle of **see¹**

see off *vb* **1** to be present at the departure of (a person going on a journey): *your sisters came to see you off* **2** *informal* to cause to leave or depart, esp. by force

seep *vb* to leak through slowly; ooze **seepage** *n*
WORD ORIGIN Old English *sīpian*

seer *n* a person who can supposedly see into the future

seersucker *n* a light cotton fabric with a slightly crinkled surface
WORD ORIGIN Hindi *śīrśakar*

seesaw *n* **1** a plank balanced in the middle so that two people seated on the ends can ride up and down by pushing on the ground with their feet **2** an up-and-down or back-and-forth movement ▷ *vb* **3** to move up and down or back and forth alternately
WORD ORIGIN reduplication of *saw*, alluding to the movement from side to side, as in sawing

seethe *vb* **seething, seethed** **1** to be in a state of extreme anger or indignation without publicly showing these feelings **2** (of a liquid) to boil or foam **seething** *adj*
WORD ORIGIN Old English *sēothan*

see through *vb* **1** to perceive the true nature of: *it was difficult to see through people* **2** to remain with until the end or completion: *not all of them saw it through* **3** to help out in a time of need or trouble: *he helped see her through her divorce* ▷ *adj* **see-through 4** (of clothing) made of thin cloth so that the wearer's body or underclothes are visible

segment *n* **1** one of several parts or sections into which an object is divided **2** *maths* **a** a part of a circle cut off by an intersecting line **b** a part of a sphere cut off by an intersecting plane or planes ▷ *vb* **3** to cut or divide into segments **segmental** *adj* **segmentation** *n*
WORD ORIGIN Latin *segmentum*

segregate *vb* **-gating, -gated** **1** to set apart from others or from the main group **2** to impose segregation on (a racial or minority group)
WORD ORIGIN Latin *se-* apart + *grex* a flock

segregation *n* **1** the practice or policy of creating separate facilities within the same society for the use of a racial or minority group **2** the act of segregating **segregational** *adj* **segregationist** *n*

seigneur *n* a feudal lord, esp. in France **seigneurial** *adj*
WORD ORIGIN Old French

seine (sane) *n* **1** a large fishing net that hangs vertically in the water by means of floats at the top and weights at the bottom ▷ *vb* **seining, seined 2** to catch (fish) using this net
WORD ORIGIN Old English *segne*

seismic *adj* relating to or caused by earthquakes
WORD ORIGIN Greek *seismos* earthquake

seismograph *n* an instrument that records the intensity and duration of earthquakes **seismographer** *n* **seismography** *n*
WORD ORIGIN Greek *seismos* earthquake + -GRAPH

seismology *n* the branch of geology concerned with the study of earthquakes **seismologist** *n*
WORD ORIGIN Greek *seismos* earthquake + -LOGY

seismometer *n* same as **seismograph**

seize *vb* seizing, seized **1** to take hold of forcibly or quickly; grab **2** to take immediate advantage of: *real journalists would have seized the opportunity* **3** to take legal possession of **4** (sometimes foll. by *on* or *upon*) to understand quickly: *she immediately seized his idea* **5** to affect or fill the mind of suddenly: *a wild frenzy seized her* **6** to take by force or capture: *the rebels seized a tank factory* **7** (often foll. by *up*) (of mechanical parts) to become jammed through overheating
WORD ORIGIN Old French *saisir*

seizure *n* **1** *pathol* a sudden violent attack of an illness, such as an epileptic convulsion **2** the act of seizing: *a seizure of drug traffickers' assets*

seldom *adv* rarely; not often
WORD ORIGIN Old English *seldon*

select *vb* **1** to choose (someone or something) in preference to another or others ▷ *adj* **2** chosen in preference to others **3** restricted to a particular group; exclusive: *a select audience* **selector** *n*
WORD ORIGIN Latin *seligere* to sort

select committee *n* a small committee of Members of Parliament, set up to investigate and report on a specified matter

selection *n* **1** a selecting or being selected **2** a thing or number of things that have been selected **3** a range from which something may be selected: *a good selection of reasonably priced wines* **4** *biol* the process by which certain organisms or individuals are reproduced and survive in preference to others

selective *adj* **1** tending to choose carefully or characterized by careful choice: *they were selective in their reading* **2** of or characterized by selection **selectively** *adv* **selectivity** *n*

selenium *n* *chem* a nonmetallic element used in photocells, solar cells, and in xerography. Symbol: Se
WORD ORIGIN Greek *selēnē* moon

self *n, pl* selves **1** the distinct individuality or identity of a person or thing **2** a person's typical bodily make-up or personal characteristics: *back to my old self after the scare* **3** one's own welfare or interests: *he only thinks of self* **4** an individual's consciousness of his or her own identity or being ▷ *pron* **5** *not standard* myself, yourself, himself, or herself: *setting goals for self and others*
WORD ORIGIN Old English

self- *combining form* **1** (used with many main words to mean) of oneself or itself: *self-defence* **2** (used with many main words to mean) by, to, in, due to, for, or from the self: *self-employed; self-respect* **3** (used with many main words to mean) automatic or automatically: *self-propelled*

self-abnegation *n* the denial of one's own interests in favour of the interests of others

self-absorption *n* preoccupation with oneself to the exclusion of others **self-absorbed** *adj*

self-abuse *n* Old-fashioned masturbation

self-addressed *adj* addressed for return to the sender

self-aggrandizement *or* **self-aggrandisement** *n* the act of increasing one's own power, wealth, or importance

self-appointed *adj* having assumed authority without the agreement of others: *self-appointed moralists*

self-assertion *n* the act of putting forward one's own opinions or demanding one's rights, esp. in an aggressive or confident manner **self-assertive** *adj*

self-assurance *n* confidence in oneself, one's abilities, or one's judgment **self-assured** *adj*

self-catering *adj* (of accommodation) for tenants providing and preparing their own food

self-centred *or US* **self-centered** *adj* totally preoccupied with one's own concerns

self-certification *n* (in Britain) the completion of a form by a worker stating that his or her absence was due to sickness

self-coloured *or US* **self-colored** *adj* **1** having only a single and uniform colour: *a self-coloured tie* **2** (of cloth or wool) having the natural or original colour

self-confessed *adj* according to one's own admission: *a self-confessed addict*

self-confidence *n* confidence in oneself, one's abilities, or one's judgment **self-confident** *adj*

self-conscious *adj* embarrassed or ill at ease through being unduly aware of oneself as the object of the attention of others **self-consciously** *adv* **self-consciousness** *n*

self-contained *adj* **1** containing within itself all parts necessary for completeness **2** (of a flat) having its own kitchen, bathroom, and toilet not shared by others

self-control *n* the ability to control one's feelings, emotions, or reactions **self-controlled** *adj*

self-deception *or* **self-deceit** *n* the act or an instance of deceiving oneself

self-defence *or US* **self-defense** *n* **1** the act or skill of defending oneself against physical attack **2** the act of defending one's actions, ideas, or rights

self-denial *n* the repression or sacrifice of one's own desires **self-denying** *adj*

self-determination *n* **1** the ability to make a decision for oneself without influence from outside **2** the right of a nation or people to determine its own form of government **self-determined** *adj*

self-discipline *n* the act of controlling or power to control one's own feelings, desires, or behaviour **self-disciplined** *adj*

self-drive *adj* relating to a hired vehicle that is driven by the hirer

self-educated *adj* educated through one's own efforts without formal instruction

self-effacement *n* the act of making oneself or one's actions seem less important than they are because of modesty or timidity **self-effacing** *adj*

self-employed *adj* earning one's living in one's own business, rather than as the employee of another

self-esteem *n* respect for or a favourable opinion of oneself

self-evident *adj* so obvious that no proof or explanation is needed **self-evidently** *adv*

self-explanatory *adj* understandable without explanation

self-expression *n* the expression of one's own personality or feelings, esp. in the creative arts **self-expressive** *adj*

self-government *n* the government of a country, nation, or community by its own people **self-governing** *adj*

self-help *n* **1** the use of one's own abilities and resources to help oneself without relying on the assistance of others **2** the practice of solving one's problems within a group of people with similar problems

self-image *n* one's own idea of oneself or sense of one's worth

self-important *adj* having an unduly high opinion of one's own importance **self-importance** *n*

self-improvement *n* the improvement of one's position, skills, or education by one's own efforts

self-indulgent *adj* tending to allow oneself to have or do things that one enjoys **self-indulgence** *n*

self-interest *n* **1** one's personal interest or advantage **2** the pursuit of one's own interest **self-interested** *adj*

selfish *adj* **1** caring too much about oneself and not enough about others **2** (of behaviour or attitude) motivated by self-interest **selfishly** *adv* **selfishness** *n*

selfless *adj* putting other people's interests before one's own **selflessly** *adv* **selflessness** *n*

self-made *adj* having achieved wealth or status by one's own efforts

self-opinionated *adj* clinging stubbornly to one's own opinions

self-pity *n* pity for oneself, esp. when greatly exaggerated **self-pitying** *adj*

self-pollination *n* *bot* the transfer of pollen from the anthers to the stigma of the same flower

self-possessed *adj* having control of one's emotions or behaviour, esp. in difficult situations **self-possession** *n*

self-preservation *n* the instinctive behaviour that protects one from danger or injury

self-propelled *adj* **1** (of a vehicle) driven by its own engine rather than drawn by a locomotive, horse, etc. **2** (of a rocket

S

launcher or artillery piece) mounted on a motor vehicle **self-propelling** adj

self-raising adj (of flour) having a raising agent, such as baking powder, already added

self-realization or **-isation** n the fulfilment of one's own potential or abilities

self-regard n **1** concern for one's own interest **2** proper esteem for oneself

self-reliance n reliance on oneself or one's own abilities **self-reliant** adj

self-reproach n the act of finding fault with or blaming oneself

self-respect n a feeling of confidence and pride in one's own abilities and worth **self-respecting** adj

self-restraint n control imposed by oneself on one's own feelings, desires, or actions

self-righteous adj thinking oneself more virtuous than others **self-righteousness** n

self-sacrifice n the giving up of one's own interests for the wellbeing of others **self-sacrificing** adj

selfsame adj the very same: *this was the selfsame woman I'd met on the train*

self-satisfied adj smug and complacently satisfied with oneself or one's own actions **self-satisfaction** n

self-sealing adj **1** (of an envelope) sealable by pressure alone **2** (of a tyre) automatically sealing small punctures

self-seeking n **1** the act or an instance of seeking one's own profit or interests ▷ adj **2** inclined to promote only one's own profit or interests: *self-seeking politicians* **self-seeker** n

self-service adj **1** of or denoting a shop or restaurant where the customers serve themselves and then pay a cashier ▷ n **2** the practice of serving oneself and then paying a cashier

self-serving adj continually seeking one's own advantage, esp. at the expense of others

self-starter n **1** an electric motor used to start an internal-combustion engine **2** a person who is strongly motivated and shows initiative at work

self-styled adj using a title or name that one has given oneself, esp. without right or justification; so-called: *the self-styled leader of the rebellion*

self-sufficient adj able to provide for or support oneself without the help of others **self-sufficiency** n

self-supporting adj **1** able to support or maintain oneself without the help of others **2** able to stand up or hold firm without support, props, or attachments

self-willed adj stubbornly determined to have one's own way, esp. at the expense of others

self-winding adj (of a wristwatch) having a mechanism which winds itself automatically

sell vb **selling, sold 1** to exchange (something) for money **2** to deal in (objects or property): *he sells used cars* **3** to give up or surrender for a price or reward: *to sell one's honour* **4 sell for** to have a specified price: *they sell for 10 pence*

each **5** to promote the sale of (objects or property): *sex sells cigarettes* **6** to gain acceptance of: *he'll sell an idea to a producer* **7** to be in demand on the market: *his books did not sell well enough* **8 sell down the river** *informal* to betray **9 sell oneself a** to convince someone else of one's potential or worth **b** to give up one's moral standards for a price or reward **10 sell someone short** *informal* to undervalue someone ▷ n **11** the act or an instance of selling: *the hard sell* ▶ See also **sell off, sell out, sell up** > **seller** n
WORD ORIGIN Old English *sellan* to give, deliver

sell-by date n **1** *Brit* the date printed on packaged food specifying the date after which the food should not be sold **2 past one's sell-by date** beyond one's prime

sell off vb to sell (remaining items) at reduced prices

Sellotape n **1** *trademark* a type of transparent adhesive tape ▷ vb **-taping, -taped 2** to seal or stick using adhesive tape

sell out vb **1 a** to dispose of (something) completely by selling **b** (of items for sale) to be bought up completely: *these tickets will sell out in minutes* **2** *informal* to abandon one's principles, standards, etc. **3** *informal* to betray in order to gain an advantage or benefit ▷ n **sellout 4** *informal* a performance of a show etc. for which all tickets are sold **5** a commercial success **6** *informal* a betrayal

sell-through adj of the sale of prerecorded video cassettes, without their first being for hire only

sell up vb *chiefly Brit & Austral* to sell all one's goods or property

selvage or **selvedge** n a specially woven edge on a length of fabric to prevent it from unravelling **selvaged** adj
WORD ORIGIN SELF + EDGE

selves n the plural of **self**

semantic adj **1** of or relating to the meanings of words **2** of or relating to semantics
WORD ORIGIN Greek *sēma* a sign

semantics n the branch of linguistics that deals with the study of meaning

semaphore n **1** a system of signalling by holding two flags in different positions to represent letters of the alphabet ▷ vb **-phoring, -phored 2** to signal (information) by semaphore
WORD ORIGIN Greek *sēma* a signal + *-phoros* carrying

semblance n outward or superficial appearance: *some semblance of order had been established*
WORD ORIGIN Old French *sembler* to seem

semen n the thick whitish fluid containing spermatozoa that is produced by the male reproductive organs and ejaculated from the penis
WORD ORIGIN Latin: seed

semester n either of two divisions of the academic year
WORD ORIGIN Latin *semestris* half-yearly

semi n *Brit, Austral, & S African informal* short for **semidetached** (sense 2)

semi- prefix **1** half: *semicircle* **2** partly or almost: *semiprofessional* **3** occurring twice in a specified period: *semiweekly*
WORD ORIGIN Latin

semiannual adj **1** occurring every half-year **2** lasting for half a year

semiarid adj denoting land that lies on the edges of a desert but has a slightly higher rainfall (above 300 mm) so that some farming is possible

semiautomatic adj **1** (of a firearm) self-loading but firing only one shot at each pull of the trigger ▷ n **2** a semiautomatic firearm

semibreve n *music* a note, now the longest in common use, with a time value that may be divided by any power of 2 to give all other notes

semicircle n **1** one half of a circle **2** anything having the shape or form of half a circle **semicircular** adj

semicolon n the punctuation mark (;) used to separate clauses or items in a list, or to indicate a pause longer than that of a comma and shorter than that of a full stop

semiconductor n *physics* a substance, such as silicon, which has an electrical conductivity that increases with temperature

semiconscious adj not fully conscious **semiconsciousness** n

semidetached adj **1** (of a house) joined to another house on one side by a common wall ▷ n **2** *Brit* a semidetached house: *the mock Georgian semidetached*

semifinal n the round before the final in a competition **semifinalist** n

seminal adj **1** highly original and influential: *seminal thinkers* **2** potentially capable of development **3** of semen: *seminal fluid* **4** *biol* of seed
WORD ORIGIN Latin *semen* seed

seminar n **1** a small group of students meeting regularly under the guidance of a tutor for study and discussion **2** one such meeting
WORD ORIGIN Latin *seminarium* a nursery garden

seminary n, pl **-naries** a college for the training of priests **seminarian** n
WORD ORIGIN Latin *seminarium* a nursery garden

semiotics n the study of human communication, esp. communication using signs and symbols **semiotic** adj
WORD ORIGIN Greek *sēmeion* a sign

semipermeable adj (of a cell membrane) allowing small molecules to pass through but not large ones

semiprecious adj (of certain stones) having less value than a precious stone

semiprofessional adj **1** (of a person) engaged in an activity or sport part time for pay **2** (of an activity or sport) engaged in by semiprofessional people ▷ n **3** a semiprofessional person

semiquaver n *music* a note having the time value of one-sixteenth of a semibreve

semirigid adj (of an airship) maintaining shape by means of a main supporting keel and internal gas pressure

S

Volapuk

Volapuk, or Volapük, is an artificial language invented by Johann Schleyer (1831–1912), a Catholic priest in Baden, Germany. He claimed that God had told him in a dream to create an international language and so, in 1880, with the stated aim of creating a language that was 'capable of expressing thought with the greatest clearness and accuracy', he constructed Volapuk from words from English, German, and Latin, bound by a set of grammatical rules. Its name was taken from *vol*, based on English *world*, and *pük*, speech, based on English *speak*.

Schleyer borrowed and often modified words to be shorter, perhaps to one or two syllables. Thus *calendar* became *kaled*, *deficiency* became *def*, *example* became *sam*. While some borrowings might be recognizable from the source language (for example *dog*, *man*), many have been altered in such a way that their origin is not obvious, with *vol* and *pük* often cited as examples. However, as his intention was to create a language that was internationally acceptable, it is likely that Schleyer deliberately made links to his source languages less evident.

Schleyer invented Volapuk with the intention that it should be easy to learn, but its grammar has been criticized for its complexity. Volapuk nouns have four cases: nominative, genitive, dative, and accusative, with a different inflectional ending for the singular and plural of each case. Many root nouns can have prefixes, suffixes, or other particles added, and so a root word can have a large number of related variations. The prefix *sma-*, for example, is formed from *smalik*, small; the word for 'nest' is *smabed* ('little bed'). *Mat* ('marriage') can become *matan* ('spouse'), *matel* ('husband'), *mated* ('marriage'), *matadit* ('divorce'), etc. Compounding is also used to form words, but this process involves another grammatical complexity: in compound words, the first element is usually connected to the second by the singular genitive ending -*a*, hence *Volapük*, strictly 'of world language'. However, the -*e* dative and the -*i* accusative endings can also be used as connective elements in compounds, or the words may be linked straightforwardly without additional letters.

Verbs are marked for tense, voice, aspect, mood, person, number, and gender. These are indicated by different prefixes and inflectional endings; for instance from the infinitive *fidön* ('to eat') you can construct *aifidob* ('I eat', ie 'am in the habit of eating'), *vom fidof* ('the woman is eating'), *fidol* ('you are eating'), *efidol* ('you have eaten'), *pafidol* ('you are being eaten'), and so on. Theoretically, a verb in Volapuk can have thousands of forms, although in practice a far smaller number would be used, and verb agreement only taken so far as to prevent ambiguity. Adjectives are formed by the suffix -*ik* (eg *beatik* 'happy' and *manik* 'masculine') and usually follow the noun. If an adjective follows the noun, it does not agree with it, but if it precedes the noun, or is separated from it by other words, it does agree.

The modern Volapuk alphabet contains 27 letters. It uses the Roman alphabet, but does not have 'q' or 'w', and includes the additional vowels 'ä', 'ö', and 'ü'. Schleyer did not include letter 'r' in his original Volapuk, believing it would be difficult for Japanese and Chinese speakers to pronounce, so 'r' was generally changed to 'l' in adopted words; thus English *rose* became *lol* (not *los*, as 's' is reserved in word-final positions to indicate plurals in Volapuk). However, 'r' was included in a 1929 revision of the language proposed by Arie de Jong (1865–1912), and some words were correspondingly revised, such as *lilöm* ('rain') to *rein*. Letters are not always pronounced as one would expect in English. Letter 'c' is pronounced as the 'ch' in *chat* or the 'j' in *joke*, 'z' as the 'ts' in *bats* or 'ds' in *beds*. The letter 'e' corresponds to the vowel sound 'ay', as in *plate*; 'i' represents the vowel sound 'ee' as in *feet*. Vowel sounds are never diphthongized, so vowels beside each other are sounded separately, with a word such as *seid* (seat) pronounced 'se-eed'.

At its peak in the late 1880s, Volapuk had an estimated 100,000 speakers. However, it was soon to be overtaken by other artificial languages with fewer vowel sounds, especially Esperanto. Time has not been kind to either the propagation or the reputation of Volapuk: in 2000, it was estimated that there were only 20 to 30 speakers of the language in the world, and the word has come to mean 'nonsense' in expressions in certain languages, for example Danish and, not surprisingly, Esperanto.

semiskilled *adj* partly skilled or trained but not sufficiently so to perform specialized work

Semite *n* a member of the group of peoples who speak a Semitic language, such as the Jews and Arabs **WORD ORIGIN** New Latin *semita* descendant of Shem, eldest of Noah's sons

Semitic *n* **1** a group of languages that includes Arabic, Hebrew, and Aramaic ▷ *adj* **2** of this group of languages **3** of any of the peoples speaking a Semitic language, esp. the Jews or the Arabs **4** same as **Jewish**

semitone *n* the smallest interval between two notes in Western music represented on a piano by the difference in pitch between any two adjacent keys **semitonic** *adj*

semitrailer *n Austral* a large truck in two separate sections joined by a pivoted bar. Also called: **semi**

semitropical *adj* bordering on the tropics; nearly tropical **semitropics** *pl n*

semivowel *n phonetics* a vowel-like sound that acts like a consonant, such as the sound *w* in *well*

semolina *n* the large hard grains of wheat left after flour has been milled, used for making puddings and pasta **WORD ORIGIN** Italian *semolino*

Semtex *n* a pliable plastic explosive

SEN (in Britain) State Enrolled Nurse

Sen. *or* **sen. 1** senate **2** senator **3** senior

senate *n* the main governing body at some universities **WORD ORIGIN** Latin *senatus* council of the elders

Senate *n* the upper chamber of the legislatures of Australia, the US, Canada, and many other countries

senator *n* a member of a Senate **senatorial** *adj*

send *vb* **sending, sent 1** to cause (a person or thing) to go or be taken or transmitted to another place: *send a cheque or postal order* **2** **send for** to dispatch a request or command for (someone or something): *she had sent for me* **3** to cause to go to a place or point: *the bullet sent him flying into the air* **4** to bring to a state or condition: *his schemes to send her mad* **5** to cause to happen or come: *the thunderstorm sent by the gods* **6** *old-fashioned, slang* to move to excitement or rapture: *this music really sends me* **sender** *n* **WORD ORIGIN** Old English *sendan*

send down *vb* **1** *Brit* to expel from a university **2** *informal* to send to prison

sendoff *n* **1** *informal* a show of good wishes to a person about to set off on a journey or start a new career ▷ *vb* **send off 2** to dispatch (something, such as a letter) **3** *sport* (of a referee) to dismiss (a player) from the field of play for some offence

send up *informal vb* **1** to make fun of by doing an imitation or parody ▷ *n* **send-up 2** a parody or imitation

senescent *adj formal* growing old **senescence** *n* **WORD ORIGIN** Latin *senescere* to grow old

seneschal (**sen**-ish-al) *n history* a steward of the household of a medieval

prince or nobleman **WORD ORIGIN** Old French

senile *adj* mentally or physically weak or infirm on account of old age **senility** *n* **WORD ORIGIN** Latin *senex* an old man

senior *adj* **1** higher in rank or length of service **2** older in years: *senior citizens* **3** *education* of or designating more advanced or older pupils or students ▷ *n* **4** a senior person **WORD ORIGIN** Latin: older

Senior *adj chiefly US* being older than someone of the same name: *Joe Yule Senior*

senior aircraftman *n* an ordinary rank in the Royal Air Force

senior citizen *n* an old person, esp. a pensioner

seniority *n, pl* **-ties 1** the state of being senior **2** degree of power or importance in an organization from length of continuous service

senior service *n Brit* the Royal Navy

senna *n* **1** a tropical plant with yellow flowers and long pods **2** the dried leaves and pods of this plant, used as a laxative **WORD ORIGIN** Arabic *sanā*

señor (sen-**nyor**) *n* a Spanish form of address equivalent to *sir* or *Mr*

señora (sen-**nyor**-a) *n* a Spanish form of address equivalent to *madam* or *Mrs*

señorita (sen-nyor-**ee**-ta) *n* a Spanish form of address equivalent to *madam* or *Miss*

sensation *n* **1** the power of feeling things physically: *I lose all sensation in my hands* **2** a physical feeling: *a burning sensation in the throat* **3** a general feeling or awareness: *a sensation of vague resentment* **4** a state of excitement: *imagine the sensation in Washington!* **5** an exciting person or thing: *you'll be a sensation* **WORD ORIGIN** Late Latin *sensatus* endowed with feelings

sensational *adj* **1** causing intense feelings of shock, anger, or excitement: *sensational allegations* **2** *informal* extremely good: *the views are sensational* **3** of the senses or sensation **sensationally** *adv*

sensationalism *n* the deliberate use of sensational language or subject matter to arouse feelings of shock, anger, or excitement **sensationalist** *adj, n*

sense *n* **1** any of the faculties (sight, hearing, touch, taste, and smell) by which the mind receives information about the external world or the state of the body **2** the ability to perceive **3** a feeling perceived through one of the senses: *a sense of warmth* **4** a mental perception or awareness: *a sense of security* **5** ability to make moral judgments: *a sense of honour* **6** (*usually pl*) sound practical judgment or intelligence: *a man lost his senses and killed his wife* **7** reason or purpose: *no sense in continuing* **8** general meaning: *he couldn't understand every word but he got the sense of what they were saying* **9** specific meaning; definition: *the three senses of the word* **10** **make sense** to be understandable or practical ▷ *vb* **sensing, sensed 11** to perceive without the evidence of the

senses: *he sensed that she was impressed* **12** to perceive through the senses **WORD ORIGIN** Latin *sentire* to feel

senseless *adj* **1** having no meaning or purpose: *a senseless act of violence* **2** unconscious **senselessly** *adv* **senselessness** *n*

sense organ *n* a part of the body that receives stimuli and transmits them as sensations to the brain

sensibility *n, pl* **-ties 1** (*often pl*) the ability to experience deep feelings **2** (*usually pl*) the tendency to be influenced or offended: *its sheer callousness offended her sensibilities* **3** the ability to perceive or feel

sensible *adj* **1** having or showing good sense or judgment **2** (of clothing and footwear) practical and hard-wearing **3** capable of receiving sensation **4** capable of being perceived by the senses **5** perceptible to the mind **6** *literary* aware: *sensible of your kindness* **sensibly** *adv* **WORD ORIGIN** Latin *sentire* to feel

sensitive *adj* **1** easily hurt; tender **2** responsive to feelings and moods **3** responsive to external stimuli or impressions **4** easily offended or shocked **5** (of a subject or issue) liable to arouse controversy or strong feelings **6** (of an instrument) capable of registering small differences or changes in amounts **7** *photog* responding readily to light: *a sensitive emulsion* **8** *chiefly US* connected with matters affecting national security **sensitively** *adv* **sensitivity** *n* **WORD ORIGIN** Latin *sentire* to feel

sensitize *or* **-tise** *vb* **-tizing, -tized** *or* **-tising, -tised** to make sensitive **sensitization** *or* **-tisation** *n*

sensor *n* a device that detects or measures a physical property, such as radiation

sensory *adj* relating to the physical senses

sensual *adj* **1** giving pleasure to the body and senses rather than the mind: *soft sensual music* **2** having a strong liking for physical, esp. sexual, pleasures **3** of the body and senses rather than the mind or soul **sensualist** *n* **WORD ORIGIN** Latin *sensus* feeling

sensuality *n* **1** the quality or state of being sensual **2** enjoyment of physical, esp. sexual, pleasures

sensuous *adj* **1** pleasing to the senses of the mind or body: *the sensuous rhythms of the drums* **2** (of a person) appreciating qualities perceived by the senses **sensuously** *adv*

sent *vb* the past of **send**

sentence *n* **1** a sequence of words constituting a statement, question, or a command that begins with a capital letter and ends with a full stop when written down **2** **a** the decision of a law court as to what punishment is passed on a convicted person **b** the punishment passed on a convicted person ▷ *vb* **-tencing, -tenced 3** to pronounce sentence on (a convicted person) in a law court **sentential** *adj* **WORD ORIGIN** Latin *sententia* a way of thinking

sentantious *adj formal* **1** trying to sound wise **2** making pompous remarks about morality **sentantiously** *adv* **WORD ORIGIN** Latin *sentantiosus* full of meaning

sentient (**sen**-tee-ent, **sen**-shent) *adj* capable of perception and feeling **sentience** *n* **WORD ORIGIN** Latin *sentiens* feeling

sentiment *n* **1** a mental attitude based on a mixture of thoughts and feelings: *anti-American sentiment* **2** (*often pl*) a thought, opinion, or attitude expressed in words: *his sentiments were echoed by subsequent speakers* **3** feelings such as tenderness, romance, and sadness, esp. when exaggerated: *a man without the softness of sentiment* **WORD ORIGIN** Latin *sentire* to feel

sentimental *adj* **1** feeling or expressing tenderness, romance, or sadness to an exaggerated extent **2** appealing to the emotions, esp. to romantic feelings: *she kept the ring for sentimental reasons* **sentimentalism** *n* **sentimentalist** *n* **sentimentality** *n* **sentimentally** *adv*

sentimentalize *or* -**lise** *vb* -**lizing,** -**lized** *or* -**lising,** -**lised** to make sentimental or behave sentimentally

sentimental value *n* the value of an article to a particular person because of the emotions it arouses

sentinel *n old-fashioned* a sentry **WORD ORIGIN** Old French *sentinelle*

sentry *n, pl* -**tries** a soldier who keeps watch and guards a camp or building **WORD ORIGIN** perhaps from obsolete *centrinel* sentinel

sentry box *n* a small shelter with an open front in which a sentry stands during bad weather

SEO search engine optimization

sepal *n bot* a leaflike division of the calyx of a flower **WORD ORIGIN** New Latin *sepalum*

separable *adj* able to be separated

separate *vb* -**rating,** -**rated** **1** to act as a barrier between: *the narrow stretch of water which separates Europe from Asia* **2** to part or be parted from a mass or group **3** to distinguish: *it's what separates the women from the boys* **4** to divide or be divided into component parts **5** to sever or be severed **6** (of a couple) to stop living together ▷ *adj* **7** existing or considered independently: *a separate issue* **8** set apart from the main body or mass **9** distinct or individual **separately** *adv* **separateness** *n* **separator** *n* **WORD ORIGIN** Latin *separare*

separates *pl n Brit, Austral, & NZ* clothes, such as skirts, blouses, and trousers, that only cover part of the body and are designed to be worn together or separately

separate school *n* (in certain Canadian provinces) a school for a large religious minority financed by provincial grants in addition to the education tax

separation *n* **1** the act of separating: *the separation of child from mother* **2** *family law* the living apart of a married couple without divorce **3** a mark, line, or object that separates one thing from another

separatist *n* a person who advocates the separation of his or her own group from an organization or country **separatism** *n*

sepia *adj* dark reddish-brown, like the colour of very old photographs **WORD ORIGIN** Latin: a cuttlefish

sepoy *n* (formerly) an Indian soldier in the service of the British **WORD ORIGIN** Urdu *sipāhī*

sepsis *n* poisoning caused by the presence of pus-forming bacteria in the body **WORD ORIGIN** Greek: a rotting

sept *n* a clan, esp. in Ireland or Scotland **WORD ORIGIN** perhaps variant of *sect*

Sept. September

September *n* the ninth month of the year **WORD ORIGIN** Latin: the seventh (month)

septennial *adj* **1** occurring every seven years **2** lasting seven years **WORD ORIGIN** Latin *septem* seven + *annus* a year

septet *n* **1** a group of seven performers **2** a piece of music for seven performers **WORD ORIGIN** Latin *septem* seven

septic *adj* of or caused by harmful bacteria **septicity** *n*

septicaemia *or* **septicemia** (sep-tis-**see**-mee-a) *n* an infection of the blood which develops in a wound **WORD ORIGIN** Greek *sēptos* decayed + *haima* blood

septic tank *n* a tank in which sewage is decomposed by the action of bacteria

septuagenarian *n* **1** a person who is between 70 and 79 years old ▷ *adj* **2** between 70 and 79 years old **WORD ORIGIN** Latin *septuaginta* seventy

Septuagint (**sept**-yew-a-jint) *n* the ancient Greek version of the Old Testament, including the Apocrypha **WORD ORIGIN** Latin *septuaginta* seventy

septum *n, pl* -**ta** *biol, anat* a dividing partition between two tissues or cavities, such as in the nose **WORD ORIGIN** Latin *saeptum* wall

septuple *vb* -**pling,** -**pled** **1** to multiply by seven ▷ *adj* **2** seven times as much or as many **3** consisting of seven parts ▷ *n* **4** a quantity or number seven times as great as another **WORD ORIGIN** Latin *septem* seven

sepulchral (sip-**pulk**-ral) *adj* **1** gloomy and solemn, like a tomb or grave **2** of a sepulchre

sepulchre *or US* **sepulcher** (**sep**-pulk-er) *n* **1** a burial vault, tomb, or grave ▷ *vb* -**chring,** -**chred** *or US* -**chering,** -**chered** **2** to bury in a sepulchre **WORD ORIGIN** Latin *sepulcrum*

sepulture (**sep**-pult-cher) *n* the act of placing in a sepulchre

sequel *n* **1** a novel, play, or film that continues the story of an earlier one **2** anything that happens after or as a result of something else: *there was an amusing sequel to this incident* **WORD ORIGIN** Latin *sequi* to follow

sequence *n* **1** an arrangement of two or more things in a successive order **2** the successive order of two or more things: *chronological sequence* **3** an action or event

that follows another or others **4** *maths* an ordered set of numbers or other quantities in one-to-one correspondence with the integers 1 to *n* **5** a section of a film forming a single uninterrupted episode ▷ *vb* **6** to arrange in a sequence **WORD ORIGIN** Latin *sequi* to follow

sequential *adj* happening in a fixed order or sequence

sequester *vb* **1** to seclude: *he could sequester himself in his own home* **2** *law* same as **sequestrate** **WORD ORIGIN** Late Latin *sequestrare* to surrender for safekeeping

sequestrate *vb* -**trating,** -**trated** *law* to confiscate (property) temporarily until creditors are satisfied or a court order is complied with **sequestration** *n* **sequestrator** *n*

sequin *n* a small piece of shiny metal foil used to decorate clothes **sequined** *adj* **WORD ORIGIN** Italian *zecchino*

sequoia *n* a giant Californian coniferous tree **WORD ORIGIN** after *Sequoya*, a Native American scholar

seraglio (sir-**ah**-lee-oh) *n, pl* -**raglios** **1** the part of a Muslim house or palace where the owner's wives live **2** a Turkish sultan's palace **WORD ORIGIN** Italian *serraglio* animal cage

seraph *n, pl* -**raphim** *theol* a member of the highest order of angels **seraphic** *adj* **WORD ORIGIN** from Hebrew

Serb *adj, n* same as **Serbian**

Serbian *adj* **1** of Serbia ▷ *n* **2** a person from Serbia **3** the dialect of Serbo-Croat spoken in Serbia

Serbo-Croat *or* **Serbo-Croatian** *n* **1** the chief official language of Serbia and Croatia ▷ *adj* **2** of this language

serenade *n* **1** a piece of music played or sung to a woman by a lover **2** a piece of music suitable for this **3** an orchestral suite for a small ensemble ▷ *vb* -**nading,** -**naded** **4** to sing or play a serenade to (someone) **WORD ORIGIN** French

serendipity *n* the gift of making fortunate discoveries by accident **WORD ORIGIN** from the fairy tale *The Three Princes of Serendip*, in which the heroes possess this gift

serene *adj* **1** peaceful or calm **2** (of the sky) clear or bright **serenely** *adv* **serenity** *n* **WORD ORIGIN** Latin *serenus*

serf *n* (esp. in medieval Europe) a labourer who could not leave the land on which he worked **serfdom** *n* **WORD ORIGIN** Latin *servus* a slave

serge *n* a strong fabric made of wool, cotton, silk, or rayon, used for clothing **WORD ORIGIN** Old French *sarge*

sergeant *n* **1** a noncommissioned officer in the armed forces **2** (in Britain, S Africa, Australia, and NZ) a police officer ranking between constable and inspector **WORD ORIGIN** Old French *sergent*

sergeant at arms *n* a parliamentary or court officer responsible for keeping order

sergeant major *n* a noncommissioned officer of the highest rank in the army

serial *n* **1** a story published or broadcast in instalments at regular intervals **2** a publication that is regularly issued and consecutively numbered ▷ *adj* **3** of, in, or forming a series: *serial pregnancies* **4** published or presented as a serial **serially** *adv*
WORD ORIGIN Latin *series* series

serialize *or* **-ise** *vb* **-izing, -ized** *or* **-ising, -ised** to publish or present in the form of a serial **serialization** *or* **-isation** *n*

serial killer *n* a person who commits a number of murders

serial monogamy *n* the practice of having a number of long-term romantic or sexual partners in succession

serial number *n* any of the consecutive numbers given to objects in a series for identification

series *n, pl* **-ries 1** a group or succession of related things **2** a set of radio or television programmes dealing with the same subject, esp. one having the same characters but different stories **3** *maths* the sum of a finite or infinite sequence of numbers or quantities **4** *electronics* an arrangement of two or more components connected in a circuit so that the same current flows in turn through each of them: *a number of resistors in series* **5** *geol* a set of layers that represent the rocks formed during an epoch
WORD ORIGIN Latin: a row

seriocomic (seer-ee-oh-**kom**-ik) *adj* mixing serious and comic elements

serious *adj* **1** giving cause for concern: *the situation is serious* **2** concerned with important matters: *there are some serious questions that need to be answered* **3** not cheerful; grave: *I am a serious person* **4** in earnest; sincere: *he believes we are serious* **5** requiring concentration: *a serious book* **6** *informal* impressive because of its substantial quantity or quality: *serious money* **seriously** *adv* **seriousness** *n*
WORD ORIGIN Latin *serius*

serjeant *n* same as **sergeant**

sermon *n* **1** a speech on a religious or moral subject given by a clergyman as part of a church service **2** *disparaging* a serious talk on behaviour, morals, or duty, esp. a long and tedious one
WORD ORIGIN Latin *sermo* discourse

seropositive (seer-oh-**poz**-zit-iv) *adj* (of a person whose blood has been tested for a specific disease, such as AIDS) showing a significant level of serum antibodies, indicating the presence of the disease

serotonin (ser-roe-**tone**-in) *n biochem* a compound that occurs in the brain, intestines, and blood platelets and acts as a neurotransmitter

serous (**seer**-uss) *adj* of, containing, or like serum

serpent *n* **1** *literary* a snake **2** a devious person
WORD ORIGIN Latin *serpens* a creeping thing

serpentine¹ *adj* twisting like a snake

serpentine² *n* a soft green or brownish-red mineral

WORD ORIGIN so named from its snakelike patterns

serrated *adj* having a notched or sawlike edge **serration** *n*
WORD ORIGIN Latin *serratus* saw-shaped

serried *adj literary* in close formation: *the serried ranks of fans*
WORD ORIGIN Old French *serré* close-packed

serum (**seer**-um) *n* **1** the yellowish watery fluid left after blood has clotted **2** this fluid from the blood of immunized animals used for inoculation or vaccination **3** *physiol, zool* any clear watery animal fluid
WORD ORIGIN Latin: whey

serval *n* a slender African wild cat with black-spotted tawny fur

servant *n* **1** a person employed to do household work for another person **2** a person or thing that is useful or provides a service: *a distinguished servant of this country*
WORD ORIGIN Old French: serving

serve *vb* **serving, served 1** to be of service to (a person, community, or cause); help **2** to perform an official duty or duties: *he served on several university committees* **3** to attend to (customers) in a shop **4** to provide (guests) with food or drink: *he served dinner guests German wine* **5** to provide (food or drink) for customers: *breakfast is served from 7 am* **6** to provide with something needed by the public: *the community served by the school* **7** to work as a servant for (a person) **8** to go through (a period of police or military service, apprenticeship, or imprisonment) **9** to meet the needs of: *they serve a purpose* **10** to perform a function: *the attacks only served to strengthen their resolve* **11** (of a male animal) to mate with (a female animal) **12** *tennis, squash, etc.* to put (the ball) into play **13** to deliver (a legal document) to (a person) **14 serve someone right** *informal* to be what someone deserves, esp. for doing something stupid or wrong ▷ *n* **15** *tennis, squash, etc.* short for **service** (sense 12)
WORD ORIGIN Latin *servus* a slave

server *n* **1** *computers* a computer or program that supplies data to other machines on a network **2** a person who serves

service *n* **1** an act of help or assistance **2** an organization or system that provides something needed by the public: *a consumer information service* **3** a department of public employment and its employees: *the diplomatic service* **4** the installation or maintenance of goods provided by a dealer after a sale **5** availability for use by the public: *the new plane could be in service within fifteen years* **6** a regular check made on a machine or vehicle in which parts are tested, cleaned, or replaced if worn **7** the serving of guests or customers: *service is included on the wine list* **8** one of the branches of the armed forces **9** the serving of food: *silver service* **10** a set of dishes, cups, and plates for use at table **11** a formal religious ceremony **12** *tennis, squash, etc.* **a** the act, manner, or right of serving the ball **b** the game in which a particular player serves: *she dropped only*

one point on her service ▷ *adj* **13** of or for the use of servants or employees: *a service elevator* **14** serving the public rather than producing goods: *service industries* ▷ *vb* **-vicing, -viced 15** to provide service or services to **16** to check and repair (a vehicle or machine) **17** (of a male animal) to mate with (a female animal)
▶ See also **services**
WORD ORIGIN Latin *servitium* condition of a slave

serviceable *adj* **1** performing effectively: *serviceable boots* **2** able or ready to be used: *five remaining serviceable aircraft* **serviceability** *n*

service area *n* a place on a motorway with a garage, restaurants, and toilets

service charge *n* a percentage added to a bill in a hotel or restaurant to pay for service

service flat *n* a flat where domestic services are provided by the management

serviceman *n, pl* **-men 1** a person in the armed services **2** a man employed to service and maintain equipment **servicewoman** *fem n*

service road *n Austral & Brit* a narrow road running parallel to a main road that provides access to houses and shops situated along its length

services *pl n* **1** work performed in a job: *the OBE for her services to the community* **2 the services** the armed forces **3** a system of providing the public with something it needs, such as gas or water

service station *n* **1** a place that sells fuel, oil, and spare parts for motor vehicles **2** same as **service area**

serviette *n* a table napkin
WORD ORIGIN Old French

servile *adj* **1** too eager to obey people; fawning **2** of or suitable for a slave **servility** *n*
WORD ORIGIN Latin *servus* slave

serving *n* a portion of food

servitor *n archaic* a servant or attendant

servitude *n formal* **1** slavery or bondage **2** the state or condition of being completely dominated
WORD ORIGIN Latin *servus* a slave

servomechanism *n* a device which converts a small force into a larger force, used esp. in steering mechanisms

sesame (**sess**-am-ee) *n* a plant of the East Indies, grown for its seeds and oil, which are used in cooking
WORD ORIGIN Greek

sessile *adj* **1** (of flowers or leaves) having no stalk **2** (of animals such as the barnacle) fixed in one position
WORD ORIGIN Latin *sessilis* concerning sitting

session *n* **1** any period devoted to a particular activity **2** a meeting of a court, parliament, or council **3** a series or period of such meetings **4** a school or university term or year **sessional** *adj*
WORD ORIGIN Latin *sessio* a sitting

sestet *n* **1** *prosody* the last six lines of a sonnet **2** same as **sextet** (sense 1)
WORD ORIGIN Italian *sesto* sixth

set¹ *vb* **setting, set 1** to put in a specified position or state: *I set him free* **2 set to** *or*

Hugh MacDiarmid: a Scots Modernist

Hugh MacDiarmid was the pen name of Christopher Murray Grieve. He was born in Langholm, near the Scottish Borders, in 1892, and worked as a journalist before embarking on a career as a poet in the 1920s. Though he had served in the Royal Army Medical Corps during World War I, he soon became a devoted Scottish Nationalist, and his most famous poems are heavily influenced by the Scots language.

Though MacDiarmid is famous for having written in a Scottish dialect, his earliest poems are in Standard English. Even when writing of Scottish themes and settings, as in 'The Wind-Bags', his spelling and grammar are consistent with English south of the Border, apart from an occasional *aye*. It was only later that MacDiarmid began employing a Scottish literary language, as is seen in the opening lines from 'The Dying Earth' (1923):

> *Pitmirk the nicht: God's waukrife yet*
> *An' lichtnin'-like his glances flit*
> *An' sair, sair are the looks he gies*
> *The auld earth as it dees.*

This language is commonly referred to as *Lallans*, and it approximates the speech of the Scottish lowlands, which scholars now simply call *Scots* (the language of the Scottish Highlands would be Gaelic).

The language of MacDiarmid's poems, however, is not Scots as it was actually spoken. Rather, MacDiarmid wrote in a self-styled 'synthetic Scots'. The term 'synthetic' was not intended to be derogatory; rather it connotes its Greek root *suntithenai*, meaning 'to put together' or 'create'. Synthetic Scots was literally a synthesis of Scots words and pronunciations both current and archaic, from any and all regions of Scotland (and, frequently, a solid basis of plain old Standard English). For example, in the above passage, *God*, *yet*, *his*, *glances*, *flit*, *looks*, and *earth* are all southern English (as are more than half the words in the stanza). Though *an'* is at best a phonetic re-spelling of an informal pronunciation of *and* (one that is, in fact, common to all varieties of English), *dees* ('dies'), *gies* ('gives'), *auld* ('old'), *sair* ('sore'), *nicht* ('night'), and *waukrife* ('wakeful, restless') are all legitimate Scots vocabulary, the latter two words being somewhat less common than the others. However, *pitmirk* ('dark as the/a pit') is MacDiarmid's own coinage, and though *lichtnin'* ('lightning') is a logical formation based on Scots *licht* ('light'), it is not attested in the *Scottish National Dictionary*, and is likely a MacDiarmid innovation.

The criticism of synthetic Scots, dubbed 'plastic Scots' by its detractors, is that it is not a natural language. No one speaks or ever has spoken Scots as presented in the poetry of MacDiarmid or Lallans writers.

MacDiarmid's writing in Scots culminated with his most famous poem, *A Drunk Man Looks at the Thistle*. MacDiarmid takes his image from Walt Whitman's 'Song of Myself', in which the narrator contemplates a blade of grass as the starting point of a lengthy ode to burgeoning American literary culture. The thistle is a traditional emblem of Scotland, but having the narrator drunk sets a sarcastic, even satirical tone to the poem. Indeed, MacDiarmid takes the opportunity to criticize the Romanticized tartanry he sees usurping serious Scottish culture. 'Forbye, the stuffie's no the real MacKay,' he writes, 'And aa that's Scotch aboot it is the name.'

In his later poems, MacDiarmid returned to writing in English. One poem in particular from this period sheds light on the synthetic Scots of his previous work. *In Memoriam James Joyce* is MacDiarmid's long elegy to the great Irish modernist. In it, he focuses his praise not on *Ulysses* but on *Finnegans Wake*, Joyce's experimental novel written in his own synthetic 'dream-language', combining elements of as many real-world languages as Joyce could squeeze in. That MacDiarmid should see himself Joyce's peer in this regard suggests that synthetic Scots was never intended to be a natural or 'realistic' language. Rather, it was a wholly artistic language, derived from and inspired by real Scots, but existing above and beyond it, a conscious rejection of what MacDiarmid perceived to be the influence of English culture. In this respect, MacDiarmid's work is not only an expression of Scottish nationalism, but also of Scottish Modernism.

on to bring (something) into contact with (something else): *three prisoners set fire to their cells* **3** to put into order or make ready: *set the table* **4** to make or become firm or rigid: *before the eggs begin to set* **5** to put (a broken bone) or (of a broken bone) to be put into a normal position for healing **6** to adjust (a clock or other instrument) to a particular position **7** to arrange or establish: *to set a date for diplomatic talks; it set the standards of performance* **8** to prescribe or assign (a task or material for study): *the examiners have set 'Paradise Lost'* **9** to arrange (hair) while wet, so that it dries in position **10** to place a jewel in (a setting): *a ring set with diamonds* **11** to provide music for (a poem or other text to be sung) **12** *printing* **a** to arrange (type) for printing **b** to put (text) into type **13** to arrange (a stage or television studio) with scenery and props **14** **set to** or **on** to value (something) at a specified price or worth: *he set a high price on his services* **15** (of the sun or moon) to disappear beneath the horizon **16** (of plants) to produce (fruits or seeds) or (of fruits or seeds) to develop **17** to place (a hen) on (eggs) to incubate them **18** (of a gun dog) to turn in the direction of game birds ▷ *n* **19** the act of setting **20** a condition of firmness or hardness **21** manner of standing; posture: *the set of his shoulders* **22** the scenery and other props used in a play or film **23** same as **sett** ▷ *adj* **24** fixed or established by authority or agreement: *set hours of work* **25** rigid or inflexible: *she is set in her ways* **26** unmoving; fixed: *a set expression on his face* **27** conventional or stereotyped: *she made her apology in set phrases* **28** **set in** (of a scene or story) represented as happening at a certain time or place: *a European film set in Africa* **29** **set on** or **upon** determined to (do or achieve something): *why are you so set upon avoiding me?* **30** ready: *all set to go* **31** (of material for study) prescribed for students' preparation for an examination ▸ See also **set about, set against**, etc.
WORD ORIGIN Old English *settan*

set² *n* **1** a number of objects or people grouped or belonging together: *a set of slides* **2** a group of people who associate with each other or have similar interests: *the tennis set* **3** *maths* a collection of numbers or objects that satisfy a given condition or share a property **4** a television or piece of radio equipment **5** the scenery and other props used in a dramatic production, film, etc. **6** *sport* a group of games or points in a match, of which the winner must win a certain number **7** a series of songs or tunes performed by a musician or group on a given occasion: *the front row spent the rest of the set craning their necks*
WORD ORIGIN Old French *sette*

set about *vb* **1** to start or begin **2** to attack

set against *vb* **1** to balance or compare **2** to cause to be unfriendly to: *the war set brother against brother*

set aside *vb* **1** to reserve for a special purpose **2** to discard or reject

set back *vb* **1** to delay or hinder **2** *informal* to cost (a person) a specified amount ▷ *n* **setback 3** anything that delays progress

set down *vb* **1** to record in writing **2** *Brit* to allow (passengers) to get off a bus etc.

set forth *vb formal or archaic* **1** to state or present (an argument or facts) **2** to start out on a journey: *he set forth on foot*

set in *vb* **1** to begin and continue for some time: *decadence has set in* **2** to insert

set off *vb* **1** to start a journey **2** to cause (a person) to act or do something, such as laugh **3** to cause to explode **4** to act as a contrast to: *blue suits you, sets off the colour of your hair*

set on or **upon** *vb* to attack or cause to attack: *they set the dogs on him*

set out *vb* **1** to present, arrange, or display **2** to give a full account of: *the policy was set out in an interview with the BBC* **3** to begin or embark on an undertaking, esp. a journey

set piece *n* **1** a work of literature, music, or art, intended to create an impressive effect **2** *football, hockey, etc.* an attacking move from a corner or free kick

set square *n* a thin flat piece of plastic or metal in the shape of a right-angled triangle, used in technical drawing

sett or **set** *n* **1** a badger's burrow **2** a small rectangular paving block made of stone
WORD ORIGIN variant of SET¹ (noun)

settee *n* a seat, for two or more people, with a back and usually with arms; couch
WORD ORIGIN from SETTLE²

setter *n* a large long-haired dog originally bred for hunting

set theory *n maths* the branch of mathematics concerned with the properties and interrelationships of sets

setting *n* **1** the surroundings in which something is set **2** the scenery, properties, or background used to create the location for a stage play or film **3** a piece of music written for the words of a text **4** the decorative metalwork in which a gem is set **5** the plates and cutlery for a single place at a table **6** one of the positions or levels to which the controls of a machine can be adjusted

settle¹ *vb* **-tling, -tled 1** to put in order: *he settled his affairs before he died* **2** to arrange or be arranged firmly or comfortably: *he settled into his own chair by the fire* **3** to come down to rest: *a bird settled on top of the hedge* **4** to establish or become established as a resident: *they eventually settled in Glasgow* **5** to establish or become established in a way of life or a job **6** to migrate to (a country) and form a community; colonize **7** to make or become quiet, calm, or stable **8** to cause (sediment) to sink to the bottom in a liquid or (of sediment) to sink thus **9** to subside: *the dust settled* **10** (sometimes foll. by *up*) to pay off (a bill or debt) **11** to decide or dispose of: *to settle an argument* **12** (often foll. by *on* or *upon*) to agree or fix: *they settled on an elementary code* **13** (usually foll. by *on* or *upon*) to give (a title or property) to a person by gift or legal deed: *he settled his property on his wife* **14** to decide (a legal dispute) by agreement without court action: *they settled out of court*
WORD ORIGIN Old English *setlan*

settle² *n* a long wooden bench with a high back and arms, sometimes having a storage space under the seat
WORD ORIGIN Old English *setl*

settle down *vb* **1** to make or become quiet and orderly **2** **settle down to** to remove all distractions and concentrate on: *we settled down to a favourite movie* **3** to adopt an orderly and routine way of life, esp. after marriage

settle for *vb* to accept or agree to in spite of dissatisfaction

settlement *n* **1** an act of settling **2** a place newly settled; colony **3** subsidence of all or part of a building **4** an official agreement ending a dispute **5** *law* **a** an arrangement by which property is transferred to a person's possession **b** the deed transferring such property

settler *n* a person who settles in a new country or a colony

set to *vb* **1** to begin working **2** to start fighting ▷ *n* **set-to 3** *informal* a brief disagreement or fight

set-top box *n* a device which converts the signals from a digital television broadcast into a form which can be viewed on a standard television set

set up *vb* **1** to build or construct: *the soldiers had actually set up a munitions factory* **2** to put into a position of power or wealth **3** to begin or enable (someone) to begin (a new venture): *he set up a small shop* **4** to begin or produce: *to set up a nuclear chain reaction* **5** to establish: *Broad set up a world record* **6** *informal* to cause (a person) to be blamed or accused **7** to restore the health of: *a pub lunch set me up nicely* ▷ *n* **setup 8** *informal* the way in which anything is organized or arranged **9** *slang* an event the result of which is prearranged

seven *n* **1** the cardinal number that is the sum of one and six **2** a numeral, 7 or VII, representing this number **3** something representing or consisting of seven units ▷ *adj* **4** amounting to seven: *seven weeks* **seventh** *adj, n*
WORD ORIGIN Old English *seofon*

sevenfold *adj* **1** having seven times as many or as much **2** composed of seven parts ▷ *adv* **3** by seven times as many or as much

seven seas *pl n old-fashioned* all the oceans of the world

seventeen *n* **1** the cardinal number that is the sum of ten and seven **2** a numeral, 17 or XVII, representing this number **3** something representing or consisting of seventeen units ▷ *adj* **4** amounting to seventeen: *seventeen children* **seventeenth** *adj, n*

seventh heaven *n* a state of supreme happiness

seventy *n, pl* **-ties 1** the cardinal number that is the product of ten and seven **2** a numeral, 70 or LXX, representing this number **3** something representing or consisting of seventy units ▷ *adj* **4** amounting to seventy: *seventy countries* **seventieth** *adj, n*

sever *vb* **1** to cut right through or cut off (something): *it accidentally severed the electrical cable* **2** to break off (a tie or relationship) **severable** *adj* **severance** *n*

WORD ORIGIN Latin *separare* to separate

several *adj* **1** more than a few: *I spoke to several doctors* **2** *formal* various or separate: *the members with their several occupations* **3** *formal* distinct or different: *misfortune visited her three several times*
WORD ORIGIN Medieval Latin *separalis*

severally *adv* individually or separately: *the Western nations severally rather than jointly decided that they would have to act without Russia*

severance pay *n* compensation paid by a firm to an employee who has to leave because the job he or she was appointed to do no longer exists

severe *adj* **1** strict or harsh in the treatment of others: *a severe parent* **2** serious in appearance or manner: *a severe look; a severe hairdo* **3** very intense or unpleasant: *severe chest pains; the punishments are severe* **4** causing discomfort by its harshness: *severe frost* **5** hard to perform or accomplish: *a severe challenge* **severely** *adv* **severity** *n*
WORD ORIGIN Latin *severus*

Seville orange *n* a bitter orange used to make marmalade
WORD ORIGIN after *Seville* in Spain

Sèvres (**sev**-ra) *n* a kind of fine French porcelain
WORD ORIGIN after *Sèvres*, near Paris

sew *vb* **sewing, sewed; sewn** *or* **sewed** **1** to join with thread repeatedly passed through with a needle **2** to attach, fasten, or close by sewing ▸ See also **sew up**
WORD ORIGIN Old English *sēowan*

sewage *n* waste matter or excrement carried away in sewers or drains

sewage farm *n* a place where sewage is treated so that it can be used as manure or disposed of safely

sewer *n* a drain or pipe, usually underground, used to carry away surface water or sewage
WORD ORIGIN Old French *essever* to drain

sewerage *n* **1** a system of sewers **2** the removal of surface water or sewage by means of sewers

sewing *n* **1** a piece of fabric or an article, that is sewn or to be sewn **2** the act of fastening together (pieces of fabric, etc.) with needle and thread

sewing machine *n* a machine that sews material with a needle driven by an electric motor

sewn *vb* a past participle of **sew**

sew up *vb* **1** to fasten or mend completely by sewing **2** *informal* to complete or negotiate successfully: *the deal was sewn up just before the deadline*

sex *n* **1** the state of being either male or female **2** either of the two categories, male or female, into which organisms are divided **3** sexual intercourse **4** feelings or behaviour connected with having sex or the desire to have sex **5** sexual matters in general ▸ *adj* **6** of sexual matters: *sex education* **7** based on or resulting from the difference between the sexes: *sex discrimination* ▸ *vb* **8** to find out the sex of (an animal)
WORD ORIGIN Latin *sexus*

sexagenarian *n* **1** a person who is between 60 and 69 years old ▸ *adj*

2 between 60 and 69 years old
WORD ORIGIN Latin *sexaginta* sixty

sex appeal *n* sexual attractiveness

sex chromosome *n* either of the chromosomes that determine the sex of an animal

sexism *n* discrimination against the members of one sex, usually women **sexist** *n, adj*

sexless *adj* **1** neither male nor female **2** having no sexual desires **3** sexually unattractive

sex object *n* someone, esp. a woman, regarded only in terms of physical attractiveness and not as a person

sexology *n* the study of sexual behaviour in human beings **sexologist** *n*

sextant *n* an instrument used in navigation for measuring angular distance, for example between the sun and the horizon, to calculate the position of a ship or aircraft
WORD ORIGIN Latin *sextans* one sixth of a unit

sextet *n* **1** a group of six performers **2** a piece of music for six performers **3** a group of six people or things
WORD ORIGIN variant of *sestet*

sexton *n* a person employed to look after a church and its churchyard
WORD ORIGIN Medieval Latin *sacristanus* sacristan

sextuple *vb* **-pling, -pled** **1** to multiply by six ▸ *adj* **2** six times as much or as many **3** consisting of six parts ▸ *n* **4** a quantity or number six times as great as another
WORD ORIGIN Latin *sextus* sixth

sextuplet *n* one of six children born at one birth

sexual *adj* **1** of or characterized by sex **2** (of reproduction) characterized by the union of male and female reproductive cells **3** of or relating to the differences between males and females **sexuality** *n* **sexually** *adv*

sexual harassment *n* the unwelcome directing of sexual remarks, looks, or advances, usually at a woman in the workplace

sexual intercourse *n* the sexual act in which the male's erect penis is inserted into the female's vagina, usually followed by the ejaculation of semen

sex up *vb* *informal* to make (something) more exciting

sexy *adj* **sexier, sexiest** *informal* **1** sexually exciting or attractive: *a sexy voice* **2** interesting, exciting, or trendy: *a sexy project; a sexy new car* **sexiness** *n*

SF *or* **sf** science fiction

SFA Scottish Football Association

SFO (in Britain) Serious Fraud Office

Sg *chem* seaborgium

S. Glam South Glamorgan

Sgt. Sergeant

sh *interj* be quiet!

shabby *adj* **-bier, -biest** **1** old and worn in appearance **2** wearing worn and dirty clothes **3** behaving in a mean or unfair way: *shabby manoeuvres* **shabbily** *adv* **shabbiness** *n*
WORD ORIGIN Old English *sceabb* scab

shack *n* **1** a roughly built hut ▸ *vb* **2** **shack up with** *slang* to live with (a lover)
WORD ORIGIN perhaps from dialect *shackly* ramshackle

shackle *n* **1** one of a pair of metal rings joined by a chain for securing someone's wrists or ankles **2** **shackles** anything that confines or restricts freedom: *free from the shackles of its feudal past* **3** a metal loop or link closed by a bolt, used for securing ropes or chains ▸ *vb* **-ling, -led** **4** to fasten with shackles **5** to restrict or hamper: *an economy shackled by central control*
WORD ORIGIN Old English *sceacel*

shad *n, pl* **shad** *or* **shads** a herring-like food fish
WORD ORIGIN Old English *sceadd*

shade *n* **1** relative darkness produced by blocking out sunlight **2** a place sheltered from the sun by trees, buildings, etc. **3** something used to provide a shield or protection from a direct source of light, such as a lamp shade **4** a shaded area in a painting or drawing **5** any of the different hues of a colour: *a much darker shade of grey* **6** a slight amount: *a shade of reluctance* **7** **put someone** *or* **something in the shade** to be so impressive as to make another person or thing seem unimportant by comparison **8** *literary* a ghost ▸ *vb* **shading, shaded** **9** to screen or protect from heat or light **10** to make darker or dimmer **11** to represent (a darker area) in (a painting or drawing), by graded areas of tone, lines, or dots **12** to change slightly or by degrees
WORD ORIGIN Old English *sceadu*

shades *pl n* **1** *slang* sunglasses **2** **shades of** a reminder of: *shades of Margaret Thatcher*

shading *n* the graded areas of tone, lines, or dots, indicating light and dark in a painting or drawing

shadow *n* **1** a dark image or shape cast on a surface when something stands between a light and the surface **2** a patch of shade **3** the dark portions of a picture **4** a hint or faint trace: *a shadow of a doubt* **5** a person less powerful or vigorous than his or her former self **6** a threatening influence: *news of the murder cast a shadow over the village* **7** a person who always accompanies another **8** a person who trails another in secret, such as a detective ▸ *adj* **9** *Austral & Brit* designating a member or members of the main opposition party in Parliament who would hold ministerial office if their party were in power: *the shadow chancellor* ▸ *vb* **10** to cast a shade or shadow over **11** to make dark or gloomy **12** to follow or trail secretly
WORD ORIGIN Old English *sceadwe*

shadow-box *vb* *boxing* to box against an imaginary opponent for practice **shadow-boxing** *n*

shadowy *adj* **1** (of a place) full of shadows; shady **2** faint or dark like a shadow: *a shadowy figure* **3** mysterious or not well known: *the shadowy world of espionage*

shady *adj* **shadier, shadiest** **1** full of shade; shaded **2** giving or casting shade **3** *informal* of doubtful honesty or legality: *shady business dealings* **shadiness** *n*

S

shaft n **1 a** a spear or arrow **b** its long narrow stem **2 shaft of wit** or **humour** a clever or amusing remark **3** a ray or streak of light **4** the long straight narrow handle of a tool or golf club **5** a revolving rod in a machine that transmits motion or power **6** one of the bars between which an animal is harnessed to a vehicle **7** archit the middle part of a column or pier, between the base and the capital **8** a vertical passageway through a building for a lift **9** a vertical passageway into a mine
WORD ORIGIN Old English sceaft

shag[1] n **1** coarse shredded tobacco **2** a matted tangle of hair or wool ▷ adj **3** (of a carpet) having long thick woollen threads
WORD ORIGIN Old English sceacga

shag[2] n a kind of cormorant
WORD ORIGIN special use of SHAG[1] (with reference to its crest)

shag[3] vb **shagging, shagged** Brit, Austral, & NZ slang **1** taboo to have sexual intercourse with (a person) **2 shagged out** exhausted
WORD ORIGIN origin unknown

shaggy adj **-gier, -giest 1** having or covered with rough unkempt fur, hair, or wool: shaggy cattle **2** rough and untidy **shagginess** n

shagreen n **1** the skin of a shark, used as an abrasive **2** a rough grainy leather made from certain animal hides
WORD ORIGIN French chagrin

shah n a ruler of certain Middle Eastern countries, esp. (formerly) Iran
WORD ORIGIN Persian: king

shake vb **shaking, shook, shaken 1** to move up and down or back and forth with short quick movements **2** to be or make unsteady **3** (of a voice) to tremble because of anger or nervousness **4** to clasp or grasp (the hand) of (a person) in greeting or agreement: they shook hands **5 shake on it** informal to shake hands in agreement or reconciliation **6** to wave vigorously and angrily: he shook his fist **7** (often foll. by up) to frighten or unsettle **8** to shock, disturb, or upset: he was badly shaken but unharmed **9** to undermine or weaken: a team whose morale had been badly shaken **10** US & Canad informal to get rid of **11** music to perform a trill on (a note) **12 shake one's head** to indicate disagreement or disapproval by moving the head from side to side ▷ n **13** the act or an instance of shaking **14** a tremor or vibration **15 the shakes** informal a state of uncontrollable trembling **16** informal a very short period of time: in half a shake **17** music same as **trill** (sense 1) **18** short for **milk shake** ▷ See also **shake down, shake off, shake up**
WORD ORIGIN Old English sceacan

shake down vb **1** to go to bed, esp. in a makeshift bed ▷ n **shakedown 2** a makeshift bed

shake off vb **1** to remove or get rid of: I have been trying to shake off the stigma for some time **2** to escape from; get away from: they switched to a blue car in a bid to shake off reporters

shaker n **1** a container used for shaking a powdered substance onto something:

a flour shaker **2** a container in which the ingredients of alcoholic drinks are shaken together

Shakespearean or **Shakespearian** adj **1** of William Shakespeare, English dramatist and poet, or his works ▷ n **2** a student of or specialist in Shakespeare's works

shake up vb **1** to mix by shaking **2** to reorganize drastically **3** informal to shock mentally or physically: the thunderstorm really shook me up ▷ n **shake-up 4** informal a radical reorganization, such as the reorganization of employees in a company

shako (**shack**-oh) n, pl **shakos** a tall cylindrical peaked military hat with a plume
WORD ORIGIN Hungarian csákó

shaky adj **shakier, shakiest 1** weak and unsteady, esp. due to illness or shock **2** uncertain or doubtful: their prospects are shaky **3** tending to shake or tremble **shakily** adv

shale n a flaky sedimentary rock formed by compression of successive layers of clay
WORD ORIGIN Old English scealu shell

shall vb, past **should 1** (with 'I' or 'we' as subject) used as an auxiliary to make the future tense: we shall see you tomorrow **2** (with 'you', 'he', 'she', 'it', 'they', or a noun as subject) **a** used as an auxiliary to indicate determination on the part of the speaker: you shall pay for this! **b** used as an auxiliary to indicate compulsion or obligation, now esp. in official documents **3** (with 'I' or 'we' as subject) used as an auxiliary in questions asking for advice or agreement: what shall we do now?; shall I shut the door?
WORD ORIGIN Old English sceal

▤ USAGE
▤ The usual rule given for the use of
▤ shall and will is that where the
▤ meaning is one of simple futurity,
▤ shall is used for the first person of the
▤ verb and will for the second and third:
▤ I shall go tomorrow; they will be there now.
▤ Where the meaning involves
▤ command, obligation, or
▤ determination, the positions are
▤ reversed: it shall be done; I will definitely go.
▤ However, shall has come to be largely
▤ neglected in favour of will, which has
▤ become the commonest form of the
▤ future in all three persons.

shallot (shal-**lot**) n a small, onion-like plant used in cooking for flavouring
WORD ORIGIN Old French eschaloigne

shallow adj **1** having little depth **2** not involving sincere feelings or serious thought **3** (of breathing) consisting of short breaths ▷ n **4** (often pl) a shallow place in a body of water **shallowness** n
WORD ORIGIN Middle English shalow

sham n **1** anything that is not genuine or is not what it appears to be **2** a person who pretends to be something other than he or she is ▷ adj **3** not real or genuine ▷ vb **shamming, shammed 4** to fake or feign (something); pretend: he made a point of shamming nervousness
WORD ORIGIN origin unknown

shaman (**sham**-man) n **1** a priest of shamanism **2** a medicine man or witch doctor of a similar religion
WORD ORIGIN Russian

shamanism (**sham**-man-iz-zum) n a religion of northern Asia, based on a belief in good and evil spirits who can be influenced or controlled only by the shamans **shamanist** n, adj

shamble vb **-bling, -bled 1** to walk or move along in an awkward shuffling way ▷ n **2** an awkward or shuffling walk **shambling** adj, n
WORD ORIGIN perhaps from shambles, referring to legs of a meat vendor's table

shambles n **1** a disorderly or badly organized event or place: the bathroom was a shambles **2** chiefly Brit a butcher's slaughterhouse **3** old-fashioned any scene of great slaughter
WORD ORIGIN Middle English shamble table used by meat vendors

shambolic adj informal completely disorganized

shame n **1** a painful emotion resulting from an awareness of having done something wrong or foolish **2** capacity to feel such an emotion: have they no shame? **3** loss of respect; disgrace **4** a person or thing that causes this **5** a cause for regret or disappointment: it's a shame to rush back **6 put to shame** to show up as being inferior by comparison: his essay put mine to shame ▷ interj **7** S African informal **a** an expression of sympathy **b** an expression of pleasure or endearment ▷ vb **shaming, shamed 8** to cause to feel shame **9** to bring shame on **10** (often foll. by into) to force someone to do something by making him or her feel ashamed not to: he was finally shamed into paying the bill
WORD ORIGIN Old English scamu

shamefaced adj embarrassed or guilty **shamefacedly** adv
WORD ORIGIN earlier shamefast

shameful adj causing or deserving shame: a shameful lack of concern **shamefully** adv

shameless adj **1** having no sense of shame: a shameless manipulator **2** without decency or modesty: a shameless attempt to stifle democracy **shamelessly** adv

shammy n, pl **-mies** informal a piece of chamois leather
WORD ORIGIN variant of chamois

shampoo n **1** a soapy liquid used to wash the hair **2** a similar liquid for washing carpets or upholstery **3** the process of shampooing ▷ vb **-pooing, -pooed 4** to wash (the hair, carpets, or upholstery) with shampoo
WORD ORIGIN Hindi chāmpo

shamrock n a small clover-like plant with three round leaves on each stem: the national emblem of Ireland
WORD ORIGIN Irish Gaelic seamróg

shandy n, pl **-dies** a drink made of beer and lemonade
WORD ORIGIN origin unknown

shanghai slang vb **-haiing, -haied 1** to force or trick (someone) into doing something **2** history to kidnap (a man) and force him to serve at sea **3** Austral &

Politics and News Language

Politics is the acquisition of power through persuasion. One way that politicians gain and use power is to select the content, timing, and delivery of news. It follows that, since politics is a primary source of news, the jargon of newsgathering must be taken into account. Terms such as *off the record*, *not for attribution*, *authoritative sources*, *backgrounder*, *sound bite*, *plant*, *leak*, and *spin* all have to do with how political diction and rhetoric frame news in the public mind.

Politicians notoriously employ bromides, clichés, and weasel words. However, this may not necessarily reflect an inability to use language eloquently. Such language is more likely to be an attempt to appeal to the prevailing instincts and attitudes of voters. Politicians seek to erect a *big tent* of voters, or at least as large a tent as possible. Some clever politicians harness a common phrase by reversing its connotations. Thus a Canadian social-democrat politician, David Lewis, once spoke of the wealthy as *corporate welfare bums*.

For George Orwell in his essay 'Politics and the English Language' (1946), pretentiousness, prolixity, and vagueness were moral failures, which he later satirized as *Newspeak* in his novel *Nineteen Eighty-Four*. Another Orwellian coinage, *Big Brother*, was the smiling mask of totalitarianism. Like *Kafkaesque*, the adjective *Orwellian* has come to be a descriptor of dystopia. The abuse of language, Orwell's essay notes, was a way 'to make lies sound truthful and murder respectable, and to give an appearance of solidity to pure wind'.

As the writer William Safire has pointed out, most American presidencies are marked by a characterizing word or slogan created by speechwriters or by other figures: Theodore Roosevelt (*bully pulpit*, *muckraker*), Woodrow Wilson (*self-determination*), Herbert Hoover (*rugged individualism*), Franklin D Roosevelt (*day of infamy*, *fireside chat*, *happy warrior*), Dwight Eisenhower (*brinksmanship*, *domino theory*), Lyndon Baines Johnson (*war on poverty*), Ronald Reagan (*star wars*, *evil empire*), and George W Bush (*axis of evil*). No Presidential period was more linguistically fruitful than Richard Nixon's, when the Watergate affair provided *cover-up*, *enemies list*, *dirty tricks*, *executive privilege*, *smoking gun*, and *stonewall*, and the combining form *–gate*, which would later be applied to scandals concerning everything from Iran to nannies.

In each decade of the twentieth century, words were coined that anticipated enormous political developments. Thus the 1900s gave us *propaganda*, *Realpolitik*, the *Middle East*, and *Palestinian*; the 1910s *appeasement* and the *atomic bomb*; the 1920s the *Iron Curtain* and *isolationism*; the 1930s *telegenic* and the *American Dream*; the 1940s the *Cold War*; the 1950s *disinformation* and *privatization*, the 1960s the *nanny state*, the 1970s *global warming* and *politically correct*; the 1980s the *chattering classes* and *zero-tolerance*; and the 1990s *people's* as an all-purpose term for decentralized power. Of these concepts, *political correctness* probably had the widest impact on general language use. Even as sexual terms became franker and more widespread, euphemisms proliferated and racially biased terms became taboo. Across the decades, politicians successively spoke of the *Negro*, the *Black*, in the United States the *African American*, and the *person of colour*. Meanwhile, the consciousness-raising notion of *black power* returned in the form of *grey power*, and an elderly person of any pigmentation became a *senior citizen*.

In some respects, politics is the animal kingdom. Its terminology gives us not only various forms of horse (*war horse*, *dark horse*, *stalking horse*) but also *hawks*, *doves*, *lame ducks*, *fat cats*, and *bird dogs*. Sometimes politicians have to *eat crow* or, adopting a different diet, make after-dinner speeches on the *rubber-chicken circuit*. Politics also can bring an obscure little word to everyone's lips. *Chad*, a paper fragment caused by a hole punched in a piece of paper, became notorious in the disputed 2000 American Presidential election. Florida vote-counters had to decide whether a card ballot was fully punched. In dealing with the dilemma, a specialized terminology sprang up. A chad could be *hanging*, *swinging*, *pregnant*, *dimpled*, or even a *trichad*. Politics deals with one vote at a time.

NZ to shoot with a catapult ▷ n **4** *Austral & NZ* a catapult
WORD ORIGIN senses 1 and 2 after the city of *Shanghai*; senses 3 and 4 from Scots dialect *shangie, shangan* cleft stick

shank n **1** the part of the leg between the knee and the ankle **2** a cut of meat from the top part of an animal's shank **3** the long narrow part of a tool, key, spoon, etc.
WORD ORIGIN Old English *scanca*

shanks's pony *or US* **shanks's mare** n *informal* one's own legs as a means of transport
WORD ORIGIN from *shank*, the lower part of the leg

shan't shall not

shantung n a heavy Chinese silk with a knobbly surface
WORD ORIGIN after province of NE China

shanty¹ n, pl **-ties** a small rough hut; crude dwelling
WORD ORIGIN Canadian French *chantier* cabin built in a lumber camp

shanty² *or* **chanty** n, pl **-ties** a rhythmic song originally sung by sailors when working
WORD ORIGIN French *chanter* to sing

shantytown n a town of poor people living in shanties

shape n **1** the outward form of an object, produced by its outline **2** the figure or outline of the body of a person **3** organized or definite form: *to preserve the union in its present shape* **4** the specific form that anything takes on: *a gold locket in the shape of a heart* **5** pattern or mould **6** condition or state of efficiency: *in poor shape* **7** **take shape** to assume a definite form ▷ vb **shaping, shaped** **8** (often foll. by *into* or *up*) to receive or cause to receive shape or form: *spinach shaped into a ball* **9** to mould into a particular pattern or form **10** to devise or develop: *to shape a system of free trade* ▶ See also **shape up**
WORD ORIGIN Old English *gesceap*, literally: that which is created

shapeless adj **1** (of a person or object) lacking a pleasing shape: *a shapeless dress* **2** having no definite shape or form: *a shapeless mound* **shapelessness** n

shapely adj **-lier, -liest** (esp. of a woman's body or legs) pleasing or attractive in shape **shapeliness** n

shape up vb *informal* **1** to progress or develop satisfactorily **2** to develop a definite or proper form **3** to start working efficiently or behaving properly: *shape up or face the sack*

shard n a broken piece or fragment of pottery, glass, or metal
WORD ORIGIN Old English *sceard*

share¹ n **1** a part or portion of something that belongs to or is contributed by a person or group **2** (*often pl*) any of the equal parts into which the capital stock of a company is divided ▷ vb **sharing, shared** **3** (often foll. by *out*) to divide and distribute **4** to receive or contribute a portion of: *we shared a bottle of mineral water* **5** to join with another or others in the use of (something): *a programme about four women sharing a house* **6** to go through (a similar experience)

as others: *we have all shared the nightmare of toothache* **7** to tell others about (something) **8** to have the same (beliefs or opinions) as others: *universal values shared by both east and west*
WORD ORIGIN Old English *scearu*

share² n short for **ploughshare**
WORD ORIGIN Old English *scear*

shareholder n the owner of one or more shares in a company

share index n an index showing the movement of share prices

sharemilker n NZ a person who works on a dairy farm belonging to someone else and gets a share of the proceeds from the sale of the milk

sharia n the body of doctrines that regulate the lives of Muslims
WORD ORIGIN Arabic

shark n **1** a large, usually predatory fish with a long body, two dorsal fins, and rows of sharp teeth **2** *disparaging* a person who swindles or extorts money from other people
WORD ORIGIN origin unknown

sharkskin n a smooth glossy fabric used for sportswear

sharp adj **1** having a keen cutting edge **2** tapering to an edge or point **3** involving a sudden change in direction: *a sharp bend on a road; a sharp rise in prices* **4** moving, acting, or reacting quickly: *sharp reflexes* **5** clearly defined: *a sharp contrast* **6** quick to notice or understand things; keen-witted **7** clever in an underhand way: *sharp practices* **8** bitter or harsh: *a sharp response* **9** shrill or penetrating: *a sharp cry of horror* **10** having a bitter or sour taste **11** (of pain or cold) acute or biting: *a sharp gust of wind* **12** *music* **a** (of a note) raised in pitch by one semitone: F *sharp* **b** (of an instrument or voice) out of tune by being too high in pitch **13** *informal* neat and stylish: *a sharp dresser* ▷ adv **14** promptly **15** exactly: *at ten o'clock sharp* **16** *music* **a** higher than a standard pitch **b** out of tune by being too high in pitch: *she sings sharp* ▷ n **17** *music* **a** an accidental that raises the pitch of a note by one semitone. Symbol: ♯ **b** a note affected by this accidental **18** *informal* a cheat; a cardsharp **sharpish** adj **sharply** adv **sharpness** n
WORD ORIGIN Old English *scearp*

sharpen vb to make or become sharp or sharper **sharpener** n

sharper n a person who cheats or swindles; fraud

sharpshooter n a skilled marksman

sharp-tongued adj very critical or sarcastic

sharp-witted adj very intelligent and perceptive

shat vb *taboo* a past tense and past participle of **shit**

shatter vb **1** to break suddenly into many small pieces **2** to damage badly or destroy: *to shatter American confidence* **3** to upset (someone) greatly: *the whole experience shattered me* **shattering** adj
WORD ORIGIN origin unknown

shattered adj *informal* **1** completely exhausted **2** badly upset: *he was shattered by the separation*

shave vb **shaving, shaved; shaved** or **shaven 1** to remove (the beard or hair) from (the face, head, or body) by using a razor or shaver **2** to remove thin slices from (wood or other material) with a sharp cutting tool **3** to touch (someone or something) lightly in passing ▷ n **4** the act or an instance of shaving **5** the removal of hair from a man's face by a razor **6** a tool for cutting off thin slices **7** **close shave** *informal* a narrow escape
WORD ORIGIN Old English *sceafan*

shaver n **1** an electrically powered razor **2** *old-fashioned* a young boy

Shavian (**shave-ee-an**) adj **1** of or like George Bernard Shaw, Irish dramatist noted for his sharp wit, or his works ▷ n **2** an admirer of Shaw or his works

shaving n **1** a thin slice of something such as wood, which has been shaved off ▷ adj **2** used when shaving: *shaving foam*

shawl n a piece of woollen cloth worn over the head or shoulders by a woman or wrapped around a baby
WORD ORIGIN Persian *shāl*

she pron **1** (refers to) the female person or animal previously mentioned or in question: *she is my sister* **2** (refers to) something regarded as female, such as a car, ship, or nation ▷ n **3** (refers to) a female person or animal
WORD ORIGIN Old English *sīe*

sheaf n, pl **sheaves 1** a bundle of papers tied together **2** a bundle of reaped corn tied together ▷ vb **3** to bind or tie into a sheaf
WORD ORIGIN Old English *scēaf*

shear vb **shearing, sheared** *or Austral & NZ sometimes* **shore; sheared** or **shorn 1** to remove (the fleece) of (a sheep) by cutting or clipping **2** to cut or cut through (something) with shears or a sharp instrument **3** *engineering* to cause (a part) to break or (of a part) to break through strain or twisting ▷ n **4** breakage caused through strain or twisting ▶ See also **shears** > **shearer** n
WORD ORIGIN Old English *sceran*

shearing shed n *Austral & NZ* a farm building with equipment for shearing sheep

shears pl n **a** large scissors, used for sheep shearing **b** a large scissor-like cutting tool with flat blades, used for cutting hedges

sheath n, pl **sheaths 1** a case or covering for the blade of a knife or sword **2** *biol* a structure that encloses or protects **3** *Brit, Austral, & NZ* same as **condom 4** a close-fitting dress
WORD ORIGIN Old English *scēath*

sheathe vb **sheathing, sheathed 1** to insert (a knife or sword) into a sheath **2** to cover with a sheathe or sheathing

sheathing n any material used as an outer layer

sheaves n the plural of **sheaf**

shebeen *or* **shebean** n *Scot, Irish, & S African* a place where alcoholic drink is sold illegally
WORD ORIGIN Irish Gaelic *sībīn* beer of poor quality

shed¹ n **1** a small, roughly made building used for storing garden tools, etc.

2 a large barnlike building used for various purposes at factories, train stations, etc.: *a locomotive shed*
WORD ORIGIN Old English *sced*

shed² *vb* **shedding, shed 1** to get rid of: *250 workers shed by the company* **2 shed tears** to cry **3 shed light on** to make (a problem or situation) easier to understand **4** to cast off (skin, hair, or leaves): *the trees were already beginning to shed their leaves* **5** to cause to flow off: *this coat sheds water* **6** to separate or divide (a group of sheep)
WORD ORIGIN Old English *sc(e)ādan*

sheen *n* a glistening brightness on the surface of something: *grass with a sheen of dew on it*
WORD ORIGIN Old English *sciēne*

sheep *n, pl* **sheep 1** a cud-chewing mammal with a thick woolly coat, kept for its wool or meat ▸ Related adjective: **ovine 2** a timid person **3 like sheep** (of a group of people) allowing a single person to dictate their actions or beliefs **4 separate the sheep from the goats** to pick out the members of a group who are superior in some respects **sheeplike** *adj*
WORD ORIGIN Old English *scēap*

sheep-dip *n* **1** a liquid disinfectant and insecticide in which sheep are immersed **2** a deep trough containing such a liquid

sheepdog *n* **1** a dog used for herding sheep **2** a breed of dog reared originally for herding sheep

sheepfold *n* a pen or enclosure for sheep

sheepish *adj* embarrassed because of feeling foolish **sheepishly** *adv*

sheepshank *n* a knot made in a rope to shorten it temporarily

sheepskin *n* the skin of a sheep with the wool still attached, used to make clothing and rugs

sheer¹ *adj* **1** absolute; complete: *sheer amazement* **2** perpendicular; very steep: *the sheer rock face* **3** (of textiles) light, delicate, and see-through ▷ *adv* **4** steeply: *the cliff drops sheer to the sea*
WORD ORIGIN Old English *scīr*

sheer² *vb* **sheer off** *or* **away (from) a** to change course suddenly **b** to avoid an unpleasant person, thing, or topic
WORD ORIGIN origin unknown

sheet¹ *n* **1** a large rectangular piece of cloth used as an inner bed cover **2** a thin piece of material such as paper or glass, usually rectangular **3** a broad continuous surface or layer: *a sheet of ice* **4** a newspaper ▷ *vb* **5** to provide with, cover, or wrap in a sheet **6** (often foll. by *down*) to rain very heavily
WORD ORIGIN Old English *scīete*

sheet² *n naut* a line or rope for controlling the position of a sail
WORD ORIGIN Old English *scēata* corner of a sail

sheet anchor *n* **1** *naut* a large strong anchor for use in an emergency **2** a person or thing that can always be relied on

sheeting *n* any material from which sheets are made

sheet metal *n* metal formed into a thin sheet by rolling or hammering

sheet music *n* music printed on individual sheets of paper

sheikh *or* **sheik** (**shake**) *n* **a** the head of an Arab tribe, village, or family **b** (in Muslim communities) a religious leader **sheikhdom** *or* **sheikdom** *n*
WORD ORIGIN Arabic *shaykh* old man

sheila *n Austral & NZ old-fashioned informal* a girl or woman
WORD ORIGIN from the girl's name *Sheila*

shekel *n* **1** the monetary unit of Israel **2 shekels** *informal* money
WORD ORIGIN Hebrew *sheqel*

shelduck *or masc* **sheldrake** *n, pl* **-ducks, -duck** *or* **-drakes, -drake** a large brightly coloured wild duck of Europe and Asia
WORD ORIGIN probably from dialect *sheld* pied

shelf *n, pl* **shelves 1** a board fixed horizontally against a wall or in a cupboard, for holding things **2** a projecting layer of ice or rock on land or in the sea **3 off the shelf** (of products in shops) sold as standard **4 on the shelf** put aside or abandoned; used esp. of unmarried women considered to be past the age of marriage
WORD ORIGIN Old English *scylfe* ship's deck

shelf life *n* the length of time a packaged product will remain fresh or usable

shell *n* **1** the protective outer layer of an egg, fruit, or nut **2** the hard outer covering of an animal such as a crab or tortoise **3** any hard outer case **4** the external structure of a building, car, or ship, esp. one that is unfinished or gutted by fire **5** an explosive artillery projectile that can be fired from a large gun **6** a small-arms cartridge **7** *rowing* a very light narrow racing boat **8 come** *or* **bring out of one's shell** to become *or* help to become less shy and reserved ▷ *vb* **9** to remove the shell or husk from **10** to attack with artillery shells ▸ See also **shell out** > **shell-like** *adj*
WORD ORIGIN Old English *sciell*

she'll she will *or* she shall

shellac *n* **1** a yellowish resin used in varnishes and polishes **2** a varnish made by dissolving shellac in alcohol ▷ *vb* **-lacking, -lacked 3** to coat with shellac
WORD ORIGIN *shell + lac*

shellfish *n, pl* **-fish** *or* **-fishes** a sea-living animal, esp. one that can be eaten, having a shell

shell out *vb informal* to pay out or hand over (money)

shell shock *n* a nervous disorder characterized by anxiety and depression that occurs as a result of lengthy exposure to battle conditions **shell-shocked** *adj*

shell suit *n Brit* a lightweight tracksuit made of a waterproof nylon layer over a cotton layer

Shelta *n* a secret language based on Gaelic, used by some travelling people in Ireland and Britain
WORD ORIGIN origin unknown

shelter *n* **1** something that provides cover or protection from weather or

danger **2** the protection given by such a cover ▷ *vb* **3** to take cover from bad weather **4** to provide with a place to live or a hiding place: *to shelter refugees*
WORD ORIGIN origin unknown

sheltered *adj* **1** protected from wind and rain **2** protected from unpleasant or upsetting experiences: *a sheltered childhood* **3** specially designed to provide a safe environment for the elderly, handicapped, or disabled: *sheltered housing*

shelve¹ *vb* **shelving, shelved 1** to put aside or postpone: *to shelve a project* **2** to place (something, such as a book) on a shelf **3** to provide with shelves: *to shelve a cupboard* **4** to dismiss (someone) from active service
WORD ORIGIN from *shelves*, plural of *shelf*

shelve² *vb* **shelving, shelved** to slope away gradually
WORD ORIGIN origin unknown

shelves *n* the plural of **shelf**

shelving *n* **1** material for shelves **2** shelves collectively

shenanigans *pl n informal* **1** mischief or nonsense **2** trickery or deception
WORD ORIGIN origin unknown

shepherd *n* **1** a person employed to tend sheep **2** *Christianity* a clergyman when considered as the moral and spiritual guide of the people in the parish ▷ *vb* **3** to guide or watch over (people) **shepherdess** *fem n*
WORD ORIGIN SHEEP + HERD

shepherd's pie *n* a baked dish of minced meat covered with mashed potato

Sheraton *adj* denoting light and elegant furniture made by or in the style of Thomas Sheraton, English furniture maker

sherbet *n* **1** *Brit, Austral, & NZ* a fruit-flavoured slightly fizzy powder, eaten as a sweet or used to make a drink **2** *US, Canad, & S African* same as **sorbet**
WORD ORIGIN Turkish *şerbet*

sheriff *n* **1** (in the US) the chief elected law-enforcement officer in a county **2** (in Canada) a municipal officer who enforces court orders and escorts convicted criminals to prison **3** (in England and Wales) the chief executive officer of the Crown in a county, having chiefly ceremonial duties **4** (in Scotland) a judge in a sheriff court **5** (in Australia) an officer of the Supreme Court
WORD ORIGIN Old English *scīrgerēfa*

sheriff court *n* (in Scotland) a court having powers to try all but the most serious crimes and to deal with most civil actions

Sherpa *n, pl* **-pas** *or* **-pa** a member of a Tibetan people living on the southern slopes of the Himalayas

sherry *n, pl* **-ries** a pale or dark brown fortified wine, originally from southern Spain
WORD ORIGIN Spanish *Xeres*, now *Jerez*, in Spain

Shetland pony *n* a very small sturdy breed of pony with a long shaggy mane and tail

shibboleth *n* **1** a slogan or catch phrase, usually considered outworn, that characterizes a particular party or sect:

the shibboleth of Western strategy **2** a custom, phrase, or use of language that reliably distinguishes a member of one group or class from another **WORD ORIGIN** word used in the Old Testament by the Gileadites as a test word for the Ephraimites, who could not pronounce *sh*

shickered *adj Austral & NZ, old-fashioned slang* drunk **WORD ORIGIN** Yiddish *shicker* liquor

shied *vb* the past of **shy**¹ or **shy**²

shield *n* **1** a piece of defensive armour carried in the hand or on the arm to protect the body from blows or missiles **2** any person or thing that protects, hides, or defends: *a wind shield* **3** *heraldry* a representation of a shield used for displaying a coat of arms **4** anything that resembles a shield in shape, such as a trophy in a sports competition ▷ *vb* **5** to protect, hide, or defend (someone or something) from danger or harm: *an industry shielded from competition* **WORD ORIGIN** Old English *scield*

shift *vb* **1** to move from one place or position to another **2** to pass (blame or responsibility) onto someone else: *he was trying to shift the blame to me* **3** to change (gear) in a motor vehicle **4** to remove or be removed: *no detergent can shift these stains* **5** *US* to change for another or others **6** *slang* to move quickly ▷ *n* **7** the act or an instance of shifting **8 a** a group of workers who work during a specific period **b** the period of time worked by such a group **9** a method or scheme **10** a loose-fitting straight underskirt or dress **WORD ORIGIN** Old English *sciftan*

shiftless *adj* lacking in ambition or initiative

shifty *adj* **shiftier, shiftiest** looking deceitful and not to be trusted **shiftiness** *n*

shillelagh (shil-**lay**-lee) *n* (in Ireland) a heavy club **WORD ORIGIN** Irish Gaelic *sail* cudgel + *éille* thong

shilling *n* **1** a former British coin worth one twentieth of a pound, replaced by the 5p piece in 1970 **2** a former Australian coin, worth one twentieth of a pound **3** the standard monetary unit in several E African countries **WORD ORIGIN** Old English *scilling*

shillyshally *vb* **-shallies, -shallying, -shallied** *informal* to be indecisive **WORD ORIGIN** shill I shall I, reduplication of shall I

shim *n* **1** a thin strip of material placed between two close surfaces to fill a gap ▷ *vb* **shimming, shimmed 2** to fit or fill up with a shim **WORD ORIGIN** origin unknown

shimmer *vb* **1** to shine with a faint unsteady light ▷ *n* **2** a faint unsteady light **shimmering** or **shimmery** *adj* **WORD ORIGIN** Old English *scimerian*

shin *n* **1** the front part of the lower leg **2** a cut of beef including the lower foreleg ▷ *vb* **shinning, shinned 3** shin up to climb (something, such as a rope or pole) by gripping with the hands or arms and the legs and hauling oneself up **WORD ORIGIN** Old English *scinu*

shinbone *n* the nontechnical name for **tibia**

shindig or **shindy** *n, pl* **-digs** or **-dies** *slang* **1** a noisy party or dance **2** a quarrel or brawl **WORD ORIGIN** variant of *shinty*

shine *vb* **shining, shone 1** to give off or reflect light **2** to direct the light of (a lamp or torch): *I shone a torch at the ceiling* **3** *pt & pp* **shined** to make clean and bright by polishing: *they earned money by shining shoes* **4** to be very good at something: *she shone in most subjects; she shone at school* **5** to appear very bright and clear: *her hair shone like gold* ▷ *n* **6** brightness or lustre **7 take a shine to someone** *informal* to take a liking to someone **WORD ORIGIN** Old English *scīnan*

shiner *n informal* a black eye

shingle¹ *n* **1** a thin rectangular tile laid with others in overlapping rows to cover a roof or a wall **2** a woman's short-cropped hairstyle ▷ *vb* **-gling, -gled 3** to cover (a roof or a wall) with shingles **4** to cut (the hair) in a short-cropped style **WORD ORIGIN** Latin *scindere* to split

shingle² *n* coarse gravel found on beaches **WORD ORIGIN** Scandinavian

shingles *n* a disease causing a rash of small blisters along a nerve **WORD ORIGIN** Medieval Latin *cingulum* girdle

shingle slide *n* NZ the loose stones on a steep slope

Shinto *n* a Japanese religion in which ancestors and nature spirits are worshipped **Shintoism** *n* **Shintoist** *n, adj* **WORD ORIGIN** Japanese: the way of the gods

shinty *n* **1** a game (of Scottish origin) like hockey but with taller goals **2** *pl* **-ties** the stick used in this game **WORD ORIGIN** perhaps Scottish Gaelic *sinteag* a pace

shiny *adj* **shinier, shiniest 1** bright and polished **2** (of clothes or material) worn to a smooth and glossy state by continual wear or rubbing

ship *n* **1** a large seagoing vessel with engines or sails **2** short for **airship** or **spaceship 3 when one's ship comes in** when one has become successful ▷ *vb* **shipping, shipped 4** to send or transport by any carrier, esp. a ship **5** *naut* to take in (water) over the side **6** to bring or go aboard a vessel: *to ship oars* **7** (often foll. by *off*) *informal* to send away: *they were shipped off to foreign countries* **8** to be hired to serve aboard a ship: *I shipped aboard a Liverpool liner* **WORD ORIGIN** Old English *scip*

shipboard *adj* taking place or used aboard a ship: *a shipboard romance*

shipbuilder *n* a person or company that builds ships **shipbuilding** *n*

shipmate *n* a sailor who serves on the same ship as another

shipment *n* **1** goods shipped together as part of the same lot: *a shipment of arms* **2** the act of shipping cargo

shipper *n* a person or company that ships

shipping *n* **1** the business of transporting freight, esp. by ship **2** ships collectively: *all shipping should stay clear of the harbour*

shipshape *adj* **1** neat or orderly ▷ *adv* **2** in a neat and orderly manner

shipwreck *n* **1** the destruction of a ship at sea **2** the remains of a wrecked ship **3** ruin or destruction: *the shipwreck of the old science* ▷ *vb* **4** to wreck or destroy (a ship) **5** to bring to ruin or destruction

shipwright *n* someone, esp. a carpenter, who builds or repairs ships

shipyard *n* a place where ships are built and repaired

shire *n* **1** *Brit* a county **2** *Austral* a rural area with an elected council **3 the Shires** the Midland counties of England **WORD ORIGIN** Old English *scīr* office

shire horse *n* a large powerful breed of working horse

shirk *vb* to avoid doing (work or a duty); to be negligent: *no-one shirks when he's around* **shirker** *n* **WORD ORIGIN** probably from German *Schurke* rogue

shirt *n* **1** an item of clothing worn on the upper part of the body, usually with a collar and sleeves and buttoning up the front **2 keep your shirt on** *informal* keep your temper **3 put one's shirt on something** *informal* to bet all one has on something **WORD ORIGIN** Old English *scyrte*

shirt-lifter *n derogatory slang* a homosexual

shirtsleeve *n* **1** the sleeve of a shirt **2 in one's shirtsleeves** not wearing a jacket

shirt-tail *n* the part of a shirt that extends below the waist

shirtwaister or *US* **shirtwaist** *n* a woman's dress with a tailored bodice resembling a shirt

shirty *adj* **shirtier, shirtiest** *slang* bad-tempered or annoyed

shish kebab *n* a dish of small pieces of meat and vegetables grilled on a skewer **WORD ORIGIN** Turkish *şiş kebab*

shit *taboo vb* **shitting, shitted, shit** or **shat 1** to defecate ▷ *n* **2** faeces; excrement **3** *slang* rubbish; nonsense **4** *slang* a worthless person ▷ *interj* **5** *slang* an exclamation of anger or disgust **shitty** *adj* **WORD ORIGIN** Old English *scītan* to defecate

shiver¹ *vb* **1** to tremble from cold or fear ▷ *n* **2** a tremble caused by cold or fear **3 the shivers** a fit of shivering through fear or illness **shivering** *n, adj* **shivery** *adj* **WORD ORIGIN** Middle English *chiveren*

shiver² *vb* **1** to break into fragments ▷ *n* **2** a splintered piece **WORD ORIGIN** Germanic

shoal¹ *n* **1** a large group of fish swimming together **2** a large group of people or things **WORD ORIGIN** Old English *scolu*

shoal² *n* **1** a stretch of shallow water **2** a sandbank or rocky area, esp. one that can be seen at low water ▷ *vb* **3** to make or become shallow **WORD ORIGIN** Old English *sceald* shallow

Scottish Dialect in Canadian English

Since *Nova Scotia* translates as 'New Scotland', and the province has an official tartan, it is a good place from which to assess the Scottish impact on Canada. Like the Irish, their fellow Gaels, Scots made a great impact on Canada's history and, additionally, on its language.

Along with the French, Scots were the first settlers of the *Maritime Provinces*, and helped to form the ethnic mix of what was first a French, then a British, colony. Included in the mix were the Acadian French, the indigenous *Mi'kmaq*, and the Blacks who came from the United States as *United Empire Loyalists* in the wake of the American Revolution, only to be badly treated on arrival. In Lunenburg along the South Shore, Germans (called 'Dutch', after *Deutsch*), settled, distinctive in their culture and in how they spoke English.

But it was the Scots, Calvinist and Catholic alike, who asserted themselves. Especially in the north and east, they cleared forests to make farmland, started emporiums, and founded universities. Many were former crofters, displaced by the Scottish upheavals that followed the eighteenth-century Jacobite rebellions and, later, by the Clearances, during which age-old tenant holdings were combined en bloc to create grazing lands for sheep.

At the height of the fur trade that followed wilderness exploration across vast tracts of northern and western Canada as far as British Columbia, Scots dominated. After the American Revolution, the *UEL*, mainly Scotch-Irish, otherwise called Ulster Scots, settled in New Brunswick, in Montreal and the Eastern Townships of Lower Canada (Quebec), and in southern Upper Canada (Ontario). The Scots of the Red River Settlement around present-day Winnipeg intermarried with French and aboriginals, forming a new people, the *Métis*. After the self-sufficient colony of Nova Scotia reluctantly entered Confederation in 1867, Scots became the new nation's leaders in commercial, educational, and political life: Canada's first two prime ministers, Sir John A Macdonald and Sir Alexander Mackenzie, were Scottish-born.

On Canadian farms, Scottish words such as *puckle*, a small indefinite amount, were in everyday use. Before Canada's population became largely urban, many young people from farms and small towns sought to make good in Montreal and Toronto, or gravitated to the United States. Among those Scottish who were US bound were James Naismith, born in what is now Almonte near Ottawa, who invented basketball, or the prolific economist and writer John Kenneth Galbraith, from the hamlet of Iona Station in southern Ontario. Galbraith published a delightful memoir of his upbringing, aptly named *The Scotch*.

Language change, culture's running mate, kept pace with demographic movements. Leading up to Confederation, Scottish Gaelic was widely spoken in Cape Breton, Prince Edward Island, and elsewhere in British North America. Except in Cape Breton, where people still take part in an annual *mod*, a cultural festival, and play the fiddle at *ceilidh* parties, Gaelic greatly shrank as a living language, though it left linguistic deposits in many place names. Standard English is in any case well-stocked with common words derived from Scottish and Irish Gaelic, or from Lowland Scots: *caddie, reel, whisky, twig* (to understand), *pet, bog, keen, brisk, brat, phony, slob, shanty, slogan*, and of course *clan*. The non-Gaelic Canadianism *storm-stayed* has a Scottish origin. The Scottish *bursary*, a scholarship, became in Canada refined to a scholarship based on financial need or other non-academic criteria. Of special relevance is *bannock*, the sense of which evolved from the unleavened Scottish oatmeal cake to what Canadians first came to know as the mixture of flour, water, and fat baked over a campfire.

The Scottish origins of the inventor Alexander Graham Bell are well-known, but Canada and the United States also claim him. He immigrated to Canada in 1870 and lived in Brantford, Ontario. After he moved to the United States, he became the first practical inventor of the telephone, among many other things. In his later years, he lived increasingly in Baddeck, Cape Breton, where he and others developed the hydrofoil and a biplane that, in 1908, made the first manned flight in the British Empire. He built an estate there overlooking Lake Bras d'Or, and fittingly named it after the Gaelic *Beinn Bhreagh*, Beautiful Mountain.

shock[1] *vb* **1** to cause (someone) to experience extreme horror, disgust, or astonishment: *the similarity shocked me* **2** to cause a state of shock in (a person) ▷ *n* **3** a sudden and violent blow or impact **4 a** a sudden and violent emotional disturbance **b** something causing this **5** *pathol* a condition in which a person's blood cannot flow properly because of severe injury, burns, or fright **6** pain and muscular spasm caused by an electric current passing through a person's body **shocker** *n* **WORD ORIGIN** Old French *choc*

shock[2] *n* **1** a number of grain sheaves set on end in a field to dry ▷ *vb* **2** to set up (sheaves) in shocks **WORD ORIGIN** probably Germanic

shock[3] *n* a thick bushy mass of hair **WORD ORIGIN** origin unknown

shock absorber *n* any device designed to absorb mechanical shock, esp. one fitted to a motor vehicle to reduce the effects of travelling over bumpy surfaces

shocking *adj* **1** *informal* very bad or terrible: *a shocking match at Leicester* **2** causing dismay or disgust: *a shocking lack of concern* **3 shocking pink** (of) a very bright shade of pink

shockproof *adj* capable of absorbing shock without damage

shock tactics *pl n* the use of unexpected or unexpectedly forceful methods to carry out a plan

shock therapy *or* **treatment** *n* the treatment of certain mental conditions by passing an electric current through the patient's brain

shod *vb* the past of **shoe**

shoddy *adj* **-dier, -diest 1** made or done badly or carelessly: *shoddy goods* **2** of poor quality; shabby **shoddily** *adv* **shoddiness** *n* **WORD ORIGIN** origin unknown

shoe *n* **1** one of a matching pair of coverings shaped to fit the foot, made of leather or other strong material and ending below the ankle **2** anything resembling a shoe in shape, function, or position **3** short for **horseshoe 4 be in a person's shoes** *informal* to be in another person's situation ▷ *vb* **shoeing, shod 5** to fit (a horse) with horseshoes **WORD ORIGIN** Old English *scōh*

shoehorn *n* a smooth curved piece of metal or plastic inserted at the heel of a shoe to ease the foot into it

shoelace *n* a cord for fastening shoes

shoemaker *n* a person who makes or repairs shoes or boots **shoemaking** *n*

shoestring *n* **1** same as **shoelace 2** *informal* a very small amount of money: *the theatre will be run on a shoestring*

shoetree *n* a long piece of metal, plastic, or wood, put into a shoe or boot to keep its shape

shone *vb* a past of **shine**

shonky *adj* **-kier, -kiest** *Austral & NZ informal* unreliable or unsound

shoo *interj* **1** go away!: used to drive away unwanted or annoying animals or people ▷ *vb* **shooing, shooed 2** to drive away by crying 'shoo' **WORD ORIGIN** imitative

shook *vb* the past tense of **shake**

shoot *vb* **shooting, shot 1** to hit, wound, or kill with a missile fired from a weapon **2** to fire (a missile or missiles) from a weapon **3** to fire (a weapon) **4** to hunt game with a gun for sport **5** to send out or be sent out quickly and aggressively: *he shot questions at her* **6** to move very rapidly: *the car shot forward* **7** to go or pass quickly over or through: *he was trying to shoot the white water* **8** to slide or push into or out of a fastening: *she shot the bolt quickly* **9** (of a plant) to sprout (a new growth) **10** to photograph or film **11** *sport* to hit or kick the ball at goal ▷ *n* **12** the act of shooting **13** a new growth or sprout of a plant **14** *chiefly Brit* a meeting or party organized for hunting game with guns **15** an area where game can be hunted with guns **16** *informal* a photographic assignment: *a fashion shoot in New York* **WORD ORIGIN** Old English *scēotan*

shooter *n* **1** a person or thing that shoots **2** *slang* a gun

shooting gallery *n* a long narrow room where people practise shooting

shooting star *n* *informal* a meteor

shooting stick *n* a walking stick with a spike at one end and a folding seat at the other

shoot-out *n* **1** a gunfight **2** short for **penalty shoot-out**

shoot up *vb* **1** to grow or increase rapidly: *crime rates have shot up; as my peers started to shoot up, I stopped growing* **2** *slang* to inject oneself with heroin or another strong drug

shop *n* **1** a place for the sale of goods and services **2** a place where a specified type of work is done; workshop: *a repair shop* **3 all over the shop** *informal* scattered everywhere: *his papers were all over the shop* **4 shut up shop** to close business at the end of the day or permanently **5 talk shop** *informal* to discuss one's business or work on a social occasion ▷ *vb* **shopping, shopped 6** (often foll. by *for*) to visit a shop or shops in order to buy (goods) **7** *Brit, Austral, & NZ slang* to inform on (someone), esp. to the police **shopper** *n* **WORD ORIGIN** Old English *sceoppa* stall

shop around *vb* *informal* **1** to visit a number of shops or stores to compare goods and prices **2** to consider a number of possibilities before making a choice

shop assistant *n* a person who serves in a shop

shop floor *n* **1** the production area of a factory **2** workers, esp. factory workers, as opposed to management

shopkeeper *n* a person who owns or manages a shop **shopkeeping** *n*

shoplifter *n* a customer who steals goods from a shop **shoplifting** *n*

shopping *n* **1** the act of going to shops and buying things **2** things that have been bought in shops

shopping centre *n* **1** a complex of stores, restaurants, and sometimes banks, usually under the same roof **2** the area of a town where most of the shops are situated

shopping list *n* **1** a written list of things to be bought when out shopping **2** any list of things desired or demanded: *a long shopping list of amendments to the treaty*

shopping mall *n* a large enclosed shopping centre

shopping plaza *n* a shopping centre, usually a small group of stores built as a strip

shopsoiled *adj* slightly dirty or faded, from being displayed in a shop

shop steward *n* a trade-union official elected by his or her fellow workers to be their representative in dealing with their employer

shoptalk *n* conversation about one's work, carried on outside working hours

shopwalker *n* *Brit* (esp. formerly) a person employed by a department store to assist sales personnel and help customers

shore[1] *n* **1** the land along the edge of a sea, lake, or wide river ▷ Related adjective: **littoral 2** land, as opposed to water: *150 yards from shore* **3 shores** a country: *foreign shores* **WORD ORIGIN** probably from Middle Low German, Middle Dutch *schōre*

shore[2] *n* **1** a prop placed under or against something as a support ▷ *vb* **shoring, shored 2 shore up a** to prop up (an unsteady building or wall) with a strong support **b** to strengthen or support (something weak): *lower interest rates to shore up the economy* **WORD ORIGIN** Middle Dutch *schōre*

shoreline *n* the edge of a sea, lake, or wide river

shorn *vb* a past participle of **shear**

short *adj* **1** of little length; not long **2** of little height; not tall **3** not lasting long **4** not enough: *the number of places laid at the table was short by four* **5 short of** or **on** lacking in: *short of cash; short on detail* **6** concise: *a short book* **7** (of drinks) consisting chiefly of a spirit, such as whisky **8** (of someone's memory) lacking the ability to retain a lot of facts **9** (of a person's manner) abrupt and rather rude: *Kemp was short with her* **10** (of betting odds) almost even **11** *finance* **a** not possessing at the time of sale the stocks or commodities one sells **b** relating to such sales, which depend on falling prices for profit **12** *phonetics* (of a vowel) of relatively brief duration **13** (of pastry) crumbly in texture **14 in short supply** scarce **15 short and sweet** brief and to the point **16 short for** a shortened form of ▷ *adv* **17** abruptly: *to stop short* **18 be caught short** to have a sudden need to go to the toilet **19 go short** not to have enough **20 short of** except: *they want nothing short of his removal from power* ▷ *n* **21** a drink of spirits **22** a short film shown before the main feature in a cinema **23** same as **short circuit 24 for short** *informal* as a shortened form: *cystic fibrosis, CF for short* **25 in short** briefly ▷ *vb* **26** to short-circuit ▷ See also **shorts** > **shortness** *n* **WORD ORIGIN** Old English *sceort*

shortage *n* not enough of something needed

shortbread *n* a rich crumbly biscuit made with butter

shortcake *n* **1** shortbread **2** a dessert made of layers of biscuit or cake filled with fruit and cream

short-change *vb* **-changing, -changed 1** to give (someone) less than the correct change **2** *slang* to treat (someone), unfairly, esp. by giving less than is expected

short circuit *n* **1** a faulty or accidental connection in an electric circuit, which deflects current through a path of low resistance, usually causing the failure of the circuit ▷ *vb* **short-circuit 2** to develop a short circuit **3** to bypass (a procedure): *she wrote to them direct and short-circuited the job agency* **4** to hinder or frustrate (a plan)

shortcoming *n* a fault or weakness

shortcrust pastry *n* a type of pastry with a crisp but crumbly texture

short cut *n* **1** a route that is shorter than the usual one **2** a way of saving time or effort

shorten *vb* to make or become short or shorter

shortening *n* butter or other fat, used in pastry to make it crumbly

shortfall *n* **1** failure to meet a requirement **2** the amount of such a failure; deficit

shorthand *n* a system of rapid writing using simple strokes and other symbols to represent words or phrases

short-handed *adj* (of a company or organization) lacking enough staff to do the required work

shorthand typist *n* a person skilled in the use of shorthand and in typing

shorthorn *n* a member of a breed of cattle with short horns

short list *n* **1** Also called (Scot): **short leet** a list of suitable candidates for a job or prize, from which the successful candidate will be selected ▷ *vb* **short-list 2** to put (someone) on a short list

short-lived *adj* lasting only for a short time: *his authority was short-lived*

shortly *adv* **1** in a short time; soon **2** spoken in a cross and impatient manner

shorts *pl n* **1** trousers reaching the top of the thigh or partway to the knee **2** *chiefly US & Canad* men's underpants

short shrift *n* brief and unsympathetic treatment

short-sighted *adj* **1** unable to see faraway things clearly **2** not taking likely future developments into account: *a short-sighted approach to the problem* **short-sightedness** *n*

short-tempered *adj* easily angered

short-term *adj* of, for, or lasting a short time

short-termism *n* the tendency to concentrate on short-term gains, often at the expense of long-term success

short wave *n* a radio wave with a wavelength in the range 10–100 metres

short-winded *adj* tending to run out of breath easily

shot¹ *n* **1** the act or an instance of firing a gun or rifle **2** *sport* the act or an instance of hitting, kicking, or throwing the ball **3** small round lead pellets used in shotguns **4** a person with specified skill in shooting: *my father was quite a good shot* **5** *informal* an attempt: *a second shot at writing a better treaty* **6** *informal* a guess **7 a** a single photograph **b** an uninterrupted sequence of film taken by a single camera **8** *informal* an injection of a vaccine or narcotic drug **9** *informal* a drink of spirits **10** the launching of a rocket or spacecraft to a specified destination: *a moon shot* **11** *sport* a heavy metal ball used in the shot put **12 like a shot** without hesitating **13 shot in the arm** *informal* something that brings back energy or confidence **14 shot in the dark** a wild guess
WORD ORIGIN Old English *scot*

shot² *vb* **1** the past of **shoot** ▷ *adj* **2** (of textiles) woven to give a changing colour effect **3** streaked with colour: *dark hair shot with streaks of grey*

shotgun *n* a gun for firing a charge of shot at short range

shot put *n* an athletic event in which contestants hurl a heavy metal ball called a shot as far as possible **shot-putter** *n*

should *vb* the past tense of **shall**: used to indicate that an action is considered by the speaker to be obligatory (*you should go*) or to form the subjunctive mood (*I should like to see you; if I should die; should I be late, start without me*)
WORD ORIGIN Old English *sceolde*

☰ **USAGE**
☰ *Should* has, as its most common
☰ meaning in modern English, the
☰ sense *ought* as in *I should go to the*
☰ *graduation, but I don't see how I can.*
☰ However, the older sense of the
☰ subjunctive of *shall* is often used with
☰ *I* or *we* to indicate a more polite form
☰ than *would: I should like to go, but I can't.*
☰ In much speech and writing, *should*
☰ has been replaced by *would* in contexts
☰ of this kind, but it remains in formal
☰ English when a conditional
☰ subjunctive is used: *should he choose to*
☰ *remain, he would be granted asylum.*

shoulder *n* **1** the part of the body where the arm, wing, or foreleg joins the trunk **2** a cut of meat including the upper part of the foreleg **3** the part of an item of clothing that covers the shoulder **4** the strip of unpaved land that borders a road **5 a shoulder to cry on** a person one turns to for sympathy with one's troubles **6 put one's shoulder to the wheel** *informal* to work very hard **7 rub shoulders with someone** *informal* to mix with someone socially **8 shoulder to shoulder a** side by side **b** working together ▷ *vb* **9** to accept (blame or responsibility) **10** to push with one's shoulder: *he shouldered his way through the crowd* **11** to lift or carry on one's shoulders **12 shoulder arms** *mil* to bring one's rifle vertically close to one's right side
WORD ORIGIN Old English *sculdor*

shoulder blade *n* either of two large flat triangular bones one on each side of the back part of the shoulder

shoulder strap *n* a strap worn over the shoulder to hold up an item of clothing or to support a bag

shouldn't should not

shout *n* **1** a loud call or cry **2** *informal* one's turn to buy a round of drinks ▷ *vb* **3** to cry out loudly **4** *Austral & NZ informal* to treat (someone) to (something, such as a drink)
WORD ORIGIN probably from Old Norse *skúta* taunt

shout down *vb* to silence (someone) by talking loudly

shove *vb* **shoving, shoved 1** to give a violent push to **2** to push (one's way) roughly **3** *informal* to put (something) somewhere quickly and carelessly: *shove it into the boot* ▷ *n* **4** a rough push
WORD ORIGIN Old English *scúfan*

shovel *n* **1** a tool for lifting or moving loose material, consisting of a broad blade attached to a large handle **2** a machine or part of a machine resembling a shovel in function ▷ *vb* **-velling, -velled** *or US* **-veling, -veled 3** to lift or move (loose material) with a shovel **4** to put away large quantities of (something) quickly: *shovelling food into their mouths*
WORD ORIGIN Old English *scofl*

shove off *vb informal* to go away; depart

show *vb* **showing, showed; shown** *or* **showed 1** to make, be, or become visible or noticeable: *to show an interest; excitement showed on everyone's face* **2** to present for inspection: *someone showed me the plans* **3** to demonstrate or prove: *evidence showed that this was the most economical way* **4** to instruct by demonstration: *she showed me how to feed the pullets* **5** to indicate: *the device shows changes in the pressure* **6** to behave towards (someone) in a particular way: *to show mercy* **7** to exhibit or display works of art, goods, etc.: *three artists are showing at the gallery* **8** to present (a film or play) or (of a film or play) to be presented **9** to guide or escort: *he offered to show me around* **10** *informal* to arrive ▷ *n* **11** a theatrical or other entertainment: *a magic show* **12** a display or exhibition: *a show of paintings* **13** something done to create an impression: *a show of indignation* **14** vain and conspicuous display: *it was nothing but mere show* **15** *slang chiefly Brit* a thing or affair: *jolly good show* ▶ See also **show off, show up**
WORD ORIGIN Old English *scēawian*

show business *n* the entertainment industry. Also (informal): **show biz**

showcase *n* **1** a setting in which something is displayed to best advantage: *a showcase for young opera singers* **2** a glass case used to display objects in a museum or shop

showdown *n informal* a major confrontation that settles a dispute

shower *n* **1 a** a kind of bathing in which a person stands upright and is sprayed with water from a nozzle **b** a device, room, or booth for such bathing **2** a brief period of rain, hail, sleet, or snow **3** a sudden fall of many small light objects: *a shower of loose gravel* **4** *Brit slang* a worthless or contemptible group of people **5** *US, Canad, Austral, & NZ* a party held to honour and present gifts to a prospective bride or prospective mother ▷ *vb* **6** to take a shower **7** to sprinkle

with or as if with a shower: *the walkers were showered by volcanic ash* **8** to present (someone) with things liberally: *he showered her with presents* **showery** *adj*
WORD ORIGIN Old English *scūr*

showing *n* **1** a presentation, exhibition, or display **2** manner of presentation

showjumping *n* the sport of riding horses in competitions to demonstrate skill in jumping **showjumper** *n*

showman *n, pl* **-men 1** a person skilled at presenting anything in an effective manner **2** a person who presents or produces a show **showmanship** *n*

shown *vb* a past participle of **show**

show off *vb* **1** to exhibit or display (something) so as to invite admiration: *he was eager to show off his new car* **2** *informal* to flaunt skills, knowledge, or looks in order to attract attention or impress people ▷ *n* **show-off 3** *informal* a person who flaunts his or her skills, knowledge, or looks in order to attract attention or impress people

showpiece *n* **1** anything displayed or exhibited **2** something admired as a fine example of its type: *an orchestral showpiece*

showplace *n* a place visited for its beauty or interest

showroom *n* a room in which goods for sale, esp. cars or electrical or gas appliances, are on display

show up *vb* **1** to reveal or be revealed clearly **2** to expose the faults or defects of (someone or something) by comparison **3** *informal* to put (someone) to shame; embarrass **4** *informal* to arrive

showy *adj* **showier, showiest 1** colourful, bright in appearance, and very noticeable, and perhaps rather vulgar: *showy jewellery* **2** making an imposing display **showily** *adv* **showiness** *n*

shrank *vb* a past tense of **shrink**

shrapnel *n* **1** an artillery shell containing a number of small pellets or bullets which it is designed to scatter on explosion **2** fragments from this type of shell
WORD ORIGIN after H. *Shrapnel*, who invented it

shred *n* **1** a long narrow piece torn off something **2** a very small amount: *not a shred of truth* ▷ *vb* **shredding, shredded** or **shred 3** to tear into shreds **shredder** *n*
WORD ORIGIN Old English *scrēad*

shrew *n* **1** a small mouselike animal with a long snout **2** a bad-tempered nagging woman **shrewish** *adj*
WORD ORIGIN Old English *scrēawa*

shrewd *adj* intelligent and making good judgments **shrewdly** *adv* **shrewdness** *n*
WORD ORIGIN from *shrew* (obsolete verb) to curse, from *shrew*

shriek *n* **1** a high-pitched scream ▷ *vb* **2** to utter (words or sounds) in a high-pitched tone
WORD ORIGIN probably from Old Norse *skrækja* to screech

shrift *n* see **short shrift**
WORD ORIGIN Old English *scrift* penance

shrike *n* a bird with a heavy hooked bill, which kills small animals by

dashing them on thorns
WORD ORIGIN Old English *scrīc* thrush

shrill *adj* **1** (of a sound) sharp and high-pitched ▷ *vb* **2** to utter (words or sounds) in a shrill tone **shrillness** *n* **shrilly** *adv*
WORD ORIGIN origin unknown

shrimp *n* **1** a small edible shellfish with a long tail and a pair of pincers **2** *informal* a small person ▷ *vb* **3** to fish for shrimps
WORD ORIGIN probably Germanic

shrine *n* **1** a place of worship associated with a sacred person or object **2** a container for sacred relics **3** the tomb of a saint or other holy person **4** a place that is visited and honoured because of its association with a famous person or event: *he'd come to worship at the shrine of Mozart*
WORD ORIGIN Latin *scrinium* bookcase

shrink *vb* **shrinking, shrank** or **shrunk; shrunk** or **shrunken 1** to become or cause to become smaller, sometimes because of wetness, heat, or cold **2 shrink from a** to withdraw or move away through fear: *they didn't shrink from danger* **b** to feel great reluctance (to perform a task or duty) ▷ *n* **3** *slang* a psychiatrist
WORD ORIGIN Old English *scrincan*

shrinkage *n* **1** the fact of shrinking **2** the amount by which anything decreases in size, value, or weight

shrink-wrap *vb* **-wrapping, -wrapped** to package (a product) in a flexible plastic wrapping which shrinks about its contours to seal it

shrivel *vb* **-velling, -velled** or *US* **-veling, -veled** to become dry and withered
WORD ORIGIN probably Scandinavian

shroud *n* **1** a piece of cloth used to wrap a dead body **2** anything that hides things: *a shroud of smoke* ▷ *vb* **3** to hide or obscure (something): *shrouded in uncertainty; shrouded by smog*
WORD ORIGIN Old English *scrūd* garment

Shrove Tuesday *n* the day before Ash Wednesday
WORD ORIGIN Old English *scrīfan* to confess one's sins

shrub *n* a woody plant, smaller than a tree, with several stems instead of a trunk **shrubby** *adj*
WORD ORIGIN Old English *scrybb*

shrubbery *n, pl* **-beries 1** an area planted with shrubs **2** shrubs collectively

shrug *vb* **shrugging, shrugged 1** to draw up and drop (the shoulders) as a sign of indifference or doubt ▷ *n* **2** the action of shrugging
WORD ORIGIN origin unknown

shrug off *vb* **1** to treat (a matter) as unimportant **2** to get rid of (someone)

shrunk *vb* a past tense and past participle of **shrink**

shrunken *vb* **1** a past participle of **shrink** ▷ *adj* **2** reduced in size

shudder *vb* **1** to shake or tremble suddenly and violently from horror or fear **2** (of a machine) to shake violently ▷ *n* **3** a shiver of fear or horror
WORD ORIGIN Middle Low German *schöderen*

shuffle *vb* **-fling, -fled 1** to walk or move (the feet) with a slow dragging motion **2** to mix together in a jumbled mass: *the chairman shuffled his papers* **3** to mix up (playing cards) so as to change their order ▷ *n* **4** an instance of shuffling **5** a rearrangement: *a shuffle of top management* **6** a dance with short dragging movements of the feet
WORD ORIGIN probably from Low German *schüffeln*

shufti *n* *slang chiefly Brit* a look; peep
WORD ORIGIN from Arabic

shun *vb* **shunning, shunned** to avoid deliberately
WORD ORIGIN Old English *scunian*

shunt *vb* **1** to move (objects or people) to a different position **2** *railways* to transfer (engines or carriages) from track to track ▷ *n* **3** the act of shunting **4** a railway point **5** *electronics* a conductor connected in parallel across a part of a circuit to divert a known fraction of the current **6** *informal* a collision where one vehicle runs into the back of another
WORD ORIGIN perhaps from Middle English *shunen* to shun

shush *interj* **1** be quiet! hush! ▷ *vb* **2** to quiet (someone) by saying 'shush'
WORD ORIGIN imitative

shut *vb* **shutting, shut 1** to move (something) so as to cover an opening: *shut the door* **2** to close (something) by bringing together the parts: *Ridley shut the folder* **3 shut up** to close or lock the doors of: *let's shut up the shop* **4 shut in** to confine or enclose **5 shut out** to prevent from entering **6** (of a shop or other establishment) to stop operating for the day: *the late-night rush after the pubs shut* **7** *adj* closed or fastened ▶ See also **shutdown, shut off**, etc.
WORD ORIGIN Old English *scyttan*

shutdown *n* **1** the closing of a factory, shop, or other business ▷ *vb* **shut down 2** to discontinue operations permanently

shuteye *n* *slang* sleep

shut off *vb* **1** to cut off the flow or supply of **2** to turn off and stop working: *I shut off the car engine* **3** to isolate or separate: *ghettoes shut off from the rest of society*

shut out *vb* **1** to keep out or exclude **2** to conceal from sight: *blinds were drawn to shut out the sun*

shutter *n* **1** a hinged doorlike cover, usually one of a pair, for closing off a window **2 put up the shutters** to close business at the end of the day or permanently **3** *photog* a device in a camera that opens to allow light through the lens so as to expose the film when a photograph is taken ▷ *vb* **4** to close or equip with a shutter or shutters

shuttle *n* **1** a bus, train, or aircraft that makes frequent journeys between two places which are fairly near to each other **2** a bobbin-like device used in weaving to pass the weft thread between the warp threads **3** a small bobbin-like device used to hold the thread in a sewing machine ▷ *vb* **-tling, -tled 4** to travel back and forth
WORD ORIGIN Old English *scytel* dart, arrow, from *sceotan* to shoot

Yorkshire Dialect

Yorkshire was historically the largest of the English counties, divided into three ridings (from *thriding*, an old word for 'a third' – which accounts for the absence of a South Riding to go with the North, East, and West Ridings). Since 1974, the historic county has been knocked about a bit, and Yorkshire no longer exists as unit of a local government, having been split into several smaller authorities. However, there is still a strong identification with the concept of Yorkshireness, and people from the region are more likely to tell you that they come from Yorkshire than from 'the East Riding of Yorkshire', or whatever newfangled county they officially reside in.

A sense of local pride and a stubborn attachment to tradition have always been part of the Yorkshire make-up. (The county's cricket team persisted in picking only players who were born in the county long after the other counties had taken to recruiting star players from overseas.) No true Yorkshireman would ever concede that another place could be better than Yorkshire, and while the rivalry with Lancashire is strong – dating back to the 'Wars of the Roses' when the House of Lancaster vied with the House of York for the English crown – the Yorkshireman's contempt is more often directed at 'soft southerners' who drink lager instead of bitter and would prefer to visit an art gallery than watch a game of rugby league.

Yorkshire people are notoriously blunt and take pleasure in 'calling a spade a spade'. This reputation for forthrightness is enhanced by the language they use, which tends to be direct and unadorned, and is pronounced with characteristically flat vowels.

Glimpses of an older form of Yorkshire dialect can be found in the novels of the Brontë sisters, who lived in Haworth. In Emily Brontë's *Wuthering Heights* (published in 1847) the servant Joseph speaks almost exclusively in dialect, saying things such as, 'I hed aimed to dee, wheare I'd sarved fur sixty year' ('I had aimed to die where I had served for sixty years'). Much of this 19th-century dialect is naturally unfamiliar to modern ears, although elements of it, such as the omission of 's' from the plural form in 'sixty year', clearly linger in modern Yorkshire speech.

Another archaic form that persists in current Yorkshire speech is the use of the second-person pronouns *thou* (often pronounced and written as *tha*) and *thee*. These pronouns can be heard in some well-known Yorkshire phrases, such as 'Th'art nobbut a lad' ('You are only a child') and the valediction 'I'll sithee' ('I'll see you'). Also archaic is the tendency for reflexive pronouns to end in '-sen' rather than '-self', so that *myself* is rendered as *missen*, and a hyperactive child might be told, 'Stop makkin' an exhibition o' thissen!'

Besides the preservation of archaic forms, Yorkshire speech is also notable for its predilection for eliminating unnecessary letters. The word *the* is often reduced to a single letter, *t'*, so that on a Friday night you might go out 'to t' pub' or 'to t' cinema'. Similarly, the word *of* may be reduced to *o'*.

The dropping of the letter 'h' before a vowel, although not exclusive to Yorkshire, is widely observed, so that *horse* is pronounced *'oss* and *happen* is pronounced *'appen*. The latter word is often used at the start of sentence with the same meaning as *perhaps*, as in 'Happen I'll see thee tomorrow'.

Yorkshire folk can often be recognized by their distinctive vocabulary. They tend to talk of *lads* and *lasses* rather boys and girls, while people are often referred to as *folk*. Other words that are characteristic of Yorkshire speech include *aye* ('yes'), *nowt* ('nothing'), *owt* ('anything'), *brass* ('money'), and *snap* ('food' or, more specifically, 'a packed lunch').

As with other regional dialects, there are concerns that the traditional Yorkshire dialect is being watered down as people from the county travel more widely and are exposed to other forms of English through the media of film and television. Yet any episode of *Emmerdale* or *Last of Summer Wine* should be enough to demonstrate that there remains much that is distinctive about the way the people of Yorkshire speak.

shuttlecock *n* a rounded piece of cork or plastic with feathers stuck in one end, struck to and fro in badminton

shut up *vb* **1** *informal* to stop talking or cause (someone) to stop talking: often used in commands **2** to confine or imprison (someone)

shy¹ *adj* **1** not at ease in the company of others **2** easily frightened; timid **3** shy of cautious or wary of **4** reluctant or unwilling: *camera-shy; workshy* ▷ *vb* **shies, shying, shied 5** to move back or aside suddenly from fear: *with a terrified whinny the horse shied* **6** shy away from to draw back from (doing something), through lack of confidence ▷ *n, pl* **shies 7** a sudden movement back or aside from fear **shyly** *adv* **shyness** *n*
WORD ORIGIN Old English *scēoh*

shy² *vb* **shies, shying, shied 1** to throw (something) ▷ *n, pl* **shies 2** a quick throw
WORD ORIGIN Germanic

Shylock *n* an unsympathetic and demanding person to whom one owes money
WORD ORIGIN after the heartless usurer in Shakespeare's *The Merchant of Venice*

si *n music* same as **te**

Si *chem* silicon

SI see **SI unit**

Siamese *n, pl* **-mese 1** same as **Siamese cat** ▷ *adj, n, pl* **-mese 2** (formerly) same as **Thai**

Siamese cat *n* a breed of cat with cream fur, dark ears and face, and blue eyes

Siamese twins *pl n* twins born joined together at some part of the body

sibilant *adj* **1** having a hissing sound ▷ *n* **2** *phonetics* a consonant, such as *s* or *z*, that is pronounced with a hissing sound
WORD ORIGIN Latin *sibilare* to hiss

sibling *n* a brother or sister
WORD ORIGIN Old English: a relative

sibyl *n* (in ancient Greece and Rome) a prophetess **sibylline** *adj*
WORD ORIGIN Greek *Sibulla*

sic¹ *adv* thus: inserted in brackets in a text to indicate that an odd spelling or reading is in fact what was written, even though it is or appears to be wrong
WORD ORIGIN Latin

sic² *vb* **sicking, sicked 1** to attack: used only in commands to a dog **2** to urge (a dog) to attack (someone)
WORD ORIGIN dialect variant of *seek*

sick *adj* **1** vomiting or likely to vomit **2** physically or mentally unwell **3** of or for ill people: *sick pay* **4** deeply affected with mental or spiritual distress: *sick at heart* **5** mentally disturbed **6** *informal* making fun of death, illness, or misfortune: *a sick joke* **7** sick of or sick and tired of *informal* disgusted by or weary of: *I'm sick of this town* ▷ *vb* **8** *informal* same as **vomit**
WORD ORIGIN Old English *sēoc*

sickbay *n* a room for the treatment of sick people, for example on a ship

sicken *vb* **1** to make (someone) feel nauseated or disgusted **2** sicken for to show symptoms of (an illness)

sickening *adj* **1** causing horror or disgust: *sickening scenes of violence*

2 *informal* extremely annoying **sickeningly** *adv*

sickie *n informal* a day of sick leave from work

sickle *n* a tool for cutting grass and grain crops, with a curved blade and a short handle
WORD ORIGIN Old English *sicol*

sick leave *n* leave of absence from work through illness

sickly *adj* **-lier, -liest 1** weak and unhealthy **2** (of a person) looking pale and unwell: *sickly pallor* **3** unpleasant to smell, taste, or look at **4** showing excessive emotion in a weak and rather pathetic way: *a sickly tune* ▷ *adv* **5** suggesting sickness: *sickly pale* **sickliness** *n*

sickness *n* **1** a particular illness or disease: *sleeping sickness* **2** the state of being ill or unhealthy: *absent from work due to sickness* **3** a feeling of queasiness in the stomach followed by vomiting

side *n* **1** a line or surface that borders anything **2** *geom* a line forming part of the perimeter of a plane figure: *a square has four sides* **3** either of two parts into which an object, surface, or area can be divided: *the right side and the left side* **4** either of the two surfaces of a flat object: *write on both sides of the page* **5** the sloping part of a hill or bank **6** either the left or the right half of the body, esp. the area around the waist: *he took a nine millimetre bullet in the side* **7** the area immediately next to a person or thing: *at the side of my bed* **8** a place within an area identified by reference to a central point: *the south side of the island* **9** the area at the edge of something, as opposed to the centre: *the far side of the square* **10** aspect or part: *there is a positive side to truancy* **11** one of two or more contesting groups or teams: *the two sides will meet in the final* **12** a position held in opposition to another in a dispute **13** a line of descent through one parent: *a relative on his father's side* **14** *informal* a television channel **15** *Brit slang* conceit or cheek: *to put on side* **16** on one side apart from the rest **17** on the side in addition to a person's main work: *she did a little public speaking on the side* **18** side by side close together **19** side by side with beside or near to **20** take sides to support one party in a dispute against another ▷ *adj* **21** situated at the side: *the side entrance* **22** less important: *a side issue* ▷ *vb* **siding, sided 23** side with to support (one party in a dispute)
WORD ORIGIN Old English *sīde*

sideboard *n* a piece of furniture for a dining room, with drawers, cupboards, and shelves to hold tableware

sideboards *or esp. US & Canad* **sideburns** *pl n* a man's whiskers grown down either side of the face in front of the ears

sidecar *n* a small passenger car attached to the side of a motorcycle

side-effect *n* **1** a usually unwanted effect caused by a drug in addition to its intended one **2** any additional effect, usually an undesirable one: *the unforeseen side-effects of the end of the Cold War*

sidekick *n informal* a close friend or associate

sidelight *n* **1** *Brit* either of two small lights at the front of a motor vehicle **2** either of the two navigational lights used by ships at night

sideline *n* an extra job in addition to one's main job

sidelines *pl n* **1** *sport* **a** the lines that mark the side boundaries of a playing area **b** the area just outside the playing area, where substitute players sit **2** on the sidelines **a** only passively involved: *on the sidelines of the modern world* **b** waiting to join in an activity

sidelong *adj* **1** directed to the side; oblique ▷ *adv* **2** from the side; obliquely

sidereal (side-**eer**-ee-al) *adj* of or determined with reference to the stars: *the sidereal time*
WORD ORIGIN Latin *sidus* a star

side-saddle *n* **1** a riding saddle originally designed for women in skirts, allowing the rider to sit with both legs on the same side of the horse ▷ *adv* **2** on a side-saddle

sideshow *n* **1** an event or incident considered less important than another: *a mere sideshow compared to the war on the Russian front* **2** a small show or entertainment offered along with the main show at a circus or fair

side-splitting *adj* causing a great deal of laughter

sidestep *vb* **-stepping, -stepped 1** to step out of the way of (something) **2** to dodge (an issue) ▷ *n* **side step 3** a movement to one side, such as in dancing or boxing

sideswipe *n* **1** an unexpected criticism of someone or something while discussing another subject **2** a glancing blow along or from the side ▷ *vb* **-swiping, -swiped 3** to make a sideswipe

sidetrack *vb* to distract (someone) from a main subject

sidewalk *n US & Canad* a raised space alongside a road, for pedestrians

sideways *adv* **1** moving, facing, or inclining towards one side **2** from one side; obliquely **3** with one side forward ▷ *adj* **4** moving or directed to or from one side

side whiskers *pl n* same as **sideboards**

siding *n* a short stretch of railway track connected to a main line, used for loading and unloading freight and storing engines and carriages

sidle *vb* **-dling, -dled** to walk slowly and carefully, not wanting to be noticed
WORD ORIGIN obsolete *sideling* sideways

SIDS sudden infant death syndrome; cot death

siege *n* **1** a military operation carried out to capture a place by surrounding and blockading it **2** a similar operation carried out by police, for example to force people out of a place **3** lay siege to to subject (a place) to a siege
WORD ORIGIN Old French *sege* a seat

siemens *n, pl* **siemens** the SI unit of electrical conductance
WORD ORIGIN after E. W. von *Siemens*, engineer

sienna *n* **1** a natural earth used as a reddish-brown or yellowish-brown pigment ▷ *adj* **2 burnt sienna** reddish-brown **3 raw sienna** yellowish-brown **WORD ORIGIN** after *Siena*, Italian city

sierra *n* a range of mountains with jagged peaks in Spain or America **WORD ORIGIN** Spanish, literally: saw

sies (**siss**) *interj S African informal* same as **sis²**

siesta *n* an afternoon nap, taken in hot countries **WORD ORIGIN** Spanish

sieve (**siv**) *n* **1** a utensil with a mesh through which a substance is sifted or strained ▷ *vb* **sieving, sieved 2** to sift or strain through a sieve **WORD ORIGIN** Old English *sife*

sift *vb* **1** to sieve (a powdery substance) in order to remove the coarser particles **2** to examine (information or evidence) carefully to select what is important **WORD ORIGIN** Old English *siftan*

sigh *vb* **1** to draw in and audibly let out a deep breath as an expression of sadness, tiredness, longing, or relief **2** to make a sound resembling this **3 sigh for** to long for **4** to say (something) with a sigh ▷ *n* **5** the act or sound of sighing **WORD ORIGIN** Old English *sīcan*

sight *n* **1** the ability to see; vision ▶ Related adjective: **visual 2** an instance of seeing **3** the range of vision: *the cemetery was out of sight* **4** anything that is seen **5** point of view; judgment: *nothing has changed in my sight* **6** *informal* anything unpleasant to see: *she looked a sight in the streetlamps* **7** a device for guiding the eye in aiming a gun or making an observation with an optical instrument **8** an aim or observation made with such a device **9 sights** anything worth seeing: *the great sights of Barcelona* **10 a sight** *informal* a great deal: *it's a sight warmer than in the hall* **11 a sight for sore eyes** a welcome sight **12 catch sight of** to glimpse **13 know someone by sight** to be able to recognize someone without having ever been introduced **14 lose sight of a** to be unable to see (something) any longer **b** to forget: *we lose sight of priorities* **15 on sight** as soon as someone or something is seen **16 set one's sights on** to have (a specified goal) in mind **17 sight unseen** without having seen the object concerned: *he would have taken it sight unseen* ▷ *vb* **18** to see (someone or something) briefly or suddenly: *the two suspicious vessels were sighted* **19** to aim (a firearm) using the sight **WORD ORIGIN** Old English *sihth*

sighted *adj* not blind

sightless *adj* blind

sight-read *vb* **-reading, -read** to sing or play (music in a printed form) without previous preparation **sight-reading** *n*

sightscreen *n cricket* a large white screen placed near the boundary behind the bowler, which helps the batsman see the ball

sightseeing *n informal* visiting famous or interesting sights in a place **sightseer** *n*

sigma *n* **1** the 18th letter in the Greek alphabet (Σ, σ) **2** *maths* the symbol Σ, indicating summation

sign *n* **1** something that indicates a fact or condition that is not immediately or outwardly observable: *a sign of tension* **2** a gesture, mark, or symbol intended to convey an idea or information **3** a board or placard displayed in public and intended to advertise, inform, or warn **4** a conventional mark or symbol that has a specific meaning, for example £ for pounds **5** *maths* **a** any symbol used to indicate an operation: *a minus sign* **b** a symbol used to indicate whether a number or expression is positive or negative **6** a visible indication: *no sign of the enemy* **7** an omen **8** *med* any evidence of the presence of a disease or disorder **9** *astrol* short for **sign of the zodiac** ▷ *vb* **10** to write (one's name) on (a document or letter) to show its authenticity or one's agreement **11** to communicate using sign language **12** to make a sign to someone so as to convey an idea or information **13** to engage or be engaged by signing a contract: *he signed for another team* ▶ See also **sign away, sign in**, etc. **WORD ORIGIN** Latin *signum*

signal *n* **1** any sign, gesture, sound, or action used to communicate information **2** anything that causes immediate action: *this is the signal for a detailed examination of the risk* **3 a** a variable voltage, current, or electromagnetic wave, by which information is conveyed through an electronic circuit **b** the information so conveyed ▷ *adj* **4** *formal* very important: *a signal triumph for the government* ▷ *vb* **-nalling, -nalled** *or US* **-naling, -naled 5** to communicate (information) by signal **signally** *adv* **WORD ORIGIN** Latin *signum* sign

signal box *n* a building from which railway signals are operated

signalman *n, pl* **-men** a railwayman in charge of the signals and points within a section

signatory (**sig**-na-tree) *n, pl* **-ries 1** a person, organization, or state that has signed a document such as a treaty ▷ *adj* **2** having signed a document or treaty

signature *n* **1** a person's name written by himself or herself, used in signing something **2** a distinctive characteristic that identifies a person or animal **3** *music* a sign at the beginning of a piece to show key or time **4** *printing* a sheet of paper printed with several pages, which when folded becomes a section of a book **WORD ORIGIN** Latin *signare* to sign

signature tune *n* a piece of music used to introduce a particular television or radio programme

sign away *vb* to give up one's right to (something): *she will sign away all rights to these pictures*

signboard *n* a board carrying a sign or notice, often to advertise a business or product

signet *n* a small seal used to make documents official **WORD ORIGIN** Medieval Latin *signetum*

signet ring *n* a finger ring engraved with an initial or other emblem

significance *n* **1** the effect something is likely to have on other things: *an event of important significance in British history* **2** meaning: *the occult significance of the symbol*

significant *adj* **1** very important **2** having or expressing a meaning **significantly** *adv*

significant figures *pl n maths* **1** the figures of a number that express a magnitude to a specified degree of accuracy: *3.141 59 to four significant figures is 3.142* **2** the number of such figures: *3.142 has four significant figures*

signify *vb* **-fies, -fying, -fied 1** to indicate or suggest **2** to stand as a symbol or sign for: *a blue line on the map signified a river* **3** to be important **WORD ORIGIN** Latin *signum* a mark + *facere* to make

sign in *vb* **1** to sign a register on arrival at a place **2** to admit (a nonmember) to a club or institution as a guest by signing a register on his or her behalf

signing *n* a system of communication using hand and arm movements, such as one used by deaf people. Also called: **sign language**

sign off *vb* to announce the end of a radio or television programme

sign of the zodiac *n astrol* any of the 12 areas into which the zodiac is divided

sign on *vb* **1** *Austral & Brit* to register and report regularly at an unemployment-benefit office **2** to commit oneself to a job or activity by signing a form or contract

signor (see-**nyor**) *n* an Italian form of address equivalent to *sir* or *Mr*

signora (see-**nyor**-a) *n* an Italian form of address equivalent to *madam* or *Mrs*

signorina (see-nyor-**ee**-na) *n* an Italian form of address equivalent to *madam* or *Miss*

sign out *vb* to sign a register to indicate that one is leaving a place

signpost *n* **1** a road sign displaying information, such as the distance to the next town **2** an indication as to how an event is likely to develop or advice on what course of action should be taken ▷ *vb* **3** to mark (the way) with signposts

sign up *vb* **1** to agree to do a job or course by signing a document **2 sign someone up** to hire (someone) officially to do a job **3** to enlist for military service

sik *adj Austral slang* excellent

Sikh (**seek**) *n* **1** a member of an Indian religion that teaches that there is only one God ▷ *adj* **2** of the Sikhs or their religious beliefs or customs **Sikhism** *n* **WORD ORIGIN** Hindi: disciple

silage (**sile**-ij) *n* a fodder crop harvested while green and partially fermented in a silo

silence *n* **1** the state or quality of being silent **2** the absence of sound **3** refusal or failure to speak or communicate when expected: *he's broken his silence on the issue* ▷ *vb* **-lencing, -lenced 4** to cause (someone or something) to become silent **5** to put a stop to: *a way of silencing criticism*

silencer *n* any device designed to reduce noise, for example one fitted to the exhaust system of a motor vehicle or one fitted to the muzzle of a gun

S

silent *adj* **1** tending to speak very little **2** failing to speak or communicate when expected: *they remained silent as minutes passed* **3** producing no noise: *the silent room* **4** not spoken: *silent reproach* **5** (of a letter) used in the spelling of a word but not pronounced, such as the *k* in *know* **6** (of a film) having no soundtrack **silently** *adv*
WORD ORIGIN Latin *silere* to be quiet

silhouette *n* **1** the outline of a dark shape seen against a light background **2** an outline drawing, often a profile portrait, filled in with black ▷ *vb* **-etting, -etted 3** to show (something) in silhouette
WORD ORIGIN after E. de *Silhouette*, politician

silica *n* a hard glossy mineral, silicon dioxide, which occurs naturally as quartz and is used in the manufacture of glass
WORD ORIGIN Latin *silex* hard stone

silicate *n* mineral a compound of silicon, oxygen, and a metal

silicon *n* **1** chem a brittle non-metallic element: used in transistors, solar cells, and alloys. Symbol: Si ▷ *adj* **2** denoting an area of a country that contains much high-technology industry: *the Silicon Glen*
WORD ORIGIN from *silica*

silicon chip *n* same as **chip** (sense 3)

silicone *n* chem a tough synthetic material made from silicon and used in lubricants, paints, and resins

silicosis *n* pathol a lung disease caused by breathing in silica dust

silk *n* **1** the fine soft fibre produced by a silkworm **2** thread or fabric made from this fibre **3 silks** clothing made of this **4** Brit **a** the gown worn by a Queen's (or King's) Counsel **b** informal a Queen's (or King's) Counsel **c** take **silk** to become a Queen's (or King's) Counsel
WORD ORIGIN Old English *sioloc*

silken *adj* **1** made of silk **2** literary smooth and soft: *her silken hair*

silk-screen printing *n* same as **screen process**

silkworm *n* a caterpillar that spins a cocoon of silk

silky *adj* **silkier, silkiest 1** soft, smooth, and shiny **2** (of a voice or manner) smooth and elegant **silkiness** *n*

sill *n* **1** a shelf at the bottom of a window, either inside or outside a room **2** the lower horizontal part of a window or door frame
WORD ORIGIN Old English *syll*

silly *adj* **-lier, -liest 1** behaving in a foolish or childish way **2** old-fashioned unable to think sensibly, as if from a blow **3** cricket (of a fielding position) near the batsman's wicket: *silly mid-off* ▷ *n, pl* **-lies 4** informal a foolish person **silliness** *n*
WORD ORIGIN Old English *sælig* (unattested) happy

silo *n, pl* **-los 1** an airtight pit or tower in which silage or grain is made and stored **2** an underground structure in which missile systems are sited for protection
WORD ORIGIN Spanish

silt *n* **1** a fine sediment of mud or clay deposited by moving water ▷ *vb* **2 silt up** to fill or choke up with silt: *the channels have been silted up*
WORD ORIGIN probably Old Norse

Silurian (sile-**yoor**-ee-an) *adj* geol of the period of geological time about 425 million years ago, during which fishes first appeared
WORD ORIGIN after *Silures*, a Welsh tribe who opposed the Romans

silvan *adj* same as **sylvan**

silver *n* **1** a precious greyish-white metallic element: used in jewellery, tableware, and coins. Symbol: Ag **2** a coin or coins made of silver **3** any household articles made of silver **4** short for **silver medal** ▷ *adj* **5** greyish-white: *silver hair* **6** (of anniversaries) the 25th in a series: *Silver Jubilee; silver wedding* ▷ *vb* **7** to coat with silver or a silvery substance: *a company that silvers their own mirrors* **8** to cause (something) to become silvery in colour: *the sun silvered the tarmac*
WORD ORIGIN Old English *siolfor*

silverbeet *n* Austral & NZ a beet of Australia and New Zealand with edible spinach-like leaves

silver birch *n* a tree with silvery-white peeling bark

silverfish *n, pl* **-fish** or **-fishes 1** a small wingless silver-coloured insect **2** a silver-coloured fish

silver goal *n* soccer (in certain competitions) a goal scored in a full half of extra time, counting as the winner if it is the only goal scored in the full half or full period of extra time

silver lining *n* a hopeful side of an otherwise desperate or unhappy situation

silver medal *n* a medal of silver awarded to a competitor who comes second in a contest or race

silver plate *n* **1** a thin layer of silver deposited on a base metal **2** articles, such as tableware, made of silver plate **silver-plate** *vb*

silver screen *n* informal films collectively or the film industry

silverside *n* a cut of beef from below the rump and above the leg

silversmith *n* a craftsman who makes or repairs items made of silver

silver thaw *n* Canad **1** a freezing rainstorm **2** same as **glitter** (sense 7)

silverware *n* items, such as tableware, made of or plated with silver

silvery *adj* **1** having the appearance or colour of silver: *her silvery eyes* **2** having a clear ringing sound: *a cascade of silvery notes*

silviculture *n* the cultivation of forest trees
WORD ORIGIN Latin *silva* woodland + CULTURE

sim *n* a computer game that simulates an activity such as flying or playing a sport

simian *adj* **1** of or resembling a monkey or ape ▷ *n* **2** a monkey or ape
WORD ORIGIN Latin *simia* an ape

similar *adj* **1** alike but not identical **2** geom (of two or more figures)

different in size or position, but with exactly the same shape **similarity** *n* **similarly** *adv*
WORD ORIGIN Latin *similis*

▤ **USAGE**
As should not be used after *similar*: *Wilson held a similar position to Jones* (not *a similar position as Jones*); *the system is similar to the one in France* (not *similar as in France*).

simile (**sim**-ill-ee) *n* a figure of speech that likens one thing to another of a different category, introduced by *as* or *like*
WORD ORIGIN Latin: something similar

similitude *n* formal likeness; similarity

simmer *vb* **1** to cook (food) gently at just below boiling point **2** (of violence or conflict) to threaten to break out: *revolt simmering among rural MPs* ▷ *n* **3** the state of simmering
WORD ORIGIN perhaps imitative

simmer down *vb* informal to calm down after being angry

simnel cake *n* Brit a fruit cake with marzipan, traditionally eaten during Lent or at Easter
WORD ORIGIN Latin *simila* fine flour

simony (**sime**-on-ee) *n* Christianity the practice of buying or selling Church benefits such as pardons
WORD ORIGIN after *Simon Magus*, a biblical sorcerer who tried to buy magical powers

simoom *n* a hot suffocating sand-laden desert wind
WORD ORIGIN Arabic *samūm* poisonous

simper *vb* **1** to smile in a silly and mannered way **2** to say (something) with a simper ▷ *n* **3** a simpering smile **simpering** *adj*
WORD ORIGIN origin unknown

simple *adj* **1** easy to understand or do: *in simple English; simple exercises* **2** plain and not elaborate: *a simple red skirt; a simple answer* **3** not combined or complex: *simple diagnostic equipment* **4** leading an uncomplicated life: *I am a simple man myself* **5** sincere or frank: *a simple apology* **6** of humble background: *the simple country girl* **7** informal mentally retarded **8** straightforward: *a simple matter of choice* **9** music denoting a time where the number of beats per bar may be two, three, or four **simplicity** *n*
WORD ORIGIN Latin *simplex* plain

simple fraction *n* maths a fraction in which the numerator and denominator are both whole numbers

simple fracture *n* a fracture in which the broken bone does not pierce the skin

simple interest *n* finance interest paid only on the original amount of a debt

simple-minded *adj* **1** (of people) naive and unsophisticated **2** (of opinions or explanations) not taking the complexity of an issue or subject into account **simple-mindedness** *n*

simple sentence *n* a sentence consisting of a single main clause

simpleton *n* a foolish or stupid person

simplify *vb* **-fies, -fying, -fied 1** to make (something) less complicated **2** maths to reduce (an equation or fraction) to its simplest form **simplification** *n*

Words from Literature
part 25

soliloquize *v* when an actor soliloquizes in a play he or she speaks to himself or herself rather than to another actor
> "A new servitude! There is something in that," I soliloquized (mentally, be it understood; I did not talk aloud)
> *Jane Eyre* Charlotte Brontë

sough *n* a drain or a ditch
> as you may have noticed the sough that runs from the marshes
> *Wuthering Heights* Emily Brontë

spirit *n* the non-physical part of a person which is believed to remain alive after their death
> that I might raise up spirits when I please
> *Doctor Faustus* 1.5 Christopher Marlowe

spleen *n* a type of sadness or depression which was thought to only affect the wealthy
> yet here I could plainly discover the true seeds of spleen
> *Gulliver's Travels* Jonathan Swift

spondulicks *n* a slang word which means money
> not for all his spondulicks and as much more on top of it
> *The Adventures of Huckleberry Finn* Mark Twain

stalled of *v* to be stalled of something is to be bored with it
> I'm stalled of doing naught
> *Wuthering Heights* Emily Brontë

stanchion *n* a pole, or bar that stands upright and is used as a buidling support
> and slid down a stanchion
> *The Adventures of Huckleberry Finn* Mark Twain

stang *n* another word for pole, which was an old measurement
> These fields were intermingled with woods of half a stang
> *Gulliver's Travels* Jonathan Swift

starling *n* a wall built around the pillars that support a bridge
> There were states of the tide when, having been down the river, I could not get back through the eddy-chafed arches and starlings of old London Bridge
> *Great Expectations* Charles Dickens

starting *n* twitching or night-time movements of the body
> with midnight's startings
> *On His Mistress* John Donne

stomacher *n* a panel at the front of a dress
> but send her aunt the pattern of a stomacher
> *Emma* Jane Austen

stoop *v* swoop
> Once a kite hovering over the garden made a stoop at me
> *Gulliver's Travels* Jonathan Swift

succedaneum *n* a substitute
> But as a succedaneum
> *The Prelude* William Wordsworth

suet *n* a hard animal fat used in cooking
> and your jaws are too weak For anything tougher than suet
> *Alice's Adventures in Wonderland* Lewis Carroll

sultry *adj* unpleasant or risky
> for it was getting pretty sultry for us
> *The Adventures of Huckleberry Finn* Mark Twain

summerset *n* an old spelling of somersault.
> I have seen him do the summerset
> *Gulliver's Travels* Jonathan Swift

surfeit *v* to surfeit in something is to have far too much of it, or to overindulge in it to an unhealthy degree
> He surfeits upon cursed necromancy
> *Doctor Faustus* chorus Christopher Marlowe

WORD ORIGIN Latin *simplus* simple + *facere* to make

simplistic *adj* (of an opinion or interpretation) too simple or naive

≡ USAGE
≡ Since *simplistic* already has *too* as part ≡ of its meaning, it is tautologous to ≡ talk about something being *too* ≡ *simplistic* or *over-simplistic*.

simply *adv* **1** in a simple manner: *an interesting book, simply written* **2** merely; just: *he's simply too slow* **3** absolutely: *a simply enormous success*

simulate *vb* -lating, -lated **1** to pretend to feel or perform (an emotion or action); imitate: *I tried to simulate anger* **2** to imitate the conditions of (a situation), as in carrying out an experiment: *we can then simulate global warming* **3** to have the appearance of: *the wood had been painted to simulate stone* **simulated** *adj* **simulation** *n*

WORD ORIGIN Latin *simulare* to copy

simulator *n* a device that simulates specific conditions for the purposes of research or training: *a flight simulator*

simultaneous *adj* occurring or existing at the same time **simultaneously** *adv* **simultaneity** *n*

WORD ORIGIN Latin *simul* at the same time

simultaneous equations *pl n maths* a set of equations that are all satisfied by the same values of the variables, the number of variables being equal to the number of equations

sin¹ *n* **1** the breaking of a religious or moral law **2** any offence against a principle or standard **3** **live in sin** *old-fashioned, informal* (of an unmarried couple) to live together ▷ *vb* **sinning, sinned 4** to commit a sin **sinner** *n*

WORD ORIGIN Old English *synn*

sin² *maths* sine

SIN (in Canada) Social Insurance Number

sin bin *n slang* (in ice hockey etc.) the area in which players must sit for a specified period after committing a serious foul

since *prep* **1** during the period of time after: *one of their worst winters since 1945* ▷ *conj* **2** continuously from the time given: *they've been standing in line ever since she arrived* **3** for the reason that; because ▷ *adv* **4** from that time: *I have often been asked since*

WORD ORIGIN Old English *siththan*

≡ USAGE
≡ See at **ago**.

sincere *adj* genuine and honest: *sincere concern* **sincerely** *adv* **sincerity** *n*

WORD ORIGIN Latin *sincerus*

sine *n* (in trigonometry) the ratio of the length of the opposite side to that of the hypotenuse in a right-angled triangle

WORD ORIGIN Latin *sinus* a bend

sinecure (**sin**-ee-cure) *n* a paid job that involves very little work or responsibility

WORD ORIGIN Latin *sine* without + *cura* care

sine die (**sin**-ay **dee**-ay) *adv* without fixing a day for future action or meeting

WORD ORIGIN Latin, literally: without a day

sine qua non (**sin**-ay kwah **non**) *n* an essential requirement

WORD ORIGIN Latin, literally: without which not

sinew *n* **1** *anat* a tough fibrous cord connecting muscle to bone **2** *literary* physical strength

WORD ORIGIN Old English *sinu, seonu*

sinewy *adj* lean and muscular

sinful *adj* **1** having committed or tending to commit sin: *I am a sinful man* **2** being a sin; wicked: *sinful acts*

sing *vb* **singing, sang, sung 1** to produce musical sounds with the voice **2** to perform (a song) **3** (of certain birds and insects) to make musical calls **4** **sing of** to tell a story in song about: *the minstrels sang of courtly love* **5** to make a humming, ringing, or whistling sound: *the arrow sang past his ear* **6** (of one's ears) to be filled with a continuous ringing sound **7** to bring (someone) to a given state by singing: *I sang him to sleep* **8** *slang chiefly US* to act as an informer ▸ See also **sing out** ▷ **singer** *n* **singing** *adj, n*

WORD ORIGIN Old English *singan*

≡ USAGE
≡ See at **ring¹**.

sing. singular

singe *vb* **singeing, singed 1** to burn slightly without setting alight; scorch: *it singed his sheepskin* ▷ *n* **2** a slight burn

WORD ORIGIN Old English *sengan*

Singhalese *n, pl* -lese, *adj* same as **Sinhalese**

singing telegram *n* **1** a service by which a person is employed to present greetings to someone on a special occasion by singing **2** the greetings presented in this way **3** the person who presents the greetings

single *adj* **1** existing alone; solitary: *the cottage's single chimney* **2** distinct from others of the same kind: *every single housing society* **3** designed for one user: *a single room* **4** unmarried **5** even one: *there was not a single bathroom* **6** (of a flower) having only one circle of petals **7** **single combat** a duel or fight involving two individuals ▷ *n* **8** a hotel bedroom for one person **9** a gramophone record, CD, or cassette with a short recording of music on it **10** *cricket* a hit from which one run is scored **11 a** *Brit* a pound note or coin **b** *US & Canad* a dollar bill **12** a ticket valid for a one-way journey only ▷ *vb* -gling, -gled **13** **single out** to select from a group of people or things: *the judge had singled him out for praise* ▸ See also **singles**

WORD ORIGIN Old French *sengle*

single-breasted *adj* (of a jacket or coat) having the fronts overlapping only slightly and with one row of buttons

single cream *n Brit* cream which has a relatively low fat content and does not thicken when beaten

single-decker *n Brit informal* a bus with only one passenger deck

single entry *n* a book-keeping system in which all transactions are entered in one account only

single file *n* a line of people, one behind the other

single-handed *adj* **1** alone; unaided: *a single-handed raid on the enemy camp* ▷ *adv* **2** unaided or working alone: *she had to take on the world single-handed* **single-handedly** *adv*

single-minded *adj* having one purpose or aim only; dedicated **single-mindedly** *adv* **single-mindedness** *n*

single-parent family *n* a family consisting of one parent and his or her child or children living together, the other parent being dead or permanently absent

singles *pl n sport* a match played with one person on each side

singles bar *n* a bar that is a social meeting place for single people

singlet *n Brit & NZ* a man's sleeveless vest

single ticket *n* same as **single** (sense 12)

singleton *n cards* the only card of a particular suit held by a player

singly *adv* one at a time; one by one

sing out *vb* to call out loudly

sing-song *n* **1** an informal group singing session ▷ *adj* **2** (of a voice) having a repetitive rise and fall in tone

singular *adj* **1** *grammar* (of a word or form) denoting only one person or thing: *a singular noun* **2** remarkable; extraordinary: *one of the singular achievements* **3** unusual; odd: *a lovable but very singular old woman* ▷ *n* **4** *grammar* the singular form of a word **singularity** *n* **singularly** *adv*

WORD ORIGIN Latin *singularis* single

Sinhalese *or* **Singhalese** *n* **1** *pl* -lese a member of a people living mainly in Sri Lanka **2** the language of this people ▷ *adj* **3** of this people ▸ See also **Sri Lankan**

sinister *adj* **1** threatening or suggesting evil or harm: *a sinister conspiracy* **2** *heraldry* of, on, or starting from the bearer's left side

WORD ORIGIN Latin: on the left-hand side, considered by Roman augurs to be the unlucky one

sink *vb* **sinking, sank, sunk 1** to submerge (in liquid) **2** to cause (a ship) to submerge by attacking it with bombs, torpedoes, etc. **3** to appear to descend towards or below the horizon **4** to make or become lower in amount or value: *sterling sank to a record low against the Deutschmark* **5** to move or fall into a lower position, esp. due to tiredness or weakness: *she sank back in her chair* **6** **sink into** to pass into a lower state or condition, esp. an unpleasant one: *to sink into debt* **7** (of a voice) to become quieter **8** to become weaker in health **9** to dig (something sharp) into a solid object: *she sank her teeth into the steak* **10** *informal* to drink (a number of alcoholic drinks) **11** to dig, drill, or excavate (a hole or shaft) **12** to drive (a stake) into the ground **13** **sink in** *or* **into** to invest (money) in (a venture) **14** *golf, snooker* to hit (the ball) into the hole or pocket: *he finally sank the shot for a bogey* ▷ *n* **15** a fixed basin in a kitchen or bathroom, with a water supply and drainpipe ▷ *adj* **16** *informal* (of a housing estate or school) deprived or having low standards of achievement

WORD ORIGIN Old English *sincan*

sinker *n* a weight attached to a fishing line or net to cause it to sink in water

sink in *vb* (of a fact) to become fully understood: *the euphoria started to wear off as the implications of it all sank in*

sinking fund *n* a fund set aside to repay a long-term debt

Sinn Féin (shin fane) *n* an Irish Republican political movement linked to the IRA
WORD ORIGIN Irish Gaelic: we ourselves

Sino- *combining form* Chinese: *Sino-European*; *Sinology*
WORD ORIGIN Late Latin *Sinae* the Chinese

Sinology (sine-ol-a-jee) *n* the study of Chinese history, language, and culture **Sinologist** *n*

sinuous *adj literary* **1** full of curves **2** having smooth twisting movements: *sinuous dances* **sinuosity** *n*
WORD ORIGIN Latin *sinuosus* winding

sinus (sine-uss) *n anat* a hollow space in bone, such as one in the skull opening into a nasal cavity
WORD ORIGIN Latin: a curve

sinusitis *n* inflammation of the membrane lining a sinus, esp. a nasal sinus

Sioux (soo) *n* **1** *pl* **Sioux** a member of a group of Native American peoples, formerly living over a wide area from Lake Michigan to the Rocky Mountains **2** any of the languages of these peoples

sip *vb* **sipping, sipped** **1** to drink (a liquid) in small mouthfuls ▷ *n* **2** an amount sipped **3** an instance of sipping
WORD ORIGIN probably from Low German *sippen*

siphon *or* **syphon** *n* **1** a tube which uses air pressure to draw liquid from a container **2** same as **soda siphon** ▷ *vb* **3** **siphon off** **a** to draw (liquid) off through a siphon **b** to redirect (resources or money), esp. dishonestly, into other projects or bank accounts
WORD ORIGIN Greek

sir *n* a polite term of address for a man
WORD ORIGIN variant of SIRE

Sir *n* a title placed before the name of a knight or baronet: *Sir David Attenborough*

sire *n* **1** a male parent of a horse or other domestic animal **2** *archaic* a respectful form of address used to a king ▷ *vb* **siring, sired** **3** to father
WORD ORIGIN Old French

siren *n* **1** a device that gives out a loud wailing sound as a warning or signal **2** **Siren** *Greek myth* a sea nymph whose singing lured sailors to destruction on the rocks **3** a woman who is attractive but dangerous to men
WORD ORIGIN Greek *seirēn*

sirloin *n* a prime cut of beef from the upper part of the loin
WORD ORIGIN Old French *surlonge*

sirocco *n, pl* **-cos** a hot stifling wind blowing from N Africa into S Europe
WORD ORIGIN Italian

sis[1] *n informal* short for **sister**

sis[2] *or* **sies** (siss) *interj S African informal* an exclamation of disgust
WORD ORIGIN Afrikaans

sisal (size-al) *n* a stiff fibre obtained from a Mexican plant and used for making rope
WORD ORIGIN after *Sisal*, a port in Mexico

siskin *n* a yellow-and-black finch
WORD ORIGIN Middle Dutch *sīseken*

sissy *or* **cissy** *n, pl* **-sies** **1** an effeminate, weak, or cowardly person ▷ *adj* **2** effeminate, weak, or cowardly
WORD ORIGIN from SIS[1]

sister *n* **1** a woman or girl having the same parents as another person **2** a female fellow member of a group, race, or profession **3** a female nurse in charge of a ward **4** *chiefly RC Church* a nun ▷ *adj* **5** of the same class, origin, or design, as another: *its sister paper*
WORD ORIGIN Old English *sweostor*

sisterhood *n* **1** the state of being sisters or like sisters **2** a religious group of women **3** a group of women united by a common interest or belief

sister-in-law *n, pl* **sisters-in-law** **1** the sister of one's husband or wife **2** one's brother's wife

sisterly *adj* of or like a sister; affectionate

Siswati *n* a language of Swaziland

sit *vb* **sitting, sat** **1** to rest one's body upright on the buttocks: *she had to sit on the ground* **2** to cause (someone) to rest in such a position: *they sat their grandfather in the shade* **3** (of an animal) to rest with the rear part of its body lowered to the ground **4** (of a bird) to perch or roost **5** **sit on** (of a bird) to cover its eggs so as to hatch them **6** to be located: *the bank sits in the middle of the village* **7** to pose for a painting or photograph **8** to occupy a seat in some official capacity: *no police representatives will sit on the committee* **9** (of a parliament or court) to be in session **10** to remain unused: *his car sat in the garage* **11** (of clothes) to fit or hang in a certain way: *that dress sits well on you* **12** to take (an examination): *he's sitting his finals* **13** (*in combination*) to look after a specified person or thing for someone else: *is someone going to dog-sit for you?* **14** **sit for** *chiefly Brit* to be a candidate for (a qualification): *he sat for a degree in medicine* **15** **sit tight** *informal* **a** to wait patiently **b** to maintain one's position firmly ▶ See also **sit back**, **sit down**, etc.
WORD ORIGIN Old English *sittan*

sitar *n* an Indian stringed musical instrument with a long neck and a rounded body
WORD ORIGIN Hindi

sit back *vb* to relax or be passive when action should be taken: *we can't just sit back and let this dreadful situation continue*

sitcom *n informal* (on television or radio) a comedy series involving the same characters in various everyday situations: *yet another unfunny sitcom set in Liverpool*

sit down *vb* **1** to adopt or cause (someone) to adopt a sitting position **2** **sit down under** to suffer (insults or humiliations) without resistance ▷ *n* **sit-down** **3** a short rest sitting down ▷ *adj* **sit-down** **4** (of a meal) eaten while sitting down at a table

sit-down strike *n* a strike in which workers refuse to leave their place of employment until a settlement is reached

site *n* **1** the piece of ground where something was, is, or is intended to be located: *a building site; a car park is to be built on the site of a Roman fort* **2** same as **website** ▷ *vb* **siting, sited** **3** to locate (something) on a specific site
WORD ORIGIN Latin *situs* position

sit-in *n* **1** a protest in which the demonstrators sit in a public place and refuse to move ▷ *vb* **sit in** **2** **sit in for** to stand in as a substitute for (someone) **3** **sit in on** to be present at (a meeting) as an observer

sitka spruce *n* a tall North American spruce tree, now often grown in Britain
WORD ORIGIN after *Sitka*, a town in Alaska

sit on *vb informal* to delay action on: *they are sitting on their information*

sit out *vb* **1** to endure to the end: *just sit it out, and it will pass eventually* **2** to take no part in (a dance or game)

sitter *n* **1** a person posing for his or her portrait or photograph **2** same as **baby-sitter** **3** (*in combination*) a person who looks after a specified person or thing for someone else: *a house-sitter*

sitting *n* **1** a continuous period of being seated at some activity: *you may not be able to complete it in one sitting* **2** one of the times when a meal is served, when there is not enough space for everyone to eat at the same time: *the second sitting* **3** a period of posing for a painting or photograph **4** a meeting of an official body to conduct business ▷ *adj* **5** current: *a sitting member of Congress* **6** seated: *a sitting position*

sitting duck *n informal* a person or thing in a defenceless or vulnerable position

sitting room *n* a room in a house or flat where people sit and relax

sitting tenant *n* a tenant occupying a house or flat

situate *vb* **-ating, -ated** *formal* to place or position
WORD ORIGIN Late Latin *situare* to position

situation *n* **1 a** state of affairs **b** a complex or critical state of affairs **2** location and surroundings **3** social or financial circumstances **4** a position of employment

▤ **USAGE**
Situation is often used in contexts in which it is redundant or imprecise. Typical examples are: *the company is in a crisis situation* or *people in a job situation*. In the first example, *situation* does not add to the meaning and should be omitted. In the second example, it would be clearer and more concise to substitute a phrase such as *people at work*.

situation comedy *n* same as **sitcom**

sit up *vb* **1** to raise oneself from a lying position into a sitting one **2** to remain out of bed until a late hour **3** *informal* to become suddenly interested: *make the world sit up and take notice* ▷ *n* **sit-up** **4** a physical exercise in which the body is brought into a sitting position from one of lying on the back

SI unit *n* any of the units (metre, kilogram, second, ampere, kelvin, candela, mole, and those derived from them) adopted for international use under the Système International d'Unités, now employed for all scientific and most technical purposes

Siva *n* a Hindu god, the Destroyer

six *n* **1** the cardinal number that is the sum of one and five **2** a numeral, 6 or VI, representing this number **3** something representing or consisting of six units **4** *cricket* a score of six runs, obtained by hitting the ball so that it crosses the boundary without bouncing **5** **at sixes and sevens** in a state of confusion **6** **knock someone for six** *informal* to upset or overwhelm someone completely **7** **six of one and half a dozen of the other** a situation in which there is no real difference between the alternatives ▷ *adj* **8** amounting to six: *six days* **sixth** *adj, n* **WORD ORIGIN** Old English *siex*

sixfold *adj* **1** having six times as many or as much **2** composed of six parts ▷ *adv* **3** by six times as many or as much

Six Nations Championship *n rugby union* an annual competition involving national sides representing England, France, Ireland, Italy, Scotland, and Wales

six-pack *n informal* **1** a package containing six units, esp. six cans of beer **2** a highly developed set of abdominal muscles in a man

sixpence *n* (formerly) a small British, Australian and New Zealand coin worth six old pennies, or 2½ pence

six-pointer *n informal* a football match between two teams in similar positions in the league table, which gains the winning team three points and denies the losing team three points

six-shooter *n US informal* a revolver that fires six shots without reloading

sixteen *n* **1** the cardinal number that is the sum of ten and six **2** a numeral, 16 or XVI, representing this number **3** something representing or consisting of sixteen units ▷ *adj* **4** amounting to sixteen: *sixteen years* **sixteenth** *adj, n*

sixth form *n* (in England and Wales) the most senior form in a secondary school, in which pupils over sixteen may take A levels or retake GCSEs **sixth-former** *n*

sixth sense *n* the supposed ability of knowing something instinctively without having any evidence for it

sixty *n, pl* **-ties 1** the cardinal number that is the product of ten and six **2** a numeral, 60 or LX, representing this number **3** something representing or consisting of sixty units ▷ *adj* **4** amounting to sixty: *sixty seconds* **sixtieth** *adj, n*

sizable *or* **sizeable** *adj* quite large

size¹ *n* **1** the dimensions, amount, or extent of something **2** large dimensions, amount, or extent: *I was overwhelmed by the sheer size of the city* **3** one of a series of standard measurements for goods: *he takes size 11 shoes* **4** *informal* state of affairs as summarized: *that's about the size of it* ▷ *vb*

sizing, sized 5 to sort (things) according to size **WORD ORIGIN** Old French *sise*

USAGE
The use of -size and -sized after *large* or *small* is redundant, except when describing something which is made in specific sizes: *a large* (not *large-size*) *organization*. Similarly, *in size* is redundant in the expressions *large in size* and *small in size*.

size² *n* **1** a thin gluey substance that is used as a sealer ▷ *vb* **sizing, sized 2** to treat (a surface) with size **WORD ORIGIN** origin unknown

sized *adj* of a specified size: *average-sized*

USAGE
See at **size**.

size up *vb informal* to make an assessment of (a person or situation)

sizzle *vb* **-zling, -zled 1** to make a hissing sound like the sound of frying fat **2** *informal* to be very hot: *the city was sizzling in a hot summer spell* **3** *informal* to be very angry ▷ *n* **4** a hissing sound **sizzling** *adj* **WORD ORIGIN** imitative

sjambok (**sham**-bock) *S African n* **1** a whip or riding crop made of hide ▷ *vb* **-bokking, -bokked 2** to beat with a sjambok **WORD ORIGIN** Malay *tjambok*

SK Saskatchewan

skanky *adj* **skankier, skankiest** *slang* **1** dirty or unattractive **2** promiscuous

skate¹ *n* **1** same as **ice skate** or **roller skate 2** **get one's skates on** *informal* to hurry ▷ *vb* **skating, skated 3** to glide on or as if on skates **4** **skate on thin ice** to place oneself in a dangerous situation **skater** *n* **skating** *n* **WORD ORIGIN** Old French *éschasse* stilt

skate² *n, pl* **skate** *or* **skates** a large edible marine fish with a broad flat body **WORD ORIGIN** Old Norse *skata*

skateboard *n* **1** a narrow board mounted on roller-skate wheels, usually ridden while standing up ▷ *vb* **2** to ride on a skateboard **skateboarding** *n*

skate round *or* **over** *vb* to avoid discussing or dealing with (a matter) fully: *friends and admirers skated round the question*

skean-dhu (**skee**-an-**doo**) *n* a dagger worn in the sock as part of Highland dress **WORD ORIGIN** Gaelic *sgian* knife + *dhu* black

skedaddle *vb* **-dling, -dled** *informal* to run off hastily **WORD ORIGIN** origin unknown

skein *n* **1** a length of yarn or thread wound in a loose coil **2** a flock of geese in flight **WORD ORIGIN** Old French *escaigne*

skeleton *n* **1** the hard framework of bones that supports and protects the organs and muscles of the body **2** the essential framework of any structure: *a metal skeleton supporting the roof and floors* **3** *informal* an extremely thin person or animal **4** an outline consisting of bare essentials: *the mere skeleton of a script* **5** a small steel-frame sledge for racing

down an ice-covered run **6** the sport of racing small steel-frame sledges down an ice-covered run **7** **skeleton in the cupboard** *or* **closet** an embarrassing or scandalous fact from the past that is kept secret ▷ *adj* **8** reduced to a minimum: *a skeleton staff* **skeletal** *adj* **WORD ORIGIN** Greek: something dried up

skeleton key *n* a key designed so that it can open many different locks

skelm *n S African informal* a villain or crook **WORD ORIGIN** Afrikaans

skeptic *n US & archaic* same as **sceptic**

skerry *n, pl* **-ries** *Scot* a rocky island or reef **WORD ORIGIN** Old Norse *sker*

sketch *n* **1** a quick rough drawing **2** a brief descriptive piece of writing **3** a short funny piece of acting forming part of a show **4** any brief outline ▷ *vb* **5** to make a quick rough drawing (of) **6** **sketch out** to make a brief description of: *they sketched out plans for the invasion* **WORD ORIGIN** Greek *skhedios* unprepared

sketchbook *n* a book of blank pages for sketching on

sketchy *adj* **sketchier, sketchiest** giving only a rough or incomplete description **sketchily** *adv*

skew *adj* **1** having a slanting position ▷ *n* **2** a slanting position ▷ *vb* **3** to take or cause to take a slanting position: *our boat skewed off course* **4** to distort or misrepresent: *the takeover bid has skewed last month's figures* **WORD ORIGIN** Old French *escuer* to shun

skewbald *adj* **1** marked with patches of white and another colour ▷ *n* **2** a horse with this marking **WORD ORIGIN** origin unknown

skewed *adj* distorted or biased because of prejudice or lack of information: *a skewed conception of religion*

skewer *n* **1** a long pin for holding meat together during cooking ▷ *vb* **2** to fasten or pierce with or as if with a skewer **WORD ORIGIN** probably from dialect *skiver*

skewwhiff *adj informal* crooked or slanting

ski *n, pl* **skis** *or* **ski 1** one of a pair of long runners that are used, fastened to boots, for gliding over snow ▷ *vb* **skiing, skied** *or* **ski'd 2** to travel on skis **skier** *n* **skiing** *n* **WORD ORIGIN** Norwegian

skid *vb* **skidding, skidded 1** (of a vehicle or person) to slide sideways while in motion ▷ *n* **2** an instance of skidding **WORD ORIGIN** origin unknown

skidoo *n, pl* **-doos** *Canad* same as **snowmobile** **WORD ORIGIN** Ski-Doo, originally a trademark

skid row *n slang chiefly US & Canad* a poor and neglected area of a city, inhabited by down-and-outs

skiff *n* a small narrow boat for one person **WORD ORIGIN** French *esquif*

ski jump *n* a steep snow-covered slope ending in a horizontal ramp from which skiers compete to make the longest jump

Klingon

Languages, jargons, and argots invented by writers do not usually have much of a life beyond the specific work of fiction in which their creators intend them to be used. The 'newspeak' spoken by obedient party members in George Orwell's *1984* and the 'Nadsat' slang used by violent delinquents in Anthony Burgess's *A Clockwork Orange* are familiar to many but few if any admirers of either book have attempted to learn these constructed languages and converse in them with other like-minded souls. Fans of *Star Trek*, however, are a different breed. Some 'Trekkies' (or 'Trekkers' as they prefer to be known) have taken their love for the long-running sci-fi show to a remarkable, some might say absurd, level by learning Klingon, the language of a race of warrior humanoid aliens who have appeared regularly in *Star Trek* since it was first shown on television in 1966.

In the original series of *Star Trek* the Klingons spoke in English – although their language was referred to in one episode as 'Klingonese' – and it wasn't until the first feature film in 1979 that they were heard speaking their native tongue (later known in Klingon as *tlhIngan Hol*). James Doohan, the actor who portrayed chief engineer Montgomery 'Scottie' Scott, made up some words on set for scenes requiring Klingon and from these humble beginnings the language was born. The third instalment of the film series, *The Search for Spock* (1984), required more Klingon dialogue but this time a professional linguist was employed. Marc Okrand, a lecturer in linguistics and an expert on Native American languages, took Doohan's original invented words and from them constructed an entire language for the most feared adversaries of Captain Kirk and his crew. The invented tongue sounded harsh, alien, and guttural but was still straightforward enough for actors playing the Klingons to pronounce.

Such was the interest in the alien language among Trekkers that Okrand decided to compile a Klingon dictionary, the first edition of which was published in 1985. This slender work of reference (at the time Klingon had only a few thousand words in its vocabulary) was not just a list of words, however, as it also featured notes on grammar and pronunciation. The dictionary was expected to sell only as a novelty item to a small number of devotees, but over the years has sold hundreds of thousands of copies and is the point of entry for those who have a genuine desire to speak the language of Qo'noS (pronounced 'Kronos'), the home planet of the Klingons.

Since the dictionary's publication, Klingon has steadily attracted the attention of linguists and *Star Trek* fans alike, so much so that by 2006 the *Guinness Book of Records* claimed that Klingon was the world's most widely spoken invented language, beating Esperanto into second place. Klingon even has a scholarly institution dedicated to the language's study. The Klingon Language Institute (KLI) was formed in 1992 as a non-profit organization and holds an annual five-day conference or *qep'a'* ('great meeting') at which members of the Institute, of which there over 2000 in over 50 countries, convene to discuss the language, attend lectures, and even complete scholastic exercises and tests. The KLI's motto is *qo'mey poSmoH Hol*, which means 'Language opens worlds'.

Members of the Institute have worked on a number of notable translation projects including Klingon versions of the Bible and two Shakespeare plays, *Hamlet* and *Much Ado About Nothing*. Undertaking such work can be difficult as English is such a rich language while Klingon's lexicon is very small, but Marc Okrand regularly coins new words in response to requests from Klingon speakers.

One such speaker, the computational linguist d'Armond Speers, even attempted to teach his young son Klingon. The infant was initially responsive to the alien tongue but eventually ceased communication in Klingon as he could hold conversations only with his father. He was also frustrated by the narrowness of the vocabulary, the Klingons being a warrior race with little interest in the toys and other things with which a child might amuse himself. It is perhaps this lack of vocabulary that will keep Klingon, for the time being at least, of interest only to committed *Star Trek* fans.

skilful or US **skillful** adj having or showing skill **skilfully** or US **skillfully** adv

ski lift n a series of chairs hanging from a power-driven cable for carrying skiers up a slope

skill n **1** special ability or expertise enabling one to perform an activity very well **2** something, such as a trade, requiring special training or expertise **skilled** adj
WORD ORIGIN Old Norse *skil* distinction

skillet n **1** a small frying pan **2** chiefly Brit a long-handled cooking pot
WORD ORIGIN origin unknown

skim vb **skimming, skimmed 1** to remove floating material from the surface of (a liquid): *skim any impurities off the surface* **2** to glide smoothly over (a surface) **3** to throw (a flat stone) across a surface, so that it bounces: *two men skimmed stones on the surface of the sea* **4** (often foll. by *through*) to read (a piece of writing) quickly and without taking in the details
WORD ORIGIN Middle English *skimmen*

skimmed or **skim milk** n milk from which the cream has been removed

skimp vb **1** to be extremely sparing or supply (someone) sparingly **2** to do (something) carelessly or with inadequate materials
WORD ORIGIN perhaps a combination of SCANT + SCRIMP

skimpy adj **skimpier, skimpiest** inadequate in amount or size; scant

skin n **1** the tissue forming the outer covering of the body **2** a person's complexion: *sallow skin* **3** any outer layer or covering: *potato skin* **4** a thin solid layer on the surface of a liquid: *custard with a thick skin on it* **5** the outer covering of a furry animal, removed and prepared for use **6** a container for liquids, made from animal skin **7 by the skin of one's teeth** by a narrow margin **8 get under one's skin** informal to annoy one **9 no skin off one's nose** informal not a matter that concerns one **10 save one's skin** to save one from death or harm **11 skin and bone** extremely thin **12 thick** or **thin skin** an insensitive or sensitive nature ▷ vb **skinning, skinned 13** to remove the outer covering from (fruit, vegetables, dead animals, etc.) **14** to injure (a part of the body) by scraping some of the skin off: *I had skinned my knuckles* **15** slang to swindle **skinless** adj
WORD ORIGIN Old English *scinn*

skin-deep adj not of real importance; superficial: *beauty is only skin-deep*

skin diving n underwater swimming using only light breathing apparatus and without a special diving suit **skin-diver** n

skin flick n slang a pornographic film

skinflint n a very mean person
WORD ORIGIN referring to a person so greedy that he or she would skin (swindle) a flint

skin graft n a piece of skin removed from one part of the body and surgically grafted at the site of a severe burn or other injury

skinhead n **1** a member of a group of White youths, noted for their closely cropped hair, aggressive behaviour, and overt racism **2** a closely cropped hairstyle

skinny adj **-nier, -niest** extremely thin

skint adj slang without money, esp. only temporarily
WORD ORIGIN variant of *skinned*

skintight adj (of garments) fitting tightly over the body; clinging

skip¹ vb **skipping, skipped 1** to move lightly by hopping from one foot to the other **2** to jump over a skipping-rope **3** to cause (a stone) to skim over a surface or (of a stone) to move in this way **4** to pass over or miss out; omit: *I skipped a few paragraphs* **5 skip through** informal to read or deal with (something) quickly or without great effort or concentration **6 skip it!** informal it doesn't matter! **7** informal to miss deliberately: *she skipped the class* **8** informal chiefly US, Canad, & Austral to leave (a place) in a hurry: *he skipped town three years later* ▷ n **9** a skipping movement or action
WORD ORIGIN probably from Old Norse

skip² n **1** a large open container for transporting building materials or rubbish **2** a cage used as a lift in mines
WORD ORIGIN variant of *skep* a beehive

ski pants pl n stretch trousers, worn for skiing or leisure, which are kept taut by straps under the feet

skipper n **1** the captain of a ship or aircraft **2** the captain of a sporting team ▷ vb **3** to be the captain of
WORD ORIGIN Middle Low German, Middle Dutch *schipper* shipper

skipping n the act of jumping over a rope held either by the person jumping or by two other people, as a game or for exercise

skipping-rope n a rope that is held in the hands and swung round and down so that the holder or others can jump over it

skirl Scot & N English dialect n **1** the sound of bagpipes ▷ vb **2** (of bagpipes) to give out a shrill sound
WORD ORIGIN probably from Old Norse

skirmish n **1** a brief or minor fight or argument ▷ vb **2** to take part in a skirmish
WORD ORIGIN Old French *eskirmir*

skirt n **1** a woman's or girl's garment hanging from the waist **2** the part of a dress or coat below the waist **3** a circular hanging flap, for example round the base of a hovercraft **4** Brit & NZ a cut of beef from the flank **5** bit of skirt offensive slang a girl or woman ▷ vb **6** to lie along or form the edge of (something): *a track skirting the foot of the mountain* **7** to go around the outer edge of (something): *we skirted the township* **8** to avoid dealing with (an issue): *I was skirting around the real issues*
WORD ORIGIN Old Norse *skyrta* shirt

skirting board n a narrow board round the bottom of an interior wall where it joins the floor

ski stick or **pole** n one of a pair of sharp pointed sticks used by skiers to gain speed and maintain balance

skit n a short funny or satirical sketch
WORD ORIGIN probably Scandinavian

skite Austral & NZ vb **1** to boast ▷ n **2** a boast

ski tow n a device for pulling skiers uphill, usually a motor-driven rope grasped by the skier while riding on his or her skis

skittish adj **1** playful or lively **2** (of a horse) excitable and easily frightened
WORD ORIGIN probably from Old Norse

skittle n **1** a bottle-shaped object used as a target in a game of skittles **2 skittles** a bowling game in which players knock over as many skittles as possible by rolling a wooden ball at them
WORD ORIGIN origin unknown

skive vb **skiving, skived** (often foll. by *off*) Brit informal to avoid work or responsibility **skiver** n
WORD ORIGIN origin unknown

skivvy chiefly Brit often disparaging n, pl **-vies 1** a female servant who does menial work; drudge **2** Austral & NZ a garment resembling a sweater with long sleeves and a polo neck ▷ vb **-vies, -vying, -vied 3** to work as a skivvy
WORD ORIGIN origin unknown

skolly or **skollie** n, pl **-lies** S African a hooligan, usually one of a gang
WORD ORIGIN origin unknown

skookum adj W Canad strong or brave
WORD ORIGIN Chinook

skua n a large predatory gull living in cold marine regions
WORD ORIGIN Faeroese *skúgvur*

skulduggery or US **skullduggery** n informal underhand dealing to achieve an aim
WORD ORIGIN origin unknown

skulk vb **1** to move stealthily, so as to avoid notice **2** to lie in hiding; lurk
WORD ORIGIN from Old Norse

skull n **1** the bony framework of the head **2** informal the head or mind: *that would have penetrated even your thick skull*
WORD ORIGIN probably from Old Norse

skull and crossbones n a picture of the human skull above two crossed bones, formerly on the pirate flag, now used as a warning of danger or death

skullcap n a closely fitting brimless cap

skunk n, pl **skunks** or **skunk 1** a mammal with a black-and-white coat and bushy tail, which gives out a foul-smelling fluid when attacked **2** informal an unpleasant or unfair person
WORD ORIGIN from a Native American language

sky n, pl **skies 1** the upper atmosphere as seen from earth **2 praise to the skies** praise rather excessively ▷ vb **skies, skying, skied 3** informal to hit (a ball) high in the air: *the blond-haired forward skied the ball high over the bar*
WORD ORIGIN Old Norse *skȳ* cloud

sky-blue adj bright clear blue

skydiving n the sport of jumping from an aircraft and falling freely or performing manoeuvres before opening the parachute **skydiver** n

sky-high adj, adv **1** very high: *most firms are no longer willing to pay sky-high prices* **2 blow sky-high** to destroy completely

skyjack vb to hijack (an aircraft)
WORD ORIGIN SKY + HIJACK

skylark n 1 a lark that sings while soaring at a great height ▷ vb 2 old-fashioned to play or frolic

skylight n a window placed in a roof or ceiling to let in daylight

skyline n 1 the line at which the earth and sky appear to meet 2 the outline of buildings, trees, or hills, seen against the sky

Skype n trademark a system that enables audiovisual communication over the internet

skyrocket n 1 same as **rocket** (sense 1) ▷ vb 2 informal to rise very quickly

skyscraper n a very tall building

skyward adj 1 towards the sky ▷ adv also **skywards** 2 towards the sky

slab n 1 a broad flat thick piece of wood, stone, or other material 2 informal a package containing 24 cans of beer
WORD ORIGIN origin unknown

slack¹ adj 1 not tight, tense, or taut: the slack jaw hung open 2 careless in one's work 3 (esp. of water) moving slowly 4 (of trade) not busy ▷ n 5 a part that is slack or hangs loose: take up the slack 6 a period of less busy activity ▷ vb 7 to neglect one's duty or work in a lazy manner: stop slacking, you pair! 8 (often foll. by off) to loosen or slacken ▶ See also **slacks** > **slackness** n
WORD ORIGIN Old English slæc, sleac

slack² n small pieces of coal with a high ash content
WORD ORIGIN probably Middle Low German slecke

slacken vb (often foll. by off) 1 to make or become looser 2 to make or become slower or less intense: to slacken the pace of reform

slacker n a person who evades work or duty; shirker

slacks pl n old-fashioned casual trousers

slag n 1 the waste material left after metal has been smelted 2 Brit & NZ, Slang a sexually immoral woman ▷ vb **slagging, slagged** 3 Brit, Austral, & NZ slang (often foll. by off) to criticize in an unpleasant way: I don't think anyone can slag it off **slagging** n **slaggy** adj
WORD ORIGIN Middle Low German slagge

slag heap n a pile of waste matter from metal smelting or coal mining

slain vb the past participle of **slay**

slake vb **slaking, slaked** 1 literary to satisfy (thirst or desire) 2 to add water to (lime) to produce calcium hydroxide
WORD ORIGIN Old English slacian

slalom n skiing, canoeing a race over a winding course marked by artificial obstacles
WORD ORIGIN Norwegian

slam¹ vb **slamming, slammed** 1 to close violently and noisily 2 to throw (something or someone) down violently 3 slang to criticize harshly: his new proposals were slammed by the opposition 4 to strike with violent force: he slammed the ball into the back of the net ▷ n 5 the act or noise of slamming
WORD ORIGIN Scandinavian

slam² n the winning of all (**grand slam**) or all but one (**little slam**) of the 13 tricks at bridge
WORD ORIGIN origin unknown

slam dunk n 1 basketball a scoring shot in which the player jumps up and forces the ball down through the basket 2 informal a task so easy that success in it is deemed a certainty ▷ vb **slam-dunk** 3 basketball to jump up and force (a ball) through a basket

slammer n **the slammer** slang prison

slander n 1 law a false and damaging statement about a person 2 the crime of making such a statement ▷ vb 3 to utter slander (about) **slanderous** adj
WORD ORIGIN Old French escandle

slang n 1 informal language not used in formal speech or writing and often restricted to a particular social group or profession ▷ vb 2 to use insulting language to (someone) **slangy** adj
WORD ORIGIN origin unknown

slanging match n an angry quarrel in which people trade insults

slant vb 1 to lean at an angle; slope 2 to write or present (information) in a biased way ▷ n 3 a sloping line or position 4 a point of view, esp. a biased one: a right-wing slant on the story 5 **on a** or **the slant** sloping ▷ adj 6 oblique; sloping **slanting** adj **slantwise** adv
WORD ORIGIN Scandinavian

slap n 1 a sharp blow or smack with something flat, such as the open hand 2 the sound made by or as if by such a blow 3 **slap and tickle** Brit old-fashioned informal sexual play 4 **a slap in the face** an unexpected rejection or insult 5 **a slap on the back** congratulations ▷ vb **slapping, slapped** 6 to strike sharply with something flat, such as the open hand 7 to bring (something) down forcefully: he slapped down a fiver 8 (usually foll. by against) to strike (something) with a slapping sound 9 informal to cover with quickly or carelessly: she slapped on some make-up 10 **slap on the back** to congratulate ▷ adv informal 11 exactly: slap in the middle 12 **slap into** forcibly or abruptly into: he ran slap into the guard
WORD ORIGIN Low German slapp

slap-bang adv informal 1 directly or exactly: he's on holiday in LA and has run slap-bang into a famous face 2 forcefully and abruptly: he'd gone and run slap-bang into the watchman

slapdash adv 1 carelessly or hastily ▷ adj 2 careless or hasty

slap-happy adj **-pier, -piest** informal cheerfully careless

slaphead n slang a bald person
WORD ORIGIN from SLAP + HEAD

slapstick n rough and high-spirited comedy in which the characters behave childishly

slap-up adj Brit informal (esp. of meals) large and expensive

slash vb 1 to cut (a person or thing) with sharp sweeping strokes 2 to make large gashes in: I slashed the tyres of his van 3 to reduce drastically: to slash costs 4 to criticize harshly ▷ n 5 a sharp sweeping stroke 6 a cut made by such a stroke 7 same as **solidus** 8 Brit slang the act of urinating

WORD ORIGIN origin unknown

slasher n Austral & NZ a tool or tractor-drawn machine used for cutting scrub or undergrowth in the bush

slat n a narrow thin strip of wood or metal, such as used in a Venetian blind
WORD ORIGIN Old French esclat splinter

slate¹ n 1 a dark grey rock that can be easily split into thin layers and is used as a roofing material 2 a roofing tile of slate 3 (formerly) a writing tablet of slate 4 chiefly US & Canad a list of candidates in an election 5 **wipe the slate clean** forget about past mistakes or failures and start afresh 6 **on the slate** Austral & Brit informal on credit ▷ vb **slating, slated** 7 to cover (a roof) with slates 8 chiefly US to plan or schedule: another exercise is slated for tomorrow **slaty** adj
WORD ORIGIN Old French esclate fragment

slate² vb **slating, slated** informal chiefly Brit & Austral to criticize harshly: the new series was slated by the critics **slating** n
WORD ORIGIN probably from Old French esclate fragment

slattern n old-fashioned a dirty and untidy woman **slatternliness** n **slatternly** adj
WORD ORIGIN probably from dialect slatter to slop

slaughter n 1 the indiscriminate or brutal killing of large numbers of people 2 the savage killing of a person 3 the killing of animals for food ▷ vb 4 to kill indiscriminately or in large numbers 5 to kill brutally 6 to kill (animals) for food 7 informal (in sport) to defeat easily
WORD ORIGIN Old English sleaht

slaughterhouse n a place where animals are killed for food

Slav n a member of any of the peoples of E Europe or the former Soviet Union who speak a Slavonic language
WORD ORIGIN Medieval Latin Sclavus a captive Slav

slave n 1 a person legally owned by another for whom he or she has to work without freedom, pay, or rights 2 a person under the domination of another or of some habit or influence: a slave to party doctrine 3 informal a badly-paid person doing menial tasks ▷ vb **slaving, slaved** 4 (often foll. by away or over) to work very hard for little or no money
WORD ORIGIN Medieval Latin Sclavus a Slav (the Slavonic races were frequently conquered in the Middle Ages)

slave-driver n 1 a person who makes people work very hard 2 (esp. formerly) a person forcing slaves to work

slaver¹ (slay-ver) n 1 (esp. formerly) a dealer in slaves 2 history a ship used in the slave trade

slaver² (slav-ver) vb 1 to dribble saliva 2 (often foll. by over) to drool (over someone), making flattering remarks ▷ n 3 saliva dribbling from the mouth 4 informal nonsense
WORD ORIGIN probably from Low German

slavery n 1 the state or condition of being a slave 2 the practice of owning slaves 3 hard work with little reward

slave trade *n* the buying and selling of slaves, esp. the transportation of Black Africans to America and the Caribbean from the 16th to the 19th centuries

slavish *adj* **1** of or like a slave **2** imitating or copying exactly without any originality: *a slavish adherence to the conventions of Italian opera* **slavishly** *adv*

Slavonic *or esp. US* **Slavic** *n* **1** a group of languages including Bulgarian, Russian, Polish, and Czech ▷ *adj* **2** of this group of languages **3** of the people who speak these languages

slay *vb* **slaying, slew, slain** *archaic or literary* to kill, esp. violently **slayer** *n*
WORD ORIGIN Old English *slēan*

sleaze *n informal* behaviour in public life considered immoral, dishonest, or disreputable: *political sleaze*

sleazy *adj* **-zier, -ziest** dirty, rundown, and not respectable: *a sleazy hotel* **sleaziness** *n*
WORD ORIGIN origin unknown

sledge¹ *or esp. US & Canad* **sled** *n* **1** a vehicle mounted on runners, drawn by horses or dogs, for transporting people or goods over snow **2** a light wooden frame used, esp. by children, for sliding over snow ▷ *vb* **sledging, sledged 3** to travel by sledge
WORD ORIGIN Middle Dutch *sleedse*

sledge² *n* short for **sledgehammer**

sledgehammer *n* **1** a large heavy hammer with a long handle, used for breaking rocks and concrete ▷ *adj* **2** crushingly powerful: *the sledgehammer approach*
WORD ORIGIN Old English *slecg* a large hammer

sleek *adj* **1** smooth, shiny, and glossy: *sleek blond hair* **2** (of a person) elegantly dressed
WORD ORIGIN variant of *slick*

sleep *n* **1** a state of rest during which the eyes are closed, the muscles and nerves are relaxed, and the mind is unconscious **2** a period spent sleeping **3** the substance sometimes found in the corner of the eyes after sleep **4** a state of inactivity, like sleep **5** *poetic* death ▷ *vb* **sleeping, slept 6** to be in or as in the state of sleep **7** to be inactive or unaware: *their defence slept as we scored another try* **8** to have sleeping accommodation for (a certain number): *the villa sleeps ten* **9** *poetic* to be dead **10 sleep on it** to delay making a decision about (something) until the next day, in order to think about it ▷ See also **sleep around, sleep in,** etc.
WORD ORIGIN Old English *slēpan*

sleep around *vb informal* to have many sexual partners

sleeper *n* **1** a railway sleeping car or compartment **2** one of the blocks supporting the rails on a railway track **3** a small plain gold ring worn in a pierced ear lobe to prevent the hole from closing up **4** *informal* a person or thing that achieves success after an initial period of obscurity

sleep in *vb* to sleep longer than usual

sleeping bag *n* a large well-padded bag for sleeping in, esp. outdoors

sleeping car *n* a railway carriage with small rooms containing beds for passengers to sleep in

sleeping partner *n* a partner in a business who shares in the financing but does not take part in its management

sleeping pill *n* a pill containing a drug that induces sleep

sleeping policeman *n Brit* a bump built across a road to prevent motorists from driving too fast

sleeping sickness *n* an infectious, usually fatal, African disease transmitted by the bite of the tsetse fly, causing fever and sluggishness

sleepless *adj* **1** (of a night) one during which one does not sleep **2** unable to sleep **3** *chiefly poetic* always active **sleeplessness** *n*

sleep off *vb informal* to get rid of by sleeping: *go home and sleep it off*

sleepout *n NZ* a small building for sleeping in

sleep out *vb* to sleep in the open air

sleepover *n* and occasion when a person stays overnight at a friend's house

sleep together *vb* to have sexual intercourse and, usually, spend the night together

sleepwalk *vb* to walk while asleep **sleepwalker** *n* **sleepwalking** *n*

sleep with *vb* to have sexual intercourse and, usually, spend the night with

sleepy *adj* **sleepier, sleepiest 1** tired and ready for sleep **2** (of a place) without activity or excitement: *a sleepy little town* **sleepily** *adv*

sleet *n* **1** partly melted falling snow or hail or (esp. US) partly frozen rain ▷ *vb* **2** to fall as sleet
WORD ORIGIN Germanic

sleeve *n* **1** the part of a garment covering the arm **2** a tubelike part which fits over or completely encloses another part **3** a flat cardboard container to protect a gramophone record **4 up one's sleeve** secretly ready: *he has a few more surprises up his sleeve* **sleeveless** *adj*
WORD ORIGIN Old English *slīefe, slēfe*

sleigh *n* **1** same as **sledge¹** (sense 1) ▷ *vb* **2** to travel by sleigh
WORD ORIGIN Dutch *slee*

sleight (**slite**) *n old-fashioned* skill or cunning
WORD ORIGIN Old Norse *slǣgth*

sleight of hand *n* **1** the skilful use of the hands when performing magic tricks **2** the performance of such tricks

slender *adj* **1** (esp. of a person's figure) slim and graceful **2** of small width relative to length or height **3** small or inadequate in amount or size: *a slender advantage*
WORD ORIGIN origin unknown

slept *vb* the past of **sleep**

sleuth (rhymes with **tooth**) *n informal* a detective
WORD ORIGIN Old Norse *slōth* a trail

slew¹ *vb* the past tense of **slay**

slew² *or esp. US* **slue** *vb* **1** to slide or skid sideways: *the bus slewed across the road* ▷ *n* **2** the act of slewing
WORD ORIGIN origin unknown

slice *n* **1** a thin flat piece or wedge cut from something: *a slice of tomato* **2** a share or portion: *the biggest slice of their income* **3** a kitchen tool having a broad flat blade: *a fish slice* **4** *sport* a shot that causes the ball to go to one side, rather than straight ahead ▷ *vb* **slicing, sliced 5** to cut (something) into slices **6** (usually foll. by *through*) to cut through cleanly and effortlessly, with or as if with a knife **7** (usually foll. by *off, from* or *away*) to cut or be cut (from) a larger piece **8** *sport* to play (a ball) with a slice
WORD ORIGIN Old French *esclice* a piece split off

slick *adj* **1** (esp. of speech) easy and persuasive: *a slick answer* **2** skilfully devised or executed: *a slick marketing effort* **3** *informal chiefly US & Canad* shrewd; sly **4** *informal* well-made and attractive, but superficial: *a slick publication* **5** *chiefly US & Canad* slippery ▷ *n* **6** a slippery area, esp. a patch of oil floating on water ▷ *vb* **7** to make smooth or shiny: *long hair slicked back with gel*
WORD ORIGIN probably from Old Norse

slide *vb* **sliding, slid 1** to move smoothly along a surface in continual contact with it: *doors that slide open* **2** to slip: *he slid on his back* **3** (usually foll. by *into, out of* or *away from*) to pass or move smoothly and quietly: *she slid out of her seat* **4** (usually foll. by *into*) to go (into a specified condition) gradually: *the republic will slide into political anarchy* **5** (of a currency) to lose value gradually **6 let slide** to allow to change to a worse state by neglect: *past chairmen have undoubtedly let things slide* ▷ *n* **7** the act or an instance of sliding **8** a small glass plate on which specimens are placed for study under a microscope **9** a photograph on a transparent base, mounted in a frame, that can be viewed by means of a projector **10** a smooth surface, such as ice, for sliding on **11** a structure with a steep smooth slope for sliding down in playgrounds **12** *chiefly Brit* an ornamental clip to hold hair in place **13** the sliding curved tube of a trombone that is moved in and out to allow different notes to be played
WORD ORIGIN Old English *slīdan*

slide rule *n* a device formerly used to make mathematical calculations consisting of two strips, one sliding along a central groove in the other, each strip graduated in two or more logarithmic scales of numbers

slide show *n* **1** any display in the form of a series of static images, such as photographic transparencies on a slide projector or images on a computer screen ▷ *adj* **slide-show 2** presented as a series of static images: *slide-show presentation*

sliding scale *n* a variable scale according to which things such as wages or prices alter in response to changes in other factors

slight *adj* **1** small in quantity or extent: *a slight improvement* **2** not very important or lacking in substance: *her political career was honourable but relatively slight* **3** slim and delicate ▷ *vb* **4** to insult (someone) by behaving rudely; snub ▷ *n* **5** an act of snubbing (someone) **slightly** *adv*

Margaret Atwood

Margaret Eleanor Atwood was born in 1939 in Ottawa, Ontario. Her father was a field entomologist, and she spent much of her childhood in the bush of Northern Quebec. She studied at the University of Toronto, where she wrote her first published volume of poetry. After spells of living in the United States and Europe, she returned to Toronto where she now lives with the writer Graeme Gibson and their daughter, Jess.

Atwood is widely considered to be Canada's most eminent contemporary writer. She has written several volumes of poems; short stories; children's books; and literary criticism, including *Survival: A Thematic Guide to Canadian Literature* (1972). It is for her novels, however, that Atwood is best known. These have gained both popular appeal and critical acclaim: *The Handmaid's Tale* (1985) won the Arthur C Clarke Award for best science fiction, and was shortlisted for the Booker Prize; *Cat's Eye* (1988), *Alias Grace* (1996) and *Oryx and Crake* (2003) were also shortlisted for the Booker; and *The Blind Assassin* (2000) won this prestigious award.

The variety and scope of Atwood's writing means that it cannot be easily categorized. She has experimented with a range of genres: science fiction, or what she prefers to call 'speculative fiction', in *The Handmaid's Tale* and *Oryx and Crake*; historical fiction in *Alias Grace*, the story of a nineteenth-century woman convicted for murder; fairy tale in several of her poems and short stories, such as her retelling of 'Bluebeard's Egg' in the collection of that title (1983); and gothic romance in *Lady Oracle* (1976).

Atwood's most popular novel, *The Handmaid's Tale*, is a dystopian fantasy about a futuristic society, the Republic of Gilead, in which freedom is severely constrained, and people have functions rather than individuality. The narrator, Offred, is a concubine; in a society in which the birth rate has plummeted, she is a 'two-legged womb', valued solely for her capacity to bear children. Denied freedom, choice, privacy, and even a name ('Offred' is simply a patronymic, 'Of Fred'), she creates a private space for herself through her memories and inner narrative. Offred's story ends ambiguously, and is followed by a set of 'historical notes', the transcript of a lecture given over a hundred years after the time-setting of the novel. The lecturer, a male professor, describes the discovery of Offred's story, which is said to be the transcript of a tape recording, and may or may not be genuine.

Several of the themes of *The Handmaid's Tale* typify Atwood's work as a whole. One is the construction of the self through memory. This is central to *Surfacing* (1972), in which a young woman descends into and resurfaces from madness through a piecing together of her past. In *Cat's Eye*, the narrator, a middle-aged artist, grapples with her childhood experiences of bullying. In both of these novels, and in *The Handmaid's Tale*, memories are central and yet unreliable: Offred writes of her memories that they are 'reconstructions', while the narrator of *Surfacing* reminds herself 'I have to be more careful about my memories. I have to be sure they're my own ...' A related theme is Atwood's ongoing exploration of the relationship between narrative, narrator and reader, evident in the 'postmodern' and uncertain ending of *The Handmaid's Tale*, and more recently in the complex layered narratives of *The Blind Assassin*.

An issue which is central to Atwood's work is her exploration of gender politics. This is evident from her first novel, *The Edible Woman* (1969), about a newly engaged woman's estrangement from her own body and identity. Yet Atwood does not think of herself as (only) a feminist: 'I would not deny the adjective,' she once said, 'but I don't consider it inclusive.' Even *The Handmaid's Tale* is not simply about the subjugation of women, but of humanity. In the Republic of Gilead, men too are denied freedom; homosexuals and priests, among others, are executed for their 'crimes'.

Atwood's work is too inclusive to be narrowly classified. She once said that the reason for writing and reading novels is that 'they force you to imagine what it's like to be somebody else.' Her success in doing just that is what gives her works such lasting appeal.

WORD ORIGIN Old Norse *slēttr* smooth

slim *adj* **slimmer, slimmest 1** (of a person) attractively thin **2** small in width relative to height or length: *a slim book* **3** poor; meagre: *a slim chance of progress* ▷ *vb* **slimming, slimmed 4** to make or become slim by diets and exercise **5** to reduce in size: *that would slim the overheads* **slimmer** *n* **slimming** *n*
WORD ORIGIN Dutch: crafty

Slim *n* the E African name for **AIDS**
WORD ORIGIN from its wasting effects

slime *n* **1** soft runny mud or any sticky substance esp. when disgusting or unpleasant **2** a thick, sticky substance produced by some fish, slugs, and fungi
WORD ORIGIN Old English *slīm*

slimy *adj* **slimier, slimiest 1** of, like, or covered with slime **2** pleasant and friendly in an insincere way

sling¹ *n* **1** med a wide piece of cloth suspended from the neck for supporting an injured hand or arm **2** a rope or strap by which something may be lifted **3** a simple weapon consisting of a strap tied to cords, in which a stone is whirled and then released ▷ *vb* **slinging, slung 4** *informal* to throw **5** to carry or hang loosely from or as if from a sling: *her shoulder bag was slung across her chest* **6** to hurl with or as if with a sling
WORD ORIGIN probably from Old Norse

sling² *n* a sweetened mixed drink with a spirit base: *gin sling*
WORD ORIGIN origin unknown

slingback *n* a shoe with a strap instead of a complete covering for the heel

sling off at *vb Austral & NZ informal* to mock and jeer

slink *vb* **slinking, slunk** to move or act in a quiet and secretive way from fear or guilt
WORD ORIGIN Old English *slincan*

slinky *adj* **slinkier, slinkiest** *informal* **1** (of clothes) figure-hugging **2** moving in an alluring way

slip¹ *vb* **slipping, slipped 1** to lose balance and slide unexpectedly: *he slipped on some leaves* **2** to let loose or be let loose: *the rope slipped from his fingers* **3** to move smoothly and easily: *small enough to slip into a pocket* **4** to place quickly or stealthily: *he slipped the pistol back into his holster* **5** to put on or take off easily or quickly: *we had slipped off our sandals* **6** to pass out of (the mind or memory) **7** to move or pass quickly and without being noticed: *we slipped out of the ballroom* **8** to make a mistake **9** to decline in health or mental ability **10** to become worse or lower: *sales had slipped below the level for June of last year* **11** to dislocate (a disc in the spine) **12** to pass (a stitch) from one needle to another without knitting it **13 let slip a** to allow to escape **b** to say unintentionally ▷ *n* **14** a slipping **15** a mistake or oversight: *one slip in concentration that cost us the game* **16** a woman's sleeveless undergarment, worn under a dress **17** same as **slipway 18** *cricket* a fielding position a little behind and to the offside of the wicketkeeper **19 give someone the slip** to escape from someone ▸ See also **slip up**
WORD ORIGIN Middle Low German or Dutch *slippen*

slip² *n* **1** a small piece of paper: *the registration slip* **2** a cutting taken from a plant **3** a young slim person: *a slip of a girl*
WORD ORIGIN probably Middle Low German, Middle Dutch *slippe* to cut

slip³ *n* clay mixed with water to a thin paste, used for decorating or patching a ceramic piece
WORD ORIGIN Old English *slyppe* slime

slipe *n* NZ wool removed from the pelt of a slaughtered sheep by immersion in a chemical bath
WORD ORIGIN Middle English *slype* to skin

slipknot *n* a nooselike knot tied so that it will slip along the rope round which it is made

slip-on *adj* **1** (of a garment or shoe) without laces or buttons so as to be easily and quickly put on ▷ *n* **2** a slip-on garment or shoe

slipped disc *n pathol* a painful condition in which one of the discs which connects the bones of the spine becomes displaced and presses on a nerve

slipper *n* a light soft shoe for indoor wear **slippered** *adj*

slippery *adj* **1** liable or tending to cause objects to slip: *the road was slippery* **2** liable to slip from one's grasp: *a bar of slippery soap* **3** not to be trusted: *slippery politicians* **slipperiness** *n*

slippy *adj* **-pier, -piest** *informal or dialect* same as **slippery** (senses 1, 2) **> slippiness** *n*

slip road *n Brit* a short road connecting a motorway to another road

slipshod *adj* **1** (of an action) done in a careless way without attention to detail: *a slipshod piece of research* **2** (of a person's appearance) untidy and slovenly

slip-slop *n S African* same as **flip-flop**

slipstream *n* the stream of air forced backwards by an aircraft or car

slip up *informal* **1** to make a mistake ▷ *n* **slip-up 2** a mistake

slipway *n* a large ramp that slopes down from the shore into the water, on which a ship is built or repaired and from which it is launched

slit *n* **1** a long narrow cut or opening ▷ *vb* **slitting, slit 2** to make a straight long cut in (something)
WORD ORIGIN Old English *slītan* to slice

slither *vb* **1** to move or slide unsteadily, such as on a slippery surface **2** to move along the ground in a twisting way: *a snake slithered towards the tree* ▷ *n* **3** a slithering movement **slithery** *adj*
WORD ORIGIN Old English *slid(e)rian*

sliver (**sliv-ver**) *n* **1** a small thin piece that is cut or broken off lengthwise ▷ *vb* **2** to cut into slivers
WORD ORIGIN obsolete *sliven* to split

Sloane Ranger *n informal* (in Britain) a young upper-class woman having a home in London and in the country, characterized as wearing expensive informal clothes
WORD ORIGIN from *Sloane Square*, London + *Lone Ranger*, cowboy hero

slob *n informal* a lazy and untidy person **slobbish** *adj*

WORD ORIGIN Irish Gaelic *slab* mud

slobber *vb* **1** to dribble (liquid or saliva) from the mouth **2 slobber over** to behave in an excessively sentimental way towards (someone) ▷ *n* **3** liquid or saliva spilt from the mouth **slobbery** *adj*
WORD ORIGIN Middle Low German, Middle Dutch *slubberen*

slob ice *n Canad* sludgy masses of floating sea ice

sloe *n* **1** the small sour blue-black fruit of the blackthorn **2** same as **blackthorn**
WORD ORIGIN Old English *slāh*

sloe-eyed *adj* having dark almond-shaped eyes

slog *vb* **slogging, slogged 1** to work hard and steadily **2** to make one's way with difficulty: *we slogged our way through the snow* **3** to hit hard ▷ *n* **4** long exhausting work **5** a long and difficult walk: *a slog through heather and bracken* **6** a heavy blow
WORD ORIGIN origin unknown

slogan *n* a catchword or phrase used in politics or advertising
WORD ORIGIN Gaelic *sluagh-ghairm* war cry

sloop *n* a small sailing ship with a single mast
WORD ORIGIN Dutch *sloep*

slop *vb* **slopping, slopped 1** (often foll. by *about*) to splash or spill (liquid) **2 slop over** *informal chiefly US & Canad* to be excessively sentimental ▷ *n* **3** a puddle of spilt liquid **4 slops** liquid refuse and waste food used to feed animals, esp. pigs **5** (often *pl*) *informal* liquid food
WORD ORIGIN Old English *-sloppe*

slope *n* **1** a stretch of ground where one end is higher than the other **2 slopes** hills or foothills **3** any slanting surface **4** the angle of such a slant ▷ *vb* **sloping, sloped 5** to slant or cause to slant **6** (esp. of natural features) to have one end or part higher than another: *the bank sloped sharply down to the river* **7 slope off** or **away** *informal* to go quietly and quickly in order to avoid something or someone **8 slope arms** *mil* (formerly) to hold (a rifle) in a sloping position against the shoulder
WORD ORIGIN origin unknown

slop out *vb* (of prisoners) to empty chamber pots and collect water

sloppy *adj* **-pier, -piest 1** *informal* careless or untidy: *sloppy workmanship* **2** *informal* excessively sentimental and romantic **3** wet; slushy **sloppily** *adv* **sloppiness** *n*

slosh *vb* **1** *informal* to throw or pour (liquid) carelessly **2** (often foll. by *about* or *around*) *informal* **a** to shake or stir (something) in a liquid **b** (of a person) to splash (around) in water or mud **3** (usually foll. by *about* or *around*) *informal* to shake (a container of liquid) or (of liquid in a container) to be shaken **4** *Brit slang* to deal a heavy blow to ▷ *n* **5** the sound of splashing liquid **6** slush **7** *Brit slang* a heavy blow **sloshy** *adj*
WORD ORIGIN variant of SLUSH

sloshed *adj slang chiefly Brit & Austral* drunk

slot *n* **1** a narrow opening or groove, such as one in a vending machine for inserting a coin **2** *informal* a place in a series or scheme: *the late-night slot when people stop watching TV* ▷ *vb* **slotting, slotted 3** to make a slot or slots in **4** (usually foll. by *in* or *into*) to fit or be fitted into a slot: *I slotted my card into the machine* **WORD ORIGIN** Old French *esclot* the depression of the breastbone

sloth (rhymes with **both**) *n* **1** a slow-moving shaggy-coated animal of Central and South America, which hangs upside down in trees by its long arms and feeds on vegetation **2** *formal* laziness, esp. regarding work **WORD ORIGIN** Old English *slǣwth*

slothful *adj* lazy and unwilling to work

slot machine *n* a machine, esp. for vending food and cigarettes or featuring an electronic game on which to gamble, worked by placing a coin in a slot

slouch *vb* **1** to sit, stand, or move with a drooping posture ▷ *n* **2** a drooping posture **3 be no slouch** *informal* be very good or talented: *he was no slouch himself as a negotiator* **WORD ORIGIN** origin unknown

slouch hat *n* a soft hat with a brim that can be pulled down over the ears

slough¹ (rhymes with **now**) *n* **1** a swamp or marshy area **2** (rhymes with **blue**) *US & Canad* a large hole where water collects **3** despair or hopeless depression **WORD ORIGIN** Old English *slōh*

slough² (**sluff**) *n* **1** any outer covering that is shed, such as the dead outer layer of the skin of a snake ▷ *vb* **slough off 2** to shed (an outer covering) or (of an outer covering) to be shed: *the dead cells would slough off* **3** to get rid of (something unwanted or unnecessary): *she tried hard to slough off her old personality* **WORD ORIGIN** Germanic

Slovak *adj* **1** of Slovakia ▷ *n* **2** a person from Slovakia **3** the language of Slovakia

sloven *n* a person who is always untidy or careless in appearance or behaviour **WORD ORIGIN** origin unknown

Slovene *adj* **1** Also: **Slovenian** of Slovenia ▷ *n* **2** a person from Slovenia **3** the language of Slovenia

slovenly *adj* **1** always unclean or untidy **2** negligent and careless: *to write in such a slovenly style* ▷ *adv* **3** in a slovenly manner **slovenliness** *n*

slow *adj* **1** taking a longer time than is usual or expected **2** lacking speed: *slow movements* **3** adapted to or producing slow movement: *the slow lane* **4** (of a clock or watch) showing a time earlier than the correct time **5** not quick to understand: *slow on the uptake* **6** dull or uninteresting: *the play was very slow* **7** not easily aroused: *he is slow to anger* **8** (of business) not busy; slack **9** (of a fire or oven) giving off low heat **10** *photog* requiring a relatively long time of exposure: *a slow film* ▷ *adv* **11** in a slow manner ▷ *vb* **12** (often foll. by *up* or *down*) to decrease or cause to decrease in speed or activity **slowly** *adv* **WORD ORIGIN** Old English *slāw* sluggish

slowcoach *n informal* a person who moves or works slowly

slow motion *n* **1** *films, television* action that is made to appear slower than normal by filming at a faster rate or by replaying a video recording more slowly ▷ *adj* **slow-motion 2** of or relating to such action **3** moving at considerably less than usual speed

slow virus *n* a type of virus that is present in the body for a long time before it becomes active or infectious

slowworm *n* a legless lizard with a brownish-grey snakelike body

sludge *n* **1** soft mud or snow **2** any muddy or slushy sediment **3** sewage **sludgy** *adj* **WORD ORIGIN** probably related to SLUSH

slug¹ *n* a mollusc like a snail but without a shell **WORD ORIGIN** probably from Old Norse

slug² *n* **1** a bullet **2** *printing* a line of type produced by a Linotype machine **3** *informal* a mouthful of alcoholic drink, esp. spirits: *he poured out a large slug of Scotch* **WORD ORIGIN** probably from SLUG¹ (with allusion to the shape of the animal)

slug³ *vb* **slugging, slugged 1** *chiefly US & Canad* to hit very hard ▷ *n* **2** *US & Canad* a heavy blow **WORD ORIGIN** probably from SLUG² (bullet)

sluggard *n old-fashioned* a very lazy person **WORD ORIGIN** Middle English *slogarde*

sluggish *adj* **1** lacking energy **2** moving or working at slower than the normal rate: *the sluggish waters of the canal*

sluice *n* **1** a channel that carries a rapid current of water, with a sluicegate to control the flow **2** the water controlled by a sluicegate **3** same as **sluicegate 4** *mining* a sloping trough for washing ore ▷ *vb* **sluicing, sluiced 5** to draw off or drain with a sluice **6** to wash with a stream of water **7** (often foll. by *away* or *out*) (of water) to run or flow from or as if from a sluice **WORD ORIGIN** Old French *escluse*

sluicegate *n* a valve or gate fitted to a sluice to control the rate of flow of water

slum *n* **1** an overcrowded and badly maintained house **2** (often *pl*) a poor rundown overpopulated section of a city ▷ *vb* **slumming, slummed 3** to visit slums, esp. for curiosity **4 slum it** to temporarily and deliberately experience poorer places or conditions **slummy** *adj* **WORD ORIGIN** origin unknown

slumber *literary vb* **1** to sleep ▷ *n* **2** sleep **slumbering** *adj* **WORD ORIGIN** Old English *slūma*

slump *vb* **1** (of commercial activity or prices) to decline suddenly **2** to sink or fall heavily and suddenly: *she slumped back with exhaustion* ▷ *n* **3** a severe decline in commercial activity or prices; depression **4** a sudden or marked decline or failure: *a slump in demand for oil* **WORD ORIGIN** probably Scandinavian

slung *vb* the past of **sling¹**

slunk *vb* the past of **slink**

slur *vb* **slurring, slurred 1** to pronounce or say (words) unclearly **2** to make insulting remarks about **3** *music* to sing

or play (successive notes) smoothly by moving from one to the other without a break **4** (often foll. by *over*) to treat hastily or carelessly ▷ *n* **5** an insulting remark intended to damage someone's reputation **6** a slurring of words **7** *music* **a** a slurring of successive notes **b** the curved line ⌢ or ⌣ indicating this **WORD ORIGIN** probably from Middle Low German

slurp *informal vb* **1** to eat or drink (something) noisily ▷ *n* **2** a slurping sound **WORD ORIGIN** Middle Dutch *slorpen* to sip

slurry *n, pl* **-ries** a thin watery mixture of something such as cement or mud **WORD ORIGIN** Middle English *slory*

slush *n* **1** any watery muddy substance, esp. melting snow **2** *informal* sloppily sentimental language or writing **slushy** *adj* **WORD ORIGIN** origin unknown

slush fund *n* a fund for financing political or commercial corruption

slut *n offensive* a promiscuous woman **sluttish** *adj* **WORD ORIGIN** origin unknown

sly *adj* **slyer, slyest** *or* **slier, sliest 1** (of a person's remarks or gestures) indicating that he or she knows something of which other people may be unaware: *she had the feeling they were poking sly fun at her* **2** secretive and skilled at deception: *a sly trickster* **3** roguish: *sly comedy* ▷ *n* **4 on the sly** secretively: *they were smoking on the sly behind the shed* **slyly** *adv* **WORD ORIGIN** Old Norse *slœgr* clever

Sm *chem* samarium

smack¹ *vb* **1** to slap sharply **2** to strike loudly or to be struck loudly **3** to open and close (the lips) loudly to show pleasure or anticipation ▷ *n* **4** a sharp loud slap, or the sound of such a slap **5** a loud kiss **6** a sharp sound made by the lips in enjoyment **7 smack in the eye** *informal* a snub or rejection ▷ *adv informal* **8** directly; squarely: *smack in the middle* **9** sharply and unexpectedly: *he ran smack into one of the men* **WORD ORIGIN** probably imitative

smack² *n* **1** a slight flavour or suggestion (of something): *the smack of loss of self-control* ▷ *vb* **2 smack of a** to have a slight smell or flavour (of something) **b** to have a suggestion (of something): *it smacks of discrimination* **WORD ORIGIN** Old English *smæc*

smack³ *n* a slang word for **heroin** **WORD ORIGIN** perhaps from Yiddish *schmeck*

smack⁴ *n* a small single-masted fishing vessel **WORD ORIGIN** Dutch *smak*

smacker *n slang* **1** a loud kiss **2** a pound note or dollar bill

small *adj* **1** not large in size or amount **2** of little importance or on a minor scale: *a small detail* **3** mean, ungenerous, or petty: *a small mind* **4** modest or humble: *small beginnings* **5 feel small** to be humiliated **6** (of a child or animal) young; not mature **7** unimportant or trivial: *a small matter* **8** (of a letter) written or printed in lower case rather

as a capital ▷ *adv* **9** into small pieces: *cut it small* ▷ *n* **10** the small narrow part of the back **11** **smalls** *informal chiefly Brit* underwear **smallish** *adj* **smallness** *n*
WORD ORIGIN Old English *smæl*

small beer *n informal chiefly Brit* people or things of no importance

small change *n* coins of low value

small fry *pl n* **1** people regarded as unimportant **2** young children

small goods *pl n Austral & NZ* meats bought from a delicatessen, such as sausages

smallholding *n* a piece of agricultural land smaller than a farm **smallholder** *n*

small hours *pl n* the early hours of the morning, after midnight and before dawn

small intestine *n anat* the narrow, longer part of the alimentary canal, in which digestion is completed

small-minded *adj* having narrow selfish attitudes; petty

smallpox *n* a contagious disease causing fever, a rash, and blisters which usually leave permanent scars

small print *n* details in a contract or document printed in small type, esp. when considered as containing important information that people may regret not reading

small-scale *adj* of limited size or scope

small screen *n* **the small screen** television, esp. in contrast to cinema: *despite his film success, he has achieved little on the small screen*

small talk *n* light conversation for social occasions

small-time *adj informal* operating on a limited scale; minor: *a small-time smuggler*

smarm *vb Brit informal* **1** to bring (oneself) into favour (with) **2** *old-fashioned* (often foll. by *down*) to flatten (the hair) with oil
WORD ORIGIN origin unknown

smarmy *adj* **smarmier, smarmiest** unpleasantly flattering or polite

smart *adj* **1** clean and neatly dressed **2** intelligent and shrewd **3** quick and witty in speech: *a smart talker* **4** (of places or events) fashionable; chic: *smart restaurants* **5** vigorous or brisk: *a smart pace* **6** causing a sharp stinging pain **7** (of a weapon) containing an electronic device which enables it to be guided to its target: *a smart bomb* ▷ *vb* **8** to feel or cause a sharp stinging physical or mental pain: *I was still smarting from the insult* ▷ *n* **9** a stinging pain or feeling ▷ *adv* **10** in a smart manner ▸ See also **smarts** ▷ **smartly** *adv* **smartness** *n*
WORD ORIGIN Old English *smeortan* be painful

smart alec *n informal* a person who thinks he or she is an expert on every subject; know-all

smart card *n* a plastic card with integrated circuits used for storing and processing computer data

smarten *vb* (usually foll. by *up*) to make or become smart

smarts *pl n slang chiefly US* know-how, intelligence, or wits: *the street smarts of the old crooks*

smash *vb* **1** to break into pieces violently and noisily **2** (often foll. by *against, through* or *into*) to throw or crash (against) violently, causing shattering: *his head smashed against a window* **3** to hit or collide forcefully and suddenly **4** *racket sports* to hit (the ball) fast and powerfully with an overhead stroke **5** to defeat or destroy: *the police had smashed a major drug ring* ▷ *n* **6** an act or sound of smashing **7** a violent collision of vehicles **8** *racket sports* a fast and powerful overhead stroke **9** *informal* a show, record or film which is very popular with the public ▷ *adv* **10** with a smash
WORD ORIGIN probably imitative

smash-and-grab *adj informal* of a robbery in which a shop window is broken and the contents removed

smasher *n informal chiefly Brit* a person or thing that is very attractive or outstanding

smashing *adj informal chiefly Brit* excellent or first-rate

smash-up *informal n* **1** a bad collision or crash involving motor vehicles ▷ *vb* **smash up 2** to damage to the point of complete destruction: *two men smashed up a bar*

smattering *n* a slight or superficial knowledge: *I knew a smattering of Russian*

smear *vb* **1** to spread with a greasy or sticky substance **2** to apply (a greasy or sticky substance) thickly **3** to rub so as to produce a smudge **4** to spread false and damaging rumours (about) ▷ *n* **5** a dirty mark or smudge **6** a false but damaging rumour spread by a rival or enemy **7** *med* a small amount of a substance smeared onto a glass slide for examination under a microscope **smeary** *adj*
WORD ORIGIN Old English *smeoru* a smear

smear test *n med* same as **Pap test**

smell *vb* **smelling, smelt** or **smelled 1** to perceive the scent of (a substance) with the nose **2** to have a specified kind of smell: *it smells fruity; your supper smells good* **3** (often foll. by *of*) to emit an odour (of): *the place smells of milk and babies* **4** to give off an unpleasant odour **5** (often foll. by *out*) to detect through instinct: *I smell trouble* **6** to use the sense of smell; sniff **7** **smell of** to indicate or suggest: *anything that smells of devaluation* ▷ *n* **8** the sense by which scents or odours are perceived ▸ Related adjective: **olfactory 9** an odour or scent **10** the act of smelling
WORD ORIGIN origin unknown

smelling salts *pl n* a preparation containing crystals of ammonium carbonate, used to revive a person feeling faint

smelly *adj* **smellier, smelliest** having a nasty smell **smelliness** *n*

smelt¹ *vb* to extract (a metal) from (an ore) by heating
WORD ORIGIN Middle Low German, Middle Dutch *smelten*

smelt² *n, pl* **smelt** or **smelts** a small silvery food fish
WORD ORIGIN Old English *smylt*

smelt³ *vb* a past tense and past participle of **smell**

smelter *n* an industrial plant in which smelting is carried out

smile *n* **1** a facial expression in which the corners of the mouth are turned up, showing amusement or friendliness ▷ *vb* **smiling, smiled 2** to give a smile **3** **smile at a** to look at with a kindly expression **b** to look with amusement at **4** **smile on** or **upon** to regard favourably: *fortune smiled on us today* **5** to express by a smile: *he smiled a comrade's greeting*
WORD ORIGIN probably from Old Norse

smiley *adj* **1** cheerful **2** depicting a smile ▷ *n* **3** a group of symbols depicting a smile, or other facial expression, used in e-mail

smirch *vb* **1** to disgrace **2** to dirty or soil ▷ *n* **3** a disgrace **4** a smear or stain
WORD ORIGIN origin unknown

smirk *n* **1** a smug smile ▷ *vb* **2** to give such a smile
WORD ORIGIN Old English *smearcian*

smite *vb* **smiting, smote; smitten** or **smit** *archaic Bible* **1** to strike with a heavy blow **2** to affect severely: *hunger smites him again* **3** to burden with an affliction in order to punish: *God smote the enemies of the righteous* **4** **smite on** to strike abruptly and with force: *the sun smote down on him*
WORD ORIGIN Old English *smītan*

smith *n* **1** a person who works in metal: *goldsmith* **2** see **blacksmith**
WORD ORIGIN Old English

smithereens *pl n* shattered fragments
WORD ORIGIN Irish Gaelic *smidirín*

smithy *n, pl* **smithies** the workshop of a blacksmith; forge

smitten *vb* **1** a past participle of **smite** ▷ *adj* **2** deeply affected by love (for)

smock *n* **1** a loose overall worn to protect the clothes **2** a loose blouselike garment worn by women **3** a loose protective overgarment decorated with smocking, worn formerly by farm workers ▷ *vb* **4** to gather (material) by sewing in a honeycomb pattern
WORD ORIGIN Old English *smocc*

smocking *n* ornamental needlework used to gather material

smog *n* a mixture of smoke and fog that occurs in some industrial areas **smoggy** *adj*
WORD ORIGIN SMOKE + FOG

smoke *n* **1** the cloudy mass that rises from something burning **2** the act of smoking tobacco **3** *informal* a cigarette or cigar **4** **go up in smoke a** to come to nothing **b** to burn up vigorously ▷ *vb* **smoking, smoked 5** to give off smoke: *a smoking fireplace* **6 a** to draw the smoke of (burning tobacco) into the mouth and exhale it again **b** to do this habitually **7** to cure (meat, cheese, or fish) by treating with smoke
WORD ORIGIN Old English *smoca*

Smoke *n* **the Smoke** *informal* short for **Big Smoke**

smokeless *adj* having or producing little or no smoke: *smokeless fuel*

smokeless zone *n* an area where only smokeless fuels may be used

Kurt Vonnegut

Kurt Vonnegut knew that humour is a serious business. In fact, mordant satire is as much part of his fiction as his celebrated wry or wistful comedy: he lamented environmental degradation and bitterly opposed his country's military involvement in Vietnam and Iraq, often expressing shame at being an American. He declared himself to be a pacifist, socialist, and humanist.

Vonnegut was born in 1922 into a prosperous, long-established German-American family in Indianapolis, Indiana. The life that followed was beset by personal tragedies: the suicide of his mother; the deaths of a sister and brother-in-law within days, which led to his adoption of three nephews; the psychotic breakdown of a son; a house fire in which he nearly perished and which destroyed many of his papers. Depressive, he once attempted suicide. But it was a public tragedy that most obviously affected his work: the British carpet-bombing raid in 1945 that largely obliterated the German city of Dresden. A prisoner of war, Vonnegut survived the firestorm, and the cataclysm led him to write his best-known novel, *Slaughterhouse-Five, or The Children's Crusade*. Vonnegut had studied chemistry, mechanical engineering, and anthropology, giving him a scientific background that few fiction writers have. But, no matter what alternative universes and vast space-time shifts he deployed – the events of *Galápagos* are related by the narrator a million years after they take place – he resisted the label of a science-fiction writer. Fantasy was mixed with autobiographical allusions, and one recurring character, Kilgore Trout, introduced in *God Bless You, Mr. Rosewater, or Pearls Before Swine*, is an authorial surrogate.

During the 1960s, Vonnegut gained a huge vogue among college youth for his absurdist cosmology, his loathing for big-business corporatism, and his anti-authoritarianism. Dystopian though his views were ('Our planet's immune system is trying to get rid of people,' he observed), he invoked the countervailing forces of decency and kindness. In the epigraph for the novel *Bluebeard: The Autobiography of Rabo Karabekian (1916–1988)* he quotes from a letter his son Mark sent him: 'We are here to help each other get through this thing, whatever it is.' In his late nonfiction book *A Man Without a Country*, he notes that tiny pleasures shore up the individual against nihilistic despair: 'We are here on Earth to fart around.'

A hallmark of Vonnegut's style is the repeated ironic use of a banal catch phrase, tagline, or slogan, most famously in *Slaughterhouse-Five*, in which the comment 'So it goes' always follows a death. In *Galápagos*, he repeats 'big brain', sarcastically referring to the so-called superiority of human beings' large brains; all the characters who die in the course of the novel invariably appear with an asterisk next to their names. (Vonnegut would disapprove of the preceding sentence, since the semi-colon was one of his stylistic bugbears: 'Here is a lesson in creative writing. First rule: Do not use semicolons. They are transvestite hermaphrodites representing absolutely nothing. All they do is show you've been to college.')

Vonnegut was a freethinker about organized religion. In *Mother Night*, a character notes, 'Say what you will about the sweet miracle of unquestioning faith, I consider a capacity for it terrifying and absolutely vile.' He invented sects such as 'Bokononism' in *Cat's Cradle* and the 'Church of God the Utterly Indifferent' in *The Sirens of Titan*. Yet he said, 'If it weren't for the message of mercy and pity in Jesus' Sermon on the Mount, I wouldn't want to be a human being. I would just as soon be a rattlesnake.' He had unflinching faith in what, in an author's note to *Bluebeard*, he called the 'mudpies of art'. The subtitle of *Slaughterhouse-Five* reflected his view that soldiers were babies.

'We are children,' he liked to say. His childlike playfulness extended to the graphic arts, since he sometimes illustrated his books with felt-tip drawings, as in *Slaughterhouse-Five* and *Breakfast of Champions, or Goodbye Blue Monday*. The title character of *God Bless You, Mr. Rosewater* says, 'Hello, babies. Welcome to Earth. It's hot in the summer and cold in the winter. It's round and wet and crowded. At the outside, babies, you've got about a hundred years here. There's only one rule that I know of, babies – "God damn it, you've got to be kind."'

smoke out vb **1** to drive (a person or animal) out of a hiding place by filling it with smoke **2** to bring (someone) out of secrecy and into the open: *they smoked out the plotters*

smoker n **1** a person who habitually smokes tobacco **2** a train compartment where smoking is permitted

smoke screen n **1** something said or done to hide the truth **2** *mil* a cloud of smoke used to provide cover for manoeuvres

smokestack n a tall chimney that carries smoke away from a factory

smoko *or* **smokeho** (**smoke**-oh) n, pl **-kos** *or* **-hos** *Austral & NZ informal* **1** a short break from work for tea or a cigarette **2** refreshment taken during this break

smoky adj **smokier, smokiest 1** filled with or giving off smoke, sometimes excessively: *smoky coal or wood fires* **2** having the colour of smoke **3** having the taste or smell of smoke **4** made dirty or hazy by smoke **smokiness** n

smolt n a young salmon at the stage when it migrates from fresh water to the sea
WORD ORIGIN Scots

smooch *slang* vb **1** (of two people) to kiss and cuddle **2** *Brit* to dance very slowly with one's arms around another person or (of two people) to dance together in such a way ▷ n **3** the act of smooching
WORD ORIGIN dialect *smouch*, imitative

smoodge *or* **smooge** vb **smoodging, smoodged** *or* **smooging, smooged** *Austral & NZ* **1** same as **smooch** (sense 1) **2** to attempt to gain favour through flattery

smooth adj **1** having an even surface with no roughness, bumps, or holes **2** without obstructions or difficulties: *smooth progress towards an agreement* **3** without lumps: *a smooth paste* **4** free from jolts and bumps: *a smooth landing* **5** not harsh in taste; mellow: *an excellent smooth wine* **6** charming or persuasive but possibly insincere ▷ adv **7** in a smooth manner ▷ vb **8** (often foll. by *down*) to make or become even or without roughness **9** (often foll. by *out* or *away*) to remove in order to make smooth: *smoothing out the creases* **10** to make calm; soothe **11** to make easier: *Moscow smoothed the path to democracy* ▷ n **12** the smooth part of something **13** the act of smoothing **smoothly** adv
WORD ORIGIN Old English *smōth*

smoothie n **1** *slang* a man who is so confident, well-dressed, and charming that one is suspicious of his motives and doubts his honesty **2** a smooth thick drink made from fresh fruit and yoghurt, ice cream, or milk

smooth over vb to ease or gloss over: *their fears are now being smoothed over*

smooth-talking adj confident and persuasive but not necessarily honest or sincere

smorgasbord n a variety of savoury dishes served as hors d'oeuvres or as a buffet meal
WORD ORIGIN Swedish

smote vb the past tense of **smite**

smother vb **1** to extinguish (a fire) by covering so as to cut it off from the air **2** to suffocate **3** to surround or overwhelm (with): *she smothered him with her idea of affection* **4** to suppress or stifle: *he smothered an ironic chuckle* **5** to cover over thickly: *ice cream smothered with sauce*
WORD ORIGIN Old English *smorian* to suffocate

smoulder *or US* **smolder** vb **1** to burn slowly without flames, usually giving off smoke **2** (of emotions) to exist in a suppressed state without being released
WORD ORIGIN origin unknown

SMS short message system: used for sending data to mobile phones

smudge vb **smudging, smudged 1** to make or become smeared or soiled ▷ n **2** a smear or dirty mark **3** a blurred form or area: *the dull smudge of a ship* **smudgy** adj
WORD ORIGIN origin unknown

smug adj **smugger, smuggest** very pleased with oneself; self-satisfied **smugly** adv **smugness** n
WORD ORIGIN Germanic

smuggle vb **-gling, -gled 1** to import or export (goods that are prohibited or subject to taxation) secretly **2** (often foll. by *into* or *out of*) to bring or take secretly: *he was smuggled out of the country unnoticed* **smuggler** n **smuggling** n
WORD ORIGIN Low German *smukkelen*

smut n **1** stories, pictures, or jokes relating to sex or nudity **2** a speck of soot or a dark mark left by soot **3** a disease of cereals, in which black sooty masses cover the affected parts **smutty** adj
WORD ORIGIN Old English *smitte*

Sn *chem* tin
WORD ORIGIN New Latin *stannum*

snack n **1** a light quick meal eaten between or in place of main meals ▷ vb **2** to eat a snack
WORD ORIGIN probably from Middle Dutch *snacken*

snack bar n a place where light meals or snacks are sold

snaffle n **1** a mouthpiece for controlling a horse ▷ vb **-fling, -fled 2** *Brit, Austral, & NZ informal* to steal or take **3** to fit or control (a horse) with a snaffle
WORD ORIGIN origin unknown

snafu (snaf-**foo**) *chiefly mil slang* n **1** confusion or chaos regarded as the normal state ▷ adj **2** confused or muddled up, as usual
WORD ORIGIN s(ituation) n(ormal): a(ll) f(ucked) u(p)

snag n **1** a small problem or difficulty: *one possible snag in his plans* **2** a sharp projecting point that may catch on things **3** a small hole in a fabric caused by a sharp object **4** a tree stump in a river bed that is a danger to navigation ▷ vb **snagging, snagged 5** to tear or catch on a snag
WORD ORIGIN Scandinavian

snail n a slow-moving mollusc with a spiral shell
WORD ORIGIN Old English *snæg(e)l*

snail mail *informal* n **1** conventional post, as opposed to e-mail **2** the conventional postal system ▷ vb **snail-mail 3** to send by the conventional postal system, rather than by e-mail

snail's pace n a very slow speed

snake n **1** a long scaly limbless reptile **2** Also: **snake in the grass** a person, esp. a colleague or friend, who secretly acts against one ▷ vb **snaking, snaked 3** to glide or move in a winding course, like a snake
WORD ORIGIN Old English *snaca*

snakebite n **1** the bite of a snake **2** a drink of cider and lager

snake charmer n an entertainer who appears to hypnotize snakes by playing music

snakes and ladders n a board game in which players move counters along a series of squares by means of dice, going up the ladders to squares nearer the finish and down the snakes to squares nearer the start

snaky adj **snakier, snakiest 1** twisting or winding **2** treacherous

snap vb **snapping, snapped 1** to break suddenly, esp. with a sharp sound **2** to make or cause to make a sudden sharp cracking sound: *he snapped his fingers* **3** to move or close with a sudden sharp sound: *I snapped the lid shut* **4** to move in a sudden or abrupt way **5** to give way or collapse suddenly under strain: *one day someone's temper will snap* **6** to panic when a situation becomes too difficult to cope with: *he could snap at any moment* **7** (often foll. by *at* or *up*) to seize suddenly or quickly **8** (often foll. by *at*) (of animals) to bite at suddenly **9** to speak (words) sharply and angrily **10** to take a photograph of **11 snap one's fingers at** *informal* to defy or dismiss contemptuously **12 snap out of it** *informal* to recover quickly, esp. from depression or anger ▷ n **13** the act of breaking suddenly or the sound of a sudden breakage **14** a sudden sharp sound **15** a clasp or fastener that closes with a snapping sound **16** a sudden grab or bite **17** a thin crisp biscuit: *brandy snaps* **18** *informal* an informal photograph taken with a simple camera **19** see **cold snap 20** *Brit & NZ* a card game in which the word *snap* is called when two similar cards are turned up ▷ adj **21** done on the spur of the moment: *snap judgments* ▷ adv **22** with a snap ▷ interj **23** *a cards* the word called while playing snap *b* a cry used to draw attention to the similarity of two things ▶ See also **snap up**
WORD ORIGIN Middle Dutch *snappen* to seize

snapdragon n a plant with spikes of colourful flowers that can open and shut like a mouth; antirrhinum

snap fastener n same as **press stud**

snapper n a food fish of Australia and New Zealand with a pinkish body covered with blue spots

snappy adj **-pier, -piest 1** smart and fashionable: *snappy designs* **2** Also: **snappish** (of someone's behaviour) irritable, unfriendly, and cross **3** brisk or lively: *short snappy movements* **4 make it snappy** *slang* hurry up! **snappiness** n

snapshot n same as **snap** (sense 18)

snap up vb to take advantage of eagerly and quickly: *the tickets have been snapped up*

snare¹ *n* **1** a trap for birds or small animals, usually a flexible loop that is drawn tight around the prey **2** anything that traps someone or something unawares ▷ *vb* **snaring, snared 3** to catch in or as if in a snare **WORD ORIGIN** Old English *snearе*

snare² *n music* a set of strings fitted against the lower head of a snare drum, which produces a rattling sound when the drum is beaten **WORD ORIGIN** Middle Dutch *snaer* or Middle Low German *snare* string

snare drum *n music* a small drum fitted with a snare

snarl¹ *vb* **1** (of an animal) to growl fiercely with bared teeth **2** to speak or say (something) fiercely: *he snarled out a command to a subordinate* ▷ *n* **3** a fierce growl or facial expression **4** the act of snarling **WORD ORIGIN** Germanic

snarl² *n* **1** a complicated or confused state ▷ *vb* **3 snarl up** to become, be, or make tangled, confused or complicated: *the line became snarled up on the propeller; the postal service was snarled up at Christmas* **WORD ORIGIN** from Old Norse

snarl-up *n informal* a confused, disorganized situation such as a traffic jam

snatch *vb* **1** to seize or grasp (something) suddenly: *she snatched the paper* **2** (usually foll. by *at*) to attempt to seize suddenly **3** to take hurriedly: *these players had snatched a few hours sleep* **4** to remove suddenly: *she snatched her hand away* ▷ *n* **5** an act of snatching **6** a small piece or incomplete part: *snatches of song* **7** a brief spell: *snatches of sleep* **8** *slang chiefly US* an act of kidnapping **9** *Brit slang* a robbery: *a wages snatch* **WORD ORIGIN** Middle English *snacchen*

snazzy *adj* **-zier, -ziest** *informal* (esp. of clothes) stylish and flashy **WORD ORIGIN** origin unknown

sneak *vb* **1** to move quietly, trying not be noticed **2** to behave in a cowardly or underhand manner **3** to bring, take, or put secretly: *we sneaked him over the border* **4** *informal chiefly Brit & NZ* (esp. in schools) to tell tales ▷ *n* **5** a person who acts in an underhand or cowardly manner ▷ *adj* **6** without warning: *a sneak attack* **sneaky** *adj* **WORD ORIGIN** Old English *snīcan* to creep

sneakers *pl n US, Canad, Austral, & NZ* canvas shoes with rubber soles

sneaking *adj* **1** slight but nagging: *a sneaking suspicion* **2** secret: *a sneaking admiration* **3** acting in a cowardly and furtive way

sneak thief *n* a burglar who sneaks into houses through open doors and windows

sneer *n* **1** a facial expression showing distaste or contempt, typically with a curled upper lip **2** a remark showing distaste or contempt ▷ *vb* **3** to make a facial expression of scorn or contempt **4** to say (something) in a scornful manner **sneering** *adj, n* **WORD ORIGIN** origin unknown

sneeze *vb* **sneezing, sneezed 1** to expel air from the nose suddenly and without control, esp. as the result of irritation in the nostrils ▷ *n* **2** the act or sound of sneezing **WORD ORIGIN** Old English *fnēosan* (unattested)

sneeze at *vb informal* to ignore or dismiss lightly: *the money's not to be sneezed at*

snib *n Scot & NZ* the catch of a door or window

snick *n* **1** a small cut in something; notch **2** *cricket* a glancing blow off the edge of the bat ▷ *vb* **3** to make a small cut or notch in (something) **4** *cricket* to hit (the ball) with a snick **WORD ORIGIN** probably Scandinavian

snicker *n, vb chiefly US & Canad* same as **snigger** **WORD ORIGIN** probably imitative

snide *or* **snidey** *adj* (of comments) critical in an unfair and nasty way **WORD ORIGIN** origin unknown

sniff *vb* **1** to inhale through the nose in short audible breaths **2** (often foll. by *at*) to smell by sniffing ▷ *n* **3** the act or sound of sniffing **sniffer** *n* **WORD ORIGIN** imitative

sniff at *vb* to express contempt or dislike for

sniffer dog *n* a police dog trained to locate drugs or explosives by smell

sniffle *vb* **-fling, -fled 1** to sniff repeatedly when the nasal passages are blocked up ▷ *n* **2** the act or sound of sniffling

sniffles *or* **snuffles** *pl n* **the sniffles** *informal* a cold in the head

sniff out *vb* to discover after some searching: *they eventually sniffed out a suitable Parliamentary seat for him*

sniffy *adj* **-fier, -fiest** *informal* contemptuous or scornful

snifter *n* **1** *informal* a small quantity of alcoholic drink **2** a pear-shaped brandy glass **WORD ORIGIN** origin unknown

snig *vb* **snigging, snigged** *Austral & NZ* to drag (a felled log) by a chain or cable **WORD ORIGIN** English dialect

snigger *n* **1** a quiet and disrespectful laugh kept to oneself ▷ *vb* **2** to utter such a laugh **WORD ORIGIN** variant of *snicker*

snip *vb* **snipping, snipped 1** to cut with small quick strokes with scissors or shears ▷ *n* **2** *informal chiefly Brit* a bargain **3** the act or sound of snipping **4** a small piece snipped off **5** a small cut made by snipping **WORD ORIGIN** Low German, Dutch *snippen*

snipe *n, pl* **snipe** *or* **snipes 1** a wading bird with a long straight bill ▷ *vb* **sniping, sniped** (often foll. by *at*) **2** to shoot (someone) from a place of hiding **3** (often foll. by *at*) to make critical remarks about **sniper** *n* **WORD ORIGIN** Old Norse *snīpa*

snippet *n* a small scrap or fragment: *the odd snippet of knowledge*

snitch *slang vb* **1** to act as an informer **2** to steal small amounts ▷ *n* **3** an informer **WORD ORIGIN** origin unknown

snitchy *adj* **snitchier, snitchiest** *NZ informal* bad-tempered or irritable

snivel *vb* **-velling, -velled** *or US* **-veling, -veled 1** to cry and sniff in a self-pitying way **2** to say (something) tearfully; whine **3** to have a runny nose ▷ *n* **4** the act of snivelling **WORD ORIGIN** Middle English *snivelen*

snob *n* **1** a person who tries to associate with those of higher social status and who hates those of a lower social status **2** a person who feels smugly superior with regard to his or her tastes or interests: *a cultural snob* **snobbery** *n* **snobbish** *adj* **WORD ORIGIN** origin unknown

snoek (**snook**) *n* a South African edible marine fish **WORD ORIGIN** Afrikaans, from Dutch: pike

snoep (**snoop**) *adj S African informal* mean or tight-fisted **WORD ORIGIN** Afrikaans: greedy

snog *Brit, NZ, & S African slang vb* **snogging, snogged 1** to kiss and cuddle ▷ *n* **2** the act of kissing and cuddling **WORD ORIGIN** origin unknown

snood *n* a pouchlike hat loosely holding a woman's hair at the back **WORD ORIGIN** Old English *snōd*

snook *n* **cock a snook at** *Brit* **a** to make a rude gesture at (someone) by putting one thumb to the nose with the fingers of the hand outstretched **b** to show contempt for (someone in authority) without fear of punishment **WORD ORIGIN** origin unknown

snooker *n* **1** a game played on a billiard table with 15 red balls, six balls of other colours, and a white cue ball **2** a shot in which the cue ball is left in a position such that another ball blocks the target ball ▷ *vb* **3** to leave (an opponent) in an unfavourable position by playing a snooker **4** to put someone in a position where he or she can do nothing **WORD ORIGIN** origin unknown

snoop *informal vb* **1** (often foll. by *about* or *around*) to pry into the private business of others ▷ *n* **2** the act of snooping **3** a person who snoops **snooper** *n* **snoopy** *adj* **WORD ORIGIN** Dutch *snoepen* to eat furtively

snooty *adj* **snootier, snootiest** *informal* behaving as if superior to other people; snobbish **WORD ORIGIN** from *snoot* nose

snooze *informal vb* **snoozing, snoozed 1** to take a brief light sleep ▷ *n* **2** a nap **WORD ORIGIN** origin unknown

snore *vb* **snoring, snored 1** to breathe with snorting sounds while asleep ▷ *n* **2** the act or sound of snoring **WORD ORIGIN** imitative

snorkel *n* **1** a tube allowing a swimmer to breathe while face down on the surface of the water **2** a device supplying air to a submarine when under water ▷ *vb* **-kelling, -kelled** *or US* **-keling, -keled 3** to swim with a snorkel **WORD ORIGIN** German *Schnorchel*

snort *vb* **1** to exhale air noisily through the nostrils **2** to express contempt or annoyance by snorting **3** to say with a snort **4** *slang* to inhale a powdered drug

S

through the nostrils ▷ n **5** a loud exhalation of air through the nostrils to express contempt or annoyance: *Clare gave a snort of disgust*
WORD ORIGIN Middle English *snorten*

snot n *usually considered vulgar* **1** mucus from the nose **2** *slang* an annoying or disgusting person
WORD ORIGIN Old English *gesnot*

snotty adj **-tier, -tiest** *considered vulgar* **1** dirty with nasal discharge **2** having a proud and superior attitude **3** *slang* contemptible; nasty **snottiness** n

snout n **1** the projecting nose and jaws of an animal **2** anything projecting like a snout: *the snout of a gun* **3** *slang* a person's nose
WORD ORIGIN Germanic

snow n **1** frozen vapour falling from the sky in flakes **2** a layer of snow on the ground **3** a falling of snow **4** *slang* cocaine ▷ vb **5** (with 'it' as subject) to be the case that snow is falling: *it's snowing today* **6** to fall as or like snow **7** **be snowed in** or **up** or **over** to be covered by or confined with a heavy fall of snow **8** **be snowed under** to be overwhelmed, esp. with paperwork **snowy** adj
WORD ORIGIN Old English *snāw*

snowball n **1** snow pressed into a ball for throwing ▷ vb **2** to increase rapidly in size or importance: *production snowballed between 1950 and 1970* **3** to throw snowballs at

snowberry n, pl **-ries** a shrub grown for its white berries

snow-blind adj blinded for a short time by the intense reflection of sunlight from snow **snow blindness** n

snowboard n a shaped board, like a skateboard without wheels, on which a person stands to slide across the snow **snowboarding** n

snowbound adj shut in or blocked off by snow

snowcap n a cap of snow on top of a mountain **snowcapped** adj

snowdrift n a bank of deep snow driven together by the wind

snowdrop n a plant with small drooping white bell-shaped flowers

snowfall n **1** a fall of snow **2** *meteorol* the amount of snow that falls in a specified place and time

snowflake n a single crystal of snow

snow goose n a North American goose with white feathers and black wing tips

snow line n (on a mountain) the altitude above which there is permanent snow

snowman n, pl **-men** a figure like a person, made of packed snow

snowmobile n a motor vehicle for travelling on snow, esp. one with caterpillar tracks and front skis

snowplough or esp. US **snowplow** n a vehicle for clearing away snow

snowshoe n a racket-shaped frame with a network of thongs stretched across it, worn on the feet to make walking on snow less difficult

snowstorm n a storm with heavy snow

SNP Scottish National Party

Snr or **snr** senior

snub vb **snubbing, snubbed 1** to insult (someone) deliberately ▷ n **2** a deliberately insulting act or remark ▷ adj **3** (of a nose) short and turned up
WORD ORIGIN Old Norse *snubba* to scold

snub-nosed adj having a short turned-up nose

snuff[1] vb **1** to inhale through the nose **2** (esp. of an animal) to examine by sniffing ▷ n **3** a sniff
WORD ORIGIN probably Middle Dutch *snuffen* to snuffle

snuff[2] n finely powdered tobacco for sniffing up the nostrils
WORD ORIGIN Dutch *snuf*

snuff[3] vb **1** (often foll. by *out*) to put out (a candle) **2** to cut off the charred part of (a candle wick) **3** (usually foll. by *out*) *informal* to put an end to **4** **snuff it** *Austral & Brit informal* to die ▷ n **5** the burned portion of the wick of a candle
WORD ORIGIN origin unknown

snuffbox n a small container for holding snuff

snuffle vb **-fling, -fled 1** to breathe noisily or with difficulty **2** to say or speak through the nose **3** to cry and sniff in a self-pitying way ▷ n **4** an act or the sound of snuffling **snuffly** adj
WORD ORIGIN Low German or Dutch *snuffelen*

snug adj **snugger, snuggest 1** comfortably warm and well protected; cosy: *safe and snug in their homes* **2** small but comfortable: *a snug office* **3** fitting closely and comfortably ▷ n **4** (in Britain and Ireland) a small room in a pub **snugly** adv
WORD ORIGIN Swedish *snygg* tidy

snuggery n, pl **-geries** a cosy and comfortable place or room

snuggle vb **-gling, -gled** to nestle into (a person or thing) for warmth or from affection
WORD ORIGIN from SNUG

so[1] adv **1** to such an extent: *the river is so dirty that it smells* **2** to the same extent as: *she is not so old as you* **3** extremely: *it's so lovely* **4** also: *I can speak Spanish and so can you* **5** thereupon: *and so we ended up in France* **6** in the state or manner expressed or implied: *they're happy and will remain so* **7** **and so on** or **forth** and continuing similarly **8** **or so** approximately: *fifty or so people came to see me* **9** **so be it** an expression of agreement or resignation **10** **so much a** a certain degree or amount (of) **b** a lot (of): *it's just so much nonsense* **11** **so much for a** no more need be said about **b** used to express contempt for something that has failed: *so much for all our plans* ▷ conj (often foll. by that) **12** in order (that): *to die so that you might live* **13** with the consequence (that): *he was late home, so that there was trouble* **14** **so as** in order (to): *to diet so as to lose weight* **15** *not standard* in consequence: *she wasn't needed, so she left* **16** **so what!** *informal* that is unimportant ▷ pron **17** used to substitute for a clause or sentence, which may be understood: *you'll stop because I said so* ▷ adj **18** true: *it can't be so* ▷ interj **19** an exclamation of surprise or triumph
WORD ORIGIN Old English *swā*

In formal English, *so* is not used as a conjunction to indicate either purpose (*he left by a back door so he could avoid photographers*) or result (*the project was abandoned so his services were no longer needed*). In the former case *to* or *in order to* should be used instead, and in the latter case *and so* or *and therefore* would be more acceptable. The expression *so therefore* should not be used.

so[2] n *music* same as **soh**

soak vb **1** to put or lie in a liquid so as to become thoroughly wet **2** (usually foll. by *in* or *into*) (of a liquid) to penetrate or permeate **3** (usually foll. by *in* or *up*) to take in; absorb: *white clay soaks up excess oil* ▷ n **4** a soaking or being soaked **5** *slang* a person who drinks very heavily **soaking** n, adj
WORD ORIGIN Old English *sōcian*

so-and-so n, pl **so-and-sos** *informal* **1** a person whose name is not specified **2** *euphemistic* a person regarded as unpleasant; a name used in place of a swear word: *you're a dirty so-and-so*

soap n **1** a compound of alkali and fat, used with water as a cleaning agent **2** *informal* short for **soap opera** ▷ vb **3** to apply soap to
WORD ORIGIN Old English *sāpe*

soapbox n a crate used as a platform for making speeches

soap opera n an on-going television or radio serial about the daily lives of a group of people
WORD ORIGIN so called because manufacturers of soap were typical sponsors

soapstone n a soft mineral used for making table tops and ornaments

soapsuds pl n foam or lather produced when soap is mixed with water

soapy adj **soapier, soapiest 1** containing or covered with soap: *a soapy liquid* **2** like soap in texture, smell, or taste: *the cheese had a soapy taste* **3** *slang* flattering or persuasive **soapiness** n

soar vb **1** to rise or fly upwards into the air **2** (of a bird or aircraft) to glide while maintaining altitude **3** to rise or increase suddenly above the usual level: *television ratings soared*
WORD ORIGIN Old French *essorer*

sob vb **sobbing, sobbed 1** to cry noisily, breathing in short gasps **2** to speak with sobs ▷ n **3** the act or sound of sobbing
WORD ORIGIN probably from Low German

sober adj **1** not drunk **2** tending to drink only moderate quantities of alcohol **3** serious and thoughtful: *a sober and serious fellow* **4** (of colours) plain and dull **5** free from exaggeration: *a fairly sober version of what happened* ▷ vb **6** (usually foll. by *up*) to make or become less drunk **sobering** adj
WORD ORIGIN Latin *sobrius*

sobriety n the state of being sober

sobriquet or **soubriquet** (so-brik-ay) n a nickname
WORD ORIGIN French *soubriquet*

sob story n a tale of personal misfortune or bad luck intended to arouse sympathy

Ebonics

E bonics (a word formed from a blend of *ebony* and *phonics*) is the name used mainly in the popular media for what linguists would call African-American Vernacular English, that is a variety of English typically spoken by working-class African-Americans. It differs from Standard American English in several ways, including pronunciation, speech patterns, idioms, and vocabulary.

Its origins are probably as old as the first arrivals of native Africans as slaves in the Americas, and it has been suggested that some of its characteristics can be traced to West African linguistic traits. However, the lack of extensive written records before the late 19th century makes accurate etymology all but impossible.

In the 20th century it was widely acknowledged in the United States that a Black vernacular was in existence, with examples becoming known to the mainstream largely through popular music (a trend that has continued): the 'Jazz talk' or 'Jive' that became *hip* for White enthusiasts to indulge in. The term 'Ebonics' was first used in the 1970s, but it only became more widely known over twenty years later. In 1996, the school board of Oakland, a city in the state of California, was the first official body to recognize Ebonics as a legitimate language. In a resolution it stated:

'As in the case of Asian-American, Latino-American, Native American and all other pupils in this District who come from backgrounds or environments where a language other than English is dominant, African-American pupils shall not, because of their race, be subtly dehumanized, stigmatized, discriminated against, or denied.'

The Oakland board propounded the belief that not only should African-American children not be discouraged or pedantically corrected when speaking in Ebonics, but that they should be given access to teaching in the language both for its own value and as an aid to learning standard English. However, widespread recognition of the legitimacy of Ebonics has not inevitably followed. Like many examples of dialect or slang it has been attacked by critics as being nothing more than a substandard, imperfect form of English, propagating the language of the criminal underclass and lending a spurious glamour to an apparent lack of education.

Critics of Ebonics from within the Black community in America have argued that its recognition as a valid language does not mean that it must achieve acceptance in wider society. They would say that with unemployment among African-Americans being disproportionately large in comparison with the wider community, it would further disadvantage job applicants if they insisted on using Ebonics on an application form or in an interview. Modern urban Black people in the professions are unlikely to speak Ebonics in their normal working day, even if they enjoy using it at other times. Indeed, in film and television drama this dichotomy is often exploited to comic effect with middle-class African-Americans lapsing into Ebonics to show that they are still *down* with the *hood* (ie connected with their origins).

As far as pronunciation is concerned, Ebonics reflects a largely Southern influence, no matter where the speakers happen to be, from New York or California. For example, 'for sure' in Ebonics would be *fo sho,* and 'more' becomes *mo.* This is partly due to the post-World War II influx of southern African-Americans to the more industrialized northern and western cities in search of better employment and living opportunities. Also, as the Black communities were usually isolated or even ghettoized, accents and forms of pronunciation were preserved that would otherwise have been diluted naturally in adapting to a new environment.

Typical patterns of speech include the dropping of elements that would be included in standard English, such as in *We working hard* instead of 'We're working hard', or *Who you talking to?* instead of 'Who are you talking to?' This simplifying of tenses is one of the traits of Ebonics that has been stigmatized as 'lazy' English. Another is the metathesis in pronunciation in which, for example, 'ask' becomes *ax.*

Vocabulary and idioms in Ebonics change with the generations, just as with any language, with one era's *hepcat* ('fashionable person') giving way to the hip-hop *playa.* Ebonics is rich in terms of praise, like *def, dope, phat,* or *fly,* but is often attacked for perpetuating misogyny (as in calling any woman a *ho*).

Soc. *or* **soc.** 1 socialist 2 society

soca (**soak**-a) *n* a mixture of soul and calypso music popular in the E Caribbean

so-called *adj* called (in the speaker's opinion, wrongly) by that name: *so-called military experts*

soccer *n* a game in which two teams of eleven players try to kick or head a ball into their opponents' goal, only the goalkeeper on either side being allowed to touch the ball with his hands **WORD ORIGIN** *Assoc(iation Football)*

sociable *adj* 1 friendly and enjoying other people's company 2 (of an occasion) providing the opportunity for relaxed and friendly companionship **sociability** *n* **sociably** *adv*

social *adj* 1 living or preferring to live in a community rather than alone 2 of or relating to human society or organization 3 of the way people live and work together in groups: *social organization* 4 of or for companionship or communal activities: *social clubs* 5 of or engaged in social services: *a social worker* 6 relating to a certain class of society: *social misfits* 7 (of certain species of insects) living together in organized colonies: *social bees* ▷ *n* 8 an informal gathering **socially** *adv* **WORD ORIGIN** Latin *socius* a comrade

Social Charter *n* a proposed declaration of the rights, minimum wages, etc. of workers in the European Union

social climber *n* a person who tries to associate with people from a higher social class in the hope that he or she will be thought also to be upper-class

social contract *or* **compact** *n* an agreement among individuals to cooperate for greater security, which results in the loss of some personal liberties

social democrat *n* 1 a person who is in favour of a market or mixed economy but believes the State must play an active role in ensuring social justice and equality of opportunity 2 (formerly) a person who believed in the gradual transformation of capitalism into democratic socialism **social democracy** *n*

social exclusion *n* *sociol* the failure of society to provide certain people with those rights normally available to its members, such as employment, health care, education, etc.

social fund *n* (in Britain) a social security fund from which loans or payments may be made to people in cases of extreme need

social inclusion *n* *sociol* the provision of certain rights to all people in society, such as employment, health care, education, etc.

social intelligence *n* the ability to form rewarding relationships with other people

socialism *n* a political and economic theory or system in which the means of production, distribution, and exchange are owned by the community collectively, usually through the state **socialist** *n, adj*

socialite *n* a person who goes to many events attended by the rich, famous, and fashionable

socialize *or* **-lise** *vb* **-lizing, -lized** *or* **-lising, -lised** 1 to meet others socially 2 to prepare for life in society 3 *chiefly US* to organize along socialist principles **socialization** *or* **-lisation** *n*

social networking site *n* a website that allows subscribers to interact, esp. by forming online communities based around shared interests, experiences, etc.

social science *n* the systematic study of society and of human relationships within society **social scientist** *n*

social security *n* state provision for the welfare of the elderly, unemployed, or sick, through pensions and other financial aid

social services *pl n* welfare services provided by local authorities or a state agency for people with particular social needs

social studies *n* the study of how people live and organize themselves in society

social welfare *n* 1 social services provided by a state for the benefit of its citizens 2 (in New Zealand) a government department concerned with pensions and benefits for the elderly, the sick, etc.

social work *n* social services that give help and advice to the poor, the elderly, and families with problems **social worker** *n*

society *n, pl* **-ties** 1 human beings considered as a group 2 a group of people forming a single community with its own distinctive culture and institutions 3 the structure, culture, and institutions of such a group 4 an organized group of people sharing a common aim or interest: *a dramatic society* 5 the rich and fashionable class of society collectively 6 *old-fashioned* companionship: *I enjoy her society* **WORD ORIGIN** Latin *societas*

Society of Friends *n* the Quakers

Society of Jesus *n* the religious order of the Jesuits

socioeconomic *adj* of or involving economic and social factors

sociology *n* the study of the development, organization, functioning, and classification of human societies **sociological** *adj* **sociologist** *n*

sociopolitical *adj* of or involving political and social factors

sock¹ *n* 1 a cloth covering for the foot, reaching to between the ankle and knee and worn inside a shoe 2 **pull one's socks up** *informal* to make a determined effort to improve 3 **put a sock in it** *slang* be quiet! **WORD ORIGIN** Greek *sukkhos* a light shoe

sock² *slang vb* 1 to hit hard ▷ *n* 2 a hard blow **WORD ORIGIN** origin unknown

socket *n* 1 a device into which an electric plug can be inserted in order to make a connection in a circuit 2 *anat* a bony hollow into which a part or

structure fits: *the hip socket* **WORD ORIGIN** Anglo-Norman *soket* a little ploughshare

Socratic *adj* of the Greek philosopher Socrates, or his teachings

Socratic method *n* *philosophy* the method of instruction used by Socrates, in which a series of questions and answers lead to a logical conclusion

sod¹ *n* 1 a piece of grass-covered surface soil; turf 2 *poetic* the ground **WORD ORIGIN** Low German

sod² *slang chiefly Brit* *n* 1 an unpleasant person 2 *jocular* a person, esp. an unlucky one: *the poor sod hasn't been out for weeks* 3 **sod all** *slang* nothing ▷ *interj* 4 **sod it** an exclamation of annoyance **sodding** *adj* **WORD ORIGIN** from *sodomite*

soda *n* 1 a simple compound of sodium, such as sodium carbonate or sodium bicarbonate 2 same as **soda water** 3 *US & Canad* a sweet fizzy drink **WORD ORIGIN** perhaps from Arabic

soda bread *n* a type of bread raised with sodium bicarbonate

soda fountain *n* *US & Canad* 1 a counter that serves soft drinks and snacks 2 a device dispensing soda water

soda siphon *n* a sealed bottle containing soda water under pressure, which is forced up a tube when a lever is pressed

soda water *n* a fizzy drink made by charging water with carbon dioxide under pressure

sodden *adj* 1 soaking wet 2 (of someone's senses) dulled, esp. by excessive drinking **WORD ORIGIN** *soden*, obsolete past participle of *seethe*

sodium *n* *chem* a very reactive soft silvery-white metallic element. Symbol: Na **WORD ORIGIN** from SODA

sodium bicarbonate *n* a white soluble crystalline compound used in fizzy drinks, baking powder, and in medicine as an antacid

sodium carbonate *n* a colourless or white soluble crystalline compound used in the manufacture of glass, ceramics, soap, and paper, and as a cleansing agent

sodium chlorate *n* a colourless crystalline compound used as a bleaching agent, antiseptic, and weedkiller

sodium chloride *n* common table salt; a soluble colourless crystalline compound widely used as a seasoning and preservative for food and in the manufacture of chemicals, glass, and soap

sodium hydroxide *n* a white strongly alkaline solid used in the manufacture of rayon, paper, aluminium, and soap

sodomite *n* a person who practises sodomy

sodomy *n* anal intercourse committed by a man with another man or a woman **WORD ORIGIN** after *Sodom*, Biblical city, noted for its depravity

Sod's Law n informal a humorous saying stating that if something can go wrong or turn out inconveniently it will

sofa n a long comfortable seat with back and arms for two or more people
WORD ORIGIN Arabic suffah

soft adj 1 easy to dent, shape, or cut: soft material 2 not hard; giving way easily under pressure: a soft bed 3 fine, smooth, or fluffy to the touch: soft fur 4 (of music or sounds) quiet and pleasing 5 (of light or colour) not excessively bright or harsh 6 (of a breeze or climate) temperate, mild, or pleasant 7 with smooth curves rather than sharp edges: soft focus 8 kind or lenient, often to excess 9 easy to influence or make demands on 10 informal feeble or silly; simple: soft in the head 11 not strong or able to endure hardship 12 (of a drug) nonaddictive 13 informal requiring little effort; easy: a soft job 14 chem (of water) relatively free of mineral salts and therefore easily able to make soap lather 15 loving and tender: soft words 16 phonetics denoting the consonants c and g when they are pronounced sibilantly, as in cent and germ 17 **soft on a** lenient towards: he was accused of being soft on criminals **b** experiencing romantic love for ▷ adv 18 in a soft manner: to speak soft ▷ interj 19 archaic quiet! **softly** adv
WORD ORIGIN Old English sōfte

softball n a game similar to baseball, played using a larger softer ball

soft-boiled adj (of an egg) boiled for a short time so that the yolk is still soft

soft coal n same as **bituminous coal**

soft drink n a nonalcoholic drink

soften vb 1 to make or become soft or softer 2 to make or become more sympathetic and less critical: the farmers softened their opposition to the legislation 3 to lessen the severity or difficulty of: foreign relief softened the hardship of a terrible winter **softener** n

soft furnishings pl n curtains, hangings, rugs, and covers

softhearted adj kind and sympathetic

softie or **softy** n, pl **softies** informal a person who is easily hurt or upset

soft option n the easiest of a number of choices

soft palate n the fleshy part at the back of the roof of the mouth

soft-pedal vb **-dalling, -dalled** or US **-daling, -daled** 1 to deliberately avoid emphasizing (something): he was soft-pedalling the question of tax increases ▷ n **soft pedal** 2 a pedal on a piano that softens the tone

soft sell n a method of selling based on subtle suggestion and gentle persuasion

soft-soap vb informal to flatter (a person)

soft-spoken adj speaking or said with a soft gentle voice

soft touch n informal a person who is easily persuaded to perform favours for, or lend money to, other people

software n computers the programs used with a computer

softwood n the wood of coniferous trees

soggy adj **-gier, -giest** 1 soaked with liquid: a soggy running track 2 moist and heavy: a soggy sandwich **sogginess** n
WORD ORIGIN probably from dialect sog marsh

soh n music the fifth note of any ascending major scale

soigné or fem **soignée** (swah-nyay) adj neat, elegant, and well-dressed: the soignée deputy editor of Vogue
WORD ORIGIN French

soil¹ n 1 the top layer of the land surface of the earth 2 a specific type of this material: sandy soil 3 land, country, or region: the first US side to lose on home soil
WORD ORIGIN Latin solium a seat, confused with solum the ground

soil² vb 1 to make or become dirty or stained 2 to bring disgrace upon: he's soiled our reputation ▷ n 3 a soiled spot 4 refuse, manure, or excrement
WORD ORIGIN Old French soillier

soiree (swah-ray) n an evening social gathering
WORD ORIGIN French

sojourn (soj-urn) literary n 1 a short stay in a place ▷ vb 2 to stay temporarily: he sojourned in Basle during a short illness
WORD ORIGIN Old French sojorner

sol¹ n music same as **soh**

sol² n chem a liquid colloidal solution

solace (sol-iss) n 1 comfort in misery or disappointment: it drove him to seek increasing solace in alcohol 2 something that gives comfort or consolation: his music was a solace to me during my illness ▷ vb **-lacing, -laced** 3 to give comfort or cheer to (a person) in time of sorrow or distress
WORD ORIGIN Old French solas

solar adj 1 of the sun: a solar eclipse 2 operating by or using the energy of the sun: solar cell
WORD ORIGIN Latin sol the sun

solarium n, pl **-lariums** or **-laria** a place with beds equipped with ultraviolet lights used for giving people an artificial suntan
WORD ORIGIN Latin: a terrace

solar plexus n 1 anat a network of nerves behind the stomach 2 not in technical use the vulnerable part of the stomach beneath the diaphragm

solar system n the system containing the sun and the planets, comets, and asteroids that go round it

sold vb 1 the past of **sell** ▷ adj 2 **sold on** slang enthusiastic and uncritical about

solder n 1 an alloy used for joining two metal surfaces by melting the alloy so that it forms a thin layer between the surfaces ▷ vb 2 to join or mend or be joined or mended with solder
WORD ORIGIN Latin solidare to strengthen

soldering iron n a hand tool with a copper tip that is heated and used to melt and apply solder

soldier n 1 **a** a person who serves or has served in an army **b** a person who is not an officer in an army ▷ vb 2 to serve as a soldier **soldierly** adj
WORD ORIGIN Old French soudier

soldier of fortune n a man who seeks money or adventure as a soldier; mercenary

soldier on vb to continue one's efforts despite difficulties or pressure

sole¹ adj 1 being the only one; only 2 not shared; exclusive: sole ownership
WORD ORIGIN Latin solus alone

sole² n 1 the underside of the foot 2 the underside of a shoe 3 the lower surface of an object ▷ vb **soling, soled** 4 to provide (a shoe) with a sole
WORD ORIGIN Latin solea sandal

sole³ n, pl **sole** or **soles** an edible marine flatfish
WORD ORIGIN Latin solea a sandal (from the fish's shape)

sole charge school n NZ a country school with only one teacher

solecism (sol-iss-iz-zum) n formal 1 a minor grammatical mistake in speech or writing 2 an action considered not to be good manners **solecistic** adj
WORD ORIGIN Greek soloikos speaking incorrectly

solely adv 1 only; completely: an action intended solely to line his own pockets 2 without others

solemn adj 1 very serious; deeply sincere: my solemn promise 2 marked by ceremony or formality: a solemn ritual 3 serious or glum: a solemn look on her face **solemnly** adv
WORD ORIGIN Latin sollemnis appointed

solemnity n, pl **-ties** 1 the state or quality of being solemn 2 a solemn ceremony or ritual

solemnize or **-nise** vb **-nizing, -nized** or **-nising, -nised** 1 to celebrate or perform (a ceremony, esp. of marriage) 2 to make solemn or serious **solemnization** or **-nisation** n

solenoid (sole-in-oid) n a coil of wire, usually cylindrical, in which a magnetic field is set up by passing a current through it **solenoidal** adj
WORD ORIGIN French solénoïde

sol-fa n short for **tonic sol-fa**

solicit vb 1 formal to seek or request, esp. formally: she was brushed aside when soliciting his support for the vote 2 to approach a person with an offer of sex in return for money **solicitation** n
WORD ORIGIN Latin sollicitare to harass

solicitor n Brit, Austral, & NZ a lawyer who advises clients on matters of law, draws up legal documents, and prepares cases for barristers

Solicitor General n, pl **Solicitors General** (in Britain) the law officer of the Crown ranking next to the Attorney General (in Scotland to the Lord Advocate) and acting as his assistant

solicitous adj formal 1 anxious about someone's welfare 2 eager **solicitousness** n
WORD ORIGIN Latin sollicitus anxious

solicitude n formal anxiety or concern for someone's welfare

solid adj 1 (of a substance) in a physical state in which it resists changes in size and shape; not liquid or gaseous 2 consisting of matter all through; not hollow 3 of the same substance all through: solid gold 4 firm, strong, or substantial: the solid door of a farmhouse

S

5 proved or provable: *solid evidence* **6** law-abiding and respectable: *solid family men* **7** (of a meal or food) substantial **8** without interruption; continuous or unbroken: *solid bombardment* **9** financially sound: *a solid institution* **10** strongly united or established: *a solid marriage* **11** *geom* having or relating to three dimensions **12** adequate; sound, but not brilliant: *a solid career* **13** of a single uniform colour or tone ▷ *n* **14** *geom* a three-dimensional shape **15** a solid substance **solidity** *n* **solidly** *adv*
WORD ORIGIN Latin *solidus* firm

solidarity *n, pl* **-ties** agreement in interests or aims among members of a group; total unity

solid geometry *n* the branch of geometry concerned with three-dimensional figures

solidify *vb* **-fies, -fying, -fied 1** to make or become solid or hard **2** to make or become strong or unlikely to change: *a move that solidified the allegiance of our followers* **solidification** *n*

solid-state *adj* (of an electronic device) using a semiconductor component, such as a transistor or silicon chip, in which current flow is through solid material, rather than a valve or mechanical part, in which current flow is through a vacuum

solidus *n, pl* **-di** a short oblique stroke used in text to separate items, such as *and/or*

soliloquize or **-quise** *vb* **-quizing, -quized** or **-quising, -quised** to say a soliloquy

soliloquy *n, pl* **-quies** a speech made by a person while alone, esp. in a play
WORD ORIGIN Latin *solus* sole + *loqui* to speak

≡ USAGE
≡ *Soliloquy* is sometimes wrongly used ≡ where *monologue* is meant. Both words ≡ refer to a long speech by one person, ≡ but a *monologue* can be addressed to ≡ other people, whereas in a *soliloquy* the ≡ speaker is always talking to himself ≡ or herself.

solipsism *n philosophy* the doctrine that the self is the only thing known to exist **solipsist** *n*
WORD ORIGIN Latin *solus* alone + *ipse* self

solitaire *n* **1** a game played by one person, involving moving and taking pegs in a pegboard with the object of being left with only one **2** a gem, esp. a diamond, set alone in a ring **3** *chiefly US* patience (the card game)
WORD ORIGIN French

solitary *adj* **1** experienced or performed alone: *a solitary dinner* **2** living a life of solitude: *a solitary child* **3** single; alone: *the solitary cigarette in the ashtray* **4** having few friends; lonely **5** (of a place) without people; empty ▷ *n, pl* **-taries 6** a person who lives on his or her own; hermit **7** *informal* short for **solitary confinement**: *I can't put him back in solitary* **solitariness** *n*
WORD ORIGIN Latin *solitarius*

solitary confinement *n* isolation of a prisoner in a special cell

solitude *n* the state of being alone

solo *n, pl* **-los 1** a piece of music or section of music for one performer: *a trumpet solo* **2** any performance by an individual without assistance ▷ *adj* **3** performed by an individual without assistance: *a solo dance* **4** Also: **solo whist** a card game in which each person plays on his or her own ▷ *adv* **5** by oneself; alone: *to fly solo across the Atlantic* **soloist** *n*
WORD ORIGIN Latin *solus* alone

Solomon *n* any person considered to be very wise
WORD ORIGIN after 10th-century BC king of Israel

Solomon's seal *n* a plant with greenish flowers and long waxy leaves

so long *interj* **1** *informal* farewell; goodbye ▷ *adv* **2** *S African slang* for the time being; meanwhile

solo parent *n NZ* a parent bringing up a child or children alone

solstice *n* either the shortest day of the year (**winter solstice**) or the longest day of the year (**summer solstice**)
WORD ORIGIN Latin *solstitium* the standing still of the sun

soluble *adj* **1** (of a substance) capable of being dissolved **2** (of a mystery or problem) capable of being solved **solubility** *n*

solute *n chem* the substance in a solution that is dissolved
WORD ORIGIN Latin *solutus* free

solution *n* **1** a specific answer to or way of answering a problem **2** the act or process of solving a problem **3** *chem* a mixture of two or more substances in which the molecules or atoms of the substances are completely dispersed **4** the act or process of forming a solution **5** the state of being dissolved: *the sugar is held in solution*
WORD ORIGIN Latin *solutio* an unloosing

solve *vb* **solving, solved** to find the explanation for or solution to (a mystery or problem) **solvable** *adj*
WORD ORIGIN Latin *solvere* to loosen

solvent *adj* **1** having enough money to pay off one's debts **2** (of a liquid) capable of dissolving other substances ▷ *n* **3** a liquid capable of dissolving other substances **solvency** *n*
WORD ORIGIN Latin *solvens* releasing

solvent abuse *n* the deliberate inhaling of intoxicating fumes from certain solvents

somatic *adj* of or relating to the body as distinct from the mind: *somatic symptoms*
WORD ORIGIN Greek *sōma* the body

sombre or *US* **somber** *adj* **1** serious, sad, or gloomy: *a sombre message* **2** (of a place) dim or gloomy **3** (of colour or clothes) dull or dark **sombrely** or *US* **somberly** *adv*
WORD ORIGIN Latin *sub* beneath + *umbra* shade

sombrero *n, pl* **-ros** a wide-brimmed Mexican hat
WORD ORIGIN Spanish

some *adj* **1** unknown or unspecified: *some man called for you* **2** an unknown or unspecified quantity or number of: *I've got some money* **3 a** a considerable number or amount of: *he lived some years afterwards* **b** a little: *show some respect*

4 *informal* an impressive or remarkable: *that was some game!* ▷ *pron* **5** certain unknown or unspecified people or things: *some can teach and others can't* **6** an unknown or unspecified quantity of something or number of people or things: *he will sell some in his pub* ▷ *adv* **7** approximately: *some thirty pounds*
WORD ORIGIN Old English *sum*

somebody *pron* **1** some person; someone ▷ *n, pl* **-bodies 2** a person of great importance: *he was a somebody*
≡ USAGE
≡ See at **everyone**.

someday *adv* at some unspecified time in the future

somehow *adv* **1** in some unspecified way **2** for some unknown reason: *somehow I can't do it*

someone *pron* some person; somebody
≡ USAGE
≡ See at **everyone**.

someplace *adv US & Canad informal* same as **somewhere**

somersault *n* **1** a leap or roll in which the head is placed on the ground and the trunk and legs are turned over it ▷ *vb* **2** to perform a somersault
WORD ORIGIN Old French *soubresault*

something *pron* **1** an unspecified or unknown thing; some thing: *there was something wrong* **2** an unspecified or unknown amount: *something less than a hundred* **3** an impressive or important person, thing, or event: *isn't that something?* **4 something else** *slang chiefly US* a remarkable person or thing ▷ *adv* **5** to some degree; somewhat: *he looks something like me*

-something *n combining form* a person whose age can approximately expressed by a specific decade: *twentysomethings*
WORD ORIGIN from the US television series *thirtysomething*

sometime *adv* **1** at some unspecified point of time ▷ *adj* **2** former: *a sometime actress*
≡ USAGE
≡ The form *sometime* should not be used ≡ to refer to a fairly long period of time: ≡ *he has been away for some time* (not *for* ≡ *sometime*).

sometimes *adv* now and then; from time to time

someway *adv* in some unspecified manner

somewhat *adv* rather; a bit: *somewhat surprising*

somewhere *adv* **1** in, to, or at some unknown or unspecified place, point, or amount: *somewhere down south; somewhere between 35 and 45 per cent* **2 getting somewhere** *informal* making progress

somnambulism *n formal* the condition of walking in one's sleep **somnambulist** *n*
WORD ORIGIN Latin *somnus* sleep + *ambulare* to walk

somnolent *adj formal* drowsy; sleepy **somnolence** *n*
WORD ORIGIN Latin *somnus* sleep

son *n* **1** a male offspring **2** a form of address for a man or boy who is younger than the speaker **3** a male who comes from a certain place or one closely

Romance

Looking for romance? What is romance anyway? Latin lovers? Perhaps the Romance languages really are the languages of Love: maybe the Portuguese, Spanish, Italians, Romanians, Catalans, and French are all doomed to express themselves in exaggerated Mills and Boon style, their hands on their hearts and a rose in their teeth. All those languages are what Latin mutated into as the Romans lost their political grip on the world. Latin was still the language of the learned, but the everyday language, called Romance, was what people used to buy and sell things, sing songs, and tell stories in. In French, a *roman* is a novel; in Spanish a *romance* is a ballad.

Romantic love itself goes back a long way, much further than its name. Poets in ancient times expressed their feelings for their girlfriends and lovers in verse, and sculptors expressed other people's love in carefully worked portraits in stone or marble, like those of the emperor Hadrian's wife Sabrina, or his tragically drowned boyfriend Antinous. The Roman poet Ovid, who lived two thousand years ago, wrote a story about a man who was desperate to find a soulmate, but was so fed up with the dissolute women around him that he sculpted a hyper-realistic statue, which he groped longingly. Here's a translation of this passage:

He pays her compliments, and brings her
presents that all girls like: shells and polished
pebbles, little birds, pretty flowers and jewels.
He dresses her up and puts rings on her fingers.
He gives her a long necklace and pearl earrings,
and a bra. It all suits her, but she still looks
better in the nude. He arranges the statue
carefully on a bed with purple bedclothes, and
calls her 'my love', and rests her neck on a
feather pillow, as if she could feel the softness.

What happens next, of course, is that she comes to life, and the two of them live happily ever after. You might say they were made for each other, but actually only one of them was. Notice how well Ovid knew his subject: if a man wants to woo a girl romantically, then he'd better flatter her profusely and give her expensive presents, preferably designer jewellery. The underwear may be out of place in the early stages of this process.

This story has been retold many times, in *Pygmalion* by George Bernard Shaw, which became *My Fair Lady*, and *Educating Rita*, with Julie Walters as the mouldable innocent and Michael Caine as her sculptor. The romantic element starts with a creator falling in love with their creation, and ends with the creation achieving some independence and loving the creator back – or in more modern versions, going off with somebody else, which is the antithesis of romance. Romance is in the realm of fantasy, a rejection of the humdrum messiness of real life.

In the nineteenth century, people started creating paintings, poems, and music that were described as 'romantic'. But since 'romance' has existed from time immemorial, what changed? Romantic art seems to be about stressing the feelings, speaking straight to the heart without bothering about the head. In this sense, it's entirely in tune with romance as expressed by the ancients. Shelley's poem *Ozymandias*, Caspar Friedrich with his brooding landscapes, and the stirring strains of Mendelssohn and Brahms are all heavily laden with feeling. What seems to have gone by the board is humour. There's plenty of feeling going on in classical painting and poetry, but it's not quite so grand and self-important.

The pendulum has now swung back, and we live in a more ironic world, post-modern and in most ways post-romantic. Romance is mainly the province of Hollywood and chick lit. Nevertheless, people still read horoscopes in the hopes of finding a heartthrob, someone to set their pulse racing, someone who will be their perfect partner. In teenagers especially, romance colours their expectations and leads them to do things they will later regret. But how dull the world would be without romance, however fictitious it may be!

connected with a certain thing: *a good son of the church* ▸ Related adjective: **filial**
WORD ORIGIN Old English *sunu*

Son *n Christianity* the second member of the Trinity, Jesus Christ

sonar *n* a device that locates objects by the reflection of sound waves: used in underwater navigation and target detection
WORD ORIGIN *so(und) na(vigation and) r(anging)*

sonata *n* a piece of classical music, usually in three or more movements, for piano or for another instrument with or without piano
WORD ORIGIN Italian

son et lumière (**sonn** ay loom-yair) *n* an entertainment staged at night at a famous building or historical site, at which its history is described by a speaker accompanied by lighting effects and music
WORD ORIGIN French, literally: sound and light

song *n* **1** a piece of music with words, composed for the voice **2** the tuneful call made by certain birds or insects **3** the act or process of singing: *he broke into song* **4** **for a song** at a bargain price **5** **make a song and dance** *informal* to make an unnecessary fuss
WORD ORIGIN Old English *sang*

songbird *n* any bird that has a musical call

songololo (song-gol-**loll**-o) *n, pl* -**los** *S African* a kind of millipede
WORD ORIGIN Nguni (language group of southern Africa) *ukusonga* to roll up

songstress *n* a female singer of popular songs

song thrush *n* a common thrush that repeats each note of its song

sonic *adj* of, involving, or producing sound
WORD ORIGIN Latin *sonus* sound

sonic barrier *n* same as **sound barrier**

sonic boom *n* a loud explosive sound caused by the shock wave of an aircraft travelling at supersonic speed

son-in-law *n, pl* **sons-in-law** the husband of one's daughter

sonnet *n prosody* a verse form consisting of 14 lines with a fixed rhyme scheme and rhythm pattern
WORD ORIGIN Old Provençal *sonet* a little poem

sonny *n* a familiar, often patronizing, term of address to a boy or man

sonorous *adj* **1** (of a sound) deep or rich **2** (of speech) using language that is unnecessarily complicated and difficult to understand; pompous **sonority** *n*
WORD ORIGIN Latin *sonor* a noise

soon *adv* **1** in or after a short time; before long **2** **as soon as** at the very moment that: *as soon as he had closed the door* **3** **as soon ... as** used to indicate that the first alternative is slightly preferable to the second: *they'd just as soon die for him as live*
WORD ORIGIN Old English *sōna*

sooner *adv* **1** the comparative of **soon**: *I only wish I'd been back sooner* **2** rather; in preference: *he would sooner leave the party than break with me* **3** **no sooner ... than** immediately after or when: *no sooner had*

he spoken than the stench drifted up **4** **sooner or later** eventually

≣ **USAGE**
≣ When is sometimes used instead of
≣ *than* after *no sooner*, but this use is
≣ generally regarded as incorrect: *no*
≣ *sooner had he arrived than* (not *when*) *the*
≣ *telephone rang.*

soot *n* a black powder formed by the incomplete burning of organic substances such as coal **sooty** *adj*
WORD ORIGIN Old English *sōt*

sooth *n* **in sooth** *archaic or poetic* in truth
WORD ORIGIN Old English *sōth*

soothe *vb* **soothing, soothed 1** to make (a worried or angry person) calm and relaxed **2** (of an ointment or cream) to relieve (pain) **soothing** *adj*
WORD ORIGIN Old English *sōthian* to prove

soothsayer *n* a person who makes predictions about the future; prophet

sop *n* **1** a small bribe or concession given or made to someone to keep them from causing trouble: *a sop to her conscience* **2** *informal* a stupid or weak person **3** **sops** food soaked in a liquid before being eaten ▸ *vb* **sopping, sopped 4** **sop up** to soak up or absorb (liquid)
WORD ORIGIN Old English *sopp*

sophism *n* an argument that seems reasonable but is actually false and misleading
WORD ORIGIN Greek *sophisma* ingenious trick

sophist *n* a person who uses clever but false arguments **sophistic** *adj*
WORD ORIGIN Greek *sophistēs* a wise man

sophisticate *vb* **-cating, -cated 1** to make (someone) less natural or innocent, such as by education **2** to make (a machine or method) more complex or refined ▸ *n* **3** a sophisticated person **sophistication** *n*
WORD ORIGIN Latin *sophisticus* sophistic

sophisticated *adj* **1** having or appealing to fashionable and refined tastes and habits: *a sophisticated restaurant* **2** intelligent, knowledgeable, or able to appreciate culture and the arts: *a sophisticated concert audience* **3** (of machines or methods) complex and using advanced technology

sophistry *n* **1** the practice of using arguments which seem clever but are actually false and misleading **2** *pl* **-ries** an instance of this

sophomore *n chiefly US & Canad* a second-year student at a secondary (high) school or college
WORD ORIGIN probably from earlier *sophum*, variant of *sophism*

soporific *adj* **1** causing sleep ▸ *n* **2** a drug that causes sleep
WORD ORIGIN Latin *sopor* sleep

sopping *adj* completely soaked; wet through. Also: **sopping wet**

soppy *adj* **-pier, -piest** *informal* foolishly sentimental: *a soppy love song* **soppily** *adv*

soprano *n, pl* **-pranos 1** the highest adult female voice **2** the voice of a young boy before puberty **3** a singer with such a voice **4** the highest or second highest instrument in a family of instruments ▸ *adj* **5** denoting a

musical instrument that is the highest or second highest pitched in its family: *the soprano saxophone* **6** of or relating to the highest female voice, or the voice of a young boy: *the part is quite possibly the most demanding soprano role Wagner ever wrote*
WORD ORIGIN Italian

sorbet (**saw**-bay) *n* a flavoured water ice
WORD ORIGIN French, from Arabic *sharbah* a drink

sorcerer *or fem* **sorceress** *n* a person who uses magic powers; a wizard
WORD ORIGIN Old French *sorcier*

sorcery *n, pl* **-ceries** witchcraft or magic
WORD ORIGIN Old French *sorcerie*

sordid *adj* **1** dirty, depressing, and squalid: *a sordid backstreet in a slum area* **2** relating to sex in a crude or unpleasant way: *the sordid details of his affair* **3** involving immoral and selfish behaviour: *the sordid history of the slave trade*
WORD ORIGIN Latin *sordidus*

sore *adj* **1** (of a wound, injury, etc.) painfully sensitive; tender **2** causing annoyance and resentment: *a sore point* **3** upset and angered: *she's still sore about last night* **4** *literary* urgent; pressing: *in sore need of firm government* ▸ *n* **5** a painful or sensitive wound or injury ▸ *adv* **6** **sore afraid** *archaic* greatly frightened
WORD ORIGIN Old English *sār*

sorely *adv* greatly: *sorely disappointed*

sorghum *n* a grass grown for grain and as a source of syrup
WORD ORIGIN Italian *sorgo*

sorority *n, pl* **-ties** *chiefly US* a society of female students
WORD ORIGIN Latin *soror* sister

sorrel *n* a plant with bitter-tasting leaves which are used in salads and sauces
WORD ORIGIN Old French *surele*

sorrow *n* **1** deep sadness or regret, associated with death or sympathy for another's misfortune **2** a particular cause of this ▸ *vb* **3** *literary* to feel deep sadness (about death or another's misfortunes); mourn **sorrowful** *adj* **sorrowfully** *adv*
WORD ORIGIN Old English *sorg*

sorry *adj* **-rier, -riest 1** (often foll. by *for* or *about*) feeling or expressing pity, sympathy, grief, or regret: *I'm sorry about this* **2** in bad mental or physical condition: *a sorry state* **3** poor: *a sorry performance* ▸ *interj* **4** an exclamation expressing apology or asking someone to repeat what he or she has said
WORD ORIGIN Old English *sārig*

sort *n* **1** a class, group, or kind sharing certain characteristics or qualities **2** *informal* a type of character: *she was a good sort* **3** a more or less adequate example: *a sort of dream machine* **4** **of sorts** *or* **of a sort a** of a poorer quality: *she was wearing a uniform of sorts* **b** of a kind not quite as intended or desired: *it was a reward, of sorts, for my efforts* **5** **out of sorts** not in normal good health or temper **6** **sort of** as it were; rather: *I sort of quit; sort of insensitive* ▸ *vb* **7** to arrange (things or people) according to class or type **8** to put (something) into working order; fix **9** to arrange (computer information) by machine in an order

the user finds convenient
WORD ORIGIN Latin *sors* fate
≡ **USAGE**
≡ See at **kind²**.

sort code *n* a sequence of numbers printed on a cheque or bank card identifying the branch holding the account

sortie *n* **1** a short or relatively short return trip **2** (of troops) a raid into enemy territory **3** an operational flight made by a military aircraft ▷ *vb* **-tieing, -tied 4** to make a sortie
WORD ORIGIN French

sort out *vb* **1** to find a solution to (a problem): *did they sort out the mess?* **2** to take or separate (things or people) from a larger group: *to sort out the wheat from the chaff* **3** to organize (things or people) into an orderly and disciplined group **4 sort someone out** to deal with a person, especially an awkward one **5** *informal* to punish or tell off (someone)

SOS *n* **1** an international code signal of distress in which the letters SOS are repeatedly spelt out in Morse code **2** *informal* any call for help

so-so *adj* **1** neither good nor bad ▷ *adv* **2** in an average or indifferent way

sot *n* a person who is frequently drunk **sottish** *adj*
WORD ORIGIN Old English *sott*

sotto voce (sot-toe **voe**-chay) *adv* with a soft voice
WORD ORIGIN Italian

sou *n* **1** a former French coin of low value **2** *old-fashioned* a very small amount of money: *the tax man never saw a sou from this income*
WORD ORIGIN French

soubrette (soo-**brett**) *n* a minor female role in comedy, often that of a pert maid
WORD ORIGIN French

soubriquet *n* same as **sobriquet**

soufflé (soo-**flay**) *n* a light fluffy dish made with beaten egg whites and other ingredients such as cheese or chocolate
WORD ORIGIN French

sough (rhymes with **now**) *vb* *literary* (of the wind) to make a sighing sound
WORD ORIGIN Old English *swōgan*

sought (sawt) *vb* the past of **seek**

souk (sook) *n* an open-air marketplace in Muslim countries
WORD ORIGIN Arabic *sūq*

soul *n* **1** the spiritual part of a person, regarded as the centre of personality, intellect, will, and emotions: believed by many to survive the body after death **2** the essential part or fundamental nature of anything: *the soul of contemporary America* **3** deep and sincere feelings: *you've got no soul* **4** Also called: **soul music** a type of Black music using blues and elements of jazz, gospel, and pop **5** a person regarded as a good example of some quality: *the soul of prudence* **6** a person: *there was hardly a soul there* **7 the life and soul** *informal* a person who is lively, entertaining, and fun to be with: *the life and soul of the campus*
WORD ORIGIN Old English *sāwol*

soul-destroying *adj* (of an occupation or situation) very boring and repetitive

soul food *n* *informal* food, such as chitterlings and yams, which is traditionally eaten by African-Americans

soulful *adj* expressing deep feelings: *a soulful performance of one of Tchaikovsky's songs*

soulless *adj* **1** lacking human qualities; mechanical: *soulless materialism* **2** (of a person) lacking in sensitivity or emotion

soul mate *n* a person with whom one gets along well because of having shared interests and experiences

soul-searching *n* deep examination of one's actions and feelings

sound¹ *n* **1** anything that can be heard; noise **2** *physics* mechanical vibrations that travel in waves through the air, water, etc. **3** the sensation produced by such vibrations in the organs of hearing **4** the impression one has of something: *I didn't really like the sound of it* **5 sounds** *slang* music, esp. rock, jazz, or pop ▷ *vb* **6** to make or cause (an instrument, etc.) to make a sound **7** to announce (something) by a sound: *guns sound the end of the two minutes silence* **8** to make a noise with a certain quality: *her voice sounded shrill* **9** to suggest (a particular idea or quality): *his argument sounded false* **10** to pronounce (something) clearly: *to sound one's r's* ▶ See also **sound off**
WORD ORIGIN Latin *sonus*

sound² *adj* **1** free from damage, injury, or decay; in good condition **2** firm or substantial: *sound documentary evidence* **3** financially safe or stable: *a sound investment* **4** showing good judgment or reasoning; wise: *sound advice* **5** morally correct; honest **6** (of sleep) deep and uninterrupted **7** thorough: *a sound defeat* ▷ *adv* **8 sound asleep** in a deep sleep **soundly** *adv*
WORD ORIGIN Old English *sund*

sound³ *vb* **1** to measure the depth of (a well, the sea, etc.) **2** *med* to examine (a part of the body) by tapping or with a stethoscope ▶ See also **sound out**
WORD ORIGIN Old French *sonder*

sound⁴ *n* a channel between two larger areas of sea or between an island and the mainland
WORD ORIGIN Old English *sund*

soundalike *n* a person or thing that sounds like another, often well-known, person or thing

sound barrier *n* a sudden increase in the force of air against an aircraft flying at or above the speed of sound

sound bite *n* a short pithy sentence or phrase extracted from a longer speech for use on television or radio: *complicated political messages cannot be properly reduced to fifteen-second sound bites*

soundcard *n* a printed circuit board inserted into a computer, enabling the output and manipulation of sound

sound effects *pl n* sounds artificially produced to make a play, esp. a radio play, more realistic

sounding board *n* a person or group used to test a new idea or policy

soundings *pl n* **1** measurements of the depth of a river, lake, or sea **2** questions asked of someone in order to find out

his or her opinion: *soundings among colleagues had revealed enthusiasm for the plan*

sound off *vb* to speak angrily or loudly

sound out *vb* to question (someone) in order to discover his or her opinion: *you might try sounding him out about his family*

soundproof *adj* **1** (of a room) built so that no sound can get in or out ▷ *vb* **2** to make (a room) soundproof

soundtrack *n* the recorded sound accompaniment to a film

sound wave *n* a wave that carries sound

soup *n* **1** a food made by cooking meat, fish, or vegetables in a stock **2 in the soup** *slang* in trouble or difficulties **soupy** *adj*
WORD ORIGIN Old French *soupe*

soupçon (**soop**-sonn) *n* a slight amount; dash
WORD ORIGIN French

souped-up *adj* *slang* (of a car, motorbike, or engine) adjusted so as to be faster or more powerful than normal

soup kitchen *n* a place where food and drink are served to needy people

sour *adj* **1** having a sharp biting taste like the taste of lemon juice or vinegar **2** made acid or bad, such as when milk ferments **3** (of a person's mood) bad-tempered and unfriendly **4 go** or **turn sour** to become less enjoyable or happy: *the dream has turned sour* ▷ *vb* **5** to make or become less enjoyable or friendly: *relations soured shortly after the war* **sourly** *adv*
WORD ORIGIN Old English *sūr*

source *n* **1** the origin or starting point: *the source of discontent among fishermen* **2** any person, book, or organization that provides information for a news report or for research **3** the area or spring where a river or stream begins ▷ *vb* **4** to establish a supplier of (a product, etc.) **5** (foll. by *from*) to originate from
WORD ORIGIN Latin *surgere* to rise

source code *n* *computers* the original form of a computer program before it is converted into a machine-readable code

sour cream *n* cream soured by bacteria for use in cooking

sour grapes *n* the attitude of pretending to hate something because one cannot have it oneself

sourpuss *n* *informal* a person who is always gloomy, pessimistic, or bitter

souse *vb* **sousing, soused 1** to plunge (something) into water or other liquid **2** to drench **3** to steep or cook (food) in a marinade ▷ *n* **4** the liquid used in pickling **5** the act or process of sousing
WORD ORIGIN Old French *sous*

soused *adj* *slang* drunk

soutane (soo-**tan**) *n* *RC Church* a priest's robe
WORD ORIGIN French

south *n* **1** one of the four cardinal points of the compass, at 180° from north **2** the direction along a line of latitude towards the South Pole **3 the south** any area lying in or towards the south ▷ *adj* **4** situated in, moving towards, or facing the south **5** (esp. of the wind) from the south ▷ *adv* **6** in, to, or towards the south

WORD ORIGIN Old English *sūth*

South *n* **1 the South a** the southern part of England **b** (in the US) the Southern states that formed the Confederacy during the Civil War **c** the countries of the world that are not technically and economically advanced ▷ *adj* **2** of or denoting the southern part of a country, area, etc.

South African *adj* **1** of the Republic of South Africa ▷ *n* **2** a person from the Republic of South Africa

southbound *adj* going towards the south

southeast *n* **1** the direction midway between south and east **2 the southeast** any area lying in or towards the southeast ▷ *adj also* **southeastern 3** of or denoting that part of a country or area which lies in the southeast **4** situated in, moving towards, or facing the southeast **5** (esp. of the wind) from the southeast ▷ *adv* **6** in, to, or towards the southeast **southeasterly** *adj, adv, n*

Southeast *n* the southeast of Britain, esp. the London area

southeaster *n* a strong wind or storm from the southeast

southerly *adj* **1** of or in the south ▷ *adv, adj* **2** towards the south **3** from the south: *light southerly winds*

southern *adj* **1** situated in or towards the south **2** facing or moving towards the south **3** (*sometimes cap*) of or characteristic of the south or South **southernmost** *adj*

Southerner *n* a person from the south of a country or area, esp. England or the US

southern hemisphere *n* that half of the globe lying south of the equator

southern lights *pl n* same as **aurora australis**

southpaw *informal n* **1** any left-handed person, esp. a boxer ▷ *adj* **2** left-handed

South Pole *n* the southernmost point on the earth's axis, at a latitude of 90°S, which has very low temperatures

South Seas *pl n* the seas south of the equator

southward *adj, adv also* **southwards 1** towards the south ▷ *n* **2** the southward part or direction

southwest *n* **1** the direction midway between west and south **2 the southwest** any area lying in or towards the southwest ▷ *adj also* **southwestern 3** of or denoting that part of a country or area which lies in the southwest **4** situated in, moving towards, or facing the southwest **5** (esp. of the wind) from the southwest ▷ *adv* **6** in, to, or towards the southwest **southwesterly** *adj, adv, n*

Southwest *n* the southwestern part of Britain, esp. Cornwall, Devon, and Somerset

southwester *n* a strong wind or storm from the southwest

souvenir *n* an object that reminds one of a certain place, occasion, or person; memento
WORD ORIGIN French

sou'wester *n* **1** a seaman's hat with a broad brim that covers the back of the neck **2** same as **southwester**
WORD ORIGIN a contraction of SOUTHWESTER

sovereign *n* **1** the Royal ruler of a country **2** a former British gold coin worth one pound sterling ▷ *adj* **3** independent of outside authority; not governed by another country: *a sovereign nation* **4** supreme in rank or authority: *a sovereign queen* **5** *old-fashioned* excellent or outstanding: *a sovereign remedy for epilepsy*
WORD ORIGIN Old French *sovrain*

sovereignty *n, pl* **-ties 1** the political power a nation has to govern itself **2** the position or authority of a sovereign

soviet *n* (in the former Soviet Union) an elected government council at the local, regional, and national levels
WORD ORIGIN Russian *sovyet*

Soviet *adj* **1** of the former Soviet Union ▷ *n* **2** a person from the former Soviet Union

sow¹ *vb* **sowing, sowed; sown** *or* **sowed 1** to scatter or plant (seed) in or on (the ground) so that it may grow: *sow sweet peas in pots; farmers sow their fields with fewer varieties* **2** to implant or introduce: *to sow confusion among the other members*
WORD ORIGIN Old English *sāwan*

sow² *n* a female adult pig
WORD ORIGIN Old English *sugu*

soya bean *or US & Canad* **soybean** *n* a plant whose bean is used for food and as a source of oil
WORD ORIGIN Japanese *shōyu*

soy sauce *n* a salty dark brown sauce made from fermented soya beans, used in Chinese cookery

sozzled *adj Brit, Austral, & NZ informal* drunk
WORD ORIGIN origin unknown

spa *n* a mineral-water spring or a resort where such a spring is found
WORD ORIGIN after *Spa*, a watering place in Belgium

space *n* **1** the unlimited three-dimensional expanse in which all objects exist **2** an interval of distance or time between two points, objects, or events **3** a blank portion or area **4** unoccupied area or room: *barely enough space to walk around* **5** the region beyond the earth's atmosphere containing other planets, stars, and galaxies; the universe ▷ *vb* **spacing, spaced 6** (often foll. by *out*) to place or arrange (things) at intervals or with spaces between them
WORD ORIGIN Latin *spatium*

space age *n* **1** the period in which the exploration of space has become possible ▷ *adj* **space-age 2** very modern, futuristic, or using the latest technology: *a space-age helmet*

space-bar *n* a bar on a typewriter that is pressed in order to leave a space between words or letters

space capsule *n* the part of a spacecraft in which the crew live and work

spacecraft *n* a vehicle that can be used for travel in space

spaced-out *adj informal* vague and dreamy, as if influenced by drugs

Space Invaders *n trademark* a video game in which players try to defend themselves against attacking enemy spacecraft

spaceman *or fem* **spacewoman** *n, pl* **-men** *or fem* **-women** a person who travels in space

space probe *n* a small vehicle equipped to gather scientific information, normally transmitted back to earth by radio, about a planet or conditions in space

spaceship *n* (in science fiction) a spacecraft used for travel between planets and galaxies

space shuttle *n* a manned reusable spacecraft designed for making regular flights

space station *n* a large manned artificial satellite used as a base for scientific research in space and for people travelling in space

spacesuit *n* a sealed protective suit worn by astronauts

space-time *or* **space-time continuum** *n physics* the four-dimensional continuum having three space coordinates and one time coordinate that together completely specify the location of an object or an event

spacious *adj* having or providing a lot of space; roomy **spaciousness** *n*

spade¹ *n* **1** a tool for digging, with a flat steel blade and a long wooden handle **2 call a spade a spade** to speak plainly and frankly
WORD ORIGIN Old English *spadu*

spade² *n* **1 a spades** the suit of playing cards marked with a black leaf-shaped symbol **b** a card with one or more of these symbols on it **2** *offensive* a Black person **3 in spades** *informal* in plenty: *all you need is talent in spades*
WORD ORIGIN Italian *spada* sword, used as an emblem on playing cards

spadework *n* dull or routine work done as preparation for a project or activity

spadix (**spade**-ix) *n, pl* **spadices** (**spade**-ice-eez) *bot* a spike of small flowers on a fleshy stem
WORD ORIGIN Greek: torn-off frond

spaghetti *n* pasta in the form of long strings
WORD ORIGIN Italian

spaghetti junction *n* a junction between motorways with a large number of intersecting roads
WORD ORIGIN from the nickname of the Gravelly Hill Interchange, Birmingham

spaghetti western *n* a cowboy film made in Europe by an Italian director

spake *vb archaic* a past tense of **speak**

spam *vb* **spamming, spammed** *computers slang* to send unsolicited e-mail simultaneously to a number of newsgroups on the internet
WORD ORIGIN from the repeated use of the word *Spam* in a popular sketch from the British television show *Monty Python's Flying Circus*

Spam *n trademark* a cold meat made from pork and spices

span *n* **1** the interval or distance between two points, such as the ends of

A Brief History of Literature
part 3

Today, the majority of creative writing is prose fiction (or, possibly, screenplays), and though some critics would argue that much of this is mediocre, still they would have to concede and we think of fiction as an 'art' and of writers as 'artists'. More importantly, we think of artists as exceptional, creative persons, invested with some inherent aptitude to create art which the majority does not possess. This was not always the case.

Though the Ancient Romans accepted the concept of divinely inspired 'natural' artists (they thought of Homer as one such), most of the Roman poets chalked their successes up to scrupulous study and meticulous revision: poetry was a product of knowledge, rather than inspiration.

Like all movements in art and culture, this idea went in and out of fashion, but it gained prominence again in Britain in the eighteenth century: the Enlightenment or 'Age of Reason'. This period saw such literary giants as Alexander Pope, Jonathan Swift, and the great Dr Samuel Johnson; talented poets though they were, these people are equally renowned for their education and wit (both of which are on full display in their verse). Although the image of the artist as a divinely inspired creature would not gain true currency again until the Romantic Period (the age of Byron, Keats, and Shelley), the Enlightenment poets did share one thing in common with our contemporary view of art: originality.

The earliest 'literary' language evolved from necessity: the words and lines had to be memorable because, before the invention of writing, there was no other way to preserve them. Even so, poems and tales were not remembered and recited verbatim, but committed to memory through 'formulas', fixed expressions that could be fitted into any given context. Also, the stories themselves were not 'original creations' but rather the inherited history and mythology of a culture.

Composing literature with 'formulaic' phrases seems anathema to the modern view of art: don't writers now seek to avoid hackneyed formulas? And don't critics berate them if their prose is full of clichés? Well, yes, but that doesn't mean that the modern approach to literary language didn't evolve from the ancient one.

By the Middle Ages, writing systems were firmly established throughout Europe, even if they were the province of the elite and lacked the standardization that modern languages possess. But the literary style of the earlier, oral culture did not disappear overnight. On the contrary, formulaic expressions were such a fixture of literary language that poets composing in writing employed them even though they didn't need to. They even made it into prose, as can be seen in Mallory's *Morte D'Arthur*, which uses formulaic expressions to give his prose version of Arthurian Legend the feel of an earlier, 'oral' epic.

Although this may seem backward-looking, it actually demonstrates that, as early as the Middle Ages, authors were putting a lot of effort into the style of their works. There was an accepted literary tone they felt obliged to adopt.

As the Middle Ages gave way to the Renaissance, formulaic expression loosened its grip and writers took pride in finding new solutions to the problem of fitting meaning to rhyme and metre (aided, no doubt, by the rediscovered Classical texts). This, again, did not usher in a preference for originality overnight, but it did begin a trend of literary virtuosity. Shakespeare, for example, took many of his plots from history, but he clothed them in language the likes of which the world has not seen since.

So in the Age of Reason it is no surprise that the great poets would devote their efforts to finding new, original ways of moulding their thought into poetic expression, or, as Pope has it, 'what oft was thought but ne'er so well expressed'. As poetry eventually gave way to the novel as the dominant literary form, so this studied originality carried over into prose.

a bridge **2** the complete extent: *that span of time* **3** short for **wingspan** **4** a unit of length based on the width of a stretched hand, usually taken as nine inches (23 cms) ▷ *vb* **spanning, spanned** **5** to stretch or extend across, over, or around: *her career spanned fifty years; to span the Danube* **WORD ORIGIN** Old English *spann*

spangle *n* **1** a small piece of shiny material used as a decoration on clothes or hair; sequin ▷ *vb* **-gling, -gled** **2** to cover or decorate (something) with spangles **WORD ORIGIN** Middle English *spange* clasp

Spaniard *n* a person from Spain

spaniel *n* a dog with long drooping ears and a silky coat **WORD ORIGIN** Old French *espaigneul* Spanish (dog)

Spanish *adj* **1** of Spain ▷ *n* **2** the official language of Spain, Mexico, and most countries of South and Central America ▷ *pl n* **3 the Spanish** the people of Spain

Spanish fly *n* a beetle, the dried body of which is used in medicine

Spanish Main *n* **1** the N coast of South America **2** the Caribbean Sea, the S part of which was frequented by pirates

spank *vb* **1** to slap (someone) with the open hand, on the buttocks or legs ▷ *n* **2** such a slap **WORD ORIGIN** probably imitative

spanking¹ *n* a series of spanks, usually as a punishment for children

spanking² *adj* **1** *informal* outstandingly fine or smart: *spanking new uniforms* **2** very fast: *a spanking pace*

spanner *n* **1** a tool for gripping and turning a nut or bolt **2 throw a spanner in the works** *informal* to cause a problem that prevents things from running smoothly **WORD ORIGIN** German *spannen* to stretch

spanspek *n* *S African* a cantaloupe melon **WORD ORIGIN** Afrikaans

spar¹ *n* a pole used as a ship's mast, boom, or yard **WORD ORIGIN** Old Norse *sperra* beam

spar² *vb* **sparring, sparred** **1** *boxing, martial arts* to fight using light blows for practice **2** to argue with someone ▷ *n* **3** an argument **WORD ORIGIN** Old English

spar³ *n* a light-coloured, crystalline, easily split mineral **WORD ORIGIN** Middle Low German

spare *adj* **1** extra to what is needed: *there are some spare chairs at the back* **2** able to be used when needed: *a spare parking space* **3** (of a person) tall and thin **4** (of a style) plain and without unnecessary decoration or details; austere: *a spare but beautiful novel* **5** *Brit slang* frantic with anger or worry: *the boss went spare* ▷ *n* **6** an extra thing kept in case it is needed ▷ *vb* **sparing, spared** **7** to stop from killing, punishing, or injuring (someone) **8** to protect (someone) from (something) unpleasant: *spare me the sermon* **9** to be able to afford or give: *can you spare me a moment to talk?* **10 not spare oneself** to try one's hardest **11 to spare** more than is required: *a few hours to spare*

WORD ORIGIN Old English *sparian*

spare part *n* a replacement piece of mechanical or electrical equipment kept in case the original component becomes damaged or worn

spareribs *pl n* a cut of pork ribs with most of the meat trimmed off

spare tyre *n* **1** an additional tyre kept in a motor vehicle in case of puncture **2** *slang* a roll of fat just above the waist

sparing *adj* (sometimes foll. by *of*) economical (with): *she was mercifully sparing in her use of jargon* **sparingly** *adv*

spark *n* **1** a fiery particle thrown out from a fire or caused by friction **2** a short flash of light followed by a sharp crackling noise, produced by a sudden electrical discharge through the air **3** a trace or hint: *a spark of goodwill* **4** liveliness, enthusiasm, or humour: *that spark in her eye* ▷ *vb* **5** to give off sparks **6** to cause to start; trigger: *the incident sparked off an angry exchange* **WORD ORIGIN** Old English *spearca*

sparkie *n* *Brit, Austral, NZ informal* electrician

sparkle *vb* **-kling, -kled** **1** to glitter with many bright points of light **2** (of wine or mineral water) to be slightly fizzy **3** to be lively, witty, and intelligent ▷ *n* **4** a small bright point of light **5** liveliness and wit **sparkling** *adj* **WORD ORIGIN** Middle English *sparklen*

sparkler *n* **1** a type of hand-held firework that throws out sparks **2** *informal* a sparkling gem; esp. a diamond

spark plug *n* a device in an internal-combustion engine that ignites the fuel by producing an electric spark

sparring partner *n* **1** a person who practises with a boxer during training **2** a person with whom one has friendly arguments

sparrow *n* a very common small brown or grey bird which feeds on seeds and insects **WORD ORIGIN** Old English *spearwa*

sparrowhawk *n* a small hawk which preys on smaller birds

sparse *adj* small in amount and spread out widely: *a sparse population* **sparsely** *adv* **WORD ORIGIN** Latin *sparsus*

Spartan *adj* **1** of or relating to the ancient Greek city of Sparta **2** (of a way of life) strict or simple and with no luxuries: *Spartan accommodation* ▷ *n* **3** a citizen of Sparta **4** a person who leads a strict or simple life without luxuries

spasm *n* **1** a sudden tightening of the muscles, over which one has no control **2** a sudden burst of activity or feeling: *a spasm of applause; sudden spasms of anger* **WORD ORIGIN** Greek *spasmos* a cramp

spasmodic *adj* taking place in sudden short spells: *spasmodic bouts of illness* **spasmodically** *adv*

spastic *n* **1** a person who has cerebral palsy, and therefore has difficulty controlling his or her muscles ▷ *adj* **2** affected by involuntary muscle contractions: *a spastic colon* **3** suffering from cerebral palsy **WORD ORIGIN** Greek *spasmos* a cramp

spat¹ *n* a slight quarrel **WORD ORIGIN** probably imitative

spat² *vb* a past of **spit¹**

spate *n* **1** a large number of things happening within a period of time: *a spate of bombings* **2** a fast flow or outpouring: *an incomprehensible spate of words* **3 in spate** *chiefly Brit* (of a river) flooded **WORD ORIGIN** origin unknown

spathe *n* *bot* a large leaf that surrounds the base of a flower cluster **WORD ORIGIN** Greek *spathē* a blade

spatial *adj* of or relating to size, area, or position: *spatial dimensions* **spatially** *adv*

spats *pl n* cloth or leather coverings formerly worn by men over the ankle and instep **WORD ORIGIN** obsolete *spatterdash* a long gaiter

spatter *vb* **1** to scatter or splash (a substance, esp. a liquid) in scattered drops: *spattering mud in all directions* **2** to sprinkle (an object or a surface) with a liquid ▷ *n* **3** the sound of spattering **4** something spattered, such as a spot or splash **WORD ORIGIN** imitative

spatula *n* a utensil with a broad flat blade, used in cooking and by doctors **WORD ORIGIN** Latin: a broad piece

spawn *n* **1** the jelly-like mass of eggs laid by fish, amphibians, or molluscs ▷ *vb* **2** (of fish, amphibians, or molluscs) to lay eggs **3** to cause (something) to be created: *the depressed economy spawned the riots* **WORD ORIGIN** Anglo-Norman *espaundre*

spay *vb* to remove the ovaries from (a female animal) **WORD ORIGIN** Old French *espeer* to cut with the sword

speak *vb* **speaking, spoke, spoken** **1** to say words; talk **2** to communicate or express (something) in words **3** to give a speech or lecture **4** to know how to talk in (a specified language): *I don't speak French* **5 on speaking terms** on good terms; friendly **6 so to speak** as it were **7 speak one's mind** to express one's opinions honestly and plainly **8 to speak of** of a significant nature: *no licensing laws to speak of* **WORD ORIGIN** Old English *specan*

speakeasy *n, pl* **-easies** *US* a place where alcoholic drink was sold illegally during Prohibition

speaker *n* **1** a person who speaks, esp. someone making a speech **2** a person who speaks a particular language: *a fluent Tibetan and English speaker* **3** same as **loudspeaker**

Speaker *n* the official chairman of a law-making body

speak for *vb* **1** to speak on behalf of (other people) **2 speak for itself** to be so obvious that no further comment is necessary: *his work on the convention speaks for itself* **3 speak for yourself!** *informal* do not presume that other people agree with you!

speak up *or* **out** *vb* **1** to state one's beliefs bravely and firmly **2** to speak more loudly and clearly

spear¹ *n* **1** a weapon consisting of a long pole with a sharp point ▷ *vb* **2** to pierce (someone or something) with a spear or other pointed object: *she took her fork and speared an oyster from its shell*
WORD ORIGIN Old English *spere*

spear² *n* **1** a slender shoot, such as of grass **2** a single stalk of broccoli or asparagus
WORD ORIGIN probably variant of *spire*

spearhead *vb* **1** to lead (an attack or a campaign) ▷ *n* **2** the leading force in an attack or campaign

spearmint *n* a minty flavouring used for sweets and toothpaste, which comes from a purple-flowered plant

spec *n* **on spec** *informal* as a risk or gamble: *I still tend to buy on spec*

special *adj* **1** distinguished from or better than others of its kind: *a special occasion* **2** designed or reserved for a specific purpose: *special equipment* **3** not usual; different from normal: *a special case* **4** particular or primary: *a special interest in gifted children* **5** relating to the education of children with disabilities: *a special school* ▷ *n* **6** a product, TV programme, etc. which is only available or shown at a certain time: *a two-hour Christmas special live from Hollywood* **7** a meal, usually at a low price, in a bar or restaurant **8** short for **special constable** ▷ **specially** *adv*
WORD ORIGIN Latin *specialis*

≡ **USAGE**
≡ See at **especial**.

Special Branch *n* (in Britain and S Africa) the department of the police force that is concerned with political security

special constable *n* a person recruited for occasional police duties, such as in an emergency

special delivery *n* the delivery of a piece of mail outside the time of a scheduled delivery, for an extra fee

special effects *pl n films* techniques used in the production of scenes that cannot be achieved by normal methods: *the special effects and make-up are totally convincing*

specialist *n* **1** a person who is an expert in a particular activity or subject **2** a doctor who concentrates on treating one particular category of diseases or the diseases of one particular part of the body: *an eye specialist* ▷ *adj* **3** particular to or concentrating on one subject or activity: *a specialist comic shop*

speciality *or esp. US & Canad* **specialty** *n, pl* **-ties 1** a special interest or skill **2** a service, product, or type of food specialized in

specialize *or* **-lise** *vb* **-lizing, -lized** *or* **-lising, -lised 1** (often foll. by *in*) to concentrate all one's efforts on studying a particular subject, occupation, or activity: *an expert who specializes in transport* **2** to modify (something) for a special use or purpose: *plants have evolved and specialized in every type of habitat* **specialization** *or* **-lisation** *n*

special licence *n Brit* a licence allowing a marriage to take place without following all the usual legal procedures

specialty *n, pl* **-ties** *chiefly US & Canad* same as **speciality**

specie *n* coins as distinct from paper money
WORD ORIGIN Latin *in specie* in kind

species *n, pl* **-cies** *biol* one of the groups into which a genus is divided, the members of which are able to interbreed
WORD ORIGIN Latin: appearance

specific *adj* **1** particular or definite: *a specific area of economic policy* **2** precise and exact: *try and be more specific* ▷ *n* **3 specifics** particular qualities or aspects of something: *the specifics of the situation* **4** *med* any drug used to treat a particular disease **specifically** *adv* **specificity** *n*
WORD ORIGIN Latin *species* kind + *facere* to make

specification *n* **1** a detailed description of features in the design of something: *engines built to racing specification* **2** a requirement or detail which is clearly stated: *the main specification was that a good degree was required* **3** the specifying of something

specific gravity *n physics* the ratio of the density of a substance to the density of water

specific heat capacity *n physics* the quantity of heat required to raise the temperature of unit mass of a substance by one degree centigrade

specify *vb* **-fies, -fying, -fied 1** to state or describe (something) clearly **2** to state (something) as a condition: *the rules specify the number of prisoners to be kept in each cell*
WORD ORIGIN Medieval Latin *specificare* to describe

specimen *n* **1** an individual or part regarded as typical of its group or class **2** *med* a sample of tissue, blood, or urine taken for analysis **3** *informal* a person: *I'm quite a healthy specimen*
WORD ORIGIN Latin: mark, proof

specious (**spee**-shuss) *adj* apparently correct or true, but actually wrong or false
WORD ORIGIN Latin *species* outward appearance

speck *n* **1** a very small mark or spot **2** a small or tiny piece of something: *a speck of fluff*
WORD ORIGIN Old English *specca*

speckle *vb* **-ling, -led 1** to mark (something) with speckles ▷ *n* **2** a small mark or spot, such as on the skin or on an egg **speckled** *adj*
WORD ORIGIN Middle Dutch *spekkel*

specs *pl n informal* short for **spectacles**

spectacle *n* **1** a strange, interesting, or ridiculous scene **2** an impressive public show: *the opening ceremony of the Olympics was an impressive spectacle* **3 make a spectacle of oneself** to draw attention to oneself by behaving foolishly
WORD ORIGIN Latin *spectare* to watch

spectacles *pl n* a pair of glasses for correcting faulty vision

spectacular *adj* **1** impressive, grand, or dramatic ▷ *n* **2** a spectacular show **spectacularly** *adv*

spectate *vb* **-tating, -tated** to be a spectator; watch

spectator *n* a person viewing anything; onlooker
WORD ORIGIN Latin *spectare* to watch

spectator ion *n chem* an ion which is present in a mixture but plays no part in a reaction

spectre *or US* **specter** *n* **1** a ghost **2** an unpleasant or menacing vision in one's imagination: *the spectre of famine* **spectral** *adj*
WORD ORIGIN Latin *spectrum*

spectrometer (speck-**trom**-it-er) *n physics* an instrument for producing a spectrum, usually one in which wavelength, energy, or intensity can be measured

spectroscope *n physics* an instrument for forming or recording a spectrum by passing a light ray through a prism or grating

spectrum *n, pl* **-tra 1** *physics* the distribution of colours produced when white light is dispersed by a prism or grating: violet, indigo, blue, green, yellow, orange, and red **2** *physics* the whole range of electromagnetic radiation with respect to its wavelength or frequency **3** a range or scale of anything such as opinions or emotions
WORD ORIGIN Latin: image

speculate *vb* **-lating, -lated 1** to form opinions about something, esp. its future consequences, based on the information available; conjecture: *it is too early to speculate about Jackie getting married* **2** to buy securities or property in the hope of selling them at a profit **speculation** *n* **speculative** *adj* **speculator** *n*
WORD ORIGIN Latin *speculari* to spy out

sped *vb* a past of **speed**

speech *n* **1** the ability to speak: *the loss of speech* **2** spoken language: *Doran's lack of coherent speech* **3** a talk given to an audience: *a speech to parliament* **4** a person's manner of speaking: *her speech was extremely slow* **5** a national or regional language or dialect: *Canadian speech*
WORD ORIGIN Old English *spēc*

speech day *n* (in schools) an annual day on which prizes are presented and speeches are made by guest speakers

speechify *vb* **-fies, -fying, -fied** to make a dull or pompous speech

speechless *adj* **1** unable to speak for a short time because of great emotion or shock **2** unable to be expressed in words: *speechless disbelief*

speech therapy *n* the treatment of people with speech problems

speed *n* **1** the quality of acting or moving fast; swiftness **2** the rate at which something moves or happens **3** a gear ratio in a motor vehicle or bicycle: *five-speed gearbox* **4** *photog* a measure of the sensitivity to light of a particular type of film **5** *slang* amphetamine **6 at speed** quickly **7 up to speed a** operating at an acceptable level **b** in possession of all the necessary information ▷ *vb* **speeding, sped** *or* **speeded 8** to move or go somewhere quickly **9** to drive a motor vehicle faster than the legal limit ▶ See also **speed up**
WORD ORIGIN Old English *spēd* (originally: success)

S

speedboat n a high-speed motorboat

speed camera n a camera for photographing vehicles breaking the speed limit

speed limit n the maximum speed at which a vehicle may legally travel on a particular road

speedo n, pl **speedos** informal a speedometer

speedometer n a dial in a vehicle which shows the speed of travel

speed trap n a place on a road where the police check that passing vehicles are not being driven at an illegally high speed

speed up vb to accelerate or cause to accelerate

≡ **USAGE**
≡ The past tense and past participle of
≡ speed up is speeded up not sped up.

speedway n **1** the sport of racing on light powerful motorcycles round cinder tracks **2** US, Canad, & NZ the track or stadium where such races are held

speedwell n a small blue or pinkish-white flower

speedy adj **speedier, speediest 1** done without delay **2** (of a vehicle) able to travel fast **speedily** adv

speleology n the scientific study of caves
WORD ORIGIN Latin spelaeum cave

spell¹ vb **spelling, spelt** or **spelled 1** to write or name in correct order the letters that make up (a word): how do you spell that name? **2** (of letters) to make up (a word): c-a-t spells cat **3** to indicate (a particular result): share price slump spells disaster ► See also **spell out**
WORD ORIGIN Old French espeller

spell² n **1** a sequence of words used to perform magic **2** the effect of a spell: the wizard's spell was broken **3 under someone's spell** fascinated by someone
WORD ORIGIN Old English spell speech

spell³ n **1** a period of time of weather or activity: the dry spell; a short spell in prison **2** a period of duty after which one person or group relieves another **3** Scot, Austral, & NZ a period of rest
WORD ORIGIN Old English spelian to take the place of

spellbinding adj so fascinating that nothing else can be thought of: his spellbinding speeches

spellbound adj completely fascinated; as if in a trance

spellchecker n computers a program that highlights any word in a word-processed document that is not recognized as being correctly spelt

spelling n **1** the way a word is spelt: the British spelling of 'theatre' **2** a person's ability to spell: my spelling used to be excellent

spell out vb **1** to make (something) as easy to understand as possible: to spell out the implications **2** to read with difficulty, working out each word letter by letter

spelt vb a past of **spell¹**

spend vb **spending, spent 1** to pay out (money) **2** to pass (time) in a specific way or place: I spent a year in Budapest **3** to concentrate (effort) on an activity: a lot of energy was spent organizing the holiday **4** to use up completely: the hurricane spent its force **spending** n
WORD ORIGIN Latin expendere

spendthrift n **1** a person who spends money wastefully ► adj **2** of or like a spendthrift: a spendthrift policy

spent vb **1** the past of **spend** ► adj **2** used up or exhausted

sperm n **1** pl **sperms** or **sperm** one of the male reproductive cells released in the semen during ejaculation **2** same as **semen**
WORD ORIGIN Greek sperma

spermaceti (sper-ma-**set**-ee) n a white waxy substance obtained from the sperm whale
WORD ORIGIN Medieval Latin sperma ceti whale's sperm

spermatozoon (sper-ma-toe-**zoe**-on) n, pl -**zoa** same as **sperm** (sense 1)
WORD ORIGIN Greek sperma seed + zōion animal

spermicide n a substance, esp. a cream or jelly, that kills sperm, used as a means of contraception **spermicidal** adj
WORD ORIGIN SPERM + Latin caedere to kill

sperm oil n an oil obtained from the head of the sperm whale, used as a lubricant

sperm whale n a large whale which is hunted for spermaceti and ambergris
WORD ORIGIN short for SPERMACETI WHALE

spew vb **1** to vomit **2** to send or be sent out in a stream: the hydrant spewed a tidal wave of water
WORD ORIGIN Old English spīwan

SPF sun protection factor: an indicator of how a sun cream, lotion, etc. protects the skin from the harmful rays of the sun

sphagnum n a moss which is found in bogs and which decays to form peat
WORD ORIGIN Greek sphagnos

sphere n **1** geom a round solid figure in which every point on the surface is equally distant from the centre **2** an object having this shape, such as a planet **3** a particular field of activity **4** people of the same rank or with shared interests: a humbler social sphere
WORD ORIGIN Greek sphaira

spherical adj shaped like a sphere

spheroid n geom a solid figure that is almost but not exactly a sphere

sphincter n anat a ring of muscle surrounding the opening of a hollow organ and contracting to close it
WORD ORIGIN Greek sphingein to grip tightly

sphinx n **1** one of the huge statues built by the ancient Egyptians, with the body of a lion and the head of a man **2** a mysterious person

Sphinx n **1** the huge statue of a sphinx near the pyramids at El Cîza in Egypt **2** Greek myth a monster with a woman's head and a lion's body, who set a riddle for travellers, killing them when they failed to answer it. Oedipus answered the riddle and the Sphinx then killed herself
WORD ORIGIN Greek

spice n **1 a** an aromatic substance, such as ginger or cinnamon, used as flavouring **b** such substances collectively **2** something that makes life or an activity more exciting ► vb **spicing, spiced 3** to flavour (food) with spices **4** (often foll. by up) to add excitement or interest to (something): they spiced their letters with pointed demands
WORD ORIGIN Old French espice

spick-and-span adj very neat and clean
WORD ORIGIN obsolete spick spike + span-new absolutely new, like a freshly cut spike

spicy adj **spicier, spiciest 1** strongly flavoured with spices **2** informal slightly scandalous: spicy new story lines

spider n a small eight-legged creature, many species of which weave webs in which to trap insects for food **spidery** adj
WORD ORIGIN Old English spīthra

spider monkey n a tree-living monkey with very long legs, a long tail, and a small head

spiel n a prepared speech made to persuade someone to buy or do something
WORD ORIGIN German Spiel play

spigot n **1** a stopper for the vent hole of a cask **2** a wooden tap fitted to a cask
WORD ORIGIN probably from Latin spica a point

spike¹ n **1** a sharp-pointed metal object: a high fence with iron spikes **2** anything long and pointed: a hedgehog bristling with spikes **3** a long metal nail **4 spikes** sports shoes with metal spikes on the soles for greater grip ► vb **spiking, spiked 5** to secure or supply (something) with spikes: spiked shoes **6** to drive a spike or spikes into **7** to add alcohol to (a drink) **spiky** adj
WORD ORIGIN Middle English spyk

spike² n bot **1** an arrangement of flowers attached at the base to a long stem **2** an ear of grain
WORD ORIGIN Latin spica ear of corn

spikenard n **1** a fragrant Indian plant with rose-purple flowers **2** an ointment obtained from this plant
WORD ORIGIN Medieval Latin spica nardi

spill¹ vb **spilling, spilt** or **spilled 1** to pour from or as from a container by accident **2** (of large numbers of people) to come out of a place: rival groups spilled out from the station **3** to shed (blood) **4 spill the beans** informal to give away a secret ► n **5** informal a fall from a motorbike, bike, or horse, esp. in a competition **6** an amount of liquid spilt **spillage** n
WORD ORIGIN Old English spillan to destroy

spill² n a splinter of wood or strip of paper for lighting pipes or fires
WORD ORIGIN Germanic

spillikin n Brit a thin strip of wood, cardboard, or plastic used in spillikins

spillikins n Brit a game in which players try to pick each spillikin from a heap without moving the others

spin vb **spinning, spun 1** to revolve or cause to revolve quickly **2** to draw out and twist (fibres, such as silk or cotton) into thread **3** (of a spider or silkworm) to form (a web or cocoon) from a silky

Irish English

Although Ireland has its own ancient Gaelic language, known as Irish, it is a language now spoken on a daily basis by only a very small percentage of the population. While there are many historical reasons for the decline of Irish and the predominance of English in Ireland today, the change is widely believed to have begun with the reconquest of Ireland in the sixteenth century by the Tudors, setting in motion events which saw the imposition of English law and language, and the settlement of English, Scottish, and Welsh colonists in Ireland.

Irish English is a generic term that covers three main varieties of English in use in Ireland, varieties which have a long historical association and link to each other in various ways. These are *Anglo-Irish*, which derives from the English of the seventeenth-century settlers from England, *Ulster Scots* (or *Ulster English*), a form of lowland Scots spoken in the north of the island, and *Hiberno-English*, used by people with Irish as their ancestral language. There are differences as well as similarities between these varieties: for example, a feature known as 'singular concord', where a singular verb ending in '-s' is used with a plural noun (as in 'These children breaks things') is more commonly found in the Ulster Scots of the north.

Most Irish accents are rhotic, prononuncing the 'r' after the vowel in words such as *hard* and *water*. Other characteristic pronunciation patterns include differentiation between the 'w' sound in *wire* and the 'wh' sound in *where*. Irish accents also display a general tendency to use more aspiration with 'd', 'p', and 't', giving them a 'breathy' quality. There are also characteristic pronunciations of vowels: the 'ay' sound in words such as *gave* and *came* might be altered to sound as 'gev' and 'kem', while *tea* or *meat* may sound closer to 'tay' or 'mate'.

Irish English also displays a number of characteristic syntactical constructions. Prepositional constructions are common where they would not be used in British English or other varieties: 'They had a bit of drink on them'; 'I'm bad with the earache'. The latter example also illustrates an extended use of the definite article, common in Irish English. Reflexive personal pronouns may be used to refer to someone, sometimes implying a negative view of the person or their action: 'Wasn't it herself told me that earlier?'

Many syntactical variations from British English can be compared with constructions in Irish (Gaelic) syntax. Irish has no words that directly translate as 'yes' and 'no', and Irish English often answers a question by repeating the verb: 'Isn't this great?' 'It is'. The word 'after' may be added to a present participle to form a pluperfect tense (which again does not exist in Irish): 'They asked me if I wanted lunch, but I was after having a sandwich.' A similar construction is used for an event in the immediate past, and is known as the 'hot news perfect': 'I'm just after coming from the town.'

The influence of the Irish language is also apparent in Irish English vocabulary. Words that have been incorporated into the English spoken in Ireland include *omadhaun* (fool) from the Irish *amadán*; *clabber* (mud) from *clabar*; *dingen* (very good) from *daingean* (secure). The influence of twelfth-century Anglo-Norman invasion and settlement is still apparent in *gossoon*, often used in rural areas to mean 'a boy', which derives from the French *garçon*. The vocabulary spoken in the north of Ireland shows the influence of Scots, for example *drout* (from Scots *drouth*, thirst) and *forenenst* (in front of). Other unique usages have developed: *grand* to mean 'good' or 'well'; *gam* meaning 'leg'.

Irish and Irish English have left their mark on other varieties of English. Established words in British English include *banshee* (from Irish *bean sídhe*, 'woman of the fairy mound'), *galore* (from *go leór*, 'to sufficiency') and *smithereens* (from *smidirín*, 'a tiny fragment'). Emigration from Ireland to mainland Britain has brought Irish usages into particular dialects, for example the second person plural pronoun *yous* which has established itself in areas around Liverpool and Glasgow. In more recent years, television and advertising have brought Irish words to an even wider audience, and usages that have now been embraced in British English include *hooley*, a lively party, *crack* or *craic*, meaning 'boisterous entertainment', and *feck* – a euphemistic pronunciation of a common expletive.

fibre that comes out of the body **4 spin a yarn** to tell an unlikely story **5** *sport* to throw, hit, or kick (a ball) so that it spins and changes direction or changes speed on bouncing **6** same as **spin-dry 7** to grow dizzy: *her head was spinning* **8** *informal* to present information in a way that creates a favourable impression ▷ *n* **9** a fast rotating motion **10** a flight manoeuvre in which an aircraft flies in a downward spiral **11** *sport* a spinning motion given to a ball **12** *informal* a short car drive taken for pleasure **13** *informal* the presenting of information in a way that creates a favourable impression ▷ See also **spin out** ▷ **spinning** *n*
WORD ORIGIN Old English *spinnan*

spina bifida *n* a condition in which part of the spinal cord protrudes through a gap in the backbone, sometimes causing paralysis
WORD ORIGIN New Latin: split spine

spinach *n* a dark green leafy vegetable
WORD ORIGIN Arabic *isfānākh*

spinal column *n* same as **spine** (sense 1)

spinal cord *n* the thick cord of nerve tissue within the spine, which connects the brain to the nerves of the body

spin bowler *n cricket* same as **spinner** (sense 1a)

spindle *n* **1** a rotating rod that acts as an axle **2** a rod with a notch in the top for drawing out, twisting and winding the thread in spinning
WORD ORIGIN Old English *spinel*

spindly *adj* **-dlier, -dliest** tall, thin, and frail

spin doctor *n informal* a person who provides a favourable slant to a news item or policy on behalf of a political personality or party
WORD ORIGIN from the spin given to a ball in sport to make it go in the desired direction

spindrift *n* spray blown up from the sea
WORD ORIGIN Scots variant of *spoondrift*, from *spoon* to scud + DRIFT

spin-dry *vb* **-dries, -drying, -dried** to dry (clothes) in a spin-dryer

spin-dryer *n* a device that removes water from washed clothes by spinning them in a perforated drum

spine *n* **1** the row of bony segments that surround and protect the spinal cord **2** the back of a book, record sleeve, or video-tape box **3** a sharp point on the body of an animal or on a plant **spinal** *adj*
WORD ORIGIN Latin *spina* thorn

spine-chiller *n* a frightening film or story **spine-chilling** *adj*

spineless *adj* **1** behaving in a cowardly way **2** (of an animal) having no spine

spinet *n* a small harpsichord
WORD ORIGIN Italian *spinetta*

spinifex *n* a coarse spiny Australian grass

spinnaker *n* a large triangular sail on a racing yacht
WORD ORIGIN probably from *spin*, but traditionally from Sphinx, the yacht that first used this type of sail

spinner *n* **1** *cricket* **a** a bowler who specializes in spinning the ball with his or her fingers to make it change direction when it bounces or strikes the batsman's bat **b** a ball that is bowled with a spinning motion **2** a small round object used in angling to attract fish to the bait by spinning in the water **3** a person who makes thread by spinning

spinneret *n* an organ through which silk threads come out of the body of a spider or insect

spinney *n chiefly Brit* a small wood: *the hollow tree in the spinney*
WORD ORIGIN Old French *espinei*

spinning jenny *n* an early type of spinning frame with several spindles

spinning wheel *n* a wheel-like machine for spinning at home, having one hand- or foot-operated spindle

spin-off *n* **1** a product or development that unexpectedly results from activities designed to achieve something else: *new energy sources could occur as a spin-off from the space effort* **2** a television series involving some of the characters from an earlier successful series

spin out *vb* **1** to take longer than necessary to do (something) **2** to make (money) last as long as possible

spinster *n* an unmarried woman **spinsterish** *adj*
WORD ORIGIN Middle English, in the sense a woman who spins

spiny *adj* **spinier, spiniest** (of animals or plants) covered with spines

spiracle (spire-a-kl) *n zool* a small blowhole for breathing through, such as that of a whale
WORD ORIGIN Latin *spiraculum* vent

spiraea *or esp. US* **spirea** (spire-ee-a) *n* a plant with small white or pink flowers
WORD ORIGIN Greek *speiraia*

spiral *n* **1** *geom* a plane curve formed by a point winding about a fixed point at an ever-increasing distance from it **2** something that follows a winding course or that has a twisting form **3** *econ* a continuous upward or downward movement in economic activity or prices ▷ *adj* **4** having the shape of a spiral: *a spiral staircase* ▷ *vb* **-ralling, -ralled** *or US* **-raling, -raled 5** to follow a spiral course or be in the shape of a spiral **6** to increase or decrease with steady acceleration: *oil prices continue to spiral* **spirally** *adv*
WORD ORIGIN Latin *spira* a coil

spire *n* the tall cone-shaped structure on the top of a church
WORD ORIGIN Old English *spīr* blade

spirit¹ *n* **1** the nonphysical aspect of a person concerned with profound thoughts and emotions **2** the nonphysical part of a person believed to live on after death **3** a shared feeling: *a spirit of fun and adventure* **4** mood or attitude: *fighting spirit* **5** a person's character or temperament: *the indomitable spirit of the Polish people* **6** liveliness shown in what a person does: *it has been undertaken with spirit* **7** the feelings that motivate someone to survive in difficult times or live according to his or her beliefs: *someone had broken his spirit* **8 spirits** an emotional state: *in good spirits* **9** the way in which something, such as a law or an agreement, was intended to be interpreted: *they acted against the spirit of the treaty* **10** a supernatural being, such as a ghost ▷ *vb* **-riting, -rited 11 spirit away** *or* **off** to carry (someone or something) off mysteriously or secretly
WORD ORIGIN Latin *spiritus* breath, spirit

spirit² *n* **1** (*usually pl*) distilled alcoholic liquor, such as whisky or gin **2** *chem* **a** a solution of ethanol obtained by distillation **b** the essence of a substance, extracted as a liquid by distillation **3** *pharmacol* a solution of a volatile oil in alcohol
WORD ORIGIN special use of SPIRIT¹

spirited *adj* **1** showing liveliness or courage: *a spirited rendition of Schubert's ninth symphony; a spirited defence of the government's policy* **2** characterized by the mood as specified: *high-spirited; mean-spirited*

spirit gum *n* a solution of gum in ether, used to stick on false hair

spirit lamp *n* a lamp that burns methylated or other spirits instead of oil

spirit level *n* a device for checking whether a surface is level, consisting of a block of wood or metal containing a tube partially filled with liquid set so that the air bubble in it rests between two marks on the tube when the block is level

spiritual *adj* **1** relating to a person's beliefs as opposed to his or her physical or material needs **2** relating to religious beliefs **3 one's spiritual home** the place where one feels one belongs ▷ *n* **4** Also called: **Negro spiritual** a type of religious folk song originally sung by Black slaves in the American South **spirituality** *n* **spiritually** *adv*

spiritualism *n* the belief that the spirits of the dead can communicate with the living **spiritualist** *n*

spirituous *adj* containing alcohol

spirogyra (spire-oh-**jire**-a) *n* a green freshwater plant that floats on the surface of ponds and ditches
WORD ORIGIN Greek *speira* a coil + *guros* a circle

spit¹ *vb* **spitting, spat** *or* **spit 1** to force saliva out of one's mouth **2** to force (something) out of one's mouth: *he spat tobacco into an old coffee can* **3** (of a fire or hot fat) to throw out sparks or particles violently and explosively **4** to rain very lightly **5** (*often foll. by out*) to say (words) in a violent angry way **6** to show contempt or hatred by spitting **7 spit it out!** *informal* a command given to someone to say what is on his or her mind ▷ *n* **8** same as **spittle 9** *informal chiefly Brit* same as **spitting image**
WORD ORIGIN Old English *spittan*

spit² *n* **1** a pointed rod for skewering and roasting meat over a fire or in an oven **2** a long narrow strip of land jutting out into the sea
WORD ORIGIN Old English *spitu*

spit and polish *n informal* thorough cleaning and polishing

spite *n* **1** deliberate nastiness **2 in spite of** regardless of: *he loved them in spite of*

their shortcomings ▷ vb **spiting, spited 3** to annoy (someone) deliberately, out of spite: *it was to spite his father* **spiteful** *adj* **spitefully** *adv*
WORD ORIGIN variant of DESPITE

spitfire *n* a woman or girl who is easily angered

spitting image *n informal* a person who looks very like someone else
WORD ORIGIN from *spit* likeness

spittle *n* the fluid that is produced in the mouth; saliva
WORD ORIGIN Old English *spætl* saliva

spittoon *n* a bowl for people to spit into

spitz *n* a stockily built dog with a pointed face, erect ears, and a tightly curled tail
WORD ORIGIN from German

spiv *n Brit, Austral, & NZ slang* a smartly dressed man who makes a living by underhand dealings; black marketeer
WORD ORIGIN dialect *spiving* smart

splash *vb* **1** to scatter (liquid) on (something) **2** to cause (liquid) to fall or (of liquid) to be scattered in drops **3** to display (a photograph or story) prominently in a newspaper ▷ *n* **4** a splashing sound **5** an amount splashed **6** a patch (of colour or light) **7 make a splash** *informal* to attract a lot of attention **8** a small amount of liquid added to a drink
WORD ORIGIN alteration of *plash*

splashdown *n* **1** the landing of a spacecraft on water at the end of a flight ▷ *vb* **splash down 2** (of a spacecraft) to make a splashdown

splash out *vb* to spend a lot of money on a treat or luxury: *she planned to splash out on a good holiday*

splatter *vb* **1** to splash (something or someone) with small blobs ▷ *n* **2** a splash of liquid

splay *vb* to spread out, with ends spreading out in different directions: *her hair splayed over the pillow*
WORD ORIGIN short for DISPLAY

splayfooted *adj* same as **flat-footed**

spleen *n* **1** a spongy organ near the stomach, which filters bacteria from the blood **2** spitefulness or bad temper: *we vent our spleen on drug barons*
WORD ORIGIN Greek *splēn*

spleenwort *n* a kind of fern that grows on walls

splendid *adj* **1** very good: *a splendid match* **2** beautiful or impressive: *a splendid palace* **splendidly** *adv*
WORD ORIGIN Latin *splendere* to shine

splendiferous *adj facetious, old-fashioned* grand in appearance
WORD ORIGIN Latin *splendor* radiance + *ferre* to bring

splendour *or US* **splendor** *n* **1** beauty or impressiveness **2 splendours** the impressive or beautiful features of something: *the splendours of the Emperor's Palace*

splenetic *adj literary* irritable or bad-tempered
WORD ORIGIN from SPLEEN

splice *vb* **splicing, spliced 1** to join up the trimmed ends of (two pieces of wire, film, or tape) with an adhesive material **2** to join (two ropes) by interweaving

the ends **3 get spliced** *informal* to get married
WORD ORIGIN probably from Middle Dutch *splissen*

splint *n* a piece of wood used to support a broken bone
WORD ORIGIN Middle Low German *splinte*

splinter *n* **1** a small thin sharp piece broken off, esp. from wood ▷ *vb* **2** to break or be broken into small sharp fragments
WORD ORIGIN Middle Dutch

splinter group *n* a number of members of an organization, who split from the main body and form an independent group of their own

split *vb* **splitting, split 1** to break or cause (something) to break into separate pieces **2** to separate (a piece) or (of a piece) to be separated from (something) **3** (of a group) to separate into smaller groups, through disagreement: *the council is split over rent increases* **4** (often foll. by *up*) to divide (something) among two or more people **5** *slang* to leave a place **6 split on** *slang* to betray; inform on: *he didn't tell tales or split on him* **7 split one's sides** to laugh a great deal ▷ *n* **8** a gap or rift caused by splitting **9** a division in a group or the smaller group resulting from such a division **10** a dessert of sliced fruit and ice cream, covered with whipped cream and nuts: *banana split* ▷ *adj* **11** divided (especially in opinion, etc.) **12** having a split or splits: *split ends* ▶ See also **splits, split up**
WORD ORIGIN Middle Dutch *splitten*

split infinitive *n* (in English grammar) an infinitive used with another word between *to* and the verb, as in *to really finish it*. This is often thought to be incorrect

≡ **USAGE**
≡ The traditional rule against placing
≡ an adverb between *to* and its verb is
≡ gradually disappearing. Although it is
≡ true that a split infinitive may result
≡ in a clumsy sentence (*he decided to firmly
≡ and definitively deal with the problem*), this
≡ is not enough to justify the absolute
≡ condemnation that this practice has
≡ attracted. Indeed, very often the most
≡ natural position of the adverb is
≡ between *to* and the verb (*he decided to
≡ really try next time*) and to change it would
≡ result in an artificial and awkward
≡ construction (*he decided really to try next
≡ time*). The current view is therefore
≡ that the split infinitive is not a
≡ grammatical error. Nevertheless,
≡ many writers prefer to avoid splitting
≡ infinitives in formal written English,
≡ since readers with a more traditional
≡ point of view are likely to interpret
≡ this type of construction as incorrect.

split-level *adj* (of a house or room) having the floor level of one part about half a storey above that of the other

split pea *n* a pea dried and split and used in soups or as a vegetable

split personality *n* **1** the tendency to change mood very quickly **2** a disorder in which a person's mind appears to have separated into two or more personalities

splits *n* (in gymnastics and dancing) the act of sitting with both legs outstretched, pointing in opposite directions, and at right angles to the body

split second *n* **1** an extremely short period of time; instant ▷ *adj* **split-second 2** made in an extremely short time: *split-second timing*

splitting *adj* (of a headache) extremely painful

split up *vb* **1** to separate (something) into parts; divide **2** (of a couple) to end a relationship or marriage **3** (of a group of people) to go off in different directions ▷ *n* **split-up 4** the act of separating

splodge *or US* **splotch** *n* **1** a large uneven spot or stain ▷ *vb* **splodging, splodged 2** to mark (something) with a splodge or splodges
WORD ORIGIN alteration of earlier *splotch*

splurge *n* **1** a bout of spending money extravagantly ▷ *vb* **splurging, splurged 2** (foll. by *on*) to spend (money) extravagantly: *they rushed out to splurge their pocket money on chocolate*
WORD ORIGIN origin unknown

splutter *vb* **1** to spit out (something) from the mouth when choking or laughing **2** to say (words) with spitting sounds when choking or in a rage **3** to throw out or to be thrown out explosively: *sparks spluttered from the fire* ▷ *n* **4** the act or noise of spluttering
WORD ORIGIN variant of SPUTTER

Spode *n* china or porcelain manufactured by the English potter Josiah Spode or his company

spoil *vb* **spoiling, spoilt** *or* **spoiled 1** to make (something) less valuable, beautiful, or useful **2** to weaken the character of (a child) by giving it all it wants **3** (of oneself) to indulge one's desires: *go ahead and spoil yourself* **4** (of food) to become unfit for consumption **5 be spoiling for** to have an aggressive urge for: *he is spoiling for a fight* ▶ See also **spoils**
WORD ORIGIN Latin *spolium* booty

spoilage *n* an amount of material that has been spoilt: *new ways to reduce spoilage*

spoiler *n* **1** a device fitted to an aircraft wing to increase drag and reduce lift **2** a similar device fitted to a car

spoils *pl n* **1** valuables seized during war **2** the rewards and benefits of having political power

spoilsport *n informal* a person who spoils the enjoyment of other people

spoke¹ *vb* the past tense of **speak**

spoke² *n* **1** a bar joining the centre of a wheel to the rim **2 put a spoke in someone's wheel** *Brit & NZ* to create a difficulty for someone
WORD ORIGIN Old English *spāca*

spoken *vb* **1** the past participle of **speak** ▷ *adj* **2** said in speech: *spoken commands* **3** having speech as specified: *quiet-spoken* **4 spoken for** engaged or reserved

spokesman, spokesperson *or* **spokeswoman** *n, pl* **-men, -people** *or* **-women** a person chosen to speak on behalf of another person or group

spoliation n the act or an instance of plundering: *the spoliation of the countryside* **WORD ORIGIN** Latin *spoliare* to plunder

spondee n *prosody* a metrical foot of two long syllables **spondaic** adj **WORD ORIGIN** Greek *spondē* ritual offering of drink

sponge n **1** a sea animal with a porous absorbent elastic skeleton **2** the skeleton of a sponge, or a piece of artificial sponge, used for bathing or cleaning **3** a soft absorbent material like a sponge **4** Also called: **sponge cake** a light cake made of eggs, sugar, and flour **5** Also called: **sponge pudding** *Austral & Brit* a light steamed or baked spongy pudding **6** a rub with a wet sponge ▷ vb **sponging, sponged** **7** (often foll. by *down*) to clean (something) by rubbing it with a wet sponge **8** to remove (marks) by rubbing them with a wet sponge **9** (usually foll. by *off* or *on*) to get (something) from someone by taking advantage of his or her generosity: *stop sponging off the rest of us!* **spongy** adj **WORD ORIGIN** Greek *spongia*

sponge bag n a small waterproof bag for holding toiletries when travelling

sponger n *informal, derogatory* a person who lives off other people by continually taking advantage of their generosity

sponsor n **1** a person or group that promotes another person or group in an activity or the activity itself, either for profit or for charity **2** *chiefly US & Canad* a person or firm that pays the costs of a radio or television programme in return for advertising time **3** a person who presents and supports a proposal or suggestion **4** a person who makes certain promises on behalf of a person being baptized and takes responsibility for his or her Christian upbringing ▷ vb **5** to act as a sponsor for (someone or something) **sponsored** adj **sponsorship** n **WORD ORIGIN** Latin *spondere* to promise solemnly

spontaneous adj **1** not planned or arranged; impulsive: *a spontaneous celebration* **2** occurring through natural processes without outside influence: *a spontaneous explosion* **spontaneously** adv **spontaneity** n **WORD ORIGIN** Latin *sponte* voluntarily

spontaneous combustion n *chem* the bursting into flame of a substance as a result of internal oxidation processes, without heat from an outside source

spoof *informal* n **1** an imitation of a film, TV programme, etc. that exaggerates in an amusing way the most memorable features of the original **2** a good-humoured trick or deception ▷ vb **3** to fool (a person) with a trick or deception **WORD ORIGIN** made-up word

spook *informal* n **1** a ghost **2** a strange and frightening person ▷ vb **3** to frighten: *it was the wind that spooked her* **spooky** adj **WORD ORIGIN** Dutch

spool n a cylinder around which film, thread, or tape can be wound **WORD ORIGIN** Germanic

spoon n **1** a small shallow bowl attached to a handle, used for eating, stirring, or serving food **2** **be born with a silver spoon in one's mouth** to be born into a very rich and respected family ▷ vb **3** to scoop up (food or liquid) with a spoon **4** *old-fashioned slang* to kiss and cuddle **WORD ORIGIN** Old English *spōn* splinter

spoonbill n a wading bird with a long flat bill

spoonerism n the accidental changing over of the first sounds of a pair of words, often with an amusing result, such as *hush my brat* for *brush my hat* **WORD ORIGIN** after W. A. *Spooner*, clergyman

spoon-feed vb **-feeding, -fed** **1** to feed (someone, usually a baby) using a spoon **2** to give (someone) too much help

spoor n the trail of an animal **WORD ORIGIN** Afrikaans

sporadic adj happening at irregular intervals; intermittent: *sporadic bursts of gunfire* **sporadically** adv **WORD ORIGIN** Greek *sporas* scattered

spore n a reproductive body, produced by nonflowering plants and bacteria, that develops into a new individual **WORD ORIGIN** Greek *spora* a sowing

sporran n a large pouch worn hanging from a belt in front of the kilt in Scottish Highland dress **WORD ORIGIN** Scottish Gaelic *sporan* purse

sport n **1** an activity for exercise, pleasure, or competition: *your favourite sport* **2** such activities collectively: *the minister for sport* **3** the enjoyment gained from a pastime: *just for the sport of it* **4** playful or good-humoured joking: *I only did it in sport* **5** *informal* a person who accepts defeat or teasing cheerfully **6** **make sport of someone** to make fun of someone **7** an animal or plant that is very different from others of the same species, usually because of a mutation **8** *Austral & NZ informal* a term of address between males ▷ vb **9** *informal* to wear proudly: *sporting a pair of bright yellow shorts* ▷ See also **sports** **WORD ORIGIN** variant of Middle English *disporten* to disport

sporting adj **1** of sport **2** behaving in a fair and decent way **3** **a sporting chance** reasonable likelihood of happening: *a sporting chance of winning*

sportive adj playful or high-spirited

sports adj **1** of or used in sports: *a sports arena* ▷ n **2** Also called: **sports day** *Brit* a meeting held at a school or college for competitions in athletic events

sports car n a fast car with a low body and usually seating only two people

sportscast n *US* a programme of sports news **sportscaster** n

sports jacket n a man's casual jacket, usually made of tweed. Also called: *US, Austral, & NZ* **sports coat**

sportsman n, pl **-men** **1** a man who plays sports **2** a person who plays by the rules, is fair, and accepts defeat with good humour **sportsman-like** adj **sportsmanship** n

sportsperson n a person who plays sports

sportswear n clothes worn for sport or outdoor leisure wear

sportswoman n, pl **-women** a woman who plays sports

sporty adj **sportier, sportiest** **1** (of a person) interested in sport **2** (of clothes) suitable for sport **3** (of a car) small and fast **sportily** adv **sportiness** n

spot n **1** a small mark on a surface, which has a different colour or texture from its surroundings **2** a location: *a spot where they could sit* **3** a small mark or pimple on the skin **4** a feature of something that has the attribute mentioned: *the one bright spot in his whole day; the high spot of our trip* **5** *informal* a small amount: *a spot of bother* **6** *informal* an awkward situation: *I'm sometimes in a spot* **7** a part of a show, TV programme, etc. reserved for a specific performer or type of entertainment **8** short for **spotlight** (sense 1) **9** **in a tight spot** in a difficult situation **10** **knock spots off someone** to be much better than someone **11** **on the spot** **a** immediately: *he decided on the spot to fly down* **b** at the place in question: *the expert weapons man on the spot* **c** in an awkward situation: *the British government will be put on the spot* **12** **soft spot** a special affection for someone: *a soft spot for older men* ▷ vb **spotting, spotted** **13** to see (something or someone) suddenly **14** to put stains or spots on (something) **15** (of some fabrics) to be prone to marking by liquids: *silk spots easily* **16** to take note of (the numbers of trains or planes observed) **17** (of scouts, agents, etc.) to look out for (talented but unknown actors, sportspersons, etc.) **18** *Brit* to rain lightly **WORD ORIGIN** from German

spot check n a quick unplanned inspection

spotless adj **1** perfectly clean **2** free from moral flaws: *a spotless reputation* **spotlessly** adv

spotlight n **1** a powerful light focused so as to light up a small area **2** **the spotlight** the centre of attention: *the spotlight moved to the president* ▷ vb **-lighting, -lit** or **-lighted** **3** to direct a spotlight on (something) **4** to focus attention on (something)

spot-on adj *informal* absolutely correct; very accurate: *they're spot-on in terms of style*

spotted adj **1** having a pattern of spots **2** marked with stains

spotted dick n *Brit* suet pudding containing dried fruit

spotter n a person whose hobby is watching for and noting numbers or types of trains or planes

spotty adj **-tier, -tiest** **1** covered with spots or pimples **2** not consistent; irregular in quality: *a rather spotty performance* **spottiness** n

spouse n a person's partner in marriage **WORD ORIGIN** Latin *sponsus, sponsa* betrothed man or woman

spout vb **1** (of a liquid or flames) to pour out in a stream or jet **2** *informal* to talk about (something) in a boring way or without much thought ▷ n **3** a projecting tube or lip for pouring liquids **4** a stream or jet of liquid:

Slang

S lang is difficult to define with precision. It might be described as a very informal variety of language that is not appropriate to or is 'outside' standard language, with a history and characteristics that set it apart from other language. It is sometimes perceived as comprising mainly obscene or vulgar words but, while some slang terms might be offensive to some, slang is a much wider category. Language being as it is, the boundaries are fluid – one person might consider a particular word vaguely informal, while another might consider it slang.

The word *slang* itself first appeared in the 18th century and referred to underworld cant or argot, the specialized language already long used by criminals and their associates to ensure confidentiality and exclusivity. Examples of such cant include *glimmer* ('fire') and *panny* ('a burglary'), and some terms that have crept into modern usage, such as *flog* ('to whip') and *shoplift* (someone who steals wares). The origin of the word *slang* is unknown, but it has been hypothesized that it comes from *sling*, or combines elements of phrases such as *rogues' language* or *beggars' language*. This perception of slang, and by extension its users, as being of a lower social status continues to this day.

Today, some of the language of the criminal underworld, eg *jumper* (a thief who steals from offices) might still be termed slang; indeed, a lot of slang is still related to what might be considered 'low' behaviour such as illegal drug use, drunkenness, or (illicit) sexual activity. However, members of any social group, be it college students or soldiers (for whom a *stripey* might be 'a sergeant') might use their own slang vocabulary and idioms primarily to identify themselves as belonging to that group. As in the past, slang terms are often invented as a reaction to authority, by people who see themselves, not always by choice, as being on the outskirts of mainstream society. Black cultures in the United States of America are rich in slang, for example *kicks* for 'shoes', and the kudos attached to such slang often means it is borrowed by other groups such as students. Although not necessarily a conscious attempt at a 'secret code', slang used by one social group might very well be unintelligible to another: older people, for instance, are likely to be bewildered by much of the slang used by teenagers.

Although limited comprehensibility is its main *raison d'être*, slang also has to be memorable, and so it tends to be metaphorical and often very visual in nature. In addition, slang can display some adventurous plays on sound as well as image. Cockney rhyming slang is one of the most widely recognized forms of slang, using one familiar image to replace another, so *plates = plates of meat = feet*. Rhyming also characterizes slang terms used more widely, eg *cop shop* ('police station'), and onomatopoeia is another favoured device: *barf*, meaning 'vomit', is just one example of this.

Although the word *slang* did not appear until the 18th century, that is not to say there were no very informal usages before then. In its contemporary definition, slang can be traced at least as far back as Chaucer who, in the 14th century, used *bones* to mean 'dice' and *bouse* to mean 'alcoholic beverage' – a term still used today. However, such staying power is not a general characteristic of slang, which tends to be transitory in nature. Many terms quickly become obsolete or change meaning (eg *sweet*, which meant 'easy' in US college culture in the 1980s, but later came to mean 'excellent').

Given its colourful history, it is no surprise that slang has long attracted the interest of linguists: numerous glossaries of cant had been published before 1676, the year Elisha Coles became the first lexicographer to include canting terms in a general English dictionary. Slang is still covered in such dictionaries, although always to a limited extent, as much is too ephemeral or group-specific to be either known by or useful to a wider audience. In the 18th and 19th centuries, notable dictionaries of slang were published by the likes of Francis Grose, John Camden Hotten, and John Farmer and WE Henley; more recently, comprehensive works by Eric Partridge and Jonathon Green have received critical recognition. The study of slang in 'respectable' circles often raises the question of slang being 'tamed', but slang continues to appear and disappear, without prescriptive rules, in every language.

a spout of steaming water **5 up the spout** slang **a** ruined or lost: *the motor industry is up the spout* **b** pregnant
WORD ORIGIN Middle English *spouten*

spouting *n* NZ **a** a rainwater downpipe on the outside of a building **b** such pipes collectively

sprain *vb* **1** to injure (a joint) by a sudden twist ▷ *n* **2** this injury, which causes swelling and temporary disability
WORD ORIGIN origin unknown

sprang *vb* a past tense of **spring**

sprat *n* a small edible fish like a herring
WORD ORIGIN Old English *sprott*

sprawl *vb* **1** to sit or lie with one's arms and legs spread out **2** to spread out untidily over a large area: *the pulp mill sprawled over the narrow flats* ▷ *n* **3** the part of a city or town that has not been planned and spreads out untidily over a large area: *the huge Los Angeles sprawl* **sprawling** *adj*
WORD ORIGIN Old English *spreawlian*

spray[1] *n* **1** fine drops of a liquid **2 a** a liquid under pressure designed to be discharged in fine drops from an aerosol or atomizer: *hair spray* **b** the aerosol or atomizer itself **3** a number of small objects flying through the air: *a spray of bullets* ▷ *vb* **4** to scatter in fine drops **5** to squirt (a liquid) from an aerosol or atomizer **6** to cover with a spray: *spray the crops* **sprayer** *n*
WORD ORIGIN Middle Dutch *sprāien*

spray[2] *n* **1** a sprig or branch with buds, leaves, flowers, or berries **2** an ornament or design like this
WORD ORIGIN Germanic

spray gun *n* a device for spraying fine drops of paint, etc.

spread *vb* **spreading, spread 1** to open out or unfold to the fullest width: *spread the material out* **2** to extend over a larger expanse: *the subsequent unrest spread countrywide* **3** to apply as a coating: *spread the paste evenly over your skin* **4** to be displayed to its fullest extent: *the shining bay spread out below* **5** to send or be sent out in all directions or to many people: *the news spread quickly; the sandflies that spread the disease* **6** to distribute or be distributed evenly: *we were advised to spread the workload over the whole year* **7 spread out** (of people) to increase the distance between one and other (to widen the scope of a search, for example) ▷ *n* **8** a spreading; distribution, dispersion, or expansion: *the spread of higher education* **9** informal a large meal **10** informal the wingspan of an aircraft or bird **11** informal chiefly US & Canad a ranch or other large area of land **12** a soft food which can be spread: *cheese spread* **13** two facing pages in a book or magazine **14** a widening of the hips and waist: *middle-age spread*
WORD ORIGIN Old English *sprædan*

spread-eagled *adj* with arms and legs outstretched

spreadsheet *n* a computer program for manipulating figures, used for financial planning

spree *n* a session of overindulgence, usually in drinking or spending money
WORD ORIGIN Scots *spreath* plundered cattle

sprig *n* **1** a shoot, twig, or sprout **2** an ornamental device like this **3** NZ a stud on the sole of a soccer or rugby boot **sprigged** *adj*
WORD ORIGIN Germanic

sprightly *adj* **-lier, -liest** lively and active **sprightliness** *n*
WORD ORIGIN obsolete *spright*, variant of SPRITE

spring *vb* **springing, sprang** or **sprung; sprung 1** to jump suddenly upwards or forwards **2** to return or be returned into natural shape from a forced position by elasticity: *the coil sprang back* **3** to cause (something) to happen unexpectedly: *the national coach sprang a surprise* **4** (usually foll. by *from*) to originate; be descended: *this motivation springs from their inborn curiosity; Truman sprang from ordinary people* **5** (often foll. by *up*) to come into being or appear suddenly: *new courses will spring up* **6** to provide (something, such as a mattress) with springs **7** informal to arrange the escape of (someone) from prison ▷ *n* **8** the season between winter and summer **9** a leap or jump **10** a coil which can be compressed, stretched, or bent and then return to its original shape when released **11** a natural pool forming the source of a stream **12** elasticity **springlike** *adj*
WORD ORIGIN Old English *springan*

spring balance or esp. US **spring scale** *n* a device that indicates the weight of an object by the extension of a spring to which the object is attached

springboard *n* **1** a flexible board used to gain height or momentum in diving or gymnastics **2** anything that makes it possible for an activity to begin: *the meeting acted as a springboard for future negotiations*

springbok *n, pl* **-bok** or **-boks 1** a S African antelope which moves in leaps **2** a person who has represented S Africa in a national sports team
WORD ORIGIN Afrikaans

spring chicken *n* **1** a young chicken, which is tender for cooking **2 he** or **she is no spring chicken** informal he or she is no longer young

spring-clean *vb* **1** to clean (a house) thoroughly, traditionally at the end of winter ▷ *n* **2** an instance of this **spring-cleaning** *n*

spring onion *n* a small onion with a tiny bulb and long green leaves, eaten in salads

spring roll *n* an Oriental dish consisting of a savoury mixture rolled in a thin pancake and fried

spring tide *n* either of the two tides at or just after new moon and full moon: the greatest rise and fall in tidal level

springtime *n* the season of spring

springy *adj* **springier, springiest** (of an object) having the quality of returning to its original shape after being pressed or pulled **springiness** *n*

sprinkle *vb* **-kling, -kled 1** to scatter (liquid or powder) in tiny drops over (something) **2** to distribute over (something): *a dozen mud huts sprinkled around it* **sprinkler** *n*
WORD ORIGIN probably from Middle Dutch *sprenkelen*

sprinkling *n* a small quantity or amount: *a sprinkling of diamonds*

sprint *n* **1** athletics **a** a short race run at top speed **b** a fast run at the end of a longer race **2** any quick run ▷ *vb* **3** to run or cycle a short distance at top speed **sprinter** *n*
WORD ORIGIN Scandinavian

sprit *n* naut a light pole set diagonally across a sail to extend it
WORD ORIGIN Old English *sprēot*

sprite *n* **1** (in folklore) a fairy or elf **2** an icon in a computer game which can be manoeuvred around the screen
WORD ORIGIN Latin *spiritus* spirit

spritsail *n* naut a sail mounted on a sprit

spritzer *n* a tall drink of wine and soda water
WORD ORIGIN German *spritzen* to splash

sprocket *n* **1** Also called: **sprocket wheel** a wheel with teeth on the rim, that drives or is driven by a chain **2** a cylindrical wheel with teeth on one or both rims for pulling film through a camera or projector
WORD ORIGIN origin unknown

sprout *vb* **1** (of a plant or seed) to produce (new leaves or shoots) **2** (often foll. by *up*) to begin to grow or develop ▷ *n* **3** a new shoot or bud **4** same as **Brussels sprout**
WORD ORIGIN Old English *sprūtan*

spruce[1] *n* **1** an evergreen pyramid-shaped tree with needle-like leaves **2** the light-coloured wood of this tree
WORD ORIGIN obsolete *Spruce* Prussia

spruce[2] *adj* neat and smart
WORD ORIGIN perhaps from *Spruce leather*; see SPRUCE[1]

spruce up *vb* **sprucing, spruced** to make neat and smart

sprung *vb* a past tense and the past participle of **spring**

spry *adj* **spryer, spryest** or **sprier, spriest** active and lively; nimble
WORD ORIGIN origin unknown

spud *n* informal a potato
WORD ORIGIN obsolete *spudde* short knife

spume *n* literary **1** foam or froth on the sea ▷ *vb* **spuming, spumed 2** (of the sea) to foam or froth
WORD ORIGIN Latin *spuma*

spun *vb* **1** the past of **spin** ▷ *adj* **2** made by spinning: *spun sugar; spun silk*

spunk *n* **1** old-fashioned, informal courage or spirit **2** chiefly Brit vulgar slang semen **3** Austral & NZ informal a sexually attractive person, especially a male **spunky** *adj*
WORD ORIGIN Scottish Gaelic *spong* tinder, sponge

spur *n* **1** an incentive to get something done **2** a sharp spiked wheel on the heel of a rider's boot used to urge the horse on **3** a sharp horny part sticking out from a cock's leg **4** a ridge sticking out from a mountain side **5 on the spur of the moment** suddenly and without planning; on impulse **6 win one's spurs** to prove one's ability ▷ *vb* **spurring, spurred 7** (often foll. by *on*) to encourage (someone)
WORD ORIGIN Old English *spura*

spurge *n* a plant with milky sap and small flowers
WORD ORIGIN Latin *expurgare* to cleanse

spurious *adj* not genuine or real
WORD ORIGIN Latin *spurius* of illegitimate birth

spurn *vb* to reject (a person or thing) with contempt
WORD ORIGIN Old English *spurnan*

spurt *vb* **1** to gush or cause (something) to gush out in a sudden powerful stream or jet **2** to make a sudden effort ▷ *n* **3** a short burst of activity, speed, or energy **4** a sudden powerful stream or jet
WORD ORIGIN origin unknown

sputnik *n* a Russian artificial satellite
WORD ORIGIN Russian, literally: fellow traveller

sputter *vb, n* same as **splutter**
WORD ORIGIN Dutch *sputteren*, imitative

sputum *n, pl* **-ta** saliva, usually mixed with mucus
WORD ORIGIN Latin

spy *n, pl* **spies 1** a person employed to find out secret information about other countries or organizations **2** a person who secretly keeps watch on others ▷ *vb* **spies, spying, spied 3** (foll. by *on*) to keep a secret watch on someone **4** to work as a spy **5** to catch sight of (someone or something); notice
WORD ORIGIN Old French *espier*

spyglass *n* a small telescope

spy out *vb* to discover (something) secretly

spyware *n computers* software surreptitiously installed in a computer via the internet to gather and transmit information about the user

sq. square

SQL *n* a computer programming language that is used for database management
WORD ORIGIN structured query language

Sqn. Ldr. squadron leader

squab *n, pl* **squabs** *or* **squab** a young bird yet to leave the nest
WORD ORIGIN probably Germanic

squabble *vb* **-bling, -bled 1** to quarrel over a small matter ▷ *n* **2** a petty quarrel
WORD ORIGIN probably Scandinavian

squad *n* **1** the smallest military formation, usually a dozen soldiers **2** any small group of people working together: *the fraud squad* **3** *sport* a number of players from which a team is to be selected
WORD ORIGIN Old French *esquade*

squadron *n* the basic unit of an air force
WORD ORIGIN Italian *squadrone* soldiers drawn up in square formation

squadron leader *n* a fairly senior commissioned officer in the air force; the rank above flight lieutenant

squalid *adj* **1** dirty, untidy, and in bad condition **2** unpleasant, selfish, and often dishonest: *this squalid affair*
WORD ORIGIN Latin *squalidus*

squall¹ *n* a sudden strong wind or short violent storm
WORD ORIGIN perhaps a special use of SQUALL²

squall² *vb* **1** to cry noisily; yell ▷ *n* **2** a noisy cry or yell
WORD ORIGIN probably Scandinavian

squalor *n* **1** dirty, poor, and untidy physical conditions **2** the condition of being squalid
WORD ORIGIN Latin

squander *vb* to waste (money or resources)
WORD ORIGIN origin unknown

square *n* **1** a geometric figure with four equal sides and four right angles **2** anything of this shape **3** an open area in a town bordered by buildings or streets **4** *maths* the number produced when a number is multiplied by itself: *9 is the square of 3, written 3²* **5** *informal* a person who is dull or unfashionable **6 go back to square one** to return to the start because of failure or lack of progress ▷ *adj* **7** being a square in shape **8 a** having the same area as that of a square with sides of a specified length: *2,500 square metres of hillside* **b** denoting a square having a specified length on each side: *a cell of only four square metres* **9** straight or level: *I don't think that painting is square* **10** fair and honest: *a square deal* **11** *informal* dull or unfashionable **12** having all debts or accounts settled: *if I give you 50 pence, then we'll be square* **13 all square** on equal terms; even in score **14 square peg in a round hole** *informal* a misfit ▷ *vb* **squaring, squared 15** *maths* to multiply (a number or quantity) by itself **16** to position so as to be straight or level: *bravely he squared his shoulders* **17** to settle (a debt or account) **18** to level the score in (a game) **19** to be or cause to be consistent: *it would not have squared with her image* ▷ *adv* **20** *informal* same as **squarely** ▸ See also **square off, square up**
WORD ORIGIN Old French *esquare*

square-bashing *n Brit mil slang* marching and other drill on a parade ground

square bracket *n* either of a pair of characters [ ], used to separate a section of writing or printing from the main text

square dance *n* a country dance in which the couples are arranged in squares

square leg *n cricket* a fielding position on the on side, at right angles to the batsman

squarely *adv* **1** directly; straight: *he looked her squarely in the eye* **2** in an honest and frank way: *you should face squarely anything that worries you*

square meal *n* a meal which is large enough to leave the eater feeling full: *we gave him his first square meal in days*

square off *vb* to stand up as if ready to start boxing or fighting

square-rigged *adj naut* having sails set at right angles to the keel

square root *n* a number that when multiplied by itself gives a given number: *the square roots of 4 are 2 and -2*

square up *vb* **1** to settle bills or debts **2 square up to** to prepare to confront (a problem or a person)

squash¹ *vb* **1** to press or squeeze (something) so as to flatten it **2** to overcome (a difficult situation), often with force **3 squash in** *or* **into** to push or force (oneself or a thing) into a confined space **4** to humiliate (someone) with a sarcastic reply ▷ *n* **5** *Austral & Brit* a drink made from fruit juice or fruit syrup diluted with water **6** a crowd of people in a confined space **7** Also called: **squash rackets** a game for two players played in an enclosed court with a small rubber ball and long-handled rackets
WORD ORIGIN Old French *esquasser*

squash² *n, pl* **squashes** *or* **squash** *chiefly US & Canad* a marrow-like vegetable
WORD ORIGIN from a Native American language

squashy *adj* **squashier, squashiest** soft and easily squashed

squat *vb* **squatting, squatted 1** to crouch with the knees bent and the weight on the feet **2** *law* to occupy an unused building to which one has no legal right ▷ *adj* **3** short and thick ▷ *n* **4** a building occupied by squatters
WORD ORIGIN Old French *esquater*

squatter *n* an illegal occupier of an unused building

squaw *n offensive* a Native American woman of N America
WORD ORIGIN from a Native American language

squawk *n* **1** a loud harsh cry, esp. one made by a bird **2** *informal* a loud complaint ▷ *vb* **3** to make a squawk
WORD ORIGIN imitative

squeak *n* **1** a short high-pitched cry or sound **2 a narrow squeak** *informal* a narrow escape or success ▷ *vb* **3** to make a squeak **4 squeak through** *or* **by** to pass (an examination), but only just **squeaky** *adj* **squeakiness** *n*
WORD ORIGIN probably Scandinavian

squeaky clean *adj* **1** (of hair) washed so clean that wet strands squeak when rubbed **2** completely clean **3** *informal, derogatory* (of a person) cultivating a virtuous and wholesome image

squeal *n* **1** a long high-pitched yelp ▷ *vb* **2** to make a squeal **3** *slang* to inform on someone to the police **4** *informal chiefly Brit* to complain loudly **squealer** *n*
WORD ORIGIN Middle English *squelen*, imitative

squeamish *adj* easily shocked or upset by unpleasant sights or events
WORD ORIGIN Anglo-French *escoymous*

squeegee *n* a tool with a rubber blade used for wiping away excess water from a surface
WORD ORIGIN probably imitative

squeeze *vb* **squeezing, squeezed 1** to grip or press (something) firmly **2** to crush or press (something) so as to extract (a liquid): *squeeze the tomato and strain the juice; freshly squeezed lemon juice* **3** to push (oneself or a thing) into a confined space **4** to hug (someone) closely **5** to obtain (something) by great effort or force: *to squeeze the last dollar out of every deal* ▷ *n* **6** a squeezing **7** a hug **8** a crush of people in a confined space **9** *chiefly Brit & NZ* a restriction on borrowing made by a government to control price inflation **10** an amount extracted by squeezing: *a squeeze of lime* **11 put the squeeze on someone** *informal*

S

to put pressure on someone in order to obtain something
WORD ORIGIN Old English *cwȳsan*

squelch *vb* **1** to make a wet sucking noise, such as by walking through mud **2** *informal* to silence (someone) with a sarcastic or wounding reply ▷ *n* **3** a squelching sound **squelchy** *adj*
WORD ORIGIN imitative

squib *n* **1** a firework that burns with a hissing noise before exploding **2 damp squib** something expected to be exciting or successful but turning out to be a disappointment
WORD ORIGIN probably imitative of a light explosion

squid *n, pl* **squid** *or* **squids** a sea creature with ten tentacles and a long soft body
WORD ORIGIN origin unknown

squiffy *adj* **-fier, -fiest** *Brit informal* slightly drunk: *a bit squiffy*
WORD ORIGIN origin unknown

squiggle *n* a wavy line **squiggly** *adj*
WORD ORIGIN perhaps SQUIRM + WIGGLE

squill *n* a Mediterranean plant of the lily family
WORD ORIGIN Greek *skilla*

squint *vb* **1** to have eyes which face in different directions **2** to glance sideways ▷ *n* **3** an eye disorder in which one or both eyes turn inwards or outwards from the nose **4** *informal* a quick look; glance: *take a squint at the map* ▷ *adj* **5** *informal* not straight; crooked
WORD ORIGIN short for *asquint*

squire *n* **1** a country gentleman in England, usually the main landowner in a country community **2** *informal chiefly Brit* a term of address used by one man to another **3** *history* a knight's young attendant ▷ *vb* **squiring, squired** **4** *old-fashioned* (of a man) to escort (a woman)
WORD ORIGIN Old French *esquier*

squirm *vb* **1** to wriggle **2** to feel embarrassed or guilty ▷ *n* **3** a wriggling movement
WORD ORIGIN imitative

squirrel *n* a small bushy-tailed animal that lives in trees
WORD ORIGIN Greek *skiouros*, from *skia* shadow + *oura* tail

squirt *vb* **1** to force (a liquid) or (of a liquid) to be forced out of a narrow opening **2** to cover or spatter (a person or thing) with liquid in this way ▷ *n* **3** a jet of liquid **4** a squirting **5** *informal* a small or insignificant person
WORD ORIGIN imitative

squish *vb* **1** to crush (something) with a soft squelching sound **2** to make a squelching sound ▷ *n* **3** a soft squelching sound **squishy** *adj*
WORD ORIGIN imitative

Sr 1 (after a name) senior **2** Señor **3** *chem* strontium

Sri Lankan *adj* **1** of Sri Lanka ▷ *n* **2** a person from Sri Lanka

SRN (formerly in Britain) State Registered Nurse

SS 1 an organization in the Nazi party that provided Hitler's bodyguard, security forces, and concentration-camp guards **2** steamship
WORD ORIGIN (sense 1) German

Schutzstaffel protection squad

SSL *computers* secure sockets layer: a protocol for encrypting and transmitting sensitive data securely over the internet

St 1 Saint **2** Street

st. stone

stab *vb* **stabbing, stabbed 1** to pierce with a sharp pointed instrument **2** (often foll. by *at*) to make a thrust (at); jab **3 stab someone in the back** to do harm to someone by betraying him or her ▷ *n* **4** a stabbing **5** a sudden, usually unpleasant, sensation: *a stab of jealousy* **6** *informal* an attempt: *you've got to have a stab at it* **7 stab in the back** an act of betrayal that harms a person **stabbing** *n*
WORD ORIGIN Middle English *stabbe* stab wound

stability *n* the quality of being stable: *the security and stability of married life*

stabilize *or* **-lise** *vb* **-lizing, -lized** *or* **-lising, -lised** to make or become stable or more stable **stabilization** *or* **-lisation** *n*

stabilizer *or* **-liser** *n* **1** a device for stabilizing a child's bicycle, an aircraft, or a ship **2** a substance added to food to preserve its texture

stable[1] *n* **1** a building where horses are kept **2** an organization that breeds and trains racehorses **3** an organization that manages or trains several entertainers or athletes ▷ *vb* **-bling, -bled 4** to put or keep (a horse) in a stable
WORD ORIGIN Latin *stabulum* shed

stable[2] *adj* **1** steady in position or balance; firm **2** lasting and not likely to experience any sudden changes: *a stable environment* **3** having a calm personality; not moody **4** *physics* (of an elementary particle) not subject to decay **5** *chem* (of a chemical compound) not easily decomposed
WORD ORIGIN Latin *stabilis* steady

staccato (stak-**ah**-toe) *adj* **1** *music* (of notes) short and separate **2** consisting of short abrupt sounds: *the staccato sound of high-heels on the stairs* ▷ *adv* **3** in a staccato manner
WORD ORIGIN Italian

stack *n* **1** a pile of things, one on top of the other **2** a large neat pile of hay or straw **3 stacks** a large amount: *there's still stacks for us to do* **4** same as **chimney stack** *or* **smokestack 5** an area in a computer memory for temporary storage ▷ *vb* **6** to place (things) in a stack **7** to load or fill (something) up with piles of objects: *Henry was watching her stack the dishwasher* **8** to control (a number of aircraft) waiting to land at an airport so that each flies at a different altitude
WORD ORIGIN Old Norse *stakkr* haystack

stack up *vb* to compare with someone or something else: *how does this stack up against what you have?*

stadium *n, pl* **-diums** *or* **-dia** a large sports arena with tiered rows of seats for spectators
WORD ORIGIN Greek *stadion*

staff *n, pl for senses 1 and 2* **staffs**; *for senses 3 and 4* **staffs** *or* **staves 1** the people employed in a company, school, or organization **2** *mil* the officers

appointed to assist a commander **3** a stick with some special use, such as a walking stick or an emblem of authority **4** *music* a set of five horizontal lines on which music is written and which, along with a clef, indicates pitch ▷ *vb* **5** to provide (a company, school, or organization) with a staff
WORD ORIGIN Old English *stæf*

staff nurse *n* (in Britain) a qualified nurse ranking just below a sister or charge nurse

Staffs Staffordshire

staff sergeant *n mil* a noncommissioned officer in an army or in the US Air Force or Marine Corps

stag *n* the adult male of a deer
WORD ORIGIN Old English *stagga*

stag beetle *n* a beetle with large branched jaws

stage *n* **1** a step or period of development, growth, or progress **2** the platform in a theatre where actors perform **3 the stage** the theatre as a profession **4** the scene of an event or action **5** a part of a journey: *the last stage of his tour around France* **6** short for **stagecoach 7** *Austral & Brit* a division of a bus route for which there is a fixed fare ▷ *vb* **staging, staged 8** to present (a dramatic production) on stage: *to stage 'Hamlet'* **9** to organize and carry out (an event)
WORD ORIGIN Old French *estage* position

stagecoach *n* a large four-wheeled horse-drawn vehicle formerly used to carry passengers and mail on a regular route

stage direction *n* an instruction to an actor, written into the script of a play

stage door *n* a door at a theatre leading backstage

stage fright *n* feelings of fear and nervousness felt by a person about to appear in front of an audience

stagehand *n* a person who sets the stage and moves props in a theatre

stage-manage *vb* **-managing, -managed** to arrange (an event) from behind the scenes

stage manager *n* a person who supervises the stage arrangements of a production at a theatre

stage-struck *adj* having a great desire to act

stage whisper *n* **1** a loud whisper from an actor, intended to be heard by the audience **2** any loud whisper that is intended to be overheard

stagflation *n* inflation combined with stagnant or falling output and employment
WORD ORIGIN STAGNATION + INFLATION

stagger *vb* **1** to walk unsteadily **2** to amaze or shock (someone): *it staggered her that there was any liaison between them* **3** to arrange (events) so as not to happen at the same time: *staggered elections* ▷ *n* **4** a staggering **staggering** *adj* **staggeringly** *adv*
WORD ORIGIN dialect *stacker*

staggers *n* a disease of horses and other domestic animals that causes staggering

Words from Literature
part 26

surtout *n* a long close-fitting overcoat
He wore a long black surtout reaching nearly to his ankles
The Old Curiosity Shop Charles Dickens

swath *n* the width of corn cut by a scythe
while thy hook Spares the next swath
Ode to Autumn John Keats

sylvan *adj* sylvan means belonging to the woods
Sylvan historian
Ode on a Grecian Urn John Keats

taction *n* touch
Without being roused by some external taction upon the organs of speech and hearing
Gulliver's Travels Jonathan Swift

Tag and Rag and Bobtail *phrase* an insulting term for lower-class people
"No," said he; "not till it got about that there was no protection on the premises, and it come to be considered dangerous, with convicts and Tag and Rag and Bobtail going up and down."
Great Expectations Charles Dickens

tallow *n* hard animal fat that is used to make candles and soap
and a lot of tallow candles
The Adventures of Huckleberry Finn Mark Twain

tan *v* to tan means to beat or whip
and if I catch you about that school I'll tan you good
The Adventures of Huckleberry Finn Mark Twain

tanyard *n* the tanyard is part of a tannery, which is a place where leather is made from animal skins
hid in the old tanyard
The Adventures of Huckleberry Finn Mark Twain

tarry *adj* tarry means the colour of tar or black
his tarry pig-tail
Treasure Island Robert Louis Stevenson

thereof *adv* from there
By all desires which thereof did ensue
On His Mistress John Donne

thick with, be *phrase* if you are thick with someone you are very close. It is often used to describe people who are planning something secret
Hasn't he been thick with Mr Heathcliff lately?
Wuthering Heights Emily Brontë

thimble *n* a thimble is a small cover used to protect the finger while sewing
The paper had been sealed in several places by a thimble
Treasure Island Robert Louis Stevenson

thirtover *adj* an old word which means obstinate or that someone is very determined to do want they want and can not be persuaded to do something in another way
I have been living on in a thirtover, lackadaisical way
Tess of the D'Urbervilles Thomas Hardy

timbrel *n* a tambourine
What pipes and timbrels?
Ode on a Grecian Urn John Keats

tin *n* slang for money or cash
Then the plain question is, an't it a pity that this state of things should continue, and how much better would it be for the old gentleman to hand over a reasonable amount of tin, and make it all right and comfortable
The Old Curiosity Shop Charles Dickens

tincture *n* a medicine made with alcohol and a small amount of a drug
with ink composed of a cephalic tincture
Gulliver's Travels Jonathan Swift

tithe *n* a tithe is a tax paid to the church
and held farms which, speaking from a spiritual point of view, paid highly-desirable tithes
Silas Marner George Eliot

towardly *adj* a towardly child is dutiful or obedient
and a towardly child
Gulliver's Travels Jonathan Swift

staging *n* a temporary support used in building

stagnant *adj* **1** (of water) stale from not moving **2** unsuccessful or dull from lack of change or development **WORD ORIGIN** Latin *stagnans*

stagnate *vb* -nating, -nated to become inactive or unchanging: *people in old age only stagnate when they have no interests* **stagnation** *n*

stag night *or* **party** *n* a party for men only, held for a man who is about to get married

stagy *or US* **stagey** *adj* stagier, stagiest too theatrical or dramatic

staid *adj* serious, rather dull, and old-fashioned in behaviour or appearance **WORD ORIGIN** obsolete past participle of STAY

stain *vb* **1** to discolour (something) with marks that are not easily removed **2** to dye (something) with a lasting pigment ▷ *n* **3** a mark or discoloration that is not easily removed **4** an incident in someone's life that has damaged his or her reputation: *a stain on his character* **5** a liquid used to penetrate the surface of a material, such as wood, and colour it without covering up the surface or grain **WORD ORIGIN** Middle English *steynen*

stained glass *n* glass that has been coloured for artistic purposes

stainless steel *n* a type of steel that does not rust, as it contains large amounts of chromium

stair *n* **1** one step in a flight of stairs **2** a series of steps: *he fled down the back stair* ▸ See also **stairs** **WORD ORIGIN** Old English *stæger*

staircase *n* a flight of stairs, usually with a handrail or banisters

stairs *pl n* a flight of steps going from one level to another, usually indoors

stairway *n* a staircase

stairwell *n* a vertical shaft in a building that contains a staircase

stake[1] *n* **1** a stick or metal bar driven into the ground as part of a fence or as a support or marker **2 be burned at the stake** to be executed by being tied to a stake in the centre of a pile of wood that is then set on fire ▷ *vb* **staking, staked 3** to lay (a claim) to land or rights **4** to support (something, such as a plant) with a stake **WORD ORIGIN** Old English *staca* stake, post

stake[2] *n* **1** the money that a player must risk in order to take part in a gambling game or make a bet **2** an interest, usually financial, held in something: *a 50% stake in a new consortium* **3 at stake** at risk **4 stakes a** the money that a player has available for gambling **b** a prize in a race or contest **c** a horse race in which all owners of competing horses contribute to the prize ▷ *vb* **staking, staked 5** to risk (something, such as money) on a result **6** to give financial support to (a business) **WORD ORIGIN** origin unknown

stakeholder *n* **1** a person or group not owning shares in an enterprise but having an interest in its operations, such as the employees, customers, or local community ▷ *adj* **2** relating to policies intended to allow people to participate in decisions made by enterprises in which they have a stake: *stakeholder economy*

stakeout *n* **1** slang chiefly US & Canad a police surveillance of an area or house ▷ *vb* **stake out 2** slang chiefly US & Canad to keep an area or house under surveillance **3** to surround (a piece of land) with stakes

stalactite *n* an icicle-shaped mass of calcium carbonate hanging from the roof of a cave: formed by continually dripping water **WORD ORIGIN** Greek *stalaktos* dripping

stalagmite *n* a large pointed mass of calcium carbonate sticking up from the floor of a cave: formed by continually dripping water from a stalactite **WORD ORIGIN** Greek *stalagmos* dripping

stale *adj* **1** (esp. of food) no longer fresh, having being kept too long **2** (of air) stagnant and having an unpleasant smell **3** lacking in enthusiasm or ideas through overwork or lack of variety **4** uninteresting from having been done or seen too many times: *such achievements now seem stale today* **5** no longer new: *her war had become stale news* **staleness** *n* **WORD ORIGIN** probably from Old French *estale* motionless

stalemate *n* **1** a chess position in which any of a player's moves would place his king in check: in this position the game ends in a draw **2** a situation in which further action by two opposing forces is impossible or will not achieve anything; deadlock **WORD ORIGIN** obsolete *stale* standing place + CHECKMATE

Stalinism *n* the policies associated with Joseph Stalin, general secretary of the Communist Party of the Soviet Union 1922–53, which resulted in rapid industrialization, state terror as a means of political control, and the abolition of collective leadership **Stalinist** *n, adj*

stalk[1] *n* **1** the main stem of a plant **2** a stem that joins a leaf or flower to the main stem of a plant **WORD ORIGIN** probably from Old English *stalu* upright piece of wood

stalk[2] *vb* **1** to follow (an animal or person) quietly and secretly in order to catch or kill them **2** to pursue persistently and, sometimes, attack (a person with whom one is obsessed, often a celebrity) **3** to spread over (a place) in a menacing way: *danger stalked the streets* **4** to walk in an angry, arrogant, or stiff way **stalker** *n* **WORD ORIGIN** Old English *bestealcian*

stalking-horse *n* something or someone used to hide a true purpose; pretext

stall[1] *n* **1** a small stand for the display and sale of goods **2** a compartment in a stable or shed for a single animal **3** any small room or compartment: *a shower stall* ▷ *vb* **4** to stop (a motor vehicle or its engine) or (of a motor vehicle or its engine) to stop, by incorrect use of the clutch or incorrect adjustment of the fuel mixture **WORD ORIGIN** Old English *steall* a place for standing

stall[2] *vb* to employ delaying tactics towards (someone); be evasive **WORD ORIGIN** Anglo-French *estale* bird used as a decoy

stallion *n* an uncastrated male horse, usually used for breeding **WORD ORIGIN** Old French *estalon*

stalls *n* **1** the seats on the ground floor of a theatre or cinema **2** (in a church) a row of seats, divided by armrests or a small screen, for the choir or clergy

stalwart (**stawl**-wart) *adj* **1** strong and sturdy **2** loyal and reliable ▷ *n* **3** a hard-working and loyal supporter: *local party stalwarts* **WORD ORIGIN** Old English *stælwirthe* serviceable

stamen *n* the part of a flower that produces pollen **WORD ORIGIN** Latin: the warp in an upright loom

stamina *n* energy and strength sustained while performing an activity over a long time **WORD ORIGIN** Latin: the threads of life spun out by the Fates, hence energy

stammer *vb* **1** to speak or say (something) with involuntary pauses or repetition, as a result of a speech disorder or through fear or nervousness ▷ *n* **2** a speech disorder characterized by involuntary repetitions and pauses **WORD ORIGIN** Old English *stamerian*

stamp *n* **1** a printed paper label attached to a piece of mail to show that the required postage has been paid **2** a token issued by a shop or business after a purchase that can be saved and exchanged for other goods sold by that shop or business **3** the action or an act of stamping **4** an instrument for stamping a design or words **5** a design, device, or mark that has been stamped **6** a characteristic feature: *the stamp of inevitability* **7** Brit informal a national insurance contribution, formerly recorded by a stamp on an official card **8** type or class: *men of his stamp* ▷ *vb* **9** (often foll. by on) to bring (one's foot) down heavily **10** to walk with heavy or noisy footsteps **11** to characterize: *a performance that stamped him as a star* **12 stamp on** to subdue or restrain: *all of which have stamped on dissent* **13** to impress or mark (a pattern or sign) on **14** to mark (something) with an official seal or device **15** to have a strong effect on: *a picture vividly stamped on memory* **16** to stick a stamp on (an envelope or parcel) **WORD ORIGIN** probably from Old English *stampian*

stampede *n* **1** a sudden rush of frightened animals or of a crowd ▷ *vb* -peding, -peded **2** to run away in a stampede **WORD ORIGIN** Spanish *estampar* to stamp

stamping ground *n* a favourite meeting place

stamp out *vb* **1** to put an end to (something) by force; suppress: *an attempt to stamp out democracy* **2** to put out by stamping: *I stamped out my cigarette*

stance *n* **1** an attitude towards a particular matter: *a tough stance in the trade talks* **2** the manner and position in which a person stands **3** *sport* the position taken when about to play the ball
WORD ORIGIN Latin *stare* to stand

stanch (stahnch) *vb* same as **staunch²**
WORD ORIGIN Old French *estanchier*

stanchion *n* a vertical pole or bar used as a support
WORD ORIGIN Old French *estanchon*

stand *vb* **standing, stood 1** to be upright **2** to rise to an upright position **3** to place (something) upright **4** to be situated: *the property stands in a prime position* **5** to have a specified height when standing: *the structure stands sixty feet above the river* **6** to be in a specified position: *Turkey stands to gain handsomely* **7** to be in a specified state or condition: *how he stands in comparison to others* **8** to remain unchanged or valid: *the Conservatives were forced to let much of the legislation stand* **9 stand at** (of a score or an account) to be in the specified position: *now the total stands at nine* **10** to tolerate or bear: *Christopher can't stand him* **11** to survive: *stand the test of time* **12** (often foll. by for) to be a candidate: *to stand for president* **13** *informal* to buy: *to stand someone a drink* **14 stand a chance** to have a chance of succeeding **15 stand one's ground** to face a difficult situation bravely **16 stand trial** to be tried in a law court ▷ *n* **17** a stall or counter selling goods: *the hot dog stand* **18** a structure at a sports ground where people can sit or stand **19** the act or an instance of standing **20** a firmly held opinion: *its firm stand on sanctions* **21** US & Austral a place in a law court where a witness stands **22** a rack on which coats and hats may be hung **23** a base, support, or piece of furniture in or on which articles may be held or stored: *a guitar stand* **24** an effort to defend oneself or one's beliefs against attack or criticism: *a last stand against superior forces* **25** *cricket* a long period at the wicket by two batsmen **26** see **one-night stand** ▸ See also **stand by, stand down**, etc.
WORD ORIGIN Old English *standan*

standard *n* **1** a level of quality: *cuisine of a high standard* **2** an accepted example of something against which others are judged or measured: *the work was good by any standard* **3** a moral principle of behaviour **4** a flag of a nation or cause **5** an upright pole or beam used as a support: *a lamp standard* **6** a song that has remained popular for many years ▷ *adj* **7** of a usual, medium, or accepted kind: *a standard cost* **8** of recognized authority: *a standard reference book* **9** denoting pronunciations or grammar regarded as correct and acceptable by educated native speakers
WORD ORIGIN Old French *estandart* gathering place

standard assessment tasks *pl n* (in Britain) national standardized tests for assessing school pupils

standard-bearer *n* **1** a leader of a movement or party **2** a person who carries a flag in battle or in a march

Standard English *n* *linguistics* the style of English that is regarded as correct and acceptable by educated native speakers

standard gauge *n* **1** a railway track with a distance of 56½ inches (1.435 m) between the lines: used on most railways ▷ *adj* **standard-gauge 2** denoting a railway with a standard gauge

Standard Grade *n* **1** (in Scotland) an examination designed to test skills and application of knowledge, replacing the O Grade **2** a pass in an examination at this level

standardize or **-dise** *vb* **-dizing, -dized** or **-dising, -dised** to make (things) standard: *to standardize the preparation process* **standardization** or **-disation** *n*

standard lamp *n* a tall electric lamp that has a shade and stands on a base

standard of living *n* the level of comfort and wealth of a person, group, or country

standard time *n* the official local time of a region or country determined by the distance from Greenwich of a line of longitude passing through the area

stand by *vb* **1** to be available and ready to act if needed: *stand by for firing* **2** to be present as an onlooker or without taking any action: *the military police stood by watching idly* **3** to be faithful to: *his wife will stand by him* ▷ *n* **stand-by 4** a person or thing that is ready for use or can be relied on in an emergency **5 on stand-by** ready for action or use ▷ *adj* **stand-by 6** not booked in advance but subject to availability: *stand-by planes*

stand down *vb* to resign or withdraw, often in favour of another

stand for *vb* **1** to represent: *AIDS stands for Acquired Immune Deficiency Syndrome* **2** to support and represent (an idea or a belief): *to stand for liberty and truth* **3** *informal* to tolerate or bear: *I won't stand for this!*

stand in *vb* **1** to act as a substitute: *she stood in for her father* ▷ *n* **stand-in 2** a person who acts as a substitute for another

standing *adj* **1** permanent, fixed, or lasting: *it was a standing joke* **2** used to stand in or on: *standing room only* **3** *athletics* (of a jump or the start of a race) begun from a standing position ▷ *n* **4** social or financial status or reputation: *her international standing* **5** duration: *a friendship of at least ten years' standing*

standing order *n* **1** an instruction to a bank to pay a fixed amount to a person or organization at regular intervals **2** a rule or order governing the procedure of an organization

standoff *n* **1** US & Canad the act or an instance of standing off or apart **2** a deadlock or stalemate ▷ *vb* **stand off 3** to stay at a distance

standoffish *adj* behaving in a formal and unfriendly way

stand out *vb* **1** to be more impressive or important than others of the same kind: *his passing ability stood out in this game* **2** to be noticeable because of looking different: *her long fair hair made her stand out*

from the rest **3** to refuse to agree or comply: *a hero who stood out against foreign domination*

standpipe *n* *chiefly Brit* a temporary vertical pipe installed in a street and supplying water when household water supplies are cut off

standpoint *n* a point of view from which a matter is considered

standstill *n* a complete stoppage or halt: *all traffic came to a standstill*

stand to *vb* **1** *mil* to take up positions in order to defend against attack **2 stand to reason** to be obvious or logical: *it stands to reason you will play better*

stand up *vb* **1** to rise to one's feet **2** *informal* to fail to keep a date with (a boyfriend or girlfriend): *sometimes he would stand me up* **3** to be accepted as satisfactory or true: *the decision would not stand up in court* **4 stand up for** to support or defend **5 stand up to a** to confront or resist (someone) bravely **b** to withstand and endure (something, such as criticism) ▷ *adj* **stand-up 6** (of a comedian) telling jokes alone to an audience **7** done while standing: *a stand-up breakfast* **8** (of a fight or row) angry and unrestrained **9** stand-up comedy or a stand-up comedian

stank *vb* a past tense of **stink**

Stanley knife *n* *trademark* a type of knife with a thick metal handle with a short, very sharp, replaceable blade
WORD ORIGIN after F. T. *Stanley*, businessman

stanza *n* *prosody* a verse of a poem
WORD ORIGIN Italian: halting place

staphylococcus (staff-ill-oh-**kok**-uss) *n, pl* **-cocci** (-**kok**-eye) a bacterium occurring in clusters and including many species that cause disease
WORD ORIGIN Greek *staphulē* bunch of grapes + *kokkos* berry

staple¹ *n* **1** a short length of wire bent into a square U-shape, used to fasten papers or secure things ▷ *vb* **-pling, -pled 2** to secure (things) with staples
WORD ORIGIN Old English *stapol* prop

staple² *adj* **1** of prime importance; principal: *the staple diet of a country* ▷ *n* **2** something that forms a main part of the product, consumption, or trade of a region **3** a main constituent of anything: *the personal reflections which make up the staple of the book*
WORD ORIGIN Middle Dutch *stapel* warehouse

stapler *n* a device used to fasten things together with a staple

star *n* **1** a planet or meteor visible in the clear night sky as a point of light **2** a hot gaseous mass, such as the sun, that radiates energy as heat and light, or in some cases as radio waves and X-rays ▸ Related adjectives: **astral, sidereal, stellar 3** stars same as **horoscope** (sense 1) **4** an emblem with five or more radiating points, often used as a symbol of rank or an award: *the RAC awarded the hotel three stars* **5** same as **asterisk 6** a famous person from the sports, acting, or music professions **7 see stars** to see flashes of light after a blow on the head ▷ *vb* **starring, starred 8** to feature (an actor or actress) or (of

an actor or actress) to be featured as a star: *he's starred in dozens of films* **9** to mark (something) with a star or stars
WORD ORIGIN Old English *steorra*

starboard *n* **1** the right side of an aeroplane or ship when facing forwards ▷ *adj* **2** of or on the starboard
WORD ORIGIN Old English *stēorbord*, literally: steering side

starch *n* **1** a carbohydrate forming the main food element in bread, potatoes, and rice: in solution with water it is used to stiffen fabric **2** food containing a large amount of starch ▷ *vb* **3** to stiffen (cloth) with starch
WORD ORIGIN Old English *sterced* stiffened

starchy *adj* **starchier, starchiest 1** of or containing starch **2** (of a person's behaviour) very formal and humourless

star-crossed *adj* (of lovers) destined to misfortune

stardom *n* the status of a star in the entertainment or sport world

stare *vb* **staring, stared 1** (often foll. by *at*) to look at for a long time **2 stare one in the face** to be glaringly obvious ▷ *n* **3** a long fixed look
WORD ORIGIN Old English *starian*

starfish *n, pl* **-fish** *or* **-fishes** a star-shaped sea creature with a flat body and five limbs

star fruit *n* same as **carambola**

stargazer *n informal* an astrologer **stargazing** *n*

stark *adj* **1** harsh, unpleasant, and plain: *a stark choice* **2** grim, desolate, and lacking any beautiful features: *the stark landscapes* **3** utter; absolute: *in stark contrast* ▷ *adv* **4** completely: *stark staring bonkers* **starkly** *adv* **starkness** *n*
WORD ORIGIN Old English *stearc* stiff

stark-naked *adj* completely naked. Also (informal): **starkers**
WORD ORIGIN Middle English *stert naket*, literally: tail naked

starlet *n* a young actress who has the potential to become a star

starlight *n* the light that comes from the stars

starling *n* a common songbird with shiny blackish feathers and a short tail
WORD ORIGIN Old English *stærlinc*

starlit *adj* lit by starlight

Star of David *n* a symbol of Judaism, consisting of a star formed by two interlaced equilateral triangles

starry *adj* **-rier, -riest 1** (of a sky or night) full of or lit by stars **2** of or like a star or stars: *a starry cast*

starry-eyed *adj* full of unrealistic hopes and dreams; naive

Stars and Stripes *n* the national flag of the United States of America

star sign *n astrol* the sign of the zodiac under which a person was born

Star-Spangled Banner *n* **1** the national anthem of the United States of America **2** same as **Stars and Stripes**

star-studded *adj* featuring many well-known performers: *a star-studded premiere*

start *vb* **1** to begin (something or to do something); come or cause to come into

being: *to start a war; this conflict started years ago* **2** to set or be set in motion: *he started the van* **3** to make a sudden involuntary movement from fright or surprise; jump **4** to establish; set up: *to start a state lottery* **5** to support (someone) in the first part of a career or activity **6** *Brit informal* to begin quarrelling or causing a disturbance: *don't start with me* **7 to start with** in the first place ▷ *n* **8** the first part of something **9** the place or time at which something begins **10** a signal to begin, such as in a race **11** a lead or advantage, either in time or distance, in a competitive activity: *he had an hour's start on me* **12** a slight involuntary movement from fright or surprise: *I awoke with a start* **13** an opportunity to enter a career or begin a project **14 for a start** in the first place ▸ See also **start off, start on**, etc.
WORD ORIGIN Old English *styrtan*

starter *n* **1** *chiefly Brit* the first course of a meal **2 for starters** *slang* in the first place **3** a device for starting an internal-combustion engine **4** a person who signals the start of a race **5** a competitor in a race or contest **6 under starter's orders** (of competitors in a race) waiting for the signal to start

startle *vb* **-tling, -tled** to slightly surprise or frighten someone **startling** *adj*
WORD ORIGIN Old English *steartlian* to kick, struggle

start off *vb* **1** to set out on a journey **2** to be or make the first step in (an activity): *beginners should start off with a walking programme* **3** to cause (a person) to do something, such as laugh

start on *vb Brit informal* to pick a quarrel with: *they started on me*

start out *vb* **1** to set out on a journey **2** to take the first steps in a career or on a course of action: *I started out as a beautician; it started out as a joke*

start up *vb* **1** to come or cause (something, such as a business) to come into being; found **2** to set (something) in motion: *she started up the car*

starve *vb* **starving, starved 1** to die from lack of food **2** to deliberately prevent (a person or animal) from having any food **3** *informal* to be very hungry: *we're both starving* **4 starve of** to deprive (someone) of something needed: *the heart is starved of oxygen* **5 starve into** to force someone into a specified state by starving: *an attempt to starve him into submission* **starvation** *n*
WORD ORIGIN Old English *steorfan* to die

Star Wars *n* (in the US) a proposed system of artificial satellites armed with lasers to destroy enemy missiles in space

stash *informal vb* **1** (often foll. by *away*) *informal* to store (money or valuables) in a secret place for safekeeping ▷ *n* **2** a secret store, usually of illegal drugs, or the place where this is hidden
WORD ORIGIN origin unknown

state *n* **1** the condition or circumstances of a person or thing **2** a sovereign political power or community **3** the territory of such a community **4** the sphere of power in such a community:

matters of state **5** (*often cap*) one of a number of areas or communities having their own governments and forming a federation under a sovereign government, such as in the US or Australia **6** (*often cap*) the government, civil service, and armed forces **7 in a state** *informal* in an emotional or very worried condition **8 lie in state** (of a body) to be placed on public view before burial **9 state of affairs** circumstances or condition: *this wonderful state of affairs* **10** grand and luxurious lifestyle, as enjoyed by royalty, aristocrats, or the wealthy: *living in state* ▷ *adj* **11** controlled or financed by a state: *state ownership* **12** of or concerning the State: *state secrets* **13** involving ceremony: *a state visit* ▷ *vb* **stating, stated 14** to express (something) in words
WORD ORIGIN Latin *stare* to stand

State Enrolled Nurse *n* (in Britain) a nurse who has completed a two-year training course

statehouse *n NZ* a rented house built by the government

stateless *adj* not belonging to any country: *stateless refugees*

stately *adj* **-lier, -liest** having a dignified, impressive, and graceful appearance or manner: *the Rolls-Royce approached him at a stately speed* **stateliness** *n*

stately home *n Brit* a large old mansion, usually one open to the public

statement *n* **1** something stated, usually a formal prepared announcement or reply **2** *law* a declaration of matters of fact **3** an account prepared by a bank at regular intervals for a client to show all credits and debits and the balance at the end of the period **4** an account containing a summary of bills or invoices and showing the total amount due **5** the act of stating

state of the art *n* **1** the current level of knowledge and development achieved in a technology, science, or art ▷ *adj* **state-of-the-art 2** the most recent and therefore considered the best; up-to-the-minute: *state-of-the-art computers*

State Registered Nurse *n* (formerly in Britain) a nurse who has completed an extensive three-year training course

stateroom *n* **1** a private room on a ship **2** *chiefly Brit* a large room in a palace, etc. used on ceremonial occasions

States *pl n* **the States** *informal* the United States of America

state school *n* a school funded by the state, in which education is free

statesman *n, pl* **-men** an experienced and respected political leader **statesmanship** *n*

static *adj* **1** not active, changing, or moving; stationary **2** *physics* (of a weight, force, or pressure) acting but causing no movement **3** *physics* of forces that do not produce movement ▷ *n* **4** hissing or crackling or a speckled picture caused by interference in the reception of radio or television transmissions **5** electric sparks or crackling produced by friction

Word Histories
part 12

Squaw has been at the centre of a raging controversy in recent years, with activists in the US alleging that the term derives from the Mohawk word for the female genitals, and is thus a gross insult to Native American women. This has led to a campaign to remove the word from various US placenames. In fact, 'squaw' comes from Massachuset, one of the Algonquin languages, and simply means 'woman'; the other Algonquin languages have related words with the same meaning. So the association with female genitals is simply false. This does not mean, however, that the word does not carry an offensive connotation. While it is not offensive in Algonquin, and while various Native American peoples use the term in English to describe their traditional practices, such as the Navajo Squaw Dance, the word undoubtedly carries a dehumanizing overtone when used to simply describe a Native American woman. Equivalents such as 'Jewess' and 'Negress' have passed out of general use for the same reason.

Starboard comes from Old English *steorbord*, which means 'steering side'. This is because boats were formerly steered with a paddle held over the right-hand side of the boat.

A **Steeplechase** was originally a horse race across country using a distant church steeple as the landmark to aim for as the finishing point of the race.

Stoic behaviour mirrors that advocated by the Stoics a school of philosophers in ancient Greece.

Suede: In French, *gants de Suède* means 'gloves from Sweden'. The gloves were called 'Swedish gloves' because they were first made there.

Swashbuckling: *Swashbuckling* originally meant 'making a noise by 'swashing' or banging your sword against your 'buckler' or shield.

Tarmac is short for *tarmacadam*, from the surname of John McAdam (1756–1836), the Scottish road engineer who greatly improved the state of British roads and invented the process of making road surfaces from a layer of small stones on top of larger stones.

Teddy bear: 'Teddy bears' are named after the American president Theodore (Teddy) Roosevelt (1859–1919), who was keen on bear-hunting.

Tip is sometimes said to be an acronym for 'To Insure Promptness'. 'Insure', rather than 'ensure', should alert us to this story's shaky foundations; like most supposed acronym etymologies, this one isn't true. 'Tip', in the sense of a small gift for service, probably comes from thieves' cant, and may be connected to the verb 'tap'.

Titan: In Greek mythology, the *Titans* were a family of twelve giants, the children of Uranus and Gaia.

Tory comes from Irish *toraidhe* or *toiridhe*, meaning 'outlaw' or 'robber'. The name was first given to Irish outlaws who harassed the English in Ireland, and then came to be applied to members of the English political faction that opposed the exclusion of the Roman Catholic James, Duke of York, from succession to the throne. Thereafter 'Tory' remained as a political label for those of a conservative outlook, as opposed to the more reformist Whigs.

Troll: An interesting example of recent folk etymology is the evolution of 'troll' on the internet. In internet discussion forums, a troll is someone who deliberately tries to provoke a heated argument. When the term first appeared in the 1990s, it was applied to the provocative message that achieved this; the person who posted it was 'trolling', in the sense of 'fishing' for angry responses. Fairly soon, though, the person who posted such messages was labelled a 'troll', the usage clearly influenced by the malevolent creature of folklore and mythology.

Tulip comes from Turkish *tulbend*, meaning 'turban', because of the shape of the flowers.

Tycoon comes from Japanese *taikun*, meaning 'great lord'. It was a term of respect given to the Japanese shoguns, the hereditary military commanders who were for centuries the real rulers of Japan although nominally subordinate to the emperors.

WORD ORIGIN Greek *statikos* causing to stand

static electricity *n* same as **static** (sense 5)

statics *n* the branch of mechanics concerned with the forces producing a state of equilibrium

statin *n med* any of several drugs that inhibit the production of cholesterol

station *n* **1** a place along a route or line at which a bus or train stops to pick up passengers or goods **2** the headquarters of an organization such as the police or fire service **3** a building with special equipment for some particular purpose: *power station; a filling station* **4** a television or radio channel **5** *mil* a place of duty **6** position in society: *he had ideas above his station* **7** *Austral & NZ* a large sheep or cattle farm **8** the place or position where a person is assigned to stand: *every man stood at his station* ▷ *vb* **9** to assign (someone) to a station
WORD ORIGIN Latin *statio* a standing still

stationary *adj* not moving: *a line of stationary traffic*
WORD ORIGIN Latin *stationarius*

≡ **USAGE**
≡ Avoid confusion with **stationery**.

stationer *n* a person or shop selling stationery
WORD ORIGIN Medieval Latin *stationarius* a person having a regular station, hence a shopkeeper

stationery *n* writing materials, such as paper, envelopes, and pens
≡ **USAGE**
≡ Avoid confusion with **stationary**.

stationmaster *n* the senior official in charge of a railway station

Stations of the Cross *pl n RC Church* **1** a series of 14 crosses with pictures or carvings, arranged around the walls of a church, to commemorate 14 stages in Christ's journey to Calvary **2** a series of 14 prayers relating to each of these stages

station wagon *n US, Austral, & NZ* an estate car

statistic *n* a numerical fact collected and classified systematically **statistical** *adj* **statistically** *adv* **statistician** *n*

statistics *n* **1** the science dealing with the collection, classification, and interpretation of numerical information ▷ *pl n* **2** numerical information which has been collected, classified, and interpreted
WORD ORIGIN originally: science dealing with facts of a state, from New Latin *statisticus* concerning state affairs

statuary *n* statues collectively

statue *n* a sculpture of a human or animal figure, usually life-size or larger
WORD ORIGIN Latin *statuere* to set up

statuesque (stat-yoo-**esk**) *adj* (of a woman) tall and well-proportioned; like a classical statue

statuette *n* a small statue

stature *n* **1** height and size of a person **2** the reputation of a person or their achievements: *a batsman of international stature* **3** moral or intellectual distinction
WORD ORIGIN Latin *stare* to stand

status *n* **1** a person's position in society **2** the esteem in which people hold a person: *priests feel they have lost some of their status in society* **3** the legal or official standing or classification of a person or country: *the status of refugees; Ireland's non-aligned status* **4** degree of importance
WORD ORIGIN Latin: posture

status quo *n* the existing state of affairs
WORD ORIGIN literally: the state in which

status symbol *n* a possession regarded as a mark of social position or wealth

statute *n* **1** a law made by a government and expressed in a formal document **2** a permanent rule made by a company or other institution
WORD ORIGIN Latin *statuere* to set up, decree

statute law *n* **1** a law made by a government **2** such laws collectively

statutory *adj* **1** required or authorized by law **2** (of an offence) declared by law to be punishable

staunch¹ *adj* strong and loyal: *a staunch supporter* **staunchly** *adv*
WORD ORIGIN Old French *estanche*

staunch² *or* **stanch** *vb* to stop the flow of (blood) from someone's body

stave *n* **1** one of the long strips of wood joined together to form a barrel or bucket **2** a stick carried as a symbol of office **3** a verse of a poem **4** *music* same as **staff** ▷ *vb* **staving, stove** **5** **stave in** to burst a hole in something
WORD ORIGIN from *staves*, plural of STAFF

stave off *vb* **staving, staved** to delay (something) for a short time: *to stave off political rebellion*

staves *n* a plural of **staff** or **stave**

stay¹ *vb* **1** to continue or remain in a place, position, or condition: *to stay away; to stay inside* **2** to lodge as a guest or visitor temporarily: *we stay with friends* **3** *Scot & NZ* to reside permanently; live **4** to endure (something testing or difficult): *you have stayed the course this long* ▷ *n* **5** the period spent in one place **6** the postponement of an order of a court of law: *a stay of execution*
WORD ORIGIN Old French *ester*

stay² *n* something that supports or steadies something, such as a prop or buttress
WORD ORIGIN Old French *estaye*

stay³ *n* a rope or chain supporting a ship's mast or funnel
WORD ORIGIN Old English *stæg*

stay-at-home *adj* **1** (of a person) enjoying a quiet, settled, and unadventurous life ▷ *n* **2** a stay-at-home person

staycation (stay-**kay**-shun) *n informal* a holiday in which leisure activities are pursued while staying at one's own home
WORD ORIGIN from *stay¹* + (VA)CATION

staying power *n* endurance to complete something undertaken; stamina

stays *pl n* old-fashioned corsets with bones in them

staysail *n* a sail fastened on a stay

STD 1 sexually transmitted disease **2** *Brit, Austral, & S African* subscriber trunk dialling **3** *NZ* subscriber toll dialling

STD code *n Brit* a code preceding a local telephone number, allowing a caller to dial direct without the operator's help
WORD ORIGIN s(ubscriber) t(runk) d(ialling)

stead *n* **1 stand someone in good stead** to be useful to someone in the future **2** *rare* the function or position that should be taken by another: *I cannot let you rule in my stead*
WORD ORIGIN Old English *stede*

steadfast *adj* dedicated and unwavering **steadfastly** *adv* **steadfastness** *n*

steady *adj* **steadier, steadiest** **1** firm and not shaking **2** without much change or variation: *we're on a steady course* **3** continuous: *a steady decline* **4** not easily excited; sober **5** regular; habitual: *the steady drinking of alcohol* ▷ *vb* **steadies, steadying, steadied** **6** to make or become steady ▷ *adv* **7** in a steady manner **8 go steady** *informal* to date one person regularly ▷ *n, pl* **steadies 9** *informal* one's regular boyfriend or girlfriend ▷ *interj* **10** a warning to keep calm or be careful **steadily** *adv* **steadiness** *n*
WORD ORIGIN from *stead*

steady state *n physics* the condition of a system when all or most changes or disturbances have been eliminated from it

steak *n* **1** a lean piece of beef for grilling or frying **2** a cut of beef for braising or stewing **3** a thick slice of pork, veal, or fish
WORD ORIGIN Old Norse *steik* roast

steakhouse *n* a restaurant that specializes in steaks

steal *vb* **stealing, stole, stolen** **1** to take (something) from someone without permission or unlawfully **2** to use (someone else's ideas or work) without acknowledgment **3** to move quietly and carefully, not wanting to be noticed: *my father stole up behind her* **4 steal the show** (of a performer) to draw the audience's attention to oneself and away from the other performers **5** to obtain or do (something) stealthily: *I stole a glance behind* ▷ *n* **6** *US, Canad, & NZ informal* something acquired easily or at little cost
WORD ORIGIN Old English *stelan*

stealth *n* **1** moving carefully and quietly, so as to avoid being seen **2** cunning or underhand behaviour ▷ *adj* **3** (of technology) able to render an aircraft almost invisible to radar **4** disguised or hidden **stealthy** *adj* **stealthily** *adv*
WORD ORIGIN Old English *stelan* to steal

stealth tax *n* an indirect tax, such as a tax on fuel or pension plans, esp. one of which people are unaware or one that is felt to be unfair

steam *n* **1** the vapour into which water changes when boiled **2** the mist formed when such vapour condenses in the atmosphere **3** *informal* power, energy, or speed **4 let off steam** *informal* to release pent-up energy or feelings

5 pick up steam *informal* to gather momentum ▷ *adj* **6** operated, heated, or powered by steam: *a steam train* ▷ *vb* **7** to give off steam **8** (of a vehicle) to move by steam power **9** *informal* to proceed quickly and often forcefully **10** to cook (food) in steam **11** to treat (something) with steam, such as in cleaning or pressing clothes **12 steam open** *or* **off** to use steam in order to open or remove (something): *let me steam open this letter* ▷ See also **steam up**
WORD ORIGIN Old English *stēam*

steam engine *n* an engine worked by steam

steamer *n* **1** a boat or ship driven by steam engines **2** a container with holes in the bottom, used to cook food by steam

steam iron *n* an electric iron that uses steam to take creases out of clothes

steamroller *n* **1** a steam-powered vehicle with heavy rollers used for flattening road surfaces during road-making ▷ *vb* **2** to make (someone) do what one wants by overpowering force

steamship *n* a ship powered by steam engines

steam up *vb* **1** to cover (windows or glasses) or (of windows or glasses) to become covered with steam **2 steamed up** *slang* excited or angry

steamy *adj* **steamier, steamiest 1** full of steam **2** *informal* (of books, films, etc.) erotic

steatite (stee-a-tite) *n* same as **soapstone**
WORD ORIGIN Greek *stear* fat

steed *n* *archaic* or *literary* a horse
WORD ORIGIN Old English *stēda* stallion

steel *n* **1** an alloy of iron and carbon, often with small quantities of other elements **2** a steel rod used for sharpening knives **3** courage and mental toughness ▷ *vb* **4** to prepare (oneself) for coping with something unpleasant: *he had steeled himself to accept the fact* **steely** *adj*
WORD ORIGIN Old English *stēli*

steel band *n* *music* a band of people playing on metal drums, popular in the West Indies

steel-grey *adj* dark bluish-grey

steel wool *n* a mass of fine steel fibres, used for cleaning metal surfaces

steelworks *n* a factory where steel is made **steelworker** *n*

steep¹ *adj* **1** having a sharp slope **2** *informal* (of a fee, price, or demand) unreasonably high; excessive **steeply** *adv* **steepness** *n*
WORD ORIGIN Old English *stēap*

steep² *vb* **1** to soak or be soaked in a liquid in order to soften or cleanse **2 steeped in** filled with: *an industry steeped in tradition*
WORD ORIGIN Old English *stēpan*

steepen *vb* to become or cause (something) to become steep or steeper

steeple *n* a tall ornamental tower on a church roof
WORD ORIGIN Old English *stēpel*

steeplechase *n* **1** a horse race over a course with fences to be jumped **2** a track race in which the runners have to leap hurdles and a water jump ▷ *vb* **-chasing, -chased 3** to race in a steeplechase
WORD ORIGIN so called because it originally took place cross-country, with a church tower serving as a landmark for the riders in the race

steeplejack *n* a person who repairs steeples and chimneys

steer¹ *vb* **1** to direct the course of (a vehicle or vessel) with a steering wheel or rudder **2** to direct the movements or course of (a person, conversation, or activity) **3** to follow (a specified course): *the Dutch government steered a middle course* **4 steer clear of** to avoid
WORD ORIGIN Old English *stīeran*

steer² *n* a castrated male ox or bull
WORD ORIGIN Old English *stēor*

steerage *n* **1** the cheapest accommodation on a passenger ship **2** steering

steering committee *n* a committee set up to prepare and arrange topics to be discussed, and the order of business, for a government, etc.

steering wheel *n* a wheel turned by the driver of a vehicle in order to change direction

steersman *n, pl* **-men** the person who steers a vessel

stein (stine) *n* an earthenware beer mug
WORD ORIGIN German *Stein*, literally: stone

stela (steal-a) *or* **stele** (steal-ee) *n, pl* **stelae** (steal-ee) *or* **steles** an upright stone slab or column decorated with figures or inscriptions, common in prehistoric times
WORD ORIGIN Greek *stēlē*

stellar *adj* **1** relating to the stars **2** *informal* outstanding or immense: *stellar profits*
WORD ORIGIN Latin *stella* star

stem¹ *n* **1** the long thin central part of a plant **2** a stalk that bears a flower, fruit, or leaf **3** the long slender part of anything, such as a wineglass **4** *linguistics* the form of a word that remains after removal of all inflectional endings ▷ *vb* **stemming, stemmed 5 stem from** originate from: *this tradition stems from pre-Christian times*
WORD ORIGIN Old English *stemn*

stem² *vb* **stemming, stemmed** to stop or hinder the spread of (something): *to stem the flow of firearms*
WORD ORIGIN Old Norse *stemma*

stem cell *n* *histology* an undifferentiated embryonic cell that gives rise to specialized cells, such as blood, bone, etc.

stemmed *adj* having a stem: *long-stemmed roses*

stench *n* a strong and very unpleasant smell
WORD ORIGIN Old English *stenc*

stencil *n* **1** a thin sheet with a cut-out pattern through which ink or paint passes to form the pattern on the surface below **2** a design or letters made in this way ▷ *vb* **-cilling, -cilled** *or US* **-ciling, -ciled 3** to make (a design or letters) with a stencil
WORD ORIGIN Old French *estenceler* to decorate brightly

Sten gun *n* a light sub-machine-gun
WORD ORIGIN S & T (initials of the inventors) + -en, as in Bren gun

stenographer *n* *US & Canad* a shorthand typist
WORD ORIGIN Greek *stenos* narrow + *graphein* to write

stent *n* a surgical implant used to keep an artery open

stentorian *adj* (of the voice) very loud: *a stentorian tone*
WORD ORIGIN after Stentor, a herald in Greek mythology

step *n* **1** the act of moving and setting down one's foot, such as when walking **2** the distance covered by such a movement **3** the sound made by such a movement **4** one of a sequence of foot movements that make up a dance **5** one of a sequence of actions taken in order to achieve a goal **6** a degree or rank in a series or scale **7** a flat surface for placing the foot on when going up or down **8** manner of walking: *he moved with a purposeful step* **9 steps a** a flight of stairs, usually out of doors **b** same as **stepladder 10** a short easily travelled distance: *Mexico and Brazil were only a step away* **11 break step** to stop marching in step **12 in step a** marching or dancing in time or at the same pace as other people **b** *informal* in agreement: *in step with the West on this issue* **13 out of step a** not marching or dancing in time or at the same pace as other people **b** *informal* not in agreement: *out of step with the political mood* **14 step by step** gradually **15 take steps** to do what is necessary (to achieve something) **16 watch one's step a** *informal* to behave with caution **b** to walk carefully ▷ *vb* **stepping, stepped 17** to move by taking a step, such as in walking (often foll. by *on*) **18** to place or press the foot; tread **19** to walk a short distance: *please step this way* **20 step into** to enter (a situation) apparently without difficulty: *she stepped into a life of luxury* ▷ See also **step down**, **step in**, etc.
WORD ORIGIN Old English *stepe, stæpe*

Step *n* **1** a set of aerobic exercises which consists of stepping on and off a special box of adjustable height ▷ *adj* **2** denoting this type of exercise: *Step aerobics*

stepbrother *n* a son of one's stepmother or stepfather

stepchild *n, pl* **-children** a stepson or stepdaughter

stepdaughter *n* a daughter of one's husband or wife by an earlier relationship

step down *vb* *informal* to resign from a position

stepfather *n* a man who has married one's mother after the death or divorce of one's father

stephanotis (stef-fan-note-iss) *n* a tropical climbing shrub with sweet-smelling white flowers
WORD ORIGIN Greek: fit for a crown

step in *vb* *informal* to intervene (in a quarrel or difficult situation)

stepladder *n* a small folding portable ladder with a supporting frame

stepmother *n* a woman who has married one's father after the death or divorce of one's mother

step on *vb* **1** to place or press one's foot on (something): *he stepped on the brakes* **2** *informal* to behave badly towards (a person in a less powerful position) **3** **step on it** *informal* to go more quickly; hurry up

step out *vb* **1** to leave a room briefly **2** to walk quickly, taking long strides

step-parent *n* a stepfather or stepmother

steppes *pl n* wide grassy plains without trees
WORD ORIGIN Old Russian *step* lowland

stepping stone *n* **1** one of a series of stones acting as footrests for crossing a stream **2** a stage in a person's progress towards a goal: *it was a big stepping stone in his career*

stepsister *n* a daughter of one's stepmother or stepfather

stepson *n* a son of one's husband or wife by an earlier relationship

step up *vb* **1** *informal* to increase (something) by stages; accelerate **2** **step up to the plate** *US & Canad* **a** *baseball* to move into batting position **b** to come forward and take responsibility for something

stereo *adj* **1** (of a sound system) using two or more separate microphones to feed two or more loudspeakers through separate channels ▷ *n, pl* **stereos** **2** a music system in which sound is directed through two speakers **3** sound broadcast or played in stereo

stereophonic *adj* same as **stereo** (sense 1)
WORD ORIGIN Greek *stereos* solid + *phōnē* sound

stereoscopic *adj* having a three-dimensional effect: *stereoscopic vision*

stereotype *n* **1** a set of characteristics or a fixed idea considered to represent a particular kind of person **2** an idea or convention that has grown stale through fixed usage ▷ *vb* **-typing, -typed** **3** to form a standard image or idea of (a type of person)
WORD ORIGIN Greek *stereos* solid + TYPE

sterile *adj* **1** free from germs **2** unable to produce offspring **3** (of plants) not producing or bearing seeds **4** lacking inspiration or energy; unproductive **sterility** *n*
WORD ORIGIN Latin *sterilis*

sterilize *or* **-lise** *vb* **-lizing, -lized** *or* **-lising, -lised** to make sterile **sterilization** *or* **-lisation** *n*

sterling *n* **1** British money: *sterling fell by almost a pfennig* ▷ *adj* **2** genuine and reliable; first-class: *he has a reputation for sterling honesty*
WORD ORIGIN probably Old English *steorra* star, referring to a small star on early Norman pennies

sterling silver *n* **1** an alloy containing at least 92.5 per cent of silver **2** articles made of sterling silver

stern¹ *adj* **1** strict and serious: *he's a very stern taskmaster* **2** difficult and often

unpleasant: *the stern demands of the day* **3** (of a facial expression) severe and disapproving **sternly** *adv*
WORD ORIGIN Old English *styrne*

stern² *n* the rear part of a boat or ship
WORD ORIGIN Old Norse *stjörn* steering

sternum *n, pl* **-na** *or* **-nums** a long flat bone in the front of the body, to which the collarbone and most of the ribs are attached
WORD ORIGIN Greek *sternon*

steroid *n* *biochem* an organic compound containing a carbon ring system, such as sterols and many hormones

sterol *n* *biochem* a natural insoluble alcohol such as cholesterol and ergosterol
WORD ORIGIN shortened from *cholesterol, ergosterol,* etc.

stertorous *adj* (of breathing) laboured and noisy
WORD ORIGIN Latin *stertere* to snore

stet *vb* **stetting, stetted** **1** used as an instruction to indicate to a printer that certain deleted matter is to be kept **2** to mark (matter) in this way
WORD ORIGIN Latin, literally: let it stand

stethoscope *n* *med* an instrument for listening to the sounds made inside the body, consisting of a hollow disc that transmits the sound through hollow tubes to earpieces
WORD ORIGIN Greek *stēthos* breast + *skopein* to look at

Stetson *n trademark* a felt hat with a broad brim and high crown, worn mainly by cowboys
WORD ORIGIN after John *Stetson,* American hat maker

stevedore *n chiefly US* a person employed to load or unload ships
WORD ORIGIN Spanish *estibador* a packer

stew *n* **1** a dish of meat, fish, or other food, cooked slowly in a closed pot **2** in **a stew** *informal* in a troubled or worried state ▷ *vb* **3** to cook by long slow simmering in a closed pot **4** *informal* (of a person) to be too hot **5** to cause (tea) to become bitter or (of tea) to become bitter through infusing for too long **6** **stew in one's own juice** to suffer, without help, the results of one's actions
WORD ORIGIN Middle English *stuen* to take a very hot bath

steward *n* **1** a person who looks after passengers and serves meals on a ship or aircraft **2** an official who helps to supervise a public event, such as a race **3** a person who administers someone else's property **4** a person who manages the eating arrangements, staff, or service at a club or hotel **5** see **shop steward** ▷ *vb* **6** to act as a steward (of)
WORD ORIGIN Old English *stigweard* hall keeper

stewardess *n* a female steward on an aircraft or ship

stewed *adj* **1** (of food) cooked by stewing **2** *Brit* (of tea) bitter through having been left to infuse for too long **3** *slang* drunk

stick¹ *n* **1** a small thin branch of a tree **2** **a** a long thin piece of wood **b** such a piece of wood shaped for a special purpose: *a walking stick; a hockey stick*

3 a piece of something shaped like a stick: *a stick of cinnamon* **4** *slang* verbal abuse, criticism: *they gave me a lot of stick* **5** **the sticks** a country area considered backward or unsophisticated: *places out in the sticks* **6** **sticks** pieces of furniture: *these few sticks are all I have* **7** *informal* a person: *not a bad old stick* **8** **get hold of the wrong end of the stick** to misunderstand a situation or an explanation completely
WORD ORIGIN Old English *sticca*

stick² *vb* **sticking, stuck** **1** to push (a pointed object) or (of a pointed object) to be pushed into another object **2** to fasten (something) in position by pins, nails, or glue: *she just stuck the label on* **3** to extend beyond something else; protrude: *he stuck his head out of the door* **4** *informal* to place (something) in a specified position: *stick it in the oven* **5** to fasten or be fastened by or as if by an adhesive **6** to come or be brought to a standstill: *stuck in a rut; two army lorries stuck behind us* **7** to remain for a long time: *the room that sticks in my mind the most* **8** *slang chiefly Brit* to tolerate; abide: *you couldn't stick it for more than two days* **9** **be stuck** *informal* to be at a loss for; to be baffled or puzzled: *I'm stuck; stuck for words*
▶ See also **stick around, stick by,** etc.
WORD ORIGIN Old English *stician*

stick around *vb informal* to remain in a place, often when waiting for something

stick by *vb* to remain faithful to: *she's stuck by me for sixty years*

sticker *n* a small piece of paper with a picture or writing on it that can be stuck to a surface

sticking plaster *n* a piece of adhesive material used for covering slight wounds

stick insect *n* a tropical insect with a long thin body and legs, which looks like a twig

stick-in-the-mud *n informal* a person who is unwilling to try anything new or do anything exciting

stickleback *n* a small fish with sharp spines along its back
WORD ORIGIN Old English *sticel* prick, sting + BACK

stickler *n* a person who insists on something: *a stickler for punctuality*

stick out *vb* **1** to (cause to) project from something else: *she stuck her tongue out at me* **2** *informal* to endure (something unpleasant): *she would stick it out for a year* **3** **stick out a mile** *or* **like a sore thumb** *informal* to be very obvious **4** **stick out for** to continue to demand (something), refusing to accept anything less

stick to *vb* **1** to adhere or cause (something) to adhere to: *the soil sticks to the blade* **2** to remain faithful to (a person, promise, or rule) **3** not to move away from: *stick to the agreement*

stick-up *n slang chiefly US* a robbery at gunpoint; hold-up

stick up for *vb informal* to support or defend (oneself, another person, or a principle)

sticky *adj* **stickier, stickiest** **1** covered with a substance that sticks to other things: *sticky little fingers* **2** intended to

Virginia Woolf and Modernism

In literary criticism, Virginia Woolf tends to be considered more readable (and thus more frequently read) than her Modernist brethren. Her biography no doubt contributes to her enduring appeal. She was a member of the influential Bloomsbury Group, a gaggle of writers, artists, and intellectuals who lived and operated in and around the Bloomsbury area of London in the inter-war years. Along with her husband, Leonard Woolf, she founded the Hogarth Press, which published works by other Modernist authors including TS Eliot. She endured a lifelong struggle with mental illness, placing her in the ever-popular 'tortured artist' category, and she died by her own hand, which gives her life and work a melodramatic poignancy she shares with the likes of Sylvia Plath and Anne Sexton.

Although her non-fiction essay *A Room of One's Own* (1929) is the standard required text in schools, Woolf's most distinguished work is the experimental novel *Mrs Dalloway* (1925). Because this novel makes use of the stream-of-consciousness technique, and because it narrates the events of a single, ordinary day in the lives of its protagonists, it is often compared to James Joyce's masterpiece *Ulysses* (1922). It would be wrong, however, to assume that Woolf's novel is a mere imitation of Joyce's. In the first place, *Mrs Dalloway* is less than two hundred pages long; *Ulysses* is nearly eight hundred. This difference in length is indicative of the two authors' approaches. Joyce's book has eighteen chapters, each narrating one hour of the day. Woolf took no such structured approach; her book contains no chapter divisions at all, and she was not at all concerned with providing such a comprehensive catalogue of hours. Furthermore, Joyce based each chapter of *Ulysses* on a different episode of Homer's *Odyssey*, and wrote each chapter in a radically different style. There is no such underlying subtext to *Mrs Dalloway*, and the narrative style only differs in that certain sections follow the perspective of different characters (usually Clarissa Dalloway herself and the melancholic war veteran Septimus Smith). Thus Woolf's prose style remains fluid and impressionistic throughout, while Joyce's is parodic, precise, and constantly evolving.

A greater difference between the two works lies in the issues they confront. Woolf is one of the twentieth century's most important feminist authors, but while Joyce's Molly Bloom is a strong and fascinating character, feminism was never one of Joyce's sympathies – the author notoriously detested intellectual women. Both novels include discussion of suicide, but in *Ulysses* it is merely part of Bloom's back-story; in *Mrs Dalloway*, it is one of the novel's most prominent themes. While Woolf and Joyce share an interest in sexuality, their approaches to this topic could not be more different. Joyce is far more determined to confront sex head-on, and while some of his descriptions (for example, Leopold Bloom's activities on the strand) would be euphemistic by today's standards, the scenes at the brothel remain bold and even shocking, and the novel was once banned from the United States by obscenity laws. Woolf's 'sex scenes' are depicted through the fog of poetic dissembling language, and rely on knowing readers to pick up on her subtle cues. Although they make for more pleasant reading, one does have the impression of a genius mind trying desperately to struggle against a prudish, upper-class upbringing.

It is genteel manners – or the lack thereof – which constitutes the greatest difference between the two literary giants. The Joyce family had fallen into poverty while James was still a young boy. Virginia Woolf was wealthy and highly-educated. Clarissa Dalloway is, like her creator, well-educated and well-off. *Ulysses*, on the other hand, focuses exclusively on the working classes. This focus comes through in the unflinching portrayal of crude language, bodily functions, sex, and violence which Woolf so famously found distasteful (once referring to *Ulysses* as 'calculated indecency'). No one swears or defecates in *Mrs Dalloway*.

We must not forget that Virginia Woolf herself constituted a kind of underclass: as a woman of the early twentieth century, she was barred from many opportunities she would have had if she had been born a man. Nonetheless *Mrs Dalloway*, beautiful and poignant though it is, reads like a Modernist experiment written by (and, presumably, for) the rebellious children of the upper-classes. *Ulysses*, by contrast, despite its infamous difficulty, is a novel for and about ordinary people.

stick to a surface: *sticky labels* **3** *informal* difficult or painful: *a sticky meeting* **4** (of weather) unpleasantly warm and humid **stickiness** *n*

sticky wicket *n* **on a sticky wicket** *informal* in a difficult situation

stiff *adj* **1** firm and not easily bent **2** moving with pain or difficulty: *stiff and aching joints* **3** not moving easily: *the door is stiff* **4** difficult or severe: *a stiff challenge; stiff penalties* **5** formal and not relaxed **6** fairly firm in consistency; thick **7** powerful: *a stiff breeze* **8** (of a drink) containing a lot of alcohol ▷ *n* **9** *slang* a corpse ▷ *adv* **10** completely or utterly: *I was bored stiff* **stiffly** *adv* **stiffness** *n*
WORD ORIGIN Old English *stíf*

stiffen *vb* to make or become stiff or stiffer

stiff-necked *adj* proud and stubborn

stifle *vb* **-fling, -fled 1** to stop oneself from expressing (a yawn or cry) **2** to stop (something) from continuing: *the new leadership stifled all internal debate* **3** to feel discomfort and difficulty in breathing **4** to kill (someone) by preventing him or her from breathing
WORD ORIGIN probably from Old French *estouffer* to smother

stifling *adj* uncomfortably hot and stuffy

stigma *n, pl* **stigmas** *or* **stigmata 1** a mark of social disgrace: *a stigma attached to being redundant* **2** *bot* the part of a flower that receives pollen **3** **stigmata** *Christianity* marks resembling the wounds of the crucified Christ, believed to appear on the bodies of certain people
WORD ORIGIN Greek: brand

stigmatize *or* **-tise** *vb* **-tizing, -tized** *or* **-tising, -tised** to regard as being shameful

stile *n* a set of steps in a wall or fence to allow people, but not animals, to pass over
WORD ORIGIN Old English *stigel*

stiletto *n, pl* **-tos 1** Also called: **spike heel, stiletto heel** a high narrow heel on a woman's shoe or a shoe with such a heel **2** a small dagger with a slender tapered blade
WORD ORIGIN Italian: little dagger

still¹ *adv* **1** continuing now or in the future as in the past: *she still loved the theatre* **2** up to this or that time; yet **3** even or yet: *still more pressure on the government* **4** even then; nevertheless: *the baby has been fed and still cries* **5** quietly or without movement: *keep still* ▷ *adj* **6** motionless; stationary **7** undisturbed; silent and calm **8** (of a soft drink) not fizzy ▷ *n* **9** *poetic* silence or tranquillity: *the still of night* **10** a still photograph from a film ▷ *vb* **11** to make or become quiet or calm **12** to relieve or end: *Fowler stilled his conscience* **stillness** *n*
WORD ORIGIN Old English *stille*

still² *n* an apparatus for distilling spirits
WORD ORIGIN Latin *stilla* a drip

stillborn *adj* **1** (of a baby) dead at birth **2** (of an idea or plan) completely unsuccessful **stillbirth** *n*

still life *n, pl* **still lifes 1** a painting or drawing of objects such as fruit or flowers **2** this kind of painting or drawing

still room *n Brit* **1** a room in which distilling is carried out **2** a room for storing food in a large house

stilt *n* **1** either of a pair of long poles with footrests for walking raised from the ground **2** a long post or column used with others to support a building above ground level
WORD ORIGIN Middle English *stilte*

stilted *adj* (of speech, writing, or behaviour) formal or pompous; not flowing continuously or naturally

Stilton *n trademark* a strong-flavoured blue-veined cheese
WORD ORIGIN named after *Stilton*, Cambridgeshire

stimulant *n* **1** a drug, food, or drink that makes the body work faster, increases heart rate, and makes sleeping difficult **2** any stimulating thing ▷ *adj* **3** stimulating

stimulate *vb* **-lating, -lated 1** to encourage to start or progress further: *a cut in interest rates should help stimulate economic recovery* **2** to fill (a person) with ideas or enthusiasm: *books satisfy a part of the intellect that needs to be stimulated* **3** *physiol* to excite (a nerve or organ) with a stimulus **stimulation** *n*
WORD ORIGIN Latin *stimulare*

stimulating *adj* **1** inspiring new ideas or enthusiasm **2** (of a physical activity) making one feel refreshed and energetic; invigorating

stimulus (**stim**-myew-luss) *n, pl* **-li** (**-lie**) **1** something that acts as an incentive to (someone) **2** something, such as a drug or electrical impulse, that is capable of causing a response in a person or an animal
WORD ORIGIN Latin: a cattle goad

sting *vb* **stinging, stung 1** (of certain animals and plants) to inflict a wound on (someone) by the injection of poison **2** to cause (someone) to feel a sharp physical pain: *her hand was stinging* **3** to offend or upset (someone) with a critical remark: *I was stung by what he said* **4** to provoke (a response) by angering: *the consulate would be stung into convulsive action* **5** *informal* to cheat (someone) by overcharging ▷ *n* **6** a skin wound caused by stinging **7** pain caused by or as if by a sting **8** a mental pain: *the sting of memory* **9** the sharp pointed organ of certain animals or plants used to inject poison **10** *slang* a deceptive trick **11** *slang* a trap set up by the police to entice a person to commit a crime, thereby producing evidence **stinging** *adj*
WORD ORIGIN Old English *stingan*

stinging nettle *n* same as **nettle** (sense 1)

stingray *n* a flat fish with a jagged whiplike tail capable of inflicting painful wounds

stingy *adj* **-gier, -giest** very mean **stinginess** *n*
WORD ORIGIN perhaps from *stinge*, dialect variant of STING

stink *n* **1** a strong unpleasant smell **2 make** *or* **create** *or* **kick up a stink** *slang* to make a fuss ▷ *vb* **stinking, stank** *or* **stunk; stunk 3** to give off a strong unpleasant smell **4** *slang* to be thoroughly bad or unpleasant: *the script stinks, the casting stinks* **stinky** *adj*
WORD ORIGIN Old English *stincan*

stink bomb *n* a small glass globe used by practical jokers: it releases a liquid with a strong unpleasant smell when broken

stinker *n slang* a difficult or very unpleasant person or thing

stinking *adj* **1** having a strong unpleasant smell **2** *informal* unpleasant or disgusting ▷ *adv* **3 stinking rich** *informal* very wealthy

stink out *vb* **1** to drive (people) away by a foul smell **2** *Brit & NZ* to cause (a place) to stink: *I won't have it stinking the car out!*

stint *vb* **1** to be miserly with (something): *don't stint on paper napkins* ▷ *n* **2** a given amount of work
WORD ORIGIN Old English *styntan* to blunt

stipend (**sty**-pend) *n* a regular salary or allowance, esp. that paid to a member of the clergy **stipendiary** *adj*
WORD ORIGIN Latin *stipendium* tax

stipple *vb* **-pling, -pled** to draw, engrave, or paint (something) using dots or flecks
WORD ORIGIN Dutch *stippelen*

stipulate *vb* **-lating, -lated** to specify (something) as a condition of an agreement **stipulation** *n*
WORD ORIGIN Latin *stipulari*

stir¹ *vb* **stirring, stirred 1** to mix up (a liquid) by moving a spoon or stick around in it **2** to move slightly **3 stir from** to depart (from one's usual or preferred place) **4** to get up after sleeping **5** to excite or move (someone) emotionally **6** to move (oneself) quickly or vigorously; exert (oneself) **7** to wake up: *to stir someone from sleep* ▷ *n* **8** a stirring **9** a strong reaction, usually of excitement: *she created a stir wherever she went* ► See also **stir up**
WORD ORIGIN Old English *styrian*

stir² *n chiefly US slang* prison: *in stir*
WORD ORIGIN Romany *stariben* prison

stir-crazy *adj slang* mentally disturbed as a result of being in prison

stir-fry *vb* **-fries, -frying, -fried 1** to cook (food) quickly by stirring it in a wok or frying pan over a high heat ▷ *n, pl* **-fries 2** a dish cooked in this way

stirrer *n informal* a person who deliberately causes trouble

stirring *adj* causing emotion, excitement, and enthusiasm

stirrup *n* a metal loop attached to a saddle for supporting a rider's foot
WORD ORIGIN Old English *stig* step + *ráp* rope

stirrup cup *n chiefly Brit* a cup containing an alcoholic drink offered to riders before a fox hunt

stirrup pump *n* a hand-operated pump, the base of which is placed in a bucket of water: used in fighting fires

stir up *vb* **1** to cause (leaves or dust) to rise up and swirl around **2** to set (something) in motion: *that fact has stirred up resentment*

stitch n **1** a link made by drawing a thread through material with a needle **2** a loop of yarn formed around a needle or hook in knitting or crocheting **3** a particular kind of stitch **4** informal a link of thread joining the edges of a wound together **5** a sharp pain in the side caused by running or exercising **6** in stitches informal laughing uncontrollably **7** not a stitch informal no clothes at all ▷ vb **8** to sew or fasten (something) with stitches **stitching** n
WORD ORIGIN Old English stice sting

stitch up vb **1** to join by stitching **2** slang to incriminate by manufacturing evidence **3** slang to prearrange in a clandestine manner ▷ n **stitch-up 4** slang a matter that has been prearranged clandestinely

stoat n a small brown N European mammal related to the weasel: in winter it has a white coat and is then known as an ermine
WORD ORIGIN origin unknown

stock n **1** the total amount of goods kept on the premises of a shop or business **2** a supply of something stored for future use **3** finance **a** the money raised by a company through selling shares entitling their holders to dividends, partial ownership, and usually voting rights **b** the proportion of this money held by an individual shareholder **c** the shares of a specified company or industry **4** farm animals bred and kept for their meat, skins, etc. **5** the original type from which a particular race, family, or group is descended **6** the handle of a rifle, held by the firer against the shoulder **7** a liquid produced by simmering meat, fish, bones, or vegetables, and used to make soups and sauces **8** a kind of plant grown for its brightly coloured flowers **9** old-fashioned the degree of status a person has **10** see **laughing stock 11** in stock stored on the premises or available for sale or use **12** out of stock not immediately available for sale or use **13** take stock to think carefully about a situation before making a decision ▷ adj **14** staple; standard: stock sizes in clothes **15** being a cliché; hackneyed: the stock answer ▷ vb **16** to keep (goods) for sale **17** to obtain a store of (something) for future use or sale: to stock up on food **18** to supply (a farm) with animals or (a lake or stream) with fish ▸ See also **stocks**
WORD ORIGIN Old English stocc tree trunk

stockade n an enclosure or barrier of large wooden posts
WORD ORIGIN Spanish estacada

stockbreeder n a person who breeds or rears farm animals

stockbroker n a person who buys and sells stocks and shares for customers and receives a percentage of their profits **stockbroking** n

stock car n a car that has been strengthened and modified for a form of racing in which the cars often collide

stock cube n a small solid cube made from dried meat or vegetables, used to add flavouring to stew, soup, etc.

stock exchange n **1 a** a highly organized market for the purchase and sale of stocks and shares, operated by professional stockbrokers and market makers according to fixed rules **b** a place where stocks and shares are traded **2** the prices or trading activity of a stock exchange: the stock exchange has been rising

stockholder n an owner of some of a company's stock

stockinette n a machine-knitted elastic fabric
WORD ORIGIN perhaps from stocking-net

stocking n a long piece of close-fitting nylon or knitted yarn covering the foot and part or all of a woman's leg
WORD ORIGIN dialect stock stocking

stockinged adj in one's stockinged feet wearing stockings, tights, or socks but no shoes

stocking stitch n alternate rows of plain and purl in knitting

stock in trade n a person's typical behaviour or usual work: practicality is the farmer's stock in trade

stockist n Brit commerce a dealer who stocks a particular product

stock market n same as **stock exchange**

stockpile vb **-piling, -piled 1** to store a large quantity of (something) for future use ▷ n **2** a large store gathered for future use

stockpot n Brit & NZ a pot in which stock for soup is made

stockroom n a room in which a stock of goods is kept in a shop or factory

stock route n Austral & NZ a route designated for droving farm animals, so as to avoid traffic

stocks pl n history an instrument of punishment consisting of a heavy wooden frame with holes in which the feet, hands, or head of an offender were locked

stock-still adv absolutely still; motionlessly

stocktaking n **1** the counting and valuing of goods in a shop or business **2** a reassessment of a person's current situation and prospects

stocky adj **stockier, stockiest** (of a person) short but well-built **stockily** adv **stockiness** n

stockyard n a large yard with pens or covered buildings where farm animals are sold

stodge n Brit, Austral, & NZ informal heavy and filling starchy food
WORD ORIGIN perhaps blend of STUFF + podge a short plump person

stodgy adj **stodgier, stodgiest 1** (of food) full of starch and very filling **2** (of a person) dull, serious, or excessively formal **stodginess** n
WORD ORIGIN from STODGE

stoep (stoop) n (in South Africa) a verandah
WORD ORIGIN Afrikaans

stoic (stow-ik) n **1** a person who suffers great difficulties without showing his or her emotions ▷ adj **2** same as **stoical**

Stoic n **1** a member of the ancient Greek school of philosophy which believed that virtue and happiness could be achieved only by calmly accepting Fate ▷ adj **2** of or relating to the Stoics **Stoicism** n
WORD ORIGIN Greek stoa porch

stoical adj suffering great difficulties without showing one's feelings **stoically** adv **stoicism** (stow-iss-iz-zum) n

stoke vb **stoking, stoked 1** to feed and tend (a fire or furnace) **2** to excite or encourage (a strong emotion) in oneself or someone else
WORD ORIGIN from STOKER

stokehold n naut the hold for a ship's boilers; fire room

stoker n a person employed to tend a furnace on a ship or train powered by steam
WORD ORIGIN Dutch stoken to stoke

stole¹ vb the past tense of **steal**

stole² n a long scarf or shawl, worn by women
WORD ORIGIN Greek stolē clothing

stolen vb the past participle of **steal**

stolid adj showing little or no emotion or interest in anything **stolidity** n **stolidly** adv
WORD ORIGIN Latin stolidus dull

stoma (stow-ma) n, pl **stomata** (stow-ma-ta) **1** bot a pore in a plant leaf that controls the passage of gases into and out of the plant **2** zool a mouth or mouthlike part
WORD ORIGIN Greek: mouth

stomach n **1** an organ inside the body in which food is stored until it has been partially digested **2** the front of the body around the waist **3** desire or appetite: he still has the stomach for a fight ▷ vb **4** to put up with: liberals could not stomach the rest of the package
WORD ORIGIN Greek stoma mouth

stomachache n pain in the stomach, such as from indigestion. Also called: **stomach upset, upset stomach**

stomacher n history a decorative V-shaped panel of stiff material worn over the chest and stomach mainly by women

stomach pump n med a pump with a long tube used for removing the contents of a person's stomach, for instance after he or she has swallowed poison

stomp vb to tread or stamp heavily
WORD ORIGIN variant of STAMP

stompie n S African slang **1** a cigarette butt **2** a short man
WORD ORIGIN Afrikaans stomp stump

stone n **1** the hard nonmetallic material of which rocks are made **2** a small lump of rock **3** Also called: **gemstone** a precious or semiprecious stone that has been cut and polished **4** a piece of rock used for some particular purpose: gravestone; millstone **5** the hard central part of fruits such as the peach or date **6** pl **stone** Brit a unit of weight equal to 14 pounds or 6.350 kilograms **7** pathol a hard deposit formed in the kidney or bladder **8** heart of stone a hard or unemotional personality **9** leave no stone unturned to do everything possible to achieve something ▷ *adj* **10** made of stoneware: *the polished stone planter* ▷ *vb* **stoning, stoned 11** to throw stones at (someone), for example as a punishment **12** to remove the stones from (a fruit) **WORD ORIGIN** Old English *stān*

Stone Age *n* a phase of human culture identified by the use of tools made of stone

stonechat *n* a songbird that has black feathers and a reddish-brown breast **WORD ORIGIN** from its cry, which sounds like clattering pebbles

stone-cold *adj* **1** completely cold ▷ *adv* **2 stone-cold sober** completely sober

stoned *adj slang* under the influence of drugs or alcohol

stone-deaf *adj* completely deaf

stone fruit *n* same as **drupe**

stoneground *adj* **1** (of flour) made by crushing grain between two large stones **2** made with stoneground flour: *stoneground wholemeal bread*

stonemason *n* a person who is skilled in preparing stone for building

stone's throw *n* a short distance

stonewall *vb* **1** to deliberately prolong a discussion by being long-winded or evasive **2** *cricket* (of a batsman) to play defensively

stoneware *n* a hard type of pottery, fired at a very high temperature

stonewashed *adj* (of clothes or fabric) given a worn faded look by being washed with many small pieces of stone

stonework *n* any structure or part of a building made of stone

stonkered *adj NZ slang* completely exhausted or beaten; whacked **WORD ORIGIN** from *stonker* to beat, of unknown origin

stony *or* **stoney** *adj* **stonier, stoniest 1** (of ground) rough and covered with stones: *the stony path* **2** (of a face, voice, or attitude) unfriendly and unsympathetic **stonily** *adv*

stony-broke *adj slang* completely without money

stood *vb* the past of **stand**

stooge *n* **1** an actor who feeds lines to a comedian or acts as the butt of his jokes **2** *slang* someone who is taken advantage of by someone in a superior position **WORD ORIGIN** origin unknown

stool *n* **1** a seat with legs but no back **2** waste matter from the bowels **WORD ORIGIN** Old English *stōl*

stool pigeon *n* an informer for the police

stoop¹ *vb* **1** to bend (the body) forward and downward **2** to stand or walk with head and shoulders habitually bent forward **3 stoop to** to lower one's normal standards of behaviour; degrade oneself: *no real journalist would stoop to faking* ▷ *n* **4** the act, position, or habit of stooping **stooping** *adj* **WORD ORIGIN** Old English *stūpian*

stoop² *n US* an open porch or small platform with steps leading up to it at the entrance to a building **WORD ORIGIN** Dutch *stoep*

stop *vb* **stopping, stopped 1** to cease from doing (something); discontinue **2** to cause (something moving) to halt or (of something moving) to come to a halt **3** to prevent the continuance or completion of (something) **4** (often foll. by *from*) to prevent or restrain: *I stopped her from going on any further* **5** to keep back: *no agreement to stop arms supplies* **6 stop up** to block or plug: *to stop up a pipe* **7** to stay or rest: *we stopped at a camp site for a change* **8** to instruct a bank not to honour (a cheque) **9** to deduct (money) from pay **10** *informal* to receive (a blow or hit) **11** *music* to alter the vibrating length of (a string on a violin, guitar, etc.) by pressing down on it at some point with the finger **12 stop at nothing** to be prepared to do anything; be ruthless ▷ *n* **13** prevention of movement or progress: *you can put a stop to it quite easily* **14** the act of stopping or the state of being stopped: *the car lurched to a stop* **15** a place where something halts or pauses: *a bus stop* **16** the act or an instance of blocking or obstructing **17** a device that prevents, limits, or ends the motion of a mechanism or moving part **18** *Brit* a full stop **19** *music* a knob on an organ that is operated to allow sets of pipes to sound **20 pull out all the stops** to make a great effort **WORD ORIGIN** Old English *stoppian* (unattested)

stopbank *n NZ* an embankment to prevent flooding

stopcock *n* a valve used to control or stop the flow of a fluid in a pipe

stopgap *n* a thing that serves as a substitute for a short time until replaced by something more suitable

stop off *vb* (often foll. by *at*) to halt and call somewhere on the way to another place

stopover *n* **1** a break in a journey ▷ *vb* **stop over 2** to make a stopover

stoppage *n* **1** the act of stopping something or the state of being stopped: *a heart stoppage* **2** a deduction of money, such as taxation, from pay **3** an organized stopping of work during industrial action

stoppage time *n chiefly Brit* same as **injury time**

stopper *n* a plug for closing a bottle, pipe, etc.

stop press *n* news items inserted into a newspaper after the printing has been started

stopwatch *n* a watch which can be stopped instantly for exact timing of a sporting event

storage *n* **1** the act of storing or the state of being stored **2** space for storing **3** *computers* the process of storing information in a computer

storage device *n* a piece of computer equipment, such as a magnetic tape or a disk in or on which information can be stored

storage heater *n* an electric device that accumulates and radiates heat generated by cheap off-peak electricity

store *vb* **storing, stored 1** to keep, set aside, or gather (things) for future use **2** to place furniture or other possessions in a warehouse for safekeeping **3** to supply or stock (certain goods) **4** *computers* to enter or keep (information) in a storage device ▷ *n* **5** a shop (in Britain usually a large one) **6** a large supply or stock kept for future use **7** short for **department store 8** a storage place, such as a warehouse **9** *computers chiefly Brit* same as **memory** (sense 7) **10 in store** about to happen; forthcoming: *you've got a treat in store* **11 set great store by something** to value something as important ▶ See also **stores** **WORD ORIGIN** Old French *estor*

storehouse *n* **1** a building where goods are stored **2** a collection of things or ideas: *a storehouse of memories*

storeroom *n* a room in which things are stored

stores *pl n* supply or stock of food and other essentials for a journey

storey *or esp. US* **story** *n, pl* **-reys** *or* **-ries** a floor or level of a building **WORD ORIGIN** Anglo-Latin *historia* picture, probably from the pictures on medieval windows

stork *n* a large wading bird with very long legs, a long bill, and white-and-black feathers **WORD ORIGIN** Old English *storc*

storm *n* **1** a violent weather condition of strong winds, rain, hail, thunder, lightning, etc. **2** a violent disturbance or quarrel: *a storm of protest from the opposition* **3** (usually foll. by *of*) a heavy discharge of bullets or missiles **4 take a place by storm a** to capture or overrun a place by a violent attack **b** to surprise people, but receive their praise, by being extremely successful at something ▷ *vb* **5** to attack or capture (a place) suddenly and violently **6** to shout angrily **7** to move or rush violently or angrily: *she stormed into the study* **WORD ORIGIN** Old English

storm centre *n* **1** the centre of a storm, where pressure is lowest **2** the centre of any disturbance or trouble

storm door *n* an additional door outside an ordinary door, providing extra protection against wind, cold, and rain

storm trooper *n* a member of the paramilitary wing of the Nazi Party

stormy *adj* **stormier, stormiest 1** (of weather) violent with dark skies, heavy rain or snow, and strong winds **2** involving violent emotions: *a stormy affair*

stormy petrel *or* **storm petrel** *n* **1** a small sea bird with dark feathers and paler underparts **2** a person who brings trouble

story¹ *n, pl* **-ries 1** a description of a chain of events told or written in prose or verse **2** Also called: **short story** a piece of fiction, shorter and usually less detailed than a novel **3** Also called: **story line** the plot of a book or film **4** a news report **5** the event or material for such a report **6** *informal* a lie **WORD ORIGIN** Latin *historia*

story² *n, pl* **-ries** *chiefly US* same as **storey**

S

Organizational Jargon

Every profession has its specialized terms, but when professional life takes organizational form, it often acquires much bafflegab and gobbledygook. Abetted by marketers and consultants, this form of communication obscures rather than clarifies, whether through e-mail memos, the minutes of meetings, invoices, press releases, or job advertisements. It often seems as if the aim is to invert systematically all the principles of plain speech and clear writing. The idea is to impress, not express.

Euphemisms are rife. When companies are *right-sized,* fired or laid-off employees are *transitioned out,* their jobs declared *redundant,* though, to soften the blow, they are said to have made *a significant contribution* and are *wished well in their future endeavours.* Some, however, are hired, not fired. In such cases, an organization's *Human Resources* department advertises a job vacancy in a manner applicable to robots, though the robots are expected to apply *passion* to their tasks. Once hired, they will work as *team players* or *partners,* with whom they have *relationships.* Using *best practices* and a *business model,* they *strategize, optimize, facilitate,* and *expedite outcomes* for their *stakeholders. Proactive,* they will *go forward,* guided by an organization's *mission statement.*

Corporate-speak is like a conspiracy to complicate the lives of lexicographers. Ordinary nouns become verbs: actions *impact* or *implement.* Yet verbs can become nouns, as in *deliverables,* and plurals are favoured, especially the plurals of abstract nouns, as in *synergies.* Adjectives become nouns: *transparency, availability, functionality.* A long verb becomes a longer noun: *reallocation, realignment, transformation, promotion, convergence, innovation, reconfiguration.* The writer uses (better, *utilizes*) the passive tense rather than the active. The suffixes *-ize* and *-ing* form verbal actions, verbs and gerunds, extended with *-ation: focalize, maximizing, regularization.* Favoured suffixes included *-centred,* as in *patient-centred initiatives* and *friendly,* as in *user-friendly.*

To the organizational mind, groups of clients are divided into *segments* or *sectors.* A business does not grow; rather, one *grows* a business. All growth, viewed *holistically,* is *organic.* People don't live in a place, but in an *environment* in which a client has a food, beverage, or service *experience. Key* is a keyword, as is *value:* a *value proposition* based on *shared values* leads to *value creation.* Problems are never problems: they are *issues* for those who have *difficulties.* As many ideas as possible are packed into a sentence. Adding to the portentous effect, the omnipresent use of PowerPoint® software in making verbal presentations accounts for a hail of bullets, each • preceding an item on anything like a list. The practice makes statements appear punchy, usually belied by the text that follows the bullet.

When corporate masters make speeches, they are prone to pleonasms: the use of many words when one will do, resulting in statements like *At this point in time* the *close proximity* we have to the *basic essentials* will *as a general rule* affect the *final outcome.* Weasel words become escape clauses to hedge any statement: *more or less; and/or; about* or *approximately; adequate, appropriate, applicable* or *as required* or *warranted; depending on* or *as circumstances dictate; in general* or *in most cases* or *instances; relevant, typically,* or *usually* or *when possible.* It is a universe of variables, and the corporate person tries to cover them all.

Of course, not all messages are so formally circumlocutory. Metaphors, the indispensable ingredients of everyday speech, become clichéd buzz phrases when members of an organization talk to one another. One gives another a *heads-up* about someone who is a *loose cannon.* Easily tapped customers or donors become *low-hanging fruit;* a situation is depicted as *win-win;* to use one's imagination is to *think outside the box, take it to the next level,* or *push the envelope.* Whether people use opaque jargon or employ hackneyed phrases, they assert their status as members of an in-group, or perhaps just want to show off.

Although it is easy to pillory and parody corporate stylistic excesses, and many have done so, such pratfalls of prose may have more to do with errors of thought than of language misuse. Abusers of English may wish to deceive by shrouding a message in fog. Less charitably, it may be supposed that they simply don't know what they're talking about.

storybook n **1** a book containing stories for children ▷ adj **2** better or happier than in real life: *a storybook romance*

stoup or **stoop** (stoop) n a small basin in a church for holy water
WORD ORIGIN from Old Norse

stoush *Austral & NZ slang* vb **1** to hit or punch (someone) ▷ n **2** fighting or violence
WORD ORIGIN origin unknown

stout adj **1** solidly built or fat **2** strong and sturdy: *stout footwear* **3** brave or determined: *we met unexpectedly stout resistance* ▷ n **4** strong dark beer
stoutly adv
WORD ORIGIN Old French *estout* bold

stouthearted adj old-fashioned determined or brave

stove¹ n **1** same as **cooker** (sense 1) **2** any apparatus for heating, such as a kiln
WORD ORIGIN Old English *stofa* bathroom

stove² vb a past tense and past participle of **stave**

stovepipe n a pipe that takes fumes and smoke away from a stove

stow vb (often foll. by *away*) to pack or store (something)
WORD ORIGIN Old English *stōwian* to keep

stowage n **1** space, room, or a charge for stowing goods **2** the act of stowing

stowaway n **1** a person who hides aboard a ship or aircraft in order to travel free ▷ vb **stow away 2** to travel in such a way: *he stowed away on a ferry*

strabismus n pathol same as **squint** (sense 3)
WORD ORIGIN Greek *strabismos*

straddle vb -dling, -dled **1** to have one leg or part on each side of (something) **2** *US & Canad informal* to be in favour of both sides of (an issue or argument)
WORD ORIGIN from *stride*

Stradivarius n a violin manufactured in Italy by Antonio Stradivari (?1644–1737) or his family

strafe vb strafing, strafed to machine-gun (an enemy) from the air
WORD ORIGIN German *strafen* to punish

straggle vb -gling, -gled **1** to spread out in an untidy and rambling way: *the town straggled off to the east* **2** to linger behind or wander from a main line or part
straggler n **straggly** adj
WORD ORIGIN origin unknown

straight adj **1** continuing in the same direction without bending; not curved or crooked **2** even, level, or upright **3** in keeping with the facts; accurate **4** outright or candid: *a straight rejection* **5** in continuous succession **6** (of an alcoholic drink) undiluted **7** not wavy or curly: *straight hair* **8** in good order **9** (of a play or acting style) straightforward or serious **10** honest, respectable, or reliable **11** *slang* heterosexual **12** *slang* conventional in views, customs, or appearance **13** *informal* no longer owing or being owed something: *if you buy the next round we'll be straight* ▷ adv **14** in a straight line or direct course **15** immediately; at once: *get straight back here* **16** in a level or upright position: *he sat up straight* **17** continuously; uninterruptedly: *we waited for three hours straight* **18** (often foll. by *out*) frankly; candidly: *she asked me straight out* **19** **go straight** *informal* to reform after having been a criminal **20** **straight away** or **straightaway** at once ▷ n **21** a straight line, form, part, or position **22** *Brit* a straight part of a racetrack **23** *slang* a heterosexual person
WORD ORIGIN Old English *streccan* to stretch

straighten vb (sometimes foll. by *up* or *out*) **1** to make or become straight **2** to make (something) neat or tidy

straighten out vb to make (something) less complicated or confused

straight face n a serious facial expression which hides a desire to laugh **straight-faced** adj

straight fight n a contest between two candidates only

straightforward adj **1** (of a person) honest, frank, and open **2** (of a task) easy to do

straight man n an actor who acts as the butt of a comedian's jokes

strain¹ n **1** tension or tiredness resulting from overwork or worry **2** tension between people or organizations: *there are signs of strain between the economic superpowers* **3** an intense physical or mental effort **4** the damage resulting from excessive physical exertion **5** a great demand on the emotions, strength, or resources **6** a way of speaking: *he would have gone on in this strain for some time* **7** *physics* the change in dimension of a body caused by outside forces **8** **strains** *music* a theme, melody, or tune ▷ vb **9** to subject (someone) to mental tension or stress **10** to make an intense effort: *the rest were straining to follow the conversation* **11** to use (resources) to, or beyond, their limits **12** to injure or damage (oneself or a part of one's body) by overexertion: *he appeared to have strained a muscle* **13** to pour (a substance) through a sieve or filter **14** **strain at** to push, pull, or work with violent effort (on something) **15** to draw (something) taut or be drawn taut
WORD ORIGIN Latin *stringere* to bind tightly

strain² n **1** a group of animals or plants within a species or variety, distinguished by one or more minor characteristics **2** a trace or streak: *a strain of ruthlessness in their play*
WORD ORIGIN Old English *strēon*

strained adj **1** (of an action, expression, etc.) not natural or spontaneous **2** (of an atmosphere, relationship, etc.) not relaxed; tense

strainer n a sieve used for straining sauces, vegetables, or tea

strait n **1** (often pl) a narrow channel of the sea linking two larger areas of sea **2** **straits** a position of extreme difficulty: *in desperate straits*
WORD ORIGIN Old French *estreit* narrow

straitened adj **in straitened circumstances** not having much money

straitjacket n **1** a strong canvas jacket with long sleeves used to bind the arms of a violent person **2** anything which holds back or restricts development or freedom: *exporters are wrapped in a straitjacket of regulations*

strait-laced or **straight-laced** adj having a strict code of moral standards; puritanical

strand¹ vb **1** to leave or drive (ships or fish) ashore **2** to leave (someone) helpless, for example without transport or money ▷ n **3** *chiefly poetic* a shore or beach
WORD ORIGIN Old English

strand² n **1** one of the individual fibres of string or wire that form a rope, cord, or cable **2** a single length of string, hair, wool, or wire **3** a string of pearls or beads **4** a part of something; element: *the many disparate strands of the Anglican Church*
WORD ORIGIN origin unknown

stranded adj stuck somewhere and unable to leave

strange adj **1** odd or unexpected **2** not known, seen, or experienced before; unfamiliar **3** **strange to** inexperienced (in) or unaccustomed (to): *they are in some degree strange to it* **strangely** adv **strangeness** n
WORD ORIGIN Latin *extraneus* foreign

stranger n **1** any person whom one does not know **2** a person who is new to a particular place **3** **stranger to** a person who is unfamiliar with or new to something: *Paul is no stranger to lavish spending*

strangle vb -gling, -gled **1** to kill (someone) by pressing his or her windpipe; throttle **2** to prevent the growth or development of: *another attempt at strangling national identity* **3** to stifle (a voice, cry, or laugh) by swallowing suddenly: *the words were strangled by sobs* **strangler** n
WORD ORIGIN Greek *strangalē* a halter

stranglehold n **1** a wrestling hold in which a wrestler's arms are pressed against his opponent's windpipe **2** complete power or control over a person or situation

strangulate vb -lating, -lated **1** *pathol* to constrict (a hollow organ or vessel) so as to stop the flow of air or blood through it: *a badly strangulated hernia* **2** same as **strangle** ▷ **strangulation** n

strap n **1** a strip of strong flexible material used for carrying, lifting, fastening, or holding things in place **2** a loop of leather or rubber, hanging from the roof in a bus or train for standing passengers to hold on to **3** short for **shoulder strap 4** **the strap** a beating with a strap as a punishment ▷ vb **strapping, strapped 5** to tie or bind (something) with a strap
WORD ORIGIN variant of STROP

straphanger n *informal* a passenger in a bus or train who has to travel standing and holding on to a strap

strapless adj (of women's clothes) without straps over the shoulders

strapped adj **strapped for** *slang* badly in need of: *strapped for cash*

strapping adj tall, strong, and healthy-looking: *a strapping young lad*
WORD ORIGIN from strap (in the archaic sense: to work vigorously)

strata *n* the plural of **stratum**

▤ USAGE
Strata is sometimes wrongly used as a singular noun: *this stratum* (not *strata*) *of society is often disregarded.*

stratagem *n* a clever plan to deceive an enemy
WORD ORIGIN Greek *stratēgos* a general

strategic (strat-**ee**-jik) *adj* **1** planned to achieve an advantage; tactical **2** (of weapons, esp. missiles) directed against an enemy's homeland rather than used on a battlefield **strategically** *adv*

strategy *n, pl* -**gies** **1** a long-term plan for success, such as in politics or business **2** the art of the planning and conduct of a war **strategist** *n*
WORD ORIGIN Greek *stratēgia* function of a general

strath *n Scot* a flat river valley
WORD ORIGIN Scottish & Irish Gaelic *srath*

strathspey *n* **1** a Scottish dance with gliding steps, slower than a reel **2** music for this dance
WORD ORIGIN after *Strathspey*, valley of the River Spey

stratified *adj* **1** (of rocks) formed in horizontal layers of different materials **2** *sociol* (of a society) divided into different classes or groups **stratification** *n*
WORD ORIGIN New Latin *stratificare* to form in layers

stratocumulus (strat-oh-**kew**-myew-luss) *n, pl* -**li** (-lie) *meteorol* an unbroken stretch of dark grey cloud

stratosphere *n* the atmospheric layer between about 15 and 50 km above the earth

stratum (**strah**-tum) *n, pl* -**ta** (-ta) **1** any of the distinct layers into which certain rocks are divided **2** a layer of ocean or atmosphere marked off naturally or decided arbitrarily by man **3** a social class
WORD ORIGIN Latin: something strewn

stratus (**stray**-tuss) *n, pl* -**ti** (-tie) a grey layer cloud
WORD ORIGIN Latin: strewn

straw *n* **1** dried stalks of threshed grain, such as wheat or barley **2** a single stalk of straw **3** a long thin hollow paper or plastic tube, used for sucking up liquids into the mouth **4 clutch at straws** to turn in desperation to something with little chance of success **5 draw the short straw** to be the person chosen to perform an unpleasant task ▷ *adj* **6** made of straw: *straw baskets*
WORD ORIGIN Old English *strēaw*

strawberry *n, pl* -**ries** a sweet fleshy red fruit with small seeds on the outside
WORD ORIGIN Old English *strēawberige*

strawberry blonde *adj* **1** (of hair) reddish-blonde ▷ *n* **2** a woman with such hair

strawberry mark *n* a red birthmark

straw-coloured *adj* pale yellow: *straw-coloured hair*

straw poll or **vote** *n* an unofficial poll or vote taken to find out the opinion of a group or the public on some issue

strawweight *n* a professional boxer weighing up to 105 pounds (47 kg). Also called: **mini-flyweight**

stray *vb* **1** to wander away from the correct path or from a given area **2** to move away from the point or lose concentration **3** to fail to live up to certain moral standards: *her man had strayed* ▷ *n* **4** a domestic animal that has wandered away from its home **5** *old-fashioned* a lost or homeless child ▷ *adj* **6** (of a domestic animal) having wandered away from its home **7** random or separated from the main group of things of their kind: *stray bombs and rockets*
WORD ORIGIN Old French *estraier*

streak *n* **1** a long thin stripe or trace of some contrasting colour **2** (of lightning) a sudden flash **3** a quality or characteristic: *a nasty streak* **4** a short stretch of good or bad luck: *a losing streak* **5** *informal* an instance of running naked through a public place ▷ *vb* **6** to mark (something) with a streak or streaks: *sweat streaking the grime of his face* **7** to move quickly in a straight line **8** *informal* to run naked through a public place **streaked** or **streaky** *adj* **streaker** *n*
WORD ORIGIN Old English *strica*

stream *n* **1** a small river **2** any steady flow of water or other liquid **3** something that resembles a stream in moving continuously in a line or particular direction: *the stream of traffic* **4** a fast and continuous flow of speech: *the constant stream of jargon* **5** *Brit, Austral, & NZ* a class of school children grouped together because of similar ability ▷ *vb* **6** to pour in a continuous flow: *rain streamed down her cheeks* **7** (of a crowd of people or traffic or a herd of animals) to move in unbroken succession **8** to float freely or with a waving motion: *a flimsy pink dress that streamed out behind her* **9** *Brit & NZ* to group (school children) in streams **streaming** *n* **streamlet** *n*
WORD ORIGIN Old English *strēam*

streamer *n* **1** a long coiled ribbon of coloured paper that unrolls when tossed **2** a long narrow flag

streaming *n computers* a method of sending video or audio material over the internet so that the receiving system can process and play it almost simultaneously

streamline *vb* -**lining**, -**lined** **1** to improve (something) by removing the parts that are least useful or profitable **2** to make (an aircraft, boat, or vehicle) less resistant to flowing air or water by improving its shape **streamlined** *adj*

street *n* **1** a public road that is usually lined with buildings, esp. in a town: *Sauchiehall Street* **2** the part of the road between the pavements, used by vehicles **3** the people living in a particular street **4 on the streets** homeless **5 right up one's street** *informal* just what one knows or likes best **6 streets ahead of** *informal* superior to or more advanced than
WORD ORIGIN Old English *strēt*

streetcar *n US & Canad* a tram

street cred or **credibility** *n* a command of the styles, knowledge, etc. associated with urban youngsters who are respected by their contemporaries: *having children was the quickest way to lose your street cred*

street value *n* the price that would be paid for goods, esp. illegal ones such as drugs, by the final user: *cocaine with a street value of £2m was seized at Heathrow airport*

streetwalker *n* a prostitute who tries to find customers in the streets

streetwise *adj* knowing how to survive or succeed in poor and often criminal sections of big cities

strength *n* **1** the state or quality of being physically or mentally strong **2** the ability to withstand great force, stress, or pressure **3** something regarded as valuable or a source of power: *his chief strength is rocketry* **4** potency or effectiveness, such as of a drink or drug **5** power to convince: *the strength of this argument* **6** degree of intensity or concentration of colour, light, sound, or flavour: *a medium-strength cheese* **7** the total number of people in a group: *at full strength; 50 000 men below strength* **8 go from strength to strength** to have ever-increasing success **9 on the strength of** on the basis of or relying upon
WORD ORIGIN Old English *strengthu*

strengthen *vb* to become stronger or make (something) stronger

strenuous *adj* requiring or involving the use of great energy or effort **strenuously** *adv*
WORD ORIGIN Latin *strenuus* brisk

streptococcus (strep-toe-**kok**-uss) *n, pl* -**cocci** (-**kok**-eye) a bacterium occurring in chains and including many species that cause disease
WORD ORIGIN Greek *streptos* crooked + *kokkos* berry

streptomycin *n med* an antibiotic used in the treatment of tuberculosis and other bacterial infections
WORD ORIGIN Greek *streptos* crooked + *mukēs* fungus

stress *n* **1** mental, emotional, or physical strain or tension **2** special emphasis or significance **3** emphasis placed upon a syllable by pronouncing it more loudly than those that surround it **4** *physics* force producing a change in shape or volume ▷ *vb* **5** to give emphasis to (a point or subject): *she stressed how difficult it had been* **6** to pronounce (a word or syllable) more loudly than those surrounding it **stressful** *adj*
WORD ORIGIN shortened from *distress*

stressed-out *adj informal* suffering from anxiety or tension

stretch *vb* **1 stretch over** or **for** to extend or spread over (a specified distance): *the flood barrier stretches for several miles* **2** to draw out or extend (something) or to be drawn out or extended in length or area **3** to distort or lengthen (something) or to be distorted or lengthened permanently **4** to extend (the limbs or body), for example when one has just woken up **5** (often foll. by *out* or *forward, etc.*) to reach or hold out (a part of one's body) **6** to reach or suspend (a rope, etc.) from one place to another **7** to draw (something) tight;

S

tighten **8** (usually foll. by *over*) to extend in time: *a dinner which stretched over three consecutive evenings* **9** to put a great strain upon (one's money or resources) **10** to make do with (limited resources): *the Walkers decided to stretch their budget* **11** to extend (someone) to the limit of his or her abilities **12** to extend (someone) to the limit of his or her tolerance **13 stretch a point** to make an exception not usually made ▷ *n* **14** the act of stretching **15** a large or continuous expanse or distance: *this stretch of desert* **16** extent in time **17** a term of imprisonment **18 at a stretch** chiefly Brit & NZ **a** with some difficulty; by making a special effort **b** at one time: *for hours at a stretch they had no conversation* ▷ *adj* **19** (of clothes) able to be stretched without permanently losing shape: *a stretch suit* **stretchy** *adj*
WORD ORIGIN Old English *streccan*

stretcher *n* a frame covered with canvas, on which an ill or injured person is carried

stretcher-bearer *n* a person who helps to carry a stretcher

strew *vb* **strewing, strewed, strewn** to scatter (things) over a surface
WORD ORIGIN Old English *streowian*

strewth *interj* informal an expression of surprise or alarm
WORD ORIGIN alteration of *God's truth*

stria (**strye**-a) *n, pl* **striae** (**strye**-ee) geol a scratch or groove on the surface of a rock crystal
WORD ORIGIN Latin: a groove

striation *n* **1** an arrangement or pattern of striae **2** same as **stria** ▷ **striated** *adj*

stricken *adj* badly affected by disease, pain, grief, etc.: *flood-stricken areas*
WORD ORIGIN past participle of STRIKE

strict *adj* **1** severely correct in attention to behaviour or morality: *a strict disciplinarian* **2** following carefully and exactly a set of rules: *she is a strict vegetarian* **3** (of a rule or law) very precise and requiring total obedience: *a strict code of practice* **4** (of a meaning) exact: *this is not, in the strictest sense, a biography* **5** (of a punishment, etc.) harsh or severe **6** complete; absolute: *strict obedience* **strictly** *adv* **strictness** *n*
WORD ORIGIN Latin *strictus* drawn tight

stricture *n* formal a severe criticism
WORD ORIGIN Latin *strictura* contraction

stride *n* **1** a long step or pace **2** the length of such a step **3** a striding walk **4** progress or development: *he has made great strides in regaining his confidence* **5** a regular pace or rate of progress: *it put me off my stride* **6 take something in one's stride** to do something without difficulty or effort ▷ *vb* **striding, strode, stridden 7** to walk with long steps or paces **8 stride over** or **across** to cross (over a space or an obstacle) with a stride
WORD ORIGIN Old English *strīdan*

strident *adj* **1** (of a voice or sound) loud and harsh **2** loud, persistent, and forceful: *a strident critic of the establishment* **stridency** *n*
WORD ORIGIN Latin *stridens*

strife *n* angry or violent struggle; conflict
WORD ORIGIN Old French *estrif*

strike *vb* **striking, struck 1** (of employees) to stop work collectively as a protest against working conditions, low pay, etc. **2** to hit (someone) **3** to cause (something) to come into sudden or violent contact with something **4 strike at** to attack (someone or something) **5** to cause (a match) to light by friction **6** to sound (a specific note) on a musical instrument **7** (of a clock) to indicate (a time) by the sound of a bell **8** to affect (someone) deeply in a particular way: *he never struck me as the supportive type* **9** to enter the mind of: *a brilliant thought struck me* **10** (of a poisonous snake) to injure by biting **11** past participle **struck** or **stricken** to change into (a different state): *struck blind* **12** to be noticed by; catch: *the heavy smell of incense struck my nostrils* **13** to arrive at (something) suddenly or unexpectedly: *to strike on a solution* **14** to afflict (someone) with a disease: *she has been struck down by breast cancer* **15** to discover a source of (gold, oil, etc.) **16** to reach (something) by agreement: *to strike a deal* **17** to take up (a posture or an attitude) **18** to take apart or pack up: *to strike camp* **19** to make (a coin) by stamping it **20 strike home** to achieve the desired effect **21 strike it rich** informal to have an unexpected financial success ▷ *n* **22** a stopping of work, as a protest against working conditions, low pay, etc.: *a one-day strike* **23** an act or instance of striking **24** a military attack, esp. an air attack on a target on land or at sea: *a pre-emptive strike* **25** baseball a pitched ball swung at and missed by the batter **26** tenpin bowling the knocking down of all the pins with one bowl **27** the discovery of a source of gold, oil, etc.
▷ See also **strike off, strike out, strike up**
WORD ORIGIN Old English *strīcan*

strikebreaker *n* a person who tries to make a strike fail by working or by taking the place of those on strike

strike off *vb* to remove the name of (a doctor or lawyer who has done something wrong) from an official register, preventing him or her from practising again

strike out *vb* **1** to score out (something written) **2** to start out or begin: *I'm going to strike out for town*

strike pay *n* money paid to strikers by a trade union

striker *n* **1** a person who is on strike **2** soccer an attacking player

strike up *vb* **1** to begin (a conversation or friendship) **2** (of a band or an orchestra) to begin to play (a tune)

striking *adj* **1** attracting attention; impressive: *her striking appearance* **2** very noticeable: *a striking difference* **strikingly** *adv*

Strimmer *n* trademark an electrical tool for trimming the edges of lawns

Strine *n* a humorous transliteration of Australian pronunciation, as in *Gloria Soame* for *glorious home*
WORD ORIGIN a jocular rendering of the Australian pronunciation of *Australian*

string *n* **1** thin cord or twine used for tying, hanging, or binding things **2** a group of objects threaded on a single strand: *a string of pearls* **3** a series of things or events: *a string of wins* **4** a tightly stretched wire or cord on a musical instrument, such as the guitar, violin, or piano, that produces sound when vibrated **5 the strings** music **a** violins, violas, cellos, and double basses collectively **b** the section of an orchestra consisting of such instruments **6** a group of characters that can be treated as a unit by a computer program **7 with no strings attached** (of an offer) without complications or conditions **8 pull strings** informal to use one's power or influence, esp. secretly or unofficially ▷ *adj* **9** composed of stringlike strands woven in a large mesh: *a string bag* ▷ *vb* **stringing, strung 10** to hang or stretch (something) from one point to another **11** to provide (something) with a string or strings **12** to thread (beads) on a string **13** to extend in a line or series: *towns strung out along the valley* **stringlike** *adj*
WORD ORIGIN Old English *streng*

string along *vb* informal **1 string along with** to accompany: *I'll string along with you* **2** to deceive (someone) over a period of time: *she had only been stringing him along*

string bean *n* same as **runner bean**

string course *n* archit an ornamental projecting band along a wall

stringed *adj* (of musical instruments) having strings

stringent (**strin**-jent) *adj* requiring strict attention to rules or detail: *all have particularly stringent environmental laws* **stringency** *n*
WORD ORIGIN Latin *stringere* to bind

stringer *n* archit **1** a long horizontal timber beam that connects upright posts **2** a journalist employed by a newspaper on a part-time basis to cover a particular town or area

string quartet *n* music **1** a group of musicians consisting of two violins, one viola, and one cello **2** a piece of music composed for such a group

string up *vb* informal to kill (a person) by hanging

stringy *adj* **stringier, stringiest 1** thin and rough: *stringy hair* **2** (of meat or other food) tough and fibrous

stringy-bark *n* an Australian eucalyptus with a fibrous bark

strip[1] *vb* **stripping, stripped 1** to take (the covering or clothes) off (oneself, another person, or thing) **2 a** to undress completely **b** to perform a striptease **3** to empty (a building) of all furniture **4** to take something away from (someone): *they were stripped of their possessions* **5** to remove (paint) from (a surface or furniture): *she stripped the plaster from the kitchen walls* **6** (often foll. by *down*) to dismantle (an engine or a mechanism) into individual parts ▷ *n* **7** the act or an instance of undressing or of performing a striptease
WORD ORIGIN Old English *bestrīepan* to plunder

strip[2] *n* **1** a long narrow piece of something **2** short for **airstrip 3** Brit, Austral, & NZ the clothes a sports team plays in
WORD ORIGIN Middle Dutch *stripe* stripe

Vanished Words

The English language is not a stable system. New words are continually being added to it, but at the same time the existing words are not guaranteed to survive. Many have fallen out of use over the centuries, with the result that modern readers can often only understand the works of writers such as Chaucer, Spenser, and Shakespeare with the help of a glossary.

There are several reasons why a word can slip out the language. Some words perhaps never had a firm grip on the language in the first place. This is the case with certain 'inkhorn terms' that were coined by people with an acquaintance of Greek and Latin, but which may never have been used in a meaningful sentence. This may account for the demise of words such as *decacuminated* ('having had the top cut off'), *lectual* ('causing a person to be confined to bed'), *nuciform* ('nut-shaped'), and *neogamist* ('a recently married person'). All of these have appeared in English dictionaries in the past, and all of them can be justified on etymological grounds. Yet for one reason or another people have managed to get by pretty well without them, and they have been quietly discarded.

Other words fall out of use because the thing they refer to becomes obsolete. The word *scavilones* entered the English language in the 16th century as a type of undergarment worn by men. When fashions changed and the garment was no longer worn, the word itself was doomed to disappear. A similar fate awaited various weapons: if you are not familiar with such words as *curtalax* (a short sword) and *lancegay* (a type of spear), it is because military technology has moved on, and there is no longer any need for anyone except historians to talk about these things.

English has also become a more homogeneous language since the advent of mass communication in the 20th century. As people have become accustomed to speaking with people from other regions, their vocabulary has become more standardized, and many dialect words have fallen out of use. Hence there is little evidence for current use of some quaint regional words such as *wapper-eyed* ('blinking'), *whinnock* ('a milk pail'), and *zoozoo* ('a wood pigeon').

Other words were designed from the outset to have a short shelf-life. Slang words are not meant to be widely understood, but rather to be the currency of a few people who are in the know. Some of these words may escape into general use, but others are quite likely to disappear within a generation. Some historical slang is extremely colourful: a *slip-string* was someone considered worthy of being hanged, a *poodle-faker* was a ladies' man, the *wiffle-woffles* meant a state of melancholia, while *doofunnies* were small items carried about in the pockets of a cowboy.

A look back at some of the words that have vanished from the language may fill the modern-day speaker of English with a sense that some of the poetry has fallen out of the language. There are numerous vanished words which could do excellent service if they were to be restored: it would surely be a fine thing to revive such terms of abuse as *dizzard* and *doddypoll* (both meaning 'a stupid person'), and to be able to accuse an officious person of being *spoffish*.

Of course, there is a sense in which such words have not vanished altogether. As long as a word is recorded somewhere, it remains accessible for future generations. Such words are still of interest to historians of English, and they may even have a second life in historical fiction (as happened when Sarah Waters seized on *fingersmith*, an obsolete word for a pickpocket, as the title of her 2002 novel set in the criminal underworld of Victorian London).

And there is always the slight possibility that a vanished word may return to favour. The word *fascinator*, referring to a lightweight decoration worn on the head at formal occasions, seemed to have disappeared from use by the end of the 20th century. However, a change in ladies' fashions suddenly revived the concept, and now the word is heard ubiquitously as the name of a must-have accessory for weddings.

strip cartoon *n* a sequence of drawings in a newspaper or magazine, telling an amusing story or an adventure

strip club *n* a club in which striptease performances take place

stripe¹ *n* **1** a long band of colour that differs from the surrounding material **2** a chevron or band worn on a uniform to indicate rank ▷ *vb* **striping, striped 3** to mark (something) with stripes **striped, stripy** or **stripey** *adj* **WORD ORIGIN** probably from Middle Dutch *strīpe*

stripe² *n* a stroke from a whip, rod, or cane **WORD ORIGIN** from Middle Low German *strippe*

strip lighting *n* a method of electric lighting that uses fluorescent lamps in long glass tubes

stripling *n* a teenage boy or young man

stripper *n* **1** a person who performs a striptease **2** a tool or liquid for removing paint or varnish

strip-search *vb* **1** (of police, customs officials, etc.) to strip (a prisoner or suspect) naked to search him or her for drugs or smuggled goods ▷ *n* **2** a search that involves stripping a person naked

striptease *n* an entertainment in which a person gradually undresses to music

strive *vb* **striving, strove, striven** to make a great effort: *to strive for a peaceful settlement* **WORD ORIGIN** Old French *estriver*

strobe *n* short for **strobe lighting** or **stroboscope**

strobe lighting *n* a flashing beam of very bright light produced by a perforated disc rotating in front of a light source

stroboscope *n* an instrument producing a very bright flashing light which makes moving people appear stationary **WORD ORIGIN** Greek *strobos* a whirling + *skopein* to look at

strode *vb* the past tense of **stride**

stroganoff *n* a dish of sliced beef cooked with onions and mushrooms, served in a sour-cream sauce. Also called: **beef stroganoff WORD ORIGIN** after Count *Stroganoff*, Russian diplomat

stroke *vb* **stroking, stroked 1** to touch or brush lightly or gently ▷ *n* **2** a light touch or caress with the fingers **3** *pathol* rupture of a blood vessel in the brain resulting in loss of consciousness, often followed by paralysis and damage to speech **4** a blow, knock, or hit **5** an action or occurrence of the kind specified: *a fantastic stroke of luck; a stroke of intuition* **6 a** the striking of a clock **b** the hour registered by this: *at the stroke of twelve* **7** a mark made by a pen or paintbrush **8** same as **solidus**: used esp. when dictating or reading aloud **9** the hitting of the ball in sports such as golf or cricket **10** any one of the repeated movements used by a swimmer **11** a particular style of swimming, such as the crawl **12** a single pull on the oars in rowing **13 at a stroke** with one action **14 not a stroke (of work)** no work at all **WORD ORIGIN** Old English *strācian*

stroll *vb* **1** to walk about in a leisurely manner ▷ *n* **2** a leisurely walk **WORD ORIGIN** probably from dialect German *strollen*

stroller *n US & Canad* a chair-shaped carriage for a baby

strong *adj* **stronger, strongest 1** having physical power **2** not easily broken or injured; solid or robust **3** great in degree or intensity; not faint or feeble: *a strong voice; a strong smell of explosive* **4** (of arguments) supported by evidence; convincing **5** concentrated; not weak or diluted **6** having a powerful taste or smell: *strong perfume* **7** (of language) using swear words **8** (of a person) self-confident: *a strong personality* **9** committed or fervent: *a strong believer in free trade* **10** important or having a lot of power or influence: *a strong left-wing tendency within the university* **11** very competent at a particular activity: *they sent a very strong team to the Olympics* **12** containing or having a specified number: *the 700-strong workforce* **13** (of an accent) distinct and indicating where the speaker comes from **14** (of a relationship) stable and likely to last **15** having an extreme or drastic effect: *strong discipline* **16** (of a colour) very bright and intense **17** (of a wind, current, or earthquake) moving fast or intensely **18** (of an economy, an industry, a currency, etc.) growing, successful, or increasing in value ▷ *adv* **19 come on strong** *informal* **a** to show blatantly that one is sexually attracted to someone **b** to make a forceful or exaggerated impression **20 going strong** *informal* working or performing well; thriving **strongly** *adv* **WORD ORIGIN** Old English *strang*

strong-arm *adj informal* involving physical force or violence: *strong-arm tactics*

strongbox *n* a box in which valuables are locked for safety

strong drink *n* alcoholic drink

stronghold *n* **1** an area in which a particular belief is shared by many people: *a Labour stronghold* **2** a place that is well defended; fortress

strong-minded *adj* not easily persuaded to change beliefs or opinions

strong point *n* something at which one is very good: *diplomacy wasn't his strong point*

strongroom *n* a specially designed room in which valuables are locked for safety

strontium *n chem* a soft silvery-white metallic element: the radioactive isotope **strontium-90** is used in nuclear power sources and is a hazardous nuclear fallout product. Symbol: Sr **WORD ORIGIN** after *Strontian*, in Scotland, where discovered

strop *n* a leather strap for sharpening razors **WORD ORIGIN** Greek *strophos* cord

stroppy *adj* **-pier, -piest** *informal* bad-tempered or deliberately awkward **WORD ORIGIN** from *obstreperous*

strove *vb* the past tense of **strive**

struck *vb* a past of **strike**

structural *adj* **1** of or having structure or a structure **2** of or forming part of the structure of a building **3** *chem* of or involving the arrangement of atoms in molecules: *a structural formula* **structurally** *adv*

structuralism *n* an approach to social sciences and to literature which sees changes in the subject as caused and organized by a hidden set of universal rules **structuralist** *n, adj*

structure *n* **1** something that has been built or organized **2** the way the individual parts of something are made, built, or organized into a whole **3** the pattern of interrelationships within an organization, society, etc. **4** an organized method of working, thinking, or behaving **5** *chem* the arrangement of atoms in a molecule of a chemical compound **6** *geol* the way in which a rock is made up of its component parts ▷ *vb* **-turing, -tured 7** to arrange (something) into an organized system or pattern: *a structured school curriculum* **WORD ORIGIN** Latin *structura*

strudel *n* a thin sheet of filled dough rolled up and baked: *apple strudel* **WORD ORIGIN** from German

struggle *vb* **-gling, -gled 1** to work or strive: *the old regime struggled for power; he struggled to keep the conversation flowing* **2** to move about violently in an attempt to escape from something restricting **3** to fight with someone, often for possession of something **4** to go or progress with difficulty **5 struggle on** to manage to do (something) with difficulty ▷ *n* **6** something requiring a lot of exertion or effort to achieve **7** a fight or battle **8 the struggle** *S African* the concerted opposition to apartheid **struggling** *adj* **WORD ORIGIN** origin unknown

strum *vb* **strumming, strummed 1** to play (a stringed instrument) by sweeping the thumb or a plectrum across the strings **2** to play (a tune) in this way **WORD ORIGIN** probably imitative

strumpet *n archaic* a prostitute or promiscuous woman **WORD ORIGIN** origin unknown

strung *vb* the past of **string**

strung up *adj informal* tense or nervous: *you sound a bit strung up*

strut *vb* **strutting, strutted 1** to walk in a stiff proud way with head high and shoulders back; swagger ▷ *n* **2** a piece of wood or metal that forms part of the framework of a structure **WORD ORIGIN** Old English *strūtian* to stand stiffly

strychnine (**strik**-neen) *n* a very poisonous drug formerly used in small quantities as a stimulant **WORD ORIGIN** Greek *strukhnos* nightshade

Stuart *adj* of or relating to the royal house that ruled Scotland from 1371 to 1714 and England from 1603 to 1714

stub *n* **1** a short piece remaining after something has been used: *a cigarette stub* **2** the section of a ticket or cheque which the purchaser keeps as a receipt ▷ *vb* **stubbing, stubbed 3** to strike (one's toe or foot) painfully against a hard surface **4 stub out** to put out (a cigarette or cigar) by pressing the end against a surface **WORD ORIGIN** Old English *stubb*

stubble *n* **1** the short stalks left in a field where a crop has been harvested **2** the short bristly hair on the chin of a man who has not shaved for a while **stubbly** *adj* **WORD ORIGIN** Old French *estuble*

stubble-jumper *n Canad slang* a prairie grain farmer

stubborn *adj* **1** refusing to agree or give in **2** persistent and determined **3** difficult to handle, treat, or overcome: *the most stubborn dandruff* **stubbornly** *adv* **stubbornness** *n* **WORD ORIGIN** origin unknown

stubby *adj* **-bier, -biest** short and broad

STUC Scottish Trades Union Congress

stucco *n* **1** plaster used for coating or decorating outside walls ▷ *vb* **-coing, -coed 2** to apply stucco to (a building) **WORD ORIGIN** Italian

stuck *vb* **1** the past of **stick²** ▷ *adj* **2** *informal* baffled by a problem or unable to find an answer to a question **3 be stuck on** *slang* to feel a strong attraction to; be infatuated with **4 get stuck in** *informal* to perform a task with determination

stuck-up *adj informal* proud or snobbish

stud¹ *n* **1** a small piece of metal attached to a surface for decoration **2** a fastener consisting of two discs at either end of a short bar, usually used with clothes **3** one of several small round objects attached to the sole of a football boot to give better grip ▷ *vb* **studding, studded 4** to decorate or cover (something) with or as if with studs: *apartment houses studded with satellite dishes* **WORD ORIGIN** Old English *studu*

stud² *n* **1** a male animal, esp. a stallion kept for breeding **2** Also: **stud farm** a place where animals are bred **3** the state of being kept for breeding purposes **4** *slang* a virile or sexually active man **WORD ORIGIN** Old English *stōd*

student *n* **1** a person following a course of study in a school, college, or university **2** a person who makes a thorough study of a subject: *a keen student of opinion polls* **WORD ORIGIN** Latin *studens* diligent

studied *adj* carefully practised or planned: *studied calm*

studio *n, pl* **-dios 1** a room in which an artist, photographer, or musician works **2** a room used to record television or radio programmes or to make films or records **3 studios** the premises of a radio, television, record, or film company **WORD ORIGIN** Italian

studio couch *n* a backless couch that can be converted into a double bed

studio flat *n Brit* a flat with one main room and, usually, a small kitchen and bathroom. Also called: **studio apartment**

studious (**styoo**-dee-uss) *adj* **1** serious, thoughtful, and hard-working

2 precise, careful, or deliberate **studiously** *adv* **WORD ORIGIN** Latin *studiosus* devoted to

study *vb* **studies, studying, studied 1** to be engaged in the learning or understanding of (a subject) **2** to investigate or examine (something) by observation and research **3** to look at (something or someone) closely; scrutinize ▷ *n, pl* **studies 4** the act or process of studying **5** a room used for studying, reading, or writing **6** (*often pl*) work relating to a particular area of learning: *environmental studies* **7** an investigation and analysis of a particular subject **8** a paper or book produced as a result of study **9** a work of art, such as a drawing, done for practice or in preparation for another work **10** a musical composition designed to develop playing technique **WORD ORIGIN** Latin *studium* zeal

stuff *n* **1** substance or material **2** any collection of unnamed things **3** the raw material of something **4** subject matter, skill, etc.: *this journalist knew his stuff* **5** woollen fabric **6 do one's stuff** *informal* to do what is expected of one ▷ *vb* **7** to pack or fill (something) completely; cram **8** to force, shove, or squeeze (something somewhere): *I stuffed it in my briefcase* **9** to fill (food such as poultry or tomatoes) with a seasoned mixture **10** to fill (a dead animal's skin) with material so as to restore the shape of the live animal **11** *slang* to frustrate or defeat **12 get stuffed!** *Brit, Austral, & NZ slang* an exclamation of anger or annoyance with someone **13 stuff oneself** or **one's face** to eat a large amount of food **WORD ORIGIN** Old French *estoffe*

stuffed shirt *n informal* a pompous or old-fashioned person

stuffed-up *adj* having the passages of one's nose blocked with mucus

stuffing *n* **1** a mixture of ingredients with which poultry or meat is stuffed before cooking **2** the material used to fill and give shape to soft toys, pillows, furniture, etc.; padding

stuffy *adj* **-ier, -iest 1** lacking fresh air **2** old-fashioned and very formal: *an image of stuffy tradition* **stuffiness** *n*

stultify *vb* **-fies, -fying, -fied** to dull (the mind) by boring routine **stultifying** *adj* **WORD ORIGIN** Latin *stultus* stupid + *facere* to make

stumble *vb* **-bling, -bled 1** to trip and almost fall while walking or running **2** to walk in an unsteady or unsure way **3** to make mistakes or hesitate in speech **4 stumble across** or **on** or **upon** to encounter or discover (someone or something) by accident ▷ *n* **5** an act of stumbling **WORD ORIGIN** Middle English *stomble*

stumbling block *n* any obstacle that prevents something from taking place or progressing

stump *n* **1** the base of a tree trunk left standing after the tree has been cut down or has fallen **2** the part of something, such as a tooth or limb, that remains after a larger part has been removed **3** *cricket* any of three

upright wooden sticks that, with two bails laid across them, form a wicket ▷ *vb* **4** to baffle or confuse (someone) **5** *cricket* to dismiss (a batsman) by breaking his wicket with the ball **6** *chiefly US & Canad* to campaign or canvass (an area), by political speech-making **7** to walk with heavy steps; trudge **WORD ORIGIN** Middle Low German

stump up *vb Brit informal* to give (the money required)

stumpy *adj* **stumpier, stumpiest** short and thick like a stump; stubby

stun *vb* **stunning, stunned 1** to shock or astonish (someone) so that he or she is unable to speak or act **2** (of a heavy blow or fall) to make (a person or an animal) unconscious **WORD ORIGIN** Old French *estoner* to daze

stung *vb* the past of **sting**

stunk *vb* a past of **stink**

stunner *n Brit, Austral, & NZ informal* a person or thing of great beauty

stunning *adj informal* very attractive or impressive **stunningly** *adv*

stunt¹ *vb* to prevent or slow down (the growth or development of a plant, animal, or person) **stunted** *adj* **WORD ORIGIN** Old English: foolish

stunt² *n* **1** an acrobatic or dangerous piece of action in a film or television programme **2** anything spectacular or unusual done to gain publicity ▷ *adj* **3** of or relating to acrobatic or dangerous pieces of action in films or television programmes: *a stunt man* **WORD ORIGIN** origin unknown

stupefaction *n* the state of being unable to think clearly because of tiredness or boredom

stupefy *vb* **-pefies, -pefying, -pefied 1** to make (someone) feel so bored and tired that he or she is unable to think clearly **2** to confuse or astound (someone) **stupefying** *adj* **WORD ORIGIN** Old French *stupefier*

stupendous *adj* very large or impressive **stupendously** *adv* **WORD ORIGIN** Latin *stupere* to be amazed

stupid *adj* **1** lacking in common sense or intelligence **2** trivial, silly, or childish: *we got into a stupid quarrel* **3** unable to think clearly; dazed: *stupid with tiredness* **stupidity** *n* **stupidly** *adv* **WORD ORIGIN** Latin *stupidus*

stupor *n* a state of near unconsciousness in which a person is unable to behave normally or think clearly **WORD ORIGIN** Latin

sturdy *adj* **-dier, -diest 1** (of a person) healthy, strong, and unlikely to tire or become injured **2** (of a piece of furniture, shoes, etc.) strongly built or made **sturdily** *adv* **WORD ORIGIN** Old French *estordi* dazed

sturgeon *n* a bony fish from which caviar is obtained **WORD ORIGIN** Old French *estourgeon*

stutter *vb* **1** to speak (a word or phrase) with involuntary repetition of initial consonants ▷ *n* **2** the tendency to involuntarily repeat initial consonants while speaking **stuttering** *n* **WORD ORIGIN** Middle English *stutten*

S

sty *n, pl* **sties** a pen in which pigs are kept
WORD ORIGIN Old English *stīg*

stye *or* **sty** *n, pl* **styes** *or* **sties** inflammation of a gland at the base of an eyelash
WORD ORIGIN Old English *stīgend* swelling + *ye* eye

Stygian (stij-jee-an) *adj* *chiefly literary* dark or gloomy
WORD ORIGIN after the *Styx*, a river in Hades

style *n* **1** a form of appearance, design, or production: *I like that style of dress* **2** the way in which something is done: *a new style of command* **3** elegance or refinement of manners and dress: *he has bags of style* **4** a distinctive manner of expression in words, music, painting, etc.: *a painting in the Expressionist style* **5** popular fashion in dress and looks: *the old ones had gone out of style* **6** a fashionable or showy way of life: *the newly rich could dine in style* **7** the particular kind of spelling, punctuation, and design followed in a book, journal, or publishing house **8** *bot* the stemlike part of a flower that bears the stigma ▷ *vb* **styling, styled** **9** to design, shape, or tailor: *neatly styled hair* **10** to name or call: *Walsh, who styled himself the Memory Man*
WORD ORIGIN Latin *stilus* writing implement

styling mousse *n* a light foam applied to the hair before styling in order to hold the style

stylish *adj* smart, fashionable, and attracting attention **stylishly** *adv*

stylist *n* **1** a hairdresser who styles hair **2** a person who performs, writes, or acts with great attention to the particular style he or she employs

stylistic *adj* of the techniques used in creating or performing a work of art: *there are many stylistic problems facing the performers of Baroque music* **stylistically** *adv*

stylized *or* **-lised** *adj* conforming to an established stylistic form

stylus *n* a needle-like device in the pick-up arm of a record player that rests in the groove in the record and picks up the sound signals
WORD ORIGIN Latin *stilus* writing implement

stymie *vb* **-mieing, -mied** **1** to hinder or foil (someone): *the President was stymied by a reluctant Congress* ▷ *n, pl* **-mies** **2** *golf* (formerly) a situation in which an opponent's ball is blocking the line between the hole and the ball about to be played
WORD ORIGIN origin unknown

styptic *adj* **1** used to stop bleeding: *a styptic pencil* ▷ *n* **2** a styptic drug
WORD ORIGIN Greek *stuphein* to contract

suave (swahv) *adj* (esp. of a man) smooth, confident, and sophisticated **suavely** *adv*
WORD ORIGIN Latin *suavis* sweet

sub *n* **1** short for **subeditor, submarine, subscription** *or* **substitute 2** *Brit informal* an advance payment of wages or salary. Formal term: **subsistence allowance** ▷ *vb* **subbing, subbed 3** to act as a substitute

sub- *or before r* **sur-** *prefix* **1** situated under or beneath: *subterranean* **2** secondary in rank; subordinate: *sublieutenant* **3** falling short of; less than or imperfectly: *subarctic; subhuman* **4** forming a subdivision or less important part: *subcommittee*
WORD ORIGIN Latin

subaltern *n* a British army officer below the rank of captain
WORD ORIGIN Latin *sub-* under + *alter* another

subaqua *adj* of or relating to underwater sport: *subaqua swimming*

subatomic *adj* *physics* of, relating to, or being one of the particles making up an atom

subcommittee *n* a small committee consisting of members of a larger committee and which is set up to look into a particular matter

subconscious *adj* **1** happening or existing without one's awareness ▷ *n* **2** *psychol* the part of the mind that contains memories and motives of which one is not aware but which can influence one's behaviour **subconsciously** *adv*

subcontinent *n* a large land mass that is a distinct part of a continent, such as India is of Asia

subcontract *n* **1** a secondary contract by which the main contractor for a job puts work out to another company ▷ *vb* **2** to let out (work) on a subcontract **subcontractor** *n*

subculture *n* a group of people within a society or class with a distinct pattern of behaviour, beliefs, and attitudes

subcutaneous (sub-cute-**ayn**-ee-uss) *adj* *med* beneath the skin

subdivide *vb* **-viding, -vided** to divide (a part of something) into smaller parts **subdivision** *n*

subdue *vb* **-duing, -dued** **1** to overcome and bring (a person or people) under control by persuasion or force **2** to make (feelings, colour, or lighting) less intense
WORD ORIGIN Latin *subducere* to remove

subeditor *n* a person who checks and edits text for a newspaper or other publication

subgroup *n* a small group that is part of a larger group

subheading *n* the heading of a subdivision of a piece of writing

subhuman *adj* lacking the intelligence or decency expected of a human being

subject *n* **1** the person, thing, or topic being dealt with or discussed **2** any branch of learning considered as a course of study **3** a person, object, idea, or scene portrayed in a work of art **4** *grammar* a word or phrase that represents the person or thing performing the action of the verb in a sentence; for example, *the cat* in the sentence *The cat catches mice* **5** a person or thing that undergoes an experiment or treatment **6** a person under the rule of a monarch or government: *Zambian subjects* ▷ *adj* **7** being under the rule of a monarch or government: *a subject race* **8 subject to a** showing a tendency towards: *they are expensive and subject to over-runs in cost and time* **b** exposed or vulnerable to: *subject to ridicule* **c** conditional upon: *pay is subject to negotiation* ▷ *adv* **9 subject to** under the condition that something takes place: *my visit was agreed subject to certain conditions* ▷ *vb* (sub-**ject**) **10 subject to a** to cause (someone) to experience (something unpleasant): *they were subjected to beatings* **b** to bring under the control or authority (of): *to subject a soldier to discipline* **subjection** *n*
WORD ORIGIN Latin *subjectus* brought under

subjective *adj* **1** of or based on a person's emotions or prejudices ▷ *n* **2** *grammar* the grammatical case in certain languages that identifies the subject of a verb **subjectively** *adv*

sub judice (sub **joo**-diss-ee) *adj* before a court of law: *he declined to comment on the case saying it was sub judice*
WORD ORIGIN Latin

subjugate *vb* **-gating, -gated** to bring (a group of people) under one's control **subjugation** *n*
WORD ORIGIN Latin *sub-* under + *jugum* yoke

subjunctive *grammar* *adj* **1** denoting a mood of verbs used when the content of the clause is being doubted, supposed, or feared true, for example *were* in the sentence *I'd be careful if I were you* ▷ *n* **2** the subjunctive mood
WORD ORIGIN Latin *subjungere* to add to

sublet *vb* **-letting, -let** to rent out (property which one is renting from someone else)

sublieutenant *n* a junior officer in a navy

sublimate *vb* **-mating, -mated** *psychol* to direct the energy of (a strong desire, esp. a sexual one) into activities that are socially more acceptable **sublimation** *n*
WORD ORIGIN Latin *sublimare* to elevate

sublime *adj* **1** causing deep emotions and feelings of wonder or joy **2** without equal; supreme **3** of great moral, artistic, or spiritual value ▷ *n* **4** the sublime something that is sublime ▷ *vb* **-liming, -limed** **5** *chem, physics* to change directly from a solid to a vapour without first melting **sublimely** *adv*
WORD ORIGIN Latin *sublimis* lofty

subliminal *adj* resulting from or relating to mental processes of which the individual is not aware: *the subliminal message*
WORD ORIGIN Latin *sub* below + *limen* threshold

sub-machine-gun *n* a portable automatic or semiautomatic gun with a short barrel

submarine *n* **1** a vessel which can operate below the surface of the sea ▷ *adj* **2** existing or located below the surface of the sea: *submarine cables* **submariner** *n*

submerge *vb* **-merging, -merged** **1** to put or go below the surface of water or another liquid **2** to involve totally: *she submerged herself in her work* **submersion** *n*
WORD ORIGIN Latin *submergere*

submersible *adj* **1** capable of operating under water ▷ *n* **2** a small vessel designed to operate under water

SCRABBLE
Three-Letter Words, part 8
SIK–UTU

SIK	Australian slang for excellent	**STY**	pigpen
SIM	simulation game on a computer	**SUB**	short for subeditor
SIN	offence or transgression	**SUD**	singular form of suds
SIP	drink in small mouthfuls	**SUE**	start legal proceedings against
SIR	polite term of address for a man	**SUI**	of himself, herself, itself
SIS	short for sister	**SUK**	open-air marketplace
SIT	rest one's body on the buttocks and thighs	**SUM**	result of addition, total
SIX	one more than five	**SUN**	star around which the earth revolves
SKA	type of West Indian pop music	**SUP**	swallow liquid
SKI	snow sport	**SUQ**	open-air marketplace
SKY	upper atmosphere	**SUR**	above
SLY	crafty	**SUS**	become aware of
SMA	Scots word for small	**SWY**	gambling game
SNY	side channel of a river	**SYE**	strain something
SOB	weep with convulsive gasps	**SYN**	Scots word for since
SOC	feudal right to hold court	**TAB**	small flap or projecting label
SOD	(piece of) turf	**TAD**	small bit or piece
SOG	soak	**TAE**	Scots word for to
SOH	musical term	**TAG**	label bearing information
SOL	liquid colloidal solution	**TAI**	(as in tai chi chuan) Chinese system of callisthenics
SOM	monetary unit	**TAJ**	tall conical cap
SON	male offspring	**TAK**	Scots word for take
SOP	concession to pacify someone	**TAM**	short for tam-o'-shanter
SOS	plural form of so	**TAN**	coloration of the skin
SOT	habitual drunkard	**TAO**	philosophical term
SOU	former French coin	**TAP**	knock lightly
SOV	sovereign	**TAR**	thick black liquid
SOW	scatter or plant	**TAS**	cup, goblet, or glass
SOX	informal spelling of socks	**TAT**	tatty or tasteless article(s)
SOY	(as in soy sauce) salty dark brown sauce	**TAU**	19th letter of the Greek alphabet
SPA	resort with a mineral-water spring	**TAV**	22nd letter of the Hebrew alphabet
SPY	obtain secret information	**TAW**	convert skins into leather
SRI	title of respect	**TAX**	compulsory payment levied
		TAY	Irish dialect word for tea
		TEA	drink

TEC	short for detective	**TRY**	make an effort or attempt
TED	dry hay	**TSK**	expression of disapproval
TEE	small peg for golf	**TUB**	open round container
TEF	grass grown for its grain	**TUG**	pull hard
TEG	two-year-old sheep	**TUI**	New Zealand bird
TEL	large mound formed from accumulated rubbish	**TUM**	stomach
TEN	one more than nine	**TUN**	large beer cask
TES	plural form of te	**TUP**	male sheep
TET	9th letter of the Hebrew alphabet	**TUT**	sound of mild reprimand
TEW	toil	**TUX**	short for tuxedo
TEX	unit of weight	**TWA**	two
THE	definite article	**TWO**	one more than one
THO	short for though	**TWP**	stupid
THY	of or associated with you (thou)	**TYE**	trough used in mining
TIC	spasmodic muscular twitch	**TYG**	cup with two handles
TID	girl	**UDO**	perennial plant
TIE	fasten with string	**UDS**	'God's' or 'God save'
TIG	children's game	**UEY**	u-turn
TIL	another name for sesame	**UFO**	flying saucer
TIN	soft metallic element	**UGH**	exclamation of disgust
TIP	narrow or pointed end of anything	**UGS**	plural form of ug
TIS	plural form of ti	**UKE**	short for ukulele
TIT	small songbird	**ULE**	rubber tree
TIX	tickets	**ULU**	type of knife
TOC	communication code for T	**UMM**	sound of hesitation
		UMP	short for umpire
TOD	unit of weight	**UMU**	type of oven
TOE	digit of the foot	**UNI**	short for university
TOG	unit of thermal resistance	**UNS**	plural form of un
		UPO	upon
TOM	male cat	**UPS**	plural form of up
TON	unit of weight	**URB**	urban area
TOO	also, as well	**URD**	type of plant with edible seeds
TOP	highest point or part	**URE**	extinct wild ox
TOR	high rocky hill	**URN**	container for the ashes of the dead
TOT	small child	**URP**	dialect word for vomit
TOW	drag, esp by means of a rope	**USE**	put into service or action
TOY	something designed to be played with	**UTA**	type of lizard
		UTE	utility vehicle
		UTS	plural form of ut
		UTU	reward

submission *n* **1** an act or instance of capitulation **2** the act of submitting (something) **3** something submitted, such as a proposal **4** the state in which someone has to accept the control of another person

submissive *adj* showing quiet obedience **submissively** *adv* **submissiveness** *n*

submit *vb* **-mitting, -mitted 1** to accept the will of another person or a superior force **2** to send (an application or proposal) to someone for judgment or consideration **3** to be voluntarily subjected (to medical or psychiatric treatment)
WORD ORIGIN Latin *submittere* to place under

subnormal *adj* **1** less than the normal: *subnormal white blood cells* **2** *no longer in technical use* having a lower than average intelligence ▷ *n* **3** *no longer in technical use* a subnormal person

subordinate *adj* **1** of lesser rank or importance ▷ *n* **2** a person or thing that is of lesser rank or importance ▷ *vb* **-nating, -nated 3** (usually foll. by *to*) to regard (something) as less important than another: *the army's interests were subordinated to those of the air force* **subordination** *n*
WORD ORIGIN Latin *sub-* lower + *ordo* rank

subordinate clause *n grammar* a clause that functions as an adjective, an adverb, or a noun rather than one that functions as a sentence in its own right

suborn *vb formal* to bribe or incite (a person) to commit a wrongful act
WORD ORIGIN Latin *subornare*

subplot *n* a secondary plot in a novel, play, or film

subpoena (sub-**pee**-na) *n* **1** a legal document requiring a person to appear before a court of law at a specified time ▷ *vb* **-naing, -naed 2** to summon (someone) with a subpoena
WORD ORIGIN Latin: under penalty

sub-post office *n* (in Britain) a post office which is run by a self-employed agent for the Post Office

subprime *adj* **1** (of a loan) made to a borrower with a poor credit rating: *subprime mortgage* ▷ *n* **2** such a loan

sub rosa (sub **rose**-a) *adv literary* in secret
WORD ORIGIN Latin, literally: under the rose; in ancient times a rose was hung over a table as a mark of secrecy

subroutine *n* a section of a computer program that is stored only once but can be used at several different points in the program

subscribe *vb* **-scribing, -scribed 1** (usually foll. by *to*) to pay (money) as a contribution (to a charity, for a magazine, etc.) at regular intervals **2 subscribe to** to give support or approval to: *I do not subscribe to this view* **subscriber** *n*
WORD ORIGIN Latin *subscribere* to write underneath

subscript *printing adj* **1** (of a character) written or printed below the line ▷ *n* **2** a subscript character

subscription *n* **1** a payment for issues of a publication over a specified period of time **2** money paid or promised, such as to a charity, or the fund raised in this way **3** *Brit, Austral, & NZ* the membership fees paid to a society **4** an advance order for a new product

subsection *n* any of the smaller parts into which a section may be divided

subsequent *adj* occurring after; succeeding **subsequently** *adv*
WORD ORIGIN Latin *subsequens*

subservient *adj* **1** overeager to carry out someone else's wishes **2** of less importance or rank: *the subservient role of women in society* **subservience** *n*
WORD ORIGIN Latin *subserviens*

subset *n* a mathematical set contained within a larger set

subside *vb* **-siding, -sided 1** to become less loud, excited, or violent **2** to sink to a lower level **3** (of the surface of the earth) to cave in; collapse **subsidence** *n*
WORD ORIGIN Latin *subsidere* to settle down

subsidiarity *n* the principle of taking political decisions at the lowest practical level

subsidiary *n, pl* **-aries 1** Also called: **subsidiary company** a company which is at least half owned by another company **2** a person or thing that is of lesser importance ▷ *adj* **3** of lesser importance; subordinate
WORD ORIGIN Latin *subsidiarius* supporting

subsidize *or* **-dise** *vb* **-dizing, -dized** *or* **-dising, -dised** to aid or support (an industry, a person, a public service, or a venture) with money

subsidy *n, pl* **-dies 1** financial aid supplied by a government, for example to industry, or for public welfare **2** any financial aid, grant, or contribution
WORD ORIGIN Latin *subsidium* assistance

subsist *vb* **subsist on** to manage to live: *to subsist on a diet of sausage rolls* **subsistence** *n*
WORD ORIGIN Latin *subsistere* to stand firm

subsistence farming *n* a type of farming in which most of the produce is consumed by the farmer and his family

subsoil *n* the layer of soil beneath the surface soil

subsonic *adj* being or moving at a speed below that of sound

substance *n* **1** the basic matter of which a thing consists **2** a specific type of matter with definite or fairly definite chemical composition: *a fatty substance* **3** the essential meaning of a speech, thought, or written article **4** important or meaningful quality: *the only evidence of substance against him* **5** material possessions or wealth: *a woman of substance* **6 in substance** with regard to the most important points
WORD ORIGIN Latin *substantia*

substandard *adj* below an established or required standard

substantial *adj* **1** of a considerable size or value: *a substantial amount of money* **2** (of food or a meal) large and filling

3 solid or strong: *substantial brick pillars* **4** *formal* available to the senses; real: *substantial evidence* **5** of or relating to the basic material substance of a thing **substantially** *adv*

substantiate *vb* **-ating, -ated** to establish (a story) as genuine **substantiation** *n*

substantive *n* **1** *grammar* a noun or pronoun used in place of a noun ▷ *adj* **2** having importance or significance: *substantive negotiations between management and staff* **3** of or being the essential element of a thing
WORD ORIGIN Latin *substare* to stand beneath

substitute *vb* **-tuting, -tuted 1** (often foll. by *for*) to take the place of or put in place of another person or thing **2** *chem* to replace (an atom or group in a molecule) with (another atom or group) ▷ *n* **3** a person or thing that takes the place of another, such as a player who takes the place of a team-mate **substitution** *n*
WORD ORIGIN Latin *substituere*

≡**USAGE**
Substitute is sometimes wrongly used where *replace* is meant: *he replaced* (not *substituted*) *the worn tyre with a new one.*

substitution reaction *n chem* the replacing of an atom or group in a molecule by another atom or group

substrate *n biol* the substance upon which an enzyme acts
WORD ORIGIN Latin *substratus* strewn beneath

substructure *n* **1** a structure that forms a part of anything **2** a structure that forms a foundation or framework for a building

subsume *vb* **-suming, -sumed** *formal* to include (something) under a larger classification or group: *an attempt to subsume fascism and communism under a general concept of totalitarianism*
WORD ORIGIN Latin *sub-* under + *sumere* to take

subtenant *n* a person who rents property from a tenant **subtenancy** *n*

subtend *vb geom* to be opposite (an angle or side)
WORD ORIGIN Latin *subtendere* to extend beneath

subterfuge *n* a trick or deception used to achieve an objective
WORD ORIGIN Latin *subterfugere* to escape by stealth

subterranean *adj* **1** found or operating below the surface of the earth **2** existing or working in a concealed or mysterious way: *the resistance movement worked largely by subterranean methods*
WORD ORIGIN Latin *sub* beneath + *terra* earth

subtext *n* **1** an underlying theme in a piece of writing **2** a message which is not stated directly but can be inferred

subtitle *n* **1 subtitles** *films* a written translation at the bottom of the picture in a film with foreign dialogue **2** a secondary title given to a book or play ▷ *vb* **-tling, -tled 3** to provide subtitles for (a film) or a subtitle for (a book or play)

subtle adj **1** not immediately obvious: *a subtle change in his views* **2** (of a colour, taste, or smell) delicate or faint: *the subtle aroma* **3** using shrewd and indirect methods to achieve an objective **4** having or requiring the ability to make fine distinctions: *a subtle argument* **subtly** adv
WORD ORIGIN Latin *subtilis* finely woven

subtlety n **1** pl **-ties** a fine distinction **2** the state or quality of being subtle

subtract vb **1** maths to take (one number or quantity) away from another **2** to remove (a part of something) from the whole **subtraction** n
WORD ORIGIN Latin *subtrahere* to draw away from beneath

subtropical adj of the region lying between the tropics and temperate lands

suburb n a residential district on the outskirts of a city or town
WORD ORIGIN Latin *sub-* close to + *urbs* a city

suburban adj **1** of, in, or inhabiting a suburb **2** *mildly disparaging* conventional and unexciting

suburbanite n a person who lives in a suburb

suburbia n suburbs or the people living in them considered as a distinct community or class in society

subvention n formal a grant or subsidy, for example one from a government
WORD ORIGIN Late Latin *subventio* assistance

subversion n the act or an instance of attempting to weaken or overthrow a government or an institution

subversive adj **1** intended or intending to weaken or overthrow a government or an institution ▷ n **2** a person engaged in subversive activities

subvert vb to bring about the downfall of (something existing by a system of law, such as a government)
WORD ORIGIN Latin *subvertere* to overturn

subway n **1** Austral & Brit an underground passage for pedestrians to cross a road or railway **2** an underground railway

subzero adj lower than zero: *subzero temperatures*

succeed vb **1** to achieve an aim **2** to turn out satisfactorily: *Grandfather's plan succeeded* **3** to do well in a specified field: *how to succeed in show biz* **4** to come next in order after (someone or something): *the first shock had been succeeded by a different kind of gloom* **5** to take over (a position) from (someone): *Henry VIII succeeded to the throne in 1509; he will be succeeded as president by his deputy* **succeeding** adj
WORD ORIGIN Latin *succedere* to follow after

success n **1** the achievement of something attempted **2** the attainment of wealth, fame, or position **3** a person or thing that is successful
WORD ORIGIN Latin *successus* an outcome

successful adj **1** having a favourable outcome **2** having attained fame, wealth, or position **successfully** adv

succession n **1** a number of people or things following one another in order **2** the act or right by which one person succeeds another in a position **3** in succession one after another: *the third time in succession*

successive adj following another or others without interruption: *eleven successive victories* **successively** adv

successor n a person or thing that follows another, esp. a person who takes over another's job or position

succinct adj brief and clear: *a succinct answer to this question* **succinctly** adv
WORD ORIGIN Latin *succinctus*

succour or US **succor** n **1** help in time of difficulty ▷ vb **2** to give aid to (someone in time of difficulty)
WORD ORIGIN Latin *succurrere* to hurry to help

succubus n, pl **-bi** a female demon fabled to have sex with sleeping men
WORD ORIGIN Latin *succubare* to lie beneath

succulent adj **1** (of food) juicy and delicious **2** (of plants) having thick fleshy leaves or stems ▷ n **3** a plant that can exist in very dry conditions by using water stored in its fleshy tissues **succulence** n
WORD ORIGIN Latin *sucus* juice

succumb vb **succumb to a** to give way to the force of or desire for (something) **b** to die of (a disease)
WORD ORIGIN Latin *succumbere*

such adj **1** of the sort specified or understood: *such places* **2** so great or so much: *such a mess* ▷ adv **3** extremely: *such a powerful friend* ▷ pron **4** a person or thing of the sort specified or understood: *such is the law of the land; fruitcakes and puddings and such* **5** as such in itself or themselves: *the Nordic countries are not lifting sanctions as such* **6** such as for example: *other socialist groups, such as the Fabians*
WORD ORIGIN Old English *swilc*

such and such adj **1** specific, but not known or named: *such and such a percentage* ▷ n **2** a specific, but not known or named, person or thing: *you have not taken such and such into account*

suchlike n **1** such or similar things: *shampoos, talcs, and suchlike* ▷ adj **2** of such a kind; similar: *astrology and suchlike nonsense*

suck vb **1** to draw (a liquid) into the mouth through pursed lips **2** to take (something) into the mouth and moisten, dissolve, or roll it around with the tongue: *suck a mint* **3** to extract liquid from (a solid food): *he sat sucking orange segments* **4** to draw in (fluid) as if by sucking: *the mussel sucks in water* **5** to drink milk from (a mother's breast); suckle **6** (often foll. by *down* or *in*, etc.) to draw (a thing or person somewhere) with a powerful force **7** slang to be contemptible or disgusting ▷ n **8** a sucking
WORD ORIGIN Old English *sūcan*

sucker n **1** slang a person who is easily deceived or swindled **2** slang a person who cannot resist something: *he's a sucker for fast cars* **3** zool a part of the body of certain animals that is used for sucking or sticking to a surface **4** a rubber cup-shaped device attached to objects allowing them to stick to a surface by suction **5** bot a strong shoot coming from a mature plant's root or the base of its main stem

suck into vb to draw (someone) into (a situation) by using a powerful pressure or inducement: *to be sucked into a guerrilla war*

suckle vb **-ling, -led** to give (a baby or young animal) milk from the breast or udder or (of a baby or young animal) to suck milk from its mother's breast or udder

suckling n a baby or young animal that is still sucking milk from its mother's breast or udder

suck up to vb informal to flatter (a person in authority) in order to get something, such as praise or promotion

sucrose (soo-kroze) n chem sugar
WORD ORIGIN French *sucre* sugar

suction n **1** the act or process of sucking **2** the force produced by drawing air out of a space to make a vacuum that will suck in a substance from another space
WORD ORIGIN Latin *sugere* to suck

Sudanese adj **1** of the Sudan ▷ n, pl **-nese 2** a person from the Sudan

sudden adj **1** occurring or performed quickly and without warning ▷ n **2** all of a sudden without warning; unexpectedly **suddenly** adv **suddenness** n
WORD ORIGIN Latin *subitus* unexpected

sudden death n sport an extra period of play to decide the winner of a tied competition: *the first player or team to go into the lead is the winner*

sudden infant death syndrome n same as **cot death**

sudoku (soo-**doh**-koo) n a logic puzzle involving the insertion of numbers so that none is repeated in the same row, column, or internal square of a larger square
WORD ORIGIN from Japanese

sudorific (syoo-dor-**if**-ik) adj **1** causing sweating ▷ n **2** a drug that causes sweating
WORD ORIGIN Latin *sudor* sweat + *facere* to make

suds pl n the bubbles on the surface of water in which soap or detergent has been dissolved; lather
WORD ORIGIN probably from Middle Dutch *sudse* marsh

sue vb **suing, sued** to start legal proceedings (against): *we want to sue the council; he sued for custody of the three children*
WORD ORIGIN Latin *sequi* to follow

suede n a leather with a fine velvet-like surface on one side
WORD ORIGIN French *gants de Suède*, literally: gloves from Sweden

suet n a hard fat obtained from sheep and cattle and used for making pastry and puddings
WORD ORIGIN Old French *seu*

suffer vb **1** to undergo or be subjected to (physical pain or mental distress) **2** suffer from to be badly affected by (an illness): *he was suffering from depression* **3** to become worse in quality; deteriorate: *his work suffered during their divorce* **4** to tolerate: *he suffers no fools*

S

5 to be set at a disadvantage: *the strongest of them suffers by comparison* **sufferer** *n* **suffering** *n*
WORD ORIGIN Latin *sufferre*

sufferance *n* **on sufferance** tolerated with reluctance: *I was there on sufferance and all knew it*

suffice (suf-**fice**) *vb* **-ficing, -ficed 1** to be enough or satisfactory for a purpose **2 suffice it to say** ... it is enough to say ...: *suffice it to say that AIDS is on the increase*
WORD ORIGIN Latin *sufficere*

sufficiency *n, pl* **-cies** an adequate amount

sufficient *adj* enough to meet a need or purpose; adequate **sufficiently** *adv*
WORD ORIGIN Latin *sufficiens*

suffix *grammar n* **1** a letter or letters added to the end of a word to form another word, such as -*s* and -*ness* in *dogs* and *softness* ▷ *vb* **2** to add (a letter or letters) to the end of a word to form another word
WORD ORIGIN Latin *suffixus* fastened below

suffocate *vb* **-cating, -cated 1** to kill or die through lack of oxygen, such as by blockage of the air passage **2** to feel uncomfortable from heat and lack of air **suffocating** *adj* **suffocation** *n*
WORD ORIGIN Latin *suffocare*

suffragan *n* a bishop appointed to assist an archbishop
WORD ORIGIN Medieval Latin *suffragium* assistance

suffrage *n* the right to vote in public elections
WORD ORIGIN Latin *suffragium*

suffragette *n* (in Britain at the beginning of the 20th century) a woman who campaigned militantly for women to be given the right to vote in public elections

suffragist *n* (in Britain at the beginning of the 20th century) a person who campaigned for women to be given the right to vote in public elections

suffuse *vb* **-fusing, -fused** to spread through or over (something): *the dawn suffused the sky with a cold grey wash* **suffusion** *n*
WORD ORIGIN Latin *suffusus* overspread with

sugar *n* **1** a sweet carbohydrate, usually in the form of white or brown crystals, which is found in many plants and is used to sweeten food and drinks **2** *informal chiefly US & Canad* a term of affection ▷ *vb* **3** to add sugar to (food or drink) to make it sweet **4** to cover with sugar: *sugared almonds* **5 sugar the pill** to make something unpleasant more tolerable by adding something pleasant **sugared** *adj*
WORD ORIGIN Old French *çucre*, from Sanskrit *śarkarā*

sugar beet *n* a beet grown for the sugar obtained from its roots

sugar cane *n* a tropical grass grown for the sugar obtained from its tall stout canes

sugar daddy *n* an elderly man who gives a young woman money and gifts in return for her company

sugar glider *n* a common phalanger that glides from tree to tree feeding on insects and nectar

sugaring off *n Canad* the boiling down of maple sap to produce sugar, traditionally a social event in early spring

sugar loaf *n* a large cone-shaped mass of hard refined sugar

sugar maple *n* a North American maple tree, grown as a source of sugar, which is extracted from the sap

sugary *adj* **1** of, like, or containing sugar: *sugary snacks* **2** (of behaviour or language) very pleasant but probably not sincere: *sugary sentiment* **sugariness** *n*

suggest *vb* **1** to put forward (a plan or an idea) for consideration: *he didn't suggest a meeting* **2** to bring (a person or thing) to the mind by the association of ideas: *a man whose very name suggests blandness* **3** to give a hint of: *her grey eyes suggesting a livelier mood than usual*
WORD ORIGIN Latin *suggerere* to bring up

suggestible *adj* easily influenced by other people's ideas

suggestion *n* **1** something that is suggested **2** a hint or indication: *the entire castle gave no suggestion of period* **3** *psychol* the process whereby the presentation of an idea to a receptive individual leads to the acceptance of that idea

suggestive *adj* **1** (of remarks or gestures) causing people to think of sex **2 suggestive of** communicating a hint of

suicidal *adj* **1** wanting to commit suicide **2** likely to lead to danger or death: *a suicidal attempt to rescue her son* **3** likely to destroy one's own career or future: *it would be suicidal for them to ignore public opinion*

suicide *n* **1** the act of killing oneself deliberately: *he tried to commit suicide* **2** a person who kills himself or herself intentionally **3** the self-inflicted ruin of one's own career or future: *such a cut would be political suicide*
WORD ORIGIN Latin *sui* of oneself + *caedere* to kill

suicide bomber *n* a terrorist who carries out a bomb attack, knowing that he or she will be killed in the explosion

suit *n* **1** a set of clothes of the same material designed to be worn together, usually a jacket with matching trousers or skirt **2** an outfit worn for a specific purpose: *a diving suit* **3** a legal action taken against someone; lawsuit **4** any of the four types of card in a pack of playing cards: spades, hearts, diamonds, or clubs **5** *slang* a business executive or white-collar worker **6 follow suit** to act in the same way as someone else **7 strong suit** *or* **strongest suit** something one excels in ▷ *vb* **8** to be fit or appropriate for: *that colour suits you* **9** to be acceptable to (someone) **10 suit oneself** to do what one wants without considering other people **suited** *adj*
WORD ORIGIN Old French *sieute* set of things

suitable *adj* appropriate for a particular function or occasion; proper **suitability** *n* **suitably** *adv*

suitcase *n* a large portable travelling case for clothing

suite *n* **1** a set of connected rooms in a hotel **2** a matching set of furniture, for example two armchairs and a settee **3** *music* a composition of several movements in the same key
WORD ORIGIN French

suitor *n* **1** *old-fashioned* a man who wants to marry a woman **2** *law* a person who starts legal proceedings against someone; plaintiff
WORD ORIGIN Latin *secutor* follower

Sukkoth (**sook**-oat) *n* an eight-day Jewish harvest festival, commemorating the period when the Israelites lived in the wilderness

sulk *vb* **1** to be silent and moody as a way of showing anger or resentment: *I went home and sulked for two days* ▷ *n* **2** a mood in which one shows anger or resentment by being silent and moody: *he was just in a sulk*

sulky *adj* **sulkier, sulkiest** moody or silent because of anger or resentment **sulkily** *adv* **sulkiness** *n*
WORD ORIGIN perhaps from obsolete *sulke* sluggish

sullen *adj* unwilling to talk or be sociable; sulky **sullenly** *adv* **sullenness** *n*
WORD ORIGIN Latin *solus* alone

sully *vb* **-lies, -lying, -lied 1** to ruin (someone's reputation) **2** to spoil or make dirty: *the stream had been sullied by the smelter's pollution*
WORD ORIGIN probably from French *souiller* to soil

sulpha drug *or US* **sulfa drug** *n pharmacol* any of a group of sulphonamides that prevent the growth of bacteria: used to treat bacterial infections

sulphate *or US* **sulfate** *n chem* a salt or ester of sulphuric acid

sulphide *or US* **sulfide** *n chem* a compound of sulphur with another element

sulphite *or US* **sulfite** *n chem* any salt or ester of sulphurous acid

sulphonamide *or US* **sulfonamide** (sulf-**on**-a-mide) *n pharmacol* any of a class of organic compounds that prevent the growth of bacteria

sulphur *or US* **sulfur** *n chem* a light yellow, highly inflammable, nonmetallic element used in the production of sulphuric acid, in the vulcanization of rubber, and in medicine. Symbol: S **sulphuric** *or US* **sulfuric** *adj*
WORD ORIGIN Latin *sulfur*

sulphur dioxide *n chem* a strong-smelling colourless soluble gas, used in the manufacture of sulphuric acid and in the preservation of foodstuffs

sulphureous *or US* **sulfureous** (sulf-**yoor**-ee-uss) *adj* same as **sulphurous** (sense 1)

sulphuric acid *n chem* a colourless dense oily corrosive liquid used in the manufacture of fertilizers and explosives

sulphurize *or* **-rise** *or US* **sulfurize** (**sulf**-yoor-rise) *vb* **-rizing, -rized** *or* **-rising, -rised** *chem* to combine with or treat (something) with sulphur or a sulphur compound

The Influence of Hindi on English

F ew English speakers whose families did not originate in South Asia can claim much of an acquaintance with Hindi, and yet we all use Hindi words in our everyday lives without thinking about it, from applying *shampoo* to our hair in the morning through to donning our *pyjamas* at night.

Yet it can be difficult to pin down exactly what we mean when we talk of 'Hindi' as a language. In its broadest sense, Hindi is a group of languages spoken in South Asia, including Urdu and Bihari, which derive from ancient Sanskrit and share much common vocabulary. In its narrowest sense, standard Hindi is a literary language within this group, used as one of the official languages of India (the other being English).

English began to rub shoulders with Hindi from the 17th century, when the East India Company set up trading posts on the Indian subcontinent. India then came under British colonial rule from 1858 to 1947 in the period known as 'the Raj' (a name that comes from a Hindi word meaning 'rule').

British soldiers, traders, and administrators in India came into contact with local Hindi words, and these began to permeate their own language. While some of these got no further than the argot of the Anglo-Indian community, others found their way back to Britain and into Standard English. Among the everyday words that English has borrowed from Hindi are *chit, cot, dinghy, khaki*, and *veranda*. In the process of adopting such words, the British often mangled the original Hindi and produced something that would fit more easily into their ideas of pronunciation. Thus *khicarī* became 'kedgeree' and *Jagannath* (the cart used to carry the image of the god Krishna) became 'juggernaut'.

The importing of Indian goods to Britain introduced some previously unfamiliar objects which naturally became known by versions of their Hindi names. Brightly patterned cloths were called *chintz*, a word formed by pluralizing the Hindi word *chīnt*, meaning 'gaily coloured'. A more hard-wearing type of cloth went by the Hindi name of *dungrī*, and so clothes made from this came to be called *dungarees*. Hindi also provided English with the word *bangle* for an ornament for the wrist (from *bangrī*) and *cummerbund* for a cloth worn around the waist (from *kamarband*).

Even things that did not get exported to Britain had to be spoken about in English, and when no English word was suitable, the local name would be used. Thus Hindi words are behind the names of many things the British encountered in India, such *cheetah, jungle*, and *sari*.

Some of the English words that originate from Hindi are quite unexpected. It is hard to imagine a more characteristically English concept than 'Blighty', but this word turns out to derive from the Hindi word *bilāyatī*, which means 'foreign land'. During World War I, a 'blighty one' was a name given to a wound that allowed the grateful recipient to return home from service; later 'Blighty' came to mean the place to where one returned. This is not the only occasion when English slang has borrowed a Hindi word: other examples – usually the product of soldiers being stationed in India – include *choky, pukka, cushy*, and *dekko*.

In 1947 the British colonists moved out of India, but that did not put an end to Hindi's influence on English. The migration of Hindi speakers into English-speaking countries has seen Hindi words continue to enter English, most notably as names of traditional Indian dishes. Lovers of Indian food have become familiar with words such as *naan, samosa, bhuna, jalfrezi, tikka, tandoori*, and *balti*. (The word *curry* itself, however, is derived from another Indian language, Tamil, and means 'sauce'.) Meanwhile, continuing interest in Eastern religion and philosophy has seen Hindi words such as *guru* and *karma* become assimilated into English.

English has much for which to thank Hindi, but linguistic borrowing is not a one-way process. The use of English as a language of administration in India and its importance in culture and technology have meant that many English words have now become part of the Hindi lexicon too.

sulphurous *or US* **sulfurous** *adj chem* **1** of or resembling sulphur **2** containing sulphur, esp. with a valence of four

sultan *n* the sovereign of a Muslim country
WORD ORIGIN Arabic: rule

sultana *n* **1** the dried fruit of a small white seedless grape **2** a sultan's wife, mother, daughter, or concubine
WORD ORIGIN Italian

sultanate *n* **1** the territory ruled by a sultan **2** the office or rank of a sultan

sultry *adj* **-trier, -triest 1** (of weather or climate) very hot and humid **2** suggesting hidden passion: *a sultry brunette*
WORD ORIGIN obsolete *sulter* to swelter

sum *n* **1** the result of the addition of numbers or quantities **2** one or more columns or rows of numbers to be added, subtracted, multiplied, or divided **3** a quantity of money: *they can win enormous sums* **4 in sum** as a summary; in short: *in sum, it's been a bad week for the government* ▷ *adj* **5** complete or final: *the sum total* ▷ *vb* **summing, summed 6** see **sum up**
WORD ORIGIN Latin *summa* the top, sum

summarize *or* **-rise** *vb* **-rizing, -rized** *or* **-rising, -rised** to give a short account of (something)

summary *n, pl* **-maries 1** a brief account giving the main points of something ▷ *adj* **2** performed quickly, without formality or attention to details: *a summary judgment* **summarily** *adv*
WORD ORIGIN Latin *summarium*

summation *n* **1** a summary of what has just been done or said **2** the process of working out a sum; addition **3** the result of such a process

summer *n* **1** the warmest season of the year, between spring and autumn **2** *literary* a time of youth, success, or happiness **summery** *adj*
WORD ORIGIN Old English *sumor*

summerhouse *n* a small building in a garden, used for shade in the summer

summer school *n* an academic course held during the summer

summer solstice *n* the time at which the sun is at its northernmost point in the sky (southernmost point in the S hemisphere), appearing at noon at its highest altitude above the horizon. It occurs about June 21 (December 22 in the S hemisphere)

summertime *n* the period or season of summer

summing-up *n* **1** a summary of the main points of an argument, speech, or piece of writing **2** concluding statements made by a judge to the jury before they retire to consider their verdict

summit *n* **1** the highest point or part of a mountain or hill **2** the highest possible degree or state; peak or climax: *the summit of success* **3** a meeting of heads of governments or other high officials
WORD ORIGIN Old French *somet*

summon *vb* **1** to order (someone) to come **2** to send for (someone) to appear in court **3** to call upon (someone) to do

something: *the authorities had summoned the relatives to be available* **4** to convene (a meeting) **5** (often foll. by *up*) to call into action (one's strength, courage, etc.); muster
WORD ORIGIN Latin *summonere* to give a discreet reminder

summons *n, pl* **-monses 1** a call or an order to attend a specified place at a specified time **2** an official order requiring a person to attend court, either to answer a charge or to give evidence ▷ *vb* **3** to order (someone) to appear in court: *three others had been summonsed for questioning*

sumo *n* the national style of wrestling of Japan, in which two contestants of great height and weight attempt to force each other out of the ring
WORD ORIGIN Japanese

sump *n* **1** a container in an internal-combustion engine into which oil can drain **2** same as **cesspool 3** *mining* a hollow at the bottom of a shaft where water collects
WORD ORIGIN Middle Dutch *somp* marsh

sumptuary *adj* controlling expenditure or extravagant use of resources
WORD ORIGIN Latin *sumptuarius* concerning expense

sumptuous *adj* magnificent and very expensive; splendid: *sumptuous decoration*
WORD ORIGIN Latin *sumptuosus* costly

sum up *vb* **1** to give a short account of (the main points of an argument, speech, or piece of writing) **2** to form a quick opinion of: *how well you have summed me up!*

sun *n* **1** the star that is the source of heat and light for the planets in the solar system ▶ Related adjective: **solar 2** any star around which a system of planets revolves **3** the heat and light received from the sun; sunshine **4 catch the sun** to become slightly suntanned **5 under the sun** on earth; at all: *there are no free lunches under the sun* ▷ *vb* **sunning, sunned 6 sun oneself** to lie, sit, or walk in the sunshine on a warm day **sunless** *adj*
WORD ORIGIN Old English *sunne*

Sun. Sunday

sunbathe *vb* **-bathing, -bathed** to lie or sit in the sunshine, in order to get a suntan **sunbather** *n* **sunbathing** *n*

sunbeam *n* a ray of sunlight

sun block *n* a chemical applied to exposed skin to block out all or almost all of the ultraviolet rays of the sun

sunburn *n* painful reddening of the skin caused by overexposure to the sun **sunburnt** *or* **sunburned** *adj*

sun cream *n* a cream applied to exposed skin to reduce the effect of the ultraviolet rays of the sun

sundae *n* ice cream topped with a sweet sauce, nuts, whipped cream, and fruit
WORD ORIGIN origin unknown

Sunday *n* the first day of the week and the Christian day of worship
WORD ORIGIN Old English *sunnandæg* day of the sun

Sunday best *n* a person's best clothes, sometimes regarded as those most suitable for wearing at church

Sunday school *n* a school for teaching children about Christianity, usually held in a church hall on Sunday

sundial *n* a device used for telling the time during the hours of sunlight, consisting of a pointer that casts a shadow onto a surface marked in hours

sundown *n US* sunset

sundries *pl n* several things of various sorts

sundry *adj* **1** several or various; miscellaneous ▷ *pron* **2** all and sundry everybody
WORD ORIGIN Old English *syndrig* separate

sunfish *n, pl* **-fish** *or* **-fishes** a large sea fish with a rounded body

sunflower *n* **1** a very tall plant with large yellow flowers **2 sunflower seed oil** the oil extracted from sunflower seeds, used as a salad oil and in margarine

sung *vb* the past participle of **sing**
USAGE
See at **ring**[1].

sunglasses *pl n* glasses with darkened lenses that protect the eyes from bright sunlight

sun-god *n* the sun considered as a god

sunk *vb* a past participle of **sink**

sunken *vb* **1** a past participle of **sink** ▷ *adj* **2** (of a person's cheeks, eyes, or chest) curving inward due to old age or bad health **3** situated at a lower level than the surrounding or usual one: *the sunken garden* **4** situated under water; submerged: *sunken ships*

sun lamp *n* a lamp that gives off ultraviolet rays, used for muscular therapy or for giving people an artificial suntan

sunlight *n* the light that comes from the sun **sunlit** *adj*

sun lounge *or US* **sun parlor** *n* a room with large windows designed to receive as much sunlight as possible

sunny *adj* **-nier, -niest 1** full of or lit up by sunshine **2** cheerful and happy

sunrise *n* **1** the daily appearance of the sun above the horizon **2** the time at which the sun rises

sunrise industry *n* any of the fast-developing high-technology industries, such as electronics

sunroof *n* a panel in the roof of a car that may be opened to let in air or sunshine

sunset *n* **1** the daily disappearance of the sun below the horizon **2** the time at which the sun sets

sunshade *n* anything used to shade people from the sun, such as a parasol or awning

sunshine *n* **1** the light and warmth from the sun **2** *Brit* a light-hearted term of address

sunspot *n* **1** *informal* a sunny holiday resort **2** a dark cool patch on the surface of the sun **3** *Austral* a small area of skin damage caused by exposure to the sun

sunstroke *n* a condition caused by spending too much time exposed to intensely hot sunlight and producing high fever and sometimes loss of consciousness

suntan *n* a brownish colouring of the skin caused by exposure to the sun or a sun lamp **suntanned** *adj*

sun-up *n US & Austral* sunrise

sup¹ *vb* **supping, supped 1** to take (liquid) by swallowing a little at a time ▷ *n* **2** a sip
WORD ORIGIN Old English *sūpan*

sup² *vb* **supping, supped** *archaic* to have supper
WORD ORIGIN Old French *soper*

super *informal adj* **1** very good or very nice: *they had a super holiday* ▷ *n Austral & NZ* **2** superannuation **3** superphosphate
WORD ORIGIN Latin: above

super- *prefix* **1** above or over: *superscript* **2** outstanding: *superstar* **3** of greater size, extent, or quality: *supermarket*
WORD ORIGIN Latin

superabundant *adj* existing in very large numbers or amount **superabundance** *n*

superannuated *adj* **1** discharged with a pension, owing to age or illness **2** too old to be useful; obsolete
WORD ORIGIN Medieval Latin *superannatus* aged more than one year

superannuation *n* **a** a regular payment made by an employee into a pension fund **b** the pension finally paid

superb *adj* extremely good or impressive **superbly** *adv*
WORD ORIGIN Latin *superbus* distinguished

Super Bowl *n American football* the championship game held annually between the best team of the American Football Conference and that of the National Football Conference

superbug *n informal* a bacterium resistant to antibiotics

supercharge *vb* **-charging, -charged 1** to increase the power of (an internal-combustion engine) with a supercharger **2** to charge (the atmosphere, a remark, etc.) with an excess amount of (tension, emotion, etc.) **3** to apply pressure to (a fluid); pressurize

supercharger *n* a device that increases the power of an internal-combustion engine by forcing extra air into it

supercilious *adj* behaving in a superior and arrogant manner **superciliously** *adv* **superciliousness** *n*
WORD ORIGIN Latin *supercilium* eyebrow

superconductivity *n physics* the ability of certain substances to conduct electric current with almost no resistance at very low temperatures **superconducting** *adj* **superconductor** *n*

supercontinent *n* a huge landmass thought to have existed in the geological past and to have split into smaller landmasses and formed the present continents

superego *n, pl* **-egos** *psychoanal* that part of the unconscious mind that governs a person's ideas concerning what is right and wrong

supererogation *n* the act of doing more work than is required

WORD ORIGIN Latin *supererogare* to spend over and above

superficial *adj* **1** not careful or thorough: *a superficial analysis* **2** only outwardly apparent rather than genuine or actual: *those are merely superficial differences* **3** (of a person) lacking deep emotions or serious interests; shallow **4** of, near, or forming the surface: *the gash was superficial* **superficiality** *n* **superficially** *adv*
WORD ORIGIN Late Latin *superficialis*

superfluous (soo-**per**-flew-uss) *adj* more than is sufficient or required **superfluity** *n*
WORD ORIGIN Latin *superfluus* overflowing

superglue *n* an extremely strong and quick-drying glue

supergrass *n Brit, Austral, & NZ* an informer who names a large number of people as terrorists or criminals, esp. one who gives this information in order to avoid being put on trial

super heavyweight *n* an amateur boxer weighing over 201 pounds (91 kg)

superhuman *adj* beyond normal human ability or experience: *a superhuman effort*

superimpose *vb* **-posing, -posed** to set or place (something) on or over something else

superintend *vb* to supervise (a person or an activity)
WORD ORIGIN Latin *super-* above + *intendere* to give attention to

superintendent *n* **1** a senior police officer **2** a person who directs and manages an organization or office

superior *adj* **1** greater in quality, quantity, or usefulness **2** higher in rank, position, or status: *he was reprimanded by a superior officer* **3** believing oneself to be better than others **4** of very high quality or respectability: *superior merchandise* **5** *formal* placed higher up: *damage to the superior surface of the wing* **6** *printing* (of a character) written or printed above the line ▷ *n* **7** a person of greater rank or status **8** see **mother superior** > **superiority** *n*
WORD ORIGIN Latin *superus* placed above

⩘ USAGE
⩘ *Superior* should not be used with *than*:
⩘ *he is a better* (not *a superior*) *poet than his*
⩘ *brother; his poetry is superior to* (not *superior*
⩘ *than*) *his brother's.*

superlative (soo-**per**-lat-iv) *adj* **1** of outstanding quality; supreme **2** *grammar* denoting the form of an adjective or adverb that expresses the highest degree of quality ▷ *n* **3** the highest quality **4** *grammar* the superlative form of an adjective or adverb
WORD ORIGIN Old French *superlatif*

superman *n, pl* **-men** any man with great physical or mental powers

supermarket *n* a large self-service shop selling food and household goods

supermodel *n* a famous and highly-paid fashion model

supernatural *adj* **1** of or relating to things that cannot be explained by science, such as clairvoyance, ghosts, etc. ▷ *n* **2** **the supernatural** forces,

occurrences, and beings that cannot be explained by science

supernova *n, pl* **-vae** or **-vas** a star that explodes and, for a few days, becomes one hundred million times brighter than the sun

supernumerary *adj* **1** exceeding the required or regular number; extra **2** employed as a substitute or assistant ▷ *n, pl* **-raries 3** a person or thing that exceeds the required or regular number **4** a substitute or assistant **5** an actor who has no lines to say
WORD ORIGIN Latin *super-* above + *numerus* number

superphosphate *n* a chemical fertilizer, esp. one made by treating rock phosphate with sulphuric acid

superpower *n* a country of very great military and economic power, such as the US

superscript *printing adj* **1** (of a character) written or printed above the line ▷ *n* **2** a superscript character

supersede *vb* **-seding, -seded 1** to take the place of (something old-fashioned or less appropriate): *cavalry was superseded by armoured vehicles* **2** to replace (someone) in function or office
WORD ORIGIN Latin *supersedere* to sit above

supersize *adj also* **supersized 1** larger than standard size ▷ *vb* **-sizes, -sizing, -sized 2** to increase the size of (something, such as a standard portion of food)

supersonic *adj* being, having, or capable of a speed greater than the speed of sound

superstar *n* an extremely popular and famous entertainer or sportsperson **superstardom** *n*

superstate *n* a large state, esp. one created from a federation of states

superstition *n* **1** irrational belief in magic and the powers that supposedly bring good luck or bad luck **2** a belief or practice based on this **superstitious** *adj*
WORD ORIGIN Latin *superstitio*

superstore *n* a large supermarket

superstructure *n* **1** any structure or concept built on something else **2** *naut* any structure above the main deck of a ship

supertanker *n* a very large fast tanker

supertax *n* an extra tax on incomes above a certain level

Super Twelve *n* an annual international southern hemisphere Rugby Union tournament between professional club sides from South Africa, Australia, and New Zealand

supervene *vb* **-vening, -vened** to happen as an unexpected development **supervention** *n*
WORD ORIGIN Latin *supervenire* to come upon

supervise *vb* **-vising, -vised 1** to direct the performance or operation of (an activity or a process) **2** to watch over (people) so as to ensure appropriate behaviour **supervision** *n* **supervisor** *n* **supervisory** *adj*
WORD ORIGIN Latin *super-* over + *videre* to see

S

supine (soo-pine) *adj formal* lying on one's back
WORD ORIGIN Latin *supinus*

supper *n* **1** an evening meal **2** a late evening snack
WORD ORIGIN Old French *soper*

supplant *vb* to take the place of (someone or something)
WORD ORIGIN Latin *supplantare* to trip up

supple *adj* **1** (of a person) moving and bending easily and gracefully **2** (of a material or object) soft and bending easily without breaking **suppleness** *n*
WORD ORIGIN Latin *supplex* bowed

supplement *n* **1** an addition designed to make something more adequate **2** a magazine distributed free with a newspaper **3** a section added to a publication to supply further information or correct errors **4** (of money) an additional payment to obtain special services ▷ *vb* **5** to provide an addition to (something), esp. in order to make up for an inadequacy: *a Saturday job to supplement her grant* **supplementary** *adj*
WORD ORIGIN Latin *supplementum*

supplicant *n formal* a person who makes a humble request
WORD ORIGIN Latin *supplicans* beseeching

supplication *n formal* a humble request for help
WORD ORIGIN Latin *supplicare* to beg on one's knees

supply *vb* **-plies, -plying, -plied 1** to provide with something required: *Nigeria may supply them with oil* ▷ *n, pl* **-plies 2** the act of providing something **3** an amount available for use; stock: *electricity supply* **4 supplies** food and equipment needed for a trip or military campaign **5** *econ* the amount of a commodity that producers are willing and able to offer for sale at a specified price: *supply and demand* **6** a person who acts as a temporary substitute ▷ *adj* **7** acting as a temporary substitute: *supply teachers* **supplier** *n*
WORD ORIGIN Latin *supplere* to complete

support *vb* **1** to carry the weight of (a thing or person) **2** to provide the necessities of life for (a family or person) **3** to give practical or emotional help to (someone) **4** to give approval to (a cause, idea, or political party) **5** to take an active interest in and be loyal to (a particular football or other sport team) **6** to establish the truthfulness or accuracy of (a theory or statement) by providing new facts **7** to speak in a debate in favour of (a motion) **8** (in a concert) to perform earlier than (the main attraction) **9** *films, theatre* to play a less important role to (the leading actor or actress) ▷ *n* **10** the act of supporting or the condition of being supported **11** a thing that bears the weight of an object from below **12** a person who gives someone practical or emotional help **13** the means of providing the necessities of life for a family or person **14** a band or entertainer not topping the bill **supportive** *adj*
WORD ORIGIN Latin *supportare* to bring

supporter *n* a person who supports a sports team, politician, etc.

suppose *vb* **-posing, -posed 1** to presume (something) to be true without certain knowledge: *I suppose it will be in the papers* **2** to consider (something) as a possible suggestion for the sake of discussion: *suppose you're arrested on a misdemeanour* **3** (of a theory) to depend on the truth or existence of: *this scenario supposes that he would do so*
WORD ORIGIN Latin *supponere* to substitute

supposed *adj* **1 supposed to** expected to: *spies aren't supposed to be nice* **2** presumed to be true without certain knowledge; doubtful: *the supposed wonders of drug therapy* **supposedly** *adv*

supposition *n* **1** an idea or a statement believed or assumed to be true **2** the act of supposing: *much of it is based on supposition*

suppositious *adj* deduced from an idea or statement believed or assumed to be true; hypothetical

suppository *n, pl* **-ries** *med* a medicine in solid form that is inserted into the vagina or rectum and left to dissolve
WORD ORIGIN Latin *suppositus* placed beneath

suppress *vb* **1** to put an end to (something) by physical or legal force **2** to prevent the circulation or publication of (information or books) **3** to hold (an emotion or a response) in check; restrain: *he could barely suppress a groan* **4** *electronics* to reduce or eliminate (interference) in a circuit **suppression** *n*
WORD ORIGIN Latin *suppressus* held down

suppressant *n* a drug that suppresses an action: *a cough suppressant*

suppurate *vb* **-rating, -rated** *pathol* (of a wound or sore) to produce or leak pus
WORD ORIGIN Latin *suppurare*

supremacy *n* **1** supreme power; dominance **2** the state or quality of being superior

supreme *adj* **1** of highest status or power: *the Supreme Council* **2** of highest quality or importance: *a supreme player* **3** greatest in degree; extreme: *supreme happiness* **supremely** *adv*
WORD ORIGIN Latin *supremus* highest

supremo *n, pl* **-mos** *informal* a person in overall authority

sur-¹ *prefix* over; above; beyond: *surcharge; surrealism*
WORD ORIGIN Old French

sur-² *prefix* see **sub-**

surcharge *n* **1** a charge in addition to the usual payment or tax **2** an excessive sum charged, often unlawfully ▷ *vb* **-charging, -charged 3** to charge (someone) an additional sum or tax **4** to overcharge (someone) for something

surd *maths n* **1** an irrational number ▷ *adj* **2** of or relating to a surd
WORD ORIGIN Latin *surdus* muffled

sure *adj* **1** free from doubt or uncertainty (in regard to a belief): *she was sure that she was still at home; I am sure he didn't mean it* **2 sure of** having no doubt, such as of the occurrence of a future state or event: *sure of winning the point* **3** reliable or accurate: *a sure sign of dry rot* **4** bound inevitably (to be or do something);

certain: *his aggressive style is sure to please the American fans* **5 sure of** or **about** happy to put one's trust in (someone): *I'm still not quite sure about her* **6 sure of oneself** confident in one's own abilities and opinions **7** not open to doubt: *sure proof* **8** bound to be or occur; inevitable: *victory is sure* **9** physically secure: *a sure footing* **10 be sure** (usually foll. by *to* or *and*) to be careful or certain (to do something): *be sure to label each jar* **11 for sure** without a doubt **12 make sure** to make certain: *make sure there is no-one in the car* **13 sure enough** *informal* in fact: *sure enough, this is happening* **14 to be sure** it has to be acknowledged; admittedly ▷ *adv* **15** *informal chiefly US & Canad* without question; certainly: *it sure is bad news* ▷ *interj* **16** *informal* willingly; yes **sureness** *n*
WORD ORIGIN Old French *seur*

sure-fire *adj informal* certain to succeed: *a sure-fire cure*

sure-footed *adj* **1** unlikely to fall, slip, or stumble **2** unlikely to make a mistake

surely *adv* **1** am I not right in thinking that? I am sure that: *surely you can see that?* **2** without doubt: *without support they will surely fail* **3** slowly but surely gradually but noticeably ▷ *interj* **4** *chiefly US & Canad* willingly; yes

surety *n, pl* **-ties 1** a person who takes legal responsibility for the fulfilment of another's debt or obligation **2** security given as a guarantee that an obligation will be met
WORD ORIGIN Latin *securitas* security

surf *n* **1** foam caused by waves breaking on the shore or on a reef ▷ *vb* **2** to take part in surfing **3** to move rapidly through a particular medium: *surfing the internet* **4** *informal* to be carried on top of something: *that guy's surfing the audience* **surfer** *n*
WORD ORIGIN probably variant of *sough*

surface *n* **1** the outside or top of an object **2** the size of such an area **3** material covering the surface of an object **4** the outward appearance as opposed to the real or hidden nature of something: *on the surface the idea seems attractive* **5** *geom* **a** the complete boundary of a solid figure **b** something that has length and breadth but no thickness **6** the uppermost level of the land or sea **7 come to the surface** to become apparent after being hidden ▷ *vb* **-facing, -faced 8** to become apparent or widely known **9** to rise to the surface of water **10** to give (an area) a particular kind of surface **11** *informal* to get up out of bed
WORD ORIGIN French

surface tension *n physics* a property of liquids, caused by molecular forces, that leads to the apparent presence of a surface film and to rising and falling in contact with solids

surfboard *n* a long narrow board used in surfing

surfeit *n formal* **1** an excessive amount **2** excessive eating or drinking **3** an uncomfortably full or sickened feeling caused by eating or drinking too much
WORD ORIGIN French *sourfait*

Leet

In 2007 the American dictionary publisher Merriam-Webster announced that *w00t* was its 'word of the year'. The word, which is an internet-slang spelling of *woot*, an exclamation of joy (especially at someone else's defeat or humiliation), was chosen by Merriam-Webster's own dictionary users and is remarkable in two respects: the use of numeric characters to represent a traditional vowel sound, and the intrusion of a previously exclusive argot into mainstream consciousness.

Woot (also spelled *w007*, \|/*007*, or simply *woot*) is an example of *Leetspeak* or *leet*, an alternative spelling system and slang developed and used by computer programmers, hackers (or *haxxorz*), and on-line gamers (*g4mzorz*).

The name *leet* is ultimately derived from standard English word *elite*, dropping the first syllable (although the variants *eleet* and *31337* also exist), which in computer programming and gaming denotes the highest level of skill and competence. The origins of *leet* go back to the 1980s, a time when the incipient internet and computer hacking really were the province of the elite; it continues to evolve, and *leet*-isms are increasingly used in more mainstream, non-computing slang and idiom.

The most striking characteristic of *leetspeak* is its frequent substitution of numbers and symbols for letters; for example, *leet* can also be spelled *l33t, l337, 1337*, or any other conceivable way, provided other users can recognize the word, and the word *leetspeak* itself can appear as *13375P34K* or even *13375?34|<*. This type of alternative spelling was probably invented in order to discuss forbidden topics on public message boards and, later, in blogs and chatrooms. This feature of *leetspeak* is frequently imitated by non-leeters, especially in computing passwords, where leet-esque numerical substitutions provide an easy way to generate a strong password (one that combines upper- and lower-case letters with numbers and symbols) which is nevertheless still memorable. Some other, non-computing sub-cultures have also adopted alternative

spellings similar to *leet*, for example the adjective *troo*, for 'true' among heavy-metal enthusiasts.

A lesser known, but no less interesting feature of *leetspeak* is its incorporation of common typographical errors as accepted variants of words. For example, *teh* has become the main way to write *the* in *leet*: 'That noob is teh suxxor' means 'That newbie really sucks'. Similarly, *pwn* has become the familiar *leet* version of *own*, meaning 'to defeat, triumph over, or humiliate utterly': 'Noob13: I's gonna pwn your 455!!!1!' means 'Newbie, I will defeat you so utterly and completely that the humiliation will follow you for the rest of your virtual life.' Although it looks vaguely Welsh, *pwn* derives from a common typo arising from the fact that the letters P and O are right next to each other on a standard Qwerty keyboard. Another such intentional misspelling is *pron*, meaning *porn* (probably harking back to the origin of *leetspeak* as a secret language for discussing forbidden topics). *Pron* has become so established among gamers that certain games are now using the word *prawn* as a pun on *pron*, especially in fictional place names associated with the virtual sex industry.

Leetspeak has also evolved its own suffixes and inflections, albeit derived from traditional English ones. For example, in standard English, the suffix *-er* can be added to a verb to form the *agent noun*, the person who performs that verb. Thus *eat* plus *-er* equals *eater*, one who eats. In *leetspeak*, verbs get the suffix *-xor*, as in *haxxor* or *h4xor* ('hacker') and *roxxor* ('rocker'). The related suffix *-zorz* was originally a plural version of this, but its meaning has evolved significantly. First, it began to be used in the singular, but it differed from *-xor* in that it was intensive: a *roxxor* may 'rock', but a *rockzorz* 'really, really rocks'. Then *-zorz* began forming adjectives ('7h47 g4m3 is sooo suckzorz') and strengthening existing nouns ('wootzorz' means 'extreme woots'). Finally, *zorz* became established as a word in its own right: as an adjective, meaning 'elite' ('My new laptop is zorz'); as an adverb, meaning 'utterly' ('I pwned that noob zorz'); and as a noun, meaning one who is truly elite ('B1FF izz teh zorz!').

surfing *n* the sport of riding towards shore on the crest of a wave by standing or lying on a surfboard

surge *n* **1** a sudden powerful increase: *a surge in spending* **2** a strong rolling movement of the sea **3** a heavy rolling motion or sound: *a great surge of people* ▷ *vb* **surging, surged 4** to move forward strongly and suddenly **5** to increase quickly and strongly **6** (of the sea) to rise or roll with a heavy swelling motion
WORD ORIGIN Latin *surgere* to rise

surgeon *n* a medical doctor who specializes in surgery

surgery *n, pl* **-geries 1** medical treatment in which a person's body is cut open by a surgeon in order to treat or remove the problem part **2** *Brit* a place where, or time when, a doctor or dentist can be consulted **3** *Brit* a time when an MP or councillor can be consulted
WORD ORIGIN Greek *kheir* hand + *ergon* work

surgical *adj* **1** involving or used in surgery **2** (of an action) performed with extreme precision: *a surgical air attack* **surgically** *adv*

surgical spirit *n* methylated spirit used medically for cleaning wounds and sterilizing equipment

surly *adj* **-lier, -liest** bad-tempered and rude
WORD ORIGIN from obsolete *sirly* haughty

surmise *vb* **-mising, -mised 1** to guess (something) from incomplete or uncertain evidence ▷ *n* **2** a conclusion based on incomplete or uncertain evidence
WORD ORIGIN Old French *surmettre* to accuse

surmount *vb* **1** to overcome (a problem) **2** to be situated on top of (something): *the island is surmounted by a huge black castle* **surmountable** *adj*
WORD ORIGIN Old French *surmonter*

surname *n* a family name as opposed to a first or Christian name
WORD ORIGIN Old French sur- over + *nom* name

surpass *vb* **1** to be greater in extent than or superior in achievement to (something or someone) **2** **surpass oneself** or **expectations** to go beyond the limit of what was expected
WORD ORIGIN French *surpasser*

surplice *n* a loose knee-length garment with wide sleeves, worn by clergymen and choristers
WORD ORIGIN Old French *sourpelis*

surplus *n* **1** a quantity or amount left over in excess of what is required **2** *accounting* an excess of income over spending ▷ *adj* **3** being in excess; extra: *surplus to requirements*
WORD ORIGIN Old French

surprise *n* **1** the act of taking someone unawares: *the element of surprise* **2** a sudden or unexpected event, gift, etc.: *this is a nice surprise* **3** the feeling of being surprised; astonishment: *to our great surprise* **4** **take someone by surprise** to capture someone unexpectedly or catch someone unprepared ▷ *adj* **5** causing

surprise: *a surprise attack* ▷ *vb* **-prising, -prised 6** to cause (someone) to feel amazement or wonder **7** to come upon or discover (someone) unexpectedly or suddenly **8** to capture or attack (someone) suddenly and without warning **9** **surprise into** to provoke (someone) to unintended action by a trick or deception **surprised** *adj* **surprising** *adj* **surprisingly** *adv*
WORD ORIGIN Old French *surprendre* to overtake

surreal *adj* very strange or dreamlike; bizarre

surrealism *n* a movement in art and literature in the 1920s, involving the combination of images that would not normally be found together, as if in a dream **surrealist** *n, adj* **surrealistic** *adj*
WORD ORIGIN French *surréalisme*

surrender *vb* **1** to give oneself up physically to an enemy after defeat **2** to give (something) up to another, under pressure or on demand: *the rebels surrendered their arms* **3** to give (something) up voluntarily to another: *he was surrendering his own chance for the championship* **4** to give in to a temptation or an influence ▷ *n* **5** the act or instance of surrendering
WORD ORIGIN Old French *surrendre*

surreptitious *adj* done in secret or without permission: *surreptitious moments of bliss* **surreptitiously** *adv*
WORD ORIGIN Latin *surrepticius* furtive

surrogate *n* **1** a person or thing acting as a substitute ▷ *adj* **2** acting as a substitute: *a surrogate father*
WORD ORIGIN Latin *surrogare* to substitute

surrogate mother *n* a woman who gives birth to a child on behalf of a couple who cannot have a baby themselves, usually by artificial insemination **surrogate motherhood** or **surrogacy** *n*

surround *vb* **1** to encircle or enclose (something or someone) **2** to exist around (someone or something): *the family members who surround him* ▷ *n* **3** *chiefly Brit* a border, such as the area of uncovered floor between the walls of a room and the carpet **surrounding** *adj*
WORD ORIGIN Old French *suronder*

surroundings *pl n* the area and environment around a person, place, or thing

surtax *n* an extra tax on incomes above a certain level

surveillance *n* close observation of a person suspected of being a spy or a criminal
WORD ORIGIN French

survey *vb* **1** to view or consider (something) as a whole: *she surveyed her purchases anxiously* **2** to make a detailed map of (an area of land) by measuring or calculating distances and height **3** *Brit* to inspect (a building) to assess its condition and value **4** to make a detailed investigation of the behaviour, opinions, etc. of (a group of people) ▷ *n* **5** a detailed investigation of the behaviour, opinions, etc. of a group of people **6** the act of making a detailed map of an area of land by measuring or

calculating distance and height **7** *Brit* an inspection of a building to assess its condition and value **surveying** *n* **surveyor** *n*
WORD ORIGIN French *surveoir*

survival *n* **1** the condition of having survived something **2** a person or thing that continues to exist in the present despite being from an earlier time, such as a custom ▷ *adj* **3** of, relating to, or assisting the act of surviving: *survival suits*

survive *vb* **-viving, -vived 1 a** to continue to live or exist **b** to continue to live or exist after (a passage of time or a difficult or dangerous experience) **2** to live after the death of (another) **survivor** *n*
WORD ORIGIN Old French *souvivre*

susceptibility *n, pl* **-ties 1** the quality or condition of being easily affected or influenced by something **2** **susceptibilities** emotional feelings

susceptible *adj* **1** **susceptible to a** giving in easily to: *susceptible to political pressure* **b** vulnerable to (a disease or injury): *susceptible to pneumonia* **2** easily affected emotionally; impressionable
WORD ORIGIN Late Latin *susceptibilis*

sushi (**soo**-shee) *n* a Japanese dish consisting of small cakes of cold rice with a topping of raw fish
WORD ORIGIN Japanese

suspect *vb* **1** to believe (someone) to be guilty without having any proof **2** to think (something) to be false or doubtful: *he suspected her intent* **3** to believe (something) to be the case; think probable: *I suspect he had another reason* ▷ *n* **4** a person who is believed guilty of a specified offence ▷ *adj* **5** not to be trusted or relied upon: *her commitment to the cause has always been suspect*
WORD ORIGIN Latin *suspicere* to mistrust

suspend *vb* **1** to hang (something) from a high place **2** to cause (something) to remain floating or hanging: *a huge orange sun suspended above the horizon* **3** to cause (something) to stop temporarily: *the discussions have been suspended* **4** to remove (someone) temporarily from a job or position, usually as a punishment
WORD ORIGIN Latin *suspendere*

suspended animation *n* a state in which the body's functions are slowed down to a minimum for a period of time, such as by freezing or hibernation

suspended sentence *n* a sentence of imprisonment that is not served by an offender unless he or she commits a further offence during a specified time

suspender belt *n* a belt with suspenders hanging from it for holding up women's stockings

suspenders *pl n* **1 a** elastic straps attached to a belt or corset, with fasteners for holding up women's stockings **b** similar fasteners attached to garters for holding up men's socks **2** *US & Canad* also called (*Brit*): **braces** a pair of straps worn over the shoulders for holding up the trousers

suspense *n* **1** a state of anxiety or uncertainty: *Sue and I stared at each other in suspense* **2** excitement felt at the

approach of the climax of a book, film, or play: *action and suspense abound in this thriller* **suspenseful** *adj*
WORD ORIGIN Medieval Latin *suspensum* delay

suspension *n* **1** the delaying or stopping temporarily of something: *the suspension of the talks* **2** temporary removal from a job or position, usually as a punishment **3** the act of suspending or the state of being suspended **4** a system of springs and shock absorbers that supports the body of a vehicle **5** a device, usually a wire or spring, that suspends or supports something, such as the pendulum of a clock **6** *chem* a mixture in which fine solid or liquid particles are suspended in a fluid

suspension bridge *n* a bridge suspended from cables that hang between two towers and are secured at both ends

suspicion *n* **1** the act or an instance of suspecting; belief without sure proof that something is wrong **2** a feeling of mistrust **3** a slight trace: *the merest suspicion of a threat* **4** **above suspicion** not possibly guilty of anything, through having a good reputation **5** **under suspicion** suspected of doing something wrong
WORD ORIGIN Latin *suspicio* distrust

suspicious *adj* **1** causing one to suspect something is wrong: *suspicious activities* **2** unwilling to trust: *I'm suspicious of his motives* **suspiciously** *adv*

suss out *vb Brit, Austral, & NZ slang* to work out (a situation or a person's character), using one's intuition
WORD ORIGIN from *suspect*

sustain *vb* **1** to maintain or continue for a period of time: *I managed to sustain a conversation* **2** to keep up the strength or energy of (someone): *one mouthful of water to sustain him; the merest drop of comfort to sustain me* **3** to suffer (an injury or loss): *he sustained a spinal injury* **4** to support (something) from below **5** to support or agree with (a decision or statement): *objection sustained* **sustained** *adj*
WORD ORIGIN Latin *sustinere* to hold up

sustainable *adj* **1** capable of being sustained **2** (of economic development or energy sources) capable of being maintained at a steady level without exhausting natural resources or causing ecological damage: *sustainable development*

sustained-release *adj* (of a pill or tablet) coated with a chemical substance that controls the dosage released into a patient's system

sustenance *n* means of maintaining health or life; food and drink

suture (soo-tcher) *n surgery* a stitch made with catgut or silk thread, to join the edges of a wound together
WORD ORIGIN Latin *suere* to sew

SUV sport (*or* sports) utility vehicle: a high-powered car with four-wheel drive, originally designed for off-road use

suzerain *n* **1** a state or sovereign that has some degree of control over a dependent state **2** (formerly) a person who had power over many people **suzerainty** *n*
WORD ORIGIN French

svelte *adj* attractively or gracefully slim; slender
WORD ORIGIN French

SW 1 southwest(ern) **2** short wave

swab *n* **1** *med* a small piece of cotton wool used for applying medication or cleansing a wound ▷ *vb* **swabbing, swabbed 2** to clean or apply medication to (a wound) with a swab **3** to clean (the deck of a ship) with a mop
WORD ORIGIN probably from Middle Dutch *swabbe* mop

swaddle *vb* **-dling, -dled** to wrap (a baby) in swaddling clothes
WORD ORIGIN Old English *swæthel* swaddling clothes

swaddling clothes *pl n* long strips of cloth formerly wrapped round a newborn baby

swag *n* **1** *slang* stolen property **2** *Austral & NZ informal* (formerly) a swagman's pack containing personal belongings
WORD ORIGIN probably Scandinavian

swagger *vb* **1** to walk or behave in an arrogant manner ▷ *n* **2** an arrogant walk or manner
WORD ORIGIN probably from *swag*

swagger stick *n* a short cane carried by army officers

swagman *n, pl* **-men** *Austral & NZ informal* a labourer who carries his personal possessions in a pack while looking for work

Swahili (swah-heel-ee) *n* a language of E Africa that is an official language of Kenya and Tanzania
WORD ORIGIN Arabic *sawāhil* coasts

swain *n archaic or poetic* **1** a male lover or admirer **2** a young man from the countryside
WORD ORIGIN Old English *swān* swineherd

swallow¹ *vb* **1** to pass (food, drink, etc.) through the mouth and gullet to the stomach **2** *informal* to believe (something) trustingly: *I was supposed to swallow the lie* **3** not to show: *I believe they should swallow their pride* **4** to make a gulping movement in the throat, such as when nervous **5** to put up with (an insult) without answering back **6** **be swallowed up** to be taken into and made a part of something: *the old centre was being swallowed up by new estates* ▷ *n* **7** the act of swallowing **8** the amount swallowed at any single time; mouthful
WORD ORIGIN Old English *swelgan*

swallow² *n* a small migratory bird with long pointed wings and a forked tail
WORD ORIGIN Old English *swealwe*

swallow dive *n* a dive in which the legs are kept straight and the arms outstretched while in the air, with entry into the water made headfirst

swallowtail *n* **1** a butterfly with a long tail-like part on each hind wing **2** the forked tail of a swallow or similar bird

swam *vb* the past tense of **swim**

swami (swah-mee) *n* a Hindu religious teacher
WORD ORIGIN Hindi *svāmī*

swamp *n* **1** an area of permanently waterlogged land; bog ▷ *vb* **2** *naut* to cause (a boat) to sink or fill with water **3** to overwhelm (a person or place) with more than can be dealt with or accommodated **swampy** *adj*
WORD ORIGIN probably from Middle Dutch *somp*

swan *n* **1** a large, usually white, water bird with a long neck ▷ *vb* **swanning, swanned 2** **swan around** *or* **about** *informal* to wander about without purpose, but with an air of superiority
WORD ORIGIN Old English

swank *informal vb* **1** to show off or boast ▷ *n* **2** showing off or boasting **swanky** *adj*
WORD ORIGIN origin unknown

swanndri (swan-dry) *n trademark, NZ* a weatherproof woollen shirt or jacket. Also called: **swannie**

swan song *n* the last public act of a person before retirement or death

swap *or* **swop** *vb* **swapping, swapped 1** to exchange (something) for something else ▷ *n* **2** an exchange
WORD ORIGIN originally, to shake hands on a bargain, strike: probably imitative

SWAPO *or* **Swapo** South-West Africa People's Organization

sward *n* a stretch of turf or grass
WORD ORIGIN Old English *sweard* skin

swarm¹ *n* **1** a group of bees, led by a queen, that has left the hive to make a new home **2** a large mass of insects or other small animals **3** a moving mass of people ▷ *vb* **4** to move quickly and in large numbers **5** to be overrun: *the place is swarming with cops*
WORD ORIGIN Old English *swearm*

swarm² *vb* **swarm up** to climb (a ladder or rope) by gripping it with the hands and feet: *the boys swarmed up the rigging*
WORD ORIGIN origin unknown

swarthy *adj* **swarthier, swarthiest** having a dark complexion
WORD ORIGIN obsolete *swarty*

swash (swosh) *n* the rush of water up a beach following each break of the waves
WORD ORIGIN probably imitative

swashbuckling *adj* having the exciting manner or behaviour of pirates, esp. those depicted in films **swashbuckler** *n*
WORD ORIGIN obsolete *swash* to make the noise of a sword striking a shield + *buckler* shield

swastika *n* **1** a primitive religious symbol in the shape of a Greek cross with the ends of the arms bent at right angles **2** this symbol with clockwise arms as the emblem of Nazi Germany
WORD ORIGIN Sanskrit *svastika*

swat *vb* **swatting, swatted 1** to hit sharply: *swatting the ball with confidence* ▷ *n* **2** a sharp blow
WORD ORIGIN dialect variant of *squat*

swatch *n* **1** a sample of cloth **2** a collection of such samples
WORD ORIGIN origin unknown

swath (swawth) *n* same as **swathe**
WORD ORIGIN Old English *swæth*

swathe *vb* **swathing, swathed 1** to wrap a bandage, garment, or piece of cloth around (a person or part of the

S

body) ▷ n **2** a long strip of cloth wrapped around something **3** the width of one sweep of a scythe or of the blade of a mowing machine **4** the strip cut in one sweep **5** the quantity of cut crops left in one sweep **6** a long narrow strip of land

WORD ORIGIN Old English *swathian*

sway vb **1** to swing to and fro: *red poppies swayed in the faint breeze* **2** to lean to one side and then the other: *entire rows swayed in time* **3** to be unable to decide between two or more opinions **4** to influence (someone) in his or her opinion or judgment ▷ n **5** power or influence **6** a swinging or leaning movement **7 hold sway** to have power or influence

WORD ORIGIN probably from Old Norse *sveigja* to bend

swear vb **swearing, swore, sworn 1** to use words considered obscene or blasphemous **2** to promise solemnly on oath; vow: *Sally and Peter swore to love and cherish each other* **3 swear by** to have complete confidence in (something) **4** to state (something) earnestly: *I swear he was all right* **5** to give evidence on oath in a law court

WORD ORIGIN Old English *swerian*

swear in vb to make (someone) take an oath when taking up an official position or entering the witness box to give evidence in court: *a new federal president was sworn in*

swear off vb to promise to give up: *I lived with memories of the gooey sundaes I've sworn off*

swearword n a word considered rude or blasphemous

sweat n **1** the salty liquid that comes out of the skin's pores during strenuous activity in excessive heat or when afraid **2** the state or condition of sweating: *he worked up a sweat* **3** slang hard work or effort: *climbing to the crest of Ward Hill was a sweat* **4 in a sweat** informal in a state of worry **5 no sweat** slang no problem ▷ vb **sweating, sweat** or **sweated 6** to have sweat come through the skin's pores, as a result of strenuous activity, excessive heat, nervousness, or fear **7** informal to suffer anxiety or distress **8 sweat blood** informal **a** to work very hard **b** to be filled with anxiety ▸ See also **sweats** ▷ **sweaty** adj

WORD ORIGIN Old English *swǣtan*

sweatband n a piece of cloth tied around the forehead or around the wrist to absorb sweat during strenuous physical activity

sweater n a warm knitted piece of clothing covering the upper part of the body

sweat lodge n (among native N American peoples) a structure in which water is poured onto hot stones to make the occupants sweat for religious or medicinal purposes

sweat off vb informal to get rid of (weight) by doing exercises

sweat out vb **sweat it out** informal to endure an unpleasant situation for a time, hoping for an improvement

sweats pl n sweatshirts and sweat suit trousers collectively

sweatshirt n a long-sleeved casual top made of knitted cotton or cotton mixture

sweatshop n a workshop where employees work long hours in poor conditions for low pay

sweat suit n a suit worn by athletes for training, consisting of a sweatshirt and trousers made of the same material

swede n a round root vegetable with a purplish-brown skin and yellow flesh

WORD ORIGIN introduced from Sweden in the 18th century

Swede n a person from Sweden

Swedish adj **1** of Sweden ▷ n **2** the language of Sweden

sweep vb **sweeping, swept 1** to clean (a floor or chimney) with a brush **2** (often foll. by *up*) to remove or collect (dirt or rubbish) with a brush **3** to move smoothly and quickly: *the car swept into the drive* **4** to spread rapidly across or through (a place): *the wave of democracy that had swept through Eastern Europe* **5** to move in a proud and majestic fashion: *the boss himself swept into the hall* **6** to direct (one's eyes, line of fire, etc.) over (a place or target) **7 sweep away** or **off** to overwhelm (someone) emotionally: *I've been swept away by my fears* **8** to brush or lightly touch (a surface): *the dress swept along the ground* **9** to clear away or get rid of (something) suddenly or forcefully: *these doubts were quickly swept aside; bridges have been swept away by the floods* **10** to stretch out gracefully or majestically, esp. in a wide circle: *the hills swept down into the green valley* **11** to win overwhelmingly in an election: *the umbrella party which swept these elections* **12 sweep the board** to win every event or prize in a contest ▷ n **13** the act or an instance of sweeping **14** a swift or steady movement: *the wide sweep of the shoulders* **15** a wide expanse: *the whole sweep of the bay* **16** any curving line or contour: *the wide sweep of the bay* **16** any curving line or contour **17** short for **sweepstake 18** chiefly Brit same as **chimney sweep 19 make a clean sweep** to win an overwhelming victory

WORD ORIGIN Middle English *swepen*

sweeper n **1** a device used to sweep carpets, consisting of a long handle attached to a revolving brush **2** soccer a defensive player usually positioned in front of the goalkeeper

sweeping adj **1** affecting many people to a great extent: *sweeping financial reforms* **2** (of a statement) making general assumptions about an issue without considering the details **3** decisive or overwhelming: *to suffer sweeping losses* **4** taking in a wide area: *a sweeping view of the area*

sweepstake or esp. US **sweepstakes** n **1** a lottery in which the stakes of the participants make up the prize **2** a horse race involving such a lottery

WORD ORIGIN originally referring to someone who *sweeps* or takes all the stakes in a game

sweet adj **1** tasting of or like sugar **2** kind and charming: *that was really sweet of you* **3** attractive and delightful: *a sweet child* **4** (of a sound) pleasant and tuneful: *sweet music* **5** (of wine) having a

high sugar content; not dry **6** fresh, clear, and clean: *sweet water; sweet air* **7 sweet on someone** fond of or infatuated with someone ▷ n **8** Brit, Austral, & NZ a shaped piece of confectionery consisting mainly of sugar **9** Brit, Austral, & NZ a dessert **sweetly** adv **sweetness** n

WORD ORIGIN Old English *swēte*

sweet-and-sour adj (of food) cooked in a sauce made from sugar and vinegar and other ingredients

sweetbread n the meat obtained from the pancreas of a calf or lamb

sweetbrier n a wild rose with sweet-smelling leaves and pink flowers

sweet corn n **1** a kind of maize with sweet yellow kernels, eaten as a vegetable when young **2** the sweet kernels removed from the maize cob, cooked as a vegetable

sweeten vb **1** to make (food or drink) sweet or sweeter **2** to be nice to (someone) in order to ensure cooperation **3** to make (an offer or a proposal) more acceptable

sweetener n **1** a sweetening agent that does not contain sugar **2** Brit, Austral, & NZ slang an inducement offered to someone in order to persuade them to accept an offer or business deal

sweetheart n **1** an affectionate name to call someone **2** old-fashioned one's boyfriend or girlfriend **3** informal a lovable or generous person

sweetie n informal **1** an affectionate name to call someone **2** Brit & NZ same as **sweet** (sense 8) **3** chiefly Brit a lovable or generous person

sweetmeat n old-fashioned a small delicacy preserved in sugar

sweet pea n a climbing plant with sweet-smelling pastel-coloured flowers

sweet pepper n the large bell-shaped fruit of the pepper plant, which is eaten unripe (**green pepper**) or ripe (**red pepper**) as a vegetable

sweet potato n a root vegetable, grown in the tropics, with pinkish-brown skin and yellow flesh

sweet spot n sport the centre area of a racquet, club, etc. from which the cleanest shots are made

sweet-talk informal vb **1** to persuade (someone) by flattery: *I thought I could sweet-talk you into teaching me* ▷ n **sweet talk 2** insincere flattery intended to persuade

sweet tooth n a strong liking for sweet foods

sweet william n a garden plant with clusters of white, pink, red, or purple flowers

swell vb **swelling, swelled; swollen** or **swelled 1** (of a part of the body) to grow in size as a result of injury or infection: *his face swelled and became pale* **2** to increase in size as a result of being filled with air or liquid: *a balloon swells if you force in more air* **3** to grow or cause (something) to grow in size, numbers, amount, or degree: *Israel's population is swelling* **4** (of an emotion) to become more intense: *his anger swelled within him*

Welsh English

The term *Wenglish* was recently coined to refer to a variety of English, used in South Wales in particular, displaying the influence of the Welsh language. *Welsh English,* however, covers those varieties used in any part of Wales, including those influenced by the language of adjacent counties in England. The use of the Celtic Welsh language itself, known as *Cymraeg* to its speakers, has declined significantly in the last two centuries, and while over a fifth of the population of Wales claim to be able to speak Welsh, English is the majority language.

The influence of Welsh is strongest in North Wales, where bilingualism is most common, but it is also evident in the English of Mid-Wales and South Wales. Vocabulary items taken from Welsh include *carreg* (a stone), *clennig* (a gift of money), *cwtch* (cuddle), *twp* (stupid), and the terms of endearment *bach* (meaning 'little') and *del*. Other words in Welsh English may be shared by some dialects in England, for example *dap* (to bounce) and *steam* (a bread bin). Standard English words that have taken on particular meanings in Wales include *tidy*, meaning 'good' or 'attractive', and *lose* meaning 'to miss', as in 'lose the train'. *Boyo*, derived from *boy*, is used as either a term of address or a reference to any man.

Syntactically, Welsh English is influenced by the grammar of Welsh. 'Foregrounding' is common, with sentence elements placed at the beginning of a sentence for emphasis: 'Tired, I am'; 'Coming on Friday, he is'. A subject pronoun, commonly omitted in the Welsh language, may also be left out in Welsh English, as in 'Saw 'im leaving'. Another legacy of Welsh is the syntactical use of the verb *do* to indicate a regular or habitual action: 'He do go to the match every week'. Whereas a similar structure might indicate emphasis in other varieties of English, it may be used in Welsh English where emphasis is not intended. The verb *be* may be omitted in a structure such as 'I'm not ready, but I will soon'. The use of *there* rather than *how* in exclamations ('There's strange it was!'), comes from a direct translation of the word *dyna* that would be used in similar constructions in Welsh. Another usage strongly associated with Welsh English is the imperative *look you* or *mind you*, used in sentences such as

'Look you, the cat has got out'. *See* may be used in a similar way: 'We were very angry, see'.

Accents can vary across Wales, and some differences can be attributed to the amount of contact with English. However, there are phonological tendencies that are common throughout the country. As in Scottish accents, there is a strong tendency to use a strong, 'rolled r' sound, and Welsh accents share the tendency of Irish accents to use more aspiration with 'd', 'p', and 't', giving them a 'breathy' quality. Vowel sounds tend to be monophthongal, with one 'pure' sound, rather than diphthongal, where a vowel sound shades into another. Where diphthongs do exist, they may be separated into distinct syllables: thus, 'poor' may be sounded 'poo-uh'.

But perhaps the most widely recognized characteristic of Welsh pronunciation is its 'sing-song' quality. Intonation in Celtic languages is commonly based on whole sentences rather than a fixed intonation of particular words, and in spoken Welsh English, there may be a rising intonation on a whole word at the end of a sentence.

There are few words in Standard English that can be said with absolute certainty to be derived from Welsh. *Flannel*, for instance, is probably from Welsh *gwlanen* (woollen fabric), and it is very probable that *penguin* is derived from *pen* (head) and *gwyn* (white). *Flummery*, originally a pudding made of oatmeal, but now an informal word for nonsense, derives from *llymru*. *Cromlech*, referring to a circle of prehistoric standing stones, is from *crom* (bent) and *llech* (flat stone), and the Welsh word for a steep-sided valley, *cwm*, has also made its way into English. The *coracle*, a small boat made of waterproofed hides, takes its name from Welsh *corwgl*; the *corgi* takes its name from *cor* (dwarf) and *ci* (dog). Occasionally, Welsh words may be used by speakers of other varieties of English when referring to Welsh customs or concepts for which there is no immediate translation, including those emotions considered so peculiarly Welsh that they defy substitution by any established term in English: the often communal emotional fervour that is *hwyl*, and *hiraeth*, a yearning for something lost or left behind.

5 (of the seas) to rise in waves **6** (of a sound) to become gradually louder and then die away ▷ *n* **7** the waving movement of the surface of the open sea **8** an increase in size, numbers, amount, or degree **9** a bulge **10** *old-fashioned, informal* a person who is wealthy, upper class, and fashionably dressed **11** *music* an increase in sound followed by an immediate dying away ▷ *adj* **12** *slang chiefly US* excellent or fine **WORD ORIGIN** Old English *swellan*

swelling *n* an enlargement of a part of the body as the result of injury or infection

swelter *vb* **1** to feel uncomfortable under extreme heat ▷ *n* **2** a hot and uncomfortable condition: *they left the city swelter for the beach* **WORD ORIGIN** Old English *sweltan* to die

sweltering *adj* uncomfortably hot: *a sweltering summer*

swept *vb* the past of **sweep**

swerve *vb* **swerving, swerved 1** to turn aside from a course sharply or suddenly ▷ *n* **2** the act of swerving **WORD ORIGIN** Old English *sweorfan* to scour

swift *adj* **1** moving or able to move quickly; fast **2** happening or performed quickly or suddenly: *a swift glance this way* **3 swift to** prompt to (do something): *swift to retaliate* ▷ *n* **4** a small fast-flying insect-eating bird with long wings **swiftly** *adv* **swiftness** *n* **WORD ORIGIN** Old English

swig *informal n* **1** a large swallow or deep drink, esp. from a bottle ▷ *vb* **swigging, swigged 2** to drink (some liquid) in large swallows, esp. from a bottle **WORD ORIGIN** origin unknown

swill *vb* **1** to drink large quantities of (an alcoholic drink) **2** (often foll. by *out*) *chiefly Brit & NZ* to rinse (something) in large amounts of water ▷ *n* **3** a liquid mixture containing waste food, fed to pigs **4** a deep drink, esp. of beer **WORD ORIGIN** Old English *swilian* to wash out

swim *vb* **swimming, swam, swum 1** to move along in water by movements of the arms and legs, or (in the case of fish) tail and fins **2** to cover (a stretch of water) in this way: *the first person to swim the Atlantic* **3** to float on a liquid: *flies swimming on the milk* **4** to be affected by dizziness: *his head was swimming* **5** (of the objects in someone's vision) to appear to spin or move around: *the faces of the nurses swam around her* **6** (often foll. by *in* or *with*) to be covered or flooded with liquid: *a steak swimming in gravy* ▷ *n* **7** the act, an instance, or a period of swimming **8 in the swim** *informal* fashionable or active in social or political activities **swimmer** *n* **swimming** *n* **WORD ORIGIN** Old English *swimman*

swimming bath *n* an indoor swimming pool

swimming costume *or* **bathing costume** *n chiefly Brit, Austral, & NZ* same as **swimsuit**

swimmingly *adv* successfully, effortlessly, or well: *everything went swimmingly*

swimming pool *n* a large hole in the ground, tiled and filled with water for swimming in

swimsuit *n* a woman's swimming garment that leaves the arms and legs bare

swindle *vb* **-dling, -dled 1** to cheat (someone) out of money **2** to obtain (money) from someone by fraud ▷ *n* **3** an instance of cheating someone out of money **swindler** *n* **WORD ORIGIN** German *schwindeln*

swine *n* **1** a mean or unpleasant person **2** *pl* **swine** same as **pig** ▷ **swinish** *adj* **WORD ORIGIN** Old English *swīn*

swine flu *n* a form of influenza occurring in swine caused by a virus capable of spreading to humans

swing *vb* **swinging, swung 1** to move backwards and forwards; sway **2** to pivot or cause (something) to pivot from a fixed point such as a hinge: *the door swung open* **3** to wave (a weapon, etc.) in a sweeping motion **4** to move in a sweeping curve: *the headlights swung along the street* **5** to alter one's opinion or mood suddenly **6** to hang so as to be able to turn freely **7** *old-fashioned, slang* to be hanged: *you'll swing for this!* **8** *informal* to manipulate or influence successfully: *it may help to swing the election* **9** (often foll. by *at*) to hit out with a sweeping motion **10** *old-fashioned* to play (music) in the style of swing **11** *old-fashioned, slang* to be lively and modern ▷ *n* **12** the act of swinging **13** a sweeping stroke or punch **14** a seat hanging from two chains or ropes on which a person may swing back and forth **15** popular dance music played by big bands in the 1930s and 1940s **16** *informal* the normal pace at which an activity, such as work, happens: *I'm into the swing of things now* **17** a sudden or extreme change, for example in some business activity or voting pattern **18 go with a swing** to go well; be successful **19 in full swing** at the height of activity **WORD ORIGIN** Old English *swingan*

swing bridge *n* a bridge that can be swung open to let ships pass through

swing by *vb informal* to go somewhere to pay a visit

swingeing (**swin**-jing) *adj chiefly Brit* severe or causing hardship: *swingeing spending cuts*

swipe *vb* **swiping, swiped 1** *informal* to try to hit (someone or something) with a sweeping blow: *he swiped at a boy who ran forward* **2** *slang* to steal (something) **3** to pass (a credit or debit card) through a machine which electronically interprets the information stored in the card ▷ *n* **4** *informal* a hard blow **WORD ORIGIN** origin unknown

swirl *vb* **1** to turn round and round with a twisting motion ▷ *n* **2** a twisting or spinning motion **3** a twisting shape **swirling** *adj* **WORD ORIGIN** probably from Dutch *zwirrelen*

swish *vb* **1** to move with or cause (something) to make a whistling or hissing sound ▷ *n* **2** a hissing or rustling sound or movement: *she turned*

with a swish of her skirt ▷ *adj* **3** *informal chiefly Brit, Austral, & NZ* smart and fashionable **WORD ORIGIN** imitative

Swiss *adj* **1** of Switzerland ▷ *n, pl* **Swiss 2** a person from Switzerland

Swiss ball *n* a very large inflatable ball made of strong elastic rubber, used for physical exercise and physiotherapy

swiss roll *n* a sponge cake spread with jam or cream and rolled up

switch *n* **1** a device for opening or closing an electric circuit **2** a sudden quick change **3** an exchange or swap **4** a flexible rod or twig, used for punishment **5** *US & Canad* a pair of movable rails for diverting moving trains from one track to another ▷ *vb* **6** to change quickly and suddenly **7** to exchange (places) or swap (something for something else) **8** *chiefly US & Canad* to transfer (rolling stock) from one railway track to another **9** see **switch off, switch on** **WORD ORIGIN** probably from Middle Dutch *swijch* twig

switchback *n* a steep mountain road, railway, or track which rises and falls sharply many times

switchboard *n* the place in a telephone exchange or office building where telephone calls are connected

switch off *vb* **1** to cause (a device) to stop operating by moving a switch or lever: *she switched off the television* **2** *informal* to become bored and stop paying attention: *when the conversation turned to house prices I switched off*

switch on *vb* **1** to cause (a device) to operate by moving a switch or lever **2** *informal* to produce (a certain type of behaviour or emotion) suddenly or automatically: *she was good at switching on the charm*

swither *Scot vb* **1** to hesitate or be indecisive ▷ *n* **2** a state of hesitation or uncertainty **WORD ORIGIN** origin unknown

swivel *vb* **-elling, -elled** *or US* **-eling, -eled 1** to turn on or swing round on a central point ▷ *n* **2** a coupling device which allows an attached object to turn freely **WORD ORIGIN** Old English *swīfan* to turn

swivel chair *n* a chair, whose seat is joined to the legs by a swivel, enabling it to be spun round

swizz *n Brit, NZ, & S African informal* a swindle or disappointment **WORD ORIGIN** origin unknown

swizzle stick *n* a small stick used to stir cocktails

swollen *vb* **1** a past participle of **swell** ▷ *adj* **2** enlarged by swelling

swoon *vb* **1** *literary* to faint because of shock or strong emotion **2** to be deeply affected by passion for (someone): *you've swooned over a string of rotten men* ▷ *n* **3** *literary* a faint **swooning** *adj* **WORD ORIGIN** Old English *geswōgen* insensible

swoop *vb* **1** (usually foll. by *down*) to move quickly through the air in a downward curve: *an owl swooped down from its perch* **2** (usually foll. by *on*) to

move suddenly and quickly towards (a place) in order to attack, arrest, or question the people inside: *nine police cars and vans swooped on the premises* ▷ *n* **3** the act of swooping
WORD ORIGIN Old English *swāpan* to sweep

swoosh *vb* **1** to make a swirling or rustling sound when moving or pouring out ▷ *n* **2** a swirling or rustling sound or movement
WORD ORIGIN imitative

swop *vb* **swopping, swopped,** *n* same as **swap**

sword *n* **1** a weapon with a long sharp blade and a short handle **2 the sword a** military power **b** death; destruction: *we will put them to the sword* **3 cross swords** to have a disagreement with someone
WORD ORIGIN Old English *sweord*

sword dance *n* a dance in which the performer dances over swords on the ground

swordfish *n, pl* **-fish** or **-fishes** a large fish with a very long upper jaw that resembles a sword

Sword of Damocles (**dam**-a-kleez) *n* a disaster that is about to take place
WORD ORIGIN after a flattering courtier forced by Dionysius, tyrant of ancient Syracuse, to sit under a sword suspended by a hair

swordplay *n* the action or art of fighting with a sword

swordsman *n, pl* **-men** a person who is skilled in the use of a sword **swordsmanship** *n*

swordstick *n* a hollow walking stick that contains a short sword

swore *vb* the past tense of **swear**

sworn *vb* **1** the past participle of **swear** ▷ *adj* **2** bound by or as if by an oath: *a sworn enemy*

swot¹ *informal vb* **swotting, swotted 1** (often foll. by *up*) to study (a subject) very hard, esp. for an exam; cram ▷ *n* **2** a person who works or studies hard
WORD ORIGIN variant of *sweat*

swot² *vb* **swotting, swotted,** *n* same as **swat**

swum *vb* the past participle of **swim**

swung *vb* the past of **swing**

sybarite (**sib**-bar-ite) *n* **1** a lover of luxury and pleasure ▷ *adj* **2** luxurious or sensuous **sybaritic** *adj*
WORD ORIGIN after *Sybaris,* ancient Greek colony in S Italy, famed for its luxury

sycamore *n* **1** a tree with five-pointed leaves and two-winged fruits **2** *US & Canad* an American plane tree
WORD ORIGIN Latin *sycomorus*

sycophant *n* a person who uses flattery to win favour from people with power or influence **sycophancy** *n* **sycophantic** *adj*
WORD ORIGIN Greek *sukophantēs*

syllabic *adj* of or relating to syllables

syllabify *vb* **-fies, -fying, -fied** to divide (a word) into syllables **syllabification** *n*

syllable *n* **1** a part of a word which is pronounced as a unit, which contains a single vowel sound, and which may or may not contain consonants: for

example, 'paper' has two syllables **2** the least mention: *without a syllable about what went on* **3 in words of one syllable** simply and plainly
WORD ORIGIN Greek *sullabē*

syllabub *n* *Austral & Brit* a dessert made from milk or cream beaten with sugar, wine, and lemon juice
WORD ORIGIN origin unknown

syllabus (**sill**-lab-buss) *n, pl* **-buses** or **-bi** (-bye) **a** the subjects studied for a particular course **b** a list of these subjects
WORD ORIGIN Late Latin

syllogism *n* a form of reasoning consisting of two premises and a conclusion, for example *some temples are in ruins; all ruins are fascinating; so some temples are fascinating* **syllogistic** *adj*
WORD ORIGIN Greek *sullogismos*

sylph *n* **1** a slender graceful girl or young woman **2** an imaginary creature believed to live in the air **sylphlike** *adj*
WORD ORIGIN New Latin *sylphus*

sylvan or **silvan** *adj* *chiefly poetic* of or consisting of woods or forests
WORD ORIGIN Latin *silva* forest

symbiosis *n* **1** *biol* a close association of two different animal or plant species living together to their mutual benefit **2** a similar relationship between different individuals or groups: *the symbiosis of the coal and railway industries* **symbiotic** *adj*
WORD ORIGIN Greek: a living together

symbol *n* **1** something that represents or stands for something else, usually an object used to represent something abstract **2** a letter, figure, or sign used in mathematics, music, etc. to represent a quantity, operation, function, etc.
WORD ORIGIN Greek *sumbolon* sign

symbolic *adj* **1** of or relating to a symbol or symbols **2** being a symbol of something **symbolically** *adv*

symbolism *n* **1** the representation of something by the use of symbols **2** an art movement involving the use of symbols to express mystical or abstract ideas **symbolist** *adj, n*

symbolize or **-lise** *vb* **-lizing, -lized** or **-lising, -lised 1** to be a symbol of (something) **2** to represent with a symbol **symbolization** or **-lisation** *n*

symmetry *n, pl* **-tries 1** the state of having two halves that are mirror images of each other **2** beauty resulting from a balanced arrangement of parts **symmetrical** *adj* **symmetrically** *adv*
WORD ORIGIN Greek *summetria* proportion

sympathetic *adj* **1** feeling or showing kindness and understanding **2** (of a person) likeable and appealing: *the film's only sympathetic character* **3 sympathetic to** showing agreement with or willing to lend support to: *sympathetic to the movement* **sympathetically** *adv*

sympathize or **-thise** *vb* **-thizing, -thized** or **-thising, -thised** ● **sympathize with a** to feel or express sympathy for: *I sympathized with this fear* **b** to agree with or support: *Pitt sympathized with these objectives* **sympathizer** or **-thiser** *n*

sympathy *n, pl* **-thies 1** (often foll. by *for*) understanding of other people's problems; compassion **2 sympathy with** agreement with someone's feelings or interests: *we have every sympathy with how she felt* **3** (often *pl*) feelings of loyalty or support for an idea or a cause: *was this where her sympathies lay?* **4** mutual affection or understanding between two people or a person and an animal
WORD ORIGIN Greek *sympatheia*

symphony *n, pl* **-nies 1** a large-scale orchestral composition with several movements **2** an orchestral movement in a vocal work such as an oratorio **3** short for **symphony orchestra 4** anything that has a pleasing arrangement of colours or shapes: *the garden was a symphony of coloured bunting* **symphonic** *adj*
WORD ORIGIN Greek *sun-* together + *phōnē* sound

symphony orchestra *n* *music* a large orchestra that performs symphonies

symposium *n, pl* **-sia** or **-siums 1** a conference at which experts or academics discuss a particular subject **2** a collection of essays on a particular subject
WORD ORIGIN Greek *sumposion* a drinking party

symptom *n* **1** *med* a sign indicating the presence of an illness or disease **2** anything that is taken as an indication that something is wrong: *a growing symptom of grave social injustice* **symptomatic** *adj*
WORD ORIGIN Greek *sumptōma* chance

synagogue *n* a building for Jewish religious services and religious instruction
WORD ORIGIN Greek *sunagōgē* a gathering

synapse *n* *anat* a gap where nerve impulses pass between two nerve cells
WORD ORIGIN Greek *sunapsis* junction

sync or **synch** *films, television, computers informal vb* **1** to synchronize ▷ *n* **2** synchronization: *the film and sound are in sync*

synchromesh *adj* **1** (of a gearbox) having a system of clutches that synchronizes the speeds of the gearwheels before they engage ▷ *n* **2** a gear system having these features
WORD ORIGIN *synchronized mesh*

synchronism *n* the quality or condition of occurrence at the same time or rate

synchronize or **-nise** *vb* **-nizing, -nized** or **-nising, -nised 1** (of two or more people) to perform (an action) at the same time: *a synchronized withdrawal of Allied forces* **2** to cause (two or more clocks or watches) to show the same time **3** *films* to match (the soundtrack and the action of a film) precisely **synchronization** or **-nisation** *n*

synchronous *adj* occurring at the same time and rate **synchrony** *n*
WORD ORIGIN Greek *sun-* together + *khronos* time

syncline *n* *geol* a downward slope of stratified rock in which the layers dip towards each other from either side

S

syncopate *vb* **-pating, -pated** *music* to stress the weak beats in (a rhythm or a piece of music) instead of the strong beats **syncopation** *n*
WORD ORIGIN Medieval Latin *syncopare* to omit a letter or syllable

syncope (**sing**-kop-ee) *n* **1** *med* a faint **2** *linguistics* the omission of sounds or letters from the middle of a word, as in *ne'er* for *never*
WORD ORIGIN Greek *sunkopē* a cutting off

syndic *n Brit* a business or legal agent of some universities or other institutions
WORD ORIGIN Greek *sundikos* defendant's advocate

syndicalism *n* a movement advocating seizure of economic and political power by the industrial working class by means of industrial action, esp. general strikes **syndicalist** *n*

syndicate *n* **1** a group of people or firms organized to undertake a joint project **2** an association of individuals who control organized crime **3** a news agency that sells articles and photographs to a number of newspapers for simultaneous publication ▷ *vb* **-cating, -cated 4** to sell (articles and photographs) to several newspapers for simultaneous publication **5** to form a syndicate of (people) **syndication** *n*
WORD ORIGIN Old French *syndicat*

syndrome *n* **1** *med* a combination of signs and symptoms that indicate a particular disease **2** a set of characteristics indicating the existence of a particular condition or problem
WORD ORIGIN Greek *sundromē*, literally: a running together

synecdoche (sin-**neck**-dock-ee) *n* a figure of speech in which a part is substituted for a whole or a whole for a part, as in *50 head of cattle* for *50 cows*
WORD ORIGIN Greek *sunekdokhē*

synergy *n* the potential ability for individuals or groups to be more successful working together than on their own
WORD ORIGIN Greek *sunergos*

synod *n* a special church council which meets regularly to discuss church affairs
WORD ORIGIN Greek *sunodos*

synonym *n* a word that means the same as another word, such as *bucket* and *pail*
WORD ORIGIN Greek *sun-* together + *onoma* name

synonymous *adj* **1** (often foll. by *with*) having the same meaning (as) **2** (foll. by *with*) closely associated (with): *a family whose name had been*

synonymous with fine jewellery

synopsis (sin-**op**-siss) *n, pl* **-ses** (-seez) a brief review or outline of a subject; summary: *they have sent me a monthly synopsis of the plot*
WORD ORIGIN Greek *sunopsis*

synoptic *adj* **1** of or relating to a synopsis **2** *Bible* of or relating to the Gospels of Matthew, Mark, and Luke **synoptically** *adv*

synovia (sine-**oh**-vee-a) *n med* a clear thick fluid that lubricates the body joints **synovial** *adj*
WORD ORIGIN New Latin

syntax *n* the grammatical rules of a language and the way in which words are arranged to form phrases and sentences **syntactic** *or* **syntactical** *adj*
WORD ORIGIN Greek *suntassein* to put in order

synthesis (**sinth**-iss-siss) *n, pl* **-ses** (-seez) **1** the process of combining objects or ideas into a complex whole **2** the combination produced by such a process **3** *chem* the process of producing a compound by one or more chemical reactions, usually from simpler starting materials
WORD ORIGIN Greek *sunthesis*

synthesize *or* **-sise** *vb* **-sizing, -sized** *or* **-sising, -sised 1** to combine (objects or ideas) into a complex whole **2** to produce (a compound) by synthesis

synthesizer *n* a keyboard instrument in which speech, music, or other sounds are produced electronically

synthetic *adj* **1** (of a substance or material) made artificially by chemical reaction **2** not sincere or genuine: *synthetic compassion* ▷ *n* **3** a synthetic substance or material **synthetically** *adv*
WORD ORIGIN Greek *sunthetikos* expert in putting together

syphilis *n* a sexually transmitted disease that causes sores on the genitals and eventually on other parts of the body **syphilitic** *adj*
WORD ORIGIN *Syphillis*, hero of a 16th-century Latin poem

syphon *n, vb* same as **siphon**

Syrian *adj* **1** of Syria ▷ *n* **2** a person from Syria

syringa *n* same as **mock orange** or **lilac**
WORD ORIGIN Greek *surinx* tube (its hollow stems were used for pipes)

syringe *n* **1** *med* a device used for withdrawing or injecting fluids, consisting of a hollow cylinder of glass or plastic, a tightly fitting piston, and a hollow needle ▷ *vb* **-ringing, -ringed 2** to wash out, inject, or spray with a

syringe: *a harmless blue dye is syringed into the uterus*
WORD ORIGIN Greek *surinx* tube

syrup *n* **1** a solution of sugar dissolved in water and often flavoured with fruit juice: used for sweetening fruit, etc. **2** a thick sweet liquid food made from sugar or molasses: *maple syrup* **3** a liquid medicine containing a sugar solution: *cough syrup*
WORD ORIGIN Arabic *sharāb* a drink

syrupy *adj* **1** (of a liquid) thick or sweet **2** excessively sentimental: *a soundtrack of syrupy violins*

system *n* **1** a method or set of methods for doing or organizing something: *a new system of production or distribution* **2** orderliness or routine; an ordered manner: *there is no system in his work* **3** the manner in which an institution or aspect of society has been arranged: *the Scottish legal system* **4 the system** the government and state regarded as exploiting, restricting, and repressing individuals **5** the manner in which the parts of something fit or function together; structure: *disruption of the earth's weather system* **6** any scheme or set of rules used to classify, explain, or calculate: *the Newtonian system of physics* **7** a network of communications, transportation, or distribution **8** *biol* an animal considered as a whole **9** *biol* a set of organs or structures that together perform some function: *the immune system* **10** one's physical or mental constitution: *the intrusion of the ME virus into my system; to get the hate out of my system* **11** an assembly of electronic or mechanical parts forming a self-contained unit: *an alarm system*
WORD ORIGIN Greek *sustēma*

systematic *adj* following a fixed plan and done in an efficient and methodical way: *a systematic approach to teaching* **systematically** *adv*

systematize *or* **-tise** *vb* **-tizing, -tized** *or* **-tising, -tised** to arrange (information) in a system **systematization** *or* **-tisation** *n*

systemic *adj biol* (of a poison, disease, etc.) affecting the entire animal or body **systemically** *adv*

systems analysis *n* the analysis of the requirements of a task and the expression of these in a form that enables a computer to perform the task **systems analyst** *n*

systole (**siss**-tol-ee) *n physiol* contraction of the heart, during which blood is pumped into the arteries **systolic** *adj*
WORD ORIGIN Greek *sustolē*

S

Figures of Speech

A figure of speech is a form of expression which deviates from the norm in order to achieve an interesting effect. Figures of speech were a central aspect of classical rhetorical theory, and were divided into *schemes* – deviations from expected arrangement of words or sounds – and *tropes* (from the Greek word for 'turns') – deviations from expected or literal meanings. One type of scheme is *alliteration*, the repetition of sounds to create a sonorous or patterned effect. For example, the first two lines of Keats' 'To Autumn':

Season of mists and mellow fruitfulness,
Close bosom-friend of the maturing sun...

Another type is *chiasmus*, where word order is inverted and balanced. This can be seen in the following line from Pope's *The Rape of the Lock*, where the adverb-verb-subject pattern of the first clause is balanced by subject-adverb-verb pattern of the second:

Smooth flow the waves, the zephyrs gently play.

However, in modern usage, the term 'figure of speech' is usually used to refer to deviations from expected meanings, and is synonymous with 'figurative language'. A *simile* is the explicit comparison between two things using *like* or *as*, for example in Robert Burns' 'My love is like a red, red rose'. A *metaphor* (from the Greek for 'a carrying over') relates two notions implicitly. For example, Shakespeare's Sonnet 73 uses the metaphor of an aging man as a tree in winter:

That time of year thou mayst in me behold
When yellow leaves, or none, or few, do hang
Upon those boughs which shake against the cold...

Extended metaphors are metaphors which are developed throughout a text. For example, Robert Frost's poem 'The Road Not Taken' is an extended metaphor of life as a path, while George Eliot's novel *Middlemarch* repeatedly uses the metaphor of human lives as a web.

A specific type of metaphor is *personification*, the treatment of a non-human form as human. In Milton's *Paradise Lost*, after Eve eats of the tree of knowledge, earth and nature are personified as sentient beings who suffer pain:

Earth felt the wound; and Nature from her seat,
Sighing through all her works gave signs of woe,
That all was lost.

Related to metaphor is *metonymy* (from the Greek for 'change of name'), where the name of one thing is substituted by something which is closely associated with it. For example, in the following line from *As You Like It*, Shakespeare metonymically refers to men and women by the clothes they wear:

I must comfort the weaker vessel, as doublet and
hose ought to show itself courageous to petticoat...

The above examples are all taken from literature, yet everyday speech also abounds in metaphor. Expressions such as 'the leg of a table' and 'I see what you mean' are often called *dead metaphors*, in that their original metaphorical force has been lost. Similarly, metonyms are frequently used without literary effect: when we say that 'the kettle is boiling', 'kettle' is a metonym for the water inside the kettle. Research over the past few decades – pioneered by George Lakoff and Mark Johnson's *Metaphors We Live By* – has explored the extent to which metaphors pervade all language and thought. For example, there is a frequent metaphorical pathway between the concept of spatial height and the concepts of happiness and health, as in phrases such as in *high spirits* and the *peak of health*.

Thus, while there is a difference between the inventive metaphors used by creative writers – which are called figures of speech – and the ingrained metaphors used in everyday language – which are not – the difference lies only in degree of novelty. Metaphor is not only a literary or rhetorical embellishment, but forms a central part of the way we think and speak.

Tt

The letter T is the twentieth letter of the English alphabet. The Romans developed this letter from the Greek letter *tau* (T, τ), which had its origins in a Semitic letter called *taw*, which was shaped like an X and meant literally 'mark'. The Greeks rotated this letter so that it consisted of a vertical stem topped by a horizontal stroke, instead of two diagonal lines.

In the Greek alphabet, the lower-case form resembled the capital, but later the stem was lengthened above the cross-stroke, so that now it stands at three-quarter height – a characteristic that it shares with F and no other letter.

T is the most frequently occurring consonant in written English, and the second most frequent of all letters – only E is used more often. The fact that T occurs in such common words as 'the', 'to', and 'it' must surely help its cause in this regard.

The shape of the capital T is replicated in a number of different objects. Most famously, a shirt with no buttons and two short sleeves bears a sufficient resemblance to the letter to have acquired the name of 'T-shirt'. A junction where two roads meet at right angles is called a 'T-junction' for similar reasons, and a 'T-bone' is a cut of meat around a section of the spine that forms a 'T' shape.

A 'T-square' is an instrument that allows draughtsmen to produce a perpendicular angle in their drawings, and the precision it allows is such that any task that is done to perfection may be said to be 'done to a T'.

In science, a 'T-cell' is a type of white blood cell that forms part of the immune system. The letter here is nothing do with the shape of the cells but rather signifies the thymus – the gland in the neck in which they are developed.

The letter T is also one of several letters that were formerly branded on convicted criminals to indicate the nature of their crimes. Thus, women found guilty of adultery were marked with an A (which is 'The Scarlet Letter' of Nathaniel Hawthorne's famous book), and persons convicted of manslaughter were branded with an M. The letter T on the thumb marked someone as a thief.

---

t *or* **T** *n, pl* **t's, T's** *or* **Ts 1** the 20th letter of the English alphabet **2 to a T a** in every detail: *that's her to a T* **b** perfectly: *that dress suits you to a T*

t tonne(s)

T 1 *chem* tritium **2** tera-

t. 1 temperature **2** ton(s)

ta *interj Brit, Austral, & NZ informal* thank you
WORD ORIGIN imitative of baby talk

Ta *chem* tantalum

TA (in Britain) Territorial Army

tab¹ *n* **1** a small flap of material, esp. one on a garment for decoration or for fastening to a button **2** any similar flap, such as a piece of paper attached to a file for identification **3** *chiefly US & Canad* a bill, esp. for a meal or drinks **4 keep tabs on** *informal* to keep a watchful eye on
WORD ORIGIN origin unknown

tab² *n* short for **tabulator**

TAB (in New Zealand) Totalisator Agency Board

tabard *n* **1** a sleeveless jacket, esp. one worn by a medieval knight over his armour **2** a short coat bearing the coat of arms of the sovereign, worn by a herald
WORD ORIGIN Old French *tabart*

Tabasco *n trademark* a very hot red sauce made from matured peppers

tabby *n, pl* **-bies 1** a cat whose fur has dark stripes or wavy markings on a lighter background ▷ *adj* **2** having dark stripes or wavy markings on a lighter background
WORD ORIGIN from the girl's name *Tabitha*, influenced by *tabby*, old kind of striped silk

tabernacle *n* **1 the Tabernacle** *Bible* the portable sanctuary in which the ancient Israelites carried the Ark of the Covenant **2** any place of Christian worship that is not called a church **3** *RC Church* a receptacle in which the Blessed Sacrament is kept
WORD ORIGIN Latin *tabernaculum* a tent

tabla *n, pl* **-bla** *or* **-blas** one of a pair of Indian drums played with the hands
WORD ORIGIN Hindi, from Arabic: drum

table *n* **1** a piece of furniture consisting of a flat top supported by legs: *a coffee table* **2** a set of facts or figures arranged in rows and columns: *a league table* **3** a group of people sitting round a table for a meal, game, etc.: *the whole table laughed* **4** *formal* the food provided at a meal or in a particular house: *he keeps a good table* **5 turn the tables** to cause a complete reversal of circumstances ▷ *vb* **-bling, -bled 6** *Austral & Brit* to submit (a motion) for discussion by a meeting **7** *US* to suspend discussion of (a proposal) indefinitely
WORD ORIGIN Latin *tabula* a writing tablet

tableau (**tab**-loh) *n, pl* **-leaux** (-loh) a silent motionless group of people arranged to represent a scene from history, legend, or literature
WORD ORIGIN French

tablecloth *n* a cloth for covering the top of a table, esp. during meals

table d'hôte (**tah**-bla **dote**) *adj* **1** (of a meal) consisting of a set number of courses with a limited choice of dishes offered at a fixed price ▷ *n, pl* **tables d'hôte** (**tah**-bla **dote**) **2** a table d'hôte meal or menu
WORD ORIGIN French: the host's table

table football *n Brit* a game based on soccer, played on a table with sets of miniature human figures mounted on rods allowing them to be tilted or spun to strike the ball. US & Canad name: **foosball**

tableland *n* a flat area of high ground; plateau

table licence *n Brit* a licence permitting the sale of alcohol with meals only

tablespoon *n* **1** a spoon, larger than a dessertspoon, used for serving food

2 Also called: **tablespoonful** the amount contained in such a spoon **3** a unit of capacity used in cooking, equal to half a fluid ounce

tablet *n* **1** a pill consisting of a compressed medicinal substance **2** a flattish cake of some substance, such as soap **3** a slab of stone, wood, etc. used for writing on before the invention of paper **4** an inscribed piece of stone, wood, etc. that is fixed to a wall as a memorial: *a tablet in memory of those who died* **WORD ORIGIN** Latin *tabula* a board

table tennis *n* a game resembling a miniature form of tennis played on a table with bats and a small light ball

table wine *n* **1** fairly cheap wine for everyday drinking with meals **2** ordinary wine, as opposed to fortified wine such as sherry or port

tabloid *n* a newspaper with fairly small pages, usually with many photographs and a concise and often sensational style **WORD ORIGIN** from *tablet*

taboo *or* **tabu** *n, pl* **-boos** *or* **-bus 1** a restriction or prohibition resulting from social or other conventions **2** a ritual prohibition, esp. of something that is considered holy or unclean ▷ *adj* **3** forbidden or disapproved-of: *a taboo subject* **WORD ORIGIN** Tongan *tapu*

tabor *n* a small drum used esp. in the Middle Ages, struck with one hand while the other held a pipe **WORD ORIGIN** Old French *tabour*

tabular *adj* arranged in parallel columns so as to form a table **WORD ORIGIN** Latin *tabula* a board

tabulate *vb* **-lating, -lated** to arrange (information) in rows and columns **tabulation** *n*

tabulator *n* a key on a typewriter or word processor that sets stops so that data can be arranged and presented in columns

tachograph *n* a device that measures the speed of a vehicle and the distance that it covers, and produces a record (**tachogram**) of its readings **WORD ORIGIN** Greek *takhos* speed + -GRAPH

tachometer *n* a device for measuring speed, esp. that of a revolving shaft **WORD ORIGIN** Greek *takhos* speed + -METER

tacit (**tass**-it) *adj* understood or implied without actually being stated: *tacit support* **WORD ORIGIN** Latin *tacitus* silent

taciturn (**tass**-it-turn) *adj* habitually silent, reserved, or uncommunicative **taciturnity** *n* **WORD ORIGIN** Latin *tacere* to be silent

tack¹ *n* **1** a short sharp-pointed nail with a large flat head **2** Brit & NZ a long loose temporary stitch used in dressmaking ▷ *vb* **3** to fasten (something) with a tack or tacks: *the carpet needs to be tacked down* **4** Brit & NZ to sew (something) with long loose temporary stitches ▶ See also **tack on** **WORD ORIGIN** Middle English *tak* fastening, nail

tack² *n* **1** *naut* the course of a boat sailing obliquely into the wind, expressed in terms of the side of the boat against which the wind is blowing: *on the port tack* **2** a course of action or a policy: *telling her to get off my back hadn't worked, so I took a different tack* ▷ *vb* **3** *naut* to steer (a boat) on a zigzag course, so as to make progress against the wind **WORD ORIGIN** from *tack* rope used to secure a sail

tack³ *n* riding harness for horses, including saddles and bridles **WORD ORIGIN** from *tackle*

tackies *or* **takkies** *pl n, sing* **tacky** S African *informal* tennis shoes or plimsolls **WORD ORIGIN** origin unknown

tackle *vb* **-ling, -led 1** to deal with (a problem or task) in a determined way **2** to confront (someone) about something: *I intend to tackle both management and union on this issue* **3** to attack and fight (a person or animal) **4** *sport* to attempt to get the ball away from (an opposing player) ▷ *n* **5** *sport* an attempt to get the ball away from an opposing player **6** the equipment required for a particular sport or occupation: *fishing tackle* **7** a set of ropes and pulleys for lifting heavy weights **8** *naut* the ropes and other rigging aboard a ship **WORD ORIGIN** Middle English

tack on *vb* to attach or add (something) to something that is already complete: *an elegant mansion with a modern extension tacked on at the back*

tack room *n* a room in a stable building in which bridles, saddles, etc. are kept

tacky¹ *adj* **tackier, tackiest** slightly sticky **tackiness** *n* **WORD ORIGIN** earlier *tack* stickiness

tacky² *adj* **tackier, tackiest** *informal* **1** vulgar and tasteless: *tacky commercialism* **2** shabby or shoddy: *tacky streets* **tackiness** *n* **WORD ORIGIN** origin unknown

taco (**tah**-koh) *n, pl* **tacos** Mexican cookery a tortilla folded into a roll with a filling and usually fried **WORD ORIGIN** from Mexican Spanish, from Spanish: literally, a bite to eat

tact *n* **1** a sense of the best and most considerate way to deal with people so as not to upset them **2** skill in handling difficult situations **tactful** *adj* **tactfully** *adv* **tactless** *adj* **tactlessly** *adv* **tactlessness** *n* **WORD ORIGIN** Latin *tactus* a touching

tactic *n* a move or method used to achieve an aim or task: *he has perfected dissent as a tactic to further his career.* See also **tactics**

tactical *adj* **1** of or employing tactics: *a tactical advantage* **2** (of missiles, bombing, etc.) for use in limited military operations **tactically** *adv*

tactical voting *n* (in an election) the practice of voting for a candidate or party one would not normally support in an attempt to prevent an even less acceptable candidate or party being elected

tactics *n* **1** *mil* the science of the detailed direction of forces in battle to achieve an aim or task ▷ *pl n* **2** the

plans and methods used to achieve a particular short-term aim **tactician** *n* **WORD ORIGIN** Greek *tassein* to arrange

tactile *adj* of or having a sense of touch: *the tactile sense* **WORD ORIGIN** Latin *tactilis*

tadpole *n* the aquatic larva of a frog or toad, which develops from a limbless tailed form with external gills into a form with internal gills, limbs, and a reduced tail **WORD ORIGIN** Middle English *tadde* toad + *pol* head

TAFE (in Australia) Technical and Further Education

taffeta *n* a thin shiny silk or rayon fabric used esp. for women's clothes **WORD ORIGIN** Persian *tāftah* spun

taffrail *n* *naut* a rail at the back of a ship or boat **WORD ORIGIN** Dutch *taffereel* panel

tag¹ *n* **1** a piece of paper, leather, etc. for attaching to something as a mark or label: *the price tag* **2** a point of metal or plastic at the end of a cord or lace **3** a brief trite quotation **4** an electronic device worn by a prisoner under house arrest so that his or her movements can be monitored **5** *slang* a graffito consisting of a nickname or personal symbol ▷ *vb* **tagging, tagged 6** to mark with a tag ▶ See also **tag along, tag on** **WORD ORIGIN** origin unknown

tag² *n* **1** a children's game in which one player chases the others in an attempt to touch one of them, who will then become the chaser ▷ *vb* **tagging, tagged 2** to catch and touch (another child) in the game of tag. Also: **tig** **WORD ORIGIN** origin unknown

Tagalog (tag-**gah**-log) *n* a language spoken in the Philippines

tag along *vb* to accompany someone, esp. when uninvited: *I tagged along behind the gang*

tag end *n* the last part of something: *at the tag end of the Ice Age*

tagetes (taj-**eat**-eez) *n, pl* **-tes** any of a genus of plants with yellow or orange flowers, including the French and African marigolds **WORD ORIGIN** Latin *Tages*, a god of ancient Etruria

tagliatelle (tal-yat-**tell**-ee) *n* a form of pasta made in narrow strips **WORD ORIGIN** Italian

tag on *vb* to add at the end of something: *a throwaway remark, tagged on at the end of a casual conversation*

tahini (tah-**hee**-nee) *n* a paste made from ground sesame seeds, used esp. in Middle Eastern cookery **WORD ORIGIN** from Arabic

t'ai chi (tie **chee**) *n* a Chinese system of exercises and self-defence characterized by slow rhythmic movements **WORD ORIGIN** Chinese *t'ai chi ch'uan* great art of boxing

taiga (**tie**-ga) *n* the belt of coniferous forest extending across much of subarctic North America, Europe, and Asia

taikonaut *n* an astronaut from the People's Republic of China

WORD ORIGIN from Cantonese *taikon(g)* cosmos

tail¹ *n* **1** the rear part of an animal's body, usually forming a long thin flexible part attached to the trunk ▸ Related adjective: **caudal 2** any long thin part projecting or hanging from the back or end of something: *the waiter produced menus from beneath the tail of his coat* **3** the last part: *the tail of the procession* **4** the rear part of an aircraft **5** *astron* the luminous stream of gas and dust particles driven from the head of a comet when it is close to the sun **6** *informal* a person employed to follow and spy upon another **7 turn tail** to run away **8 with one's tail between one's legs** completely defeated and demoralized ▸ *adj* **9** at the back: *tail feathers* ▸ *vb* **10** *informal* to follow (someone) stealthily ▸ See also **tail off, tails** > **tailless** *adj*

WORD ORIGIN Old English *tægel*

tail² *n law* the limitation of an estate or interest to a person and his or her descendants

WORD ORIGIN Old French *taille* a division

tailback *n Brit* a queue of traffic stretching back from an obstruction

tailboard *n* a removable or hinged rear board on a lorry or trailer

tail coat *n* a man's black coat which stops at the hips at the front and has a long back split into two below the waist

tailgate *n* **1** same as **tailboard 2** a door at the rear of a hatchback vehicle ▸ *vb* **3** to drive very close behind (a vehicle) **tailgater** *n*

tail-light *or* **tail lamp** *n* same as **rear light**

tail off *or* **away** *vb* **1** to decrease gradually: *orders tailed off* **2** (of someone's voice) to become gradually quieter and then silent

tailor *n* **1** a person who makes, repairs, or alters outer garments, esp. menswear ▸ Related adjective: **sartorial** *vb* **2** to cut or style (a garment) to satisfy specific requirements **3** to adapt (something) so as to make it suitable: *activities are tailored to participants' capabilities* **tailored** *adj*

WORD ORIGIN Old French *taillier* to cut

tailorbird *n* a tropical Asian warbler that builds a nest by sewing together large leaves using plant fibres

tailor-made *adj* **1** (of clothing) made by a tailor to fit exactly **2** perfect for a particular purpose: *I'm tailor-made for the role*

tailpiece *n* **1** a piece added at the end of something, for example a report **2** a decorative design at the end of a chapter **3** a piece of wood to which the strings of a stringed musical instrument are attached at its lower end

tailpipe *n* a pipe from which exhaust gases are discharged, esp. in a motor vehicle

tailplane *n* a small horizontal wing at the tail of an aircraft to help keep it stable

tails *pl n* **1** *informal* same as **tail coat** ▸ *interj, adv* **2** with the side of a coin

uppermost that does not have a portrait of a head on it

tailspin *n* **1** *aeronautics* same as **spin** (sense 10) **2** *informal* a state of confusion or panic

tailwind *n* a wind blowing from behind an aircraft or vehicle

taint *vb* **1** to spoil or contaminate by an undesirable quality: *tainted by corruption* ▸ *n* **2** a defect or flaw **3** a trace of contamination or infection **tainted** *adj*

WORD ORIGIN Old French *teindre* to dye

taipan *n* a large poisonous Australian snake

WORD ORIGIN Aboriginal

take *vb* **taking, took, taken 1** to remove from a place, usually by grasping with the hand: *he took a fifty-dollar note from his wallet* **2** to accompany or escort: *he took me home* **3** to use as a means of transport: *we took a taxi* **4** to conduct or lead: *that road takes you to Preston* **5** to obtain possession of (something), often dishonestly: *they had taken everything most precious to us* **6** to seize or capture: *her husband had been taken by the rebels* **7** (in games such as chess or cards) to win or capture (a piece, trick, etc.) **8** to choose or select (something to use or buy): *I'll take the green one, please* **9** to put an end to: *he took his own life* **10** to require (time, resources, or ability): *this would have taken years to set up* **11** to use as a particular case: *take a friend of mine for example* **12** to find and make use of (a seat, flat, etc.) **13** to accept the duties of: *the legitimate government will take office* **14** to receive in a specified way: *my mother took it calmly* **15** to receive and make use of: *she took the opportunity to splash her heated face* **16** to eat or drink: *all food substances are toxic if taken in excess* **17** to perform (an action, esp. a beneficial one): *she took a deep breath* **18** to accept (something that is offered or given): *she took a job as a waitress* **19** to put into effect: *taking military action simply* **20** to make (a photograph) **21** to write down or copy: *taking notes* **22** to work at or study: *taking painting lessons* **23** to do or sit (a test, exam, etc.) **24** to begin to experience or feel: *he took an interest in psychoanalysis* **25** to accept (responsibility, blame, or credit) **26** to accept as valid: *I take your point* **27** to stand up to or endure: *I can't take this harassment any more* **28** to wear a particular size of shoes or clothes: *what size of shoes do you take?* **29** to have a capacity of or room for: *the Concert Hall can take about 2500 people* **30** to ascertain by measuring: *she comes after breakfast to take her pulse and temperature* **31** to subtract or deduct: *take seven from eleven* **32** to aim or direct: *he took a few steps towards the door* **33** (of a shop, club, etc.) to make (a specified amount of money) from sales, tickets, etc.: *films that take no money at the box office* **34** to have or produce the intended effect: *the dye hasn't taken on your shoes* **35** (of seedlings) to start growing successfully **36 take account of** *or* **take into account** see **account** (sense 9) **37 take advantage of** see **advantage** (sense 4) **38 take care** see **care** (sense 10) **39 take care of** see **care** (sense 11) **40 take it** to assume or believe: *I take it that means they don't want to*

leave **41 take part in** see **part** (sense 17) **42 take place** see **place** (sense 20) **43 take upon oneself** to assume the right or duty (to do something) **44 take your time** use as much time as you need ▸ *n* **45** *films, music* one of a series of recordings from which the best will be selected **46** *informal chiefly US* a version or interpretation: *Minnelli's bleak take on the story* ▸ See also **take after, take against**, etc.

WORD ORIGIN Old English *tacan*

take after *vb* to resemble in appearance or character: *he takes after his grandfather*

take against *vb informal* to start to dislike, esp. for no good reason: *I took against her right from the start*

take apart *vb* **1** to separate (something) into its component parts: *once I'd taken the clock apart I couldn't fit the bits together again* **2** *informal* to criticize severely

take away *vb* **1** to remove or subtract: *the lymph glands are taken away and examined under a microscope* **2** to detract from or lessen the value of (something): *the fact that he beat his wife doesn't take away from his merits as a writer* ▸ *prep* **3** minus: *six take away two is four* ▸ *adj* **takeaway 4** *Brit, Austral, & NZ* sold for consumption away from the premises: *takeaway food* ▸ *n* **takeaway** *Brit, Austral, & NZ* **5** a shop or restaurant that sells such food **6** a meal sold for consumption away from the premises

take back *vb* **1** to retract or withdraw (something said or promised): *I take back what I said about him* **2** to regain possession of **3** to return for exchange or a refund: *shopkeepers are often reluctant to take back unsatisfactory goods* **4** to accept (someone) back into one's home, affections, etc.: *I'll only take you back if you promise to behave* **5** to remind (one) of the past: *this takes me back to my childhood*

take down *vb* **1** to record in writing **2** to dismantle or remove **3** to reduce (someone) in power or arrogance: *I do think he needed taking down a peg or two*

take for *vb informal* to consider or suppose to be, esp. mistakenly: *what kind of mug do you take me for?*

take-home pay *n* the remainder of one's pay after income tax and other compulsory deductions have been made

take in *vb* **1** to understand: *I was too tired to take in all of what was being said* **2** *informal* to cheat or deceive: *don't be taken in by his charming manner* **3** to include: *this tour takes in the romance and history of Salzburg, Vienna, and Munich* **4** to receive into one's house: *his widowed mother lived by taking in boarders* **5** to make (clothing) smaller by altering the seams **6** to go to: *taking in a movie*

taken *vb* **1** the past participle of **take** ▸ *adj* **2 taken with** enthusiastically impressed by

take off *vb* **1** to remove (a garment) **2** (of an aircraft) to become airborne **3** *informal* to set out on a journey: *taking off for the Highlands* **4** *informal* to become successful or popular: *the record took off after being used in a film* **5** to deduct (an amount) from a price or total **6** to withdraw or put an end to: *the bus service has been taken off because of lack of demand*

The Influence of German on English

❛ Whenever the literary German dives into a sentence, that is the last you are going to see of him until he emerges on the other side of his Atlantic with his verb in his mouth,' Mark Twain said. Leaving aside the word order that Twain struggled with, German has the same genetic origins as English.

Added to this shared linguistic inheritance are historical factors: German-speakers were world leaders in science, technology, and the humanities before 1900, and became a tremendous political and military force after it. Germany fought two world wars, during which words like *storm troopers, panzer, flak, U-boat,* and *strafe* became common in English, as well as the *Third Reich*, the *Nazis*, and *Gestapo*, while people suffered well-founded *Angst* and *Weltschmerz*. Anti-German feeling ran so high in North America during World War I that the Canadian town *Berlin* was renamed *Kitchener* and, in the United States, *sauerkraut* became *liberty cabbage*.

The most versatile survivor was *blitz*, from *Blitzkrieg*, 'lightning war', which became applied to marketing campaigns and rushes by American football linebackers. The *Kaiser* lent his name to a bread roll, joining menu items such as *schnitzel, strudel, muesli, pretzel, kirsch,* and *lager*. The *hamburger* and *frankfurter* became fast-food staples; *wursts* (*bratwurst, liverwurst*) were offered at *delicatessens*.

Germans had long lived in the United States. As early as the 17th century, religious dissenters fled to the then-*hinterland* of Pennsylvania. Two centuries after the Dutch, shiploads of Germanic immigrants disembarked, including many Jews who spoke Yiddish, which had a largely German vocabulary.

The modern industrial world is inconceivable without German or Austrian discoveries or inventions: the chemical elements *zinc* and *nickel*, the *diesel* engine, the mineral *quartz*, the *klieg light*, the *Geiger counter*, the *Doppler effect*, the *Fahrenheit* temperature scale, the units of the *ohm, gauss,* and *hertz,* and a miracle drug: *aspirin*. The study of mind was advanced by Austrians, *Freud* and *Adler*, and a Swiss German, *Jung*, who gave their names to entire schools of psychology.

The Germans are serious about recreation, and skiing and mountaineering are rife with German terms: *abseil, alpenstock, mogul, schussing.* For the lighter-hearted *wandervogel*, whose *wanderlust* ends in a *wanderjahr*, it's *wunderbar*. Dog-fanciers select their best friend from the *dachshund* (or *wiener dog*), the *Doberman pinscher*, the *schnauzer*, the *Weimaraner*, the *Rottweiler*, the *spitz*, and the *poodle*. However, the pet-owner might opt for a *hamster*. Musicians had fewer choices: the *alphorn, flugelhorn*, or *glockenspiel*, though they had a vocal alternative: they could sing *lieder* – or *yodel*.

German peoples have long valued high culture, but their vocabulary has supplied English with many common lowlife terms. A consumer product may be *ersatz* or *dreck*, liable to go *on the fritz* or even *kaput*. Entertainment may be *glitzy, schmaltzy,* or *kitschy*. A person may be a *dummkopf*, a *bum*, a *loafer* or, through Yiddish, a *klutz, schmuck,* or *shyster*. To this unlovely cast may be added a *poltergeist*, who possesses *Schadenfreude*, a delight in others' misfortunes.

Because Germans were philological pioneers, they made an impact on how spelling guides speaking. The *schwa*, phonetically rendered as /ə/, is the weak, neutral vowel sound found in unstressed syllables, like the 'u' in *occur*. The diacritical *umlaut* (¨) over a vowel indicates that the letter should be transliterated with an added 'e'. With its usual inconsistency, English sometimes retains the umlaut (*föhn*), drops it (*doppelganger*), or transliterates (*loess*), just as it retains German capitalization (*Neanderthal*) or dispenses with it (*lederhosen* was once *Lederhosen.*)

Given the great German philosophers, it's sometimes supposed that their language bestowed special advantages for abstract thought. After all, they conceived words like *Weltanschauung* and *zeitgeist* and, in literary studies, *Bildungsroman* and *leitmotif*. Certainly, the German propensity for compounding words was convenient in condensing concepts. Not to be outdone, English often forms words by attaching German affixes like *über-* (an operatic diva may be an '*über* soprano'), *-fest* (*filmfest, gabfest*) and *–meister* (*schlockmeister*). Still, German is best at compounding. Mark Twain justly observed, 'Some German words are so long that they have a perspective.'

7 *informal* to mimic (someone) ▷ *n* **takeoff 8** the act or process of making an aircraft airborne **9** *informal* an act of mimicry

take on *vb* **1** to employ or hire **2** to assume or acquire: *his eyes took on a strange intensity* **3** to agree to do: *he took on the job of treasurer* **4** to compete against: *we must take on our foreign competitors*

take out *vb* **1** to remove (something) from a place: *she took a comb out of her bag* **2** to obtain: *she took out American citizenship in 1937* **3** to escort or go out with (someone) on a social trip: *can I take you out for a meal some time?* **4** *informal* to kill, destroy, or maim: *most of the enemy's air defences have been taken out* **5 take it** or **a lot out of** *informal* to sap the energy or vitality of **6 take it out on** *informal* to vent one's anger on ▷ *adj, n* **takeout 7** *chiefly US & Canad* same as **takeaway** (senses 4, 5, 6)

take over *vb* **1** to gain control or management of **2** to become responsible for (a job) after another person has stopped doing it: *I'll take over the driving if you want a break* **3 take over from** to become more successful or important than (something), and eventually replace it: *CDs have more or less taken over from records* ▷ *n* **takeover 4** the act of gaining control of a company by buying its shares **5** the act of seizing and taking control of something: *the rebel takeover in Ethiopia*

taker *n* a person who agrees to take something that is offered: *there's only one sweet left – any takers?*

take to *vb* **1** to form a liking for **2** to start using or doing (something) as a habit: *I took to studying the published records of his life*

take up *vb* **1** to occupy or fill (space or time): *looking after the baby takes up most of my time* **2** to adopt the study, practice, or activity of: *I took up architecture* **3** to shorten (a garment) **4** to accept (an offer): *I'd like to take up your offer of help* **5 take up on a** to accept what is offered by (someone): *I might just take you up on that offer* **b** to discuss (something) further with (someone): *I'd like to take you up on that last point* **6 take up with a** to discuss (an issue) with (someone): *take up the matter with the District Council more seriously* **b** to begin to be friendly and spend time with (someone): *he's already taken up with the woman he would marry*

taking *adj* charming, fascinating, or intriguing

takings *pl n* receipts; earnings

talaq or **talak** *n* a form of divorce under Islamic law in which the husband repudiates the marriage by saying 'talaq' three times
WORD ORIGIN Arabic

talc or **talcum** *n* **1** same as **talcum powder 2** a soft mineral, consisting of magnesium silicate, used in the manufacture of ceramics, paints, and talcum powder
WORD ORIGIN Persian *talk*

talcum powder *n* a powder made of purified talc, usually scented, used to dry or perfume the body

tale *n* **1** a report, account, or story: *everyone had their own tale to tell about the flood* **2** a malicious piece of gossip **3 tell tales a** to tell fanciful lies **b** to report malicious stories or trivial complaints, esp. to someone in authority **4 tell a tale** to reveal something important **5 tell its own tale** to be self-evident
WORD ORIGIN Old English *talu*

talent *n* **1** a natural ability to do something well: *the boy has a real talent for writing* **2** a person or people with such ability: *he is the major talent in Italian fashion* **3** *informal* attractive members of the opposite sex collectively: *there's always lots of talent in that pub* **4** any of various ancient units of weight and money
talented *adj*
WORD ORIGIN Greek *talanton* unit of money

talent scout *n* a person whose occupation is the search for talented people, such as sportsmen or performers, for work as professionals

talisman *n, pl* -**mans** a stone or other small object, usually inscribed or carved, believed to protect the wearer from evil influences **talismanic** *adj*
WORD ORIGIN Medieval Greek *telesma* ritual

talk *vb* **1** to express one's thoughts or feelings by means of spoken words **2** to exchange ideas or opinions about something: *they were talking about where they would go on holiday* **3** to give voice to; utter: *he was talking rubbish* **4** to discuss: *the political leaders were talking peace* **5** to reveal information: *she was ready to talk* **6** to be able to speak (a language or style) in conversation: *the ferry was full of people talking French* **7** to spread rumours or gossip **8** to be effective or persuasive: *money talks* **9** to get into a particular condition or state of mind by talking: *I had talked myself hoarse* **10 now you're talking** *informal* at last you're saying something agreeable **11 you can** or **can't talk** *informal* you are in no position to comment or criticize ▷ *n* **12** a speech or lecture: *a talk on local government reform* **13** an exchange of ideas or thoughts: *we had a talk about our holiday plans* **14** idle chatter, gossip, or rumour **15** (*often pl*) a conference, discussion, or negotiation ▷ See also **talk back, talk down**, etc.
talker *n*
WORD ORIGIN Middle English *talkien*

talkative *adj* given to talking a great deal

talkback *n* NZ a broadcast in which telephone comments or questions from the public are transmitted live

talk back *vb* to answer (someone) rudely or cheekily

talk down *vb* **1 talk down to** to speak to (someone) in a patronizing manner **2** to give instructions to (an aircraft) by radio to enable it to land

talkie *n* *informal* an early film with a soundtrack

Talking Book *n trademark* a recording of a book, designed to be used by the blind

talking head *n* (on television) a person, shown only from the shoulders up, who speaks without illustrative material

talking point *n* something that causes discussion or argument: *his appointment as manager was a major talking point in football circles*

talking-to *n informal* a scolding or telling-off

talk into *vb* to persuade (someone) to do something by talking to him or her: *don't let anyone talk you into buying things you don't want*

talk out *vb* **1** to resolve (a problem) by talking: *we won't reach a compromise unless we can talk out our differences* **2** Brit to block (a bill) in parliament by discussing it for so long that there is no time to vote on it **3 talk out of** to dissuade (someone) from doing something by talking to him or her

talk round *vb* **1** to persuade (someone) to agree with one's opinion or suggestion: *he didn't want to go, but I talked him round* **2** to discuss (a subject) without coming to a conclusion

tall *adj* **1** of greater than average height **2** having a specified height: *five feet tall*
WORD ORIGIN Middle English

tallboy *n* Brit a high chest of drawers made in two sections placed one on top of the other

tall order *n informal* a difficult or unreasonable request

tallow *n* a hard fatty animal fat used in making soap and candles

tall poppy syndrome *n* Austral & NZ *informal* a tendency to disparage any person who is conspicuously successful

tall ship *n* a large square-rigged sailing ship

tall story *n informal* an unlikely and probably untrue tale

tally *vb* -**lies**, -**lying**, -**lied 1** to agree with or be consistent with something else: *this description didn't seem to me to tally with what we saw* **2** to keep score ▷ *n, pl* -**lies 3** any record of debit, credit, the score in a game, etc. **4** an identifying label or mark **5** a stick used (esp. formerly) as a record of the amount of a debt according to the notches cut in it
WORD ORIGIN Latin *talea* a stick

tally-ho *interj* the cry of a participant at a hunt when the quarry is sighted

Talmud *n Judaism* the primary source of Jewish religious law **Talmudic** *adj* **Talmudist** *n*
WORD ORIGIN Hebrew *talmūdh* instruction

talon *n* a sharply hooked claw, such as that of a bird of prey
WORD ORIGIN Latin *talus* ankle

tamarillo *n, pl* -**los** a shrub with a red oval edible fruit

tamarind *n* a tropical evergreen tree with fruit whose acid pulp is used as a food and to make beverages and medicines
WORD ORIGIN Arabic *tamr hindī* Indian date

tamarisk *n* a tree or shrub of the Mediterranean region and S Asia, with scalelike leaves, slender branches, and feathery flower clusters
WORD ORIGIN Latin *tamarix*

tambour *n* an embroidery frame, consisting of two hoops over which the fabric is stretched while being worked **WORD ORIGIN** French

tambourine *n music* a percussion instrument consisting of a single drum skin stretched over a circular wooden frame with pairs of metal discs that jingle when it is struck or shaken **WORD ORIGIN** from Old French

tame *adj* **1 a** (of an animal) changed by humans from a wild state into a domesticated state **b** (of an animal) not afraid of or aggressive towards humans **2** (of a person) tending to do what one is told without questioning or criticizing it **3** mild and unexciting: *the love scenes are fairly tame by modern standards* ▷ *vb* **taming, tamed 4** to make (an animal) tame; domesticate **5** to bring under control; make less extreme or dangerous: *many previously deadly diseases have been tamed by antibiotics* **WORD ORIGIN** Old English *tam*

Tamil *n* **1** *pl* **-ils** *or* **-il** a member of a people of S India and Sri Lanka **2** the language of the Tamils ▷ *adj* **3** of the Tamils

tam-o'-shanter *n* a Scottish brimless woollen cap with a bobble in the centre **WORD ORIGIN** after the hero of Burns's poem *Tam o' Shanter*

tamp *vb* to force or pack (something) down by tapping it several times: *he tamped the bowl of his pipe* **WORD ORIGIN** probably from obsolete *tampin* plug for gun's muzzle

tamper *vb* (foll. by *with*) **1** to interfere or meddle with without permission: *someone has been tampering with the locks* **2** to attempt to influence someone, esp. by bribery: *an attempt to tamper with the jury* **WORD ORIGIN** alteration of *temper* (verb)

tampon *n* an absorbent plug of cotton wool inserted into the vagina during menstruation **WORD ORIGIN** French

tan¹ *n* **1** a brown coloration of the skin caused by exposure to ultraviolet rays, esp. those of the sun ▷ *vb* **tanning, tanned 2** (of a person or his or her skin) to go brown after exposure to ultraviolet rays **3** to convert (a skin or hide) into leather by treating it with a tanning agent **4** *slang* to beat or flog ▷ *adj* **5** yellowish-brown **WORD ORIGIN** Medieval Latin *tannare*

tan² *maths* tangent

tandem *n* **1** a bicycle with two sets of pedals and two saddles, arranged one behind the other for two riders **2 in tandem** together or in conjunction: *the two drugs work in tandem to combat the disease* ▷ *adv* **3** one behind the other: *Jim and Ruth arrived, riding tandem* **WORD ORIGIN** Latin *tandem* at length

tandoor *n* a type of Indian clay oven **WORD ORIGIN** Urdu

tandoori *adj* cooked in a tandoor: *tandoori chicken*

tang *n* **1** a strong sharp taste or smell: *we could already smell the tang of the distant sea* **2** a trace or hint of something: *there was a tang of cloves in the apple pie* **3** the pointed end of a tool, such as a knife or chisel, which fits into the handle **tangy** *adj* **WORD ORIGIN** Old Norse *tangi* point

tangata whenua (**tang**-ah-tah **fen**-noo-ah) *pl n* NZ **1** the original

Polynesian settlers in New Zealand **2** descendants of the original Polynesian settlers **WORD ORIGIN** Māori: people of the land

tangent *n* **1** a line, curve, or plane that touches another curve or surface at one point but does not cross it **2** (in trigonometry) the ratio of the length of the opposite side to that of the adjacent side of a right-angled triangle **3 go off at a tangent** suddenly take a completely different line of thought or action ▷ *adj* **4** of or involving a tangent **5** touching at a single point **WORD ORIGIN** Latin *linea tangens* the touching line

tangential *adj* **1** only having an indirect or superficial relevance: *Hitler's vegetarianism only has a tangential link with the policies of the Nazis* **2** of or being a tangent: *a street tangential to the market square* **tangentially** *adv*

tangerine *n* **1** the small orange-like fruit, with a sweet juicy flesh, of an Asian tree ▷ *adj* **2** reddish-orange **WORD ORIGIN** *Tangier*, a port in Morocco

tangi (**tang**-ee) *n* NZ **1** a Māori funeral ceremony **2** *informal* a lamentation

tangible *adj* **1** able to be touched; material or physical **2** real or substantial: *tangible results* **tangibility** *n* **tangibly** *adv* **WORD ORIGIN** Latin *tangere* to touch

tangle *n* **1** a confused or complicated mass of things, such as hair or fibres, knotted or coiled together: *a tangle of wires* **2** a complicated problem or situation ▷ *vb* **-gling, -gled 3** to twist (things, such as hair or fibres) together in a confused mass **4** to come into conflict: *the last thing she wanted was to tangle with the police* **5** to catch or trap in a net, ropes, etc.: *the string of the kite had got tangled in the branches* **tangled** *adj* **WORD ORIGIN** Middle English *tangilen*

tango *n, pl* **-gos 1** a Latin-American dance characterized by long gliding steps and sudden pauses **2** music for this dance ▷ *vb* **-going, -goed 3** to perform this dance **WORD ORIGIN** American Spanish

taniwha (**tun**-ee-fah) *n* NZ a mythical Māori monster that lives in rivers and lakes **WORD ORIGIN** Māori

tank *n* **1** a large container for storing liquids or gases **2** an armoured combat vehicle moving on tracks and armed with guns **3** Also called: **tankful** the quantity contained in a tank **WORD ORIGIN** Gujarati (language of W India) *tānkh* artificial lake

tankard *n* a large one-handled beer-mug, sometimes fitted with a hinged lid **WORD ORIGIN** Middle English

tanked up *adj slang chiefly Brit* very drunk

tanker *n* a ship or lorry for carrying liquid in bulk: *an oil tanker*

tank farming *n* same as **hydroponics** ▷ **tank farmer** *n*

tannery *n, pl* **-neries** a place or building where skins and hides are tanned

tannic *adj* of, containing, or produced from tannin or tannic acid

tannie (**tun**-nee) *n S African* a title of respect used to refer to an elderly woman **WORD ORIGIN** Afrikaans, literally: aunt

tannin *n* a yellowish compound found in many plants, such as tea and grapes, and used in tanning and dyeing. Also called: **tannic acid**

Tannoy *n trademark, Brit* a type of public-address system

tansy *n, pl* **-sies** a plant with yellow flowers in flat-topped clusters **WORD ORIGIN** Greek *athanasia* immortality

tantalize *or* **-lise** *vb* **-lizing, -lized** *or* **-lising, -lised** to tease or make frustrated, for example by tormenting (someone) with the sight of something that he or she wants but cannot have **tantalizing** *or* **-lising** *adj* **tantalizingly** *or* **-lisingly** *adv* **WORD ORIGIN** after *Tantalus*, a mythological king condemned to stand in water that receded when he tried to drink it and under fruit that moved away when he reached for it

tantalum *n chem* a hard greyish-white metallic element that resists corrosion. Symbol: Ta **WORD ORIGIN** after *Tantalus* (see TANTALIZE), from the metal's incapacity to absorb acids

tantalus *n Brit* a case in which bottles of wine and spirits may be locked with their contents tantalizingly visible

tantamount *adj* **tantamount to** equivalent in effect to: *the raid was tantamount to a declaration of war* **WORD ORIGIN** Anglo-French *tant amunter* to amount to as much

tantrum *n* a childish outburst of bad temper **WORD ORIGIN** origin unknown

Taoiseach (**tee**-shack) *n* the Prime Minister of the Irish Republic

Taoism (rhymes with **Maoism**) *n* a Chinese system of religion and philosophy advocating a simple honest life and noninterference with the course of natural events **Taoist** *n, adj*

tap¹ *vb* **tapping, tapped 1** to knock lightly and usually repeatedly: *she tapped gently on the door* **2** to make a rhythmic sound with the hands or feet by lightly and repeatedly hitting a surface with them: *he was tapping one foot to the music* ▷ *n* **3** a light blow or knock, or the sound made by it **4** the metal piece attached to the toe or heel of a shoe used for tap-dancing **5** same as **tap-dancing** **WORD ORIGIN** Middle English *tappen*

tap² *n* **1** *Brit, Austral, & NZ* a valve by which the flow of a liquid or gas from a pipe can be controlled. Usual US word **faucet 2** a stopper to plug a cask or barrel **3** a concealed listening or recording device connected to a telephone **4** *med* the withdrawal of fluid from a bodily cavity: *a spinal tap* **5 on tap a** *informal* ready for use **b** (of drinks) on draught rather than in bottles ▷ *vb* **tapping, tapped 6** to listen in on (a telephone conversation) secretly by making an illegal connection **7** to obtain something useful or desirable from (something): *a new way of tapping the sun's energy* **8** to withdraw liquid from (something) as if through a tap: *to tap a cask of wine* **9** to cut into (a tree) and draw off sap from it **10** *Brit, Austral, & NZ informal* to obtain (money or information) from (someone) **11** *informal* to make an illicit attempt to recruit (a player or employee bound by an existing contract) **WORD ORIGIN** Old English *tæppa*

tapas (tap-ass) *pl n* (in Spanish cookery) light snacks or appetizers, usually eaten with drinks **WORD ORIGIN** Spanish *tapa* cover, lid

tap-dancing *n* a style of dancing in which the performer wears shoes with metal plates at the heels and toes that make a rhythmic sound on the stage as he or she dances **tap-dancer** *n* **tap dance** *n*

tape *n* **1** a long thin strip of cotton or linen used for tying or fastening: *a parcel tied with pink tape* **2 a** short for **magnetic tape b** a spool or cassette containing magnetic tape, and used for recording or playing sound or video signals: *he put a tape into his stereo* **c** the music, speech, or pictures which have been recorded on a particular cassette or spool of magnetic tape **3** a narrow strip of plastic which has one side coated with an adhesive substance and is used to stick paper, etc. together: *sticky tape* **4** a string stretched across the track at the end of a race course **5** short for **tape measure** ▷ *vb* **taping, taped 6** Also: **tape-record** to record (speech, music, etc.) on magnetic tape **7** to bind or fasten with tape **8 have a person** or **situation taped** *Austral & Brit informal* to have full understanding and control of a person or situation **WORD ORIGIN** Old English *tæppe*

tape deck *n* **1** the part of a tape recorder which supports the spools or cassettes, and contains the motor and the playback, recording, and erasing heads **2** the unit in a hi-fi system which fulfils the same function

tape drive *n* a machine for storing or transferring information from a computer onto tape

tape measure *n* a tape or length of metal marked off in centimetres or inches, used for measuring

taper *vb* **1** to become narrower towards one end **2 taper off** to become gradually less: *treatment should be tapered off gradually* ▷ *n* **3** a long thin fast-burning candle **4** a narrowing **WORD ORIGIN** Old English *tapor*

tape recorder *n* an electrical device used for recording and reproducing sounds on magnetic tape

tape recording *n* **1** the act of recording sounds on magnetic tape **2** the magnetic tape used for this: *a tape recording of the interview* **3** the sounds so recorded

tapestry *n, pl* **-tries 1** a heavy woven fabric, often in the form of a picture, used for wall hangings or furnishings **2** same as **needlepoint** (sense 1). **3** a colourful and complicated situation that is made up of many

different kinds of things: *the rich tapestry of Hindustani music* **WORD ORIGIN** Old French *tapisserie* carpeting

tapeworm *n* a long flat parasitic worm that inhabits the intestines of vertebrates, including man

tapioca *n* a beadlike starch made from cassava root, used in puddings **WORD ORIGIN** S American Indian *tipioca* pressed-out juice

tapir (tape-er) *n* a piglike mammal of South and Central America and SE Asia, with a long snout, three-toed hind legs, and four-toed forelegs **WORD ORIGIN** S American Indian *tapiira*

tappet *n* a short steel rod in an engine which moves up and down transferring movement from one part of the machine to another **WORD ORIGIN** from TAP¹

taproom *n* *old-fashioned* the public bar in a hotel or pub

taproot *n* the main root of plants such as the dandelion, which grows straight down and bears smaller lateral roots

tar¹ *n* **1** a dark sticky substance obtained by distilling organic matter such as coal, wood, or peat **2** same as **coal tar** ▷ *vb* **tarring, tarred 3** to coat with tar **4 tar and feather** to cover (someone) with tar and feathers as a punishment **5 tarred with the same brush** having, or regarded as having, the same faults **tarry** *adj* **WORD ORIGIN** Old English *teoru*

tar² *n informal* a seaman **WORD ORIGIN** short for *tarpaulin*

tarakihi (tarr-a-kee-hee) *or* **terakihi** (terr-a-kee-hee) *n* a common edible sea fish of New Zealand waters **WORD ORIGIN** Māori

taramasalata *n* a creamy pale pink pâté, made from the eggs of fish, esp. smoked cod's roe, and served as an hors d'oeuvre **WORD ORIGIN** Modern Greek

tarantella *n* **1** a peasant dance from S Italy **2** music for this dance **WORD ORIGIN** Italian

tarantula *n* **1** a large hairy spider of tropical America with a poisonous bite **2** a large hairy spider of S Europe **WORD ORIGIN** Medieval Latin

tarboosh *n* a felt or cloth brimless cap, usually red and often with a silk tassel, formerly worn by Muslim men **WORD ORIGIN** Arabic *tarbūsh*

tardy *adj* **-dier, -diest 1** occurring later than it is expected to or than it should: *he spent the weekend writing tardy thank-you letters* **2** slow in progress, growth, etc.: *we made tardy progress across the ice* **tardily** *adv* **tardiness** *n* **WORD ORIGIN** Latin *tardus* slow

tare¹ *n* **1** the weight of the wrapping or container in which goods are packed **2** the weight of a vehicle without its cargo or passengers **WORD ORIGIN** Arabic *tarah* something discarded

tare² *n* **1** any of various vetch plants of Eurasia and N Africa **2** *Bible* a weed, thought to be the darnel **WORD ORIGIN** origin unknown

target *n* **1** the object or person that a weapon, ball, etc. is aimed at: *the station was an easy target for an air attack* **2** an object at which an archer or marksman aims, usually a round flat surface marked with circles **3** a fixed goal or objective: *our sales figures are well below target* **4** a person or thing at which criticism or ridicule is directed: *the Chancellor has been the target of much of the criticism* ▷ *vb* **-geting, -geted 5** to direct: *an advertising campaign targeted at gay men* **6** to aim (a missile) **WORD ORIGIN** Old French *targette* a little shield

tariff *n* **1 a** a tax levied by a government on imports or occasionally exports **b** a list of such taxes **2** a list of fixed prices, for example in a hotel **3** *chiefly Brit* a method of charging for services such as gas and electricity by setting a price per unit **WORD ORIGIN** Arabic *ta'rīfa* to inform

Tarmac *n* **1** *trademark* a paving material made of crushed stone bound with a mixture of tar and bitumen, used for a road or airport runway **2 the tarmac** the area of an airport where planes wait and take off or land: *we had to wait for an hour on the tarmac* ▷ *vb* **tarmac, -macking, -macked 3** to apply Tarmac to (a surface) **WORD ORIGIN** TAR + MAC(ADAM)

tarn *n* *chiefly Brit* a small mountain lake **WORD ORIGIN** from Old Norse

tarnish *vb* **1** (of a metal) to become stained or less bright, esp. by exposure to air or moisture **2** to damage or taint: *the affair could tarnish the reputation of the prime minister* ▷ *n* **3** a tarnished condition, surface, or film on a surface **tarnished** *adj* **WORD ORIGIN** Old French *ternir* to make dull

taro *n, pl* **-ros** a plant with a large edible rootstock **WORD ORIGIN** Tahitian & Polynesian

tarot (tarr-oh) *n* **1** a special pack of cards, now used mainly for fortune-telling **2** a card in a tarot pack with a distinctive symbolic design **WORD ORIGIN** French

tarpaulin *n* **1** a heavy waterproof canvas coated with tar, wax, or paint **2** a sheet of this canvas, used as a waterproof covering **WORD ORIGIN** probably from TAR¹ + PALL¹

tarragon *n* a European herb with narrow leaves, which are used as seasoning in cooking **WORD ORIGIN** Old French *targon*

tarry *vb* **-ries, -rying, -ried** *old-fashioned* **1** to delay or linger: *I have no plans to tarry longer than necessary* **2** to stay briefly: *most people tarried only a few hours before moving on* **WORD ORIGIN** origin unknown

tarsal *anat adj* **1** of the tarsus or tarsi ▷ *n* **2** a tarsal bone

tarseal *n* *NZ* **1** the bitumen surface of a road **2 the tarseal** the main highway

tarsier *n* a small nocturnal primate of the E Indies, which has very large eyes

tarsus *n, pl* **-si 1** the bones of the ankle and heel collectively **2** the corresponding part in other mammals and in amphibians and reptiles

Words from Literature
part 27

toy *n* toys are things which are considered to have little importance, value, or significance
> purchase my life from them bysome bracelets, glass rings, and other toys
> *Gulliver's Travels* Jonathan Swift

tract *n* a religious pamphlet or leaflet
> and Joe Harper got a hymn-book and a tract
> *The Adventures of Huckleberry Finn* Mark Twain

train-oil *n* train-oil is oil from whale blubber
> The train-oil and gunpowder were shoved out of sight in a minute
> *Wuthering Heights* Emily Brontë

tribulation *n* the suffering or difficulty you experience in a particular situation
> Amy was learning this distinction through much tribulation
> *Little Women* Louisa May Alcott

trivet *n* a three-legged stand for resting a pot or kettle
> a pocket-knife in his right; and a pewter pot on the trivet
> *Oliver Twist* Charles Dickens

trot line *n* a fishing line to which a row of smaller fishing lines are attached
> when he got along I was hard at it taking up a 'trot' line
> *The Adventures of Huckleberry Finn* Mark Twain

troth *n* an oath or pledge
> I wonder, by my troth
> *The Good-Morrow* John Donne

truckle *n* a truckle bedstead is a bed that is on wheels and can be slid under another bed to save space
> It rose under my hand, and the door yielded. Looking in, I saw a lighted candle on a table, a bench, and a mattress on a truckle bedstead.
> *Great Expectations* Charles Dickens

trump *n* a trump is a good, reliable person who can be trusted
> This lad Hawkins is a trump, I perceive
> *Treasure Island* Robert Louis Stevenson

tucker *n* a frilly lace collar which is worn around the neck
> Whereat Scrooge's niece's sister – the plump one with the lace tucker: not the one with the roses – blushed.
> *A Christmas Carol* Charles Dickens

tureen *n* a large bowl with a lid from which soup or vegetables are served
> Waiting in a hot tureen!
> *Alice's Adventures in Wonderland* Lewis Carroll

turnkey *n* a prison officer; jailer
> As we came out of the prison through the lodge, I found that the great importance of my guardian was appreciated by the turnkeys, no less than by those whom they held in charge.
> *Great Expectations* Charles Dickens

turnpike *n* gates or some other barrier set across a road to prevent passage until a toll had been paid
> There was a gate to prevent people travelling further along the road until the toll had been paid. Traddles, whom I have taken up by appointment at the turnpike, presents a dazzling combination of cream colour and light blue; and both he and Mr. Dick have a general effect about them of being all gloves.
> *David Copperfield* Charles Dickens

twas *contraction* it was
> twas but a dream of thee
> *The Good-Morrow* John Donne

tyrannize *v* to bully or force people to do things against their will
> for people would soon cease coming there to be tyrannized over and put down
> *Treasure Island* Robert Louis Stevenson

'un *pron* a slang term for one, usually used to refer to a person
> She's been thinking the old 'un
> *David Copperfield* Charles Dickens

WORD ORIGIN Greek *tarsos* flat surface, instep

tart¹ *n* **1** a pastry case, often having no top crust, with a sweet filling, such as jam or custard **2** *chiefly US* a small open pie with a fruit filling
WORD ORIGIN Old French *tarte*

tart² *adj* **1** (of a flavour) sour or bitter **2** sharp and hurtful: *he made a rather tart comment* **tartly** *adv* **tartness** *n*
WORD ORIGIN Old English *teart* rough

tart³ *n* *informal* a sexually provocative or promiscuous woman: *you look like a tart*. See also **tart up**
WORD ORIGIN from *sweetheart*

tartan *n* **1** a design of straight lines, crossing at right angles to give a chequered appearance, esp. one associated with a Scottish clan **2** a fabric with this design
WORD ORIGIN origin unknown

tartar¹ *n* **1** a hard deposit on the teeth **2** a brownish-red substance deposited in a cask during the fermentation of wine
WORD ORIGIN Medieval Greek *tartaron*

tartar² *n* a fearsome or formidable person
WORD ORIGIN from *Tartar*

Tartar or **Tatar** *n* **1** a member of a Mongoloid people who established a powerful state in central Asia in the 13th century, now scattered throughout Russia and central Asia ▷ *adj* **2** of the Tartars
WORD ORIGIN Persian *Tātār*

tartaric *adj* of or derived from tartar or tartaric acid

tartaric acid *n* a colourless crystalline acid which is found in many fruits

tartar sauce *n* a mayonnaise sauce mixed with chopped herbs and capers, served with seafood

tartine *n* an open sandwich, esp. one with a rich or elaborate topping
WORD ORIGIN French

tartrazine (tar-*traz*-zeen) *n* an artificial yellow dye used as a food additive

tart up *vb* *Brit informal* **1** to decorate in a cheap and flashy way: *the shops were tarted up for Christmas* **2** to try to make (oneself) look smart and attractive

Tarzan *n* *informal, often ironic* a man with great physical strength, agility, and virility
WORD ORIGIN after the hero of stories by E. R. Burroughs

task *n* **1** a specific piece of work required to be done **2** an unpleasant or difficult job or duty **3 take to task** to criticize or rebuke
WORD ORIGIN Old French *tasche*

taskbar *n* a row of selectable buttons and icons typically running along the bottom of a computer screen, displaying information such as the names of running programs

task force *n* **1** a temporary grouping of military units formed to undertake a specific mission **2** any organization set up to carry out a continuing task

taskmaster *n* a person who enforces hard or continuous work

Tasmanian devil *n* a small flesh-eating marsupial of Tasmania

Tass *n* (formerly) the principal news agency of the Soviet Union

tassel *n* a tuft of loose threads secured by a knot or knob, used to decorate a cushion, piece of clothing, etc.
WORD ORIGIN Old French

taste *n* **1** the sense by which the flavour of a substance is distinguished by the taste buds **2** the sensation experienced by means of the taste buds **3** a small amount eaten, sipped, or tried on the tongue **4** a brief experience of something: *a taste of the planter's life* **5** a liking for something: *a taste for puns* **6** the ability to appreciate what is beautiful and excellent: *she's got very good taste in clothes* **7** a person's typical preferences as displayed by what they choose to buy, enjoy, etc.: *the film was good but a bit violent for my taste* **8** the quality of not being offensive or bad-mannered: *that remark was in rather poor taste* ▷ *vb* **tasting, tasted 9** to distinguish the taste of (a substance) by means of the taste buds: *I've got a stinking cold and can't taste anything* **10** to take a small amount of (a food or liquid) into the mouth, esp. in order to test the flavour **11** to have a flavour or taste as specified: *the pizza tastes delicious* **12** to have a brief experience of (something): *they have tasted democracy and they won't let go*
WORD ORIGIN Old French *taster*

taste bud *n* any of the cells on the surface of the tongue, by means of which the sensation of taste is experienced

tasteful *adj* having or showing good social or aesthetic taste: *tasteful decor* **tastefully** *adv*

tasteless *adj* **1** lacking in flavour: *the canteen serves cold, tasteless pizzas* **2** lacking social or aesthetic taste: *a room full of tasteless ornaments; a tasteless remark* **tastelessly** *adv* **tastelessness** *n*

taster *n* **1** a person employed to test the quality of food or drink by tasting it **2** a sample of something intended to indicate what the entire thing is like: *the entrance hall was filled with flowers, giving a taster of the splendours in the main exhibition*

tasty *adj* **tastier, tastiest** having a pleasant flavour

tat *n* *Brit* tatty or tasteless articles

ta-ta *interj* *chiefly Brit informal* goodbye
WORD ORIGIN origin unknown

Tatar *n, adj* same as **Tartar**

tater *n* *Brit dialect* a potato

tattered *adj* **1** ragged or torn: *a tattered old book* **2** wearing ragged or torn clothing: *the tattered refugees*

tatters *pl n* **1** torn ragged clothing **2 in tatters a** (of clothing) torn in several places **b** (of an argument, plan, etc.) completely destroyed

tatting *n* **1** an intricate type of lace made by looping a thread of cotton or linen with a hand shuttle **2** the work of producing this
WORD ORIGIN origin unknown

tattle *vb* **-tling, -tled 1** to gossip or chatter ▷ *n* **2** gossip or chatter **tattler** *n*
WORD ORIGIN Middle Dutch *tatelen*

tattletale *n* *chiefly US & Canad* a scandalmonger or gossip

tattoo¹ *n, pl* **-toos 1** a picture or design made on someone's body by pricking small holes in the skin and filling them with indelible dye ▷ *vb* **-tooing, -tooed 2** to make pictures or designs on (a person's skin) by pricking and staining it with indelible colours **tattooed** *adj* **tattooist** *n*
WORD ORIGIN Tahitian *tatau*

tattoo² *n, pl* **-toos 1** (formerly) a signal by drum or bugle ordering soldiers to return to their quarters **2** a military display or pageant **3** any drumming or tapping
WORD ORIGIN Dutch *taptoe*

tatty *adj* **-tier, -tiest** worn out, shabby, or unkempt
WORD ORIGIN Scots

taught *vb* the past of **teach**

taunt *vb* **1** to tease or provoke (someone) with jeering remarks ▷ *n* **2** a jeering remark **taunting** *adj*
WORD ORIGIN French *tant pour tant* like for like

Taurus *n* *astrol* the second sign of the zodiac; the Bull
WORD ORIGIN Latin

taut *adj* **1** stretched tight: *the cable must be taut* **2** showing nervous strain: *he was looking taut and anxious* **3** (of a film or piece of writing) having no unnecessary or irrelevant details: *a taut thriller*
WORD ORIGIN Middle English *tought*

tauten *vb* to make or become taut

tautology *n, pl* **-gies** the use of words which merely repeat something already stated, as in *reverse back* **tautological** or **tautologous** *adj*
WORD ORIGIN Greek *tautologia*

tavern *n* **1** old-fashioned a pub **2** *US, Canad, Austral, & NZ* a place licensed for the sale and consumption of alcoholic drink
WORD ORIGIN Latin *taberna* hut

tawdry *adj* **-drier, -driest** cheap, showy, and of poor quality: *tawdry Christmas decorations*
WORD ORIGIN Middle English *seynt Audries lace*, finery sold at the fair of St Audrey

tawny *adj* brown to brownish-orange
WORD ORIGIN Old French *tané*

tawny owl *n* a European owl having a reddish-brown plumage and a round head

tawse *n* *Scot* a leather strap with one end cut into thongs, formerly used by schoolteachers to hit children who had misbehaved
WORD ORIGIN probably plural of obsolete *taw* strip of leather

tax *n* **1** a compulsory payment to a government to raise revenue, levied on income, property, or goods and services ▷ *vb* **2** to levy a tax on (people, companies, etc.) **3** to make heavy demands on: *the task taxed his ingenuity and patience* **4 tax someone with** to accuse someone of: *he was taxed with parochialism and meanness* **taxable** *adj* **taxing** *adj*
WORD ORIGIN Latin *taxare* to appraise

taxation *n* the levying of taxes or the condition of being taxed

tax avoidance *n* reduction of tax liability by lawful methods

tax-deductible *adj* legally deductible from income or wealth before tax assessment

tax disc *n* (in Britain) a small disc of paper which must be displayed on a vehicle to show that the tax due on it for that year has been paid

tax evasion *n* reduction of tax liability by illegal methods

tax-free *adj* not needing to have tax paid on it: *a tax-free lump sum*

tax haven *n* a country or state having a lower rate of taxation than elsewhere

taxi *n, pl* **taxis** **1** Also called: **cab, taxicab** a car that may be hired, along with its driver, to carry passengers to any specified destination ▷ *vb* **taxiing, taxied** **2** (of an aircraft) to move along the ground, esp. before takeoff and after landing
WORD ORIGIN *taximeter cab*

taxidermy *n* the art of preparing, stuffing, and mounting animal skins so that they have a lifelike appearance **taxidermist** *n*
WORD ORIGIN Greek *taxis* arrangement + *derma* skin

taximeter *n* a meter fitted to a taxi to register the fare, based on the length of the journey

taxi rank *n* a place where taxis wait to be hired

taxman *n, pl* **-men** **1** a collector of taxes **2** *informal* a tax-collecting body personified: *he was convicted of conspiring to cheat the taxman*

taxonomy *n* **1** the branch of biology concerned with the classification of plants and animals into groups based on their similarities and differences **2** the science or practice of classification **taxonomic** *adj* **taxonomist** *n*
WORD ORIGIN Greek *taxis* order + *nomia* law

taxpayer *n* a person or organization that pays taxes

tax relief *n* a reduction in the amount of tax a person or company has to pay

tax return *n* a declaration of personal income used as a basis for assessing an individual's liability for taxation

tax year *n* a period of twelve months used by a government as a basis for calculating taxes

Tb *chem* terbium

TB tuberculosis

tba *or* **TBA** to be arranged

tbc *or* **TBC** to be confirmed

T-bone steak *n* a large choice steak cut from the sirloin of beef, containing a T-shaped bone

tbs. *or* **tbsp.** tablespoon(ful)

Tc *chem* technetium

te *n music* (in tonic sol-fa) the seventh note of any ascending major scale

Te *chem* tellurium

tea *n* **1 a** a drink made by infusing the dried chopped leaves of an Asian shrub in boiling water: *would you like a cup of tea?* **b** the dried chopped leaves of an Asian shrub used to make this drink: *could you get some tea at the grocer's?* **c** the Asian shrub on which these leaves grow

2 *Brit, Austral, & NZ* the main evening meal **3** *chiefly Brit* a light meal eaten in mid-afternoon, usually consisting of tea and cakes, sometimes with sandwiches **4** a drink like tea made from other plants: *mint tea*
WORD ORIGIN Ancient Chinese *d'a*

tea bag *n* a small bag containing tea leaves, infused in boiling water to make tea

teacake *n chiefly Brit* a flat bun, usually eaten toasted and buttered

teach *vb* **teaching, taught** **1** to tell or show (someone) how to do something **2** to give instruction or lessons in (a subject) to (students) **3** to cause to learn or understand: *life has taught me to seize the day* **4 teach someone a lesson** to warn or punish someone: *a bully has to be taught a lesson* **teachable** *adj*
WORD ORIGIN Old English *tǣcan*

teacher *n* a person whose job is to teach others, esp. children

tea chest *n* a large light wooden box used for exporting tea or storing things in

teaching *n* **1** the art or profession of a teacher **2 teachings** the ideas and principles taught by a person, school of thought, etc.: *the teachings of the Catholic Church*

teaching hospital *n* a hospital attached to a medical school, in which students are taught and given supervised practical experience

tea cloth *n* same as **tea towel**

tea cosy *n* a covering for a teapot to keep the contents hot

teacup *n* **1** a cup out of which tea may be drunk **2** Also called: **teacupful** the amount a teacup will hold

teahouse *n* a restaurant, esp. in Japan or China, where tea and light refreshments are served

teak *n* the hard yellowish-brown wood of an East Indian tree, used for furniture making
WORD ORIGIN Malayalam (a language of S India) *tēkka*

teal *n, pl* **teals** *or* **teal** a small freshwater duck related to the mallard
WORD ORIGIN Middle English *tele*

tea leaves *pl n, sing* **tea leaf** the dried and shredded leaves of the tea shrub, esp. those left behind in a cup or teapot after tea has been made and drunk

team *n* **1** a group of players forming one of the sides in a sporting contest **2** a group of people organized to work together: *a team of scientists* **3** two or more animals working together: *a sledge pulled by a team of dogs* ▷ *vb* **4 team up with** to join with (someone) in order to work together **5 team with** to match (something) with something else: *navy skirts teamed with various coloured blouses*
WORD ORIGIN Old English *tēam* offspring

team-mate *n* a fellow member of a team

team spirit *n* willingness to cooperate as part of a team

teamster *n* **1** *US & Canad* a truck driver **2** (formerly) a driver of a team of horses

teamwork *n* the cooperative work done by a team

teapot *n* a container with a lid, spout, and handle, in which tea is made and from which it is served

tear¹ *n* **1** Also called: **teardrop** a drop of salty fluid appearing in and falling from the eye ▷ Related adjectives: **lacrimal, lachrymal, lacrymal 2 in tears** weeping
WORD ORIGIN Old English *tēar*

tear² *vb* **tearing, tore, torn** **1** to rip a hole in (something): *I tore my jumper on a nail* **2** to pull apart or to pieces: *eagles have powerful beaks for tearing flesh* **3** to hurry or rush **4** to remove or take by force: *the sacred things torn from the temples of Inca worshippers* **5 tear at someone's heartstrings** to cause someone distress or anguish **6** to injure (a muscle or ligament) by moving or twisting it violently ▷ *n* **7** a hole or split ▷ See also **tear away, tear down, tear into**
WORD ORIGIN Old English *teran*

tear away *vb* **1** to persuade (oneself or someone else) to leave: *she stood and watched, unable to tear herself away from the room* ▷ *n* **tearaway 2** *Brit* a wild or unruly person

tear down *vb* to destroy or demolish: *it will be cheaper to tear down the old house and build a new one than to repair it*

tear duct *n* a short tube in the inner corner of the eyelid, through which tears drain into the nose

tearful *adj* weeping or about to weep **tearfully** *adv*

tear gas *n* a gas that stings the eyes and causes temporary blindness, used in warfare and to control riots

tearing *adj* very urgent: *I had been in a tearing hurry to leave the camp*

tear into *vb informal* to attack vigorously and damagingly

tear-jerker *n informal* an excessively sentimental film or book

tearoom *n* **1** *chiefly Brit* a restaurant where tea and light refreshments are served **2** *NZ* a room in a school or university where hot drinks are served

tease *vb* **teasing, teased** **1** to make fun of (someone) in a provocative and often playful manner **2** to arouse sexual desire in (someone) with no intention of satisfying it **3** to raise the nap of (a fabric) with a teasel ▷ *n* **4** a person who teases **5** a piece of teasing behaviour **teasing** *adj*
WORD ORIGIN Old English *tǣsan*

teasel, teazel *or* **teazle** *n* **1** a plant of Eurasia and N Africa, with prickly heads of yellow or purple flowers **2** the dried flower head of a teasel, used, esp. formerly, for raising the nap of cloth
WORD ORIGIN Old English *tǣsel*

tease out *vb* **1** to comb (hair, flax, or wool) so as to remove any tangles **2** to extract information with difficulty: *it's not easy to tease out the differences between anxiety and depression*

teaser *n* **1** a difficult question **2** a preliminary advertisement in a campaign that makes people curious to know what product is being advertised

t

teaspoon n **1** a small spoon used for stirring tea or coffee **2** Also called: **teaspoonful** the amount contained in such a spoon **3** a unit of capacity used in cooking etc. equal to 5 ml

teat n **1** the nipple of a breast or udder **2** something resembling a teat such as the rubber mouthpiece of a feeding bottle **WORD ORIGIN** Old French *tete*

tea towel or **tea cloth** n a towel for drying dishes

tea tree n a tree of Australia and New Zealand that yields an oil used as an antiseptic

tech n *informal* a technical college

tech. **1** technical **2** technology

techie or **techy** *informal* n **1** a person who is skilled in the use of technological devices, such as computers ▷ adj **2** of, relating to, or skilled in the use of such devices

technetium (tek-**neesh**-ee-um) n *chem* a silvery-grey metallic element, produced artificially, esp. by the fission of uranium. Symbol: Tc **WORD ORIGIN** Greek *tekhnētos* man-made

technical adj **1** of or specializing in industrial, practical, or mechanical arts and applied sciences: *a technical school* **2** skilled in practical activities rather than abstract thinking **3** relating to a particular field of activity: *technical jargon* **4** according to the letter of the law: *a last-minute penalty awarded to the Irish for a technical offence* **5** showing technique: *technical perfection* **technically** adv

technical college n *Austral & Brit* an institution for further education that provides courses in art and technical subjects

technical drawing n drawing done by a draughtsman with compasses, T-squares, etc.

technicality n, pl **-ties** **1** a petty formal point arising from a strict interpretation of the law or a set of rules: *the case was dismissed on a legal technicality* **2** a detail of the method used to do something: *the technicalities of making a recording*

technical knockout n *boxing* a judgment of a knockout given when a boxer is, in the referee's opinion, too badly beaten to continue without risk of serious injury

technician n a person skilled in a particular technical field: *oil technicians*

Technicolor n *trademark* a process of producing colour film for the cinema by superimposing synchronized films of the same scene, each having a different colour filter

technikon n *S African* a technical college

technique n **1** a method or skill used for a particular task: *modern management techniques* **2** proficiency in a practical or mechanical skill: *he lacks the technique to be a good player* **WORD ORIGIN** Greek *tekhnē* skill

techno n a type of very fast disco music, using electronic sounds and having a strong technological influence

techno- *combining form* of or relating to technology: *technocrat* **WORD ORIGIN** Greek *tekhnē* skill

technocracy n, pl **-cies** government by scientists, engineers, and other experts **technocrat** n **technocratic** adj **WORD ORIGIN** Greek *tekhnē* skill + *kratos* power

technology n, pl **-gies** **1** the application of practical or mechanical sciences to industry or commerce **2** the scientific methods or devices used in a particular field: *the latest aircraft technology* **technological** adj **technologist** n **WORD ORIGIN** Greek *tekhnologia* systematic treatment

technophile n **1** a person who is enthusiastic about technology ▷ adj **2** enthusiastic about technology

technophobia n fear of using technological devices, such as computers **technophobe** n **technophobic** adj

tectonics n *geol* the study of the earth's crust and the forces that produce changes in it **WORD ORIGIN** Greek *tektōn* a builder

ted¹ vb **tedding, tedded** to shake out (hay), so as to dry it **WORD ORIGIN** Old Norse *tethja*

ted² n *Brit informal* short for **teddy boy**

teddy¹ n, pl **-dies** short for **teddy bear**

teddy² n, pl **-dies** a woman's one-piece undergarment incorporating a camisole top and French knickers **WORD ORIGIN** origin unknown

teddy bear n a stuffed toy bear **WORD ORIGIN** after *Teddy* (Theodore) Roosevelt, US president

teddy boy n (in Britain, esp. in the mid-1950s) a youth who wore mock Edwardian fashions **WORD ORIGIN** *Teddy*, from *Edward*

Te Deum (tee **dee**-um) n *Christianity* an ancient Latin hymn beginning Te Deum Laudamus (we praise thee, O God)

tedious adj boring and uninteresting **tediously** adv **tediousness** n

tedium n the state of being bored or the quality of being boring: *the tedium of a nine-to-five white-collar job* **WORD ORIGIN** Latin *taedium*

tee n **1** a support for a golf ball, usually a small wooden or plastic peg, used when teeing off **2** an area on a golf course from which the first stroke of a hole is made **3** a mark used as a target in certain games such as curling and quoits ▶ See also **tee off** **WORD ORIGIN** origin unknown

tee-hee or **te-hee** *interj* an exclamation of mocking laughter **WORD ORIGIN** imitative

teem¹ vb **teem with** to have a great number of: *the woods were teeming with snakes and bears* **WORD ORIGIN** Old English *tēman* to produce offspring

teem² vb (of rain) to pour down in torrents **WORD ORIGIN** Old Norse *tœma*

teen adj *informal* same as **teenage**

teenage adj **1** (of a person) aged between 13 and 19 **2** typical of or designed for people aged between 13 and 19: *teenage fashions*

teenager n a person between the ages of 13 and 19

teens pl n **1** the years of a person's life between the ages of 13 and 19 **2** all the numbers that end in *-teen*

teeny adj **-nier, -niest** *informal* extremely small **WORD ORIGIN** variant of *tiny*

teenybopper n *old-fashioned slang* a young teenager, usually a girl, who is a keen follower of fashion and pop music **WORD ORIGIN** *teeny* teenage + *-bopper* someone who bops

tee off vb **teeing, teed** *golf* to hit (the ball) from a tee at the start of a hole

teepee n same as **tepee**

teeter vb to wobble or move unsteadily **WORD ORIGIN** Middle English *titeren*

teeth n **1** the plural of **tooth** **2** the power to produce a desired effect: *resolution 672 had no teeth* **3** armed to the teeth very heavily armed **4** get one's teeth into to become engrossed in **5** in the teeth of in spite of: *trying to run a business in the teeth of the recession*

teethe vb **teething, teethed** (of a baby) to grow his or her first teeth

teething ring n a hard ring on which babies may bite while teething

teething troubles pl n problems arising during the early stages of a project

teetotal adj never drinking alcohol **teetotaller** n **WORD ORIGIN** reduplication of *t* + *total*

TEFL Teaching of English as a Foreign Language

Teflon n *trademark* a substance used for nonstick coatings on saucepans etc.

te-hee *interj* same as **tee-hee**

tel. telephone

tele- *combining form* **1** at or over a distance: *telecommunications* **2** television: *telegenic* **3** via telephone or television: *teleconference* **WORD ORIGIN** Greek *tele* far

telecast vb **-casting, -cast** or **-casted** **1** to broadcast by television ▷ n **2** a television broadcast **telecaster** n

telecommunications n communications using electronic equipment, such as telephones, radio, and television

telecommuting n same as **teleworking**

telegram n (formerly) a message transmitted by telegraph

telegraph n **1** (formerly) a system by which information could be transmitted over a distance, using electrical signals sent along a cable ▷ vb **2** (formerly) to send (a message) by telegraph **3** to give advance notice of (something), esp. unintentionally: *the twist in the plot was telegraphed long in advance* **4** *Canad informal* to cast (a vote) illegally by impersonating a registered voter **telegraphist** n **telegraphic** adj

telegraphy n (formerly) the science or use of a telegraph

telekinesis n movement of a body by thought or willpower, without the

Words from Shakespeare
part 16

transgress *v* to break a moral law or rule of behaviour
> Virtue that transgresses is but patched with sin
> *Twelfth Night* 1.5

troth, by my *phrase* I swear or in truth or on my word
> By my troth, Sir Toby, you must come in earlier o'
> nights *Twelfth Night* 1.3

trumpery *n* things that look expensive but are worth nothing (often clothing)
> The trumpery in my house, go bring it hither
> For stale catch these thieves *The Tempest* 4.1

twink *n* the wink of an eye or no time at all
> Ay, with a twink *The Tempest* 4.1

undo *v* to run, destroy, or bring down someone
> You have undone a man of fourscore three
> *The Winter's Tale* 4.4

varlet *n* a villain or ruffian
> Say again: where didst thou leave these varlets?
> *The Tempest* 4.1

vaward *n* the vanguard, front part or earliest
> And since we have the vaward of the day
> *A Midsummer Night's Dream* 4.1

visage *n* face
> when Phoebe doth behold
> Her silver visage in the watery glass
> *A Midsummer Night's Dream* 1.1

voice *n* a vote
> He has our voices *Coriolanus* 2.3

waggish *adj* playful
> As waggish boys in game themselves forswear
> *A Midsummer Night's Dream* 1.1

wane *v* to vanish, go down or get slighter. It is most often used to describe a phase of the moon
> but, O, methinks, how slow
> This old moon wanes
> *A Midsummer Night's Dream* 1.1

want *v* to lack or to be without
> a beast that wants discourse of reason
> Would have mourned longer *Hamlet* 1.2

warrant *v* to assure, promise, or guarantee
> I warrant your grace *As You Like It* 1.2

welkin *n* the sky or the heavens
> The starry welkin cover thou anon
> With drooping fog as black as Acheron
> *A Midsummer Night's Dream* 3.2

wench *n* a girl
> Well demanded, wench *The Tempest* 1.2

whence *adv* from where
> Whence came you, sir? *Twelfth Night* 1.5

wherefore *adv* why
> Wherefore, sweetheart? what's your metaphor?
> *Twelfth Night* 1.3

wide-chopped *adj* big-mouthed
> This wide-chopped rascal *The Tempest* 1.1

wight *n* a person
> She was a wight, if ever such wight were *Othello* 2.1

wit *n* intelligence or wisdom
> thou didst conclude hairy men plain dealers,
> without wit *The Comedy of Errors* 2.2

wits *pl n* practical intelligence
> we that have good wits have much to answer for
> *As You Like It* 4.1

wont *v* to be in the habit of doing something regularly
> When were you wont to use my sister thus?
> *The Comedy of Errors* 2.2

wooer *n* a suitor, someone who is hoping to marry
> and of a foolish knight that you brought in one
> night here to be her wooer *Twelfth Night* 1.3

wot *v* to know or learn
> for well I wot
> Thou runnest before me
> *A Midsummer Night's Dream* 3.2

application of a physical force **telekinetic** *adj*

telemetry *n* the use of electronic devices to record or measure a distant event and transmit the data to a receiver **telemetric** *adj*

teleology *n* **1** *philosophy* the doctrine that there is evidence of purpose or design in the universe **2** *biol* the belief that natural phenomena have a predetermined purpose and are not determined by mechanical laws **teleological** *adj* **teleologist** *n* **WORD ORIGIN** Greek *telos* end + -LOGY

telepathy *n* the direct communication of thoughts and feelings between minds without the need to use normal means such as speech, writing, or touch **telepathic** *adj* **telepathically** *adv* **WORD ORIGIN** Greek *tele* far + *pathos* suffering

telephone *n* **1** a piece of equipment for transmitting speech, consisting of a microphone and receiver mounted on a handset: *the telephone was ringing* **2** the worldwide system of communications using telephones: *reports came in by telephone* ▷ *vb* **-phoning, -phoned 3** to call or talk to (a person) by telephone ▷ *adj* **4** of or using a telephone: *a telephone call* **telephonic** *adj* **WORD ORIGIN** Greek *tele* far + *phōnē* voice

telephone box *n* an enclosure from which a paid telephone call can be made

telephone directory *n* a book listing the names, addresses, and telephone numbers of subscribers in a particular area

telephonist *n* a person who operates a telephone switchboard

telephony *n* a system of telecommunications for the transmission of speech or other sounds

telephoto lens *n* a lens fitted to a camera to produce a magnified image of a distant object

teleprinter *n Brit* an apparatus, similar to a typewriter, by which typed messages are sent and received by wire

Teleprompter *n trademark* a device for displaying a script under a television camera, so that a speaker can read it while appearing to look at the camera

telesales *n* the selling of a commodity or service by telephone

telescope *n* **1** an optical instrument for making distant objects appear closer by use of a combination of lenses **2** see **radio telescope** ▷ *vb* **-scoping, -scoped 3** to shorten (something) while still keeping the important parts: *a hundred years of change has been telescoped into five years* **telescopic** *adj* **WORD ORIGIN** New Latin *telescopium* far-seeing instrument

telescopic sight *n* a sight on a rifle, etc. consisting of a telescope, used for aiming at distant objects

teletext *n* a Videotex service in which information is broadcast by a television station and received on a specially equipped television set

Teletext *n trademark* (in Britain) the ITV teletext service

Teletype *n trademark* a type of teleprinter

televangelist *n US* an evangelical preacher who appears regularly on television, preaching the gospel and appealing for donations from viewers **WORD ORIGIN** tele(vision) + (e)vangelist

televise *vb* **-vising, -vised** to show (a programme or event) on television

television *n* **1** the system or process of producing a moving image with accompanying sound on a distant screen **2** Also called: **television set** a device for receiving broadcast signals and converting them into sound and pictures **3** the content of television programmes: *some people think that television is too violent nowadays* ▷ *adj* **4** of or relating to television: *a television interview* **televisual** *adj*

teleworking *n* the use of home computers, telephones, etc. to enable a person to work from home while maintaining contact with colleagues or customers **teleworker** *n*

telex *n* **1** an international communication service which sends messages by teleprinter **2** a teleprinter used in such a service **3** a message sent by telex ▷ *vb* **4** to transmit (a message) by telex **WORD ORIGIN** tel(eprinter) ex(change)

tell *vb* **telling, told 1** to make known in words; notify: *I told her what had happened* **2** to order or instruct (someone to do something): *he had been told to wait in the lobby* **3** to give an account (of an event or situation): *the President had been told of the developments* **4** to communicate by words: *he was woken at 5 am to be told the news* **5** to discover, distinguish, or discern: *she could tell that he was not sorry* **6** to have or produce an impact or effect: *the pressure had begun to tell on him* **7** *informal* to reveal secrets or gossip **8 tell the time** to read the time from a clock **9 you're telling me** *slang* I know that very well **WORD ORIGIN** Old English *tellan*

tell apart *vb* to distinguish between: *they're different colours, otherwise how would you tell them apart?*

teller *n* **1** a narrator **2** a bank cashier **3** a person appointed to count votes

telling *adj* having a marked effect or impact: *to inflict telling damage on the enemy*

tell off *vb informal* to reprimand or scold (someone) **telling-off** *n*

telltale *n* **1** a person who tells tales about others ▷ *adj* **2** giving away information: *examining the hands for telltale signs of age*

tellurian *adj* of the earth **WORD ORIGIN** Latin *tellus* the earth

tellurium *n chem* a brittle silvery-white nonmetallic element. Symbol: Te **WORD ORIGIN** Latin *tellus* the earth

telly *n, pl* **-lies** *informal* short for **television**

telomere *n genetics* either of the ends of a chromosome **WORD ORIGIN** Greek *telos* end + *meros* part

temazepam (ti-**maz**-i-pam) *n* (*sometimes cap*) a sedative in the form of a gel-like capsule, which is taken orally or melted and injected by drug users

temerity (tim-**merr**-it-tee) *n* boldness or audacity **WORD ORIGIN** Latin *temere* at random

temp *Brit informal n* **1** a person, esp. a secretary, employed on a temporary basis ▷ *vb* **2** to work as a temp

temp. 1 temperature **2** temporary

temper *n* **1** a sudden outburst of anger: *she stormed out in a temper* **2** a tendency to have sudden outbursts of anger: *you've got a temper all right* **3** a mental condition of moderation and calm: *he lost his temper* **4** a person's frame of mind: *he was in a bad temper* ▷ *vb* **5** to modify so as to make less extreme or more acceptable: *past militancy has been tempered with compassion and caring* **6** to reduce the brittleness of (a hardened metal) by reheating it and allowing it to cool **7** *music* to adjust the frequency differences between the notes of a scale on (a keyboard instrument) **WORD ORIGIN** Latin *temperare* to mix

tempera *n* a painting medium for powdered pigments, consisting usually of egg yolk and water **WORD ORIGIN** Italian *temperare* to mingle

temperament *n* a person's character or disposition **WORD ORIGIN** Latin *temperamentum* a mixing

temperamental *adj* **1** (of a person) tending to be moody and have sudden outbursts of anger **2** *informal* working erratically and inconsistently; unreliable: *the temperamental microphone* **3** of or relating to a person's temperament: *we discussed temperamental and developmental differences* **temperamentally** *adv*

temperance *n* **1** restraint or moderation, esp. in yielding to one's appetites or desires **2** abstinence from alcoholic drink **WORD ORIGIN** Latin *temperare* to regulate

temperate *adj* **1** of a climate which is never extremely hot or extremely cold **2** mild or moderate in quality or character: *try to be more temperate in your statements* **WORD ORIGIN** Latin *temperatus*

Temperate Zone *n* those parts of the earth's surface lying between the Arctic Circle and the tropic of Cancer and between the Antarctic Circle and the tropic of Capricorn

temperature *n* **1** the hotness or coldness of something, as measured on a scale that has one or more fixed reference points **2** *informal* an abnormally high body temperature **3** the strength of feeling among a group of people: *his remarks are likely to raise the political temperature considerably* **WORD ORIGIN** Latin *temperatura* proportion

tempest *n literary* a violent wind or storm **WORD ORIGIN** Latin *tempestas*

tempestuous *adj* **1** violent or stormy **2** extremely emotional or passionate: *a tempestuous relationship* **tempestuously** *adv*

template *n* a wood or metal pattern, used to help cut out shapes accurately **WORD ORIGIN** from *temple* a part in a loom that keeps the cloth stretched

temple[1] *n* a building or place used for the worship of a god or gods **WORD ORIGIN** Latin *templum*

temple[2] *n* the region on each side of the head in front of the ear and above the cheek bone **WORD ORIGIN** Latin *tempus*

tempo (tem-po) *n, pl* **-pi** (-pee) *or* **-pos** **1** rate or pace: *the slow tempo of change in an overwhelmingly rural country* **2** the speed at which a piece of music is played or meant to be played **WORD ORIGIN** Italian

temporal[1] *adj* **1** of or relating to time **2** of secular as opposed to spiritual or religious affairs: *in the Middle Ages the Pope had temporal as well as spiritual power* **3** not permanent or eternal: *a temporal view of drugs as the No. 1 social problem* **WORD ORIGIN** Latin *tempus* time

temporal[2] *adj anat* of or near the temple or temples

temporal bone *n* either of two compound bones forming the sides of the skull

temporary *adj* lasting only for a short time; not permanent: *temporary accommodation* **temporarily** *adv* **WORD ORIGIN** Latin *temporarius*

temporize *or* **-rise** *vb* **-rizing, -rized** *or* **-rising, -rised** **1** to delay, act evasively, or protract a negotiation in order to gain time or avoid making a decision: *'Well,' I temporized, 'I'll have to ask your mother'* **2** to adapt oneself to circumstances, as by temporary or apparent agreement **WORD ORIGIN** Latin *tempus* time

tempt *vb* **1** to entice (someone) to do something, esp. something morally wrong or unwise: *can I tempt you to have another whisky?* **2** to allure or attract: *she was tempted by the glamour of a modelling career* **3** **be tempted** to want to do something while knowing it would be wrong or inappropriate to do so: *many youngsters are tempted to experiment with drugs* **4** **tempt fate** *or* **providence** to take foolish or unnecessary risks **tempter** *n* **temptress** *fem n* **WORD ORIGIN** Latin *temptare* to test

temptation *n* **1** the act of tempting or the state of being tempted **2** a person or thing that tempts

tempting *adj* attractive or inviting: *it's tempting to say I told you so* **temptingly** *adv*

ten *n* **1** the cardinal number that is the sum of one and nine **2** a numeral, 10 or X, representing this number **3** something representing or consisting of ten units ▷ *adj* **4** amounting to ten: *ten years* **tenth** *adj, n* **WORD ORIGIN** Old English *tēn*

tenable *adj* **1** able to be upheld or maintained: *a tenable strategy* **2** (of a job) intended to be held by a person for a particular length of time: *the post will be tenable for three years in the first instance* **tenability** *n* **tenably** *adv* **WORD ORIGIN** Latin *tenere* to hold

tenacious *adj* **1** holding firmly: *a tenacious grasp* **2** stubborn or persistent:

tenacious support **tenaciously** *adv* **tenacity** *n* **WORD ORIGIN** Latin *tenere* to hold

tenancy *n, pl* **-cies 1** the temporary possession or use of lands or property owned by somebody else, in return for payment **2** the period of holding or occupying such property

tenant *n* **1** a person who pays rent for the use of land or property **2** any holder or occupant **WORD ORIGIN** Old French: one who is holding

tenant farmer *n* a person who farms land rented from somebody else

tenantry *n old-fashioned* tenants collectively

tench *n* a European freshwater game fish of the carp family **WORD ORIGIN** Old French *tenche*

Ten Commandments *pl n Bible* the commandments given by God to Moses on Mount Sinai, summarizing the basic obligations of people towards God and their fellow humans

tend[1] *vb* to be inclined (to take a particular kind of action or to be in a particular condition) as a rule: *she tends to be rather absent-minded* **WORD ORIGIN** Latin *tendere* to stretch

tend[2] *vb* **1** to take care of: *it is she who tends his wounds* **2 tend to** to attend to: *excuse me, I have to tend to the other guests* **WORD ORIGIN** variant of *attend*

tendency *n, pl* **-cies 1** an inclination to act in a particular way **2** the general course or drift of something **3** a faction, esp. within a political party **WORD ORIGIN** Latin *tendere* to stretch

tendentious *adj* expressing a particular viewpoint or opinion, esp. a controversial one, in very strong terms: *a somewhat tendentious reading of French history* **tendentiously** *adv*

tender[1] *adj* **1** (of cooked food) having softened and become easy to chew or cut **2** gentle and kind: *tender loving care* **3** vulnerable or sensitive: *at the tender age of 9* **4** painful when touched: *his wrist was swollen and tender* **tenderly** *adv* **tenderness** *n* **WORD ORIGIN** Old French *tendre*

tender[2] *vb* **1** to present or offer: *he tendered his resignation* **2** to make a formal offer or estimate for a job or contract: *contractors tendering for government work* ▷ *n* **3** a formal offer to supply specified goods or services at a stated cost or rate: *the government invited tenders to run television and radio services* **tenderer** *n* **tendering** *n* **WORD ORIGIN** Latin *tendere* to extend

tender[3] *n* **1** a small boat that brings supplies to larger vessels in a port **2** a wagon attached to the rear of a steam locomotive that carries the fuel and water **WORD ORIGIN** variant of *attender*

tenderfoot *n, pl* **-foots** *or* **-feet** a newcomer to a particular activity

tenderize *or* **-rise** *vb* **-rizing, -rized** *or* **-rising, -rised** to make (meat) tender, by pounding it or adding a substance to break down the fibres **tenderizer** *or* **-riser** *n*

tenderloin *n* a tender cut of pork from between the sirloin and ribs

tendon *n* a band of tough tissue that attaches a muscle to a bone **WORD ORIGIN** Medieval Latin *tendo*

tendril *n* a threadlike leaf or stem by which a climbing plant attaches itself to a support **WORD ORIGIN** probably from Old French *tendron*

tenement *n* a large building divided into several different flats **WORD ORIGIN** Latin *tenere* to hold

tenet (ten-nit) *n* a principle on which a belief or doctrine is based **WORD ORIGIN** Latin, literally: he (it) holds

tenfold *adj* **1** having ten times as many or as much **2** composed of ten parts ▷ *adv* **3** by ten times as many or as much

ten-gallon hat *n* (in the US) a cowboy's broad-brimmed felt hat with a very high crown

tenner *n Brit, Austral, & NZ informal* **1** a ten-pound or ten-dollar note **2** the sum of ten pounds or ten dollars: *it's worth a tenner at least*

tennis *n* a game played between two players or pairs of players who use a racket to hit a ball to and fro over a net on a rectangular court ▷ See also **lawn tennis, real tennis, table tennis** **WORD ORIGIN** probably from Anglo-French *tenetz* hold!

tennis elbow *n* inflammation of the elbow, typically caused by exertion in playing tennis

tenon *n* a projecting end of a piece of wood, formed to fit into a corresponding slot in another piece **WORD ORIGIN** Old French

tenor *n* **1 a** the second highest male voice, between alto and baritone **b** a singer with such a voice **c** a saxophone, horn, or other musical instrument between the alto and baritone or bass **2** a general meaning or character: *it was clear from the tenor of the meeting that the chairman's actions were very unpopular* ▷ *adj* **3** denoting a musical instrument between alto and baritone: *a tenor saxophone* **4** of or relating to the second highest male voice: *his voice lacks the range needed for the tenor role* **WORD ORIGIN** Old French *tenour*

tenpin bowling *n* a game in which players try to knock over ten skittles by rolling a ball at them

tense[1] *adj* **1** having, showing, or causing mental or emotional strain: *the tense atmosphere* **2** stretched tight: *tense muscles* ▷ *vb* **tensing, tensed 3** Also: **tense up** to make or become tense **tensely** *adv* **tenseness** *n* **WORD ORIGIN** Latin *tensus* taut

tense[2] *n grammar* the form of a verb that indicates whether the action referred to in the sentence is located in the past, the present, or the future: *'ate' is the past tense of 'to eat'* **WORD ORIGIN** Old French *tens* time

tensile *adj* of or relating to tension or being stretched: *The posts were linked by high tensile wire.*

tensile strength n a measure of the ability of a material to withstand lengthwise stress, expressed as the greatest stress that the material can stand without breaking: *the addition of linseed oil improved the tensile strength of the cricket bat*

tension n **1** a situation or condition of hostility, suspense, or uneasiness: *a renewed state of tension between old enemies* **2** mental or emotional strain: *nervous tension* **3** a force that stretches or the state or degree of being stretched tight: *keep tension on the line until the fish comes within range of the net* **4** physics a force that tends to produce an elongation of a body or structure **5** physics voltage, electromotive force, or potential difference
WORD ORIGIN Latin *tensio*

tent n **1** a portable shelter made of canvas or other fabric supported on poles, stretched out, and fastened to the ground by pegs and ropes **2** see **oxygen tent**
WORD ORIGIN Old French *tente*

tentacle n **1** a flexible organ that grows near the mouth in many invertebrates and is used for feeding, grasping, etc. **2** **tentacles** the unseen methods by which an organization or idea, esp. a sinister one, influences people and events: *the tentacles of the secret police* **tentacled** adj
WORD ORIGIN Latin *tentare* to feel

tentative adj **1** provisional or unconfirmed: *a tentative agreement* **2** hesitant, uncertain, or cautious: *their rather tentative approach* **tentatively** adv **tentativeness** n
WORD ORIGIN Latin *tentare* to test

tenterhooks pl n **on tenterhooks** in a state of tension or suspense
WORD ORIGIN Latin *tentus* stretched + HOOK

tenth adj, n see **ten**

tenuous adj insignificant or flimsy: *there is only the most tenuous evidence for it* **tenuously** adv
WORD ORIGIN Latin *tenuis*

tenure n **1** the holding of an office or position **2** the length of time an office or position lasts **3** the holding of a teaching position at a university on a permanent basis **4** the legal right to live in a place or to use land or buildings for a period of time
WORD ORIGIN Latin *tenere* to hold

tepee or **teepee** (tee-pee) n a cone-shaped tent of animal skins, formerly used by American Indians
WORD ORIGIN Sioux *tîpî*

tepid adj **1** slightly warm **2** lacking enthusiasm: *tepid applause* **tepidity** n **tepidly** adv
WORD ORIGIN Latin *tepidus*

tequila n a Mexican alcoholic spirit distilled from the agave plant
WORD ORIGIN after *Tequila*, district in Mexico

tera- combining form denoting one million million (10^{12}): *terameter*
WORD ORIGIN Greek *teras* monster

teratology (terr-a-**tol**-a-jee) n the branch of medicine concerned with the development of physical abnormalities

during the fetal or early embryonic stage
WORD ORIGIN Greek *teras* monster + -LOGY

terbium n chem a soft silvery-grey element of the lanthanide series of metals. Symbol: Tb
WORD ORIGIN after *Ytterby*, Sweden, where discovered

tercentenary or **tercentennial** adj **1** marking a 300th anniversary ▷ n, pl -**tenaries** or -**tennials** **2** a 300th anniversary
WORD ORIGIN Latin *ter* three times + CENTENARY

teredo (ter-**ree**-doh) n, pl -**dos** or -**dines** (-din-eez) a marine mollusc that bores into and destroys submerged timber
WORD ORIGIN Greek *terēdōn* wood-boring worm

tergiversate (**tur**-jiv-verse-ate) vb -**sating, -sated** formal **1** to be evasive or ambiguous **2** to change sides or loyalties **tergiversation** n **tergiversator** n
WORD ORIGIN Latin *tergiversari* to turn one's back

term n **1** a word or expression, esp. one used in a specialized field of knowledge: *he coined the term 'inferiority complex'* **2** a period of time: *a four-year prison term* **3** one of the periods of the year when a school, university, or college is open or a lawcourt holds sessions **4** the period of pregnancy when childbirth is imminent **5** maths any distinct quantity making up a fraction or proportion, or contained in a sequence, series, etc. **6** logic any of the three subjects or predicates occurring in a syllogism **7** **full term** the end of a specific period of time: *the agony of carrying the child to full term* ▷ vb **8** to name, call, or describe as being: *social workers tend to be termed lefties* ▷ See also **terms**
WORD ORIGIN Latin *terminus* end

termagant n literary an unpleasant, aggressive, and overbearing woman
WORD ORIGIN earlier *Tervagaunt*, after an arrogant character in medieval mystery plays

terminable adj capable of being terminated: *his terminable interest in the property* **terminability** n

terminal adj **1** (of an illness) ending in death **2** situated at an end, terminus, or boundary: *the terminal joints of the fingers* **3** informal extreme or severe: *terminal boredom* ▷ n **4** a place where vehicles, passengers, or goods begin or end a journey: *the ferry terminal* **5** a point at which current enters or leaves an electrical device **6** computers a device, usually a keyboard and a visual display unit, having input/output links with a computer **terminally** adv
WORD ORIGIN Latin *terminus* end

terminal velocity n physics the maximum velocity reached by a body falling under gravity through a liquid or gas, esp. the atmosphere

terminate vb -**nating, -nated** **1** to bring or come to an end: *his flying career was terminated by this crash* **2** to put an end to (a pregnancy) by inducing an abortion **3** (of the route of a train, bus, etc.) to

stop at a particular place and not go any further: *this train terminates at Leicester* **termination** n
WORD ORIGIN Latin *terminare* to set boundaries

terminology n, pl -**gies** the specialized words and expressions relating to a particular subject **terminological** adj **terminologist** n

terminus (**term**-in-nuss) n, pl -**ni** (-nye) or -**nuses** the station or town at one end of a railway line or bus route: *Vienna's Westbahnhof is the terminus for trains to France*
WORD ORIGIN Latin: end

termite n a whitish antlike insect of warm and tropical regions that destroys timber
WORD ORIGIN New Latin *termites* white ants

terms pl n **1** the actual language or mode of presentation used: *the test is carried out in plain non-engineering terms* **2** the conditions of an agreement **3** mutual relationship or standing of a specified nature: *he is on first-name terms with many of the directors* **4** **come to terms with** to learn to accept (an unpleasant or difficult situation) **5** **in terms of** as expressed by; with regard to: *he is the best cricketer we have got in fact in terms of pure ability*

tern n a gull-like sea bird with a forked tail and long narrow wings
WORD ORIGIN Old Norse *therna*

ternary adj **1** consisting of three items or groups of three items **2** maths (of a number system) to the base three
WORD ORIGIN Latin *ternarius*

Terpsichore (turp-**sick**-or-ee) n Greek myth the Muse of dance

Terpsichorean (turp-sick-or-**ee**-an) adj often used facetiously of or relating to dancing
WORD ORIGIN from *Terpsichore*, the Muse of dance in Greek mythology

Terr. **1** terrace **2** territory

terrace n **1** a row of houses, usually identical and joined together by common dividing walls, or the street onto which they face **2** a paved area alongside a building **3** a horizontal flat area of ground, often one of a series in a slope **4** **the terraces** or **terracing** Brit & NZ a tiered area in a stadium where spectators stand ▷ vb -**racing, -raced** **5** to make into terraces
WORD ORIGIN Latin *terra* earth

terraced house n Brit a house that is part of a terrace

terracotta n **1** a hard unglazed brownish-red earthenware used for pottery ▷ adj **2** made of terracotta **3** brownish-orange
WORD ORIGIN Italian, literally: baked earth

terra firma n the ground, as opposed to the sea
WORD ORIGIN Latin

terraforming n planetary engineering designed to enhance the capacity of an extraterrestrial planetary environment to sustain life
WORD ORIGIN Latin *terra* earth

terrain n an area of ground, esp. with reference to its physical character: *mountainous terrain*
WORD ORIGIN Latin *terra* earth

Canadian Versus American English

The Canada-US boundary used to be called 'the longest undefended border in the world'. Amid American concerns about homeland security in the aftermath of the terrorist attacks of September 11, 2001, the border was no longer quite so undefended.

Fortunately, words do not require passports to cross borders. Many entries in *The Dictionary of American Regional English* show that Canadians and Americans share a great many words. General dictionaries often throw up their hands at trying to distinguish them, and simply apply the label *North American*. Somewhat to Canadians' annoyance, the British tend to lump together Canada and the United States and call it *America*. To Canadians, America is the United States.

The global reach of American commerce, technology, and culture, befitting the most powerful country in the world, means that Canadians, like everyone else, will adopt many words originating in the United States. But a huge land mass ensured that Canadians came up with some words of their own; history ensured that Canadian English was a hybrid of British, American, and even French spellings, pronunciations, and usages.

Canadians generally retain the British *u* in *colour* and *honour* (American *color, honor*) and the *re* in *centre* and *theatre* (American *center, theater*), but write *tire* and *curb* (British *tyre* and *kerb*). They favour American *-ize, -yze*, not British *-ise, -yse*, endings in words like *analyze* (British *analyse*). They almost never use the American *check* for *cheque*, or *maneuver* for *manoeuvre*. Like the British, Canadians usually double the *l* and other consonants at the end of words when adding suffixes, for example, *modelling* and *traveller*, though *benefited* is one exception. Likewise, Canadians prefer the British *-ce* endings in nouns like *defence* and *offence*. They are likely to choose the British *axe, catalogue, fulfil, grey* (not American *gray*), and *woollen*.

Apart from spelling variants, entirely different words may be used across the Atlantic. Canadians and Americans get their medical prescriptions filled by *pharmacists*, the British by *chemists*. A Canadian-made car will have a *hood* and *trunk*, not a *bonnet* and *boot*. A *sidewalk* in Canada and the United States is a *pavement* in Britain. But Canadians munch *chocolate bars*, not American *candy bars*. Canadian students *write* exams, Americans *take* them, and the British *sit* them.

When British and other foreign English-speakers say that Canadians sound like Americans and talk like some residents of California and upstate New York, or notice that Canadian actors and broadcasters make an easy transition to Hollywood and US television networks, they are really saying that urban, educated Canadians broadly use one of many American accents. It is not the speech of Maine, Massachusetts, Brooklyn, or the Bronx. Still less is it a Southern drawl, a Western twang, or one of the many varieties of English spoken by African or Hispanic Americans. It is close to the standard American speech in which the *r* in words like *motor* and *father* is pronounced, *schedule* sounds like *skedule*, and *butter* sounds like *budder.* On the other hand, Canadians make *houses* sound somewhat like *howses*, not the American *hawses*.

Canadians, like Americans, play *soccer*, not *football*, reserving the latter for the game that evolved from rugby. *Canadian football*, however, differs somewhat from the American variety: the action takes place on a wider field, and the two teams have 12, not 11, players, who must gain at least 10 yards in three, not four, downs. Some words and usages in sports indicate Canadian cultural differences without being themselves Canadianisms, such as *ringette*, a hockey-like game played with a straight stick and a rubber ring, or *boxla*, box lacrosse. Terms or phrases peculiar to ice hockey, like *deke*, to deceive an opponent player with a fake shot or movement, or *rag the puck*, to waste time intentionally by controlling the puck, aren't Canadianisms, yet are used much more frequently in Canada than in the United States because hockey has the status of a national sport. For all their great popularity, American baseball, football, and basketball don't occupy the same role.

Subtleties abound. Canadians who order *brown toast* for breakfast may puzzle American restaurant servers. (Isn't toast always brown?) The Canadian breakfasters mean *wholewheat* (British *wholemeal*) toast. Another item on the US breakfast table, *Canadian bacon* (Canadian *back bacon*), is in fact an Americanism.

terra incognita (**terr**-a in-**kog**-nit-a) *n* an unexplored region
WORD ORIGIN Latin

terrapin *n* a small turtle-like reptile of N America that lives in fresh water and on land
WORD ORIGIN from a Native American language

terrarium *n* **1** an enclosed area or container where small land animals are kept **2** a glass container in which plants are grown
WORD ORIGIN Latin *terra* earth

terrazzo *n*, *pl* **-zos** a floor made by setting marble chips into a layer of mortar and polishing the surface
WORD ORIGIN Italian: terrace

terrestrial *adj* **1** of the planet earth **2** of the land as opposed to the sea or air **3** (of animals and plants) living or growing on the land **4** *television* denoting or using a signal sent over land from a transmitter on land, rather than by satellite
WORD ORIGIN Latin *terra* earth

terrible *adj* **1** very serious or extreme: *war is a terrible thing* **2** *informal* very bad, unpleasant, or unsatisfactory: *terrible books* **3** causing fear **terribly** *adv*
WORD ORIGIN Latin *terribilis*

terrier *n* any of several small active breeds of dog, originally trained to hunt animals living underground
WORD ORIGIN Old French *chien terrier* earth dog

terrific *adj* **1** very great or intense: *a terrific blow on the head* **2** *informal* very good; excellent: *a terrific book* **terrifically** *adv*
WORD ORIGIN Latin *terrere* to frighten

terrify *vb* **-fies, -fying, -fied** to frighten greatly **terrified** *adj* **terrifying** *adj* **terrifyingly** *adv*
WORD ORIGIN Latin *terrificare*

terrine (terr-**reen**) *n* **1** an oval earthenware cooking dish with a tightly fitting lid **2** the food cooked or served in such a dish, esp. pâté
WORD ORIGIN earlier form of *tureen*

territorial *adj* **1** of or relating to a territory or territories **2** of or concerned with the ownership and control of an area of land or water: *a territorial dispute* **3** (of an animal or bird) establishing and defending an area which it will not let other animals or birds into: *the baboon is a territorial species* **4** of or relating to a territorial army **territorially** *adv* **territoriality** *n*

Territorial *n* a member of a Territorial Army

Territorial Army *n* (in Britain) a reserve army whose members are not full-time soldiers but undergo military training in their spare time so that they can be called upon in an emergency

territorial waters *pl n* the part of the sea near to a country's coast, which is under the control of the government of that country

territory *n*, *pl* **-ries 1** any tract of land; district: *mountainous territory* **2** the geographical area under the control of a particular government: *the islands are Japanese territory* **3** an area inhabited and defended by a particular animal or pair of animals **4** an area of knowledge or experience: *all this is familiar territory to readers of her recent novels* **5** a country or region under the control of a foreign country: *a French Overseas Territory* **6** a region of a country, esp. of a federal state, that enjoys less autonomy and a lower status than most constituent parts of the state
WORD ORIGIN Latin *territorium* land surrounding a town

terror *n* **1** very great fear, panic, or dread **2** a person or thing that inspires great dread **3** *Brit, Austral, & NZ informal* a troublesome person, esp. a child
WORD ORIGIN Latin

terrorism *n* the systematic use of violence and intimidation to achieve political ends **terrorist** *n*, *adj*

terrorize or **-rise** *vb* **-rizing, -rized** or **-rising, -rised 1** to control or force (someone) to do something by violence, fear, threats, etc.: *he was terrorized into withdrawing his accusations* **2** to make (someone) very frightened **terrorization** or **-risation** *n* **terrorizer** or **-riser** *n*

terry *n* a fabric covered on both sides with small uncut loops, used for towelling and nappies
WORD ORIGIN origin unknown

terse *adj* **1** neatly brief and concise **2** curt or abrupt **tersely** *adv* **terseness** *n*
WORD ORIGIN Latin *tersus* precise

tertiary (**tur**-shar-ee) *adj* **1** third in degree, order, etc. **2** (of education) at university or college level **3** (of an industry) involving services, such as transport and financial services, as opposed to manufacture
WORD ORIGIN Latin *tertius*

Tertiary *adj geol* of the period of geological time lasting from about 65 million years ago to 600 000 years ago

Terylene *n trademark* a synthetic polyester fibre or fabric

TESL Teaching of English as a Second Language

tessellated *adj* paved or inlaid with a mosaic of small tiles
WORD ORIGIN Latin *tessellatus* checked

tessera *n*, *pl* **-serae** a small square tile used in mosaics
WORD ORIGIN Latin

test¹ *vb* **1** to try (something) out to ascertain its worth, safety, or endurance: *the company has never tested its products on animals* **2** to carry out an examination on (a substance, material, or system) in order to discover whether a particular substance, component, or feature is present: *baby foods are regularly tested for pesticides* **3** to put under severe strain: *the long delay tested my patience* **4** to achieve a result in a test which indicates the presence or absence of something: *he tested positive for cocaine* ▷ *n* **5** a method, practice, or examination designed to test a person or thing **6** a series of questions or problems designed to test a specific skill or knowledge: *a spelling test* **7** a chemical reaction or physical procedure for testing the composition or other qualities of a substance **8** *sport* short for **Test match 9 put to the test** to use (something) in order to gauge its usefulness or effectiveness **testable** *adj* **testing** *adj*
WORD ORIGIN Latin *testum* earthen vessel

test² *n* the hard outer covering of certain invertebrates
WORD ORIGIN Latin *testa* shell

testa (**tess**-ta) *n*, *pl* **-tae** (-tee) the hard outer layer of a seed
WORD ORIGIN Latin: shell

testaceous (test-**ay**-shuss) *adj biol* of or having a hard continuous shell
WORD ORIGIN Latin *testacens*, from TESTA

testament *n* **1** something which provides proof of a fact about someone or something: *the size of the audience was an immediate testament to his appeal* **2** *law* a formal statement of how a person wants his or her property to be disposed of after his or her death: *last will and testament* **testamentary** *adj*
WORD ORIGIN Latin *testis* a witness

Testament *n* either of the two main parts of the Bible, the Old Testament or the New Testament

testate *law adj* **1** having left a legally valid will at death ▷ *n* **2** a person who dies and leaves a legally valid will **testacy** *n*
WORD ORIGIN Latin *testari* to make a will

testator (test-**tay**-tor) *or fem* **testatrix** (test-**tay**-triks) *n law* a person who has made a will, esp. one who has died testate

test card *n* a complex pattern used to test the characteristics of a television transmission system

test case *n* a legal action that serves as a precedent in deciding similar succeeding cases

testicle *n* either of the two male reproductive glands, in most mammals enclosed within the scrotum, that produce spermatozoa
WORD ORIGIN Latin *testis* a witness (to masculinity)

testify *vb* **-fies, -fying, -fied 1** *law* to declare or give evidence under oath, esp. in court **2 testify to** to be evidence of: *a piece of paper testifying to their educational qualifications*
WORD ORIGIN Latin *testis* witness

testimonial *n* **1** a recommendation of the character or worth of a person or thing **2** a tribute given for services or achievements ▷ *adj* **3** of a testimony or testimonial: *a testimonial match*

≣ **USAGE**
≣ Testimonial is sometimes wrongly used
≣ where *testimony* is meant: *his re-election*
≣ *is a testimony* (not *a testimonial*) *to his*
≣ *popularity with his constituents.*

testimony *n*, *pl* **-nies 1** a declaration of truth or fact **2** *law* evidence given by a witness, esp. in court under oath **3** evidence proving or supporting something: *that they are still talking is a testimony to their 20-year friendship*
WORD ORIGIN Latin *testimonium*

testis *n*, *pl* **-tes** same as **testicle**

Test match *n* (in various sports, esp. cricket) an international match, esp. one of a series

testosterone *n* a steroid male sex hormone secreted by the testes

test paper *n* **1** the question sheet of a test **2** *chem* paper impregnated with an indicator for use in chemical tests

test pilot *n* a pilot who flies aircraft of new design to test their performance in the air

test tube *n* a cylindrical round-bottomed glass tube open at one end, which is used in scientific experiments

test-tube baby *n* **1** a fetus that has developed from an ovum fertilized in an artificial womb **2** a baby conceived by artificial insemination

testy *adj* **-tier, -tiest** irritable or touchy **testily** *adv* **testiness** *n*
WORD ORIGIN Anglo-Norman *testif* headstrong

tetanus *n* an acute infectious disease in which toxins released from a bacterium cause muscular spasms and convulsions
WORD ORIGIN Greek *tetanos*

tetchy *adj* **tetchier, tetchiest** cross, irritable, or touchy **tetchily** *adv* **tetchiness** *n*
WORD ORIGIN probably from obsolete *tetch* defect

tête-à-tête *n, pl* **-têtes** *or* **-tête 1** a private conversation between two people ▷ *adv* **2** together in private: *they dined tête-à-tête*
WORD ORIGIN French, literally: head to head

tether *n* **1** a rope or chain for tying an animal to a fence, post, etc. so that it cannot move away from a particular place **2 at the end of one's tether** at the limit of one's patience or endurance ▷ *vb* **3** to tie with a tether
WORD ORIGIN Old Norse *tjōthr*

tetra- *combining form* four: *tetrapod*

tetrad *n* a group or series of four
WORD ORIGIN Greek *tetras*

tetraethyl lead *n* a colourless oily insoluble liquid used in petrol to prevent knocking

tetragon *n* a shape with four angles and four sides **tetragonal** *adj*
WORD ORIGIN Greek *tetragōnon*

tetrahedron (tet-ra-**heed**-ron) *n, pl* **-drons** *or* **-dra** a solid figure with four triangular plane faces **tetrahedral** *adj*
WORD ORIGIN Late Greek *tetraedron*

tetralogy *n, pl* **-gies** a series of four related books, dramas, operas, etc.
WORD ORIGIN Greek *tetralogia*

tetrameter (tet-**tram**-it-er) *n* **1** *prosody* a line of verse consisting of four metrical feet **2** verse consisting of such lines
WORD ORIGIN Greek *tetra-* four + METER

Teuton (**tew**-tun) *n* **1** a member of an ancient Germanic people of N Europe **2** a member of any people speaking a Germanic language, esp. a German ▷ *adj* **3** Teutonic
WORD ORIGIN Latin *Teutoni* the Teutons

Teutonic (tew-**tonn**-ik) *adj* **1** characteristic of or relating to the Germans **2** of the ancient Teutons

Tex-Mex *adj* **1** combining elements of Texan and Mexican culture ▷ *n* **2** Tex-Mex music or cooking

text *n* **1** the main body of a printed or written work as distinct from items such as notes or illustrations **2** any written material, such as words displayed on a visual display unit **3** the written version of the words of a speech, broadcast or recording: *an advance text of the remarks the president will deliver tonight* **4** a short passage of the Bible used as a starting point for a sermon **5** a book required as part of a course of study: *shelves full of sociology texts* ▷ *vb* **6** to send (a text message) by mobile phone **7** to contact (a person) by means of a text message
WORD ORIGIN Latin *texere* to compose, weave

textbook *n* **1** a book of facts about a subject used by someone who is studying that subject ▷ *adj* **2** perfect or exemplary: *a textbook example of an emergency descent*

textile *n* **1** any fabric or cloth, esp. a woven one ▷ *adj* **2** of or relating to fabrics or their production: *the world textile market*
WORD ORIGIN Latin *textilis* woven

text message *n* **1** a message sent in text form, esp. by means of a mobile phone **2** a message appearing on a computer screen **text messaging** *n*

textual *adj* of, based on, or relating to, a text or texts **textually** *adv*

texture *n* **1** the structure, appearance, and feel of a substance: *curtains of many textures and colours* **2** the overall sound of a piece of music, resulting from the way the different instrumental parts in it are combined: *a big orchestra weaving rich textures* ▷ *vb* **-turing, -tured 3** to give a distinctive texture to (something) **textural** *adj*
WORD ORIGIN Latin *texere* to weave

TGV *n* (in France) a high-speed passenger train
WORD ORIGIN French *train à grande vitesse*

TGWU (in Britain) Transport and General Workers Union

Th *chem* thorium

Thai *adj* **1** of Thailand ▷ *n* **2** *pl* **Thais** *or* **Thai** a person from Thailand **3** the main language of Thailand

Thalia *n Greek myth* the Muse of comedy

thalidomide (thal-**lid**-oh-mide) *n* a drug formerly used as a sedative and hypnotic but withdrawn from use when found to cause abnormalities in developing fetuses
WORD ORIGIN *thali(mi)do(glutari)mide*

thallium *n chem* a soft highly toxic white metallic element. Symbol: Tl
WORD ORIGIN Greek *thallos* a green shoot; from the green line in its spectrum

than *conj, prep* **1** used to introduce the second element of a comparison, the first element of which expresses difference: *men are less observant than women and children* **2** used to state a number, quantity, or value in approximate terms by contrasting it with another number, quantity, or value: *temperatures lower than 25 degrees* **3** used after the adverbs *rather* and *sooner* to introduce a rejected alternative: *fruit is examined by hand, rather than by machine*

WORD ORIGIN Old English *thanne*

USAGE
In formal English, *than* is regarded as a conjunction governing an unexpressed verb: *he does it far better than I (do)*. The case of any pronoun depends on whether it is the subject or object of the unexpressed verb: *she likes him more than I (like him); she likes him more than (she likes) me*. However in ordinary speech and writing *than* is often treated as a preposition followed by the object form of a pronoun: *my brother is younger than me*.

thane *n* **1** (in Anglo-Saxon England) a nobleman who held land from the king or from a superior nobleman in return for certain services **2** (in medieval Scotland) a person of rank holding land from the king
WORD ORIGIN Old English *thegn*

thank *vb* **1** to convey feelings of gratitude to: *he thanked the nursing staff for saving his life* **2** to hold responsible: *he has his father to thank for his familiarity with the film world* **3 thank you** a polite response or expression of gratitude **4 thank goodness** *or* **thank heavens** *or* **thank God** an exclamation of relief
WORD ORIGIN Old English *thancian*

thankful *adj* grateful and appreciative **thankfully** *adv*

thankless *adj* unrewarding or unappreciated: *she took on the thankless task of organizing the office Xmas lunch* **thanklessly** *adv* **thanklessness** *n*

thanks *pl n* **1** an expression of appreciation or gratitude **2 thanks to** because of: *the birth went very smoothly, thanks to the help of the GHQ medical officer* ▷ *interj* **3** *informal* an exclamation expressing gratitude

thanksgiving *n* a formal public expression of thanks to God

Thanksgiving Day *n* (in North America) an annual holiday celebrated on the fourth Thursday of November in the United States and on the second Monday of October in Canada

that *adj* **1** used preceding a noun that has been mentioned or is already familiar: *he'd have to give up on that idea* **2** used preceding a noun that denotes something more remote: *that book on the top shelf* ▷ *pron* **3** used to denote something already mentioned or understood: *that's right* **4** used to denote a more remote person or thing: *is that him over there?* **5** used to introduce a restrictive relative clause: *a problem that has to be overcome* **6 and all that** *or* **and that** *informal* and similar or related things: *import cutting and all that* **7 that is a** to be precise **b** in other words **8 that's that** there is no more to be said or done ▷ *conj* **9** used to introduce a noun clause: *he denied that the country was suffering from famine* **10** used, usually after *so*, to introduce a clause of purpose: *he turns his face away from her so that she shall not see his tears* **11** used to introduce a clause of result: *a scene so sickening and horrible that it is impossible to describe it* ▷ *adv* **12** Also: **all that** *informal* very or particularly: *the fines imposed have not been that large*
WORD ORIGIN Old English *thæt*

USAGE
Precise writers maintain a distinction between *that* and *which*: *that* is used as a relative pronoun in restrictive clauses and *which* in nonrestrictive clauses. In *the book that is on the table is mine*, the clause *that is on the table* is used to distinguish one particular book (the one on the table) from another or others (which may be anywhere, but not on the table). In *the book, which is on the table, is mine*, the *which* clause is merely descriptive or incidental. The more formal the level of language, the more important it is to preserve the distinction between the two relative pronouns; but in informal or colloquial usage, the words are often used interchangeably.

thatch *n* **1** Also called: **thatching** a roofing material that consists of straw or reeds **2** a roof made of such a material **3** a mass of thick untidy hair on someone's head ▷ *vb* **4** to cover with thatch **thatched** *adj* **thatcher** *n*
WORD ORIGIN Old English *theccan* to cover

thaw *vb* **1** to melt or cause to melt: *snow thawing in the gutter* **2** (of frozen food) to become or cause to become unfrozen; defrost **3** (of weather) to be warm enough to cause ice or snow to melt: *it's not freezing, it's thawing again* **4** to become more relaxed or friendly: *only with Llewelyn did he thaw, let his defences down* ▷ *n* **5** the act or process of thawing **6** a spell of relatively warm weather, causing snow or ice to melt
WORD ORIGIN Old English *thawian*

THC tetrahydrocannabinol: the active ingredient in cannabis which gives it its narcotic effect

the[1] *adj (definite article)* **1** used preceding a noun that has been previously specified or is a matter of common knowledge: *those involved in the search* **2** used to indicate a particular person or object: *the man called Frank turned to look at it* **3** used preceding certain nouns associated with one's culture, society, or community: *to comply with the law* **4** used preceding an adjective that is functioning as a collective noun: *the unemployed* **5** used preceding titles and certain proper nouns: *the Middle East* **6** used preceding an adjective or noun in certain names or titles: *Alexander the Great* **7** used preceding a noun to make it refer to its class as a whole: *cultivation of the coca plant* **8** used instead of *my, your, her*, etc. with parts of the body: *swelling of tissues in the brain* **9** the best or most remarkable: *it's THE place in town for good Mexican food*
WORD ORIGIN Old English *thē*

the[2] *adv* used in front of each of two things which are being compared to show how they increase or decrease in relation to each other: *the smaller the baby, the lower its chances of survival*
WORD ORIGIN Old English *thē, thȳ*

theatre *or US* **theater** *n* **1** a building designed for the performance of plays, operas, etc. **2** a large room or hall with tiered seats for an audience: *a lecture theatre* **3** a room in a hospital equipped for surgical operations **4** the theatre drama and acting in general **5** a region in which a war or conflict takes place: *a potential theatre of war close to Russian borders* **6** *US, Austral, & NZ* same as **cinema** (sense 1)
WORD ORIGIN Greek *theatron*

theatrical *adj* **1** of or relating to the theatre or dramatic performances **2** exaggerated and affected in manner or behaviour **theatricality** *n* **theatrically** *adv*

theatricals *pl n* dramatic performances, esp. as given by amateurs

thee *pron old-fashioned* the objective form of **thou**[1]

theft *n* **1** the act or an instance of stealing: *he reported the theft of his passport* **2** the crime of stealing: *he had a number of convictions for theft*
WORD ORIGIN Old English *thēofth*

their *adj* of or associated with them: *owning their own land; two girls on their way to school*
WORD ORIGIN Old Norse *theira*

USAGE
See at **they**.

theirs *pron* **1** something or someone belonging to or associated with them: *it was his fault, not theirs* **2** **of theirs** belonging to them

theism (**thee**-iz-zum) *n* **1** belief in one God as the creator of everything in the universe **2** belief in the existence of a God or gods **theist** *n, adj* **theistic** *adj*
WORD ORIGIN Greek *theos* god

them *pron (objective)* refers to things or people other than the speaker or people addressed: *I want you to give this to them*
WORD ORIGIN Old English *thǣm*

USAGE
See at **me, they**.

theme *n* **1** the main idea or topic in a discussion or lecture **2** (in literature, music, or art) an idea, image, or motif, repeated or developed throughout a work or throughout an artist's career **3** *music* a group of notes forming a recognizable melodic unit, used as the basis of part or all of a composition **4** a short essay, esp. one set as an exercise for a student **thematic** *adj* **thematically** *adv*
WORD ORIGIN Greek *thema*

theme park *n* an area planned as a leisure attraction in which all the displays and activities are based on a particular theme, story, or idea: *a Wild West theme park*

theme tune *or* **theme song** *n* a tune or song used to introduce or identify a television or radio programme or performer

themselves *pron* **1 a** the reflexive form of *they* or *them*: *two men barricaded themselves into a cell* **b** used for emphasis: *among the targets were police officers themselves* **2** their normal or usual selves: *they don't seem themselves these days*

then *adv* **1** at that time: *he was then at the height of his sporting career* **2** after that: *let's eat first and then we can explore the town* **3** in that case: *then why did he work for you?* ▷ *pron* **4** that time: *since then the list of grievances has steadily grown* ▷ *adj* **5** existing or functioning at that time: *the then Defence Minister*

WORD ORIGIN Old English *thænne, thanne*

thence *adv formal* **1** from that place: *the train went south into Switzerland, and thence on to Italy* **2** for that reason; therefore
WORD ORIGIN Middle English *thannes*

thenceforth *or* **thenceforward** *adv formal* from that time on

theocracy *n, pl* **-cies 1** government by a god or by priests **2** a community under such government **theocrat** *n* **theocratic** *adj* **theocratically** *adv*
WORD ORIGIN Greek *theos* god + *kratos* power

theodolite (thee-**odd**-oh-lite) *n* an instrument used in surveying for measuring horizontal and vertical angles
WORD ORIGIN origin unknown

theologian *n* a person versed in the study of theology

theology *n, pl* **-gies 1** the systematic study of religions and religious beliefs **2** a specific system, form, or branch of this study: *Muslim theology* **theological** *adj* **theologically** *adv*
WORD ORIGIN Greek *theos* god + -LOGY

theorem *n* a proposition, esp. in maths, that can be proved by reasoning from the basic principles of a subject
WORD ORIGIN Greek *theōrein* to view

theoretical *or* **theoretic** *adj* **1** based on or concerned with the ideas and abstract principles relating to a particular subject rather than its practical uses: *theoretical physics* **2** existing in theory but perhaps not in reality: *the secret service is under the theoretical control of the government* **theoretically** *adv*

theoretician *n* a person who develops or studies the theory of a subject rather than its practical aspects

theorize *or* **-rise** *vb* **-rizing, -rized** *or* **-rising, -rised** to produce or use theories; speculate **theorist** *n*

theory *n, pl* **-ries 1** a set of ideas, based on evidence and careful reasoning, which offers an explanation of how something works or why something happens, but has not been completely proved: *the theory of cosmology* **2** the ideas and abstract knowledge relating to something: *political theory* **3** an idea or opinion: *it's only a theory, admittedly, but I think it's worth pursuing* **4 in theory** in an ideal or hypothetical situation: *in theory, the tax is supposed to limit inflation*
WORD ORIGIN Greek *theōria* a sight

theosophy *n* a religious or philosophical system claiming to be based on an intuitive insight into the divine nature **theosophical** *adj* **theosophist** *n*
WORD ORIGIN Greek *theos* god + *sophia* wisdom

therapeutic (ther-rap-**pew**-tik) *adj* of or relating to the treatment and cure of disease **therapeutically** *adv*
WORD ORIGIN Greek *therapeuein* to minister to

therapeutics *n* the branch of medicine concerned with the treatment of disease

therapy *n, pl* **-pies** the treatment of physical, mental, or social disorders or disease **therapist** *n*

The Language of Mobile Phones

Ernie Wise is best known for his comic partnership with Eric Morecambe but he also played a small but important role in the history of one of the modern world's most important new technologies by making Britain's first call by mobile phone on the 1st of January 1985. Despite Ernie's PR involvement, mobile telephony was slow to take off. Handsets were pricey (they cost several months' wages), battery life was short, and calling expensive, leading many people to regard the heavy and brick-sized mobile phone as a 'yuppie status symbol'.

By the late 1990s, however, the technology behind the new gadgets had become much cheaper and mobile phone sales rocketed not only in Britain but throughout the world. People found that it was 'good to talk' (as one phone company advertising slogan memorably claimed) and suddenly mobile phones were ubiquitous and people found that they couldn't live without them.

Such dependency can bring problems, however, and fear of being without one's mobile or being in a *dead zone* without a signal has been dubbed *nomophobia* (from 'no mo(bile) phobia'). The urge to grab one's mobile when hearing a ringtone on TV or at the cinema has been called *ringxiety* and some people have even been known to experience *phantom vibrations* when they erroneously imagine that their handset is buzzing. If some people can't live without their phones, others wish they hadn't been invented at all. Such sensitive souls flee from noisy conversations on cell phones – or *yell phones* – and are often found in the *quiet carriage* of trains (a feature of rail travel unknown in the pre-mobile era) hoping not to be disturbed by annoying ringtones, whether it be the Crazy Frog or the Ride of the Valkyries.

Not all mobile users are anti-social, however, and the majority can happily use their handsets quietly, choosing instead to communicate with *text messages* by *SMS* (short message service). The first text message was sent in 1992 and since then hundreds of billions have been exchanged across the ether in a strange new abbreviated language called *text speak* or *textese* (or even *txtspk*). The latter name gives the strongest clue as to the nature of the new language, being an example of the kind of *disemvowelled* word that makes up the lexicon of text speak. The tiny keypad of a mobile phone can't be typed in the manner of a computer keyboard and messages instead have to be keyed by thumb. This led the early adopters of SMS in Japan to be nicknamed the *thumb tribe* and it has also resulted in such medical ailments as *Blackberry thumb*, a painful feeling in the thumbs caused by excessive thumbing of a mobile phone keypad, especially a Blackberry (which is a type of *smart phone* that has so many applications – *apps* – that some users have become addicted).

Keying by thumb, as sufferers from Blackberry thumb might attest, is more time-consuming than standard typing and so methods have evolved for keeping the number of characters in a message to a manageable level. Words have had their vowels removed – *keyboard* becomes *kbrd*; phrases have become reduced to abbreviations – *by the way* becomes *btw*; numerals have replaced entire words or syllables – *to* becomes 2 and *great* becomes *gr8*; and expressions of emotion are conveyed by *emoticons* or *smileys* – where happiness is :-) and sadness is :-(. Keying mistakes are known as *thumbos* rather than typos and it seems that no message is complete without an abbreviated description of the sender's disposition: *lol* (laughing out loud) and *rofl* (rolling on the floor laughing) being two of the most common.

Mobile phones have certainly made communication simple and cheap, but they have also changed the way we entertain ourselves. TV talent shows are based upon voting by text message, people can watch *mobisodes* of a favourite show on their handset, and a group of people can be summoned together briefly in a *flash mob* to do something silly in a public space. The flash mob also has a more serious cousin – the *smart mob* – where people get together and campaign against or even topple an unpopular government. For this reason, surely, mobile phones can be considered a force for good, despite the occasional annoying ringtone.

WORD ORIGIN Greek *therapeia* attendance

there *adv* **1** in, at, or to that place or position: *he won't be there* **2** in that respect: *you're right there* **3 there and then** immediately and without delay: *he walked out there and then* ▷ *adj* **4 not all there** *informal* mentally defective or silly ▷ *pron* **5** that place: *to return from there* **6** used as a grammatical subject when the true subject follows the verb, esp. the verb 'to be': *there are no children in the house* **7 so there!** an exclamation, used esp. by children, that usually follows a declaration of refusal or defiance: *you can't come, so there!* **8 there you are** or **go a** an expression used when handing a person something **b** an exclamation of satisfaction or vindication ▷ *interj* **9** an expression of sympathy, for example when consoling a child: *there, there, pet!*
WORD ORIGIN Old English *thær*

USAGE
In correct usage, the verb should agree with the number of the subject in such constructions as *there is a man waiting* and *there are several people waiting*. However, where the subject is compound, it is common in speech to use the singular as in *there's a police car and an ambulance outside*.

thereabouts *or US* **thereabout** *adv* near that place, time, amount, etc.: *meet me at three o'clock or thereabouts; Methuselah lived 900 years or thereabouts*

thereafter *adv formal* from that time onwards

thereby *adv formal* by that means or consequently

therefore *adv* for that reason: *the training is long, and therefore expensive*

therein *adv formal* in or into that place or thing

thereof *adv formal* of or concerning that or it

thereto *adv formal* **1** to that or it **2** Also: **thereunto** in addition to that

thereupon *adv formal* immediately after that; at that point

therm *n Brit* a unit of heat equal to 1.055 056 × 10⁸ joules
WORD ORIGIN Greek *thermē* heat

thermal *adj* **1** of, caused by, or generating heat **2** hot or warm: *thermal springs* **3** (of garments) specially made so as to have exceptional heat-retaining qualities: *thermal underwear* ▷ *n* **4** a column of rising air caused by uneven heating of the land surface, and used by gliders and birds to gain height

thermionic valve *or esp. US & Canad* **thermionic tube** *n* an electronic valve in which electrons are emitted from a heated rather than a cold cathode

thermistor (therm-**mist**-or) *n physics* a metal-oxide rod whose resistance falls as temperature rises, used in electronic circuits and as a thermometer

thermocouple *n* a device for measuring temperature, consisting of a pair of wires of different metals joined at both ends

thermodynamics *n* the branch of physical science concerned with the

relationship between heat and other forms of energy

thermoelectric *or* **thermoelectrical** *adj* of or relating to the conversion of heat energy to electrical energy

thermometer *n* an instrument used to measure temperature, esp. one in which a thin column of liquid, such as mercury, expands and contracts within a sealed tube marked with a temperature scale

thermonuclear *adj* **1** (of a nuclear reaction) involving a nuclear fusion reaction of a type which occurs at very high temperatures **2** (of a weapon) giving off energy as the result of a thermonuclear reaction **3** involving thermonuclear weapons

thermoplastic *adj* **1** (of a material, esp. a synthetic plastic) becoming soft when heated and rehardening on cooling ▷ *n* **2** a synthetic plastic or resin, such as polystyrene

Thermos *or* **Thermos flask** *n trademark* a type of stoppered vacuum flask used to preserve the temperature of its contents

thermosetting *adj* (of a material, esp. a synthetic plastic) hardening permanently after one application of heat and pressure

thermostat *n* a device which automatically regulates the temperature of central heating, an oven, etc. by switching it off or on when it reaches or drops below a particular temperature **thermostatic** *adj* **thermostatically** *adv*

thesaurus (thiss-**sore**-uss) *n, pl* **-ruses** *or* **-ri** a book containing lists of synonyms and related words
WORD ORIGIN Greek *thēsauros* a treasury

these *adj, pron* the plural of **this**

thesis (**theess**-siss) *n, pl* **-ses** (-seez) **1** a written work resulting from original research, esp. one submitted for a higher degree in a university **2** an opinion supported by reasoned argument: *it is the author's thesis that Britain has yet to come to terms with the loss of its Empire* **3** *logic* an unproved statement put forward as a premise in an argument
WORD ORIGIN Greek: a placing

Thespian *n* **1** *often facetious* an actor or actress ▷ *adj* **2** of or relating to drama and the theatre
WORD ORIGIN after *Thespis*, a Greek poet

they *pron* (*subjective*) **1** refers to people or things other than the speaker or people addressed: *they both giggled* **2** refers to people in general: *they say he beats his wife* **3** *informal* refers to an individual person, whose sex is either not known or not regarded as important: *someone could have a nasty accident if they tripped over that*
WORD ORIGIN Old Norse *their*

USAGE
It was formerly considered correct to use *he*, *him*, or *his* after pronouns such as *everyone*, *no-one*, *anyone*, or *someone* as in *everyone did his best*, but it is now more common to use *they*, *them*, or *their*, and this use has become acceptable in all but the most formal contexts: *everyone did their best*.

thiamine *or* **thiamin** *n* vitamin B₁, a vitamin found in the outer coat of rice and other grains, a deficiency of which leads to nervous disorders and to beriberi
WORD ORIGIN Greek *theion* sulphur + VITAMIN

thick *adj* **1** having a relatively great distance between opposite surfaces: *thick slices* **2** having a specified distance between opposite surfaces: *fifty metres thick* **3** having a dense consistency: *thick fog* **4** consisting of a lot of things grouped closely together: *thick forest* **5** (of clothes) made of heavy cloth or wool: *a thick jumper* **6** *informal* stupid, slow, or insensitive **7** (of an accent) very noticeable: *each word was pronounced in a thick Dutch accent* **8** Also: **thick as thieves** *informal* very friendly **9 a bit thick** *Brit informal* unfair or unreasonable: *£2 an hour, that's a bit thick!* **10 thick with a** covered with a lot of: *glass panels thick with dust* **b** (of a voice) throaty and hard to make out: *his voice was thick with emotion* ▷ *adv* **11** in order to produce something thick: *the machine sliced the potatoes too thick* **12 lay it on thick** *informal* **a** to exaggerate a story **b** to flatter someone excessively **13 thick and fast** quickly and in large numbers: *theories were flying thick and fast* ▷ *n* **14 the thick** the most intense or active part: *in the thick of the fighting* **15 through thick and thin** in good times and bad **thickly** *adv*
WORD ORIGIN Old English *thicce*

thicken *vb* **1** to make or become thick or thicker **2** to become more complicated: *the plot thickens* **thickener** *n*

thickening *n* **1** something added to a liquid to thicken it **2** a thickened part or piece

thicket *n* a dense growth of small trees or shrubs
WORD ORIGIN Old English *thiccet*

thickhead *n slang* a stupid or ignorant person **thickheaded** *adj*

thickie *n slang* same as **thicko**

thickness *n* **1** the state or quality of being thick **2** the dimension through an object, as opposed to length or width **3** a layer: *several thicknesses of brown paper*

thicko *n, pl* **thickos** *or* **thickoes** *Brit slang* a slow-witted unintelligent person

thickset *adj* **1** stocky in build **2** planted or placed close together

thick-skinned *adj* insensitive to criticism or hints; not easily upset

thief *n, pl* **thieves** a person who steals something from another **thievish** *adj*
WORD ORIGIN Old English *thēof*

thieve *vb* **thieving**, **thieved** to steal other people's possessions **thieving** *adj*
WORD ORIGIN Old English *thēofian*

thigh *n* the part of the human leg between the hip and the knee
WORD ORIGIN Old English *thēh*

thighbone *n* same as **femur**

thimble *n* a small metal or plastic cap used to protect the end of the finger from the needle when sewing
WORD ORIGIN Old English *thymel* thumbstall

thin *adj* **thinner**, **thinnest** **1** having a relatively small distance between

opposite surfaces: *a thin mattress* **2** much narrower than it is long: *push a thin stick up the pipe in order to clear it* **3** (of a person or animal) having no excess body fat **4** made up of only a few, widely separated, people or things: *thin hair* **5** not dense: *a thin film of dust* **6** unconvincing because badly thought out or badly presented: *the evidence against him was extremely thin* **7** (of a voice) high-pitched and not very loud: *a thin squeaky voice* ▷ *adv* **8** in order to produce something thin: *roll the dough very thin* ▷ *vb* **thinning, thinned 9** to make or become thin or sparse **thinly** *adv* **thinness** *n*
WORD ORIGIN Old English *thynne*

thin client *n computers* a computer on a network where most functions are carried out on a central server

thine *old-fashioned adj* **1** (preceding a vowel) of or associated with you (thou): *if thine eye offend thee, pluck it out!* ▷ *pron* **2** something belonging to you (thou): *the victory shall be thine*
WORD ORIGIN Old English *thīn*

thing *n* **1** any physical object that is not alive: *there are very few jobs left where people actually make things* **2** an object, fact, circumstance, or concept considered as being a separate entity: *that would be a terrible thing to do* **3** an object or entity that cannot or need not be precisely named: *squares and circles and things* **4** *informal* a person or animal: *pretty little thing, isn't she?* **5** a possession, article of clothing, etc.: *have you brought your swimming things?* **6** *informal* a preoccupation or obsession: *they have this thing about policemen* **7 do one's own thing** to engage in an activity or mode of behaviour satisfying to one's personality **8 make a thing of** to exaggerate the importance of **9 the thing** the latest fashion
WORD ORIGIN Old English: assembly

thingumabob *or* **thingamabob** *n informal* a person or thing the name of which is unknown, temporarily forgotten, or deliberately overlooked. Also: **thingumajig, thingamajig, thingummy**

think *vb* **thinking, thought 1** to consider, judge, or believe: *I think that it is scandalous* **2** to make use of the mind, for example in order to make a decision: *I'll need to think about what I'm going to do* **3** to engage in conscious thought: *that made me think* **4** to be considerate enough or remember (to do something): *no other company had thought to bring high tech down to the user* **5 think much** *or* **a lot of** to have a favourable opinion of: *I don't think much of the new design* **6 think of a** to remember or recollect: *I couldn't think of your surname* **b** to conceive of or formulate: *for a long time he couldn't think of a response* **7 think twice** to consider something carefully before making a decision ▷ *n* **8** *informal* a careful open-minded assessment: *she had a long hard think* **thinker** *n*
WORD ORIGIN Old English *thencan*

thinking *n* **1** opinion or judgment: *contrary to all fashionable thinking* **2** the process of thought ▷ *adj* **3** using intelligent thought: *the thinking man's sport*

think over *vb* to ponder or consider

think-tank *n informal* a group of experts employed to study specific problems

think up *vb* to invent or devise

thinner *n* a solvent, such as turpentine, added to paint or varnish to dilute it

thin-skinned *adj* sensitive to criticism or hints; easily upset

third *adj* **1** of or being number three in a series **2** rated, graded, or ranked below the second level **3** denoting the third from lowest forward gear in a motor vehicle ▷ *n* **4** one of three equal parts of something **5** the fraction equal to one divided by three $\frac{1}{3}$ **6** the third from lowest forward gear in a motor vehicle **7** *Brit* an honours degree of the third and usually the lowest class **8** *music* the interval between one note and the note four semitones (**major third**) or three semitones (**minor third**) higher or lower than it ▷ *adv* **9** Also: **thirdly** in the third place
WORD ORIGIN Old English *thirda*

third class *n* **1** the class or grade next in value, rank, or quality to the second ▷ *adj* **third-class 2** of the class or grade next in value, rank, or quality to the second

third degree *n informal* torture or bullying, esp. as used to extort confessions or information

third-degree burn *n* a burn in which both the surface and the underlying layers of the skin are destroyed

third man *n cricket* a fielding position on the off side, near the boundary behind the batsman's wicket

third party *n* **1** a person who is involved in an event, legal proceeding, agreement, or other transaction only by chance or indirectly ▷ *adj* **third-party 2** *insurance* providing protection against liability caused by accidental injury or death of other people: *third-party cover*

third person *n* the form of a pronoun or verb used to refer to something or someone other than the speaker or the person or people being addressed

third-rate *adj* mediocre or inferior

Third Reich *n* see **Reich**

Third World *n* the developing countries of Africa, Asia, and Latin America collectively

thirst *n* **1** a desire to drink, accompanied by a feeling of dryness in the mouth and throat **2** a craving or yearning: *a thirst for knowledge* ▷ *vb* **3** to feel a thirst
WORD ORIGIN Old English *thurst*

thirsty *adj* **thirstier, thirstiest 1** feeling a desire to drink **2** causing thirst: *morris dancing is thirsty work* **3 thirsty for** feeling an eager desire for: *thirsty for information* **thirstily** *adv*

thirteen *n* **1** the cardinal number that is the sum of ten and three **2** a numeral, 13 or XIII, representing this number **3** something representing or consisting of thirteen units ▷ *adj* **4** amounting to thirteen: *thirteen people* **thirteenth** *adj, n*

thirty *n, pl* **-ties 1** the cardinal number that is the product of ten and three **2** a numeral, 30 or XXX, representing this number **3** something representing or consisting of thirty units ▷ *adj*

4 amounting to thirty: *thirty miles* **thirtieth** *adj, n*

Thirty-nine Articles *pl n* a set of formulas defining the doctrinal position of the Church of England

this *adj* **1** used preceding a noun referring to something or someone that is closer: *on this side of the Channel* **2** used preceding a noun that has just been mentioned or is understood: *this text has two chief goals* **3** used to refer to something about to be mentioned: *NPR's Anne Garrels has this report* **4** used to refer to the present time or occasion: *this week's edition of the newspaper* **5** *informal* used instead of *a* or *the* in telling a story: *see, it's about this bird who fancies you* ▷ *pron* **6** used to denote a person or thing that is relatively close: *black coral like this* **7** used to denote something already mentioned or understood: *this didn't seem fair to me* **8** used to denote something about to be mentioned: *just say this: collect Standish from the top of the fire escape* **9** the present time or occasion: *after this it was impossible to talk to him about his feelings* **10 this and that** various unspecified and trivial events or facts
WORD ORIGIN Old English *thes, thēos, this* (masculine, feminine, and neuter singular)

thistle *n* a plant with prickly-edged leaves, dense flower heads, and feathery hairs on the seeds **thistly** *adj*
WORD ORIGIN Old English *thīstel*

thistledown *n* the mass of feathery plumed seeds produced by a thistle

thither *adv formal* to or towards that place
WORD ORIGIN Old English *thider*

tho' *or* **tho** *conj, adv US or poetic* same as **though**

thole[1] *or* **tholepin** *n* one of a pair of wooden pins set upright in the gunwale on either side of a rowing boat to serve as a fulcrum in rowing
WORD ORIGIN Old English *tholl*

thole[2] *vb* **tholing, tholed** *Scot & N English* to bear or put up with

thong *n* **1** a thin strip of leather or other material **2** *Austral, US, & Canad* same as **flip-flop 3** a skimpy article of beachwear consisting of thin strips of leather or cloth attached to a piece of material that covers the genitals while leaving the buttocks bare
WORD ORIGIN Old English *thwang*

Thor *n Norse myth* the god of thunder

thorax (**thaw**-racks) *n, pl* **thoraxes** *or* **thoraces** (**thaw**-rass-seez) **1** the part of the human body enclosed by the ribs **2** the part of an insect's body between the head and abdomen **thoracic** *adj*
WORD ORIGIN Greek: breastplate, chest

thorium *n chem* a silvery-white radioactive metallic element. It is used in electronic equipment and as a nuclear power source. Symbol: Th
WORD ORIGIN after *Thor*, Norse god of thunder

thorn *n* **1** a sharp pointed woody projection from a stem or leaf **2** any of various trees or shrubs having thorns, esp. the hawthorn **3 a thorn in one's side** *or* **flesh** a source of irritation: *he was sufficiently bright at school to become a thorn in*

the side of his maths teacher **thornless** *adj*
WORD ORIGIN Old English

thorny *adj* **thornier, thorniest 1** covered with thorns **2** difficult or unpleasant: *a thorny issue*

thorough *adj* **1** carried out completely and carefully: *he needs a thorough checkup by the doctor* **2** (of a person) painstakingly careful: *he is very thorough if rather unimaginative* **3** great in extent or degree; utter: *a thorough disgrace* **thoroughly** *adv* **thoroughness** *n*
WORD ORIGIN Old English *thurh* through

thoroughbred *adj* **1** obtained through successive generations of selective breeding: *thoroughbred horses* ▷ *n* **2** a pedigree animal, esp. a horse

thoroughfare *n* a way through from one place to another: *the great thoroughfare from the Castle to the Palace of Holyrood*

thoroughgoing *adj* **1** extremely thorough **2** absolute or complete: *a thoroughgoing hatred*

those *adj, pron* the plural of **that**
WORD ORIGIN Old English *thās*, plural of *this*

thou¹ *pron old-fashioned* same as **you**: used when talking to one person
WORD ORIGIN Old English *thū*

thou² *n, pl* **thou** *informal* **1** one thousandth of an inch **2** a thousand

though *conj* **1** despite the fact that: *he was smiling with relief and happiness though the tears still flowed down his cheeks* ▷ *adv* **2** nevertheless or however: *he can't dance – he sings well, though*
WORD ORIGIN Old English *thēah*

thought *vb* **1** the past of **think** ▷ *n* **2** the act or process of thinking **3** a concept or idea **4** ideas typical of a particular time or place: *the development of Western intellectual thought* **5** detailed consideration: *he appeared to give some sort of thought to the question* **6** an intention, hope, or reason for doing something: *his first thought was to call the guard and have the man arrested*
WORD ORIGIN Old English *thōht*

thoughtful *adj* **1** considerate in the treatment of other people **2** showing careful thought: *a thoughtful and scholarly book* **3** quiet, serious, and deep in thought **thoughtfully** *adv* **thoughtfulness** *n*

thoughtless *adj* not considerate of the feelings of other people **thoughtlessly** *adv* **thoughtlessness** *n*

thousand *n, pl* **-sands** *or* **-sand 1** the cardinal number that is the product of ten and one hundred **2** a numeral, 1000 or 10³, representing this number **3** a very large but unspecified number: *thousands of bees swarmed out of the hive* **4** something representing or consisting of 1000 units ▷ *adj* **5** amounting to a thousand: *a thousand members* **thousandth** *adj, n*
WORD ORIGIN Old English *thūsend*

thrall *n* the state of being completely in the power of, or spellbound by, a person or thing: *he was held in thrall by her almost supernatural beauty*
WORD ORIGIN Old English *thrǣl* slave

thrash *vb* **1** to beat (someone), esp. with a stick or whip **2** to defeat totally: *the All Blacks thrashed England 24-3* **3** to move

about in a wild manner: *his legs stuck and he fell sideways, thrashing about wildly* **4** same as **thresh** ▷ *n* **5** *informal* a party ▷ See also **thrash out**
WORD ORIGIN Old English *therscan*

thrashing *n* a severe beating

thrash out *vb* to discuss (a problem or difficulty) fully in order to come to an agreement or decision about it: *we must arrange a meeting to thrash out the details of the scheme*

thread *n* **1** a fine strand or fibre of some material **2** a fine cord of twisted yarns, esp. of cotton, used in sewing or weaving **3** something acting as the continuous link or theme of a whole: *the thread of the story* **4** the spiral ridge on a screw, bolt, or nut **5** a very small amount (of something): *there was a thread of nervousness in his voice* **6** a very thin seam of coal or vein of ore ▷ *pl n* **threads 7** *chiefly US slang* clothes ▷ *vb* **8** to pass thread through the eye of (a needle) before sewing with it **9** to string together: *plastic beads threaded on lengths of nylon line* **10** to make (one's way) through a crowd of people or group of objects: *she threaded and pushed her way through the crowds* **threadlike** *adj*
WORD ORIGIN Old English *thrǣd*

threadbare *adj* **1** (of cloth, clothing, or a carpet) having the nap worn off so that the threads are exposed **2** having been used or expressed so often as to be no longer interesting: *threadbare ideas* **3** wearing shabby worn-out clothes

threadworm *n* a small threadlike worm that is a parasite of humans

threat *n* **1** a declaration of an intention to inflict harm: *they carried out their threat to kill the hostages* **2** a strong possibility of something dangerous or unpleasant happening: *the wet weather will bring a threat of flooding* **3** a person or thing that is regarded as dangerous and likely to inflict harm: *unemployment is a serious threat to the social order*
WORD ORIGIN Old English *thrēat*

threaten *vb* **1** to express a threat to (someone): *he threatened John with the sack* **2** to be a threat to: *he was worried about anything that might threaten the health of his child* **3** to be a menacing indication of (something): *the early summer threatened drought* **threatening** *adj* **threateningly** *adv*

three *n* **1** the cardinal number that is the sum of one and two **2** a numeral, 3 or III, representing this number **3** something representing or consisting of three units ▷ *adj* **4** amounting to three: *three days*
WORD ORIGIN Old English *thrēo*

three-decker *n* **1** a warship with guns on three decks **2** anything that has three levels, layers, or tiers

three-dimensional *or* **3-D** *adj* **1** having three dimensions **2** lifelike or realistic: *all the characters are three-dimensional*

threefold *adj* **1** having three times as many or as much **2** composed of three parts ▷ *adv* **3** by three times as many or as much

three-legged race *n* a race in which pairs of competitors run with their adjacent legs tied together

three-ply *adj* made of three thicknesses, layers, or strands

three-point turn *n* a complete turn of a motor vehicle using forward and reverse gears alternately, and completed after only three movements

three-quarter *adj* **1** amounting to three out of four equal parts of something **2** being three quarters of the normal length: *a three-quarter-length coat* ▷ *n* **3** *rugby* any of the four players between the fullback and the halfbacks

three Rs *pl n* reading, writing, and arithmetic regarded as the three fundamental skills to be taught in primary schools
WORD ORIGIN humorous spelling of *reading, 'riting, and 'rithmetic*

threescore *adj archaic* sixty

threesome *n* a group of three people

threnody *n, pl* **threnodies** *formal* a lament for the dead **threnodic** *adj* **threnodist** *n*
WORD ORIGIN Greek *thrēnōidia*

thresh *vb* **1** to beat (stalks of ripe corn, rice, etc.), either with a hand tool or by machine to separate the grain from the husks and straw **2** **thresh about** to toss and turn
WORD ORIGIN Old English *therscan*

thresher *n* any of a genus of large sharks occurring in tropical and temperate seas. They have a very long whiplike tail

threshold *n* **1** the lower horizontal part of an entrance or doorway, esp. one made of stone or hardwood **2** any doorway or entrance: *he had never been over the threshold of a pub before* **3** the starting point of an experience, event, or venture: *she was on the threshold of a glorious career* **4** the point at which something begins to take effect or be noticeable: *the threshold for basic rate tax; he has a low boredom threshold*
WORD ORIGIN Old English *therscold*

threw *vb* the past tense of **throw**

thrice *adv literary* **1** three times: *twice or thrice in a lifetime* **2** three times as big, much, etc.: *his vegetables are thrice the size of mine*
WORD ORIGIN Old English *thrīwa, thrīga*

thrift *n* **1** wisdom and caution with money **2** a low-growing plant of Europe, W Asia, and North America, with narrow leaves and round heads of pink or white flowers **thriftless** *adj*
WORD ORIGIN Old Norse: success

thrifty *adj* **thriftier, thriftiest** not wasteful with money **thriftily** *adv* **thriftiness** *n*

thrill *n* **1** a sudden sensation of excitement and pleasure: *he felt a thrill of excitement* **2** a situation producing such a sensation: *all the thrills of rafting the meandering Dordogne* **3** a sudden trembling sensation caused by fear or emotional shock ▷ *vb* **4** to feel or cause to feel a thrill **5** to vibrate or quiver **thrilling** *adj*
WORD ORIGIN Old English *thȳrlian* to pierce

thriller *n* a book, film, or play depicting crime, mystery, or espionage in an atmosphere of excitement and suspense

The Thriller

ollins English Dictionary defines a *thriller* as: 'a book, film, play, etc, depicting crime, mystery, or espionage in an atmosphere of excitement and suspense'. This makes the thriller genre a very broad category of literary fiction indeed, as most Western storytelling incorporates these elements, from heroic myth and legend to hardboiled crime novels. The term *thriller* can, therefore, be applied to much of fiction. While the mystery and detective fiction genres are closely linked to the thriller genre and often share subject matter and themes, they also have their own literary conventions, such as the central character being a sleuth, or someone skilled at investigating. Thrillers, however, can accommodate an everyman protagonist. Also, the revelatory nature of mystery writing is not an integral element of a thriller. Suspense, on the other hand, is essential. The most celebrated explanation of this narrative requirement came from Alfred Hitchcock. In a published series of interviews with François Truffaut, he explained that a scene involving a mundane conversation between two characters at a table could be used to generate either surprise or suspense depending on whether the audience knew or did not know that a bomb was beneath the table. Although Hitchcock was, of course, describing a different medium (film), the same principles hold true in literature, in that the reader must be provided by the author with enough information to generate the suspense and thus keep the reader's attention. Hence the phrase *page turner*.

Another key factor is a central character pitted against unlikely odds. The formula can be traced back to Homer's *Odyssey*, which features a hero, Odysseus, who faces seemingly insurmountable odds in his journey home to Ithaca following the siege of Troy. The theme has stood the test of time, and can be identified throughout the history of Western literature, from *The Count of Monte Cristo* by Alexandre Dumas, in which a man is falsely imprisoned and escapes to take revenge on his captors, to John Buchan's *The Thirty-Nine Steps*, in which a man is falsely accused of murder and goes on the run while becoming embroiled in a web of espionage.

Such dramatic plots mean that the thriller genre lends itself to the pulp tradition, and it is no surprise that many authors adopted pseudonyms to write more lurid material (as in the case of the prolific mystery writer Donald Westlake's violent novels written as Richard Stark). Earlier still, the same themes were present in many of the 'dime novels' that gave exaggerated accounts of outlaws and criminality in the United States, as did the 'penny dreadfuls' in Britain. Although penny dreadfuls often concerned creatures such as vampires, the thriller genre remains distinct from the horror genre in that it tends to avoid supernatural elements.

As the genre is so wide, it can be broken down into various subgenres. Crime fiction aside, categories include the spy thriller (examples include *The Spy Who Came in from the Cold* by John le Carré, *The Ipcress File* by Len Deighton, the *Bourne* series by Robert Ludlum, and of course the James Bond novels written by Ian Fleming), the legal thriller (of which the books of John Grisham including *The Firm* and *A Time to Kill* are the best-known examples), the political thriller (Graham Greene's *Our Man in Havana*), the military thriller (Tom Clancy's *The Hunt for Red October*), the religious thriller (Dan Brown's *The Da Vinci Code*), the science-fiction thriller (a notable contributor being Michael Crichton), the medical thriller (particularly the novels of Robin Cook) and the true-crime thriller (such as Truman Capote's *In Cold Blood*). Many of these titles have become bestsellers, and it is likely that the thriller genre will have a long lifespan, such is the broad appeal of its successful literary formula.

thrips *n, pl* **thrips** a small slender-bodied insect with piercing mouthparts that feeds on plant sap
WORD ORIGIN Greek: woodworm

thrive *vb* **thriving; thrived** *or* **throve; thrived** *or* **thriven 1** to do well; be successful: *Munich has thrived as a centre of European commerce* **2** to grow strongly and vigorously: *the vine can thrive in the most unlikely soils*
WORD ORIGIN Old Norse *thrífask* to grasp for oneself

thro' *or* **thro** *prep, adv informal* same as **through**

throat *n* **1** the passage from the mouth and nose to the stomach and lungs **2** the front part of the neck **3 at each other's throats** quarrelling or fighting with each other **4 cut one's own throat** to bring about one's own ruin **5 cut someone's throat** to kill someone **6 ram** *or* **force something down someone's throat** to insist that someone listen to or accept something **7 stick in one's throat** to be hard to accept: *his arrogance really sticks in my throat*
WORD ORIGIN Old English *throtu*

throaty *adj* **throatier, throatiest 1** hoarse and suggestive of a sore throat: *a throaty 40 fags-a-day bark* **2** deep, husky, or guttural: *she gives a deliciously throaty laugh*

throb *vb* **throbbing, throbbed 1** to pulsate or beat repeatedly, esp. with abnormally strong force: *her eardrums were throbbing with pain* **2** (of engines, drums, etc.) to have a strong rhythmic vibration or beat ▷ *n* **3** the act or sensation of throbbing: *he felt a throb of fear; the throb of the engines* **throbbing** *adj, n*
WORD ORIGIN imitative

throes *pl n* **1** violent pangs, pain, or convulsions: *an animal in its death throes* **2 in the throes of** struggling to cope with (something difficult or disruptive): *in the throes of a civil war*
WORD ORIGIN Old English *thrāwu* threat

thrombosis (throm-**boh**-siss) *n, pl* **-ses** (-seez) coagulation of the blood in the heart or in a blood vessel, forming a blood clot **thrombotic** (throm-**bot**-ik) *adj*
WORD ORIGIN Greek: curdling

throne *n* **1** the ceremonial seat occupied by a monarch or bishop on occasions of state **2** the rank or power of a monarch: *she came to the throne after her father was murdered*
WORD ORIGIN Greek *thronos*

throng *n* **1** a great number of people or things crowded together ▷ *vb* **2** to gather in or fill (a place) in large numbers: *streets thronged with shoppers*
WORD ORIGIN Old English *gethrang*

throstle *n poetic* a song thrush
WORD ORIGIN Old English

throttle *n* **1** a device that controls the fuel-and-air mixture entering an engine ▷ *vb* **-tling, -tled 2** to kill or injure (someone) by squeezing his or her throat **3** to suppress or censor: *the government is trying to throttle dissent*
WORD ORIGIN Middle English *throtel* throat

throttle back *vb* to reduce the speed of a vehicle or aircraft by reducing the quantity of fuel entering the engine: *throttling back the engine failed to bring the plane under control*

through *prep* **1** going in at one side and coming out at the other side of: *he drove through the West of the city* **2** occupying or visiting several points scattered around in (an area): *a journey through the Scottish Highlands* **3** as a result of: *diminished responsibility through temporary insanity* **4** during: *driving for five hours through the night* **5** for all of (a period): *it rained all through that summer* **6** *chiefly US* up to and including: *from Monday through Saturday* ▷ *adj* **7** finished: *I'm through with history* **8** having completed a specified amount of an activity: *he tried to stop the investigation halfway through* **9** (on a telephone line) connected **10** no longer able to function successfully in some specified capacity: *they are through, they haven't got a chance* **11** (of a train, plane flight, etc.) going directly to a place, so that passengers do not have to change: *the first ever through train between Singapore and Bangkok* ▷ *adv* **12** through a thing, place, or period of time: *the script gives up around halfway through* **13** extremely or absolutely: *I'm soaked through* **14 through and through** to the greatest possible extent: *the boards are rotten through and through*
WORD ORIGIN Old English *thurh*

throughout *prep* **1** through the whole of (a place or a period of time): *radio stations throughout the UK* ▷ *adv* **2** through the whole of a place or a period of time: *I led both races throughout*

throughput *n* the amount of material processed in a given period, esp. by a computer

throve *vb* a past tense of **thrive**

throw *vb* **throwing, threw, thrown 1** to hurl (something) through the air, esp. with a rapid motion of the arm **2** to put or move suddenly, carelessly, or violently: *she threw her arms round his neck* **3** to bring into a specified state or condition, esp. suddenly: *the invasion threw the region into turmoil* **4** to move (a switch or lever) so as to engage or disengage a mechanism **5** to cause (someone) to fall: *I'm riding the horse that threw me* **6 a** to tip (dice) out onto a flat surface **b** to obtain (a specified number) in this way: *one throws a 3 and the other throws a 5* **7** to shape (clay) on a potter's wheel **8** to give (a party) **9** *informal* to confuse or disconcert: *the question threw me* **10** to direct or cast (a look, light, etc.): *the lamp threw a shadow on the ceiling* **11** to project (the voice) so as to make it appear to come from somewhere else **12** *informal* to lose (a contest) deliberately **13 throw a punch** to strike, or attempt to strike, someone with one's fist **14 throw oneself at** to behave in a way which makes it clear that one is trying to win the affection of (someone) **15 throw oneself into** to involve oneself enthusiastically in **16 throw oneself on** to rely entirely upon (someone's goodwill, etc.): *the president threw himself on the mercy of the American people* ▷ *n* **17** the act or an instance of throwing **18** the distance thrown: *a throw of 90 metres* **19** (in sports such as wrestling or judo) a move which causes one's opponent to fall to the floor **20** a decorative blanket or cover **21 a throw each**: *we drank our way through a couple of bottles of claret at £12.50 a throw* ▶ See also **throwaway, throwback**, etc.
WORD ORIGIN Old English *thrāwan* to turn, torment

throwaway *adj* **1** said or done incidentally: *a throwaway line* **2** designed to be discarded after use: *throwaway cups* ▷ *vb* **throw away 3** to get rid of or discard: *try to recycle glass bottles instead of simply throwing them away* **4** to fail to make good use of: *she threw away the chance of a brilliant career when she got married*

throwback *n* **1** a person or thing that is like something that existed or was common long ago: *his ideas were a throwback to old colonial attitudes* ▷ *vb* **throw back 2** to remind someone of (something he or she said or did previously) in order to upset him or her: *he threw back at me everything I'd said the week before*

throw in *vb* **1** to add at no additional cost: *he'd got good at bargaining them down, making them throw in variations for free* **2** to contribute (a remark) in a discussion **3 throw in the towel** *informal* to give in; accept defeat ▷ *n* **throw-in 4** *soccer, etc.* the act of putting the ball back into play when it has gone over one of the sidelines, by throwing it over one's head with both hands

throw off *vb* **1** to take off (clothing) hurriedly **2** *literary* to free oneself of: *Vietnamese farmers threw off their dependency on European seed potatoes*

throw out *vb* **1** to discard or reject: *the court threw out the case* **2** to expel or dismiss, esp. forcibly: *her parents threw her out when they discovered she was pregnant*

throw over *vb old-fashioned* to leave or reject (a lover)

throw together *vb* **1** to assemble (something) hurriedly **2** (of a set of circumstances) to cause (people) to meet and get to know each other

throw up *vb* **1** *informal* to vomit **2** to give up or abandon: *he would threaten to throw up his job* **3** to construct (a building or structure) hastily **4** to produce: *these links are throwing up fresh opportunities*

thru *prep, adv, adj chiefly US* same as **through**

thrum *vb* **thrumming, thrummed 1** to strum rhythmically but without expression on (a musical instrument) **2** to make a low beating or humming sound: *the air conditioner thrummed* ▷ *n* **3** a repetitive strumming
WORD ORIGIN imitative

thrush¹ *n* any of a large group of songbirds, esp. one having a brown plumage with a spotted breast, such as the mistle thrush and song thrush
WORD ORIGIN Old English *thrÿsce*

thrush² *n* **1** a fungal disease, esp. of infants, in which whitish spots form on the mouth, throat, and lips **2** a genital infection caused by the same fungus
WORD ORIGIN origin unknown

thrust vb **thrusting, thrust 1** to push (someone or something) with force: *he took him by the arm and thrust him towards the door* **2** to force (someone) into some condition or situation: *the unemployed have been thrust into the front line of politics* **3** to force (one's way) through a crowd, forest, etc.: *Edward thrust his way towards them* **4** to stick out or up: *she thrust out her lower lip* ▷ n **5** a forceful drive, push, stab, or lunge: *the thrust of his spear* **6** a force, esp. one that produces motion **7** the propulsive force produced by the pressure of air and gas forced out of a jet engine or rocket engine **8** the essential or most forceful part: *the main thrust of the report* **9** physics a continuous pressure exerted by one part of an object against another **10** informal intellectual or emotional drive; forcefulness: *thanks to the ingenuity and enterprising thrust of this company* **WORD ORIGIN** Old Norse *thrȳsta*

thrusting adj ambitious and having great drive: *a thrusting young executive*

thud n **1** a dull heavy sound **2** a blow or fall that causes such a sound ▷ vb **thudding, thudded 3** to make or cause to make such a sound **WORD ORIGIN** Old English *thyddan* to strike

thug n a tough and violent man, esp. a criminal **thuggery** n **thuggish** adj **WORD ORIGIN** Hindi *thag* thief

thulium n chem a silvery-grey element of the lanthanide series. Symbol: Tm **WORD ORIGIN** after *Thule*, a region thought by ancient geographers to be northernmost in the world

thumb n **1** the short thick finger of the hand set apart from the others **2** the part of a glove shaped to fit the thumb **3 all thumbs** very clumsy **4 thumbs down** an indication of refusal or disapproval **5 thumbs up** an indication of encouragement or approval **6 under someone's thumb** completely under someone else's control ▷ vb **7** to touch, mark, or move with the thumb: *he thumbed the volume switch to maximum* **8** to attempt to obtain (a lift in a motor vehicle) by signalling with the thumb: *he thumbed a lift to the station* **9 thumb one's nose at** to behave in a way that shows one's contempt or disregard for: *her mother had always thumbed her nose at convention* **10 thumb through** to flip the pages of (a book or magazine) in order to glance at the contents **WORD ORIGIN** Old English *thūma*

thumb index n a series of notches cut into the fore-edge of a book to facilitate quick reference

thumbnail n **1** the nail of the thumb ▷ adj **2** concise and brief: *a thumbnail sketch*

thumbscrew n (formerly) an instrument of torture that pinches or crushes the thumbs

thumbtack n the US and Canadian term for **drawing pin**

thump n **1** the sound of something heavy hitting a comparatively soft surface **2** a heavy blow with the hand ▷ vb **3** to place (something) on or bang against (something) with a loud dull sound: *thumping the table is aggressive* **4** to hit or punch (someone): *stop that at once or I'll thump you!* **5** to throb or beat violently: *he could feel his heart thumping* **WORD ORIGIN** imitative

thumping adj slang huge or excessive: *a thumping majority*

thunder n **1** a loud cracking or deep rumbling noise caused by the rapid expansion of atmospheric gases that are suddenly heated by lightning **2** any loud booming sound: *the thunder of heavy gunfire* **3 steal someone's thunder** to lessen the effect of someone's idea or action by anticipating it ▷ vb **4** to make a loud noise like thunder: *an explosion thundered through the shaft* **5** to speak in a loud, angry manner: *'Get out of here this instant!' he thundered* **6** to move fast, heavily, and noisily: *a lorry thundered by* **thundery** adj **WORD ORIGIN** Old English *thunor*

thunderbolt n **1** a flash of lightning accompanying thunder **2** something sudden and unexpected: *his career has been no thunderbolt* **3** myth a weapon thrown to earth by certain gods **4** sport a very fast-moving shot or serve

thunderclap n **1** a loud outburst of thunder **2** something as violent or unexpected as a clap of thunder

thundercloud n a large dark electrically charged cloud associated with thunderstorms

thundering old-fashioned slang adj **1** extreme: *a thundering disgrace* ▷ adv **2** extremely: *thundering good music*

thunderous adj **1** resembling thunder in loudness: *thunderous applause* **2** threatening or angry: *a thunderous scowl*

thunderstorm n a storm with thunder and lightning and usually heavy rain or hail

thunderstruck adj amazed or shocked

thurible (thyoor-rib-bl) n same as **censer** **WORD ORIGIN** Latin *turibulum*

Thurs. Thursday

Thursday n the fifth day of the week **WORD ORIGIN** Old English *Thursdæg* Thor's day

thus adv **1** as a result or consequence: *the platforms provided a new floor and thus improved and enlarged the premises* **2** in this manner: *I sat thus for nearly half an hour* **3** to such a degree: *the competition has been almost bereft of surprise thus far* **WORD ORIGIN** Old English

thwack vb **1** to beat with something flat ▷ n **2 a** a blow with something flat **b** the sound made by it **WORD ORIGIN** imitative

thwart vb **1** to prevent or foil: *they inflicted such severe losses that they thwarted the invasion* ▷ n **2** the seat across a boat where the rower sits **WORD ORIGIN** Old Norse *thvert* across

thy adj old-fashioned belonging to or associated in some way with you (thou): *love thy neighbour* **WORD ORIGIN** variant of *thine*

thyme (time) n a small shrub with white, pink, or red flowers and scented leaves used for seasoning food **WORD ORIGIN** Greek *thumon*

thymol n a white crystalline substance obtained from thyme, used as a fungicide and an antiseptic

thymus (thigh-muss) n, pl -muses or -mi (-my) anat a small gland situated near the base of the neck **WORD ORIGIN** Greek *thumos* sweetbread

thyroid anat adj **1** of or relating to the thyroid gland **2** of or relating to the largest cartilage of the larynx, which forms the Adam's apple in men ▷ n **3** the thyroid gland **WORD ORIGIN** Greek *thureos* oblong shield

thyroid gland n anat an endocrine gland that secretes hormones that control metabolism and body growth

thyself pron old-fashioned the reflexive form of **thou**[1]

ti n music same as **te**

Ti chem titanium

tiara n **1** a semicircular jewelled headdress worn by some women on formal occasions **2** the triple-tiered crown sometimes worn by the pope **WORD ORIGIN** Greek

tibia (tib-ee-a) n, pl tibiae (tib-ee-ee) or tibias the inner and thicker of the two bones of the human leg below the knee; shinbone **tibial** adj **WORD ORIGIN** Latin: leg, pipe

tic n a spasmodic muscular twitch **WORD ORIGIN** French

tick[1] n **1** a mark (✓) used to check off or indicate the correctness of something **2** a recurrent metallic tapping or clicking sound, such as that made by a clock **3** informal a moment or instant: *won't be a tick* ▷ vb **4** to mark or check with a tick **5** to produce a recurrent tapping sound or indicate by such a sound: *the clock ticked away* **6 what makes someone tick** informal the basic motivation of a person ▸ See also **tick off, tick over** **WORD ORIGIN** Low German *tikk* touch

tick[2] n a small parasitic creature typically living on the skin of warm-blooded animals and feeding on the blood and tissues of their hosts: *a sheep tick* **WORD ORIGIN** Old English *ticca*

tick[3] n Brit & NZ informal account or credit: *a spending spree that was financed on tick* **WORD ORIGIN** from *ticket*

ticker n slang the heart

ticker tape n (formerly) a continuous paper tape on which current stock quotations were printed by machine

ticket n **1** a printed piece of paper or cardboard showing that the holder is entitled to certain rights, such as travel on a train or bus or entry to a place of public entertainment **2** a label or tag attached to an article showing information such as its price and size **3** an official notification of a parking or traffic offence **4** the declared policy of a political party **5 that's (just) the ticket** informal that's the right or appropriate thing ▷ vb -eting, -eted **6** to issue or attach a ticket or tickets to **WORD ORIGIN** Old French *etiquet*

tickets pl n S African informal death or ruin; the end

ticking n a strong cotton fabric, often striped, used esp. for mattress and pillow covers **WORD ORIGIN** probably from Middle Dutch *tīke*

tickle vb **-ling, -led 1** to touch or stroke (someone), so as to produce laughter or a twitching sensation **2** to itch or tingle **3** to amuse or please **4 tickled pink** or **to death** informal greatly pleased **5 tickle someone's fancy** to appeal to or amuse someone ▷ n **6** a sensation of light stroking or itching: *a tickle in the throat* **7** the act of tickling **8** Canad (in the Atlantic Provinces) a narrow strait **WORD ORIGIN** Middle English *titelen*

ticklish adj **1** sensitive to being tickled **2** delicate or difficult: *a ticklish problem*

tick off vb **1** to mark with a tick, esp. to show that an item on a list has been dealt with **2** informal to reprimand or scold (someone) **ticking-off** n

tick over vb **1** (of an engine) to run at low speed with the transmission disengaged **2** to run smoothly without any major changes: *the business is just ticking over*

ticktack n Austral & Brit a system of sign language, mainly using the hands, by which bookmakers transmit their odds to each other at race courses

ticktock n a ticking sound made by a clock

tidal adj **1** (of a river, lake, or sea) having tides **2** of or relating to tides: *a tidal surge*

tidal wave n **1** not in technical use same as **tsunami 2** an unusually large incoming wave, often caused by high winds and spring tides **3** a forceful and widespread movement in public opinion, action, etc.: *a tidal wave of scandals and embezzlement*

tiddler n informal **1** a very small fish, esp. a stickleback **2** a small child **WORD ORIGIN** perhaps from TIDDLY¹

tiddly¹ adj **-dlier, -dliest** Brit very small **WORD ORIGIN** childish variant of *little*

tiddly² adj **-dlier, -dliest** informal chiefly Brit slightly drunk **WORD ORIGIN** origin unknown

tiddlywinks n a game in which players try to flick discs of plastic into a cup **WORD ORIGIN** origin unknown

tide n **1** the alternate rise and fall of sea level caused by the gravitational pull of the sun and moon **2** the current caused by these changes in level: *I got caught by the tide and almost drowned* **3** a widespread tendency or movement: *the rising tide of nationalism* **4** literary or old-fashioned a season or time: *Yuletide* **WORD ORIGIN** Old English *tīd* time

tideline n the mark or line left by the tide when it retreats from its highest point

tidemark n **1** a mark left by the highest or lowest point of a tide **2** chiefly Brit & NZ a line of dirt left round a bath after the water has been drained away **3** informal chiefly Brit a dirty mark on the skin, indicating the extent to which someone has washed

tide over vb **tiding, tided** to help (someone) to get through a period of difficulty or distress: *they need some form of Social Security to tide them over*

tidings pl n information or news **WORD ORIGIN** Old English *tīdung*

tidy adj **-dier, -diest 1** neat and orderly **2** Brit, Austral, & NZ informal quite large: *a tidy sum of money* ▷ vb **-dies, -dying, -died 3** to put (things) in their proper place; make neat: *I've tidied up the toys under the bed* ▷ n, pl **-dies 4** a small container for odds and ends **tidily** adv **tidiness** n **WORD ORIGIN** (originally: timely, excellent) from *tide*

tie vb **tying, tied 1** to fasten or be fastened with string, rope, etc.: *a parcel tied with string* **2** to make a knot or bow in (something): *hang on while I tie my laces* **3** to restrict or limit: *they had children and were consequently tied to the school holidays* **4** to equal the score of a competitor or fellow candidate: *three players tied for second place* ▷ n **5** a long narrow piece of material worn, esp. by men, under the collar of a shirt, tied in a knot close to the throat with the ends hanging down the front **6** a bond or link: *he still has close ties to the town where he grew up* **7** a string, wire, etc. with which something is tied **8** Brit sport a match in a knockout competition: *whoever wins the tie will play Australia in the semifinals* **9 a** a result in a match or competition in which the scores or times of some of the competitors are the same: *a tie for second place* **b** the match or competition in which the scores or results are equal **10** a regular commitment that limits a person's freedom: *it's a bit of a tie having to visit him every day* **11** something which supports or links parts of a structure **12** US & Canad a sleeper on a railway track **13** music a curved line connecting two notes of the same pitch indicating that the sound is to be prolonged for their joint time value ▷ See also **tie in, tie up** **WORD ORIGIN** Old English *tīgan*

tie-break or **tie-breaker** n an extra game or question that decides the result of a contest that has ended in a draw

tied adj Brit **1** (of a public house) allowed to sell beer from only one particular brewery **2** (of a house) rented out to the tenant for as long as he or she is employed by the owner

tie-dye, tie-dyed or **tie and dye** adj (of a garment or fabric) dyed in a pattern by tying sections of the cloth together so that they will not absorb the dye: *a tie-dye T-shirt*

tie in vb **1** to have or cause to have a close link or connection: *there's no evidence to tie this killing in with the murder of Mrs McGowan* ▷ n **tie-in 2** a link or connection **3** a book or other product that is linked with a film or TV programme

tiepin n an ornamental pin used to pin the two ends of a tie to a shirt

tier n one of a set of rows placed one above and behind the other, such as theatre seats **WORD ORIGIN** Old French *tire*

tie up vb **1** to bind (someone or something) securely with string or rope **2** to moor (a vessel) **3** to commit (money etc.) so that it is unavailable for other uses: *people don't want to tie up their*

savings for a long period ▷ n **tie-up 4** a link or connection

tiff n a minor quarrel **WORD ORIGIN** origin unknown

tiffin n (in India) a light meal, esp. at midday **WORD ORIGIN** probably from obsolete *tiff* to sip

tiger n **1** a large Asian mammal of the cat family which has a tawny yellow coat with black stripes **2** a dynamic, forceful, or cruel person **3** a country, esp. in E Asia, that is achieving rapid economic growth **WORD ORIGIN** Greek *tigris*

tiger lily n a lily of China and Japan with black-spotted orange flowers

tiger moth n a moth with conspicuously striped and spotted wings

tiger snake n a highly venomous brown-and-yellow Australian snake

tight adj **1** stretched or drawn taut: *loosening-up of tight muscles* **2** closely fitting: *wearing a jacket that was too tight for him* **3** made, fixed, or closed firmly and securely: *a tight band* **4** constructed so as to prevent the passage of water, air, etc.: *watertight; airtight* **5** cramped and allowing very little room for movement: *they squeezed him into the tight space* **6** unyielding or stringent: *tight security* **7** (of a situation) difficult or dangerous **8** allowing only the minimum time or money for doing something: *we have been working to a tight schedule* **9** Brit, Austral, & NZ informal mean or miserly **10** (of a match or game) very close or even **11** informal drunk **12** (of a corner or turn) turning through a large angle in a short distance: *the boat skidded round in a tight turn* ▷ adv **13** in a close, firm, or secure way: *they held each other tight* **tightly** adv **tightness** n **WORD ORIGIN** Old Norse *thēttr* of close texture

tighten vb to make or become tight or tighter

tight-fisted adj unwilling to spend money; mean

tightknit adj closely integrated: *a tightknit community*

tight-lipped adj **1** unwilling to give any information; secretive: *the Minister remained tight-lipped when it came to answering the press's questions* **2** with the lips pressed tightly together, as through anger: *tight-lipped determination*

tightrope n a rope stretched taut on which acrobats perform

tights pl n a one-piece clinging garment covering the body from the waist to the feet, worn by women and also by acrobats, dancers, etc.

tigress n **1** a female tiger **2** a fierce, cruel, or passionate woman

tike n same as **tyke**

tiki (tee-kee) n a Māori greenstone neck ornament in the form of a fetus **WORD ORIGIN** Māori

tikka adj Indian cookery (of meat) marinated in spices and then dry-roasted: *chicken tikka*

tilde n a mark (˜) used in some languages to indicate that the letter

Texas English

Texans like to say of braggarts that they're 'all hat and no cattle'. Texas is all hat *and* cattle. It's the largest state in the contiguous United States in size, and the second-largest in population. No surprise, then, that broadly speaking, and Texans talk very broadly indeed, the English they speak is outsize.

Texas is so big that, as far as its English is concerned, it's both Southern and Western. In the humid subtropical Piney Woods region of East Texas, pronunciation takes its soft-spoken cue from Appalachia and the Deep South, as befits the fact that many early settlers came from there, and that this part of the state abuts Arkansas and Louisiana. In linguistic terms at least, the Texas-reared President George W Bush ('Dubya' to some) had a few points in common with Bill Clinton, his Arkansas predecessor. From the South came such features as the pronunciation of *dog* as *dawg*, the use of *y'all* for *you-all* and the verb *fixin' to* for *planning to* ('I'm fixin' to speak good Texan'), as well as the flattening of the *i*-vowel in words like *right*, *night*, and *fire* to sound like *raht, nahd*, and *far*. As in much of the South, any soft drink can be a *coke*.

Though Texas has several distinct topographical regions, most people associate it with the High Plains of cowboys and Longhorn cattle, tumbleweeds and oil wells – even if two-thirds of the state's population lives in big cities like Dallas and Houston. Here, combined with many Southern interventions, the Texas twang of the Far West comes into its own, and *horse* can sound like *hars, lord* like *lard*. A pretty girl is *purty*, barbed wire is *bob wahr*, and vowels can stretch so indefinitely (*kee-uhd* for *kid*) that *shit* is pronounced with as many as four syllables. *Pin* and *pen* sound the same. One *warshes* one's hair with shampoo, then *renches* it. You don't want to be *sorry*, that is, worthy of contempt. Words slowly slur and blend: someone may ask you, 'Hyeru?' or 'Hairyew?' to which you naturally reply, 'Fahn, hyeru?' or 'Fahn, hairyew?' With such an opening, you have no cause to be *aggravated* (annoyed), pronounced *aggervated*.

Given they are such a colourful people, it follows that Texans will have colourful locutions: a *blue norther*, a huge mass of cold air that may presage rain and wind; the barely printable *turd-floater*, a heavy downpour; enigmatic directions such as *up* or *over in through there;* the historically evocative *damnyankee*; epithets like *as handy as hip pockets on a hog*, considered a compliment, and *like a gnat in a hail storm*; and the pithily descriptive *looks like he has been rode hard and put up wet*. During the US Civil War, in which Texas sided with the Confederacy, President Lincoln issued the Emancipation Proclamation, belatedly announced in Texas, the date of which is now celebrated on 19 June as the holiday *Juneteenth*. To general English, Texas has given *maverick,* an unorthodox or independent-minded person, originally one of the cattleman Sam Maverick's unbranded cows, which were liable to stray, and has lent its name to such combinations as *Texas leaguer,* in baseball a softly hit ball that pops up and falls between the infield and outfield; the poker variety *Texas hold'em;* and *Texas gate*, a Canadianism for a cattle grid (called a *cattle guard* in the United States). *Tex-Mex* is the style of cooking associated with the long Mexican border.

The Apache and Comanche, so important in myths about pioneering days, represent only a tiny proportion of Texans. By contrast, Hispanics, some of whom had illegally crossed the Rio Grande from Mexico, are important to the economy and rapidly growing in number; for some time, Texas English has been absorbing such lexical items as *frijoles, arroyo,* and *mesa*. For centuries a sparsely inhabited extension of Mexico, briefly in the early 19th century an independent republic (hence its nickname the *Lone Star State*), Texas recently has seen migrants from across the United States and elsewhere become workers in the burgeoning high-tech, aerospace, and petrochemical industries. The newcomers doubtless will influence Texas speech. Just as likely, the seductive qualities of that speech will induce new arrivals to speak like true-born Texans.

over which it is placed is pronounced in a certain way, as in Spanish *señor*
WORD ORIGIN Spanish

tile *n* **1** a thin piece of ceramic, plastic, etc. used with others to cover a surface, such as a floor or wall **2** a rectangular block used as a playing piece in mah jong and other games **3 on the tiles** *informal* out having a good time and drinking a lot ▷ *vb* **tiling, tiled 4** to cover (a surface) with tiles **tiled** *adj* **tiler** *n*
WORD ORIGIN Latin *tegula*

tiling *n* **1** tiles collectively **2** something made of or surfaced with tiles

till¹ *conj, prep* same as **until**
WORD ORIGIN Old English *til*

≡ **USAGE**
≡ Till is a variant of *until* that is
≡ acceptable at all levels of language.
≡ Until is, however, often preferred at
≡ the beginning of a sentence in formal
≡ writing: *until his behaviour improves, he*
≡ *cannot become a member.*

till² *vb* to cultivate (land) for the raising of crops: *a constant round of sowing, tilling and harvesting* **tillable** *adj* **tiller** *n*
WORD ORIGIN Old English *tilian* to try, obtain

till³ *n* a box or drawer into which money taken from customers is put, now usually part of a cash register
WORD ORIGIN origin unknown

tillage *n* **1** the act, process, or art of tilling **2** tilled land

tiller *n naut* a handle used to turn the rudder when steering a boat
WORD ORIGIN Anglo-French *teiler* beam of a loom

tilt *vb* **1** to move into a sloping position with one end or side higher than the other: *Dave tilted his chair back on two legs* **2** to move (part of the body) slightly upwards or to the side: *Marie tilted her head back* **3** to become more influenced by a particular idea or group: *the party is tilting more and more to the right* **4** to compete against someone in a jousting contest ▷ *n* **5** a slope or angle: *a tilt to one side* **6** the act of tilting **7 a** a jousting contest, esp. in medieval Europe **b** a thrust with a lance delivered during a medieval tournament **8** an attempt to win a contest: *a tilt at the world title* **9 at full tilt** at full speed or force
WORD ORIGIN Old English *tealtian*

tilth *n* **1** the tilling of land **2** the condition of land that has been tilled

timber *n* **1** wood as a building material **2** trees collectively **3** a wooden beam in the frame of a house, boat, etc. ▷ *adj* **4** made out of timber: *timber houses* **5** of or involved in the production or sale of wood as a building material: *a timber merchant* **timbered** *adj* **timbering** *n*
WORD ORIGIN Old English

timber limit *n Canad* **1** the area to which rights of cutting timber, granted by a government licence, are limited **2** same as **timber line**

timber line *n* the geographical limit beyond which trees will not grow

timbre (**tam**-bra) *n* the distinctive quality of sound produced by a particular voice or musical instrument
WORD ORIGIN French

timbrel *n chiefly biblical* a tambourine
WORD ORIGIN Old French

Timbuktu *or* **Timbuctoo** (tim-buck-too) *n* any distant or outlandish place: *we could run our office from Timbuktu as long as there was a good fax line*
WORD ORIGIN after *Timbuktu*, town in Africa

time *n* **1** the past, present, and future regarded as a continuous whole ▸ Related adjective: **temporal 2** *physics* a quantity measuring duration, measured with reference to the rotation of the earth or from the vibrations of certain atoms **3** a specific point in time expressed in hours and minutes: *what time are you going?* **4** a system of reckoning for expressing time: *the deadline is 5:00 Eastern Time today* **5** an unspecified interval; a while: *some recover for a time and then relapse* **6** an instance or occasion: *when was the last time you saw it?* **7** a sufficient interval or period: *I need time to think* **8** an occasion or period of specified quality: *they'd had a lovely time* **9** a suitable moment: *the time has come to make peace* **10** a period or point marked by specific attributes or events: *in Victorian times* **11** *Brit* the time at which licensed premises are required by law to stop selling alcoholic drinks **12** the rate of pay for work done in normal working hours: *you get double time for working on a Sunday* **13 a** the system of combining beats in music into successive groupings by which the rhythm of the music is established **b** a specific system having a specific number of beats in each grouping or bar: *duple time* **14 against time** in an effort to complete something in a limited period **15 ahead of time** before the deadline **16 at one time a** once or formerly **b** simultaneously **17 at the same time a** simultaneously **b** nevertheless or however **18 at times** sometimes **19 beat time** to indicate the tempo of a piece of music by waving a baton, hand, etc. **20 do time** *informal* to serve a term in jail **21 for the time being** for the moment; temporarily **22 from time to time** at intervals; occasionally **23 have no time for** to have no patience with **24 in no time** very quickly **25 in one's own time a** outside paid working hours **b** at the speed of one's choice **26 in time a** early or at the appointed time: *he made it to the hospital in time for the baby's arrival* **b** eventually: *in time, the children of intelligent parents will come to dominate* **c** *music* at a correct metrical or rhythmic pulse **27 make time** to find an opportunity **28 on time** at the expected or scheduled time **29 pass the time** to occupy oneself when there is nothing else to do: *they pass their time watching game shows on television* **30 pass the time of day** to have a short casual conversation (with someone) **31 time and again** frequently **32 time of one's life** a memorably enjoyable time **33 time out of mind** from long before anyone can remember ▷ *vb* **timing, timed 34** to measure the speed or duration of: *my Porsche was timed at 128 mph* **35** to set a time for: *the attack was timed for 6 am* **36** to do (something) at a suitable time: *her*

entry could not have been better timed ▷ *adj* **37** operating automatically at or for a set time: *an electrical time switch* ▷ *interj* **38** the word called out by a publican signalling that it is closing time ▸ See also **times**
WORD ORIGIN Old English *tīma*

time and a half *n* a rate of pay one and a half times the normal rate, often offered for overtime work

time-and-motion study *n* the analysis of work procedures to work out the most efficient methods of operation

time bomb *n* **1** a bomb containing a timing mechanism that is set so that the bomb will explode at a specified time **2** something that will have a large, often damaging, effect at a later date: *the decline of the manufacturing industry is a political time bomb*

time capsule *n* a container holding articles representative of the current age, buried for discovery in the future

time clock *n* a clock with a device for recording the time of arrival or departure of an employee

time-consuming *adj* taking up a great deal of time

time exposure *n* a photograph produced by exposing film for a relatively long period, usually a few seconds

time-honoured *adj* having been used or done for a long time and established by custom

timekeeper *n* **1** a person or thing that keeps or records time, for instance at a sporting event **2** an employee with a record of punctuality as specified: *a poor timekeeper* **timekeeping** *n*

time lag *n* a gap or delay between one event and a related event that happens after it: *the time lag between the development and the marketing of new products*

timeless *adj* **1** unaffected by time or by changes in fashion, society, etc.: *the timeless appeal of tailored wool jackets* **2** eternal and everlasting: *the timeless universal reality behind all religions* **timelessness** *n*

timely *adj* **-lier, -liest,** *adv* at the right or an appropriate time

time-out *n* **1** *sport chiefly US, Canad, & Austral* an interruption in play during which players rest, discuss tactics, etc. **2 take time out** to take a break from a job or activity

timepiece *n* a device, such as a clock or watch, which measures and indicates time

timer *n* a device for measuring time, esp. a switch or regulator that causes a mechanism to operate at a specific time

times *prep* multiplied by: *ten times four is forty*

timescale *n* the period of time within which events occur or are due to occur

time-served *adj* having successfully completed an apprenticeship or period of training: *a time-served electrician*

timeserver *n* a person who changes his or her views in order to gain support or favour

time sharing *n* **1** a system of part ownership of a property for use as a holiday home whereby each participant owns the property for a particular period every year **2** a system by which users at different terminals of a computer can communicate with it at the same time

time signature *n music* a sign, usually consisting of two figures placed after the key signature, that indicates the number and length of beats in the bar

timetable *n* **1** a plan of the times when a job or activity should be done: *the timetable for the Royal Visit* **2** a list of departure and arrival times of trains or buses: *a timetable hung on the wall beside the ticket office* **3** a plan of the times when different subjects or classes are taught in a school or college: *a heavy timetable of lectures and practical classes* ▷ *vb* **-tabling, -tabled** **4** to set a time when a particular thing should be done: *the meeting is timetabled for 3 o'clock*

time value *n music* the duration of a note relative to other notes in a composition and considered in relation to the basic tempo

time warp *n* an imagined distortion of the progress of time, so that, for instance, events from the past seem to be happening in the present

timeworn *adj* **1** showing the adverse effects of overlong use or of old age: *a timeworn café* **2** having been used so often as to be no longer interesting: *a timeworn cliché*

time zone *n* a region throughout which the same standard time is used

timid *adj* **1** lacking courage or self-confidence: *a timid youth* **2** indicating shyness or fear: *a timid and embarrassed smile* **timidity** *n* **timidly** *adv*
WORD ORIGIN Latin *timere* to fear

timing *n* the ability to judge when to do or say something so as to make the best effect, for instance in the theatre, in playing an instrument, or in hitting a ball in sport

timorous (**tim**-mor-uss) *adj literary* lacking courage or self-confidence: *a reclusive timorous creature* **timorously** *adv*
WORD ORIGIN Latin *timor* fear

timpani *or* **tympani** (**tim**-pan-ee) *pl n* a set of kettledrums **timpanist** *or* **tympanist** *n*
WORD ORIGIN Italian

tin *n* **1** a soft silvery-white metallic element. Symbol: Sn **2** a sealed airtight metal container used for preserving and storing food or drink: *a cupboard full of packets and tins* **3** any metal container: *a tin of paint* **4** the contents of a tin **5** *Brit, Austral, & NZ* galvanized iron, used to make roofs ▷ *vb* **tinning, tinned** **6** to put (food) into tins
WORD ORIGIN Old English

tin can *n* a metal food container

tincture *n* a medicine consisting of a small amount of a drug dissolved in alcohol
WORD ORIGIN Latin *tinctura* a dyeing

tinder *n* dry wood or other easily-burning material used to start a fire **tindery** *adj*
WORD ORIGIN Old English *tynder*

tinderbox *n* (formerly) a small box for tinder, esp. one fitted with a flint and

steel which could be used to make a spark

tine *n* a slender prong of a fork or a deer's antler **tined** *adj*
WORD ORIGIN Old English *tind*

tinfoil *n* a paper-thin sheet of metal, used for wrapping foodstuffs

ting *n* a high metallic sound such as that made by a small bell
WORD ORIGIN imitative

ting-a-ling *n* the sound of a small bell

tinge *n* **1** a slight tint or colouring: *his skin had an unhealthy greyish tinge* **2** a very small amount: *both goals had a tinge of fortune* ▷ *vb* **tingeing** *or* **tinging, tinged** **3** to colour or tint faintly: *the sunset tinged the lake with pink* **4** **tinged with** having a small amount of a particular quality: *the victory was tinged with sadness*
WORD ORIGIN Latin *tingere* to colour

tingle *vb* **-gling, -gled** **1** to feel a mild prickling or stinging sensation, as from cold or excitement ▷ *n* **2** a mild prickling or stinging feeling **tingling** *adj* **tingly** *adj*
WORD ORIGIN probably a variant of *tinkle*

tin god *n* a self-important person

tinker *n* **1** (esp. formerly) a travelling mender of pots and pans **2** *Scot & Irish* a Gypsy **3** a mischievous child ▷ *vb* **4** **tinker with** to try to repair or improve (something) by making lots of minor adjustments
WORD ORIGIN origin unknown

tinker's damn *or* **cuss** *n* **not give a tinker's damn** *or* **cuss** *slang* not to care at all

tinkle *vb* **-kling, -kled** **1** to ring with a high tinny sound like a small bell ▷ *n* **2** a high clear ringing sound **3** *Brit informal* a telephone call **tinkly** *adj*
WORD ORIGIN imitative

tinned *adj* (of food) preserved by being sealed in a tin

tinny¹ *adj* **-nier, -niest** **1** (of a sound) high, thin, and metallic: *the tinny sound of a transistor radio* **2** cheap or shoddy: *a tinny East European car*

tinny² *adj* **-nier, -niest** *Austral & NZ slang* lucky

tin-opener *n* a small tool for opening tins

Tin Pan Alley *n* the popular music industry, esp. the more commercial aspects of it

tin plate *n* thin steel sheet coated with a layer of tin to protect it from corrosion

tinpot *adj informal* worthless or unimportant: *a tinpot dictator*

tinsel *n* **1** a decoration consisting of a piece of metallic thread with thin strips of metal foil attached along its length **2** anything cheap, showy, and gaudy: *all their tinsel and show counts for nothing* ▷ *adj* **3** made of or decorated with tinsel **4** cheap, showy, and gaudy **tinselly** *adj*
WORD ORIGIN Latin *scintilla* a spark

Tinseltown *n informal* Hollywood, the centre of the US film industry

tinsmith *n* a person who works with tin or tin plate

tint *n* **1** a shade of a colour, esp. a pale one: *his eyes had a yellow tint* **2** a colour that is softened by the addition of white: *a room decorated in pastel tints*

3 a dye for the hair ▷ *vb* **4** to give a tint to (something, such as hair)
WORD ORIGIN Latin *tingere* to colour

tintinnabulation *n* the ringing or pealing of bells
WORD ORIGIN Latin *tintinnare* to tinkle

tiny *adj* **tinier, tiniest** very small
WORD ORIGIN origin unknown

tip¹ *n* **1** a narrow or pointed end of something: *the northern tip of Japan* **2** a small piece attached to the end or bottom of something: *boot tips keep boots from getting scuffed* ▷ *vb* **tipping, tipped** **3** to make or form a tip on: *the long strips that hang down are tipped with silver cones* **tipped** *adj*
WORD ORIGIN Old Norse *typpi*

tip² *n* **1** an amount of money given to someone, such as a waiter, in return for service **2** a helpful hint or warning: *here are some sensible tips to help you avoid sunburn* **3** a piece of inside information, esp. in betting or investing ▷ *vb* **tipping, tipped** **4** to give a tip to
WORD ORIGIN origin unknown

tip³ *vb* **tipping, tipped** **1** to tilt: *he tipped back his chair* **2** **tip over** to tilt so as to overturn or fall: *the box tipped over and the clothes in it spilled out* **3** *Brit* to dump (rubbish) **4** to pour out (the contents of a container): *he tipped the water from the basin down the sink* ▷ *n* **5** a rubbish dump
WORD ORIGIN origin unknown

tip-off *n* **1** a warning or hint, esp. one given confidentially and based on inside information ▷ *vb* **tip off** **2** to give a hint or warning to: *the police had been tipped off about the robbery*

tippet *n* a scarflike piece of fur, often made from a whole animal skin, worn, esp. formerly, round a woman's shoulders
WORD ORIGIN probably from TIP¹

tipple *vb* **-pling, -pled** **1** to drink alcohol regularly, esp. in small quantities ▷ *n* **2** an alcoholic drink **tippler** *n*
WORD ORIGIN origin unknown

tipstaff *n* **1** a court official **2** a metal-tipped staff formerly used as a symbol of office

tipster *n* a person who sells tips to people betting on horse races or speculating on the stock market

tipsy *adj* **-sier, -siest** slightly drunk **tipsiness** *n*
WORD ORIGIN from TIP³

tiptoe *vb* **-toeing, -toed** **1** to walk quietly with the heels off the ground ▷ *n* **2** **on tiptoe** on the tips of the toes or on the ball of the foot and the toes: *I stood on tiptoe*

tiptop *adj, adv* of the highest quality or condition

tip-up *adj* able to be turned upwards around a hinge or pivot: *tip-up seats*

TIR International Road Transport
WORD ORIGIN French *Transports Internationaux Routiers*

tirade *n* a long angry speech or denunciation
WORD ORIGIN French

tire¹ *vb* **tiring, tired** **1** to reduce the energy of, as by exertion: *she could still do things that would tire women half her age* **2** to become wearied or bored: *he simply* stopped talking when he tired of my questions **tiring** adj

WORD ORIGIN Old English *tēorian*

tire² n US same as **tyre**

tired adj 1 weary or exhausted: *they were tired after their long journey* 2 bored of or no longer interested in something: *I'm tired of staying in watching TV every night* 3 having been used so often as to be no longer interesting: *you haven't fallen for that tired old line, have you?* **tiredness** n

tireless adj energetic and determined: *a tireless worker for charity* **tirelessly** adv

tiresome adj boring and irritating

'tis poetic or dialect it is

tissue n 1 a group of cells in an animal or plant with a similar structure and function: *muscular tissue forms 42% of the body tissue* 2 a thin piece of soft absorbent paper used as a disposable handkerchief, towel, etc. 3 short for **tissue paper** 4 an interwoven series: *a tissue of lies*

WORD ORIGIN Old French *tissu* woven cloth

tissue paper n very thin soft delicate paper used esp. to wrap breakable goods

tit¹ n any of various small European songbirds, such as the bluetit, that feed on insects and seeds

WORD ORIGIN Middle English *tite* little

tit² n 1 slang a female breast 2 a teat or nipple

WORD ORIGIN Old English *titt*

titan n a person of great strength, importance, or size: *one of the titans of the computer industry*

WORD ORIGIN after the *Titans*, a family of gods in Greek mythology

titanic adj having or requiring colossal strength: *a titanic struggle*

titanium n chem a strong white metallic element used in the manufacture of strong lightweight alloys, esp. aircraft parts. Symbol: Ti

WORD ORIGIN from *titan*

titbit or esp. US **tidbit** n 1 a tasty small piece of food 2 a pleasing scrap of scandal: *an interesting titbit of gossip*

WORD ORIGIN origin unknown

titfer n old-fashioned Brit slang a hat

WORD ORIGIN rhyming slang *tit for tat*

tit-for-tat adj done in return or retaliation for a similar act: *a spate of tit-for-tat killings*

WORD ORIGIN earlier *tip for tap*

tithe n 1 one tenth of one's income or produce paid to the church as a tax 2 a tenth or very small part of anything: *he had accomplished only a tithe of his great dream* ▷ vb **tithing, tithed** 3 to demand a tithe from 4 to pay a tithe or tithes **tithable** adj

WORD ORIGIN Old English *teogotha*

tithe barn n a large barn where, formerly, the agricultural tithe of a parish was stored

Titian (**tish**-un) adj (of hair) reddish-yellow

WORD ORIGIN from *Titian*, Italian painter, because he often used this hair colour in his paintings

titillate vb **-lating, -lated** to arouse or excite pleasurably, esp. in a sexual way

titillating adj titillation n

WORD ORIGIN Latin *titillare*

titivate vb **-vating, -vated** to make smarter or neater **titivation** n

WORD ORIGIN perhaps from *tidy* + *cultivate*

title n 1 the distinctive name of a book, film, record, etc.: *his first album bore the title 'Safe as Milk'* 2 a descriptive name or heading of a section of a book, speech, etc. 3 a book or periodical: *publishers were averaging a total of 500 new titles annually* 4 a name or epithet signifying rank, office, or function: *the job bears the title Assistant Divisional Administrator* 5 a formal designation, such as *Mrs* or *Dr* 6 sport a championship: *the Italians have won the title* 7 law the legal right to possession of property

WORD ORIGIN Latin *titulus*

titled adj having a title such as 'Lady' or 'Sir' which indicates a high social rank

title deed n a document containing evidence of a person's legal right or title to property, esp. a house or land

titleholder n a person who holds a title, esp. a sporting championship

title page n the page in a book that gives the title, author, publisher, etc.

title role n the role of the character after whom a play or film is named

titmouse n, pl **-mice** same as **tit¹**

WORD ORIGIN Middle English *tite* little + MOUSE

titrate (**tite**-rate) vb **-trating, -trated** chem to measure the volume or concentration of (a solution) by titration

WORD ORIGIN French *titrer*

titration n chem an operation in which a measured amount of one solution is added to a known quantity of another solution until the reaction between the two is complete. If the concentration of one solution is known, that of the other can be calculated

titter vb 1 to snigger, esp. derisively or in a suppressed way ▷ n 2 a suppressed laugh or snigger

WORD ORIGIN imitative

tittle n a very small amount: *it doesn't matter one jot or tittle what you think*

WORD ORIGIN Latin *titulus* title

tittle-tattle n 1 idle chat or gossip ▷ vb **-tattling, -tattled** 2 to chatter or gossip

tittup vb **-tupping, -tupped** or US **-tuping, -tuped** 1 to prance or frolic ▷ n 2 a caper

WORD ORIGIN probably imitative

titular adj 1 in name only: *titular head of state* 2 of or having a title

tizzy n, pl **-zies** informal a state of confusion or excitement

WORD ORIGIN origin unknown

T-junction n a junction where one road joins another at right angles but does not cross it

Tl chem thallium

Tm chem thulium

TN Tennessee

TNT n 2,4,6-trinitrotoluene: a type of powerful explosive

to prep 1 used to indicate the destination of the subject or object of an action: *he*

went to the theatre 2 used to introduce the indirect object of a verb: *talk to him* 3 used to introduce the infinitive of a verb: *I'm going to lie down* 4 as far as or until: *from September 11 to October 25* 5 used to indicate that two things have an equivalent value: *there are 16 ounces to the pound* 6 against or onto: *I put my ear to the door* 7 before the hour of: *17 minutes to midnight* 8 accompanied by: *dancing to a live band* 9 as compared with: *four goals to nil* 10 used to indicate a resulting condition: *burnt to death* 11 working for or employed by: *Chaplain to the Nigerian Chaplaincy in Britain* 12 in commemoration of: *a memorial to the victims of the disaster* ▷ adv 13 towards a closed position: *push the door to*

WORD ORIGIN Old English *tō*

toad n 1 an amphibian which resembles a frog, but has a warty skin and spends more time on dry land 2 a loathsome person

WORD ORIGIN Old English *tādige*

toadflax n a plant with narrow leaves and yellow-orange flowers

toad-in-the-hole n a traditional British dish made of sausages baked in a batter

toadstool n any of various poisonous funguses consisting of a caplike top on a stem

toady n, pl **toadies** 1 a person who flatters and ingratiates himself or herself in a fawning way: *a spineless political toady* ▷ vb **toadies, toadying, toadied** 2 to fawn on and flatter (someone) **toadyism** n

WORD ORIGIN shortened from *toadeater*, originally a quack's assistant who pretended to eat toads, hence a flatterer

to and fro adv, adj also **to-and-fro** 1 back and forth: *he moved his head to and fro as if dodging blows* 2 from one place to another then back again: *the ferry sailed to and fro across the river* **toing and froing** n

toast¹ n 1 sliced bread browned by exposure to heat ▷ vb 2 to brown (bread) under a grill or over a fire 3 to warm or be warmed: *toasting his feet at the fire*

WORD ORIGIN Latin *tostus* parched

toast² n 1 a proposal of health or success given to a person or thing and marked by people raising glasses and drinking together 2 a person or thing that is honoured: *his success made him the toast of the British film industry* ▷ vb 3 to propose or drink a toast to (a person or thing)

WORD ORIGIN from the spiced toast formerly put in wine

toaster n an electrical device for toasting bread

toastmaster n a person who introduces speakers and proposes toasts at public dinners

tobacco n, pl **-cos** or **-coes** an American plant with large leaves which are dried for smoking, or chewing, or made into snuff

WORD ORIGIN Spanish *tabaco*

tobacconist n Austral & Brit a person or shop that sells tobacco, cigarettes, pipes, etc.

-to-be adj about to be; future: *the bride-to-be*

Chicano

People of Hispanic ethnic origin constitute the largest ethnic minority in the United States. It is all too easy to think of them as a monolithic grouping and to pigeonhole their versions of the English language under the catch-all term 'Spanglish'. However, just as there are Hispanic Americans whose ancestry derives from the many different countries of Latin America, so are there many different varieties of Spanish-influenced English, from the Puerto Rican-influenced dialect of New York City to the Cuban-influenced dialect of Florida. These forms of English will of course share many common elements, but there are distinct local differences and Chicano is a perfect example of this.

The term *Chicano* (with the feminine *Chicana*) is used to mean an American citizen of Mexican ethnic descent. Various theories are advanced for the origin of the term, but the most widely-held belief is that is is derived from a shortening of the Spanish word *mejicano*, meaning 'Mexican'. It is not a particularly old word, and it seems to have first appeared in print in the 1940s. *Chicano* is also a term for the variety of English spoken by these people, which is common throughout the southwest of the United States, especially in California.

The southwestern American states share an extensive border with Mexico and there is a long history of migration from south to north, from the temporary visits of migrant workers to permanent immigration. It was inevitable that the children of first-generation immigrants would grow up hearing Spanish in the home from often monolingual parents while being exposed to English through education and the various forms of media that surrounded them. Extensive family networks spreading across both sides of the border guaranteed the interpenetration of English and Spanish. The border continues to be rather porous and 'wetbacks' (illegal immigrants seen as having swum the Rio Grande) still defy the US immigration authorities, known in Chicano as *La Migra*.

As with many dialects of English, Chicano is often stigmatized as 'bad' or illiterate English, spoken by people whose first language is Spanish rather than English. The association of the dialect with lower-class people and the criminal world, such as the notorious street gangs of Los Angeles, has also impaired its respectability. Speaking Chicano is sometimes seen as indicative of a lack of aspiration, with middle-class Mexican-Americans amending their speech to approximate more closely standard American English.

While the vocabulary of many Chicano speakers will inevitably contain many words borrowed from Spanish, it should not be assumed that such speakers are bilingual in the two languages. In fact, many speakers of Chicano do not speak Spanish to any level of fluency and they cannot be said to have acquired their knowledge of English as a foreign language. It is therefore claimed that Chicano is not 'broken English' but a distinct regional dialect of American English.

The Spanish influence is immediately apparent in many of the pronunciations of English words in Chicano. For example, the standard English 'i' sound, as in 'chip', in Chicano will be heard as closer to 'cheep'. Similarly, the common English word ending '-ing' will tend to lose the 'g' element and sound more like '-een', as in 'go-een' ('going'). Also, individual words and phrases of Spanish vocabulary are highly prominent in Chicano. This well-documented practice of interlingual borrowing and the ability to move naturally, often unconsciously, between different languages or dialects is often referred to by linguists as 'code-switching'. This gives rise to such constructions in Chicano as *Vamos tomorrow* ('Let's go tomorrow') or *Es muy helpful* ('He is very helpful').

A young Chicano, living, for example in the predominantly Mexican-American districts of East Los Angeles (known as *East LA* or *East Los*), may be into Chicano rap music. He may refer to his neighbourhood as the *barrio* and his friends as his *homies* (shortened from *homeboys*). His vehicle of choice might be a *lowrider*, a car that has had its suspension altered so that it sits lower on its wheels. He may be invited to the type of party known as a *quinceañera* (often shortened to *quince*), held to celebrate a girl's fifteenth birthday, and refer to people of non-Hispanic descent as *Anglos*.

toboggan *n* **1** a long narrow sledge used for sliding over snow and ice ▷ *vb* **2** to ride on a toboggan
WORD ORIGIN from a Native American language

toby *n*, *pl* **-bies** NZ a water stopcock at the boundary of a street and house section
WORD ORIGIN origin unknown

toby jug *n* chiefly Brit a beer mug or jug in the form of a stout seated man wearing a three-cornered hat and smoking a pipe
WORD ORIGIN from the name *Tobias*

toccata (tok-**kah**-ta) *n* a piece of fast music for the organ, harpsichord, or piano, usually in a rhythmically free style
WORD ORIGIN Italian

Toc H *n* a society formed after World War I to encourage Christian comradeship
WORD ORIGIN from initials of *Talbot House*, Poperinge, Belgium, its original headquarters

tocsin *n* **1** a warning signal **2** an alarm bell
WORD ORIGIN French

tod *n* **on one's tod** Brit slang by oneself; alone
WORD ORIGIN rhyming slang *Tod Sloan/alone*

today *n* **1** this day, as distinct from yesterday or tomorrow **2** the present age: *in today's world* ▷ *adv* **3** during or on this day: *I hope you're feeling better today* **4** nowadays: *this is one of the most reliable cars available today*
WORD ORIGIN Old English *tō dæge*, literally: on this day

toddle *vb* **-dling, -dled 1** to walk with short unsteady steps, like a young child **2** **toddle off** jocular to depart: *he toddled off to bed* ▷ *n* **3** the act or an instance of walking with short unsteady steps
WORD ORIGIN origin unknown

toddler *n* a young child who has only just learned how to walk

toddy *n*, *pl* **-dies** a drink made from spirits, esp. whisky, hot water, sugar, and usually lemon juice
WORD ORIGIN Hindi *tārī* juice of the palmyra palm

to-do *n*, *pl* **-dos** Brit, Austral, & NZ a commotion, fuss, or quarrel

toe *n* **1** any one of the digits of the foot **2** the part of a shoe or sock covering the toes **3** **on one's toes** alert **4** **tread on someone's toes** to offend a person, esp. by trespassing on his or her field of responsibility ▷ *vb* **toeing, toed 5** to touch or kick with the toe **6** **toe the line** to conform to expected attitudes or standards
WORD ORIGIN Old English *tā*

toecap *n* a reinforced covering for the toe of a boot or shoe

toehold *n* **1** a small space on a rock, mountain, etc. which can be used to support the toe of the foot in climbing **2** any means of gaining access or advantage: *the French car industry has lost its last toehold in America*

toenail *n* a thin hard clear plate covering part of the upper surface of the end of each toe

toerag *n* Brit slang a contemptible or despicable person

toff *n* Brit slang a well-dressed or upper-class person
WORD ORIGIN perhaps from *tuft*, nickname for a titled student at Oxford University wearing a cap with a gold tassel

toffee *n* **1** a sticky chewy sweet made by boiling sugar with water and butter **2** **can't (do something) for toffee** informal is not competent or talented at (doing something): *she couldn't dance for toffee*
WORD ORIGIN earlier *taffy*

toffee-apple *n* an apple fixed on a stick and coated with a thin layer of toffee

toffee-nosed *adj* slang snobbish or conceited

tofu *n* a food with a soft cheeselike consistency made from unfermented soya-bean curd
WORD ORIGIN Japanese

tog *n* unit for measuring the insulating power of duvets

toga (**toe**-ga) *n* a garment worn by citizens of ancient Rome, consisting of a piece of cloth draped around the body **togaed** *adj*
WORD ORIGIN Latin

together *adv* **1** with cooperation between people or organizations: *we started a company together* **2** in or into contact with each other: *he clasped his hands together* **3** in or into one place: *the family gets together to talk* **4** at the same time: 'Disgusting,' said Julie and Alice together **5** considered collectively: *the properties together were worth more as a unit* **6** old-fashioned continuously: *working for eight hours together* **7** **together with** in addition to ▷ *adj* **8** slang self-possessed, competent, and well-organized
WORD ORIGIN Old English *tōgædere*

☰ **USAGE**
☰ See at **plus**.

togetherness *n* a feeling of closeness to and affection for other people

togged up *adj* informal dressed up in smart clothes. Also: **togged out**

toggle *n* **1** a bar-shaped button inserted through a loop for fastening coats etc. **2** computers a key on a keyboard which, when pressed, will turn a function or feature on if it is currently off, and turn it off if it is currently on **3** short for **toggle switch** (sense 1)
WORD ORIGIN origin unknown

toggle switch *n* **1** an electric switch with a projecting lever that is moved in a particular way to open or close a circuit **2** same as **toggle** (sense 2)

togs *pl n* **1** Brit, Austral, & NZ informal clothes **2** Austral, NZ, & Irish a swimming costume
WORD ORIGIN probably from *toga*

toheroa (toe-a-**roe**-a) *n* a large edible mollusc of New Zealand with a distinctive flavour
WORD ORIGIN Māori

tohunga (**toe**-hung-a) *n* NZ a Māori priest
WORD ORIGIN Māori

toil *n* **1** hard or exhausting work: *hours of toil beneath the Catalan sun* ▷ *vb* **2** to work

hard: *workers toiling in the fields to produce tea for westerners to drink* **3** to move slowly and with difficulty, for instance because of exhaustion or the steepness of a slope: *Joanna toiled up the steps to the church*
WORD ORIGIN Anglo-French *toiler* to struggle

toilet *n* **1 a** a bowl fitted with a water-flushing device and connected to a drain, for receiving and disposing of urine and faeces **b** a room with such a fitment **2** old-fashioned the act of dressing and preparing oneself
WORD ORIGIN French *toilette* dress

toilet paper *n* thin absorbent paper used for cleaning oneself after defecation or urination

toilet roll *n* a long strip of toilet paper wound around a cardboard tube

toiletry *n*, *pl* **-ries** an object or cosmetic used in making up, dressing, etc.

toilette (twah-**let**) *n* same as **toilet** (sense 2)
WORD ORIGIN French

toilet water *n* liquid perfume lighter than cologne

toilsome *adj* literary requiring hard work: *a most toilsome job*

token *n* **1** a symbol, sign, or indication of something: *as a token of respect* **2** a gift voucher that can be used as payment for goods of a specified value **3** a metal or plastic disc, such as a substitute for currency for use in a slot machine **4** **by the same token** in the same way as something mentioned previously ▷ *adj* **5** intended to create an impression but having no real importance: *as a token gesture of goodwill*
WORD ORIGIN Old English *tācen*

tokenism *n* the practice of making only a token effort or doing no more than the minimum, esp. in order to comply with a law **tokenist** *adj*

token strike *n* a brief stoppage of work intended to convey strength of feeling on a disputed issue

told *vb* the past of **tell**

tolerable *adj* **1** able to be put up with; bearable **2** informal fairly good **tolerably** *adv*

tolerance *n* **1** the quality of accepting other people's rights to their own opinions, beliefs, or actions **2** capacity to endure something, esp. pain or hardship **3** the ability of a substance to withstand heat, stress, etc. without damage **4** med the capacity to endure the effects of a continued or increasing dose of a drug, poison, etc. **5** an acceptable degree of variation in a measurement or value: *the bodywork of the car is precision-engineered with a tolerance of 0.01 millimetres*

tolerant *adj* **1** accepting of the beliefs, actions, etc. of other people **2** **tolerant of** able to withstand (heat, stress, etc.) without damage

tolerate *vb* **-ating, -ated 1** to allow something to exist or happen, even although one does not approve of it: *you must learn to tolerate opinions other than your own* **2** to put up with (someone or something): *he found the pain hard to tolerate* **toleration** *n*
WORD ORIGIN Latin *tolerare* to sustain

toll[1] *vb* **1** to ring (a bell) slowly and regularly **2** to announce by tolling: *the bells tolled the Queen's death* ▷ *n* **3** the slow regular ringing of a bell
WORD ORIGIN origin unknown

toll[2] *n* **1** a charge for the use of certain roads and bridges: *the Skye bridge toll* **2** loss or damage from a disaster: *the annual death toll on the roads is about 4500* **3** **take a** *or* **its toll** to have a severe and damaging effect: *the continued stress had taken a toll on her health*
WORD ORIGIN Old English *toln*

tollgate *n* a gate across a toll road or bridge at which travellers must pay

tolu (tol-**loo**) *n* a sweet-smelling balsam obtained from a South American tree, used in medicine and perfume
WORD ORIGIN after *Santiago de Tolu*, Colombia

toluene *n* a flammable liquid obtained from petroleum and coal tar and used as a solvent and in the manufacture of dyes, explosives, etc.
WORD ORIGIN previously obtained from tolu

tom *n* **1** a male cat ▷ *adj* **2** (of an animal) male: *a tom turkey*
WORD ORIGIN from *Thomas*

tomahawk *n* a fighting axe used by the Native Americans of N America
WORD ORIGIN from a Native American language

tomato *n, pl* **-toes 1** a red fleshy juicy fruit with many edible seeds, eaten in salads, as a vegetable, etc. **2** the plant, originally from South America, on which this fruit grows
WORD ORIGIN S American Indian *tomatl*

tomb *n* **1** a place for the burial of a corpse **2** a monument over a grave **3** **the tomb** *poetic* death
WORD ORIGIN Greek *tumbos*

tombola *n* *Brit* a type of lottery, in which tickets are drawn from a revolving drum
WORD ORIGIN Italian

tomboy *n* a girl who behaves or dresses like a boy

tombstone *n* a gravestone

tome *n* a large heavy book
WORD ORIGIN Greek *tomos* a slice

tomfoolery *n* foolish behaviour

Tommy *n, pl* **-mies** *Brit, old-fashioned informal* a private in the British Army
WORD ORIGIN originally *Thomas Atkins*, name used in specimen copies of official forms

Tommy gun *n* a type of light sub-machine-gun
WORD ORIGIN in full *Thompson sub-machine-gun*, from the name of the manufacturer

tommyrot *n* *old-fashioned, informal* utter nonsense

tomorrow *n* **1** the day after today: *tomorrow's meeting has been cancelled* **2** the future: *the struggle to build a better tomorrow* ▷ *adv* **3** on the day after today: *the festival starts tomorrow* **4** at some time in the future: *they live today as millions more will live tomorrow*
WORD ORIGIN Old English *tō morgenne*

tomtit *n* *Brit* a small European bird that eats insects and seeds

tom-tom *n* a long narrow drum beaten with the hands
WORD ORIGIN Hindi *tamtam*

ton[1] *n* **1** *Brit* a unit of weight equal to 2240 pounds or 1016.046 kilograms **2** *US & Canad* a unit of weight equal to 2000 pounds or 907.184 kilograms **3** see **metric ton 4 come down on someone like a ton of bricks** to scold someone very severely ▷ *adv* **5 tons** a lot: *I've got tons of things to do before going on holiday*
WORD ORIGIN variant of *tun*

ton[2] *n* *slang chiefly Brit* a hundred miles per hour
WORD ORIGIN special use of TON[1]

tonal *adj* **1** *music* written in a key **2** of or relating to tone or tonality

tonality *n, pl* **-ties 1** *music* the presence of a musical key in a composition **2** the overall scheme of colours and tones in a painting

tone *n* **1** sound with reference to its pitch, timbre, or volume **2** *US & Canad* same as **note** (sense 6). **3** *music* an interval of two semitones, such as that between doh and ray in tonic sol-fa **4** the quality or character of a sound: *her tone was angry* **5** general aspect, quality, or style: *the tone of the conversation made him queasy* **6** high quality or style: *my car with its patches of rust lowered the tone of the neighbourhood* **7** the quality of a given colour, as modified by mixture with white or black; shade or tint **8** *physiol* the natural firmness of the tissues and normal functioning of bodily organs in health ▷ *vb* **toning, toned 9** to be of a matching or similar tone **10** to give a tone to or correct the tone of **toneless** *adj* **tonelessly** *adv*
WORD ORIGIN Greek *tonos*

tone-deaf *adj* unable to distinguish subtle differences in musical pitch

tone down *vb* to moderate in tone: *I sensed some reserve in his manner, so I toned down my enthusiasm*

tone poem *n* *music* an extended orchestral composition based on nonmusical material, such as a work of literature or a fairy tale

toner *n* **1** a cosmetic applied to the skin to reduce oiliness **2** a powdered chemical that forms the image produced by a photocopier

tone up *vb* to make or become more vigorous, healthy, etc.: *muscle tissue can be toned up*

tong *n* (formerly) a secret society of Chinese Americans
WORD ORIGIN Chinese (Cantonese) *t'ong* meeting place

tongs *pl n* a tool for grasping or lifting, consisting of two long metal or wooden arms, joined with a hinge or flexible metal strip at one end
WORD ORIGIN Old English *tange*

tongue *n* **1** a movable mass of muscular tissue attached to the floor of the mouth, used for tasting, eating, and speaking **2** a language, dialect, or idiom: *the Scots tongue* **3** the ability to speak: *taken aback, she could not find her tongue* **4** a manner of speaking: *a sharp tongue* **5** the tongue of certain animals used as food **6** a narrow strip of something that extends outwards:

a narrow tongue of flame **7** a flap of leather on a shoe **8** the clapper of a bell **9** a projecting strip along an edge of a board that is made to fit a groove in another board **10 hold one's tongue** to keep quiet **11 on the tip of one's tongue** about to come to mind **12 with (one's) tongue in one's cheek** with insincere or ironical intent
WORD ORIGIN Old English *tunge*

tongue-tie *n* a congenital condition in which movement of the tongue is limited as the result of the fold of skin under the tongue extending too close to the front of the tongue

tongue-tied *adj* speechless, esp. with embarrassment or shyness

tongue twister *n* a sentence or phrase that is difficult to say clearly and quickly, such as *the sixth sick sheikh's sixth sheep's sick*

tonguing *n* a technique of playing a wind instrument by obstructing and uncovering the air passage through the lips with the tongue

tonic *n* **1** a medicine that improves the functioning of the body or increases the feeling of wellbeing **2** anything that enlivens or strengthens: *his dry humour was a stimulating tonic* **3** Also called: **tonic water** a carbonated beverage containing quinine and often mixed with alcoholic drinks: *gin and tonic* **4** *music* the first note of a major or minor scale and the tonal centre of a piece composed in a particular key ▷ *adj* **5** having an invigorating or refreshing effect: *a tonic bath* **6** *music* of the first note of a major or minor scale
WORD ORIGIN Greek *tonikos* concerning tone

tonic sol-fa *n* a method of teaching music, by which syllables are used as names for the notes of the major scale in any key

tonight *n* **1** the night or evening of this present day: *tonight's programme examines the rise of poverty in the 1990s* ▷ *adv* **2** in or during the night or evening of this day: *I want to go out dancing tonight*
WORD ORIGIN Old English *tōniht*

toning table *n* an exercise table, parts of which move mechanically to exercise specific parts of the body of the person lying on it

tonnage *n* **1** the capacity of a merchant ship expressed in tons **2** the weight of the cargo of a merchant ship **3** the total amount of shipping of a port or nation

tonne (**tunn**) *n* a unit of mass equal to 1000 kg or 2204.6 pounds
WORD ORIGIN French

tonsil *n* either of two small oval lumps of spongy tissue situated one on each side of the back of the mouth **tonsillar** *adj*
WORD ORIGIN Latin *tonsillae* tonsils

tonsillectomy *n, pl* **-mies** surgical removal of the tonsils
WORD ORIGIN TONSIL + Greek *tomē* a cutting

tonsillitis *n* inflammation of the tonsils, causing a sore throat and fever

tonsorial *adj* *often facetious* of a barber or his trade
WORD ORIGIN Latin *tondere* to shave

t

tonsure n **1 a** (in certain religions and monastic orders) the shaving of the head or the crown of the head only **b** the part of the head left bare by such shaving ▷ vb **-suring, -sured 2** to shave the head of **tonsured** adj
WORD ORIGIN Latin tonsura a clipping

too adv **1** as well or also: I'll miss you, too **2** in or to an excessive degree: it's too noisy in here **3** extremely: you're too kind **4** US, Canad, & Austral informal used to emphasize contradiction of a negative statement: You didn't! – I did too!
WORD ORIGIN Old English tō

≡ **USAGE**
≡ See at **very**.

took vb the past tense of **take**

tool n **1 a** an implement, such as a hammer, saw, or spade, that is used by hand to help do a particular type of work **b** a power-driven instrument: machine tool **2** the cutting part of such an instrument **3** a person used to perform dishonourable or unpleasant tasks for another: the government is acting as a tool of big business **4** any object, skill, etc. used for a particular task or in a particular job: a skilled therapist can use photographs as tools ▷ vb **5** to work, cut, or form (something) with a tool
WORD ORIGIN Old English tōl

toolbar n a row or column of buttons displayed on a computer screen, allowing the user to select a variety of functions

tool-maker n a person who specializes in the production or reconditioning of machine tools **tool-making** n

tool-pusher n a person who supervises drilling operations on an oil rig

toonie or **twonie** n Canad informal a Canadian two-dollar coin

toot n **1** a short hooting sound ▷ vb **2** to give or cause to give a short blast, hoot, or whistle: motorists tooted their car horns
WORD ORIGIN imitative

tooth n, pl **teeth 1** one of the bonelike projections in the jaws of most vertebrates that are used for biting, tearing, or chewing **2** one of the sharp projections on the edge of a comb, saw, zip, etc. **3 long in the tooth** old or ageing **4 a sweet tooth** a liking for sweet food **5 tooth and nail** with great vigour and determination: the union would oppose compulsory redundancies tooth and nail ▶ See also **teeth**
WORD ORIGIN Old English tōth

toothache n a pain in or near a tooth

toothbrush n a small brush with a long handle, for cleaning the teeth

toothless adj **1** having no teeth **2** having no real power: the proposed Commission will not be as toothless as scoffers suggest

toothpaste n a paste used for cleaning the teeth, applied with a toothbrush

toothpick n a small wooden or plastic stick used for extracting pieces of food from between the teeth

tooth powder n a powder used for cleaning the teeth, applied with a toothbrush

toothsome adj delicious or appetizing in appearance, flavour, or smell

toothy adj **toothier, toothiest** having or showing numerous, large, or prominent teeth: a toothy grin

tootle vb **-tling, -tled 1** to hoot softly or repeatedly ▷ n **2** a soft hoot or series of hoots

top¹ n **1** the highest point or part of anything: the top of the stairs **2** the most important or successful position: at the top of the agenda **3** a lid or cap that fits on to one end of something, esp. to close it: he unscrewed the top from a quart of ale **4** the highest degree or point: the two people at the top of the Party **5** the most important person or people in an organization: the top of the military establishment **6** the loudest or highest pitch: she cheered and sang at the top of her voice **7** a garment, esp. for a woman, that extends from the shoulders to the waist or hips **8** the part of a plant that is above ground: nettle tops **9** same as **top gear 10 off the top of one's head** without previous preparation or careful thought **11 on top of a** in addition to: the average member of staff will get 25% on top of salary **b** informal in complete control of: we're on top of our costs and expenses and looking for other opportunities **12 over the top a** lacking restraint or a sense of proportion: you went over the top when you called her a religious maniac **b** mil over the edge of a trench ▷ adj **13** at, of, or being the top: men still hold most of the top jobs in industry ▷ vb **topping, topped 14** to put on top of (something): top your salad with a mild dressing **15** to reach or pass the top of **16** to be at the top of: her biggest hit topped the charts for six weeks **17** to exceed or surpass: his estimated fortune tops £2 billion **18 top and tail a** to trim off the ends of (fruit or vegetables) before cooking **b** to wash only a baby's face and bottom ▶ See also **top off, top out, tops**, etc.
WORD ORIGIN Old English topp

top² n **1** a toy that is spun on its pointed base **2 sleep like a top** to sleep very soundly
WORD ORIGIN Old English

topaz (toe-pazz) n a hard glassy yellow, pink, or colourless mineral used in making jewellery
WORD ORIGIN Greek topazos

top brass pl n the most important or high-ranking officials or leaders

topcoat n **1** an overcoat **2** a final coat of paint applied to a surface

top dog n informal the leader or chief of a group

top drawer n old-fashioned, informal people of the highest social standing

top dressing n a layer of fertilizer or manure spread on the surface of land **top-dress** vb

tope¹ vb **toping, toped** to drink (alcohol), usually in large quantities **toper** n
WORD ORIGIN perhaps from French toper to take a bet

tope² n a small grey shark of European coastal waters
WORD ORIGIN origin unknown

topee or **topi** (toe-pee) n same as **pith helmet**
WORD ORIGIN Hindi topī hat

top-flight adj of very high quality

topgallant n **1** a mast or sail above a topmast ▷ adj **2** of or relating to a topgallant

top gear n the highest forward ratio of a gearbox in a motor vehicle

top hat n a man's hat with a tall cylindrical crown and narrow brim, now only worn for some formal occasions

top-heavy adj unstable through being overloaded at the top

topiary (tope-yar-ee) n **1** the art of trimming trees or bushes into artificial decorative shapes **2** trees or bushes trimmed into decorative shapes ▷ adj **3** of or relating to topiary **topiarist** n
WORD ORIGIN Latin topia decorative garden work

topic n a subject of a speech, book, conversation, etc.
WORD ORIGIN Greek topos place

topical adj of or relating to current affairs **topicality** n **topically** adv

topknot n a crest, tuft, decorative bow, etc. on the top of the head

topless adj of or relating to women wearing costumes that do not cover the breasts: topless bars

top-level adj of, involving, or by those with the highest level of influence or ability: a top-level meeting

topmast n the mast next above a lower mast on a sailing vessel

topmost adj at or nearest the top

top-notch adj informal excellent or superb: top-notch entertainment

top off vb to finish or complete, esp. with some decisive action

topography n, pl **-phies 1** the surface features of a region, such as hills, valleys, or rivers: the islands are fragile, with a topography constantly changed by wind and wave **2** the study or description of such surface features **3** the representation of these features on a map **topographer** n **topographical** adj
WORD ORIGIN Greek topos a place + -GRAPHY

topology n a branch of geometry describing the properties of a figure that are unaffected by continuous distortion **topological** adj
WORD ORIGIN Greek topos a place + -LOGY

top out vb to place the highest stone on (a building)

topper n informal a top hat

topping n a sauce or garnish for food

topple vb **-pling, -pled 1** to fall over or cause (something) to fall over, esp. from a height: he staggered back against the railing and toppled over into the river **2** to overthrow or oust: few believe the scandal will topple the government
WORD ORIGIN from TOP¹ (verb)

tops slang n **1 the tops** a person or thing of top quality ▷ adj **2** excellent: Pacino's no-holds-barred performance is tops

topsail n a square sail carried on a yard set on a topmast

top-secret adj (of military or government information) classified as needing the highest level of secrecy and security

A History of English – Modern English

E nglish has long outgrown its birthplace and is now spread all over the world. The expansion of English that began as a by-product of British colonialism continues today with English serving as a standard means of international communication. It is spoken by over 300 million people as a first language and many millions more as a second language. One in five of the planet's population speaks English competently, and projections indicate that the number of people for whom English is a second language will exceed the number of native speakers within the next few years. The expansion of English has influenced its evolution. As a culture absorbs a language, the language is affected by that culture, absorbing elements of vocabulary, grammar and pronunciation from the culture's other languages, and adapting to suit their particular linguistic needs.

As a consequence of this process, English exists in countless varieties; many are well-documented but new varieties are regularly emerging and constantly evolving. Amongst all this variety, standardized forms such as British English and Canadian English exist, incorporating the more neutral (non-dialect) vocabulary and grammar of their regions, and enabling communication within and between regions. American English has arguably become a global standard due to America's considerable presence in today's mass media.

The Americanization of varieties other than American English is a cause for concern for some, certainly in Britain, where American English is seen in some quarters as the offspring who grew up and moved away, changed as a result, and is now having a worrying influence on the native youth. Such concerns over linguistic change are not new. Back in the 17th century, the Modern English period began in a similar atmosphere of anxiety over the sorry state of the language and where it might be heading. The vocabulary, already an unwieldy mix of native Anglo-Saxon words alongside Latin, French, and Scandinavian borrowings, was growing rapidly as a result of imperialist activity, with words like 'chintz' (from Hindi), and 'kayak' (from Western Canadian Inuit) entering the language. Unlike Latin and French, English had no authoritative guides in the form of dictionaries or grammar books to appeal to for direction on word meanings and correct usage, and this circumstance was a source of frustration for many contemporary writers, including Daniel Defoe and Jonathan Swift. In 1712, Swift proposed that an institution should be created for the purpose of 'ascertaining and fixing our language for ever'.

Samuel Johnson's dictionary, published in 1755, represents a landmark in the development of English, establishing as it did a methodology for the creation of further dictionaries. But by contemporary standards it was eccentric and tinged throughout by its creator's humour and prejudices.

Attention then turned to providing an authoritative grammar text, and the results, such as Lowth's *Short Introduction to English Grammar* in 1762, set the tradition which continued into the 19th century of prescribing correct usage (for example the condemning of the double negative, applied to language by analogy from mathematics) rather than describing genuine usage. The development of the sciences which began in the 19th century gave impetus to a new objective discipline of linguistics, and, at least among linguists, there was a new recognition of language as being in a constant state of change, like a living organism, and as such it could never be 'fixed' in the manner desired by Swift. The task of linguists came to be understood in terms of providing 'snapshots' of the language at a given time, or charting linguistic change and understanding its mechanisms, as opposed to providing a model of linguistic correctness.

The vocabulary of English continues to expand and evolve, spurred on by the communications and media revolution, with new words being created to express new concepts. These are often created from the existing resources of the language (*staycation*), as blends of technology terms with existing words (*podcast*), in addition to words which have bubbled to the surface from the regional varieties that produced them (*anyhoo*). Swift may not have approved, and his concerns might be shared by many in the present-day. But others might advise him to *chillax*.

topside *n* a lean cut of beef from the thigh containing no bone

topsoil *n* the surface layer of soil

topsy-turvy *adj* 1 upside down 2 in a state of confusion ▷ *adv* 3 in a topsy-turvy manner
WORD ORIGIN probably top + obsolete *tervy* to turn upside down

top up *vb* 1 to refill (a container), usually to the brim: *I topped up his glass* 2 to add to (an amount) in order to make it sufficient: *the grant can be topped up by a student loan* ▷ *n* **top-up** 3 another serving of a drink in the glass that was used for the first one: *anyone want a top-up?* ▷ *adj* **top-up** 4 serving to top something up: *a top-up loan*

toque (toke) *n* 1 a woman's small round brimless hat 2 *Canad* same as **tuque** (sense 2)
WORD ORIGIN French

tor *n chiefly Brit* a high hill, esp. a bare rocky one
WORD ORIGIN Old English *torr*

Torah *n* the whole body of traditional Jewish teaching, including the Oral Law
WORD ORIGIN Hebrew: precept

torch *n* 1 a small portable electric lamp powered by batteries 2 a wooden shaft dipped in wax or tallow and set alight 3 anything regarded as a source of enlightenment, guidance, etc.: *a torch of hope* 4 **carry a torch for** to be in love with (someone), esp. unrequitedly ▷ *vb* 5 *informal* to deliberately set (a building) on fire
WORD ORIGIN Old French *torche* handful of twisted straw

tore *vb* the past tense of **tear**²

toreador (torr-ee-a-dor) *n* a bullfighter, esp. one on horseback
WORD ORIGIN Spanish

torero (tor-**air**-oh) *n, pl* -ros a bullfighter, esp. one on foot
WORD ORIGIN Spanish

torment *vb* 1 to cause (someone) great pain or suffering 2 to tease or pester (a person or animal) in an annoying or cruel way ▷ *n* 3 physical or mental pain 4 a source of pain or suffering **tormentor** *n*
WORD ORIGIN Latin *tormentum*

tormentil *n* a creeping plant with yellow four-petalled flowers
WORD ORIGIN Old French *tormentille*

torn *vb* 1 the past participle of **tear**² ▷ *adj* 2 split or cut 3 divided or undecided, as in preference: *torn between two lovers*

tornado *n, pl* -dos or -does a rapidly whirling column of air, usually characterized by a dark funnel-shaped cloud causing damage along its path
WORD ORIGIN Spanish *tronada* thunderstorm

torpedo *n, pl* -does 1 a cylindrical self-propelled weapon carrying explosives that is launched from aircraft, ships, or submarines and follows an underwater path to hit its target ▷ *vb* -doing, -doed 2 to attack or hit (a ship) with one or a number of torpedoes 3 to destroy or wreck: *the Prime Minister warned his party against torpedoing the bill*
WORD ORIGIN Latin: crampfish (whose electric discharges can cause numbness)

torpedo boat *n* (formerly) a small high-speed warship for torpedo attacks

torpid *adj* 1 sluggish or dull: *he has a rather torpid intellect* 2 (of a hibernating animal) dormant
WORD ORIGIN Latin *torpere* to be numb

torpor *n* drowsiness and apathy

torque (tork) *n* 1 a force that causes rotation around a central point such as an axle 2 an ancient Celtic necklace or armband made of twisted metal
WORD ORIGIN Latin *torques* necklace + *torquere* to twist

torr *n, pl* torr a unit of pressure equal to one millimetre of mercury (133.3 newtons per square metre)
WORD ORIGIN after E. *Torricelli*, physicist

torrent *n* 1 a fast or violent stream, esp. of water 2 a rapid flow of questions, abuse, etc.
WORD ORIGIN Latin *torrens*

torrential *adj* (of rain) very heavy

torrid *adj* 1 (of weather) so hot and dry as to parch or scorch 2 (of land) arid or parched 3 highly charged emotionally: *a torrid affair*
WORD ORIGIN Latin *torrere* to scorch

torsion *n* the twisting of a part by equal forces being applied at both ends but in opposite directions **torsional** *adj*
WORD ORIGIN Latin *torquere* to twist

torso *n, pl* -sos 1 the trunk of the human body 2 a statue of a nude human trunk, esp. without the head or limbs
WORD ORIGIN Italian: stalk, stump

tort *n law* a civil wrong or injury, for which an action for damages may be brought
WORD ORIGIN Latin *torquere* to twist

tortilla *n Mexican cookery* a kind of thin pancake made from corn meal
WORD ORIGIN Spanish: little cake

tortoise *n* a land reptile with a heavy dome-shaped shell into which it can withdraw its head and legs
WORD ORIGIN Medieval Latin *tortuca*

tortoiseshell *n* 1 the horny yellow-and-brown mottled shell of a sea turtle, used for making ornaments and jewellery 2 a domestic cat with black, cream, and brownish markings 3 a butterfly which has orange-brown wings with black markings ▷ *adj* 4 made of tortoiseshell

tortuous *adj* 1 twisted or winding: *a tortuous route* 2 devious or cunning: *months of tortuous negotiations*
USAGE See at **torture**.

torture *vb* -turing, -tured 1 to cause (someone) extreme physical pain, esp. to extract information, etc.: *suspects were regularly tortured and murdered by the secret police* 2 to cause (someone) mental anguish ▷ *n* 3 physical or mental anguish 4 the practice of torturing a person 5 something which causes great mental distress: *she was going through the torture of a collapsing marriage* **tortured** *adj* **torturer** *n* **torturous** *adj*
WORD ORIGIN Latin *torquere* to twist

USAGE The adjective *torturous* is sometimes confused with *tortuous*. One speaks of a *torturous* experience, i.e. one that involves pain or suffering, but of a *tortuous* road, i.e. one that winds or twists.

Tory *n, pl* -ries 1 a member or supporter of the Conservative Party in Great Britain or Canada 2 *history* a member of the English political party that supported the Church and Crown and traditional political structures and opposed the Whigs ▷ *adj* 3 of or relating to a Tory or Tories **Toryism** *n*
WORD ORIGIN Irish *tóraidhe* outlaw

tosa (toe-za) *n* a large reddish dog, originally bred for fighting
WORD ORIGIN after a province on the Japanese island of Shikoku

toss *vb* 1 to throw (something) lightly 2 to fling or be flung about, esp. in a violent way: *the salty sea breeze tossing the branches of the palms* 3 to coat (food) with a dressing by gentle stirring or mixing: *her technique for tossing Caesar salad* 4 (of a horse) to throw (its rider) 5 to move (one's head) suddenly backwards, as in impatience 6 to throw up (a coin) to decide between alternatives by guessing which side will land uppermost 7 **toss and turn** to be restless when trying to sleep ▷ *n* 8 the act or an instance of tossing 9 the act of deciding between alternatives by throwing up a coin and guessing which side will land uppermost: *Essex won the toss and decided to bat first* 10 **argue the toss** to waste time and energy arguing about an unimportant point 11 **not give a toss** *informal* not to care at all
WORD ORIGIN Scandinavian

toss off *vb* 1 to do or produce (something) quickly and easily: *the tales my sister tossed off so lightly over the dusting* 2 to finish (a drink) in one swallow

toss up *vb* 1 to spin (a coin) in the air in order to decide between alternatives by guessing which side will land uppermost ▷ *n* **toss-up** 2 an instance of tossing up a coin 3 *informal* an even chance or risk: *if it's a toss-up for a top position, he gives it to the woman*

tot *n* 1 a very young child 2 a small drink of spirits
WORD ORIGIN origin unknown

total *n* 1 the whole, esp. regarded as the sum of a number of parts 2 **in total** overall: *the company employs over 700 people in total* ▷ *adj* 3 complete: *a total ban on alcohol* 4 being or related to a total: *the total number of deaths* ▷ *vb* -talling, -talled or *US* -taling, -taled 5 to amount to: *the firm's losses totalled more than $2 billion* 6 to add up: *purchases are totalled with a pencil and a notepad* **totally** *adv*
WORD ORIGIN Latin *totus* all

totalitarian *adj* 1 of a political system in which there is only one party, which allows no opposition and attempts to control everything: *a totalitarian state* ▷ *n* 2 a person who is in favour of totalitarian policies **totalitarianism** *n*

totality *n, pl* -ties 1 the whole amount 2 the state of being total

totalizator, **totalizer** or **totalisator**, **totaliser** n a machine to operate a system of betting on a racecourse in which money is paid out to the winners in proportion to their stakes

tote[1] vb **toting**, **toted** informal **1** to carry or wear (a gun) **2** to haul or carry ▸ **WORD ORIGIN** origin unknown

tote[2] n **the tote** trademark short for **totalizator**

tote bag n a large handbag or shopping bag

totem n **1** (esp. among Native Americans) an object or animal symbolizing a clan or family **2** a representation of such an object **totemic** adj **totemism** n ▸ **WORD ORIGIN** from a Native American language

totem pole n a pole carved or painted with totemic figures set up by certain North American Indians as a tribal symbol

totter vb **1** to move in an unsteady manner **2** to sway or shake as if about to fall **3** to be failing, unstable, or precarious: the world was tottering on the edge of war ▸ **WORD ORIGIN** origin unknown

tot up vb **totting**, **totted** to add (numbers) together: I'll just tot up what you owe me ▸ **WORD ORIGIN** from total

toucan n a tropical American fruit-eating bird with a large brightly coloured bill ▸ **WORD ORIGIN** Portuguese tucano

touch vb **1** to cause or permit a part of the body to come into contact with (someone or something): the baking tin is too hot to touch **2** to tap, feel, or strike (someone or something): he touched me on the shoulder **3** to come or bring (something) into contact with (something else): the plane's wheels touched the runway **4** to move or disturb by handling: we shouldn't touch anything before the police arrive **5** to have an effect on: millions of people's lives had been touched by the music of the Beatles **6** to produce an emotional response in: the painful truth of it touched her **7** to eat or drink: she hardly ever touched alcohol **8** to compare to in quality or attainment; equal or match: nothing can touch them for scope and detail **9** Brit, Austral, & NZ slang to ask (someone) for a loan or gift of money **10** to fondle in a sexual manner: I wouldn't let him touch me unless I was in the mood **11** to strike, harm, or molest: I never touched him! **12** **touch on** or **upon** to allude to briefly or in passing: these two issues may be touched upon during the talks ▸ n **13** the sense by which the texture and other qualities of objects can be experienced when they come in contact with a part of the body surface, esp. the tips of the fingers ▸ Related adjective: **tactile 14** the feel or texture of an object as perceived by this sense: she enjoyed the touch of the damp grass on her feet **15** the act or an instance of something coming into contact with the body: he remembered the touch of her hand **16** a gentle push, tap, or caress: the switch takes only the merest touch to operate **17** a small amount; trace: a touch

of luxury **18** a particular manner or style of doing something: his songs always reveal his keen melodic touch **19** a detail of some work: final touches were now being put to the plans **20** a slight attack: a touch of dysentery **21** (in sports such as football or rugby) the area outside the lines marking the side of the pitch: he kicked the ball into touch **22** the technique of fingering a keyboard instrument **23** a touch slightly or marginally: it's nice, but a touch expensive **24** **in touch a** regularly speaking to, writing to, or visiting someone **b** having up-to-date knowledge or understanding of a situation or trend **25** **lose touch a** to gradually stop speaking to, writing to, or visiting someone **b** to stop having up-to-date knowledge or understanding of a situation or trend **26** **out of touch a** no longer speaking to, writing to, or visiting someone **b** no longer having up-to-date knowledge or understanding of a situation or trend ▸ See also **touchdown, touch off, touch up** ▸ **WORD ORIGIN** Old French tochier

touch and go adj risky or critical: it was touch and go whether the mission would succeed

touchdown n **1** the moment at which a landing aircraft or spacecraft comes into contact with the landing surface **2** American football a scoring move in which an attacking player takes the ball into the area behind his opponents' goal ▸ vb **touch down 3** (of an aircraft or spacecraft) to land

touché (too-shay) interj **1** an acknowledgment that a remark or witty reply has been effective **2** an acknowledgment of a scoring hit in fencing ▸ **WORD ORIGIN** French, literally: touched

touched adj **1** moved to sympathy or emotion: I was touched by her understanding **2** slightly mad: she's a bit touched

touching adj **1** arousing tender feelings ▸ prep **2** relating to or concerning: she might talk about matters touching both of them

touch judge n one of the two linesmen in rugby

touchline n either of the lines marking the side of the playing area in certain games, such as rugby

touch off vb to cause (a disturbance, violence, etc.) to begin: the death of a teenager in police custody touched off a night of riots

touchpaper n a fuse of dark blue paper on a firework

touchstone n a standard by which judgment is made: this restaurant is the touchstone for genuine Italian cookery in Leeds

touch-type vb **-typing**, **-typed** to type without looking at the keyboard **touch-typist** n

touch up vb to enhance, renovate, or falsify (a picture) by adding extra touches to it

touchwood n something, esp. dry wood, used as tinder ▸ **WORD ORIGIN** touch (in the sense: to kindle)

touchy adj **touchier**, **touchiest 1** easily upset or irritated: he is a touchy and quick-tempered man **2** requiring careful

and tactful handling: a touchy subject **touchiness** n

touchy-feely adj informal, sometimes offensive sensitive and caring

tough adj **1** strong and difficult to break, cut, or tear: this fabric is tough and water-resistant **2** (of meat or other food) difficult to cut and chew; not tender **3** physically or mentally strong and able to cope with hardship: a tough uncompromising woman, unwilling to take no for an answer **4** rough or violent: a tough and ruthless mercenary **5** strict and firm: the country's tough drugs laws **6** difficult or troublesome to do or deal with: a tough task **7** **tough luck!** informal an expression of lack of sympathy for someone else's problems ▸ n **8** a rough, vicious, or violent person ▸ vb **9** **tough it out** informal to endure a difficult situation until it improves: criticism of his performance has reinforced his desire to tough it out **toughness** n ▸ **WORD ORIGIN** Old English tōh

toughen vb to make or become tough or tougher

toupee (too-pay) n a hairpiece worn by men to cover a bald place ▸ **WORD ORIGIN** French toupet forelock

tour n **1** an extended journey visiting places of interest along the route **2** a trip, by a band, theatre company, etc. to perform in several places **3** an overseas trip made by a cricket team, rugby team, etc. to play in several places **4** mil a period of service, esp. in one place: the regiment has served several tours in Northern Ireland ▸ vb **5** to make a tour of (a place) ▸ **WORD ORIGIN** Old French: a turn

tour de force n, pl **tours de force** a masterly or brilliant stroke or achievement ▸ **WORD ORIGIN** French, literally: feat of skill or strength

tourism n tourist travel, esp. when regarded as an industry

tourist n **1** a person who travels for pleasure, usually sightseeing and staying in hotels **2** a member of a sports team which is visiting a country to play a series of matches: the tourists were bowled out for 135 **3** the lowest class of accommodation on a passenger ship ▸ adj **4** of or relating to tourists or tourism: a popular tourist attraction **5** of the lowest class of accommodation on a passenger ship or aircraft

touristy adj informal, often disparaging full of tourists or tourist attractions

tourmaline n a hard crystalline mineral used in jewellery and electrical equipment ▸ **WORD ORIGIN** German Turmalin

tournament n **1** a sporting competition in which contestants play a series of games to determine an overall winner **2** Also: **tourney** medieval history a contest in which mounted knights fought for a prize ▸ **WORD ORIGIN** Old French torneiement

tournedos (tour-ned-doh) n, pl **-dos** (-doze) a thick round steak of beef ▸ **WORD ORIGIN** French

tourniquet (tour-nick-kay) n med a strip of cloth tied tightly round an

t

arm or leg to stop bleeding from an artery
WORD ORIGIN French

tourtière (tour-tee-**air**) n Canad a type of meat pie

tousle (rhymes with **arousal**) vb -sling, -sled to make (hair or clothes) ruffled and untidy **tousled** adj
WORD ORIGIN Low German tūsen to shake

tout (rhymes with **shout**) vb 1 to seek (business, customers, etc.) or try to sell (goods), esp. in a persistent or direct manner: he went from door to door touting for business 2 to put forward or recommend (a person or thing) as a good or suitable example or candidate: the plant was once touted as a showcase factory ▷ n 3 a person who sells tickets for a heavily booked event at inflated prices
WORD ORIGIN Old English tȳtan to peep

tow¹ vb 1 to pull or drag (a vehicle), esp. by means of a rope or cable ▷ n 2 the act or an instance of towing 3 in tow informal in one's company or one's charge or under one's influence: she had an older man in tow 4 on tow (of a vehicle) being towed
WORD ORIGIN Old English togian

tow² n fibres of hemp, flax, jute, etc. prepared for spinning
WORD ORIGIN Old English tōw

towards or US **toward** prep 1 in the direction of: towards the lake 2 with regard to: hostility towards the President 3 as a contribution to: the profits will go towards three projects 4 just before: towards evening

towbar n a rigid metal bar attached to the back of a vehicle, from which a trailer or caravan can be towed

towel n 1 a piece of absorbent cloth or paper used for drying things 2 **throw in the towel** see **throw in** (sense 3) ▷ vb -elling, -elled or US -eling, -eled 3 to dry or wipe with a towel
WORD ORIGIN Old French toaille

towelling or US **toweling** n a soft, fairly thick fabric used to make towels and dressing gowns

tower n 1 a tall, usually square or circular structure, sometimes part of a larger building and usually built for a specific purpose 2 **tower of strength** a person who supports or comforts someone else at a time of difficulty ▷ vb 3 **tower over** to be much taller than: sheer walls of limestone towered over us
WORD ORIGIN Latin turris

tower block n Brit a very tall building divided into flats or offices

towering adj 1 very tall 2 very impressive or important: his towering presence on stage 3 very intense: in a towering rage

towheaded adj having blonde or yellowish hair
WORD ORIGIN tow flax

town n 1 a large group of houses, shops, factories, etc. smaller than a city and larger than a village ▶ Related adjective: **urban** 2 the nearest town or the chief town of an area: people from town rarely went out to the farm 3 the central area of a town where most of the shops and offices are: we're going to a

pub in town tonight 4 the people of a town: the town is split over the plans for a bypass 5 built-up areas in general, as opposed to the countryside: migration from the country to the town 6 **go to town** to make a supreme or unrestricted effort 7 **on the town** visiting nightclubs, restaurants, etc.: we'd a night on the town to celebrate her promotion
WORD ORIGIN Old English tūn village

town clerk n (currently in Australia and in Britain until 1974) the chief administrative officer of a town

town crier n (formerly) a person employed to make public announcements in the streets

town hall n a large building in a town often containing the council offices and a hall for public meetings

town house n 1 a terraced house in an urban area, esp. an up-market one 2 a person's town residence as distinct from his or her country residence

townie or **townee** n chiefly Brit informal, often disparaging a resident in a town, esp. as distinct from country dwellers

town planning n the comprehensive planning of the physical and social development of a town

township n 1 a small town 2 (in South Africa) a planned urban settlement of black people or people of mixed racial descent 3 (in the US and Canada) a small unit of local government, often consisting of a town and the area surrounding it 4 (in Canada) a land-survey area, usually 36 square miles (93 square kilometres)

townsman n, pl -men an inhabitant of a town **townswoman** fem n

townspeople or **townsfolk** pl n the people who live in a town

towpath n a path beside a canal or river, formerly used by horses pulling barges

towrope n a rope or cable used for towing a vehicle or vessel

toxaemia or US **toxemia** (tox-**seem**-ya) n 1 a form of blood poisoning caused by toxins released by bacteria at a wound or other site of infection 2 a condition in pregnant women characterized by high blood pressure **toxaemic** or US **toxemic** adj
WORD ORIGIN Latin toxicum poison + haima blood

toxic adj 1 poisonous: toxic fumes 2 caused by poison: toxic effects **toxicity** n
WORD ORIGIN Greek toxikon (pharmakon) (poison) used on arrows

toxicology n the branch of science concerned with poisons and their effects **toxicological** adj **toxicologist** n

toxin n 1 any of various poisonous substances produced by microorganisms and causing certain diseases 2 any other poisonous substance of plant or animal origin

toy n 1 an object designed for children to play with, such as a doll or model car 2 an object that adults use for entertainment rather than for a serious purpose: I do use my computer: it's not just a toy ▷ adj 3 being an imitation or model of something for children to play with: a toy aeroplane 4 (of a dog) of a variety

much smaller than is normal for that breed: a toy poodle
WORD ORIGIN origin unknown

toy boy n the much younger male lover of an older woman

toy-toy or **toyi-toyi** S African n 1 a dance expressing defiance and protest ▷ vb 2 to dance in this way
WORD ORIGIN origin uncertain

toy with vb 1 to consider an idea without being serious about it or being able to decide about it: I've been toying with the idea of setting up my own firm 2 to keep moving (an object) about with one's fingers, esp. when thinking about something else: Jessica sat toying with her glass

trace vb tracing, traced 1 to locate or work out (the cause or source of something): he traced the trouble to a faulty connection 2 to find (something or someone that was missing): the police were unable to trace her missing husband 3 to discover or describe the progress or development of (something): throughout the 19th century we can trace the development of more complex machinery 4 to copy (a design, map, etc.) by putting a piece of transparent paper over it and following the lines which show through the paper with a pencil 5 to make the outline of (a shape or pattern): his index finger was tracing circles on the arm of the chair ▷ n 6 a mark, footprint, or other sign that shows that a person, animal, or thing has been in a particular place: the police could find no trace of the missing van 7 an amount of something so small that it is barely noticeable: I detected a trace of jealousy in her voice 8 a remnant of something: traces of an Iron-Age fort remain visible 9 a pattern made on a screen or a piece of paper by a device that is measuring or detecting something: a baffling radar trace **traceable** adj
WORD ORIGIN French tracier

trace element n a chemical element that occurs in very small amounts in soil, water, etc. and is essential for healthy growth

tracer n 1 a projectile that can be observed when in flight by the burning of chemical substances in its base 2 med an element or other substance introduced into the body to study metabolic processes

tracer bullet n a round of small-arms ammunition containing a tracer

tracery n, pl -eries 1 a pattern of interlacing lines, esp. one in a stained glass window 2 any fine lacy pattern resembling this

traces pl n 1 the two side straps that connect a horse's harness to the vehicle being pulled 2 **kick over the traces** to escape or defy control
WORD ORIGIN Old French trait

trachea (track-**kee**-a) n, pl -cheae (-**kee**-ee) anat, zool the tube that carries inhaled air from the throat to the lungs
WORD ORIGIN Greek

tracheotomy (track-ee-**ot**-a-mee) n, pl -mies surgical incision into the trachea, as performed when the air passage has been blocked
WORD ORIGIN TRACHEA + Greek tomē a cutting

American Popular Music

Quantitatively, the United States has the world's largest music industry. Qualitatively, the American democratic genius is most characteristically expressed through its popular song. It is no accident that many of its greatest, most original songwriters were blacks or Jews who sought to overcome poverty and prejudice. So it was that Irving Berlin, born Israel Baline, wrote 'White Christmas', the bestselling single record of all time, and that Otis Redding wrote 'Respect', a huge hit when sung by another black artist, Aretha Franklin.

In 'Respect' a woman asks for 'just a little bit' of respect from her man, implicitly a plea for black self-affirmation, which was more explicitly expressed in the Staples Singers' hit, 'Respect Yourself' ('Take the sheet off your face, boy, it's a brand new day'). American society was coming to terms with its racist past, and in their tone and attitude such songs were radically different from the eighteenth-century 'Yankee Doodle', which may first have been written to mock Americans but became a patriotic jingle, or 'Happy Birthday to You', composed by two nineteenth-century Kentucky kindergarten teachers, perhaps the most widely recognized song in English.

The chronically impoverished Stephen Foster, the greatest American songwriter of the nineteenth century, illustrates the dualities of American culture. During the Civil War era he wrote both celebrations of the South such as 'My Old Kentucky Home' and Union rallying cries such as 'We Are Coming, Father Abraham, 300,000 More'. Disillusionment about the American Dream and the reaction against patriotic chauvinism reached their peak in the 1960s, as singer-songwriters such as Bob Dylan ('Blowin' in the Wind' and 'The Times They Are a-Changin'') championed civil rights and raged against their country's involvement in the Vietnam War. Throughout its history, America's self-perception has ranged from the unblushing pride of 'America the Beautiful' and Irving Berlin's 'God Bless America' to the decidedly more ambiguous 'American Pie' by Don McLean ('Drove my chevy to the levee, / But the levee was dry') and Bruce Springsteen's 'Born in the USA'. ('...I'm a long gone daddy in the USA').

Not all American songs were about politics and the individual's place in society. Many tapped the universal theme of romantic love, or the loss of it. Novelty songs such as Roger Miller's 'Ya can't roller skate in a buffalo herd' and Jerry Livingston's 'Mairzy Doats' (when sung, the words sound like, 'Mairzy doats and dozy doats and liddle lamzy divey', but said slowly they are revealed as 'Mares eat oats and does eat oats and little lambs eat ivy') were ceaselessly inventive. Broadway musicals such as *Oklahoma!* and *West Side Story*, even those with non-American settings and characters, as in *My Fair Lady* and *The Sound of Music*, took tunes and libretti far from their European antecedents, and songs leapt from movies to the hit parade. Jerome Kern ('All the Things You Are'), Cole Porter ('I've Got You Under My Skin') and Hoagy Carmichael ('Stardust') introduced melodic sophistication and wit. Country and western music drew on British balladic roots newly bloomed in America, reaching aching poignancy in the work of Hank Williams:

Like a bird that's lost its mate in flight
I'm alone and oh so blue tonight
Like a piece of driftwood on the sea
May you never be alone like me

The same was true of folk music, especially as it took form in the hills of Appalachia, just as transatlantic, African origins were found in the blues. In a great song, music and words ineffably combine to become a poem. This perfection was achieved by such composer-lyricist teams as George and Ira Gershwin (most notably in 'Summertime' from the folk opera *Porgy and Bess*) and Harold Arlen and Johnny Mercer, who wrote 'One for My Baby (and One More for the Road)'. A verse in the anonymous 'Goodnight, Irene', alternatively, 'Irene, Goodnight', links performer and audience:

You cause me to weep, you cause me to mourn
You cause me to leave my home
But the very last words I heard her say
Was 'Please sing me one more song.'

trachoma (track-**oh**-ma) n a chronic contagious disease of the eye characterized by inflammation of the inner surface of the lids and the formation of scar tissue
WORD ORIGIN Greek trakhōma roughness

tracing n 1 a copy of something, such as a map, made by tracing 2 a line traced by a recording instrument

track n 1 a rough road or path: *a farm track* 2 the mark or trail left by something that has passed by: *the fox didn't leave any tracks* 3 a rail or pair of parallel rails on which a vehicle, such as a train, runs 4 a course for running or racing on: *a running track* 5 a separate song or piece of music on a record, tape, or CD: *Dolphy switches back to bass clarinet for the final track* 6 a course of action, thought, etc.: *I don't think you're on the right track at all* 7 an endless band on the wheels of a tank, bulldozer, etc. to enable it to move across rough ground 8 **keep** or **lose track of** to follow or fail to follow the course or progress of 9 **off the beaten track** in an isolated location: *the village where she lives is a bit off the beaten track* ▷ vb 10 to follow the trail of (a person or animal) 11 to follow the flight path of (a satellite etc.) by picking up signals transmitted or reflected by it 12 *films* to follow (a moving object) while filming ▶ See also **tracks**
▷ **tracker** n
WORD ORIGIN Old French trac

track down vb to find (someone or something) by tracking or pursuing

tracker dog n a dog specially trained to search for missing people

track event n a competition in athletics, such as sprinting, that takes place on a running track

track record n informal the past record of the accomplishments and failures of a person or organization

tracks pl n 1 marks, such as footprints, left by someone or something that has passed 2 **in one's tracks** on the very spot where one is standing: *those words stopped her in her tracks* 3 **make tracks** to leave or depart: *it was time to start making tracks*

track shoe n a light running shoe fitted with steel spikes for better grip

tracksuit n a warm loose-fitting suit worn by athletes etc. esp. during training

tract[1] n 1 a large area, esp. of land: *an extensive tract of moorland* 2 anat a system of organs or glands that has a particular function: *the urinary tract*
WORD ORIGIN Latin tractus a stretching out

tract[2] n a pamphlet, esp. a religious one
WORD ORIGIN Latin tractatus

tractable adj formal easy to control, manage, or deal with: *he could easily manage his tractable and worshipping younger brother* **tractability** n
WORD ORIGIN Latin tractare to manage

traction n 1 pulling, esp. by engine power: *the increased use of electric traction* 2 med the application of a steady pull on an injured limb using a system of weights and pulleys or splints: *he was in traction for weeks following the accident* 3 the grip that the wheels of a vehicle have on the ground: *four-wheel drive gives much better traction in wet or icy conditions*
WORD ORIGIN Latin tractus dragged

traction engine n a heavy steam-powered vehicle used, esp. formerly, for drawing heavy loads along roads or over rough ground

tractor n a motor vehicle with large rear wheels, used to pull heavy loads, esp. farm machinery
WORD ORIGIN Late Latin: one who pulls

trade n 1 the buying and selling of goods and services 2 a person's job, esp. a craft requiring skill: *he's a plumber by trade* 3 the people and practices of an industry, craft, or business 4 amount of custom or commercial dealings: *a brisk trade in second-hand weapons* 5 a specified market or business: *the wool trade* 6 **trades** the trade winds ▷ vb **trading**, **traded** 7 to buy and sell (goods) 8 to exchange: *he traded a job in New York for a life as a cowboy* 9 to engage in trade 10 to deal or do business (with) **tradable** or **tradeable** adj **trader** n **trading** n
WORD ORIGIN Low German: track, hence a regular business

trade-in n 1 a used article given in part payment for the purchase of a new article ▷ vb **trade in** 2 to give (a used article) as part payment for a new article

trademark n 1 **a** the name or other symbol used by a manufacturer to distinguish his or her products from those of competitors **b Registered Trademark** one that is officially registered and legally protected 2 any distinctive sign or mark of a person or thing: *the designer bars which have become the trademark of the city*

trade name n 1 the name used by a trade to refer to a product or range of products 2 the name under which a commercial enterprise operates in business

trade-off n an exchange, esp. as a compromise: *there is often a trade-off between manpower costs and computer costs*

trade on vb to exploit or take advantage of: *a demanding woman who traded on her poor health to get her own way*

tradescantia (trad-dess-**kan**-shee-a) n a widely cultivated plant with striped leaves
WORD ORIGIN after John Tradescant, botanist

trade secret n a secret formula, technique, or process known and used to advantage by only one manufacturer

tradesman n, pl -men 1 a skilled worker, such as an electrician or painter 2 a shopkeeper **tradeswoman** fem n

Trades Union Congress n (in Britain and South Africa) the major association of trade unions, which includes all the larger unions

trade union or **trades union** n a society of workers formed to protect and improve their working conditions, pay, etc. **trade unionism** or **trades unionism** n **trade unionist** or **trades unionist** n

trade wind n a wind blowing steadily towards the equator either from the northeast in the N hemisphere or the southeast in the S hemisphere

trading estate n chiefly Brit a large area in which a number of commercial or industrial firms are situated

tradition n 1 the handing down from generation to generation of customs, beliefs, etc. 2 the unwritten body of beliefs, customs, etc. handed down from generation to generation 3 a custom or practice of long standing 4 **in the tradition of** having many features similar to those of a person or thing in the past: *a thriller writer in the tradition of Chandler*
WORD ORIGIN Latin traditio a handing down

traditional adj of, relating to, or being a tradition **traditionally** adv

traditionalist n a person who supports established customs or beliefs **traditionalism** n

traduce vb -ducing, -duced formal to speak badly of (someone) **traducement** n **traducer** n
WORD ORIGIN Latin traducere to lead over, disgrace

traffic n 1 the vehicles travelling on roads 2 the movement of vehicles or people in a particular place or for a particular purpose: *air traffic* 3 trade, esp. of an illicit kind: *drug traffic* 4 the exchange of ideas between people or organizations: *a lively traffic in ideas* ▷ vb -ficking, -ficked 5 to carry on trade or business, esp. of an illicit kind: *he confessed to trafficking in gold and ivory* **trafficker** n
WORD ORIGIN Old French trafique

traffic island n a raised area in the middle of a road designed as a guide for traffic flow and to provide a stopping place for pedestrians crossing

traffic jam n a number of vehicles so obstructed that they can scarcely move

traffic light n one of a set of coloured lights placed at a junction to control the flow of traffic

traffic warden n Brit a person employed to supervise road traffic and report traffic offences

tragedian (traj-**jee**-dee-an) or fem **tragedienne** (traj-jee-dee-**enn**) n 1 an actor who specializes in tragic roles 2 a writer of tragedy

tragedy n, pl -dies 1 a shocking or sad event 2 a serious play, film, or opera in which the main character is destroyed by a combination of a personal failing and adverse circumstances
WORD ORIGIN Greek tragōidia

tragic adj 1 sad and distressing because it involves death or suffering: *she was blinded in a tragic accident* 2 of or like a tragedy: *a tragic hero* 3 sad or mournful: *a tragic melody* **tragically** adv

tragicomedy n, pl -dies a play or other written work having both comic and tragic elements **tragicomic** adj

trail n 1 a rough path across open country or through a forest 2 a route along a series of roads or paths that has been specially planned to let people see or do particular things: *a nature trail through the woods* 3 a print, mark, or scent left by a person, animal, or object:

a trail of blood was found down three flights of stairs **4** something that trails behind: *a vapour trail* **5** a sequence of results from an event: *a trail of mishaps* ▷ *vb* **6** to drag or stream along the ground or through the air behind someone or something: *part of her sari trailed behind her on the floor* **7** to lag behind (a person or thing): *Max had arrived as well, trailing behind the others* **8** to follow or hunt (an animal or person), usually secretly, by following the marks or tracks he, she, or it has made: *the police had trailed him the length and breadth of the country* **9** to be falling behind in a race, match or competition: *they trailed 2-1 at half-time* **10** to move wearily or slowly: *we spent the afternoon trailing round the shops* **WORD ORIGIN** Old French *trailler* to tow

trail away *or* **off** *vb* to become fainter, quieter, or weaker: *his voice trailed away*

trailblazer *n* a pioneer in a particular field **trailblazing** *adj, n*

trailer *n* **1** a road vehicle, usually two-wheeled, towed by a motor vehicle and used for carrying goods, transporting boats, etc.: *ahead of us was a tractor, drawing a trailer laden with dung* **2** the rear section of an articulated lorry **3** an extract or series of extracts from a film, TV, or radio programme, used to advertise it **4** *US & Canad* same as **caravan** (sense 1)

trailer trash *n derogatory* poor people living in trailer parks in the US

trailing *adj* (of a plant) having a long stem which spreads over the ground or hangs loosely: *trailing ivy*

train *vb* **1** to instruct (someone) in a skill: *soldiers are trained to obey orders unquestioningly* **2** to learn the skills needed to do a particular job or activity: *she was training to be a computer programmer* **3** to do exercises and prepare for a specific purpose: *he was training for a marathon* **4** to focus on or aim at (something): *the warship kept its guns trained on the trawler* **5** to discipline (an animal) to obey commands or perform tricks **6** to tie or prune (a plant) so that it grows in a particular way: *he had trained the roses to grow up the wall* ▷ *n* **7** a line of railway coaches or wagons coupled together and drawn by a engine **8** a sequence or series: *following an earlier train of thought* **9** the long back section of a dress that trails along the floor **10** **in its train** as a consequence: *economic mismanagement brought unemployment and inflation in its train* **11** **in train** actually happening or being done: *the programme of reforms set in train by the new government* ▷ *adj* **12** of or by a train: *the long train journey North* **WORD ORIGIN** Old French *trahiner*

trainbearer *n* an attendant who holds up the train of a dignitary's robe or bride's gown

trainee *n* **1** a person undergoing training ▷ *adj* **2** (of a person) undergoing training: *a trainee journalist*

trainer *n* **1** a person who coaches a person or team in a sport **2** a person who trains racehorses **3** an aircraft used for training pilots **4** *Brit* a flat-soled sports shoe of the style used by athletes when training

training *n* the process of bringing a person to an agreed standard of proficiency by practice and instruction

training shoe *n* same as **trainer** (sense 4)

train spotter *n Brit* **1** a person who collects the numbers of railway locomotives **2** *informal* a person who is obsessed with trivial details, esp. of a subject generally considered uninteresting

traipse *informal vb* **traipsing, traipsed** **1** to walk heavily or tiredly ▷ *n* **2** a long or tiring walk **WORD ORIGIN** origin unknown

trait *n* a characteristic feature or quality of a person or thing **WORD ORIGIN** French

traitor *n* a person who betrays friends, country, a cause, etc. **traitorous** *adj* **traitress** *fem n* **WORD ORIGIN** Latin *tradere* to hand over

trajectory *n, pl* **-ries** the path described by an object moving in air or space, esp. the curved path of a projectile **WORD ORIGIN** Latin *trajectus* cast over

tram *n* an electrically driven public transport vehicle that runs on rails laid into the road and takes its power from an overhead cable **WORD ORIGIN** probably from Low German *traam* beam

tramlines *pl n* **1** the tracks on which a tram runs **2** the outer markings along the sides of a tennis or badminton court

trammel *vb* **-melling, -melled** *or US* **-meling, -meled** **1** to hinder or restrict: *trammelled by family responsibilities* ▷ *n* **2** **trammels** things that hinder or restrict someone: *the trammels of social respectability* **WORD ORIGIN** Old French *tramail* three-mesh net

tramp *vb* **1** to walk long and far; hike **2** to walk heavily or firmly across or through (a place): *she tramped slowly up the beach* ▷ *n* **3** a homeless person who travels about on foot, living by begging or doing casual work **4** a long hard walk; hike: *we went for a long tramp over the downs* **5** the sound of heavy regular footsteps: *we could hear the tramp of the marching soldiers* **6** a small cargo ship that does not run on a regular schedule **7** *US, Canad, Austral, & NZ slang* a promiscuous woman **WORD ORIGIN** probably from Middle Low German *trampen*

tramping *n NZ* the leisure activity of walking in the bush **tramper** *n*

trample *vb* **-pling, -pled** **1** Also: **trample on** to tread on and crush: *three children were trampled to death when the crowd panicked and ran* **2** **trample on** to treat (a person or his or her rights or feelings) with disregard or contempt **WORD ORIGIN** from *tramp*

trampoline *n* **1** a tough canvas sheet suspended by springs or cords from a frame, which acrobats, gymnasts, etc. bounce on ▷ *vb* **-lining, -lined** **2** to exercise on a trampoline **WORD ORIGIN** Italian *trampolino*

trance *n* **1** a hypnotic state resembling sleep in which a person is unable to move or act of his or her own will **2** a dazed or stunned state **WORD ORIGIN** Latin *transire* to go over

tranche (**trahnsh**) *n* an instalment or portion, esp. of a loan or share issue: *the new shares will be offered in four tranches around the world*

trannie *or* **tranny** *n, pl* **-nies** *informal chiefly Brit* a transistor radio

tranquil *adj* calm, peaceful, or quiet **tranquilly** *adv* **WORD ORIGIN** Latin *tranquillus*

tranquillity *or US sometimes* **tranquility** *n* a state of calmness or peace

tranquillize, -lise *or US* **tranquilize** *vb* **-lizing, -lized** *or* **-lising, -lised** **1** to make or become calm or calmer **2** to give (someone) a drug to make them calm or calmer **tranquillization, -lisation** *or US* **tranquilization** *n* **tranquillizing, -lising** *or US* **tranquilizing** *adj*

tranquillizer, -liser *or US* **tranquilizer** *n* a drug that calms someone suffering from anxiety, tension, etc.

trans. **1** transitive **2** translated

trans- *prefix* **1** across, beyond, crossing, or on the other side of: *transnational* **2** changing thoroughly: *transliterate* **WORD ORIGIN** Latin

transact *vb* to do, conduct, or negotiate (a business deal) **WORD ORIGIN** Latin *transigere* to drive through

transaction *n* **1** something that is transacted, esp. a business deal **2** **transactions** the records of the proceedings of a society etc.: *an article on land use in the Niagara area taken from the 'Transactions of the Royal Canadian Institute'*

transalpine *adj* beyond the Alps, esp. as viewed from Italy

transatlantic *adj* **1** on or from the other side of the Atlantic **2** crossing the Atlantic

transceiver *n* a device which transmits and receives radio or electronic signals **WORD ORIGIN** *trans(mitter)* + *(re)ceiver*

transcend *vb* **1** to go above or beyond what is expected or normal: *a vital party issue that transcends traditional party loyalties* **2** to overcome or be superior to: *to transcend all difficulties* **WORD ORIGIN** Latin *transcendere* to climb over

transcendent *adj* **1** above or beyond what is expected or normal **2** *theol* (of God) having existence outside the created world **transcendence** *n*

transcendental *adj* **1** above or beyond what is expected or normal **2** *philosophy* based on intuition or innate belief rather than experience **3** supernatural or mystical **transcendentally** *adv*

transcendentalism *n* any system of philosophy that seeks to discover the nature of reality by examining the processes of thought rather than the things thought about, or that emphasizes intuition as a means to knowledge **transcendentalist** *n, adj*

Transcendental Meditation *n* a technique (trademarked in the US), based on Hindu traditions, for relaxing and refreshing the mind and body through the silent repetition of a special formula of words

transcribe *vb* **-scribing, -scribed 1** to write, type, or print out (a text) fully from a speech or notes **2** to make an electrical recording of (a programme or speech) for a later broadcast **3** *music* to rewrite (a piece of music) for an instrument other than that originally intended **transcriber** *n*
WORD ORIGIN Latin *transcribere*

transcript *n* **1** a written, typed, or printed copy made by transcribing **2** *chiefly US & Canad* an official record of a student's school progress

transcription *n* **1** the act of transcribing **2** something transcribed

transducer *n* any device, such as a microphone or electric motor, that converts one form of energy into another
WORD ORIGIN Latin *transducere* to lead across

transect *n biol* a sample strip of land used to monitor plant distribution and animal populations within a given area

transept *n* either of the two shorter wings of a cross-shaped church
WORD ORIGIN Latin *trans-* across + *saeptum* enclosure

transfer *vb* **-ferring, -ferred 1** to change or move from one thing, person, place, etc. to another: *he was transferred from prison to hospital* **2** to move (money or property) from the control of one person or organization to that of another: *the money has been transferred into your account* **3** (of a football club) to sell or release (a player) to another club: *he was transferred to Juventus for a world record fee* **4** to move (a drawing or design) from one surface to another ▷ *n* **5** the act, process, or system of transferring, or the state of being transferred **6** a person or thing that transfers or is transferred **7** a design or drawing that is transferred from one surface to another **8** the moving of (money or property) from the control of one person or organization to that of another **transferable** *or* **transferrable** *adj* **transference** *n*
WORD ORIGIN Latin *trans* across + *ferre* to carry

transfer station *n NZ* a depot where rubbish is sorted for recycling

transfiguration *n* a transfiguring or being transfigured

Transfiguration *n* **1** *New Testament* the change in the appearance of Christ on the mountain **2** the Church festival held in commemoration of this on August 6

transfigure *vb* **-guring, -gured 1** to change or cause to change in appearance **2** to become or cause to become more exalted
WORD ORIGIN Latin *trans-* beyond + *figura* appearance

transfix *vb* **-fixing, -fixed** *or* **-fixt 1** to make (someone) motionless, esp. with horror or shock: *they stood transfixed and revolted by what they saw* **2** to pierce (a person or animal) through with a pointed object: *the Pharaoh is shown transfixing enemies with arrows from a moving chariot*
WORD ORIGIN Latin *transfigere* to pierce through

transform *vb* **1** to change completely in form or function: *the last forty years have seen the country transformed from a peasant economy to a major industrial power* **2** to change so as to make better or more attractive: *most religions claim to be able to transform people's lives* **3** to convert (one form of energy) to another **4** *maths* to change the form of (an equation, expression, etc.) without changing its value **5** to change (an alternating current or voltage) using a transformer
WORD ORIGIN Latin *transformare*

transformation *n* **1** a change or alteration, esp. a radical one **2** the act of transforming or the state of being transformed **3** *S African* a political slogan for demographic change in the power struggle

transformer *n* a device that transfers an alternating current from one circuit to one or more other circuits, usually with a change of voltage

transfuse *vb* **-fusing, -fused 1** to inject (blood or other fluid) into a blood vessel **2** *literary* to transmit or instil
WORD ORIGIN Latin *transfundere* to pour out

transfusion *n* **1** the injection of blood, blood plasma, etc. into the blood vessels of a patient **2** the act of transferring something: *a transfusion of new funds*

transgenic *adj* (of an animal or plant) containing genetic material artificially transferred from another species

transgress *vb formal* **1** to break (a law or rule) **2** to overstep (a limit): *he had never before been known to transgress the very slowest of walks* **transgression** *n* **transgressor** *n*
WORD ORIGIN Latin *trans* beyond + *gradi* to step

transient *adj* **1** lasting for a short time only: *she had a number of transient relationships with fellow students* **2** (of a person) not remaining in a place for a long time: *the transient population of the inner city* ▷ *n* **3** a transient person or thing **transience** *n*
WORD ORIGIN Latin *transiens* going over

transistor *n* **1** a semiconductor device used to amplify and control electric currents **2** *informal* a small portable radio containing transistors
WORD ORIGIN *transfer* + *resistor*

transistorized *or* **-ised** *adj* (of an electronic device) using transistors

transit *n* **1** the moving or carrying of goods or people from one place to another **2** a route or means of transport: *transit by road* **3** *astron* the apparent passage of a celestial body across the meridian **4** **in transit** while travelling or being taken from one place to another: *in transit the fruit can be damaged* ▷ *adj* **5** indicating a place or building where people wait or goods are kept between different stages of a journey: *a transit lounge for passengers who are changing planes*
WORD ORIGIN Latin *transitus* a going over

transit camp *n* a camp in which refugees, soldiers, etc. live temporarily

transition *n* **1** the process of changing from one state or stage to another: *the transition from dictatorship to democracy* **2** *music* a movement from one key to

another **transitional** *adj*
WORD ORIGIN Latin *transitio* a going over

transition element *or* **metal** *n chem* any element belonging to one of three series of elements with atomic numbers between 21 and 30, 39 and 48, and 57 and 80 (**transition series**). They tend to have more than one valency and to form complexes

transitive *adj grammar* denoting a verb that requires a direct object: *'to find' is a transitive verb*

transitory *adj* lasting only for a short time

translate *vb* **-lating, -lated 1 a** to change (something spoken or written in one language) into another **b** to be capable of being changed from one language into another: *puns do not translate well* **2** to express (something) in a different way, for instance by using a different measurement system or less technical language: *the temperature is 30° Celsius, or if we translate into Fahrenheit, 86°* **3** to transform or convert, for instance by putting an idea into practice: *cheap crops translate into lower feed prices* **4** to interpret the significance of (a gesture, action, etc.): *I gave him what I hoped would be translated as a thoughtful look* **5** to act as a translator: *I had to translate for a party of visiting Greeks* **translatable** *adj* **translator** *n*
WORD ORIGIN Latin *translatus* carried over

translation *n* **1** a piece of writing or speech that has been translated into another language **2** the act of translating something **3** the expression of something in a different way or form: *the book's plot was radically altered during its translation to film* **4** *maths* a transformation in which the origin of a coordinate system is moved to another position so that each axis retains the same direction **translational** *adj*

transliterate *vb* **-rating, -rated** to write or spell (a word etc.) into corresponding letters of another alphabet **transliteration** *n*
WORD ORIGIN Latin *trans-* across + *littera* letter

translucent *adj* allowing light to pass through, but not transparent **translucency** *or* **translucence** *n*
WORD ORIGIN Latin *translucere* to shine through

transmigrate *vb* **-grating, -grated** (of a soul) to pass from one body into another at death **transmigration** *n*

transmission *n* **1** the sending or passing of something, such as a message or disease from one place or person to another **2** something that is transmitted, esp. a radio or television broadcast **3** a system of shafts and gears that transmits power from the engine to the driving wheels of a motor vehicle

transmit *vb* **-mitting, -mitted 1** to pass (something, such as a message or disease) from one place or person to another **2 a** to send out (signals) by means of radio waves **b** to broadcast (a radio or television programme)

Eggcorns

There is an episode of *The Simpsons* in which Marge tells a fugitive Bart to 'run like the wind' with the *wind* pronounced as in *wind up*. Lisa corrects her and Marge confesses she has only read the phrase in books. This mistake, while comic, illustrates a common source of errors in English: inherited words, phrases, and expressions whose original meaning and significance are no longer commonly known. When this happens, a speaker naturally reaches for something familiar to replace the misunderstood word.

The most famous error of this type is the *malapropism*, named after Richard Sheridan's character Mrs Malaprop (whose name is derived from the phrase *mal à propos*). The malapropism is distinguished by substituting one word for an unrelated but similar-sounding word, creating a nonsensical utterance, such as 'this report was corrugated by several other witnesses' (instead of 'corroborated by'). There is another, less famous but increasingly common and far more interesting category of this mistake: the *eggcorn*.

The term 'eggcorn' was coined in 2003 by the linguist Geoffrey Pullum, in response to a blog describing a woman who did not know the word *acorn* and instead consistently substituted *eggcorn*. This substitution does not qualify as a malapropism, because the substitution was not simply nonsensical. The speaker in question justified this usage because in shape an acorn resembles an egg in an eggcup. The blogger remarked that there was no name for this kind of linguistic mistake, and Pullum suggested calling these things 'eggcorns'.

So what, precisely, qualifies as an eggcorn? Well, like a malapropism, an eggcorn is a mistake of substituting one word for a similar-sounding word, especially in a well-known cliché or set phrase whose origin is increasingly obscure. However, an eggcorn is not merely erroneous, as a malapropism is, and it is far less likely to be humorous. In fact, many speakers are convinced the eggcorn is the 'correct' version of the phrase. Most importantly, whereas a malapropism is completely nonsensical, an eggcorn does make a certain kind of sense; that is, there is logic and creativity behind the word the speaker has chosen to substitute.

For example, one of the most famous eggcorns is *old-timer's disease* for *Alzheimer's disease*. 'Alzheimer' is the proper name of the German psychiatrist who first described the illness, so it is understandable that this word would be unfamiliar to some English speakers. As the disease commonly affects the elderly, and as its most characteristic symptom – memory loss and resultant confusion – is considered typical of the elderly, *old timer's disease* is a natural substitution, although it remains incorrect (and somewhat insulting).

Another common eggcorn is *just desserts* for *just deserts*. In contemporary English, the spelling *desert* usually means 'a region devoid of vegetation due to low rainfall'. Most English speakers are not as familiar with the now archaic meaning of 'something that is deserved or merited'. So *just deserts* are the things you justly deserve (whether as a reward or, more commonly, punishment). Most people are understandably unaware of this, especially as this sense of *desert* is pretty much restricted to this one phrase. 'Just hot and dry regions' makes no sense, so speakers naturally reach for the other option: *desserts*, sweet dishes served after one's main meal. Desserts are often given as a reward to children (and withheld as punishment), and people who have made a mistake often have to eat *humble pie* (itself an ancient eggcorn for *numble pie*, 'numbles' being the offal of a deer), so *just desserts* makes sense to many English speakers.

What makes eggcorns such a fascinating linguistic phenomenon is that, because the substitution seems to make sense (often more sense in Modern English than the archaic 'correct' word), and because the original expression or phrase reflects an outdated or uncommon usage, many people are convinced that eggcorns are correct and that the original phrases are wrong. This means that we may reach the point where, as with *straight and narrow* (originally *strait and narrow*), the mistake becomes the accepted version of the phrase, by consensus of the majority of English speakers.

3 to allow the passage of (particles, energy, etc.): *water transmits sound better than air* **4** to transfer (a force, motion, etc.) from one part of a mechanical system to another: *the chain of the bike transmits the motion of the pedals to the rear wheel* **transmittable** *adj*
WORD ORIGIN Latin *transmittere* to send across

transmitter *n* **1** a piece of equipment used for broadcasting radio or television programmes **2** a person or thing that transmits something

transmogrify *vb* **-fies, -fying, -fied** *jocular* to change or transform (someone or something) into a different shape or appearance, esp. a grotesque or bizarre one **transmogrification** *n*
WORD ORIGIN origin unknown

transmute *vb* **-muting, -muted** to change the form or nature of: *self-contempt is transmuted into hatred of others* **transmutation** *n*
WORD ORIGIN Latin *transmutare* to shift

transom *n* **1** a horizontal bar across a window **2** a horizontal bar that separates a door from a window over it
WORD ORIGIN Old French *traversin*

transparency *n, pl* **-cies 1** the state of being transparent **2** a positive photograph on transparent film, usually mounted in a frame or between glass plates, which can be viewed with the use of a slide projector

transparent *adj* **1** able to be seen through; clear **2** easy to understand or recognize; obvious: *transparent honesty* **transparently** *adv*
WORD ORIGIN Latin *trans-* through + *parere* to appear

transpire *vb* **-spiring, -spired 1** to come to light; become known **2** *not standard* to happen or occur **3** *physiol* to give off (water or vapour) through the pores of the skin, etc. **4** (of plants) to lose (water vapour) through the stomata **transpiration** *n*
WORD ORIGIN Latin *trans-* through + *spirare* to breathe

USAGE
It is often maintained that *transpire* should not be used to mean happen or occur, as in *the event transpired late in the evening*, and that the word is properly used to mean become known, as in *it transpired later that the thief had been caught*. The word is, however, widely used in the former sense, esp. in spoken English.

transplant *vb* **1** *surgery* to transfer (an organ or tissue) from one part of the body or from one person to another **2** to remove or transfer (esp. a plant) from one place to another ▷ *n* **3** *surgery* **a** the procedure involved in transferring an organ or tissue **b** the organ or tissue transplanted **transplantation** *n*

transponder *n* a type of radio or radar transmitter-receiver that transmits signals automatically when it receives predetermined signals
WORD ORIGIN *transmitter* + *responder*

transport *vb* **1** to carry or move (people or goods) from one place to another, esp. over some distance **2** *history* to exile (a criminal) to a penal colony **3** to have

a strong emotional effect on: *transported by joy* ▷ *n* **4** the business or system of transporting goods or people: *public transport* **5** *Brit* freight vehicles generally **6** a vehicle used to transport troops **7** a transporting or being transported **8** ecstasy or rapture: *transports of delight* **transportable** *adj*
WORD ORIGIN Latin *trans-* across + *portare* to carry

transportation *n* **1** a means or system of transporting **2** the act of transporting or the state of being transported **3** *history* deportation to a penal colony

transport café *n Brit* an inexpensive eating place on a main road, used mainly by long-distance lorry drivers

transporter *n* a large vehicle used for carrying cars from the factory to garages for sale

transpose *vb* **-posing, -posed 1** to change the order of (letters, words, or sentences) **2** *music* to play (notes, music, etc.) in a different key **3** *maths* to move (a term) from one side of an equation to the other with a corresponding reversal in sign: *transposing* 3 *in* x – 3 = 6 *gives* x = 6 + 3 **transposition** *n*
WORD ORIGIN Old French *transposer*

transsexual *or* **transexual** *n* **1** a person who believes that his or her true identity is of the opposite sex **2** a person who has had medical treatment to alter his or her sexual characteristics to those of the opposite sex

transship *vb* **-shipping, -shipped** to transfer or be transferred from one ship or vehicle to another **transshipment** *n*

transubstantiation *n Christianity* the doctrine that the bread and wine consecrated in Communion changes into the substance of Christ's body and blood
WORD ORIGIN Latin *trans-* over + *substantia* substance

transuranic (tranz-yoor-**ran**-ik) *adj chem* (of an element) having an atomic number greater than that of uranium

transverse *adj* crossing from side to side: *the transverse arches in the main hall of the college*
WORD ORIGIN Latin *transvertere* to turn across

transvestite *n* a person, esp. a man, who seeks sexual pleasure from wearing clothes of the opposite sex **transvestism** *n*
WORD ORIGIN Latin *trans-* across + *vestitus* clothed

trap *n* **1** a device or hole in which something, esp. an animal, is caught: *a fox trap* **2** a plan for tricking a person into being caught unawares **3** a situation from which it is difficult to escape: *caught in the poverty trap* **4** a bend in a pipe that contains standing water to prevent the passage of gases **5** a boxlike stall in which greyhounds are enclosed before the start of a race **6** a device that hurls clay pigeons into the air to be fired at **7** see **trap door 8** a light two-wheeled carriage: *a pony and trap* **9** *Brit, Austral, & NZ slang* the mouth: *shut your trap!* ▷ *vb* **trapping, trapped**

10 to catch (an animal) in a trap **11** to catch (someone) by a trick: *the police trapped the drug dealers by posing as potential customers* **12** to hold or confine in an unpleasant situation from which it is difficult to escape: *trapped in the rubble of collapsed buildings* ▶ See also **trap out**
WORD ORIGIN Old English *træppe*

trap door *n* a hinged door in a ceiling, floor, or stage

trap-door spider *n* a spider that builds a silk-lined hole in the ground closed by a hinged door of earth and silk

trapeze *n* a horizontal bar suspended from two ropes, used by circus acrobats
WORD ORIGIN French

trapezium *n, pl* **-ziums** *or* **-zia 1** a quadrilateral having two parallel sides of unequal length **2** *chiefly US & Canad* a quadrilateral having neither pair of sides parallel **trapezial** *adj*
WORD ORIGIN Greek *trapeza* table

trapezoid (**trap**-piz-zoid) *n* **1** a quadrilateral having neither pair of sides parallel **2** *US & Canad* same as **trapezium** (sense 1)
WORD ORIGIN Greek *trapeza* table

trap out *vb* **trapping, trapped** to dress or adorn
WORD ORIGIN Old French *drap* cloth

trapper *n* a person who traps animals, esp. for their furs or skins

trappings *pl n* **1** the accessories that symbolize a condition, office, etc.: *the trappings of power* **2** ceremonial harness for a horse or other animal
WORD ORIGIN probably from Old French *drap* cloth

Trappist *n* a member of an order of Christian monks who follow a rule of strict silence

trash *n* **1** foolish ideas or talk; nonsense **2** *US, Canad, NZ, & S African* unwanted objects; rubbish **3** *chiefly US, Canad, & NZ* a worthless person or group of people ▷ *vb* **4** *slang* to attack or destroy maliciously: *we've never trashed a hotel room* **trashy** *adj*
WORD ORIGIN origin unknown

trattoria (trat-or-**ee**-a) *n* an Italian restaurant
WORD ORIGIN Italian

trauma (**traw**-ma) *n* **1** *psychol* an emotional shock that may have long-lasting effects **2** *pathol* any bodily injury or wound. **traumatic** *adj* **traumatically** *adv* **traumatize** *or* **-ise** *vb*
WORD ORIGIN Greek: a wound

travail *n literary* painful or exceptionally hard work
WORD ORIGIN Old French *travaillier*

travel *vb* **-elling, -elled** *or US* **-eling, -eled 1** to go or move from one place to another **2** to go or journey through or across (an area, region, etc.): *Margaret travelled widely when she was in New Zealand* **3** to go at a specified speed or for a specified distance: *the car was travelling at 30 mph* **4** to go from place to place as a salesman **5** (of perishable goods) to withstand a journey: *not all wines travel well* **6** (of light or sound) to be transmitted or carried from one place to another: *sound travels a long distance in these conditions* **7** (of a machine or part) to move in a fixed path **8** *informal* (of a vehicle) to move rapidly ▷ n **9** the act or a means of travelling: *air travel has changed the way people live* **10** a tour or journey: *his travels took him to Dublin* **11** the distance moved by a mechanical part, such as the stroke of a piston **WORD ORIGIN** Old French *travaillier* to travail

travel agency n an agency that arranges flights, hotel accommodation, etc. for tourists **travel agent** n

traveller or US **traveler** n **1** a person who travels, esp. habitually **2** a travelling salesman **3** a Gypsy

traveller's cheque n a cheque sold by a bank, travel agency, etc. which the buyer signs on purchase and can cash abroad by re-signing it

travelling salesman n a salesman who travels within an assigned area in order to sell goods or get orders for the company he or she represents

travelogue or US **travelog** n a film or lecture on travels and travelling

travel sickness n nausea or vomiting caused by riding in a car or other moving vehicle **travel-sick** adj

traverse vb **-versing, -versed 1** to move over or back and forth over; cross: *he once traversed San Francisco harbour in a balloon* **2** to reach across **3** to walk, climb, or ski diagonally up or down a slope ▷ n **4** something being or lying across, such as a crossbar **5** the act or an instance of traversing or crossing **6** a path or road across ▷ adj **7** being or lying across **traversal** n **WORD ORIGIN** Latin *transversus* turned across

travesty n, pl **-ties 1** a grotesque imitation or mockery: *a travesty of justice* ▷ vb **-ties, -tying, -tied 2** to make or be a travesty of **WORD ORIGIN** French *travesti* disguised

travois (trav-**voy**) n, pl **-vois** (-**voyz**) *Canad* a sled used for dragging logs **WORD ORIGIN** Canadian French

trawl n **1** a large net, usually in the shape of a sock or bag, dragged at deep levels behind a fishing boat ▷ vb **2** to fish using such a net **WORD ORIGIN** Middle Dutch *traghelen* to drag

trawler n a ship used for trawling

tray n **1** a flat board of wood, plastic, or metal, usually with a rim, on which things can be carried **2** an open receptacle for office correspondence **WORD ORIGIN** Old English *trieg*

TRC n (in South Africa) Truth and Reconciliation Commission: a commission which encourages people who committed human rights abuses or acts of terror during the apartheid era to reveal the truth about their crimes in return for immunity from prosecution

treacherous adj **1** disloyal and untrustworthy: *he was cruel, treacherous, and unscrupulous* **2** unreliable or dangerous, esp. because of sudden changes: *the tides here can be very treacherous* **treacherously** adv

treachery n, pl **-eries** the act or an instance of wilful betrayal **WORD ORIGIN** Old French *trecherie*

treacle n a thick dark syrup obtained during the refining of sugar **treacly** adj **WORD ORIGIN** Latin *theriaca* antidote to poison

tread vb **treading, trod; trodden** or **trod 1** to set one's foot down on or in something: *he trod on some dog's dirt* **2** to crush or squash by treading (on): *treading on a biscuit* **3** to walk along (a path or road) **4 tread carefully** or **warily** to proceed in a delicate or tactful manner **5 tread water** to stay afloat in an upright position by moving the legs in a walking motion ▷ n **6** a way of walking or the sound of walking: *he walked, with a heavy tread, up the stairs* **7** the top surface of a step in a staircase **8** the pattern of grooves in the outer surface of a tyre that helps it grip the road **9** the part of a shoe that is generally in contact with the ground **WORD ORIGIN** Old English *tredan*

treadle (tred-dl) n a lever operated by the foot to turn a wheel **WORD ORIGIN** Old English *tredan* to tread

treadmill n **1** (formerly) an apparatus turned by the weight of men or animals climbing steps on a revolving cylinder or wheel **2** a dreary routine: *they are chained to the treadmill of a job* **3** an exercise machine that consists of a continuous moving belt on which to walk or jog

treason n **1** betrayal of one's sovereign or country, esp. by attempting to overthrow the government **2** any treachery or betrayal **treasonable** adj **treasonous** adj **WORD ORIGIN** Latin *traditio* a handing over

treasure n **1** a collection of wealth, esp. in the form of money, precious metals, or gems **2** a valuable painting, ornament, or other object: *the museum has many art treasures* **3** *informal* a person who is highly valued: *she can turn her hand to anything, she's a perfect treasure* ▷ vb **-suring, -sured 4** to cherish (someone or something) **WORD ORIGIN** Greek *thēsauros*

treasure hunt n a game in which players act upon successive clues to find a hidden prize

treasurer n a person appointed to look after the funds of a society or other organization

treasure-trove n *law* any articles, such as coins or valuable objects found hidden and without any evidence of ownership **WORD ORIGIN** Anglo-French *tresor trové* treasure found

treasury n, pl **-uries 1** a storage place for treasure **2** the revenues or funds of a government or organization

Treasury n (in various countries) the government department in charge of finance

treat vb **1** to deal with or regard in a certain manner: *her love for a man who treats her abominably* **2** to attempt to cure or lessen the symptoms of (an illness or injury or a person suffering from it): *the drug is prescribed to treat asthma* **3** to subject to a chemical or industrial process: *the wood should be treated with a preservative* **4** to provide (someone) with something as a treat: *I'll treat you to an ice cream* **5 treat of** to deal with (something) in writing or speaking: *this book treats of a most abstruse subject* ▷ n **6** a celebration, entertainment, gift, or meal given for or to someone and paid for by someone else **7** any delightful surprise or specially pleasant occasion **treatable** adj **WORD ORIGIN** Old French *tretier*

treatise (treat-izz) n a formal piece of writing that deals systematically with a particular subject **WORD ORIGIN** Anglo-French *tretiz*

treatment n **1** the medical or surgical care given to a patient **2** a way of handling a person or thing: *the party has had unfair treatment in the press*

treaty n, pl **-ties 1** a formal written agreement between two or more states, such as an alliance or trade arrangement: *the Treaty of Rome established the Common Market* **2** an agreement between two parties concerning the purchase of property **WORD ORIGIN** Old French *traité*

treble adj **1** three times as much or as many **2** of or denoting a soprano voice or part or a high-pitched instrument **3** of the highest range of musical notes: *these loudspeakers give excellent treble reproduction* ▷ n **4** a soprano voice or part or a high-pitched instrument ▷ vb **-bling, -bled 5** to make or become three times as much or as many: *sales have trebled in three years* **trebly** adv **WORD ORIGIN** Latin *triplus* threefold

treble chance n *Brit* a method of betting in football pools in which the chances of winning are related to the number of draws and the number of home and away wins forecast by the competitor

treble clef n *music* the clef that establishes G a fifth above middle C as being on the second line of the staff

tree n **1** any large woody perennial plant with a distinct trunk and usually having leaves and branches ▶ Related adjective: **arboreal** **2** see **family tree, shoetree, saddletree 3 at the top of the tree** in the highest position of a profession **treeless** adj **WORD ORIGIN** Old English *trēow*

tree creeper n a small songbird of the N hemisphere that creeps up trees to feed on insects

tree diagram n *maths* a branching diagram showing the probability of various events

tree fern n any of numerous large tropical ferns with a trunklike stem

tree kangaroo n a tree-living kangaroo of New Guinea and N Australia

tree line n same as **timber line**

tree-lined adj (of a road) having trees on either side of it: *a pleasant tree-lined avenue in Bristol*

tree surgery n the treatment of damaged trees by filling cavities, applying braces, etc. **tree surgeon** n

tree tomato n same as **tamarillo**

treetop n the highest part of a tree, where the leaves and branches are: *monkeys swung through the treetops*

t

trefoil (**tref**-foil) n **1** a plant, such as clover, with leaves divided into three smaller leaves **2** archit a carved ornament with a shape like such leaves **trefoiled** adj
WORD ORIGIN Latin trifolium three-leaved herb

trek n **1** a long and often difficult journey, esp. on foot **2** S African a journey or stage of a journey, esp. a migration by ox wagon ▷ vb **trekking, trekked 3** to make a trek
WORD ORIGIN Afrikaans

trellis n a frame made of vertical and horizontal strips of wood, esp. one used to support climbing plants **trelliswork** n
WORD ORIGIN Old French treliz fabric of open texture

tremble vb **-bling, -bled 1** to shake with short slight movements: her hands trembled uncontrollably; he felt the ground trembling beneath him **2** to experience fear or anxiety: his parents trembled with apprehension about his future **3** (of the voice) to sound uncertain or unsteady, for instance through pain or emotion ▷ n **4** the act or an instance of trembling **trembling** adj
WORD ORIGIN Latin tremere

tremendous adj **1** very large or impressive: a tremendous amount of money **2** very exciting or unusual: a tremendous feeling of elation **3** very good or pleasing: my wife has given me tremendous support **tremendously** adv
WORD ORIGIN Latin tremendus terrible

tremolo n, pl **-los** music **1** (in playing the violin or other stringed instrument) the rapid repetition of a note or notes to produce a trembling effect **2** (in singing) a fluctuation in pitch
WORD ORIGIN Italian: quavering

tremor n **1** an involuntary shudder or vibration: the slight tremor of excitement **2** a minor earthquake
WORD ORIGIN Latin

tremulous adj literary trembling, as from fear or excitement: I managed a tremulous smile **tremulously** adv
WORD ORIGIN Latin tremere to shake

trench n **1** a long narrow ditch in the ground, such as one for laying a pipe in **2** a long deep ditch used by soldiers for protection in a war: my grandfather fought in the trenches in the First World War ▷ adj **3** of or involving military trenches: trench warfare
WORD ORIGIN Old French trenche something cut

trenchant adj **1** keen or incisive: a trenchant screenplay **2** vigorous and effective: the prime minister's trenchant adoption of this issue **trenchancy** n
WORD ORIGIN Old French: cutting

trench coat n a belted raincoat similar in style to a military officer's coat

trencher n history a wooden board on which food was served or cut
WORD ORIGIN Old French trencheoir

trencherman n, pl **-men** a person who enjoys food; hearty eater

trench warfare n a type of warfare in which opposing armies face each other in entrenched positions

trend n **1** general tendency or direction: an accelerating trend towards the use of mobile phones **2** fashionable style: she set a trend for wearing lingerie as outer garments ▷ vb **3** to take a certain trend
WORD ORIGIN Old English trendan to turn

trendsetter n a person or thing that creates, or may create, a new fashion **trendsetting** adj

trendy informal adj **trendier, trendiest 1** consciously fashionable: a flat in Glasgow's trendy West End ▷ n, pl **trendies 2** a trendy person: a media trendy **trendily** adv **trendiness** n

trepidation n formal a state of fear or anxiety
WORD ORIGIN Latin trepidatio

trespass vb **1** to go onto somebody else's property without permission ▷ n **2** the act or an instance of trespassing **3** old-fashioned a sin or wrongdoing **trespasser** n
WORD ORIGIN Old French trespas a passage

trespass on or **upon** vb formal to take unfair advantage of (someone's friendship, patience, etc.): I won't trespass upon your hospitality any longer

tresses pl n a woman's long flowing hair
WORD ORIGIN Old French trece

trestle n **1** a support for one end of a table or beam, consisting of two rectangular frameworks or sets of legs which are joined at the top but not the bottom **2** Also called: **trestle table** a table consisting of a board supported by a trestle at each end
WORD ORIGIN Old French trestel

trevally (trih-**val**-lee) n, pl **-lies** Austral & NZ any of various food and game fishes
WORD ORIGIN probably alteration of cavalla, species of tropical fish

trews pl n chiefly Brit close-fitting trousers of tartan cloth
WORD ORIGIN Scottish Gaelic triubhas

tri- combining form **1** three or thrice: trilingual **2** occurring every three: triweekly
WORD ORIGIN Latin tres

triad n **1** a group of three **2** music a three-note chord consisting of a note and the third and fifth above it **triadic** adj
WORD ORIGIN Greek trias

Triad n a Chinese secret society involved in criminal activities, such as drug trafficking

trial n law an investigation of a case in front of a judge to decide whether a person is innocent or guilty of a crime by questioning him or her and considering the evidence **2** the act or an instance of trying or proving; test or experiment: the new drug is undergoing clinical trials **3** an annoying or frustrating person or thing: young children can be a great trial at times **4** a motorcycling competition in which the skills of the riders are tested over rough ground **5 trials** a sporting competition for individual people or animals: horse trials **6 on trial a** undergoing trial, esp. before a court of law **b** being tested, for example before a commitment to purchase: I only have the car out on trial ▷ adj **7** on a temporary basis while being tried out or tested: a trial run ▷ vb

trialling, trialled 8 to test or make experimental use of: the idea has been trialled in several schools
WORD ORIGIN Anglo-French trier to try

trial and error n a method of discovery based on practical experiment and experience rather than on theory: raising her children has been a matter of trial and error

trial balance n book-keeping a statement of all the debit and credit balances in the double-entry ledger

triallist or **trialist** n **1** a person who takes part in a competition **2** sport a person who takes part in a preliminary match or heat held to determine selection for a team or event

triangle n **1** a geometric figure with three sides and three angles **2** any object shaped like a triangle: a triangle of streets running up from the river **3** music a percussion instrument that consists of a metal bar bent into a triangular shape, played by striking it with a metal stick **4** any situation involving three people or points of view: a torrid sex triangle **triangular** adj
WORD ORIGIN TRI- + Latin angulus corner

triangulate vb **-lating, -lated** to survey (an area) by dividing it into triangles

triangulation n a method of surveying in which an area is divided into triangles, one side (the base line) and all angles of which are measured and the lengths of the other lines calculated by trigonometry

Triassic adj geol of the period of geological time about 230 million years ago
WORD ORIGIN Latin trias triad

triathlon n an athletic contest in which each athlete competes in three different events: swimming, cycling, and running **triathlete** n
WORD ORIGIN TRI- + Greek athlon contest

tribalism n loyalty to a tribe, esp. as opposed to a modern political entity such as a state

tribe n **1** a group of families or clans believed to have a common ancestor **2** informal a group of people who do the same type of thing: a tribe of German yachtsmen **tribal** adj
WORD ORIGIN Latin tribus

tribesman n, pl **-men** a member of a tribe

tribulation n great distress: the tribulations of a deserted wife
WORD ORIGIN Latin tribulare to afflict

tribunal n **1** a special court or committee that is appointed to deal with a particular problem: an industrial tribunal investigating allegations of unfair dismissal **2** a court of justice
WORD ORIGIN Latin tribunus tribune

tribune n **1** a person who upholds public rights **2** (in ancient Rome) an officer elected by the plebs to protect their interests
WORD ORIGIN Latin tribunus

tributary n, pl **-taries 1** a stream or river that flows into a larger one: Frankfurt lies on the River Main, a tributary of the Rhine **2** a person, nation, or people that pays tribute ▷ adj **3** (of a stream or river) flowing into a larger stream **4** paying tribute: Egypt was formerly a tributary province of the Turkish Empire

The Influence of Hebrew on English

Hebrew is one of the oldest languages in the world, the language in which the sacred writings of Judaism (part of which form the Old Testament of the Christian Bible) were written. Both the Christian and Jewish traditions have brought words of Hebrew origin into modern English.

Although the English translators of the Old Testament also knew the text in its Greek and Latin translations, the original Hebrew peeps out at various places in the best-known English versions, and from there it has often found its way into the wider English language.

Some Hebrew words came to be regarded as holy, and so they were retained when the Bible was translated. The word *amen* ('so be it') survived into English in its original Hebrew form, while words such as *hallelujah* ('praise the Lord') and *hosanna* ('save now, we pray') have experienced slight changes in form in their journey into English. The Old Testament is also the route by which words of Hebrew origin such as *messiah* ('anointed one'), *cherub*, and *sabbath* came into English.

Not all words that come into English from the Old Testament have an overtly religious flavour. The words *behemoth* and *leviathan* both come originally from the Book of Job, and seem to have been adopted because translators of the Bible could find no suitable English alternatives for the Hebrew words *behemoth* (a plural form of *behemah*, meaning 'beast'), and *liwyathan*. The word *shibboleth*, meaning 'slogan' or 'watchword', remained untranslated in the English version of the Book of Judges, because it is essential to the story of the Ephraimites, who gave themselves away to their enemies from Gilead by pronouncing the word – which literally means 'an ear of corn' – as *sibboleth*, because they were unable to articulate the 'sh' sound.

Some Hebrew words come from the Old Testament into English by rather circuitous routes. The spice *cinnamon* takes its name ultimately from the Hebrew word *qinnamown*, but came into English via Greek, Latin and French. A similar journey saw the Hebrew word *yōbhēl*, meaning 'ram's horn', emerge in English as *jubilee*. (Every fiftieth year a ram's horn was blown to announce the start of a year in which Hebrew slaves were to be liberated and property was to be restored to its owners.) The final form of this word in English is influenced by the Latin verb *jubilare* ('to rejoice'), but its origins are undeniably Hebrew.

Hebrew words have also come into English as terms relating to the Jewish religion. More esoteric words such as *mikvah* ('a pool used for ritual purification') and *kashruth* ('the condition of being fit for ritual use') are probably familiar only to members of the Jewish faith or keen players of Scrabble anxious to find ways of disposing of the troublesome K tile. However, words such as *rabbi* (literally meaning 'my great one'), *shalom* ('peace'), and *kosher* ('correct') are familiar even to non-Jews, and in the case of *kosher*, the word has acquired an informal use in English that is much more wide-ranging than its original meaning of 'conforming to religious law'.

Wider Jewish culture has introduced ideas such as the *kibbutz* (from a Hebrew word meaning 'gathering'), while some Hebrew words have come into English through the intermediary of Yiddish, as in the case of *chutzpah* and *maven*.

A Hebrew word that has a surprising legacy in English is *shēkhār*, which means 'strong drink'. This word occurs in Yiddish as *shikker*, from which we get the slang word *shickered*, which is used primarily in Australia and New Zealand and means 'drunk'. However, the Hebrew word also entered Greek as *sikera*, and via Latin came into French as *cisdre*, which was applied to a particular type of strong drink brewed from apples. So it is that the influence of Hebrew on English extends beyond the language of the Old Testament and of Judaism and can be detected even in something as apparently unconnected with religion as cider.

tribute *n* **1** something given, done, or said as a mark of respect or admiration **2** a payment by one ruler or state to another, usually as an acknowledgment of submission **3** something that shows the merits of a particular quality of a person or thing: *the car's low fuel consumption is a tribute to the quality of its engine* **WORD ORIGIN** Latin *tributum*

trice *n* **in a trice** in a moment: *she was back in a trice* **WORD ORIGIN** originally, at one tug, from *trice* to haul up

triceps *n* the muscle at the back of the upper arm **WORD ORIGIN** Latin

trichology (trick-ol-a-jee) *n* the branch of medicine concerned with the hair and its diseases **trichologist** *n* **WORD ORIGIN** Greek *thrix* hair

trichromatic *or* **trichromic** *adj* **1** having or involving three colours **2** of or having normal colour vision **trichromatism** *n*

trick *n* **1** a deceitful or cunning action or plan: *she was willing to use any dirty trick to get what she wanted* **2** a joke or prank: *he loves playing tricks on his sister* **3** a clever way of doing something, learned from experience: *an old campers' trick is to use three thin blankets rather than one thick one* **4** an illusory or magical feat or device **5** a simple feat learned by an animal or person **6** a deceptive illusion: *a trick of the light* **7** a habit or mannerism: *she had a trick of saying 'oh dear'* **8** *cards* a batch of cards played in turn and won by the person playing the highest card **9 do the trick** *informal* to produce the desired result **10 how's tricks?** *slang* how are you? ▷ *vb* **11** to defraud, deceive, or cheat (someone) **trickery** *n* **WORD ORIGIN** Old French *trique*

trickle *vb* **-ling, -led 1** to flow or cause to flow in a thin stream or drops: *tears trickled down her cheeks* **2** to move slowly or in small groups: *voters trickled to the polls* ▷ *n* **3** a thin, irregular, or slow flow of something: *a trickle of blood* **WORD ORIGIN** probably imitative

trickle-down *adj* of the theory that granting concessions like tax cuts to the rich will benefit all levels of society by stimulating the economy

trick out *vb* to dress up: *tricked out in chauffeur's rig*

trickster *n* a person who deceives or plays tricks

tricky *adj* **trickier, trickiest 1** involving snags or difficulties: *a tricky task* **2** needing careful handling: *a tricky situation* **3** sly or wily: *a tricky customer* **trickily** *adv* **trickiness** *n*

tricolour *or US* **tricolor** (trick-kol-lor) *n* a flag with three equal stripes in different colours, esp. the French or Irish national flags

tricycle *n* a three-wheeled cycle **tricyclist** *n*

trident *n* a three-pronged spear **WORD ORIGIN** Latin *tridens* three-pronged

tried *vb* the past of **try**

triennial *adj* occurring every three years **triennially** *adv*

WORD ORIGIN TRI- + Latin *annus* year

trier *n* a person or thing that tries

trifle[1] *n* **1** a thing of little or no value or significance **2** *Brit, Austral, & NZ* a cold dessert made of sponge cake spread with jam or fruit, soaked in sherry, covered with custard and cream **3 a trifle** to a small extent or degree; slightly: *he is a trifle eccentric* **WORD ORIGIN** Old French *trufle* mockery

trifle[2] *vb* **trifling, trifled** ● **trifle with** to treat (a person or his or her feelings) with disdain or disregard

trifling *adj* insignificant, petty, or frivolous: *a trifling misunderstanding*

trig. trigonometry

trigger *n* **1** a small lever that releases a catch on a gun or machine **2** any event that sets a course of action in motion: *his murder was the trigger for a night of rioting* ▷ *vb* **3** Also: **trigger off** to set (an action or process) in motion: *various factors can trigger off a migraine* **WORD ORIGIN** Dutch *trekker*

trigger-happy *adj* *informal* too ready or willing to use guns or violence: *trigger-happy border guards*

trigonometry *n* the branch of mathematics concerned with the relations of sides and angles of triangles, which is used in surveying, navigation, etc. **WORD ORIGIN** Greek *trigōnon* triangle

trig point *n* a point on a hilltop etc. used for triangulation by a surveyor

trike *n* *informal* a tricycle

trilateral *adj* having three sides

trilby *n, pl* **-bies** a man's soft felt hat with an indented crown **WORD ORIGIN** after *Trilby*, the heroine of a novel by George Du Maurier

trill *n* **1** *music* a rapid alternation between a note and the note above it **2** a shrill warbling sound made by some birds: *the canary's high trills* ▷ *vb* **3** (of a bird) to make a shrill warbling sound **4** (of a person) to talk or laugh in a high-pitched musical voice **WORD ORIGIN** Italian *trillo*

trillion *n* **-lions** *or* **-lion 1** the number represented as one followed by twelve zeros (10^{12}); a million million **2** (in Britain, originally) the number represented as one followed by eighteen zeros (10^{18}); a million million million ▷ *adj* **3** amounting to a trillion: *a trillion dollars* **trillionth** *n, adj* **WORD ORIGIN** French

trillium *n* a plant of Asia and North America that has three leaves at the top of the stem with a single white, pink, or purple three-petalled flower **WORD ORIGIN** New Latin

trilobite (trile-oh-bite) *n* a small prehistoric marine arthropod, found as a fossil **WORD ORIGIN** Greek *trilobos* having three lobes

trilogy (trill-a-jee) *n, pl* **-gies** a series of three books, plays, etc. which form a related group but are each complete works in themselves **WORD ORIGIN** Greek *trilogia*

trim *adj* **trimmer, trimmest 1** neat and spruce in appearance: *trim lace curtains*

2 attractively slim: *his body was trim and athletic* ▷ *vb* **trimming, trimmed 3** to make (something) neater by cutting it slightly without changing its basic shape: *his white beard was neatly trimmed* **4** to adorn or decorate (something, such as a garment) with lace, ribbons, etc.: *a cotton camisole neatly trimmed with lace* **5 a** to adjust the balance of (a ship or aircraft) by shifting cargo etc. **b** to adjust (a ship's sails) to take advantage of the wind **6** to reduce or lower the size of: *the company has trimmed its pretax profits forecast by $2.3 million* **7** to alter (a plan or policy) by removing parts which seem unnecessary or unpopular: *the government would rather trim its policies than lose the election* **8 trim off** or **away** to cut so as to remove: *trim off most of the fat before cooking the meat* ▷ *n* **9** a decoration or adornment: *a black suit with scarlet trim* **10** the upholstery and decorative facings of a car's interior **11** good physical condition: *he had always kept himself in trim* **12** a haircut that neatens but does not alter the existing hairstyle **WORD ORIGIN** Old English *trymman* to strengthen

trimaran (trime-a-ran) *n* a boat with one smaller hull on each side of the main hull **WORD ORIGIN** tri- + (cata)maran

trimming *n* **1** an extra piece added to a garment for decoration: *a pink nightie with lace trimming* **2 trimmings** usual or traditional accompaniments: *bacon and eggs with all the trimmings*

Trinitarian *n* **1** a person who believes in the doctrine of the Trinity ▷ *adj* **2** of or relating to the Trinity **Trinitarianism** *n*

trinitrotoluene *n* the full name for **TNT**

trinity *n, pl* **-ties** a group of three people or things **WORD ORIGIN** Latin *trinus* triple

Trinity *n* *Christianity* the union of three persons, the Father, Son, and Holy Spirit, in one God

trinket *n* a small or worthless ornament or piece of jewellery **WORD ORIGIN** origin unknown

trio *n, pl* **trios 1** a group of three people or things **2** a group of three instrumentalists or singers **3** a piece of music for three performers **WORD ORIGIN** Italian

trip *n* **1** a journey to a place and back, esp. for pleasure: *they took a coach trip round the island* **2** a false step; stumble **3** the act of causing someone to stumble or fall by catching his or her foot with one's own **4** *informal* a hallucinogenic drug experience **5** a catch on a mechanism that acts as a switch ▷ *vb* **tripping, tripped 6** Also: **trip up** to stumble or cause (someone) to stumble **7** Also: **trip up** to trap or catch (someone) in a mistake **8** to walk lightly and quickly, with a dancelike motion: *I could see Amelia tripping along beside him* **9** *informal* to experience the effects of a hallucinogenic drug **WORD ORIGIN** Old French *triper* to tread

tripartite *adj* involving or composed of three people or parts **tripartism** *n*

tripe *n* **1** the stomach lining of a cow or pig used as a food **2** *Brit, Austral, & NZ informal* nonsense or rubbish
WORD ORIGIN Old French

Tripitaka (trip-it-**tah**-ka) *n* the three collections of books making up the Buddhist scriptures
WORD ORIGIN Pali (an ancient language of India) tri three + pitaka basket

triple *adj* **1** made up of three parts or things: *a triple murder* **2** (of musical time or rhythm) having three beats in each bar **3** three times as great or as much: *a triple brandy* ▷ *vb* -**pling**, -**pled** **4** to make or become three times as much or as many: *the company has tripled its sales over the past five years* ▷ *n* **5** something that is, or contains, three times as much as normal **6** a group of three **triply** *adv*
WORD ORIGIN Latin triplus

triple jump *n* an athletic event in which the competitor has to perform a hop, a step, and a jump in a continuous movement

triple point *n chem* the temperature and pressure at which a substance can exist as a solid, liquid, and gas

triplet *n* **1** one of three children born at one birth **2** a group of three musical notes played in the time that two would normally take **3** a group or set of three similar things

triplicate *adj* **1** triple ▷ *vb* -**cating**, -**cated** **2** to multiply or be multiplied by three ▷ *n* **3** in triplicate written out three times: *my request to interview the commander had to be made in triplicate* **triplication** *n*
WORD ORIGIN Latin triplicare to triple

tripod (**tripe**-pod) *n* **1** a three-legged stand to which a camera can be attached to hold it steady **2** a three-legged stool, table, etc.
WORD ORIGIN TRI- + Greek pous a foot

tripos (**tripe**-poss) *n Brit* the final honours degree examinations at Cambridge University
WORD ORIGIN Latin tripus tripod

tripper *n chiefly Brit* a tourist

triptych (**trip**-tick) *n* a set of three pictures or panels, usually hinged together and often used as an altarpiece
WORD ORIGIN TRI- + Greek ptux plate

trireme (**try**-ream) *n* an ancient Greek warship with three rows of oars on each side
WORD ORIGIN TRI- + Latin remus oar

trismus *n pathol* the state of being unable to open the mouth because of sustained contractions of the jaw muscles, caused by tetanus. Nontechnical name: **lockjaw**
WORD ORIGIN Greek trismos a grinding

triste (**treest**) *adj* old-fashioned sad
WORD ORIGIN French

trite *adj* (of a remark or idea) commonplace and unoriginal
WORD ORIGIN Latin tritus worn down

tritium *n* a radioactive isotope of hydrogen. Symbol: T or ^{3}H
WORD ORIGIN Greek tritos third

triumph *n* **1** the feeling of great happiness resulting from a victory or major achievement **2** an outstanding success, achievement, or victory: *the concert was a musical triumph* **3** (in ancient Rome) a procession held in honour of a victorious general ▷ *vb* **4** to gain control or success: *triumphing over adversity* **5** to rejoice over a victory **triumphal** *adj*
WORD ORIGIN Latin triumphus

triumphant *adj* **1** feeling or displaying triumph: *her smile was triumphant* **2** celebrating a victory or success: *the general's triumphant tour round the city* **triumphantly** *adv*

triumvir (try-**umm**-vir) *n* (esp. in ancient Rome) a member of a triumvirate
WORD ORIGIN Latin

triumvirate (try-**umm**-vir-rit) *n* **1** a group of three people in joint control of something: *the triumvirate of great orchestras which dominates classical music in Europe* **2** (in ancient Rome) a board of three officials jointly responsible for some task

trivalent *adj chem* **1** having a valency of three **2** having three valencies **trivalency** *n*

trivet (**triv**-vit) *n* **1** a three-legged stand for holding a pot, kettle, etc. over a fire **2** a short metal stand on which hot dishes are placed on a table
WORD ORIGIN Old English trefet

trivia *n* petty and unimportant things or details

trivial *adj* of little importance: *a trivial matter* **triviality** *n* **trivially** *adv*
WORD ORIGIN Latin trivialis common

trivialize or -**lise** *vb* -**lizing**, -**lized** or -**lising**, -**lised** to make (something) seem less important or complex than it is

trochee (**troke**-ee) *n prosody* a metrical foot of one long and one short syllable **trochaic** *adj*
WORD ORIGIN Greek trekhein to run

trod *vb* the past tense and a past participle of **tread**

trodden *vb* a past participle of **tread**

troglodyte *n* a person who lives in a cave
WORD ORIGIN Greek trōglodutēs one who enters caves

troika *n* **1** a Russian coach or sleigh drawn by three horses abreast **2** a group of three people in authority: *a troika of European foreign ministers*
WORD ORIGIN Russian

Trojan *adj* **1** of ancient Troy or its people ▷ *n* **2** a person from ancient Troy **3** a hard-working person

Trojan Horse *n* **1** *Greek myth* the huge wooden hollow figure of a horse used by the Greeks to enter Troy **2** a trap or trick intended to undermine an enemy

troll[1] *n* (in Scandinavian folklore) a supernatural dwarf or giant that dwells in a cave or mountain
WORD ORIGIN Old Norse: demon

troll[2] *vb angling* to fish by dragging a lure through the water
WORD ORIGIN Old French troller to run about

troll[3] *internet* *n* **1** a person who posts deliberately inflammatory messages on an internet discussion board ▷ *vb* **2** to post such a message

trolley *n* **1** a small table on casters used for carrying food or drink **2** a wheeled cart or stand used for moving heavy items, such as shopping in a supermarket or luggage at a railway station **3** *Brit* see **trolley bus** **4** *US & Canad* see **trolley car** **5** a device, such as a wheel, that collects the current from an overhead wire, to drive the motor of an electric vehicle **6** *Austral & Brit* a low truck running on rails, used in factories, mines, etc.
WORD ORIGIN probably from TROLL[2]

trolley bus *n* a bus powered by electricity from two overhead wires but not running on rails

trolley car *n US & Canad* same as **tram**

trollop *n derogatory* a promiscuous or slovenly woman
WORD ORIGIN origin unknown

trombone *n* a brass musical instrument with a sliding tube which is moved in or out to alter the note played **trombonist** *n*
WORD ORIGIN Italian

trompe l'oeil (tromp luh-ee) *n, pl* **trompe l'oeils** (tromp luh-ee) **1** a painting etc. giving a convincing illusion that the objects represented are real **2** an effect of this kind
WORD ORIGIN French, literally: deception of the eye

troop *n* **1** a large group: *a troop of dogs* **2** troops soldiers: *troops have been maintaining an unusually high profile* **3** a subdivision of a cavalry or armoured regiment **4** a large group of Scouts made up of several patrols ▷ *vb* **5** to move in a crowd: *we trooped into the room after her* **6** *mil chiefly Brit & Austral* to parade (a flag or banner) ceremonially: *trooping the colour*
WORD ORIGIN French troupe

trooper *n* **1** a soldier in a cavalry regiment **2** *US & Austral* a mounted policeman **3** *US* a state policeman **4** a cavalry horse **5** *informal chiefly Brit* a troopship

troopship *n* a ship used to transport military personnel

trope *n* a word or expression used in a figurative sense
WORD ORIGIN Greek tropos style, turn

trophy *n, pl* -**phies 1** a cup, shield, etc. given as a prize **2** a memento of success, esp. one taken in war or hunting: *stuffed animal heads and other hunting trophies* ▷ *adj* **3** *informal* regarded as a highly desirable symbol of wealth or success: *a trophy wife*
WORD ORIGIN Greek tropaion

tropic *n* **1** either of the lines of latitude at about 23½°N (**tropic of Cancer**) and 23½°S (**tropic of Capricorn**) of the equator **2** the tropics that part of the earth's surface between the tropics of Cancer and Capricorn: *the intense heat and humidity of the tropics*
WORD ORIGIN Greek tropos a turn; from the belief that the sun turned back at the solstices

tropical *adj* belonging to, typical of, or located in, the tropics: *tropical rainforests* **tropically** *adv*

tropism *n* the tendency of a plant or animal to turn or curve in response to an external stimulus
WORD ORIGIN Greek tropos a turn

troposphere n the lowest layer of the earth's atmosphere, about 18 kilometres (11 miles) thick at the equator to about 6 km (4 miles) at the Poles **WORD ORIGIN** Greek *tropos* a turn + SPHERE

trot vb **trotting, trotted 1** (of a horse) to move in a manner faster than a walk but slower than a gallop, in which diagonally opposite legs come down together **2** (of a person) to move fairly quickly, with small quick steps ▷ n **3** a medium-paced gait of a horse, in which diagonally opposite legs come down together **4** a steady brisk pace **5 on the trot** *informal* one after the other: *ten years on the trot* **6 the trots** *slang* diarrhoea **WORD ORIGIN** Old French

Trot n *chiefly Brit informal* a follower of Trotsky

troth (rhymes with **growth**) n *archaic* **1** a pledge of fidelity, esp. a betrothal **2 in troth** truly **WORD ORIGIN** Old English *trēowth*

trot out vb *informal* to repeat (old information or ideas) without fresh thought: *the government trots out the same excuse every time*

Trotskyist or **Trotskyite** adj **1** of the theories of Leon Trotsky (1879–1940), Russian Communist, which call for a worldwide revolution by the proletariat ▷ n **2** a supporter of Trotsky or his theories **Trotskyism** n

trotter n **1** the foot of a pig **2** a horse that is specially trained to trot fast

troubadour (**troo**-bad-oor) n a travelling poet and singer in S France or N Italy from the 11th to the 13th century who wrote chiefly on courtly love **WORD ORIGIN** French

trouble n **1** difficulties or problems: *I'd trouble finding somewhere to park* **2** a cause of distress, disturbance, or pain: *we must be sensitive to the troubles of other people* **3** disease or a problem with one's health: *ear trouble* **4** a state of disorder, ill-feeling, or unrest: *the police had orders to intervene at the first sign of trouble* **5** effort or exertion to do something: *they didn't even take the trouble to see the film before banning it* **6** a personal weakness or cause of annoyance: *his trouble is that he's constitutionally jealous* **7 in trouble a** likely to be punished for something one has done: *in trouble with the public prosecutor* **b** pregnant when not married **8 more trouble than it's worth** involving a lot of time or effort for very little reward: *making your own pasta is more trouble than it's worth* ▷ vb **-bling, -bled 9** to cause trouble to **10** to make an effort or exert oneself: *he dismissed the letters as forgeries without troubling to examine them* **11** to cause inconvenience or discomfort to: *sorry to trouble you!* **troubled** adj **WORD ORIGIN** Old French *troubler*

troublemaker n a person who causes trouble, esp. between people **troublemaking** adj, n

troubleshooter n a person employed to locate and deal with faults or problems **troubleshooting** n, adj

troublesome adj causing trouble

trouble spot n a place where there is frequent fighting or violence: *the Balkans have long been one of the major European trouble spots*

troublous adj *literary* unsettled or agitated

trough (**troff**) n **1** a long open container, esp. one for animals' food or water **2** a narrow channel between two waves or ridges **3** a low point in a pattern that has regular high and low points: *the trough of the slump in pupil numbers was in 1985* **4** *meteorol* a long narrow area of low pressure **5** a narrow channel or gutter **WORD ORIGIN** Old English *trōh*

trounce vb **trouncing, trounced** to defeat (someone) utterly **WORD ORIGIN** origin unknown

troupe (**troop**) n a company of actors or other performers **WORD ORIGIN** French

trouper n **1** a member of a troupe **2** an experienced person: *Bette plays a showbiz trouper*

trouser adj **1** of or relating to trousers: *trouser legs* ▷ vb **2** *Brit slang* to take (something, esp. money), often surreptitiously or unlawfully

trousers pl n a garment that covers the body from the waist to the ankles or knees with a separate tube-shaped section for each leg **WORD ORIGIN** Scottish Gaelic *triubhas* trews

trousseau (**troo**-so) n, pl **-seaux** (-so) the clothes, linen, and other possessions collected by a bride for her marriage **WORD ORIGIN** Old French

trout n, pl **trout** or **trouts** any of various game fishes related to the salmon and found chiefly in fresh water in northern regions **WORD ORIGIN** Old English *trūht*

trove n see **treasure-trove**

trowel n **1** a hand tool resembling a small spade with a curved blade, used by gardeners for lifting plants, etc. **2** a similar tool with a flat metal blade, used for spreading cement or plaster on a surface **WORD ORIGIN** Latin *trulla* a scoop

troy weight or **troy** n a system of weights used for precious metals and gemstones in which one pound equals twelve ounces **WORD ORIGIN** after the city of *Troyes*, France, where first used

truant n **1** a pupil who stays away from school without permission **2 play truant** to stay away from school without permission ▷ adj **3** being or relating to a truant: *a truant schoolkid* **truancy** n **WORD ORIGIN** Old French: vagabond

truce n a temporary agreement to stop fighting or quarrelling **WORD ORIGIN** plural of Old English *trēow* pledge

truck[1] n **1** *Brit* a railway wagon for carrying freight **2** a large motor vehicle for transporting heavy loads **3** any wheeled vehicle used to move goods ▷ vb **4** *chiefly US* to transport goods in a truck **WORD ORIGIN** perhaps from *truckle* a small wheel

truck[2] n **1** *history* the payment of wages in goods rather than in money **2 have no truck with** to refuse to be involved with: *the opposition will have no truck with the planned cut in pensions* **WORD ORIGIN** Old French *troquer* (unattested) to barter

trucker n a long-distance lorry driver

truckie n *Austral & NZ informal* a truck driver

truckle vb **-ling, -led** to yield weakly or give in: *he accused the government of truckling to the right-wing press* **WORD ORIGIN** from obsolete *truckle* to sleep in a truckle bed

truckle bed n *chiefly Brit* a low bed on wheels, stored under a larger bed

truculent (**truck**-yew-lent) adj defiantly aggressive or bad-tempered **truculence** n **truculently** adv **WORD ORIGIN** Latin *trux* fierce

trudge vb **trudging, trudged 1** to walk or plod heavily or wearily ▷ n **2** a long tiring walk **WORD ORIGIN** origin unknown

true adj **truer, truest 1** in accordance with the truth or facts; factual: *not all of the stories about her are true* **2** real or genuine: *he didn't want to reveal his true feelings* **3** faithful and loyal: *a true friend* **4** accurate or precise: *he looked through the telescopic sight until he was convinced his aim was true* **5** (of a compass bearing) according to the earth's geographical rather than magnetic poles: *true north* **6 come true** to actually happen: *fortunately his gloomy prediction didn't come true* ▷ n **7 in** or **out of true** in or not in correct alignment ▷ adv **8** truthfully or rightly: *I'd like to move to Edinburgh, true, but I'd need to get a job there first* **WORD ORIGIN** Old English *trīewe*

true-blue adj **1** staunchly loyal ▷ n **true blue 2** *chiefly Brit & Austral* a staunch royalist or Conservative

true-life adj taken directly from reality: *true-life TV horror stories*

truelove n the person that one loves

true north n the direction from any point along a meridian towards the North Pole

truffle n **1** a round fungus which grows underground and is regarded as a delicacy **2** Also called: **rum truffle** a sweet flavoured with chocolate or rum **WORD ORIGIN** French *truffe*

trug n *Brit* a long shallow basket for carrying garden tools, flowers, etc. **WORD ORIGIN** perhaps variant of *trough*

truism n a statement that is clearly true and well known

truly adv **1** in a true, just, or faithful manner **2** really: *a truly awful poem*

trump[1] n **1** same as **trump card** ▷ vb **2** *cards* to beat a card by playing a card which belongs to a suit which outranks it **3** to outdo or surpass: *she trumped his news by announcing that she had been picked for the Olympic team* ▸ See also **trumps** **WORD ORIGIN** variant of *triumph*

trump[2] n *archaic* or *literary* **1** a trumpet or the sound produced by one **2 the last trump** the final trumpet call on the Day of Judgment **WORD ORIGIN** Old French *trompe*

Pidgins and Creoles

What happens when mutually unintelligible languages collide? The explorers and colonizers dispatched by European empire-builders found out, and so did the native peoples with whom they came in contact, whether in tropical or subtropical Africa, the Indian Ocean, Oceania, or the Americas. Once the shock of contact was over, the strangers had to communicate. Often the result was a simplified language in which traders and slavers could talk to their suppliers, customers, or slaves.

This second language, known as a *pidgin*, gets down to basics. It may have grown from the blend of two or more languages, but it took its impetus from the speech of the socially dominant group. Speakers learned to express themselves in simplified forms and norms: sign language became amplified to include a limited number of useful nouns and verbs, and a simple grammar grew to connect them. A preposition might double as another part of speech. Inflections were scant. Words or syllables might be repeated to indicate plurals or some form of increase. The meaning of everything said often depended on social context. Pidgins are highly functional, dedicated to getting things done.

A pidgin may not always evolve into a *creole* language, but it often does, and sometimes in a single generation. Considered as peoples, Creoles were the descendants of Europeans – English, French, Dutch, Spanish, and Portuguese – who lived in the new lands and called it home, though in Brazil they could be the descendants of West Africans. As languages, creoles are not necessarily European in origin: creoles based on Arabic or Malay also exist. In some cases, a creole could become important as a lingua franca shared by other language groups. Structurally, creoles tended at first to resemble pidgins in having a simple subject-verb-object grammar. Questions and answers could rely on verbal intonation, not syntax, and there might be no distinction between the active and passive voice of verbs. Once again their foundation was from the more powerful classes, with many contributions from a dominated underclass. Over time they could become stable, self-sufficient languages, or become de-creolized dialects of the standard language

from which they started.

That creoles can be found scattered across the Caribbean, and even on mainland South and North America, demonstrates their staying power. Papiamento, based on Dutch, Portuguese, and Spanish, is spoken on the ABC Islands of Aruba, Bonaire, and Curaçao. Since they warred for centuries in the Caribbean, England and France left linguistic markers. The English were responsible for the formation of Guyanan Creole and Jamaican Patois, and their influence swept as far north as the mid-Atlantic seaboard of the United States, where Gullah is spoken on islands along the coast of northern Florida, Georgia, and South Carolina. Forms of French Creole can be found not just in the historically French islands of Martinique and Guadeloupe, but also in the former English colonies of Trinidad and Tobago, Dominica, and St Lucia. But Haiti was the most notable French redoubt: some eight million speak Haitian Creole, the largest creole-speaking population in the world. It is the nation's official language, as is the English-derived Tok Shin in Papua New Guinea.

Since colonies gained independence, creoles have vastly increased their prestige in the eyes of speakers, scholars, and onlookers. The scholars have hotly disputed what characterizes pidgins and creoles, and how they arose, declined, or flourished. What they can agree on is that a creole or pidgin differs from a *dialect*, a form of a standard language that is peculiar to a region or a social group, and from a *mixed language*, in which a speaker of two languages freely mixes elements of both.

Given the tangled history of exploiters and the exploited, pidgins and creoles have often been regarded as the n'er-do-well cousins of standard languages, or as their debased or degenerate dialects. But Anglophones should remind themselves that when they ineffectually try to order something in a foreign shop, they likely speak in rudimentary pidgin. They could also remember that, in the view of some linguists, Middle English was a creole, since it superimposed a huge lexicon of French on the structure and popular vocabulary of Anglo-Saxon. If they're right, Chaucer wrote in creole.

trump card *n* **1** any card from the suit that ranks higher than any other suit in one particular game **2** an advantage, weapon, etc. that is kept in reserve until needed: *the President hoped to use his experience of foreign affairs as a trump card in the election.* Also called: **trump**

trumped up *adj* (of charges, excuses, etc.) made up in order to deceive

trumpery *n, pl* **-eries 1** something useless or worthless ▷ *adj* **2** useless or worthless
WORD ORIGIN Old French *tromperie* deceit

trumpet *n* **1** a valved brass musical instrument consisting of a narrow tube ending in a flare **2** a loud sound such as that of a trumpet: *the elephant gave a loud trumpet* **3 blow one's own trumpet** to boast about one's own skills or good qualities ▷ *vb* **-peting, -peted 4** to proclaim or state forcefully: *almost every one of the party's loudly trumpeted election claims is untrue* **5** (of an elephant) to make a loud cry **trumpeter** *n*
WORD ORIGIN Old French *trompette*

trumps *pl n* **1** *cards* any one of the four suits that outranks all the other suits for the duration of a deal or game **2 turn up trumps** (of a person) to bring about a happy or successful conclusion, esp. unexpectedly

truncate *vb* **-cating, -cated** to shorten by cutting **truncated** *adj* **truncation** *n*
WORD ORIGIN Latin *truncare*

truncheon *n chiefly Brit* a small club, esp. one carried by a policeman
WORD ORIGIN Old French *tronchon* stump

trundle *vb* **-dling, -dled** to move heavily on or as if on wheels: *a bus trundled along the drive*
WORD ORIGIN Old English *tryndel* circular or spherical object

trundle bed *n US, Canad, & NZ* a low bed on wheels, stored under a larger bed

trundler *n* **1** *NZ* a golf or shopping trolley **2** a child's pushchair

trunk *n* **1** the main stem of a tree **2** a large strong case or box used to contain clothes when travelling and for storage **3** a person's body excluding the head, neck, and limbs; torso **4** the long nose of an elephant **5** *US* the boot of a car
▸ See also **trunks**
WORD ORIGIN Latin *truncus*

trunk call *n chiefly Brit & Austral* a long-distance telephone call

trunk line *n* **1** a direct link between two distant telephone exchanges or switchboards **2** the main route or routes on a railway

trunk road *n Brit* a main road, esp. one maintained by the central government

trunks *pl n* shorts worn by a man for swimming

truss *vb* **1** to tie or bind (someone) up **2** to bind the wings and legs of (a fowl) before cooking ▷ *n* **3** *med* a device for holding a hernia in place **4** a framework of wood or metal used to support a roof, bridge, etc. **5** a cluster of flowers or fruit growing at the end of a single stalk
WORD ORIGIN Old French *trousse*

trust *vb* **1** to believe that (someone) is honest and means no harm: *my father warned me never to trust strangers* **2** to feel that (something) is safe and reliable: *I don't trust those new gadgets* **3** to entrust (someone) with important information or valuables: *she's not somebody I would trust with this sort of secret* **4** to believe that (someone) is likely to do something safely and reliably: *I wouldn't trust anyone else to look after my child properly* **5** to believe (a story, account, etc.) **6** to expect, hope, or suppose: *I trust you've made your brother welcome here* ▷ *n* **7** confidence in the truth, worth, reliability, etc. of a person or thing; faith: *he knew that his father had great trust in him* **8** the obligation of someone in a responsible position: *he was in a position of trust as her substitute father* **9 a** a legal arrangement whereby one person looks after property, money, etc. on another's behalf **b** property that is the subject of such an arrangement **10** (in Britain) a self-governing hospital, group of hospitals, or other body that operates as an independent commercial unit within the National Health Service **11** *chiefly US & Canad* a group of companies joined together to control the market for any commodity ▷ *adj* **12** of or relating to a trust or trusts: *trust status*
WORD ORIGIN Old Norse *traust* help, support, confidence

trustee *n* **1** a person who administers property on someone else's behalf **2** a member of a board that manages the affairs of an institution or organization

trustful or **trusting** *adj* characterized by a readiness to trust others **trustfully** or **trustingly** *adv*

trust fund *n* money, securities, etc. held in trust

trustworthy *adj* (of a person) honest, reliable, or dependable

trusty *adj* **trustier, trustiest 1** faithful or reliable: *his trusty steed* ▷ *n, pl* **trusties 2** a trustworthy convict to whom special privileges are granted

truth *n* **1** the quality of being true, genuine, or factual: *there is no truth in the allegations* **2** something that is true: *he finally learned the truth about his parents' marriage* **3** a proven or verified fact, principle, etc.: *some profound truths about biology have come to light*
WORD ORIGIN Old English *trīewth*

truthful *adj* **1** telling the truth; honest **2** true; based on facts: *a truthful answer* **truthfully** *adv* **truthfulness** *n*

try *vb* **tries, trying, tried 1** to make an effort or attempt: *you must try to understand* **2** to sample or test (something) to see how enjoyable, good, or useful it is: *I tried smoking once but didn't like it* **3** to put strain or stress on (someone's patience) **4** to give pain, affliction, or vexation to: *sometimes when I've been sorely tried, my temper gets a little out of hand* **5 a** to investigate (a case) in a court of law **b** to hear evidence in order to determine the guilt or innocence of (a person) ▷ *n, pl* **tries 6** an attempt or effort **7** *rugby* a score made by placing the ball down behind the opposing team's goal line
WORD ORIGIN Old French *trier* to sort

≡ USAGE
The use of *and* instead of *to* after *try* is very common, but should be avoided in formal writing: *we must try to prevent* (not *try and prevent*) *this happening.*

trying *adj* upsetting, difficult, or annoying

try on *vb* **1** to put on (a garment) to find out whether it fits **2 try it on** *informal* to attempt to deceive or fool someone ▷ *n* **try-on 3** *Brit informal* something done to test out a person's tolerance etc.

try out *vb* **1** to test (something), esp. to find out how good it is ▷ *n* **tryout 2** *chiefly US & Canad* a trial or test, for example of an athlete or actor

trysail *n* a small fore-and-aft sail set on a sailing vessel to help keep her head to the wind in a storm

tryst *n archaic or literary* **1** an arrangement to meet, esp. secretly **2** a meeting, esp. a secret one with a lover, or the place where such a meeting takes place
WORD ORIGIN Old French *triste* lookout post

tsar or **czar** (**zahr**) *n* (until 1917) the emperor of Russia. Also: **tzar** ▷ **tsarist** or **czarist** *n*
WORD ORIGIN Russian, ultimately from Caesar

tsarevitch or **czarevitch** (**zahr**-rev-itch) *n* the eldest son of a Russian tsar

tsarina or **czarina** (zahr-**een**-a) *n* the wife of a Russian tsar

tsetse fly or **tzetze fly** (**tset**-see) *n* a bloodsucking African fly whose bite transmits disease, esp. sleeping sickness
WORD ORIGIN Tswana (language of southern Africa) *tse tse*

T-shirt or **tee-shirt** *n* a short-sleeved casual shirt or top
WORD ORIGIN T-shape formed when laid flat

tsotsi (**tsot**-see) *n S African* a Black street thug or gang member
WORD ORIGIN perhaps from Nguni (language group of southern Africa) *tsotsa* to dress flashily

tsp. teaspoon

T-square *n* a T-shaped ruler used for drawing horizontal lines and to support set squares when drawing vertical and inclined lines

tsunami *n* a large, often destructive, sea wave, usually caused by an earthquake under the sea
WORD ORIGIN Japanese

TT 1 teetotal **2** teetotaller **3** tuberculin-tested

tuatara (too-ah-**tah**-rah) *n* a large lizard-like New Zealand reptile
WORD ORIGIN Māori *tua* back + *tara* spine

tub *n* **1** a low wide, usually round container **2** a small plastic or cardboard container for ice cream etc. **3** *chiefly US* same as **bath** (sense 1). **4** Also called: **tubful** the amount a tub will hold **5** a slow and uncomfortable boat or ship
WORD ORIGIN Middle Dutch *tubbe*

tuba (**tube**-a) *n* a low-pitched brass musical instrument with valves
WORD ORIGIN Latin

tubby *adj* -bier, -biest (of a person) fat and short **tubbiness** *n*

tube *n* **1** a long hollow cylindrical object, used for the passage of fluids or as a container **2** a flexible cylinder of soft metal or plastic closed with a cap, used to hold substances such as toothpaste **3** *anat* any hollow cylindrical structure: *the Fallopian tubes* **4 the tube** *Brit* the underground railway system in London **5** *electronics* see **cathode-ray tube 6** *slang chiefly US* a television set **tubeless** *adj*
WORD ORIGIN Latin *tubus*

tuber (**tube**-er) *n* a fleshy underground root of a plant such as a potato
WORD ORIGIN Latin: hump

tubercle (**tube**-er-kl) *n* **1** a small rounded swelling **2** any abnormal hard swelling, esp. one characteristic of tuberculosis
WORD ORIGIN Latin *tuberculum* a little swelling

tubercular (tube-**berk**-yew-lar) *or* **tuberculous** *adj* **1** of or symptomatic of tuberculosis **2** of or relating to a tubercle

tuberculin (tube-**berk**-yew-lin) *n* a sterile liquid prepared from cultures of the tubercle bacillus and used in the diagnosis of tuberculosis

tuberculin-tested *adj* (of milk) produced by cows that have been certified as free of tuberculosis

tuberculosis (tube-berk-yew-**lohss**-iss) *n* an infectious disease characterized by the formation of tubercles, esp. in the lungs

tuberous (**tube**-er-uss) *adj* (of plants) forming, bearing, or resembling a tuber or tubers

tubing (**tube**-ing) *n* **1** a length of tube **2** a system of tubes

tub-thumper *n* a noisy or ranting public speaker **tub-thumping** *adj*, *n*

tubular (**tube**-yew-lar) *adj* **1** having the shape of a tube or tubes **2** of or relating to a tube or tubing

tubule (**tube**-yewl) *n* any small tubular structure, esp. in an animal or plant

TUC (in Britain and South Africa) Trades Union Congress

tuck *vb* **1** to push or fold into a small space or between two surfaces: *she tucked the letter into her handbag* **2** to thrust the loose ends or sides of (something) into a confining space, so as to make it neat and secure: *he tucked his shirt back into his trousers* **3** to make a tuck or tucks in (a garment) ▷ *n* **4** a pleat or fold in a part of a garment, usually stitched down **5** *Brit informal* food, esp. cakes and sweets
WORD ORIGIN Old English *tūcian* to torment

tuck away *vb informal* **1** to eat (a large amount of food) **2** to store (something) in a safe place: *we knew he had some money tucked away somewhere* **3** to have a quiet, rarely disturbed or visited location: *the chapel is tucked away in a side street*

tucker *n* **1** a detachable yoke of lace, linen, etc. formerly worn over the breast of a low-cut dress **2** *Austral & NZ informal* food **3** one's best bib and tucker *informal* one's best clothes

tuckered *adj* **tuckered out** *informal chiefly US & Canad* exhausted

tuck in *vb* **1** to put (someone) to bed and make him or her snug **2** to thrust the loose ends or sides of (something) into a confining space: *tuck in the bedclothes* **3** *informal* to eat, esp. heartily

tuck shop *n chiefly Brit* a shop in or near a school, where cakes and sweets are sold

Tudor *adj* **1** of or in the reign of the English royal house ruling from 1485 to 1603 **2** denoting a style of architecture characterized by half-timbered houses: *a Tudor cottage*

Tues. Tuesday

Tuesday *n* the third day of the week
WORD ORIGIN Old English *tīwesdæg* day of Tyr, Norse god

tufa (**tew**-fa) *n* a porous rock formed of calcium carbonate deposited from springs
WORD ORIGIN Italian *tufo*

tuff *n geol* a porous rock formed from volcanic dust or ash
WORD ORIGIN Old French *tuf*

tuffet *n* a small mound or low seat
WORD ORIGIN from *tuft*

tuft *n* a bunch of feathers, grass, hair, threads, etc. held together at the base **tufted** *adj* **tufty** *adj*
WORD ORIGIN probably from Old French *tufe*

tug *vb* **tugging, tugged 1** to pull or drag with a sharp or powerful movement: *she tugged at my arm* **2** to tow (a ship or boat) by means of a tug ▷ *n* **3** a strong pull or jerk **4** Also called: **tugboat** a boat with a powerful engine, used for towing barges, ships, etc.
WORD ORIGIN Middle English *tuggen*

tug-of-love *n* a conflict over the custody of a child between divorced parents or between the child's natural parents and its foster or adoptive parents

tug-of-war *n* **1** a contest in which two people or teams pull opposite ends of a rope in an attempt to drag the opposition over a central line **2** any hard struggle between two people or two groups

tuition *n* **1** instruction, esp. that received individually or in a small group **2** the payment for instruction, esp. in colleges or universities
WORD ORIGIN Latin *tueri* to watch over

tuktu *n Canad* another name for **caribou**

tuk-tuk *n* (in Thailand) a three-wheeled motor vehicle used as a taxi

tulip *n* **1** a plant which produces bright cup-shaped flowers in spring **2** the flower or bulb
WORD ORIGIN Turkish *tülbend* turban

tulip tree *n* a North American tree with tulip-shaped greenish-yellow flowers and long conelike fruits

tulle (**tewl**) *n* a fine net fabric of silk, rayon, etc. used to make evening dresses
WORD ORIGIN French

tumble *vb* -bling, -bled **1** to fall or cause to fall, esp. awkwardly or violently: *chairs tumbled over* **2** to roll or twist, esp. in playing: *they rolled and tumbled as wild*

beasts **3** to decrease in value suddenly: *interest rates tumbled* **4** to move in a quick and uncontrolled manner: *the crowd tumbled down the stairs* **5** to disturb, rumple, or toss around: *she was all tumbled by the fall* **6** to perform leaps or somersaults ▷ *n* **7** a fall, esp. an awkward or violent one: *he took a tumble down the stairs* **8** a somersault **tumbled** *adj*
WORD ORIGIN Old English *tumbian* dance, jump

tumbledown *adj* (of a building) falling to pieces; dilapidated

tumble dryer *or* **drier** *n* an electrically-operated machine that dries wet laundry by rotating it in warmed air inside a metal drum

tumbler *n* **1 a** a flat-bottomed drinking glass with no handle or stem **b** the amount a tumbler will hold **2** a person who performs somersaults and other acrobatic feats **3** a part of the mechanism of a lock

tumble to *vb* to understand or become aware of: *how did he tumble to this?*

tumbril *n* a farm cart that tilts backwards to empty its load, which was used to take condemned prisoners to the guillotine during the French Revolution
WORD ORIGIN Old French *tumberel*

tumescent (tew-**mess**-ent) *adj* swollen or becoming swollen

tumid (**tew**-mid) *adj rare* **1** (of an organ or part of the body) enlarged or swollen **2** pompous or fulsome in style: *a tumid tome* **tumidity** *n*
WORD ORIGIN Latin *tumere* to swell

tummy *n, pl* -mies an informal or childish word for **stomach**

tumour *or US* **tumor** (**tew**-mer) *n pathol* **a** any abnormal swelling **b** a mass of tissue formed by a new growth of cells **tumorous** *adj*
WORD ORIGIN Latin *tumere* to swell

tumult (**tew**-mult) *n* **1** a loud confused noise, such as one produced by a crowd **2** a state of confusion and excitement: *a tumult of emotions*
WORD ORIGIN Latin *tumultus*

tumultuous (tew-**mull**-tew-uss) *adj* **1** exciting, confused, or turbulent: *this week's tumultuous events* **2** unruly, noisy, or excited: *a tumultuous welcome*

tumulus (**tew**-myew-luss) *n, pl* -li (-lie) *archaeol no longer in technical usage* a burial mound
WORD ORIGIN Latin: a hillock

tun *n* a large beer cask
WORD ORIGIN Old English *tunne*

tuna (**tune**-a) *n, pl* -na *or* -nas **1** a large marine spiny-finned fish **2** the flesh of this fish, often tinned for food
WORD ORIGIN American Spanish

tundra *n* a vast treeless Arctic region with permanently frozen subsoil
WORD ORIGIN Russian

tune *n* **1** a melody, esp. one for which harmony is not essential **2** the correct musical pitch: *many of the notes are out of tune* **3** call the tune to be in control of the proceedings **4** change one's tune to alter one's attitude or tone of speech **5** in *or* out of tune with in or not in

agreement or sympathy with: *in tune with public opinion* **6 to the tune of** *informal* to the amount or extent of ▷ *vb* **tuning, tuned 7** to adjust (a musical instrument) so each string, key, etc. produces the right note **8** to make small adjustments to (an engine, machine, etc.) to obtain the proper or desired performance **9** to adjust (a radio or television) to receive a particular station or programme: *the radio was tuned to the local station* **tuner** *n*
WORD ORIGIN variant of *tone*

tuneful *adj* having a pleasant tune **tunefully** *adv*

tune in *vb* **1** to adjust (a radio or television) to receive (a station or programme) **2 tuned in to** *slang* aware of or knowledgeable about: *tuned in to European cinema*

tuneless *adj* having no melody or tune

tune up *vb* **1** to adjust (a musical instrument) to a particular pitch **2** to adjust the engine of a car, etc. to improve its performance

tungsten *n chem* a hard greyish-white metallic element. Symbol: W
WORD ORIGIN Swedish *tung* heavy + *sten* stone

tunic *n* **1** a close-fitting jacket forming part of some uniforms **2** a loose-fitting knee-length garment
WORD ORIGIN Latin *tunica*

tuning fork *n* a two-pronged metal fork that when struck produces a pure note of constant specified pitch

tunnel *n* **1** an underground passageway, esp. one for trains or cars **2** any passage or channel through or under something: *the carpal tunnel* ▷ *vb* **-nelling, -nelled** *or US* **-neling, -neled 3** to make one's way through or under (something) by digging a tunnel: *ten men succeeded in tunnelling out of the prisoner-of-war camp* **4** to dig a tunnel (through or under something): *the idea of tunnelling under the English Channel has been around for a long time*
WORD ORIGIN Old French *tonel* cask

tunnel vision *n* **1** a condition in which a person is unable to see things that are not straight in front **2** narrowness of viewpoint resulting from concentration on only one aspect of a subject or situation

tunny *n, pl* **-nies** *or* **-ny** same as **tuna**
WORD ORIGIN Latin *thunnus*

tup *n chiefly Brit* a male sheep
WORD ORIGIN origin unknown

tupik (**too**-pick) *n* a tent of seal or caribou skin used for shelter by the Inuit in summer
WORD ORIGIN Inuktitut *tupiq*

tuppence *n Brit* same as **twopence** ▷ **tuppenny** *adj*

tuque (rhymes with **fluke**) *n Canad* **1** a knitted cap with a long tapering end **2** a close-fitting knitted hat often with a tassel or pompom
WORD ORIGIN Canadian French

turban *n* **1** a head-covering worn by a Muslim, Hindu, or Sikh man, consisting of a long piece of cloth wound round the head **2** any head-covering resembling this **turbaned** *adj*
WORD ORIGIN Turkish *tülbend*

turbid *adj literary* (of water or air) full of mud or dirt, and frequently swirling around: *the turbid stream of the Loire* **turbidity** *n*
WORD ORIGIN Latin *turbare* to agitate

turbine *n* a machine in which power is produced by a stream of water, air, etc. that pushes the blades of a wheel and causes it to rotate
WORD ORIGIN Latin *turbo* whirlwind

turbocharger *n* a device that increases the power of an internal-combustion engine by using the exhaust gases to drive a turbine **turbocharged** *adj*

turbofan *n* a type of engine in which a large fan driven by a turbine forces air rearwards to increase the propulsive thrust

turbojet *n* **1** a gas turbine in which the exhaust gases provide the propulsive thrust in an aircraft **2** an aircraft powered by turbojet engines

turboprop *n* an aircraft propulsion unit where the propeller is driven by a gas turbine

turbot *n, pl* **-bot** *or* **-bots** a European flatfish, highly valued as a food fish
WORD ORIGIN Old French *tourbot*

turbulence *n* **1** a state or condition of confusion, movement, or agitation **2** *meteorol* instability in the atmosphere causing gusty air currents

turbulent *adj* **1** involving a lot of sudden changes and conflicting elements: *the city has had a turbulent history* **2** (of people) wild and unruly: *a harsh mountain land inhabited by a score of turbulent tribes* **3** (of water or air) full of violent unpredictable currents: *the turbulent ocean*
WORD ORIGIN Latin *turba* confusion

turd *n taboo* **1** a piece of excrement **2** *slang* a contemptible person
WORD ORIGIN Old English *tord*

tureen *n* a large deep dish with a lid, used for serving soups
WORD ORIGIN French *terrine* earthenware vessel

turf *n, pl* **turfs** *or* **turves 1** a layer of thick even grass with roots and soil attached: *a short turf rich in wild flowers* **2** a piece cut from this layer: *we spent the afternoon digging turves* **3** *informal* **a** the area where a person lives and feels at home: *my boyhood turf of east Cork* **b** a person's area of knowledge or influence: *when Kate is at work, she's on her own turf* **4 the turf a** a track where horse races are run **b** horse racing as a sport or industry **5** same as **peat** ▷ *vb* **6** to cover (an area of ground) with pieces of turf
WORD ORIGIN Old English

turf accountant *n Brit* same as **bookmaker**

turf out *vb informal* to throw (someone or something) out: *the residents fear a new landlord might push up rents and turf them out of their homes*

turgid (**tur**-jid) *adj* **1** (of language) pompous, boring, and hard to understand **2** (of water or mud) unpleasantly thick and brown **turgidity** *n*
WORD ORIGIN Latin *turgere* to swell

Turk *n* a person from Turkey

turkey *n, pl* **-keys** *or* **-key 1** a large bird of North America bred for its meat **2** *informal chiefly US & Canad* something, esp. a theatrical production, that fails **3 cold turkey** *slang* a method of curing drug addiction by abrupt withdrawal of all doses **4 talk turkey** *informal chiefly US & Canad* to discuss, esp. business, frankly and practically
WORD ORIGIN used at first of the African guinea fowl (because it was brought through Turkish territory), later applied by mistake to the American bird

Turkic *n* a family of Asian languages including Turkish and Azerbaijani

Turkish *adj* **1** of Turkey ▷ *n* **2** the language of Turkey

Turkish bath *n* **1** a type of bath in which the bather sweats freely in hot dry air, is then washed, often massaged, and has a cold plunge or shower **2 Turkish baths** an establishment for such baths

Turkish coffee *n* very strong black coffee

Turkish delight *n* a jelly-like sweet flavoured with flower essences, usually cut into cubes and covered in icing sugar

turmeric *n* **1** a tropical Asian plant with yellow flowers and an aromatic underground stem **2** a yellow spice obtained from the root of this plant
WORD ORIGIN Old French *terre merite* meritorious earth

turmoil *n* disorder, agitation, or confusion: *a period of political turmoil and uncertainty*
WORD ORIGIN origin unknown

turn *vb* **1** to move to face in another direction **2** to rotate or move round **3** to operate (a switch, key, etc.) by twisting it **4** to aim or point (something) in a particular direction: *they turned their guns on the crowd* **5** to change in course or direction: *the van turned right into Victoria Road* **6** (of a road, river, etc.) to have a bend or curve in it **7** to perform or do (something) with a rotating movement: *a small boy was turning somersaults* **8** to change so as to become: *he turned pale* **9** to reach, pass, or progress beyond in age, time, etc.: *she had just turned fourteen* **10** to find (a particular page) in a book: *turn to page 78* **11** to look at the other side of: *turning the pages of a book* **12** to shape (wood, metal, etc.) on a lathe **13** (of leaves) to change colour in autumn **14** to make or become sour: *the milk is starting to turn* **15** to affect or be affected with nausea or giddiness: *that would turn the strongest stomach* **16** (of the tide) to start coming in or going out **17 turn against** to stop liking (something or someone previously liked): *people turned against her because she became so dictatorial* **18 turn into** to become or change into: *my mother turned our house into four apartments* **19 turn loose** to set (an animal or a person) free **20 turn someone's head** to affect someone mentally or emotionally **21 turn to a** to direct or apply (one's attention or thoughts) to **b** to stop doing or using one thing and start doing or using (another): *I turned to*

Cockney Dialect

London's importance in British history is without question. It is Britain's largest city, the country's political, financial, and administrative capital, and is associated with royalty, nobility, the civil service, high finance, and high culture. However, London is also home to one of Britain's best-known working-class communities, whose accent, vocabulary, and culture have been immortalized in countless books, plays, musicals, films, and television series over the years: the Cockneys.

The word 'Cockney' is not quite as old as London itself but comes from the Middle English *cokenay* which meant 'a pampered child'. It was used in this sense in Chaucer's *Canterbury Tales* (c. 1386) but by the sixteenth century it had come to mean a town-dweller ignorant of the harsh realities of life. This contemptuous word gradually narrowed its meaning and by the seventeenth century it had come to indicate a person from one particular part of one particular city: the East End of London. Indeed, one writer of the time narrowed down the definition even further and claimed that 'Cockney' could be applied only to someone born within the sound of Bow Bells (the bells of St Mary-le-Bow church), a definition that is familiar to this day.

Later a number of noted writers made famous the speech patterns of the East End of London, including Charles Dickens, Rudyard Kipling, and George Bernard Shaw. The latter wrote *Pygmalion* (1913), a play in which a professor of phonetics, Henry Higgins, tries to pass off a Cockney flower girl, Eliza Doolittle, as an aristocrat. In the musical version of the play, *My Fair Lady* (1956), Higgins memorably drills Eliza to say 'In Hertford, Hereford, and Hampshire hurricanes hardly happen' without dropping her aitches. This is one of Cockney's best known features – although some East Enders attempt to 'hypercorrect' their speech by adding an 'h' to words that don't need one: 'hambitious' (ambitious) and 'hever' (ever), for example.

Other characteristics of the Cockney accent include the glottal stop, where the 't' in words such as 'rental' and 'flatter' is dropped; the use of 'f' instead of 'th', where 'thirty' becomes 'firty'; the use of 'v' instead of 'th', where 'mother' becomes 'muvver'; and the use of the 'linking R', where 'r' is inserted into words such as 'drawing' so that it is pronounced 'drawring'.

Cockney vocabulary is a colourful mix of words and phrases from various sources. From armed forces slang picked up overseas are *ackers* (probably from Arabic *fakka*, meaning 'small change'), *shufti* (from Arabic, meaning 'a look'), *cushty* (from Hindi *khush* 'pleasure', indicating pleasure or approval), *dekko* (from Hindi, meaning 'a look'), and *doolally* (meaning 'mad', and derived from the Indian town of Deolali where a British Army psychiatric hospital was located). From Romany there is *mush* (mate). Euphemisms are also characteristic, with a number for 'God' including *Gordon Bennett* (an American motor-racing promoter) and *Cor Blimey* (derived from 'God blind me').

Most celebrated of all, however, is Cockney rhyming slang, where an everyday word is replaced by a word or phrase with which it rhymes. Some well known examples are *frog and toad* (road), *apples and pears* (stairs), and *dog and bone* (phone). Those wishing to take a closer *butcher's hook* (look) into the subject will find that modern Cockney rhyming slang also has a penchant for taking people from the public eye and turning them into rhyming phrases. Some recent examples of this are *Lionel Blairs* (flares), *Ayrton Senna* (tenner), and *Britney Spears* (beers).

The vibrancy of Cockney culture and language make it attractive to many people who are not from London's East End, and a recent contemptuous coinage is the *Mockney* who apes the speech patterns and lifestyles of Cockneys despite not having been born near the sound of Bow Bells. Such individuals, whether they be film directors, pop stars, or chefs, are perhaps envious of the 'lovable rogue' image of Cockneys and wish to imitate noted fictional 'cheeky chappies' such as Private Walker from *Dad's Army*, Del Trotter from *Only Fools and Horses*, and Arthur Daley from *Minder*. This image of the East End's inhabitants has been around since the days of the music hall and, like dropped aitches and rhyming slang, shows no sign of disappearing.

photography from writing **c** to appeal or apply to (someone) for help, advice, etc. ▷ *n* **22** the act of turning **23** a movement of complete or partial rotation: *a turn of the dial* **24** a change of direction or position **25** same as **turning** (sense 1). **26** the right or opportunity to do something in an agreed order or succession: *it was her turn to play next* **27** a change in something that is happening or being done: *events took an unhappy turn* **28** a period of action, work, etc. **29** a short walk, ride, or excursion **30** natural inclination: *a liberal turn of mind* **31** distinctive form or style: *she'd a nice turn of phrase* **32** a deed that helps or hinders someone: *I'm trying to do you a good turn* **33** a twist, bend, or distortion in shape **34** a slight attack of an illness: *she's just having one of her turns* **35** *music* a melodic ornament that alternates the main note with the notes above and below it, beginning with the note above, in a variety of sequences **36** a short theatrical act: *tonight's star turn* **37** *informal* a shock or surprise: *you gave me rather a turn* **38** **done to a turn** *informal* cooked perfectly **39** **turn and turn about** one after another; alternately ▶ See also **turn down, turn in**, etc.
turner *n*
WORD ORIGIN Old English *tyrnan*

turnaround *or* **turnabout** *n* a complete change or reversal: *a prompt economic turnaround*

turncoat *n* a person who deserts one cause or party to join an opposing one

turn down *vb* **1** to reduce (the volume, brightness, or temperature of something): *turn the heat down* **2** to reject or refuse: *the invitation was turned down* **3** to fold down (sheets, etc.)

turn in *vb informal* **1** to go to bed for the night **2** to hand in: *turning in my essay* **3** to hand (a suspect or criminal) over to the police: *his own brother turned him in*

turning *n* **1** a road, river, or path that turns off the main way **2** the point where such a way turns off **3** the process of turning objects on a lathe

turning circle *n* the smallest circle in which a vehicle can turn

turning point *n* a moment when a decisive change occurs

turnip *n* a vegetable with a large yellow or white edible root
WORD ORIGIN Latin *napus*

turnkey *n old-fashioned* a jailer

turn off *vb* **1** to leave (a road or path): *turning off the main road* **2** (of a road or path) to lead away from (another road or path): *a main street with alleys twisting and turning off it* **3** to cause (something) to stop operating by turning a knob, pushing a button, etc. **4** *informal* to cause disgust or disinterest in (someone): *keeping kids from getting turned off by mathematics* ▷ *n* **turn-off 5** a road or other way branching off from the main thoroughfare **6** *informal* a person or thing that causes dislike

turn on *vb* **1** to cause (something) to operate by turning a knob, pushing a button, etc.: *turn on the radio, please* **2** to attack (someone), esp. without warning: *the Labrador turned on me*

3 *informal* to produce suddenly or automatically: *turning on that bland smile* **4** *slang* to arouse emotionally or sexually **5** to depend or hinge on: *the match turned on three double faults by Sampras* ▷ *n* **turn-on 6** *slang* a person or thing that causes emotional or sexual arousal

turn out *vb* **1** to cause (something, esp. a light) to stop operating by moving a switch **2** to produce or create: *turning out two hits a year* **3** to force (someone) out of a place or position: *turned out of office* **4** to empty the contents of (something): *the police ordered him to turn out his pockets* **5** to be discovered or found (to be or do something): *he turned out to be a Finn* **6** to end up or result: *how interesting to see how it all turned out!* **7** to dress and groom: *she is always very well turned out* **8** to assemble or gather: *crowds turned out to see him* **9 turn out for** *informal* to make an appearance, esp. in a sporting competition: *he was asked to turn out for Liverpool* ▷ *n* **turnout 10** a number of people attending an event: *there has been a high turnout of voters in elections in Bulgaria* **11** the quantity or amount produced

turn over *vb* **1** to change position, esp. so as to reverse top and bottom **2** to shift position, for instance by rolling onto one's side: *he turned over and went straight to sleep* **3** to consider carefully: *as I walked, I turned her story over* **4** to give (something) to someone who has a right to it or to the authorities: *the police ordered him to turn over the files to them* **5** (of an engine) to start or function correctly: *when he pressed the starter button, the engine turned over at once* **6** *slang* to rob: *the house had been turned over while they were out* ▷ *n* **turnover 7 a** the amount of business done by a company during a specified period **b** the rate at which stock in trade is sold and replenished **8** a small pastry case filled with fruit or jam: *an apple turnover* **9** the number of workers employed by a firm in a given period to replace those who have left

turnpike *n* **1** *history* a barrier across a road to prevent vehicles or pedestrians passing until a charge (toll) had been paid **2** *US* a motorway for use of which a toll is charged
WORD ORIGIN *turn + pike* a spike

turnstile *n* a mechanical barrier with arms that are turned to admit one person at a time

turntable *n* **1** the circular platform in a record player that rotates the record while it is being played **2** a circular platform used for turning locomotives and cars

turn up *vb* **1** to arrive or appear: *few people turned up* **2** to find or discover or be found or discovered: *a medical checkup has only turned up a sinus infection* **3** to increase the flow, volume, etc. of: *he turned up the radio* ▷ *n* **turn-up 4** *Brit* the turned-up fold at the bottom of some trouser legs **5 a turn-up for the books** *informal* an unexpected happening

turpentine *n* **1** a strong-smelling colourless oil distilled from the resin of some coniferous trees, and used for thinning paint, for cleaning, and in medicine **2** a semisolid mixture of resin and oil obtained from various

conifers, which is the main source of commercial turpentine **3** *not in technical usage* any one of a number of thinners for paints and varnishes, consisting of fractions of petroleum
WORD ORIGIN Latin *terebinthina*

turpitude *n formal* depravity or wickedness: *newspapers owned by proprietors whose moral turpitude far exceeded anything chronicled in their pages*
WORD ORIGIN Latin *turpitudo* ugliness

turps *n* short for **turpentine** (senses 1, 3)

turquoise *adj* **1** greenish-blue ▷ *n* **2** a greenish-blue precious stone
WORD ORIGIN Old French *turqueise* Turkish (stone)

turret *n* **1** a small tower that projects from the wall of a building, esp. a castle **2** (on a tank or warship) a rotating structure on which guns are mounted **3** (on a machine tool) a turret-like steel structure with tools projecting from it that can be rotated to bring each tool to bear on the work **turreted** *adj*
WORD ORIGIN Latin *turris* tower

turtle *n* **1** an aquatic reptile with a flattened shell enclosing the body and flipper-like limbs adapted for swimming **2 turn turtle** (of a boat) to capsize
WORD ORIGIN French *tortue* tortoise

turtledove *n* an Old World dove noted for its soft cooing and devotion to its mate
WORD ORIGIN Old English *turtla*

turtleneck *n* a round high close-fitting neck on a sweater or a sweater with such a neck

Tuscan *adj* of a style of classical architecture characterized by unfluted columns
WORD ORIGIN from *Tuscany*, a region in central Italy

tusk *n* a long pointed tooth in the elephant, walrus, and certain other mammals **tusked** *adj*
WORD ORIGIN Old English *tūsc*

tussle *n* **1** an energetic fight, struggle, or argument: *she resigned following a protracted boardroom tussle* ▷ *vb* **-sling, -sled 2** to fight or struggle energetically
WORD ORIGIN Middle English *tusen* to pull

tussock *n* a dense tuft of grass or other vegetation **tussocky** *adj*
WORD ORIGIN origin unknown

tut *interj, n, vb* **tutting, tutted** short for **tut-tut**

tutelage (tew-till-lij) *n formal* **1** instruction or guidance, esp. by a tutor **2** the state of being supervised by a guardian or tutor
WORD ORIGIN Latin *tueri* to watch over

tutelary (tew-till-lar-ee) *adj literary* **1** having the role of guardian or protector **2** of a guardian

tutor *n* **1** a teacher, usually one instructing individual pupils **2** (at a college or university) a member of staff responsible for the teaching and supervision of a certain number of students ▷ *vb* **3** to act as a tutor to (someone) **tutorship** *n*
WORD ORIGIN Latin: a watcher

tutorial *n* **1** a period of intensive tuition given by a tutor to an individual student or to a small group of students ▷ *adj* **2** of or relating to a tutor

tutti *adj, adv music* to be performed by the whole orchestra, choir, etc. **WORD ORIGIN** Italian

tutti-frutti *n, pl* **-fruttis** an ice cream or other sweet food containing small pieces of candied or fresh fruits **WORD ORIGIN** Italian, literally: all the fruits

tut-tut *interj* **1** an exclamation of mild reprimand, disapproval, or surprise ▷ *vb* **-tutting, -tutted 2** to express disapproval by the exclamation of 'tut-tut' ▷ *n* **3** the act of tut-tutting: *his bright red tennis shorts provoked a few tut-tuts from the traditionalists*

tutu *n* a very short skirt worn by ballerinas, made of projecting layers of stiffened material **WORD ORIGIN** French

tuxedo *n, pl* **-dos** a dinner jacket **WORD ORIGIN** after a country club in *Tuxedo Park*, New York

TV television

TVEI *Brit* technical and vocational educational initiative: a national educational scheme in which pupils gain practical experience in technology and industry, often through work placement

twaddle *n* **1** silly, trivial, or pretentious talk or writing ▷ *vb* **-dling, -dled 2** to talk or write in a silly or pretentious way **WORD ORIGIN** earlier *twattle*

twain *adj, n archaic* two **WORD ORIGIN** Old English *twēgen*

twang *n* **1** a sharp ringing sound produced by or as if by the plucking of a taut string **2** a strongly nasal quality in a person's speech: *a high-pitched Texas twang* ▷ *vb* **3** to make or cause to make a twang: *a bunch of angels twanging harps* **twangy** *adj* **WORD ORIGIN** imitative

twat *n Brit, Austral, & NZ taboo slang* **1** the female genitals **2** a foolish person **WORD ORIGIN** origin unknown

tweak *vb* **1** to twist or pinch with a sharp or sudden movement: *she tweaked his ear* **2** *informal* to make a minor alteration ▷ *n* **3** the act of tweaking **4** *informal* a minor alteration **WORD ORIGIN** Old English *twiccian*

twee *adj informal* excessively sentimental, sweet, or pretty **WORD ORIGIN** from *tweet*, affected pronunciation of *sweet*

tweed *n* **1** a thick woollen cloth produced originally in Scotland **2 tweeds** a suit made of tweed **WORD ORIGIN** probably from *tweel*, Scots variant of *twill*

tweedy *adj* **tweedier, tweediest 1** of, made of, or resembling tweed **2** showing a fondness for a hearty outdoor life, often associated with wearers of tweeds

tweet *interj* **1** an imitation of the thin chirping sound made by small birds ▷ *vb* **2** to make this sound **3** to write a short message on the Twitter website ▷ *n* **4** a thin chirping sound **5** a short message posted on the Twitter website **WORD ORIGIN** imitative

tweeter *n* a loudspeaker used in high-fidelity systems for the reproduction of high audio frequencies

tweezers *pl n* a small pincer-like tool used for tasks such as handling small objects or plucking out hairs **WORD ORIGIN** obsolete *tweeze* case of instruments

twelfth *adj* **1** of or being number twelve in a series ▷ *n* **2** number twelve in a series **3** one of twelve equal parts of something

Twelfth Day *n* January 6, the twelfth day after Christmas and the feast of the Epiphany

twelfth man *n* a reserve player in a cricket team

Twelfth Night *n* **a** the evening of January 5, the eve of Twelfth Day **b** the evening of Twelfth Day itself

twelve *n* **1** the cardinal number that is the sum of ten and two **2** a numeral, 12 or XII, representing this number **3** something representing or consisting of twelve units ▷ *adj* **4** amounting to twelve: *twelve months* **WORD ORIGIN** Old English *twelf*

twelvemonth *n archaic chiefly Brit* a year

twelve-tone *adj* of or denoting the type of serial music which uses as its musical material a sequence of notes containing all 12 semitones of the chromatic scale

twenty *n, pl* **-ties 1** the cardinal number that is the product of ten and two **2** a numeral, 20 or XX, representing this number **3** something representing or consisting of twenty units ▷ *adj* **4** amounting to twenty: *twenty minutes* **twentieth** *adj, n*

Twenty20 *n* form of one-day cricket in which each side bats for twenty overs

twenty-four-seven or **24/7** *adv informal* constantly or all the time: *consultants would no longer be available 24/7* **WORD ORIGIN** from twenty-four hours a day, seven days a week

twerp or **twirp** *n informal* a silly, stupid, or contemptible person **WORD ORIGIN** origin unknown

twice *adv* **1** two times; on two occasions or in two cases: *I've met her only twice* **2** double in degree or quantity: *twice as big* **WORD ORIGIN** Old English *twiwa*

twiddle *vb* **-dling, -dled 1** to twirl or fiddle, often in an idle way: *twiddling the knobs of a radio* **2 twiddle one's thumbs a** to rotate one's thumbs around one another, when bored or impatient **b** to be bored, with nothing to do ▷ *n* **3** an unnecessary decoration, esp. a curly one **WORD ORIGIN** probably *twirl* + *fiddle*

twig¹ *n* a small branch or shoot of a tree **twiggy** *adj* **WORD ORIGIN** Old English *twigge*

twig² *vb* **twigging, twigged** *informal* to realize or understand: *I should have twigged it earlier* **WORD ORIGIN** origin unknown

twilight *n* **1** the soft dim light that occurs when the sun is just below the horizon after sunset **2** the period in which this light occurs: *soon after twilight we started marching again* **3** a period in which strength, importance, etc. is gradually declining: *the twilight of his political career* ▷ *adj* **4** of or relating to the period towards the end of the day: *the twilight shift* **5** of or being a period of decline: *he spent most of his twilight years working on a history of France* **6** denoting irregularity and obscurity: *a twilight existence* **twilit** *adj* **WORD ORIGIN** Old English *twi-* half + LIGHT

twilight zone *n* any indefinite or intermediate condition or area: *the twilight zone between sleep and wakefulness*

twill *n* a fabric woven to produce an effect of parallel diagonal lines or ribs in the cloth **WORD ORIGIN** Old English *twilic* having a double thread

twin *n* **1** one of a pair of people or animals conceived at the same time **2** one of a pair of people or things that are identical or very similar ▷ *vb* **twinning, twinned 3** to pair or be paired together **WORD ORIGIN** Old English *twinn*

twin bed *n* one of a pair of matching single beds

twin-bedded *adj* (of a room in a hotel etc.) containing two single beds

twine *n* **1** string or cord made by twisting fibres together ▷ *vb* **twining, twined 2** to twist or wind together: *she twined the flowers into a garland* **3 twine round** or **around** to twist or wind around: *she twined her arms around her neck* **WORD ORIGIN** Old English *twīn*

twin-engined *adj* (of an aeroplane) having two engines

twinge *n* **1** a sudden brief darting or stabbing pain **2** a sharp emotional pang: *a twinge of conscience* **WORD ORIGIN** Old English *twengan* to pinch

twinkle *vb* **-kling, -kled 1** to shine brightly and intermittently; sparkle **2** (of the eyes) to sparkle, esp. with amusement or delight ▷ *n* **3** a flickering brightness; sparkle **WORD ORIGIN** Old English *twinclian*

twinkling *n* **in the twinkling of an eye** in a very short time

twinset *n* a matching jumper and cardigan

twin town *n* a town that has cultural and social links with a foreign town: *Nuremberg is one of Glasgow's twin towns*

twirl *vb* **1** to move around rapidly and repeatedly in a circle **2** to twist, wind, or twiddle, often idly: *twirling the glass in her hand* ▷ *n* **3** a whirl or twist **4** a written flourish **WORD ORIGIN** origin unknown

twist *vb* **1** to turn one end or part while the other end or parts remain still or turn in the opposite direction: *never twist or wring woollen garments* **2** to distort or be distorted **3** to wind or twine: *the wire had been twisted twice* **4** to force or be forced out of the natural form or position: *I twisted my knee* **5** to change the meaning of; distort: *he'd twisted the truth to make himself look good* **6** to revolve or

rotate: *he twisted the switch to turn the radio off* **7** to wrench with a turning action: *he twisted the wheel sharply* **8** to follow a winding course: *the road twisted as it climbed* **9** to dance the twist **10 twist someone's arm** to persuade or coerce someone ▷ *n* **11** the act of twisting: *she gave a dainty little twist to her parasol* **12** something formed by or as if by twisting: *there's a twist in the cable* **13** a decisive change of direction, aim, meaning, or character: *the latest revelations give a new twist to the company's boardroom wranglings* **14** an unexpected development in a story, play, or film **15** a bend: *a twist of the mountain road* **16** a distortion of the original shape or form **17** a jerky pull, wrench, or turn **18 the twist** a dance popular in the 1960s, in which dancers vigorously twist the hips **19 round the twist** *slang* mad or eccentric **twisty** *adj*
WORD ORIGIN Old English

twisted *adj* (of a person) cruel or perverted

twister *n Brit* a swindling or dishonest person

twit¹ *vb* **twitting, twitted** *Brit* to poke fun at (someone)
WORD ORIGIN Old English *ætwītan*

twit² *n informal* a foolish or stupid person
WORD ORIGIN from TWIT¹

twitch *vb* **1** (of a person or part of a person's body) to move in a jerky spasmodic way: *his left eyelid twitched involuntarily* **2** to pull (something) with a quick jerky movement: *she twitched the curtains shut* ▷ *n* **3** a sharp jerking movement, esp. one caused by a nervous condition
WORD ORIGIN Old English *twiccian* to pluck

twitcher *n Brit informal* a bird-watcher who tries to spot as many rare varieties as possible

twitchy *adj* **twitchier, twitchiest** nervous, worried, and ill-at-ease: *he was twitchy with anticipation*

twitter *vb* **1** (esp. of a bird) to utter a succession of chirping sounds **2** to talk rapidly and nervously in a high-pitched voice: *novelists who twittered about how much they admired him* **3** to write a short message on the Twitter website ▷ *n* **4** the act or sound of twittering **5 Twitter** *trademark* a website where people can post short messages about their current activities **6 in a twitter** in a state of nervous excitement **twitterer** *n* **twittering** *n* **twittery** *adj*
WORD ORIGIN imitative

two *n* **1** the cardinal number that is the sum of one and one **2** a numeral, 2 or II, representing this number **3** something representing or consisting of two units **4 in two** in or into two parts: *cut the cake in two and take a bit each* **5 put two and two together** to reach an obvious conclusion by considering the evidence available **6 that makes two of us** the same applies to me ▷ *adj* **7** amounting to two: *two years*
WORD ORIGIN Old English *twā*

twoccing or **twocking** *n Brit slang* the act of breaking into a motor vehicle and driving it away **twoccer** or **twocker** *n*

WORD ORIGIN from T(aking) W(ithout) O(wner's) C(onsent), the legal offence

two-dimensional *adj* **1** having two dimensions **2** somewhat lacking in depth or complexity: *a modern audience is unable to tolerate two-dimensional characters*

two-edged *adj* **1** (of a remark) having both a favourable and an unfavourable interpretation, such as *she looks nice when she smiles* **2** (of a knife, saw, etc.) having two cutting edges

two-faced *adj* deceitful or hypocritical: *he's a two-faced liar and opportunist*

twofold *adj* **1** having twice as many or as much **2** composed of two parts ▷ *adv* **3** by twice as many or as much

two-four *n Canad informal* a box containing 24 bottles of beer

two-handed *adj* **1** requiring the use of both hands **2** requiring the participation of two people: *a two-handed transatlantic yacht race*

twopence or **tuppence** (**tup**-pence) *n Brit* **1** the sum of two pennies **2** the slightest amount: *I don't care twopence who your father is*

twopenny or **tuppenny** (**tup**-pen-ee) *adj chiefly Brit* **1** cheap or tawdry **2** worth or costing two pence **3 not care a twopenny damn** to not care at all

two-piece *adj* **1** consisting of two separate parts, usually matching, such as a woman's suit or swimsuit ▷ *n* **2** such an outfit

two-ply *adj* made of two thicknesses, layers, or strands

two-sided *adj* **1** having two sides: *two-sided paper* **2** having two aspects or interpretations: *an ambivalent two-sided event*

twosome *n* a group of two people

two-step *n* **1** an old-time dance in duple time: *the next dance was the Military Two-Step* **2** music for this dance

two-stroke *adj* of an internal-combustion engine whose piston makes two strokes for every explosion

Two Thousand Guineas *n* **the Two Thousand Guineas** an annual horse race for three-year-olds, run at Newmarket

two-time *vb* **-timing, -timed** *informal* to deceive (a lover) by having an affair with someone else **two-timer** *n*

two-way *adj* **1** moving in, or allowing movement in, two opposite directions: *two-way traffic* **2** involving mutual involvement or cooperation: *two-way communication* **3** (of a radio or transmitter) capable of both transmission and reception of messages

TX Texas

tycoon *n* a businessman of great wealth and power
WORD ORIGIN Japanese *taikun* great ruler

tyke or **tike** *n* **1** *Brit, Austral, & NZ informal* a small or cheeky child **2** *Brit dialect* a rough ill-mannered person
WORD ORIGIN Old Norse *tík* bitch

tympani *pl n* same as **timpani**

tympanic membrane *n anat* the thin membrane separating the external ear from the middle ear; eardrum

tympanum *n, pl* **-nums** or **-na 1** *anat* **a** the cavity of the middle ear **b** same as **tympanic membrane 2** *archit* the recessed space between the arch and the lintel above a door **tympanic** *adj*
WORD ORIGIN Greek *tumpanon* drum

Tynwald (**tin**-wold) *n* the Parliament of the Isle of Man
WORD ORIGIN Old Norse *thing* assembly + *vollr* field

type *n* **1** a kind, class, or category of things, all of which have something in common **2** a subdivision of a particular class; sort: *it is more alcoholic than most wines of this type* **3** the general characteristics distinguishing a particular group: *the old-fashioned type of nanny* **4** *informal* a person, esp. of a specified kind: *a seagoing type* **5** a block with a raised character on it used for printing **6** text printed from type; print ▷ *vb* **typing, typed 7** to write using a typewriter or word processor **8** to be a symbol of or typify **9** to decide the type of; classify
WORD ORIGIN Greek *tupos* image

typecast *vb* **-casting, -cast** to cast (an actor or actress) in the same kind of role continually

typeface *n* the size and style of printing used in a book, magazine, etc.

typescript *n* any typewritten document

typeset *vb* **-setting, -set** *printing* to set (text for printing) in type

typesetter *n* a person who sets type; compositor

typewriter *n* a machine which prints a letter or other character when the appropriate key is pressed

typewritten *adj* typed on a typewriter or word processor

typhoid *pathol n* **1** short for **typhoid fever** ▷ *adj* **2** of or relating to typhoid fever: *typhoid vaccines*

typhoid fever *n* an acute infectious disease characterized by high fever, spots, abdominal pain, etc. It is spread by contaminated food or water

typhoon *n* a violent tropical storm, esp. one in the China Seas or W Pacific
WORD ORIGIN Chinese *tai fung* great wind

typhus *n* an acute infectious disease transmitted by lice or mites and characterized by high fever, skin rash, and severe headache
WORD ORIGIN Greek *tuphos* fever

typical *adj* **1** being or serving as a representative example of a particular type; characteristic: *a typical working day* **2** considered to be an example of some undesirable trait: *it was typical that he should start talking almost before he was inside the room* **typically** *adv*
WORD ORIGIN Greek *tupos* image

typify *vb* **-fies, -fying, -fied 1** to be typical of or characterize: *the beers made here typify all that is best about the independent brewing sector* **2** to symbolize or represent: *a number of dissident intellectuals, typified by Andrei Sakharov*

typing *n* **1** the work or activity of using a typewriter or word processor **2** the skill of using a typewriter quickly and accurately

Spoonerisms and Malapropisms

Ask the average person to give you an example of metathesis and you will probably be treated to a blank stare. However, if you narrow this down and specify that you require a spoonerism, which is a form of metathesis, then most people will happily trot out their favourite examples. The Rev WA Spooner (1844–1930), Warden of New College, Oxford, was prone to the verbal infelicity of accidentally transposing the initial consonants of a pair of words. Long after the quality of his lectures has been forgotten, fame of an unlooked-for sort will forever be his while people enjoy the comical effect of a spoonerism. Here are a few of the better-known examples that have been attributed to him (no doubt spuriously in some cases):

'The Kinquering Congs Their Titles Take'

'horny-handed tons of soil (for 'sons of toil')'

'Sir, you have tasted two whole worms; you have hissed all my mystery lectures and have been caught fighting a liar in the quad; you will leave Oxford by the town drain.'

'You will find as you grow older that the weight of rages will press harder and harder upon the employer.'

'We all know what it is to have a half-warmed fish within us.'

This kind of thing is obviously too good not to be taken advantage of, and over the generations many comedians, professional and otherwise, have dreamed up innumerable deliberate spoonerisms, often in the form of jokes beginning 'What's the difference between ...?', as in 'What's the difference between (the name of some famous woman one dislikes) and the Panama Canal? The Panama Canal is a busy ditch ...'. One of the most bandied-about, not to mention cleanest, is the witticism 'I'd rather have a bottle in front of me than a frontal lobotomy', which is as likely to appear on a T-shirt as in a list of quotations attributed to Dorothy Parker.

Like the spoonerism, another form of laughable word confusion known as the malapropism takes its title from the surname of its most famous proponent. In this case the person involved is fictional: Mrs Malaprop, a character in a play, *The Rivals*, by the Irish dramatist Richard Brinsley Sheridan, first performed in 1775. The lady in question (whose name derives from the French phrase *mal à propos*, meaning 'not to the purpose') was given to confusing the meanings of long and fancy-sounding words, substituting one word for another to nonsensical and ludicrous effect. Some examples from the play include:

'No caparisons (for 'comparisons'), miss, if you please.'

'As headstrong as an allegory (for 'alligator') on the banks of the Nile.'

'Sure, if I reprehend ('comprehend') any thing in this world it is the use of my oracular ('vernacular') tongue, and a nice derangement ('arrangement') of epitaphs ('epithets')!'

'Then, sir, she should have a supercilious ('superficial') knowledge in accounts; – and as she grew up, I would have her instructed in geometry ('geography'), that she might know something of the contagious ('contiguous') countries.'

Sheridan may have given the malapropism a name, but it would be wrong to assume that he invented it. Indeed, it had been a recognized method of raising a laugh in the theatre long before his day. Shakespeare often put malapropisms into the mouths of his comic characters such as Dogberry in *Much Ado About Nothing*, who declares, among other things, that 'Comparisons are odorous (ie 'odious').'

Comic writers and performers in subsequent centuries continued to use malapropisms liberally. This kind of humour has a double edge, in that not only is the character uttering such nonsense exposed as being ridiculously ignorant or pretentious, but the audience can also bask in the warm glow of feeling superior, confident that *they* would never commit such a verbal faux pas.

Some malapropisms have become so well known as to constitute catchphrases. For example, many people will deliberately say 'cast nasturtiums' instead of 'cast aspersions' but no-one knows for sure how this particular mix-up originated. Such immediately recognized usages are part of the shared everyday conversational humour that plays a vital part in enlivening banal conversation or, as signals of a move towards more informal communication, breaking the ice between strangers.

typist *n* a person who types letters, reports, etc., esp. for a living

typo *n, pl* **-pos** *informal* a typographical error

typography *n* **1** the art or craft of printing **2** the style or quality of printing and layout in a book, magazine, etc. **typographical** *adj* **typographically** *adv*

tyrannical *adj* of or like a tyrant; unjust and oppressive

tyrannize *or* **-ise** *vb* **-nizing, -nized** *or* **-nising, -nised** to rule or exercise power (over) in a cruel or oppressive manner: *he dominated and tyrannized his younger brother*

tyrannosaurus (tirr-ran-oh-**sore**-uss) *or* **tyrannosaur** *n* a large two-footed flesh-eating dinosaur common in North America in Cretaceous times **WORD ORIGIN** Greek *turannos* tyrant + *sauros* lizard

tyranny *n, pl* **-nies 1 a** government by a tyrant **b** oppressive and unjust government by more than one person **2** the condition or state of being dominated or controlled by something that makes unpleasant or harsh demands: *the tyranny of fashion drives many women to diet although they are not overweight* **tyrannous** *adj*

tyrant *n* **1** a person who governs oppressively, unjustly, and arbitrarily **2** any person who exercises authority in a tyrannical manner: *a domestic tyrant* **WORD ORIGIN** Greek *turannos*

tyre *or US* **tire** *n* a ring of rubber, usually filled with air but sometimes solid, fitted round the rim of a wheel of a road vehicle to grip the road **WORD ORIGIN** earlier *tire*, probably archaic variant of *attire*

tyro *n, pl* **-ros** a novice or beginner **WORD ORIGIN** Latin *tiro* recruit

tzar *n* same as **tsar**

tzatziki (tsat-**see**-kee) *n* a Greek dip made from yogurt, chopped cucumber, and mint **WORD ORIGIN** Modern Greek

tzetze fly *n* same as **tsetse fly**

Uu

The letter U is the twenty-first letter of the English alphabet. In the Roman alphabet U and V were different forms of the same letter, which was used as both a vowel and a consonant. The rounded form of the letter was used in more informal writing and in the middle of words. By the sixteenth century this form came to be used exclusively as a vowel, while the pointed form V was reserved for use as a consonant, so that the two were effectively different letters. Nevertheless, their common origin is reflected in the fact they sit side by side in the modern alphabet.

The Roman letter had originally developed from the Greek letter *upsilon* (Y, υ), which has the distinction of being the ancestor of no fewer than three of our letters: not only U and V were derived from it, but also Y.

In Burma or Myanmar, the single letter U is used in male names as a title of respect. Perhaps the best known bearer of this title was U Thant, the former Secretary-General of the United Nations.

The terms 'U' and 'non-U' were used in the 20th century as indicators of social rank. In this terminology the letter U stands for 'upper-class', and certain words whose use was indicative of the upper class (such as 'wireless' and 'cycle') were considered 'U', whereas their demotic counterparts ('radio' and 'bike') were 'non-U'. This distinction was first made by an academic called Alan Ross, but it was especially associated with the novelist Nancy Mitford, who made it the subject of a book called *Noblesse Oblige* in 1956.

The letter U is apt to be called on to describe anything that curves back on itself in the shape of a letter U. A U-turn is a manoeuvre that sends a person back in the direction from which they came, while a U-bend is a curved portion of pipe that stands beneath a sanitary fitting.

The German submarines of World War II were shaped nothing like a letter U, but were nevertheless known as U-boats. The name of these craft was simply a short form of the German name for a submarine: *Unterseeboot*.

U 1 (in Britain) universal (used to describe a film certified as suitable for viewing by anyone) **2** *chem* uranium ▷ *adj* **3** *Brit informal* (of language or behaviour) characteristic of the upper class

UB40 *n* **1** (in Britain) a registration card issued to an unemployed person **2** *informal* (in Britain) a person registered as unemployed

ubiquitous (yew-**bik**-wit-uss) *adj* being or seeming to be everywhere at once **ubiquity** *n*
WORD ORIGIN Latin *ubique* everywhere

U-boat *n* a German submarine
WORD ORIGIN German *Unterseeboot* undersea boat

Ubuntu *n* S African humanity or fellow feeling; kindness
WORD ORIGIN Nguni (language group of southern Africa)

uc *printing* upper case

UCAS (in Britain) Universities and Colleges Admissions Service

UCCA (formerly, in Britain) Universities Central Council on Admissions

UCW (in Britain) Union of Communications Workers

udder *n* the large baglike milk-producing gland of cows, sheep, or goats, with two or more teats
WORD ORIGIN Old English *ūder*

UDI Unilateral Declaration of Independence

UEFA Union of European Football Associations

UFO unidentified flying object

ugh (**uhh**) *interj* an exclamation of disgust, annoyance, or dislike

UGLI *n, pl* **-LIS** *or* **-LIES** *trademark* a yellow citrus fruit: a cross between a tangerine, grapefruit, and orange
WORD ORIGIN probably an alteration of *ugly*, from its wrinkled skin

ugly *adj* **uglier, ugliest 1** so unattractive as to be unpleasant to look at **2** very unpleasant and involving violence or aggression: *an ugly incident in which one man was stabbed* **3** repulsive or displeasing: *ugly rumours* **4** bad-tempered or sullen: *an ugly mood* **ugliness** *n*
WORD ORIGIN Old Norse *uggligr* dreadful

ugly duckling *n* a person or thing, initially ugly or unpromising, that becomes beautiful or admirable
WORD ORIGIN from *The Ugly Duckling* by Hans Christian Andersen

UHF *radio* ultrahigh frequency

UHT ultra-heat-treated (milk or cream)

UK United Kingdom

ukase (yew-**kaze**) *n* (in imperial Russia) a decree from the tsar
WORD ORIGIN Russian *ukaz*

Ukrainian *adj* **1** of Ukraine ▷ *n* **2** a person from Ukraine **3** the language of Ukraine

ukulele *or* **ukelele** (yew-kal-**lay**-lee) *n* a small four-stringed guitar
WORD ORIGIN Hawaiian, literally: jumping flea

ulcer *n* an open sore on the surface of the skin or a mucous membrane
WORD ORIGIN Latin *ulcus*

ulcerated *adj* made or becoming ulcerous **ulceration** *n*

ulcerous *adj* of, like, or characterized by ulcers

ulna *n, pl* **-nae** *or* **-nas** the inner and longer of the two bones of the human forearm or of the forelimb in other vertebrates **ulnar** *adj*
WORD ORIGIN Latin: elbow

ulster *n* a man's heavy double-breasted overcoat
WORD ORIGIN *Ulster*, the northernmost province of Ireland

Ulsterman *or fem* **Ulsterwoman** *n, pl* **-men** *or* **-women** a person from Ulster

ult. ultimo

ulterior (ult-**ear**-ee-or) *adj* (of an aim, reason, etc.) concealed or hidden: *an ulterior motive*
WORD ORIGIN Latin: further

ultimate *adj* **1** final in a series or process: *predictions about the ultimate*

u

destination of modern art **2** highest, supreme, or unchallengeable: *he has the ultimate power to dismiss the Prime Minister* **3** fundamental or essential: *a believer in the ultimate goodness of man* **4** most extreme: *genocide is the ultimate abuse of human rights* **5** final or total: *she should be able to estimate the ultimate cost* ▷ *n* **6** **the ultimate** in the best example of: *the ultimate in luxury holidays* **ultimately** *adv*
WORD ORIGIN Latin *ultimus* last, distant

ultimatum (ult-im-**may**-tum) *n* a final warning to someone that they must agree to certain conditions or requirements, or else action will be taken against them: *Britain declared war after the Nazis rejected the ultimatum to withdraw from Poland*

ultimo *adv* in or during the previous month. It is rare except when abbreviated to ult. in formal correspondence: *your communication of the 1st ultimo*
WORD ORIGIN Latin: on the last

ultra *n* a person who has extreme or immoderate beliefs or opinions
WORD ORIGIN Latin: beyond

ultra- *prefix* **1** beyond a specified extent, range, or limit: *ultrasonic* **2** extremely: *ultraleftist*
WORD ORIGIN Latin

ultraconservative *adj* **1** highly reactionary ▷ *n* **2** a reactionary person

ultrahigh frequency *n* a radio frequency between 3000 and 300 megahertz

ultramarine *n* **1** a blue pigment originally made from lapis lazuli ▷ *adj* **2** vivid blue
WORD ORIGIN Latin *ultra* beyond + *mare* sea; because the lapis lazuli from which the pigment was made was imported from Asia

ultramodern *adj* extremely modern

ultramontane *adj* **1** on the other side of the mountains, usually the Alps, from the speaker or writer **2** of a movement in the Roman Catholic Church which favours supreme papal authority ▷ *n* **3** a person from beyond the Alps **4** a member of the ultramontane party of the Roman Catholic Church

ultrasonic *adj* of or producing sound waves with higher frequencies than humans can hear **ultrasonically** *adv*

ultrasonics *n* the branch of physics concerned with ultrasonic waves

ultrasound *n* ultrasonic waves, used in echo sounding, medical diagnosis, and therapy

ultrasound scan *n* an examination of an internal bodily structure by the use of ultrasonic waves, esp. for diagnosing abnormality in a fetus

ultraviolet *n* **1** the part of the electromagnetic spectrum with wavelengths shorter than light but longer than X-rays ▷ *adj* **2** of or consisting of radiation lying in the ultraviolet: *ultraviolet light*

ultra vires (ult-ra **vire**-eez) *adv, adj* beyond the legal power of a person or organization
WORD ORIGIN Latin, literally: beyond strength

ululate (**yewl**-yew-late) *vb literary* **-lating, -lated** to howl or wail **ululation** *n*
WORD ORIGIN Latin *ululare*

umbel *n* a type of compound flower in which the flowers arise from the same point in the main stem and have stalks of the same length, to give a cluster with the youngest flowers at the centre **umbellate** *adj*
WORD ORIGIN Latin *umbella* a sunshade

umbelliferous *adj* of or denoting a plant with flowers in umbels, such as fennel, parsley, carrot, or parsnip
WORD ORIGIN Latin *umbella* a sunshade + *ferre* to bear

umber *n* **1** a type of dark brown earth containing ferric oxide (rust) ▷ *adj* **2** dark brown to reddish-brown
WORD ORIGIN French (*terre d'*)*ombre* or Italian (*terra di*) *ombra* shadow (earth)

umbilical (um-**bill**-ik-kl) *adj* of or like the navel or the umbilical cord

umbilical cord *n* the long flexible cordlike structure that connects a fetus to the placenta

umbilicus (um-**bill**-ik-kuss) *n anat* the navel
WORD ORIGIN Latin: navel, centre

umbra *n, pl* **-brae** *or* **-bras** a shadow, usually the shadow cast by the moon onto the earth during a solar eclipse
WORD ORIGIN Latin: shade

umbrage *n* **take umbrage** to take offence
WORD ORIGIN Latin *umbra* shade

umbrella *n* **1** a portable device used for protection against rain, consisting of a light canopy supported on a collapsible metal frame mounted on a central rod **2** a single organization, idea, etc. that contains or covers many different organizations or ideas **3** anything that has the effect of a protective screen or general cover: *under the umbrella of the Helsinki security conference* ▷ *adj* **4** containing or covering many different organizations, ideas, etc.: *an umbrella group of nationalists and anti-communists* **umbrella-like** *adj*
WORD ORIGIN Italian *ombrella*, from *ombra* shade

UMF *n trademark* a standard for the level of antibacterial agent possessed by manuka honey

umiak, oomiak *or* **oomiac** (**oo**-mee-ak) *n* a large open boat made of stretched skins, used by Inuit
WORD ORIGIN Inuktitut

umlaut (**oom**-lout) *n* **1** the mark (¨) placed over a vowel, esp. in German, indicating change in its sound **2** (esp. in Germanic languages) the change of a vowel brought about by the influence of a vowel in the next syllable
WORD ORIGIN German, from *um* around + *Laut* sound

umlungu (oom-**loong**-goo) *n S African* a White man: used esp. as a term of address
WORD ORIGIN Nguni (language group of southern Africa)

umpire *n* **1** an official who ensures that the people taking part in a game follow the rules; referee ▷ *vb* **-piring, -pired** **2** to act as umpire in a game

WORD ORIGIN Old French *nomper* not one of a pair

umpteen *adj informal* very many: *the centre of umpteen scandals* **umpteenth** *n, adj*
WORD ORIGIN *umpty* a great deal + *-teen* ten

UN United Nations

un-¹ *prefix (freely used with adjectives, participles, and their derivative adverbs and nouns: less frequently used with certain other nouns)* not; contrary to; opposite of: *uncertain; untidiness; unbelief; untruth*
WORD ORIGIN Old English *on-, un-*

un-² *prefix forming verbs* **1** denoting reversal of an action or state: *uncover; untie* **2** denoting removal from, release, or deprivation: *unharness*
WORD ORIGIN Old English *un-, on-*

unabashed *adj* not ashamed or embarrassed

unabated *adv* without any reduction in force: *the storm continued unabated*

unable *adj* **unable to** not having the power, ability, or authority to; not able to

unabridged *adj* (of a book or text) complete and not shortened or condensed

unacceptable *adj* too bad to be accepted; intolerable

unaccompanied *adj* **1** not having anyone with one: *unaccompanied female travellers should take care* **2** (of singing or a musical instrument) not being accompanied by musical instruments

unaccountable *adj* **1** without any sensible explanation: *for some unaccountable reason I got on the wrong bus* **2** not having to justify or answer for one's actions to other people: *the secret service remains unaccountable to the public* **unaccountably** *adv*

unaccounted *adj* **unaccounted for** unable to be found or traced: *four people were killed in the floods, and eleven remain unaccounted for*

unaccustomed *adj* **1** **unaccustomed to** not used to: *unaccustomed to such behaviour* **2** not familiar: *moments of unaccustomed freedom*

unacknowledged *adj* **1** ignored or not accepted as true or existing **2** not officially recognized as being important

unacquainted *adj* **unacquainted with** not knowing about; unfamiliar with

unadopted *adj Brit* (of a road) not maintained by a local authority

unadorned *adj* not decorated; plain

unadulterated *adj* **1** completely pure, with nothing added: *fresh unadulterated spring water* **2** (of an emotion) not mixed with anything else: *a look of unadulterated terror*

unadventurous *adj* not taking chances or trying anything new

unaffected¹ *adj* unpretentious, natural, or sincere

unaffected² *adj* not influenced or changed

unafraid *adj* not frightened or nervous

unaided *adv* without any help or assistance; independently: *he could not walk unaided for months after the accident*

unalienable *adj law* same as **inalienable**

English in New England

A popular anecdote about the word *Yankee* tells us that its meaning depends entirely on whom you ask. *Yankee* is synonymous with *American* for many people outside the United States. Within the United States, a *Yankee* is a native of New England, the north-easternmost region of the United States. If you're a Southerner, however, and hail from one of the states that seceded in the 19th-century Civil War, a *Yankee* is anyone from one of the Northern states that remained in the Union. And if you're a resident of New England, you either own the title *Yankee* or you attribute it to someone who lives further north or east than you do.

Nearly everything that can be said about *Yankee* can be said about the English spoken in New England: what it is depends entirely on whom you ask. As its name attests, New England was and in some ways still is the most accurate mirror of England in all the United States. It was settled almost entirely by English speakers (English Protestants seeking religious freedom in various movements, starting in the early 17th century). But New England – and its brand of English – have now had 400 years to develop apart from the mother country. The English spoken there today is not a unified dialect, any more than the mother tongue is on its own soil. Nevertheless, there are some similarities that set apart the dialects of New England from those spoken in the rest of the United States.

Perhaps because of its strong association with England and the prestige that attaches to its early settlers, the speech of New England alone among American dialects still has a slightly patrician ring to many American ears. Another contributing factor to this phenomenon is the fact that New England quickly became the intellectual centre of the fledgling United States – a distinction that it maintains today, with the presence of its most respected private schools, and two of its oldest and most prestigious universities: Harvard and Yale. Finally, it certainly did not detract from the lofty status of New England that America's first two great lexicographers – Joseph Worcester and Noah Webster – were born, lived most of their lives, and died in New England.

A standout feature of many New England dialects today – and one that may give it a familiar ring to speakers of British English - is that it is non-rhotic. In less technical talk, that means that the consonant 'r' is not pronounced when it follows a vowel at the end of a word or syllable, just as is the case in RP and in many other British dialects: thus *caw* for *car*, *hawraw* for *horror*. This aspect of New England speech, however, exists today mainly in coastal communities, and much more prominently among working-class speakers.

Another prominent feature of New England dialects is the persistence of 'broad a' in some words whose pronunciation has gone to 'short a' or a 'long a' in many other American dialects – again, just as you will find in some British dialects today. In New England, you rhyme *tomato* with *gelato*, not with *potato*, and you rhyme *aunt* with *flaunt*, not with *ant*. Anyone in the United States who wishes to send up a high-flown New England accent has only to drop their r's and broaden their a's to achieve the intended effect.

An anecdote from the diary of Thomas Hutchinson, the British royal governor of colonial Massachusetts from 1771 to 1774, illustrates how some words changed their meanings after arrival on New World shores. Speaking with King George III, Hutchinson used *corn* in its New World sense, meaning *maize*. 'What corn?' asked the King. 'Indian corn,' explained Hutchinson. For Americans of the time, the modifying *Indian* was gone, and *maize* had become *corn*. Though not as precisely documented, several other high-frequency words fared similarly in the New World: *store* (replacing *shop*), *lumber* (for cut timber), *dry goods* (denoting textiles, not edible commodities), and *rock* (retaining its British meaning but also synonymous with *stone* for most speakers).

As the earliest centre for commerce in the United States, New England provided the backdrop for all of these words to develop their New World meanings, which spread to all other American dialects as settlement moved west. Americans now use these words without awareness of their New England roots, but a few words still distinguish New England varieties of English today: *tonic* for fizzy drink (whereas most Americans call it *pop* or *soda pop*); *hero sandwich* for *submarine sandwich*; and *frappe* for *milk shake*.

unalike *adj* not similar; different

unalloyed *adj literary* not spoiled by being mixed with anything else

unalterable *adj* not able to be changed

unambiguous *adj* having a clear meaning which can only be interpreted in one way

un-American *adj* **1** not in accordance with the aims, ideals, or customs of the US **2** against the interests of the US **un-Americanism** *n*

unanimous (yew-**nan**-im-uss) *adj* **1** in complete agreement **2** characterized by complete agreement: *unanimous approval* **unanimity** *n* **unanimously** *adv*
WORD ORIGIN Latin *unus* one + *animus* mind

unannounced *adv* without warning: *she turned up unannounced*

unanswerable *adj* **1** having no possible answer **2** so obviously correct that disagreement is impossible

unappealing *adj* unpleasant or off-putting

unappetizing *adj* tasting, looking, or smelling unpleasant to eat

unappreciated *adj* not given the respect or recognition that is deserved

unapproachable *adj* discouraging friendliness; aloof

unarguable *adj* so obviously correct that disagreement is impossible

unarmed *adj* **1** not carrying any weapons: *they were shooting unarmed peasants* **2** not using any weapons: *unarmed combat*

unashamed *adj* not embarrassed, esp. when doing something some people might find offensive: *unashamed greed* **unashamedly** *adv*

unasked *adv* **1** without being asked to do something: *he opened the door unasked* ▷ *adj* **2** (of a question) not asked, although sometimes implied

unassailable *adj* not able to be destroyed or overcome: *an unassailable lead*

unassisted *adj* without help from anyone else

unassuming *adj* modest or unpretentious

unattached *adj* **1** not connected with any specific body or group **2** not engaged or married

unattainable *adj* not able to be achieved; impossible

unattended *adj* not being watched or looked after: *unattended baggage*

unattractive *adj* not attractive or appealing

unauthorized *or* **-ised** *adj* done or made without official permission

unavailable *adj* not able to be met, obtained, or contacted

unavailing *adj* useless or futile

unavoidable *adj* unable to be avoided or prevented **unavoidably** *adv*

unaware *adj* **1** not aware or conscious: *unaware of my surroundings* ▷ *adv* **2** not standard same as **unawares**

unawares *adv* **1** by surprise: *death had taken him unawares* **2** without knowing: *had he passed her, all unawares?*

unbalanced *adj* **1** lacking balance **2** mentally deranged **3** biased; one-sided: *his unbalanced summing-up*

unbearable *adj* not able to be endured **unbearably** *adv*

unbeatable *adj* not able to be bettered

unbecoming *adj* **1** unattractive or unsuitable: *unbecoming garments* **2** not proper or appropriate to a person or position: *acts unbecoming of university students*

unbeknown *adv* (foll. by *to*) without the knowledge of (a person): *unbeknown to her family she had acquired modern ways.* Also (esp. Brit): **unbeknownst**
WORD ORIGIN UN-² + *beknown* known

unbelievable *adj* **1** too unlikely to be believed **2** extremely impressive; marvellous **3** *informal* terrible or shocking **unbelievably** *adv*

unbeliever *n* a person who does not believe in a religion

unbend *vb* **-bending, -bent** to become less strict or more informal in one's attitudes or behaviour

unbending *adj* rigid or inflexible: *an unbending routine*

unbiased *adj* not having or showing prejudice or favouritism; impartial

unbidden *adj literary* not ordered or asked; voluntary or spontaneous: *unbidden thoughts came into Catherine's mind*

unbind *vb* **-binding, -bound** **1** to set free from bonds or chains **2** to unfasten or untie

unblemished *adj* not spoiled or tarnished: *smooth unblemished skins*

unblinking *adj* looking at something without blinking

unblock *vb* to remove a blockage from; clear or free

unblushing *adj* immodest or shameless

unbolt *vb* to unfasten a bolt of a door

unborn *adj* not yet born

unbosom *vb* to relieve oneself of secrets or feelings by telling someone
WORD ORIGIN UN-² + *bosom* (in the sense: centre of the emotions)

unbounded *adj* having no boundaries or limits

unbowed *adj* not giving in or submitting: *the battered but as yet unbowed general secretary*

unbreakable *adj* not able to be broken; indestructible

unbridled *adj* (of feelings or behaviour) not restrained or controlled in any way: *unbridled passion*

unbroken *adj* **1** complete or whole **2** continuous: *I slept for eight unbroken hours* **3** not disturbed or upset: *an unbroken night* **4** (of a record) not improved upon **5** (of animals, esp. horses) not tamed

unburden *vb* to relieve one's mind or oneself of a worry or trouble by telling someone about it

uncalled-for *adj* unnecessary or unwarranted: *uncalled-for comments*

uncanny *adj* **1** weird or mysterious: *an uncanny silence* **2** beyond what is normal: *an uncanny eye for detail* **uncannily** *adv* **uncanniness** *n*

uncared-for *adj* not cared for; neglected

uncaring *adj* showing no concern for other people's suffering and hardship

unceasing *adj* continuing without a break; never stopping

unceremonious *adj* **1** relaxed and informal: *she greeted him with unceremonious friendliness* **2** abrupt or rude: *the answer was an unceremonious 'no'* **unceremoniously** *adv*

uncertain *adj* **1** not able to be accurately known or predicted: *an uncertain future* **2** not definitely decided: *they are uncertain about the date* **3** not to be depended upon: *an uncertain career* **4** changeable: *an uncertain sky* **uncertainty** *n*

unchallenged *adj, adv* done or accepted without being challenged: *seventy years of unchallenged rule; her decisions went unchallenged*

unchangeable *adj* not able to be altered

unchanged *adj* remaining the same

uncharacteristic *adj* not typical **uncharacteristically** *adv*

uncharitable *adj* unkind or harsh **uncharitably** *adv*

uncharted *adj* **1** (of an area of sea or land) not having had a map made of it, esp. because it is unexplored **2** unknown or unfamiliar: *a whole uncharted universe of emotions*

unchecked *adj* **1** not prevented from continuing or growing: *unchecked population growth* **2** not examined or inspected ▷ *adv* **3** without being stopped or hindered: *the virus could spread unchecked* **4** without being examined or inspected: *the drugs passed unchecked through airport security*

unchristian *or* **un-Christian** *adj* not in accordance with Christian principles

uncial (**un**-see-al) *adj* **1** of or written in letters that resemble modern capitals, as used in Greek and Latin manuscripts of the third to ninth centuries ▷ *n* **2** an uncial letter or manuscript
WORD ORIGIN Late Latin *unciales litterae* letters an inch long

uncivil *adj* impolite, rude or bad-mannered **uncivilly** *adv*

uncivilized *or* **-lised** *adj* **1** (of a tribe or people) not yet civilized **2** lacking culture or sophistication

unclassified *adj* **1** not arranged in any specific order or grouping **2** (of official information) not secret

uncle *n* **1** a brother of one's father or mother **2** the husband of one's aunt **3** a child's term of address for a male friend of its parents **4** *slang* a pawnbroker
WORD ORIGIN Latin *avunculus*

unclean *adj* lacking moral, spiritual, or physical cleanliness

unclear *adj* confusing or hard to understand

Uncle Sam *n* a personification of the government of the United States
WORD ORIGIN apparently a humorous interpretation of the letters stamped on army supply boxes during the War of 1812: *US*

Uncle Tom *n informal, offensive* a Black person whose behaviour towards White people is regarded as servile
WORD ORIGIN from *Uncle Tom's Cabin* by H. B. Stowe

unclothed *adj* not wearing any clothes; naked

uncluttered *adj* not containing anything unnecessary; austere and simple

uncoil *vb* to unwind or untwist

uncomfortable *adj* **1** not physically relaxed: *he was forced to sit in an uncomfortable cross-legged position* **2** not comfortable to be in or use: *an uncomfortable chair* **3** causing discomfort or unease: *the uncomfortable truth* **uncomfortably** *adv*

uncommitted *adj* not bound to a specific opinion, course of action, or cause

uncommon *adj* **1** not happening or encountered often **2** in excess of what is normal: *an uncommon amount of powder*

uncommonly *adv* **1** in an unusual manner or degree **2** extremely: *an uncommonly good humour*

uncommunicative *adj* disinclined to talk or give information

uncomplaining *adj* doing or tolerating something unpleasant or difficult without complaint: *uncomplaining devotion*

uncomplicated *adj* simple and straightforward

uncomplimentary *adj* not expressing respect or praise; insulting

uncomprehending *adj* not understanding what is happening or what has been said

uncompromising *adj* not prepared to compromise; inflexible **uncompromisingly** *adv*

unconcealed *adj* not hidden or disguised: *a look of unconcealed hatred*

unconcern *n* apathy or indifference

unconcerned *adj* **1** not interested in something and not wanting to become involved **2** not worried or troubled **unconcernedly** (un-kon-**sern**-id-lee) *adv*

unconditional *adj* without conditions or limitations: *an unconditional ceasefire* **unconditionally** *adv*

unconfirmed *adj* not yet proved to be true: *unconfirmed reports of a major accident*

uncongenial *adj* (of a place or condition) unpleasant and unfriendly

unconnected *adj* not linked to each other: *a series of unconnected incidents*

unconscionable *adj* **1** unscrupulous or unprincipled: *an unconscionable charmer* **2** excessive in amount or degree: *unconscionable number of social obligations*

unconscious *adj* **1** unable to notice or respond to things which one would normally be aware of through the senses; insensible or comatose **2** not aware of one's actions or behaviour: *unconscious of his failure* **3** not realized or intended: *unconscious duplicity* **4** coming from or produced by the unconscious: *unconscious mental processes* ▷ *n* **5** *psychoanal* the part of the mind containing instincts, impulses, and ideas that are not available for direct examination **unconsciously** *adv* **unconsciousness** *n*

unconstitutional *adj* forbidden by the rules or laws which state how an organization or country must function

uncontrollable *adj* **1** unable to be restrained or prevented: *a fit of uncontrollable giggles* **2** (of a person) wild and unmanageable in behaviour: *he became violent and uncontrollable* **uncontrollably** *adv*

unconventional *adj* not conforming to accepted rules or standards

unconvinced *adj* not certain that something is true or right: *I remained unconvinced by his arguments*

unconvincing *adj* (of a reason, argument, etc.) not good enough to convince people that something is true or right

uncooked *adj* raw

uncooperative *adj* not willing to help other people with what they are trying to do

uncoordinated *adj* **1** not joining or functioning together properly to form a whole **2** (of a person) not able to control his or her movements properly; clumsy

uncork *vb* to remove the cork from a bottle

uncorroborated *adj* not supported by other evidence or proof

uncountable *adj* existing in such large numbers that it is impossible to say how many there are: *uncountable millions*

uncouple *vb* **-pling, -pled** to disconnect or become disconnected

uncouth *adj* lacking in good manners, refinement, or grace **WORD ORIGIN** Old English *un-* not + *cūth* familiar

uncover *vb* **1** to remove the cover or top from **2** to reveal or disclose: *they have uncovered a plot to overthrow the government* **uncovered** *adj*

uncritical *adj* not making a judgment about the merits or morality of something

uncrowned *adj* **1** having the powers, but not the title, of royalty **2** (of a king or queen) not yet crowned

unction *n* **1** *chiefly RC & Eastern Churches* the act of anointing with oil in sacramental ceremonies **2** oily charm **3** an ointment **4** anything soothing **WORD ORIGIN** Latin *unguere* to anoint

unctuous *adj* pretending to be kind and concerned but obviously not sincere **WORD ORIGIN** Latin *unctum* ointment

uncultured *adj* not knowing much about art, literature, etc.

uncut *adj* **1** not shortened or censored **2** not cut **3** (of precious stones) not having shaped and polished surfaces

undamaged *adj* not spoilt or damaged; intact

undaunted *adj* not put off, discouraged, or beaten

undeceive *vb* **-ceiving, -ceived** to reveal the truth to someone previously misled or deceived

undecided *adj* **1** not having made up one's mind **2** (of an issue or problem) not agreed or decided upon

undeclared *adj* not acknowledged for tax purposes

undemanding *adj* not difficult to do or deal with: *an undemanding task*

undemonstrative *adj* not showing emotions openly or easily

undeniable *adj* **1** unquestionably true **2** of unquestionable excellence: *of undeniable character* **undeniably** *adv*

under *prep* **1** directly below; on, to, or beneath the underside or base of: *under the bed* **2** less than: *in just under an hour* **3** lower in rank than: *under a general* **4** subject to the supervision, control, or influence of: *under communism for 45 years* **5** in or subject to certain circumstances or conditions: *the bridge is still under construction; under battle conditions* **6** in (a specified category): *he had filed Kafka's 'The Trial' under crime stories* **7** known by: *under their own names* **8** planted with: *a field under corn* **9** powered by: *under sail* ▷ *adv* **10** below; to a position underneath **WORD ORIGIN** Old English

under- *prefix* **1** below or beneath: *underarm; underground* **2** insufficient or insufficiently: *underemployed* **3** of lesser importance or lower rank: *undersecretary* **4** indicating secrecy or deception: *underhand*

underachieve *vb* **-achieving, -achieved** to fail to achieve a performance appropriate to one's age or talents **underachiever** *n*

underactive *adj* less active than is normal or desirable: *an underactive thyroid gland*

underage *adj* below the required or standard age, usually below the legal age for voting or drinking: *underage sex*

underarm *adj* **1** *sport* denoting a style of throwing, bowling, or serving in which the hand is swung below shoulder level **2** below the arm ▷ *adv* **3** in an underarm style

underbelly *n, pl* **-lies 1** the part of an animal's belly nearest the ground **2** a vulnerable or unprotected part, aspect, or region

underbrush *n Austral, US, & Canad* same as **undergrowth**

undercarriage *n* **1** the wheels, shock absorbers, and struts that support an aircraft on the ground and enable it to take off and land **2** the framework supporting the body of a vehicle

undercharge *vb* **-charging, -charged** to charge too little for something

underclass *n* a class beneath the usual social scale consisting of the most disadvantaged people, such as the long-term unemployed

underclothes *pl n* same as **underwear**. Also called: **underclothing**

undercoat *n* **1** a coat of paint applied before the top coat **2** *zool* a layer of soft fur beneath the outer fur of animals such as the otter ▷ *vb* **3** to apply an undercoat to a surface

undercook *vb* to cook for too short a time or at too low a temperature

undercover *adj* done or acting in secret: *an undercover investigation*

undercurrent *n* **1** a current that is not apparent at the surface **2** an underlying opinion or emotion

undercut *vb* **-cutting, -cut 1** to charge less than a competitor in order to

u

obtain trade **2** to undermine or render less effective: *the latest fighting undercuts diplomatic attempts to find a peaceful solution* **3** to cut away the under part of something

underdeveloped *adj* **1** immature or undersized **2** (of a country or its economy) lacking the finance, industries, and organization necessary to advance

underdog *n* a person or team in a weak or underprivileged position

underdone *adj* insufficiently or lightly cooked

underemployed *adj* not fully or adequately employed

underestimate *vb* **-mating, -mated** **1** to make too low an estimate of: *the trust had underestimated the cost of work* **2** to not be aware or take account of the full abilities or potential of: *the police had underestimated him* ▷ *n* **3** too low an estimate **underestimation** *n*

≡ **USAGE**
≡ *Underestimate* is sometimes wrongly
≡ used where *overestimate* is meant: *the*
≡ *importance of his work cannot be*
≡ *overestimated* (not *cannot be*
≡ *underestimated*).

underexpose *vb* **-posing, -posed** *photog* to expose (a film, plate, or paper) for too short a time or with insufficient light **underexposure** *n*

underfed *adj* not getting enough food to be healthy

underfelt *n* thick felt laid under a carpet to increase insulation

underfoot *adv* **1** underneath the feet; on the ground **2** *trample or crush* **underfoot a** to damage or destroy by stepping on **b** to treat with contempt

undergarment *n* a garment worn under clothes

undergo *vb* **-going, -went, -gone** to experience, endure, or sustain: *he underwent a three-hour operation*
WORD ORIGIN Old English *undergān*

undergraduate *n* a person studying in a university for a first degree

underground *adv* **1** below ground level: *moles digging underground* **2** secretly: *several political parties had to operate underground for many years* ▷ *adj* **3** beneath the ground: *an underground bunker* **4** secret; clandestine: *an underground organization* **5** (of art, film, music, etc.) avant-garde, experimental, or subversive ▷ *n* **6** a movement dedicated to overthrowing a government or occupation forces **7** (often preceded by *the*) an electric passenger railway operated in underground tunnels

undergrowth *n* small trees and bushes growing beneath taller trees in a wood or forest

underhand *adj also* **underhanded 1** sly, deceitful, and secretive **2** *sport* same as **underarm** ▷ *adv* **3** in an underhand manner or style

underinsured *adj* not insured for enough money to cover the replacement value of the goods covered

underlay *n* felt or rubber laid under a carpet to increase insulation and resilience

underlie *vb* **-lying, -lay, -lain 1** to lie or be placed under **2** to be the foundation, cause, or basis of: *the basic unity which underlies all religion*

underline *vb* **-lining, -lined 1** to put a line under **2** to emphasize

underling *n derogatory* a subordinate

underlying *adj* **1** not obvious but detectable: *the deeper and underlying aim of her travels* **2** fundamental; basic: *an underlying belief* **3** lying under: *the underlying layers of the skin*

undermanned *adj* not having enough staff to function properly

undermentioned *adj* mentioned below or later

undermine *vb* **-mining, -mined 1** to weaken gradually or insidiously: *morphia had undermined his grasp of reality* **2** (of the sea or wind) to wear away the base of cliffs

underneath *prep* **1** under or beneath: *a table underneath an olive tree* ▷ *adv* **2** under or beneath: *the chest of drawers was scratched underneath* ▷ *adj* **3** lower ▷ *n* **4** a lower part or surface
WORD ORIGIN Old English *underneothan*

undernourished *adj* lacking the food needed for health and growth **undernourishment** *n*

underpaid *adj* not paid as much as the job deserves

underpants *pl n* a man's undergarment covering the body from the waist or hips to the thighs

underpass *n* **1** a section of a road that passes under another road or a railway line **2** a subway for pedestrians

underpay *vb* **-paying, -paid** to pay someone insufficiently **underpayment** *n*

underpin *vb* **-pinning, -pinned 1** to give strength or support to: *the principles that underpin his political convictions* **2** to support from beneath with a prop: *to underpin a wall* **underpinning** *n*

underplay *vb* to achieve (an effect) by deliberate lack of emphasis

underprivileged *adj* **1** lacking the rights and advantages of other members of society; deprived ▷ *n* **2** **the underprivileged** underprivileged people regarded as a group

underrate *vb* **-rating, -rated** to not be aware or take account of the full abilities or potential of **underrated** *adj*

underscore *vb* **-scoring, -scored** same as **underline**

undersea *adj, adv* below the surface of the sea

underseal *n* **1** a special coating applied to the underside of a motor vehicle to prevent corrosion ▷ *vb* **2** to apply such a coating to a motor vehicle

undersecretary *n, pl* **-taries** a senior civil servant or junior minister in a government department

undersell *vb* **-selling, -sold** to sell at a price lower than that of another seller

undersexed *adj* having weaker sexual urges than is considered normal

undershirt *n US & Canad* an undergarment covering the body from the shoulders to the hips

undershoot *vb* **-shooting, -shot** *aviation* to land an aircraft short of a runway

underside *n* the bottom or lower surface

undersigned *n* **the undersigned** the person or people who have signed at the foot of a document, statement, or letter

undersized *adj* smaller than normal

underskirt *n* a skirtlike garment worn under a skirt or dress; petticoat

understaffed *adj* not having enough staff to function properly

understand *vb* **-standing, -stood 1** to know and comprehend the nature or meaning of: *I understand what you are saying* **2** to know what is happening or why it is happening: *in order to understand the problems that can occur* **3** to assume, infer, or believe: *I understand he is based in this town* **4** to know how to translate or read: *don't you understand Russian?* **5** to be sympathetic to or compatible with: *she needed him to understand her completely* **understandable** *adj* **understandably** *adv*
WORD ORIGIN Old English *understandan*

understanding *n* **1** the ability to learn, judge, or make decisions **2** personal opinion or interpretation of a subject: *my understanding of what he said* **3** a mutual agreement, usually an informal or private one ▷ *adj* **4** kind, sympathetic, or tolerant towards people

understate *vb* **-stating, -stated 1** to describe or portray something in restrained terms, often to obtain an ironic effect **2** to state that something, such as a number, is less than it is **understatement** *n*

understood *vb* **1** the past of **understand** ▷ *adj* **2** implied or inferred **3** taken for granted

understudy *n, pl* **-studies 1** an actor who studies a part so as to be able to replace the usual actor if necessary **2** anyone who is trained to take the place of another if necessary ▷ *vb* **-studies, -studying, -studied 3** to act as an understudy to

undertake *vb* **-taking, -took, -taken 1** to agree to or commit oneself to something or to do something: *I undertook the worst job in gardening* **2** to promise to do something

undertaker *n* a person whose job is to look after the bodies of people who have died and to organize funerals

undertaking *n* **1** a task or enterprise **2** an agreement to do something **3** *informal* the practice of overtaking on an inner lane a vehicle which is travelling in an outer lane

undertone *n* **1** a quiet tone of voice **2** something which suggests an underlying quality or feeling: *an undertone of anger*

undertow *n* a strong undercurrent flowing in a different direction from the surface current, such as in the sea

undervalue *vb* **-valuing, -valued** to value a person or thing at less than the true worth or importance

underwater *adj* **1** situated, occurring, or for use under the surface of the sea, a lake, or a river ▷ *adv* **2** beneath the surface of the sea, a lake, or a river

Words from Literature
part 28

undistinguished *adj* undiscriminating or incapable of making a distinction between good and bad things
> their undistinguished appetite to devour everything
> *Gulliver's Travels* Jonathan Swift

use *n* habit
> Though use make you apt to kill me
> *The Flea* John Donne

vacant *adj* vacant usually means empty, but here Wordsworth uses it to mean carefree
> To vacant musing, unreproved neglect
> *The Prelude* William Wordsworth

valetudinarian *n* one too concerned with his or her own health.
> for having been a valetudinarian all his life
> *Emma* Jane Austen

vamp *v* vamp means to walk or tramp somewhere
> Well, vamp on to Marlott, will 'ee
> *Tess of the D'Urbervilles* Thomas Hardy

vapours *n* the vapours is an old term which means unpleasant and strange thoughts, which make the person feel nervous and unhappy
> and my head was full of vapours
> *Robinson Crusoe* Daniel Defoe

vegetable *n* plant
> the other vegetables are in the same proportion
> *Gulliver's Travels* Jonathan Swift

venturesome *adj* if you are venturesome you are willing to take risks
> he must be either hopelessly stupid or
> a venturesome fool
> *Wuthering Heights* Emily Brontë

verily *adj* really or truly
> though I believe verily
> *Robinson Crusoe* Daniel Defoe

vicinage *n* an area or the residents of an area
> and to his thought the whole vicinage was haunted
> by her
> *Silas Marner* George Eliot

victuals *pl n* victuals means food
> grumble a little over the victuals
> *The Adventures of Huckleberry Finn* Mark Twain

vintage *n* vintage in this context means wine
> Oh, for a draught of vintage!
> *Ode to a Nightingale* John Keats

virtual *adj* here virtual means powerful or strong
> had virtual faith
> *The Prelude* William Wordsworth

vittles *n* a slang word which means food
> There never was such a woman for givin' away
> vittles and drink
> *Little Women* Louisa May Alcott

voided straight *phrase* an old expression which means emptied immediately
> see the rooms be voided straight
> *Doctor Faustus* 4.1 Christopher Marlowe

wainscot *n* wood panel lining in a room so wainscoted means a room lined with wooden panels
> in the dark wainscoted parlor
> *Silas Marner* George Eliot

walking the plank *phrase* walking the plank was a punishment in which a prisoner would be made to walk along a plank on the side of the ship and fall into the sea, where they would be abandoned
> about hanging, and walking the plank
> *Treasure Island* Robert Louis Stevenson

wanting *adj* wanting means lacking or missing
> wanting two fingers of the left hand
> *Treasure Island* Robert Louis Stevenson

wanting, I was not *phrase* I was not wanting means I did not fail
> I was not wanting to lay a foundation of religious
> knowledge in his mind
> *Robinson Crusoe* Daniel Defoe

under way adj **1** in progress; taking place: this test is already under way **2** naut in motion in the direction headed

underwear n clothing worn under other garments, usually next to the skin

underweight adj weighing less than is average, expected, or healthy

underwent vb the past tense of **undergo**

underworld n **1** criminals and their associates **2** Greek and Roman myth the regions below the earth's surface regarded as the abode of the dead

underwrite vb -writing, -wrote, -written **1** to accept financial responsibility for a commercial project or enterprise **2** to sign and issue an insurance policy, thus accepting liability **3** to support **underwriter** n

undeserved adj not earned or deserved

undesirable adj **1** not desirable or pleasant; objectionable ▷ n **2** a person considered undesirable

undetected adj not having been discovered: an undetected cancer

undeterred adj not put off or dissuaded

undeveloped adj **1** not yet mature or adult **2** (of land) not built on or used for commercial or agricultural purposes

undies pl n Brit, Austral, & NZ informal women's underwear

undignified adj foolish or embarrassing

undiluted adj **1** (of a liquid) not having any water added to it; concentrated **2** not mixed with any other feeling or quality: undiluted hatred

undiminished adj not lessened or decreased: his admiration for her remained undiminished

undine (un-deen) n a female water spirit

WORD ORIGIN Latin unda a wave

undisciplined adj behaving badly, with a lack of self-control

undisguised adj shown openly; not concealed: undisguised curiosity

undismayed adj not upset about something; undaunted

undisputed adj unquestionably true or accurately described: Mao became undisputed leader of China

undistinguished adj not particularly good or bad; mediocre

undisturbed adj **1** quiet and peaceful: an undisturbed village **2** uninterrupted: three hours' undisturbed work **3** not touched, moved, or used by anyone: the wreck has lain undisturbed for centuries

undivided adj **1** total and whole-hearted: her undivided attention **2** not separated into different parts or groups

undo vb -doing, -did, -done **1** to open, unwrap or untie **2** to reverse the effects of: all the work of the congress would be undone **3** to cause the downfall of

undoing n **1** ruin; downfall **2** the cause of someone's downfall: his confidence was his undoing

undone¹ adj not done or completed; unfinished

undone² adj **1** ruined; destroyed **2** unfastened; untied

undoubted adj beyond doubt; certain or indisputable **undoubtedly** adv

undreamed or **undreamt** adj (often foll. by of) not thought of or imagined

undress vb **1** to take off the clothes of oneself or another ▷ n **2** in a state of undress naked or nearly naked **3** informal or ordinary working clothes or uniform **undressed** adj

undue adj greater than is reasonable; excessive: undue attention

USAGE
The use of undue in sentences such as there is no cause for undue alarm is redundant and should be avoided.

undulate vb -lating, -lated **1** to move gently and slowly from side to side or up and down **2** to have a wavy shape or appearance **undulation** n
WORD ORIGIN Latin unda a wave

unduly adv excessively

undying adj never ending; eternal

unearned adj **1** not deserved **2** not yet earned

unearned income n income from property or investments rather than work

unearth vb **1** to discover by searching **2** to dig up out of the earth

unearthly adj **1** strange, unnatural, or eerie: unearthly beauty **2** ridiculous or unreasonable: the unearthly hour of seven in the morning **unearthliness** n

unease n **1** anxiety or nervousness: my unease grew when she was not back by midnight **2** dissatisfaction or tension: unease about the government's handling of the affair

uneasy adj **1** (of a person) anxious or apprehensive **2** (of a condition) precarious or insecure: an uneasy peace **3** (of a thought or feeling) disquieting **uneasily** adv **uneasiness** n

uneatable adj (of food) so rotten or unattractive as to be unfit to eat

uneconomic adj not producing enough profit

uneconomical adj not economical; wasteful

uneducated adj not educated well or at all

unemotional adj (of a person) not displaying any emotion

unemployable adj unable or unfit to keep a job

unemployed adj **1** without paid employment; out of work **2** not being used; idle ▷ pl n **3** people who are out of work: the long-term unemployed

unemployment n **1** the condition of being unemployed **2** the number of unemployed workers: unemployment rose again last month

unemployment benefit n (formerly, in the British National Insurance scheme, and currently, in New Zealand) a regular payment to an unemployed person

unencumbered adj not hindered or held back: unencumbered by the responsibilities of childcare

unending adj not showing any signs of ever stopping

unendurable adj too unpleasant to bear

unenthusiastic adj not keen about or interested in (something)

unenthusiastically adv

unenviable adj (of a task) so difficult, dangerous, or unpleasant that one is glad not to have to do it oneself: the unenviable task of phoning the parents of the dead child

unequal adj **1** not equal in quantity, size, rank, or value **2** unequal to inadequate for: he felt unequal to the job **3** not offering all people or groups the same opportunities and privileges: the unequal distribution of wealth **4** (of a contest) having competitors of different ability **unequally** adv

unequalled or US **unequaled** adj greater, better, or more extreme than anything else of the same kind

unequivocal adj completely clear in meaning; unambiguous **unequivocally** adv

unerring adj never mistaken; consistently accurate

UNESCO United Nations Educational, Scientific, and Cultural Organization

unethical adj morally wrong

uneven adj **1** (of a surface) not level or flat **2** not consistent in quality: an uneven performance **3** not parallel, straight, or horizontal **4** not fairly matched: the uneven battle

uneventful adj ordinary, routine, or quiet **uneventfully** adv

unexampled adj without precedent

unexceptionable adj not likely to be criticized or objected to

unexceptional adj usual, ordinary, or normal

unexciting adj slightly dull and boring

unexpected adj surprising or unforeseen **unexpectedly** adv

unexplained adj strange or unclear because the reason for it is not known

unexpurgated adj (of a piece of writing) not censored by having allegedly offensive passages removed

unfailing adj continuous or reliable: his unfailing enthusiasm **unfailingly** adv

unfair adj **1** unequal or unjust **2** dishonest or unethical **unfairly** adv **unfairness** n

unfaithful adj **1** having sex with someone other than one's regular partner **2** not true to a promise or vow **unfaithfulness** n

unfamiliar adj **1** not known; strange: an unfamiliar American accent **2** unfamiliar with not acquainted with: anyone who is unfamiliar with the language **unfamiliarity** n

unfashionable adj not popular or in vogue

unfasten vb to undo, untie, or open or become undone, untied, or opened

unfathomable adj too strange or complicated to be understood: pugs exert a powerful, unfathomable hold over their owners

unfavourable or US **unfavorable** adj **1** making a successful or positive outcome unlikely: unfavourable weather conditions **2** disapproving: an unfavourable opinion **unfavourably** or US **unfavorably** adv

unfeeling adj without sympathy; callous

unfettered *adj* not limited or controlled: *unfettered competition*

unfinished *adj* **1** incomplete or imperfect **2** (of paint) without an applied finish

unfit *adj* **1** unqualified for or incapable of a particular role or task: *an unfit mother; he was unfit to drive* **2** unsuitable: *this meat is unfit for human consumption* **3** in poor physical condition

unfitted *adj* unsuitable: *unused to and unfitted for any form of manual labour*

unflappable *adj* *informal* (of a person) not easily upset **unflappability** *n*

unfledged *adj* **1** (of a young bird) not having developed adult feathers **2** immature and inexperienced

unflinching *adj* not shrinking from danger or difficulty

unfold *vb* **1** to open or spread out from a folded state **2** to reveal or be revealed: *a terrible truth unfolds* **3** to develop or be developed: *the novel unfolds through their recollections*

unfollow *vb* to choose to no longer receive someone's updates on the Twitter website

unforeseen *adj* surprising because not expected

unforgettable *adj* making such a strong impression that it is impossible to forget **unforgettably** *adv*

unforgivable *adj* too bad or cruel to be excused

unforgiving *adj* **1** unwilling to forgive other people's mistakes or wrongdoings **2** (of a machine) allowing little or no opportunity for mistakes to be corrected **3** harsh: *an unforgiving and desolate landscape*

unformed *adj* in an early stage of development; not fully developed or thought out

unforthcoming *adj* not inclined to speak, explain, or communicate

unfortunate *adj* **1** caused or accompanied by bad luck: *an unfortunate coincidence* **2** having bad luck: *my unfortunate daughter* **3** regrettable or unsuitable: *an unfortunate choice of phrase* ▷ *n* **4** an unlucky person **unfortunately** *adv*

unfounded *adj* (of ideas, fears, or allegations) not based on facts or evidence

unfreeze *vb* -freezing, -froze, -frozen **1** to thaw or cause to thaw **2** to relax restrictions or controls on (trade, the transfer of money, etc.): *Congress is considering unfreezing US aid to Jordan*

unfriend *or* **defriend** *vb* to choose to no longer be friends with someone on the social networking site Facebook

unfriendly *adj* -lier, -liest not friendly; hostile

unfrock *vb* to deprive (a person in holy orders) of the status of a priest

unfulfilled *adj* not satisfied

unfurl *vb* to unroll or spread out (an umbrella, flag, or sail) or (of an umbrella, flag, or sail) to be unrolled or spread out

unfurnished *adj* not containing any furniture

ungainly *adj* -lier, -liest lacking grace when moving **ungainliness** *n*
WORD ORIGIN dialect *gainly* graceful

ungenerous *adj* **1** mean or overly thrifty **2** (of a remark or thought) unfair or harsh

ungodly *adj* -lier, -liest **1** wicked or sinful **2** *informal* unreasonable or outrageous: *at this ungodly hour* **ungodliness** *n*

ungovernable *adj* **1** (of an emotion) not able to be controlled or restrained: *an ungovernable rage* **2** (of a country or area) not able to be effectively governed, esp. because of unrest or violence: *years of religious conflict had made much of the island ungovernable*

ungracious *adj* not polite or friendly, esp. when being offered praise or thanks

ungrammatical *adj* not following the rules of grammar

ungrateful *adj* not showing or offering thanks for a favour or compliment

unguarded *adj* **1** unprotected **2** open or frank: *one unguarded briefing* **3** incautious or careless: *an unguarded moment*

unguent (**ung**-gwent) *n* *literary* an ointment
WORD ORIGIN Latin *unguere* to anoint

ungulate (**ung**-gyew-lit) *n* a hoofed mammal
WORD ORIGIN Latin *ungula* hoof

unhallowed *adj* **1** not consecrated or holy: *unhallowed ground* **2** sinful or wicked

unhand *vb* old-fashioned or literary to release from one's grasp

unhappy *adj* -pier, -piest **1** sad or depressed **2** unfortunate or wretched **unhappily** *adv* **unhappiness** *n*

unharmed *adj* not hurt or damaged in any way

unhealthy *adj* -healthier, -healthiest **1** likely to cause illness or poor health: *unhealthy foods such as hamburger and chips* **2** not very fit or well **3** caused by or looking as if caused by poor health: *a thin unhealthy look about him* **4** morbid or unwholesome: *an unhealthy interest in computer fraud* **unhealthiness** *n*

unheard *adj* not listened to; unheeded: *all my warnings went unheard*

unheard-of *adj* **1** without precedent: *an unheard-of phenomenon* **2** highly offensive: *unheard-of behaviour*

unheeded *adj* noticed but ignored: *their protests went unheeded*

unhelpful *adj* doing nothing to improve a situation

unheralded *adj* not announced beforehand

unhindered *adj* **1** not prevented or obstructed: *unhindered access* ▷ *adv* **2** without being prevented or obstructed: *he was able to go about his work unhindered*

unhinge *vb* -hinging, -hinged to make a person mentally deranged or unbalanced **unhinged** *adj*

unholy *adj* -lier, -liest **1** immoral or wicked **2** *informal* outrageous or unnatural: *this unholy mess* **unholiness** *n*

unhook *vb* **1** to unfasten the hooks of a garment **2** to remove something from a hook

unhurried *adj* done at a leisurely pace, without any rush or anxiety

unhurt *adj* not injured in an accident, attack, etc.

unhygienic *adj* dirty and likely to cause disease or infection

uni *n* *Brit, Austral, & NZ informal* short for **university**

uni- *combining form* of, consisting of, or having only one: *unilateral*
WORD ORIGIN Latin *unus* one

unicameral *adj* of or having a single legislative chamber: *Denmark's unicameral parliament, known as the Folketing*

UNICEF United Nations Children's Fund

unicellular *adj* (of organisms) consisting of a single cell

Unicode *n* *computers* a character set for all languages

unicorn *n* a legendary creature resembling a white horse with one horn growing from its forehead
WORD ORIGIN Latin *unus* one + *cornu* a horn

unicycle *n* a one-wheeled vehicle driven by pedals, used in a circus **unicyclist** *n*

unidentified *adj* **1** not able to be recognized; unknown: *unidentified gunmen* **2** anonymous or unnamed: *the house of an unidentified Scottish businessman* **unidentifiable** *adj*

uniform *n* **1** a special identifying set of clothes for the members of an organization, such as soldiers ▷ *adj* **2** regular and even throughout: *the mixture must be beaten to a uniform consistency* **3** alike or like: *uniform green metal filing cabinets* **uniformity** *n* **uniformly** *adv*
WORD ORIGIN Latin *unus* one + *forma* shape

unify *vb* -fies, -fying, -fied to make or become one; unite **unification** *n*
WORD ORIGIN Latin *unus* one + *facere* to make

unilateral *adj* made or done by only one person or group: *unilateral action* **unilateralism** *n*

unilingual *adj* **1** of or relating to only one language **2** *chiefly Canad* knowing only one language ▷ *n* **3** *chiefly Canad* a person who knows only one language

unimaginable *adj* so unusual, great, or extreme that it is difficult to imagine or understand: *the unimaginable vastness of space*

unimaginative *adj* not having or showing much imagination

unimpeachable *adj* completely honest and reliable

unimpeded *adj* not stopped or disrupted by anything

unimportant *adj* trivial or insignificant

uninhabitable *adj* not able to support human life: *an uninhabitable wasteland*

uninhabited *adj* having no people living in or on it: *an uninhabited island*

uninhibited *adj* behaving freely and naturally, without worrying what other people will think

uninitiated *pl n* the uninitiated people who have no special knowledge or experience: *no easy way for the uninitiated to find out what the internet can do*

uninspired *adj* not particularly good or exciting

uninspiring *adj* not likely to make people interested or excited

unintelligible *adj* impossible to make out or understand; incomprehensible: *an unintelligible London accent*

unintended *adj* (of an action or its consequences) not planned or intended: *sometimes drugs have unintended side-effects*

unintentional *adj* (of an action) not done deliberately; accidental: *unintentional discrimination* **unintentionally** *adv*

uninterested *adj* having or showing no interest in someone or something

USAGE
See at **disinterested**.

uninteresting *adj* boring or dull

uninterrupted *adj* continuous, with no breaks or interruptions: *uninterrupted applause*

uninvited *adj* **1** not having been asked: *uninvited guests* ▷ *adv* **2** without having been asked: *he sat down uninvited on the side of the bed*

union *n* **1** the act of merging two or more things to become one, or the state of being merged in such a way **2** short for **trade union 3** an association of individuals or groups for a common purpose: *the Scripture Union* **4 a** an association or society: *the Students' union* **b** the buildings of such an organization **5** marriage or sexual intercourse **6** *maths* a set containing all the members of two given sets **7** (in 19th-century England) a workhouse maintained by a number of parishes ▷ *adj* **8** of a trade union
WORD ORIGIN Latin *unus* one

unionism *n* **1** the principles of trade unions **2** adherence to the principles of trade unions **unionist** *n, adj*

Unionist *n* a supporter of union between Britain and Northern Ireland

unionize or **-ise** *vb* **-izing, -ized** or **-ising, -ised** to organize workers into a trade union **unionization** or **-isation** *n*

Union Jack or **Union flag** *n* the national flag of the United Kingdom, combining the crosses of Saint George, Saint Andrew, and Saint Patrick

unique (yew-**neek**) *adj* **1** being the only one of a particular type **2 unique to** concerning or belonging to a particular person, thing, or group: *certain dishes are unique to this restaurant* **3** without equal or like **4** *informal* remarkable **uniquely** *adv*
WORD ORIGIN Latin *unicus* unparalleled

USAGE
Unique is normally taken to describe an absolute state, i.e. one that cannot be qualified; thus something is either *unique* or *not unique*; it cannot be *rather unique* or *very unique*. However *unique* is sometimes used informally to mean remarkable or unusual, and this makes it possible to use comparatives or intensifiers with it, although many people object to this use.

unisex *adj* (of clothing, a hairstyle, or hairdressers) designed for both sexes

unisexual *adj* **1** of one sex only **2** (of an organism) having either male or female reproductive organs but not both

unison *n* **1 in unison** at the same time as another person or other people: *smiling and nodding in unison* **2** (usually preceded by *in*) complete agreement: *to act in unison* **3** *music* a style, technique, or passage in which all the performers sing or play the same notes at the same time
WORD ORIGIN Latin *unus* one + *sonus* sound

UNISON *n* a British trade union consisting mainly of council and hospital workers

unit *n* **1** a single undivided entity or whole **2** a group or individual regarded as a basic element of a larger whole: *the clan was the basic unit of Highland society* **3** a mechanical part or small device that does a particular job: *a waste disposal unit* **4** a team of people that performs a specific function, and often also their buildings and equipment: *a combat unit* **5** a standard amount of a physical quantity, such as length or energy, used to express magnitudes of that quantity: *the year as a unit of time* **6** *maths* the digit or position immediately to the left of the decimal point **7** a piece of furniture designed to be fitted with other similar pieces: *bedroom units* **8** NZ a self-propelled railcar **9** *Austral & NZ* short for **home unit**
WORD ORIGIN from *unity*

Unitarian *n* **1** a person who believes that God is one being and rejects the Trinity ▷ *adj* **2** of Unitarians or Unitarianism **Unitarianism** *n*

unitary *adj* **1** consisting of a single undivided whole: *a unitary state* **2** of a unit or units

unit cost *n* the actual cost of producing one article

unite *vb* **uniting, united 1** to make or become an integrated whole: *conception occurs when a sperm unites with the egg* **2** to form an association or alliance: *the opposition parties united to fight against privatization* **3** to possess (a combination of qualities) at the same time: *he manages to unite charm and ruthlessness*
WORD ORIGIN Latin *unus* one

united *adj* **1** produced by two or more people or things in combination: *a united effort* **2** in agreement: *we are united in our opposition to these proposals* **3** in association or alliance

United Kingdom *n* a kingdom of NW Europe, consisting of the island of Great Britain together with Northern Ireland

United Nations *n* an international organization of independent states, formed to promote peace and international security

unit price *n* the price charged per unit

unit trust *n* *Austral & Brit* an investment trust that issues units for public sale and invests the money in many different businesses

unity *n, pl* **-ties 1** the state of being one **2** mutual agreement: *unity of intention* **3** the state of being a single thing that is composed of separate parts, organizations, etc.: *moves towards church unity* **4** *maths* the number or numeral one
WORD ORIGIN Latin *unus* one

Univ. University

univalent *adj chem* same as **monovalent**

universal *adj* **1** of or relating to everyone in the world or everyone in a particular place or society: *the introduction of universal primary education* **2** of, relating to, or affecting the entire world or universe: *the universal laws of physics* **3** true and relevant at all times and in all situations: *there may be no single universal solution* ▷ *n* **4** something which exists or is true in all places and all situations: *universals such as beauty and justice* **universality** *n* **universally** *adv*

USAGE
The use of *more universal* as in *his writings have long been admired by fellow scientists, but his latest book should have more universal appeal* is acceptable in modern English usage.

universal joint or **coupling** *n* a form of coupling between two rotating shafts allowing freedom of movement in all directions

universe *n* **1** the whole of all existing matter, energy, and space **2** the world
WORD ORIGIN Latin *universum* the whole world

university *n, pl* **-ties 1** an institution of higher education with authority to award degrees **2** the buildings, members, staff, or campus of a university
WORD ORIGIN Medieval Latin *universitas* group of scholars

Unix (**yew**-nicks) *n trademark* an operating system found on many types of computer

unjust *adj* not fair or just

unjustifiable *adj* inexcusably wrong or unfair

unjustified *adj* not necessary or reasonable

unkempt *adj* **1** (of the hair) uncombed or dishevelled **2** untidy or slovenly: *an unkempt appearance*
WORD ORIGIN Old English *uncembed*, from *cemban* to comb

unkind *adj* unsympathetic or cruel **unkindly** *adv* **unkindness** *n*

unknowing *adj* unaware or ignorant: *unknowing victims of fraud*

unknown *adj* **1** not known, understood, or recognized **2** not famous: *a young and then unknown actor* **3 unknown quantity** a person or thing whose action or effect is unknown or unpredictable ▷ *n* **4** an unknown person, quantity, or thing ▷ *adv* **5 unknown to someone** without someone being aware: *unknown to him, the starboard engine had dropped off*

unlawful *adj* not permitted by law; illegal

unleaded *adj* (of petrol) containing less tetraethyl lead, in order to reduce environmental pollution

unlearn *vb* **-learning, -learned** or **-learnt** to try to forget something learnt or to discard accumulated knowledge

unlearned (un-**lurn**-id) *adj* ignorant or uneducated

unlearnt or **unlearned** *adj* **1** denoting knowledge or skills innately present rather than learnt **2** not learnt or taken notice of: *unlearnt lessons*

Word Histories
part 13

Ultramarine comes from Latin *ultramarinus*, meaning 'from beyond the sea'. It was given this name because the blue mineral, lapis lazuli, that the pigment was made from was imported from Asia.

Undermine: 'Undermining' is originally a military term, denoting the practice in warfare of digging mines or tunnels under enemy fortifications in order to make them collapse.

Vaccine comes from Latin *vacca*, meaning 'a cow'. At a time when many people were dying of smallpox, the English surgeon Edward Jenner (1749–1823) noted that people who had contracted cowpox, a relatively mild disease caught from cattle, were immune to smallpox. He therefore advocated inoculation with the cowpox virus as a means of immunizing against smallpox.

Vet: In Latin *veterinae* means 'animals used for pulling carts and ploughs'.

Wake: An urban myth, propagated over the internet, insists that the object of a wake was to watch in case the corpse woke up – hence the name. According to this story, live burials were so common in earlier centuries, due to coma victims being taken for dead, that relatives began to sit around the corpse for some time after death to ensure that the deceased really was dead! In reality, the wakefulness indicated in this wake is on the part of those watching over the corpse to ensure that the body is undisturbed before burial.

Walnut comes from Old English *walh-hnutu* meaning 'foreign nut'. The walnut is an Asian tree that was not introduced into Britain until the 15th or 16th century, and so walnuts originally were imported from abroad.

Welsh rarebit, a fancy name for cheese on toast, was originally a slur against the Welsh. 'Welsh' was used as a synonym for inferior in England, and 'rarebit' was originally 'rabbit', snootily implying that Wales was so poor in resources that the Welsh had to make do with cheese on toast instead of game.

Whisky: The word 'whisky' comes from Scottish Gaelic *uisge beatha*, meaning 'water of life'. Whisky is not the only alcoholic 'water of life': 'aqua vitae', which means 'water of life' in Latin, is an old name for brandy, and there is also in Scandinavia a strong alcoholic drink called 'aquavit' or 'akvavit'.

Wormwood: comes from the Old English name for the plant, *wormod*, which refers to neither worms nor wood. As a relatively obscure word, *wormod* was broken down into two recognizable elements by folk etymology, despite the fact that these elements have nothing to do with its meaning.

Xenophobia: 'Xenophobia' comes from the Greek words *xenos*, meaning 'stranger', and *phobos*, meaning 'fear'.

Ye: The 'ye' on faux-archaic signs like 'Ye Old English Tea Shoppe' stems from a misinterpretation of Middle English texts, where the runic letter thorn (Þ), which is pronounced 'th', was mistaken for a 'y'. A kind of visual folk etymology has taken place, resulting in 'ye' being used instead of 'the' by writers who wish to create a quaintly archaic effect.

Yoga comes from Sanskrit *yoga*, meaning 'union'. The practice of yoga was intended to produce a mystical union between the practitioner and the Supreme Being.

Although **Yuletide** is an archaic word virtually synonymous with 'Christmas-time', Yule (Old English *geola*) was actually a pagan festival. It went on for twelve days around the time of the winter solstice.

Zany comes from Italian *zanni*, meaning 'clown'. 'Zann'. is the Venetian form of the Italian name *Giovanni*, meaning 'John', and was the name often given to comic characters in medieval Italian plays.

Zombie comes from an African word *zumbi*, meaning a 'fetish' or 'good-luck charm'.

unleash *vb* to set loose or cause (something bad): *to unleash war*

unleavened (un-**lev**-vend) *adj* (of bread) made without yeast or leavening

unless *conj* except under the circumstances that; except on the condition that: *you can't get in unless you can prove you're over eighteen*

unlettered *adj* uneducated or illiterate

unlike *adj* **1** not similar; different ▷ *prep* **2** not like or typical of: *unlike his brother, he could not control his weight* **unlikeness** *n*

unlikely *adj* not likely; improbable **unlikeliness** *n*

unlimited *adj* **1** apparently endless: *there was unlimited coffee* **2** not restricted or limited: *unlimited access to the rest of the palace*

unlisted *adj* **1** not entered on a list **2** (of securities) not quoted on a stock exchange **3** *Austral, US, & Canad* not listed in a telephone directory by request

unlit *adj* **1** (of a fire, cigarette, etc.) not lit and therefore not burning **2** (of a road) not having any streetlights switched on

unload *vb* **1** to remove cargo from a ship, lorry, or plane **2** to express worries or problems by telling someone about them **3** to remove the ammunition from a gun

unlock *vb* **1** to unfasten a lock or door **2** to release or let loose: *the revelation unlocked a flood of tears*

unlooked-for *adj* unexpected or unforeseen

unloose *or* **unloosen** *vb* -loosing, -loosed *or* -loosening, -loosened to set free or release

unlovable *adj* too unpleasant or unattractive to be loved

unloved *adj* not loved by anyone

unlovely *adj* unpleasant in appearance or character

unlucky *adj* **1** having bad luck or misfortune: *an unlucky man* **2** caused by bad luck or misfortune: *an unlucky coincidence* **3** regarded as likely to bring about bad luck: *an unlucky number* **unluckily** *adv*

unmade *adj* **1** (of a bed) with the bedclothes not smoothed and tidied **2** (of a road) not surfaced with tarmac **3** not yet made

unmake *vb* -making, -made to undo or destroy

unman *vb* -manning, -manned **1** to cause to lose courage or nerve **2** to make effeminate

unmanageable *adj* difficult to use, deal with, or control, esp. because it is too big

unmanly *adj* **1** not masculine or virile **2** cowardly or dishonourable

unmanned *adj* **1** having no personnel or crew: *the border posts were unmanned* **2** (of an aircraft or spacecraft) operated by automatic or remote control

unmannerly *adj* lacking manners; discourteous **unmannerliness** *n*

unmarked *adj* **1** having no signs of damage or injury **2** not having any identifying signs or markings: *an unmarked police car*

unmarried *adj* not married

unmask *vb* **1** to remove the mask or disguise from **2** to expose or reveal the true nature or character of

unmatched *adj* **1** not equalled or surpassed: *his pace is unmatched by any other modern player* **2** not coordinated or forming a set with anything else: *three unmatched chairs*

unmentionable *adj* unsuitable as a topic of conversation

unmercifully *adv* excessively and relentlessly: *the young boy is hounded unmercifully*

unmistakable *or* **unmistakeable** *adj* clear or unambiguous **unmistakably** *or* **unmistakeably** *adv*

unmitigated *adj* **1** not reduced or lessened in severity or intensity **2** total and complete: *unmitigated boredom*

unmolested *adv* without disturbance or interference: *the enemy aircraft passed overhead unmolested*

unmoved *adj* not affected by emotion; indifferent

unmoving *adj* still and motionless

unmusical *adj* **1** (of a person) unable to appreciate or play music **2** (of a sound) harsh and unpleasant

unnamed *adj* **1** not mentioned by name; anonymous: *an unnamed government spokesman* **2** not known or described clearly enough to be named: *unnamed fears*

unnatural *adj* **1** strange and slightly frightening because it is not usual; abnormal: *an unnatural silence* **2** not in accordance with accepted standards of behaviour: *an unnatural relationship* **3** affected or forced: *a determined smile which seemed unnatural* **4** inhuman or monstrous: *unnatural evils* **unnaturally** *adv*

unnecessary *adj* not essential, or more than is essential **unnecessarily** *adv*

unnerve *vb* -nerving, -nerved to cause to lose courage, confidence, or self-control: *he unnerves me* **unnerving** *adj*

unnoticed *adj* without being seen or noticed

unnumbered *adj* **1** countless; too many to count **2** not counted or given a number

UNO United Nations Organization

unobtainable *adj* impossible to get

unobtrusive *adj* not drawing attention to oneself or itself; inconspicuous

unoccupied *adj* **1** (of a building) without occupants **2** unemployed or idle **3** (of an area or country) not overrun by foreign troops

unofficial *adj* **1** not authorized or approved by the relevant organization or person: *an unofficial strike* **2** not confirmed officially: *unofficial reports of the minister's resignation*

unorganized *or* -**nised** *adj* **1** not arranged into an organized system or structure **2** (of workers) not unionized

unorthodox *adj* **1** (of ideas, methods, etc.) unconventional and not generally accepted **2** (of a person) not conventional in beliefs, behaviour, etc.

unpack *vb* **1** to remove the packed contents of a case **2** to take something out of a packed container

unpaid *adj* **1** without a salary or wage: *unpaid overtime* **2** still to be paid: *unpaid bills*

unpalatable *adj* **1** (of food) unpleasant to taste **2** (of a fact, idea, etc.) unpleasant and hard to accept

unparalleled *adj* not equalled; supreme

unpardonable *adj* unforgivably wrong or rude

unparliamentary *adj* not consistent with parliamentary procedure or practice

unperson *n* a person whose existence is officially denied or ignored

unpick *vb* to undo the stitches of a piece of sewing

unpin *vb* -pinning, -pinned **1** to remove a pin or pins from **2** to unfasten by removing pins

unplanned *adj* not intentional or deliberate

unplayable *adj sport* **1** (of a ball) thrown too fast or too skilfully to be hit **2** (of a pitch or course) too badly affected by rain or frost to be used

unpleasant *adj* not pleasant or agreeable **unpleasantly** *adv* **unpleasantness** *n*

unplug *vb* -plugging, -plugged to disconnect a piece of electrical equipment by taking the plug out of the socket

unplugged *adj* using acoustic rather than electric instruments: *an unplugged version of the song*

unplumbed *adj* **1** not measured **2** not understood in depth

unpolished *adj* **1** not polished **2** not elegant or refined

unpopular *adj* generally disliked or disapproved of **unpopularity** *n*

unpractised *or US* **unpracticed** *adj* not experienced or skilled: *an unpractised surgical technique*

unprecedented *adj* never having happened before: *an unprecedented decision*

unpredictable *adj* not easy to predict or foresee

unprejudiced *adj* free from bias; impartial

unprepared *adj* surprised or put at a disadvantage by something because you are not ready to deal with it

unprepossessing *adj* not very attractive or appealing

unpretentious *adj* modest, unassuming, and down-to-earth

unprincipled *adj* lacking moral principles; unscrupulous

unprintable *adj* unsuitable for printing for reasons of obscenity, libel, or indecency

unproductive *adj* not producing any worthwhile results: *unproductive talks*

unprofessional *adj* not behaving according to the standards expected of a member of a particular profession

unprofitable *adj* **1** not making a profit **2** not producing any worthwhile results: *an unprofitable line of thinking*

u

unpromising *adj* not likely to turn out well

unprompted *adj* doing without being urged by anyone else; spontaneous

unpronounceable *adj* (of a name or word) too difficult to say

unprotected *adj* not defended or protected from harm

unprovoked *adj* carried out without any cause or reason: *an unprovoked attack*

unpunished *adj* without suffering or resulting in a penalty: *the guilty must not go unpunished; such crimes should not remain unpunished*

unputdownable *adj* (of a book, usually a novel) so gripping that one wants to read it at one sitting

unqualified *adj* 1 lacking the necessary qualifications 2 having no conditions or limitations: *an unqualified denial* 3 total or complete: *unqualified admiration*

unquestionable *adj* not to be doubted; indisputable **unquestionably** *adv*

unquestioned *adj* accepted by everyone without doubt or disagreement: *an engineer of unquestioned genius*

unquestioning *adj* accepting a belief or order without thinking about or doubting it in any way: *unquestioning obedience* **unquestioningly** *adv*

unquiet *adj* *chiefly literary* anxious or uneasy

unquote *interj* an expression used to indicate the end of a quotation that was introduced with the word 'quote'

unravel *vb* **-velling, -velled** *or US* **-veling, -veled** 1 to separate something knitted or woven into individual strands 2 to become separated into individual strands 3 to explain or solve: *we unravelled the secrets*

unreactive *adj* (of a substance) not readily partaking in chemical reactions

unread *adj* 1 (of a book or article) not yet read 2 (of a person) having read little

unreadable *adj* 1 unable to be read or deciphered; illegible 2 too difficult or dull to read

unreal *adj* 1 existing only in the imagination or giving the impression of doing so: *an unreal quality* 2 insincere or artificial **unreality** *n*

unrealistic *adj* 1 not accepting the facts of a situation and not dealing with them in a practical way: *he had unrealistic expectations of his son* 2 not true to life: *an unrealistic portrayal of Scottish life* **unrealistically** *adv*

unreasonable *adj* 1 unfair and excessive: *an unreasonable request* 2 refusing to listen to reason **unreasonably** *adv*

unreasoning *adj* not controlled by reason; irrational

unrecognizable *or* **-nisable** *adj* changed or damaged so much that it is hard to recognize

unrecognized *or* **-nised** *adj* not properly identified or acknowledged: *her talents went unrecognized during her lifetime*

unregenerate *adj* unrepentant or unreformed

unrelated *adj* not connected with each other: *a series of unrelated mishaps*

unrelenting *adj* 1 refusing to relent or take pity 2 not diminishing in determination, effort, or force

unreliable *adj* not able to be trusted or relied on

unremitting *adj* never slackening or stopping

unrepentant *adj* not ashamed of one's beliefs or actions

unrequited *adj* (of love) not returned

unreserved *adj* 1 complete and without holding back any doubts: *unreserved support* 2 open and forthcoming in manner 3 not booked or not able to be booked: *all the seats are unreserved* **unreservedly** (un-riz-**zerv**-id-lee) *adv*

unresolved *adj* not satisfactorily solved or concluded: *the mystery of her death remains unresolved*

unresponsive *adj* not reacting or responding

unrest *n* 1 a rebellious state of discontent 2 an uneasy or troubled state

unrestrained *adj* not controlled or limited: *the unrestrained use of state power*

unrestricted *adj* not limited by any laws or rules

unrewarding *adj* not giving any satisfaction

unrighteous *adj* sinful or wicked

unripe *adj* not fully matured

unrivalled *or US* **unrivaled** *adj* having no equal; matchless

unroll *vb* 1 to open out or unwind: *I unrolled the map* 2 (of a series of events or period of time) to happen or be revealed or remembered one after the other

unruffled *adj* 1 calm and unperturbed 2 smooth and still: *unruffled ponds*

unruly *adj* **-lier, -liest** difficult to control or organize; disobedient or undisciplined **unruliness** *n*

unsaddle *vb* **-dling, -dled** 1 to remove the saddle from a horse 2 to cause to fall or dismount from a horse

unsafe *adj* 1 dangerous 2 (of a criminal conviction) based on inadequate or false evidence

unsaid *adj* not said or expressed

unsaleable *adj* unable to be sold

unsatisfactory *adj* not good enough

unsaturated *adj* 1 *chem* (of an organic compound) containing a double or triple bond and therefore capable of combining with other substances 2 (of a fat, esp. a vegetable fat) containing a high proportion of fatty acids with double bonds

unsavoury *or US* **unsavory** *adj* objectionable or distasteful: *an unsavoury divorce*

unscathed *adj* not harmed or injured

unscheduled *adj* not planned or intended

unscramble *vb* **-bling, -bled** 1 to sort out something confused or disorderly 2 to restore a scrambled message to an intelligible form **unscrambler** *n*

unscrew *vb* 1 to loosen a screw or lid by turning it 2 to unfasten something by removing the screws which fasten it: *the mirror had been unscrewed and removed*

unscripted *adj* spoken without a previously prepared text

unscrupulous *adj* prepared to act in a dishonest or immoral manner

unseasonable *adj* 1 (of the weather) inappropriate for the season 2 inappropriate or unusual for the time of year: *an unseasonable dip in the sea*

unseat *vb* 1 to throw or displace from a seat or saddle 2 to depose from office or position

unseeded *adj* (of a player in a sport) not given a top player's position in the opening rounds of a tournament

unseeing *adj* not noticing or looking at anything: *staring with unseeing eyes*

unseemly *adj* not according to expected standards of behaviour **unseemliness** *n*

unseen *adj* 1 hidden or invisible: *an unseen organist was practising* 2 mysterious or supernatural: *unseen powers* ▷ *adv* 3 without being seen; unnoticed: *the thief entered unseen* ▷ *n* 4 a passage which is given to students for translation without them having seen it in advance

unselfish *adj* concerned about other people's wishes and needs rather than one's own **unselfishly** *adv* **unselfishness** *n*

unsettle *vb* **-tling, -tled** 1 to change or become changed from a fixed or settled condition 2 to confuse or agitate a person or the mind

unsettled *adj* 1 lacking order or stability: *an unsettled time* 2 disturbed and restless: *your child will feel unsettled and insecure* 3 constantly changing or moving from place to place: *his wandering unsettled life* 4 (of an argument or dispute) not resolved 5 (of a debt or bill) not yet paid

unshakable *or* **unshakeable** *adj* (of beliefs) utterly firm and unwavering

unshaken *adj* (of faith or feelings) not having been weakened

unshaven *adj* (of a man who does not have a beard) having stubble on his chin because he has not shaved recently

unsheathe *vb* **-sheathing, -sheathed** to pull a weapon from a sheath

unshockable *adj* not likely to be upset by anything seen, heard, or read

unsightly *adj* unpleasant to look at; ugly **unsightliness** *n*

unsigned *adj* (of a letter etc.) anonymous

unskilled *adj* not having or requiring any special skill or training

unsociable *adj* (of a person) not fond of the company of other people

unsocial *adj* 1 not fond of the company of other people 2 (of the hours of work of a job) falling outside the normal working day

unsolicited *adj* given or sent without being asked for: *unsolicited advice; unsolicited junk mail*

unsophisticated *adj* 1 (of a person) lacking experience or worldly wisdom 2 lacking refinement or complexity: *unsophisticated fighter aircraft*

unsound *adj* 1 unhealthy or unstable: *of unsound mind* 2 based on faulty ideas: *unsound judgment* 3 not firm: *unsound*

u

foundations **4** not financially reliable: *his business plan was unsound*

unsparing *adj* **1** very generous; lavish **2** harsh or severe **unsparingly** *adv*

unspeakable *adj* **1** incapable of expression in words: *unspeakable gratitude* **2** indescribably bad or evil: *unspeakable atrocities* **unspeakably** *adv*

unspoiled *adj* **1** not damaged or harmed **2** (of a place) attractive and not having changed for a long time

unspoken *adj* not openly expressed: *unspoken fears; an unspoken agreement*

unsporting *adj* not following the principles of fair play

unstable *adj* **1** not firmly fixed and likely to wobble or fall: *an unstable pile of books* **2** likely to change suddenly and create difficulties or danger: *the unstable political climate* **3** (of a person) having abrupt changes of mood or behaviour **4** *chem, physics* readily decomposing

unsteady *adj* **1** not securely fixed: *unsteady metal posts* **2** (of a manner of walking, standing, or holding) shaky or staggering **unsteadily** *adv* **unsteadiness** *n*

unstinting *adj* generous and gladly given: *unstinting praise*

unstoppable *adj* impossible to prevent from continuing or developing

unstrap *vb* **-strapping, -strapped** to undo the straps fastening (something) in position

unstructured *adj* without formal or systematic organization

unstuck *adj* **1** freed from being stuck, glued, or fastened **2** **come unstuck** to suffer failure or disaster

unstudied *adj* natural or spontaneous: *her unstudied elegance and grace*

unsubstantial *adj* **1** lacking weight or firmness **2** having no material existence

unsubstantiated *adj* not yet confirmed or proved to be true: *unsubstantiated rumours*

unsuccessful *adj* not achieving success

unsuitable *adj* not right or appropriate for a particular purpose

unsuited *adj* **1** not appropriate for a particular task or situation: *a likeable man unsuited to a military career* **2** (of a couple) having different personalities or tastes and unlikely to form a lasting relationship: *they are totally unsuited to each other*

unsung *adj* not appreciated or honoured: *an unsung hero*

unsure *adj* **1** lacking assurance or self-confidence **2** uncertain or undecided: *he was unsure who was really in charge*

unsurpassed *adj* better or greater than anything else of its kind

unsuspected *adj* **1** not known to exist: *an unsuspected talent* **2** not under suspicion

unsuspecting *adj* having no idea of what is happening or about to happen

unsweetened *adj* having no sugar or other sweetener added

unswerving *adj* not turning aside; constant

unsympathetic *adj* **1** not feeling or showing sympathy **2** unpleasant and unlikeable **3** (foll. by *to*) opposed or hostile to

untamed *adj* not brought under human control; wild: *an untamed wilderness*

untangle *vb* **-gling, -gled** to free from tangles or confusion

untapped *adj* not yet used or exploited: *untapped mineral reserves*

untaught *adj* **1** without training or education **2** acquired without instruction

untenable *adj* (of a theory, idea, etc.) impossible to defend in an argument

unthinkable *adj* **1** so shocking or unpleasant that one cannot believe it to be true **2** unimaginable or inconceivable

unthinking *adj* **1** thoughtless and inconsiderate **2** done or happening without careful consideration: *an unthinking reflex* **unthinkingly** *adv*

untidy *adj* **-dier, -diest** not neat; messy and disordered **untidily** *adv* **untidiness** *n*

untie *vb* **-tying, -tied** to unfasten or free something that is tied

until *conj* **1** up to a time that: *he lifted the wire until it was taut* **2** before (a time or event): *until the present crisis, they weren't allowed into the country* ▷ *prep* **3** (often preceded by *up*) in or throughout the period before: *up until then I'd never thought about having kids* **4** before: *Baker does not get to Israel until Sunday*

WORD ORIGIN earlier *untill*

USAGE
The use of *until such time as* (as in *industrial action will continue until such time as our demands are met*) is unnecessary and should be avoided: *industrial action will continue until our demands are met*. See also at **till**.

untimely *adj* **1** occurring before the expected or normal time: *his untimely death* **2** inappropriate to the occasion or time: *an untimely idea to raise at the United Nations* **untimeliness** *n*

unto *prep archaic* to
WORD ORIGIN from Old Norse

untold *adj* **1** incapable of description: *untold misery* **2** incalculably great in number or quantity: *untold millions* **3** not told

untouchable *adj* **1** above criticism, suspicion or punishment **2** unable to be touched ▷ *n* **3** a member of the lowest class in India, whose touch was formerly regarded as defiling to the four main castes

untouched *adj* **1** not changed, moved, or affected: *a sleepy backwater untouched by mass tourism* **2** not injured or harmed: *the Cathedral survived the war untouched* **3** (of food or drink) not eaten or consumed **4** emotionally unaffected: *he was untouched by the news of his uncle's death*

untoward *adj* **1** causing misfortune or annoyance **2** unfavourable: *untoward reactions* **3** out of the ordinary; out of the way: *nothing untoward had happened*

untrained *adj* without formal or adequate training or education

untrammelled *or US* **untrammeled** *adj* able to act freely and without restrictions

untried *adj* **1** not yet used, done, or tested **2** (of a prisoner) not yet put on trial

untroubled *adj* calm and unworried

untrue *adj* **1** incorrect or false **2** disloyal or unfaithful

untrustworthy *adj* unreliable and not able to be trusted

untruth *n* a statement that is not true; lie

untruthful *adj* **1** (of a person) given to lying **2** (of a statement) not true **untruthfully** *adv*

untutored *adj* **1** without formal education **2** lacking sophistication or refinement

unusable *adj* not in good enough condition to be used

unused *adj* **1** not being or never having been used **2** (foll. by *to*) not accustomed to

unusual *adj* uncommon or extraordinary **unusually** *adv*

unutterable *adj* incapable of being expressed in words **unutterably** *adv*

unvarnished *adj* not elaborated upon; plain: *an unvarnished account of literary life*

unvarying *adj* always staying the same; unchanging

unveil *vb* **1** to ceremonially remove the cover from a new picture, statue, plaque, etc. **2** to make public a secret **3** to remove the veil from one's own or another person's face

unveiling *n* **1** a ceremony involving the removal of a veil covering a statue **2** the presentation of something for the first time

unvoiced *adj* **1** not expressed or spoken **2** *phonetics* voiceless

unwaged *adj* (of a person) not having a paid job

unwanted *adj* not wanted or welcome

unwarranted *adj* not justified or necessary

unwary *adj* not careful or cautious and therefore likely to be harmed **unwarily** *adv* **unwariness** *n*

unwavering *adj* (of a feeling or attitude) remaining firm and never weakening

unwelcome *adj* unpleasant and unwanted

unwell *adj* not healthy; ill

unwept *adj* not wept for or lamented

unwholesome *adj* **1** harmful to the body or mind: *unwholesome food* **2** morally harmful: *unwholesome dreams* **3** unhealthy-looking **4** (of food) of inferior quality

unwieldy *adj* too heavy, large, or awkward to be easily handled

unwilling *adj* **1** reluctant **2** done or said with reluctance **unwillingly** *adv* **unwillingness** *n*

unwind *vb* **-winding, -wound** **1** to slacken, undo, or unravel: *Paul started to unwind the bandage* **2** to relax after a busy or tense time: *we go out to unwind after work*

unwise *adj* foolish; not sensible **unwisely** *adv*

Register

Register is a term used in linguistics to refer to the varieties of language used in particular social situations or particular subject areas. Register can refer to the specific language used in, for example, legal or scientific fields (in the 'field of discourse') but, arguably, most often refers to levels of language that might vary with the more general context or might be determined by the social situation of the participants (the 'manner of discourse' or 'tenor'). By this definition, formal language or slang, for example, may be called registers. Many of the labels presented alongside words and phrases in this dictionary give information about their register.

Different registers may display differences in vocabulary, syntax, and pronunciation, and they have different pragmatic rules, for example, the expected level of politeness or the acceptability of interruption. The most broad, and perhaps the most widely recognized, registers are *formal* and *informal* (although some textbooks use the term *tenor* or *style* to refer to the degree of formality). It is worth noting here that the method of communication – the 'mode of discourse' – can also affect register: written texts, unless they are in a deliberately informal style, tend to be more formal in register. That said, an email is likely to be less formal than a letter, even if intended for the same recipient. Ultimately, however, the relative formality of any piece of speech or writing will usually depend on what is considered 'appropriate' in a given situation.

In an academic piece, a business letter, or a conversation with someone in authority, for example, a formal register may be more appropriate. This may be characterized by complex sentences, impersonal language, and passive constructions (*Something must be done about this*), full-out words and phrases with no contractions or spoken elisions (*did not* rather than *didn't*), and Standard English grammar and vocabulary, with no dialect words or regionalisms. However, there are no clearly demarcated boundaries between formal and informal language, and words and usages may be considered to have varying degrees of formality: *require*, rather than *need*, may be considered

quite formal, but *dwell*, rather than *live*, perhaps even more so.

An informal register may be used between participants in a discourse who are very familiar with each other and/or are social peers. Informal language may be characterized by shorter sentences, active constructions, and personal references (*I'm going to do something about this*), abbreviations and contractions or spoken elisions ('*cause* rather than *because*), words and usages that are considered colloquial or non-Standard (*take off* rather than *leave*), and the usages of particular regions or social groups. Just as there can be degrees of formality, there can varying levels of informality. Slang, for instance, is very informal language, some of which may be specific to a particular social group and limited in its distribution. It is likely to be used only with people whom the speaker knows very well.

Registers determined by the field of discourse include the likes of religious, medical, and legal language, and some of these are abstruse enough to have gained names that suggest they are languages in their own right, eg *legalese* or *greenspeak* (the language of ecology). Such registers can involve the specialist language of a particular activity, known as *jargon*. The computing terms *shareware* and *open source*, and the legal terms *appellant* and *defeasance*, for example, can be considered jargon and therefore belonging to a particular register. As with relative formality, appropriateness also plays a part in when and where such registers are used. Those involved in a particular field will understand, and expect to hear, the specific language employed in it, whereas people outside that field might struggle to comprehend what is being said.

Given this need for appropriateness, a person may change register according to context and audience; a person who uses slang with friends could be capable of using formal or technical language with an employer. This shifting between registers is called *code-switching* in linguistics, with a *code* being either a language or a variety of it. Most people who employ code-switching can do so adeptly, sometimes without even being aware they are making skilful linguistic choices.

unwitting *adj* 1 not intentional 2 not knowing or conscious **unwittingly** *adv* **WORD ORIGIN** Old English *unwitende*

unwonted *adj* out of the ordinary; unusual

unworkable *adj* impractical and certain to fail: *unworkable proposals for reform*

unworldly *adj* 1 not concerned with material values or pursuits 2 lacking sophistication; naive

unworn *adj* 1 not having deteriorated through use or age 2 (of a garment) never having been worn

unworried *adj* not bothered or perturbed

unworthy *adj* 1 not deserving or meriting: *a person deemed unworthy of membership* 2 (often foll. by *of*) beneath the level considered befitting (to): *unworthy of a prime minister* 3 lacking merit or value **unworthiness** *n*

unwrap *vb* **-wrapping, -wrapped** to remove the wrapping from something or (of something wrapped) to have the covering removed

unwritten *adj* 1 not printed or in writing 2 operating only through custom: *an unwritten code of conduct*

unyielding *adj* remaining firm and determined

unzip *vb* **-zipping, -zipped** to unfasten the zip of a garment or (of a zip or a garment with a zip) to become unfastened

up *prep* 1 indicating movement to a higher position: *go up the stairs* 2 at a higher or further level or position in or on: *a shop up the road* ▷ *adv* 3 to an upward, higher, or erect position: *the men straightened up from their digging* 4 indicating readiness for an activity: *up and about* 5 indicating intensity or completion of an action: *he tore up the cheque* 6 to the place referred to or where the speaker is: *a man came up to me* 7 **a** to a more important place: *up to the city* **b** to a more northerly place: *pensioners who were going up to Norway* **c** to or at university 8 above the horizon: *the sun came up* 9 appearing for trial: *up before the judge* 10 having gained: *ten pounds up on the deal* 11 higher in price: *beer has gone up again* 12 **all up with someone** *informal* over for or hopeless for someone 13 **something's up** *informal* something strange is happening 14 **up against** having to cope with: *look what we're up against now* 15 **up for** being a candidate or applicant for: *he's up for the job* 16 **up to a** occupied with; scheming: *she's up to no good* **b** dependent upon: *the decision is up to you* **c** equal to or capable of: *are you up to playing in the final?* **d** as far as: *up to his neck in mud* **e** as many as: *up to two years' credit* **f** comparable with: *not up to my usual standard* 17 **what's up?** *informal* **a** what is the matter? **b** what is happening? ▷ *adj* 18 of a high or higher position 19 out of bed: *aren't you up yet?* 20 (of a period of time) over or completed: *the examiner announced that their time was up* 21 of or relating to a train operating to a more important place: *the up platform* ▷ *vb* **upping, upped** 22 to increase or raise 23 **up and** *informal* to do something suddenly: *he upped and left her* ▷ *n* 24 a high point: *when the ups come along you have to enjoy them* 25 **on the up and up a** *Brit* trustworthy or honest **b** *Brit, Austral, & NZ* on an upward trend: *our firm's on the up and up* **WORD ORIGIN** Old English *upp*

≣ **USAGE**
≣ The use of *up* before *until* is redundant
≣ and should be avoided: *the talks will*
≣ *continue until* (not *up until*) *March 23.*

up-and-coming *adj* likely to be successful in the future; promising

upbeat *adj* 1 *informal* cheerful and optimistic: *the upbeat atmosphere of a thriving metropolis* ▷ *n* 2 *music* **a** an unaccented beat **b** the upward gesture of a conductor's baton indicating this

upbraid *vb* to scold or reproach **WORD ORIGIN** Old English *upbrēdan*

upbringing *n* the education of a person during his or her formative years

upcoming *adj* coming soon: *the upcoming election*

upcountry *adj* 1 of or from the interior of a country ▷ *adv* 2 towards or in the interior of a country

update *vb* **-dating, -dated** 1 to bring up to date 2 inform; relay the most recent information to

upend *vb* to turn or set or become turned or set on end

upfront *adj* 1 open and frank 2 (of money) paid at the beginning of a business arrangement ▷ *adv* **up front** 3 at the front; (in sport) in attack: *Liverpool's strikers dominated up front* 4 at the beginning of a business arrangement; in advance: *we charge up front*

upgrade *vb* **-grading, -graded** 1 to promote a person or job to a higher rank 2 to raise in value, importance, or esteem

upheaval *n* a strong, sudden, or violent disturbance

uphill *adj* 1 sloping or leading upwards 2 requiring a great deal of effort: *an uphill struggle* ▷ *adv* 3 up a slope ▷ *n* 4 *S African* a difficulty

uphold *vb* **-holding, -held** 1 to maintain or defend against opposition 2 to give moral support to **upholder** *n*

upholster *vb* to fit chairs or sofas with padding, springs, and covering **upholstered** *adj* **upholsterer** *n*

upholstery *n* the padding, springs, and covering of a chair or sofa

upkeep *n* 1 the act or process of keeping something in good repair 2 the cost of maintenance

upland *adj* of or in an area of high or relatively high ground: *an upland wilderness*

uplands *pl n* an area of high or relatively high ground: *the uplands of Nepal*

uplift *vb* 1 to raise or lift up 2 to raise morally or spiritually 3 *Scot* to collect or pick up ▷ *n* 4 the act or process of bettering moral, social, or cultural conditions ▷ *adj* 5 (of a bra) designed to lift and support the breasts **uplifting** *adj*

upload *vb* to transfer (data or a program) from one computer's memory into that of another

upmarket *adj* expensive and of superior quality

upon *prep* 1 on 2 up and on: *they climbed upon his lap for comfort* **WORD ORIGIN** *up* + *on*

upper *adj* 1 higher or highest in physical position, wealth, rank, or status 2 **Upper** *geol* denoting the late part of a period or formation: *Upper Cretaceous* ▷ *n* 3 the part of a shoe above the sole 4 **on one's uppers** *Brit, Austral, & NZ* very poor; penniless

upper-case *adj* denoting capital letters as used in printed or typed matter

upper class *n* 1 the highest social class; aristocracy ▷ *adj* **upper-class** 2 of the upper class

upper crust *n* *Brit, Austral, & NZ informal* the upper class

uppercut *n* a short swinging upward punch delivered to the chin

upper hand *n* the position of control: *the hardliners have gained the upper hand*

Upper House *n* the smaller and less representative chamber of a two-chamber parliament, for example the House of Lords or a Senate

uppermost *adj* 1 highest in position, power, or importance ▷ *adv* 2 in or into the highest place or position

uppish *adj* *Brit informal* uppity

uppity *adj* *informal* snobbish, arrogant, or presumptuous **WORD ORIGIN** *up* + fanciful ending

upright *adj* 1 vertical or erect 2 honest or just ▷ *adv* 3 vertically or in an erect position ▷ *n* 4 a vertical support, such as a post 5 short for **upright piano** 6 the state of being vertical **uprightness** *n*

upright piano *n* a piano which has a rectangular vertical case

uprising *n* a revolt or rebellion

up-river *adj, adv* nearer the source of a river: *we sailed slowly up-river; the village of Juffure, four days up-river*

uproar *n* 1 a commotion or disturbance characterized by loud noise and confusion 2 angry public criticism or debates: *the decision to close the railway led to an uproar*

uproarious *adj* 1 very funny 2 (of laughter) loud and boisterous

uproot *vb* 1 to pull up by or as if by the roots 2 to displace (a person or people) from their native or usual surroundings 3 to remove or destroy utterly: *we must uproot all remnants of feudalism*

ups and downs *pl n* alternating periods of good and bad luck or high and low spirits

upscale *informal adj* (**up-**skale) 1 of or for the upper end of an economic or social scale; upmarket ▷ *vb* (up-**skale**), **-scaling, -scaled** 2 to increase the scale of

upset *adj* 1 emotionally or physically disturbed or distressed ▷ *vb* **-setting, -set** 2 to turn or tip over 3 to disrupt the normal state or progress of: *bad weather upset their plans* 4 to disturb mentally or emotionally 5 to make physically ill: *it still seems to upset my stomach* ▷ *n* 6 an unexpected defeat or reversal, as in a contest or plans

7 a disturbance or disorder of the emotions, mind, or body **upsetting** adj

upset price n chiefly Scot, US, & Canad the lowest price acceptable for something that is for sale by auction, usually a house

upshot n the final result or conclusion; outcome **WORD ORIGIN** up + shot

upside down adj **1** with the bottom where the top would normally be; inverted **2** informal confused or jumbled ▷ adv **3** in an inverted fashion **4** in a chaotic manner or into a chaotic state: recent events have turned many people's lives upside down **WORD ORIGIN** by folk etymology, from upsodown

upsides adv informal chiefly Brit (foll. by with) equal or level with, as through revenge

upstage adv **1** on, at, or to the rear of the stage ▷ adj **2** at the back half of the stage ▷ vb **-staging, -staged 3** to move upstage of another actor, forcing him or her to turn away from the audience **4** informal to draw attention to oneself and away from someone else

upstairs adv **1** to or on an upper floor of a building **2** informal to or into a higher rank or office ▷ n **3** an upper floor ▷ adj **4** situated on an upper floor: an upstairs bedroom

upstanding adj **1** of good character **2** upright and vigorous in build

upstart n a person who has risen suddenly to a position of power and behaves arrogantly

upstream adv, adj in or towards the higher part of a stream; against the current

upsurge n a rapid rise or swell

upswing n **1** econ a recovery period in the trade cycle **2** any increase or improvement

upsy-daisy or **upsadaisy** interj an expression of reassurance, usually used to a child, eg when it stumbles or is being lifted up **WORD ORIGIN** originally up-a-daisy

uptake n **1** quick or slow on the uptake informal quick or slow to understand or learn **2** the use or consumption of something by a machine or part of the body: the uptake of oxygen into the blood

upthrust n **1** an upward push **2** geol a violent upheaval of the earth's surface

uptight adj informal **1** nervously tense, irritable, or angry **2** unable to express one's feelings

up-to-date adj modern or fashionable: an up-to-date kitchen

up-to-the-minute adj the latest or most modern possible: up-to-the-minute news about what's on in town

uptown US & Canad adj, adv **1** towards, in, or relating to some part of a town that is away from the centre ▷ n **2** such a part of town, esp. a residential part

upturn n **1** an upward trend or improvement ▷ vb **2** to turn or cause to turn over or upside down

UPVC unplasticized polyvinyl chloride

upward adj **1** directed or moving towards a higher place or level ▷ adv also

upwards 2 from a lower to a higher place, level, or condition **3 upward** or **upwards of** more than (the stated figure): a crowd estimated at upward of one hundred thousand people

upward mobility n movement from a lower to a higher economic and social status

upwind adv **1** into or against the wind **2** towards or on the side where the wind is blowing ▷ adj **3** going against the wind **4** on the windward side

Urania n Greek myth the Muse of astronomy

uranium (yew-**rain**-ee-um) n chem a radioactive silvery-white metallic element of the actinide series. It is used chiefly as a source of nuclear energy by fission of the radioisotope **uranium 235.** Symbol: U **WORD ORIGIN** from Uranus, from the fact that the element was discovered soon after the planet

Uranus n **1** Greek myth a god; the personification of the sky **2** the seventh planet from the sun **WORD ORIGIN** Greek Ouranos heaven

urban adj **1** of or living in a city or town **2** relating to modern pop music of African-American origin, such as hip-hop **WORD ORIGIN** Latin urbs city

urbane adj polite, elegant, and sophisticated in manner **WORD ORIGIN** Latin urbanus of the town

urbanity n the quality of being urbane

urbanize or **-nise** vb **-nizing, -nized** or **-nising, -nised** to make a rural area more industrialized and urban **urbanization** or **-nisation** n

urchin n **1** a mischievous child **2** see **sea urchin** **WORD ORIGIN** Latin ericius hedgehog

Urdu (**oor**-doo) n an Indic language of the Indo-European family which is an official language of Pakistan and is also spoken in India **WORD ORIGIN** Hindustani (zabāni) urdū (language of the) camp

urea (**yew**-ree-a) n a white soluble crystalline compound found in urine **WORD ORIGIN** Greek ouron urine

ureter (yew-**reet**-er) n the tube that carries urine from the kidney to the bladder **WORD ORIGIN** Greek ourein to urinate

urethra (yew-**reeth**-ra) n the tube that in most mammals carries urine from the bladder out of the body **WORD ORIGIN** Greek ourein to urinate

urethritis (yew-rith-**rite**-iss) n inflammation of the urethra causing a discharge and painful urination **urethritic** adj

urge n **1** a strong impulse, inner drive, or yearning ▷ vb **urging, urged 2** to plead with or press someone to do something: he urged his readers to do the same **3** to advocate earnestly and persistently: I have long urged this change **4** (often foll. by on) to force or hasten onwards: something very powerful urged him on **WORD ORIGIN** Latin urgere

urgent adj **1** requiring speedy action or attention: an urgent inquiry **2** earnest and

forceful: she heard loud urgent voices in the corridor **urgency** n **urgently** adv **WORD ORIGIN** Latin urgere to urge

uric (**yew**-rik) adj of or derived from urine

uric acid n a white odourless crystalline acid present in the blood and urine

urinal n **1** a sanitary fitting, used by men for urination **2** a room containing urinals

urinary adj anat of urine or the organs that secrete and pass urine

urinary bladder n a membranous sac that can expand in which urine excreted from the kidneys is stored

urinate vb **-nating, -nated** to excrete urine **urination** n

urine n the pale yellow fluid excreted by the kidneys, containing waste products from the blood. It is stored in the bladder and discharged through the urethra **WORD ORIGIN** Latin urina

urinogenital (yew-rin-oh-**jen**-it-al) adj same as **urogenital**

URL uniform resource locator: a standardized address of a location on the internet

urn n **1** a vaselike container, usually with a foot and a rounded body **2** a vase used as a container for the ashes of the dead **3** a large metal container, with a tap, used for making and holding tea or coffee **WORD ORIGIN** Latin urna

urogenital (yew-roh-**jen**-it-al) or **urinogenital** adj of the urinary and genital organs and their functions. Also: **genitourinary**

urology (yew-**rol**-a-jee) n the branch of medicine concerned with the urinary system and its diseases

ursine adj of or like a bear **WORD ORIGIN** Latin ursus a bear

us pron (objective) **1** refers to the speaker or writer and another person or other people: the bond between us **2** refers to all people or people in general: this table shows us the tides **3** informal me: give us a kiss! **4** formal same as **me**: used by monarchs **WORD ORIGIN** Old English ūs ☰ **USAGE** ☰ See at **me**.

US or **U.S.** United States

USA or **U.S.A.** United States of America

usable adj able to be used **usability** n

usage n **1** regular or constant use: a move to reduce pesticide usage **2** the way in which a word is actually used in a language **3** a particular meaning or use that a word can have **WORD ORIGIN** Latin usus a use

USB Universal Serial Bus: a standard for connection sockets on computers and other electronic equipment

USB drive n computers a small portable data storage device with a USB connection

use vb **using, used 1** to put into service or action; employ for a given purpose: use a garden fork to mix them together **2** to choose or employ regularly: what sort of toothpaste do you use? **3** to take advantage

of; exploit: *I used Jason and he used me*
4 to consume or expend: *a manufacturing plant uses 1000 tonnes of steel a month* ▷ *n* **5** the act or fact of using or being used: *large-scale use of pesticides* **6** the ability or permission to use **7** need or opportunity to use: *the Colombian government had no use for them* **8** usefulness or advantage: *there is no use in complaining* **9** the purpose for which something is used **10 have no use for a** to have no need of **b** to have a contemptuous dislike for **11 make use of a** to employ; use **b** to exploit (a person) ▸ See also **use up** ▷ **user** *n*
WORD ORIGIN Latin *usus* having used

use-by date *n* the date on packaged food after which it should not be sold

used *adj* second-hand: *it was a used car*

used to *adj* **1** accustomed to: *I am used to being a medical guinea pig* ▷ *vb* **2** used as an auxiliary to express habitual or accustomed actions or states taking place in the past but not continuing to be the case in the present: *he used to vanish into his studio for days*

≡ **USAGE**
≡ The most common negative form of
≡ *used to* is *didn't used to* (or *didn't use to*),
≡ but in formal contexts *used not to* is
≡ preferred.

useful *adj* **1** able to be used advantageously or for several purposes **2** *informal* commendable or capable: *a useful hurdler* **usefully** *adv* **usefulness** *n*

useless *adj* **1** having no practical use **2** *informal* ineffectual, weak, or stupid: *I'm useless at most things* **uselessly** *adv* **uselessness** *n*

Usenet *n computers* a vast collection of newsgroups that follow agreed naming, maintaining, and distribution practices

user-friendly *adj* easy to familiarize oneself with, understand, and use

username *n computers* a name that someone uses for identification purposes when logging onto a computer or certain computer applications

use up *vb* to finish a supply of something completely

U-shaped valley *n* a steep-sided valley caused by glacial erosion

usher *n* **1** an official who shows people to their seats, as in a church **2** a person who acts as doorkeeper in a court of law ▷ *vb* **3** to conduct or escort **4** (foll. by *in*) to happen immediately before something or cause it to happen; herald: *the French Revolution ushered in a new age*

WORD ORIGIN Old French *huissier* doorkeeper

usherette *n* a woman assistant in a cinema, who shows people to their seats

USP *marketing* unique selling proposition (or point)

USSR Union of Soviet Socialist Republics: a former state in E Europe and N Asia, covering the area now composed of Russia, Ukraine, Kazakhstan and a number of smaller states

usual *adj* **1** of the most normal, frequent, or regular type: *the usual assortment of stories* ▷ *n* **2** ordinary or commonplace events: *the dirt was nothing out of the usual* **3 as usual** as happens normally **4 the usual** *informal* the habitual or usual drink **usually** *adv*

WORD ORIGIN Latin *usus* use

usurp (yewz-**zurp**) *vb* to seize a position or power without authority **usurpation** *n* **usurper** *n*

WORD ORIGIN Latin *usurpare* to take into use

usury (**yewz**-yoor-ree) *n, pl* **-ries** *old-fashioned* **1** the practice of loaning money at an exorbitant rate of interest **2** an unlawfully high rate of interest **usurer** *n*

WORD ORIGIN Latin *usura* usage

UT Utah

ute *n Austral & NZ informal* a utility truck

utensil *n* a tool or container for practical use: *cooking utensils*

WORD ORIGIN Latin *utensilia* necessaries

uterine *adj* of or affecting the womb

uterus (**yew**-ter-russ) *n, pl* **uteri** (**yew**-ter-rye) *anat* a hollow muscular organ in the pelvic cavity of female mammals, which houses the developing fetus; womb

WORD ORIGIN Latin

utilidor (yew-**till**-lid-or) *n Canad* above-ground insulated casing for pipes carrying water, sewerage and electricity in permafrost regions

WORD ORIGIN utility + -dor, from Greek *dōron* gift

utilitarian *adj* **1** useful rather than beautiful **2** of utilitarianism ▷ *n* **3** an advocate of utilitarianism

utilitarianism *n ethics* the doctrine that the right thing to do is that which brings about the greatest good for the greatest number

utility *n, pl* **-ties** **1** usefulness **2** something useful **3** a public service,

such as water or electricity ▷ *adj* **4** designed for use rather than beauty: *utility fabrics*

WORD ORIGIN Latin *utilitas* usefulness, from *uti* to use

utility room *n* a room with equipment for domestic work like washing and ironing

utility truck *n Austral & NZ* a small truck with an open body and low sides

utilize *or* **-lise** *vb* **-lizing, -lized** *or* **-lising, -lised** to make practical or worthwhile use of **utilization** *or* **-lisation** *n*

utmost *adj* **1** of the greatest possible degree or amount: *the utmost seriousness* **2** at the furthest limit: *the utmost point* ▷ *n* **3** the greatest possible degree or amount: *I was doing my utmost to comply*

WORD ORIGIN Old English *ūtemest*

Utopia (yew-**tope**-ee-a) *n* any real or imaginary society, place, or state considered to be perfect or ideal **Utopian** *adj*

WORD ORIGIN coined by Sir Thomas More in 1516 as the title of his book that described an imaginary island representing the perfect society, literally: no place, from Greek *ou* not + *topos* a place

utter¹ *vb* **1** to express something in sounds or words: *she hadn't uttered a single word* **2** *criminal law* to put counterfeit money or forged cheques into circulation

WORD ORIGIN Middle Dutch *ūteren* to make known

utter² *adj* total or absolute: *utter amazement* **utterly** *adv*

WORD ORIGIN Old English *ūtera* outer

utterance *n* **1** something expressed in speech or writing **2** the expression in words of ideas, thoughts, or feelings

uttermost *adj, n* same as **utmost**

U-turn *n* **1** a turn, made by a vehicle, in the shape of a U, resulting in a reversal of direction **2** a complete change in policy

UV ultraviolet

UV-A *or* **UVA** *n* ultraviolet radiation with a range of 320-380 nanometres

UV-B *or* **UVB** *n* ultraviolet radiation with a range of 280-320 nanometres

uvula (**yew**-view-la) *n* the small fleshy part of the soft palate that hangs in the back of the throat **uvular** *adj*

WORD ORIGIN Medieval Latin, literally: a little grape

uxorious (ux-or-ee-uss) *adj* excessively fond of or dependent on one's wife

WORD ORIGIN Latin *uxor* wife

u

Common Spelling Errors

English spelling can sometimes seem to be a chaotic affair. The spellings of words such as *choir*, *colonel*, *laugh*, and *yacht* bear such little relation to the way that words are pronounced in spoken English that learners are likely to throw up their hands in despair.

Part of the trouble is that there is a mismatch between the number of letters in the alphabet (26) and the number of sounds in the language (generally reckoned to be about 44). If every letter represented one sound and one sound only, you could write out words very easily once you knew which letter represented which sound. Some languages (such as Italian) are quite like this, and present few surprises with regard to spelling once you know how each sound is written.

But in English the same letter can have several different sounds, and the same sound can be represented by several sets of different letters. The vowel sound in *cart*, *palm*, *clerk*, and *heart* is written differently in each of the four words. You simply have to know which word uses which pattern of letters.

Most native speakers of English learn how to navigate such spelling oddities at an early stage, but few native speakers become infallible. Certain features of English spelling are particularly apt to trip up writers.

It is quite common, for example, for a writer to be foxed by the fact that two words sound alike but have different spellings and to write *there* instead of *their*, or *hear* instead of *here*. Among the pairs that are most liable to be confused are *complement* and *compliment*, *currant* and *current*, *desert* and *dessert*, and *principle* and *principal*. This type of error is particularly likely to slip past a computer's spellchecker as the computer can't guess which of the two words the writer meant to use.

Another common spelling problem is caused by words which might plausibly be spelt using a single or double letter. Words such as *committee*, *necessary*, and *broccoli* present a real problem from this point of view, as there is more than one place where the writer needs to decide whether a single or double letter is required.

Then there are the words that contain silent letters. Who would imagine *indict* would be spelt with a 'c' or *diaphragm* with a 'g'? Often these silent letters were sounded in the original form of a word, and have remained in the written form of the word after the pronunciation has been simplified. But knowing that is not likely to help someone trying to spell *excerpt* or *abscess* for the first time.

Finally, English spellers have to deal with any number of words that are borrowed from other languages and preserve the original language's spelling system, which may use letters to make sounds that they would never make in natural English words. So the spellings of originally French words such as *chalet*, *rendezvous*, and *manoeuvre* are almost impossible to guess for someone who is only familiar with English spelling rules.

All of these factors can make English words tricky to spell. Precisely because they are common sources of error, however, careful spellers will be on the lookout for them. If people know that a word is hard they may take the trouble to memorize its spelling. They may even use some sort of mnemonic to help remember it (such as thinking that 'a committee should have as many members as possible' to help you to remember to use two sets of double consonants in *committee*).

Some of the most frequently misspelt words are not, in fact, the ones that present especially unusual combinations of letters, but ones that lull writers into a false sense of security. A writer may naturally assume that *liquefy* is spelt like *liquid*, and use an 'i' instead of an 'e'. There is an obvious tendency to assume that *minuscule* begins with the prefix *mini-*, since it refers to things of small size. We get used to words that end in *-cede*, such as *concede*, *recede*, *precede*, and *intercede*, so why would it occur to us that *supersede* would not follow the same pattern? On such occasions, you might be better off not knowing so much if you want to stay out of the trap.

Vv

The letter V is the twenty-second letter of the English alphabet. In the Roman alphabet U and V were different forms of the same letter, which was used as both a vowel and a consonant. The pointed form of the letter was used in inscriptions and at the start of words. By the sixteenth century this form came to be used exclusively as a consonant, while the rounded form was used as a vowel. Both forms were derived from the Greek letter *upsilon* (Y,υ).

During World War II, the letter V became a totemic letter for the Allies. The slogan of 'V for Victory' was popularized, and the Morse code signal for this letter (three dots followed by a dash) was incorporated into the BBC's propaganda broadcasts to occupied countries of Europe. Winston Churchill also did his bit for the letter with his trademark 'V-sign' salute, made by extending two fingers from the fist with the palm facing out. (The same sign made with palm facing inwards is a notable gesture of contempt, which one story traces to medieval English archers taunting their French foes by demonstrating their undiminished ability to draw the string of a bow.)

The letter V did not have uniformly happy associations for the Allies, however. The V_1 and V_2 were rockets trained against the south of England from Germany. The letter V in the names of these weapons here represents the German word *Vergeltungswaffe*, which means 'weapon of retaliation'.

The letter V is also associated with several things that resemble the letter in shape. A 'V-neck' on a sweater requires no explanation, while the cylinders of an engine can be described as, for example, V8 or V_{12} if they are arranged in two rows set at an acute angle to each other in the manner of a letter V.

The practice of using V to represent the number five in Roman numerals can also be attributed to the simplicity of its shape, which made it a suitable character for marking on wood. When tallies were being kept a single stroke represented one unit, but as the size of a tally increased it became useful to mark every fifth unit with an extra mark so that the total could be easily reckoned. Thus a mark with two strokes at an acute angle came to represent the number five.

V **1** *chem* vanadium **2** volt **3** the Roman numeral for five

V. **1** verb **2** verse **3** versus **4** volume

VA Virginia

vac *n* *Brit informal* short for **vacation**

vacancy *n, pl* **-cies** **1** an unoccupied job or position: *he had heard of a vacancy for a librarian* **2** an unoccupied room in a hotel or guesthouse: *the last hotel we tried had a vacancy* **3** the state of being unoccupied

vacant *adj* **1** (of a toilet, room, etc.) unoccupied or not being used: *I sat down in a vacant chair* **2** (of a job or position) unfilled at the present time **3** having or suggesting a lack of interest or understanding: *he sat there staring at me with a vacant look* **4** (of a period of time) not set aside for any particular activity: *two slots in his programme have been left vacant* **vacantly** *adv*
    WORD ORIGIN Latin *vacare* to be empty

vacate *vb* **-cating, -cated** **1** to cause (something) to be empty by leaving: *do you wish us to vacate the room?* **2** to give up (a job or position)

vacation *n* **1** *Brit & S African* a time of the year when the universities or law courts are closed **2** *US, Canad, & Austral* same as **holiday** (sense 2)
    WORD ORIGIN Latin *vacatio* freedom

vaccinate *vb* **-nating, -nated** to inject (someone) with a vaccine in order to protect them against a disease: *children vaccinated against meningitis* **vaccination** *n*

vaccine *n* **1** *med* a substance made from the germs that cause a disease which is given to people to prevent them getting the disease **2** *computers* a piece of software that detects and removes computer viruses from a system
    WORD ORIGIN Latin *variolae vaccinae* cowpox (source of the first smallpox vaccine), from *vacca* a cow

vacillate (**vass**-ill-late) *vb* **-lating, -lated** to keep changing one's mind or opinions about something: *he vacillated between republican and monarchist sentiments* **vacillation** *n*
    WORD ORIGIN Latin *vacillare* to sway

vacuity *n* an absence of intelligent thought or ideas: *I suggested to one of his advisers that his vacuity was a handicap in these debates*

vacuous *adj* **1** lacking in intelligent ideas **2** showing no sign of intelligence or understanding: *her smile was vacuous but without malice*
    WORD ORIGIN Latin *vacuus* empty

vacuum *n, pl* **vacuums** *or* **vacua** **1** a space which contains no air or other gas **2** a vacant place or position that needs to be filled by someone or something else: *the army moved in to fill the power vacuum* **3** short for **vacuum cleaner** ▷ *vb* **4** to clean (something) with a vacuum cleaner
    WORD ORIGIN Latin *vacuus* empty

vacuum cleaner *n* an electric machine which sucks up dust and dirt from carpets and upholstery **vacuum cleaning** *n*

vacuum flask *n* a double-walled flask with a vacuum between the walls that keeps drinks hot or cold

vacuum-packed *adj* (of food) packed in an airtight container in order to preserve freshness

vacuum tube *or* **valve** *n* same as **valve** (sense 3)

vade mecum (**vah**-dee **make**-um) *n* a handbook carried for immediate use when needed
    WORD ORIGIN Latin, literally: go with me

vagabond *n* a person who travels from place to place and has no fixed home or job
    WORD ORIGIN Latin *vagari* to roam

vagary (**vaig**-a-ree) *n, pl* **-garies** an unpredictable change in a situation or in someone's behaviour: *I was unused to the vagaries of the retailer's world*
    WORD ORIGIN probably from Latin *vagari* to roam

V

vagina (vaj-**jine**-a) *n* the passage in most female mammals that extends from the neck of the womb to the external genitals **vaginal** *adj*
WORD ORIGIN Latin: sheath

vagrant (**vaig**-rant) *n* **1** a person who moves from place to place and has no regular home or job ▷ *adj* **2** wandering about **vagrancy** *n*
WORD ORIGIN probably from Old French *waucrant*

vague *adj* **1** not expressed or explained clearly: *he thought of his instructions, so vague and imprecise* **2** deliberately withholding information: *he was rather vague about the whole deal* **3** (of a sound or shape) unable to be heard or seen clearly: *he heard some vague sound from downstairs* **4** (of a person) not concentrating or thinking clearly: *she was mumbling to herself in a vague way* **5** not clearly established or known: *it was a vague rumour which would fade away and be forgotten* **vaguely** *adv* **vagueness** *n*
WORD ORIGIN Latin *vagus* wandering

vain *adj* **1** excessively proud of one's appearance or achievements **2** senseless or unsuccessful: *he made a vain attempt to lighten the atmosphere* ▷ *n* **3 in vain** without achieving the desired effects or results: *the old man searched in vain for his son* **vainly** *adv*
WORD ORIGIN Latin *vanus*

vainglorious *adj* boastful or proud: *his vainglorious posturing had earned him numerous powerful enemies*

valance (**val**-lenss) *n* a short piece of decorative material hung round the edge of a bed or above a window
WORD ORIGIN perhaps after *Valence* in SE France

vale *n* *literary* a valley
WORD ORIGIN Latin *vallis* valley

valediction (val-lid-**dik**-shun) *n* a farewell speech **valedictory** *adj*
WORD ORIGIN Latin *vale* farewell + *dicere* to say

valence (**vale**-enss) *n* *chem* the ability of atoms and chemical groups to form compounds

valency *or esp. US & Canad* **valence** *n, pl* -cies *or* -ces *chem* the number of atoms of hydrogen that an atom or chemical group is able to combine with in forming compounds
WORD ORIGIN Latin *valere* to be strong

valentine *n* **1** a card sent, often anonymously, as an expression of love on Saint Valentine's Day, February 14 **2** the person to whom one sends such a card
WORD ORIGIN after Saint *Valentine*

valerian *n* a plant with small white or pinkish flowers and a medicinal root
WORD ORIGIN Medieval Latin *valeriana (herba)* (herb) of Valerius

valet *n* **1** a male servant employed to look after another man ▷ *vb* **-eting, -eted 2** to act as a valet (for) **3** to clean the bodywork and interior of (a car) as a professional service
WORD ORIGIN Old French *vaslet* page

valeta *or* **veleta** (vel-**lee**-ta) *n* an old-time dance in triple time
WORD ORIGIN Spanish *veleta* weather vane

valetudinarian (val-lit-yew-din-**air**-ee-an) *n* **1** a person who is chronically sick **2** a person who continually worries about his or her health **valetudinarianism** *n*
WORD ORIGIN Latin *valetudo* state of health

Valhalla *n* *Norse myth* the great hall of Odin where warriors who die as heroes in battle dwell eternally
WORD ORIGIN Old Norse *valr* slain warriors + *höll* hall

valiant *adj* very brave: *it was a valiant attempt to rescue the struggling victim* **valiantly** *adv*
WORD ORIGIN Latin *valere* to be strong

valid *adj* **1** based on sound reasoning: *I think that's a very valid question* **2** legally acceptable: *she must produce a valid driving licence* **3** important or serious enough to say or do: *religious broadcasting has a valid purpose* **validity** *n*
WORD ORIGIN Latin *validus* robust

validate *vb* **-dating, -dated 1** to prove (a claim or statement) to be true or correct **2** to give legal force or official confirmation to **validation** *n*

valise (val-**leez**) *n* *old-fashioned* a small suitcase
WORD ORIGIN Italian *valigia*

Valium *n trademark* a drug used as a tranquillizer

Valkyrie (**val**-keer-ee) *n* *Norse myth* any of the beautiful maidens who take the dead heroes to Valhalla
WORD ORIGIN Old Norse *valr* slain warriors + *kyrja* chooser

valley *n* a long stretch of land between hills, often with a river flowing through it
WORD ORIGIN Latin *vallis*

valour *or US* **valor** *n literary* great bravery, esp. in battle **valorous** *adj*
WORD ORIGIN Latin *valere* to be strong

valuable *adj* **1** worth a large amount of money: *his house was furnished with valuable antique furniture* **2** of great use or importance: *the investigations will provide valuable information* ▷ *n* **3 valuables** valuable articles of personal property, such as jewellery

valuation *n* **1** a formal assessment of how much something is worth: *they will arrange a valuation on your house* **2** the price arrived at by the process of valuing

value *n* **1** the desirability of something, often in terms of its usefulness or exchangeability **2** an amount of money considered to be a fair exchange for something: *50 kilos of cocaine with a high street value* **3** something worth the money it cost: *the set meal was value for money* **4 values** the moral principles and beliefs of a person or group **5** *maths* a particular number or quantity represented by a figure or symbol **6** *music* short for **time value** ▷ *vb* **-uing, -ued 7** to assess the worth or desirability of (something) **8** to hold (someone or something) in high regard **valued** *adj* **valueless** *adj* **valuer** *n*
WORD ORIGIN Latin *valere* to be worth

value-added tax *n* *Brit & S African* see **VAT**

value judgment *n* a personal opinion about something based on an

individual's beliefs and not on facts which can be checked or proved

valve *n* **1** a part attached to a pipe or tube which controls the flow of gas or liquid **2** *anat* a small flap in a hollow organ, such as the heart, that controls the flow and direction of blood **3** a closed tube through which electrons move in a vacuum **4** *zool* one of the hinged shells of an oyster or clam **5** *music* a device on some brass instruments by which the effective length of the tube may be varied
WORD ORIGIN Latin *valva* a folding door

valvular *adj* of or relating to valves: *valvular heart disease*

vamoose *vb* **-moosing, -moosed** *slang chiefly US* to leave a place hurriedly
WORD ORIGIN Spanish *vamos* let's go

vamp[1] *informal n* **1** a sexually attractive woman who seduces men ▷ *vb* **2** (of a woman) to seduce (a man)
WORD ORIGIN short for *vampire*

vamp[2] *vb* **vamp up** to make (a story, piece of music, etc.) seem new by inventing additional parts
WORD ORIGIN Old French *avantpié* the front part of a shoe

vampire *n* (in European folklore) a corpse that rises nightly from its grave to drink the blood of living people
WORD ORIGIN from Magyar

vampire bat *n* a bat of Central and South America that feeds on the blood of birds and mammals

van[1] *n* **1** a road vehicle with a roof and no side windows used to transport goods **2** *Brit* a closed railway wagon used to transport luggage, goods, or mail
WORD ORIGIN shortened from *caravan*

van[2] *n* short for **vanguard**

vanadium *n chem* a silvery-white metallic element used to toughen steel. Symbol: V
WORD ORIGIN Old Norse *Vanadís*, epithet of the goddess Freya

Van Allen belt *n* either of two belts of charged particles which surround the Earth
WORD ORIGIN after J. A. *Van Allen*, physicist

vandal *n* someone who deliberately causes damage to personal or public property **vandalism** *n*
WORD ORIGIN from the name of a Germanic tribe of the 3rd and 4th centuries AD

vandalize *or* **-lise** *vb* **-lizing, -lized** *or* **-lising, -lised** to cause damage to (personal or public property) deliberately

Van der Hum *n S African* a liqueur made from tangerines
WORD ORIGIN origin uncertain but possibly derived from the humorous uncertainty of the name, equivalent of *whatshisname*

Vandyke beard *n* a short pointed beard
WORD ORIGIN after Sir Anthony *Van Dyck*, Flemish painter

vane *n* **1** one of the blades forming part of the wheel of a windmill, a screw propeller, etc. **2** short for **weather vane**
WORD ORIGIN Old English *fana*

V

vanguard n **1** the leading division or units of an army **2** the most advanced group or position in scientific research, a movement, etc.: *a distinguished architect in the vanguard of his profession* **WORD ORIGIN** Old French *avant-garde* advance guard

vanilla n **1** a flavouring for food such as ice cream, which comes from the pods of a tropical plant **2** a flavouring extract prepared from the beans of this plant and used in cooking ▷ *adj* **3** flavoured with vanilla: *vanilla essence* **4** *slang* ordinary or conventional: *a vanilla kind of guy* **WORD ORIGIN** Spanish *vainilla* pod

vanish vb **1** to disappear suddenly: *the choppers vanished from radar screens at dawn yesterday* **2** to cease to exist: *the old landmarks had vanished* **WORD ORIGIN** Latin *evanescere* to evaporate

vanishing cream n *old-fashioned* a cosmetic cream that is colourless once applied

vanishing point n the point in the distance where parallel lines appear to meet

vanity n **1** a feeling of pride about one's appearance or ability **2** pl **-ties** something about which one is vain: *it's one of my vanities that I can guess scents* **WORD ORIGIN** Latin *vanitas* emptiness

vanity case n a small bag for holding cosmetics

vanity unit n a hand basin built into a surface, usually with a cupboard below it

vanquish vb *literary* to defeat (someone) in a battle, contest, or argument **WORD ORIGIN** Latin *vincere*

vantage n a state, position, or opportunity offering advantage **WORD ORIGIN** Old French *avantage* advantage

vantage point n a position that gives one an overall view of a scene or situation

vapid adj dull and uninteresting: *their publications were vapid and amateurish* **vapidity** n **WORD ORIGIN** Latin *vapidus*

vapor n US same as **vapour**

vaporize or **-rise** vb **-rizing, -rized** or **-rising, -rised** (of a liquid or solid) to change into vapour **vaporization** or **-risation** n

vaporous adj resembling or full of vapour

vapour or US **vapor** n **1** a mass of tiny drops of water or other liquids in the air, which appear as a mist **2** the gaseous form of a substance that is usually a liquid or a solid **3** **the vapours** *old-fashioned* a feeling of faintness, dizziness, and depression **WORD ORIGIN** Latin *vapor*

variable adj **1** likely to change at any time: *variable weather* **2** *maths* having a range of possible values ▷ *n* **3** something that is subject to variation **4** *maths* an expression that can be assigned any of a set of values **variability** n **variably** adv **WORD ORIGIN** Latin *variare* to diversify

variance n **at variance** not in agreement: *the real record is at variance with the public record*

variant adj **1** differing from a standard or type: *variant spellings* ▷ *n* **2** something that differs from a standard or type

variation n **1** something presented in a slightly different form: *his books are all variations on a basic theme* **2** a change in level, amount, or quantity: *there was a variation in the figures* **3** *music* the repetition of a simple tune with the addition of new harmonies or a change in rhythm: *Variations on a Hussar's Song*

varicoloured or US **varicolored** adj having many colours

varicose adj of or resulting from varicose veins: *a varicose ulcer* **WORD ORIGIN** Latin *varix* a swollen vein

varicose veins pl n veins, usually in the legs, which have become knotted, swollen, and sometimes painful

varied adj of different types, sizes, or quantities: *these young men and women would be of varied backgrounds*

variegated adj having patches or streaks of different colours: *variegated holly* **variegation** n

variety n, pl **-ties 1** the state of being diverse or various **2** different things of the same kind: *I'm cooking the mince with a variety of vegetables* **3** a particular type of something in the same general category: *this variety of pear is extremely juicy* **4** *taxonomy* a race whose distinct characters do not justify classification as a separate species **5** a type of entertainment consisting of short unrelated acts, such as singing, dancing, and comedy **WORD ORIGIN** Latin *varietas*

varifocal adj of a lens that is gradated to permit any length of vision between near and distant

varifocals pl n a pair of spectacles with varifocal lenses

various adj **1** several different: *there are various possible answers to this question* **2** of different kinds: *the causes of high blood pressure are various and complicated* **variously** adv **WORD ORIGIN** Latin *varius* changing

≡ USAGE
≡ The use of *different* after *various* should
≡ be avoided: *the disease exists in various*
≡ *forms* (not in *various different forms*).

varlet n *old-fashioned* **1** a menial servant **2** a rascal **WORD ORIGIN** Old French *vaslet*

varmint n *informal* an irritating or obnoxious person or animal **WORD ORIGIN** dialect variant of *varmin* vermin

varnish n **1** a liquid painted onto a surface to give it a hard glossy finish **2** a smooth surface, coated with or as if with varnish **3** an artificial, superficial, or deceptively pleasing manner or appearance: *those who aspired to become civil servants acquired a varnish of university education* **4** *chiefly Brit* short for **nail varnish** ▷ *vb* **5** to apply varnish to **6** to try to make (something unpleasant) appear more attractive: *when did we start equivocating, camouflaging, varnishing the truth?* **WORD ORIGIN** Old French *vernis*

varsity n, pl **-ties** *old-fashioned & informal* short for **university**

vary vb **varies, varying, varied 1** to change in appearance, character, or form **2** to be different or cause to be different: *the age of appearance of underarm and body hair varies greatly from person to person* **3** to give variety to: *you can vary the type of exercise you do* **4** to change in accordance with another variable: *an individual's calorie requirement varies with age, sex, and physical activity* **varying** adj **WORD ORIGIN** Latin *varius* changing

vas n, pl **vasa** *anat, zool* a vessel or tube that carries a fluid **WORD ORIGIN** Latin: vessel

vascular adj *biol, anat* of or relating to the vessels that conduct and circulate body fluids such as blood or sap **WORD ORIGIN** Latin *vas* vessel

vas deferens n, pl **vasa deferentia** *anat* either of the two ducts that convey sperm from the testicles to the penis **WORD ORIGIN** Latin *vas* vessel + *deferens* carrying away

vase n a glass or pottery jar used as an ornament or for holding cut flowers **WORD ORIGIN** Latin *vas* vessel

vasectomy n, pl **-mies** surgical removal of all or part of the vas deferens as a method of contraception **WORD ORIGIN** VAS + Greek *tomē* a cutting

Vaseline n *trademark* petroleum jelly, used as an ointment or a lubricant

vassal n **1** (in feudal society) a man who gave military service to a lord in return for protection and often land **2** a person, nation, or state dominated by another **vassalage** n **WORD ORIGIN** Medieval Latin *vassus* servant

vast adj unusually large in size, degree, or number **vastly** adv **vastness** n **WORD ORIGIN** Latin *vastus* deserted

vat n a large container for holding or storing liquids **WORD ORIGIN** Old English *fæt*

VAT (in Britain and S Africa) value-added tax: a tax levied on the difference between the cost of materials and the selling price of a commodity or service

Vatican n **1** the Pope's palace, in Rome **2** the authority of the Pope **WORD ORIGIN** Latin *Vaticanus (mons)* Vatican (hill)

vaudeville n variety entertainment consisting of short acts such as song-and-dance routines and comic turns **WORD ORIGIN** French

vault¹ n **1** a secure room where money and other valuables are stored safely **2** an underground burial chamber **3** an arched structure that forms a roof or ceiling **4** a cellar for storing wine **WORD ORIGIN** Old French *voute, voulte*

vault² vb **1** to jump over (something) by resting one's hands on it or by using a long pole ▷ *n* **2** the act of vaulting **vaulter** n **WORD ORIGIN** Italian *voltare* to turn

vaulted adj being or having an arched roof: *an atmospheric vaulted dining room*

vaulting¹ n the arrangement of ceiling vaults in a building

vaulting² adj excessively confident: *a vaulting ambition for the highest political office*

Polari

Polari is an unusual form of slang, in that it has always been predominantly identified not with a particular part of the country or social class but with a specific way of life, ie showbusiness.

As its alternative name, Parlyaree, would suggest, it has Mediterranean, more specifically Italian, overtones and is thought to derive from *parlare*, an Italian verb meaning 'to speak'. The Mediterranean has always been a highway for peoples of different races and languages, and it is thought that the origins of Polari lie in the *lingua franca* by which seagoers of many diverse mother tongues sought to communicate with one another. Sailors are great transporters of linguistic terms from one port to another, and the first appearances in English of individual expressions in Polari have been traced to the talk of English mariners in the 16th century. The Italianate influence is clearly shown in such terms as *omi* ('man'), *dona* ('woman'), *bona* ('good'), *mangarly* ('food'), and *carsey* ('house'). Thus the *omi of the carsey* was 'the man of the house' and *bona mangarly* meant 'good food'.

This secret language was taken up by actors, showmen, and other travelling players in an era when this mode of earning a living was seen as existing only a hair's breadth above the level of common criminality. As with any other group on the fringes of society, seen as suspicious if not actually threatening, these entertainers often felt the need to disguise what they were saying to one another from the ears of the legitimate world. An itinerant lifestyle brought many of them into contact with Gypsies, another marginal section of society, and many terms in Polari were borrowed from Romany. The more widely used backslang (backwards pronunciation of standard English vocabulary) also influenced Polari, with terms such as *eek* ('face', shortened from 'ecaf') and *riah* ('hair').

It was in the 19th century that Polari became more strongly identified with the gay community, which has traditionally been much associated with showbusiness. At a period when homosexuality was against the law and openly gay people were rigorously punished, it was inevitable that homosexual activity had to be 'kept underground' and the ready-made canting language of Polari was widely adopted by gay men even when they were not in the business of professional entertainment.

In the 20th century acting and other forms of performance were increasingly accepted as (fairly) respectable professions, and the use of Polari became more a badge of belonging and a source of amusement to practitioners rather than a necessary camouflage. It was therefore to its use among the gay community that Polari owed its continued survival.

It became more widely exposed in the 1960s when a popular BBC radio programme, *Round the Horne*, featured a couple of camp characters, Julian and Sandy, who peppered their conversation with Polari terms, much of the humour deriving from the 'straight' listeners failing to realize how risqué some of the repartee could be. Soon more people than ever could decode phrases like *How bona to vada your dolly old eek* ('How nice to see your pretty face') or *Vada the lallies on that dona* ('Look at that woman's legs'). Perhaps this popularization contributed to the slang's demise, as the more people who can understand the veiled references of a secret language, the less utility it has for its intended purpose.

As late as the 1990s, the English singer Morrissey entitled one of his albums *Bona Drag* (meaning 'good clothes') and released a single called *Piccadilly Palare*, but this was more of a nod to a passing generation rather than a celebration of a vibrant language and the 21st century has seen a decline in the use of Polari other than as a quaint curiosity.

Some Polari terms have survived by having successfully crossed over into more general slang usage, such as *naff* (meaning 'bad') and *khazi* or *carsey* (the Polari for 'house', specialized to mean 'toilet'), and many people who glibly use these terms my well be unaware of their origin. *Zhoozh* or *zhoosh* is another example, and this term meaning 'to tidy' or 'improve the look of' something is the common parlance of hairdressers, decorators, style gurus, and commentators in many television 'makeover' reality shows.

vaunt *vb* **1** to describe or display (one's success or possessions) boastfully ▷ *n* **2** a boast **vaunted** *adj*
WORD ORIGIN Latin *vanus* vain

vb verb

VC **1** Vice Chancellor **2** Victoria Cross **3** *history* Vietcong: the Communist-led guerrilla force of South Vietnam

V-chip *n* a device within a television set that allows the set to be programmed not to receive transmissions that have been classified as containing sex, violence, or obscene language

vCJD variant Creutzfeldt-Jakob disease

VCR video cassette recorder

VD venereal disease

VDU visual display unit

veal *n* the meat from a calf, used as food
WORD ORIGIN Latin *vitulus* calf

vector *n* **1** *maths* a variable quantity, such as force, that has magnitude and direction **2** *pathol* an animal, usually an insect, that carries a disease-producing microorganism from person to person
WORD ORIGIN Latin: carrier

Veda (**vay**-da) *n* any or all of the most ancient sacred writings of Hinduism **Vedic** *adj*
WORD ORIGIN Sanskrit: knowledge

veer *vb* **1** to change direction suddenly: *the plane veered off the runway and careered through the perimeter fence* **2** to change from one position or opinion to another: *her feelings veered from tenderness to sudden spurts of genuine love* ▷ *n* **3** a change of course or direction
WORD ORIGIN Old French *virer*

veg *n informal* a vegetable or vegetables

vegan (**vee**-gan) *n* a person who does not eat meat, fish, or any animal products such as cheese, butter, etc.

vegeburger *or* **veggieburger** *n* a flat cake of chopped vegetables or pulses that is grilled or fried and served in a roll

vegetable *n* **1** a plant, such as potato or cauliflower, with parts that are used as food **2** *informal* someone who is unable to move or think, as a result of brain damage ▷ *adj* **3** of or like plants or vegetables
WORD ORIGIN Late Latin *vegetabilis* animating

vegetable marrow *n* a long green vegetable which can be cooked and eaten

vegetable oil *n* any of a group of oils that are obtained from plants

vegetal *adj* of or relating to plant life

vegetarian *n* **1** a person who does not eat meat or fish ▷ *adj* **2** excluding meat and fish: *a vegetarian diet* **vegetarianism** *n*

vegetate *vb* -tating, -tated to live in a dull and boring way with no mental stimulation

vegetation *n* plant life as a whole

vegetative *adj* **1** of or relating to plant life or plant growth **2** (of reproduction) characterized by asexual processes

veggie *informal n* **1** a vegetable **2** a vegetarian ▷ *adj* **3** vegetarian: *a veggie cookbook*

veggieburger *n* same as **vegeburger**

vehement *adj* **1** expressing strong feelings or opinions **2** (of actions or gestures) performed with great force or energy **vehemence** *n* **vehemently** *adv*
WORD ORIGIN Latin *vehemens* ardent

vehicle *n* **1** a machine such as a bus or car for transporting people or goods **2** something used to achieve a particular purpose or as a means of expression: *the newspaper was a vehicle for explaining government policies* **3** *pharmacol* an inactive substance mixed with the active ingredient in a medicine **4** a liquid, such as oil, in which a pigment is mixed before it is applied to a surface **vehicular** *adj*
WORD ORIGIN Latin *vehere* to carry

veil *n* **1** a piece of thin cloth, usually as part of a hat or headdress, used to cover a woman's face **2** something that conceals the truth: *a veil of secrecy* **3 take the veil** to become a nun ▷ *vb* **4** to cover or conceal with or as if with a veil
WORD ORIGIN Latin *velum* a covering

veiled *adj* (of a comment or remark) presented in a disguised form: *it was a thinly veiled criticism*

vein *n* **1** any of the tubes that carry blood to the heart **2** a thin line in a leaf or in an insect's wing **3** a clearly defined layer of ore or mineral in rock **4** an irregular streak of colour in marble, wood, or cheese **5** a distinctive trait or quality in speech or writing: *critics have exposed a strong vein of moralism in the poem* **6** a temporary mood: *we're in a very humorous vein tonight* **veined** *adj*
WORD ORIGIN Latin *vena*

Velcro *n trademark* a type of fastening consisting of one piece of fabric with tiny hooked threads and another with a coarse surface that sticks to it

veld *or* **veldt** *n* the open country of South Africa including landscapes which are grassy, bushy, or thinly forested
WORD ORIGIN Afrikaans: field

veldskoen, velskoen (**felt**-skoon) *n* S African a sturdy ankle boot
WORD ORIGIN Afrikaans

veleta *n* same as **valeta**

vellum *n* **1** a fine calf, kid, or lamb parchment **2** a strong good-quality paper that resembles vellum
WORD ORIGIN Old French *velin* of a calf

velocipede (vel-**loss**-sip-peed) *n* an early form of bicycle
WORD ORIGIN Latin *velox* swift + *pes* foot

velocity (vel-**loss**-it-ee) *n, pl* -ties the speed at which something is moving in a particular direction
WORD ORIGIN Latin *velox* swift

velour *or* **velours** (vel-**loor**) *n* a silk or cotton cloth similar to velvet
WORD ORIGIN Latin *villus* shaggy hair

velouté (vuh-**loo**-tay) *n* a rich white sauce made from stock, eggs, and cream
WORD ORIGIN French, literally: velvety

velskoen *n* same as **veldskoen**

velvet *n* **1** a fabric with a thick close soft pile on one side **2** the furry covering of the newly formed antlers of a deer ▷ *adj* **3** made of velvet **4** soft or smooth like velvet **5 an iron fist** *or* **hand in a velvet glove** determination concealed by a gentle manner **velvety** *adj*

WORD ORIGIN Old French, from Latin *villus* shaggy hair

velveteen *n* a cotton fabric that resembles velvet

venal (**vee**-nal) *adj* **1** willing to accept bribes in return for acting dishonestly: *venal politicians* **2** associated with corruption or bribery: *venal greed* **venality** *n*
WORD ORIGIN Latin *venum* sale

vend *vb* to sell (goods)
WORD ORIGIN Latin *vendere* to sell

Venda *n* **1** *pl* -da *or* -das a member of a Negroid people of southern Africa, living chiefly in NE South Africa **2** the language of this people

vendetta *n* **1** a long-lasting quarrel between people or organizations in which they attempt to harm each other: *it's an inexplicable vendetta against the firm and its directors* **2** a private feud between families in which members of one family kill members of the other family in revenge for earlier murders
WORD ORIGIN Italian

vending machine *n* a machine that automatically dispenses food, drinks, or cigarettes when money is inserted

vendor *n* **1** a person who sells goods such as newspapers or hamburgers from a stall or cart **2** *chiefly law* a person who sells property

veneer *n* **1** a thin layer of wood or plastic used to cover the surface of something made of cheaper material **2** a deceptive but convincing appearance: *nobody penetrated his veneer of modest charm*
WORD ORIGIN Old French *fournir* to furnish

venerable *adj* **1** (of a person) entitled to respect because of great age or wisdom **2** (of an object) impressive because it is old or important historically **3** *RC Church* a title given to a dead person who is going to be declared a saint **4** *Church of England* a title given to an archdeacon
WORD ORIGIN Latin *venerari* to venerate

venerate *vb* -ating, -ated to hold (someone) in deep respect **venerator** *n*
WORD ORIGIN Latin *venerari*

veneration *n* a feeling of awe or great respect: *George Gershwin is worthy of the veneration accorded his classical counterparts*

venereal (vin-**ear**-ee-al) *adj* **1** transmitted by sexual intercourse: *venereal infections* **2** of the genitals: *venereal warts*
WORD ORIGIN Latin *venus* sexual love

venereal disease *n* a disease, such as syphilis, transmitted by sexual intercourse

Venetian *adj* **1** of Venice, a port in NE Italy ▷ *n* **2** a person from Venice

Venetian blind *n* a window blind made of thin horizontal slats

vengeance *n* **1** the act of killing, injuring, or harming someone for revenge **2 with a vengeance** to a much greater extent or with much greater force than expected: *my career was beginning to take off with a vengeance*
WORD ORIGIN Old French, from Latin *vindicare* to punish

vengeful *adj* wanting revenge

V

venial (**veen**-ee-al) *adj* easily excused or forgiven: *venial sins*
WORD ORIGIN Latin *venia* forgiveness

venison *n* the flesh of a deer, used as food
WORD ORIGIN Old French *venaison*

Venn diagram *n maths* a drawing which uses circles to show the relationships between different sets
WORD ORIGIN after John Venn, logician

venom *n* **1** a feeling of great bitterness or anger towards someone **2** the poison that certain snakes and scorpions inject when they bite or sting **venomous** *adj* **venomously** *adv*
WORD ORIGIN Latin *venenum* poison, love potion

venous (**vee**-nuss) *adj* of or relating to veins
WORD ORIGIN Latin *vena* vein

vent¹ *n* **1** a small opening in something through which fresh air can enter and fumes can be released **2** the shaft of a volcano through which lava and gases erupt **3** the anal opening of a bird or other small animal **4 give vent to** to release (an emotion) in an outburst: *she gave vent to her misery and loneliness* ▷ *vb* **5** to release or express freely: *consumers vented their anger on the group by boycotting its products* **6** to make vents in
WORD ORIGIN Old French *esventer* to blow out

vent² *n* a vertical slit in the lower hem of a jacket
WORD ORIGIN Latin *findere* to cleave

ventilate *vb* **-lating, -lated 1** to let fresh air into (a room or building) **2** to discuss (ideas or feelings) openly: *ultra-rightists ventilated anti-Semitic sentiments* **ventilation** *n*
WORD ORIGIN Latin *ventilare* to fan

ventilator *n* an opening or device, such as a fan, used to let fresh air into a room or building

ventral *adj* relating to the front part of the body **ventrally** *adv*
WORD ORIGIN Latin *venter* abdomen

ventricle *n anat* **1** a chamber of the heart that pumps blood to the arteries **2** any one of the four main cavities of the brain **ventricular** *adj*
WORD ORIGIN Latin *ventriculus*

ventriloquism *n* the ability to speak without moving the lips so that the words appear to come from another person or from another part of the room **ventriloquist** *n*
WORD ORIGIN Latin *venter* belly + *loqui* to speak

venture *n* **1** a project or activity that is risky or of uncertain outcome **2** a business operation in which there is the risk of loss as well as the opportunity for profit ▷ *vb* **-turing, -tured 3** to do something that involves risk or danger: *I thought it wise to venture into foreign trade* **4** to dare to express (an opinion) **5** to go to an unknown or dangerous place **6** to dare (to do something): *you have asked me so often to come to your place that I ventured to drop in* **venturer** *n*
WORD ORIGIN variant of *adventure*

venture capital *n* money provided for investment in new commercial enterprises **venture capitalist** *n*

Venture Scout *or* **Venturer** *n* a member of the senior branch of the Scouts

venturesome *adj* willing to take risks

venue *n* a place where an organized gathering, such as a concert or a sporting event, is held
WORD ORIGIN Latin *venire* to come

Venus *n* **1** the Roman goddess of love **2** the planet second nearest to the sun

Venus's flytrap *or* **Venus flytrap** *n* a plant that traps and digests insects between hinged leaves

veracious *adj* habitually truthful
WORD ORIGIN Latin *verus* true

veracity *n* **1** habitual truthfulness **2** accuracy

verandah *or* **veranda** *n* **1** an open porch attached to a house **2** NZ a continuous overhead canopy outside shops that gives shelter to pedestrians
WORD ORIGIN Portuguese *varanda* railing

verb *n* a word that is used to indicate the occurrence or performance of an action or the existence of a state, for example *run*, *make*, or *do*
WORD ORIGIN Latin *verbum* word

verbal *adj* **1** of or relating to words: *verbal skills* **2** spoken rather than written: *a verbal agreement* **3** *grammar* of or relating to a verb **verbally** *adv*

verbalism *n* an exaggerated emphasis on the importance of words

verbalize *or* **-lise** *vb* **-lizing, -lized** *or* **-lising, -lised** to express (an idea or feeling) in words

verbal noun *n grammar* a noun derived from a verb, for example *smoking* in the sentence *smoking is bad for you*

verbatim (verb-**bait**-im) *adv* **1** using exactly the same words: *I'll repeat it verbatim* ▷ *adj* **2** using exactly the same words: *a verbatim account*
WORD ORIGIN Medieval Latin: word by word

verbena *n* a plant with red, white, or purple sweet-smelling flowers
WORD ORIGIN Latin: sacred bough used by the priest in religious acts

verbiage *n* the excessive use of words
WORD ORIGIN Latin *verbum* word

verbose (verb-**bohss**) *adj* using more words than is necessary **verbosity** *n*

verdant *adj literary* covered with green vegetation
WORD ORIGIN from Latin *viridis* green

verdict *n* **1** the decision made by a jury about the guilt or innocence of a defendant **2** an opinion formed after examining the facts
WORD ORIGIN Latin *vere dictum* truly spoken

verdigris (**ver**-dig-reess) *n* a green or bluish coating which forms on copper, brass, or bronze that has been exposed to damp
WORD ORIGIN Old French *vert de Grice* green of Greece

verdure *n literary* flourishing green vegetation
WORD ORIGIN from Latin *viridis* green

verge¹ *n* **1** a grass border along a road **2 on the verge of** having almost reached (a point or condition) **3** an edge or rim ▷ *vb* **verging, verged 4 verge on** to be near to: *she was verging on hysteria*
WORD ORIGIN Latin *virga* rod

verge² *vb* **verging, verged** to move in a specified direction: *verging towards the Irish Sea*
WORD ORIGIN Latin *vergere*

verger *n chiefly Church of England* **1** a church official who acts as caretaker **2** an official who carries the rod of office before a bishop or dean in ceremonies and processions
WORD ORIGIN Latin *virga* rod, twig

verify *vb* **-fies, -fying, -fied 1** to check the truth of (something) by investigation **2** to prove (something) to be true **verifiable** *adj* **verification** *n*
WORD ORIGIN Latin *verus* true + *facere* to make

verily *adv literary* truly: *for verily, this was their destiny*
WORD ORIGIN from *very*

verisimilitude *n* the appearance of truth or reality
WORD ORIGIN Latin *verus* true + *similitudo* similitude

veritable *adj* rightly called; real: *a veritable mine of information* **veritably** *adv*

verity *n, pl* **-ties** a true statement or principle
WORD ORIGIN Latin *verus* true

vermicelli (ver-me-**chell**-ee) *n* **1** very fine strands of pasta, used in soups **2** tiny chocolate strands used as a topping for cakes or ice cream
WORD ORIGIN Italian: little worms

vermiform *adj* shaped like a worm

vermiform appendix *n anat* same as **appendix**

vermilion *adj* **1** orange-red ▷ *n* **2** mercuric sulphide, used as an orange-red pigment; cinnabar
WORD ORIGIN Late Latin *vermiculus* insect from which red dye was prepared

vermin *pl n* **1** small animals collectively, such as insects and rodents, that spread disease and damage crops **2** unpleasant people **verminous** *adj*
WORD ORIGIN Latin *vermis* worm

vermouth (**ver**-muth) *n* a wine flavoured with herbs
WORD ORIGIN German *Wermut* wormwood

vernacular (ver-**nak**-yew-lar) *n* **1** the commonly spoken language or dialect of a particular people or place ▷ *adj* **2** in or using the vernacular
WORD ORIGIN Latin *vernaculus* belonging to a household slave

vernal *adj* of or occurring in spring **vernally** *adv*
WORD ORIGIN Latin *ver* spring

vernier (**ver**-nee-er) *n* a small movable scale in certain measuring instruments such as theodolites, used to obtain a fractional reading of one of the divisions on the main scale
WORD ORIGIN after Paul *Vernier*, mathematician

veronica *n* a plant with small blue, pink, or white flowers
WORD ORIGIN Medieval Latin, perhaps from the name *Veronica*

v

verruca (ver-**roo**-ka) *n pathol* a wart, usually on the sole of the foot
WORD ORIGIN Latin: wart

versatile *adj* having many different skills or uses **versatility** *n*
WORD ORIGIN Latin *versare* to turn

verse *n* **1** a division of a poem or song **2** poetry as distinct from prose **3** one of the short sections into which chapters of the books of the Bible are divided **4** a poem
WORD ORIGIN Latin *versus* furrow, literally: a turning (of the plough)

versed *adj* **versed in** knowledgeable about or skilled in

versify *vb* **-fies, -fying, -fied 1** to put (something) into verse **2** to write in verse **versification** *n* **versifier** *n*
WORD ORIGIN Latin *versus* verse + *facere* to make

version *n* **1** a form of something, such as a piece of writing, with some differences from other forms **2** an account of something from a certain point of view: *so far there's been no official version of the incident* **3** an adaptation, for example of a book or play into a film
WORD ORIGIN Latin *vertere* to turn

verso *n, pl* **-sos 1** the left-hand page of a book **2** the back of a sheet of printed paper
WORD ORIGIN New Latin *verso (folio)* (the leaf) having been turned

versus *prep* **1** (in a sporting competition or lawsuit) against **2** in opposition to or in contrast with: *man versus machine*
WORD ORIGIN Latin: turned (in the direction of), opposite

vertebra (**ver**-tib-bra) *n, pl* **-brae** (-bree) one of the bony segments of the spinal column **vertebral** *adj*
WORD ORIGIN Latin

vertebrate *n* **1** an animal with a backbone, such as a fish, amphibian, reptile, bird, or mammal ▷ *adj* **2** having a backbone

vertex (**ver**-tex) *n, pl* **-tices** (-tiss-seez) **1** the highest point **2** *maths* **a** the point on a geometric figure where the sides form an angle **b** the highest point of a triangle
WORD ORIGIN Latin: top

vertical *adj* **1** at right angles to the horizon: *the vertical cliff* **2** straight up and down: *a vertical cut* **3** *econ* of or relating to associated or consecutive, though not identical, stages of industrial activity: *the purchase of a chain of travel agents by a leading tour operator will increase vertical integration in the holiday industry* ▷ *n* **4** a vertical line or direction **vertically** *adv*
WORD ORIGIN from Latin *vertex* top, pole of the sky

vertiginous *adj* producing dizziness

vertigo *n pathol* a sensation of dizziness felt because one's balance is disturbed, sometimes experienced when looking down from a high place
WORD ORIGIN Latin: a whirling round

vervain *n* a plant with long slender spikes of purple, blue, or white flowers
WORD ORIGIN Latin *verbena* sacred bough

verve *n* great enthusiasm or liveliness
WORD ORIGIN Latin *verba* words, chatter

very *adv* **1** used to add emphasis to adjectives and adverbs that are able to be graded: *I'm very happy; he'll be home very soon* ▷ *adj* **2** used with nouns to give emphasis or exaggerated intensity: *the very end of his visit; the very thing I need*
WORD ORIGIN Old French *verai* true

⌷ USAGE
In strict usage adverbs of degree such as *very, too, quite, really,* and *extremely* are used only to qualify adjectives: *he is very happy; she is too sad.* By this rule, these words should not be used to qualify past participles that follow the verb *to be,* since they would then be technically qualifying verbs. With the exception of certain participles, such as *tired* or *disappointed,* that have come to be regarded as adjectives, all other past participles are qualified by adverbs such as *much, greatly, seriously,* or *excessively: he has been much (not very) inconvenienced; she has been excessively (not too) criticized.*

very high frequency *n* a radio-frequency band lying between 30 and 300 megahertz

Very light *n* a coloured flare for signalling at night
WORD ORIGIN after Edward W. *Very,* naval ordnance officer

vesicle *n biol* **1** a small sac or cavity, esp. one filled with fluid **2** a blister
WORD ORIGIN Latin *vesica* bladder, sac

vespers *n* an evening service in some Christian churches
WORD ORIGIN Latin *vesper* the evening star

vessel *n* **1** a ship or large boat **2** an object used as a container for liquid **3** *biol* a tubular structure in animals and plants that carries body fluids, such as blood and sap
WORD ORIGIN Latin *vas*

vest *n* **1** *Brit* an undergarment covering the top half of the body **2** *Austral, US, & Canad* a waistcoat ▷ *vb* **3** **vest in** to settle (power or property) on: *by the power vested in me, I pronounce you man and wife* **4** **vest with** to bestow on: *the sponsorship has vested these matches with a new interest*
WORD ORIGIN Latin *vestis* clothing

vestal *adj* **1** chaste or pure ▷ *n* **2** a chaste woman
WORD ORIGIN Latin *Vestalis* virgin priestess of the goddess Vesta

vestal virgin *n* (in ancient Rome) one of the virgin priestesses dedicated to the goddess Vesta and to maintaining the sacred fire in her temple

vested *adj property law* having an existing right to the immediate or future possession of property

vested interest *n* **1** a strong personal interest someone has in a matter because he or she might benefit from it **2** *property law* an existing right to the immediate or future possession of property

vestibule *n* a small entrance hall
WORD ORIGIN Latin *vestibulum*

vestige (**vest**-ij) *n* **1** a small amount or trace **2** *biol* an organ or part that is a small nonfunctional remnant of a functional organ in an ancestor
WORD ORIGIN Latin *vestigium* track

vestigial (vest-**ij**-ee-al) *adj* remaining after a larger or more important thing has gone: *a strong seam of vestigial belief*

vestments *pl n* **1** ceremonial clothes worn by the clergy at religious services **2** robes that show authority or rank
WORD ORIGIN Latin *vestire* to clothe

vestry *n, pl* **-tries** a room in a church used as an office by the priest or minister
WORD ORIGIN probably Old French *vestiarie* wardrobe

vet¹ *n* **1** short for **veterinary surgeon** ▷ *vb* **vetting, vetted 2** to make a careful check of (a person or document) for suitability: *guests have to be vetted and vouched for*

vet² *n US, Canad, Austral, & NZ* short for **veteran**

vetch *n* **1** a climbing plant with blue or purple flowers **2** the beanlike fruit of the vetch, used as fodder
WORD ORIGIN Latin *vicia*

veteran *n* **1** a person who has given long service in some capacity **2** a soldier who has seen a lot of active service **3** a person who has served in the military forces ▷ *adj* **4** long-serving: *the veteran American politician*
WORD ORIGIN Latin *vetus* old

veteran car *n Austral & Brit* a car built before 1919, esp. before 1905

veterinarian *n US, Canad, & Austral* a veterinary surgeon

veterinary *adj* relating to veterinary science
WORD ORIGIN Latin *veterinae* draught animals

veterinary medicine *or* **science** *n* the branch of medicine concerned with the treatment of animals

veterinary surgeon *n Brit* a person qualified to practise veterinary medicine

veto (**vee**-toe) *n, pl* **-toes 1** the power to prevent legislation or action proposed by others: *no single state has a veto* **2** the exercise of this power ▷ *vb* **-toing, -toed 3** to refuse consent to (a proposal, such as a government bill) **4** to prohibit or forbid: *the Sports Minister vetoed the appointments*
WORD ORIGIN Latin: I forbid

vex *vb* to cause (someone) to feel annoyance or irritation **vexing** *adj* **vexation** *n*
WORD ORIGIN Latin *vexare* to jolt (in carrying)

vexatious *adj* vexing

vexed *adj* **1** annoyed and puzzled **2** much debated: *the vexed question of pay*

VHF *or* **vhf** *radio* very high frequency

VHS Video Home System: a video cassette recorder system using half-inch magnetic tape

VI Vancouver Island

via *prep* **1** by way of; through: *he fled to London via Crete* **2** by means of: *working from home and keeping in touch with office life via a video link-up*
WORD ORIGIN Latin

viable *adj* **1** able to be put into practice: *the party has failed to propose a viable alternative* **2** (of seeds or eggs) capable of growth **3** (of a fetus) sufficiently

Inuit and English

Those who make their home in the Arctic do not deserve the fallacies that have grown around their lives and languages. It's sometimes supposed that, because they were less technologically advanced traditionally than those in industrial societies, their languages must be likewise 'primitive'. In fact, grammar and syntax of languages in the Eskimo-Aleut family are as complex and sophisticated as they are in, say, English and French, just as their carvings and sculptures are artworks of a high order. If these people had fewer words, they were, given the landscape and climate, the words they needed.

An even more pervasive canard is the notion that Arctic native peoples have multiple words for *snow*. Their languages are *polysynthetic*, that is, nouns are added to create a compound unit that might amount to a phrase in another language. The variety of these constructions led the anthropologist Edward Sapir and linguist Benjamin Lee Whorf to suppose that Eskimo-Aleut languages, in fact all languages, express separate and distinct views of reality, a romantic theory often called *linguistic relativism*. Some began to believe that Arctic speakers did not conceptualize what fell from the sky as snow, but understood it as separate kinds of precipitation. In effect, this idea confuses the snowflake of words with the blizzard of a worldview.

The Canadian poet Al Purdy has called the Arctic 'the land of permanent ice cream'. Poetic licence's allusion to whiteness aside, snow is actually not much of a linguistic factor, since little snow falls inside much of the Arctic Circle, though admittedly what falls stays on the ground or sea ice, or blows around. As the subject of technical vocabulary, ice is much more important.

The conceptual confusion extends to terms for the people who speak related Eskimo-Aleut languages and who live and speak in Alaska, the Far East of Siberia, the Far North of Canada, and Greenland. The *Aleut*, from whom the name of the language family derives, represent only a tiny population living near the Bering Strait. *Eskimo* as a term for a people is considered pejorative in Canada and Greenland. Alaskan and Siberian groups speak various forms of *Yupik*; in Alaska, Inuit speakers call themselves the *Inupiat or Inupiaq,* in US legal parlance, *Native Alaskans.* In Canada, the people are grouped among *Native Canadians* and termed the *Inuit*, of which the singular is *Inuk*, and speak *Inuktitut.* The Inuit in Greenland speak *Greenlandic* or *Kalaallit,* their official language, and their writing script is in the Latin alphabet, not in the Inuktitut syllabary devised and used in Canada.

Though *anorak* is Greenlandic in origin and *parka* comes from Aleut, most of the words of the widely scattered Arctic populations that have passed into standard English, like *igloo* and *kayak,* derive from Inuktitut. Interestingly, the canine *husky* comes from the same linguistic root as *Eskimo*, sometimes translated as 'eater of raw flesh'. Some English words merely relate to features of Inuit culture, like the sled-hauling *Eskimo dog*, a husky, and *Eskimo roll*, a manoeuvre by which a kayak is turned from upright to capsized to upright again, as well as *throat-singing,* a form of singing in which two women face each other and vocalize with deep-throated sounds. Others, like the trademarked *Eskimo pie*, a chocolate-coated bar of ice cream, make playful assumptions about Inuit life.

Apart from providing many northern place names, Inuktitut has had an impact on Canadian English and a few words have had a vogue outside the Arctic, like *Chimo!,* a greeting, often a toast, and *Ookpik*, an owl-like doll originally made from sealskin. To the category of regionalisms generally belong *amatik* and *atigi,* types of parka; *angakok*, a shaman or healer; *komatik*, a sled; *qiviut*, soft, fine-fibred wool taken from the underbelly of a muskox; *ulu*, a knife; *umiak*, a large, open, flat-bottomed boat; and *kaboona*, a non-Inuit person. Yupik supplies *mukluk*, a winter boot with a thick rubber sole and high fabric upper, originally made from sealskin or caribou hide, not to be confused with the Inuktitut *muktuk*, whale blubber used as food.

In Inuktitut, *kattingolartut* means 'growling dogs'. In Yupik, *qimugglugpag* means a small rocky bluff, literally 'big bad dog'. Perhaps the differing words for *dog* in Inuktitut and Yupik signify separate views of reality, though it's unlikely.

developed to survive outside the uterus **viability** n
WORD ORIGIN Latin *vita* life

viaduct n a bridge for carrying a road or railway across a valley
WORD ORIGIN Latin *via* way + *ducere* to bring

Viagra n *trademark* a drug that allows increased blood flow into the penis, used to treat impotence in men

vial n same as **phial**
WORD ORIGIN Greek *phialē* a bowl

viands pl n *old-fashioned* food
WORD ORIGIN Latin *vivenda* things to be lived on

viaticum n, pl **-ca** or **-cums** *Christianity* Holy Communion given to a person dying or in danger of death
WORD ORIGIN Latin *viaticus* belonging to a journey

vibes pl n *informal* **1** the emotional reactions between people **2** the atmosphere of a place **3** short for **vibraphone**

vibrant (**vibe**-rant) adj **1** full of energy and enthusiasm **2** (of a voice) rich and full of emotion **3** (of a colour) strong and bright **vibrancy** n
WORD ORIGIN Latin *vibrare* to agitate

vibraphone n a musical instrument with metal bars that resonate electronically when hit

vibrate vb **-brating, -brated 1** to move backwards and forwards rapidly **2** to have or produce a quivering or echoing sound **3** *physics* to undergo or cause to undergo vibration **vibratory** adj
WORD ORIGIN Latin *vibrare*

vibration n **1** a vibrating **2** *physics* **a** a periodic motion about an equilibrium position, such as in the production of sound **b** a single cycle of such a motion

vibrato n, pl **-tos** *music* a slight rapid fluctuation in the pitch of a note

vibrator n a device for producing a vibratory motion, used for massage or as a sex aid

viburnum (vie-**burn**-um) n a subtropical shrub with white flowers and berry-like fruits
WORD ORIGIN Latin

Vic. Victoria (Australian state)

vicar n **1** *Church of England* a priest who is in charge of a parish **2** *RC Church* a church officer acting as deputy to a bishop **vicarial** adj
WORD ORIGIN Latin *vicarius* a deputy

vicarage n the house where a vicar lives

vicar apostolic n *RC Church* a clergyman with authority in missionary countries

vicar general n, pl **vicars general** an official appointed to assist the bishop in his administrative duties

vicarious (vik-**air**-ee-uss) adj **1** felt indirectly by imagining what another person experiences: *vicarious satisfaction* **2** undergone or done as the substitute for another: *vicarious adventures* **3** delegated: *vicarious power* **vicariously** adv
WORD ORIGIN Latin *vicarius* substituted

Vicar of Christ n *RC Church* the Pope as Christ's representative on earth

vice[1] n **1** an immoral or evil habit or action: *greed is only one of their vices* **2** a habit regarded as a weakness in someone's character: *one of his few vices is cigars* **3** criminal activities involving sex, drugs, or gambling
WORD ORIGIN Latin *vitium* a defect

vice[2] or US **vise** n a tool with a pair of jaws for holding an object while work is done on it
WORD ORIGIN Latin *vitis* vine, plant with spiralling tendrils

vice[3] adj serving in the place of; being next in importance to: *the vice chairman*
WORD ORIGIN Latin *vicis* interchange

vice admiral n a senior commissioned officer in certain navies

vice chancellor n the chief executive or administrator at a number of universities

vicegerent n a person appointed to exercise all or some of the authority of another
WORD ORIGIN VICE[3] + Latin *gerere* to manage

vice president n an officer ranking immediately below a president and serving as his or her deputy **vice-presidency** n

viceregal adj **1** of a viceroy **2** *chiefly Austral & NZ* of a governor or governor general

viceroy n a governor of a colony or country who represents the monarch
WORD ORIGIN VICE[3] + French *roi* king

vice squad n a police division responsible for the enforcement of gaming and prostitution laws

vice versa adv the other way round: *there were attacks on northerners by southerners and vice versa*
WORD ORIGIN Latin: relations being reversed

Vichy water (**vee**-shee) n a natural mineral water from Vichy in France which is supposed to be good for the health

vicinity (viss-**in**-it-ee) n the area immediately surrounding a place
WORD ORIGIN Latin *vicinus* neighbouring

vicious adj **1** cruel or violent: *vicious attacks* **2** forceful or ferocious: *she gave the chair a vicious jerk* **3** intended to cause hurt or distress: *vicious letters* **4** (of an animal) fierce or hostile **viciously** adv **viciousness** n
WORD ORIGIN Latin *vitiosus* full of faults

vicious circle n a situation in which an attempt to resolve one problem creates new problems that recreate the original one

vicissitudes (viss-**iss**-it-yewds) pl n changes in circumstance or fortune
WORD ORIGIN Latin *vicis* change

victim n **1** a person or thing that suffers harm or death **2** a person who is tricked or swindled **3** a living person or animal sacrificed in a religious rite
WORD ORIGIN Latin *victima*

victimize or **-mise** vb **-mizing, -mized** or **-mising, -mised** to punish or discriminate against (someone) selectively or unfairly **victimization** or **-misation** n

victor n **1** a person or nation that has defeated an enemy in war **2** the winner of a contest or struggle

WORD ORIGIN Latin, from *vincere* to conquer

victoria n **1** a large sweet red-and-yellow plum **2** a light four-wheeled horse-drawn carriage with a folding hood
WORD ORIGIN after Queen *Victoria*

Victoria Cross n the highest decoration for bravery in battle awarded to the British and Commonwealth armed forces

Victorian adj **1** of or in the reign of Queen Victoria of Great Britain and Ireland (1837–1901) **2** characterized by prudery or hypocrisy **3** of or relating to Victoria (the state or any of the cities) ▷ n **4** a person who lived during the reign of Queen Victoria **5** an inhabitant of Victoria (the state or any of the cities)

Victoriana pl n objects of the Victorian period

victorious adj **1** having defeated an enemy or opponent: *the victorious allies* **2** of or characterized by victory: *a victorious smile*

victory n, pl **-ries 1** the winning of a war or battle **2** success attained in a contest or struggle
WORD ORIGIN Latin *victoria*

victual vb **-tualling, -tualled** or US **-tuaing, -tualed** *old-fashioned* to supply with or obtain victuals **victualler** or US **-tualer** n
WORD ORIGIN Latin *victus* sustenance

victuals (**vit**-tals) pl n *old-fashioned* food and drink

vicuna (vik-**kew**-na) n **1** a S American mammal like the llama **2** the fine cloth made from its wool
WORD ORIGIN Spanish

vide (**vie**-dee) see: used to direct a reader to a specified place in a text or in another book
WORD ORIGIN Latin

videlicet (vid-**deal**-ee-set) adv namely: used to specify items
WORD ORIGIN Latin

video n, pl **-os 1** the recording and showing of films and events using a television set, video tapes, and a video recorder **2** short for **video cassette** **3** short for **video cassette recorder** ▷ vb **videoing, videoed 4** to record (a television programme or an event) on video ▷ adj **5** relating to or used in producing televised images
WORD ORIGIN Latin *videre* to see

video cassette n a cassette containing video tape

video cassette recorder n a device for recording and playing back television programmes and films

video game n a game that can be played by using an electronic control to move symbols on the screen of a visual display unit

video nasty n a film, usually specially made for video, that is explicitly horrific and pornographic

videophone n a communications device by which people can both see and speak to each other

video recorder n short for **video cassette recorder**

V

video tape *n* **1** magnetic tape used mainly for recording the video-frequency signals of a television programme or film ▷ *vb* **video-tape, -taping, -taped 2** to record (a film or programme) on video tape

Videotex *n trademark* same as **Viewdata**

videotext *n* a means of providing a written or graphical representation of computerized information on a television screen

vie *vb* **vying, vied** to compete (with someone): *the sisters vied with each other to care for her* **WORD ORIGIN** probably Old French *envier* to challenge

Vietnamese *adj* **1** of Vietnam ▷ *n* **2** *pl* **-ese** a person from Vietnam **3** the language of Vietnam

view *n* **1** opinion, judgment, or belief: *in my view that doesn't really work* **2** an understanding of or outlook on something: *a specific view of human history* **3** everything that can be seen from a particular place or in a particular direction: *there was a beautiful view from the window* **4** vision or sight, esp. range of vision: *as they turned into the drive, the house came into view* **5** a picture of a scene **6** the act of seeing or observing **7** **in view of** taking into consideration **8** **on view** exhibited to the public **9** **take a dim or poor view of** to regard (something) unfavourably **10** **with a view to** with the intention of ▷ *vb* **11** to consider in a specified manner: *they viewed the visit with hardly disguised apprehension* **12** to examine or inspect (a house or flat) carefully with a view to buying it **13** to look at **14** to watch (television) **WORD ORIGIN** Latin *videre* to see

Viewdata *n trademark* a videotext service linking users to a computer by telephone, enabling shopping, ticket booking, etc. to be done from home

viewer *n* **1** a person who views something, esp. television **2** a hand-held device for looking at photographic slides

viewfinder *n* a device on a camera that lets the user see what will be included in the photograph

viewpoint *n* **1** a person's attitude towards something **2** a place from which one gets a good view

vigil (**vij**-ill) *n* **1** a night-time period of staying awake to look after a sick person, pray, etc. **2** *RC Church, Church of England* the eve of certain major festivals **WORD ORIGIN** Latin: alert

vigilance *n* careful attention

vigilance committee *n* (in the US) a self-appointed body of citizens organized to maintain order

vigilant *adj* on the watch for trouble or danger **WORD ORIGIN** Latin *vigilare* to be watchful

vigilante (vij-ill-**ant**-ee) *n* a person who takes it upon himself or herself to enforce the law **WORD ORIGIN** Spanish, from Latin *vigilare* to keep watch

vignette (vin-**yet**) *n* **1** a short description of the typical features of something **2** a small decorative illustration in a book **3** a photograph or drawing with edges that are shaded off **WORD ORIGIN** French, literally: little vine (frequently used to embellish a text)

vigorous *adj* **1** having physical or mental energy **2** displaying or performed with vigour: *vigorous exercise* **vigorously** *adv*

vigour *or US* **vigor** *n* **1** physical or mental energy: *the vigour of his invective astonished MPs* **2** strong healthy growth **WORD ORIGIN** Latin *vigor*

Viking *n* any of the Scandinavians who raided by sea most of N and W Europe from the 8th to the 11th centuries **WORD ORIGIN** Old Norse *víkingr*

vile *adj* **1** morally wicked: *a vile regime* **2** disgusting: *the vile smell of the man* **3** unpleasant or bad: *I had a vile day at work* **vilely** *adv* **vileness** *n* **WORD ORIGIN** Latin *vilis* cheap

vilify (**vill**-if-fie) *vb* **-fies, -fying, -fied** to speak very badly of (someone) **vilification** *n* **WORD ORIGIN** Latin *vilis* worthless + *facere* to make

villa *n* **1** a large house with gardens **2** *Brit* a house rented to holiday-makers **WORD ORIGIN** Latin: a farmhouse

village *n* **1** a small group of houses in a country area **2** the inhabitants of such a community **villager** *n* **WORD ORIGIN** Latin *villa* a farmhouse

villain *n* **1** a wicked or evil person **2** the main wicked character in a novel or play **WORD ORIGIN** Late Latin *villanus* worker on a country estate

villainous *adj* of or like a villain

villainy *n, pl* **-lainies** evil or vicious behaviour

villein (**vill**-an) *n* (in medieval Europe) a peasant who was directly subject to his lord, to whom he paid dues and services in return for his land **villeinage** *n* **WORD ORIGIN** see VILLAIN

villus *n, pl* **villi** *zool, anat* **1** any of the numerous finger-like projections of the mucous membrane lining the small intestine of many vertebrates **2** any of the finger-like projections formed in the placenta of mammals **WORD ORIGIN** from Latin: shaggy hair

vim *n informal* vigour and energy **WORD ORIGIN** Latin *vis* force

vinaigrette *n* salad dressing made from oil and vinegar with seasonings **WORD ORIGIN** French

vindaloo *n, pl* **-loos** a type of very hot Indian curry **WORD ORIGIN** perhaps from Portuguese *vin d'alho* wine and garlic sauce

vindicate *vb* **-cating, -cated 1** to clear (someone) of guilt or suspicion **2** to provide justification for: *the arrests may vindicate the strong-arm tactics* **vindication** *n* **WORD ORIGIN** Latin *vindex* claimant

vindictive *adj* **1** maliciously seeking revenge **2** characterized by spite or ill will **vindictively** *adv* **vindictiveness** *n* **WORD ORIGIN** Latin *vindicare* to avenge

vine *n* **1** a plant, such as the grapevine, with long flexible stems that climb by clinging to a support **2** the stem of such a plant **viny** *adj* **WORD ORIGIN** Latin *vinea* vineyard

vinegar *n* **1** a sour-tasting liquid made by fermentation of beer, wine, or cider, used for salad dressing or for pickling **2** bad temper or spitefulness: *the vinegar in her pen is often a welcome seasoning to duller news* **vinegary** *adj* **WORD ORIGIN** French *vin* wine + *aigre* sour

vineyard (**vinn**-yard) *n* an area of land where grapes are grown **WORD ORIGIN** Old English *wīngeard*

vingt-et-un (**van**-tay-**uhn**) *n* same as **pontoon²** **WORD ORIGIN** French, literally: twenty-one

viniculture *n* the process or business of growing grapes and making wine **viniculturist** *n* **WORD ORIGIN** Latin *vinum* wine + CULTURE

vino (**vee**-noh) *n, pl* **-nos** *informal* wine **WORD ORIGIN** Spanish or Italian: wine

vinous (**vine**-uss) *adj* of or characteristic of wine **WORD ORIGIN** Latin *vinum* wine

vintage *n* **1** the wine obtained from a particular harvest of grapes **2** the harvest from which such a wine is obtained **3** a time of origin: *an open-necked shirt of uncertain vintage* ▷ *adj* **4** (of wine) of an outstandingly good year **5** representative of the best and most typical: *a vintage Saint Laurent dress* **WORD ORIGIN** Latin *vindemia*

vintage car *n* a car built between 1919 and 1930

vintner *n* a wine merchant **WORD ORIGIN** Latin *vinetum* vineyard

vinyl (**vine**-ill) *n* **1** any of various strong plastics made by the polymerization of vinyl compounds, such as PVC **2** conventional records made of vinyl as opposed to compact discs ▷ *adj* **3** *chem* of or containing the monovalent group of atoms CH_2CH-: *vinyl chloride* **4** of or made of vinyl: *vinyl tiles* **WORD ORIGIN** Latin *vinum* wine

viol (**vie**-oll) *n* a stringed musical instrument that preceded the violin **WORD ORIGIN** Old Provençal *viola*

viola¹ (vee-**oh**-la) *n* a bowed stringed instrument of the violin family, slightly larger and lower in pitch than the violin **WORD ORIGIN** Italian

viola² (**vie**-ol-la) *n* a variety of pansy **WORD ORIGIN** Latin: violet

viola da gamba (vee-**oh**-la da **gam**-ba) *n* the second largest and lowest member of the viol family **WORD ORIGIN** Italian, literally: viol for the leg

violate *vb* **-lating, -lated 1** to break (a law or agreement): *he violated export laws* **2** to disturb rudely or improperly: *these men who were violating her privacy* **3** to treat (a sacred place) disrespectfully **4** to rape **violation** *n* **violator** *n* **WORD ORIGIN** Latin *violare* to do violence to

violence *n* **1** the use of physical force, usually intended to cause injury or destruction **2** great force or strength in action, feeling, or expression **WORD ORIGIN** Latin *violentus* violent

violent *adj* **1** using or involving physical force with the intention of causing injury or destruction: *violent clashes with government supporters* **2** very intense: *I took a violent dislike to him* **3** sudden and forceful: *a violent explosion* **violently** *adv*

violet *n* **1** a plant with bluish-purple flowers ▷ *adj* **2** bluish-purple **WORD ORIGIN** Latin *viola*

violin *n* a musical instrument, the highest member of the violin family, with four strings played with a bow **WORD ORIGIN** Italian *violino* a little viola

violinist *n* a person who plays the violin

violist (vee-**oh**-list) *n* a person who plays the viola

violoncello (vie-oll-on-**chell**-oh) *n, pl* -los same as **cello** **WORD ORIGIN** Italian

VIP very important person

viper *n* a type of poisonous snake **WORD ORIGIN** Latin *vipera*

virago (vir-**rah**-go) *n, pl* -goes *or* -gos an aggressive woman **WORD ORIGIN** Latin: a manlike maiden

viral (**vie**-ral) *adj* of or caused by a virus

virgin *n* **1** a person, esp. a woman, who has never had sexual intercourse **2** a person who is inexperienced in a specified field: *a ski virgin* ▷ *adj* **3** not having had sexual intercourse **4** fresh and unused: *he found a scrap of virgin paper in a sea of memoranda* **5** not yet cultivated, explored, or exploited by people: *virgin territory* **WORD ORIGIN** Latin *virgo*

Virgin *n* **1 the Virgin** same as **Virgin Mary 2** a statue or picture of the Virgin Mary

virginal[1] *adj* **1** like a virgin **2** extremely pure or fresh

virginal[2] *n* an early keyboard instrument like a small harpsichord **WORD ORIGIN** probably Latin *virginalis* virginal, perhaps because it was played largely by young ladies

Virgin Birth *n Christianity* the doctrine that Jesus Christ was conceived solely by the direct intervention of the Holy Spirit so that Mary remained a virgin

Virginia creeper *n* a climbing plant with leaves that turn red in autumn

virginity *n* the condition or fact of being a virgin

Virgin Mary *n* the Virgin Mary *Christianity* Mary, the mother of Christ

Virgo *n astrol* the sixth sign of the zodiac; the Virgin **WORD ORIGIN** Latin

virile *adj* **1** having the traditional male characteristics of physical strength and a high sex drive **2** forceful and energetic: *a virile Highland fling* **virility** *n* **WORD ORIGIN** Latin *virilis* manly

virology *n* the branch of medicine concerned with the study of viruses **virological** *adj*

virtual *adj* **1** having the effect but not the appearance or form of: *the investigation has now come to a virtual standstill* **2** *computers* designed so as to extend the potential of a finite system beyond its immediate limits: *virtual memory* **3** of or relating to virtual reality **WORD ORIGIN** Latin *virtus* virtue

virtually *adv* almost or nearly: *he is virtually a prisoner in his own palace*

virtual reality *n* a computer-generated environment that seems real to the user

virtue *n* **1** moral goodness **2** a positive moral quality: *the virtue of humility* **3** an advantage or benefit: *the added virtue of being harmless* **4** chastity, esp. in women **5 by virtue of** by reason of; because of: *they escaped execution by virtue of their high rank* **WORD ORIGIN** Latin *virtus* manliness, courage

virtuoso *n, pl* -si *or* -sos **1** a person with exceptional musical skill **2** a person with exceptional skill in any area ▷ *adj* **3** showing exceptional skill or brilliance: *a virtuoso performance* **virtuosity** *n* **WORD ORIGIN** Italian: skilled

virtuous *adj* **1** morally good **2** (of a woman) chaste **virtuously** *adv*

virulent (**vir**-yew-lent) *adj* **1** extremely bitter or hostile **2 a** (of a microorganism) very infectious **b** (of a disease) having a violent effect **3** extremely poisonous or harmful: *the most virulent poison known to man* **virulence** *n* **WORD ORIGIN** Latin *virulentus* full of poison

virus *n* **1** a microorganism that is smaller than a bacterium and can cause disease in humans, animals, or plants **2** *informal* a disease caused by a virus **3** *computers* an unsanctioned and self-replicating program which, when activated, corrupts a computer's data and disables its operating system **WORD ORIGIN** Latin: slime, poisonous liquid

visa *n* an official stamp in a passport permitting its holder to travel into or through the country of the government issuing it **WORD ORIGIN** Latin: things seen

visage (**viz**-zij) *n chiefly literary* **1** face **2** appearance **WORD ORIGIN** Latin *visus* appearance

vis-à-vis (veez-ah-**vee**) *prep* in relation to **WORD ORIGIN** French: face-to-face

viscera (**viss**-er-a) *pl n anat* the large internal organs of the body collectively **WORD ORIGIN** Latin: entrails

visceral *adj* **1** of or affecting the viscera **2** instinctive rather than rational: *visceral hatred of the neighbours*

viscid (**viss**-id) *adj* sticky **WORD ORIGIN** Latin *viscum* mistletoe, birdlime

viscose *n* **1** a sticky solution obtained by dissolving cellulose **2** rayon made from this material **WORD ORIGIN** Latin *viscum* birdlime

viscosity *n, pl* -ties **1** the state of being viscous **2** *physics* the extent to which a fluid resists a tendency to flow

viscount (**vie**-count) *n* (in the British Isles) a nobleman ranking below an earl and above a baron **viscountcy** *n* **WORD ORIGIN** Old French *visconte*

viscountess (**vie**-count-iss) *n* **1** a woman holding the rank of viscount **2** the wife or widow of a viscount

viscous *adj* (of liquids) thick and sticky

vise *n US* same as **vice**[2]

Vishnu *n* a Hindu god, the Preserver

visibility *n* **1** the range or clarity of vision: *visibility was good, despite rain* **2** the condition of being visible

visible *adj* **1** able to be seen **2** able to be perceived by the mind: *a visible and flagrant act of aggression* **visibly** *adv* **WORD ORIGIN** Latin *visibilis*

vision *n* **1** the ability to see **2** a vivid mental image produced by the imagination: *I kept having visions of him being tortured* **3** a hallucination caused by divine inspiration, madness, or drugs: *visions of God* **4** great perception of future developments: *what he had instead of charisma was vision* **5** the image on a television screen **6** a person or thing of extraordinary beauty **WORD ORIGIN** Latin *visio* sight, from *videre* to see

visionary *adj* **1** showing foresight: *a visionary statesman* **2** idealistic but impractical **3** given to having visions **4** of or like visions ▷ *n, pl* -naries **5** a visionary person

visit *vb* -siting, -sited **1** to go or come to see (a person or place) **2** to stay with (someone) as a guest **3** *old-fashioned* (of a disease or disaster) to afflict **4 visit on** *or* **upon** to inflict (punishment) on **5 visit with** *US informal* to chat with (someone) ▷ *n* **6** the act or an instance of visiting **7** a professional or official call **8** a stay as a guest **WORD ORIGIN** Latin *visitare* to go to see

visitant *n* **1** a ghost or apparition **2** a migratory bird temporarily resting in a particular region

visitation *n* **1** an official visit or inspection **2** a punishment or reward from heaven **3** an appearance of a supernatural being

Visitation *n* **a** the visit made by the Virgin Mary to her cousin Elizabeth (Luke 1: 39–56) **b** the Church festival commemorating this, held on July 2

visiting hours *pl n* the times when visitors are allowed to see someone in a hospital or other institution: *many prisoners' wives complain about the short visiting hours*

visitor *n* a person who visits a person or place

visitor's passport *n* a British passport, valid for one year, that grants access to some countries, usually for a restricted period

visor (**vize**-or) *n* **1** a transparent flap on a helmet that can be pulled down to protect the face **2** a small movable screen attached above the windscreen in a vehicle, used as protection against the glare of the sun **3** a peak on a cap **WORD ORIGIN** Old French *vis* face

vista *n* **1** an extensive view **2** a wide range of possibilities or future events: *the vista of opportunity* **WORD ORIGIN** Italian

visual *adj* **1** done by or used in seeing **2** capable of being seen **visually** *adv* **WORD ORIGIN** Latin *visus* sight

visual aids *pl n* objects to be looked at that help the viewer to understand or remember something

visual display unit *n computers* a device with a screen for displaying data held in a computer

JK Rowling

Joanne Rowling is famous for two things: her enormously successful *Harry Potter* books (written under the name 'JK Rowling') and her own fairytale life story. Rowling was born in Gloucestershire in 1965, and began to write stories at an early age. She took a degree in French and Classics, and then moved to Portugal to teach English as a Foreign Language, where she met her first husband. After their separation, Rowling moved to Edinburgh with their daughter, where she started writing the *Harry Potter* books while living on state benefits. From these humble beginnings, Rowling has become one of the most successful writers of our time and one of the wealthiest women in Britain.

What is it that has made the *Harry Potter* series such a world-wide success? These tales of the education of a young wizard are based on a mixture of literary traditions. They are, in part, versions of the school story, a genre that developed in the nineteenth century and was very popular in the twentieth. *Harry Potter* has all the ingredients of a successful school story: friendships and rivalries; school sports (with the interesting modification that the wizarding sport *Quidditch* is played in the air); rules and rule-breaking; and, not least, the appealing concept of the self-contained boarding school. (Hogwarts, with its moving staircases and secret passageways, is a school in which any child would want to live.) However, *Harry Potter* is also a very modern school story where, in the later volumes, teenage sexuality begins to emerge in a way that was not found in the earlier gender-segregated and innocent versions of the genre. Another ingredient in the mix is the story of the orphaned child: Harry Potter, like David Copperfield, Jane Eyre, and many others, is an orphan who must discover his identity and past in order to develop as a character.

Primarily, however, *Harry Potter* is a fantasy series. In some ways, it is based on traditional fantasy characters found in children's books: the witches and wizards wear robes, fly on broomsticks, and make potions in cauldrons. However, a lot of its success derives from the fact that, unlike many fantasy realms, the magical world of *Harry Potter* intersects and overlaps with the real world. This results in some of the most inventive and enjoyable features of the books, such as the portals between the worlds (which are always ordinary, such as a deserted telephone kiosk or an old boot) and the 'Muggles' – unmagical people – who are too blinkered to see the magic around them.

It could be argued that the melding of genres in *Harry Potter* is one of the reasons for its success, although it has been criticized: AS Byatt described the series as 'made up of intelligently patchworked derivative motifs from all sorts of children's literature'. Perplexed by the appeal of the books to adults, Byatt also criticized their superficial magic: there is, for example, no particular reason that the Forbidden Forest is dangerous except that we are told so. Other critics have mentioned the often formulaic nature of the books, and the caricatured quality of some of the characters, particularly the unbelievably callous Dursleys. In some ways, however, it is the uneven nature of the series that makes it so interesting. The early books are most certainly written for children, filled with fights with trolls and spells to make one's classmates vomit slugs. However, as the series progresses, both Harry and the books grow up. Deeper and more disturbing elements of the magical world emerge, such as the Dementors, which suck out positive emotions and leave depression and despair in their wake. The series also becomes more political: much of the evil of the final books is caused by the bureaucracy and narrow-mindedness of the 'Ministry for Magic'. The characters become less black-and-white: for example, Draco Malfoy is a caricature rival in the early books, but becomes a sympathetic and torn character at the end.

Whatever one's evaluation of the *Harry Potter* series, there is no doubt about its impact on modern culture. *Muggle* has entered the English vocabulary as a general word meaning 'an unskilful, mundane, ordinary person', while there are few people in the English-speaking world who would not understand a reference to *Quidditch* or *Hogwarts*.

visualize or **-lise** vb **-lizing, -lized** or **-lising, -lised** to form a mental image of (something not at that moment visible) **visualization** or **-lisation** n

vital adj **1** essential or highly important: *marriage isn't such a vital part of his life* **2** energetic or lively: *the epitome of vital youthful manhood* **3** necessary to maintain life: *the vital organs* ▷ n **4 vitals** the bodily organs, such as the brain and heart, that are necessary to maintain life **vitally** adv **WORD ORIGIN** Latin *vita* life

vitality n physical or mental energy

vitalize or **-lise** vb **-lizing, -lized** or **-lising, -lised** to fill with life or vitality **vitalization** or **-lisation** n

vital statistics pl n **1** population statistics, such as the numbers of births, marriages, and deaths **2** informal the measurements of a woman's bust, waist, and hips

vitamin n one of a group of substances that occur naturally in certain foods and are essential for normal health and growth **WORD ORIGIN** from Latin *vita* life + AMINE

vitiate (vish-ee-ate) vb **-ating, -ated** **1** to spoil or weaken the effectiveness of (something) **2** to destroy the legal effect of (a contract) **vitiation** n **WORD ORIGIN** Latin *vitiare* to injure

viticulture n the cultivation of grapevines **WORD ORIGIN** Latin *vitis* vine

vitreous adj **1** of or like glass **2** of or relating to the vitreous humour **WORD ORIGIN** Latin *vitrum* glass

vitreous humour or **body** n a transparent gelatinous substance that fills the eyeball between the lens and the retina

vitrify vb **-fies, -fying, -fied** to change into glass or a glassy substance **vitrification** n

vitriol n **1** language expressing bitterness and hatred **2** sulphuric acid **WORD ORIGIN** Latin *vitrum* glass, referring to the glossy appearance of the sulphates

vitriolic adj (of language) severely bitter or harsh

vituperative (vite-tyew-pra-tiv) adj bitterly abusive **vituperation** n **WORD ORIGIN** Latin *vituperare* to blame

viva¹ interj long live (a specified person or thing) **WORD ORIGIN** Italian, literally: may (he) live!

viva² Brit n **1** an examination in the form of an interview ▷ vb **vivaing, vivaed** **2** to examine (a candidate) in a spoken interview **WORD ORIGIN** from VIVA VOCE

vivace (viv-vah-chee) adj music to be performed in a lively manner **WORD ORIGIN** Italian

vivacious adj full of energy and enthusiasm

vivacity n the quality of being vivacious

vivarium n, pl **-riums** or **-ria** a place where live animals are kept under natural conditions **WORD ORIGIN** Latin *vivus* alive

viva voce (vive-a voh-chee) adv, adj **1** by word of mouth ▷ n **2** same as **viva²** (sense 1) **WORD ORIGIN** Medieval Latin, literally: with living voice

vivid adj **1** very bright: *a vivid blue sky* **2** very clear and detailed: *vivid memories* **3** easily forming lifelike images: *a vivid imagination* **vividly** adv **vividness** n **WORD ORIGIN** Latin *vividus* animated

vivify vb **-fies, -fying, -fied** **1** to bring to life **2** to make more vivid or striking **WORD ORIGIN** Latin *vivus* alive + *facere* to make

viviparous (viv-**vip**-a-russ) adj giving birth to living offspring, as most mammals do **WORD ORIGIN** Latin *vivus* alive + *parere* to bring forth

vivisection n the performing of experiments on living animals, involving cutting into or dissecting the body **vivisectionist** n **WORD ORIGIN** Latin *vivus* living + *sectio* a cutting

vixen n **1** a female fox **2** Brit, Austral, & NZ informal a spiteful woman **WORD ORIGIN** related to Old English *fyxe*, feminine of *fox*

viz adv namely: used to specify items: *I had only one object, viz, to beat the Germans* **WORD ORIGIN** abbreviated from Latin *videlicet* namely

vizier (viz-**zeer**) n a high official in certain Muslim countries **WORD ORIGIN** Turkish *vezīr*

vizor n same as **visor**

VLF or **vlf** radio very low frequency

V neck n **a** a neck on a garment that comes down to a point, like the letter V **b** a sweater with a neck like this **V-neck** or **V-necked** adj

vocab n short for **vocabulary**

vocable n linguistics a word regarded simply as a sequence of letters or spoken sounds **WORD ORIGIN** Latin *vocare* to call

vocabulary n, pl **-laries** **1** all the words that a person knows **2** all the words contained in a language **3** the specialist terms used in a given subject **4** a list of words in another language with their translations **5** a range of symbols or techniques as used in any of the arts or crafts: *the building's vocabulary of materials, textures, and tones* **WORD ORIGIN** Latin *vocabulum* vocable

vocal adj **1** of or relating to the voice: *vocal pitch* **2** expressing one's opinions clearly and openly: *a vocal minority with racist views* ▷ n **3 vocals** the singing part of a piece of jazz or pop music **vocally** adv **WORD ORIGIN** Latin *vox* voice

vocal cords pl n either of two pairs of membranous folds in the larynx, of which the lower pair can be made to vibrate and produce sound by forcing air from the lungs over them

vocalist n a singer with a pop group

vocalize or **-lise** vb **-lizing, -lized** or **-lising, -lised** **1** to express with or use the voice **2** to make vocal or articulate: *vocalize your discontent* **3** phonetics to articulate (a speech sound) with voice **vocalization** or **-lisation** n

vocation n **1** a specified profession or trade **2 a** a special urge to a particular calling or career, esp. a religious one **b** such a calling or career **WORD ORIGIN** Latin *vocare* to call

vocational adj directed towards a particular profession or trade: *vocational training*

vocative n grammar a grammatical case used in some languages when addressing a person or thing **WORD ORIGIN** Latin *vocare* to call

vociferate vb **-rating, -rated** to exclaim or cry out about (something) noisily **vociferation** n **WORD ORIGIN** Latin *vox* voice + *ferre* to bear

vociferous adj loud and forceful: *a vociferous minority* **vociferously** adv

VOD video on demand: an interactive TV system that allows the viewer to select content and view it at a time of his or her own choosing

vodka n a clear alcoholic spirit originating in Russia, made from potatoes or grain **WORD ORIGIN** Russian

voetsak or **voetsek** (**foot**-sak) interj S African, offensive informal an expression of dismissal or rejection **WORD ORIGIN** Afrikaans, from Dutch *voort se ek* forward, I say, commonly applied to animals

vogue n **1** the popular style at a given time **2 in vogue** fashionable ▷ adj **3** fashionable: *a vogue word* **voguish** adj **WORD ORIGIN** French

voice n **1** the sound made by the vibration of the vocal cords, esp. when modified by the tongue and mouth **2** a distinctive tone of the speech sounds characteristic of a particular person: *he can recognize her voice* **3** the ability to speak or sing: *he had at last found his voice* **4** the condition or quality of a person's voice: *her voice was kind* **5** the musical sound of a singing voice: *what I have is a good voice and a great love of lyrics* **6** the expression of feeling or opinion: *there was a chorus of dissenting voices* **7** a right to express an opinion: *the party should now move towards a system which will give every member an equal voice* **8** grammar a category of the verb that expresses whether it is active or passive **9** phonetics the sound characterizing the articulation of several speech sounds, that is produced when the vocal cords are vibrated by the breath **10 with one voice** unanimously ▷ vb **voicing, voiced** **11** to express verbally: *anyone with an objection has a chance to voice it* **12** to articulate (a speech sound) with voice **WORD ORIGIN** Latin *vox*

voiced adj phonetics articulated with accompanying vibration of the vocal cords, for example 'b' in English

voiceless adj **1** without a voice **2** phonetics articulated without accompanying vibration of the vocal cords, for example 'p' in English

voice mail n an electronic system for the transfer and storage of telephone messages, which can then be dealt with by the user at his or her convenience

voice-over n the voice of an unseen commentator heard during a film

void *n* **1** a feeling or condition of loneliness or deprivation **2** an empty space or area ▷ *adj* **3** having no official value or authority, because the terms have been broken or have not been fulfilled: *the race was declared void and rerun* **4** *old-fashioned or literary* empty: *behold, the tomb is void!* **5 void of** devoid of or without: *the fact of being punished becomes void of all moral significance* ▷ *vb* **6** to make ineffective or invalid **7** to empty **8** to discharge the contents of (the bowels or bladder)
WORD ORIGIN Latin *vacare* to be empty

voile (**voyl**) *n* a light semitransparent dress fabric
WORD ORIGIN French: veil

voip *n informal* voice-over internet protocol: a system for converting analogue signals to digital so that telephone calls may be made over the internet

vol. volume

volatile (**voll**-a-tile) *adj* **1** (of circumstances) liable to sudden change **2** (of people) liable to sudden changes of mood and behaviour **3** (of a substance) changing quickly from a solid or liquid form to a vapour **volatility** *n*
WORD ORIGIN Latin *volare* to fly

volatilize *or* **-lise** *vb* **-lizing, -lized** *or* **-lising, -lised** to change from a solid or liquid to a vapour **volatilization** *or* **-lisation** *n*

vol-au-vent (**voll**-oh-von) *n* a very light puff pastry case with a savoury filling
WORD ORIGIN French, literally: flight in the wind

volcanic *adj* **1** of or relating to volcanoes: *volcanic ash* **2** displaying sudden violence or anger: *their boisterous and often volcanic behaviour*

volcano *n, pl* **-noes** *or* **-nos** **1** an opening in the earth's crust from which molten lava, ashes, dust, and gases are ejected from below the earth's surface **2** a mountain formed from volcanic material ejected from a vent
WORD ORIGIN Italian, from Latin *Volcanus* Vulcan, Roman god of fire

vole *n* a small rodent with a stocky body and a short tail
WORD ORIGIN short for *volemouse*, from Old Norse *vollr* field + *mus* mouse

volition *n* **1** the ability to decide things for oneself **2 of one's own volition** through one's own choice **volitional** *adj*
WORD ORIGIN Latin *volo* I will

volley *n* **1** the simultaneous firing of several weapons **2** the bullets fired **3** a burst of questions or critical comments **4** *sport* a stroke or kick at a moving ball before it hits the ground ▷ *vb* **5** to fire (weapons) in a volley **6** *sport* to hit or kick (a moving ball) before it hits the ground
WORD ORIGIN French *volée* a flight

volleyball *n* a game in which two teams hit a large ball backwards and forwards over a high net with their hands

volt *n* the SI unit of electric potential; the potential difference between two points on a conductor carrying a current of 1 ampere, when the power dissipated between these points is 1 watt

WORD ORIGIN after Count Alessandro *Volta*, physicist

voltage *n* an electromotive force or potential difference expressed in volts

voltaic *adj* same as **galvanic** (sense 1)

volte-face (volt-**fass**) *n, pl* **volte-face** a reversal of opinion
WORD ORIGIN Italian *volta* turn + *faccia* face

voltmeter *n* an instrument for measuring voltage

voluble *adj* talking easily and at length **volubility** *n* **volubly** *adv*
WORD ORIGIN Latin *volubilis* turning readily

volume *n* **1** the magnitude of the three-dimensional space enclosed within or occupied by something **2** an amount or total: *the volume of trade between the two countries; the volume of military traffic* **3** loudness of sound **4** the control on a radio etc. for adjusting the loudness of sound **5** a book: *a slim volume* **6** one of several books that make up a series **7** a set of issues of a magazine over a specified period
WORD ORIGIN Latin *volumen* a roll

volumetric *adj* of or using measurement by volume: *a simple volumetric measurement*

voluminous *adj* **1** (of clothes) large and roomy **2** (of writings) extensive and detailed

voluntary *adj* **1** done or undertaken by free choice: *voluntary repatriation* **2** done or maintained without payment: *voluntary work* **3** (of muscles) having their action controlled by the will ▷ *n, pl* **-taries** **4** *music* a composition, usually for organ, played at the beginning or end of a church service **voluntarily** *adv*
WORD ORIGIN Latin *voluntarius*

volunteer *n* **1** a person who offers voluntarily to do something **2** a person who freely undertakes military service ▷ *vb* **3** to offer (oneself or one's services) by choice and without being forced **4** to enlist voluntarily for military service **5** to give (information) willingly **6** to offer the services of (another person)

voluptuary *n, pl* **-aries** a person devoted to luxury and sensual pleasures
WORD ORIGIN Latin *voluptas* pleasure

voluptuous *adj* **1** (of a woman) sexually alluring because of the fullness of her figure **2** pleasing to the senses: *voluptuous yellow peaches* **voluptuously** *adv* **voluptuousness** *n*

volute *n* a spiral or twisting shape or object, such as a carved spiral scroll on an Ionic capital
WORD ORIGIN Latin *volvere* to roll up

vomit *vb* **-iting, -ited** **1** to eject (the contents of the stomach) through the mouth **2** to eject or be ejected forcefully ▷ *n* **3** the partly digested food and drink ejected in vomiting
WORD ORIGIN Latin *vomitare* to vomit repeatedly

voodoo *n* **1** a religion involving ancestor worship and witchcraft, practised by Black people in the West Indies, esp. in Haiti ▷ *adj* **2** of or relating to voodoo: *a voodoo curse*
WORD ORIGIN from West African

voorkamer (foor-**kahm**-er) *n S African* the front room of a house
WORD ORIGIN Afrikaans

voracious *adj* **1** eating or craving great quantities of food **2** very eager or insatiable in some activity: *a voracious collector* **voraciously** *adv* **voracity** *n*
WORD ORIGIN Latin *vorare* to devour

vortex (**vor**-tex) *n, pl* **-tices** (-tiss-seez) **1** a whirling mass or motion, such as a whirlpool or whirlwind **2** a situation which draws people into it against their will: *the vortex of other people's problems* **vortical** *adj*
WORD ORIGIN Latin: a whirlpool

votary *n, pl* **-ries** **1** *RC Church, Eastern Churches* a person who has dedicated himself or herself to religion by taking vows **2** a person devoted to a cause **votaress** *fem n*
WORD ORIGIN Latin *votum* a vow

vote *n* **1** a choice made by a participant in a shared decision, esp. in electing a candidate **2** the right to vote **3** the total number of votes cast **4** the opinion of a group of people as determined by voting: *the draft should be put to the vote at a meeting of the Council* **5** a body of voters or voters collectively: *the youth vote* ▷ *vb* **voting, voted** **6** to make a choice by vote **7** to authorize or allow by voting: *the organizing committee voted itself controversial new powers* **8** to declare oneself as being (something or in favour of something) by voting: *I've always voted Labour* **9** *informal* to declare by common opinion: *he was voted hotelier of the year for the third time*
WORD ORIGIN Latin *votum* a solemn promise

vote down *vb* to decide against or defeat in a vote: *a proposed British resolution was voted down*

voter *n* a person who can or does vote

votive *adj* done or given to fulfil a vow
WORD ORIGIN Latin *votivus* promised by a vow

vouch *vb* **vouch for a** to give personal assurance about: *I can vouch for the man, he's a relative by marriage* **b** to give supporting evidence for or be proof of: *his presence alone vouches for the political nature of the trip*
WORD ORIGIN Latin *vocare* to call

voucher *n* **1** a ticket or card used instead of money to buy specified goods: *a gift voucher* **2** a document recording a financial transaction
WORD ORIGIN Old French *vo(u)cher* to summon

vouchsafe *vb* **-safing, -safed** **1** *old-fashioned* to give or grant: *she has powers vouchsafed to few* **2** to offer assurances about; guarantee: *he absolutely vouchsafed your integrity*
WORD ORIGIN *vouch* + *safe*

vow *n* **1** a solemn and binding promise **2 take vows** to enter a religious order and commit oneself to its rule of life by the vows of poverty, chastity, and obedience ▷ *vb* **3** to promise or decide solemnly: *she vowed to fight on; I solemnly vowed that some day I would return to live in Europe*
WORD ORIGIN Latin *votum*

vowel *n* **a** a voiced speech sound made with the mouth open and the stream of

V

breath unobstructed by the tongue, teeth, or lips, for example *a* or *e* **b** a letter representing this **WORD ORIGIN** Latin *vocalis (littera)*, from *vox* voice

vox pop *n Brit* interviews with members of the public on a radio or television programme

vox populi *n* public opinion **WORD ORIGIN** Latin: the voice of the people

voyage *n* **1** a long journey by sea or in space ▷ *vb* **-gaging, -gaged 2** to go on a voyage: *in this story he voyages to Ireland* **voyager** *n* **WORD ORIGIN** Latin *viaticum* provision for travelling

voyageur (voy-ahzh-**ur**) *n* **1** formerly a French or Métis canoeman who transported furs from trading posts in the North American interior **2** (in Canada) a woodsman, guide, trapper, boatman, or explorer, esp. in the North **WORD ORIGIN** French: voyager

voyeur *n* a person who obtains sexual pleasure from watching people undressing or having sexual intercourse **voyeurism** *n* **voyeuristic** *adj* **WORD ORIGIN** French, literally: one who sees

VPL *jocular* visible panty line

VPN virtual private network: a network that uses the internet to transfer information using secure methods

VR virtual reality

vrou (**froh**) *n S African* an Afrikaner woman, esp. a married woman **WORD ORIGIN** Afrikaans

vs versus

VSA (in New Zealand) Voluntary Service Abroad

V-sign *n* **1** (in Britain and Australia) an offensive gesture made by sticking up the index and middle fingers with the palm of the hand inwards **2** a similar gesture with the palm outwards meaning victory or peace

VSO (in Britain) Voluntary Service Overseas

VSOP very special (*or* superior) old pale: used of brandy or port

VT Vermont

VTOL vertical takeoff and landing

VTR video tape recorder

Vulcan *n* the Roman god of fire

vulcanite *n* a hard black rubber produced by vulcanizing natural rubber with sulphur

vulcanize *or* **-nise** *vb* **-nizing, -nized** *or* **-nising, -nised** to treat (rubber) with sulphur under heat and pressure to improve elasticity and strength **vulcanization** *or* **-nisation** *n* **WORD ORIGIN** after *Vulcan*, Roman god of fire

vulgar *adj* **1** showing lack of good taste, decency, or refinement: *vulgar tabloid sensationalism* **2** denoting a form of a language spoken by the ordinary people, rather than the literary form **vulgarly** *adv* **WORD ORIGIN** Latin *vulgus* the common people

vulgar fraction *n* same as **simple fraction**

vulgarian *n* a vulgar person, usually one who is rich

vulgarism *n* a coarse or obscene word or phrase

vulgarity *n, pl* **-ties 1** the condition of being vulgar **2** a vulgar action or phrase

vulgarize *or* **-rise** *vb* **-rizing, -rized** *or* **-rising, -rised 1** to make vulgar **2** to make (something little known or difficult to understand) popular **vulgarization** *or* **-risation** *n*

Vulgar Latin *n* any of the dialects of Latin spoken in the Roman Empire other than classical Latin

Vulgate *n* the fourth-century Latin version of the Bible

vulnerable *adj* **1** able to be physically or emotionally hurt **2** easily influenced or tempted **3** *mil* exposed to attack **4** financially weak and likely to fail: *this company could be vulnerable in a prolonged economic slump* **5** *bridge* (of a side that has won one game towards rubber) subject to increased bonuses or penalties **vulnerability** *n* **WORD ORIGIN** Latin *vulnus* a wound

vulpine *adj* **1** of or like a fox **2** clever and cunning **WORD ORIGIN** Latin *vulpes* fox

vulture *n* **1** a very large bird of prey that feeds on flesh of dead animals **2** a person who profits from the misfortune and weakness of others **WORD ORIGIN** Latin *vultur*

vulva *n* the external genitals of human females **WORD ORIGIN** Latin: covering, womb, matrix

vuvuzela *n S African* an elongated plastic instrument that football fans blow to make a loud trumpeting noise **WORD ORIGIN** from Zulu

vying *vb* the present participle of **vie**

V

SCRABBLE
Three-Letter Words, part 9
UVA–ZZZ

UVA grape or berry	**WAI** in New Zealand, water	**WOX** obsolete form of the verb to wax	**YON** that or those over there
VAC short for vacation	**WAN** pale and sickly-looking	**WRY** drily humorous	**YOS** plural form of yo
VAE bay or narrow creek	**WAP** strike	**WUD** Scots word for wood	**YOU** person or people addressed
VAG vagrant	**WAR** fighting between nations	**WUS** casual term of address	
VAN motor vehicle for transporting goods	**WAS** part of the verb to be	**WYE** the letter Y	**YOW** variant of ewe
VAR unit of reactive power	**WAT** Thai Buddhist monastery or temple	**WYN** rune equivalent to English W	**YUG** one of the four ages of mankind
VAS vessel or tube that carries a fluid	**WAW** sixth letter of the Hebrew alphabet	**XIS** plural form of xi	**YUK** expression of dislike or disgust
VAT large container for liquids	**WAX** solid shiny fatty or oily substance	**YAD** pointer used for reading the Torah	**YUM** expression of delight
VAU sixth letter of the Hebrew alphabet	**WAY** manner or method	**YAE** Scots word meaning one or a single	**YUP** informal affirmative statement
VAV sixth letter of the Hebrew alphabet	**WEB** net spun by a spider	**YAG** artificial crystal	**YUS** plural form of yu
VAW 6th letter of the Hebrew alphabet	**WED** marry	**YAH** exclamation of derision or disgust	**ZAG** change direction sharply
VEE the letter V	**WEE** small or short	**YAK** Tibetan ox with long shaggy hair	**ZAP** kill (by shooting)
VEG short for vegetable	**WEM** womb or belly	**YAM** tropical root vegetable	**ZAS** plural form of za
VET check the suitability of	**WEN** cyst on the scalp	**YAP** bark with a high-pitched sound	**ZAX** small axe for cutting slates
VEX frustrate, annoy	**WET** covered or soaked with water		**ZEA** type of grass
VIA by way of	**WEX** wax	**YAR** nimble	**ZED** the letter Z
VID video	**WEY** measurement of weight	**YAW** turn from side to side while moving	**ZEE** the letter Z
VIE compete (with someone)	**WHA** Scots word for who	**YAY** exclamation of approval	**ZEK** Soviet prisoner
VIG interest on a loan	**WHO** which person	**YEA** yes	**ZEL** Turkish cymbal
VIM force, energy	**WHY** for what reason	**YEH** yes	**ZEP** type of long sandwich
VIN French wine	**WIG** artificial head of hair	**YEN** monetary unit of Japan	**ZEX** tool for cutting roofing slate
VIS power, force, or strength	**WIN** come first in a competition	**YEP** affirmative statement	**ZHO** Tibetan breed of cattle
VLY low marshy ground	**WIS** know or suppose	**YES** expresses consent	**ZIG** change direction sharply
VOE bay or narrow creek	**WIT** clever humour	**YET** up until then or now	**ZIN** short form of zinfandel
VOL short for volume	**WIZ** accomplished person, whizz	**YEW** evergreen tree	
VOR (in dialect) warn	**WOE** grief	**YEX** hiccup, belch	**ZIP** fastener with two rows of teeth
VOW solemn and binding promise	**WOF** fool	**YGO** archaic form of the verb to go	**ZIT** spot or pimple
VOX voice or sound	**WOG** Australian word meaning influenza	**YID** offensive word for a Jew	**ZIZ** short sleep
VUG small cavity in a rock or vein	**WOK** bowl-shaped Chinese cooking pan	**YIN** Scots word for one	**ZOA** plural form of zoon
VUM swear, vow	**WON** monetary unit	**YIP** emit a high-pitched bark	**ZOL** South African slang for a cannabis cigarette
WAB Scots word for web	**WOO** seek the love or affection of	**YOB** bad-mannered aggressive youth	**ZOO** place where live animals are kept
WAD small mass of soft material	**WOP** strike or beat	**YOD** 10th letter of the Hebrew alphabet	**ZOS** plural form of zo
WAE old form of woe	**WOS** plural form of wo		**ZUZ** silver coin of ancient Palestine
WAG move rapidly from side to side	**WOT** wit, to know	**YOK** chuckle	**ZZZ** informal word for sleep
	WOW exclamation of astonishment	**YOM** day	

Ww

The letter W is the twenty-third letter of the English alphabet. It is one of two letters (the other being J) that were not used by the Romans but were added to their alphabet at a later date.

In Latin, the sound that we now associate with W was represented by the letter V. As the sound that we now associate with V was not used at all, this did not cause any difficulty. In languages that used both the /w/ and /v/ sounds, however, V became overworked, and it became necessary to distinguish between the different sounds. In early English writing this was done by using a symbol borrowed from the Runic alphabet called 'wyn' to show the /w/ sound, but by the thirteenth century, this had been superseded. Writers found it easier simply to write two letter V's or U's together (V and U being regarded as two forms of the same letter at this time). The shape of the letter has remained the same, and its name reflects its origin as a 'double U'.

The early association of W with letter U can still be perceived in the way that the letter has a secret life as a vowel. In words such as 'lawn' and 'town' the W acts just like U, combining with the preceding vowel to make a distinctive sound.

Many European languages still manage pretty well without a W. In French, Italian, and Spanish, W is an exotic letter, occurring only in a handful of words borrowed from English, such as *whisky* and *watt*.

In English, however, W is well established, and is particularly notable for being the first letter in many interrogative words. Journalists are taught that a good story should be based on the 'five W's': who?, what?, why?, where?, and when? The answers to these questions should be presented to a reader in the first paragraph of any news story. Rather annoyingly, there is a sixth key question – how? – which also needs to be asked, but which does not fit neatly into the scheme.

Fewer in number, but also worthy of note, were the 'three W's', the feared West Indian batting trio of Clyde Walcott, Frank Worrell, and Everton Weekes who were a dominant force in world cricket in the 1950s.

---

w *cricket* **a** wicket **b** wide

W 1 *chem* tungsten
WORD ORIGIN German *Wolfram* **2** watt **3** West(ern)

WA 1 Washington (state) **2** Western Australia

wacko *chiefly US & Canad informal adj* **1** mad or eccentric ▷ *n, pl* **wackos 2** a mad or eccentric person
WORD ORIGIN from WACKY

wacky *adj* **wackier, wackiest** *slang* odd, eccentric, or crazy: *a wacky idea* **wackiness** *n*
WORD ORIGIN dialect: a fool

wad *n* **1** a small mass of soft material, such as cotton wool, used for packing or stuffing **2** a roll or bundle of banknotes or papers
WORD ORIGIN Late Latin *wadda*

wadding *n* a soft material used for padding or stuffing

waddle *vb* **-dling, -dled 1** to walk with short steps, rocking slightly from side to side ▷ *n* **2** a swaying walk
WORD ORIGIN from *wade*

waddy *n, pl* **-dies** a heavy wooden club used by Australian Aborigines

wade *vb* **wading, waded 1** to walk slowly and with difficulty through water or mud **2 wade in** *or* **into** to begin doing (something) in an energetic way: *wading into the fray* **3 wade through** to

proceed with difficulty through: *a stack of literature to wade through*
WORD ORIGIN Old English *wadan*

wader *n* a long-legged bird, such as the heron or stork, that lives near water and feeds on fish. Also called: **wading bird**

waders *pl n* long waterproof boots which completely cover the legs, worn by anglers for standing in water

wadi (**wod**-dee) *n, pl* **-dies** a river in N Africa or Arabia, which is dry except in the rainy season
WORD ORIGIN Arabic

wafer *n* **1** a thin crisp sweetened biscuit, often served with ice cream **2** *Christianity* a round thin piece of unleavened bread used at Communion **3** *electronics* a small thin slice of germanium or silicon that is separated into numerous individual components or circuits
WORD ORIGIN Old French *waufre*

wafer-thin *adj* very thin: *wafer-thin meat*

waffle¹ *n* a square crisp pancake with a gridlike pattern
WORD ORIGIN Dutch *wafel*

waffle² *informal chiefly Brit, Austral, & NZ vb* **-fling, -fled 1** to speak or write in a vague and wordy manner ▷ *n* **2** vague and wordy speech or writing
WORD ORIGIN origin unknown

waft *vb* **1** to move gently through the air as if being carried by the wind: *the scent*

of summer flowers gently wafting through my window ▷ *n* **2** a scent carried on the air
WORD ORIGIN Middle Dutch *wachter* guard

wag¹ *vb* **wagging, wagged 1** to move rapidly and repeatedly from side to side or up and down: *Franklin wagged his tail* ▷ *n* **2** an instance of wagging
WORD ORIGIN Old English *wagian*

wag² *n old-fashioned* a humorous or witty person **waggish** *adj*
WORD ORIGIN origin unknown

Wag *n informal* the wife or girlfriend of a famous sportsperson

wage *n* **1** Also: **wages** the money paid in return for a person's work, esp. when paid weekly or daily rather than monthly: *a campaign for higher wages* ▷ *vb* **waging, waged 2** to engage in (a campaign or war)
WORD ORIGIN Old French *wagier* to pledge

wager *n* **1** a bet on the outcome of an event or activity ▷ *vb* **2** to bet (something, esp. money) on the outcome of an event or activity
WORD ORIGIN Old French *wagier* to pledge

waggle *vb* **-gling, -gled** to move with a rapid shaking or wobbling motion
WORD ORIGIN from WAG¹

wagon *or* **waggon** *n* **1** a four-wheeled vehicle used for carrying heavy loads,

sometimes pulled by a horse or tractor **2** an open railway freight truck **3** a lorry **4 on the wagon** *informal* abstaining from alcoholic drink **wagoner** or **waggoner** *n*
WORD ORIGIN Dutch *wagen*

wagtail *n* a small songbird of Eurasia and Africa with a very long tail that wags up and down when it walks

Wagyu (wag-yoo) *n* **1** any of several Japanese breeds of beef cattle, raised to produce Kobe beef **2** another name for **Kobe beef**

wahine (wah-**hee**-nay) *n* NZ a Māori woman, esp. a wife
WORD ORIGIN Māori

wahoo *n* a large food and game fish of tropical seas

waif *n* a person, esp. a child, who is, or who looks as if he or she might be, homeless or neglected
WORD ORIGIN Anglo-Norman

wail *vb* **1** to utter a prolonged high-pitched cry of pain or sorrow ▷ *n* **2** a prolonged high-pitched cry of pain or sorrow **wailing** *n, adj*
WORD ORIGIN from Old Norse

wain *n poetic* a farm cart
WORD ORIGIN Old English *wægn*

wainscot *n* a wooden covering on the lower half of the walls of a room. Also: **wainscoting**
WORD ORIGIN Middle Low German *wagenschot*

waist *n* **1** *anat* the narrow part of the body between the ribs and the hips **2** the part of a garment covering the waist
WORD ORIGIN origin unknown

waistband *n* a band of material sewn on to the waist of a garment to strengthen it

waistcoat *n* a sleeveless upper garment which buttons up the front and is usually worn by men over a shirt and under a jacket

waistline *n* **1** an imaginary line around the body at the narrowest part of the waist **2** the place where the upper and lower part of a garment are joined together

wait *vb* **1** to stay in one place or remain inactive in expectation of something: *the delegates have to wait for a reply* **2** to be temporarily delayed: *the celebrations can wait* **3** (of a thing) to be ready or be in store: *waiting for her on the library table was the latest Jilly Cooper novel* ▷ *n* **4** the act or a period of waiting **5 lie in wait for a** to prepare an ambush for **b** to be ready or be in store for ▶ See also **wait on, wait up**
WORD ORIGIN Old French *waitier*

Waitangi Day *n* February 6, the national day of New Zealand commemorating the Treaty Of Waitangi in 1840

waiter *n* a man who serves people with food and drink in a restaurant

waiting game *n* **play a waiting game** to postpone taking action or making a decision in order to gain an advantage

waiting list *n* a list of people waiting for something that is not immediately available: *a long waiting list for heart surgery*

waiting room *n* a room in which people can wait, for example at a railway station or doctor's surgery

wait on *vb* **1** to serve (people) with food and drink in a restaurant **2** to look after the needs of: *they were waited on by a manservant* ▷ *interj* **3** NZ stop! hold on!. Also (for senses 1, 2): **wait upon**

waitress *n* **1** a woman who serves people with food and drink in a restaurant ▷ *vb* **2** to work as a waitress

wait up *vb* to delay going to bed in order to wait for someone or something: *when he's late, she waits up for him*

waive *vb* **waiving, waived** to refrain from enforcing or claiming (a rule or right)
WORD ORIGIN Old French *weyver*

waiver *n* the act or an instance of voluntary giving up a claim or right

waka *n* NZ a Māori canoe

wake¹ *vb* **waking, woke, woken** **1** Also: **wake up** to become conscious again or bring (someone) to consciousness again after a sleep **2 wake up** to make (someone) more alert after a period of inactivity **3 wake up to** to become aware of: *the world did not wake up to this tragedy until many people had died* **4 waking hours** the time when a person is awake: *he often used his waking hours to write music* ▷ *n* **5** a watch or vigil held over the body of a dead person during the night before burial
WORD ORIGIN Old English *wacian*

≡ **USAGE**
≡ Where there is an object and the sense
≡ is the literal one *wake* (*up*) and *waken* are
≡ the commonest forms: *I wakened him;*
≡ *I woke him* (*up*). Both verbs are also
≡ commonly used without an object: *I*
≡ *woke up. Awake* and *awaken* are preferred
≡ to other forms of *wake* where the sense
≡ is a figurative one: *he awoke to the danger.*

wake² *n* **1** the track left by a ship moving through water **2 in the wake of** following soon after: *the arrests come in the wake of the assassination*
WORD ORIGIN Scandinavian

wakeful *adj* **1** unable to sleep **2** without sleep: *wakeful nights* **3** alert: *wakeful readiness* **wakefulness** *n*

waken *vb* to become conscious again or bring (someone) to consciousness again after a sleep

≡ **USAGE**
≡ See at **wake**.

walk *vb* **1** to move on foot at a moderate rate with at least one foot always on the ground **2** to pass through, on, or over on foot: *to walk a short distance* **3** to walk somewhere with (a person or a dog) **4 walking on air** very happy and excited **5 walk the streets** to wander about, esp. when looking for work or when homeless ▷ *n* **6** a short journey on foot, usually for pleasure **7** the action of walking rather than running **8** a manner of walking: *a proud slow walk* **9** a place or route for walking **10 walk of life** social position or profession: *people from all walks of life were drawn to her* ▶ See also **walk into, walk out**, etc. **walker** *n*
WORD ORIGIN Old English *wealcan*

walkabout *n* **1** an occasion when royalty, politicians, or other celebrities walk among and meet the public **2 go walkabout** *Austral* **a** to wander through the bush as a nomad **b** *informal* to be lost or misplaced **c** *Informal* to lose one's concentration

walkie-talkie *n* a small combined radio transmitter and receiver that can be carried around by one person

walking stick *n* a stick or cane carried in the hand to assist walking

walk into *vb* to encounter unexpectedly: *the troop reinforcements had walked into a trap*

Walkman *n trademark* a small portable cassette player with headphones

walk-on *adj* (of a part in a film or play) small and not involving speaking

walk out *vb* **1** to leave suddenly and without explanation, usually in anger **2** (of workers) to go on strike **3 walk out on** *informal* to abandon or desert ▷ *n* **walkout 4** a strike by workers

walkover *n* **1** *informal* an easy victory ▷ *vb* **walk over 2** to mistreat or bully; take advantage of: *if you don't make your mark early, people will walk all over you*

walkway *n* **1** a path designed for use by pedestrians **2** a passage or pathway between two buildings

wall *n* **1** a vertical structure made of stone, brick, or wood, with a length and height much greater than its thickness, used to enclose, divide, or support ▶ Related adjective: **mural 2** anything that suggests a wall in function or effect: *a wall of elm trees; a wall of suspicion* **3** *anat* any lining or membrane that encloses a bodily cavity or structure: *cell walls* **4 drive someone up the wall** *slang* to make someone angry or irritated **5 go to the wall** *informal* to be financially ruined **6 have one's back to the wall** *informal* to be in a very difficult situation, with no obvious way out of it ▷ *vb* **7** to surround or enclose (an area) with a wall **8 wall in** or **up** to enclose (someone or something) completely in a room or place **walled** *adj*
WORD ORIGIN Old English *weall*

wallaby *n, pl* **-bies** a marsupial of Australia and New Guinea that resembles a small kangaroo
WORD ORIGIN Aboriginal *wolabā*

wallah (**woll**-a) *n informal* a person involved with or in charge of a specified thing: *rickshaw wallahs*
WORD ORIGIN Hindi *-wālā*

wallaroo *n* a large stocky Australian kangaroo of rocky regions

wall bars *pl n* a series of horizontal bars attached to a wall and used in gymnastics

wallet *n* a small folding case, usually of leather, for holding paper money and credit cards
WORD ORIGIN Germanic

walleye *n* a fish with large staring eyes

walleyed *adj* having eyes with an abnormal amount of white showing because of a squint
WORD ORIGIN Old Norse *vagleygr*

wallflower *n* **1** a plant grown for its clusters of yellow, orange, red, or purple fragrant flowers **2** *informal* a woman who does not join in the dancing at a party or dance because she has no partner

W

Walloon (wol-**loon**) n **1** a French-speaking person from S Belgium or the neighbouring part of France **2** the French dialect of Belgium ▷ adj **3** of the Walloons
WORD ORIGIN Germanic

wallop informal vb **1** to hit hard ▷ n **2** a hard blow
WORD ORIGIN Old French waloper to gallop

walloping informal n **1** a severe physical beating ▷ adj **2** large or great: a walloping amount of sodium

wallow vb **1** to indulge oneself in some emotion: they wallow in self-pity **2** to lie or roll about in mud or water for pleasure ▷ n **3** the act or an instance of wallowing **4** a muddy place where animals wallow
WORD ORIGIN Old English wealwian to roll (in mud)

wallpaper n **1** a printed or embossed paper for covering the walls of a room ▷ vb **2** to cover (walls) with wallpaper

wall-to-wall adj (of carpeting) completely covering a floor

wally n, pl -**lies** Brit slang a stupid or foolish person
WORD ORIGIN from the name Walter

walnut n **1** an edible nut with a hard, wrinkled, light brown shell **2** a tree on which walnuts grow **3** the light brown wood of a walnut tree, used for making furniture
WORD ORIGIN Old English walh-hnutu foreign nut

walrus n, pl -**ruses** or -**rus** a mammal of cold northern seas, with two tusks that hang down from the upper jaw, tough thick skin, and coarse whiskers
WORD ORIGIN Dutch: whale horse

waltz n **1** a ballroom dance in triple time in which couples spin round as they progress round the room **2** music for this dance ▷ vb **3** to dance a waltz **4** informal to move in a relaxed and confident way: he waltzed over to her table to say hello
WORD ORIGIN German Walzer

wampum (**wom**-pum) n (formerly) money used by Native Americans of N America, made of shells strung or woven together
WORD ORIGIN Native American wampompeag

wan (rhymes with **swan**) adj **wanner**, **wannest** very pale, as a result of illness or unhappiness **wanly** adv
WORD ORIGIN Old English wann dark

WAN computers wide area network

wand n **1** a rod used by a magician when performing a trick or by a fairy when casting a spell **2** a hand-held electronic device which is pointed at or passed over an item to read the data stored there
WORD ORIGIN Old Norse vöndr

wander vb **1** to walk about in a place without any definite purpose or destination **2** (often foll. by off) to leave a place where one is supposed to stay: kids wander off **3** (of the mind) to lose concentration ▷ n **4** the act or an instance of wandering **wanderer** n **wandering** adj, n
WORD ORIGIN Old English wandrian

wanderlust n a great desire to travel

wane vb **waning**, **waned 1** to decrease gradually in size, strength, or power: the influence of the extremists is waning **2** (of the moon) to show a gradually decreasing area of brightness from full moon until new moon ▷ n **3** **on the wane** decreasing in size, strength, or power: his fame was on the wane **waning** adj
WORD ORIGIN Old English wanian

wangle vb -**gling**, -**gled** informal to get (something) by cunning or devious methods: I've wangled you both an invitation
WORD ORIGIN origin unknown

wanigan (**wonn**-ig-an) n Canad **1** a watertight box or chest used by canoeists or lumberjacks to hold provisions **2** a sled or boat for carrying camping supplies
WORD ORIGIN from a Native American language

wank taboo slang vb **1** (of a man) to masturbate ▷ n **2** an instance of masturbating
WORD ORIGIN origin unknown

wanker n taboo slang a worthless or stupid person

wannabe or **wannabee** adj **1** wanting to be, or be like, a particular person or thing: a wannabe actress ▷ n **2** a person who wants to be, or be like, a particular person or thing

want vb **1** to feel a need or longing for: I want a job **2** to wish or desire (to do something): we did not want to get involved **3** Brit, Austral, & NZ to have need of or require (doing or being something): what will you do when it wants cleaning? **4** informal should or ought (to do something): the last person you want to hire is someone who is desperate for a job **5** **want for** to be lacking or deficient in: they were convinced I was wealthy and wanted for nothing ▷ n **6** something that is needed, desired, or lacked: attempts to satisfy a number of wants **7** a lack, shortage, or absence: for want of opportunity **8** **in want of** needing or lacking: the Chinese peasant farmer may be in want of a roof, a job, a doctor nearby
WORD ORIGIN Old Norse vanta to be deficient

wanted adj being searched for by the police in connection with a crime that has been committed

wanting adj **1** lacking: I would be wanting in charity if I did not explain the terms **2** not meeting requirements or expectations: she compares herself to her sister and finds herself wanting

wanton adj **1** without motive, provocation, or justification: sheer wanton destruction **2** (of a person) maliciously and unnecessarily cruel **3** old-fashioned (of a woman) sexually unrestrained or immodest ▷ n **4** old-fashioned a sexually unrestrained or immodest woman
WORD ORIGIN Middle English wantowen unruly

WAP n Wireless Application Protocol: a system that allows mobile phone users to access the internet and other information services

wapiti (**wop**-pit-tee) n, pl -**tis** a large North American deer, now also found in New Zealand

WORD ORIGIN from a Native American language

war n **1** open armed conflict between two or more countries or groups: this international situation led to war **2** a particular armed conflict: the American war in Vietnam **3** any conflict or contest: a trade war **4** **have been in the wars** informal to look as if one has been in a fight ▷ adj **5** relating to war or a war: the war effort; a war correspondent ▷ vb **warring**, **warred 6** to conduct a war **warring** adj
WORD ORIGIN Old Northern French werre

waratah n an Australian shrub with crimson flowers

warble vb -**bling**, -**bled** to sing in a high-pitched trilling voice
WORD ORIGIN Old French werbler

warbler n any of various small songbirds

war crime n a crime committed in wartime in violation of the accepted customs, such as ill-treatment of prisoners **war criminal** n

war cry n **1** a rallying cry used by combatants in battle **2** a slogan used to rally support for a cause

ward n **1** a room in a hospital for patients requiring similar kinds of care: the maternity ward **2** one of the districts into which a town, parish, or other area is divided for administration or elections ▷ Also called: **ward of court** law a person, esp. a child whose parents are dead, who is placed under the control or protection of a guardian or of a court ▶ See also **ward off** ▷ **wardship** n
WORD ORIGIN Old English weard protector

-ward suffix **1** (forming adjectives) indicating direction towards: a backward step **2** (forming adverbs) chiefly US & Canad same as -**wards**
WORD ORIGIN Old English -weard

warden n **1** a person who is in charge of a building, such as a youth hostel, and its occupants **2** a public official who is responsible for the enforcement of certain regulations: a game warden **3** the chief officer in charge of a prison
WORD ORIGIN Old French wardein

warder or fem **wardress** n chiefly Brit a prison officer
WORD ORIGIN Old French warder to guard

ward off vb to prevent (something unpleasant) from happening or from causing harm: to ward off the pangs of hunger; to ward off cancer cells

wardrobe n **1** a tall cupboard, with a rail or hooks on which to hang clothes **2** the total collection of articles of clothing belonging to one person: your autumn wardrobe **3** the collection of costumes belonging to a theatre or theatrical company
WORD ORIGIN Old French warder to guard + robe robe

wardrobe mistress n the woman in charge of the costumes in a theatre or theatrical company **wardrobe master** masc n

wardroom n the quarters assigned to the officers of a warship, apart from the captain

Roald Dahl

Roald Dahl was born in 1916 in Llandaff, Wales, to Norwegian parents. Many of his life-shaping childhood experiences – the death of his father and sister when he was three years old, the summers he spent with his family in Norway hearing stories about trolls and other mythical creatures, and his less than idyllic experiences at boarding school – are recounted in his autobiography *Boy* (1984). Dahl served in the Royal Air Force in World War II, and then began publishing fiction in the 1950s. After a life marred by tragedy – one of his sons suffered brain damage as a baby, and one of his daughters died at the age of seven – Dahl died of leukaemia in 1990.

His first publications were the short stories which he wrote for magazines such as *Harper* and *The New Yorker*. These stories, which gained widespread renown when adapted into the television series *Tales of the Unexpected* (1979–1988), are often terse, macabre, and darkly comic. One of the most famous is 'Lamb to the Slaughter' (first published in 1953), in which a young woman kills her husband with a frozen leg of lamb, then roasts the lamb and serves it to the policemen who come to investigate the crime. The story ends with the policemen speculating over what the murder weapon might have been, and saying that it was probably 'right under our very noses'; we hear the young woman giggling in the other room.

However, it is on his children's fiction that Dahl's fame rests. His first success was *James and the Giant Peach* (1961 US; 1967 UK), shortly followed by *Charlie and the Chocolate Factory* (1964 US; 1967 UK). Other masterpieces were *Danny the Champion of the World* (1970), *Fantastic Mr Fox* (1970), *The BFG* (1982), *The Witches* (1983), and *Matilda* (1988), several of which have been made into films. Dahl uses all the right ingredients to make his books appealing to children. They are inventive and imaginative: what child would not fall in love with the sweet edible grass, the choco-late river, or the boat hollowed out of a giant boiled sweet in *Charlie and the Chocolate Factory*? Their playful use of language is perhaps best seen in *The BFG*, where the Big Friendly Giant of the title laments, 'Words is oh such a twitch-tickling problem to me all my life....As I am telling you before, I know exactly what words I am wanting to say, but somehow or other they is always getting squiff-squiddled around.'

The BFG is replete with coinages such as *scrumdiddlyumptious*, *sloshflunking* and *gungswizzled*, in the tradition of children's classics such as Lewis Carroll's *Alice in Wonderland*. Dahl also seems to understand a child's sense of humour: one chapter of *The BFG*, for example, is devoted to the pleasures of *whizzpopping* (farting).

Furthermore, there is often a subversive and irreverent treatment of adults and authority: most of Dahl's books feature at least one mean and stupid adult who comes to a bad end. On the other hand, most of his books also present at least one adult character as a model parent or grandparent, such as the kindly grandmother in *The Witches*, the effervescent Grandpa Joe in *Charlie and the Chocolate Factory*, and the creative and inspiring father in *Danny the Champion of the World*. Another central aspect of the books which appeals to Dahl's young readers is their strong sense of fairness and morality. The underdog always triumphs: the mistreated fox family succeed in duping the cruel farmers in *Fantastic Mr Fox*, while it is Charlie Bucket, poor and good-hearted, who earns the chocolate factory, while the spoiled and brattish children get turned into giant blueberries or sent down rubbish chutes.

Dahl has been criticized for the subversiveness and the rather harsh morality found in his children's books. However, if children are to be the judges then Dahl's works are a resounding success, perhaps because, as Dahl explained in an interview not long before his death, 'My lucky thing is I laugh at exactly the same jokes that children laugh at.'

-wards *or* **-ward** *suffix* forming adverbs indicating direction towards: *a step backwards*
WORD ORIGIN Old English *-weardes*

ware *n* articles of the same kind or material: *crystal ware.* See also **wares**
WORD ORIGIN Old English *waru*

warehouse *n* a place where goods are stored prior to their sale or distribution

wares *pl n* goods for sale

warfare *n* **1** the act of conducting a war **2** a violent or intense conflict of any kind: *class warfare*

war game *n* **1** a tactical exercise for training military commanders, in which no military units are actually deployed **2** a game in which model soldiers are used to create battles in order to study tactics

warhead *n* the front section of a missile or projectile that contains explosives

warhorse *n* **1** (formerly) a horse used in battle **2** *informal* a veteran soldier or politician

warlike *adj* **1** of or relating to war: *warlike stores and equipment* **2** hostile and eager to have a war: *a warlike nation*

warlock *n* a man who practises black magic
WORD ORIGIN Old English *wǣrloga* oath breaker

warlord *n* a military leader of a nation or part of a nation

warm *adj* **1** feeling or having a moderate degree of heat **2** giving heat: *warm clothing* **3** (of colours) predominantly red or yellow in tone **4** kindly or affectionate: *warm embraces* **5** *informal* near to finding a hidden object or guessing facts, for example in a children's game ▷ *vb* **6** to make warm **7 warm to a** to become fonder of: *I warmed to him when he defended me* **b** to become more excited or enthusiastic about: *he had warmed to his theme* ▶ See also **warm up** ▷ **warmly** *adv* **warmness** *n*
WORD ORIGIN Old English *wearm*

warm-blooded *adj* **1** (of an animal, such as a mammal or a bird) having a constant body temperature, usually higher than the surrounding temperature **2** having a passionate nature **warm-bloodedness** *n*

warm-down *n* light exercises performed to aid recovery from strenuous physical activity

war memorial *n* a monument to people who have died in a war, esp. local people

warm front *n meteorol* the boundary between a warm air mass and the cold air it is replacing

warm-hearted *adj* kind, affectionate, or sympathetic

warming pan *n* a long-handled pan filled with hot coals, formerly pulled over the sheets to warm a bed

warmonger *n* a person who encourages warlike ideas or advocates war **warmongering** *n*

warmth *n* **1** the state of being warm **2** affection or cordiality: *the warmth of their friendship*

warm up *vb* **1** to make or become warm or warmer **2** to prepare for a race,
sporting contest, or exercise routine by doing gentle exercises immediately beforehand **3** (of an engine or machine) to be started and left running until the working temperature is reached **4** to become more lively: *wait until things warm up* **5** to reheat (food that has already been cooked) ▷ *n* **warm-up 6** a preparatory exercise routine

warn *vb* **1** to make (someone) aware of a possible danger or problem **2** to inform (someone) in advance: *you'd better warn your girlfriend that you'll be working at the weekend* **3 warn off** to advise (someone) to go away or not to do something
WORD ORIGIN Old English *wearnian*

warning *n* **1** a hint, threat, or advance notice of a possible danger or problem **2** advice not to do something ▷ *adj* **3** giving or serving as a warning: *warning signs* **warningly** *adv*

warp *vb* **1** (esp. of wooden objects) to be twisted out of shape, for example by heat or damp **2** to distort or influence in a negative way: *love warps judgment* ▷ *n* **3** a fault or an irregularity in the shape or surface of an object **4** a fault or deviation in someone's character **5** see **time warp 6** the yarns arranged lengthways on a loom through which the weft yarns are woven **warped** *adj*
WORD ORIGIN Old English *wearp* a throw

war paint *n* **1** paint applied to the face and body by certain North American Indians before battle **2** *informal* cosmetics

warpath *n* **on the warpath a** preparing to engage in battle **b** *informal* angry and looking for a fight or conflict

warrant *n* **1** an official authorization for some action or decision: *Scotland Yard today issued a warrant for the arrest of this man* **2** a document that certifies or guarantees something, such as a receipt or licence ▷ *vb* **3** to make necessary: *we've no hard evidence to warrant a murder investigation*
WORD ORIGIN Old French *guarant*

warrant officer *n* an officer in certain armed services with a rank between those of commissioned and noncommissioned officers

Warrant of Fitness *n* NZ a six-monthly certificate required for a motor vehicle certifying that it is mechanically sound

warrantor *n* a person or company that provides a warranty

warranty *n, pl* **-ties** a guarantee or assurance that goods meet a specified standard or that the facts in a legal document are as stated
WORD ORIGIN Anglo-French *warantie*

warren *n* **1** a series of interconnected underground tunnels in which rabbits live **2** an overcrowded building or area of a city with many narrow passages or streets: *a mountainous concrete warren of apartments*
WORD ORIGIN Anglo-French *warenne*

warrigal *Austral n* **1** a dingo ▷ *adj* **2** wild

warrior *n* a person who is engaged in or experienced in war
WORD ORIGIN Old French *werreieor*

warship *n* a ship designed for naval warfare

wart *n* **1** a firm abnormal growth on the skin caused by a virus **2 warts and all** including faults: *she loves him warts and all* **warty** *adj*
WORD ORIGIN Old English *weart(e)*

warthog *n* a wild African pig with heavy tusks, wartlike lumps on the face, and a mane of coarse hair

wartime *n* **1** a time of war ▷ *adj* **2** of or in a time of war: *the wartime coalition*

wary (**ware**-ree) *adj* **warier, wariest** cautious or on one's guard: *be wary of hitchhikers* **warily** *adv* **wariness** *n*
WORD ORIGIN Old English *wær* aware, careful

was *vb* (with 'I', 'he', 'she', 'it', or a singular noun as subject) the past tense of **be**
WORD ORIGIN Old English *wæs*

wash *vb* **1** to clean (oneself, part of one's body, or a thing) with soap or detergent and water **2** (of a garment or fabric) to be capable of being washed without damage or loss of colour **3** to move or be moved in a particular direction by water: *houses may be washed away in floods* **4** (of waves) to flow or sweep against or over (a surface or object), often with a lapping sound **5** *informal* to be acceptable or believable: *the masculine pride argument won't wash now when so many women go out to work* ▷ *n* **6** the act or process of washing **7** all the clothes etc. to be washed together on one occasion **8** a thin layer of paint or ink: *a pale wash of blue* **9** the disturbance in the air or water produced at the rear of an aircraft, boat, or other moving object: *we were hit by the wash of a large vessel* **10 come out in the wash** *informal* to become known or apparent in the course of time ▶ See also **wash down, wash out, wash up** ▷ **washable** *adj*
WORD ORIGIN Old English *wæscan, waxan*

Wash. Washington (state)

washbasin *n* a small sink in a bathroom, used for washing the face and hands. Also: **wash-hand basin**

wash down *vb* **1** to have a drink with or after (food or medicine): *a large steak, washed down with coffee* **2** to wash from top to bottom: *she washed down the staircase*

washed out *adj* **1** exhausted and lacking in energy **2** faded or colourless

washed up *adj informal* no longer as successful or important as previously: *she stands discredited, her career probably washed up*

washer *n* **1** a flat ring of rubber, felt, or metal used to provide a seal under a nut or bolt or in a tap or valve **2** *informal* a washing machine **3** a person who washes things, esp. as a job: *chief cook and bottle washer* **4** *Austral* a small piece of towelling cloth used to wash the face

washerwoman *n, pl* **-women** a woman who washes clothes as a job

washing *n* all the clothes etc. to be washed together on one occasion

washing machine *n* a machine for washing clothes and bed linen in

washing soda *n* crystalline sodium carbonate, used as a cleansing agent

washing-up *n* the act of washing used dishes and cutlery after a meal

wash out *vb* **1** Also: **wash off** to remove or be removed by washing: *the rain washes* the red dye out of the cap **2** to wash the inside of (a container) ▷ *n* **washout** **3** *informal* a total failure or disaster **4** *NZ* a part of a road or railway washed away by floodwaters

washroom *n US & Canad* a toilet

washstand *n* a piece of furniture designed to hold a basin for washing the face and hands in

wash up *vb* **1** to wash used dishes and cutlery after a meal **2** *US & Canad* to wash one's face and hands

washy *adj* **washier, washiest** **1** overdiluted or weak **2** lacking intensity of colour: *a washy blend of pale brown and pale grey*

wasn't was not

wasp *n* a common stinging insect with a slender black-and-yellow striped body **WORD ORIGIN** Old English *wæsp*

Wasp *or* **WASP** (in the US and Canada) White Anglo-Saxon Protestant: a person descended from N European, usually Protestant stock, forming a group often considered to be the most dominant and privileged in N American society

waspish *adj* bad-tempered or spiteful: *waspish comments*

wasp waist *n* a very narrow waist **wasp-waisted** *adj*

wassail *n* **1** (formerly) a toast drunk to a person during festivities **2** a festivity involving a lot of drinking **3** hot spiced beer or mulled wine drunk at such a festivity ▷ *vb* **4** **go wassailing** to go from house to house singing carols at Christmas **WORD ORIGIN** Old Norse *ves heill* be in good health

wastage *n* **1** the act of wasting something or the state of being wasted: *wastage of raw materials* **2** reduction in the size of a workforce by retirement, redundancy, etc.

≡ **USAGE**
≡ *Waste* and *wastage* are to some extent
≡ interchangeable, but many people
≡ think that *wastage* should not be used
≡ to refer to loss resulting from human
≡ carelessness, inefficiency, etc.: *a waste*
≡ (not *a wastage*) *of time, money, effort,* etc.

waste *vb* **wasting, wasted** **1** to use up thoughtlessly, carelessly, or unsuccessfully **2** to fail to take advantage of: *let's not waste an opportunity to see the children* **3** **be wasted on** to be too good for; not be appreciated by: *fine brandy is wasted on you* **4** **waste away** to lose one's strength or health: *wasting away from unrequited love* ▷ *n* **5** the act of wasting something or the state of being wasted: *a waste of time* **6** something that is left over because it is in excess of requirements **7** rubbish: *toxic waste* **8** *physiol* matter discharged from the body as faeces or urine **9** **wastes** a region that is wild or uncultivated ▷ *adj* **10** rejected as being useless, unwanted, or worthless: *waste products* **11** not cultivated or productive: *waste ground* **12** *physiol* discharged from the body as faeces or urine: *waste matter* **13** **lay waste** *or* **lay waste to** to devastate or destroy: *the Bikini atoll, laid waste by nuclear tests* **WORD ORIGIN** Latin *vastare* to lay waste

wasted *adj* **1** unnecessary or unfruitful: *wasted effort* **2** pale, thin, and unhealthy: *the hunched shoulders and the wasted appearance of his body*

wasteful *adj* causing waste: *wasteful expenditure* **wastefully** *adv*

wasteland *n* **1** a barren or desolate area of land **2** something that is considered spiritually, intellectually, or aesthetically barren: *the TV wasteland*

wastepaper basket *n* a container for paper discarded after use

waster *n* *informal* a lazy or worthless person

wasting *adj* reducing the vitality and strength of the body: *a pernicious wasting illness*

wastrel *n* *literary* a lazy or worthless person

watap (wat-**tahp**) *n* a stringy thread made by Native Americans from the roots of conifers **WORD ORIGIN** from a Native American language

watch *vb* **1** to look at or observe closely and attentively **2** to look after (a child or a pet) **3** to maintain a careful interest in or control over: *it reminds me to watch my diet* **4** **watch for** to be keenly alert to or cautious about: *the vigilant night watchman hired to watch for thieves* **5** **watch it!** be careful! ▷ *n* **6** a small portable timepiece worn strapped to the wrist or in a waistcoat pocket **7** the act or an instance of watching **8** *naut* any of the periods, usually of four hours, during which part of a ship's crew are on duty **9** **keep a close watch on** to maintain a careful interest in or control over: *he keeps a close watch on party opinion* **10** **keep watch** to be keenly alert to danger; keep guard **11** **on the watch** on the lookout ▶ See also **watch out, watch over** > **watcher** *n* **WORD ORIGIN** Old English *wæccan*

watchable *adj* interesting, enjoyable, or entertaining: *watchable films*

watchdog *n* **1** a dog kept to guard property **2** a person or group that acts as a guard against inefficiency or illegality

watchful *adj* **1** carefully observing everything that happens **2** **under the watchful eye of** being closely observed by **watchfully** *adv* **watchfulness** *n*

watchmaker *n* a person who makes or mends watches and clocks

watchman *n, pl* **-men** a man employed to guard buildings or property

watch-night service *n* **a** (in Protestant churches) a service held on the night of December 24, to mark the arrival of Christmas Day **b** (in Protestant churches) a service held on the night of December 31, to mark the passing of the old year

watch out *vb* to be careful or on one's guard

watch over *vb* to look after or supervise: *her main ambition is still to watch over the family*

watchstrap *n* a strap attached to a watch for fastening it round the wrist. Also called (US and Canad): **watchband**

watchtower *n* a tower on which a

sentry or sentinel keeps watch

watchword *n* a slogan or motto: *quality, not quantity, is the watchword*

water *n* **1** a clear colourless tasteless liquid that is essential for plant and animal life, that falls as rain, and forms seas, rivers, and lakes ▶ Related adjectives: **aquatic, aqueous 2** any area of this liquid, such as a sea, river, or lake **3** the surface of such an area of water: *four-fifths of an iceberg's mass lie below water* **4** the level of the tide: *at high water* **5** *physiol* **a** any fluid discharged from the body, such as sweat, urine, or tears **b** the fluid surrounding a fetus in the womb **6** **hold water** (of an argument or idea) to be believable or reasonable **7** **of the first water** of the highest quality or the most extreme degree: *he's a scoundrel of the first water* **8** **pass water** to urinate **9** **water under the bridge** events that are past and done with ▷ *vb* **10** to moisten or soak with water: *keep greenhouse plants well watered* **11** to give (an animal) water to drink **12** (of the eyes) to fill with tears: *our eyes were watering from the fumes* **13** (of the mouth) to fill with saliva in anticipation of food ▶ See also **water down** > **waterless** *adj* **WORD ORIGIN** Old English *wæter*

water bed *n* a waterproof mattress filled with water

water biscuit *n* a thin crisp unsweetened biscuit, usually eaten with butter or cheese

water buffalo *n* a large black oxlike draught animal of S Asia, with long backward-curving horns

water cannon *n* a machine that pumps a jet of water through a nozzle at high pressure, used to disperse crowds

water chestnut *n* the edible tuber of a Chinese plant, used in Oriental cookery

water closet *n* *old-fashioned* a toilet. Abbrev: **WC**

watercolour *or US* **watercolor** *n* **1** a kind of paint that is applied with water rather than oil **2** a painting done in watercolours

water-cooled *adj* (of an engine) kept from overheating by a flow of water circulating in a casing

watercourse *n* the channel or bed of a river or stream

watercress *n* a plant that grows in ponds and streams, with strong-tasting leaves that are used in salads and as a garnish

water cycle *n* *geol* the circulation of the earth's water, in which water from the sea evaporates, forms clouds, falls as rain or snow, and returns to the sea by rivers

water diviner *n* a person who can locate the presence of water underground with a divining rod

water down *vb* **1** to weaken (a drink or food) with water **2** to make (a story, plan, or proposal) weaker and less controversial **watered-down** *adj*

waterfall *n* a cascade of falling water where there is a vertical or almost vertical step in a river

waterfowl *n, pl* **-fowl** a bird that swims on water, such as a duck or swan

W

waterfront n the area of a town or city next to an area of water, such as a harbour or dockyard

waterhole n a pond or pool in a desert or other dry area, used by animals as a drinking place

water ice n ice cream made from frozen fruit-flavoured syrup

watering can n a container with a handle and a spout with a perforated nozzle, used to sprinkle water over plants

watering hole n facetious slang a pub

watering place n 1 a place where people or animals can find drinking water 2 Brit a spa or seaside resort

water jump n a ditch or brook over which athletes or horses must jump in a steeplechase

water level n 1 the level reached by the surface of an area of water 2 same as **water line**

water lily n a plant with large leaves and showy flowers that float on the surface of an area of water

water line n the level to which a ship's hull will be immersed when afloat

waterlogged adj 1 saturated with water: waterlogged meadows 2 (of a boat) having taken in so much water as to be likely to sink

water main n a principal supply pipe in an arrangement of pipes for distributing water to houses and other buildings

watermark n 1 a mark impressed on paper during manufacture, visible when the paper is held up to the light 2 a line marking the level reached by an area of water

water meadow n a meadow that remains fertile by being periodically flooded by a stream

watermelon n a large round melon with a hard green rind and sweet watery reddish flesh

water pistol n a toy pistol that squirts a stream of water

water polo n a game played in water by two teams of seven swimmers in which each side tries to throw a ball into the opponents' goal

water power n the power of flowing or falling water to drive machinery or generate electricity

waterproof adj 1 not allowing water to pass through: waterproof trousers ▷ n 2 chiefly Brit a waterproof garment, such as a raincoat ▷ vb 3 to make waterproof: the bridge is having its deck waterproofed

water rat n same as **water vole**

water rate n a charge made for the public supply of water

water-resistant adj (of a fabric or garment) having a finish that resists the absorption of water

watershed n 1 the dividing line between two adjacent river systems, such as a ridge 2 an important period or factor that serves as a dividing line: a watershed in history

waterside n the area of land beside a river or lake

watersider n NZ a person employed to load and unload ships

water-ski n 1 a type of ski used for gliding over water ▷ vb -skiing, -skied or -ski'd 2 to ride over water on water-skis while holding a rope towed by a speedboat **water-skier** n **water-skiing** n

water softener n a device or substance that removes the minerals that make water hard

waterspout n a tornado occurring over water, which forms a column of water and mist

water table n the level below which the ground is saturated with water

watertight adj 1 not letting water through: watertight compartments 2 without loopholes or weak points: a watertight system

water tower n a storage tank mounted on a tower so that water can be distributed at a steady pressure

water vapour n water in a gaseous state, esp. when due to evaporation at a temperature below the boiling point

water vole n a small ratlike animal that can swim and lives on the banks of streams and ponds

waterway n a river, canal, or other navigable channel used as a means of travel or transport

water wheel n a large wheel with vanes set across its rim, which is turned by flowing water to drive machinery

water wings pl n an inflatable rubber device shaped like a pair of wings, which is placed under the arms of a person learning to swim

waterworks n 1 an establishment for storing, purifying, and distributing water for community supply ▷ pl n 2 informal chiefly Brit euphemistic the urinary system 3 **turn on the waterworks** informal to begin to cry deliberately, in order to attract attention or gain sympathy

watery adj 1 of, like, or containing water: a watery discharge 2 (of eyes) filled with tears 3 insipid, thin, or weak: a watery sun had appeared

watt (**wott**) n the SI unit of power, equal to the power dissipated by a current of 1 ampere flowing across a potential difference of 1 volt **WORD ORIGIN** after J. Watt, engineer

wattage n the amount of electrical power, expressed in watts, that an appliance uses or generates

wattle (**wott**-tl) n 1 a frame of rods or stakes interwoven with twigs or branches used to make fences 2 a loose fold of brightly coloured skin hanging from the throat of certain birds and lizards 3 an Australian acacia tree with dense golden, yellow or cream flowers ▷ adj 4 made of, formed by, or covered with wattle: a wattle fence **WORD ORIGIN** Old English watol

wattle and daub n a building material consisting of interwoven twigs plastered with a mixture of clay and water

wave vb **waving**, **waved** 1 to move (one's hand) to and fro as a greeting 2 to direct (someone) to move in a particular direction by waving: I waved him on 3 to hold (something) up and move it from side to side in order to attract attention 4 to move freely to and fro: flowers waving in the wind ▷ n 5 one of a sequence of ridges or undulations that moves across the surface of the sea or a lake 6 a curve in the hair 7 a sudden rise in the frequency or intensity of something: a wave of sympathy 8 a widespread movement that advances in a body: a new wave of refugees 9 a prolonged spell of some particular type of weather: a heat wave 10 the act or an instance of waving 11 physics an energy-carrying disturbance travelling through a medium or space by a series of vibrations without any overall movement of matter 12 **make waves** to cause trouble **WORD ORIGIN** Old English wafian

waveband n a range of wavelengths or frequencies used for a particular type of radio transmission

wave down vb to signal to (the driver of a vehicle) to stop

wavelength n 1 physics the distance between two points of the same phase in consecutive cycles of a wave 2 the wavelength of the carrier wave used by a particular broadcasting station 3 **on the same wavelength** informal having similar views, feelings, or thoughts

waver vb 1 to hesitate between possibilities; be indecisive 2 to swing from one thing to another: she wavered between annoyance and civility 3 (of a voice or stare) to become unsteady 4 to move back and forth or one way and another: the barrel of the gun began to waver **wavering** adj **WORD ORIGIN** Old Norse vafra to flicker

wavey n Canad a snow goose or other wild goose **WORD ORIGIN** from a Native American language

wavy adj **wavier, waviest** having curves: wavy hair; a wavy line

wax¹ n 1 a solid fatty or oily substance used for making candles and polish, which softens and melts when heated 2 short for **beeswax** or **sealing wax** 3 physiol a brownish-yellow waxy substance secreted by glands in the ear ▷ vb 4 to coat or polish with wax **waxed** adj **waxy** adj **WORD ORIGIN** Old English weax

wax² vb 1 to increase gradually in size, strength, or power: trading has waxed and waned with the economic cycle 2 (of the moon) to show a gradually increasing area of brightness from new moon until full moon 3 to become: he waxed eloquent on the disadvantages of marriage **WORD ORIGIN** Old English weaxan

waxed paper or **wax paper** n paper treated or coated with wax or paraffin to make it waterproof

waxen adj 1 resembling wax in colour or texture: his face is waxen and pale 2 made of, treated with, or covered with wax: a waxen image

waxeye n a small New Zealand bird with a white circle round its eye

waxwork n a life-size lifelike wax figure of a famous person

waxworks n a museum or exhibition of wax figures

W

The Influence of Scandinavian Languages on English

Scandinavian words formed part of the vocabulary of English even before the first Norse-speaking Viking raiders ventured across the North Sea in the 8th century. The Anglo-Saxons, who were the first speakers of English, spoke a language that was closely related to Old Norse, so many Norse words were present in the earliest recorded forms of English in the 5th century. The influence of Norse was greatly increased when the Vikings overran large parts of Britain, and it continued even after they were expelled in the 11th century.

Although Old Norse did not contribute as many words to English as French or Latin did, many of the words that it did contribute are now fundamental to the language. These include very common verbs such as *run, call, work, get,* and *give,* adjectives such *hot* and *low,* words for parts of the body (*arm, leg, skin, skull*), and names of the days of the week: *Tuesday, Wednesday, Thursday* and *Friday* are named after the Norse deities Tiw, Woden, Thor, and Freya respectively.

Many words of Norse origin point to a culture in which life was brutish and short. Old Norse is at the root of the names of several weapons (*club, gun, knife*), besides *slaughter, ransack,* and *die*. On the other hand, we are also indebted to it for some more pacific concepts, such as *game, plough,* and *law.*

The Norse language also lives on in many British place names. Anywhere whose name ends in *-by* ('town'), *-thorp* ('village'), or *-ness* ('headland') is likely to have a Viking heritage, and there are plenty of such places in Eastern England, such as Derby, Scunthorpe, and Skegness (Scottish place names such as Loch Ness, however, come from Gaelic).

The assimilation of words from Scandinavia did not come to an abrupt end when the Vikings (itself a Norse word meaning 'sea pirate') were driven out. Many words that entered English in the Middle Ages can be traced back to Scandinavian origins: *lift, skip,* and *smile* in the 13th century; *bubble, craze,* and *tatter* in the 14th; *leak, silt,* and *slug* in the 15th; *fumble, hug,* and *sprint* in the 16th. The general legacy is a group of short words with a plethora of hard vowels (*bank, bat, kick, muck, mug, rug, rump*), whereas words of French origin are likely to be longer and more melodious.

The number of Scandinavian words entering English has declined in recent centuries as the language has drawn on a much wider range of influences. Nevertheless, most of the modern Scandinavian languages that are the descendants of Old Norse (Swedish, Danish, Norwegian, Icelandic and Faroese) have left their mark in some way.

Swedish words that have come into widespread use in English include *ombudsman, orienteering, smorgasbord* (literally a 'sandwich table'), and *Aga,* the latter being a shortened form of the name of the original Swedish manufacturer *Svenskaa Aktiebolaget Gasackumulator*. The chemical element tungsten was originally a Swedish word meaning 'heavy stone', while *rutabaga* ('root bag') has caught on in American English as the name for the root vegetable that the British call a 'swede'.

Fewer modern Danish words have found their way into English. Perhaps the most familiar is *Lego,* the construction toy that was developed in Denmark and whose name was taken from the Danish phrase *leg godt* which means literally 'play well'.

Norwegian has made a greater impression, however, most notably in the field of winter sports, where it is the source of the words *ski* and *slalom*. We can also thank Norwegian for *fjord* ('narrow inlet of the sea') and *gravlax* ('dry-cured salmon'), as well as the names of several animals including *lemming, krill,* and the mythical *kraken*. More recently, the Norwegian and Danish words for the numbers 15 and 18 have been adopted by scientists as the source of the prefixes *femto-* and *atto-,* which indicate units that are respectively 10^{-15} and 10^{-18} the size of a standard unit, as in *femtosecond* or *attometre*.

Even Icelandic has contributed the word *geyser,* which not only refers to the thermal springs found in that country but has also come to be used in British English as the name for a domestic gas water heater.

way *n* **1** a manner, method, or means: *a new way of life; a tactful way of finding out* **2** a characteristic style or manner: *we are all special in our own way* **3** **ways** habits or customs: *he had a liking for British ways* **4** an aspect or detail of something: *the tourist industry is in many ways a success story* **5** a choice or option, for example in a vote: *he thought it could go either way* **6** a route or direction: *the shortest way home* **7** a journey: *you could buy a magazine to read on the way* **8** distance: *they are a long way from Paris* **9** space or room for movement or activity: *you won't be in his way* **10** **by the way** incidentally: *by the way, I've decided to leave* **11** **by way of a** serving as: *by way of explanation* **b** by the route of: *I went by way of my family home* **12** **get one's own way** to have things exactly as one wants them to be **13** **give way a** to collapse or break **b** to yield or concede: *I tried to make him understand but he did not give way an inch* **14** **give way to a** to be replaced by: *my first feelings of dismay have given way to comparative complacency* **b** to show (an emotion) unrestrainedly **c** to slow down or stop when driving to let (another driver) pass **15** **go out of one's way** to take considerable trouble: *he had gone out of his way to reassure me* **16** **have it both ways** to enjoy two things that would normally be mutually exclusive **17** **in a bad way** *informal* in a poor state of health or a poor financial state **18** **in a way** in some respects **19** **in no way** not at all **20** **make one's way** to proceed or go: *he decided to make his way back in the dark* **21** **on the way out** *informal* becoming unfashionable **22** **out of the way a** removed or dealt with so as to be no longer a hindrance **b** remote **23** **under way** having started moving or making progress ▷ *adv* **24** *informal* far or by far: *that is way out of line*
WORD ORIGIN Old English *weg*

waybill *n* a document stating the nature, origin, and destination of goods being transported

wayfarer *n old-fashioned* a traveller

waylay *vb* **-laying, -laid** **1** to lie in wait for and attack **2** to intercept (someone) unexpectedly

way-out *adj old-fashioned, informal* extremely unconventional

waypoint *n* the co-ordinates of a specific location as defined by a GPS

ways and means *pl n* **1** the methods and resources for accomplishing something **2** the money and the methods of raising the money needed for the functioning of a political unit

wayside *adj* **1** *old-fashioned* situated by the side of a road: *wayside shrines* ▷ *n* **2** **fall by the wayside** to be unsuccessful or stop being successful: *thousands of new diets are dreamed up yearly – many fall by the wayside*

wayward *adj* erratic, selfish, or stubborn **waywardness** *n*
WORD ORIGIN AWAY + -WARD

Wb *physics* weber

WC *or* **wc** *n* a toilet

we *pron (used as the subject of a verb)* **1** the speaker or writer and another person or other people: *we arrived in Calais* **2** all

people or people in general: *it's an unfair world we live in* **3** *formal* same as **I**: used by monarchs and editors
WORD ORIGIN Old English *wē*

weak *adj* **1** lacking in physical or mental strength **2** (of a part of the body) not functioning as well as is normal: *a weak heart* **3** liable to collapse or break: *weak bridges* **4** lacking in importance, influence, or strength: *a weak government* **5** (of a currency or shares) falling in price or characterized by falling prices **6** lacking in moral strength; easily influenced **7** not convincing: *weak arguments* **8** lacking strength or power: *his voice was weak* **9** not having a strong flavour: *weak coffee* **weakly** *adv*
WORD ORIGIN Old English *wāc* soft

weaken *vb* to become or make weak or weaker

weak-kneed *adj informal* lacking strength, courage, or resolution

weakling *n* a person who is lacking in physical or mental strength

weak-minded *adj* **1** lacking willpower **2** of low intelligence; foolish

weakness *n* **1** the state of being weak **2** a failing in a person's character: *his weakness is his impetuosity* **3** a self-indulgent liking: *a weakness for gin*

weal[1] *n* a raised mark on the skin produced by a blow
WORD ORIGIN from Old English *walu* ridge

weal[2] *n old-fashioned* prosperity or wellbeing: *the public weal*
WORD ORIGIN Old English *wela*

wealth *n* **1** the state of being rich **2** a large amount of money and valuable material possessions: *redistribution of wealth* **3** a great amount or number: *a wealth of detail*
WORD ORIGIN Middle English *welthe*

wealthy *adj* **wealthier, wealthiest** **1** having a large amount of money and valuable material possessions **2** **wealthy in** having a great amount or number of: *a continent exceptionally wealthy in minerals*

wean *vb* **1** to start giving (a baby or young mammal) food other than its mother's milk **2** to cause (oneself or someone else) to give up a former habit: *they are unable to wean themselves from the tobacco habit* **weaning** *n*
WORD ORIGIN Old English *wenian* to accustom

weapon *n* **1** an object used in fighting, such as a knife or gun **2** anything used to get the better of an opponent: *having a sense of humour is a weapon of self-defence*
WORD ORIGIN Old English *wǣpen*

weaponry *n* weapons regarded collectively

wear *vb* **wearing, wore, worn** **1** to carry or have (a garment or jewellery) on one's body as clothing or ornament **2** to have (a particular facial expression): *she wore a scowl of frank antagonism* **3** to style (the hair) in a particular way: *she wears her hair in a braid* **4** to deteriorate or cause to deteriorate by constant use or action **5** *informal* to accept: *he won't be given a top job – the Party wouldn't wear it* **6** **wear thin** to lessen or become weaker: *his patience began to wear thin* **7** **wear well** to remain

in good condition for a long time ▷ *n* **8** clothes that are suitable for a particular time or purpose: *evening wear; beach wear* **9** deterioration from constant or normal use **10** the quality of resisting the effects of constant use ▶ See also **wear down, wear off, wear out** > **wearable** *adj* **wearer** *n*
WORD ORIGIN Old English *werian*

wear and tear *n* damage or loss resulting from ordinary use

wear down *vb* **1** to make shorter by long or constant wearing or rubbing: *the back of his heels were worn down* **2** to overcome gradually by persistent effort: *to wear down the enemy*

wearing *adj* causing exhaustion and sometimes irritation

wearisome *adj* causing fatigue and irritation

wear off *vb* to have a gradual decrease in effect or intensity: *the cocaine injection was beginning to wear off*

wear out *vb* **1** to make or become unfit for use through wear: *my red trousers are worn out* **2** *informal* to exhaust: *the afternoon's races and games had worn him out*

weary *adj* **-rier, -riest** **1** very tired; lacking energy **2** caused by or suggestive of weariness: *he managed a weary smile* **3** causing exhaustion: *a long weary struggle* **4** **weary of** discontented or bored with: *he was weary of the war* ▷ *vb* **-ries, -rying, -ried** **5** to make weary **6** **weary of** to become discontented or bored with: *he seems to have wearied of her possessiveness* **wearily** *adv* **weariness** *n* **wearying** *adj*
WORD ORIGIN Old English *wērig*

weasel *n, pl* **-sels** *or* **-sel** a small meat-eating mammal with reddish-brown fur, a long body and neck, and short legs
WORD ORIGIN Old English *wesle*

weather *n* **1** the day-to-day atmospheric conditions, such as temperature, cloudiness, and rainfall, affecting a specific place **2** **make heavy weather of** *informal* to carry out (a task) with great difficulty or needless effort **3** **under the weather** *informal* feeling slightly ill ▷ *vb* **4** to undergo or cause to undergo changes, such as discoloration, due to the action of the weather **5** to come safely through (a storm, problem, or difficulty)
WORD ORIGIN Old English *weder*

weather-beaten *adj* **1** tanned by exposure to the weather: *a crumpled weather-beaten face* **2** worn or damaged as a result of exposure to the weather

weatherboard *n* a timber board that is fixed with others in overlapping horizontal rows to form an exterior cladding on a wall or roof **weatherboarded** *adj*

weathercock *n* a weather vane in the shape of a cock

weather eye *n* **keep a weather eye on** to keep a careful watch on: *keep a weather eye on your symptoms*

weathering *n* the breakdown of rocks by the action of the weather

weatherman *n, pl* **-men** a man who forecasts the weather on radio or television **weather girl** *fem n*

weatherproof *adj* able to withstand exposure to weather without deterioration: *a weatherproof roof*

weather vane *n* a metal object on a roof that indicates the direction in which the wind is blowing

weave *vb* **weaving, wove** or **weaved, woven** or **weaved** **1** to form (a fabric) by interlacing yarn on a loom **2** to make (a garment or a blanket) by this process **3** to construct (a basket or fence) by interlacing cane or twigs **4** to compose (a story or plan) by combining separate elements into a whole **5** to move from side to side while going forward: *to weave in and out of lanes* **6** **get weaving** *informal* to hurry ▷ *n* **7** the structure or pattern of a woven fabric: *the rough weave of the cloth* **weaver** *n* **weaving** *n* **WORD ORIGIN** Old English *wefan*

web *n* **1** a mesh of fine tough threads built by a spider to trap insects **2** anything that is intricately formed or complex: *a web of relationships* **3** a membrane connecting the toes of some water birds and water-dwelling animals such as frogs **4** **the web** (*often cap*) short for **World Wide Web** ▷ *adj* **5** of or situated on the World Wide Web: *a web server; web pages* **webbed** *adj* **WORD ORIGIN** Old English *webb*

web address *n* another name for **URL**

webbing *n* a strong fabric that is woven in strips and used under springs in upholstery or for straps

webcam *n* a camera that transmits still or moving images over the internet

webcast *n* a broadcast of an event over the internet

weber (**vay**-ber) *n* the SI unit of magnetic flux (the strength of a magnetic field over a given area) **WORD ORIGIN** after W. E. *Weber*, physicist

web-footed *or* **web-toed** *adj* (of certain animals or birds) having webbed feet that aid swimming

weblog *n* a person's online journal

webmail *n* an e-mail system that allows account holders to access mail via an internet site rather than by downloading it onto a computer

website *n* a group of connected pages on the World Wide Web containing information on a particular subject

Web 2.0 *n* the internet viewed as a medium in which interactive experience plays a more important role than simply accessing information

wed *vb* **wedding, wedded** *or* **wed** **1** *old-fashioned* to take (a person) as a husband or wife; marry **2** to unite closely: *to wed folklore and magic* **WORD ORIGIN** Old English *weddian*

Wed. Wednesday

wedded *adj* **1** of marriage: *wedded bliss* **2** firmly in support of an idea or institution: *wedded to the virtues of capitalism*

wedding *n* **1** a marriage ceremony **2** a special wedding anniversary, esp. the 25th (**silver wedding**) or 50th (**golden wedding**)

wedding breakfast *n* the meal usually served after a wedding ceremony or just before the bride and bridegroom leave for their honeymoon

wedding cake *n* a rich iced fruit cake, with one, two, or more tiers, which is served at a wedding reception

wedding ring *n* a plain ring, usually made of a precious metal, worn to indicate that one is married

wedge *n* **1** a block of solid material, esp. wood or metal, that is shaped like a narrow V in cross section and can be pushed or driven between two objects or parts of an object in order to split or secure them **2** a slice shaped like a wedge: *a wedge of quiche* **3** *golf* a club with a wedge-shaped face, used for bunker or pitch shots **4** **drive a wedge between** to cause a split between (people or groups) **5** **the thin end of the wedge** anything unimportant in itself that implies the start of something much larger ▷ *vb* **wedging, wedged** **6** to secure (something) with a wedge **7** to squeeze into a narrow space: *a book wedged between the bed and the table* **WORD ORIGIN** Old English *wecg*

wedge-tailed eagle *n* a large brown Australian eagle with a wedge-shaped tail

Wedgwood *n trademark* a type of fine pottery with applied decoration in white on a coloured background **WORD ORIGIN** after Josiah *Wedgwood*, potter

wedlock *n* **1** the state of being married **2** **born out of wedlock** born when one's parents are not legally married **WORD ORIGIN** Old English *wedlāc*

Wednesday *n* the fourth day of the week **WORD ORIGIN** Old English *Wōdnes dæg* Woden's day

wee¹ *adj Brit, Austral, & NZ* small or short **WORD ORIGIN** Old English *wǣg* weight

wee² *informal n* **1** an instance of urinating ▷ *vb* **weeing, weed** **2** to urinate. Also: **wee-wee** **WORD ORIGIN** origin unknown

weed *n* **1** any plant that grows wild and profusely, esp. among cultivated plants **2** *slang* **a** marijuana **b** **the weed** or **the evil weed** tobacco **3** *informal* a thin weak person ▷ *vb* **4** to remove weeds from (a garden) **WORD ORIGIN** Old English *wēod*

weedkiller *n* a chemical or hormonal substance used to kill weeds

weed out *vb* to separate out, remove, or eliminate (an unwanted element): *to weed out the thugs*

weedy *adj* **weedier, weediest** **1** *informal* thin or weak: *sick and weedy children* **2** full of weeds: *weedy patches of garden*

week *n* **1** a period of seven consecutive days, esp. one beginning with Sunday **2** a period of seven consecutive days from a specified day: *a week from today* **3** the period of time within a week that is spent at work **WORD ORIGIN** Old English *wice, wicu*

weekday *n* any day of the week other than Saturday or Sunday

weekend *n* Saturday and Sunday

weekly *adj* **1** happening once a week or every week: *a weekly column* **2** determined or calculated by the week: *weekly earnings* ▷ *adv* **3** once a week or

every week: *report to the police weekly* ▷ *n, pl* **-lies** **4** a newspaper or magazine issued every week

weeny *adj* **-nier, -niest** *informal* very small; tiny **WORD ORIGIN** from **WEE¹**

weep *vb* **weeping, wept** **1** to shed tears; cry **2** to ooze liquid: *the skin cracked and wept; the label is weeping black ink in the rain* ▷ *n* **3** a spell of weeping: *together we had a good weep* **WORD ORIGIN** Old English *wēpan*

weeping willow *n* a willow tree with graceful drooping branches

weepy *informal adj* **weepier, weepiest** **1** liable or tending to weep ▷ *n, pl* **weepies** **2** a sentimental film or book

weevil *n* a beetle with a long snout that feeds on plants **WORD ORIGIN** Old English *wifel*

wee-wee *n, vb* **-weeing, -weed** *informal chiefly Brit* same as **wee²**

weft *n* the yarns woven across the width of the fabric through the lengthways warp yarns **WORD ORIGIN** Old English

weigh *vb* **1** to have weight as specified: *the tree weighs nearly three tons* **2** to measure the weight of **3** to consider carefully: *the President now has to weigh his options* **4** to be influential: *the authorities did not enter my mind or weigh with me* **5** **weigh anchor** to raise a ship's anchor **6** **weigh out** to measure out by weight ▷ See also **weigh down, weigh in,** etc. **WORD ORIGIN** Old English *wegan*

weighbridge *n* a machine for weighing vehicles by means of a metal plate set into a road

weigh down *vb* **1** (of a heavy load) to impede the movements of **2** (of a problem or difficulty) to worry (someone) a great deal

weigh in *vb* **1** (of a boxer or jockey) to be weighed to check that one is of the correct weight for the contest **2** *informal* to contribute to a discussion or conversation: *he weighed in with a few sharp comments* ▷ *n* **weigh-in** **3** *sport* the occasion of checking the competitors' weight before a boxing match or a horse race

weigh on *vb* to be oppressive or burdensome to: *the expectations that weigh so heavily on diplomats' wives*

weight *n* **1** the heaviness of an object, substance, or person **2** *physics* the vertical force experienced by a mass as a result of gravitation **3 a** a system of units used to express weight: *metric weight* **b** a unit used to measure weight: *the kilogram is the weight used in the metric system* **4 a** an object of known heaviness used for weighing objects, substances, or people **b** an object of known heaviness used in weight training or weightlifting to strengthen the muscles **5** any heavy load: *with a weight of fish on their backs* **6** force, importance, or influence: *they want their words to carry weight* **7** an oppressive force: *the weight of expectation* **8** **pull one's weight** *informal* to do one's full share of a task **9** **throw one's weight about** *informal* to act in an aggressive authoritarian manner ▷ *vb* **10** to add weight to; make heavier

11 to slant (a system) so that it favours one side rather than another **WORD ORIGIN** Old English *wiht*

weighting *n* Brit an allowance paid to compensate for higher living costs: *salary includes Inner London weighting*

weightless *adj* **1** seeming to have very little weight or no weight at all **2** seeming not to be affected by gravity, as in the case of astronauts in an orbiting spacecraft **weightlessness** *n*

weightlifting *n* the sport of lifting barbells of specified weights in a prescribed manner **weightlifter** *n*

weight training *n* physical exercise using light or heavy weights in order to strengthen the muscles

weighty *adj* **weightier, weightiest** **1** important or serious: *weighty matters* **2** very heavy

weigh up *vb* to make an assessment of (a person or situation)

weir *n* **1** a low dam that is built across a river to divert the water or control its flow **2** a fencelike trap built across a stream for catching fish in **WORD ORIGIN** Old English *wer*

weird *adj* **1** strange or bizarre **2** suggestive of the supernatural; uncanny **weirdly** *adv* **weirdness** *n* **WORD ORIGIN** Old English *(ge)wyrd* destiny

weirdo *n, pl* **-dos** *informal* a person who behaves in a bizarre or eccentric manner

welch *vb* same as **welsh**

welcome *vb* **-coming, -comed** **1** to greet the arrival of (a guest) cordially **2** to receive or accept (something) gladly: *I would welcome a chance to speak to him* ▷ *n* **3** the act of greeting or receiving someone or something in a specified manner: *the President was given a warm welcome* ▷ *adj* **4** gladly received or admitted: *I wouldn't want to stay where I'm not welcome* **5** encouraged or invited: *you are welcome to join us at one of our social events* **6** bringing pleasure: *a welcome change* **7 you're welcome** an expression used to acknowledge someone's thanks **welcoming** *adj* **WORD ORIGIN** Old English *wilcuma*

weld *vb* **1** to join (two pieces of metal or plastic) by softening with heat and hammering or by fusion **2** to unite closely: *the diverse ethnic groups had been welded together by the anti-Fascist cause* ▷ *n* **3** a joint formed by welding **welder** *n* **WORD ORIGIN** obsolete *well* to melt, weld

welfare *n* **1** health, happiness, prosperity, and general wellbeing **2** financial and other assistance given, usually by the government, to people in need **WORD ORIGIN** WEL(L)¹ + FARE

welfare state *n* a system in which the government undertakes responsibility for the wellbeing of its population, through unemployment insurance, old age pensions, and other social-security measures

well¹ *adv* **better, best** **1** satisfactorily or pleasingly: *well proportioned* **2** skilfully: *I played well for the last six holes* **3** thoroughly: *make sure the chicken is well cooked* **4** comfortably or prosperously:

he has lived well from his various nautical exploits **5** suitably or fittingly: *you can't very well refuse* **6** intimately: *darling Robert, I know him so well* **7** favourably: *it will go down very well with all the people who support him* **8** by a considerable margin: *well over half; she left well before tea* **9** very likely: *the claim may well be true* **10** *informal* extremely: *well cool* **11 all very well** used ironically to express discontent or annoyance: *that's all very well, but I'm left to pick up the pieces* **12 as well a** in addition **b** with equal effect: used to express indifference or reluctance: *I might as well go out* **13 as well as** in addition to **14 just as well** fortunate or appropriate: *it's just as well I didn't spend all my money* ▷ *adj* **15** in good health: *I'm not feeling well* **16** satisfactory or acceptable: *all was well in the aircraft* ▷ *interj* **17 a** an expression of surprise, indignation, or reproof: *well, what a cheek!* **b** an expression of anticipation in waiting for an answer or remark: *well, what do you think?* **WORD ORIGIN** Old English *wel*

well² *n* **1** a hole or shaft bored into the earth to tap a supply of water, oil, or gas **2** an open shaft through the floors of a building, used for a staircase ▷ *vb* **3** to flow upwards or outwards: *tears welled up into my eyes* **WORD ORIGIN** Old English *wella*

we'll we will *or* we shall

well-advised *adj* prudent or sensible: *you would be well-advised to cooperate with me*

well-appointed *adj* (of a room or building) equipped or furnished to a high standard

well-balanced *adj* sensible and emotionally stable

well-behaved *adj* having good manners; not causing trouble or mischief

well-being *n* the state of being contented and healthy: *a sense of well-being*

well-born *adj* belonging to a noble or upper-class family

well-bred *adj* having good manners; polite

well-built *adj* strong and well-proportioned

well-connected *adj* having influential or important relatives or friends

well-disposed *adj* inclined to be sympathetic, kindly, or friendly towards a person or idea

well-done *adj* **1** made or accomplished satisfactorily **2** (of food, esp. meat) cooked very thoroughly

well-founded *adj* having a sound basis in fact: *a well-founded fear of persecution*

well-groomed *adj* having a smart tidy appearance

well-grounded *adj* having a sound basis in fact: *well-grounded suspicions*

wellhead *n* **1** the source of a well or stream **2** a source, fountainhead, or origin

well-heeled *adj* *informal* wealthy

wellies *pl n* Brit, NZ, & Austral *informal* Wellington boots

well-informed *adj* knowing a lot about a great variety of subjects or about one particular subject

Wellington boots *or* **wellingtons** *pl n* long rubber boots, worn in wet or muddy conditions **WORD ORIGIN** after the 1st Duke of Wellington, soldier and statesman

well-intentioned *adj* having good or kindly intentions, usually with unfortunate results

well-known *adj* widely known; famous

well-meaning *adj* having or indicating good intentions, usually with unfortunate results

well-nigh *adv* almost: *a well-nigh impossible task*

well-off *adj* **1** moderately wealthy **2** in a fortunate position: *some people don't know when they are well-off*

well-preserved *adj* not showing signs of ageing: *amazingly well-preserved for a man of 70*

well-read *adj* having read and learned a lot

well-rounded *adj* **1** desirably varied: *his well-rounded team* **2** rounded in shape or well developed: *a voluptuous well-rounded lady*

well-spoken *adj* having a clear, articulate, and socially acceptable accent and way of speaking

wellspring *n* a source of abundant supply: *the wellspring of truth*

well-thought-of *adj* liked and respected

well-to-do *adj* moderately wealthy

well-versed *adj* knowing a lot about a particular subject

well-wisher *n* a person who shows benevolence or sympathy towards a person or cause

well-worn *adj* **1** (of a word or phrase) having lost its meaning or force through being overused **2** having been used so much as to show signs of wear: *well-worn leather*

welly *n* **1** *informal* same as **Wellington boot** **2** Brit *slang* energy or commitment: *give it some welly!*

welsh *or* **welch** *vb* **welsh on** to fail to pay (a debt) or fulfil (an obligation) **WORD ORIGIN** origin unknown

Welsh *adj* **1** of Wales ▷ *n* **2** a Celtic language spoken in some parts of Wales ▷ *pl n* **3 the Welsh** the people of Wales **WORD ORIGIN** Old English *Wēlisc, Wǣlisc*

Welshman *or fem* **Welshwoman** *n, pl* **-men** *or* **-women** a person from Wales

Welsh rarebit *n* melted cheese, sometimes mixed with milk or seasonings, served on hot toast. Also called: **Welsh rabbit**

welt *n* **1** a raised mark on the skin produced by a blow **2** a raised or strengthened seam in a garment **WORD ORIGIN** origin unknown

welter *n* a confused mass or jumble: *a welter of facts* **WORD ORIGIN** Middle Low German, Middle Dutch *weltern*

welterweight *n* a professional boxer weighing up to 147 pounds (66.5 kg) or an amateur boxer weighing up to 67 kg

wen *n* *pathol* a cyst on the scalp **WORD ORIGIN** Old English *wenn*

Words from Literature
part 29

ward *n* a ward is, usually, a child who has been put under the protection of the court or a guardian for his or her protection
> I call the Wards in Jarndcye. The are caged up with all the others.
> *Bleak House* Charles Dickens

waylay *v* to waylay someone is to lie in wait for them or to intercept them
> I must go up the road and waylay him
> *The Adventures of Huckleberry Finn* Mark Twain

weazen *n* weazen is a slang word for throat. It means shrivelled
> "You with a uncle too! Why, I knowed you at Gargery's when you was so small a wolf that I could have took your weazen betwixt this finger and thumb and chucked you away dead"
> *Great Expectations* Charles Dickens

wery *adv* a mispronunciation of very
> Be wery careful o' vidders all your life
> *Pickwick Papers* Charles Dickens

wherry *n* wherry is a small swift rowing boat for one person
> It was flood tide when Daniel Quilp sat himself down in the wherry to cross to the opposite shore.
> *The Old Curiosity Shop* Charles Dickens

whether *prep* whether means which of the two in this example
> we came in full view of a great island or continent (for we knew not whether)
> *Gulliver's Travels* Jonathan Swift

whetstone *n* a whetstone is a stone used to sharpen knives and other tools
> I dropped pap's whetstone there too
> *The Adventures of Huckleberry Finn* Mark Twain

wicket *n* a wicket is a little door in a larger entrance
> Having rested here, for a minute or so, to collect a good burst of sobs and an imposing show of tears and terror, he knocked loudly at the wicket;
> *Oliver Twist* Charles Dickens

without *conj* without means unless
> You don't know about me, without you have read a book by the name of The Adventures of Tom Sawyer
> *The Adventures of Huckleberry Finn* Mark Twain

wittles *n* a mispronunciation of vittles, which means food
> I live on broken wittles – and I sleep on the coals
> *David Copperfield* Charles Dickens

words, to have *phrase* if you have words with someone you have a disagreement or an argument
> I do not want to have words with a young thing like you.
> *Black Beauty* Anna Sewell

workhouse *n* workhouses were places where the homeless were given food and a place to live in return for doing very hard work
> "And the Union workhouses?" demanded Scrooge. "Are they still in operation?"
> *A Christmas Carol* Charles Dickens

yawl *n* a yawl is a small boat kept on a bigger boat for short trips. Yawl is also the name for a small fishing boat
> She sent out her yawl, and we went aboard
> *The Adventures of Huckleberry Finn* Mark Twain

yeomanry *n* a collective term for the middle classes involved in agriculture
> The yeomanry are precisely the order of people with whom I feel I can have nothing to do
> *Emma* Jane Austen

yonder *adv* yonder means over there
> all in the same second we seem to hear low voices in yonder!
> *The Adventures of Huckleberry Finn* Mark Twain

wench *n old-fashioned* **1** *facetious* a girl or young woman **2** a prostitute or female servant
WORD ORIGIN Old English *wencel* child

wend *vb* to make (one's way) in a particular direction: *it's time to wend our way back home*
WORD ORIGIN Old English *wendan*

Wendy house *n* a small toy house for a child to play in
WORD ORIGIN after *Wendy*, the girl in J. M. Barrie's play *Peter Pan*

wensleydale *n* a white cheese with a flaky texture
WORD ORIGIN after *Wensleydale*, North Yorkshire

went *vb* the past tense of **go**

wept *vb* the past of **weep**

were *vb* the form of the past tense of **be**: used after *we, you, they*, or a plural noun, or as a subjunctive in conditional sentences
WORD ORIGIN Old English *wēron, wæron*

USAGE
Were, as a remnant of the past subjunctive in English, is used in formal contexts in clauses expressing hypotheses (*if he were to die, she would inherit everything*), suppositions contrary to fact (*if I were you, I would be careful*), and desire (*I wish he were there now*). In informal speech, however, *was* is often used instead.

we're we are

weren't were not

werewolf *n, pl* **-wolves** (in folklore) a person who can turn into a wolf
WORD ORIGIN Old English *wer* man + *wulf* wolf

west *n* **1** one of the four cardinal points of the compass, at 270° clockwise from north; the direction along a line of latitude towards the sunset **2 the west** any area lying in or towards the west ▷ *adj* **3** situated in, moving towards, or facing the west **4** (esp. of the wind) from the west ▷ *adv* **5** in, to, or towards the west
WORD ORIGIN Old English

West *n* **1 the West a** the western part of the world contrasted historically and culturally with the East **b** (esp. formerly) the non-Communist countries of Europe and America contrasted with the Communist states of the East ▷ *adj* **2** of or denoting the western part of a country or region

westbound *adj* going towards the west

westerly *adj* **1** of or in the west ▷ *adv, adj* **2** towards the west **3** from the west: *a westerly wind*

western *adj* **1** situated in or towards the west **2** facing or moving towards the west **3** (*sometimes cap*) of or characteristic of the west or West ▷ *n* **4** a film or book about cowboys in the western states of the US in the 19th century **westernmost** *adj*

Western *adj* (esp. formerly) of or characteristic of the Americas and the parts of Europe not under Communist rule

Westerner *n* a person from the west of a country or region

western hemisphere *n* the half of the globe that contains the Americas

westernize or **-nise** *vb* **-nizing, -nized** or **-nising, -nised** to influence or make familiar with the customs or practices of the West **westernization** or **-nisation** *n*

West Indian *adj* **1** of the West Indies ▷ *n* **2** a person from the West Indies

Westminster *n* the British Houses of Parliament

westward *adj, adv also* **westwards** **1** towards the west ▷ *n* **2** the westward part or direction

wet *adj* **wetter, wettest** **1** moistened, covered, or soaked with water or some other liquid **2** not yet dry or solid: *wet paint* **3** rainy: *the weather was cold and wet* **4** *Brit & NZ informal* feeble or foolish **5 wet behind the ears** *informal* immature or inexperienced ▷ *n* **6** rainy weather **7** *Brit informal* a feeble or foolish person **8** *Brit informal* a Conservative politician who supports moderate policies ▷ *vb* **wetting, wet** or **wetted** **9** to make wet: *wet the brush before applying the paint* **10** to urinate in (one's clothes or bed) **11 wet oneself** to urinate in one's clothes **wetly** *adv* **wetness** *n*
WORD ORIGIN Old English *wēt*

wet blanket *n informal* a person whose low spirits or lack of enthusiasm have a depressing effect on others

wet dream *n* an erotic dream accompanied by an emission of semen

wether *n* a male sheep, esp. a castrated one
WORD ORIGIN Old English

wetland *n* an area of marshy land

wet nurse *n* (esp. formerly) a woman hired to breast-feed another woman's baby

wet room *n* a type of waterproofed room with a drain in the floor often serving as an open-plan shower

wet suit *n* a close-fitting rubber suit used by skin-divers and yachtsmen to retain body heat

W. Glam West Glamorgan

whack *vb* **1** to hit hard: *that lad whacked him over the head with a bottle* **2** (usually foll. by *in* or *on*) *informal* to put something onto or into (something else) with force or abandon: *whack on some sunscreen* ▷ *n* **3** a hard blow or the sound of one: *a whack with a blunt instrument* **4** *informal* a share: *he took his whack of that money* **5 have a whack** to make an attempt **6 out of whack** *informal* out of order or out of condition: *my body is just a little out of whack*
WORD ORIGIN imitative

whacked *adj informal* completely exhausted

whacking *n* **1** *old-fashioned* a severe beating ▷ *adv* **2** *Brit, Austral, & NZ informal* extremely: *a whacking great elm*

whale *n* **1** a very large fishlike sea mammal that breathes through a blowhole on the top of its head **2 have a whale of a time** *informal* to enjoy oneself very much
WORD ORIGIN Old English *hwæl*

whalebone *n* a thin strip of a horny material that hangs from the upper jaw of some whales, formerly used for stiffening corsets

whalebone whale *n* any whale with a double blowhole and strips of whalebone between the jaws instead of teeth, including the right whale and the blue whale

whaler *n* **1** a ship used for hunting whales **2** a person whose job is to hunt whales

whaling *n* the activity of hunting and killing whales for food or oil

wham *interj informal* an expression indicating suddenness or forcefulness: *suddenly, wham! you are caught up right in the middle of it*
WORD ORIGIN imitative

whammy *n, pl* **-mies** *informal* a devastating setback: *the double whammy of drugs and divorce*

wharepuni (for-rep-poon-ee) *n NZ* (in a Māori community) a tall carved building used as a guesthouse
WORD ORIGIN Māori

wharf *n, pl* **wharves** or **wharfs** a platform along the side of a waterfront for docking, loading, and unloading ships
WORD ORIGIN Old English *hwearf*

wharfie *n Austral & NZ* a dock labourer

what *pron* **1** used in requesting further information about the identity or categorization of something: *what was he wearing?; I knew what would happen* **2** the person, thing, people, or things that: *all was not what it seemed* **3** used in exclamations to add emphasis: *what a creep!* **4 what for?** for what reason? **5 what have you** other similar or related things: *qualifications, interests, profession, what have you* ▷ *adj* **6** used with a noun in requesting further information about the identity or categorization of something: *what difference can it make now?* **7** to any degree or in any amount: *they provided what financial support they could*
WORD ORIGIN Old English *hwæt*

USAGE
The use of *are* in sentences such as *what we need are more doctors* is common, although many people think *is* should be used: *what we need is more doctors*.

whatever *pron* **1** everything or anything that: *I can handle whatever comes up* **2** no matter what: *whatever you do, keep your temper* **3** *informal* other similar or related things: *a block of wood, rock, or whatever* **4** an intensive form of *what*, used in questions: *whatever gave you that impression?* ▷ *adj* **5** an intensive form of *what: I can take whatever actions I deem necessary* **6** at all: *there is no foundation whatever for such opinions*

whatnot *n informal* other similar or related things: *groceries, wines, and whatnot*

whatsoever *adj* at all: used for emphasis after a noun phrase that uses words such as *none* or *any: there is nothing whatsoever wrong with your heart; it can be used at any time and under any circumstances whatsoever*

wheat *n* **1** a kind of grain used in making flour and pasta **2** the plant from which this grain is obtained
WORD ORIGIN Old English *hwēte*

wheatear *n* a small northern songbird with a white rump
WORD ORIGIN from *white* + *arse*

wheaten *adj* made from the grain or flour of wheat: *wheaten bread*

wheat germ *n* the vitamin-rich middle part of a grain of wheat

wheatmeal *n* a brown flour intermediate between white flour and wholemeal flour

wheedle *vb* **-dling, -dled 1** to try to persuade (someone) by coaxing or flattery: *wheedling you into giving them their way* **2** to obtain (something) in this way: *she wheedled money out of him* **wheedling** *adj, n*
WORD ORIGIN origin unknown

wheel *n* **1** a circular object mounted on a shaft around which it can turn, fixed under vehicles to enable them to move **2** anything like a wheel in shape or function: *the steering wheel; a spinning wheel* **3** something that is repeated in cycles: *the wheel of fashion would turn, and the clothes would be back in style* **4 at** or **behind the wheel** driving a vehicle ▷ *vb* **5** to push (a bicycle, wheelchair, or pram) along **6** to turn in a circle **7 wheel and deal** to operate shrewdly and sometimes unscrupulously in order to advance one's own interests **8 wheel round** to change direction or turn round suddenly ▶ See also **wheels**
WORD ORIGIN Old English *hwēol, hweowol*

wheelbarrow *n* a shallow open box for carrying small loads, with a wheel at the front and two handles

wheelbase *n* the distance between the front and back axles of a motor vehicle

wheelchair *n* a special chair on large wheels, for use by people who cannot walk properly

wheel clamp *n* a device fixed onto one wheel of an illegally parked car to prevent the car being driven off

wheelhouse *n* an enclosed structure on the bridge of a ship from which it is steered

wheelie *n* a manoeuvre on a cycle or skateboard in which the front wheel or wheels are raised off the ground

wheelie bin *n Brit, Austral, & NZ* a large container for household rubbish, mounted on wheels so that it can be moved more easily

wheeling and dealing *n* shrewd and sometimes unscrupulous moves made in order to advance one's own interests **wheeler-dealer** *n*

wheels *pl n* **1** *informal* a car **2** the main force and mechanism of an organization or system: *the wheels of the economy* **3 wheels within wheels** a series of intricately connected events or plots

wheelwright *n* a person whose job is to make and mend wheels

wheeze *vb* **wheezing, wheezed 1** to breathe with a rasping or whistling sound ▷ *n* **2** a wheezing breath or sound **3** *Brit old-fashioned slang* a trick or plan: *a glorious tax wheeze* **wheezy** *adj*
WORD ORIGIN probably from Old Norse *hvǣsa* to hiss

whelk *n* an edible sea creature with a strong snail-like shell
WORD ORIGIN Old English *weoloc*

whelp *n* **1** a young wolf or dog **2** *offensive* a youth ▷ *vb* **3** (of an animal) to give birth

WORD ORIGIN Old English *hwelp*

when *adv* **1** at what time?: *when are they leaving?* ▷ *conj* **2** at the time at which: *he was twenty when the war started* **3** although: *he drives when he could walk* **4** considering the fact that: *how did you pass the exam when you hadn't studied for it?* ▷ *pron* **5** at which time: *she's at the age when girls get interested in boys*
WORD ORIGIN Old English *hwanne, hwænne*

≡ USAGE
≡ When should not be used loosely as
≡ a substitute for *in which* after a noun
≡ which does not refer to a period of
≡ time: *paralysis is a condition in which* (not
≡ *when*) *parts of the body cannot be moved.*

whence *conj old-fashioned or poetic* from what place, cause, or origin: *he would then ask them whence they came*
WORD ORIGIN Middle English *whannes*

≡ USAGE
≡ The expression *from whence* should be
≡ avoided, since *whence* already means
≡ from which place: *the tradition whence*
≡ (not *from whence*) *such ideas flowed.*

whenever *conj* **1** at every or any time that: *the filly was trained to stop whenever a jockey used a whip* ▷ *adv* **2** no matter when: *I am eager to come whenever you suggest* **3** *informal* at an unknown or unspecified time: *the 16th, 17th, or whenever* **4** an intensive form of *when*, used in questions: *if we can't exercise restraint now, whenever can we?*

where *adv* **1** in, at, or to what place, point, or position?: *where are we going?; I know where he found it* ▷ *pron* **2** in, at, or to which place: *he found a sandwich bar where he could get a snack* ▷ *conj* **3** in the place at which: *he should have stayed where he was doing well*
WORD ORIGIN Old English *hwǣr*

whereabouts *pl n* **1** the place, esp. the approximate place, where a person or thing is: *the whereabouts of the president are unknown* ▷ *adv* **2** approximately where: *whereabouts will you go?*

whereas *conj* but by contrast: *she was crazy about him, whereas for him it was just another affair*

whereby *pron* by or because of which: *the process whereby pests become resistant to pesticides*

wherefore *n* **1 the whys and wherefores** the reasons or explanation: *the whys and wherefores of the war* ▷ *conj* **2** *old-fashioned or formal* for which reason

wherein *old-fashioned or formal adv* **1** in what place or respect?: *wherein lies the truth?* ▷ *pron* **2** in which place or thing: *the mirror wherein he had been gazing*

whereof *old-fashioned or formal adv* **1** of what or which person or thing? ▷ *pron* **2** of which person or thing: *I know whereof I speak*

whereupon *conj* at which point: *they sentenced him to death, whereupon he fainted*

wherever *pron* **1** at, in, or to every place or point which: *I got a wonderful reception wherever I went* ▷ *conj* **2** in, to, or at whatever place: *wherever they went, the conditions were harsh* ▷ *adv* **3** no matter where: *we're going to find him, wherever he is* **4** *informal* at, in, or to an unknown or unspecified place: *the jungles of Borneo or*

wherever **5** an intensive form of *where*, used in questions: *wherever have you been?*

wherewithal *n* **the wherewithal** the necessary funds, resources, or equipment: *the wherewithal for making chemical weapons*

whet *vb* **whetting, whetted 1 whet someone's appetite** to increase someone's desire for or interest in something: *she gave him just enough information to whet his appetite* **2** *old-fashioned* to sharpen (a knife or other tool)
WORD ORIGIN Old English *hwettan*

whether *conj* **1** used to introduce an indirect question: *he asked him whether he had seen the hunter* **2** used to introduce a clause expressing doubt or choice: *you are entitled to the assistance of a lawyer, whether or not you can afford one; we learn from experience, whether good or bad*
WORD ORIGIN Old English *hwæther*

whetstone *n* a stone used for sharpening knives or other tools

whew *interj* an exclamation of relief, surprise, disbelief, or weariness

whey (**way**) *n* the watery liquid that separates from the curd when milk is clotted, for example in making cheese
WORD ORIGIN Old English *hwǣg*

which *adj* **1** used with a noun in requesting that the particular thing being referred to is further identified or distinguished: *which way had he gone?; a questionnaire to find out which shops local consumers use* **2** any out of several: *you have to choose which goods and services you want* ▷ *pron* **3** used in requesting that the particular thing being referred to is further identified or distinguished: *which of these occupations would be suitable for you?* **4** used in relative clauses referring to a thing rather than a person: *a discovery which could have lasting effects* **5** and that: *her books were all over the dining table, which meant we had to eat in the kitchen*
WORD ORIGIN Old English *hwelc*

≡ USAGE
≡ See at **that**.

whichever *adj* **1** any out of several: *choose whichever line you feel more comfortable with* **2** no matter which: *whichever bridge you take, pause mid-stream for a look up and down the river* ▷ *pron* **3** any one or ones out of several: *delete whichever is inapplicable* **4** no matter which one or ones: *whichever you choose, you must be consistent throughout*

whiff *n* **1** a passing odour: *I got a whiff of her perfume* **2** a trace or hint: *the first whiff of jealousy*
WORD ORIGIN imitative

Whig *n* **1** a member of a British political party of the 18th–19th centuries that sought limited political and social reform and provided the core of the Liberal Party ▷ *adj* **2** of or relating to Whigs **Whiggism** *n*
WORD ORIGIN probably from *whiggamore*, one of a group of 17th-century Scottish rebels

while *conj* **1** at the same time that: *anti-inflammatory remedies may be used to alleviate the condition while background factors are investigated* **2** at some point during the time that: *her father had died while she was gone* **3** although or whereas: *while she* *tossed and turned, he fell into a dreamless sleep* ▷ *n* **4** a period of time: *I'd like to stay a while* **WORD ORIGIN** Old English *hwīl*

while away *vb* **whiling, whiled** to pass (time) idly but pleasantly

whilst *conj chiefly Brit* same as **while**

whim *n* a sudden, passing, and often fanciful idea
WORD ORIGIN origin unknown

whimper *vb* **1** to cry, complain, or say (something) in a whining plaintive way ▷ *n* **2** a soft plaintive whine
WORD ORIGIN imitative

whimsical *adj* unusual, playful, and fanciful: *a whimsical story* **whimsically** *adv*

whimsy *n* **1** *pl* **-sies** a fanciful or playful idea: *they thought sparing the rod a foolish whimsy* **2** capricious or playful behaviour: *sudden flights of whimsy*
WORD ORIGIN from *whim*

whin *n chiefly Brit* same as **gorse**
WORD ORIGIN from Old Norse

whine *n* **1** a long high-pitched plaintive cry or moan **2** a peevish complaint ▷ *vb* **whining, whined 3** to whinge or complain **4** to issue a long high-pitched moan **whiner** *n* **whining** *adj, n*
WORD ORIGIN Old English *hwīnan*

whinge *Brit, Austral, & NZ informal vb* **whingeing, whinged 1** to complain in a moaning manner ▷ *n* **2** a complaint **whinger** *n*
WORD ORIGIN Old English *hwinsian* to whine

whinny *vb* **-nies, -nying, -nied 1** (of a horse) to neigh softly or gently ▷ *n, pl* **-nies 2** a gentle or low-pitched neigh
WORD ORIGIN imitative

whip *n* **1** a piece of leather or rope attached at one end to a stiff handle, used for hitting people or animals **2 a** a member of a political party who is responsible for urging members to attend Parliament to vote on an important issue **b** a notice sent to members of a political party by the whip, urging them to attend Parliament to vote in a particular way on an important issue **3** a dessert made from egg whites or cream beaten stiff: *raspberry whip* ▷ *vb* **whipping, whipped 4** to hit with a whip **5** to hit sharply: *strands of hair whipped across her cheeks* **6** *informal* to move or go quickly and suddenly: *machine-gun bullets whipped past him* **7** to beat (cream or eggs) with a whisk or fork until frothy or stiff **8** to rouse (someone) into a particular condition: *politicians and businessmen have whipped themselves into a panic about never-ending recession* **9** *informal* to steal (something) ▶ See also **whip out, whip-round, whip up** ▷ **whipping** *n*
WORD ORIGIN perhaps from Middle Dutch *wippen* to swing

whip bird *n Austral* a bird with a whistle ending in a whipcrack note

whip hand *n* **the whip hand** an advantage or dominating position: *buyers have the whip hand over estate agents*

whiplash *n* **1** a quick lash of a whip **2** short for **whiplash injury**

whiplash injury *n* an injury to the neck resulting from the head being suddenly thrust forward and then snapped back, for example in a car crash

whip out *or* **off** *vb* to take (something) out or off quickly and suddenly: *she whipped off her glasses*

whipper-in *n, pl* **whippers-in** a huntsman's assistant who manages the hounds

whippersnapper *n old-fashioned* a young impertinent overconfident person

whippet *n* a small slender dog similar to a greyhound
WORD ORIGIN perhaps based on *whip it!* move quickly!

whipping boy *n* a person who is expected to take the blame for other people's mistakes or incompetence

whip-round *n informal* an impromptu collection of money

whipstock *n* the handle of a whip

whip up *vb* **1** to excite or arouse: *to get people all whipped up about something; to whip up enthusiasm* **2** *informal* to prepare quickly: *she had whipped up a rich sauce*

whir *n, vb* **whirring, whirred** same as **whirr**

whirl *vb* **1** to spin or turn round very fast **2** to seem to spin from dizziness or confusion: *my mind whirled with half-formed thoughts* ▷ *n* **3** the act or an instance of whirling: *he grasps her by the waist and gives her a whirl* **4** a round of intense activity: *the social whirl of Paris* **5** a confused state: *my thoughts are in a whirl* **6 give something a whirl** *informal* to try something new
WORD ORIGIN Old Norse *hvirfla* to turn about

whirligig *n* **1** a spinning toy, such as a top **2** same as **merry-go-round 3** anything that whirls

whirlpool *n* a powerful circular current of water, into which objects floating nearby are drawn

whirlwind *n* **1** a column of air whirling violently upwards in a spiral ▷ *adj* **2** done or happening much more quickly than usual: *a whirlwind tour of France*

whirr *or* **whir** *n* **1** a prolonged soft whizz or buzz: *the whirr of the fax machine* ▷ *vb* **whirring, whirred 2** to produce a prolonged soft whizz or buzz **whirring** *n, adj*
WORD ORIGIN probably from Old Norse

whisk *vb* **1** to move or take somewhere swiftly: *I was whisked away in a police car* **2** to brush away lightly: *the waiter whisked the crumbs away with a napkin* **3** to beat (cream or eggs) with a whisk or fork until frothy or stiff ▷ *n* **4** the act or an instance of whisking: *a whisk of a scaly tail* **5** a utensil for beating cream or eggs until frothy or stiff
WORD ORIGIN Old Norse *visk* wisp

whisker *n* **1** any of the long stiff hairs that grow out from the sides of the mouth of a cat or other mammal **2** any of the hairs growing on a man's face, esp. on the cheeks or chin **3 by a whisker** by a very small distance or

amount: *we missed him by a whisker* **whiskered** *or* **whiskery** *adj*
WORD ORIGIN Old Norse *visk* wisp

whiskey *n* Irish or American whisky

whisky *n, pl* **-kies** a strong alcoholic drink made by distilling fermented cereals, esp. in Scotland
WORD ORIGIN Scottish Gaelic *uisge beatha* water of life

whisky-jack *n Canad* same as **Canada jay**

whisper *vb* **1** to speak or say (something) very softly, using the breath instead of the vocal cords **2** to make a low soft rustling sound: *the leaves whispered* ▷ *n* **3** a low soft voice: *her voice sank to a whisper* **4** *informal* a rumour: *I just picked up a whisper on this killing* **5** a low soft rustling sound: *a whisper of breeze in the shrubbery* **whispered** *adj*
WORD ORIGIN Old English *hwisprian*

whist *n* a card game for two pairs of players
WORD ORIGIN perhaps from *whisk*, referring to the whisking up of the tricks

whist drive *n* a social gathering where whist is played

whistle *vb* **-tling, -tled 1** to produce a shrill sound by forcing breath between pursed lips **2** to produce (a tune) by making a series of such sounds **3** to signal (to) by whistling or blowing a whistle: *the doorman whistled a cruising cab* **4** to move with a whistling sound: *a shell whistled through the upper air* **5** (of a kettle or train) to produce a shrill sound caused by steam being forced through a small opening **6** (of a bird) to give a shrill cry **7 whistle in the dark** to try to keep up one's confidence in spite of being afraid ▷ *n* **8** the act or sound of whistling: *he gave a whistle of astonishment* **9** a metal instrument that is blown down its end to produce a tune, signal, or alarm: *he played the tin whistle; the referee's whistle* **10** a device in a kettle or a train that makes a shrill sound by means of steam under pressure **11 blow the whistle on** *informal* to reveal and put a stop to (wrongdoing or a wrongdoer): *to blow the whistle on corrupt top-level officials* **12 wet one's whistle** *informal* to have a drink
WORD ORIGIN Old English *hwistlian*

whistle-blower *n Informal* a person who informs on someone or puts a stop to something

whistle for *vb informal* to expect in vain: *he could whistle for his vote in the future*

whistle-stop *adj* denoting a tour, esp. a campaign tour by a political candidate, in which short stops are made at many different places

whit *n* **not a whit** not at all: *it does not matter a whit*
WORD ORIGIN probably variant of obsolete *wight* a person

Whit *n* **1** short for **Whitsuntide** ▷ *adj* **2** of Whitsuntide: *Whit Monday*

white *adj* **1** having no hue, owing to the reflection of all or almost all light; of the colour of snow **2** pale, because of illness, fear, shock, or another emotion: *white with rage* **3** (of hair) having lost its colour, usually from age **4** (of coffee or

Seventeenth-Century English Poetry

John Milton was supposed to have pronounced the letter *r* very hard, so he might have rolled words characterizing his chaotic century: revolution, regicide, republic, and restoration. The most erudite, multilingual, and technically gifted poet of his generation, he rushed home from travels on the Continent in 1639 'to embark in a troubled sea of noises and hoarse disputes'. He promoted the Parliamentary cause against Charles I, defended the execution of the king at the end of the English Civil War, and became Oliver Cromwell's 'Secretary for Foreign Tongues' and all-round polemicist. Then, blind, ill with gout, troubled by rebellious daughters, his political allies defeated by the Stuarts' restoration, for a time in danger of execution himself, he dictated the nearly 11,000 orotund lines of *Paradise Lost*.

In some respects, Milton was centuries ahead of his time. He published pamphlets championing freedom of the press (although by this he meant the Protestant, not the Roman Catholic, press) and divorce (in the midst of a rocky first marriage). He was a poetic revolutionary, too, writing the epics *Paradise Lost*, *Paradise Regained*, and *Samson Agonistes* in the metrically novel blank verse: five-beat, ten-syllable lines with no terminal rhymes. With the Bible and the Latin classics practically memorized, he invoked the pagan 'Heavenly Muse' to recount Original Sin. In *Paradise Lost*, a sonorous marvel of dramatic pacing, Milton keeps monotony at bay: he alters words and subverts word order ('unvoyageable gulf obscure'), mixes parts of speech ('grinned horrible'), and compounds epithets ('night-warbling bird'). He expands poetic diction with neologisms or archaic words that later became common: 'hue', 'murky', 'carol', 'humid', 'fervid', 'jubilant', 'ire', 'bland', 'reluctant', 'palpable', and 'ornate'.

An assistant to Milton, and like Milton a parliamentarian and secretary to Cromwell, was Andrew Marvell. A moderate with Royalist sympathies, Marvell may have helped to save Milton's life after the Restoration. Though he shared his friend's satirical proclivities, his lyrical ease, grace, and sense of paradox were all his own. Due to the comments of John Dryden, Milton's admirer, and later to Samuel Johnson (who called Milton 'an acrimonious and surly republican'), we think of Marvell and contemporaries such as John Donne as 'the Metaphysical Poets'.

Born a Catholic, blessed with money, Donne led an adventurous, much-travelled early life. But after he secretly married his patron's 17-year-old niece, he was jailed briefly, and endured disgrace and poverty. Later his father-in-law became reconciled with him, and James I appointed him royal chaplain. A reluctant Anglican priest at first, Donne became the greatest preacher of his day. In hand-circulated manuscripts, he wrote death-haunted 'Holy Sonnets' ('I run to death, and death meets me as fast') and extraordinary prose 'Devotions', in one of which occur the famous words 'Any Man's death diminishes me, because I am involved in Mankind; And therefore never send to know for whom the bell tolls; It tolls for thee.'

Donne's poetry builds on densely layered metaphors, elaborated conceits, paradox, and hyberbole. He often begins shockingly ('Batter my heart, three-personed God...'). With jagged metre, awkward rhymes ('forbids' and 'eye-lids' in 'Satire 3') and knotty, convoluted imagery, he is obsessed with decay and change: many poems centre on anniversaries, memorials, and obsequies. Emotions are rooted in outlandish images. In 'Metempsychosis' he likens a whale and a holder of high office. He melds the sacred and the erotic in an ongoing dialectic; physical desire is yoked to spiritual yearning.

Donne's visionary mysticism led to equally devout, less rhetorically wrenched lyrics by George Herbert, Henry Vaughan, and Richard Crashaw. Clearer, lighter, more direct, and more secular lyrics came from courtiers, Royalist sympathizers, or equivocators such as Robert Herrick, Richard Lovelace, Thomas Carew, Sir John Suckling, and Edmund Waller. The century had begun with poets who regarded themselves as the poetic heirs of Shakespeare: Milton and the polymath and playwright Ben Jonson wrote verse homages to him. But the century became dogmatically maddened. Sir Isaac Newton, whose greatest scientific work was done before the end of it, spent much more time working on theology than on the theory of gravitation.

tea) with milk or cream **5** (of wine) made from pale grapes or from black grapes separated from their skins **6** denoting flour, or bread made from flour, that has had part of the grain removed ▷ *n* **7** the lightest colour; the colour of snow **8** the clear fluid that surrounds the yolk of an egg **9** *anat* the white part of the eyeball **10** anything white, such as white paint or white clothing: *a room decorated all in white* ▸ See also **whites** >**whiteness** *n* **whitish** *adj*
WORD ORIGIN Old English *hwīt*

White *n* **1** a member of a light-skinned race ▷ *adj* **2** of or relating to a White or Whites

whitebait *n* **1** the young of herrings, sprats, or pilchards, cooked and eaten whole **2** any of various small silvery fishes of Australia and New Zealand and of North American coastal regions of the Pacific

white blood cell *n* same as **leucocyte**

whitecaps *pl n* waves with white broken crests

white-collar *adj* denoting workers employed in professional and clerical occupations

white dwarf *n* a small, faint, very dense star

white elephant *n* a possession that is unwanted by its owner

white feather *n* a symbol of cowardice

white fish *n* a sea fish with white flesh that is used for food, such as cod or haddock

white flag *n* a signal of surrender or to request a truce

whitefly *n, pl* **-flies** a tiny whitish insect that is harmful to greenhouse plants

White Friar *n* a Carmelite friar

white gold *n* a white lustrous hard-wearing alloy containing gold together with platinum or other metals, used in jewellery

white goods *pl n* large household appliances, such as refrigerators and cookers

white heat *n* **1** intense heat that produces a white light **2** *informal* a state of intense emotion: *the white heat of hate*

white hope *n informal* a person who is expected to accomplish a great deal: *the great white hope of Polish cinema*

white horses *pl n* same as **whitecaps**

white-hot *adj* **1** at such a high temperature that white light is produced **2** *informal* in a state of intense emotion: *white-hot agony*

White House *n* the US president and the executive branch of the US government: *the White House reviewed the report*
WORD ORIGIN after the official home of the US president in Washington DC

white lie *n* a small lie, usually told to avoid hurting someone's feelings

white light *n* light that contains all the wavelengths of the visible spectrum, as in sunlight

white matter *n* the whitish tissue of the brain and spinal cord, consisting mainly of nerve fibres

white meat *n* meat, such as chicken or pork, that is light in colour when cooked

whiten *vb* to make or become white or whiter **whitener** *n* **whitening** *n*

white noise *n* noise that has a wide range of frequencies of uniform intensity

whiteout *n* an atmospheric condition in which blizzards or low clouds make it very difficult to see

white paper *n* an official government report which sets out the government's policy on a specific matter

white pepper *n* a hot seasoning made from the seeds of the pepper plant with the husks removed

White Russian *adj* **1** (formerly) of Byelorussia, an administrative division of the W Soviet Union: now Belarus ▷ *n* **2** (formerly) a person from Byelorussia **3** (formerly) the language of Byelorussia

whites *pl n* white clothes, as worn for playing cricket

white sauce *n* a thick sauce made from flour, butter, seasonings, and milk or stock

white slave *n* a girl or woman forced or sold into prostitution **white slavery** *n*

white spirit *n* a colourless liquid obtained from petroleum and used as a substitute for turpentine

White supremacy *n* the theory or belief that White people are superior to people of other races **White supremacist** *n, adj*

white tie *n* **1** a white bow tie worn as part of a man's formal evening dress ▷ *adj* **white-tie** **2** denoting an occasion when formal evening dress should be worn: *tickets for the white-tie Shelley Ball*

white trash *n* poor White people living in the United States, esp. in the South

whitewash *n* **1** a mixture of lime or chalk in water, for whitening walls and other surfaces **2** an attempt to conceal the unpleasant truth: *the report was a whitewash* ▷ *vb* **3** to cover with whitewash **4** to conceal the unpleasant truth about **whitewashed** *adj*

whitewood *n* a light-coloured wood often prepared for staining

whither *conj old-fashioned or poetic* to what place or for what purpose: *they knew not whither they went*
WORD ORIGIN Old English *hwider, hwæder*

whiting (**white**-ing) *n* **1** a white-fleshed food fish of European seas **2** *Austral* any of several marine food fishes

whitlow *n* an inflamed sore on the end of a finger or toe
WORD ORIGIN originally *white + flaw*

Whitsun *n* **1** short for **Whitsuntide** ▷ *adj* **2** of Whit Sunday or Whitsuntide

Whit Sunday *n* the seventh Sunday after Easter
WORD ORIGIN Old English *hwīta sunnandæg* white Sunday

Whitsuntide *n* the week that begins with Whit Sunday

whittle *vb* **-tling, -tled** **1** to make (an object) by cutting or shaving pieces from (a piece of wood) with a small knife **2** **whittle down** *or* **away** to reduce in size or effectiveness gradually: *my self-confidence had been whittled away to almost nothing*
WORD ORIGIN Old English *thwītan* to cut

whizz *or* **whiz** *vb* **whizzing, whizzed** **1** to move with a loud humming or buzzing sound: *the bullets whizzed overhead* **2** *informal* to move or go quickly: *the wind surfers fairly whizzed along the water* ▷ *n, pl* **whizzes** **3** a loud humming or buzzing sound **4** *informal* a person who is extremely good at something: *he's a whizz on finance* **5** *slang* amphetamine
WORD ORIGIN imitative

whizz kid *or* **whiz kid** *n informal* a person who is outstandingly able and successful for his or her age

who *pron* **1** which person: *who are you?; he didn't know who had started it* **2** used at the beginning of a relative clause referring to a person or people already mentioned: *he is a man who can effect change*
WORD ORIGIN Old English *hwā*

☰ USAGE
☰ See at **whom**.

WHO World Health Organization

whoa *interj* a command used to stop horses or to slow down someone who is moving or talking too fast

whodunnit *or* **whodunit** (hoo-**dun**-nit) *n informal* a novel, play, or film about the solving of a murder mystery

whoever *pron* **1** the person or people who: *whoever bought it for you has to make the claim* **2** no matter who: *I pity him, whoever he is* **3** *informal* other similar or related people or person: *your best friend, your neighbours, or whoever* **4** an intensive form of *who*, used in questions: *whoever thought of such a thing?*

whole *adj* **1** constituting or referring to all of something: *I'd spent my whole allowance by Saturday afternoon* **2** unbroken or undamaged ▷ *adv* **3** in an undivided or unbroken piece: *truffles are cooked whole* **4** *informal* completely or entirely: *a whole new theory of treatment* ▷ *n* **5** all there is of a thing: *the whole of my salary* **6** a collection of parts viewed together as a unit: *taking Great Britain as a whole* **7** **on the whole** **a** taking all things into consideration: *on the whole he has worked about one year out of twelve* **b** in general: *on the whole they were not successful* **wholeness** *n*
WORD ORIGIN Old English *hāl*

wholefood *n* **1** food that has been refined or processed as little as possible ▷ *adj* **2** of or relating to wholefood: *a wholefood diet*

wholehearted *adj* done or given with total sincerity or enthusiasm: *wholehearted support* **wholeheartedly** *adv*

wholemeal *adj Austral & Brit* **1** (of flour) made from the entire wheat kernel **2** made from wholemeal flour: *wholemeal bread*

whole number *n maths* a number that does not contain a fraction, such as 0, 1, or 2

wholesale *n* **1** the business of selling goods in large quantities and at lower prices to retailers for resale **2** relating to such business: *wholesale prices* **3** extensive or indiscriminate: *the*

W

wholesale destruction of forests ▷ *adv* **4** by or through the wholesale business: *we buy beef wholesale* **5** extensively or indiscriminately: *buffalo were slaughtered wholesale* **wholesaler** *n*

wholesome *adj* **1** physically beneficial: *wholesome food* **2** morally beneficial: *a wholesome attitude of the mind* **WORD ORIGIN** from *whole* healthy

whole-wheat *adj* *US & Canad* same as **wholemeal**

wholly *adv* completely or totally

whom *pron* the objective form of *who*: *whom will you tell?; he was devoted to his wife, whom he married in 1960* **WORD ORIGIN** Old English *hwām*

USAGE
It was formerly considered correct to use *whom* whenever the objective form of *who* was required. This is no longer thought to be necessary and the objective form *who* is now commonly used, even in formal writing: *there were several people there who he had met before.* *Who* cannot be used directly after a preposition – the preposition is usually displaced, as in *the man (who) he sold his car to.* In formal writing *whom* is preferred in sentences like these: *the man to whom he sold his car.* There are some types of sentence in which *who* cannot be used: *the refugees, many of whom were old and ill, were allowed across the border.*

whomever *pron* the objective form of *whoever*: *this law limits an employer's right to employ whomever he wants*

whoop *vb* **1** to cry out in excitement or joy **2 whoop it up** *informal* to indulge in a noisy celebration ▷ *n* **3** a loud cry of excitement or joy **WORD ORIGIN** imitative

whoopee *old-fashioned informal interj* **1** an exclamation of joy or excitement ▷ *n* **2 make whoopee a** to indulge in a noisy celebration **b** to make love

whooping cough *n* an acute infectious disease mainly affecting children, that causes coughing spasms ending with a shrill crowing sound on breathing in

whoops *interj* an exclamation of mild surprise or of apology

whopper *n informal* **1** an unusually large or impressive example of something: *Deauville's beach is a whopper* **2** a big lie

whopping *informal adj* **1** unusually large: *a whopping 40 per cent* ▷ *adv* **2** extremely: *it's a whopping great gamble*

whore (**hore**) *n* a prostitute or promiscuous woman: often a term of abuse **WORD ORIGIN** Old English *hōre*

whorehouse *n informal* a brothel

whorl *n* **1** *bot* a circular arrangement of leaves or flowers round the stem of a plant **2** *zool* a single turn in a spiral shell **3** anything shaped like a coil **WORD ORIGIN** probably variant of *whirl*

who's who is *or* who has

whose *pron* **1** of whom? belonging to whom?: used in direct and indirect questions: *whose idea was it?; I wondered whose it was* **2** of whom or of which: used as a relative pronoun: *Gran had sympathy for anybody whose life had gone wrong*

WORD ORIGIN Old English *hwæs*, genitive of *hwā* who + *hwæt* what

whosoever *pron old-fashioned or formal* same as **whoever**

why *adv* **1** for what reason?: *why did he marry her?; she avoided asking him why he was there* ▷ *pron* **2** for or because of which: *you can think of all kinds of reasons why you should not believe it* ▷ *n, pl* **whys 3 the whys and wherefores** see **wherefore** (sense 1) ▷ *interj* **4** an exclamation of surprise, indignation, or impatience: *why, I listen to you on the radio twice a week* **WORD ORIGIN** Old English *hwȳ, hwī*

WI 1 Wisconsin **2** *Brit & NZ* Women's Institute

wick *n* **1** a cord through the middle of a candle, through which the fuel reaches the flame **2 get on someone's wick** *Austral & Brit slang* to annoy someone **WORD ORIGIN** Old English *wēoce*

wicked *adj* **1** morally bad: *the wicked queen in 'Snow White'* **2** playfully mischievous or roguish: *let's be wicked and go skinny-dipping* **3** dangerous or unpleasant: *there was a wicked cut over his eye* **4** *slang* very good **wickedly** *adv* **wickedness** *n* **WORD ORIGIN** Old English *wicca* sorcerer, *wicce* witch

wicker *adj* made of wickerwork: *a wicker chair* **WORD ORIGIN** from Old Norse

wickerwork *n* a material consisting of slender flexible twigs woven together

wicket *n cricket* **1** either of two sets of three stumps stuck in the ground with two wooden bails resting on top, at which the batsman stands **2** the playing space between these **3** the act or instance of a batsman being got out **WORD ORIGIN** Old French *wiket*

wicketkeeper *n cricket* the fielder positioned directly behind the wicket

wicking *adj* acting to move moisture by capillary action from the inside to the surface: *wicking fabric*

wide *adj* **1** having a great extent from side to side: *the wide main street* **2** having a specified extent from side to side: *three metres wide* **3** covering or including many different things: *a wide range of services* **4** covering a large distance or extent: *the proposal was voted down by a wide margin* **5** (of eyes) opened fully ▷ *adv* **6** to a large or full extent: *he swung the door wide* **7 far and wide** see **far** (sense 7) ▷ *n* **8** *cricket* a ball bowled outside the batsman's reach, which scores a run for the batting side **widely** *adv* **WORD ORIGIN** Old English *wīd*

wide-angle lens *n* a lens on a camera which can cover a wider angle of view than an ordinary lens

wide-awake *adj* fully awake

wide-eyed *adj* **1** innocent or naive **2** surprised or frightened: *wide-eyed astonishment* ▷ *adv* **3** in a frightened, surprised, or excited manner: *they looked at me wide-eyed*

widen *vb* to make or become wide or wider

wide open *adj* **1** open to the full extent: *the main door was wide open* **2** exposed or vulnerable: *he was leaving himself wide open to problems*

wide-ranging *adj* covering or including many different things or subjects: *a wide-ranging review*

widespread *adj* affecting an extensive area or a large number of people: *widespread damage; widespread public support*

widgeon *n* same as **wigeon**

widget *n* **1** *informal* any small device, the name of which is unknown or forgotten **2** a small device in a beer can which, when the can is opened, releases nitrogen gas into the beer, giving it a head **3** a small computer program that can be installed on and executed from the desktop of a personal computer **WORD ORIGIN** changed from GADGET

widow *n* a woman whose husband has died and who has not remarried **widowhood** *n* **WORD ORIGIN** Old English *widewe*

widowed *adj* denoting a person, usually a woman, whose spouse has died and who has not remarried

widower *n* a man whose wife has died and who has not remarried

widow's weeds *pl n old-fashioned* the black mourning clothes traditionally worn by a widow **WORD ORIGIN** from Old English *wēd* a band worn in mourning

width *n* **1** the extent or measurement of something from side to side **2** the distance across a rectangular swimming bath, as opposed to its length

wield *vb* **1** to handle or use (a weapon or tool) **2** to exert or maintain (power or influence) **WORD ORIGIN** Old English *wieldan, wealdan*

wife *n, pl* **wives** the woman to whom a man is married **wifely** *adj* **WORD ORIGIN** Old English *wīf*

Wi-Fi *n computers* a system of wireless access to the internet

wig *n* an artificial head of hair **WORD ORIGIN** from *periwig*

wigeon *or* **widgeon** *n* a wild marshland duck **WORD ORIGIN** origin unknown

wigging *n Brit old-fashioned slang* a reprimand **WORD ORIGIN** origin unknown

wiggle *vb* **-gling, -gled 1** to move with jerky movements from side to side or up and down: *she wiggled her toes in the cool water* ▷ *n* **2** a wiggling movement or walk **WORD ORIGIN** Middle Low German, Middle Dutch *wiggelen*

wigwam *n* a Native American's tent, made of animal skins **WORD ORIGIN** Native American *wīkwām*

wiki *computers n* **1** a website, or page within one, whose content can be edited freely by anyone with access to a web browser ▷ *adj* **2** of or relating to the software which facilitates such open editing: *wiki technology* **WORD ORIGIN** from Hawaiian *wiki-wiki* quick

wilco *interj* an expression in signalling and telecommunications, indicating that a message just received will be complied with

W

WORD ORIGIN abbreviation for *I will comply*

wild *adj* **1** (of animals or birds) living in natural surroundings; not domesticated or tame **2** (of plants) growing in a natural state; not cultivated **3** uninhabited and desolate: *wild country* **4** living in a savage or uncivilized way: *a wild mountain man* **5** lacking restraint or control: *a wild party* **6** stormy or violent: *a wild windy October morning* **7** in a state of extreme emotional intensity: *wild with excitement* **8** without reason or substance: *wild accusations* **9** **wild about** *informal* very enthusiastic about: *his colleagues aren't all that wild about him* ▷ *adv* **10** **run wild** to behave without restraint: *she was allowed to run completely wild* ▷ *n* **11** **the wild** a free natural state of living: *creatures of the wild* **12** **the wilds** a desolate or uninhabited region: *the wilds of Africa* **wildly** *adv* **wildness** *n*
WORD ORIGIN Old English *wilde*

wild card *n* **1** *sport* a player or team that is allowed to take part in a competition despite not having met the normal qualifying requirements **2** *computers* a character that can be substituted for any other in a file

wildcat *n, pl* **-cats** *or* **-cat** **1** a wild European cat that looks like a domesticated cat but is larger and has a bushy tail **2** *informal* a quick-tempered person ▷ *adj* **3** *chiefly US* risky and financially unsound: *a wildcat operation*

wildcat strike *n* a strike begun by workers spontaneously or without union approval

wildebeest *n, pl* **-beests** *or* **-beest** same as **gnu**
WORD ORIGIN Afrikaans

wilderness *n* **1** a wild uninhabited uncultivated region **2** a confused mass or tangle: *a wilderness of long grass and wild flowers* **3** a state of being no longer in a prominent position: *a long spell in the political wilderness*
WORD ORIGIN Old English *wildēornes*, from *wildēor* wild beast

wildfire *n* **spread like wildfire** to spread very quickly or uncontrollably

wild flower *n* any flowering plant that grows in an uncultivated state

wildfowl *pl n* wild birds, such as grouse and pheasants, that are hunted for sport or food

wild-goose chase *n* a search that has little or no chance of success

wildlife *n* wild animals and plants collectively

wild rice *n* the dark-coloured edible grain of a North American grass that grows on wet ground

Wild West *n* the western US during its settlement, esp. with reference to its lawlessness

wiles *pl n* artful or seductive tricks or ploys
WORD ORIGIN from Old Norse *vēl* craft

wilful *or US* **willful** *adj* **1** determined to do things in one's own way: *a wilful and insubordinate child* **2** deliberate and intentional: *wilful misconduct* **wilfully** *adv*

will¹ *vb, past* **would** **1** used as an auxiliary to make the future tense: *he will go on trial*

on October 7 **2** to express resolution: *they will not consider giving up territories* **3** to express a polite request: *will you please calm Mummy and Daddy down* **4** to express ability: *many essential oils will protect clothing from moths* **5** to express probability or expectation: *his followers will be relieved to hear that* **6** to express customary practice: *boys will be boys!* **7** to express desire: *go in very small steps, if you will*
WORD ORIGIN Old English *willan*

≡ USAGE
≡ See at **shall**.

will² *n* **1** a strong determination: *a fierce will to survive* **2** desire or wish: *a referendum to determine the will of the people* **3** a document setting out a person's wishes regarding the disposal of his or her property after death **4** **at will** when and as one chooses: *customers can withdraw money at will* ▷ *vb* **willing, willed** **5** to try to make (something) happen by wishing very hard for it: *she willed herself not to cry* **6** to wish or desire: *if he wills it, we will meet again* **7** to leave (property) in one's will: *the farm had been willed to her*
WORD ORIGIN Old English *willa*

willies *pl n* **give someone the willies** *slang* to make someone nervous or frightened
WORD ORIGIN origin unknown

willing *adj* **1** favourably disposed or inclined: *I'm willing to hear what you have to say* **2** keen and obliging: *willing volunteers* **willingly** *adv* **willingness** *n*

will-o'-the-wisp *n* **1** someone or something that is elusive or deceptively alluring: *their freedom was just a will-o'-the-wisp* **2** a pale light that is sometimes seen over marshy ground at night
WORD ORIGIN *Will*, short for *William* + *wisp* twist of hay burning as a torch

willow *n* a tree that grows near water, with thin flexible branches used in weaving baskets and wood used for making cricket bats
WORD ORIGIN Old English *welig*

willowherb *n* a plant with narrow leaves and purplish flowers

willow pattern *n* a pattern in blue on white china, depicting a Chinese landscape with a willow tree, river, bridge, and figures

willowy *adj* slender and graceful

willpower *n* strong self-disciplined determination to do something

willy *n, pl* **-lies** *Brit, Austral, & NZ informal* a childish or jocular word for **penis**

willy-nilly *adv* **1** in a haphazard fashion; indiscriminately: *spending taxpayers' money willy-nilly* **2** whether desired or not
WORD ORIGIN Old English *wile hē, nyle hē* will he or will he not

willy wagtail *n* *Austral* black-and-white flycatcher

willy-willy *n* *Austral* a small tropical dust storm
WORD ORIGIN from a native Australian language

wilt *vb* **1** (of a flower or plant) to become limp or drooping **2** (of a person) to lose strength or confidence
WORD ORIGIN perhaps from obsolete *wilk* to wither

Wilts Wiltshire

wily *adj* **wilier, wiliest** sly or crafty

wimp *informal* *n* **1** a feeble ineffective person ▷ *vb* **2** **wimp out of** to fail to do (something) through lack of courage **wimpish** *or* **wimpy** *adj*
WORD ORIGIN origin unknown

WIMP *computers* windows, icons, menus (or mice), pointers: denoting a type of user-friendly screen display used on small computers

wimple *n* a piece of cloth draped round the head to frame the face, worn by women in the Middle Ages and now by some nuns
WORD ORIGIN Old English *wimpel*

win *vb* **winning, won** **1** to achieve first place in (a competition or race) **2** to gain (a prize or first place) in a competition or race **3** to gain victory in (a battle, argument, or struggle) **4** to gain (sympathy, approval, or support) ▷ *n* **5** *informal* a success, victory, or triumph: *three consecutive wins* ▶ See also **win over** ▷ **winnable** *adj*
WORD ORIGIN Old English *winnan*

wince *vb* **wincing, winced** **1** to draw back slightly, as if in sudden pain ▷ *n* **2** the act of wincing
WORD ORIGIN Old French *wencier, guenchir* to avoid

winch *n* **1** a lifting or hauling device consisting of a rope or chain wound round a barrel or drum ▷ *vb* **2** to haul or lift using a winch: *two men were winched to safety by a helicopter*
WORD ORIGIN Old English *wince* pulley

wind¹ *n* **1** a current of air moving across the earth's surface **2** a trend or force: *the chill wind of change* **3** the power to breathe normally, esp. during or after physical exercise: *if you feel tired during the exercise, persevere – you'll soon get a second wind* **4** gas in the stomach or intestines **5** *informal* foolish or empty talk: *political language is designed to give an appearance of solidity to pure wind* **6** **break wind** to release intestinal gas through the anus **7** **get wind of** *informal* to find out about: *the media finally got wind of her disappearance* ▷ *adj* **8** *music* of or relating to wind instruments: *the wind section* ▷ *vb* **winding, winded** **9** to cause (someone) to be short of breath: *he fell with a thud that left him winded* **10** to cause (a baby) to bring up wind after feeding **windless** *adj*
WORD ORIGIN Old English

wind² *vb* **winding, wound** **1** to twist (something flexible) round some object: *a sweatband was wound round his head* **2** to tighten the spring of (a clock or watch) by turning a key or knob **3** to follow a twisting course: *a narrow path wound through the shrubbery* ▶ See also **wind down, wind up** ▷ **winding** *adj, n*
WORD ORIGIN Old English *windan*

windbag *n* *slang* a person who talks a lot but says little of interest

windblown *adj* blown about by the wind: *windblown hair*

windbreak *n* a fence or a line of trees that gives protection from the wind by breaking its force

windcheater *n* *chiefly Brit* a warm jacket with a close-fitting knitted neck, cuffs, and waistband

Newfoundland English

Although Vikings set foot on the rocky island of Newfoundland by the eleventh century, if not before, the origins of Newfoundland English date from the exploitation of one of the world's great foodstocks, the cod of the Grand Banks lying off its shores, as well as stocks found inshore. From the early sixteenth century onward, ships from northern Europe made seasonal voyages, and settlement of the island gradually followed, largely confined to the shorelines of innumerable deepwater bays and inlets. The settlers and their servants chiefly arrived from Ireland and the West Country of England. Over the centuries Newfoundland went from a British colony to a self-governing Dominion to a province of Canada. For much of this time, Newfoundland was dually dependent on the mercies of the fish stocks and its far-off political masters.

Features of Newfoundland society included an educational system of schools run by religious denominations, notably the Roman Catholic church; sharp class divisions between the merchant elite of St. John's, the capital, and the rest of the population; the isolation of many ports only reachable by water. The isolation of communities especially resulted in a fantastic variety of pronunciations, grammar, and spellings. *Field* may be pronounced *fiel'*, *squall* as *squaw*. Present-tense verbs may take *-s* or *-es*: 'I thinks this is true.' *Ticklace*, the Atlantic kittiwake, is spelled at least 10 different ways, including as *tickle-ass*. The homogeneity of Newfoundland's ethnic stock and its proud status as an island (except for Labrador, which lies on the subarctic mainland) yielded the lively and idiosyncratic dialect recorded in the fine *Dictionary of Newfoundland English*. It is the most distinctive regional variety of Canadian English.

Many Newfoundlandisms are outside the scope of this dictionary. The vocabulary borrowed from the native languages with whom settlers, traders, and trappers came in contact, for example, *adikey*, an Inuit outer garment, and *tabanask*, a small sled. An abundance of nautical or fishing-related terms came from seafarers who set out from the Atlantic seaboard from Nova Scotia to New England, not to mention those from other parts of the world. Birds, beasts, and plants took on vivid coloration: *bedlamer* is an immature seal, a *gozzard* is a merganser, a *starrigan* is a small, young evergreen. Some words were dialect survivors from the United Kingdom hinterland adapted to the conditions of the new environment: *droke*, a steep-sided valley, or a belt of trees; *dwy*, a brief flurry or shower. Some apparently evolved on the island: *caplin*, a smelt-like fish much used for bait; *janny*, a person who takes part in costumed group activities at Christmas; *nunny-bag*, a knapsack; and *livyer*, a permanent resident. Common words may combine (*outport*, any coastal settlement other than St. John's); general words may denote more specific ones (just as *scotch* is always *whisky* in Scotland, *codfish* is always *fish* in Newfoundland). A verse from the song 'I's the b'y' (I'm the boy), an unofficial anthem like Australia's 'Waltzing Matilda', conveys a few of many common words that have special senses:

> Sods and rinds to cover your flake
> Cake and tea for supper
> Codfish in the spring o' the year
> Fried in maggoty butter.

Rind is a long strip of bark, usually spruce or fir, used for many purposes. A *flake* is a platform built on poles and spread with boughs for drying codfish on land. *Cake* is ship's biscuit or hardtack.

In recent decades, the collapse of the sealing industry and, especially, the cod fishery, destroyed an entire way of life; it also made hundreds of specialized terms obsolete. The rise of offshore oil-drilling has not enriched the language as the fishery had, but it has made Newfoundland, 'The Rock', much less impoverished. Newfoundland retains a vibrant community of writers, artists, and quirky, independent-minded thinkers. After the bitterly contested plebiscite in 1949 that brought it into the Canadian Confederation, its citizens have become Canadians, yet remain, like Acadians and Quebecois, a unique people. *I's the b'y* suggests the ebullience and resilience of this people and their wordstock:

> I's the b'y that builds the boat
> And I's the b'y that sails her
> I's the b'y that catches the fish
> And brings them home to Lizer.

wind chill *n* the serious chilling effect of wind and low temperature

wind down *vb* **1** to move downwards by turning a handle: *he wound down the rear window* **2** (of a clock or watch) to slow down before stopping completely **3** to relax after a stressful or tiring time: *I have not had a chance to wind down from a busy day* **4** to diminish gradually: *trading wound down for the day*

winded *adj* temporarily out of breath after physical exercise or a blow to the stomach

windfall *n* **1** a piece of unexpected good fortune, esp. financial gain **2** a fruit blown off a tree by the wind

windfall tax *n* a tax levied on profits made from the privatization of public utilities

wind farm *n* a large group of wind-driven generators for electricity supply

wind gauge *n* same as **anemometer**

winding sheet *n* a sheet in which a dead person is wrapped before being buried

wind instrument *n* a musical instrument, such as a flute, that is played by having air blown into it

windjammer *n* *history* a large merchant sailing ship

windlass *n* a machine for lifting heavy objects by winding a rope or chain round a barrel or drum driven by a motor **WORD ORIGIN** Old Norse *vindāss*

windmill *n* **1** a building containing machinery for grinding corn or for pumping, driven by sails that are turned by the wind **2** *Brit* a toy consisting of a stick with plastic vanes attached, which revolve in the wind

window *n* **1** an opening in a building or a vehicle containing glass within a framework, which lets in light and enables people to see in or out **2** the display area behind a glass window in a shop **3** a transparent area in an envelope which reveals the address on the letter inside **4** an area on a computer screen that can be manipulated separately from the rest of the display area, for example so that two or more files can be displayed at the same time **5** a period of unbooked time in a diary or schedule **WORD ORIGIN** Old Norse *vindauga* wind eye

window box *n* a long narrow box, placed on a windowsill, in which plants are grown

window-dressing *n* **1** the art of arranging goods in shop windows in such a way as to attract customers **2** an attempt to make something seem better than it is by stressing only its attractive features: *do you think that the president's calling for an investigation is window-dressing, or do you think he actually means to do something?* **window-dresser** *n*

windowpane *n* a sheet of glass in a window

window seat *n* **1** a seat below a window **2** a seat beside a window in a bus, train, or aircraft

window-shopping *n* looking at goods in shop windows without intending to buy anything

windowsill *n* a shelf at the bottom of a window, either inside or outside a room

windpipe *n* a nontechnical name for **trachea**

windscreen *n* *Brit, Austral, & NZ* the sheet of glass that forms the front window of a motor vehicle

windscreen wiper *n* *Brit, Austral, & NZ* an electrically operated blade with a rubber edge that wipes a windscreen clear of rain

windshield *n* *US & Canad* the sheet of glass that forms the front window of a motor vehicle

windshield wiper *n* *US & Canad* an electrically operated blade with a rubber edge that wipes a windshield clear of rain

windsock *n* a cloth cone mounted on a mast, used esp. at airports to indicate the direction of the wind

windsurfing *n* the sport of riding on water using a surfboard steered and propelled by an attached sail **windsurfer** *n*

windswept *adj* **1** exposed to the wind: *the vast windswept plains* **2** blown about by the wind: *his hair was looking a bit windswept*

wind tunnel *n* a chamber through which a stream of air is forced, in order to test the effects of wind on aircraft

wind up *vb* **1** to bring to a conclusion: *we want to wind this conflict up as quickly as possible* **2** *informal* to dissolve (a company) and divide its assets among creditors **3** to tighten the spring of (a clockwork mechanism) by turning a key or knob **4** to move (a car window) upwards by turning a handle **5** *informal* to end up: *to wind up in the hospital* **6** *informal* to make nervous or tense: *as crisis after crisis broke, I became increasingly wound up* **7** *Brit, Austral, & NZ slang* to tease or annoy: *that really used to wind my old man up something rotten* ▷ *adj* **wind-up** **8** operated by clockwork: *a wind-up toy* ▷ *n* **wind-up** **9** a light-hearted hoax **10** the finish

windward *chiefly naut adj* **1** of or in the direction from which the wind blows ▷ *n* **2** the windward direction ▷ *adv* **3** towards the wind

windy *adj* **windier, windiest** **1** denoting a time or conditions in which there is a strong wind: *a windy day* **2** exposed to the wind: *the windy graveyard* **3** long-winded or pompous: *his speeches are long and windy* **4** *old-fashioned slang* frightened

wine *n* **1 a** an alcoholic drink produced by the fermenting of grapes with water and sugar **b** an alcoholic drink produced in this way from other fruits or flowers: *dandelion wine* ▷ *adj* **2** dark purplish-red ▷ *vb* **wining, wined** **3 wine and dine** to entertain (someone) with wine and fine food **WORD ORIGIN** Latin *vinum*

wine bar *n* a bar that specializes in serving wine and usually food

wine box *n* a cubic carton containing wine, with a tap for dispensing

wine cellar *n* **1** a cellar where wine is stored **2** the stock of wines stored there

wineglass *n* a glass for wine, usually with a small bowl on a stem with a flared base

wing *n* **1** one of the limbs or organs of a bird, bat, or insect that are used for flying **2** one of the two winglike supporting parts of an aircraft **3** a projecting part of a building: *converting the unused east wing into a suitable habitation* **4** a faction or group within a political party or other organization: *the youth wing of the African National Congress* **5** *Brit* the part of a car body surrounding the wheels **6** *sport* **a** either of the two sides of the pitch near the touchline **b** same as **winger** **7 wings** *theatre* the space offstage to the right or left of the acting area **8 in the wings** ready to step in when needed **9 on the wing** flying **10 spread one's wings** to make fuller use of one's abilities by trying new experiences: *he increasingly spread his wings abroad* **11 take someone under one's wing** to look after someone **12 take wing** to fly away ▷ *vb* **13** to fly: *a lone bird winging its way from the island* **14** to move through the air: *sending a shower of loose gravel winging towards the house* **15** to shoot or wound in the wing or arm **16** to provide with wings **winged** *adj* **wingless** *adj* **WORD ORIGIN** Old Norse *vængr*

wing chair *n* an easy chair with side pieces extending forward from a high back

wing commander *n* a middle-ranking commissioned officer in an air force

winger *n* *sport* a player positioned on a wing

wing nut *n* **1** a threaded nut with two flat projections which allow it to be turned by the thumb and forefinger **2** a foolish or insane person

wingspan *n* the distance between the wing tips of a bird, insect, bat, or aircraft

wink *vb* **1** to close and open one eye quickly as a signal **2** (of a light) to shine brightly and intermittently; twinkle ▷ *n* **3** the act or an instance of winking, esp. as a signal **4** a twinkling of light **5** *informal* the smallest amount of sleep: *I didn't sleep a wink last night* **6 tip someone the wink** *Brit, Austral, & NZ informal* to give someone a hint or warning **WORD ORIGIN** Old English *wincian*

winkle *n* **1** an edible shellfish with a spirally coiled shell ▷ *vb* **-kling, -kled** **2 winkle out** *informal chiefly Brit* **a** to obtain (information) from someone who is not willing to provide it: *try to winkle the real problem out of them* **b** to coax or force out: *he somehow managed to winkle him out of his room*

winkle-pickers *pl n old-fashioned* shoes with very pointed narrow toes

winner *n* **1** a person or thing that wins **2** *informal* a person or thing that seems sure to be successful

winning *adj* **1** gaining victory: *the winning side* **2** charming or attractive: *her winning smiles*

winnings *pl n* the money won in a competition or in gambling

winnow *vb* **1** to separate (grain) from (chaff) by a current of air **2** (often foll. by *out*) to separate out (an unwanted element): *the committee will need to winnow out the nonsense* **WORD ORIGIN** Old English *windwian*

wino (**wine**-oh) *n, pl* **winos** *informal* a destitute person who habitually drinks cheap wine

win over *vb* to gain the support or consent of: *his robust performance won over his critics*

winsome *adj literary* charming or attractive: *a winsome smile*
WORD ORIGIN Old English *wynsum*

winter *n* **1** the coldest season of the year, between autumn and spring ▷ *vb* **2** to spend the winter in a specified place: *wintering in Rome*
WORD ORIGIN Old English

wintergreen *n* an evergreen shrub from which is obtained a pleasant-smelling oil that is used medicinally and for flavouring

winter solstice *n* the time, about December 22, at which the sun is at its southernmost point in the sky

winter sports *pl n* sports held on snow or ice, such as skiing and skating

wintertime *n* the period or season of winter

wintry *adj* **-trier, -triest** **1** of or characteristic of winter: *a cold wintry day* **2** cold or unfriendly: *a wintry smile*

win-win *adj* guaranteeing a favourable outcome for everyone involved: *a win-win situation for NATO*

wipe *vb* **wiping, wiped** **1** to rub (a surface or object) lightly with a cloth or the hand, in order to remove dirt or liquid from it **2** to remove by wiping: *she made a futile attempt to wipe away her tears* **3** to erase a recording from (a video or audio tape) ▷ *n* **4** the act or an instance of wiping: *a quick wipe*
WORD ORIGIN Old English *wīpian*

wipe out *vb* to destroy or get rid of completely: *a hail storm wipes out a wheat crop in five minutes*

wiper *n* short for **windscreen wiper**

wire *n* **1** a slender flexible strand of metal **2** a length of this used to carry electric current in a circuit **3** a long continuous piece of wire or cable connecting points in a telephone or telegraph system **4** *old-fashioned informal* a telegram ▷ *vb* **wiring, wired** **5** to fasten with wire **6** to equip (an electrical system, circuit, or component) with wires **7** *informal* to send a telegram to **8** to send by telegraph: *they wired the money for a train ticket*
WORD ORIGIN Old English *wīr*

wired *adj* **1** *slang* excitable or edgy, usually from stimulant intake: *I don't want coffee, I'm wired enough as it is* **2** using computers to send and receive information, esp. via the internet

wire-haired *adj* (of a dog) having a rough wiry coat

wireless *n* **1** *old-fashioned* same as **radio** ▷ *adj* **2** *computers* communicating without connecting wires: *wireless application protocol*

wire netting *n* a net made of wire, used for fencing

wiretapping *n* the practice of making a connection to a telegraph or telephone wire in order to obtain information secretly

wireworm *n* a destructive wormlike beetle larva

wiring *n* the network of wires used in an electrical system, device, or circuit

wiry *adj* **wirier, wiriest** **1** (of a person) slim but strong **2** coarse and stiff: *wiry grass*

wisdom *n* **1** the ability to use one's experience and knowledge to make sensible decisions or judgments **2** accumulated knowledge or learning: *the wisdom of Asia and of Africa*
WORD ORIGIN Old English *wīsdōm*

wisdom tooth *n* any of the four molar teeth, one at the back of each side of the jaw, that are the last of the permanent teeth to come through

wise¹ *adj* **1** possessing or showing wisdom: *a wise move* **2 none the wiser** knowing no more than before: *I left the conference none the wiser* **3 wise to** *informal* aware of or informed about: *they'll get wise to our system; he put him wise to the rumour* **wisely** *adv*
WORD ORIGIN Old English *wīs*

wise² *n old-fashioned* way, manner, or respect: *in no wise*
WORD ORIGIN Old English *wīse* manner

-wise *adv suffix* **1** indicating direction or manner: *crabwise* **2** with reference to: *moneywise*
WORD ORIGIN Old English *-wisan*

wiseacre *n* a person who wishes to seem wise
WORD ORIGIN Middle Dutch *wijsseggher* soothsayer

wisecrack *informal n* **1** a clever, amusing, sometimes unkind, remark ▷ *vb* **2** to make such remarks **wisecracking** *adj*

wise guy *n informal* a person who likes to give the impression of knowing more than other people

wise up *vb* **wising, wised** *slang* (often foll. by *to*) to become aware (of) or informed (about)

wish *vb* **1** to want or desire (something impossible or improbable): *he wished he'd kept quiet* **2** to desire or prefer to be or do something: *the next person who wished to speak* **3** to feel or express a hope concerning the welfare, health, or success of: *we wished him well* **4** to greet as specified: *I wished her a Merry Christmas* ▷ *n* **5** a desire, often for something impossible or improbable: *a desperate wish to succeed as a professional artist* **6** something desired or wished for: *your wishes will come true* **7** the expression of a hope for someone's welfare, health, or success: *give him our best wishes*
WORD ORIGIN Old English *wȳscan*

wishbone *n* the V-shaped bone above the breastbone of a chicken or turkey

wishful *adj* desirous or longing: *she seemed wishful of prolonging the discussion*

wishful thinking *n* an interpretation of the facts as one would like them to be, rather than as they are: *was it wishful thinking, or had the enemy lost heart?*

wish list *n* a list of things desired by a person or organization: *the government's wish list*

wish on *vb* to want (something unpleasant) to be experienced by: *I wouldn't wish that wretched childhood on anyone*

wishy-washy *adj informal* lacking in character, force, or colour

wisp *n* **1** a thin, delicate, or filmy piece or streak: *little wisps of cloud* **2** a small untidy bundle, tuft, or strand: *a wisp of hair* **3** a slight trace: *a wisp of a smile*
WORD ORIGIN origin unknown

wispy *adj* **wispier, wispiest** thin, fine, or delicate: *grey wispy hair*

wisteria *n* a climbing plant with large drooping clusters of blue, purple, or white flowers
WORD ORIGIN after Caspar *Wistar*, anatomist

wistful *adj* sadly wishing for something lost or unobtainable **wistfully** *adv* **wistfulness** *n*

wit¹ *n* **1** the ability to use words or ideas in a clever, amusing, and imaginative way **2** a person possessing this ability **3** practical intelligence: *do credit me with some wit* ▶ See also **wits**
WORD ORIGIN Old English *witt*

wit² *vb* **to wit** (used to introduce a statement or explanation) that is to say; namely
WORD ORIGIN Old English *witan*

witblits (**vit**-blits) *n S African* an illegally distilled strong alcoholic drink
WORD ORIGIN Afrikaans *wit* white + *blits* lightning

witch *n* **1** (in former times) a woman believed to possess evil magic powers **2** a person who practises magic or sorcery, esp. black magic **3** an ugly or wicked old woman
WORD ORIGIN Old English *wicce*

witchcraft *n* the use of magic, esp. for evil purposes

witch doctor *n* a man in certain tribal societies who is believed to possess magical powers, which can be used to cure sickness or to harm people

witchetty grub *n* a wood-boring edible Australian caterpillar

witch hazel *n* a medicinal solution made from the bark and leaves of a N American shrub, which is put on the skin to treat bruises and inflammation

witch-hunt *n* a rigorous campaign to expose and discredit people considered to hold unorthodox views on the pretext of safeguarding the public welfare

with *prep* **1** accompanying; in the company of: *the captain called to the sergeant to come with him* **2** using; by means of: *unlocking the padlock with a key* **3** possessing or having: *a woman with black hair; the patient with angina* **4** concerning or regarding: *be gentle with me* **5** in a manner characterized by: *I know you will handle it with discretion* **6** as a result of: *his voice was hoarse with nervousness* **7** following the line of thought of: *are you with me so far?* **8** having the same opinions as; supporting: *are you with us or against us?*
WORD ORIGIN Old English

withdraw *vb* **-drawing, -drew, -drawn** **1** to take out or remove: *he withdrew an envelope from his pocket* **2** to remove (money) from a bank account or savings

w

account **3** to leave one place to go to another, usually quieter, place: *he withdrew into his bedroom* **4** (of troops) to leave or be pulled back from the battleground **5** to take back (a statement) formally **6 withdraw from** to give up: *they withdrew from the competition*
WORD ORIGIN *with*, in the sense: away from

withdrawal *n* **1** the act or an instance of withdrawing **2** the period that a drug addict goes through after stopping using drugs, during which he or she may experience symptoms such as tremors, sweating, and vomiting ▷ *adj* **3** of or relating to withdrawal from an addictive drug: *withdrawal symptoms*

withdrawn *vb* **1** the past participle of **withdraw** ▷ *adj* **2** extremely reserved or shy

wither *vb* **1** to make or become dried up or shrivelled: *the leaves had withered but not fallen* **2** to fade or waste: *deprived of the nerve supply the muscles wither* **3** to humiliate (someone) with a scornful look or remark **withered** *adj*
WORD ORIGIN probably variant of *weather* (verb)

withering *adj* (of a look or remark) extremely scornful

withers *pl n* the highest part of the back of a horse, between the shoulders
WORD ORIGIN earlier *widersones*

withhold *vb* **-holding, -held** to keep back (information or money)

within *prep* **1** in or inside: *within the hospital grounds* **2** before (a period of time) has passed: *within a month* **3** not beyond: *within the confines of a low budget; he positioned a low table within her reach* ▷ *adv* **4** *formal* inside or internally: *a glimpse of what was hidden within*

without *prep* **1** not accompanied by: *I can't imagine going through life without him* **2** not using: *our Jeep drove without lights* **3** not possessing or having: *four months without a job; a lot of them came across the border without shoes* **4** in a manner showing a lack of: *without reverence* **5** while not or after not: *she sat without speaking for some while* ▷ *adv* **6** *formal* outside: *seated on the graveyard without*

withstand *vb* **-standing, -stood** to resist or endure successfully: *our ability to withstand stress*

witless *adj* **1** *formal* lacking intelligence or sense **2 scared witless** extremely frightened

witness *n* **1** a person who has seen or can give first-hand evidence of some event: *the only witness to a killing* **2** a person who gives evidence in a court of law: *a witness for the defence* **3** a person who confirms the genuineness of a document or signature by adding his or her own signature **4** evidence proving or supporting something: *the Church of England, that historic witness to the power of the Christian faith* **5 bear witness to** to be evidence or proof of: *the high turn-out bore witness to the popularity of the contest* ▷ *vb* **6** to see, be present at, or know at first hand: *I have witnessed many motor-racing accidents* **7** to be the scene or setting of: *the 1970s witnessed an enormous increase in*

international lending **8** to confirm the genuineness of (a document or signature) by adding one's own signature **9 witness to** *formal* to confirm: *our aim is to witness to the fact of the empty tomb*
WORD ORIGIN Old English *witnes*

witness box *or esp. US* **witness stand** *n* the place in a court of law where witnesses stand to give evidence

wits *pl n* **1** the ability to think and act quickly: *when he was sober his wits were razor-sharp* **2 at one's wits' end** at a loss to know what to do **3 have one's wits about one** to be able to think and act quickly **4 live by** *or* **on one's wits** to gain a livelihood by craftiness rather than by hard work **5 scared out of one's wits** extremely frightened

witter *vb* *chiefly Brit informal* to chatter or babble pointlessly or at unnecessary length
WORD ORIGIN origin unknown

witticism *n* a witty remark

wittingly *adv* intentionally and knowingly

witty *adj* **-tier, -tiest** clever and amusing **wittily** *adv*

wives *n* the plural of **wife**

wizard *n* **1** a man in fairy tales who has magic powers **2** a person who is outstandingly gifted in some specified field: *a financial wizard*
WORD ORIGIN from *wise*

wizardry *n* **1** magic or sorcery **2** outstanding skill or accomplishment in some specified field: *technological wizardry*

wizened (**wiz**-zend) *adj* shrivelled, wrinkled, or dried up with age

WMD *n* weapon(s) of mass destruction

woad *n* a blue dye obtained from a European plant, used by the ancient Britons as a body dye
WORD ORIGIN Old English *wād*

wobbegong *n* an Australian shark with brown-and-white skin

wobble *vb* **-bling, -bled** **1** to move or sway unsteadily **2** to shake: *she was having difficulty in controlling her voice, which wobbled about* ▷ *n* **3** a wobbling movement or sound
WORD ORIGIN Low German *wabbeln*

wobbly *adj* **-blier, -bliest** **1** unsteady **2** trembling ▷ *n* **3 throw a wobbly** *slang* to become suddenly angry or upset

wodge *n* *informal* a thick lump or chunk: *my wodge of Kleenex was a sodden ball*
WORD ORIGIN from *wedge*

woe *n* **1** *literary* intense grief **2 woes** misfortunes or problems: *economic woes* **3 woe betide someone** someone will or would experience misfortune: *woe betide anyone who got in his way*
WORD ORIGIN Old English *wā, wē*

woebegone *adj* sad in appearance
WORD ORIGIN *woe* + obsolete *bego* to surround

woeful *adj* **1** extremely sad **2** pitiful or deplorable: *a woeful lack of understanding* **woefully** *adv*

wok *n* a large bowl-shaped metal Chinese cooking pot, used for stir-frying
WORD ORIGIN Chinese (Cantonese)

woke *vb* the past tense of **wake¹**

woken *vb* the past participle of **wake¹**

wold *n* a large area of high open rolling country
WORD ORIGIN Old English *weald* wood

wolf *n, pl* **wolves** **1** a predatory doglike wild animal which hunts in packs **2** *old-fashioned informal* a man who habitually tries to seduce women **3 cry wolf** to give false alarms repeatedly: *if you cry wolf too often, people will take no notice* ▷ *vb* **4 wolf down** to eat quickly or greedily: *they will wolf down kidneys but refuse tongue*
WORD ORIGIN Old English *wulf*

wolfhound *n* a very large dog, formerly used to hunt wolves

wolf whistle *n* **1** a whistle produced by a man to express admiration of a woman's appearance ▷ *vb* **wolf-whistle, -whistling, -whistled** **2** to produce such a whistle

wolverine *n* a large meat-eating mammal of Eurasia and North America with very thick dark fur
WORD ORIGIN earlier *wolvering*, from *wolf*

wolves *n* the plural of **wolf**

woman *n, pl* **women** **1** an adult female human being **2** adult female human beings collectively: *the very image of woman pared of the trappings of 'femininity'* **3** an adult female human being with qualities associated with the female, such as tenderness or maternalism: *she's more woman than you know* **4** a female servant or domestic help **5** *informal* a wife or girlfriend ▷ *adj* **6** female: *a woman doctor*
WORD ORIGIN Old English *wīfmann*

womanhood *n* **1** the state of being a woman: *young girls approaching womanhood* **2** women collectively: *Asian womanhood*

womanish *adj* (of a man) looking or behaving like a woman

womanizer *or* **-niser** *n* a man who has casual affairs with many women

womanizing *or* **-nising** *n* (of a man) the practice of indulging in casual affairs with women

womankind *n* all women considered as a group

womanly *adj* possessing qualities generally regarded as typical of, or appropriate to, a woman

womb *n* the nontechnical name for **uterus**
WORD ORIGIN Old English *wamb*

wombat *n* a furry heavily-built plant-eating Australian marsupial
WORD ORIGIN Aboriginal

women *n* the plural of **woman**

womenfolk *pl n* **1** women collectively **2** a group of women, esp. the female members of one's family

Women's Liberation *n* a movement promoting the removal of inequalities based upon the assumption that men are superior to women. Also called: **women's lib**

won *vb* the past of **win**

wonder *vb* **1** to think about something with curiosity or doubt: *I wonder why she did that* **2** to be amazed: *I did wonder at her leaving valuable china on the shelves* ▷ *n*

Scrabble Words with the Power Tiles

The highest-scoring tiles in Scrabble are J, Q, X, and Z, with J and X scoring eight points each, while Q and Z are worth ten points each. These are known as the 'power tiles', and they are the most potent weapons in the Scrabble player's arsenal, but need to be carefully deployed. This isn't always a matter of using them in a long word – a carefully positioned short word can be just as good a move. It's worth learning all of the two- and three-letter words using power tiles to get some easy high scores. There are too many words from four to eight letters to remember, but it is good to know some that begin or end in a power tile because that is a standard length between a double or triple letter square and a double or triple word square on the board.

There is only one J tile in Scrabble, so any word with two Js (eg HAJJ or JUJU) requires a blank tile. When trying to use a J word for parallel play, remember that there are only two two-letter words with J – JA and JO. Like Q, J is not as flexible as X or Z, so it is wise to try to use it as soon as it arrives on your rack rather than hold onto it hoping for a better score later. Don't forget unusual combinations like the FJ in FJELD and FJORD, or the DJ in DJIN, DJINN, and their plurals. There are also a number of words that contain a JR combination, including BAJRA, BAJRI, and HIJRA, and these can be useful.

Along with Z, Q is the highest-scoring letter in Scrabble. Unlike Z, Q can be tricky to use because the majority of words that contain Q also require a U. However, you shouldn't keep holding onto the Q in the hope you might get a U to go with it. It is better to play it as soon as possible and there are a number of words that contain Q but no U which can help: FAQIR, INQILAB, NIQAB, QABALA, QABALAH, QADI, QAID, QANAT, QASIDA, QAT, QAWWAL, QI, QIBLA, QIGONG, QINDAR, QINTAR, QIS, QOPH, QORMA, QWERTY, SHEQEL, TALAQ, TRANQ, TSADDIQ, TZADDIQ, WAQF, YAQONA.

There is only one two-letter word with Q, QI, which is very useful as you are likely to have an I either on your rack or on the board. It's also worth committing the few three-letter Q words to memory: QAT, QIS, QUA, SUQ. If you are lucky enough to have Q and U on your rack, or a U is available on the board, then the four- or five-letter Q words are most likely to get you the best scores. It can help to remember some of them in sets such as QUAD, QUID, QUOD and QUINA, QUINE, QUINO.

X is perhaps the most versatile of the power tiles, simply because of the extensive number of two- and three-letter words that contain it. It can reap many points through parallel play, especially if the X falls on a premium square, because there is a two-letter word for every vowel, ie AX, EX, OX, XI, XU. It is fairly easy to spot words that end in X, so it's worth learning a few words that begin with X when a board may not favour X-ending words (eg XENIA, XENON, XYST). Of all the power tiles, the X is the only one that is worth holding back in the hope of getting a better score later, providing you can score reasonably well with your other tiles meanwhile.

Z scores the same as Q: ten points. But is an easier letter to use primarily because of the two two-letter words (ZA, ZO). Generally you should look to play it sooner rather than later. It is worth familiarizing yourself with some unusual three-, four-, and five-letter words with the Z, especially those with low-scoring letters (eg ZEA, ZOA, ZEIN, ZILA, ZONAE, ZANTE). There are a few Z words that also contain another power tile (JIZ, JAZY, ZAX, ZEX, QUIZ). Although these appear to be very useful, in practice if you have two power tiles on your rack, it can be wiser to play them separately over two turns to maximize your score. There are also quite a few words with a double Z (eg BUZZ, FUZZ, and WHIZZ).

With these and other judicious uses of the power tiles, you can capitalize on their high-scoring potential.

3 something that causes surprise or awe: *it's a wonder she isn't speechless with fright* **4** the feeling of surprise or awe caused by something strange: *the wonder of travel* **5 do** or **work wonders** to achieve spectacularly good results **6 no** or **small wonder** it is not surprising: *no wonder you're going broke* ▷ *adj* **7** causing surprise or awe because of spectacular results achieved: *a new wonder drug for treating migraine* **wonderingly** *adv* **wonderment** *n* **WORD ORIGIN** Old English *wundor*

wonderful *adj* **1** extremely fine; excellent: *I've been offered a wonderful job* **2** causing surprise, amazement, or awe: *a strange and wonderful phenomenon* **wonderfully** *adv*

wonderland *n* **1** an imaginary land of marvels or wonders **2** an actual place of great or strange beauty: *the apartment was a wonderland of design and colour*

wondrous *adj old-fashioned* or *literary* causing surprise or awe; marvellous

wonky *adj* **-kier, -kiest** *Brit, Austral, & NZ slang* **1** shaky or unsteady: *wonky wheelbarrows; wonky knees* **2** insecure or unreliable: *his marriage is looking a bit wonky* **WORD ORIGIN** dialect *wanky*

wont (rhymes with **dont**) *old-fashioned adj* **1** accustomed: *most murderers, his police friends were wont to say, were male* ▷ *n* **2** a usual practice: *she waded straight in, as was her wont* **WORD ORIGIN** Old English *gewunod*

won't will not

woo *vb* **wooing, wooed 1** to coax or urge: *it will woo people back into the kitchen* **2** *old-fashioned* to attempt to gain the love of (a woman) **wooing** *n* **WORD ORIGIN** Old English *wōgian*

wood *n* **1** the hard fibrous substance beneath the bark in trees and shrubs, which is used in building and carpentry and as fuel ▸ Related adjective: **ligneous 2** an area of trees growing together that is smaller than a forest: *a track leading into a wood* ▸ Related adjective: **sylvan 3** *golf* a long-shafted club with a wooden head ▷ *adj* **4** made of, using, or for use with wood: *wood fires* ▸ See also **woods** **WORD ORIGIN** Old English *widu, wudu*

wood alcohol *n* same as **methanol**

woodbine *n* a wild honeysuckle with sweet-smelling yellow flowers

woodcarving *n* **1** a work of art produced by carving wood **2** the act or craft of carving wood

woodcock *n* a large game bird with a long straight bill

woodcut *n* a print made from a block of wood with a design cut into it

woodcutter *n* a person who cuts down trees or chops wood

wooded *adj* covered with woods or trees

wooden *adj* **1** made of wood **2** lacking spirit or animation: *the man's expression became wooden* **woodenly** *adv*

wooden spoon *n* a booby prize, esp. in sporting contests

woodland *n* **1** land that is mostly covered with woods or trees ▷ *adj* **2** living in woods: *woodland birds*

woodlouse *n, pl* **-lice** a very small grey creature with many legs that lives in damp places

woodpecker *n* a bird with a strong beak with which it bores into trees for insects

wood pulp *n* pulp made from wood fibre, used to make paper

woodruff *n* a plant with small sweet-smelling white flowers and sweet-smelling leaves **WORD ORIGIN** Old English *wudurofe*

woods *pl n* closely packed trees forming a forest or wood

woodsman *n, pl* **-men** a person who lives in a wood or who is skilled at woodwork or carving

woodwind *music adj* **1** of or denoting a type of wind instrument, such as the oboe ▷ *n* **2** the woodwind instruments of an orchestra

woodwork *n* **1** the parts of a room or house that are made of wood, such as the doors and window frames: *stark white walls and blue woodwork* **2** the art or craft of making objects from wood **3 crawl out of the woodwork** to appear suddenly and in large numbers: *intellectuals and environmentalists crawled out of the woodwork*

woodworm *n* **1** a beetle larva that bores into wooden furniture or beams **2** the damage caused to wood by these larvae

woody *adj* **woodier, woodiest 1** (of a plant) having a very hard stem **2** (of an area) covered with woods or trees

woof¹ *n* same as **weft** **WORD ORIGIN** Old English *ōwef*

woof² *n* an imitation of the bark of a dog

woofer *n* a loudspeaker used in high-fidelity systems for the reproduction of low audio frequencies

wool *n* **1** the soft curly hair of sheep and some other animals **2** yarn spun from this, used in weaving and knitting **3** cloth made from this yarn **4 pull the wool over someone's eyes** to deceive someone **WORD ORIGIN** Old English *wull*

woolgathering *n* idle or absent-minded daydreaming

woollen or US **woolen** *adj* **1** made of wool or of a mixture of wool and another material **2** relating to wool: *woollen mills* ▷ *n* **3 woollens** woollen clothes, esp. knitted ones

woolly or US **wooly** *adj* **-lier, -liest 1** made of or like wool **2** confused or indistinct: *woolly ideas* ▷ *n, pl* **-lies 3** a woollen garment, such as a sweater

woolshed *n Austral & NZ* a large building in which sheep shearing takes place

woomera *n* a notched stick used by Australian Aborigines to aid the propulsion of a spear

woozy *adj* **woozier, wooziest** *informal* feeling slightly dizzy **WORD ORIGIN** origin unknown

wop-wops *pl n NZ informal* remote rural areas

Worcester sauce (**wooss**-ter) or **Worcestershire sauce** *n* a sharp-tasting sauce, made from soy sauce, vinegar, and spices

Worcs Worcestershire

word *n* **1** the smallest single meaningful unit of speech or writing ▸ Related

adjective: **lexical 2** a brief conversation: *I would like a word with you* **3** a brief statement: *a word of warning* **4** news or information: *let me know if you get word of my wife* **5** a solemn promise: *he had given his word as a rabbi* **6** a command or order: *he had only to say the word and they'd hang him* **7** *computers* a set of bits used to store, transmit, or operate upon an item of information in a computer **8 by word of mouth** by spoken rather than by written means: *their reputation spreads by word of mouth* **9 in a word** briefly or in short: *in a word, we've won* **10 my word!** Also: **upon my word!** *old-fashioned* an exclamation of surprise or amazement **11 take someone at his** or **her word** to accept that someone really means what he or she says: *they're willing to take him at his word when he says he'll change* **12 take someone's word for it** to believe what someone says **13 the last word** the closing remark of a conversation or argument, often regarded as settling an issue **14 the last word in** the finest example of: *the last word in comfort* **15 word for word** using exactly the same words: *he repeated almost word for word what had been said* **16 word of honour** a solemn promise ▷ *vb* **17** to state in words: *the questions have to be carefully worded* ▸ See also **words** **WORD ORIGIN** Old English

Word *n* **the Word** the message and teachings contained in the Bible

-word *n combining form* (preceded by 'the' and an initial letter) a euphemistic way of referring to a word by its first letter because it is considered to be unmentionable by the user: *the c-word, meaning cancer*

word game *n* any game involving the discovery, formation, or alteration of a word or words

wording *n* the way in which words are used to express something: *the exact wording of the regulation has still not been worked out*

word-perfect *adj* able to repeat from memory the exact words of a text one has learned

word processing *n* the storage and organization of text by electronic means, esp. for business purposes

word processor *n* an electronic machine for word processing, consisting of a keyboard, a VDU incorporating a microprocessor, and a printer

words *pl n* **1** the text of a song, as opposed to the music **2** the text of an actor's part **3 have words** to have an argument or disagreement **4 in other words** expressing the same idea in a different, more understandable, way **5 put into words** to express in speech or writing: *she was reluctant to put her thoughts into words*

wordy *adj* **wordier, wordiest** using too many words, esp. long words: *wordy explanations*

wore *vb* the past tense of **wear**

work *n* **1** physical or mental effort directed to doing or making something **2** paid employment at a job, trade, or profession **3** duties or tasks: *I had to*

delegate as much work as I could **4** something done or made as a result of effort: *a work by a major artist* **5** the place where a person is employed: *accidents at work* **6** *physics old-fashioned* the transfer of energy occurring when a force is applied to move a body **7 at work** working or in action: *the social forces at work in society* ▷ *adj* **8** of or for work: *work experience* ▷ *vb* **9** to do work; labour: *no-one worked harder than Arnold* **10** to be employed: *she worked as a waitress* **11** to make (a person or animal) labour **12** to operate (a machine or a piece of equipment) **13** (of a machine or a piece of equipment) to function, esp. effectively: *he doesn't have to know how things work* **14** (of a plan or system) to be successful **15** to cultivate (land) **16** to move gradually into a specific condition or position: *he picked up the shovel, worked it under the ice, and levered* **17** to make (one's way) with effort: *he worked his way to the top* **18** *informal* to manipulate to one's own advantage: *they could see an angle and they'd know how to work it* ▸ See also **work off**, **works**, etc.
WORD ORIGIN Old English *weorc*

workable *adj* **1** able to operate efficiently: *a workable solution* **2** able to be used: *a workable mine*

workaday *adj* commonplace or ordinary: *workaday surroundings*

workaholic *n* a person who is obsessed with work

workbench *n* a heavy table at which a craftsman or mechanic works

worker *n* **1** a person who works in a specified way: *a hard worker* **2** a person who works at a specific job: *a government worker* **3** an employee, as opposed to an employer **4** a sterile female bee, ant, or wasp, that works for the colony

work ethic *n* a belief in the moral value of work

workforce *n* **1** the total number of workers employed by a company **2** the total number of people available for work: *the local workforce*

workhorse *n* a person or thing that does a lot of work, esp. dull or routine work: *this plane is the workhorse of most short-haul airlines*

workhouse *n* (formerly, in England) a public institution where very poor people did work in return for food and accommodation

working *adj* **1** having a job: *the working mother* **2** concerned with, used in, or suitable for work: *working conditions* **3** capable of being operated or used: *a working mechanism* ▷ *n* **4** a part of a mine or quarry that is or has been used **5 workings** the way that something works: *the workings of the human brain*

working capital *n* the amount of capital that a business has available to meet the day-to-day cash requirements of its operations

working class *n* **1** the social group that consists of people who earn wages, esp. as manual workers ▷ *adj* **working-class 2** of or relating to the working class: *a working-class neighbourhood*

working day *or esp. US & Canad* **workday** *n* **1** a day when people normally go to work: *the last working day of the week* **2** the part of the day allocated to work: *the long working day of twelve to fourteen hours*

working party *n* a committee established to investigate a problem

workload *n* the amount of work to be done, esp. in a specified period: *a heavy workload*

workman *n, pl* **-men** a man who is employed to do manual work

workmanlike *adj* skilfully done: *a neat workmanlike job*

workmanship *n* the degree of skill with which an object is made: *shoddy workmanship*

workmate *n* *informal* a person who works with another person; fellow worker

work of art *n* **1** a piece of fine art, such as a painting or sculpture **2** an object or a piece of work that has been exceptionally skilfully made or produced: *the doll was truly a work of art*

work off *vb* to get rid of, usually by effort: *he went along to the tennis club and worked off his pique there*

work on *vb* to try to persuade or influence (someone)

work out *vb* **1** to solve, find out, or plan by reasoning or calculation: *working out a new budget* **2** to happen in a particular way: *he decided to wait and see how things worked out* **3** to be successful or satisfactory: *the dates never worked out* **4** to take part in physical exercise **5 work out at** to be calculated at (a certain amount): *the return on capital works out at 15 per cent* ▷ *n* **workout 6** a session of physical exercise for training or to keep fit

work over *vb* *slang* to give (someone) a severe beating: *whoever worked her over did a thorough job*

works *n* **1** a place where something is manufactured: *a chemical works* ▷ *pl n* **2** the sum total of a writer's or artist's achievements considered together: *the works of Goethe* **3 the works** *slang* everything associated with a particular subject or thing: *traditional Indian music, sitars, the works*

worksheet *n* a sheet of paper containing exercises to be completed by a student

workshop *n* **1** a room or building where manufacturing or other manual work is carried on **2** a group of people engaged in intensive study or work in a creative or practical field: *a writers' workshop*

workshy *adj* not inclined to work; lazy

work station *n* **1** an area in an office where one person works **2** *computers* a component of an electronic office system consisting of a VDU and keyboard

worktable *n* a table at which writing, sewing, or other work may be done

worktop *n* a surface in a kitchen, usually the top of a fitted kitchen unit, which is used for food preparation. Also: **work surface**

work-to-rule *n* a form of industrial action in which employees keep strictly to their employers' rules, with the result of reducing the work rate

work up *vb* **1** to make angry, excited, or upset: *he worked himself up into a rage* **2** to build up or develop: *I'd worked up a thirst* **3** to work on (something) in order to improve it: *there was enough material to be worked up into something publishable* **4 work one's way up** to make progress: *he worked his way up in the catering trade* **5 work up to** to develop gradually towards: *the fete worked up to a climax around lunch time*

world *n* **1** the earth as a planet **2** the human race; people generally: *providing food for the world* **3** any planet or moon, esp. one that might be inhabited **4** a particular group of countries or period of history, or its inhabitants: *the Arab world; the post-Cold War world* **5** an area, sphere, or realm considered as a complete environment: *the art world; the world of nature* **6** the total circumstances and experience of a person that make up his or her life: *there may not ever be a place for us in your world* **7 bring into the world** to deliver or give birth to (a baby) **8 come into the world** to be born **9 for all the world** exactly or very much: *they looked for all the world like a pair of newly-weds* **10 in the world** used to emphasize a statement: *she didn't have a worry in the world* **11 man *or* woman of the world** a man *or* woman who is experienced in social or public life **12 worlds apart** very different from each other: *this man and I are worlds apart* ▷ *adj* **13** of or concerning the entire world: *the world championship*
WORD ORIGIN Old English *w(e)orold*

world-class *adj* being as good as anyone else in the world in a particular field: *he has the makings of a world-class batsman*

World Cup *n* an international competition held between national teams in various sports, most notably association football

worldly *adj* **-lier, -liest 1** not spiritual; earthly or temporal: *as a simple monk he had no interest in politics and other worldly affairs* **2** of or relating to material things: *all his worldly goods* **3** wise in the ways of the world; sophisticated: *a suave, worldly, charming Frenchman* **worldliness** *n*

worldly-wise *adj* wise in the ways of the world; sophisticated

world music *n* popular music of a variety of ethnic origins and styles

world-shaking *adj* of enormous significance; momentous: *world-shaking events*

World War I *n* the war (1914–18) between the Allies (principally France, Russia, Britain, Italy, Australia, Canada, and the US) and the Central Powers (principally Germany, Austria-Hungary, and Turkey). Also: **First World War**

World War II *n* the war (1939–45) between the Allies (Britain, France, Australia, Canada, the US, and the Soviet Union) and the Axis (Germany, Italy, and Japan). Also: **Second World War**

world-weary *adj* no longer finding pleasure in life

worldwide *adj* applying or extending throughout the world

World Wide Web *n* *computers* a vast network of hypertext files, stored on computers throughout the world, that

W

can provide a computer user with information on a huge variety of subjects

worm n **1** a small invertebrate animal with a long thin body and no limbs **2** an insect larva that looks like a worm **3** a despicable or weak person **4** a slight trace: *a worm of doubt* **5** a shaft on which a spiral thread has been cut, for example in a gear arrangement in which such a shaft drives a toothed wheel **6** *computers* a type of virus ▷ *vb* **7** to rid (an animal) of worms in its intestines **8 worm one's way a** to go or move slowly and with difficulty: *I had to worm my way out sideways from the bench* **b** to get oneself into a certain situation or position gradually: *worming your way into my good books* **9 worm out of** to obtain (information) from someone who is not willing to provide it: *it took me weeks to worm the facts out of him* ▸ See also **worms**
· **WORD ORIGIN** Old English *wyrm*

WORM n *computers* write once read many (times): an optical disk which enables users to store their own data

wormcast n a coil of earth or sand that has been excreted by a burrowing worm

worm-eaten adj eaten into by worms: *worm-eaten beams*

wormhole n a hole made by a worm in timber, plants, or fruit

worms n a disease caused by parasitic worms living in the intestines

wormwood n a plant from which a bitter oil formerly used in making absinthe is obtained
WORD ORIGIN Old English *wormōd, wermōd*

wormy adj **wormier, wormiest** infested with or eaten by worms

worn vb **1** the past participle of **wear** ▷ adj **2** showing signs of long use or wear: *the worn soles of his boots* **3** looking tired and ill: *that worn pain-creased face*

worn-out adj **1** worn or used until threadbare, valueless, or useless **2** completely exhausted: *worn-out by their exertions*

worried adj concerned and anxious about things that may happen **worriedly** adv

worrisome adj *old-fashioned* causing worry

worry vb **-ries, -rying, -ried 1** to be or cause to be anxious or uneasy **2** to annoy or bother: *don't worry yourself with the details* **3** (of a dog) to frighten (sheep or other animals) by chasing and trying to bite them **4 worry away at** to struggle with or work on (a problem) ▷ *n, pl* **-ries 5** a state or feeling of anxiety: *he was beside himself with worry* **6** a cause for anxiety: *having a premature baby is much less of a worry these days* **worrier** n
WORD ORIGIN Old English *wyrgan*

worry beads pl n a string of beads that supposedly relieves nervous tension when fingered or played with

worrying adj causing concern and anxiety

worse adj **1** the comparative of **bad 2 none the worse for** not harmed by (adverse events or circumstances) **3 the worse for wear** *informal* in a poor condition; not at one's best: *returning the*

worse for wear from the pub ▷ n **4 for the worse** into a worse condition: *taking a turn for the worse* ▷ adv **5** the comparative of **badly 6 worse off** in a worse condition, esp. financially
WORD ORIGIN Old English *wiersa*

worsen vb to make or become worse **worsening** adj, n

worship vb **-shipping, -shipped** or US **-shiping, -shiped 1** to show profound religious devotion to (one's god), for example by praying **2** to have intense love and admiration for (a person) ▷ n **3** religious adoration or devotion **4** formal expression of religious adoration, for example by praying **5** intense love or devotion to a person **worshipper** n
WORD ORIGIN Old English *weorthscipe*

Worship n **Your** or **His** or **Her Worship** *chiefly Brit* a title for a mayor or magistrate

worshipful adj feeling or showing reverence or adoration

worst adj, adv **1** the superlative of **bad** or **badly** ▷ n **2** the least good or the most terrible person, thing, or part: *the worst is yet to come* **3 at one's worst** in the worst condition or aspect of a thing or person: *the British male is at his worst in July and August* **4 at worst** in the least favourable interpretation or conditions: *all the questions should ideally be answered 'no', or at worst 'sometimes'* ▷ vb **5** *old-fashioned* to defeat or beat
WORD ORIGIN Old English *wierrest*

worsted (**wooss**-tid) n a close-textured woollen fabric used to make jackets and trousers
WORD ORIGIN after *Worstead*, a district in Norfolk

worth prep **1** having a value of: *the fire destroyed property worth $200 million* **2** worthy of; meriting or justifying: *if a job is worth doing, it's worth doing well* **3 worth one's weight in gold** extremely useful or helpful; very highly valued **4 worth one's while** worthy of spending one's time or effort on something: *they needed a wage of at least £140 a week to make it worth their while returning to work* ▷ n **5** monetary value: *the corporation's net worth* **6** high quality; value: *the submarine proved its military worth during the Second World War* **7** the amount of something that can be bought for a specified price: *$10 billion worth of property*
WORD ORIGIN Old English *weorth*

worthless adj **1** without value or usefulness: *worthless junk bonds* **2** without merit: *he sees himself as a worthless creature* **worthlessness** n

worthwhile adj sufficiently important, rewarding, or valuable to justify spending time or effort on it

worthy adj **-thier, -thiest 1** deserving of admiration or respect: *motives which were less than worthy* **2 worthy of** deserving of: *he would practise extra hard to be worthy of such an honour* ▷ n, pl **-thies 3** often *facetious* an important person **worthily** adv **worthiness** n

would vb **1** used as an auxiliary to form the past tense or subjunctive mood of **will**: *he asked if she would marry him; that would be delightful* **2** to express a polite

offer or request: *would you like some lunch?* **3** to describe a habitual past action: *sometimes at lunch time I would choose a painting to go and see*
▤ **USAGE**
▤ See at **should**.

would-be adj wanting or pretending to be: *would-be brides*

wouldn't would not

wound¹ n **1** an injury to the body such as a cut or a gunshot injury **2** an injury to one's feelings or reputation ▷ vb **3** to cause an injury to the body or feelings of **wounding** adj
WORD ORIGIN Old English *wund*

wound² vb the past of **wind²**

wove vb a past tense of **weave**

woven vb a past participle of **weave**

wow interj **1** an exclamation of admiration or amazement ▷ n **2** *slang* a person or thing that is amazingly successful: *he would be an absolute wow on the chat shows* ▷ vb **3** *slang* to be a great success with: *the new Disney film wowed festival audiences*
WORD ORIGIN Scots

wowser n *Austral & NZ slang* **1** a fanatically puritanical person **2** a teetotaller
WORD ORIGIN dialect *wow* to complain

wp word processor

WPC (in Britain) woman police constable

wpm words per minute

WRAC (in Britain) Women's Royal Army Corps

wrack¹ n same as **rack²**
WORD ORIGIN Old English *wræc* persecution
▤ **USAGE**
▤ The use of the spelling *wrack* rather than *rack* in sentences such as *she was wracked by grief* or *the country was wracked by civil war* is very common but is thought by many people to be incorrect.

wrack² n seaweed that is floating in the sea or has been washed ashore
WORD ORIGIN probably from Middle Dutch *wrak* wreckage

WRAF (in Britain) Women's Royal Air Force

wraith n *literary* a ghost **wraithlike** adj
WORD ORIGIN Scots

wrangle vb **-gling, -gled 1** to argue noisily or angrily ▷ n **2** a noisy or angry argument
WORD ORIGIN Low German *wrangeln*

wrap vb **wrapping, wrapped 1** to fold a covering round (something) and fasten it securely: *a small package wrapped in brown paper* **2** to fold or wind (something) round a person or thing: *she wrapped a handkerchief around her bleeding palm* **3** to fold, wind, or coil: *she wrapped her arms around her mother* **4** to complete the filming of (a motion picture or television programme) ▷ n **5** *old-fashioned* a garment worn wrapped round the shoulders **6** (in the filming of a motion picture or television programme) the end of a day's filming or the completion of filming **7** a type of sandwich consisting of filling rolled up in a flour tortilla **8** *Brit slang* a small

The Lord's Prayer in English

One way to show how English has changed over its history is to examine a passage that occurs in each phase of the language's development. The Biblical passage known as *The Lord's Prayer* is one of the most frequently recited prayers in Christianity and has been translated into many languages, including Old, Middle, and Early Modern English.

One of the most recent versions comes from the New International Version of the Bible (1978).

> Our Father in heaven,
> hallowed be your name,
> your kingdom come,
> your will be done
> on earth as it is in heaven.
> Give us today our daily bread.
> Forgive us our debts,
> as we also have forgiven our debtors.
> And lead us not into temptation,
> but deliver us from the evil one.
> (Matthew 6:9-13)

There is more than one version of the *Lord's Prayer* in Old English. The following comes from the 9th century AD and is in West Saxon dialect, which became the literary standard for Old English until the Norman Conquest. A gloss is provided below each line:

> þu ure fæder, þe eart on heofonum, sie þin nama
> ȝehalgod.
> *thou our father, who art in heaven, be thine name*
> *hallowed*
> Cume þin rice. Sie þin wylla on eorþan swa swa on
> heofonum.
> *come thine kingdom. Be thine will on earth just as in*
> *heaven.*
> Syle us todæȝ urne dæȝhwamlican hlaf.
> *sell us today our day-which-ly loaf*
> And forȝief us ure ȝyltas swa swa we forȝiefaþ
> þæm þe wið us agyltaþ
> *and forgive us our guilts, just as we forgive them who*
> *against us become guilty.*
> And ne læd þu nu us on costnunge, ac alies us fram
> yfele
> *and not lead you now us into temptation, but loose us*
> *from evil.*

Some noticeable features of the language include the runic character *thorn* (þ) in place of *th*; the vowel *ash* (æ) in words that have *a* in Modern English (eg 'fæder' for *father*); the letter *yogh* (3), which in Old English represented the letter *g* before the vowels *e* and *i*; and the prefix ȝe- in the past participle 'ȝehalgod' (*hallowed* or *holied*).

There are even more versions of the *Lord's Prayer* in Middle English than in Old English, as in Middle English regional variation was the norm. The following Middle English version comes from the Midlands dialect of the late 14th century. As it is much nearer to Modern English, no gloss is necessary.

> Oure fadir, þat art in heuenys, halewid be þi
> name. Þi kyngdom come to. Be þi wile don ase
> in heuene and in erþe. Ȝiue to us þis day oure
> breed ouer oþer substaunse. And forȝiue to us
> oure dettes, as and we forȝiuen to oure det-
> touris. And leede us not into temptaciouns, but
> delyuere us from yuel.

This version is much more understandable to a modern reader; however, there are still some noticeably different features. The letters þ and 3 have been retained from Old English, though æ has disappeared; the letter *u* is used both for the vowel and for the consonant *v*; vowels are doubled when they are long, as in *breed* ('bread'), while a final -*e* is pronounced as a syllable, rather than indicating a long vowel (*wile* means 'will,' not 'wile'). Also, some French vocabulary has entered the language, replacing earlier Germanic words, such as *dettes* ('debts') for *gyltas* ('guilts') and *temptaciouns* ('temptations') for *costnunge*.

Finally we have an Early Modern version, from the *Book of Common Prayer* (1549). Though a half-century earlier, it is close to the King James Version, which many still think of as the 'typical' Biblical language.

> Our Father, which art in heaven, Hallowed be
> thy Name. Thy kingdom come. Thy will be
> done, in earth as it is in heaven. Give us this
> day our daily bread. And forgive us our tres-
> passes, As we forgive them that trespass
> against us. And lead us not into temptation;
> But deliver us from evil.

packet of an illegal drug in powder form: *a wrap of heroin* **9 keep something under wraps** to keep something secret
WORD ORIGIN origin unknown

wraparound *adj* **1** (of a skirt) designed to be worn wrapped round the body **2** extending in a curve from the front round to the sides: *wraparound shades*

wrap party *n* a party held by cast and crew to celebrate the completion of filming of a motion picture or television programme

wrapper *n* a paper, foil, or plastic cover in which a product is wrapped: *a single sweet wrapper*

wrapping *n* a piece of paper, foil, or other material used to wrap something in

wrap up *vb* **1** to fold paper, cloth, or other material round (something) **2** to put warm clothes on: *remember to wrap up warmly on cold or windy days* **3** *informal* to finish or settle: *he will need 60 to 90 days to wrap up his current business dealings* **4** *slang* to stop talking **5 wrapped up in** giving all one's attention to: *wrapped up in her new baby*

wrasse *n* a brightly coloured sea fish
WORD ORIGIN Cornish *wrach*

wrath (**roth**) *n old-fashioned or literary* intense anger **wrathful** *adj*
WORD ORIGIN Old English *wrǣththu*

wreak *vb* **1 wreak havoc** to cause chaos or damage: *this Australian sun will wreak havoc with your complexions* **2 wreak vengeance on** to take revenge on
WORD ORIGIN Old English *wrecan*

Ξ **USAGE**
Ξ See at **wrought**.

wreath *n, pl* **wreaths 1** a ring of flowers or leaves, placed on a grave as a memorial or worn on the head as a garland or a mark of honour **2** anything circular or spiral: *a wreath of smoke*
WORD ORIGIN Old English *writha*

wreathe *vb* **wreathing, wreathed** *literary* **1 wreathed in a** surrounded by: *wreathed in pipe smoke* **b** surrounded by a ring of: *wreathed in geraniums* **2 wreathed in smiles** smiling broadly

wreck *vb* **1** to break, spoil, or destroy completely **2** to cause the accidental sinking or destruction of (a ship) at sea ▷ *n* **3** something that has been destroyed or badly damaged, such as a crashed car or aircraft **4** a ship that has been sunk or destroyed at sea **5** a person in a poor mental or physical state
WORD ORIGIN from Old Norse

wreckage *n* the remains of something that has been destroyed or badly damaged, such as a crashed car or aircraft

wrecker *n* **1** a person who destroys or badly damages something: *a marriage wrecker* **2** (formerly) a person who lured ships on to the rocks in order to plunder them **3** *chiefly US, Canad, & NZ* a person whose job is to demolish buildings or dismantle cars **4** *US & Canad* a breakdown van

wreckers *pl n NZ* a business which sells material from demolished cars or buildings

wren *n* a very small brown songbird
WORD ORIGIN Old English *wrenna*

Wren *n informal* (formerly, in Britain and certain other nations) a member of the former Women's Royal Naval Service
WORD ORIGIN from abbreviation WRNS

wrench *vb* **1** to twist or pull (something) violently, for example to remove it from something to which it is attached: *he grabbed the cable and wrenched it out of the wall socket* **2** to move or twist away with a sudden violent effort: *she wrenched free of his embrace* **3** to injure (a limb or joint) by a sudden twist ▷ *n* **4** a violent twist or pull **5** an injury to a limb or joint, caused by twisting it **6** a feeling of sadness experienced on leaving a person or place: *it would be a wrench to leave Essex after all these years* **7** a spanner with adjustable jaws
WORD ORIGIN Old English *wrencan*

wrest *vb* **1** to take (something) away from someone with a violent pull or twist **2** to seize forcibly by violent or unlawful means: *she must begin to wrest control of the army and the police*
WORD ORIGIN Old English *wrǣstan*

wrestle *vb* **-tling, -tled 1** to fight (someone) by grappling and trying to throw or pin him or her to the ground, often as a sport **2 wrestle with** to struggle hard with (a person, problem, or thing): *I wrestled with my conscience* **wrestler** *n*
WORD ORIGIN Old English *wrǣstlian*

wrestling *n* a sport in which each contestant tries to overcome the other either by throwing or pinning him or her to the ground or by forcing a submission

wretch *n old-fashioned* **1** a despicable person **2** a person pitied for his or her misfortune
WORD ORIGIN Old English *wrecca*

wretched (**retch**-id) *adj* **1** in poor or pitiful circumstances: *a vast wretched slum* **2** feeling very unhappy **3** of poor quality: *the wretched state of the cabbages* **4** *informal* undesirable or displeasing: *what a wretched muddle* **wretchedly** *adv* **wretchedness** *n*

wriggle *vb* **-gling, -gled 1** to twist and turn with quick movements: *he wriggled on the hard seat* **2** to move along by twisting and turning **3 wriggle out of** to avoid (doing something that one does not want to do): *he wriggled out of donating blood* ▷ *n* **4** a wriggling movement or action
WORD ORIGIN Middle Low German *wriggeln*

wring *vb* **wringing, wrung 1** Also: **wring out** to squeeze water from (a cloth or clothing) by twisting it tightly **2** to twist (a neck) violently **3** to clasp and twist (one's hands) in anguish **4** to grip (someone's hand) vigorously in greeting **5** to obtain by forceful means: *to wring concessions from the army* **6 wring someone's heart** to make someone feel sorrow or pity
WORD ORIGIN Old English *wringan*

wringer *n* same as **mangle²** (sense 1)

wringing *adv* **wringing wet** extremely wet

wrinkle *n* **1** a slight ridge in the smoothness of a surface, such as a crease in the skin as a result of age ▷ *vb*

-kling, -kled 2 to develop or cause to develop wrinkles **wrinkled** *or* **wrinkly** *adj*
WORD ORIGIN Old English *wrinclian* to wind around

wrist *n* **1** the joint between the forearm and the hand **2** the part of a sleeve that covers the wrist
WORD ORIGIN Old English

wristwatch *n* a watch worn strapped round the wrist

writ *n* a formal legal document ordering a person to do or not to do something
WORD ORIGIN Old English

write *vb* **writing, wrote, written 1** to draw or mark (words, letters, or numbers) on paper or a blackboard with a pen, pencil, or chalk **2** to describe or record (something) in writing: *he began to write his memoirs* **3** to be an author: *he still taught writing, but he didn't write* **4** to write a letter to or correspond regularly with someone: *don't forget to write!* **5** *informal chiefly US & Canad* to write a letter to (someone): *I wrote him several times* **6** to say or communicate in a letter or a book: *in a recent letter a friend wrote that everything costs more in Russia now* **7** to fill in the details for (a cheque or document) **8** *computers* to record (data) in a storage device **9 write down** to record in writing: *write it down if you find it too embarrassing to talk about*
WORD ORIGIN Old English *wrītan*

write off *vb* **1** *accounting* to cancel (a bad debt) from the accounts **2** to dismiss from consideration: *he wrote her off as a tense woman* **3** to send a written request (for something): *he wrote off for leaflets on the subject* **4** *informal* to damage (a vehicle) beyond repair ▷ *n* **write-off 5** *informal* a vehicle that is damaged beyond repair

write out *vb* **1** to put into writing or reproduce in full form in writing **2** to remove (a character) from a television or radio series: *another actress is to be written out of the BBC soap*

writer *n* **1** a person whose job is writing; author **2** the person who has written something specified: *the writer of this letter is pretty dangerous*

write up *vb* **1** to describe fully, complete, or bring up to date in writing: *she would write up her diary in bed* ▷ *n* **write-up 2** a published account of something, such as a review in a newspaper or magazine: *I see the Herald didn't give you a very good write-up*

writhe *vb* **writhing, writhed** to twist or squirm in pain: *writhing in agony*
WORD ORIGIN Old English *wrīthan*

writing *n* **1** something that has been written: *the writing on the outer flap was faint* **2** written form: *permission in writing* **3** short for **handwriting 4** a kind or style of writing: *creative writing* **5** the work of a writer: *Wilde never mentioned chess in his writing*

written *vb* **1** the past participle of **write** ▷ *adj* **2** recorded in writing: *written permission*

WRNS (in Britain, formerly) Women's Royal Naval Service

wrong *adj* **1** not correct or accurate: *the wrong answers* **2** acting or judging in error; mistaken: *do correct me if I'm wrong*

W

3 not in accordance with correct or conventional rules or standards; immoral: *this group argues that even gently slapping a child is wrong* **4** not intended or appropriate: *I ordered the wrong things; you've picked the wrong time to ask such questions* **5** being a problem or trouble: *come on, I know when something's wrong* **6** not functioning properly: *there's something wrong with the temperature sensor* **7** denoting the side of cloth that is worn facing inwards ▷ *adv* **8** in a wrong manner: *I guessed wrong* **9 get someone wrong** to misunderstand someone: *don't get me wrong, I'm not making threats* **10 get something wrong** to make a mistake about something: *he had got his body language wrong* **11 go wrong a** to turn out badly or not as intended **b** to make a mistake **c** (of a machine) to stop functioning properly: *pilots must be able to react instantly if the automatic equipment suddenly goes wrong* ▷ *n* **12** something bad, immoral, or unjust: *how can such a wrong be redressed?* **13 in the wrong** mistaken or guilty ▷ *vb* **14** to treat (someone) unjustly **15** to think or speak unfairly of (someone) **wrongly** *adv*
WORD ORIGIN Old English *wrang* injustice

wrongdoing *n* immoral or illegal behaviour **wrongdoer** *n*

wrong-foot *vb* **1** *sport* to play a shot in such a way as to catch (an opponent) off-balance: *he constantly wrong-footed his opponent with fine passing* **2** to gain an advantage over (someone) by doing something unexpected: *China wrong-footed Vietnam by supporting the peace plan*

wrongful *adj* unjust or illegal: *wrongful imprisonment* **wrongfully** *adv*

wrong-headed *adj* constantly and stubbornly wrong in judgment

wrote *vb* the past tense of **write**

wroth *adj* old-fashioned or literary angry
WORD ORIGIN Old English *wrāth*

wrought (**rawt**) *vb* **1** old-fashioned a past of **work** ▷ *adj* **2** metallurgy shaped by hammering or beating: *wrought copper and brass*

≣ USAGE
≣ Wrought is sometimes used as if it were
≣ the past tense and past participle of
≣ *wreak*, as in *the hurricane wrought havoc in*
≣ *coastal areas.* Many people think this
≣ use is incorrect.

wrought iron *n* a pure form of iron with a low carbon content, often used for decorative work

wrung *vb* the past of **wring**

WRVS (in Britain) Women's Royal Voluntary Service

wry *adj* **wrier, wriest** *or* **wryer, wryest**
1 drily humorous; sardonic: *wry amusement* **2** (of a facial expression) produced by twisting one's features to denote amusement or displeasure: *a small wry smile twisted the corner of his mouth* **wryly** *adv*
WORD ORIGIN Old English *wrīgian* to turn

wrybill *n* a New Zealand plover whose bill is bent to one side enabling it to search for food beneath stones

wryneck *n* a woodpecker that has a habit of twisting its neck round

wt. weight

WTO World Trade Organization

wuss (**woos**) *or* **wussy** *n, pl* **wusses** *or* **wussies** *slang chiefly US* a feeble or effeminate person
WORD ORIGIN perhaps from PUSSY[1]

WV West Virginia

WWI World War One

WWII World War Two

WWW World Wide Web

WY Wyoming

wych-elm *or* **witch-elm** *n* a Eurasian elm with long pointed leaves
WORD ORIGIN Old English *wice*

WYSIWYG *n, adj computers* what you see is what you get: referring to what is displayed on the screen being the same as what will be printed out

W

Xx

The letter X is the twenty-fourth letter of the English alphabet. It has its origins in the Greek letter *xi* (Ξ,ξ), and achieved its current form in the Etruscan alphabet of pre-Roman Italy, from where it was adopted by the Romans.

The letter corresponds to the shape of a diagonal cross and is one of only four letters that are both horizontally and vertically symmetrical (the others being H, I, and O). The simplicity of its shape led to its use as a mark by the illiterate, and so it is used to indicate preference on ballot papers and to mark an important place on the map, which gives us the saying that 'X marks the spot'. Although few people sign their names as X in an era of universal literacy, there remains a convention for writing the letter X on greeting cards and messages to indicate a kiss.

Another connotation of the letter arises from its former use in the cinema to indicate a film that is suitable for viewing only by adults. Since 1982 films of this type have been officially designated as '18', but this change has not broken the association of the letter X with sex and violence, and something that is regarded as explicit or gratuitously violent may still be referred to as 'X-rated'.

As the letter X represents a sound made by two consonants /ks/ it is not natural for words to begin with an X in English or most other languages. There are fewer English words beginning with X than with any other letter, and most of these are formed from four Greek prefixes: *xantho-* ('yellow'), *xeno-* ('foreign'), *xero-* ('dry'), and *xylo-* ('wood').

Possibly because it is so uncommon to find words that begin with X, the letter has achieved a certain mystique. This is further enhanced by the convention of mathematicians to use lower-case *x* as the symbol for an unknown factor in an algebraic formula (a practice first used by Descartes). As a result we talk about 'the X factor' as the intangible quality that can bring about success for a project or individual. It is not surprising that the makers of a drama series about investigators looking into events that may have been caused by aliens alighted on the title of *The X Files* – no other letter would have produced the required effect.

---

x *maths* **1** (along with *y* and *z*) an unknown quantity **2** the multiplication symbol

X **1** indicating an error, a choice, or a kiss **2** indicating an unknown, unspecified, or variable factor, person, or thing: *Miss X* **3** the Roman numeral for ten **4** (formerly) indicating a film that may not be publicly shown to anyone under 18: since 1982 replaced by symbol 18

X-chromosome *n* the sex chromosome that occurs in pairs in the females of many animals, including humans, and as one of a pair with the Y-chromosome in males

Xe *chem* xenon

xenon *n chem* a colourless odourless gas found in minute quantities in the air. Symbol: Xe
WORD ORIGIN Greek: something strange

xenophobia (zen-oh-**fobe**-ee-a) *n* hatred or fear of foreigners or strangers **xenophobic** *adj*
WORD ORIGIN Greek *xenos* foreign + *phobos* fear

xerography (zeer-**og**-ra-fee) *n* a photocopying process in which an image of the written or printed material is electrically charged on a surface and attracts oppositely charged dry ink particles which are then fixed by heating **xerographic** *adj*
WORD ORIGIN Greek *xēros* dry + -GRAPHY

Xerox (**zeer**-ox) *n trademark* **1** a machine for copying printed material **2** a copy made by a Xerox machine ▷ *vb* **3** to produce a copy of (a document) using such a machine

Xhosa (**kawss**-a) *n* **1** *pl* **-sa** *or* **-sas** a member of a Black people living in the Republic of South Africa **2** the language of this people **Xhosan** *adj*

Xmas (**eks**-mass) *n informal* short for **Christmas**
WORD ORIGIN from the Greek letter *chi* (X), first letter of *Khristos* Christ

XML extensible markup language: a computer language used in text formatting

X-rated *adj* **1** (formerly, in Britain) (of a film) considered suitable for viewing by adults only **2** *informal* involving bad language, violence, or sex: *an X-rated conversation*

X-ray *or* **x-ray** *n* **1** a stream of electromagnetic radiation of short wavelength that can pass through some solid materials **2** a picture produced by exposing photographic film to X-rays: used in medicine as a diagnostic aid, since parts of the body, such as bones, absorb X-rays and so appear as opaque areas on the picture ▷ *vb* **3** to photograph, treat, or examine using X-rays

X-ray diffraction *n physics* the scattering of X-rays on contact with matter, resulting in changes in radiation intensity, which is used for studying atomic structure

xylem (**zile**-em) *n bot* a plant tissue that conducts water and mineral salts from the roots to all other parts
WORD ORIGIN Greek *xulon* wood

xylene (**zile**-lean) *n chem* a hydrocarbon existing in three isomeric forms, all three being colourless flammable volatile liquids used as solvents and in the manufacture of synthetic resins, dyes, and insecticides
WORD ORIGIN Greek *xulon* wood

xylitol *n chem* an artificial sweetener produced from xylose and used esp. in chewing gum

xylophone (**zile**-oh-fone) *n music* a percussion instrument consisting of a set of wooden bars played with hammers **xylophonist** *n*
WORD ORIGIN Greek *xulon* wood

xylose *n* a white crystalline sugar derived from wood and straw

English and the Opera

Opera is the complete collaborative art form, combining music, theatre, and sometimes dance. Words are often the forgotten part of this complex mix. In fact, opera-goers usually can make out only some of the words sung, even in a language they know. When the words are in Italian, opera's most-used language, an entire *libretto* (an Italian word meaning 'little book') can sound like variations on a vowel. Given the absurd or crazed plots of many operas, some might argue that it doesn't matter.

But, since many operas are based on literary works, words still count, whether in the poetry of lyrics in operatic *arias*, or the prose of *recitative* (dialogue and narrative sung in the rhythm of speech). Some measure of justice is restored in the *musical theatre*, a lineal descendant of opera, since we tend to identify famous Broadway musicals or Covent Garden operettas with their conjoined writer-composer teams: *Gilbert and Sullivan, Rogers and Hammerstein, Lerner and Loewe*. Of course, a few artists, such as Stephen Sondheim, or his operatic predecessors Richard Wagner and Hector Berlioz, composed both words and music. How the creators of musicals are credited usually reflect disparate authorship; separate people often compose the music, write the lyrics, and provide the *book*, the spoken dialogue and stage directions. Earlier, it had been a significant moment in the evolution of the musical when solos and duets began to be used, not just to make melodic statements, but to advance a story.

Occasionally, great composers get absorbed intellectually by whether the music comes first, or the words. Richard Strauss's final opera, *Capriccio*, called 'A Conversation Piece for Music', centres on characters who debate this topic. (When we remember that in his opera Strauss quotes the music of other composers – and himself – and that he collaborated on the libretto, the issue becomes even more complicated.) Strauss's heroine must decide whether she prefers one suitor, a poet, or another, a composer. The two are challenged to collaborate on an opera that, we may speculate, will turn out to be a mirror image of the opera being performed. In any event, it is a duel between the rival claimants, text and music. In the end the heroine, unable to choose, sings that the two are inseparable. And so they are, at least in opera.

In the latter part of the twentieth century, it began to dawn on the producers of pure opera that audiences should be given some idea of what was going on in front of them. Lotfi Mansouri solved the problem in 1983 when, in a Canadian Opera Company production of Strauss's *Elektra*, he introduced *surtitles*, in which words, translated or not, are projected on a screen above a theatre's proscenium. Lest this distract an audience, some opera houses use seatback screens, the system of the *electronic libretto*.

Directly related to intelligibility is the debate about whether an opera should be translated or presented in its original language. In eighteenth-century London, the German-born George Frederick Handel composed operas in Italian for English speakers, leading Samuel Johnson to call them 'irrational and exotic entertainments', a characterization that is still applicable. A century later, Wagner strongly urged that his operas be translated for the English audience, thus treating it to Wotan's interminable ruminations about his motives and past in the Ring Cycle. Intelligibility has its costs.

Opera shares some of its terminology (*diva, bel canto, falsetto, vibrato*) with other vocal music, but a few terms have wider currency. The Wagnerian *leitmotif*, a single or multiple recurring theme, has been applied equally to novels by James Joyce and the soundtracks of Hollywood movies. Even the word 'opera' itself has an afterlife in compounds such as *soap opera* and *rock opera*. The latter term describes such ambitious projects as *Tommy*, created by rock band The Who. Soap operas on daytime TV got their name because the radio serials that preceded them were sponsored by soap makers, and the daily doings of their dramatic characters take on the exaggerations of opera. True enough. If, for example, a heroine passionately falls in love with her fiancé's law partner but then dreads telling him because she has learned that he just spent a wild romantic weekend with her mother, the resemblance to the typical plots of grand opera becomes uncanny.

Yy

The letter Y is the twenty-fifth letter of the English alphabet. Like U and V, it has its origins in a Greek letter called *upsilon* (Y,υ), the ancestor of which was a Semitic letter called *waw* that represented a hook.

The early Roman alphabet used the upsilon as the basis for its letter U or V, which could denote both a vowel and consonant. It had no need for a Y as a separate letter, and ended with the letter X. Later, after the Romans had conquered Greece, the letter Y was added (together with Z) at the end of the alphabet, but was used only to transliterate the letter upsilon in words that were imported from the Greeks. The Romans pronounced this letter like their I, and so Y was called *I Graeca* or 'the Greek I'. To this day, the name of this letter in French, Spanish, and several other languages means 'Greek I'.

In English, Y has the unique distinction of being used as both a vowel (in words such as 'shy' and 'system') and a consonant (in words such as 'year' and 'beyond'). In early written English a distinction was made between the vowel and consonant, and a character called *yogh* (shaped a little like a figure 3) was used for the consonant sound. However, this character disappeared with the advent of the printing press as it did not feature in the fonts that British printers imported from Europe. Thus Y acquired its dual purpose.

The advent of printing also spelt the death knell for the letter called *thorn* (þ), which had been used in early English to represent the consonant sound at the start of words such as 'this' and 'the'. Before the convention of writing this sound as TH was established, printers employed the underused Y as a substitute for thorn, which led to spellings such as 'Ye olde inn' – although the word was still pronounced 'the'.

In more recent times, an inverted form of the letter Y, with one of the branches of the letter forming a flap, has featured in a style of men's underpants, which thus came to be known as Y-fronts.

---

y *maths* (along with *x* and *z*) an unknown quantity

Y 1 an unknown, unspecified, or variable factor, number, person, or thing **2** *chem* yttrium

Y2K *n informal* name for the year 2000 AD (esp. referring to the millennium bug)

ya *interj S African* yes

yabby *n, pl* -bies *Austral* **1** a small freshwater crayfish **2** a marine prawn used as bait
WORD ORIGIN from a native Australian language

yacht (**yott**) *n* **1** a large boat with sails or an engine, used for racing or pleasure cruising ▷ *vb* **2** to sail or cruise in a yacht **yachting** *n, adj*
WORD ORIGIN obsolete Dutch *jaghte*

yachtsman *or fem* **yachtswoman** *n, pl* -men *or* -women a person who sails a yacht

yack *n, vb* same as **yak²**

yah *interj* **1** *informal* same as **yes 2** an exclamation of derision or disgust

yahoo *n, pl* -hoos a crude, brutish, or obscenely coarse person
WORD ORIGIN after the brutish creatures in *Gulliver's Travels*

yahweh *or* **yahveh** *n Bible* a personal name of god
WORD ORIGIN Hebrew YHVH, with conjectural vowels

yak¹ *n* a Tibetan ox with long shaggy hair
WORD ORIGIN Tibetan *gyag*

yak² *slang n* **1** noisy, continuous, and trivial talk ▷ *vb* **yakking, yakked 2** to talk continuously about unimportant matters
WORD ORIGIN imitative

yakka *n Austral & NZ informal* work
WORD ORIGIN from a native Australian language

Yale lock *n trademark* a type of cylinder lock using a flat serrated key
WORD ORIGIN after L. *Yale*, inventor

yam *n* **1** a twining plant of tropical and subtropical regions, cultivated for its starchy roots which are eaten as a vegetable **2** the sweet potato
WORD ORIGIN Portuguese *inhame*

yammer *informal vb* **1** to whine in a complaining manner ▷ *n* **2** a yammering sound **3** nonsense or jabber
WORD ORIGIN Old English *geōmrian* to grumble

Yang *n* see **Yin and Yang**

yank *vb* **1** to pull (someone or something) with a sharp movement: *I yanked myself out of the water* ▷ *n* **2** a sudden pull or jerk
WORD ORIGIN origin unknown

Yank *n slang* a person from the United States

Yankee *n* **1** *slang* same as **Yank 2** a person from the Northern United States ▷ *adj* **3** of or characteristic of Yankees
WORD ORIGIN perhaps from Dutch *Jan Kees* John Cheese, nickname for English colonists

yap *vb* **yapping, yapped 1** to bark with a high-pitched sound **2** *informal* to talk at length in an annoying or stupid way ▷ *n* **3** a high-pitched bark **4** *slang* annoying or stupid speech **yappy** *adj*
WORD ORIGIN imitative

yarborough *n bridge, whist* a hand in which no card is higher than nine
WORD ORIGIN supposedly after the second earl of *Yarborough*, said to have bet a thousand to one against its occurrence

yard¹ *n* **1** a unit of length equal to 3 feet (0.9144 metre) **2** *naut* a spar slung across a ship's mast to extend the sail
WORD ORIGIN Old English *gierd* rod, twig

yard² *n* **1** a piece of enclosed ground, often adjoining or surrounded by a building or buildings **2** an enclosed or open area where a particular type of work is done: *a shipbuilding yard* **3** *Austral, US, & Canad* the garden of a house **4** *US & Canad* the winter pasture of deer, moose, and similar animals
WORD ORIGIN Old English *geard*

Yard *n* **the Yard** *Brit informal* short for **Scotland Yard**

yardarm *n naut* the outer end of a ship's yard

yardstick *n* **1** a measure or standard used for comparison: *there's no yardstick for judging a problem of this sort* **2** a graduated measuring stick one yard long

yarmulke (**yar**-mull-ka) *n* a skullcap worn by Jewish men
WORD ORIGIN Yiddish

yarn *n* **1** a continuous twisted strand of natural or synthetic fibres, used for knitting or making cloth **2** *informal* a long involved story **3** **spin a yarn** *informal* to tell such a story
WORD ORIGIN Old English *gearn*

yarrow *n* a wild plant with flat clusters of white flowers
WORD ORIGIN Old English *gearwe*

yashmak *n* a veil worn by a Muslim woman to cover her face in public
WORD ORIGIN Arabic

yaw *vb* **1** (of an aircraft or ship) to turn to one side or from side to side while moving ▷ *n* **2** the act or movement of yawing
WORD ORIGIN origin unknown

yawl *n* **1** a two-masted sailing boat **2** a ship's small boat
WORD ORIGIN Dutch *jol* or Middle Low German *jolle*

yawn *vb* **1** to open one's mouth wide and take in air deeply, often when sleepy or bored **2** to be open wide as if threatening to engulf someone or something: *the doorway yawned blackly open at the end of the hall* ▷ *n* **3** the act or an instance of yawning **yawning** *adj*
WORD ORIGIN Old English *geonian*

yaws *n* an infectious disease of tropical climates characterized by red skin eruptions
WORD ORIGIN Carib

Yb *chem* ytterbium

Y-chromosome *n* the sex chromosome that occurs as one of a pair with the X-chromosome in the males of many animals, including humans

yd yard (measure)

YDT Yukon Daylight Time

ye¹ (**yee**) *pron old-fashioned or dialect* you
WORD ORIGIN Old English *gē*

ye² *adj* (*definite article*) *old-fashioned or jocular* the: *ye olde Rose and Crown pub*
WORD ORIGIN a misinterpretation of *the*, written with the old letter thorn (þ), representing *th*

yea *interj* **1** *old-fashioned* yes ▷ *adv* **2** *old-fashioned or literary* indeed or truly: *they wandered about the church, yea, even unto the altar*
WORD ORIGIN Old English *gēa*

yeah *interj informal* same as **yes**

year *n* **1** the time taken for the earth to make one revolution around the sun, about 365 days **2** the twelve months from January 1 to December 31 **3** a period of twelve months from any specified date **4** a specific period of time, usually occupying a definite part or parts of a twelve-month period, used for some particular activity: *the financial year* **5** a group of people who have started an academic course at the same time **6** **year in, year out** regularly or monotonously, over a long period

7 years a a long time: *the legal case could take years to resolve* **b** age, usually old age: *a man of his years*
WORD ORIGIN Old English *gēar*

USAGE
In writing spans of years, it is important to choose a style that avoids ambiguity. The practice adopted in this dictionary is, in four-figure dates, to specify the last two digits of the second date if it falls within the same century as the first: *1801–08; 1850–51; 1899–1901*. In writing three-figure BC dates, it is advisable to give both dates in full: *159–156BC*, not *159–56BC* unless of course the span referred to consists of 103 years rather than three years. It is also advisable to specify BC or AD in years under 1000 unless the context makes this self-evident.

yearbook *n* a reference book published once a year containing details of events of the previous year

yearling *n* an animal that is between one and two years old

yearly *adj* **1** occurring, done, or appearing once a year or every year **2** lasting or valid for a year: *the yearly cycle* ▷ *adv* **3** once a year

yearn *vb* **1** to have an intense desire or longing: *he often yearned for life in a country town* **2** to feel tenderness or affection: *I yearn for you* **yearning** *n, adj*
WORD ORIGIN Old English *giernan*

yeast *n* a yellowish fungus used in fermenting alcoholic drinks and in raising dough for bread **yeasty** *adj*
WORD ORIGIN Old English *giest*

yebo *interj S African informal* yes
WORD ORIGIN Zulu *yebo* yes, I agree

yell *vb* **1** to shout, scream, or cheer in a loud or piercing way ▷ *n* **2** a loud piercing cry of pain, anger, or fear
WORD ORIGIN Old English *giellan*

yellow *n* **1** the colour of a lemon or an egg yolk **2** anything yellow, such as yellow clothing or yellow paint: *painted in yellow* ▷ *adj* **3** of the colour yellow; of the colour of a lemon or an egg yolk **4** *informal* cowardly or afraid **5** having a yellowish complexion ▷ *vb* **6** to make or become yellow or yellower **yellowish** or **yellowy** *adj*
WORD ORIGIN Old English *geolu*

yellow-belly *n, pl* -**bellies** *slang* a coward **yellow-bellied** *adj*

yellow card *n soccer* a piece of yellow pasteboard raised by a referee to indicate that a player has been booked for a serious violation of the rules

yellow fever *n* an acute infectious tropical disease causing fever and jaundice, caused by certain mosquitoes

yellowfin tuna *n* a large marine food fish of tropical and subtropical waters

yellowhammer *n* a European songbird with a yellowish head and body
WORD ORIGIN origin unknown

Yellow Pages *pl n trademark* a telephone directory that lists businesses under the headings of the type of business or service they provide

yellow streak *n informal* a cowardly or weak trait

yelp *vb* **1** to utter a sharp or high-pitched cry of pain ▷ *n* **2** a sharp or high-pitched cry of pain
WORD ORIGIN Old English *gielpan* to boast

yen¹ *n, pl* **yen** the standard monetary unit of Japan
WORD ORIGIN Japanese *en*

yen² *informal n* **1** a longing or desire ▷ *vb* **yenning, yenned** **2** to have a longing
WORD ORIGIN perhaps from Chinese *yän* a craving

yeoman (**yo**-man) *n, pl* -**men** *history* a farmer owning and farming his own land
WORD ORIGIN perhaps from *yongman* young man

yeoman of the guard *n* a member of the ceremonial bodyguard (**Yeomen of the Guard**) of the British monarch

yeomanry *n* **1** yeomen collectively **2** (in Britain) a former volunteer cavalry force

yep *interj informal* same as **yes**

yes *interj* **1** used to express consent, agreement, or approval, or to answer when one is addressed **2** used to signal someone to speak or keep speaking, enter a room, or do something ▷ *n* **3** an answer or vote of *yes* **4** a person who answers or votes *yes*
WORD ORIGIN Old English *gēse*

yes man *n* a person who always agrees with his or her superior in order to gain favour

yesterday *n* **1** the day before today **2** the recent past ▷ *adv* **3** on or during the day before today **4** in the recent past

yesteryear *formal or literary n* **1** last year or the past in general ▷ *adv* **2** during last year or the past in general

yet *conj* **1** nevertheless or still: *I'm too tired to work, yet I have to go on* ▷ *adv* **2** up until then or now: *this may be her most rewarding book yet* **3** still: *yet more work to do* **4** now (as contrasted with later): *not ready for that yet* **5** eventually in spite of everything: *I'll break your spirit yet!* **6** **as yet** up until then or now
WORD ORIGIN Old English *gīeta*

yeti *n* same as **abominable snowman**
WORD ORIGIN Tibetan

yew *n* an evergreen tree with needle-like leaves, red berries, and fine-grained elastic wood
WORD ORIGIN Old English *īw*

Y-fronts *pl n trademark* men's or boys' underpants that have a front opening within an inverted Y shape

YHA (in Britain) Youth Hostels Association

yid *n slang, offensive* a Jew
WORD ORIGIN probably from *Yiddish*

Yiddish *n* **1** a language derived from High German, spoken by Jews in Europe and elsewhere by Jewish emigrants, and usually written in the Hebrew alphabet ▷ *adj* **2** of this language
WORD ORIGIN German *jüdisch* Jewish

yield *vb* **1** to produce or bear **2** to give as a return: *some of his policies have yielded large savings* **3** to give up control of; surrender **4** to give way, submit, or surrender, through force or persuasion: *the players*

y

finally yielded to the weather **5** to agree (to): *governments too weak to say no repeatedly yielded to petitions for charters* **6** to grant or allow: *to yield right of way* ▷ *n* **7** the amount produced

WORD ORIGIN Old English *gieldan*

yielding *adj* **1** compliant or submissive **2** soft or flexible: *he landed on a yielding surface rather than rock or board*

Yin and Yang *n* two complementary principles of Chinese philosophy: Yin is negative, dark, and feminine, Yang is positive, bright, and masculine

WORD ORIGIN Chinese *yin* dark + *yang* bright

yippee *interj* an exclamation of joy, pleasure, or anticipation

YMCA Young Men's Christian Association

yo *interj* an expression used as a greeting or to attract someone's attention

WORD ORIGIN origin unknown

yob or **yobbo** *n, pl* **yobs** or **yobbos** Brit, Austral, & NZ slang a bad-mannered aggressive youth **yobbish** *adj*

WORD ORIGIN perhaps back slang for *boy*

yodel *vb* **-delling, -delled** or US **-deling, -deled** **1** to sing with abrupt changes back and forth between the normal voice and falsetto, as in folk songs of the Swiss Alps ▷ *n* **2** the act or sound of yodelling **yodeller** or US **yodeler** *n*

WORD ORIGIN German *jodeln* (imitative)

yoga *n* **1** a Hindu system of philosophy aiming at spiritual, mental, and physical wellbeing by means of deep meditation, prescribed postures, and controlled breathing **2** a system of exercising involving such meditation, postures, and breathing

WORD ORIGIN Sanskrit: a yoking

yogi *n* a person who practises or is a master of yoga

yogurt or **yoghurt** *n* a slightly sour custard-like food made from milk curdled by bacteria, often sweetened and flavoured with fruit

WORD ORIGIN Turkish

yoke *n, pl* **yokes** or **yoke** **1** a wooden frame with a bar put across the necks of two animals to hold them together so that they can be worked as a team **2** a pair of animals joined by a yoke **3** a frame fitting over a person's shoulders for carrying buckets **4** an oppressive force or burden: *people are still suffering under the yoke of slavery* **5** a fitted part of a garment to which a fuller part is attached ▷ *vb* **yoking, yoked** **6** to put a yoke on **7** to unite or link

WORD ORIGIN Old English *geoc*

yokel *n disparaging* a person who lives in the country, esp. one who appears simple and old-fashioned

WORD ORIGIN perhaps from dialect *yokel* green woodpecker

yolk *n* the yellow part in the middle of an egg that provides food for the developing embryo

WORD ORIGIN Old English *geoloca*

Yom Kippur *n* an annual Jewish holiday celebrated as a day of fasting, with prayers of penitence

WORD ORIGIN Hebrew *yōm* day + *kippūr* atonement

yon *adj* **1** *chiefly Scot & N English dialect* that: *yon dog* ▷ *adv* **2** yonder: *he flicked glances hither and yon* ▷ *pron* **3** that person or thing: *yon was a pretty sight*

WORD ORIGIN Old English *geon*

yonder *adv* **1** over there ▷ *adj* **2** situated over there: *a tree at yonder waterfall*

WORD ORIGIN Old English *geond*

yonks *pl n informal* a very long time: *he must have been planning this for yonks*

WORD ORIGIN origin unknown

yoo-hoo *interj* a call to attract a person's attention

yore *n* of yore a long time ago: *in days of yore*

WORD ORIGIN Old English *geāra*

yorker *n cricket* a ball bowled so as to pitch just under or just beyond the bat

WORD ORIGIN probably after the *Yorkshire* County Cricket Club

Yorkist *English history n* **1** a supporter of the royal House of York, esp. during the Wars of the Roses ▷ *adj* **2** of or relating to the supporters or members of the House of York

Yorks. Yorkshire

Yorkshire pudding *n* a baked pudding made from a batter of flour, eggs, and milk, often served with roast beef

WORD ORIGIN from *Yorkshire*, county in NE England

you *pron* **1** (refers to) the person or people addressed: *can I get you a drink?* **2** (refers to) an unspecified person or people in general: *stick to British goods and you can't go wrong* ▷ *n* **3** *informal* the personality of the person being addressed: *that hat isn't really you*

WORD ORIGIN Old English *ēow*

≡ **USAGE**
≡ See at **me.**

you'd you had *or* you would

you'll you will *or* you shall

young *adj* **1** having lived or existed for a relatively short time **2** having qualities associated with youth: *their innovative approach and young attitude appealed to him* **3** of or relating to youth: *he'd been a terrorist himself in France in his young days* **4** of a group representing the younger members of a larger organization: *Young Conservatives* ▷ *n* **5** young people in general: *that never seems very important to the young* **6** offspring, esp. young animals: *a deer suckling her young* **youngish** *adj*

WORD ORIGIN Old English *geong*

youngster *n* a young person

your *adj* **1** of, belonging to, or associated with you: *ask your doctor to make the necessary calls* **2** of, belonging to, or associated with an unspecified person or people in general: *it is not right to take another baby to replace your own* **3** *informal* used to indicate all things or people of a certain type: *these characters are not your average housebreakers*

WORD ORIGIN Old English *ēower*

you're you are

yours *pron* **1** something belonging to you: *my reputation is better than yours* **2** your family: *a blessed Christmas to you and yours* **3** used in closing phrases at the end of a letter: *yours sincerely; yours faithfully* **4** of yours belonging to you: *that husband of yours*

yourself *pron, pl* **-selves** **1 a** the reflexive form of you **b** used for emphasis: *you've stated publicly that you yourself use drugs* **2** your normal self: *you're not yourself today*

yours truly *pron informal* I or me

WORD ORIGIN from the closing phrase of letters

youth *n* **1** the period between childhood and maturity **2** the quality or condition of being young, immature, or inexperienced: *his youth told against him in the contest* **3** a young man or boy **4** young people collectively: *there is still hope for today's youth* **5** the freshness, vigour, or vitality associated with being young

WORD ORIGIN Old English *geogoth*

youth club *n* a club that provides leisure activities for young people

youthful *adj* **1** vigorous or active: *the intermediate section was won by a youthful grandmother* **2** of, relating to, possessing, or associated with youth: *youthful good looks* **youthfully** *adv* **youthfulness** *n*

youth hostel *n* an inexpensive lodging place for young people travelling cheaply

YouTube *n* a website on which subscribers can post video files

you've you have

yowl *vb* **1** to produce a loud mournful wail or cry ▷ *n* **2** a wail or howl

WORD ORIGIN Old Norse *gaula*

yo-yo *n, pl* **-yos** **1** a toy consisting of a spool attached to a string, the end of which is held while it is repeatedly spun out and reeled in ▷ *vb* **yo-yoing, yo-yoed** **2** to change repeatedly from one position to another

WORD ORIGIN originally a trademark for this type of toy

yrs **1** years **2** yours

YST Yukon Standard Time

YT Yukon Territory

YTS (in Britain) Youth Training Scheme

ytterbium (it-**terb**-ee-um) *n chem* a soft silvery element that is used to improve the mechanical properties of steel. Symbol: Yb

WORD ORIGIN after *Ytterby*, Swedish quarry where discovered

yttrium (**it**-ree-um) *n chem* a silvery metallic element used in various alloys and in lasers. Symbol: Y

WORD ORIGIN see YTTERBIUM

yuan *n, pl* **-an** the standard monetary unit of the People's Republic of China

WORD ORIGIN Chinese *yüan* round object

yucca *n* a tropical plant with spiky leaves and white flowers

WORD ORIGIN from a Native American language

yucky or **yukky** *adj* **yuckier, yuckiest** or **yukkier, yukkiest** *slang* disgusting or nasty

WORD ORIGIN from *yuck*, exclamation of disgust

Yugoslav *adj* **1** of the former Yugoslavia ▷ *n* **2** a person from the former Yugoslavia

Yule *n literary or old-fashioned* Christmas or the Christmas season: *Yuletide*

WORD ORIGIN Old English *geōla*, originally a pagan feast lasting 12 days

y

The Influence of Indian Languages on English

Britain first established a presence in India with the founding of a permanent trading post in the early 17th century. The area under British control was steadily expanded until at its height it encompassed over half of the subcontinent. In 1876 Queen Victoria was proclaimed Empress of India, and British rule (known as the Raj) did not come to an end until independence was granted in 1948. English became the language of administration and education but the effects of its long side-by-side existence with the many indigenous languages and dialects were by no means one-sided, and a great many originally Indian expressions became absorbed into English.

It was inevitable that the British who lived in India for any length of time, whether as merchants, government employees, members of the Indian Army, or *memsahibs* overseeing a household of servants, would have to learn at least a handful of terms in a native language in order to communicate with Indians who spoke little or no English.

In food and drink, for example, several terms were both imported into the English language and into Britain with the return of those who had lived in the subcontinent. These include the various spicy dishes collectively known as *curry* (from a Tamil term meaning 'sauce'), the pickle called *chutney* (from Hindi), *mango* (from Tamil), *tiffin*, *toddy* (from Hindi), *cheroot* (ie a cigar, from Tamil), and *punch* (the drink, probably from Hindi). Even in the late 20th century 'old India hands' in Britain would refer to their whisky and soda or gin and tonic as a *chota peg* ('short drink', from Hindi).

One of the major commodities that was cheaply produced for the British market in India was cloth of various kinds and qualities. This trade gave English such terms as *chintz* (from Hindi), *calico* (originally from the Indian town of Calicut), and *seersucker* (from Hindi). As well as fabrics, the names of several kinds of clothing were borrowed, including *jodhpurs* (named after the north-west Indian town of Jodhpur), and *pyjamas* (from Urdu). Similarly, in terms of personal adornment, the word *bangle* comes from a Hindi term.

Life in India often involved types of dwelling-place that were unknown in the British Isles, and it is to India that we owe such terms as *bungalow* (from Hindi, originally meaning a Bengali style of house) and *veranda* (from Hindi). In their leisure hours Brits in India would often take to the water in a *dinghy* (from Hindi or Bengali) or even a *catamaran* (from Tamil).

Some of these terms had a limited lifespan, particularly those originating in the Indian Army, which was divided up after the Partition of India in 1947. For example, any British serviceman in the subcontinent would at one time have freely referred to his rifle as a *bundook* (from Hindi), and he would know exactly what the sergeant meant if he told him to *get a jildi on* (ie hurry up, from a Hindi word meaning 'speed'). He would refer to any man as a *wallah* (from Hindi), particularly when identifying him by his means of earning a living (eg a *dhobi wallah* washed people's clothes, and a *punka wallah* manually operated a fan used to cool a room). Above all he might dream of the cooling breezes of *Blighty* (from a Hindi term meaning 'foreign land').

On the other hand, some expressions which have survived the test of time, often because there was no direct English equivalent, include *shampoo, pundit, guru, loot,* and *juggernaut* (all from Hindi). Most people still talk about a *cushy* (from Hindi) job, and recognize when something is *pukka* (again from Hindi). If we never achieve *nirvana* (from Sanskrit) we may just put that down to *karma* (also Sanskrit).

Such was the prevalence of Indian terms in 19th-century English that a dictionary was considered necessary: Yule and Burnell's *Glossary of Colloquial Anglo-Indian Words and Phrases* (1886). This volume's subtitle was *Hobson-Jobson*, which was a term used for the borrowing of words or pronunciations from one language into another. This term has the distinction of being an example of itself, as 'Hobson-Jobson' was originally a somewhat dull British ear's interpretation of *ya Hasan! ya Husayn!*, an Arabic lament for the grandsons of Mohammed.

yummy *slang adj* **-mier, -miest**
1 delicious or attractive: *yummy sauces*
▷ *interj* **2** Also: **yum-yum** an exclamation indicating pleasure or delight, as in anticipation of delicious food
WORD ORIGIN yum-yum (imitative)

yuppie *n* **1** a young highly-paid professional person, esp. one who has a fashionable way of life ▷ *adj* **2** typical of or reflecting the values of yuppies: *a yuppie accessory*
WORD ORIGIN y(oung) u(rban) or u(pwardly mobile) p(rofessional)

yuppify *vb* **-fies, -fying, -fied** to make yuppie in nature: *Mount Pleasant was being yuppified* **yuppification** *n*

YWCA Young Women's Christian Association

y

Zz

The letter Z is the twenty-sixth and final letter of the English alphabet. Ideas on how to pronounce the name of this letter are governed by where you come from: in the United States the preferred pronunciation is 'zee', but most other English-speakers say 'zed'. At one time the letter could be called 'izzard', but this name is now sadly obsolete. Z entered the Roman alphabet as a form of the Greek letter *zeta* (Z,ζ), which was based on a Semitic letter called *zayin*, literally meaning 'dagger'. In the early Greek alphabet, *zeta* came in seventh position, and was probably pronounced more like /zd/ than /z/.

The original Roman alphabet followed the Greek in including the letter Z in seventh position. But the Romans had little use for the letter, and when they came up with the much more useful letter G, Z was unceremoniously kicked out to make way. It was later reinstated at the end of the alphabet, but it was only used in transliterations of Greek words that used a *zeta*.

In English, too, Z has remained a peripheral and somewhat exotic letter. As an initial, it occurs mainly in loanwords (such as 'ziggurat') and foreign place names (such as 'Zanzibar'). In Scrabble it ranks alongside Q as one of the most difficult letters to play and scores a premium of ten points.

The notion that the letter was regarded as something of an anomaly may be behind its memorable use in Act Two of Shakespeare's *King Lear*, when the Duke of Kent excoriates against the steward Oswald with the words, 'Thou whoreson zed, thou unnecessary letter!'

Various attempts have been made to expand the use of Z, however. When the letter *yogh* became obsolete with the arrival of printing, Z was introduced into Scottish words such as 'capercailzie'. However, English printers opted to use a Y instead for this consonant. American English has consistently used Z in spellings such as 'realize' and 'organize' where the British fashion has traditionally been to favour an S, but the tendency to use Z has become more widespread, and most British dictionaries now use the Z for the primary spelling of such words.

---

z *or* **Z** *n, pl* **z's, Z's** *or* **Zs 1** the 26th and last letter of the English alphabet **2 from A to Z** see **a** (sense 3)

z *maths* (along with *x* and *y*) an unknown quantity

Z *chem* atomic number

zabaglione (zab-al-**lyoh**-nee) *n* a dessert made of egg yolks, sugar, and wine, whipped together
WORD ORIGIN Italian

zany (**zane**-ee) *adj* **zanier, zaniest** comical in an endearing way
WORD ORIGIN Italian dialect *Zanni*, nickname for *Giovanni* John; traditional name for a clown

zap *vb* **zapping, zapped** *slang* **1** to kill, esp. by shooting **2** to change television channels rapidly by remote control **3** to move quickly
WORD ORIGIN imitative

zeal *n* great enthusiasm or eagerness, esp. for a religious movement
WORD ORIGIN Greek *zēlos*

zealot (**zel**-lot) *n* a fanatic or an extreme enthusiast **zealotry** *n*

zealous (**zel**-luss) *adj* extremely eager or enthusiastic **zealously** *adv*

zebra *n, pl* **-ras** *or* **-ra** a black-and-white striped African animal of the horse family
WORD ORIGIN Old Spanish: wild ass

zebra crossing *n Brit* a pedestrian crossing marked by broad black and white stripes: once on the crossing the pedestrian has right of way

zebu (**zee**-boo) *n* a domesticated ox of Africa and Asia, with a humped back and long horns
WORD ORIGIN French

zed *n* the British and New Zealand spoken form of the letter *z*

zee *n* the US spoken form of the letter *z*

Zeitgeist (**tsite**-guyst) *n* the spirit or general outlook of a specific time or period
WORD ORIGIN German, literally: time spirit

Zen *n* a Japanese form of Buddhism that concentrates on learning through meditation and intuition

Zend-Avesta *n* the Zoroastrian scriptures (the **Avesta**), together with the traditional interpretive commentary known as the **Zend**

zenith *n* **1** the point in the sky directly above an observer **2** the highest or most successful point of anything: *he was at the zenith of his military career* **zenithal** *adj*
WORD ORIGIN Arabic *samt arrās* path over one's head

zephyr (**zef**-fer) *n* a soft gentle breeze
WORD ORIGIN Greek *zephuros* the west wind

Zeppelin *n* a large cylindrical rigid German airship of the early 20th century
WORD ORIGIN after Count von *Zeppelin*, its designer

zero *n, pl* **-ros** *or* **-roes 1** the cardinal number between +1 and −1 **2** the symbol, o, representing this number **3** the line or point on a scale of measurement from which the graduations commence **4** the lowest point or degree: *my credibility is down to zero* **5** nothing or nil **6** the temperature, pressure, etc. that registers a reading of zero on a scale ▷ *adj* **7** amounting to zero: *zero inflation* **8** *meteorol* (of visibility) limited to a very short distance ▷ *vb* **-roing, -roed 9** to adjust (an instrument or scale) so as to read zero
WORD ORIGIN Arabic *sifr* empty

zero gravity *n* the state of weightlessness

zero hour *n* **1** *mil* the time set for the start of an operation **2** *informal* a critical time, usually at the beginning of an action

zero in on *vb* **1** to aim a weapon at (a target) **2** to concentrate one's attention on

zero-rated *adj* denoting goods on which the buyer pays no value-added tax

zest *n* **1** invigorating or keen excitement or enjoyment: *he has a zest for life and a quick intellect* **2** added interest, flavour, or charm: *he said that she would provide a new zest for his government* **3** the peel of an

z

orange or lemon, used as flavouring **zestful** *adj*
WORD ORIGIN French *zeste*

Zeus *n* *Greek myth* the ruler of the gods

ziggurat *n* (in ancient Mesopotamia) a temple in the shape of a pyramid
WORD ORIGIN Assyrian *ziqqurati* summit

zigzag *n* **1** a line or course having sharp turns in alternating directions ▷ *adj* **2** formed in or proceeding in a zigzag ▷ *adv* **3** in a zigzag manner ▷ *vb* **-zagging, -zagged** **4** to move in a zigzag
WORD ORIGIN German *zickzack*

zilch *n* *informal* nothing
WORD ORIGIN origin unknown

zillion *n, pl* **-lions** or **-lion** (*often pl*) *informal* an extremely large but unspecified number: *there are zillions of beautiful spots to visit*
WORD ORIGIN after *million*

Zimmer *n trademark* a tubular frame with rubber feet, used as a support to help disabled or infirm people walk

zinc *n chem* a brittle bluish-white metallic element that is used in alloys such as brass, to form a protective coating on metals, and in battery electrodes. Symbol: Zn
WORD ORIGIN German *Zink*

zinc ointment *n* a medicinal ointment consisting of zinc oxide, petroleum jelly, and paraffin

zinc oxide *n chem, pharmacol* a white insoluble powder used as a pigment and in making zinc ointment

zing *n* **1** *informal* the quality in something that makes it lively or interesting **2** a short high-pitched buzzing sound, like the sound of a bullet or vibrating string
WORD ORIGIN imitative

zinnia *n* a plant of tropical and subtropical America, with solitary heads of brightly coloured flowers
WORD ORIGIN after J. G. *Zinn*, botanist

Zion *n* **1** the hill on which the city of Jerusalem stands **2 a** the modern Jewish nation **b** Israel as the national home of the Jewish people **3** *Christianity* heaven

Zionism *n* a political movement for the establishment and support of a national homeland for Jews in what is now Israel **Zionist** *n, adj*

zip *n* **1** Also called: **zip fastener** a fastener with two parallel rows of metal or plastic teeth, one on either side of a closure, which are interlocked by a sliding tab **2** *informal* energy or vigour **3** a short sharp whizzing sound, like the sound of a passing bullet ▷ *vb* **zipping, zipped** **4** (often foll. by *up*) to fasten with a zip **5** to move with a sharp whizzing sound: *bullets zipped and*

ricocheted all around us **6** to hurry or rush
WORD ORIGIN imitative

zip code *n* the US equivalent of **postcode**
WORD ORIGIN z(one) i(mprovement) p(lan)

zipper *n* *US & Canad* same as **zip** (sense 1)

zippy *adj* **-pier, -piest** *informal* full of energy

zircon *n mineral* a hard mineral consisting of zirconium silicate, used as a gemstone and in industry
WORD ORIGIN German *Zirkon*

zirconium *n chem* a greyish-white metallic element, occurring chiefly in zircon, that is exceptionally corrosion-resistant. Symbol: Zr

zit *n slang* a spot or pimple

zither *n* a musical instrument consisting of numerous strings stretched over a flat box and plucked to produce notes **zitherist** *n*
WORD ORIGIN Greek *kithara*

zloty *n, pl* **-tys** or **-ty** the standard monetary unit of Poland
WORD ORIGIN Polish: golden

Zn *chem* zinc

zodiac *n* **1** an imaginary belt in the sky within which the sun, moon, and planets appear to move, and which is divided into 12 equal areas called **signs of the zodiac**, each named after the constellation which once lay in it **2** *astrol* a diagram, usually circular, representing this belt **zodiacal** *adj*
WORD ORIGIN Greek *zōidion* animal sign, from *zōion* animal

zombie or **zombi** *n, pl* **-bies** or **-bis** **1** a person who appears to be lifeless, apathetic, or totally lacking in independent judgment **2** a corpse brought to life by witchcraft
WORD ORIGIN W African *zumbi* good-luck fetish

zone *n* **1** a region, area, or section characterized by some distinctive feature or quality: *a demilitarized zone* **2** *geog* one of the divisions of the earth's surface according to temperature **3** a section on a transport route **4** *maths* a portion of a sphere between two parallel lines intersecting the sphere **5** *NZ* a catchment area for a specific school ▷ *vb* **zoning, zoned** **6** to divide (a place) into zones for different uses or activities **zonal** *adj* **zoning** *n*
WORD ORIGIN Greek *zōnē* girdle

zonked *adj* *Brit, Austral, & NZ slang* **1** highly intoxicated with drugs or alcohol **2** exhausted
WORD ORIGIN imitative

zoo *n, pl* **zoos** a place where live animals are kept, studied, bred, and exhibited to the public
WORD ORIGIN from *zoological garden*

zooid (**zoh**-oid) *n* **1** any independent animal body, such as an individual of a coral colony **2** a cell or body, produced by an organism and capable of independent motion, such as a gamete
WORD ORIGIN Greek *zōion* animal

zool. **1** zoological **2** zoology

zoological garden *n* the formal term for **zoo**

zoology *n* the study of animals, including their classification, structure, physiology, and history **zoological** *adj* **zoologist** *n*
WORD ORIGIN Greek *zōion* animal + -LOGY

zoom *vb* **1** to move very rapidly: *the first rocket zoomed into the sky* **2** to increase or rise rapidly: *stocks zoomed on the American exchange* **3** to move with or make a continuous buzzing or humming sound ▷ *n* **4** the sound or act of zooming **5** a zoom lens
WORD ORIGIN imitative

zoom in or **out** *vb photog, films, television* to increase or decrease rapidly the magnification of the image of a distant object by means of a zoom lens

zoom lens *n* a lens system that can make the details of a picture larger or smaller while keeping the picture in focus

zoophyte (**zoh**-a-fite) *n* any animal resembling a plant, such as a sea anemone
WORD ORIGIN Greek *zōion* animal + *phuton* plant

Zoroastrianism (zorr-oh-**ass**-tree-an-iz-zum) or **Zoroastrism** *n* the religion founded by the ancient Persian prophet Zoroaster, based on the concept of a continuous struggle between good and evil **Zoroastrian** *adj*

zounds *interj* *old-fashioned* a mild oath indicating surprise or indignation
WORD ORIGIN euphemistic shortening of *God's wounds*

Zr *chem* zirconium

zucchetto (tsoo-**ket**-toe) *n, pl* **-tos** *RC Church* a small round skullcap worn by clergymen and varying in colour according to the rank of the wearer
WORD ORIGIN Italian

zucchini (zoo-**keen**-ee) *n, pl* **-ni** or **-nis** *chiefly US, Canad, & Austral* a courgette
WORD ORIGIN Italian

Zulu *n* **1** *pl* **-lus** or **-lu** a member of a tall Black people of Southern Africa **2** the language of this people

zygote *n* the cell resulting from the union of an ovum and a spermatozoon
WORD ORIGIN Greek *zugōtos* yoked

Z